International Dictionary of Architects and Architecture - 1

ARCHITECTS

International Dictionary of Architects and Architecture - 1

ARCHITECTS

EDITOR
RANDALL J. VAN VYNCKT

EUROPEAN CONSULTANT
DOREEN YARWOOD

PHOTO and GRAPHIC RESEARCHER
SUHAIL BUTT

St J

St James Press

Detroit   London   Washington D.C.

STAFF

Randall J. Van Vynckt, *Editor*
Doreen Yarwood, *European Consultant*
Suhail Butt, *Photo and Graphic Researcher*
Jim Kamp, *Project Editor*
Linda Irvin, *Contributing Editor*
Paul E. Schellinger, *Associate Editor*

Cynthia Baldwin, *Art Director*
Barbara J. Yarrow, *Graphic Services Supervisor*
Kathleen Hourdakis, *Designer*
C. J. Jonik, *Keyliner*

Mary Beth Trimper, *Production Director*
Evi Seoud, *Assistant Production Manager*
Shanna P. Heilveil, *Production Assistant*

Margaret A. Chamberlain, *Permissions Supervisor*
Pamela A. Hayes and Keith Reed, *Permissions Associates*
Arlene Johnson and Barbara Wallace, *Permissions Assistants*

Cover photo: Wexler Center for the Arts, by Peter Eisenman. Courtesy of Kevin Fitzsimons/Wexler Center for the Arts

Library of Congress Cataloging-in-Publication Data
International dictionary of architects and architecture / editor, Randall J. Van Vynckt;
European consultant, Doreen Yarwood; photo and graphic researcher, Suhail Butt.
p. cm.
Includes bibliographical references and indexes.
Contents: v. 1. Architects — v. 2. Architecture
ISBN 1-55862-089-3 (set: not sold sep.): $250.00. — ISBN 1-55862-087-7
(v. 1). — ISBN 1-55862-088-5 (v. 2).
1. Architects—Biography—Dictionaries. 2. Architecture—Dictionaries.
I. Yarwood, Doreen. II. Butt, Suhail.
NA40.I48 1993
720'.9—dc20   93-13431
                                                                                      CIP

A CIP catalogue record of this book is available from the British Library.

Printed in the United States of America.
Published simultaneously in the United Kingdom.

The trademark **ITP** is used under license.

CONTENTS

INTRODUCTION

Scope

The *International Dictionary of Architects and Architecture* features 523 architects and 467 buildings and sites that have figured prominently in Western architectural history. The *Architects* volume covers architects, theorists and engineers, as well as personalities involved in architectural decoration, landscape design and urban planning. Many buildings and sites in the *Architecture* volume were selected to compensate for coverage that simply could not be provided in the *Architects* volume. Arranged geographically, the *Architecture* volume covers a range of periods and styles, from Ancient Greece to examples of postmodernism and deconstruction, and includes Classical sites, cathedrals, buildings, and other works whose architects generally are not known. The geographic ordering of the *Architecture* volume is intended to provide users with a convenient means of accessing related works.

Selection

The selection of subjects was based on original research, published sources, many writers who served as de facto advisers, and Doreen Yarwood, who shared her valuable experience of more than forty years of canvassing European architecture. Despite the size of this dictionary, the space is nonetheless limited in terms of the entire spectrum of architectural history, especially in terms of the depth of information we intended to provide for each topic; we therefore decided to limit our focus to architects and architecture within what has been considered the Western tradition. This dictionary, then, should serve as a valuable complement to original sources, monographs and reference works that deal with the wealth of architecture that has been promulgated within this tradition. Notable within our presentation of this Western realm are many important buildings and architects from areas of Eastern Europe that often have been excluded from English-language reference books, but that have recently become more accessible.

Entry Content

Entries in the *International Dictionary of Architects and Architecture* contain the following information:

- HEADNOTES: Compiled by the editor and his staff from a number of different sources as well as from information supplied by contributors, headnotes provide key information at a glance. The content varies according to volume:

  - *Architects*—Begins with biographical data, including nationality, birth and death locations and dates, educational background, and principal affiliations. Next follows a concise chronology of the architect's major built works.

► *Architecture*—Features dates of construction, architect(s) if known, and listings of notable additions or alterations.

● BIBLIOGRAPHIC CITATIONS: The dictionary's thousands of bibliographic citations—books and articles ranging from the general to the specific—were selected to aid everyone from the beginning student to the more advanced researcher.

► *Architects*—Contains chronological lists of books and/or articles by the architect as well as alphabetical lists (by author or, if unavailable, by title) of books and/or articles about the architect.

► *Architecture*—Features books and articles about a specific site or building.

● SIGNED CRITICAL ESSAYS: Some 220 international contributors knowledgeable about their respective subjects wrote the original essays in both volumes. Averaging about 1000 words, the essays discuss the key developments in an architect's life and career or the design, construction and impact of an architectural masterwork. Since the essays reflect each writer's scholarship and orientation, the approach to the subject matter ranges from detailed, matter-of-fact reporting to impressionistic musings. To learn more about any contributor, refer to the "Notes on Contributors" in the back of each volume.

● ILLUSTRATIONS: The *Dictionary* is highlighted by 964 photographs and 169 floor plans. Providing a wealth of information in their own right, these 1,133 illustrations appear in the majority of entries in *Architects* and **all** of the entries in *Architecture*.

Indexes

The Geographic, Building, and Architect indexes in these two volumes were designed to provide significant assistance in pinpointing desired information and in relating various architects to their buildings, and vice-versa.

Special Thanks

During the final months of book preparation, several people made special efforts to help complete *International Dictionary of Architects and Architecture*. Those who helped with final proofing and headnote compilation and coding include assistant editors Joanna Brod, Pamela S. Dear, Jeff Hill, Thomas F. McMahon, Terrie A. Rooney, Aarti D. Stephens, Linda Tidrick, Brandon R. Trenz and Roger M. Valade III along with associate editors Shelly Andrews, Elizabeth A. Des Chenes, Kathleen J. Edgar, Marie Ellavich, David M. Galens, Motoko Huthwaite, Mark F. Mikula, Michelle M. Motowski, Susan R. Reicha, Kenneth R. Shepherd, Deborah A. Stanley, Polly A. Vedder and Thomas Wiloch. In addition, "Notes on Contributors" was compiled by associate editor Mary K. Ruby and all photo captions were prepared by assistant editor Jane M. Kelly.

LIST OF ARCHITECTS

Aalto, Alvar
Adam, Robert
Adam, William
Adelcrantz, Carl Fredrik
Alberti, Leon Battista
Albini, Franco
Aleijadinho
Alessi, Galeazzo
Almqvist, Osvald
Ammann, Othmar
Ammannati, Bartolomeo
Ando, Tadao
Andrews, John
Antoine, Jacques-Denis
Apollodorus of Damascus
Archer, Thomas
Arnolfo di Cambio
Arup, Ove
Asam Brothers
Ashbee, C. R.
Asplund, Erik Gunnar
Atwood, Charles Bowler
Austin, Henry
Bacon, Henry
Bähr, Georg
Baker, Herbert
Banfi, Belgiojoso, Peresutti and Rogers (BBPR)
Barnes, Edward Larrabee
Barrágan, Luis
Barry, Charles
Basevi, George
Basile, Ernesto
Bazhenov, Vasili Ivanovich
Behnisch, Günther
Behrens, Peter
Bélanger, François-Joseph
Belluschi, Pietro
Benjamin, Asher
Bentley, John Francis
Berlage, Hendrik Petrus
Bernini, Giovanni Lorenzo
Bindesbøll, Michael Gottlieb
Blondel, Jacques-François
Bodley, George Frederick
Boffrand, Germain
Bofill, Ricardo
Bogardus, James
Böhm, Dominikus

Böhm, Gottfried
Bonomi, Joseph
Borromini, Francesco
Botta, Mario
Boullée, Etienne-Louis
Bramante, Donato
Breuer, Marcel
Bridgeman, Charles
Brodrick, Cuthbert
Brongniart, Alexandre-Théodore
Brown, Capability
Bruce, William
Brunel, Isambard K.
Brunelleschi, Filippo
Bryggman, Erik
Bulfinch, Charles
Buontalenti, Bernardo
Burges, William
Burle Marx, Roberto
Burlington, Earl of
Burn, William
Burnham, Daniel H.
Burton, Decimus
Burton, James
Butterfield, William
Cameron, Charles
Campbell, Colen
Candela, Felix
Carr, John
Carrère and Hastings
Castellamonte, Carlo
Chalgrin, Jean-François
Chambers, William
Chermayeff, Serge Ivan
Churriguera Family
Coates, Wells
Cockerell, C. R.
Cockerell, Samuel Pepys
Coducci, Mauro
Comper, John Ninian
Cormier, Ernest
Cortona, Pietro da
Costa, Lucio
Cram, Ralph Adams
Cret, Paul Philippe
Cuvilliés, François
Cuypers, P. J. H.
Dakin, James H.

Howells, John Mead
Hunt, Richard Morris
Hurtado, Francisco
Iktinos
Isozaki, Arata
Jacobsen, Arne
Jahn, Helmut
Japelli, Giuseppe
Jefferson, Thomas
Jenney, William Le Baron
Jensen-Klint, Peder Vilhelm
Johnson, Philip
Jones, Inigo
Jones, Owen
Juvarra, Filippo
Kahn, Albert
Kahn, Ely Jacques
Kahn, Louis
Kallikrates
Karfík, Vladimír
Kent, William
Kleihues, Josef-Paul
Klenze, Leo von
Knobelsdorff, Georg Wenzeslaus von
Kotěra, Jan
Krier, Leon
Krier, Rob
Kroll, Lucien
Labrouste, Henri
Lafever, Minard
Langhans, Carl Gotthard
Lasdun, Denys
Latrobe, Benjamin H.
Laugier, Marc-Antoine
Laurana, Luciano
Laves, Georg Friedrich
Le Brun, Charles
Lechner, Ödön
Le Corbusier
Ledoux, Claude-Nicolas
Lemercier, Jacques
L'Enfant, Pierre Charles
Le Nôtre, André
Leonardo da Vinci
Lescaze, William
Lescot, Pierre
Lethaby, William Richard
Le Vau, Louis
Leverton, Thomas
Lienau, Detlef
Ligorio, Pirro
Lodoli, Carlo
Lombardo, Pietro
Longhena, Baldassare
Loos, Adolf
Louis, Victor
Lubetkin, Berthold
Ludovice, João Frederico
Lurçat, André
Lutyens, Edwin Landseer
Mackintosh, Charles Rennie

Maderno, Carlo
Maekawa, Kunio
Maiano, Giuliano da
Maki, Fumihiko
Mansart, François
Marchionni, Carlo
Markelius, Sven
Matthew, Robert Hogg
May, Hugh
Maybeck, Bernard
McIntire, Samuel
McKim, Mead and White
Meier, Richard
Melnikov, Konstantin
Mendelsohn, Erich
Michelangelo
Michelozzo di Bartolomeo
Mies van der Rohe, Ludwig
Mills, Robert
Mnesikles
Montuori, Eugenio
Moore, Charles W.
Moosbrugger, Caspar
Morgan, Julia
Morris, William
Moser, Karl
Mulholland, Roger
Mullett, Alfred B.
Nash, John
Nervi, Pier Luigi
Nesfield, William Eden
Neumann, Johann Balthasar
Neutra, Richard
Niemeyer, Oscar
Nolli, Giovanni Battista
Notman, John
Nowicki, Matthew
Nyrop, Martin
O'Gorman, Juan
Olbrich, Joseph Maria
Oliveira, Mateus Vicente de
Olmsted, Frederick Law
Oppenord, Gilles-Marie
Östberg, Ragnar
Otto, Frei
Oud, J. J. P.
Paesschen, Hans Hendrik van
Paine, James
Palladio, Andrea
Parker and Unwin
Parler Family
Parris, Alexander
Paxton, Joseph
Peabody and Stearns
Pearce, Edward Lovett
Pearson, John Loughborough
Pei, I. M.
Pelli, Cesar
Percier and Fontaine
Perrault, Claude
Perret, Auguste

Geographic Index

A listing of architects according to the country in which their principal works were constructed.

Ancient Greece and Rome

Apollodorus of Damascus
Hermogenes
Hippodamos of Miletos
Iktinos
Kallikrates
Mnesikles
Rabirius
Vitruvius

Argentina

Testa, Clorindo

Australia

Andrews, John
Seidler, Harry

Austria

Ferstel, Heinrich von
Fischer von Erlach, Johann Bernhard
Hansen, Theophilus
Hildebrandt, Johann Lukas von
Hoffmann, Josef
Hollein, Hans
Krier, Rob
Loos, Adolf
Olbrich, Joseph Maria
Prandtauer, Jacob
Semper, Gottfried
Sitte, Camillo
Wagner, Otto

Belgium

Horta, Victor
Kroll, Lucien
Van de Velde, Henry

Brazil

Aleijadinho
Burle Marx, Roberto
Costa, Lucio
Niemeyer, Oscar
Reidy, Affonso
Warchavchik, Gregori

Canada

Cormier, Ernest
Erickson, Arthur
Safdie, Moshe

Czechoslovakia

Dientzenhofer, Kilian Ignaz
Fuchs, Bohuslav
Gočár, Josef
Havlíček, Josef
Karfík, Vladimír
Kotěra, Jan
Santini-Aichel, Johann

Denmark

Bindesbøll, Gottlieb
Fisker, Kay
Hansen, C. F.
Hansen, Hans Christian
Jacobsen, Arne
Jensen-Klint, Peder Vilhelm
Nyrop, Martin
Petersen, Carl
Utzon, Jørn

England

Adam, Robert
Archer, Thomas

Arup, Ove
Ashbee, C. R.
Baker, Herbert
Barry, Charles
Basevi, George
Bentley, John Francis
Bodley, George Frederick
Bonomi, Joseph
Bridgeman, Charles
Brodrick, Cuthbert
Brown, Capability
Brunel, Isambard K.
Burges, William
Burlington, Earl of
Burton, Decimus
Burton, James
Butterfield, William
Campbell, Colen
Carr, John
Chambers, William
Coates, Wells
Cockerell, C. R.
Cockerell, Samuel Pepys
Comper, John Ninian
Dance, George the Elder
Dance, George the Younger
Ellis, Peter
Emberton, Joseph
Erskine, Ralph
Foster, Norman
Fry, E. Maxwell
Gibberd, Frederick
Gibbs, James
Harrison, Thomas
Hawksmoor, Nicholas
Henry of Reyns
Holden, Charles
Holland, Henry
Jones, Inigo
Jones, Owen
Kent, William
Krier, Leon
Lasdun, Denys
Lethaby, William Richard
Leverton, Thomas
Lubetkin, Berthold
Lutyens, Edwin
Matthew, Robert Hogg
May, Hugh
Morris, William
Nash, John
Nesfield, W. Eden
Paine, James
Parker, Barry (Parker and Unwin)
Paxton, Joseph
Pearson, John Loughborough
Pratt, Roger
Prior, Edward
Pugin, A. W. N.
Repton, Humphry
Roberts, Henry

Rogers, Richard
Ruskin, John
Salvin, Anthony
Scott, George Gilbert
Scott, Giles Gilbert
Scott, M. H. Baillie
Shaw, Richard Norman
Smirke, Robert
Smithson, Alison
Smithson, Peter
Smythson, Robert
Soane, John
Spence, Basil
Stirling, James
Street, George Edmund
Stuart, James
Talman, William
Taylor, Robert
Telford, Thomas
Townsend, Charles Harrison
Unwin, Raymond (Parker and Unwin)
Upjohn, Richard
Vanbrugh, John
Voysey, Charles F. A.
Waterhouse, Alfred
Webb, Aston
Webb, Philip Speakman
Wilkins, William
William of Sens
Williams, Owen
Wood, John the Elder (Wood Family)
Wood, John the Younger (Wood Family)
Wren, Christopher
Wyatt, James
Wyatville, Jeffry
Yevele, Henry
Yorke, F. R. S.

Finland

Aalto, Alvar
Bryggman, Erik
Engel, Carl Ludwig
Ervi, Aarne
Pietilä, Reima and Raili
Ruusuvuori, Aarno
Saarinen, Eliel
Sonck, Lars Eliel

France

Antoine, Jacques-Denis
Bélanger, François-Joseph
Blondel, Jacques-François
Boffrand, Germain
Boullée, Etienne-Louis
Brongniart, Alexandre-Théodore
Chalgrin, Jean-François
De Brosse, Salomon

De Cotte, Robert
De l'Orme, Philibert
De Wailly, Charles
Du Cerceau Family
Durand, J. N. L.
Eiffel, Gustave
Fontaine, Pierre-François-Léonard (Percier and Fontaine)
Gabriel, Ange-Jacques
Garnier, Charles
Garnier, Tony
Gondouin, Jacques
Guimard, Hector
Hardouin-Mansart, Jules
Haussmann, Georges-Eugène
Hennebique, François
Hittorff, Jacques Ignace
Labrouste, Henri
Laugier, Marc-Antoine
Le Brun, Charles
Le Corbusier
Ledoux, Claude-Nicolas
Lemercier, Jacques
Le Nôtre, André
Lescot, Pierre
Le Vau, Louis
Louis, Victor
Lurçat, André
Mansart, François
Oppenord, Gilles-Marie
Percier, Charles (Percier and Fontaine)
Perrault, Claude
Perret, Auguste
Primaticcio, Francesco
Prouvé, Jean
Rondelet, Jean-Baptiste
Soufflot, Jacques-Germain
Tschumi, Bernard
Vauban, Sébastien le Prestre de
Villard de Honnecourt
Viollet-le-Duc, Eugène Emmanuel

Germany

Asam Brothers
Bähr, Georg
Behnisch, Günther
Behrens, Peter
Böhm, Dominikus
Böhm, Gottfried
Cuvilliés, François
Dientzenhofer Brothers
Du Ry, Simon
Eiermann, Egon
Endell, August
Erdmannsdorff, Friedrich Wilhelm von
Feuchtmayer, Josef Anton
Fischer, Johann Michael
Gilly, Friedrich
Gropius, Walter
Gärtner, Friedrich von

Häring, Hugo
Hilberseimer, Ludwig
Höger, Fritz
Holl, Elias
Kleihues, Josef-Paul
Klenze, Leo von
Knobelsdorff, Georg Wenzeslaus von
Langhans, Carl Gotthard
Laves, Georg Friedrich
Mendelsohn, Erich
Neumann, Johann Balthasar
Otto, Frei
Parler Family
Pöppelmann, Matthaeus D.
Scharoun, Hans
Schickhardt, Heinrich
Schinkel, Karl Friedrich
Schlüter, Andreas
Taut, Bruno
Thumb, Michael
Thumb, Peter
Ungers, Oswald Mathias
Weinbrenner, Friedrich
Zimmermann Brothers
Zuccalli, Enrico

Hungary

Lechner, Ödön

Ireland

Deane, Thomas (Deane and Woodward)
Deane, Thomas Newenham (Deane and Woodward)
Gandon, James
Mulholland, Roger
Pearce, Edward Lovett
Woodward, Benjamin (Deane and Woodward)

Italy

Alberti, Leon Battista
Albini, Franco
Alessi, Galeazzo
Ammannati, Bartolomeo
Arnolfo di Cambio
Banfi, Gianluigi (Banfi, Belgiojoso, Peresutti and Rogers)
Basile, Ernesto
Belgiojoso, Lodovico (Banfi, Belgiojoso, Peresutti and Rogers)
Bernini, Giovanni Lorenzo
Borromini, Francesco
Bramante, Donato
Brunelleschi, Filippo
Buontalenti, Bernardo

Castellamonte, Carlo
Coducci, Mauro
Cortona, Pietro da
D'Aronco, Raimondo
Del Duca, Giacomo
De Rossi, Giovanni Antonio
Fanzago, Cosimo
Filarete, Il
Fontana, Carlo
Francesco di Giorgio
Fuga, Ferdinando
Galilei, Alessandro
Ghiberti, Lorenzo
Giulio Romano
Gruppo 7
Guarini, Guarino
Japelli, Giuseppe
Juvarra, Filippo
Laurana, Luciano
Leonardo Da Vinci
Ligorio, Pirro
Lodoli, Carlo
Lombardo, Pietro
Longhena, Baldassare
Maderno, Carlo
Maiano, Giuliano da
Marchionni, Carlo
Michelangelo
Michelozzo di Bartolomeo
Montuori, Eugenio
Nervi, Pier Luigi
Nolli, Giovanni Battista
Palladio, Andrea
Peresutti, Enrico (Banfi, Belgiojoso, Peresutti and Rogers)
Peruzzi, Baldassare
Piacentini, Marcello
Piranesi, Giovanni Battista
Ponti, Gio
Porta, Giacomo della
Pozzo, Andrea
Raguzzini, Filippo
Rainaldi, Carlo
Raphael
Ricchino, Francesco
Rogers, Ernesto Nathan (Banfi, Belgiojoso, Peresutti and Rogers)
Rossellino, Bernardo
Rossi, Aldo
Rossi, Mattia de
Sangallo, Antonio da, the Younger
Sangallo, Guiliano da
Sanmicheli, Michele
Sansovino, Jacopo
Sant'Elia, Antonio
Scamozzi, Vincenzo
Scarpa, Carlo
Serlio, Sebastiano
Sommaruga, Giuseppe
Terragni, Giuseppe
Valadier, Giuseppe

Vanvitelli, Luigi
Vasari, Giorgio
Vignola, Giacomo Barozzi da
Vittone, Bernardo

Japan

Ando, Tadao
Isozaki, Arata
Maekawa, Kunio
Maki, Fumihiko
Raymond, Antonin
Shinohara, Kazuo
Tange, Kenzo

Mexico

Barrágan, Luis
O'Gorman, Juan
Villagran Garcia, José

Netherlands

Bakema, Jacob B. (Van den Broek and Bakema)
Berlage, Hendrik Petrus
Brinkman, Johannes Andreas (Van der Vlugt and Brinkman)
Cuypers, P. J. H.
De Key, Lieven
De Keyser, Hendrick
De Klerk, Michel
Dudok, Willem Marinus
Duiker, Johannes
Hertzberger, Herman
Oud, J. J. P.
Paesschen, Hans Hendrik van
Post, Pieter
Rietveld, Gerrit
Van Campen, Jacob
Van den Broek, Johannes Hendrik (Van Den Broek and Bakema)
Van der Vlugt, Leendert Cornelius (Van Der Vlugt and Brinkman)
Van Doesburg, Theo
Van Eyck, Aldo
Vingboons, Justus
Vingboons, Philips

Norway

Grosch, Christian Heinrich

Portugal

Ludovice, João Frederico

Oliveira, Mateus Vicente de
Torralva, Diogo de

Russia

Bazhenov, Vasili Ivanovich
Cameron, Charles
Ginsburg, Moisei
Melnikov, Konstantin
Quarenghi, Giacomo
Rastrelli, Bartolomeo
Rossi, Karl Ivanovich
Shchusev, Aleksei V.
Shekhtel, Fedor
Thomon, Thomas de
Ton, Konstantin A.
Vesnin Brothers
Zakharov, Adrian D.

Scotland

Adam, William
Bruce, William
Burn, William
Hamilton, Thomas
Mackintosh, Charles Rennie
Playfair, William Henry
Rennie, John
Smith, James
Thomson, Alexander

Spain

Bofill, Ricardo
Churriguera Family
Domènech, Lluís
Gaudí, Antonio
Gil de Hontañón, Rodrigo
Gomez de Mora, Juan
Guas, Juan
Herrera, Juan de
Hurtado, Francisco
Rodríguez, Ventura
Sert, Josep Lluís
Siloe, Diego de
Simón de Colonia
Toledo, Juan Bautista de
Tomé, Narciso
Vazquez, Lorenzo
Villanueva, Juan de

Sweden

Adelcrantz, Carl Fredrik
Almqvist, Osvald
Asplund, Erik Gunnar

Markelius, Sven Gottfrid
Östberg, Ragnar
Tengbom, Ivar
Tessin Family

Switzerland

Botta, Mario
Moser, Karl
Moosbrugger, Caspar

Turkey

Sinan

United States

Abramovitz, Max (Harrison and Abramovitz)
Ammann, Othmar
Atwood, Charles
Austin, Henry
Bacon, Henry
Barnes, Edward Larrabee
Belluschi, Pietro
Benjamin, Asher
Bogardus, James
Breuer, Marcel
Bulfinch, Charles
Burnham, Daniel H.
Candela, Felix
Carrère, John Mervin (Carrère and Hastings)
Chermayeff, Serge Ivan
Cram, Ralph Adams
Cret, Paul Philippe
Dakin, James H.
Davis, Alexander Jackson
Downing, A. J.
Eames, Charles O.
Eidlitz, Leopold
Eisenman, Peter
Elmslie, George Grant
Flagg, Ernest
Fuller, R. Buckminster
Furness, Frank
Gallier, James, Sr.
Gehry, Frank O.
Gilbert, Cass
Gill, Irving
Giurgola, Romaldo
Godefroy, Maximilian
Goff, Bruce
Goodhue, Bertram Grosvenor
Graves, Michael
Greene, Charles and Henry
Griffin, Walter Burley
Gwathmey, Charles
Hadfield, George

Harrison, Peter
Harrison, Wallace K. (Harrison and Abramovitz)
Hastings, Thomas (Carrère and Hastings)
Haviland, John
Hejduk, John
Holabird, William (Holabird and Roche)
Hood, Raymond M.
Howe, George
Howells, John Mead
Hunt, Richard Morris
Jahn, Helmut
Jefferson, Thomas
Jenney, William Le Baron
Johnson, Philip
Kahn, Albert
Kahn, Ely Jacques
Kahn, Louis I.
Lafever, Minard
Latrobe, Benjamin H.
L'Enfant, Pierre Charles
Lescaze, William
Lienau, Detlef
Maybeck, Bernard
McIntire, Samuel
McKim, Charles Follen (McKim, Mead and White)
Mead, William Rutherford (McKim, Mead and White)
Meier, Richard
Merrill, John (Skidmore, Owings and Merrill)
Mies van der Rohe, Ludwig
Mills, Robert
Moore, Charles
Morgan, Julia
Mullett, Alfred B.
Neutra, Richard
Notman, John
Nowicki, Matthew
Olmsted, Frederick Law
Owings, Nathaniel (Skidmore, Owings and Merrill)
Parris, Alexander
Peabody, Robert Swain (Peabody and Stearns)
Pei, I. M.
Pelli, Cesar
Platt, Charles Adams
Pope, John Russell
Post, George Browne
Potter, Edward T.
Potter, William A.
Price, Bruce

Renwick, James
Richardson, H. H.
Roche, Kevin
Roche, Martin (Holabird and Roche)
Roebling, John Augustus
Roebling, Washington Augustus
Rogers, Isaiah
Root, John Wellborn
Rudolph, Paul Marvin
Saarinen, Eero
Schindler, R. M.
Skidmore, Louis (Skidmore, Owings and Merrill)
Sloan, Samuel
Soleri, Paolo
Stearns, John Goddard (Peabody and Stearns)
Stern, Robert A. M.
Stone, Edward Durell
Strickland, William
Sturgis, John Hubbard
Sturgis, Russell
Sullivan, Louis
The Architects Collaborative (TAC)
Thornton, William
Tigerman, Stanley
Town, Ithiel
Trumbauer, Horace
Van Brunt, Henry
Van Osdel, John Mills
Vaux, Calvert
Venturi, Robert
Walter, Thomas U.
Wank, Roland
White, Stanford
Wright, Frank Lloyd
Yamasaki, Minoru
Young, Ammi B.

Venezuela

Villanueva, Carlos Raúl

Yugoslavia

Plečnik, Jože

International Dictionary of Architects and Architecture - 1
ARCHITECTS

AALTO, Alvar.

Finnish. Born in Kuortane, near Jyväskylä, Finland, 3 February 1898. Died in Helsinki, Finland, 11 May 1976. Married Aino Marsio (died in 1949), 1924; two children; married Elissa Mäkiniemi, 1952. Studied at Helsinki Polytechnic, 1916-21. Worked as an exhibition designer in Göteborg, Sweden, then in Tampere and Turku, Finland, 1921-22; practiced privately in Jyväskylä, Finland, 1923-27, then in Turku, 1927-33, and Helsinki, 1933-76. Professor of experimental architecture, Massachusetts Institute of Technology, Cambridge, Massachusetts, U.S.A., 1946-47. Member, Academy of Finland, 1955; honorary member, Akademie der Künste, Berlin; honorary fellow, American Institute of Architects; Gold Medal, Royal Institute of British Architects, 1957.

Chronology of Works
All in Finland unless noted

1923-24	Railway Employees Housing, Jyväskylä
1924-25	Workers Club, Jyväskylä
1925	Civil Guard House, Seinäjoki
1927	Municipal Hospital, Alajärvi
1927-29	Civil Guard House, Jyväskylä
1927-29	Parish Church, Muurame
1927-29	Southwestern Agricultural Cooperative, Turku
1933-35	Municipal Library, Viipuri
1928-29	Standard Apartment for Tapani, Turku
1928-30	Newspaper Plant and Offices, Turun Sanomat, Turku
1929	700th Anniversary Fair, Turku (with Erik Bryggman)
1929-33	Tuberculosis Sanatorium, Paimio
1934-36	Alvar Aalto House, Helsinki
1937	Finnish Pavilion, World's Fair, Paris, France
1937	Savoy Restaurant, Helsinki
1937-38	Villa Mairea, Noormarkku
1938-40	Finnish Pavilion, World's Fair, New York, U.S.A.
1938-40	Terraced Housing, Kauttua
1941	Kokemäki River Valley Master Plan
1944	Stromberg Housing Development, Vaasa
1944-45	Rovaniemi Town Plan
1944-47	Stromberg Meter Factory and Terrace Housing, Vaasa
1946-49	Baker Dormitory, Massachusetts Institute of Technology, Cambridge, Massachusetts, U.S.A.
1950-52	Town Hall, Säynätsalo
1952-56	National Pension Bank, Helsinki
1953-55	Alvar Aalto House, Muuratsalo
1953-55	Rautatalo Office Building, Helsinki
1953-56	Alvar Aalto Studio, Munkkiniemi
1955-64	Finnish Institute of Technology, Otaniemi (main building)
1956-58	Vuoksenniska Church, Imatra
1956-59	Maison Louis Carre, Bazoches sur Guyonne, France
1958-60	Parish Church, Seinäjoki
1958-63	Cultural Center, Wolfsburg, Germany
1958-65	Civic Center, Seinäjoki
1959-62	Central Finnish Museum, Jyväskylä
1956-62	Enso-Gutzeit Company Headquarters, Helsinki
1961-89	Opera House, Essen, Germany
1962-75	Finlandia Hall Concert and Convention Center, Helsinki
1963-68	Library, Rovaniemi
1965-70	Library, Mount Angel Benedictine College, Mount Angel, Oregon, U.S.A.
1969-73	Art Museum, Aalborg, Denmark
1972-78	Riola Parish Center, Bologna, Italy
1972-78	Theater, Rovaniemi

Publications

BOOKS BY AALTO

An Experimental Town. Cambridge, Massachusetts, 1940.
Post-War Reconstruction: Rehousing Research in Finland. New York, 1941.
Synopsis. Stuttgart, 1970.

ARTICLES BY AALTO

''The Humanizing of Architecture.'' *Technology Review* (Cambridge, Massachusetts, November 1940). Reprinted in *Architectural Forum* (December 1940).
''The Decadence of Public Buildings.'' *Arkkitehti* 9/10 (1953).
''Diversity, Relevance and Representation in Architecture.'' *Architectural Record* (June 1982).

BOOKS ABOUT AALTO

BAIRD, GEORGE: *Alvar Aalto.* New York, 1970.
BLASER, WERNER: *Alvar Aalto als Designer.* Stuttgart, 1982.
CRESTI, CARLO: *Alvar Aalto.* Florence, 1975.
DUNSTER, DAVID (ed.): *Alvar Aalto.* New York, 1979.
FELIX, ZDENEK (ed.): *Alvar Aalto: das architektonische Werk* Exhibition catalog. Essen, West Germany, 1979.
FLEIG, KARL (ed.): *Alvar Aalto 1922-1978.* 3 vols. Zürich, London, and New York, 1963-78.
FUTAGAWA, YUKIO ET AL: *Alvar Aalto.* Tokyo, 1968, revised English edition as *Alvar Aalto* by George Baird and Yukio Futagawa. London, 1970.
GIRSBERGER, H.: *Alvar Aalto.* London, 1963.
GROAK S., and RAUTSI, J.: *The Alvar Aalto Guide.* Princeton, New Jersey, 1989.
GROAK, STEVEN; HEIHONEN, LIISA; and PORPHYRIOS, DEMETRI: *Alvar Aalto, Architectural Monographs 4.* London, 1978.

Alvar Aalto: Town Hall, Säynätsalo, Finland, 1950-52

GUTHEIM, FREDERICK A.: *Alvar Aalto*. New York, 1960.

McANDREW, J., and BREINES, S.: *Alvar Aalto: Architecture and Furniture*. New York, 1938.

MIKKOLA, KIRMO (ed.): *Alvar Aalto versus the Modern Movement*. Helsinki, 1981.

MOSSO, LEONARDO: *L'opera di Alvar Aalto*. Exhibition catalog. Milan, 1965.

MOSSO, LEONARDO: *Alvar Aalto*. Helsinki, 1967.

NEUENSCHWANDER, EDOUARD and CLAUDIA: *Alvar Aalto and Finnish Architecture*. London and New York, 1954.

PALLASMAA, JUHANI (ed.): *Alvar Aalto Furniture*. Helsinki, 1984.

PAULSSON, THOMAS: *Scandinavian Architecture*. London, 1959.

PEARSON, DAVID PAUL: *Alvar Aalto and the International Style*. London, 1989.

PORPHYRIOS, DEMETRI: *Sources of Modern Eclecticism: Studies on Alvar Aalto*. London, 1982.

QUANTRILL, MALCOLM: *Alvar Aalto: A Critical Study*. New York, 1983.

RUBINO, LUCIANO: *Aino and Alvar Aalto: tutto il design*. Rome, 1980.

RUUSUVUORI, AARNE (ed.): *Alvar Aalto, 1898-1976*. Exhibition catalog, Helsinki, 1978.

SALOKORPI, ASKO: *Modern Architecture in Finland*. London, 1970.

SCHILDT, GÖRAN: *Alvar Aalto*. 3 vols. New York, 1984-91.

SCHILDT, GÖRAN (ed): *Sketches, Alvar Aalto*. Cambridge, Massachusetts, and London, 1978.

SCHILDT, GÖRAN, and MOSSO, LEONARDO: *Alvar Aalto*. Jyväskylä, Finland, 1962.

SCHILDT, GÖRAN: *Det vita bordet: Alvar Aaltos ungdom och grundlagganda konstnarlis ideer*. Stockholm, 1982.

WICKBERG, NILS ERIK: *Finnish Architecture*. Helsinki, 1962.

ARTICLES ABOUT AALTO

"Aalto Revisited." *Architectural Forum*. (April 1966).

"Alvar Aalto: Finland's Modern Master." *Architectural Forum* (April 1938).

"Alvar Aalto: His Life, Work and Philosophy." Special issue of *L'Architecture d'ujourd'hui* (June, 1977).

"Alvar Aalto: The Man and His Work." Special issue of *Arkkitehti* Nos. 7/8 (1976).

"Alvar Aalto." *Progressive Architecture* 58 (April 1977): 53-77.

"Alvar Aalto." Special issue of *Architectural Association Quarterly* 3 (1978).

"Alvar Aalto." Special issue of *Space Design* (January/February 1977).

BAIRD, GEORGE: "Reflections on the Influence of Alvar Aalto." *Canadian Architect* (May 1977).

BANHAM, REYNER: "The One and the Few: The Rise of Modern Architecture in Finland." *Architectural Review* (April 1957): 243-259.

BURCHARD, JOHN E.: "Finland and Architect Aalto." *Architectural Record* 125 (January 1959).

HITCHCOCK, HENRY-RUSSELL: "Aalto versus Aalto: The Other Finland." *Perspecta* No. 9/10 (1965): 132-166.

HODGKINSON, P.: "Finlandia Hall, Helsinki." *Architectural Review* (June 1972): 341-343.

KAY, JANE HOLTZ: "Aalto Ego" *Building Design* (August 1973).

KLIMENT, ROBERT M.: "Alvar Aalto in Context." *Architectural Record* (September 1981).

MENDINI, ALESSANDRO: "L'Opera di Alvar Aalto." *Casabella* (November 1965).

MOSSO, LEONARDO (ed.): "Alvar Aalto." *Architecture d'aujourd'hui* special issue (June 1977).

OYARZUM, FERNANDO PEREZ: "Alvar Aalto in Barcelona Again." *Arquitecturas bis* (April-June 1981).

RACE, E.: "Trends in Factory-Made Furniture." *Architectural Review* No. 617 (1948).

RICHARDS, JAMES M.: "Hvitträsk." *Architectural Review* 139, No. 828 (February 1966): 152-154.

SALOKORPI, ASKO: "Currents and Undercurrents in Finnish Architecture." *Apollo* (May 1982).

SANTINI, CARLO, and SCHILDT, GÖRAN: "Alvar Aalto from Sunila to Imatra: Ideas, Projects and Buildings." *Zodiac* 3 (1958): 27-82.

SANTINI, CARLO: "Il lungo cammino di Alvar Aalto." *Domus* (January 1951).

SHAND, P. MORTON: "The Work of Alvar Aalto." *Architectural Review* (September 1931).

SHAND, P. MORTON: "The Library at Viipuri, Eastern Finland." *Architectural Review* 79 (March 1936): 107-114.

SHAND, P. MORTON: "Tuberculosis Sanatorium, Paimio, Finland." *Architectural Review* (September 1933): 85-90.

SHARP, DENNIS: "Aalto and his Influence." *Architecture and Building* (December 1957): 476-79.

SMITHSON, ALISON and PETER: "Alvar Aalto." *Arkkitehti* (August 1976).

SMITHSON, PETER: "Alvar Aalto and the Ethos of the Second Generation." *Arkkitehti* Nos. 7/8 (1967).

SUHONEN, PEKKA: "Aalto Literature: Architecture in Buildings and Ideas." *Arkkitehti* No. 2 (1980).

VENTURI, ROBERT, et al.: "On Aalto." *Quaderna* (April/June 1983).

VENTURI, ROBERT: "Learning from Aalto." *Progressive Architecture* (April 1977).

*

Though Alvar Aalto is considered a modern architect, his architecture exhibits a carefully maintained balance of complex forms, spaces and elements, and a traditionalism rooted in the cultural heritages and physical environment of Finland. Unlike his contemporaries, Aalto did not rely on industrialized processes as a compositional technique, but forged an architecture influenced by a broad spectrum of concerns. Aalto's architecture manifests an understanding of the psychological needs of modern society, the particular qualities of the Finnish milieu, and the historical, technical and cultural traditions of Scandinavian architecture. To achieve these qualities, Aalto began with simple formal propositions, which received multiple layers of expression through the process of design. This stands in contrast to current tendencies, which are based upon complex theoretical foundations, yet achieve only single-dimension realization.

Even as a student, Aalto desired to be the architectural "top dog." Given his provincial background, this might have appeared as idle boasting, but he had a competitive personality and an ability to quickly seize a situation. Entering Helsinki Polytechnic in 1916, Aalto became a protégé of Armas Lindgren (partner of Eliel Saarinen and Herman Gesellius during the National Romantic era), and was further influenced by Polytechnic instructors Usko Nyström and Carolus Lindberg. Upon graduation in 1921, Aalto sought employment with Gunnar Asplund in Stockholm, though he settled for a position with Arvid Bjerke in Göteborg.

When Aalto opened his Jyväskylä office in 1923, a classical revival was flowering throughout Scandinavia. The work of Asplund and Ragnar Östberg, coupled with the simplicity of the vernacular architecture of northern Italy, provided the major sources for expression for Finnish architects. Aalto quickly mastered its tenets. His buildings of that period—the Workers Club in Jyväskylä (1924-25), the Seinäjoki Civil Guards Complex (1925), the Jyväskylä Civil Guards Building (1927) and the Muurame Church (1927-29)—are composed of simple, well-proportioned volumes rendered in stucco or wood, with sparse decoration and selective use of classical elements. While securing local commissions, Aalto also followed the normal Finnish practice of participating in architectural competitions. Among his best designs of the period are several unbuilt competition entries, including the church proposals for Jämsä (1925), Töölö (1927) and Viinikka (1927). Qualities emerged in both built works and competitive entries that foretold themes that occurred in Aalto's later work: courtyards acted as primary organizing devices for his buildings, unique program elements often received elaborate volumetric expression, and there was a sense of whimsy and playfulness in his details.

In 1924 Aalto married the architect Aino Marsio (1894-1949), who was an equal partner in their work until her death in 1949. Aino's influence informed building design as well as the creation of furniture and applied art objects, and together husband and wife formed a symbiotic unit, complementing and contrasting one another.

Winning the 1927 competition for the Southwestern Agricultural Cooperative Building in Turku was of major importance for the Aaltos. Moving the office soon after to the more cosmopolitan city of Turku, the couple developed numerous contacts that proved important to their development. Friendships with Erik Bryggman, coupled with Turku's proximity to Sweden, led to associations with Asplund, Sven Markelius and the continental architectural avant-garde. Aalto became an active polemicist advancing the cause of modern architecture in Finland. Attending the 1929 CIAM (Congrès Internationaux d'Architecture Moderne) meeting, and traveling regularly throughout Europe, set him among the most knowledgeable of Finnish architects on "modern architecture." Hilding Ekelund commented wryly on Aalto's quick mastery of functionalist ideas in a 1930 essay: "With the same ardent enthusiasm as the academics of the 1880s drew Roman baroque portals, Gothic pinnacles, etc., in their sketch books for use in their architectural practice, Alvar Aalto noses out new, rational-technical details from all over Europe which he then makes use of and transforms with considerable skill."

Aalto's understanding of the avant-garde design tenets was demonstrated in the evolution of his work from the austere classicist Southwestern Agricultural Cooperative (1927-29) toward a full expression of the formal and theoretical canons of "functionalism" (the Finnish term for modernism) witnessed in the Turku Standard Apartment Block (1929) and *Turun Sanomat* Newspaper building (1928-30). The *Turun Sanomat* was the first Finnish building to incorporate Le Corbusier's "five points of a new architecture," while Turku's Seventh Centenary Exhibition (designed with Erik Bryggman) and the Paimio Tuberculosis Sanatorium (1929-33) witnessed Aalto's awareness of Russian constructivism, the Dutch De Stijl, and the work of Johannes Duiker, André Lurçat and Laszlo Moholy-Nagy. This activism did not always sit well with the more conservative of the Finnish architectural community, and once during a Society of Finnish Architects social event, Aalto was accused of being a "Bolshevik."

The six years spent in Turku saw Aalto's reputation change from that of provincial practitioner to one of international stature. Furniture design contributed significantly to that enhanced reputation. Beginning with the stackable chair for the Agricultural Cooperative, by the time the Paimio Sanatorium was complete, the famous continuously curving, bent plywood chair had evolved. Moving their office to Helsinki in 1933 in hopes that the capital would provide more commissions, the Aaltos initially spent more time doing competition entries and developing furniture and glassware designs. The curved, free forms of those applied designs emerged as architectural elements, spaces and forms beginning in the mid-1930s. In that important period of transition, Aalto's work assumed a more tactile and picturesque posture, becoming less machine-like in imagery. Coupled with a rekindled interest in Finnish vernacular building traditions and a concern for the alienated individual within modern mass society, these changes signaled Aalto's movement away from the technical functionalism of the early 1930s to a more personal style, which achieved maturity after World War II.

Specific architectural concerns and elements emerged that formed a continuity of thought and expression throughout the remainder of Aalto's career. The presence of an exterior courtyard space or a court-like interior atrium became a principal organizational strategy in Aalto's work. The Viipuri Library (1927-35) and the Finnish Pavilion for the 1937 Paris World's Fair incorporated an interior court, while the Villa Mairea (1937-38) was ordered around an exterior courtyard. The conical skylights illuminating the Viipuri reading room and Paris Pavilion exhibition area provided a sense of externality to each space, and were precursors to the numerous forms Aalto developed for bringing natural light into his spaces. The Viipuri reading room includes staircases, landings and handrails as dynamic elements celebrating human action and movement. Sinuousity appears: an important compositional theme in Aalto's work, as witnessed in the undulating ceiling of the Viipuri Library meeting room, the three-story flowing display wall in the Finnish Pavilion for the 1939 New York World's Fair, and the figural geometries found in the plan of the Villa Mairea. Exploring the tectonic possibilities of the undulating surface, he demonstrated a unique sensitivity to the dynamics of the sinuous element in architecture. Aalto's material vocabulary became more expressive and textural. Wood and brick, among other materials, created a tactility and richness of surface and expression complementing the formal changes in Aalto's work. These changes codify the qualities now so inextricably associated with his oeuvre. Moreover, they exist at a multiplicity of scales of realization in his buildings. The sinuous element is not merely a building element or spatial construct, but assumes another presence as furniture, glassware, light fixture, and door handle and handrail.

Between 1945 and the early 1960s, Aalto enjoyed an incredibly productive period—one lauded as being uniquely Finnish in feeling. Characterized by the use of red brick, copper and wood, exemplary works include the Säynätsalo Town Hall (1950-52), Jyväskylä Teachers College (1953-56), and Technical Institute in Otaniemi (1956-64); and in Helsinki, the Public Pensions Institute (1952-56), Rautatalo Building (1953-56) and House of Culture (1955-58). The picturesque massing of these buildings, their responsiveness to site, the juxtaposition of materials and textural effects, the rich manipulation of natural light, and concern for detail too, demonstrate Aalto's maturity. The themes of the late 1930s evolved and solidified, achieving a calm, self-assured realization. The atrium or courtyard continued to be an essential organizational strategy. From the small courtyards in Aalto's summer house (1953) and studio (1955) to the plaza spaces in the Säynätsalo Town Hall and House of Culture, to the agora of the Teachers College, Aalto used the exterior court to order and regulate these complexes. Similarly, the multilevel skylighted atria found in the Rautatalo Building, Public Pensions Institute and the Teachers College assumed the quality of protected external spaces. The large serpentine walls of the Massachusetts Institute of Technology's Baker House Dormitory (1946-49) and the House of Culture spoke of sinuosity with new vitality. Several competition entries transformed the undulating line into the fan-shaped plans and forms of numerous Aalto libraries, housing complexes and auditoriums.

The last 20 years of Aalto's practice, beginning with the Vuoksenniska Church (1956-58), produced a more complex, expressive architecture contrasting with the "bronze" imagery of the 1940s and 1950s. There is thematic continuity with his earlier work—light, sinuosity, courtyards and tactility still figured importantly in the designs—yet more explicit references to classical and romantic ordering sensibilities emerged at that time. Eschewing the simple duality of pairing organic and geometric elements, these works seem to fuse both classical restraint and romantic exuberance. The Seinäjoki Civic Complex (1958-65), the Wolfsburg Cultural Complex (1958-63), Finlandia Hall (1962-65), the Rovaniemi Library (1968) and the Riola Church (1966-78), along with Vuoksenniska, represent the best work of the late period.

During his 50-year career, Aalto developed a rich and complex architectural language that explored the full range of expressive means available to the architect. His concerns were architectural ones addressed through the process of designing and building. The unique variety of architectural responses he created resulted from the fact that he never forgot the role and purpose of the architect. Alvar Aalto believed architecture to be an affirmative act, and the architect's purpose to design and build. Through responsive and responsible design, Aalto was able to create an architecture that was extremely humane, yet profoundly tangible.

—WILLIAM C. MILLER

ADAM, Robert.

Scottish. Born in Kirkcaldy, Scotland, 3 July 1728. Died in London, 3 March 1792. Father was the architect William Adam (1689-1748); brothers included the architects John Adam (1721-92) and James Adam (1732-94). Entered Edinburgh University, 1743. Apprenticed to his father, 1746-48; formed partnership with John Adam, 1748; traveled in Italy and Dalmatia, 1754-57; established own office, London, 1758; served as architect of the King's Works, 1761-69, and as surveyor of Chelsea Hospital, London, 1765. Fellow, Royal Society, 1761; Member of Parliament for Kinross, 1769.

Chronology of Works
All in England unless noted
* Approximate dates
† Work no longer exists

1758-61	Hatchlands, Surrey (interiors)
1759-60	Admiralty Screen, London
1759-71	Harewood House, Yorkshire (interiors and exterior modifications)
1760ff.	Croome Court, Worcestershire (interiors and garden buildings)

1760-67*	Compton Verney, Warwickshire (additions and alterations)
1761-69	Syon House, Middlesex (interior remodeling)
1760-71*	Kedleston Hall, Derbyshire (south front, interiors, and garden buildings)
1761-64	Shardeloes, Buckinghamshire (interiors and portico)
1761-64	Bowood House, Wiltshire (portico, interiors, and offices)†
1761-80	Osterley Park, Middlesex (remodeling)
1764	Bowood Mausoleum, Wiltshire†
1761-68*	Lansdowne House, Berkeley Square, London
1762-66	Mersham-le-Hatch, Kent
1762-71	Ugbrooke Park, Devon
1763	Croome Church, Worcestershire
1763-66	19 Arlington Street, London (alterations)†
1763-66	Audley End, Essex (interiors)
1764-66	Coventry House, Piccadilly, London (interiors)
1765-85	Nostell Priory, Yorkshire (interiors and north wing)
1766-67	Auchencruive House, Ayr, Scotland (interiors)
1766-67	Strawberry Hill, Middlesex (round room interior)
1766-74	Luton Hoo, Bedfordshire (interiors later rebuilt)
1767-69	Kenwood House, Hampstead, London (remodeling and additions)
1767-71	Shire Hall, Hertford, Hertfordshire
1767-85*	Newby Hall, Yorkshire (additions and remodeling)
1768-71	Clerk House, Duchess Street, London (remodeling)†
1768-72	The Adelphi, London†
1768-79	Saltram, Devon (interiors)
1769-74	Pulteney Bridge, Bath
1770*	British Coffee House, London
1770-74	Chandos House, London
1770-75*	Lowther Village, Westmoreland
1770-75	Mansfield Street, London
1770-75	Northumberland House, The Strand, London†
1770-78*	Mellerstain, Berwickshire, Scotland
1770-80*	Alnwick Castle, Northumberland (interiors and outbuildings)
1771-75	Headfort House, County Meath, Ireland (interiors)
1771-75	Wedderbrun Castle, Berwickshire, Scotland
1771-77*	Stowe, Buckinghamshire (south front design; altered when built)
1771-78*	Apsley House, Piccadilly, London (later remodeled)
1772-74	Royal Society of Arts, London
1772-76	Wynn House, 20 St. James's Square, London
1773-74	Derby House, 23 Grosvenor Square, London†
1773-76	Home House, 20 Portman Square, London
1774	Fête Pavilion, The Oaks, Surrey†
1774-92	Register House, Edinburgh, Scotland
1775-76	Theatre Royal, Drury Lane, London (remodeling and facade)
1775-77	Etruscan Rooms, Osterley
1776	Mistley Church, Essex†
1776-80*	Portland Place, London
1777-78	Roxburghe House, Hanover Square, London (remodeling)†
1777-79	Wormleybury, Hertfordshire (interiors)
1777-90	Culzean Castle, Ayrshire, Scotland
1778	Auchencruive House, Ayrshire, Scotland (tower)
1778	David Hume Monument, Old Calton Burying Ground, Edinburgh, Scotland
1780-88*	Cumberland House, 86 Pall Mall, London†

1780-82	Oxenfoord Castle, Midlothian, Scotland
1784-85	Brasted Place, Kent
1789	Mausoleum, Castle Upton, County Antrim, Ireland
1789-91	Newliston, West Lothian, Scotland
1789-91	Seton Castle, East Lothian, Scotland
1789-93	University of Edinburgh, Scotland (completed later in modified fashion)
1790-91	Airthrey Castle, Stirling, Scotland
1790-91	Archerfield House, East Lothian, Scotland (interiors)†
1790-92	Dunbar Castle, East Lothian, Scotland
1790-94	Fitzroy Square, London
1790-96	Belleville House (also known as Balavil House), Inverness, Scotland
1790-1800*	Gosford House, East Lothian, Scotland
1791	Walkinshaw House, Renfrew, Scotland†
1791-93*	Balbardie House, West Lothian, Scotland
1791-93	Dalkeith Bridge, Midlothian, Scotland
1791-94	Trades House, Glasgow, Scotland
1791-95	Royal Infirmary, Glasgow, Scotland†
1791-96	Mauldsley Castle, Lanark, Scotland†
1791-1807	Charlotte Square, Edinburgh, Scotland
1792-94	St. George's Episcopal Chapel, Edinburgh, Scotland
1793-94	Tron Church, Glasgow, Scotland
1796-98	Assembly Rooms, Glasgow, Scotland

Publications

BOOKS BY ADAM

Ruins of the Palace of the Emperor Diocletian at Spalatro. London, 1764.
The Works in Architecture of Robert and James Adam. With James Adam. Vols. 1-2, London, 1773-79; Vol. 3, London, 1822.

BOOKS ABOUT ADAM

BEARD, GEOFFREY: *Decorative Plasterwork in Great Britain.* London, 1975.
BEARD, GEOFFREY: *Georgian Craftsmen and Their Work.* London, 1966.
BEARD, GEOFFREY: *The Work of Robert Adam.* New York, 1978.
BOLTON, ARTHUR T.: *The Architecture of Robert and James Adam.* 2 vols. London, 1922.
Classical Architecture: A Comprehensive Handbook to the Tradition of Classical Style. New York, 1991.
CROFT-MURRAY, EDWARD: *Decorative Painting in England: 1537-1837.* 2 vols. London, 1962-71.
FITZGERALD, PERCY: *Robert Adam.* London, 1904.
FLEMING, JOHN: *Robert Adam and His Circle in Edinburgh and Rome.* London, 1962.
HARRIS, EILEEN: *The Furniture of Robert Adam.* London, 1963.
HUSSEY, CHRISTOPHER: *English Country Houses: Mid-Georgian, 1760-1800.* London, 1956.
LEES-MILNE, JAMES: *The Age of Adam.* London, 1947.
MUSGRAVE, CLIFFORD: *Adam and Hepplewhite and other Neo-Classical Furniture.* 1966.
ORESKO, ROBERT: *The Works in Architecture of Robert and James Adam.* 1975.
ROWAN, ALISTAIR J.: *Designs for Castles and Country Villas by Robert and James Adam.* London, 1985.
RYKWERT, JOSEPH and ANNE: *Robert and James Adam: The Men and the Style.* London, 1985.

Robert Adam: Syon House, Middlesex, England, 1761-69

SERVICE, ALASTAIR: *The Architects of London*. London, 1979.

STILLMAN, DAMIE: *The Decorative Work of Robert Adam*. London, 1966.

SWARBRICK, JOHN: *Robert Adam and His Brothers: Their Lives, Work and Influence on English Architecture, Decoration and Furniture*. London, 1915.

SWARBRICK, JOHN: *The Works in Architecture of Robert and James Adam*. London, 1959.

TOMLIN, MAURICE: *Catalogue of Adam Period Furniture*. London, 1972.

YARWOOD, DOREEN: *Robert Adam*. London, 1970.

YOUNGSON, A. J.: *The Making of Classical Edinburgh*. Edinburgh, 1968.

ARTICLES ABOUT ADAM

BEARD, GEOFFREY: "New Light on Adam's Craftsmen." *Country Life* 131 (1962): 1098-1100.

BEARD, GEOFFREY: "Robert Adam's Craftsmen." *Connoisseur Year Book* 26-32 (1958).

BOLTON, ARTHUR T.: "Robert Adam as a Bibliographer, Publisher and Designer of Libraries." *Transactions of the Bibliographical Society* 14 (1915-17).

BOLTON, ARTHUR T.: "The Classical and Romantic Compositions of Robert Adam." *Architectural Review* 57 (January-May 1925).

CRAIG, MAURICE: "Burlington, Adam and Gandon." *Journal of the Warburg and Courtauld Institutes* 17 (1954): 381-382.

FLEMING, JOHN: "An Italian Sketchbook by Robert Adam, Clérisseau and Others." *Connoisseur* 146 (December 1960): 186-194.

FLEMING, JOHN: "The Journey to Spalatro." *Architectural Review* 123 (February 1958): 102-107.

FLEMING, JOHN: "Robert Adam, the Grand Tourist." *Cornhill Magazine* No. 1004 (Summer 1955): 118-137.

FLEMING, JOHN: " 'Retrospective View' by John Clerk of Eldin with Some Comments on Adam's Castle Style." In JOHN SUMMERSON (ed.): *Concerning Architecture: Essays Presented to Nikolaus Pevsner*. London, 1968.

FLEMING, JOHN: "Robert Adam's Castle Style." *Country Life* 143 (23 and 30 May 1968): 1356-1359; 1443-1447.

KIMBALL, FISKE: "Clérisseau and Adam." *Architectural Review* 117 (April 1955): 272-273.

MACAULAY, JAMES: "Robert Adam's Northern Castles." In *The Gothic Revival*. London, 1975.

OPPRÉ, PAUL: "Robert Adam's Picturesque Compositions." *Burlington Magazine* 80 (1942).

ROWAN, ALISTAIR J.: "After the Adelphi: Forgotten Years in the Adam Brothers' Practice." *Journal of the Royal Society of Arts* 122 (September 1974): 659-710.

STEEGMAN, J., and ADAMS, C. K.: "The Iconography of Robert Adam." *Architectural Review* 91 (1942).

STILLMAN, DAMIE: "Robert Adam and Piranesi." In D. FRASER (ed.): *Essays in the History of Architecture Presented to Rudolf Wittkower*. London, 1967.

TAIT, A. A.: "The Picturesque Drawings of Robert Adam." *Master Drawings* 9 (1971): 161-171.

UDY, D.: "The Furniture of James Stuart and Robert Adam." *Discovering Antiques* No. 42 (1971).

*

Like his brothers John (1721-92) and James (1734-94), Robert Adam trained in the Edinburgh office of their father William (1688-1748), Scotland's leading architect, whose work had earned him a fortune, and the friendship and trust of Edinburgh's intellectual and political elite. Robert left Scotland in 1754, aged 26, for what would be a particularly fruitful grand tour. After two years in Rome, where he enjoyed the friendship and tutelage of Charles-Louis Clérisseau (1721-80) and Giovanni Battista Piranesi (1720-78), Adam led an expedition to record the *Ruins of the Palace of the Emperor Diocletian at Spalato* (Split), published in 1764. Having benefited from the companionship of two of the most inventive and knowledgeable architects of the century, and having made a spectacular and important contribution to classical archaeology, Adam settled in 1758 in London, where he was eventually joined by his brother James. The two worked in partnership, but Robert's was the dominant artistic personality.

Adam first made his name with the replanning and decoration of country houses such as Syon House in London (begun in 1761), nearby Osterley Park (begun in 1761), Kenwood House in London (1767-69), Kedleston Hall in Derby (after 1759) and Newby Hall in Yorkshire (1767-85). Many of these had been built, or begun, during the mania for construction that was part of Palladianism; others were older. Adam built very few houses during the first decade of his career. Later the brothers planned speculative housing developments—most notoriously the Adelphi (1768-72), comprising several streets of houses on the Thames Embankment, which almost ruined them—and in the 1770s built grander town houses, among them Wynn House, St. James's Square (1771-75); Derby House, Grosvenor Square (1773-74, demolished); and Home House, Portman Square (1773-77), whose plans ingeniously triumphed over the restraints of expensive London sites: Wynn's was only 46 feet wide.

The "Adam style" of furniture and interior design became synonymous with a particularly graceful and unemotional synthesis of antique Greek and Roman, and Italian Renaissance decorative motifs such as flowers, grotesques, key meanders, Vitruvian scrolls, feathers and egg-and-dart moldings. Adam collected these devices in Italy, where he had filled dozens of notebooks, and from publications. The actual number of these motifs is surprisingly small, but by stylizing and then recombining them in different sizes, materials and colors, Adam used them to immensely imaginative effect. As John Summerson pointed out, Adam was "reconstructing a system of [classical] Roman interior decoration," of which he believed that the 16th-century Italians had more examples available to them for study than their modern successors.

Adam was indeed a precociously neoclassical architect, but classifying him as such forces us to reconsider what "classicism" then comprised, in a way that has important ramifications for the history of the movement as a whole. His exteriors, first, generally avoid the matrix of the pedimented temple front so beloved by the Palladians. The double portico at Osterley, although pedimented, in fact quotes the Augustan Porticus Octaviae, a rectangular colonnaded enclosure; Kedleston's south facade (ca. 1761), one of Adam's few early exteriors, is composed around the triumphal-arch motif he favored, and which he used most magnificently on the entrance front of the University of Edinburgh (now the Old College, begun in 1789). Adam, who wrote very little about his art, seems to have made a distinction between secular and religious antique architecture, and drew upon the former for his own secular designs. He did so with his customary disinclination to obey the rules for their own sake—a selective attitude that was itself an important part of neoclassicism—and in accordance with his often-quoted definition of "movement," which "is meant to express, the rise and fall, the advance and recess, with other diversity of form, in the different parts of a building, so as to add greatly to the picturesque of the composition'' (from the *Works in Architecture of Robert and James Adam,* published in installments in 1773 and 1779).

Adam's neoclassicism also embraced, oddly enough, the castellated country-house style he pursued in such mock fortresses as Culzean Castle, Ayrshire (1777-90), whose forbidding exterior is negated by perfectly regular and convenient internal arrangements, which have the usual exquisitely classical finishing. A score of such houses were built, most in Scotland, and as many more were planned. Some were built new, but others were reworkings of old Scottish tower houses, like Culzean and Oxenfoord Castle (1780-82), whose bartizans were carried up to the eaves and down to the ground to form turrets. Mellerstain (begun in 1770), the largest of the early castles, is a battlemented box, but the last and the best, Seton, East Lothian (begun in 1790), well exemplifies the ''movement'' of the Adam aesthetic.

The castles form a distinct group, both stylistically and iconographically: cheap to build, the style was undoubtedly appropriate to Scotland, and was pleasantly suggestive of a long ancestry that had fought gloriously to defend the comforts within. However, the Adams were, after all, experts at inserting neoclassical rooms into medieval shells. The plan of quadrangular Syon, for example, goes back to the building's origins as a Bridgettine conventual cloister of 1431. Constrained by the exterior walls and existing floor levels, the Adams made a suite of rooms not only in the ''antique'' style, as the duke of Northumberland had specified, but shaped with classical prototypes in mind: the entrance hall, for example, was a basilica articulated with a Doric order. The form of Mellerstain, whose interiors were also of course neoclassical, was probably influenced by Syon.

The castles' exteriors should also be understood as neoclassical, not neo-Gothic: strictly speaking, Seton has no medieval features at all. In his *Analytical Inquiry into the Principles of Taste* (1805), Richard Payne Knight (1750-1824) explicitly defended the combination, at his own Downton Castle, Herefordshire (begun in 1773), of ''what are called Gothic towers and battlements without, with Grecian columns and entablatures within,'' partly on the grounds that there was nothing distinctively medieval about towers and battlements, which had been known in antiquity. Similarly, in the early 1790s, Adam's friend and brother-in-law John Clerk of Eldin (1728-1812) wrote ''Of the Rise of British Architecture,'' which remained in manuscript until published in the 1960s. Clerk of Eldin, and doubtless the Adams, believed that Roman fortifications on the Scottish borders were the origin of a ''Romano-British'' style, exclusively applied to domestic and defensive buildings, that coexisted with the pointed-arch, ecclesiastical Gothic. He explicitly placed houses like Culzean within a very long tradition of British classicism.

The prison was the other building type to which the castellated style was most commonly applied at the end of the 18th century. Penal reformers insisted that prison facades should stand, like posters, as deterrents to potential criminals. These buildings could do so by connoting the medieval and antique fortresses which, it was well known, had contained dungeons of the most horrific type. Of course, prisons built in this style, like Adam's Edinburgh Bridewell (1791), did not contain dungeons: once again, a venerable exterior belied the modernity within. The plan of the Bridewell, which in its provision for central ''inspection,'' or surveillance, reflects Adam's correspondence with Jeremy Bentham, author of the *Panopticon* (1791), suggests that Adam, had he been a bit younger, could have become an extremely interesting institutional architect, and certainly the only one with the wit and character to cope with Bentham. With Edinburgh University, the Bridewell forms part of a group

of fine late projects—including Charlotte Square in Edinburgh's New Town (1791) and the Glasgow Royal Infirmary (begun in 1792)—with which Robert and James Adam fed their native country's appetite for fine houses and public buildings, and the rivalry of Edinburgh and Glasgow, work that James continued after his brother's death.

—CHRISTINE STEVENSON

ADAM, William.

Scottish. Born in Kirkcaldy, Scotland, 30 October 1689. Died on 24 June 1748. Married to Mary Robertson, 1716; sons included the architects Robert and James Adam. Worked independently.

Chronology of Works
All in Scotland

1721-26	Floors Castle, Roxburghshire
1723-27	Mavisbank, Midlothian (with John Clerk)
1723-48	Hopetoun House, West Lothian
1724-26	Lawers, Perthshire
1725-26	Mellerstain, Berwickshire
1725-28	Dalmahoy House, Midlothian
1726-30	The Drum, Midlothian
1726-32	Arniston, Midlothian
1730*	Yester House, East Lothian
1730-32	Robert Gordon's Hospital, Aberdeen
1731	Cumbernauld House, Lanarkshire
1731-43	Chatelherault, Lanarkshire
1732-35	Haddo House, Aberdeenshire
1732-45	University Library, Glasgow
1733	Hamilton Church, Bamff
1735-39	Duff House, Bamff
1738-48	Royal Infirmary, Edinburgh
1745-48	Inverary Castle, Argyllshire (to designs of Roger Morris)

Publications

BOOKS BY ADAM

The Vitruvius Scoticus. 2 vols. Edinburgh, 1720-40; 1810.

BOOKS ABOUT ADAM

DUNBAR, J. G.: *The Historic Architecture of Scotland.* 1966.
FLEMING, JOHN: *Robert Adam and His Circle.* London, 1962.
GIFFORD, JOHN: *William Adam 1689-1748: A Life and Times of Scotland's Universal Architect.* Edinburgh, 1989.
TAIT, A. A.: *The Landscape Garden in Scotland.* Edinburgh, 1980.

ARTICLES ABOUT ADAM

ROWAN, ALISTAIR: ''William Adam and Co.'' *Journal of the Royal Society of Arts* 122 (1974): 659-678.

*

William Adam, the leading Scottish architect of his day, provides a chronological if not stylistic link between the work of William Bruce and that of his own sons, Robert and James Adam. Whereas Bruce had suffered professionally because of his Jacobite sympathies, Adam carried himself as a Presbyterian Whig, and therefore received the support of the government and the new aristocracy of the Scottish Enlightenment. Like his sons, Adam was not only an architect, but was also a building contractor and an entrepreneur. It was he who built Inveraray Castle for the duke of Argyll to designs by Roger Morris (1745) and who, after a visit to Holland, first manufactured pantiles in Scotland. Thus, his fortune was based as much, if not more, on his business acumen as on his architecture.

As an architect Adam lacked the refined taste of his English contemporaries, and his work sometimes displays a Vanbrugh-esque heaviness and theatricality, which suggest its provincial provenance. He had received no special training and had undertaken no grand tour. His father, although of minor gentry stock, worked as a builder in Kirkaldy, Fife, and it was from that background that Adam rose. The patronage of such men as the earl of Stair and Sir John Clark of Penicuik provided him with introductions into Edinburgh society and opportunities for political advancement. As a result, the majority of his commissions were for country houses, and his public buildings, with the exception of the Town Houses in Aberdeen (1729), Dundee (1732) and Haddington (1742), remained comparatively few.

William Adam's position between Bruce and the brothers Adam is best shown at Hopetoun House, where his reworking of Bruce's double-pile house was, in turn, reworked by his own sons. He removed Bruce's pedimented east front and replaced it with a facade of giant Corinthian pilasters surmounted by an attic story and balustrade. Adam's intended central portico was never built, and the concave, colonnaded side wings with which he flanked his facade lack conviction: had Bruce's convex colonnade been allowed to remain, the strength of the whole east front would have been significantly greater. As it is, it seems to drain to distant end pavilions. Although begun in 1736, while Adam's sons were still boys, these pavilions display a reserve that is at odds with the main facade and indeed is more representative of the sons' later work. Yet the cupolas which surmount the pavilions are heavy and more suggestive of the father. The two versions of the east elevation can be easily compared: Bruce's is illustrated in Colen Campbell's *Vitruvius Britannicus* (1717) and Adam's in his own posthumous publication, *Vitruvius Scoticus* (1812). But if Adam's work can be criticized for being ill-considered, it should be remembered that, as architect, contractor and landscape designer, his responsibilities at Hopetoun were wide.

Adam probably came closest to the restraint of Bruce in his building of Dalmahoy House in 1725 for George Dalrymple, youngest son of Lord Stair. Like Bruce's earlier Craigiehall House (ca. 1695) or Mertoun House (1703), this is a double-pile house of three stories, but composed of seven bays, arranged awkwardly in a 1-4-2 rhythm. The facade, broken by a heavy stringcourse, is surmounted by a deep cornice and square balustrade rather than eaves, which Bruce would have used. At the other end of the scale might be Arniston, a house built for Robert Dundas in 1726, where the nine-bay entrance facade is flanked by small pavilions in the more contemporary Palladian manner. Yet, internally, the double-height, arcaded salon was richly plastered by Joseph Enzer in a manner more reminiscent of Andrea Palladio than English Palladianism, but really representative of neither.

Adam's best work was done when in harmony with another mind: here the significance of Sir John Clerk, "Scotland's Lord Burlington," can be recognized. Adam built Mavisbank House in 1723-27 to Clerk's specification. It is of five bays, the three in the center pushing forward below a pediment, and is linked to side pavilions. The house, compact and rather vertical, suggests the Mauritshuis at The Hague (1633); perhaps this house

represents a memory of Adam's journey to Holland, for, as in the Dutch example, the upper-floor windows are as tall as those of the *piano nobile,* their pediments alternately triangular and segmental. However, quoins replace pilasters, and a balustrade runs along the cornice.

These three houses, Dalmahoy, Arniston and Mavisbank, were all begun within a three-year period when Adam was in his mid-30s, and are among the earliest of his works. Yet, together with Hopetoun House, they would have formed the backbone for what he surely regarded as a prospectus of his own work as much as an account of the new architecture of Scotland, *Vitruvius Scoticus.* For when he started collecting subscriptions for that book in 1727, he had only 10 designs to his name: such was his confidence.

—NEIL JACKSON

ADELCRANTZ, Carl Fredrik.

Swedish. Born in Stockholm, Sweden, 1 March 1716. Died in Stockholm, 3 January 1796. Father was the architect Göran Josua Adelcrantz (1668-1739). Studied with C. G. Tessin; study trip to Italy and France, 1739-44. Appointed supervisor of palace building in Stockholm, 1741, and Hofintendant, 1750; named Oberintendant for buildings (with C. J. Cronstedt from 1757-67); director, Painting and Sculpture Academy, 1768. Freiherr, 1766; Präses, Swedish Royal Art Academy, 1767. Resigned his posts in 1795.

Chronology of Works
All in Sweden
* Approximate dates
† Work no longer exists

1753	Theater, Ulriksdal (remodeling of the riding master's quarters)
1763*	Kina Slott (Chienese Pavilion), Drottningholm, near Stockholm
1764*	Theater, Drottningholm
1768-74	Adolf-Friedrichskirche, Stockholm (dome built 1776-83)
1777-82	Royal Opera House, Stockholm†
n.d.	Fredrikshof Palace, Stockholm (remodeling)
n.d.	Klarakirche, Stockholm (remodeling)
n.d.	Chancellery, Stockholm (remodeling)

Publications

BOOKS ABOUT ADELCRANTZ

FOGELMARCK, STIG: *Carl Fredrik Adelcrantz Arkitekt.* Stockholm, 1957.
SETTERWALL, ÅKE C. E.; FOGELMARCK, STIG; and GYLLENSVÄRD, BO: *The Chinese Pavilion at Drottningholm.* Malmö, Sweden, 1974.

ARTICLES ABOUT ADELCRANTZ

FOGELMARCK, STIG: "Gustav III's Opera." *Samfundet Sankt Eriks Årsbok* (1949): 95-150.

*

The needs of the late 18th-century Swedish court for festive buildings were well served by Carl Fredrik Adelcrantz. While as superintendent of buildings for the state from 1757 until 1795 he had many responsibilities and was awarded many honors, he is probably best known for the Chinese Pavilion and the Court Theater at Drottningholm. The first was a gift from King Adolf Fredrik to Queen Lovisa Ulrika. The second was built at the behest of the queen when the previous theater at Drottningholm, built in 1753, burned in 1762. By early experience Adelcrantz was well prepared for these assignments.

His father, Göran Josuae Adelcrantz, had been royal architect until forced out politically in 1727. Soured by that experience, he tried to direct his son toward a career in the civil service. On his father's death in 1739, however, Carl Fredrik turned to his real interest, architecture, which he had cultivated in the course of a more prosaic education. Having received a stipend, he traveled to Germany, Holland, France and Italy, returning to Sweden in 1743. This enabled him to see for himself the works of Palladio, Scamozzi, Serlio and Vignola that he already knew from the books by these masters and others in his father's extensive architectural library. Along with those books were many on the theater.

The elder Adelcrantz had been much interested in theater, and owned an extensive library of dramatic literature as well. He wrote for the theater and translated Racine's *Esther* into Swedish, the first of such translations of French plays. He had even acted in the old theater at Stockholm Castle, the Lejonkulan, remodeled from Queen Christina's lion's den. Architecture and the theater were part of the household in which young Adelcrantz was raised, and so must have been an awareness of court life. A portrait of him as a young man, wearing a powdered wig and embroidered coat, shows him with courtly bearing and genial manner.

After several years of work for the court under the architect Carl Hårleman, Adelcrantz made another trip to Italy, and from this his diary survives, filled with notes—in Swedish, French and Italian—and sketches. The studies show great observation of detail and also awareness of plans and sections, some including shadows cast by colonnettes, moldings and carvings. One especially careful sketch is a study of the Teatro San Carlo in Naples, where he recorded a number of dimensions.

On his return to Sweden, Adelcrantz carried out the first of his theatrical commissions in 1753, that of remodeling the riding master's quarters at Ulriksdal to serve as a theater. There he filled up the long room of the riding school with a stage and arranged adjoining rooms for parties and receptions, the whole decorated in the French Rococo taste characteristic of his early work. Ulriksdal is just outside Stockholm, and the theater there was reached more easily than the first one at Drottningholm, built in the same year.

For the Chinese Pavilion at Drottningholm 10 years later, Adelcrantz put forth his most exotic and playful touches. It is actually a small group of buildings on a rise at the end of a park. It consists of a main block with curved wings and dependencies, plus four separate small buildings. Drawing probably on William Chambers' *Designs for Chinese Buildings,* published in 1757, he gave the roofs a Chinese tilt, and used many Chinese motifs in the decoration of the interior. This may well have been intended to console Lovisa Ulrika for the loss of her theater, which had burned in 1762.

Adelcrantz had two more theaters to design, the one at Drottningholm in 1764, and the Royal Opera in Stockholm in 1777, each having different requirements. For Drottningholm he had to provide a more intimate setting, where the royal family might take part in performances and the entire household attend. He wisely decided upon a severely plain exterior next to the baroque main palace. The building is remarkably well preserved, with more than 30 original stage sets, and the seats still marked

for their proper occupants. Vestibules, reception rooms, and quarters for the actors were included, all of them furnished in the French manner.

The Royal Opera, unfortunately destroyed in 1892, was planned as a much more stately structure, befitting its site across from the Royal Palace and facing a princely palace opposite on the plaza. Shaping his plans to the needs of his royal patrons, Adelcrantz gave them a private entrance on the side toward the Royal Palace. The public entrance, facing the plaza, was through a central portico, with a giant order of columns rising above the rusticated ground level, while pilasters framed the window bays on either side. In this design Adelcrantz inclined more to French classicism than to the Rococo, and by 1783 his work was beginning to show the emerging neoclassicism, as witnessed by designs for the Royal Mint.

In many ways Adelcrantz's work showed an unusual flexibility and a strong sense of the appropriate. He furnished stately designs for churches and houses. Altars and pulpits might be more elaborate, and his designs for organ cases are lively with scrolls, garlands and putti. A unique task came in 1771 when he had to plan the catafalque and lying-in-state on the death of King Adolf Fredrik.

Near the end of Adelcrantz's life, he fell into financial difficulties and resigned his several official posts. What remains of his work today is marked by the refinement and good nature revealed in the early portrait.

—MARIAN C. DONNELLY

ALBERTI, Leon Battista.

Italian. Born in Genoa, Italy, 18 February 1404. Died in Rome, April 1472. Family banned from Florence until 1428. Studied in Padua with Gasparino Barsizia of Bergamo, 1412-14; received doctorate in law, University of Bologna, 1428. Employed in papal service as cultural adviser and architectural director, 1447.

Chronology of Works
All in Italy

1444-51	Palazzo Rucellai, Florence
1450ff.	Tempio Malatestiano (San Francesco), Rimini (uncompleted)
1458-71	Santa Maria Novella, Florence (facade)
1460-67	Rucellai Chapel, San Pancrazio, Florence
1460ff.	San Sebastiano, Mantua
1470-72	Sant'Andrea, Mantua (not completed until 1481)
1470	Santissima Annunziata, Florence (tribuna; not completed until 1481)

Publications

BOOKS BY ALBERTI

Kleinere kunsttheoretische Schriften. Edited by H. Janitschek. Vienna, 1877.
The Ten Books on Architecture (English translation of *De re aedificatoria* by James Leoni; edited by Joseph Rykwert). London, 1955.
Leon Battista Alberti: L'Architettura. Edited by Giovanni Orlandi and Paolo Portoghesi. Milan, 1966.
The Albertis of Florence: Leon Battista Alberti's Della famiglia. Lewisburg, Pennsylvania, (ca. 1441) 1971.
On Painting and Sculpture. With introduction and notes by Cecil Grayson. London, 1972.

The Ten Books of Architecture, The 1755 Leoni Edition. 1986.
On The Art of Building in Ten Books. Edited by Joseph Rykwert. Cambridge, Massachusetts, 1989.

BOOKS ABOUT ALBERTI

ACCADEMIA NAZIONALE DEI LINCEI, ROME: *Convegno internazionale indetto nel V centenario di Leon Battista Alberti (Roma-Mantova-Firenze, 25-29 aprile 1972).* Rome, 1974.

BEHN, IRENE: *Leone Battista Alberti als Kunstphilosoph.* Strasbourg, 1911.

BONUCCI, A.: *Opere volgari di L. B. Alberti.* Florence, 1847.

BORSI, FRANCO: *Leon Battista Alberti: The Complete Works.* New York, 1989.

CLARK, KENNETH: *Leon Battista Alberti on Painting.* London, 1944.

DEZZI BARDESCHI, MARCO: *La facciata di Santa Maria Novella.* Pisa, 1970.

FLEMMING, W.: *Die Begründung der modernen Aesthetik und Kunstwissenschaft durch Leon Battista Alberti.* Leipzig, 1916.

GADOL, JOAN: *Leon Battista Alberti: Universal Man of the Early Renaissance.* Chicago and London, 1969.

GENGARO, MARIA LUISA: *Leon Battista Alberti teorico e architetto del rinascimento.* Milan, 1939.

GUZZO, A.: *Leon Battista Alberti.* Naples, 1919.

HOFFMANN, PAUL: *Studien zu Leon Battista zehn Büchern De Re Aedificatoria.* Frankenberg i. S., Germany, 1883.

JARZOMBEK, MARK: *On Leon Baptista Alberti: His Literary and Aesthetic Theories.* Cambridge, Massachusetts, 1990.

JOHNSON, EUGENE J.: *S. Andrea in Mantua: The Building History.* London, 1975.

LAMOUREUX, RICHARD E.: *Alberti's Church of San Sebastiano in Mantua.* London and New York, 1979.

LEONI, GIACOMO: *The Architecture of Leon Battista Alberti.* London, 1726.

LONDI, E.: *Leon Battista Alberti architetto.* Florence, 1906.

LÜCKE, H. K.: *Alberti Index.* 4 vols. Munich, 1975.

MANCINI, GIROLAMO: *Vita di Leone Battista Alberti.* Florence, 1911.

MARANI, ERCOLANI (ed.): *Il Sant'Andrea di Mantova e Leon Battista Alberti.* Mantua, 1974.

MICHEL, PAUL-HENRI: *Un ideal humain au XVme siècle; la pensée de L. B. Alberti.* Paris, 1930.

Omaggio ad Alberti. Vol. 1 in *Studi e documenti di architettura.* Florence, 1972.

ORSINI, L.: *Il Tempio Malatestiano.* Milan, 1915.

RICCI, CORRADO: *Leon Battista Alberti architetto.* Turin, 1917.

RICCI, CORRADO: *Il Tempio Malatestiano.* Milan and Rome, 1925.

SCHULZ, ANNE MARKHAM: *The Sculpture of Bernardo Rossellino and His Workshop.* Princeton, New Jersey, 1977.

SEITZ, F.: *San Francesco in Rimini.* Berlin, 1893.

SEMPRINI, G.: *Leon Battista Alberti.* Milan, 1927.

Sigismondo Pandolfo Malatesta e il suo tempio. Vicenza, Italy, 1970.

VENTURI, ADOLFO: *L. B. Alberti.* Rome, 1923.

VERGA, CORRADO: *Un altro malatestiano.* Crema, Italy, 1977.

WESTFALL, CARROLL WILLIAM: *In This Most Perfect Paradise: Alberti, Nicholas V, and the Invention of Conscious Urban Planning in Rome, 1447-55.* London and University Park, Pennsylvania, 1974.

WITTKOWER, RUDOLF: *Architectural Principles in the Age of Humanism.* London, 1952.

ARTICLES ABOUT ALBERTI

BIALOSTOCKI, J.: "The Power of Beauty: A Utopian Idea of Leone Battista Alberti." *Studien zur Toskanischen Kunst: Festschrift für Ludwig Heinrich Heydenreich zum 23 März 1963.* Munich, 1964.

BROWN, BEVERLY LOUISE: "The Tribuna of SS. Annunziata in Florence." Ph.D. dissertation. Northwestern University, Evanston, Illinois, 1978.

BURNS, HOWARD: "A Drawing by L. B. Alberti." *Architectural Design* 49, Nos. 5-6 (1979): 45-56.

CHAMBERS, DAVID SANDERSON: "Sant'Andrea at Mantua and Gonzaga Patronage: 1460-1472." *Journal of the Warburg and Courtauld Institutes* 40 (1977): 99-127.

DEHIO, GEORG: "Die Bauprojekte Nikolaus V und Leon Battista Alberti." *Repertorium für Kunstwissenschaft* 3 (1880).

DEZURKO, EDWARD R.: "Alberti's Theory of Form and Function." *Art Bulletin* 39 (1957): 142-145.

DEZZI BARDESCHI, MARCO: "Il complesso monumentale di San Pancrazio a Firenze e il suo restauro." *Quaderni dell'Istituto di Storia dell' Architettura* 13, Nos. 73-78 (1966): 1-66.

EDEN, W. A.: "Studies in Urban Theory: The 'De Re Aedificatoria' of L. B. Alberti." *Town Planning Review* 19 (1943): 10-28.

FORSTER, KURT W.: "The Palazzo Rucellai and Questions of Typology in the Development of Renaissance Buildings." *Art Bulletin* 58 (1976): 109-113.

GRAYSON, CECIL: "Notes on the Texts of Some Vernacular Works of Leon Battista Alberti." *Rinascimento* 3 (1952): 211-244.

GRAYSON, CECIL: "Studi su Leon Battista Alberti." *Rinascimento* 4 (1953): 45-62.

GRAYSON, CECIL: "The Humanism of Alberti." *Italian Studies* 12 (1957): 37-56.

GRAYSON, CECIL: "Leon Battista Alberti: Architect." *Architectural Design* 49, Nos. 5-6:7-17.

GRAYSON, CECIL: "The Composition of L. B. Alberti's *Decem libri de re aedificatoria.*" *Münchner Jahrbuch der bildenden Kunst* 11 (1960): 152-161.

HORSTER, MARITA: "Brunelleschi und Alberti in ihrer Stellung zur römischen Antike." *Mitteilungen des Kunsthistorischen Instituts in Florenz* 17 (1973): 29-64.

HUBALA, ERICH: "L. B. Albertis Langhaus von Sant'Andrea in Mantua." Pp. 83-120 In *Festschrift für Kurt Badt zum 70. Geburtstage.* Berlin, 1961.

KENT, F. W.: "The Letters Genuine and Spurious of Giovanni Rucellai." *Journal of the Warburg and Courtauld Institutes* 37 (1974): 342-349.

KLOTZ, HEINRICH: "L. B. Albertis 'De re aedificatoria' in Theorie und Praxis." *Zeitschrift für Kunstgeschichte* 32 (1969): 93-103.

KRAUTHEIMER, RICHARD: "Alberti and Vitruvius." *Acts of the 20th International Congress of the History of Art* 2 (1961): 42-52.

KRAUTHEIMER, RICHARD: "Alberti's Templum Etruscum." In *Studies in Early Christian, Medieval, and Renaissance Art.* New York, 1963.

LORENZ, HELMUT: "Zur Architektur L. B. Albertis: Die Kirchenfassaden." *Wiener Jahrbuch für Kunstgeschichte* 29 (1976): 65-100.

MACK, CHARLES RANDALL: "The Rucellai Palace: Some New Proposals." *Art Bulletin* 56 (1974): 517-529.

MAGNUSON, TORGIL: "The Project of Nicholas V for Rebuilding the Borgo Leonino in Rome." *Art Bulletin* 36 (June 1954): 89-115.

MITCHELL, CHARLES: "The Imagery of the Tempio Malatestiano." *Studi Romagnoli* 2 (1951): 77-90.

MITCHELL, CHARLES: "An Early Christian Model for the Tempio Malatestiano." In PETER BLOCK (ed.): *Intuition und Kunstwissenschaft: Festschrift für Hanns Swarzenski*. Berlin, 1973.

NAREDI-RAINER, PAUL VON: "Bemerkungen zur Säule bei L. B. Alberti." *Jahrbuch des Kunsthistorischen Instituts der Universität Graz* 11 (1976): 51-61.

ONIANS, JOHN: "Alberti and Filarete. A Study in their Sources." *Journal of the Warburg and Courtauld Institutes* 34 (1971): 96-114.

PARRONCHI, ALESSANDRO: "Otto piccoli documenti per la biografia dell'Alberti." *Rinascimento* 12 (1972): 229-235.

PETRINI, MARIO: "L'Uomo di Alberti." *Belgafor* 6 (1951): 665-674.

PREYER, BRENDA: "The Rucellai Loggia." *Mitteilungen des Kunsthistorischen Instituts in Florenz* 21 (1977): 183-198.

PREYER, BRENDA: "The Rucellai Palace." Pp. 155-225 in *Giovanni Rucellai ed il suo Zibaldone II: A Florentine Patrician and His Palace*. London, 1981.

RITSCHER, ERNST: "Die Kirche S. Andrea in Mantua." *Zeitschrift für Bauwesen* 49:1-20, 181-200.

RYKWERT, JOSEPH (ed.): "Leon Battista Alberti." *Architectural Design* Profile no. 21.

SCHÄDLICH, C.: "L. B. Albertis Schönheitsdefinition und ihre Bedeutung für die Architekturtheorie." *Wissenschaftliche Zeitschrift Hochschule Weimar* 5, No. 4 (1957-58): 217-284.

SUMMERSON, JOHN: "Antitheses of the Quattrocento." In *Heavenly Mansions and Other Essays on Architecture*. London, 1949.

TEUBNER, HANS: "Das Langhaus der SS. Annunziata in Florenz." *Mitteilungen des Kunsthistorischen Instituts in Florenz* 22 (1978): 27-60.

VAGNETTI, LUIGI: "Concinnitas; riflessioni sul significato di un termine albertiano." *Studi e documenti di architettura* 2 (1973): 137-161.

WITTKOWER, RUDOLF: "Alberti's Approach to Antiquity in Architecture." *Journal of the Warburg and Courtauld Institutes* 4, Nos. 1-2 (1940-41): 1-18.

*

Leon Battista Alberti most nearly represents the Renaissance concept of "the universal man." Born in Genoa, the son of an exiled Florentine patrician, Alberti received a humanist education (at Padua and at the University of Bologna) and devoted his life to rediscovering, interpreting, propagating and surpassing the achievements of antiquity. His assimilation of classical material was manifested with the 1424 publication of his play *Philodoxeus,* an accomplished forgery purporting to be a rediscovered manuscript. Once revealed as his own, *Philodoxeus* was offered as proof of Alberti's own scholarly attainments. Throughout his life, Alberti continued to author a wide variety of treatises dealing with civic, social and philosophic themes.

The ban on his family was lifted in 1428, and Alberti journeyed to Florence to wonder at the extraordinary cultural events taking place. Stimulated by contact with the leading intellectuals as well as by admiration for Florence's new wave of artists, Alberti began to devote considerable attention to artistic matters. Although examples of his sculpture and painting are either known or are mentioned by such writers as Giorgio Vasari, most of his artistic efforts remained theoretical (*De statua* and *De pictura,* both of which were issued in 1435). In *De pictura,* the Italian version of which he dedicated to Filippo Brunelleschi

in 1436, Alberti offered the first written demonstration of perspective. His admiration for Brunelleschi and his recognition of the leading role architecture had to play in the revitalization of the antique spirit turned his attention toward architecture. Unlike Brunelleschi, who achieved his theoretical distinction through practical application, Alberti came to architecture through theoretical speculation and a deliberate antiquarian zeal.

Alberti's growing fascination with the physical as well as the literary survivals of the ancient world led him quite naturally to Rome, where he found employment in the papal service. During the flight from Rome of Pope Eugenius IV, Alberti returned to Florence (1434-36) and then traveled with the papal party to Bologna (1436), and to the Council of Ferrara in 1438. While in Ferrara, he attracted the attention of Lionello d'Este, who possibly employed him (1443) to design the pedestal (the Arco del Cavallo) for an equestrian monument to Niccolo d'Este and the bell tower of the city's cathedral.

Alberti's *Descriptio urbis Romae,* dating from 1443, was a landmark in archaeological topography, displaying the author's knowledge of the principles of ancient cartography as well as the new Renaissance concepts of proportional relationships. During his student days in Bologna, Alberti had formed a friendship with Tommaso Parentucelli, and with the succession of that humanist to the papal throne in 1447 as Pope Nicholas V, Alberti attained an unofficial position as cultural adviser and architectural director for the great renewal projects which the new pope hoped to initiate. By way of stimulation, Alberti presented to the pope in 1452 his monumental *De re aedificatoria,* at which he had been at work since the mid-1440s. The main purposes of this book were to modernize the ancient architectural advice of Vitruvius (a copy of whose writings Alberti was to loan Pope Pius II in 1459), to extol the merits of ancient architectural practices, to offer helpful building advice to his aristocratic readers, and to explain how the principles of rational Roman urban design could be put into contemporary and systematic practice. For Alberti, architecture assumed a moral character transcending the individual elements in building. Architecture became the domain of the architect (and enlightened patron) and not the stonemason.

Alberti's actual contribution to the variety of architectural projects initiated or contemplated by Pope Nicholas, in his attempt to reawaken the majesty of the papacy, remains problematic. Giorgio Vasari claimed to have owned a drawing by Alberti for a covered way over the Ponte Sant'Angelo. Perhaps Alberti also designed the little chapel that once stood at its entrance. A recently discovered drawing of a bath building, annotated in Alberti's own hand, may have been done in conjunction with a thermal spa palace begun for Pope Nicholas near Viterbo in 1454. Alberti's involvement with the architectural programs of Nicholas V remained, like the majority of the programs themselves, theoretical. All of what actually was executed was simply a first stage of restoration; the next stage of actual building was never implemented. Included in this projected phase was to be an extensive reconstruction of the papal palace at the Vatican, the laying out of three porticoed streets leading through the *borgo* district to the Basilica of St. Peter, and, most stupendously, the complete reconstruction of the old basilica. These never-executed plans anticipated the later programs of Popes Sixtus IV, Julius II, Sixtus V and Alexander VII.

At the same time he was serving as an architectural adviser to Pope Nicholas, Alberti was also preparing plans (mostly at long distance) for the reconstruction of the church of San Francesco in Rimini, which, as the Tempio Malatestiano, was intended to serve as a sort of humanistic mortuary for Sigismondo Malatesta and his court. Alberti's involvement with this

Leon Battista Alberti: Sant'Andrea, Mantua, Italy, 1470-72

project began in 1450. He proceeded to encase the medieval church (the interior was renewed by Matteo de' Pasti) in a classicizing shell, the flanks of which, with their sepulchral niches, recall the rhythms of a Roman aqueduct as well as the Mausoleum of Theodoric and the blind arcuation along the sides of the Mausoleum of Galla Placida and San Apolinare in Classe, all in nearby Ravenna. The front was deliberately modeled after an ancient triumphal arch. In this project, Alberti was at his most archaeological. The upper story of the facade, left incomplete when work was suspended in 1461, can be reconstructed based on a foundation medal cast by de' Pasti in 1450, a drawing showing the actual construction in progress, and an illustrated and autographed letter from Alberti to de' Pasti in 1454 (Morgan

Library, New York) showing Alberti's new proposal for volutes along the roof line of the facade (a relationship to Brunelleschi's intentions for Santo Spirito in Florence has yet to be explored). The medal shows Alberti's unrealized intention of terminating the nave in a great ribbed hemispherical dome.

Alberti was in Florence during the reign of Calixtus III where he worked for Giovanni Rucellai on completing (1458-71) the facade of the medieval church of Santa Maria Novella, blending the Gothic beginnings with a harmonious upper story inspired by the Romanesque church of San Miniato ai Monte. He may also have been involved in formulating ideas for the facade of Rucellai's new family palace (actually built under the direction of Bernardo Rossellino, ca. 1460-62). While in Florence on that occasion, he may have begun rebuilding the apse of San Martino a Gangalandi (from which he enjoyed the benefices), employing, once more, an updated refrain taken from San Miniato.

Alberti reentered papal service under the humanist Pope Pius II. His involvement with the Benediction Loggia at the Vatican and in plans for rebuilding the papal birthplace of Pienza is conjectural, although Pienza certainly reflects, in miniature, many of the unrealized intentions for Nicholas V's Rome. Alberti accompanied Pope Pius to Mantua in 1459, stopping in Florence, where he received another commission from Giovanni Rucellai, this time to design a barrel-vaulted mausoleum chapel at San Pancrazio containing a pilaster-articulated "reproduction" of the Holy Sepulcher in Jerusalem. Work began about 1460 and was completed by 1467. In Mantua, Alberti reaffirmed his connections with the Gonzaga family (his initial Latin edition of *De Pictura* had been dedicated to Gianfrancesco Gonzaga). For Marquis Lodovico Gonzaga, Alberti began (1460) the building of San Sebastiano. The unfinished facade of this church, articulated by pilasters and an arch that penetrates the pediment, has suggested to some an illusionary temple front, but its intended appearance remains problematic. Alberti may have drawn his antiquarian inspiration from the Roman arch at Orange, the Tomb of Annia Regilla near Rome, Diocletian's Palace at Split, or, more likely, from the facade of the Tomb of the Cercenii south of Rome. The ground-plan of San Sebastiano also relates to the cruciform plan of this tomb as well as to the Greek Library of Hadrian's Villa at Tivoli. What precisely Alberti had intended for the interior of this Greek-cross-plan church is uncertain; several varieties of domes to crown the crossing recently have been suggested.

With the death of Pope Pius in 1464, Alberti left the papal service and devoted himself to fulfilling assignments for his Gonzaga clients. Another Gonzaga commission brought Alberti back to Florence in 1470 to take over from Michelozzo the direction of work on the great rotunda at the end of the church of Santissima Annunziata. Alberti's involvement at the inception of the project in 1445 also has been suggested. The tribune is modeled after Rome's Minerva Medica via Brunelleschi's unfinished Santa Maria degli Angeli. Alberti's contributions to the Renaissance progression toward centrality unfortunately are obscured by later embellishments.

In 1470 Alberti offered his services again to the Gonzaga, this time in connection with an enormous plan to rebuild the church of Sant'Andrea in Mantua. It was to be his crowning architectural accomplishment. There, Alberti combined temple front and triumphal arch motifs for the facade and carried this concept into the interior to articulate the entrances of the major and minor chapels opening off the aisleless and barrel-vaulted nave. In the great space of Sant'Andrea, Alberti came the closest to reconstituting the form and spirit of ancient architecture. Unfortunately, the architect was dead before the cornerstone could be laid in June 1472.

—CHARLES R. MACK

ALBINI, Franco.

Italian. Born in Robbiate, Como, Italy, 17 October 1905. Died in Milan, 1 November 1977. Married; Son is the architect Marco Albini. Received diploma in architecture from Polytechnic, Milan, 1929. Practiced privately in Milan from 1930; partners Franca Helg, from 1952, Antonio Piva, from 1962, and Marco Albini, from 1965. Lecturer, American-Italian Commission of Cultural Exchanges, Rome, 1954-63; professor of architectural composition, Polytechnic, Milan, 1963-77. Member, UNESCO Commission for Renewal of the Museums of the United Arab Republic, 1968-69; member of CIAM (Congrès Internationaux d'Architecture Moderne).

Chronology of Works
All in Italy unless noted

1936	Fabio Filzi Quarter Project (with R. Camus and G. Palanti)
1936	Room for One Person, Milan Triennale Exhibit
1937	Palace of Italian Civilization Project, EUR, Rome
1938	Milano Verde Urban Project, Milan (with Camus, Palanti, G. Pagano and G. Mazzoleni)
1938	Villa Pestarini, Piazza Tripoli, Milan
1950-61	Palazzo Bianco, Genoa (renovation)
1950	Istituto Nazionale Assicurazioni Office Building, Parma
1952	Tesoro di San Lorenzo, Genoa (renovation)
1952-61	Palazzo Rosso, Genoa (renovation)
1952-62	Municipal Offices, Genoa
1955	Valleta Cambiaso Public Gardens and Sports Grounds, Genoa
1955-56	Villa Olivetti, Ivrea
1957	Istituto Nazionale Assicurazioni Housing Estate, Scandino, Reggio Emilia
1957-61	La Rinascente Department Store, Rome
1962-63	Metro Stations, Milan (with Franca Helg)
1963-75	Sant'Agostino Museum, Genoa
1964-67	Hotel, Santa Cesarea Terme, Calabria
1965-72	Graeco-Roman Museum, Alexandria, Egypt
1967	Thermal Bath Building, Salsomaggiore Terme
1968	Breuil Center, Cervinia
1968-69	Master Plan, Egyptian Museum and Egyptian Museum Cultural Center, Cairo Villa, Cremella, Como
1968-70	Brionvega Storage, Display and Office Buildings, Arzano, Padua and Florence
1969-70	Medieval Tower, Montecatini Val Cecina (conversion)
1969-74	Civic Museum, Eremitani Cloister, Padua (conversion)
1971-72	Palladio Exhibition Plan, Basilica, Vicenza
1971-73	Villas, Daverio
1972	Office and picture gallery, Sforza Castle, Milan (conversion)
1974	Kindergarten, Sassuolo, Modena (with A. Pastorini)

Publications

BOOKS ABOUT ALBINI

ARGAN, GIULIO CARLO: *Franco Albini*. Milan, 1962.

BENEVOLO, LEONARDO: *Storia dell'architettura moderna*. 2 vols. Bari, Italy, 1960.

FOSSATI, PAOLO: *Design in Italia 1945-1972*. Milan, 1972.

Franco Albini 1905-1977: Architettura per un museo. Exhibition catalog. Rome, 1980.

GREGOTTI, VITTORIO: *New Directions in Italian Architecture*. New York, 1968.

GREGOTTI, VITTORIO: *Orientamente nuovi nell'architettura italiana*. Milan, 1970.

HELG, FRANCA: *Franco Albini 1930-1970*. London, 1981.

KIDDER SMITH, G. E.: *The New Architecture of Europe*. New York and London, 1961.

LEET, S. (ed.): *Franco Albini: Architecture and Design*. Princeton, New Jersey, 1989.

MAZZOCCHI, MARIA GRAZIA: *Architettura*. Exhibition catalog. Milan, 1979.
MOSCHINI, F.: *Franco Albini*. London, 1979.
PICA, AGNOLDOMENICO: *Architettura italiana ultima/Recent Italian Architecture*. Milan, 1959.
PICA, AGNOLDOMENICO: *Forme nuove in Italia*. Milan and Rome, 1957.
SETA, CESARE DE: *La cultura architettonica in Italia tra le due guerre*. Bari, Italy, 1972.

ARTICLES ABOUT ALBINI

"Contemporary Italian Architects." *Notiziario culturale italiano* (May 1963).
D'ALFONSO, E.: "Realismo e architettura povera." *Casabella* No. 352 (1970).
FERRARI, ALBERTO: "Bourgeois, Architect, Reserved and a Poet—The Work of Franco Albini." *Modo* (April 1980).
SAMONÀ, GIUSEPPE: "Franco Albini e la cultura architettonica in Italia." *Zodiac* 3 (1958): 83-115.
SARTORIS, ALBERTO: "The Rationalist Franco Albini." *Domus* (February 1980).
TENTORI, F.: "Recent Works by Albini-Helg." *Zodiac* 14 (1965).
"The Work of Franco Albini." *Architettura* Special issue (October 1979).

*

Franco Albini, an Italian architect active before and after World War II, was recognized as much for his work on displays and museum installations as for his buildings. He was born in Robbiate, Como, and educated at the Politecnico in Milan; he received his diploma in 1929 and opened a practice a year later. Work came almost immediately, his first important building being that for the Istituto Nazionale delle Assicurazione in Milan in 1935. That building showed a form of design that became essential to all of Albini's work: the language of Ludwig Mies van der Rohe and the Bauhaus tempered by the idea of an Italian tradition of design; that approach allowed him to move beyond the stricter limits that were favored by the rationalist movement in Italy.

Albini was noted in the Milan Triennales of 1933 and 1936, and it was in the latter year that he designed the Appartamenti Minetti in Milan and, with Renato Camus and Giancarlo Palanti, the much-praised Fabio Filzi Workers' Housing Estate in the Viale Argonne in Milan; the Fabio Filzi housing won the Silver Medal in the Paris International Exhibition of 1937. World War II led to a slowing of his practice, but by the early 1950s he was fully back at work, most notably with the Albergo Pirovano in Cervinia (1949-50), which looked to Walter Gropius and the Sommerfeld House, and the building for the Istituto Nazionale delle Assicurazioni in Parma (1950), which was immediately recognized as one of the first significant postwar buildings in Italy.

Other important projects followed, the Uffici Comunali in Genoa (1952-61) and La Rinascente Department Store (1957-61) on the Piazza Fiume in Rome. The offices in Genoa are attached to an older Renaissance structure, the Palazzo Doria-Tursi, which has a large double-loggia courtyard. The new building by Albini is set into a hill on three sides, the fourth being open with a view, over the old palazzo, to Genoa and the sea beyond; Albini's plan continued the slightly turning axis of the whole. A 19th-century elevator tower connects this complex to the lower parts of the city. The whole ensemble is filled out with elegant, gentle details.

The design of the Rinascente Department Store in Rome, done in collaboration with one of his partners, Franca Helg, went through many stages, but in its final form it is a simple steel-frame building. However, the forms of this frame are so emphasized, as critics noted, that they look like the timbers of an old Japanese temple. Around and amidst the frame are set exposed, precast walls, windowless for the most part, carrying within them the service elements, such as air-conditioning, all ending at the appropriate floors and with the contents defining the size of each external unit. This leads to a patterning of forms that serves to enliven the otherwise simple, even dull profile; the shadows of the spandrels above and thin horizontal white bands at head height on each floor provide further accent. This building, so Paolo Portoghesi could claim in 1962, was an argument against vulgarity and approximation, and a model for all designers.

Albini was also involved with many problems of interior design, working in 1962-63 on a number of stations for the Milan metropolitan railway system and remodeling, with great success, the interiors of two Renaissance palace museums in Genoa, the Palazzo Bianco (1950) and the Palazzo Rosso (1952-61). With Helg, he later worked on reordering the Villetta Cambiaso (1955-61). Albini was also responsible for some interesting furniture designs, most notably a set of chairs done with Helg.

Albini never proposed a theory of architecture, but from his editorship for many years of the journal *Casabella-Costruzioni,* he was able to bring together a group of architects who were sympathetic to his way of working. That way of working, as Manfredo Tafuri suggested at a conference about Albini held in 1960, was a way of accommodating the best of the architectural traditions of Italy with its present social and political realities.

—DAVID CAST

ALEIJADINHO.

Brazilian. Born Antonio Francisco Lisboa near Ouro Prêto, Brazil, 1738. Died in 1814. Apprenticed to his father, a Portuguese stonemason.

Chronology of Works
All in Brazil
* Approximate dates

1766-76	São Francisco de Assis Church, Ouro Prêto (completion)
1767-79	Nossa Senhora do Carmo Church, Ouro Prêto
1769-71	Nossa Senhora do Carmo Church, Sabara
1774-1820*	Sān Francisco de Assis Church, Sān João del Rei
1777-1805	Nosso Senhor do Bom Jesus de Matosinhos Church, Congonhas do Campo (sanctuary, courtyard, and statuary)
1778	Nosso Senhor do Bom Jesus Church, Ouro Prêto (facade decoration)

Publications

BOOKS ABOUT ALEIJADINHO

BAZIN, GERMAIN: *L'architecture religieuse baroque au Brésil*. 2 vols. Paris, 1956-59.
BAZIN, GERMAIN: *Aleijadinho et la sculpture baroque au Brésil*. Paris, 1963.

Aleijadinho: Nosso Senhora do Bom Jesus de Matosinhos Church, Congonhas do Campo, Brazil, 1777-1805

BRÉTAS, RODRIGO JOSÉ FERREIRA: *Antônio Francisco Lisboa-O Aleijadinho*. Rio de Janeiro, 1951.
KUBLER, G.; SORIA, M.: *Art and Architecture in Spain and Portugal and Their American Dominions 1500-1800*. Harmondsworth, 1959.

ARTICLES ABOUT ALEIJADINHO

BURY, JOHN B.: "Estilo Aleijadinho and the Churches of Eighteenth Century Brazil." *Architectural Review* 111 (February 1952): 92-100.

MARIANNO FILHO, JOSÉ: "Da participação de Antonio Fancisco Lisboa na arquitetura sacra Mineira." *Estudos de Arte Brasileira* (1942): 45-53.
SMITH, ROBERT C.: "The Colonial Architecture of Minas Gerais in Brazil." *Art Bulletin* 21 (June 1939): 110-159.

*

Antonio Francisco Lisboa, "O Aleijadinho" ("Little Cripple"), has been called the "greatest architect and sculptor Brazil has produced." His achievement rests on the brilliance and quantity of his work in both these media, and in his miraculous ability to turn out numerous masterpieces despite the fact that he suffered from a debilitating disease that plagued his career and grew worse with age. According to some accounts, the disease (possibly leprosy or syphilis) caused the artist gradually to lose not only his toes and fingers, but his skin and vision as well. Although much of our knowledge about his illness is based on legends and contemporary accounts, most scholars agree that the mulatto artist must have suffered intensely during the last 40 years of his life: he had to be carried to and from his work sites, and sculpt with tools strapped to the stubs of his wrists.

Aleijadinho was the illegitimate son of the Portuguese architect Manuel Francisco Lisboa and a black slave girl. His father taught him the basics of architectural design and construction, but Aleijadinho learned the stone-carver's trade from the Brazilian sculptor Francisco Xavier de Brito. Although Aleijadinho's origin and color meant that he was excluded from the local artists' guilds and could accept commissions only through intermediaries, his genius was widely recognized. By the late 1770s he was the leading practitioner of the Brazilian Baroque-Rococo style.

The historical background of Aleijadinho's achievement was the discovery of gold in the interior captaincy of Minas Gerais in the early 1690s (and diamonds in 1729). The concerted exploitation of these mineral resources gave rise to a group of mining settlements focused around the town of Vila Rica (today Ouro Preto). By 1700 the town had a population of about 60,000 and had become the capital of Minas captaincy. The wealth from the mines created a building boom: in and around the capital, new churches, monasteries and municipal buildings were erected using slave labor and craftsmen who flocked to the region from all over Brazil. Commissions were abundant, and talented artists were respected and sought after. The hills of Minas provided the materials for these artists—gold for the decorators of church interiors, soft soapstone for the sculptors. It has been observed that for all the misfortunes of his personal life, Aleijadinho was fortunate indeed for having such a plentiful supply of the highly malleable soapstone: a harder material might have precluded his incredible sculptural achievement.

Had Aleijadinho not suffered from a crippling disability, his artistic output would still seem prodigious to us today. Among his many works, which included numerous chapels, altars, doors and facades, the Church of São Francisco in Ouro Preto (1766-94) stands out as one of his superior achievements. There the architect worked out a plastic unity of rich volumetric complexity by recessing the cylindrical towers in an undulant plane well behind that of the main portal. The effect is one of greater verticality in the frontispiece and greater interpenetration of the towers' monumental form and the interior space of the nave. In the chevet, Aleijadinho placed the pulpits in the chancel arch, thereby resolving a circulation problem and making possible, through the suppression of the nave corridors, a greater spatial unity. The lateral elevations are enriched by the opening up to the outside of the tribunes above the sanctuary, which became arcaded verandas. Though similar manipulations are found in contemporaneous church architecture in Portugal, Aleijadinho's works are noteworthy for their softer, more undulating character, made possible in part by the material used.

Aleijadinho's masterpiece is the open-air sanctuary of the Church of Bom Jesus de Matosinhos in the little town of Congonhas de Campo near Ouro Preto. There, more than 60 years old and at the painful height of his affliction, he carved his psychically intense, 10-foot-tall statues of the 12 prophets. Monumentally guarding the entrance to the church, these sculptures alone, in their expressive sculptural presence and touching pathos, could have established his reputation for posterity. Below the church he designed 10 little chapels in a garden lined by rows of giant royal palm trees. Within these he carved life-size wooden figures depicting the stations of the cross. At Congonhas Aleijadinho achieved a plastically rich, characteristically Baroque synthesis of media that combines theatrical drama and solemn religious ritual in a unified architectural ensemble of penetrating power.

—DAVID K. UNDERWOOD

ALESSI, Galeazzo.

Italian. Born in Perugia, Italy, in 1512. Died in Porta Sole, 30 December 1572. Studied with the architect/painter Giovanni Battista Caporali, Giulio Danti, and possibly Michelangelo.

Chronology of Works
All in Italy

1542-44	Rocca Paolina (loggia and Stanze)†
1546	Sant'Angelo della Pace (loggia, later oratory)
1547	Palazzo dei Priori (loggia)
1547*	Santa Maria del Popolo (nowCamera di Commercio)
1547	Via Nuova, Perugia
1548	Villa Giustiniani (laterCambiaso)
1549-72	Santa Maria di Carignano (not completed until 1603)
1551-53	Porta del Molo
1555ff.	Villa Grimaldi (later Sauli), Genoa†
1557	Palazzo Marino
1561	San Barnaba, Milan
1562-66*	Sacro Monte di Varallo (porta maggiore and chapel of Adam and Eve), Varallo
1564	Auditorio delle Scuole Canobiane, Milan†
1567	Church of San Pietro (wooden tabernacle)†
1567-68	Duomo, Perugia (southern portal)
1568	Santa Maria degli Angeli, Assisi
1568	Santa Maria presso San Celso, Milan
1570	San Francesco, Assisi (bronze tabernacle)
1570-72	Palazzo dei Priori (renovation)
1571	San Pietro (Chiostro delle Stelle), Perugia
1571	San Rufino, Assisi (renovation)

Publications

BOOKS BY ALESSI

Libro dei misteri: Progetto di pianificazione urbanistica, architettonica e figurativa del Sacro Monte di Varallo in Valsesia (1565-1569). 2 vols. Bologna, 1974.

BOOKS ABOUT ALESSI

BROWN, NANCY A. HOUGHTON: *The Milanese Architecture of Galeazzo Alessi.* New York, 1980.
Galeazzo Alessi: Catalogo della mostra di fotografie, rilievi, disegni. Genoa, Italy, 1974.
HEYDENREICH, LUDWIG H., and LOTZ, WOLFGANG: *Architecture in Italy: 1400-1600.* Harmondsworth, England, 1974.
NEGRI, E.: *Galeazzo Alessi a Genova.* Genoa, 1957.

ARTICLES ABOUT ALESSI

BRIGGS, MARTIN SHAW: ''Architects of the Later Renaissance in Italy: Galeazzo Alessi.'' *Architectural Review* 38 (August 1915): 26-31.

BROWN, NANCY A. HOUGHTON: ''The Church of St. Barnaba
in Milan.'' *Arte Lombarda* 9, No. 2 (1964): 62-94; 10, No.
1 (1965): 65-98.
KÜHN, G: ''Galeazzo Alessi und die Genuesische Architektur im
16. Jahrhundert.'' *Jahrbuch für Kunstwissenschaft* (1929).
PERONI, ADRIANO: ''Architetti manieristi nell'Italia settentrio-
nale: Pellegrino Tibaldi e Galeazzo Alessi.'' *Bollettino del
Centro Internazionale di Studi di Architettura ''Andrea Palladio''* 9 (1967).
ROCCO, GIOVANNI: ''Galeazzo Alessi a Milano.'' *Atti del IV
Convegno di Storia dell'Architettura* (Milan, 1939).

*

Galeazzo Alessi was the leading architect of Genoa and Milan
in the mid-16th century, known even beyond those cities from
the publication of many of his designs by Peter Paul Rubens
in *Palazzi di Genova,* printed first in 1622 and again in 1652.

Alessi's first commission was for the Rocca Paolina (1542-
44), and, from what we know of it, the design seems to have
reflected the rather restrained style of Antonio da Sangallo, who

was working in the area; Alessi's first surviving work, done in
1546, a loggia turned later into the oratory of Sant'Angelo della
Pace, also was designed in that style.

While working in his hometown of Perugia, Alessi met Bartolommeo Sauli, a Genoese banker and the apostolic treasurer in
Perugia and Umbria, and it was he perhaps who encouraged
Alessi to go to Genoa and work on the memorial church of
Sauli's family, Santa Maria di Carignano. This was Alessi's
first important building, but its history is halting and complicated. The commission was placed in 1549, work beginning in
1552 and continuing on and off for the rest of the century, the
dome not being finished until 1603. The plan, a Greek cross
set within a square, from which the apse protrudes slightly,
was based upon the plans for St. Peter's by Michelangelo and
Sangallo. Here, however, the major dome at the crossing is
surrounded by four more domes and two *campanili* (four were
planned), which reach almost to the height of the major dome,
while the others barely rise above the line of the roof. The
crossing piers are massive, yet the dome is hardly wider than
the arms of the crossing, so it serves more as a vertical accent
above the junction of the arms rather than as the center of the

Galeazzo Alessi: Villa Cambiaso (formerly Villa Giustiniani), Genoa, Italy, 1548

building. Outside, each of the arms of the cross has attached facades, great pilasters carrying pediments with large lunette windows. Not all was done as Alessi intended, and much sculptural ornament was added in the 17th century. But the effect of Alessi's design is there, with its peculiarities of decoration and scale; together with Todi and Montepulciano, this is one of the grandest centrally planned churches of the 16th century.

Alessi was also busy with secular works. The suburban villa of Luca Giustiniani (now the Villa Cambiaso) was begun in 1548, and reflected something of the Palazzo Farnese in Rome, if made more symmetrical and axial. The exterior decoration, as we would now expect, is very rich: paired Doric columns on pedestals support paired Corinthian pilasters, which, in turn, support paired segments of a solid parapet at each wing. And in a loggia on the second floor, Alessi set a range of herms, dense vegetal friezes, and decorative vault and niche patterns.

Alessi's great opportunity came in 1550, when the doge of Genoa issued a decree ordering the layout of a new street, on the model of a classical city, in an area on the outskirts of the city that was comparatively vacant. This was the Strada Nuova; there, between 1558 and 1570, some 11 palaces were built (15 are there now) in what was perhaps the first such organized street of independent, block-like structures in Italy, all different in their details and designed by different architects, yet governed by a simple, rational plan, which, according to Giorgio Vasari, was by Alessi. Alessi's own designs for such buildings are remarkable. In 1555 he began work on the Villa Grimaldi, which had some notable gardens and fountains, and lavish decorations. He continued that manner in a building in Milan in 1557 for a Genoese banker, Tomaso Marino; it was a vast town house, as large as anything being built at the time in Rome. The facade is, at one level, highly disciplined, yet the subordinate elements seem so rich as almost to swallow up the idea of the structure. Also, the pattern of window articulation moves from a richness of the lower sections—in which a Doric order is set around windows with massive keystones and broken columns—to a comparatively plain section at the highest level, where, for all the plainness, the pilasters end in a curious reverse U-shape where capitals should be. In the courtyard every pair of columns supports an architrave, which serves as the impost block for a round-headed arcade above. Again Alessi set up a contrast between the plainer Doric columns and the Ionic piers above: all this is filled out with lions' heads on the brackets over the Doric columns (masculine), and with caryatids in the Ionic (feminine) upper story.

Soon after this, in 1568, Alessi produced a design for the Church of Santa Maria presso San Celso, a building of the scale of the Palazzo Marino, but work there, which was not begun until after Alessi's death, was carried out by Martino Bassi. Many changes were made, most obviously in the use of sculptural ornament, which Alessi had set in the upper two stories of the whole church, but which Bassi confined to smaller, isolated sections; also, the height of the obelisques that Alessi had set around the roofline was reduced. Alessi had long been involved with some of the church reforms, notably at the Church of San Barnaba (1561) built for the newly instituted Barnabite Order. The idea he demonstrated there, of making a firm division between the nave, the presbytery and the choir, was codified later by Saint Charles Borromeo in his *Instructiones* (1575). Alessi also worked on Milan Cathedral and, in this new spirit of religious art, on the project for the Sacro Monte at Varallo (1562-66).

Alessi spent his last years back in Perugia, and the work he did there then, the Chiostro delle Stelle at San Pietro and the renovation of the Cathedral of San Rufino, both 1571, seems more restrained than his earlier projects. What Alessi had contributed to the traditional love in Lombardy of decorated surfaces had become more controlled. And the effect of his work, like that of Pirro Ligorio, a similar designer in Rome, yielded for a while in the tradition of architecture to the austere and authoritative models of Michelangelo and Vignola.

—DAVID CAST

ALMQVIST, Osvald.

Swedish. Born in Trankil, near Karlstad, Värmland, Sweden, 2 October 1884. Died in Stockholm, 6 April 1950. Attended Royal Institute of Technology, Stockholm, 1904-08, and Royal Academy of Arts, Stockholm, 1909-10. Founded Klara School of Architecture, with others, Stockholm, 1910; worked for Ivar Tengbom in Stockholm, 1910-11; in partnership with Gustaf Linden, Stockholm, 1911-13; in private practice, Stockholm, 1913-16; architect and engineer for Stora Kopparbergs Bergslag Company Domnarvet Ironworks, Dalecarlia, 1916-20; returned to private practice, Stockholm, 1920; head of Committee on Standardization of Kitchen Equipment, 1922-34; town-planning adviser to Södertälje, 1940-48.

Chronology of Works
All in Sweden unless noted

1911-13	Apartment Building, Stockholm (with Gustaf Linden)
1911-13	Hotel, Nyköping (with Gustaf Linden)
1916-20	Bergslagsbyn Workers' Village at Domnarvet Ironworks, Dalecarlia
1917-21	Forshuvudforsen Power Station (with Vattenbyggnadsbyran)
1924	Elementary School, Sundsvall
1925-28	Hammarforsen Power Station (with Vattenbyggnadsbyran)
1925-28	Krangforsen Power Station (with Vattenbyggnadsbyran)
1929	Chenderoh Power Station, Malaya (with Vattenbyggnadsbyran and Rendel, Palmer and Tritton)
1930	Terrace houses, furniture and industrial products in concrete, Stockholm Exhibition
1931	Town plan for Stockholm (with Sigurd Lewerentz)
1931-32	Workshop Training School, Domnarvet, Dalecarlia
1933-36	Vocational School, Lulea
1939-40	Plan for Aarsta suburb of Stockholm (with Albert Lilienthal)

Publications

BOOKS BY ALMQVIST

Byggnadsplaner för bostadsområden: Ñgra allmänna synpunkter. Stockholm, 1921.
Domnarvets industriskolas nybyggnad. Stockholm, 1933.
Köket och ekonomiqavdelningen i mindrebostadslägenheter. Stockholm, 1934.

ARTICLES BY ALMQVIST

Numerous articles in *Byggmästaren*, Stockholm.

BOOKS ABOUT ALMQVIST

LINN, BJÖRN: *Osvald Almqvist: En arkitekt och hans arbete.* Stockholm, 1967.

*

Osvald Almqvist's early education, first at the Royal Institute of Technology, and then at the Royal Academy of Fine Arts in Stockholm, led him to establish (with Sigurd Lewerentz and others) in 1910 the Klara School of Architecture in Stockholm—with Carl Bergsten, Ragnar Östberg, Ivar Tengbom and Carl Westman as teachers. The main themes explored at the short-lived school (where Erik Gunnar Asplund also studied) were concerned with a rediscovery of the vernacular and national traditions of Swedish architecture and design, as part of an awareness of national identity asserting itself throughout Europe at the time.

Almqvist traveled and worked in Belgium and Germany, before settling in Stockholm to work with Ivar Tengbom from 1910 to 1911, after which he formed a practice with Gustaf Linden. By then, Almqvist had become interested in the theories of Camillo Sitte, and his work moved away from the academic classicism that had been taught at the Academy. Since the summer of 1910 he had become an enthusiastic student of the timber-framed buildings of Sweden, and was steeped in the language of traditional structures, forms and details. His early work at Nyköping with Linden owes much to medieval apartment blocks and traditional vernacular buildings.

Almqvist entered an unfinished scheme for the Stockholm Woodland Cemetery Competition in 1914; this was won by Asplund and Lewerentz, but Almqvist's design seems to have exercised a powerful influence on the later realization of the project. The fact that the design was submitted in a sketchy state was an early indication of Almqvist's distressing inability to make decisions, and of a reluctance to commit himself, tendencies that were to become more acute as the years passed. His partnership with Linden was dissolved, and Almqvist became architect and engineer to the Domnarvet Ironworks in 1916. For Domnarvet he created Bergslagsbyn, a model village for workers that incorporated some of the lessons learned from Swedish vernacular housing and from the traditional townscapes of medieval Europe, mixed with a strong dose of theory from the works of Sitte.

From 1917, however, Almqvist's work changed in character, and his Forshuvudforsen Hydroelectric Power Station (completed in 1921) owes little to period precedent. Possibly his collaboration with Vattenbyggnadsbyran influenced this change of direction, for their hydroelectric power stations at Hammarforsen and Krangforsen (both 1925-28) are free of any reference to the past.

From that time, Almqvist was to evolve his theory of sanitary aesthetics that would help designers to avoid inessentials, and would promote solutions derived from first principles and from a clear analysis of necessity, function, structure, materials and detail. In the years following 1922 he designed standard kitchen components, and his ideas were consolidated in the publications of the Swedish kitchen standards in 1934. These standards have been the basis for much that is now taken for granted in domestic utilities.

He collaborated with Lewerentz in the redevelopment competition for Jönköping in 1928, and the project won first prize. Almqvist's most celebrated expression of the principles of utility was his design for the Chenderoh Hydroelectric Power Station in Malaya (1929) which he evolved in collaboration with Vattenbyggnadsbyran and Rendel, Palmer and Tritton of London. The success of this project made Almqvist an international authority on the design of power stations.

Almqvist prepared several designs for the Stockholm Exhibition of 1930, including a house, furniture and a prefabricated cast-iron stair that became a classic. In 1931 he again worked with Lewerentz, this time on a town plan for Stockholm, and the two architects collaborated on a competition project for a museum at Malmö in 1932. In later years, Almqvist ran a small practice, and became acting head of the Stockholm Parks Development in 1936, a post he relinquished two years later when it became clear that his administrative abilities and tendency to procrastinate made him unsuitable for the job. His last works were concerned with the planning of the Årsta district of Stockholm (with Albert Lilienthal), and with the planning of the town of Södertälje (1940-48).

In 1950 Almqvist succumbed to the lung disease that had plagued him since 1921. He left many drawings of small projects that reflected his lifelong interest in Swedish vernacular housing and in the problems of designing for ordinary people and everyday life.

—JAMES STEVENS CURL

AMMANN, Othmar.

Swiss. Born in Switzerland, 1879. Died in 1965. Received civil engineering degree from the Swiss Federal Institute of Technology, 1902. Moved to the United States, 1904; worked for the engineer John Mayer; worked for C. C. Schneider, 1907; worked for the Hudson River Bridge Company, 1912; joined the Port of New York Authority, 1925; returned to private practice, 1939; partnership with Charles Whitney, 1946.

Chronology of Works
All in the United States

1912ff.	Hellgate Bridge, New York City
1931	Bayonne Bridge, New York City
1931	George Washington Bridge, New York City
1932ff.	Triborough Bridge, New York City
1930s	Bronx-Whitestone Bridge, New York City
1964	Verrazano-Narrows Bridge, New York City (date completed)

Publications

ARTICLES BY AMMANN

"The George Washington Bridge: General Conception and Development of Design." *Transactions of the American Society of Civil Engineers* 97 (1933).
"The Hudson River Bridge at New York between Fort Washington and Fort Lee." *Proceedings of the Connecticut Society of Civil Engineers* (1928): 47-74.
"Present Status of Designs of Suspension Bridges with Respect to Dynamic Wind Action." *Boston Society of Civil Engineers* 40 (1953).

BOOKS ABOUT AMMANN

BILLINGTON, DAVID P.: *The Tower and the Bridge: The New Art of Structural Engineering.* Princeton, New Jersey, 1983.

STÜSSI, FRITZ: *Othmar H. Ammann: Sein Beitrag zur Entwicklung des Brückenbaus.* Basel, 1974.

ARTICLES ABOUT AMMANN

GIES, JOSEPH: "The Biggest Bridge: The Verrazano-Narrows." In *Wonders of the Modern World.* New York, 1966.

*

The Verrazano Narrows Bridge, perhaps the most majestic bridge in New York Harbor, was the last of many bridges designed by engineer Othmar Ammann. For many years the Verrazano was the longest suspension bridge in the world, spanning the Narrows between Brooklyn and Staten Island at a record-breaking 4,260 feet. Ammann built the bridge for Robert Moses as an independent consulting engineer, after a long career working for the Port of New York Authority (now the Port Authority of New York and New Jersey) and the Triborough Bridge Authority.

During a 35-year period, Ammann designed every major bridge in the New York area—the Bayonne, the George Washington, the Triborough, the Bronx-Whitestone and the Verrazano Narrows—and helped transform the landscape of the region. All of Ammann's bridges are superb engineering and architectural landmarks, and they are all the more remarkable because they were designed by one man.

Ammann, who received his civil engineering degree from the Swiss Federal Institute of Technology in 1902, first became involved in the design and construction of steel bridges in Frankfurt, Germany, and was steered to America by a former teacher. Soon after his arrival in the United States in 1904, Ammann was hired by John Mayer, a consulting engineer who specialized in railroad bridges.

Ammann made his first mark, however, in 1907, when a cantilever bridge across the St. Lawrence River near Quebec collapsed, killing 79 workmen. Then 28 years old and employed by the Pennsylvania Steel Company, Ammann offered his assistance to C. C. Schneider, who had been hired to investigate the disaster. After heading the inquiry for Schneider, Ammann continued to work for him for several years.

In 1912 Ammann went to work for the Hudson River Bridge Company, headed by Gustav Lindenthal, where he served as deputy chief engineer on the construction of the Hellgate Bridge across the East River in New York. Lindenthal envisioned a bridge crossing the Hudson River at 57th Street in New York, while Ammann maintained the belief that Washington Heights was a superior location.

In 1925 Ammann joined the agency then known as the Port of New York Authority, established only four years earlier. Among Ammann's first projects for the authority was the design and construction of the Bayonne Bridge, spanning the Kill Van Kull between Staten Island and Bayonne, New Jersey. His graceful, parabolic, two-hinged, steel-arch design received worldwide acclaim. At the time of its completion in 1931, the Bayonne Bridge was the longest steel-arch suspension bridge in the world—and it remained so for almost 50 years.

The George Washington Bridge, which also opened in 1931, was an even greater engineering and architectural achievement. Completed on time and within budget, the 3,500-foot-long bridge had a span twice the length of any existing suspension bridge. As Ammann had previously envisioned, it connected Washington Heights with Fort Lee, New Jersey. The bridge displays an excellence of proportion in the long central span and short side spans, as well as in the shallow curve of the cables. The heavy steel framework of the arched towers, originally intended to be clad in masonry but left exposed, conveys classical form with a machine aesthetic.

Ammann's concern with economy and simplicity led to his invention of flexible stiffening trusses, which saved $10 million, or about 17 percent of the total costs of the original bridge. The construction of the George Washington Bridge also demonstrated that the most critical factor in a bridge's cost was not the length of span but the expense of the foundations and the traffic capacity. Anticipating future growth in the region, Ammann's design provided for the addition of a second roadway, which was completed in 1957.

By the early 1930s Ammann had established a national reputation, and was asked to assist on a number of projects across the nation, including the Golden Gate Bridge in San Francisco. In 1932 Robert Moses, then head of the Triborough Bridge Authority, asked Ammann and his team of Port Authority engineers to complete the design of the Triborough Bridge, a tremendous undertaking intended to connect Manhattan, Queens and the Bronx. Ammann cut $2 million from the cost of the bridge by eliminating one of the two proposed decks, dropping the proposed granite facing and reducing the number of supporting piers.

That bridge was followed by another bridge designed by Ammann for Moses—the Bronx-Whitestone Bridge, which was intended to channel traffic to and from the 1939 World's Fair. Ammann's slender suspension span embodied an elegance of outline and detail, and was the first bridge to use shallow plate girders as stiffeners rather than the customary deep trusses. The bridge exhibited relatively high levels of vertical motion under strong winds, however, and following the Tacoma Narrows Bridge disaster in 1940, measures were taken to strengthen the Bronx-Whitestone by adding diagonal stays and by widening the roadway.

In 1939, at the age of 60, Ammann returned to private practice as a consulting engineer. Although he wished only enough work for himself and his son Werner, the firm grew, and in 1946 he entered a partnership with Milwaukee engineer Charles Whitney. Today the firm of Ammann and Whitney is one of the leading engineering firms in the world, with projects—including bridges, highways, floating drydocks and airports—throughout the world.

Moses called on Ammann once more, after rejecting a baroque design for the Verrazano Narrows Bridge. Then 80 years old, Ammann revised the design to produce the streamlined suspension bridge, which was completed in 1964. In a report to the New York Academy of Sciences on the design, Ammann commented that he had applied aesthetic considerations to the form of the struts at the top and below the deck, and to the structural makeup of the shafts and struts to create a pleasing appearance.

Again and again, Ammann had skillfully demonstrated that aesthetics could be combined with economy. His death in 1965 brought to an end the golden era of bridge building in New York.

—BETH SULLEBARGER

AMMANNATI, Bartolomeo.

Italian. Born in Settignano, near Florence, Italy, 18 June 1511. Died in Florence, 22 April 1592. Married the poet Laura Battiferri, 1550. Studied with Baccio Bandinelli, Florence, and with Jacopo Sansovino, Venice; studied Michelangelo's tombs for

Bartolomeo Ammannati: Palazzo Pitti, Florence, Italy, 1560ff.

the Medici Chapel at San Lorenzo, Florence. Worked in Padua, 1544-46, then in Rome, ca. 1550-60, and finally in Florence.

Chronology of Works
All in Italy

1544-46	Triumphal Archway, Palazzo Benavides
1545	Benavides Tomb, Padua
1550-53	San Pietro in Montorio (Del Monte Chapel)
1551-55	Villa Giulia, Rome (with Giorgio Vasari, Giacomo Barozzi da Vignola, and Michelangelo)
1553	Palazzo Firenze, Rome
1557-75	Palazzo Griffoni, Florence
1558-59	Laurentian Library, Florence (execution of Michelangelo's model for the staircase)
1560ff	Palazzo Pitti, Florence (enlargements and alterations)
1567-70	Ponte Santa Trinita
1572	Tempietto della Vittoria, near Arezzo
1575	Houses, Arte della Lana, Florence
1575	Madonna del Umilità, Pistoia (restoration of cupola)
1576	Villa Medici, Rome [attributed]
1578	Palazzo Provinciale, Lucca
1579-85	Jesuit College and Church of San Giovannino, Florence
1581	Collegio Romano, Rome [attributed]
1592	Church of Santa Maria in Gradi, Arezzo

Publications

BOOKS BY AMMANNATI

La città. Rome, 1970.

BOOKS ABOUT AMMANNATI

ANDRES, GLENN M.: *The Villa Medici in Rome*. 2 vols. New York, 1976.
FOSSI, MAZZINO: *Bartolomeo Ammannati: Architetto*. Florence, 1967.
KINNEY, PETER: *The Early Sculpture of Bartolomeo Ammannati*. New York, 1976.

ARTICLES ABOUT AMMANNATI

BARSALLI, I. BELLI: "Problemi sulla tarda architettura di B. Ammannati: Il palazzo pubblico di Lucca." *Palladio* 1-2 (1960).
BAYER, F.: "La construction de la Villa Medicis." *Revue d'art antique et moderne* 51 (1927): 3-14, 109-120.
BETTINI, G.: "Note sui soggiorni veneti di B. Ammannati." *Arti* 3 (1937).
BIAGI, L.: "Di Bartolommeo Ammannati e di alcune sue opere." *Arte* 26 (1923).
GABBRIELLI, A.: "Su B. Ammannati." *Critica d'arte* 2 (1937).

KRIEGBAUM, E.: ''Ein verschollenes-Brunnenwerk des B. Ammannati.'' *Mitteilungen des Kunsthistorischen Instituts in Florenz* (August 1929).

PIRRI, P.: ''L'architetto B. Ammannati i Gesuiti.'' *Archivum historicum S. J.* 12 (1943).

SANPAOLESI, P.: ''La vita vasariana del Sansovino e l'Ammannati.'' In *Atti del Convegno Internazionale IV Centenario Prima Edizione delle ''Vite'' del Vasari.* Florence, 1952.

VENTURI, ADOLFO: ''Bartolomeo Ammannati.'' Vol. 11, part 2, pp. 212-350 in *Storia dell arte italiana*. Milan, 1939.

VODOZ, E.: ''Studien zum architektonischen Werk des Bartolomeo Ammannati.'' *Mitteilungen des Kunsthistorischen Instituts in Florenz* 6 (1941): 1-141.

WITTKOWER, RUDOLF: ''Michelangelo's Biblioteca Laurenzia.'' In *Idea and Image*. London, 1978.

*

Bartolomeo Ammannati was primarily a Mannerist sculptor. As an architect, he designed the elegant and graceful Ponte Santa Trinità in Florence (1567-70), which was destroyed by the retreating German forces in 1944 and subsequently rebuilt. With Giacomo da Vignola (1507-73; also known as Giacomo Barozzi) and his fellow Tuscan, Giorgio Vasari (1511-74), Ammannati played some part, as yet not fully codified, in the design of the Villa Giulia in Rome between 1551 and 1555. In Florence he enlarged and altered the garden facade of the Pitti Palace (1560), the semi-official residence of the grand dukes of Tuscany. His garden facade is heavily rusticated, both subtle and obvious in its use of rustication as supports and as arched lintels. In Florence he completed the Palazzo Griffoni (1557) and supervised the building of Michelangelo's vestibule staircase at the Laurentian Library. Outside Florence, Ammannati's other known works include the Tempietto della Vittoria near Arezzo (1572) and the Palazzo Provinciale in Lucca (1578), where the frontispiece is composed of a Serlian loggia drawn in part from the Serlian loggia used by Vasari at the Uffizi in Florence. Ammannati broke no new ground in his few original designs; he was, instead, a highly competent, if not inspired, architect, whose career fell entirely within the span of Romano-Tuscan Mannerism.

Mannerism in architecture has been neither completely analyzed nor fully acknowledged as a distinct architectural style. However, profound changes took place in architectural design between 1515 and 1590 in Rome, Florence and other northern Italian cities—changes that transformed the architecture of the High Renaissance into something which was quite similar yet quite different from its sources. It was in that period and in those places that Ammannati worked; his architecture is deeply and wholly Mannerist.

All Late Renaissance architects followed the theories of Vitruvius (first century B.C.), Leon Battista Alberti (1404-72) and other architectural authors, such as Antonio di Pietro Averlino Filarete (ca. 1400-69), Francesco di Giorgio Martini (1439-1502) and even Leonardo. They knew the books of Sebastiano Serlio (1475-1554), Vignola and even Andrea Palladio (1508-80). They believed that they were sharing in an on-going tradition, yet their architecture is often labeled ''Mannerist'' to distinguish it from the works of preceding generations. Vasari acknowledged that he and his contemporaries had discovered the true manner, the proper ''maniera'' of building. Vasari believed he and his fellow architects to be the heirs of the Renaissance, not rebels against it; they were, in their own thoughts, the continuation not the contradiction of that linear development. It is now generally accepted that Mannerism, as a movement in Italian art, spans a period of some eighty years.

The beginnings and the end are both temporally fluid, and the style, the ''Stylish Style'' (as it may be termed), began simultaneously in both Rome and Florence and was based on the works of Raphael and his circle, and especially on the works of Michelangelo. The spread of the style into northern Italy, and eventually into northern Europe, was aided by the political upheavals of the first third of the cinquecento. The Sack of Rome in 1527 and the siege of Florence caused a wholesale movement of artists from those centers to the more secure courts of the smaller states of the North. Eventually some artists returned to Rome, while others remained in their new homes practicing the style learned in Rome during the heady days of Pope Leo X. Some returned to Florence or were called home to take up service in the court of Cosimo I de'Medici after he had become the second duke of that city.

Mannerism, then, reflects a particular historical period which, in itself, differs from the period of the High Renaissance but developed out of the High Renaissance; it was responsive to the changes that had taken place in Italy between the reigns of Pope Leo X (Medici) and Pope Clement VII (Medici). The style reflects the changing political, social and aesthetic mores and practices of post-invasion Italy. The arts of the period all share this ability to reflect those changes that had taken place, rapidly and painfully, in Italian life. Those changes, which were all-encompassing, caused the emphasis to be placed on some traits of the art of the High Renaissance at the expense of others.

Rudolf Wittkower, in his magisterial essay ''Michelangelo's Biblioteca Laurenziana,'' adumbrates the salient characteristics of Mannerist architecture. He refers to those characteristics as ''the problem of Mannerism,'' since the characteristics listed are quite different from those which mark and define the architecture of the High Renaissance. In his dissection of the architecture of Florence before and after the establishment of the Medici duchy, Wittkower isolates the following features: ambiguity, conflict, duality of function, inversion and permutation. Ambiguity is described as an attempt to work out the architecture according to one system which immediately leads to another; the resulting ambivalence creates doubt and tension. Conflict is described as a restless fluctuation between opposite extremes, which is true both of the parts and of the whole. Duality of function is one of the ''fundamental laws'' of Mannerist architecture as members may seem to have divergent functions apart from the roles typically assigned the Orders. Inversion forbids a vertical reading of the facade; the eye is led to wander from side to side and up and down. The movement thus provoked can be called ambiguous. Permutation indicates a constant shifting of forms and parts into seemingly other forms and parts, thus a pilaster strip appears to become a wall, while a wall itself may invoke a feeling of ambiguous movement by becoming a recessed plane.

Mannerism in architecture can be said to be characterized by a sharp contrast between two artistic principles, the classic and the anti-classic, wherein the structure is dissolved and there is either a crushing emphasis on, or a visual elimination of, mass. There is a movement toward the exploitation of, or the denial of the idea of load or of apparent stability. The style exploits contradictory elements in a facade; it employs harshly rectilinear forms and emphasizes a type of nervous or arrested movement. This denial of stability extends to a denial of the wall itself as the surface of the wall is either heavily rusticated or over-refined, and brutally direct rustication occurs in combination with an excess of attenuated delicacy. All these elements represent the anti-classical strain in Mannerist architecture which led to the breaking-up of the logical, spatial relations of Renaissance architecture.

The classical face of Mannerism can be found in the dependence on the classic works of the Renaissance and in its dependence on the use of the classical Orders. The classic and the anti-classic co-existed in Mannerist architecture in a profound, unbalanced equilibrium. Indeed, Mannerism "was an attempt to sever art from the surface realities of life and to pursue it, not to a logical, but rather to an intuitive conclusion," as Wittkower noted. The Mannerism practiced in Florence during the reign of Cosimo I produced an architecture that was as dependent on Roman models as it was on local ones. Because the regime was essentially quite conservative, Florentine Mannerism was also conservative.

It is possible to determine something of Ammannati's style—conservative, Florentine, Mannerist—in his addition to the Pitti Palace. This addition to the palace was made to the cube-like structure attributed to Filippo Brunelleschi (1377-1446), which was heavily rusticated and set the tone for the whole new composition. The scheme devised for the extension was based on the typical Roman or Florentine town palace, centered on its cortile. However, Ammannati departed from this scheme by eliminating the rear portion of the cube-like block, thereby opening up the cortile to the gardens beyond. His play on the original form was quite subtle, as the first range of the cortile is closed on all four sides, the second range, the piano nobile—taking advantage of a difference in the ground level—eliminates the rear section, opening up the upper floors to a view of the gardens and creating the effect of a pavilion set between two wings or of a French-style *coeur d'honneur*. The uppermost floor continues this U-shaped pattern and is capped by a broad cornice which unites the wings to the central facade, emphasizing the projection of the wings from the inner facade. Ammannati succeeded in fusing the town palace and the country villa, as the cortile facade faces the expanse of the lower Boboli Gardens, looking directly to the open-air theater which forms the closure of the vista across the formal lawn-beds which continue the outer lines of the projecting wings. A fountain was placed on the roof of the lower range of the cortile, marking the transition from palace to garden and from inner to outer space. If Brunelleschi's stoney facade presents an image of fortified urban grandeur, Ammannati's garden facade presents an image of courtly arcadian grace, while continuing the rustication of the principal street facade.

It is in the arrangement of the elements of the cortile facade and in his use of rustication that Ammannati achieved his greatest success while also supplying an exemplary instance of Mannerist architecture. Nearly the entire surface is rusticated, engaged columns are banded and each bay is framed by bands of rustication acting as arches or lintels. The bays grow more complex as they proceed from side to center and from lower to upper and a complex rhythm is set up in the alternating distribution of arched and straight-headed windows. The central bay of each range is broader than the side bays; they contain pseudo-Serlian arches with blind side-bays and windows set in a portion of the central arch. The ranges of the cortile facade are arcuated in the "Colosseum" fashion while the garden facades of the enframing wings bear rusticated pilasters below and banded semi-round columns above. The lower range carries a simple ovolo cornice; the upper, a rusticated lintel acting as a flattened arch. The upper corners of the wings transform the quoins into banded pilasters carrying a dentilated cornice below the pitched eaves. The cortile facade contains one window per bay per floor and the facade of the wings contain two windows per bay, one above the other, creating the effect of a four-story building set behind the two-story trabeation so that the wings, which are actually close together, seem twice as high as the central block which appears much deeper and in greater recess due to the optical effect.

Ammannati's work at the Pitti fully reflects Wittkower's definition of Mannerist architectural features: ambiguity, conflict, duality of function, inversion and permutation. Vasari says of Ammannati that he "as architect, is giving his attention, with much honor and praise to the fabric of the Pitti in which work he has had a great opportunity to show the worth and grandeur of his mind."

—DONALD FRICELLI

ANDO, Tadao.

Japanese. Born in Osaka, Japan, 13 October 1941. Married Yumiko Kato, 1970; one son. Self-taught in architecture, 1962-69; traveled in the United States, Europe and Africa, 1962-70. Founder-director of Tadao Ando Architect and Associates, Osaka, 1969; has taught in the United States as visiting professor at Yale University, 1987, at Columbia University, 1988, and at Harvard University, 1990.

Chronology of Works
All in Japan unless noted

1973	Tomishima House, Oyodo, Osaka
1974	Tatsumi House, Taisho, Osaka
1974	Hiraoka House, Takarazuka, Hyogo
1974	Shibata House, Ashiya, Hyogo
1975	Soseikan (Yamaguchi/Twin House), Takarazuka, Hyogo
1976	Azuma House (Row-House Sumiyoshi), Sumiyoshi, Osaka
1976	Hirabayashi House, Suita, Osaka
1976	Bansho House, Nishi-Kamo, Aichi
1977	Manabe Residence (Tezukayama House), Abeno, Osaka
1977	Matsumoto House, Ashiya, Hyogo
1978	Ishihara House (Glass-Block House), Ikuno, Osaka
1978	Okusu House, Setagaya, Tokyo
1979	Horiuchi House (Glass-Block Wall), Sumiyoshi, Osaka
1979	Matsutani House, Fushimi, Kyoto
1979	Ohnishi House, Sumiyoshi, Osaka
1979	Ueda House, Soja, Okayama
1980	Steps (commercial complex), Takamatsu, Kagawa
1980	Matsumoto House, Wakayama
1980	Kitano Ivy Court, Chuo, Kobe
1980	Fuku House, Wakayama
1980	Katayama House, Nihinomiya, Hyogo
1981	Koshino House, Ashiya, Hyogo
1982	Tadao Ando and Associates Studio, Oyodo, Osaka
1982	Ishii House, Hammamatsu, Shizuoka
1982	Bigi Atelier Building, Shibuya, Tokyo
1982	Soseikan Tea-House, Takarazuka, Hyogo
1982	Akabane House, Setagaya, Tokyo
1982	Rokko Housing, Nada, Kobe
1983	Ryukotsushin Building, Shinjuku, Tokyo
1983	Kaneko House, Shibuya, Tokyo
1984	Uejo House, Suita, Osaka
1984	Iwasa House, Ashiya, Hyogo
1984	Koreyasu House, Toyonaka, Osaka
1984	Ota House, Takahashi, Okayama
1984	Minamibayashi House, Ikoma, Nara

Tadao Ando: Chapel on Mount Rokko, Kobe, Japan, 1986

1984	Time's Building, Nakagyo, Kyoto
1985	Bigi Aobadai Building, Meguro, Tokyo
1985	Bigi Atelier House, Shibuya, Tokyo
1985	Nakayama House, Nara
1985	Bal Mon-Petit-Chou Building, Sakyo, Kyoto
1986	Kidosaki House ('K House'), Setagaya, Tokyo
1986	Chapel on Mount Rokko, Kobe, Hyogo
1988	Chapel on the Water, Tomamu, Hokkaido
1988	I House (guest-house), Asiya, Hyogo
1988	Galleria Akka, Chuo-ku, Osaka
1989	Children's Museum, Hyogo
1989	Raika Headquarters Building, Suminoe, Osaka
1989	Natsukawa Memorial Hall, Hikone, Shiga
1989	Church of the Light, Ibaraki, Osaka
1990	Museum of Literature, Himeji, Hyogo
1990	Collezione, Tokyo
1991	Water Temple, Awaji Island
1992	Forest of Tombs Museum, Kumamoto Prefecture
1992	Children's Seminar House, Himeji, Hyogo
1992	Japanese Room, Chicago Art Institute, Illinois, U.S.A.
1992	Japan Pavilion, Expo '92, Seville, Spain
1992-	Rokko Housing II, Kobe

Publications

BOOKS BY ANDO

Tadao Ando. Tokyo, 1981.
Tadao Ando: Monographies. Paris, 1982.
Tadao Ando: Buildings, Projects, Writings. New York, 1984.

Tadao Ando: The Yale Studio and Current Works. New York, 1989

ARTICLES BY ANDO

"A Wedge in Circumstances." *Japan Architect* (June 1977).
"Conforming to the Environment." *Japan Architect* (August 1977).
"New Relations between Space and the Person." *Japan Architect*, October/November 1977).
"Blank Space on the Site." *Japan Architect* (May 1978).
"The Wall as Territorial Delineation." *Japan Architect* (June 1978).
"The Emotionally Made Architectural Spaces of Tadao Ando." *Japan Architect* (April 1980).
"Steps Upward Through Light." *Japan Architect* (July 1980).
"From Self-Enclosed Modern Architecture Toward Universality." *Japan Architect* (May 1982).
"Sun Place." *Japan Architect* (September 1982).
"The Simple Relationship Between Human Beings and Space" [interview]. *Architectes* (March 1983).
"Space Determined by Concrete Blocks." *Japan Architect* (October 1983).
"Town House at Kujo." *Japan Architect* (November/December 1983).
"Twin Wall." *Japan Architect* (August 1984).

BOOKS ABOUT ANDO

BOGNAR, BOTAND: *Contemporary Japanese Architecture: Its Development and Challenge.* New York, 1985.

BOGNAR, BOTAND: *Tadao Ando*. London, 1990.
BOGNAR, BOTAND: *The New Japanese Architecture*. New York, 1990.
CHASLIN, FRANCOIS; ISOZAKI, ARATA; GREGOTTI, VITTORIO AND OTHERS: *Tadao Ando-Minimalisme*. Paris, 1982.
FIELDS, D. (ed.): *Tadao Ando—Dormant Lines*. New York, 1991.
FRAMPTON, KENNETH (ed.): *Tadao Ando: Buildings, Projects, Writings*. New York, 1984.
FRAMPTON, KENNETH: *Tadao Ando*. Exhibition catalogue. New York, 1991.
FUTAGAWA, YUKIO (ed.): *Tadao Ando*. Tokyo, 1987.

ARTICLES ABOUT ANDO

BOGNAR, BOTOND: "Latest Work of Tadao Ando." *Architectural Review* (November 1982).
BOGNAR, BOTOND: "Tadao Ando: A Redefinition of Space, Time and Existence." *Architectural Design* (May 1981).
Croquis, special issue (July-September 1990).
Japan Architect, special issue (May 1982).
Japan Architect, special issue 1 (1991).
LAMARRE, F.: "Tadao Ando—The Beauty of Simplicity." *Architecture* (September 1982).
PETERS, D.: "Tadao Ando—A Japanese Architect of the New Wave." *Baumeister* (January 1982).
Space Design, special issue (June 1981).
"Tadao Ando: Recent Works and Projects.' *Japan Architect* (April 1988).
"Tadao Ando: Abstraction Serving Reality." *Progressive Architecture* (February 1990).
TAKEYAMA, KIYOSHI: "Tadao Ando: Heir to a Tradition." *Perspecta* 20 (1983).
TAKI, KOJI: "Architects and Builders: The Work of Fumihiko Maki and Tadao Ando." *Japan Architect* (November/December 1983).

One of the most prolific and accomplished architects in Japan and the world today, Tadao Ando has produced and continues to turn out an exceptionally original and high quality architecture. His work is capable of responding sensitively but also critically to the chaotic Japanese urban environment while capturing the poetics of changing natural phenomena and the appeal of the landscape. The hardly more than two-decade and, in many respects, unusual career of this Osaka-based architect has been marked from the very beginning by growing achievements and their continued recognition; Ando is recipient of the Annual Prize of the Architectural Institute of Japan (1980), the Award of the Japanese Ministry of Education (1986), Mainichi Art Prize (1987), Isoya Yoshida Award (1988), as well as the prestigious Alvar Aalto Medal (1985), the Gold Medal by the French Academy of Architecture (1989) and the Danish Carlsberg Architectural Prize (1992), among others. He has held exhibitions all over the world, including the Museum of Modern Art, New York (1991), and taught at universities such as Yale, Columbia and Harvard. His works have been published in every major international architectural magazine and journal as well as in several books.

A self-educated architect, Ando established his office in Osaka in 1969 and began to develop a radically new line of architecture characterized by the simple but powerful use of unfinished reinforced concrete structures: walls, trabeated pergolas, and so on. The geometrical simplicity of his small buildings, however, were always to conceal, and eventually reveal, a subtlety and richness in spatial articulation and experiential

qualities which continue to distinguish his designs to this day. His first widely acclaimed work, the revolutionary Row House in Sumiyoshi, Osaka (1976), represented as much a new architectural paradigm as a critical social commentary. In response to the deteriorating urban conditions in the 1970s of congestion, pollution and lack of privacy, Ando single-handedly pioneered what became known as "defensive architecture."

In order to protect the inhabitants, his early, small residences turned their backs toward the hostile city, hiding behind solid, unyielding walls hardly broken by openings. Opposing the sensory overload and volatility of the outside world, the *minimalist* designs of the Tezukayama House (1977), the Glass-Block House (1978), both in Osaka, and the Koshino Residence (1981) in Ashiya, in addition to the earlier Row House, all emphasized the tranquility of traditional *sukiya*-style architecture and the courtyard arrangement of the urban residence or *machiya*. Ando's buildings thus simultaneously revealed not only an explicit opposition to increasingly hedonistic contemporary lifestyles and conformist postmodern architecture, but also a strong affinity with the simplicity and "primitivism" of the Japanese vernacular.

In pursuing his goals, Ando found a powerful ally in nature, which was rapidly squeezed out by the reckless megapolitan developments in Japan. The incorporation of small courtyards has become an indispensable strategy and element in just about every work of his. Courtyards introduce the elementary forces of nature—wind, rain, sky, and so on—in a direct, even provocative, way, while the natural phenomena of light and shadow are revealed in a poetically abstract manner in the realm of the human habitat and the domain of architecture. The interiors of Ando's buildings—by virtue of their intensive dialogue with nature, poetic aspirations, layering of space evocative of the traditional notion of emptiness or void *(mu)*, and choreographed movement through the building—consistently attain both ritualistic qualities and the attributes of "hermetic," microcosmic worlds.

Continuing to conceive his architecture primarily in exposed reinforced concrete, and capitalizing on his interest and artistry in imparting intangible qualities through substantial materiality and tectonic articulation, Ando in the 1980s has expanded his repertoire by successfully transcribing many of the features of his earlier designs into larger, public complexes, fast increasing in number. Yet, somewhat similar to the changing attitude of most other Japanese architects, his explicitly negative stance toward the city has been attenuated, while he has not abandoned an implicitly critical position altogether. Therefore, although the courtyard arrangement reappears, often as a system of small plazas within various urban projects and commercial and office buildings, it is now articulated so as to assure more open overall spatial compositions than before. As best exemplified in the Rokko Housing in Kobe (1982 & 92), Festival in Naha (1984), Time's in Kyoto (1984 & 91), Galleria Akka in Osaka (1988) and Collezione in Tokyo, (1990), Ando's outstanding new architecture engages the surrounding built environment more actively, yet still selectively.

In recent years Ando has also undertaken numerous significant cultural and ecclesiastical commissions: three Christian churches and a Buddhist temple, in addition to several museums, art galleries, educational buildings, and others, including the uniquely shaped Japanese Pavilion at the 1992 Seville Expo in Spain. As most of these projects are situated in attractive, even pastoral settings, they have prompted yet another shift of emphasis in Ando's increasingly rich architectural vocabulary.

In the spectacular designs of the Chapel on Mt. Rokko in Kobe (1986), Church on the Water in Hokkaido (1988), Church with Light in Ibaragi, Osaka (1989), Water Temple on Awaji

Island (1991), or the Children's Museum complex in Himeji (1989 & 92) and Forest of Tombs Museum in Kumamoto Prefecture (1992), Ando has complemented his previous modes of integrating architecture into its natural environment by responding not only to the landscape, but also to the land. Such "architecturalization of nature" by Ando—beyond his use of light, wind and water—is achieved through the incorporation of earth or the soil as another "architectural" element, insofar as some of these buildings are designed with sunken courtyards, extensive subterranean realms and/or are buried considerably in the ground or under earthworks.

The significance of Ando's work therefore resides, to a large degree, in the fact that while consistently maintaining his own architectural style, he has also been able to demonstrate a ceaseless capacity to engender an astonishing variety in solutions, thereby broadening the range and profundity of human experience. As the number and diversity of his commissions increase, along with his popularity both at home and abroad, Ando is expected to continue making outstanding contributions to contemporary architecture.

—BOTOND BOGNAR

ANDREWS, John.

Australian. Born in Sydney, New South Wales, Australia, 29 October 1933. Married Rosemary Randall, 1958; four children. B.Arch., University of Sydney, 1956; M.Arch., Graduate School of Design, Harvard University, 1958. Worked for Edwards Madigan Torzillo, Sydney, 1957; John B. Parkin and Don Mills, Toronto, Canada, 1958-62; principal, John Andrews Architects, Toronto, since 1962, and John Andrews International Pty. Ltd., Sydney, since 1972; member of staff, 1962-69, and chairman, 1967-69, School of Architecture, University of Toronto. Fellow, Royal Architectural Institute of Canada, Royal Australian Institute of Architects, and American Institute of Architects; Associate, Royal Institute of British Architects; Gold Medal, Royal Australian Institute of Architects, 1980.

Chronology of Works
All in Australia unless noted

1963	Scarborough College, stage 1, Military Road, Scarborough, Ontario, Canada
1965	Bellmere Public School, Scarborough, Ontario, Canada
1965	Student Housing Complex B, University of Guelph, Ontario, Canada
1965	African Place, Expo '67, Montreal, Quebec, Canada
1967	Weldon Library, University of Western Ontario, London, Ontario, Canada
1967	Plan, Metro Centre, Toronto, Ontario, Canada
1967	Miami Seaport Passenger Terminal, Miami, Florida, U.S.A.
1967	Student Residence, Brock University, St. Catherines, Ontario, Canada
1967	Plan, Yorkdale Shopping Centre, Toronto, Ontario, Canada
1968	Gund Hall, Harvard Graduate School of Design, Harvard University, Cambridge, Massachusetts, U.S.A.
1968	Cameron Offices, Canberra
1968	Smith College Art Complex, Northampton, Massachusetts, U.S.A.
1969	David Mirvish Gallery, Toronto, Ontario, Canada
1969	Scarborough College, stage II, Scarborough, Ontario, Canada
1970	School of Art, Kent State University, Kent, Ohio, U.S.A.
1970	Canadian National Tower, Metro Centre, Toronto, Ontario, Canada
1970	American Express Tower (formerly King George Tower), Sydney
1970	Student Residence, Australian National University, Canberra
1973	Chemical Engineering Building, University of Queensland, Brisbane
1975	School of Australian Environmental Studies, Griffith University, Brisbane
1975	Little Bay Housing, Sydney
1976	Educational Resource Centre, Kelvin Grove College of Advanced Education, Brisbane
1976	Belconnen Bus Terminal, Canberra
1977	Woden College of Technical and Further Education, Canberra
1978	Resource Material Centre, Ipswich College of Technical and Further Education, Queensland
1978	Andrews Farmhouse, Eugowra, New South Wales
1978	Union Building, Royal Melbourne Institute of Technology, Melbourne
1980	Intelsat Headquarters Building, Washington, D.C., U.S.A.
1980	Garden Island Parking Structure, Woolloomooloo Bay, Sydney
1981	Hyatt Regency Hotel, Perth
1982	Physics, Chemistry and Common Teaching Building, Australian Defence Forces Academy, Canberra
1984	World Congress Centre, Melbourne
1985	Darling Harbour Convention Centre, Sydney
1985	Adelaide Exhibition Hall, Adelaide
1986	Octagon Office Building, Parramatta, New South Wales
1986	Padbury High School, Perth
1988	No. 2 Bond Street Office Building, Sydney

Publications

BOOKS BY ANDREWS

Architecture: A Performing Art. With Jennifer Taylor. Sydney, 1980.

ARTICLES ABOUT ANDREWS

Architecture and Urbanism, special issue (May 1974).
"Conversations with the John Andrews Architects." *Progressive Architecture* (February 1972).
"Design and Process: Four Projects by the John Andrews Office." *Architectural Record* (February 1970).
"Eugowra Classical." *Architectural Review* (June 1982).
"Five Projects by John Andrews International." *Canadian Architect* (July 1976).
FRAMPTON, KENNETH: "Scarborough College." *Architectural Design* (April 1967).
"John Andrews International: Two Projects." *Architecture Australia* (January 1988).

"Notes from Down Under" [interview]. *Canadian Architect* (June 1976).

ROBERTSON, J. T.: "Architecture as Urban Precinct: An Office Block by John Andrews." *Architectural Record* (October 1980).

"Serious in Sydney." *Architectural Review* (June 1989).

TAYLOR, JENNIFER: "Civil Service City." *Architectural Review* (March 1978).

"Uncommon Sense: Intelsat Headquarters." *Architectural Record* (October 1985).

WITZIG, JOHN: "A. A. Interview." *Architecture in Australia* (June 1975).

*

Sydney-born John Andrews is one of the most outstanding architects of contemporary Australia. His education included a scholarship to the Gradulate School of Design at Harvard University, where he was exposed to the teaching of Siegfried Giedion and Josep Luis Sert.

Through an unsuccessful competition that he and three fellow students at Harvard entered for the Toronto City Hall in 1958, Andrews was invited to join the Toronto office of John B. Parkin Associates, where he stayed for three years. Commencing from the basic classicism of Ludwig Mies van der Rohe to which the firm adhered, Andrews gradually developed his own style. He was drawn to vernacular architecture through an "architectural pilgrimage" to Europe, Russia, the Middle East and India. His realization of the importance of adaptation to climate, evident from his early design for Canadian conditions, was strengthened by what he saw, and this approach to design for the environment has shown up in all his subsequent work.

Andrews' breakthrough was the design of a new satellite college for the University of Toronto at Scarborough (1962). In association with Page & Steel, Andrews worked with the contours and developed structures connecting the various units of humanities, science, and administration. There Andrews expressed his conviction that a building should be a natural consequence of the social, economical and climatic constructional requirements. In *John Andrews: Architecture as Performing Art,* the architect is quoted on this point: "The greatest success of Scarborough College as a built form is its ability to allow the users to create their own community learning environment."

The success of Scarborough College led to a small primary school for the nearby residential district of Bellmere. This was a single-story development of repetitive unit classrooms with pyramid roofs, grouped around a main hall. Again the social function of the building was visible, and the climatic response was characterized by the northern light in each classroom.

The continuity of Scarborough and the cellular structure of Bellmere appeared at the students' residences at Guelph University (1965). The requirement of housing 1,760 students was realized by a well-structured system of social grouping arranged along a diamond grid with courtyards. Jennifer Taylor commented in *Australian Architecture Since 1960* that "low-height, walk-up circulation, elevated streets, multiple points of entry, repetitive groupings of standard units or clusters, and close contact with the outside environment persists in Andrew's work today wherever sites permit."

In 1967 Andrews was appointed professor and chairman of the Department of Architecture at the University of Toronto. At the same time, several major commissions took place, including the African Place of Expo '67 in Montreal. That pavilion was a series of one-story rooms with trusses supporting folded roofs, and the modules could be added or subtracted as required. A reverse wind-scoop was provided to each roof for ventilation. Andrews noted, "African Place is one of the purest responses I have made. . . . The design arose complete and simply from the response to the client's requirements, site conditions and the need of exhibition space. . . . One can see that an African village has to meet many of these same conditions, a conglomerate of spaces capable of growth and change to meet unpredicted needs" *(Australian Architecture Since 1960).*

The Miami Passenger Terminal (1967) was another demonstration of Andrews' design principles. The problem called for the solution of both the functional requirements of a sea terminal and a symbol of the gateway to Miami. Andrews used a linear multilevel structure with several nodal points where facilities were provided. A curved roof was used to dramatize the ocean, and the shape was derived according to aerodynamic principles against hurricanes. Andrews pointed out: "The number of ships using the terminal tripled even before the first five nodes were constructed. . . . The solution is straightforward, electing what was in essence a simple problem of transportation" *(John Andrews: Architecture as Performing Art).*

Perhaps the most controversial building by Andrews is Gund Hall at Harvard. Commissioned in 1968, the project coincided with the height of the student movement of the 1960s, and Gund Hall became a focus of protest, or "scapegoat," as some have suggested. Andrews began the project with the belief that the disciplines of the Harvard Graduate School of Design should not be compartmentalized, but totally exposed for all to see. This was expressed by the vast studio with its stepped levels covered by a sloping tubular trussed roof. Students working in their individual spaces were made aware of the activities of the whole school, and vice-versa. The roof was deliberately kept low so that students were made to look downward. There Andrews abandoned massive walls, raised the structure on columns, and enclosed it with glass, with consequential heating and cooling problems. In spite of protests and demands from all quarters, Andrews' design was by-and-large unchanged, except for omission of louvers for ventilation, and the opening up of the building for public access. Gund Hall is a reminder of the steadfastness of an architect who stood by his principles of design.

Andrews returned to Australia toward the end of 1968 upon the invitation of the Australian National Capital Development Commission to design a government complex known as Cameron Offices, which would accommodate 4,000 workers with office space of 600,000 square feet. Completed in 1977, Cameron Offices was designed on a linear pedestrian system around open courts, along which low-rise buildings were developed. Andrews strived to alleviate the impersonal nature of offices by the creation of landscaped courts with which the workers could identify, and to break down the complex into manageable units. The office buildings themselves were sufficiently open to accommodate unforeseen changes, and additions could be made to the urban system without destroying the whole. It was a successful urban system applied to buildings. Various themes of the Australian landscape were used for the courts, giving them a sense of distinctiveness.

The commission of the King George Tower (now American Express Tower, 1976) in Sydney was the first tall building for Andrews. Departing from the Miesian approach prevalent in Australia in the mid-1960s, he designed a concrete tower with a strong service core forming a corner of the triangular plan, while the three elevations were protected from the harsh Australian sun with a unique light tubular structure supporting anti-sun glass. The triangular plan gave frontal space removed from the crowded street corner, thereby donating a valuable urban court for downtown Sydney. Integration between the tower and this space was by means of a lower-level structure of shops, which took advantage of pedestrian movement.

In the Chemical Engineering Building at the University of Queensland (1976), the offices, laboratories and workshops were organized by means of well-defined bays, and the activities of the department were expressed by the articulation of the building. The Resource Centre of Kelvin Grove College of Advanced Education of 1976 (now the Queensland University of Technology, Kelvin Grove Campus) provided for pedestrian movement at the ground level of the building; the large building was designed to fit comfortably on the relatively small site, and relates well to the existing buildings and courtyards. The School of Australian Environmental Studies (1978) at Griffith University near Brisbane is a stepped rectilinear building of compact design, with controlled circulation around two large courtyards.

Andrews' success in urban design was seen at the Merlin Hotel in Perth (1984), a large commercial development of 2.5 hectares. The strong crucifix form was said to be a "microcosm of a city," with giant atria and courts creating an environment distinct from the surrounding streets. Typical of Andrews' work, the building was based on a comprehensive series of precincts and spaces as an expression of organized urban life.

As an architect, John Andrews has not been compelled to follow any particular tradition. His international practice and absence from Australia during his formative years has set him apart from his contemporaries. He has developed his own approach to architecture after a series of experiments. His understanding of the climatic, social, economic and constructional influences on architecture has enabled him to find appropriate solutions for the design problems at hand.

—B. P. LIM

ANTOINE, Jacques-Denis.

French. Born in Paris, 6 August 1733. Died in Paris, 24 August 1801. Appointed architect of the Royal Mint, 1766. Member, Académie Royale d'Architecture, 1776; imprisoned, 1793-94; elected to the Institut, 1799.

Chronology of Works
All in France unless noted

1760	Theatre, Comédie Française, Paris
1765	St. Nicolas-du-Chardonnet, Paris (facade)
1766-68	Church, Charny, Seine-et-Marne
1768-74	Hôtel Brochet-de-Saint-Prest, Paris
1768-75	The Mint, quai Conti, Paris
1760s	Hospital of Charity, Paris†
1770	Hôtel de Jaucourt, Paris
1770-72	Château de Herces a Berchère-sur-Vesgre, Eure-et-Loire, France
1772-75	Chapel of the Communion, Saint-Nicholas-des-Champs, Paris
1773	Berwick Palace, Madrid, Spain (stairway, interior decorations, and gardens)†
1776	Rochefoucauld Asylum, Paris
1782	Château du Buisson-du-Mai a Saint Aquilin-de-Pacy, Eure
1782?	Château a Kirn-Kyrbourg, Palatinate, Germany (château and gardens)
1782-84	Chapel of the Visitation to Nancy, Meurthe-et-Moselle
1782-85	Palais de Justice, Paris (stairway, waiting hall, and archives)†
1790-92	The Mint, Bern, Switzerland

Publications

BOOKS ABOUT ANTOINE

BRAHAM, ALLAN: *The Architecture of the French Enlightenment.* Berkeley, California, and Los Angeles, 1980.
HAUTECOEUR, LOUIS: *Histoire de l'architecture classique en France.* Vol. 4. Paris, 1952.
LAULAN, R.: *L'École Militaire de Paris.* Paris, 1950.
LUSSAULT, N.: *Notice historique sur défunt J. D. Antoine.* Paris, 1801.
MAZEROLLE, FERNAND: *L'hotel des Monnaies, les bâtiments, le musée, les ateliers.* Paris, 1907.

ARTICLES ABOUT ANTOINE

LE BRETON, JOACHIM: "Notice sur la vie et les travaux de J. D. Antoine." *Magazine encyclopédique* (de Millin) 22 (1803).
MAZEROLLE, FERNAND: "Jacques-Denis Antoine: Architecte de la Monnaie, 1733-1801." *Réunion des Sociétés des Beaux-Arts des Départements* (1897): 1038-1050.
MOSSER, MONIQUE: "L'hôtel des Monnaies de Paris: Oeuvre de J. D. Antoine." *Information d'histoire de l'art* 6, No. 2 (1971): 94-99.

*

Jacques-Denis Antoine was a French architect active in Paris in the years immediately before the Revolution. The son of a carpenter, Antoine did not receive any formal academic training, working first in the building trades and learning what he knew of construction from his family. By the age of 20 he was already well established as a contractor, in time becoming what was then termed an *expert-entrepreneur*. And throughout his life he was always highly regarded for his technical skill and for the efficiency with which he worked as an architect. Yet he also studied the older masters, traveling to Italy in 1777-78, in particular studying the works of Andrea Palladio, Michele Sanmicheli and Michelangelo. We do not know exactly when his career as an architect began, but in 1760 he won recognition for a very inventive project for the theater of the Comédie Française that had a semicircular facade, following the line of the auditorium itself.

In 1766 Antoine was appointed architect of the new Royal Mint, the Hôtel des Monnaies. This project had a complex history. The first plan had been for additions to be made to the Place Louis XV of Ange-Jacques Gabriel, and it was perhaps with the help of Gabriel that Antoine produced a design there for these additions to be placed around two enclosed courtyards, to the rear of a colonnaded building. But that project was halted in 1767, and the site of the whole complex was shifted to a more central and convenient site at the old Hôtel de Conti, on the Seine. There, the formal challenge was remarkable, since on the river front the site faced the Louvre, and to the side it was flanked by Louis Le Vau's Collège de France. What Antoine did, to make his design worthy of the setting, was to turn the Hôtel back to front, setting the main building along the river. The courtyard then lay immediately behind this river wing, with the foundry and the subsidiary court and workshops arranged

Jacques-Denis Antoine: The Mint, Paris, France, 1768-75

beyond that quite ingeniously within the irregular, triangular site of the old hotel. The service entrance was to the left, in the rue Guénégaud, where the minting shops lay; this wing was heavily rusticated, and carried with it that suggestion of fortification quite customary, since the time of Jacopo Sansovino's Mint in Venice, in what might be called the architecture of coinage. The effect of this whole scheme was to separate the administrative wing from the executive offices and to ensure that the river front should be, as a contemporary biographer put it, "the symbol representing national opulence." This was a public building new of its kind. The front was emphatically horizontal, extending some 11 bays to each side of the central frontispiece, unbroken but for three small balconies; at the center, in place of the pediment above the entrance, there was an attic story, punctuated by six statues that represented the virtues of government: Peace, Commerce, Prudence, Law, Strength and Abundance.

After the success of that project, Antoine was named in 1776 a member of the Académie Royale d'Architecture, holding two official positions, one as *contrôleur des hôtels des monnaies du royaume*, the other as architect of the Révérands Pères de la Charité, for whom he designed several hospitals. He was also entrusted, after the dismissal of Claude-Nicolas Ledoux in 1787, with completing the construction of the Barrières de Fermiers Généraux. Antoine was by then very successful, serving also a number of wealthy patrons and designing for them well-built yet somewhat severe residences, like the Hôtel Brochet de Saint-Prest (1768-74), the Hôtel de Jaucourt (1770), the Château de Herces in Berchères-sur-Vesgre (1770-72) and the Château du Buisson-du-Mai in Saint-Aquiline-de-Pacy (1782). He was interested still in public buildings, preparing designs

for several projects—the Corn Exchange, the Discount Bank, the National Assembly—and plans for the restoration of the Panthéon. He worked out also some extensive schemes for the redevelopment of the île de laCité and for the joining of the Louvre to the Tuileries.

It is interesting to look at his ecclesiastical projects, few though these were; freed of what duty required, Antoine seems to have been able in these designs to exercise the full range of his imagination. At the circular Eglise Conventuelle at Nancy he worked out a design that was completely windowless. At the hospital of the monastery of the Charité, a work of the 1760s, he designed a portico that seems to have had the first Doric columns in France set on the ground without any base moldings.

When the Revolution came, Antoine was required to replace his colleague, Claude-Nicolas Ledoux as architect of the Paris tollhouses, something he found extremely awkward because of his admiration of Ledoux's work. In 1799, after the death of Etienne-Louis Boullée, Antoine was elected to the Institut, where he was very active for the two remaining years of his life. It was an appropriately distinguished conclusion to a distinguished career.

—DAVID CAST

APOLLODORUS of DAMASCUS.

Roman. Born in Damascus, first third of second century. Chief architect of Roman Emperor Trajan; subsequently worked with

Emperor Hadrian; also a master engineer and bridge builder, and may have been a major sculptor.

Chronology of Works

105*	Bridge across the Danube at Drobeta (Turnu-Severin), Romania†
109	Trajan's Baths, Rome (date of opening)
112	Trajan's Forum (date of consecration; works include the Basilica Ulpia, the two libraries, the Markets, the construction of the helical Column, and perhaps the sculpture)
n.d.	Odeion of Trajan, Rome

Publications

BOOKS ABOUT APOLLODORUS

DE FINE LICHT, KJELD: *Untersuchungen an den Trajansthermen zu Rom.* Hafniae, Denmark, 1974.
MACDONALD, W. L.: *The Architecture of the Roman Empire.* New Haven, Connecticut, 1965.

ARTICLES ABOUT APOLLODORUS

BLANCKENHAGEN, PETER H. VON: ''The Imperial Fora.'' *Journal of the Society of Architectural Historians* 13 no. 4 (1954): 21-26.
HEILMEYER, WOLF-DIETER: ''Apollodoros von Damaskus, der Architekt des Pantheon.'' *Jahrbuch des deutschen archäologischen Instituts* 90 (1975): 316-347.

*

Apollodorus is generally credited with planning of the Trajanic expansion of the Imperial Fora in Rome. As such, he would have been responsible for three major monuments: the Forum of Trajan, the Column of Trajan, and the nearby market complex on the slopes of the Esquiline hill. The planning of this monumental complex was a substantial undertaking, one of the major steps in the urban renewal of Rome, the logical continuation of Augustus' plan a century before to change Rome from a city of brick to a city of marble. The area chosen was in the very heart of the ancient city and required some topographical rearrangement; an inscription on the column records that the column's height is equal to the amount of hill that was removed to build the forum. In this sense, Apollodorus built a typically imperial complex: vast, grand, and imposing in every sense, including the imposition of topographical order on an unruly environment.

Apollodorus proved a worthy match for the topographical difficulties and produced two very different architectural complexes. In the newly excavated valley he created an axially planned, highly propagandistic display area. On the slope of the hill, he built an irregularly terraced, ad-hoc arrangement of functional interiors for the market area. Much in the innovation was in the separation of function. That at that point in Roman architectural planning (100-113 A.D.) there could be such great differentiation between forum and market indicates how far the forum form had developed from its humble beginnings as an open market space, an outdoor area for trade and assembly.

The forum area itself was planned as a triumphal complex, paid for with the fruits of conquest. Only partially excavated

today, it can be reconstructed with the aid of literary evidence and contemporary numismatic representations. It was rigidly axial, with a longitudinal axis that led the visitor through a progression of closed and open spaces to a climactic view. The progression was from triumphal arch, to a vast colonnaded courtyard, through a lofty basilica (on the cross axis), to a smaller courtyard framed by two libraries and punctuated by the vertical mass of the column of Trajan (serving as both historical document and emperor's tomb). This last courtyard eventually became the forecourt for the imposing facade of the Temple of the Deified Trajan. The forum expressed Roman order and power; the viewer moved through lavishly decorated spaces where architecture and sculpture provided constant reminders of the triumph of Rome and Trajan (in that order). The program insisted on the primacy of Rome as civilizing force. *This* was not a utilitarian space; it was an ideological statement expressed by Apollodorus with all the self-assurance and arrogance of the high empire. The forum was a monument that was both universal and personal, a testament to an emperor and his empire at a moment when the two were seen as inseparable and indivisible.

There could have been no more dramatic contrast than to go from forum to the nearby markets where Apollodorus had created an introspective, structurally innovative complex. Casually arranged in multiple levels on the slope, the galleries of shops were cast from brick-faced concrete to create a series of powerful, groin-vaulted spaces. The architecture was functional, spare, stripped of ornament and affectation. Surfaces did not detract from the clarity of space and the power of form. The massive structures were so beautifully integrated into the slope of the hill (and originally masked by the forum) that from the valley it would have been impossible to anticipate the amount of enclosed space. The markets themselves were not shops in the true sense, and the market can in no way be likened to a modern shopping mall; in this case, the rooms were storage areas for the redistribution of staple commodities. There, Apollodorus proved himself a master of improvisation by responding to the needs of function, enclosing vast amounts of space effortlessly and indiscernibly.

Unfortunately, Apollodorus proved himself less adept at political improvisation. If the famous anecdote recounted by Cassius Dio can be trusted, he will also remain famous as a paradigm for the power of the Roman patron over the artist. Having criticized the architectural pretensions of the future emperor Hadrian, Apollodorus paid with his life for his lack of tact and foresight.

—P. GREGORY WARDEN

ARCHER, Thomas.

British. Born in 1668. Died in London, England, May 1743. Married Anne Chaplin. Educated at Trinity College, Oxford, 1686-89. Groom Porter, 1705; Comptrollership of Customs, Newcastle, 1715.

Chronology of Works
All in England
* *Approximate dates*

1702	Chatsworth House, Derbyshire (Cascade House)
1704-05	Chatsworth House, Derbyshire (north front)
1705	Cliveden House, Buckinghamshire
1707-10	Haythrop House, Oxfordshire

1709-11	Garden Pavilion, Wrest Park, Bedfordshire
1710-12	Roehampton House, Wandsworth, Surrey
1710-15	St. Philip's Church, Birmingham
1713-28	St. John's Church, Smith Square, Westminster, London
1713-30	St. Paul's Church and Rectory, Deptford, London
1715*	Hale House, Hampshire
1716-17	Russell House, 43 King Street, Covent Garden, London
1717-18	Monmouth House, Soho Square, London [attributed]†
1720*	Marlow Place, Buckinghamshire [attributed]
1725*	Harcourt House, 1 Cavendish Square†

Publications

BOOKS ABOUT ARCHER

DOWNES, KERRY: *English Baroque Architecture*. London, 1966.
LEES-MILNE, JAMES: *English Country Houses: Baroque*. London, 1970.
SERVICE, ALASTAIR: *The Architects of London*. London, 1979.
WHIFFEN, MARCUS: *Thomas Archer: Architect of the English Baroque*. Los Angeles, 1973.

ARTICLES ABOUT ARCHER

JACKSON-STOPS, G.: "The Cliveden Album: Drawings by Archer, Leoni and Gibbs." *Architectural History* 19 (1976).
PINKERTON, G.: "The Parish Church of St. Paul Deptford." *Architectural Review* 51 (1922).

*

After some 200 years of negative critical opinion, the architectural works of Thomas Archer have come to receive a more understanding, if not wildly enthusiastic, appraisal. Not formally trained as an architect, and busied during his career by government posts, Archer produced a body of work that is not large, but does cover most of the important genres of buildings in early-18th-century England. Country houses, city houses, churches and garden pavilions are all represented by more than one example; only the larger commissions of governmental and university buildings are conspicuous by their absence. And even this limit to his range was not the conviction of his contemporaries, because he was counted among a group of architects whom officials considered inviting to submit designs for the Radcliffe Library at Oxford.

With John Vanbrugh and Nicholas Hawksmoor, Archer represents the brief ascendancy of a Baroque style in English architecture. The fundamentals of the style derived from the architecture of Christopher Wren, with whom Vanbrugh and Hawksmoor had close associations early in their careers. Archer's designs were distinguished by his greater employment of elements drawn from the architecture of the Catholic Baroque. This strain in Archer usually is traced to his journey through south Germany, Austria and Italy in the early 1690s, more than 10 years before his first known building. But as the specific elements (broken pediments, elaborate moldings around windows and Corinthian capitals with reversed volutes) appeared regularly throughout his career and would have been accessible in England in published examples, it is safest to take these as evidence that Archer shared something of the Catholic Baroque's preference for complexity and drama over classical restraint and propriety.

In both his ecclesiastical and domestic architecture, Archer was fond of giant classical orders to unify elevations and add a sense of grandeur. But his churches were, if anything, more complex and ornate than his aristocratic houses. His two churches built in compliance with the 1711 Act of Parliament calling for 50 new churches in London and its suburbs (only 12 were built) were symbolic assertions of the newly won political power of the Tories, and the dominating religious and social presence of the state church within the increasingly populated suburbs. St. John's, Westminster, demonstrates how effectively Archer could apply his own flamboyant style to the religious political and social issues of the commission. In contrast to Wren's task of 40 years earlier in the rebuilding after the Great Fire, Archer was free from the constraints of a preexisting site and local traditions. Set as the centerpiece of a newly developed square, St. John's stood apart from and dominated its neighborhood. It appears externally as a Greek cross, each of its four faces confronting one of the four streets giving access to the square.

The two stories of arched windows are unified in typical Archer fashion by a giant order, here Doric. Both arms are gabled, ending in split pediments on the north and south, smaller tabernacles flanked by volutes on the east and west. The entire design approximates two crossing, pseudoperipteral temples. Masking the reentrant angles are convex quadrant walls, which, in addition to their curving form, are set off from the arms they link by heavily rusticated masonry. The simple skyline is broken only by the four enormous towers, ornamented in the Corinthian order and ending (in the original design) in pairs of pyramidal finials. With their piercing arches and spiking tops, they perhaps were meant to accommodate themselves to the Gothic forms of nearby Westminster Abbey.

The balancing of the forms of the two arms is fully realized in plan. The east-west arm takes the form of a large rectangle rounded at the corners and with rectangular extensions on the short ends. These are the chancel at the east (required by the commission) and its mirror, if less functional, space at the west. The north-south arm, inconspicuous on the interior, is more richly ornamented externally and provides for entrance porticoes. Had the staircases been executed to Archer's design, the north-south arm would have replicated the shape of the east-west, with the rounded corners and the chancel projection picked up in the similarly shaped staircase.

If the exterior responds to the opportunities of the church's siting, the interior concerns itself with liturgy in an appropriately grand setting. Only a groin vault at the very center continues the lines of the two crossing arms. Otherwise, the interior is treated as a galleried hall on the east-west axis. The giant order of the exterior is repeated, but the effect is more richly ornamental, Corinthian columns supporting a plaster vault that extends east and west, and smaller Ionic columns supporting galleries that run the length of the interior.

As effectively as St. John's manifests the spirit of the 1711 Act, it stands as a nocturne, rather than an aubade for this type of architecture. Even before St. John's was completed, a new generation of architects in England had seized the reins of fashion. For them, those features in Archer's designs that were closest to continental manifestations of the Baroque— complex overlapping of surfaces, interpenetration of parts, and a taste for the grand gesture—were the very ones that made his buildings most unacceptable. Ironically, those Palladians did share with Archer an openness to foreign—specifically Italian—architectural influences, though of a much different sort.

—BRIAN MADIGAN

ARNOLFO DI CAMBIO.

Italian. Born in Colle Val d'Elsa, near Florence, Italy, 13th century. Died in Colle Val d'Elsa, 1310. Worked in the workshop of Nicola Pisano, Siena, 1265-68; moved to Rome with Angevin court; master mason, Florence Cathedral, from 1296.

Chronology of Works
All in Italy
* Approximate dates

1294-1310	Santa Croce, Florence (not completed until 1442)
1296-1310	Santa Maria del Fiore, Florence
1299-1310	Palazzo della Signoria, Florence (not completed until 1323)

Publications

BOOKS ABOUT ARNOLFO

BRAUNFELS, WOLFGANG: *Der Dom von Florenz.* Olten, Germany, 1964.

PAATZ, WALTER: *Werden und Wesen der Trecento-Architektur in Toskana: Die grossen Meister als Schöpfer einer neuen Baukunst: Die Meister von Santa Maria Novella; Niccolò Pisano; Giovanni Pisano; Arnolfo di Cambio und Giotto.* Burg bei Main, Germany, 1937.

PAATZ, WALTER and ELISABETH: *Die Kirchen von Florenz: Ein kunstgeschichtliches Handbuch.* 6 vols. Frankfurt, 1940-1954.

ROMANINI, ANGIOLA MARIA: *Arnolfo di Cambio e lo stil nuovo del gotico italiano.* Milan, 1969.

TRACHTENBERG, MARVIN: *The Campanile of Florence Cathedral: "Giotto's Tower."* New York, 1971.

WHITE, JOHN: *Art and Architecture in Italy: 1250-1400.* Baltimore, 1966.

ARTICLES ABOUT ARNOLFO

KELLER, G.: "Der Bildhauer Arnolfo di Cambio und seine Werkstatt." *Jahrbuch der Preussischen Kunstsammlungen* (1934-35).

METZ, P.: "Die Florentiner Domfassade des Arnolfo di Cambio." *Jahrbuch der Preussischen Kunstsammlungen* (1938).

SAALMAN, HOWARD: "Santa Maria del Fiore, 1294-1418." *Art Bulletin* (1964): 472-500.

TOKER, FRANKLIN: "Arnolfo's S. Maria del Fiore: A Working Hypothesis." *Journal of the Society of Architectural Historians* 42 (May 1983): 101-120.

TOKER, FRANKLIN: "Florence Cathedral: The Design Stage." *Art Bulletin* 60 (1978): 214-231.

*

Toward the end of the 13th century, Florence must have seemed a metropolis to contemporary observers. The city was undergoing a massive expansion, and was seized in a ferment of innovation visible in the numerous construction sites. Florence was a powerful magnet for the provinces, and the city was filled with artists. The guilds seemed to compete in signing them up for commissions. Renovation projects all over Florence brought the artists face to face with the wealth of the past, forging a new aesthetic. A revolution was taking place in all art forms. On the one hand, Cimabue and Duccio dedicated their work to the transformation of the splendid though static iconography of Romanesque art to suit the needs of the Gothic, which propelled classical models toward a new conception of space. On the other hand, Dante was laying the foundations of a new Italian language, synthesizing classical culture with contemporary concerns. The Gothic style came to full expression during that time, best exemplified in such new buildings as the Bargello at Santa Maria Novella and in enlargements of complexes such as San Pier Maggiore. It was in that artistic ferment that Arnolfo di Cambio, nourished by an unprecedented artistic impulse, developed as an artist and an architect.

Born in Colle Val D'Elsa, he moved to Florence in 1245, following in the footsteps of his father, who was also a skilled architect. After brief stays in Siena and Perugia, where he perfected his skills as a sculptor to rank with Nicola Pisano, Arnolfo left for Rome. There, under the patronage of the Angevin court, he executed a number of exceptionally beautiful sepulchral monuments for the churches of San Giovanni in Laterano, San Paolo and Santa Cecilia. When in Rome he also had the opportunity to deepen his knowledge of ancient Roman and Etruscan art, which was to have a lasting influence on his work. Having matured as an artist, Arnolfo returned to Florence, where the need for talented architects would allow him to play a primary role in the transformation of the city's appearance.

Arnolfo was retained as the architect of the new cathedral, Santa Maria del Fiore, the first of many architects engaged with the building, which took centuries to complete. He constructed a wooden model of his design, which, unfortunately, has been lost. It seems that Andrea Bonaiute substantially recreated the model in his fresco in the Sala Capitolare at Santa Maria Novella, though in more pronounced Gothic form. In Bonaiute's portrayal, the church has flying buttresses to support the central nave, a large number of spires around the apsidal group, and decorations on the vault ribs, the cupola and the lantern.

Arnolfo's highly sculptural facade, recognizable in the Our Lady of Mercy fresco in the Bigallo, was subsequently modified by Giotto and eventually demolished in 1588. The perimeter walls, founded and constructed by Arnolfo, were also demolished following later enlargements of the temple.

Frequent floods and an inadequate drainage system required a reconstruction of the Piazza San Giovanni (later the Piazza del Duomo), where the new cathedral was under construction. Arnolfo raised the level of the square, covering the brick pavement with a stone pavement, which still exists. The elevation of the square involved moving a number of marble and sandstone arches along the walls of the baptistery. These walls were then clad with green and white marble. Arnolfo's changes were designed to harmonize visually with the surrounding area, especially with the old Cathedral of Santa Reparata, which was preserved until the roofs of the new Cathedral of Santa Maria del Fiore were in place. The new appearance of the square, however, set the tone for the new cathedral.

Between 1284 and 1300, there was not a single major construction project in Florence with which Arnolfo was not in some way involved. He built the outer ring of the city walls, with doors still intact today. He built the brick loggia with a cantilevered roof, later transformed into the Orsanmichele by Francesco Talenti. He renovated and expanded the Florentine Badia. He also laid the foundations for the Church of Santa Croce, giving the building an amplitude of form and proportions which place it squarely in the Gothic tradition. The monumentality of Arnolfo's work was a prelude to new cultural directions, distancing architecture from older types, still adhered to in such contemporary buildings as Santa Maria Novella or Santa Trinità. At the Palazzo dei Signori, Arnolfo was able to incorporate several existing structures into the new building, using them as supports for the tower. (A similar procedure had been followed

Arnolfo di Cambio: Santa Croce, Florence, Italy, 1294-1310

for the earlier projects of the Palazzo del Podesta and the Poppi Castle.) The demolition of houses owned by the Ghibelline Uberti family helped set off the imposing facade of the palace, creating a spacious piazza in front of it.

Most likely, Arnolfo had come into contact with Etruscan art during his time in Rome, Siena and Perugia, and possibly also while working on the foundations of his buildings. An Etruscan influence is detectable in the solemn fixity of his sculpture. Examples are the Madonna intended for the cathedral facade, the classicizing Saint Reparata, and the statue of Saint Timothy in the tabernacle of San Paolo. The latter, animated by an unusual dynamism, seems to allude to a statue of Saint Tiburtius in the tabernacle of Santa Cecilia at Trastevere, in its schematic plasticity and in the counterpoised movement of the horse and the saint's head.

The cult of the Madonna was gathering force in Florence, and a race to renovate and enlarge all churches dedicated to the Virgin began. Arnolfo enlarged the Church of Santa Maria Maggiore, connecting the two lateral naves in order to make it into the grandest church in Florence dedicated to the Virgin Mary. In order to emphasize the Madonna sculpture, it was housed in the niches of the facade. Thus, a typically medieval conception of Mary had a strong impact on everyday life by contributing to the Renaissance reevaluation of women.

—GIULIANO CHELAZZI
Translated from the Italian by Terri L. Stough

ARUP, Ove.

British. Born to Danish parents in Newcastle upon Tyne, England, 16 April 1895. Died in London, 1988. Married Ruth Sorenson, 1925; three children. Studied at University of Copenhagen, Denmark, B.A., 1916; studied civil engineering, Royal Technical College, Copenhagen, 1916-22. Designer, Chri and Nielsen, Hamburg, Germany, 1922-23; designer, 1923-25, and chief designer, 1925-34, Christiani and Nielsen, London; chief designer, J. L. Kier and Company, London, 1934-38; director, Arup Designers Ltd., London, and Arup and Arup Ltd. (with his cousin), 1938-46; independent engineering consultant, 1946-49; senior partner, Ove Arup and Partners, London, from 1949, and Arup Associates, London, from 1963.

Chronology of Works
All in England

1963	Kingsgate Footbridge, Durham
1964-67	Wolfson Building, Oxford
1967	Maltings Concert Hall, Snape, Suffolk
1970-76	Bush Lane House, London
1977-80	Lloyd's Headquarters Building, London

Publications

BOOKS BY ARUP

Design, Cost, Construction and Relative Safety of Trench, Surface, Bombproof and Other Air Raid Shelters. London, 1939.
London's Shelter Problem. London, 1940.
Safe Housing in Wartime. London, 1941.
Ove Arup and Partners 1946-86. London, 1986.

ARTICLES BY ARUP

"Subsidence under the Tidal Pressures." *Structural Engineer* No. 12 (1929).
"Planning in Reinforced Concrete." *Architectural Design* Nos. 9 and 10 (1935).
"Reinforced Concrete." *Architects' Yearbook* (1945).
"Shell Construction." *Architectural Design* No. 11 (1947).
"Modern Architecture: The Structural Fallacy." *Listener* No. 1375 (1955).
"Design and Construction of the Printing Works at Debden." With Howard Robertson and others. *Structural Engineer* No. 4 (1956).
"A Discussion about Future Developments in Building Techniques." *Architectural Design* No. 11 (1957).
"The Architect and the Engineer." With E. D. J. Matthews. *Journal of the Institution of Civil Engineers* (August 1959).
"Foreword" to COLIN FABER: *Candela, The Shell Builder.* New York, 1963.
"Discussion of Form and Structure in Engineering." *Journal of the Institution of Civil Engineers* (October 1964).
"Problems and Progress in the Construction of the Sydney Opera House." *Civil Engineering and Public Works Review* No. 703 (1965).
"Art and Architecture: The Architect-Engineer Relationship." *Royal Institute of British Architects Journal* (August 1966).
"The Evolution and Design of the Concourse at the Sydney Opera House." *Journal of the Institution of Civil Engineers* No. 4 (1968).
"The Potential of Prestressed Concrete." *Concrete* No. 6 (Slough, Buckinghamshire, 1970).
"I Am Not a Prophet." *Contract Journal* No. 4761 (1970).

"Sydney Opera House." With G. Z. Zunz. *Civil Engineering* No. 12 (1971).
"Built Environment Professions: What's in a Name?" *Built Environment* (March 1975).
"I Only Used Ordinary, Plain Common Sense." *New Civil Engineer* (April 1975).
"FIP 8th Congress." *Concrete* (Slough, Buckinghamshire, May 1978).
"Development of English Architecture." *Erhvervs bladet* (Copenhagen, June 1979).
"My Architectural Theory." *Royal Institute of British Architects Journal* (November 1980).
"Arup Associations." *Architectural Review* (January 1980).
"Arup on Arup Associates." *Architects' Journal* (17 June 1991).
Numerous articles and reports in the *Arup Journal*.

BOOKS ABOUT ARUP

BIRKS, T.: *Building, the New Universities.* Newton Abbot, England, 1972.
BRAWNE, MICHAEL: *Arup Associates: The Biography of an Architectural Practice.* London, 1983.
BRAWNE, MICHAEL: *University Planning and Design.* London, 1967.
DREW, PHILIP: *Third Generation: The Changing Meaning of Architecture.* London, 1972.
TAYLOR, NICHOLAS, and BOOTH, PHILIP: *Cambridge New Architecture.* London, 1970.

ARTICLES ABOUT ARUP

"Arup Associates." *Architecture and Urbanism* (December 1977).
"Arup's First Ten Years." *Architecture Plus* (November/December 1974).
"Grand Master: The Career of Sir Ove Arup and His Influence on Post-1930 Architecture." *Building* (7 October 1976).
"The Award Winners: A Profile of Arup Associates." *Building Design* (11 June 1976).
CARROLL, R.: "Berthold Lubetkin and Ove Arup: A Study of a Unique Partnership." Thesis. University of Newcastle, England, 1976.
HANCOCK, GRAHAM: "Piece Work." *Building Design* (5 September 1975).
"Ove Arup Talks to Peter Rawstone." *Royal Institute of British Architects Journal* No. 4 (1965).
PAWLEY, MARTIN: "From Gorillas at the Zoo to Aussies at the Opera [interview]." *Building Design* (May 1970).
PAWLEY, MARTIN: "Task Force from the Past." *Building Design* (25 June 1982).
SHERRAT, J.: "Ove Arup and his Collaboration with Berthold Lubetkin." Thesis. St. Andrew's University, Fife, Scotland, 1982.
"Sir Ove Arup [interview]." *Building* (October 1977).

*

Ove Arup was the founder of Ove Arup and Partners, the leading British firm of structural engineers, and through much of his long life he was the most respected member of his profession. Wise, calm and kind, he combined engineering brilliance with the ability to head a large international organization. A modest man, he often claimed that his only skill was to choose brilliant partners and assistants; but these colleagues all speak of him with affection as the guiding father figure of the firm.

Ove Arup: Kingsgate Footbridge, Durham, England, 1963

Arup read philosophy and mathematics at the University of Copenhagen before studying as a civil engineer. He worked for Christiani and Nielsen from 1923 to 1934, first in Hamburg and then in London; most of that work was on docks and civil engineering projects. His interest in reinforced concrete led him to move to J. L. Kier as a director, and he worked there from 1934 to 1938.

In 1933 Arup advised the architects Tecton on the structure of the Highpoint 1 flats, pioneering the use of slip-form shuttering. That was the beginning of a long relationship with Tecton, and happened at a time when modern architects were looking to reinforced concrete as a building material that was appropriate for the new architecture. Arup worked with Tecton again on Highpoint 2 and the Finsbury Health Centre, but the most spectacular result of the collaboration was the Penguin Pool at London Zoo, with two interlocking ramps that brought a playfulness to architecture not usually associated with reinforced concrete or with modern design. In 1938 Ove Arup set up the firm of Arup and Arup, engineers and contractors, but at the end of World War II, he left to set up his own firm of consulting engineers.

Once he had formed his own practice, Arup was free to develop the interest in modern architecture that had grown from his prewar work with Tecton. Tecton itself continued to give him work, but the first spectacular job was a bus station in Dublin with Michael Scott as architect. Built at a time of Europewide shortages and general impoverishment in design, the Dublin Bus Shelter was a milestone, a cheerful building with its clear simplicity and wavy concrete roof that, in typical Arup manner, was both stylish and structurally efficient.

The Arup office grew and worked with inventive architects on a world scale. The Sydney Opera House, begun in 1957, stretched the firm's skills to the limit. The opera house was the subject of an international competition won by Arup's fellow Dane Jørn Utzon with a design that was dramatic, endearing and extraordinarily difficult to build. The breakthrough in design development came when Arup's partner Ronald Jenkins developed a geometry for the great shells that now glisten over Sydney Harbor. The Arup firm again put its knowledge and skills at the disposal of competition winners when Renzo Piano and Richard Rogers won the competition for the Centre Pompidou in Paris in 1973. Later works, continuing the evolution of inventive structures and working with imaginative architects, are the Mound Stand at Lords Cricket Ground, London, with Michael Hopkins as architect, and the Hong Kong and Shanghai Bank in Hong Kong with Foster Associates.

Arup presided over his growing firm, which increased in excellence as its reputation for innovative design attracted the brightest of engineering graduates. One design by Ove Arup himself, a footbridge in Durham, bridges the River Wear on a beautiful site below Durham Cathedral. In order to avoid the expense of constructing formwork over the water, the bridge was built in two halves, each over its own riverbank, and each half was then rotated until the ends met over the river. The form of the bridge makes clear its method of erection. The Durham bridge, more than any other structure, reveals Arup's preferences for lovingly exposed reinforced concrete, a form that explains structure and construction, and for a lightness and delicacy all controlled by a skilled eye.

The reputation of the Arup office was such that by the mid-1950s it began to receive architectural commissions and to have architects on the payroll. In 1963, under the leadership of Philip Dowson, a multidisciplinary design team called Arup Associates was set up. This practice grew to include many famous designers—Peter Foggo, Richard Frewer, Derek Sugden and others. With Arup's background perceived as being in engineering, it was natural that the early commissions were for industrial buildings, and the design practice first came to fame with the construction of a series of cool Miesian industrial and research buildings for CIBA at Duxford near Cambridge.

More prestigious commissions followed, with university buildings at Oxford and Cambridge. An 18-story tower block at Bracknell took Arup Associates into low-cost housing, and in 1969 the firm began a series of spacious buildings near Portsmouth to become the British home of the IBM Corporation. Arup Associates' "Horizon Project," a large industrial plant in Nottingham for Imperial Tobacco, with a bold framed structure was completed in 1971; this was followed by Gateway 1, an office building in Basingstoke for Wiggins Teape, with a stepped section so that each floor opened onto a generous garden, and the Heavy Plate Shop for the Royal Navy at Portsmouth, with a massive frame of plate girders exposed externally.

In 1978 the offices for Lloyd's of London on a riverside site in Chatham marked a shift of style to softer forms and more traditional materials, a trend continued in the CEGB Headquarters at Bedminster Down, near Bristol, where the interiors verge on the folksy. A second building for Wiggins Teape at Basingstoke is a major study in energy conservation and a return to simple geometry. Simple geometry again comes to the fore in the beautiful Finsbury Avenue office building, the first stage of the Broadgate development; later buildings are granite-faced and lack the distinction of the earlier building, but they have given to the city of London its most successful urban space in many years.

—JOHN WINTER

ASAM BROTHERS.

Bavarian. Cosmas Damian Asam: Born in Benediktbeuern, 28 September 1686. Died in Kloster Weltenburg, May 1739. Egid Quirin Asam: Born in Tegernsee, 1 September 1692. Died in Mannheim, 29 April 1750. Father was Johannes Georg Asam (1649-1711), a leading Bavarian fresco painter. Abbot Quirin Millon sent the brothers to Rome upon the death of their father, 1711: C. D. studied there with (Pierleone) Giuseppe Ghezzi, and won prize from the Accademia di San Luca, 1714; E. Q. completed his sculpture apprenticeship with Andreas Faistenberger in Munich, 1716; C. D. engaged to Maria Anna Mörl (died 1731), 1717; one son; engaged to Maria Ursula Ettenhofer, 1732. The brothers named court painter and court sculptor to the prince at Freising, 1724; both named to Kurbayerischen Kammerdienern, 1730; C. D. named by Kurfurst Karl Philipp von der Pfalz to Kurpfälzischen Hofkammerrat; C. D. was also Kurmainzischen Hofkammerrat; the brothers executed most of their works jointly, C. D. as painter, and E. Q. as sculptor and fresco artist.

Chronology of Works

All in Germany unless noted
* Approximate dates
† Work no longer exists
C. D. Asam—frescoes:

1714-16	Benedictine Abbey, Ensdorf
1715	Dreifaltigkeitskirche, Munich
1716-21	Benedictine Abbey, Michelfeld
1717-20	Benedictine Abbey, Weingarten
1726-28	Benedictine Abbey, Brevnov, Czechoslovakia
1728	Schlosskapelle, Mannheim†
1730	Schloss, Alteglofsheim
1732	Schlosskapelle, Ettlingen
1732-36	Santa Maria de Victoria, Ingolstadt [attributed]
1733	Benedictine Priory Church, Wahlstatt, Silesia
1734	Landhaus, Innsbruck, Austria

E. Q. Asam:

1733	St. Peter, Munich (Four Fathers of the Church)
1738	St. Anna am Lehel, Munich (side altars)†
1740	Pilgrimage Church, Maria Dorfen (high altar)†
1747-48	Church, Sandizell (altar sculptures)
1747-50	Jesuit Church, Mannheim (ceiling frescoes)†

C. D. and E. Q. Asam:

1708-10	Maria-Hilf-Kirche, Freistadt (frescoes, executed with father)
1715	Abbey Church, Ensdorf
1717-25	Augustinian Priory Church, Rohr
1720*	Cistercian Abbey, Aldersbach (frescoes and stuccoes)
1722-23	Parish Church of St. Jakobi, Innsbruck, Austria (frescoes and stuccoes)
1722-37	Cistercian Abbey, Fürstenfeldbruck (decoration)
1723-24	Cathedral, Freising (decoration)
1724-26	Benedictine Abbey, Einsiedeln, Switzerland (decoration)
1727	Heilig-Geistkirche, Munich (frescoes)
1729	St. Anna am Lehel, Munich (decoration)†
1729-35	Premonstratensian Abbey, Osterhofen (decoration)
1731-33	St. Emmeran Benedictine Abbey, Regensburg
1733-40s	St. John Nepomuk, Munich
1735-38	Johanniskapelle (Cathedral), Freising
1736-40	Ursulinenkirche, Straubing

Publications

BOOKS ABOUT THE ASAM BROTHERS

BAUER, RICHARD et al.: *St. Johann Nepomuk im Licht der Quellen.* Munich, 1977.

BAUER, RICHARD and DISCHINGER, GABRIELE: *Die Asamkirchen in München.* Munich, 1981.

BOURKE, JOHN: *Baroque Churches of Central Europe.* 2nd ed., London, 1962.

FEULNER, ADOLF: *Bayerisches Rokoko.* Munich, 1923.

HALM, PHILIPP MARIA: *Die Künstlerfamilie der Asam.* Munich, 1896.

HANFSTAENGL, ERIKA: *Kosmas Damian Asam.* Munich, 1939.

HANFSTAENGL, ERIKA: *Die Brüder Cosmas Damian und Egid Quirin Asam.* Munich and Berlin, 1955.

HITCHCOCK, HENRY-RUSSELL: *Rococo Architecture in Southern Germany.* London, 1968.

LIEB, NORBERT: *Barockkirchen zwischen Donau und Alpen.* Munich, 1953; 4th ed., 1976.

LIEB, NORBERT and SAUERMOST, HEINZ JÜRGEN: *Münchens Kirchen.* Munich, 1973.

MITTERWIESER, ALOIS: *Herkunft, Aufstieg und Niedergang der Künstlerfamilie Asam.* 1935.

RUPRECHT, BERNHARD and MULBE, WOLF VON DER: *Die Brüder Asam: Sinn und Sinnlichkeit im Bayerischen Barock.* Regensburg, 1980.

TINTELNOT, HANS: *Die Barocke Freskomalerei in Deutschland: Ihre Entwicklung und europäische Wirkung.* Munich, 1951.

ARTICLES ABOUT THE ASAM BROTHERS

HITCHCOCK, HENRY-RUSSELL: ''The Brothers Asam and the Beginnings of Bavarian Rococo Church Architecture.'' *Journal of the Society of Architectural Historians* 24-25 (Part I: October 1965; Part II: March 1966): 187-228; 3-49.

*

Cosmas Damian Asam was first and foremost a painter of frescoes, and his younger brother, Egid Quirin, was primarily a sculptor. Both designed parts of buildings, and so can be regarded as architects as well. They were capable of executing fine stuccowork, and indeed could turn their accomplished hands to varieties of creative endeavor.

The brothers were the sons of Georg Asam (1649-1711), who was himself the leading Bavarian fresco-painter responsible for the decoration of the vault over the crossing in the Benedictine Abbey of Tegernsee. The two brothers were taken under the wing of the abbot of Tegernsee after their father's death and were sent to study in Rome. Cosmas Damian won a prize for a painting in 1713, and when the brothers returned to Bavaria shortly afterward, they quickly found themselves in demand as decorators of churches. C.D. Asam worked in the Benedictine Abbey Church at Ensdorf in 1714, and the Italian influence was at once apparent in a composition involving crowds of figures leading to a small oculus in the middle of the ceiling. It was his next commission, for the frescoes in the Dreifaltigkeitskirche in Munich, that brought him fame: the great fresco in the crossing that features the glorification of the Trinity (a favorite subject of the time), and its spectacular mastery of illusion and perspective, brought the young man much work.

In 1714 he began his labors at the Benedictine Abbey of Weltenburg, and it is there that the Roman influences are strongly evident. The great nave of the church is elliptical on plan, and most of the light sources are invisible, while the marbles and golds recall Bernini's Sant'Andrea al Quirinale in Rome. Bernini's ellipse, however, has the longer axis parallel to the plane of the high altar, while Asam placed his high altar on the longer axis. From 1721 C.D. was joined at Weltenburg by his brother, and a remarkable partnership produced its first masterpiece of pure theater.

Dark, brooding, passionate and mysterious, the lighting and the deep tones of the coloring combine to create an atmosphere of great emotional intensity. The eye is drawn to the high altar as though to a stage, and indeed the theatrical effects are startling, for E.Q. Asam's St. George on horseback charging out of the sun, killing the dragon with what looks like a golfing umbrella, and rescuing the maiden who rushes offstage, is straight from a Baroque opera: one can imagine the music of Handel, in a florid aria ablaze with trumpets, to accompany the heroic deed. The group is set against a blaze of golden light within an aediculated arrangement featuring four Solomonic columns. Above, the elliptical gallery has a sculptured figure of C.D. Asam himself, leaning over the rail and smiling at us, as it were, to study our reactions to his creation. This gallery frames the ceiling fresco, a composition of enormous verve and grandeur, and conceals the lighting from the windows around the cupola. The gallery is also the divide between the spiritual realms above and the earthly world below.

C.D. Asam by 1718 was also working on the frescoes at Weingarten in Württemberg, but it was at Rohr from 1717 to 1725 that the brothers once more created a theatrical tour de force in the Assumption group above the high altar: there the sarcophagus has been opened, its lid leaning against the drapes behind, while in the air above, the Virgin ascends to Heaven, borne aloft by angels. The sculptured group, with the startled figures around the open sarcophagus, is held within an aedicule featuring the composite order that supports a broken segmental pediment, in the center of which are clouds, putti, and a burst of glory featuring the Trinity. This amazing achievement is largely the work of E.Q. Asam.

The scale of the Rohr aedicule is huge, and the coloring is dark, while at Weltenburg the aedicule is less overpowering in scale, and there is no upward sweep of the sculptured figures. Yet at both altars, the suggestions of a proscenium and of a spectacular theatrical effect are inescapable. At Rohr and Weltenburg, the overwhelming influences came from the Baroque of the Rome of Bernini.

C.D. Asam worked on the frescoes at Fürstenfeldbruck from 1722, and in that year and in 1723 the brothers worked on the decorations of the Pfarrkirche St. Jakobi in Innsbruck, in which certain early Rococo tendencies are present. These Rococo aspects became more overt in the work of the Asams from 1724 at Einsiedeln in Switzerland, where C.D. Asam carried out the frescoes, and E.Q. the stuccowork.

At Osterhofen the Asams provided decorations of incomparable richness with a pronounced Rococo flavor. The generous niches at the eastern quadrants of the nave have altar compositions employing gigantic crowns over sculptural groups that feature the enthroned Madonna and Child with saints and the holy kin. As with E.Q. Asam's other sculpture, the effect is overwhelming, and at the high altar the influence of Bernini's work is paramount, with the four Solomonic columns similar to those of Michelfeld and Weltenburg.

Two other stunning interiors, those of St. Emmeran in Regensburg and Santa Maria de Victoria in Ingolstadt (1730s), may be mentioned before the dark and justly celebrated drama of St. John Nepomuk in Munich, the brothers' major contribution to late Baroque and early Rococo in Bavaria, in which superlative lighting effects combine with the high drama of the *Gnadenstuhl* over the altar.

Between 1736 and 1741 the Asams produced their charming and fantastic interior of the Ursulinenkirche at Straubing, although C.D. died in 1739. This church is small and is constructed on a quatrefoil ground plan. There, the characteristic lighting from above, especially in the sanctuary, where the cornice separates the heavenly realms from those of the earth, can be found, with the Berniniesque altarpieces.

The Asams had a masterly understanding of lighting, theatrical effects, color, perspective, composition and sheer power of emotion in their designs. They took the Roman Baroque devices of the ellipse and of the high drama of the Bernini St. Theresa group in Santa Maria della Vittoria in Rome, and carried the ideas many stages further, creating in their later works Rococo themes, but never losing the power to amaze and to move the emotions.

—JAMES STEVENS CURL

ASHBEE, C. R.

British. Born Charles Robert Ashbee in Isleworth, near London, England, 1863. Died in 1942. Apprenticed in architecture with G. F. Bodley and Thomas Garner; founded Guild and School of Handicraft, 1888 (school moved to Chipping Camden, Gloucestershire, in 1902; ceased in 1908); opened architectural office, 1890; founded Essex Press.

Chronology of Works
All in England
† Work no longer exists

1894-1913	37-39, 71-73 and 75 Cheyne Walk, London (all but 38 and 39 destroyed)
1899-1901	The Wodehouse, Wombourne, Staffordshire (additions)
1903	The High House, Sheep Street, Chipping Campden, Gloucestershire
1904	Woodroffe House, Westington, Chipping Campden, Gloucestershire (additions)
1906	52 industrial cottages around Birchfield Road, Ellesmere Port, Cheshire
1906-07	Norman Chapel, Broad Campden, Gloucestershire (restoration and additions)
1907	Byways, Yarnton, Oxfordshire
1911	1049-54 Squirrel's Heath Avenue, Romford, Essex

Publications

BOOKS BY ASHBEE

An Endeavor Towards the Teaching of J. Ruskin and W. Morris. London, 1901.
A Book of Cottages and Little Houses. London, 1906.
Craftsmanship in Competitive Industry. London, 1908.
Modern English Silverwork. London, 1909.
Should We Stop Teaching Art? London, 1911.

BOOKS ABOUT ASHBEE

C. R. Ashbee and the Guild of Handicraft. Cheltenham, 1981.
CRAWFORD, ALAN: *C. R. Ashbee, Architect, Designer, and Romantic Socialist.* New Haven, Connecticut, and London, 1985.
DAVEY, PETER: *Arts and Crafts Architecture.* London, 1980.
McCARTHY, FIONA: *C. R. Ashbee in the Cotswolds.* London, 1981.
NAYLOR, GILLIAN: *The Arts and Crafts Movement.* London, 1990.
RICHARDSON, MARGARET: *The Craft Architects.* London, 1983.

ARTICLES ABOUT ASHBEE

PEVSNER, NIKOLAUS: "William Morris, C. R. Ashbee and the Twentieth Century." *Manchester Review* 7 (1956): 437-458.

*

C.R. Ashbee is possibly better known as an English Arts and Crafts designer of furniture and cabinetry, metalwork including silverware and jewelry, leatherwork, enameling, bookbinding and printing than he is as an architect. His total architectural output, all done in the Queen Anne revival and its vernacular offshoots, amounted to fewer than 60 built works, mostly residential.

An avid reader of John Ruskin while a student of history at King's College, Cambridge, Ashbee adopted socialist as well as Arts and Crafts principles. Channeling his ideals, he decided to become an architect under George Frederick Bodley, the Ruskinian Gothic revivalist. Living at Toynbee Hall, the university settlement in the slums of London's East End, he gave lectures on the writings of Ruskin and in an adjacent building began the School and Guild of Handicrafts during 1888. In 1891, the guild moved further east to Essex House, where it expanded from metal and cabinetwork to include other crafts; the Essex Press began there. Finally the guild moved to Chipping Campden, a medieval village constructed in the local stone tradition of the Cotswolds, where it effectively ceased to exist in 1908. Ashbee worked in collaboration with the craftsmen and had a major share in all designing. As an architect, was responsible for the interiors and furniture of his own buildings. His cabinets were simple but bold boxes, unadorned by moldings but equipped with oversized hinges, locks and handles. Inlays, usually flowers, were simple and flush. In addition to an occasional piano cabinet, he designed church fittings. He produced elegant loop-handled silver dishes, tazzas, mounted decanters, boxes and jewelry with gemstones and enameling.

Ashbee was also instrumental in the founding of the British preservation movement after the demolition of the Old Palace of James I at Bromley-le-Bow, and he established a Watch Committee to begin a systematic list of London buildings. Starting at Aldgate, one of 26 slices of London that he and his helpers intended to survey, Ashbee's survey ultimately led to the publication by the London County Council of the many volumes comprising *The Survey of London*.

Ashbee opened his architecture office in September 1890, and one of his earliest commissions was for a chapel and entrance which he sympathetically added to the 17th-century, Dutch-inspired Wombourne Wodehouse in Staffordshire (1899-1901). There he designed in the indigenous form of the existing house. Ashbee is, however, best remembered for his work along the embankment of the River Thames in Chelsea at Cheyne Walk. There, at the turn of the century, was a village adjacent to London where a few artists and men of letters lived. Over the years, he built seven houses along the embankment (numbers 37-39, 71-73, and 75, built from 1894 to 1913), although only two, numbers 38 and 39, remained after bomb damage in World War II. All were designed in the Queen Anne idiom, in which brickwork and stucco were juxtaposed, and oriels and bays protruded; irregular-shaped windows were leaded, while other windows were flush casements or dormers; there were decorative details, cornices, ironwork, and even small sculptures as part of the designs. The first house (1894) was for his mother and two sisters on the site of the old Ancient Magpie and Stump Inn, which had burned. This house was referred to as the Magpie and Stump, and Ashbee moved his office there. The interiors in particular reflected the hand of Ashbee, especially as he hired his own craftsmen in order to have close control of the work, and the guild built much of the furniture. As a whole, Ashbee's row of Cheyne Walk residences had the flavor of traditional buildings, added one to another over a long period of time to form a streetscape.

During the five years after the guild moved to Chipping Campden, Ashbee was responsible for 16 buildings and conversions for the village, including remodeling the old silk mill for the craftsmen. One mile away at Broad Campden, he converted an old Norman chapel and adjacent medieval priesthouse into a home for Ananda Coomaraswami and his wife; eventually that building became the Ashbee home, the lower level of the chapel serving as the library, with the music room above. All of his work in that area of Gloucestershire was in the spirit and context of what already existed.

Ashbee visited the United States on several occasions. He liked the spirit of Cornell University in Ithaca, New York, thought the Illinois houses of Frank Lloyd Wright and the California houses of Greene and Greene were the most beautiful in America, and felt the furniture from the Greenes' workshop was outstanding. Wright visited Chipping Campden in 1909 and two years later invited Ashbee to write the introduction to *Frank Lloyd Wright: Ausgeführte Bauten* (Berlin: Wasmuth, 1911). Ashbee praised the indigenous American qualities of Wright's architecture as being midwestern Arts and Crafts architecture suited to the prairie environment.

—LAWRENCE WODEHOUSE

ASPLUND, Erik Gunnar.

Swedish. Born in Stockholm, Sweden, 22 September 1885. Died in Stockholm, 20 October 1940. Married Gerda Sellman, 1918 (divorced); married Ingrid Katarina Kling, 1934. Studied architecture at Royal Institute of Technology, Stockholm, 1905-09; studied at the Klara Academy of Architecture under Bergsten, Tengbom, Westman, Östberg, 1910-11. Assistant lecturer, 1912-13, special instructor in ornamental art, 1917-18, and professor of architecture, 1931-40, Royal Institute of Technology, Stockholm. Editor, *Arkitektur*, Stockholm, 1917-20.

Chronology of Works
All in Sweden unless noted

1912-18	Karlshamn Secondary School, Karlshamn
1913	Villa Selander, Örnsköldsvik
1913	Sturegarden, Nyköping
1914	Ruth Villa, Kuusankoski, Finland
1915-24	Carl Johan Elementary School, Göteborg
1917	Workers' Emergency Dwellings, Stockholm
1917-18	Snellman Villa, Djursholm, near Stockholm
1917-21	Lister County Court House, Sölvesborg
1918-20	Woodland Chapel, South Cemetery, Stockholm
1920-28	City Library, Stockholm
1921	Prince Oscar Bernadotte's Family Vault, North Cemetery, Stockholm
1921	Cemetery, Almunge (extension)
1922	Bridge and road approaches, Klevaliden
1922-23	Skandia Cinema, Stockholm
1922-24	Woodland Cemetery Offices, South Cemetery, Stockholm
1924-25	Admiral Sten Ankarcrona's Family Vault, North Cemetery, Stockholm
1924-29	Cemetery, Oxelösund
1926-28	Hjalmar Rettig's Family Vault, North Cemetery, Stockholm
1927-35	City Library Park, Stockholm
1928-30	Design, Stockholm Exhibition
1931	Swedish Society of Arts and Crafts, Stockholm (reconstruction and interiors)
1933-35	Bredenberg Department Store, Stockholm
1933-37	State Laboratory for Biological Research, Stockholm
1934-37	Göteborg Law Courts, Göteborg (rebuilding and extension)
1935-37	Chapel, Oxelösund
1935-40	Woodland Crematorium, South Cemetery, Stockholm
1936-40	Kviberg Cemetery Crematorium, Göteborg
1937	Asplund Summer Residence (Stennäs House), Sorunca Parish, Stockholm

Publications

BOOKS BY ASPLUND

Acceptera. With Wolter Gahn, Sven Markelius, Gregor Paulsson, Eskil Sundahl and Uno Åhrén. Stockholm, 1931.

ARTICLES BY ASPLUND

Writings in *Arkitektur*, 1917-20, and *Byggmästaren*, 1920-40.

BOOKS ABOUT ASPLUND

AHLBERG, HAKON: *Gunnar Asplund Arkitekt, 1885-1940: Ritningar, Skisser, och Fotografier.* Stockholm, 1943.
AHLBERG, HAKON: *Swedish Architecture of the Twentieth Century.* London, 1925.
Asplund: 1885-1940. Exhibition catalog. Stockholm, 1985.
CALDENBY, CLAES, and HUTLIN, OLOF (eds.): *Asplund.* New York, 1986.
CRUICKSHANK, DAN (ed.): *Erik Gunnar Asplund.* London, 1988.
DE MARÉ, ERIC: *Gunnar Asplund: A Great Modern Architect.* London, 1955.
ENGFORS, CHRISTINA (ed.): *Lectures and Briefings from the International Symposium on the Architecture of Erik Gunnar Asplund.* Stockholm, 1986.
FRAMPTON, KENNETH, and FUTAGAWA, YUKIO: *Modern Architecture: 1920-1945.* New York, 1983.
Gunnar Asplund 1885-1940: The Dilemma of Classicism. Exhibition catalog. London, 1988.
HOLMDAHL, GUSTAV; LIND, SVEN IVAR; and ÖDEEN, KJELL (eds.): *Gunnar Asplund Architect, 1885-1940.* Stockholm, 1950.
NAGY, ELEMÉR: *Erik Gunnar Asplund.* Budapest, 1974.
PAAVILAINEN, SIMO (ed.): *Nordic Classicism 1910-1930.* Exhibition catalog. Helsinki, 1982.
WREDE, STUART: *The Architecture of Erik Gunnar Asplund.* Cambridge, Massachusetts, 1980.
ZEVI, BRUNO: *Erik Gunnar Asplund.* Milan, 1948.
ZEVI, BRUNO: *Verso un'architettura organica.* Milan, 1945.

ARTICLES ABOUT ASPLUND

AHLBERG, HAKON: "The Crematorium in Stockholm." *Byggmästaren* No. 19 (1940).
ÅHRÉN, UNO: "Reflexioner i Stadsbiblioteket." *Byggmästaren* (1928).
BLOMBERG, ERIK: "Stadsbiblioteket i Stockholm." *Svenska slöjdforeningnens arsbok* (1928).
BRAVO, LUIS: "The Dwelling of Man Beneath the Stars." *2C Construction de la Ciudad* (Barcelona, November 1981).

Erik Gunnar Asplund: Woodland Crematorium, Stockholm, Sweden, 1935-40

"E. G. Asplund: In Memoriam." *Arkkitehti* Nos. 11/12 (1940).

"Erik Gunnar Asplund, September 22, 1885-October 20, 1940." *Space Design* Special issue (October 1982).

FARIELLO, FRANCESCO: "The Work of E. G. Asplund." *Architettura* (October 1942).

GRAVES, MICHAEL: "The Swedish Connection." *Journal of Architectural Education* (1975).

MIRO, FRANCISCO MITJANS, and FISAC, MIGUEL: "The First Discovery of Asplund." *Quaderns* (October 1981).

PAAVILAINEN, SIMO: "Stuart Wrede, Hakon Ahlberg and the Architecture of Gunnar Asplund." *Arkkitehti* No. 5 (1981).

PODESTA, ATTILO: "L'ultima opera di Asplund." *Casabella* (September 1941).

SHAND, P. MORTON: "E. Gunnar Asplund: A Tribute." *Architectural Review* (May 1941).

SHAND, P. MORTON: "E. Gunnar Asplund." *Architectural Association Journal* (January 1959).

SPARK, D. M.: "Gunnar Asplund." Dissertation. University of Newcastle, England, 1959.

TREIB, MARC: "Woodland Cemetery—A Dialogue of Design and Meaning." *Landscape Architecture* 76, No. 2 (March/April 1986): 42-49.

"Woodland Crematorium, Stockholm, 1935-40; Woodland Chapel, 1918-20; Stockholm Public Library, 1920-28." *Global Architecture* No. 62 (1982).

WREDE, STUART: "Asplund: Form and Metaphor." *Progressive Architecture* (February 1980).

WREDE, STUART: "Landscape and Architecture: The Work of Erik Gunnar Asplund." *Perspecta* 20 (1983): 195-214.

ZEVI, BRUNO: "Sweden's First Functionalist." *Architectural Record* (April 1938).

The work of Erik Gunnar Asplund, one of the most influential Scandinavian architects of the first half of the 20th century, evolved from National Romanticism through the spare Nordic classicism of the 1920s. By 1930 he had embraced canonical modernism, only to embark in the late 1930s on a more personal path influenced by traditional architecture and a desire for increased symbolic content in his work. Asplund had the ability to create a sense of place in his architecture, manifesting directly the context in which his buildings were situated by manipulating landscape elements as forcefully as architectural ones.

Though Asplund began studying architecture in 1905 at the Royal Institute of Technology, upon his return from a traveling scholarship to Germany in 1909, he helped establish the Klara School, an independent academy of design. With fellow students Osvald Almqvist, Erik Karlstrand, Sigurd Lewerentz, Josef Östlin and M. Wernstedt, Asplund sought to supplant the normative neoclassic academic training of the period with more contemporaneous processes and techniques. The Klara students invited Carl Bergsten, Ragnar Östberg, Ivar Tengbom and Carl Westman as their tutors, thus ensuring a romantic sensibility that acknowledged the influence of Scandinavian vernacular design and handicrafts. Vernacular and traditional sources of expression had influenced Nordic architecture since the turn of the 20th century, creating the style known as National Romanticism.

The National Romantic influences of Westman and Östberg, but most particularly Östberg's ability to combine symmetrical facade composition with informal plan organization, informed Asplund's early work. The villa project for Ivar Asplund (1911), the Karlshamn School (1912), the Villa Rosenberg (1912) and the Villa Ruth (1914) are all characterized by a vernacular imagery created by using traditional board-and-batten siding or stucco-rendered walls, tile-covered gable-roof forms, and carefully placed and proportioned window and door openings.

Asplund continued to use vernacular imagery, but classical motifs began to appear in his work. This resulted, in part, from a six-month journey to the Mediterranean begun in the autumn of 1913. The first-place entry for the Woodland Cemetery competition (1915), designed in collaboration with Sigurd Lewerentz, was a strongly romantic composition maximizing the naturalistic features of the site. Asplund's Woodland Chapel (1918-19) blended romanticism and classicism; the simple, steeply pitched roof recalls Swedish vernacular buildings, while the austere Doric portico, domed interior space and white stucco walls reference classicism. The Villa Snellman (1917-18), located in the Stockholm suburb of Djursholm, combined these two qualities, while demonstrating Asplund's mastery of the compositional techniques found in Östberg's villa designs. In the simple, taut-skinned stuccoed form is housed a series of uniquely crafted rooms and spaces. The villa, which continued the Nordic tradition of L-shaped plan orders in domestic design, is also indebted to Danish architect Kay Fisker's earlier Villa Friis. In the Lister County Courthouse (1917-21), the classic-romantic dialogue continued, but the detail qualities assumed a more idiosyncratic, even mannered, character. Three competition entries for urban projects, the Göta Square (1917) and Gustaf Adolf Square (1918), both in Göteborg, and the Royal Chancellery (1922) in Stockholm, indicate that Asplund's sensitivity in designing buildings within the historical context of the city was equal to that within the natural landscape. Only recently have Asplund's urban design proposals received the analysis they deserve, most especially the Royal Chancellery competition entry.

Paralleling the development of classicism in Scandinavia during the 1920s, the classical-romantic duality of Asplund's earlier work gave way to a more explicit expression of classical principles. The work of this period represents a serious attempt at innovation within the context of classicism, rather than a nascent eclecticism. Two buildings in Stockholm, the Skandia Cinema (1922-23) and the Public Library (1920-28), along with the Swedish Pavilion for the 1925 Paris Exhibition, demonstrated his leadership position in this Nordic movement. Whereas the Skandia Cinema and the Swedish Pavilion project a certain playful and idiosyncratic use of classical elements and motifs, the Public Library has a simplicity and austerity reminiscent of the neoclassical architecture of the French Enlightenment. Although the initial design for the library was explicitly classical, with coffered dome, columnar entry porticoes and palazzo-like facade treatment, the built work, while maintaining the same organizational *parti*, was abstracted into two simple volumetric elements: cube and cylinder. Preceded by a large reflecting pool, the building sits slightly rotated in its park-like setting, adding further monumentality to the austere volumes. The cylinder houses a great rotunda containing the tiered, open-stack lending hall, a monumental clerestoried space that recalls the work of Etiènne-Louis Boullée. Exterior and interior surfaces are rendered in stucco, with finely proportioned openings and excellently crafted and integrated sculptural detail that provides the building with a subtle power.

The Stockholm Public Library marked the end of Nordic classicism in Asplund's work, for "functionalism," as modernism was termed in Scandinavia, began to appear in Sweden. His 1930 Stockholm Exhibition, which celebrated the emergence of functionalism in Sweden, represented a fundamental change in sensibility. The design for the exhibition complex underwent three phases, the last occurring after Asplund traveled to the Continent to visit extant examples of the new "modern" architecture. The Stockholm Exhibition not only epitomized the

mechanistic aesthetics of modernism but served as a propaganda instrument for its social programs. But unlike many modernist compositions, which were isolated objects sitting in green, park-like settings, Asplund's complex assumed a more dense, urban form. The light, machine-like pavilions were tied together by such traditional urban elements as squares, concourses, cul-de-sacs and garden courtyards. The tall constructivist-inspired advertising mast was combined with light steel structures holding signs and flags that provided a festive quality to the exhibition.

Although Asplund designed the Bredenberg Department Store (1933-35) in a functionalist vocabulary, the State Bacteriological Laboratories (1933-37) signaled a move away from the canons of modernism. In his last two major commissions, the Göteborg Law Courts Annex (originally won in competition in 1913, redesigned in 1925, and finalized and built between 1935 and 1936), and the Woodland Crematorium (1935-40), Asplund's reaction to functionalism solidified.

Asplund's Law Courts addition to Nicodemus Tessin's building of 1672 accepted the urban, neoclassic context of Gustaf Adolf Square as binding. Initially conceived of as a direct extension of the original facade, in the final design Asplund attempted the difficult proposition of developing a facade that would form a dialogue between the old and the new. The facade facing the square appears as two frames, a symmetrical neoclassic one and a modern structural grid, that embrace a yellow fenestrated plane layered behind them. The yellow plane provides a common inner surface binding the traditional and modern outer structures. In plan, Asplund repeated Tessin's U-shaped building order in a twofold manner. First, an interior atrium was formed that extended the existing light court into his composition. Second, Asplund's plan order mirrored Tessin's, for similar room and corridor widths extend between old and new. The interior atrium, composed of a delicate concrete framework and staircases, and superbly detailed wood paneling, has a timeless quality transcending stylistic preferences.

Beneath the powerful Swedish sky, a monumental vista is presented those approaching Asplund's Woodland Crematorium: a composition of strategically positioned architectural elements—processional walk, wall, loggia, cross, and meditation grove on raised mound—placed within a gently sloping landscape that is contained by dark forest edges. The naturalistic aspects of the site appear dominant, for the buildings seem subordinate to the landscape. But Asplund did more than enhance the site features; he recrafted a former gravel pit into a resonant dialogue between building and site. The vitality of this dialogue is facilitated by the open vistas that frame and articulate the presence of architectural objects, as they stand discretely and statically in the space of the site. It is the architectural elements, in fact, which gather the sky and earth together, establishing the place of human action in the setting. Leading to the classical loggia crowning the ensemble, a long, low wall roots the complex to the rolling landscape. The loggia is balanced in space by the tree-bedecked meditation mound, while the wayfarer's cross acts as a vertical counterpoint between the two. The roof of the loggia slopes down to an opening at its center over an impluvium, while the sculpture "Resurrection" ascends through this opening. The cave-like interior of the main chapel contrasts with the openness of the loggia, and also refers to the earthen hill of the meditation grove, which recalls ancient burial mounds.

At the time of his death in 1940, Asplund had, as witnessed in the Law Courts Annex and the Woodland Crematorium, developed a strategy of resistance to modernism's reliance on universal technique. These works, as with those completed or remaining on the drawing board after his death— the Kviberg

Crematorium in Göteborg (1936-40), the crematorium in Skövde (1937-40) and the Social Welfare Offices project in Stockholm (1938-39)—represent a tactic that included reincorporating the vital heritages of the past, as well as revitalizing the experiential and tactile capacities of architecture. Asplund's was a resonant architecture that eschewed the trivializing potential of a nostalgic, or allusion-based, architecture.

—WILLIAM C. MILLER

ATWOOD, Charles.

American. Born Charles Bowler Atwood in Millbury, Massachusetts, 8 May 1848. Died 19 December 1895. Studied at Lawrence Scientific School, Harvard University, Cambridge, Massachusetts. Draftsman for Ware and Van Brunt, Boston; established his own office in Boston, 1872; designer, Herter Brothers, New York, 1875; established his own office in New York; joined D. H. Burnham and Company, Chicago, 1891; designer for World's Columbian Exposition, Chicago, 1893; became a partner in Burnham and Company, 1893.

Chronology of Works
All in the United States
† Work no longer exists

1872	State Mutual Assurance Company Building, Worcester, Massachusetts
1874	City Hall, Holyoke, Massachusetts
1879-81	W. H. Vanderbilt Houses, New York City (with Herter Brothers and John B. Snook)†
1884	W. Seward Webb and H. McK. Twombly Houses, New York City†
1886-88	Mrs. Mark Hopkins House, Great Barrington, Massachusetts (completion)
1892-93	Marshall Field Retail Store Annex, Chicago, Illinois
1893	Fine Arts Building, World's Columbian Exposition, Chicago, Illinois (rebuilt as the Museum of Science and Industry)
1893	Terminal, Peristyle and other structures, World's Columbian Exposition, Chicago, Illinois†
1894-95	Ellicott Square Building, Buffalo, New York
1894-95	Reliance Building, Chicago, Illinois
1895-96	Fisher Building, Chicago, Illinois

Publications

BOOKS ABOUT ATWOOD

APPLEBAUM, STANLEY: *The Chicago World's Fair of 1893: A Photographic Record.* New York, 1980.
BADGER, REID: *The Great American Fair: The World's Columbian Exposition and American Culture.* Chicago, 1979.
BURG, DAVID F.: *Chicago's White City of 1893.* Lexington, Kentucky, 1976.
CONDIT, CARL W.: *The Chicago School of Architecture.* Chicago, 1964.
HINES, THOMAS S.: *Burnham of Chicago: Architect and Planner.* London, 1974.

HOFFMANN, DONALD: *The Architecture of John Wellborn Root.* Baltimore, 1973.
JOHNSON, ROSSITER (ed.): *A History of the World's Columbian Exposition Held in Chicago in 1893.* 4 vols. New York, 1897.
JORDY, WILLIAM H.: *American Buildings and Their Architects.* Vol. 3, *Progressive and Academic Ideals at the Turn of the Twentieth Century.* Garden City, New York, 1972.
MOORE, CHARLES: *Daniel Burnham: Architect, Planner of Cities.* 2 vols. Boston, 1921.
SCHUYLER, MONTGOMERY: *American Architecture and Other Writings.* Edited by William H. Jordy and Ralph Coe. 2 vols. Cambridge, Massachusetts, 1961.

ARTICLES ABOUT ATWOOD

BURNHAM, DANIEL H.: "Charles Bowler Atwood." *Inland Architect and News Record* 26, no. 6 (January 1896): 56-57.
JENKINS, CHARLES E.: "A White Enameled Building." *Architectural Record* 4, no. 3 (January-March 1895): 299-306.
KARLOWICZ, TITUS M.: "Notes on Columbian Exposition's Manufactures and Liberal Arts Building." *Journal of the Society of Architectural Historians* 33 (October 1974): 214-18.
MOORE, CHARLES: "Lessons of the Chicago World's Fair: An Interview with the Late Daniel H. Burnham." *Architectural Record* 33, no. 2 (1913): 34-44.
REBORI, A. N.: "The Work of Burnham & Root, D. H. Burnham & Co. and Graham, Burnham & Co." *Architectural Record* 38, no. 1 (July 1915): 31-168.
SCHUYLER, MONTGOMERY: "Architecture in Chicago: D. H. Burnham & Co." No. 2, Part 2 of "Great American Architects Series." *Architectural Record* 5 (December 1895): 49-71.
SCHUYLER, MONTGOMERY: "Last Words About The World's Fair." *Architectural Record* 3, no. 3 (January-March 1894): 291-301.
SITZENSTOCK, ROBERT P.: "Evolution of the High-Rise Office Building." *Progressive Architecture* 44, no. 9 (September, 1963): 146-57.
WOLTERSDORF, ARTHUR: "A Portrait Gallery of Chicago Architects: III. Charles B. Atwood." *Western Architect* 33, no. 8 (1924): 89-94.

*

During his brief, five-year association with Daniel Burnham in the 1890s, Charles Atwood influenced the look of the World's Columbian Exposition of 1893 and the emerging commercial style of D.H. Burnham and Company. "A great user of books," in Burnham's words, Atwood took an academic approach to design that helped establish Renaissance classicism as the favored Burnham office style. Two office buildings by Atwood for Burnham, the Reliance (1894-95) and Fisher (1895-96) buildings, are among the triumphs of the Chicago School, soaring towers of glass and terra-cotta that represented a step forward in opening up the facade of the metal frame skyscraper. Atwood's troubled personal life—a son who died in childhood, a failed marriage, drug addiction—remains obscure, but it led to his dismissal by Burnham in December 1895, and his death less than two weeks later at age 46.

Before moving to Chicago in 1891, Atwood had established a reputation on the East Coast as a talented but erratic designer, mainly of upper-class residences, while working for Ware and

Van Brunt, Herter Brothers, and occasionally on his own. Primarily an interior-decorating firm, Herter Brothers employed Atwood and John B. Snook to design the double houses (1879-81) built for William H. Vanderbilt on Fifth Avenue in New York City. Built at a cost of $2 million and known for their ostentatiously elaborate interiors, the Vanderbilt houses were admired by many but also criticized as brownstone boxes with confused lines and uncoordinated exterior ornament.

Atwood's brilliance as a designer and draftsman brought him success in competitions, but few of them resulted in commissions. His competition entries from the 1880s show a progressively greater and more confident use of classical forms. Atwood's 1881 competitive entry for the New York Produce Exchange, essentially a High Victorian Gothic composition with contrasting bands of color, a corner turret, and dormers, incorporated the three-part traceried windows typical of Venice in the early Renaissance. The stylistic vocabulary of his competitive design for an addition to the New York Municipal Building (1888) was thoroughly Renaissance, with a distinctly French touch in the handling of the corner pavilions, which had pyramidal roofs and elaborate frontispieces.

Hired in April 1891 to replace John Root as principal designer in Burnham's office, Atwood was almost immediately appointed designer-in-chief for the 1893 World's Fair. His stylistic preferences made him an ideal choice to implement the decision to use classicism to unify the fair's monochrome white Court of Honor. Atwood ultimately designed 60 structures for the fair, as well as numerous ornamental features. Atwood's fair buildings, particularly the Fine Arts Building (rebuilt in permanent materials beginning in 1929 as the Museum of Science and Industry) and the Peristyle that closed the eastern end of the Court of Honor, were extravagantly praised by his contemporaries. The American sculptor Augustus Saint-Gaudens pronounced the Fine Arts Building unequaled since the Parthenon.

Atwood drew on a variety of antique and Renaissance sources for his fair buildings. He prided himself on the accuracy of his details, at one point sending a subordinate to Boston solely to measure a plaster cast of the Erechtheion. Atwood's Terminal Railroad Station at the fair was based on Roman bath buildings, a scheme that subsequently became common for railroad stations, as in the main waiting room of McKim, Mead and White's Pennsylvania Station in New York City (1902-11). The Peristyle too had Roman antecedents, with a triumphal arch used as the centerpiece of the composition, flanked by Corinthian colonnades that ran to Atwood's Music Hall and Casino, identical buildings in an Italian Renaissance idiom.

At the close of the fair in 1893, Burnham made Atwood a partner in his firm, according him a 27% share in profits and full responsibility for matters of design. Atwood designed several major commercial buildings in the two years that remained to him, and also worked on early plans for the redevelopment of Chicago's lakefront as parkland.

Atwood's Marshall Field Annex (1892-93), one of the few commissions accepted by Burnham while the fair work was under way, had already marked a departure from Root's use of eclectic, nonarchaeological ornament and dark hues. The annex, clad in light-colored granite at the base and gray-white brick and terra-cotta above, resembled an Italian Renaissance palazzo grown to nine stories. The building's metal frame carried a heavily rusticated exterior with a deep and elaborate cornice. Atwood's design for the Ellicott Square Building in Buffalo (1894) continued in the classical vein of the fair and the Field Annex. Occupying a whole city block, the 10-story building had the cubic solidity of the Field Annex and employed the same pale palette. Here the cladding was of off-white brick

and terra-cotta with heavily accented entrances in a French Renaissance vein.

In the 14-story Reliance Building and 18-story Fisher Building, both in Chicago, Atwood culminated one line of development in Chicago School skyscraper design. Adopting the idea of shallowly projecting bays from Holabird and Roche's Tacoma Building in Chicago (1887), Atwood dramatically increased the glazed area in his two towers and reduced the terra-cotta cladding to a minimum. In the Reliance, slender mullions and spandrel panels with restrained French Gothic ornament surround large panes of glass. The unbroken horizontal lines of the spandrels balance the vertical thrust of the bays. The Gothic decoration of the salmon-colored Fisher is more elaborate, but the use of continuous colonnettes makes for a pronounced verticality. The effect in both buildings is of tremendous lightness and openness.

From 1895 until World War I, the commercial work of the Burnham office followed the classicizing direction indicated in the Ellicott Square Building. The relatively heavy modeling of the Marshall Field Annex was replaced in most of Burnham's later office buildings by flat wall planes and more restrained decoration. Atwood's influence on the Burnham office perhaps can be observed most clearly in monumental structures, such as the Field Museum in Chicago (1911-19), which is a respectful reworking of the 1893 Fine Arts Building. Following Root's death in 1891, Burnham seemed ready for a new aesthetic direction, and Atwood and the other classically oriented eastern architects who designed for the World's Fair provided it.

—ROBERT W. BLYTHE

AUSTIN, Henry.

American. Born in Mt. Carmel, Connecticut, 4 December 1804. Died on 17 December 1891. Worked as carpenter's apprentice, and trained in office of Town and Davis, New York. Opened own office in New Haven, Connecticut, 1837.

Chronology of Works
All in the United States
† *Work no longer exists*

1842-45	Yale College Library (now Dwight Chapel), New Haven, Connecticut
1845-48	James Dwight Dana House, New Haven, Connecticut
1848-49	Railroad Station, New Haven, Connecticut†
1848-49	Gate, Grove Street Cemetery, New Haven, Connecticut
1850	Moses Yale Beach House, Wallingford, Connecticut†
1858	First Congregational Church, Danbury, Connecticut [attributed]†
1859-63	Morse-Libby House, Portland, Maine
1861-62	City Hall, New Haven, Connecticut
1879-80	W. J. Clark House, Branford, Connecticut

Publications

BOOKS ABOUT AUSTIN

BROWN, ELIZABETH MILLS: *New Haven: A Guide to Architecture and Urban Design.* New Haven, Connecticut, 1976.

DANA, ARNOLD G. (ed.): *New Haven, Old and New, 1641-1974.* Collection of 152 vols. at New Haven Historical Society, n.d.

Henry Austin: City Hall, New Haven, Connecticut, 1861-62

KELLEY, BROOKS MATHER: *New Haven Heritage: An Area of Historic Houses on Hillhouse Avenue and Trumbull Street.* New Haven, Connecticut, 1974.

New Haven Architecture. Washington, D.C., 1970.

SEYMOUR, GEORGE DUDLEY: *New Haven.* New Haven, Connecticut, 1942.

*

As an architect working in the 19th century's climate of archaeological revivals, Henry Austin showed a remarkable agility matched by consummate skill. From his training with Ithiel Town in the 1820s to the end of his career, Austin mastered numerous styles, beginning with the Greek Revival, then moving to the Italianate and ending with the Stick Style. While his use of various styles may have deliberately coincided with their popularity, he met the needs of his clients and left a legacy of buildings that are remembered today as prime examples of 19th century revivalism.

His architectural education with Town and sometime collaboration with the firm of Town and Davis emphasized the importance of classical proportion mixed with the romanticism and exoticism of the Gothic. Yet Austin broke free from a stringent reliance on his mentors' work by using his own talents in later years to conjure associations through a variety of styles on different types of buildings. Austin practiced architecture at a time of phenomenal growth in the United States. The mid-19th century saw the erection of numerous public structures such as city halls, railroad stations, universities and cemeteries, as well as private homes which allowed the architect to exercise his imagination.

Perhaps the best way to understand Austin's work is to look at some of his commissions in New Haven, Connecticut, where many of his buildings remain standing. After working for Town, Austin opened his own office in New Haven in 1837 and remained there (with the exception of a temporary office in Hartford from 1840 to 1841) until his death. Austin began his career designing small Greek Revival houses. However, he quickly moved on to other styles, beginning with the Yale Library (now Dwight Chapel), built from 1842 to 1845. The Gothic Revival structure paid tribute to Town and Davis' new building for New York University (1832-37), which in turn was based on King's Chapel in Cambridge, England. Austin's building more accurately reproduced King's Chapel in design, but it placed greater emphasis on verticality and utilized local dark brownstone. In both his building and that of Town and Davis, one sees that the use of the Gothic was becoming associated with universities, rather than just churches, perhaps in an attempt to lend a sense of European antiquity to the country's relatively young institutions of learning. However, it is significant that the romanticism of the Yale Library's Gothic pinnacles saved the structure from being torn down in the 1930s and led its saviors to convert it into a chapel.

From the Gothic Revival, Austin ventured into the Egyptian Revival. He used this style only once, but his work was hailed as a success. His massive gate for the Grove Street Cemetery (1848-49) is an excellent example of the use of this style to connote funerary associations as well as to express life everlasting. The heavy battered pylons flank two thick columns topped by papyrus capitals, which are carved into hard, flat-planed edges, enlivening the stoic structure. Lest one should miss the symbolism of the work, the words "The Dead Shall Be Raised" are engraved in the lintel. The gate displays Austin's dexterity in working with mass and volume; the ponderous columns literally squeeze the spaces between them.

The industrial revolution provided new building types for Austin to exploit. As construction of railroads progressed, so too did the construction of railroad stations. However, no single style had been attached to such structures, which by the late 1840s were among the largest of 19th-century buildings. Austin contributed his own ideas to the type by using evocative and highly inventive elements for the station in New Haven (1848-49; heavily damaged by fire in 1894). The building has been described as both Italianate and Oriental. The large central hall and its arched windows are Italianate, while the central tower and two end towers recall Chinese and Indian architecture, respectively. The adaptation of Eastern styles for the station connected the act of travel with the idea of exploring new, exotic places, even if one were only taking the 80-mile train ride to New York City.

Always keeping in touch with the pulse of fashion, Austin designed the New Haven City Hall in 1861 at the vanguard of the High Victorian Gothic movement. His building, facing the lower end of the New Haven Green, acted as a foil to the Georgian and Gothic Revival churches and the Greek Revival State Capitol on the green. The exterior's multicolored stone surface with a variety of pinnacles and a clock tower contrasted dramatically with the surrounding buildings. The interior carried on this decorativeness with what was described as one of the finest High Victorian iron stairs in America. This building marked the beginning of the High Victorian Gothic in the United

States, which competed with the French Second Empire as the dominant style of the late 19th century.

Despite the acclaim which the New Haven City Hall received, Austin moved on to other styles. For domestic architecture, he utilized the Italianate style, relying on his architectural skill to produce houses that were well proportioned, but intriguing in their irregular massing and off-center towers. The Morse-Libby House in Portland, Maine (1859), an excellent example of this style, displays Austin's interest in manipulating mass and volume to create an exterior that changes as light and shadow play across the surface. While the asymmetrical plan creates a number of separate parts, the building comes together in a unified whole.

Austin's practice peaked in the late 1850s, but he continued working until about 1880. His last buildings were wooden houses incorporating elements of the new Stick Style. As an architect, Austin continued working in different modes, mastering each one and sometimes making up his own through a mixture of elements, to create buildings that remain as evocative as they were in their own time.

—JULIE NICOLETTA

BACON, Henry.

American. Born in Watseka, Illinois, 26 November 1866. Died on 14 February 1924. Brother was the architect and interior designer Francis Henry Bacon (1856-1940). Studied at University of Illinois, Champaign-Urbana, 1884. Worked as draftsman, Chamberlin and Whidden, Boston, 1885, then joined McKim, Mead and White, New York; won Rotch Traveling Scholarship and traveled to Europe, 1889-91; worked again for McKim, Mead and White, 1891-97; partnership with James Brite (died in 1942) as Brite and Bacon, 1897; opened own office, 1902. Gold Medal, American Institute of Architects, 1923.

Chronology of Works
All in the United States

1891	Hall of History, American University, Washington, D.C.
1897-1901	"Chesterwood" (home and studio for Daniel Chester French), the Berkshires, Massachusetts
1897-1907	Melvin Memorial, Concord, Massachusetts
1898	Public Library, Jersey City, New Jersey
1906	Danforth Memorial Library, Paterson, New Jersey
1908	Eclectic Society Building, Middletown, Connecticut
1911-22	Lincoln Memorial, Washington, D.C.
1913-15	Trask Memorial Fountain, Saratoga, New York
1915	Court of the Seasons, Pan-Pacific Exposition, San Francisco, California

Publications

BOOKS ABOUT BACON

FLETCHER, BANISTER: *A History of Architecture.* 4th. ed. New York, 1977.
HITCHCOCK, HENRY-RUSSELL: *Architecture: Nineteenth and Twentieth Centuries.* Baltimore, 1958.
KIDNEY, WALTER C.: *The Architecture of Choice: Eclecticism in America, 1880-1930.* New York, 1974.
SCULLY, VINCENT: *American Architecture and Urbanism.* New York, 1969.
TALLMADGE, THOMAS E.: *The Story of Architecture in America.* 3d. ed., rev. New York, 1936.

Henry Bacon is chiefly remembered as the designer of the Lincoln Memorial in Washington, D.C. (1911-22). Largely trained in architects' offices (Chamberlin and Whidden, Boston, 1885-88; McKim, Mead and White, New York, 1888-89), Bacon won recognition early for his drawing ability and his skill in the design of classical elements. The great influence on his career was his older brother Francis Henry Bacon (1856-1940),

an architect and interior designer of considerable classical learning who had taken part in an archaeological expedition in Asia Minor in the early 1880s. When Henry won the Rotch Travelling Scholarship in 1889, he spent much of the next two years in Greece and Asia Minor studying classical remains.

Henry Bacon worked for the prestigious firm of McKim, Mead and White as a design assistant, principally to Charles McKim, from 1891 to 1897. He contributed substantially to some of the firm's most important designs of the period, including that of the Rhode Island State House (1891-1903), buildings at the World's Columbian Exposition of 1893, the Brooklyn Museum (begun the same year) and, later, the J. P. Morgan Library (1902-06). Indeed, once suspects that Bacon's taste and training were in part the stimulus behind the shift toward a cool, white classicism in the work of the office (especially Stanford White) around the turn of the century. But, feeling like "a cog in the wheel" of the huge McKim, Mead and White practice, Bacon left it in 1897 and determined never again to work for others or have others design for him. Except for a brief partnership (1897-1903) with the like-minded James Brite, Bacon always worked on his own thereafter, on a select number of commissions for which he did most of the drawing and designing himself, and supervising a small staff of trusted assistants. This accounts for the relatively small scale and exquisitely high standards of design and supervision that marked all his work, consisting largely of residences, public libraries, collegiate buildings and savings banks—some of the building types most characteristic of the age.

Still more to Bacon's liking was the design of architectural settings for monuments and memorials, of which he did more than a hundred, ranging from diminutive tombstones, *stelae* and memorial plaques to temple-like mausolea, such as that of Marcus Hanna in Lake View Cemetery, Cleveland (1904-06). Such structures—small, ideal rather than practical, and ornamental in a reserved, classical way—suited his temperament and practice perfectly, and were the basis for the commission for the far-larger Lincoln Memorial. In many of his monumental projects Bacon collaborated with sculptors, including Augustus Saint-Gaudens and Daniel Chester French, whom he met through McKim, Mead and White. The friendship and collaboration between French and Bacon were especially close: Bacon designed the sculptor's summer home and studio, Chesterwood, in the Berkshires (1897-1901); and the pair worked together on more than 50 projects for monuments and memorials—some, such as the Melvin Memorial in Concord, Massachusetts (1897-1907), and the Trask Memorial Fountain in Saratoga, New York (1913-15), quite as remarkable in their own way as the Lincoln Memorial itself.

In August 1911 the commission created by Congress to build a memorial to Abraham Lincoln in Washington invited Bacon to be its consulting architect, and he accepted. Such a memorial, terminating the axis of the Mall at the Potomac River and serving as the pivot for a new driveway along the river to Rock Creek Park and a memorial bridge to

Arlington, had been proposed by the Senate Park Commission (or McMillan Commission) in 1901-02, but no action had been taken on the proposal. Late in 1911 Bacon presented a design for a temple-like memorial to Lincoln of white marble, raised on a mound and stepped platform and surrounded by a peristyle of fluted Doric columns. Somewhat unexpectedly a design competition with another talented young architect, John Russell Pope, was staged, in which Pope put forward several striking yet probably impractical schemes for memorials to Lincoln. But Bacon's design (modified somewhat) was selected, and Congress authorized its building in early 1913. Despite a slow start, caused by a change of administrations (the Democrat Woodrow Wilson took office in 1913), and a maddening series of interruptions owing to wartime shortages and the need to stop work on the memorial at an advanced stage to underpin the foundations of its approaches, the building was completed and dedicated in May 1922.

From the beginning the Lincoln Memorial was acclaimed as a triumph. For his achievement the American Institute of Architects awarded Bacon its Gold Medal in 1923, a judgment at which few architects (Louis Sullivan among them) demurred. Political and architectural conservatives praised the classical memorial and French's seated marble colossus of Lincoln inside for the dignity with which they represented the beloved president, while a few years later modernist architects hailed the white purity, austerity and geometric abstraction of the Lincoln Memorial. The public for its part took to it immediately, visiting the memorial in droves and canonizing it as a shrine not just to Lincoln but to the American democracy he had come to represent. The memorial was the backdrop for the action in Frank Capra's ultrapatriotic film *Mister Smith Goes to Washington* (1939), and, thanks to events like the opera singer Marian Anderson's Easter concert on the steps in 1939 and the rally for the March on Washington held there in August 1963, the Lincoln Memorial was invested with particular associations with racial justice.

As for Bacon, although he died less than a year after winning the Gold Medal and so did not have the chance to follow up his achievement in the Lincoln Memorial—at the time of his death, he had been proposed as the designer of a new United States Supreme Court and a National Gallery of Art— his design for the Lincoln Memorial had demonstrated how demanding, yet rich and rewarding, classicism could be in the hands of one who knew it intimately. In effect, his career bridged the gap between the romantic neoclassicism and scientific archaeology of the 19th century and the building needs of a burgeoning American society in the 20th century.

—CHRISTOPHER THOMAS

BÄHR, Georg.

Saxon. Born in Fürstenwalde, near Lauenstein, Saxony, 1666. Died in Dresden, 16 March 1738. Apprenticed as a carpenter; was master carpenter of Dresden by 1705.

Chronology of Works
All in eastern Germany
† *Work no longer exists*

1705-08	Church, Loschwitz (near Dresden)
1713-16	Church, Schmiedeberg
1719-21	Church, Forchheim
1722-43	Frauenkirche, Dresden (completed by Johann Georg Schmidt)†
1725-26	Church, Hohnstein

Publications

BOOKS ABOUT BÄHR

BARTH, A.: *Zur Baugeschichte der Dresdner Kreuzkirche.* Dresden, 1907.
HEMPEL, EBERHARD: *Baroque Art and Architecture in Central Europe.* Harmondsworth, England, 1965.
Der Kirchenbau des Protestantismus. Berlin, 1893.
LÖFFLER, F.: *Das alte Dresden.* Dresden, 1955.
POPP, HERMANN: *Die Architektur der Barock- und Rokokozeit in Deutschland und der Schweiz.* Stuttgart, 1924.
The Splendor of Dresden: Five Centuries of Art Collecting. Exhibition catalog. New York, 1978.
SPONSEL, J. L.: *Die Frauenkirche zu Dresden.* Dresden, 1893.

ARTICLES ABOUT BÄHR

FISCHER, HORST: "Forschungen zu Georg Bähr und dem Sächsischen Barock." Dissertation. Technische Universität, Dresden, 1965.

*

The destruction of Dresden, the incomparable Baroque capital city of Saxony, in 1945, was one of the worst disasters ever to befall the architectural heritage of Europe. Among the casualties of that terrible catastrophe was the Frauenkirche, or Protestant Church of Our Lady, built in 1722-43 to designs by Georg Bähr, who was *Ratszimmermeister* (master carpenter) to the city of Dresden. Distinctions between master craftsmen and architects were often nebulous before the rise of "professionalism" in the 19th century, and there are many examples of 18th-century craftsmen who designed buildings and can be considered to have functioned as architects too. On the strength of the Frauenkirche alone, Bähr must be counted as an architect, and an architect of genius at that, who, in this stupendous church, demonstrated his mastery of geometry, form, space, planning, structure, materials and architectural effects.

This great building was probably the finest centrally planned Protestant church ever created, although it was not by any means the first. The traditional cruciform or basilican arrangement was not particularly well suited to Protestant worship: Protestantism does not involve the need for processional ways or the kind of ecclesiastical show demonstrated in the most elaborate ceremonies of the Roman Catholic Church. Protestant worship is more static, with a congregation that does not move about, and which is addressed by a clergyman from a pulpit that ideally is centrally placed. Cruciform or basilican plans were not readily adaptable for galleries, and much potential space was wasted in such building types. Tiered galleries arranged as though round a theater could accommodate large numbers of people with economy of means. For Protestant services, therefore, the tendency was to shorten the arms of the cross so that a more centralized plan was created, and this arrangement became the concern of many architects in the Netherlands and in northern Germany. The Silesian Nikolaus Goldmann, who died a professor of architecture in Leiden in 1665, had commenced writing a treatise on architecture, which was completed by Leonhard Christian Sturm (1669-1729) as *Vollständige Anweisung aller Arten von Kirchen* (1718). In this influential text the *Zentralbau* was recommended for Protestant churches so that a congregation could see and hear the preacher better, and Sturm suggested that the beauty of the building should derive from its form rather than from its ornament or surface decoration.

Centralized Protestant churches, or "temples," as they were often called, derived partly from those round churches of the

Georg Bähr: Frauenkirche, Dresden, Germany, 1722-43

early Middle Ages, partly from the Pantheon-like forms that were supposed, in many 17th-century illustrations, to represent a memory of the Temple in Jerusalem, and partly from the needs of congregational forms of worship. French Protestant and Netherlandish ideas penetrated far into Protestant Germany, influencing the designs of the Parochial Church in Berlin by Johann Arnold Nering (1693), of the Parish Church of Hehlen in Westphalia (1697-98) by Hermann Korb, of the elliptical church in Nürnberg (1718), of the Garrison Church at Potsdam (with galleries, organ pipes behind the pulpit, and altar in front [*Kanzelaltar*]), and of the noblest of all such churches, Bähr's Frauenkirche in Dresden.

The plan of the Frauenkirche was essentially a circle within a square, with the chancel set in a partial ellipse, and with staircases in all four corners, set diagonally, over which were inventive towers. Eight great piers carried the steep stone-vaulted dome with its immense lantern. Set between the piers were three tiers of galleries: the fronts of the lowest tier were glazed in to form boxes, rather like theatrical arrangements, known as *Ranglogen, Hoflogen* or *Bettstübchen* (little bed-rooms). Steps led up to the altar, and organ pipes towered behind, emphasizing the sense of theater. This mighty temple, with seats for almost four thousand people, featured prominently in the views of Dresden by Bernardo Bellotto (1720-80): it was the greatest achievement of a specifically Protestant type of church architecture, and, while there were other centrally planned Protestant places of worship such as the Pauluskirche at Frankfurt-am-Main and the Ostkerk in Middelburg in the Netherlands, Bähr's masterpiece outstrips all others as a supreme work of architecture.

The Frauenkirche stood in a large square, the Neumarkt, and was an object in space, as James Gibbs' Radcliffe Camera is in Radcliffe Square, Oxford (the buildings are approximately contemporary). Like the Oxford building, the Frauenkirche was an immense and assured composition, bold and grand enough to succeed as a major work of architecture and in townscape terms. Not only was the church a stupendous building, dominating its square, but the huge dome contributed to the skyline of Dresden when seen from across the Elbe.

Bähr was also responsible for various buildings for the Lutheran Church in his capacity as municipal architect-carpenter. When the elector of Saxony became king of Poland in 1697, converting to Roman Catholicism in the process, the Protestant ethos of Saxony fractured. Bähr's buildings, and especially his Frauenkirche, were architectural statements of great splendor designed to demonstrate the importance of a continuing Protestant tradition in spite of a Catholic court. Baroque architecture in Germany is mostly associated with the building activities in the Roman Catholic lands after the strife of the Thirty Years' War. The Dresden Frauenkirche demonstrates how the Baroque style could be adapted for use in a Protestant church: on the strength of this one building, its architect can be regarded as one of the most important designers of the period in all Germany.

—JAMES STEVENS CURL

BAKER, Herbert.

British. Born in Cobham, Kent, England, 9 June 1862. Died in Cobham, Kent, 4 February 1946. Married Florence Edmeades, 1904; four children. Studied at Royal Academy School of Architecture, London, 1879-81; articled to his cousin, the architect Arthur Baker, 1879-82. Worked for Ernest George and Harold Peto, London, 1882-87; opened office in Gravesend, Kent, 1890; moved to Cape Town, South Africa, 1892, and appointed as architect to Cecil Rhodes; opened office in Johannesburg, 1902; returned to London in 1913, and practiced there until his death; worked with Edwin Lutyens at New Delhi, India, 1913-31; principal architect to Imperial War Graves Commission, 1918-28; architect to Bank of England, from 1921. Fellow, Royal Institute of British Architects, 1900; founder member, South African Society of Architects, 1901; associate, 1922, and member, 1932, Royal Academy; Gold Medal, Royal Institute of British Architects, 1927; knighted, 1926.

Chronology of Works
All in South Africa unless noted
* Approximate dates

1882-87	Waterside House, Westgate-on-Sea, Kent, England
1882-87	Redroofs, Streatham Common, London, England
1892-1902	Housing, Somerset West, Cape Town
1894	St. Andrew's Church, Newlands
1893-95	Groote Schuur (Cecil Rhodes House), Rondebosch, South Africa (rebuilt after a fire in 1897)
1902	Rhodes Building, Cape Town
1904	New Government Buildings, Bloemfontein, Orange Free State
1904*	Northwards (Lace House), Parktown, Johannesburg
1905-07	Government House and Union Buildings, Pretoria
1908	Rhodes Memorial, near Cape Town
1908-10*	Villa Arcadia, Parktown, Johannesburg
1909	Railway Station, Pretoria
1911	Rhodes University College, Cape Town
1913	Union Buildings, Pretoria
1913-26	Secretariat, Legislative and Staff Buildings, New Delhi, India (with Edwin Lutyens)
1918-28	Numerous war cemeteries in Belgium and France, and war memorial structures in England
1921-39	Bank of England, London, England (reconstruction)
1925	India House, London, England
1934	Scott Polar Research Institute, Cambridge, England
1935	South Africa House, London, England
1936-41	Royal Empire Society, London, England

Publications

BOOKS BY BAKER

Plas Mawr, Conway, North Wales. With Arthur Baker. London, 1888.
Cecil Rhodes by His Architect. London, 1934.
Architecture and Personalities. London, 1944.

ARTICLES BY BAKER

"The Origin of Old Cape Architecture." In ALYS FANE TROTTER: *Old Colonial Houses of the Cape of Good Hope.* London, 1900.
"The Architectural Needs of South Africa." *State* (May 1909).
"Architecture and Town Planning." *South African Architect* (August 1911).

BOOKS ABOUT BAKER

DAY, E. HERMITAGE: *The Cathedral of St. George, Cape Town.* Cape Town, 1939.
GREIG, DOREEN: *Herbert Baker in South Africa.* Cape Town, 1970.
IRVING, ROBERT G.: *Indian Summer: Lutyens, Baker, and Imperial Delhi.* New Haven, Connecticut, 1982.

ARTICLES ABOUT BAKER

CHRISTENSEN, E. A.: "Government Architecture and British Imperialism: Edwardian Architects in London, Pretoria and New Delhi (1882-1931)." Dissertation. Northwestern University, Evanston, Illinois, 1991.
"The New Delhi. The Work of Sir Edwin Lutyens and Sir Herbert Baker." *Architectural Review* 60 (1926): 216-225.

*

In 1892, a young Herbert Baker left London for the Cape Colony, during a period of escalating British imperialist activity in southern Africa. There, Baker established himself as the foremost architect of the region, first as the protégé of the capitalist and politician Cecil Rhodes, and later in connection with Lord Milner in the Transvaal. Under their aegis, Baker understood his task as that of creating an appropriate architecture for a nascent British South African culture, an architecture that would

Herbert Baker: Union Buildings, Pretoria, South Africa, 1913

often play an integral role in the politics of the region. Initially drawing inspiration for his work from memories of English vernacular architecture, the lessons of the Arts and Crafts movement, and a close study of Cape Dutch architecture and furniture, he increasingly mixed elements drawn from these as well as other sources with the classicism of the Italian Renaissance, forging a distinctive manner of high-quality building which he would later adapt for buildings in Rhodesia, Kenya, India, and finally England.

Throughout his career, Baker was closely associated with a network of British politicians and capitalists in South Africa, who formed the core of his clientele. Cecil Rhodes gave shape and direction to his early career; Baker was devoted to him to the extent that he later published an idealized tribute of this controversial imperialist, *Cecil Rhodes by his Architect* (1934). For Rhodes, he restored Groote Schuur at Rondebosch (1893-95), adding to the residence a two-story wing containing bedrooms, bathrooms, a billiard room and servant spaces. The addition was connected to the original building by means of a columned *stoep* at the back, which gave access to extensive gardens. After the house burned in 1897, he rebuilt it again according to Rhodes' instructions.

Rhodes intended Groote Schuur not only to serve as his residence, but to stimulate interest in Cape Dutch architecture, furniture and silver, an integral part of his plan to create a distinctive British culture in southern Africa. Thus, the house has thick brick walls plastered and whitewashed within and without, featuring a simplified version of high picturesque Dutch gables and twisted barley-sugar chimneys. The traditional thatched roof was replaced with one of thick, handmade English

tile to discourage further fire damage. Inside, white walls stand in pleasing contrast to extensive teak woodwork employed throughout for doors, the main staircase, wall paneling and massive support beams. The light fixtures, such as chandeliers and sconces, are the work of George Ness, patterned after Cape Dutch examples. To complete the ensemble, the furniture consists of old colonial pieces—some constructed of lustrous South African stinkwood—mixed with contemporary furniture fashioned at Cape Town specifically for the house.

Work on Groote Schuur gave Baker direction not only politically, but aesthetically, as he labored to establish a practice in Cape Town. As an architect who subscribed to the Arts and Crafts ideal of high-quality craftsmanship and the use of the best local materials, he was faced with a difficult struggle: to replace the relatively cheap prefabricated building parts from abroad, then widely employed in construction in the colony, with quality materials and workmanship. To that end, Baker trained his own craftsmen, ensuring that the cutting of the stone, the making of bricks, the preparation of timber, and the fashioning of all furniture, joinery and metalwork for his buildings would be conducted to his specifications. As a result, his buildings, whether domestic, ecclesiastical or civic, exhibit very-high-quality workmanship down to the smallest detail.

Baker left the Cape in 1902 for Johannesburg, at the invitation of Lord Milner, then Governor-General of the former Boer republics. In Johannesburg, he was associated closely with the "Milner kindergarten," a group of young Oxford graduates engaged in the task of reconstruction after the Boer War. Through these political connections Baker gained numerous commissions for houses for mining magnates, residences that reveal him as a supremely successful domestic architect. He was particularly skillful in creating carefully detailed, intimate and romantic houses that blend harmononiously with their sites: for example, Northwards (ca. 1904), a huge stone mansion containing more than 40 rooms, constructed in Parktown for Colonel John Dale Lace and wife Jos; and Villa Arcadia, (ca. 1908-10), an enomous Italianate villa surrounded by extensive gardens, created in Parktown for Lionel and Florence Philips. Indeed, by 1910 *The Times* could assert that he built '...'' so many private dwellings that it may be said that a 'Baker House' has become part of the indispensable equipment of a South African magnate.''

It was a government commission in Pretoria, the Union Buildings, that gained Baker an international reputation. In 1909 Jan Christian Smuts and Louis Botha, leaders of the colonial Transvaal government, commissioned Baker to construct monumental buildings to house new government offices in Pretoria, the new administrative capital of the country after the 1910 unification of South Africa. Further, these buildings were intended to symbolize in stone the unification of the British and the Dutch in South Africa.

To solve the problem, Baker placed a U-shaped complex of colored sandstone halfway up Meintjes Kop on a natural, narrow rock platform overlooking the city. The buildings consist of two identical porticoed blocks modeled loosely on Italian Renaissance palazzi. These blocks are connected by a semicircular colonnade enclosing a small, paved amphitheater overlooking a series of terraced gardens. Twin towers complete the building, affording a striking silhouette that can be seen to effect throughout the city.

Based on the success of the Union Buildings, Baker gained the prestigious appointment of joint architect to New Delhi, where he would collaborate with his longtime friend Edwin Lutyens on the design of the new imperial capital of British India. Like the Union Buildings, it was a commission of considerable political significance in imperial affairs.

Beginning work in 1913, Baker was mainly responsible for the design of the North and South Secretariats in the government complex, and a circular, columned legislative building located off Rajpath at an angle to the main complex. The Secretariats, built of white and red sandstone, stand on a raised platform on either side of an elegant garden court, which terminates in Lutyens' imposing Government House. Each Secretariat consists of a long block containing three floors of offices; on the exterior, each features multiple columned porticoes topped by *chattris*, a large central dome surrounded by *chattris*, and a high tower. Although the Secretariats are rather awkward in the relation of various parts to the whole, they provide an impressive, awe-inspiring silhouette from a distance.

In designing these buildings, Baker mixed classical architecture with Indian decorative and structural elements, utilizing the *jaali*, a pierced-stone lattice or window screen; the *chajja*, a wide, protecting stone slab for a cornice; and the *chattris*, an open columned turret shaded with *chajjas*. This combination of Western and Eastern architectural elements would, according to politicians, signal increased Indian participation in government.

Baker's career continued to prosper after he left South Africa to set up practice in London in about 1912-13. There, his political connections brought him an appointment as a principal architect to the Imperial War Graves Commission from 1917, an appointment as architect to the Bank of England in 1921, and commissions for a host of buildings of various types, including India House at Aldwyeh (1925) and South Africa House (1935) on Trafalgar Square. Baker won many honors and was knighted in 1926.

Despite historians' interest in Baker's work, many aspects of his career remain obscure and are now the subject of further extensive research. Indeed, his architecture, particularly in South Africa, deserves to become better known, as his work—consistently exhibiting a high degree of craftmanship and warmth of human scale—was an architecture in the best Arts and Crafts tradition, and often played an integral role in the political life of the British Empire at its zenith.

—ELLEN A. CHRISTENSEN

BANFI, BELGIOJOSO, PERESUTTI and ROGERS (BBPR).

Italian. Partnership established in Milan, Italy, 1932, by Gianluigi Banfi (born in Milan, 1910; died 1945), Lodovico Belgiojoso (born in Milan, 1909), Enrico Peressutti (born in 1908; died in Milan, 1975) and Ernesto Nathan Rogers (born in Trieste, 1909; died in 1969).

Chronology of Works
All in Italy
† Work no longer exists

1933	Casa del Sabato per gli Sposi, *Triennale*, Milan (exhibition project; with Portaluppi, Fontana and Chiesa)
1934	Palazzo del Littorio, *Mostra della rivoluzione fascista*, Rome (exhibition project; with Luigi Figini, Gino Pollini and Luigi Danusso)
1936	Villa Venosta, Gornate Olona, Varese (conversion)
1936-37	Master plan for the Aosta Valley, Italy (with others)
1937	Central Post Office Building, EUR Quarter, Rome
1937	Italian Shipping Companies' Floating Pavilion, World's Fair, Paris, France (with P. Zappa, M. Russo, and L. Fontana)
1938	Sanatorium Building (Heliotherapy Clinic), Legnano
1940	San Simpliciano Cloisters, Milan (restoration; with E. Radice Fossati)
1946	Monument to the Victims of German Concentration Camps, Monumental Cemetery, Milan
1956-63	Sforza Castle, Milan (renovations)
1955-58	Torre Velasca, Milan (renovations)
1966	Banca Commerciale Italiana Building, Via Ruggero Settimo, Palermo, Sicily (with R. Guttuso, S. Bassani, R. Chiavelli, and G. Lanzani)
1967	Housing development, Via Beato Angelico, Milan
1967	Andreatta Apartment Building, Pinzolo, Trento
1967	Apartment and Office Building, Via Stampa, Milan
1968	Hispano-Olivetti Showrooms, Piazza de Espana, Madrid, Spain (with R. Casals and A. Rodriguez)
1969	Piazzale Meda Offices, Milan
1969	Chase Manhattan Bank, Milan
1969	Giornale di Sicilia Building, Via Lincoln, Palermo, Sicily
1970	Gabriele d'Annunzio University, Chieti, Italy (with F. Ordanini and W. Passarella)
1974	Spaltenna Castle, Gaiole in Chianti (conversion)
1975	Memorial to the Victims of Nazi Concentration Camps, Auschwitz, Poland
1977	Stock Exchange Building, Milan (conversion)

Banfi, Belgiojoso, Peresutti and Rogers: Torre Velasca, Milan, Italy, 1955-58

Publications

BOOKS ABOUT BBPR

BONFANTI, EZIO and PORTA, MARCO: *Città, museo e architettura: Il gruppo BBPR nella cultura architettonica italiana 1932-1970*. Florence, 1973.

CRISPOLTI, ENRICO (ed.): *Immaginazione megastrutturale dal futurismo a oggi*. Venice, 1979.

DE FEO, GIOVANNA and VALERIANI, ENRICO: *Architetture italiane degli anni '70*. Exhibition catalog. Rome, 1981.

DE SETA, CESARE: *La cultura archietonnica in Italia tra le due guerre*. Rome, 1972.

PIVA, ANTONIO (ed.): *BBPR a Milano*. Exhibition catalog. Milan, 1982.

*

A partnership of Gian Luigi Banfi, Ludovico Barbiano di Belgiojoso, Enrico Peressutti and Ernesto Nathan Rogers was formed in 1932, the year of their graduation from Milan Polytechnic. A youthful visionary spirit prompted these architects early in their careers to reject the Polytechnic's neoclassical lessons and instead to look to modern European architects for references (especially Walter Gropius, Le Corbusier and Ludwig Mies van der Rohe). Their abstract formal language in the 1930s also contained traces of architectural tradition. In this, they resembled some of their Italian contemporaries, such as Giuseppe Terragni, Luigi Figini, Gino Pollini, Cesare Cattaneo and others.

After World War II, the surviving three members—Belgiojoso, Peressutti and Rogers—continued the activity of the group, producing some of the pivotal works of that period by combining poetic references to tradition and preexisting architectural context with a formal vocabulary of modern architecture. In this way, BBPR became a bond between the avant-garde beginnings of modernism and its critical redefinition in the later part of this century. Their design sensitivity was reflected not only in architecture, but also in interior and industrial design, and urban planning. Parallel to their professional activity, the members of BBPR were continually active as prolific writers and teachers, especially Rogers, with his major contributions to architectural journalism as the editor of *Quadrante, Domus,* and *Casabella-Continuità.*

The early years of BBPR Group bear resemblance to the Gruppo 7, six years their predecessors: formation of the group during the last year of university studies, rejection of the neoclassical formulas (already in their thesis projects at the Polytechnic), regard for mid-European abstract architecture and the strong formal influence of those sources. BBPR Group's major contribution in that period was the spreading of modern concepts in Italy. A witty Weekend House for the Newlyweds (1933) was reminiscent of the work of Gropius, as was the project for the Palazzo del Littorio competition in 1934 (in collaboration with Figini and Pollini). This abstract composition of rectangular volumes was double-coded, with the asymmetrical honorific forecourt elevated on the monumental esplanade overlooking the street. Early respect for history was also present in urban plans: the master plan for Pavia retained the monuments of the city, although not the urban fabric, which the architects proposed to demolish, following Le Corbusier's urban theories.

The group became internationally known with the Sanatorium at Legnano (built 1937-38, demolished 1956) which clearly adhered to mid-European modernism. Some of their work in the second half of the 1930s departed partially from the precepts of modernism. The Post Office at EUR '42 (1937) bore a similarity to the works of the northern school of Italian rationalism, displaying a monumental and symbolic grid. The Floating Pavilion at the Paris World's Fair in 1937 presented a freer experimentation with architectural forms, while a conversion project for Villa Venosta (1936) prompted the contemplation of the relationship between the existing and new architecture, a theme which was the forte of BBPR Group's postwar projects. Sensitivity to tradition permeated another one of their works—the restoration of the San Simpliciano monastery in 1940.

In the prewar years BBPR Group was sympathetic to the Fascist Party, as were most other architects in Italy, only to experience a disappointment during the war years. Rogers was forced to leave for Switzerland; Banfi and Belgiojoso were sent to Mauthausen concentration camp in 1944, where Banfi died in April of the following year. BBPR's design for the Monument to the Victims of German Concentration Camps (1946) was a powerfully fragile and elegant object that had its formal roots in the symbolic grids of Italian prewar rationalism.

During the 1950s BBPR Group created their most historically significant works. Renovation of the Sforza Castle in 1956 and the building of the Torre Velasca in 1958 resulted in controversy because of the perceived noncompliance with the emerging dogmas of modernism. Torre Velasca unified a concern for the "preexisting environment," 20th-century technology, and a poetic and free exploration of architectural form. Its roots were in the tradition of modernism, historical formal vocabulary and expressionism.

The late 1950s and 1960s were a period of ups and downs in the firm's work, but in 1969 BBPR created one final masterpiece, less revolutionary than Torre Velasca, but compositionally better executed. The Chase Manhattan Bank Building in Milan is a modern building respectful of its urban fabric, which contains subtle references to architectural tradition. This was the last major work of the old BBPR. Rogers died in 1969, and Peressutti in 1975. Belgiojoso continued to practice.

—DRAŽEN ČAČKOVIĆ

BARNES, Edward Larrabee.

American. Born in Chicago, Illinois, 22 April 1915. Married Mary Elizabeth Coss, 1944; one son. Studied at Harvard University, M.Arch., 1942. Lieutenant, United States Navy, 1942-47. Private practice, New York City, since 1949. Has taught at the Pratt Institute, Brooklyn, New York, 1954-59, Yale University, 1957-64, and several other universities; since 1978, member of the visiting committee, Graduate School of Design, Harvard University; member, advisory council, Trust for Public Land, since 1984. Fellow, American Institute of Architects.

Chronology of Works
All in the United States unless noted

1949   Whitelaw Reid Residence, Purchase, New York
1950-51 Osborn Residence and Studio, Salisbury, Connecticut
1954-61 Camp Bliss, Fishkill, New York
1957   Straus House, Pound Ridge, New York
1958-65 Capitol Towers Apartments, Sacramento, California (with Wurster, Bernardi and Emmons, and DeMars and Reay)
1961-62 Haystack Mountain School of Arts and Crafts, Deer Isle, Maine
1961   Dormitories, St. Paul's School, Concord, New Hampshire
1963   Cowles House, Wayzata, Minnesota
1963-71 Music, Art and Library Building and Faculty Apartments, Emma Willard School, Troy, New York
1963-74 Master plan and major buildings, State University of New York at Potsdam
1964   W. D. Richards Elementary School, Columbus, Indiana
1966-87 Christian Theological Seminary, Indianapolis, Indiana
1967-79 Master plan and major buildings, State University of New York at Purchase.
1971   New England Merchants National Bank Building, Boston
1971   Walker Art Center, Minneapolis, Minnesota
1972   Crown Center (office and retail complex), Kansas City, Missouri
1974   Sarah M. Scaife Gallery, Carnegie Institute, Pittsburgh, Pennsylvania
1974   IBM World Trade Center, Mount Pleasant, New York
1976-   Indiana University/Purdue University Master plan and major buildings, Indianapolis, Indiana
1976   Chicago Botanic Gardens, Glencoe, Illinois
1976   Visual Art Center, Bowdoin College, Brunswick, Maine
1976   Cathedral of the Immaculate Conception, Burlington, Vermont
1979   Conservatory restoration, New York Botanical Garden, Bronx, New York
1981   Asia Society Gallery, New York
1982   Office Building, 535 Madison Avenue, New York
1983   IBM World Headquarters, 590 Madison Avenue, New York

1983-84 Dallas Museum of Art, Dallas, Texas
1983-89 Fuqua School of Business, Duke University, Durham, North Carolina
1984   Private Residence, Dallas, Texas
1984   Mathematics and Computer Center, Amherst College, Massachusetts
1985   Museum of Art, Fort Lauderdale, Florida
1986   Office Building, 599 Lexington Avenue, New York
1988   Minneapolis Sculpture Garden, Minneapolis, Minnesota
1989   Knoxville Museum of Art, Knoxville, Tennessee
1990   Katonah Museum of Art, Katonah, New York
1991   Allen Library, University of Washington, Seattle
1991-93 Judiciary Office Building, Washington, D.C

Publications

ARTICLES BY BARNES

"Defence Housing." *Task* 2 (1941).
"The Design Process." *Perspecta* 5 (1959).
"Control of Graphics Essential to Good Shopping Center Design." *Architectural Record* (June 1962).
"Remarks on Continuity and Change." *Perspecta* 9/10 (1965).

BOOKS ABOUT BARNES

DIAMONSTEIN, BARBARALEE (ed.): *American Architecture Now.* New York, 1979.
Edward Larrabee Barnes Museum Designs. Exhibition catalog. Katonah, New York, 1987.

ARTICLES ABOUT BARNES

"Architect Ed Barnes: Toward Simpler Details, Simpler Forms and Greater Unity." *Architectural Forum* (August 1963).
"Barnes Gratia Artis." *Progressive Architecture* (March 1975).
BLAKE, PETER: "Brick-on-Brick and White-on-White." *Architecture Plus* 2 (July/August 1974).
DEITZ, PAULA: "The IBM Garden Plaza." *Architectural Record* (May 1984).
DILLON, DAVID: "Blend of Modernism and Regionalism." *Architecture* (May 1986).
"Edward Larrabee Barnes." *Space Design* (July 1985).
FRIEDMAN, M.: "Walker Art Center." *Design Quarterly* 81 (1971).
FRIEDMAN, M., and TREIB, M. "Minneapolis Sculpture Garden." *Design Quarterly* 141 (1988).
KOERBLE, BARBARA: "Design Clarity and Urban Synthesis." *Architecture* 78 (February 1989)
"Lines and Volume: Two Recent Projects from the Boards of Edward Larrabee Barnes." *Progressive Architecture* (April 1969).
MERKEL, JAYNE: "Building on Tradition: The Late 20th Century Campus." *Inland Architect* (July/August 1987).
"Minimal Sculpture Inside and Out: The New Walker Art Museum by Edward Larrabee Barnes." *Architectural Record* 150 (July 1971).
"A Neo-Richardson Romanesque Cathedral by Edward Larrabee Barnes." *Architectural Record* (January 1979).
SMITH, HERBERT: "A Paradoxical Neighbor." *Architectural Record* (February 1988).
VILADAS, P.: "Minneapolis Sculpture Garden." *Progressive Architecture* 69 (November 1988).

Continuity is the word that best summarizes Edward Larrabee Barnes' design approach and the development of his practice during 40 years. His education at Harvard's Graduate School of Design emphasized clarity and functionality, qualities which have always remained present in his work. At Harvard, Marcel Breuer's influence was strong, and his concept of binuclear functionalism has shaped Barnes' house designs throughout his career.

Following his visit to the Greek island of Mykonos in the late 1950s, Barnes adapted the village vernacular concepts he observed there, disciplining them with rigorous geometry. At that time, he made an emphatic break with Breuer's multiplicity of design elements, and began approaching his designs in the 1960s with a heightened simplicity, reducing the expression of interior and exterior walls to continuous expanses of single materials. The forms of his buildings grew increasingly simple and boldly geometric, evoking the prime forms of Le Corbusier. Yet Barnes also extracted from village architecture the concept of contextual design that related buildings to their surroundings and gracefully accommodated their sites. The Haystack Mountain School of Arts and Crafts (1962) and St. Paul's School Dormitories (1961) were the most notable early examples of Barnes' new approach. Barnes' designs grew increasingly reductive in the 1960s, when his expanded firm undertook numerous academic projects. That period culminated in the monumental severity of the State University of New York at Purchase campus (1968) and the minimalist sculptural forms of the Walker Art Center in Minneapolis (1971).

While office towers would become the high-profile work of the firm during the 1980s, it is in the design of private residences that Barnes has consistently excelled. His early house designs were primarily developed at one horizontal level raised upon a stone base or on piles to ride above the site. These houses grew increasingly complex as extended wings interlocked the houses with their sites, as in the Straus House (1957). In contrast to the long horizontal wings of the Cowles House (1963), the Hilltop House (1965) and subsequent houses grew vertically, their spacial development expressed in distinct towers, In addition, the Hilltop House and Barnes' Dallas Residence (1984) are fully integrated into their pitched sites, containing entrances and outdoor courts at different levels. Both the Dallas Residence and a Garden Library in Virginia (1983) are further distinguished by Barnes' subtle evocation of the starkly modern compositions of the Mexican architect Luis Barragán.

Barnes' reputation as a designer of art museums has grown since the completion of the highly acclaimed Walker Art Center in 1971. While Barnes has completed numerous museums in the intervening years, he has never surpassed the Walker Art Center, which 20 years later is still one of the most appealing environments for contemporary art in the United States. The Walker has recently been enhanced by Barnes' design for a remarkable urban sculpture garden (1988). Barnes' approach to the museum as building type is characteristically understated in the minimal detailing within the galleries, and is complemented by his attention to open visual flow aided by continuous materials and wall surfaces (''flow is as important as form''), well-proportioned gallery spaces, and daylighting deployed through perimeter light coves and light wells. Barnes' affinity for white interiors creates what he terms a ''light sandwich'' of the gallery spaces in which objects are bathed in soft reflected light. His willingness to subordinate the interiors of his museums as a simple background to art installations is frequently paired with a more monumental exterior treatment to achieve a civic presence. The dignified and somber exterior of the Dallas Museum of Art (1984) exemplifies this, yet the visual continuity within the museum created through glazed openings to the outdoor sculpture garden makes the museum less insular than it might appear from the outside.

Throughout his career, Barnes has sought to create new compositions by selecting and assimilating the best design features of early masters and other historical sources. However, he has never abandoned modernist design principles, and during the 1980s, he was one of the few prominent architects who resisted adopting the more literal historicism of the postmodernists. Yet recently even Barnes' office has made forays into a more overtly historicist approach in buildings such as the Allen Library at the University of Washington in Seattle (1991), which features neo-Gothic gables and finials, and the neoclassical Beaux-Arts-inspired Judicial Office Building in Washington, D.C. (scheduled for completion in 1993). Both of these projects are atypical of the Barnesian aesthetic, and reflect the emerging voices of Barnes' longtime partners, such as John M. Y. Lee, who now shares the firm's name.

Barnes was one of the first of his generation to act as a leading proponent of contextual design. His influence was established not only through the body of his published work, but also through his contact with young emerging architects who worked in his office, then went on to put contextual ideas into practice as they established their own firms. For this reason, Barnes has been described as the dean of the ''Grays,'' an appellation used to distinguish this group of architects who are concerned with architecture as an integral part of society. During the 1960s, Barnes was one of the leading architects to break away from the cubical massing of the International Style with the diagonal forms of his shed-roofed buildings at the Haystack Mountain School of Arts and Crafts (1962).

A unique synthesis has gradually developed in Barnes' work, in which the lyrical romanticism dating back to his woodland houses of the 1950s is tempered by an ascetic modernist vocabulary. While Barnes' residential commissions have more frequently permitted the indulgence of a romantic vision, his urban office towers are exercises in pure form. A progressively complex shaping of the prismatic volumes of his New York City office towers (535 Madison Avenue, IBM 590 Madison Avenue, and 599 Lexington Avenue) is used to create setbacks and to relate them to surrounding buildings. The precise geometry of Barnes' buildings is accentuated by the skin stretched tautly over surface planes to emphasize volume, forming an elegant sheath that is exactingly detailed. When applied to office designs, such as the IBM World Trade Center in Mount Pleasant, New York (1974), an almost crystalline quality is expressed in the precise and smoothly flowing contours of mullion-free butt-jointed glass and polished stone spandrels. Barnes' office towers are the embodiment of the Late Modern development of the thin-skinned tower as a taut technological membrane. Barnes does not always successfully mitigate a sometimes overbearing monumentality created by broad expanses of unrelieved planar surfaces, yet the power of his boldly sculpted forms has lent continuing vigor to Late Modern expression. In a period characterized by architectural complexity and postmodern eclecticism, Barnes' clean, elemental buildings are his quiet affirmation of restraint, clarity and continuity.

—BARBARA KOERBLE

BARRÁGAN, Luis.

Mexican. Born in Guadalajara, Jalisco, Mexico, in 1902. Died in Mexico, 22 November 1988. Engineering diploma, Guadalajara, 1925; self-taught as an architect; traveled in Spain and France, 1924-26; attended Le Corbusier's lectures in Paris, 1931-32.

Luis Barrágan: Gilardi House, Mexico City, Mexico, 1976

Practiced in Guadalajara, 1927-36; builder of speculative housing, Mexico City, 1936-40; concentrated on planning studies and real estate, 1940-45; founder-director (with J. A. Bustamante), Jardines del Pedregal de San Angel, Mexico City, 1945-52; partner, with Raul Ferrera, Luis Barrágan y Raul Ferrera Arquitectos, 1976-88. Member, Mexican Academy of Architects; Fellow, American Institute of Architects; Pritzker Prize, 1980.

Chronology of Works
All in Mexico

1928	Enrique Aguilar House, Guadalajara
1928	E. Gonzalez Luna House, Guadalajara
1929	Children's Playground, Parque de la Revolucion, Guadalajara
1936-40	Apartment Building, Plaza Melchor Ocampo, Mexico City
1940	Painters' studios building, Plaza Melchor Ocampo, Mexico City
1945	Three private gardens, Avenida San Jeronimo, San Angel, Mexico City
1945-50	El Pedregal, Mexico City (landscape and residential plan)
1947	Barragán House, Tacubaya, Mexico City
1950	Eduardo Prieto Lopez House, El Pedregal, Mexico City
1950	Jardines del Pedregal, Mexico City
1955	Hotel Pierre Marquez gardens, Acapulco
1955	Chapel of the Sacramentarian Capuchins, Mexico City
1957	Satellite City Towers, Queretaro Highway, Mexico City (with Mathias Goeritz)
1959	Las Arboledas, El Pedregal, Mexico City
1959	Gálvez House, Mexico City
1964	Los Clubes master plan, public landscaping, and building code, Mexico City
1968	Egerstrom House and other buildings, Mexico City
1976	Gilardi House, Tacubaya, Mexico City (with Raul Ferrera and Alberto Chauvet)

Publications

ARTICLES BY BARRÁGAN

"Gardens for Environment—Jardines del Pedregal." *Journal of the American Institute of Architects* (April 1952).
"The Construction and Enjoyment of a Garden Accustoms People to Beauty, to Its Instinctive Use, Even to Its Accomplishment." *Via 1: Ecology in Design* (Philadelphia, 1968).

BOOKS ABOUT BARRÁGAN

AMBASZ, EMILIO: *The Architecture of Luis Barragán* [exhibition catalog]. New York, 1976.
BORN, ESTHER: *The New Architecture in Mexico*. New York, 1937.
DE ANDA, ENRIQUE (ed.): *Luis Barragán, clásico del silencio*. Colombia, 1989.
FUTAGAWA, YUKIO (ed.): *GA 48: House and Atelier for Luis Barragán*. Tokyo, 1979.
HITCHCOCK, HENRY-RUSSELL: *Latin American Architecture since 1945*. New York, 1955.
KIRBY, ROSINA GREENE: *Mexican Landscape Architecture—From the Street and from Within*. Tucson, Arizona, 1972.
MYERS, I. E.: *Mexico's Modern Architecture*. New York, 1952.
SMITH, CLIVE BAMFORD: *Builders in the Sun: Five Mexican Architects*. New York, 1967.

ARTICLES ABOUT BARRÁGAN

AMBASZ, EMILIO: "Imponderable Substance: Luis Barragán's Casa Gilardi in Mexico." *Progressive Architecture* (September 1980).
"Designing for a Dry Climate (Barragán)." *Progressive Architecture* 52 (August 1971).
DOHNERT, HORST: "Arbeiten von Luis Barragán, Mexico." *Baukunst und Werkform* (Darmstadt, West Germany, November 1954).
GARDUNO, M. SCHJETAN: "Luis Barragán and His Works." *Arquitectura Mexico* (September/October 1978).
"The Haunting Art of Luis Barragán." *Progressive Architecture* (June 1980).
"The Influential Lyricist of Mexican Culture." *Landscape Architecture* (January 1982).
"Jardines del Pedregal, Mexico City" and "House by Luis Barragán, Architect." *Arts and Architecture* (August 1951).
"Luis Barragán." *Arquitectura Mexico* (January/February 1977).
"Luis Barragán—Alchemist of Architecture." *Arkkitehti* 4 (1980).
"Master Designer, Luis Barragán." *Interiors* (December 1963).
"Mexican Villas: Luis Barragán, Architect." *Architectural Record* (September 1931).
"I muri di Luis Barragán." *Domus* (November 1968).
"Modern Mexican Architecture." *Process: Architecture* (July 1983).
"Recent Work of a Mexican Architect—Luis Barragán." *Architectural Record* (January 1935).

SAINT ALBANS, MARY: "The Gardens of Pedregal." *Modern Mexico* (April 1946).

SALVAT, JORGE: "Luis Barragán" [interview]. *Archetype* (Autumn 1980).

"The Shaping of Space with Simple Means." *Deutsche Bauzeitung* (November 1983).

"The Works and Background of Luis Barragán." *Architecture and Urbanism* (August 1980).

*

The implied homogeneity of "International Style" modern architecture was in a process of disintegration even as it was first defined by Henry-Russell Hitchcock and Philip Johnson in 1932: Functionalism, a key component of this mode, should logically consider local climate, culture, and available materials and techniques, and thus introduce elements of site-specificity. Modern functionalism's chief polemicist, Le Corbusier, had gone so far as to suggest a dialectical position, in which spiritual and intellectual needs are answered along with material ones. The mature work of Luis Barragán should be understood as an outgrowth of this position, wherein the character of a people and a place, in tradition and transition, could inform a tangible, utilizable modern form.

In a 1951 California address, Barragán voiced his ideas regarding architecture's role in the modern world: A properly conceived garden, he said, "leads a man to the common use of beauty ... and causes (him) to fall in an atmosphere of spontaneous meditation ... helps ... in the development of personality and in avoiding standardization of the mind." These themes were echoed in his 1980 Pritzker Prize acceptance speech, in which he defined religion and myth, mystery, silence, serenity and nostalgia as among the elements considered in his work. Terms like these are inevitably brought into any discussion of Barragán. They are fine and evocative, but their overuse has tended to de-emphasize not only the physical and economic forces which any built architecture—including Barragán's—must address, but also the pragmatic, modern sensibility that afforded his work such resonance.

The common conception of Barragán as mystic naif should be approached cautiously. He is frequently described, for example, as a "self-trained architect"; in fact, he completed his course of studies in engineering and architecture at Guadalajara, and only the inopportune closing of the school while he was away on a self-guided European "study tour" kept him from obtaining his degree. Any monastic character about his life—privacy being among the greatest luxuries in a city of 18 million—was financed through shrewd real estate speculation. Stated another way, Barragán knew as well as any architect that an environment need be no less tranquil for modern convenience.

In a decidedly Moorish vein, with details culled from the Alhambra in Granada, Spain, and illustrations found in the books of French writer/gardener Ferdinand Bac, Barragán built his first Guadalajaran houses and gardens. The best of these, and the one most indicative of his later direction, was the house for Enfrain González Luna. Narrow circulation channels there lead into open living areas, while movement between zones is accompanied by transitions from subdued to intensified—though still indirect—natural lighting. The effect is comparable to that often found in Moorish and Hispanic religious buildings. Barragán was intrigued by the frequent intersections of spirituality and eroticism, and referred to this system as a sort of "architectural strip-tease"; with his characteristic tendency to rework an idea over long periods of time, he used it again 50 years later in the Gilardi House. At the Gilardi, entry immediately offers one the choice of vertical or lateral movement—up a skylit stairwell, or down a tunnel-like hall lit by opaque yellow slit windows. The humidity grows palpable as one moves down this hall. At its terminus is a discreetly lit indoor pool/dining room area, with walls painted sky blue and cherry red. For all the silent austerity of the composition, its effect is somehow explosive, like silent film footage of a crashing sea.

Until his receipt of the Pritzker Prize in 1980, Barragán was generally better known for landscapes than buildings. (See, for example, Emilio Ambasz's 1976 book.) For Barragán himself there was little fundamental difference between buildings and gardens: "Landscape architecture is architecture without ceilings," he once said. Nonetheless, his mature regionalistic style coalesced in landscape design. After moving to Mexico City late in 1935 to take part in the construction boom then going on there, Barragán spent four years building speculative housing, much of it financed from his own pocket and all done in a strict International Style format. Between 1940 and 1944 he withdrew from speculation to create for himself a group of private, meditational gardens. With a delicacy oddly complementary to the rugged landscapes that were his raw material, he inlaid paths, gates, terraces, ponds and benches. These gardens were remarkable for the way in which Barragán, fresh from the front lines of the International Style, explored in them the specificity of a natural place and the use of a modern man could make of it.

From these gardens grew Barragán's most famous design: the subdivision El Pedregal. The purchase of a building lot in El Pedregal carried with it strictly stated regulations regarding the preservation of local lava formations and indigenous plants, and urging the employment of contemporary, non-colonial architectural styles. To demonstrate the possibilities of the place, Barragán collaborated with German emigré architect Max Cetto on two houses and gardens. (Mathias Goeritz, another European emigré with whom Barragán collaborated throughout the 1950s, was brought in to carry out certain sculptural elements; Goeritz's expressive minimalism was in profound sympathy with Barragán's own, and their exchange of ideas can readily be seen in the many similarities between Goeritz's El Eco Theatre and Barragán's roughly concurrent chapel at Tlalpan.) El Pedregal was a huge success; lots sold briskly and land values skyrocketed. Barragán grew rich and watched as new owners cleared their lots of the jagged rock to plant formal gardens before mock haciendas and châteaux. His regulations, however, seem to have been more on the order of salesmanship than naivete; he must have known from the beginning that he could exercise no real control over the property once sold, but that such regulations would serve to advertise the development, to heighten its aura of exclusivity and modern good taste. In all fairness, it should be pointed out that in a later residential development, Los Clubes, Barragán did take steps to maintain his building code; there the project was limited to about 30 households, with a strong neighborhood association organized to enforce standards.

By 1960 El Pedregal had been drastically altered, but like other ravaged arcadias it remains pristine in the abstract, fragmentary world of photography. Barragán met photographer Armando Salas Portugal in 1944 and hired him to take promotional shots of El Pedregal. Salas Portugal worked for the architect up into the 1970s, and it is chiefly through his images that Barragán's efforts are known; in few other instances, in fact, has general knowledge of a major architect's work been so dependent upon the view from a single lens. Photography allowed Barragán's often-frangible structures to be captured before time, climate, neglect and misuse began taking their toll. This fragility, both real and metaphorical, is related to what Barragán defined as the surrealist element in his work. The architect collected books of surrealist art, and a moody, theatrical stillness, like that of Giorgio De Chirico, Salvador Dali or Balthus, pervades places like the plazas of Las Arboledas—a mood only heightened by decay.

In his work after 1940, Barragán demonstrated a synthesis of the varied influences of which he had previously availed himself: Mexican vernacular, International Style and Mediterranean images were sublimated and given dream-like juxtaposition. In the 1968 Egerstrom House, for example, there appears a particular Corbusian motif: the sort of punctured wall with which Barragán had opened the roof terraces of many of his 1930s International Style buildings (e.g., the Painter's Studios at Plaza Melchor Ocampo). At the Egerstrom House, however, this wall has a rough adobe-like texture and an enormously exaggerated scale, is painted a glaring pink and reflected in the mirror stillness of a horse pool. We are given the architect's memory of the motif, rather than the motif itself, and in memory it has merged seamlessly with another wall, glimpsed in a distant childhood, of a brightly painted village hut.

By 1893 the French critic G.-Albert Aurier could already say, "It is mysticism alone that can save our society from brutalization, sensualism and utilitarianism." Barragán would have agreed with Aurier; but if Barragán was a mystic, he was also keenly aware of the realities of his age. The impact of his architecture arises from its assertion of an individual identity in the face of globally homogenizing forces of commerce and technology. That assertion—and awareness of the need to make it—lies at the heart of his modernity, and serves as the source of his influence upon that architecture which since World War II has attempted to locate itself within the modern world.

—KEITH EGGENER

BARRY, Charles.

British. Born in London, England, 23 May 1795. Died in London, 12 May 1860. Sons included the architects Charles Barry, Jr. (1824-1900), and Edward Middleton Barry (1830-80). Articled to the Middleton and Bailey firm of surveyors, 1810-16; traveled to France, Italy, Greece and the Near East, 1816-19; opened office in London, 1819. Member, Royal Academy; Fellow, Royal Society; Gold Medal, Royal Institute of British Architects, 1850; knighted, 1852.

Chronology of Works
All in England unless noted
† *Work no longer exists*

1822-25	St. Matthew's Church, Campfield, Manchester†
1822-26	All Saints' Church, Stand, Lancashire
1824-28	St. Peter's Church, Brighton
1824-35	Royal Institution of Fine Arts, Manchester (now the City Art Gallery)
1825-27	Buile Hill, Pendleton, Lancashire
1827-28	Brunswick Chapel, Hove, Sussex
1829-30	Thomas Attree Villa, Brighton
1829-32	Travellers' Club, Pall Mall, London
1833-37	Royal College of Surgeons, London (alterations)
1833-37	King Edward VI School, Birmingham (decorative detailing by A. W. N. Pugin)†
1834-49	Trentham Hall, Staffordshire (additions and gardens)†
1834-57	Bowood House, Wiltshire (alterations, additions and gardens)
1835-39	Kingston Lacy, Dorset (alterations)
1835-60	Houses of Parliament, London (completed by his son Edward Middleton Barry in 1870; decorative detailing by A. W. N. Pugin)
1836-39	Athenaeum, Manchester
1837	Walton House, Walton-on-Thames, Surrey (additions)†
1837-39	Unitarian Chapel, Upper Brook Street, Manchester
1837-41	Reform Club, Pall Mall, London
1838-43	Lancaster House, London (alterations)
1839	Trafalgar Square, London
1841	Pentonville Prison, London (facade)
1842	Highclere Castle, Hampshire (alterations)
1842-48	British Embassy, Istanbul, Turkey
1843-45	Holy Trinity Church, Hurstpierpoint, Sussex
1843-50	Harewood House, Yorkshire (alterations and gardens)
1844-46	Board of Trade, London (enlargement and remodeling)
1844-50	Dunrobin Castle, Sutherland (reconstruction with W. Leslie)
1845-47	12, 18-19, and 20, Kensington Palace Gardens, London
1847-57	Bridgewater House, St. James's, London
1854-55	Canford Manor, Dorset (additions)
1848-54	Shrubland Park, Suffolk (alterations, additions and gardens)
1850-51	Cliveden, Buckinghamshire (reconstruction)
1850*	Kiddington Hall, Oxfordshire (remodeling)
1855	Schools, Dowlais, Glamorgan, Wales
1859-62	Town Hall, Halifax, Yorkshire (interior by Edward Middleton Barry)

Publications

BOOKS ABOUT BARRY

BARRY, ALFRED: *Memoir of the Life and Works of the Late Sir Charles Barry.* 2nd ed. London, 1867.
BOASE, T. S. R.: *English Art 1800-1870.* Oxford, 1959.
DIXON, ROGER, and MUTHESIUS, STEFAN: *Victorian Architecture.* New York and Toronto, 1978.
FERRIDAY, PETER (ed.): *Victorian Architecture.* London, 1963.
HITCHCOCK, HENRY-RUSSELL: *Early Victorian Architecture in Britain.* 2 vols. New York, 1954.
LEEDS, WILLIAM HENRY: *The Travellers' Club House.* London, 1839.
PORT, M. H. (ed.): *The Houses of Parliament.* New Haven, Connecticut, and London, 1976.
PORT, M. H.: "The New Houses of Parliament." In H. M. COLVIN (ed.): *The History of the King's Works.* Vol. 6. London, 1973.
SERVICE, ALASTAIR: *The Architects of London.* London, 1979.
WHIFFEN, MARCUS: *The Architecture of Sir Charles Barry in Manchester and Neighbourhood.* Manchester, 1950.

ARTICLES ABOUT BARRY

BINNEY, MARCUS: "The Travels of Sir Charles Barry." *Country Life* 146 (28 August, 4-11 September 1969): 494-498, 550-552, 622-624.
DENT, A. R.: "Barry and the Greek Revival." *Architecture* 5th Series, 3 (1924-25): 225.
GIROUARD, MARK: "Charles Barry: A Centenary Assessment." *Country Life* (13 October 1960).
WYATT, MATTHEW DIGBY: 'On the Architectural Career of Sir Charles Barry." *Royal Institute of British Architects Transactions* (1859-60): 118-137.

Charles Barry: Houses of Parliament, London, England, 1835-60

Charles Barry succeeded John Soane in the leadership of the late Georgian architectural profession in England. Articled to a practice occupied chiefly in surveying, Barry acquired a thorough grounding in the business side of architecture, but had to teach himself the artistic. He invested his paternal inheritance in a three-year grand tour of France, Italy, Greece, Turkey and Egypt, in the course of which he made valuable contacts among the English aristocracy.

Barry's position, however, was based upon his success in public competitions, a dominant feature of the new market economy in architecture. His first victories were in contractual competitions for Gothic churches, then proliferating by the bounty of the government's million-pound grant, but ironically a type of which he had made little study. Later, he developed an office in which design problems were discussed between the architect and his team of assistants, and effective contributions were made by experts in engineering, draftsmanship and constructional practice. Barry retained overall control, and the completed buildings were fully his in a way that is not always true of the products of such a major contemporary office as George Gilbert Scott's. Barry's early experience of competition showed him the need to invest time, effort and also money in order to attain success. He drew on his Italian experience for the Travellers' Club (1829); but in 1835 he visited Belgium specifically to study Gothic town halls in preparation for the Houses of Parliament competition, in which he also employed a specialist (A.W.N. Pugin) to draw the designs.

He also favored another aspect of the contemporary market economy: the development of contracting in gross. This form of lump-sum contract, covering all building trades and agreed on the basis of competitive tenders, had developed during Barry's early years, and he employed it at the Travellers' Club,

Birmingham Grammar School, the Reform Club, and the first two contracts for portions of the Houses of Parliament.

His travels and public successes brought Barry into contact with rich aristocrats, who commissioned him to work on their country houses. Unlike many of the rivals of his later days, Barry sustained the many-sided practice characteristic of the late Georgian age. Again, typically late-Georgian, he was ready to work in the style that his client demanded. Although he clearly had his preferences, and—along with Soane—was responsible for introducing the astylar Italian into London architecture in his Travellers' Club, he was a more-than-competent Gothic designer, as proved by his Birmingham Grammar School (1833), designed prior to his employment of Pugin. Some ascribe his success in the competition of 1835 to Pugin for the most important English building of the century, the Gothic Houses of Parliament. Pugin's brilliant draftsmanship was clearly a factor; but essentially it was the quality of planning and composition that assured Barry's victory, skills that he had already mastered in the Travellers' Club and Birmingham Grammar School.

Whether in Gothic or classical styles, Barry achieved a mastery of the picturesque that made clients seek his services in laying out significant space, in town as well as in country. Thus in 1839 he was entrusted by the government with laying out the key area in front of the National Gallery, London (Trafalgar Square), where by clever manipulation of levels he was able to mitigate the defect of the gallery's lack of height. Similarly, at Shrubland Park, Suffolk (1848), he used the fall of the ground effectively in a series of Italianate terraces and flights of stairs. Massive terraces at Harewood (where he transformed a mansion by John Carr and Robert Adam into an Italianate palazzo) at once elevated the house and created a platform for viewing a celebrated picturesque landscape (1843). The use of asymmetrical towers, preferably seen for their full height, was a notable, much-copied element of his design vocabulary, from Walton-on-Thames (1837) to Halifax Town Hall (1859), but first and most familiar in the Houses of Parliament, where the low-lying situation of the building made towers essential to render the building significant. He disliked elevating the center and sought a massive rectangular silhouette: that bounding by immediately visible continuous lines that John Ruskin distinguished as the essential means of achieving nobility and sublimity.

Inevitably in an old-established society like the England of the 1830s, much of an architect's work was the revamping of existing buildings. Most of Barry's country-house practice was of this nature. Although the client had by then superseded the patron, Barry was fortunate in establishing a relationship with the outstandingly rich ducal family of Sutherland. For them, he remodeled and landscaped Trentham, Staffordshire, in the severe Italianate of his clubs (from 1834); completed their London seat, Stafford (formerly York, and now Lancaster) House; designed extensions at Dunrobin, Sutherlandshire, in a chateau style; reconstructed Cliveden, Buckinghamshire, after a fire, and built Bridgewater House, London (these two in his later, much-enriched Italian). For Lord Carnarvon he transformed Highclere, Hampshire, a sober Georgian mansion, into a highly ornamented, towered and turreted quasi-Elizabethan prodigy house, creating an influential pattern for country houses of the mid-century decades (*e.g.*, Somerleyton, Mentmore and Bylaugh).

Much of Barry's public work was also alteration. In 1844 he was commissioned to rebuild the offices of the Board of Trade and the Privy Council (Soane, 1823-27). Raising the structure a story and breaking the entablature above Soane's re-used columns, he created the greater massiveness and richness looked for in the 1840s. Born and bred in London, opposite the old Palace of Westminster, he was always much exercised by the problems of metropolitan improvement, devising many projects that remained unrealized, though nonetheless influential.

The need for a larger Board of Trade flowed from the onset of industrialization. This created opportunities in the way of public buildings for new industrial cities and accommodation offering all the facilities of an aristocratic town house for the new clubs of men of similar interests. After experimenting in Grecian (Manchester Royal Fine Arts Institution, 1824), Barry devised a model that met these several needs admirably: the refined astylar Italian palazzo, characterized by an unusually large proportion of wall to void and a dominating cornice; the plan focused on a *cortile* rather than a staircase. His Travellers' Clubhouse (1829) introduced the style in London; the Manchester Athenaeum (1836), larger and more severe— after the Palazzo Farnese—set the pattern in the provinces for the great textile warehouses. The Reform Club (for Liberal politicians), an improved version of the Manchester Athenaeum, its severe rectangularity striving powerfully for sublimity, became the prototype for monumental commercial architecture—the insurance offices and banking houses of the city. As a clubhouse, the Reform set new standards of capacity, comfort and convenience. Barry retained the Roman central courtyard (introduced in the Travellers'), but to meet English conditions, he turned it into a central hall with a glazed roof. The main staircase he tucked ingeniously to one side, using mirrors and marbles to give it the requisite grandeur. So successful was his adaptation of the *cortile* that he subsequently used it in Highclere Castle, Bridgewater House and Halifax Town Hall. It was widely copied: a great central hall giving access to all the other major rooms or offices was obviously convenient in a public building; but in country houses, too, it was welcomed for its splendor

and adaptability, despite its tendency to bring into collision groups of users whom contemporary architects sought to keep apart: family, guests, servants, children. It obviated long dark corridors, reduced the amount of external walling necessary, and facilitated early, gravity-fed forms of central heating, so that it became one of the two dominant country-house plans of the period.

Beyond his outstanding powers of planning and composition, Barry possessed personal qualities that enabled him to flourish as a great public architect. Buoyed by an innate optimism, essential if he were to realize his projects (which he was constantly refining) in the face of the obstacles incessantly raised, he was pliable and accommodating with the commissions and committees that played so powerful a role in matters of public architecture, careful not to say too much (unlike the loquacious George Gilbert Scott). He was, however, governed by a steely inner determination to achieve his purposes, so he was not always too scrupulous about the means employed. Thus, in revising the competition designs of the Houses of Parliament to secure parliamentary approval, he removed much of the ornament that had attracted the judges but frightened thrifty-minded M.P.s, knowing that he could easily replace it once he had secured the commission. Toward the end of his life, he agreed to contracts for work on the parliament buildings against the explicit directions of the minister of public works. His alleged suppression after Pugin's death of letters to the latter is consistent with this character, but to complete that building required an element of ruthlessness in the architect. And in fighting, he fought not only for himself and his works, but for the independence of the architectural profession.

—M. H. PORT

BASEVI, George.

British. Born in London, England, 1 April 1794. Died in Ely, 16 October 1845 (fell to death while inspecting Ely Cathedral). Benjamin Disraeli was a cousin. Studied with Dr. Burney, Greenwich, then with John Soane, 1811; studied abroad in Italy and Greece, 1816-19. Began practice in London, 1820; surveyor to the Guardian Assurance Company, 1821; superintendant on Belgrave Square for W. and G. Haldimand, 1825-40; appointed surveyor for the Trustees of Smith's Charity Estate, 1829. Fellow of the Royal Institute of British Architects, the Royal Society and the Society of Antiquaries; exhibited at the Royal Academy six times between 1820 and 1837.

Chronology of Works
All in England
* Approximate dates
† Work no longer exists

1820*	Gatcombe Park, Gloucestershire (alterations)
1822-25	St. Thomas' Church, Stockport, Cheshire (chancel added in 1890)
1823-24	St. Mary's Church, Greenwich, Kent†
1825-40	Houses, Belgrave Square, London (except for corner mansions)
1826-27	West Side, Garden Quadrangle, Balliol College, Oxford (upper story added in 1926)
1827-30	Alexander Square, London (for the Thurloe Estate)
1827-32	Painswick House, Gloucestershire (alterations and additions)
1832	Dr. Fryer's Almshouses, Stamford, Lincolnshire
1832	Truesdale's Hospital, Stamford, Lincolnshire
1833ff.	Pelham Crescent and Place, Brompton Crescent (now

	Egerton Crescent), Walton Place, London (for the Trustees of Dr. Smith's Charity Estate)
1833-36	Parish Church, Hove, Sussex (reconstruction)
1834	Beechwood, Highgate, London (for his brother Nathaniel Basevi)
1834	Middlesex Hospital, London (expansion)†
1836	St. Mary's Hall School, Hove, Sussex
1836-45	Fitzwilliam Museum, Cambridge (completed by C. R. Cockerell, 1845-48, and E. M. Barry, 1870-75)
1838	Hankey Family Tomb, General Cemetery of All Souls, Kensal Green
1838	Longhills Hall, near Lincoln
1839-40	St. Saviour Church, Walton Place, Chelsea (north aisle added in 1878, and chancel added in 1890)
1840-41	Holy Trinity Church, Twickenham, Middlesex (chancel and transepts added in 1863)
1840-41	National Schools, Twickenham, Middlesex†
1843	Thurloe Square, London (for the Thurloe Estate)
1843-44	St. Jude's Church, Chelsea†
1843-44	Conservative Club, St. James's, London (with Sydney Smirke)
1844-45	Parson's Almshouses, Ely, Cambridgeshire
1845	Prison, Ely, Cambridgeshire (addition)
1845-46	House of Correction, Wisbech, Cambridgeshire†
1845-46	St. Matthew, Eye, Northamptonshire (steeple added in 1857)

Publications

BOOKS ABOUT BASEVI

BOLTON, A. T.: *The Portrait of Sir John Soane*. 1927.
STROUD, DOROTHY: *The Thurloe Estate*. 1959.
STROUD, DOROTHY: *The South Kensington Estate of Henry Smith's Charity*. 1975

ARTICLES ABOUT BASEVI

BASEVI, W. H. F.: "The Grand Tour of an Architect." *The Architect* (7 July-1 September 1922).
HOBHOUSE, HERMIONE: "The Building of Belgravia." *Country Life* 145 (1969): 1154-57, 1312-14.

*

George Basevi was one of several pupils of John Soane (who thought a great deal of his abilities and promise), and he was probably the most successful in later life. From 1816, when he set off for a tour of Italy and Greece, Basevi imbibed knowledge of a huge number and variety of buildings, and returned to London armed with skills that were admirably suited to the increasingly eclectic tastes of the times. From 1820, when he set up his own practice in London, he produced several important designs, notably the splendid houses in Belgrave Square (1825-40), the layout and many terraces on the Thurloe Estate (1827-45), and, from 1833, the elegant Pelham Crescent, Pelham Place, Egerton Crescent and Walton Place for the Trustees of the Smith's Charity Estate, all in London. In these fine designs he demonstrated his ability to enliven the standard terraces of houses and squares of late-Georgian times with elements derived from a variety of classical sources.

He often used doors with iron-studded frames, based on 17th-century illustrations of the great doors of the Pantheon in Rome, and on patterns used by Soane at his own house and at the Bank of England. Basevi's treatment of the unified stucco-fronted facades of terraces and crescents included austere Greco-Roman detailing in which variations on the palm-leaf capital can be found, and indeed his impeccable understanding and application of classicism, while clearly based on antique precedents, is freely, sensitively and inventively apparent in most of his London work, without any suggestion of slavish archaeological or antiquarian bias. Soane's influence is clear in the way in which Basevi handled the problems of proportion and architectural nuance; he paraphrased and omitted where necessary, but always displayed a sure architectonic touch. His guidance of the development of the Smith's Charity Estate in South Kensington was of a very high professional order, for there he was responsible for the production of designs of real distinction. In fact his work there stands out for its quality, originality without outrageousness, and well-mannered, scholarly and inventive élan.

Like many of his contemporaries, Basevi could turn his hand to Gothic churches (most of which were undeniably dull) and Tudor almshouses (of which Dr. Fryer's and Truesdale's Hospital, both in Stamford, Lincolnshire, and both of 1832, are his most pretty and assured designs). Although there is no documentary evidence, the sumptuous Rock Terrace (1841) and Rock House (1842), also in Stamford, may be by Basevi. These most interesting designs, realized for Richard Newcombe, are very unusual and vigorous examples of free classicism, showing all the hallmarks of Basevi's work in South Kensington. There is strong visual evidence that they are probably from drawings by Basevi, for the plans, details and architecture are all assured and of very high quality, indicating that the hand of a master was at work. Certainly these exquisite designs in Stamford are fully comparable with the best of Basevi's London houses, and, in some respects, are even more free, mature and assured in their virtuosity.

While his work on country houses is worthy of little remark, his Fitzwilliam Museum in Cambridge (1836-45), completed by C.R. Cockerell and E.M. Barry, is a major work of the early Victorian period in which his mastery of a free mix of Greco-Roman detailing is displayed. At the Fitzwilliam, Basevi's designs heralded the new taste for opulence as an antidote to the cool, severe Greek Revival that had been de rigueur for many public buildings during the first decades of the 19th century. The imposing pedimented octastyle portico at the Fitzwilliam, extended as colonnades terminating in boldly modeled pavilions, is a theme derived from the Roman Capitolinum at Brescia. The overall effect is luxurious and peculiarly rich, conveying a sense of vigorous sculptured enrichment, which C.R. Cockerell also employed in his designs.

Basevi could handle many building types, and was responsible for the family tomb of J.A. Hankey (1838) in the General Cemetery of All Souls, Kensal Green, which was published in A. W. Hakewill's *Modern Tombs gleaned from the Public Cemeteries of London* (1851).

He was also responsible, in association with Sydney Smirke (1787-1877), for the designs of two London clubhouses: the Conservative (1843-44) in St. James' Street and the Carlton (1854-56) in Pall Mall. The Conservative Club was a grand essay featuring superimposed orders, while the Carlton took the theme further, quoting elements from Jacopo Sansovino's Library of St. Mark in Venice in its sumptuous facades. Basevi's part in the later clubhouse was confined to the earliest proposals, for he fell to his death in 1845 while inspecting the western tower of Ely Cathedral. Had he lived longer, he could well have produced buildings of even greater distinction, and been a formidable adversary of the shriller elements within the Gothic camp.

—JAMES STEVENS CURL

BASILE, Ernesto.

Italian. Born in Palermo, Italy, 31 January 1857. Died in 1932. Apprenticed with his father, the architect Giovanni Battista Filippo Basile (1825-91). Assistant instructor in architecture, Scuola di Applicazione, Rome, 1877; director, Istituto Royale di Belle Arti; professor of architecture, Istituto Royale di Belle Arti; professor of architecture, University of Palermo.

Chronology of Works
All in Italy
† *Work no longer exists*

1891-92	Pavilions, National Exhibition, Palermo†
1893-96	Palazzo Bordonaro, Palermo
1894	Ribaudo Kiosk, Piazza Teatro Massimo, Palermo
1897	Vicari Kiosk, Palermo
1899	Raccuglia Family Funeral Monument, Palermo
1899	Villino Florio all'Olivuzza, Palermo
1899-1900	Grand Hotel Villa Igiea, Palermo
1901	Utveggio House, Palermo
1902	Palazzina Vanoni, Rome
1902-27	Palazzo Montecitorio (now the House of Parliament), Rome (extension)
1903	Villino Basile, Palermo
1903	Villino Fassini, Palermo†
1904	City Hall, Licata
1906	Palazzo Bruno di Belmonte, Spaccaforno
1907	Electric Power Station, Caltagirone
1907-12	Cassa di Risparmio Vittorio Emanuele, Palermo
1912	Assicurazioni Generali Venezia, Palermo
1914	Municipal Palace, Reggio Calabria
1915	Ribaudo's Kiosk, Piazza Castelnuovo, Palermo
1924	Villino Gregorietti, Mondello
1926-27	Casa di Risparmio Vittorio Emanuele, Messina
1928	Santa Rosalia Church, Palermo

Publications

BOOKS BY BASILE

Architettura, dei suoi principi e del suo rinnovamento. 1882. Reprint: Palermo, 1981.

BOOKS ABOUT BASILE

BORSI, FRANCO: *L'architettura dell'Unità d'Italia.* Florence, 1966.
CARONIA ROBERTI, SALVATORE: *Ernesto Basile e cinquant' anni di architettura in Sicilia.* Palermo, 1935.
DAMIGELLA, ANNA MARIA: *Il liberty nella Sicilia orientale.* Palermo, 1976.
MEEKS, CARROLL L. V.: *Italian Architecture: 1750-1914.* New Haven, Connecticut, 1966.
NICOLETTI, MANFREDI: *L'architettura Liberty in Italia.* Rome and Bari, Italy, 1978.
PEVSNER, NIKOLAUS, and RICHARDS, J. M. (eds.): *The Anti-Rationalists.* London, 1973.
PIRRONE, GIANNI: *Palermo Liberty.* Rome, 1971.
PIRRONE, GIANNI: *Studi e schizzi di E. Basile.* Palermo, 1976.
RUSSELL, FRANK (ed.): *Art Nouveau Architecture.* London, 1979.
SESSA, ETTORE: *Mobile e arredi di Ernesto Basile nella produzione Ducrot.* Palermo, 1980.
ZEVI, BRUNO: *Storia dell'architettura moderna.* Turin, 1950.

ARTICLES ABOUT BASILE

NICOLETTI, MANFREDI: "Art Nouveau in Italy." Pp. 32-62 in J. M. RICHARDS and NIKOLAUS PEVSNER (eds.): *The Anti-Rationalists.* London, 1973.
PIACENTINI, MARCELLO: "Ernesto Basile." *Architettura e arti decorative* 11 (1932): 507.
ZINO, VITTORIO: "La cultura architettonica in Sicilia, dall'Unità alla prima guerra mondiale." *Casa* 6 (1959): 96-119.

*

Ernesto Basile was one of the most prolific art nouveau, or Liberty, designers in Italy. His work always oscillated, however, between an interest in international art nouveau currents and a studied eclecticism, including his native Sicilian tradition, depending on the patrons and locations of his commissions.

His early works are best described as electric. Two Roman projects he worked on with his father, Giovanni Battista Filippo Basile, the first competition for the Monument to Victor Emanuel (1881) and the first competition for the new Parliament Building (1889), betray a confident use of the classical vocabulary. After the death of the elder Basile, Ernesto took over his father's position as architect of the classicizing Teatro Massimo (completed in 1897) and his father's chair in architecture at the University of Palermo.

Basile often incorporated references to the multilayered Sicilian artistic heritage in his works. His National Monument to the Battle of Calatafimi (1885), for example, echoes the Doric order of the nearby Temple of Segesta. Basile's first public work of consequence, the National Exposition in Palermo (1891-92), a stunning combination of Gothic, Renaissance and Norman forms, firmly established his reputation. In another work from that period, the Palazzo Bordonaro (1893-96), Basile made references to the Florentine quattrocento, including the tower, which became a leitmotif in many of his projects.

The tower form was, in fact, the basis for the octagonal Ribaudo Kiosk in Palermo (1894), considered by some scholars to be the first work of Liberty architecture in Italy. The later Vicari Kiosk in Palermo (1897) incorporated elements from Islamic architecture. While these two works show Basile forging a personal vision of the art nouveau language, some of his works reflect the European avant-garde. The Raccuglia family funeral monument in Palermo (1899), for example echoes the work of Victor Horta, with its sinuous lines and floral motifs.

Basile's very personal version of international architectural currents is best seen in works like the Grand Hotel Villa Igea in Palermo (1899-1900), commissioned by Ignazio Florio, one of the architect's most important clients. An addition to an existing building, the hotel features some of Basile's most creative designs, including the still largely intact dining room. There, Basile created a dramatically flowing space filled with his dynamic designs for furniture and applied wall and ceiling decoration. In 1898 Basile had begun a fruitful collaboration with the Ducrot firm for the production of furniture and fabric, thus allowing him to mass-produce for a larger audience. His designs were featured at the Ducrot exhibit at the First International Arts Exposition in 1902 in Turin, through which the architect gained important international exposure. In addition, his reputation was considerably bolstered by favorable criticism of his work in the English journal *The Studio* in 1903.

This fusion of interior and exterior design animates the Villino Florio all'Olivuzza in Palermo (1899), a wildly eclectic work featuring elements from classical, art nouveau, Romanesque and Islamic architecture. The architect's own house, the Villino Basile in Palermo (1903), is one of the simplest of his Liberty designs, including the by-then-ubiquitous tower, along with smooth white surfaces brought to life by very few decorative details, and a lively play of rusticated stone at the base. Two other projects can be mentioned in this context. The City Hall of Licata (1904), an intensely personal interpretation of art nouveau currents, includes a Norman-Sicilian clock tower housing a startlingly original iron bell frame. A similarly striking corner tower is the focal point of the Palazzo Bruno di Belmonte in Spaccaforno (1906), an eclectic incorporating another of Basile's favorite motifs, a rusticated base and crowning window treatment.

Basile is best known, however, not for these exuberantly eclectic small-scale projects, but for his most public work, the Parliment Building in Rome (1902-27), an addition to Giovanni Lorenzo Bernini's Palazzo Montecitorio. In 1883 and 1889, Basile had entered the competitions for this building with his father. After determining the project too costly, the government decided on an addition to the existing building, and hand-picked Basile for the commission. The resulting building, while perhaps not Basile's most representative work, was surely his most important in terms of patron and political significance. It both deferred to Bernini's Palazzo Montecitorio and succeeded in combining Liberty detailing with classical forms in a design of considerable daring. The architect, in effect, was able to place comfortably an eclectic, yet simple, building in the heart of the Italian capital. In doing so, he created a new type of government building, antirhetorical and discreet, in a city populated by the heavy, classicizing structures created to house the various government offices of the recently unified Italian state.

The critic R. Savarese perhaps best defined Basile's work, when he spoke in 1902 of the "clearly Latin, traditional and personal" language that was opposed to "Northern utilitarianism." From the bold eclecticism of his Sicilian and Roman houses to the personal "Floreale" designs of his furniture and interiors, Basile created a unique architectural language that was at once Sicilian, Italian and European.

—ELLEN R. SHAPIRO

BAZHENOV, Vasili Ivanovich.

Russian. Born in Malojaroslavian area of Kaluga, Russia, 1 March 1737. Died in St. Petersburg, Russia, 2 August 1799. Studied at the architectural school of Prince Dmitri Uchtomski, from 1751, then at Moscow University; began studying at the Art Academy in St. Petersburg, 1758; apprenticed to Bartolomeo Rastrelli, 1760; sent to study with Charles de Wailly in Paris, 1761; subsequent travel to Italy; returned to St. Petersburg in 1765, where he was named captain of artillery for the court. Elected to the Academy, 1784; eventually named vice-president of the Academy by Czar Paul.

Chronology of Works
All in Russia
† Work no longer exists

1767ff.	Kremlin, Moscow (head of reconstruction project)
1775	Khodynskoye Field, near Moscow (remodeling)†
1784-86	Pashkov House, Moscow
1796ff.	St. Michael's (Engineers') Castle, St. Petersburg
n.d.	Palace and Buildings at Tsaritsyno, near Moscow
n.d.	Dolgov House, Moscow (since altered)
n.d.	Yushkov House, Moscow
n.d.	Skorbyashchenskaya Church, Moscow (bell tower)

Vasili I. Bazhenov may be claimed as the most inventive and visionary architect that Russia produced in the "Petersburg age," perhaps in any age—a man of wide-ranging intellect, sense of mission, varied artistic abilities and painstaking technical skills. His contribution to early neoclassicism has universal importance. Yet he is inadequately known and appreciated, even in Russia, primarily because ill fortune dogged his career and prevented the realization of his greatest commissions; like his contemporaries, Etienne-Louis Boullée and Claude-Nicolas Ledoux, a major part of Bazhenov's legacy is in his plans and ideas. Scarcely more than a half dozen of his building projects survive, and doubt surrounds several of these.

Born to an impoverished family near Moscow, he was brought up in the city (his father worked in a Kremlin office), sensed his vocation early, and managed to study under two major Late Baroque architects and teachers: D. Ukhtomsky in Moscow, then S. Chevakinsky in Petersburg. He was sent by the Academy of Arts to study in Paris and Italy, where he had the unusual honor of election to the academies of Rome, Florence and Bologna. On his return to St. Petersburg he failed (through intrigue?) to be chosen for a professorship at the academy, of which at the end of his life he became vice president. His first independent works of that period (e.g., the Kamennovstrovsky Palace) have not survived in their original form.

In 1767 he was put in charge of the reconstruction of the Moscow Kremlin, whose dilapidated condition had disturbed Catherine II at her recent coronation there. He headed a large team, with the other great Moscow architect of early neoclassicism, M. Kazakov, as second in command (the latter's noble Senate building, 1776, is now the only visible result of the whole endeavor). Bazhenov's scheme, several times reworked and eventually embodied in a magnificent scale model, was of breathtaking grandeur. A vast palace, with a main frontage more than 600 yards long above the Moskva River, would be integrated with the Kremlin's chief ancient structures. The great Ionic colonnade binding the two upper stories of the facade over a severe rustication would have had a sober magnificence comparable only with Diocletian's Palace at Split. Elsewhere, Bazhenov's lifelong predilection for the juxtaposition and intersection of circular, oval, polygonal and rectilinear forms is apparent. Though much painstaking preliminary work was done, the scheme was abandoned (to Bazhenov's mortification) at the end of the Russo-Turkish War (1774), for unclear reasons, although cost must have been prominent.

Bazhenov's talents, however, were almost immediately redirected to two further large-scale projects. The first involved the remodeling of the Khodynskoye Field outside Moscow for the victory celebrations in summer 1775. Surviving drawings (by Kazakov) and a letter from Catherine to Baron von Grimm show that this was no less than a grandiose "symbolic landscape," with the Black Sea represented by a lake carrying ships, and towns and fortresses represented by various fanciful buildings.

Though the architecture on Khodynskoye Field was temporary and the whole landscape ephemeral, it was stylistically important for the commission on which Bazhenov embarked immediately afterward: the planning of a palace and many subsidiary buildings for the empress at Tsaritsyno, south of Moscow. The style was Gothic—a very early instance of such a revival anywhere in Europe, surprising in Russia (with no indigenous Gothic tradition), and probably unique for its scale at that date; the whole was picturesquely disposed in an undulating wooded park with lakes. After 10 years that project, too, was abandoned: Bazhenov's almost-complete palace was razed, and Kazakov was commissioned to rebuild it in his own drier and less convincing brand of Gothic (this also remains a shell); in the other buildings, however, more of Bazhenov's original, ceaselessly inventive and picturesque work survives than is the case anywhere else. Similarities of style can be found in certain churches and park buildings, also with individualistic late-18th-century mock Gothic—fused with old Russian—features, in the vicinity of Moscow, and have set unresolved problems for scholars. Among these works the gates at Mikhalkovo are almost certainly Bazhenov's work.

As a leading Freemason, Bazhenov came into sharp court disfavor in the mid-1780s. He turned to private commissions in Moscow: there survive the Dolgov House (with alterations), the prominent Yushkov House with a splendid rounded, colonnaded corner between two severe street facades meeting at a 90-degree angle, the beautiful round bell tower of the Skorbyashchenskaya Church, and above all, the Pashkov House (1784-86), dramatically placed on a slope facing the southwest angle of the Kremlin. Records of its construction were destroyed in the fire of 1812, so Bazhenov's authorship has to be inferred on stylistic grounds (there are echoes of the Kremlin project). It was listed as his work in the 1830s, and the attribution is not nowadays seriously doubted. As well as the lofty, domed central block, there are elegant pavilions, gateways and other structures.

Catherine's son and heir, Paul, generally favored those his mother disfavored (and was close to the Freemasons); Bazhenov's last major project was Paul's Petersburg residence, the St. Michael's (later known as Engineers') Castle, begun in late 1796. It is an uningratiating yet fascinating building, a reinterpretation in neoclassical terms of the moated defensive castle desired by the fearful and suspicious Paul. A fundamentally square ground plan contains an octagonal courtyard; the projecting chapel is crowned with one of Petersburg's three great golden flèches. Bazhenov, already ill when the castle was begun, did not live to witness its completion; decorative additions by his assistant, V. Brenna, now somewhat detrimentally mask the severity of its forms. Paul was murdered in the building by his courtiers in 1801, before the walls had fully dried. Its sumptuous detached pavilions are Bazhenov's final masterpiece.

Bazhenov's genius is not easy to summarize; each of his known projects tackled a new problem in a new way. Though in one sense a luminary of international neoclassicism, he stood apart from its relaxed and genial development in the hands of Kazakov and subsequent Russian architects of the period; he was at heart a Mannerist (his hero was Michelangelo). He also strongly felt his Russianness: in a highly interesting memorandum dating from the inauguration of the Kremlin project the young Bazhenov listed his predilections in architecture, with strong emphasis on the ''Moscow Baroque'' period (ca. 1680-1700). The polychrome laciness of his ''Gothic'' detailing is fundamentally Old Russian in inspiration, his work as a whole a strange link between the Muscovite, the Baroque and the modern ages.

—R. R. MILNER-GULLAND

BEHNISCH, Günther.

German. Born in Lockwitz bei Dresden, 12 June 1922. Studied engineering at the Technische Hochschule, Stuttgart, 1947-51, Dip.Ing. In practice with Bruno Lambart, Stuttgart, 1952-56; in private practice, Stuttgart, 1956-66; formed Behnisch and Partner, Stuttgart, 1966. Professor, Technische Hochschule, Darmstadt, from 1975.

Chronology of Works
All in Germany

1963	Fachhochschule (State Technical College), Ulm
1967-72	Olympic Buildings, Munich (with Frei Otto)
1969	In den Berglen School, Oppelsbohm
1973	Auf dem Schafersfeld Grammar School, Lorch (stage I)
1979-82	Auf dem Schafersfeld Grammar School, Lorch (stage II)
1980-82	Professional School, Herrenberg
1987	University Library, Eichstaett

Publications

BOOKS BY BEHNISCH

Buildings of 19th-Century Paris. Darmstadt, 1974.
Buildings of 19th-Century England. Darmstadt, 1976.
Backsteinbauten. Darmstadt, 1977.

BOOKS ABOUT BEHNISCH

Behnisch and Partner: Buildings and Projects. Stuttgart, 1975.
JOEDICKE, JURGEN (ed.): *Architektur in Deutschland '83.* Stuttgart, 1984.

*

Günther Behnisch is of the German tradition of Hugo Häring (1882-1958) and Hans Scharoun (1893-1972). His work, which until recently was miscategorized as deconstructivism, can be explained clearly in relation to the German organic tradition. Behnisch himself acknowledges that he shares with both Häring and Scharoun the belief that any architectural expression should be given the opportunity to arise out of the nature of the task. In his view, architecture should not be directed by any preconception. Every task should have its own architecture, and each building must necessarily be seen as a political act. The architecture of Günther Behnisch and his office does not deny the possibility of functional expression, nor does it exhibit the abstract formalism or personal subjectivity that can be found in many contemporary projects.

Behnisch's architecture documents the essential characteristics of the German organic tradition: aggregative planning, geometrical irregularity and aperspective space. The building does not conceptually follow one order system, such as a monotonous grid system that rules and organizes the building as a whole. Behnisch buildings, similar to those of Alvar Aalto, who used the same conceptual strategies, are composed of a series of independent elements which maintain their own identity and establish a sense of place. These disparate parts often have their own structure, but still contribute to the overall concept. This strategy is recognizable particularly in Hans Scharoun's projects. His Geschwister Scholl School in Lünen (1956-62) and the proposal for a housing project for the elderly (1952) in Berlin-Tiergarten show independent elements linked by an irregular internal circulation system. These projects reflect the human needs of their occupants, and the spatial organizations reflect social organization. They document clearly that Scharoun was more concerned with the social impact of a project than with its technical or artistic merit. This concern is shown by Behnisch, who believes that each building part should be independent, symbolizing the individual in a democratic society.

This point of view does not inform Behnisch's early work. Projects during the 1950s and 1960s like the Fachhochschule at Ulm (1963) and the Fachhochschule at Aalen (1968) were the result of rather monotonous building systems, which were limited in their development and expression. But that period was a time when Behnisch developed his technical skills, and those projects allowed him to express such skills with confidence. From 1967 to 1972 this experience allowed him, in collaboration with Frei Otto, to execute the Munich Olympic buildings with cable roofs of unprecedented size. The integration of landscape and buildings at Munich might be read as the transition toward an architecture that documents the freedom of its elements. At the schools "In den Berglen" near Oppelsbohm (1969) and the Progymnasium at Lorch (1973), both of which are based on a polygonal system, Behnisch employed the experience of the earlier grid systems but also started to break up the regular arrangement; this was especially true of Lorch.

From that point, the planning of Behnisch and Partners became freer. This freedom was and is exposed through geometrical irregularity, necessary to express the individual elements of a project. This notion overcomes any determining grid system or any other system that is rooted in history. Here Behnisch clearly acknowledges Häring's concept of the "Neues Bauen," which attempted to overcome any preconceived geometries and moved toward an organic expression. For Häring, basic abstract forms were not original natural shapes, they were abstract and derived from Häring's understanding of intellectual laws that were translated into form and shape. However, this concept did not mean that Häring totally abandoned geometry in his planning process.

The other important similarity in the conceptual approach of Häring, Scharoun and Behnisch is the notion of aperspective space. Aperspective space rejects the static nature of the general perspective, in which traditional understanding is a preferred position for the viewer. By eliminating the preferred position, the aperspective space becomes four-dimensional. The constantly changing position of the viewer breaks the recognizable picture into smaller fragments and adds time as the fourth dimension to the spatial experience.

Behnisch used this concept at the University Library at Eichstätt (1987). This highly complex building contains faculty offices, teaching spaces and the library itself. Behnisch designed three-story wings to the north and the east that contain the administrative offices, a large radial element to the south containing the library, and one-story wings to the west, which contain reading rooms and additional offices. The building is not monolithic, nor is it formally harmonized. The free arrangement of the building parts creates interior connection spaces that are similar to the spaces in Scharoun's school. The space between the north wing and the library, for instance, contains the main staircase, which dominates its environment with dynamic impact. This is one of the most noticeable strategies of the German organic tradition.

In addition to Scharoun's Häring's influence on Behnisch's planning and spatial development, it must be mentioned that their work in the area of construction and technology was clearly different. Behnisch's concern with the relationship between the structure and the skin shows the influence of Johannes Duiker, while his work with layering facades and the expression of lightness are clearly influenced by Egon Eiermann and Ludwig Mies van der Rohe. Behnisch's high degree of control—his office is closely involved with every stage of the building—creates a more flexible and extended design process. This approach to planning, which includes a long development process characterized by the transformation and manipulation of the initial proposal, allows Behnisch to develop and execute projects that involve more complex order systems. These systems also include the notion of constant transformation, which addresses the question of the building's life span. What is otherwise a weakness becomes a strength in an architecture that has no end and does not establish itself as a fashionable object. It is this kind of architecture that reflects the social commitment in the work of Behnisch and Partners.

—UWE DROST

BEHRENS, Peter.

German. Born in Hamburg, Germany, 14 April 1868. Died in Berlin, 27 February 1940. Married Lili Kramer. Studied at Karlsruhe and Düsseldorf Art Schools. Founder member, Munich Sezession, 1893; co-formed Art Colony, Darmstadt, 1899; head of Düsseldorf Art School, 1903; designer to electrical combine AEG, Berlin, 1907; established own firm, Berlin, 1907; director, Academy of Art, Düsseldorf, 1921-22; director of architecture, Vienna Academy, Vienna, Austria, 1922; director, Department of Architecture, Prussian Academy, Berlin, 1936-40.

Chronology of Works
All in Germany unless noted

1900-01	Behrens House, Künstler-Kolonie, Darmstadt
1905-06	Obernauer House at Sankt Johann, near Saarbrücken
1906-07	Crematorium, Delstern, near Hagen, Westphalia
1908-09	Schröder House, Hagen-Eppenhausen, Westphalia
1909-10	AEG Turbine Factory, Huttenstrasse, Berlin (with Karl Bernhard)
1909-12	AEG Works, Berlin Light Engine Factory, Berlin High Tension Factory, Berlin Small Motor Factory, Berlin Large Machinery Assembly Hall, Berlin Humboldthain Complex, Berlin Workers' Housing, Berlin
1910	Cuno House, Hagen-Eppenhausen, Westphalia
1910-12	Goedecke House, Hagen-Eppenhausen, Westphalia
1911-12	AEG New Factory for Electric Railway Equipment, Berlin
1911-12	German Embassy, St. Petersburg, Russia
1911-12	Mannesmann Office Building, Düsseldorf
1911-12	Wiegand House, Berlin
1911-13	Gas Works, Frankfurt
1911-20	Continental Rubber Company Office Building, Hannover
1914	Frank and Lehmann Commercial Building, Cologne
1915-17	EGH Housing and Factory, Nationale Automobil AG, Berlin
1917	Werkbund Exhibition, Bern, Switzerland
1920-21	Deutsche Werft Housing, Altona
1920-24	Administrative Building, IG Farben AG Dye Works (now Höchst Werke), Frankfurt-am-Main
1921-25	Hoag Steelworks, Oberhausen
1923-26	"New Ways" House, Northampton, England
1924-25	St. Peter's Monastery, Salzburg, Austria
1924-29	Three Low-income Housing Blocks, Vienna, Austria
1926-27	Terrace House Apartments, Weissenhofsiedlung, Stuttgart
1929-30	Kurt Lewin House, Berlin
1929-31	Office Buildings, Alexanderplatz, Berlin
1931-32	Clara Ganz Villa, Kronberg im Taunus
1932-34	Austrian State Tobacco Factory, Linz, Austria (with Alexander Popp)

Publications

BOOKS BY BEHRENS

Feste des Lebens und der Kunst: Eine Betrachtung des Theaters als höchsten Kultursymbols. Leipzig, 1900.
Ein Dokument deutscher Kunst: Die Ausstellung der Künstler-Kolonie in Darmstadt 1901. Munich, 1901.
Behrens Schrift. Offenbach am Main, Germany, 1902.
Beziehungen der künstlerischen und technischen Probleme. Berlin, 1917.
Vom sparsamen Bauen: Ein Beitrag zur Siedlungsfrage. With Heinrich de Fries. Berlin, 1918.
Das Ethos und die Umlagerung der künstlerischen Probleme. Darmstadt, 1920.
Terrassen am Hause. Stuttgart, 1927.

ARTICLES BY BEHRENS

"Über den Zusammenhang des baukünstlerischen Schaffens mit der Technik." In *Berlin, Kongress für Asthetik und allgemeine Kunstwissenschaft* (Stuttgart, 1914).
"Über die Beziehungen der künstlerischen und technischen Probleme." *Wendingen* 3 (1920): 4-20.
"The Work of Josef Hoffmann." *Architecture* 2 (London, 1923): 589-599.
"Seeking Aesthetic Worth in Industrial Buidings." *American Architect* 128 (1925): 475-479.
"Administration Buildings for Industrial Plants." *American Architect* 128 (1925): 167-174.
"Die Baukunst und das Leben." *Baugilde* No. 16 (1932).
"Die Baugesinnung des Faschismus." *Neue Linie* (November 1933): 11-13.

BOOKS ABOUT BEHRENS

BILANCIONI, GUGLIELMO: *Il Primo Behrens: origini del moderno in architettura.* Florence, 1981.
BRANCHESI, LIDA: *Peter Behrens.* Rome, 1965.
BUDDENSIEG, TILMANN, and ROGGE, HENNING: *Industriekultur. Peter Behrens and the AEG, 1907-1914.* Cambridge, Massachusetts, 1984.
BUDERATH, BERNARD (ed.): *Peter Behrens: Umbautes Licht.* Frankfurt-am-Main and Munich, 1990.
CREMERS, PAUL JOSEPH: *Peter Behrens: Sein Werk von 1909 bis zur Gegenwart.* Essen, 1928.
GRIMME, KARL MARIA (ed.): *Peter Behrens und seine Wiener akademische Meisterschule.* Vienna, 1930.
HAENLE, ERICH, and TSCHARMANN, HEINRICH: *Das Einzelwohnhaus der Neuzeit.* Leipzig, 1906.
HOEBER, FRITZ: *Peter Behrens.* Munich, 1913.
HOEPER, FRIEDRICH: *Die Kunst Peter Behrens.* Berlin, 1909.
HOEPFNER, WOLFRAM, and NEUMEYER, FRITZ: *Nicht gebaute Architektur: Peter Behrens und Fritz Schumacher als Kirchenplaner in Hagen.* Mainz, 1979.
HOEPFNER, WOLFRAM; NEUMEYER, FRITZ; et al.: *Das Haus Wiegand.* Mainz, 1979.
KADATAZ, H. J.: *Peter Behrens.* Leipzig, 1977.
LE CORBUSIER: *Etude sur le mouvement d'art décoratif en Allemagne.* La Chaux-de-Fonds, Switzerland, 1912.
LUX, JOSEPH AUGUST: *Das neue Kunstgewerbe in Deutschland.* Leipzig, 1908.
MEIER-GRAEFE, JULIUS: *Entwicklungsgeschichte der modernen Kunst.* Stuttgart, 1904.
MEYER-SCHÖNBRUNN, F.: *Peter Behrens.* Dortmund, 1913.
NORBERG-SCHULZ, CHRISTIAN: *Casa Behrens, Darmstadt.* Rome, 1980.

Peter Behrens und Nürnberg. Exhibition catalog. Munich, 1980.
SCHEFFLER, KARL: *Moderne Baukunst.* Berlin, 1907.
SEIPE, E.: *Das Gesellenhaus und eine städtebauliche Studie von Peter Behrens in Neuss.* Neuss, Germany, 1961.
SHARP, DENNIS (ed.): *The Rationalists: Theory and Design in the Modern Movement.* London, 1978.
WEBER, WILHELM (ed.): *Peter Behrens (1868-1940).* Exhibition catalog. Kaiserslautern, Germany, 1966.
WINDSOR, ALAN: *Peter Behrens, Architect and Designer.* London and New York, 1981.

ARTICLES ABOUT BEHRENS

ANDERSON, STANFORD: "Peter Behrens and the New Architecture of Germany: 1900-1917." Dissertation. Columbia University, New York. Published in part in *Architectural Design* 29, No. 2, and in *Oppositions* Nos. 11, 21, 23.
ANDERSON, STANFORD: "Peter Behrens's Changing Concept of Life as Art." *Architectural Design* 39 (February 1969): 72-78.
ANDERSON, STANFORD: "Modern Architecture and Industry: Peter Behrens and the AEG Factories." *Oppositions* No. 23 (1981): 53-83.
BUDDENSIEG, TILMANN, and ROGGE, HENNING: "Peter Behrens and the AEG Architecture." *Lotus* 12 (September 1976): 90-127.
MURET, L. MIOTTO: "Peter Behrens." *Architecture* (April 1976).
NIEMEYER, W.: "Peter Behrens und die Raumästhetik seiner Kunst." *Dekorative Kunst* (1906-07): 137-165.
"Peter Behrens and the Rathenhaus AEG." *Casabella* (April 1981).
"Peter Behrens: Haus Behrens 1901." *Architectural Design* No. 1/2 (1980).
POSENER, JULIUS: "L'oeuvre de Peter Behrens." *Architecture d'aujourd'hui* (March 1934): 8-29.
ROGERS, ERNESTO NATHAN, et al.: "Peter Behrens." *Casabella continuità* No. 240, special issue (1960).
SHAND, P. MORTON: "Peter Behrens." *Architectural Review* (September 1934): 39-42.
SHAND, P. MORTON: "The Machine: Peter Behrens." *Architectural Association Journal* 75 (1959): 173-178.

*

Like his contemporary Henry Van de Velde, Peter Behrens was originally an artist. Around the turn of the century, he began to occupy himself with architecture and industrial production. In a short time, Behrens became the leading personality in German architecture and a pioneer in industrial design. Behrens' work in these areas became the precursor of German functionalism between the wars, and it is hardly surprising that three of the main figures of modern architecture—Le Corbusier, Walter Gropius and Ludwig Mies van der Rohe—sought him out and worked for him.

Behrens' architectural work initially remained within the Jugendstil. In 1899 Behrens had been invited to join the artists' colony in Darmstadt by the archduke Ernst Ludwig, where, following Van de Velde's example, he built his own house (1901). This house, including the interior decoration, was designed in a subdued form of Jugendstil. Besides the influence of Van de Velde, that of Charles Rennie Mackintosh is visible. But Behrens left Darmstadt in 1903, and became director of the Düsseldorf Arts and Crafts School, at the recommendation

Peter Behrens: AEG Turbine Factory, Berlin, Germany, 1909-10

of Herman Muthesius. With his departure from Darmstadt, Behrens also left the Jugenstil behind, and turned to classical architecture. That turn was not too surprising, since classicism had also offered a new source of inspiration to other architects coming out of the Jugendstil, such as Josef Hoffmann. Behrens' stylistic reorientation was not a matter of nostalgia, however, but amounted to a new interpretation of classical ideas. The houses Obenauer in Saarbrücken (1905-06) and Cuno in Eppenhausen (1908-09) bear witness to Behrens' abstract reworking of classical architecture. The crematorium in Hagen (1906-07) also has a clear connection to a classical idiom combined with allusions to the forms of the Florentine proto-Renaissance. The severe, temple-like grouping of the crematorium building mass anticipated the later forms of his industrial buildings.

In 1907 Behrens was offered the position of consultant to the Allgemeine Elektricitäts-Gesellschaft (AEG) in Berlin. Behrens' acquaintance with Walther Rathenau, one of the factory's directors, was of great importance. Both were convinced of the liberating potential of modern technology and of the necessity of a collaboration between artists and industry. It is no coincidence that the Deutscher Werkbund— which sought to improve the quality of industrial production—was founded in the same year (1907). The new position in Berlin meant a significant expansion of Behrens' activities. Besides residential designs and exhibition pavilions, he was charged with the design of industrial buildings and products. By far the best-known example of his industrial buildings is the AEG Turbine Hall in Berlin (1908-09), where Behrens pursued, in his own words, a "new beauty in harmony with the spirit of our time." The most important innovation was Behrens' conception of the commission as an artistic rather than purely utilitarian project. He

incorporated the support elements, the 22 gigantic iron columns, as structural elements into the facade, consciously setting them on plates that project 30 centimeters from the wall plane. A massive concrete gable carried by corner pylons dominates the short principal facade. In reality, however, these corner supports do not have a function in the support system, but were used for their function in the facade design. They give the facade a classical temple-like appearance.

In later industrial buildings, Behrens also pursued a worthy and humane appearance through contemporary means, which made it possible to integrate industrial architecture into the urban context. The Kleinmotorenfabrik on the Voltastrasse in Berlin (1911-13) and the former NAG Building in Berlin (1915-16) are good examples. In buildings for industrial headquarters, such as Continental AG in Hannover and Mannesmann in Düsseldorf (both 1911-12), Behrens hid the functional divisions behind a monumental classicistic facade. In government buildings, particularly the German Embassy in St. Petersburg, Russia (1911-12), his classicism became even more naturalistic.

Besides his work in architecture, Behrens did work in design, principally for AEG. His range was broad: letterheads, advertisements, lamps, electromotors, clocks, ventilators, dentists' drills and railway locomotives. The integration of the design of all products was new, and so was the style itself, which became a distinctive "AEG style." Instead of traditional, added-on decoration, Behrens started out from serial production, which requires effective design. This does not mean, however, that he simply took over existing forms. He was of the opinion that an electromotor should look like a birthday present, that is to say that Behrens designed the necessary cover for electrical appliances according to the image of contemporary industrial form, rather than as a craft decoration.

After World War I, Behrens became professor and director of the Architecture School of the Vienna Academy. Besides a modest contribution to Vienna's housing projects (Winarsky-hof, 1924-26), he was occupied with a variety of commissions. His conception of architecture changed. For big projects, such as the I. G. Farben headquarters in Hoechst (1920-24), for example, Behrens often used the expressionist idiom then prevalent in Germany, accentuating vertical wall articulation. The architectural solution for the Gutehoffnungshütte in Oberhausen (1921-26), with its cubic composition of the building mass underlining the horizontals, displays an alternative approach. Behrens' terrace houses for the Weissenhofsiedlung in Stuttgart were conceived in the same spirit. The country house "New Ways" in Northampton, England (1923), shows the severe classical composition of his early years, in spite of the cubic, unornamented form.

Behrens' most important creative period came in the years before World War I. His attention to industrial design and his understanding of a modern formal idiom ensure him a unique position in the history of architecture.

—OTAKAR MÁČEL
Translated from the German by Marijke Rijsberman

BÉLANGER, François-Joseph.

French. Born in Paris, France, 1744. Died in Paris, 5 January 1818. Married Mlle. Delvieux. Studied architecture at the Académie Royale d'Architecture, 1764-65. Imprisoned for a year as a royalist during the Revolution.

Chronology of Works
All in France unless noted
* Approximate dates

1770	Château de Baudour, Belgium (remodeling)
1770	Château de Beloeil, Belgium (landscaping)
1770	Hôtel de Brancas, Paris
1773	Hôtel des Gardes, Versailles
1777	Pavillon de Bagatelle, Bois de Boulogne, Paris
1777-79	Château de Maison, Neuilly-sur-Seine (remodeling)
1780*	Folie St. James and Garden, Neuilly-sur-Seine
1786-88	Three houses, rue Saint Georges, Paris
1796	Hôtel des Menus Plaisirs, Paris (restoration)
1799	Bibliothèque Nationale, Paris (extension)
1800-15	Bélanger House, Santeny
1808-13	Halle au Blé, Paris (dome)

Publications

ARTICLES BY BÉLANGER

"Eloge de Brongniart." *Journal des arts et sciences et de la littérature* (June 1813).
"Lettres sur les arts par un ami des artistes." *Journal de Paris* (1777).

BOOKS ABOUT BÉLANGER

BRAHAM, ALLAN: *The Architecture of the French Enlightenment.* Berkeley, California, and Los Angeles, 1980.
DUCHESNE, HENRI-GASTON: *Histoire du Bois de Boulogne: Le château de Bagatelle.* Paris, 1909.
KAUFMANN, EMIL: *Architecture in the Age of Reason: Baroque and Post-Baroque in England, Italy, France.* Cambridge, Massachusetts, 1955.
STERN, JEAN: *A l'ombre de Sophie Arnould. François Joseph Bélanger.* 2 vols. Paris, 1930.

ARTICLES ABOUT BÉLANGER

WIEBENSON, DORA: "The Two Domes of the Halle au Blé in Paris." *Art Bulletin* (June 1973): 262-279.

François-Joseph Bélanger was an architect active in France at the end of the 18th century who was noted also for his work in the applied arts and in landscape design. Born to a Parisian haberdasher, Bélanger was educated, like Claude-Nicolas Ledoux and Alexandre-Théodore Brongniart, at the Collège de Beauvais, studying physics with Abbé Nollet, and then training as an architect with Julien David Leroy at the Académie Royale d'Architecture. Bélanger was also a protégé of the comte de Caylus and perfected his craftsmanship with Pierre Contant d'Ivry.

Bélanger's professional career began in 1767 when he was appointed draftsman to the *Menus-Plaisirs du Roi*, where he designed a jewelry cupboard for Marie Antoinette. In 1769 he met Sophie d'Arnould, the prima donna of the Paris Opéra, and was introduced by her to a number of wealthy clients; among them were the prince de Ligne, for whom he worked on designs for the gardens of the Château de Beloeil in Belgium, and the comte de Lauraguais, who commissioned from him in 1770 a bathhouse designed as a *pavillon à l'antique* for his Hôtel de Brancas in Paris. Lauraguais was a frequent visitor to England, having his own stables at Newmarket. And Bélanger visited England on at least one occasion, a notebook of which is still preserved with his various sketches of English buildings. Bélanger was not the first to introduce the English garden into France, but he did much to encourage it, most notably at the famous sites of Beloeil, Bagatelle, Neuilly and Méréville.

Bélanger also did well with another client, the comte d'Artois, the younger brother of Louis XVI and another confirmed Anglophile; in 1777 Bélanger bought the post at d'Artois' *premier architecte*. The most significant work Bélanger did for d'Artois was the Pavillon de Bagatelle, constructed—to win a bet—in 64 days. This building, like that of the bathhouse for Lauraguais, was praised for the invention of its interiors, and especially the main bedroom, where military emblems appeared everywhere: the room itself was conceived of as a tent, and the details in it included a cannon raised on end to support the chimneypiece and heaps of cannonballs and grenades for the stoves. The scale of the building, as befitted so self-conscious a project, was deliberately too mean for its owner's proper rank. The main access to Bagatelle was along a winding road that was designed, when the house was built, by a Scottish landscape gardener, Thomas Blaikie, who was busy on the site until the time of the Revolution. Nearby, Bélanger created a park for another patron, Claude Baudard de St.James, the son of a financier. There Bélanger built a small brick house and designed a large park, full of pavilions, kiosks, and grottoes and swings, the most famous of them the "Grand Rocher." This so-called "Eighth Wonder of the World" was a massive rock designed to accommodate a bathroom, reservoir, grotto and gallery. Bélanger then designed a garden in the shadow of the Bastille, again for the comte d'Artois. With the painter Hubert Robert he worked at Méréville, the most lavish of all the prerevolutionary gardens, for the court banker Jean-Joseph de Laborde. Bélanger also designed some houses in Paris, now known only from engravings; the most remarkable may have been the house for Talleyrand (1792), which—though still in the classical style— shows just how much the precepts and practices of Renaissance architecture had been softened.

Bélanger's fortunes during the Revolution were mixed. In 1789 he was elected to the States General for the district of St. Joseph, but he was also imprisoned briefly on suspicion of having helped some of the émigrés. In 1796 he joined the staff of the newly formed Monuments Publics, and he was for a while the architect of the Bibliothèque Nationale; however, it was not a time of great productivity. His last two works were very different from anything he had done earlier. One was a slaughterhouse at Rochechouart; the other, the dome of the Halle au Blé in Paris (1808-13), was the first such iron-and-glass structure known in Western architecture. The dome was not well received, and the end of Bélanger's life was marked by disputes, including his publication of an anonymous booklet that attacked the administration of public buildings under Jarente de la Bruyère. With the restoration of the Bourbon dynasty, however, he was again in demand and honored, admitted to the Légion d'Honneur; he organized a number of public decorations, most notably that of the entry of Louis XVIII into Paris in 1814. Bélanger died in 1818 and was buried in the Cemetery of Père Lachaise; his epitaph was nicely grand, recording that he was "superior to [William] Kent in the gardens of Mereville/ worthy follower of Michelangelo in the cupola of the Halle au Blé.''

—DAVID CAST

BELLUSCHI, Pietro.

American. Born in Ancona, Italy, 18 August 1899. Immigrated to the United States, 1923. Studied at the University of Rome, 1919-22; Cornell University, Ithaca, New York, 1924. Worked with A. E. Doyle and Associates, Portland, Oregon, 1925-42 (partner from 1933); in private practice, Portland, 1943-50; dean of the School of Architecture and Planning, Massachusetts Institute of Technology, Cambridge, 1951-65; in private practice, Boston, Massachusetts, and Portland, Oregon, from 1965. Gold Medal, American Institute of Architects, 1972.

Chronology of Works
All in the United States

1928	Eastside Office, Pacific Telephone and Telegraph Company, Portland, Oregon
1928	Corbett Residence, Portland, Oregon
1930-38	Portland Art Museum (additions), Oregon
1936	Belluschi House, Portland, Oregon
1938	Sutor House, Portland, Oregon
1939-41	St. Thomas More Chapel, Portland, Oregon
1940	Joss House, Portland, Oregon
1941	Platt House, Portland, Oregon
1941	Kerr House, Gearhart, Oregon
1944-48	Equitable Life Assurance Building, Portland, Oregon
1950	Zion Lutheran Church, Portland, Oregon
1950	Central Lutheran Church, Portland, Oregon
1955-70	Julliard School of Music, Lincoln Center, New York City (with Eduardo Catalano and Helge Westermann)

Publications

BOOKS ON BELLUSCHI

FORD, JAMES, and KATHERINE MORROW FORD: *The Modern House in America*. New York, 1940.
GUBITOSI, CAMILLO, and ALBERTO IZZO (eds.): *Pietro Belluschi: Buildings and Plans*. Rome, 1974.
STUBBLEPINE, JO (ed.): *The Northwest Architecture of Pietro Belluschi*. New York, 1953.

Pietro Belluschi, trained as an engineer in Italy and the United States, has enjoyed a long and successful career as both a practicing architect and an educator. The designer of numerous commercial, domestic and religious structures throughout the United States, Belluschi is one of the most respected architects of the American Northwest. Belluschi was most productive during the period from 1930 to 1950, and his contribution to the development of American architecture was recognized by the American Institute of Architects in 1972, when he was awarded its Gold Medal. Although Belluschi's commercial designs often reflected the concepts of the burgeoning International Style, his domestic and religious work revealed an interest in regional traditions and native materials.

After settling in Portland, Oregon, in 1925, Belluschi found employment with the firm of Albert E. Doyle, a prominent Northwest architect. By 1927 Belluschi was given the title of chief designer, and in 1933 he became a partner. At a time when American architects were beginning to seek new forms and alternatives to traditional, historicizing ornament, the Doyle firm maintained strong links to the Beaux-Arts tradition. Belluschi's work for the firm during the 1920s was solidly within that tradition, as exemplified by two works from 1928: the Eastside Office of Pacific Telephone and Telegraph Company, designed in an English Renaissance mode, and the Hamilton Corbett Residence, conceived as a Georgian Revival mansion.

An addition to the Portland Art Museum begun in 1930 can be seen as a transitional work within Belluschi's oeuvre. Early studies for the building reveal his continued reliance on historical style, but as constructed, the Ayer Wing was without any referential ornament. Belluschi's straightforward use of brick and travertine, in conjunction with strip windows, was seen at the time as thoroughly modern. His design for the 1938 Hirsch Wing of the museum was noted for its skylighted sculpture court. Belluschi's continued use of rich materials such as travertine and the overall simplicity of the structure prompted comparisons between his work and that of European modernist Ludwig Mies van der Rohe.

During the 1930s, the Doyle firm turned its attention to the design of domestic structures, due mostly to the lack of major public commissions during the Depression. As a result, Belluschi began to develop a regional style appropriate to the terrain of western Oregon. After designing his own house in 1936, he went on to design such significant Northwest dwellings as the Jennings Sutor House (1938), the Joss House (1940), the Platt House (1941), all in Portland, and the Kerr House (1941) in Gearhart. Each house featured an open plan sheltered by a broad, overhanging roof; through the use of natural woods, such as cedar and spruce, Belluschi carefully integrated building and site. Despite the simplicity of his domestic work, Belluschi did not draw parallels between his designs and those of the International Style modernists. Whereas the International Style sought that which was new, modern and unencumbered by history, Belluschi ultimately sought an expression which was traditional, rooted in the vernacular language of the region and constructed of local materials. In this respect, Belluschi's work can be linked to the domestic architecture of Frank Lloyd Wright, who also experimented with the creation of a regional architectural identity. One of the clearest expressions of this is seen in Wright's Robie House in Chicago (1907-09), where the flatness of the prairie is echoed in the sweeping horizontal lines of the design.

Belluschi's interest in regional types is also evident in his church designs from the late 1930s and 1940s. In his 1939-41 design for St. Thomas More Chapel in Portland, unfinished wood, became the dominant construction material and means of both exterior and interior ornament. For the exterior, Belluschi employed knotty-pine lap siding and cedar shingles, while he finished the interior with cedar walls and fir flooring. Exposed beams and columns served as the only interior enlivenment. The design of St. Thomas More brought Belluschi national acclaim, and his later designs for Zion Lutheran Church and Central Lutheran Church, both erected in 1950 in Portland, also emphasized regional materials assembled in a vernacular mode.

A sharp contrast to Belluschi's domestic and religious buildings is provided by his design for the Equitable Life Assurance Building in Portland (1944-48), an early example of the International Style tower type. The Equitable was distinguished as the first aluminum-clad skyscraper enclosing a concrete frame. Other innovative features employed at the Equitable Building included double-glazed, green-tinted window panels and a sealed, climate-controlled interior environment. This building was the first in a series of numerous corporate towers to embrace such aesthetic and industrial advances of the International Style, the most prominent of which was Mies van der Rohe and Philip Johnson's Seagram Building in New York City (1956-58).

In 1950 Belluschi was invited to serve as the dean of the School of Architecture and Planning at the Massachusetts Institute of Technology. This was an especially prestigious appointment, as MIT is the oldest and most established school of architecture in the country. Serving as dean until 1965, Belluschi continued to practice architecture simultaneously, most often in collaboration with a team of architects. His most significant project from that period was the design of the Juilliard School of Music at Lincoln Center in New York City (1955-70). Completed in association with architects Eduardo Catalano and Helge Westermann, the school was designed to function as a total learning complex, incorporating four theaters, classrooms and studios.

—MEREDITH ARMS

BENJAMIN, Asher.

American. Born in Greenfield, Massachusetts, 5 June 1771. Died on 25 June 1845. Apprenticed in Suffield, Connecticut. Opened own office, Boston, 1803.

Chronology of Works
All in the United States
* Approximate dates
† Work no longer exists

1796*	Luke Baldwin House, Brookfield, Massachusetts†
1796*	Samuel Hinckley House, Northampton, Massachusetts†
1797	William Coleman House, Greenfield, Massachusetts
1797	Leavitt-Hovey House, Greenfield, Massachusetts
1797-98	First Deerfield Academy Building (Memorial Hall), Massachusetts
1799*	Hubbard House, Windsor, Vermont
1799-1800	Old South Meetinghouse, Windsor, Vermont
1800*	Fullerton House, Windsor, Vermont (rebuilt in New Canaan, Connecticut)
1800*	Harriet Lane House, Windsor, Vermont
1802	United States Marine Hospital, Charlestown, Massachusetts†
1805	African Meetinghouse, Boston, Massachusetts
1806	West Church, Boston, Massachusetts
1806-09	Exchange Coffee House, Boston, Massachusetts†
1807	Charles Street Meetinghouse, Boston, Massachusetts
1807-08	Double house, 54-55 Beacon Street, Boston, Massachusetts
1808	James Smith Colburn Houses, Boston, Massachusetts
1808	Fourth Meetinghouse, First Church, Boston, Massachusetts†
1811-12	First Parish Church, Northampton, Massachusetts†
1812-14	Center Church, New Haven, Connecticut
1817	Rhode Island Union Bank, Newport, Rhode Island†
1818	Ward Nicholas Boylston House, Princeton, Massachusetts
1825	Olive Street Congregational Church, Nashua, New Hampshire†
1828	Houses, 70-75 Beacon Street, Boston, Massachusetts
1830	Isaac Munson House, South Wallingford, Vermont
1832	Cambridgeport Town Hall, Cambridge, Massachusetts†
1833-34	Asher Benjamin Houses, 7-9 West Cedar Street, Boston, Massachusetts
1834	Thatcher Magoun House, Medford, Massachusetts†
1835	Lexington-Concord Battle Monument, Peabody, Massachusetts
1836	William Ellery Channing House, Boston, Massachusetts
1836	George Shattuck Monument, Mount Auburn Cemetery, Cambridge, Massachusetts
1836	F.O.J. Smith House, Westbrook, Maine†
1838-39	Fifth Universalist Church, Boston, Massachusetts
1840	Unitarian Meetinghouse (Third Religious Society), Dorchester, Massachusetts†
1841-42	Edmund Hastings House, Medford, Massachusetts†

Publications

BOOKS BY BENJAMIN

The Country Builder's Assistant. Greenfield, Massachusetts, 1797.
The American Builder's Companion; or, A New System of Architecture. Boston, 1806.
The Rudiments of Architecture. Boston, 1814.
The Practical House Carpenter. Boston, 1830.
The Practice of Architecture. Boston, 1833.
The Builder's Guide; or, Complete System of Architecture. Boston, 1839.
The Elements of Architecture. Boston, 1843.

BOOKS ABOUT BENJAMIN

EMBURY, AYMAR (ed.): *Asher Benjamin.* New York, 1917.

ARTICLES ABOUT BENJAMIN

BACH, RICHARD F.: "Asher Benjamin Revived." *American Architect* 112 (19 December 1917): 449-450.

"Bible of Classicism: The Influence on Today's Decoration of Asher Benjamin's *Builders' Companion.*" *House and Garden* 77 (June 1940): 46-49.

BISHER, CATHERINE W.: "Asher Benjamin's *Practical House Carpenter* in North Carolina." *Carolina Comments* 27 (3 May 1979): 66-74.

BOOTH, VINCENT R.: "Restoration of the Old First Church of Bennington, Vermont." *Old-Time New England* (January 1940).

CANDEE, RICHARD M.: "Three Architects of Early New Hampshire Mill Towns." *Journal of the Society of Architectural Historians* 30 (1971): 155-163.

COMSTOCK, HELEN: "Windsor House at New Canaan, Connecticut." *Antiques* 58 (1950): 462-467.

CONGDON, HERBERT WHEATON: "Our First Architectural School?" *Journal of the American Institute of Architects* 13 (1950): 139-140.

CROCKER, MARY WALLACE: "Asher Benjamin: The Influence of His Handbooks on Mississippi Buildings." *Journal of the Society of Architectural Historians* 38 (1979): 266-270.

CUMMINGS, ABBOTT LOWELL: "An Investigation of the Sources, Stylistic Evolution, and Influence of Asher Benjamin's *Builder's Guides.*" Ph.D. dissertation. Ohio State University, Columbus, Ohio, 1950.

DEAN, NANCY REISTER: "Asher Benjamin's Nashua Years." Master's thesis. Brown University, Providence, Rhode Island, 1963.

GREENE, JOHN GARDNER: "The Charles Street Meetinghouse, Boston." *Old-Time New England* 30 (January 1940): 86-93.

HADDON, R. W.: "Mr. Embury's Asher Benjamin." *Architectural Record* 42 (August 1917): 181-184.

HALL, LOUISE: "First Architectural School? No! But . . ." *Journal of the American Institute of Architects* 14 (1950): 79-82.

HOWE, FLORENCE THOMPSON: "Asher Benjamin: Country Builder's Assistant." *Antiques* 40 (1941): 364-366.

HOWE, FLORENCE THOMPSON: "More About Asher Benjamin." *Journal of the Society of Architectural Historians* 13 (October 1954): 16-19.

KIRKER, HAROLD: "The Boston Exchange Coffee House." *Old-Time New England* 52 (Summer 1961): 11-13.

MINOT, WILLIAM: "*The Builder's Guide* by Asher Benjamin, Architect." *North American Review* 52 (1841): 301-320.

O'DONNELL, THOMAS E.: "Asher Benjamin: A Pioneer Writer of Architectural Books." *Architecture* 54 (December 1926): 375-378.

QUINAN, JACK: "Asher Benjamin and American Architecture" and "The Boston Exchange Coffee House." *Journal of the Society of Architectural Historians* 38 (1979): 244-256, 256-262.

QUINAN, JACK: "Asher Benjamin as an Architect in Windsor, Vermont." *Vermont History* 62 (1974): 181-194.

QUINAN, JACK: "The Architectural Style of Asher Benjamin." Ph.D. dissertation. Brown University, Providence, Rhode Island, 1973.

REINHARDT, ELIZABETH W., and GRADY, ANNE A.: "Asher Benjamin in East Lexington, Massachusetts." *Old-Time New England* 67 (Winter-Spring 1977): 23-35.

STURGES, WALTER KNIGHT: "The Black House, Ellsworth—An Asher Benjamin House in Maine." *Antiques* 65:398-400.

THOMPSON, FLORENCE: "More about Asher Benjamin." *Journal of the Society of Architectural Historians* 13 (October 1954).

TOMLINSON, JULIETTE: "Asher Benjamin—Connecticut Architect." *Connecticut Antiquarian* 6 (1954): 26-29.

VAN METER, MARY: "A New Benjamin Church in Boston." *Journal of the Society of Architectural Historians* 38 (1979): 262-266.

VOYE, NANCY S.: "Asher Benjamin's West Church: A Model for Change." *Old-Time New England* 67 (Summer-Fall 1976): 7-15.

*

The internationally admired image of an early-19th-century New England rural town, with comfortable, block-like "Late Colonial" houses dominated by a white-spired church, is generally believed to be the product of talented and aesthetically sensitive, though formally untrained, local housewrights and "mechanicks." Though this is in essence true, an architect was the source for the designs for many of these buildings throughout New England and even into Ohio. Asher Benjamin published America's first builder's guide, *The Country Builders' Assistant,* in 1797, in the Connecticut River Valley town of Greenfield, Massachusetts, when he was just beginning his own practice of architecture. It and six subsequent titles were issued in 47 editions between 1797 and 1856 (some posthumously). Used by several generations of other architects and builders, the books were clear, practical, and heavily illustrated in architectural styles from the Late Georgian and the Federal architecture of Charles Bulfinch (1763-1844), who was Benjamin's chief model, to later, Greek Revival architecture. His publications, which he continually revised to improve and keep up with stylistic trends, offered a new, American architecture to a growing population fired by their new independence; not only were houses needed, but new meetinghouses and churches for the old and established as well as the various emerging religious societies.

Although many buildings designed by Benjamin are no longer extant, there are enough to demonstrate his architectural skill. Bostonians are proud of Benjamin's African Meetinghouse (1805), West Church (1806) and Charles Street Meetinghouse (1807); domestic architecture such as the double house at 54-55 Beacon Street (1807-08) and the block of houses from 70-75 Beacon Street (1828)—all surrounding the base of Beacon Hill; the William Ellery Channing house at 83 Mount Vernon Street (1836) near the top of Beacon Hill; the Fifth Universalist Church on Warrenton Street (1838-39, now the Charles Playhouse); and the handsome spire of the First Church in Roxbury (ca. 1806). Two of his earliest Boston buildings—the African Meetinghouse and the Charles Street Meetinghouse—served Beacon Hill's black community. And the first house he designed for himself was also on Charles Street. (It is now gone, though the second still exists at 9 West Cedar Street.)

Benjamin's ambitious, innovative seven-story Exchange Coffee House (1806-09) in Boston was America's first example of hotel architecture, though called "too high and disproportioned" at the time. (It burned in 1818 and was replaced by a smaller, much more traditional building.) In spite of the criticism, he designed buildings for other notable Boston clients until 1825, when, bankrupt, he fled creditors and appeared soon in Nashua, New Hampshire, selling paint and acting as a mill agent.

Both Nashua and Windsor, Vermont, where Benjamin was active earlier in his career, still have a representative array of buildings designed by him. The architecturally highly significant central town green of New Haven, Connecticut, features three famous early-19th-century churches, one of which is Benjamin's Center Church (1812-14). But aside from these and the Boston buildings, most of the other ones still extant are in the Connecticut Valley; Deerfield Academy's first building, Memorial Hall, was designed by Benjamin in 1797—the year he designed the Coleman and Leavitt-Hovey houses and published his first builder's guidebook in nearby Greenfield.

Benjamin is credited with two other innovations. He designed and built the first circular staircase in New England, for the Hartford, Connecticut, state capitol building designed by Bulfinch (1795), and he proposed an architectural school in Windsor, Vermont, in 1802. Excepting James Hoban's advertisement for an evening school in Charlestown, South Carolina, in 1790, Benjamin's would have been the first such school in the United States. Whether or not he ever held classes in Windsor or later in Boston, a number of architects such as Ithiel Town, Solomon Willard, Robert Henry Eddy, Elias Carter and Samuel Shepherd claimed to have studied with him. Benjamin also was among the noted architects who endorsed the founding of the American Institution of Architects (now the American Institute of Architects) in New York in 1836.

Architectural historian Abbott Lowell Cummings sparked the academic interest in Benjamin with a doctoral thesis at Ohio State University in 1951 on the sources, evolution and influence of the architect's guidebooks. He considered Benjamin's fourth book, *Practical House Carpenter,* issued in 21 recorded reprintings, "the most popular American handbook of the nineteenth century." Such widely admired New England churches as Lavius Fillmore's First Church in Bennington, Vermont, and First Church in Middlebury, Vermont, were based on a Benjamin plate; many Greek Revival iron fences and balconies on Beacon Hill were inspired by other plates. The proliferation of the domestic "Greek temple," especially its particular characteristics in the Connecticut Valley, are due to Benjamin's influence. Jack Quinan has pointed out that Benjamin's designs could be made easily with an ordinary wood lath, thereby avoiding the more difficult curvilinear elements of design.

Benjamin is generally regarded as a major architect, though not the equal of Bulfinch, and some architectural historians consider Benjamin more significant than Salem's Samuel McIntire. Richard H. Pratt cited Benjamin's books (and those of the less well-known Minard Lafever) as partly responsible for the "ill-fated parade" of the decline of American architecture in the first half of the 19th century. However, in a society which to this day, two centuries later and with an abundance of architectural schools, builds expensive houses without benefit of architectural advice, the handy, practical, easily procured and understood books of Asher Benjamin provided early-19th-century housewrights with creditable, professional guides. Regional derivations from the illustrated plates, though sometimes ill scaled and awkward, enrich the American architectural heritage.

—BETTINA A. NORTON

BENTLEY, John Francis.

British. Born in Doncaster, England, January 1839. Died 2 March 1902. Married; one son was an architect. Converted to Roman Catholic faith in 1862. Apprenticed with George Gordon Place at Loversall Church; worked with a firm of mechanical engineers, Manchester; worked for firm of Winslow and Holland, London, 1855; articled to Henry Clutton (1819-93), London, 1857; opened his own office in London, 1862; traveled to Italy and France, 1894-95, and to the United States, 1898.

Chronology of Works
All in England

1861	Church of St. Francis of Assisi, Notting Hill, London (begun by Henry Clutton)
1863	Nathaniel Westlake House, Lancaster Road, Nottingdale
1871	Distillery, Finsbury, London
1875-88	Convent of the Sacred Heart, Hammersmith, London
1876-84	St. John's Seminary, Hammersmith, London
1883-90	Church of the Holy Rood, Watford, Hertfordshire
1885	Cottage, Bainbridge, Yorkshire
1885	Corpus Christi Church, Brixton, London
1886-88	St. John's Preparatory School, Beaumont, Old Windsor, Berkshire
1891-93	Redemptorist Monastery, London
1894-1903	Westminster Cathedral, London
1880s-1890s	Ecclesiastical furniture and fittings

Publications

BOOKS ABOUT BENTLEY

BUTLER, A. S. G.: *John Francis Bentley.* 1961.
FERRIDAY, PETER: (ed.): *Victorian Architecture.* London, 1963.
LETHABY, W.R. and SWAINSON, HAROLD: *The Church of Sancta Sophia Constantinople: A Study of Byzantine Building.* London, 1894.
L'HOPITAL, WINEFRIDE DE: *Westminster Cathedral and Its Architect.* London, 1919.
SCOTT-MONCRIEFF, W.: *John Francis Bentley.* London, 1924.
SERVICE, ALASTAIR: *The Architects of London.* London, 1979.
VAUGHAN, HERBERT A.: *Letters of Herbert Cardinal Vaughan to Lady Herbert of Lea, 1867 to 1903.* London, 1942.
VICTORIA AND ALBERT MUSEUM: *Victorian Church Art.* London, 1971.
Victorian Church Art. Exhibition catalog. London, 1971.
Westminster Cathedral and Bentley, 1902. (RIBA Manuscripts)

*

John Bentley visited the Great Exhibition in London in 1851, an experience that made a vivid impression on the boy, and helped to awaken in him an interest in art and architecture. In 1853 the superb medieval church of St. George in Doncaster (a building to which Bentley was devoted) burned down, and young Bentley made a detailed model of the building in order to raise funds for its rebuilding. In fact a new church, designed by George Gilbert Scott, was erected, and Bentley haunted the site, drawing everything, and eventually assisting the clerk of works. The young man gained further experience at Loversall Church under the architect George Gordon Place of Newark. In 1855 Bentley entered the London office of the builders Winslow & Holland, where his draftsmanship techniques improved. Richard Holland recognized talent when he saw it, however, and he sent Bentley to join the office of Henry Clutton (1819-93) in 1857; there Bentley imbibed a sound knowledge of Continental Gothic.

John Francis Bentley: Westminster Cathedral, London, England, 1894-1903

By 1858, when Bentley's drawings for a church at Heigham were prepared, it was clear he had become familiar with Italian Gothic, and by 1861 he demonstrated his mastery of polychrome decoration in a drawing exhibited at the Royal Academy: the influence of William Burges had become marked.

During the late 1850s Bentley supervised the building of the sedilia and chapel at the Jesuit Church in Farm Street and the construction of the tiny Church of St. Francis of Assisi, Notting Dale, London. By 1860 Bentley had determined to set up his own practice, and he made a study of the contents of the Architectural Museum (founded by John Ruskin, George Gilbert Scott, William Burges and others) and of the monuments in Westminster Abbey.

In 1862 Bentley took the fateful step of entering the Roman Catholic Church, and assumed the additional name of Francis when he was baptized in the new baptistery he himself had designed for Clutton's Church of St. Francis of Assisi at Notting Dale.

Bentley embraced his new spiritual life with ardor and developed numerous clerical friendships, especially among the Oblates of St. Charles Borromeo, founded in Bayswater by Dr.

Manning in 1857. His first commission from the Oblates was for the additions and embellishments of the Notting Dale church, a task which he carried out with great taste and sensitivity: indeed, the exquisite baptistry and altars for this church, executed in collaboration with Thomas Earp of Lambeth and N. H. J. Westlake, are among the best designs he ever did.

Then followed a series of commissions for the Roman Catholic Church. Gradually, Bentley moved away from Franco-Italian Gothic to a more native variety, culminating in his great Church of the Holy Rood, Watford, Hertfordshire (1883-90), brilliantly conceived on a very tight site, and in style that was a firmly English mix of Decorated and Perpendicular Gothic, treated with enormous skill. The materials were flint facings with dressings of Bath stone. Exquisite were the high altar and reredos, rood loft and rood, while the painted decoration of the church conjured a vision of late-medieval richness of the finest quality. Throughout, this marvelous ensemble had a care for detail lavished on it, and the furnishings, fixtures and glass were of the very best.

Gradually, Bentley's taste, like that of his great contemporary G. F. Bodley, moved toward a revival of English Gothic, and his essays in the design of fittings based on Perpendicular precedents were breathtakingly beautiful. His architecture tended to become somewhat flat and angular, heralding that very robust Late Gothic of the Edwardian period.

In his domestic work, Bentley showed a remarkable inventiveness. For Westlake, he designed an extraordinary dwelling at the corner of Lancaster Road, Notting Hill, which had an arcaded loggia on the third floor and many other features that made it one of the most unusual designs of the period.

At Bainbridge in Yorkshire, Bentley built in 1885 a two-story cottage in a free style, yet with 17th-century features, that had certain affinities with later, more celebrated examples of the Domestic Revival. His designs for ecclesiastical furniture and fittings in the 1880s and 1890s often showed the influence of Arts and Crafts ideas, and there are even some pieces with art nouveau and Jacobean strapwork in evidence.

A late-19th-century search for a "real" architecture freed from the tyranny of Gothic led Bentley to his masterpiece, the Roman Catholic Cathedral at Westminster (1894-1903). This Italo-Byzantine building, with its red-and-white striped exterior influenced, no doubt, by R. Norman Shaw's New Scotland Yard, represents the culmination of Bentley's scholarly achievement. Here the Byzantine architecture of St. Mark's in Venice, San Vitale and other churches in Ravenna, the Romanesque Duomo in Pisa, the Domkirche in Speier, the church of Sant'Ambrogio in Milan, the Certosa in Pavia and many other great Churches, including Hagia Sophia in Constantinople, are the precedents for aspects of what is a truly original design. Here Early Christian, Romanesque and Byzantine elements fuse with the free styles of Late Victorian England in a tour-de-force of enormous emotional power and imagination. Spatially, Westminster Cathedral is stupendous and sublime, while the delightful carvings and details are a virtual conspectus of work by some of the best Arts and Crafts personalities of the Edwardian and later periods.

In the words of Cardinal Vaughan, Bentley was "no copyist and no slave to tradition. Whatever he produced was stamped with his own individuality; it was alive and original; and he had a genius for taking infinite pains with detail." Bentley was unquestionably one of the most interesting and inventive of British architects of the second half of the 19th century. His three greatest works are his miniatures at the Church of St. Francis of Assisi (Continental Gothic), the Church of the Holy Rood at Watford (East Anglian Late Gothic) and Westminster Cathedral. In the last building, a synthesis of many themes is firmly made and indissolubly connected within a work of the highest integrity and quality.

—JAMES STEVENS CURL

BERLAGE, Hendrik Petrus.

Dutch. Born in Amsterdam, Netherlands, 21 February 1856. Died in The Hague, 12 August 1934. Married Marie Bienfait, 1887. Studied painting at the Rijksakademie van Beeldende Kunsten, Amsterdam, 1874-75, and architecture at the Eidgenössische Technische Hochschule, Zurich, 1875-78; traveled in Germany, 1879, and in Italy, 1880-81. Worked in Arnhem, Netherlands, 1879, and later in the office of Theodorus Sanders, Amsterdam, 1881-84; in partnership with Sanders, 1884-89; practiced privately in Amsterdam and The Hague, 1889-1934. Gold Medal, Royal Institute of British Architects, 1932.

Chronology of Works
All in the Netherlands unless noted
† Work no longer exists

1883-84	De Hoop Restaurant/Hotel, Amsterdam (with Theodorus Sanders)†
1884-86	Focke and Meltzer Store, Amsterdam (with Sanders)
1891-92	E. D. Pijzel House, Amsterdam
1892-94	De Algemeene General Life Insurance Building, Amsterdam†
1894	G. Heymans House, Groningen
1894-95	De Nederlanden van 1845 Insurance Company Building, Amsterdam
1895-96	De Nederlanden van 1845 Insurance Company Building, The Hague
1897-1903	Stock Exchange [Beurs], Amsterdam
1898	Villa Henny, The Hague
1898-1900	Diamond Workers' Union Building, Amsterdam
1900	Villa Parkwijk, Amsterdam†
1900-17	Plan, Amsterdam South
1906	Voorwaarts Workers' Cooperative Building, Rotterdam
1910	De Nederlanden van 1845 Insurance Company Building, Rotterdam†
1910-13	Workers' Housing, Tolstraat, Amsterdam
1911-13	Workers' Housing, Algemeene Woningbouwvereeniging, Transvaalbuurt, Amsterdam
1912-15	Workers' Housing, Javaplein, Amsterdam
1913	Berlage House, The Hague
1913	Simons House, Prinsevinkenpark, The Hague
1914	Meddens and Son, Hofweg, The Hague
1914-16	Holland House, London
1914-20	St. Hubertus Hunting Lodge, Otterlo
1924-27	De Nederlanden van 1845 Insurance Company Building (with A. D. N. van Gendt and W. N. van Vliet), The Hague
1925	Mercatorplein, Amsterdam-West
1925-26	First Church of Christ, Scientist, The Hague (with Phil Zwart)
1925-32	Amsterdamse Bank, Rembrandtplein, Amsterdam
1926	Berlage Bridge, Amsterdam
1926	Zorgvliet, The Hague
1927-35	Municipal Museum, The Hague
1929	Town Hall, Usquert
1930	De Nederlanden van 1845 Insurance Company Building, Utrecht

Publications

BOOKS BY BERLAGE

Over Stijl in Bouw- en Meubelkunst. Rotterdam, 1904. 2nd ed., 1908. 3rd ed., 1917.
Gedanken über Stil in der Baukunst. Leipzig, 1905.
Grundlagen und Entwicklung der Architektur. Berlin and Rotterdam, 1908.
Studies over Bouwkunst, Stil en Samenleving. Rotterdam, 1910.
Een drietal Lezingen in Amerika gehouden. Rotterdam, 1912.
Amerikaansche Reisherinneringen. Rotterdam, 1913.
Schoonheid en Samenleving. Rotterdam, 1919. 2nd ed., 1924.
L'art et la société. Brussels, 1921.
De Ontwikkeling der moderne Bouwkunst in Holland. Amsterdam, 1925.
Het wezen der Bouwkunst en haar geschiedenis: aesthetische beschouwingen. Haarlem, 1934.

Hendrik Petrus Berlage: Stock Exchange [Beurs], Amsterdam, Netherlands, 1897-1903

ARTICLES BY BERLAGE

"Over Architectuur." *Tweemaandelijks Tijdschrift* 11 (1896).
"Frank Lloyd Wright." *Wendingen* 11 (special issue, 1921).

BOOKS ABOUT BERLAGE

DE BAZEL, K. P. C., et al.: *Dr. H. P. Berlage en zijn Werk.* Festschrift, 60th birthday. Rotterdam, 1916.
EISLER, M.: *Der Baumeister Berlage.* 1921.
GRATAMA, J.: *Dr H. P. Berlage, Bouwmeester.* Festschrift, 70th birthday. Rotterdam, 1925.
GRINBERG, DONALD: *Housing in the Netherlands 1900-1940.* 1977.
HAVELAAR, J.: *Dr H. P. Berlage.* Amsterdam, ca. 1927.
OUD, J. J. P.: *Het Hofplein van Dr. Berlage.* Rotterdam, 1922.
POLANO, S.: *Hendrik Petrus Berlage: Complete Works.* New York, 1988.
REININK, ADRIAAN WESSEL: *Amsterdam en de Beurs van Berlage: Reacties van Tijdgenoten.* The Hague, 1975.
SINGELENBERG, PIETER: *H. P. Berlage: Idea and Style—The Quest for Modern Architecture.* Utrecht, 1972.

ARTICLES ABOUT BERLAGE

"Berlage, Dudok and Weeber." *Wonen-TA BK* special issue (January 1983).
GRASSI, G.: "Un architetto e una città: Berlage ad Amsterdam" and "Immagine di Berlage." *Casabella* No. 249 (March 1961).

"H. P. Berlage." *Bouwkundig Weekblad Architectura* No. 51 special issue (1934).
SEARING, HELEN: "Berlage and Housing, 'the most significant modern building type'." *Nederlands Kunsthistorisch Jaarboek* 25 (1974): 133-179.

*

Next to P. J. H. Cuypers (1827-1921), the architect of the Rijksmuseum and the Central Station in Amsterdam, Hendrik Petrus Berlage can be considered the most important Dutch architect at the end of the 19th century. He was born in 1856 in Amsterdam, where he also began studying art at the Academy of Fine Arts. After a year he decided to leave that school for the Eidgenössische Technische Hochschule in Zurich, Switzerland, where he received most of his architectural education. The influence of the teachings of the former director of the Swiss school, Gottfried Semper, can be retraced not only in Berlage's early buildings but also in most of his writings. Another influence on Berlage's thinking—in many ways completely different from Semper—was that of the French architect Eugène-Emmanuel Viollet-le-Duc. It was the peculiar combination of these two major architectural theorists in the 19th century, along with some Dutch sources, that enabled Berlage to find a way out of historicism toward modernism.

Berlage's career was all but smooth, and was marked by a continuous search for a style of architecture that would be appropriate for his time. He began working in the studio of an engineer, Theodor Sanders, with whom he designed some projects that showed an interest in town-planning issues. Together they participated in the competition for the Amsterdam Stock Exchange in 1884.

In 1889 Berlage opened his own studio. His projects from that period continued to show a total dependency on historical styles. Only in the project for a *"monument historique"* conceived for the celebration of the 100th anniversary of the French Revolution did Berlage put the notion of historical styles into a statement that reflected a crisis of architectural language.

The office for the insurance company De Algemeene in Amsterdam (1891-94; enlarged in 1901-05, but since destroyed) marked an important change in Berlage's work. Influenced by a collaboration with the painter Antoon Derkinderen, he began a search for monumentality in architecture. The office, with its heavy, impressive facade, was the first result. Other buildings in which the scope was to achieve a certain monumentality—especially with the help of the block form—were the buildings for the insurance company De Nederlanden in Amsterdam (1894-95; enlarged in 1910-11) and in The Hague (1895-96; enlarged in 1901-02 and 1908-09), and the office of the Syndicate of Diamond-Cutters (ANDB), also in Amsterdam (1897-1900).

Contemporary with those office buildings were a couple of private houses in which the architect tried to arrive at *Wohnlichkeit* (hominess), which meant that the facade didn't have a representative function but was adapted to the inside. The best such example is the house for the philosopher Heymans in Groningen (1893-95).

In those years, Berlage elaborated his theory of an "impressionistic" architecture, which had nothing to do with impressionism in painting. Berlage believed that an architect should not preoccupy himself with ornament and other details, but should concentrate on the effect of volumes and mass. According to Berlage, ornament should be limited only to those areas where it was sure to be noticed. This theory of Berlage's, formulated in the conference "Bouwkunst en Impressionisme" (1894), was derived from that of the "pure visibility" of Gustav Fechner, Heinrich Wölfflin, Adolf Hildebrand and others.

The most remarkable work of Berlage, and a central element in his ouvre, is the Stock Exchange in Amsterdam (1896-1903), a project which was built after two competitions had led to no result. Thanks to this building, Berlage became an internationally renowned architect. The various designs for the building show a process of growing simplification. The actual building, which is characterized by *Sachlichkeit,* is a compendium of the architectonic and urbanistic problems with which Berlage was struggling. The different elevations reflect these problems and conflicts clearly: whereas the south and east fronts express monumentality, the others—in an attempt to connect the building with the existing city—are irregular and composed of more volumes. Berlage gave a dominant position to the massive tower, which catches the eye as one looks from the Dam (the central square in Amsterdam) toward the central Station. The tower pulls the spectator toward the square in front of the Stock Exchange, and to the main entrance.

A major contradiction is to be found between the ground plan and two main elevations. The theorist J. L. M. Lauwerijks noted in 1903 that whereas the ground plan is disposed on a grid pattern, the two elevations are built according to a system based on the Egyptian triangle. It is a demonstration that Berlage had not achieved the "unity in plurality" that was so dear to him. There is more unity to be found in Berlage's idealistic and utopian designs, such as those for the Beethovenhuis (1907-08), the Wagnertheater (1910) and the Pantheon der Menschheid (Pantheon of Humanity, 1915).

Another crucial building in Berlage's oeuvre is the Municipal Museum in The Hague. The first project dates from 1919-20, but a second design was executed from 1928 until the architect's death in 1934. There is an interesting difference between the two projects. The first still shows an architectural language close to that of the Stock Exchange, but in the second version the volumetric elevation is stressed. The building would have been inconceivable without W. M. Dudok's Town Hall in Hilversum, begun in 1915. Berlage experimented with Dudok's method of stacking volumes, and transformed it into a result that has the same "bareness" of Dudok's masterpiece. Berlage's interest in volumetric composition was already noticeable in his design for the Christian Science Church in The Hague (1925-26).

Although Berlage began his career in Amsterdam, it was The Hague that offered him the most opportunities. In 1907 he was asked to project a general plan for the expansion of the city. Instead of creating an organic plan, which would have permitted an easy flow of traffic, Berlage conceived a plan made of parts. These parts formed the "rooms" of the city, familiar places that would make easy orientation possible, and with which the inhabitants could identify. He combined elements of the garden city with elements of a more compact city. Berlage even copied the plan of Karlsruhe in Germany, and inserted a design by K. P. C. de Bazel for a world city.

Berlage also designed plans for the cities of Amsterdam (1901-05 and 1914-17), Utrecht (1920), Batavia in Indonesia (1923-25) and Groningen (1927-28). It would be wrong, however, to put too much emphasis on his importance as a town planner: for Berlage, towns existed above all only because of architecture.

—HERMAN VAN BERGEIJK

BERNINI, Giovanni Lorenzo.

Italian. Born in Naples, Italy, 7 December 1598. Died in Rome, 28 November 1680. Son of the sculptor Pietro Lorenzo Bernini. Trained in his father's workshop in Rome. Elected president of the Academy of St. Luke by 1621; master of the Royal Foundry, 1623, and architect to St. Peter's, 1629; prepared designs for Louis XIV's rebuilding of the Louvre, Paris, 1665.

Chronology of Works
All in Italy
* *Approximate dates*

1624-26	Santa Bibiana, Rome (renovation)
1624-33	St. Peter's, Rome (baldacchino)
1627-29	Barcaccia Fountain, Piazza di Spagna, Rome
1627-41	St. Peter's, Rome (reliquary loggias)
1627-47	St. Peter's, Rome (Tomb of Urban III)
1629-40*	Palazzo Barberini, Rome (with others)
1630	Santa Maria in Aracoeli, Rome (Catafalque for Carlo Barberini)
1634-39	Cappella dei Re Magi, Palazzo di Propaganda Fide, Rome
1634-35	San Paolo, Bologna (high altar)
1636-43	Santa Maria in Via Lata, Rome (apse and high altar)
1637-42	St. Peter's, Rome (campanili)
1638	Palazzo del Quirinale, Rome (benediction loggia)
1640-44	San Lorenzo in Damaso, Rome (apse decoration)
1640-47	Raimondi Chapel, San Pietro in Montorio, Rome
1641-49	Santa Maria Nova, Rome (confessio)
1642-43	Triton Fountain, Piazza Barberini, Rome

1644	Api Fountain, Rome	

1644   Api Fountain, Rome
1644   Palazzo di Propaganda Fide, Rome (north facade)
1645-48 St. Peter's, Rome (decoration of nave)
1647-51 Cornaro Chapel, Santa Maria della Vittoria, Rome
1648-51 Four Rivers Fountain, Piazza Navona, Rome
1649-50 Alaleona Chapel, Santi Domenico e Sisto, Rome
1651-54 Moro Fountain, Rome
1652-54 Chapel of Saint Barbara, Cathedral, Rieti
1652-56 Chigi Chapel, Santa Maria del Popolo, Rome (restoration)
1653-55 Palazzo di Montecitorio (Ludovisi), Rome
1655ff. Santa Maria del Popolo, Rome (restoration of interior and facade)
1656-58 Porta del Popolo, Rome (restoration)
1656-59 Quirinal Palace, Rome (extension)
1656-67 Piazza di San Pietro, Rome
1657-66 Cathedral Pietri, St. Peter's, Rome
1658-61 San Tommaso di Villanova, Castel Gondalfo, Rome
1658-63 Arsenal, Civitavecchia
1658-64 Chigi Chapel, Cathedral, Siena
1658-70 Sant'Andrea al Quirinale, Rome
1660-63* De Silva Chapel, Sant'Isidoro, Rome
1660-66 Fonseca Chapel, San Lorenzo in Lucina, Rome
1662-64 Santa Maria dell'Assunzione, Ariccia
1663-66 Scala Regia, Vatican Palace, Rome
1664-66 Palazzo Chigi (later Odescalchi), Rome (reconstruction)
1668-70 Ponte Sant'Angelo, Rome (reconstruction and decoration)
1671-75 Altieri Chapel, San Francesco a Ripa, Rome
1671-78 St. Peter's, Rome (Tomb of Alexander VII)
1673-74 Chapel of the Holy Sacrament, St. Peter's, Rome (decoration)

Publications

BOOKS ABOUT BERNINI

BALDINUCCI, FILIPPO: *Vita del Cavaliere Bernini*. Rome, 1682; Milan, 1948; as *Life of Gian Lorenzo Bernini*, translated by Catherine Enggass. University Park, Pennsylvania, 1966.

BAUER, GEORGE C.: *Bernini in Perspective*. Englewood Cliffs, New Jersey, 1976.

BERNINI, DOMENICO: *Vita del Cavalier Gio. Lorenzo Bernini*. Rome, 1713; Ann Arbor, Michigan, 1980.

BIRINDELLI, MASSIMO: *La machina heroica: Il disegno di Gianlorenzo Bernini per piazza San Pietro*. Rome, 1980.

BORSI, FRANCO: *Il palazzo di Montecitorio*. Rome, 1967.

BORSI, FRANCO: *La chiesa di S. Andrea al Quirinale*. Rome, 1967.

BORSI, FRANCO: *Bernini architetto*. Milan, 1980.

BRAUER, HEINRICH, and WITTKOWER, RUDOLF: *Die Zeichnungen des Gianlorenzo Bernini*. 2 vols. New York, 1970.

FAGIOLO DELL'ARCO, MAURIZIO, and FAGIOLO DELL'ARCO, MARCELLO: *Bernini: Una introduzione al gran teatro del Barocco*. Rome, 1967.

FAGIOLO DELL'ARCO, MAURIZIO, and CARANDINI, SILVIA: *L'effemero barocco*. 2 vols. Rome, 1977-78.

FAGIOLO, MAURIZIO: *Bernini: Architecture, Sculpture and Painting—The Creator of the Baroque*. 1981.

FRÉART, PAUL, SIEUR DE CHANTELOU: *Journal du Voyage en France du Cavalier Bernin*. Paris, 1885.

GOULD, C. *Bernini in France: An Episode in Seventeenth Century History*. Princeton, New Jersey, 1982.

HIBBARD, HOWARD: *Bernini*. Harmondsworth, England, 1965.

KITAO, TIMOTHY K.: *Circle and Oval in the Square of St. Peter's: Bernini's Art of Planning*. New York, 1974.

LAVIN, IRVING: *Bernini and the Crossing of St. Peter's*. New York, 1968.

LAVIN, IRVING: *Bernini and the Unity of the Visual Arts*. 2 vols. New York, 1980.

LAVIN, IRVING ET AL: *Drawings by Gianlorenzo Bernini from the Museum der Bildenden Künste Leipzig*. Princeton, New Jersey, 1981.

PANE, R.: *Gianlorenzo Bernini, Architetto*. Venice, 1953.

VARRIANO, J.: *Italian Baroque and Rococo Architecture*. New York, 1986.

WITTKOWER, RUDOLF: *Art and Architecture in Italy 1600-1750*. 3rd. ed., Baltimore and Harmondsworth, England, 1973.

WITTKOWER, RUDOLF: *Gian Lorenzo Bernini, The Sculptor of the Roman Baroque*. 3rd ed., Ithaca, New York, 1981.

ARTICLES ABOUT BERNINI

BAUER, G.: "Gian Lorenzo Bernini: The Development of an Architectural Iconography." Ph.D. dissertation. Princeton University, Princeton, New Jersey, 1974.

BLUNT, ANTHONY: "The Palazzo Barberini: the Contributions of Maderno, Bernini and Pietro da Cortona." *Journal of the Warburg and Courtauld Institutes* 21 (1958): 256-287.

CONNORS, J.: "Bernini's S. Andrea al Quirinale: Payments and Planning." *Journal of the Society of Architectural Historians* 41 (March 1982): 15-37.

FICHERA, FRANCESCO: "Juvarra tra Bernini e Borromini." *Quadrivio* 49 (1935).

FROMMEL, C. L.: "S. Andrea al Quirinale: genesi e struttura." In *Gianlorenzo Bernini architetto e l'architettura europea del sei-settecento*, ed. Gianfranco Spagnesi and Marcello Fagiolo. Rome, 1983.

HAGER, HELLMUT: "Bernini, Mattia de Rossi and the Church of S. Bonaventura at Monterano." *Architectural History* 21 (1978): 68-78.

HAGER, HELLMUT: "Gian Lorenzo Bernini e la ripresa dell' Alto Barocco nell'architettura del Settecento Romano." In *Atti del Convegno Bernini e il Barocco Europeo*. Rome, 1981.

KIRWIN, W. CHANDLER: "Bernini's Baldacchino Reconsidered." *Römisches Jahrbuch für Kunstgeschichte* 19 (1981): 143-171.

MARDER, T.: "The Evolution of Bernini's Designs for the facade of Sant'Andrea al Quirinale: 1658-76." *Architectura* 20, vol. 21: 108-132.

SMYTH-PINNEY, J. M.: "The Geometrics of S. Andrea al Quirinale." *Journal of the Society of Architectural Historians* XLVIII (1989): 53-65.

WITTKOWER, RUDOLF: "Palladio and Bernini." In *Palladio and English Palladianism*. London, 1974.

*

Giovanni Lorenzo Bernini was the son of the Florentine sculptor Pietro Bernini. The family moved from Naples to Rome in about 1606, where Giovanni Lorenzo entered the service of Cardinal Scipione Borghese as a sculptor, then worked for the first of eight pontiffs, Paul V Borghese (1605-21). Bernini became an expansive courtier, much at ease with princely patrons. He was also patronized by Cardinal Maffeo Barberini, who later became Pope Urban VIII (1623-44). This service led to his earliest grand project, the gilded bronze

Giovanni Lorenzo Bernini: St. Peter's Square, Rome, Italy, 17th century

canopy in the Basilica of St. Peter (1624-33), marking the high altar and grave of its onomastic saint and first pope. The *baldacchino* was supported by twisted columns modeled on those preserved from Constantine's first basilica and inspired by Old Testament descriptions of the Temple of King Solomon in Jerusalem. In its almost 10 stories, the *baldacchino* appears as a building within a building, too grand to be considered just a work of sculpture. It blurs the borders between sculpture and architecture. It encloses an important space, yet its ebullient character is more in the tenor of Bernini's sculpture, for he took a more conservative approach to his architecture. He worked on this early project with the assistance of Francesco Borromini.

During those same years, the discovery of the remains of Saint Bibiena led the pope to commission a facade for her church (1624-26), which represented Bernini's first independent architectural undertaking. He created a square facade of two stories with three flat bays above three arcuated bays. Superimposed clustered pilasters added a planar restraint. They supported a broken pediment to create a central vertical axis. Bernini's use of the more slender Ionic order was iconographically appropriate for a church dedicated to a female martyr.

On the death of Carlo Maderno in 1629, Bernini succeeded him as architect of St. Peter's. Bernini's other projects at the time included a cataflque for the funeral of Cardinal Barberini and a high altar for the Chruch of San Paolo in Bologna. He also succeeded Maderno in the construction of the Palazzo Barberini, again with the assistance of Borromini, but the contributions of each are not easily distinguished. From the evidence of drawings, Bernini's participation appears to have been decorative.

Bernini had also inherited Maderno's project for the bell towers to flank the facade of St. Peter's. They had reached the height of the facade when progress was halted with the discovery of an underground stream threatening the stability of the tower on the south side (or viewer's left when facing the facade). As the office of the Fabbrica was determined to proceed with the project, Bernini presented a wooden model for towers in late 1636 that were even larger and more expensive than Maderno's. The south tower was up by mid-1641, then removed because it looked too small. It is known from drawings, a painting and engravings. Work on the north tower halted with the death of the pope in 1644. The decision of Urban VIII's successor, Innocent X Pamphili, to terminate the project in 1646 badly damaged Bernini's reputation.

Bernini turned to other projects in the 1640s, such as the Raimondi Chapel in San Pietro in Montorio, where he utilized white marble and hidden windows to highlight the altar. He worked at Santa Maria in Via Lata (1636-43) and designed the *Confessio* for Saint Francesca Romana in Santa Maria Nova (1641-49).

With the ascendency of the Chigi pope, Alexander VII (1655-67), Bernini began to design the piazza of the Vatican basilica. The heavy-handed approach typical of papal city planning schemes involved the demolition of Raphael's Palazzo dell'Aquila and Paul V's clock tower at the entrance to the Vatican. The sloping site was suitable for the intended multiple uses of the space, both civic and religious. A large area was needed to accommodate pilgrims, and to contain the crowds at papal appearances from the pope's apartments to the north, and especially at Easter to witness his blessing *urbi et orbi* from the central balcony of the basilica's facade. Bernini's choice of a transverse oval plan offered better views of both locations when the papal *epiphania* took place. Too, the broader roads and increased reliance on coaches with teams of two and four horses required larger spaces throughout the city.

Bernini's integration of his new piazza with Maderno's old facade involved a brilliant conflation of elements as a solution to several problems. The liberties taken with the classical orders by Italian architects in the 16th century paved the way for Bernini. He defined the periphery of the piazza space with a stout colonnade of the Tuscan order supporting an Ionic frieze. By his use of the latter, Bernini created an unbroken horizontal that tied the piazza together visually and created a sense of compression as it abutted the cathedral's facade. The use of Tuscan columns placed the meeting of vertical and horizontal at a lower point on the broad facade in a further attempt to emphasize its verticality.

The piazza began with a trapezoidal space extended as a colonnade from the facade of St. Peter's, with the narrow base of the trapezoid tangential to an oval at its short axis. Bernini had depicted the colonnade in a crude sketch as analogous to the arms of the church embracing its faithful. A short loggia was to complete the oval extension of the colonnade at the far end of the piazza opposite the facade, but not connecting with it physically, thereby leaving two openings. The obelisk, which had been set in place by Domenico Fontana for Sixtus V in 1586, became a visual fulcrum for the space of the piazza, aligning the transverse axis of the oval with the facade. The oval itself was a fusion of two circles, the centers of which were used to align the columns in the arcs of the colonnade. The colonnade circumscribing the piazza was comprised of four sets of parallel columns more widespaced at the center to create a covered loggia for carriage and pedestrian traffic. Bernini sought the sense of awe and exhilaration in ancient Roman piazzas, such as that at the Pantheon, engendered by the sudden opening of space as one meandered through the winding streets of Rome, and underscored by the play of water in fountains. Bernini moved Carlo Maderno's fountain to the north and installed a counterpart in the oval's south cusp. The present vista from the facade to the Tiber was a result of Mussolini's planning in 1936.

Bernini's many fountain projects, such as the Barcaccia, (1627-29) in the Piazza di Spagna, the Triton (1642) in the Piazza Barberini, and the Four Rivers of Piazza Navona (1648-51), were more sculptural than architectural, but also grand engineering projects. The plentiful sources of water in Rome simplified problems of hydraulic engineering for Bernini

From 1663 to 1666, Bernini devoted his attention to the staircase, or Scala Regia, linking the papal apartments with the Vatican basilica at its narthex and north colonnade. It presented a problem because the corridor's walls were not parallel. This was cleverly corrected by Bernini, who created a double colonnade within the corridor, varying the thickness of the columns, their height and their distance from the wall in an optical solution. The columns also added a processional air, and Bernini's use of directed light at the landings gave the impression of *epiphania*. At the foot of the staircase, he placed papal arms with trumpeting personifications of Fame above the entrance arch adjacent to his own marble figures of Constantine on a rearing horse to add a note of grandeur, and to reinforce the physical ascent of the staircase both visually and symbolically.

Bernini initiated work on a trio of churches in the late 1650s. He utilized a number of similar elements for the interior articulation of all three structures, such as the combination of ribs and coffers in the domes, which had been an innovation of Pietro da Cortona. Bernini made his coffers diminish in size as they rose within the cupola to reinforce the illusion of height in the

Giovanni Lorenzo Bernini: Sant'Andrea al Quirinale, Rome, Italy, 1658-70

dome, an approach used earlier by Borromini in his San Carlo alle Quattro Fontane (1638-41).

Bernini donated his services in the construction of Sant' Andrea al Quirinale (1658-70) for Jesuit novices, its expenses financed by Camillo Pamphili. Domenico Bernini, in his biography of his father's career, identified the church as Bernini's favorite work of architecture. Bernini labored under the conditions of a shallow site near Borromini's daring San Carlo alle Quattro Fontane, and of restrictions in height to preserve the view from the Quirinal Palace opposite. He chose a transverse oval for its plan. The use of a short axis to align the altar with the entrance responded to the demands of the shallow site, and created liturgical immediacy. Bernini placed paired chapels to the left and right of the altar with piers situated at the apogee of the long axis. He distinguished the altar bay with a pediment supported by paired, freestanding and engaged columns. Bernini filled the broken gable of the pediment with Antonio Raggi's figure of Saint Andrew ascending on a bank of clouds to the oval oculus of the dome. He decorated the latter with hexagonal coffers and 10 ribs continuing the vertical sweep of the 10 pilasters from the floor level, interrupted only by the continuous horizontal of the entablature. In honor of Saint Andrew and appropriate for the Jesuit missions, rose-colored, veined marble alluded to the blood of martyrdom which earned the heavenly splendor symbolized by the gilded stucco in the dome. Bernini's fenestration is visible at the base of the dome on the interior but appears sunken within the drum from the exterior in an approach similar to Borromini's at San Carlo.

Sant'Andrea has the grandeur and appearance of monumentality of so many Italian Baroque churches, but in reality it is modest in size. Bernini's exterior is both stark and bold. Two pilasters support a triangular gable and serve as a frame for two freestanding columns. These sustain a convex roof-entablature with a broken scroll pediment framing the Pamphili arms.

Bernini's San Tommaso di Villanova (1658-61) is situated near the pontifical palace at Castel Gondalfo, the summer residence of the pope just 30 miles south of Rome. The occasion for its construction was the canonization of the saint in 1658. Bernini devised a modest Greek-cross plan with a square crossing. In the interior, his combination of colored marbles with gilded stucco coffers and ribs above, and the low drum with eight windows matched the usage at Sant' Andrea. Windows in the dome rest on a circular entablature supported by pendentives at the corners of the crossing. Bernini's flat treatment of the exterior's cross arms is reminiscent of the Renaissance austerity of Giuliano da Sangallo's Santa Maria delle Carceri in Prato (1485). Superimposed pilasters of the Tuscan order support projecting entablatures at each level of a two-story elevation with a triangular pediment above.

For Santa Maria dell'Assunzione (1662-64), opposite the Chigi family palace in Ariccia, Bernini used the Pantheon (which he was renovating, 1656-67) as a point of departure. His facade is a portico of triple arches separated by Tuscan pilasters with a triangular pediment above. The stark exterior offers a contrast to the finely modulated interior. The church proper has a circular drum supporting a dome, with eight ribs and hexagonal coffers leading to the oculus of the lantern. The vertical emphasis of the interior is borne by eight fluted Corinthian pilasters interrupted by the unbroken circle of the entablature. The circular plan with its multiplicity of chapels tends to de-emphasize the main altar. On completion of the church, the Chigi commissioned Bernini to remodel their palace in Rome (1664-66).

The Palazzo Chigi was expanded by Nicola Salvi (1697-1751) when the Odescalchi family purchased it in 1745, but Bernini's original intentions are known from surviving engravings. He created a facade of 13 bays in a three-story elevation with quoins at the ends of recessed wings, their horizontal rustication emphasizing the verticality of the seven central bays. These Bernini defined with eight colossal-order pilasters. In its regal elegance, the Palazzo Chigi became the exemplar of Bernini's palace architecture.

—EDWARD J. OLSZEWSKI

BINDESBØLL, Gottlieb.

Danish. Born Michael Gottlieb Bindesbøll in Ledöje, Seeland, 5 September 1800. Died in Copenhagen, Denmark, 14 July 1856. Studied architecture at the Kunstakademie, Copenhagen; traveled to Germany and France, 1822-23; studied in Italy and Greece, 1834-38. Worked in Copenhagen, 1838-47; building inspector for the duchy of Holstein, 1847; building inspector for Jutland, 1849; practiced in Copenhagen, 1851-56; professor of architecture, Kunstakademie, Copenhagen, 1856.

Chronology of Works
All in Denmark unless noted

1839	Thorvaldsen Studio, Nysø
1839-47	Thorvaldsen Museum, Copenhagen
1844	Bathing Establishment, Klampenborg
1850-51	Jutland Asylum, near Århus
1850-52	Church, Hobrø
1851-53	City Hall, Thisted
1852	City Hall, Flensburg, Germany
1853-54	City Hall, Stege
1853-55	Medical Association Housing Project, Copenhagen
1853-57	Hospital, Oringe
1855-56	City Hall, Naestved
1856-58	Royal Veterinary and Agricultural School, Copenhagen (main block)

Publications

BOOKS ABOUT BINDESBØLL

BRAMSEN, HENRIK: *Gottlieb Bindesbøll: Liv og Arbejder.* Copenhagen, 1959.
BRUUN, CHARLES and FENGER, L. P.: *Thorvaldsens Musaeums Historie.* Copenhagen, 1892.
MILLECH, KNUD: *Bindesbølls Museum.* Copenhagen, 1960.
MILLECH, KNUD: *J. D. Herholdt og Universitets-bibliotekt i Fiolstraede.* Copenhagen, 1961.
WANSCHER, VILHELM: *Arkitekten G. Bindesbøll.* Copenhagen, 1903.

ARTICLES ABOUT BINDESBØLL

JØRGENSEN, LISBET BALSLEV: "Thorvaldsen's Museum: A National Monument." *Apollo* New Series 96, Part 1 (July-September 1972): 198-205.
KOCH, M.: "M. Gottlieb Bindesbølls mobler i Thorvaldsens Museum." *Meddelelser fra Thorvaldsens Museum* (1948).
WANSCHER, VILHELM: "Gottlieb Bindesboll." *Artes* 1 (1932).

*

M. G. Bindesbøll was the romantic individualist among the architects of his day. Stylistically audacious, he used many different forms of expression, depending on the nature of the project and its literary and historical resonances; but he managed to impart a distinctive stamp to all his work, a personal signature unusual in an historicizing era. Bindesbøll lived in a period of transition, when neoclassicism still dominated in Denmark, though without its initial vigor: it was as conservative and absolute as the monarchy, which also had its critics. Bindesbøll solved many of the architectural problems posed by the requirements of an expanding new state, which had been established by the Constitution of 1849. His short career produced relatively few—but significant—buildings, many of them for the state. His last works mark out a style that has been called objective for its concision and economy of material and form; these would be important models for Danish functionalism.

Originally trained as a millwright, Bindesbøll chose mathematics and physics when given the chance to pursue academic study. Interestingly, H. C. Ørsted, the discoverer of electromagnetism, chose the youth as a traveling companion on a European tour. During the trip Bindesbøll became interested in architecture, which he began to study in 1823. He served as the court architect J. H. Koch's clerk of works while still at the Copenhagen Academy of Art: a promising student, he won all the academy's prizes between 1824 and 1833, including the Major Gold Medal and its travel scholarship. After his return from Greece and Rome he won the competition to build a museum for Bertel Thorvaldsen's sculptures (1839-47). He was the Jutland inspector of buildings from 1849 to 1851, when he was called back to the capital. Not until 1847 did he become a member of the Art Academy, and it was only in 1856, shortly before his death, that he was appointed as the professor of architecture there: his significance for the next generation of architects lay exclusively in his executed buildings.

Thorvaldsen's Museum was his first project and his masterpiece, perhaps the most interesting Danish building of the 19th

Gottlieb Bindesbøll: Thorvaldsen Museum, Copenhagen, Denmark, 1839-47

century, with which Bindesbøll ranged himself among the most original and creative architects of the period. Greek and Italian antiquity was clearly inspirational, but Bindesbøll's empirical approach to his models, the personal contrivances, the richness of his colors and the surprising details put the museum into a special class. A distinctive portal motif with battered sides, probably of Etruscan origin, dominates the western entrance facade to grand effect; it is reiterated in the windows of the side walls. The interior glitters with the colors of Pompeiian-style murals and floor mosaics; but it is the painted exterior that is most extraordinary. Against a background of warm ocher the building's structural frame is outlined in clear blue, green and white. A painted frieze runs around three sides of the building, over the socle. This original idea was carried out by the painter Jørgen Sonne: the frieze shows the long journey Thorvaldsen's sculptures had made from Rome to Copenhagen. The museum is one of the very few 19th-century exhibition buildings in which the then-intense debate about the relationship between architecture and art was actually resolved; Bindesbøll's is a vibrant and original house for works of art. The museum also made an important contribution to the international, and otherwise predominantly theoretical, discussion about poly-chromy in architecture.

As the inspector of buildings for Jutland, Bindesbøll built a church for Hobro (1850-52) in a Gothic style, where pinnacle gables provide the dominant theme; the tower, ostentatiously placed at the east of the church, nonetheless shows the selectivity of his neo-Gothicism. His interest in the Netherlandish Renais-sance—Kronborg Castle, he declared, was his favorite build-ing—is apparent in the Stege Town Hall (1853-54).

Also from that period is his design for a mental hospital, the Jutland Asylum north of Århus (1850-51), a project Bindesbøll

inherited from his predecessor, F. F. Friis. The chief physician of the hospital was Harald Selmer, a pioneer of Danish psychiatry. Collaboration between doctor and architect resulted in a hospital whose modernity placed Denmark among the nations leading in the institutional care of the insane. The surrounding landscape was shaped so the patients could benefit from "that humanizing influence which landscape and the external forms of daily life can also give to the healthy psyche." The traditional Danish manor type clearly determined the overall plan of the complex. A limited budget resulted in simple, uniform buildings in yellow and red brick and red roof tiles, sparsely decorated and accented only by shaped gables. The buildings symmetrically unfold themselves dog-leg fashion from a central wing that held the doctors' apartments, chapel, dispensary, mortuary, library and assembly hall. The complex's center axis was the border be-tween the male and female divisions of the hospital. The central block and side wings are two stories, but the furthest wings, originally for disruptive patients, are one story. The layout of the wings and their reciprocal relations represented Bindesbøll's most important contribution to the project: by such simple means, and with his appreciation for the surrounding landscape, he created an institution that inspires a mood of affection and peace, one entirely devoid of monumentality.

The plans for another mental hospital, St. Hans in Roskilde (1852-53), were never executed. Bindesbøll's development of this building type culminated at Oringe Mental Hospital on Zealand (1854-57), built after his death. The buildings are en-tirely free of historicism, and the hospital stands as a free experiment in line and form shaped around the elements found in the two earlier projects and the planning principles established there.

The Medical Association's housing block at Østerbro, Copenhagen (1853-55), was built as a philanthropic venture. The two-story terrace for the poor was designed with Bindesbøll's usual care: light and air were freely admitted into the small apartments, whose exteriors conform to the urban street aesthetic. The building represents an early example of English influence. Copenhagen's Veterinary and Agricultural College (1856), finished after Bindesbøll's death, is more emphatic than most of his late works, with its large, arched windows, the crow-step gables and the semicircular projection of the auditorium. This well-integrated building offers a fine conclusion to his career.

Bindesbøll had no pupils at the time of his death. He was an individualist whose buildings were certainly inspirational, but did not lend themselves to imitation. Thorvaldsen's Museum, though a successful, vibrant work of art, is something unique—and matchless. A clear line can be traced from the hospitals to modern buildings like those at Århus University (begun in 1932). Twentieth-century architects have used Bindesbøll's experience in their cultivation of an institutional form with human proportions, openness and contact with the natural surroundings, as well as a formal language that is not vociferous or loud, but in its soft way inspires true confidence.

—WIVAN MUNK-JØRGENSEN
Translated from the Danish by Christine Stevenson

BLONDEL, Jacques-François.

French. Born in Rouen, France, 8 January 1705. Died in Paris, 9 January 1774. Father was the architect Jean François Blondel (1681-1756). Studied with his uncle, the architect François Blondel II (1683-1748). Opened architecture school in Paris, 1739; professor at Académie Royale d'Architecture, 1756; practiced in Metz, 1764-76.

Chronology of Works
All in France
* Approximate dates
† Work no longer exists

1745	Port St. Martin, Paris (decoration)
1748	Archbishop's Palace, Cambrai
1748	Blondel House, Paris (remodeling)
1748	Gallery, Hôtel de Choiseul, Paris (decoration)
1761-71	Cathedral, Metz (principal portal)†
1767*	Cathedral, Strasbourg (aubette and screen)

Publications

BOOKS BY BLONDEL

De la Distribution des Maisons de Plaisance et de la Décoration des Edifices en General. 2 vols. 1737-38. Reprint: Farnborough, England 1967.
Disours sur la Manière d'Etudier L'Architecture, et les Arts qui sont Relatifs a celui de Bastir. Paris, 1747.
*L'Architecture François, ou Recueil de Plans, d'Elévations, Coupes et Profils....*8 vols. 1752-56. Reprint: Paris,1904-05.
Discours sur la Nécessité de l'Etude de l'Architecture. Paris, 1754.
De l'Utilité de Joindre à l'Etude de l'Architecture, celle des Sciences et des Arts qui lui Sont Relatifs. Paris, 1771.
L'Homme du Monde Eclairé par les Arts. 1774. Reprint: Geneva, 1973.
Cours d'Architecture. With Pierre Patte. 9 vols. Paris, 1771-77.

ARTICLES BY BLONDEL

Numerous articles on architecture in volumes 1-7 of the *Encyclopédie*, ed. by Denis Diderot and Jean le Rond d'Alembert. Paris, 1750-76.

BOOKS ABOUT BLONDEL

BAROZZIO DE VIGNOLE, JACQUES: *Livre Nouveau ou Règles des Cinq Ordres d'Architecture...,Nouvellement Revu...par monsieur B*** Architecte du Roy....*Paris, 1767.
BRAHAM, ALAN: *The Architecture of the French Enlightenment.* Berkeley, California, 1980.
ERIKSON, SVEND: *Early Neo-Classicism in France.* London, 1974.
GALLET, MICHEL: *Stately Mansions: Eighteenth Century Paris Architecture.* New York, 1972.
KAUFMANN, EMIL: *Architecture in the Age of Reason: Baroque and Post-Baroque in England, Italy, and France.* New York, 1955.
LEJEAUX, JEANNE: *La Place d'Armes de Metz.* Strasbourg, France, 1927.
PROST, AUGUSTE: *Jacques-François Blondel at Son Oeuvre.* Metz, France, 1860.

ARTICLES ABOUT BLONDEL

COURAJOD, LOUIS: 'Introduction: L'Enseignement de l'Art Français aux Différentes Epoques de son Histoire.' Pages LXDVII-LXXIX in *L'Ecole Royale des Elèves Protégés.* Paris, 1874.
DAZALLIER D'ARGENVILLE, A. N.: 'Jacques-François Blondel.' Vol. 1, pp. 467-73 in *Vies des Fameux Architectes depuis la Renaissance des Arts, avec une Description de leurs Ouvrages.* Reprint. Geneva, (1787)1972.
FRANQUE, FRANÇOIS: 'Eloge de J-F Blondel.' *Journal des Beaux-Arts et des Sciences* (March 1774): 559-70.
HARRINGTON, KEVIN: 'Architectural Relationships: Changing Ideas on Architecture in the Encyclopedie, 1750-1775.' Unpublished Ph.D. dissertation, Cornell University, Ithaca, New York, 1981.
HERRMANN, WOLFGANG: 'Jacques-François Blondel.' Appendix 9 in *Laugier and 18th Century French Theory.* London, 1962.
KAUFMANN, EMIL: 'The Contribution of J-F Blondel to Mariette's *Architecture François.*' *Art Bulletin* 31 (1949): 58-59.
LEJEAUX, JEANNE: 'Jacques-François Blondel: Professeur d'Architecture.' *L'Architecture* 40 (1927): 23-27.
LEJEAUX, JEANNE: 'La Cathédrale de 1750 à 1870 et l'Oeuvre de Blondel à Metz.' Chapter 2 in Marcel Aubert (ed.), *La Cathédrale de Metz.* Paris, 1931.
LENITRE, G.: 'J-F Blondel, et l'Architecture Français.' *L'Architecte* 5 (1910).
MIDDLETON, ROBIN: 'Jacques-François Blondel and the *Cours d'Architecture.*' *Journal of the Society of Architectural Historians* 18 (1959).
STURGES, W. KNIGHT: 'Jacques-François Blondel.' *Journal of the Society of Architectural Historians* 11 (1952).

*

Jacques-François Blondel was an architect and teacher of architecture, active in France in the middle years of the 18th century. Born in Rouen into a family of architects, he began his formal study with his uncle, learning also to draw and engrave; in addition, he worked with Gilles Marie Oppenord. From all his training, and from the books he read and the buildings he studied,

Blondel acquired a considerable knowledge and a great respect for the traditions of French design and architecture. He did not travel outside France, but familiar as he was with the published sources, he knew all that had been done recently, especially in Italy and England. He did not build much, and the little work he was responsible for was mostly outside of Paris, as with the Archbishop's House at Cambrai (1748) and the details he added in the Cathedrals of Metz and Strasbourg (late 1760s); he also produced some designs for the reorganization of Metz.

From the very beginning of his career, Blondel was actively involved with publishing books on architecture. And in 1743, despite great opposition from the Académie Royale d'Architecture, he took the remarkable step of opening an independent school of architecture in Paris, located on the rue de la Harpe. This was immediately popular, for the teaching was less conservative than that offered at the Académie; his school attracted students not only from France, such as Etienne Louis Boullée, Claude-Nicolas Ledoux and Charles de Wailly, but even foreigners who spread his ideas in their own countries, the most notable of these being the Englishman William Chambers.

Blondel's fundamental innovation was the establishment of a carefully organized curriculum that sought to include a great range of both theory and technique. The training was fixed for all the students, and it contained not only the study of so familiar a topic for architecture as proportion, but also training in such practical subjects as engineering and calculus that would allow students, of whatever experience and abilities, to complete all that was appropriate and possible for them. All this was based on three general principles. The first was an idea of rational analysis in the solving of architectural problems; the second was the idea of the significance of the particular problem, or program, in the construction of the general solution, relating this also to the other solutions of the problem; and the third was an emphasis on the importance of detail, from the very beginning to the end of any task.

Blondel himself was conservative in his tastes, the architect most satisfying to him being perhaps Ange-Jacques Gabriel. But he showed no preference for one style over another, emphasizing rather that for every project there was a rational solution, whatever the details used to give form to this. Much of what Blondel said might seem vague, phrases and words such as ''taste united to rule,'' ''symmetry,'' ''liveliness in planning and silhouette'' and, perhaps most elusively, ''bienséance'' or ''suitability.'' Yet however much or little these terms might mean by themselves, combined as they were with a devotion to the French classical tradition of architecture and especially to François Mansart, whom Blondel called ''the god of architecture,'' they fostered among those who followed a new style of rational and abstract architecture that, in the work of Boullée and Ledoux, might have been too advanced for Blondel's own particular tastes.

Blondel's methods were admitted by the Académie itself when in 1762 he was appointed to be its professor. And in the 12 volumes of his *Cours d'architecture,* based on his lectures and completed in the 1770s by his assistant Pierre Patte, the whole range and method of his teaching were laid out for all to read. Beyond his professional architecture students, Blondel sought to reach other audiences, most obviously professionals and craftsmen in the building trades, to whom he offered his classes on Sundays. He also conducted public lectures on architectural theory and led tours of buildings, completed and under construction, for both amateurs and, perhaps more important, for the bureaucrats of government who, of course, had a vital role in the commissioning and supervision of government buildings. Blondel's reasoning was simple: he believed that if there was a wider audience of sophisticated and reasoning patrons, unreason and mere fashion would be less likely to pass muster. Taste based on reason was, by his account, crucial to the whole purpose of architecture. And if this made light of the idea of genius, Blondel hardly cared; he considered the vast majority of cases where such genius was held to be the source of creative activity to be instances where the architect was unwilling to think and reason deeply. The social order required, in Blondel's analysis, more from reason than from any individual license.

All this theory Blondel promulgated in every way he could, and his influence can be recognized in a number of ways. He wrote, in the 1750s and 1760s, a number of entries in the *Encyclopédie,* and it is to such a source that we can trace the reflection of Blondel's ideas in someone such as Denis Diderot. Blondel's work was familiar also to Jean François Marmontel, another contributor to the encyclopedia, and secretary too of the marquis de Marigny in the royal bureaucracy. In William Chambers, who attacked the idea of absolute rules in architecture and asked instead for reason, we have an instance of all this theory translated into particular architectural actions. So too in Ledoux's book, *L'architecture Considérée sous le Rapport de l'Art des Moeurs et de la Legislation* (1804), where architecture is understood in terms of the laws and customs of a people, rather than through any absolute principles. The influence of Blondel's ideas was perhaps as much a reflection of his personality as of his mind. He was described always as generous and friendly and devoted to his students.

—DAVID CAST

BODLEY, George Frederick.

British. Born in Hull, England, 1827. Died in England, 21 October 1907. Studied with George Gilbert Scott, 1840; traveled to France. Partner with Thomas Garner (1839-1906), 1869-97. Royal Academy; Gold Medal, Royal Institute of British Architects, 1899.

Chronology of Works
All in England unless noted

1855-75	St. John the Baptist Church, France Lynch, Gloucestershire
1859-62	All Saints Church, Selsley, Gloucestershire
1861-63	St. Martin-on-the-Hill Church, Scarborough, Yorkshire
1863	All Saints Church, Dedworth, Berkshire
1863-65	St. Wilfred's Church, Hayward's Heath, Sussex
1863-69	All Saints Church, Cambridge
1865-70	St. Saviour Church, Dundee
1867	Vicarage, St. Martin-on-the-Hill Church, Scarborough, Yorkshire
1868-70	St. John the Baptist Church, Tue Brook, Liverpool
1870-74	St. Augustine's Church, Pendlebury, Lancashire
1872-79	Holy Angels Church, Hoar Cross, Staffordshire
1876-79	Master's Lodge, University College, Oxford
1879	3 Chelsea Embankment, London
1883-84	St. Germain's Church, Roath, Cardiff, Wales
1884-91	Hewell Grange, Worcestershire
1886-89	St. Mary's Church, Clumber, Nottinghamshire
1889-1909	St. John the Baptist Church, Epping, Essex
1890-91	Queens' College Chapel, Cambridge
1894-99	St. Mary's Church, Eccleston, Chestershire
1902	Holy Trinity Church, Prince Consort Road, London

1906   Cathedral of SS. Peter and Paul, Washington, D.C.,
              U.S.A. (built 1910-76)

Publications

BOOKS ABOUT BODLEY

ANSON, PETER F.: *Fashions in Church Furnishings: 1840-1940.*
    London, 1960.
CLARKE, BASIL F. L.: *Church Builders of the Nineteenth Cen-
    tury.* London, 1938.
EASTLAKE, CHARLES L.: *A History of the Gothic Revival.*
    London, 1872.
FAWCETT, JANE (ed.): *Seven Victorian Architects.* University
    Park, Pennsylvania, 1976.
SEWTER, A. C.: *The Stained Glass of Morris and His Circle.*
    2 vols. New Haven, Connecticut, and London, 1974-75.

ARTICLES ABOUT BODLEY

ADDLESHAW, G. W. O.: ''Architects, Sculptors, Painters, Crafts-
    men, 1660-1960, Whose Work Is to Be Seen in York Minis-
    ter.'' *Architectural History* 10 (1967): 89-119.
BRANDON-JONES, JOHN: ''Letters of Philip Webb and his Con-
    temporaries.'' *Architectural History* 8 (1965): 52-72.
SIMPSON, F. M.: ''George Frederick Bodley.'' *Journal of the
    Royal Institute of British Architects* Series 3, 15 (1908): 145-
    158.
THOMPSON, PAUL: *The Work of William Morris.* New York,
    1967.
VEREY, DAVID: ''The Victorian Architects' Work in Glouces-
    tershire.'' *Transactions of the Bristol and Gloucestershire
    Archaeological Society* 92 (1973): 5-11.
WARREN, EDWARD: ''The Life and Work of George Frederick
    Bodley.'' *Journal of the Royal Institute of British Architects*
    Series 3, 17 (1910): 305-340.

No architect of the second half of the 19th century was more
successful or more prolific than George Frederick Bodley (1827-
1907), whose churches in the Gothic style represent the climax
of the Gothic revival in England. He was deeply impressed
with John Ruskin's writings and the work of his friend, William
Butterfield, which directly influenced his bold, muscular, original work of the 1850s and 1860s. The heaviness of Bodley's
High Victorian work evolved by the early 1870s to typical Late
Victorian designs that featured magnificently decorated simple
spaces.

Bodley's mature style emerged in 1862 with the design of
the small French Gothic-style church of All Saints, Selsley,
Gloucestershire, a building typical of his High Victorian phase.
The building is composed of three masses, two major and one
minor. The major masses are the vertical tower mass and the
horizontal main body of the church containing the nave and
chancel. The minor mass, containing the sacristy and organ loft,
mediates between and enriches the two major forms. The effect
of the exterior is very simple; yet it is picturesque. Its appeal
depends upon the drama of the occult balance of the massive
geometric units, especially the relationship of vertical to horizontal masses, and the play of repeating design elements at
different scales.

This church, unlike Bodley's later churches, has minimal
constructional color or painted decoration. It depends for its
effect upon the strength and vigor of its spaces and forms, and
the effect is very strong, masculine and simple. The splendid

glass from the studio of William Morris complements the architecture.

Although Bodley was an architect of considerable ability, his
greatest talent was as a decorator of churches. His talent in this
area lay in his ability to see the interior as a whole and to be
able to bring all decoration—patterns, fittings, glass— into a
harmonious unit. In order to do this, he kept tight control over
every design decision, often even designing altar vessels and
vestments.

The Church of St. John the Baptist, Tue Brook, built in 1868,
remains one of the few existing examples where the sumptuous
unity of his decorative style can be seen and studied. At Tue
Brook, a comprehensive, sensitive restoration has been completed, and the church today is as bright and fresh as it was a
century ago.

The exterior of the church gives no hint of the glorious
decoration to be found inside. Though large and pleasing in its
form, there is nothing especially distinguished about its exterior.
It is an architecturally simple High Victorian church with a
west steeple and spire, a long nave with lower side aisles and
clerestory above, and a lower chancel, all built in a restrained
Decorated style.

The interior plan and resulting space are architecturally as
simple and straightforward as the exterior form. What truly
astonishes the modern visitor to St. John the Baptist, Tue Brook,
however, is the amazing variety of surface patterns which cover
virtually all of the church's interior surfaces. Even more astonishing is the unity of decorative effect achieved in spite of the
variety of devices utilized.

The weight of the structure is de-emphasized on the interior of
the church, mainly through the utilization of painted, decorative
devices. The stone construction is expressed in the interior only
in the piers, arches and lower wall surfaces. It is of two colors,
gray-beige and pinkish-tan, and is laid in alternating courses
of various heights. The stone seems very thin; it has a two-
dimensional rather than a three-dimensional character. The stenciled patterns painted on the plaster upper wall surfaces continue
to the intersections of the wall planes. In consequence, neither
stone nor plaster has any apparent thickness; two-dimensional
patterns dominate every surface; even the stone wainscot appears to have its pattern painted on.

A variety of stenciled Morris-like patterns are used to decorate
the plaster wall surfaces. Elegant stenciled borders separate
different wall patterns and mark intersections of walls and ceilings. The dark ceiling panels and the projecting beams and
purlins are decorated with stenciled medallions.

The focus of the nave space is on the rood screen, through
which is seen the richly decorated chancel. The delicacy of
Bodley's screen suggests spatial separation without obscuring
view.

Pattern complexity and color richness increase in the chancel.
Gilt, red and navy replace the restrained colors of the nave and
aisles. The carpet that leads to the altar, the railing of the screen,
the drapery of the altar and the walls of the chancel on either
side of the reredos use these colors in patterns borrowed from
Safavid Persia. The upper walls of the chancel are decorated
in a complex foliate stenciled pattern that is paisley-like in
effect. The chancel ceiling is paneled much like the nave ceiling
but features gold star medallions against a teal background—
a stylized variation of the Gothic and early Renaissance ''starry
sky'' pattern.

The decorative patterns of St. John the Baptist, Tue Brook, do
more than decorate the space; they establish its very character.
Without them the space would seem heavy and ponderous,
because the rhythm of its structural components is slow and the
amount of wall as opposed to window is great. In contrast, the

decorative patterns are small-scaled, and their rhythms are lively and fast. In consequence, the space is lightened and humanized in scale. The color scheme and consistent overall character of the decoration give the space visual unity. The concentration of pattern complexity and color richness in the chancel area establishes its preeminence in the hierarchy of the building's spaces and focuses the attention of worshippers upon it.

Bodley's style changed dramatically in the 1870s. The change in his style is demonstrated by the Church of Holy Angels, Hoar Cross, Staffordshire (1872-1879). His austere, blunt, highly original High Victorian work changed to luxuriant, exceedingly refined, essentially derivative Late Victorian work. In his early work, Bodley meant to create something new; at Hoar Cross he intended to show what perfection was obtainable within the rubrics of English late medieval decoration and architecture.

Holy Angels seems to be a perfect 14th-century church. The only clue to its 19th-century origin is the perfection of its fabric. It is magnificent in its elegance and beauty, but it has little in common with Bodley's earlier work. The blocky muscular forms have given way to attenuated verticality; pattern and color have been replaced by monochromatic stone. Bodley, perhaps due to the influence of Thomas Garner, his new partner, had entered a new period that was essentially derivative and elegant rather than creative and bold, yet it is for the beauty of his Late Victorian churches that Bodley is primarily remembered today.

—C. MURRAY SMART, JR.

Germain Boffrand: Hôtel de Soubise, Paris, France, 1732-39

BOFFRAND, Germain.

French. Born in Nantes, France, 5 July 1667. Died in Paris, 18 March 1754. Father was the architect/sculptor Jean Boffrand. Studied sculpture with François Girardon and architecture with Jules Hardouin-Mansart. Joined the Département des Ponts-et-Chaussées, 1730s.

Chronology of Works
All in France unless noted

1700	Hôtel LeBrun, Paris
1702-22	Château, Lunéville, Lorraine
1704-05	Hôtel d'Argenton, Paris†
1704-06	Hunting Lodge, Bouchefort, near Brussels, Belgium†
1708	Château de Bugnéville, Lorraine†
1709-11	Petit Luxembourg, Paris
1710-12	Château de Croismare, Lorraine†
1711-14	Hôtel de Duras, Paris
1711-17	La Malgrange, near Nancy†
1712	Château de Commercy, Lorraine (central pavilion)
1712	Château d'Haroué, Lorraine
1712	Hôtel de Craon, Nancy
1712-14	Hôtel du Premier Président, Palais de Justice, Paris (renovation)†
1713-15	Hôtel de Torcy (now German Embassy), Paris
1715-22	Palais Ducal, Nancy†
1715-25	Arsenal, Paris (addition)
1717	Maison du Prince de Rohan, St.-Ouen, near Paris†
1725-27	Notre-Dame, Paris (restoration)
1729	Pavilion of the duchess of Maine, Arsenal, Paris
1730-47	St. Jacques, Lunéville [attributed]
1732-39	Hôtel de Soubise, Paris (oval salons)
1733-40	Well and Reservoir, Hospital, Bicêtre, near Paris
1746-51	Foundling Hospital, Paris†

Publications

BOOKS BY BOFFRAND

Livre d'architecture. Paris, 1745.

BOOKS ABOUT BOFFRAND

BABELON, JEAN-PIERRE: *Musée de l'histoire de France.* Vol. 1 in *Historiques et description des bâtiments des Archives Nationales.* Paris, 1958.

BLOMFIELD, REGINALD: *A History of French Architecture from the Death of Mazarin to the Death of Louis XV: 1661-1774.* London, 1921.

BLONDEL, JACQUES-FRANÇOIS: *L'architecture française.* 4 vols. 1752-56.

HAUTECOEUR, LOUIS: *Histoire de l'architecture classique en France.* Vols. 3 and 4. Paris, 1950 and 1952.

HERRMANN, WOLFGANG: *Laugier and Eighteenth Century French Theory.* London, 1962.

KALNEIN, WEND, and LEVEY, MICHAEL: *Art and Architecture of the Eighteenth Century in France.* Harmondsworth, England, 1972.

KAUFMANN, EMIL: *Architecture in the Age of Reason.* Cambridge, Massachusetts, 1955.

KIMBALL, FISKE: *Le Style Louis XV.* Paris, 1949.

KIMBALL, FISKE: *The Creation of the Rococo.* New York, 1943.

MOREY, MATHIEU PROSPER: *Notice sur la vie et les oeuvres de Germain Boffrand.* Nancy, France, 1866.

PATTE, PIERRE: *Discours sur l'architecture.* Paris, 1754.

PATTE, PIERRE: *Monuments érigés à la gloire de Louis XV.* Paris, 1765.

ARTICLES ABOUT BOFFRAND

BABELON, JEAN-PIERRE: "Les façades sur jardin des palais Rohan-Soubise." *Revue de l'art* 4 (1969): 66-73.

BABELON, JEAN-PIERRE: "Le palais de l'Arsenal à Paris." *Bulletin monumental* 128 (1970): 267-310.

BOUDON, FRANÇOISE: "Urbanisme et spéculation à Paris au XVIII siècle: Le terrain de l'Hôtel de Soissons." *Journal of the Society of Architectural Historians* 32 (1973): 267-307.

COCHE DE LA FERTÉ, ETIENNE: "Le Faubourg Saint Germain dans l'Orient séditieux." *Oeil* 176-177 (1969): 20-27.

GARMS, JÖRG: "Studien zu Boffrand." Ph.D. dissertation, University of Vienna, 1962.

GARMS, JÖRG: "Boffrand à l'église de la Merci." *Bulletin de la Société d'Histoire de l'Art Français* (1964): 184-187.

GARMS, JÖRG: "L'aménagement du parvis de Notre Dame par Boffrand." *Art de France* 4 (1964): 153-157.

GARMS, JÖRG: "Les projets de Mansart et de Boffrand pour le Palais Ducal de Nancy." *Bulletin monumental* 125 (1967): 231-246.

GARMS, JÖRG: "Projects for the Pont Neuf and the Place Dauphine in the First Half of the 18th Century." *Journal of the Society of Architectural Historians* 26 (1967): 102-113.

GARMS, JÖRG: "Der Grundriss der Malgrange I von Boffrand." *Wiener Jahrbuch für Kunstgeschichte* 22 (1969): 184-188.

GRANET, SOLANGE: "Le livre de vérité de la Place Louis XV." *Bulletin de la Société d'Histoire de l'Art Français* (1961): 107-113

MIDDELTON, ROBIN D.: "The Abbé de Cordemoy and the Gothic Ideal." *Journal of the Warburg and Courtauld Institutes* 25 (1962): 278-320.

*

Germain Boffrand was the most significant French architect of the first half of the 18th century. He was a valid link between the legacy of Jules Hardouin-Mansart and the architecture of Étienne-Louis Boullée, and he recovered forms and motifs of the 17th-century architect Louis Le Vau to reinvigorate the major architectural types of the period of Louis XV. After leaving the Bâtiments du Roi in 1699, Boffrand was extremely active in building and remodeling Parisian town houses while simultaneously cultivating an international reputation. He designed important works for the nobility of Lorraine, including the duke, for the elector Max Emmanuel of Bavaria, and he was even consulted by Johann Balthasar Neumann concerning the Schönborn residence at Würzburg. After a severe financial setback in 1719, Boffrand concentrated more on administration and teaching. In the 1730s he began a fruitful career with the Départment des Ponts-et-Chaussées (Department of Bridges and Roads) and assembled theoretical essays eventually published as the *Livre d'Architecture* (1745). Although Boffrand was an active and respected member of the Académie Royale d'Architecture, his theory and practice were attempts to expand the academic vocabulary. Unfortunately, a complete study relating Boffrand's theory to his buildings has not been written.

All of Boffrand's major town houses were built in the first two decades of the 18th century. His first effort, the Hôtel Le Brun, is a freestanding Palladian block with a minimum of decoration. The severity of Boffrand's facades distinguishes his work from that of his contemporaries. In general, Boffrand's facades are articulated through an arrangement of unadorned blocks, variations in fenestration, and a limited application of Régence motifs. At the Hôtel Le Brun, a Doric entablature and pediment offset the simplicity of the wall and provide touches of the *grand goût* which reflect the station and taste of owner Charles Le Brun, the *Premier Peintre du roi* (First Painter).

In his later *hôtels*, Boffrand appears to have incorporated elements from his theory. He believed that *convenance* and *commodité* were first principles of architecture, and in his search for flexibility of planning he reached back to the 17th century of France and Italy. Although based on a traditional town-house plan, the Hôtel Amelot contains an oval court that is picked up in the disposition of the *corps de logis,* and mandates an annular procession off the central axis. Combined with the spatial variety and the emphasis on curvilinear form, a new concept of planning is suggested. The elevation draws on those of Giovanni Lorenzo Bernini, and implies that Boffrand saw in the Italian architect something that is essentially French. The court facade is a pyramidal build-up of forms toward the concave *corps de logis,* which is distinguished by a giant order of pilasters. It is based on Bernini's Palazzo Chigi-Odescalchi in Rome, with a raised center section and two lower wings. The central emphasis, however, is counterbalanced by a continuous horizontal entablature.

The originality of Boffrand's plans and elevations is most evident in his *maisons de plaisance,* some of which were not realized but were published in his *Livre.* There, ideas latent in his hôtel and château design, such as centrifugal movement and picturesque articulation of the facade, are expressed more fully. Typically, the plans consist of a symmetrical core around which he developed a sophisticated system of axes and cross axes. The facades incorporate a fretwork-like balance of mass and void, verticals and horizontals.

These projects particularly exhibit an innovative treatment of elements derived from tradition. Bouchefort, a hunting pavilion for Max Emmanuel, belongs to a long line of centrally planned pavilions beginning with those of Andrea Palladio, but its spatial variety and dynamism make it unique. Malgrange, although primarily a retreat, required a number of public functions similar to those of a château, and the two solutions demonstrate Boffrand's facility in combining plan types to accommodate the patrons' needs. The first project, and the one actually executed, was a monumental enlargement of the plan of Vaux-le-Vicomte, with an enormous elevation reminiscent of a street facade and derived from Jules Hardouin-Mansart's backdrops for the Places des Victoire and Vosges. A second project for Malgrange consisted of a circular core similar to Bouchefort with four radiating wings, a plan similar to some by Jacques Androuet Du Cerceau, but retrieved through J. B. Fischer von Erlach's plan for the Gartenpalais Althann in Vienna. The facade corresponds to the work of Antoine Le Pautre and Bernini, although the "crown" is supported by Gothic buttressing.

That a building should express its function and the status of its owner was a commonly held notion evolved from the Vitruvian idea of decorum, and was at the basis of the mid-century concept of character. Boffrand expanded this theory of character in a section of his treatise paralleling the rules of literature (rather than painting) as expressed in Horace's *Ars Poesis* with the rules of architecture. Boffrand's concept of character encompassed both iconographic and aesthetic aspects that indicated the building's use and the character of its patron, but also embraced an affective quality that instilled a particular emotion in the observer. Moreover, Boffrand believed that each building should possess a single character that would act as a unifying force in the design. The primary means of achieving character is proportion, aided by composition and ornament. Each order has a character based on its proportion, but the order itself is unnecessary as long as the appropriate proportion is retained. Boffrand's divorcing of proportion from the orders was a major contribution to 18th-century theory. Yet the "character" of

Boffrand's own buildings still stems, traditionally, from the orders.

Boffrand's abstracting principles generated a pure concept of classical architecture that allowed him to absorb nonclassical styles; he could thus extend the repertoire of forms beyond the boundaries set by academic tradition. For example, at the Château de Haroué, Boffrand synthesized Palladian and medieval vocabularies by simplifying the elements to their basic geometric essentials.

Boffrand's fusion of the Greek and Gothic was theoretically expressed in the *Nouveau Traité* of the Abbé de Cordemoy and described by Robin Middleton. Although the prototype of Boffrand's chapel at Lunéville was Hardouin-Mansart's chapel at Versailles, the changes Boffrand made to his model originated in Cordemoy's description of the ideal church: disengaged columns supporting a straight entablature, a quality of lightness from a reduction of wall mass, and an expression of structure. Boffrand earlier explored the importance of the column as a support independent of the wall, but it exists in its purest form in this chapel, which carried important implications for Jacques Germain Soufflot's Ste. Genèvieve.

In the civic projects that Boffrand designed at the end of his life, he became increasingly concerned with pictorial values. Many aspects of his earlier work foreshadow ideas which would be assimilated into the picturesque, but it was not until his urban schemes that Boffrand examined the scenic function of architecture and its interaction with the environment. At the Forum des Halles (one of his projects for the Place Louis XV), Boffrand used columns as architectonic "trees" to create allées that delimit the courts but also allow for their interpenetration with one another and with the surrounding space. In conjunction with his plan to create an urban square in front of Nôtre-Dame de Paris, Boffrand designed a giant portico for the Hôpital des Enfants-Trouvés which is inappropriate for that building type but necessary for visual impact and to establish a relationship with the cathedral.

Boffrand was also responsible for several important Rococo interiors; especially well known is the oval Salon de la Princesse in the Hôtel de Soubise. But Boffrand's most significant contribution was the expansion of academic principles in both theory and practice which established key concepts that would be appropriated and developed at the end of the century by his student Étienne-Louis Boullée.

—PATRICIA LYNN PRICE

BOFILL, Ricardo.

Spanish. Born in Barcelona, Spain, 5 December 1939. Son of the architect Emilio Bofill. Studied at French Institute of Barcelona, until 1955; studied at Escuela Tecnica Superior de Arquitectura, Barcelona, 1955-56; studied at Geneva School of Architecture, Switzerland, 1957-60. Founded Taller de Arquitectura, Barcelona, 1960; opened offices in Paris, 1971; also has offices in New York City. Fellow, American Institute of Architects, 1985.

Chronology of Works

1963-65	Schenkel Apartment Building, Calle Nicaragua 99, Spain
1963-65	Two apartment buildings, Calle J. S. Bach 4, Barcelona, Spain
1964-72	Barrio Gaudi Residential Complex, Reus, Spain
1966-68	La Manzanera (Xanadu) Apartment House, Calpe, Spain
1966-68	Kafka's Castle vacation apartments, Barcelona, Spain
1970-75	Walden 7 Residential Complex, Barcelona, Spain
1972-75	Les Arcades du Lac, St. Quentin en Yvelines, France
1973-74	Le Viaduc housing, St. Quentin en Yvelines, France
1973-75	La Fabrica, Barcelona, Spain (renovation of cement factory into multi-house facility
1978-80	Houari Boumedienne Agricultural Village, Abadla, Algeria
1978-83	Les Espaces d'Abraxas, Marne-la-Vallée, France
1978-84	La Place du Nombre d'Or complex (first part of the 'Antigone' new quarter), Montpellier, France
1979-85	Les Echelles du Baroque housing development, Paris, France
1981-85	Green Crescent housing and municipal development (Les Colonnes de Saint Christophe), Cergy-Pontoise, France
1984	PA Soder Crescent housing, Stockholm, Sweden
1985-89	Swift Headquarters, near Brussels, Belgium
1987	Shepherd School of Music, Rice University, Houston, Texas, U.S.A.
1989	Office Tower, 77 West Wacker Drive, Chicago, Illinois, U.S.A.
1989-92	Olympic Village, Barcelona, Spain

Publications

BOOKS BY BOFILL

Hacia una formalizacion de la Ciudad en el Espacio. Barcelona, 1968.
CEEX 1, City in Space Experience. Barcelona, 1970.
L'Architecture d'un homme. Paris, 1978.
El Taller y la critica. Barcelona, 1981.
Los Espacios de Abraxas-El Palacio-El Teatro-El Arco. Paris, 1981.
Projets Français 1978-81: La Cité—histoire et technologie [exhibition catalog]. Paris, 1981.
Los Jardines del Turia [catalog]. Valencia, 1982.
Taller de Arquitectura: City Design, Industry and Classicism. Barcelona, 1984.
Espaces d'une vie. Paris, 1989.

ARTICLES BY BOFILL

"Sobre la situación actual de la arquitectura Española." *Zodiac* 15 (1965).
"Xanadu, residence d'Alicante, laboratoire Granollers." *Architecture d'aujourd'hui* 139 (1968).
"Taller de Arquitectura." *GA Document* (Winter 1981).
"La Cimenterie." *Architecture d'aujourd'hui* 213 (1981).

BOOKS ABOUT BOFILL

FUTAGAWA, YUKIO (ed.): *GA 19: Taller de Arquitectura.* Tokyo, 1980.
———— (photos): *Ricardo Bofill.* New York, 1985.

GOYTISOLO, JOSE AGUSTIN: *Taller de Arquitectura.* Barcelona, 1977.

JAMES, WARREN A. (ed.): *Ricardo Bofill/Taller de Arquitectura: Buildings and Projects 1960-1985.* New York, 1986.

ARTICLES ABOUT BOFILL

Architecture and Urbanism (December 1976).

BOFILL, ANNA: "Taller de Arquitectura." *Wonen-TA/BK* (Heerlen, Netherlands, April 1979).

BROADBENT, G.: "The Taller of Bofill." *Architectural Review* (November 1975).

————: "The Road to Xanadu and Beyond." *Progressive Architecture* 9 (1975).

CARANDELL, JOSEP MARIA: "Barrio Gaudi." *Architectural Forum* (May 1971).

ELLIS, CHARLOTTE: "Bofill's Gargantuan Brand of Classicism in Montparnasse." *Architecture* (September 1986).

HODGKINSON, PETER: "Xanadu." *Architectural Design* (July 1968).

JENCKS, CHARLES: "Ricardo Bofill—Palace of Abraxas, Theatre and Arch, Marne la Vallée." *Architectural Design* (February 1982).

SCHILLING, RUDOLF: "Ricardo Bofill, ein Star der Postmoderne." *Tages Anzeiger Magazin* (24 April 1982).

SCULLY, VINCENT: "Ricardo Bofill: Radical Classicism of the Spanish Architect's Housing Projects." *Architectural Digest* (April 1988).

*

Short on formal architectural education but fortunate enough to have a father who is a contractor/builder, Ricardo Bofill founded in 1960 what became known as the Taller de Arquitectura (Architecture Workshop). This latter office was the designing arm of the architect's father's (Emilio Bofill) already established building concern. A very young Bofill (he was 21 years old) was allowed, together with a group of friends, to transform their workshop into a sort of playpen, metaphorically speaking. To some extent this helped set the stage for the flamboyant work which continues to be built.

Barcelona, the capital city of Catalonia, has always been a city of political resistance, against the domination of a right-wing dictatorship based in central Madrid since the 1940s. By the 1960s Catalans were openly defiant, not only politically but also socially, by going against conservative mores. In this context, a movement coalesced, comprised of members of the upper middle class and the educated elite, known as "*la gauche divine*," which included young as well as established figures from the arts, literature, media and architecture. Within it, representing part of the architectural community, was Bofill and his band (notably among them, Anna Bofill, Peter Hodgkinson, Manolo Nuñez Yanowsky and the Llistosella brothers). They took advantage of the circumstances to issue manifestos, direct films, write reviews, make public pronouncements and cause controversy. Architecture, for them, was public relations and image making first, and building design and construction concerns second.

Ironically, some of the best buildings by the Taller are from that period. They exhibit an unabashed sense of built bravura, naïveté and child-like originality. As the commissions got bigger, from single-family and apartment houses to housing complexes and vacation condominiums, the work became progressively more daring. In Barcelona proper, two buildings deserve notice: the apartment houses at 99 Nicaragua Street (1963-65) and at the Plaza San Gregorio (1963-1965) are examples of

what Kenneth Frampton has called "critical regionalism." This is an architecture which takes a critical stance on regionalism by using local building techniques— "the poetics of revealed construction"—without resorting to vernacular forms. Both buildings are built of native brick but have angled profiles in plan and in elevation, recalling at times the spirit of the work of master Catalan architect Antonio Gaudí.

Two later buildings show the shifting emphasis of the Taller's work: Xanadu (1966-68) and the Red Wall (1974-75), built as vacation apartment complexes in Alicante, south of Valencia. They use standard masonry construction and are painted bright green and red, respectively, with equally exotic and suggestive names. Building technique was no longer as important as the scenographic effect these buildings produced, with their geometric forms and agitated profiles. They were indeed photogenic buildings. While the two earlier buildings in the city were widely respected by critics and received local and national attention, it was the latter two that launched Bofill's international reputation. These buildings were photographed, published, exhibited and discussed worldwide. The architect claimed mass housing was possible with desirable results—low cost, easy construction, expandable modules, sensuous architecture and so on. However, these were chic second apartments for the elite, not public housing for the full-time poor.

In 1975, after a brief and widely published liaison with the French president's daughter, Bofill was awarded the Les Halles commission in Paris. The scheme called for a central park with edges defined by linear housing of classical parentage—in keeping with the character of Paris. A portion was built, and President Valéry Giscard d'Estaing pronounced Bofill "the greatest living architect in the world," but opposition from other political factions had it torn down. The French establishment wanted local architects, not a foreigner, to benefit from this once-in-a-generation opportunity in central Paris. In its place an architecturally stylistic zoo was built by numerous architects, and remains to this day a political embarrassment.

Bofill was, in compensation, given several commissions to design and build publicly subsidized housing in the growing new towns surrounding Paris. Out of that campaign another generation of buildings emerged, with prefabrication techniques as the necessary salient feature, given their vast scale and need to economize. Les Arcades du Lac, completed in 1982, Les Espaces d'Abraxas (1978-83) and the Green Crescent (1981-85) are examples of that period. The first one, as the name implies, was built near a rectangular man-made lake, with a portion of the housing actually on the water, like an aqueduct. Four stories high, with flat roofs and simple, prefabricated concrete panels, Les Arcades du Lac was a first for Bofill, and the results were amateurish with gratuitous monumentality.

Les Espaces d'Abraxas, with a smaller site and denser program requirements, generated a fortress-like complex with two buildings, nine and 18 stories, forming a court. Within it, a nine-story *arc de triomphe*, with apartments ("for exhibitionists"), was built with the leftover concrete panels. The project posed so powerfully an oppressive image that it was featured in Terry Gilliam's film *Brazil* (1986) as the housing complex where the protagonist lives in a not-so-distant Orwellian future. The last building, the Green Crescent, featured hollow, precast concrete columns six stories high to recall a vast colonnade, with reflective glass infill between them. This building too was used in film, Eric Rohmer's *L'ami de mon amie* (*Boyfriends and Girlfriends* in the U.S.) of 1988. One actress likens it to living in a palace—although, as the name suggests, it is shaped like the Royal Crescent in Bath, England.

Ricardo Bofill: Les Espaces d'Abraxas, Marne-le-Vallée, France, 1978-83

Bofill's early experience in filmmaking served him well in creating ideal stage sets. They work well on film and photographs, but up close, detailing is often crude, while building forms, classical in plan, are rigidly simple, resulting in really unconvincing housing for real people. The Brobdingnagian scale common to them rendered the buildings unreal. However, Bofill successfully contributed to the then ongoing debate on postmodernism versus modernism. Postmodernism had to do with recovering a sense of place, popular identifications, and architectural history. Contextualism was accommodated since Bofill was building in France, "a monumental culture," and the French "liked monumentality"; humanist principles were addressed via classicism, "the universal language of the world"; and history was applied, especially the "lessons of the Renaissance," with allusions and "homages" to Michelangelo, Alberti, Borromini, et al. It was a new architecture of "sound bites."

While this work, barely 10 years old, is aging prematurely and poorly (panels are sagging and loosing their finish), more recent work continues along those very lines, except the mono-programmatic quality (always housing) of the work has changed as well as the locations for it. From Barcelona, Bofill has expanded his practice with representative offices in Paris and New York, from where he can direct his brand of prefabricated gigantic classicism. Building architecture was never this easy. A revealing fact is that the concrete molds used in one project are used repeatedly in numerous others, in Warholian fashion, facilitating and speeding construction, but reducing the architect's job to sketching in 15 minutes napkin-sized floor plans for buildings all over the world, and to full-time jet-setting public relations. The rest is taken care of by draftsmen, engineers and contractors, without the architect ever having to invent or

bother with it again—a version of *"la gauche divine"* at a global scale, perhaps, where fame is more important than architecture.
—WARREN A. JAMES

BOGARDUS, James.

American. Born in Catskill, New York, 14 March 1800. Died in New York City, 13 April 1874. Established foundry in New York City, 1848. Was also an inventor who held numerous patents. Awards.

Chronology of Works
All in the United States
† Work no longer exists

1848	Laing Stores, New York City†
1848-49	Bogardus Foundry and Manufactory, New York City†
1851	Fire Tower, New York City†
1853	Fire Tower, New York City†
1854	Harper and Brothers Printing Plant, New York City†
1855	Fire Tower, New York City†
1855	McCullough Shot Tower, New York City†

Publications

BOOKS BY BOGARDUS

Cast Iron Buildings: Their Construction and Advantages. New York, 1856.

BOOKS ABOUT BOGARDUS

CONDIT, CARL W.: *American Building: Materials and Techniques from the First Colonial Settlements to the Present.* Chicago, 1968.

ARTICLES ABOUT BOGARDUS

BANNISTER, TURPIN C.: "Bogardus Revisited." *Journal of the Society of Architectural Historians* 15-16 (1956-57).
WEISMAN, WINSTON: "Commercial Palaces of New York 1854-1875." *Art Bulletin* (December 1954).

*

Known as the father of the cast-iron building, James Bogardus' talent perhaps went beyond his architectural achievements. He originated many "devices," including cotton-spinning machines, gas meters, clocks and mechanical pencils. His practical inventions in architecture included creation of structural cast-iron skeleton frames and prefabricated building parts that could be assembled "on the site" of construction. A true pioneer in mechanical engineering, he furthered and developed wrought iron and, later, steel construction that ultimately led to the skyscrapers of the 20th century.

Bogardus began his career as a mechanical inventor in his early 20s, when he went to New York City. In 1828 he won a gold medal for his invention of an eight-day clock. That was followed in 1830 by his mechanical devices to improve machines for the spinning of cotton thread; in 1831 he designed a sugar mill, followed in 1832 by a clock-striking device, and in 1835 by an "eversharp-pencil" placed in a metal tube.

There followed a sojourn to England, where he won $2,000 from the British Government for his invention of an engraving machine. Between 1840 and 1847, Bogardus, back in America, continued his inventions. Most notable were a mill to grind white lead paint oxide, a dynamo-meter used in engines, and a mill to powder rice.

By the late 1840s, he began to take an interest in structural designs. And in 1848 he substituted cast-iron columns for masonry of the exterior walls to support a building's floors. This led to a five-story factory built in 1848 in New York. The following year (1849), he obtained a patent to erect the first entire cast-iron building. Everything in this structure was made of wrought iron—floors, beams and plates, tie-rods and roof trusses. Between 1850 and 1880, he developed a prefabricated metal system for warehouses, office buildings and department stores. Among the finest structures incorporating these devices were the Laing Stores, New York, (ca. 1848), and the print factory for Harper and Brothers at Franklin Square, New York (1854). The latter followed plans of the architect John B. Corlies. There Bogardus designed its facade of glass and iron columns and arches to follow the Venetian Renaissance mode. In his book titled *Cast Iron Buildings: Their Construction and Advantages* (1853), he wrote the following in the third-person style: "Mr. Bogardus first conceived the idea of emulating [the rich architectural designs of antiquity] in modern times, by the aid of cast-iron."

Like his 18th-century predecessor, Daniel Badger (a foundryman who, as early as 1772, had a similar idea in the use of metals for building construction), he conceived cast iron as a panacea which would ultimately "satisfy all demands of both the engineer and the artist." He even wanted to employ this for residential structures, as he wrote further in his treatise: "Mr. Bogardus firmly believes that had his necessities required him to construct a dwelling house rather than a factory [this method] would be now as popular for this purpose, as it is for stores."

The Harper Building was a glass shell upheld by a metal frame of cast-iron girders, wrought-iron ties, hollow-cast iron columns, and wrought-iron floor beams. Its source of manufacture was the Trenton Iron Works of New Jersey.

Bogardus' most innovative work, replete with imagination and physical inventiveness, was for the Crystal Palace, New York Exposition (1853) and subsequent iron towers (1855). The proposed exposition design showed a tower (a fire lookout and general observatory) and a huge projected coliseum (60 feet in height with columns and arches demarking its many stories). The coliseum would have had catenary rods to support a hanging roof made of rolled, sheet iron—devices which were more appropriate for bridge construction. He even designed an elevator to lift viewers to the top of the tower. Although the project never came to fruition (a more historical mode was selected), it paved the way for the designs later incorporated in skyscraper construction of the Chicago school.

In 1855 Bogardus had built the McCullough Shot and Lead Company, New York. The appearance was a vertical octagonal prism made of eight columns tethered by iron beams and bolted. Its interior space had brick wall facings framed by columns and panel beams. Again, his inventiveness prophetized the curtain walls of the International Style developed at the Bauhaus by Walter Gropius and associates.

Most of Bogardus' major achievements occurred in the 1850s. Sometimes called the "universal man" who could "unite," as the noted architectural historian Sigfried Giedion wrote in his book *Space, Time and Architecture*, "in his own life the greatest number of different *kinds* of activity, the man who was at once artist, scientist, engineer."

—GEORGE M. COHEN

BÖHM, Dominikus.

German. Born in Jettingen, near Ulm, Germany, 23 October 1880. Died in Cologne, 3 August 1955. Son of an architect; married Maria Schreiber; three sons, including the architect Gottfried Böhm (born in 1920). Apprenticed with his father; studied at the Bauschule, Augsburg, and at the Technische Hochschule, Stuttgart, under Theodor Fischer. Private practice in Cologne, 1925-55; partner with Gottfried Böhm, 1952-55; instructor, Bauschule, Bingen, 1907; instructor, 1907-25, and professor, Kunstgewerbeschule, Offenbach, 1914-26; professor, Kölner Werkschule, Cologne, 1926-35, 1945-50. First prize, International Cathedral Competition, San Salvador, 1953; commander, Order of St. Sylvester, Vatican, 1953.

Chronology of Works
All in Germany unless noted
† *Work no longer exists*

1919-20	St. Joseph's Church, Offenbach am Main (temporary structure)†
1921-27	St. John the Baptist Church, Neu-Ulm
1922-23	SS. Peter and Paul Church, Dettingen am Main (with Martin Weber)
1921-24	Abbey of St. Benedict, Vaals, Netherlands (with Weber)
1924-26	Church of Christ the King, Mainz-Bischofsheim
1929-31	Catholic Seminary, Limburg an der Lahn
1929-31	St. Camillus Asthma Hospital and Church, Mönchengladbach
1930-31	St. Joseph's Church, Hindenburg
1930-32	Caritas Institute Hospital Church of St. Elisabeth, Cologne
1930-32	St. Engelbert's Church, Cologne
1931	Summer Church, Norderney
1931-32	Dominikus Böhm House, Cologne
1934-36	St. Engelbert's Church, Essen
1935	St. Marien's Church, Nordhorn-Frenswegen
1936	Heart of Jesus Church, Bremen-Neustadt
1937-39	Holy Cross Church, Dülmen
1938-40	St. Wolfgang's Church, Regensburg
1939-40	Dominikus Böhm House, Jettingen
1948-50	St. Joseph's Church, Duisburg (reconstruction)
1949-51	St. Martin's Church, Cochem (reconstruction)
1950-51	Roman Catholic Church, Geilenkirchen-Hünshofen (reconstruction, with Gottfried Böhm)
1953-54	Church of Mary the Queen, Cologne-Marienburg
1955-56	St. Joseph's Church, Cologne-Rodenkirchen

Publications

BOOKS ABOUT BÖHM

HABBEL, JOSEF (ed.): *Dominikus Böhm, ein deutscher Baumeister*. Regensburg, Germany, 1943.

HOFF, AUGUST: *Dominikus Böhm*. Berlin, 1930.

HOFF, AUGUST; MUCK, HERBERT; and THOMA, RAIMUND: *Dominikus Böhm: Leben und Werk*. Munich, 1962.

MAGUIRE, ROBERT, and MURRAY, KEITH: *Modern Churches of the World*. New York, 1965.

SCHELL, HUGO: *20th Century Church Architecture in Germany*. Munich, 1974.

STALLING, GESINE: *Studien zu Dominikus Böhm*. Bern, Switzerland, and Frankfurt, 1974.

Dominikus Böhm: St. John the Baptist, Neu-Ulm, Germany, 1921-27

ARTICLES ABOUT BÖHM

"Brief Biographies of German and Swiss Architects Distinguished for Church Design." *Bauen und Wohnen* (November 1958).

"Documents of 20th Century Architecture: Priests' Seminary of the Diocese of Limburg." *Architekt* (April 1978).

"Dominikus Böhm (1880-1955)." *Bauwelt* (7 November 1980).

"Dominikus Böhm." *Moderne Bauformen* (August 1940).

HOFF, AUGUST: "Kirchenbau und Planung von Dominikus and Gottfried Böhm." *Bauen und Wohnen* (December 1949).

LÜTZELER, HEINRICH: "Dominikus Böhm—Siebzig Jahre Alt." *Das Münster* 3 (1950): 294-299.

"St. Joseph's Church, Hindenburg, Germany." *Architectural Forum* 63 (August 1935): 108-116.

SCHWARZ, RUDOLF: "Dominikus Böhm und sein Werk." *Moderne Bauformen* 26 (1927): 226-240.

SCHWARZ, RUDOLF: "Dominikus Böhm—Kirchbauten aus vier Jahrzehnten." *Baukunst und Werkform* 8 (February 1955): 72-131.

*

Dominikus Böhm was the pathbreaking architect of the new Catholic church architecture in Germany. His early designs, up to about 1920, displayed Early Christian, Romanesque and Gothic motifs, but also those of the so-called Jesuit style, against a background of southern German neoclassicism. In those designs, Böhm was apparently not concerned with adaptations of historic styles, but with the typology of Christian religious architecture and the design solutions best suited to the Catholic liturgy.

Böhm came to modernism in the early 1920s through abstraction. In spite of modernist forms, the building types— mostly three-nave basilicas—remained conventional. Examples are the temporary wooden Church of St. Josef at Offenbach (1919) and its massive counterpart, the Church of Sts. Peter and Paul at Dettingen (1922), which was celebrated at the time as the first modern church in Germany. The St. Benedict Abbey at Vaals in the Netherlands (1921-23) is similar to the local masonry churches on the exterior. In the interior, where expressionist architectural thought is conveyed with the aid of Gothic motifs, however, Böhm's mastery of reinforced concrete becomes apparent. The design of the circular choir was particularly forward-looking from a liturgical point of view, in that the participants in the Eucharist could form a three-quarter circle around the altar.

The "*circumstatio*," or gathering of the congregation around the altar, is the leading thought of the project "Circumstantes" (1922), which is significant from the point of view of form and motif. The plan of the church is elliptical. The altar is located in the eastern focal point of the ellipse, surrounded by a circle of slender columns, which leads up to the crowning lantern. The spatially centralizing design expresses the Christocentric liturgy. The seating area west of the altar, however, retains characteristics of longitudinal plans, in spite of the centralized plan. The pillars of the outer ring of supports also create a focus on the altar area, and thus unite the congregation at the same time that they create a procession ambulatory.

Until about 1929, Böhm realized the ideas of the liturgical movement and of the renewed awareness of the congregation in his work. An expressionist architecture, working with Gothic vault forms and the Baroque dynamism of monumental massing in folds, cell vaults and high arches, was given form against the modernist background and with materials such as plastered wire fabric, pressed concrete, cast concrete and reinforced concrete (St. John the Baptist, Neu-Ulm, 1926; Christkönig, Mainz-Bischofsheim, 1926; Frielingsdorf, 1927). Catholic church architecture was conceived, in neoromantic fashion, as a symbol, as "spatial embodiment of the faith" and as the "body of the congregation." The interior of such a "*Gesamtkunstwerk*" shields the faithful from the outside world, and concentrates on the irrational experience of transcendence. By means of the church exterior, the Catholic faith was to have an effect on the world.

After 1928, Böhm's designs were determined by the "Neues Bauen" approach and by rationalism. The Immaculate Chapel for the Cologne Press Exhibition of 1928 was the turning point. A circular masonry base carries a ring of slender pillars with mirrored glass in between. A statue of the Virgin Mary stands at the center. An aspect of Böhm's work also present in his public buildings and industrial architecture is apparent here. The churches of the following years, in exposed or masonry-clad concrete, achieved an effect of tense balance between large, undivided wall spaces and powerful punched round arches and windows, even while they retain a traditional typology. Prominent examples are the Church of St. Elisabeth at Köln-Hohenlind (1928), the Church of St. Josef at Hindenburg (1930) and the Church of St. Engelbert at Essen (1935). These buildings undoubtedly also express the contemporary view of Early Christian community life. The monumental arcades are not stylistic quotations in these churches, in spite of all the allusions to Roman and Romanesque architecture. They are applied, rather, as elementary forms that lend the buildings a certain suprahistorical validity and a sacred aura. It is these buildings in particular that influenced the German church architects Rudolf Schwarz and Emil Steffan.

The Church of St. Engelbert in Köln-Riehl (1931) was an exception in that phase of Böhm's career. The commission specified that the building was to have a centralized plan and building annexes. A steep tent dome—a reinforced-concrete shell in the form of a citrus juicer—is folded over eight parabolic skeletal walls. The grand staircase in front of the church and the choir, set back somewhat from the center, creates a certain degree of direction in spite of the central plan. The expressive qualities of the star-shaped parabolic folds in the interior hark back to the expressive spatial creations of the 1920s.

Although dismissed from his teaching position by the National Socialists, Böhm was able to continue building in a modernist spirit for religious and private clients into the 1940s. In the decade following the war, Dominikus Böhm and his son Gottfried were much sought after to design reconstructions of damaged churches as well as numerous new constructions. They were in demand for their abstract recreations of previous buildings, for the masterful artistic contrasts between the old and the new in their designs, and also for their inclusive abilities in the area of religious arts and crafts work. A number of Gothicizing vaults of plaster-covered wire fabric or concrete shell date from this period, of which the Church of St. Martin at Cochem (1949-51) may serve as an example; there were ornamented roof membranes as well, as at Geilenkirchen-Hünshofen (1950). With his use of rounded arch openings and rose windows simply set into the wall surface, Dominikus Böhm responded even more pointedly to the specific requirements of religious architecture. Böhm's architectural ideal always sought to do justice to the materials used, and pursued a monumental simplicity and a suprahistorical connection of modern architectural thought with traditional motifs. His later work was cautiously enriched with elements inspired by the International

Style and with explicit historic reminiscences and quotations from his own earlier work. All these qualities made Böhm the ideally suited architect for moderately progressive church circles, which sought in the ideals of Early Christianity an answer to the experience of fascism and war. The aesthetic qualities of Böhm's architecture consequently became an ethical postulate for his clients.

—MICHAEL HESSE
Translated from the German by Marijke Rijsberman

BÖHM, Gottfried.

German. Born in Offenbach am Main, Germany 23 January 1920; son of the architect Dominikus Böhm. Married Elisabeth Haggenmüller, 1948; four children. Engineering diploma, Technische Hochschule, Munich, 1946; studied at Academy of Sculptural Art, Munich, 1947. Worked as assistant to his father, 1947-50; assistant to architect Rudolph Schwarz, Cologne, 1950; assistant architect to C. Baumann, New York City, 1951; partner with father, Cologne, 1952-55; private practice in Cologne since 1955; professor of architecture, Institute of Technology, Aachen, since 1963; has also taught in the United States. Pritzker Prize, 1986.

Chronology of Works
All in Germany unless noted

1949	St. Columba's Church, Cologne
1955	Church in Ching Liau, Taiwan
1957	Herz Jesu Church, Schildgen, near Cologne
1958	St. Christopher's Church, Oldenburg
1958	Queen of Grace Church, Kassel-Wilhelmshohe
1959	Corpus Christi Parish Center, Porz-Urbach, near Cologne
1959	St. Joseph Parishioners' Center, Kierspe
1962	Church of the Pilgrimages, Neviges
1962	Housing for the elderly, Garath, Düsseldorf
1963	Children's Village, Refrath, Bensberg
1963	Church of the Annunciation, Impekoven
1964	Town Hall, Bensberg
1965	St. Ludwig Church, Saarlouis
1965	Children's Village, near Lake Bracciano, Italy
1966	Dr. Paul Böhm House, Munich
1967	City Center Plan, Bensberg
1969	Housing Complex, Chorweiler, Cologne
1969	Cathedral restoration, Trier
1969	Diocesan Museum, Paderborn
1970-80	Housing and Commercial Development, Bad Godesberg, Bonn
1972	Pilgrimage Church, Wigratzbad
1973	City Hall and Cultural Center, Bocholt
1977	Community Center, Kettwig, Essen
1977	Town Hall, Rheinberg
1981	Single-Family Terraced Housing, Porz-Zündorf, near Cologne
1984	Baufirma Züblin Headquarters Building, Stuttgart
1987	Renovation, Saarbrücken Castle, Saarbrücken
1988	Assembly Hall, Folkwang School, Essen Werden, Norderhein
1989	University Library and Auditorium, Mannheim
1990	Der Heumarkt, Cologne

Publications

ARTICLES BY BÖHM

"Die Gewebedecke." In *Neue Baumethoden 1,* ed. by H. Hoffmann, Stuttgart, 1949.

BOOKS ABOUT BÖHM

DARIUS, VERONIKA: *Der Architekt Gottfried Böhm: Bauten der sechziger Jahre.* Düsseldorf, 1988.
Der Baumeister Gottfried Böhm (booklet). Wuppertal, Germany, 1968.
RAEV, SVETLOZAR (ed.): *Gottfried Böhm: Bauten und Projekte 1950-1980.* Cologne, 1982.
RAEV, SVETLOZAR (ed.): *Gottfried Böhm: Lectures, Buildings, Projects.* Stuttgart and Zurich, 1988.
SCHWARTZ, FRITZ: *Die Architektur von Gottfried Böhm* (thesis). Eidgenössische Technische Hochschule, Zurich (1977).
WEISNER, U.; PEHNT, W.; and SACK, M.: *Zusammenhänge: Der Architekt Gottfried Böhm* (exhibition catalog). Bielefeld, Germany, 1984.

ARTICLES ABOUT BÖHM

Architecture and Urbanism, special issue (March 1978).
Architecture and Urbanism, special issue (September 1990).
CHELAZZI, GIULIANO: "An Expressionist Presence: Gottfried Böhm." *L'Architettura* (April 1974).
GENDERS, CHARLIE: "Gottfried Böhm." *Architect* (The Hague) 11 (1980).
KUMP, HANS: "Der Architekt Gottfried Böhm." *Bauen und Wohnen* 9 (1980).
SCHIRMBECK, EGON: "Observations on the Architectural Work of Gottfried Böhm." *Bauen und Wohnen* (November 1977).

*

Gottfried Böhm belongs to the exceptions of postwar architecture, in that his entire oeuvre, in opposition to the philosophies of modernism, bears witness to architecture's expressive potential. Long before the rise of postmodernism, Böhm's work demonstrated that architecture did not have to forgo the multiplicity and wealth of meaning it is capable of— without reverting to historical styles.

Gottried Böhm was born in 1920, and was formed as an architect by his father, Dominikus Böhm (1880-1955), who was one of the most well-known German expressionist architects. During his time in his father's office, from 1947 to 1955, he was involved with church designs, such as that of St. Columba Church in Cologne, which were conceived as independent variations on the structural principles of expressionist architecture. In the course of the 1950s, Gottfried Böhm developed an almost exotic architectural style. At Herz-Jesu in Schildgen (1957-60), hidden from view behind high walls, geometrical forms like cubes, cones and cylinders were synthesized into an outlandish monastic architecture with a mysterious effect.

Gottfried Böhm: Church of the Pilgrimages, Neviges, Germany, 1962

One of his principal works is the Pilgrimage Church at Neviges (1962-64), which may be considered the most important religious structure of the postwar period, together with Le Corbusier's Ronchamp. At the end of a pilgrimage road that heightens the visitor's expectations, the church proper, conceived as an expressive architectural sculpture, comes into view. With its 35 meters, the building has a cathedral-like height, a crystalline split roof, interior galleries that recall archaic and dramatically staged lighting. Out of these elements, Böhm created a church of rare charm. Cave and crystal, two topoi of German expressionism, are utilized at Neviges in a surprising new fashion. The vertical emphasis, moreover, plays with another expressionist concept—that of the *"Stadtkrone,"* a building situated and designed in such a way as to function like the crown of the urban landscape.

Besides the Pilgrimage Church at Neviges, Böhm did designs for the Bensberg Town Hall in 1962 (built in 1964-67), which are similar in conception. Böhm connected the remains of a medieval fort situated on a ridge with a concrete structure of a highly sculptural design, accented by a bizarre tower. As an angular, sculptural *Stadtkrone,* Böhm's building opened a dialogue, unusual at the time, with its medieval context. The Bensberg Town Hall may be considered an early example of contextualism, the style that combines a respect for tradition with independently conceived modern structures.

In a long series of projects, Böhm demonstrated the potential diversity of historically contextualized architecture. For the Diocesan Museum at Paderborn (1969-71), he created a transparent hall, which is self-consciously opposed to the Gothic hall of the neighboring cathedral. Following the expressive plasticity of Böhm's earlier work, the Paderborn Diocesan Museum introduced a series of more slender and graceful buildings, culminating in the renovations of the castle at Saarbrücken (1979). Böhm did not propose a reconstruction of F.J. Stengel's Baroque building, but rather an addition in the form of filigree-like central bay, recalling greenhouses in its weightlessness. Böhm's glass house, with colorfully painted interior walls, imparts a festive and elegant air to the Saarbrücken building that it did not have before. Böhm was also successful in bringing out the superior quality of a historical building, heightening it even, in the alteration of the Abbey at Essen-Werden, which houses the Folkwang School for Music, Theater and Dance. For this project, he did not merely adapt the existing structure to new purposes, but created spatial works of art of a high quality in the application of a highly imaginative aesthetic.

Among Böhm's critical encounters with history, city restoration projects take up a special place. On a gigantic open site at Dudweiler (1979), he created a charming city center with a marketplace and the rotunde of a town house. The Prager Platz in Berlin, destroyed during World War II, will regain its grand urban character with Böhm's design (1978, in preparation). The design includes transparent towerhouses that paraphrase, in an unusual manner, an architectural tradition typical of Berlin. The city of Cologne, destroyed during the war and disfigured by postwar architecture, will have rebuilt one of its important squares when Böhm's Heumarkt design (1980) is carried to completion. The completed Maritim Hotel on the Heumarkt recalls the galleries of 19th-century architecture with its glass hall. The design refers to a historical building type in the same way that the Rautenstrauch-Joest Museum (of Anthropology) does. Böhm's museum (in preparation) is a multipartite tower, which enriches the silhouette of Cologne's city front along the Rhine with a significant architectonic sign.

With all its diversity, Gottfried Böhm has been building up an oeuvre in which expressiveness and complexity are unfailing constants. It is precisely its expressiveness which constitutes his specific contribution to the architecture of the second half of the 20th century.

—RICHARD HÜTTEL
Translated from the German by Marijke Rijsberman

BONOMI, Joseph.

British. Born in Rome, Italy, 19 January 1739. Died in London, England, 9 March 1808. Married Rosa Florini, 1775; three sons. Educated at Collegio Romano, Rome. Worked for Robert and James Adam, London, 1767; assisted Thomas Leverton; associate, Clementine Academy at Bologna; associate, Academy of St. Luke, Rome; established practice, London, 1784. Honorary Architect to St. Peter's, Rome, 1776.

Chronology of Works
All in England unless noted
* Approximate dates
† Work no longer exists

1782-88*	Packington Hall, Warwickshire
1782-90*	Montagu House (Great Room), Portman Square, London†
1784-88	Dale Park, Sussex†
1786-91	Stansted House, Sussex (with James Wyatt)†
1789-90	Bavarian Chapel, Warwick Street, London†
1789-92	Great Packington Church, Warwickshire
1789-94	Longford Hall, Shropshire
1792-93	Barrells, Warwickshire†
1793-96	Spanish Chapel, Manchester Square, London†
1793-1800	Eastwell Park, Kent†
1794	Mausoleum, Blickling, Norfolk
1796*-97	Lambton Hall, County Durham†
1796-99	Laverstoke Park, Hampshire
1799	Sandling House, Kent†
1803-06	Roseneath Castle, Dumbartonshire, Scotland†

Publications

ARTICLES ABOUT BONOMI

"The Life and Works of Joseph Bonomi." *Architect, Engineer and Surveyor* (1843): 70-71.
PAPWORTH, WYATT: "Memoir." *Transactions of the Royal Institute of British Architects* 19 (1868-69): 123-34.

*

Joseph Bonomi was the son of a prominent family who occupied "dignified stations in the church and the civil departments" at Rome; his brother, Don Carlo, was professor of divinity at the Collegio di Propaganda Fide. Bonomi was educated at the Collegio Romano and later joined the Marchese Teodoli, a nobleman devoted to the study and practice of architecture. Bonomi probably met Robert and James Adam in Rome, and may have accompanied Robert Adam and Charles-Louis Clérisseau to the Roman palace of Diocletian at Split, Dalmatia (1757), and James Adam to Paestum (1763). He came to England in 1767 to work for the Adams and remained with them for several years, apparently in the capacity of a draftsman, contributing the accomplished perspectives of interiors for *The Works in Architecture,* Volumes I (1773) and II (1778). He joined Thomas

Leverton's office in the 1770s, assisting the latter with an Adam-like house at the northwest corner of Lincoln's Inn Fields, and with the building of Bedford Square.

In 1783 Bonomi returned to Rome, where he was elected associate of the Clementine Academy, Bologna, and of the Roman Accademia di San Luca. The following year he went back to England and quickly established himself as a fashionable designer of country houses, and was even noticed by Jane Austen in *Sense and Sensibility*. Bonomi's houses were dignified and uncomprisingly austere with coarse detailing; they were marked by a vigor and insensitivity of handling, and were often awkwardly proportioned. He liked massive porticoes, two-story or semicircular, raised or approached by ramps. Longford Hall, Shropshire (1789-94) for R. Leake), had a Doric portico with an architrave cornice, and was remarkable for the earliest use of a porte cochere. Eastwell Park, Kent (1793-1800), for George Finch Hatton), had the unconventional arrangement of a five-column portico, emphasizing that this porte cochere was to be entered laterally. His most important and last executed work, Roseneath, Dumbartonshire (1803-06, for the duke of Argyll, gutted by fire in 1947 and demolished in 1961) had most of these rather disagreeable features. His plans were often dull and interior decoration simple with (occasionally) neoclassical features such as casts from the antique. His 1782 "Design for the Great Drawing Room for Mrs Montagu, Portman Square," with a richly ornamented segmental ceiling springing from a cornice carried by Corinthian columns, seems to have been based on James Stuart's earlier intentions. His design for a gallery at Townley House (1789 for Charles Townley) had colored marbles on floor and walls and Adamish arabesques on the vaulted ceiling.

Bonomi was associated with the early Greek Revival in his use of Greek Doric orders. His remarkable church at Great Packington (1789-90 for the fourth earl of Aylesford, who was "much his patron") was his most radical building and an early appearance of the Greek Doric Paestum order; he had earlier, with James Wyatt, used a primitivistic, unfluted Greek Doric at Stansted House, Sussex (1786-91 for Richard Barwell, destroyed by fire in 1900). He detested the Gothic style and denounced it as having caused the "total corruption of medieval architecture throughout Europe," at the same time lamenting the revival of "such absurdities in this country."

Bonomi exhibited regularly at the Royal Academy (1783-1806) and in 1789 was elected an associate by the casting vote of the then-President, Sir Joshua Reynolds. Bonomi's knowledge of perspective encouraged Reynolds to try and secure his election to full academician in 1790 to qualify him for the vacant seat of professor of perspective. When this was opposed, Reynolds temporarily resigned from the presidency.

Bonomi maintained lifelong links with Italy. In 1776 he designed an elegant sacristy for St. Peter's and, in 1803, failed to be appointed architect to the king of Naples. In 1804 he was elected honorary architect to St. Peter's, Rome, by the Congregation of Cardinals.

—MOIRA RUDOLF

BORROMINI, Francesco.

Italian. Born in Bissone, near Como, Italy, 25 September 1599. Died in Rome, 2 August 1667. Father was G. D. Castelli-Borromini, architect to the Visconti family of Milan. Studied sculpture in Milan, from 1608; apprenticed with his kinsman

Carlo Maderno in Rome, from about 1620. Assistant to Giovanni Lorenzo Bernini at St. Peter's, Rome, 1630-33.

Chronology of Works
All in Italy
* Approximate dates

1619-33	St. Peter's, Rome (decorative details and various additions)
1623	Sant'Andrea della Valle, Rome (lantern)
1623-24	Carlo Maderno Tomb, San Giovanni dei Fiorentini, Rome
1624	Monte di Pietà, Rome (campanile)
1628-32	Palazzo Barberini, Rome (decorative details)
1634-42	San Carlo alle Quattro Fontane, Rome
1637-50	Oratory and Residence of the Filippini, Rome (from work begun by Maruscelli)
1638-39	Santa Lucia in Selci, Rome (Cappella Landi)
1638-42	Santi Apostoli, Naples (Filomarini Altar)
1638-43	Palazzo Carpegna, Rome
1642-62	Sant'Ivo alla Sapienza, Rome
1643-46	Santa Maria dei Sette Dolori, Rome
1646	Pamphili Gallery, Rome
1646-50	San Giovanni in Laterano, Rome (rebuilding of nave and aisles)
1646-56	Palazzo Falconieri, Rome (remodeling and enlargement)
1647	Palazzo di Spagna, Rome (staircase remodeling)
1650	Ceva Memorial, Lateran Baptistery, Rome
1650*	Palazzo Ciustiani, Rome (portal and remodeling)
1650*	Villa Giustriani al Laterano, Rome (facade remodeling)
1650-53	Palazzo Spada-Capodiferro, Rome (colonnade, piazza and remodeling)
1652-67	Collegio di Propaganda Fide, Rome
1653-57	Sant'Agnese in Piazza Navona, Rome (completions; based on plans by Rainaldi)
1653-67	Sant'Andrea delle Fratte, Rome (unfinished cupola and campanile)
1655ff.	Lateran Tombs, Rome
1657	Lateran Baptistery, Rome (frieze)
1659	Piazza Sant'Agostino, Rome
1659	San Giovanni in Oleo, Rome (remodeling)
1660-66	Biblioteca Alessandrina alla Sapienza, Rome
1661-62	Palazzo del Banco di Santo Spirito a Piazza Monte Giordano, Rome (later Palazzo Spada)
1663-66	Collegio Innocenziano a Piazza Navona, Rome
1665-67	San Carlo alle Quattro Fontane, Rome (lower story of facade)
1667*	Villa Falconieri, Frascati

Publications

BOOKS BY BORROMINI

Opus Architectonicum. 1720-25. With Virgilio Spada. Reprint: London, 1964.

BOOKS ABOUT BORROMINI

ACCADEMIA NAZIONALE DI SAN LUCA: *Studi sul Borromini.* Rome, 1967.
ANTONAZZI, GIOVANNI: *Il Palazzo di Propaganda.* Rome, 1979.

Francesco Borromini: Sant'Ivo alla Sapienza, Rome, Italy, 1642-62

ARGAN, GIULIO CARLO: *Borromini*. Verona, 1952.

BLUNT, ANTHONY: *Borromini*. Harmondsworth, England, 1979.

CONNORS, JOSEPH: *Borromini and the Roman Oratory: Style and Society*. Cambridge, Massachusetts, 1980.

DE BERNARDI FERRERO, DARIA: *L'opera di Francesco Borromini nella letteratura artistica e nelle incisioni dell'otà barocca*. Turin, 1967.

EIMER, GERHARD: *La fabbrica di S. Agnese in Navona*. Stockholm, 1970.

HEIMBÜRGER RAVALLI, MINNA: *Architettura, scultura e arte minori nel barocco italiano. Ricerche nell'Archivio Spada*. Florence, 1977.

HEMPEL, EBERHARD: *Francesco Borromini*. Vienna, 1924.

HIBBARD, HOWARD: *Carlo Maderno and Roman Architecture 1580-1630*. London, 1971.

MARTINELLI, FIORAVANTI: *Roma nel seicento*. Florence (1660-1662) 1969.

NEPPI, LIONELLO: *Palazzo Spada*. Rome, 1975.

PIAZZO, MARCELLO DEL (ed.): *Ragguagli Borrominiani, Mostra Documentaria*. Rome, 1968.

PORTOGHESI, PAOLO: *Borromini nella cultura europea*. Rome, 1964.

PORTOGHESI, PAOLO: *Borromini. Architettura come linguaggio*. Rome and Milan, 1967.

PORTOGHESI, PAOLO: *Disegni di Francesco Borromini*. Rome, 1967.

PORTOGHESI, PAOLO: *The Rome of Borromini*. New York, 1968.

SEDLMAYR, HANS: *Die Architektur Borrominis*. Berlin, 1939.

STEINBERG, LEO: *Borromini's San Carlo alle Quattro Fontane: A Study in Multiple Form and Architectural Symbolism*. New York, 1977.

THELEN, HEINRICH: *Francesco Borromini: Die Handzeichnungen*. Graz, Austria, 1967.

THELEN, HEINRICH: *Zur Entstehungsgeschichte der Hochalter-Architektur von St. Peter in Rom*. Berlin, 1967.

WITTKOWER, RUDOLF: *Art and Architecture in Italy 1600-1750*. 3rd. ed., Baltimore and Harmondsworth, England, 1973.

ARTICLES ABOUT BORROMINI

FICHERA, FRANCESCO: "Juvarra tra Bernini e Borromini." *Quadrivio* 49 (1935).

GÜTHLEIN, KLAUS: "Quellen aus dem Familienarchiv Spada zum römischen Barock." *Römisches Jahrbuch für Kunstgeschichte* 18 (1979): 173-246.

INCISA DELLA ROCCHETTA, GIOVANNI: "Un dialogo del: Virgilio Spada sulla fabbrica dei Filippini." *Archivo della Societa Romana di Storia Patria* 90 (1967): 165-211.

OST, HANS: "Borrominis römische Universitätskirche S. Ivo alla Sapienza." *Zeitschrift für Kunstgeschichte* 30 (1967): 101-142.

PREIMESBERGER, RUDOLF: "Pontiflex romanus per Aeneam praesignatus: Die Galleria Pamphilj und ihre Fresken." *Römisches Jahrbuch für Kunstgeschichte* 16 (1976): 221-288.

WITTKOWER, RUDOLF: "Francesco Borromini, his Character and Life." *Studies in the Italian Baroque*. London, 1975.

Unlike his contemporaries, Giovanni Lorenzo Bernini, Pietro da Cortona, Carlo Rainaldi and Martino Longhi, Francesco Borromini challenged the traditional Renaissance approach to architectural design, returning almost exclusively to Michelangelo, to the architecture of imperial Rome, and to nature for his inspiration. Though Michelangelo was his hero, it was not Michelangelo's forms that Borromini utilized, but rather his principles of design. Borromini's concept of nature was mathematical, following Galileo, who had taught that the language of nature is mathematics and that its pictographs are circles, triangles and other geometrical figures. This view led Borromini to work out his plans through complex geometrical manipulation, often overlapping circles, triangles and ellipses to create interactive, dynamic spatial units dramatically different from the additive spatial modules of Renaissance practice.

In about 1620, Borromini began his career as an architectural draftsman for his kinsman Carlo Maderno, mostly designing decorative elements for St. Peter's Basilica and the Palazzo Barberini. When Bernini took over as architect of St. Peter's upon Maderno's death a decade later, Borromini continued to work as "assistant to the architect." Borromini came to architecture as a builder and trained specialist; he was disdainful of Bernini's lack of technical knowledge and jealous of his success, and consequently the relationship lasted only until 1633, when Borromini set out on his own. Although Borromini was involved throughout his career with a variety of palazzo and villa designs, including, most notably, the Villa Falconieri at Frascati, it is for his ecclesiastical work that he is best known.

Borromini's great opportunity to establish himself as an architect came, in 1634, with the commission to design the Monastery of San Carlo alle Quattro Fontane for the order of the Spanish Discalced Trinitarians in Rome. This church, along with Cortona's contemporary church of SS. Luca e Martina, inaugurated the Roman High Baroque period and is truly one of its masterpieces. It achieves Baroque richness and complexity using exclusively architectural means; the limited resources of the Trinitarians did not allow for use of the rich materials that characterize Bernini's Church of Sant'Andrea just down the block.

Both cloister and church illustrate Borromini's fascination with geometrical manipulation. The cloister begins as a simple rectangular space. In it is inserted a two-story octagon defined by columns of alternating wide and narrow spacing; at the lower level the wide bays carry arches, while the narrow bays have straight entablatures. At the corners, the entablatures, and the wall segments above them, bulge inward as if the mass of the building were pressing into the open space.

The plan of the church retains the central octagonal spatial unit defined by pairs of columns, but the diagonal wall segments they define are straight rather than curved. It is, instead, the walls of the larger bays on the longitudinal and cross axes that are curved. These bow out to form narthex, sanctuary and side chapels. The straight walls are fixed and solid, the curved walls plastic and membranous; equilibrium is created between dynamic space and solid structure. The effect is as if the space were pushing the wall membrane out between the rigid piers anchoring the corners of the nave. The space has a dynamic, pulsating character at the ground level that is in contrast to the simple elliptical dome that constitutes the upper zone of the church.

At the same time that he was involved with San Carlino, Borromini was also engaged in the design for the Oratory of San Filippo Neri. He received the commission in 1637; it was an extremely important one, for the oratory was to be part of the ensemble of the Church of Santa Maria in Vallicella, the mother church of the new Oratorian order, popularly referred to as the Chiesa Nuova. Although the word "oratory" refers specifically to the chamber to be used for musical performances, which is the most important element of the plan, the commission included the entire monastic complex (except for the preexisting church and the large sacristy adjacent to it.)

The most interesting part of the design is the facade. Borromini used very thin bricks laid up with hardly any mortar. The design is not done in the sculptural, Michelangelesque manner that he used at San Carlino, but instead emphasizes its single, slow, curving plane. Anthony Blunt described it this way: "Instead of being a mass of masonry curving in and out, it has the springiness of a sheet of metal which has been slightly curved under pressure. It is totally non-monumental, but it is maturely Baroque in that it forces the eye of the observer to move across it along determined lines."

Shortly after the body of the Church of San Carlo alle Quattro was completed, Borromini received the commission that was to produce his masterpiece—the design of the church for the Roman university, Sant'Ivo della Sapienza.

In Sant'Ivo, Borromini produced an exceptionally successful example of a complex, centralized church plan created by overlapping geometric figures. Six circles are drawn on a six-pointed star made by superimposing one equilateral triangle upon another. Segments of the resulting diagram yield all elements of the plan, which begins with a convex curve where one of the outer circles intersects a triangle, which yields to a straight wall segment, which intersects with a concave curve from one of the inner circles, which leads to another straight wall segment, and so on around the interior perimeter of the space.

The space that results from this play of geometry epitomizes the Baroque fascination with movement. Semicircular bays alternate with sharply angular ones which focus upon convex wall segments; interior space exerting outward pressure seems to be restrained by exterior space pushing in. Clusters of three giant-order Corinthian pilasters form piers that hold the opposing spatial forces in equilibrium and support an entablature that runs unbroken around the space. The mass of the enclosing wall is emphasized by the niches that are carved into it.

Above the entablature the bays and the pilasters of the ground plan continue up to form the dome, where the complex geometry of the ground plan is resolved into a hemispherical space by means of doubly curved surfaces, aedicular window frames and camouflaging sculptural ornament. The pilasters are gathered up into a simple pattern which radiates from the circular aperture of the lantern that marks the center of the church. Complex forms have evolved into a single simple one. The result is magical. The apparent geometry of the space seems to change as one's direction of view changes.

The renown Borromini gained from San Carlo and Sant'Ivo soon brought him two other important ecclesiastical commissions—the renovation of the great Early Christian basilica and first church of Rome, San Giovanni in Laterano, and the completion of Carlo Rainaldi's Church of Sant'Agnese on the Piazza Navona. San Giovanni was in danger of collapse, but inasmuch as it was one of the venerated pilgrimage churches of the city, Pope Innocent X insisted that its fabric be retained. Beginning in 1646, Borromini converted it into a modern Baroque building by literally encasing the old structure of the nave and its four flanking aisles in new material. Borrowing the interlocking triumphal-arch arrangement consisting of solid piers with niches alternating with bays with tall arched openings that had been used since the design of Sant'Andrea in Mantua by Leon Battista Alberti in the mid-15th century, Borromini encased consecutive pairs of columns in the old basilica in broad new piers.

Giant-order Corinthian pilasters run through all three wall zones to carry the cornice that surrounds the space and establishes its unity. Borromini continued the triumphal arch motif from side wall to side wall around the entrance wall of the nave by placing pier units on the diagonal across the two corners. Borromini intended for the nave to be vaulted, but the vault was never built; only the inner aisle was vaulted.

San Giovanni in Laterano is perhaps most interesting as a demonstration of Borromini's skill as a decorator. The countless tombs of clerics that had filled the aisles of the old basilica had to be rearranged and rehoused in new monuments appropriate to their new architectural setting. For them Borromini designed new settings using *putti,* architectural forms, and floral and vegetable motifs, combined in fresh new ways.

At Sant'Agnese, Borromini inherited a Greek-cross plan that was already under construction when he was appointed to replace Rainaldi as architect of Innocent X's family church on the Piazza Navona in 1653. Borromini made only minor modifications to the plans, but he dramatically changed the form, and hence the appearance, of the church. Instead of the broad dome carried on a rather low drum planned by Rainaldi, Borromini designed an extremely tall, slender silhouette having a dome modeled on that at St. Peter's carried on a high drum. The pedimented portal is located in the center of a gentle concave depression that is anchored at each end by piers carrying tall, open towers that frame the drum and dome. As Michelangelo had done at St. Peter's, the entablature of the portal is extended through all parts of the facade, creating the appearance of an attic above the main story below. In *Art and Architecture in Italy 1600-1750,* Rudolph Wittkower said of Sant'Agnese: "The church must be regarded as the High Baroque revision of the centralized plan for St. Peter's. . . . From the late sixteenth century onwards may be observed a progressive reduction of mass and weight, a heightening of the drum at the expense of the vault, and a growing elegance of the sky-line. All this reached a kind of finality in the dome of S. Agnese . . . here dome and towers form a grand unit, perfectly balanced in scale. Never before had it been possible for a beholder to view at a glance such a rich and varied group of towers and dome while at the same time experiencing the spell of the intense spatial suggestions: he feels himself drawn into the cavity of the facade, above which looms the concave mass of the drum."

Borromini received few new commissions following the death of his papal patron, Innocent X, in 1655. Most of the final 12 years of his life were devoted to projects already in hand. The most significant of these was the design for the building to house the college dedicated to the preparation of Roman Catholic missionaries, the Colegio di Propaganda Fide. The most interesting space by far is the chapel dedicated to the Three Kings or "Re Magi." The chapel is much simpler in plan and spatial geometry than any of Borromini's earlier ecclesiastical spaces. However, it is just as interesting, but for different reasons. The plan is a rectangle with chamfered corners and is similar to the plans of the Oratory and the nave of San Giovanni in Laterano. What is different is the manner in which the wall has been dissolved, to create a space that seems to be defined by a cage of vertical and horizontal linear elements. Twelve piers decorated with giant-order Ionic columns surround the space. Behind them, smaller Doric pilasters carry an entablature that defines a clerestory "gallery" of generous windows that break up into the giant-order entablature, visually extending the large openings to chapels in the lower zone into the zone of the clerestory. The giant-order pilasters support ribs that move diagonally across the shallow vaulted ceiling to different positions on the opposite or adjacent sides. The space seems to flow between and around the elements of a cage. The wall, as weight and mass, has been defeated.

—C. MURRAY SMART, JR.

BOTTA, Mario.

Swiss. Born in Mendrisio, Switzerland, 1 April 1943. Apprentice building draftsman, office of Carloni and Camenisch, Lugano, 1958-61; studied at the Liceo Artistico, Milan, 1961-64; studied at the Istituto Universitario di Architettura, Venice, 1964-69, Dip.Arch. 1969. Assistant to Le Corbusier, Venice and Paris, 1965; private practice in Lugano, since 1969; professor, École Polytechnique Fédérale, Lausanne, since 1983.

Chronology of Works
All in Switzerland unless noted

1965-67	Single-family House, Stabio
1972-77	Secondary School, Morbio Inferiore, Ticino
1973	Single-family House, Riva San Vitale
1975-76	Single-family House, Ligornetto
1976-78	Municipal Gymnasium, Balerna
1976-79	Library, Capuchin Convent, Lugano
1977-79	Craft Center, Balerna
1977-82	Administration Building, Staatsbank, Fribourg
1979	Single-family house, Pregassona
1981	Casa Rotunda, Stabio
1981	Administration and Commercial Building, Lugano

Mario Botta: Bank of Gothard Offices, Lugano, Switzerland, 1982

1982 Single-family House, Viganello
1982 Bank of Gothard offices, Lugano
1982 André Malraux House of Culture, Chambéry, France
1983-84 Single-family House, Morbio Superiore
1989- Museum of Modern Art, San Francisco, California, U.S.A.

Publications

ARTICLES BY BOTTA

"Architecture and Environment." *Architecture and Urbanism* (June 1979).
"Une Maison Familiale Encore!" *Werk, Bauen und Wohnen* 5 (1980).
"Swiss Transmission and Exaggerations" [interview]. *Skyline* 2/8 (1980).
"Ein Raum for Guernika." *Werk, Bauen und Wohnen* 11 (1981).
"Architecture Means Giving Form to History" [interview]. *Arkkitehti* 79 nos. 4/5 (1982).
"Casa a Stabio." *Rivista tecnica* 2 (1982).
"L'albero come eccezione." *Lotus* 31 (1982).
"Il teatro e la città" [interview]. *Casabella* (November 1983).
"Architecture and Morality" [interview]. *Perspecta* 20 (1983).
"Interview with Emilio Ambasz." *Domus* (May 1983).
"The Neo-Rationalists Are Coming" [interview]. *Interior Design* (June 1983).
"Una visita al nuovo Lingotto" [interview]. *Casabella* (May 1984).

BOOKS ABOUT BOTTA

BROWN-MANRIQUE, GERARDO: *The Ticino Guide.* Princeton, New Jersey, 1989.
DAL CO, FRANCESCO: *Mario Botta: Architetture 1960-1985.* Milan, 1985; English translation, New York, 1986.
FUTAGAWA, YUKIO (ed.): *GA Architect 3: Mario Botta.* Tokyo, 1984.
NICOLIN, PIERLUIGI: *Mario Botta: Buildings and Projects 1961-1982.* New York, 1984.
OESCHLIN, WERNER: *Mario Botta, Architectures 1980-90.* Barcelona, 1991.
ROTA, ITALO (ed.): *Mario Botta: Architecture and Projects in the 70s.* London, 1981.
SANGUINETI, E., et al.: *Mario Botta: La casa rotonda.* Milan, 1982.
WREDE, STUART: *Mario Botta.* New York, 1986.
WATARI, E. (ed.): *Mario Botta: Watari-Um Projects in Tokyo 1985-1990.* New York, 1991.

ARTICLES ABOUT BOTTA

ALFIERI, BRUNO: "Una casa nel Ticino." *Lotus* 5 (1978).
Architecture and Urbanism, extra edition (September 1986).
ARNELL, PETER: "Mario Botta—Transalpine Rationalist." *Architectural Record* (June 1982).
"Contemporary Architects 14: Mario Botta." *Architecture and Urbanism* (June 1979).
DEN HOLLANDER, JORD: "Mario Botta—One of the Ticino Architects." *Architect* (The Hague, June 1979).
HEDGEPETH, MICHAEL: "Visit by Mario Botta." *Archetype* 4 (1980).
"Intellectual Tradition—Mario Botta." *Space Design* 3 (1981).
JENCKS, CHARLES: "Mario Botta and the New Tuscanism." *Architectural Design* 53, Nos. 9/10 (1983).

KNOBEL, LANCE: "Botta." *Architectural Review* (July 1981).
————: "Botta in the City." *Architectural Review* (May 1983).
"Mario Botta and the School of Ticino." *Oppositions* (Fall 1978).
"Mario Botta—architetto ticinese." *Ottagono* (September 1980).
"Mario Botta: Critique." *Progressive Architecture* (July 1982).
"Mario Botta—A Portrait." *Domus* (September 1981).
"Mario Botta—Works and Projects." *Casabella* (June 1976).
McTEAGUE, M.: "Botta: Themes and Variations." *Architecture South Africa* (January/February 1984).
PELISSIER, A., and MORITA, K.: "Mario Botta Talks on Recent Works." *Architecture and Urbanism* (April 1983).
SARTORIS, ALBERTO: "On the Architectural Drawings by Mario Botta." *GA Gallery* (September 1984).
Space Design, special issue (August 1984).
STRZALA, R. F.: "Mario Botta: Portrait of an Architect in Ticino." *Yorkshire Architect* (Sunderland, January/February 1983).
VILADAS, PILAR: "Botta on Botta's Chair." *Progressive Architecture* (May 1983).
Werk, special issue, "Einfamilienhäuser—Ferienhäuser" (January 1969).
Werk, Bauen und Wohnen, special issue (January/February 1983).
ZARDINI, MIRKO: "Mario Botta." *Architecture and Urbanism* (January 1989).

*

In just two decades since graduating from the school of architecture in Venice, Mario Botta has established himself as a major influence upon contemporary architecture.

While in Venice, Botta had the good fortune to find employment with Le Corbusier on the Venice Hospital project and with Louis Kahn on his convention center exhibition. Both architects exerted a large influence upon Botta, as did Carlo Scarpa, his mentor at architecture school. Of the three, Kahn's influence was most profound; Kahn had been trained in Beaux-Arts principles of axial planning, and his expression of materials and their structural meaning is reflected most particularly in Botta's earlier work, a series of one-off houses set in the Swiss landscape. Their preoccupation is formal and contextual; there are none of the wider social concerns so evident, for example, in the work of Botta's Dutch contemporaries.

By contrast, Botta has established an architectural language confined to a program of houses commissioned by a wealthy bourgeoisie, ironically reflecting Le Corbusier's early career. Given the context of clientele and location, it is hardly surprising that the language thus evolved has much to do with tradition; in their monumentality the houses echo the vernacular buildings of Botta's native Ticino Canton; most embody a powerful image of symmetry (suggesting Kahn's Beaux-Arts influence) but are not doggedly subservient to its logical outcome; Botta's ability to insert dynamic components within the strong framework of geometrical order owes much to Le Corbusier; finally, the obsession with detail and texture reflects Scarpa's influence.

Where Botta's work has made its own contribution is not only in its contextualism but also as a convincing synthesis of the distinct attitudes pursued by his mentors. Nor is Botta constrained by modernist dogma; contextualism is heightened by a sense of historical continuity, form is not generated by function, and his architectural expression avoids any notion of clear structural expression. Nevertheless, all of Botta's work is imbued with an immense clarity largely borne of geometries in plan, section and elevation which create a sense of order and hierarchy.

The house at Riva San Vitale (1973) is a monumental cuboid form, square on plan but with an asymmetrically disposed staircase and huge voids and fissures to the elevations. The house at Ligornetto (1976), similarly monumental, employs a centrally disposed slot, suggested the influence of Robert Venturi, as does Botta's house at Pregassona (1979).

Even more divorced from any notion of structural expression is the house at Stabio (1981), a hugely scaled brick drum with a top-lit galleried slot at its diameter. The carefully organized fenestration is set back deep into the structure, heightening the stark contrast of solid and void. Massive sections of cantilevered masonry give no hint of structural support. Botta's most rigorous classical composition is his house in Viganello (1982). The main elevation, with its stepped masonry, is redolent of a Palladian staircase leading to the *piano nobile,* which of course it is not. A semicircular glazed barrel vault covers a centrally disposed terrace, while a top-lit undulating wall at the rear of the plan evokes Le Corbusier's ''. . . forms brought together in light.''

Such adherence to symmetry is again demonstrated at Morbio Superiore, Switzerland (1983), but there the plan allows for plastic elements to interplay freely with the overriding geometrical discipline, another reference to Le Corbusier. An interesting variation for corner plots is evident at Breganozona (1984) and Morbio Inferiore (1986). The corner locations have generated diagonal axes around which symmetrical plans are organized.

The sense of the monumental pervades Botta's work whether the program is domestic, social, commercial or civic. His large-scale projects have been few, but all exhibit the same confidence of his domestic work. The school at Morbio Inferiore (1977) was the result of a competition success, and ingeniously reconciled the conflicting geometries of classroom block and gymnasium by means of an amphitheater. Botta's acute concern for place and context led to his library at Capuchin Monastery, Lugano, (1976-79) being placed underground so as not to compete with existing 17th-century buildings.

Later large-scale commissions, most notably the Bank of Gothard, Lugano (1982), pursue Botta's contextualism. This huge complex is expressed as four linked pavilions, whose planning and elevational treatment evoke his previous houses, again emphasizing the importance of these domestic commissions for exploring a formal language.

Botta's real contribution to contemporary architecture has been by synthesis: the recognition that a fitting architectural language for our time may emerge from harnessing modernism to vernacular tradition.

—A. PETER FAWCETT

BOULLÉE, Etienne-Louis.

French. Born in Paris, France, 12 February 1728. Died in Paris, 6 February 1799. Father was the architect Louis-Claude Boullée; mother was Marie-Louise Boucher, probably related to the painter François Boucher. Studied with Jacques-François Blondel, Pierre-Etienne Lebon, Jean-Laurent Legeay and Germain Boffrand. Professor in Paris, from 1747. Appointed general controller of buildings, Hôtel des Invalides, 1778. Member, Académie Royale d'Architecture, 1762.

Chronology of Works
All in France

1752-54	Altar for the Chapelle du Clavaire and the Chapelle de la Vierge, Église St. Roch, Paris†
1762	Maison Tourolle, Paris (decorations)
1763	Chapelle St. Geneviève, Église St. Roch, Paris
1763-66	Hôtel Alexandre, Paris
1764	Hôtel de Monville, Paris†
1764-66	Château de Chaville, Paris†
1768-70	Hôtel de Pernon, Paris†
1769-71	Hôtel de Thun, Paris†
1774-79	Hôtel de Brunoy, Paris†
1780-82	Prison de la Grande Force, Paris†

Publications

BOOKS BY BOULLÉE

Architektur. German translation by Hanna Böck, with commentary by Adolf Max Vogt. Zürich, 1987.

BOOKS ABOUT BOULLÉE

BRAHAM, ALLAN: *The Architecture of the French Enlightenment.* Berkeley, California, and Los Angeles, 1980.

COULON, M.: *Etienne-Louis Boullée, architecte des Bâtiments du Roi.* Thesis. Paris, 1947.

ETLIN, RICHARD A.: ''Cities of the Dead: From Charnel House to Elysium in Eighteenth-Century Paris.'' Cambridge, Massachusetts, 1983.

KAUFMANN, EMIL: ''Etienne Louis Boullée.'' *Art Bulletin* 21, No. 3 (1939): 212-227.

KAUFMANN, EMIL: *Three Revolutionary Architects: Boullée, Ledoux, and Lequeu.* Philadelphia, 1952.

KAUFMANN, EMIL: *Architecture in the Age of Reason: Baroque and Post-Baroque in England, Italy, France.* Cambridge, Massachusetts, 1955.

LANKEIT, KLAUS: *Der Tempel der Vernunft: Unveröffentlichte Zeichnungen von Etienne-Louis Boullée.* Basel and Stuttgart, 1968.

LE CAMUS DE MÉZIERES, NICOLAS: *Le Génie de l'architecture ou l'Analogie de cet art avec nos sensations.* Paris, 1780.

LEMAGNY, J. C.: *Visionary Architects: Boullée, Ledoux, Lequeu.* Austin, Texas, 1990.

PÉROUSE DE MONTCLOS, JEAN-MARIE (ed.): *Etienne-Louis Boullée, Architecture, Essai sur l'art.* Paris, 1968.

PÉROUSE DE MONTCLOS, JEAN-MARIE: *Etienne-Louis Boullée, 1728-1799: De l'architecture classique à l'architecture révolutionnaire.* Paris, 1969.

PÉROUSE DE MONTCLOS, JEAN-MARIE: *Etienne-Louis Boullée, 1728-1799; Theoretician of Revolutionary Architecture.* New York, 1974.

ROSENAU, HELEN (ed.): *Boullée's Treatise on Architecture.* London, 1953.

ROSENAU, HELEN: *Boullée and His Visionary Architecture.* London, 1976.

ROSSI, ALDO (ed.): *Etienne-Louis Boullée, Architettura. Saggio sull'arte.* Padua, Italy, 1967.

STAROBINSKI, JEAN: *The Invention of Liberty; 1700-1789.* Geneva, 1964.

SZAMBIEN, WERNER: ''Notes sur le Recueil d'Architecture privée de Boullée (1792-1796).'' *Gazette des beaux-arts* 97 (1981): 111-124.

VOGT, ADOLF MAX: *Boullées Newton-Denkmal: Sakralbau und Kugelidee.* Basel and Stuttgart, 1969.

Etienne-Louis Boullée's importance as a teacher and a visionary architect far exceeds the importance of his building career. His teaching position in Paris (since 1747) and his membership in the *Académie Royale d'Architecture* (since 1762) steered him toward theoretical writings and drawings, which became the only means of expression left to him during the revolutionary period. As a passionate teacher, Boullée influenced an entire generation of students, including Jean-François-Thérèse Chalgrin, Alexandre-Théodore Brogniart and Jean-Nicolas-Louis Durand.

From 1740 to 1746, Boullée trained with different architects, such as Jacques-François Blondel and Jean-Laurent Legeay, from whom he assimilated the principles of the French classical tradition of the 17th and 18th centuries. From 1762 to 1778, Boullée worked only on private châteaux and hôtels. Most were demolished, but 18th-century prints and guidebooks recorded Boullée's most famous hôtels, such as the Hôtel Alexandre (1763, still existing), the Hôtel de Monville (1764) and the Hôtel de Brunoy (1774). Along with Claude-Nicolas Ledoux, Charles de Wailly and Marie-Joseph Peyre the Elder, Boullée pioneered a new form of domestic architecture in the 1760s. He designed the main unit of the hôtel as a horizontal compact block and monumentalized it with a giant order. Wings were covered with trellis work or hidden by blind walls to set off the volume of the main unit in such a way that it looked like a pavilion. With this composition, Boullée reinterpreted the Palladian villa type.

Boullée played a definitive role in the anti-Rococo movement of the 1760s by reintroducing 17th-century classical tradition in interior design. His contemporaries recognized the brilliance of his decoration. In addition to this reform, Boullée (like Ledoux) decorated rooms to evoke a mood appropriate for their function, an approach described by Jean-François Bastide in *La Petite Maison* (1753) and Nicolas Le Camus de Mézières in *Le Génie d'Architecture* (1780). The main innovation credited to Boullée is his attention to lighting, a theme that he began to develop in his domestic architecture and then further explored in his visionary drawings. In order to design his facade as compactly as possible and to avoid a monotonous repetition of windows, Boullée used skylights to create varied light effects.

The relation between architecture and nature was another theme that Boullée developed first in his domestic architecture and later in his visionary drawings. For example, Boullée envisioned the Hôtel de Brunoy in Paris as a temple to the goddess Flora. He linked the garden and the house both thematically and physically: he treated the back of the house as a temple raised on a podium of steps and topped by the statue of Flora, while wings were hidden under trelliswork. A small garden extended toward the Champs-Elysées, allowing the passerby to admire the entire composition.

With his appointment as general controller of buildings at the Hôtel des Invalides (1778), Boullée ceased to work for private clients and interceded in the planning of several public buildings until 1782. But from 1778 to 1788, he created drawings that represent the most original part of his oeuvre. According to Jean-Marie Pérouse de Montclos, Boullée's drawings, intended to illustrate his treatise *Architecture. Essai sur l'Art* (ca. 1790, published in 1953), can be separated into two categories: the projects for public competitions and the reworking of those building types for teaching purposes.

Boullée's renderings of his official projects and visionary drawings relied on picturesque effects and a sense of the monumental inspired by Roman antique architecture and the Baroque grandeur of Giovanni Lorenzo Bernini. The official projects that Boullée submitted, such as the remodeling of the Palace of Versailles (1780), the opera house of the Palais Royal (1781) and the public library (1784), were designed in this new manner,

but it was with his drawings of imaginary projects that Boullée revealed his originality to its greatest extent. Using bold geometrical forms, the repetition of the same element (the column) and little ornament other than light and shadow, he created a new genre of visionary composition.

Boullée's visionary buildings drew on the universal and eclectic sources of neoclassical culture: the 16th-century records of antique tombs and monuments, such as those of Jacques Androuet du Cerceau the Elder; the 18th-century imaginary reconstructions of antique architecture, such as those of Viel de Saint-Maux; G. B. Piranesi's imaginary illustrations of antiquity; and archaeological and travel accounts describing civilizations predating ancient Greece and Rome. This new historical relativism paralleled the rising interest in the effect of architecture on the sentiments and its didactic and moral power as experienced through sensations, a theory based on John Locke, Etienne de Condillac and Claude-Adrien Helvétius.

Boullée's architectural treatise, *Architecture. Essai sur l'Art*, was his ultimate statement and provided unity to his work. It begins with Boullée's definition of beauty, which is based on the three properties that he observed in nature: symmetry, regularity and variety; all three combine to produce harmony and proportion. In his doctrine titled "Théorie des Corps," Boullée describes the influence of volumes on our senses, such as the sphere which calls to mind order and perfection, and contrasts it with irregular volumes that invoke confusion. Transposing his observations from nature to architecture, Boullée then defines the character of a building as its impression on the human senses. In an analogy between architecture and nature, he borrows the pictorial effect of each season—the quality of light, the variety of colors and shapes, concealment and exposure—and transplants them into his architecture. In this way Boullée develops a whole architectural rhetoric in which images are displayed that elicit particular emotions, such as the image of grandeur for a palace, sadness for a tomb, or strength for a military building. Boullée's architecture, like the polarity of the seasons between life and death, is dedicated to the living and the dead. Public and funerary buildings are, for the most part, organized on a centralized plan that develops into precise and simple geometric volumes. With its rigor, Boullée's architecture recalls some points of the Abbé Laugier's reductionist doctrine: the elimination of unnecessary ornament, the use of freestanding columns carrying a straight entablature, and the use of a barrel vault over a rectangular plan. If Boullée sees nature as his source of inspiration, he also integrates it into some of his projects: the monument dedicated to the Supreme Being is a mountain (a natural pyramid) adorned only by a temple used as a pedestal.

Like Ledoux's, Boullée's architecture not only speaks but edifies. Boullée's choice to focus on public building for study, assembly and worship indicates his interest in an ethical role for architecture, encouraged by his readings of Jean-Jacques Rousseau, Helvétius and Denis Diderot. He emulated both palaces and antique buildings to achieve a sense of grandeur and dignity as described in his treatise. By referring to the concept of grandeur, Boullée alluded to Greco-Roman literary models that the French public upheld as a paradigm for the stoic and virtuous life.

—ANITA POLETTI-ANDERSON

BRAMANTE, Donato.

Italian. Born Donato di Angelo di Antonio/da Urbino/Pascuccio in Monte Asdrualdo (now Fermignano), near Urbino, 1444. Died 11 April 1514. May have trained as painter of perspective with Mantegna; student of Piero della Francesca. Worked with Leonardo da Vinci in Milan; entered service of Duke Ludovico, 1479; appointed consultant to Pavia Cathedral, 1488; fled from Milan to Rome, 1499.

Chronology of Works
All in Italy
* Approximate dates
† Work no longer exists

1478ff*	Santa Maria presso San Satiro, Milan (renovation and additions)
1488ff.	Pavia Cathedral (as consultant)
1492ff.	Piazza, Vignevano
1492ff.	Santa Maria delle Grazie (tribune)
1492	Canonica of San Ambrogio, Milan
1497	Santa Maria Nascente, Abbiategrasso (entrance)
1497-98ff.	Sant' Ambrogio, Milan (cloisters)
1500-04	Santa Maria della Pace, Rome (cloister)
1502*	Tempietto of San Pietro in Montorio, Rome
1504?	Belvedere Court
1505-06	St. Peter's, Rome (demolition and partial reconstruction of the old basilica)
1505-09	Santa Maria del Popolo (choir)
1508-09	Palazzo Caprini (House of Raphael), Rome†
1509ff.	Santi Celso e Giuliano†
1509ff.	Sant' Eligio [attributed]†
1513	Tegurio, Rome (shelter for St. Peter's Tomb)†

Publications

BOOKS ABOUT BRAMANTE

ACKERMAN, JAMES S.: *The Cortile del Belvedere*. Rome, 1954.
BARONI, C.: *L'architettura da Bramante al Ricchino*. Milan, 1941.
BELTRAMI, L.: *Bramante a Milano*. Milan, 1912.
BORSI, FRANCO: *Bramante*. Milan, 1989.
BRUSCHI, ARNALDO: *Bramante*. London, 1977.
CAROTTI, G.: *Le opere di Leonardo, Bramante e Raffaello*. Milan, 1905.
CESARIANO, CESARE: *Di Lucio Vitruvio Pollione de architectura*. 1521. Reprint: New York and London, 1968.
Congresso internazionale de studi bramanteschi. Rome, 1974.
DENKER NESSELRATH, CHRISTIANE: *Die Säulenordnungen bei Bramante*. Worms, 1990.
FÖRSTER, OTTO H.: *Bramante*. Vienna and Munich, 1956.
KERBER, OTTMAR: *Von Bramante zu Lucas von Hildebrandt*. Stuttgart, 1947.
MARI, A.: *Della vita e delle opere di Bramante da Urbino*. Ferrara, 1889.
VOGEL, J.: *Bramante und Raphael*. Leipzig, 1910.

ARTICLES ABOUT BRAMANTE

ALBERTINI, FRANCESCO: "Opusculum de mirabilibus urbis Romae." 1510. Reprinted in PETER MURRAY (ed.): *Five Early Guides to Rome and Florence*. Farnsborough, England, 1972.
HUSKINSON, J. M.: "The Crucifixion of St. Peter." *Journal of the Warburg and Courtauld Institutes* 32 (1969): 135-161.
MURRAY, PETER: "Bramante Milanese: The Prints and Drawings." *Arte Lombarda* 7, No. 1 (1962): 25-42.
MURRAY, PETER: "Leonardo and Bramante: Leonardo's Approach to Anatomy and Architecture and Its Effect on Bramante." *Architectural Review* 134 (1963): 346-351.
MURRAY, PETER: "Menicantonio, du Cerceau, and the Towers of St. Peter's." In *Studies in Renaissance and Baroque Art Presented to Anthony Blunt*. London, 1967.
PEDRETTI, CARLO: "Newly Discovered Evidence of Leonardo's Association with Bramante." *Journal of the Society of Architectural Historians* 32 (1973): 223-237.

*

Giorgio Vasari, in his *Lives of the Artists,* wrote that Bramante produced an ideal plan for the Church of St. Peter's, but that incompetent architects later ruined it. Ultimately their mistakes were corrected by Michelangelo, who improved Bramante's plan. Vasari's anecdote is symptomatic of the high esteem afforded Bramante during the 16th century. Simply stated, he was unsurpassed as an architect and, at least in Vasari's view, only Michelangelo would prove his superior.

Bramante's fame was founded on his ability to rival the architecture of antiquity. He was the only architect of the High Renaissance, with the possible exception of Raphael, who was considered the equal of the ancients. Sebastiano Serlio, in his *Books on Architecture* (1537) wrote that ". . . he revived the good architecture which had been buried from the days of the Ancients until now." Andrea Palladio, in his *Four Books on Architecture* (1570), delivered a comparable encomium: ". . . Bramante was the first to bring to light the good and beautiful architecture which had been hidden from the time of the Ancients." Both authors included wood engravings of Bramante's Roman buildings side by side with the famed monuments of antiquity. Not only was Bramante considered the equal of the ancients, but he was perceived to be the originator of a new ideal.

Donato de Angelo di Antonio early acquired his nickname of Bramante. Little is known about his early years, not even his date of birth, but he probably received some formal education. Attempts have been made to locate Bramante's early architectural activity at the Ducal Palace in Urbino, under construction during the 1460s and 1470s. In particular, the Chapel of the Perdono, the Ducal Study and the Church of San Bernardino are occasionally attributed to Bramante. However, there is no evidence of Bramante's continuing presence in Urbino, except for the proximity of his native town, which simply would indicate an early familiarity with Luciano Laurana's architecture at the Palazzo Ducale, and perhaps the works of Francesco di Giorgio.

He is first documented in Bergamo, in 1477, where he painted a figurative frieze for the facade of the Palazzo del Podesta. In 1481, one of his drawings was transformed into an engraved model for painters to carry out. Therefore, it seems reasonable to accept contemporary accounts of Bramante's first training as a painter of perspective, under the shadow of Andrea Mantegna and as a student of Piero della Francesca. About 1479, he entered the service of Duke Ludovico Sforza, and by 1482 he had taken up more or less permanent residence in Milan, where he turned increasingly to architecture. He came into close contact with Leonardo da Vinci, who had arrived shortly after Bramante, also to work for the duke. In 1488 Bramante worked as a consultant at the Pavia Cathedral, and in 1490 he advised on the crossing tower of the Milan Cathedral. At that point in his career, he was established as an expert of architectural matters. Ducal projects at Vigevano resulted in Bramante planning the town piazza and surrounding streets, as well as illusionistic paintings from about 1492 to 1494. The rebuilding of the cloisters at the medieval Church of Sant' Ambrogio took place during his final years in Milan.

Donato Bramante: Tempietto of San Pietro in Montorio, Rome, Italy, ca. 1502

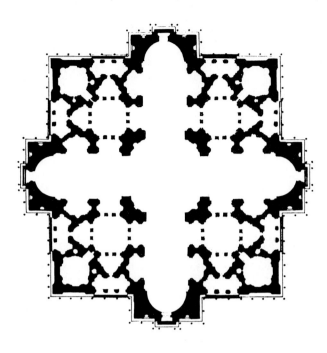

ST. PETER'S, ROME

Although over fifty years old, Bramante had yet to reach the pinnacle of his career. Absolute recognition would come with the works of his Roman years. Yet the assured manipulation of space that characterized his later architecture would have been unthinkable without the groundwork laid in Milan. There, Bramante had been introduced to Vitruvius and, thus, to the crucial connection between architectural theory and practice. In pursuit of the ideal form, his investigations of centralized church plans paralleled studies in the manuscript pages of Leonardo da Vinci. Although it is impossible to establish formal collaboration, there remains little doubt that cross-fertilization of ideas shaped Bramante's lifelong preoccupation with an architecture based on conceptual draftsmanship, harmonious proportion and perspective views. And Bramante must have influenced Leonardo, for it was during that period that the latter commenced writing a treatise on architecture. Bramante surely examined the Early Christian "antiquities" in Lombardy first-hand and, like Leonardo, studied descriptions of Hagia Sofia. However, this hospitable environment was to vanish in 1499 when the French invaded Lombardy, ending Sforza rule.

Bramante had moved permanently to Rome by 1500, although documented absences from Milan in 1492 and 1493 suggest prior trips. Certainly the sobriety of his later Milanese works, particularly the Doric cloister at Sant' Ambrogio, can be seen as a prelude to his Roman period. Vasari related that Bramante worked under Antonio da Sangallo the Elder on the corridor in the Vatican Borgo and executed a fresco at the Lateran for the Holy Year 1500. More significant, Bramante had the resources to devote himself to study, drawing and measuring antiquities as far south as Naples. Then the succession of Julius II in 1503 secured Bramante's ascendancy. Few of Bramante's Roman buildings exist as he intended them, but his projects survive in the form of numerous drawings (both autograph and variants), in the testimony of his contemporaries, and in his

influence on a younger generation. Among the architects who trained in his Roman workshop were Antonio da Sangallo the Younger, Jacopo Sansovino, Baldassare Peruzzi and Raphael.

A chronological survey of selected works by Bramante begins in Milan, where he rebuilt the Church of Santa Maria presso San Satiro in stages. San Satiro was an early medieval structure approximating a Greek-cross plan. Perhaps as early as 1478 Bramante began the renovation of the centralized church, attaching a rectangular oratory with a barrel vault and central dome. A second building campaign, from 1482 to 1486, resulted in an example of Bramante's early ability to forge classical solutions from unconventional design problems. With the decision to convert the oblong church into a basilica, he devised a Latin-cross plan, with the transformation of the extant building into a transept and the construction of a wide nave. In the interior, Bramante introduced illusionistic perspective in the nearly flat choir to suggest depth, a technical tour-de-force typical of his expertise as a painter. The wide barrel vault over the nave rests in lateral walls articulated by giant pilasters, recalling the interior of Sant' Andrea in Mantua. Bramante could have studied Leon Battista Alberti's plan, then in construction, on his way to Milan. Like Alberti, Bramante employed classically inspired motif's throughout the interior, such as the coffering in the dome at the crossing.

Bramante experimented with newly formulated ideas about centralized church plans at Santa Maria delle Grazie, also in Milan, during the 1490s. He worked on the eastern end—in the area of the crossing, choir and transepts—with the result that a spacious tribune emerged at the end of the extant Gothic nave. In the interior, illumination floods the crossing, revealing the harmonious proportions and classical detailing of the decoration. The exterior of the tribune shows the massing of semicircular apses around a rectangular core, all topped by a massive drum. Bramante's interest in the fusion of geometrical forms, carried out on a grand scale, is implicit in the monumental tribune, which was to serve as a mausoleum for the Sforza family. Carried out after Bramante's departure, the decoration of the exterior conflicts with the classical inspiration of the whole.

Bramante's Tempietto in Rome was his greatest achievement. The small, circular building evolved from a highly personal interpretation of the antique, but the harmony of the architecture made it the symbol of a universal ideal. Only an architect with a profound understanding of antiquity could have resurrected a purely classical form, albeit using the syntax of the Renaissance. Properly speaking, the Tempietto was neither a church nor, naturally, a temple. Instead, it functioned as a martyrium, marking the presumed site of St. Peter's crucifixion on the Janiculum. The property, adjoining the Church of San Pietro in Montorio, belonged to the Spanish Franciscans. It is likely that Bramante was engaged by Ferdinand and Isabella of Spain as early as 1502, the date on a commemorative inscription, but it is difficult to know at what point construction ceased. He may have continued to work on the project intermittently during the decade. Although the essential structure of the small temple is finished, the circular peristyle planned by Bramante to frame the building was never begun.

Today the Tempietto stands in a narrow courtyard. The impression of its monumentality results from the classical conception, rather than the scale of the building, which is diminutive. The circular plan, so dear to Renaissance theorists, evoked the perfection of ancient Rome. Not only did it have pagan antecedents, but it also had Early Christian roots, as in the centralized churches of Lombardy familiar to Bramante. Bramante employed the Doric order for the colonnade, including a correct entablature with metopes and triglyphs. He surely followed the advice of Vitruvius, who recommended the Doric temple as appropriate to heroic, male gods. Serlio acknowledged that connection in Book IV of his treatise, when he credited Bramante with adapting the Doric temple to Christian purposes. Additionally, Bramante transformed the ancient motifs found on metopes into liturgical symbols, synthesizing the classical with the Christian in the details of the restrained decoration.

In the new Church of St. Peter's, Bramante sought to resurrect the physical authority of imperial Rome, and to imbue it with equally potent Christian symbolism. The church was to be a fitting monument to the "Prince of the Apostles," Saint Peter, in the form of a centralized martyrium. Julius II, elected pope in October 1503, viewed himself as the fitting successor to the first pope, and he probably solicited plans from Bramante as soon as the next year. Without a doubt, Julius II embarked upon the project in concert with Bramante. The Julian program called for building projects on a vast scale for the express purpose of restoring Rome to the position of *caput mundi*. Architect and patron conceived of the rebuilding of St. Peter's as the key element.

Bramante was the first architect to work on St. Peter's since Bernardo Rossellino followed Alberti's scheme for renovating the Constantinian basilica in the mid-15th century. Whereas the Early Renaissance architect had rebuilt the choir to the west, Bramante's proposal required the demolition of the old church and the imposition of a totally new plan. The foundation stone was laid in April 1506. Work commenced at the four giant piers of the crossing but did not progress far before the pope's death in 1513, and Bramante's the next year. Reports of structural problems, specifically cracks in the piers and arches, indicated Bramante's lack of expertise in the technology of vaulting. His early plans show a giant dome, like the Pantheon, resting on narrow piers, supports later enlarged by other architects. Nevertheless, the position and height of the piers established the scale of the building, and even as the church evolved over the course of the next century, Bramante's plan lay at the core. His sensitive revival of ancient motifs, in the coffering of the connecting arches and the Corinthian pilasters at the crossing, imbue the interior with a classical integrity, apparent even with layers of modern decoration.

Various stages of the project survive in drawings from the circle of Bramante. The most finished is an autograph presentation drawing, the so-called Parchment Plan (Uffizi A1), probably dating to 1506. In the same year, Caradosso, the papal medalist, struck a foundation medal with a corresponding elevation. Bramante's drawing represents half of a ground plan that would have consisted of a Greek cross with four minor Greek crosses in the arms. The crossing is vaulted by an immense, hemispherical dome, with the minor crosses supporting smaller domes. Towers rise at the corners. Despite their reliability, the Parchment Plan and the medal do not seem to represent the final solution. To the contrary, the quantity of alternative designs stemming from Bramante's ideas suggests that both architect and pope experimented continually with other forms. The decision to build a purely centralized church seems to have remained in contention, for a second type emerges in the drawings proposing a central plan with a nave extension. Serlio illustrated this type, although he attributed the design to Raphael, Bramante's successor as architect of St. Peter's. Yet both church plans are consistent with Bramante's own oeuvre: a centralized martyrium (like the Tempietto) and a basilican plan combined with a centralized tribune (like Santa Maria delle Grazie in Milan). It is also important to acknowledge that Bramante envisioned a piazza, blocked out in sketches, as the ideal urban setting for the new basilica.

Bramante's vision of city planning depended on a corresponding fusion of architecture with perspectival design and symbolic function, whether religious or political. His role in the rebuilding of Rome, fostered by Julius II, has only recently emerged in the analysis of specific projects. For example, the pope directed Bramante to plan a residential district along the axis of the new Via Giulia, extending from the Pons Triumphalis to the Ponte Sisto. A new judicial center, the Palazzo dei Tribunali (1508-09), was planned around an enormous courtyard, with the Church of San Biagio, on a variation of the Greek-cross plan, to the rear. A piazza was to rise in front of the huge palace block, near the midpoint of Via Giulia, extending as far as the Palazzo della Vecchia Cancelleria. The scale of such urban projects matched the ambitions of both architect and patron, but not their means. Yet the plans for the Via Giulia represented but one link in a comprehensive network of streets for the new Rome.

Raphael painted a portrait of Bramante, his teacher and friend, as Euclid in the *School of Athens* in the Stanza della Segnatura. The pairing of the early-16th-century architect and the ancient geometer epitomizes the contemporary view of Bramante. He was recognized for reviving the principles of antiquity in his buildings and, as did Euclid, he taught theoretical truths to his followers.

—EUNICE D. HOWE

BREUER, Marcel.

American. Born in Pécs, Hungary, 22 May 1902. Died in New York City, 1 July 1981. Married Martha Erps, 1926; married Constance Crocker, 1940; two children. Immigrated to the United States in 1937; naturalized in 1944. Educated at Allami Föreáiskola, Pécs, 1912-20; Bauhaus, Weimar, Germany, 1920-24. Master of the Bauhaus, Weimar, 1924, and Dessau, Germany, 1925-28. Architect and planner in Dessau, 1925-28, Berlin, 1928-31, and London (in partnership with F. R. S. Yorke), 1935-36; associate professor, Harvard University School of Design, Cambridge, Massachusetts, 1937-46; principal, Marcel Breuer and Associates, Cambridge, Massachusetts, 1937-46, and New York City, 1946-76. Fellow, American Institute of Architects; Gold Medal, American Institute of Archtiects, 1968; Grande Medaille d'Or, French Academy of Architecture, 1976.

Chronology of Works
All in the United States unless noted

1924-28	Prototype steel furniture and interchangeable cabinet units
1932	Harnischmacher House I, Wiesbaden, Germany
1935-36	Doldertal Apartments, Zurich, Switzerland (with Roth Brothers)
1936	Isokon Laminated Furniture, England (with F. R. S. Yorke)
1936	Gane's Exhibition Pavilion, Bristol, England (with Yorke)
1937	Isokon Bar, London, England (with Yorke)
1938	Wheaton College Art Center, Norton, Massachusetts, (with Walter Gropius)
1938	Gropius House, Lincoln, Massachusetts (with Gropius)
1938	Haggerty House, Cohasset, Massachusetts (with Gropius)
1939	Breuer House I, Lincoln, Massachusetts

Marcel Breuer: Harnischmacher House I, Wiesbaden, Germany, 1932

1940	Chamberlain Cottage, Wayland, Massachusetts (with Gropius)
1943	Wartime Housing, New Kensington, Pittsburgh, Pennsylvania (with Gropius)
1945	Geller House, Lawrence, Long Island, New York
1947	Breuer House II, New Canaan, Connecticut
1950	Co-op Dormitory, Vassar College, Poughkeepsie, New York
1952-58	UNESCO Headquarters, Paris, France (with Pier Luigi Nervi and Bernard Zehrfuss)
1953-70	St. John's Abbey and University, Collegeville, Minnesota (with H. Smith)
1954-57	Institute for Advanced Study Housing, Princeton, New Jersey (with R. F. Gatje)
1957	De Bijenkorf Store, Rotterdam, Netherlands (with A. Elzas)
1958	United States Embassy, The Hague, Netherlands
1959	Convent of the Annunciation, Bismarck, North Dakota (with H. Smith)
1961	IBM Research Center, Le Gaude, Var, France (with Gatje)
1966	Whitney Museum, New York City (with H. Smith)
1969	Engineering Building, Yale University, New Haven, Connecticut
1970	Cleveland Museum of Art, Cleveland, Ohio (with H. Smith)
1975	Australian Embassy, Paris, France (with Harry Seidler and M. Jossa)
1977	Federal Courthouse and Offices, Columbia, South Carolina (with H. Beckbard and others)

Publications

BOOKS BY BREUER

Sun and Shadow: The Philosophy of an Architect. Edited by Peter Blake. New York, 1955.

ARTICLES BY BREUER

"Das Innere de Hauses." *Bauwelt* (May 1931).
"Aus einem Vortrag . . . gehalten im Kunstgewerbemuseum Zürich." *Werk* No. 19 (1932).

"Where Do We Stand?" *Architectural Review* (April 1935).
"Architecture and Material." *Circle: International Survey of Constructive Art* (1937).
"What Is Modern Architecture?." *Museum of Modern Art Bulletin* (Spring 1948).
"Les buts de l'architecture." *Architecture, formes et fonctions* 9 (1962-63): 6-29.
"Genesis of Design." Pp. 120-125 in GYORGY KEPES (ed.): *The Man-made Object.* New York, 1966.

*

Marcel Breuer was one of the pioneers of the Modern Movement in architecture, important as an architect, as a teacher and as a furniture designer.

Born in Hungary, Breuer moved to Vienna in 1920 as an art student, but at the Art Academy he found the conservative teaching irrelevant and boring, and he looked around for a more exciting, innovative establishment. He found his ideal in Walter Gropius and the new Weimar Bauhaus, and enrolled as one of its first students when he was still only 18 years old. Four years later he was master in charge of the Bauhaus furniture workshops, and it was as a furniture designer that the young Breuer first made his mark. In the Bauhaus workshops, Breuer invented and developed tubular steel furniture, and most of the tubular steel furniture manufactured throughout the world is based on his original designs. In 1925 the Bauhaus moved to Dessau, with a new building designed by Gropius; Breuer was commissioned to design all the furniture and fittings for the building, and the new workshops gave him scope to expand his ideas and his teaching.

At the age of 26, Breuer left the Bauhaus and set up an architectural practice in Berlin. Younger than the earlier pioneers like Gropius or Ludwig Mies van der Rohe, and brought up with the modern outlook at the Bauhaus, Breuer did not need to proclaim his modernity. He had no need to turn each project into a manifesto; he could simply build sanely and well using the architecture of the time. So his buildings are usually gentler, more practical and better built than most modern buildings of a similar date. Breuer also had the confidence to build in natural materials, breaking away from the hard white cubes that were de rigueur for modern architects in the 1920s and 1930s.

From his background as a furniture designer, Breuer brought a fascination with mass production and the repetition of identical factory-made units, and all his life he produced projects for large buildings and housing developments employing mass-produced elements. It was as a designer of single houses, however, that Breuer was at his best. During his early practice in Berlin, he designed the Harnismacher house, built at Wiesbaden in 1932 and unfortunately destroyed during the war. The Harnismacher house must have been one of the most livable of the early modern houses, with sensible planning, generous sun-terraces, colored fabrics and rich materials— chrome and shiny wood.

The coming of the Nazis made Germany an unsympathetic place for modern architects, and Breuer, like so many students and teachers from the Bauhaus, had to leave Germany if he wished to develop his ideas. Siegfried Giedion, historian and enthusiastic supporter of modern architecture, invited Breuer to Zurich to design two blocks of flats in collaboration with local architects A. & E. Roth. The design was a development of the Harnismacher house; gentler and more elegant, it was indicative of Breuer's growth as a designer.

In 1935, Breuer went to London and set up in practice with F.R.S. Yorke. The mid-1930s were the golden age of modern architecture in England, as the local architects of the nascent Modern Movement teamed up with world-famous emigrés from Hitler's Germany—Erich Mendelsohn, Gropius, Arthur Korn and Breuer himself. Breuer and Yorke designed and built a few houses. They were of very high quality and continued the Breuer direction of increasing gentleness and the use of natural materials—the giving of a softly smiling face to the International Style. The key year was 1936. A seaside house at Angnering-on-Sea had its main floor raised to give sea views, and it was very much the International Style villa of white cube raised on stilts. Two houses for masters at Eton College kept the cube and the rigorous geometry of the International Style, but returned to the English tradition of building in exposed brickwork. With the Gane Pavilion, an exhibition house for a furniture manufacturer in Bristol, Breuer and Yorke took the natural-materials route a step further by building in stone. In 1937 they built the Isokon Bar in London's Hampstead—for 20 years a meeting place for architects and artists.

The connection with Isokon took Breuer back to his first love—designing furniture. For Jack Pritchard of Isokon, Breuer designed chairs, tables, shelves, and the best-known, the bent ply reclining chair, which is among the most famous 20th-century chairs and is still in production. That chair sums up Breuer's virtues in that it is comfortable and constructed of a traditional material used in a technically sophisticated way.

Meanwhile, Breuer's old Bauhaus mentor Walter Gropius had become professor at Harvard. In 1937 he invited Breuer to join him as partner in his practice and as a teacher at Harvard. At Harvard, Gropius and Breuer trained many of those who were to dominate American architecture in the next generation—I.M. Pei, Philip Johnson, Paul Rudolph, John Johansen, Ed Barnes and the Australian Harry Seidler.

In their practice at Cambridge, Massachusetts, Gropius and Breuer each designed themselves houses in Lincoln, a suburb of Boston; they also designed houses for some of the area's prominent families: the Haggertys, the Fords and the Franks. These houses were random stonework and white painted timber, a happy combination of the traditions of European modernism and the traditional architecture of New England. In a little weekend cottage for the Chamberlains, they went a step further in the softening of modern architecture and built in unpainted wood.

After the war Breuer left Gropius and opened his own office in New York. He built himself an exquisite house in New Canaan, Connecticut, and for a decade constructed a series of houses that were a delight—habitable, comfortable and beautiful—culminating in an exhibition house in the garden of New York's Museum of Modern Art. The impact of Breuer's postwar houses on the American lifestyle was probably greater than any other architect at that time.

Success brought fame, and fame brought big commissions. UNESCO in Paris, an abbey church in Minnesota, offices for IBM, the Whitney Museum of American Art in Manhattan. These large structures, which often have quality, never rise to the standard of the best houses, and it is for the houses and the furniture that Breuer is best remembered.

—JOHN WINTER

BRIDGEMAN, Charles.

British. English landscape architect. Died in 1738. Worked under Henry Vanbrugh and the Royal Gardener Henry Wise at Blenheim, 1709; appointed Wise's assistant, 1726; collaborated with Wise on gardens at Eastbury, Claremont and Stowe; royal gardener to King George II and Queen Caroline, 1728-38; also worked at Hampton Court, Kensington, Hyde Park and Richmond, 1726-38; worked for private patrons at Blenheim, Eastbury, Wimpole, Marble Hill and Stowe. Joined St. Luke's Club for artists, 1726.

Chronology of Works
All in England
* Approximate dates
† Work no longer exists

1715*	Gardens at Chiswick [attributed]
1715-late	Gardens at Stowe†
1720s	
1715-20*	Gardens at Rousham†
1726-38	Gardens at Hampton Court, Kensington, St. James and Richmond

Publications

BOOKS ABOUT BRIDGEMAN

WHATELY, THOMAS: *Observations on Modern Gardening.* 1770.
WILLIS, PETER: *Charles Bridgeman and the English Landscape Garden.* London, 1977.

*

When one thinks of 18th-century English garden design, names such as William Kent and Lancelot "Capability" Brown come to mind before that of Charles Bridgeman. However, Bridgeman probably had more influence on the development of the English landscape garden than either of his famous successors. Bridgeman is known for his rather formal, geometric garden plans, which came out of the tradition of Renaissance and Baroque Italian and French gardens. These gardens were characterized by such features as parterres, kitchen gardens, geometric

Charles Bridgeman: Gardens at Stowe, Buckinghamshire, England, 1715-late 1720s

lakes and ponds, and straight avenues leading one through the grounds.

Bridgeman, while utilizing some of these elements in his designs, introduced new transitional features that preceded the freer plans of Kent and Brown. The most significant innovation attributed to Bridgeman is the "ha-ha," a low ditch physically delineating the boundary of the garden, but having the added feature of being invisible to the viewer. Thus, the ha-ha, which supposedly derives its names from one's astonished expression upon discovering the hidden ditch ("ah-ah"), marked the border of one's property, while bridging the garden with the "wilderness" of the English landscape beyond. Another significant change was Bridgeman's use of *pattes d'oie,* avenues that directed the visitor's view toward specific focal points either within the garden or outside its limits. Though virtually nothing of Bridgeman's work exists today, plans and descriptions provide an idea of the appearance of his gardens.

Little is known about Bridgeman's early life or training. He appeared on the scene in 1709 at Blenheim, working under the direction of John Vanbrugh, the architect, and Henry Wise, the royal gardener. From those two men, Bridgeman was exposed to the massive grandeur and sensuous formality of the Baroque as well as an architectural approach to gardens. He continued to collaborate with Vanbrugh at Eastbury, Claremont and Stowe until 1726, the year of Vanbrugh's death. During that period, Bridgeman had a hand in the design of many of the most important English gardens of the time, including Chiswick, Stowe, Rousham and Hampton Court.

Bridgeman's participation at Chiswick, circa 1715, is questionable, though his presence there was asserted by Thomas Whately in his *Observations on Modern Gardening* (1770). Indeed, Bridgeman's inclusion in the circles of Alexander Pope and Lord Burlington would suggest such a presence, particularly in the early stages of the garden's design. Further evidence pointing to Bridgeman's influence at Chiswick is seen in the use of garden buildings as the focal points of radiating allées and rectangular pools. However, Lord Burlington's own strong interest in garden design and the fact that the account books provide no confirmation of Bridgeman's activity there leave the matter a mystery.

We do know that Bridgeman was the first gardener to work at Stowe, around 1715, when he was called in by Lord Cobham to work on the landscape while Vanbrugh made alterations to the house and garden buildings. At Stowe, Bridgeman's formal gardens were confined primarily to the southwestern side of the manor house. However, the surrounding land was a blend of the formal and the informal. Long straight walks and geometric pools were set out with broad lawns and mounts commanding spectacular views of the countryside. Bridgeman continued to work at Stowe into the late 1720s, and was joined there by James Gibbs (Vanbrugh's replacement) in 1726. Nevertheless, much of Bridgeman's work was short-lived; beginning in 1738, Kent began to make the garden more naturalistic, and Bridgeman's work was virtually destroyed.

We have a better idea of Bridgeman's influence at Rousham (circa 1715-20), thanks to a plan dating from about 1715. The plan shows Bridgeman's mixture of precise garden forms with more irregular groves. It also reveals his skill at "enlarging" a relatively small garden by using winding paths through wooded areas, which occasionally open onto theatrical glades, providing prospects looking out beyond the bounds of the garden itself. When Kent began redesigning the garden in 1737, he transformed many of the straight walks and geometric areas into freer, more natural areas, but he did maintain much of Bridgeman's early layout. Features that survived Kent's changes at Rousham include a bowling green on the garden side of the house, a serpentine walk through the wilderness to the Cold Bath, and the straight Elm Walk. The well-known Venus Vale was created by Bridgeman, but Kent altered it by changing the location of the path leading to it and adding statues that contribute to the thematic focus of the garden as it exists today.

Bridgeman's successes at Stowe and Rousham led to his appointment as Henry Wise's partner in the royal gardens in 1726. Two years later, with his succession to royal gardener to George II, Bridgeman became responsible for the gardens of Hampton Court, Kensington, St. James' Park and Richmond. At those sites, Bridgeman continued to merge the formal garden with more progressive elements. Such examples are the Serpentine in Hyde Park and the Round Pond in Kensington Garden.

Unlike his successors, Bridgeman seems to have had little interest in design theory or to have associated his work with any cultural or political cause. Nor did he develop the emblematic or associational qualities of garden design, which became popular under Kent in such areas as the Elysian Fields at Stowe. Bridgeman was more concerned in bridging the formality of 17th-century Italian gardens with the illusion of unlimited space in his innovative use of ha-ha's and prospects. Yet, in those changes, Bridgeman may have encouraged the rise of nationalism, which made the *jardin anglais* a symbol of English pride in the latter half of the 18th century.

—JULIE NICOLETTA

BRODRICK, Cuthbert.

British. Born in Hull, England, 1822. Died in England, 1905. Traveled in France, 1844. Apprenticed with Henry Francis Lockwood (1811-78).

Chronology of Works
All in England
*Approximate dates
†Work no longer exists

1852	Royal Institution, Hull†
1853-58	Town Hall, Leeds
1860	Hydropathic Establishment (now College of Housecraft), Ilkley, Yorkshire
1860-63	Corn Exchange, Leeds
1862	Town Hall, Hull (parts since re-used in a memorial at Brantingham, Yorkshire)
1862*	Warehouse, King Street, Leeds†
1863-67	The Cliffs (now Grand Hotel), Scarborough, Yorkshire
1865-68	Mechanics' Institute (now theater), Leeds
1866	Turkish Baths, Cookridge Street, Leeds†

Publications

BOOKS ABOUT BRODRICK

DIXON, ROGER, and MUTHESIUS, STEFAN: *Victorian Architecture.* New York and Toronto, 1978.
LINSTRUM, DEREK: *West Yorkshire: Architects and Architecture.* London, 1978.
WILSON, T. B.: *Two Leeds Architects: Cuthbert Brodrick and George Corson.* Leeds, 1937.

ARTICLES ABOUT BRODRICK

LINSTRUM, DEREK: "Architecture of Cuthbert Broderick." *Country Life* 141 (1967): 1379-1381.
"Obituary of Cuthbert Broderick." *Builder* 88 (1905): 272.

*

Of the 16 proposals for a new town hall submitted in the 1852 competition at Leeds, the assessor, Sir Charles Barry, chose that of an inexperienced 27-year-old architect from Hull, Cuthbert Brodrick, who succeeded in designing and building one of the most important and acclaimed civic structures in Victorian England. Having thereby established his reputation as an architect, Brodrick was throughout his career extremely independent in terms of style and is, therefore, difficult to classify, even in considering his masterpiece, the Leeds town hall. In its massing it suggests, principally, the English Baroque of John Vanbrugh, yet it is also vaguely reminiscent of earlier romantic classicism.

There are even hints of Brodrick's French leanings, developed undoubtedly during his travels in France in 1844 at the age of 21.

In 1854 Brodrick revised his plans for the Leeds town hall, adding a tower at the suggestion of Barry, and construction began in August 1853. The south and principal facade consists of a deeply recessed portico of Corinthian columns flanked by projecting wings. The massive columns, 65 feet high, support a plain classical entablature that rings the entire building, topped off by a balustrade on all four sides. Double rows of windows pierce the walls of the wings flanking the entrance portico, and thus soften the monumental grandeur of the entrance by providing a contrasting human scale, which is reinforced by the horizontal band dividing the facade into halves. On the side walls windows are separated by pilasters extending the full length of the facade. Brodrick was particularly skillful in playing off such elements against each other, for example, the divided and layered wall against the uninterrupted flow of columns and pilasters. It was in the adroit handling of such details that Brodrick managed to recall the massing of the romantic classical tradition, while prefiguring the Neo-Baroque style that emerged soon after in town halls such as John Belcher's at Colchester.

Baroque treatment characterizes the roof level with its balustrade and stone vases placed at frequent intervals, creating a lively visual landscape above the impressive facades. Near the building's four corners, and behind the balustrades, rise small square structures, which not only provide additional visual variety, but house a sophisticated air-circulation system for the interior. Brodrick was the first town hall builder in England to plan such practical and necessary mechanical systems as an integral part of the structure. Likewise, he was the first to provide for all the specific office spaces required by city administration, relating them to the movement of the public and staff through carefully arranged corridors, all situated around the central hall. In this regard alone Brodrick revolutionized English town hall planning, which had not been noted for its attention to such mundane but essential details.

The attic that rises from the roof articulates the great hall below. Forward of the attic and centered on the entrance vestibule rises a striking tower—the first on a major English town hall since the turn of the century. The monumental, yet somewhat simple, facade provides a massive, solid and classical base from which the tower rises, surely the most successful aspect of the exterior design.

Brodrick's particular talent for playing off disparate architectural elements reveals itself most clearly in his handling of the base of the tower. Its rows of Corinthian columns support an entablature crowned with a balustrade carrying small stone vases. The base of the tower replicates and plays off against the entire facade below it. Similarly the concave surfaces of the tower contrast sharply with the flat expanse of facades below them. Resulting from the interplay of such details and from Brodrick's overall massing of elements is a building reminiscent of both Christopher Wren and Vanbrugh, yet also prophetic of later Edwardian Neo-Baroque.

As one enters the portico, a spacious vestibule situated directly beneath the tower provides a striking introduction to the great hall just beyond. With its vast, vaulted ceiling, this hall could accommodate 8,000 people for special occasions. At its north end an apse contains the stage and organ. Brodrick's hall at Leeds is derivative of Harvey Lonsdale Elmes' at Liverpool, which had become a prototype for town hall construction throughout England. As at Liverpool, crown and civil courts are included, in Leeds at the northern end of the building. Interestingly, at the time of construction there were not needed, but Brodrick convinced the town fathers to allow him to incorpo-

Cuthbert Brodrick: Town Hall, Leeds, England 1853-58

rate the courts into his plan in the hope that Leeds would grow enough in importance and stature to become the seat of the assize courts. This came to pass a few years later, no doubt due in part to the prestige confirmed upon Leeds by its new, impressive town hall.

Opulent detail, superior craftsmanship and first-rate materials became Brodrick's hallmark. Minton tiles grace the entrance vestibule floor; John Thomas executed the sculptures, and J.C. Crace decorated the great hall and other interior spaces. Unfortunately, his work has been painted over, and the proportions of the great hall itself were ruined by the inclusion of a gallery at a later date. Dedicated by Queen Victoria and Prince Albert, the Leeds town hall was highly acclaimed in its time. Brodrick's achievement there directly inspired three other important town halls, at Morley, Portsmouth and Bolton.

As a result of his success at Leeds, Brodrick was one of only six architects invited to submit designs for the National Gallery in London. In Leeds itself he executed three other notable buildings—the Calverly Street Baths (1866), the Mechanic's Institute (1865), now a theater, and the Corn Exchange (1860-63). The latter was consciously anachronistic for 1860 since it

strongly evoked romantic classicism with its rusticated walls penetrated by arches at regular intervals. With its vast interior and simple massing, Brodrick created a commercial building as successful and impressive as its civic counterpart, the town hall. Typical of Brodrick's other efforts, the Corn Exchange eludes stylistic classification.

Brodrick's resort hotel, the Cliffs, now the Grand Hotel, at Scarborough, Yorkshire (1863-67), was built just before his retirement. Overlooking steep cliffs along the sea, it reveals, more than his other efforts, Brodrick's French inclinations. The mansard roof and conical domes at each corner create a unique silhouette at the roof line. The result is a sort of Anglicized French Second Empire mansard roof, typical of Brodrick's best work in that it is visually successful, masterfully detailed and difficult to classify within the usual stylistic categories. Shortly after completion of the hotel, Brodrick retired from architecture, moved to Paris, and in retirement devoted himself to landscape painting. The town hall and Corn Exchange at Leeds remain as the best examples of his diverse, complex achievements in architecture.

—FRANCIS J. GREENE

BROGNIART, Alexandre-Théodore.

French. Born in Paris, France, 15 February 1739. Died in Paris, 6 June 1813. Studied with Jacques-François Blondel and Etienne-Louis Boullée. Succeeded Boullée as architect at the Hôtel des Invalides and the École Militaire; appointed to Conseil des Bâtiments Civiles, 1795; named as consultant for the Panthéon; also worked as porcelain designer for Sèvres.

Chronology of Works
All in France
† Work no longer exists

1769-73	Hôtel de Mme. de Montesson, Paris†
1771	Hôtel de Taillepied de Bondi, Paris†
1772-74	Hôtel du Duc d'Orléans, Paris†
1774-77	Hôtel de Monaco, Paris
1775	Hôtel de Bouret de Vézelay, Paris†
1779-82	Monastery of Saint Louis d'Antin, Paris
1780-81	Hôtel de Montesquiou, Paris
1781	Hôtel de Bourbon-Condé, Paris
1781	Maison Brogniart, Paris
1785-86	École Militaire, Paris (stables and observatory; after plans by Ange Jacques Gabriel)
1787	Hôtel Masserano, Paris
1788-89	Hôtel de Boisgelin, Paris
1792	Château de Trilbardon, Seine et Marne
1797	Hôtel Montesson, Romainville†
1805	Père Lachaise Cemetery, Paris
1808	Petits Appartements, Saint-Cloud (interior decoration)†
1808-13	Stock Exchange, Paris (not completed until 1825)

Publications

BOOKS BY BROGNIART

Plans du Palais de la Bourse de Paris et du cimetière Mont-Louis. Paris, 1814.

BOOKS ABOUT BROGNIART

ANDIA, BÉATRICE DE: *De Bagatelle à Monceau, 1778-1978: Les Folies du XVIII Siècle à Paris.* Paris, 1978.
ANDIA, BÉATRICE DE: *Le Faubourg Saint-Germain: La Rue de Grenelle.* Paris, 1980.
BIVER, MARIE LOUISE: *Le Paris de Napoléon.* Paris, 1963.
BRAHAM, ALLAN: *The Architecture of the French Enlightenment.* Berkeley, California, and Los Angeles, 1980.
EGBERT, DONALD DREW: *The Beaux-Arts Tradition in French Architecture.* Princeton, New Jersey, 1980.
ERIKSEN, SVEND: *Early Neo-Classicism in France.* London, 1974.
FREGNAC, CLAUDE, and ANDREWS, WAYNE: *Great Houses of Paris.* New York, 1979.
GALLET, MICHEL: *Demeures Parisiennes: L'époque de Louis XVI.* Paris, 1964.
GALLET, MICHEL: *Claude-Nicolas Ledoux.* Paris, 1980.
HAUTECOEUR, LOUIS: *Histoire de l'architecture classique en France.* Vols. 4 and 5. Paris, 1952 and 1953.
Jardins en France: 1760-1820. Paris, 1978.
KALNEIN, WEND GRAF, and LEVEY, MICHAEL: *Art and Architecture of the Eighteenth Century in France.* Harmondsworth, England, 1972.

KAUFMANN, EMIL: *Architecture in the Age of Reason: Baroque and Post-Baroque in England, Italy, France.* Cambridge, Massachusetts, 1955.
LAUNAY, LOUIS DE: *Une grande famille de savants: Les Brongniart.* Paris, 1940.
MOSSER, MONIQUE, et al.: *Alexandre-Théodore Brongniart, 1739-1813.* Paris, 1986.
PÉROUSE DE MONTCLOS, JEAN MARIE: *Etienne-Louis Boullée, 1728-1799: De l'architecture classique à l'architecture révolutionnaire.* Paris, 1969.
RIVIERE, CLÉRY: *Un village de Brie au XVIII siècle: Mauperthuis.* Paris, 1939.
ROSENBLUM, ROBERT: *Transformations in Late Eighteenth Century Art.* Princeton, New Jersey, 1967.
SILVESTRE DE SACY, JACQUES: *Alexandre Théodore Brongniart 1739-1813: sa vie et son oeuvre.* Paris, 1940.
Soufflot et son temps. Paris, 1980.
WIEBENSON, DORA: *The Picturesque Garden in France.* Princeton, New Jersey, 1978.

ARTICLES ABOUT BROGNIART

ETLIN, RICHARD A.: "Landscapes of Eternity: Funerary Architecture and the Cemetery, 1793-1781." *Oppositions* 8 (1977): 14-31.
HÉBERT, MONIQUE: "Les demeures du duc d'Orléans et de Madame de Montesson à la Chaussée d'Antin." *Gazette des beaux-arts* 64 (1964): 161-176.
OTTOMEYER, HANS: "Autobiographies d'architectes Parisiens: 1759-1811." *Bulletin de la Société de l'Histoire de Paris et de l'Ile de France* 98 (1974): 141-206.
PLARISET, FRANÇOIS-GEORGES: "L'architecte Brongniart, les activités à Bordeaux et à La Réole (1793-1795)." *Bulletin et mémoires de la Société Archéologique de Bordeaux* 62 (1962): 1-59.

*

Alexandre Théodore Brongniart was an architect active in Paris in the years immediately before the Revolution. He came from a distinguished family, his father being a professor at the Collège de Pharmacie, his mother a relative of a famous chemist, the Comte de Fourcroy. His teachers were Jacques François Blondel and Etienne Louis Boullée, with whom he studied in about 1760. He competed unsuccessfully for several of the Académie prizes from 1762 to 1765 and then began work for Boullée, whose influence is clearly visible in Brongniart's early buildings. Brongniart's subsequent career is associated mainly with two particular patrons, the Orléans and Condé families, and the development of two parts of Paris, the northern section of the Chaussée d'Antin and the area around the Invalides.

In 1769 Brongniart began a financial relationship with Jean-François le Tellier, who had bought a large plot of land to the east of the rue Chaussée d'Antin; this was resold to the marquise de Montesson, who, having just come into money on the death of her husband, commissioned Brongniart to build a house for her on the site. The house itself, the Hôtel de Montesson, is fairly modest in scale and recalls the earlier houses of Boullée, if perhaps less rigid in appearance. Madame de Montesson was also the mistress of the duc d'Orléans, and Brongniart was then asked to design a large house for him. This house is set, like a country palace, in a large garden, and with a theater; a circular salon forms the center of the plan, and around it are arranged rooms that seem, in the variety and extravagance of their forms, almost at odds with the severe elevations Brongniart gave his design. The garden front has a plain attic, set above a screen of Tuscan columns that are doubled at the center and the sides. This was in north Paris. In the south, Brongniart designed a number of buildings, beginning with the hôtel of the princess de Monaco. This has a very simple plan, and the facade is like that of the pavilion of the duc d'Orléans, with a low Tuscan colonnade and a curved projection at the center, which serves as the portico for the building. The garden front is richer, filled with huge Corinthian columns. And inside is a curved staircase, attached to the rear wall of the entrance vestibule, that leads up to the landing of the principal floor. Another building in that area is the Hôtel de Bourbon-Condé, built in 1781 for the daughter of the prince de Condé; the style there is unpretentious and simple, perhaps as the simple and unpretentious owner requested.

On occasion Brongniart could produce extremely severe designs; this is true of his plans for the Capuchin Monastery, now part of the Lycée Condorcet, that he designed in 1779 for the new parish of Chaussée d'Antin. This has a famous courtyard, articulated with baseless Tuscan columns that were perhaps a model for the painter Jacques-Louis David; the facade has a simple, central portico, flanked also by Tuscan columns that are surmounted by an entablature that rides above the simple, rusticated walls of the front.

Brongniart's career was only temporarily disrupted by the Revolution. In 1781 he had been able to join the Académie, enjoying an active social life with figures like Hubert Robert and Madame Vigée-Lebrun. In those years he also was busy completing the outbuildings of the École Militaire and laying out the roads in front of the Invalides. But because of his connections with the family of Orléans, when the Revolution came, he lost his posts at the École Militaire and the Invalides, and in 1792 he was forced to sell his rich collection of art, which included several pieces by Clodion. He moved for a while to Bordeaux, but returned to Paris in 1795, exhibiting that year at the Salon. In 1800 he took employment at the porcelain factory at Sèvres, which had been revived by Napoleon, designing china and furniture; his famous piece the "Table des Marechaux," made for Napoleon in 1808, is now in Buckingham Palace, London. Brongniart's architectural career was revived a year later when he was appointed *inspecteur des travaux publiques*, and it was in that position that he laid out the plan of the cemetery of Père Lachaise in 1805. In 1808 he presented a design for the Bourse, or Temple du Commerce. There, with sensible adaptability, he took the older neoclassicism he had previously used and adapted it to the taste Napoleon had for Roman Corinthian temples. Brongniart died in 1813, just before the restoration of the monarchy, and was buried, appropriately enough, in the cemetery he himself had designed.

—DAVID CAST

BROWN, Capability.

British. Born Lancelot Brown in Kirkhale, Northumberland, England, 1716. Died in Hampton, 6 February 1783. Gardener to Sir William Loraine, Kirkharle, 1732; head gardener to Lord Cobham, Stowe, 1741; consulting landscape gardener, 1749; partnership with Henry Holland, 1771; Master Gardener, Hampton Court, 1764.

Chronology of Works
All in England
* *Approximate dates*

1742	Wotton, Buckinghamshire
1745	Newnham Paddox (house and landscaping)
1750-52	Warwick Castle, Warwickshire (castle renovations and landscaping)
1750-52	Croome, Worcestershire (house and landscaping)
1751	Packington, Warwickshire
1754	Petworth Park, Sussex
1754	Burghley, Northamptonshire (house and landscaping)
1757	Bowood, Wiltshire
1757	Longleat, Wiltshire
1758	Harewood, Yorkshire
1759	Ashridge, Hertfordshire
1760*	Alnwick, Northumberland
1760	Chatsworth, Derbyshire
1760	Corsham, Wiltshire (house and landscaping)
1761	Castle Ashby, Northamptonshire
1762	Temple Newsam, Yorkshire
1763	Redgrave, Suffolk (house and landscaping)
1763	Milton Abbey, Dorset (and village landscaping)
1764	Broadlands, Hampshire (house and landscaping)
1764	Luton Hoo, Bedfordshire
1764	Richmond Park, Surrey (alterations)
1766	Blenheim Park, Oxfordshire
1766	Sandbeck, Yorkshire
1766	Thorndon, Essex
1767	Ashburnham, Sussex
1767	Wimpole, Cambridgeshire
1768	Fiserwick, Staffordshire (house and landscaping)
1769-70	Claremont, Surrey (house and landscaping; with Henry Holland)
1771	Brocklesby, Lincolnshire
1773	Wardour Castle, Wiltshire
1774	Benham, Berkshire (house and landscaping; with Holland)
1775	Sherborne Castle, Dorset

Publications

BOOKS ABOUT BROWN

HUSSEY, CHRISTOPHER: *English Gardens and Landscapes, 1700-1750.* London, 1967.
HYAMS, EDWARD: *Capability Brown and Humphry Repton.* 1971.
REPTON, HUMPHRY: *Theory and Practice of Landscape Gardening.* 1803.
STROUD, DOROTHY: *Capability Brown.* London, 1950; rev. ed. 1975.
TURNER, ROGER: *Capability Brown and The Eighteenth Century English Landscape.* New York, 1985.
WALPOLE, HORACE: *Essay on Modern Gardening.* London, 1785.

ARTICLES ABOUT BROWN

CLARKE, GEORGE: "Lancelot Brown's Work at Stowe." *The Stoic* (Stowe [England] School Magazine) (1971).

*

Lancelot Brown, the 18th-century English landscape architect nicknamed "Capability" at an early point in his career and thus known throughout the rest of his life, created a style of landscape architecture so removed from European garden traditions that his natural, untamed domestic parks signalized a new national style identified from his time onward as "*jardin anglais.*" Unlike the European formal, geometric garden style,

Capability Brown: Blenheim Park, Oxfordshire, England, 1766

which was based on a visual formula of linear and aerial perspective, Brown approached gardening from a literary angle, referring to his landscape additions as various forms of grammatical punctuation.

In the richly verdant English countryside, Brown designed and fabricated landscapes that followed the natural flow of land according to the different regions of the country in which he worked, but he put various elements together so discreetly that these landscapes did not appear contrived. Although he had no formal architectural training, Brown occasionally had the opportunity to build new houses, which, like the houses set in his landscape projects, were the key features or focal points of his total settings, and were compatible with his garden schemes in every way.

During his extremely successful career as a landscape architect, Brown moved upward from a reputed humble beginning to become a wealthy landowner and royal gardener in Whig-dominated 18th-century England. His clients were aristocratic landowners whose influence, derived from their wealth and political power, added impact to the growth of Brown's popularity in England, from where the style spread onto the Continent, which had been dominated in the previous century by the French formal style of André Le Nôtre.

After learning basic gardening skills in the early 1730s during an apprenticeship to Sir William Loraine in his native Northumberland, Brown quickly began his move up the social ladder. Nearly a decade later in 1739, he worked for about a year for a new patron, Sir Richard Grenville, at Wotton in Oxfordshire before attracting the attention of the more powerful Lord Cobham, master of Stowe Park in Buckinghamshire. In 1740 Cobham brought Brown to Stowe, where the latter served as undergardener to William Kent. At Stowe, under the tutelage of Kent, as on Loraine's humble estate in Northumberland, Brown learned many new techniques in both landscape and architectural design. Stowe, however, though significant for Brown as a learning workshop, did not offer him the autonomy to create new designs and experiment with the ideas learned from Kent and the work of Kent's predecessor, Charles Bridgeman.

Brown left Stowe in 1741 and settled in Hammersmith near London to establish his own practice. His first commission, for the sixth earl of Coventry at Croome Court in Worcestershire,

was significant because it included not only the landscape but also the design and construction of a new house. This opportunity to plan the site of the house as a focal point of the landscape demonstrated Brown's vision of a landscape as a total integration of building and grounds in a natural, harmonious and picturesque whole so subtle that the presence of the human hand in the operation was not visible.

The Palladian house Brown built at Croome Court clearly reflected his knowledge of Kent's architectural contributions to the Palladian circle of the earl of Burlington (Richard Boyle), while his complex landscape involving the use of water announced one of the primary features of his evolving garden style. There he transformed a marshy setting into a picturesque park by using culverts to divert water flow into an artificial river away from the house site.

In 1756 Brown began a 26-year-long project for Lord Exeter of Burghley House in Northamptonshire. In one of his most important commissions, Brown added to the Tudor house built for the first earl of Exeter, lord high treasurer to Elizabeth I, and converted much of the earlier formal garden into his own vast natural park. His architectural projects at Burghley included a lodge, a bathhouse/banqueting hall, an orangery, conservatory, and a large masonry bridge over the lake he created to extend approximately 30 acres south of the house.

A second major Tudor estate Brown transformed was Longleat in Wiltshire. Brown began working there for Lord Weymouth in 1757; again a formal garden, in this case one in the Italian Renaissance style like the decorative details of the house, yielded to Brown's winding new park, where he planted many new species of trees in plentiful supply. The effect at Longleat, as at Burghley, was to add a soft focus of greenery as a backdrop for the sharp edges of the crisply detailed Tudor house. His clumps of trees provide visual resting places around the house, which rises up to the rigid vertical projections of its Tudor roofline.

Brown's conversion of the large park surrounding the large country house, built as a military monument to the first duke of Marlborough at Blenheim in Oxfordshire for the fourth duke in the 1760s, added significantly to his reputation because of the fame of Blenheim Palace. John Vanbrugh had anticipated Brown's picturesque landscape vision in his own intentions for the setting of the expansive palace. Vanbrugh's plan to retain the old Woodstock Manor on the hill above the River Glyme so that it could be seen from the palace as a curiosity did not survive his disputes with the first duchess, but it did demonstrate a clear affinity with the natural park Brown created later. In his turn, Brown established a real function for Vanbrugh's bridge over the Glyme, which had remained a serious point of contention between the duchess and Vanbrugh until his resignation in 1716. In Vanbrugh's time, the Glyme was only a small stream and was dwarfed by the bridge, which he planned as the grand entrance to the north facade of the palace. Brown's solution to the problem was to form a large lake on each side of the bridge by damming the Glyme. The scale of his lake, which can be judged best in aerial views, now balances the massive bridge. Less successful at Blenheim, however, was Brown's wide, sweeping south lawn, which he produced by demolishing Henry Wise's formal military garden designed, like the house, to honor the first duke's victory at Blenheim. In extremely dry weather the outlines of the original garden are visible still on the plain south lawn.

At Corsham Court in Wiltshire, Brown expanded Paul Metheun's house to provide exhibition space for a large art collection by building stylistically consistent additions to the wings of the existing Jacobean house. He also carried out his typical landscape consisting of pleasure walks and waterways formed by applying his skills in engineering and hydraulics.

Another important patron was the first duke of Northumberland, who commissioned Brown to revise the park at Alnwick Castle in Northumberland and Syon Park near London. Brown created broad, romantic and picturesque parks to serve as scenic backdrops for the neoclassical masterpieces of the interiors Robert Adam was producing at Syon, and which Adam and James Paine together were forming at Alnwick. Although documents reveal no specific reference to any acquaintanceship of Brown and Adam, the two designers probably crossed paths, because these are only two instances in which both worked for the same patron simultaneously.

For the British hero of India, Lord Robert Clive, Brown built a Palladian house at Claremont in Esher on the site of an earlier house by Vanbrugh that Clive had had demolished for Brown's design. The house was Brown's primary concern there, for, although he added to the gardens, the landscape had been revised earlier by William Kent. Clive's selection of Brown's house design over a design by William Chambers suggests that Brown's architectural career was not merely a sideline to his landscape design, but was a real vocation in which he could have competed successfully without his gardening business.

An abbreviated list of other major landscapes by Brown includes some of the most famous place names in England; Warwick Castle in Warwickshire, Chatsworth in Derbyshire, Holkham Hall in Norfolk, Audley End in Essex, Wimbledon Park near London, Broadlands near London, Temple Newsam in Leeds and Prior Park in Bath. The distance Brown traveled to become England's premier landscape architect can be measured in miles of English countryside and in the measure of esteem paid him by his patrons. One group of aristocratic friends of Brown sought a royal appointment for him in 1757 and repeated the request in 1758. Those requests were ignored by George II, but George III awarded the honor in 1764, naming Brown surveyor of His Majesty's Gardens and Waters at Hampton Court. There Brown planted a grapevine known as the Great Vine, but otherwise he made only minimal changes in the royal garden. In addition to a salary, Brown was provided with a residence called Wilderness House near the Lion Gate; he also later acquired a modest house of his own at Fenstanton in Huntingdonshire.

Brown's continued success and his genial relationships with his patrons suggest that he was an easygoing, cooperative artist. A rare exception to his pleasant encounters with clients was the case of Ambrose Dickens, who refused to pay part of a bill for extra work. Brown then publicly tore up the bill in a fit of pique. A second damper on his otherwise brilliant career occurred in 1772, when William Chambers, whose house design for Clive had been rejected in favor of Brown's, launched a virulent and unprovoked personal attack on Brown in *A Dissertation on Oriental Gardening,* a mixed book of unoriginal ideas about Eastern gardens and a series of fanciful thoughts. Brown, however, was supported by friends and survived the attack, which reflected worse on Chambers.

Although Capability Brown had a long and distinguished career in both architecture and landscape design, his fame is linked to the natural style of landscape he created and popularized. His name alone conjures up visions of natural parks consisting of lakes flowing in serpentine lines through wild clumps of trees and pleasure walks around a grand house, like punctuation marks in a literary masterpiece.

—JOYCE M. DAVIS

BRUCE, William.

Scottish. Born in Perthshire, Scotland, ca. 1630. Died on 1 January 1710. Father was Robert Bruce; married Mary Halket, Pitfirrane, 1660; married Magdalene Clerk, 1770. Clerk of the Bills, Scotland, 1681; receiver of fines; commissioner of excise in Fife; Justice of the Peace, Kinross, 1673; parliamentary commissioner for Kinross-shire; member of the Privy Council for Scotland, 1685-86; Surveyor-general and overseer of the King's Buildings in Scotland, 1671-78; worked independently.

Chronology of Works
All in Scotland
* *Approximate dates*
† *Work no longer exists*

1668*-74	Balcaskie House, Fife (remodeling)
1670*-77	Thirlestane Castle, Berwickshire (remodeling)
1671-79	Holyroodhouse, Edinburgh (rebuilding)
1672-74	Brunstane House, Midlothian (remodeling)
1673-74	Lauder Church, Berwickshire
1673-77	Lethington (now Lennoxlove) East Lothian
1676*-84	Dunkeld House, Perthshire
1679	Moncreiffe House, Perthshire [attributed]†
1680-82	The Exchange, Edinburgh†
1686-93	Kinross House, Kinross-shire
1695*-99	Craigiehall House, West Lothian
1699-1703	Hopetoun House, West Lothian
1702-07	Auchindinny, Midlothian
1703ff.	Mertoun House, Berwickshire
1703-05	The Town House, Stirlingshire
1709*-10	House of Nairne, Perthshire (not completed until 1712)†

Publications

BOOKS ABOUT BRUCE

DUNBAR, JOHN G.: *Sir William Bruce.* Exhibition catalog. Edinburgh, 1970.
DUNBAR, JOHN G.: *The Architecture of Scotland.* Rev. ed. London, 1966.

FENWICK, H.: *Architect Royal, The Life and Works of Sir William Bruce 1630-1710*. Kineton, England, 1970.
MYLNE, ROBERT SCOTT: *The Master Masons to the Crown of Scotland and their Works*. Edinburgh, 1893.

*

William Bruce's importance lies in the seminal role he played in the introduction of Renaissance architecture to Scotland. As such he might be regarded as a Scottish Inigo Jones—but later. Indeed, Daniel Defoe referred to him as the "Kit Wren of Scotland," although a comparison of his work with that of Roger Pratt (Coleshill, 1649) or Hugh May (Cornbury Park, ca.1666-77), both "gentlemen architects," would be more appropriate.

Like both Pratt and May, Bruce's fortunes were linked to the Restoration Court, but after the accession of James VII and II (1686) he became distrusted; then, following the Glorious Revolution of 1688, he was regarded with actual hostility, being imprisoned for his Jacobite sympathies on more than one occasion. So it is not surprising that his architectural fortunes waned a little during the latter part of his life: he did no more public work of significance but continued to work on his house at Kinross (1686-93) and to build for a number of sympathetic Scottish aristocracy and gentry.

Bruce's architectural successes came in the years following the Restoration in 1660. Up to that time he had built nothing and, apparently, had no architectural training, although much ferrying to and fro between Scotland, England, Holland and probably France, all in the cause of the Restoration, had doubtlessly exposed him to the new and erudite architecture of the Enlightenment. Thus, the significance of his position in Scottish architecture is as much in the influence he had on others through his connections with the court and his circle of learned friends as it was in the buildings he built during the 1670s and 1680s. With the exception of Holyroodhouse (1671-79) and the Exchange (1680) in Edinburgh, and Lauder Church, Berwickshire (1673), all his work was on country houses.

It was not, however, until 1676 that Bruce had his first opportunity to build a completely new country house on an open site—Dunkeld House, built for the first marquess of Atholl. There, unencumbered by previous works, Bruce turned to the new style and produced a small, cubic building right out of the pages of Sebastiano Serlio's *Tutte l'Opera di Architettura e Prospetiva* (1619) or Peter Paul Rubens' *Palazzi di Genova* (1622). Yet, strangely or perhaps fortuitously, Bruce added angle turrets: the house was garrisoned during the 1745 Rebellion. Moncreiffe House, Perthshire (1679), followed the same format—five central bays, one side bay, astylar, hip-roofed and cupolaed—and could have been a dry run for his own Kinross House, site leveling for which began the same year.

Kinross House shows Bruce at his best. Between the walls and pavilions of his extensive gardens, the five central bays of the west facade, encompassing a small, pedimented entrance portico, are set back between two articulated side wings, each of three bays with flanking, giant Corinthian pilasters. Above the heavy entablature, small attic-story windows are squeezed in between the strong cornice and the heavy, hipped roof, with its surmounting cluster of chimneys and central cupola. It is double-pile designs like this, and Craigiehall House and Mertoun, which draw comparisons with Pratt and May in England.

Hopetoun House, near Edinburgh, was, however, somewhat different. Built for Charles Hope, the first earl of Hopetoun, in 1699-1703, it is again a double-pile arrangement, but taken far beyond the scale of even Kinross House. At Hopetoun the central entrance has developed into a double-story portico, its pediment breaking the statued parapet. The roof is clearly expressed as three separate, hipped elements, the central one bearing not only a cupola but also a surrounding balustrade. So far so good—a development of a theme. But as if this was not enough, Bruce designed two convex and colonnaded side wings to the east front. The effect of these was to give an abrupt change of scale from the west front and to give the approaching visitor a sense of scale dominated by the bulging side wings. None of this remains: the present east front was rebuilt by the Adam dynasty in the 18th century.

Bruce's other and earlier work was on existing buildings, and there he was inclined to work within the Scottish tower-house vernacular. His own house, Balcaskie (1668-76), shows a little Renaissance sensitivity in the entrance arch with its surmounting Serlian window, and, similarly, the great Doric entrance on the west front of what is perhaps his best-known work, the Palace of Holyroodhouse, is classical but of copy-book correctness. There he even duplicated James V's 16th-century northwest tower in the interest of continuity and symmetry. Had Bruce been given free rein at Holyroodhouse, he could have far exceeded the novelty of Hopetoun and even produced something approaching John Vanbrugh's later Blenheim Palace (1705-16) for scale, siting and picturesque sensitivity. But instead he compromised and copied.

—NEIL JACKSON

BRUNEL, Isambard K.

British. Born Isambard Kingdom Brunel in Portsmouth, England, 1806. Died in 1859. Father was the engineer Marc Isambard Brunel. Studied mathematics and watchmaking at the Lycée Henri IV in Paris. Entered father's office, 1822; appointed chief engineer for Great Western Railway, 1833; also involved in shipbuilding.

Chronology of Works
All in England

1829-62	Clifton Suspension Bridge, Bristol
1837	Great Western Hotel, Bristol (with Richard Shackleton Pope)
1838	Railway Bridge, Maidenhead, Berkshire
1839-40	Temple Meads Station, Bristol (with Matthew Digby Wyatt)
1852-54	Paddington Station, London (with Matthew Digby Wyatt)
1859	Royal Albert Bridge over the Tamar River, Saltash, Cornwall

Publications

BOOKS BY BRUNEL

The Life of Isambard Kingdom Brunel, Civil Engineer. London, 1870.

BOOKS ABOUT BRUNEL

BILLINGTON, DAVID P.: *The Tower and the Bridge: The New Art of Structural Engineering*. Princeton, New Jersey, 1983.
NOBLE, CELIA BRUNEL: *The Brunels: Father and Son*. London, 1938.
PUGSLEY, ALFRED (ed.): *The Works of Isambard Kingdom Brunel: An Engineering Appreciation*. New York, 1980.
ROLT, L. T. C.: *Isambard Kingdom Brunel*. London, 1957.

ARTICLES ABOUT BRUNEL

HITCHCOCK, HENRY-RUSSELL: "Brunel and Paddington." *Architectural Review* 109 (1951): 240-246.

*

The best-known of the Victorian architect-engineers, Isambard K. Brunel's legacy to modernity lay in his confident recasting of timeworn conceptions of fitness, efficiency and beauty in meeting the challenge of new technology, in particular the expanded use of iron. It is as a mechanical and structural engineer, as the designer of a great railroad system, greater bridges and the largest iron ships then built, that Brunel is famed.

Although lacking formal engineering education (he studied mathematics and watchmaking at the Lycée Henri Quatre in Paris for three years), Brunel was the son of one of the great project engineers of the early 19th century—Marc Brunel, whose tunnel under the Thames River was the wonder of the age and provided young Isambard with his first opportunity for design and oversight on a major civil engineering project.

Isambard Brunel's career spanned the "heroic age" of engineering, when many problems were addressed for the first time, often with a greater sense of aesthetic purpose than later commercial values would deem warranted. As the newly appointed engineer of the Great Western Railway in 1833 at the age of 27, Brunel had a *tabula rasa* before him—in the first 11 years of the company, he surveyed the line of the railroad, determined its famous "broad-gauge" track, encouraged experiment and improvements to the locomotives, drove the two-mile-long Box Tunnel between Chippenham and Bath, designed the world's longest-span flat-arch brick bridge (over the Thames at Maidenhead), introduced a limited measure of standardization in the design of some 26 station buildings between London and Bristol, and, with Matthew Digby Wyatt, laid out the company town of Swindon (including 300 cottages for railway employees and their families).

Wyatt also worked with Brunel on the great train station *cum* shed at Paddington (1854). Brunel's initial letter to Wyatt asking the architect to collaborate on the station is telling of Brunel's view of the engineering/architecture relationship: "I am going to design . . . a Station after my own fancy; that is, with engineering roofs, etc . . . such a thing will be entirely *metal* as to all the general forms . . .; it almost of necessity becomes an Engineering Work, but, to be honest, even if it were not, it is a branch of architecture of which I am fond, and *of course,* believe myself fully competent for; but for *detail* of ornamentation I neither have time nor knowledge . . ."

And indeed, today one can clearly see Wyatt's cast-iron decorative work bolted on to the webs of the wrought-iron ribs of the train shed roof—an appliqué of historicizing detail with little organic connection to the sweep of the arches. (Similarly, Brunel's Bristol Temple Meads station of 1839-40 has a 72-foot span roof that appears to be a hammer-beam system, but is actually a tied, pointed arch.)

His biographer, L. T. C. Rolt, aptly noted that Brunel resisted subordinating engineering to commercial considerations, and "considered every project with which he was associated in isolation as an engineering perfectionist." At the beginning of the railroad era, systematization had little precedent, and perhaps there was no pressing need for it. Brunel and his peers acted under certain constraints—the limited power of the early locomotives for one, a constricted understanding of dynamic stress loading for another—but were free to build as their engineering vision saw fit; that vision often was a very grand one indeed.

Brunel submitted the whole system of railroad transportation to a searching reappraisal. The "broad-gauge" tract Brunel designed for the Great Western Railway is a prime example of his approach: He studied the problem of obtaining adequate speed from the limited locomotive power available, and decided that the largest possible wheels should be used, placing them outside the locomotive and cars, rather than under them, to avoid having the cars unsuitably high. This required wider tracks—the celebrated "broad gauge," with tracks 7 feet apart, in contrast to the more common (then as today) 4-foot 8½-inch gauge.

The broad gauge gave the Great Western Railway a reputation for speed and smoothness, but prevented connection with other British railroads, most of whom had accepted the 4-foot 8½-inch standard, and it was not until 1892 that the Great Western bowed to commercial pressures and converted to the norm.

As an architect, Brunel stuck to the historicizing styles so prevalent in his time, but his engineer's approach—emphasizing efficiency and planning—often brought results where design quality alone could not ensure them. An example was his unitized field hospital for Renkioi in the Crimea (1855). Shipped from England fully equipped with tarred wooden sewers, mechanical ventilation and polished tin roof and wall sheathing, this prefabricated structure owed its success as much to Brunel's prowess in organizing its shipment and his forethought on its erection as to the design itself.

This engineer's approach ensured the continued functionality of his designs long after their appearance had gone out of fashion. Thus the railway village at Swindon is one of the best examples of planned urban development in England, while remaining firmly within the bounds of financial realism (unlike such later "company towns" as the Lever Company's Port Sunlight of 1888). His most celebrated bridge, the Royal Albert Bridge at Saltash (1857-59), continues in service today.

The Saltash Bridge serves as a good example, too, of the fact that although Brunel made the best use he could of theory and calculation, his final reliance had to be placed on the results of tests to destruction. Brunel could accurately determine live and dead loads, but he could make only generous allowance for the dynamic stresses induced by rocking locomotives—and wind, with its attendant torsional effects on suspension bridges, was always the great unknown.

Brunel pioneered several strength tests and preservation methods (for bridge timber), but always in response to specific, immediate problems, not to advance theoretical knowledge; it was his insistence on development through logical analysis, even when that meant going to the limits of the technology of his time, that constituted Brunel's chief legacy to the profession of engineering.

—PRESTON THAYER

BRUNELLESCHI, Filippo.

Italian. Born in Florence, Italy, in 1377. Died, 1446. Father was public official in Florence; mother was related to Spini and Aldobrandini families. Master goldsmith, 1404; apprenticed with Toscanelli; taught geometric laws and one-point perspective (students included Piero della Francesca, Fra Angelico and Masaccio); member, Florentine city council; studied in Rome with Donatello.

Chronology of Works
All in Italy
* *Approximate dates*

1417/18-46　Cathedral of Santa Maria del Fiore, Florence (cupola, lantern and *tribune morte*)

Filippo Brunelleschi: Cathedral, Florence, Italy, 14th century

1418*	Church of San Lorenzo, Florence
1418-29	Church of San Lorenzo, Florence (sacristy)
1419	Ospedale degli Innocenti, Florence
1420s	Barbadori Chapel, Church of Santa Felicita, Florence
1420s-40s	Palazzo di Parte Guelfa, Florence (upper story; not completed)
1425*-28	Pazzi Chapel, Church of Santa Croce, Florence (executed after 1442)
1429	Uffizi del Monte, Palazzo Becchio, Florence
1434	Church of Santa Maria degli Angeli, Florence (not completed)
1436*	Church of Santo Spirito, Florence (completed after Brunelleschi's death)

Publications

BOOKS ABOUT BRUNELLESCHI

ARGAN, GIULIO C.: *Brunelleschi*. Milan, 1955; 1978.

BATTISTI, EUGENIO: *Filippo Brunelleschi*. Milan, 1976.

BOZZONI, CORRADO and CARBONARA, GIOVANNI: *Filippo Brunelleschi: Saggio di Bibliografia*. 2 vols. Rome, 1977-78.

BRUCKER, GENE: *The Civic World of Early Renaissance Florence*. Princeton, New Jersey, 1977.

CABLE, CAROLE: *Brunelleschi and His Perspective Panels*. Monticello, Illinois, 1981.

CARLI, E.: *Brunelleschi*. Florence, 1950.

FABRICZY, CORNELIUS VON: *Filippo Brunelleschi*. Stuttgart, 1892.

FANELLI, GIOVANNI: *Brunelleschi*. Florence, 1977.

Filippo Brunelleschi: L'uomo e l'artista. Mostra documentaria. Florence, 1977.

FLORENCE, GALLERIA DEGLI UFFIZI, GABINETTO DEI DISEGNI E DELLE STAMPE: *Disegni di fabbriche brunelleschiane*. Florence, 1977.

FOLMESICS, HANS: *Brunelleschi: Ein Beitrag zur Entwicklungsgeschichte der Frührenaissance-Architektur*. Vienna, 1915.

GINORI-CONTI, PIERO: *La Basilica di S. Lorenzo di Firenze, e la famiglia Ginori*. Florence, 1940.

GIOVANNI, FANELLO: *Brunelleschi*. 1980.

GORI-MONTANELLI, LORENZO: *Brunelleschi e Michelozzo*. Florence, 1957.

HYMAN, ISABELLE (ed.): *Brunelleschi in Perspective*. Englewood Cliffs, New Jersey, 1974.

HYMAN, ISABELLE: *Fifteenth Century Florentine Studies: The Palazzo Medici and a Ledger for the Church of San Lorenzo*. New York, 1977.

KENT, DALE: *The Rise of the Medici: Faction in Florence, 1426-1434*. Oxford, 1978.

KLOTZ, H.: *Die Frühwerke Brunelleschis und die mittelalterliche Tradition*. Berlin, 1970; as *Filippo Brunelleschi: The Early Works and the Medieval Tradition*. New York, 1990.

LUPORINI, EUGENIO: *Brunelleschi: Forma e ragione*. Milan, 1964.

MANETTI, ANTONIO: *The Life of Brunelleschi*. University Park, Pennsylvania, 1970.

MORENI, DOMENICO: *Vita di Filippo di Ser Brunelleschi... Scritta da Filippo Baldinucci*. Florence, 1812.

PRAGER, FRANK D. and SCAGLIA, GUSTINA: *Brunelleschi: Studies of His Technology and Inventions*. Cambridge, Massachusetts, 1970.

RAGGHIANTI, CARLO L.: *Filippo Brunelleschi: Un uomo, un universo*. Florence, 1977.

SAALMAN, HOWARD: *Filippo Brunelleschi: The Cupola of Santa Maria del Fiore: Studies in Architecture XX*. London, 1980.

SANPAOLESI, PIERO: *Brunelleschi*. Milan, 1962.

SANPAOLESI, PIERO: *La cupola di S. Maria del Fiore. Il progetto. La costruzione*. Florence, 1941; 1977.

ARTICLES ABOUT BRUNELLESCHI

ARGAN, GIULIO CARLO: "The Architecture of Brunelleschi and the Origins of Perspective Theory in the Fifteenth Century." *Journal of the Warburg and Courtauld Institutes* 9 (1946): 96-121.

BENEVOLO, LEONARDO; CHIEFFI, STEFANO; and MAZZETTI, GIULIO: "Indagine sul S. Spirito di Brunelleschi." *Quaderni dell' Istituto di Storia dell' Architettura, Università di Roma* 15:85-90 (1968).

BRUSCHI, ARNOLDO: "Considerazioni sulla 'Maniera matura' del Brunelleschi: Con un'appendice sulla Rotonda degli Angeli." *Palladio*, New Series 22 (1972): 89-126.

HEYDENREICH, LUDWIG HEINRICH: "Spätwerke Brunelleschis." *Jahrbuch der preussischen Kunstsammlungen* 52 (1931): 1-28.

HOFFMANN, VOLKER: "Brunelleschis Architektursystem." *Architectura* 1 (1971): 54-71.

HORSTER, MARITA: "Brunelleschi und Alberti in ihrer Stellung zur Römischen Antike." *Mitteilungen des Kunsthistorischen Instituts in Florenz*, 17 (1973): 29-64.

KEMP, MARTIN: "Science, Non-science and Nonsense: The Interpretation of Brunelleschi's Perspective." *Art History* 1 No. 2 (1978): 134-161.

MAINSTONE, ROWLAND: "Brunelleschi's Dome." *Architectural Review* 162 (1977): 156-166.

MOLHO, ANTHONY: "Three Documents Regarding Filippo Brunelleschi." *Burlington Magazine* 119 (1977): 851-852.

NYBERG, D.: "Brunelleschi's Use of Proportion in the Pazzi Chapel." *Marsyas* VII (1957).

PICA, A.: "La cupola di S. Maria del Fiore e la collaborazione Brunellesco-Ghiberti." *Emporium* 97 (1943): 70ff.

SAALMAN, HOWARD: "Filippo Brunelleschi: Capital Studies." *Art Bulletin* 40 (1958).

SAALMAN, HOWARD: "Early Renaissance Architectural Theory and Practice in Antonio Filarete's Tratto di Architettura." *Art Bulletin* 41 (1959): 89-106.

SAALMAN, HOWARD: "San Lorenzo: The 1434 Chapel Project." *Burlington Magazine* 120 (1978): 361-364.

SANPAOLESI, PIERO: "Ipotesi sulla conoscenze matematiche, statiche e meccaniche del Brunelleschi." *Belle Arti* 2 (1951): 25-54.

WADDY, PATRICIA: "Brunelleschi's Design for S. Maria degli Angeli in Florence." *Marsyas* 15 (1970-72): 36-45.

ZERVAS, DIANE FINIELLO: "Filippo Brunelleschi's Political Career." *Burlington Magazine* 121 (1979): 630-639.

*

Toward the end of the 14th century, Florence experienced a period of exceptional artistic growth. The city was one great workshop, producing a cityscape still visible today. An extraordinary attempt to break with medieval art and architecture was undertaken. Every detail of 14th-century Florentine architecture testified to the indefatigable search for a new, sublime aesthetic, as well as a desire to avoid French and German influences. A continuous process of artistic evolution—beginning with the Gothic style already transformed by the work of Arnolfo di Cambio—spawned numerous architectural innovations. This process led to the construction by Filippo Brunelleschi of the cupola and its drum over the central transept of Florence Cathedral.

Brunelleschi was trained as a goldsmith and had a particular interest in drawing. He developed a great interest in technical innovation, being dissatisfied from the beginning with traditional technology. He spent much time in the early years with Paolo Toscanelli, a merchant, doctor, scientist and mathematician, who taught him the laws of geometry. From those laws Brunelleschi developed the principles of one-point perspective, sharpening also the instruments of correct perspective representation. He did a great number of perspective drawings of Florentine scenes, the most well-known of which is his drawing of the Piazza San Giovanni. He also taught his new findings on perspective to fellow artists such as Piero della Francesca, Fra Angelico and Masaccio, his favorite pupil and friend. The new vision of the world inherent in the development of correct perspective representation has been well described by G. C. Argan: "Perspective neither uncovers, creates, nor invents space. Rather, it is an essentially critical method or process that can be applied to the spatial data of architecture, reducing it to proportion or to reason. The Platonic influence predominates over Aristotelianism, in the synthesis of longitudinal and central diagrams into a perspective of contemplation, a perspective that leads, theoretically, to a single point."

Brunelleschi's friendship with Donatello was of particular significance to the former's development as an artist and architect. The work of both artists was fueled by a similar restlessness, and they had similar aspirations. They were the creators of a dramatic and intensely human art, forming the link between the static archaism of the Gothic tradition and the humanist search for harmony. However, there are also some marked differences between these artists' works. Donatello's Christ, shaken with pain, is a personification of inconsolable suffering, harking back to medieval types. Brunelleschi's Christ, on the other hand, stretched out in an unending moment of abandon, is already the expression of a Renaissance sensibility. A similar aesthetic is evident in Brunelleschi's well-known Paradise Door: the work testifies to Donatello's influence in the exceptional vibrancy of the figures, which are set off by the architecture of the door. The parallel planes exploit the contrast between light and shadow in such a way as to create an unusual impression of depth. The figures still have 14th-century connotations, but the work has a unified vision, reaching for infinity, which is characteristic of the Renaissance. The disjunctions in Brunelleschi's art are symptoms of his vitality and of an unusual process of artistic maturation.

Brunelleschi, accompanied by Donatello, spent several years in Rome, immersing himself in a study of antiquity, and paying special attention to the triumphs of Roman engineering. He made drawings of a great many ancient buildings, including baths, basilicas, amphitheaters and temples, particularly studying the construction of architectural elements, such as vaults and cupolas. The object of his archaeological researches, however, was not to learn to reproduce Roman architecture, but to enrich the architecture of his own time and to perfect his engineering skills.

The design and construction of the drum and cupola of the Cathedral in Florence clearly demonstrate the results of his archaeological studies. The cupola, contributing significantly to the splendor of the whole building, had been conceived when the foundations for the building were laid. At the moment of conception, however, it was not at all clear how the work could be realized. For the construction of the drum, Brunelleschi had to learn all the mason's secrets, and understand the properties of brick, since brick proved to be the most versatile and stable

material for structures of such large dimensions. These are facts he gleaned from his study of Roman remains.

Brunelleschi also designed the cupola of the octagonal Baptistery, this one with a double shell. The exceptional dimensions of the drum posed unusual construction problems, which Brunelleschi resolved with a brick structure laid in a rotating herringbone pattern. The drum consisted of eight segments interconnected with ribs deflecting the cupola's enormous weight. The construction was completed without the use of scaffolding, and with a minimum of building equipment, by using a system of concentric circles. To compensate for a lack of workers, traditionally employed to form a human assembly line, Brunelleschi also designed a number of new machines.

The red outer shell of the cupola, constructed to protect the weight-bearing structure, carries the marble lantern. The cupola demonstrates the nature of Brunelleschi's construction practices and his perspective theory. His predilection for central plans is clearly visible in the order of the apsidal group, studded with cupolas and loggias. Viewing the building from behind, one anticipates a round and compact temple, similar to the Church of Santa Maria degli Angeli, which also had an octagonal plan and dimensions similar to those of the Baptistery.

Among the other basilicas Brunelleschi built, the Church of the Santi Apostoli, with its wide arcades rhythmically ordered by crenellated cornices, may be considered as a point of departure. At the Church of San Lorenzo, the sequence of the columns surmounted with noble, ornate capitals imparts a more measured rhythm to the corniced arcades. Proportions in this building are studied and controlled, down to the smallest detail. The new Church of Santo Spirito—constructed in more ample and monumental form right next to the older structure—expands the internal space of the tall lateral chapels and the transept colonnade which intersects with the colonnade of the central nave, in such a way as to form an airy ambulatory. The high windows give the interior such an intense luminosity and vibrant serenity that Giorgio Vasari called it "the most perfect temple of Christianity."

The sacristy of San Lorenzo and the Pazzi Chapel could be considered of secondary importance were it not for their stylistic perfection, which elevates the buildings to the first rank in architectural history. The Pazzi Chapel is situated on the longitudinal axis of Arnolfo di Cambio's cloister. It consists of a structure with a central plan, covered with a 12-sided cupola. The sail-like cupola is fitted by steps onto the elongated square plan of the transept, so as to achieve the greatest thickness in perspective. It is preceded by a barrel-vaulted portico, which has a principal perspective determined exactly by the golden section. The resulting architectural image is characterized by an exceptional composition of solids and voids, mediated by the purposeful use of cornices.

Brunelleschi's secular architecture, deriving from the typical 14th-century Tuscan palace, must be considered in terms of its urban location. The Palazzo Pitti was originally limited to the development of the seven central windows, and closely resembled the Palazzo Strozzi in its centralized and compact form. It was a representative palace that dominated the vast piazza in front of it. The palace of the Guelph party, on the other hand, being confined to a narrow site in the crowded center of the city, uses rows of windows and stringcourses to enhance the perspective from all vantage points.

Brunelleschi's technological ideals, applied in a variety of forms in all his buildings, coalesced into an exceptional sensitivity to considerations of urban planning. In this respect, Brunelleschi was a bit of a "magus," as Giovanni Michelucci described him. To hazard a more daring comparison, it places him in the same league with that master of modern architecture, Ludwig Mies van der Rohe.

—GIULIANO CHELAZZI
Translated from the Italian by Terri L. Stough

BRYGGMAN, Erik.

Finnish. Born in Turku, Finland, 7 February 1891. Died in Turku, 21 December 1955. Married Agda Grönberg, 1918; one daughter. Studied at Turku School of Art, 1906-09, and Obo Svenska Klassika Lyceum, Turku, 1910; diploma from Institute of Technology, Helsinki, 1916. Worked for Valter Jung, Helsinki, 1916-23; practiced privately in Turku, 1923-1955.

Chronology of Works
All in Finland

1929	Design, 7th Centenary of Turku exhibition, Turku (with Alvar Aalto)
1935	Öbo Akademi Library Book Tower, Turku
1936-56	Ǩren Student Building, Turku
1937	Vierumäki Sports Institute, Heinola
1941	Resurrection Chapel, Turku
1952	Water Tower and Supply Plant, Riihimäki

Publications

BOOKS BY BRYGGMAN

Turun siunauskappeli. Turun, Finland, 1948.

BOOKS ABOUT BRYGGMAN

PIIRONEN, ESA: *Erik Bryggman.* Exhibition catalog. Turku, Finland, 1967.
RICHARDS, J. M.: *800 Years of Finnish Architecture.* Newton Abbot, England, 1978.
STIGELL, ANNA-LISA: *Erik Bryggman.* Ekenäs, Finland, 1965.
WICKBERG, NILS ERIK: *Finnish Architecture.* Helsinki, 1962.

ARTICLES ABOUT BRYGGMAN

"Chapel at Öbo." *Architectural Review* No. 617 (1948).
"Finnische Landhäuser." *Monatshefte für Baukunst und Städtebau* No. 10 (1936).
"Geschäftshaus Sampo in Turku" and "Sportakademie Vierumäki." *Werk* No. 3/4 (1940).
MOSSO, LEONARDO: "L'opera di Erik Bryggman nella storia dell'architettura finlandese." *Atti SJA* (Turin, December 1958).
RUBINO, LUCIANO: "The Last 100 Years—The Masters." *Ville giardini* (June 1979).

*

The Finnish architect Erik Bryggman showed an early love for drawing, which led him to take classes at Turku Art School while attending the Classical Lyceum. He matriculated in 1910. During his studies at the Helsinki School of Architecture he traveled in Scandinavia and central and southern Europe. He qualified for architectural practice in 1916 and worked until 1921 in the Helsinki office of Valter Jung. His former teacher, Armas Lindgren, asked him to make measured drawings for the restoration of Turku's medieval cathedral, and that enabled

him to return to the city of his birth. He established his office there in 1923. A prodigious worker, Bryggman carried out projects ranging from villas, single-family homes, apartment blocks and museums to town plans, municipal institutions, freedom monuments and burial chapels. It is surprising, perhaps, that his office never employed more than half a dozen people.

Turku in the 1920s, with its largely Swedish-speaking population, was soon to become a microcosm of developments in Nordic architecture. Bryggman, who had visited the Baltic Exhibition in Malmö as a student, was keenly aware of the subtle change from classicism to functionalism taking place in the works of the Swedish architects Sigurd Lewerentz, Gunnar Asplund and Sven Markelius. He remarked on the Italian influences in Lewerentz's 1913 design for Bergaliden Crematorium in Helsingborg. Moved by his lifelong interest in the design of sacred buildings, Bryggman entered two competitions in 1919. One was for Helsinki Crematorium, the other for a funeral chapel in Viipuri. He won second prize in each. These projects showed a marked departure from the National Romantic style of the earlier generation that produced the rich buildings of Eliel Saarinen and Lars Sonck. The small scale, nonaxial plans, perimeter walls, surface voids, unadorned stucco walls and saddle roofs brought to mind Italian vernacular architecture. Bryggman utilized these elements in a way that suited the kind of project at which he became adept: apartment buildings, villas and small-scale institutional buildings. Riitta Nikula, head of research at the Museum of Finnish Architecture, holds that Bryggman's "Atrium apartment building of 1927 and the Hospits Betel hotel located opposite, with its chapel, form the most Italianate urban architectural setting ever created in Finland."

The arrival of Alvar Aalto in Turku in 1927 brought Bryggman in contact with his younger colleague, and they collaborated on the design of the 1929 Turku Exposition. Bryggman's serious and unassertive manner left him in the shadow of Aalto, who had a more gregarious disposition. One year later, Bryggman was awarded the Grand Prix at the Antwerp World Fair for his Finnish Pavilion, a birch plywood functionalist design he had been given only a week to produce.

The next buildings of note, the Åbo Akademi Book Tower, the Swedish-speaking university's innovative library block (1935), and Vierumäki Sports Institute in Heinola (1937), marked his success as a functionalist, and earned Bryggman the unanimous approval of his architectural contemporaries. That period also saw the start of a decade-long association with Schauman plywood factories. He designed a variety of small dwellings for industry in eastern Finland, as well as workers' housing for the shipping and cotton-spinning industries.

Bryggman's entry "Sub specie aeternitatis" in the architectural competition for a burial chapel in Turku won first prize, after the assessors recalled three entries for further development. Delayed by the Finnish-Russian Winter War, the Resurrection Chapel was completed in 1941, and is a brilliant testament to Bryggman's mature years. The fortuitously-phased construction of the work allowed the architect to deepen the levels of symbolism, invest each article with the design attention it deserved, and leave the imprint of his own hand on the fabric of the building (he set the stones that adorn external walls).

Any description does little to convey the air of peace-inspired-by-beauty pervading this chapel. Every visible element carries a message speaking powerfully to visitors, whether they believe in the afterlife or not. The attention given to the experience of death and mourning, the way the shattered psyche of the bereaved is helped to accept death through a dignified sequence of rites for the deceased, the successful creation of the environment in which the events occur—all were foreseen by the architect and duly integrated in the design.

Erik Bryggman: Resurrection Chapel, Turku, Finland, 1941

Described by Asko Salokorpi as "the quintessential monument to the Romantic movement of the 1940s," the Resurrection Chapel, due to Bryggman's breadth of vision, stands above any building of his contemporaries. While others may win admiration for the genius of their technical prowess, this work of art has a quality lifting it above the merely technical, giving it a certain spiritual beauty not discernible in any other church built in the Evangelical-Lutheran building renaissance of postwar decades. The 1984 renovation of the chapel by the Turku office of Laiho-Pulkkinen-Raunio Architects in association with the architect's daughter, Carin Bryggman, is well done and worthy of the master architect. The Resurrection Chapel has regained the pristine beauty of its early days.

In 1936 Bryggman began a two-stage project for the Kåren student building. It had a gymnasium, festivities hall, small library and offices. Typical of Bryggman's low-key approach, he moved his working office into the building, while he was designing the later stage. Completed in 1956, after Bryggman's death, the new building added a five-story hostel and student union quarters, restaurants, music room and meeting room accessible from the second level of the original building.

Bryggman's last major work was a water tower completed in 1952 for the town of Riihimäki. The tower flanks the municipal swimming pool that was part of a sports park planned by Yrjö Lindegren, the architect of Helsinki's Olympic Stadium. The water tower is distinguished by the lightness of its appearance even though it holds 880 cubic meters of water. It was intended that the two lower floors serve as a glass museum (Riihimäki was an important center of artistic glass products), but the space was given to the State Handicraft Training Institute. The penthouse became an attractive cafeteria and viewing platform that drew further income, and the building enjoyed popular acclaim. Thus, Bryggman showed how even such a prosaic construction as a water tower can have human dimensions, and serve more than a purely utilitarian purpose.

—DESMOND O'ROURKE

BULFINCH, Charles.

American. Born in Boston, Massachusetts, 8 August 1763. Died on 4 April 1844. Educated at Harvard University, 1778-81. Toured Europe, 1785-87. Accountant for local merchant, Boston, 1787; began working as an architect, Boston; supervising architect for United States Capitol building, Washington, D.C., 1817.

Chronology of Works
All in the United States
* Approximate dates
† Work no longer exists

1787-88	Hollis Street Church, Boston, Massachusetts†
1789	Washington Arch, Boston, Massachusetts†
1790-91	Beacon Hill Memorial Column, Boston, Massachusetts†
1791-92	Joseph Coolidge, Sr., House, Boston, Massachusetts†
1791-93	Congregational Church, Pittsfield, Massachusetts†
1792-93	Joseph Barrell House, Somerville, Massachusetts†
1793	Charles Bulfinch House, Boston, Massachusetts†
1793-94	Theater, Boston, Massachusetts†
1793-94	Tontine Crescent, Boston, Massachusetts†
1793-96	State House, Hartford, Connecticut

1795-96	Harrison Gray Otis House I, Boston, Massachusetts
1795-97	State House, Boston, Massachusetts
1795-99	Elias Hasket Derby House, Salem, Massachusetts†
1796	James Swan House, Dorchester, Massachusetts†
1796	Perez Morton House, Roxbury, Massachusetts
1798	United States Bank, Boston, Massachusetts†
1799-1801	Almshouse, Boston, Massachusetts†
1800-02	Harrison Gray Otis House II, Boston, Massachusetts
1800-03	Church of the Holy Cross, Boston, Massachusetts†
1802-04	New North Church, Boston, Massachusetts (St. Stephen's Church)
1803	Suffolk Insurance Office, Boston, Massachusetts†
1803-04	Thomas Amory House, Boston, Massachusetts
1803-05	Park Row, Boston, Massachusetts
1803-08	India Wharf, Boston, Massachusetts†
1804-05	Thomas Perkins House, Boston, Massachusetts†
1804-05	State Prison, Charlestown, Massachusetts†
1804-05	Swan Houses, Boston, Massachusetts
1805-08	Harrison Gray Otis House III, Boston, Massachusetts
1809	Boylston Hall and Market, Boston, Massachusetts†
1810-12	Colonnade, Boston, Massachusetts†
1810-12	Suffolk County Courthouse, Boston, Massachusetts†
1812	Third Latin School, Boston, Massachusetts†
1813-14	University Hall, Harvard University, Cambridge, Massachusetts
1814	New South Church, Boston, Massachusetts†
1814-15	Blake-Tuckerman Houses, Boston, Massachusetts†
1816	Church of Christ, Lancaster, Massachusetts
1817-18	Person Hall, Andover, Massachusetts
1818-23	Massachusetts General Hospital, Boston, Massachusetts
1818-29	United States Capitol, Washington, D.C. (rebuilding and completion)
1821-22	Unitarian Church, Washington, D.C.†
1827-28	Federal Penitentiary, Washington, D.C.†
1829-32	State House, Augusta, Maine (alterations)

Publications

BOOKS ABOUT BULFINCH

BROWN, GLENN: *History of the United States Capitol.* Washington, D.C., 1900-03.

BULFINCH, ELLEN SUSAN: *The Life and Times of Charles Bulfinch, Architect.* Boston and New York, 1896.

HITCHCOCK, HENRY-RUSSELL, and SEALE, WILLIAM: *Temples of Democracy: The State Capitols of the USA.* New York, 1976.

KIRKER, HAROLD, and KIRKER, JAMES: *Bulfinch's Boston, 1787-1817.* New York, 1964.

KIRKER, HAROLD: *The Architecture of Charles Bulfinch.* Cambridge, Massachusetts, 1978.

MORISON, SAMUEL E.: *The Life and Letters of Harrison Gray Otis.* 2 vols. Cambridge, Massachusetts, 1913.

PLACE, CHARLES A.: *Charles Bulfinch, Architect and Citizen.* Boston and New York, 1925.

QUINCY, JOSIAH: *A Municipal History of the Town and City of Boston during Two Centuries.* Boston, 1852.

Charles Bulfinch: State House, Boston, Massachusetts, 1795-97

ARTICLES ABOUT BULFINCH

BROWN, FRANK CHOUTEAU: "The Joseph Barrell Estate, Somerville, Massachusetts; Charles Bulfinch's First Country House." *Old-Time New England* 38 (January 1948): 53-62.

"Charles Bulfinch, the First American Architect." *Architecture* 52 (December 1925): 431-436.

FORBES, JOHN D.: "Shepley, Bulfinch, Richardson and Abbott, Architects: An Introduction." *Journal of the Society of Architectural Historians* 17 (1958): 19-31.

FREW, JOHN: "Bulfinch on Gothic." *Journal of the Society of Architectural Historians* 45 (June 1986): 161-163.

HOWELLS, JOHN MEAD: "Charles Bulfinch, Architect." *American Architect* 93 (June 1908): 195-200.

KIRKER, HAROLD, and KIRKER, JAMES: "Charles Bulfinch: Architect as Administrator." *Journal of the Society of Architectural Historians* 22 (March 1963): 29-35.

NEWCOMB, REXFORD G.: "Charles Bulfinch, First American-born Architect of Distinction." *Architect* 9 (December 1927): 289-293.

PICKENS, BUFORD: "Wyatt's Pantheon, the State House in Boston and a New View of Bulfinch." *Journal of the Society of Architectural Historians* 29 (May 1970): 124-131.

PIERSON, WILLIAM H., JR.: "American Neoclassicism—The Traditional Phase: Charles Bulfinch." In *American Buildings and Their Architects: The Colonial and Neo-Classical Styles*. Garden City, New York, 1970.

ROTHSCHILD, L.: "A Triumphal Arch by Charles Bulfinch." *Old-Time New England* 29 (April 1939): 161-162.

SHANNON, M. A. S.: "Architecture of Charles Bulfinch." *American Magazine of Art* 17 (August 1925): 431-437.

STODDARD, R.: "A Reconstruction of Charles Bulfinch's First Federal Street Theater, Boston." *Winterthur Portfolio* 6 (1970).

WILLARD, A. R.: "Charles Bulfinch, the Architect." *New England Magazine* 3 (November 1890): 273-299.

*

Charles Bulfinch, America's first native-born professional architect, had the capability to combine the colonial Georgian manner and the English Adamite style into a refined neoclassical expression. Some say he developed a national style that was simple, frugal and dignified. Certainly, he was unique in that he employed, almost exclusively, drawings in the construction of his themes. In addition, he actually supervised the construction of his buildings, making certain that his designs were interpreted as he had originally planned them. Finally, he showed a deep sensitivity toward materials used and their function both aesthetically and physically.

After graduating from Harvard in 1781, Bulfinch came under the guidance and influence of Thomas Jefferson. In effect, Jefferson told him to go abroad and study historical styles firsthand. Thus, from 1785 to 1787 Bulfinch traveled in England, France and Italy. In England he noted the neoclassical work of the architects James and Robert Adam, as well as James Wyatt, William Chambers and John Soane. And in France, he observed carefully the country's unique methods of city planning—its function and organization.

When he returned to Boston, he became an accountant for a local merchant. That position, ironically, allowed him time to further his then-independent study of architecture. Bulfinch became what is known as an "amateur-gentleman-architect."

One of his initial commissions was the Old State House in Hartford, Connecticut (1793-96), America's first public structure since the Revolutionary War. It reveals a Late Georgian grace and elegance coupled with a dignified, classic simplicity and overall formality. Well proportioned in design, its brick facade displayed a colonnade (with paired columns at the end) raised on a blind arcade. A wooden balustrade is accentuated by Grecian urns, and all are crowned by a dominant cupola, which was added later.

There followed his most recognized civic work, the Massachusetts State House in Boston (1795-97). Located on fashionable Beacon Hill, the building reveals definite European sources in plan and elevation. This is seen in its emulation of the center portion of Somerset House in London (1776-86) by William Chambers. In addition to the classical designs of Chambers, Bulfinch followed plans by the Frenchman Ange-Jacques Gabriel for the Ministry of the Navy on the Place de la Concorde in Paris (completed in 1763). These European neoclassical architects' influence on Bulfinch pushed American architecture into an equal status with England and France. The so-called "time lag" between old-world and new-world styles was beginning to disappear.

In the area of urban planning Bulfinch's Franklin Place in Boston (1793-95) proved to be a most exciting and innovative concept. Based on an ellipse, made of two similar crescent-shapes, the theme was to have 16 town houses which would face and be connected to each other. Pictorially, the houses, located on a plot about 500 feet on each side, were to look out on an oval with grass and trees. However, Bulfinch had difficulties with his financial backers. As a result, only one end of the ellipse was completed, the Tontine Crescent (1793-94). This end was made up of four double homes, not a crescent, and a theater was placed at the east end of the project. The structures were based on Robert Adam's two half circles at Portland Place in London and on crescent themes Bulfinch had seen at Bath in England. Unfortunately, Tontine Crescent was razed in 1858. Yet its concept and idea introduced neoclassical city planning to America.

The adventurous Tontine Crescent project, with less than half its houses occupied, ultimately led to Bulfinch's bankruptcy. That forced him into a new role—political in nature— as chairman of the Boston Board of Selectmen and police superintendent. Those duties, so remote from architecture, dealt on a day-to-day level with people and their immediate economic problems. This led Bulfinch to design such "public" structures as the Boston Almshouse (1799-1801). The work shows the influence of James Wyatt. There followed the Suffolk County Courthouse (1810-12) and later the State Prison in Charlestown, Massachusetts (1804-05). Their neoclassical details were combined with heavy iron balconies with granite. The courthouse was said to be almost Greek Revival in appearance.

Bulfinch's school buildings, the Third Latin School, Boston (1812), and Harvard's University Hall, Cambridge (1813-14), were made of Chelmsford granite. He followed these academic themes with the neoclassical designs for New South Church (1814) and Massachusetts General Hospital (1818-23), both in Boston, which were deemed to be pure Greek Revival in treatment and plan. In fact, New South Church reflected ancient Roman buildings with its octagonal spaces and plans based on James Gibbs' St. Martin-in-the-Fields, London (1721-26), as well as its use of Roman Doric that Bulfinch had seen and also displayed in St. Chad's Church in Shrewsbury, Massachusetts (1796).

Bulfinch's achievements in town planning included leveling part of Beacon Hill so his earlier State House would stand free from neighboring houses. Parkways, malls, wharves, marketplaces and streets were also developed at that time. Such themes as the India Wharf (1803-08), Park Row (1803-05) and the Colonnade (1810-12) reshaped Boston's complex and cluttered colonial appearance into one of neoclassical purity and physical formalism. In addition, his many Beacon Hill residences echoed neoclassical structures in England and France. The most noteworthy was the first Harrison Gray Otis House (1795-96). Its foursquare mass, hipped-roof line, pronounced Palladian facade window, corner rooms and central hallway reflected colonial Georgian themes. However, Bulfinch imbued it with a neoclassical appearance by using recessed arches on the ground floor and a balustrade above. There followed the third Otis House (1805-08), also in Boston. This structure displayed more of a typical Federal style with its huge windows, pilasters and bracketed entablature.

Bulfinch's most noted religious work was the Church of Christ, Lancaster, Massachusetts (1816). The pronounced "coeval arches" of its portico (added later) and the narrow brick piers redefined statements already made at the State House, Boston. The church's belfry-cupola reflected Donato Bramante's Tempietto in Rome (1503). In essence, the Church of Christ was the personification of Bulfinch's neoclassical designs in its overall simplicity, purity of form and mass—all situated on a grassy, tree-filled knoll.

In 1817 President James Monroe appointed Bulfinch to replace Benjamin H. Latrobe as official architect to rebuild the United States Capitol in Washington, D.C., after it was burned by the British in 1814. There, Bulfinch designed the western portico with terrace and steps, the old Library of Congress (burned in 1851), the dome (later replaced by Thomas V. Walter's wrought-iron dome), and much of the grounds surrounding the Capitol.

Bulfinch's last major commission was the Maine State House in Augusta (1829-32, altered 1851). Its appearance again mirrored the earlier state houses in Hartford and Boston. However, stone was used instead of brick.

Throughout the rest of his life, Bulfinch continued to perfect the neoclassical manner into one of refinement and physical simplicity. Up until his death, he worked in a mode that was sincere, academically coherent and sound. He utilized materials—stone, brick and iron—to achieve an aesthetic and structural end. Truly, Bulfinch could be called "an architect's architect."

—GEORGE M. COHEN

BUONTALENTI, Bernardo.

Italian. Born in Florence, Italy, in 1531. Died in 1608. Orphaned and adopted by the Medici Court, 1547. Entire working career spent in the service of Medici grand dukes, including as military architect and supervisor of canals and rivers in Tuscany; named architect of the Uffizi, 1574.

Chronology of Works
All in Italy
* Approximate dates
† Work no longer exists

1560	Fortress, Porto Ferraio
1561*-65	Medici Villa, Seravezza
1565	Fortress, Porto Ercole
1565	Fortress, Terra del Sole
1567-74	Bianca Cappello House, Florence (renovation)
1569ff.	Medici Villa and Gardens, Pratolino†
1571	Bastion for Fortress, Pistoia
1571	Fortress, San Piero, Sieve
1574	Baldachin, Florence (for funeral of Cosimo I)†
1574	Casino Mediceo, Florence
1574	Santa Trinità, Florence (altar stairs and choir; now in Santo Stefano)
1575	Fortress, Pistoia
1575-90	Medici Villa, Petraia, Florence
1576/ 1587-89	Fortress, Livorno
1578-83	Villa, Poggio Francoli
1580	Porta delle Suppliche, Uffizi, Florence
1583	Loggia dei Lanzi, Florence (roof garden)†
1583-88	Granducal Palace, Pisa
1583-93	Grotta Grande, Pitti Palace, Florence
1584	Santa Trinità, Florence (cloister)
1585	Medici Villa, La Magia
1586	Theater, Uffizi, Florence
1586	Tribuna, Uffizi, Florence
1587ff.*	Capela dei Principi, San Lorenzo, Florence
1587	Medici Villa, Marignole
1588	Palazzo Vecchio, Florence (additions)
1592	Medici Villa, Castello
1592	Santa Trinità, Florence (facade)
1593-1600	Palazzo Non-Finito, Florence
1594	Corsini Palace, Florence
1594	Medici Villa, Artimino
1594-95	Belvedere Villa, Pitti Palace, Florence (remodeling)
1596	Santa Maria Maggiore, Florence (organ loft)
1605	Loggia dei Banchi, Pisa

Publications

BOOKS ABOUT BUONTALENTI

BERTI, LUCIANO: *Il principe dello studiolo: Francesco I dei Medici e la fine del rinascimento fiorentino.* Florence, 1967.

BOTTO, IDA MARIA: *Mostra di disegni di Bernardo Buontalenti (1531-1608).* Exhibition catalog. Florence, 1968.

FARA, AEMILIO: *Buontalenti: architettura e teatro.* Florence, 1979.

NAGLER, ALOIS: *Theatre Festivals of the Medici: 1539-1637.* New Haven, Connecticut, 1964.

VENTURI, ADOLFO: "Bernardo Buontalenti." Vol. II, Part 2: 455-546 in *Storia dell'arte italiana.* Milan, 1939.

*

Bernardo Buontalenti was the chosen architect of the Medici family in the second half of the 16th century, and his work for them over the years covered all parts of the courtly life: civil and military projects, sculpture, pyrotechnics, mechanical displays, court pageants. His style, to fit the style of a court, was rich and elegant, most especially in his use of ornament. He displayed his talent best in architectural detailing such as that at the Porta delle Suppliche in Florence's Uffizi (1580), where he set a broken V-shaped pediment over the door, surmounted by a portrait of Duke Cosimo I; this design was dependent in part on what Michelangelo had done at the tombs in the New Sacristy, picking up from there perhaps an allusion to death and to the idea of commemoration.

Buontalenti, who was adopted at the age of 16 by the Medici, worked first as a military architect, a vocation he continued throughout his life. He worked especially on fortresses built throughout the Medicis' territory, most notably the Porto Ferraio (1560), Terra del Sole and Porto Ercole (1565), and works at Pistoia (1575) and Livorno (1576, 1587-89). In 1563 Buontalenti went with Prince Francesco de' Medici to Spain, whose friendship ensured his continued employment; in 1568 he was also placed in charge of all the canals and rivers in Tuscany. His first major architectural work was the remodeling of a medieval house in Florence on the Via Maggio for the mistress of Francesco, Bianca Capello; this was a restrained design, though it included some windows on the ground floor where details of bats and shells were cleverly set within traditional frames.

Buontalenti began his masterpiece, the villa and gardens at Pratolini, near Florence, in 1569. The site was extremely difficult to work with, the nearest water being some five miles away; the design of the villa itself—which we know best from a painting by Giusto Utens, since the building was remodeled in the early 19th century—was not unlike that of Giuliano da Sangallo for the Medici villa at Poggio a Caiano, done almost 100 years earlier. It included a tall base, like that at Caiano, which lifted the structure up to take advantage of the sunlight; the apartments inside, set on separate sides of a great hall, were like those at Caiano and also at the residential wing recently completed by Bartolommeo Ammanati at the Palazzo Pitti in Florence. The gardens were set down the slope of the land and filled with an informal arrangement of fountains, water courses, statues and grottoes, which, once built, were taken to be the equal of anything at the Villa d'Este at Tivoli.

Villa design remained one of Buontalenti's particular concerns, especially since the Medici chose to live for much of the year outside the city. The villas nearest to Florence were most elaborate, being used for the entertainment of the Medici themselves or to impress foreign dignitaries; those further off were plainer. Much of this work, it must be noted, involved the remodeling of extant buildings, so it is often difficult to know exactly what Buontalenti did in each instance. At the villa at Seravezza (ca. 1561-65), his contribution was perhaps in the simple massing and the window rhythms; at La Magia (1585) and Marignole (1587) all he could do was turn what was there into simple hunting lodges; at Petraia (1575-90) he transformed a castellated structure into a compact block. While some alterations were made to the building at Castello (1592), the garden was the main center of attention, the work there being completed later by Giorgio Vasari. One important project was at Artimino (1594), a hunting lodge which was altered to accommodate the whole court and there again the design was based on Caiano; while bastions were added to the exterior without any apparent purpose, inside all was at once elegant and functional.

In Florence itself Buontalenti was always busy. In 1594 he remodeled a small villa at the Palazzo Pitti, the Belvedere, making it a retreat for the Medici from which they could look down on the city and the countryside, back and front. For the funeral of Cosimo I in 1574, he designed an elegant baldachin, based on Spanish models, with a pyramidal canopy at the top, surmounted at the corners by figures set on volutes, as Michelangelo had done in the New Sacristy.

Buontalenti also made designs for the many theatrical productions at the Medici court: in 1565 he worked with Vasari on some *intermezzi* performed at the Palazzo Vecchio; in 1568 he designed costumes for Baldassare Lancia's production of *La Vedova;* and in the *intermezzi* done for the wedding of Ferdinando in 1589 he included an artificial mountain that was made to collapse at the end.

In 1574 Buontalenti succeeded Vasari as architect of the Uffizi. His most important work there is the Tribuna (1586), taken from Vitruvius' account of the Tower of the Winds in Athens, a hanging garden with fountains on the roof of the Loggia dei Lanzi (1583), and a staircase in the west arm that permitted access to the gallery and artists' workshops on the top floor. He also designed the Grotta Grande at the Palazzo Pitti (1583-93), where pumice stone covered the vestige of the pediment, and, inside, satyrs and other figures lurked, lit by hidden sources of illumination.

Of all his other projects, perhaps the most inventive was the small design of the stairs at Santa Trinita (1574), now in Santo Stefano; there the balustrades taper downward, rather than up, and the steps, which are rolled like volutes, are too narrow to be used, being there only for their visual effect, with the route to the altar being from either side. Buontalenti was busy the last years of his life with the great Capella dei Principi in San Lorenzo, the funerary chapel of the Medici. But for all the time, some 60 years, that he had spent in the service of the Medici, he was forgotten in his old age: if a letter of 1606 to Duke Ferdinando is to be believed, he lived out his old age deprived of food and neglected.

—DAVID CAST

BURGES, William.

British. Born in London, England, 1827. Died in London, 1881. Father was the civil engineer Alfred Burges. Trained as engineer, then apprenticed in architecture with Edward Blore (1787-1879) and Matthew Digby Wyatt (1820-77).

Chronology of Works
All in England unless noted

1857	Design for Crimean Memorial Church, Constantinople, Turkey (unexecuted)
1859-60	Gayhurst House, Buckinghamshire (additions)
1859-77	Waltham Abbey, Essex (restoration)
1861-62	All Saints Church, Fleet, Hampshire
1863-76	St. Finbar's Cathedral, Cork, Ireland
1864-79	Chapel and Hall, Worcester College, Oxford
1866	Warehouse, 46 Upper Thames Street, London
1866-68	Holy Trinity Church, Templebrady, Cork, Ireland
1867-68	St. Michael's Church, Lowfield Heath, Surrey
1868-81	St. Faith's Church, Stoke Newington, London
1868-81	Cardiff Castle, Wales (reconstruction and additions)
1869-71	Knightshayes Court, Devon
1871-72	Christ Church, Skelton, Yorkshire
1871-78	St. Mary's Church, Studley Royal, Yorkshire
1872-77	Speech Room, Harrow School, London
1873-82	Trinity College, Hartford, Connecticut, U.S.A. (built to Burges' designs)
1875-81	Castel Coch, near Cardiff, Wales
1876-81	Tower House (Burges House), 9 Melbury Road, Kensington, London

Publications

BOOKS BY BURGES

Art Applied to Industry. London, 1865.

BOOKS ABOUT BURGES

CROOK, J. MORDAUNT, et al.: *The Strange Genius of William Burgess.* Cardiff, Wales, 1981.
CROOK, J. MORDAUNT: *William Burges and the High Victorian Dream.* Chicago and London, 1981.

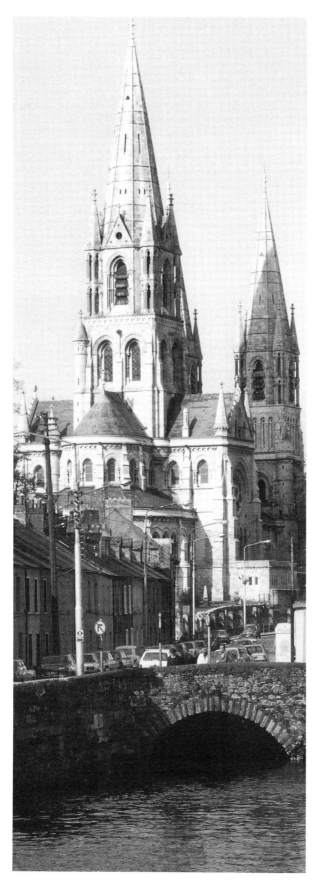

William Burges: St. Finbar's Cathedral, Cork, Ireland, 1863-76

DIXON, ROGER, and MUTHESIUS, STEFAN: *Victorian Architecture*. New York and Toronto, 1978.

FERRIDAY, PETER (ed.): *Victorian Architecture*. London, 1963.

GIROUARD, MARK: *The Victorian Country House*. Oxford, 1971.

PULLEN, A.: *Architectural Designs of William Burges*. London, 1883-87.

ARTICLES ABOUT BURGES

CROOK, J. MORDAUNT: "Knightshayes, Devon: Burges versus Grace." *National Trust Yearbook* 1 (1975-76): 44-55.

CROOK, J. MORDAUNT: "Patron Extraordinary: John, 3rd Marquess of Bute." In P. HOWELL (ed.): *Victorian South Wales*. London, 1970.

HANDLEY-READ, C.: "Cork Cathedral." *Architectural Review* 107 (1967): 422-430.

HANDLEY-READ, C.: "Notes on William Burges's Painted Furniture." *Burlington Magazine* 105 (1963): 496-509.

*

No architect responded more creatively or forcefully to the new High Victorian muscular Gothic style than did William Burges; yet his impact upon the development of architecture has been negligible. Burges' work is certainly strong and massive, but it is not characterized by rational design, constructional polychromy or honest expression of function. Burges believed that Gothic architecture was an architecture of figures and subjects achieving its impact through the synthesis of figural sculpture, painting and stained glass into the building fabric. He felt strongly that the poetry of a building lay in its decoration.

Moreover, Burges was as much an artist, a furniture designer and a decorator as he was an architect. Working closely with the artists and craftsmen who executed the various parts of his buildings, he controlled every detail of the work. Consequently, his buildings were so special, so individual, that they defied imitation and exist outside the mainstream of architectural development.

As a personal, intuitive, creative artist, Burges was interested almost exclusively in appearances and effects. Three Burges characteristics can be seen over and over in his work. First, he was a hopeless romantic who sought to escape from the reality of life in industrial Britain through medieval fantasy. Second, he could never resist architectural play-acting and visual humor. Third, he liked things to be larger than life, huge in scale. He was the great 19th-century master of scale manipulation; he could imbue small things—buildings, spaces, objects—with size, strength and power far in excess of reality. Yet he managed to balance fantasy with common sense and sound architectural judgment. Although his work was extremely experimental, it was disciplined by a thorough grasp of construction practice. He had an archaeologist's knowledge of Gothic architecture, yet he felt free to borrow widely from history, combining and reinterpreting traditional elements in fresh new ways. He could function equally well in both the Gothic and classical styles; like Christopher Wren and Nicholas Hawksmoor before him, he varied his style to suit the situation.

Burges' work is invariably bold, sculptural, and highly personal and distinctive; it is easily recognizable. He was unique in his age in his ability to handle plain walls and simple geometric shapes with consummate assurance. He was the inspired decorator of his era. Because private means allowed him to restrict his practice and because he was fortunate in having clients with the money, taste and patience to allow him to give his personal attention to every design detail, Burges put his own stamp on every part of each building he designed. In fact, Burges' wealthy clients were willing to give their architect carte blanche to design whatever he thought appropriate. From 1868 until his death in 1881, Burges spent a considerable portion of his time on the design and decoration of just two projects—Cardiff Castle and Castel Coch— for the third marquess of Bute, the richest man in the world at that time.

Burges postulated a set of rules to govern the design of "modern Gothic" architecture. First, he preached "regularity." He felt that an unbridled enthusiasm for the picturesque had produced buildings that looked as if they had been "shaken around in a hat" (*Art Applied to Industry,* 1865). He believed that a strong organizational system should govern plan and form arrangement.

Burges' other rules dealt mostly with design detail or the use of materials. He loved color and made an eloquent plea for the return of color to the modern city; however, he believed that color should be used sparingly and carefully in order to avoid the "piebald" appearance of much contemporary work that featured multi-colored brick and tile patterns. He despised small-scale, fretful detail that obscured major architectural elements. He believed that nothing should be done to compromise understanding of the nature and strength of building forms and materials. He made the aesthetic of the sublime rather than the aesthetic of the picturesque preeminent in his work.

Burges established his reputation as an architect through his participation in several important design competitions, most notably the competition for the design of the Church of Ireland cathedral, St. Finbar's, in Cork—a church that is one of the true masterpieces of the muscular Gothic style. In its form and plan it is as bold, vigorous and powerful as any other High Victorian church. Its monumental quality is particularly interesting considering the cathedral's small physical size.

Burges' design for the exterior demonstrates amazing virtuosity in the manipulation of scale, material and mass to monumental effect. From a distance St. Finbar's gives the appearance of a great French cathedral transported to Ireland. It dominates its city as its French counterparts do theirs; yet it is less than half the French cathedrals' typical length or height. J. Mordaunt Crook described it as exuding weight, power and majesty. In *William Burges and the High Victorian Dream,* he wrote, "It crouches, heavily muscled, like some tumescent beast, waiting to spring."

Burges was able to accomplish this architectural miracle by careful proportioning of all parts, by utilization of an ordering grid that affected the design of all facade elements, by skillful optical manipulation of the ordering geometry, by the choice of an exterior wall material that reflects light and reveals form regardless of atmospheric conditions, and by the marriage of architectural form and sculpture in a uniquely successful way.

Burges' skill as an interior designer is demonstrated by the interiors of the two churches built in North Yorkshire as memorials to Frederick Grantham Vyner—the churches of Christ the Consoler, Skelton-on-Ure, and St. Mary, Studley Royal—which are his most celebrated ecclesiastical works. Their interiors are richly sculptural; they play a delicate inner architectural system against a massive architectural envelope; they use similar materials and a similar color scheme; their figurative sculpture and stained glass are as fine as any produced during the Victorian age; and their sanctuaries are treated as golden reliquaries safely contained within, and detached from, their enclosing stone walls. They are examples of Victorian medievalism at its very best and most romantic.

—C. MURRAY SMART, JR.

BURLE MARX, Roberto.

Brazilian. Born in São Paulo, Brazil, 4 August 1909. Studied Brazilian flora privately at Dahlen Botanical Gardens, Berlin, Germany,1928-29; self-taught in landscape design. Director of parks, Recife, Brazil, 1935-37; private practice in Rio de Janeiro since 1937; has also worked as painter and as designer of jewelry, tapestries, stage scenery and sculptural reliefs.

Chronology of Works
All in Brazil unless noted

1934	Public Gardens, Recife
1938	Roof Gardens, Ministry of Education and Health Building (now Palacio da Cultura), Rio de Janeiro
1943	Pampulha Park and Gardens, Belo Horizonte
1948	Odette Monteiro Gardens, Correias, Petropolis
1948	Burton Tremaine House, Santa Barbara, California, U.S.A.
1950	Hotel Amazonas, Manaus
1951	Galeao Airport, Rio de Janeiro
1951	PDF Building, Rio de Janeiro
1954	Museum of Modern Art, Rio de Janeiro
1955	Imperial Museum, Petropolis
1956	Lindoia Park, São Paulo State
1956	Hacienda Monte Sacro, Valencia, Spain
1957	Parque del Este, Caracas, Venezuela
1961	Gloria-Flamengo Park, Rio de Janeiro
1963	UNESCO Gardens, Paris, France
1965	Biological Reserve, Jacarepagua, Guanabara
1966	Civic Center, Curitiba
1968	Brazilian Embassy, Washington, D.C., U.S.A.
1969	Petrobras Headquarters, Rio de Janeiro
1970	Copacabana Promenade, Rio de Janeiro
1970	Ministry of Justice, Brasilia
1972	Brasilia Square, Quito, Ecuador
1972	Planalto Palace, Brasilia
1972	Ministry of Development, Brasilia
1972	Petrobras Building and Terminal, Santa Teresa, Rio de Janeiro
1976	Abbey of Santa Maria, São Paulo
1976	Restaurant, Conservatory and Recreational Park, Brasilia
1977	Civic Center, Curitiba

Publications

BOOKS BY BURLE MARX

Rino Levi, with Nestor Goulart Reis Filho. Milan, 1974.

ARTICLES BY BURLE MARX

"Gardens and Ecology: A Personal View." *Plan* 10 (Johannesburg, 1973).
"Landscape Gardening." *Arts and Architecture* (July 1954).

BOOKS ABOUT BURLE MARX

BARDI, P. M., and M. GAUTHEROT: *The Tropical Gardens of Burle Marx.* New York and London, 1964.
MOTTA, F. L.: *Roberto Burle Marx e a nova visão da paisagem,* São Paulo, 1984; 3rd ed., 1986.

ARTICLES ABOUT BURLE MARX

EMANUEL, M.: "Roberto Burle Marx." *Landscape Design* (August 1979).

"The Gardens of Roberto Burle Marx." *Royal Architectural Institute of Canada Journal* (February 1952).

HESS, ALAN: "Burle Marx: A Shaky Legacy." *Landscape Architecture* (April 1992).

KERNER, MIGUEL THOMAS: "Robert Burle Marx: Parks, Gardens, Towns, Squares, Beaches." *Architettura* (April 1976).

KORFF, ALICE GRAEME: "Roberto Burle Marx of Brazil." *American Institute of Architects Journal* (May 1965).

PLAYFAIR, GUY: "The Versatility of Burle Marx." *Architectural Review* (November 1964).

"Roberto Burle Marx: Art and Landscape." *Architectural Record* (October 1954).

*

"His life is a permanent process of experimentation and creation. The work of the botanist, the gardener, the landscape architect is nourished by the work of the plastic artist, the graphic designer, and the painter, and vice-versa, in a continual give and take." Lúcio Costa, the author of these words, has been one of Roberto Burle Marx's greatest admirers and probably the most sensitive observer of his development as an artist. More important, Costa was a formative influence on Burle Marx's career. It was he who encouraged the young student to take up painting and design, just as he had stimulated Oscar Niemeyer to conceive spaces and structures. It might be said that Costa provided the fertile soil in which Burle Marx's painterly landscape art took root and flowered.

Today Burle Marx is known around the world as one of the premier landscape architects of the modern age. For many, he is *the* creator of modern landscape design, and his historical importance in the field places him alongside the likes of André Le Nôtre and Lancelot "Capability" Brown. Burle Marx is to landscape design in the 20th century what these men were to the Baroque garden: his profound significance lies in his having creatively synthesized the concerns and materials of environmental design with the formal and methodological problems of modernism. Just as Le Nôtre expressed an appropriately French, 17th-century, Cartesian vision of the landscape, Burle Marx's approach is similarly rooted in the philosophical concerns of 20th-century science and art. For Burle Marx, the art of composing the natural environment must be founded on the expertise of the positive scientist. A thorough botanical knowledge of the plant species and their ecological settings is a fundamental prerequisite for the creation of landscape art. But so too is an understanding of the painter's art of composition.

Burle Marx claims that he did not really "discover" the tropical exuberance, plastic richness and ecological complexity of the flora of his native Brazil until he visited the Botanical Gardens at Dahlem, Germany, in 1928. Grouped according to geographic area, the tropical plants in this garden came as a revelation to the student who had been trained to see as a painter. There too he began to appreciate the importance of plant associations within specific ecosystems. Henceforth he became the champion of Brazilian flora, committing himself not only to its study and conservation, but to its aesthetic celebration through his own landscape art. The plants of Brazil became the colors on the landscapist's palette.

The key to Burle Marx's synthesis has thus been his identification of the working methods of the landscape architect and scientifically trained environmentalist with those of the modern painter. It has been observed that Burle Marx's canvas is the earth, and his colors are the plants themselves. Thus, the major difference between the painter and the landscapist is the different materials each uses to achieve his artistic composition. But Burle Marx always treats plants with the specificity of the scientist, and never in the general terms of mere "vegetation" that is of interest for possessing certain qualities or colors. The plant is appreciated for its plastic as well as its individual organic (or specific botanical and ecological) qualities, and an appreciation of the former depends entirely on a knowledge of the latter.

In his mature works and writings, however, Burle Marx suggests that the parallel between the painter and the landscape architect should not be pushed too far. He recognizes the unique features of landscape design that distinguish it from the art of the painter and bring it more into the realm of the architect: three-dimensionality, the importance of the time-space dimension for experiencing and thus appreciating the garden; the changing impact of the sun, its light and the elements. Moreover, the landscape designer, he acknowledges, participates in a willful act of utopian reform: that of attempting to restore a paradise lost to the overly developed, industrialized world of the 20th century. For Burle Marx, this attempt has meant the effort to improve the quality of life of the city dweller through the creation of public parks and small pockets of tropical Eden on the rooftops, in the private gardens, and along the shorelines and byways of Latin America's cities.

Many of Burle Marx's best-known works have been created in the context of collaborative architectural projects with Oscar Niemeyer and others (the gardens for the Ministry of Education and Health Building in Rio de Janeiro, the Pampulha complex, and the Ministry of Justice in Brasília, for example). A 70-hectare state park and recreation area, the Parque del Este in Caracas, Venezuela (begun in 1957), also involved collaboration with a whole team of specialists including architects, botanists, zoologists and horticulturalists. Such large-scale public park commissions provided Burle Marx with ample artistic freedom and the opportunity to participate in the creation of entire environments within a specific urban and public context. In these we see the painterly botanist, environmental designer and social reformer rolled into one.

Two of Burle Marx's most celebrated Brazilian creations are the bayfront Glória-Flamengo Park and the decorative pavements for the sidewalks along Copacabana Beach in Rio de Janeiro. In the pavement designs, Burle Marx used small, variously shaped rocks of black, white and brown, artfully pieced together (following the ancient techniques of "Portuguese mosaic") into swirling patterns of color that echo the waves of the sea. There he demonstrated that Brazilian stone could be as powerful a natural element in landscape design as tropical plants themselves. His most famous private garden, that for the residence of Mrs. Odette Monteiro in Correias (1948), raises an issue that is at the heart of Burle Marx's intellectual and artistic quest: where does art end and nature begin? The role of the landscapist in the project is to plant in such a way as to make the formal composition around the house appear to introduce the natural environment around it and thus be at one with it.

Perhaps the ultimate statement of this intention is found in his own estate in Guaratiba, near Rio de Janeiro. Both a botanical laboratory and aesthetic showcase, Burle Marx's home is an ecologically complex synthesis of built structures, carefully grouped flora and wild tropical vegetation surrounding a winding hillside walkway. The element of visual surprise is present at every bend in the path, but it is often difficult, to the layman perhaps impossible, to know which of the incidents are "natural" and which were planted by Burle Marx. His manipulation of this natural landscape is informed by both aesthetic and didactic intentions: in bringing out the lush natural beauty of

Earl of Burlington: Chiswick House, Middlesex, London, England, ca. 1730

tropical species in all their exuberant plasticity and color, Burle Marx seeks to instruct the viewer about the harmonious natural groupings of the plants and to call attention to the importance of valuing and conserving Brazil's sensitive ecosystems. In a nation faced with the increasing devastation of its greatest ecological resource, the Amazon, Burle Marx's call for environmental education and conservation is of no small importance.

—DAVID K. UNDERWOOD

BURLINGTON, Earl of.

British. Born Richard Boyle, Third Earl of Burlington, on 25 April 1694. Died on 4 December 1753. Toured Italy, 1714-15; returned to Italy to study the works of Andrea Palladio in Vicenza, 1719. Worked independently in England.

Chronology of Works
All in England
* Approximate dates
† Work no longer exists

1721*	Mountrath House, London†
1721	Tottenham Park, Wiltshire
1722-30	Dormitory, Westminster School, London
1723	Wade House, London†
1728*-30	Northwick Park, Worcestershire (remodeling)
1730*	Chiswick House, London (with William Kent)
1730*	Richmond House, London (partial rebuilding)
1730*-32*	Foxhall House, Charlton, Sussex
1731-32*	Assembly Rooms, York
1747ff.*	Kirby Hall, Northamptonshire (with Roger Morris)

Publications

BOOKS BY BURLINGTON

Fabbriche Antiche disegnate da Andrea Palladio. 1730.

BOOKS ABOUT BURLINGTON

Apollo of the Arts, Lord Burlington and his Circle. Exhibition catalog. Nottingham, 1973.
CHARLTON, JOHN: *A History and Description of Chiswick House and Gardens*. London, 1958.
LEES-MILNE, JAMES: *Earls of Creation*. London, 1962.
NEAVE, DAVID: *Londesborough: History of an East Yorkshire Estate Village*. Londesborough, England, 1977.
RYKWERT, JOSEPH: *The First Moderns, The Architects of the Eighteenth Century*. Cambridge, Massachusetts, and London, 1980.
SAXL, F., and WITTKOWER, RUDOLF: *British Art and the Mediterranean*. London, 1969.
SERVICE, ALASTAIR: *The Architects of London*. London, 1979.
SINGLETON, W. A.: *Studies in Architectural History*. London, 1954. WHEATLEY, HENRY B.: *London Past and Present*. London, 1891.

WILLIS, PETER: *Charles Bridgeman and the English Landscape Garden*. London, 1977.

WITTKOWER, RUDOLF: *The History of the York Assembly Rooms*. York, n.d.

WITTKOWER, RUDOLF: *Palladio and English Palladianism*. London, 1974.

ARTICLES ABOUT BURLINGTON

CRAIG, MAURICE: "Burlington, Adam and Gandon." *Journal of the Warburg and Courtauld Institutes* 17 (1954): 381.

GOODALL, IAN H.: "Lord Burlington's 'Piazza'." *Annual Report of the York Georgian Society* (1970).

"Hogarth against Burlington." *Architectural Review* (August 1964).

KIMBALL, FISKE: "Burlington Architectus." *Royal Institute of British Architects Journal* 34-35 (15 October 1927).

LEES-MILNE, JAMES: "Lord Burlington in Yorkshire" *Architectural Review* (July 1945).

WITTKOWER, RUDOLF: "Lord Burlington and William Kent." *Archaeological Journal* 102 (1945). Reprinted in *Palladio and English Palladianism*. London, 1974.

WITTKOWER, RUDOLF: "Pseudo-Palladian Elements in English Neo-Classical Architecture." *Journal of the Warburg Institute* 6 (1943).

"Young Lord Burlington." *Country Life* (30 June 1960).

*

Lord Burlington is responsible for the English study of classical architecture according to the precepts of Renaissance architect and theorist Andrea Palladio (1508-80). In turn, Palladio's ideas were based on those of Roman architect and theorist Vitruvius (active 43-30 B.C.), whose treatise on Greco-Roman architecture was the only complete work extant from that time.

Palladio's definition of beauty dealt with the concordance and conformity of parts, both to each other and to the whole. Palladian concepts were inspired by rules from the ancients: propriety and rationality were dominant. Guided but not confined by these rules, Palladio's buildings were interpretations rather than reproductions of classical buildings.

One of the earliest English followers of Palladio, Inigo Jones (1573-1652) influenced Burlington to the extent that the latter enticed his protégé William Kent to publish *Designs of Inigo Jones* (1727). Burlington also obtained Jones' gateway for his Chiswick gardens. But long before that, Burlington had received a firsthand introduction to antiquity during his initial grand tour of the Continent (1714-15).

Upon his return, he hired another Palladian, Colen Campbell (1679-1729), as architect for the facade of Burlington House and some of its rooms (1718-29). Like Palladio, Campbell extolled the simplicity of ancient works, the classical use of square and circle as the most perfect forms, an emphasis on cubic quality, and a reduction in excessive ornamentation. His buildings display subsidiary parts and focal points, frequently a central portico. Burlington's association with Campbell, just subsequent to the latter's publication of *Vitruvius Britannicus* in 1715 and 1717, influenced his second tour (1719), which involved a direct study of Palladio's architecture and the acquisition of 60 original drawings, along with a number of books and prints.

Approval of Palladian style not only expressed a wish to depart from the dramatic Baroque works of architects like Christopher Wren and John Vanbrugh, it also reflected the political realities of the day. Newly elected, the Whig party encouraged strong public sentiment against the French, Catholicism, absolutism and the court architecture of the earlier-ruling Tories.

Turning to Inigo Jones, an English architect, exhibited a resurgence of national pride. But the rational rules of Palladian architecture also reflected a concept particularly in favor at the beginning of the 18th century.

Burlington remained faithful to the spirit of Palladio through his emphasis on geometric parts and on proportions that emphasized the relationship of modules. While assembled into a whole, individual parts remained distinct. An example of this can be found in one of Burlington's early buildings, Tottenham Park, Wiltshire. The simplicity that he and Campbell espoused was especially evident in their symmetrical plans—another distinctive Palladian characteristic. Burlington's interest in Palladio's use of columns can also be found in the gardens at Chiswick, where Burlington employed a screen of trees in similar manner to his preceptor's use of columns at San Giorgio Maggiore in Venice.

Unlike some so-called Palladians, Burlington did not just add details of a Palladian type (e.g., Diocletian or Venetian windows, or pedimented porticoes)—he created in the *spirit* of his teacher. He was so well versed in Palladio's doctrine that he could synthesize new applications from classical concepts, putting Palladio's ideas on Egyptian halls for entertainment and Roman basilicas to work in his own design for the Assembly Rooms at York (1730). Even measurements missing in Palladio's original description were extrapolated from the first English translation of Palladio's *Quattro libri dell'architettura* (provided by Giacomo Leoni in 1715-20) to provide the York Assembly with 18 columns on each side appropriate to a Roman basilica, and six columns on each end as befitting an Egyptian hall. And while Palladio himself did not seem to have departed from symmetrical arrangements of rooms, he did acknowledge asymmetry in his plans for Roman thermae. Burlington provided a flowing organization to his rooms, changing from the circle and square to include ovals in his plans, providing variety to the sequence of rooms.

Similarly, in keeping with Palladio's approach to architecture, Burlington favored a rusticated basement contrasted with large, clear areas of wall above. But by that point, Burlington had developed this idea, of movement from heaviness and complexity at the bottom toward lightness, clarity and simplicity toward the top, to include a new form of staircase at the front of Chiswick—something alien to Palladio and his Villa Rotonda.

Burlington's influence extended beyond providing designs. His so-called "School of Athens" was responsible for an interest in Palladian architecture by a number of young, reputable architects who worked for Burlington at various times: Henry Flitcroft, Isaac Ware, Stephen Wright and Daniel Garrett. Public taste was further influenced when these men were put in positions that allowed them to provide designs for public buildings. Burlington advised his portégé William Kent and amateur architects who were either building for themselves or consulting for others. Burlington's only known publication was *Fabbriche Antiche disegnate da Andrea Palladio* (1730), in which he published some of the Palladio drawings he had found at Villa Maser. The book also included many of his own ideas and certain illustrations of windows often used in his designs. Ironically, while Burlington himself had been inspired by an English translation of Palladio's ideas, his own work, penned in Italian, had little influence on others.

Some critics have charged that Burlington practiced architecture in an academic manner: that his careful separation, clarity of form, and otherwise painstaking designs resulted in cold and abstract structures. Justification for this charge is found in Chiswick Villa (circa 1725), a close imitation of Palladio's Villa Rotonda, and also in the garden facade of General Wade's residence (1723), precisely copied from one of Palladio's unbuilt houses. It is also due to Burlington's own insistence on historical accuracy when he used classical architecture or when he interpreted Palladio.

—TERESA S. WATTS

BURN, William.

Scottish. Born in Edinburgh, Scotland, 20 December 1789. Died 15 February 1870. Father was Scottish architect Robert Burn (1752-1815), whose practice he took over around 1820. Married Eliza MacVicar; several children. Studied with Robert Smirke (1781-1867), London, 1808-12; established office in Edinburgh, 1812; partner with his pupil David Bryce (1803-76), 1841-50; opened office in London, 1844; later became partner with his nephew, J. MacVicar Anderson (1834-1915), who continued the practice after Burn's death; consultant architect to the Government in Scotland, 1850s. Institute of British Architects, 1835.

Chronology of Works
All in Scotland unless noted
†*Work no longer exists*

1813-16	North Leith Parish Church, Edinburgh
1815-18	St. John's Episcopal Church, Edinburgh
1817-18	Custom House, Greenock
1818-26	Saltoun Hall, East Lothian
1820-24	Blairquhan, Ayr
1822-24	Carstairs House, Lanark
1823-24	Edinburgh Academy, Edinburgh
1824	Strathendry House, Leslie, Fife
1824-26	Camperdown House, Angus
1824-27	Snaigow House, Perth†
1825-28	John Watson's School (now the National Gallery of Modern Art), Edinburgh
1826-27	Fettercairn House, Kincardine
1826-27	Garscube House, Dunbarton†
1828-32	Dupplin Castle, Perth†
1829-30	Tyninghame House, East Lothian
1829-36	Milton Lockhart, Lanark†
1832-34	Madras College, St. Andrews, Fife
1834	New Club, Edinburgh†
1834-35	County Hall, Castle, Inverness
1834-39	Crichton Royal Lunatic Asylum, Dumfries
1835	Stenhouse, Stirling†
1838-55	Harlaxton Manor, Lincolnshire, England (interiors and additions)
1839-41	Stoke Rochford Hall, Lincolnshire, England
1839-43	Muckross Abbey, Kerry, Ireland
1839-44	Falkland House, Fife
1839-44	Whitehill Hall, Edinburgh
1844	Revesby Abbey, Lincolnshire, England
1844-46	Dartrey, Monaghan, Ireland†
1848-52	Idsworth, Hampshire, England
1849-52	Poltalloch, Inverness†
1851-52	Dunira, Perth†
1851-53	Buchanan House, Stirling†
1851-55	Sandon Hall, Staffordshire, England
1856	Fonthill House, Wiltshire, England†
1856-61	Lynford Hall, Norfolk, England
1857-59	Montague House, Whitehall Gardens, London, England†
1865-68	Whittlebury Lodge, Northamptonshire, England

Publications

PUBLICATIONS BY BURN

A Report Relative to Proposed Approaches from the South and West of the Old Town of Edinburgh. With Thomas Hamilton. Edinburgh, 1824.

BOOKS ABOUT BURN

FIDDLES, VALERIE, and ROWAN, ALISTAIR (compilers): *David Bryce, 1803-1876.* Edinburgh, 1976.
GIROUARD, MARK: *The Victorian Country House.* New Haven, Connecticut, and London, 1971.
HITCHCOCK, HENRY-RUSSELL: *Early Victorian Architecture in Britain.* 2 vols. New Haven, Connecticut, and London, 1954.
HUSSEY, CHRISTOPHER: *English Country Houses: Late Georgian, 1800-1840.* London, 1958.
KERR, ROBERT: *The English Gentleman's House.* London, 1864.
LINDSAY, IAN GORDON: *Georgian Edinburgh.* Edinburgh, 1948.
MACAULEY, JAMES: *The Gothic Revival: 1745-1845.* Glasgow and London, 1975.
WALKER, DAVID: ''William Burn: The Country House in Transition.'' In JANE FAWCETT (ed.): *Seven Victorian Architects.* University Park, Pennsylvania, 1976.

ARTICLES ABOUT BURN

DONALDSON, T. L.: ''Memoir, William Burn.'' *Royal Institute of British Architects Transactions* (1869-70): 121-129.
MACLACHLAN, JOHN: ''Edinburgh Architects.'' *Builder* (1882): 667-668.

*

Of the group of Scottish architects, including William Playfair, Thomas Hamilton and William Stark, who were practicing in Edinburgh in the first half of the 19th century and who gave to Europe one of the most memorable townscapes to result from the British preoccupation with styles and with the picturesque, William Burn may not have been the most imaginative nor the most creative, but he was certainly the most prolific. Following a period of four years in London as a pupil of Robert Smirke, he established a practice in Edinburgh in 1812, which by 1830 had become the largest in Scotland.

Burn's principal early commissions were for public buildings, but by the 1830s he had built up a reputation as a designer of country houses in the Jacobean style. It was with this type of building that he was to be mainly concerned for the rest of his long working life. In 1841 he suffered a breakdown, probably due to overwork, but quickly recovered. In 1844, by which time he had taken David Bryce into partnership—one of several of his pupils, including Richard Norman Shaw, who were to become famous architects in their own right—he moved to London, leaving Bryce in charge of the Edinburgh office. From London he was able to give proper attention to the many commissions for country houses he was receiving from English clients. He became one of the most sought-after architects for this type of building, and was particularly noted for the care he took to ensure that his clients' wishes were fully satisfied. Perhaps for this reason he was regarded by some of his architectural contemporaries as more of a businessman than an architect, but a serious examination of his work would quickly have revealed that judgment to be unjust.

From the very beginning, Burn produced work in a wide variety of styles. His North Leith Church (1813-16), in what is now part of Edinburgh, is neoclassical. Its front consists of a two-story rectangular block of five bays with a full-height Ionic portico, tetrastyle, fronting the central three bays. The effect is similar to that of a country house, but a Gibbsian steeple consisting of a three-stage tower plus a spire is placed centrally over the entrance and serves to mark the building as a parish church. St. John's Church (1815-18) in Edinburgh's Princes Street is an essay in Perpendicular Gothic and, considering its date, is exceptionally faithful in both spirit and detailing to the medieval original. Edinburgh Academy (1823-24) and John Watson's School (1825) are Greek Revival buildings of similar appearance. John Watson's, the larger of the two, is a long E-plan building of two stories plus basement. A central Doric portico, hexastyle, is flanked by wings of seven bays each, with the end three bays of both being brought forward to form pavilions. Ornamentation of the wings is confined to a continuation of the Doric frieze of the portico along the entire width of the building and the addition of pilasters to the end pavilions. The overall effect is one of solemnity and sobriety, which was no doubt thought appropriate for an educational establishment in the Presbyterian "Athens of the North."

Burn built or altered a large number of country houses during his early years in practice. As with his churches and public buildings, he employed the full range of styles that were then thought appropriate. Saltoun (1818-26) is castellated Gothic; Camperdown (1824-26), Greek Revival; Garscube (1826-27), Tudor Gothic, and Strathendry (1824), Jacobean; all were competently executed country houses from that period. Tyninghame (1829-30), in East Lothian, is a house which is of particular interest. This was in fact a remodeling of an existing building and was Burn's first serious essay in what was to become a Scottish Baronial style. There he combined aspects of Scottish vernacular—steeply pitched roofs, "crow-stepped" gables, wallhead gables and circular turrets—with Tudor and Jacobean elements such as mullioned windows and tall prominent chimneys. The overall effect is lively and romantic.

The buildings mentioned above are a small representative sample of Burn's early work. They demonstrate that he was undoubtedly a competent architect capable of providing buildings in a range of styles. They also demonstrate that although most of his buildings were fairly standard essays in their various idioms, he was not without some capacity for invention and innovation.

Following his move to London in 1844, Burn made a specialty of country house design, particularly Elizabethan and Jacobean mansions. He attracted an enormous volume of work and was especially noted for the ingenuity, complexity and convenience of the plans he produced.

Burn has entered the history books as a Greek Revival architect who practiced in Scotland. This is perhaps justified, as it may be said that buildings such as John Watson's School were among his finest works. It is a fact, however, that a very large body of his later work was produced in England and that this, as well as his early work, covered the full range of idioms that were fashionable at the time, from late neoclassicism to Gothic,

Elizabethan and Jacobean. Perhaps Burn's most significant contribution to British architecture was in fact his pioneer work in the revival of the Scottish vernacular. It was Burn who first developed this revival into the Scottish Baronial style, which became very popular in the second half of the 19th century, and whose principal exponent was Burn's pupil David Bryce.

—A. J. MACDONALD

BURNHAM, Daniel H.

American. Born Daniel Hudson Burnham in Henderson, New York, 1846. Died in Heidelberg, Germany, 1 June 1912. Educated at city schools, Chicago, Illinois; studied with private tutor, Bridgewater, Massachusetts. Entered large mercantile house, Chicago, 1868; apprenticeship, Loring and Jenney office, Chicago; partnership with Gustave Laureau; draftsman, Carter, Drake and Wight, 1872; partnership with John Wellborn Root (1850-91) as Burnham and Root, 1873-91; opened own office, 1891; appointed c hairman of the Commission of Fine Arts, Washington, D.C., 1910. Elected to Chicago chapter of the American Institute of Architects, 1884, of which he became a fellow in 1887, and president in 1894.

Chronology of Works
All in the United States
† *Work no longer exists*

1874	Sherman House, Chicago†
1881-82	Montauk Building, Chicago†
1881-83	Calumet Clubhouse, Chicago†
1883-85	Montezuma Hotel, Las Vegas, Nevada
1885-86	Ayer House, Chicago†
1885-87	Rookery Building, Chicago
1886-87	Art Institute, Chicago†
1887	Train Station, Kewanee†
1887-88	Lakeview Presbyterian Church, Chicago
1888-89	Valentine House, Chicago†
1888-90	DeKoven House, Chicago
1888-90	Rand-McNally Building, Chicago†
1888-90	Society for Savings Bank, Cleveland, Ohio
1889-91	Monadnock Building, Chicago
1890-91	Herald Building, Chicago†
1890-91	Mills Building, San Francisco, California
1890-92	Equitable Building, Atlanta, Georgia†
1890-92	Masonic Temple, Chicago†
1890-92	Women's Building, Chicago†
1890-94	Reliance Building, Chicago (with Charles B. Atwood)
1892-93	World's Columbian Exposition, Chicago (master plan with Frederick Law Olmsted)
1893-1902	Marshall Field Department Store, Chicago
1898-1902	Union Station, Pittsburgh, Pennsylvania
1903	Railway Exchange Building, Chicago
1903	Flatiron (Fuller) Building, New York City
1903-07	Union Station, Washington, D.C.
1905	Orchestra Hall, Chicago
1909	Wanamaker's Department Store, Philadelphia, Pennsylvania
1910-11	People's Gas Building, Chicago
1912	Filene's Department Store, Boston, Massachusetts

Publications

BOOKS BY BURNHAM

The World's Columbian Exposition: The Final Official Report of the Director of Works. Chicago, 1898.
Plan of Chicago. With Edward Bennett. Chicago, 1909.

ARTICLES BY BURNHAM

"Charles Bowler Atwood." *Inland Architect and News Record* 26, No. 6 (1896): 56-57.

BOOKS ABOUT BURNHAM

The Architectural Work of Graham, Anderson, Probst and White ... and their Predecessors D. H. Burnham and Co. and Graham. 2 vols. London, 1933.
CONDIT, CARL W.: *The Chicago School of Architecture: A History of Commercial and Public Building in the Chicago Area, 1875-1925.* Chicago, 1964.
HINES, THOMAS S.: *Burnham of Chicago, Architect and Planner.* New York, 1974.
HOFFMANN, DONALD: *The Architecture of John Wellborn Root.* Baltimore, 1973.
MONROE, HARRIET: *John Wellborn Root: A Study of His Life and Work.* Boston and New York, 1896.
MOORE, CHARLES: *Daniel Burnham: Architect, Planner of Cities.* 2 vols. Boston, 1921.
ZUKOWSKY, JOHN; CHAPPELL, SALLY KITT; and BRUEG-MANN, ROBERT: *The Plan of Chicago: 1909-1979.* Exhibition catalog. Chicago, 1979.

ARTICLES ABOUT BURNHAM

BESS, PHILIP: "Big Plans, Divine Details: The Burnham Plan and Citywide Development in Modern Chicago." *Inland Architect* 34, No. 2 (March/April 1990): 56-63.
MOORE, CHARLES: "Lessons of the Chicago World's Fair: An Interview with the Late Daniel H. Burnham." *Architectural Record* 33, No. 1 (1913): 34-44.
REBORI, ANDREW N.: "The Work of Burnham & Root, D. H. Burnham & Co. and Graham, Burnham & Co." *Architectural Record* 38, No. 1 (July 1915): 32-168.
SCHUYLER, MONTGOMERY: "Architecture in Chicago: D. H. Burnham & Co." *Architectural Record* 5 (December 1895): 49-71.

*

Recognized as the impresario of turn-of-the-century American architecture and planning, Daniel H. Burnham demonstrated an acute ability to organize architectural activity at a grand scale and to catalyze productivity among others. He built one of the largest architectural firms in the United States, having operated several offices and developed numerous highly influential and large-scale urban plans. Burnham won fame as the orchestrator of the World's Columbian Exposition of 1893, held in Chicago to celebrate the 400th anniversary of the arrival of Christopher Columbus in the New World. Willis Polk, Burnham's assistant, compiled a paragraph from the titan's speeches and writings; it includes the legendary statement that best summarizes Burnham's entrepreneurial spirit: "Make no little plans, they have no magic to stir men's blood."

Born in 1846 in upstate New York to Edwin and Elizabeth Burnham, who were practicing Swedenborgians, Burnham moved to Chicago with his family when he was eight. He attended the New Church School of the Worcestors in Waltham, Massachusetts, and also received tutoring from Tilly Brown Hayward in Bridgewater, Massachusetts. His social and drawing skills exceeded his scholastic standing.

After deciding to explore the field of architecture, Burnham entered the Chicago office of Loring and Jenney in 1867, where he worked for William Le Baron Jenney. In 1868 he ventured west to try his hand at silver speculation and gold prospecting in Nevada, but he failed at that. Upon returning to Chicago in 1870 he ran for the office of state senator and lost. Next he entered into a partnership with the architect Gustave Laureau; that lasted for only a short period, for the great fire of 1871 brought ruin to the firm. Burnham's next professional step was significant: he joined Carter, Drake and Wight, where he gained a deeper appreciation of scholarship in architecture and where he met John Wellborn Root, with whom he formed his own professional partnership in 1873.

As administrator, coordinator of business development and cultivator of clients, Burnham, with his talents with words and pencil, became the practical and promotional partner, while Root, who received his early architectural training in the New York office of James Renwick, was versatile, romantic and original. Together they achieved great success in the heady period that followed the fire by filling the need for architectural leadership in Chicago that became evident by 1880. In 1881 the firm relocated to offices in the Montauk Building, which they had recently designed, and where they installed a drafting staff of 60, earning commissions throughout the United States.

Burnham and Root's early commissions included the John B. Sherman House in Chicago (1874), which led to other commissions, including the Edward Ayer House (1886) and Reginald DeKoven House (1890). The Sherman commission was important in another significant aspect, because Burnham married Sherman's daughter Margaret. That early period reflects a widely accepted preference for Queen Anne style residences, heavily influenced by the domestic designs in England of Richard Norman Shaw and for the Richardsonian Romanesque in commercial buildings.

By 1891, the year in which Root died unexpectedly, the firm had to its name 200 buildings in Chicago and 50 in other cities. From then until 1894 the firm's name was simply Daniel H. Burnham, and from 1894 until his death in 1912 the firm's name was D. H. Burnham and Company; during this latter 18-year period, the firm created more than 60 buildings and 11 parks in Chicago alone.

The most significant buildings were commercial in nature. They began with the Montauk Building in Chicago (1881-82), to which the term "skyscraper" was first applied. It was indeed a forerunner of buildings that contained true skyscraper construction, and was the first tall building in Chicago to achieve commercial success. Containing fireproofed iron beams, the 10-story building rested on the first example of floating-raft foundations. In the 11-story Rookery (1886), Burnham is said to have established the pattern for the greatly influential floor plan, a hollow rectangle, that became the prototype for early commercial-style buildings in Chicago. In technological terms the Rookery is transitional, with load-bearing masonry walls along the public facades at the corner of Adams and La Salle streets and with lighter walls supported at ground level along the alleys by cast-iron columns with wrought-iron spandrel beams. The spirit is Richardsonian, with a wall composition closely related to that of H. H. Richardson's Marshall Field Wholesale Store (1886), and the interior court is faced with highly reflective white-glazed brick. In San Francisco the 10-story Mills Building (1890-91) is similar in plan and, like the Rookery, has an arcaded facade.

Unlike almost all historical precedents, the 16-story Monadnock Building in Chicago (1889-91) is a lesson in unified design. As the tallest building with exterior load-bearing walls in the world, it features chamfered corners that widen toward the building's outward-flaring cove cornice, an inwardly sloping wall and undulating oriel windows, and a magnificently plastic effect achieved by unusually narrow mortar joints and compound curves. The Masonic Temple Building was constructed at almost the same time; at 22 stories it was the tallest building in the world, marked by its picturesque sloping roof and gabled attic stories. It served as the model for Philip Johnson and John Burgee's 190 South La Salle Street, built in the mid-1980s.

Buildings designed by Burnham's firm after Root's death began to abandon Root's interest in the ruggedness of the Romanesque in favor of either a clear expression of the structural frame or, more often, the persistence of an eclectic Beaux-Arts classicism, as revived by Burnham in his prescribed style for the World's Columbian Exposition. The southeast quadrant of Marshall Field's Department Store in Chicago (1893; originally the annex) and Wanamaker's in Philadelphia (1909) both graft the surface details of enlarged Renaissance palazzi onto facades that refer closely to Richardson's Marshall Field Wholesale Store. Additional well-planned department stores designed by the firm include Selfridge's in London (1906), Gimbel's in New York City (1909) and Filene's in Boston (1912).

Charles Atwood replaced Root as chief designer in Burnham's firm, and his design for the Reliance Building in Chicago (1894) is greatly admired. It set a construction record with the erection in only 15 days of the wind-braced framework of its top 10 stories, designed by Edward C. Shankland. Aesthetically it achieved even more: its Chicago windows and delicate Gothic-inspired, attenuated mullions form an almost pure curtain wall enclosure. The 18-story Fisher Building (1895-96) is similar; both exhibit Gothic ornament and, more important, large expanses of glass and terra-cotta stretched tightly over a skeleton frame, achieving an open, dematerialized outer wall.

In New York the celebrated image of the Flatiron Building (1903; also known as the Fuller Building) exploits its triangular site and thus integrates two primary factors in the history of Burnham's career: an interest in the commercial style and in the effects of urban design parameters. Also from that period is the 17-story Railway Exchange Building in Chicago (1903-04), clad in gleaming white terra-cotta and featuring an undulating wall of oriel windows that recall the Monadnock Building, oculi in the top story, and low-relief classical urns, goddesses and festoons.

Among the last of Burnham's commercial buildings in Chicago is the People's Gas Building (1910-11). Its richly ornamental terra-cotta wall, like a low-relief tapestry, set between two-story, monolithic granite columns and a colonnaded attic, exaggerates the horizontality of the building. With its emphasis on the corners and grand scale, the People's Gas Building displays ironically a distinctly baronial classicism.

Incorporated in 1890 in Chicago, the World's Columbian Exposition appointed Root as consulting architect, Frederick Law Olmsted as landscape architect and Burnham as chief of construction. The exposition projected Burnham onto the national scene. With its exalted interpretation of classicism and tendency toward imperial allusions, the fair represented the apotheosis of the American Renaissance. It was unique in its scale and unity of expression, Burnham having sanctioned a robust synthesis of Greek and Roman classicism and having entrusted the design to a national array of architects, many of whom were trained at the École des Beaux-Arts in Paris; Richard Morris Hunt, McKim, Mead and White, Peabody and Stearns, George Browne Post and Louis H. Sullivan were among those

invited to design its buildings. The initial plan was drawn by Henry S. Codman, an assistant to Frank Lloyd Wright, in cooperation with Burnham and Root. Olmsted chose the site in the marshy lagoon that was to become Jackson Park. The result was nothing less than the birth of modern American city planning.

Employing uniform cornice heights and an arcaded module, the buildings at the fair featured interconnected utilities and services as well as the large-scale use of water and electric lighting reflected in lagoons. The Beaux-Arts principles of ensemble, strong axes and axial planning reigned, to be relieved only by the picturesque wooded island for the Japanese pavilion. Burnham called it his plaster dream city; it became known as the "White City" because of the mass of classical stucco buildings created for it. Critics called it imperialistic, bemoaned its academic reading of classicism and textbook classical detail, and felt it abandoned the progressive ideals of the commercial style.

The fair initiated the last phase of Burnham's career, and perhaps the most important—his participation in the City Beautiful movement, an attempt to bring order to urban America in response to expansion and modernization. He sensed in the national mood a desire for uniformity and academic order. He developed plans for Washington, D.C., Cleveland's Civic Center with Brunner and Carrère, the Civic Center in San Francisco, and Manila and Baguio, the summer capital of the Philippines. In the age of reform Burnham captured the national spirit in architectonic terms.

In 1901 the Senate Park Commission, as the result of a resolution by Senator James McMillan of Michigan, appointed Burnham as chair, to work with Charles McKim and Frederick Law Olmsted, Jr., to restore the grand gestures of Pierre Charles L'Enfant's 1791 plan for Washington, D.C., which was supposedly inspired by André Le Nôtre's Baroque design for Louis XIV's Versailles. Burnham drew on the lessons of the World's Columbian Exposition with the reclamation of the Mall, the planning of buildings around the Capitol and the White House, and the development of interconnected parks. Stemming from an initial proposal in the same year, Burnham's firm designed Union Station (1903-07). Its fully realized Beaux-Arts design exhibits a five-part facade with central focus on a triple-arched entrance that leads to a monumental barrel-vaulted waiting room.

Working with Edward H. Bennett, Burnham produced his most famous document, the Plan of Chicago (1906-09). As a result of the World's Columbian Exposition, civic officials and people of commerce recognized the value of large-scale plans, with orderly groups of buildings, parks and transportation arteries. With the support of the Merchants and Commercial Clubs, Burnham and Bennett prepared the plan and presented it to a group that would later establish the Chicago Plan Committee. Burnham wrote that he developed the plan to save the city from the "chaos incident to rapid growth." It addressed four basic aspects of civic life: dwelling, work, transportation and recreation. It included boulevards radiating from a civic center, city and county park systems, bilevel riverfront drives, a ring system of boulevards and preservation of the lakefront. It was indeed a comprehensive regional plan and included the establishment of the Forest Preserve District and the creation of Humboldt, Garfield and Columbus Parks, which represent perhaps the best of Jens Jensen's landscape design achievements.

The Plan of Chicago established precedents for all of the elements of 20th-century urban planning. Despite its dignity and boldness, the plan's weakness lies perhaps in its excessive formal organization in the absence of an accompanying reorganization of community life. Lewis Mumford criticized it as an "accessory of business."

Greatly honored toward the end of his life, Burnham was appointed First Chairman of the national Commission of Fine Arts by President William Howard Taft in 1910; the commission recommended Potomac Park in Washington, D.C., as the location for the Lincoln Memorial. Burnham joined the prestigious Century Club in New York City, and both Harvard and Yale universities gave him honorary degrees. Traveling in Europe in 1912, he died suddenly in Heidelberg, Germany, and is memorialized in Graceland Cemetery in Chicago.

—PAUL GLASSMAN

BURTON, Decimus.

British. Born in 1800. Died in London, England, 14 December 1881. Trained in the office of his father, the builder James Burton; studied under George Maddox; attended Royal Academy Schools, 1871. Worked independently. Fellow of the Royal Society; fellow, Society of Antiquaries; vice president, Royal Institute of British Architects.

Chronology of Works
All in England unless noted
† *Work no longer exists*

n.d.	Cornwall Terrace, Regent's Park, London
1822	Clarence Terrace, Regent's Park, London
1823-27	Colosseum, Regent's Park, London†
1825	Hyde Park Screen, London
1825	Hertford Villa, Regent's Park, London
1829*	Holy Trinity, Kent
1827-30	Athenaeum Club, London
1827-40*	Calverley Estate, Kent
1828-31	Beulah Spa, London†
1835-43	Port of Fleetwood, Lancashire
1836-40	Great Conservatory, Chatsworth, Derbyshire
1844-48	Palm Stove, Royal Botanic Gardens, Kew (with Richard Turner)
1845-46	Winter Garden Conservatory, Regent's Park, London (with Turner)†
1859-62	Temperate House Conservatory, Royal Botanic Gardens, Kew

Publications

BOOKS ABOUT BURTON

ELMES, JAMES: *Metropolitan Improvements; or London in the Nineteenth Century.* London, 1827.
SERVICE, ALASTAIR: *The Architects of London.* London, 1979.
SUMMERSON, JOHN: *Georgian London.* 3rd ed. Cambridge, Massachusetts, 1945; 1978.

ARTICLES ABOUT BURTON

HONOUR, HUGH: "The Regent's Park Colosseum." *Country Life* 113 (1953): 22-24.
HUSSEY, CHRISTOPHER: "Grimston Park, Yorkshire." *Country Life* 87 (1940): 276-280.
JONES, R. F.: "The Life and Works of Decimus Burton." *Architectural Review* (1905).
McRAE, J. F.: "Burton's Tunbridge Wells." *Architect's Journal* 65 (1927): 214-216, 249-250.
MONKHOUSE, C.: "Fleetwood, Lancashire." *Country Life* 158 (1975): 126-128, 290-293.

NARES, GORDON: "The Athenaeum." *Country Life* 109 (1951): 1018-1022.
RAMSEY, STANLEY C.: "The Athenaeum Club, London." *Architectural Review* 34 (1913): 54-58.
TAYLOR, G. C.: "Holme House, Regent's Park." *Country Life* 86 (1939): 444-448.
TAYLOR, G. C.: "A House in Regent's Park." *Country Life* 87 (1940): 416-418.

*

Decimus Burton was most fortunate in that his entry into the architectural profession was at the highest level. His father, James, had been John Nash's principal supporter in the Regent's Park and Street scheme. In gratitude, Nash took Decimus into his office and allowed him to design Cornwall and Clarence Terraces. These structures were to give the impression of great palaces overlooking the park, as at Versailles, providing country-house views from within, yet having the convenience of a house in the city. Burton's watercolor rendering for Clarence Terrace reveals his talents as a painter in a technique reminiscent of J.M. Gandy. As built, however, the richly ornamented Greco-Roman design was much simplified. His other Regent's Park designs were equally imaginative. Grove House was an adaptation of the asymmetric porches of the Erechtheion to the form of a villa, and was widely published at home and abroad (the American architect Ithiel Town copied it in New Haven, Connecticut). The Colosseum, one of Burton's most ambitious works, was actually the Pantheon with Parthenon Doric portico and had a wooden dome larger than that of St. Paul's Cathedral. Its interior was painted with a vast panorama of London viewed from the original ball and cross atop St. Paul's, which had just been removed during renovations.

After Napoleon's defeat in 1815, an effort was made to supplant Paris by London as a new Rome, a center of empire. A processional way into the city leading to Buckingham Palace was conceived, with triumphal arches at key locations, like those used to welcome returning emperors. Burton's Hyde Park Corner Facade and Green Park Entrance, together with Nash's Marble Arch (originally in front of Buckingham Palace), were intended to fulfill this symbolic concept. King George IV actually signed Burton's drawings for the two archways, but in reality the archways were underscaled (especially when compared with Paris' Arc de Triomphe), and their original intention has long since been forgotten.

Burton's indirect connections to the Crown through Nash paid off in another way. He was invited by J.W. Croker, privy council to the king, to be on the founding committee of the Athenaeum, a club for men with artistic and literary tastes, and was soon chosen to design a new building. The result was one of the most elegant of such clubhouses, with its Parthenon sculptural frieze and gilded figure of Athena over the entrance. This was to be the zenith of Burton's career, the end of a period during which he created his best work, all in the classical style, while still in his twenties. He had become prominent but was not a leading architect in the sense of John Soane or Nash, by whose work he had indeed been influenced. After 1830, the climate of patronage for Burton in London changed—Nash had fallen into disrepute, and George IV had died. From that time on, he received more than half of his commissions from members of the Athenaeum, many of them for country house designs or alterations. Other opportunities lay in speculative building on inland and coastal estates soon to become much more accessible through a new railway network.

In 1823, Burton had already designed Holwood, a villa in Kent for John Ward, an early member of the Athenaeum. From 1827 on, he developed Ward's Calverley Estate at Tunbridge Wells. This was a speculative attempt to compensate for the decline of this inland spa in the face of the growing popularity of the coastal resorts. Burton took the Regent's Park scheme's basic ideas, placing classical terraces on the regular sections of the plan and villas within a landscaped park, following the picturesque practice of Humphry Repton and Nash. The 24 villas arranged in a crescent are interesting permutations of the type established by Nash's Cronkhill (1802) and are in the Regency classical, Italianate and Gothic styles. The use of brown local stone and lack of ornamental detail give the whole a rather severe, drab look and, except for the Gothic villas, the buildings need the light color of Regent's Park stucco. In those years (1827-40), Burton employed the same styles in about a dozen larger country houses nearby in Kent and Sussex. His seven churches also date from that period—all in the Gothic style, they are essentially of the Georgian meeting-hall type done over in simplified Gothic detail. Had he been allowed to build them in the classical style, his reputation would doubtless have been enhanced.

The new seaport of Fleetwood (for another Athenaeum member) was an ambitious town planning scheme intended to take advantage of Lancashire's industrial wealth and provide a terminus for the new railway journey north to Scotland. Burton designed it right after his Calverley Estate and used the same severe classical style in local stone for the commercial buildings, terraced housing and two lighthouses. He provided a number of other schemes for estate development between 1830 and 1850, but few of them materialized. His 1840 rebuilding of Grimston Park, Yorkshire, in an Italianate style was the most ambitious example of his later country house work.

During those years he became *the* architect most associated with the design of large conservatories. He was supervising architect for the great Palm House erected at Chatsworth in 1836, but the structure was conceived by Joseph Paxton. For the newly founded Royal Botanic Society, he designed a large iron-and-glass Winter Garden for Regent's Park's Inner Circle. This was built in 1846-46 in a simpler form by the Dublin ironmaster Richard Turner, and patronized by Queen Victoria. In the meantime, both Burton and Turner submitted designs for a Palm House in the Royal Botanic Gardens at Kew. The final bubble-like design of 1844 was by Burton, although the overall layout was suggested by Turner. It still ranks as the most beautiful of all the 19th-century conservatories. By comparison, Burton's later (1859) large Temperate House at Kew is very conventional, being conceived in essentially a rectilinear architectural form.

—PETER BOHAN

BURTON, James.

British. Born in 1761. Died in St. Leonard's, Kent, England, 31 March 1837. Partnership with James Dalton; speculative builder, 1785; worked independently; Master of Tylers' and Bricklayers' Company, 1801-21; Sheriff of Kent, 1810.

Chronology of Works
All in England
† *Work no longer exists*

1784	Leverian Museum, London†
1792-1802	Foundling Estate, London (housing)
1798-1803	Bedford Estate, London (housing)
1802	Russell Institution, London†
1807-16	Skinners' Estate, London (housing)
1808-14	Lucas Estate, London (housing)
1817-24	Regent's Street buildings, London†
1818	The Holme, Regent's Park, London (with Decimus Burton)
1818-23	Eyre Estate, London (housing)
1822	York Terrace, London (eastern Half)
1825	Chester Terrace, London
1828-32	St. Leonard's-on-Sea, Sussex (Hotel, James Burton House, Baths†, Assembly Rooms, South Lodge, Clock Tower, St. Leonard's Church†, Gloucester Lodge, Quarry House, North Lodge)

Publications

BOOKS ABOUT BURTON

BAINES, J. MANWARING: *Burton's St. Leonards.* Hastings, England, 1956.
OLSEN, DONALD J.: *Town Planning in London: The Eighteenth and Nineteenth Centuries.* New Haven, Connecticut, 1964.
SUMMERSON, JOHN: *Georgian London*, 1945; 3rd ed. 1978.

ARTICLES ABOUT BURTON

MONKHOUSE, CHRISTOPHER: "St. Leonards." *Country Life* 21-28 February 1974).

*

Until the middle of the 20th century, James Burton's work was largely overshadowed by that of his architect son Decimus—James was usually considered to be only a speculative builder. But he was the architect of his own new town, St. Leonard's-on-Sea, for which a number of his designs survive. These reveal an imagination at least as inventive as his son's. In his first few years of building in Southwark (1785-92), he increased his assets eightfold by dint of a boldness and shrewdness that he would exhibit throughout his life. Later portraits of him suggest a man of keen intelligence and engaging personality. Doubtless this would explain the large number of connections that he had with people of influence.

His own rise to wealth and prominence resulted from his willingness to take risks: he became the principal speculative builder on the estates of London's Bloomsbury region between 1792 and 1816, despite the fact that during the early years of the Napoleonic Wars other builders had faced ruin, particularly because of a rapid rise in the cost of building materials. (With the threat of invasion by the French in 1803, he raised a whole volunteer regiment of his workmen and was made a lieutenant-colonel in charge of these Loyal British Artificers.) The planning of the Bloomsbury estates followed established 18th-century London practice, but the facades of the long terraced streets, squares and one crescent built by Burton have an austerity that some find monotonous but others find pleasing. This simplicity was partly the product of the Building Act of 1774, which had standardized the individual houses of these terraces.

When he had a freer hand, Burton tried to give architectural distinction to some of the facades by emphasizing a central bay with pilasters and attic detail. His first major architectural design for which we have an image was his Russell Institution (1802), a social center, on the Bedford estate. It was illustrated in Britton and Pugin's *Public Buildings of London* (1825), where it was described as "large, massy and with a novel aspect." Built of brick with a stucco facade, it had a Greek Doric portico projecting from a simple, closed rectangular block.

While Burton was pushing to complete building on the Skinners' and Lucas estates, the greatest speculative proposal of them all appeared, the Regent's Park scheme, using Crown lands. John Nash, the *prince regent's* favorite architect, had designed the layout, but he had no supporters until James Burton came in on the project; Burton built seven sections of Regent's Street and four of the Regent's Park terraces between 1817 and 1824. In gratitude, Nash took Burton's son Decimus under his wing and allowed him to design two of those four terraces, thus giving the young man an auspicious start to his career. In addition, James Burton was given a choice site for his own new house right on the park's Inner Circle—as it turned out, very few other freestanding villas were built within the park. Designed by him in 1818, the Holme is essentially a two-story block with Corinthian entrance portico and corresponding rotunda on the other side, overlooking the park's serpentine lake.

The Regent's Park scheme had a telling influence on both James and Decimus Burton as a model for estate developments undertaken elsewhere by both men. James, already in his sixties, took it to the Channel coast, where he poured his 40 years of accumulated experience and wealth into the planning and building of a completely new town, St. Leonard's-on-Sea. Long residential terraces faced the seafront, with a hotel at center, all with classically detailed facades; more modest streets were built behind them. Blocks of these marina terraces on both sides of center incorporated one-story, covered colonnades of cast-iron Doric columns for the shelter of shopping pedestrians, as in Nash's Regent Street Quadrant. A central wooded valley, like a park, had a few villas within it. These and other peripheral buildings erected after 1830 were designed in the new styles considered to be more appropriate to their picturesque settings, such as Italianate, rustic, Tudor and castellated Gothic. Some of Burton's surviving renderings show the public buildings as originally intended: the Baths, with a superposed Egyptoid obelisk at the center of a long closed block; the Assembly Rooms, a Doric prostyle temple with flanking wings; and the big East Boundary Archway, uniting two Doric lodges, taken from Piranesi. They also show the influences of Claude-Nicolas Ledoux and J.N.L. Durand. Burton's own house on the West Marina has a front directly inspired by the east facade of the Louvre.

Burton, following the Regent's Park idea, had made St. Leonard's-on-Sea largely residential in nature, with an appeal to the professional and upper classes, but in this instance his business acumen took second place to his desire to see his vision realized. Had he created a seaside resort for vacationers from the big city, his town doubtless would have flourished, especially after the advent of railway travel in the 1830s. Instead, because the town was not really self-supporting, it gradually merged with the popular resort of Hastings to its east, and lost its separate identity. His son Decimus was never in favor of the St. Leonard's scheme and held aloof from it during his father's lifetime. Yet for James Burton there were other kinds of reward: in 1834 he had the honor of being invited to dinner at his own new house there by the young Princess Victoria. Three years later she became queen—in the same year in which he died.

—PETER BOHAN

BUTTERFIELD, William.

British. Born in London, England, 1814. Died in 1900. Apprenticed to a builder in Pimlico, 1831; articled to architect E. L. Blackburne, 1833-36; assistant to an architect in Worcester; worked in office of William and Henry Inwood; opened independent practice in London, 1840; joined Cambridge Camden Society, 1842. Gold Medal, Royal Institute of British Architects, 1884.

Chronology of Works
All in England unless noted

1842	Highbury Chapel, Bristol
1844-45	St. Savior Church and Vicarage, Coalpit Heath, Gloucestershire
1844-73	St. Augustine's College, Canterbury, Kent
1847-78	Anglican Cathedral, Adelaide, Australia
1847-90	St. Ninian's Anglican Cathedral, Perth, Scotland
1849	SS. James and Anne, Alfington, Devon
1849-51	Cathedral of the Isles, Cumbrae, Bute
1849-59	All Saints, Margaret Street, London
1850-52	Osnaburgh Street Convent, London
1850-63	St. Dunstan's Abbey, Plymouth, Devon
1853-54	Churches, vicarages and schools, Cowick, Hensall, Pollington (Balne) and Wykeham, Yorkshire
1853-56	Milton Ernest Hall, Bedfordshire
1854-55	All Saints, Braishfield, Hampshire
1854-55	Langley Church and School, near Maidstone, Kent
1854-56	St. Mary, Milton, near Banbury, Oxfordshire
1854-57	Balliol College Chapel, Oxford
1855-57	St. James, Waresley, Huntingdonshire
1856-58	St. Mary, Etal, Northumberland
1856-60	Bamford Church and Parsonage, Derbyshire
1858-84	Rugby School, Warwickshire (additions)
1859-62	School, Castle Hill, Devon
1862-66	St. Cross, Clayton, Manchester
1863-68	Royal Hampshire County Hospital, Winchester
1864-66	St. Augustine, Penarth, Cardiff, Wales
1865-66	St. Anne, Dropmore, Buckinghamshire
1865-68	Church, Elerch, Cardiff, Wales
1865-74	All Saints, Babbacombe, Devon
1867-83	Keble College, Oxford
1870-75	St. Mary Brookfield, London
1870-77	St. Augustine, Queen's Gate, London
1876-91	St. Mark Dundela, Belfast, Ireland
1877-87	Grammar School, Exeter, Devon
1877-91	St. Paul's Anglican Cathedral, Melbourne, Australia
1878	St. Michael's Home, Axebridge, Devon
1880-83	The Chanter's House, Ottery St. Mary, Devon

Publications

BOOKS BY BUTTERFIELD

Instrumenta Ecclesiastica. 2 vols. London, 1850-52.

BOOKS ABOUT BUTTERFIELD

DIXON, ROGER, and MUTHESIUS, STEFAN: *Victorian Architecture.* New York and Toronto, 1978.
EASTLAKE, CHARLES L.: *A History of the Gothic Revival.* London, 1872.
FERRIDAY, PETER (ed.): *Victorian Architecture.* London, 1963.
SERVICE, ALASTAIR: *The Architects of London.* London, 1979.
THOMPSON, PAUL: *William Butterfield.* London, 1981.

ARTICLES ABOUT BUTTERFIELD

HITCHCOCK, HENRY-RUSSELL: ''Ruskin or Butterfield: Victorian Gothic at the Mid-Century.'' In *Early Victorian Architecture in Britain*. New York, 1954.

SUMMERSON, JOHN: ''William Butterfield.'' *Architectural Review* 64 (1945).

SUMMERSON, JOHN: ''William Butterfield, or the Glory of Ugliness.'' In *Heavenly Mansions and Other Essays on Architecture*. London, 1949.

*

William Butterfield, ascetic, High Churchman, favorite of the Ecclesiological Society and builder of its model church, All Saints, Margaret Street, has been alternately praised and derided both in his own time and since. He remains, however, the architect synonymous with the development of the High Victorian Gothic movement in architecture. Practically trained and inclined, this most English of the architects of that movement used an applied eclecticism in the evolution of his idiosyncratic architecture. Beginning in a form of qualified historicism, his style developed at the peak of his career into a truly inventive fusion of historicism and modernity.

This transition encompassed a progressive reduction of emphasis on mass in his work and a correspondingly increased emphasis on line. This is seen in an architecture that when viewed in its entirety seeks a balance between the picturesque and the sublime, but which is never willful. It is an architecture that has been likened in its controlled dissonance to the poetry of Gerard Manley Hopkins, who admired it and rightly sensed in it an overriding order that was not always apparent to Butterfield's contemporaries.

Butterfield's architectural evolution may be seen by comparing the Coalpit Heath Church and Vicarage of 1844, the latter independently important as the progenitor of the domestic work of Philip Webb, William Eden Nesfield and Richard Norman Shaw, with key buildings designed by Butterfield in the 1850s and 1860s. The buildings of the 1840s, while picturesque in form and setting, still show vestiges of their classical heritage; they are additive rather than organic in form, and show only slight variations of texture and color. In contrast, the buildings designed in the early 1850s, such as St. Thomas, Leeds, show the beginnings of experimentation in constructional polychromy in designs that favor forms derivative of the circle and the unifying effect of a continuous ridge line and uninterrupted wall plane.

Butterfield's sense of design for place was evidenced in this period by two buildings: his sensibility to landscape at Cumbrae College, and to the constraints of an urban setting at All Saints, Margaret Street, an urban minster whose design resulted from addressing both functional and symbolic needs. The latter building, which includes a choir school and clergy house as well as the church on a small contained site, shows Butterfield's ingenuity in planning, massing and spatial manipulation in a complex that exploits the limitations of the site and the constraints imposed by the brief to achieve an architecture that successfully emphasizes internal proportion at the expense of external irregularity.

The emphasis on surface and volume evident in the work of the 1850s, akin to John Ruskin's notions of the bounding line and the wall-veil, was progressively replaced by the increasing importance given to line in the designs of the 1860s. This is evident at All Saints, Babbacombe, with its linear enclosure echoed in the internal detail and decoration of the building. Constructional polychromy using both natural and machine-made materials to describe separately both external mass and interior space evolved in Butterfield's work from the audacious, naive and developing experiment of All Saints, Margaret Street, to its namesake at Babbacombe; this development echoes the transition from an emphasis on mass to one on line in the form of these two buildings.

The importance of Margaret Street, however, cannot be overrated. There Butterfield showed conclusively that historicism need not be used literally, and that it was possible to blend its intelligent and inventive use with modern technology to achieve an original and rational result. Butterfield sought in his work to reconcile the conflicting demands of a precedent perceived as relevant with the requirements of function and available technology, and this is nowhere clearer than in his choice of materials and their application. He made the use of brick respectable for both exteriors and interiors, as it came to predominate over stone in his work of the late 1850s and 1860s. He combined it with stone externally and used it glazed and unglazed internally in decorative schemes that also incorporated encaustic tiles, terra-cotta and mastic in incised decoration, as well as granites and marbles. These materials were variously combined in bands, diapers and checkers designed both to contrast with and complement structure and form, with use frequently being made of local brick and stone. Butterfield's use of these devices culminated in the 1870s in his design for Keble College, and particularly in that for the chapel. There, in a controlled picturesque composition dominated by the horizontal elements of long rooflines, stone bands and string courses, the patterning of brick and stone became a continuously varied texture designed to provide relief to the wall surfaces and a reaction against the plain surfaces of his earlier designs.

Butterfield's sense of functionality also decreed that his buildings be designed for commodity and firmness as well as delight. In a Butterfieldian building the chimneys work and the flashings are designed with the same care as the interior decoration and the liturgical fittings. Moreover, the chimneys are likely to find equal expression with the buttresses in the building's form. Butterfield's architecture has been variously described as mannered, cranky, sadomasochistic and deliberately ugly. Of these epithets, that of mannerism may be fairly admitted, but only in the sense that implies an inventive use of relevant precedent as a genuine response to the spirit of the age. For Butterfield the times called for a realistic, functional and unsentimental architecture, which in the final analysis may more fairly be called dissonant.

—R. J. MOORE

C

CAMERON, Charles.

Scottish. Born in Scotland, 1743. Died in St. Petersburg, Russia, 1812. Apprenticed to his father, the builder Walter Cameron, 1760; studied under Isaac Ware, London, until 1766. Worked independently in London ca. 1770-77; moved to St. Petersburg at the invitation of Catherine II, 1778; remained court architect until 1796; dismissed by Emperor Paul, 1796, then recalled to the Russian court and appointed architect to the admiralty by Alexander I, 1802.

Chronology of Works
All in Russia
* Approximate dates

1780-84	First-Fifth Apartments, Summer Palace, Tsarskoe Selo
1781-96	Pavlovsky Palace and Park, Pavlovsk
1782-85	Agate Pavilion, Summer Palace, Tsarskoe Selo
1782-87	Cathedral of St. Sophia, Summer Palace, Tsarskoe Selo
1783-85	Cameron Gallery, Summer Palace, Tsarskoe Selo
1785-96	Garden Pavilions and Town, Pavlovsky Palace, Pavlovsk
1787*	Bakhtchi-Serai, Crimea
1790s	Batourin, Crimea
1804	St. Andrew's Cathedral, Kronstadt (redesigned by Adrian D. Zakharov)
1804-05	Naval Hospital, Oranienbaum

Publications

BOOKS ABOUT CAMERON

LOUKOMSKI, G. K.: *Charles Cameron.* London, 1943.
RAE, ISOBEL: *Charles Cameron, Architect to the Court of Russia.* 1971.
RICE, T. TALBOT and TAIT, A. A. (eds.): *Charles Cameron.* Exhibition catalog. Edinburgh and London, 1968.

Charles Cameron was a Scottish architect, responsible for introducing into Russia in the late 18th century an English version of neoclassical architecture that satisfied perfectly the needs of the newly Europeanized monarchs, Catherine II and, later, Alexander I.

Cameron was apprenticed first in 1760 to his father Walter Cameron, a carpenter and builder; subsequently he became the pupil of the neo-Palladian architect Isaac Ware, who, like Cameron's father, was a member of the London Carpenters' Company. When Ware died in 1766, Cameron decided to continue the project Ware had begun: a new edition of Lord Burlington's *Fabbriche Antiche.* Cameron went to Rome to correct and finish the drawings by Palladio that Burlington had used in his book. This resulted in *The Baths of the Romans explained and illustrated, with the Restorations of Palladio corrected and improved,* published in 1772, a careful and scholarly work with identical texts in French and English, containing a rich and usable catalog of neoclassical ornaments and designs; new editions appeared in 1774 and 1775. While in Rome, Cameron also had come into contact with Charles-Louis Clérisseau, an important figure in the making of neoclassical taste.

With his book Cameron doubtless hoped to secure the support of patrons in England (he dedicated it for that purpose to Lord Bute), but on his return he seems to have gained little work in England; we have record only of his working on a house in Hanover Square, London, in 1770-74 with his father and others for a Jervoise Clarke. Otherwise, there are only stories of disputes and misbehavior, a suit against his father that led to the elder Cameron's imprisonment, and some activities with one of Ware's daughters, something still held against him in 1791 when he was being considered for membership of the newly established Architects' Club.

Cameron's publications had attracted Catherine II, however, and she invited him to work for her; from the time he arrived in Russia in 1778 until her death in 1796, Cameron was her principal architect. He made alterations and additions at the Palace of Tsarskoe Selo, near St. Petersburg, from 1779 onward, most notably the Agate Pavilion and the colonnaded gallery, known now as the Cameron Gallery, which seems to have been quite closely modeled on a room at West Wycombe Park, Buckinghamshire. From 1782 to 1785 he worked for Grand Duke Paul at the Palace of Pavlovsk, including in the designs for the surrounding buildings a theater and some Grecian temples, the first such to be built in Russia. He then worked in the Crimea at the Palace of the empress at Bakhtchi-Serai, probably around 1787. But after Catherine's death, Cameron was dismissed from office by Emperor Paul, who was intent on reversing all of his mother's policies.

Cameron seems then to have endured financial difficulties for a time, though he may have been able to get work from private patrons; by one story he returned for a while to England. By 1800, however, he was back at Tsarskoe Selo, working on the design of the Pavilion of the Three Graces and the Elizabeth Gallery for the dowager empress, and in 1802, the new emperor, Alexander I, appointed him architect to the Admiralty, though it is not clear how much Cameron did in that position. Ten years later he was dead, his widow dispersing his books and his drawings, the main collection of which are now in the Hermitage State Museum in Leningrad.

Cameron was a competent and well-trained architect, but not as subtle as his contemporary Robert Adam, or as accomplished a draftsman as his successor in Russia, Giacomo Quarenghi. But the apartments he designed at the royal palaces were of a splendor that was very effective, especially in their use of color: red columns set against green jasper walls with gilt, bronze capitals that suggested a kind of polychromy many others in

Russia were to follow. And the rooms at Tsarskoe Selo are among the most elegant such spaces in Europe, Cameron taking pains also to design every piece of furniture for the buildings in his charge. His work there was not unlike the model suggested by Adam, but what Adam had to achieve in paint and plaster, Cameron—in the richer context of the Russian court—was able to carry out with the most expensive of stones and materials.

—DAVID CAST

CAMPBELL, Colen.

Scottish. Born in Nairnshire, Scotland, 1676. Died in London, England, probably on 13 September 1729. Educated and practiced as a lawyer in Scotland; admitted to Faculty of Advocates, Edinburgh, 1702; studied with the Scottish architect James Smith (ca. 1645-1731), with whom he may have traveled in Italy; subsequently published *Vitruvius Britannicus*, which inspired the English Palladian movement. Chief clerk and deputy surveyor of the Works, Scotland, 1718-19; became architect to th e Prince of Wales and Lord Burlington, 1719; succeeded John Vanbrugh (1664-1726) as surveyor at Greenwich Hospital, London, 1726.

Chronology of Works
All in England unless noted
* Approximate dates
† Work no longer exists

1711-12	Shawfield Mansion, Glasgow, Scotland†
1714-20*	Wanstead House, Essex†
1716-17	House for Sir Charles Hotham, Beverley, Yorkshire†
1717-24	Rolls House, Chancery Lane, London†
1718	Ebberston Lodge, near Scarborough, Yorkshire
1718-19	Gateway, Burlington House, Piccadilly, London (also remodeled the front)†
1718-23	31-34 Old Burlington Street, London
1719	Nine houses on the Rolls Estate, London†
1719-21	Burlington School for Girls, Boyle Street, London†
1720-28	Newby Park (now Baldersby Park), Yorkshire
1720-24*	Stourhead, Wiltshire (wings added in 1793-95, and portico in 1841)
1722-25*	Mereworth Castle, Kent
1722-35	Houghton Hall, Norfolk (completed by others)
1724	Pembroke House, Whitehall, London (rebuilt in 1757)†
1724	House for John Plumptre, Stoney Street, London†
1725*	Waverley Abbey, Surrey (wings added ca. 1750, plus later alterations)
1726	76 Brook Street, London (No. 76, Campbell's own house, survives)
1726	78 Brook Street, London
1726-27	Compton Place, Eastbourne, Sussex
1728	House for Stamp Brooksbank, Hackney, Middlesex†

Publications

BOOKS BY CAMPBELL

Vitruvius Britannicus or The British Architect. 3 vols. London, 1715-25. Reprint: New York, 1967.
Andrea Palladio's Five Orders of Architecture. London, 1728-29.

BOOKS ABOUT CAMPBELL

BREMAN, P. and ADDIS, D.: *Guide to Vitruvius Britannicus.* New York, 1972.
HARRIS, JOHN: *Catalogue of the Drawings Collection of the RIBA: Colen Campbell.* Farnborough, England, 1972.
STUTCHBURY, H. E.: *The Architecture of Colen Campbell.* Manchester, England, 1967.

ARTICLES ABOUT CAMPBELL

BOYNTON, L.: "Newby Park, Yorkshire: The First Palladian Villa in England." In COLVIN, H. M. and HARRIS, JOHN (eds.): *The Country Seat: Studies in the History of the British Country House Presented to Sir John Summerson.* London, 1970.
COLVIN, H. M.: "A Scottish Origin for English Palladianism?" *Architectural History* 17 (1974): 5-13.
CONNOR, T. P.: "The Making of Vitruvius Britannicus." *Architectural History* 20 (1977): 14-30.
CONNOR, T. P.: "Colen Campbell as Architect to the Prince of Wales." *Architectural History* 22 (1979): 64-71.
GOODFELLOW, G. L. M.: "Colin Campbell's Shawfield Mansion in Glasgow." *Journal of the Society of Architectural Historians* 23, No. 3 (1964): 123-128.
GOODFELLOW, G. L. M.: "Colin Campbell." *Architectural Review* 140 (August 1966): 145-146.
GOODFELLOW, G. L. M.: "Colin Campbell's Last Years." *Burlington Magazine* 111 (April 1969): 185-191.

*

Colen Campbell inherited private means in Scotland, and trained as a lawyer in that country, being admitted to the Faculty of Advocates in Edinburgh in 1702; it appears that he was highly thought of in his profession. It is not known exactly when Campbell transferred his efforts from the law to architecture, for in 1717, when he designed the Rolls House in Chancery Lane in London, he was still described as a "Doctor of Laws." The transition may have been gradual, enabling him to keep his feet in both camps, for architecture was not then regarded as a profession with the clout accorded to law.

Campbell traveled in Italy (the precise dates are not known), and seems to have been associated with the Scottish architect James Smith (ca. 1645-1731), probably as a pupil. Smith is known to have traveled in Italy, and it was probably he who directed Campbell toward a study of the works of Andrea Palladio, who was to be the most important exemplar in Campbell's career. In 1712 Campbell presented a design for an ambitious domed church intended to be erected in Lincoln's Inn Fields at the behest of "Persons of Quality," and he also submitted in that year several designs to the Commissioners for Building Fifty New Churches. Campbell may have enjoyed aristocratic patronage before he met Lord Burlington, for he prepared plans for Ardkinglas House, Argyll, clearly based on Palladio's Villa Emo; these were preserved among the duke of Argyll's papers at Inveraray Castle. Coming from the higher echelons of Scottish society himself, Campbell was in a favored position, enhanced by his legal training and a keen eye, not only for architecture, but for the main chance.

It was as the evangelist of the Palladian style that Campbell made his reputation. His *Vitruvius Britannicus,* ostensibly a book about contemporary British architecture, was in fact a proselytizing volume intended to promote antique simplicity in design by reference to the works of Palladio and Inigo Jones (who had first introduced the Palladian manner to England in the reign of King James I). Palladianism was seen as a reaction

Colen Campbell: Mereworth Castle, Kent, England, ca. 1722-25

to the excesses and licentiousness of the Baroque manner that had reigned supreme from the time of Christopher Wren, but the timing of the publication was very fortunate. The Jacobite Rising in Scotland occurred in 1715, and the Hanoverian Succession had just placed King George I on the throne in 1714. It was necessary to suggest both a beginning and a sense of continuity, and the architecture of Palladio struck the right chords. It had been the style of Inigo Jones, introduced before the upheavals of the Civil War and the commonwealth, and therefore suggested a continuity with the legitimate Stuart line from 1603. But it could also become, by being associated with the Whig oligarchy and with the Hanoverian Succession, a sort of official architecture, reconciling the past and the future, and demonstrating that King George really was the successor of James I in spite of the claims of the pretender. Campbell's *Vitruvius Britannicus* was dedicated, significantly, to King George I, as was Giacomo Leoni's edition of Palladio's *I Quattro Libri,* also of 1715. Campbell's book came out in 1715, 1717 and 1725, with a later edition of 1731. It surveyed, in a great series of plates, British architecture from the time of Inigo Jones, and included works by Campbell himself. Thus the book not only promoted Palladianism, in the sense of a British architecture that had been influenced by that of Palladio, but was a puff for Campbell as an architect, for all his own significant works were illustrated, as well as several designs dedicated to prominent Whigs.

Campbell became chief clerk and deputy surveyor of the Works in 1718, but in 1719 lost these offices because he was associated with the corrupt William Benson, surveyor general of the Works. That does not seem to have harmed him, however, for he was appointed architect to the Prince of Wales, and in 1719 Lord Burlington, whose passion was architecture, employed

Campbell to redesign in the Palladian style his own Burlington House in Piccadilly.

Campbell acquired several influential patrons, including John Aislabie, Henry Hoare, the earl of Pembroke and Sir Robert Walpole, for whom he carried out various works, and in 1726 he succeeded John Vanbrugh as surveyor of Greenwich Hospital. After his successful *Vitruvius Britannicus* he published a revised version of Palladio's *First Book of Architecture* in 1728, reissued in 1729 as *The Five Orders of Architecture* with additional plates by Campbell himself.

Campbell was one of the most important figures of the Palladian movement. His Wanstead House (1714-20) was a Palladian palace, in scale as grand as Blenheim or Castle Howard, but strictly classical rather than Baroque. It was the great prototype of English country houses for the next century. Wanstead had an impressively severe exterior, with a hexastyle portico set on a rusticated base. This *piano nobile* effect, like the portico, was derived from Palladio, and indeed the portico was the first on any English country house. Palladio mistakenly thought that villas in antiquity had porticoes, and his error was perpetuated in British Palladianism, which is curious, since although a portico might be agreeable in Italy, it would be an expensive luxury in the colder climes of Britain.

Campbell's work at Houghton in Norfolk was an exercise in turning an earlier country house into a Palladian structure by means of a portico, Venetian windows and other motifs. Mereworth Castle in Kent (1722-25) was the first and closest English version of the Villa Capra (La Rotonda) at Vicenza; at Newby Park in Yorkshire (1720-28) and Stourhead in Wiltshire (1720-24), he designed the models for a type of small but thoroughly designed country house based on Palladio's originals in Italy. So Campbell's importance lies in the fact that between 1715 and 1725 he laid the foundations of British Palladianism in his publications and his buildings, and it was he who established the movement's most characteristic motifs, elements and forms.

By the time of Campbell's early death in September 1729, Palladianism was firmly established as a preferred style; the Baroque manner of John Vanbrugh, Nicholas Hawksmoor, James Gibbs and Thomas Archer had become unfashionable, and the tyranny of "Taste" had begun. The triumph of Palladianism, though avidly promoted by Burlington, was largely the result of the early efforts of Campbell, who must be regarded as one of the most influential and important figures in 18th-century architecture.

—JAMES STEVENS CURL

CANDELA, Felix

American. Born in Madrid, Spain, 27 January 1910. Married 1) Eladia Martin; 2) Dorothy Davies; children. Educated at the Escuela Superior de Arquitectura, Madrid, 1927-35; Academia de Bellas Artes de San Fernando, Spain, 1936. Immigrated to Mexico in 1939; immigrated to the United States, 1971; naturalized, 1978. Architect, Agricultural Colony, Chihuahua, Mexico, 1939-40; partner, Candela and Bringas, Acapulco, Mexico, 1940-41; assistant architect, Jesus Marti and Associates, Mexico City, 19 41-44; private practice, Mexico City, 1944-49; founder-president, Cubiertas ALA S.A., design and construction company, Mexico City, 1950-69; associate architect, Praeger-Kavanagh-Waterbury, New York, 1969-71; private practice, Chicago, Illinois, 1971-79; private practice, Madrid, since 1980; consultant architect, Project Planning Association, Toronto, Canada, since 1977; consultant architect, IDEA Center, Athens, Greece, since 1978; professor of architecture, National University, Mexico City, 1953-70; taugh t widely in the United States, including as professor of architecture, 1971-78, and since 1978 professor emeritus, University of Illinois at Chicago.

Chronology of Works
All in Mexico unless noted

1949	Experimental Funicular Vaults, San Bartolo, Mexico City
1950	Fernández Factory, San Bartolo, Mexico City
1952	Cosmic Ray Pavilion, University City, Mexico City
1952	Umbrella prototype, Tecamachalco, Mexico City
1953	Hidalgo School, Unidad Modelo, Mexico City
1953-55	Church of the Miraculous Virgin, Navarte, Mexico City
1954	Río Warehouse, Linda Vista, Mexico City
1955	Lederle Laboratories, Coapa, Mexico City
1955	Civic Center Auditorium, Ciudad Sahagun, Hidalgo
1955	Celestino Warehouse, Vallejo
1955	Cabero Warehouse, Vallejo
1955	Champagnac Church, Las Charcas, Guatemala
1955	High Life Factory, Coyoacan, Mexico City
1955	Borges House, Havana, Cuba
1956	Church of San Antonio de las Huertas, Tacuba, Mexico City (with Enrique de la Mora)

Felix Candela: Cosmic Ray Pavilion, Mexico City, Mexico, 1952

1957	Texas Instruments Factory, Dallas, Texas, U.S.A. (with O'Neil Ford and Associates)
1958	Centro Electrónico, University City, Mexico City
1958	Restaurant, Xochimilco, Mexico City (with J. Alvarez Ordonez)
1958	Auditorium and Restaurant, Casino de la Selva, Cuernavaca
1958-59	Open Chapel, Lomas de Cuernavaca (with Guillermo Rossell)
1959	Church of San José Obrero, Monterrey (with Enrique de la Mora)
1960	Bacardi Bottling Plant, Queretaro, Tlalnepantla
1960	Chapel of San Vicente de Paul, Coyoacan, Mexico City (with Enrique de la Mora)
1963	John Lewis Warehouse, Stevenage, Hertfordshire, England (with Yorke, Rosenberg and Mardall)
1968	Olympic Stadium, Mexico City (with E. Castaneda and A. Peyri)

Publications

ARTICLES BY CANDELA

"Simple Concrete Shell Structures." *American Concrete Institute Journal* (December 1951).

"Structural Digressions on Style." *Espacio* (May 1953).

"The Shell as Space Encloser." *Arts and Architecture* (January 1955).

"A New Way to Span Space." *Architectural Forum* (November 1955).

"Shell Concrete Construction in Mexico." *Municipal Journal* (March 1956).

"Lezione di Modestia di Felix Candela." *Architettura* (August 1957).

"Understanding the Hyperbolic Paraboloids." *Architectural Record* (July 1958).

"Felix Candela." *Arquitectura* (October 1959).

"Design and Construction in Mexico: Shell Construction." *Industrial Building* (September 1961).

"Une seule conscience pour l'oeuvre à créer." *Architecture d'aujourd'hui* (December 1961/January 1962).

"Architettura e strutturalismo." *Casabella* 306 (1966).

"Shell Structure Development." *Canadian Architect* (January 1967).

"The Heritage of Maillart." *Archithese* 6 (1973).

BOOKS ABOUT CANDELA

FABER, COLIN: *Candela: The Shell Builder*. New York and London, 1963.

SMITH, CLIVE BAMFORD: *Builders in the Sun: Five Mexican Architects*. New York, 1967.

ARTICLES ABOUT CANDELA

"Candela: Recent Works." *Zodiac* (October 1973).

CAMPBELL, BETTY: "Felix Candela." *Guilds' Engineer* 13 (1962).

"Felix Candela." *Concrete Quarterly* (April/June 1957).

McCOY, ESTHER: "The New University City of Mexico." *Arts and Architecture* (September 1953).

NICOLETTI, MANFREDI: "Incontro con Felix Candela" *Architettura* (February 1957).

"Modern Mexican Architecture." *Process: Architecture* (July 1983).

"Shell Concrete Today." *Architectural Forum* (August 1954).

"Two Generations of Engineering Architecture: Felix Candela and Santiago Calatrava." *World Architecture* 13 (1991).

"Wizard of the Shells." *Architectural Forum* (November 1959).

"The Work of Felix Candela." *Progressive Architecture* (July 1955).

*

Among the long list of honors awarded to Felix Candela, perhaps the most intriguing is his appointment, in 1961-62, as Charles Eliot Norton Professor of Poetry at Harvard University. This seems an extraordinary circumstance for a man who calls himself neither poet, artist nor architect, but a building contractor—a man who once modestly claimed that his "greatest satisfaction" came "not in having achieved certain spectacular structures . . . but in having helped in a small way to solve the problem of covering habitable spaces economically."

Candela studied architecture and engineering in his native Madrid, where he witnessed the pioneering work in laminar structures of Eduardo Torroja. An officer in the Republican army, he was forced to flee Franco's Spain and set out for Mexico in 1939. There, with his brother Antonio, he eventually established his own firm, Cubiertas Ala, which specialized, by the late 1940s, in thin-shell concrete vaulting. It should be noted that shell construction is most effectively accomplished with a monolithic material that can be used to create membrane-like surfaces of even thickness and distribution of stress. In Candela's case this material was concrete, hand-poured or gun-sprayed into straight timber formwork, and reinforced with steel rods or wire mesh. Strength in shells is arrived at through shape rather than mass, and within this narrow constructional mode,

Candela formulated an impressive array of shapes: long and short barrel vaults, conoids, hypers, cones, domes and various other partial spheres, as well as flat, umbrella, prismatic and undulating slabs.

Candela was one of a number of architects practicing in the late 1940s and 1950s whose work exchanged the "universal" Miesian grid and glass curtain wall for an individualized language of fluid shapes. Though many of his works are highly sculptural—notably the lotus-like restaurant at Xochimilco, and the sweeping and magnificently sited chapel at Lomas de Cuernavaca—he lambasted the "willful" formal flamboyance and exaggerated scale of contemporary projects like Brasília, the Sydney Opera House and Eero Saarinen's TWA Terminal in New York. He likewise criticized the International Style as a formal movement, void of underlying structural advance. For the most part, Candela's original designs, before being embellished by other designers, have been small in scale and free of components not essential to their structure or function. In their flowing, curvilinear lines, these buildings adhere to a rational underpinning no less rigorous than the Miesian grid. For Candela like Mies, structure, not form or function, stands first in the Vitruvian triad.

Candela has said "Architects are my best clients." Though he did sometimes work as architect, engineer, builder and even foreman on a single project—as with his 1954 Church of the Miraculous Virgin in Mexico City—much of the activity of his firm involved engineering consultation geared toward making workable and affordable schemes devised by other architects. (Among his most frequent clients were the architects Enrique de la Mora and Fernando Lopez Carmona.) Often receiving more credit for a final design than the firm that consulted him, Candela himself has admitted to preferring many of his works "before the architecture is added," when the shell is pure space enclosing form, unencumbered by walls or windows.

With Mexico's low labor costs and scarcity of structural steel, Candela's concrete shells and slabs proved economical as well as unusual, and thus came to widespread usage during the country's post-World War II boom years. The first project to gain him international attention was the 1952 Cosmic Rays Pavilion for the University City of Mexico. Due to the nature of the experiments to be carried out within, the building's program called for a roof with a then-unheard-of thickness of just 1.5 centimeters; Candela achieved this with a hand-poured concrete funicular vault composed of two intersecting hyperbolic paraboloids. The resulting roof, whose thickness is about half that of a cigarette filter's length, was strong enough so that a man could jump on it without it collapsing. (This was actually tried in one test.) Amid the overwhelming scale and strict rectilineal configuration of the university campus, Candela's effort, likened in form by some to a covered wagon, is a humble but striking little gem. Offers to build and lecture at home and abroad immediately followed, and Candela found himself at the forefront of contemporary work in shell design.

With a self-professed love of the intellectual exercise offered by calculation, Candela has nonetheless favored a design approach based on practice and intuition. He advised against analysis and the limitations imposed by established mathematical theories when he wrote: "The irrational or intuitive methods of design might not be so illogical afterall. They depend on the capricious and sporadic functioning of the subconscious, but, as a geometrician, I am inclined to believe them to be the only way to really design anything." Better, he suggested, to build according to one's hard-fought sense of rightness and possibility, and to bend formulas after the fact, in order to explain what has already happened. This was precisely the course he adopted with the Church of the Miraculous Virgin, whose 3.7-centimeter-thick warped hyperbolic paraboloid shells were invented and drawn up inside of a week, with calculations made on site during construction.

The Church of the Miraculous Virgin bears many formal similarities to the fantastic schemes of early German expressionists like Erich Mendolsohn, and like them, Candela too looked back to the creations of the great Gothic master builders. He admired Gothic architecture for having taken stone to the limits of its structural potential. Referring to a model for his own philosophy of design, Candela noted that "the imposing stone vaults of Gothic cathedrals . . . were built without the help of differential calculus but, instead, with a great . . . sense of equilibrium and sound judgement of the play of forces, qualities more necessary indeed to a real builder than full knowledge of mathematical intricacies." But, he went on, ". . . no Gothic cathedral could be built today. The most lenient Building Department would consider it quite unsafe."

A variety of factors caused Candela's building activity to slow down in the early 1960s. Though revered as a theorist, he did encounter some resistance to his untraditional methods, particularly in areas with more stringent building codes than Mexico's. Prestigious chairs were offered to him by European and American universities, and the architect found less time to devote to the practice of architecture. As with all "shaped" architecture—R. Buckminster Fuller's domes and the birds and tortoise shells of Eero Saarinen and Jorn Utzon—Candela's shells were unfeasible for multi-story applications, and therefore unfavorable to dense urban environments. Candela's career peaked alongside a vision of a future in which we would all travel by rocket or monorail, and some of his lesser creations now bear the dated aspect of Cadillac tailfins. But with economical means and an obvious and delighted curiosity as to the possibilities of materials, he could still bring visual grace to buildings of the most prosaic function—warehouses, factories and garages. Of all the architects building during the 1950s, Felix Candela, engineer and poet, came as close as any to reconciling the science and the art of architecture.

—KEITH EGGENER

CARR, John.

British. Born in Horbury, near Wakefield, Yorkshire, England, May 1723. Died on 22 February 1807. Father was the stone mason Robert Carr. Mostly self-taught in architecture. Worked independently, Yorkshire; city chamberlain, York, 1766; sheriff, York, 1767; alderman, York, 1769; Lord Mayor, York, 0; magistrate for the West Riding. Member, London Architects' Club.

Chronology of Works
All in England unless noted
* Approximate dates
† Work no longer exists

1748	Huthwaite Hall, Yorkshire
1750-54	Arncliffe Hall, Ingleby Arncliffe, Yorkshire
1754-57	Racestand, York†
1756	Church, Ravenfield
1757-64	Everingham Hall, Yorkshire
1757-64	Lytham Hall, Lancashire
1759-71	Harewood House (staterooms designed by Robert Adam), Yorkshire
1760-63	Church, Kirkleathan, Yorkshire
1760-67	Tabley Hall, Cheshire
1762-68	Constable Burton Hall, Yorkshire
1763-65	Castlegate House, York
1766	Royds House, Halifax, Yorkshire
1767-71	Thoresby House, Nottinghamshire†
1769-71	Infirmary, Leeds, Yorkshire
1770-81	Denton Park, Yorkshire
1770-99	Hospital of San Antonio, Oporto, Portugal
1771	Chesters, Hexham, Northumberland
1772	Aston Hall, Yorkshire
1772-77	County Assize Courts, York
1773	Rutherford Bridge
1773	Greta Bridge, Yorkshire
1774	Leventhorpe Hall, near Leeds, Yorkshire
1774-76	Town Hall, Newark, Nottinghamshire
1774-77	County Lunatic Asylum, York
1776	Norton Place, Bishop Norton, Lincolnshire
1776	Basildon Park, Berkshire
1776-77	County Hospital, Lincoln
1777	Racestand, Nottingham†
1777-81	Racestand, Doncaster†
1777-80	Middleton Lodge, Middleton Tyas
1779-81	Thornes House, Wakefield†
1780	Wiganthorpe Hall, Malton; Yorkshire
1780-73	Female Prison, York
1780*-90	Crescent, Buxton, Derbyshyire
1781-85	Raby Castle, Durham
1781-86	Grimston Garth, Aldbrough, Yorkshire
1782-84	Church, Ossington, Nottinghamshire
1783-85	Clifton House, Rotherham
1786-89	Eastwood House, Rotherham†
1786-90	Farnley Hall, Otley
1791-93	Church, Horbury
1797-1804	Bridge, Ferrybridge, Yorkshire
1799-1807	Coolattin Park, Shillelagh, Ireland
1800-03	Morton Bridge, Yorkshire

Publications

BOOKS ABOUT CARR

BRADSHAW, JOHN and HALL, IVAN: *John Carr of York*. Exhibition catalog. Hull, England, 1973.
YORK GEORGIAN SOCIETY: *The Works in Architecture of John Carr.* York, England, 1973.

ARTICLES ABOUT CARR

DAVIES, ROBERT: "A Memoir of John Carr, Esq., Formerly of York, Architect." *Yorkshire Archaeological and Topographical Journal* 4 (1877): 202-213.
HALL, IVAN: "John Carr: A New Approach" *York Georgian Society's Report* (1972).
INGAMELLS, JOHN: "Portraits of John Carr." *City of York Art Gallery Quarterly* 34 (1971).
KITSON, S. D.: "Carr of York." *Royal Institute of British Architects Journal* (22 January 1910).
WRAGG, R. B. and M.: "Carr in Portugal." *Architectural Review* 125 (1959).
WRAGG, R. B.: "John Carr of York." *Journal of the W. Yorkshire Society of Architects* (December 1957 and March 1958).
WRAGG, R. B.: "John Carr: Bridgemaster." *York Georgian Society's Report* (1957).
WRAGG, R. B.: "John Carr: Early Years and the Meeting with Robert Adam." *Journal of West Riding Society of Architects* 17 (1957).

WRAGG, R. B.: "John Carr: Gothic Revivalist." *Studies in Architectural History* (1956).

WRAGG, R. B.: "John Carr: Late Life and Achievements." *Journal of West Riding Society of Architects* 17 (1957).

*

John Carr of York was the epitome of the successful provincial architect in 18th-century England, preeminent in his own area but not confined to it: he was also the prime example in the second half of the century of the craft-based architect from the building trades who was to "leave off his apron" and become a "gentleman" practitioner—a process which, as a result of the development of the architectural profession during that period, could take effect more completely in his case than it had with comparable figures from earlier generations. He is, therefore, a representative figure of some significance.

Born at Horbury, near Wakefield in Yorkshire, Carr was the son of a stonemason and quarry-owner—trades that had also been practiced by his grandfather and great-grandfather—and was himself trained as a mason. As an architect he appears to have been largely self-taught, although in his early years he did have the benefit of a brief contact with Lord Burlington: one of Carr's first commissions was the erection of Kirby Hall, Yorkshire (1747-55, demolished), a house designed by Lord Burlington and Roger Morris. "I have got a clever fellow of a mason at the head of my works," wrote the owner of the house, Stephen Thompson. From that unpretentious but not insubstantial background, Carr rose to become the leading architect in Yorkshire and the north of England for more than half a century, with a practice that also extended as far afield as Ireland and Portugal. His standing is reflected in the fact that in 1770 he served as lord mayor of the city of York—an office he is said to have filled "with becoming dignity and hospitality"—while in his later years he acquired a country estate and at his death left a substantial fortune. He also became the only provincial member of the London Architects' Club when it was founded in 1791.

That membership confirms that Carr was known and respected in architecturally sophisticated circles, but his success among the north-country gentry who formed the bulk of his clients rested on a reputation for practical reliability and "good taste" rather than on any spark of genius. He was an assured exponent of the established Palladian manner, whose buildings exemplified the best of Georgian craftsmanship, but he was hardly an innovative designer. At Constable Burton Hall, Yorkshire (circa 1762-68), he created a competent specimen of an Anglo-Palladian villa—not a new idea by that time—while some of his subsequent country houses, such as Denton Park, Yorkshire (1770-81), and Basildon House, Berkshire (1776), can be regarded as containing references to the villa theme; however, other examples—notably Lytham Hall, Lancashire (1757-64); Harewood House, Yorkshire (1759-71); and Tabley House, Cheshire (circa 1760-67)—were more strongly influenced by the traditional "double-pile" form. Of his many handsome urban and public buildings, perhaps the most memorable is the Crescent at Buxton, Derbyshire (circa 1780-90), inspired by John Wood's Royal Crescent at Bath. Carr's interior decoration was of high quality, but subsequent to, rather than setting, the fashion—Rococo in his earlier works, such as Heath Hall, Yorkshire (circa 1754), and later neoclassical in the manner of Robert Adam, as at Farnley Hall in the same county (1786-90).

Occasionally, however, Carr did achieve a more individual form of expression. At Raby Castle, County Durham (1781-85), he created a powerfully dramatic Gothic entrance hall that is among the most remarkable of all 18th-century interiors in this idiom, while his triangular Grimston Garth, Yorkshire (1781-86), is a delightful geometrical fantasy in Gothic dress. Finally, in his church at Horbury (1791-93), he combined an orthodox mixture of restrained Palladian and neoclassical detail with an ingeniously modeled main volume with broad apsidal ends and temple-fronted cross-axis, and a striking western tower with a sequence of diminishing stages distantly reminiscent of James Gibbs' St. Martin-in-the-Fields. Built by Carr at his own expense as a gift to his native village, this fine church is an appropriate monument to his success.

—PETER LEACH

CARRÈRE and HASTINGS.

CARRÈRE, John Mervin.
American. Born in Rio de Janeiro, Brazil, 9 November 1858. Died on 1 March 1911. Studied at the Institute Breitenstein in Switzerland; studied at the École des Beaux-Arts in Paris, graduated 1882. Joined McKim, Mead and White, New York, 1883; opened office with Thomas Hastings, New York, 1886; appointed chief architect for the Pan American Exposition, Buffalo, New York, 1901. Fellow, American Institute of Architects, 1891; director and instructor at the American Academy at Rome.

HASTINGS, Thomas.
American. Born in New York City, 1 March 1860. Died in New York, 23 October 1929. Studied at Columbia University, New York; studied at École des Beaux-Arts, Paris. Joined McKim, Mead and White, New York, 1884; opened office with John M. Carrère, New York, 1886. Fellow, American Institute of Architects, 1892; Gold Medal, Royal Institute of British Architects, 1922; Chevalier of Legion of Honor, France.

Chronology of Works
All in the United States unless noted

1886-88	Ponce de León Hotel, St. Augustine, Florida
1889-90	Laurel-in-the-Pines Hotel, Lakewood, New Jersey
1893-94	Hotel Jefferson, Richmond, Virginia
1894	Sloane Townhouse, New York City
1898	First Church of Christ Scientist, New York City
1901	Staten Island Ferry Terminals, New York City
1902	Blair Building, New York City
1902-11	New York Public Library, New York City
1903-06	Richmond Borough Hall, New York City
1904-11	Manhattan Bridge and Approaches, New York City
1905-10	Arden House, New York City
1907-09	New Theater (Century Theater), New York City
1911-12	U.S. Rubber Building, New York City
1913-14	Henry Clay Frick House, New York City
1913-19	Richmond County Courthouse, Richmond, Virginia
1919-20	Liggett Building, New York City
1919-21	Cunard Building, New York City (with Benjamin W. Morris)
1920-22	Fisk Building, New York City
1924	Macmillan Building, New York City
1925-26	Devonshire House, Piccadilly, London, England
1926	Standard Oil Building, New York City

Publications

BOOKS ABOUT CARRÈRE and HASTINGS

GRAY, DAVID: *Thomas Hastings, Architect.* Boston, 1933.
Hotel Ponce de León. St. Augustine, Florida, n.d.
REED, HENRY HOPE: *The New York Public Library, Its Architecture and Decoration.* New York, 1986.

ARTICLES ABOUT CARRÈRE and HASTINGS

"The Work of Messrs. Carrère and Hastings." *Architectural Record* 27 (January 1910): 1-20.

Best known today as the architects of the magisterial New York Public Library, the firm of Carrère and Hastings was one of the most prominent in New York in the first decades of the 20th century, using an adaptation of French academic classicism in a variety of modern buildings.

John Merven Carrère, born in Brazil to a prosperous coffee merchant from Baltimore, Maryland, spent his early years in Rio de Janeiro, but at the age of 14 was sent to study at the Institute Breitenstein in Grenchen, Switzerland. His early propensity for drawing led to studies in architecture at the École des Beaux-Arts in Paris, where he met Thomas Hastings, also a student. Carrère studied in the ateliers of Victor Robert, Charles Laisne and Léon Ginain, and received his *diplôme* in 1882. Carrère then settled in New York City, entering the office of McKim, Mead and White.

Hastings, born in New York City, was the son of a prominent Presbyterian minister. After a brief period at Columbia University, Hastings went to Paris, where he was admitted to the École des Beaux-Arts, studying in the atelier of Jules André and earning his *diplôme* in 1884. When Hastings returned to New York in 1884, and began working for McKim, Mead and White, he renewed his acquaintance with Carrère.

In 1886 the two men left McKim, Mead and White to form their own partnership, designing several private residences. Their career was launched as the result of being selected by Henry M. Flagler (a friend of Hastings' father) to design a luxurious resort hotel in St. Augustine, Florida. The Ponce de Leon Hotel (1886-87) was an expansive symmetrical composition with an artistic fusion of Moorish, Spanish and Renaissance elements, incorporating electric illumination throughout. At Flagler's request, the architects used a unique form of concrete construction incorporating local coquina stone made up of shell and coral. Flagler soon followed that commission with three more for a more modest hotel, the Alcazar (1888), and two churches—Grace Methodist (1887) and the memorial Presbyterian Church (1890)—all in St. Augustine.

The firm's earliest work in the 1890s, whether commercial office high-rises, churches or country residences, was elaborately embellished with heavy and overscaled ornament. Examples include the Central Congregational Church, Providence, Rhode Island (1891), the Jefferson Hotel, Richmond, Virginia (1893), and the Edison Building, New York City (1903). The most unusual product of those years was their Spanish Renaissance design submitted in the competition for the huge Cathedral of St. John the Divine, New York City (1889).

Gradually, however, the firm's work became more restrained in tone, drawing increasingly from late French Baroque or French academic classic sources. One example was their double-width town house in New York City for H. T. Sloane (1894). During the late 1890s, Carrère and Hastings drew from both French Baroque and American Georgian sources for several large country estates they designed, notably the Giraud Foster estate, Lenox, Massachusetts (1897), and the Blair estate at Peapack, New Jersey (1898). For their massive First Church of Christ Scientist, New York City (1898), they took inspiration from James Gibbs' St. Martin-in-the-Fields in London. Again for Flagler the firm designed a palatial summer residence, Whitehall, at Palm Beach, Florida (1901-02), combining a Roman Doric portico with spacious French Baroque interiors.

The partners used this restrained classicism also for several tall office blocks, including the 15-story Blair Building, New York City (1902), and the Traders Block, Toronto, Canada (1905); for these they followed the three-part formula of base, body and crown that was gaining popularity in Chicago and New York at the turn of the century. The structural complexities of these and other large buildings (such as the New York Public Library) were handled by Owen Brainard (1865-1919), who was the engineer for the firm. Having joined Carrère and Hastings in 1892, Brainard was made a partner in 1901 but withdrew to establish his own engineering consulting practice in 1904, although he continued as engineer for all of the later buildings by Carrère and Hastings. While carrying out office blocks and costly country homes, Carrère and Hastings also designed a block of simple classical speculative houses in Clifton, New Jersey (1900), for George W. Vanderbilt. The playfully exuberant character of the partners' early work reappeared in their bridges, gardens and decorative work for the Pan-American Exposition in Buffalo, New York (1901), for which Carrère was chief architect and planner.

At the turn of the century, Carrère and Hastings were busy with perhaps the single most important building they created, the New York Public Library. Won by the architects in a celebrated competition in 1897, the project was not finished until 1911. Recognizing that the library was likely to represent the pinnacle of their career, Carrère and Hastings lavished particular care on the planning and embellishment of this building; indeed, it was the apex of Carrère's achievement, for he was killed in an automobile accident in March 1911, just two months short of the dedication of his masterwork.

The New York Public Library was created by the amalgamation of two large private libraries begun in the early 19th century. The older was the collection of fur merchant and financier John Jacob Astor (1763-1848), begun in 1830 and opened to readers in 1852. The second was the more specialized collection put together by wealthy bachelor James Lenox from 1835 to 1870. Eventually his collection grew so large that he commissioned Richard Morris Hunt to erect a special building for a scholarly reference library at Fifth Avenue and 70th Street. Collection development of these private libraries diminished dramatically after the deaths of their founders. In 1886 wealthy railroad attorney and New York political figure Samuel Jones Tilden (1814-86) died, and left $2 million for the creation of a public library in New York. Tilden's trustees included several influential and intensely public-spirited lawyers who were also trustees of both Astor's and Lenox's estates. During the same years, too, the beginnings of a small public municipal circulating library had been made. It then occurred to these lawyers and other public leaders that the Tilden bequest would best be used as a book-buying fund for development of a great public library, to be created by merging the Astor and Lenox collections with the circulating library, forming a rich collection serving not only the general public but scholars as well. In May 1895 the New York Public Library, Astor, Lenox and Tilden Foundations were created.

A superb site for a permanent building to house the amalgamated collections was at 42nd Street and Fifth Avenue, where the antiquated Croton Aqueduct Reservoir was to be demolished.

There, at the very heart of the city, an entire city block was available, located at the nexus of public transportation. On the eastern half of this site the new library could be built, with a park behind it providing possible future expansion space.

The library trustees learned much from the ongoing difficulties in the design and construction of the Boston Public Library, for the trustees of the Boston Library had dismissed their librarian's advice and kept changing their minds regarding internal requirements even as McKim, Mead and White built the shell of the building. The New York trustees therefore appointed John Shaw Billings (1838-1913) in December 1895 as director to shape the program of the new library and the basic conceptual organization of the proposed building. Noted as a scholar, manager and skilled public servant, Billings worked with the library trustees to persuade the state of New York to raze the Croton Reservoir in 1897.

In the meantime Billings began to sketch out, literally, the novel arrangement he had in mind for the library. In essence, the new building would be a rectangular block, roughly 350 by 225 feet, with layers of dense book stacks across the back, and two light courts centered in each half of the rectangle. On the ground floor would be a major central entrance at the front, leading to an exhibition room between the internal light courts. Around the outer part of the building on the ground floor (excluding the stacks) would be various rooms and collections which had the heaviest public use. On the second floor would be special collections and reading rooms, in addition to staff offices (again with the stacks at the rear). On the third and uppermost floor, additional special collections would be at the front and sides of the building, but to the rear, spanning the entire width of the building, would be two spacious public reading rooms, altogether measuring 297 feet long by 78 feet wide, and 51 feet high, served by a circulation area at the center. In the middle of this circulation area, and running down through the core of the book stacks, would be a system of dumbwaiters for bringing the requested titles up to the circulation desk. With this arrangement, Billings reasoned, serious readers and scholars would gain the best light, the greatest quiet, and peaceful isolation from the curious public in the elevated reading rooms, while collections most heavily used by the general public would be on the ground floor.

An initial public competition for the library design was announced in May 1897, and produced 88 entries. From those initial entrants, six architects were selected to continue in the second competition, to be joined by an additional six architects invited by the library's executive committee. From the first competition, the executive committee selected these six competitors: J. H. Freedlander; Haydel and Shepard; Hornbostel, Wood and Palmer; Howard and Cauldwell; W. Wheeler Smith associated with Walker and Morris; and Whitney Warren. For the six invited architects, the Committee first selected McKim, Mead and White, and then listed George B. Post, Cyrus Eidlitz, Carrère and Hastings, Peabody and Stearns, and Charles C. Haight. Ernest Flagg was considered but ultimately was not selected.

The second competition program was distributed to the selected architects in August 1897, with drawings due November 1. The jury was made up of three architects (Walter Cook, Cass Gilbert and Edgar V. Seeler) and three library trustees, plus Billings. Although the trustees had expected much from McKim, Mead and White, that firm's third-place entry was not nearly as well developed as that of Howard and Cauldwell, who were ranked second, and significantly inferior to that of Carrère and Hastings, which was ranked first.

The basic internal disposition of spaces, determined by Billings, was clearly and dramatically announced on the exterior of the building by Carrère and Hastings, demonstrating how their Parisian training enabled them to express internal function through external massing. The projecting central pavilion, with its tall triple arches, was clearly the entrance, and its deep recesses anticipated the large lobby within. On the front facade, the large arched windows expressed the presence on the first floor of the large public reading rooms for children's books and periodicals. The large pediments visible from the front carried the eye to the rear, where the elevated arcade at the top of the rear wall expressed the internal reading rooms. Perhaps the most strikingly modern aspect of the rear facade was the lower section of tall masonry wall, opened up by narrow slits where slender windows admitted light into the internal iron book stacks. Even adamant proponents of International Modernism later admired this direct expression of internal function of the book stacks. Although planned by the architects (following Billings' instructions) to accommodate the most modern assessment of library service, the building was structurally conservative, with solid marble walls and cut stone vaults.

During 1902-11, as work on the New York Public Library progressed slowly, Carrère and Hastings pursued a busy practice in other areas as well. As a result of both winning the library competition, and Carrère's activities in connection with the Pan-American Exposition, the firm became active in the design of public buildings and memorials that were austerely classic in character but graced with a delicate finesse in massing and ornamentation. Included in that group of buildings were the Richmond Borough Hall, New York City (1903-07), the McKinley Monument in Buffalo, New York (1903), the approaches and architectural work for the Manhattan Bridge, New York City (1905), and the L-shaped group of colonnaded buildings comprising Woolsey and Memorial Hall at Yale University (1901-02). Perhaps most impressive in the group was the pair of marble office buildings the firm designed around the United States Capitol—the Senate Offices (1905) and the House of Representatives Offices (1906). Both office blocks were low and deliberately subdued in character so as to elegantly frame but not usurp the Capitol.

More lavishly decorated in the French Baroque style were several theaters and theater interiors, including the Empire Theater (1903) and the New Theater (later Century Theater, 1906-09), both in New York City. The festive quality of the firm's work was strikingly evident in its agriculture building for the St. Louis World's Fair in 1904, and even more on the playful Tower of Jewels for the Panama Pacific Exposition, San Francisco (1914-15), done by Hastings alone.

When Carrère died in 1911, he and Hastings were completing the design for the City Hall of Portland, Maine. Working in association with John Calvin Stevens, they achieved a balanced composition combining American Colonial form and massing with a French Renaissance character. Before his death, Carrère had been increasingly active in city planning, serving on planning commissions for the cities of Cleveland, Ohio (1904), Grand Rapids, Michigan (published in 1909), and Hartford, Connecticut (published in 1912). He was offered but declined the post of supervising architect of the United States Treasury Department.

After 1911 Hastings continued to run the office, maintaining the original firm name. The chaste but elegant classicism of the firm's earlier work was continued in the Richmond County Courthouse, Staten Island, New York (1919), and the French-inspired residence of Henry Clay Frick (1914) that occupied the site of Richard Morris Hunt's Lenox Library on Fifth Avenue in New York City. It also was evident in the Memorial Amphitheater in the National Cemetery at Arlington, Virginia (1917).

In later years Hastings associated himself with other architects in the design of large office buildings in southern Manhattan,

New York City, such as the Cunard Building (with B. W. Morris, 1919). For the Standard Oil Building in New York City (1922-23), Hastings was associated with the firm of Shreve, Lamb and Blake. In designing the soaring 42-story Ritz Tower (1925), Hastings worked with Emery Roth. Among Hastings' last works was the large Devonshire House, London, England (1925-27), a palatial apartment complex done in association with English architect Charles Herbert Reilly. Another indication of Hastings' regard in England was the award of the Royal Gold Medal by the Royal Institute of British Architects in 1922. Particularly distinguished among Hastings' last works was the Knoedler Gallery, New York City (1926).

—LELAND M. ROTH

CASTELLAMONTE, Carlo.

Italian. Born in 1550/60. Died in 1639/40. Son was the architect Amedeo Castellamonte. Assistant to Ascanio Vitozzi; practiced in Turin from 1602; appointed as ducal engineer, 1615.

Chronology of Works
All in Italy

1598	Sanctuary, Vicoforte di Mondovi (with Ascanio Vitozzi)
1602	Eremo dei Camaldolesi, Turin
1604	Church of the Arciconfraternità del SS. Sudario dei Piemontesi, Rome (altered)
1604	Oratory, San Rocco, Turin
1619	San Carlo, Turin (with M. Valperga)
1635-38	Santa Cristina, Turin
1639	Piazza San Carlo, Turin

Publications

BOOKS ABOUT CASTELLAMONTE

BOGGIO, C.: *Gli architetti Carlo ed Amedeo di Castellamonte.* Turin, 1896.

CARBONERI, NINO: *Ascanio Vitozzi: Un architetto tra manierismo e barocco.* Rome, 1966.

MARINI, GIUSEPPE LUIGI: *L'architettura barocca in Piemonte: La provincia di Torino.* Turin, 1963.

POMMER, RICHARD: *Eighteenth Century Architecture in Piedmont.* New York and London, 1967.

SCOTTI, AURORA: *Ascanio Vitozzi: Ingegnere ducale a Torino.* Florence, 1969.

ARTICLES ABOUT CASTELLAMONTE

BERTAGNA, U.: ''Vicende costruttive delle chiese del Corpus Domini e dello Spirito Santo in Torino.'' *Palladio* 23-25 (1974-76): 75-113.

BRINO, G.; DE BERNARDI, A.; and GARDANO, G. (eds.): *L'opera di Carlo e Amedeo di Castellamonte.* Turin, 1966.

COLLOBI, L.: ''Carlo di Castellamonte, primo ingegnere del duca di Savoia.'' *Bollettino storico bibliografico subalpino.* Turin, 1937.

LOTZ, WOLFGANG: ''Die ovalen Kirchenräume des Cinquecento.'' *Römisches Jahrbuch für Kunstgeschichte* 7 (1955): 9-99.

PROMIS, CARLOS: ''Gli ingegneri militari.'' *Miscellanea di storia italiana* 12 (1871): 584-591.

Carlo Castellamonte was an architect and engineer active in Turin at the beginning of the 17th century, when the city was enlarged and modernized under Carlo Emanuele I. The first stages of this architectural program had been begun by Ascanio Vitozzi, and it was with Vitozzi that Castellamonte, a member of the Cogneno branch of the Castellamonte counts, began his work; indeed, he continued to use some of Vitozzi's designs after the latter's death in 1615.

Castellamonte worked in two areas, practical and administrative. In 1615 he was made engineer to the duke; in 1627 he was appointed member of the Council of the Fabriche and Fortificazioni; and at the end of his life, in 1637, he was given additional posts as superintendent of fortresses, councillor of state and lieutenant of architecture. The role Castellamonte played from those positions as intermediary between the duke and the city councillors in all matters of building was extremely important—if a cause of jealousy from his colleagues—and in this sense Castellamonte can be seen to have made a fundamental contribution to the urban development of Turin.

His style as an architect was based, not surprisingly, on Vitozzi, who had been able in some small way, as in the church of Santa Maria in Vicoforte di Mondovi (begun in 1596), where Castellamonte also worked, to bring to Piedmont elements of the new architecture in Rome; to this Castellamonte added something of Andrea Palladio's style. And if the results were not especially interesting in simple buildings, it served Castellamonte very well for the larger-scale designs he laid out.

Castellamonte worked on several individual buildings in Turin, most notably the two churches of San Carlo (1619), with the help of Maurizio Valperga, and Santa Christina (1635-38). These two buildings on the famous Piazza San Carlo, both of which have single-aisled, rectangular plans, are set at the opening into the square like the churches in the Piazza del Popolo in Rome. Both, it must be noted, have facades of a later date: Santa Christina was completed by Filippo Juvarra in 1715, and San Carlo by Ferdinando Caronesi in 1834. The piazza that Castellamonte designed was square, as necessitated by what is essentially a grid plan of the streets of Turin. But the piazza was enlivened by these two churches and filled with elegant palaces that were set all around, their articulation ending at street level with doubled columns. Some of the most notable families of Turin lived on this new piazza, among them the *marchesi* Havard de Senantes and their heirs, the Isnardi di Caraglio; their palace, now the Solaro del Borgo, suggests perhaps more than any of the other surviving buildings the original intentions of Castellamonte. The piazza underwent much reconstruction in the 19th century, and it was at that time that the statue of Emanule Filiberto by Carlo Marochetti was set in the center. The piazza also damaged in World War II, but enough remains to show why it was praised so much by its first foreign visitors.

Castellamonte also worked, in the 1630s, on the Piazza San Giovanni in front of the cathedral. However, for all his success in Turin, Castellamonte spent more of his time working for the duke on military projects, most notably at the fortresses he rebuilt at Verrua, Momigliano and Savigliano; he possibly also was involved with the rebuilding of the castle at Moncaliere. He worked on one particularly interesting project in Turin at the Eremo dei Camaldolesi, established in 1601 by Carlo Emanuele I; the first designs were by Vitozzi, and Castellamonte used them in the 1630s when he continued the work with Valperga. Castellamonte was also very interested in hydraulics, the record we have of this being a manuscript of 161 titled *Parere sopra la fabrica dell'imboccatura da farsi al naviglio che scorre da Ivrea a Vercelli.* Castellamonte's son, Amadeo, followed in his father's footsteps, working notably on the Valentino Villa in the 1630s; the hands there of Carlo and his son are difficult to distinguish.

—DAVID CAST

CHALGRIN, Jean-François.

French. Born Jean-François-Thérèse Chalgrin in Paris, France, 1739. Died in Paris, 20 January 1811. Studied with Etienne-Louis Boullée and Giovanni Nicolo Servandoni; won Prix de Rome at École des Beaux-Arts, 1758. Elected to Académie d'Architecture, 1770; promoted to first class of the Académie, 1791; architect to the comte de Provence, 1775; intendant des bâtiments to the comte d'Artois, 1779 (imprisoned during the Revolution for these royal connections); i nspecteur des travaux de la ville de Paris under Pierre Louis Moreau-Desproux, 1763; appointed member of the Conseil des Bâtiments, 1795. Succeeded Charles de Wailly in the Institut de France.

Chronology of Works
All in France
† Work no longer exists
* Approximate dates

1767-70   Hôtel de St. Florentin, Paris (designed by Ange-Jacques Gabriel)
1768-75   St. Philippe-du-Roule, Paris
1776-88   St. Sulpice, Paris (completion of project begun by Servandoni)
1780-84   Collège de France, Paris
1781-84   Gardens of the Comtesse de Provence, Paris†
1784   Music Pavilion of the Comtesse de Provence, Paris
1786ff.   Gardens and Pavilion of Madame de Balbi, Versailles†
1787-   Palais du Luxembourg, Paris (remodeling)
1803*
1806-36   Arc de Triomphe, Paris

Publications

BOOKS BY CHALGRIN

Plan, coupes et élévations de l'église de St. Philippe du Roule. Paris, n.d.

BOOKS ABOUT CHALGRIN

BRAHAM, ALLAN: *The Architecture of the French Enlightenment.* Berkeley, California, and Los Angeles, 1980.
GAEHTGENS, THOMAS W.: *Napoleons Arc de Triomphe.* Göttingen, Germany, 1974.
GALLET, MICHEL: *Paris' Domestic Architecture of the Eighteenth Century.* London, 1972.
HAUTECOEUR, LOUIS: *Histoire de l'architecture classique en France.* Vol. 4. Paris, 1952.
RICE, HOWARD C.: *L'Hôtel de Langéac: Jefferson's Paris Residence.* Monticello, Virginia, 1947.

ARTICLES ABOUT CHALGRIN

GAEHTGENS, THOMAS W.: "Four Newly Discovered Designs for the Arc de Triomphe by J-F Chalgrin." *Print Review* 5 (1976): 58-68.
SCOTT, BARBARA: "Madame's Pavillon de Musique." *Apollo* 95 (1972): 390-399.

*

Born of a poor family, Jean-François-Thérèse Chalgrin became one of the foremost architects in France, carrying forward the neoclassical aesthetic fulfilled by Germain Foufflot's Church of Ste. Geneviève, now the Panthéon. Chalgrin began his architectural studies as a pupil of Giovanni Nicolo Servandoni, who had designed the Church of St. Sulpice in 1732, which, with its emphasis on freestanding columns and horizontal lintels, was the first major monument in Paris to reflect the new aesthetic toward antique architecture. Chalgrin pursued his studies under Etienne-Louis Boullée, who championed an even more rigorous and austere neoclassicism based on pure geometric forms and dramatic lighting. After winning the Prix de Rome at the École des Beaux-Arts in 1758, Chalgrin traveled to Italy, where he studied firsthand the monuments of antiquity while also coming into contact with other progressive architects such as Soufflot.

Returning to France in 1763, Chalgrin became Inspecteur des Travaux de la Ville de Paris under Pierre Louis Moreau-Desproux. As such, Chalgrin was responsible for the construction of the Hôtel de St. Florentin (1767-70) which had been designed by Ange-Jacques Gabriel to frame his two palaces to the north of the Place de la Concorde, and to act as a subtle transition between them and the surrounding urbanscape. Chalgrin's original contribution to the design was the hôtel's main doorway and the court's portal screen, which consisted of a pair of freestanding Doric columns supporting a plain entablature. This project already betrays Chalgrin's commitment to a more severe classical style if compared with the delicate refinement of Gabriel's architecture.

Soon after the completion of the Hôtel de St. Florentin, Chalgrin was admitted to the Académie Royale d'Architecture. At the same time, he began his long association with the nobility, serving as *premier architecte* to the comte de Provence in 1775 (the future Louis XVIII), and as *intendant des bâtiments* to the comte d'Artois in 1779. In 1764 the comte de St. Florentin again commissioned Chalgrin to design a new church, St. Philippe-du-Roule, in the burgeoning western part of the city, where so many private *hôtels particuliers* were being constructed. It would become the basilican-type church par excellence, bringing to fruition earlier efforts at arriving at a church worthy of antiquity, efforts spearheaded by the theorists Jean Louis de Cordemoy and Abbé Laugier, and by the architect Pierre Contant d'Ivry. The latter had already designed the Church of the Madeleine in 1761 along a strict classical model, utilizing freestanding columns and a straight entablature. His design was modified, however, by Alexandre-Pierre Vignon in 1807.

Although two other basilican churches were also being constructed at the time, Louis-Francois Trouard's St. Symphorien (1764-70) and Nicolas-Marie Potain's St. Louis of St. Germain-en-Laye (1764-87), it was Chalgrin's example that defined the type and which influenced similar efforts throughout Europe through the first half of the 19th century. Plans for St. Philippe-du-Roule were approved in 1768, and the church was substantially finished seven years later.

The facade of St. Philippe du Roule is articulated by a squat, recessed Tuscan portico composed of a four-column peristyle, and topped by a triangular pediment. The central door is deeply

Jean-François Chalgrin: St. Philippe-du-Roule, Paris, France, 1768-75

recessed within the portico, and is less visible than the aisle doors flanking it. The facade reveals at first glance the interior disposition of the church, which is composed of a high nave and two lower aisles of narrow proportions terminating in two small square chapels. The nave consists of a coffered barrel vault supported by a range of freestanding Ionic columns, which continue around the curve of the apse as engaged columns. Chalgrin eschewed ribs, cross vaults or lunettes in order to preserve the purity and severity of the nave. Furthermore, he eliminated the traditional transepts, further emphasizing the volumetric purity and simplicity of the building.

Although loosely based on Early Christian basilicas, the Parisian examples were much smaller and intimate if compared with their antique prototypes, which had been built on the gigantic scale of Roman classical temples. Chalgrin's interior organization differed as well, as evident in the uninterrupted coffered barrel vault, and in the continuation of the colonnade around the apse. Furthermore, there were no side chapels, but altars in niches beneath the windows. Characterized by its simplicity and cubic appearance, devoid of traditional religious architectural iconography such as deambulatory,

flanking towers or dome, Chalgrin's basilica was divorced from everything that had theretofore made church architecture a complex undertaking. Chalgrin had intended, however, to construct a stone vault supported by flying buttresses that were to be visible on the exterior. A lighter and more economical wooden vault was installed instead.

Antoine Chrysostôme Quatremère de Quincy, the *secrétaire perpétuel* of the Académie des Beaux-Arts from 1816 to 1839, was a champion of antique art and praised it as a worthy model for contemporary French architecture. His *Notice sur Chalgrin* (1816) praised the new character of St. Philippe-du-Roule with its frank adoption of the Early Christian basilican plan. Gone were the complexities and vagaries of the Baroque program with its heavy piers, rich ornamentation and convoluted, arcuated architecture, which had until then dominated church architecture. In addition, Chalgrin's model, modest in scale and economical, was ideally suited for the construction of neighborhood churches for a growing Parisian population. By contrast, Soufflot's monumental church of Ste. Genevieve, with its dome and transepts, was felt to be too far removed from the antique.

While working on St. Philippe-du-Roule, Chalgrin was also involved with the completion of St. Sulpice, which had been begun by his teacher, Servandoni. Between 1776 and 1788, Chalgrin built the north tower and fluted the columns of the porch, giving the facade a more severe classical look than Servandoni had originally intended.

Although imprisoned during the Revolution on account of his ties to the nobility, Chalgrin survived to work on prestigious commissions for both the young republic and the empire. Although involved with the renovation of the Palais du Luxembourg as early as 1787, Chalgrin's major work at the palace dates to 1803, when he transformed its interior for the use of the senate, constructing a great semicircular debating chamber, the Salle du Senat, at the back of the palace. Chalgrin's amphitheater was completely remodeled in 1837 by his pupil Alphonse-Henri de Gisors.

The Arc de Triomphe, designed in 1806, was Chalgrin's last important commission before his death in 1811. He conceived it in the grandeur of Roman prototypes with freestanding columns, statues and bas-relief panels. Its gigantic size and commanding position at the heights of the Champs-Elysées would make it visible from key points in the capital, with the Place de la Concorde and the Louvre directly on axis. Napoleon, however, favored a simpler, more austere arch, free of columns and superfluous decoration. It was this stripped-down version which was finally completed in 1836 by Abel Blouet, who added a rather heavy attic to the top of the arch, altering Chalgrin's classical balance. By its completion, the arch's function, to celebrate Napoleon's victorious armies, was broadened to memorialize the armies of the republic as well. It remains today the most hallowed symbol of national aspirations.

—MARC VINCENT

CHAMBERS, William.

British. Born in Gothenburg, Sweden, 23 February 1723. Died in London, England, 8 March 1796. Married Catherine More in Rome, March 1753; at least one daughter. Trained at Jacques-François Blondel's École des Arts, Paris; at 17, traveled to India, China and elsewhere in the Far East, followed by educational trips to Paris, Italy and Holland. Established practice in England, 1755; architectural tutor to the Prince of Wales (later King George III); appointed one of two joint architects (Robert Adam was the other) at the Office of Works, 1761; member of the French Académie (Architecture), 1763; named comptroller of the Works, 1769, then surveyor general and comptroller, 1782; member of the Swedish Academy of Sciences, 1766, and Knight of the Polar Star (Sweden), 1770; Fellow of the Royal Society.

Chronology of Works
All in England unless noted
* Approximate dates
† Work no longer exists

1749	House of Confucius, Kew Gardens, Surrey
1757	Garden works completed, Kew Gardens, Surrey
1757-59	Wilton House, Wiltshire (triumphal arch, casino, rock bridge, library interior)
1757-60	Goodwood House, Sussex (additions)
1757-62	Orangery and Pagoda, Kew Gardens, Surrey
1758-75	Marino House, near Dublin, Ireland (additions and alterations)†
1758-76	Casino, Marino House, near Dublin, Ireland
1760-64*	The Hoo, Kimpton, Hertfordshire (bridge, gateway, house interior alterations)†
1760-68	Parksted, Roehampton, Surrey
1760*	Castle Hill, Dorset†
1762	Temple of Romulus and Remus, Coleby Hall, near Ingatestone, Essex
1762-73	Buckingham House (Palace), London (remodeling)†
1763-68	Duddingston House, Midlothian, Scotland
1763-75	Charlemont House, Dublin, Ireland
1764-70	Berners Street Town Houses, London†
1765-74	Gower House, Whitehall, London†
1765-75*	Peper Harrow, Surrey
1765*	Newby Park, Yorkshire (pheasantry, menagerie, internal alterations)
1765*	Teddington Grove, Middlesex†
1766	Woodstock Town Hall, Oxfordshire
1766-75*	Blenheim Palace, Oxfordshire (internal decoration, Bladon Bridge, Temples of Flora and Diana, Tuscan gateway)
1767-68	Barton Hall (library), Great Barton, Suffolk†
1767-70	Cobham Hall, Kent (general restoration and alterations)
1767-72	Woburn Abbey, Bedfordshire (south wing and some interiors)
1768	Observatory, Richmond Gardens, Surrey
1768-72	Ampthill Park, Bedfordshire (additions and redecoration)
1769-71	Milton House, Park Lane, London (additions)
1769-72	St. Andrew's Square, No. 26, Edinburgh, Scotland
1770-71	Rathfarnham Castle, County Dublin, Ireland (interiors)
1770-72	House for John Calcraft, Knightsbridge, London†
1770*	Danson Hill, Kent (internal alterations, bridge, temple)
1770*	Exclamation Gate, Castle Howard, Yorkshire
1771-74	Dundas House, Edinburgh, Scotland
1771-74	Marlborough House, St. James's, London (addition of attic and alterations)
1771-74	Melbourne House, Piccadilly, London
1771-76	Milton Abbey, Dorset
1772	Chinese Temple, Amesbury House, Wiltshire
1772	Theatre Royal, Liverpool†
1772	Trinity House Chapel, Hull, Yorkshire†
1772-73	White House, Kew, Surrey (alterations)†
1775-86	Theater, Trinity College, Dublin, Ireland
1775-86	Chapel, Trinity College, Dublin, Ireland
1776-79	Queen's Lodge, Windsor Castle, Berkshire†
1776-1801	Somerset House, Strand, London (completed by James Wyatt)
1777	Trent Place, Middlesex
1778	Hedsor Lodge, Buckinghamshire†
1779-82	Lower Lodge, Windsor Castle, Berkshire

Publications

BOOKS BY CHAMBERS

Designs of Chinese Buildings. 1757. Reprint: New York, 1968.
Treatise on Civil Architecture. 1759; 3rd ed., as *A Treatise on the Decorative Part of Civil Architecture*, 1791. Edited by J. Gwilt, 1825. Reprint: New York, 1968.

William Chambers: Somerset House, London, England, 1776-1801

Plans, Elevations, Sections and Perspective Views of the Gardens and Buildings at Kew in Surrey. 1763. Reprint: Farnborough, England, 1966.
Dissertation on Oriental Gardening. 1772. Reprint: Farnborough, England, 1972.

BOOKS ABOUT CHAMBERS

EDWARDS, A. T.: *Sir William Chambers.* London, 1924.
HARRIS, JOHN: *Sir William Chambers.* London, 1970.
MASON, WILLIAM: *An Heroic Epistle to Sir William Chambers.* 1773. Reprint: Farnborough, England, 1972.
SERVICE, ALASTAIR: *The Architects of London.* London, 1979.

ARTICLES ABOUT CHAMBERS

BEARD, GEOFFREY W.: "A New Design by Chambers." *Architectural Review* (September 1953).
"Chambers at Kew." *Apollo* (August 1963).
HARDWICK, T.: "Memoir of the Life of Sir William Chambers." *Treatise on Civil Architecture,* 1825.
HARRIS, JOHN: "Sir William Chambers and His Paris Album." *Architectural History* (1963): 54-90.
MARTIENSSEN, H. M.: "Chambers as a Professional Man." *Architectural Review* (April 1964).

*

William Chambers was born in Sweden, where his father, John, a Scottish merchant, was established. William was sent to Ripon in Yorkshire for his early education, but at 16 he returned to Sweden, where he began a career as a merchant in the Swedish East India Company. In the 1740s he traveled to Bengal and China (where he sketched many buildings) on the company's ships, and had time on the long voyages to study modern languages, the arts and (especially) civil architecture. Between the periods when he undertook his Far Eastern journeys, he visited England, Scotland, the Netherlands, Flanders and France.

Chambers had gathered sufficient funds by 1749 to give up his work in commerce and trade in order to devote himself entirely to architecture, and he commenced his training at Jacques-François Blondel's (1705-74) École des Arts in Paris (opened 1743); Blondel was later to subscribe to his pupil's *Civil Architecture* in 1759. In 1750 Chambers traveled to Italy, where he spent the next five years, mostly in Rome, although he also saw Naples, Florence, Bologna, Venice, Vicenza, Genoa, Milan and Turin. While he was in Rome he was taught by Charles-Louis Clérisseau (1721-1820), who had also trained at Blondel's school. Chambers appears to have lodged with Clérisseau at some time, but the two men quarreled later. Chambers was also taught by Laurent Pécheux, and imbibed much of the essence of French neoclassicism from the works of men such as Jean Laurent Le Geay (ca. 1710-ca. 1786) and Louis-Joseph Le Lorrain (1715-59). During his time in Rome he became known to visiting Englishmen on the grand tour, and established a sound reputation for good taste and sense among them.

By 1755 Chambers was back in England. Through contacts he was recommended to the third earl of Bute (1713-92) as tutor in architecture to the Prince of Wales. Chambers had arrived.

During his stay in Rome, Chambers had made a design for a mausoleum in memory of Frederick, Prince of Wales (1707-51), his royal pupil's father. This probably created a suitable confidence in Chambers on the part of the Princess Dowager Augusta of Wales (died 1772), and she commissioned Chambers to design the gardens for her house at Kew; he duly carried out the work, embellishing the grounds with temples and gardenbuildings, some classical and some in the chinoiserie style (including the famous Pagoda). Chambers celebrated these buildings in 1763 by bringing out a lavish folio, dedicated to his royal patron, and titled *Plans, Elevations, Sections and Perspective Views of the Gardens and Buildings at Kew in Surrey*. It was not Chambers' first publishing venture, however, for in 1757 he had brought out *Designs of Chinese Buildings, Furniture, Dresses, etc.,* and the first part of the important *Treatise on Civil Architecture* had appeared in 1759, a volume that was intended to be a selective collection "from mountains of promiscuous Materials" of "Sound Precepts and Good Designs." This justly celebrated volume on the use of the classical orders and ornament went into another edition in 1768, and the "considerably augmented" third edition of 1791 was titled *A Treatise on the Decorative Part of Civil Architecture.*

Chambers went to the Office of Works as one of two architects appointed by the Crown: his colleague was Robert Adam (1728-92). In 1769 Chambers succeeded Henry Flitcroft (1697-1769) as comptroller of the Works, and in 1782 he was appointed surveyor-general and comptroller. In his official capacity Chambers was a first-class administrator and an architect of great talent. He carried out modernization at Buckingham Palace for his erstwhile pupil (by then King George III), and designed the Rococo state coach, which is still used at coronations. His grandest work as a public architect was unquestionably Somerset House, commenced in 1776, by which time he had been created a Knight of the Polar Star by the king of Sweden, and was allowed by George III to assume the rank and title of an English knight as well. Other distinctions included membership in the Swedish Academy of Sciences, corresponding membership in the French Academy of Architecture, and a fellowship of the Royal Society. He was a founder of the Royal Academy of Arts, and exhibited regularly at the Society of Arts from 1761 to 1768, and at the Academy from 1769 to 1777.

In his architectural work Chambers evolved a judicious mix of French neoclassicism and English Palladian Revival, and never lost touch with advanced French stylistic tendencies, as is apparent at Somerset House. In 1774 he revisited Paris, and corresponded with Julien-David Le Roy and Charles de Wailly. Chambers' eclecticism was fastidious and wide-ranging, and he admired Andrea Palladio and Vincenzo Scamozzi, seeing their works as more chaste and simple than the "luxuriant," "bold" and "licentious" manner of Michelangelo and Gievanni Lorenzo Bernini, both of whom he studied. Although the publications of James Stuart and Nicholas Revett were starting to herald the Greek Revival, Chambers resisted what he termed "Attic Deformity," and he was equally out of sympathy with things Gothick. His one foray into Gothick was at Milton Abbey, Dorset (1771-76), and he carried out that commission only at the insistence of Lord Milton; it is clear Chambers disliked His Lordship as much as the "vast ugly Gothic house," but he appears to have been the author of the layout of the charming model village of Milton Abbas (1774-80).

At Kew, Chambers demonstrated that he could have the lightest of touches when he chose, and his delightful chinoiseries and Moresque essays contrasted with the almost severe Franco-Palladian style he adopted for such architectural works as the Casino at Marino, near Dublin, for James, fourth viscount and first earl of Charlemont (1728-99) of 1758-76. Chambers' *Designs of Chinese Buildings* was an important sourcebook, and his *Dissertation on Oriental Gardening* (1772) was a sustained denunciation of the style of landscape gardening evolved by Lancelot "Capability" Brown (1716-83), thinly disguised as an argument to prove the superiority of Chinese landscape gardening over European designs. The *Dissertation* may have been prompted by Brown's success in getting the commission to design Claremont, Lord Clive's house in Surrey, for Chambers had also provided a scheme. Certainly the *Dissertation* was somewhat bombastic in tone, and its claims to scholarship were somewhat thin, as many of the descriptions were lifted from the works of others. Chambers' chinoiserie was attacked in an anonymous pamphlet of 1773, now known to have been by the satirist William Mason (1717-97), and that squib did Chambers' reputation no good at all. Nevertheless, Chambers was regarded as the most successful English architect of the second half of the 18th century, while his Somerset House was seen as the greatest architectural work of the reign of George III by no less an authority than James Fergusson (1808-86), who also detected an influence of Inigo Jones in the Strand front of Somerset House.

Among Chambers' pupils the most distinguished was undoubtedly James Gandon (1743-1823), whose Custom House in Dublin displays clear Chambersian themes in its dignified and deeply modeled facades.

—JAMES STEVENS CURL

CHERMAYEFF, Serge Ivan

American. Born Sergius Ivan Issakovitch, in Grozny, Azerbaidzhan, Russia, 8 October 1900; immigrated to England, 1910: naturalized, 1928; immigrated to the United States, 1939: naturalized, 1946. Married Barbara Maitland; sons are the graphic artist Ivan Chermayeff and the architect Peter Chermayeff. Educated at Royal Drawing Society School and Harrow School, London, 1910-17; studied art and architecture at various schools in Germany, Austria, France and the Netherlands, 1922-25. Worked as a journalist for the Amalgamated Press, London, 1918-23; chief designer, E. Williams Ltd. decorators, London, 1924-27; director of modern art development, Waring and Gillow, London, 1928-29; established own firm, 1930; partnership with the architect Eric Mendelsohn, 1933-36; private architectural practice, London, 1937-39, San Francisco, 1940-41, and New York, 1942-46. Chairman, Department of Design, and professor of architecture, Brooklyn College, 1942-46; in practice, New York City, 1946-51; president, Inst itute of Design, Chicago, 1946-51; lecturer, Massachusetts Institute of Technology, Cambridge, 1953-62; professor of architecture, Harvard Graduate School of Design, 1953-62; professor, Yale University, 1962-71, emeritus since 1971. Gropius Lecturer, Harvard University, Cambridge, Massachusetts, 1974.

Chronology of Works
All in England unless noted

1930   Cambridge Theatre, London (interior)
1932-34   British Broadcasting Corporation, London (interiors)

Serge Ivan Chermayeff: Chermayeff House, Bentley Wood, Halland, Sussex, 1939

1933	Shann House, Rugby, Warwickshire
1934-35	De La Warr Pavilion, Bexhill-on-Sea, Sussex (with Eric Mendelsohn)
1935	Nimmo House, Chalfont St. Giles, Buckinghamshire (with Mendelsohn)
1935-36	Cohen House, Old Church Street, Chelsea, London (with Mendelsohn)
1936	House, Frinton Park, Essex (with Mendelsohn)
1937	W. and A. Gilbey Offices, London
1938	Ciro Jewelry Shop, 48 Old Bond Street, London
1938	Imperial Chemical Industries Research Laboratory, Manchester
1939	Chermayeff House, Bentley Wood, Halland, Sussex
1942	Walter Horn House, Marin County, California, U.S.A.
1945-72	Mayhew House, Oakland, California, U.S.A.
1951	Chermayeff Family Compound, Truro, Massachusetts, U.S.A.
1952	Payson House, Portland, Maine, U.S.A.
1953	Sigerson House, Truro, Massachusetts, U.S.A.
1953	Wilkinson House, Truro, Massachusetts, U.S.A.
1956	O'Connor House, Truro, Massachusetts, U.S.A.
1962	Chermayeff House, New Haven, Connecticut, U.S.A.

Publications

BOOKS BY CHERMAYEFF

Report on the Future Development of Diamond K. Ranch. Cambridge, Massachusetts, 1955.
The Shape of Privacy. Cambridge, Massachusetts, 1955.

Community and Privacy: Toward a New Architecture of Humanism. With Christopher Alexander. New York, 1963; Tokyo and London, 1966.
Advanced Studies in Urban Environments. With Alexander Tzonis. New Haven, Connecticut, 1967.
Synopsis of Conclusions and Record of Progress: The Chermayeff Studio. Edited by W. Mitchell. New Haven, Connecticut, 1967.
The Shape of Community: Realization of Human Potential. With Alexander Tzonis. New York, 1970; London, 1971.
Verse of Anger and Affection, 1957-1973. Orleans, Massachusetts, 1973.
Design and the Public Good: Selected Writings by Serge Chermayeff 1930-1970. Edited by Richard Plunz. Cambridge, Massachusetts, 1982.

ARTICLES BY CHERMAYEFF

"Thinking Before Acting." *American Institute of Architects Journal* (April 1980).

BOOKS ABOUT CHERMAYEFF

PLUNZ, RICHARD: *Projects and Theories of Serge Chermayeff*. Cambridge, Massachusetts, 1972.
TAYLOR, A. J. P.; JEFFEY, IAN; et al.: *Thirties: British Art and Design Before the War*. London, 1979.

ARTICLES ABOUT CHERMAYEFF

"Chermayeff: Ahead of His Time." *Architects' Journal* (1 October 1980).
"House at Chalfont St. Giles." *Architectural Review* (November 1935).
"House near Halland, Sussex." *Architects' Journal* (16 February 1939).
"Leisure at the Seaside." *Architectural Review* (July 1936).
"Serge Chermayeff." *Designer* (December 1980).
"Time and Chermayeff." *Architectural Review* (June 1960).

*

Serge Chermayeff's great importance is that when he was one of a small, but very influential, band of modern architects practicing in England in the 1930s.

In 1910 he was sent to school in England, and left Harrow seven years later. But the Russian Revolution cut off the family funds that supported him, and left him in England. In 1924 Chermayeff started work as an interior designer. He became interested in the modern furniture being designed in Europe, and in 1928 he organized the first exhibition of modern furniture in England; this exhibition was held in Waring and Gillow's London store, and Chermayeff became director of its modern-furniture department. Many interior design commissions followed, mostly carried out through Waring and Gillow, the most important ones being the interiors for the Cambridge Theatre and for the new BBC Broadcasting House.

After opening his own office in London in 1930, Chermayeff built the Shann House at Rugby (1933), an early Modern Movement house. The Shann House was a simple white cube constructed of eight-inch reinforced-concrete walls, enriched by a three-quarter-circle balcony cantilevered out at first-floor level and a curved terrace below.

In 1933 Chermayeff formed a partnership with Erich Mendelsohn, already a world-famous architect, but a Jew and hence an early refugee from Nazi Germany. Such immigrants were not permitted to practice on their own in England and sought sympathetic local architects with whom to work. The Mendelsohn and Chermayeff partnership proved very successful, but ended with Mendelsohn's emigration to Israel in 1936. The most important building by this partnership was the De La Warr Pavilion on the seafront at Bexhill, Suxxes (1933-35). Won in open competition, it was one of a handful of public buildings built in the 1930s by modern architects, and it may well have been the seaside setting and holiday use which made such a building acceptable at the time. Two wings, one fully glazed and one solid, flank a semicircular reinforced-concrete stair tower that is glazed and balconied, a truly marvelous space and a jeu d'esprit showing just what reinforced concrete can do.

The De La Warr Pavilion was followed by two luxurious houses. The first of these, the Nimmo House at Shrub's Wood, Chalfont St. Giles, Buckinghamshire, was built for the manufacturer of Aspro pain reliever. Set in an old landscape park, the Nimmo House has a beauty of setting and a luxury of materials and finish unmatched by comparable houses. Generous terraces with curving retaining walls tie the house to the land, but the house itself is a pure white box, with ribbon windows, pilotis and a sweeping staircase showing the architects' delight in reinforced concrete. The Cohen House, completed in 1937 in Chelsea's Old Church Street, stands next to a house of the same date by Walter Gropius and Maxwell Fry, so London could see a whole length of street by modern architects. The Cohen House is built of brick, which is exposed in the plinth, but above ground-floor level all is rendered and painted. This house has the semicircular terrace, the luxurious finishes and the spacious

planning of the Nimmo House—and a squash court to complete the luxury life-style. The Cohen House is built with its front elevation at the back of the sidewalk and with only service rooms on the street side; this gives it a more forebidding aspect than the Nimmo House, but the garden elevation is generous and open.

Following the departure of Mendelsohn, Chermayeff's first important commission was a new office building for Gilbey's Gin in London's Camden Town. A simple seven-story block with a dark tiled plinth and white render above, it gains great élan by a slight curve on plan outward at the corner. At a time when modern buildings were often trying to break away from the corridor street, Chermayeff gave us an exemplar in street architecture.

In 1934 Chermayeff designed his masterpiece, a house for his own family at Bentley Wood, Halland, Sussex, but the local authority did not approve the design, and it was 1938 before the house was built. Set in a beautiful landscape, with a garden by Christopher Tunnard focusing on a reclining figure by Henry Moore, the house is two stories high, and like the Cohen House has all the rooms looking out in one direction. The similarity ends there, however, for Bentley Wood is a timber house, with main beams of jarrah and outside facing of unpainted western red cedar. The main elevation has a continuous balcony with all infill of glass, and a matching timber frame standards in the landscape, framing views. This outside frame and the house are linked with walls that extend beyond the house to enclose garages and service rooms, and to make courtyards which foreshadow his later American houses.

Chermayeff did not enjoy his beautiful house for long. In 1938 he built a large dyestuff plant near Manchester for ICI, and, with Europe moving toward war, he set sail for America. In 1940 Chermayeff commenced practice in California, where he built a house in Marin County (1942) and another in Oakland (1945). He then moved to the East Coast and built more houses, notably his own at Truro, Massachusetts, but the quality never again reached that of his English work. It is as a teacher that Chermayeff is known in America.

In 1942 he was appointed chairman of the Department of Art at Brooklyn College; there he formed a Department of Design, a pioneering venture at that time. In 1946, following the death of Laszlo Moholy-Nagy, he was appointed president of the Chicago Institute of Design, and he expanded the curriculum to embrace architecture and environmental design. In 1951 he taught at MIT, then moved to Harvard, where he reorganized the first-year program. In 1963 he moved to Yale as director of the master's class in environmental design.

—JOHN WINTER

CHURRIGUERA FAMILY.

Spanish. Three brothers, José Benito de Churriguera (1665-1725), Joaquin de Churriguera (1674-1724), and Alberto de Churriguera (1676-1750), sons of Jose Simon Churriguera, a sculptor from Barcelona.

Chronology of Works
All in Spain
† *Work no longer exists*

1686-87 Ayala Chapel, Cathedral, Segovia (retable; José Benito de Churriguera)
1689 Catafalque, Funeral of Maria Louise of Orleans, Madrid (José Benito de Churriguera)

Churriguera Family: Cathedral, Salamanca, Spain, 18th century

1692-94	Church of San Esteban, Salamanca (retables; José Benito de Churriguera)
1701-04	Church of San Salvador, Legañes (retables; José Benito de Churriguera)
1702	Church Santa Clara, Salamanca (Joaquin Churriguera)
1709-13	Nuevo Baztan (José Benito de Churriguera)
1709-13	Juan de Goyeneche House, Madrid (José Benito de Churriguera)
1710-15	Church of San Sebastian, Madrid (retable; José Benito de Churriguera)†
1714-24	Cathedral, Salamanca (crossing dome; Joaquin Churriguera)
1715	Hospederia, Colegio de Anaya (Joaquin Churriguera)
1717	Collegio de Calatrava, Salamanca (Joaquin Churriguera)
1724-33	Cathedral, Salamanca (choir; Alberto de Churriguera)
1725-26	Cathedral, Plasencia (retable of the Assumption; Alberto de Churriguera)
1729	Cathedral, Valladolid (west facade; Alberto de Churriguera)
1731-38	Parish Church, Orgaz (Alberto de Churriguera)
1738-47	Church of St. Thomas, Rueda (Alberto de Churriguera)

Publications

BOOKS ABOUT THE CHURRIGUERAS

CHUECA GOITIA, FERNANDO: *La catedral nueva de Salamanca*. Spain, 1951.

GUTIERREZ DE CEBALLOS, ALFONSO RODRIGUEZ: *Los Churriguera*. Madrid, 1971.
GUTIERREZ DE CEBALLOS, ALFONSO RODRIGUEZ: *El Colegio de la Orden Militar de Calatrava de la Universidad de Salamanca*. Salamanca, 1972.
IGARTUA MENDIA, MARIA TERESA: *Desarrollo del Barroco en Salamanca*. Madrid, 1972.
KUBLER, G. and SORIA, M.: *Art and Architecture in Spain and Portugal and their American Dominions 1500-1800*. Pelican History of Art. Harmondsworth, 1959.
KUBLER, GEORGE: *Arquitectura de los Siglos XVII y XVIII*. Madrid, 1957.

ARTICLES ABOUT THE CHURRIGUERAS

BONET CORREA, ANTONIO: "Los retablos de las Calatravas de Madrid." *Archivo Español de Arte* 35, No. 137 (1962): 21-49.
GARCIA Y BELLIDO, A.: "Estudios del barroco español, avances para un monografía de los Churrigueras." *Archivo Español de Arte y Arqueologia* 5, No. 13 (1929): 21-86.
GUTIERREZ DE CEBALLOS, ALFONSO RODRIGUEZ: "Los retablos de la parroquia de San Salvador de Legañes." *Archivo Español de Arte* 45, No. 177 (1972): 23-32.
VERRIE, E. P.: "Los barceloneses Xuriguera." Vol. 8 in *Divulgacion Historica*. Barcelona, 1949.

*

The traces of the Churriguera family are identified with José Rates y Dalmau of Barcelona, who migrated to Madrid and joined a son or stepson, also a Catalan, who had previously come to Madrid, José Simon Churriguera (?-1679).

Of the sons of José Simon Churriguera, three contributed substantially to the cultural advancement of art and architecture of Spain and the New World during the 17th and 18th centuries. The family created a new architectural style, the Churrigueresque, an expression of Spanish Baroque architecture and sculpture characterized by a lavish, even fantastic, but harmonious, decorative exuberance. Their architectural signatures are richly garlanded spiral columns.

José Benito de Churriguera (1665-1725), Joaquín de Churriguera (1674-1724) and Alberto de Churriguera (1676-1750) began their artistic careers under the tutelage of their father and a family acquaintance, José Ximines Donoso, who were painters, architects and sculptors of wooden altarpieces or retables. The sons were also well schooled by their father through an exposure to drawings, engravings, books and personal observations of the arts.

José Benito, the eldest son, became head of the family on the death of José Rates in 1684, and began his practice in 1689 with a few altarpieces derived from the indigenous Catalan foliated surfaces, tori and *bocelón* moldings. The first important commission was undertaken collaboratively with a Madrid architect, Juan de Ferraras, in 1686-90, for a retable in the Ayale Chapel, the *sagrario* or parish church of the Cathedral of Segovia. That work was composed of paired Solomonic columns, gilded in imitation of tasseled fabric, under a canopy of brightly colored simulated fabric.

José Benito was the winner of a competition in 1689 to erect a catafalque for the funeral of the first wife of Charles II, Queen Maria Louisa of Orléans. The monument was composed of eight *estípies* rising from a projecting console symmetrically surrounding the four-sided base.

José Benito was appointed *ayuda trazador de las obras reals,* or assistant designer for the royal works, and in essence was the architectural draftsman, without salary, working for the chief designer, Teodoro Ardemáns (1664-1726). José Benito became salaried in 1696, but he and Ardemáns became rivals, which encouraged Churriguera to find a private patron.

His work continued with the retable of San Esteban at Salamanca in 1692. Payment from his patron included a monthly salary for two years to José Benito's wife, Isabel de Palomares, and provision for his food and shelter in the monastery of Salamanca. In addition, José Benito constructed the retable of the Virgin of the Rosary in the north transept between 1693 and 1694. In 1702 José Benito received the contract to construct the retable designed by Manuel de Arredondo in San Salvadore in the city of Leganes.

José Benito's patron, Juan de Goyeneche, a banker, commissioned him from 1709 through 1713 to plan the town of Nuevo Baztar and to design and build the buildings. The town plan avoids the traditional rigid symmetry of the Renaissance gridiron plan and aligned squares, and instead follows a broken axis comprising three plazas, a palace and a church creating an off-center block. This plan is considered the most original and ambitious work of urban design in 18th-century Spain. The two-tower, high, narrow church facade counters the long, narrow palace influenced by the architectural design concepts of Andrea Palladio and Juan de Herrera. The facade of the church is composed of two columns—each resting symmetrically on a stylobate on each side of the arched entrance—that support an elaborate entablature, which in turn supports a niche with a carved figure and highly sculptured pilasters carrying a pediment. Above this pediment are a finial and a second pediment located on a receding plane.

José Benito also built a town house for his patron Goyeneche, which is now the Academia de San Fernando in Madrid. Although José Benito's architectural career developed late and his commissions were not numerous, he contributed to the new orders of design often associated with the visual animation of the Baroque and to ideas breaking with the traditional symmetrical town planning of that time in Spain.

Joaquín de Churriguera pursued the artistic ideology of his elder brother in a conservative spirit, relying on the less extravagant Plateresque architectural expression. His talents extended to his work at Salamanca Cathedral, beginning in 1702 and continuing until his death in 1724. In 1714 Joaquín was appointed master of works of the cathedral. His commissions included the retable of Santa Clara (1702) in collaboration with Pedro de Gamboa, the Hospederia of the Colegio de Anay (1715), the Colegio de Calatrava (1717) and the crossing dome, later dismantled, of Salamanca Cathedral (1714-24).

The youngest of the brothers, Alberto de Churriguera, worked under the direction of his brothers. His work was frequently overshadowed by theirs, and he did not emerge as an independent talent until after their deaths in 1724 and 1725. The choir closing in Salamanca Cathedral is his earliest known work, undertaken in 1724. He created the retable of the Assumption for the Cathedral of Plasencia in 1725-26.

In 1728 Alberto was commissioned by the town council to design the Plaza Mayor for Salamanca, the primary public open space in the city; it compared favorably with the public plazas of Cordova, Madrid and Valladolid. The plan is not related to axial symmetry, is closed to passage as a thoroughfare, is handsomely planned and designed to offer a visual relationship between the vertical and the horizontal proportions. The square is animated with a continuous rhythmic arcade at the ground floor, with the upper three levels punctuated in an orderly manner with evenly spaced window openings aligned with the arches below, and molding bands delineating each of the upper three floors. The major buildings incorporated in the inside periphery

of the square are the Town Hall and the Royal Pavilion designed in the spirit of the neo-Plateresque.

Alberto designed the upper level of the west facade of the Cathedral of Valladolid in 1729. In 1731 he was commissioned to design the Parish Church at Orgaz. Alberto renounced his position as chief architect to the Cathedral of Salamanca in 1738 in reaction to his disapproval of a tower designed by Pedro de Ribera for the church. His final commissions were for the Parish Church at Orgaz (1738), St. Thomas at Rueda (1738-40) and the Church of the Assumption at Rueda (1738-47).

The facade of the Church of the Assumption was designed with a sense of visual austerity. The portal, dedicated to the Assumption of the Virgin, is flanked by two massive towers, each constructed from cut stone with a rectangular opening near the ceiling level of the first floor and an oculus at the upper level of the second floor. The towers are covered with conical roofs. The portal, which has a larger oval oculus above, is flanked with stone pilasters and is highly carved with sprays, plumes and curved moldings, with the Trinity as the uppermost element.

During the reign of Philip II (1556-89) and throughout much of the rule of the House of Austria, there was a spirit of political unity that existed only with the unity in religion. As a result of this ideology of the authorities, liturgical architecture was restricted to classical elements and icons. After Philip II's reign, there was a gradual relaxation of the restrictions on Eucharistic embellishments, and more elaborate artistic expressions were introduced. The Baroque (17th century), the Plateresque (late 15th and early 16th centuries), and the Churrigueresque (17th and 18th centuries) became the predominant architecture of the places of worship.

The Churrigueresque period originating in Spain with the Churriguera family was introduced to New Spain through the mission and parish churches. The Mexican Churrigueresque, although deriving from the works of the Churriguera family, like much of the architecture of the New World has little relevance to the original style. It is characterized by lavish decorative recurrent features incorporating richly garlanded spiral columns and pilasters. Some more successful examples of buildings identified with the period include the Cathedral at Zacatecas (1752), Valenciana of Guanajuato (1765-88), St. Sebastian and St. Prisca of Taxco (1748).

—GORDON ECHOLS

COATES, Wells.

Canadian. Born to Canadian parents in Tokyo, Japan, 17 December 1895. Died in London, England, 17 June 1958. Married Marion Grove, 1927 (separated); one daughter. Studied at the University of British Columbia, Vancouver, Canada, 1914-16, 1919-21, B.S., then at the University of London, 1922-24, Ph.D. Worked as journalist for the *Daily Express*, London and Paris, 1923-26; worked in Adams and Thompson office with Maxwell Fry, London, 1924; engineer/architect, Chrysede Textiles Company, London and Cornwall, 1927-28; private practice as designer and architect, London, 1929-39, 1945-52; partnership with David Pleydell-Bouverie, 1933-34; partnership with Patrick Gwynne, 1935-39; partnership with Jacqueline Tyrwhitt, 1949-52; partnership with Michael Lyell, 1954-56; private practice, London, 1956-58. Founder member, MARS (Modern Architectural Research) Group, London, 1933; Fellow, Royal Institute of British Architects; member, Royal Architectural Institute of Canada; Associate, Royal Society of Arts, 1944; Royal Designer for Industry, 1944; Master of the Faculty of

Design for Industry, 1951-53; Officer, Order of the British Empire, 1944.

Chronology of Works
All in England

1932-33   Lawn Road Flats, London
1934   Sunspan House (design, with David Pleydell-Bouverie; fifteen houses built in England between 1935 and 1938)
1935   Embassy Court, Brighton
1935   Studio flat, 18 Yeoman's Row, Knightsbridge, London
1938   10 Palace Gate, Kensington, London
1938   The Homewood House, Esher, Surrey (with Patrick Gwynne)
1951   "Telekinema," South Exhibition, Festival of Britain, London
1956   House, Thames Ditton, Surrey (with Michael Lyell)
1956   House, West Wittering, Sussex (with Michael Lyell)

Publications

ARTICLES BY COATES

"Critics: A Reader's Way to Reconcile Their Unfriendliness." *Architects Journal* (11 February 1931).
"Inspiration from Japan" and "Material for Architecture." *Architects' Journal* (4 November 1931).
"Furniture Today—Furniture Tomorrow." *Architectural Review* (July 1932).
"Response to Tradition." *Architectural Review* (November 1932).
"Modern Shops and Modern Materials." *Building* (December 1932).
"Design in Modern Life: Modern Dwellings for Modern Needs." With Geoffrey Boumphrey. *Listener* (24 May 1933).
"Planning in Section." *Architectural Review* (August 1937).
"The Conditions for an Architecture for Today." *Architectural Association Journal* (April 1938): 447-457.
"Planning the Festival of Britain Telekinema." *British Kinematography* (April 1951).
"The Cine-Theatre Today and Tomorrow." *Atti e rassegna tecnica della società degli ingegnieri e degli architetti* (Turin, December 1952).
"The Film Theatre of the Future." *Ideal Kinema* (26 May 1953).
"Graduation Banquet Address." *Royal Architectural Institute of Canada Journal* (June 1959).

BOOKS ABOUT COATES

CANTACUZINO, SHERBAN: *Wells Coates*. London, 1978.
COHN, LAURA (ed.): *Wells Coates*. Oxford, 1979.
COLLINS, MICHAEL (ed.): *Hampstead in the Thirties*. Exhibition catalog, London, 1974.
HOGBEN, CAROL (ed.): *The Wireless Show*! Exhibition catalog. Oxford, 1979.
JACKSON, ANTHONY: *The Politics of Architecture: A History of Modern Architecture in Britain*. London, 1970.
MILLER, DUNCAN: *Interior Decorating*. London, 1937.
READ, HERBERT (ed.): *Unit One: The Modern Movement in English Architecture, Painting and Sculpture*. London, 1934.
WEBB, M.: *Architecture in Britain Today*. London, 1969.

YORKE, F. R. S., and GIBBERD, FREDERICK: *The Modern Flat*. London, 1950.

ARTICLES ABOUT COATES

BANHAM, REYNER: "Isokon Flats." *Architectural Review* (July 1955).
BOUMPHREY, GEOFFREY: "The Designers: Wells Coates." *Architectural Review* (January 1936).
"The Double Tragedy of Architect Wells Coates." *House and Garden* (September 1980).
FRY, E. MAXWELL: "English Architecture from the Thirties." *Architect's Yearbook* 8 (London 1957).
OZANNE, ANDREW: "Frontiersman of the Heroic Age." *Royal Institute of British Architects Journal* (September 1979).
PEVSNER, NIKOLAUS: "Broadcasting Comes of Age: The Radio Cabinet 1919-1949." *Architectural Review* (May 1940).
RICHARDS, J. M.: "Wells Coates 1895-1958." *Architectural Review* (December 1958): 357-360.
STANTON, CORIN HUGHES: "The Complete Coates—Exhibition at the Museum of Modern Art in Oxford." *Building Design* 13 July 1979).

*

Born in Japan in 1895 of missionary parents, Wells Coates was one of the pioneer modern architects of the 1930s. He always valued his Japanese upbringing, with its love of visual things and its sensitivity to the cultured life. His further education in engineering at the University in Vancouver was followed by a period as a fighter pilot at the end of World War I, and it was his training for this that first took him to England. Returning to England after the war, he took a Ph.D. in "The Gases of the Diesel Engine," and then worked as a journalist, mostly for the *Daily Express.*

Coates drifted into architecture by way of interiors and industrial design. Outwardly a self-confident man, he declared that the sensitivity of a Japanese upbringing, followed by an engineering education, was a better training for a modern architect than an architecture school. Throughout the 1930s, Coates designed radio cabinets and electric convector heaters for Ekco, designs that were best-sellers and among the finest industrial designs of their time.

The great breakthrough into architectural design came when Jack and Molly Pritchard purchased a site in Lawn Road, Hampstead, in 1929, with the intention of building some houses. Coates designed houses for them, but over time the brief changed, and by 1932 the intention was to build a five-story block of minimally sized service apartments. The idea was typical of the social idealism of the early 1930s, and of the deliberate attempt to create new life-styles in new surroundings. Halfway between flats and hotels, the dwellings were small, but room service was always available. It was seen as a way of life where household chores could be refined away. The resulting building, completed in 1933 as the first major reinforced-concrete domestic building in England, was immediately recognized as a landmark, both socially and architecturally. As a building it was the first major British example of the new European architecture of white concrete, horizontal balconies and minimalist detailing. Socially it became home to many famous people, particularly refugees from Nazi Germany. It was a manifesto building, and Coates never compromised. It has all the gusto of such a building—together with the many technical shortcomings that affected the "white architecture."

The Lawn Road flats were followed by two other apartment buildings, built at Brighton and Kensington. Embassy Court on the seafront at Brighton was completed only a year after Lawn Road; eleven stories high amidst its four- and five-story Regency neighbors, it shares with them a painted finish and a good sense of proportion. Lacking the arrogance and manifesto quality of Lawn Road, it fits in well on the Brighton seafront. The third block of flats, built in Palace Gate, Kensington, in 1939, is altogether softer, with precast concrete cladding and teak window frames giving a sense of luxury absent in the earlier buildings. The great innovation at Palace Gate is in the section, where two floors of living rooms share the same height as three floors of bedrooms, thus breaking out into spatial complexity and elegance rarely found in apartment buildings.

Parallel with the interest in apartment building ran an interest in the suburban house. Coates built two beautiful houses, one at Esher and one near Southend, but his real interest lay in developing techniques that would mechanize the construction of houses, and this he achieved with the "Sunspan" house. Planned on the diagonal with a great curved window on the sunny side, the Sunspan houses had walls, floors and roofs constructed of dovetail steel sheeting secured to both sides of steel framing members; however, the aesthetic of the Modern Movement in England at that time resulted in the houses having a smooth white finish, so they look like concrete and the innovatory nature of the construction is not visible. The first Sunspan house was built at the *Daily Mail* Ideal Home Exhibition of 1934, and was then marketed, with variations to suit the size of the house and the site, but always with the same basic plan layout and the same structural system. Fifteen Sunspan houses were built and, unlike some other novel structural systems of the time, they have worn well and are generally in good condition 55 years later.

After World War II, Coates was full of optimism and creative ideas, but the success of the 1930s eluded him. His one postwar built work, the Telekinima built on London's South Bank as part of the 1951 Festival of Britain, was inventive in construction and in section, but curiously weak in physical form. To a younger generation of architects who looked upon Coates as an old master, the Telekinima was a great disappointment.

During his latter years Coates spent much of this time in Canada. Plans for apartment blocks and for new towns show his continued enthusiasm, but all came to nothing. Parallel with these designs were his developments of the "wingsail," intended to improve the performance of small sailing boats; he constructed a wingsail catamaran on the Norfolk Broads in 1946 and later built a larger craft on the Thames; given the right wind, they performed well, but like many experiments which were not backed by enough research and testing, they had limitations.

—JOHN WINTER

COCKERELL, C. R.

British. Born Charles Robert Cockerell in London, England, 27 April 1788. Died in London, 17 September 1863. Father was the architect Samuel Pepys Cockerell (1753-1827); married Anne Rennie, daughter of the civil engineer John Rennie, 1828; son was the architect Frederick Pepys Cockerell (1833-78). Studied with his father, then at Westminster; apprenticed with Robert Smirke (1781-1867), 1809; traveled in Italy and Greece, 1810-17; worked independently; appointed surveyor of St. Paul's Cathedral, 1819; architect to the Bank of England, 1833; professor of architecture, 1840. Royal Academy, 1836. Gold Medal, Royal Institute of British Architects, 1848 (first recipient); president, Royal Institute of British Architects, 1860.

Chronology of Works
All in England unless noted
† *Work no longer exists*

1819-36	Oakly Park, Shropshire (remodeling)
1821-23	Literary and Philosophical Institution, Bristol
1821-29	Lough Crew, County Meath, Ireland†
1823-25	Hanover Chapel, London†
1824-29	National Monument, Edinburgh, Scotland
1827-28	Lodge, Wynnstay, Denbigh, Wales
1827-33	Langton House, Dorset†
1829-30	Holy Trinity Chapel, Hotwells, Bristol
1831-32	Westminster Life and British Fire Office, London†
1836-42	University Library, Cambridge
1837-39	London and Westminster Bank, Lothbug, London†
1839-42	Sun Fire and Life Assurance, Threadneedle Street, London†
1840-41	Chapel, Killerton Park, Devon
1841-45	Ashmolean Museum and Taylorian Institute, Oxford
1842-45	Caversfield House, Oxfordshire†
1844-47	Bank of England, Liverpool
1844-47	Bank of England, Manchester
1844-47	Bank of England, Bristol
1846-49	Bank Chambers, Cook Street, Liverpool†
1847-56	St. George's Hall, Liverpool (completion)
1855-57	London and Globe Insurance, Dale Street, Liverpool (with F. P. Cockerell)

Publications

BOOKS BY COCKERELL

Antiquities of Athens and other Places of Greece, Sicily, etc., supplementary to *The Antiquities of Athens* by Stuart and Revett. London, 1830.
Iconography of the West Front of Wells Cathedral. Oxford and London, 1851.
The Temples of Jupiter Panhellenius at Aegina, and of Apollo Epicurius at Bassae near Phigalein at Arcadia. London, 1860.
A Descriptive Account of the Sculptures of the West Front of Wells Cathedral photographed for the Architectural Photographic Association. London, 1862.
Travels in Southern Europe and the Levant, 1810-1817. Edited by S. P. Cockerell. London, 1903.

ARTICLES BY COCKERELL

"The Architectural Works of William of Wykeham." *Proceedings of the Archaeological Institute at Winchester* (1845).
"On the Painting of the Ancients." *Civil Engineer and Architect's Journal* 22 (1859): 42-44, 88-91.

BOOKS ABOUT COCKERELL

CROOK, J. MORDAUNT: *The Greek Revival.* London, 1971.
FERRIDAY, PETER (ed.): *Victorian Architecture.* London, 1963.
MIDDLETON, ROBIN D., and WATKIN, DAVID: *Neoclassical and 19th Century Architecture.* 2 vols. New York, 1980.
WATKIN, DAVID: *The Life and Work of C. R. Cockerell.* London, 1974.

ARTICLES ABOUT COCKERELL

BRYDON, J. M.: "The Work of Prof. Cockerell, R. A." *Royal Institute of British Architects Journal* 3rd series, 7 (1899-1900): 349-368.

CARR, GERALD L.: "C. R. Cockerell's Hanover Chapel." *Journal of the Society of Architectural Historians* 39 (December 1980): 265-285.

COCKERELL, R. P.: "The Life and Works of C. R. Cockerell, R. A." *Architectural Review* 12 (1902): 43-47, 129-146.

HARRIS, JOHN: "C. R. Cockerell's 'Ichnographica Domestica'." *Architectural History* 14 (1971): 5-29.

SPIERS, R. P.: "Cockerell's Restorations of Ancient Rome." *Architectural Review* 29 (1911): 123-128.

*

Charles Robert Cockerell was the most inventive and creative of English 19th-century neoclassical architects, bringing English neoclassicism to its apogee of scholarship and imagination. The son of the architect S.P. Cockerell, he began his architectural education while still a child; he completed his apprenticeship with Robert Smirke, one of England's most notable neoclassicists and the designer of the British Museum.

In the early decades of the 19th century, England's 18th-century Rome and Italian Renaissance-based neoclassicism gave way to a new form of neoclassicism, the Greek Revival. After Cockerell's apprenticeship, his interest in things classical led him to travel to Italy, Greece and Asia Minor, where he participated in the excavations of the Temple of Jupiter Panhellenius on the island of Aegina and the Temple of Apollo Epicurius at Bassae. His archaeological work in Greece caused him to appreciate the sculptural form of Greek buildings and to give his own work a similar character. It was this feature that more than anything else set his work apart from that of other Greek Revivalists.

Cockerell held true to the forms of classical antiquity and as a scholar, archaeologist and academic fiercely defended the use of classical forms for public buildings against the attacks of those who favored Neo-Gothic as the appropriate national style for Victorian Britain.

Early in the 19th century, neoclassicists, including Cockerell, discovered that Greek buildings had originally been enlivened with brightly colored, painted decoration. Cockerell liked and wanted colored decoration; he accepted John Ruskin's recommendation to make color an integral part of architectural construction inasmuch as paint did not hold up well in the British climate.

His first important commission—he succeeded John Soane as architect of the Bank of England—led, in 1837, to commissions for a number of bank buildings, including the first new bank in London formed as a joint stock company, the London and Westminster Bank in Lothbury. That building's facade treatment—a two-story rusticated block with rectangular fenestration, capped by a massive cornice carried by colossal engaged columns, with a third story set back behind the block of the lower mass—was the basis for the design of a number of banks in London and elsewhere. When a four-story building was called for, as at the Sun Fire and Life Assurance Building, he repeated the whole London and Westminster Bank design, but set it upon

C. R. Cockerell: Ashmolean Museum, Oxford, England, 1841-45

a heavy, rusticated base story. Particularly influential were his branch banks for the Bank of England in Liverpool, Manchester and Bristol. The smaller nature of those buildings made it possible for Cockerell to develop, using the forms described above, a facade reminiscent of Roman Baroque church facades, in contrast to the Renaissance palazzo bank facades favored by most designers of the time.

Cockerell's typical bank was pedimented, with a three-bay, two-story portico composed of colossal columns, usually in antis, set close or engaged to the building wall, and carrying a horizontal entablature. A third story was inserted between the cornice and the pediment. Entry was usually on the central axis. The portal was accentuated by a round-headed window in the third story, giving the facade a decidedly Palladian character. An exception to this pattern was the branch bank in Bristol, where Cockerell employed unusual paired entries in the outer solid bays.

Cockerell's most notable building—the Ashmolean Museum and Taylorian Institute at Oxford (1841-1845)—is one of the most interesting, and one of the last, examples of Greek Revival public architecture built in Britain. This building has a dual purpose, as a museum to house the university's collection of antiquities and as an institute to teach foreign languages. Cockerell introduced in this design an unorthodox Ionic capital that he had discovered at the Temple of Apollo at Bassae; the scroll between the volutes is rounded rather than straight, and all volutes are placed on the diagonals.

Cockerell, unlike other Greek Revival architects, was willing to enrich his Greek architecture with details and ideas from other periods and styles. The composition of the facade of the Taylorian Institute is based on the Roman triumphal arch. The columns stand free from the wall, and their entablatures break forward above them in the manner of Baroque building. The division of the facade with a two-story colossal order carrying an attic story that functions as a giant cornice was used by Michelangelo in the design of St. Peter's Basilica and Jacopo Sansovino in his Loggetta in Venice. Cockerell also used Baroque planning principles here. The intersection of the cross-axis that marks the entrance to the Taylorian Institute with the central axis on which the museum entrance is placed controls most plan decisions. The building is identifiably Victorian in its multicolored stonework, eclectic borrowings, strongly plastic modeling of the facades, and the introduction of exterior color. The interior features casts of the classical friezes Cockerell helped excavate at Bassae.

The death of Harvey Lonsdale Elmes in 1847 resulted in Cockerell's receiving the commission to complete St. George's Hall in Liverpool. The exterior form of the building is Elmes' design, but the interior is largely Cockerell's. St. George's Hall is perhaps Britain's best neoclassical building. Its exterior and its interior are equally fine. Its great hall, based on the Baths of Caracalla, repeats the colossal order of the exterior in a series of red granite columns that carry an ornately coffered vault. The floor is covered in multicolored Minton tiles. Its detail is rich, fanciful and polychrome. The effect of the interior is not nearly so severely neoclassical as is the exterior. Most attractive is Cockerell's circular, domed concert hall with its undulating, latticed balcony supported by graceful female caryatids, and its unorthodox pilasters featuring lyres and muses and carrying a handsome frieze of griffons.

Cockerell received the first Royal Gold Medal of the Royal Institute of British Architects in 1848. There is no record of his having trained apprentices in his office; however, he delivered a series of brilliant lectures as professor at the Royal Academy from 1841 to 1856. But it is his architecture that has brought him lasting fame. Middleton and Watkin, in their discussion of

Cockerell's work, say, "[In its presence,] we feel at once that we are in the presence of a man possessed of a profound intelligence, who thinks architecturally with a persuasive conviction and authority."

—C. MURRAY SMART, JR.

COCKERELL, Samuel Pepys.

British. Born in 1753. Died in London, England, 12 July 1827. Father was John Cockerell; son was C. R. Cockerell. Pupil of Sir Robert Taylor. District surveyor, St. George's, Hanover Square, 1774; clerk of works, Tower of London, 1775; clerkship, Newmarket; inspector of repairs to the Admirality, 1785; surveyorship of the Foundling and Pulteney estates, London, 1788; surveyorship, Victualling Office, 1791; surveyorship, East India Company, 1806; surveyor, sees of Canterbury and London, 1811-1 9; surveyor of St. Paul's Cathedral, 1811-1819. Co-founder, Architects' Club, 1791.

Chronology of Works
All in England unless noted
† *Work no longer exists*

1786-88	Admiralty House, London
1788-93	Daylesford House, Gloucestershire
1792	Tickencote Parish Church, Rutlandshire
1792-95	Gore Court, Tunstall†
1792-97	Church of St. Mary's, Banbury
1793-95	Middleton Hall, Carmarthenshire, Wales†
1796-98	Church of St. Martin Outwich, London†
1802-03	Church of St. Anne's, Soho, London (tower)
1804-05	Westminster Guildhall, London†
1805*	Sezincote House, Gloucestershire
1819-32	St. James' Square, London

Publications

BOOKS ABOUT COCKERELL

HUSSEY, CHRISTOPHER: *English Country Houses: Late Georgian, 1800-1840*. London, 1958.
WATKIN, DAVID: *The Life and Work of C. R. Cockerell*. London, 1974.

ARTICLES ABOUT COCKERELL

BETJEMAN, JOHN: "Sezincote, Moreton-in-Marsh, Gloucestershire: Its Situation, History, and Architecture Described." *Architectural Review* 69 (1931): 161-166.
HUSSEY, CHRISTOPHER: "Sezincote." *Country Life* (13 May and 20 May 1939).
NORTON, PAUL F.: "Daylesford: S. P. Cockerell's Residence for Warren Hastings." *Journal of the Society of Architectural Historians* 22 (1963): 127-133.

*

Not a man of letters, Samuel Pepys Cockerell was nevertheless proud of his literary ancestor on his mother's side, the English diarist Samuel Pepys (1633-1703). Cockerell, orphaned at an

Samuel Pepys Cockerell: Sezincote House, Gloucestershire, England, ca. 1805

early age, began his own distinguished career when at age 15 he became an apprentice to the prominent London architect Robert Taylor. Cockerell presumably began as little more than an errand boy, but he showed a talent that led Taylor to train him in the business of architecture as well as in its aesthetic delights. Upon Taylor's death in 1788, Cockerell took over the business, which included lucrative surveyorships (in charge of architectural needs for large estates, churches and public offices).

Cockerell matured as an architect toward the end of the Georgian era, when forms of classical style were still in vogue, though changes were in the air that would soon bewilder both architects and public. When Cockerell and John Soane arrived on the London scene, they were off on a new tack that could include not only an interest in Greek originals, but also a romantic desire to use Gothic forms and even the outlandish Indian. To be sure, the mid-19th century brought even greater confusion. Yet in London and shires where wealthy families lived, plain Georgian mansions were no longer acceptable. They had to be fashionable in the latest mode. The most interesting designs by Cockerell were the unusual ones that caused more than normal comment when erected. In other words, Cockerell still is significant today, not for the wealth and stature he gained through his profession, but rather for his interest in introducing something new to England.

Of Cockerell's many architectural works, half a dozen qualify as innovative, either in detail or in a broader way. The earliest of these was Daylesford House, Gloucestershire (1788-93), designed with numerous ornaments, both inside and out, that relate to the Indian style. The appropriateness of that style lay in the fact that the design was for Warren Hastings, who had just retired as governor-general of India. Cockerell's other, more ambitious use of the Indian style was at Sezincote, Gloucestershire, where he built a house completely Indianized on the exterior in 1805 for his brother Sir Charles Cockerell. Sir Charles was a nabob who had profited considerably from his many years spent in India. He too had retired to England, and asked his brother to make the Indian design. Curiously, the Indian decor of the exterior covers an unadulterated Georgian mansion. So the romance of India was grafted onto a totally traditional plan, satisfying both master and mistress.

Although not the first architect to introduce ancient Greek orders to England—that had already been done by James Stuart

in the 1750s—Cockerell took a great interest in the new discoveries of ancient temples in Italy and Greece. Thus, at Middleton Hall, Carmichaelshire (1793), he built a new mansion with a Greek Ionic portico; for the new Westminster Guildhall, London (1804), he constructed a Greek Doric portico.

Cockerell rebuilt the Church of St. Martin Outwich, London (1796-98, demolished), in a distinctly French style of the most recent vintage. Whether he saw published views of buildings designed by the eminent French architect Claude-Nicolas Ledoux, or whether he visited Paris in the 1790s, is not known. In any case, the emphasis on horizontal courses of stone, and the arch whose voussoirs at their outer edges become more horizontally accented courses, plus the use of a simplified pilaster order, are all characteristic of Ledoux's work.

The Architects' Club was founded by George Dance the Younger, James Wyatt, Henry Holland and Cockerell in 1791. It was mainly social in the beginning, as the members met for dinner once a month. When more members were added, and some rejected, what was purely pleasure became more business-like. Discussions centered on professional ethics and procedures with serious implications. Owing to persistent squabbles, the club finally disbanded, but not until after it became clear that some kind of an architect's organization was advisable, if not inevitable. In 1835 just such an organization was formed, the Institute of British Architects.

Several factors explain Cockerell's professional successes and the respect accorded him by all those he had dealings with. He was determined to succeed. He had a desire to design good buildings appropriate to the clients' needs. He was honest in the use of building materials and in dealings with clients. The only complaints against him came from men whose own reputations were already in doubt. That Cockerell was levelheaded and honest is borne out by the number of professional committees and juries he served on, and the number of cases of dispute that he was asked to help settle. At his command were not only his good character, but also his strong professional grounding in all aspects of design and construction. Several of Cockerell's apprentices became architects of high standing, including William Porden, C. H. Tatham, Cockerell's own son Charles, and Benjamin Henry Latrobe, who became the best American architect between 1798 and 1820.

—PAUL F. NORTON

Mauro Coducci: Palazzo Loredan on the Grand Canal, Venice, Italy, 1502-04

CODUCCI, Mauro.

Italian. Born in Lenna, near Bergamo, Italy, ca. 1440. Died in Venice, April 1504. Married Antoniola; two sons were architects.

Chronology of Works
All in Italy
*Approximate dates

1469-79	Church of San Michele in Isola, Venice
1479*-82	Palazzo Zorzi at San Severo, Venice (remodeling)
1482-90	San Pietro di Castello, Venice (bell tower)
1483-91	Church of San Zaccaria, Venice (facade and completion of the interior)
1490-95	Scuola Grande di San Marco, Santi Giovanni e Paolo, Venice (great staircase and completion of facade)
1490-95	Church of Santa Maria Formosa, Venice (rebuilding)
Before 1493	Palazzo Lando (Corner-Spinelli) on the Grand Canal, Venice
1497-1504	Church of San Giovanni Crisostomo (San Zuan Grisostomo) at Rialto, Venice
1498-1504	Scuola Grande di San Giovanni Evangelista (great staircase), Venice
1502-04	Palazzo Loredan (not completed until 1509; also called Palazzo *Non Nobis* or Vendramin-Calergi) on the Grand Canal, Venice

Publications

BOOKS ABOUT CODUCCI

ANGELINI, LUIGI: *Le opere in Venezia di Mauro Codussi*. Milan, 1945.

ANGELINI, LUIGI: *Un artista ignoto per secoli. L'architetto bergamasco Mauro Codussi e le sue opere in Venezia (1440-1504)*. Bergamo, Italy, 1962.

HOWARD, DEBORAH: *The Architectural History of Venice*. New York, 1981.

LORENZETTI, G.: *Venezia ed il suo estuario.* Venice, 1926.

McANDREW, JOHN: *Venetian Architecture of the Early Renaissance.* Cambridge, Massachusetts, and London, 1980.

PAOLETTI, PIETRO: *L'architettura e la scultura del rinascimento in Venezia.* Venice, 1893-97.

PUPPI, LIONELLO, and PUPPI, LOREDANA OLIVATO: *Mauro Codussi.* Milan, 1977.

ARTICLES ABOUT CODUCCI

CARBONERI, NINO: "Mauro Codussi." *Bollettino del Centro Internazionale di Studi di Architettura "Andrea Palladio"* 6/2 (1964): 188-198.

BELLAVITIS, GIORGIO: "La condizione spaziale di Venezia nell'opera prima di Mauro Coducci." *Psicon* 3, No. 6 (January-March 1976): 109-115.

LIEBERMAN, RALPH: "Review of *Mauro Codussi* by Lionello Puppi and Loredana Olivato Puppi." *Journal of the Society of Architectural Historians* 38 (1979): 387-390.

SOHM, PHILIP L.: "The Staircases of the Venetian Scuole Grandi and Mauro Coducci." *Architectura* 8 (1978): 125-149.

*

Mauro Coducci, or by another transliteration of his legal name, Codussi, was the first true Renaissance architect in Venice, most famous now perhaps for the Palazzo Loredan. He was born at Lenna, in the Valle Brembana north of Bergamo; nothing is known either of his youth or his training as an architect, though he seems to have retained his ties with Lombardy all the time he worked in Venice, returning to his home near Bergamo almost every winter.

He may well have known the Capella Colleoni in Bergamo Cathedral that was built by Giovanni Antonio Amadeo between 1470 and 1473 in the new, modern style. But in his very first commission, that for the Camaldolese Monastery Church of San Michele in Isola, completed under his supervision between 1469 and 1479, Coducci showed immediately the range of his inventiveness and, at the same time, what his sources were. The facade, with its curved central pediment, flanked by two half-curves at the side, was derived perhaps from Matteo de' Pasti's foundation medal for the unfinished Tempio Malatestiano in Rimini by Leon Battista Alberti; the smooth, sharply cut stone blocks of the front seem to fit the pattern on the Palazzo Rucellai in Florence, also by Alberti; the rusticated pilasters recall the Palazzo Piccolimini at Pienza; yet in its scale and proportion and order—the elements that lead scholars to call this a humanist building—San Michele suggests something of what could be seen in the great Palazzo Ducale at Urbino, which was reaching a stage of completion at that time.

Coducci was busy with several further commissions in the 1480s and 1490s: the remodeling of the Palazzo Zorzi (1479-82), completion of the Benedictine Abbey Church of San Zaccaria (1483-91), the rebuilding of the Parish Church of Santa Maria Formosa (1490-95), and the completion of the Scuola Grande di San Marco (1490-95). In all of these projects, in varying ways, Coducci continued his concern with the new style of Renaissance architecture. But his reputation rests on three projects done after these, San Giovanni Evangelista (1498-1504), San Giovanni Cristostomo (1497-1504) and the Palazzo Loredan (1502-04, completed 1509).

The commission for San Giovanni Evangelista, built in conscious rivalry of the Scuola di San Marco, begun by the Lombardi and then completed by Coducci, was an expansive and expensive design, with a grand staircase of broadening flights of steps, saucer domes above them, which lead to an upper landing where there is a square room opening under a dome. It was about that time that Coducci was also at work on the Church of San Giovanni Crisostomo which, like San Michele, had a facade of three curved pediments. Yet everything was done differently there: the piers are taller, the capitals are more richly decorated, and the interior of the church, filled with much more light than the usual darkness of medieval Venetian churches, is a simple yet extraordinarily eloquent space, a centrally domed cube, opening up with four arches into the equivalent arms of the Greek cross, with four smaller domed compartments at the corners. Something of this design can be seen in the church of Santa Maria Formosa, a building Coducci had rebuilt a few years earlier. But there were deeper chapels there and larger bays; what San Giovanni Crisostomo represents is a comprehensively articulated scheme of great delicacy and authority that was to become a model for north Italian church architecture for the next 50 years.

Coducci's last great work was the Palazzo Loredan, also known as the Palazzo Non Nobis, or Vendramin-Calergi, set on the Grand Canal, begun in 1502 but completed after his death by his sons. This building was recognized immediately in Venice as signaling a new range of grander secular, urban architecture. The Palazzo Loredan has a balanced and subtly centralized front, of some three levels, each diminishing as they rise. A parade of arches and loggias moves from the lower level with three bays on the canal to what is in effect a scheme of five bays on the two higher floors, all realised with a strength of articulation that would not have been out of place in Rome or Florence. Yet if set against the model of such Roman and Florentine palaces of the time, the Palazzo Vidoni-Cafarelli, for example, it is clear that the Palazzo Loredan, in both its frontage and plan, was based on a type of design seen, for example, at the Fondaco dei Turchi, that went back to Byzantine, even Roman predecessors: the roofs ending in gables, the *porticato* or water entrance on the ground floor, a courtyard behind, and the first story occupied by a great hall, the other rooms being distributed at the side and on the topmost floor. It was on and around such a model that Coducci set the design of the Palazzo Loredan, and very successfully, as it was to remain the scheme in Venice for such buildings for centuries afterward.

—DAVID CAST

COMPER, John Ninian.

Scottish. Born in Aberdeen, Scotland, 1864. Died in 1960. Attended Trinity College, Cambridge; attended the Ruskin School, Oxford, 1882. Articled to the architect George F. Bodley, 1883; partnership with William Bucknell, 1888-1905.

Chronology of Works

1888-90	St. Margaret's Church, Aberdeen, Scotland (extensions)
1891	Chapel (for the Community of St. Margaret), Aberdeen, Scotland
1893-1903	St. Wilfrid's, Cantley, Yorkshire, England (restoration)
1896	Workshouse Chapel, Oundle, Northamptonshire, England
1897	St. Mary's, Egmanton, Nottinghamshire, England (restoration)
1898	St. Peter Mancroft, Norwich, Norfolk, England (restoration)

1898-1905	St. Braemar, Aberdeenshire, Scotland
1902-03	St. Cyprian (Clarence Gate), St. Marylebone, London, England
1904	St. John's Home Chapel, Cowley, Oxford, England
1904-05	St. Crispin, Yerendawna, India
1904-31	St. Mary Wellingborough, Northampshire, England
1907	All Saints Church, Margaret Street, London, England (restoration)
1908	St. Margaret's (Founder's Asile), Aberdeen, Scotland
1909-11	Westminster Abbey, London, England (windows of abbots and kings; not completed until 1961)
1909-11	St. Mary, Rochedale, Lancashire, England
1909-11	Wimbourne St. Giles, Dorset, England (restoration)
1911	Oriel College, Oxford University, Oxford, England (hall restoration)
1912	St. Gilbert and St. Hugh, Gosberton Clough, Lincolnshire, England
1913-34	Wymondham Abbey, Norfolk, England (altar screen)
1914	St. John the Baptist, Lound, Suffolk, England (restoration)
1917	Stanton Chyantry, St. Alban, Holborn, London, England
1919-24	St. Andrew and St. George, Rosyth, Fife, Scotland
1928	Welsh National Memorial, Cardiff, Wales
1930	Church, Rothiemurcas, Inverness, Scotland
1930	House of Prayer Chapel, Burnham Beeches, Buckinghamshire, England
1931	Westminster Abbey, London, England (Warrior's Chapel)
1936-43	Cathedral Church of St. Andrew, Aberdeen, Scotland (chancel)
1937	St. Philip's Cosham, Portsmouth, England
1952	Westminster Hall, London, England (Parliamentary War Memorial window)
1959	Shrine of Our Lady of Walsingham, Norfolk, England (altar and reredos; with William Bucknall)

Publications

BOOKS BY COMPER

The Resonableness of the Ornaments Rubric Illustrated by a Comparison of the German and English Altars. London, 1897.

Further Thoughts on the English Altar, or Practical Considerations on the Planning of a Modern Church. Cambridge, England, 1933.

The Atmosphere of a Church. London, 1940.

Of the Christian Altar and the Buildings Which Contain It. London, 1950.

ARTICLES ABOUT COMPER

ANSON, PETER F.: "The Work of John Ninian Comper: A Pioneer Architect of the Modern Liturgical Revival." *Fashions in Church Furnishings.* London, 1937.

BETJEMAN, JOHN: "A Note on J. N. Comper: Heir to Butterfield and Bodley." *Architectural Review* 85 (1939): 79-82.

FENWICK, HUBERT: "Sir Ninian Comper (1864-1960): Last of the Ecclesiologists." *Anglican World* (1964).

It was usual until recently to see John Ninian Comper as an architect distant from the main current of architectural design, and one whose long career caused him to be regarded as a Victorian Gothic revivalist—and thus a reactionary figure—well into the second half of the 20th century. Only in recent years has his contribution to modern church architecture been appreciated.

His early career, as apprentice to a leading Victorian church architect, George Frederick Bodley, gave him a sound basis for his later work. Commencing practice immediately upon leaving Bodley, he is best known for the series of large churches for the Anglo-Catholic wing of the Anglican Church, which reflected his consuming passion for Catholic worship and the architecture that was necessary to express the spiritual values and ritualist nature of worship.

His early work is regarded as among his best. Comper himself regarded St. Cyprian, Marylebone (1902-03), as a definitive statement of his position. There is an early glimpse of his major influence on church design in that the altar is visible from all parts of the church, but "set apart" by gilded screens. He described St. Cyprian as a "lantern and the Altar." The critics of the time regarded it as an indivudalistic and mannerist interpretation of Gothic. This early assessment gave him a reputation that followed him for the rest of his life.

His career took on a curious dichotomy: in addition to designing new churches, he became a church decorator and furnisher. The immense scale of this side of his work can be judged, as he has been credited with the design of about 800 windows. This intervention into existing churches greatly influenced his architectural design. This can be seen, especially, in his development of the "English" altar, where he developed an eclectic architectural expression. His historical research led him to a love of medieval imagery, while his design work not only demonstrated a classical sense of discipline, but also a mastery of classical detail in the design of his altars and ciboria.

Comper's most splendid church is St. Mary's, Wellingborough (1904-31). A lesser designer could not have exercised the control over the diverse elements which Comper used at St. Mary's. The ciborium is classical in form, while a feature of the nave is plaster lierne vaulting with suspended pendants, reflecting the fan vaulting at Cambridge and Windsor. Comper regarded it "as much Italian as English and English as Italian." Yet there, with its mixture of styles, as in other of his major churches, Comper argued that "Unity by Inclusion" was as applicable to architecture as it was to other conceptual philosophies that strive to deal with cultural diversity. His palette was extended by visits to northern Europe and to Rome, which strengthened his views on the need for Mass-centered liturgy and his resolution to make the altar the focal point in church architecture.

In the development of Anglican church architecture in the 20th century, the liturgical revival is now seen to have been a major influence. Yet, because of the stylistic nature of his work, Comper is not regarded as one of the pioneers. Fundamentally, he can now be seen to be a major contributor to architectural progress in ecclesiastical work. He was the first architect in the modern period to investigate the relationship between the congregation and the altar. The placing of the altar in a central position as a liturgical focus was his major contribution to the development of the church plan, and was a clear break from the traditions of the Oxford movement.

His parish church at St. Philip, Cosham, Portsmouth, most clearly expresses his principle of liturgically orientated design. Once again, classical columns support a Gothic-inspired but nonstructural vault. The scheme is successful because of the artistic skill and control of detail which produced an elegance unmatched in contemporary architecture, and which paradoxically tended to disguise the originality of the underlying work.

Comper's approach to Eucharistic worship has influenced the form of almost all Anglican church buildings in Britain since 1950 and anticipated the sense of cultural aspects of Vatican II. Toward the end of his career he was taken up by John Betjeman, among others, who recognized his innovative talent and the delicacy of his architectural forms. The neoromantics who have become influential in church design regard Comper as an important figure, possibly the last Gothic revivalist. He is one who is yet to be given due recognition as a significant figure in modern church architecture, and whose standard of perfection and elegance of craftsmanship are fully in accord with the great cultural heritage of the Anglo-Catholic tradition.

—K. H. MURTA

CORMIER, Ernest.

Canadian. Born 1885. Died 1980. Trained as engineer in Montreal; studied at École des Beaux-Arts, Paris; spent two years in Rome; received diploma, 1917. Practiced as engineer and architect; design consultant for the United Nations Headquarters, New York City. Taught at the École Polytechnique of Montreal, 1925-54. Officer, Order of Canada, 1975.

Chronology of Works
All in Canada unless noted
† *Work no longer exists*

1922	Debrulé Building, Montreal (with J. O. Marchand)
1922	Ecole des Beaux Arts de Montréal
1922	École St.-Arsène, Montreal
1923	Église Sainte Marguerite-Marie, Montreal
1923-26	Criminal Court of Montreal (with L. A. Amos and C. J. Saxe)
1924-26	Chambre de Commerce, Montreal (with J. E. C. Daoust)†
1924-50	Université de Montréal, Montreal
1925-26	St. John the Baptist Church, Pawtucket, Rhode Island, U. S. A.
1925-28	Église St. Ambroise, Montreal (unfinished)
1926-27	Notre Dame of the Sacred Heart, Central Falls, Rhode Island, U. S. A.
1928	Pointe-aux-Trembles Airport, Montreal
1930-31	Cormier House, Montreal
1934-35	Église St. Louis de France, Montreal (modifications)
1938-50	Supreme Court of Canada, Ottawa
1943-44	Hospice-Orphélinat, Sorel, Quebec
1945-48	Hôtel Dieu, Sorel, Quebec
1948	St. Michael's College, Toronto
1949	Basilian Seminary, Toronto (modifications)
1950-58	National Printing Bureau, Ottawa
1952	General Assembly Building, United Nations, New York City, U. S. A. (entrance door)
1957-60	Grande Séminaire de Québec, Québec City (interior remade to house the National Archives of Quebec)

Publications

ARTICLES BY CORMIER

"Les plans de l'Université de Montréal." *Architecture, Bâtiment, Construction* (January 1947): 16-30.

BOOKS ABOUT CORMIER

GOURNAY, ISABELLE (ed.): *Ernest Cormier and the Université de Montréal.* Cambridge, Massachusetts, 1990.

Ernest Cormier strove to borrow from the avant-garde forms he saw when he studied and traveled in Europe, but he also wanted to maintain strong links with the French Beaux-Arts traditions of rationality and decorum. As a result, he was a very deliberate designer, paying special attention to appropriate forms for given functions and physical conditions. This is not to say that he always insisted that form follow function, for some of his buildings look far more like art deco and the geometrical branch of art nouveau than anything in the International Style.

Cormier's taste for extremely restrained decor and expensive materials is most clearly revealed in his own house at 1418, avenue des Pins, Montréal (1930-31). The building is composed of several intersecting cubic volumes, which gives a severe first impression. A more leisurely investigation reveals a charming but intellectually rigorous study strongly influenced by art deco. The front of the home is a bit foreboding: a plain doorway is surmounted by a cantilevered projection slightly set back from the flanking planes. The two-story window in the studio and library block to the right is similarly stepped back, and the only other articulation of the facade is a set of low reliefs in vertical bands moving from the centers of the window and door openings to the flat roofline. A smaller projection to the left encloses the kitchen, but it is left resolutely blank on the facade.

The interior is equally spartan, but there Cormier spared no expense in his selection of sumptuous materials. The inlaid floors contain curving decorative bands that now look oddly like intersecting baseball laces, and the banded walls display an occasional sculpture designed specifically for a given placement. Decor is otherwise strictly a matter of gracefully balanced arrangements of plain masses and volumes. At strategic points, simple cylinders rhyme with the four great columns supporting the entire structure at the intersection of the semicircular staircase and the studio, which itself takes up well over one quarter of the ground floor. These enormous columns are nothing more than larger cylinders clad in highly polished, dark marble. Equally striking in its barren elegance is the nearby dining room; its very high ceiling, tightly controlled fixtures and stoically inorganic furnishings make it look more like a corporate boardroom than a place to eat. Characteristic of the more private parts of the house is the main bedroom, whose walls are covered entirely by a simple drapery.

The rear of the building provides a surprising contrast, for there on a sloping lot lies a geometrical garden softened by greenery. Most odd, and really rather incongruous, is a medieval-looking cylindrical tower faced in rustic stone and topped with a high cone of cedar shakes. When one turns to look past it, back at the house, it contrasts violently with the flat roof and plan window surrounds of the garden facade, which here resemble those of the early work of Adolf Loos and Walter Gropius.

More expressive of Cormier's rationalist, public spirit is his major work, the Université de Montréal (1924-50). The consensus is that this complex reflects both his Art Deco and International Style interests, and reveals his background in both engineering and traditional Beaux-Arts architecture. The exterior is a massive symmetrical complex of numerous interlocking wings, each of which is nearly 500 feet long, spreading from a central tower. The top of the tower is a spherical observatory between

Ernest Cormier: Université de Montreal, Montreal, Canada, 1924-50

four massed corners, rather reminiscent of Joseph Maria Olbrich's *Sezession* building in Vienna. The face of the tower, and most of the rest of the structure, is treated with tall vertical bands on slightly staggered planes, creating a maximum of movement in a vocabulary of sobriety and rationalism. Some of the spaces housing services along the roofline are stepped back and side to side to add what Cormier called a "picturesque silhouette," although the overall effect he sought was "practical utility and rigid rationality." The various wings of the complex are placed at different heights on the sloping terrain to reveal the configuration of the whole complex from a distance.

Apart from that, the disposition of the various elements of the building—the Faculty of Sciences on one side, that of Medicine on the other, and the administration and library facing an implied court of honor at the center—shows Cormier's functionalist interest in maximizing the usefulness of spaces in a nonetheless traditional framework. Laboratory spaces are standardized, outpatient services and dispensaries are placed with separate entrances at the street level—whereas labs and teaching areas are not, signifying the ultimate unity of the Faculties—and services are rationalized wherever possible. (Only the heating system is fully concealed, beneath the tower.)

Decoration is entirely a matter of the arrangement of plain forms; the exterior is mostly concrete covered by a brick revetment, and the windows are all quite plain, with variations in size only where their function demands them. There are a few ceremonial areas in the interior where more expensive materials could be justified. Some of these recall the interior of Auguste Perret's Théâtre des Champs-Elysées, suggesting richness in the absence of actual ornament or "superfluous motifs."

Among Cormier's other well-known works is the Supreme Court building in Ottawa, which had to be a variation on a theme already established in the vast parliamentary complex. As a result, he followed the pattern of a Beaux-Arts structure with a high mansard roof, giving some individuality to the principal street facade by recessing it between two projecting pavilions and adding a colossal stripped-classical order. Typically, he was personally involved at every stage of the design, ensuring, for example, that even relatively minor elements, like the octagonal decorations inset into important doors, were rationally carried into the interior from the outside, in this case from a small park carefully placed opposite a principal entrance.

Other designs include a skyscraper-type tower for the Hôtel Windsor, the rather more modern Hôtel-Dieu de Sillery, the Greek Revival Palais de Justice in Montréal, the Neo-Gothic St. Michael's College in the University of Toronto, and some churches of relatively conventional design, apart from the handling of some details (e.g., St. John the Baptist in Pawtucket, Rhode Island, and the rather Richardsonian St. Ambroise in Montréal). Cormier was generally less inventive in these, but he remained respected enough to be named Officer of the Order of Canada in 1975.

—ROBERT J. BELTON

CORTONA, Pietro da.

Italian. Born in Cortona, Italy, in 1596. Died in Rome, in 1669. Father was Giovanni Berrettini, a carver of decoration who was versed in architecture; uncle was Francesco Berrettini, an architect in Cortona. Studied painting with Andrea Commodi, Florence; entered studio of the Florentine Baccio Ciarpi, Rome,

1614. Set up own studio, and began working for the Tuscan nobleman Marcello Sacchetti; employed mainly by Ferdinando II, 1637-47; traveled to Paris, France, for work at the Louvre, 1644; began working for Pope Alexander VII, 1655.

Chronology of Works

All in Rome, Italy unless noted
† *Work no longer exists*

1626-27	Villa Sacchetti, Castel Fusano (gallery and chapel frescoes; later the Villa Chigi)
1627	San Lorenzo fuori le mura (left side aisle and the monument to Barclay and Guglielmi)
1628-39	Palazzo Barberini (riding court, chapel, and gallery, and salon ceiling frescoes)
1633	San Lorenzo in Damaso (decoration)
1633-35	Chapel of the Immaculate Conception, San Lorenzo in Damasco
1634-69	Santi Luca e Martina
Mid-1630s	Villa Sacchetti del Pigneto, near Rome†
1637-47	Palazzo Pitti (restoration and additions; completed in 1661 by Ciro Ferri)
1645	San Firenze, Florence (executed and modified by others)†
1647-65	Santa Maria in Vallicella
1651-54	Pamphilj Gallery (fresco)
1656	Chapel of the Sacrament, San Marco
1656-57	Quirinal Palace (Gallery of Alexander VII)
1656-59	Santa Maria della Pace (piazza, facade, and interior redecoration)
1658-62	Santa Maria in Via Lata (facade and crypt)
1662	Francesco da Cortona House, Via della Pedacchia
1668	San Carlo al Corso (cupola)
1668	Gavotti Chapel, San Nicola di Tolentino

Publications

BOOKS BY CORTONA

Trattato della pittura e scultura: Uso et abuso loro. With Giandomenico Ottonelli. 1652; with introduction and notes by Vittorio Casale, Treviso, Italy, 1973.

BOOKS ABOUT CORTONA

ARCHIVIO DI STATO DI ROMA: *Pietro da Cortona. Mostra documentaria. Itinerario.* Rome, 1969.

BRIGANTI, GIULIANO: *Pietro da Cortona o della pittura barocca.* Florence, 1962.

CAMPBELL, M.: *Pietro da Cortona at the Pitti Palace: A Study of the Planetary Rooms and Related Projects.* Princeton, New Jersey, 1976.

FABBRINI, NARCISO: *Vita del Cav. Pietro Berrettini da Cortona pittore ed architetto.* Cortona, Italy, 1896.

LUGARI, GIOVANNI BATTISTA: *La via della Peddacchia e la casa di Pietro da Cortona.* Rome, 1885.

NOEHLES, KARL: *La Chiesa dei Santi Luca e Martina nell'opera di Pietro da Cortona.* Rome, 1970.

THELEN, HEINRICH: *Francesco Borromini: Die Handzeichnungen.* Graz, Austria, 1967.

WITTKOWER, RUDOLF: *Art and Architecture in Italy: 1600-1750.* 3rd ed., Harmondsworth, England, 1973.

ARTICLES ABOUT CORTONA

BLUNT, ANTHONY: "The Palazzo Barberini: the Contributions of Maderno, Bernini and Pietro da Cortona." *Journal of the Warburg and Courtauld Institutes* 21 (1958): 256-287.

CASALE, VITTORIO: "Pietro da Cortona e la Cappella del Sacramento in San Marco a Roma." *Commentari* 20 (1969): 93-108.

CHIARINI, MARCO and NOEHLES, KARL: "Pietro da Cortona a Palazzo Pitti: Un episodio ritrovato." *Bollettino d'Arte* 52 (1967): 233-239.

COFFEY, CAROLINE: "Pietro da Cortona's Project for the Church of San Firenze in Florence." *Mitteilungen des Kunsthistorischen Instituts in Florenz* 22 (1978): 85-118.

JACOB, SABINE: "Pierre de Cortone et la décoration de la galerie d'Alexandre VII au Quirinal." *Revue de l'Art* 11 (1971): 42-54.

NOEHLES, K.: "Die Louvre-Projekte von Pietro da Cortona und Carlo Rainaldi." *Zeitschrift für Kunstgeschichte* XXIV (1961): 40.

NOEHLES, KARL: "Architekturprojekte Cortonas." *Münchner Jahrbuch der bildenden Kunst* 20 (1969): 171-206.

NOEHLES, KARL: "Der Hauptaltar von Santo Stefano in Pisa: Cortona, Ferri, Silvani, Foggini." *Giessener Beiträge zur Kunstgeschichte* 1 (1970): 87-123.

OST, HANS: "Studien zu Pietro da Cortonas Umbau von S. Maria della Pace." *Römisches Jahrbuch für Kunstgeschichte* 13 (1971): 231-285.

POSSE, HANS: "Das Deckenfresko des Pietro da Cortona im Palazzo Barberini und die Deckenmalerie in Rom." *Jahrbuch der Preussischen Kunstsammlungen* 40 (1919): 93-118, 126-173.

RASY, ELISABETTA: "Pietro da Cortona: I progetti per la Chiesa Nuova di Firenze." In *Architettura barocca a Roma.* Maurizio and Rome, Italy, 1972.

VITZTHUM, WALTER: "A Comment on the Iconography of Pietro da Cortona's Barberini Ceiling." *Burlington Magazine* 103 (1961): 427-434.

WIRBIRAL, NORBERT: "Contributi alle ricerche sul Cortonismo in Roma: I pittori della Galleria di Alessandro VII nel Palazzo del Quirinale." *Bollettino d'Arte* 45 (1960): 123-165.

WITTKOWER, RUDOLF: "Pietro da Cortona's Project for Reconstructing the Temple of Palestrina." In *Studies in the Italian Baroque.* London, 1935; 1975.

*

Together with Giovanni Lorenzo Bernini and Francesco Borromini, Pietro da Cortona was one of the great figures of the Roman Baroque. Born Pietro Berrettini in 1596 in the town of Cortona, whence his cognomen, he came from an artistic background. His father was a stonecarver, and an uncle was an architect. Pietro received his early training as a painter in Cortona and Florence. By 1611 he was in Rome, where he served his apprenticeship before setting up his own studio. He received patronage first from the Mattei family, for whose Roman palace he painted frescoes in 1622-23. In 1623 he began work on frescoes for Santa Bibbiana as part of a campaign of the rebuilding of that church directed by Bernini. Even at that early point in his career, his work was distinctive in its use of color, modeling and pictorial construction. Later in the same decade he designed two villas for the Sacchetti family, one at Castelfusano and the other in the Pigneto di Roma. The latter building is known today only through reproductions; its garden facade was marked by a highly plastic composition of building elements, platforms and stairs. Although apparently his first architectural

Pietro da Cortona: Santi Luca e Martina, Rome, Italy, 1635-50

essay, the Villa del Pigneto clearly presaged the novelty and boldness of Pietro's mature works.

Pietro's reputation as a fresco painter was assured when, again under the direction of Bernini, he executed the ceiling of the great salon of Palazzo Barberini (1633-39). For this setting he designed one of the largest and most innovative fresco compositions to be painted before or since. Of huge dimensions, the painting is constructed in quadratura, that is, with an illusionistic architectural frame, which divides the surface into five panels. Closest to the observer, fully realized figures are disposed upon a cornice, seemingly in front of the painted architecture, which is itself decorated with sculptural supporters and ancient reliefs, all painted; in the spaces framed by the painted architecture, in turn, are scenes developed in atmospheric perspective. The subject of the whole is the triumph of Divine Providence and of the Barberini, the latter represented by the three bees of their coat of arms flying to heaven at the center of the composition. The combination in a single work of sacred content, dynastic allegory, and technical mastery was unprecedented, and its influence was to be felt in great palaces throughout Europe for the next century and more.

As the ceiling of the great salon at Palazzo Barberini was under way, Pietro simultaneously produced the design for SS. Luca e Martina, a new church erected at the corner of the ancient Forum Romanum. Carried out principally in 1635-50, the church is in plan a Greek cross, slightly elongated on the principal axis, the cross superimposed on a square and surmounted by a dome on a high drum. The piers of the crossing below the dome are pilastered and angled to the center, increasing the dome's diameter and emphasizing the reference to the plan of St. Peter's. The walls of the arms of the cross retreat from fully expressed columns, reversing the plastic order of the crossing piers. Above, vaults and dome are described by powerful ribs against which the curved surfaces are coffered in contrasting diagonal and hexagonal patterns. The overall effect of the interior, carried out from base to crown in counterreformatory white, is at once complex, forceful and pure.

Externally, modern demolitions have left the building inappropriately isolated from its former surroundings, but the view of the entrance front is much as it was originally. The facade is in two stories of equal width, narrow and high, with a bulging, flattened center confined by emphatic edges. The detailing is exceptionally complex. At the edges pilasters stand in front of the surface, and at the center columns are sunk into the mass; between edges and center the wall plane moves unpredictably forward and back. The system of the interior is hinted at but not revealed, and the statement to the observer is one of barely restrained force. Following his demonstration of mastery of figural composition in the colossal fresco at Palazzo Barberini, Pietro showed that he was equally a master of the abstract language of architecture at SS. Luca e Martina.

In the 1640s Pietro was commissioned by the Medici family to decorate the principal rooms of Palazzo Pitti in Florence. His work there, involving architectural decor, stucco figures and illusionistic frescoes, represented a step beyond his achievement at Palazzo Barberini. The decorations of the Planetary Rooms—dedicated to the realms of Venus, Apollo, Mars, Jupiter and Saturn—deal not with the specifics of dynastic allegory, as before, but with the universals of the education and duties of the wise ruler. In particular the combination of classical iconography and richness of decor create an impression of overwhelming splendor. The interiors of princely palaces from that moment on owed a debt to Pietro's work at Palazzo Pitti.

Returning to Rome, Pietro executed a variety of commissions, among which the huge fresco program at Santa Maria in Vallicella occupied him during the years 1647-51 and again in 1655-65, while during the years 1651-54 there were frescoes for Palazzo Pamphili. In 1656, he designed a new facade for Santa Maria della Pace. A small church in the heart of medieval Rome, Santa Maria della Pace was built in the 1490s, probably to a design by a Florentine architect. Donato Bramante had designed the adjacent monastic courtyard, and the church interior was decorated with frescoes by Raphael, among others. The problem for Pietro was to create an impressive effect in an extremely confined space. His solution was to open up a small piazza by cutting away parts of the foreground buildings. With an enlarged space at his disposal, Pietro then challenged the observer's expectations by spreading the new facade left and right, claiming both adjacent buildings and streets, while pushing a semicircular porch into the center of the new piazza. In the result the newly created space is both open and crowded, and totally dominated by the new facade.

The lower order of the facade is in Tuscan Doric, the upper order Ionic, respecting the usage of Bramante's adjacent cortile. In most other respects the new facade departs totally from classical practice. The detailing of the porch is of the simplest design, perhaps referring to Bramante's Tempietto, but the story above, superficially representing the nave behind it, combines emphatic edges with a compressed and flattened convex center, together with an array of columns and pilasters whose relations to a constantly shifting wall plane are almost incomprehensible. The side wings at the lower level are flat, while at the second story they follow reentrant curves in plan, increasing the visual projection of the central unit. The final result gives the impression of a building perfectly blended with its setting and simultaneously bursting out of its spatial confines, exuberant and dramatic to a high degree. At the same time descriptive and indescribable, the facade of Santa Maria della Pace combined flat and curving surfaces into a dynamic and unified whole that was to be definitive of the Baroque for the next century. Equally important, as an addition to an existing structure, Pietro's design took the final step in the process of separating the facade from any necessary relationship to the building behind it, assigning it an independent role in dominating its foreground space and thereby the responses of the participant observer.

At Santa Maria in Via Lata (1658-62), Pietro applied a vestibule and facade to a small church facing onto the Corso, Rome's principal street. A columned porch in two stories, confined between narrow, pilastered flanks, terminates in an arcuated center beneath a triangular pediment, a clear reference to Roman imperial usage. Despite the cramped site, Pietro's facade was at once simple and grandiose, and in a manner so classical that it can only be called high Hellenistic.

In 1664 Pietro submitted designs for the new Louvre, but they did not meet with favor in Paris. Before his death in 1669 he designed the dome for San Carlo al Corso (1668), which shows his late manner in architecture, massive and sober, and even more than his earlier works combines forcefulness with control.

Pietro's achievements in various media—fresco painting, the decorated ensemble, architecture—all in their own ways displayed technical ability and inventiveness of the highest order. Had Pietro's work been judged in only one medium he would have deserved his fame. His ability to excel in so many areas marked him as outstanding even among the greatest artists of seventeenth-century Rome. But beyond his technical mastery, Pietro showed in his work a dramatic intensity and controlled forcefulness unmatched in the work of his contemporaries. It was no accident that Pietro da Cortona received the distinction, so often awarded, so rarely earned, of being hailed as a second Michelangelo.

—BERNARD M. BOYLE

COSTA, Lucio.

Brazilian. Born in Toulon, France, 27 February 1902. Married Julieta Guimaraes; two daughters. Early education in England and Switzerland; studied at the Escola Nacional de Belas Artes, Rio de Janeiro, Brazil, 1917-22. Private practice, Rio de Janeiro, since 1924; director, National School of Fine Arts, Rio de Janeiro, 1930-31; consultant architect, Servico do Patrimonio Historico e Artistico Nacional, since 1937. Honorary member, Royal Institute of British Architects; American Institute of Arch itects; Académie d'Architecture, France; commandeur, Légion d'Honneur, France.

Chronology of Works
All in Brazil unless noted

1932	Alfredo Schwartz House, Rio de Janeiro (with Gregori Warchavchik)
1932	San Miguel Church restoration, Rio Grande Do Sul
1936-43	Ministry of Education and Health [now the Palacio da Cultura], Rio de Janeiro (with Le Corbusier, Oscar Niemeyer, Affonso Eduardo Reidy, Jorge Machado Moreira)
1939	Brazilian Pavilion, World's Fair, New York, U.S.A. (with Oscar Niemeyer)
1942	Hungria Machado House, Rio de Janeiro
1943	Saavedra House, Correias
1944	Park Hotel, Friburgo
1948-54	Eduardo Guinle Apartments, Rio de Janeiro
1955	Brazilian Pavilion, Cité Universitaire, Paris, France
1956	Master plan for Brasília
1968	Master plan for Barra da Tijuca, Rio de Janeiro

Publications

BOOKS BY COSTA

Arquitectura Carioca. Rio de Janeiro, 1952.
The Architect and Contemporary Society. Venice, 1952.
About My Work in Brazil. Rio de Janeiro, 1958.
Scientific and Technological Humanism. Cambridge, Massachusetts, 1961.
Sôbre Arquitetura. Pôrto Alegre, Brazil, 1962.
Biblioteca Educacion y Cultura, vol. 10: Arquitetura. Rio de Janeiro,1980.

ARTICLES BY COSTA

"A Necessary Documentation." *Revista do Serviço do Patrimônio Histórico Artistico"* 1 (1938).
"Portuguese-Brazilian Furniture." *Revista do Serviço do Patrimônio Histórico Artistico"* 3 (1940).
"Jesuit Architecture in Brazil." *Revista do Serviço do Patrimônio Histórico Artistico* 5 (1941).
"L'urbaniste défend sa capitale." *Architecture: Formes et fonctions* 14 (1968).
"Manifestation normale de vie." *Architecture: Formes et Fonctions* 15 (1969).
"Lúcio Costa por ele mesmo." *Jornal do Brasil* (27 February 1982).

BOOKS ABOUT COSTA

BULLRICH, FRANCISCO: *New Directions in Latin American Architecture.* New York, 1969.
EVENSON, NORMA: *Two Brazilian Capitals: Architecture and Urbanism in Rio de Janeiro and Brasília.* New Haven, Connecticut, 1973
GAZENCO, J. O., and SCARONE, M. M.: *Lúcio Costa.* Buenos Aires, 1959.
HOLSTON, JAMES: *The Modernist City: An Anthropological Critique of Brasília.* Chicago, 1989.
MAGALHAES, A., and FELDMAN, E.: *Doorway to Brasilia.* Philadelphia, 1959.
MINDLIN, HENRIQUE: *Modern Architecture in Brazil.* New York, 1956.

ARTICLES ABOUT COSTA

"Brasilia: Monument van het modernisme." *Architect* 20/11 (The Hague, November 1989).
"Lucio Costa: Notes for a Revolutionary Biography." *Summa* (April 1983).
"Lucio Costa—Brazilian Town Planner." *Metropolis* (Paris, November/December 1974).
"Lúcio Costa e as Casas do Poeta." *Projeto* 125 (September 1989).
"Lúcio Costa: A Vanguarda Permeada com a Tradicão" [interview]. *Projeto* 104 (October 1987).
"XIIIo Congresso Brasileiro de Arquitetos Lúcio Costa." *Projeto* 146 (October 1991).

*

Lúcio Costa's vision of a modern Brazilian architecture that could be progressive, functional, and at the same time respectful of the forms and practices of Luso-Brazilian tradition has distinguished him as the father of modernism in Brazil and the spiritual leader of the country's most creative avant-garde. His fundamental contribution to the evolution of modernism in Brazil has been made in three distinct but related areas of professional activity: historic preservation, theoretical and academic reform, and architecture and urban planning.

A major theme in Costa's career has been his persistent interest in the traditional architecture that was brought by the Portuguese colonizers and adapted to its new Brazilian context during the 17th and 18th centuries. Costa's relentless effort to safeguard Brazil's colonial architectural heritage through his involvement with the national organization for the preservation of the historic patrimony (Serviço do Patrimônio Histórico e Artístico Nacional), and his equally important attempt to integrate colonial building traditions into a modern Brazilian architecture that would be appropriate to the technology and society of the 20th century—these have been his most characteristic undertakings.

A second, and no less important, project has been his championing of Le Corbusier's functionalism and his sanctioning of that architect's theoretical writings, especially *Vers une Architecture*, as the "bible of architecture" for young Brazilian architects. Taking as his points of departure this Corbusian doctrine and his own profound admiration for colonial architecture, beginning in 1930-31 Costa argued for an alternative to the historicist neocolonial style that was then in vogue in Rio de Janeiro's Escola Nacional de Belas Artes. Initially supportive of the fashionable style, Costa was led, primarily through his profound reflection on Le Corbusier's theories, to perceive the weaknesses and contradictions inherent in the use of a historical style in a 20th-century context. But he parted company with Le

Corbusier and the European rationalists for the apparent total disrespect for the past that he perceived in their doctrines. What Costa admired most in colonial Brazilian architecture was not its decoration, but the functional simplicity of its technical and aesthetic solutions and the structural and material frankness of its building processes. For Costa, Corbusian functionalism was thus not a rigid model to be slavishly copied, but a liberating force that provided a disciplining alternative to the superficialities of fashionable facades and historical styles deemed technically and socially inappropriate to modern times. As such it provided a means to establish a new synthesis between traditional and modern architecture in Brazil. The colonial heritage provided an anchor that would give Costa's brand of functionalism a distinctly Brazilian character.

Coinciding with the political revolution of October 1930, Costa's desire for a new aesthetic alternative for Brazil led him to spearhead the revision of the outdated curriculum of Rio's beaux-arts academy. His reform gave the students of the school the option of attending either the courses of the older professors, who were retained in their original positions, or the courses of a group of younger instructors who, contracted from outside the academy, were advocates of avant-garde modernism. At first the reform was a great success: students flocked to the new classes, and the rivalry between the old teachers and the new presented the students with a clear contrast of the different teachings and options open to them. Nominated director of the reformed school in December 1930, Costa, then barely 29 years old, had launched a campaign that, initially at least, was successful in exposing Brazil's architecture students to the teachings and works of modernists such as Gregori Warchavchik, one of the first to design frankly modern buildings in Brazil. Soon, however, Costa faced considerable opposition from the older professors and their professional supporters, and through a series of protests and a cunning legalistic manipulation of the school's bylaws, José Marianno Filho and his colleagues, the leaders of the old neocolonial camp, forced Costa to step down in September 1931.

Costa's resignation, however, masked a *de facto* victory for the avant-garde. After a six-month student strike in support of the reforms, the creative talents of the young generation followed Costa's example in seeking a new solution for Brazilian architecture. This effort, as well as Costa's desire for a uniquely Brazilian synthesis, was realized perhaps most brilliantly in the Ministry of Education and Health Building in Rio de Janeiro (1936-43). The project was a collaborative venture that involved Costa's supervision of a design team confronted with the task of creating Brazil's first monumental public palace in the manner of Le Corbusier, who had been invited to Brazil as a consultant for the project in 1936. But by 1939 the team had evolved well beyond Le Corbusier's initial proposals, and Costa passed the mantle of creative leadership on to his ex-draftsman Oscar Niemeyer. The Ministry Building as executed is a remarkable document of the rapid aesthetic progress made by Costa and the design team influenced by him.

Costa's architectural output increased significantly after the successes of the 1930s and early 1940s. Among his most outstanding contributions were his award-winning Eduardo Guinle Apartments (1948-54) and his Brazilian Pavilion at the Cité Universitaire in Paris (1955). A year later he contributed the winning pilot plan for the new capital, Brasília, a project noteworthy for the monumental simplicity of its idea and the symbolic appropriateness with which he imbued his choice of forms and planning metaphors. Costa's accomplishments as a planner with a special sensitivity to the Brazilian landscape were again illustrated in his extensive urbanization proposals for the Barra

Ralph Adams Cram: St. Thomas' Church, New York City, New York, 1906-14

de Tijuca, a suburban resort and residential *bairro* of Rio, begun in 1968.

Known for his open and modest personality, Costa continues to inspire Brazilian architects young and old. Today he keeps a quiet watch over the increasingly commercialized Brazilian architectural scene from his apartment home on Leblon Beach.

—DAVID K. UNDERWOOD

CRAM, Ralph Adams.

American. Born in Hampton Falls, New Hampshire, 16 December 1863. Died in Boston, Massachusetts, 22 September 1942. Apprenticed with Rotch and Tilden, Boston. Opened office with Charles Wentworth (1861-97), Boston, 1887; partner, Cram Wentworth and Goodhue, and later Cram Goodhue and Ferguson, 1891-1910; continued practicing with other architects, including Frank Cleveland, Chester Godfrey and Alexander Hoyle, under the name Cram and Ferguson. Fellow, American Institute of Architects.

Chronology of Works
All in the United States unless noted

1889-92	Ide House, Williamstown, Massachusetts
1892-1913	All Saints' Church, Ashmont, Boston, Massachusetts
1896-99	Phillips Church, Exeter, New Hampshire
1897	Church of Our Savior, Middleborough, Massachusetts
1898-1900	Richmond Court Apartments, Brookline, Massachusetts

1899	Deborah Cook Sayles Public Library, Pawtucket, Rhode Island
1899-1916	St. Stephen's Church, Cohasset, Massachusetts
1900-1921	Emmanuel Church, Newport, Rhode Island
1903-14	United States Military Academy, West Point, New York
1906-14	St. Thomas' Church, New York City
1904	Harborcourt, Newport, Rhode Island
1904-31	Sweet Briar College, Virginia
1905-09	First Unitarian Church, West Newton, Massachusetts
1905-28	Calvary Church, Pittsburgh, Pennsylvania
1907-41	Euclid Avenue Church (Church of the Covenant), Cleveland, Ohio
1907-41	St. Paul's Cathedral, Detroit, Michigan
1909	Holy Cross Monastery, West Park, New York
1909-41	Rice Institute (University) Campus, Houston, Texas
1910	Japanese Garden Court, Museum of Fine Arts, Boston, Massachusetts
1910-30	St. John the Evangelist Church, Boston, Massachusetts (interior)
1911-29	Princeton University Chapel and Graduate College, Princeton, New Jersey
1911-37	Fourth Presbyterian Church, Chicago, Illinois
1912-41	House of Good Hope Church, St. Paul, Minnesota
1913-17	Swedenborgion Cathedral, Bryn Athyn, Pennsylvania
1913-25	All Saints' Church, Peterborough, New Hampshire
1913-35	Second Unitarian Church (Ruggles Street Church), Boston, Massachusetts
1914	St. Elizabeth's Chapel (Cram estate), Sudbury, Massachusetts
1914-20	Williams College Chapel and Chapin Hall, Williamstown, Massachusetts
1914-32	Phillips Exeter Academy, Exeter, New Hampshire (library, dormitories, gymnasium, inn and administration building)
1914-36	St. Anne's Convent, Arlington, Massachusetts
1915-34	Wheaton College, Norton, Massachusetts (chapel and other buildings)
1915-41	Cathedral of St. John the Divine, New York City (nave, west front, baptistery, chancel remodeling and miscellaneous buildings)
1916-31	Mercersbury Academy Chapel, Mercersburg, Pennsylvania
1917-20	Englewood Chapel, Nahant, Massachusetts
1920-28	St. George's School Chapel, Newport, Rhode Island
1921-24	First Presbyterian Church, Utica, New York
1921-29	Sacred Heart Church, Jersey City, New Jersey
1922-25	First Presbyterian Church, Tacoma, Washington
1924-26	Choate School Chapel, Wallingford, Connecticut
1926-31	Holy Rosary Church, Pittsburgh, Pennsylvania
1926-34	United States War Memorial Chapels, Belleau Wood Cemetery, Aisne-Marne and Oise-Aisne Cemetery, Fere-en-Tardenons, France
1927	Church of the Ascension, Montgomery, Alabama
1927	Provident Mutual Building, Philadelphia, Pennsylvania
1927-29	St. Paul's Church, Winston-Salem, North Carolina
1929-41	Madison Avenue Church (Christ Church), New York City
1930	Federal Building, Boston, Massachusetts
1930-39	Rollins College, Winter Park, Florida
1931-41	East Liberty Church, Pittsburgh, Pennsylvania
1935-38	Church of SS. Mary and John, Cambridge, Massachusetts

Publications

BOOKS BY CRAM

Church Building. Boston, 1901 (3rd ed., 1924).
Impressions of Japanese Architecture and the Allied Arts. New York, 1905.
Introduction to HENRY ADAMS: *Mont-Saint Michel and Chartres*. New York, 1913.
The Ministry of Art. New York, 1914.
Six Lectures on Architecture. 1917.
The Substance of Gothic. Boston, 1917 (2nd ed., 1925).
The Ruined Abbeys of Great Britain. Boston, 1927.
Impressions of Japanese Architecture and The Allied Arts. New York, 1930.
The Catholic Church and Art. New York, 1930.
My Life in Architecture. Boston, 1936.

BOOKS ABOUT CRAM

DANIEL, ANN MINER: *The Early Architecture of Ralph Adams Cram: 1889-1902*. Ann Arbor, Michigan, 1980.
HAMLIN, A. D. F.: *A Study of the Designs for the Cathedral of St. John the Divine*. New York, 1924.
MAGINNIS, C. D.: *The Work of Cram and Ferguson, Architects*. New York, 1929.
MUCCIGROSSO, ROBERT: *American Gothic: The Mind and Art of Ralph Adams Cram*. Washington, D.C., 1980.
NORTH, ARTHUR TAPPAN: *Ralph Adams Cram*. New York, 1931.
TUCCI, DOUGLASS SHAND: *Ralph Adams Cram: American Medievalist*. Boston, 1975.
TUCCI, DOUGLASS SHAND: "Ralph Adams Cram and Boston Gothic." In *Built in Boston, City and Suburbs, 1800-1950*. Boston, 1978.

ARTICLES ABOUT CRAM

SCHUYLER, MONTGOMERY: "The Works of Cram, Goodhue and Ferguson." *Architectural Record* 29: entire issue (1911).
TUCCI, DOUGLASS SHAND: "First Impressions on the Rediscovery of Two New England Galleries by Ralph Adams Cram." *Currier Gallery of Art Bulletin* (1979): 2-16.
TUCCI, DOUGLASS SHAND: "Ralph Adams Cram and Mrs. Gardner." *Fenway Court* (1975): 27-34.

*

Ralph Adams Cram, architect, lecturer and writer, was the ardent champion of Gothic architecture at the turn of the century and through the early years of the 20th century. Although best known for his churches, he also designed many other buildings, in styles other than Gothic.

Cram was born in New Hampshire to a distinguished family of limited means; his father left farming to become a Unitarian minister. Since the family could not afford to send the boy to college, he was apprenticed to the Boston architects Rotch and Tilden, among the leading practitioners of Ruskinian High Victorian Gothic in the northeastern United States. Through his employers he became well acquainted with the writings of John Ruskin and William Morris, and developed his own views about the relationship of architecture to society and about the expression of function. Eventually his reading persuaded him to embrace High Church Anglicanism. At that time Cram also came under the influence of Henry Vaughan, formerly an assistant to the English architect George F. Bodley, but practicing in Boston since 1882. Because of these influences, and following several trips to England during the 1880s, Cram became convinced that Gothic was a principle of living and design, and not merely a period style, that Gothic was not dead but simply moribund and in need of resuscitation. Cram undertook this reinvigoration of Gothic as his life mission.

In 1889 Cram took on Charles Francis Wentworth (1861-97) as a partner and formed his own office. Not long after, they received the commission for a new Episcopalian church at Ashmont, Dorchester, Boston (1891-93 ff.), whose simple, strong and forceful Gothic style brought the firm regional attention and enabled them to add to the office a young and highly gifted draftsman, Bertram Grosvenor Goodhue (1869-1924). The new firm of Cram, Wentworth and Goodhue designed several churches in the vicinity of Boston. Wentworth died early of pneumonia, and his place as business manager in the office was taken by Frank Ferguson (1861-1926) in 1897. The renamed firm continued to build churches in the Northeast, as well as a block of apartments in Brookline, Massachusetts, and a public library in Pawtucket, Rhode Island.

The rise of Cram, Goodhue and Ferguson to national prominence came with the winning of two commissions: the master plan and chapel for the United States Military Academy at West Point, New York, in 1903, and the commission for St. Thomas' Church on Fifth Avenue in New York City. These two major commissions in New York required the establishment of a second office in New York City, which Goodhue supervised; eventually this division would result in the split of the firm into two independent offices, as Goodhue endeavored to develop a more progressive and personal Gothic style.

St. Thomas' was Cram's first great success, showing how the intricacies of Late Gothic could be used to develop an urban church on a crowded site by eliminating a side aisle and presenting to the street a dramatic facade focusing on a massive corner tower. The church is also one of the best examples of the integrated arts—combining woodcarving, stonecarving, metalwork, stained glass, lighting fixtures—which Cram incorporated into all his churches and other buildings. It is no surprise, therefore, to discover that Cram was also very active in the American Arts and Crafts movement centered in Boston. Attracted to Cram's office during that time were younger architects who were to become leaders in other branches of church architecture, among them Charles D. Maginnis, who did for Catholic church design in the Northeast what Cram and his partners did for Episcopalian and Protestant churches.

Additional churches and other buildings followed, among the best of which were the Graduate School complex at Princeton University, and the chapel there (1911-29), the Fourth Presbyterian Church in Chicago (1911-37) and the large Swedenborgian Cathedral at Bryn Athyn, Pennsylvania (1913-17), all Gothic. At the same time, Cram used various interpretations of Georgian Colonial classicism in his complex for Sweet Briar College, Virginia (1904-31), the Wheaton College Chapel, Norton, Massachusetts (1915-34), his campus complex for Phillips Exeter Academy, Exeter, New Hampshire (1914-32), and the Williams College Library, Williamstown, Massachusetts (1914-22). For commissions in California, Florida and Texas, however, Cram adapted Spanish Colonial Baroque motifs. For the large Doheny Library at the University of California, Los Angeles, and the Administration Building at Rice University, Houston, Texas, Cram developed a colorful and massive interpretation of Italian Lombard Romanesque, in brick with limestone trim (1909-41). These and other variations of non-Gothic styles tended to come later in Cram's career, after 1920, when Cram and Ferguson had been operating on their own for five years. Cram also designed the exterior shell of the Federal Building, Boston (1930-39), whose art deco flourishes are among the best of the period in that city.

Cram's greatest undertaking, in terms of sheer scale and length of involvement, was his attempt to complete the looming hulk of the Cathedral of St. John the Divine, Morningside Heights, New York City. The building was begun in 1892 by Heins and Lafarge on a huge scale in a modified Byzantine-Romanesque style, but only the choir and crossing dome were roughly finished when the task was turned over to Cram in 1915. He managed to integrate his own scheme for Gothic transept arms and a vast Gothic nave with the original section of the building. Because of the expansive dimensions of the nave, and its double side aisles, Cram developed a wholly original method of doubling the cross ribs in the sexpartite vaults, as well as doubling the corresponding external flying and vertical buttresses. Notably, Cram insisted on traditional masonry construction, without resort to hidden steel reinforcements. Still under construction at the time of Cram's death in 1942, the church suffered from the change in taste toward modernism that followed World War II. Since the mid-1960s, however, as the grip of modernism has lessened and interest in preservation and historic architecture has grown, construction has resumed. The new work thus fulfills Cram's hope that architecture and its allied arts could effect social and economic betterment, for in the Harlem slums a new generation of craftsmen is being trained whose building skills can now be carried back into the neighborhoods for desperately needed rehabilitation projects.

—LELAND M. ROTH

CRET, Paul Philippe.

American. Born in Lyons, France, 21 October 1876; immigrated to the United States, 1903. Died on 8 September 1945. Studied at the École des Beaux-Arts, Lyons, and at the École des Beaux-Arts, Paris. Professor of design, University of Pennsylvania, Philadelphia, 1903; began own firm, 1907; collaborated with the firm of Zantzinger, Borie and Medary.

Chronology of Works
All in the United States unless noted
* Approximate dates
† Work no longer exists

1907-10	International Bureau of the American Republics (now Organization of American States), Washington, D.C. (with Albert Kelsey)
1914-17	Indianapolis Public Library, Indianapolis, Indiana (with Zantzinger, Borie and Medary)
1919-27	Detroit Institute of Arts, Detroit, Michigan (with Zantzinger, Borie and Medary)
1920-26	Delaware River Bridge, Philadelphia (with Ralph Modjeski)
1923-25	Barnes Foundation Gallery, Merion, Pennsylvania
1925	University Avenue Bridge, Philadelphia (with Stephen Noyes)
1926-30	Hartford County Building, Hartford, Connecticut (with Smith and Bassette)
1926-30	Rodin Museum, Philadelphia (with Jacques Gréber)

Paul Philippe Cret: Folger Shakespeare Library, Washington, DC, 1928-32

1926-33	Aisne-Marne Memorial, near Chateau-Thierry, France
1926-33	Flanders Field Chapel, Wareghem, Belgium
1926-33	Memorial, near Bellicourt, France
1927-29	Providence War Memorial, Providence, Rhode Island
1928-32	Folger Shakespeare Library, Washington, D.C.
1930-37	Naval Memorial, Gibraltar, Spain
1932-34	Federal Reserve Bank, Philadelphia
1935-37	Federal Reserve Board Building, Washington, D.C.

Publications

ARTICLES BY CRET

"Modern Architecture." Pp. 183-243 in *The Significance of the Fine Arts*. Boston, 1923.

"The Ecole des Beaux-Arts: What Its Architectural Teaching Means." *Architectural Record* 23 (1908): 367-371.

BOOKS ABOUT CRET

WHITE, THEO B.: *Paul Philippe Cret, Architect and Teacher*. Philadelphia, 1973.

ARTICLES ABOUT CRET

GROSSMAN, ELIZABETH G.: "Paul Philippe Cret: Rationalism and Imagery in American Architecture." Ph.D. dissertation. Brown University, Providence, Rhode Island, 1980.

SWALES, FRANCIS S.: "Draftsmanship and Architecture, as Exemplified by the Work of Paul P. Cret." *Pencil Points* 9 (1928): 688-704.

VAN ZANTEN, DAVID: "Le Systeme des Beaux-Arts." *Architectural Design* 48, No. 5 (1978): 11-12, 66-79.

*

In 1903, at the age of 27, Paul Philippe Cret emigrated from France to the United States to teach architectural design at the University of Pennsylvania. Under his tenure as chief design critic, Penn's School of Architecture was recognized as the best in the country—a distinction that was to continue in the 1950s and 1960s under the influence of Cret's most famous student, Louis I. Kahn. During his lifetime, Cret was granted the most prestigious honors awarded by his profession, including gold medals from the American Institute of Architects and the New York Architectural League. Ralph Adams Cram, the leading practitioner of the Gothic style, praised Cret's Indianapolis Public Library (1928-32) as "the most beautiful secular building produced in modern times, complete in its planning, organization, scale and beauty."

Cret's views on architectural education were solicited by the leading American educators, and his architectural theory was widely published and discussed. Cret's renown was due to his unique ability to utilize his French Beaux-Arts training and French sensibilities toward tradition and historicism, and apply them with skill and finesse to modern architectural problems and issues.

The École des Beaux-Arts stressed the application of a universal and rational system that organized building parts into a sequence of hierarchically arranged spaces. These were differentiated by function and given aesthetic meaning through a universally recognized ornamental vocabulary, appropriate to the building's character and function. Although Cret was aware of contemporary architectural trends toward an art nouveau aesthetic, he was not swayed by it, because of its antidecorative qualities that prevented the viewer from quickly apprehending the underlying architectural mass. For Cret, ornament should never detract from the architectonic quality of the building. He remained faithful to the more profound and deeply rooted classical architectural tradition, which transcended temporary taste and fashion. It was that tradition, learned at the École des Beaux-Arts, which Cret would expound in the United States.

Cret's first American building, now known as the Pan American Union Building (1907-10), was designed in association with Albert Kelsey, and was the result of a competition for the International Bureau of the American Republics in Washington, D.C. The white marble edifice betrays Cret's Beaux-Arts training in its three-arched entryway and rich sculptural decoration. Already, however, Cret had departed from traditional monumental planning by eschewing the French tripartite pavilion formula and adopting instead a relatively blocky and rectangular volume. Furthermore he incorporated an interior patio following the entrance vestibule, complete with a movable glass roof. Cret believed that a building's program was its most important aspect and that it should guide planning and architectural decision. Accordingly, the headquarters of a pan-American political assembly should reflect its Hispanic roots—albeit in a modern fashion.

In his later buildings, Cret further distanced himself from the decorative aspects of Beaux-Arts architecture, to concentrate on the effect of light and shadow on largely undecorated surfaces, letting the architectonic mass and poche of the building carry its expressive meaning and significance. He remained faithful, however, to Beaux-Arts conceptions of planning, hierarchy and character. The Indianapolis Public Library (1914-17), in association with Zantzinger, Borie and Medary, and the Hartford County Building (1926-30), with Smith and Bassette, illustrate Cret's shift in aesthetics from the massive, windowless flanking pavilions framing a monumental Doric colonnade—as seen in Indianapolis—to the blocky rectangular mass of the Hartford building articulated chiefly by square piers.

Cret's Detroit Institute of Arts (1919-27), in association with Zantzinger, Borie and Medary, is a mixture of traditional Beaux-Arts planning and innovative interior decoration. Organized around a central courtyard, the gallery space is divided into three clearly defined exhibition areas, for European, Asiatic and American art, with an auditorium on axis behind the courtyard. The gallery space was praised for its decoration, corresponding to the style of the artworks on display in the particular rooms. Such a correlation between art and architecture underscores Cret's belief in the importance of the latter as a contributing agent to the museum's educational function. In addition, the museum's exterior massing, through its Beaux-Arts emphasis on character and hierarchy, reflects its interior organization. A one-story rusticated facade with a triple-arched entrance is dominated by the central hall, whose roof is visible from the street, and which announces its function as an important gathering area. Furthermore, the outdoor sculpture and niches prepare the visitors for the artistic experience waiting for them inside.

The Folger Shakespeare Library in Washington, D.C., built between 1928 and 1932, just after the Detroit museum, was seen by contemporaries as Cret's most modern work to date. Its smooth, unified volumetric composition, articulated by fluted

pilasters and sculptured panels, illustrates the degree to which Cret had assimilated key features of the modern aesthetic as defined by Henry-Russell Hitchcock and Philip Johnson in their 1932 book *The International Style: Architecture Since 1922,* which accompanied a seminal exhibition on modern architecture. The authors had declared that architecture should emphasize volumes in space as opposed to mass, that its composition should be guided by regularity and repetition, such as ribbon windows, and that it should be free of ornament. In an article in the *Architectural Forum* of August 1933 titled "Ten Years of Modernism," Cret stated that "on the whole, the modernist trend has been useful. It has forcefully focused our attention on some principles of composition, not new to be sure, but somewhat neglected during the past hundred years, such as the value of restraint, the value of designing volumes instead of merely decorating surfaces, and the value of empty surfaces as elements of composition."

It was Cret's broad definition of modern architecture, and his ability to weld together divergent architectural principles that distinguished him from his contemporaries. Unlike the narrow definition of the International Style as expounded by Hitchcock and Johnson, Cret believed that architecture should reflect both the needs and ideals of its time, and should therefore express aesthetic, moral and emotional values, in addition to the strictly functional ones. Thus, Cass Gilbert's neo-Gothic Woolworth Building skyscraper in New York (1910-13) and the Philadelphia Savings Fund Society Building by George Howe and William Lescaze (1929-32), the first International Style skyscraper in America, were both modern because they answered, in their plan and configuration, modern conditions and demands. The style of their facades was merely a question of taste and not of modernity. It was Cret's insistence on emotional content, such as derived from Gilbert's "Cathedral of Commerce" that was the Woolworth Building, coupled with the presence of familiar, and thus reassuring, architectural elements that underlay his approach to building.

Unlike Bauhaus architects, Cret believed that architecture was the product of forces beyond human control and that it could not be forcefully and artificially imposed from without. Cret defined these forces as the persistent legacy of the past kept for sentimental or aesthetic reasons. Cret viewed the eclecticism of his age as a natural consequence of both its advanced state, requiring many different services, and of its political constitution, being essentially democratic and pluralistic. The Federal Reserve Board Building in Washington, D.C. (1935-37), testifies to Cret's success in inventing an architectural vocabulary appropriate for new governmental agencies founded under the New Deal such as the Federal Reserve System. The Board Building is characterized by an unrelenting rhythm of smooth piers, and a strong rectangularity, broken only by a central projecting portico. Contemporaries likened it to Robert Mills' severe neoclassical vocabulary, making it appropriate for federal architecture.

Besides designing monumental public architecture, Cret was also involved in the design of formidable works of engineering, such as the Delaware River Bridge, constructed with the engineer Ralph Modjeski. Now known as the Benjamin Franklin Bridge, it was the longest suspension bridge in the world when completed in 1926 in time for Philadelphia's sesquicentennial celebration. Cret's anchorages are masterful examples of his interpretation of bridges as important signposts in the urban scene, symbolizing not just movement across rivers, but marking that movement in a manner appropriate to their surroundings. The massive Piranesi-like rusticated anchorages in tandem with the monumental pylons at the entrances give the impression of strength and solidity, in contrast to the seemingly light steel suspension cables. Although engineering could lay the groundwork, only architecture, as a fine art, had the power to impart meaning and expression.

Indeed, Cret felt himself to be an heir to the great architectural tradition dating back to the classical French tradition of the 17th century. Although practicing in the United States, a country characterized by an unrelenting belief in progress and modernity, he never abandoned what he understood to be the essential characteristic of architecture: its ability to move the senses. Although pragmatic and open to technical advancement, he was reluctant to abandon time-tested architectural formulas which he felt were still appropriate. Architecture evolved very slowly and could not be changed overnight, as the Bauhaus aesthetic pretended. Cret's careful, measured approach to architectural design is reflected in the quiet grandeur and monumentality of his buildings.

—MARC VINCENT

CUVILLIÉS, François.

Belgian. Born in Soignies-en-Hainaut, near Brussels, Belgium, 1695. Died in 1768. Son was the architect François-Joseph-Ludwig Cuvilliés (1731-77). Entered the service of Max II Emmanuel, elector of Bavaria from 1679 to 1726, as court dwarf, 1706; worked for him as military engineer; studied architecture in Paris, 1720-24, partly with Nicolas-François Blondel (1683-1756); appointed court architect, 1725, to join the current court architect, Joseph Effner (1687-1745); served as supervising architect to electoral court in Munich, 1730-53; became director of architecture for Elector Maximilian III Joseph, 1763.

Chronology of Works
All in Germany
* Approximate dates
† Work no longer exists

1726-32	Palais Piosasque de Non, Munich†
1728-37	Yellow Apartment and Falkenlust, Schloss Augustusburg, Brühl
1729ff.	Reiche Zimmer, Residenz, Munich (decoration)
1733-37	Palais Königsfeld, Munich
1734-39	Amalienburg, Nymphenburg Palace, near Munich
1738*	High Altar, Church, Diessen
1734	Bad Mergentheim
1747ff.	Schloss Haimhausen, near Munich
1750-52	Schloss Wilhelmstal, near Kassel
1750-53	Theater, Residenz, Munich
1756-57	Main Salon, Schloss Nymphenburg, near Munich (reconstruction)
1767	Theatinerkirche (St. Kajetan), Munich (central section of facade)
n.d.	Church of St. Michael, Berg-am-Laim (begun by Johann Michael Fischer)
n.d.	Abbey Church, Schäftlarn

Publications

BOOKS BY CUVILLIÉS

Livres de Cartouches. Series I, 1738ff.; Series II, 1745ff.; Series III, 1756ff.

BOOKS ABOUT CUVILLIÉS

BRAUNFELS, WOLFGANG: *François de Cuvilliés.* Würzburg, Germany, 1938.

Kurfürst Clemens August, Landesherr und Mäzen des 18. Jahrhunderts. Ausstellung im Schloss Augustusburg zu Brühl, 1961. Cologne, 1961.

HAGER, LUISA: *Nymphenburg: Schloss, Park und Burgen.* Munich, 1955.

HANSMANN, WILFRIED: *Schloss Falkenlust.* Cologne, 1973.

LIEB, NORBERT: *Barockkirchen zwischen Donau und Alpen.* 2nd ed. Munich, 1958.

MELLENTHIN, HORST: *François Cuvilliés' Amalienburg: Ihr Bezug zur französischen Architekturtheorie.* Munich, 1989.

THON, CHRISTINA: *Johann Baptist Zimmermann als Stukkator.* Munich, 1977.

WOLF, FRIEDRICH: *François de Cuvilliés: Der Architekt und Dekorschöpfer.* Munich, 1967.

ARTICLES ABOUT CUVILLIÉS

HANSMANN, WILFRIED: ''Die Stuckdecken des Gelben Appartements im Schloss Augustusburg zu Brühl.'' *Beiträge zur rheinischen Kunstgeschichte und Denkmalpflege* 16 (1970): 241-268.

LAING, ALASTAIR: Pp. 281-287 in Anthony Blunt (ed.), *Baroque and Rococo: Architecture & Decoration.* New York, 1978.

*

Jean-François-Vincent-Joseph Cuvilliés had an astonishing career, for at the age of 11 he entered the service of Max II Emmanuel, elector of Bavaria from 1679 to 1726 (who was exiled at the court of King Louis XIV from 1704 to 1714), as the court dwarf, traveling in the elector's entourage through France and accompanying Max-Emmanuel during his stay at the luxurious French court.

When the elector was able to return to Munich, Cuvilliés, who had imbibed many architectural and decorative stimuli in France and in the low Countries, worked as a military engineer. Such was his aptitude, however, that the elector sent him to Paris from 1720 to 1724 to study architecture. This he did, apparently partly under François Blondel (1683-1756), the influential architect and architectural theorist, and in 1725 was appointed court architect with Joseph Effner (1687-1745), who had trained under Germain Boffrand in Paris, and who had been court architect from 1715. Thus there was a strong French influence among the designers of buildings for the electoral court.

One of Cuvilliés' first major jobs from 1728 was at Schloss Augustusburg at Brühl in the Rhineland, where he took over as architect from Johann Conrad Schlaun (1695-1773), who had commenced building the palace in 1725 for the Elector Clemens August, prince-archbishop of Cologne, also a member of the Bavarian ruling house. Clemens August was devoted to the taste of chinoiserie, and employed Cuvilliés to design his *indianisches Kabinett* and the charming little hunting lodge of Falkenlust at Brühl. In the Schloss itself, Cuvilliés designed many of the delicious Rococo interiors, and in these projects French, German and chinoiserie Rococo exoticisms were exquisitely executed for the aesthetically minded elector. At Brühl, too, Cuvilliés may have designed the *chinesisches Haus* for the pheasantry of the park, erected before 1750, and probably around 1730.

On the death of Max II Emmanuel, Cuvilliés did not immediately become chief architect to the new Bavarian elector, Karl

François Cuvilliés: Amalienburg, Nymphenburg Palace, Munich, Germany, 1734-39

Albrecht (1726-45), who later became Emperor Karl VII. Until about 1729 Cuvilliés was more closely involved with the building activities of Clemens August, but by 1730 he was confirmed in his position as the supervising architect to the electoral court in Munich, a position he held until 1753. In the period during which Cuvilliés wielded his influence, the Rococo style enjoyed a triumphant progress in Bavaria, beginning with the decorations of the Reiche Zimmer in the Munich Residenz, carried out from 1729, and recognized before their partial destruction as among the finest Rococo work in all Europe.

Shortly afterward Cuvilliés built the Palais Königsfeld in Munich (1733-37), a restrained and refined building in the Rococo style that contrasted mightily with the heavier, more deeply modeled style of the Baroque, which Cuvilliés and his contemporaries caused to be superseded.

On the grounds of the Nymphenburg Palace outside Munich, Cuvilliés designed and built what was to become his most celebrated work of architecture, the Amalienburg, which is perhaps the greatest of all masterpieces of the Franco-German Rococo style. The Amalienburg (1734-39) is a single-story pavilion with a large circular room in the center expressed as a curve in the middle of the facade. It takes its name from the Electress Amalia, and is really a hunting lodge set in the woodlands that were planted for the rearing of pheasants near the Nymphenburg itself. The rooms are simply arranged on either side of the central salon, over which is a balcony with a light wrought-iron rail from which pheasants could be shot: this elegant *tir aux faisans* crowns the low curved shape of the roof of the circular central room. The exterior is restrained, refined and very Gallic, while the interiors, with their delicately colored and modeled Rococo and chinoiserie decorations, are charming in their subtlety and grace.

In 1738 Cuvilliés published his *Livre de Cartouches,* which consisted of 30 suites of six plates each, and included cartouches, frames, designs for ceilings, and elevations of the interiors of rooms complete with paneling and furniture. From 1745 a second series was published that included more cartouches, panels of ornament, furniture designs, vases, mirrors, chandeliers, picture frames and much else. The third series, of 1756 and after, consisted of architectural designs.

He was involved in the building of the church of St. Michael at Berg-am-Laim, begun by J. M. Fischer; some time earlier Cuvilliés had provided designs for the Abbey Church of Schäftlarn, and around 1738 he designed the superb high altar at Fischer's church at Diessen.

Cuvilliés was consulted by aristocratic and princely patrons in many parts of Germany, and was involved at Bad Mergentheim in 1734 and at Kassel in 1749. Most of his great works were in Munich, where he served the electors well. Almost as celebrated as the Amalienburg, for example, is the exquisite Residenz Theater in Munich (1750-53), one of the great triumphs of German Rococo. The auditorium, in the form of the traditional 18th-century Italian opera house, is lavishly embellished with carved *putti,* caryatids, swags, trophies and representations of musical instruments, with many bursting and frothing cartouches (in the design of which Cuvilliés was a master). There is much gilding, and the coloring is richly red. This small theater was very badly damaged in 1944, but was rebuilt in 1958.

As late as 1767, after he had been appointed director of architecture to the Elector Maximilian III Joseph (1745-77) in 1763, Cuvilliés completed the central section of the facade of the Theatinerkirche (St. Kajetan) in Munich, which had been begun by Agostino Barelli in 1663, and was loosely based on Sant'Andrea della Valle in Rome, the mother church of the Theatine Order. Enrico Zuccalli took over the supervision in

1667. Cuvilliés' twin-towered facade is majestic and wide, and the three-stage towers are capped with voluted cupolas: the two-story front itself, with its superimposed orders, is pronouncedly Roman, quite unlike the earlier, lighter French-influenced work of the Walloon architect.

Cuvilliés' son, François-Joseph-Ludwig (1731-77), trained in Paris, and like his father studied under Jacques-François Blondel (1705-74), who ran his own teaching establishment until he became professor at the Académie Royale de l'Architecture in 1762. Cuvilliés the Younger produced many remarkable designs in which the Rococo and neoclassical styles merged.

The elder Cuvilliés brought to the Rococo real genius, and elevated it beyond mere decoration. His work transcends that of many of his contemporaries, and he gave Europe one building of rare and absolute perfection: the Amalienburg. He was a master of the asymmetrical, and he exploited the sparkling effects of modeled waterfalls, webs, cartouches and emblems. It is clear he was familiar with French published sources and that he knew the work of François Boucher, Jacques de Lajoue and Juste-Aurèle Meissonier, among many other French Rococo artists. It is known, for example, that he revisited Paris in 1754-55. Cuvilliés the Younger reissued many of his father's designs in his *École de l'Architecture Bavaroise,* published from 1770 in Munich, and which was intended to illustrate aspects of Bavarian architecture. By the 1770s, though, Rococo was becoming old-fashioned, and neoclassicism was gaining ground.

It is tragic that we do not have more surviving work by the elder Cuvilliés: changes of taste and, above all, the catastrophe of World War II have wreaked havoc upon his works. We are fortunate, however, to have the handful of exquisite designs left.

—JAMES STEVENS CURL

CUYPERS, P. J. H.

Dutch. Born in Roermond, Netherlands, in 1827. Died in 1921. Son was the architect Joseph Cuypers. Architectural training at the Academy in Antwerp, Belgium; won Prix d'Excellence, 1849. Began own practice in Roermond, 1850; formed partnership with Stoltenberg, 1852; founded the Rijksmuseum School (later the Quellinus School), Amsterdam, 1865.

Chronology of Works
All in the Netherlands unless noted
† Work no longer exists

1850-52	P. J. H. Cuypers House, Maastrichterweg, Roermond
1855-62	St. Lambertus, Veghel
1858-1908	St. Servaas, Maastricht (restoration)
1859	St. Catharina, Eindhoven
1864-73	St. Willibrordus-buiten-de-Veste, Amsterdam†
1865	St. Barbara, Breda
1870-73	Heilig Hart, Vondelstraat, Amsterdam
1870-84	Minster, Roermond (restoration)
1872-75	Cathedral, Mayence, Germany (restoration)
1873-1900	Nieuwe Kerk, Delft (restoration)
1875	St. Jacobus Major, Parkstraat, The Hague
1876	Houses, 36-42 and 75 Vondelstraat, Amsterdam
1876-85	Rijksmuseum and Director's House, Amsterdam
1878-80	Houses, 3-7 Vondelstraat, Amsterdam
1881-85	St. Bonifacius, Leeuwarden
1883-86	Fountain Count William II of Holland, Binnenhof, The Hague

P. J. H. Cuypers: Central Station, Amsterdam, Netherlands, 1885-89

1884-85	Oud-Leyerhoven II House, Tesselschadestraat-Vondelstraat, Amsterdam
1885-89	Central Station, Amsterdam (with A. L. Van Gendt)
1886	St. Josef, Groningen (with Joseph Cuypers)
1886-1917	Onze Lieve Vrouwekerk, Maastricht (restoration; with Joseph Cuypers)
1887	Maria-Magdalena Church, Spaarndammerstraat, Amsterdam
1890-92	St. Vitus, Hilversum (K. P. C. de Bazel, surveyor)
1891-96	Château de Haar, Haarzuilens (restoration; with Joseph Cuypers)
1897	St. Petrus, Oisterwijk

Publications

BOOKS BY CUYPERS

Le château de Haar à Haarzuylens. With Frans Luyten. Utrecht, 1910.

BOOKS ABOUT CUYPERS

CUYPERS, J. T. J.: *Het Werk van Dr. P. J. H. Cuypers, 1827-1917.* Amsterdam, 1917.
ROSENBERG, H. P. R.: *De 19de-eeuwse kerkelijke bouwkunst in Nederland.* The Hague, 1972.
STUERS, VICTOR DE: *Holland op zijn smalst.* Bussum, Netherlands, 1873.

Petrus Josephus Hubertus Cuypers, a Dutch architect active in the second half of the 19th century, is known most for his design of the Rijksmuseum in Amsterdam and his influence as a teacher on the next generation of architects, such as Hendrik Berlage and Karel de Bazel. Cuypers was born in Roermond, a town in the Roman Catholic province of Limburg. After training as an architect at the Academy in Antwerp, Belgium, which he left in 1849 with the Prix d'Excellence, Cuypers went to Paris to study the work of the medievalist Eugène-Emmanuel Viollet-le-Duc. Viollet-le-Duc's idea of the proper effect of architecture and the relationship between form and structure, together with the similar notions of A.W.N. Pugin in England, had interested Cuypers ever since he learned of those concepts from Josef Alberdingk Thijn, a Catholic intellectual in Antwerp.

In 1850 Cuypers was back in Roermond, however, and it was there that he designed his first building, the P.J.H. Cuypers House, Maastrichterweg. Two years later he founded a school in Roermond, the studio Cuypers and Stoltenberg, which produced during the next few years a range of furniture, sculpture and decoration for ecclesiastical commissions; these opportunities occurred because in 1853 the episcopal hierarchy was restored in the Netherlands, and the Catholics required a number of new buildings since, as in England, the Protestants kept the old medieval churches.

Cuypers designed several such churches, most notably St. Lambertus, Veghel (1855-62), St. Catherina, Eindhoven (1859), and the vast St. Willibrordus-buiten-de-Veste Amsterdam (1864). This last church was later expanded, but even in its first conception it was a remarkable and exuberant design, with a large central tower and spire at the crossing, two smaller towers at the back and a pair of flanking towers at the front. The brick, slate and cast-iron church was filled with rich decorations, including patterns on the brick, frescoes and ornaments. Like the work of Pugin and Viollet-le-Duc, the design of St. Willibrordus was governed by what was considered to be an honesty in materials and a reasoning in the structure. Such an example was to have an extraordinary influence on later architects.

Cuypers was also involved in the restoration of medieval buildings, including the church at Roermond (1870), the Cathedral of Mayence in Germany (1872) and the Nieuwe Kerk in Delft (1873); like Viollet-le-Duc, he often brought these buildings to a state of perfection they had never enjoyed in their medieval history. He was encouraged in his efforts by Victor de Stuers, who, from 1875 onward, was in charge of arts and sciences at the ministry of the interior, and paid much attention to all the restoration of the monuments of the old Netherlands.

Cuypers' greatest achievements, though, were in his new architecture. In 1865 he moved to Amsterdam, where he founded another school for the study of applied arts, the Rijksmuseum School, or, as it was later called, the Quellinus School. In 1876 he received the commission for the Rijksmuseum. He designed a vast and imposing structure that was very close to its models in England: one especially notable influence was the University Museum in Oxford by Deane and Woodward, which Cuypers had noted on an 1862 trip to England to view the work of Pugin and George Gilbert Scott. The Rijksmuseum's plan is in two parts, with wings set around courtyards that were then filled in, on each side of a great central hall. Two great towers mark the front and smaller blocks at the corners. The whole is in brick, decorations and all, but the roofs and the interior galleries, like those at Oxford, are cast-iron. The whole effect, like that of the museums in England, was at once traditional and modern.

There were other commissions, that for the Central Station in Amsterdam (1885), which he designed with A.L. Van Gendt, and a number of commissions he carried out with his son, Joseph Cuypers: the Church of St. Joseph, Groningen (1886), the restoration of the Onze Lieve Vrouwekerke, Maastricht (1886), and his last significant commission, a rather free re-creation of the Château de Haar at Haarzuilens (1891).

Cuypers influenced several generations, also through the practice of his nephew, Eduard Cuypers, who had in his studio a number of young assistants who were to become the leading architects of the Amsterdam school: Michel de Klerk, J. M. van der Mey and Piet Kramer.

—DAVID CAST

D

DAKIN, James H.

American. Born in New York, 1808. Died on 10 May 1852. Brother was the architect Charles Dakin. Apprentice draftsman, Town and Davis, 1829; joined Charles Dakin's firm, New Orleans, Louisiana, 1835. Co-founded American Institution of Architects, 1836.

Chronology of Works
All in the United States
† Work no longer exists

1833-34	Rockaway Marine Pavilion, New York†
1833-37	New York University, New York City†
1834	First Presbyterian Church, Troy, New York
1834-36	Bank of Louisville, Louisville, Kentucky
1836	Barton Academy, Mobile, Alabama (with James Gallier, Sr., and Charles Dakin)
1836-37	Government Street Presbyterian Church, Mobile, Alabama (with Gallier and Charles Dakin)
1836-37	United States Hotel, Mobile, Alabama†
1838-40	St. Patrick's Church, New Orleans, Louisiana
1839	State Arsenal, New Orleans, Louisiana
1842	Gayoso House Hotel, Memphis, Tennessee†
1843	Medical College of Louisiana, New Orleans, Louisiana†
1843-44	Canal Bank, New Orleans, Louisiana
1847-55	University of Louisiana, New Orleans, Louisiana†
1847-52	Louisiana State Capitol, Baton Rouge, Louisiana
1848-81	United States Custom House, New Orleans, Louisiana (with others)

Publications

BOOKS ABOUT DAKIN

ANDREWS, WAYNE: *American Gothic: Its Origins, Its Trials, Its Triumphs.* New York, 1975.

CARROTT, RICHARD G.: *Egyptian Revival: Its Sources, Monuments, and Meanings, 1808-1858.* Berkeley, California, 1978.

GALLIER, JAMES, SR.: *Autobiography of James Gallier, Architect.* Paris, 1864.

GEBHARD, DAVID, and NEVINS, DEBORAH (eds.): *200 Years of American Architectural Drawing.* New York, 1977.

HAMLIN, TALBOT F.: *Greek Revival Architecture in America.* New York, 1944.

PATRICK, JAMES A.: *Architecture in Tennessee: 1768-1897.* Knoxville, Tennessee, 1980.

SCULLY, ARTHUR, JR.: *James Dakin, Architect: His Career in New York and the South.* Baton Rouge, Louisiana, 1973.

ARTICLES ABOUT DAKIN

ANDREWS, WAYNE: "American Gothic." *American Heritage* (October 1971): 26-33.

DAVIES, JANE B.: "A. J. Davis' Projects for a Patent Office Building, 1832-1834." *Journal of the Society of Architectural Historians* 24 (1965): 229-251.

LAUGHLIN, CLARENCE JOHN: "Louisiana Fantasy." *Architectural Review* 141 (1967): 330, 383-386.

PATTON, GLENN: "Chapel in the Sky: Origins and Edifices of the University of the City of New York." *Architectural Review* 145 (1969): 177-180.

*

James Harrison Dakin was one of America's most creative early 19th century architects and an imaginative interpreter of romantic classicism. A skilled practitioner in the Greek Revival style, Dakin also experimented successfully with the Egyptian and Gothic Revivals. His designs were characteristically well proportioned but not slavishly archaeological.

A native of Dutchess County, New York, who was initially trained as a carpenter, Dakin began his architectural career in 1829 with Town and Davis in New York City. A brilliant draftsman, Dakin produced exquisite drawings and renderings in a style remarkably similar to that of his mentor Alexander Jackson Davis. By 1832 Dakin was made a full partner, and the firm was renamed Town, Davis and Dakin.

Many of Dakin's early designs incorporated signature elements of Town and Davis: the pilastrade—a screen divided by pilasters; Davisean windows—multistory openings that spanned the entire space between pilasters; and the distyle *in-antis* facade. For example, the Perry House in Brooklyn (1832, demolished), the earliest commission that can definitely be credited to Dakin, displayed some of those elements. This Greek Revival mansion consisted of a two-story central block flanked by one-story wings with pilastrades and Davisean windows. Its facade was modeled after Ithiel Town's Bowers House.

Early on, however, Dakin demonstrated his ability to work in other styles. His design for New York University (1833-37), with interior details by Davis, was one of the earliest examples of Collegiate Gothic, which became the traditional style for educational buildings in the United States.

For the Bank of Louisville, Kentucky (1834-36), one of Dakin's best works, he ingeniously combined Greek Revival with Egyptian motifs. Dakin produced a monumental distyle *in-antis* facade, substituting a cast-iron anthemion for a pediment and battering the side walls. On the interior, he dramatized the banking hall with an unusual elliptical, coffered dome. Arthur Scully, Jr., observed that this was "the least archaeological building ever designed by a Greek Revival architect."

Dakin's importance as a draftsman and designer was reflected in the publication in 1835 of eight of his drawings in *Illustrated Views in New York* by Theodore Fay. Dakin's influence on builders was greatly increased by the inclusion of numerous of his designs in two of Minard Lafever's books, *The Modern Builder's Guide* (1833) and *The Beauties of Modern Architecture* (1835).

Seeking greater opportunities, Dakin left New York for New Orleans in 1835, where he joined James Gallier, Sr., and his brother Charles Dakin, both of whom he had hired for Town and Davis. Gallier soon went off on his own, and the Dakin brothers established Dakin and Dakin. While Charles maintained an office in Mobile, Alabama, James became one of the busiest architects in New Orleans, building speculative housing projects as well as major public buildings, including the Greek Revival State Arsenal (1839) and the Gothic Revival St. Patrick's Church (1838-40).

Dakin's career was set back by a dispute over construction of the church and a bankruptcy following the Panic of 1837, but only temporarily. Among his later projects in New Orleans were the Canal Bank (1843-44) and the Medical College of Louisiana (1843), both Greek Revival designs. Dakin's building for the Medical College closely resembled the Perry House of a decade earlier in its plan and proportions. In 1847-55 he incorporated the original building in a much grander E-shaped complex when the Medical College was absorbed by the University of Louisiana, which subsequently became Tulane University.

Dakin designed a number of major hotels during his career, all in the Greek Revival style, including the Rockaway Marine Pavilion (1833-34), a sprawling resort hotel on Long Island, New York; the Verandah Hotel in New Orleans (1836), with the prototype of the iron balconies, so characteristic of that city, that covered the entire sidewalk; the huge United States Hotel in Mobile (1836-37), crowned by a low dome; and the great Gayoso House Hotel in Memphis (1842), with its imposing Corinthian portico. Although he did not eclipse Isaiah Rogers, "the father of the American Hotel," Dakin's success in this building type was notable.

Dakin is perhaps best known for the Louisiana State Capitol in Baton Rouge (1847-50, rebuilt 1880-82). In form and detail, it resembles a Tudor Gothic palace, but with a light stucco finish rather than brick. The choice of the Gothic style was controversial, but it demonstrates Dakin's concern with stylistic innovation. In his diary, Dakin commented that a design in the Grecian or Roman style "would unavoidably appear to be a mere copy of some other edifice already erected and often repeated in every city and town in our Country." His desire for distinction was borne out. The Louisiana State Capitol has been described by Arthur Scully, Jr., as "one of the finest examples of secular Gothic design in America during the Revival Period," and it is one of only two state capitols in that style.

Dakin was also conscientious in applying technological innovations, as demonstrated in his handling of the United States Customs House in New Orleans, for which he supervised construction from 1848 to 1851. He argued that the plan for the building, previously drawn by Alexander T. Wood, should be revised to substitute a cast-iron frame for masonry groin vaults, as well as to provide more light and air. Although his proposals were supported unanimously by a panel of leading architects, including Isaiah Rogers, local politics blocked his recommendations. Rather than capitulate, Dakin resigned his post, reflecting his strict adherence to the highest professional standards.

An indication of Dakin's prestige was the invitation in 1836 by Thomas U. Walter to join with a select group of architects in forming the American Institution of Architects (the forerunner of the American Institute of Architects.) Although the initial organization was short-lived, Dakin's membership indicated that he was one of the dozen leading architects of the day. His ability to create original compositions using the Greek, Gothic and Egyptian Revival vocabularies, particularly as seen in the Bank of Louisville, prompted Talbot Hamlin to describe his work as "forceful" and "brilliant."

—BETH SULLEBARGER

DANCE, George the Elder.

British. Born in London, England, 1695. Died in 1768. Father was Giles Dance, a stonemason; married Elizabeth Gould, daughter of surveyor James Gould, 1719; son was George Dance, Jr., also an architect. Apprenticed to his father. Clerk of the Works, City of London, and surveyor of Bridge House Estate, 1735.

Chronology of Works
All in England unless noted
* Approximate dates
† Work no longer exists

1725-29	St. Botolph's Church, Bishopsgate, London (rebuilding, with James Gould)
1730	Gould Square, London (with James Gould)
1734-37	Fleet Market, London†
1737-40	St. Leonard's Church, Shoreditch, London
1737-42	Mansion House, London
1737	Skinners' Hall, Dowgate Hill, London
1740-43	Market House, Coleraine, County Londonderry, Ireland†
1741-44	St. Botolph's Church, Aldgate, London
1743-46	St. Matthew's Church, Bethnal Green, London
1746	Lambs Conduit, Holborn, London†
1747-50	Corn Market, Mark Lane, London†
1748	Cowper's Court, Smithfield, London (two coffee houses and two residences for the second Earl Cowper)†
1748-51*	Surgeons Hall, Old Bailey, London†
1750-51	St. Luke's Hospital, Old Street, London
1751	Gable in the southeast transept of the Canterbury Cathedral (rebuilding)
1754-55	St. Mary's Church, Faversham, Kent (rebuilding of nave)
1758-66	London Bridge (rebuilding, with Robert Taylor)†
1765-66	Great Synagogue, Duke's Place, Aldgate, London†

Publications

BOOKS ABOUT DANCE

CURL, JAMES STEVENS: *The Londonderry Plantation 1609-1914: The History, Architecture, and Planning of the Estates of the City of London and its Livery Companies in Ulster.* Chichester, England, 1986.
PERKS, SYDNEY: *The History of the Mansion House.* Cambridge, England, 1922.
STROUD, DOROTHY: *George Dance, Architect: 1741-1825.* London, 1971.

ARTICLES ABOUT DANCE

STRATTON, A.: "Two Forgotten Buildings by the Dances." *Architectural Review* 40 (1916): 21.

George Dance, Senior, was the son of Giles Dance, mason of London and freeman of the Merchant Taylor's Company. George joined his father in the business of Messrs Dance & Co., and was also made free of the Merchant Taylor's Company in 1725, when he was described as a ''stonecutter'' of Moorfields. Thus, like Robert Taylor (1714-88), Dance had close connections with the City of London, and his status was further enhanced when in 1719 he married Elizabeth, daughter of James Gould (died 1734), surveyor to the South Sea Company, and former associate of Colen Campbell (1676-1729). From 1725 to 1729 Dance and Gould joined forces to rebuild the Church of St. Botolph, Bishopsgate, and the two men may have been involved in the laying out of Gould Square in 1730.

In 1735 Dance was appointed clerk of the works to the City of London and surveyor of the Bridge House Estate. His status as clerk of the works gave him a monopoly on the city's architectural commissions, and in 1737 his designs for the new Mansion House were accepted; these included a handsome portico on a podium and a very grand interior. It is a source of considerable speculation as to why Dance should have prevailed over architects of the status of James Gibbs, Giacomo Leoni and John James, but it is clear that his advantage as clerk was such to ensure that he got the job. One amusing story relates to the submission of a design by Lord Burlington, based on the work of Andrea Palladio. The Court of Common Council rejected the design on the grounds that Palladio was a Papist. There may indeed be a grain of truth in this, for the City of London had lost considerable sums through its Ulster Estates being severely damaged in the course of the 17th century in the Great Rebellion of 1641 and during the Jacobite Wars from 1689, so Papists were certainly regarded with less than favor in the city. However, the explanation is much more mundane: the holder of the post of clerk of the works to the city had a great advantage over any other candidate, no matter how distinguished. In any case, Dance rose to the occasion with a design for the Mansion House that had a certain quality of civic dignity, although Burlington's opinion of it was very low. The ''Egyptian'' Hall in the Mansion House was rightly regarded as a fine example of the type, much admired in the first half of the 18th century.

Dance's architectural style was influenced by the work of Christopher Wren and James Gibbs, and by the omnipresent Palladianism promoted by Burlington and his circle with such success. Dance's Church of St. Leonard, Shoreditch (1736-40), for example, has a steeple that clearly owes much to Wren's St. Mary-le-Bow, but there is another, more severe and antique note in the front of the church with its five-bay, four-column giant Tuscan order and pediment forming the grave and noble prostyle portico.

Among other works carried out by Dance were the Fleet Market (1734-37), redecorations of parts of the interior of the Skinners' Hall (1737), the Church of St. Botolph, Aldgate (1741-44), St. Matthew's Church, Bethnal Green (1743-46), Lamb's Conduit, Holborn (1746), the Corn Market, Mark Lane (1747-50), Cowper's Court, Smithfield; two houses and two coffee houses (1748), the Surgeon's Hall, Old Bailey (ca. 1748-51), St. Luke's Hospital, Old Street (1750-51), alterations to London Bridge including the removal of houses on it (1756-66), and the Great Synagogue, Aldgate (1765-66).

For the Honourable Irish Society, Dance designed the Market House with Court House for the City of London's settlement at Coleraine, County Londonderry, erected from 1742 to 1744. This was two stories high with a courtroom on the first floor above an arcaded ground floor (described and illustrated in James Stevens Curl, *The Londonderry Plantation 1609-1914*, pp. 420-21).

There is no question but that Dance was a man of great diligence and integrity. He was able to hand over his office to his son, George Dance, Junior (1741-1825), before he died. The younger Dance was a great architect, whose masterpiece was Newgate Prison (1770-80). All in all, however, the elder Dance's work was characterized by a certain stolid and respectable Georgian mien, not without nobility, and not without spirit, but with one foot in the backward-looking ''Wrenaissance'' and one in a tentative Palladian manner.

Dance was buried in the Church of St. Luke, Old Street, a building on which he had worked as a mason 40 years before, and which had been designed by his rival John James (ca. 1672-1746) in collaboration with Nicholas Hawksmoor (ca. 1661-1736).

—JAMES STEVENS CURL

DANCE, George the Younger.

British. Born in London, England, 1741. Died 14 January 1825. Youngest son of the architect George Dance the Elder (1695-1768). Architectural training in Italy, 1758-64; member of the Accademia di San Lucca, Rome. Succeeded his father as clerk of city works, London, 1768; drafted the Building Act with the architect Robert Taylor, 1774; master of Merchant Taylor's Company; professor of architecture, 1798-1806. Original member of the Royal Academy, 1768; fellow of the Royal Society and Society of Antiquaries.

Chronology of Works
All in England
* *Approximate dates*
† *Work no longer exists*

1765-67	All Hallows Church, London Wall, London
1767-68	Crescent, Circus and America Square, Minories, London
1768	Pitzhanger Manor, Ealing (additions)
1769-78	Newgate Prison, London†
1768-1816	Finsbury Estate Development, London
1769-74	Sessions House, Old Bailey, London†
1777-79	Guildhall, London (Council Chamber)†
1779*-81	Cranbury, Hampshire (additions)
1782-85	St. Luke's Hospital, London†
1785	Borough Compter, London
1786-94	Lansdowne House, London†
1787-89	Giltspur Street Compter, London†
1787-89	Guildhall, London (chamberlain's court)†
1788-89	Boydell's Shakespeare Gallery, London†
1788-89	Guildhall, London (facade)
1788-89	Honey Lane Market, London†
1789-90	St. Bartholemew-the-Less, London (nave)
1790-1807	Skinner Street, Holborn, London†
1793-95	Martin's Bank, Lombard Street, London†
1793-1804	Pickett Place, The Strand, London†
1795-96	Mansion House, London (alterations)
1795-97	Guildhall, London (Justice Rooms)†
1796-1802	West India Docks and Limestone Canal, London
1796-1810	Alfred Place, London (with north and south crescents)†
1798	Billingsgate Market, London†

1802-08	Cole Orton Hall, Leicestershire,
1803-06	Stratton Park, Hampshire (remodeling; portico survives)†
1804-05	Theatre Royal, Bath
1805-13	Royal College of Surgeons, London
1806	All Saints Church, East Stratton, Hampshire (rebuilding)
1806-07	Cottages, East Stratton, Hampshire
1806-08	St. Mary's Church, Micheldever, Hampshire
1807-09	House, 143 Piccadilly, London
1812*	Laxton Hall, Northamptonshire (additions)
1812-17	Ashburnham Place, Sussex†
1814-15	Kidbrooke, Sussex (alterations)

Publications

BOOKS ABOUT DANCE

George Dance the Elder and Younger. Exhibition catalog. Shoreditch, England, 1972.

SERVICE, ALASTAIR: *The Architects of London.* London, 1979.

STROUD, DOROTHY: *George Dance, Architect: 1741-1825.* London, 1971.

TEYSSOT, GEORGES: *Città e utopia nell'illuminismo inglese: George Dance il giovane.* Rome, 1974.

ARTICLES ABOUT DANCE

ANGELL, SAMUEL: "Sketch of the Professional Life of George Dance, Architect." *Builder* 5 (1847): 333-335.

BLOMFIELD, REGINALD: "The Architect of Newgate." *Studies in Architecture* (1905).

"George Dance." *Official Architect* (August 1949).

HUGO-BRUNT, MICHAEL: "George Dance as Town-Planner (1768-1814)." *Journal of the Society of Architectural Historians* 14 (1955): 13-22.

KALMAN, H. D.: "George Dance the Younger." Ph.D. dissertation. Princeton University, New Jersey, 1972.

ROSENAU, HELEN: "George Dance the Younger." *Journal of the Royal Institute of British Architects* 3rd series, 54 (August 1947): 502-507.

*

In terms of sheer stylistic audacity, the younger George Dance must be counted among the most original English architects of all time, as well as an Enlightenment figure whose international stature still needs to be defined. That he is not better known is, however, understandable. His father, George the Elder (1695-1768), and he between them held the clerkship of works to the City of London for more than 80 years: the son often returned to rehouse or repair institutions and buildings the father had served, among them St. Luke's Hospital, Newgate Prison, the Corporation (later Royal College) of Surgeons and the Mansion House, and their careers were not disentangled until the 20th century. Dance's major institutional buildings, Newgate Prison (1769-78) and St. Luke's Hospital for the Insane on Old Street (1782-79), are now demolished and were anyway almost instantly discredited by a new breed of professional reformer that distrusted architects' pretensions to institutional expertise. Dance's planning of the City of London's streets, squares, crescents and waterfronts was less spectacular in scope, and included dwellings more modest than John Nash's later work to the west. Above all, Dance was overshadowed by the work of his friend and, briefly, pupil John Soane (1753-1837).

It now seems clear, as John Summerson pointed out, that the "Soane style" is actually the creation of two men. In the years from 1791 to 1806, when he was often working closely with Dance, Soane worked out some of his favorite systems and motifs, but the same incised ornament, top-lighting from oculi, and wafer-thin pendentives arcing smoothly into vaults had already appeared in Dance's designs for such Guildhall interiors as the Common Council Chamber (1777-78) and for Cranbury Park, Hampshire (completed in 1781). Soane hinted at a more fundamental debt in the third of his *Lectures* as professor of architecture at the Royal Academy, in discussing the famous entablature inside All Hallow's London Wall (rebuilt in 1765-67), which Dance reduced to a frieze and minimal cornice. Soane was at first shocked, he claimed, by the omission of the architrave, but then concluded that "not only the eye was pleased but the judgement was satisfied with this example of refined taste." We are left to assume that the great reductionist had been set on his path.

Dance's decision was a matter of "taste" in the widest sense. To his great friend Joseph Faringdon, Dance once "derided the prejudice of limiting Designs in Architecture within certain rules which in fact, though held out as laws had never been satisfactorily explained." The re-examination of orthodoxy in terms of what was demanded by rationality and need was the project of the European Enlightenment, in which Dance represented English architecture. He did so not only by virtue of his critical and selective eye, but for his cheerful willingness to shock with strange, hybrid styles, on the one hand, and no style at all on the other. Thus James Wyatt (1747-1813), hardly a stickler himself, thought that Dance had "quitted grammatical art for Fancies" at the south front of the Guildhall (designed in 1788). Dance produced an extraordinary facade which managed simultaneous nods at the Gothic architecture of the 15th-century original, and that of Mughal India (possibly in an acknowledgment, correct in principle, that the two styles were both influenced by Islamic architecture).

With regard to Newgate Prison, however, Wyatt spoke of a "specimen of true taste in design," and Soane, more precisely, of "characteristic beauties." In other words, Newgate was not beautiful—it was terrifying, but the character of terror was beautifully imparted with very little reference to architectural style as conventionally understood. With the rebuilding of Newgate, England's largest prison, Dance won international fame: it was one of the few English buildings to be represented in J. N. L. Durand's taxonomy of building types, the *Recueil et parallèle des édifices de tout genre* (1800). Construction began in 1770; ten years later, the Gordon rioters burned the building down, and it was rebuilt with few alterations. John Howard had in the meantime begun to publish his exhaustive surveys of institutional buildings: Newgate's plan was not what would soon be defined as progressive—with prisoner wards, not cells, it was just as conducive to the formation of subcultures as its predecessor. It was for its architectural character that it was ranked among the masterpieces of the century by Dance's contemporaries. As Reginald Blomfield wrote in 1905, "The task before [Dance] was to get some architectural quality out of a gigantic wall," 300 feet long on the south front. In fact, in an early design (April 1768), Dance provided huge expanses of completely blank, rusticated wall on each side of the central Keeper's House. This was apparently too much even for a frugal building committee, and the contract elevation of the following year reveals more incident. Dance added one obvious emblem of confinement, relief festoons of fetters in panels above the two prisoners' entrances; and, on each side, two large blind tabernacles (in which statues from the old Newgate were eventually installed) within arches. This device's form and rustication were adapted from quite different contexts, Andrea Palladio's Palazzo Thiene in Vicenza (after 1542) and Giulio Romano's Palazzo del Tè (begun in 1525) and own house (ca. 1540) at Mantua. Newgate's introverted, menacing character as civil fortress and deterrent was not troubled by these grimly elegant quotations. Dance once told Faringdon that "Architecture unshackled would afford to the greatest genius the greatest opportunity of producing the most powerful efforts of the human mind." That realization, combined with genial self-confidence, historical sophistication and a fine mind, took him very far.

—CHRISTINE STEVENSON

D'ARONCO, Raimondo.

Italian. Born in Genoa, Italy, 1857. Died in San Remo, Italy, 1932. Father was a building contractor. Apprenticed as a mason in Graz, Austria, for three years; attended the Accademia delle Belli Arte, Venice. Professor of design, Accademia delle Belli Arte, Genoa, 1880; moved to Turkey, where he was official architect to Sultan Abdul Hamid II, 1894-98; elected to Italian parliament, 1910; associated with the Politecnico, Naples, 1911-17.

Chronology of Works
† *Work no longer exists*

1896	Tophane Fountain, Istanbul, Turkey
1902	Pavilions for Turin Exhibition, Turin, Italy†
1903	Mosque in Karakeny Square, Galata, Turkey
1903	Pavilion of Fine Arts, National Exhibition, Udine, Italy
1905	Italian Embassy Summer Residence, Therapia, Turkey
1907	Fountain and Library, Yildiz, Turkey
1907	Santoro House, Istanbul, Turkey
1908-32	Palazzo Comunale, Udine, Italy

Publications

BOOKS ABOUT D'ARONCO

NICOLETTI, MANFREDI: *Raimondo D'Aronco*. Milan, 1955.
NICOLETTI, MANFREDI: *D'Aronco e l'architettura liberty*. Bari, Italy, 1982.
PEVSNER, NIKOLAUS, and RICHARDS, J. M. (eds.): *The Anti-Rationalists*. London, 1973.
RUSSELL, FRANK (ed.): *Art Nouveau Architecture*. London, 1979.

There is very little in the early work of Raimondo D'Aronco to hint at the dramatic change that was to take place in the direction of his career in middle age. In an initial series of competitions and expositions that he entered throughout Italy when he was young, he consistently produced highly competent but relatively unoriginal designs in the Beaux-Arts style that was then so popular. In 1894, however, a happy accident of history took him to Turkey, and in the 15 years that followed, he paradoxically seemed to find the ideal atmosphere for the expression of a previously untested talent, working within a social and cultural context that was totally foreign to his own.

At the time of his introduction to that culture, Istanbul had long since passed its zenith as the center of the Ottoman Empire,

but it had also just embarked on a campaign of modernization that was intended to end its long isolation from the West. A series of reforms, or *Tanzimat,* had been enacted in 1827, and those new laws radically altered the Oriental customs and manners of the city, and quickened the pace of modernization. New railways, including the celebrated Orient Express, were being built to connect the Ottoman capital to Europe, and the wealth of trade that they made possible began to transform what had been a walled, medieval city.

A great deal of that transformation was taking place in the Beyoglu district of Pera, where many of D'Aronco's buildings were located. The foreign banks that were attracted by the new wealth were just beginning to operate there, and the entrepreneurs who followed settled in that district to be near the banks. Abdul Hamid II, who initially commissioned D'Aronco to work for him, was only the fourth sultan to live outside of the Topkapi Palace, which traditionally had served as the royal household since Mehmet the Conqueror had had it built soon after the conquest of Constantinople in 1453. By having D'Aronco extend the Yeldiz Palace, the sultan was clearly reiterating his wish to continue to break with the past and to adopt a foreign style.

In addition to the inspiration provided by the novel and exotic setting, as well as by the heady atmosphere of wealth and transformation that then prevailed in Istanbul, D'Aronco also seems to have experienced what his biographer Manfredi Nicoletti called a "crisis of conscience" following the Chicago World's Columbian Exposition of 1893, and the excitement caused by Louis Sullivan's Transportation Building there. In forsaking the stolid conservatism of the Beaux-Arts for the organic vitality of art noveau at that point in his life, D'Aronco was apparently not only responding to the example of the man whom Frank Lloyd Wright had called "*lieber Meister,*" but was also reflecting an upsurge in that new aesthetic direction on the Continent as well.

In Austria, where D'Aronco had traveled extensively while still in architecture school, the *Künstlerkolonie* of Joseph Olbrich and the Vienna Secession movement were in full swing at the turn of the century, and artists like Antonio Gaudí, Hector Guimard, Victor Horta and Gustav Klimt were at the peak of their creativity. Prior to, and eventually in tandem with, the more radical and far-reaching efforts of the Modern Movement to break through the ponderous eclecticism that had dominated the late 19th century, art nouveau sought a return to natural forms in the belief that they alone could purify and simplify architecture.

As interpreted by D'Aronco, however, that search took on a deeper and far more contextual dimension, making him one of the first Western architects working in the Middle East to attempt to translate sympathetically regional forms into a more internationally intelligible language. His initial attempts in that direction, such as a convalescent home in a district of Istanbul called Sisli (1899), were tentative yet commendable forays into previously uncharted territory that had to wait for others, such as Sedat Hakki Eldem and Doğan Kuban, for full analysis.

Several houses along the Bosporus that followed the convalescent-home project also showed D'Aronco's growing awareness of and sensitivity to vernacular forms. Each of these houses demonstrated his development of the structural invention that is typical of the traditional Turkish house, where long roof overhangs, or *cikma,* evolved as a result of narrow, irregular village streets and building lots of various sizes, allowing builders to change the shape and area of the upper stories of a house while adhering to a restricted property line on the ground floor.

The masterpiece of D'Aronco's time in Istanbul, however, and perhaps of his entire career, is the Şeyh Zafir Tomb in Yildiz. The building, which actually utilizes a Mamluk building type called a *sabil-kuttab* by combining a mausoleum with a library and public fountain, was coincidentally built soon after a meeting between Olbrich and D'Aronco in Paris in 1900. Improbably, but quite convincingly, the building marries art nouveau plasticity with an Islamic and ultimately Altaic typology, and brings out the best attributes of each. Interesting parallels may also be seen in both the rendering techniques and regionalism of this work and several of the early projects of Frank Lloyd Wright, who also attempted to evolve new forms out of existing vernacular styles. While the tomb in Yildiz and a small number of other projects that followed it are all that remain of D'Aronco's translations, Wright went on to work out that same theme in his Prairie houses, with far more notoriety.

Prior to leaving Turkey in 1910, D'Aronco was able to expand on his growing interest in regionalism by designing a hospital in Medina, Saudi Arabia, which was still part of the Ottoman Empire. The impressive evidence of his adaptability seen in this project did not continue on his return to Italy, however, leaving but limited testimony to this gifted architect's considerable talent standing in Turkey today.

—JAMES STEELE

DAVIS, Alexander Jackson.

American. Born in New York, 1803. Died in 1892. Educated at Antique School, Philosophical Society (later merged with Academy of Design), and at the Athenaeum, Boston, 1827; later at the American Academy of Fine Arts and New York Drawing Association, New York. Served as apprentice designer under Josiah R. Bradley, New York; draftsman, Ithiel Town's office, New York; partner with Town, New York, 1828; opened own office, New York, 1844.

Chronology of Works
All in the United States
* Approximate dates
† Work no longer exists

1829-31	Highwood (Sachem's Wood), New Haven, Connecticut†
1831-32	West Presbyterian Church, New York City (with Ithiel Town)†
1831-33*	Aaron N. Skinner House, New Haven, Connecticut
1831-33	Samuel Ward House, New York City (with Town)†
1831-35	Indiana State Capitol, Indianapolis, Indiana (with Town)†
1832-34*	Glen Ellen, Towson, Maryland (with Town)†
1833-40	North Carolina State Capitol, Raleigh, North Carolina (with Town and others)
1833-42	United States Customhouse, New York City (with Town and Others)
1834-48	Lunatic Asylum, Blackwell's Island, New York City (partially built, by others)
1835-36	Lyceum of Natural History, New York City (with Town)†
1835-36	Abby Salisbury House, New Haven, Connecticut†
1835-37	Dutch Reformed Church, Newburgh, New York (with Russell Warren)
1835-37	New York University Chapel, New York City†
1835-38	First Unitarian Church, New Bedford, Massachusetts (with Warren)
1836	Wyllys Warner House, New Haven, Connecticut†
1836-37	Mary Prichard House, New Haven, Connecticut
1836-39	Belmont, New Haven, Connecticut†

1836-51	Blithewood, Barrytown, New York (remodeling and new structures)†
1838-40	Millbrook, Tarrytown, New York†
1837-67	Lyndhurst, Tarrytown, New York
1841	Federal Vanderburgh Cottage, Rhinecliff, New York†
1842-44	Samuel E. Lyon House, White Plains, New York†
1842-44	Wadsworth Atheneum, Hartford, Connecticut (facade, with Town)
1842-49	Kenwood, Albany, New York†
1843-44	Henry H. Elliot House and Robert C. Townsend House, New York City†
1843-44	Church of the Holy Cross, Troy, New York (with N. B. Warren)
1843-67	Montgomery Place, Barrytown, New York (additions and new structures; some work survives)
1844	Henry Delamater Cottage, Rhinebeck, New York
1844	Blandwood, Greensboro, North Carolina (remodeling)
1844-45	W. Coventry H. Waddell House, New York City†
1844-52	University of North Carolina, Chapel Hill, North Carolina (additions and Smith Hall)
1845-46	London Terrace, New York City†
1845-47*	William J. Rotch House, New Bedford, Massachusetts
1845-48	Belmead, Powhatan County, Virginia
1845-48	John Cox Stevens House, New York City†
1846-47	Charles A. Davis House, New York City†
1846-47*	Henry A. Kent House, Brooklyn, New York†
1846-48	Walnut Wood, Bridgeport, Connecticut†
1847-48	James W. Phillips House and Charles C. Taber House, New York City†
1848	Lewis B. Brown House, Rahway, New York†
1848	Academy, Rome, New York†
1848-49	County Courthouse, Powhatan, Virginia
1848-49	Malbone, Newport, Rhode Island
1848-61	Virginia Military Institute, Lexington, Virginia (some work survives)
1849	Cottage Lawn, Oneida, New York
1850-52	Belmont, near Belleville, New Jersey†
1850-52	Elm Street Arsenal, New York City†
1850-52	Loudoun, Lexington, Kentucky
1850-55	North Carolina Hospital for the Insane, Raleigh, North Carolina (some work survives)
1851-52	Locust Grove, Poughkeepsie, New York (remodeling, with Morse)
1851-52	Winyah, New Rochelle, New York
1851-53	Yale College Alumni Hall, New Haven, Connecticut†
1851-54	Hawkwood, Green Springs, Virginia
1852-54	Whitby, Rye, New York
1853-54	Town Hall and Courthouse, Bridgeport, Connecticut (since altered)
1853-63	Edgewater, Barrytown, New York (addition and new structures; some work survives),
1854-55	John Munn House, Utica, New York
1854-57	Grace Hill, Brooklyn, New York
1854-57	Ingleside, Dobbs Ferry, New York
1856-59	Chambers Building, Davidson College, Davidson, North Carolina†
1858-60	Castlewood, West Orange, New Jersey
1857-66	Llewellyn Park, West Orange, New Jersey (gatehouses and other structures; some work survives)
1858-59	House of Mansions, New York City†
1859-74	Sans Souci, New Rochelle, New York

Publications

BOOKS BY DAVIS

Rural Residences. New York, 1838.

BOOKS ABOUT DAVIS

ANDREWS, WAYNE: *Architecture, Ambition and Americans: A Social History of American Architecture.* New York, 1964.
DUNLAP, WILLIAM: *History of the Rise and Progress of the Arts of Design in the United States.* Boston, 1918.
NEWTON, ROGER HALE: *Town and Davis, Architects: Pioneers in American Revivalist Architecture, 1812-1870.* New York, 1942.
PECK, AMELIA (ed.): *Alexander Jackson Davis, American Architect 1803-1882.* New York, 1992.
PIERSON, WILLIAM H., JR.: "American Neoclassicism: The Greek Revival." In *American Buildings and Their Architects: The Colonial and Neo-Classical Styles.* Garden City, New York, 1978.
PIERSON, WILLIAM H., JR.: "Alexander Jackson Davis and the Picturesque." In *American Buildings and Their Architects: Technology and the Picturesque: The Corporate and Early Gothic Styles.* Garden City, New York, 1978.

ARTICLES ABOUT DAVIS

ALLCOTT, JOHN V.: "Architect A. J. Davis in North Carolina: His Launching at the University." *North Carolina Architect* 20, Nos. 11-12 (1973): 10-15.
ANDREWS, WAYNE: "Alexander Jackson Davis." *Architectural Review* 109 (May 1951): 307-312.
CARD, M.: "Alexander Jackson Davis and the Printed Specification." *College Art Journal* 12 (Summer 1953): 354-359.
DAVIES, JANE B.: "A. J. Davis' Projects for a Patent Office Building, 1832-1834." *Journal of the Society of Architectural Historians* 24 (1965): 229-251.
DAVIES, JANE B.: "Alexander J. Davis: Architect of Lyndhurst." *Historic Preservation* 17, No. 2 (1965): 54-59.
DAVIES, JANE B.: "Gothic Revival Furniture Designs of Alexander J. Davis." *Antiques* 111 (1977): 1014-1027.
DONNELL, EDNA: "A. J. Davis and the Gothic Revival." *Metropolitan Museum Studies* 5 (September 1936): 183-233.

*

At a time when most native American architects entered the profession through the building trades or by apprenticeship to a practicing architect, A. J. Davis' early training and sensibilities were those of an artist. He probably studied at the American Academy of Fine Arts (perhaps with painter John Trumbull), at the New York Association of Artists and at the Antique School of the National Academy of Design. Throughout his life, Davis remained part of an artistic and intellectual milieu that included the painters of the Hudson River school and writer Washington Irving. Davis' aptitude for watercolor rendering and perspective drawing strongly affected his design process. Perhaps because he drew so well, Davis' strength was design, not theory, and many of his best buildings were composed around their perspective or "pictorial" effects.

In 1829 architect Ithiel Town made Davis his partner; it was the first notable architectural partnership in the United States. Davis' brilliant design and drawing abilities compensated for Town's lack thereof; to the partnership Town brought maturity, engineering experience and business acumen. While building his patented lattice-truss bridges all over the country, Town

acquired an extensive array of clients. From their New York office the firm conducted a national architectural practice which Davis continued even after the termination of the partnership in 1835 (renewed again briefly in 1842-43). Though the majority of Davis' buildings are in the New York area, he eventually had clients as far south as New Orleans, as far west as Michigan, Ohio and Kentucky, and along the eastern seaboard in Maryland, Virginia and North Carolina.

Davis' personality presents an interesting dichotomy: that of a romantic artist driven by highly organized working methods. He was, for example, the first American architect to use standardized, printed specifications, and the meticulousness of his surviving office records makes him one of the best-documented architects of the 19th century.

Davis' designs present a complex amalgam of international influences, combined with a keen sense of American vernacular traditions, social customs and environmental factors. His inspiration usually began with the pages of European architectural publications. Though Davis never left the United States, Town traveled in Europe (1829 and 1843), and collected an art, architecture and engineering library in excess of 10,000 volumes, the largest of its kind in America of the period. These books kept Davis abreast of international developments. While he worked in all the historical revival styles current in the early 19th century, and on a great range of building types, Davis' most original contributions occurred in three categories: his Greco-Italianate institutional buildings, his picturesque-Gothic country houses, and his small Gothic and Italianate villas and cottages.

In the 1830s Town and Davis contributed significantly to the refinement of Greek Revival architecture in America. They designed state capitols for Connecticut, Indiana and North Carolina, and submitted competition designs for the Ohio Statehouse which probably influenced its final form. These edifices, and their New York Customs House, exhibited Greek temple exteriors of traditional trabeated structure, often with amphiprostyle porticoes, but with the colonnades of the flanks reduced to huge square pilasters or *antae* (later called "pilastrades"). Davis eventually invented a unique window to be used between the pilasters. It ran in a continuous vertical plane, embracing several stories, the floor levels marked on the exterior only by shallow wooden panels nearly flush with the glass. He called these "Davisean" windows; they represent his contribution to the problem of transforming Greek temples into functional public buildings. Though the exteriors of Town and Davis' public buildings were of a severe, trabeated, Grecian character, the interiors invariably contained sophisticated vaults and domes based on Roman arcuated structure.

Realizing the limited potential of the Greek temple units with their trabeated exteriors, Davis began to experiment with designs that fused classical sources from antiquity to the Renaissance. During the 1840s and 1850s, he used Etruscan-Italianate temples as the central units of institutional complexes composed of interconnecting pavilions and wings, often intended to enclose huge central courtyards. Davis derived the multipart elevations from Andrea Palladio's villas, and punctuated them with "Davisean" windows. Among the best of this type were the Pauper Lunatic Asylum on Blackwell's Island, New York City; the North Carolina Hospital for the Insane at Raleigh; and Davidson College, North Carolina. These complexes were highly flexible and additive, allowing construction in stages as the institution they housed grew, or as public funding for expansion became available.

Davis also excelled at designing large Gothic Revival villas. He developed striking elevations by synthesizing the forms and details he found in early-19th-century publications on English

Gothic architecture by such authors as John Britton and Augustus Charles Pugin. These details he composed with the organic asymmetry advocated by English picturesque-landscape theorists such as Richard Payne Knight, Uvedale Price and Humphry Repton. Surprisingly, Davis developed his Gothic villa plans by a system of geometric addition and subdivision which he probably took from the *Précis des Leçons d'Architecture* (1802-05) of French rational-classical architect J.N.L. Durand. From his somewhat remote position in America, but with wide access to European publications, Davis fused French and English sources in ways that never would have occurred to the architects of either country.

Davis' large Gothic villas displayed greater sensitivity to site and landscape conditions than any previous American domestic architecture. He wrapped the villa exteriors with carefully integrated veranda systems, which he called "umbrages." These created interpenetrating zones of exterior and interior space, and captured fine landscape views. He also developed a typology of villa plans for specific sites. For limited suburban sites he used a frontally oriented plan with centralized circulation; for expansive suburban or rural sites a sculptural Greek-cross plan; and for his numerous clients with Hudson River or other riverfront sites, a "river plan" consisting of a Latin cross with short and long axes, the short axis containing the entry, the long axis containing the major public rooms and laid out parallel to the twin lines of the public road at the front of the site, and the river behind. Davis developed the opposing road and river elevations into striking asymmetrical compositions of different characters, the road fronts closed and castle-like, the river fronts open and airy. Among Davis' most important surviving Gothic villas are Lyndhurst in Tarrytown, New York, Belmead in Powhatan County, Virginia, Ingleside and Whitby in Westchester County, New York, and Loudoun in Lexington, Kentucky. Davis also designed large Italianate villas, such as Grace Hill in Brooklyn, using many of the same design principles as his Gothic villas. The organic asymmetry, landscape orientation and spatial fluidity of Davis' picturesque villas formed his major contributions to American domestic architecture. His legacy is evident in the Shingle and Prairie style houses of the late 19th and early 20th centuries.

While Davis adapted European historical styles to American circumstances with great facility, he also looked carefully at American vernacular traditions. He was the first American architect to celebrate the nature of wood as a material. He designed prototypical "log cabins" with the rustic porticoes of primitive classical temples, and often employed the vertical board-and-batten siding of utilitarian vernacular structures in his designs for cottages.

Though Davis published a few of his cottage and villa designs in *Rural Residences* (1837-38), his only book, his designs gained much wider circulation through the publications of prolific landscape gardener Andrew Jackson Downing. Many of Davis' designs for "pointed style" Gothic cottages and "bracketed" Italianate villas appeared in Downing's journal, *The Horticulturist,* and in his popular pattern books, such as *Cottage Residences* (1842) and *The Architecture of Country Houses* (1850). This publicity greatly expanded Davis' practice, resulted in countless emulations of his designs by regional builders and architects, and made him the most influential architect of suburban and country houses in 19th-century America.

Though Davis lived until 1892, his career ended in the 1860s. Several factors conspired against him. Downing died in 1852, leaving Davis with nowhere to publish his designs. His practice had become precariously dependent upon country-house commissions in the North, and upon his southern commissions for both domestic and public buildings. The Civil War (1861-65)

terminated his southern practice, and the increasing urbanism of the North reduced the market for country houses. Davis found it impossible to reenter the urban practice he had neglected. His training in 18th-century picturesque theory and the historical revival styles was not suitable to the structural, programmatic and stylistic complexities required in later-19th-century urban buildings. Davis' old-fashioned mode of self-guided architectural education through European books could not compete with the numerous European immigrant architects arriving in late-19th-century America, with American architects like Richard Morris Hunt or H. H. Richardson trained at the École des Beaux-Arts, or with the establishment of formal architectural training in American universities beginning in the 1860s. One of the country's most creative designers from 1830 to 1860, Davis exerted no significant influence from 1860 to 1892.

Since the 1940s, scholarly interest in Davis has evolved, abetted by the 1964 acquisition of Lyndhurst, his largest Gothic villa, by the National Trust for Historic Preservation. Davis' papers survive in great quantities in public collections, but the number and geographical extent of his commissions have presented scholars with a formidable task of evaluation, and a truly satisfying and comprehensive monograph on his work has yet to appear.

—PATRICK SNADON

DEANE and WOODWARD.

Irish. Thomas Deane: Born 1792. Died 1871. Mayor of Cork. Knighted, 1830. Partner of Benjamin Woodward (1815-61). Deane was partner with his son, Thomas Newenham Deane (1828-99), from 1850.

Chronology of Works
† *Work no longer exists*

1845-50	Queen's College (now University College), Cork, Ireland
1847-50	Lunatic Asylum, Killarney, Ireland
1853-57	Trinity College Museum, Dublin, Ireland
1855-57	Dundrum Police Court and Barracks, Dublin, Ireland
1855-58	Crown Life Insurance Offices, Bridge Street, London†
1855-61	Museum of Natural History, Oxford, England
1856	Llysdulas (house), near Llanwennlyfo, Anglesey, Wales†
1856-57	Union Society Rooms, Oxford, England
1856-58	St. Anne's Parochial Schools, Dublin, Ireland†
1857	Government Offices Competition Design, London, England
1857	Oxford Union, Oxford, England
1857-59	Dundrum Schools, Dublin, Ireland
1857-59	Middleton Hall, Oxford, England
1857ff.	Brownsbarn, Thomastown, Ireland
1858ff.	Clontra, County Dublin, Ireland
1858ff.	Glandore, County Dublin, Ireland
1858-59	St. Austin's Abbey, County Carlow, Ireland
1858-61	Kildare Street Club, Dublin, Ireland
1858-62	Kilkenny Castle, Ireland (alterations)
1859-61	15 Upper Philmore Gardens, London, England†
1860-62	Trinity College Library, Dublin, Ireland

Deane and Woodward: Museum of Natural History, Oxford, England, 1855-61

Works by Thomas Newenham Deane:

1861-64   Cathedral (Church of Ireland), Tuam, Galway, Ireland
1862-65   Meadow Building, Christ Church College, Oxford, England
1885-90   National Library and Museum, Dublin, Ireland (with his son, Thomas Manley Deane)

Publications

BOOKS ABOUT DEANE and WOODWARD

ACLAND, HENRY, and RUSKIN, JOHN: *The Oxford Museum.* London, 1859.
BLAU, EVE: *Ruskinian Gothic: The Architecture of Deane and Woodward, 1845-1861.* Princeton, New Jersey, 1982.
COOK, E. T., and WEDDERBURN, ALEXANDER (eds.): *The Works of John Ruskin.* 39 vols. London, 1903-12.
EASTLAKE, CHARLES: *A History of the Gothic Revival.* London, 1872.
HERSEY, GEORGE L.: *High Victorian Gothic: A Study in Associationism.* Baltimore, 1972.
HITCHCOCK, HENRY-RUSSELL: *Early Victorian Architecture in Britain.* New York, 1954.
MUTHESIUS, STEFAN: *The High Victorian Movement in Architecture 1850-1870.* London, 1972.
RICHARDSON, DOUGLAS: *Gothic Revival Architecture in Ireland.* New York, 1978.

ARTICLES ABOUT DEANE and WOODWARD

CURRAN, C. P.: "Benjamin Woodward, Ruskin, and the O'Sheas." *Studies* 29 (1940): 255-268.
FERRIDAY, PETER: "The Oxford Museum." *Architectural Review* 132 (1962): 409-416.

*

When Thomas Deane and Benjamin Woodward took over the architectural practice of Deane's father, Sir Thomas Deane, in Cork in the 1850s, they introduced a Ruskinian Gothic style different in form and theory from evolving High Victorian Gothic. These two young architects were the earliest exponents of John Ruskin's precepts. The firm's most famous building is the Oxford University Museum; most accounts of Victorian architecture also include discussion of the Oxford Union (if only for its Pre-Raphaelite murals) and the Crown Life Company office building in London. Unfortunately, however, the bulk of the firm's work was done in Ireland and is often ignored by historians.

Deane and Woodward interpreted Ruskin's writings to call for an independent style that is essentially a symmetrical, classicized, polychromatic Venetian Gothic. The Ruskinian Gothic style they developed, which is exemplified in the Oxford Museum, took its use of particular materials, surface patterns and carved decoration from Ruskin's writings. However, Woodward, not Ruskin, was the driving force behind the program, planning, siting, composition, structural engineering and fenestration of the firm's buildings. Hence, he was the driving force behind the creation of the style associated with Deane and Woodward . Until Woodward joined the firm in 1845, its buildings, both neoclassical and neo-gothic, had been prosaic and provincial. Woodward brought to the firm's designs a new vitality, intensity and originality.

The first project produced by the firm that reveals Woodward's influence was the design for the Queen's College in Cork, (1845-50). The external massing of the building is dramatic; the examination hall, library and entry tower, all buttressed and battlemented, create an impressive asymmetrical effect on the crest of the hill on which the college is sited. Inside the quadrangle, the effect is different; all is calm, regular and at a much smaller scale. Structural determinism plays a major part in the design. The buttresses are structural, not just decorative, and the great variety of wooden roofs gives character to the ensemble. Many details are drawn from A. W. N. Pugin's published illustrations of collegiate buildings. These details were conceived separately from the plan and basic massing, and were added as the building was constructed. Consequently, the ornament there, and in the firm's subsequent buildings, is appropriate, diverse and spontaneous. Most important is that Queen's College, Cork, established the principle of expressive functional design that was to be the hallmark of the firm's work.

In 1850, T. N. Deane joined the firm, and in the following year both he and Woodward were made partners. Gradually Sir Thomas Deane turned over the management of the firm to his son and the design of the firm's commissions to Woodward. Shortly thereafter, the firm's fame was assured through the design of Trinity College Library in Dublin (1853-57). The building organizes its 10 lecture rooms, two exhibition galleries and a drawing school into a single block with symmetrical massing and a nearly symmetrical plan. The roof is low, the outline is regular, and the ornament is restrained. The building is designed to complement its Palladian neighbors. The style is eclectic. Although most decorative features are borrowed from 14th- and 15th-century Venetian palazzi, Ruskin's four favorite styles—Pisan Romanesque, early   Gothic of the western Italian republics, Venetian Gothic and English Decorated Gothic—are all present in one way or another. Although the building does not articulate its functional parts, it is nevertheless associationally and functionally expressive. Deane and Woodward chose to express the museum as storehouse of knowledge by designing it as a single monumental block.

The Trinity College Museum was the first physical expression of Ruskin's architectural teachings and was much admired by Ruskin himself. Its expressive use of architectural ornament, honest use of materials, simplified forms, clarity of outline, regular plan, new preoccupation with surface decoration, and balanced composition were radically different from the picturesque High Victorian Gothic style as practiced by William Butterfield, G. E. Street and others.

The firm's most famous work, the Oxford University Museum of Physical Sciences (1855-61), owes much to the Trinity College Museum in its symmetry, monumentality and containment. The organization of the interior spaces is also similar; in both buildings a small, centrally located foyer leads to a large skylit central hall around which subsidiary spaces are arranged peripherally. However, the character of the vast exhibition gallery that is the central space of the Oxford Museum, with its forest of iron columns supporting a glass roof, is very different from the more classical central hall in the Dublin building: also, the peripheral circulation system is much more efficient than the central-axis system employed in the Trinity College Museum.

Critics disagreed as to the style of the Oxford building; some called it Veronese Gothic; others maintained it to be English Early Decorated. The museum's steep gabled roofs, central tower, dormers and regular fenestration, however, are obvious historic references to northern medieval cloth and town halls, and the arcaded central court recalls the courtyards of Italian palaces by way of Charles Barry's Reform Club. As in the Trinity College Museum, the Oxford Museum reflects Ruskin's ideas concerning form, proportion, decoration and monumentality. His illustrations in *The Stones of Venice* and *Examples of the Architecture of Venice* were the models for the exterior windows and the gallery arcades. The building adheres to Ruskin's prescription for adopting the forms of Northern Gothic and decorating them with Italian details.

There is no question that the spirit of the Oxford Museum is closer to the mainstream of High Victorian Gothic architecture than is the Trinity College Museum. The constructional polychromy, angularity, flat wall surfaces, steep roofs and asymmetrical dependencies are consistent with the work of Butterfield, for instance. Yet the building materials, especially the exposed "Gothic" iron structure, the Venetian Gothic references and the elaborate carved surface relief decoration are derived directly from Ruskin.

Critics of the day were more interested in the building's modernity than they were in its style. In particular, the iron-and-glass structure of its central exhibition court was seen as an innovative combination of modern building materials and techniques with a historic style, Gothic, that was associated with the English psyche. The Oxford Museum, was regarded as proof positive that the Gothic style could accommodate large-scale public buildings as effectively as it could churches and houses. It was the precursor of countless Gothic monumental public buildings, and it pioneered the integration of modern engineering and the Gothic style. Although nothing similar to the Gothicized iron-and-glass roof was attempted again, the museum as a type was the progenitor of countless town halls and museums built during the High Victorian period.

—C. MURRAY SMART, JR.

DE BROSSE, Salomon.

French. Born in Verneuil-sur-Oise, 1571. Died in 1626. Father was the architect Jean de Brosse; mother was daughter of the architect Jacques I Androuet du Cerceau; also related to the architect Charles du Ry, who became his principal assistant. Trained in Verneuil. Worked for his uncle, Jacques II Androuet du Cerceau, after 1585.

Chronology of Works
All in France
* Approximate dates
† Work no longer exists

1600-08	Château of Verneuil, Oise (completion)†
1608*-15	Château of Montceaux, Seine-et-Marne (completion)†
1611-12	Hôtel de Soissons, Paris (enlargement)†
1611-19*	Château of Blérancourt, Aisne†
1612ff.	Hôtel de Bouillon, Paris (enlargement)†
1613	Château of Coulommiers-en-Brie, Seine-et-Marne†
1614ff.*	Luxembourg Palace, Paris (later altered)
1615	Hôtel Bégnine-Bernard, Paris (enlargement)†
1616	St. Gervais, Paris (west front)
1618ff.	Salle des Pas Perdus, Palais de Justice, Paris
1618	Palais du Parlement (now Palais de Justice), Rennes (principal front and rooms)
1623	Temple, Charenton†

Publications

BOOKS ABOUT DE BROSSE

BLOMFIELD, REGINALD: *A History of French Architecture, from the Reign of Charles VII till the Death of Mazarin.* London, 1911.

BLUNT, ANTHONY: *Art and Architecture in France 1500-1700.* 2nd ed. Baltimore, 1970.

BROCHARD: *Saint Gervais.* Paris, 1938.

COOPE, ROSALYS: *Salomon de Brosse and the Development of the Classical Style in French Architecture 1565-1630.* London, 1972.

HUSTIN, A.: *Le Palais du Luxembourg.* Paris, 1904.

MAROT, JEAN: *Recueil des plans, profils et élévations de plusiers palais, châteaux, églises, sépultures, grotes et hostels bâtis dans Paris.* 1665. Facsimile ed.: Farnsborough, England, 1969.

PANNIER, JACQUES: *Un architecte français au commencement du XVII siècle: Salomon de Brosse.* Paris, 1911.

*

Despite the brevity of his career, Salomon de Brosse holds an important position in the history of French architecture. His work, mostly done in the second decade of the 17th century, stands at the transition from Mannerism to classicism, and prepared the way for such classicist architects as François Mansart. Unlike his Mannerist predecessors, de Brosse thought in terms of mass rather than surface decoration, crafting a style that combined a classical monumentality with a severe sobriety. Much of our knowledge of de Brosse's work derives from drawings and engravings, not all of them reliable, since few of his buildings survive, none in an unaltered state. His small oeuvre includes Parisian hôtels, public buildings and churches, and he left a significant heritage in these types. However, his châteaux, and particularly the Palais du Luxembourg, constitute his most important contribution.

Son of the architect Jean de Brosse and connected to the Du Cerceau family of architects through his mother, he served his apprenticeship within his own family. De Brosse got a late start as an architect, because of the Wars of Religion, which created such turmoil toward the end of the 16th century that virtually all building activity stopped. His earliest documented work, at the châteaux of Montceaux and Verneuil, was done around the turn of the century. Although the exact nature of his contribution to those projects is unclear, Verneuil was to have considerable importance for his later work. Echoes of the courtyard plan and of the elevation are to be found in the more important later châteaux. He returned to Montceaux later, having been put in charge of its completion (1608-ca. 1615). The entrance pavilion, though in ruins, and the facade of the forecourt chapel of that château survive, the latter showing the clear influence of Sebastiano Serlio and Giacomo Barozzi da Vignola. At the same time he worked on Montceaux, de Brosse received a number of commissions to enlarge Parisian hôtels, most notably the Hôtel de Soissons (1611-12) and the Hôtel de Begnine-Bernard (1615). His Vignolesque *portes cocheres* for those two hôtels, which have both been destroyed, quickly became famous.

More important commissions of the 1610s were for the design of the Château de Blérancourt (1611-19) and for the Château de Coulommiers-en-Brie (1613, destroyed). Coulommiers was the more conventional of the two in that it adhered to the customary French U-plan with a screen wall to close off the court, rather similar to Verneuil. Interestingly, the severity of the entirely rusticated exterior at Coulommiers was counterbalanced by the highly elaborate courtyard facades, which recalled

Salomon De Brosse: Luxembourg Palace, Paris, France, ca. 1614ff.

Pierre Lescot's classicist Louvre designs. Blérancourt is in many ways more interesting, because it used a wingless block plan with four corner pavilions. The block plan had occasionally been used on a small scale in France, but is more properly considered an Italian model. It was mainly known in France from the engravings of Serlio and Jacques Androuet du Cerceau the Elder, de Brosse's grandfather. The block plan entered the French tradition through the example of Blérancourt, which was taken up by François Mansart. Blérancourt was built for a very knowledgeable patron, Charlotte de Vieuxpont, who was an admirer of Vignola and a collector of architectural drawings. In the contract, she demanded an unusual correctness in the design of classical details. The influence of Lescot's Louvre is again apparent in the design of the elevations. The simple and refined articulation set the tone for the development of later French classical architecture. Parts of Blérancourt have been rebuilt after its destruction in World War I.

Both Blérancourt and Coulommiers anticipated de Brosse's masterwork, the Palais du Luxembourg in Paris. The Luxembourg was built for Maria de'Medici, and the rustication of the whole building presumably was a concession to her wish for an imitation of the Palazzo Pitti in Florence, her childhood home. De Brosse began work on the Palais du Luxembourg in 1615 but did not finish it, being dismissed for financial mismanagement in 1624. However, the palace was largely completed to his design, though later much altered. It has been described as a combination of the plans of Coulommiers and Blérancourt, in that the main block resembles the latter, while wings and a screen like those at Coulommiers are added to the main block. The entrance pavilion, with its fine circular domed vestibule, and the wing pavilions are the least altered and give the best indication of the original appearance of de Brosse's

work. One of the most important innovations of the Luxembourg was the creation of a full set of apartments in the corner pavilions, which came to dominate the interior planning of French châteaux. De Brosse doubled the corner pavilions to accommodate the apartments, which had the unfortunate result of creating an asymmetrical side elevation. He also designed the interiors, none of which survive, and laid out the garden, which was principally distinguished by its simplicity and the sparing use of statuary. Later development in the area has made the gardens rather smaller and less balanced than they originally were.

De Brosse's other Parisian work of that period is the west facade of the Church of St. Gervais (1616-21). The height of this Gothic church provided the occasion for the first use of the three superimposed classical orders in a church front. The result, recalling Vignola's Church of Il Gesù in Rome and work by Philibert de l'Orme, is surprisingly felicitous. De Brosse's only complete church building, the Temple des Huguenots at Charenton, does not survive, but engravings were made by Jean Marot before its destruction. The colossal church with three naves and continuous double galleries seems to have been based on Vitruvius' description of a basilica, and was built on a rectangular plan. It had some influence on later Protestant church building in northern Europe. The Temple des Huguenots, in combination with the usual severity of de Brosse's style, is probably responsible for the fact that the architect is sometimes credited with the invention of a ''Huguenot style.''

De Brosse's other surviving major work is the Palais de Justice de Bretagne at Rennes (1618), which may perhaps be accounted the first work of French classicism. The design for the Palais de Justice is based on Primaticcio's Aile de la Belle Cheminée at the Palais du Fontainebleau, which in turn was inspired by Vignola's classicism. Uncharacteristically, the building emphasizes surface and volume, rather than plasticity and mass. The result is characterized by a crisp clarity of line, combining monumentality with a certain lightness. Unfortunately, the original proportions of the facade have been spoiled by the removal of the front steps and the terrace.

Although some critics have seen in de Brosse a more rational and less imaginative student of the Mannerist Jacques Androuet du Cerceau the Elder, his essential achievement was his continuation and development of the work of Lescot and Vignola, which brought French architecture closer to classicism and strongly influenced the architecture of François Mansart, the chief architect of the next generation.

—MARIJKE RIJSBERMAN

DE COTTE, Robert.

French. Born in Paris, 1656. Died 15 July 1735. Married the sister-in-law of the architect Jules Hardouin-Mansart. Originally trained as a stonemason. Worked in the office of Jules Hardouin-Mansart, 1676; assistant to Hardouin-Mansart as royal architect, 1682; succeeded Hardouin-Mansart as royal architect, 1708-33.

Chronology of Works
All in France unless noted
† Work no longer exists
* Approximate dates

1690*-1750	Hôtel des Invalides, Paris (additions and alterations; with Jules Hardouin-Mansart)
1699	Hôtel des Mousquetaires Noirs, Paris (with Hardouin-Mansart)†
1699	Place Vendôme, Paris
1700-35	Abbey of St.-Denis, Paris (not completed until 1765)
1703	Hôtel de Pontchartrain, Paris (interior remodeling)†
1706	Hôtel de Beauvais, Paris (remodeling)†
1708-09	Ste. Croix, Orléans (west portal; constructed after 1742)
1708-10	Chapel, Versailles (decoration)
1708-14	Notre Dame, Paris (decoration)
1708*-22	Cathedral, Montauban (additions to portal)
1710	Hôtel du Lude, Paris†
1711	Château de Chanteloup†
1711-13	Hôtel d'Estrées, Paris
1713-15	Château, Bonn, Germany (additions)
1713-19	Hôtel de Vrillière, Paris (remodeling)
1714	Hôtel de Caumont, Aix-en-Provence
1715*	Château of Tilburg, Netherlands
1715	Pompe de la Samaritaine, Paris†
1715-23	Château of Poppelsdorf, Bonn, Germany
1716-19	Hôtel du Maine, Paris†
1716-20	Hôtel des Mousquetaires Gris, Paris†
1717	Hôtel de Bourvalais, Paris (remodeling)
1719	Château d'Eau, Paris†
1719-20	Palais Episcopaux, Châlons-sur-Marne (unfinished)
1720-22	Palais Bourbon, Paris
1721-22	Robert de Cotte House, Paris†
1721-35	Cabinet des Medailles, Bibliothèque du Roi, Paris (with Jules Robert de Cotte; not completed until 1741)
1724-35	Palais Episcopaux, Verdun (not completed until 1739)
1727-35	Palais Thurn and Taxis, Frankfurt, Germany†
1729-32	Hunting Lodge, Compiègne
1731*-32	Chapel of the Charité, Paris (portal; partially destroyed)
1731*-35	St. Roch, Paris (portal; not completed until 1738)
1731-35	Palais des Rohan, Strasbourg (not completed until 1742)
1734	Hôtel d'Armagnac, Paris

Publications

BOOKS ABOUT DE COTTE

BLONDEL, JACQUES FRANCOIS: *L'architecture française.* 4 vols. Paris, 1752-56.

Exposition de dessins et de souvenirs de Robert de Cotte, premier architecte du roi (1656-1735). Paris, 1937.

GUIFFREY, JULES: *Comptes des bâtiments du roi sous le règne de Louis XIV, 1664-1715.* 5 vols. Paris, 1881-1901.

HAUTECOEUR, LOUIS: *Histoire de l'architecture classique en France.* Vols. 2 and 3. Paris, 1948 and 1950.

JESTAZ, BERTRAND: *Le voyage d'Italie de Robert de Cotte.* Paris, 1966.

KALNEIN, WEND GRAF, and LEVEY, MICHAEL: *Art and Architecture of the Eighteenth Century in France.* Baltimore, 1972.

KALNEIN, WEND GRAF: *Das Kürfürstliche Schloss Clemensruhe in Poppelsdorf.* Düsseldorf, Germany, 1956.

LÜBBECKE, FRIED: *Das Palais Thurn und Taxis in Frankfurt am Main.* Frankfurt, 1955.

LUDMANN, JEAN-DANIEL: *Le Palais Rohan de Strasbourg.* Strasbourg, 1979.

MARCEL, PIERRE: *Inventaire des papiers manuscripts du cabinet de Robert de Cotte.* Paris, 1906.

MARIE, ALFRED: *Versailles au temps de Louis XIV, Mansart et de Cotte.* Paris, 1976.

REINHARDT, URSULA: *Die bischöflichen Residenzen von Châlons-sur-Marne, Verdun und Strasbourg. Ein Beitrag zum Werk des ersten königlichen Architekten Robert de Cotte (1656-1735).* Basel, 1972.

ARTICLES ABOUT DE COTTE

BRUNEL, GEORGES: ''Würzburg: Les Contacts entre Balthasar Neumann et Robert de Cotte.'' *Actes du XXII Congrès International d'Histoire de l'Art (Budapest, 1969).* Budapest, 1972.

CHRIST, YVAN: ''Ce Saint-Denis méconnu: Un chef d'oeuvre du classicisme français.'' *Jardin des arts* 134 (1966): 12-23.

D'IBERVILLE-MOREAU, JOSÉ-LUC: ''Robert de Cotte: His Career as an Architect and the Organization of the Services des Bâtiments.'' Ph.D. dissertation, University of London, 1972.

GARDES, GILBERT: ''La Décoration de la Place Royale de Louis le Grand (Place Bellecour) à Lyon, 1686-1783.'' *Bulletin des musées et monuments Lyonnais* 5 (1974-75): 185-388.

HAUTTMAN, MAX: ''Die Entwürfe Robert-de-Cottes für Schloss Schleissheim.'' *Münchener Jahrbuch* 6 (1911): 256-276.

NEUMAN, ROBERT: ''French Domestic Architecture in the Early 18th Century: The Town Houses of Robert de Cotte.'' *Journal of the Society of Architectural Historians* 39 (May 1980): 128-144.

NEUMAN, ROBERT: ''Robert de Cotte and the Baroque Ecclesiastical Façade in France.'' *Journal of the Society of Architectural Historians* 44 (October 1985): 250-265.

NEUMAN, ROBERT: ''Robert de Cotte: Architect of the Late Baroque.'' Ph.D. dissertation. University of Michigan, Ann Arbor, 1978.

RAUCH-ELKAN, ANNELISE: ''Acht Pläne und ein Baumémoire Robert de Cottes für Schloss Tilburg in Brabant.'' *Brabantia* (2 February 1958):43-52.

*

Robert de Cotte was one of the most important architects and designers in France in the early years of the 18th century. We do not know much about his beginnings, but apparently he first worked as an entrepreneur and a contractor for masonry. By 1676 he was in the office of Jules Hardouin-Mansart, who became the first architect for Louis XIV. de Cotte, having married that architect's sister-in-law, became his assistant in 1682 in the Service des Bâtiments du Roi. When Hardouin-Mansart was named Surintendant des Bâtiments in 1699, and enlarged the Bureau des Desseins to make offices at Versailles, Marly and Paris, de Cotte was made second in command, or *architecte ordinaire*, and director of both the Départment de Paris—the most important part of the whole organization—and the Académie Royale d'Architecture.

When Hardouin-Mansart died in 1708, de Cotte was, naturally, appointed to succeed him as *premier architecte*, a position he held for 25 years. But Louis XIV, faced in those years with the costs of his military campaigns, was stretched for money and held little interest in architecture. This forced de Cotte and the staffs of his offices to direct their attention to other political and cultural centers to replace Versailles—namely Paris and the provincial capitals of France and even foreign courts. This is known from the records of the offices de Cotte supervised, now preserved in the Bibliothèque Nationale and the Bibliothèque de l'Institut de France in Paris, where design after design may be seen, all done by the staff of the offices, but with notes by de Cotte, recording his continual presence and involvement.

De Cotte's work, as we might expect, was indebted to the example of Hardouin-Mansart, most notably in the various urban designs he supervised. This began at the Place Vendôme, where Hardouin-Mansart had been responsible for the first design, but the final, octagonal plan was one fixed by de Cotte. The same pattern was repeated at the Place du Dôme des Invalides; this had been worked out by Hardouin-Mansart as early as 1676, but when in 1698 the square was being finished, de Cotte, as overseer of the work, was able—even though his plan was not used—to fix the final form of the square. At Lyons, at the Place Bellecour, Hardouin-Mansart's rather visionary project was completely rejected and that of de Cotte, which was simpler and more practical, was the one accepted and built.

The projects by de Cotte for hôtels and town houses date from 1710 onward, and especially after the 1720s with the expansion west of the boundaries of Paris. There again he followed the example of Hardouin-Mansart, though he was able to make whatever variations on this type that expense and propriety required. At the Hôtel du Lude (1710), everything was subordinated to an idea of display; at the Hôtel d'Estrées (1711-13), the plan was concerned more with convenience, with various apartments available for various functions, and the exterior was simple and clear. This was true also of the designs for the Hôtel de Torcy (ca. 1713) and the Hôtel du Maine (1716-19), where in the elevations de Cotte was able to establish the elements most delicately, and set together the end pavilions and the entrance front under a large, simple roof. De Cotte did little with the interiors, leaving them to designers like Pierre le Pautre and François Antoine Vassé. It was about this time that de Cotte also undertook the building of three episcopal palaces outside Paris, one at Châlons-sur-Marne (1719-20), one at Verdun (1724-35) and another at Strasbourg (1731-35), where, as necessary for such buildings, there was a clear sense of hierarchy: the apartment of the bishop was modest, but that for the king, the Grand Appartement, was more lavish, and at Strasbourg was set along the river side of the building.

De Cotte also prepared several palace designs for European nobility, outside France, though few were built; all seem to have been modeled on Versailles, with longitudinal axes in the plans and radiating avenues in the gardens, and in the buildings themselves, one of several variations: a simple block, as at the Château de Rivoli (ca. 1700) for the duke of Savoy; a U-shaped plan, as at Chanteloup (1711) for Princess Orsini; and a central plan, like that at the Château of Poppelsdorf in Bonn (1715-23), or that of the Château of Tilburg in the Netherlands (ca. 1715), which was like the Italianate form found in France in the earlier years of the Renaissance. All these plans had very imposing state rooms, but unlike the designs of the previous century, they also had a more functional arrangement in the private rooms and connecting corridors that could offer some privacy. In 1715 de Cotte also planned two palaces outside Madrid for Philip V of Spain, the grandson of Louis XIV. The plan of what was called Buenretiro I was for a U-shaped building, that of Buenretiro II was of a vast cross, set in a square; the latter plan could accommodate two sets of apartments—joined by a single suite of dressing rooms—that would be inhabited alternately in summer and winter.

Few churches were built in the 18th century, but de Cotte was put in charge of two great decorative projects at the end of the reign of Louis XIV: the chapel at Versailles (1708-10) and the choir of Notre-Dame (1708-14), for which in the end the designs used were largely the work of Pierre le Pautre. Interestingly, for the facade of the Cathedral of Orléans, de Cotte produced a design in the Late Gothic style (1708-09). His most successful ecclesiastical design was perhaps that for the portal of St. Roch, Paris (1731-35), which had something of the aedicular facade of a Roman church, but which referred also to the model of St. Gervais, Paris (1635), by Salomon de Brosse or the Dôme of the Invalides (1680-91) by Hardouin-Mansart.

De Cotte also built several large complexes, with walls punctuated only by an almost monotonous repetition of windows, dormers and blind arches, as in the wings he and Hardouin-Mansart added at the Hôtel des Invalides (ca. 1690-1750) and the pair of garrisons erected in Paris for the Mousquetaires Noires (1699) and the Mousquetaires Gris (1716-1720). Yet in a manner not unlike that of John Vanbrugh, his contemporary in England, de Cotte could also exploit the austerity of these formal elements, as in the monastic quarters built at St.-Denis (1700-65), producing a design that impressed many of his contemporaries for its monumental size and great sweeping spaces. What de Cotte was able always to design was a simple, balanced form of architecture that seemed to work especially well for his new clients who required not only comfort but a proper and modest setting for the public life of which they were a part.

—DAVID CAST

DE KEY, Lieven.

Dutch. Born in Ghent, Belgium, ca. 1560. Died in Haarlem, Netherlands, in 1627. Trained as a stonemason. Worked in England during the Spanish domination of the Netherlands; moved to Haarlem, 1590. Municipal architect of Haarlem, from 1593.

Lieven De Key: Meat Hall, Haarlem, Netherlands, 1602-03

Chronology of Works
All in the Netherlands

1593	St. Bavo Church (Vont Chapel), Haarlem
1594	Town Hall, Leyden (new facade)
1595-98	Weighhouse, Haarlem [attributed]
1597	Gemeenlandshuis, Leyden
1597	Town Hall, Haarlem (staircase)
1602-03	Meat Hall, Haarlem
1613	Nieuwe Kerk Tower, Haarlem
1616-20	Town Hall, Haarlem (extension)
1625	Frans Loenenhofje, Haarlem (porch)

Publications

BOOKS ABOUT DE KEY

FOCKEMA ANDREAE, S. J.; KUILE, E. H.; and HEKKER, R. C.: *De bouwkunst na de Middeleeuwen*. Vol. 2 in *Duizend jaar bouwen in Nederland*. Amsterdam, 1957.

HITCHCOCK, HENRY-RUSSELL: *Netherlandish Scrolled Gables of the Sixteenth and Early Seventeenth Centuries*. New York, 1978.

ROSENBERG, JAKOB; SLIVE, SEYMOUR; and TER KUILE, E. H.: *Dutch Art and Architecture 1600-1800*. Harmondsworth, England, 1977.

VERMEULEN, FRANS A. J.: *Handboek tot de Geschiedenis der Nederlandsche Bouwkunst*. 3 vols. The Hague, 1928-41.

ARTICLES ABOUT DE KEY

JANSSEN, C. F.: "Lieven de Key: Bouwmeester van Haarlem." *Bouw* 16 (1961): 754-757 .

LALEMAN, M. C.: "Joos Roman en Lieven de Key." *Vlaanderen* 153 (July-August 1976).

TER KUILE, E. H.: "De werkzaamheden van Lieven de Key te Haarlem." *Oud Holland* 55 (1938): 245-252.

TER KUILE, E. H.: "Overheidsbouw te Leiden: 1588-1632." *Oudheidkundig Jaarboek* 7 (1939): 83-87.

Lieven de Key and Hendrick de Keyser were the two principal architects of the final Late Renaissance phase of architectural style called International Mannerism occurring about 1600. De Key practiced mainly as the municipal architect of Haarlem, while de Keyser was his counterpart in Amsterdam. With their deaths, the Dutch version of the style came to an end, and was replaced by an interest in a more classicizing version of the Baroque.

Originally a stonemason, de Key spent an unknown period of years working in England before he arrived in 1591 in Haarlem, where he remained in the service of the city for the rest of his life. De Key's Mannerist style was taken from the highly decorative and rather florid engravings of the Flemish painter and engraver Hans Vredeman de Vries (1526/27-1606), who worked in Flanders, Holland, Denmark and northern Germany. De Key translated ideas from Vredeman de Vries' fanciful collection of large, playful, heavy architectural forms into a three-dimensional reality. The usual Mannerist decorations such as strapwork, cartouches, scrolls, herms and other freely interpreted classical forms were applied with liveliness by de Key to the traditional Netherlandish large, steeply gabled rectangular block.

De Key is most noted for two structures: the Haarlem Meat Hall (1602-03) and the Nieuwe Kerk Tower (1613). In the Meat Hall, de Key took the traditional block and created a richly ornamented example of his personal style. The high-pitched, steep gables which are so distinctive of the area provided de Key with a perfect opportunity to exercise the urge to enliven surfaces. Each gable is divided horizontally into six stages of varying height. These stages are marked by strongly projecting stringcourses and by wide, but strangely thin, quoins at the corners. Complex finials are attached to these corners at two levels, and the peak is crowned by another. Even taller and more complex finials crown the three dormers on each long elevation. Smaller and less assertive decoration fills wall space in *horror vaccui* fashion. An arched and exaggerated rusticated entrance on a gable facade fills the entire center-third of the wall up to architrave level.

The Nieuwe Kerk Tower was originally designed by de Key as part of the medieval Church of St. Anna. The work now rises above the famous Nieuwe Kerk designed by Jacob van Campen (1645), which replaced the medieval church. Exemplifying the vigorous outline associated with de Key's work, the tower and spire crown one of the most famous works by the classicizing Baroque architect van Campen. While the spire may seem to provide merely a clash of contrast, the effect is satisfying. The church is low and plain, in severe contrast to the ornate spire, but the effect is one of each complimenting the other. The tower itself rises in stages which are fairly plain, unusual for de Key. The top is completed by a heavy, ornate balustrade. Above it, the high spire forms a complex series of expanding and contracting shapes which narrow to a peak. The individual parts display de Key's familiar heaviness and complexity. Van Campen created a transition between the two parts, church and tower, by designing an attic with a Doric entablature. Such lively and imaginative work was the end of an era. The taste which succeeded it in the Dutch Republic was for a more sober art.

—ANN STEWART BALAKIER

DE KEYSER, Hendrick.

Dutch. Born in Utrecht, Netherlands, 15 May 1565. Died in Amsterdam, 15 May 1621. Sons, Thomas, Pieter and Willem, were also noted architects, sculptors and painters. Trained as a stonemason. Appointed municipal sculptor and architect of Amsterdam, 1594.

Chronology of Works
All in the Netherlands
* Approximate dates
† Work no longer exists

1606-14	Zuiderkerk, Amsterdam
1608-11	Exchange, Amsterdam†
1609	Weigh House, Hoorn
1618	Town Hall, Delft
1620*	Bartolotti's House, 170-172 Herengracht, Amsterdam [attributed]
1620	Mint Tower (rebuilding), Amsterdam
1620-23	Noorderkerk, Amsterdam
1620-38	Westerkerk, Amsterdam

Publications

BOOKS BY DE KEYSER

Architectura moderna. Amsterdam, 1631. Facsimile edition: Soest, Netherlands, 1971.

BOOKS ABOUT DE KEYSER

HITCHCOCK, HENRY-RUSSELL: *Netherlandish Scrolled Gables of the Sixteenth and Early Seventeenth Centuries.* New York, 1978.
NEURDENBURG, ELISABETH: *Hendrick de Keyser: Beeldhouwer en Bouwmeester van Amsterdam.* Amsterdam, 1929.
OZINGA, M. D.: *De Protestantsche Kerkenbouw in Nederland van Hervorming tot franschen Tijd.* Amsterdam, 1929.
ROSENBERG, JAKOB; SLIVE, SEYMOUR; and TER KUILE, E. H.: *Dutch Art and Architecture: 1600-1800.* 3rd ed. Harmondsworth, England, 1977.
VERMEULEN, FRANS A. J.: *Handboek tot de Geschiedenis der Nederlandsche Bouwkunst.* 3 vols. The Hague, 1928-41.

*

Hendrik de Keyser, an architect active in Holland in the early 17th century, is noted most for his two churches, the Zuiderkerk and the Westerkerk, which still stand as landmarks in the profile of Amsterdam. De Keyser was trained as a stonemason, and works of sculpture from his hand survive, most notably the Tomb of Prince William I (1618) in the Nieuwe Kerk in Delft, an accomplished if slightly uninventive example of Late Mannerist decoration that harks back to the French tombs of Francesco Primaticcio. But de Keyser's greater attention went always to architecture. In 1594 he was appointed municipal sculptor and architect to Amsterdam, an important opportunity since the city was expanding rapidly at that time.

His first commission was for the Zuiderkerk (South Church), a Protestant church that was begun in 1606 and completed eight years later. For the Zuiderkerk, de Keyser suggested the form of a basilica, a rectangle with two nonprojecting transepts, a tunnel vault over the nave, and no choir; all this was planned in a simple classical order, with Tuscan columns along the nave. The main focus, as befitted a Protestant church, was on the pulpit, rather than on the altar. The spire was set to the side, and there de Keyser worked out a somewhat loose but striking ascent of niches, columns and pediments that could stand as a reminiscence of a Gothic tower, but one clothed in appropriately classical forms.

Hendrik De Keyser: Zuiderkerk, Amsterdam, Netherlands, 1606-14

De Keyser repeated this same general pattern in the Westerkerk (West Church, begun in 1620), yet perhaps more successfully. For if in the Zuiderkerk the use of classical architecture was labored and sometimes awkward, here the scale and simplicity of the interior spaces is different, looking forward to the assured and balanced classicism of Jacob van Campen in the next generation. The plan is of a perfect rectangle with two transepts; again the focus is on the pulpit, and again the tower, set outside at the west end and reminiscent of a Gothic spire, is articulated with a mass of classical elements, more rationally organized perhaps than at the Zuiderkerk.

De Keyser did much other work in Amsterdam. In 1608 he designed the large Exchange building, based on the Royal Exchange in London, then some 40 years old, which itself had been built by a Flemish architect. He also designed a number of houses for merchants, most notably the so-called Bartolotti's House, Nos. 170-172 Herengracht. He added details to the towers of the fortifications of the city, including the Mint Tower (1620-23). And he also rebuilt the Town Hall of Delft in 1618 with a facade that is reminiscent of the playful surface design of the French architect Jacques Androuet du Cerceau, whose work de Keyser might have noted when working on the Tomb of Prince William in the same city.

This influence is a token of de Keyser's importance, for more than any of his contemporaries, such as Lieven de Key in Haarlem, de Keyser was open to foreign influences; these he used very well, spreading a type of new Protestant architecture through Holland that shows up, for example, in the Town Hall at Klundert (1621). Whether his influence spread farther afield, even to England, is a matter of debate. The London city churches of Christopher Wren seem immediately similar; however, it is not clear if Wren knew of de Keyser's work. John Summerson, for example, thinks Vitruvius was more of a force than what he calls de Keyser's loose and provincial classicism. But de Keyser was certainly well celebrated, and the book by Salomon de Bray, *Architectura Moderna*, published in 1631, is in effect a monograph on his work and an advertisement for it.

The work of de Keyser's family should also be mentioned. His son Thomas de Keyser (1596/97-1667) was a leading portrait painter in Amsterdam before Rembrandt, and municipal architect to the city from 1662. Two other sons, Pieter de Keyser (1595-1676) and Willem de Keyser (1603-78), were also both architects and sculptors. Willem spent some time in England, working initially with Nicholas Stone (1587-1647), a mason for Inigo Jones at the Banqueting House in 1620 who had himself been trained with de Keyser and became his son-in-law.

—DAVID CAST

DE KLERK, Michel.

Dutch. Born in Amsterdam, Netherlands, 1884. Died in Amsterdam, 1923. Studied at the Industrial School, Amsterdam; mainly self-taught as an architect. Worked in the studio of the architect P.J.H. Cuijpers, Amsterdam, 1898-1910; collaborated with P. Kramer, Amsterdam, 1911-16; in private practice, Amsterdam, 1916-23.

Chronology of Works
All in the Netherlands

1911-12	Hillehuis Apartment Block, Amsterdam
1913-15	Eigen Haard Housing Estate, Amsterdam (stage I)
1914	Veerhoff-Kothe House, Hilversum

1915-20	Eigen Haard Housing Estate, Amsterdam (stages II and III)
1920-22	De Dageraad Housing Estate, Amsterdam
1920-22	Flower Auction Building, Aalsmeer-Oosteinde
1921-22	Housing on the Vrijheidslaan, Amsterdam
1923	Country House, Wassenaer
1923	Barendsen House, Aalsmeer-Oosteinde

Publications

BOOKS ABOUT DE KLERK

DE WIT, WIM: *The Amsterdam School.* Cambridge, Massachusetts, 1983.

FRANK, SUZANNE: *Michel De Klerk 1884-1923, Architect of the Amsterdam School.* New York, 1984.

ARTICLES ABOUT DE KLERK

SEARING, HELEN: "Eigen Haard: Workers' Housing and the Amsterdam School." *Architectura* 2 (1971): 148-175.

Michel de Klerk's work was completely involved with the decorative and expressionist aspects of architecture. His spirit, rather than his introverted personality, was the driving force behind the group of architects who became known as the Amsterdam school.

De Klerk was fortunate to be employed, from the age of 13, for 12 years in the office of Ed Cuypers, the nephew of P. J. H. Cuypers, who designed the Rijksmuseum in Amsterdam. Due to Ed Cuypers' foreign visits, the young De Klerk became familiar with the decorative designs of the Dutch Indies. His skill as a draftsman and artist was acknowledged by his colleagues, and he became a past-master in the design of brick detailing.

The description "Amsterdam school" was first noted in a critical article on the work of De Klerk and his friends following the 1915 exhibition of the society Architectura et Amicitae. The focus for the criticism was a design by J. M. van der Mey, Piet Kramer and De Klerk for the shipping company offices Het Scheepvaarthuis. The design contained symbolic representation, the rich use of decorative motifs and, overall, a Gothic formal expression.

At the time De Klerk distanced himself from the values of H. P. Berlage, who was the leading figure of rationalism and abstraction in Dutch architecture. De Klerk wrote a review in which he criticized Berlage's work as being uninventive and restrained in formal expression, and he even claimed that Berlage did "not understand the play and the language of forms."

In contrast, critics of De Klerk and the Amsterdam school felt that the work of what they thought to be "sensational" and "facade" architects would not last. To an extent, the label of "facade" architect was true for De Klerk, whose reputation was based upon the formal expression of social housing. It has been said that De Klerk's expression was that of the "icing" on a rather mean cake of constrained dwelling types. Yet, that is too critical, because the people who lived in buildings he designed were genuinely appreciative of his work.

The creative period of De Klerk's life occurred during the decade from 1913, when he began work on three housing blocks at the Spaarndammerplantsoen in Amsterdam. Of these blocks, those for the housing society Eigen Haard indicated the formal strength of his architecture. Possibly there was an influence from Joseph Maria Olbrich in the earlier blocks: certainly the

qualities of empathy in design motifs is expressed, and there is an influence from Indonesian design in the detailing. Although De Klerk is probably most famed as the designer of the Eigen Haard schemes, the design work he did for the De Dageraad housing society as a part of Berlage's plan for Amsterdam South is considered by many to be his best work. This scheme comprises two mirror-image blocks in which flats in the form of villas produce a terrace with brick, tile and timber detailing in a notably polychromatic expression.

Often De Klerk's design ideas were either too expressionist or too expensive to construct. One idea prepared for the De Dageraad society proposed three-story-high, sail-like, billowing forms to be built in brickwork. Although he had to modify that design to an angular but decorative expression, he was able to use the design as an oriel bay in a later work. At De Dageraad, he collaborated on part of the scheme with Piet Kramer, in particular on the design of access tower blocks composed of curved plan forms.

De Klerk was also an accomplished designer of furniture and interiors in a decorative style possibly developed from the Dutch Nieuwe Kunst style. In his later architectural work, however, his designs indicated an influence from organic expressionism. The two designs that should be noted in this context were particularly elegant. They both date from the final year of his life, 1923. One design for a rowing clubhouse, De Hoop, was built on the Amstel in Amsterdam but no longer exists; the other project, for a flower market, remained in design form. These organic works had a quality of unity in the plastic expression possibly lacking in his earlier designs.

Undoubtedly De Klerk's suicide in November 1923 on his 39th birthday took away the creative spirit of the Amsterdam school. De Klerk indicated a continuity in decorative styles over the first quarter of the century, from his "art nouveau" competition design of 1907 to the decorative details of 1923. An overt influence from German expressionism is seldom apparent, except in the later work, such as the design for the flower market, which showed some influence from Erich Mendelsohn.

The reproduction of that scheme and housing work by De Klerk in *Wendingen*, a magazine of the decorative arts which was produced by the society Architectura et Amicitae, provided strong images from which the Amsterdam school drew inspiration. De Klerk was both a visionary and a romantic manipulator of formal devices, especially in the context of urban composition.

—E. S. BRIERLEY

DEL DUCA, Giacomo.

Italian. Born in Cefalù, Sicily, ca. 1520. Died 1604. Known also as Jacopo Siciliano. Trained as a sculptor; turned to architecture at the age of 50. Worked in the Roman workshop of Rafaello de Montelepo, then as assistant to Michelangelo; employed as sculptor for tomb of Pope Julius II, 1542; appointed architect to the city of Messina, 1592.

Chronology of Works
All in Italy
* *Approximate dates*
† *Work no longer exists*

1561-65	Porta Pia, Rome (mascherone and stemma; with Michelangelo)
1564-68	Farnese Tabernacle, Rome
1568	Swiss Guards' Chapel, Vatican City, Rome (works in stone)

1570	Savelli Tomb, San Giovanni in Laterano, Rome
1573-74	Porta San Giovanni, Rome
1573-75	Santa Maria in Trivio, Rome (complex)
1573-77	Santa Maria di Loreto, Rome (drum, dome, and lantern)
1575-77	Trajan's Column, Rome (enclosure)
1575-83	Public Works, Rome
1576	Orti Farnesiani, Rome (wall enclosure)
1582	Palazzo Cornaro, Rome
1582	Parish Church, Compagno (presbytery and choir)
1582	Santa Maria Imperatrice, Rome (restoration)
1582-85	Castle, Bracciano (gates and secret garden)
1584-86	Palazzo Farnese, Caprarola (garden, basement, and front piazza)
1584-86	Palazzo Restituti, Caprarola (garden, basement, and front piazza)
1585*	Santi Quirico e Giulitta, Rome (restructuring)†
1586*	Garden of Cardinal Pio, Palazzo Rivaldi, Rome
1586*	Villa Mattei, Rome†
1586-87	Mattei Chapel, Aracoeli, Rome
1586-87	Villa Mattei, Monte Mario, Rome†
1592-1604	San Giovanni di Malta, Messina (tribune)
1599	Palazzo Senatorio, Messina (sea facade)

Publications

BOOKS ABOUT DEL DUCA

BENEDETTI, SANDRO: *Giacomo del Duca e l'architettura del cinquecento*. Rome, 1973.

ARTICLES ABOUT DEL DUCA

SCHWAGER, KLAUS: "Unbekannte Zeichnungen Jacopo del Ducas. Ein Beitrag zur Michelangelo-Nachfolge." *Akten des 21. Internationalen Kongresses für Kunstgeschichte in Bonn 1964* Vol. 2 (Berlin, 1967): 56-64.

*

Giacomo del Duca remains an intriguing figure in Roman architecture of the later 16th century. Sparse biographical information combines with scattered visual evidence to suggest an inventive, possibly eccentric mind. Del Duca's documented association with Michelangelo (1475-1564) makes the scarcity of knowledge about his career even more perplexing, for the young sculptor apparently absorbed his master's design principles. As an architect, del Duca was well versed in the classical vocabulary, completely reworking motifs, introducing them into preexisting buildings and creating complex formal relationships.

Giacomo del Duca trained as a sculptor, but turned to architecture when he was about 50 years old. By 1542, he had moved from his native Sicily to Rome, where he was employed as a sculptor on the tomb of Julius II. During the 1560s, he was still active as a sculptor. Not until the following decade did he emerge as an architect, garnering a number of important commissions in Rome, including churches, palaces and villas. He was listed as an architect in the "Congregazione dei Virtuosi al Pantheon" in 1578, and he competed for commissions in Sixtine Rome during the 1580s. By the next decade, he had returned to Sicily. His works from this late period have suffered damage from earthquakes and bombing, but the tribune of San Giovanni di Malta, Messina, designed in collaboration with the Florentine Camillo Camilliani in 1590-92, survives.

Trained as a sculptor and active as an architect, del Duca was known also as a poet. However, his literary work already

had disappeared by 1642, the date of Giovanni Baglione's *Vite dei pittori, scultori ed architetti*. Baglione, who is our most loquacious informant, relates that del Duca was an architect who worked in the grand manner, and that he was an unorthodox personality, ingenious and energetic. In addition, Baglione lists an impressive number of works from del Duca's hand. Some, such as the Tomb of Elena Savelli (died 1570) in San Giovanni in Laterano, can be connected to del Duca on the basis of supporting evidence. In other attributions, like the central windows of the Capitoline and Conservator's Palaces, Baglione seems to have confused del Duca with his contemporary, Giacomo della Porta (c. 1537-1602). It is likely that del Duca was an accomplished draftsman—polished architectural drawings survive for the Chapel of the Mattei (1582-86) in Santa Maria in Aracoeli—and his linear architectural forms suddenly found a champion in Francesco Borromini during the Baroque.

Del Duca's relationship with Michelangelo was the crucial factor in his transformation from a second-string sculptor to an independent architect. Michelangelo was his friend as well as his teacher, and after the master died in 1564, his heirs corresponded with del Duca about a tabernacle left in the planning stages. Del Duca, assisted by Jacopo Rocchetto, proceeded to complete a bronze ciborium after Michelangelo's model for the church of Santa Maria degli Angeli. Later acquired by the Farnese family and now in the Naples Museum, the ciborium has low reliefs based on Michelangelo's drawings and an architectural framework decorated with classical motifs.

Del Duca also participated in his master's architectural commissions. He worked on the Porta Pia (1561-65) and received payment in 1562 for the papal coat-of-arms carved in marble for the exterior of the gate. He gained unusual insight into Michelangelo's ideas on urban planning, as demonstrated years later when he was commissioned by Gregory XIII to design the Porta San Giovanni (1573-74). The later gate has heavy, rusticated blocks forming the archway and flanking pilasters. It adheres to a type formulated by Sebastiano Serlio but developed in Michelangelo's drawings for his own urban projects. Except for Tiberio Calcagni, Michelangelo's assistant who seems to have been active primarily as a draftsman, Giacomo del Duca was the only follower in Rome to become an architect. Other architects of his generation—Giacomo della Porta and Guidetto Guidetti, for example—were influenced by Michelangelo, but del Duca alone continued to reinterpret the Florentine master's repertoire.

The small church of Santa Maria in Trivio at the Trevi Fountain was reconstructed by del Duca on the site of an earlier church. The simple plan is based on a rectangle with a wide nave, shallow chapels and a raised altar, in keeping with other Counter-Reformation churches. The tall, narrow facade, dated 1575, has a colossal order of Ionic pilasters, an attic story and a pedimental temple front, flanked by obelisks, at the top. The resemblance of the two-order facade to designs by della Porta is superficial; the elongated proportions and ornamental motifs suggest the enduring influence of Michelangelo, 11 years after his death. Del Duca inserted windows between the pilasters and in the attic, with niches and suspended surrounds distributed over the remaining surface. He devised an unusual pediment for the central door, with broken scrolls looped over the tympanum, and a hanging bracket intersecting the base—a motif that Borromini would later sketch.

The other major church commissioned from del Duca in Rome was Santa Maria di Loreto in Trajan's Forum. It had been begun early in the century by Antonio da Sangallo, who had supervised construction of the base of the octagonal drum. Del Duca added the bell tower and the side doors (1573-677), which have details reminiscent of Michelangelo's Porta Pia. To cover the earlier vaulting, del Duca designed a double-shell dome, extravagant in its scale and ornamentation. Again he drew inspiration from Michelangelo, although here from his Florentine works, for the window surrounds in the drum. An oversized lantern embellished with anthropomorphic details is a curious reinterpretation of the lantern projected by Michelangelo for St. Peter's. Executed in 1592, it was probably designed by del Duca before his departure for Sicily.

The eccentricities of del Duca's architecture perturbed some of his contemporaries. Yet, patrons like the Mattei and the Farnese families must have valued the ingenuity of his architecture, which extended even to landscape design, as in his works at the Farnese Palace in Caprarola (1584-86). It is true that an emphasis on contour and verticality, features characteristic of the Mannerist investigation of complex form, appear in del Duca's work. Yet, his approach to architectural design was inherently individualistic, an attitude fostered and elevated to prominence by his mentor, Michelangelo.

—EUNICE D. HOWE

DE L'ORME, Philibert.

French. Born in Lyons, France, June 1514. Died in Paris, 8 January 1570. Father was the master mason Jean de l'Orme, and uncle was a military engineer, also named Jean de l'Orme. Studied architecture in Rome, 1533-36. Began practicing architecture in Lyons, 1536; moved to Paris, 1538; architect to the dauphin, 1545; architect to King Henri II, 1547-59; after Henri's death, worked for Charles IX, and for Catherine de' Medici.

Philibert De l'Orme: Château d'Anet, France, 1547-55

Chronology of Works
All in France
† Work no longer exists
* Approximate dates

1536	Gallery, Hôtel de Bullioud, Lyons
1541-44	Château de St. Maur, near Paris†
1547-55	Chateau d'Anet (corps-de-logis, 1547-48; east wing and chapel, 1549-52; west wing, 1551-52; entrance wing, 1552-54)
1547-56	Arsenal of the King, Paris†
1547-58	Tomb of François I, St. Denis (with François Carmoy, François Marchand and Pierre Bontemps)
1547*-59	Château de Saint-Léger
1548-55	Château de Madrid, Paris (completion of upper stories)†
1548-56	Château de Vincennes, Paris (completion of chapel and gallery)
1548-59	Château de Fontainebleau
1548-59	Château de St. Léger-en-Yvelines (grand gallery, chapel, pavilions)†
1548-59	Hôtel des Tournelles, Paris (fountain, triumphal arch, stables, décor for banqueting hall)†
1549	Collaboration, décor for Entry of Henri II into Paris and Coronation of Catherine de' Medici at St.-Denis†
1550	Urn for the heart of François I, St. Denis (with Pierre Bontemps)
1552-55	Chapel, Villers-Cotterêts†
1554-58	Hôtel de Philibert de l'Orme, Paris†
1555-57	Building and gallery, Abbey of Montmartre, Paris†
1556-57	Bridge, Château de Chenonceau
1557	Château de la Muette, St. Germain-en-Laye (upper story)†
1557-59	Château-Neuf, St. Germain-en-Laye†
1563-70	Château de St. Maur (enlargement)†
1564-69	Notre-Dame, Paris (repair of vaults and enlargement of cloister)
1564-70	Palais des Tuileries, Paris†

Publications

BOOKS BY DE L'ORME

Nouvelles Inventions pour Bien Bastir et à Petits Fraiz. Paris, 1576.
Architecture de Philibert de l'Orme. Paris, 1626.

BOOKS ABOUT DE L'ORME

ANDROUET DU CERCEAU THE ELDER, JACQUES: *Les plus excellents bastiments de France.* 2 vols. Paris, 1576-79.
BERTY, ADOLPHE: *Les grands architectes français de la Renaissance.* Paris, 1860.
BLOMFIELD, REGINALD: *A History of French Architecture.* London, 1911.
BLUNT, ANTHONY: *Art and Architecture in France; 1500-1700.* Harmondsworth, England, 1953.
BLUNT, ANTHONY: *Philibert de l'Orme.* London, 1958.
BOUDON, F., and BLECON, J.: *Philibert Delorme et le château royal de Saint-Léger-en-Yvelines.* Paris, 1985.
BOURGEOIS, A.: *Le château d'Anet, restauration du cryptoportique et du perron.* Paris, 1877.
BRION-GUERRY, LILIANE: *Philibert de l'Orme.* New York, 1955.
CHEVALIER, M. L'ABBÉ C.: *Lettres et devis de Philibert de l'Orme.* In *Archives Royales de Chenonceau.* Paris, 1864.

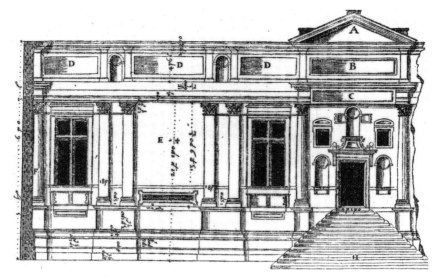

Philibert De l'Orme: Château de Saint Maur, France, 1541-44

CLOUZOT, H.: *Philibert de l'Orme*. Paris, 1910.

GÉBELIN, FRANÇOIS: *Les Châteaux de la Renaissance*. Paris, 1927.

HAUTECOEUR, LOUIS: *Histoire de l'architecture classique en France*. Vol. 1, part 2. Rev. ed. Paris, 1965.

JAMES, G. P. R.: *De l'Orme*. 3 vols. London, 1830.

MAYER, MARCEL: *Le Château d'Anet*. Paris, 1953.

PFNOR, R. and DU CLEUZIOU, H.: *Monographie du château d'Anet*. Paris, 1867.

PRÉVOST, JEAN: *Philibert Delorme*. Paris, 1948.

ROUSSEL, P. D.: *Histoire et description du château d'Anet depuis le dixième siècle jusqu'à nos jours*. Paris, 1875.

ROUX, A.: *Le château d'Anet*. Paris, 1911.

VACHON, MARIUS: *Philibert De L'Orme*. Paris, 1887.

WITTKOWER, RUDOLF: *Architectural Principles in the Age of Humanism*. New York, 1949.

ARTICLES ABOUT DE L'ORME

CLOUZOT, HENRI: "Philibert de l'Orme: Grand Architecte du Roi mégiste." In *Revue du Seizième Siècle*. Paris, 1917.

GUILLAUME, J.: "Le Traité de De l'Orme." *Les Traités d'architecture de la Renaissance*. Tours, France, 1982.

HÉLIOT, P.: "Documents inédits sur le château d'Anet." *Mémoires de la Société nationale des Antiquaires de France*. Vol. 9, no. 2 (1951): 257-69.

HERBET, J.: "Les Travaux de Philibert Delorme à Fontainebleau." *Annales de la Société Historique et Archéologique du Gâtinais* 12 (1894):153-163

MONTAIGLON, ANATOLE DE: "Philibert et Jean Delorme, architectes." *Archives de l'Art Français*, Series 2, 2 (1862): 314-336.

PORCHER, JEAN: "Les premières constructions de Philibert Delorme au château d'Anet." *Bulletin de la société de l'histoire de l'art français*. 1939.

POTIÉ, P.: "Le Projet constructif de Philibert de l'Orme.": In XAVIER MALVERTI (ed.): *L'idée constructive en architecture*. Paris, 1987.

SANABRIA, SERGIO: "From Gothic to Renaissance Stereotomy: The Design Methods of Philibert de l'Orme and Alonso de Vandelvira." *Technology and Culture* 30, No. 2 (1989): 266-299.

Philibert de l'Orme transformed French architecture by brilliantly integrating the lessons of Italy with the constructional virtuosity of the French master mason's workshop. No less decisive for the practice of architecture in France was his unprecedented control of royal architectural design under Henri II and subsequent publication of his landmark treatise on architecture.

Philibert and his brother Jean trained under their father Jean de l'Orme, a master mason in Lyons. Philibert de l'Orme mastered stereotomy, the art of cutting stones to fit vaults and squinches, and carpentry for creating timber trusses. He also learned to manage a large work site, once boasting of having supervised 300 workers at 15 years of age. The widely held notion that he had contact with humanist circles in Lyons is only a surmise.

By 1533 de l'Orme was in Rome. There he garnered a thorough understanding of the classical orders from a survey of the principal ancient monuments, such as the Theater of Marcellus, the Pantheon, the Colosseum and the Temple of Castor and Pollux. Though no autograph drawings by de l'Orme are known, many of the woodcuts included in the section on the orders in his treatise, published some 30 years later, record the study of antique ornament made during his Roman trip.

Attempts to connect de l'Orme with contemporary Italian architects, such as Antonio da Sangallo the Younger, Giulio Romano and Michelangelo, are based only on stylistic connections. Despite his claim to have been employed by Pope Paul III, de l'Orme hardly mentions a contemporary Italian building or architect in his writings, ignoring even the massive rebuilding of St. Peter's. His discussion in his treatise of Donato Bramante's spiral staircase of the Belvedere at the Vatican reveals his ambivalent attitude. With a mason's eye, de l'Orme criticized the use of brick over stone, an entablature instead of sloping arches, and the level capitals and bases of the columns which do not follow the ascent of the spiral.

Upon returning to Lyons from Italy in 1536, de l'Orme received his first notable commission. This was a gallery for the town house of Antoine Bullioud, the treasurer of Brittany. The corridor provided access across a small court separating two wings of the house. To preserve the court and a wellhead, de l'Orme cantilevered the three bays of the third-story gallery on corbels and extended the passage between two turrets supported by magnificent squinches. The solution was practical, efficient and determined by his experience as a master mason. He displayed his acquaintance with Rome by employing window frames with segmental and triangular pediments and applying pilasters of two orders, Doric below and Ionic above. The manner in which the window pediments overlap the pilaster shafts recalls the door from the vestibule to the reading room of the Laurentian Library and suggests that de l'Orme took note of Michelangelo's work on a visit to Florence.

After the death of his father in 1538, de l'Orme moved to Paris. On the grounds of the secularized monastery of Saint-Maur outside the city, he built for Cardinal Jean du Bellay, François I's ambassador to Rome, a single-story residence with a rectangular court and facades articulated with a single order. The arrangement was like Giulio Romano's Palazzo del Tè in Mantua, which de l'Orme may have visited just before its completion in 1536, perhaps while traveling with du Bellay's entourage. For his Italophile patron, de l'Orme stripped away most of the exterior elements which characterized the typical French château, such as turrets, towers and high-pitched roofs with dormers. Saint-Maur was the exact contemporary of Sebastiano Serlio's equally remarkable Château d'Ancy-le-Franc and Grand Ferrare at Fontainebleau.

The Château de Saint-Maur brought de l'Orme to the attention of Henri II and the royal favorite Diane de Poitiers, for whom he built the châteaux of Saint-Léger and Anet, respectively. These shared with Saint-Maur the same basic U-shaped layout with a lower entrance wing enclosing a rectangular court. At Anet, however, a long, fortified wall extended in front of not one, but three courts. In the center, de l'Orme placed an entrance gate flanked by terraces and trapezium angle pavilions, the latter inspired by Baldassare Peruzzi or Antonio da Sangallo the Younger. The barrel-vaulted entrance vestibule of the gate reflects the entry to Sangallo's Palazzo Farnese in Rome. Strong French elements emerged as well, such as brick walls trimmed in stone, turrets, high-pitched roofs and squinches.

At Anet, de l'Orme translated antique elements into a French idiom. To buttress the foundations of the *corps de logis,* begun by an unknown predecessor, he recreated an antique cryptoporticus with complex stone vaults. The chapel remains a tour-de-force of stereotomy and is one of four centralized chapels de l'Orme designed for châteaux, including others at Saint-Léger, Villers-Cotterêts and Saint-Germain-en-Laye. Chimneys like sarcophagi surmount the extraordinary entrance gate, a triumphal arch whose clock and astronomical instruments gauged the hours and the movement of heavenly bodies while measuring the patron's devotion to both her late husband and her royal suitor.

De l'Orme adopted for the *corps de logis* the kind of entrance motif with tiers of paired columns which Pierre Lescot and Jean Goujon were then using at the Louvre (the one royal building not under de l'Orme's supervision). At Anet, de l'Orme transformed the motif into a tower of Doric, Ionic and Corinthian columns harking back to the Colosseum. His application of the orders was in no way thoroughly canonical, however. Instead of the Composite or Corinthian orders commonly used on Roman triumphal arches, he preferred a Doric order for the entrance gate at Anet and an Ionic order for the tomb of François I at Saint-Denis, the latter patterned after either the Arch of Septimus Severus or the Arch of Constantine in Rome.

As Henri II's overseer of royal buildings between 1547 and 1559, until the 17th century the only architect to occupy that position, de l'Orme worked on most royal buildings. At Fontainebleau he completed the Gallery of Henri II with an Italian-style coffered wood ceiling and an elaborate mantel. In the Court du Cheval-Blanc at Fontainebleau he constructed a staircase of twin curving flights, a solution developed for the garden façades of both Saint-Maur and Anet. The Château-Neuf at Saint-Germain-en-Laye was a festival site which departed from de l'Orme's standard château plan by deploying a forecourt before a *corps de logis* with apartments in four angle pavilions. Having grown rich from royal benefices, de l'Orme designed his own house in Paris consisting of two blocks, without orders, separated by a court.

During the 1560s de l'Orme worked for Queen Catherine de'Medici at the Château de Saint-Maur and the new Palais des Tuileries just outside the Paris city walls. Returning to Saint-Maur, which Catherine had acquired from the heirs of Jean du Bellay, de l'Orme expanded the living quarters by adding angle pavilions with apartments. On the facades of the Tuileries he used a novel type of column, the shafts of which were punctuated with highly decorative bands of ornament. The interior staircase, supported entirely on squinches and encircling an open stairwell, culminated his work in stone and fostered a long tradition.

De l'Orme fell from grace after the accidental death of Henri II in 1559. Bitter about his forced retirement, he pledged "instead of learning to build (*édiffier*) châteaux and houses, I will learn to teach (*édiffier*) men (*Instruction*)." In his first publication, the *Nouvelles inventions pour bien bastir et à petits fraiz* (*Innovations for Better and Cheaper Building*) of 1561, he proposed a practical alternative to trusses made with increasingly scarce large timbers, substituting instead overlapping short pieces of wood secured with pegs. He had tested the invention in the mid-1550s at a pall-mall court for Catherine de' Medici's Château de Montceaux and the roof of the Château de la Muette at Saint-Germain-en-Laye.

De l'Orme complemented his treatise on timber construction with one on stereotomy, including it as part of his *Premier tome de l'architecture* (*First Volume on Architecture*) of 1567. A complete set of woodcuts revealed the art of the master mason's workshop by demonstrating for the first time how to determine scientifically the various shapes of stones required for complex vaults and squinches. Among the examples, he included the famous "Grand Vis" or spiral staircase at Saint-Gilles-du-Gard, a marvel of French stonecutting, and his own cabinet on squinches designed for the garden facade at Anet.

Woodcuts illustrating the attributes appropriate to an architect begin and end the *Architecture*. These sum up de l'Orme's vision of the architect as a humanist immersed in the texts and monuments of antiquity. In the section of the *Architecture* explicating the orders, however, de l'Orme clearly states that ancient sources such as the writings of Vitruvius or Roman monuments provide no absolute rule and must be balanced by two guides: divine proportions derived from the Temple and House of Solomon, Ezekiel's vision of the Temple, and Noah's Ark described in the Old Testament, and, ultimately, the architect's own expert judgment.

An emphasis on the architect's creative freedom permitted de l'Orme to include his own variants of the standard orders. One was a column simulating a pruned trunk. The pruned tree used as a support was part of the late-medieval vocabulary, and de l'Orme could have seen a 15th-century example in the tower of Jean sans Peur in Paris, though he may have known the type used by Bramante in the Portico della Canonica at Sant'Ambrogio in Milan. The tree column may have reflected Vitruvius' statement of wooden prototypes for the orders, though de l'Orme was silent about that.

The second invention de l'Orme called "French columns." Like the timber vaulting system, these solved a material problem. French stone precluded monolithic shafts, and de l'Orme proposed decorating the breaks between the drums with bands of ornament. He may have seen antique precedents, but he presented the columns as his own conception. He first used a Corinthian version on the portico of the chapel in the park at Villers-Cotterêts (also significant as the earliest application of the temple front in France). The label "French columns" was both a challenge to the antique canon of the orders and a flattery to de l'Orme's patron Catherine de'Medici, to whom the treatise was dedicated and for whose Palais des Tuileries he employed such columns in the Ionic mode.

Little of de l'Orme's built work survives. The gallery in Lyons, the tomb of François I at Saint-Denis, the gate and chapel at Anet and the entrance tower of that château (now at the École des Beaux-Arts in Paris) are the most important. The legacy of his plans and elevations is immediately apparent in the buildings of Salomon de Brosse and François Mansart. A great many vaults, stairs, domes and bridges crafted of precisely cut stone owe something to him. The French rationalist tradition has its roots in de l'Orme's work. His treatise, the first by a French architect, inspired writings on construction from Mathurin Jousse (1627) to Jean-Baptiste Rondelet (1802). Jacques-Germain Soufflot's Sainte-Geneviève (Panthéon) in Paris (1756-90) is a distant heir. Jacques-Guillaume Legrand and Jacques Molinos revived de l'Orme's timber truss system for the colossal dome of the Halle au Blé in Paris (1782-83), inspiring Thomas Jefferson in the United States and David Gilly in Germany. Three centuries after de l'Orme's death, Eugène-Émmanuel Viollet-le-Duc recognized the 16th-century architect's continued relevance as a compelling practitioner and theoretician whose "thoroughly sound taste . . . and severity in point of principles" would benefit modern architecture (*Entretiens sur l'architecture,* 1858-72).

—MAURICE S. LUKER III

DE ROSSI, Giovanni Antonio.

Italian. Born in Rome, Italy, 1616. Died in Rome, 9 October 1695. Father was a stonecutter. Trained with Francesco Peparelli, Rome. Served as architect of a number of hospitals in Rome, 1640s; stimatore of the Apostolic Office under Pope Innocent X, 1644-55; architect of the papal palaces under Pope Clement XI, 1670-76.

Chronology of Works
All in Italy
* *Approximate dates*

1636-50	Santa Maria della Cima, Genzano, near Rome (with Francesco Peparelli)
1640-43	Santa Maria in Publicolis, Rome (rebuilding)
1642	Palazzo del Bufalo (completion of work begun by Peparelli)
1643-45	Santa Maria Porta Paradisi, Rome (restoration)
1646-76	San Rocco, Rome (restoration)
1650-54	Palazzo Altieri, Rome
1650*	San Francesco di Paola, Rome (alteration)
1651-57	Cappella della Madonna delle Grazie, San Rocco, Rome
1655-56	L'Ospedale delle Donne, San Giovanni in Laterano, Rome
1655-57	Cathedral, Tivoli (sacristy)
1656-60	Cappella, Palazzo della Monte di Pietà , Rome (completion of work begun by Peparelli)
1657*	Palazzo Gambirasi, Rome (alteration)
1658-67*	Palazzo d'Aste, Rome
1659-60	Palazzo Nuñez-Torlonia, Rome
1660*-62	Palazzo Muti Bussi, Via Aracoeli, Rome (courtyard and staircase)
1665	Palazzo Celsi

1670	Palazzo Baccelli, Rome†
1670-72	Palazzo Santacroce, Rome (enlargement)
1670-76	Palazzo Altieri, Rome (enlargement)
1671-76	Villa Altieri, Rome
1674ff.	Cappella Lancellotti, San Giovanni in Laterano, Rome
1674-95	Palazzo Carpegna, Rome
1676-86	Santa Maria in Campo Marzio, Rome (rebuilding)
1677	Palazzo Nari, Rome (doorway, entrance vestibule, and staircase)
1678	Palazzo Celsi, Rome (doorway and stairhall)
1678*	Palazzo Gomez, Rome
1680-95	High Alter, San Francesco di Paola ai Monti
1681-88	San Pantaleo, Rome
1695ff.	Santa Maria Maddalena, Rome (additions; completed in 1699 by Giulio Carlo Quadri and Francesco Antonio Bufalini)

Publications

BOOKS ABOUT DE ROSSI

BELLI BARSALI, ISA: *Ville di Roma: Lazio I.* Milan, 1970.

BORSI, FRANCO, et al.: *Santa Maria in Campo Marzio.* Rome, 1987.

BOSI, M.: *Santa Maria in Campo Marzio.* Rome, 1961.

EIMER, GERHARD: *La fabbrica di S. Agnese in Navona.* 2 vols. Stockholm, 1970-71.

FAGIOLO DELL'ARCO, M., and CARANDINI, S.: *L'effimero barocco: Strutture della festa nella Roma del seicento.* 2 vols. Rome, 1977-78.

MALLORY, NINA A.: *Roman Rococo Architecture from Clement XI to Benedict XIV (1700-1758).* New York, 1977.

MORTARI, LUISA: *S. Maria Maddalena.* Rome, 1969.

PASCOLI, LEONE: *Vite de'pittori, scultori ed architetti.* Vol. 1. Rome, 1730.

PIERACCINI, GIOVANNI, et al.: *Palazzo Bonaparte a Roma.* Rome, 1981.

PORTOGHESI, PAOLO: *Roma barocca.* Cambridge, Massachusetts, 1970.

SCHIAVO, ARMANDO: *Palazzo Altieri.* Rome, 1964.

SPAGNESI, GIANFRANCO: *Giovanni Antonio de Rossi architetto romano.* Rome, 1964.

WITTKOWER, RUDOLF: *Art and Architecture in Italy: 1600-1750.* Harmondsworth, England, 1980.

ARTICLES ABOUT DE ROSSI

ANTINORI, ALOISIO: "Alcune notizie sulla villa Altieri all'Esquilino e sull'attività di Giovanni Antonio de Rossi architetto romano." *Bollettino d'arte* 71 (1986): 113-128.

BLUNT, ANTHONY: "Roman Baroque Architecture: The Other Side of the Medal." *Art History* 3 (1980): 61-80.

HABEL, DOROTHY METZGER: "Alexander VII and the Private Builder: Two Case Studies in the Via del Corso Development." *Journal of the Society of Architectural Historians* 49 (September 1990): 293-309.

HAGER, HELLMUT: "Contributi dall'opera di Giovanni Antonio de Rossi per S. Maria in Campo Marzio a Roma." *Commentari* 28 (1967): 329-339.

HAGER, HELLMUT: "Zur Planungs- und Baugeschichte der Zwillingskirchen auf der Piazza del Popolo: S. Maria di Montesanto und S. Maria dei Miracoli in Rom." *Römisches Jahrbuch für Kunstgeschichte* 11 (1967-68): 189-306.

SPAGNESI, GIANFRANCO: "Due opere del primo decennio di atività (1640-1650) dell'architetto Giovanni Antonio de

Rossi.'' *Quaderni dell'Istituto di Storia dell'Architettura 5*, Nos. 52-53 (1962): 8-23.

TAFURI, MANFREDO: ''Un inedito di Giovanni Antonio de Rossi: Il Palazzo Carpegna a Carpegna.'' *Palatino* 11, No. 2 (1967): 133-140.

*

Giovanni Antonio de Rossi is often lumped together with architects of similar rank working in and around Rome in the middle of the 17th century. This group, which also includes the older Giovanni Battista Soria (1581-1651), Vincenzo (fl. 1626-ca.1663) and Felice (ca.1626-77) Della Greca and Antonio del Grande (1625-71), active in the midst of the major Roman Baroque personalities—Giovanni Lorenzo Bernini (1598-1680), Francesco Borromini (1599-1967); Pietro da Cortona (1597-1669) and Carlo Rainaldi (1611-91)—was responsible for a vast number of relatively modest projects in and around Rome. De Rossi's contribution is especially significant in the area of Roman palace design, where his considerable talents as a site planner are clearly demonstrated. In this context he is also credited with the introduction of an inventive vocabulary of architectural details related to, but not slavishly derived from, the works of Borromini and Cortona.

Born in Rome, the son of a northern Italian stonecutter, de Rossi apprenticed with Francesco Peparelli (died in 1641), who seems to have introduced de Rossi to the basic formulas of Roman church and palace design as well as to a number of influential patrons, among them members of the Santacroce family. De Rossi inherited a number of Peparelli's patrons after his master's death; moreover, by the 1640s those connections led to de Rossi's appointment as architect of a number of the hospitals in the city and, thereby, his introduction to the group of governors of those institutions, many of whom hired de Rossi for their private building campaigns. He was also connected with colleagues in the trade; through his association with Girolamo Rainaldi, for example, de Rossi held the position of *stimatore* of the Apostolic Office under Pope Innocent X Pamphili (1644-55). In the 1670s, as a favored architect of the Altieri, he was elected architect of the papal palaces under Pope Clement XI Altieri (1670-76).

For the most part, de Rossi's church architecture, if modest in scale, is impressive for its problem solving. Most notable of his sacred designs is the restoration of San Rocco, the design for the rebuilding of Santa Maria in Campo Marzio and the solution for the nave of Santa Maria Maddalena. At San Rocco, de Rossi may have been responsible for a reorientation of the church from the original 16th-century building campaign. But his work is most readily identifiable in the context of the architecture of the side aisles, the side chapels, the presbytery and the sacristy. In the case of the three-bay side aisles, de Rossi introduced an ingenious adaptation of Carlo Maderno's design for the aisles added to St. Peter's (1609-26). The effect, determined in large measure by the use of freestanding columns that carry arches defined as segmental pediments, is rich and monumental.

The church of Santa Maria in Campo Marzio offered de Rossi his only opportunity to design an entire church structure. Enlisted to replace the earlier church fabric, and in so doing to reorganize the monastery complex, de Rossi introduced an unusual solution in which the church, encased in a self-contained setting and accessible from a small atrium, accommodates the inherited character of the neighborhood, not in the way of furnishing a traditional facade-as-backdrop, but rather by introducing a more organic structure that follows the established network of streets and even helps to preserve this. For example,

from the Via della Maddalena, the apse of Santa Maria in Campo Marzio, furnishing a broad convex plane, and the rectangular volumes above marking the arms of the Greek-cross plan of the church together signal the junction of the street with the Via degli Uffici del Vicario at Piazza Santa Maria in Campo Marzio.

De Rossi's problem solving is also apparent in what must have been his last commission, the design of the nave of Santa Maria Maddalena. In this case, the architect was asked to adapt his scheme for the nave to the chancel and transept completed in the early 1670s by Carlo Fontana (1638-1714). His solution—an elongated octagon allowing for two side chapels on each side, as well as transitional spaces for the entrance and before the transept, is highly original and complements by opposition the dry and predictable nature of Fontana's earlier work.

Of much greater consequence for the history of Roman Baroque and Rococo architecture are de Rossi's numerous palace designs. With the exception of his work for the Altieri family, de Rossi's palace architecture answered the needs of upper-class patrons whose property holdings were considerably more modest and whose households were far more intimate than was the case with the great baronial and papal families of Baroque Rome. De Rossi made a career of working for that class of patron, and in so doing he introduced significant variations into the tradition of Roman palace architecture. His introduction to the problem of palace design was certainly at the hand of Peparelli, with whom de Rossi worked on modifications to the Palazzo del Buffalo at Piazza Colonna and on the design of the Palazzo Santacroce at the present-day Piazza Benedetto Cairoli. Both of these are standard examples of the rather dry and repetitious palace type established by Giacomo della Porta in the later 16th century and popularized by Carlo Maderno in the early 17th century. But de Rossi departed from that tradition with designs such as those for the Palazzo D'Aste and Palazzo Muti-Bussi. In both of these palaces, de Rossi demonstrated his ingenuity in site planning.

At the Palazzo D'Aste he worked in concert with his patron Francesco Bonaventura D'Aste, a noted hospital governor, to accommodate the palace design to its critical location at the southern tip of the Via del Corso. De Rossi, acknowledging the peculiarly narrow site as well as the corridor of the Corso and the open venue of the Piazza San Marco, altered the orientation of prior development on the site from the Corso to the Piazza San Marco, and eliminated the standard central courtyard in favor of an atrium that gives onto the minor, east facade of the block. This also afforded the development of the relatively narrow piazza facade (it is only five bays wide) as the major facade of the palace. As if taking his cue from the Carnival festivities staged along the Corso and Piazza San Marco, de Rossi introduced a fresh vocabulary of architectural detail; here, the palace corners, marked by a sequence of three stories of highly inventive pilaster orders, are textured and rounded. The decorative overhang is complemented by the appearance of modified segmental and pagoda-like pediments over the windows of the upper stories. The standard Roman window of appearances, hardly appropriate for the palace of Cavaliere D'Aste, was replaced by a wooden *palco,* or balcony, at the corner with the Corso offering front-row seats for the Carnival races and various ceremonial parades staged throughout the year. In all, the Palazzo D'Aste is an elegant signorial palace, and de Rossi can be credited with introducing this alternative palace into the Roman architectural cityscape.

The Palazzo Muti-Bussi is another example of de Rossi's inventive planning. Unfortunately, the context for the Palazzo Muti-Bussi, originally fronting the Piazza d'Aracoeli, has been lost as a result of modern alterations to this area of the city at the base of the Capitoline hill. Originally, the palace—remarkable for its hexagonal plan alone—was organized with a main axis that pierced the palace and its central courtyard straight through, opening a vista of the facade of the Church of San Venanzio beyond. The attention to site, in concert with the reduction of the scale of these buildings, and the care lavished on architectural details of the surfaces opened the way for the exploration of smaller-scale, private building throughout the city in the early 18th century.

The overbearing attention by modern historians to the architectural feats of the Baroque masters Bernini, Borromini and Cortona has meant that architects of de Rossi's stature have remained relatively unexplored. In a recent attempt to establish the position of these so-called minor figures in the larger context of Roman Baroque architecture, Anthony Blunt (1980) chose the label ''non'' or ''anti''-Baroque for the architecture of de Rossi and his colleagues. However, this tag, intended to suggest the alternative nature of their work, suggests that these were architects working outside of conventional taste, and yet de Rossi was certainly an architect whose designs were sought after, and whose language of architecture evidenced his ready participation in the Baroque mentality as it appeared in Rome in the 17th century.

—DOROTHY METZGER HABEL

DE WAILLY, Charles.

French. Born in Paris, France, 1730. Died in Paris, 1798. Trained with Giovanni Nicolo Servandoni and Jean Laurent Le Geay. First prize, Grand Prix de Rome, 1752; studied at French Academy in Rome, 1754-56. Dual career as builder and painter-architect. Member of Académie Royale d'Architecture, 1767; member of Académie de Peinture et de Sculpture, 1771.

Chronology of Works
All in France

1762-70	Hôtel d'Argenson, Paris (interior)†
1764-69	Château de Montmusard, near Dijon†
1769	Chapel of the Resting Place, Versailles†
1769-78	Château des Ornes, Poitou (renovation)†
1769-82	Théâtre de l'Odéon, Paris (with Marie-Joseph Peyre)
1772-73	Palazzo Spinola, Genoa, Italy (interior)†
1774-78	Hôtel de Voltaire, rue Richelieu, Paris†
1776-78	Hôtels de Pajou et de Charles de Wailly, Paris†
1778	Chapel of the Virgin, St. Sulpice, Paris (redecoration)
1780	St. Leu-St. Gilles, Paris (crypt)
1784	La Comédie Italienne, Paris (interior)

Publications

BOOKS ABOUT DE WAILLY

BRAHAM, ALLAN: *The Architecture of the French Enlightenment.* Berkeley, California, and Los Angeles, 1980.
GALLET, MICHEL: *Charles de Wailly 1730-1798.* Paris, 1979.
HAUTECOEUR, LOUIS: *Histoire de l'architecture classique en France.* 4 vols. Paris, 1943-52.
LE ROI, J. A.: *Histoire des rues de Versailles.* Paris, 1861.
MOSSER, MONIQUE, and RABREAU, DANIEL: *Charles De Wailly: Peintre-architecte dans l'Europe des lumières.* Exhibition catalog. Paris, 1979.

ARTICLES ABOUT DE WAILLY

BRAHAM, ALLAN: ''Charles de Wailly and Early Neo-Classicism.'' *Burlington Magazine* 109 (1972): 670-685.
FOUCART-BORVILLE: ''Les projets de Charles de Wailly par la gloire de la cathédrale d'Amiens et de Victor Louis pour le maître-antel de la cathédrale de Noyen.'' *Bulletin de la Société de l'Histoire de l'Art Français* (1974): 131-144.
GALLET, MICHEL: ''Un projet de Charles de Wailly pour la Comédie Française.'' *Bulletin du Musée Carnavalet* No. 1 (1965): 2-13.
RABREAU, DANIEL: ''Charles De Wailly dessinateur (1730-1798).'' *Information d'histoire de l'art* No. 5 (1972): 219-228.
STEINHAUSER, MONIKA, and RABREAU, DANIEL: ''Le Théâtre de l'Odéon de Charles De Wailly et Marie-Joseph Peyre, 1767-1782.'' *Revue de l'art* 16 (1973): 9-49.

*

In terms of style, Charles de Wailly cannot be classified easily. He lived at a time when archaeological interest in antiquity certainly was popular. The result of that interest, the neoclassical style, was a rational approach to the architecture of the ancients. De Wailly was a student of Jacques François Blondel, whose restraint and symmetry made the ''noble simplicity'' of the ancients even more discreet, and de Wailly's works have sometimes been seen as cold and isolated. But his style was also influenced by the visionary antiquarianism of Jean Laurent LeGeay and Giovanni Battista Piranesi, especially their grandiose views of Roman antiquity, which emphasized monumentality through oblique perspective and strong contrast of light and shade. A third strong influence, the Roman Baroque, was dramatic and theatrical; de Wailly had spent a number of years copying such masterpieces as Giovanni Lorenzo Bernini's ''Cathedra Petri.'' De Wailly's use of strong contrasts of light and shade, smoke and mirrors, long vistas and multiple columns created grandiose schemes.

Architectural hyperbole dominated de Wailly's early ideas. A stage designer, he favored dramatic devices: dark foregrounds, excessive ornamental statuary, triumphal arches and multiple levels of elliptically shaped colonnades. Each may be found in the ''Facade of a Palace,'' his neoclassical entry in the Grand Prix de Rome (1752) for which he was awarded first prize. (A generous sort, de Wailly shared his award, a three-year Roman stipend, with fellow competitor Pierre-Louis Moreau-Desproux.)

De Wailly followed the ancient concept of using circle and oval to provide an ideal sense of beauty. His design for the Temple des Arts in the duke de Marigny's gardens at Ménars uses a large central circle with three smaller perimeter circles interpenetrating its circumference. The Château at Montmusard uses circles to provide integration and logical progression. He used overlapping circles along an axis for the Théâtre Français (now Odéon) and the Théâtre de la Réunion des Arts, both in Paris, and for his plans for Wilhelmshöhe Castle in Germany. This same idea continued to dominate his design proposals for the castle (none of which were executed), in which a series of circular forms from the exterior fountains progress through the courtyard colonnade into a central round salon. Similarly, ovals were applied to the staircase at the Château des Ormes and the Hôtel de la Villette. This return to the ancients for basic forms would have met with Blondel's approval.

A number of de Wailly's designs are in the Roman Baroque mode, exemplified by his dramatic and grandiose interior for the Palazzo Spinola in Genoa, Italy (1772-73). Contrasts of light and shade enhance its drama. The grandeur and excitement of

Bernini's work were resurrected in new form; interiors are encrusted with all types of decoration, including repeated arches supported by de Wailly's own elegant slender columns, large wall mirrors placed to extend the illusion of endless space, and vases, one evocative of Piranesi. De Wailly was never as fanatical as some of his French compatriots in their desire to recreate pure Greco-Roman buildings. While he used classical motifs and columns, he lacked the cool classical integrity of Blondel: his presentation was more theatrical, and he loved ornament too much to leave it out.

A lighter spirit of Roman Baroque can often be found in his works, particularly his love of tall columns—a direct consequence of his studies with LeGeay—which he used to create a sense of movement, receding and projecting rather than just articulating.

De Wailly provided not only architectural drawings but also decoration: sculpture for churches and vases. His designs for furniture, exhibited at the Salon from about 1761, demonstrate a clear and simple style; the publication of his *Première suite de Vases inventée et gravée par Dewailly* also indicates his eminence in this field. As might be expected, de Wailly was also consulted by others, including the marquis de Marigny, regarding the acquisition of appropriate sculpture. His ability to combine opposing styles was as adroit in sculpture as in architecture. Like the work of LeGeay, his altar at Amiens Cathedral is Baroque in its painterly effects and sense of drama, but classical in that the identity of its separate parts is retained.

De Wailly's expert drawings provide the contemporary scholar with a concise understanding of his intentions. This talent made him highly successful at a time when there was an acknowledged overabundance of architects. His dramatic use of lighting, often from one specific source to the side, created theatrical settings. Like Piranesi and LeGeay, he created a sense of proportion by "peopling" his architectural drawings. Building exteriors were shown surrounded by landscapes; his works often had the look of a *vedute* painting.

A man of varying talents, de Wailly was an architect who decorated interiors, designed vases, sculpture and furniture, painted scenes, and provided ideas for landscape gardens. While such multiplicity is remarkable, it is even more unusual to have it recognized by one's peers: de Wailly was the sole architect to gain acceptance into the Academy of Painting and Sculpture.

—TERESA S. WATTS

DIENTZENHOFER BROTHERS.

Bavarian. Several architects from a family in Aibling, Bavaria. Georg: Born in 1643. Died in Waldsassen, 2 February 1689. Wolfgang: Born in 1648. Died in 1706. Christoph: Born in 1655. Died in Prague, 20 June 1722. Married Anna Aichbauer, 1685; son was the architect Kilian Ignaz Dientzenhofer (1689-1751; see separate entry). [Johann] Leonhard: Born in 1660. Died in Bamberg, 26 November 1707. Johann: Born in 1663. Died in Bamberg, 20 July 1726. Son was Justus Heinrich Dientzenhofer (1702-4 4), court architect at Bamberg. Christoph and Johann settled in Prague in 1675; Johann named chief court architect at Pommersfelden in 1707, succeeding his brother Leonhard. Their sister Anna went with them to Prague, where she married the architect Abraham Leuthner (died in 1700); it was Leuthner who gave the brothers a start in architecture. All brothers trained as masons, and only Johann received a formal education in architecture.

Chronology of Works

Georg: All in Germany:

1682-89	Cistercian Monastery (execution of Abraham Leuthner's design), Waldsassen
1684-89	Jesuit College, Amberg
1685-89	Pilgrimage Church, Kappel (rebuilding)
1686-93	St. Martin's, Bamberg

Wolfgang: All in Germany:

1690-95	Benedictine Church and Monastery, Michelfeld
1691-1706	Abbey Church, Speinshart
1693-99	Salesian Church and Convent, Amberg
1695ff.	Abbey Church, Ensdorf
1705-07	Pilgrimage Church (Frauenbrunndl), Straubing

Christoph: All in Czechoslovakia:

1690ff.	Benedictine Monastery, Tapla, Czechoslovakia
1699-1712	St. Joseph's Church, Oborĭištĕ
1700-13	Chapel, Castle, Smiřice
1703-11	St. Nicholas in the Old Town, Prague
1707-11	St. Clare's Church, Cheb
1709ff.	Ascension of the Holy Virgin Church, Nova Paka
1710-15	St. Margaret's Church, Břevnov
1717-23	Our Lady of Loreto, Hradčany, Prague

Leonhard: All in Germany:

1686-1704	Monastery, Ebrach
1689-93	St. Martin's Church (design by Georg)
1695-1705	Monastery, Banz (completed by Johann)
1696-1702	St. Michael on the Michelsberg (completed by Johann)
1697-1703	New Residenz, Bamberg
1698ff.	Monastery, Schöntal (completed by Bernhard Schiesser)
1704	Church of the Holy Savior, Castle Weiher, Hollfeld

Johann: All in Germany:

1704-12	Stiftskirche (Cathedral), Fulda
1707-13	Stadtschloss (City Palace), Fulda
1710ff.	Schloss Bieberstein, Fulda
1710-19	Abbey Church, Banz
1711-18	Schloss Weissenstein, Pommersfelden
1713	Böttingerhaus, Bamberg
1714-19	Schloss Schrottenberg, Reichmannsdorf
1715-18	Church, Litzldorf
1716-22	Concordia Castle, Bamberg
1723	Schloss, Kleinheubach

Publications

BOOKS ABOUT THE DIENTZENHOFER BROTHERS

FRANZ, HEINRICH GEBHARD: *Die Kirchenbauten des Christoph Dientzenhofer*. Brno, Czechoslovakia, Munich and Vienna, 1942.

FRANZ, HEINRICH GEBHARD: *Die deutsche Barockbaukunst Mährens*. Munich, 1943.

FRANZ, HEINRICH GEBHARD: *Studien zur Barockarchitektur in Böhmen und Mähren*. Brno, Czechoslovakia, 1943.

HAGER, WERNER: *Die Bauten des deutschen Barocks: 1690-1770*. Jena, Germany, 1942.

Johann Dientzenhofer: Abbey Church, Banz, Germany, 1710-19

HEMPEL, EBERHARD: *Baroque Art and Architecture in Central Europe.* Harmondsworth, England, 1977.

HOFFMANN, JOSEF: *Der Barock in Nordwestböhmen.* Carlsbad, Czechoslovakia, 1898.

KREISEL, HEINRICH: *Das Schloss zu Pommersfelden.* Munich, 1953.

NEUMANN, JAROMIR: *Česky barok.* Prague, 1969.

NORBERG-SCHULZ, CHRISTIAN: *Baroque Architecture.* New York, 1972.

NORBERG-SCHULZ, CHRISTIAN: *Late Baroque and Rococo Architecture.* New York, 1974.

POCHE, EMANUEL and PREISS, PAVEL: *Pražské paláce.* Prague, 1973.

SCHMERBER, HUGO: *Beiträge zur Geschichte der Dientzenhofer.* Prague, 1900.

SCHNELL, HUGO: *Die Stiftskirche Waldsassen.* Munich, 1961.

SWOBODA, KARL MARIA (ed.): *Barock in Böhmen.* Munich, 1964.

ZIMMER, HANS: *Die Dientzenhofer.* Germany, 1976.

ARTICLES ABOUT THE DIENTZENHOFER BROTHERS

FRANZ, HEINRICH GEBHARD: "Die Klosterkirche Banz und die Kirchen Balthasar Neumanns in ihrem Verhältnis zur böhmischen Barockbaukunst." *Zeitschrift für Kunstwissenschaft* 1 (1947): 54-72.

*

The Dientzenhofer Brothers comprised a remarkable quintet of talent. All gifted architects, there were five brothers, all sons of Georg Dientzenhofer: these were Georg, Johann Leonhard, Christoph, Johann and Wolfgang. The family came from the district of Bad Aibling near Rosenheim in Bavaria, but most of their greatest works (especially those of Christoph and his son Kilian Ignaz) were in Franconia and Bohemia, and their importance lies in their ingenious adaptations of themes introduced by Francesco Borromini and Guarino Guarini.

Georg Dientzenhofer's younger brothers Christoph and Johann settled in Prague around 1675, and Christoph returned there for permanent residence in 1686 after a spell working with Georg at the great Cistercian Stiftskirche Waldsassen (1681-1704), but the Dientzenhofers only assisted Abraham Leuthner, who was the architect-in-charge. There are three elliptical vaults over the nave, and three bays open into side chapels arched over to form galleries. There is a vestigial transept, and the church is very long, very high and very narrow: it is more like a Vorarlberg church than the rest of the Dientzenhofers' oeuvre, but Waldsassen is important in that it was one of the first splendid German Baroque churches, with a rare globe tabernacle on the hugh altar designed by Karl Stilp, a local man. While Christoph went back to Prague, Johann went to Rome, where he remained for some time.

Not far to the northwest of Waldsassen is the remarkable Pilgrimage Church of Kappel (1685-89), rebuilt to designs by Georg Dientzenhofer while he was working at Waldsassen. The plan consists of three apses separated by wall piers, and is symbolic of the church's dedication to the Holy Trinity: yet the basis of the plan in the center is really an equilateral triangle formed by the arched openings of each apse. There are three slender circular towers at each intersection of the apses (that is, associated with the wall piers), and there is a low lean-to aisle around the main body of the church to hold the stations of the cross and to accommodate the pilgrims. Over the center of the half-circle of each apse is a tall circular lantern capped by an onion dome. As each of the three staircase towers at the intersection of the apses also has an inventive onion dome on top, the total effect of the exterior is curiously exotic and oriental. Georg was also responsible for St. Martin's in Bamberg (1686-93), which took the theme of the Michaelskirche in Munich and transferred it into an expression of High Baroque architecture. A feature of the church is the rectangular "cupola" over the crossing that leads to the narrower choir.

Wolfgang Dientzenhofer was responsible for the Premonstratensian Abbey Church of Speinshart (1691-1706), a *Wandpfeilerkirche,* with a three-bay nave, two-bay choir and twin towers; this church like Waldsassen, owes much to the Vorarlberg type, except that the balconies are set very high. Speinshart is significant for its rich stucco ornamentation.

Johann Dientzenhofer's first great church was the Stiftskirche (now the Dom) at Fulda (1704-12), the burial place of St. Boniface, the English missionary martyred in Friesland in 755. The west altar dedicated to the saint was of great historical significance, and the new building was therefore orientated toward it, with the main facade facing east. Johann Dientzenhofer was recalled from Rome when the prince-abbot decided to pull down the old Romanesque building, and the Roman influence shows in Dientzenhofer's treatment of the nave, with its repetitive triumphal-arch themes, echoing St. Peter's, Il Gesù and Sant' Ignazio in Rome, and even memories of Leon Battista Alberti's Andrea in Mantua. The chief and most obvious connection between the nave of Fulda and Roman exemplars is Borromini's work at San Giovanni in Laterano: this Borromini source is of singular importance in any consideration of the work of the Dientzenhofers.

Johann Dientzenhofer was called to Pommersfelden in 1711, having been named Hofbaumeister in 1707 in succession to his brother Johann Leonhard; there, he built Schloss Weissenstein, one of the greatest Baroque palaces in Franconia. At the same time, he was involved in the building of the Benedictine Abbey Church of Banz (1710-19), a structure which exploits the possibilities of ellipses in the plan, undulating galleries and a complex system of intersecting vaults. The Banz church is clearly derived from the convent church of St. Joseph in Obořiště (1699-1712) and from the church of St. Clare in Cheb (1707), both by Christoph Dientzenhofer. Obořiště in turn owes much to the church of Santa Maria dell' Immacolata Concezione in Turin by Guarini (1673), but the main front with its concave center derives from Borromini, while the segmental pediment over the entrance (the so-called "Dientzenhofer motif") had been used by Georg Dientzenhofer, but again comes from Roman models. At Banz the segment over the entrance recurs, but it has a break-back, and is set on a convex curved plan. Johann Leonhard designed the monastery buildings at Banz, but does not appear to have had a hand in the genesis of the church itself.

Christoph's church at Obořiště, the castle chapel at Smiřice, the church of St. Niklas in Prague-Kleinseite (Sv. Mikuláš, Praha Malá Strana) of 1703-11, the church of St. Clare in Cheb (1707), and the church of St. Margaret at Břevnov (Sv. Markéta, Praha-Břevnov) of 1710-15, all demonstrate the assured mixing of motifs derived from Borromini and Guarini. Undulating curves and segmental pediments on columns or pilasters are much in evidence. It was at Smiřice that Christoph Dientzenhofer mixed Guarini's plan of San Lorenzo in Turin with the wall-pier system of the Vorarlberg school, producing an extraordinarily effective amalgam of centralized and longitudinal spaces. The exterior, with its convex and concave forms, writhes and undulates in an almost alarming fashion. St. Niklas on the Kleinseite has wall piers with chapels between them over which are undulating galleries, while the nave itself consists essentially of three interpenetrating ellipses that are hinted at by the obliquely positioned pilasters set against the piers. The result is that conventional "bays" break down, and a kind of syncopated rhythm is set up, a theme that was later developed by Balthasar Neumann at Vierzehnheiligen. Christoph Dientzenhofer stands revealed as an original architect of genius, taking ideas from Borromini, Guarini, and Johann Lukas von Hildebrandt's church at Gabel a stage further.

Christoph's last great work was in fact the church of St. Margaret in Prague-Břevnov, which contains a series of interlocking ellipses similar to those at St. Niklas, but this time the nave consists of two transverse ellipses with smaller ellipses at each end. Even the exterior, with its swaying crowning entablatures on madly swinging gables and its lively architectural modeling, comprises a vigorous ensemble of imaginatively treated motifs coming together in an harmonious entity.

Unforgettable, too, is the beautiful facade of Our Lady of Loreto on the Hradčany (1717-23). This enchanting composition, with its elegant central belfry, is probably one of the most delicately and subtly modeled works of central European Baroque architecture ever conceived.

Thus, of the five brothers, at least three can be counted as among the first rank of Baroque architects in Franconia and Bohemia, while the son of Christoph, Kilian Ignaz, was unquestionably one of the most talented of this remarkable architectural dynasty.

—JAMES STEVENS CURL

DIENTZENHOFER, Kilian Ignaz.

Bohemian. Born in Prague, 1 September 1689. Died in Prague, 18 December 1751. Father was the architect Christoph Dientzenhofer (1655-1722); married twice; 19 children. Trained with his father; studied and worked in Vienna, 1707-17, including with Johann Lukas von Hildebrandt (1688-1745); began professional career in Prague, 1717.

Chronology of Works
All in Czechoslovakia

1715-20	Villa Amerika, Prague
1720-26	Nativity of the Virgin Church, Nicov
1720-28	St. John Nepomuk on the Hradčany, Prague
1720-30	Churches near Broumov (attributed, with others)
1721-24	Loreto, Hradčany, Prague
1723-25	Church and Convent of the Elizabethines, Prague
1723-31	St. Edwige Church and Monastery, Wahlstatt
1724-26	St. Adalbert Church, Počáply
1724-31	St. Thomas in the Lesser Town, Prague (rebuilding)
1725-28	Villa Portheim, Prague
1725-31	St. Bartholomew's Church, Prague
1726-38	Benedictine Monastery, Broumov
1729-39	St. John Nepomuk on the Rock, Prague
1730-37	Karolin War Invalids Hospice, Prague (unfinished)
1731-37	St. Mary Magdalen, Karlsbad
1732-34	Imperial Hospital with Chapel on the Hradčany, Prague
1732-35	St. Clement, Odelená Voda
1732-35	St. Francis Xavier, Opařany
1732-37	St. Nicholas in the Old Town, Prague
1733	Church, Dobrá Voda (with others)
1733	Church, Nepomuk (with others)
1734-43	Ursuline Convent, Kutná Hora (unfinished)
1736	St. Charles Borromeo, Prague (with others)
1737	St. Catherine, Prague (with others)

1737-51	St. Nicholas in the Lesser Town, Prague (dome and bell tower)
1739-40	Břevov Monastery, Prague (gateway and additions)
1739-42	Sts. Peter and Paul, Březno
1743-51	Chapel of the Holy Cross in Stodulky, Prague
1743-51	Silva-Tarouca Palace, Prague
1745	Calvary Chapel, Radnice
1746	Church, Dolni Ročov (with others)
1746-48	St. Florian, Kladno
1747	Loreto Sanctuary Cloisters, Prague
1747-51	St. Martin, Chválenice
1748	Church, Přeštice (with others)
1748-51	St. John the Baptist, Paštiky

Publications

BOOKS ABOUT DIENTZENHOFER

FRANZ, HEINRICH GEBHARD: *Die deutsche Barockbaukunst Mährens*. Munich, 1943. FRANZ, HEINRICH GEBHARD: *Studien zur Barockarchitektur in Böhmen und Mähren*. Brno, Czechoslovakia, Munich and Vienna, 1943.

FRANZ, HEINRICH GEBHARD: *Bauten und Baumeister der Barockzeit in Böhmen*. Leipzig, 1962.

GRUNDMANN, GÜNTHER: *Das ehemalige Benediktinerkloster Wahlstatt*. Berlin, 1944.

HAGER, WERNER: *Die Bauten des deutschen Barocks: 1690-1770*. Jena, Germany, 1942.

HEGEMANN, HANS W.: *Die deutsche Barockbaukunst Böhmens*. Munich, 1943.

HEMPEL, EBERHARD: *Baroque Art and Architecture in Central Europe*. Harmondsworth, England, 1977.

HOFFMANN, JOSEF: *Der Barock in Nordwestböhmen*. Carlsbad, Czechoslovakia, 1898.

MADL, KAREL B.: *Die Ville Amerika*. Prague, 1890.

NEUMANN, JAROMIR: *Česky barok*. Prague, 1969.

NORBERG-SCHULZ, CHRISTIAN: *Kilian Ignaz Dientzenhofer e il barocco boemo*. Rome, 1968.

NORBERG-SCHULZ, CHRISTIAN: *Late Baroque and Rococo Architecture*. New York, 1974.

POCHE, EMANUEL and PREISS, PAVEL: *Pražské paláce*. Prague, 1973.

SCHMERBER, HUGO: *Beiträge zur Geschichte der Dientzenhofer*. Prague, 1900.

SCHNELL, HUGO: *Die Stiftskirche Waldsassen*. Munich, 1961.

SWOBODA, KARL MARIA (ed.): *Barock in Böhmen*. Munich, 1964.

ZIMMER, HANS: *Die Dientzenhofer*. Germany, 1976.

ARTICLES ABOUT DIENTZENHOFER

KORECKY, MIROSLAV: "Zur Architektur und zum Deckenfresko des Kirchenschiffs von St. Niklas auf der Prager Kleinseite." *Wandmalereien des Spätbarocks* (1958).

MENZEL, BEDA: "Christoph und Kilian Ignaz Dientzenhofer im Dienste der Äbte von Brewnow-Braunau." *Jahrbuch des deutschen Riesengebirgsvereins* (1934).

SCHMIDT, ADALBERT and BLASCHKA, ANTON: "Ein Beitrag zur Lebensgeschichte Kilian Ignaz Dientzenhofers und seiner Familie." *Mitteilungen des Vereins für Geschichte der deutschen in Böhmen* (1930).

Kilian Ignaz Dientzhofer: St. Nicholas in the Old Town, Prague, Czechoslovakia, 1732-37

Killian Ignaz Dientzenhofer was the son of Christoph Dientzenhofer (1655-1722), and came from a Bavarian family of architects hailing from the district of Bad Aibling near Rosenheim. Father and son settled in Prague, and carried out most of their important works in Bohemia. The chief influences on Christoph and Kilian Ignaz were the designs of Francesco Borromini and Guarino Guarini, and they exploited the possibilities of convex and concave curves, undulating entablatures, complex vaulting systems and sequences of differently shaped spaces.

Kilian Ignaz trained under his father and later with the great Johann Lukas von Hildebrandt (1688-1745), and he may have been responsible for the completion of Hildebrandt's Piaristenkirche Maria Treu in Vienna much later. Dientzenhofer's first independent building, the Villa Amerika in Prague (1715-20), has clear Hildebrandtian echoes in the two-tier roof (which has more than a slight chinoiserie hint about it): the modeling above the windows is lavishly inventive, with keystones and urns standing on *ancones* breaking into the *supercilia* of the architraves, powerfully evocative Mannerist-Baroque devices.

He collaborated with his father in the building of the extraordinary and delicate Prague Loreto at Hradčany (1721-24), an enchanting composition with a central belfry over the great doorway. With the Ursuline church of St. Johann Nepomuk, also on the Hradčany in Prague (St. Johann Nepomuk, Prag-Burgstadt), of 1720, the basic arrangement of Hildebrandt's church of St. Lawrence at Gabel is repeated, but the central space is a square with the corners beveled off, two small rectangular transepts, and two more rectangular compartments, one for the vestibule and one for the chancel. There is a square tower placed over the west end. This church and Wallfahrtskirche Mariae Geburt in Nitzau (Nicov) represent the earliest independently designed churches of Dientzenhofer. At Nicov (1720-26), however, the transepts are segmental on plan, and there are twin towers on either side of a concave front with an attic gable. In both these designs the Hildebrandt Gabel plan, influenced by Guarini, is cleverly merged with the Dientzenhofer family's favorite *Wandpfeilerkirche* theme. Nicov has a remarkably clear architectonic plan: the main space is defined within subsidiary

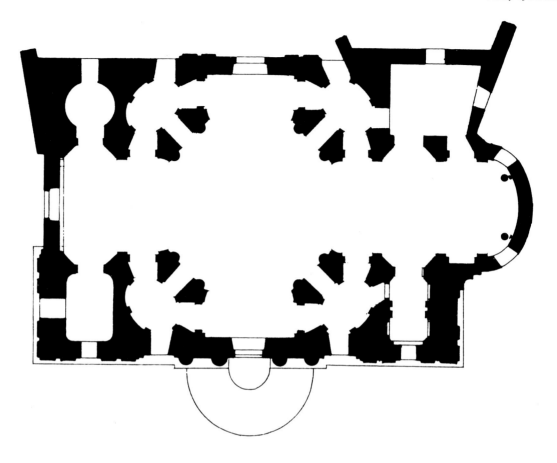

spaces all around it, and it must be one of the very first examples of what the Germans call *Zweischaligkeit.*

In his next major ecclesiastical building, the monastery church of St. Edwige (or Hedwig) at Wahlstatt in Silesia (1723-31), Dientzenhofer employed what are basically ellipses in his plan: a large ellipse with the axis of the church coincident with the longer axis of the ellipse, then two smaller ellipses with their long axes at right angles to that of the church, and an apsidal chancel. Twin towers flank a convex frontispiece. The walls of the ellipses have clusters of piers and columns breaking up the wall surfaces and carrying complex vaulting systems above. Clusters of pilasters are employed in the upper order of the exterior, in the towers and on the attic story, while the broken and swaying pediments of the front seem to suggest a mighty force pushing upward in the center.

Then, in 1724, Dientzenhofer began the small but important church of St. Adalbert in Potschapl (Počáply) near Theresienstadt (Terezín). The plan is again Hildebrandtian, is not unlike that of St. Johann Nepomuk on the Hradčany, and consists of a tower square on plan, an ellipse with its short axis conciding with that of the church, a large space with the corners beveled off and made convex, and the remaining sides of the square also made convex, than another ellipse parallel to the first one, then another square compartment containing the sanctuary. The convex interiors of the central element are expressed as concave walls outside.

The arrangement at Počáply was repeated at the great church of St. Johann Nepomuk am Felsen (Sv. Jan na Scalce) in Prague (1729-39), probably Kilian Ignaz Dientzenhofer's best-known work. Nowhere else are the Baroque rhetoric, drama and plastic modeling so admirably expressed. The plan consists of an elliptical vestibule (the short axis of which coincides with that of the church), an octagonal central space with convex sides, an elliptical choir and an apsidal sanctuary. As in Počáply the interior convexes are expressed by means of concaves outside. The church is approached by a dramatic double staircase which lands on a platform in front of the convex front with its engaged giant order of Tuscan columns and pilasters carrying a Doric entablature and a segmental pediment partially broken in the middle. The front is in fact a gigantic aedicule set between two two-stage towers, which are placed diagonally to the main axis, thus heightening the drama of the composition. The spires of these towers have the elaborate tiered roofs derived from Hildebrandt's architecture.

Concave-convex elements are again found in the plan between the twin two-stage towers of the church of St. Maria Magdalena in Karlsbad (Sv. Majdaléna, Karlový Vary), and the composition of the facade is beautifully proportioned. On plan, the disposition of the elements is not unlike that of St. Johann Nepomuk am Felsen, except that the centralized space reads more like an ellipse with three chapels on each side of the longer axis and separated by wall piers. The chancel and the vestibule (the latter between the towers) are separated from the central space by means of two transitional zones with convex sides internally. The entire interior, with its unifying giant order of engaged composite columns and pilasters, and the swinging, writhing entablature, is very clearly influenced by Borromini's work, notably at San Carlo alle Quattro Fontane in Rome. The Karlsbad church was built between 1731 and 1737.

With St. Nikolaus in der Altstadt (Sv. Mikuláš Staré Město) in Prague (1732-37), Dientzenhofer created a masterwork of astonishing originality and fluency. Basically, it consists of a central square (again with the corners beveled off), with four rectangular spaces around this, and small elliptical spaces behind the pierced-corner piers on the diagonals; on the longer axis of the church are two more rectangles with beveled corners, and beyond one of them is a further rectangle with a half-elliptical sanctuary. The main facade is flanked by twin two-stage towers, but it is not at the end of the long axis of the church, but parallel to it. The towers are separated from the heroic central element by means of lower panels which are pierced by *oeil-de-boeuf* windows and crowned by segmental pediments. The central frontispiece has two pairs of engaged Ionic columns carrying entablatures over which are semiellipti-cal pediments, so these two pairs form aedicules on either side of the lively and cleverly modeled Baroque doorway, over which is a semicircular-headed window framed with Mannerist-Baroque ornament of the most exuberant kind. Gesticulating mitered bishops stand between each pair of columns supported on *ancones* startlingly placed on the dies of the pedestals. Crowning the whole composition is the extraordinary form of the clerestory (for it cannot be described as a cupola or a dome), with its carefully articulated straight sides and recessed convex corners, capped by another two-tier roof in the Hildebrandtian manner, over which is a lantern.

Dientzenhofer added the beautiful cupola and made other alterations to his father's church of St. Nikolaus auf der Kleinseite (Sv. Mikuláše in Malá Strana). Inside he used the trick of aedicules becoming the solids, and outside the elegant cupola is polygonal. In this late and great achievement of the 1750s Dientzenhofer displayed his great sensitivity. That he was also capable of strong modeling, creating huge tensions in the juxtaposition of concave and convex forms, indicating crushing weight by means of heavy entablatures, making em-phatic gestures in the fluent rhetoric of the Baroque, and crash-ing elements together in an architectural equivalent of huge dissonances is evident in his enormous output. Limited space cannot do justice to this towering genius of the Baroque in central Europe, for Dientzenhofer deserves a study on a grander scale than anything he has been accorded so far. Now that Czechoslovakia's frontiers are more open than they were, Dient-zenhofer's buildings will become better known: they deserve to be, for in so many ways he surpassed Hildebrandt, Borromini, Guarini, and his own father.

—JAMES STEVENS CURL

DOMÈNECH, Lluís.

Spanish. Born in Lluís Domènech i Montaner in Barcelona, Spain, 1850. Died 1923. Studied at the Escuela de Arquitectura, Madrid, graduated 1873. In private practice, Barcelona, 1878 until his death in 1923; active in discovering and promoting Catalan heritage. Director of School of Architecture, Barcelona, 1900-19; parliamentary representative, from 1901; founded Workshop of Decorative Arts; president of Athenaeum Club seven times.

Chronology of Works
All in Spain
† *Work no longer exists*

1880	Editorial Montaner i Simón, Barcelona
1885-96	Palau Montaner, Barcelona
1887	Casino, Riera Sant Domènec, Canet de Mar
1887-88	Café Restaurant de l'Exposició (now the Zoologi-cal Museum), Barcelona
1888	Hotel Internacional, Barcelona†
1889-92	Comillas Seminary, Santander (rebuilding and in-terior decoration)
1890	Marqués de Comillas Monument, Santander
1895-98	Thomas House, 291-293 Carrer Mallorca, Barce-lona (later altered)
1897-1919	Pere Mata Institute, Reus, Tarragona
1900	Rull House, 27 Carrer Sant Joan, Reus, Tarragona
1901	Navàs House, 7 Plaça Espanya, Reus, Tarragona
1902	Lamadrid House, 113 Carrer Girona, Barcelona
1902-03	Espanya Restaurant, Barcelona
1902-10	Hospital of St. Paul, Barcelona (first wing)
1902-12?	Gran Hotel (now Institut Nacional de Previsión), Palma de Mallorca
1905	Lleó Morera House, 35 Passeig de Gràcia, Barce-lona (later altered)
1905-08	Palau de la Música Catalana, Barcelona
1908-10	Fuster House, 132 Passeig de Gràcia, Barcelona
1913-16	Solà House, Firal, Olot, Girona
1914	Restaurant, near the Santuario de la Misericordia, Canet de Mar, Barcelona

Publications

BOOKS ABOUT DOMÈNECH

BOHIGAS, ORIOL, et al.: *Lluís Domènech i Muntaner*. Barcelona, 1973.
BOHIGAS, ORIOL: *Once arquitectos*. Barcelona, 1976.
BORRÀS, MARIA LLUISA: *Lluís Domènech i Montaner*. Barce-lona, 1970.
MACKAY, DAVID: *Modern Architecture in Barcelona 1854-1939*. Barcelona, 1989.
PEVSNER, NIKOLAUS, and RICHARDS, J. M. (eds.): *The Anti-Rationalists*. London, 1973.
RUSSELL, FRANK (ed.): *Art Nouveau Architecture*. London, 1979.

ARTICLES ABOUT DOMÈNECH

BOHIGAS, ORIOL: ''Luis Domènech y Montaner 1850-1923.'' *Architectural Review* (December 1967): 426-436.
Cuadernos de arquitectura Nos. 52-53: entire issue (1963).
RAFOLS, J. B.: ''Lo decorativo en la obra de Domènech i Mon-taner.'' *Cuadernos de arquitectura* 97-102 (1956).
SOSTRES MALUQUER, JOSE MARIA: ''Luis Domènech y Mon-taner a través de un edificio cincuentenario.'' *Revista nacio-nal de arquitectura* 202 (1958): 26-30.

The Catalan architect Lluís Domènech represents in his life, work and writings, much more trenchantly than Antoni Gaudi (two years his junior), the political, social, commercial and cultural aspirations of the new urban bourgeoisie growing up in mid-19th-century Barcelona. He graduated as an architect in 1873, when the debate between a centralist government in Ma-drid and federalist movements in Barcelona was at its most acute. Domènech was squarely in the middle of these arguments; he was seven times president of the Atheneum club, the cultural powerhouse of Catalan separatism, director of the School of Architecture in Barcelona from 1900, and parliamentary repre-sentative for the city from 1901.

Some of his basic convictions about the civic role of architec-ture in the modern nation-state were already contained in his essay *In Search of a National Architecture*, which he published in Catalan in 1878 at the age of 28. From his tentative conclu-sions emerge two main points. A national style cannot be achieved through academic classicism, and only partially through medieval archaeology, in this case Catalan Gothic and Hispano-Islamic forms. The proposed national style must visibly weld together the past and the future; it must accommodate the two technologies, look to the correspondence of form and function, and root itself in what can roughly be defined as the national cultural heritage; for him this meant in essence Catalonia, not Spain. In later years he saw this in England in the work of M. H. Baillie Scott; in Germany, Joseph Olbrich; in Belgium, Victor Horta; and in Austria, Otte Wagner and Baumann. If there were any faults in Domènech's arguments, he confesses to committing them in the name of eclecticism.

He built two good examples of the stylistic transition between eclecticism and the more socially and historically self-conscious style which later acquired the name of *Modernisme* in Catalonia. The first is an industrial building, a family printing business, the Editorial Muntaner i Simó, set on one of the main streets in downtown Barcelona (1880-85). It is basically a workshop with an attached street facade in brick, not upmarket stone. This is the architectural equivalent of the language of the populace, Catalan, the brick of the rural farmhouse, striped with decorative bands of Mudejar motifs over large expansive windows on the ground floor, topped with Romanesque arches, and a near continuous run of smaller square windows on the upper floor where the typesetting was carried out. The main entrance, centrally situated, leads to an internal patio, around which the two-story building wraps itself in a U shape. It was one of the first structures in the city to use steel beams, and this expression of the modern age is echoed in the heraldic device in brick at top center of the facade: the bird, the book and three large interlocking cogwheels.

The second building was an element in the famous Universal Exhibition of 1888, in which Domènech, as an assistant architect, made his name: the Café Restaurant in the Ciutadela Park (1887-88). This has come down to us as a canonical representation of the eclectic style. It is a massive two-story near-cube of brick, wrapped around with double-leaf walls. Where they cross at the corners, four towers arise. The whole may echo the form of a Gothic town palace, but the dominant impression is of smooth, solid brick planes relieved by a frieze of blue and white porcelain shields at roof level, topped by pinnacles of yellow ceramics. Inside one can see how the large open dining spaces, with exposed arching steel trusses on the upper story, have dictated the external shape.

The best expression of political and cultural Catalanism is to be found in the *Palau de la Música Catalana* (1888-1905)—note the term ''palace'' and the adjective ''Catalan.'' This is a concert hall in central Barcelona, so studded with symbolic devices that the eye does not at first perceive that it is a glass box in a brick frame. Domènech worked, as in the Café Restaurant, from the inside out. On a corner site he created two symmetrical facades in brick and ceramic, which start as flat planes but are then punctured, broken inward and studded with projections reminiscent of the work of Charles Rennie Mackintosh. The building has three successive units: one, a vestibule on the corner with large depressed arches leading to a monumental staircase that gives on to the circulation areas; two, the auditorium—held in a steel frame, beams and uprights of laminated steel, with the sides glassed in like a modern curtain wall—with a roof pierced by an enormous rectangular ceiling light with a conical center drop in colored glass; and three, the stage area set under twin sculptured columns at either side of the proscenium arch, the rooted tree at one side and the rolling clouds ridden by the Valkyrie on the other. Around the back of the orchestral stage are highly colored bas-reliefs of the muses, and across the whole play wide ranges of symbolic colors from the lateral windows. This is not a building that an architect brought up in the 1930s will find easy to digest. It takes much time and understanding of the historical context.

One other building in the sphere of public health enshrines the civic sense of responsibility of the Catalan ruling classes, the Hospital de Sant Pau (1902-11). By the very nature of the exercise, the technical aspect dominates the cultural, but does not exclude it. The shape and the form were determined by a medical debate, not yet resolved, about whether a hospital should be concentrated into a single building or split into an articulated series of wards. Domènech chose to construct isolated pavilions in brick above ground and link them at a subterranean level, where the operating theaters were located. Gardens were then planted round the pavilions. Thus the functional heart of the hospital is not visible at ground level. The composition of the whole, administrative unit and pavilions, occupies four blocks of the Cerdà grid pattern, but turned around at 45 degrees. Inside, brick vaulting and flat tile paneling predominate. This ornamentation is of broad sweeping floral patterns which enhance the spaciousness of high-roofed wards, and high windows throw light on them without disturbing the patient at ground level. Similar handling of institutional architecture can be found in the Pere Mata mental hospital (1897-1919). He also worked in the domestic scale, in the Lleò Morera house (1905) and the Casa Fuster (1908-10) in which one can see remarkable simplifications of traditional elements like capital and cornice.

Domènech's architectural work cannot be separated from his civic activities. He was steeped in archaeology and heraldry; he founded a workshop of decorative arts, and widened the horizons of architecture with his remarkable *Historia general del arte* (1886-1907). In short, he gave the Catalan bourgeoisie an architecture that expressed both the best, and the worst, of its civic pride.

—ROBERT B. TATE

DOWNING, A. J.

American. Born Andrew Jackson Downing in the United States, 1815. Died aboard the Hudson steamer *Henry Clay*, 1852. Self-taught in architecture. Left school to work in the family owned nursery, 1831; became sole proprietor of the nursery, 1837-46; partnership with Calvert Vaux, 1850-52; also collaborated with Frederick Law Olmstead. Consultant on numerous landscaping projects, including the Mall in Washington, D. C.

Publications

BOOKS BY DOWNING

A Treatise on the Theory and Practice of Landscape Gardening Adapted to North America. New York and London, 1841.
Cottage Residences, Rural Architecture and Landscape Gardening. New York and London, 1842; rev. ed., 1873.
Landscape Architecture. New York, 1844.
The Architecture of Country Houses, including Designs for Cottages, Farmhouses and Villas. New York, 1850.
Rural Essays. New York, 1853.

BOOKS ABOUT DOWNING

DUNLAP, WILLIAM: *History of the Rise and Progress of the Arts of Design in the United States.* 3 vols. Boston, 1918.
KOWSKY, FRANCIS R.: *The Architecture of Frederick Clarke Withers and the Progress of the Gothic Revival after 1850.* Middletown, Connecticut, 1980.

STEIN, ROGER B.: *John Ruskin and Aesthetic Thought in America, 1840-1900.* Cambridge, Massachusetts, 1967.

VAUX, CALVERT: *Villas and Cottages.* New York, 1857.

ARTICLES ABOUT DOWNING

DOWNS, ARTHUR CHANNING: "Downing's Newburgh Villa." *Bulletin of the Association for Preservation Technology* 4 (1972): 1-113.

PATTEE, SARAH LEWIS: "Andrew Jackson Downing and His Influence on Landscape Architecture in America." *Landscape Architecture* 19 (January 1929): 79-83.

PIERSON, WILLIAM H., JR.: "Andrew Jackson Downing: Villa, Cottage, and Landscape." In *American Buildings and Their Architects: Technology and the Picturesque, The Corporate and Early Gothic Styles.* Garden City, New York, 1978.

SCHUYLER, DAVID: "Rural Values and Urban America: The Social Thought of Andrew Jackson Downing." Ph.D. dissertation. University of North Carolina, 1976.

SCULLY, VINCENT J., JR.: "American Villas, Inventiveness in the American Suburb from Downing to Wright." *Architectural Review* 115 (March 1954): 163-179.

SCULLY, VINCENT J., JR.: "Romantic Rationalism and the Expression of Structure in Wood: Downing, Wheeler, Gardner, and the 'Stick Style,' 1840-1876." *Art Bulletin* 35 (June 1953): 121-142.

TATUM, GEORGE B.: "Andrew Jackson Downing: Arbiter of American Taste, 1815-1852." Ph.D. dissertation. Princeton University, Princeton, New Jersey, 1950.

*

A. J. Downing referred to himself as a "rural architect." Uninterested in the advancement of "high design" in buildings, he sought to promote what he viewed as "good taste" for the American middle class, a sector of society previously uncatered to by architects. Downing believed in accommodating progressive systems in residential designs, and his influence was spread through his pattern books and extensive writings. Numerous dwellings attest to the impact of these works, and to this day dominate the landscape of the continental United States.

Downing was never formally trained as an architect. Raised in a rural environment near the Hudson River in New York, he taught himself in the pubic libraries of the area; he was strongly influenced by the works of John Ruskin and A. W. N. Pugin, and particularly by Francis Goodwin's *Rural Architecture.* Downing developed a romantic yearning for the nonurban environment, and in the picturesque found an inherently American ideal. For him the nation had been established in a wilderness, and urbanization seemed an unnatural and inhuman course, with its dense population and industrial concentrations.

In *Cottage Residences* (1842), Downing expressed his desire to become an arbiter of taste for the middle classes: "I wish to inspire all persons with a love of beautiful forms . . . to appreciate the superior charm of the tasteful cottage or villa, and the well-designed and neatly kept garden or grounds, full of beauty and harmony, not the less beautiful and harmonious, because simple and limited, and to become aware that the superior forms, and the higher and more refined enjoyment derived from them, may be had at the same cost and with the same labor as a clumsy dwelling, and its uncouth and ill-designed accessories." He further felt that "[it was] a barrier against vice, immorality, and bad habits." He discussed the appropriateness of ornament, color and spatial planning. Thus, Downing established a moral position in his philosophy of architecture.

Downing's rural residence or "cottage" would be designed in keeping with the character of the site. The proposed considerations for the planning of the site incorporated images of residences in appropriate landscape settings. He deemed the trend for utilizing classical elements advisable only for grand public architecture, and completely incompatible and inappropriate in the rural dwelling. Romantic and irrational styles such as Gothic, Italian Villa or Elizabethan he would promote, provided that the style was specific to the use. Such specific residences discussed by Downing included a suburban cottage for a small family, a small farmhouse and a cottage for a clergyman.

According to Downing, residences should be asymmetrically planned, irregular and uncontrolled. Downing advocated the appropriate placement of spaces and their adjacencies in order to plan for their optimal utilization and accommodation of function. Color was important, as structures should harmonize with their environment. White was inappropriate for the exterior. Instead, earth tones were recommended. Downing also discussed innovations in technology as applied to buildings, including the recommendation for the institution of indoor plumbing. Thus, Downing may be credited with the widespread modernization of living environments, and thereby significantly improving the creature comforts of the common man.

Through the prolific availability of his writings and plans, Downing established the norms for familiar residential designs, and as such his cottage was adopted throughout the country. His plans, readily available through publication, became prototypes for suburban residences, and were reinterpreted many times over. Downing's designs were thus adopted as vernacular types. With the advent of steam power, industrial production of building components made standardized elements and ornamentation abundant and inexpensive. This advancement furthered the "vernacularization" of Downing's designs.

In addition to his contributions to American architecture, Downing is further recognized as a significant figure in the history of landscape architecture. His belief that the environment impacts behavior, and that the greatest benefit to mankind can be gained in a rural setting, inspired his advocacy of the creation of public parks in congested urban settings; he was consulted in the design of numerous landscapes, including the plan for the first urban park in the United States, the Mall in Washington D.C.

By advocating spaces for rural retreat, Downing convinced city dwellers of the importance of public open spaces, and elaborate parks within urban centers. Through numerous publications, including *Treatise on the Theory and Practice of Landscape Architecture and Gardening Adapted to North America, with Remarks on Rural Architecture* (1841), *The Architecture of Country Houses* (1850) and *Rural Essays* (1853), rather than through his own completed projects, he introduced the middle class to design, and to the possibilities of providing themselves many of the luxuries previously reserved only for the more affluent. Although Downing left few monuments of his own design, his legacy can be seen throughout the landscape of America.

—ANDREA URBAS

DU CERCEAU FAMILY.

French. Jacques Androuet Du Cerceau I (born 1510/12; died ca. 1584): settled in Orléans, late 1540s, where he opened an architectural workshop and began a family of architects, including his eldest son, Baptiste Androuet Du Cerceau (born 1544/47; died 1590). Baptiste entered the service of Henri III, 1575; succeeded Pierre Lescot as architect of the Louvre, 1578.

Jacques Androuet Du Cerceau (born ca. 1550; died 16 September 1614), the second son of Jacques I, became architect to Henri IV a fter the death of his brother Baptiste. Charles Androuet Du Cerceau (died 1606), the third son of Jacques I, directed building projects in Châtellerault. Jean Androuet Du Cerceau (born ca. 1585; died after 1649), the son of Baptiste Androuet Du Cerceau, trained with his cousin, Salomon de Brosse, later working with de Brosse at the Luxembourg Palace; succeeded Antoine Métivier as architect to Louis XIII, 1617.

Chronology of Works
All in France
* Approximate dates
† Work no longer exists

1568ff	Château, Verneuil (Jacques Androuet Du Cerceau I, with others)†
1570s	Château, Charleval (Jacques Androuet Du Cerceau I, with others)†
1578-82	Louvre, Paris (Baptiste Androuet Du Cerceau; extension of the Square Court)
1578-1604	Pont Neuf, Paris (Baptiste Androuet Du Cerceau; alterations)
1605-13	Grand Gallery, Louvre, Paris (Jacques Androuet Du Cerceau II)†
1614*	Luxembourg Palace, Paris (Jean Androuet du Cerceau, with Salomon de Brosse)
1632	Hôtel de Sully, Paris (Jean Androuet du Cerceau) [attributed]
1638*	Hôtel de Bretonvilliers, Paris (Jean Androuet du Cerceau; left wing; continued by Le Vau after 1638)

Publications

BOOKS BY JACQUES ANDROUET DU CERCEAU I

Les trois livres d'architecture. Paris, 1559-72.
Les plus excellents bastiments de France. Paris, 1576-1607.

BOOKS ABOUT THE DU CERCEAU FAMILY

BERTY, ADOLPHE: *Les grands architectes français.* Paris, 1860.
CHEVALLEY, D. A.: *Der grosse Tuilerienentwurf in der Überlieferung Ducerceaus.* Frankfurt, 1973.
THOMSON, DAVID: *Jacques et Baptiste Androuet du Cerceau: Recherches sur l'architecture française 1545-1590.* Paris, 1982.
VON GEYMÜLLER, H.: *Les Du Cerceau, leur vie, leur oeuvre.* Paris, 1887.

ARTICLES ABOUT THE DU CERCEAU FAMILY

BOUDON, F.: "Les livres d'architecture de Jacques Androuet Du Cerceau." Pp. 367-396 in JEAN GUILLAUME (ed.): *Les traités d'architecture de la Renaissance.* Paris, 1988.
COOPE, ROSALYS: "The Château of Montceaux-en-Brie." *Journal of the Warburg and Courtauld Institutes* 22 (1959).
MURRAY, PETER: "Menicantonio, du Cerceau, and the Towers of St. Peter's." In *Studies in Renaissance and Baroque Art Presented to Anthony Blunt.* London, 1967.
TOESCA, ILARIA: "Drawings by Jacques Androuet Du Cerceau the Elder in the Vatican Library." *Burlington Magazine* 98 (1956): 153-57.

*

Jacques Androuet Du Cerceau was the founder and most accomplished member of a family of French artists active in the 16th and 17th centuries. A Huguenot, he worked for both Protestant and Catholic court circles, and rode out the Wars of Religion at Montargis, castle of Renée de France, duchess of Ferrara. Very little is known about Du Cerceau personally or about his early career, although he is thought to have traveled to Italy in the early 1540s with Georges d'Armagnac, French ambassador to Rome. At the end of the decade Du Cerceau settled in Orléans, where he opened an atelier. He designed the festival architecture for Henri II's entry into the city, but worked primarily as an engraver rather than an architect. His contemporaries referred to Du Cerceau as an "architect," but the term might refer solely to his work as a draftsman and ornamentalist.

Even in his own lifetime, Du Cerceau's fame and success derived primarily from his graphic work. The publications of Orléans, mostly free interpretations of antique and Renaissance motifs, reflected his early interest in Italy. Eventually, Du Cerceau would subordinate his Italian-based art to a native standard, and from the 1560s on he experimented with synthesizing French and Italian designs.

By 1559 Du Cerceau was in Paris, where he published his *Premier Livre d'architecture.* Dedicated to Henri II, it initiated his contact with the royal family. From that point, Du Cerceau's work was a direct result of royal support and reflected the political and aesthetic ambitions of the court. In the preface, Du Cerceau stated his intent to revitalize French architecture and eliminate the need for foreign architects—in essence, to elevate and unify French domestic design. Consequently, the *Premier Livre* was a handbook for the mason and patron, containing a series of plans, elevations and perspectives representing 50 town houses, accompanied by a text describing measurements, materials and expenses. Du Cerceau was alleged to have designed for a range of economic classes, but in truth he was concerned primarily with the wealthy patron. Earlier architectural treatises had neglected domestic architecture, and Du Cerceau remedied this. Attempting to place his work within a larger Vitruvian context, he labeled his plates in Latin and published a Latin edition simultaneously with the French.

The *Premier Livre* was practical rather than theoretical, but many of the first designs came directly from Sebastiano Serlio, whose "True Sixth Book" was available in manuscript form. These initial plans were traditional and may have influenced contemporary town houses, although the lack of surviving 16th-century examples makes this difficult to gauge. The larger designs at the end of the book were characterized by creative manipulations of simple geometric forms with a strong emphasis on centralized planning.

In the first book Du Cerceau showed a limited interest in furthering a particular style, and the decorative effect of the elevations springs from a combination of units and a limited application of traditional ornament. But in the *Second Livre* of 1561, he provided models for highly decorated features such as pavilions and dormers that may augment the stripped-down models provided in Book I. The fact that there are two different volumes denotes a separation of structure and ornament alien to the Italian tradition, but which was common in early French classicism.

The *Troisieme Livre* (1572) followed the publication of the treatises of Philibert Delorme and Andrea Palladio, and while it was still primarily a manual, there was a greater concern for the aesthetic impact of a building. Thirty-eight country houses were presented in plates that include both decorative details and landscape designs. In addition to purely invented plans, there were many inspired by Italian and French prototypes. While retaining the marked separation of plan and elevation,

Du Cerceau combined three-dimensional forms along a complex development of axes rather than relying on the generation of two-dimensional geometric figures.

Du Cerceau published *Les plus excellents bastiments de France* in 1576-1579, although there are indications he had been planning such a survey much earlier. The two-volume work assembled 30 contemporary châteaux and their histories, and probably related to a widening current of French nationalism in the late 16th century. This collection is our best record of French Renaissance châteaux, but it is not a purely objective one. The plates display considerable accuracy, but Du Cerceau modified and completed the unfinished buildings according to his own taste. He showed a development beyond his earlier publications and unveiled a new court architecture derived from the infusion of French models with imperial Roman scale. Many of these are, in effect, ideal plans that embody an emotional rather than built reality.

One should acknowledge the engravings as precious works of art in themselves and as an important contribution to the formation of taste. Du Cerceau was the first in France to use copper engravings rather than woodcuts, which allow for finer detailing and more subtlety, and could better articulate his ideas. Engraving in copper became a major medium for French architectural illustration.

There is an unresolved question regarding Du Cerceau's responsibility for the designs of the châteaux of Verneuil and Charleval, both of which appear in *Les plus excellents bastiments*. Traditionally attributed to Du Cerceau on stylistic grounds, they have also been assigned alternatively to his son, son-in-law and, in the case of Charleval, itinerant Italians. Although the question of Charleval is still open, Rosalys Coope has amassed a great deal of circumstantial evidence that Du Cerceau was indeed the architect of Verneuil.

Commissioned in 1568 by Philippe de Boulainvilliers, who desired ''*quelque oeuvre singulier,*'' Verneuil began as a grand and somewhat eccentric example of a French château. It was sold in 1575 to the duc de Nemours, son-in-law of Renée de France, and to whom Du Cerceau would later dedicate his *Livre des edifices antique romanes* (1584). As Coope notes, this change of ownership initiated a modification of the original concept toward a more simple, unified and coherent design based on architectural rather than ornamental principles.

Verneuil is important as a source of motifs, as the birthplace of Salomon de Brosse, and for the harmony it embodies between architecture and landscape. The château is part of a complex processional arrangement of forecourts, terraces and gardens integrated on a single central axis following a sloping site. It is contemporary with the Villa d'Este in Tivoli and more directly inspired by Italian spatial design than the work of Delorme.

Charleval continued this enlarged concept of a building. Begun as a hunting lodge for Charles IX, its enormous scale is analagous to, and even surpasses, Serlio's enlargement of the Louvre (Book 6) and Jean Bullant's scheme for Chenonceau. Charleval is an almost hyperrational magnification of Renaissance geometric design, and its unparalleled openness and intricacy anticipated Andre Le Nôtre's work at Vaux-le-Vicomte and Versailles.

The megalomaniacal scale and excessive ornament displayed at both Charleval and Verneuil are considered by modern scholars to be evidence of Du Cerceau's Mannerism, although the scale may have evolved from the breakdown of values in the period. He did directly borrow motifs from Italian Mannerists working at Fontainebleau, but whether or not they retain their iconographical import is unclear. Du Cerceau also lavished attention on elements such as staircases that particularly interested Mannerist artists. More important, he also shared in a special artistic approach based on an imaginative and facile manipulation of specifically classical models. As defined by Shearman, Mannerism requires a highly accomplished norm against which the artist may react and, in essence, compete. Although the creation of capricious variations on a theme had been a method of Du Cerceau in his earliest work at Orléans, it was only in his late drawings and engravings that he exploited two specific canons: Denate Bramante and Philibert Delorme. From Bramante, Du Cerceau derived a number of highly artificial and decorative facades. He exhibited a distinctly different attitude toward the work of other Italian artists such as Palladio and Filarete, who had a strong effect on his designs but were not treated as received doctrine. The buildings of Delorme triggered a more three-dimensional exploration of French architectural elements, and it may be through his play with Delorme's achievement that Du Cerceau initiated a French Mannerism dependent upon the Italian, but nonetheless unique.

Very little solid information is available on the three sons of Du Cerceau. Baptiste, the eldest, was a major architect in Paris at the end of the 16th century. He may be responsible for several châteaux outside Paris that exploited the decorative and planning ideas of his father. His major work was for Henri III, whose service he entered in 1575. In 1578 Baptiste succeeded Pierre Lescot as architect of the Louvre and completed the west part of the south wing of the Square Court in 1582. Baptiste succeeded Jean Bullant at the Valois Mausoleum and may have modified its design for structural reasons. He was heavily involved in numerous religious projects initiated by the intermittently penitent Henri III, including the design of a monastery for the Château de Madrid. Baptiste contributed to urban projects realized after his death, including changes to the initial design of the Pont Neuf.

Jacques Androuet Du Cerceau II, who began his career at Charleval and Tours, became architect to Henri IV after the death of his brother Baptiste, and was placed in charge of royal houses. He completed part of the ''Grand Galerie,'' joining the Louvre and Tuileries in a manner inspired by the work of his father and Bullant. The gallery was later demolished by Hector Lefuel.

The youngest son, Charles, directed two major building projects, a bridge and town house, in Châtellerault.

Jean Androuet Du Cerceau, the son of Baptiste, spent the early part of his career in the atelier of his cousin, Salomon de Brosse, with whom he worked at the Luxembourg Palace. He succeeded Antoine Métivier as architect to Louis XIII in 1617, and was a domestic architect in Paris from the 1620s to 1640s, when the Marais and Île St. Louis were developed. The themes behind Jean's town-house plans were elucidated in the writings of Pierre Le Muet (1623) and Louis Savot (1624).

The earliest town house authored by Jean was the Hôtel de Sully, although this attribution is based solely on stylistic analogies. Named for the minister of Henri IV who purchased the property in 1634, it is considered a prototype of the Parisian *hôtel* in the early 17th century. The plan is a more regularized version of the Hôtel Carnavalet, derived from Serlio's Grand Ferrare, and related to the simpler plans of Le Muet. The court facade flaunts a profusion of heavy ornament drawn from the ''Flemish Baroque,'' and contrasts with the strict simplicity of the street facade.

About 10 years after, Jean began the Hôtel de Bretonvilliers, one of the first town houses built after Louis XIII purchased the Île Notre Dame (later the Île St. Louis). Only the left wing was built by 1638, when a new contract was drawn and the building was continued by Louis Le Vau. The Hôtel de Bretonvilliers responded to the planning requirements of a new economic class, such as a greater differentiation of functions, and there was a more sophisticated development of axes than in the Hôtel de Sully. Once again, the facade was richly decorated with sculpture.

Jean Du Cerceau replaced Delorme's staircase in the Cour du Cheval Blanc at Fontainebleau with a complicated version of a horseshoe shape popular in the period of Louis XIII. It is similar to that at the Château de Cany-Barville, with the two wings resting on sloping vaults. In the early 1630s Jean designed some fortifications with his cousin Paul de Brosse and Charles du Rys, and began a new bridge, the Pont au Change, with Denis Laud and Mathieu Du Ry.

—PATRICIA LYNN PRICE

DUDOK, Willem Marinus.

Dutch. Born in Amsterdam, Netherlands, 6 July 1884. Died in Hilversum, Netherlands, 6 April 1974. Studied at Royal Military Academy, Breda, 1902-05. Municipal engineer, Leiden, 1913-14; director of municipal works, Hilversum, 1915-27; municipal architect, Hilversum, from 1927. Gold Medal, Royal Institute of British Architects, 1935; Gold Medal, American Institute of Architects, 1955; Officer, Order of the Oranje Nassau, Netherlands; Knight of the Order of the Nederlandse Leeuw; Officer, Order of the Crown of Belgium.

Chronology of Works
All in the Netherlands unless noted
†*Work no longer exists*

1916	Secondary School, Leiden
1917	Leidse Dagblad Offices, Leiden
1918	Residential development, 1st Municipal Quarter, Hilversum
1920	Rembrandt School, Hiversum
1921	Dr. H. Babinck School, Hilversum
1921	Residential development, 4th Municipal Quarter, Hilversum
1923	Abattoir, Hilversum
1925	Jan van der Heyden School, Hilversum
1925	Minckelers School, Hilversum
1926	Juliana School, Hilversum
1926	Fabritius School, Hilversum
1926	Dudok House, Hilversum
1927-39	Dutch Student House, Cité Universitaire, Paris, France
1928	Ruysdael School, Hilversum
1928-30	De Bijenkork Department Store, Rotterdam†
1928-31	Town Hall, Hilversum
1930	Johannes Calvijn School, Hilversum
1930	Valerius School, Hilversum
1931	Snellius School, Hilversum
1934-35	HAV Bank, Schiedam
1936	Aquatic Sports Pavilion, Hilversum
1938	De Burgh Garden City, Eindhoven
1939	Erasmushuis Office and Apartment Building, Rotterdam
1939	De Nederlanden van 1945 Insurance Company Office Building, Arnhem
1941	Municipal Theater, Utrecht
1947-51	Royal Dutch Steelworks Offices, Velsen

Publications

ARTICLES BY DUDOK

"Foreword." *Hilversum: A Short Introduction to the Recent Plans of Extension*. Hilversum, Netherlands 1924.
Texts in *Moderne Bouwkunst in Nederland*. Edited by H. P. Berlage, J. Gratema and others. 20 vols. Rotterdam, 1932-35.
Lectures in *Willem M. Dudok*. Edited by G. Stuiveling, F. Bakker-Schut and others. Amsterdam, 1954.

BOOKS ABOUT DUDOK

CRAMER, MAX; VAN GRIEKEN, HANS; and PRONE, H.: *W. M. Dudok: 1884-1974*. Exhibition catalog. Amsterdam, 1981.
FRIEDHOFF, G.: *W. M. Dudok*. Amsterdam, 1930.
HAAGSMA, IDS (ed.): *Amsterdam Bouwen, 1880-1980*. Utrecht and Antwerp, 1981.
MAGNÉE, R. N. H. (ed.): *Willem M. Dudok*. Amsterdam, 1954.
SOERGEL, HERMANN: *Wright, Dudok, Mendelsohn*. Munich, 1926.
STUIVELING, G.; BAKKER-SCHUT, F.; et al.: *Willem M. Dudok*. Amsterdam, 1954.
VAN BERGEIJK, HERMAN: *Willem Marinus Dudok: Architect and Urban Designer*. Laren, Netherlands, 1992.

ARTICLES ABOUT DUDOK

"Baukunst des Auslandes: Holland." *Deutsche Bauzeitung* (April 1937).
"Berlage, Dudok and Weeber." *Wonen-TA BK* (Herleen, Netherlands). Special issue (January 1983).
DE MEYER, JAN: "Willem Marinus Dudok." *Bouwkundig Weekblad* (23 November 1940).
"Exhibition of the Work of Architect Dudok." *Polytechnisch Tijdschrift* (May 1981).
"Forty Years of Hilversum." *Town and Country Planning* (November 1955).
FUTAGAWA, YUKIO (ed.): "Town Hall, Hilversum, Netherlands 1928-1931." *Global Architecture* No. 58 (1981).
"Hilversum Town Hall." *Architecture and Urbanism* (May 1982).
JORDAN, R. F.: "Dudok and the Repercussions of His European Influence." *Architectural Review* (April 1954): 236-241.
MOSER, KARL: "Neue holländische Architektur: Bauten von W. M. Dudok, Hilversum." *Werk* 9 (1922): 205-214.
PADOVAN, RICHARD: "Willem Dudok 1884-1974." *Architectural Review* (June 1974).
WILSON, RICHARD GUY: "Willem Dudok—Modernist But Not Mainstream." *American Institute of Architects Journal* (August 1982).

*

Willem Marinus Dudok was one of the most remarkable architects in the Netherlands, especially during the period between the two world wars. Although he hardly participated in the discussions about modern architecture in the 1920s, he was nevertheless an important transitional figure between traditional and modern building. Far from the main centers of architectural culture, Amsterdam and Rotterdam, he was a peripheral master, known for the outstanding quality of his work in Hilversum. He arrived in that town after a short career in the army and a position as architect for the city of Leiden. Besides doing work for the city, he collaborated with J. J. P. Oud, who remained

Willem Marinus Dudok: Town Hall, Hilversum, Netherlands, 1928-31

a lifetime friend. Together they built workers' housing in Leiderdorp (1914-15) and the office for the *Leids Dagblad* (1916-17), which shows an expressive use of brick.

From 1915 until 1954, Dudok was in charge of the Public Works Council of Hilversum, and as such was responsible for the design of many public buildings, including schools, slaughterhouses, cemeteries and police stations. Thanks to those buildings and his many residential designs in Hilversum, he could define the future townscape to a great extent. Dudok pleaded for a close, concentrated city which would not extend beyond a certain limit and would be bound in form. For him, the prospect of indefinite growth was a nightmare.

Although Dudok designed some exceptional buildings, such as the Dutch Student House at the Cité Universitaire in Paris (1927-39) and the department store De Bijenkorf in Rotterdam (1928-30, destroyed), which has big glass walls, his name is attached above all to one outstanding building, the Hilversum Town Hall (1915-31). With this work the architect became internationally recognized: the complex articulation of volumes (which substitutes for ornament), the moderate architectural language in which functionalism is combined with romanticism,

and the use of the traditional building material brick (the famous yellow Dudok-brick) are features that characterize much of Dudok's later architecture. The first ideas for the town hall date back to 1916. Dudok made designs in the style of H. P. Berlage and the Amsterdam school before he finally reached the definite solution for this building, which was to become a mecca for many young architects. In many ways Dudok tried to arrive at an architecture that showed characteristics of the Amsterdam school—neoplasticism and functionalism.

Besides his work for Hilversum, Dudok had the opportunity to plan and build in many other cities. Due to the fact that attention has always been focused on the Hilversum Town Hall, these other projects have remained almost completely in the shadows. The HAV-Bank in Schiedam (1931-35), the offices for *De Nederlanden* in Arnhem (1937-39) and the Theater in Utrecht (1937-41), all of which were crucial to Dudok's development before 1940, are hardly considered, yet they constitute masterworks in Dutch architectural history. A second aspect of his work comprises the various town-planning proposals that he was asked to elaborate for cities such as Hilversum (from 1915 onward), The Hague (1934-42 and 1945-52), Alkmaar

(1942-43), Velsen (1945-52) and Zwolle (1948-53). Although his plans were not always executed, they have left their traces. Besides, for Dudok, the relationship between city planning and architecture was always very close, as most of his projects demonstrate.

His working method was from the large to the small. The first sketches of a building were usually perspectives that would show the visual effect of the object in the cityscape. If we walk through the Town Hall of Hilversum, we have the sensation of going through a city that was projected according to Leon Battista Alberti's principle that a house should be a small city, and the city a big house. In his town planning, Dudok was influenced by Camillo Sitte, too.

Dudok's little-noticed buildings after World War II include the administration building for the Royal Dutch Steelworks at Velsen (1947-51), along with the magnificent glass bridge over the street and the Town Hall for the same city (1949-65). At the end of his career, after having left his position in Hilversum, Dudok worked on a large number of projects for a real estate agent. Although the quality of these projects remained high, especially compared with the architectural poverty in the Netherlands in those days, they never had the innovative character of his work from before the war. Because of their clarifying simplicity, they lack the tension between building volumes that was prevalent in his earlier work.

—HERMAN VAN BERGEIJK

DUIKER, Johannes.

Dutch. Born in the Hague, Netherlands, 1 March 1890. Died in Amsterdam, 23 February 1935. Graduated from Delft Technical University, 1913. Partnership with Bernard Bijvoet (1889-1979), Amsterdam, 1916-35. Member, De Stijl; member, De 8 en Opbouw.

Chronology of Works
All in the Netherlands

1917-19	Karenhuizen Housing for the Elderly, Alkmaar
1918	Housing and shops, Thomsonplein 10-15, The Hague
1920	Terrace housing, J. v. Oldenbarneveldelaan, The Hague
1920	Housing Development, Scheveningselaan, Kijkduin, The Hague
1922	Villas, Kijkduin, The Hague
1922-31	Technical School, Scheveningen
1924	Country House, Stommerkade 64, Aalsmeer
1924-25	Copper Rods Fund Soap Factory, Diemerbrug
1925	Chemist's Shop, Haltestraat 8, Zandvoort
1926-28	Zonnestraal Sanatorium Complex, Hilversum (with Bernard Bijvoet)
1927-30	Open-Air Public School, Cliostraat, Amsterdam
1927-30	Nirvana Flats, Benoordenhoutseweg and Willem Witsenplein, The Hague (with Wiebenga)
1934	Handelsblad-Cineac Cinema, Amsterdam
1934-36	Grand Hotel Gooiland, Hilversum (completed by Bijvoet)

Publications

BOOKS BY DUIKER

Hoogbouw. Rotterdam, 1930.

ARTICLES BY DUIKER

Several in *De 8 en Opbouw* (1932-35).

BOOKS ABOUT DUIKER

BOGA, J. (ed.): *Bernard Bijvoet and Johannes Duiker 1890-1935*. Zurich, n.d.
MOLEMA, JAN: *Duiker*. Rotterdam, 1989.

ARTICLES ABOUT DUIKER

JELLES, E. J., and ALBERTS, C. A.: "Duiker." *Forum* 22, Nos. 5-6, special issues (November 1971-January 1972).
VICKERY, ROBERT: "Bijvoet and Duiker." *Perspecta* 13/14 (1971): 130-161.
"Zonnestraal." *Forum* 16, entire issue (January 1962).

*

In a life tragically cut short at 45, Johannes Duiker's oeuvre understandably represents a modest output in terms of sheer volume. However, three buildings—all of which embrace the wider concerns of education, health care and entertainment—have ensured Duiker's place in the development of mainstream 20th-century Dutch architecture. These are the Open Air School, Cliostraat, in Amsterdam; the Zonnestraal Sanatorium in Hilversum; and the Handelsblad-Cineac Cinema in Amsterdam.

A true progressive, Duiker was a member of the loosely knit De Stijl group, whose ideas developed apace during World War I, when Holland remained neutral, thereby gaining ground on similar groups in France, Germany and Russia whose activities were to some extent interrupted and eclipsed by the war. Duiker was also closely associated with the functionalist Opbouw group and its radical journal, *De 8 en Opbouw*. Established in 1920 in Rotterdam, Opbouw's concern for "universality" had strong parallels in Piet Mondrian's view that abstract art could embrace similar goals.

Like many of his contemporaries, Duiker in his early career succumbed to the immense influence which Frank Lloyd Wright had exerted upon the Low Countries after publication of the celebrated Wasmuth volumes. However, Duiker's country house at Aalsmeer (1924, with Bernard Bijvoet) represented a dramatic departure, particularly in its informal assembly of monopitches. The horizontal weatherboarding and strip windows meeting at the corners, together with the freestanding, cylindrical, drum-like staircase tower, were more redolent of international modernism than any of his earlier Wright-inspired work.

Even more akin to the International Style, and particularly to Russian constructivism, was his Zonnestraal Sanatorium, Hilversum (1928). This is an assured masterwork, where the latest reinforced-concrete technology was harnessed to industrial glazing techniques to produce a fitting response to progressive movements in health care which prescribed an abundance of sunlight and fresh air. The flat-roofed ward blocks radiate in a butterfly plan from a central block for administration and medical care to produce an almost Beaux-Arts axiality. In detail,

Johannes Duiker: Open-Air Public School, Amsterdam, Netherlands, 1927-30

the building achieves a degree of precision that reinforces the clarity of its formal expression. The nautical flavor of roof-terrace balustrades and drum-like stairs that punctuate the smooth white facades owe much to the architectural vocabulary of Le Corbusier's Parisian houses from the period.

An adherence to a symmetrical organization of the plan is also evident at the Amsterdam Open Air school (1930). The main four-story classroom is square on plan with reinforced-concrete floor slabs supported on tapered beams springing from a regular grid of concrete columns. A central stair with lobby is disposed diagonally and thus heightens the impact of the open terraces that engage with it. These terraces form a quarter of each floor plan, evidence of a strict formalism, which gives way to a more relaxed arrangement of the associated single-story block. The expression of the building is functionalist *in extremis*. Floor slabs are connected with full-height glazing, which is simply omitted to signal the open terraces. The effect is chasm-like and in hindsight not altogether satisfactory, but its strictly functionalist ethos devoid of any superfluous gesture found favor with architects of a similar persuasion.

Less serious was the Cineac Cinema, Amsterdam (1934), which nevertheless harnessed precisely the same architectural language to a more frivolous program of public entertainment. A smooth white cube with indented corner like the Open Air School conceals a surprising egg-shaped auditorium. Hugely scaled electronic signs advertising the building's cinematic function owe much to Russian constructivist projects of the previous decade. However, the Cineac evinces the same confidence and élan of Duiker's previous work.

Other projects including Hilversum's Grand Hotel and A.V.R.O. Radio Station were completed after Duiker's death, and suggest a career poised for further success had it not been so curtailed.

Duiker's short career was a testament to the successful confluence of avant-garde architecture and an optimistic society: interwar Holland was the catalyst for such progressive attitudes, which, in spite of the horrific interlude of World War II, survive today in the work of architects like Aldo Van Eyck and Herman Hertzberger.

—A. PETER FAWCETT

DURAND, J. N. L.

French. Born Jean-Nicolas-Louis Durand in Paris, France, 18 September 1760. Died in France, 31 December 1834. Studied at the Collège de Montaigu; studied architecture with Pierre Panseron, École Militaire, and at the Académie d'Architecture with Jean Perronet and Etienne Louis Boullée; won second place in Prix de Rome competitions, 1779 and 1780. Began working for Boullée as draftsman, 1776; professor of architecture at the new École Polytechnique, 1795-1834.

Chronology of Works
In France

1788   Hôtel Lathuille, rue du Faubourg-Poissonnière, Paris

Publications

BOOKS BY DURAND

Recueil et parallèle des édifices de tout genre, anciens et modernes. 2 vols. Paris, 1800.
Précis des leçons d'architecture données à l'École royale polytechnique. 2 vols. Paris, 1802-05.

BOOKS ABOUT DURAND

BRAHAM, ALLAN: *The Architecture of the French Enlightenment.* Berkeley, California, and Los Angeles, 1980.
COLLINS, PETER: *Changing Ideals in Modern Architecture.* London, 1965.
HAUTECOEUR, LOUIS: *Histoire de l'architecture classique en France.* Paris, 1953.
JANINOT, JEAN-FRANCOIS: *Vues pittoresques des principaux édifices de Paris.* Paris, 1792.
KAUFMANN, EMIL: *Architecture in the Age of Reason: Baroque and Post-Baroque in England, Italy, France.* Cambridge, Massachusetts, 1955.
KRAFFT, JEAN CHARLES, and RANSONNETTE, NICOLAS (eds.): *Plans, coupes, élévations des plus belles maisons et des hôtels construits à Paris et dans les environs.* Paris, 1802.
RONDELET, ANTOINE: *Notice historique sur la vie et les ouvrages de J. N. L. Durand.* Paris, 1835.
SZAMBIEN, WERNER: *Jean-Nicolas-Louis Durand, 1760-1834: De l'imitation à la norme.* Paris, 1984.
VILLARI, SERGIO: *J. N. L. Durand.* New York, 1990.

ARTICLES ABOUT DURAND

HERNANDEZ, A.: "J. N. L. Durand's Architectural Theory." *Perspecta* 12 (1969).

*

J.N.L. Durand taught and wrote: he built very little. The Hôtel Lathuille on the rue du Faubourg-Poissonnière (1788) in Paris, however, symbolizes his whole career. Its plan and elevations appeared in two publications by Johann Karl Krafft and in a somewhat simplified version in Durand's own *Précis* of 1802.

The building is a severe, almost featureless, rectangular pile, covered by a hipped roof; two stories face its entrance court and three stories face its garden. Four doric columns, unfluted except for a few inches at the base and top of the shaft, mark the court entrance. Two windows flank the portal; there are

three windows in the upper story directly under the eaves. Other than round-arched French doors spanning the intervals between the columns, all other embellishments including pediments and pilasters, are absent.

Four equally severe doric columns form the entrance of the garden side; there, however, Durand relieved the austerity with a rusticated basement story and caryatids directly above each of the columns. The caryatids, in high relief, separate three windows. Each caryatid stands flat-footed, hands folded across her lap, demurely looking down.

A rigid symmetry governs the plan. A stair with a salon behind forms the axis of the first floor, and although specific functions are designated to rooms, such as *chambre à coucher* and *salle à manger,* no indication of use is seen in their shape or size. They simply echo each other on either side of the axial spaces. Although Durand designated one room as the kitchen (main floor) and another as the bath (garden level), he made no mention of plumbing or any other technical device.

The house, therefore, suggests the clientele for whom it was destined: a moderately wealthy bourgeois with practical inclinations and "correct" tastes. To Durand, his house suggested an austere beauty that stood in contrast to the wasteful opulence of the ancien régime. He wrote: "Of all the arts, architecture is the most expensive; it is costly to build private residences; it is enormously expensive to construct public buildings even when both have been conceived with wisdom; and if one follows prejudice, caprice, or routine, the expenses will be incalculable." He observed that this impracticality of opulence could be seen in Versailles: "The château of Versailles, this edifice in which one finds rooms without number and no entrance; thousands of columns and no colonnade; a vast expanse without grandeur; an extreme richness without magnificence, is a striking example of this truth."

To Durand, certain basic truths or principles governed all architecture, and an architect, whether designing a palace or a cabin, either followed them or doomed his project to failure. Durand's truths derived from a tradition of classical French rationalism and the revolutionary milieu in which he lived.

The son of a cobbler, Durand rose from humble circumstances. He attended the Collège de Montaigu and studied architecture with Pierre Panseron of the École Militaire; Jean Perronet, founder of the École des Ponts et Chaussées, and Étienne-Louis Boullée, for whom he became a draftsman. He entered the Académie d'architecture, winning second place in the Prix de Rome competitions of 1779 and 1780. By 1795, in the midst of the revolutionary period, Durand had enough prestige and sufficient contacts to be appointed professor of architecture at the newly established (1793) École Polytechnique. He taught there until his death. His association with engineers determined his architectural views, which had little sympathy with either orthodox neoclassicism or romantic attitudes.

He felt that adherence to the authority of the antique was ridiculous, because the ancients themselves varied architectural forms extensively, generally in response to functional and structural requirements. He found the notion that the classical orders reflected human proportions and sexual qualities (Doric, masculine; Ionic, feminine; Corinthian, virginal) to be ludicrous. He contemptuously dismissed Père Laugier's romantic theory that the temple evolved from a primitive hut.

His immediate inspiration came from the great visionary architects of the revolutionary era, of whom his teacher Boullée was a principal representative. Boullée's compositions embodied great monumental, often Piranesi-like effects, however, and Durand would have none of that. To him architecture existed as a practical craft in which beauty occurred as a by-product. The architect had two fundamental tasks: he must, with a given sum, make a building as convenient and solid as possible—a primary necessity of private structures; the requirements of a structure being given—especially true of public buildings—he must build as cheaply as possible. Durand maintained that an architect must consider the building traditions of a culture and, in order not to shock, might make reference to historic styles. He hoped to familiarize architects, engineers, stage designers, landscape painters and others with a range of styles, each drawn to scale, in his *Recueil*.

Durand believed, however, that in essence the form of a building derived from its purpose and the materials of its construction. The architect's plans expressed the structure's function. In this way, each kind of building revealed its individual character. The elevation grew out of the plan naturally.

As to planning itself, Durand insisted that the architect employ grid paper. He could therefore control every aspect of the design, establishing the principal axes, adjusting proportions and dimensions, and coordinating plan and elevation.

Ornament was a useless extravagance, according to Durand, and should seldom, if ever, be applied to buildings. The very dynamics of construction produced a pleasing effect. Thus a wall, thickened at certain points to buttress vaults, created a naturally occurring decoration. Stories and points of support might be emphasized by string courses and Doric pilasters. Buildings expressing their structure in this manner need not be boring, and Durand illustrated many of the infinite variations possible in his *Précis*. When employing columns, the architect must use them for actual support; Durand could not abide sham.

Durand illustrated his ideas by redesigning the Panthéon in Paris, which he found deficient both in grandeur and structural stability. Had Jacques-Germain Soufflot used a shallow Roman dome, supported on a cylindrical wall and buttressed by a ring of freestanding Doric columns, the result would have had no structural problems, been more economical and, as a result, visually much more powerful, Durand noted.

Durand realized that his engineering students could spend little time studying architecture, yet, ironically, he wrote, engineers designed the greatest number and types of structures employed by society. He therefore created a clear and succinct system of instruction.

He divided his course into three parts. In the first, the students considered the constituent parts of a building, such as walls, doors, arcades, engaged and isolated supports (pilasters and columns), pillars, floors, roofs and terraces. At that stage, one also studied the manner in which these elements were used, their materials and proper proportions. The second part involved the combination of these elements into buildings or parts of buildings, such as porticoes, porches, vestibules and various kinds of rooms in general ensembles. Students undertook the study of grander compositions in the third part: there they made a quick study of urban planning, looking at the approaches to cities, their entrances, streets and squares. Most important would be the design of particular types of structures, such as public buildings relating to governing, health, pleasure and security, as well as private houses in the city, apartment buildings, country houses, farms and hostelries.

Durand taught that necessity, economy and convenience dictated the ultimate form of an edifice. Nevertheless, he still approached all problems from a classical, almost Platonic, point of view. He preferred the simplest possible forms: a square was preferable to a parallelogram, and a circle to both. Basic geometric shapes were simpler, hence more economical to build. Also, a function, enclosed by a pure geometric form, revealed itself in the elevation of a building, giving a structure its unique character. All plans *must* be symmetrical with clearly defined axial spaces, because axial and symmetrical planning assured

an efficient, economical building. Durand was a functionalist, but a *classical* functionalist.

Most important, he devised a teachable system. His methods and models were taken up in other countries, particularly Germany, and other engineering schools. In 1829, the École Centrale des Arts et Manufactures adopted Durand's system; there, many foreign students, including the American architect William Le Baron Jenney, imbibed Durand's system.

Durand thus seemed to anticipate much of the Modern Movement that followed in the 19th and 20th centuries. Fragments of his teaching can be found in the ideas of Henri Labrouste and Eugène Viollet-le-Duc. Statements made by Le Corbusier regarding fenestration and other forms deriving from structure often sound similar to Durand's. Both Ludwig Mies van der Rohe and Frank Lloyd Wright disposed simple geometric forms on grids. Durand's own pure forms suggest Adolf Loos and Tony Garnier.

Durand nevertheless manifested conservative tendencies. Most of the examples used in his *Précis* were simplifications of designs made by academically inclined architects. He advocated only traditional materials. He advised that little or no iron be used in vaulting, despite the fact that French builders had used wrought iron in ingenious ways since the 17th century. Durand professed an admiration for Andrea Palladio, and, like Palladio, he compressed his functions within symmetrical schemes. Later functionalist architects from Viollet-le-Duc through the Bauhaus and Wright exploited the asymmetries suggested by a building's purposes.

Durand expressed the Enlightenment: he approached each problem with reason and clarity of purpose. Although he did not go beyond his time, others picked up and developed many of the implications of his thinking.

—THEODORE TURAK

DU RY, Simon.

German. Born Simon Louis du Ry in Kassel, Germany, 13 January 1726. Died 23 August 1799. Father was Charles-Louis du Ry, chief court architect to Landgrave Frederick I; grandfather was Paul du Ry, court architect to Landgrave Karl of Hessen-Kassel; great-grandfather was Mathurin du Ry, a court architect in Paris. Trained as architect by his father; further training with the Swedish court architect Karl Hårleman, Stockholm, 1746-48; studied with Jacques François Blondel, Paris, 1748-52; study tour in Italy, 1753-56. Succeeded his father as chief court architect at Kassel; became professor of architecture, Collegium Carolinum, Kassel, 1766; appointed court building counselor, 1776; appointed chief building director of Kassel, 1785; director, Academy of Architecture, and vice-president and secretary, Academy of Arts, 1795.

Chronology of Works
All in Germany
† *Work no longer exists*

1768-71	Jungken Palace (later White Palace), Kassel, Hesse†
1769-79	Fridericanium Museum (later rebuilt), Kassel, Hesse†
1770-72	French Hospital, Kassel, Hesse†
1770-74	Geistliches Haus, Kassel, Hesse†
1770-74	St. Elisabeth's Church, Kassel, Hesse†
1771-75	Oberneustadt Town Hall, Kassel, Hesse†
1775-84	Schloss Hüffe, near Minden, Westphalia
1776-83	Schloss Fürstenberg, Westphalia

1786-92	Landgrave's Palace, Weissenstein, near Kassel, Hesse
1787-88	Schloss Montcheri, Hofgeismar, Hesse
1792	Monopteron, Hofgeismar, Hesse

Publications

BOOKS ABOUT DU RY

BOEHLKE, HANS-KURT: *Simon Louis du Ry als Stadtbaumeister Landgraf Friedrichs II. von Hessen Kassel.* Kassel, 1958.

GERLAND, OTTO: *Paul, Charles und Simon Louis du Ry: Eine Künstlerfamilie der Barockzeit.* Stuttgart, 1895.

GUTKIND, E. A.: *Urban Development in Central Europe.* London, 1964.

HEMPEL, EBERHARD: *Baroque Art and Architecture in Central Europe.* Baltimore, 1965.

*

Simon Louis du Ry came from a family of architects who had originated in France and eventually settled in Kassel, Germany. He received his initial training from his father, Charles du Ry, studied in Stockholm (1746-48) under Swedish court architect Carl Hårleman and then in Paris at Jacques François Blondel's own school (1748-52). This was followed by three years in Italy (1753-56), where he examined the buildings of Rome, studied the works of Andrea Palladro in Vicenza, and inspected the excavations at Herculaneum.

All these influences produced an adaptable architect who could blend structures with their settings and with surrounding architecture. In addition, his studies with Blondel enabled him to achieve simplicity and purity while still providing "character" to his buildings, and also to make his architecture appear appropriate to its purpose. Following in the footsteps of his father and grandfather, Paul du Ry (1640-1714), Simon du Ry was made Kassel's court architect in 1767, in service to Landgrave Friedrich II. He obtained many commissions through his diligence and was rewarded with numerous memberships and directorships. Many of his most important works are located in Kassel, once considered by Georg Forster to be the most beautiful city, where du Ry helped implement Friedrich II's policies for improving the town through urban planning. A Tischbein portrait depicts him with the plans for that area.

The two central components of the development were the Königsplatz circus and the Friedrichsplatz square. Du Ry designed the buildings on the Königsplatz with uniform building heights but with diverse decorations. The Friedrichsplatz, planned and executed as a large rectangle, forms the necessary connections between the countryside, the new upper city and other squares and circuses in the city itself. A new military parade ground on its southern side creates a view in that direction. The simplicity of the plan is emphasized by a double row of lime trees around the garden, with open space in front of the Museum Fridericianum. Du Ry's buildings are united: the museum dominates the middle of the long side of the square and is flanked by two wings—St. Elisabeth's Church (no longer extant) on one side and the palatial residence of von Jungken, a cabinet minister, on the other. Landscape, in the form of trees, provides natural bridges between the three.

The Museum Fridericianum is severe and ponderous, possibly because of its serious purpose. Du Ry did not follow the English custom of placing such an edifice on a high plinth, but attempted to convey public accessibility by directly connecting its entrance (an Ionic, pedimented portico) to the street. The entablature is severely simple, while the balustrade provides a sense of decoration to the top, further accentuated by vases marking the progression toward the middle. The central attic area behind the gable is decorated with classically draped statues. This is a restrained form of Baroque art, containing classical elements in its distribution of parts and use of columns, pilasters and walls.

Flanking the museum, du Ry's private chapel of St. Elisabeth for the Roman Catholic convert Friedrich II is a simple classical facade with applied pilasters, more like a palace than like a church, in accordance with Friedrich's promise not to build any Catholic churches. As befits a wing, the flat and relatively smooth exterior is simpler than the museum's strongly silhouetted skyline and pronounced facade. On entering the chapel, one is impressed by splendid South German decoration and the surprising two-story dome at the center.

A much more grandiose style was employed for the landgrave's Palace at Weissenstein. Influences of English Palladianism, French neoclassicism and the Italian Baroque are evident. Du Ry began by building new wings at an angle of 45 degrees to the main structure, replacing the old pavilions which had been at right angles. These wings, each oriented to face the mountain, demonstrate a special quality found in du Ry's works: they are made to look taller by utilizing narrow intercolumniation. Vases surmounting the balustrade continue the visual vertical idea. The ends of the wings are rounded off with projecting semicircular apses, another unique embellishment. Their ground floors consist of arched, rusticated areas and sets of stairs leading into the structures. Du Ry provided smooth transitions between the parts of the buildings, rounding corners and breaking up the rooflines.

The design of the additions at Weissenstein, exploiting the view of Carlsberg Mountain and its gardens, points to the sensitivity of an architect who cleverly emphasized the various projects which had cost his patron a great deal of money: ornamental temples, statues, vases, busts and lines of hedges. Friedrich II had not at first planned to replace the main building, but his successor, Wilhelm IX, was so enamored with the renovations that a new center for the structure was commissioned. Unfortunately, du Ry was not chosen to complete his masterpiece; that honor went to Heinrich Christoph Jussow (1754-1825).

Basing his work on English garden buildings which had been made popular by William Chambers, du Ry was responsible for a number of structures for the gardens of Wilhelmshöhe, notably Felseneck (a small mountain retreat) and the Chinese Village; he was also involved in changing the gardens' strictly symmetrical, axial layout to one with more wandering paths.

While hardly revolutionary in spirit, du Ry did introduce the neoclassical ideas of England and France to his community. His arena of operations was necessarily limited: Kassel was somewhat old-fashioned in its architecture, and his patrons had definite aesthetic ideas. Within that framework, du Ry managed to produce some elegant designs; his buildings and town plans are simple and well proportioned. Neither overly grandiose nor excessively austere, his works, especially his larger structures, are imbued with a Baroque quality.

—TERESA S. WATTS

EAMES, Charles O.

American. Born in St. Louis, Missouri, 17 June 1907. Died in St. Louis, Missouri, 21 August 1978. Married Ray Kaiser, 1941. Studied architecture at Washington University, St. Louis, 1924-26. In private practice, St. Louis, 1930-34; traveled and worked in Mexico, 1934-35; returned to private practice in St. Louis, 193536; fellow, then head of Department of Experimental Design, Cranbrook Academy, Bloomfield Hills, Michigan, 1936-40; partnership with his wife in Los Angeles, California, 1942-45, and then in Venice, California, 1945-78; consulting designer to Herman Miller Inc, Los Angeles, from 1947. Lecturer, California Institute of Technology, Pasadena, 1953-56; Charles Eliot Norton Professor of Poetry, Harvard University, Cambridge, Massachusetts, 1970. Gold Medal, American Institute of Architects, 1957; Gold Medal, Royal Institute of British Architects, 1979.

Chronology of Works
All in the United States

1945-49	Charles Eames Residence, Pacific Palisades, California (with Eero Saarinen)
1945-50	John Entenza Residence, Pacific Palisades, California (with Eero Saarinen)
1947-49	Herman Miller Showroom, Beverly Hills, California
1956	Lounge Chair and Ottoman (design)
1964	IBM Exhibit, World's Fair, New York

Publications

BOOKS BY EAMES

A Computer Perspective. Cambridge, Massachusetts, 1973.
The World of Franklin and Jefferson. Exhibition catalog. Los Angeles, 1976.

ARTICLES BY EAMES

"Design Today." *Arts and Architecture* (September 1941).
"Organic Design." *Arts and Architecture* (December 1941).
"General Motors Revisited." *Architectural Forum* (June 1971).

BOOKS ABOUT EAMES

CAPLAN, RALPH, and MORRISON, PHILIP: *Connections: The work of Charles and Ray Eames.* Los Angeles, 1976.
CLARK, ROBERT JUDSON: *Design in America: The Cranbrook Vision 1925-1950.* Exhibition catalog. New York, 1983.
DREXLER, ARTHUR: *Charles Eames: Furniture from the Design Collection.* Exhibition catalog. New York, 1973.
McCOY, ESTHER: *Case Study Houses, 1945-1962.* 2nd ed. Los Angeles, 1977.

NEWHART, JOHN; NEWHART, MARILYN; and EAMES, RAY: *Eames Design: The Work of the Office of Charles and Ray Eames.* New York, 1989.
RUBINO, LUCIANO: *Ray and Charles Eames: il collectivo della fantasia.* Rome, 1981.

ARTICLES ABOUT EAMES

BARONI, DANIELE: "Form and Its Double." *Ottagono* (June 1981).
"Case Study House for 1949: Designed by Charles Eames." *Arts and Architecture* 66, No. 12 (1949): 26-39.
"Case Study Houses 8 and 9 by Charles Eames and Eero Saarinen, Architects." *Arts and Architecture* 62, No. 12 (1945): 43-51.
"Case Study Houses No. 8 and No. 9, Architects, Charles Eames and Eero Saarinen." *Arts and Architecture* 65, No. 3 (1948): 39-41.
"Charles Eames—Scholar and Architect." *MD: Moebel Interior Design* (September 1980).
"Dallo studio di Eames." *Domus* No. 402 (1963): 26-42.
"Eames Celebration." *Architectural Design* 36, No. 9, special issue (September 1966): 432-471.
"The Eames House." *Arts and Architecture* No. 2 (1983).
GOLDBERGER, PAUL: "The Keen, Loving Eye of Charles Eames." *Art News* 77, No. 8 (October 1978): 135-136.
"Golden Connections." *Building* (6 April 1979).
GUELFT, OLGA: "Charles Eames 1907-1978." *Interiors* (October 1978).
HILL, MIKE: "Eames' Epitaph." *Building Design* (11 February 1983).
KAUFMANN, EDGAR, JR.: "Chairs, Eames and Chests." *Art News* 49, No. 3 (1950): 36-40.
McCOY, ESTHER: "An Affection for Objects." *Progressive Architecture* 54 (August 1973): 64-67.
McCOY, ESTHER: "Charles and Ray Eames." *Design Quarterly* 98-99 (1975): 21-29.
McCOY, ESTHER: "Charles Eames, A Personal Memoir." *Progressive Architecture* (January 1979).
McCULLOGH, JANE: "Some Thoughts about Eames." *Zodiac* No. 8 (1961).
MILLER, J. R.: "Mathematica." *Industrial Design* (May 1961).
NELSON, GEORGE: "Design in America: The Last 25 Years." *Interiors* (November 1965).
NOYES, ELIOT: "Charles Eames." *Arts and Architecture* 63 (September 1946): 26-44.
SCHRADER, PAUL: "Poetry of Ideas: The Films of Charles Eames." *Film Quarterly* (Spring 1970).
SMITHSON, PETER: "Charles Eames." *Journal of the Royal Institute of British Architects* 85, No. 11 (October 1978).
"Three Chairs/Three Records of the Design Process." *Interiors* (April 1958).
WINTER, JOHN: "Charles Eames." *Architectural Review* (October 1978).

Because Charles Eames did so many things and did them equally well, it is possible that his reputation as one of the 20th century's most influential designers will be somewhat tenuous. Descriptive terms such as architect, furniture designer, graphic artist and filmmaker just suggest the scope of his design skills and the range of his interests. For Eames, design was "a plan for arranging elements in such a way as to best accomplish a particular purpose." The very inclusiveness of his definition reinforces the idea that for him design knew no limits: the boundaries of design were the boundaries of the problem itself.

Charles Ormond Eames, Jr., was the second child of a railroad security officer who was also an amateur photographer; there was not much in Eames' early life to suggest the future breadth of his interests. The same was true for his adolescence, when he held what could be described—for the time—as a youngster's usual assortment of part-time jobs: printer's devil, drugstore factotum, steelmill laborer. Prior to entering Washington University in St. Louis on an architecture scholarship, Eames spent the summer designing lighting fixtures for a local firm. Other summers were spent in the employ of architects in St. Louis.

Upon graduation and after marrying a student whom he met at the university, Eames opened an architectural office with Charles M. Gray. Their practice remained small during what were the Depression's early years, and the office closed in 1934. Returning to St. Louis after a trip to Mexico, Eames opened an office with Robert T. Walsh. One of their commissions, St. Mary's Church, Helena, Arkansas (1935), was published in *Architectural Forum* and seen by Eliel Saarinen (1873-1950), who wrote to express his admiration for the work. In 1938 Eames accepted a fellowship from Saarinen to study architecture and design at the Cranbrook Academy of Art near Detroit, Michigan. The list of his classmates reads like a "Design Who's Who." Joining the Cranbrook faculty in 1940, Eames headed the industrial design department. With Eero Saarinen (1910-61), Eliel's son, Eames entered the Museum of Modern Art's "Organic Design in Home Furnishings" competition (1940), winning first prize in two categories. While conceived for mass production, their furniture designs surpassed current understanding of the idea of furniture in terms of fabrication techniques and materials employed. This characteristic of innovation marks all of Eames' work, as does the freshness with which he approached problem solving in general.

Divorcing his wife in 1941, Eames married Bernice "Ray" Kaiser (1912-88) in June of the same year, their marriage forming the basis of a design partnership whose work is of enduring quality and influence. It is not so much that they were willing to tackle any design problem, it is how they achieved their solutions that makes them so remarkable. Without preconception, but strongly influenced by mass-production techniques, their work manifests a clarity and an originality that is, at once, arresting and provocative. This is especially true of their molded plywood furniture. Here material and form work together, resulting in designs that are lightweight, functional and expressive of their means of production. The work is of such quality and innovation as to place Eames firmly in the Modern Movement.

In addition to countless furniture designs—some existing only as prototypes—Eames designed his own home (1945-49), many important exhibitions, produced numerous graphic designs, toys, and a series of perceptive and thought-provoking films on a variety of subjects. The films cover a large intellectual and aesthetic spectrum, with some designed to communicate mathematical concepts simply *(Powers of Ten)*, to delight the soul of the child in us all *(Toccata for Toy Trains)*, or to inform *(De Gaulle Sketch)*. Common to all the films is a simplicity that belies their content and structure: they are carefully crafted with apparent effortlessness, but one is never made aware of means. It is the same with the furniture, especially his most famous design, the Lounge Chair (1956). In fact, this quality is to be found in everything Eames designed. He brought an openness to every problem that can only be described as childlike, fresh and receptive to new possibilities.

Though by nature taciturn, Eames was nevertheless willing to place his efforts in a larger historical context. When asked if design is the creation of an individual, his response is a model of reticence: "No—because to be realistic one must always admit the influence of those who have gone before." In retrospect, we can see how true this is in his work, strongly influenced as it was by virtue of his close association with both Saarinens and his second wife, Ray. His was an original talent of imposing clarity and proportions, and, justly, his name is synonymous with the word "designer."

—DAVID SPAETH

EIDLITZ, Leopold.

American. Born in Prague, Bohemia (now Czech Republic), 10 March 1823. Died on 21 March 1906. Educated at Vienna Polytechnic. Draftsman, Richard Upjohn office, New York, 1843; opened practice in New York; appointed to advisory board on the State Capitol, Albany, New York, 1875. Cofounder, American Institute of Architects, 1857.

Chronology of Works
All in the United States
* Approximate dates
† Work no longer exists

1846-48	St. George's Church, New York City
1847	Wooster Street Synagogue, New York City
1848	P. T. Barnum House, Bridgeport, Connecticut†
1849-54	First Church of Christ, New London, Connecticut
1851	Eidlitz Residence, New York City†
1851-52	Fifth Avenue Presbyterian Church, New York City†
1851-52	St. George's Rectory, New York City
1853-55	St. Peter's, New York City
1854	Willoughby House, Newport, Rhode Island
1854-55	City Hall, Springfield, Massachusetts*
1856-57	Continental Bank, New York City†
1856-59	Second Congregational Church, Greenwich, Connecticut
1857	American Exchange Bank, New York City†
1858*	Hamilton Ferry House, Brooklyn, New York†
1858-59	Broadway Tabernacle, New York City†
1859-67	Christ Church, St. Louis, Missouri
1860-61	Brooklyn Academy of Music, Brooklyn, New York†
1860-61	Produce Exchange, New York City†
1865	Masonic Temple, Troy, New York†
1866-68	Temple Emanu-El, New York City (with Henry Fernback)†
1867-68	St. Peter's Chapel, New York City
1868-70	Parish House and Church of the Pilgrims, Brooklyn, New York
1869	Brooklyn Union Building, Brooklyn, New York†
1870	Decker Building, New York City†
1870-75	Church of the Holy Trinity, New York City†

1872	Children's Aid Society, Newsboys' Lodging House, New York City†
1872	St. George's Chapel, New York City†
1875	Dry Dock Savings Bank, New York City†
1875-85	State Capitol, Albany, New York (with H. H. Richardson and Frederick Law Olmsted)
1876-78	"Tweed" Courthouse, New York City (south wing)
1886-88	St. George's Clergy House, New York City
1884-85	Cooper Union, New York City (reconstruction)
1890	Asylum, Ward's Island, New York†
1890	Asylum Buildings, Central Islip, New York†

Publications

BOOKS BY EIDLITZ

A Viaduct Railway for the City of New York. With John W. Serrell. New York, 1870.
The Nature and Function of Art, More Especially of Architecture. New York, 1881.
Big Wages and How to Earn Them. New York, 1887.

ARTICLES BY EIDLITZ

"Christian Architecture." *Crayon* 5, No. 2 (1858): 53-55.
Speech at the first annual dinner of the American Institute of Architects. *Crayon* 5, No. 4 (1858): 109-111.
"On Style." *Crayon* 5 (1858): 139-142.
"Cast Iron and Architecture." *Crayon* 6, No. 1 (1859): 20-24.
"The Architect." *Crayon* 6, No. 3 (1859): 99-100.
Crayon 6, No. 5 (1859): 150-151.
"On Aesthetics in Architecture." *Crayon* 8, Nos. 4-5 (1861): 89-91; 111-113.
"The Vicissitudes of Architecture." *Architectural Record* 1, No. 4 (1892): 471-484.
"The Architect of Fashion." *Architectural Record* 3, No. 4 (1894): 347-353.
"Competitions—The Vicissitudes of Architecture." *Architectural Record* 4, No. 2 (1894): 147-156.
"The Educational Training of Architects." *Journal of the Royal Institute of British Architects* Series 3, 4 (1897): 213-217, 462-468.

BOOKS ABOUT EIDLITZ

JORDY, WILLIAM H., and COE, RALPH (eds.): *American Architecture and Other Writings.* Cambridge, Massachusetts, 1961.
ROSEBERRY, CECIL R.: *Capitol Story.* Albany, New York, 1964.

ARTICLES ABOUT EIDLITZ

BROOKS, H. ALLEN: "Leopold Eidlitz: 1823-1908." M. A. thesis. Yale University, New Haven, Connecticut, 1955.
ERDMANN, BIRUTA: "Leopold Eidlitz's Architectural Theories and American Transcendentalism." Ph.D. dissertation. University of Wisconsin, Madison, 1977.
LEVINE, NEIL A.: "The Idea of Frank Furness' Buildings." M. A. thesis. Yale University, New Haven, Connecticut, 1967.
McFARLAND, H. H.: "History and Descriptive Sketch of the Church of the Pilgrims." *Congregational Quarterly* (January 1871).

SCHUYLER, MONTGOMERY: "The Capitol of New York." *Scribner's Monthly* 19, No. 2 (1879): 161-178.
SCHUYLER, MONTGOMERY: "A Great American Architect: Leopold Eidlitz." *Architectural Record* 24 (September 1908).
SCHUYLER, MONTGOMERY: "The Work of Leopold Eidlitz." *Architectural Record* 24 (October-November 1908).

*

Leopold Eidlitz, Prague-born, Vienna Polytechnic-educated, arrived in New York City in 1843, and found ready acceptance in Richard Upjohn's office. The English-born Upjohn was the leading exponent of the Gothic Revival; Eidlitz had his roots in the Austrian-Viennese tradition of medievalism and the Romanesque, and in the contemporary pluralistic romantic revival trends of Austrian architecture. By 1848, St. George's Church in New York City (1846-48; spires completed in 1856) by Eidlitz and Otto Blesch offered the most vigorous expression of the Viennese-German *Rundbogenstil,* and predated H.H. Richardson's early experiments in Romanesque in the 1860s.

Eidlitz's role in shaping American architectural theory commenced with the founding of the American Institute of Architects in 1857. A group of 13 practicing architects, among them Eidlitz, Upjohn (who became the first president of the AIA) and Richard Morris Hunt, were drawn together by a shared discontent with contemporary architectural practice and architectural education. In 1858, at the first anniversary dinner of the AIA, the 35-year-old Eidlitz was the third speaker. In "The Day We Celebrate," he proclaimed a far-reaching theoretical program for American architecture. It was essentially a discourse on nature, showing affinities with Ralph Waldo Emerson's transcendentalist manifesto *Nature* (1836). The papers given at the AIA were published in the *Crayon* between 1858 and 1861.

Eidlitz was the most prolific writer of the AIA. He was a great stylist in the poetical use of language and a brilliant orator. His writings expressed a blending of the observations of the architect, the contemplation of a philosopher and the ideality of a poet. Theoretically, by observing the changes and developments of the seasons—the life, growth and decay of the flora and fauna—the architects, as Eidlitz suggested in his address, should express ". . . the sweet harmonies of Nature and reproduce them in their monuments of Art." Eidlitz depended heavily on the use of analogies (biological and geological) in order to emphasize the organic unity (physical and spiritual) that bound together nature, man and art. His metaphorical celebration of nature and art was Emersonian.

Eidlitz, like Horatio Greenough in the 1840s, was an outspoken critic of classicism and the Renaissance. The sculptor Greenough came to his brand of structural functionalism through Emerson. All three writers used similar aesthetic terminology when they discussed the laws of nature and nature-based organic structuring systems in manmade creations. In "Cast Iron and Architecture" (*The Crayon,* 6, January 1859), Eidlitz spiritualized the materiality of stone: "Nature herself has made all her strongholds of stone." The First Congregational Church in New London, Connecticut, (1849-54) reflected that ideology. He did not believe in machine technology and dismissed iron as a suitable building material. But a fragment of an undated drawing by Eidlitz for the New York Crystal Palace (Avery Architectural Library, Columbia University) shows an advanced engineering knowledge in the methods of wire-cable suspension bridge construction. The 1850s was a period of experimentation in metal construction, but Eidlitz's first important commercial building, the American Exchange Bank in New York City (1857, demolished) was built in stone. In theory, Eidlitz transcended the historical limitations of style, but visually his buildings failed to communicate his theories. Eidlitz had plenty of critics, among them Henry Van Brunt, whose technological determinism did not agree with Eidlitz's organic theory.

The Crayon articles laid the foundation for Eidlitz's *The Nature and Function of Art, More Especially of Architecture* (1881), which remains an all-encompassing treatise of American architectural theory and aesthetics, and of cultural history as well. What makes this book of such exceptional critical interest is the encyclopedic range and number of comparisons with other philosophers that extends from Plato and Winckelmann to Kant and Hegel; inspirational echoes from Charles Darwin to Herbert Spencer; parallelisms and appropriations from Emerson and Greenough to Viollet-le-Duc that suggest themselves to a critic who has studied the book. Van Brunt's review of the book was unfavorable. The most important tribute to Eidlitz as a thinker and architectural theoretician came from the Chicago architect John Wellborn Root in 1888. According to Root, it was Eidlitz, not Louis H. Sullivan, who must be permanently acknowledged as the first practicing architect to celebrate nature as the source of and as the unending support for an organic expression in architecture. Eidlitz's writings were central to the direction that Sullivan's organic functionalism took in the late 1880s. In the 1890s, Eidlitz continued to publish in the *Architectural Record* (1892-94), and in the *Journal of the Royal Institute of British Architects* (1897-98). *Big Wages and How to Earn Them* (published under the assumed name "A. Foreman" in 1887), provides an understanding of Eidlitz as a social critic and cultural theorist.

Eidlitz's buildings—Christ Church Cathedral in St. Louis (1859-67), Second Congregational Church in Greenwich, Connecticut (1856-59), Temple Emanu-El in New York City (1866-68, in association with Henry Fernbach; demolished in 1927)—were critically acclaimed when they were built. Two of the most innovative urban projects—the New York Crystal Palace and the proposal for New York Elevated Railway (circa 1859, in association with John J. Serrell)—were never built. The Assembly Chamber of the State Capitol at Albany, New York (1876-82, in association with H.H. Richardson, Frederick Law Olmsted and the painter William Morris Hunt), was Eidlitz's last major commission.

"We are in a state of transition," said Eidlitz in 1894, and then he summed up: "The pioneers of the revival of medieval art are passing away one after another, and there are no successors to fill their places. . . ." That, however, was not the end of the line of Eidlitz's organic functionalist ideology. After Eidlitz, Sullivan became the dominant figure in American architectural theory, but the principal theoretician, orator and publicist of organic functionalism was Frank Lloyd Wright.

—BIRUTA ERDMANN

EIERMANN, Egon.

German. Born in Neuendorf, near Berlin, Germany, 29 September 1904. Died in Baden-Baden, West Germany, 19 July 1970. Married Brigitte Feyerabendt, 1954; two children (one from previous marriage). Studied at the Technische Hochschule, Charlottenburg, Berlin, under Hans Poelzig (1869-1936), 1923-27. Worked in architectural office of Rudolf Karstadt Company, Hamburg, 1927-28, and for BEWAG, Berlin, 1928-30; private practice, Berlin, 1934-45, and Karlsruhe, 1947-70. Chairman,

Olympic buildings ju ry, Munich, 1968. Dean of architecture faculty, Technical University, Karlsruhe, 1947-70. Member, Akademie der Künste, Berlin, from 1955; honorary member, Zentralvereinigung der Architekten Österreichs, Vienna, 1960; honorary corresponding member, Royal Institute of British Architects, 1963; Grand Prize, Bund Deutscher Architekten, 1968.

Chronology of Works
All in Germany unless noted
† *Work no longer exists*

1929-30	Berlin Electricity Company Transformer Station, Berlin
1937-39	Dega AG Buildings, Berlin
1939-41	Märkische Metallbau GmbH Building, Oranienburg
1948-52	Ciba AG Buildings, Wehr (with Robert Hilgers)
1949-51	Handkerchief Weaving Mill, Blumberg (with Hilgers)
1950-53	Vereinigte Seidenweberei AG, Krefeld (with Hilgers)
1951-52	Merkur Stores, Heilbronn, Stuttgart and Reutlingen (with Hilgers)
1952-56	Matthaus Church, Pforzheim (with Hilgers)
1953-55	Burda-Moden Buildings, Offenburg
1955-57	Volkshilfe Lebensversicherung AG Offices, Cologne

(with Hilgers)

1957	Apartment Block, Interbau Housing Exhibition, Berlin (with Hilgers)
1957-63	Kaiser Wilhelm Memorial Church, Berlin
1958-61	Neckermann KG Mail Order Facilities, Frankfurt (with Hilgers)
1958-61	Steel Works Administration Building, Offenburg (with Hilgers)
1958-64	German Embassy Chancery, Washington, D.C., U.S.A. (with Eberhard Brandl)
1959-60	Egon Eiermann House, Baden-Baden
1965-69	Bundestag Member's Building, Bonn
1967-72	IBM Administration Building, Stuttgart
1968-72	Olivetti Headquarters, Frankfurt

Publications

BOOKS BY EIERMANN

Planungsstudie Verwaltungsgebäude am Beispiel für die IBM-Deutschland. With Heinz Kuhlmann. Stuttgart, 1967.

ARTICLES BY EIERMANN

"Der arbeitende Mensch und die Technik." *Baukunst und Werkform* No. 1 (1947).
"Einige Bermerkungen über Technik und Bauform." *Baukunst und Werkform* No. 1 (1947).
"Neubau der Kanzlei der Deutschen Botschaft in Washington, D.C.." *Architektur und Wohnform* No. 74 (1966).

BOOKS ABOUT EIERMANN

KOENIG, G. K.: *Architettura tedesca del secondo dopoguerra.* Bologna, 1965.

SCHIRMER, WULF (ed.): *Egon Eiermann 1904-1970: Bauten und Projekte*. Stuttgart, 1984.
ZECHLIN, H. J.: *Landhäuser*. Tübingen, 1951.

ARTICLES ABOUT EIERMANN

"Egon Eiermann (1904)-1970)." *Bauwelt* (12 October 1970).
"Egon Eiermann 1904-1970." *Architektur und Wohnenwelt* (12 October 1970).
"Egon Eiermann." *Architecture Plus* (September 1973).
"Headquarters of Olivetti-Germany" and "Headquarters of IBM-Germany." *Architecture and Urbanism* 4 (June 1974): 99-103.
LEITL, ALFONS: "Vom Sauerteig des Künstlerischen: Zu den Arbeiten von Professor Egon Eiermann." *Baukunst und Werkform* (April 1951).
ROSENTHAL, H. WERNER: "Egon Eiermann 1904-1970." *Journal of the Royal Institute of British Architects* 78 (January 1971): 41.

*

Egon Eiermann is known primarily for his industrial buildings. However, the full range of his work is far more encompassing. Eiermann's work must be viewed in perspective along with the history of Germany and the interruption of many architects' work during World War II. Eiermann was born in 1904 in Neuendorf at the periphery of Berlin, when the empire of Wilhelm II was at its strongest, and Berlin was one of the sparkling and most promising cities of the world. As a 14-year-old, Eiermann experienced the collapse of existing monarchy and the establishment of the republic in Germany. In 1927 he received his diploma from the Technische Hochschule of Berlin-Charlottenburg.

Eiermann was strongly influenced by the excited atmosphere of the 1920s in Berlin, as well as by the architecture of Karl-Friedrich Schinkel, whose presence was still felt even after many years of political change. Heinrich Tessenow and Hans Poelzig were Eiermann's most influential teachers. Poelzig in particular had a deep impact on the young Eiermann. Poelzig's personality, his belief in common harmony between the inside and the outside of a building, and his view of humanity as a wonderful influence became characteristic of Eiermann's work. Eiermann's buildings document clearly his own personality. He avoided any architectural gesture and any pathos or pomp. He was suspicious of any building that had a monumental intention or could be seen as sculpture. Eiermann never proposed utopian urban strategies, nor did he propose the then-so-common dwelling machines. His work is distinguished by a highly developed sensibility that is based completely on the harmony of proportions. Eiermann's work is characterized by its transparency and lightness, documenting its question of any architecture that does not believe in eternity.

Eiermann's use of steel elevated this material to another level. For Eiermann, building in steel represented the aristocratic principles of building, which featured the highest level of precision. Eiermann believed in the 45-degree angle, which seemed to violate natural existence. However, as much as he was concerned with the function of a proposed solution, he was also concerned with the overall scheme and its response to nature. Eiermann's work is immediately associated with the basic ideas of form, order, precision, a love for detail, and logic, which were as important to him as clarity, honesty and truth. These ideas could, at best, establish the harmony and beauty of an overall scheme which depends on its individual elements. Eiermann was not interested in creating beauty, but in designing an appropriate functional solution, which for him had its own harmony and beauty.

A retrospective of Eiermann's work must be divided into two major parts. Even though there is very little documentation left of his early years in Berlin, that time period must be named as the basis of Eiermann's architecture. During those years he designed and built several residential buildings. The expected outbreak of World War II and the demands of the armaments industry put a hold on private building activity. At that time Eiermann had to look for other opportunities to build, and he turned to the building tasks of industry, whose strong functional requirements for building he eagerly embraced. His early work, such as the power plant for the power company of Berlin (BEWAG) and the competition proposal for the new justice building in Berlin, clearly show the influence of his former teacher, Hans Poelzig.

The years after World War II saw Germany in desperate need of housing. With his buildings and housing projects, Eiermann tried to introduce introverted dwellings even in high-density projects. He rejected any false understanding of ownership, which he saw as a hindrance for development. In his mind people did not have to look for modern architecture, but for a new form of living altogether. Most characteristic in Eiermann's architecture is the additive notion, which exists as a theme throughout his opus. The additive is, in Eiermann's case, not to be understood as a line of similar elements, but as a principle of order. His architecture must be seen as a whole in which each individual element is clearly addressed so that the overall scheme becomes transparent and readable. This notion can be recognized in any project of any scale; the chimneys of the power plants are detached and freestanding, the entrance roofs float freely from any pressure in front of the building mass, and the detailing of stairs and their railings documents this notion as well.

Eiermann understood architecture as the synthesis between the creative and rational notion and believed that clarity and honesty, even of the smallest detail, are architecture's most important virtues. He saw the architect's task as that of collecting and creating order in an objective, rational way. This notion seems to have been developed in self-protection, as illustrated by the process projects, which often changed from an expressive solution to a very simple one, which was what Eiermann understood as the "true" design. Eiermann's churches, office buildings and department stores, all of which were defined by their functional and rational conditions, demonstrate this principle. This uniform development is perhaps shown best in his office buildings such as the German IBM Headquarters in Stuttgart and the high-rise building for the delegates of the German Parliament in Bonn, both strongly influenced by Ludwig Mies van der Rohe's early proposals for Berlin as well as his buildings in New York and Chicago.

Eiermann's other significant buildings are the West German Embassy in Washington, D.C. (1958-64), the Kaiser-Wilhelm Memorial Church in Berlin (1957-63) and the mail-order house for the Josef Neckermann Cooperative in Frankfurt-am-Main (1958-61). Eiermann was also actively involved with designing furniture and household articles. As a teacher at the Technical University of Karlsruhe, where he taught beginning in 1947, Eiermann influenced hundreds of students through his strong personality and his equally strong beliefs, which were relentless and sometimes extremely closed-minded. Egon Eiermann was an architect who was not influenced by any fashionable movement in architecture. He must be viewed as a conservative architect who was uninterested in any architecture that attempted to surprise and impress through the constant production of new and sensational solutions.

—UWE DROST

EIFFEL, Gustave.

French. Born in Dijon, France, 1832. Died in 1923. Studied at the École Centrale des arts et Manufactures, graduated 1855. Worked under the railroad engineer Charles Nepveu; joined the Pauwels Group with Nepveu; opened own firm at Levallois-Perret, 1866; established metal-working ateliers in Paris, 1870.

Chronology of Works
All in France unless noted

1866-67	Universal Exhibition, Paris (with J. B. Krantz)
1868-69	Railway Viaducts, Gannat-Commentry Line, Massif Central
1871-73	Railway Viaducts, built in France and exported to Spain and Portugal, Austria, Rumania, Egypt, Peru, and Bolivia
1875	Railway Station, Pest, Hungary
1876	Bon Marché Department Store, Paris (with L. C. Boileau)
1877-78	Douro Bridge (Maria-Pia Bridge), Porto, Portugal
1880-84	Garabit Viaduct, Masif Central
1883	Tardes Viaduct, Massif Central
1884	Observatory Cupola, Nice
1885	Statue of Liberty, New York (metal superstructure only; sculptor, Bartholdi)
1887	Panama Canal Works, Panama (initial plans, adapted and carried out by others)
1887-89	Eiffel Tower, Paris

Publications

BOOKS BY EIFFEL

Mémoire sur les épreuves des arcs métalliques de la Galérie des Machines du Palais de l'Exposition Universelle de 1867. Paris, 1867.
Les grands constructions métalliques. Paris, 1888.
Notice sur le Viaduc de Garabit. Paris, 1888.
La Tour Eiffel en 1900. Paris, 1902.

BOOKS ABOUT EIFFEL

BESSET, MAURICE: *Gustave Eiffel.* Paris, 1957.
BILLINGTON, DAVID P.: *The Tower and the Bridge: The New Art of Structural Engineering.* Princeton, New Jersey, 1983.
BRAIBANT, CHARLES: *Histoire de la Tour Eiffel.* Paris, 1964.
DEYDIER, ÉLIE: *Le Viaduc de Garabit.* Paris, 1960.
HARRISS, JOSEPH: *The Tallest Tower: Eiffel and the Belle Epoque.* Boston, 1975.
IGOT, Y.: *Gustave Eiffel.* Paris, 1961.
LOYRETTE, HENRI: *Gustave Eiffel.* 1985.
PONCETTON, FRANÇOIS: *Eiffel: Le magicien du fer.* Paris, 1939.
PRÉVOST, JEAN: *Eiffel.* Paris, 1929.

*

As a leading structural engineer of a period that celebrated the rise of engineering, Gustave Eiffel earned accolades for his

Gustav Eiffel: Eiffel Tower, Paris, France, 1887-89

dozens of bridges as well as architectural structures. Yet these achievements are nearly eclipsed by his eponymous Tower. It was perhaps because his extraordinary wrought-iron arch-and-truss bridges were outspanned by suspension bridges and soon outdated by steel construction that they were lost in the shadow of the Eiffel Tower's remarkable height and powerful symbolism. Nonetheless, Gustave Eiffel deserves recognition for all of his achievements.

After graduating from Paris' École Centrale des Arts et Manufactures in 1855, Eiffel worked under the tutelage of the eccentric railroad engineer Charles Nepveu. Both were soon hired by the Pauwels Group, a Belgian industrial conglomerate. On his first major project, Eiffel administrated construction on the Bordeaux bridge, an early example of compressed-air foundations. There the young engineer first showed his talent for speedy and innovative administration of complex projects. After six successful years with the Pauwels Group, Eiffel opened his own firm at Levallois-Perret in 1866.

The Exhibition of 1867 provided the firm with an early precedent-setting commission. Eiffel would go on to produce two major halls for the 1878 Exhibition and the Eiffel Tower as centerpiece of the 1889 event. Another early commission also foreshadowed the tower. The Viaduct of la Sioule, commissioned in 1867, explored the wind resistance of tapered pylons, whose form and structure directly prefigured the Eiffel Tower.

Before the Tower, Eiffel was perhaps best known for his many bridges, one of which he won in competition in 1875, collaborating with Théophile Seyrig and Henry de Dion. Four firms submitted designs to span Portugal's precipitous Douro River Valley. Not necessarily the prettiest, Eiffel's design was the cheapest by far, and was matched with an ingenious construction technique, Eiffel's specialty. Piers were built on each side of the river, and arch and deck were constructed from each side, meeting in the middle. The design consists of varying-height piers descending the valley and a single, two-radius central arch, all supporting a continuous deck.

Success of the Douro Bridge led directly to the commission for the Garrabit Viaduct over the Truyère River without the usual competitive bidding. The 564-meter bridge was touted by Eiffel as the largest work in the world, due to its unprecedented 89-meter-high piers.

In architecture, Eiffel's endeavors soon went beyond exhibition halls. His 13,000-square-meter railway station at Pest, Hungary (1875), though perhaps architecturally undistinguished, was one of the earliest combined uses of masonry and iron, with its simple, monumental iron gable and surrounding masonry pavilions. As consulting engineer, Eiffel brought the light and airiness made possible by exposed wrought iron to other building types such as department stores and a synagogue in Paris. "Why," asked Eiffel, "should we disguise the industrial nature of iron, even in the city?"

Eiffel in his time exemplified the rising presence of engineers and their technical aesthetic in the realm of architecture. His fame and expertise with wind resistance garnered the commission from sculptor Auguste Bartholdi to design the Statue of Liberty's structural skeleton.

As for the Eiffel Tower, it hardly matters that the idea and first sketches came from Emile Nougier and Maurice Koechlin, two of Eiffel's engineers. Their sketches drew upon Eiffel's own work in wind-resistant pylons. Eiffel nonetheless bought the patent from his employees and personally assumed all liability for the project. By that time, Eiffel was widely acknowledged as the only engineer who could manage the Herculean tasks of engineering, production and construction from the single-page sketch Nougier and Koechlin provided. The surgical efficiency of the two-year construction period is its own remarkable epic.

The tower was as controversial as it now is famous, referred to variously as "a masterpiece of the builder's art" and "Our Lady of second-hand merchandise." It epitomized the debate that once polarized "technical" and "architectural" arts, while apotheosizing the industry of the French Republic.

What had seemed a tenuous justification to build the world's tallest structure became a second career for Eiffel. Having answered the Eiffel Tower's foes by saying that it would be useful for studies of aerodynamics and wind resistance, Eiffel spent the last 20 years of his career performing such studies from the tower, as well as designing wind tunnels and airplane wings. His efforts garnered the Smithsonian Institution's Gold Medal in Aviation, the first to be awarded after the Wright brothers medal.

Eiffel's involvement in an early aborted attempt to build a canal across Panama first placed him under indictment due to botched financial dealings beyond his control. The mortified Eiffel was eventually exonerated and later even praised by subsequent engineers on the project who cited his work as crucial to their own success. It seems remarkable that a man best known for one monument was involved in so many engineering milestones of his time.

—CHARLES ROSENBLUM

EISENMAN, Peter.

American. Born in Newark, New Jersey, 11 August 1932. Studied at Cornell University, Ithaca, New York, 1951-55, B.Arch.; Columbia University, New York, 1959-60, M.S.Arch.; Cambridge University, Cambridge, England, 1960-63, Ph.D. in theory of design. Worked for Percival Goodman, New York, 1957-58; worked with The Architects Collaborative (TAC), Cambridge, Massachusetts, 1959; has taught at Cambridge University, Princeton University and Cooper Union, New York. Cofounder of CASE (Conference of Architects for the Study of the Environment), 1964; founder-director, Institute for Architecture and Urban Studies, New York City, 1967-82; editor, *Oppositions* magazine, 1973-82.

Chronology of Works
All in the United States unless noted

1967-68	House I: Barenholtz House, Princeton, New Jersey
1969-70	House II: Falk House, Hardwick, Vermont
1969-70	House III: Miller House, Lakeville, Connecticut
1972	House VI: Frank House, Cornwall, Connecticut
1975	House X: Aronoff House, Bloomfield Hills, Michigan
1981-87	Apartments, Kochstrasse, Berlin, Germany
1985-89	Wexner Center for the Visual Arts, Ohio State University, Columbus
1987-89	Bio Center, Frankfurt-am-Main, Germany
1987-89	Guardiola House, Bay of Cadiz, Spain
1989-92	Columbus Convention Center, Columbus, Ohio
1993	College of Design, Architecture, Art and Planning, University of Cincinnati, Ohio

Publications

BOOKS BY EISENMAN

Giuseppe Terragni. Cambridge, Massachusetts, 1985.
House of Cards. New York, 1985.

Peter Eisenman: Wexner Center for the Visual Arts, Columbus, Ohio, 1985-89

ARTICLES BY EISENMAN

"Towards an Understanding of Form in Architecture." *Architectural Design* (October 1963).
"The Big Little Magazine: Perspecta 12 and the Future of the Architectural Past." *Architectural Forum* (October 1969); reprinted in *Casabella* (January 1970).
"Notes on Conceptual Architecture I." *Design Quarterly* 78/79 (1970); reprinted in *Casabella* (December 1971).
"Ordinariness and Light." *Architectural Forum* (May 1971).
"From Golden Lane to Robin Hood Gardens; or, If You Follow the Yellow Brick Road You May Not Get to Golders Green." *Architectural Design* (September 1972); reprinted in *Oppositions* (September 1973).
"Notes on Conceptual Architecture II." In *Arquitectura: historia y teoria de los signos.* Barcelona, 1973.
"Notes on Conceptual Architecture IIA." *Environmental Design Research* (Stroudsburg, Pennsylvania) Vol. II (1973).
"Cardboard Architecture." *Casabella* (February 1973).
"From Adolf Loos to Bertold Brecht." *Progressive Architecture* (May 1974).
"Real and English: Destruction of the Box I." *Oppositions* (October 1974).
"White and Gray." With Robert A. M. Stern. *Architecture and Urbanism* 52 (April 1975).
"Post Functionalism." *Oppositions* (Fall 1976).
"Behind the Mirror: On the Writings of Philip Johnson." *Oppositions* (Fall 1977).
"Three Texts for Venice." *Domus* (November 1980).
"Aspects of Modernism." *Cahiers de la recherche architecturale* (Roquevaire, France, November 1982).

BOOKS ABOUT EISENMAN

FRAMPTON, KENNETH, and ROWE, COLIN: *Five Architects: Eisenman, Graves, Gwathmey, Hejduk, Meier.* New York, 1972.
JENCKS, CHARLES: *The New Moderns.* London, 1990.
JOHNSON, P., and WIGLEY, M.: *Deconstructionist Architecture.* Exhibition Catalog. New York, 1988.

ARTICLES ABOUT EISENMAN

Architecture and Urbanism, special issue (January 1980).
Architecture and Urbanism, special issue (August 1988).
Architecture and Urbanism, special issue (January 1990).
BESS, PHILIP: "Peter Eisenman and the Architecture of the Therapeutic." *Inland Architect* 34/3 (May/June 1990).
Croquis, special issue (December 1989).
"Eisenman/Hejduk." *Wonen-TA/BK* (Heerlen, Netherlands), special issue (November 1980).
GANDELSONAS, MARIO: "On Reading Architecture: Eisenman and Graves, an Analysis." *Progressive Architecture* (March 1972).
GOLDBLATT, D.: "The Dislocation of the Architectural Self." *Journal of Aesthetics and Art Criticism* (Fall 1991).
"Peter Eisenman: Recent Projects." *Architectural Design* 59 (1989).
"Peter Eisenman" [interview]. *Connaissance des arts* (October 1990).
"Peter Eisenman." *Architecture d'aujourd'hui* (February 1992).
"Recent Projects of Peter Eisenman." *Architecture and Urbanism* (September 1991).

On 11 August 1982, at the celebration of his fiftieth birthday in his New York office, Peter Eisenman made a short speech, to wit: "I spent my first fifty years working for the Institute [for Architecture and Urban Studies (IAUS)]; the next fifty years will be devoted to our architectural practice." Whereas this account is not entirely accurate (Eisenman's term at the Institute was fifteen years), it is true that since 1982 Eisenman has completed a few large-scale projects, as opposed to his single family houses of the 1960s and 1970s. His life's work centers on his active participation in architecture and planning by means of talks given throughout the world and writing. His production of several books and numerous articles in journals such as *Architectural Forum* is commensurate with his Ph.D. degree from Cambridge University. Eisenman works alone, with his office staff, and in collaboration with artists (e.g., Michael Heizer), philosophers (e.g., William Gass), and editors (e.g., Cynthia Davidson, his wife). For Eisenman, the architect is humanistic, someone versed in all the arts and sciences, not limited to the nitty gritty of building; at the same time, he enjoys seeing his conceptual designs realized.

As a child Eisenman was not a leader, but he became one before he founded and directed the Institute in 1967. He was a lieutenant in the Korean war during the fifties, and during the mid-sixties he organized the Conference of Architects for the Study of the Environment, meetings for which took place at the Museum of Modern Art (MoMA) in New York. With the help of Arthur Drexler, director of MoMA, and Colin Rowe, Eisenman's former mentor from Cambridge, the IAUS became registered by New York State. Assisted by Amelio Ambasz, his student at Princeton, Eisenman developed the Charter for the Institute which stated the aim of joining the camps of academia and the architectural office, blending ideas with skills. (This was not dissimilar to the aims of the Beaux-Arts in 19th- and early 20th-century Paris.) Under the auspices of trustees and with the participation of fellows and students, the Institute produced, among other things, many publications. The two most prominent were the journal *Oppositions* (the name was coined by Duarte Cabral de Melo and alluded to Eisenman's dialectical way of thinking) and the newspaper *Skyline* (named by Andrew MacNair to connote coverage of architectural news of New York). Both publications bore high standards and favored the avant-garde, resisting both functionalism and postmodernism in architecture. Although many names would have to be added to indicate the enormous contributions of others at the Institute, it must be remembered that Eisenman was involved in developing all Institute projects. As Kenneth Frampton, the second prime mover of the Institute, said in 1980, just before the Institute folded, "There would be no Institute without Peter; without Peter there would be no magazine."

Eisenman's architectural practice began at Princeton where he was able to oversee the completion of an antique toy museum. Influenced by Le Corbusier (1887-1965; pseud. for Charles–Édouard Jeanneret), Giuseppe Terragni (1904-42) and Andrea Palladio (1508-80), this pavilion developed into a highly original statement. Starting as a cube, the form was layered and punctuated in space by columns, beams, planes, and slots. The transformational process which Eisenman created became a unique architectural language with grammatical rules that were highly intellectual, in concert with Noam Chomsky's linguistics and the strategies of chess. There were other houses to follow, which are partly explained and illustrated in *Five Architects* (1972), *House X* (1982) and *House of Cards* (1985), each of which was initiated by Eisenman.

It was only with his later works, after he opened an office in 1982, that Eisenman achieved recognition by a larger segment of society. His Wexner Center was large in scale and received considerable press attention. It stands as a monument to deconstruction or decomposition as well as to his response to the site as contrasted with some disregard of earlier landscaping. Eisenman really expresses his involvement with deconstruction in more recent projects, e.g., his solution for the Cincinnati College of Design, Architecture, Art, and Planning. His consideration of a design's relation to its context also appears in "Choral Works" (with French deconstructionist philosopher Jacques Derrida; b. 1930) in which he includes a segment of a Parisian fortification at Parc de la Villette.

Now that Eisenman heads Eisenman Architects, he is again a director but not in the usual sense of an institutional director. He travels more frequently and thus does not have as much time for the young people who gather to learn from him at the office. However, as before, Eisenman is charismatic and still has keen interest in dissimilar areas of life; these now include deconstruction philosophy, the surreal films of David Lynch, and the Ohio State University football team and marching band. And the latter's throbbing rhythms captures in sound the dynamics of volumes in Eisenman's architecture.

—SUZANNE S. FRANK

ELLIS, Peter.

British. Born in England, 1804. Died in England, 1884.

Chronology of Works
All in England

1864   Oriel Chambers, Water Street, Liverpool
1866   No. 16 Cook Street, Liverpool

Publications

BOOKS ABOUT ELLIS

HITCHCOCK, HENRY-RUSSELL: *Architecture: Nineteenth and Twentieth Centuries.* 4th ed. Baltimore, 1977.
HUGHES, JAMES QUENTIN: *Seaport.* London, 1964.
PEVSNER, NIKOLAUS: *The Buildings of England: Lancashire—The Industrial and Commercial North.* Harmondsworth, England, 1969.

*

Peter Ellis was an architect in Liverpool in the middle of the 19th century, long forgotten but praised now for the radically functional aspect of his designs. What he built was not well received: a writer in *The Builder* in 1866 described his office at Oriel Chambers as "a vast abortion" and "an agglomeration of protruding plate glass bubbles," and it was perhaps this sort of comment that dissuaded any later clients from placing commissions with Ellis. Ellis practiced as an architect for another 18 years, but by 1867 the entry for him in *Gore's Dictionary* described him also as a "civil engineer," and in the 1884 edition, this term precedes that of "architect." Ellis is known to have designed only two works, Oriel Chambers (1864) and an office building at 16 Cook Street (1866), completed at the moment of the unfavorable notice in *The Builder.*

Oriel Chambers is set on the corner of Water Street and Covent Garden, the plan having a central courtyard; along the Covent Garden side the facade is divided into cast-iron-framed bays, each fourth bay sealed by a stone wall and a chimney breast. The courtyard has deeper rooms, with stanchions set in

from the facade, making it almost a curtain glass construction. This is in itself remarkable, but the building is unusual in other ways also. So far as we know, it was the first modern office block designed solely to house the offices of a business, without warehouses attached or a factory space. And the design, far more certainly than any other building of the time, seems to embody within itself an expression of the materials of which it was made. The structure consists of a cast-iron frame made of arched, inverted T-beams, supported on H-section stanchions, the sections between these T-beams being spanned by shallow brick arches with a filling of concrete at the top to support the floors. This was a system of support that had been used in warehouses in Liverpool earlier in that century, but at Oriel Chambers the frame was kept inside, and the supporting stanchions were not disguised or decorated in any way. The facade in the courtyard is also completely without decoration, and the bottom panels of the long, projecting windows are filled with stone slabs, slotted between the frames, to form a type of cladding. All this allows a far larger area of the external surface to be glass, the oriels letting as much daylight as possible in this cloudy northern city to enter through the top and the sides as well as through the front. And for this also, Ellis' use of a modified Gothic style was an advantage over the more-usual classical forms where the surface of the wall was always more significant than the openings. This open aspect of Ellis' design is even more evident on the courtyard facade, where, with no decoration to block them, long bands of glass project uninterrupted except by the stone cross walls at each third bay. It should be noted that on the Covent Garden side, originally of some 12 bays, a sympathetic extension was built in 1959 by the firm of James and Bywater, replacing a section damaged in World War II.

After Oriel Chambers, 16 Cook Street seems perhaps rather modest. It is a narrow, high, three-bay building, each bay ending in a triplet of stepped, arched tops. But the courtyard is remarkable, for a whole wall and a tight spiral staircase that runs up the full height of the building are sheathed almost entirely in glass, with only the thinnest of mullions separating the panels; the mullions are T-shaped to receive the glass on the outer edge and are formed in the shape of a bulbous spiral on the inner side. And the back is asymmetrical, the arrangement of the windows, wall surface and chimney foreshadowing the work of the Free Architecture Movement in England in the 1900s.

All this can be seen as a further stage of the aesthetics of iron-frame construction, predicted by John Ruskin and begun with the building of the Crystal Palace. However, Ellis worked in the provinces, and it was the more traditional Gothic style of architects such as Alfred Waterhouse that was admired by those in the 1870s and 1880s in Liverpool. Even a more sympathetic critic like Charles Reilly, dean of the Architectural School in Liverpool in the 1920s, could only call Oriel Chambers "logical and disagreeable" and "a cellular habitation for the human insect." We judge these elements now very differently.

—DAVID CAST

ELMSLIE, George Grant.

American. Born in Huntley, Scotland, 1871. Died in 1952. Family moved to Chicago, 1884. Educated in Chicago Public Schools. Joined office of J. Lyman Silsbee, 1888; joined firm of Adler and Sullivan, Chicago, 1889; became head draftsman when Frank Lloyd Wright left the firm in 1893; partner, with William Purcell and George Feick, Purcell Feick and Elmslie, Chicago, 1909-13; partner, with Purcell, Purcell and Elmslie,

Chicago, 1913-22; continued working in Chicago after Purcell left the firm, from 1922.

Chronology of Works
All in the United States
Purcell and Elmslie:

1913	Edna S. (William Gray) Purcell House, Minneapolis, Minnesota
1915	E. S. Hoyt House, Red Wing, Minnesota
1913	Madison State Bank, Madison, Minnesota
1913-14	Community House and Parsonage, First Congregational Church, Eau Claire, Wisconsin
1914	First State Bank, LeRoy, Minnesota
1914	Edison Shop, San Francisco, California
1914	Margaret Little House, Berkeley, California
1914-15	Harold C. Bradley House, Madison, Wisconsin
1915	C. T. Backus House, Minneapolis, Minnesota
1915-16	Henry Babson Service Buildings, Riverside, Illinois
1915-17	Woodbury County Courthouse, Sioux City, Iowa (with William L. Steele)
1916	Louis Heitman House, Helena, Montana
1916	Farmers and Merchants State Bank, Hecter, Minnesota
1916	Offices for Alexander International Leather and Belting Corporation, Philadelphia, Pennsylvania
1917-18	Factories, Alexander International Leather and Belting Corporation, New Haven, Connecticut
1917	Charles Wiethoff House, Minneapolis, Minnesota
1918	William Gray Purcell Bungalow, Rose Valley, Pennsylvania
1917-20	First National Bank, Adams, Minnesota

George Grant Elmslie:

1921-24	Old Second National Bank, Aurora, Illinois
1922	American National Bank, Aurora, Illinois
1922-24	Capital Building and Loan Association, Topeka, Kansas
1925-26	Congregational Church, Western Springs, Illinois
1926	Healy Chapel, Aurora, Illinois
1929	Forbes Hall, Yankton College, Yankton, South Dakota
1936	Oliver Morton School, Hammond, Indiana (with William S. Hutton)

Publications

ARTICLES BY ELMSLIE

"Sullivan Ornamentation." *Journal of the American Institute of Architects* 6 (1946): 155-158.
"The Chicago School: Its Inheritance and Bequest." *Journal of the American Institute of Architects* 18 (1952): 32-40.

ARTICLES BY PURCELL AND ELMSLIE

"Illustrating the Work of Purcell, Feick and Elmslie, Architects." *Western Architect* 19, No. 1 (special issue, 1913)
"Illustrating in this Issue the Work of Purcell and Elmslie, Architects." *Western Architect* 21, No. 1 (1915): 1-20.
"Illustrating the Work of Purcell and Elmslie." *Western Architect* 22, No. 1 (special issue, 1915).

BOOKS ABOUT PURCELL AND ELMSLIE

ANDREWS, WAYNE: *Architecture, Ambition, and Americans.* Rev. ed. New York, 1978.
BROOKS, HAROLD ALLEN: *The Prairie School: Frank Lloyd Wright and His Midwest Contemporaries.* Toronto, 1972.
CONDIT, CARL W.: *The Chicago School of Architecture.* Chicago, 1964.
GEBHARD, DAVID: *A Guide to the Existing Buildings of Purcell and Elmslie.* 1960.
GEBHARD, DAVID: *Purcell and Elmslie: Architects.* Exhibition catalog. Minneapolis, 1953.
GEBHARD, DAVID: *The Work of Elmslie and Purcell: Architects.* Park Forest, Illinois, 1965.
SPENCER, BRIAN A. (ed.): *The Prairie School Tradition.* New York, 1979.
ZABEL, CRAIG: *American Public Architecture: European Roots and Native Expressions.* University Park, Pennsylvania, 1989.

ARTICLES ABOUT PURCELL AND ELMSLIE

GEBHARD, DAVID: "Louis Sullivan and George Grant Elmslie." *Journal of the Society of Architectural Historians* 19 (1960): 62-68.
HAMLIN, TALBOT F.: "George Grant Elmslie and the Chicago Scene." *Pencil Points* 22 (1941): 575-586.
HOFFMANN, D. L.: "Elmslie's Topeka Legacy." *Prairie School Review* 1, Fourth Quarter (1964).

With a career that spanned some 50 years, divided into four periods—20 of those in the employ of Louis Sullivan, a highly productive 13 years in partnership with William Purcell, another decade in private practice, and his last working years again designing for others—George Grant Elmslie's development covers the entire range of the Prairie school era. Like his mentor, Louis Sullivan, Elmslie not only advocated designs free of historical illusions and rejected the traditional building typology, but also produced original decorative schemes for both the interiors and exteriors of his buildings. In fact, Elmslie's design interests were even broader than those of Sullivan, with the younger man designing type, decorative patterns and advertising brochures. For his own use and for a limited number of clients, he also produced ornate yet delicate textiles for domestic use.

It is difficult to assess Elmslie's contributions while in Sullivan's employ (1889-1909), in part because the senior designer was unlikely to share credit with those he saw as merely carrying out his plans, in part because the younger man had such a feel for original design that, like Frank Lloyd Wright before him, his own early work reflected and merged with that of the master. Further, since Elmslie and Wright shared an office in the Adler and Sullivan firm's suite, for a few years in the early 1890s, either of the two younger men might actually have worked on any given project. With the breakup of the Adler and Sullivan firm and the departure of Wright, however, Elmslie had an increasingly personal stake in the design of such major buildings as the Guaranty Building. He was all but a design partner in the great National Farmers' Bank, completed before unfulfilling work in the Sullivan office caused him to go out on his own.

When Purcell, Feick and Elmslie began their partnership, many of their projects were small businesses and banks, and the rest of their commissions came in the form of domestic architecture. Elmslie and—for half a year in 1903—Purcell had worked on the small-town bank projects of Sullivan and had a ready model for such important projects as their Merchants

Bank of Winona, Minnesota (1911-12). The bank is a well-proportioned blend of Sullivan-influenced plan and organization with an overhead skylight, interior brick piers and planters that show the influence of Oak Park Prairie school homes that Purcell knew so well from his neighbor Wright. The design was no slavish imitation, though, with a steel frame that permitted great walls of glass and with the building rising without a visible base.

It is in domestic architecture, both large and modest-sized houses built throughout the Midwest, that Elmslie and his partner Purcell (George Feick left the firm in 1913, never having had a major role in the design process) made their widest contribution to the growth of the Prairie school. In many of the smaller homes Elmslie designed the furnishings and even the tapestries, involving his wife in completing the embroidery and other textiles from his designs.

Like other followers of the crafts aesthetic, Elmslie often used stained or even unfinished wood, plaster walls without paper, and an abundant use of leaded glass in geometric shapes that replicate the basic forms of the house itself. Though Purcell and Elmslie certainly were part of a larger movement, particular characteristics mark their work. Whether in the one-story houses, the larger homes or the commercial structures, Elmslie's main and consistent contribution seems to have been in conceiving the wall as a thin curtain or membrane, flat and geometric, with little of the three-dimensional ornamentation found in the work of his contemporaries. In the Edison Shop in Chicago (1912), a commercial reconstruction project, the flat sections of wall and ceiling are joined by continuous bands of trim, and similarly divided floors. Combined with small, elongated geometric fixtures on the walls, the unified interior prefigured both International School and art deco design that were to burst on the American architectural scene one to two decades later.

Both Elmslie and Purcell enjoyed their work, combining the self-confidence of Sullivan with an ability to work easily together and, on larger projects, with others, as witnessed by their collaboration on the Woodbury County Courthouse in Sioux City, Iowa. Living in different cities and working for—but independently of—the architect of record, they were able to harmonize the diverse parts and uses of a major civic structure while respecting the initial design.

The partners also shared an interest in promulgating functionalist and craftsman-derived ideas, and wrote as forcibly if not as poetically as Sullivan. With the *Western Architect* as their major forum, they wrote and designed the type and borders for several articles, illustrating each piece with plates of their own work. They, like Sullivan, spoke of the value of innovation and freedom, and in the strong polemic of "The Statics and Dynamics of Architecture" (1913) expressed the greatest scorn for those who relied for inspiration on such conventions of traditional architecture as the column.

After Purcell's ill health and the advent of World War I forced the dissolution of the partnership, Elmslie continued on his own. His designs tended to repeat or modify earlier ones, however, and the majority of his commissions were for business rather than residential use. Several of his last major designs were for schools in the Chicago suburbs, and though the basis of patronage gave less freedom to his design impulse, he managed to combine the strong geometry of many of his best early buildings with a rejuvenated and refined sense of ornamentation. His reputation seemed to die with his retirement late in the 1930s, but renewed research and interest in the Prairie school and other American developments of the early 20th century have resurrected Elmslie as an innovative and effective architect with a complex, holistic approach to design.

—DAVID M. SOKOL

EMBERTON, Joseph.

British. Born in Audley, Staffordshire, England, 1889. Died in 1956. Studied at the Kensington (now Royal) College of Art, graduated in 1913. In partnership with Percy Westwood, 1922-26; in private practice, from 1926.

Chronology of Works
All in England
† *Work no longer exists*

1924-25	Lion Kiosk; Nobel Hall; State Express House; Main Avenue Kiosk; and Lakeside Kiosk; British Empire Exhibition, Wembley (with P. J. Westwood)†
1925-26	House, Weybridge, Surrey
1928	Madelon Chaumet Shop, Berkeley Street, London†
1929-30	New Empire Hall, Olympia, Hammersmith Road, London
1931	Royal Corinthian Yacht Club, Burnham-on-Crouch, Essex
1933	Universal House, Southwark
1934-50	Pleasure Beach, Blackpool
1936	Simpson's Store, Piccadilly, London
1939	Casino, Blackpool
1939	H.M.V. Store, Oxford Street, London

Publications

BOOKS ABOUT EMBERTON

IND, ROSEMARY: *Joseph Emberton.* London, 1982-1983.

ARTICLES ABOUT EMBERTON

IND, ROSEMARY: "The Architecture of Pleasure: Joseph Emberton's Work at Blackpool." *Architectural Association Quarterly* 8, No. 3 (1976): 51-59.

REILLY, CHARLES H.: "Some Younger Architects of Today: Joseph Emberton." *Building* (August 1931): 348-356.

*

Joseph Emberton's Royal Corinthian Yacht Club at Burnham-on-Crouch (1931) was the only example of British architecture chosen by Henry-Russell Hitchcock and Philip Johnson to be included in their "Modern Architecture: International Exhibition" held at the Museum of Modern Art in New York during 1932. Hitchcock and Johnson's book, *The International Style,* published the same year, also included the yacht club. This building, together with a store for Simpson's, the gentleman's outfitter in Piccadilly, London, and the Blackpool Casino, made Emberton the most significant British architect working in the International Style.

Emberton was educated at the Kensington (now Royal) College of Art under W.R. Lethaby and Beresford Pite, earning his certificate of architecture in 1913. He always claimed that he never learned anything, meaning a philosophy of design, in his training. Instead, he was strongly influenced after World War I by Thomas Tait, partner in the firm of Burnet and Tait, a designer in the Moderne idiom for whom Emberton worked. Emberton became conversant with modern architecture in Europe during the 1920's, mostly in Holland, France and Spain. He is known to have seen and admired the Van Nelle Factory in Rotterdam (1927-29) by Brinkman and Van der Vlugt, and the Open Air School in Amsterdam (1930) by Johannes Duiker.

Emberton began a practice with Percy Westwood in 1922, but practiced on his own from 1926. His commissions then and for the remainder of his life consisted mainly of shops, exhibition pavilions and advertising kiosks, each streamlined and monolithic, with curved sheets of glass, multicolored neon signage and strip lighting, and metal window frames, handrails and furniture.

His New Empire Hall at Olympia in west London (1929) was slightly expressionist, being monumental and symmetrical on its main facade, and, in fact, typical of Thomas Tait's Moderne architecture. Emberton's first design for the Yacht Club, however, exhibited at the Royal Academy in 1930, was closer to the modern idiom. Even so, travel in Europe led him to redesign the Yacht Club, and he built it as a steel-framed structure on concrete piles and platform, with floor-to-ceiling windows on almost all of three sides and a starter's box on the roof, accessed by a standard metal spiral stair. In correspondence with Emberton, Philip Johnson expressed dislike of the spiral stair and the sloping windows in the staircase located in one rear corner of the building. Emberton agreed with Johnson on the spiral stair, but justified the sloping windows as openings in a four-and-one-half-inch, non-load-bearing brick wall; they could be any shape. Here, then, was a full-fledged building from England in the International Style. Thereafter, Emberton did not look back.

Universal House in Southwark (1933), just south of the Thames, was a steel-frame building with concrete floors and upstands, the whole exterior covered in Vitrolite glass, a concrete sandwich with cork infill and ventilation holes to prevent condensation. The reason given for a glass building, one of only a half-dozen in Britain at that time, was that it was near to a railroad station at a period when locomotives were coal-fired. It was assumed that the glass would be self-cleaning and admit the maximum amount of daylight.

Simpson's (1936), on the south side of Piccadilly in London, was five stories high and faced north. Emberton retained Felix Samuely, an innovative engineer, who designed a welded steel frame, which unfortunately had to be modified to suit local building regulations. The owner of the site made a further limitation, demanding Portland stone as the external finish. Emberton therefore stretched glass windows across the width of the building between strips of Portland stone, and in bronze channels he hid colored neon strips at each level in combinations of blue, red and green; each combination provided a different effect, which was most successful at night. A glass-block canopy cantilevered out from the facade, and black granite with curved glass above was used in the entrance display area. Internally there was a unity of design in the sympathetic use of material. The travertine marble staircase, lighted by a wall of glass between concrete mullions, had well-designed light fixtures by Emberton, who was responsible for all built-in furniture and some of the metal furnishings, although some examples by Alvar Aalto and others were to be found. Simpson's and a pharmaceutical store called Timothy White's at Southsea were exhibited in 1937 at the Museum of Modern Art exhibition called "Modern Architecture in Britain."

The Blackpool Casino (1939) was devoted mainly to facilities where one thousand people could be seated in the main banqueting hall. It was a three-story building plus basement for billiards, circular in plan. Some details, such as the stair tower, were inspired by Erich Mendelsohn and Serge Chermayeff's Bexhill Pavilion (1934-36), but the Emberton touch was there, most notably in the color schemes, where off-whites, ivories and grays were highlighted by red columns, tomato red and cream staircase handrails, and scarlet leather seats at the bar of the soda fountain.

After World War II, Britain found the modern expression in architecture to be economical in its materials and construction and socially acceptable for public housing and other amenities. Finsbury Borough Council in London had built modern structures prior to 1951, the year in which it asked Emberton to design a six-story slab block called Stuart House on Killick Street. He projected other schemes for Y-shaped blocks, and even suggested an arrangement of such blocks within the devastated landscape surrounding St. Paul's Cathedral in London.

Emberton's main contribution was limited to the decade prior to World War II, however, when the International Style in Britain related more to an idiom acceptable to the wealthy and educated, and for a very select number of commissions unrelated to the social consciousness of modern architecture in Europe.

—LAWRENCE WODEHOUSE

ENDELL, August.

German. Born in Berlin, Germany, 12 April 1871. Died in Berlin, 1924. Studied in Tübingen and Munich. Director, Breslau Academy, 1918.

Chronology of Works
All in Germany
† *Work no longer exists*

1896-97	Elvira Photographic Studio, Munich†
1898	Sanatorium, Wyk auf Führ
1901	Buntes Theater, Berlin
1904	Schule für Formkunst, Berlin
1905-06	Neumannsche Festival Hall, Berlin
1906-07	Apartment House, 32 Kastanienallee, Westend, Berlin
1908	Apartment House 17 Eichenallee, Westend, Berlin
1909	Salamander Shops, Westend, Berlin (interiors)
1910-11	Apartment House Kühl, 14 Akazienallee, Westend, Berlin
1912-13	Racetrack, Mariendorf, Berlin
1914	Railway Dining Car, Werkbund Exposition, Cologne

Publications

BOOKS BY ENDELL

Um die Schönheit: Eine Paraphrase über die Münchener Kunstausstellung in 1896. Munich, 1896.
Die Schönheit der grossen Stadt. Stuttgart, 1908.

ARTICLES BY ENDELL

"Möglichkeit und Ziele einer neuen Architektur." *Deutsche Kunst und Dekoration* 1 (1897-98): 141-153.
"Formenschönheit und dekorative Kunst." In TIM BENTON, CHARLOTTE BENTON, and DENNIS SHARP (eds.): *Architecture and Design: 1890-1939.* New York, 1975 (originally published in 1898).
"Architektonische Erstlinge." *Die Kunst* 2 (1900): 297-317.

BOOKS ABOUT ENDELL

HEUSS, THEODOR: *Das Haus der Freundschaft in Konstantinopel: Ein Wettbewerb Deutscher Architekten.* Munich, 1918.

KILLY, HERTA ELISABETH; PFANKUCH, PETER; and SCHEPER, DIRK: *Poelzig-Endell-Moll und die Breslauer Kunstakademie: 1911-1932*. Berlin, 1965.

SEMBACH, KLAUS-JÜRGEN (ed.): *August Endell: Der Architekt des Photoateliers Elvira 1871-1925*. Exhibition catalog. Munich, 1977.

ARTICLES ABOUT ENDELL

FUCHS, GEORG: ''Das 'Bunte Theater' von August Endell'' and ''Originalität und Tradition.'' *Deutsche Kunst und Dekoration* 9 (1901-02): 275-289; 290-96.

GREEN, PETER: ''August Endell.'' *Architectural Association Quarterly*, Vol. 9, No. 4 (1977): 36-44.

SCHEFFLER, KARL: ''August Endell.'' *Kunst und Künstler* 5 (1907): 314-24.

SCHEFFLER, KARL: ''Neue Arbeiten von August Endell.'' *Kunst und Künstler* 11 (1913): 350-59.

*

August Endell is among the most underrated architects in the history of modern architecture. His career evolved at the decisive moment when historicism was replaced by developments that ultimately led to modernism. His work demonstrates what art nouveau could contribute to the International Style. However, Endell's impact was more theoretical than artistic. From the beginning of his career, he deplored the lack of ideals, which he saw as the main reason for architects' escape into eclecticism. He believed, rather, that the present should be the basis of architecture.

Like many representatives of the art nouveau style, he derived his earliest designs from the observation of nature and its principles. His later development was characterized by simplicity and strength. His last designs were created out of a building's purpose and static requirements, and the architectonic form derived from tectonic considerations, eliminating applied ornamentation. The decreasing ornamental emphasis was replaced by an increasing priority given to spatial concerns. Endell attempted to enclose and vivify space as the main element of architecture.

Endell's major influence on later developments was exerted through his theory. He originally embraced a position against pure functionalism, because he did not consider a structural skeleton enough to establish architectural form. His design theory also emphasized an architecture that would not continue the practice of individually modified application of old forms. Rather, he promoted ''an art with forms which signify nothing, represent nothing and remind us of nothing, which arouse our souls as deeply and as strongly as music has been able to do.''

Endell's entire career was a quest for the power of forms. In this enterprise, he pressed for the artistic aspects of architectural design. In his opinion, the effect of forms was related neither to memory, nor to associations, nor to subconscious perception of their essence. Influenced by Theodor Lipps' theory of empathy and Hermann Obrist's insistence on the visionary origins of artistic creation, Endell advocated an education intended to teach one to see forms properly by way of ingraining a feeling for form. He believed that through empathic perception, forms would exert power on the mind and awaken novel sensations and feelings. Theories of perception and the psychology of art were the cornerstones of Endell's designs. His art can rightfully be interpreted as the expression of philosophical astonishment. He admonished the public to stop thinking and start feeling. He explained this theory in two seminal articles published in 1898 and 1899, which dealt primarily with linear forms. He stated that perception is based on time (= length of line) and tension (= thickness). Endell even drew up a table that listed nuances of emotions called forth by the various tempos and intensities of lines, and demonstrated its application in the perception of straight-line architectural details.

Based on these theoretical convictions, Endell's work was sensual. His designs derived from the practical application of the possibilities offered by the psychology of perception to aesthetic experience. In his major building, the Elvira Photostudio in Munich (1896-97), he handled forms and materials with total freedom. The aim of the ornamentation was the creation of an emotional effect on the viewer, rejecting an anecdotal or educational approach.

Endell saw the world as having two faces: the objective and the visual. He clearly understood that nature and art are two different media. While art—and ornamentation—derives from nature, it goes beyond pure imitation. Art is the agent that liberates the visual impression from the perception of the objective world. In turn, it allows different comprehensions of the objective world. This visual impression is capable of raising the ugliest object to the level of beauty. Hence, the artist needs to pursue the poetic potential of design. The visual impression is directly tied to human faculties of perception. Human experience, especially the spatial one, is the central agent of visual impression. Consequently, the essential element of architecture is not form, but its obverse, space.

Endell's ornamental vocabulary was intended to elicit an artistic sensation of space. An aesthetic sensation of the void could be created by establishing an atmospheric quality through decorative details. His linear ornamentation and its appeal to the senses were the features by which this two-dimensional design element created a spatial illusion in the viewer. Through ornamentation, walls and ceilings lost their traditional support functions and were transformed into space. In this respect, Endell managed to create architecture that expressed a general vitality.

His early work was characterized by ornamentation in linear configurations. Length, thickness, directional thrust, frequency and shape of the various lines established rhythmic patterns. Details were treated individually. In his later work, including even a grandstand for a horse racetrack, he attempted to simplify his design by creating an overall rhythm by way of repetition and sequencing.

August Endell's main contribution to future architects was his credo that elementary forms are effective without relying on historical, biological or anecdotal associations. He sought to demonstrate the emotional qualities inherent in proportional relationships. These ideas exerted a powerful influence on many expressionist artists and architects, and provided a viable emotional alternative to the intellectual, functionalist design theory of the International Style.

—HANS R. MORGENTHALER

ENGEL, Carl Ludwig.

German. Born in Berlin, Germany, 1778. Died in Helsinki, Finland, 1840. Studied at the Berlin School of Architecture, and studied briefly in Italy. Town architect of Tallinn, Estonia, 1809; moved to Turku, Finland, 1814; appointed architect for the reconstruction of Helsinki, 1816; comptroller of public works, Helsinki, 1824.

Carl Ludwig Engel: Venha Church, Helsinki, Finland, 1826

Chronology of Works
All in Finland

1818-22	Senate Square, Helsinki
1822	Guards' Barracks, Kasarmitori Square, Helsinki
1824-26	Holy Trinity Church, Helsinki
1826	Venha Church (Old Church), Helsinki
1827	Church, Lapua
1827-33	City Hall, Helsinki
1828-32	Main Building, University of Helsinki
1830-40	Lutheran Cathedral, Helsinki
1836	Country House, Vuojoki
1836-45	Library, University of Helsinki
1840	Town Hall, Pori (not completed until 1841)
1840	Orthodox Church, Turku (not completed until 1945)

Publications

BOOKS ABOUT ENGEL

MEISSNER, CARL: *Carl Ludwig Engel, deutscher Baumeister in Finnland*. Berlin, 1937.

RICHARDS, J. M.: *A Guide to Finnish Architecture*. London, 1966.

RICHARDS, J. M.: *800 Years of Finnish Architecture*. Newton Abbot, England, 1978.

SUOLAHTI, EINO E.: *Helsinki: A City in a Classic Style*. Helsinki, 1973.

WICKBERG, NILS E.: *Carl Ludwig Engel*. Berlin, 1970.

ARTICLES ABOUT ENGEL

EPP, H.: ''Carl Ludwig Engel, Ein deutscher Baumeister in Reval und Helsinki.'' *Der Deutsche im Osten* 6 (1943).

NEUMANN, M.: ''Klassizismus in Finnland. Zu den Arbeiten Carl Ludwig Engels.'' *Zentralblatt der Bauverwaltung* 62 (1942).

PÖYKKÖ, KALEVI: ''Helsinki's Neo-Classical Center.'' *Apollo* 115, No. 243 (May 1982): 354-360.

*

Carl Ludwig Engel's reputation as one of the leading neoclassical architects in Europe rests primarily on his work in Helsinki and to a lesser extent elsewhere in Finland. He came to this, however, by a circuitous route.

He was born in the Charlottenburg suburb of Berlin, studied briefly in Italy, but received his principal architectural education under Friedrich Gilly (1772-1800) in the newly founded Bauakademie in Berlin. There he was a fellow student with Karl Friedrich Schinkel (1781-1841), his slightly younger contemporary, who was to build his own great reputation in Germany. By Gilly both young men were trained in the principles of French neoclassicism, with its emphasis on geometry and simplicity.

For a short time Engel worked for the Prussian government, but the Prussian army fell to Napoleon in October 1806, the government fled to Königsberg, and Engel was out of work. By 1809 he was appointed town architect of Reval (now Tallinn) in Estonia. That position proved to be not very lucrative, and Engel applied for a leave of absence in 1814 and found employment in Turku, Finland. There he met Johan Albert Ehrenström, chairman of the committee to reconstruct Helsinki after the devastating fire of 1808. Engel went on to work in St. Petersburg, but he had so impressed Ehrenström that the latter arranged for his appointment as architect for the reconstruction by Czar Alexander I in 1816.

The grandeur of newly or nearly completed civic buildings in the Russian capital was not lost upon the architect then coming into his maturity. For such buildings as the Mining Institute (1806-11), the Admiralty (1806-15) and the Exchange (1806-18), the Russian architects were drawing upon the massive elements of the Greek Doric. While Engel was to use other orders for his major works in Finland, he was surely impressed by the monumentality of building in St. Petersburg.

Then came the virtually unprecedented opportunity. At the time of the fire in 1808 Helsinki was simply a port town, the capital of Finland then being in Turku. Plans for rebuilding were dramatically changed in 1812 when Czar Alexander I moved the capital to Helsinki to have the government farther from Sweden, which had been forced to cede Finland to Russia in 1809. The plan that had been developed by the time of Engel's appointment still governs the center of the city today. A height rising to the north from the south harbor was chosen for a public square, with a wide esplanade extending to the west from the harbor on the lower ground. It was up to Engel to furnish this grand scheme with buildings of sufficient dignity and grandeur.

What he did for the public square, now called the Senate Square, is a story in itself (see Vol. 2: Finland, Helsinki, Senate Square). It occupied Engel for the rest of his life but was far from the only work that he undertook. Enlarging the site chosen for the square meant demolishing the wooden Church of Ulrika Eleanora, and Engel provided a place for a new church to replace it at another site. The Old Church, as it is now called, was built to his designs on a rise just beyond the western end of the Esplanade. With its cemetery, it is now in a tree-shaded park between Lönnrotinkatu and Bulevardi. By that time Engel had been appointed controller of public works, in 1824, and from his office designs for churches and town halls were sent all over Finland. The design for the Old Church, a low wooden structure with classical porticoes and a domed turret in the center, was a type that was used, with variations, in the provincial towns. Although some of the churches, such as the one built at Lapua in Ostrobothnia (1827), were probably not by the architect himself, there is little doubt as to the source of inspiration.

The other major area for design from Engel's office was town halls. As it happened, Helsinki never received a town hall to his plans. The first intention was to remodel the old one, located on the public square, but changes in plan caused it to be torn down, and a house on the south side of the square was remodeled for the purpose. For other towns, Lapeentra (1829) and Pori (1841), for example, the conventional model was used. Local builders had designs from the Office of Public Works which they used in constructing centralized buildings with hipped roofs and central turrets, all embellished with neoclassical detail.

Engel's career was, therefore, primarily devoted to public works, from his first commissions in Berlin to those in Reval, and finally to his monumental contributions to the creation of the capital in Helsinki. Scholarly opinion is divided as to whether these contributions were founded on his early education under Gilly or were more importantly shaped by what he had seen in St. Petersburg. The truth is probably somewhere in between. His dedication to the use of classical traditions was complete, and he expressed firm disapproval of the neo-Gothic. He worked with basically simple underlying forms, each building distinctive in his handling of proportion and detail. James M. Richards attributes to his influence the restrained character of much subsequent Finnish architecture.

—MARIAN C. DONNELLY

ERDMANNSDORFF, Friedrich Wilhelm von.

German. Born in Dresden, Germany, 18 May 1736. Died in Dessau, 9 March 1800. Studied at University of Wittenberg, 1754-57; study trips to England and Holland in 1763, and Italy in 1761-63, 1765-66, 1770-71. Patronized by Prince Leopold Friedrich Franz of Anhalt-Dessau. Summoned by King Friedrich Wilhelm II in 1787 to Berlin. Further travel throughout Germany and Italy, 1787-90.

Chronology of Works
All in Germany
† *Work no longer exists*

1767-68	Interiors of Town Palace, Dessau
1769-73	Wörlitzer Castle, Wörlitz Garden buildings, Wörlitz
1774-80	Schloss Luisium, near Dessau
1777	Court Theater, Dessau
1778	Round Temple, Gotha

1780	Schloss Georgium
1780s	Sans Souci, Potsdam (redesign of king's rooms)
1787	Cemetery Gateway, Dessau
1787-89	Royal Palace, Berlin (King's Rooms)
1793-94	Stables, Coach House, Orangery and Guard House, Dessau
1794	Theater, Magdeburg
1795	Town Hall, Wörlitz

Publications

BOOKS ABOUT ERDMANNSDORFF

GROTE, L.: *Führer durch den Wörlitzer Park.* Dessau, 1929.

HARKEN, MARIELUISE: *Erdmannsdorff und seine Bauten in Wörlitz.* Wörlitz, Germany, 1973.

RIESENFELD, ERICH PAUL: *Friedrich Wilhelm von Erdmannsdorff, der Baumeister des Herzogs Leopold Friedrich Franz von Anhald-Dessau.* Berlin, 1913.

STAATLICHE SCHLÖSSER UND GÄRTEN, WÖRLITZ: *Der Englische Garten zu Wörlitz.* Berlin, 1987.

*

Friedrich Wilhelm von Erdmannsdorff was a cultivated gentleman and friend of princes. He studied mathematics, history, philology, natural sciences and philosophy at the University of Wittenberg in 1754-57, and 1756 met Prince Franz of Anhalt-Dessau (1740-1817), with whose fortunes his career was to be so intimately bound. From 1757, in fact, Erdmannsdorff was employed as adviser on artistic matters as well as agent and architect in the service of the prince.

Erdmannsdorff was sent to Italy in 1761, and in 1763 the prince and his architect traveled in England and the Netherlands. In 1765-66 the two men again visited Italy, and in Rome they met Charles-Louis Clerisseau and the great J. J. Winckelmann. Indeed, Erdmannsdorff saw Winckelmann almost every day, and the latter was indefatigable in his enthusiasm and energies to show off the Roman collections to his German friends. Early in 1766 Erdmannsdorff traveled to Naples, where he met William Hamilton, who was building up his impressive collection of Greek vases; later Erdmannsdorff saw the Greek temples at Paestum, so the stimuli he received were firmly in tune with the mood of the times, and his education in antique remains was as up-to-date as possible. The two Germans then returned to Saxony by a roundabout route, visiting France, England, Scotland and Ireland on the way.

In 1767 Erdmannsdorff designed the interiors of the town palace at Dessau, in which he demonstrated his mastery of the neo-antique style, clearly not uninfluenced by the works if William Chambers and Robert Adam in Britain. Erdmannsdorff's masterpiece, however, is Schloss Wörlitz, built for the prince some miles from Dessau in 1769-73. It is an Anglo-Palladian villa with elevations very like those of Claremont in Surrey (also designed in 1769), but the plan at Wörlitz is closer to Palladio than to English Palladian exemplars. The central part of the house is an open court, and the entrance hall is a miniature Pantheon. Much of the decoration derives from Robert Wood's *The Ruins of Palmyra* (1753) and from the Roman house contiguous to the Villa Negroni in Rome. Chimneypieces owe much to G. B. Piranesi.

If the house itself is charming, the gardens at Wörlitz are enchanting, and are partially influenced by Stowe, Stourhead and even Kew, with a strong dash of French design as well, for one of the odder features is the Rousseau-Insel of 1782, an island planted with poplars and embellished with a cenotaph: it is based on the Île des Peupliers at Ermenonville. The prince had met Jean-Jacques Rousseau in 1775, and of course the image of the island was celebrated. Prince Franz was sympathetic to the ideals of the Enlightenment, and was both an Anglophile and an admirer of things French. With Erdmannsdorff, he created a landscaped park in the "English" style at Wörlitz as an expression of modernity and progressive ideas. Erdmannsdorff designed the garden buildings at Wörlitz, including the Pantheon, the Temple of Flora, the Temple of Venus (in which Greek Doric was used) and the Villa Hamilton, all of which had pretty neoclassical interiors that demonstrated the architect's sureness of touch with antique themes.

Erdmannsdorff was also responsible for Schloss Luisium near Dessau (1774-80), another charming little building with neoclassical interiors of the most delicate design. While building was proceeding, Erdmannsdorff visited England again in 1775. When he returned, he designed the theater in the Residenz at Dessau (1777), the round temple in the park at Gotha (1778), and around 1780 Schloss Georgium and various garden buildings.

Friedrich Wilhelm von Erdmannsdorff: Wörlitzer Castle, Wörlitz, Germany, 1769-73

Wörlitz was very much admired for its novelty in the latter part of the 18th century. Goethe visited the gardens and made sketches there in 1778. With the labyrinth, miniature Vesuvius, small-scale version of the iron bridge at Coalbrookdale in Shropshire, temples, Gothick house, synagogue and Rousseau-Insel, the grounds at Wörlitz suggested England, France, progressive and enlightened views, liberal and advanced notions, and a strong whiff of Freemasonry, as well as poetic and elegiac moods. It was, in every sense, a garden of allusions.

When Friedrich II (the Great) of Prussia was succeeded by Friedrich Wilhelm II in 1787, the new king decided to make Berlin a great cultural center in which German art and architecture would be preeminent. In the following year he called Erdmannsdorff from Dessau, Carl Gotthard Langhans from Breslau and David Gilly from Stettin; these men formed the nucleus of a group of architects of genius who were to create the Franco-Prussian style of neoclassicism, and who were to teach new generations of designers. Erdmannsdorff redesigned in a neoclassical style the rooms where Friedrich II had lived and died in Sans Souci at Potsdam, and also remodeled the king's apartments at the Berlin Schloss. These represent distinguished neoclassical contributions that were to influence the later generation of Karl Friedrich Schinkel and his contemporaries.

In 1787 Erdmannsdorff designed the gateway to the new cemetery at Dessau (one of the earliest planned cemeteries in Germany), which incorporates Masonic allegories and motifs. In the following two years he visited Braunschweig, Italy, Weimar, Gotha, Kassel, Karlsruhe and Dresden, where he was received at court. In 1792-93 he built the stables, coach house, orangery and guardhouse at Dessau, and in 1794 the theater at Magdeburg. His last building at Wörlitz was the Rathaus (1795). From 1796 until his death in 1800 he was the first artistic director of the Dessau institute of copper engraving.

Erdmannsdorff had a widely cultured mind, and his interests ranged over frontiers and into many disciplines. As one of the best and earliest of the architects who brought the language of neoclassicism to the German lands, he is of considerable importance. He is buried in the cemetery in Dessau that he designed.

—JAMES STEVENS CURL

ERICKSON, Arthur.

Canadian. Born in Vancouver, British Columbia, Canada, 14 June 1924. Studied at the University of British Columbia, Vancouver, 1942-45; McGill University, Montreal, 1946-50, B.Arch.; awarded McLennan Travelling Scholarship for architectural research in the Middle East and Europe, 1950-53. Served in the Canadian Army, 1943-45; captain, Canadian Intelligence Corps in India, Ceylon, and Malaya, 1945. In private practice, Vancouver, 1953-62; partnership with Geoffrey Massey, Vancouver, 1963-72 ; since 1972, principal, Arthur Erickson Architects, Vancouver, Los Angeles and Toronto; since 1977, president, Arthur Erickson Associates, Vancouver, Toronto, Kuwait and Jeddah, Saudi Arabia. Has taught at the University of Oregon, Eugene, and at the University of British Columbia, Vancouver. Broadcaster, Canadian Broadcasting Corporation, 1956-62. Gold Medal, Royal Architectural Institute of Canada, 1984; Gold Medal, American Institute of Architects, 1986.

Arthur Erickson: Canadian Chancery Building, Washington, DC, 1983-89

Chronology of Works
All in Canada unless noted

1953	Smith House I, West Vancouver
1961	Danto House, Vancouver
1962	Lloyd House, Vancouver
1963	Simon Fraser University, Burnaby, British Columbia (with Geoffrey Massey)
1964	Smith House, West Vancouver
1965	MacMillan Bloedel Building, Vancouver (with F. Donaldson)
1966	Faculty Club, University of British Columbia, Vancouver (additions and alterations)
1967	Craig House, Kelowna, British Columbia
1967	Catton House, West Vancouver
1967-71	University of Lethbridge, Alberta
1968	Nelson Towers Apartments, Vancouver
1971-80	Bank of Canada, Ottawa (with Marani, Rounthwaite, and Dick)
1971-76	Museum of Anthropology, University of British Columbia, Vancouver
1972	Helmut Eppich House, West Vancouver
1973-79	Robson Square (Provincial Government Offices and Law Courts), Vancouver
19733	Arthur Erickson House, Vancouver (remodeling)
1976	Sawaber Housing Development, Kuwait
1976-80	Roy Thomson Hall, Toronto
1979	Napp Laboratories, Cambridge, England
1980	California Plaza (mixed-use development), Los Angeles, California, U. S. A.
1981	Songhees Family Townhouses and Seniors Tower, Victoria

1981	Red Deer Regional Arts Centre, Red Deer, Alberta
1982	Crown Plaza (mixed-use development), Los Angeles, California, U. S. A.
1983-89	Canadian Chancery Building, Washington, D.C., U.S.A.
1984-89	Convention Center, San Diego, California, U.S.A.
1985	Etilisat Headquarters, Abu Dhabi, United Arab Emirates
1986	Centennial Campus Master Plan, North Carolina State University, Raleigh, North Carolina, U. S. A. (with Land Design)
1986-88	Markham Municipal Building, Markham, Ontario
1987	Thunder Bay Government Office Building, Thunder Bay, Ontario (with Reginald Nalezyty)
1987	Negishi Housing, Yokohama, Japan
1988	Balboa Beach House, Newport Beach, California, U.S.A.
1988	Halperin House, Woodside, California, U.S.A.
1989	Mikage Housing, Kobe, Japan

Publications

ARTICLES BY ERICKSON

"The Weight of Heaven." *Canadian Architect* (March 1964).
"The Roots" and "A Tendency Towards Formalism." *Canadian Architect* (December 1966).
"The University; The New Visual Environment." *Canadian Architect* (January 1968).
"Architecture, Urban Development and Industrialization." *Canadian Architect* (January 1975).
"The Context for Urbanization and Industrialization." In *Towards a Quality of Life: The Role of Industrialization in the Architecture and Urban Planning of Developing Countries.* Teheran, Iran, 1976.
"Ideation as a Source of Creativity." In W. H. NEW (ed.): *A Political Art.* Vancouver, 1978.

BOOKS ABOUT ERICKSON

The Architecture of Arthur Erickson. Montreal, 1975.
The Architecture of Arthur Erickson. New York, 1988.
CAWKER, R. (ed.): *Building with Words: Canadian Architects on Architecture.* Toronto, 1981.
IGLAUER, EDITH: *Seven Stones: A Portrait of Arthur Erickson, Architect.* Seattle, Washington, 1981.
SHAPIRO, BARBARA (ed.): *Arthur Erickson: Selected Projects 1971-1985.* New York, 1985.

ARTICLES ABOUT ERICKSON

"The Design of a House." *Canadian Art* (November 1960).
DUBOIS, MACY: "Erickson." *Canadian Architect* (November 1974).
LEHRMAN, JONAS: "Museum of Anthropology: An Appraisal." *Canadian Architect* (May 1977).
MAZZARIOL, GIUSEPPE: "The Language of Erickson." *Lotus* 5 (1969).
"Meet the Architect: Arthur Erickson." In *GA Houses.* Tokyo, 1977.
NAIRN, JANET: "Vancouver's Grand New Government Center." *Architectural Record* 168/8 (1980).
ROGATNICK, ABRAHAM: "Simon Fraser University, British Columbia." *Architectural Review* 143 (1968).
SCHMERTZ, MILDRED F.: "Spaces for Anthropological Art." *Architectural Record* (May 1977).

"The University of Lethbridge: Project One." *Architectural Record*, 153/5 (1973).
"Two Universities—Simon Fraser and Lethbridge." *Domus* (June 1975).
VASTOKAS, JOAN: "Architecture as Cultural Expression: Arthur Erickson and the New Museum of Anthropology, University of British Columbia." *Arts Canada* (October/November 1976).

For Canada, whose history has been strongly colored by the concomitant influences of England, France and the United States, the issue of national identity in the arts has been problematic. Even though a distinctively "Canadian" architecture is an abstract ideal that may well be unattainable in this postmodern period, the heroic architect, both master builder and theorist, still dominates architectural discourse. Some works will be thought of as uniquely "Canadian" simply because they have been designed by Canadian architects. In the years since the Centennial (1967), Arthur Erickson's name has become synonymous with that which is contemporary and inherently Canadian about Canadian architecture. The winner of the gold medals of the Royal Architectural Institute of Canada, the French Académie d'Architecture and the American Institute of Architects, and the author of seminal works built across the geographically diverse Canadian landscape, in the United States, and in the Middle East and Japan, Erickson is, arguably, Canada's most renowned architect.

The works that brought him international attention in the late 1960s and 1970s explored an architectural language informed by three conceptual bases: responsiveness to environmental context, sensitivity to cultural traditions, and craftsmanlike approaches to contemporary constructive technology. Transcendent qualities of light, tradition and place resonate in Erickson's work, defying categorizations of style in a legacy of design that spans over 30 years.

It is remarkable that Erickson evolved an architectural expression that defies conventional description. His professional training at McGill University was cast in the then-influential model of the Bauhaus. When he entered architectural practice in Vancouver in 1953, the International Style was emerging forcefully in North America, but Erickson resisted its prescriptions for a universal machine aesthetic. Erickson appreciated the Miesian ideal of structural honesty and formal efficiency, but his intuitive response to environmental context indicates that he did not subscribe to the International Style's blatant rejection of regional and cultural specificity. Erickson sought a different theoretical point of departure, vested in the land, its climate and culture, which he found in the precedents of Frank Lloyd Wright and nurtured through an experiential approach to historic architecture of both the eastern and the western traditions.

A broad definition of context is the touchstone for Erickson's conceptual framework. According to the architect, context comprises not only the obvious matters of topography, orientation, climate and surrounding structures, but also the more elusive ones—the general character of the site and the quality of light. Site has to be understood before it can be enhanced with architecture.

Profound regard for sense of place is apparent in Erickson's first internationally acclaimed work, the Simon Fraser University (Burnaby, British Columbia, 1963), executed with Geoffrey Massey, his partner from 1963 to 1972. There, Erickson created an academic village of great richness, featuring a covered mall which ceremoniously leads to an introspective academic quadrangle. In section, the complex responds to the topography of the natural landscape, and the buildings, visually rooted to the land, evoke the surrounding mountains. Also precedent-setting are the sculptural handling of concrete and facile manipulation of structure.

The principles that governed the design of Simon Fraser University were adapted to a very different environmental context, the Canadian prairie, in the University of Lethbridge (1967). Although clearly informed by the earlier project, this design is mindful of the severity of the prairie's climate and the brilliance of its light. The expansive concrete building becomes an intimate part of its landscape, horizontally attenuated and embracing the land.

The site-sensitive solutions of Simon Fraser University and the University of Lethbridge are paralleled in Erickson's residential work. Of particular note are the second Smith House (West Vancouver, 1964), the plan of which was manipulated to reveal its site and planar glass elevations conceived to afford unrestricted visual connection with the landscape. The richly vegetated site is a rhetorical source for the huge wood beams that frame the house. Similarly, the Helmut Eppich House (West Vancouver, 1972) merges naturalistically with the land through the creation of stepped terraces that extend laterally across the site. In both cases, interior space and materials were calculated to take maximum advantage of natural light.

By the mid-1970s, Canadian architecture had matured and diversified, evidencing new technologies, regional specificity and concern for public life. Two of Erickson's finest works figure in this evolution, the University of British Columbia Anthropology Museum (Vancouver, 1976) and the Vancouver Law Courts and Robson Square Redevelopment (1979). Clearly a cultural text, the Anthropology Museum weds tangible features of site with abstract constructs of meaning. A profound regard for the traditions of Canada's native people was implicit in Erickson's concept: he has noted that the design of the museum was influenced by the image of a photograph depicting an early Indian village between the edge of the forest and the edge of the sea (Edith Iglauer, *Seven Stones*. Built to house relics of the Northwest Coast Haida, Kwakiutl and Nootka tribes, the building is characterized by the rhythm of its constructive elements, concrete posts and beams, in a progressively changing series of proportions that echo the formal qualities of the totems it contains. Outside, the building silhouette creates, on a grand scale, a form reminiscent of the Haida house. Great glass walls punctuated by a muscular, yet organic, concrete structure render the museum one with its site. The tectonic and imagistic character of the Anthropology Museum differs considerably from that of the Law Courts, the result of the architect's acute sense of place.

Erickson has observed that "the urban site is a . . . problematic design exercise. . . . The success of an urban building is dependent upon its relationship to its neighbors and the spaces around it." From the urban context emerged Erickson's works which subscribed most closely to the tenets of modernism, including the MacMillan Bloedel Building (Vancouver, 1965) and the Bank of Canada (Ottawa, 1971-80). In its late-modern celebration of structure, the Law Courts derive from this tradition. There, Erickson captured the traditional monumentality of the courthouse in a dialogue between its glass and steel space-frame spine and its formal, concrete terraced massing. Outside, Erickson's sculptural, stage-set-like orchestration of the urban landscape both enhances the dynamics of the city center and counteracts its density with intimate spaces. Again, the sensitive response to northwest light and facile sectional integration of building and site characterize Erickson's work. In a very different context, the Law Court's linearity of plan and transparency

of form are reflected in a later work, the San Diego Convention Center (1989).

For many years Erickson was an outspoken critic of postmodernism. He decried its nostalgic impulses, and advocated adherence to the vernacular and utilitarian traditions in North American architecture. However, recent works indicate that "when the context made it pertinent to do so, the new eclecticism freed (him) to render more literally the classical canons" (*The Architecture of Arthur Erickson*, p. 184). For Erickson, employing classicism involves juxtaposing abstract spatial arrangements against historically derived details, and merging traditional expectations with modern technologies. His Markham Municipal Building (1986-88) combines classical elements, a rotunda and an encompassing colonnade, in a composition that strives for invitation without ceremony. His 1988 competition entry for Chicago's Harold Washington Library Center derived from the paradigmatic classical athenaeum. Perhaps the most controversial of the architect's recent work is the Canadian Chancery (Washington, D.C., 1983-89).

A highly contextual response to the neoclassicism of Washington, D.C.'s federal architecture, Erickson's building makes overt references to its neighbors along Pennsylvania Avenue, including I. M. Pei's National Gallery East Wing. Requiring far less space than the site afforded, the chancery clings to Pennsylvania Avenue, but its volume is generously disposed around a unifying courtyard. Seemingly oppositional architectural texts occur in its literally classical rotunda, representational courtyard colonnade of fifty-foot-high aluminum columns, and abstract fenestration and stepped terraces; only the latter are reminiscent of the architect's earlier work. The chancery is both a thoughtful response to site and symbol, and a postmodern burlesque of classicism.

Erickson is among the few architects whose careers have spanned the period from the singularly authoritative modernism of the 1950s to the pluralistic postmodernism of the 1980s. It should not be surprising that he has bridged the gulf between abstract and referential vocabularies of architectural design. His work has always seemed uniquely removed from the self-limiting jargon of style; transcendent principles rather than period fashions have been the touchstones of his theories. A survey of Erickson's work presents a natural evolution of his design ideology—an architectural language informed by a broadly constructed definition of natural, human-made and cultural contexts, vested in the uniqueness of place, its land and its light. Through his concomitant concerns for site, space and materials, Erickson has continually achieved, "a contemporary evocation of the spirit of past experience, involving a merger of utility, culture and beauty of place." Erickson's architecture thus overarches the theoretical camps of the second half of the 20th century, establishing him as one of the few of this era's architects whose work achieves an instinctively North American character.

—ETHEL S. GOODSTEIN

ERSKINE, Ralph.

British. Born in Mill Hill, London, 24 February 1914. Married Ruth Monica Francis, 1939; three children. Studied at Regent Street Polytechnic, London, 1932-37, Dip. Arch., 1937; Royal Academy of Arts, Stockholm, 1944-45. In private practice, Drottningholm, Sweden, since 1946; guest professor, Eidgenössische Technische Hochschule, Zurich, 1964-65, and McGill University, Montreal, 1967-68. Member of Team 10 since 1959. Made Commander, Order of the British Empire, 1978. Gold Medal, Royal I nstitute of British Architects, 1987.

Chronology of Works
All in Sweden unless noted

1941-42	Erskine House, Lissma, near Stockholm
1945	Housing development for workers, Gyttorp
1946-47	Town plan and housing, Storviks-Hammarby
1947-48	Mattress Factory, Köping
1948-50	Skiing Hotel/Center, Borgafjäll
1950-53	Cardboard Factory, Fors, near Avesta
1953	Paper-pulp Factory, Storviks-Hammarby
1954	Apartment buildings, Växjö
1955-56	Engström House, Sorunda, Isle of Lisö, near Nynäshamn
1956	*Verona* barge conversion to Erskine offices, Drottningholm
1958	Ideal Subarctic Town, Lappland (project)
1961	Primary School, Gyttorp
1961	Gadelius House, Lidingö, near Stockholm
1961-62	Ortdrivaren Housing Development, Kiruna
1962	Nordmark House, near Södertälje
1962-72	Barberaren Housing Estate, Sandviken
1963	LKAB Staff Housing, Svappavaara
1963	Erskine House and Studio, Drottningholm
1967-69	Post-Graduate College, Clare Hall, Cambridge, England
1969-72	Killingworth Housing Estate, near Newcastle upon Tyne, England
1969-81	Byker Housing Estate, Newcastle upon Tyne, England
1970-76	Studlands Park Housing Estate, Newmarket, Suffolk, England
1973-74	Plan for the development of the Old City, Resolute Bay, Northwest Territories, Canada
1973-77	Eaglestone Housing Estate, Milton Keynes, Buckinghamshire, England
1973-78	Bruket Housing Estate, Sandviken
1974-82	Library and Student Center, Frescati University, Stockholm
1976	Multiple Staff Housing, Resolute Bay, Northwest Territories, Canada
1981-86	Malminkartano Housing, Helsinki, Finland
1983	SAS Building, Bromma
1983-	Housing, Graz, Austria
1983-	Ekerö Center, Tappstrom
1985-86	Myrstuguberget Housing, Huddinge, near Stockholm
1987-90	Office Building at Lilla Bommen, Göteborg
1988-91	Larson Office Building, Hammersmith, London, England (with Vernon Gracie)

Publications

ARTICLES BY ERSKINE

"Town Planning in the Swedish Subarctic." *Habitat* (November/December 1960).
"The Challenge of the High Latitudes" and "Community Design for Production, for Publication, or for People." *Royal Architectural Institute of Canada Journal* (1964).
"Architecture and Town Planning in the North." *Polar Record* (Cambridge) 89 (1968).
"Climate." *Werk* 4 (1969).
"8 Riposte a 8 domande." *Architettura* (November 1974).
"Working on Projects Abroad" and "Byker." With J. Sjostrom. *Arkitektur* (October 1976).
"On the Situation of the Architect." *Bauen und Wohnen* (January 1977).

"Byker: New Building Best Solution." *Arkitektur* (February 1977).
"Nya Bruket: Daynursery in Sandviken." *Arkitektur* (August 1977).
"The Loyal Architecture." *Arkitektur* (June 1979).
"Architecture in a Cold Climate." *RIBA Journal* (October 1980).
"Democratic Architecture." *RSA Journal* (September 1982).

BOOKS ABOUT ERSKINE

COLLYMORE, PETER: *The Architecture of Ralph Erskine*. London, 1982.
EGELIUS, MATS: *Ralph Erskine, Architect*. Stockholm, 1990.
FUTAGAWA, YUKIO (ed.): *GA 55: The Byker Redevelopment*.

ARTICLES ABOUT ERSKINE

AMERY, COLIN: "Byker by Erskine." *Architectural Review* (December 1974).
Architectural Design, special issue, 47/11-12 (1977).
Architettura, special issue (November 1974).
Arkitektur, special issue, 81/7 (1981).
Bauen und Wohnen, special issue (January 1977).
BENTON, CHARLOTTE: "Erskine's Evolution." *Building Design* (November 1984).
COLLYMORE, PETER: "Erskine's Allhus." *Architectural Review* (November 1981).
Deutsche Bauzeitung, special issue, 3 (1983).
EGELIUS, MATS: "Ralph Erskine, The Human Architect." *Architectural Design* (November/December 1977).
"Erskine Experience." *Architectural Review* (March 1988).
POSENER, JULIUS: "The Way Leads to Ralph Erskine." *Architekt* (October 1982).
"Ralph Erskine Talks to AJ." *Architects' Journal* (3 March 1976).
World Architecture, special issue, 6 (1990).

*

Born in 1914 and raised in north London, Ralph Erskine moved to Sweden as a young man and has become the most famous living architect in that country. Erskine, whose parents were Fabian socialists, studied at a Quaker School. Social ideals and concerns from those sources stayed with him and became a dominant theme in his architecture. After studying at the Regent Street Polytechnic, Erskine went to Sweden, attracted by that country's commitment to modern architecture and to the welfare state. He was not disappointed and has made Sweden his home since 1939.

Stranded in Sweden by World War II, Erskine lost his job with a Stockholm firm of architects. During the following period of hardship, he designed wooden cabins in remote areas. Eventually a farmer in Lissma gave him a piece of land, on which Erskine and his wife, Ruth, built their own house in 1941-42. That little house shows many of the interests that were to remain with the architect—love of the great outdoors, an irregular plan with walls at odd angles, a fascination with climatic and insulation problems, a clear examination of functional requirements often leading to unconventional solutions.

After the war, Erskine entered numerous Swedish architectural competitions and was quite successful. The resulting architect's office could not be contained in the tiny Lissma house, and in 1946 the Erskines moved to the island of Drottningholm, west of Stockholm. They worked and lived there in a rented house until 1963, when they built a new house and office. For many years Erskine and his colleagues would decamp each summer, working for that period in a converted Thames barge which they would sail to Rago, a three-day voyage away from Stockholm. For Erskine, home life and work life are not totally separable, and both should be enjoyable and lively. In time the office grew to be too large for the barge and then too large for the studio by the house; so another building was purchased. But Erskine is not a man to enjoy being the head of a large organization, and in 1981 he broke the office in two; Erskine and a few of his staff moved back into the studio next to the house, while the rest of the office formed a semi-independent cooperative called Arken-Erskinearkitekterna and moved to central Stockholm.

Architecturally, Erskine has plowed a lonely furrow. His buildings are readily identifiable, usually by their quirky geometry. But the quirkiness is never willful. Erskine is a true functionalist. His interests are various and have been consistent. First, participation: working with and trying to understand the users of the building. Second, climate: a fascination with weather and the environment and using its requirements to help give form to the building. Third, social relevance: the office turns down work that it does not consider beneficial to society. Fourth, antimonumentality: architecture is for use, not for the glory of state, church or corporation. Hence an avoidance of the hard geometry of much contemporary architecture. Fifth, small is beautiful: village scale is human scale; garden cities are preferable to dense urbanity, but they degenerate into suburbia without community centers, clinics and pubs.

A housing development at Gyttorp, completed in 1945, was Erskine's first major commission. A row of seven houses, with curved barrel-vault roofs, were set staggered to give privacy. They are friendly houses, with an emphasis on the individual dwellings. A mattress factory at Koping took the barrel-vault roof to a larger and more elegant project. Numerous housing developments followed, but the most memorable image from Erskine's work of the 1950s is the Engstrom House. A 16-sided dome of 3-millimeter steel with 100 Rockwool insulation, it is a design for a cold climate and virtually disappears under the snow in winter.

In 1961 the mining town of Kiruna in Lappland gave Erskine an opportunity to study the appropriate form and technology for building in a very cold climate, and those concepts were further developed in 1973 at Resolute Bay in the Canadian Northwest. At Resolute Bay, the Erskine office participated with the indigenous Inuit Eskimos and the whites operating the airfield and weather station, and saw its role in bringing these two groups together in a development where the worst effects of the hostile climate could be mitigated by the form of the buildings.

In 1968 Cambridge University's Clare Hall constructed a postgraduate seminar building to Erskine's design, bringing him back to England. Gentle, complex and functional, it had a great impact on English architects at the time. But more was to come. The Byker development in Newcastle, begun in the following year, gave a new and optimistic image to public housing and to high-rise living just as those concepts were going out of favor. Known as the ''Byker Wall'' because of its great curved block shielding the site from the north and from a planned motorway, it created pleasant low-rise housing in the shelter of the wall. Erskine extended his English triumph with the construction, in 1990, of an office building by London's Hammersmith flyover, where the social needs and pleasures of office workers received the same warm response as had been shown to the residents of the housing developments.

—JOHN WINTER

ERVI, Aarne.

Finnish. Born Aarne Adrian Elers in Forssa, Finland, 19 May 1910 (adopted the surname Ervi in 1935). Died in Helsinki, 26 September 1977. Married Naemi Inkeri Hanninen, 1935 (divorced, 1957); married Rauni Maria Erika Luoma, 1957; three children. Studied at the Helsingin Suomaleinen Yhteiskoulu, Helsinki, 1930; Technical University of Helsinki, 1930-35, Dip.Arch. Assistant architect, City Planning Building Office, Helsinki, 1934; worked in the office of Alvar Aalto, Helsinki, 1935, and Toivo Paatela, Helsinki, 1937; in private practice, Helsinki, 1938 until his death in 1977. Worked in the Standardization Department, Finnish Rebuilding Office, Helsinki, 1942-44; director, Standardization Institute, Association of Finnish Architects, 1942-45; director, City Planning Office, Helsinki, 1965-68. Special instructor, Central School of Arts and Crafts, Helsinki, 1937-38; instructor, Technical University of Helsinki, 1943-46. Assistant editor, *Arkkitehti*, Helsinki, 1937-43.

Chronology of Works
All in Finland

1939	Apartment building, Lauttesaarentie 7, Helsinki
1941	Institute of Economics
1947-53	Voimatalo Commercial and Office Building, Helsinki (with Tapani Nironen)
1949-54	Oulujoki Oy Power Plants, and their housing areas, at Pyhäkoski, Jyhämä, Nuojua, and Pälli
1950	Ervi House, Kuusisaari, Helsinki
1950-57	Helsinki University Institute, Porthania, Helsinki
1952-56	Library, Main Building, and Institute of Natural Sciences, Turku University, Turku
1952-64	Town center, houses, apartments, and row housing, Tapiola Garden City, Espoo
1962	Apartment building, Kaivopuisto, Helsinki
1966	Municipal Office Building, Tampere
1968-70	Töölö Library, Helsinki
1969	Kaleva Insurance Company Offices, Espoo
1974	Tapiola Garden Hotel, Espoo

Publications

ARTICLES BY ERVI

''Bybyggerne bag Tapiola.'' *Arkitektur* 6, No. 2 (April 1962): 43-54.

BOOKS ABOUT ERVI

BECKER, H. J. and SCHLOTE, W.: *Esempi di pianificiazione edilizia in Finlandia.* Milan, 1960.
Finnish Building. Exhibition catalog, Helsinki, 1953.
RICHARDS, J. M.: *800 Years of Finnish Architecture.* London, 1978.
SAIVO, PIRKKA: *Modern Finland.* Helsinki, 1956.
SALOKORPI, ASKO: *Modern Architecture in Finland.* London, 1970.
SOLLA, PENTTI: *Aarne Ervi arkkitehtuuria.* Helsinki, 1970.
HERTZEN, HEIKKI VON, and SPREIREGEN, PAUL D.: *Building a New Town: Finland's New Garden City, Tapiola.* Cambridge, Massachusetts, 1971.
TEMPEL, EGON: *New Finnish Architecture.* London, 1968.
WICKBERG, NILS ERIK: *Finnish Architecture.* Helsinki, 1959.

Aarne Ervi: Töölö Library, Helsinki, Finland, 1968-70

ARTICLES ABOUT ERVI

"Centre de Tapiola, cité satellite d'Helsinki." *Architecture d'aujourd'hui* No. 101 (1962).

"Libraries in Finland." *Architektura* (August 1975).

"Nouveau bâtiments de l'Université de Turku." *Architecture d'aujourd'hui* No. 93 (1960-61).

PENTTILA, TIMO and VON HERTZEN, HEIKKI: "Aarne Ervi in Memoriam." *Arkkitehti* No. 7 (1977).

SOLLA, PENTTI: "Aarne Ervi: Ein Ritter der alten Schule." *Deutsche Bauzeitung* No. 9 (1968).

"Terassenhaus, Tapiola." *Architektur und Wohnform* No. 4 (1967).

Finnish architects were well versed in the International Style from its earliest days. Alvar Aalto's seminal works in that vein, the offices for Turun Sanomat and Paimio Sanatorium, broke on the European scene in 1928 and 1929. The young Aarne Ervi graduated from high school the following year, and entered Helsinki Technical University to study architecture. After his studies, he became an assistant for the town-planning course. He also taught design at the Institute for Industrial Design, and later building technology at the Technical University (1935-37). He founded his own architectural practice in 1938.

Ervi is described by his colleague Timo Penttilä as follows: "He was not a theorist. For him, architecture and life had a close influence on each other. . . . He very deliberately invested architecture with graceful rhythms since he was no stranger to liveliness or charm. . . . If he enjoyed the name of being ultramodern for his use of new technology, he was equally

adept with log, slate, and the traditional turf sod roof. Bombast of any kind was foreign to him. . . . His architecture focussed on people. . . . He sketched spaces around people, making sure that the spaces would allow freedom of movement and be congenial, aesthetically pleasing" (Timo Penttilä, translated from the Finnish text in the journal *Arkkitehti* 7/1977, p. 10).

It is no surprise then that Ervi's first prewar design to be built was an apartment house (1939) at Lauttasaarentie 7, Helsinki. A bank branch is set into the gentle slope at ground level; the facade is broken with the angular projections of living-room windows to catch the evening sun. Each dwelling was provided with a balcony, an innovation for the period. The penthouse is set back from the eaves, cleverly reducing the mass of the building from the vantage point of the street-level observer.

After World War II, Ervi first built his house (1950), then his office (1962) on Kuusisaari's eastern shore. The low, single-story building cluster is almost indistinguishable from its leafy surroundings. Ervi was a caring and genial employer who saw to it that his staff availed themselves of the swimming pool he had built for his family. He is remembered late in life opening his own door without ceremony to welcome foreigners wishing to meet him.

The course of Ervi's architecture was dictated in the early years by works he designed on Oulujoki River for the evolving hydroelectric industry. Those ambitious projects comprised not only power stations but housing and support facilities for working staff who lived there all year round. Giant power stations at Pyhäkoski (1949), Jylhämä (1950), Pälli (1953) and Nuojua (1954) made him articulate in treating huge geometric planes, such as turbine and generator halls, with their massive areas of wall and flat roof. Ervi's skill was to integrate form and materials by applying the principles of the International Style to the function the building served. Small gems of architectural dwelling design can be found in the adjacent houses built for staff engineers, for instance at Imatra (1951).

A major development for the University of Turku (1954-59) was the next scheme of note designed by Ervi. His work at the time was characterized by clean facades with full-height windows, lime-sand brick or composite stone cladding, and low-pitched, copper-clad roofing. The prefabricated elements in the multipurpose Helsinki University Porthania Building (1957) have a fluted, colored aggregate surface, and have weathered well. Ervi's mastery was shown in the way he could make academic buildings so attractive to students that they were believed to spend all their waking hours under the same roof. Students found accommodations for their studies, exercise and nourishment, and a cafeteria terrace that was popular as a place for socializing in the sun.

Ervi's magnum opus was the competition he won for the design of Tapiola, a suburb of Helsinki that became renowned as a paragon of town planning. He converted a disused quarry, the focus of the new suburb, into a large pool in his first-prize entry (1954). He also contributed to the design of individual elements: a central office tower, a swimming hall, cinema, shops and an apartment block east of the center. The enclosed Heikintori shopping mall on the pedestrian route connecting the central tower with vehicular traffic was an innovation of Ervi's that became the hub of the later retail development serving the surrounding area. The last piece in Tapiola's plan, the Espoo Cultural Center (Arto Sipinen, 1989), was added 40 years after the tower with its conspicuous lantern roof was begun.

Ervi returned to the theme of dwelling design with the 12-family housing development on Myllytie in the Kaivopuisto district of Helsinki (1962). It is a twin-cluster development with separate central stairwells and a common leisure area at roof level in addition to generous balcony space.

The architect's great skill in the design of public buildings reappeared in the Töölö borough library, Helsinki (1970). The south facade presents a graceful curve toward the adjacent park, where a monument to the composer Jean Sibelius stands. The main reading room is protected by remote-controlled awnings that can be lowered as a shield from the sun. The children's library has its own outdoor courtyard bordered by the park. A side entrance lets one directly into a public reading room with periodicals and newspapers. The third floor is used for public lectures and of instrumental-music recitals, while a music library at penthouse level is equipped with audio booths. The oval staircase with its natural skylight is a joy to the eye.

Ervi became a member of the Finnish Academy of Technical Sciences in 1965, received the honorary title of Doctor of Sciences in Stuttgart in 1966, and was named a professor in 1967. He did not write much about architecture. Penttilä recounts that "Ervi kept his own prejudices under the careful control of reason. He never assented to an easy but mediocre solution, nor did he ever dogmatically set limits to anything that could possibly be done. He brought his buoyant good humour to planning tasks. Sarcasm he rarely used. Scepticism and cynicism were completely foreign to his nature." Ervi's insights were at least the equal of Aalto's: his innate modesty allowed him to be great without expecting credit for it from his contemporaries. This quality made him all the more approachable and popular, a rare achievement in a profession crowded with artists who are convinced that buildings are monuments to their makers.

—DESMOND O'ROURKE

F

FANZAGO, Cosimo.

Italian. Born in Clusone, near Bergamo, Italy, in 1591. Died in Naples, 13 February 1678. Moved to Naples, 1608. In partnership with Angelo Landi, 1612-20.

Chronology of Works

All in Italy unless noted
* Approximate dates
† Work no longer exists

1620*-38	Santa Maria delle Anime del Purgatorio, Naples (facade and interior decoration)
1622-57	Ascensione a Chiaia, Naples
1623-56	Certosa di San Martino, Naples (cloister, facade, and interior; completion of work begun in 1591 by Giovanni Antonio Dosio)
1628-78	Santa Maria dei Monti, Naples (not completed until 1714)
1629-34	San Nicola al Lido, Venice (high altar)
1630	Santissima Trinità delle Monache (facade)
1632ff.	Palazzo Caviano, Naples
1633-36	Church of the Augustinian Nuns, Salamanca, Spain (additions)
1633-50	Chapels of Sant'Ignazio and San Francesco Saverio, Gesù Nuovo, Naples
1634-39	Fontana Medina, Naples
1634-78	San Giuseppe dei Vecchi a San Potito, Naples (not completed until 1724)
1635-41	Santi Severino e Sosio, Naples (high altar)
1637-60	Guglia di San Gennaro, Naples
1637ff.	Chapel of Sant'Antonio di Padova, San Lorenzo Maggiore, Naples
1638-53	Santa Maria della Sapienza, Naples (facade)
1639ff.	Santa Maria degli Angeli alle Croci, Naples (high altar and facade)
1640*-45	Gesù e Maria, Pescostanzo (high altar)
1640-78	San Giorgio Maggiore, Naples
1642-44	Palazzo Donn'Anna, Naples
1643-45	Cappella Cacace, San Lorenzo Maggiore, Naples
1643-60	San Giuseppe degli Scalzi a Pontecorvo, Naples
1645	Abbey Church, Naples (high altar)†
1647ff.	Palazzo Sitgliano, Naples
1649	Santo Spirito dei Napoletani, Rome (facade)†
1649-52	Santa Maria in Via Latia, Rome
1650*	San Domenico Maggiore, Naples (high altar)
1650-52	San Lorenzo in Lucina, Rome (decoration and high altar)†
1650-53	Fontana Sellaro, Naples
1650-62	Santa Teresa a Chiaia, Naples
1651-78	Santa Maria Egiziaca a Pizzofalcone (not completed until 1717)
1652ff.	Palazzo Maddaloni, Naples
1653-78	Santa Maria Maggiore (La Pietrasanta), Naples
1658	Fontana del Sebeto, Naples
1660*	San Ferdinando, Naples (facade)
1664*	Mastrelli Chapel, Santa Maria delle Anime del Purgatorio, Naples

Publications

BOOKS ABOUT FANZAGO

BLUNT, ANTHONY: *Neapolitan Baroque and Rococo Architecture.* London, 1975.
DOMINICI, BERNARDO DE': *Vite de' pittori, scultori, et architetti napoletani.* 3 vols. Naples, 1742-43.
EIMER, GERHARD: *La fabbrica di S. Agnese in Navona: Römische Architekten, Bauherren, und Handwerker im Zeitalter des Nepotismus.* 2 vols. Stockholm, 1970-71.
FOGACCIA, PIERO: *Cosimo Fanzago.* Bergamo, 1945.
PANE, ROBERTO: *Architettura dell'età barocca in Napoli.* Naples, 1939.
PORTOGHESI, PAOLO: *Roma Barocca: The History of an Architectonic Culture.* Cambridge, Massachusetts, 1970.
SALERNO, LUIGI; SPEZZAFERRO, LUIGI; and TAFURI, MANFREDO: *Via Giulia: Una utopia urbanistica dell'500.* Rome, 1973.
TASSI, FRANCESCO MARIA: *Vite de' pittori, scultori, e architetti bergamaschi.* 2 vols. 1793. Reprint: 1969-70.
WINTHER, ANNEMARIE: *Cosimo Fanzago und die Neapler Ornamentik des 17. und 18. Jahrhunderts.* Bremen, Germany, 1973.
WITTKOWER, RUDOLF: *Art and Architecture in Italy 1600 to 1750.* 3rd ed., Harmondsworth, England, 1980.

ARTICLES ABOUT FANZAGO

BOSEL, RICHARD: "Cosimo Fanzago a Roma." *Prospettiva* 15 (1978): 29-40.
BRAUEN, FRED: "Fanzago's Commission as Royal Chief Engineer." *Storia dell'arte* 26 (1976): 61-72.
CANTONE, GAETANA: "Il complesso conventuale di S. Maria Egiziaca a Pizzofalcone." *Napoli nobilissima* 8 (1969): 93-106.
MADRUGA REAL, ANGELA: "Cosimo Fanzago en las Agustinas de Salamanca." *Goya* 125 (1975): 291-297.
WEISE, GEORG: "Il repertorio ornamentale del Barocco napoletano di Cosimo Fanzago e il suo significato per la genesi del Rococo (I-V)." *Antichità viva* 13 (1974), No. 4:40-53, No. 5:32-41; 14 (1975), No. 1:24-31, No. 5:27-35; 16 (1977), No. 5:42-51.

*

Cosimo Fanzago, the most famous Neapolitan architect of the 17th century, was born in 1591 near Bergamo, but moved to

Naples in 1608 to live with his uncle after the death of his father. Fanzago began his professional career in 1612 when he created a partnership with the Florentine sculptor Angelo Landi that lasted until Landi's death in 1620. All of Fanzago's work during that early period consisted of sculptural rather than architectural commissions, which is important in understanding his later architecture, known for its extremely sculptural and decorative detail rather than its structural innovations. Fanzago spent all of his career in Naples except for a few short trips to Rome, Montecassino and the Veneto. In his early career Fanzago worked mainly on sculptural decorations and altars in churches; then, in the middle of his career, he received more than a dozen commissions to build churches, while at the end of his career his work became more varied, including churches, chapels and a number of domestic palaces.

One of Fanzago's earliest but most important works was the completion of the cloister of the Certosa of San Martino in Naples in 1623. This cloister was begun by Giovanni Antonio Dosio about 1591, and Fanzago was mainly responsible for the sculptural decoration. In each corner of the courtyard, Fanzago built paired doorways ornately decorated with half-length figures growing out of shallow niches above the door frames. While the decorative detail derives from the Florentine Mannerism of Bernardo Buontalenti, known by Fanzago through Angelo Landi, the use of half-length figures protruding from a wall is Lombard in origin, and can be found in Leone Leoni's Casa degli Omenoni in Milan (1565). Fanzago's Lombard origins clearly influenced this sculptural style of architecture that he introduced into Naples.

One of Fanzago's most important contributions to architectural sculpture was his invention of a new type of freestanding altar that separates the church sanctuary from the monks' choir. The new altar first appeared in the Benedictine Church of San Nicola on the Lido in Venice, a documented work by Fanzago dated 1629. It is unclear how Fanzago received that commission so unrelated to his work in Naples, but his trip to Venice was instrumental in the development of this altar type that then became popular in Naples. The separation of the sanctuary from the choir was an idea already worked out by Andrea Palladio in his Church of Il Redentore in Venice from the 1570s. In Il Redentore, Palladio separated the choir, used by the Capuchin monks, from the tribune, used for votive gatherings, by a large choir screen of columns. Fanzago developed his freestanding altar from that idea, but by creating a huge altar with doors on either side to separate the spaces, Fanzago gave room for ample sculpted decoration. In Naples, this altar type can be seen in Fanzago's Santa Maria degli Angeli alle Croce from the later 1620s, San Domenico Maggiore (1640s) and Santa Maria la Nova (1645-47), and it continued to be used in Naples through the 18th century.

Fanzago's churches are difficult to study because so many of them were remodeled or rebuilt in later centuries. He clearly preferred the Greek-cross-plan church, however, which can be seen in his most important church, Santa Maria Egiziaca in Naples, begun in the 1650s but finished only in 1717. Although the interior of the church is circular, the large piers in the nave are beveled to create an octagonal area similar to Carlo Rainaldi's Church of Sant'Agnese in Rome (ca. 1652). Fanzago's Church of Santa Maria Maggiore in Naples, begun in 1653 and built completely to his design, shows a cross-shaped plan within a rectangle, and his two churches of the Anime di Purgatorio and San Francesco Saverio from about 1660 both continued with this development of a centralized plan.

The Church of Santa Teresa a Chiaia in Naples (1650-62) is important in Fanzago's oeuvre for its incredibly detailed exterior as well as the large staircase that stretches across the facade.

These broad staircases also appear on the facades of Fanzago's Church of Santa Maria degli Angeli alle Croci, begun in 1639 but completed in the next century, and his Santi Trinità delle Monache. The use of an exterior stairway became popular in Naples and continued to be used during the 18th century.

Fanzago is also known for his work on various chapels, such as in the Gesù Nuovo in Naples, where he decorated the chapels of Sant'Ignazio and San Francesco Saverio between 1633 and 1650. There Fanzago created a unity between sculpture, decoration and architecture that parallels Giovanni Lorenzo Bernini's unification of the three media in his Roman work from that period. Fanzago also shared with Bernini a preference for richly colored marbles in his church interiors. Fanzago's intricate floor marbles in the interior of the Certosa of San Martino, remodeled in the early 1630s, interact with the extensive fresco program done in part by Giovanni Lanfranco, Giovanni Battista Caracciolo and Guido Reni. It is there that Fanzago invented the complexity of pavement design that appeared throughout his career.

The most innovative of Fanzago's palaces, all of which date to the latter part of his career, is his Palazzo Donn'Anna in Naples (1642-44); it was never completed, and was partially destroyed by an earthquake about 40 years later. There Fanzago built an impressively huge three-story loggia facade with beveled corners unique to that building, thus allowing a vista toward the sea from the unprecedented facade design.

Fanzago can be seen as an architect who always thought as a sculptor, influenced by his early training in sculpture derived from Florentine Mannerism, and the highly sculptural architecture found in Lombardy in the Renaissance, as well as the dynamic, coloristic work of Bernini, his contemporary in Rome. Although Fanzago's career remains inadequately studied, his diversity in media, huge output of work and long career merit his fame as the most important architect working in Naples in the Baroque age.

—ALLISON PALMER

FERSTEL, Heinrich von.

Austrian. Born in Vienna, Austria, 7 July 1828. Died in Vienna, 14 July 1883. Studied at the Vienna Polytechnical Institute, 1847, and the Architecture School of the Academy of Fine Arts, Vienna, 1847-50. In the studio of his uncle, Friedrich Stache, 1851-53. Worked independently in Vienna from 1855.

Chronology of Works
All in Austria unless noted

1853-55	Schloss Türmitz, near Teplitz, Czechoslovakia
1856-60	Nationalbank, Vienna
1856-79	Votivkirche, Vienna
1860-61	Villa Wisgrill, Traunsee
1860-62	Pollak Apartment Building, Vienna
1861-63	Bergl Palace, Brno, Czechoslovakia
1862-77	Catholic Church, Teplitz, Czechoslovakia
1863-67	Protestant Church, Brno, Czechoslovakia
1863-69	Palace Ludwig Viktor, Vienna
1864	Villa Ferstel, Grinzing, Vienna
1864-68	Wertheim Palace, Vienna
1868-70	Administration Building of the State Railway Company, Vienna†
1868-70	Wertheim Apartment Building, Vienna
1868-71	Österreichisches Museum für Kunst und Industrie, Vienna

Heinrich von Ferstel: Votivkirche, Vienna, Austria, 1856-79

1869-72	Chemical Institute of the University of Vienna, Vienna
1870-72	Villa Wartholz, Reichenau
1870-72	Zentralanstalt für Meteorologie und Erdmagnetismus, Vienna
1870-73	Leon Apartment Building, Schottenring, Vienna
1870-73	Maximiliansgymnasium, Vienna
1871-72	Primary School, Grinzing, Vienna
1871-72	Villa Tauber, Traunsee
1872-73	Weiss Apartment Building, Vienna
1873-74	Casino of the *Cottageverein*, Vienna
1873-74	Villa Jacobson, Reichenau
1873-75	Apartment Building of Allgemeine Österreichische Baugesellschaft, Vienna
1873-75	Liechtenstein Garden Palace, Vienna
1873-83	University of Vienna, Vienna (not completed until later)
1874-76	Kunstgewerbeschule, Vienna
1874-76	Leon Apartment Building, Kärntnerstrasse, Vienna
1875-76	Leon Apartment Building, Wipplingerstrasse, Vienna
1875-76	Villa Gerbitz, Grinzing, Vienna†
1875-77	Linder Apartment Building, Vienna
1875-77	Wiener Baugesellschaft Apartment Building, Vienna
1877-78	Benischko Apartment Building, Vienna
1878-79	Presbytery of the Votivkirche, Vienna
1880-81	Hollitzer Apartment Building, Vienna
1880-83	Administration Building of the Austro-Hungarian Lloyd, Trieste, Italy
1880-84	City Hall, Tiflis, Russia (now Georgia)
1880-84	Winter Palace of Archduke Ludwig Viktor, Klessheim, near Salzburg
1882-84	Leon Apartment Building, Ebendorferstrasse, Vienna

Publications

BOOKS BY FERSTEL

Das bürgerliche Wohnhaus und das Wiener Zinshaus. Brochure. With Rudolph Eitelberger. Vienna, 1860.
Denkschrift aus Anlass des Konkurrenzprojektes für das Reichsratsgebäude in Berlin. 1882.
Brief an Theophil Hansen zu dessen 70. Geburtstag. 1883.
Über Styl und Mode. Vienna, 1883.

BOOKS ABOUT FERSTEL

EGGERT, KLAUS: *Die Ringstrasse.* Vienna and Hamburg, 1971.
EITELBERGER, RUDOLPH: *Kunst und Künstler Wiens.* Vienna, 1879.
GURLITT, C.: *Die deutsche Kunst des 19. Jahrhunderts.* Berlin, 1899.
MIGNOT, CLAUDE: *Architektur des 19. Jahrhunderts.* Stuttgart, 1983.
THAUSING, M.: *Die Votivkirche in Wien.* Vienna, 1879.
VON FALKE, J.: *Heinrich Freiherr von Ferstel.* Festschrift. Vienna, 1884.
VON LÜTZOW, C., and TISCHLER, L.: *Wiener Neubauten—Unter Mitwirkung der Architekten Heinrich von Ferstel, etc.* Vienna, 1879.
WAGNER-RIEGER, R.: *Wiens Architektur im 19. Jahrhundert.* Vienna, 1970.
WAGNER-RIEGER, R., and KRAUSE, W. (eds.): *Historismus und Schlossbau.* Munich, 1975.
WANZENBÖCK, H., and SCHIEFER, H.: *Die Ringstrasse: Als Wien zur Weltstadt wurde.* Vienna, 1988.
WIBIRAL, N., and MIKULA, R.: *Heinrich von Ferstel.* Wiesbaden, 1974.

ARTICLES ABOUT FERSTEL

WIBIRAL, NORBERT: ''Heinrich von Ferstel und der Historismus in der Baukunst des 19. Jahrhunderts.'' Ph.D. dissertation, University of Vienna, 1953.

*

Heinrich von Ferstel made a definitive break with the Gothic-Romantic style of his early work only with the palace for the archduke Ludwig Viktor on the Schwarzenbergplatz in Vienna (1864-69). His first independent commission, which marked the beginning of his career in Bohemia, was Schloss Turmitz near Teplitz (1853-55) for Count Nostiz, a building in the Gothic style.

The career of the architect Heinrich von Ferstel is indissolubly bound up with the program for the expansion and beautification of the Vienna city center. He was one of the architects who contributed to the development of the so-called Ringstrasse style, beginning with the Votivkirche, for which he won a competition in 1855. As a consequence of financial difficulties and frequent changes, the church itself took 13 years to complete. It bears a close relationship to French cathedral Gothic, with its two-tower facade, ambulatory and radial chapels, here applied as the ideal forms of timeless validity. The church has a distinctly Viennese local character, however, which is expressed in the harmony and balance of the regularly ordered wealth of forms. Unity is wrought out of diversity, and equilibrium out of contrast. Ferstel transformed the dynamically conceived Gothic elements into a harmonious unity all his own, and thus designed the most important neo-Gothic building in Vienna. The Votivkirche also made Ferstel a favorite with the Viennese public.

The architect already achieved recognition during the construction of the Votivkirche, receiving several honors and a great many commissions. In 1855, for instance, he took first prize in the competition for the National Bank (completed in 1860). Early in the 1860s Ferstel made a trip to Italy, which seems to have prompted the break with the romanticism of his early work. His later work shows the influence of classic forms, particularly as these had been understood in Italian Renaissance architecture. The change was unmistakably apparent for the first time in the palace for Ludwig Viktor on the Schwarzenbergplatz and also in the Wertheim Palace (1864-68) facing it. Both buildings lie at the central intersection of two important urban axes, and are similar in articulation, height and ornamentation.

During the great building era of Vienna's urban expansion, Ferstel received two commissions that were to become the chief works of his oeuvre. The Österreichisches Museum für Kunst und Industrie was constructed between 1868 and 1871. It was built out of brick, in an Italian Renaissance style. In the design, the architect sought to give symbolic expression to the relationship of the arts and crafts to the other arts. The powerful opposition between the dynamic of the center and corners on the one hand and the connecting elements on the other strongly contributes to the monumental plasticity of the building. The museum forms a contrast to the neighboring Kunstgewerbeschule (1874-76), also by Ferstel, with its refined relief effect. In both buildings and also in the Chemical Institute for the University of Vienna (completed in 1871), Ferstel's personal predilections, such as his preference for sgraffito decoration and rich figurative terra-cotta ornamentation, asserted themselves.

Ferstel's second masterpiece is the University of Vienna on the Ringstrasse, begun in 1873 but completed only after the architect's death. In the design of this building, which uses the monumental forms of the Italian High Renaissance, the architect's Italian impressions from his travels of 1870-71 and 1875-76 are unmistakable. The individually conceived wings are ordered around an arcaded *cour d'honneur,* which forms the center of the layout and of the entire complex. The richly articulated facade has a central bay and a projecting loggia. One recognizes the design principle, typical of historicism, of massing toward the center. The emphasis on the upper levels and the discharge of architectural dynamics in a fan shape also contribute to the effect. The public spaces, which display the rich rhythmical divisions of all the building's interiors, are located behind the loggia. The forward wings, which are crowned with domes, define the sides of the building and simultaneously establish a connection with the parts of the building lying further back. By means of these wings, Ferstel gave the design a dramatically heightened organic character. The individual masses seem to shift their weight toward each other, creating a balance between flat surface and plasticity, between horizontals and verticals. The library and the main staircase are further highlights in Ferstel's grand artistic achievement, which has been seen as the beginning of a new era in the history of the University.

In the final years of his career, Ferstel returned to the Italian Gothic, in works such as the Tiflis Town Hall in Georgia (Russia), the office building for the Austrian-Hungarian Lloyd at Trieste, and the high altar for the Viennese Schottenkirche. However, elements from Georgian and Armenian architecture were integrated into the style. To complete the picture of Ferstel's inclusive activity as an architect, his unexecuted competition designs must also be mentioned, such as those for the Academy Building in Budapest (1861), for the Parliament Building in Vienna (1865), for the Hofmuseen (1866), and particularly those for the Berlin Reichstag. Ferstel's numerous memoranda accompanying the construction of his buildings, most of them published in the *Wiener Bauzeitung,* and a brochure of 1860, written with Rudolf von Eitelberger, also had considerable influence in professional circles.

As the most important exponent of the revival of Renaissance architecture, in the style of Donato Bramante in particular, Heinrich von Ferstel belonged to the leading architects of the so-called Vienna style. This form of architecture transcended a mere historicizing eclecticism in the creative re-experience of bygone styles, and placed the personality of the architect in a foreground position.

—CAROLIN BAHR
Translated from the German by Marijke Rijsberman

FEUCHTMAYER, Josef Anton.

German. Born in Linz, Germany, 1696. Died in Mimmenhausen, 2 January 1770. Father was the sculptor Franz Joseph Feuchtmayer. Trained in decoration by his father and the masters Diego Carlone and Paul Egell. Worked chiefly in the Lake Constance (Bodensee) area.

Chronology of Works
All in Germany
* Approximate dates

1720-24*	Choir stalls in church and carvings in summer sacristy, Weingarten
1728-31	Church of St. Peter, Black Forest (main portal and statues for high altar)
1730	Altars, Einsiedeln
1733	Benedictine Abbey, Engelberg (high altar and side altars)
1742-43	Schlosskapelle, Meersburg (decoration and altar)
1747-50	Pilgrimage Church and Cistercian Priory, Neu-Birnau (interiors; with Peter Thumb)
1762-68	Stiftskirche, St. Gallen (decoration of the confessional, and choir stalls and altars)
1763-64	Schloss Zeil, Wurttenberg (high altar)

Joseph Anton Feuchtmayer, a member of a Wessobrunn family, worked as a woodcarver, stuccoer and sculptor in the vicinity of the Bodensee. Feuchtmayer spent part of his youth at Salem, where his father worked on the decorations of the Schloss, and where he himself was to be involved for a number of years. From his father and his masters (Diego Carlone and Paul Egell) he learned the craft, that he perfected to become the quintessential Rococo decorator.

His first masterpieces can be identified as the choir stalls in the church and the carvings in the Summer Sacristy at Weingarten, designed and carved when he was only 24. From 1728 to 1731 he made the statues for the high altar in Peter Thumb's Church of St. Peter in the Black Forest, some 10 miles east of Freiburg, and also provided the other altars in the building. In his faces, especially those representing older personalities, Feuchtmayer created vivid images, not unlike antique theatrical masks, a tendency that first occurred in the series of the Zähringer dukes in St. Peter's Church.

At the Benedictine Abbey of Engelberg (designed by Johannes Rueff) of 1730-37, some 15 miles south of the Lake of Luzern, Feuchtmayer made the high altar and side altars of 1733. Three years earlier he had worked on some of the altars at Einsiedeln, and in those artifacts were hints of what was to come. Feuchtmayer's complete decoration of the Schlosskapelle at Meersburg (1741-1743) demonstrated his mastery of the Rococo style. The stunning stucco crucifix there shows that he was no mere decorator, content with a profusion of frothy scrollwork, but a sculptor of genius, capable of moving the spirit and emotions in very profound ways: there is only a cloth blowing between the shapely legs of the Christ, and the figure itself is almost shakingly beautiful and elegant, while also iconographically unusual in its realistic and almost erotic pose.

Feuchtmayer's most celebrated work is the two-story interior of the pilgrimage church and Cistercian priory of Neu-Birnau on the northern shore of the Bodensee, which he carried out with Peter Thumb from 1747 to 1750. There he showed that he was a stuccoer of great verve and élan, but he was also a designer, a sculptor and a maker of complete altarpieces: the contract documents relating to Neu-Birnau specifically refer to payments made to Feuchtmayer for side altars, stucco capitals, and a design for the high altar. At Neu-Birnau he also provided the confessionals, some of the stations of the cross, pew ends, carved keystones, *stucchi* and gilding for the galleries, and statues.

And it was in his statuary at Neu-Birnau that Feuchtmayer achieved greatness. The figures have a physical presence, a ruggedness, a sense of movement (especially in the way the bodies seem to turn) that raise them high above much of the contemporary sculpture of the Rococo period. The celebrated putto known as the *Honigschlecker* on the St. Bernard altar has enormous charm, and yet demonstrates Feuchtmayer's disconcerting ability to create an almost shocking, intensely moving realism. This realism is also demonstrated in the figures of Joachim, Anne, Elisabeth and Zacharias on the high altar, yet there the realism becomes theatrical, for it is more than real, and, in lesser hands, might verge on caricature.

At Neu-Birnau Feuchtmayer's fully mature, individual and developed style is evident. The friendly, pouting, cheerful putti, first demonstrated earlier at Weingarten, are present, but at Neu-Birnau their dimpled figures have an exotic quality that cannot fail to delight. Feuchtmayer is revealed in this great church as the most Rococo of all sculptors, with a strong tendency toward the grotesque and unusual. Often his work verges on the erotic: just as the undraped right flank of that extraordinary crucifix at Meersburg exploits the elegance of a well-turned thigh, so are the right thighs of figures in the Augustinermuseum in Freiburg and the small figure at Neu-Birnau exposed, with only a cord laid over them.

The stations of the cross at Neu-Birnau have unrestrained, jubilant Rococo scrolls and froths, which Feuchtmayer also exploited in the scenes for the life of Christ on the confessionals in Stiftskirche St Gallen, where he also carried out the choir stalls and altars from 1760 to 1770. Ecstatic hovering putti are found in the Martinskapelle in Nenzingen, and Feuchtmayer's devotional figures in the Pfarrkirche at Mimmenhausen cannot fail to involve the heart and mind. It was at Mimmenhausen that Feuchtmayer died, and there he was commemorated by a monument designed and made by his talented pupil, Johann Georg Dirr.

—JAMES STEVENS CURL

FILARETE, Il.

Italian. Born Antonio di Pietro Averlino, in Florence, Italy, ca. 1400. Died in Rome, ca. 1469. Named Il Filarete (a lover of virtue) by Italian painter, architect, and biographer Giorgio Vasari (1511-74). Worked as a sculptor until ca. 1450; probably trained as a bronze worker. Expelled from Rome, 1448; moved to Venice, then to Milan, ca. 1450; became the ducal engineer in Milan.

Chronology of Works
All in Italy
† *Work no longer exists*

1433-55	Old Saint Peter's, Rome (central doors)
1447-48	Tomb of Cardinal Chaves, San Giovanni in Laterno, Rome†
1451-57	Castello Sforzesco di Porta Giovia, Milan (gate tower)†
1457	Cathedral, Bergamo (since altered)
1460-65	Ospedale Maggiore, Milan

Publications

BOOKS BY FILARETE

FILARETE (ANTONIO AVERLINO): *Treatise on Architecture.* Translated by John R. Spencer. 2 vols. New Haven, Connecticut, 1965.

Il Filarete: Ospedale Maggiore, Milan, Italy, 1460-65

BOOKS ABOUT FILARETE

BELTRAMI, LUCA: *Il Castello di Milano.* Milan, 1894.
BELTRAMI, LUCA: *La "Cà del Duca" sul Canal grand.* Milan, 1900.
BIAGETTI, VINCENZINA: *L'Ospedale Maggiore di Milano.* Milan, 1937.
CAIMI, GAETANO: *Notizie storiche del Grand 'ospitale di Milano.* Milan, 1857.
HEYDENREICH, LUDWIG H., and LOTZ, WOLFGANG: *Architecture in Italy 1600-1750.* New York, 1974.
LAZZARONI, MICHELE, and MUÑOZ, ANTONIO: *Filarete, scultore e architetto del secolo XV.* Rome, 1908.
OETTINGEN, W. VON: *A. Averlino Filarete's Traktat über die Baukunst.* Vienna, 1890.
TIGLER, PETER: *Die Architekturtheorie des Filarete.* Berlin, 1963.
VON MOOS, STANISLAUS: *Kastell, Palast, Villa: Studien zur italienischen Architektur des 15 und 16. Jh.* Zurich, 1970.

ARTICLES ABOUT FILARETE

Arte Lombarda. New Series 38-39, entire issue.
BASCAPÉ, GIACOMO C.: "Il progresso dell'assistenza ospedaliera nel sec. XV e gli ospedali 'a crociera." *Tecnica ospedaliera* 1 (1936): 9-21.
CRIPPA, G.: "Inediti sul Duomo di Bergamo dal Filarete al Fontana." *Bergamo arte* 2 (1971): 21-30.
DAL CANTON, GIUSEPPINA: "Architettura del Filarete ed architettura veneziana: campione di un palazzo del 'trattato' filaretiano." *Arte Lombarda* 18 (1973): 103-115.

DOHME, R.: ''Filarete's Traktat von der Architektur.'' *Jahrbuch der königlich-Preussischen Kunstsammlungen* 1 (1880): 225-241.

FABRICZY, CORNELIUS VON: ''Ein Brief Antonio Averulinos, gennant Filarete.'' *Repertorium für Kunstwissenschaft* 27 (1904): 188-189.

FRANCO, FAUSTO: ''L'interpolazione del Filarete trattista fra gli artefici del Rinascimento architettonici a Venezia.'' Pp. 267-280 in *Atti del IV Convegno nazionale di storia dell'architettura*. Milan, 1939.

GRASSI, LILIANA: ''Aspetti nuovi dell'antico Ospedale Maggiore sistemato ad uso dell'Università di Milano.'' *Arte Lombarda* New Series 1 (1955): 136-145.

LANG, S.: ''Sforzinda, Filarete and Filelfo.'' *Journal of the Warburg and Courtauld Institutes* 35 (1972): 391-397.

ONIANS, JOHN: ''Alberti and Filarete. A Study in their Sources.'' *Journal of the Warburg and Courtauld Institutes* 34 (1971): 96-114.

SAALMAN, HOWARD: ''Early Renaissance Architectural Theory and Practice in Antonio Filarete's *Trattato di Architettura*.'' *Art Bulletin* 41 (1959): 80-109.

SALMI, MARIO: ''Antonio Averlino detto il Filarete e l'architettura lombarda del primo Rinascimento.'' In *Atti del Primo Congresso nazionale di storia dell'architettura*, 1936.

SCURATI-MANZONI, PIETRO: ''Lo svillupo degli edifici rinascimentale a pianta centrale in Lombardia.'' *Archivo storico Lombardo* 7 (1969):193-209.

SINUSI, S.: ''Razionalità e immaginazione in Filarete.'' *Reviste studi salernitani* 7 (1971): 281-296.

SPENCER, JOHN R.: ''Filarete and Central-plan Architecture.'' *Journal of the Society of Architectural Historians* 17 (1958): 10-18.

SPENCER, JOHN R.: ''Filarete and the Cà del duca.'' *Journal of the Society of Architectural Historians* 35 (1976): 219-222.

SPENCER, JOHN R.: ''The Cà del Duca in Venice and Benedetto Ferrini.'' *Journal of the Society of Architectural Historians* 29 (1970): 3-8.

THOENES, C.: ''Sostegno e adornamento. Zur sozialen Symbolik der Säulenordnung.'' *Kunstchronik* (1972): 343-344.

ZAREBSKA, TERESA: ''L'abitazione colletiva nella teoria urbanistica italiana del XV e XVI secolo.'' *Urbanistica* 31-35 (1965).

*

Il Filarete (a lover of virtue or *virtù*), an architect and writer on architecture, was probably trained as a bronze worker; his career began with a commission to produce a pair of bronze doors for the central portals of Old St. Peter's in Rome. The work began in 1433; by 1455 the doors were ready and set in place; later they were taken down when the fabric of the old church was demolished, enlarged and then set in place in 1620 as the doors for the new basilica.

In 1447 Filarete received the commission to build the tomb of Cardinal Chaves of Portugal in San Giovanni in Laterano in Rome, the freestanding design of which was based on the Arch of Janus near San Giorgio in Velabro. But problems erupted. In 1448 Filarete was accused of attempting to steal the head of John the Baptist, arrested, tortured and expelled from Rome, leaving the sculptural decoration of the tomb unfinished. He moved then to Venice, but when hostilities broke out between that city and Florence he was expelled and went to Milan, arriving perhaps in early 1450.

There he became the ducal engineer, and for the next 15 years he worked on a range of architectural projects in both Milan and Lombardy. In 1451 he was at work on the gate tower at what is now the Castello Sforzesco (later destroyed but reconstructed by Luca Beltrami between 1893 and 1904). In 1457 he was given leave to build a new cathedral for Bergamo, and though he was soon back in Milan, his designs were followed faithfully; however, the building was modified by Carlo Fontana in 1620 and completely redone in 1853. In 1460 Filarete began his major work in the city, the Ospedale Maggiore (Great Hospital); five years later one part of the plan was completed, but although work continued until about 1500 under the direction of Giuniforte Solari, only one of the two crosses of Filarete's original plan was built.

The design, which was included in 1521 by Cesare Cesariano in his edition of Vitruvius, had a long-lasting influence on hospital design in Europe, especially in France. The plan was essentially that of a rectangle of the proportions 5:2, into which at both ends a cross of equal arms was set with squares, on one side the wards being for men, the other for women, the hospital church and its forecourt being in a rectangle of the proportions 1:2. The whole building was carried out with classical details that would not have been out of place in Florence, yet also featured the more varied and exuberant coloring of the local Milanese tradition; if, in its plan, the Ospedale Maggiore embodied something of the regularity of Florentine architecture, this was used for hygiene: each arm of the cross was a long ward, and isolation areas were set aside, with air and light coming into all parts of the design.

Yet Filarete is perhaps best known now not for these buildings but for the treatise he composed on architecture, written purportedly to instruct Francesco Sforza and his heir, Galeazzo Maria, in the ways of Florentine architecture. In it, an ideal city, Sforzinda, was planned in the shape of an eight-pointed star; major streets led to the center, where the main public buildings were located; on the periphery were minor squares, each with its parish church; there was a port, Plusiapolis; housing was designed for the various classes; and the trades were located in specially restricted areas, the most noisome at the furthest points from the center. The text Filarete wrote is often awkward and uncertain—one scholar spoke of the stylistic helplessness of the *autore illiterato;* there are digressions of various kinds; the subject is not presented in the most logical way; and Sforzinda itself, as its very name implied, was the expression of an autocratic, despotic regime. But this ideal city was conceived and executed as a whole, functionally and aesthetically, every building being related to every other building, and what this embodied was a stage of planning beyond that of Leon Battista Alberti, a stage of particular historical significance. The treatise roused the interest of several important rulers; Giangaleazzo Sforza and Piero de' Medici received dedicated copies, and both Matthias Corvinus and the king of Naples had copies or translations made for them. And when, a little later, Francesco di Giorgio (1439-1501/02) and Leonardo da Vinci (1452-1519) turned their attention to the same problems, they both borrowed from these ideas of Filarete's, in the plans they envisaged for their perfect cities.

—DAVID CAST

FISCHER, Johann Michael.

German. Born in Burglengenfeld, Oberpfalz, Germany, 1691/92. Died in Munich, 6 May 1766. Father was Johann Michael Fischer, a stonemason. Married in 1725. Worked in Bohemia; clerk of the works in Brno and elsewhere in Moravia (now Czechoslovakia), 1715-16; moved to Munich, where he worked as foreman for the city mason Johann Mayr (1677-1731), 1718-19; became master mason of Munich, 1723.

Johann Michael Fischer: Benedictine Abbey Church, Zwiefalten, Germany, 1740-65

Chronology of Works

All in Germany
* Approximate dates
† Work no longer exists

1721	Stables, Schloss Lichtenberg, near Landsberg-am-Lech
1723	Monastery, Altomünster, near Augsburg
1724	Church, Kircham
1724-26	Benedictine Abbey Church, Niederaltaich (choir and sacristy)
1726*	Parish Church, Schärding
1726-40	Premonstratensian Convent Church, Osterhofen
1727-29	Church, Rinchnach
1727-37	St. Anna am Lehel, Munich (rebuilt in the 1950s)†
1730	Church, Bergkirchen
1731	Church, Unering
1732-39	Augustinian Priory Church, Diessen (redesign)
1736-51	Parish Church, Aufhausen
1735-40	Augustinian Church, Ingolstadt†
1738-51	St. Michael's Church, Berg-am-Laim
1739-48	Cistercian Abbey Church, Fürstenzell
1740-65	Benedictine Abbey Church, Zwiefalten
1748-67	Benedictine Abbey Church, Ottobeuren
1750-58	Chapel of St. Anastasia, Benediktbeuren
1751-53	Church, Bichl
1751-53	Premonstratensian Abbey Church, Schäftlarn
1755	Church, Sigmershausen
1759-63	Benedictine Abbey Church, Rott-am-Inn
1763-66	Brigittine Church, Altomünster

Publications

BOOKS ABOUT FISCHER

FEULNER, AD.: *Johann Michael Fischer.* 1922.

FEULNER, ADOLF: *Bayerisches Rokoko.* Munich, 1923.

HAGEN-DEMPF, FELICITAS: *Der Zentralbaugedanke bei Johann Michael Fischer.* Munich, 1954.

HAUTTMANN, MAX: *Geschichte der kirchlichen Baukunst in Bayern/Schwaben, und Franken/1550-1780.* Munich, Berlin, and Leipzig, 1921.

HITCHCOCK, HENRY-RUSSELL: *Rococo Architecture in Southern Germany.* London, 1968.

LIEB, NORBERT: *Johann Michael Fischer: Baumeister und Raumschöpfer im späten Barock Süddeutschlands.* Regensburg, 1982.

LIEB, NORBERT: *Barockkirchen zwischen Donau und Alpen.* 2nd ed. Munich, 1958.

LIEB, NORBERT: *Münchener Barockbaumeister.* Munich, 1941.

SCHELL, HUGO: *Gesamtverzeichnis des deutschsprachigen Schrifttums.* Munich, n.d.

SCHELL, HUGO: *Ottobeuren: Kloster und Kirche.* Munich, 1979.

ARTICLES ABOUT FISCHER

FRANZ, HEINRICH GERHARD: "Johann Michael Fischer und die Baukunst des Barock in Böhmen." *Zeitschrift für Ostforschung* (1955).

LAING, ALASTAIR and BLUNT, ANTHONY: "Central and Eastern Europe." In *Baroque and Rococo: Architecture & Decoration.* New York, 1978.

Johann Michael Fischer probably received his earliest instruction from his father, a master mason of the same name. In his twenties he worked in Bohemia and Moravia, including a time as clerk of the works in Brno. In 1718 he moved to Munich, and worked as an associate of the city master mason, Johann Mayr (1677-1731), during which time he appears to have ingratiated himself with the nobility and with society as a whole. In 1723 Fischer became a citizen of Munich and a master mason in his own right, and in 1725 he married into the Munich building trade by taking Mayr's daughter to wife. It was quite clear he had arrived, for he became a close associate of Johann Baptist Gunetzrhainer (1692-1763), once *Ingenieur* in the Electoral Office of Works, and *Hofunterbaumeister* from 1721, who also happened to be Mayr's stepson. Fischer's connections must have been impeccable, for his future clients were to include the Wittelsbach princes Clemens August, archbishop of Cologne, the prince-bishop of Regensburg, and Duke Clemens Franz in Munich.

Fischer's earliest works under Mayr seem to have been the monastic buildings of the Priory of Schlehdorf near Murnau, where the parish church, with its large centrally planned octagonal nave, may be by Mayr. By 1721, however, Fischer was designing and building the stable block of the Electoral Schloss Lichtenberg near Landsberg-am-Lech, and in 1723 he was overseeing the construction of the monastic buildings at Altomünster near Augsburg. His first independent work on a major ecclesiastical building was at the Benedictine Abbey of Niederaltaich, where he reconstructed the church, followed by two church commissions at Kirchham and Rinchnach. Then came a whole series of major buildings, starting with the Premonstratensian Convent Church at Osterhofen (1726) to the south of the Danube between Deggendorf and Vilgertshofen not far to the northwest of Passau. It is a church of great size and richness, and, like many of Fischer's works, is a "wall-pier" church (*Wandpfeilerkirche*) consisting of a five-bay rectangular nave with elliptical spaces on each side, and an apsidal chancel. There are galleries over the side chapels, but the sides of the nave space are not straight, and in fact they undulate: the faces of the piers themselves, with their Rococo capitals, are concave, while the galleries bow outward in convex curves. This in-out wavy effect has its origins in Bohemia, but the most obvious source for Fischer's wave-like rhythms is Banz, consecrated in 1719 and designed by Johann Dientzenhofer (1663-1726). Fischer was not responsible for the decorations at Osterhofen, however: the scheme was by the Asams, who provided a sumptuous high altar with four Solomonic columns, clearly derived from Giovanni Lorenzo Bernini's *baldachino* in St. Peter's in Rome, and two enormous crowned altarpieces at the eastern quadrants of the nave.

Fischer's next important commission, and one that has rightly been acclaimed as a masterpiece, was for the Augustinian Priory Church at Diessen, beside the Ammersee southwest of Munich. Fischer took over the building of the church, which had already been started by Magnus Feichtamayr, and virtually redesigned the structure from 1732. Diessen, consecrated in 1739, is of the Vorarlberg type, consisting of a four-bay rectangular nave with wall piers creating chapels on either side, a western vestibule under the organ loft, a crossing with transeptal arms that do not project beyond the walls of the aisles and which contain galleries, and an apsidal chancel. Against the east faces of the characteristic wall piers are elaborate Baroque altars with aedicules framing pictures, but throughout the church above the level of the pier capitals the spirit is entirely Rococo, and this is very much a characteristic of Fischer's work. The powerful and architectonic flavor of the building is robustly and clearly expressed up to the level of the pier capitals, and above that tidemark the Rococo stucco and delicate treatment of sculpture and fresco take over. The iron gates at the west end are exquisite too. The west front of the church is very curious, having a central giant aedicule, convex on plan, flanked by narrow concave bays and wider convex bays terminating rather weakly in single pilasters. Above the undulating entablature is an attic story with a central niche under a segmental arch, flanked by two curving sweeps terminating in urns. The *Rundogenstil* tower, set back behind the monastic buildings, is a 19th-century replacement of an earlier structure that was destroyed by lightning.

By the time Diessen was being roofed in, Fischer was involved in other commissions, notably the Church of St. Michael at Berg-am-Laim, which demonstrated his interest in the organization of interior volumes. Berg-am-Laim has a large domed central space with domed choir and short chancel, the whole with highly architectonic systems of axes, niches and entries at 45 degrees to the main axes of the central space. Similar but even more elaborate variations on this theme can be found in the ingenious designs for the Franciscan Church at Ingolstadt and in the Pilgrimage Church at Aufhausen.

Then came Fürstenzell (1739-48) and Zwiefalten (1740-65), two major commissions for abbey churches, to which occasions Fischer rose with style. Fürstenzell has a twin-towered facade with a convex front, and an attic story not unlike that of Diessen. It is a four-bay wall-pier church without a crossing and with a square-ended, two-bay choir. The corners of the nave are treated as quadrants, and the barrel vault of the nave curves down into those quadrants. Over the shallow side chapels (the altars are placed this time against the outside walls) are convex galleries over depressed vaults between the piers; these galleries are fronted with delicate Rococo grillwork of a porcelain delicacy. Piers are faced with twinned fluted pilasters: there, as in Diessen, the Rococo elements occur mainly above the line of the nave capitals, although the convex fronts of the Fürstenzell galleries have vigorous Rococo stucco moldings.

Zwiefalten is very much more articulated, starting with the west front, which again is convex with concave elements on either side, but the central section is a huge aedicule with four detached columns flanked by single pilasters, the columnar system carrying a broken pediment, over which is an elaborate gabled attic with a central niche. Inside, the nave is of four bays with wall piers defining the side chapels, and there is a vestibule under the organ loft. The transepts flank a dome over the crossing, and there are twin towers attached not to the west front but to the east ends of the transepts, so they stand sentinel on either side of the body of the church. Choir and sanctuary are set in an elongated space beyond the crossing, so the effect is one of very great length, accentuated by the proportions of the interior, with its considerable width and comparatively low ceiling. The treatment of the wall piers is stunningly architectonic, with pairs of engaged scagliola columns set against the pure white ground of the piers behind. Between the piers, with their delicious Rococo capitals, are galleries that sway out into the nave and are carried on the lightest of arches that themselves are distorted. Virtually the whole decorative scheme is Rococo. In fact, Zwiefalten is one of the finest of Fischer's many achievements, and ranks among the most beautiful of his churches.

Three more of his churches demonstrate Fischer's concerns with centralized plans. The beautiful Abbey Church at Rott-am-Inn in Bavaria, begun in 1759, has a central octagon with a dome over it, with volumes on square plans to the east and west of it, while other minor spaces are set at 45-degree angles off the main central space. The huge Benedictine Abbey Church of Ottobeuren, partly begun before Fischer was called in in 1748, has a wide apsidal crossing in the center, and the west front bows fully out like an apse between the twin towers. But Fischer was not primarily responsible for Ottobeuren: by 1755

when the dome over the crossing was complete, his contribution was that crossing and the three-quarters-engaged scagliola columns there and in the apses. At Ottobeuren the Rococo flavor is fully developed, and there is no doubt of the quality of this great building in architectural terms. In none of Fischer's churches apart from Ottobeuren is there as much Rococo decoration below the main entablature, although Zwiefalten has a fair amount, and runs Ottobeuren a close second. At Schäftlarn Abbey Church, however, charmingly decorated by J. B. Zimmermann, there is some restrained Rococo decoration, and a very homogeneous scheme in total, combined with the large centralized space. Schäftlarn's plan is curious, for its main element is a rectangular volume with a dome on top, with two narrower rectangular volumes to the east and west of the central space. The nave therefore consists of a narrow bay, a wide bay and another narrow bay, and the bays are marked by wall piers. The larger space has a transeptal arrangement containing altars on each side. Then the choir is narrower than the nave, and it too has spaces on either side between wall piers, while the chancel is a horseshoe shape. At the west end, in the center, is a single tower. It is a charming and subtle church with very interesting rhythms in its bay arrangements.

One of Fischer's last works, the Church of the Brigittines at Altomünster, is a very long building, and takes the Schäftlarn arrangement a stage further: it is divided into a large octagonal centralized nave, a smaller domed space to the east, then a long chancel and sanctuary, so there are pronounced compartments along the length of the church.

Fischer was buried in the Frauenkirche in Munich: his tombstone claimed that he had designed 32 churches, 23 monasteries and many secular works. His architecture spans the Baroque-Rococo era, and his architectonic domes, emphasizing centralized octagonal elements, which are then coupled to long, compartmentalized axial plans, are of great interest. With J. B. Neumann, Fischer was a giant among south German Baroque architects working in the first part of the 18th century, and he was extremely prolific. Most writers on 18th-century German architecture have given Fischer due credit as an architect of the greatest importance, and he is generally reckoned to be of the first rank.

—JAMES STEVENS CURL

FISCHER VON ERLACH, Johann Bernhard.

Austrian. Born in Graz, Austria, 20 July 1656. Died in Vienna, 5 April 1723. Father was the sculptor Johann Baptist Fischer. Married Sophia Konstantin Morgner, 1690; five children, including the architect Joseph Emanuel Fischer von Erlach. Went to Rome, 1671, where he studied and worked under Phillipp Schor. Returned to Vienna, 1678; chief inperial inspector of the royal buildings, from 1705.

Chronology of Works
All in Austria unless noted
* Approximate dates
† Work no longer exists

1687-89	Holy Trinity Plague column, Vienna (with others)
1687-90	Liechtenstein Palace (garden belvedere), Rossau, Vienna†
1688	Schloss Eisgrub Stables, Moravia, Czechoslovakia
1688-95	Schloss Frain (Ancestral Hall), Moravia, Czechoslovakia

1689-90	Schloss Mirabell, Salzburg (garden, vases, sculpture; attributed)
1690	Two Triumphal Arches for Joseph I, Vienna
1690-93	Althan Garden Palace, Rossau, Vienna†
1690-93	Summer Riding School; Archibishop's Stables, Salzburg
1690-96	Fountain, Krautmarkt, Brno, Czechoslovakia
1692-93	Strattmann Palace, Salzburg [attributed]
1692-97	Neuwaldegg Hunting Lodge, Salzburg
1692-1704	Church of Mariazell, Salzburg (high altar; executed by E. C. Engelbrecht and J. A. Pfeffel to Fischer von Erlach's design)
1693*	Hunting Lodge, Engelhartstetten
1693-94	Archbishop's Stables and Horse Bath, Salzburg
1694-97	Cathedral, Salzburg (spiral staircase in north tower)
1694-1702	Dreifaltigkeitskirche, Salzburg (priest's house and college)
1694-1707	Kollegienkirche, Salzburg
1694*-1709	Hospital and Church of St. John (Johannes-Spiral), Mülleck
1696-1700	City Palace of Prince Eugene of Savoy, Vienna
1696-1701	Pilgrimage Church of Maria Kirchenthal, Lofer, Salzburg
1696-1711	Schönbrunn Palace, Vienna†
1698-1700	Schloss Frain, Moravia, Czechoslovakia (chapel; attributed)
1698-1705	Batthyány Palace, Vienna
1700-1709	Kleswheim Palace, Salzburg (including garden house)
1702-06	St. Joseph's Hoher Markt, Vienna†
after 1708-14	Bohemian Chancellery, Vienna
1709-11	Dietrichstein Palace, Vienna (remodeling of facade)
1710*-15	Villa Huldenberg, Weidlingau, near Vienna†
1710-16	Trautson Garden Palace, Vienna
1712*	Schwarzenberg City Palace, Vienna†
1713-19	Gallas Palace, Prague, Czechoslovakia
1714-16	St. James Church, Prague, Czechoslovakia (sepulchral monument for Johann Wenzel Count Wratislaw von Mitrowitz)
1715-38	Karlskirche, Vienna
1716-18	Herzogenburg Convent, Lower Austria (central part of east wing, great hall and staircase)
1716*-19	Hofburg Palace, Vienna (project for revisions)†
1716-24	Elector's Chapel, Breslau Cathedral (now Wroclaw), Poland
1718-21	Herzogen Convent Church, Lower Austria (tower)
1719-23	Imperial Stables (partially executed), Vienna
1720*	Schwarzenberg Garden Palace, Vienna (alteration and interior decorations)
1722-30	Imperial Library, Hofburg Palace, Vienna

Publications

BOOKS BY FISCHER VON ERLACH

Entwurff einer historischen Architektur. Vienna, 1721. 2nd ed.: 1725. Reprint of 2nd ed., with English translation: Farnsborough, England, 1964.

BOOKS ABOUT FISCHER VON ERLACH

AURENHAMMER, HANS: *Johann Bernhard Fischer von Erlach*. Exhibition catalog. Graz, Vienna and Salzburg, 1956-57.

AURENHAMMER, HANS: *J. B. Fischer von Erlach*. London, 1973.
BUCHOWIECKI, WALTER: *Der Barockbau der ehemaligen Hofbibliothek in Wien, ein Werk J. B. Fischer von Erlach*. Vienna, 1957.
FRANZ, H. G.: *Die deutsche Barockbaukunst Mährens*. Munich, 1943.
FREY, DAGOBERT: *Fischer von Erlach*. Vienna, 1923.
GRIMSCHITZ, BRUNO: *Wiener Barockpaläste*. Vienna, 1944.
HAGEN-DEMPF, FELICITAS: *Die Kollegienkirche in Salzburg*. Vienna, 1949.
HEMPEL, EBERHARD: *Baroque Art and Architecture in Central Europe*. Harmondsworth, England, 1965.
ILG, ALBERT: *Die Fischer von Erlach*. Vienna, 1895.
KUNOTH, GEORG: *Die historische Architektur Fischers von Erlach*. Dusseldorf, 1956.
LANCHESTER, H. V.: *Fischer von Erlach*. London, 1924.
SEDLMAYR, HANS: *Österreichische Barockarchitektur, 1690-1740*. Vienna, 1930.
SEDLMAYR, HANS: *Johann Bernhard Fischer von Erlach*. Vienna and Munich, 1956.

ARTICLES ABOUT FISCHER VON ERLACH

HAGER, WERNER: "Zum Verhaltnis Fischer-Guarini." *Kunstchronik* 10 (1957): 206-208.
HASELBERGER-BLAHA, HERTA: "Die Triumphtore Bernhard Fischers von Erlachs." *Wiener Jahrbuch für Kunstgeschichte* 17 (1955): 63-85.
HEMPEL, EBERHARD: "Jugendwerke Fischers von Erlach." *Kunstchronik* 10 (1957): 338ff.
LORENZ, HELLMUT: "Das 'Lustgartengebäude' Fischers von Erlach—Variationen eines architektonischen Themas." *Wiener Jahrbuch für Kunstgeschichte* 32 (1979): 59-88.
MOISY, P.: "Fischer von Erlach et les architectes français." *Art de France* 3 (1963): 154ff.
MORPER, JOHANN JOSEPH: "Schriftum zum Fischer von Erlach." *Das Münster* 10, Nos. 1-2 (1957): 49-51.
PASSMORE, EDWARD: "Fischer von Erlach, Architect to a Monarchy." *Journal of the Royal Institute of British Architects* 58 (1951): 452-475.
SCHMIDT, J.: "Die Architekturbücher der Fischer von Erlach." *Wiener Jahrbuch für Kunstgeschichte* (1934): 152ff.
SEDLMAYR, HANS: "Die europäische Bedeutung Johann Bernhard Fischers von Erlach." *Kunstchronik* 10 (1957): 334ff.
WAGNER-RIEGER, R.: "Das Verhältnis J. B. Fischers von Erlach zur österreichischen Architektur." *Alte und moderne Kunst* 3, No. 4 (1958): 12ff.
ZACHARIAS, T.: *Joseph Emanuel Fischer von Erlach*. Vienna and Munich, 1960.

*

Johann Bernhard Fischer von Erlach was born in Graz in 1656, where his family enjoyed the patronage of the princes of Eggenberg. His father was a turner and sculptor, and had carried out works for his patrons. It was very likely under the aegis of the Eggenbergs that the young J. B. Fischer was sent to Italy, and he arrived in Rome in 1671. At first he found things difficult, but he was taken under the wing of Phillipp Schor, architect and painter at the papal court, who employed the young man as a sculptor and wax-worker to make models to Schor's designs. Fischer also studied architectural theory, and obtained a thorough grounding in the works of Vitruvius, Leon Battista Alberti, Giacomo Barozzi da Vignola, Andrea Palladio, Sebastiano Serlio and Vincenzo Scamozzi, also imbibing the essence of Roman

Johann Bernhard Fischer von Erlach: Karlskirche, Vienna, Austria, 1715-38

architecture, new and antique. Through Schor, Fischer was introduced to the papal court, to the studio of Giovanni Lorenzo Bernini, and to the artistic and intellectual circle of Queen Christina of Sweden (1626-89). However, Fischer's knowledge of Bernini's studio dates from the time it was run by Carlo Fontana, whose interest in synthesis may have prompted Fischer's own concerns in that area.

Fischer obtained first-class instruction in the design and manufacture of medals at the hands of G. F. Travani, who had been a pupil of Bernini. Fischer was also given access to the antiquities and *objets d'art* belonging to Queen Christina, and made himself familiar not only with these, but with the other great collections in Rome. Significantly, he met the Jesuit Athanasius Kircher (1602-80), the papal librarian, who had amassed a huge collection of Egyptian and Egyptianizing objects, and who clearly sparked Fischer's interest in antiquities. Other important influences were ideas emanating from France which were disseminated in the Academy in Rome, the works of Guarino Guarini, and the art theorist Pietro Bellori (ca. 1615-96), whose work on Roman triumphal arches made a deep impression on the young Austrian.

When in Rome, Fischer was introduced to *Scheinarchitektur*, or temporary buildings for festive occasions, and in 1679 and 1689 he made bronze medals for the king of Spain. Through

Johann Bernhard Fischer von Erlach: Kollegienkirche, Salzburg, Austria, 1694-1707

his Spanish connections, Schor was appointed court architect in Naples in 1683, and Fischer also moved there as Schor's assistant. That period enabled the Austrian to amass a fortune, and the thoroughly proficient architect, sculptor, medalist, archaeologist and theorist decided to return to his homeland. There is no doubt that Fischer saw his main chance, for during his stay in Italy, Austria had become a world power. Not only had the Turks been defeated in 1683, but the Holy Roman Empire was to become one of the main forces in the alliance to contain the ambitions of France.

The removal of the Turkish threat heralded a period of building. At the age of 31, a well-connected architect arrived home: he was acquainted with later Roman Baroque, and was thoroughly up-to-date in architectural theory. Very soon the imperial court recognized Fischer's qualities, and from 1687 he was employed as an architect in Vienna and Graz, where his Eggenberg connections doubtless stood him in good stead. Votive columns, reliefs, medals, carvings, snuffboxes, stucco decorations, vases, ornamental gates, belvederes and gardens originated on his drawing board, and it was not long before he was commissioned by some of the noblest families to design buildings for them.

One of his first important monuments was the Pestsäule in the Graben in Vienna, erected by the emperor in thanksgiving for deliverance from the Plague, and Fischer also designed the stucco decorations for the Hapsburg mausoleum in Graz. In 1689 Fischer was appointed as teacher of architecture and perspective to the emperor's son and heir, Joseph, who was later to become Fischer's royal and imperial patron.

For Prince Johann Adam Andreas von Liechtenstein, Fischer designed park gates and a belvedere to be erected at the palace of Rossau and at the prince's country seat of Schloss Eisgrub

in Moravia. He also designed palatial stables where his knowledge of modern French architecture was dazzlingly displayed. After his success in designing some festive triumphal arches to celebrate the entry into Vienna of young Joseph, Fischer became a member of Joseph's court in the capital in 1694. That position ensured commissions from the Austrian nobility, and from that period dates the fine Town Palace of Prince Eugen of Savoy in Vienna, in which the architect combined elements from a Roman High Baroque palazzo with aspects of French architecture. The building is exuberantly decorated with lively sculpture, and the model was clearly Bernini's Palazzo Chigi in Rome, although there are Palladian elements in the entrance hall, while the portal with balcony above derives from the *cour d'honneur* of the Château de Lignières by Louis Le Vau (1656). For Ernst Rüdiger Graf Stahremberg, Fischer designed a hunting lodge at Engelhartsstetten in 1693 which was basically a Palladian-French composition, but with an elliptical centerpiece, possibly influenced by Le Vau's Château Le Raincy.

However, while these commissions were important, the most significant early works were in Salzburg, where the prince-archbishop, Johann Ernst Graf Thun (1687-1709), called in Fischer as his architectural adviser and inspector of buildings. Under the aegis of the worthy prelate, Fischer von Erlach (he was ennobled in 1696) designed the Dreifaltigkeitskirche, Kollegienkirche, Ursulinenkirche and much else. At the Dreifaltigkeitskirche the main element is an ellipse, with its long axis that of the entrance-high altar, but the front is concave, flanked by two towers. Here Fischer von Erlach combined elements from Francesco Borromini's Sant'Agnese in Agone in the Piazza Navona in Rome, towers derived from the work of Guarino Guarini, a centerpiece taken from the work of Jules Hardouin Mansart, and the elliptical arrangement of Vignola's Santa Anna dei Palafrenieri in Rome. Here his syncretic interests are fully demonstrated. This church was completed in 1702, and heralds a full flowering of Austrian Baroque architecture. Unhappily, the towers were drastically altered, not improved, much later.

Then came the great masterpiece of the Kollegienkirche, the large church of the Benedictine University of Salzburg, designed in 1694. The plan is basically a mixture of the longitudinal and centrally planned types of church, with a cupola over the central space. The long building was emphasized by the four elliptical chapels arranged in a way that suggests Fischer von Erlach knew Rosato Rosati's Church of San Carlo ai Catinari in Rome (1611), but the Rosato plan was mixed with Jacques Lemercier's design for the Church of the Sorbonne in Paris, begun in 1635 (the Benedictine University of Salzburg had close links with the University of Paris). At the Kollegienkirche the entrance front has a convex facade set between two elegantly inventive towers with their crowning elements reminiscent of the work of Guarini and Borromini. The very grand and noble interior has, above the high altar, an extraordinary composition of clouds rising up to heaven, as the Immacolata floats upward in glory. We view this stunning vision through two great columns set on either side of the apse: the columns suggest Jachin and Boaz of Solomon's Temple, the Gates of Paradise, and the Divine Wisdom of the Church. Here a Palladian note is also struck, reminding us of the columns at the altar ends of Venetian churches. Here Fischer's concerns with syncretism come to the fore, and his mastery of sculpture (he designed all the stucco decorations) is amply demonstrated.

The same architect designed the Hospital of St. John in Salzburg, the church of which is basically a central space, all light and white, with fine decorations in the manner of Borromini—indeed the convex elements swaying into the sanctuary are reminiscent of the latter's San Carlo alle Quattro Fontane in

Rome. There are also quotations from Fontana's Lateran. Mention should also be made of the exquisite high altar Fischer von Erlach designed (erected in 1709) for the Franciscan Church in Salzburg, with its lovely Madonna by Michael Pacher and elegant superstructure with sunbursts, angels and swaying entablatures.

At the height of his career and powers at the turn of the century Johann Bernhard Fischer von Erlach was building Schloss Schönbrunn, but the War of the Spanish Succession of 1701-14 intervened, and in 1704 he began to study the architecture of the Protestant north, including Prussia, the Netherlands and England. It is likely that he met Christopher Wren, who was proposing to write a historical treatise about architecture and how it had originated in the Temple of Solomon, an idea which was close to the Austrian's heart. In 1707 Fischer von Erlach went to Venice to study Palladio, and on the accession of Joseph I as emperor he was appointed chief inspector of court buildings, in which post his work on his great *Entwurff* and his administrative duties precluded much building. Nevertheless, Fischer von Erlach was responsible for the decorations for the coronation, the emperor's marriage ceremonies, and his funeral in 1711.

On the accession of Charles VI, Fischer von Erlach gained favor with his designs for the Karlskirche, a conception that demonstrated the architect's mastery of syncretism: here biblical, imperial, antique, Solomonic, Roman Baroque and many influences coalesce. In his last years Fischer von Erlach also carried out major works for the Hofburg, including the mighty Hofbibliothek, and by the 1720s his son, Joseph Emanuel, was collaborating with him. Joseph Emanuel supervised the building of the Karlskirche, the Hofburg buildings and the imperial stables.

Johann Bernhard Fischer von Erlach was undoubtedly one of the greatest architects of the Baroque period, and many of his buildings (especially the churches) are spectacular and dramatic. He was a master of syncretism, and, like Wren, he was intensely interested in archaeology, theory, history, science and ideas. The skyline of Salzburg would be infinitely poorer without his great buildings, especially the Kollegienkirche, while the beautiful altar of the Franziskanerkirche in Salzburg must be one of the loveliest artifacts ever created in the Baroque style, and is even finer than the design for the high altar at Mariazell. In Vienna, the Karlskirche and Hofbibliothek are works of architecture of world importance and, in the case of the Karlskirche, the symbolism and syncretic mastery have no equals anywhere, for that great church is a tour-de-force by any standards. Of the unfinished schemes, the stunning first proposals for Schönbrunn have a scale and an imperial grandeur which would have eclipsed Versailles and all other palaces: it is one of the most astonishing "might-have-beens" in all architectural history. Although the Hofstall-Gebäude complex was only partially completed, an image of the grand design survives, and that, too, had an imperial nobility worthy of Roman antiquity itself. Yet it is in his mastery of the fusing of apparently disparate eclectic elements that he impresses most, displaying a breathtakingly wide scholarship, references and historical knowledge, as well as a complete control of bold strokes of design. In his use of the ellipse as a major element in his plans he had no equal, even among the great Romans of the 17th century, while the freedom of invention displayed in his decorations, sculptures and towers is entirely admirable, and deserves the greatest of respect.

Fischer von Erlach's extraordinary *Entwurff einer historischen Architektur,* published in 1721, was one of the most important architectural books of the century, and the plates were amazing interpretations of the past: they certainly influenced later designers, such as Etienne Louis Boullée, with the visions of cloud-topped pyramids with ramped sides, while the monumental scale of the engraved buildings led to some of the most astonishing flights of fancy found in French neoclassicism.

—JAMES STEVENS CURL

FISKER, Kay.

Danish. Born in Frederiksberg, Denmark, 14 January 1893. Died in Copenhagen, 21 June 1965. Studied architecture at the Academy of Fine Arts, Copenhagen, 1909-20, Dip.Arch.; traveled n Italy, France, India, China and Japan, 1920-22. Private practice, Copenhagen, 1920-30; partnership with C. F. Møller, Copenhagen, 1930-43; private practice, 1944-65. Professor of architecture, from 1936, and dean of School of Architecture, Academy of Fine Arts, Copenhagen, from 1941; also taught in th e United States and Sweden. Honorary corresponding member, Royal Institute of British Architects, 1946; member, Royal Society of Arts, London, 1948; honorary fellow, American Institute of Architects, 1955; extraordinary member, Society of Architectural Historians (U.S.), 1960, and Akademie der Künste, Berlin, 1960.

Chronology of Works
All in Denmark unless noted
† *Work no longer exists*

1918-22	Cooperative Building Society Housing, Borups Allé and Stefansgade, Copenhagen
1920-22	Hornbaekhus Cooperative Society Housing, Borups Allé, Aagade and Hornbaekgade, Copenhagen
1927	Gullofshus Housing, Artillerivej and Gullofsgade, Copenhagen
1930-32	Housing, Aaboulevarden and Rosenørns Allé, Copenhagen
1932-45	University, Aarhus (with Povl Stegmann until 1937; with C. F. Møller until 1945)
1934	Natural History Museum, Aarhus
1935	Vestersøhus I Housing, Vester Søgade, Copenhagen
1938	Vestersøhus II Housing, Vester Søgade, Copenhagen
1939-44	Stefansgaarden Housing, Stefansgade, Copenhagen (with Eske Kirstensen)
1943	Egeparken Terraced Housing, Bredevej and Lindevangen, Lyngby
1944	Svanholm Estate Farmworkers' Housing, Hornsherred
1955	National Council for Unmarried Mothers Administration Building and Home, Copenhagen
1956-57	Interbau Housing, West Berlin, Germany

Publications

BOOKS BY FISKER

Modern Danish Architecture. With F. R. Yerbury. New York, 1927.
Kobenhavnske boligtyper. With others. Copenhagen, 1936.
Danish Architectural Drawings of All Periods. With others. Copenhagen, 1947.
Danske arkitekturstrømninger 1850-1950. With Knud Millech. Copenhagen, 1951.
Monumenta architecturae danicae: Danish Architectural Drawings, 1660-1920 (ed.). With Christian Elling. Copenhagen, 1961.

Kay Fisker: University, Aarhus, Denmark, 1932-45

ARTICLES BY FISKER

"Better Dwellings." *Berlingske tidende* No. 3 (1942).
"Gunnar Asplund and Scandinavian Architecture." *Svenska Dagbladet* No. 9 (1942).
"The Danish House." *Berlingske tidende* No. 1 (1942).
"Omkring Herholdt." *Arkitekten* (1943): 49-64.
"Tre Pionerer fra Aarhundredskiftet." *Byggmästaren* 26 (1947): 221-232.
"The History of Domestic Architecture in Denmark." *Architectural Review* 104 (November 1948): 219-226.
"The Development of Architecture in Denmark." *Architecture d'aujourd'hui* (June 1949).
"Den Funktionelle Tradition." *Arkitekten* 52 (1950): 69-100.
"The Moral of Functionalism." *Magazine of Art* (February 1950).
"Den Klintske skole." *Arkitektur* 7, No. 2 (April 1963): 37-80.

BOOKS ABOUT FISKER

FABER, TOBIAS: *Arkitekten Kay Fisker: 1893-1965*. Copenhagen, 1966.
LANGBERG, HARALD: *Danmarks bygningskultur*. Copenhagen, 1955.
LANGKILDE, HANS ERLING: *Arkitekten Kay Fisker*. Copenhagen, 1960.
MØLLER, CHRISTIAN F.: *Aarhus universitets bygninger*. Århus, Denmark, 1977.
PAULSSON, GREGOR: *The New Architecture*. Copenhagen, 1920.

ARTICLES ABOUT FISKER

"Bay Region—stilens ophavsmaend." *Arkitekten* (January 1962).
"Den Klintske Skole." *Arkitekten* Special issue, 7 (April 1963).
"Kay Fisker—70 Years." *Arkitekten* Special issue, 7 (February 1963).
"Station Buildings at Bornholm." *Arkitekten* 24 (June 1980).
TINTORI, S.: "Kay Fisker, architetto danese." *Casabella* 239 (May 1960).

*

Characterized by its formal clarity and logical planning, the architecture of Kay Fisker combined inspiration from Danish vernacular buildings and early-20th-century German modernism. Remembered for his public housing complexes, Fisker's work synthesized functional appropriateness and aesthetic unity without sacrificing experiential quality. But his influence on Danish architects goes beyond these projects, for as professor and then dean of the architecture school at the Royal Academy of Fine Arts in Copenhagen, he stressed the importance of social responsibility in Danish architecture. Through his extensive lecturing he kept his colleagues and students informed of the international developments in architecture. Author of several books on Danish architecture, Fisker was a contributor to the Danish journal *Arkitekten* for 40 years.

While an architecture student at the Royal Academy, Fisker worked for Anton Rosen, a leading proponent of the art nouveau in Denmark, and then assisted Hack Kampmann (architect of the Copenhagen Police Headquarters). At Kampmann's office he met Aage Rafn, with whom he won the competitions for the train stations at Bornholm (1916) and Christianshöj (1918-19). Fisker also won the 1917 competition for the Copenhagen daily *Politiken's* summer house. These designs were based upon traditional Danish building types, and incorporated simple wooden forms, sloped tile roofs and meticulous detailing.

By 1920, Fisker had won competitions for much larger scale projects, including a residential complex for Vibenhus (1918) and the Hotel Bergen (1919). The facades of the Vibenhus project were executed in black ceramic tiles, with the door frames in polished granite. Accent was provided by the white painted frames and glazing bars of the windows. The fresco-painted interiors for the Hotel Bergen, done in collaboration with Oluf Gierløv-Knudsen, were inspired by the Thorvaldsen Museum. But it was the housing complex at Borups Allé in Copenhagen, executed from 1918-22, that established his reputation for housing planning and design. The large blocks, surrounding an interior garden court, are simple brick volumes with pitched roofs and a uniform rhythm established by the window placement. The overall effect of this complex, due to its scale and endless repetition of windows, is somewhat austere and monotonous. While such works exemplify the Nordic classicism found throughout Scandinavia after World War I, the rationalism seen in these works led Fisker toward "functionalism," as international modernism was termed in the Scandinavian countries.

Though many Danish architects moved to embrace functionalism, Fisker sought to balance modernist canon, with its preference for cubic form, with the classic demands of Danish architecture: order, rhythm, solidity, brick construction and responsiveness to climatic concerns. His competition entry for the Danish students' hostel at the Cité Universitaire in Paris (1929) conveyed a modernist austerity, yet had the more traditional sloped roof and punched window openings of Danish vernacular. Fisker, along with other Danes, worked to emancipate brick architecture from historical styles by using it to modify functionalist tenets. The results were seen in private houses as well as public architecture, and the University of Aarhus, won in competition in 1931 by Fisker, C. F. Møller and Povl Stegmann, exemplifies this synthesis.

Aarhus University sits in a handsome, rolling landscape, a complex of yellow brick buildings unified through their siting, their formal vocabulary and materials. There the open landscape is preferred, for within the complex, each building maintains its objects status in a park-like setting accented by a small stream. Simultaneously, the designers strove to enhance the seemingly "naturalistic" qualities of the setting through the romantic tactic of casually placing the buildings upon the site to achieve a picturesque relationship between landscape and architecture. The designers integrated modernist "free" planning and elemental volumetrics with traditional building shapes and roof profiles. They excluded overhangs from the pitched-roof forms in a desire to maintain a taut, cubic outline. The buildings were firmly rooted to the earth, not held aloft on thin columns. Tile roofs compliment the brick cladding, though concrete frame construction was used. The resulting simplicity of form, coupled with the asymmetrical arrangement of building elements and the pisturesque site, imbued the university buildings with a quiet monumentality. The science complex, in particular, encapsulates these qualities. Finally, simply proportioned, punched window openings provided a more traditional image, while the scale of the openings was enlarged beyond the norms often associated with tradition. This window treatment reinforced the modern quality of the simple, cubic volumes. The university design was completed after World War II, when Fisker was no longer working on the project.

In the design of Vesterøhus (1935-39), a housing complex in Copenhagen, Fisker, in collaboration with C. F. Møller, was responsible for introducing the projecting but partly recessed balcony into large housing blocks. This allowed for large balconies to regulate and accent the design of the long facades characterizing Danish urban housing. The use of larger glazing areas in housing designs also accompanied the recessed balcony development at that time. This design informed many housing projects for the next several decades. Fisker also influenced Danish housing through his teaching at the Royal Academy, for he constantly reminded architects of their social responsibility in the area of habitation.

Fisker's postwar work demonstrated the best of what is considered Danish social architecture, yet also ranged from the design of ship interiors to large housing complexes of more than one thousand units. Although he did numerous other building types, Kay Fisker will be remembered for his important contributions in housing design, and for humanizing modern architecture through the use of local tradition.

—WILLIAM C. MILLER

FLAGG, Ernest.

American. Born in Brooklyn, New York, 7 February 1857. Died in New York City, 10 April 1947. Father was Rev. Jared Flagg, rector of Grace Church in New York; brothers included Montague Flagg, architect, and Charles Noel Flagg, portrait painter. Studied at the École des Beaux-Arts, Paris, France, 1888. Opened own office in New York, 1891. Fellow, American Institute of Architects, 1926.

Chronology of Works
All in the United States
† Work no longer exists

1892-96	St. Luke's Hospital, New York City
1892-97	Corcoran Gallery of Art, Washington, D.C.
1894-98	St. Margaret Memorial Hospital, Pittsburgh, Pennsylvania
1896-97	Mills House Number 1 ("The Atrium"), New York City
1896-98	Clark Tenements, New York City†
1896-99	Singer Building, New York City†
1896-1908	United States Naval Academy, Annapolis, Maryland
1897-99	Farmington Avenue Church (Immanuel Congregational Church), Hartford, Connecticut (with George M. Bartlett)
1897-99	Ernest Flagg House ("Stone Court"), Staten Island, New York
1898-99	Fire Engine Company 33, New York City
1899	New York Fireproof Model Tenements, New York City
1899-1900	Alfred Corning Clark House, New York City†
1899-1900	O. G. Jennings House (Lycée Français), New York City (with Walter B. Chambers)
1902-04	Singer Loft Building, New York City
1903-05	Frederick G. Bourne House ("The Towers"), Dark Island, Chippewa Bay, New York
1904-06	Naval Hospital, Washington, D.C.
1905-07	Ernest Flagg House, New York City†
1906-08	Ernest Flagg Office, New York City
1906-08	Singer Tower, New York City
1906-11	Pomfret School, Connecticut

1910-11	Princeton University Press (Scribner Building), New York City
1912-13	Charles Scribner's Sons Building, New York City
1913-14	Gwynne Building, Cincinnati, Ohio
1917	"Bow-Cot," Staten Island, New York
1918	Sun Village (Emergency Fleet Corporation Housing Project), Chester, Pennsylvania
1933-37	Flagg Court, Brooklyn, New York

Publications

BOOKS BY FLAGG

Small Houses: Their Economic Design and Construction. New York, 1922.

ARTICLES BY FLAGG

"Influence of the French School on Architecture in the United States." *Architectural Record* 4 (1894): 211-228.
"The New York Tenement House Evil and Its Cure." *Scribner's Magazine* 16 (1894): 108-117.
"The Limitation of Height and Area of Buildings in New York." *American Architect and Building News* 93, No.2 (1908): 125-127.

BOOKS ABOUT FLAGG

BACON, MARDGES: *Ernest Flagg: Beaux-Arts Architect and Urban Reformer.* Cambridge, Massachusetts, 1986.

ARTICLES ABOUT FLAGG

DESMOND, HARRY W.: "The Works of Ernest Flagg." *Architectural Record* 11 (1902): 1-104.
DESMOND, HARRY W.: "A Rational Skyscraper." *Architectural Record* 15 (1904): 274-284.

*

Ernest Flagg was among the most unusual of the Beaux-Arts-trained American architects, developing a practice that included major public buildings and one of the most important early skyscrapers in New York, but also focusing on the problem of housing for the working class.

Flagg was the son of Jared Bradley Flagg, also a man of multiple talents and interests, an accomplished painter and an Episcopal clergyman. While his father was rector of Grace Church in Brooklyn Heights, New York, Ernest was born in Brooklyn. Ernest Flagg was educated in a number of private Episcopal schools, but when his father resigned his parish and turned to painting and business ventures to support the family, Ernest and his brother became office boys on Wall Street and set up several small business operations of their own. They rented tenement rooms in the working-class sections of Manhattan rather than commute from Brooklyn; this experience of slum conditions shaped the rest of Flagg's career. A few years later, when his father promoted some of the early cooperative apartment buildings erected in New York, Ernest Flagg assisted in planning them, and that involvement in innovative housing also affected the young man.

Although living in genteel poverty, Flagg was connected to socially prominent families. His cousin, Alice Moore Gwynne, married Cornelius Vanderbilt II, and his sister married Charles Scribner; both of those connections would help him later in his career. Vanderbilt requested Flagg's advice in proposed modifications to his newly built house by George B. Post. Although the modifications were not carried out, Vanderbilt was sufficiently impressed with Flagg's talent that he not only suggested that Flagg become an architect, but offered to pay the cost of education at the École des Beaux-Arts in Paris.

Flagg attended the École des Beaux-Arts from 1888 to 1891, studying in the atelier of Paul Blondel, absorbing the technique of design analysis with its emphasis on developing a clear conceptual *parti,* and also coming under the influence of the somewhat overblown Baroque style then fashionable in Paris. Soon after Flagg's return to New York, Vanderbilt was instrumental in obtaining for him the commission for St. Luke's Hospital in New York City (1891-96). At almost the same time, Flagg began work on plans for the new Corcoran Gallery of Art in Washington, D.C., a commission directed to him perhaps because of his father's connections among prominent artists. Built in 1892-97, the new Corcoran Gallery demonstrated the strong French stylistic influence on Flagg. Also French in character and in its arrangement of public spaces was Flagg's complex of buildings for the United States Naval Academy at Annapolis, Maryland (1896-1908).

Around the turn of the century, his French training in rational structural design prompted Flagg to use reinforced-concrete frames (as in the Naval Academy chapel) and to switch to metal-frame construction in commercial buildings. This was evident in the light skin of glass held in the metal frame of the Scribner Loft Building (1902-04), and most dramatically in the slender tower of the Singer Building and Tower (1896-99, 1906-08), both in New York City. Rising 612 feet, the 47-story Singer Tower was Flagg's most brilliant structural work; its narrow office tower was cross-braced at each corner to resist torsion twisting caused by winds off the harbor. It was also a dramatic illustration of the effectiveness of reducing the tall section of the building to one quarter of its total plan area, a requirement put into law by zoning ordinances in 1916.

As Flagg designed these public and commercial works, he also completed a number of fashionable urban residences, as well as several country houses on Long Island. At the same time, however, he was active in the design and construction of model tenement apartment blocks, beginning with designs for the Clark Tenements built by the City and Suburban Homes Company in New York (1896-98). During World War I, Flagg's expertise in housing design was put to use in the design of Sun Village, an Emergency Fleet Corporation housing project in Chester, Pennsylvania (1918). Flagg continued to develop designs for improved apartment blocks in New York City and Boston, Massachusetts, and in 1932 formed his own company to build the Flagg Court apartments in Brooklyn. He also explored methods of economical concrete house construction and published his designs in *Small Houses: Their Economical Design and Construction* in 1922.

—LELAND M. ROTH

FONTANA, Carlo.

Italian. Born near Como, Italy, in 1638. Died in Rome, 5 February 1714. Studied with Pietro da Cortona, Rome, 1650s; worked with Bernini in Rome. Made Accademico di Merito of the Accademia di San Luca, 1667; knighted, 1670; elected to the members of the Congregazione dei Virtuosi al Pantheon, 1694; appointed architect of St. Peter's, 1697.

Carlo Fontana: San Marcello al Corso, Rome, Italy, 1682-83

Chronology of Works
All in Italy unless noted
* Approximate dates
† Work no longer exists

1661*-67ff. Santa Maria dei Miracoli, Piazza del Popolo, Rome (with Carlo Rainaldi and Gianlorenzo Bernini)
1661*-67ff. Santa Maria di Montesanto, Piazza del Popolo, Rome (with Rainaldi and Bernini)
1664 Santi Faustino e Giovita, Rome (facade)
1665* San Biagio in Campitelli, Rome (facade and entrance vestibule)
1666-68 Santo Spirito dei Napolitani, Rome (remodeling of interior)
1670-74 Santa Margherita at Montefiascone, Rome (completion)
1670-74 Santa Marta in Piazza del Collegio Romano, Rome (remodeling and enlargement)
1671-84 Capella Ginetti, Sant'Andrea della Valle, Rome
1674 Santa Maria in Traspontina, Rome (high altar)
1675* Medieval Church, Lanuvio (remodeling)
1676-80 Palazzo Bigazzini, near Pienza†
1676-80 Palazzo Grimani, near Pienza
1680*ff. Palazzo Massimo al Campidoglio, near Pienza (remodeling and fountain in the courtyard)
1678-79 San Quirico d'Orcia, near Pienza (palace and garden)
1678-80 Santa Margherita in Trastevere, Rome
1679-80 Villa Cetinale, near Siena
1680* Villa Versaglia, Formello
1682-83 San Marcello al Corso, Rome (facade)
1682-84 Cappella Cybo, Santa Maria del Popolo, Rome

1685-87 Cappella dell' Assunta, Collegio Clementino, Rome†
1688 Cathedral, Como (dome)
1689-92 Cathedral, Bergamo (completion)
1692 Monument to Innocent XII, St. Peter's, Rome†
1692-98 St. Peter's, Rome (baptismal chapel)
1692-1702 Aqueduct, Civitavecchia (restoration)
1694-96 Palazzo Ludovisi, Rome (completion)
1696-1701 Monument to Queen Christina of Sweden, St. Peter's, Rome
1700* Convent of the Dominicans, Santa Maria Sopra Minerva, Rome (main hall of library)
1700 Palais Martinitz, Prague, Czechoslovakia
1702 Santa Maria in Trastevere, Rome (remodeling of portico and facade)
1701-04 Casa Correzionale, Rome
1708-11 Ospizio di San Michele, Rome (additions)
1702-04 San Teodoro al Palatino, Rome (restoration)
1702-08 San Spirito dei Napolitani, Rome (second remodeling of the interior and construction of a chapel for the main altar; since altered)
1703 Santa Maria dell' Umilità, Rome (facade)
1703 Casino Vaini, Rome
1703-05 Granari alle Terme, Rome (left incomplete)
1705 Palazzo Capponi, Florence
1705 Palazzo Durazzo, Genoa (stairhall and loggia opposite the near front)
1706-12 Cappella Albani, San Sebastiano fuori le mura, Rome

Publications

BOOKS BY FONTANA

FONTANA, CARLO: *Discorso del Mons. Carlo Vespignano sopra la facile riuscita di restaurare il Ponte Senatorio.* Rome, 1692.
FONTANA, CARLO: *Discorso sopra le cause delle inondazioni del Tevere.* Rome, 1696.
FONTANA, CARLO: *Descrizione della nob. Cappella della Fonte Battesimale in S. Pietro.* Rome, 1697.

BOOKS ABOUT FONTANA

BRAHAM, ALLAN, and HAGER, HELLMUT: *Carlo Fontana: The Drawings at Windsor Castle.* London, 1977.
BRAHAM, ALLAN: *Funeral Decoration in Early Eighteenth-century Rome.* London, 1975.
BRAUER, HEINRICH and WITTKOWER, RUDOLF (eds.): *Die Zeichnungen des Gianlorenzo Bernini.* Berlin, 1931.
BUCHOWIECKI, WALTER: Vol. 2 in *Handbuch der Kirchen Roms.* Vienna, 1970.
CATENA, CLAUDIO: *Guida Storico Artistica.* Rome, 1954.
CHATTARD, G. P.: *Nuova descrizione del Vaticano, o sia Palazzo Apostolico di S. Pietro.* 3 vols. Rome, 1762-1767.
COUDENHOVE-ERTHAL, EDUARD: *Carlo Fontana und die Architektur des römischen Spätbarocks.* Vienna, 1930.
DONATI, UGO: *Artisti ticinesi a Roma.* Bellinzona, Italy, 1942.
FALDA, GIOVANNI BATTISTA: *Il nuovo teatro delle fabbriche di Roma moderna.* Rome, 1665-1699.
FASOLO, FURIO: *Le chiese di Roma nel' 700, I, Trastevere.* Rome, 1949.
GARMS, JÖRG: *Il Bambin Gesù.* Rome, 1979.
GIGLI, LAURA: *San Marcello al Corso.* Rome, 1977.
GOLZIO, VINCENZO: *Documenti artistici sul Seicento nell' Archivio Chigi.* Rome, 1939.

GRASSI, LILIANA: *Provincie del Barocco e del Rococo*. Milan, 1966.

MALLORY, NINA: *Roman Rococo Architecture from Clement XI to Benedict XIV (1700-1758)*. New York, 1977.

METZGER, DOROTHY J.: *Piazza S. Ignazio, Rome in the Seventeenth and Eighteenth Centuries*. Ann Arbor, 1979.

D'ONOFRIO CESARE: *Roma val bene un' abjuria: Storie romane tra Christina di Svezia, Piazza del Popolo e l'Accademia d'Arcadia*. Rome, 1976.

PASTOR, LUDWIG VON: *The History of the Popes*. London, 1953.

DE ROSSI, DOMENICO: *Studio d'architettura civile*. 3 vols. Rome, 1702-1721.

SALERNO, LUIGI: *Piazza di Spagna*. Naples (1967).

WITTKOWER, RUDOLF: *Art and Architecture in Italy: 1600-1750*. 3d. ed. Harmondsworth, England, 1973.

ARTICLES ABOUT FONTANA

BLUNT, ANTHONY: "The Drawings of Carlo Fontana in the Royal Library at Windsor Castle." *Barocco europeo, barocco italiano, barocco salentino*. Lecce, Italy, 1969.

CONFORTI, MICHAEL: "Planning the Lateran Apostles." *Studies in Italian Art and Architecture: Memoirs of the American Academy in Rome* 35 (1980) :243-260.

COUDENHOVE-ERTHAL, EDUARD: "Römisches Stadtbaudenken zu Ende des Seicento." In *Hermann Egger: Festschrift zum 60. Geburtstag*. Graz, Austria, 1933.

COUDENHOVE-ERTHAL, EDUARD: "Zum Problem Carlo Fontana." *Wiener Jahrbuch für Kunstgeschichte*, 23 (1934): 157-158 .

CRIPPA, G.: "Inediti sul Duomo di Bergamo dal Filarete al Fontana." *Bergamo arte* 2 (1971): 21-30.

DOWLEY, FRANCIS H.: "Some Maratta Drawings at Düsseldorf." *Art Quarterly* 20 (1957): 163-179.

ENGGASS, ROBERT: "Laurentius Ottoni Rom. Vat. Basilicae Sculptor." *Storia dell' Arte* 15-16 (1972): 315-342.

HAGER, HELLMUT: "Carlo Fontana and the Jesuit Sanctuary at Loyola." *Journal of the Warburg and Courtauld Institutes* 37 (1974): 280-289.

HAGER, HELLMUT: "Carlo Fontana's Project for a Church in Honour of the 'Ecclesis Triumphans' in the Colosseum, Rome." *Journal of the Warburg and Courtauld Institutes* 36 (1973): 319-337.

HAGER, HELLMUT: "L'intervento di Carlo Fontana per le chiese dei Monasteri di Santa Marta e Santa Margherita in Trastevere." *Commentari* 25 (1974): 225-242.

HAGER, HELLMUT: "La cappella del Cardinale Alderano Cybo in Santa Maria del Popolo." *Commentari* 25 (1974a): 47-61.

HAGER, HELLMUT: "La crisi statica della cupola di S. Maria in Vallicella in Roma e i rimedi proposti da Carlo Fontana, Carlo Rainaldi e Mattia di Rossi." *Commentari* 24 (1973): 300-318.

HAGER, HELLMUT: "On a Project Ascribed to Carlo Fontana for the Façade of San Giovanni in Laterano." *Burlington Magazine* 117 (1975): 105-109.

HAGER, HELLMUT: "Un riesame di tre cappelle di Carlo Fontana a Roma." *Commentari* 27 (1976): 252-289.

HAGER, HELLMUT: "Zur Planungs und Baugeschichte der Zwillingskirchen auf der Piazza del Popolo: S. Maria di Montesanto und S. Maria dei Miracoli in Rom." *Römisches Jahrbuch für Kunstgeschichte* 11 (1967-1968): 189-306.

INCISA DELLA ROCCHETTA, GIOVANNI: "Notizie sulla fabbrica della Chiesa Collegiata di Ariccia." *Rivista dell' Istituto di Archeologia e Storia dell' Arte* 1 (1929): 281-285.

KITAO, TIMOTHY K.: "Carlo Fontana Had No Part in Bernini's Planning for the Square of St. Peter's." *Journal of the Society of Architectural Historians* 36 (1977): 85-93.

MISCIATELLI, PIERO: "Un documento inedito dell' architetto Carlo Fontana." *Repertorium für Kunstwissenschaft* 32 (1909): 247-257.

SCHIAVO, ARMANDO: "Notizie biografiche sui Fontana." *Studi Romani* 19 (1971): 56-61.

TAVASSI LA GRECA, BIANCA: "Alcuni problemi inerenti l'attivita teoricà di Carlo Fontana." *Storia dell' Arte* 29 (1977): 39-59.

WITTKOWER, RUDOLF: "Carlo Rainaldi and the Roman Architecture of the Full Baroque." *Art Bulletin* 19 (1937): 242-313.

*

Born near Como, Carlo Fontana arrived in Rome in the 1650s, where he studied with Pietro da Cortona, whom he assisted with the facade for Santa Maria della Pace. He also worked with Giovanni Lorenzo Bernini on the piazza for St. Peter's Basilica, and in 1663 on Bernini's reworking of the Vatican's Scala Regia.

Fontana's career was an active one, but, unluckily, one also susceptible to changing fortunes. Many of his projects were never carried out, and others were destroyed or remodeled after his death. Also, much of his career was spent supervising projects for other architects and designing more modest structures, such as chapels, altars and fountains, or ephemera such as the catafalque for Emperor Leopold I installed in Santa Maria dell'Anima in 1705.

Fontana's work for Pope Alexander VII-Chigi put him in contact with other members of the Chigi family. He assisted Bernini with the palace for Cardinal Flavio Chigi (1664-67) and with the palace and church at the Chigi retreat in Ariccia.

In 1662 Fontana worked on the design and execution of the facade of Sant'Andrea della Valle. He later participated in efforts on the two churches constructed to embellish the important Piazza del Popolo. Fontana replaced Carlo Rainaldi on the second of these, Santa Maria di Montesanto, in 1677, completing the dome to his own designs and finishing the church's interior decoration.

The architect's work for the Ottoboni family began with his renovation of the Fontana Paola for Pope Alexander VIII in 1690. He added a large basin to Flaminio Ponzio's five-bay facade for this socially minded pope. After Alexander's death in 1691, Fontana confirmed the structural soundness of Carlo Enrico di San Martino's plans for the Vatican tomb commissioned by Cardinal Pietro Ottoboni for his great-uncle. Fontana's drawing for the tomb niche dates from 1696 and is preserved in Windsor Castle.

His modest monument in the Vatican Basilica to Pope Innocent XII in 1692 was replaced by Filippo della Valle's grander ensemble in 1747. Fontana is better known for his design of the Vatican monument honoring Queen Christina of Sweden (1696-1701), with its large bronze medallion portrait of the queen and related relief sculpture.

Fontana's masterpiece in religious architecture was the facade for San Marcello al Corso (1682-83). Set back on the Via del Corso in a shallow but broad piazza, the church remains among the most distinguished of the many in Rome. It is striking for its concave facade, its curvature interrupted only at the center by freestanding orders that flank the central portal and advance to meet the faithful entering the piazza. The architrave is staggered to project in concert with the composite-order columns, and an aedicule breaks the segmented pediment above the entrance. Fontana placed an unbroken, triangular pediment at the apex of the structure, the second story articulated by pilasters of the same order. The pilasters of the lateral bays at ground level link with the paired pilasters in the central bay above to preserve the spreading planarity of the facade. Fontana's reliance on these planar orders in the church facade reflects Bernini's influence, whereas his independent thinking as an architect extends to the freestanding columns terminating the corners of the second story; they continue the vertical thrust of the ground-level columns below as a means of muting the horizontal spread of the facade.

Fontana's secular projects shared the same mixed success as his religious commissions. His most impressive private venture was the Palazzo Bigazzini on the Piazza San Marco, undertaken in 1676-80, just after his involvement with the Palazzo Chigi. No longer extant, the three-story palace across from the Palazzo Venezia had a facade of rusticated corners and pedimented windows, but lacked the classical orders.

Fountains seem to have been a particular success for Fontana, who was perhaps stimulated by his family name. The piazza in front of Santa Maria in Trastevere had long been the location for a water source. Pope Alexander VII ordered the fountain on site in 1659 to be remodeled in accord with Bernini's designs, but Fontana revised the huge, octagonal basin in 1692.

In 1695, again for Pope Innocent XII, Fontana began construction of a customs house, the Dogana di Terra, around the ruins of the Hadrianeum. He later supervised many restoration projects for the Albani pope, Clement XI (1700-21). In 1703-05 Fontana undertook the building of a granary warehouse as a protection against famine. The Granary of Clement XI faced the baths of Diocletian, but was never completed. In 1698 Cardinal Domenico Casanate founded the Biblioteca Casanatense and bequeathed his library to the Dominicans at Santa Maria sopra Minerva. Two years later Fontana began the construction of the library's main hall.

Two particularly grand projects that Fontana had planned were never executed. These were a trapezoidal extension of Bernini's oval piazza at St. Peter's Basilica by means of a colonnade, and the construction of a central-plan church in honor of the Christian martyrs; the latter structure was to be placed within the Colosseum, which required shoring after several of its arches collapsed during an earthquake in 1703. The design was reminiscent of Donato Bramante's Tempietto, but its atrophied towers made the church appear anemic as it rested within the Colosseum's walls.

Fontana executed numerous small projects in many of Rome's major edifices. He was responsible for the splendid bronze altar rail in Il Gesù. He designed the high altar for Santa Maria in Traspontina (1674), the portico for Santa Maria in Trastevere (1701-02), and, until his death in 1714, he supervised the project for the apostle statues to fill the nave tabernacles in San Giovanni in Laterano.

Fontana was awarded a knighthood in about 1670; he was elected *principe* of the Accademia de San Lucca in 1686 and again from 1693 to 1699, a period of elected office that eclipsed the four-year term of his master, Pietro da Cortona, earlier in the century. He was entered among the members of the Congregazione dei Virtuosi al Pantheon on 14 February 1694. Three years later Innocent XII appointed him architect of St. Peter's Basilica.

Fontana was a prolific draftsman, and scores of his drawings have survived. Filippo Juvarra and Nicola Michetti had studied with him in Rome, and Fontana influenced a generation of important architects throughout Europe.

—EDWARD J. OLSZEWSKI

FOSTER, Norman.

British. Born in Manchester, England, 1 June 1935. Married Wendy Cheesman, 1964; four children. Served in the Royal Air Force, 1953-55. Studied at the University of Manchester School of Architecture and Department of Town and Country Planning, 1956-61; Yale University School of Architecture, 1961-62, M.Arch. Partner in Foster Associates, London, since 1967. Gold Medal, Royal Institute of British Architects, 1983. Knighted, 1990.

Chronology of Works
All in England unless noted

1966-67	Reliance Controls Factory, Swindon, Wiltshire
1971	Fred Olsen Passenger Terminal and Operations Centre, Millwall, London
1971	IBM Advance Head Office, Cosham, Hampshire
1971	Computer Technology Building, Hemel Hempstead, Hertfordshire
1971	Foster Associates Studio, Fitzroy Street, London
1973	Modern Art Glass Warehouse, Thamesmead, Kent
1973	Orange Hand Shops, London, Nottingham, Brighton and Reading
1975	Willis Faber Dumas Country Head Office, Ipswich, Suffolk
1975	Palmerston Special School, Bellvale, Liverpool
1978	IBM Technical Park, Greenford, Middlesex
1978	Sainsbury Centre for the Visual Arts, University of East Anglia, Norwich
1979	Norman and Wendy Foster House, Cannon Place, Hampstead, London
1979-85	Hong Kong and Shanghai Banking Corporation Headquarters, Hong Kong
1981-91	Third London Airport, Stansted, Essex
1983	Renault UK Parts Distribution Centre, Swindon, Wiltshire
1984-92	Médiathèque, Maison Carrée, Nîmes, France
1985-91	Masterplan and Sackler Galleries at the Royal Academy of Arts, London
1986	Shop for Katharine Hamnett, London
1987-89	Offices for Stanhope Securities, Stockley Park, Uxbridge, Middlesex
1987-91	Century Tower, Tokyo, Japan
1988	Shop for Esprit, London
1988-91	Telecommunications Tower, Barcelona, Spain
1988-93	Underground Railway System, Bilbao, Spain
1988-	Kings Cross Redevelopment, London
1988-	Technology Centre and Business Promotion Centre, Duisburg, Germany
1989-91	Offices for Stanhope Properties, Bollo Lane, London
1990	Riverside Offices and Apartments, London
1990	ITN New Headquarters, London
1990	Law Faculty of Cambridge University, Cambridge
1991	Crescent Wing (addition), Sainsbury Centre for the Visual Arts, University of East Anglia, Norwich

Publications

ARTICLES BY FOSTER

"How to Design Low-Cost Flexible Quick-Build Buildings." *Building Design* (October 1973).
"Alvar Aalto 1898-1976." *RIBA Journal* (July 1976).

Norman Foster: Third London Airport, Stansted, Essex, England, 1981-91

"Foster Associates: Buildings and Projects." *Architectural Design* (September/October 1977).
"Fostering Good Relations" [interview]. *Building* (7 May 1982).

SUDJIC, DEYAN: *Norman Foster, Richard Rogers, James Stirling: New Directions in British Architecture*. London, 1986.
WILLIAMS, STEPHANIE: *Hongkong Bank: The Building of Norman Foster's Masterpiece*. London, 1989.

BOOKS ABOUT FOSTER

BEST, ALASTAIR: *Foster Associates, Buildings and Projects 1991*, ed. by Norman Foster. London, 1991.
DAVIES, COLIN: *High Tech Architecture*. New York, 1988.
DENT, ROGER N.: *Principles of Pneumatic Architecture*. London, 1971.
Foster Associates. London, 1979.
LAMBOT, IAN (ed.): *Norman Foster: Foster Associates Buildings and Projects 1964-1985*. 3 vols. London, 1990-91.
Norman Foster: Architect—Selected Works 1964-1984. Manchester, 1984.
Norman Foster: Three Themes, Six Projects. Florence, 1988
POWELL, KEN: *Stansted: Norman Foster and the Architecture of Flight*. London, 1992.

ARTICLES ABOUT FOSTER

Architecture and Urbanism, special issue (September 1975).
COLLOVA, ROBERTO: "Foster Associates—IBM UK, Cosham." *Parametro* (Bologna, February 1975).
COOK, PETER: "Unbuilt England." *Architecture and Urbanism* (October 1977).
"East Anglia Arts Centre." *Architectural Review* (December 1978).
"Engineering Design and Foster Associates." *Northern Architect* (Sunderland, England, April 1976).
"Foster Associates: Assembly Without Composition." *Casabella* (March 1973).
"Foster Associates' Recent Work." *Architectural Design* (May 1970).
"Foster's Other Side." *Architects' Journal* (21 May 1980).

"Fostering the Arts." *Architects' Journal* (April 1978).

"High-tech to Appropriate: A View of Foster Associates' Approach to Appropriate Technology." *Architectural Design* (March 1976).

"Is There Life after Norman?" *Building* (3 April 1981).

"Low-Profile School." *Architectural Review* (November, 1976).

MEADE, MARTIN K.: "Foster, Prouvé and Loos in Paris." *Architects' Journal* (9 March 1983).

"Method on a Macro Scale." *Design* (March 1981).

"Orange Hand: The Shops for Boys." *Architecture and Urbanism* (September 1973).

"Palmerston Special School in London." *Bauen und Wohnen* (Zürich, May 1977).

PECKHAM, A.: "This is the Modern World." *Architectural Digest* 49/2 (1979).

Space Design, special issue, "Foster Associates: The Architecture of the Near Future" (March 1982).

SPRING, MARTIN: "Art Shed." *Building* (April 1978).

WILLIAMS, STEPHANIE: "Stretching Glass" and "Roundabout." *Building Design* (February 1978).

*

Norman Foster, together with Richard Rogers, was the leader of the high-tech style in Britain in the 1970s and 1980s and is the country's most distinguished architect.

Educated at Manchester and at Yale, Foster teamed up with his Yale classmate Richard Rogers and others in 1963 to form the architectural practice called Team 4. That practice produced a few modest houses and then, in 1967, the Reliance Control Electronics Factory in Swindon. This building, which was rectangular in plan and placed everyone—workers and management—in a single space, had long, low proportions and a white painted Miesian steel frame. Whereas with Mies the frame was complete and static, at Reliance the beams extended beyond the skin to give the implication and the possibility of extension in all directions. It also had clearly expressed diagonal bracing. It was a compelling image and made Foster and Rogers famous, but it could not keep them together: Team 4 split up upon completion of the building in 1967.

Foster's first buildings from an independent practice showed a new and confident direction with more emphasis on jointing and less on expressed structure. A keen glider and helicopter pilot, Foster is clearly more at home with the techniques of aerospace manufacturing than he is with the conventional products of the building industry. He has tried, with more success than anyone else, to bring the technology and the delight in lightweight structures of aircraft into building, and he has done it with confidence, style and more than a hint of enjoyment. In the 1960s Skidmore, Owings and Merrill gave modern business its desired face, but the first Norman Foster buildings made all that look out of date. This passion for technology meant that his buildings really worked—the dream of modern architecture, the well-serviced, machine-made space, was at last a reality.

The terminal for Olsen Lines in London's Docklands, finished in 1971, consisted of an office and amenity building for the shipping line, and a metal tube to convey the passengers. The building had glazed ends, with the first of Foster's minimalist glass walls—reflective glazing in neoprene gaskets and nothing else. Never before had architectural form been so simplified. In the same year the IBM building was completed at Cosham in Hampshire, a short-life office building with a deep rectangular plan and a glass skin even more minimalist than that for Olsen, for there were no horizontal subdivisions to the glazing, just a single sheet of glass from ground to sky. An even shorter-life

office building was built at Hemel Hempstead in the form of a tented structure held up by air pressure. The Foster office was gaining in skill and confidence in its ability to serve its clients using techniques beyond the norm of the building industry.

The office building in Ipswich for Willis, Faber and Dumas is a three-story building with a reflective skin of unframed glass hung from the top. The plan form follows the curving streetlines, giving an array of reflections and fitting the building into the medieval road pattern in a way that had been forgotten during the long-slab-and-plaza fashion. Internally the open office areas form galleries to a great well, with the escalators rising in sequence to the roof garden at the top.

Two years after the construction of the Ipswich building, Foster Associates completed the Sainsbury Centre for the Visual Arts in nearby Norwich. A great single space like an aircraft hangar, it has a thick structural zone along its long sides and across the roof, and all services and minor rooms are kept within this structural zone to free the great space within as art gallery and restaurant. The shorter ends are totally glazed, and the roof and side walls are formed of identical panels emphasizing the hangar look. The mid-1970s were an uncomfortable time for architecture in England, with the Modern Movement losing its hold and nothing of strength appearing to take its place, so the Foster buildings at Ipswich and Norwich stand as rare masterpieces from a period of architectural disillusion.

The completion of the Hong Kong and Shanghai Bank on the Hong Kong waterfront marked the transition of Foster Associates from being a talented British firm to a major international practice. The high-rise office building had been the American building type, with American architects and American ideas carrying all before them on all continents. For Hong Kong, Foster produced a new image. Building on the Chicago joy in the structure of tall buildings, he designed a tower where the structure is clearly expressed, with its floors hanging from eight great towers. As in Rogers' Lloyd's building in London, vertical elements were brought to the edge of the plan to leave a great uninterrupted working space in the middle. The Hong Kong building sits on a regular site, however, so the order of its construction and servicing is less constrained by street lines than at Lloyd's.

The Hong Kong Bank was followed by commissions from around the globe. But wherever Foster builds, the same painstaking, well-crafted, machine-made look is present, as each new project is taken as an opportunity to perfect building as an advancing technology.

In the United Kingdom, the construction of Stansted as London's fourth airport gave the practice a new building type, with a great passenger terminal under umbrella roofs. However, at the same time, they have designed more-modest, less-exotic buildings, which indicate that the more flamboyant phase of hi-tech may be over. Two buildings in London bear this out: the firm's own offices in Battersea and the Independent Broadcasting Authority's building on Grays Inn Road. In each case the building is advanced state of the art, but the expression is minimalist rather than exuberant.

—JOHN WINTER

FRANCESCO DI GIORGIO.

Italian. Born Francesco Maurizio di Giorgio di Martini in Siena, Italy; baptized 23 September 1439. Died in or near Siena, buried 29 November 1501. Trained as an artist in the Sienese school of Lorenzo di Pietro (Il Vecchietta); first recorded as painter and

Francesco di Giorgio: Church of Santa Maria delle Grazie al Calcinaio, Cortona, Italy, 1484-90

sculptor, 1464; worked in Siena (in joint studio with Neroccio de Landi) until 1475; worked in Urbino, 1475-85; repatriated as citizen of Siena, 1485 or 89; appointed city engineer, consultant, and served on the Supreme magistracy.

Chronology of Works
All in Italy
* Approximate dates
† Work no longer exists

1474-84	Church of San Bernardino all'Osservanza, Siena
1476-82	Palazzo Ducale, Gubbio (additions)
1476-82	Palazzo Ducale, Urbino
1476*-82	Monastery of San Bernardino degli Zoccolanti, Urbino
1476-94	Cathedral, Urbino†
1476*-99*	Castle of San Leo; Castle of Mondavio; Castle of Sassocorvaro; Castle of Cagli
1482*-89	Convent of Santa Chiara, Urbino†
1482*-98	Church of San Bernardino degli Zoccolanti, Urbino
1484-90	Church of Santa Maria delle Grazie al Calcinaio, Cortona
1484-93	Palazzo degli Anziani, Ancona†
1484-1503	Palazzo del Comune, Iesi
1492-97	Castel Nuovo, Naples†
1493-1501	Church of San Sebastiano in Valle Piata, Siena (not completed until 1504)
1498-1501	Church of Santo Spirito, Siena (not completed until 1509)

Publications

BOOKS BY FRANCESCO

Book of Machines and Castles. Unpublished manuscript. London, 1474-75.
Trattato di architettura, ingegneria ed arte militare. Turin, 1475-76.
"Translation of Vitruvius." Unpublished manuscript. Florence, ca. 1476/82.
Trattato di architettura, ingegneria ed arte militare. ca. 1482/92; edited by C. Maltese. Milan, 1967.
Trattato di architettura civile e militare di Francesco di Giorgio Martini. Edited by Carlo Promis. Turin, 1841.

BOOKS ABOUT FRANCESCO

FIORE, FRANCESCO PAOLO: *Città e macchine del'400 nei disegni di Francesco di Giorgio Martini.* Florence, 1978.
HERSEY, GEORGE L.: *Alfonso II and the Artistic Renewal of Naples: 1485-1495.* New Haven, Connecticut, 1969.
PAPINI, ROBERTO: *Francesco di Giorgio architetto.* 3 vols. Florence, 1946.
ROTONDI, PASQUALE: *Francesco di Giorgio nel Palazzo Ducale di Urbino.* Milan, 1970.
VOLPE, GIANNI: *Rocche e fortificazioni del Ducato di Urbino.* Urbino, 1982.
WELLER, ALLEN S.: *Francesco di Giorgio: 1439-1501.* Chicago, 1943.

ARTICLES ABOUT FRANCESCO

BETTS, RICHARD J.: "On the Chronology of Francesco di Giorgio's Treatises: New Evidence from an Unpublished Manuscript." *Journal of the Society of Architectural Historians* 36 (1977): 3-14.

BURNS, HOWARD: "Progetti di Francesco di Giorgio per i conventi di San Bernadino e Santa Chiara di Urbino." Pp. 293-311 in *Studi Bramanteschi*. Rome, 1974.

DE LA CROIX, HORST: "Military Architecture and the Radial City Plan in Sixteenth Century Italy." *Art Bulletin* 42 (1960): 263-290.

DEZZI-BARDESCHI, MARCO: "Le rocche di Francesco di Giorgio nel Ducato di Urbino." *Castellum* 8 (1968): 97-140.

KOLB, CAROLYN: "The Francesco di Giorgio Material in the Zichy Codex." *Journal of the Society of Architectural Historians* 47 (June 1988): 132-159.

LOWIC, LAWRENCE: "The Meaning and Significance of the Human Analogy in Francesco di Giorgio's Trattato." *Journal of the Society of Architectural Historians* 42 (December 1983): 360-370.

MILLON, HENRY A.: "The Architectural Theory of Francesco di Giorgio." *Art Bulletin* 40 (1958): 257-261.

RETI, LADISLAO: "Francesco di Giorgio Martini's Treatise on Engineering and Its Plagiarists." *Technology and Culture* 4 (1963): 287-298.

*

Architect, military engineer, artificer, hydraulics expert and inventor of war machines, but also painter, sculptor, foundryman, numismatist, inlayer, miniaturist and writer of treatises, Francesco di Giorgio Martini is one of the major representatives of the early Italian Renaissance, equal if not superior to Leonardo da Vinci.

Francesco di Giorgio was held in high esteem by his contemporaries. Raphael's father, Giovanni Santi, who knew Francesco personally, considered him a "supreme architect." Giorgio Vasari described him as an "excellent architect," while Venturi called him a "universal master." For more than a century now, Francesco's eclectic architectural work has been an object of ever more thorough research. These modern revaluations place Francesco more and more firmly in the first ranks of the history of Italian art and architecture.

Francesco di Giorgio was trained as an artist in the Sienese school of Lorenzo di Pietro, also known as Vecchietta, and the school of Neroccio dei Landi, with whom he maintained a long artistic association. Hailing from the people, Francesco was essentially self-taught. He was also a tireless traveler, a person of striking curiosity and interest in novelty, who nevertheless had a strong awareness of the importance of antiquity and was a constant visitor at archaeological sites. Early in his career, Francesco made his mark on the scene of the Italian quattrocento as an original artist with a creative and prolific mind, containing within himself the imagination, curiosity about science and rational disposition typical of the Renaissance genius.

Francesco is part of the great tradition of Sienese painting, and his activity as a painter is well documented since the early years. However, he was also an excellent sculptor, or rather foundryman, such is the bravura of his bronzes. His sculptural style at first appears severe and sharp, but in fact it is incisive and energetic. Francesco's sculpture has a painterly quality, seeming almost impressionistic because of the vibrant play of light on the surfaces. Some of the sculptures, particularly *Flagellazione* and *Discordia,* also reveal his architectural interests.

After an early career as a hydraulics engineer in Siena (where he was responsible for the aqueduct, among other works), he moved to the court of Federigo da Montefeltro at Urbino, then a hotbed of artistic and cultural exchange. There he had the opportunity to put his architectural ideas into practice, beginning an illustrious career as a multifaceted architect, which brought him successes unequaled in Italy, and a fame that even his native city did not confer upon him. From the 1470s to the end of the century, Francesco di Giorgio was responsible for the work on the Ducal Palace at Urbino, taking over from Luciano Laurana. He also took on the extensive projects begun by Federigo da Montefeltro for the defense of the ducal territories extending from Marecchia to Cesano, and from the Apennines almost to the sea. (Francesco designed fortifications at Sant'Agata Feltria, San Leo, Sassofeltrio, Tavoleto, Montecerignone, Sassocorvaro, Fossombrone, Pergola, Frontone, Serra Sant'Abbondio, Cagli, Costacciaro and Gubbio, among many other places.) He was also in charge of different types of architectural commissions, such as the local ducal and noble residences at Gubbio, Fossombrone, Cagli, Mercatello and Apecchio; civic and religious buildings such as the cathedral, church and convent of San Bernardino, the convent of Santa Chiara at Urbino, and the episcopal palace at Fossombrone. In addition to the architecture, critics ascribe other works of art of great value to Francesco's time at Urbino, such as medallions and bas-reliefs.

Francesco di Giorgio's experience at Urbino can perhaps be considered as his most intense and productive period of training. According to contemporary chronicles and the artist himself, he completed 136 buildings for Montefeltro in that period. To those buildings we must add the works Francesco did for Giovanni della Rovere, in the territories of Senigallia, Mondavia, Orciano, San Costanzo and Mondolfo, and other towns in the Marche region, from the Palazzo del Governo in Ancona to the Palazzo della Signoria in Iesi. All these accomplishments, for the most part supported by documentary evidence, testify to Francesco di Giorgio's professionalism and the multiplicity of his interests, as well as his capacity to develop a variety of themes in a distinctive personal style.

Francesco di Giorgio's experience in the Marches region was certainly of fundamental importance to his career. Because of it, he was received in other cities and in cultural circles of the highest order in different areas of Italy. His background also enabled him to participate in the cultural life of the major courts, and he was sought after by all the Italian princes. At the Neapolitan court of Aragon, Francesco supervised the modernization of the walls and fortifications. He also played a principal role in the construction of Castel Nuovo, where he successfully experimented with the use of mines for military purposes. Francesco was the designer, as R. Pane has demonstrated, of the Pontano chapel and very probably also of the Church of Santa Catarina in Formiello. Most important of all is Francesco's primary role in the reconstruction of a good part of the fortifications in the Aragon territories in southern Italy, at Ortona, Monte Sant'Angelo, Manfredonia, Brindisi, Otranto, Gallipoli and Taranto, among others. On the other hand, Francesco's Milanese period was significant both for his work on the cathedrals of Milan and Padua, and for his meetings with Bramante and Leonardo.

When Francesco di Giorgio worked for the Orsini family, he continued to add to his fame as an architect, working on fortifications at Campagnano, Avezzano and other Italian cities, such as Lucignano, Lucca, Montepulciano and Florence. The Church of Calcinaio in Cortona, one of Francesco's most prestigious monuments, dates from that period. During his entire career, Francesco maintained an active and valued relationship with his native town. In fact, for many years he was chief engineer of Siena, and master of works of the cathedral there. He died in Siena in 1502.

Francesco's output, though very extensive, was all based on a clear frame of reference and on precise and highly recognizable architectural elements, such as the constant negation of symmetry. His work was also based on the recurrent use of personal architectural types and signatures, such as U-shaped or courtyard plans, spiral staircases, bands and fascias, and stone oculi. These were all conceived as an architectural language as well as personal artistic statements.

As a scientist and inventor, Francesco di Giorgio developed an enormous range and inventory of instruments and machines, which are documented in notes and drawings collected in the various copies of the *Trattati*. These inventions were part of an endless search for solutions to concrete problems, in which the aesthetic and artistic aspects are always clearly visible. The famous *macchine di guerra e di pace,* carved into the bench at the Ducal Palace at Urbino, for instance, clearly demonstrates this confluence of scientific and artistic interests. Francesco the architect and military engineer was the inventor of the mine, according to Biringuccio, but even more important was his essential contribution to the development of ramparts and forward bastions, later called ''all'italiana.'' He developed these defensive systems after extensive theoretical research, partial reformulations of Valturio's work and the great Sienese tradition of Taccola, and a long process of experimentation with transitional examples during his service with military men of the stature of Federigo da Montefeltro, and the court of Aragon, for instance.

Francesco's military architecture consists of a range of often completely original solutions, models and forms, which explore the problems of military defenses through a consideration of various architectural types. This range extends from isolated towers to ravelins; from forts conceived as war machines determined by form, number of defenders and technological apparatus to complex circuits made up of bastions, ramparts, advanced bulwarks and simple towers, capable of every type of defense, from the machicolated to the dug-out. Francesco worked out offensive-defensive schemes, with solutions that are typologically ingenious and complex geometries specific to each instance. These schemes, although sometimes still based on traditional ways of organizing a siege, were radically new, revolutionary in form, responsive in their technology to specific sites and local materials, and planned in accordance with scientific principles and the latest developments in military technology. In the final analysis, Francesco di Giorgio was responsible for an incredible legacy of military solutions and images, which endured for decades and was exported well beyond the boundaries of the Italian peninsula. This legacy became a basic and continuous point of reference for a large number of military architects of the 16th century, who faced the new and compelling problems created by the increasingly massive and widespread use of firearms.

As a theoretician, Francesco di Giorgio must be remembered for his treatises (*I Trattati,* including the first notebook, *Il Codicetto,* at the Vatican Library), and his texts on architecture, engineering and the applied arts, which make no distinction between the major and minor arts. Francesco's writing is characterized by an incredible imagination and technical ability, as well as by a rare touch in his presentation of topics ranging from ancient and modern military and civic machines to firearms; from hydraulic plants to measurements; from architectural subjects of any kind to distribution schemes. All of his theoretical work is imbued with an anthropomorphic vision, to which he relates dimensions, models and formulas, as well as geometries for urban planning, fortifications, buildings and churches, down to the most detailed elements of construction, such as columns and capitals. Francesco di Giorgio's work is not merely a body of theoretical speculation and a dynamic vision of structured architecture, characterized by an exceptional inventiveness. It is also a thorough study of antiquity (Vitruvius *in primis*), compared and reinterpreted through archaeological research and direct observation of the ancient Roman ruins.

—GIANNI VOLPE
Translated from the Italian by Luisa Guglielmotti

FRY, E. Maxwell.

British. Born Edwin Maxwell Fry in Wallasey, Cheshire, England, 2 August 1899. Died in Durham, 1987. Married Ethel Speakman, 1930 (divorced 1941); married the architect Jane Drew, 1942; one daughter. Studied at Liverpool Institute, 1910-17; joined King's Liverpool Regiment, 1917; entered Liverpool School of Architecture, Liverpool University, 1919. Worked for Carrère and Hastings, New York City, 1922; worked for town-planning firm Adams and Thompson, London, 1925-27; chief assistant, Archi tects Department, Southern Railway, London, 1927-30; partner, Adams, Thompson and Fry firm, London, 1930-34; partner, Gropius and Fry, London, 1934-36; major with Royal Engineers during World War II; town planning adviser (with Drew, Denys Lasdun and Lindsey Drake) to the resident minister, West Africa, 1944-46; established Fry, Drew and Partners, London, 1946-73; senior architect for the new capital, Chandigarh, Punjab, India, 1951-54. Cofounded MARS (Modern Architectural Research) Group, 1931; vice-presid ent, Royal Institute of British Architects, 1961-62; Gold Medal, Royal Institute of British Architects, 1964; fellow, Royal Town Planning Institute; associate, 1966, and member, 1972, Royal Academy; honorary fellow, American Institute of Architects, 1973; Commander, Order of the British Empire, 1953.

Chronology of Works
All in England unless noted
† *Work no longer exists*

1930	Ridge End House, Wentworth, Surrey
1933-34	Sassoon House, Peckham, London
1935	Little Winch House, Chipperfield, Hertfordshire
1935-36	Sun House, Hampstead, London
1936	Impington Village College, Cambridgeshire (with Walter Gropius)
1936	Levy House, Chelsea, London (with Gropius)
1936	Wood House, Shipbourne, Kent (with Gropius)
1936-38	Kensal House, Ladbroke Grove, London
1940	Cecil House, Gower Street, London
1946	Adisadel College, Cape Coast, Ghana
1946	Prempeh College, Kumasi, Ghana (with Jane Drew)
1948	Nigerian Broadcasting Company House, Kaduna, Nigeria
1950	Ashanti Secondary School, Kumasi, Ghana (with Drew)
1950	Passfield Estate, Lewisham, London
1951-56	Capital, Chandigarh, India (with Le Corbusier and Drew)
1953	Flats, Bromley Road, Lewisham, London
1953-59	University College, Ibadan, Nigeria (with Drew)
1958	Woman's Teacher Training College, Kano, Nigeria (with Drew)
1958	Teacher Training College, Wudil, Nigeria (with Drew)

1960	Liverpool University College of Engineering and Veterinary Science Building, Liverpool (with Drew)
1960	St. Patrick's School, Lagos, Nigeria
1963	Pilkington Glass Headquarters, St. Helen's, Lancashire
1963	Wates Head Office, Norbury, London
1964	Chelwood House, Gloucester Square, London
1964	Isle of Thorns College, Chelwood Gate, Sussex
1967	Woodsford Square, London
1974	Porchester Terrace, London
1975	Breadspear Crematorium, Northwood, London

Publications

BOOKS BY FRY

The Need for Planning Town and Countryside. Pamphlet. With Joan Gloag. London, 1933.
English Town Hall Architecture. London, 1934.
Fine Building. London, 1944.
Architecture for Children. With Jane B. Drew. London, 1944. Revised edition: *Architecture and the Environment.* London, 1976.
Village Housing in the Tropics. With Jane B. Drew. London, 1947.
Tropical Architecture in the Humid Zone. With Jane B. Drew. London, 1956.
Tropical Architecture in the Dry and Humid Zones. With Jane B. Drew. London, 1964.
The Bauhaus and the Modern Movement. London, 1968.
Art in a Machine Age. London, 1969.
Autobiographical Sketches. London, 1975.

ARTICLES BY FRY

"The Architect and His Time." *Architects' Year Book* No. 3 (1949): 9-12.
"Walter Gropius." *Architectural Review* (March 1955).
"A Discursive Commentary." *Architects' Year Book* No. 6 (1955): 7-10.
"English Architecture from the Thirties." *Architects' Year Book* No. 8 (1957): 53-56.
"F. R. S. Yorke: A Memoir." *Architectural Review* (July 1962).

BOOKS ABOUT FRY

HITCHINS, STEPHEN (ed.): *Fry, Drew, Knight, Creamer: Architecture.* London, 1978.
JACKSON, ANTHONY: *The Politics of Architecture.* 1970.
SERVICE, ALASTAIR: *The Architects of London.* London, 1979.

ARTICLES ABOUT FRY

COOPER, MAURICE: "Max Fry Remembers." *Building Design* (24 January 1975).
COROMINAS, MIGUEL: "Modern Architecture in England." *Arquitectura* (May 1975).
MOFFETT, NOEL: "Nigeria Today." *Royal Institute of British Architects Journal* (June 1977).
MORRIS, A. E. J., and MURPHY, CORNELIUS: "Max Fry." *Building* (31 October 1975).
PRITCHARD, JACK, and MOODY, ALAN: "The Origins of Impington." *Northern Architect* (Sutherland, England, April 1975).

As is the case with great periods of change in history, among the limited number of participants who grasp the significance of the period, there can be distinguished three stances toward that change: the conservatives, the nostalgics and the progressives; the British architectural community fell into these categories between World Wars I and II. E. Maxwell Fry was among the rare breed of the latter in English early modernism, one of the elite avant-garde of the 1920s and 1930s who could grasp the positive social implications of a world in flux. Under the guidance of Charles H. Reilly at the University of Liverpool School of Architecture, Fry was one of the first Englishmen launched into the modern world as architect and city planner. As he remembered the time, "I was cogitating in London . . . it was a lonely time. I dumbly realized I was in a period of transition." Thus Fry and the English architectural world were simultaneously wrenched from the Beaux-Arts and into the 20th century.

Fry had made the pilgrimage in 1929 to the Weissenhof siedlung in Stuttgart, and though he claimed that Ludwig Mies van der Rohe's "great classical proportions and virtues of materials" were his real inspiration, it was with another German architect that Fry was to be associated for a significant period of his life, Walter Gropius. Gropius, former director of the Bauhaus, was brought to England during the 1930s in a humanitarian gesture of the British avant-garde circle of which Fry was a member, in cohorts with architectural patron J. C. Pritchard and critic P. Morton Shand. Speaking of the period of their brief partnership as the firm Gropius and Fry, Fry said, that Gropius tended toward "the ponderous. I gave him my lyricism," but "Gropius grasped the *whole* position, the dilemma of the individual within the wider world of art."

Fry was much younger and less experienced than Gropius when the famous refugee was essentially thrust upon Fry's fledgling firm, and a certain ambivalence was apparent in Fry's feelings toward Gropius in interviews much later in Fry's life. Fry was in every sense a British gentleman, an almost self-effacing man, and Gropius' assertive personality must have been difficult for Fry to accept within his own office; Gropius may even have appropriated clients originally committed to Fry. Though it took a good portion of their three years together to forge a cohesive professional relationship, the problematic partnership of young British avant-garde and internationally renowned German Bauhaus director did eventually become, as the press releases of the day proclaimed the firm, "an innovation of unusual interest."

The overshadowing of Fry by a more dominant figure from the world of international architecture, however, prefigured the difficulty Fry was later to have with Le Corbusier at Chandigarh, India. As Fry told the story, it is a little-known fact that it was he who was first invited by the Indian government to design the city in the Punjab. When told of the added participation of Le Corbusier in the project, Fry recalled replying, "Honor and glory for you, but bitterness for me. He wants only disciples." And correct Fry was in his estimation of the situation, for history remembers only Le Corbusier's public edifices and grand master plan for Chandigarh, as Fry was relegated to the far less impressive task of housing design.

In retrospect, housing was actually an excellent milieu for Fry, for throughout his career, it was there that he excelled, as well as in the related field of school design. His earliest modern works were private homes, the best known being Sun House, Hampstead (1936), but private residences did not show Fry to his best advantage, for he was too much the social thinker rather than the aesthetician to gravitate toward the private commission. His "Fine Building," as he would later title his text on architectural theory, was public housing, an excellent example of which is extant: Kensal House in London (1936) included many amenities, such as a nursery school and clubhouse for the inhabitants. There Fry could put into practice all his beliefs about the betterment of the lower classes. Fry was a member of the old school, the liberal, upper-class benefactor. As he put it, "You can't beat aristocratic patronage. Labor never saved the chimney sweeps!" With the patronage of Lady Sassoon, he had built Sassoon House, Peckham (1934); Kensal House followed, a social demonstration project for the British gas company.

Fry understood and empathized with his proletarian clients, but never with condescension. This is evidenced by his most successful collaboration with Gropius, Impington Village College in rural Cambridgeshire (1936). At Impington, Fry worked not only with Gropius on the designs, but on the social theory with liberal patron J. C. Pritchard and education specialist Henry Morris, as he had before worked with housing specialist Elizabeth Denby at Kensal House. The Impington Village College project represented a significant social experiment in rural regeneration and education for the masses for England in the 1930s, and Gropius and Fry there gave form to ideals. This school, which set the style, program and theory for so many schools that were to follow in the next 30 years in England and America was an experiment in fresh air, light and openness for children that was truly revolutionary in its day. Of Impington, Fry stated that he was striving for "architectural clarity" and endeavoring "to dignify the villagers' education."

The kind of community spirit and sensitivity to human needs that Fry exhibited at Impington later became a part of the architect's works in West Africa, where he developed a new expertise and explored relatively uncharted architectural territory in *Tropical Architecture*. This late work, with his wife, the architect Jane Drew, won him the acclaim that meant most to him in his lifetime, an honorary degree from the University of Nigeria.

For a lifetime of socially committed architecture as founder of MARS (Modern Architectural Research Group) in the 1930s, through his work on the postwar reconstruction of England and the Festival of Britain in the 1950s, Fry was awarded the Commander of the British Empire and recognized with the gold medal of the Royal Institute of British Architects.

When asked near the end of his life by this author, "What does it mean to be modern?" Maxwell Fry replied, "To be modern means you make your own models."

—LESLIE HUMM CORMIER

FUCHS, Bohuslav.

Czechoslovakian. Born in Všechovice, Czechoslovakia, 24 March 1895. Died in Brno, Czechoslovakia, 18 September 1972. Son is the architect Kamil Fuchs. Studied at the Academy of Fine Arts, Prague, 1916-19. Worked in Jan Kotěra office, Prague, 1919-21; collaboration with Josef Štěpánek, Prague, 1921-23; architect, City Building and Planning Department, Brno, 1929; private practice, Brno, 1923-72; professor of town planning and architecture, Technic al University, Brno, 1945; architect for the Institute for the Conservation of Historic Monuments, Brno. Member, Czech Academy of Arts and Sciences, 1940; National Artist of Czechoslovakia Award, 1968; Herder Prize, Vienna, Austria, 1969.

Chronology of Works
All in Czechoslovakia

1920	Masaryk Hut, Šerlich Mount, Orlické Mountains
1921	House and Power Plant, Háj, near Mohelnice (with Josef Štěpánek)
1925	Cemetery Funeral Chapel, Brno
1925	Zeman Café, Brno
1926-27	Villas Avion, Viola and Radun, Luhacovice
1927-28	Hotel Avion, Brno
1927-28	Brno Town Pavilion, Brno Exhibition Ground
1927-28	Bohuslav Fuchs Residence, Brno
1927-28	Triple House, Czechoslovak Werkbund Housing Exhibition, Brno
1928-30	Masaryk Students' Hostel, Brno
1929-30	Elika Machová Hostel, Brno
1929-30	Spa House, Zábrdovice
1929-30	Vesna School and Girls' Home, Brno (with Joseph Polášek)
1929-31	Municipal Baths, Brno
1931	Morava Recreational Home, Tatranská Lomnica
1931	Savings Bank, Tišnov (with Jindřich Kumpošt)
1931	Savings Bank, Trebíc (with Kumpost)
1934	Sokol Gymnasium and Cinema, Jihlava
1935-37	Green Frog Thermal Bath, Trencianske Teplice
1936-37	Provincial Military Command Building, Brno
1938	Rail Post Office, Brno
1940	Vlčina Hotel, Frenštát
1968-72	Department Store, Znojmo (with Kamil Fuchs)

Publications

BOOKS BY FUCHS

Nové zónování: Urbanistická tvorba zivotního prostredí z hlediska sídelního a krajinného. Prague, 1967.

BOOKS ABOUT FUCHS

KALIDOVA, FRANTISEK: *Bohuslav Fuchs: Architectural Works in Brno.* Brno, 1970.
KUBINSZKY, MIHALY: *Bohuslav Fuchs.* Budapest, 1977.
KUDEKKA, ZDENEK: *Bohuslav Fuchs.* Prague, 1966.
ROSSMANN, ZDENEK (compiler): *Architekt Bohuslav Fuchs: 1919-1929.* Basel, 1930.

ARTICLES ABOUT FUCHS

SLAPETA, VLADIMIR (compiler): "Bohuslav Fuchs-Josef Štěpánek, Korespendence." *Zpravy Krajskeho vlastivedneho murzea v Olomovci* (1981).
WALKER, FRANK ARNEIL: "Bohuslav Fuchs." *The Architects' Journal* (7 November 1973).

*

Bohuslav Fuchs was one of the most important architects working in Czechoslovakia between the world wars. He was active mostly in Brno, the country's second-largest city, and many of his works were built there. The conditions in Brno were favorable for a modernist architect. In contrast to Prague, where modern architects often found themselves in conflict with city and preservation officials, the relationship between architects and officials was more productive in Brno, where future members of the Modern Movement had been employed by the city since the early 1920s. Fuchs, who had studied with Jan Kotěra

Bohuslav Fuchs: Hotel Avion, Brno, Czechoslovakia, 1927-28

at the Academy of Fine Arts, was called to Brno in 1923 by the city architect Jindrich Kumpošt. Both men were young— Kumpošt was 29 years old when he became city architect, and Fuchs was 28 upon his arrival in Brno—and both architects were interested in new ways of thinking about architecture and urban planning.

Fuchs' path to modern architecture was typical of the situation in Czechoslovakia at that time. His studies with Kotěra, from 1916 to 1919, were in the tradition of that architect's erstwhile teacher, Otto Wagner. After a brief period in Kotěra's office, Fuchs had to prove himself equal to his contemporaries, who were working in the Bohemian cubist style. His first projects as an independent architect were designs in the decorative cubist style. He was subsequently influenced by Dutch architecture. At first, it was the Amsterdam school and Willem Dudok, and later the group De Stijl that provided the models out of which Fuchs developed his new architectural expression. The Meat Market in Brno (1924) and the Ceremonial Hall of Brno's Central Cemetery (1925), both of brick and with accentuated cubist massing, are representative of Fuchs' ''Dutch'' period.

De Stijl's abstract formal language and Fuchs' familiarity with Le Corbusier's architecture contributed to the Czech architect's increasingly strict decisions in selecting architectonic means. The change in his style became apparent with his Zeman Café in Brno, which was completed in 1926. The whitewashed building with steel-frame windows presents a functional unity both in plan and elevation. Fuchs developed this principle further in the following years: by 1931 he had built more than 20 functionalist projects, including houses, schools, civic buildings, banks and hotels. Notable, for example, was the Hotel Avion in Brno (1927), the result of a problematic assignment. The parcel in the center of the city was very narrow, but deep (8.5 by 34 meters). In addition to the matter of a functional plan, Fuchs was challenged to achieve an acceptable disposition of space. He succeeded in creating a transparent space through the use of skylights, air shafts and mirrored walls.

Exemplary of Fuchs' residential architecture was his own house in Brno (1927-28), where he interpreted Le Corbusier's principles of the studio-house. Also being built at that time where the model houses of the Nový Dum (''New House'') development, a Czech descendant of the Weissenhofsiedlung in Stuttgart, Germany; these houses were part of the Exhibition of Contemporary Culture. In the exhibition area itself, Fuchs built the pavilion of the city of Brno. The high point of Fuchs' work in that period was the complex of the Vesna school and dormitories and the Eliška Machová Home for Girls (Brno, 1929-30), on which Fuchs collaborated with J. Polášek. The use of a cross support system in the Girls' Home block made it possible to replace the closed facade with a grid of differently colored loggias. A new and sculptural appearance had thus been achieved, opening up the facade.

The economic crisis after 1929 slowed down construction, but did not stop it altogether. Besides smaller projects, Fuchs was occupied with questions of urban planning, a kind of work he had first undertaken in the 1920s. With his traffic and communication plans for Brno (1933-35), which he did together with Kumpošt and which he later developed for the entire country, he became the pioneer of regional planning in Czechoslovakia. In the mid-1930s, Fuchs often left behind the strict orthogonal line in his designs, in favor of a curved form. For the thermal baths ''Zelená Žába'' (''green frog''), he curved one part of the building in harmony with the surrounding terrain (Trenčanske Teplice, 1935-36). The militia building in Brno has a segmented design in order to provide an optical terminus to the street.

In the mid-1930s, Fuchs participated in the reorganization of the activities of the Czech CIAM (Congrés Internationaux d'Architecture Moderne) group and in the foundation of a new professional group in Brno. With František Kalivoda, he also published a special issue about CIAM for the journal *Index*. In 1937-38 he participated in the CIAM-East conferences. The German occupation of 1939 put a quick end to that work, as it did to all construction.

After the war, Fuchs' work was honored when he was offered a chair at the Technical University in Brno (1948), but the communist regime, which saw him as a representative of bourgeois functionalism, made it very difficult for Fuchs to work. Besides a few renovations and monuments, Fuchs was not able to build much in the years after the war.

—OTAKAR MÁČEL
Translated from the German by Marijke Rijsberman

FUGA, Ferdinando.

Italian. Born in Florence, Italy, in 1699. Died in 1781, probably in Naples. Trained in sculpture and architecture under Giovanni Battista Foggini, Florence; studied architecture in Rome, 1717-26. Architect of the papal palaces under Clement XII, from 1730. Principal of the Academy of St. Luke, 1752-54.

Chronology of Works
All in Italy
*Approximate dates
† Work no longer exists

1726-27	Palazzo Cellamare, Naples (chapel)
1730-32	Quirinale Palace, Rome (renovation and expansion)
1732-37	Palazzo della Consulta, Rome
1733-37	Santa Maria dell'Orazione e Morte, Rome
1734-35	Casa di corezione feminile in the Capizio di San Michele a Ripa, Rome
1736-37	Quirinale Palace, Rome (carriage house)†
1736-54	Palazzo Corsini, Rome
1741	Santa Cecilia in Trastevere, Rome (atrium)
1741-43	Lateran Triclimium, Rome (restoration)
1741-43	Quirinale Gardens (*Caffehaus*), Rome
1741-43	Santa Maria Maggiore, Rome (facade)
1743-44	Ospedale di Santo Spirito, Rome (expansion)
1742-48	Church of Sant'Apollinare, Rome
1744	San Paolo, Calvi d'Umbria
1745	Palazzo Cenci-Bolognetti, Rome
1751-81	Albergo dei Poveri, Naples (not completed until 1819)
1763	Cemitero dei Tredici, Naples
1768*	Villa Favorita, Resena
1779	Granary, Naples†
1780*	Chiesa dei Gerolomini, Naples (facade)
1780*	Palazzo Caramanico, Naples
1780*	Palazzo Giordano, Naples

Publications

BOOKS ABOUT FUGA

BIANCHI, LIDIA: *Disegni di Ferdinando Fuga e di altri architetti del settecento*. Rome, 1955.

BLUNT, ANTHONY: *Neapolitan Baroque and Rococo Architecture*. London, 1975.

BORSI, FRANCO: *Il Palazzo della Consulta*. Rome, 1975.

HAGER, HELLMUT: *S. Maria dell'Orazione e Morte*. Rome, 1964.

Ferdinando Fuga: Palazzo della Consulta, Rome, Italy, 1732-37

MATTHIAE, GUGLIELMO: *Ferdinando Fuga e la sua opera romana*. Rome, 1952.

MILIZIA, FRANCESCO: *Memorie degli architetti antichi e moderni*. 3d. ed. Parma, Italy. 1781.

PANE, ROBERTO: *Ferdinando Fuga*. Naples, 1956.

PORTOGHESI, PAOLO: *Roma Barocca: The History of an Architectonic Culture*. Cambridge, Massachusetts, 1966.

STRAZZULLO, LUIGI (ed.): *Le lettere di Luigi Vanvitelli*. Galatine, 1976-77.

*

Ferdinando Fuga was the most successful and long-lived of the 18th-century architects whose careers began in Rome and ended in Naples. Like Luigi Vanvitelli, whose career his parallels, Fuga has usually been characterized as a transition figure from the Late Baroque to the neoclassical style that took root toward the end of the century. While a chronological overview of his works shows such a stylistic development, scholars now promote the idea that Fuga's choice of more rigidly geometric designs came less from any theoretical conviction on the part of the architect, and more from his perceptive response to the changing typological demands of civic commissions of his day. As societal needs became more complex in the late 18th century, there was a corresponding development of typologies, or reconsideration of old typologies, to house those needs; Fuga was among those architects involved in creating new civic architectural forms.

Unlike Vanvitelli, Fuga was marginally more successful in Rome, as he was employed during two relatively lengthy pontificates, those of Clement XII Corsini (1730–40) and Benedict XIV Lambertini (1740–58). Fuga's career began brilliantly

when after his architectural training in Florence under the Berniniesque sculptor and architect Giovanni Battista Foggini, and a comprehensive study of architecture in Rome from 1717 to 1726, he was summoned to Rome in 1730 when a fellow Florentine was elected Clement XII. Fuga was given the title of architect of the papal palaces at that time, and he retained that title under Clement's successor, Benedict XIV.

In that capacity, Fuga renovated the Quirinale Palace and built the nearby Palazzo della Consultà. While the facade of the latter displays Fuga's love of scenographic design, his plan for the same palace shows his sensitivity to a then-growing concern for the programmatic workings of a building.

The facade of the Palazzo della Consultà has a commanding location in Rome, and Fuga exploited this in what scholars typify as a *barochetto* design. The two-story facade has 13 bays, the central three of these comprising a slightly projected pavilion articulated with a highly decorated entry on the ground floor and the papal coat of arms on the balconied entablature. Without designing any exaggeratedly Baroque recessions or projections, Fuga gave the facade a liveliness and a subtle coloration by using well-placed rustication and sculptural elements—pediments, volutes, pilasters, balconies. For example, quoining defines the pavilion and the corners of the facade, and its horizontal rhythms are carried over the facade in the rustication around the window panels on the lower level, especially in the keystones which, like their Mannerist predecessors, break through the window pediments. Similarly, on both levels, while pilasters are used to articulate the pavilion and the corner bays, subtle layered indentations create the suggestions of pilasters, and hence order, across the entire facade. Clement XII had commanded Fuga to create a monument using decorative forms applied ''with naturalness and with reason''; Fuga provided this in his subtly scenographic design for the Palazzo della Consultà.

The plan of the palace is also lively, and somewhat less traditional. Fuga placed the main stair centrally within a trapezoidal plan, thereby straightforwardly addressing the problem of movement through the building. Renaissance and Baroque palaces, with a few exceptions—the most noted one being Giovanni Lorenzo Bernini's Palazzo Barberini—relegated the stair to the side of the central courtyard, and for the most part disregarded the importance of circulation patterns. With what could be termed a more French concern for "commodious" movement through a building, Fuga designed the Palazzo della Consultà with a central stair.

At the behest of Benedict XIV, Fuga was involved in a few church renovations. Two such designs that best illustrate the 18th-century concern for preserving monuments of the past— it was about that time that the Pantheon and the Colosseum were renovated—are Santa Maria Maggiore and Sant' Apollinare, both in Rome. In these designs, Fuga displayed an 18th-century sensitivity—if not one appreciated by architectural historians today—for earlier cultures.

In Santa Maria Maggiore, Fuga was commissioned to create a majestic facade while preserving the church's original medieval mosaics. He designed a screen—a two-story loggia in the traditional Baroque nave church form, with a crescendo of plastic forms in the center—that allows for the display of these early monuments. In the interior, probably also by Fuga, the architect retained the Early Christian basilican design, but elaborated on it by inserting majestic and properly classical Ionic columns and friezes in the nave.

The Sant' Apollinare commission was also a renovation of an earlier church, although Fuga was restricted less by the extant structure. This church served the German and Hungarian colleges, which were housed in an attached palace, and Fuga's design facilitated movement between church and palace. As Sant' Apollinare was also a nave church, Fuga embellished the longitudinal axis with six chapels, and added to each of its ends a domed foyer and an elongated apse. In plan, then, the church has three distinct spaces. Fuga's interior decoration upholds the division of spaces with its separating arches and structures allowing for different lighting effects. What unifies the spaces, though, is the structural clarity of Fuga's elements, such as the colossal pilasters, straight entablatures and incised dome ribs. The facade is a traditional basilican church facade articulated with sober pilasters, but there Fuga employed such Baroque elements as the slight bulging toward the center, and the broken pediments.

With the waning architectural commissions in Rome at mid-century, Fuga sought work with the Neapolitan monarch. The architect had established connections as early as 1726 with Naples, and he entered the service of the king in 1728. This was interrupted by Clement XII's summoning him to Rome, but after mid-century, Fuga's architectural career centered in Naples. His major commission of that period, the Albergo dei Poveri, was a state commission for a poorhouse, and it occupied the last 30 years of this life, from 1751 to 1781. This late work exhibits more than any other Fuga's use of neoclassical forms.

The scale of this project was huge in order to accommodate the specified 8,000 needy persons in the Neapolitan state, and its forms were rigidly geometric and symmetrical. The complex was laid out around a centralized church, around which four courtyards and various ranges of buildings embracing those courtyards were arranged. Its facade, like its plan, was simple and geometric, and used sparse classical vocabulary without much articulation. Traditionally, this design is considered to illustrate Fuga's conversion to neoclassicism late in his career.

However, the Albergo dei Poveri should not be considered as exemplary of a deliberate theoretical shift in Fuga's design criteria inspired by a strong conviction for anti-Baroque forms. Rather, Fuga's design there was a practical response to a public commission of the day, and speaks of a new sensibility in developing new typologies to meet new societal needs in the late 18th century.

—SUSAN M. DIXON

FULLER, R. Buckminster.

American. Born Richard Buckminster Fuller in Milton, Massachusetts, 12 July 1895. Died in Los Angeles, California, 1 July 1983. Married Anne Hewlett, 1917; two children. Studied at Harvard University, Cambridge, Massachusetts, 1913-15; United States Naval Academy, Annapolis, Maryland, 1917. Worked as president of Stockdale Building System, Chicago, Illinois, 1922-27; founder and president, 4D Company, Chicago, 1927-32; editor and publisher, *Shelter* magazine, Philadelphia, 1930-32; f ounder, director and chief engineer, Dymaxion Corporation, Bridgeport, Connecticut, 1932-36, and 1940-50; president of Geodesics Inc., Forest Hills, New York, 1949-83; also involved with numerous companies specializing in specialty structures and technology. Professor, Department of Design, Southern Illinois University, Carbondale, Illinois, 1959-75 (and emeritus 1975-83).

Chronology of Works
All in the United States unless noted
† Work no longer exists

1937	Dymaxion Bathroom Unit (patented aluminum casting)
1940	Twin Dymaxion Deployment Units, Butler Manufacturing Company
1950	Mini-Earth Sphere Geoscope, Cornell University, Ithaca, New York
1953	Ford Rotunda dome, River Rouge Plant, Dearborn, Michigan
1954	United States Air Force DEW (Distant Early Warning) Line domes along the Arctic Circle from Scandinavia and Iceland through Canada to Alaska and the Aleutian Islands.
1954	Restaurant dome, Woods Hole, Massachusetts
1958	Two domes for Union Tank Car Company, Baton Rouge, Louisiana (384-foot-diameter dome)
1958	Union Tank Car Company, Wood River, Illinois (354-foot-diameter dome)
1959	United States Pavilion, Sokolniki Park, Moscow, Russia [Soviet Union]
1959	Palais des Sports, Paris, France
1960	Botanical Garden Climatron, St. Louis, Missouri
1966	Placer County administration headquarters, California
1967	United States Pavilion, Expo '67, Montreal, Canada†
1969	Airplane Museum, Schiphol Airport, Amsterdam, Netherlands
1973	Weather radome, Mount Fuji, Tokyo, Japan

R. Buckminster Fuller: United States Pavilion, Expo '67, Montreal, Canada, 1967

Publications

BOOKS BY FULLER

4D Timelock. Chicago, 1928.
Nine Chains to the Moon. New York, 1938.
No More Secondhand God. New York, 1963.
Education Automation. New York, 1963.
Ideas and Integrities. Englewood Cliffs, New Jersey 1963.
World Design Decade Documents. With others. 1965-75.
Operating Manual for Spaceship Earth. New York, 1968.
Utopia of Oblivion. New York, 1969.
I Seem to Be a Verb, with Jerome Agel and Quentin Fiore. New York, 1970.
Buckminster Fuller to Children of Earth. New York, 1972.
Earth Inc. New York, 1973.
Synergetic Explorations in the Geometry of Thinking. With E. J. Applewhite. New York, 1975.
Pass, Not to Stay. New York, 1977.
Synergetics 2: Further Explorations in the Geometry of Thinking. With E. J. Applewhite. New York, 1979.
Buckminster Fuller Sketchbook. Philadelphia 1980.
Critical Path. With Kiyoshi Kuromiya. New York, 1980.
Grunch of Giants. New York, 1983.

BOOKS ABOUT FULLER

APPLEWHITE, E. J.: *Cosmic Fishing: An Account of Writing Synergetics with Buckminster Fuller*. New York, 1978.
HATCH, ALDEN: *Buckminster Fuller: At Home in the Universe*. New York, 1974.

KENNER, HUGH: *Bucky: A Guided Tour of Buckminster Fuller*. New York, 1973.
McHALE, JOHN: *R. Buckminster Fuller*. New York and London, 1962.
OTTO, FREI: *Tensile Structures*. Cambridge, Massachusetts, and London, 1967.
PAWLEY, MARTIN: *Buckminster Fuller*. London, 1990.
ROBERTSON, DONALD W.: *Mind's Eye of Richard Buckminster Fuller*. New York, 1974.
ROSEN, SIDNEY: *Wizard of the Dome—R. Buckminster Fuller, Designer for the Future*. Boston, 1969.
WARD, J.: *The Artifacts of R. Buckminster Fuller*. New York, 1990.

*

R. Buckminster Fuller possessed an unusually creative mind, which could synthesize efficiency and technology into unorthodox solutions to commonplace problems. He worked from the premise that it is preferable to do "more with less" and often derived his designs from paradigms in the natural world.

His primary concern was improving the built environment on a global scale, and he believed that the best way to accomplish this was to design in anticipation of future needs.

There were three key factors that motivated his desire to improve the built environment. The first was the death of his four-year-old daughter, Alexandra, from a series of epidemic diseases whose spread Fuller blamed, in part, on the deficiencies of the environment. The second resulted from Fuller's direct involvement with the construction business, which demonstrated to him the extravagance of craft labor. Third, on the brink of financial ruin in 1927, Fuller isolated himself for two years and resolved to devote his energies to a nonprofit investigation into the optimal use of the earth's limited resources. During that period, Fuller realized that since human nature could not be altered, the betterment of humankind would result only from a transformation of the built environment. He insisted that his subsequent inventions and discoveries were the byproducts, not the objectives, of his research.

Fuller gained recognition in 1927 with his design for the Dymaxion House. "Dymaxion," a combination of dynamic and maximum, was a simplified way of illustrating Fuller's desire to obtain the greatest benefit from the least use of energy. The dymaxion principle was not limited in its application to the production of housing; in 1928, Fuller developed the Dymaxion Three-Wheeled Auto. The Dymaxion House was a prefabricated, transportable "machine for living in" that was suspended from a central mast and contained its own utilities. Designed to employ contemporary developments in building materials, mass production and aircraft technology, the Dymaxion House was in direct contrast to its more aesthetically inclined European counterparts, such as the Villa Savoye (1929-30) by Le Corbusier. Although both Fuller and Le Corbusier can be viewed as looking for an architectural expression of the machine age, Fuller devised a way to place machines at the service of the inhabitants, whereas Le Corbusier was more interested in using machines to achieve his ideal of artistic perfection.

Approximately 20 years after the presentation of the Dymaxion House, Fuller developed one of the most important architectural innovations of the 20th century, the geodesic dome. The concept behind the geodesic dome was based upon Fuller's observation of a directionally oriented, or vectorial, system of forces, providing maximum strength with minimum structure, within the nested tetrahedron lattices of some organic compounds. Using the structure of nesting tetrahedron lattices as a model, Fuller formulated "energetic-synergetic geometry." Fuller combined energetic-synergetic geometry with the dome—the ideal form to him because it provides the greatest amount of space in proportion to the area of the exterior—to produce the geodesic dome: an architectural structure with no limiting dimensions.

The geodesic dome is a clear expression of Fuller's "more with less" criterion. A geodesic dome is a covered hemisphere composed of interlocking tetrahedrons made from standardized, mass-produced parts. The architectural forerunners of the geodesic dome were the crystal palaces and cast-iron buildings of the 19th century. The geodesic dome is a very flexible and versatile structure because its strength is derived from its tensile design rather than from its mass. Because he viewed shelter as a form of environmental management, Fuller wanted to develop the geodesic dome to the point where it could cover entire cities and exert complete climate control over them. To illustrate this idea, in 1950, Fuller presented a hypothetical plan to build a geodesic dome with a two-mile diameter over the midsection of Manhattan.

There were additional, less well-known inventions by Fuller. Among the first, invented during World War I, was a new type of lifesaving equipment. Other inventions, stemming from his desire to improve the built environment, included a hexagonal fourth-dimension dwelling machine; a prefabricated, modular, die-stamped bathroom; and tetrahedronal floating cities. He also devised a new world map that presents all the land masses of the earth without notable distortion. One of his last contributions to the 20th century was the system of Tensegrity Structures: skeletal structures whose tension rods are held together solely by members in compression.

Fuller did not consider himself to be an architect. He disregarded the work of most architects, whom he considered to be "exterior decorators." His appraisal of their work was that it was trivial since it did not seek to fulfill the need for shelter from an engineering viewpoint, and without conforming to the demands of style or tradition. This judgment was passed upon architects throughout history, even his most progressive contemporaries who were working within the mandates of, first, the Bauhaus and, later, the International Style.

Fuller was one of the most ingenious and unselfish thinkers of the 20th century. He devoted most of his professional life to correcting the deficiencies of the built environment on a global scale through the application of his "more with less" principle. It was his specific intention "to make man a success in the universe." He published several books and lectured extensively on the wisdom of his theories. Although his ideas were somewhat radical, Fuller was one of the significant "architects" of this century because he formulated a method of placing technology at the service of humankind.

—LORETTA LORANCE

FURNESS, Frank.

American. Born in Philadelphia, Pennsylvania, 1839. Died in Medea, Pennsylvania, 30 June 1912. Draftsman, Richard M. Hunt office, New York; employed by George D. Hewitt, Philadelphia; partnership with Allan Evans, Philadelphia. Charter member, Philadelphia chapter of the American Institute of Architects, 1868.

Chronology of Works
All in the United States
† Work no longer exists

1866-67	Unitarian Church, Germantown, Pennsylvania†
1868-70	Church of the Holy Apostles, Philadelphia
1869-71	Rodef Shalom Synagogue, Philadelphia†
1871	Northern Savings Fund Society, Philadelphia
1871-75	Pennsylvania Academy of Fine Arts, Philadelphia
1872-73	Philadelphia Warehouse Company, Philadelphia†
1873-75	Guarantee Life and Trust Company, Philadelphia†
1874	Armory for the First Troop, Philadelphia City Cavalry, Philadelphia (addition)†
1874-75	Pennsylvania Institution for the Deaf and Dumb, Philadelphia (addition)
1875-76	Thomas Hockley House, Philadelphia
1875-76	Philadelphia Zoological Gardens Elephant House, Restaurant and Gatehouses, Philadelphia (the Gatehouses remain standing)†
1876	Brazilian Pavilion, Centennial Exhibition, Philadelphia†
1876	Centennial National Bank, Philadelphia
1876-79	Provident Life and Trust Company, Philadelphia†
1877	Kensington National Bank, Philadelphia
1878-79	Church of the Redeemer for Seamen and Their Families, Philadelphia†
1879-80	Library Company of Philadelphia, Philadelphia†
1879-81	William H. Rhawn House (Knowlton), Fox Chase, Pennsylvania
1881	Clement Griscom House ("Dolobran"), Haverford, Pennsylvania
1882	Samuel Shipley House ("Winden"), West Chester, Pennsylvania
1882-84	Penn National Bank, Philadelphia†

Frank Furness: Pennsylvania Academy of Fine Arts, Philadelphia, Pennsylvania, 1871-75

1883-84	National Bank of the Republic, Philadelphia†
1883-86	First Unitarian Church and Parish House, Philadelphia
1884*	Philadelphia and Reading Railroad Depot, Graver's Lane, Chestnut Hill, Pennsylvania
1886	Baltimore and Ohio Railroad Depot, Chester, Pennsylvania†
1886-88	Baltimore and Ohio Passenger Station, Philadelphia†
1887	William Winsor House ("Hedgley"), Ardmore, Pennsylvania
1888-91	Library, University of Pennsylvania, Philadelphia
1889-91	Williamson Free School of Mechanical Trades, Elwyn, Pennsylvania
1891	Chapel, Mount Sinai Cemetery, Frankford, Pennsylvania
1892-93	Pennsylvania Railroad Station at Broad Street, Philadelphia (enlargement and renovation)†
1896-1911	Merion Cricket Club, Haverford, Pennsylvania
1897-98	Philadelphia Saving Fund Society, Philadelphia (addition)

1898	West End Trust Building, Philadelphia†
1900	Commercial Trust Building, Philadelphia
1905-07	Girard Trust Company, Philadelphia (with McKim, Mead and White)

Publications

BOOKS ABOUT FURNESS

MYERS, HYMAN: *The Architect and the Building*. Philadelphia, 1976.

O'GORMAN, JAMES F.; THOMAS, GEORGE E.; and MYERS, HYMAN: *The Architecture of Frank Furness*. Philadelphia, 1973.

THOMAS, GEORGE E.; COHEN, JEFFREY A.; and LEWIS, MICHAEL A.: *Frank Furness: The Complete Works*. New York, 1991.

ARTICLES ABOUT FURNESS

CAMPBELL, WILLIAM: "Frank Furness: An American Pioneer." *Architectural Review* (November 1951).

LEVINE, NEIL A.: "The Idea of Frank Furness' Buildings." M. A. thesis. Yale University, New Haven, Connecticut, 1967.

MASSEY, JAMES C.: "Frank Furness in the 1870s." *Charette* 43 (January 1963): 13-16.

MASSEY, JAMES C.: "Frank Furness in the 1880s." *Charette* 43 (October 1963): 25-29.

MASSEY, JAMES C.: "Frank Furness: The Declining Years, 1890-1912." *Charette* 46 (February 1966): 8-13.

VENTURI, ROBERT: "A Reaction to Complexity and Contradiction in the Work of Furness." *Pennsylvania Academy of the Fine Arts Newsletter* (Spring 1976).

*

Frank Furness forged a powerful American architecture out of the values of commerce, the new materials and manufactured products of the industrial revolution, and the expression of individualism, the great forces that shaped post-Civil War society. Twentieth-century historians, notably Lewis Mumford and Charles Whitaker, have asserted the influence of transcendentalist philosopher Ralph Waldo Emerson and native poet Walt Whitman in giving direction to the nation's arts in the decade before the Civil War, linking them through the writings of Louis Sullivan to Frank Lloyd Wright and American modernism. Rather than learning these authors' ideas solely from books, Furness encountered them directly at his family's table, for Emerson was his father's closest friend, and his brother Horace's literary work brought Whitman into the family circle. It was Emerson's call for an architecture that responded to the American present, that celebrated its industry and its landscape, and Whitman's claim of the infinite variety of the American democracy that catalyzed the insistent individualism that characterized Furness' career.

Furness began his architectural studies in the New York atelier of Richard Morris Hunt, where he encountered modern French classicism—but far enough removed from the power of the actual source to permit the exploration of other ideas, notably English free Gothic and the nascent fusion of Gothic and classic that absorbed both Hunt and the other members of the atelier. These included George B. Post, Henry Van Brunt, Charles Gambrill and William Robert Ware. During the Civil War, Furness served in the Sixth Pennsylvania Cavalry in the Virginia campaign and at Gettysburg, winning the Medal of Honor (the only architect to whom it was awarded); he then reentered Hunt's office, working as principal assistant for two years.

In 1867 he returned to his native Philadelphia, forming a partnership with John Fraser, a well-connected though uninspired designer, and George W. Hewitt, successor to the practice of John Notman. An office coup separated the young partners from Fraser at the moment when they won their first important commission, the design of the new building for the Pennsylvania Academy of the Fine Arts (1871-75). Its French mansarded form overlaid with English polychromy and massed according to the functions within gave evidence of the beginnings of a modern architecture that would address issues of program and design not through the styles of the past, but as the experimental basis of the future.

In those same years the firm built houses, churches and clubs in the vicinity of Rittenhouse Square while perfecting an ever-more-adventurous commercial architecture that transformed narrow bank facades into aggressive billboards. The Northern Savings Fund Society (1871), the Guarantee Life and Trust company (1873, demolished) and the Provident Life and Trust Company (1876, demolished) demonstrated the degree to which conventional forms could be distorted to make one bank in a row stand out. During that period, the young Louis Sullivan worked in Furness' office, an experience he would remember with warmth because of the high standards and guild-like atmosphere.

In 1875 Furness' increasing preoccupation with individual expression led to the dissolution of his partnership with Hewitt. The firm's work before the split could be characterized by the Gothic of Hewitt's apprenticeship with Notman and the abstracted neo-Greek of Furness' training with Hunt, modified by the tonality of the red brick of the Quaker City. Henceforth, though a variety of partners joined the office, it reflected Furness' interests alone. His second decade of practice peripherally explored the Queen Anne, but with a perversely original direction to ornament and ever more toward the direct expression of function given character by striking massing. In the decade of the 1880s alone, Emerson's directive that a building should look like what it is found direct expression in nearly 200 railroad stations, a dozen hospitals, libraries and numerous country houses.

Of these the most remarkable were the Philadelphia Terminal for the Baltimore and Ohio Railroad (1886) and the Library of the University of Pennsylvania (1888-91). The railroad station was complicated by its elevated entrance from the raised Walnut Street Bridge, while the trains were at grade along the banks of the Schuylkill. A heroic iron and glass porte cochere opened into an entrance tower containing a vast, unadorned wrought-and cast-iron stair that led to the main concourse. More extraordinary was the building's color. In an age when white limestone, marble and terra-cotta had changed the hue of American cities, Furness' station was red in its brick, tile, terra-cotta, sandstone and paint. These materials remained his choice well through the 1890s for the Pennsylvania Railroad's Broad Street Station (1892), the Merion Cricket Club (1896) and the Commercial Trust Building (1900).

Only in the 20th century did Furness and his Philadelphia clientele bow to the forces of classicism and the Beaux-Arts. In buildings such as the white-marble, Pantheon-derived Girard Trust Company (1905-7 with McKim, Mead and White), Furness continued to explore the themes which had interested him for two generations—clear and direct form to establish commercial identity, top lighting of the main commercial space for comfort of working and maximum drama, and the reversal of expectation in the shift from a spherical dome on the exterior to a rectangular sail vault within.

Though 20th-century taste diverged strongly from Furness' designs, it can be claimed that his strong adherence to the representation of function, his reliance on brick, and his mannerist love of expressing the ironies of modern life shaped the characteristics of Philadelphia architecture to the present. As Robert Stern pointed out, George Howe's Philadelphia Savings Fund Society shows motifs from Furness' Broad Street Station; more recently the functional expressionism of Louis Kahn's Richards Medical Research Labs at the University of Pennsylvania would be nearly inexplicable without Furness' Library, as would be the strident commercialism of Robert Venturi's "Billding-board" architecture without Furness' banks.

—GEORGE THOMAS

G

GABRIEL, Ange-Jacques.

French. Born in Paris, France, 23 October 1698. Died in Paris, 4 January 1782. Father was Jacques Gabriel, architect to King Louis XV of France. Succeeded his father as architect to the King, 1742; director of the Académie Royale.

Chronology of Works
All in France

1742-75	Palais de Versailles (renovations and additions, including completion of right wing)
1744	Place Royale, Bordeaux (completion of work by Jacques Gabriel)
1746	Château de la Muette, near St. Germain (renovations)
1747-82	Château de Compiègne (renovations and additions; completed posthumously by others)
1748-56	Church, Choisy
1749	Château de Fontainebleau (renovations, additions, and Great Pavilion)
1749	Palais de Versailles (Pavillon Français)
1749-50	Le Butard (hunting Lodge), near Versailles
1750-69	École Militaire, Paris
1751-54	Château de Fontainebleau (additions, renovation of the King's Bedroom and the Council Chamber)
1753	Hermitage, Choisy
1753-54	Palais de Versailles (dining room renovations)
1754	Louvre (additions), Paris
1755	Council Chamber, Versailles
1755	Place Louis XV, Paris (now Place de la Concorde)
1755-74	St. Hubert, near Rambouillet (additions to hunting lodge, including Great Circular Salon)
1761-70	Palais de Versailles (Petit Trianon, Opera House, and Hermitage for the Trianon)
1764	Tuileries, Paris (reconstruction of theater; with Germain Soufflot)
1772-73	Château de Fontainebleau (renovations and additions)
1773	Château de Bellevue (dining room), near Paris

Publications

BOOKS ABOUT GABRIEL

BLUNT, ANTHONY: *Art and Architecture in France 1500-1700.* 4th ed. rev. Harmondsworth, England, 1982.

BOTTINEAU, YVES: *L'art d'Ange-Jacques Gabriel à Fontainebleau 1735-1774.* Paris, 1962.

BOTTINEAU, YVES; GALLET, MICHEL; et al.: *Les Gabriel.* Paris, 1982.

BRAHAM, ALLAN: *The Architecture of the French Enlightenment.* Berkeley, California, and Los Angeles, 1980.

CHAMCHINE, B.: *Le château de Choisy.* Paris, 1910.

CONOLLY, C., and ZERBE, J.: *Les pavillons.* London, 1962.

COURTEAULT, P.: *La Place Royale de Bordeaux.* Paris, 1922.

COX, H. B.: *Ange-Jacques Gabriel (1698-1782).* London, 1926.

DESPIERRES, G.: *Les Gabriel.* Paris, 1895.

ELLING, C.: *Documents inédits concernant les projets de A.-J. Gabriel et N.-H. Jardin pour l'Eglise Frédéric à Copenhague.* Copenhagen, 1931.

ERIKSEN, SVEND: *Early Neo-Classicism in France.* London, 1974.

FELS, EDMOND FRISCH: *Ange-Jacques Gabriel: Premier architecte du roi.* Paris, 1912.

GALLET, MICHEL: *Paris Domestic Architecture of the 18th Century.* London, 1972.

GRANET, SOLANGE: *La Place de la Concorde.* Paris, 1963.

GROMORT, GEORGES: *Jacques-Ange Gabriel.* Paris, 1933.

HAUTECOEUR, LOUIS: *Histoire de l'architecture classique en France.* 7 vols. Paris, 1943-57.

KALNEIN, WEND GRAF, and LEVEY, MICHAEL: *Art and Architecture of the Eighteenth Century in France.* Harmondsworth, England, 1972.

KAUFMANN, EMIL: *Architecture in the Age of Reason: Baroque and Post-Baroque in England, Italy and France.* Cambridge, Massachusetts, 1955.

KIMBALL, FISKE: *The Creation of the Rococo.* Philadelphia, 1943. French edition: *Le style Louis XV.* Paris, 1949.

LAULAN, ROBERT: *L'Ecole Militaire de Paris: Le Monument, 1751-1788.* Paris, 1950.

RACINAIS, HENRY: *Un Versailles inconnu: Les petits appartements des rois Louis XV et Louis XVI au château de Versailles.* Paris, 1950.

TADGELL, CHRISTOPHER: *Ange-Jacques Gabriel.* London, 1978.

*

Ange-Jacques Gabriel was raised in a privileged milieu, surrounded by artists linked to the French court and related to the Mansart family, comprising the country's most illustrious architects. Gabriel himself succeeded his father, after the latter's death in 1742, as *premier architecte du roi* and director of the Académie Royale d'Architecture. These prestigious posts enabled him to influence the reign's architectural production, characterized by refinement coupled with comfort and *convenance*, while being faithful to a distinctly French classical ideal shaped primarily by Claude Perrault and François Mansart in the preceding century, and by Gabriel's contemporary, Jacques-François Blondel. Indeed, the autonomy and validity of France's own architectural tradition was underscored by the refusal of Gabriel's father to allow his son to travel to Italy for artistic studies.

Soon after his succession as *premier architecte*, Gabriel renovated the royal apartments in the châteaux of Versailles, Fontainebleau, Compiègne and Choisy, bringing them in line with contemporary standards of comfort and privacy. Most of Gabriel's work in this genre was sympathetic to the existing Rococo

Ange-Jacques Gabriel: Petit Trianon, Palais de Versailles, Versailles, France, 1761-70

decor. His Pavilion Français at Versailles (1749), however, is distinguished by freestanding Corinthian columns in the interior, marking a reaffirmation of the classical orders as integral elements in interior design.

During the 1750s Gabriel continued his father's work, begun a decade earlier, at the palace of Fontainebleau. For the facade of a new wing, Gabriel abandoned the traditional French reliance on superimposed pilasters, intimately linked to the wall and participating in its function. Instead, he utilized freestanding Doric columns that defiantly asserted their autonomy from the wall, forming an independent architectonic unit. Furthermore, the pyramidal composition favored by his father's generation was substituted by one emphasizing horizontality and breadth. Thus by mid-century, interior and exterior decoration were subject to the same architectonic rigor, characterized by clean, simple and robust forms, highlighted by simpler roof lines, continuous horizontals and a drastic reduction in curvilinear ornament. This was the *noble simplicité* so prized by Gabriel, which called for ornament to be limited to significant architectural members of the building such as orders, and door and window frames.

The emphasis on an architecture of greater authority and solidity coincided with a renewed interest in large public works, made possible by an increase in funds after the Treaty of Aix-la-Chapelle in 1748. Louis XV's building program, and Gabriel's architecture in particular, purposely echoed that of the king's great-grandfather, Louis XIV, satisfying a yearning for similar grandeur and nobility.

Two of Gabriel's major Parisian projects were designed in the 1750s: the Place Louis XV (now Place de la Concorde) and the École Militaire, although the latter was constructed to radically different designs in the 1760s. The Place de la Concorde epitomizes Gabriel's skill at utilizing the best of the French classical tradition while infusing it with new vitality and meaning. The twin palaces to the north of the square, flanking the rue Royale, are characterized by rusticated basements, of Anglo-Palladian derivation, supporting a giant order of single freestanding columns. Although based on the 17th-century Louvre colonnade by Claude Perrault, Gabriel's examples are lighter and more festive in tone, with sculptural decoration limited to the architecturally significant parts of the palaces. The Place is a masterful mélange of urban grandeur and open vistas, bordered on the east and west by the Tuileries and Elysées gardens and on the south by the Seine River. The square was not planned as a confluence of major traffic arteries, as it has become today, but as a broad promenade, isolated from the rest of the urban fabric by balustrades and large, landscaped moats crossed by bridges leading to the royal equestrian statue at the center.

Later in the 1750s, Gabriel undertook work at Versailles, designing an envelope which would have obscured completely the original Louis XIII château known as the Cour de Marbre. This grand scheme was never realized, and Gabriel completed only the palace's west wing, begun by Louis Le Vau in the 1670s, by integrating the various apartments and the early-18th-century royal chapel into a coherent and harmonious whole. As at Fontainebleau, Gabriel rejected the traditional French formula of high mansard roofs and division into distinct pavilions, and instead applied a giant Corinthian order on the homogeneous facade composed of a uniform entablature and regularly framed windows. He utilized half columns to mark the location of the royal apartments and to accent the end facades of the wings.

The following decade was marked by two of Gabriel's best-known works at Versailles, the Petit Trianon and the Opera House. The former was built for Madame de Pompadour and complete in 1764, the year of her death. It is generally considered to be the paradigm of French classical design, elegance and *bon goût*, serving as the model for countless villas around the world. The Petit Trianon is itself based on the Palladian villa characterized by a cubic or rectangular block isolated in landscape, a formula that was already well known in France, as seen in Jules Hardouin-Mansart's 12 independent pavilions at the Château of Marly, dating to 1679. Closer to Gabriel's time, Jean-Francois-Therèse Chalgrin and Mathurin Cherpital, who shared the 1748 Prix de Rome competition designs for a "*pavillion à l'angle d'une terrasse*," had designed their pavilion with the same cubic austerity and regularity, undoubtedly being familiar with similar designs in Colen Campbell's *Vitruvius Britannicus* published in England in 1715.

The novelty of Gabriel's Petit Trainon is in its harmony and diversity. Each facade is a variation on a theme, and yet does not violate the unity of the whole, characterized by simple rectangular lines, large windows and blank wall surfaces. No projecting pediments, statues or garlands disturb the wall surface. Instead, the building's relative sobriety is offset by richly carved moldings, cornices and entablatures, which contribute to the liveliness of the surface through the resultant play of light and shadow. The main facade is composed of pilasters over a rusticated basement, while the rear facade, linked to a formal garden by a large terrace, is articulated by full columns. Half columns adorn the sides. Furthermore, the architectural organization of each facade mirrors the importance of the rooms behind it, reflecting Gabriel's concern for a close rapport between exterior and interior. The latter was widely acclaimed by contemporaries for its emphasis on convenience, commodity and intimacy. The Petit Trianon is a testament to Gabriel's restrained yet refined architecture, heir to the great classical French tradition which preceded him, yet breaking new ground in its architectonic austerity and intimate interiors.

Gabriel's other important Versailles project was the palace's first permanent theater, completed in 1770. Modeled on Palladio's Teatro Olimpico, it was characterized by an elliptical plan with freestanding columns around the gallery, giving the whole an architectonic solidity in keeping with Gabriel's aesthetic. The auditorium was praised by contemporaries for its sumptuous decoration, while its stage machinery was much admired for its advanced technology. Compared with Garmain Soufflot's Lyons theater, designed a decade earlier and characterized by sobriety inside and out, the Versailles Opéra must be seen as conservative and retardataire. While Gabriel utilized sumptuous decoration, Soufflot depended on the theater's mass and volume, and not on ornament, to express architectural power and meaning.

In Paris, Gabriel's outstanding work during the 1760s was the École Militaire, founded in 1751 by Madame de Pompadour as a school for 500 destitute cadets. Both in its function, that of ameliorating the fortunes of poor soldiers, and in its location, on the western edge of the capital, the École Militaire was meant to best Louis XIV's prestigious and neighboring Hôtel des Invalides. Early plans called for a central building to be complemented by a series of pavilions and a chapel on axis at the rear of a central court—an arrangement similar to that of the Invalides and its model, the Escorial. Construction was delayed, however, until the end of the Seven Years War in 1763, and in the meantime, the school had been much reduced in scale due to budgetary constraints. The new plans consisted of a central pavilion flanked only by two smaller wings. Gabriel's design emphasized the juxtaposition of these three simple volumes of varying size. The flanking pavilions were distinguished by their rustication, while the central "château," by contrast, was smooth-faced and was articulated by a colossal Corinthian order. The revised plans also relocated all of the school's varying departments, including the chapel, library, exercise rooms, council chambers and the governor's apartments, in the central building. A similar solution had already been employed by Antoine Le Roy, in his winning 1759 Prix de Rome competition design for a riding academy, in which the chapel was situated in one of the wings, and not axially as was traditional.

The École Militaire is solid, unostentatious architecture, marked by the juxtaposition between the verticality of the colossal orders and the horizontality of the binding cornice and balcony that interrupt the giant Corinthian columns on the court side. Furthermore, solids and voids are juxtaposed as well, as seen in the simple mass of the flanking pavilions and in the plain wall surface of the main building's Champs de Mars facade contrasted to the void caused by the two-story open galleries facing the court. The dynamism and interpenetration of both solids and voids, and verticals and horizontals, foreshadow the concerns of the succeeding generation of neoclassical architects. Yet, the École Militaire is still strongly tied to the classical French tradition in its pyramidal composition and emphasis on the central pavilion, topped by a square dome as in the Louvre Palace.

Gabriel's architecture was one of moderation, synthesis and equilibrium. Originality and novelty were always held in check in favor of an overriding concern for harmony and propriety. Gabriel upheld the theories of his contemporary Jean-François Blondel, who called for a reasoned emulation of the past adapted to a specifically French interpretation, as demonstrated in the classicism of François Mansart. Gabriel's architecture reasserted the eminence of this French classical tradition at a time of great social and philosophical fermentation, marked by the publication of Voltaire's *Le Siècle de Louis XIV* in 1751 and his *Essai sur les Moeurs* five years later. Montesquieu's *Esprit des Lois* and Diderot's *Encyclopédie* were likewise published in 1751. These were the first works to criticize openly the social, religious and political status quo of the ancien régime. By contrast, Gabriel's architecture upheld the values and ideals of his king, whom he served as *premier architecte*. It is not surprising then that Gabriel's mature architecture evolved very little. After his death in 1782, Gabriel's oeuvre was criticized by the so-called revolutionary architects as being retardataire and derivative. It was only at the end of the 19th century that Gabriel's architecture, heir to the French classical tradition of the 17th century, found favor in a society imbued with nationalistic fervor.

—MARC VINCENT

GALILEI, Alessandro.

Italian. Born in Florence, Italy, 25 July 1691. Died in Rome, 21 December 1737. Married Leitia Martin. Studied architecture with Antonio Ferri and Giovanni Battista Foggini. Moved to England, 1714; returned to Florence, 1719. Architect to the Florentine Granducal court, 1720-31. Member, Accademia Etrusca, Cortona.

Alessandro Galilei: San Giovanni in Laterano, Rome, Italy, 1732-36

Chronology of Works
All in Italy unless noted
† Work no longer exists

1718	Garden Temple, All Hallows College, Drumcondra, Dublin, Ireland
1718-19	Castletown, Celbridge, County Kildare, Ireland (built in 1722-1725 by Edward L. Pearce)
1718-19	Kimbolton Castle, Huntingdonshire, England (east Portico)
1718-19	Houses, Cork and Brewer Streets, London, England†
1722-24	Galleria degli stucchi, Palazzo Cerretani, Florence
1724	Madonna del Vivaio, Scarperia (oratorio)
1725-30	Villa Venuti, Cortona (remodeling)
1726-28	Gascoigne Monument, Berwick-in-Elmet, Yorkshire, England†
1729	Santa Maria, Cortona (choir)
1730-31	San Gaggio, Florence (altar)
1731-35	Villa Corsini, Anzio (executed by Nicola Michetti)
1732-35	Corsini Chapel, San Giovanni in Laterano, Rome
1732-36	San Giovanni in Laterano, Rome (facade, east portico and penitenzieria)
1733-35	Palazzo Lateranense, Rome (west facade)
1733-35	San Giovanni dei Fiorentini, Rome (facade)

Publications

BOOKS ABOUT GALILEI

WITTKOWER, RUDOLF: *Art and Architecture in Italy: 1600-1750.* 3rd. ed. Harmondsworth, England, 1980.

ARTICLES ABOUT GALILEI

CARAFFA, FILIPPO: "La Cappella Corsini nella Basilica Lateranense (1731-1799)." *Carmelus*, 21 (1974): 281-338.
CRAIG, MAURICE; GLIN, KNIGHT OF (DESMOND FITZGERALD); and CORNFORTH, JOHN: "Castletown, Co. Kildare." *Country Life* 145 (1969): 722-726, 798-802, 882-885.

GOLZIO, VINCENZIO: "La facciata di S. Giovanni in Laterano e l'architettura del Settecento." In *Miscellanea Bibliothecae Hertzianae*. Munich, 1961.

KIEVAN, ELISABETH: "Galilei in England." *Country Life* 153 (1973): 210-212 .

KIEVAN, ELISABETH: "The Gascoigne Monument by Alessandro Galilei." *Leeds Arts Calendar* 77 (1975): 13-23.

NAVA, ANTONIO: "La storia della chiesa di S. Giovanni dei Fiorentini nei documenti del suo archivio." *Archivio della Reale Deputazione romana di storia patria*, 59 (1936): 337-362.

OSWALD, ARTHUR: "Kimbolton Castle, Huntingdonshire." *Country Life* 144 (1968).

SANPAOLESI, PIERO: "L'Oratorio del Vivaio a Scarperia: Architettura di Alessandro Galilei." In *Atti del VIII. congresso nazionale di storia dell'architettura*. Rome, 1956.

TOESCA, I.: "Alessandro Galilei in Inghilterra." *English Miscellany, III*. Rome, 1952.

TOESCA, ILARIA: "Un parere di Alessandro Galilei." *Paragone* 4, No. 39 (1953): 53-55.

ZANGHERI, LUIGI: "Apparti di Alessandro Galilei alla corte Medicea." *Antichità viva* 14, No. 1 (1975): 32-36.

*

Alessandro Galilei was one of the first Italian 18th-century architects to choose with deliberate theoretical intent to build in the neoclassical style. His architecture and his extant writings show his preference for rectilinear forms whose compositions are governed by Vitruvian principles, and complementarily, his aversion to the curvilinear and excessively ornamented style of the Baroque. Superficially, Galilei's taste seems unprecedented, for he studied architecture with two leading Florentine Baroque artists, Antonio Ferri and Giovanni Battista Foggini, both designers working in the style of Giovanni Lorenzo Bernini. Galilei's training, though, was tempered by his study of the bold geometricity of Florentine cinquecento architecture—for example, that of Michelangelo—and later by an increased interest in reevaluating and embracing the Vitruvian belief that architecture is a science, and should exhibit qualities of proportion, symmetry and functionality.

The most famous of his works and the one most exemplary of his neoclassicism is the facade for the Church of San Giovanni in Laterano in Rome (1732-36). Galilei was summoned to Rome from Florence in 1731 after the election of a fellow Florentine to pope. Clement XII Corsini patronized many Tuscan artists and architects in a conscious program to revitalize the arts in Italy, beginning in Rome. One of the major commissions given during his office was the facade for the Lateran church. Galilei received that commission after his design was chosen as best among 23 submitted in a heated competition whose entrants included such competent architects as Luigi Vanvitelli. The decision in favor of Galilei's relatively staid composition was not immediately accepted by the Accademia di San Luca, the institution that was arbiter of architectural taste in Rome. The academicians on the whole preferred the more Baroque designs of submitters such as Vanvitelli. Antoine Deriset, the first Frenchman to have served as teacher at the Accademia, was the spokesperson for the competition's judges. Deriset defended the jury's decision and Galilei's designs, an action that anticipated neoclassicism in Italy.

Stylistically, the facade of San Giovanni in Laterano clearly articulates its structural elements at the expense of applied ornament. It is a five-bay two-story building, with a central pavilion. The bays of open loggias are separated by impressive single double-height Corinthian pilasters, the facade terminating with a doubling of those pilasters. All pilasters are set upon high pedestals. The central pavilion protrudes slightly from the building—this was Galilei's concession to the contemporary taste for the Roman Baroque—and is articulated by double engaged columns. These columns are also raised on high pedestals, and are crowned by a rigidly classical pediment. This pediment interrupts a strongly profiled entablature, which is topped by a balustrade on which stand statues of saints and church fathers. With the exception of small passages of structural confusion, for example, where the central bay columns are superimposed on the giant pilasters, the facade of San Giovanni in Laterano exhibits the clear structural integrity that is termed neoclassical.

Galilei's taste was informed by a new attitude toward history prevalent in 18th-century Italy, especially in Florence. Such an attitude called for a reevaluation of the historical text, and as a corollary, the looking anew at artifacts for a more truthful gauge of the past. In such a vein, many scholars examined and critiqued passages from Vitruvius' text in light of extant architectural monuments. Such exercises were carried out by members of the Accademia Etrusca in Cortona. The Venuti brothers, founders of the academy, were known to Galilei, as they commissioned him to renovate their villa from 1725 to 1730; Galilei himself became a member of this institution. His reliance on Vitruvius for his aesthetic is apparent in both his buildings and his texts.

Another characteristic of research undertaken by the academy was its inclusion of art and objects from many eras, including, of course, the Etruscan, but also the medieval, Early Renaissance and Baroque periods. Many scholars in Tuscany and elsewhere in Italy saw history as a continuous process, and knowledge of the history of art and architecture of all ages was useful in instituting thoughtful artistic reforms. Giovanni Gaetano Bottari, a Florentine at the papal court in Rome, wrote texts which critiqued past architecture in order to facilitate such reforms; he called for a renewed truthfulness in structure, and preferred rectilinear forms. Galilei abided by Bottari's use of history in his own critique of architecture of the past in his reports on the many restorations he undertook while he was architect at the Florentine grandducal court from 1720 to 1731, and he also built in a style congruous with that called for by Bottari. (Curiously, though, Bottari did not approve of Galilei's design for the Lateran facade.)

Galilei began his architectural career in England, but returned to Florence just before the neo-Palladian movement flourished in England. Attempts to link him with the development of neoclassical tastes in England are inconclusive so far. Leaving immediately after his training in Florence, Galilei went to England in 1714 in the company of John Molesworth to continue his architectural education, and he remained there to design some churches, palaces and country houses, only a few of which were executed. While in England, Galilei moved in the circles of those with an interest in neoclassical forms. For example, he was connected with Lord Burlington, the promoter of the neo-Palladian movement, via his business association with Nicholas Dubois, the translator of Giacomo Leoni's edition of Andrea Palladio's *The Four Books of Architecture,* but their association ended before Burlington embraced neo-Palladianism. Galilei also knew Lord Shaftesbury, friend of his patron Molesworth, who at the time adamantly advocated a revival of Greek art. The neoclassical taste did not take root until after Galilei had left England, after 1718, and his involvement, if any, in the movement there was circumstantial. However, in Italy, where his architectural commissions were few, he deserves the reputation as a harbinger of the neoclassical style.

—SUSAN M. DIXON

GALLIER, James, Sr.

American. Born in Ravensdale, Ireland, 24 July 1798. Died in shipwreck off Cape Hatteras, 16 May 1868. Attended Dublin's Art School; studied building with his father. Worked in architectural and building offices, London, 1822-32; left Europe for America, worked in office of Ithiel Town and Andrew Jackson Davis, New York City, 1832; partner with Charles and James Dakin, New Orleans, 1835; opened own office, New Orleans, 1840.

Chronology of Works
All in the United States
† Work no longer exists

1835	Barton Academy, Mobile, Alabama
1835	Christ Church, New Orleans, Louisiana†
1835	Government Street Presbyterian Church, Mobile, Alabama
1835	Merchant's Exchange, New Orleans, Louisiana†
1835-36	Arcade Baths, New Orleans†

1835-36	William Nott House, New Orleans
1835-36	St. Charles Hotel, New Orleans†
1838	Thomas Hale House, New Orleans†
1838	Paloc and Dufour Houses, New Orleans
1839-40	St. Patrick's Church, New Orleans (completion)
1843	Commercial Exchange, New Orleans
1844	W. N. Mercer House (Boston Club), New Orleans
1845-50	City Hall (Gallier Hall), New Orleans

Publications

BOOKS BY GALLIER

The American Builder's General Price Book and Estimator. New York, 1833.
Autobiography of James Gallier, Architect. Paris, 1864.

BOOKS ABOUT GALLIER

CHRISTOVICH, MARY LOUISE (ed.): *New Orleans Architecture.* Gretna, Louisiana, 1972.

James Gallier, Sr.: Gallier Hall, New Orleans, Louisiana, 1845-50

HAMLIN, TALBOT: *Greek Revival Architecture in America.* New York, 1944.

HUBER, LEONARD V.: *New Orleans: A Pictorial History.* New York, 1971.

SCULLY, ARTHUR, JR.: *James Dakin, Architect: His Career in New York and the South.* Baton Rouge, Louisiana, 1973.

WILSON, SAMUEL, JR., and LEMANN, BERNARD: *The Lower Garden District.* Vol 1 of *New Orleans Architecture.* Gretna, Louisiana, 1971.

*

James Gallier, Sr., was one of the most prominent architects of the Greek Revival period in America. Gallier, together with James and Charles Dakin, was largely responsible for the dissemination of the Greek Revival style in New Orleans, where he spent the majority of his career. At a time when there was little formal distinction between the architect and the builder, Gallier's designs, which reflected a knowledgeable yet imaginative approach to the art of antiquity, earned him a lasting professional reputation.

Gallier, born in Ireland, initially learned the building trade from his father, who was a builder and an engineer. Although he was largely a student of experience, Gallier studied architectural drawing for a brief period at the School of Fine Arts in Dublin. In 1816 he worked for several months in Manchester and Liverpool, England, settling eventually in London in 1822. While in London, Gallier supervised construction of a prison for the architect William Wilkins, and the building of a group of houses for the architect John Deering. Although he began to receive small, independent commissions in London, he felt that the opportunity for success was greater in the United States.

He sailed for New York, arriving in April of 1832. In New York, Gallier became associated with James H. Dakin, a partner in the prominent firm of Town, Davis and Dakin. In 1833 he collaborated with Minard Lafever, best known for architectural handbooks such as *The Modern Builder's Guide* (1833), to produce numerous drawings for builders. Finding his work to be routine and seeking to establish his name, Gallier authored a book titled *American Builder's General Price Book and Estimator* (1833), which he modeled on contemporary English guides. He also developed a series of lectures on architectural history, which he delivered to the public. In hopes of obtaining more ambitious projects in the South, Gallier left New York in the fall of 1834 with his new partner, Charles B. Dakin, the brother of James Dakin.

Gallier and Dakin achieved almost immediate success in New Orleans, as the number of professional architects in America, and especially in the South, was limited. Within their first year of practice, they received commissions to design the St. Charles Hotel (1835-37), the Merchants Exchange (1835) and Christ Church (1835). The St. Charles Hotel was constructed on a grand scale, and featured a rectangular block with central pediment, capped by a large dome. Although the building burned in 1851, it was rebuilt according to the original design, with the exception of the dome, which was eliminated. The significance of this building as it was originally constructed lay in its similarity in scale and detail to Isaiah Rogers' Tremont House in Boston (1828-29), underscoring the relative uniformity of the Greek Revival style throughout various regions of the country. Although the partnership of Gallier and Dakin was dissolved in 1835, following the arrival in New Orleans of Dakin's brother James, Gallier continued to receive important commissions, nearly all of which he executed in the Greek Revival style.

A design for St. Patrick's Church, originally awarded to Dakin and Dakin in 1837, but completed by Gallier in 1839-40, makes plain Gallier's devotion to the Greek Revival style. When Gallier took charge of the project, following a dispute between the Dakins and church administrators, he retained the basic plan and Gothic outline of the church as envisioned by the Dakin brothers, but his alteration of the exterior details—reduction in the number of windows and virtual elimination of pinnacles—revealed his strong dependence on simplified form, a hallmark of the Greek Revival style.

One of Gallier's most prominent works was a house designed for Dr. W. Newton Mercer on Canal Street in New Orleans. Begun in 1844, the three-story, three-bay house was rectangular in plan with a hexagonal side bay. Details such as the recessed entry, framed by engaged Ionic columns and pilasters, and pedimented lintels were classically inspired and bore a strong resemblance to those found on contemporary New York City row houses, such as those designed by Lafever. Similarities in the domestic work of Gallier and Lafever, long after their separation in 1834, have been noted by Greek Revival scholars such as Talbot Hamlin.

The design of City Hall in New Orleans was one of Gallier's final projects, executed in 1845-50 before he relinquished his business to his son. Featuring an Ionic hexastyle portico and sculpted pediment, the New Orleans City Hall rivals the works of Robert Mills and William Strickland, long considered the preeminent Greek Revival architects. Following the construction of a new City Hall in the 1950s, the building was renamed Gallier Hall, a permanent reminder of the architect's significance within the city.

Shortly before his death in 1866, Gallier published his *Autobiography of James Gallier Architect* (1864). An important contribution to the understanding of the civic development of 19th-century New Orleans, the book also chronicles the practice of architecture during a critical period in the history of the field, illuminating the difficulty of establishing an architectural career at a time when there was no prescribed course of study and little professional support. While his built works are lasting monuments to the Greek Revival era in America, his autobiography is an equally compelling legacy.

—MEREDITH ARMS

GANDON, James.

Irish. Born in London, England, February 1742. Died at Canonbrook, Lucan, near Dublin, Ireland, 24 December 1823. Studied at Shipley's Drawing Academy, London; apprenticed to William Chambers, 1758, then studied at the Royal Academy Schools. Began architectural practice, 1765; workfi0in, 1781-97. Exhibited at the Society of Artists, 1765-73; fellow of the Society of Artists, 1771; won the first gold medal for architecture from the Royal Academy Schools, 1769; honorary member of the A rchitects Club, London, 1791; charter member of the Royal Irish Academy.

Chronology of Works
All in Ireland unless noted
* Approximate dates
† Work no longer exists

1768	Bishop's Palace, Ferns, County Carlow (alterations)
1770*	Mill House, Eastbourne, Sussex, England†
1770-72	County Hall, Nottingham, England

James Gandon: Four Courts, Dublin, Ireland, 1786-1802

1772	Theater, Wynnstay, Denbighshire, England†
1780-91	Custom House, Dublin
1783*	Rockingham Library, Charlemont House, Rutland Square, Dublin†
1784	Rotunda Assembly Rooms, Dublin (additions)
1784-87	Courthouse and Jail, Waterford†
1785	Coolbanagher Church and Mausoleum, County Leix
1785-89	East portico and screen wall, House of Lords, Parliament House (now Bank of Ireland), Dublin
1786	Military Infirmary, Phoenix Park, Dublin
1786-1802	Four Courts, Dublin
1790*	Abbeville, near Malahide, County Dublin (alterations and additions)
1790*	William Ashford House, Sandymount, County Dublin
1790-1800*	Emo Park, County Leix (begun)
1790-93*	Houses, Beresford Place, Dublin
1790-95*	Office court and gateway, Carriglas, County Longford
1791-94	Carlisle Bridge, Dublin†
1794	Emsworth, County Dublin
1800	King's Inns, Dublin (begun)

Publications

BOOKS BY GANDON

Six Designs of Frizes. 1767.
A Collection of Antique and Modern Ornaments. 1778.
A Collection of Frizes, Capitals and Grotesque Ornaments. 1778.

BOOKS ABOUT GANDON

CRAIG, MAURICE: *Dublin 1660-1860.* Dublin, 1980.
GANDON, JAMES, JR., and MULVANY, THOMAS (eds.): *The Life of James Gandon.* Dublin, 1846. New edition by Maruice Craig, London, 1969. McPARLAND, EDWARD: *James Gandon: Vitruvius Hibernicus.* New Haven, Connecticut, and London, 1985.

ARTICLES ABOUT GANDON

CRAIG, MAURICE: "Burlington, Adam and Gandon." *Journal of the Warburg and Courtauld Institutes* 17 (1954): 381-382.
CURRAN, CONSTANTINE: "Cooley Gandon and the Four Courts." *Journal of the Royal Society of Antiquaries of Ireland* 79 (1949): 20-25.
CURRAN, CONSTANTINE: "The Architecture of the Bank of Ireland." In FREDERICK G. HALL: *The Bank of Ireland 1783-1946.* Dublin, 1949.
MAXWELL, CONSTANTIA: "James Gandon, Architect of Georgian Dublin." *Country Life* (22 October 1948).
McPARLAND, EDWARD: "James Gandon and the Royal Exchange Competition, 1768-69." *Journal of the Royal Society of Antiquaries of Ireland* 102 (1972).
McPARLAND, EDWARD: "Emo Court, Co. Leix." *Country Life* 155 (1974): 1274-1277, 1346-1349.
McPARLAND, EDWARD: "The Early History of James Gandon's Four Courts." *Burlington Magazine* 122 (1980): 727-735.

James Gandon was apprenticed in 1758 to the great William Chambers. While with Chambers, Gandon imbibed the master's fluency in a mixture of English Palladianism and French neoclassicism.

Gandon set up his own practice in about 1765, and, with the Irishman John Wolfe (died 1793), began the publication of a continuation of Colen Campbell's *Vitruvius Britannicus,* Volume IV of which appeared in 1767, and Volume V in 1771. The later volume contained details of Gandon's designs for County Hall (begun 1770) in Nottingham (the simplified Doric facade of which suggests a French influence), but the books provided a record of contemporary English architecture rather than an overt advertisement for Gandon's own work. Publications seem to have occupied him in the 1760s and 1770s, for his *Six Designs for Frizes* came out in 1767, followed by *A Collection of Antique and Modern Ornaments* and *A Collection of Frizes Capitals and Grotesque Ornaments,* both dated 1778. Gandon was prominent as an exhibitor at the Society of Artists from 1765 to 1773, and at the Royal Academy from 1774 to 1780. Indeed, he studied at the Royal Academy schools from 1769, and won the first Gold Medal there for architecture. He also won second premium in a competition to design a new Royal Exchange for Dublin, and collected the first premium for his proposals for a new lunatic asylum for London.

The Dublin competition was of great significance, for it marked the beginnings of Gandon's connections with the capital of Ireland. Apart from winning second prize in the Royal Exchange competition, he carried out alterations at the Bishop's Palace at Ferns in County Carlow, and his first designs to be exhibited at the Royal Academy were for a villa for a "gentleman in Ireland." Through Chambers, Gandon met Lord Charlemont, the great patron of the arts in Ireland, and later he became acquainted with Lord Carlow (later the first earl of Portarlington) and with the Rt. Hon. John Beresford, who was to become chief commissioner of the Irish Revenue.

In 1781 Gandon went to Dublin to supervise the building of new docks, stores and the Custom House (which he had designed in 1780 at the behest of Lord Carlow). Gandon was successful in overcoming the immense difficulties posed by the waterlogged site, by local opposition to him personally, and by the lack of skilled labor: his great building was completed in 1791. Gandon's favorite architectural motifs were the triumphal arch and paired detached columns set into a recess in a plain wall: both motifs look back to antiquity, and the latter device is found very successfully treated in the north and south faces of the corner pavilions of the Custom House. Gandon's entablature runs over the fronts of these pavilions, without breaks, but the bases of the Doric columns project between the slabs of plain wall. The Custom House combines Palladian motifs with a severe antique gravity derived from Chambers and from French exemplars, while the cupola of the building is indebted to Christopher Wren's Greenwich Hospital. This gives a clue to Gandon's greatness, for he rejected the refined elegance of the Adam style, saw French neoclassicism as a way of reinvigorating the English Palladian tradition, and incorporated a spirited charge of powerful Baroque forms into his design: thus his Custom House is very much more monumental than is Chambers' Somerset House in London. Unfortunately, the Custom House has lost its chimneys and statues, which helped by their vertical emphases to create a transition between the scale of the monumental and serene river front and the Baroque cupola that rises behind; this is because the damage during the civil war in the 1920s was not entirely made good, and the Wrennish cupola looks rather sudden as it stands today. The end pavilions, however, owe a considerable debt to Chambers, and, with their French neoclassical vases, recall Chambers' Casino at Marino,

Clontarf. The vigorous sculpture on the building was by Edward Smyth.

Gandon added to Edward Lovett Pearce's Parliament House in Dublin the Corinthian east portico to the House of Lords and the curved screen-wall of 1785-89, as well as making designs for the western Ionic portico to the House of Commons, built 1790-92. Gandon's response to Pearce's masterpiece was nothing short of brilliant, and it is not often that the work of a late-18th-century architect enhances that of a much earlier architect with such sympathy, sensitivity and understanding.

Gandon's third great building in Dublin is the Four Courts, also sited on the north bank of the Liffey, upstream from the Custom House. It was begun in 1786, and incorporates part of a quadrangle designed in 1776-84 by Thomas Cooley (1740-84). The wonderful clarity of Gandon's plan disposes the four Courts of Law at angles of 45 degrees around the noble central rotunda (which owes not a little to the Pantheon in Rome), over which rises the grave circular room (originally intended as a library) surrounded by a peristyle of the Corinthian order. The central block has a prostyle hexastyle pedimented Corinthian portico in the center (with bays on either side that owe a debt to Wren), and the two courtyards are enclosed on the river front by arcaded screens, in the centers of which are triumphal arches: there is antique Roman grandeur indeed in the arches, the temple portico and the great rotunda, while the elements of the plan also have an antique clarity in the geometry. Again, this marvelous building suffered very severely during the civil war, and in its burning, priceless records were lost.

Gandon had actually published two versions of the Nottingham County Hall in *Vitruvius Britannicus,* and the one not built in Nottingham was resurrected as Waterford Court House (1784-86). It consisted of a large top-lit hall off which were two court rooms. The architectural character was grave and severe, incorporating Tuscan columns set between plain walls, with suggestions of the triumphal-arch theme between the colonnaded openings to the court rooms.

Of Gandon's oeuvre, not much survives intact. His embellishment of the Rotunda Assembly Rooms in Dublin (1784), the design of Coolbanagher Church and Mausoleum in County Leix for the first earl of Portarlington (1785), and the impressive stable blocks at Carriglas, County Longford (1790-95), deserve mention. Gandon graced Ireland with architecture of real distinction, and his Custom House and Four Courts rank high among British civic buildings of the 18th century.

—JAMES STEVENS CURL

GARNIER, Charles.

French. Born in France, 1825. Died in 1898. Studied at the École des Beaux Arts; Grand Prix de Rome, 1848. Traveled in the Mediterranean until 1853; returned to Paris and was given the commission for the new Opéra, 1860. Inspecteur général des bâtiments civils, 1877-96. Elected to the Institut de France, 1874; Gold Medal, Royal Institute of British Architects, 1886.

Chronology of Works
All in France unless noted

1860-75	Opéra, Paris
1872	Villa Garnier, Borgidhera, Italy
1878	Cercle de la Librairie, Paris
1878-81	Casino, Monte Carlo, Monaco

Charles Garnier: Opéra, Paris, France, 1860-75

Publications

BOOKS BY GARNIER

Histoire de l'habitation humaine.
Michel-Ange, architecte.
Monographie de l'Observatoire de Nice.
Restauration des tombeaux des rois Angevins en Italie.
A travers les Arts. Paris, 1869.
Le théâtre. Paris, 1871.
Le nouvel Opéra de Paris. 4 vols. Paris, 1878-81.

BOOKS ABOUT GARNIER

JOURDAIN, FRANTZ: *Constructions élevées au Champ de Mars par M. Ch. Garnier.* Paris, 1892.
MIDDLETON, ROBIN D., and WATKIN, DAVID: *Neo-Classical and Nineteenth Century Architecture.* New York, 1980.
STEINHAUSER, MONIKA: *Die Architektur der Pariser Oper.* Munich, 1969.

ARTICLES ABOUT GARNIER

COOLIDGE, J. R.: "Notes upon the Architectural Work of C. Garnier." *Architectural Review* (1898).
GARNIER, LOUISE: "Charles Garnier par Mme Garnier." *Architecture* 38 (1925): 377-390.
LAVEZZARI, E.: "Le nouvel Opéra." *Revue générale de l'architecture* 32 (1875): 30-33.
REVEL, J. F.: "Charles Garnier, dernier fils de la Renaissance." *Oeuil* 99 (1963).

SÉDILLE, PAUL: "Charles Garnier." *Gazette des beaux-arts* 20 (1898): 341-346.

*

Although of humble Parisian origins, Charles Garnier lived to see himself acclaimed as the architect of the most celebrated building of its day, the Opéra, inaugurated in 1875. His education and subsequent career epitomize the French Beaux-Arts system, for which Garnier was perhaps the greatest apologist. In 1842 Garnier was admitted to the École des Beaux-Arts in Paris in the atelier of a conservative neoclassical architect, Louis Hippolyte Lebas, best known for the church of Notre-Dame-de-Lorette. While there, Garnier was a draftsman for Eugène-Emmanuel Viollet-le-Duc, who at the time was completing the restoration of the basilica of Vézelay and was preparing to work on Notre-Dame in Paris. Garnier subsequently rebelled against Viollet-le-Duc's too strict rationalist/functionalist aesthetic.

Four years after his admission to the École, Garnier won its most distinguished honor, the Grand Prix de Rome, which allowed him, at the young age of 23, to travel to Italy to pursue his architectural studies. While there, he visited Venice, Siena, Pisa, Rome and Florence, and also traveled further east, to Greece and Turkey. Garnier's trip to the eastern Mediterranean was to be of critical importance in the development of his architecture, instilling in him an admiration, not for classical architecture as represented in the Parthenon, but for the Gothic-Byzantine mélange which captivated him in Sicily. This emotionally charged architecture, laden with polychromy and intricate mosaic decoration, struck a responsive chord in Garnier. His reconstitution of the Temple of Aphaia at Aegina, which

Garnier prepared for the Académie, was instructive, not for the purity of its archaic classicism, but for its irrefutable proof of polychromy in ancient architecture. Garnier was to remain faithful to this particular brand of Mediterranean architecture, and would translate it to great advantage in his mature Parisian work.

In 1854 Garnier returned to a Paris that was ebullient about Baron Georges-Eugène Haussmann's gigantic building campaign, which had just begun, and which would afford Garnier the opportunity to build a new opera house for the capital. In 1860 he was named architect of the fifth and sixth *arrondissements,* responsible for the architectural alignments of the new boulevards being pierced by Haussmann. In contrast to the latter's insistence on regular and unified street facades, Garnier's view of the city was a picturesque and animated one, shaped by his Italian experience. This interpretation would manifest itself in his Opéra, characterized by animated volumes and dazzling polychromy.

It was also in 1860 that the government announced a competition for the construction of a new opera house to replace the cramped 40-year-old opera house on rue Le Peletier. Out of the 171 projects submitted, Garnier placed fifth and was subsequently awarded the commission of his architectural career—one that would also mark its apogee. Garnier's design was distinguished by its bold volumetric composition and its plan, both of which revolutionized theater architecture. The theater's hallmark was that the interior disposition of spaces, the Grand Foyer, the auditorium and the stage were expressed on the exterior, thereby abandoning the traditional Palladian formula, which called for an undifferentiated rectangular box under a single roof. The Opéra's plan was clear and rational, and eminently functional in the ease in which spectators of varying social backgrounds were funneled to their respective seats.

For all its planning and sensitive massing, it was the Opéra's sumptuous decor, and especially its grand staircase, that at once captured critical acclaim. Its immense scale, which dwarfed the auditorium, and its rich decoration highlighted by polychromed marble, candelabras, and surrounding arcaded galleries and hallways, dazzled contemporaries accustomed to more restrained decoration. Ornamental richness was for Garnier a necessary ingredient, imparting emotional and visual depth to an architecture which had theretofore been subsumed by a cold, austere neoclassicism or by the functionalist aesthetic of Viollet-le-Duc.

The Opéra's exterior reflects Garnier's skillful blend of traditional architecture formulas and daring invention. Although loosely modeled on Claude Perrault's Louvre colonnade, that hallowed masterpiece of French classicism, Garnier's colonnade is lighter and more vibrant because of its constant interplay of light and shadow produced by the insertion of small colonnettes, by projecting and receding surfaces, and by vivid polychromy. It was Garnier's innovative manipulation of traditional French architecture that captured the popular imagination in a manner unequaled in the 19th century.

Garnier's architecture was a mixture of rationalism enlivened with emotion. He was adamant in his denunciation of the rationalist/utilitarian theories of Viollet-le-Duc, which devalued the role of the architect as artist, and emphasized engineering, technique and function. Garnier saw himself as heir to the great artist-architect tradition, as exemplified by Giovanni Lorenzo Bernini and Filippo Brunelleschi, which called for the creation of a personal vocabulary while still respecting a common classical language. The École des Beaux-Arts had taught Garnier such a system of architecture based on proven principles tested by time, yet open to improvement as befit contemporary demands and problems.

Garnier not only reacted against Viollet-le-Duc's rationalism but also against the analagous utilization of steel in architecture. Garnier believed that steel was a means, and not a principal, of construction because it was wanting in plasticity. Steel reduced two great architectural principles, the point of support and the span, to their bare minimum. Although he accepted the use of steel in fulfilling certain constructional requirements, such as in Henri Labrouste's Ste. Geneviève (1838-50) and Nationale (1854-75) libraries, Victor Baltard's Les Halles (1845-70) or Jacques Ignace Hittorff's Gare du Nord (1858-66), Garnier believed that metallic architecture, like its wood or masonry counterpart, had to partake in the prevalent architectural style or language. Garnier denied steel its inherent structural capabilities, which would eventually revolutionize building in the succeeding decades.

Garnier remained faithful to the Beaux-Arts system and aesthetic throughout his life. His opera house heralded a great flourish of Baroque Beaux-Arts academicism, whose robust yet florid classicism appealed to the Third Republic's building program consisting of official monuments such as city halls, museums, universities and train stations. The architects of these buildings, such as Julien Guadet, Jean-Louis Pascal, Emile Bénard, Georges Scellier de Gisors and Paul Nenot, had all worked under Garnier in the Opéra's drafting rooms, and although Garnier never directed an official student atelier, he effectively trained the best architects of the succeeding generation.

The Opéra, which seems to have consumed all of Garnier's creative energy, was his first—and last—masterpiece. He constructed nothing comparable to it during the following 23 years of his life. His subsequent architectural oeuvre consisted of funerary monuments, amusement palaces, such as the casino at Monte Carlo (1878-81), private Parisian office buildings and additions to his Mediterranean villa at Bordighera. Yet Garnier remained active in the architectural field—he was admitted to the Institut de France (1874), was appointed Inspecteur General des Bâtiments Civils (1877-96), was twice president of the Société centrale des Architectes (1889-91 and 1895-97), and was a member of the Commission des Monuments Historiques (1895-98). Yet Garnier will always be remembered for his Paris Opéra, testament to how an architectural system can so perfectly embody the society and culture which it serves.

—MARC VINCENT

GARNIER, Tony.

French. Born in Lyons, France, 13 August 1869; son of the architect Charles Garnier. Died in La Bédoule, France, 19 January 1948. Studied at the École National des Beaux-Arts, Lyons, 1886-89; École des Beaux-Arts, Paris, 1889-99; Prix de Rome Scholar, 1899-1904. In private practice, Lyons, 1904 until his death in 1948.

Chronology of Works
All in France

1904-05	Vacherie du Park de la Tête-d'Or, Lyons
1904-14	Cité Industrielle (project)
1908-24	Slaughterhouse and Stockyard, Lyons
1909-11	Villa Tony Garnier, St.-Rambert, Lyons
1911-27	Hôpital Grange-Blanche, Lyons
1913-18	Municipal Stadium, Lyons
1920-35	Housing Sector, Quartier des Etats-Unis, Lyons
1922-25	Monument to the War Dead, Parc de la Tête d'Or, Lyons (with the sculptor Larrive)

1927	Moncey Central Telephone Exchange, Lyons
1930-33	Textile School, Croix-Rousse, Lyons
1931-34	Hôtel de Ville, Boulogne-Billancourt (with J. H. E. Debat-Ponsan)

Publications

BOOKS BY GARNIER

Une Cité Industrielle: Etude pour la construction des villes. Paris, 1918 (2nd ed., 1932). Reprint: Princeton, New Jersey, 1989.

Les grands travaux de la ville de Lyons. Paris, 1920.

Tony Garnier: L'oeuvre complete. Paris, 1989.

BOOKS ABOUT GARNIER

BADOVICI, J., and MORANCÉ, A. (eds.): *L'oeuvre de Tony Garnier.* Paris, 1938.

BOURDEIX, P.: *Tony Garnier et son oeuvre.* Paris, 1967.

DESHAIRS, L.: *Catalogue d'exposition de Tony Garnier au Musée des Arts Décoratifs à Paris.* Paris, 1925.

HERRIOT, E., and PIESSAT, L.: *Tony Garnier 1869-1948.* Lyons, 1951.

MARIANI, R.: *Tony Garnier: Une Cité Industrielle.* New York, 1990.

PAWLOWSKI, CHRISTOPHE: *Tony Garnier et les débuts de l'urbanisme fonctionnel en France.* Paris, 1967.

Tony Garnier. Exhibition catalog. Lyons, 1970.

Tony Garnier 1869-1948. Lyons, 1951.

VERONESI, GIULIA: *Tony Garnier.* Milan, 1947.

WIEBENSON, DORA: *Tony Garnier: The Cité Industrielle.* New York and London, 1969.

ARTICLES ABOUT GARNIER

BOURDEIX, P.: "Tony Garnier: Précurseur de architecture d'aujourd'hui." *Architecture d'aujourd'hui* (March 1931).

*

Tony Garnier began his formal education as an architect in his hometown of Lyons. Between 1885 and 1889 he was enrolled at the École Nationale des Beaux-Arts, and a scholarship from that institution enabled Garnier to move to Paris and study at the École Nationale Supérieure des Beaux-Arts. While it can be argued that Garnier was profoundly influenced by the academic structure and nature of these two institutions, this overlooks the impact that growing up in Lyons had on him. At the time of his birth in 1869, Lyons was an important industrial center with special emphasis on textiles and metallurgy. Commencing in the mid-19th century, Lyons had undergone extensive urban renewal. As a child, Garnier would have observed new construction, especially in reinforced concrete, firsthand.

During the year that Garnier studied in Paris, he was exposed to the work of many architects. His studies with two unexceptional architects, Paul Blondel (1847-97) and Scellier de Gisors (1844-1905), exposed him to a simplified vocabulary of the forms and details associated with classicism. Neither of those teachers seems to have been interested in new materials or new techniques of construction, and as a result, Garnier's training at the École was well within the school's existing tradition.

There was, however, a spark, something that suggests that previous experience was not lost on Garnier. It can be found in a manifesto he submitted with the 1901 version of what would be his most important work, the plans for an industrial city. The manifesto seems to reject the classical traditions with which his architectural education was so strongly infused. In the teaching of Julien Gadget (1834-1908), a faculty member at the École, Garnier found sympathy and support, and Gadget exercised a lasting impact on Garnier and one of his fellow students, Auguste Perret (1874-1954).

The most important competition at the École was the Prix de Rome. Between 1894 and 1898, Garnier entered six times. While the emphasis was on speed, not originality, according to a recent critic of academic design at the École, Garnier's winning design still represents a high point in the Beaux-Arts approach to planning buildings and organizing space. A condition of the Prix de Rome was study in Rome at the Villa Medici, including a careful examination and conjectural reconstruction of one of the city's ancient monuments. The influence of ancient Rome is everywhere evident in Garnier's proposed Cité Industrielle.

While there is a strongly formal quality to the planning of the Cité Industrielle, especially in the use of the gridiron and major and minor axes, there is also something of the picturesque, and Garnier's work can be seen as an attempt to synthesize these two approaches to urban design. In retrospect, it is not the synthesis that is so important about his work, but his very serious attempt to design a new city predicated on technology and embracing industry.

Garnier's drawings for his industrial city, full of classical analogies and references—links to a more perfect past—were so carefully drawn that each building and building type has been considered fully and in detail. That Garnier did not include jails, churches and courts of law in his city is an indication of both the utopian nature of his proposal as well as the faith Garnier had in the power of design to alter human behavior. There were some equally practical considerations in the plan, too. For example, residential areas, scaled to the pedestrian and separated from factories and industry, were connected with other parts of the city by a tramway; green space and lush landscaping create the impression of a city in a garden, peopled with attractive and healthy families, a city rich in architectural variety and expression.

The choice and extensive use of reinforced concrete for the buildings in the Cité Industrielle as well as his attitude toward the expression of this new material, coupled with his faith in technology, place Garnier in the Modern Movement. His later work as an architect practicing in Lyons reinforces this assertion. To a large degree, Garnier's reputation suffered from the fact that *Une Cité Industrielle* was not published until 1917 and was not reissued until 1932.

—DAVID SPAETH

GÄRTNER, Friedrich von.

German. Born in Koblenz, Germany, 1792 Died in 1847. Father was the builder and architect Andreas Gärtner. Studied with Karl von Fischer, 1808-11; worked with Friedrich Weinbrenner in Karlsruhe, 1812, then with J. N. L. Durand and Charles Percier in Paris, 1812-14; grand tour to Italy, 1814-17; visited England, 1819. Taught at the Academy, Munich, 1817-27, and became professor of architecture, 1820; received part of commission for Ludwigsstrasse in Munich, 1827; trips to complete royal res idence in Athens, 1835-36.

Chronology of Works
All in Germany unless noted

1832-43 Bavarian Court and State Library, Munich
1829-44 Ludwigskirche, Munich
1835 Institute for the Blind, Munich
1835-37 Cathedral, Bamberg (restoration)
1835-39 Women's Charitable Foundation, Munich
1835-54 Universitätsplatz, Munich: University (1835-40); Georgianum (1835-40); Girls' School (1837); Siegestor (Triumphal Arch, 1843-54)
1836-41 Royal Residence, Athens, Greece
1837 Cathedral, Regensburg (restoration)
1837 Abbey, Heilbrönn (renovations)
1838-43 Offices of the Saltworks, Munich
1840 Feldherrnhalle, Munich
1842-46 Pompeian House, Aschaffenburg

Publications

BOOKS ABOUT GÄRTNER

EGGERT, KLAUS: *Friedrich von Gärtner, der Baumeister König Ludwigs I*. Munich, 1963.
HEDERER, OSWALD: *Friedrich von Gärtner 1792-1847: Leben, Werk, Schüler*. Munich, 1976.

*

Friedrich von Gärtner was very strongly influenced by the work of Leo von Klenze, and became a master of the heavily rusticated Florentine style that Klenze and King Ludwig I had introduced to Munich. Gärtner's designs showed a wide eclectic range, but could often be feeble, even sentimental, as was demonstrated by his unsatisfactory proposals for the Befreiungshalle, an 18-sided, domed building in the *Rundbogenstil* manner, the foundation stone of which was laid in 1842. Although Gärtner had ordered the marble Victories from Schwanthaler that were eventually incorporated into the building that stands near Kelheim today, Klenze completely remodeled the design in a severe neoclassical manner after Gärtner's death in 1847.

For some 20 years from 1827, Gärtner was the second-most-important architect in Munich after Klenze, and he probably had even more influence on the younger generation of architects, as Klenze remained faithful to the (by then) rather old-fashioned ideals of the Greek Revival.

Gärtner studied under Karl von Fischer from 1808 to 1811, but even more important in his development were the periods during which he worked under Friedrich Weinbrenner in Karlsruhe (1812) and under J. N. L. Durand and Charles Percier in Paris (1812-14). During his travels in Italy, he met Karl von Humboldt and the sculptor Johann Martin von Wagner, and visited the Greek temples in Paestum and Sicily, later to be recorded in his *Ansichten der am meisten erhalten griechischen Monumente Siciliens—nach der Natur und auf Stein gezeichnet von Friedrich Gärtner* (1819). This collection of lithographs stood him in good stead when he visited C. R. Cockerell in England in 1819 and was introduced to Hullmandel, the celebrated lithographer, with whom Cockerell worked. During his stay in England, Gärtner became interested in the new technologies of building being used for factories, warehouses and docks, just as Karl Friedrich Schinkel was to be captivated only a few years later.

When, in 1820, Gärtner returned to the Bavarian capital, he was appointed professor of architecture, and in 1827 was commissioned by the king to design the new Court and State

Library. This was built in 1832-43 in the Ludwigstrasse as a version of the Palazzo Pitti in Florence and contains a nobly conceived staircase with a vaulted ceiling of great magnificence. Next to the library is the Ludwigskirche (1829-44), built in an Italian Romanesque style with twin towers that recall Weinbrenner's designs for the Protestant church at Karlsruhe (1806-16).

Florentine Renaissance of the round-arched variety was again the style of the Institute for the Blind (1835), the Women's Charitable Foundation (1835-39) and the Offices of the Saltworks (1838-43), all in the Ludwigstrasse, and erected opposite the State Library and the Ludwigskirche. The Saltworks building features exposed brickwork on the facade, recalling the brick buildings of Bologna, which both Gärtner and Schinkel had studied with profit.

Gärtner also laid out the Universitätsplatz, including the University (1835-40) opposite which is the Georgianum (1835-40) and the Girls' School (1837). The ensemble was completed by the Siegestor, or triumphal arch (1843-54), which stands on the axis of the Ludwigstrasse and is modeled on the Arch of Constantine in Rome. The Siegestor, which celebrates the Bavarian army and its triumphs and is embellished with sculpture designed by J. M. von Wagner, was prompted by similar triumphal arches in Paris and London.

At the southern end of the Ludwigstrasse, Gärtner designed in 1840 the Feldherrnhalle, erected in 1841-43: it is a copy of the Loggia dei Lanzi in Florence, but shelters statues of Marshals Tilly and Wrede by Schwanthaler. This apparently disparate mix of Florentine medieval and Renaissance architecture with classical elements was deliberate, and was part of the policy of the king to make Munich a cultural capital of European importance. Besides, the Loggia dei Lanzi has certain aspects that are agreeably suggestive of a classical past and a Renaissance future.

From 1835 to 1837 Gärtner supervised the program of restoration at Bamberg Cathedral, and from 1837 he worked on the cathedral at Regensburg and on the Romanesque abbey at Heilbronn. Thus, in Gärtner, the romantic mix of classical antiquity, medieval heritage and Renaissance *Rundbogenstil* is complete. Like Schinkel and Klenze he could turn his hand with equal deftness to a variety of architectural expressions.

Of all Gärtner's designs, however, the happiest must be the Pompeian House at Aschaffenburg (1842-46). This enchanting house, built for King Ludwig, was based on the House of Castor and Pollux at Pompeii, and alludes to antiquity in the most scholarly yet inventive way. The Villa Ludwigshöhe near Edenkoben in the Palatinate is also most agreeable: it is an Italianate villa set among vineyards, with echoes of the Palazzo Chiericati in Vicenza and many other eclectic references to Italy and to the Italian Renaissance.

Gärtner was a fine romantic neoclassical architect, who could create new syntheses of antique, Romanesque and Renaissance motifs. He deserves a greater attention than he has enjoyed hitherto in countries outside Germany.

—JAMES STEVENS CURL

GAUDÍ, Antonio.

Spanish. Born Antonio Gaudí y Cornet in Reus, Catalonia, Spain, 25 June 1852. Died in Barcelona, 10 June 1926. Studied architecture at the Escola Superior d'Arquitectura, Barcelona, Spain, Dip.Arch., 1878; worked with various architects, Barcelona, 1874-82; in private practice, Barcelona, 1882 until his death in 1926.

Antonio Gaudi: Expiatory Church of the Holy Family, Sagrada
Familia, Barcelona, Spain, 1883-1926

Chronology of Works
All in Spain
* Approximate dates

1878	Furniture for Comillas Pantheon, Comillas, Santander
1878-80	Casa Vicens, Barcelona
1883-85	El Capricho Summer Villa, Comillas, Santander
1883-1926	Expiatory Church of the Holy Family, Barcelona (Sagrada Familia; work still in progress)
1884*-87	Güell Estate, Las Corts de Sarrá, Barcelona (additions)
1886-89	Palau Güell, Barcelona
1887-93	Episcopal Palace, Astorga, León (completed in 1907)
1888-90	Colegio de Santa Teresa de Jesús, Bonanova, Barcelona
1891-94	Casa Fernández y Andrés, León
1898-1904	Casa Calvet, 48 calle Caspe, Barcelona
1909-15*	Church, Güell Workers' Colony, Santa Coloma de Cervelló, Barcelona
1900-09	Villa Bell Esguard, Bonanova, Barcelona
1900-14	Park Güell, Montaña Pelada, Barcelona
1901-02	Hermenegildo Miralles Estate, Las Corts de Sarriá, Barcelona
1901-15	Cathedral, Palma de Mallorca (interior)
1904-06	Casa Batlló, Barcelona (remodeling)
1906-10	Casa Milá, Barcelona

Publications

BOOKS ABOUT GAUDÍ

BASSEGODA NONELL, JUAN: *El Gran Gaudí.* Barcelona, 1989.

BERGÓS MASSÓ, JOAN: *Antoni Gaudí, l'home i l'obra.* Barcelona, 1953. Spanish translation: 1974.

BOHIGAS, O.: *Arquitectura modernista. Gaudí e il movimento catalano.* Barcelona, 1968.

CASANELLES, ENRIC: *Nueva visión de Gaudí.* Barcelona, 1965. English edition: Greenwich, Connecticut, 1968.

COLLINS, GEORGE R.: *Antonio Gaudí.* New York, 1960.

COLLINS, GEORGE R. (compiler): *A Bibliography of Antonio Gaudí and the Catalan Movement, 1870-1930.* Vol. 10 in *Papers of the American Association of Architectural Bibliographers.* Charlottesville, Virginia, 1973.

COLLINS, GEORGE R., and BASSEGODA NONELL, JUAN: *The Designs and Drawings of Antonio Gaudí.* Princeton, New Jersey, 1983.

DALISI, R.: *Gaudí Furniture.* London, 1979.

DESCHARNES, ROBERT: *Gaudí the Visionary.* New York, 1971.

FLORES, CARLOS: *Gaudí, Jujol y el modernismo catalan.* 2 vols. Madrid, 1982.

GIEDION-WELCKER, C.: *Park Güell.* Barcelona and New York, 1966.

MACKAY, DAVID: *Modern Architecture in Barcelona 1854-1939.* Barcelona, 1989.

MARTINELL, CÉSAR: *Conversaciones con Gaudí.* Barcelona, 1951.

MARTINELL, CÉSAR: *Gaudí: His Life, His Theories, His Work.* Cambridge, Massachusetts, 1975.

PANE, ROBERTO: *Antoni Gaudí.* Milan, 1974.

PEVSNER, NIKOLAUS, and RICHARDS, J. M. (eds.): *The Anti-Rationalists.* London, 1973.

PUIG BOADA, ISIDRO: *El pensament de Gaudí: Compilació de textos i comentaris.* Barcelona, 1981.

RÀFOLS, JOSÉ F.: *Gaudí.* Barcelona, 1929.

RUSSELL, FRANK (ed.): *Art Nouveau Architecture.* London, 1979.
SOLÁ-MORALES, IGNASI DE: *Gaudí.* New York, 1984.
SWEENEY, JAMES JOHNSON, and SERT, JOSÉ LUIS: *Antonio Gaudí.* London and New York, 1961.
TORII, TOKUTOSHI: *El mundo enigmático de Gaudí.* 2 vols. Madrid, 1983.
WIEDEMAN, J.: *Gaudí. Inspiration in Architektur und Handwerk.* Munich, 1974.
ZERBST, RAINER: *Antoni Gaudí i Cornet—A Life Devoted to Architecture.* Cologne, 1988.

ARTICLES ABOUT GAUDÍ

BORRAS, MARIA LLUISA: "Casa Batllo, Casa Mila." *Global Architecture* No. 17 (1972).
HITCHCOCK, HENRY-RUSSELL: "The Work of Antoni Gaudí i Cornet." *Architectural Association Journal* (November 1958): 86-98.
ZEVI, BRUNO: "Un genio catalano: Antonio Gaudí." *Metron* No. 38 (1950): 26-53.

The architect Antonio Gaudí y Cornet lived in the intensely stimulating intellectual ferment and social unrest of Early Modern Barcelona. Industrialization of the region had expanded its economy dramatically, in sharp contrast to most of rural Spain, kindling a broad, defiant Catalan nationalist movement that sought to revive its rich medieval culture. Catalonia's most brilliant historic period began in the 12th century, when it became a major Mediterranean power. Its independence vanished with Spanish unification in the late 15th century, an arrangement Catalans never found comfortable. Their nationalism was both medievalizing and progressive, torn between recollections of a great past and conflicting visions of a brighter future. Fourteenth-century Catalan architects had tested their daring with vaults of wide span and supports of unusual slenderness in Gothic churches such as Santa María del Mar and Santa Maria del Pi in Barcelona, and the cathedrals of Palma de Mallorca and Girona. Catalan masons later developed a vernacular construction with lightweight, thin vaults of brick layers laid edge to edge and set in thick mortar beds. Gaudí developed these traditions of masonry construction through intensely original, technically sophisticated transformations.

To appreciate Gaudí's visionary work requires an approach unencumbered with the classical requirements of unity, simplicity or clear visual order. Gaudí was not a purist. He saw nothing wrong in juxtaposing unrelated systems, nor was he troubled about altering established visual orders, but he insisted on a deeper consistency based on construction and production. Thus, his floor plans often conflict with structure, as at the Palacio Güell and Casa Milá, and structural advantage regulated appearance as with the leaning Archaic Doric columns at Parc Güell or the even more precarious-looking piers at the Colonia Güell chapel, where the inclination responded to the loads. His fantastically warped surfaces improved structural efficiency while allowing traditional Catalan vaulting techniques to be used. His ceramic decorations made of broken tiles, cups and saucers used an economical waste material to extraordinary aesthetic advantage. The Gaudinian aesthetic demands the sensibility of a builder who must do rather than contemplate, and yet contemplate as he does. Gaudí was contemptuous of two-dimensional thinking generated by designing on paper, and expected his work to be experienced in space.

Gaudí's father was a coppersmith, as were both his grandfathers. Gaudí believed this had prepared him, as smiths must make volumes from flat sheets, and thus think spatially, as do architects. His plastic sensibility was also affected early by the strange rock formations of the sacred mountain of Montserrat, to whose black Virgin Gaudí was deeply devoted. The death early in his life of his mother, his older brother and his sister, and the fact that he remained a bachelor throughout his life, deprived him of the close family life that the Spanish think is important, and for which he developed an exaggerated respect. Gaudí attended school in Reus until 1868. In 1869 he moved to Barcelona, and in 1870 qualified for admission to the new school of architecture at the University of Barcelona, completing his studies eight years later. Gaudí was not a distinguished student. During that time he worked for the builder Josep Fonserè i Mestre on the important project of the Parc de la Ciutadella in Barcelona. While working for Fonserè, Gaudí failed to attend a class in strength of materials. Nonetheless, he worked the calculations for a cascade and waterworks in the park, and his professor, Joan Torras i Guardiola, gave him credit for the course. Gaudí's interest in ingenious mechanisms and technical devices was already awakened. He never shared the aversion to machinery and industry of English Arts and Crafts theorists.

In 1878 Gaudí graduated as an architect, and established himself quickly. He had just obtained a commission from City Hall for streetlights in the Plaça Reial and Pla del Palau in Barcelona. In the same year he designed a remarkable glass showcase for the Barcelonese glove manufacturer Esteban Comella for the Paris Universal Exhibition of 1878. That brought him to the attention of Eusebi Güell, who was among the wealthiest industrialists in Barcelona and an important art collector who would become his most important and influential patron. Also in 1878 Gaudí began a house for Manuel Vicens that, along with Lluís Domènech i Muntaner's contemporary Editorial Montaner i Simon, announced the birth of Catalan Modernismo. No longer historicist, the house has a dreamlike Moorish quality, with its brilliantly colored tilework alternating with bands of earth-colored rubble, verandas with latticed brick walls, irregular roofline with lookouts, and splendid wrought-iron work with the earliest art nouveau whiplash ornament in Europe. Vicens was a tile manufacturer, and Gaudí used his tiles as modular units. Gaudí often had entire walls torn out as construction progressed, judging the composition of each element as it was built. The house was enlarged in 1925 with Gaudí's approval, but in 1946 part of the lot was sold and the garden destroyed.

Before 1880 Güell commissioned Gaudí to design the furniture for the private chapel in Comillas (Santander) of his father-in-law, Antonio López, first marquis of Comillas, whose successful shipping business had paved his ascent to the aristocracy. In 1881 Gaudí designed an iron and glass garden pavilion at Comillas, a multiple-domed Mughal fantasy, for a visit of King Alfonso XII. Gaudí began attending the artistic soirées at the house of Eusebi Güell, and was soon a central figure in them. He probably learned of the English Arts and Crafts through Güell, who owned pieces from the William Morris circle.

In the early 1880s Gaudí assisted the architect Joan Martorell i Montells in several ecclesiastical designs, most importantly, the 1882 project for completing the facade of the 14th-century cathedral of Barcelona. By then Gaudí was viewed as an eccentric, following a strict vegetarian diet and taking long daily hikes to treat his rheumatism. He spoke only Catalan, pretending not to know enough Spanish, and became an ardent supporter of Catalan nationalism. His religious inclinations deepened, as he studied systematically Catholic dogma, theology and ritual.

Gaudí's planning would gradually become fraught with religious and Catalan symbolism, informed by the idea of a new social order based on a renewed church.

Gaudí apparently ventured outside Catalonia only twice. In 1887 he visited Andalusia and Morocco to study the Moslem environment for a Franciscan mission in Tangiers. In 1889 he traveled to Astorga in western Castile to supervise the construction of the episcopal palace he had designed there. Gaudí learned of European, especially Gothic, architecture through literature. He admired the theories of Eugène-Emmanuel Viollet-le-Duc, owning both his *Dictionnaire Raisonnée* and the *Entretiens.* Viollet-le-Duc interpreted the rise of the Gothic style entirely in terms of structural and functional necessity, and Gaudí owed much of his passionate interest in structure to Viollet-le-Duc.

Two projects of 1883 initiated Gaudí into the formal expression of structure. Since 1877 he had done work for the Worker's Cooperative at Mataró, and was friendly with its director, the socialist labor leader Salvador Pagés. Gaudí may have adopted some of Pagés' views, but ultimately he disavowed Pagés' anticlericalism. In 1883 Gaudí designed the textile bleaching hall at Mataró using parabolic arches of laminated timber, a system devised by Philibert de l'Orme in the 16th century. In 1883-85 Gaudí built El Capricho, a house for Máximo Díaz de Quijano, a neighbor of the marquis of Comillas. Its irregular elongated plan follows the steep slope of the site. It has a rusticated stone basement, two plain brick stories enlivened with multiple horizontal rows of rose-shaped tiles, and a dramatic, tiled corbeled cornice. An extraordinary cylindrical tower, brightly decorated with tiles and sinuous ironwork, rises above the four massive columns of the entrance portico. Above its observation platform exaggeratedly slender iron posts support a heavy-looking corbeled roof. Juan Bergós reports that while designing this tower, Gaudí considered inclining the columns to improve their stability and reduce their bulk.

In 1884, through Joan Martorell's recommendation, Gaudí received the commission for his great masterpiece, the Expiatory Temple of the Sagrada Familia, begun in 1882 by Francisco del Villar. That year he also began the gate, gatehouse and stables of the Finca Güell, Eusebi Güell's summer house in Pedralbes, now part of the University of Barcelona. The fantastic dragon gate is among the finest Spanish 19th-century wrought-iron pieces. The gatehouse exhibits an Islamic-inspired repetitive pattern in brick and stucco. Juan Bassegoda has suggested that the gate represents the dragon that protected the golden apples of the Hesperides and is part of a complex iconographic program, reminiscent of humanist gardens of the Late Renaissance.

The palace for Eusebi Güell, built in 1885-89 in an unfashionable area of Barcelona near the Ramblas, was Gaudí's first major commission. The stone facade has two parabolic arches filled with marvelous, sinuous iron grilles. A central hall three stories tall dominates the interior. Its parabolic dome, with tiny piercings simulating stars, is double-shelled. The outer shell is conical and projects high above the roof. The many fireplaces with their chimneys create a fantastic roofscape of strangely shaped and brightly tiled growths.

The Episcopal Palace of Astorga, León (1887-93), was designed for Gaudí's friend the bishop Juan Grau Vallespinós. It is a building of Gothic inspiration with a Greek-cross plan. The granite exterior with a slate roof has a severe character unexpected in Gaudí's work. This Gothicizing restraint was to inform his work until shortly after 1900. An even sparser, more economical building is the Teresan School for Girls in Barcelona (1888-90). It is a simple rectangular block, animated by a crenellated roof. The exterior is of finely executed unornamented rubble. The elegant restrained interiors express its structure of

parabolic arches. The Casa Fernández Andrés in León (1891-92) was commissioned as a result of the work in Astorga. The mixed-use building had a warehouse in the basement, business offices on the main floor, the owner's apartment on the *piano nobile,* and other apartments on the upper three floors. It is again a severe and aesthetically economical Gothicizing structure with rusticated stonework outside and very fine Catalan iron grilles.

Toward the beginning of the century Gaudí's work regained animation. The Casa Calvet in Barcelona (1898-1900) is Gaudí's most serene design for a town house. An oriel and balconies with trefoil plans and fine art nouveau ironwork enrich its flat rusticated facade. Gaudí furnished the interiors of the principal apartment with his most elegant furniture designs. The house won the annual Barcelona City Hall architecture prize in 1900. Bell Esguard (1900-08), a house on the slopes of Mount Tibidabo west of Barcelona, occupies the site of King Martin I's 13th-century summer palace. The house has a cubic profile, with a steep tower flanking the front entrance. The rubble walls culminate in a gallery, as in Catalan Gothic palaces, with battlements and a steep roof above. The attic has thin brick diaphragms on parabolic arches, an efficient and rigid roof structure.

Parc Güell (1899-1913) was Eusebi Güell's brainchild, a housing development on a hill west of Barcelona. It was intended to introduce the English garden city to well-to-do Barcelonese. Some 60 plots were envisioned, plus a market area, an esplanade, a chapel and common parklands. Four stone viaducts with inclined supports allowed a sinuous road to connect all lots without major alterations to the contours of the site. The central area, with two extraordinarily colorful oval pavilions, a monumental stair, an Archaic Doric hypostyle hall and a long curvilinear bench around a high plaza, has some of the most fluid shapes and colorful ceramics in Gaudí's oeuvre. The painter Josep Maria Jujol was largely responsible for the protocubist ceramics, constructing abstract forms out of broken fragments. The project was unsuccessful commercially and in 1923 was given to the city as a park. Gaudí himself lived from 1906 to 1925 in one of two houses built in the park, neither his design.

The unfinished chapel for the Colonia Güell, a textile workers' settlement at Santa Coloma de Cervelló (1898-1915), was Gaudí's most accomplished structural tour-de-force. Only the crypt was completed, perhaps Gaudí's finest space. The complex structure was designed with a polyfunicular model, a string replica of the building loaded with small weights. This was a tool perfected by Gaudí for determining stresses and positions of structural members. Tension in any string could be scaled proportionally to compression in the corresponding element of the building. The angles assumed by strings were those at which compression members should meet forces to avoid bending stresses. The funicular model replaced working drawings due to the three-dimensional complexity of the design.

Gaudí directed important alterations from 1903 to 1914 at the cathedral of Palma de Mallorca, one of the largest Gothic churches in Europe. Gaudí changed the arrangement of furnishings according to his view of the medieval planning altered in 17th- and 18th-century remodelings. He generally cleared the space of the huge central vessel and its aisles. He opened blocked windows and designed stained glass for them, moved the choir from the nave to the sanctuary, and designed unusual light fixtures, a baldachino, an altar, a pulpit and other furniture.

The Casa Batlló in Barcelona (1904-06) is a dramatic remodeling of an older building. There Gaudí attained complete maturity and control in his decoration. Sinuous bone-like stone members articulate three-dimensional arches in the lower two floors. The facade is flatter in the upper floors, where abstract ceramic tiles introduce a colorful ground. Wrought-iron balconies imitate masks. The roof, made of catenary arches, resembles a serpent with scale-like tiles ranging from orange to emerald green. A tower at the left with the initials of the Holy Family and a four-arm cross finial pierces the beast. The entire facade represents Saint George and the dragon, symbols of Barcelona. The commission for the nearby Casa Milá (1905-10) resulted from the construction of the Casa Batlló.

After recovering from an attack of undulant fever in 1911, Gaudí abandoned most work other than the Sagrada Familia. Construction of the church depended on alms, and funds were always short, so he often begged in the streets to raise funds. He attended daily Mass at the Church of San Felipe Neri, in the Barri Gotic. As he was walking to Mass on 7 June 1926, a trolley car struck him. He was poorly dressed, and no one recognized him, so he was taken to a paupers' ward at the Hospital de Santa Cruz, where friends found him. He never regained consciousness, and died three days later. News of his death was received as a local calamity, and his funeral procession was almost a kilometer long, with crowds of mourners along the three-kilometer funeral procession. He was buried in the crypt of his unfinished church. Revolutionary mobs destroyed most of his drawings, models and personal records in July of 1936.

—SERGIO L. SANABRIA

GEHRY, Frank O.

Canadian. Born Ephraim Goldberg, in Toronto, Ontario, Canada, 28 February 1929. Studied architecture at the University of Southern California, Los Angeles, 1949-51 and 1954, B.Arch., and city planning at Harvard University, Cambridge, Massachusetts, 1956-57. Served in the Special Services Division of the United States Army, 1955-56. Architectural designer, Victor Gruen Associates, Los Angeles, 1953-54; planner and designer, Robert and Company Architects, Atlanta, Georgia, 1955-56; designer and planner, Hideo Sasaki Associates, Boston, Massachusetts, 1957; architectural designer, Pereira and Luckman, Los Angeles, 1957-58; worked in planning, design and project direction for Victor Gruen Associates, Los Angeles, 1958-61; project designer and planner, André Remondet, Paris, France, 1961; principal, Frank O. Gehry and Associates, Los Angeles, since 1962. Has taught at the University of Southern California, University of California at Los Angeles, Yale University and Harvard University. Fell ow, American Institute of Architects, 1974; Pritzker Prize, 1989.

Chronology of Works
All in the United States unless noted

1968	O'Neill Hay Barn, San Juan Capistrano, California
1968	Joseph Magnin Store, South Coast Plaza, Costa Mesa, California
1970-72	Ron Davis Studio and House, Malibu California
1970-82	Hollywood Bowl, Hollywood, California
1973-80	Santa Monica Place (mall and parking structures), Santa Monica, California
1974	Rouse Company Headquarters, Columbia, Maryland
1977	Ruscha House, 29 Palms, California
1978	Mid-Atlantic Toyota Office, Glen Burnie, Maryland (interiors)
1978/84	Main Street Project, Venice, California
1979	Los Angeles Children's Museum, Los Angeles
1979/87	Frank O. Gehry House, Santa Monica, California
1981-84	Law School Building, Loyola University, Los Angeles
1982-84	California Aerospace Museum, Los Angeles
1982	Wosk Residence, Beverly Hills, California
1982	Goldwyn Regional Branch Library, Hollywood, California
1983	Norton House, Venice, California
1984	Edgemar Development, Santa Monica, California
1984-86	Winton Guest House, Wayzata, Minnesota
1985	Herman Miller Western Regional Facilities, Rocklin, California
1985-89	Yale Psychiatric Institute, New Haven, Connecticut
1986	Schnabel Residence, Brentwood, California
1986-89	Fishdance Restaurant, Kobe, Japan
1987-89	Vitra Furniture Museum and Factory, Weil am Rhein, Germany
1988	American Center, Paris, France
1989	Walt Disney Concert Hall, Los Angeles, California
1990	University of Minnesota Art Museum, Minneapolis

Publications

BOOKS ABOUT GEHRY

ARNELL, PETER, and BICKFORD, TED (eds.): *Frank Gehry: Buildings and Projects*. New York, 1985.
COBB, H. N., BLETTER, R. H., et al.: *The Architecture of Frank Gehry*. New York, 1986.
BOISSIERE, OLIVIER: *Gehry, SITE, Tigerman: trois portraits de l'artiste en architecture*. Paris, 1981.
BOISSIERE, OLIVIER, and FILLER, MARTIN: *The Vitra Design Museum: Frank Gehry, Architect*. New York, 1990.

ARTICLES ABOUT GEHRY

BOISSIERE, OLIVIER: "Ten Los Angeles Architects: Frank Gehry." *Domus* (March 1980).
"Davis Residence, Malibu." *GA Houses* 2 (1977).
"Deconstruction III: The Vitra Design Museum." *Architectural Design* Profile no. 87 (1990).
FILLER, MARTIN: "Gehry's Urbanism." *Skyline* (October 1982).
"Frank Gehry." *Architecture and Urbanism* (September 1989).
GOLDBERGER, PAUL: "Frank O. Gehry, Aerospace, Loyola and Norton." *Architecture and Urbanism* (January 1986).
GRANDEE, C. K.: "Catch of the Day—Fishdance Restaurant." *Architectural Record* (January 1988).
JENCKS, CHARLES: "Frank Gehry—The Deconstructivist." *Art and Design* (May 1985).
McCOY, ESTHER: "Report from the Malibu Hills." *Progressive Architecture* (December 1974).
NAIRN, JANET: "Frank Gehry: The Search for 'No Rules' Architecture." *Architectural Record* (June 1976).
"A New Wave in American Architecture: Frank O. Gehry." *Space Design* (July 1980).
NULLI, A.: "Vitra Design Museum, Weil am Rhein." *Domus* (February 1990).
SCALVINI, MARIA LUISA: "The Gehry Intersection." *Domus* (September 1982).
SHAPIRO, LINDSAY STAMM: "A Minimalist Architecture of Allusion: Current Projects of Frank Gehry." *Architectural Record* (June 1983).
"Schnabel Residence." *GA Houses* 29 (August 1990).
STEPHENS, SUZANNE: "Frank O. Gehry and Associates." *Progressive Architecture* (March 1980).

STRATHAUS, ULRIKE J.-S.: "Frank Gehry." *Werk, Bauen und Wohnen* (July/August 1984).

SUDJIC, DEYAN: "One Man and His Museum." *Blueprint* (November 1989).

VILADAS, PILAR: "Outdoor Sculpture—Winton Guest House." *Architectural Record* (December 1987).

"Vitra Design Museum" and "American Center." *GA Document* 27 (1990).

*

Frank Gehry is Canadian by birth, but Californian by adoption and training, and his postmodern populism would seem to be quintessentially America. But with highly acclaimed work completed in 1989; museums in Minnesota and Ohio; the Yale Psychiatric Institute in New Haven, Connecticut; the Fish Dance Restaurant in Kobe, Japan; and the Vitra Design Museum in Weil am Rhein, Germany, Gehry is today acknowledged as an architect of international importance. He was awarded the prestigious Pritzker Prize in Architecture for 1990.

Gehry's architecture has undergone a marked evolution from the ragtime, chain-link, plywood and corrugated-metal vernacular of his own house in Santa Monica, California (1976-78), to the distorted but pristine, painted concrete cubes of the Vitra Design Museum a decade later. Importantly, however, the work retains its ad hoc, deconstructed aesthetic so appropriate to the uncertainties of an increasingly fragmented world.

Possessing the improvisational look of process art, Gehry's work is best understood, he believes, in its relationship to painting and sculpture. His close ties with contemporary painters and sculptors who came of age in the 1960s—Robert Rauschenberg, Claes Oldenburg, Ron Davis, Robert Irwin, Richard Serra—are often cited. In fact, Gehry's pejorative attitude toward architecture as art played a part in his rejection of a promising design business after the 1972 marketing success of his "East Edges" corrugated-cardboard furniture. He felt uncomfortable in the role of industrial designer.

When Gehry's Santa Monica House was completed, its deconstructed three-dimensional collage of plywood, metal and chain link were combined with the "found object" of a 1920s house, and the ensemble was rightly compared to the collaged painted relief "combines" of Rauschenberg. In their layering of space, both painter and architect owe debts to cubism and abstract expressionism. In their often-lyrical sense for the juxtaposition of form, shape and texture, their debts are to Russian constructivism and the Dada constructs of Kurt Schwitters. With few exceptions, Gehry's work is also characterized by genuine concerns with both context and allegorical content. What is constant in his work is the dialogue between his "high" aesthetic sense for formal composition and his preference for the "low" materials of vernacular use. Aspects of Gehry's biography hold a key to these dualities.

Gehry's interior designs utilizing fish sculptures and lamps, and his Fish Dance Restaurant in Japan reflect his ongoing obsession with the image of a fish. This obsession derives not only from the nickname of "Fish" given by his anti-Semitic tormentors in high school, but also from the live fish his grandmother bought at market and kept in a bathtub for making gefilte fish. Gehry's ability to utilize the appropriate symbolic object in his architectural compositions is most successfully demonstrated in his California Aerospace Museum in Los Angeles (1982-84). Therein, a Lockheed F104 Starfighter jet hovers in mid-takeoff above the 40-foot-high hangar-like door of the facade, and a metallic, polygonal, planet-like sphere tops the museum's entrance on the north side. Gehry's association with Claes Oldenburg and his wife Coosje van Bruggen in designing the maritime imagery for Camp Good Times in the Santa Monica Mountains, California (1984-85), and the binoculars-as-entranceway for the Main Street Project in Venice, California (1975-86), for the Chiat/Day advertising agency demonstrates again the potent validity of symbolic imagery in architecture.

After Gehry's parents moved to Los Angeles in 1947, he drove a truck while attending night school at Los Angeles City College; he then worked part-time for the architectural firm of Victor Gruen while enrolled at the University of Southern California. He received his architecture degree in 1954, firmly trained in the modernism of Frank Lloyd Wright, R. M. Schindler and Richard Neutra. Drafted into the United States Army in 1955, Gehry designed furniture and "day rooms" for enlisted men at Fort Benning, Georgia. The day rooms were located in "temporary" structures covered in corrugated metal, plywood and asphalt shingles; his furniture was so popular that it was frequently transferred to the Officer's Club.

Gehry studied city planning at Harvard School of Design in 1956, where he discovered architectural history and Le Corbusier. Gehry was back in Los Angeles from 1956 to 1960 with Victor Gruen, and then spent a year in the Paris office of Andre Remondet; he opened his own firm in Los Angeles in 1962. In France he made pilgrimages to see Le Corbusier's highly sculptural Santa Maria du Haute at Ronchamp (1950-54) and his monastery, La Tourette, at Eveux (1957-60), and to medieval towns, where context is primary.

Gehry's early accomplishments set the direction for his future development. His O'Neill Hay Barn in San Juan Capistrano, California (1968), is a functional yet eloquent piece of minimalist sculpture made of the cheapest materials: telephone poles for frame, corrugated metal for siding. His Ron Davis Studio in Malibu, California (1970-72), is a large trapezoidal structure, subtly tilted and slanted inside and out to exaggerate normal perceptions. Both Davis and Gehry were concerned at the time with the use of perspective in creating optical illusions. Similar to many of Gehry's later works, such as the California Aerospace Museum and the Vitra Design Museum, the studio also combines sculptural strength on the exterior with great flexibility on the interior.

Pilar Viladas suggests that Gehry's archetypal vocabulary of cube, cone, pyramid, dome, etc., has taken two directions from the beginning. This vocabulary is combined either in "collision" architecture—as it is in the California Aerospace Museum and the Vitra Museum, where the forms look as though they were brought together in collision—or these building forms are arranged individually into the related fragments of a landscape or "village," as they are in the structures of Loyola Law School, Los Angeles (1981-84), and in his highly acclaimed Winton Guest House, Wayzata, Minnesota (1984-86). Gehry describes the latter's sculptural components with an allusion to the art of painting: "a tight complex, like a still life, like a Morandi."

Thus far, Gehry's architecture holds the dynamic tension between "high" formal compositions and "low" vernacular materials in harmonious balance.

—ANN GLENN CROWE

GHIBERTI, Lorenzo.

Italian. Born in Florence, Italy, ca. 1378. Died near Florence, 1 December 1455. Married Marsilia di Bartolomeo di Luca; sons were the artists Tommaso and Vittorio. Trained in the workshop of his stepfather, Bartoluccio; worked in Florence as goldsmith and painter.

Chronology of Works

All in Italy

1403-24 St. John the Baptist, Florence (bronze doors of the baptistery; now in Bargello Museum)

1418*-23 Santa Trinita, Florence (tomb of Onofrio Strozzi and entry portal to the sacristy)

1420-26 Cathedral, Santa Maria del Fiore, Florence (dome with Filippo Brunelleschi)

1424-52 Bronze doors ('Gates of Paradise'), Baptistery of Saint John the Baptist, Florence

Publications

BOOKS ABOUT GHIBERTI

ACKERMAN, JAMES S.: *A Bibliography of Italian Renaissance and Baroque Architecture.* Cambridge, Massachusetts, 1974.

ANDERSON, WILLIAM J.: *The Architecture of the Renaissance in Italy.* London, 1927.

BOTTARI, GIOVANNI G., and TICOZZI, STEFANO: *Raccolta di lettere sulla pittura, scultura et architettura scritte da piu celebri personaggi dei secoli XV, XVIe XVII.* Milan, 1822-25.

Lorenzo Ghiberti: I Commentarii—A Cura di Ottavio Morisani. 2 vols. Naples, 1947.

GOLDSCHEIDER, LUDWIG: *Lorenzo Ghiberti.* London, 1949.

HEYDENREICH, LUDWIG H., and LOTZ, WOLFGANG: *Architecture in Italy: 1400-1600.* Harmondsworth, England, 1974.

KRAUTHEIMER, RICHARD, and KRAUTHEIMER-HESS, TRUDE: *Lorenzo Ghiberti.* Princeton, New Jersey, 1956; 1982.

PERKINS, C. C.: *Ghiberti et son école.* Paris, 1886.

POGGI, GIOVANNI: *Il Duomo di Firenze: Document sulla decorazione della chiesa e del campanile tratti dall'archivio dell'opera.* Berlin, 1909.

Santa Maria del Fiore: La costruzione della chiesa e del campanile secondo i documenti tratti dall'archivio dell'opera secolare e da quello di stato per cura di Cesare Guasti. Florence, 1887.

SCHLOSSER, JULIUS VON: *Leben und Meinungen des florentinischen Bildners Lorenzo Ghiberti.* Basel, 1941.

ARTICLES ABOUT GHIBERTI

CLARK, KENNETH M.: "Architectural Backgrounds in Fifteenth Century Italian Painting." *Arts* 1 (1946-47).

GENGARO, M. L.: "Precisazioni su Ghiberti architetto." *Arte* 41 (1938): 280ff.

KRAUTHEIMER, RICHARD: "Ghiberti-Architetto." *Bulletin of the Allen Memorial Art Museum* 12 (1955): 484.

MARQUAND, A.: "A Terracotta Sketch by Lorenzo Ghiberti." *American Journal of Archeology* 9 (1894): 207ff.

PICA, A.: "La cupola di S. Maria del Fiore e la collaborazione Brunellesco-Ghiberti." *Emporium* 97 (1943): 70ff.

*

Although first trained as a painter and now most famous for his sculptures (the north and east doors of the Florence Baptistery; the statues of Saints John the Baptist and Matthew at Orsanmichele, Florence, and the baptismal font panels in the Siena Baptistery), Lorenzo Ghiberti also made contributions to the formation of the architectural manner of Early Renaissance Florence. Ghiberti was born the natural child of the goldsmith Bartoluccio (from whom he probably received his initial training in sculpture) but adopted the patronymic of his mother's first husband. Details of his career are known from the autobiography appended to the second of his three *Commentaries,* probably the first true work of art history, and also from the account of his life given in the mid-16th-century *Lives of the most eminent Painters, Sculptors and Architects* by Giorgio Vasari, and in a variety of contemporary notices and documents.

Ghiberti's enigmatic reputation as an architect rests upon three areas of primary involvement: his participation in what was the most celebrated architectural project of his day, the dome of Florence Cathedral; his association with a number of small architecturally related commissions, notably door frames and statue tabernacles; and the architectural renderings found in several of his bronze panels. In addition, Ghiberti is known to have projected a treatise on architecture.

The extent of Ghiberti's involvement in the Florentine cathedral dome project remains problematic. According to Antonio Manetti's *Life of Brunelleschi* (1480s), the design and construction of the dome was solely in the hands of Filippo Brunelleschi. Ghiberti's autobiography, however, claimed for himself a share equal to that of his competitor. Although he certainly overstated his case, his role may have been more significant than is generally believed, as is suggested by documents that show that he had both a position and salary similar to that enjoyed by Brunelleschi. After 1426, however, his role would appear to have become secondary to that of Brunelleschi (explained, in part, by his own absorption in work on the east baptistery doors). In addition to the important dome project, Ghiberti's name has been connected with only three actual building projects, all tenuously: the Torre del Marzocco in the harbor of Livorno (circa 1439), the wing of papal apartments erected for Pope Martin V at the monastery of Santa Maria Novella, Florence (1418-19), and the Florentine Palazzo dello Strozzino (a connection tentatively suggested by Piero Sanpaolesi at the 1978 Ghiberti Congress in Florence).

Ghiberti's most extensive and generally accepted architectural role took place at the sacristy of the church of Santa Trinita in Florence, where he designed the tomb of Onofrio Strozzi (which was executed by Niccolo di Pietro Lamberti in about 1418) with its classicizing semicircular frame; Ghiberti also was responsible for the entry portal to the room (1423) and, by stylistic association, the window frames as well. The doorway is framed by thin attached columns with Corinthian capitals whose medieval proportions, however, negate their classical details. The sacristy windows feature similarly splayed frames coupled with Gothicizing proportions and details, but the crowning pediments and dentil moldings illustrate the advent of the Renaissance revival. About the same time, Ghiberti also may have installed the doorway leading into the audience hall of the Palazzo di Parte Guelfa in Florence, distinguished by a heavily proportioned lunette arch supported by curiously medieval twisted columns.

Architectural frames appear to have been a specialty of Ghiberti's, and he has been credited with several windows from about 1405 in the tribune areas of Florence Cathedral. These windows are typified by mixed-element arches, a device that occurs also at Orsanmichele in the west door frame (circa 1410), installed by Albizzo di Piero and sometimes attributed to Niccolo Lamberti, and in the tabernacle frame for Ghiberti's statue of Saint John the Baptist for the Wool Merchants Guild (1414). Just as Ghiberti's later (1419-21) statue of Saint Matthew at Orsanmichele shows an abrupt shift toward a revived classicism, so too does the tabernacle frame for that statue. The sober, pediment-crowned niche utilizes an architectural vocabulary akin to that of the Trinita sacristy. Ghiberti's failure to fully embrace the new language of the Renaissance is illustrated by the tabernacle for his statue of Saint Stephen at Orsanmichele (1428), which seems a throwback to the Gothic manner.

The clearest notion of Ghiberti's architectural preferences, as well as the vehicle for his greatest potential impact on architectural style, can be found in several of his sculpture panels. Despite the fact that none of Ghiberti's paintings have been identified (the Birth Salver in Berlin, long attributed to Masaccio, remains an, as yet, unexplored possibility), Ghiberti's approach to relief sculpture was pictorial and, thus, afforded occasion for background architectural views. As was the case with his sculpture, his architectural language embraced both the International Gothic and the *al antica* vocabulary of the Renaissance. The various panels of his first (north) set of baptistery doors (1404-24) illustrate his evolution from Gothic to Renaissance approaches in several of the architectural settings. The differences between the architecture of his earlier "Annunciation" panel and such latter conceptions as the "Flagellation," "Christ Before Pilate" or "Pentecost" panels are as marked as is his handling of the figures and the compositions.

Ghiberti's acceptance of the new Brunelleschian stylistic innovations is most clearly seen in several of the panels of the celebrated east doors (1425-52), in particular in the "Isaac" panel, whose spacious halls and classical memberings remind one of Brunelleschi's church of San Lorenzo; the "Joseph" panel, in which the circular building recalls the Early Christian church of San Stefano Rotondo in Rome and Brunelleschi's intended articulation of the upper story of the Ospedale degli Innocenti; and the "Solomon" panel, with its central temple, which, despite the pointed vaults, reflects the portico of Brunelleschi's Pazzi Chapel. In this latter panel the totality of the architectural space looks forward to the Urbino cityscape panels associated with Francesco di Giorgio. In their architectural settings these panels also would seem to have influenced not only Benozzo Gozzoli but Fra Angelico's Chapel of Nicholas V in the Vatican.

A further development toward the sort of broader architectural compositions discussed in the *De re aedificatoria* of Leon Battista Alberti, or found in the probable intentions of Brunelleschi for the Piazza Santissima Annunziata or in Bernardo Rossellino's urbanscape at Pienza can be seen in backgrounds of the bronze panels of Ghiberti's *Reliquary of Saint Zanobious* (1432-44) in the Florence Cathedral. Certainly, Lorenzo Ghiberti's achievements as an architect were secondary to his considerable accomplishments as a sculptor, yet, despite the investigations of scholars over the last two decades, these achievements have yet to be fully appreciated and integrated into the history of the formation and evolution of Florentine Renaissance architecture.

—CHARLES R. MACK

GIBBERD, Frederick.

British. Born in Coventry, England, 7 January 1908. Died in Harlow, Essex, England, 9 January 1984. Married Dorothy Philips, 1938 (died, 1970); married Patricia Fox Edwards, 1972. Studied architecture in the office of Crouch, Butter and Savage, Birmingham, and at the Birmingham School of Architecture, 1925-29. In private practice, London, 1930 until his death in 1984: principal, Frederick Gibberd and Partners, 1950-78, and consultant, 1978-84. President, Building Centre, London, 1959-76. Fellow, Royal Institute of British Architects, 1939; member of the council, Royal Institute of British Architects, 1951-70. Commander, Order of the British Empire, 1954; knighted, 1967.

Chronology of Works
All in England

1933-36	Pullman Court, Streatham, London
1937-39	Macclesfield Nurses Home, Cheshire
1945-49	Somerfield Estate, Hackney, London
1946-63	Nuneation Town Center, Warwickshire
1946-73	Harlow New Town, Essex
1949-51	Lansbury Market, London
1950-69	Terminal Buildings, Heathrow Airport, near London
1952	Market Square, Harlow, Essex
1953-61	Ulster Hospital, Belfast
1955	College of Technology, Huddersfield, Yorkshire
1956	Bath Technical College, Somerset
1956-68	Civic Center, St. Albans, Hertfordshire
1958	Derwent Reservoir, Durham and Northumberland
1959-69	Civic Center, Doncaster, Yorkshire
1960-67	Roman Catholic Cathedral, Liverpool
1962-66	Douai Abbey, Berkshire
1964	St. George's Chapel, Heathrow Airport, near London
1964-68	Didcot Power Station, Berkshire
1966-75	Arundel Great Court, The Strand, London
1968-75	Inter-Continental Hotel, Hyde Park Corner, London
1969	Coutts Bank, The Strand, London
1969	Kielder Reservoir, Northumberland
1970-77	Central Mosque, Regent's Park, London

Publications

BOOKS BY GIBBERD

The Modern Flat. With F. R. S. Yorke. London, 1937.
The Architecture of England. London, 1938.
Harlow New Town. Harlow, Essex, 1947.
Report of the Oxford University Drama Commission: Supplementary Architectural Report. Oxford, 1948.
Design in Town and Village. With others. London, 1953.
Metropolitan Cathedral of Christ the King. London, 1968.
Sculpture in Harlow. Harlow, Essex, 1973.
Harlow Expansion 1974. Harlow, Essex, 1974.
A Tonic for the Nation—Lansbury. London, 1976.
Harlow: The Story of a New Town. With others. London, 1980.

ARTICLES BY GIBBERD

"Wall Textures." *Architectural Review* (July 1940).
"The Schools and Practice." *Architectural Review* (November 1943).
"Landscaping a New Town." *Architectural Review* (March 1948).
"Three-Dimensional Aspects of Housing Layout." *Royal Institute of British Architects Journal* (August 1948).
"Detail in Civic Design." *Town Planning Institute Journal* (March 1951).
"Expression in Modern Architecture." *Royal Institute of British Architects Journal* (January 1952).
"High Flats in Medium Sized Towns." *Royal Institute of British Architects Journal* (February 1955).
"Mark Hall Neighbourhood." *Architectural Review* (May 1955).
"Designing a New Town." *Far and Wide* (Winter 1957-58).
"New Towns in Britain." *American Institute of Architects Journal* (March 1961).
"The Landscape of Reservoirs." *Journal of the Institute of Water Engineers* (March 1961).
"Reflections on Architecture 1965." *Builder* (December 1964).

Frederick Gibberd: Harlow New Town, Essex, England, 1946-73

"The Landscaping of Reservoirs." *Architectural Review* (July 1966).

"Environmental Aspects of Boulby Mine." *Minerals and the Environment* (June 1974).

"A New Lake for Northumbria." *Country Life* (December 1974).

"Sculpture in the Landscape: The Private Garden." *Journal of the Institute of Landscape Architects* (February 1978).

"An Environmental Centre of the Year 2000." *BEE/Bulletin of Environmental Education* (January 1979).

"Harlow—The Design of a New Town." *Town Planning Review* (January 1982).

"On Making a Garden." *Royal Institute of British Architects Transactions* No. 1 (1982).

"Public Parks." *Landscape Design* (August 1982).

"Further Stages in the Making of a Notable Garden." *House and Garden* (December 1982).

BOOKS ABOUT GIBBERD

Designs of Frederick Gibberd. Exhibition catalog. Harlow, Essex, 1978.

ARTICLES ABOUT GIBBERD

ALDOUS, TONY: "The Gibberd Touch." *Architects' Journal* 167 (January 1978).

COOMBES, MICHAEL: "Sir Frederick Gibberd 1908-1984." *Building* (13 January 1984).

CRUICKSHANK, DAN: "Colchester Camouflage." *Architects' Journal* (27 August 1980).

HUXLEY, ANTHONY: "Landscape Creation of the Present." *Country Life* (18 December 1980).

"London Central Mosque." *Royal Institute of British Architects Journal* (June 1976).

LYALL, SUTHERLAND: "Arundel Great Court, Strand." *Architects' Journal* (3 November 1976).

MADGE, JAMES: "Harpur Centre, Bedford." *Architects' Journal* (11 January 1978).

"Reservoir, Harrow on the Hill." *Landscape Design* (February 1980).

WILLIAMS, STEPHANIE: "The Making of Harlow." *Building Design* (27 August 1976).

WRIGHT, LANCE: "Hotel, Hyde Park Corner." *Architectural Review* (December 1975).

*

During a career spanning more than half a century, Frederick Gibberd contributed to the development and international acclaim of postwar British architecture at several levels. His uniqueness lay in the sheer range of his activities: he was at once the visionary town planner fashioning a whole genre of "New Town" attitudes following the New Towns Act of 1947, the landscape architect acutely aware of the central role of landscape in urban design, the architect of varied but distinguished buildings, and the author of, among other works, the standard treatise on urban planning, *Town Design*.

Gibberd trained at the Birmingham School of Architecture, where he met that doyen of English modernism, F. R. S. Yorke. A shared commitment with Yorke to Continental modernism was evident in Gibberd's first major commission, Pullman Court, Streatham, London, completed in 1936. However, it was for his work at Harlow New Town in Essex from 1947 that he was to gain international recognition. To many contemporaries—particularly Berthold Lubetkin, who had recently been appointed chief architect at Peterlee New Town in County Durham, and the critic J. M. Richards—Harlow represented the antithesis of an urban ideal, with its low-density housing and folksy "People's Detailing" (a pejorative term coined by the contemporary *Architectural Review*), which owed more to English garden city principles than it did to any Continental urban manifesto.

Nevertheless, such caution in introducing Continental modernist principles reaped its benefits in the event where modest buildings accord with a mature landscape, vindicating Gibberd's strongly held views of landscape's integral role with architecture and planning. Harlow's town center, civic, educational and industrial buildings all adhered to orthodox modernist principles, reinforcing the 1951 Festival of Britain's new architecture for "everyman."

During the 1950s and 1960s, his work was varied not only in type but also in expression, suggesting that Gibberd, while firmly of modernist persuasion, also demonstrated traditional pragmatic tendencies. Such variety encompassed his Terminal

Buildings at Heathrow Airport near London (1950-69), the technical colleges at Huddersfield and Bath (appropriately clad in Bath stone) of 1955 and 1956, and a series of civic centers, of which Doncaster, Yorkshire (1959-69), was the most imposing, if somewhat heavy-handed in its execution.

Gibberd's success as a landscape architect led to the important Derwent Reservoir, Durham, commission in 1958, an exemplary case of the sensitive incorporation of a massive public utility with the landscape.

Apart from Harlow, Gibberd is best remembered for his competition-winning design for Liverpool Roman Catholic Cathedral in 1960, which owed much in its initial plan and conical form to Oscar Niemeyer's recently completed Brasilia Cathedral. Gibberd's design was lauded at the time for its uncompromising response to Edwin Lutyens' prewar crypt, but the rehabilitation of the latter architect in more recent times has since tempered that view. In spite of crude detailing and execution (in marked contrast to Basil Spence's cathedral at Coventry), the church makes a powerful statement at an urban level, where its striking silhouette contrasts starkly with that of Giles Gilbert Scott's Anglican Cathedral. At the time, Gibberd's church represented something of an oasis in a distinctly run-down part of the city.

The Liverpool success led to other ecclesiastical commissions, adding further to the enormous breadth of Gibberd's architectural practice. Particularly noteworthy was his London Central Mosque (1969-77), where Gibberd accommodated traditional mosque motifs of surprising scale in that most English of settings, Regent's Park.

The end of Gibberd's career was marked by a series of shopping centers throughout England, but most notably by the celebrated Coutts Bank, The Strand, London (1969-78), where a dramatic interior was partially enclosed by retention of an existing facade by John Nash, an early essay in conservation. Similarly urbane was the Inter-Continental Hotel at Hyde Park Corner, London (1968-75), demonstrating Gibberd at his most confident and mature but still adhering to the modernist principles which he never forsook throughout his rich and varied career.

The Kielder Reservoir, Northumberland, signaled a return to his landscape concerns, and was as successful as his Derwent and Llyn Celyn reservoirs of the previous decade.

Gibberd was also a teacher and writer; the war years saw him as a principal at the Architectural Association, London, while his prolific publication output ranged from *The Modern Flat* (with F. R. S. Yorke, 1937) to a series of articles on public parks and gardens published in the early 1980s. Among his contemporaries, Gibberd was unique not only in the sheer volume and range of his output, but also in his willingness to communicate his theoretical stance in a stream of books and articles.

For many critics, however, his work lacks the intellectual rigor, say, of Denys Lasdun, and does not match the intuitive flair of Basil Spence, but Harlow New Town and Liverpool Cathedral alone would have secured Gibberd's place in the annals of postwar British architecture.

—A. PETER FAWCETT

GIBBS, James.

Scottish. Born in Aberdeen, Scotland, 1682. Died in London, England, 5 August 1754. Studied at Scots College; pupil of

Carlo Fontana, Rome. Worked independently; surveyor, 1714; Architect of the Ordnance, Surrey, 1727.

Chronology of Works
All in England unless noted
* Approximate dates
† Work no longer exists

1710*	Mar Lodge, Alloa, Clackmannan, Scotland
1714*-23	Newcastle Monument, Westminster Abbey, London
1714-23	St. Mary-le-Strand, London
1715*	Burlington House, London (additions)
1716*-19	Cannons House, Middlesex
1716*-28	Lowther Hall, Westmoreland
1717*-28	Sudbrook Park, Surrey
1719-20	St. Clement Danes, London (steeple)
1719*-30	Walpole Hall, Cambridgeshire
1720*	Johnston's Octagonal Pavilion (Orleans House), Twickenham, Middlesex
1720*	Alexander Pope Villa, Twickenham, Middlesex
1720-21	Down Hall, Essex
1720-26	St. Martin-in-the-Fields, London (rebuilding)
1721-23	Matthew Prior Monument, Westminster Abbey, London
1721-24	Oxford Chapel, London (St. Peter's, Vere Street)
1722-30	Senate House, Cambridge
1723-25	All Saints Cathedral, Derby
1724-27	James Craggs Monument, Westminster Abbey, London
1724*-39	Tring Park, Hertfordshire
1724-49	King's College Fellows Building, Cambridge
1725*	Gubbins, Hertfordshire†
1725*-26	Whitton Park, Middlesex†
1726*-28	Gibbs Building and Boycott Pavilions, Stowe, Buckinghamshire
1728*	Hackwood Park, Hampshire
1728*-32	Kelmarsh Hall, Northamptonshire
1728-37	Mansion House, London
1728-54	St. Bartholomew's Hospital, London
1734-35	Duchess of Norfolk's House, London
1737-54	Radcliffe Library, Oxford
1739	Temple of Friendship, Stowe, Buckinghamshire
1739-41	Turner Mausoleum, Kirkleatham, Yorkshire
1740*	Hartwell House, Buckinghamshire
1741-44	Temple of Liberty, Stowe, Buckinghamshire
1741-55	Saint Nicholas Church West, Aberdeen, Scotland
1743-54	Patshull Hall and Church, Staffordshire
1744*-48	Ladies' Temple, Stowe, Buckinghamshire†
1747-48	Cobham Monument, Stowe, Buckinghamshire
1750*	Bank Hall (Town Hall), Warrington, Lancashire
1750*-55	Ragley Hall, Warwickshire

Publications

BOOKS BY JAMES GIBBS

A Book of Architecture, Containing Designs of Buildings and Ornaments. London, 1728.
Rules for Drawing the Several Parts of Architecture. London, 1732.
Bibliotheca Radcliviana. London, 1747.

BOOKS ABOUT GIBBS

DOWNES, KERRY: *English Baroque Architecture.* London, 1966.

James Gibbs: Senate House, Cambridge, England, 1722-30

FRIEDMAN, TERRY: *James Gibbs.* New Haven, Connecticut, and London, 1984.

GILLIAM, S. G.: *The Building Accounts of the Radcliffe Camera.* Oxford, 1958.

LITTLE, BRYAN: *The Life and Works of James Gibbs, 1682-1754.* London, 1955.

SERVICE, ALASTAIR: *The Architects of London.* London, 1979.

SUMMERSON, JOHN: *Architecture in Britain 1530-1830.* 7th ed. Harmondsworth, England, 1983.

WHINNEY, MARGARET: *Sculpture in Britain 1530 to 1830.* Harmondsworth, England, 1964.

WILLIS, PETER: *Charles Bridgeman and the English Landscape Garden.* London, 1977.

WILLIS, ROBERT, and CLARK, JOHN WILLIS: *The Architectural History of the University of Cambridge, and of the Colleges of Cambridge and Eton.* Cambridge, 1886.

ARTICLES ABOUT GIBBS

FIELD, JOHN: "Early Unknown Gibbs." *Architectural Review* (May 1962).

HOLLOWAY, JOHN: "A James Gibbs Autobiography." *Burlington Magazine* (May 1955).

JACKSON-STOPS, G.: "The Cliveden Album: Drawings by Archer, Leoni and Gibbs." *Architectural History* 19 (1976).

LANG, S.: "Gibbs: A Bicentenary Review of His Architectural Sources." *Architectural Review* (July 1954).

LANG, S.: "By Hawksmoor out of Gibbs." *Architectural Review* (April 1949).

MACWILLIAM, A. S.: "James Gibbs, Architect, 1682-1754." *Innes Review* 5 (1954).

OSWALD, ARTHUR: "James Gibbs and His Portraits." *Country Life Annual* (1963).

STUTCHBURY, H. E.: "Palladian Gibbs." *Transactions of the Ancient Monuments Society* New series, 7 (1960).

WHIFFEN, MARCUS: "The Progeny of St. Martin in the Fields." *Architectural Review* 100 (July 1946).

*

The Palladian and Baroque architect James Gibbs came from a Catholic family whose actual name was Gibb. The young Gibb left his native city in about 1700 to travel on the Continent, displaying an interest in architecture and drawing. He reached Rome in 1703, and entered the Scots College to prepare for the Catholic priesthood. He soon left the college, however, and took up architecture instead. Gibb trained with Carlo Fontana for a period of about five years. Fontana was the leading architect of the Late Baroque in Papal Rome, and must have been an important influence on Gibb's architecture, which was principally in the Baroque style but used some Palladian sources.

In 1709 Gibb returned to Scotland, but in 1710 he settled in London, one of the first Scotsmen to make a career in one of the important professions in England. Gibb kept quiet about his Catholicism, and added an "s" to his name to seem less Scottish. He became a friend of Christopher Wren, who admired his drawing and respected his professional training, which was unusual among English architects of that time. In 1714 Gibbs became one of the "surveyors" under the New Churches Act of 1711. The peak of Gibbs' activity came in the 1720s and 1730s, when, according to Horace Walpole, Gibbs became the most fashionable architect in England.

Gibbs' church designs were all for Protestant churches, and arranged for 18th-century Anglican worship, which emphasized preaching and had few Communion services. The Parish Church of St. Martin-in-the-Fields (1722-26) is among Gibbs' most famous buildings. The splendid steeple owes a debt to some of Wren's more elaborate steeples in the city of London. It starts with a square stage with Ionic pilasters, surmounted with a more fanciful stage with urns at the corners, which contains the clock. The steeple is finished with an octagonal lantern with Corinthian half columns and a graceful short spire. Gibbs submitted several designs for St. Martin's, among which were a number of circular designs. These were rejected for reasons of expense, and thus had no immediate influence. They were adapted in the 1790s, however, for All Saints' Church in Newcastle-on-Tyne and St. Chad's at Shrewsbury. Gibbs must have admired many buildings in Rome, notably the Church of Santa Maria della Pace by Pietro da Cortona. Its porch served as a model for that of the Church of St. Mary-le-Strand in London. Gibbs' last church designs, executed in 1741, were for the reconstruction of the Presbyterian Church of St. Nicholas at Aberdeen. Construction according to those designs was not begun until 1752, however.

Like many of his contemporaries, and not surprisingly in an architect drawing mostly on classical and classicizing sources, Gibbs had little admiration for the Gothic style. Until the Gothic Revival, which did not begin until about 1755, after Gibbs' death, the Middle Ages and Gothic architecture were generally thought of as barbaric. However, in 1725 Gibbs was asked to make a survey of the Gothic Lincoln Cathedral, which was in poor condition. He designed some "Roman" arches in the interior to provide support for the western towers, which still survive.

In 1729 Gibbs completed his designs for the new quadrangle of St. Bartholomew's Hospital in London. Only three of his proposed blocks were actually constructed, however. In the 1730s Gibbs designed and supervised the construction of the Radcliffe Library at Oxford. The circular library has a boldly ribbed dome and three-quarter columns, which recall the dome and columns of St. Peter's in Rome. The building was set above an open piazza, which could be closed off with iron gates but is now glazed in.

One of Gibbs' last works was the design for the splendid decoration of the entrance hall at Ragley Hall in Warwickshire. It is unlikely that Gibbs supervised the work himself, and the designs must have been sent up for masons, stuccoworkers and other craftsmen to render without the architect's personal supervision.

Gibbs' significance rests not only in his buildings, but also derives from his pioneering *Book of Architecture,* which was an architectural pattern book published in 1728. It was the first of such books aimed at craftsmen—masons, joiners, makers of decorative items, such as urns, fireplaces and murals—and considerably enhanced Gibbs' architectural influence. It was most useful to provincial, and indeed colonial, craftsmen, who could render the designs of an acknowledged master with the aid of the patterns. As Gibbs himself explained, the book "would be of use to such gentlemen as might be concerned in Building, especially in the remote parts of the country, where little assistance for Designs can be procured." The book also contained his unexecuted designs. The drawings in the *Book of Architecture* and in his drawings now in the Ashmolean Museum at Oxford prove Gibbs to have been an outstanding draftsman.

Gibbs' last years were spent in comparative retirement, with few architectural commissions. He died in London in 1754, leaving his large private library and many of his drawings to the Radcliffe Library at Oxford.

—BRYAN LITTLE

GILBERT, Cass.

American. Born in Zanesville, Ohio, 28 January 1858. Died in Ridgefield, Connecticut, 17 May 1934. Son was the architect Cass Gilbert, Jr. Architectural apprenticeship in St. Paul, Minnesota; studied at Massachusetts Institute of Technology, Cambridge, Massachusetts, 1879. Assistant to Stanford White of McKim, Mead and White, New York, 1880; opened office with James Knox Taylor (1857-ca. 1929), St. Paul, 1882; opened own office in St. Paul, 1892; moved office to New York City, 1905; consultin g architect for the New York Authority on the Hudson River and Kill Van Kull Bridges. President, American Institute of Architects, 1908; appointed chairman of the Council of Fine Arts by President Theodore Roosevelt.

Chronology of Works
All in the United States
* Approximate dates
† Work no longer exists

1888	Dayton Avenue Presbyterian Church, St. Paul, Minnesota
1889	Charles P. Noyes House, St. Paul, Minnesota
1895	Boston Clothing House Block, St. Paul, Minnesota
1895-1903	Minnesota State Capitol, St. Paul, Minnesota
1896	Brazer Building, Boston, Massachusetts
1899-1900	Broadway-Chambers Building, New York City
1901-07	United States Custom House, New York City
1902	Union Club, New York City
1902-04	St. Louis Art Museum, Louisiana Purchase Exposition Art Building, St. Louis, Missouri
1905-07	West Street Building, New York City
1911-13	Woolworth Building, New York City
1924-25	Chamber of Commerce Building, Washington, D.C.
1925-28	New York Life Insurance Building, New York City

Publications

BOOKS ABOUT GILBERT

GEBHARD, DAVID, and MARTINSON, TOM: *A Guide to the Architecture of Minnesota*. Minneapolis, 1977.

HITCHCOCK, HENRY-RUSSELL, and SEALE, WILLIAM: *Temples of Democracy: The State Capitols of the U.S.A.*. New York, 1976.

IRISH, SHARON L.: *Cass Gilbert's Career in New York City, 1879-1905*. Ann Arbor, Michigan, 1990.

THOMPSON, NEIL B.: *Minnesota's State Capitol: The Art and Politics of a Public Building*. St. Paul, Minnesota, 1974.

TORBERT, DONALD: *A Century of Art and Architecture in Minnesota*. Minneapolis, 1958.

WEISMAN, WINSTON: "A New View of Skyscraper History." Pp. 115-160 in EDGAR KAUFMAN, JR. (ed.): *The Rise of An American Architecture*. New York, 1970.

ARTICLES ABOUT GILBERT

JONES, ROBERT ALLEN: "Cass Gilbert, Midwestern Architect in New York." Ph.D. dissertation. Case Western Reserve University, Cleveland, Ohio, 1976.

KIRKHAM, GUY: "Cass Gilbert, Master of Style." *Pencil Points* 15:541-556 (1934).

MURPHY, PATRICIA ANNE: ''The Early Career of Cass Gilbert: 1878 to 1895.'' M. A. thesis. University of Virginia, Charlottesville, 1976.

''New York Life Insurance Company Building, New York.'' *American Architect* 135 (1929): 351-414.

SCHUYLER, MONTGOMERY: ''The New Custom House at New York.'' *Architectural Record* 20 (July 1906): 1-14.

SCHUYLER, MONTGOMERY: ''The Towers of Manhattan; and Notes on the Woolworth Building.'' *Architectural Record* 33 (February 1913): 99-122.

SWALES, F.: ''The Work of Cass Gilbert.'' *Architectural Review* 31 (1912): 3-16.

WEBER, P. J.: ''A Review of the Works of Cass Gilbert.'' *Architectural Review* 1 (30 June 1897): 42-65.

''The West Street Building.'' *Architectural Record* 22 (August 1907): 102-109.

*

The American architect Cass Gilbert began his career as a carpenter's helper and draftsman for Abraham Radcliff in St. Paul, Minnesota, in 1876. Having decided to become an architect, he went to the Massachusetts Institute of Technology; during 1880 he traveled widely in Europe, studying Roman, Gothic and Renaissance architecture. When he returned to the United States, Gilbert entered the office of McKim, Mead and White, then just beginning its rapid rise to prominence; he remained three years and quickly became one of the major assistants in the office. His role became so important that the partners planned to create a branch office, headed by Gilbert, in St. Paul, in anticipation of a series of important commissions from the Northern Pacific Railroad. When the railroad projects failed to materialize, Gilbert nonetheless remained in St. Paul and set out on his own, soon forming a partnership with a boyhood friend, James Knox Taylor. Due to a paucity of commissions, their partnership lasted only until 1892, when Taylor withdrew. At first with Taylor and then working alone, Gilbert produced a number of houses and churches in St. Paul and Minneapolis, as well as several smaller regional stations for the Northern Pacific Railroad. Meanwhile Gilbert, a skilled artist, supplemented his limited income with the sale of watercolors.

Gilbert's rise to national recognition came from his selection as architect for the new Minnesota State Capitol in 1895. The original state capitol had been built in St. Paul in 1851-53, based on designs of carpenter and joiner N. C. Prentice. Its bulky proportions, thin Doric portico and bulbous dome had never been warmly received. That wooden structure was so severely damaged by fire in 1881 that construction of a temporary structure proved necessary. When the Minnesota legislature convened in 1893, it authorized expenditure of $2 million for a permanent replacement. Influenced by the popular success of the World's Columbian Exposition in Chicago, the legislature also resolved to obtain the design for the new capitol in competition, following in large part the guidelines in the newly enacted Tarsney Act that provided for competitions for new federal government buildings. In contrast to the wording of the Tarsney Act, however, which provided that winning architects in federal competitions were to be hired as supervising architects, at the standard fee of 5 percent of the building's cost, the Minnesota legislature stipulated half that amount and specified the dimensions of the new buildings before any consideration had been given to the spaces needed within.

As the most active advocate for the American Institute of Architects in Minnesota, Gilbert met frequently with the new capitol commissioners, arguing vehemently but unsuccessfully against the substandard fees. The competition was announced and advertised, and two architects, Henry Ives Cobb of Chicago and Edmund M. Wheelright of Boston, were engaged as jurors. In October 1894, these two met with the commissioners to review the 56 sets of drawings received (Gilbert had refused to participate). Prize premiums were paid, but all drawings were returned because no entry was judged suitable for building. The program for a second competition was drawn up and this time Gilbert agreed to enter, for the legislature had voted to permit a fee of 5 percent for the supervising architect. In October 1895, the judging of the 41 new entries began. The voting among the commissioners and Wheelright (by then the sole professional juror), shifted day by day, in favor of one competitor or another; finally, however, Gilbert was unanimously awarded first prize and hired as supervising architect for the new capitol. Although excavation began four months later, the laying of the foundations and the cornerstone in July 1898 was delayed due to political and financial difficulties.

Gilbert's winning design was based closely on the Rhode Island State Capitol, begun by his mentors, McKim, Mead and White, only four years before. Essentially a long rectangular block, the capitol was to be raised on a tall basement, with projecting pavilions at each end, and larger projecting pavilions with recessed loggias at the center, all surmounted by an imposing dome clearly inspired by Michelangelo's dome on St. Peter's in Rome. Gilbert had specified marble for the body of the building as well as the dome, if funds were sufficient. The building was to be of solid masonry walls with internal supports of iron and steel. After considerable political wrangling, the commissioners voted to use Minnesota granite for the basement levels, white Georgia marble for the superstructure, and other Minnesota stones for interior foundations.

With improving general economic conditions during 1897-99 as the nation emerged from a protracted business depression, the Minnesota legislature provided additional funds for mural paintings by John La Farge, Edward Simmons, Elmer Garnsey and Edwin Howland Blashfield, and for sculptural embellishment by the celebrated sculptor Daniel Chester French. For the dome, Gilbert devised an ingenious solution, with an internal marble shell, an intermediate steel-and-masonry cone rising to support the lantern, and a self-supporting outer shell built of brick-backed marble. The intermediate cone was made waterproof and a gutter provided at the bottom, between its base and that of the outer dome shell. In this way Gilbert was able to drain away any leakage in the outer shell, thus preventing damage that could have been caused by alternate freezing and thawing during bitter Minnesota winters.

The exterior of the Minnesota capitol was finished in 1903; the building was occupied by the legislature in January 1905, and the interior was completed with all external landscaping in 1907. Altogether the project had cost $4.5 million, more than double the original appropriation, but resulted in a solid and handsome building, prized by Minnesotans as demonstrating that Minnesota was no longer a rural province on the frontier. It also propelled Gilbert to the forefront of his profession. Later, in 1922, Gilbert would draw on this success in his design for the West Virginia State Capitol in Charleston, finished in 1932 by his son, Cass Gilbert, Jr.

Buoyed by the success of the Minnesota Capitol, in 1899 Gilbert moved his office to New York, and received a number of important commissions for major commercial buildings there and in Boston, culminating in his winning the competition for the New York Custom House, New York City (1901-07), a massive block at the southern tip of Manhattan, heavily embellished inside and out. This was followed by several tall office towers in lower Manhattan, including one of 24 stories at 90 West Street (1905) using Gothic arches, clustered colonnettes,

Cass Gilbert: Minnesota State Capitol, St. Paul, Minnesota, 1895-1903

and other 14th-century details in terra cotta. This prepared him for the soaring Woolworth Building in New York City (1911-13), perhaps Gilbert's most noteworthy creation. Until 1930 the tallest building in the world, the Woolworth Building loomed above all its neighbors, celebrating its verticality with its multiplied vertical lines. Its unprecedented 55 stories rose 760 feet 6 inches to the top of the spire, exploiting and pushing to the limit the technology of steel-frame construction. Instead of rising in one massive block like Chicago skyscrapers, the Woolworth Building consisted of a tall U-shaped base out of which rose a tower, terminating in a series of setbacks and a richly embellished spire, all entirely clad in white glazed terracotta with subdued color accents. Within three years, new zoning ordinances in New York City required all future tall office blocks to be set back in a similar fashion.

Critical acclaim also came to Gilbert for his design of the focal group of buildings for the Louisiana Purchase Exposition in St. Louis, Missouri, in 1904. Its heavily scaled and richly embellished domed centerpiece, Festival Hall, was framed by cascading semicircular water terraces. After the fair, Gilbert was involved in relandscaping the grounds for a public park,

included in which was a building constructed to survive the fair; this was refitted by Gilbert to become the St. Louis Art Museum (1902-04).

Largely on the critical success of these early buildings, Gilbert was elected president of the American Institute of Architects in 1908. This was followed, two years later, by his appointment to the National Commission of Fine Arts, a body that ruled on all new federal buildings being constructed in Washington, D.C. Gilbert's involvement in Washington increased with commissions for the United States Treasury Annex (1918-19), the District's Chamber of Commerce (1924-25) and, most important, the somber white marble neoclassical building for the Supreme Court directly behind the United States Capitol building (1933-35).

Meanwhile, Gilbert received important commissions in New York and elsewhere, including the Public Library in Detroit, Michigan (1921), closely patterned after the Boston Public Library by McKim, Mead and White. For the New York Life Insurance Company in New York City (1925-28), Gilbert faced the difficult problem of erecting a large office building filling an entire city block at the northeast corner of Madison Square.

His solution was a series of setbacks at the lower level, with a tower and spire rising from its center. The building also has the dubious distinction of replacing the festive Madison Square Garden by McKim, Mead and White. Gilbert's interiors, however, incorporated those designed by Stanford White for the insurance company's former headquarters in lower Manhattan. For the New York Lawyer's Club, New York City (1930), Gilbert created a greatly restrained neo-Georgian interpretation of a London club. Gilbert's large and imposing Roman-detailed United States Courthouse in New York City (1936) was finished by his son.

One of Gilbert's last commissions is today best known for the absence of Gilbert's contribution: the George Washington Bridge at the north end of Manhattan (1927-31). Gilbert was consulting architect, with O. H. Ammann as engineer for the New York Port Authority. The heavy steel towers and cable-anchor pylons were to have been enclosed in masonry designed by Gilbert, but conditions imposed by the worsening business depression prevented completion. Today, ironically, many observers believe the bridge achieves its particular beauty specifically because the structural system is not hidden behind Gilbert's masonry.

—LELAND M. ROTH

GIL DE HONTAÑÓN, Rodrigo.

Spanish. Born in Rasines, in the province of Santander, Spain, 1500. Died in 1577. Illegitimate son of the master stonemason Juan Gil de Hontañón. Apprenticed to his father and other Castillian masters, and had become a master mason by 1526. Served as master mason of Segovia, 1526-40, and as master of Salamanca Cathedral, 1538; master at Astorga Cathedral, 1549-59.

Chronology of Works
All in Spain

1526-29	Cathedral, Segovia
1529	Church of San Sebastian, Villacastin
1533	Church of Santiago, Medina de Rioseco
1537-53	College of San Ildefonso, Alcala de Henares (facade)
1537-77	Cathedral, Salamanca
1538	Cathedral, Santiago de Compostela (cloister)
1540	Church of San Martin, Mota del Marques
1540-49	Cathedral, Ciudad Rodrigo (choir)
1544	Cathedral, Plasencia
1551	Cathedral, Astorga (south portal)
1553-57	Cathedral, Astorga (transept chapels)
1556	Monastery Church of San Esteban, Salamanca
1563-77	Cathedral, Segovia
1566-72	Church of La Magdalena, Valladolid

Publications

BOOKS ABOUT GIL DE HONTAÑÓN

ALVAREZ VILLAR, JULIAN: *El palacio de la Salina de Salamanca*. Salamanca, 1984.
CAMON AZNAR, JOSÉ: *La arquitectura plateresca*. 2 vols. Madrid, 1945.
CASASECA, ANTONIO: *Rodrigo Gil de Hontañón*. Valladolid, 1989.
CASTILLO OREJA, M. A.: *Colegio Mayor de San Ildefonso de Alcalá de Henares, génesis y desarrollo de su construcción*. Madrid, 1980.
CHUECA GOITIA, FERNANDO: *Arquitectura del siglo XVI: Ars Hispaniae*. Vol. 11. Madrid, 1953.
CHUECA GOITIA, FERNANDO: *La catedral nueva de Salamanca: Historia documental de su construcción*. Salamanca, 1951.
GARCIA, SIMON: *Compendio de arquitectura y simetria de los templos*. Salamanca, 1681. Reprint: Salamanca, 1941.
HOAG, JOHN DOUGLAS: *Rodrigo Gil de Hontañón: Gótico y renacimiento en la arquitectura española del siglo XVI*. Madrid, 1985.
KUBLER, GEORGE, and SORIA, MARTIN: *Art and Architecture in Spain and Portugal and their American Dominions, 1500-1800*. Harmondsworth, England, and Baltimore, 1959.
LOZOYA, JUAN CONTRERAS Y LOPEZ DE AYALA: *Rodrigo Gil de Hontañón en Segovia*. Santander, 1962.
PEREDA DE LA REGUERA, MANUEL (ed.): *Rodrigo Gil de Hontañón, selección y estudio*. Santander, 1951.
RODRIGUEZ G. DE CEBALLOS, ALFONSO: *La iglesia y el convento de San Esteban de Salamanca*. Salamanca, 1987.
SENDIN CALABUIG, MANUEL: *El colegio mayor del Arzobispo Fonseca en Salamanca*. Salamanca, 1977.
TORRES BALBAS, LEOPOLDO: *Arquitectura gótica*. Madrid, 1952.

ARTICLES ABOUT GIL DE HONTAÑÓN

CAMON AZNAR, JOSÉ: "La intervencion de Rodrigo Gil en el manuscrito de Simon García." *Archivo español de arte* 14 (1940-41): 300-305.
GARCIA-MURGA ALCANTARA, JUAN: "La intervención de Rodrigo Gil de Hontañón en la iglesia de Santa Maria de Guareña. *Goya* 144 (1978): 315-323.
KUBLER, GEORGE: "A Late Gothic Computation of Rib Vault Thrusts." *Gazette des beaux-arts* Series 6, 26 (1944): 135-148.
MAINSTONE, ROWLAND: "Structural Theory and Design Before 1742." *Architectural Review* (April 1968): 303-310.
NAVASCUÉS PALACIO, PEDRO: "Rodrigo Gil y los entalladores de la fachada de la universidad de Alcalá." *Archivo español de arte* 45 (1972): 103-117.
SANABRIA, SERGIO: "The Mechanization of Design in the 16th Century: The Structural Formulae of Rodrigo Gil de Hontañón." *Journal of the Society of Architectural Historians* 41 (December 1982): 281-293.
SANABRIA, SERGIO: "From Gothic to Renaissance Stereotomy: The Design Methods of Philibert de l'Orme and Alonso de Vandelvira." *Technology and Culture* 30, No. 2 (1989): 266-299.

*

Rodrigo Gil de Hontañón, the most prolific Spanish architect of the 16th century, was the illegitimate son of Juan Gil de Hontañón, Late Gothic master of the cathedrals of Salamanca, Segovia and Seville. Educated under the tutelage of his father and other distinguished Castillian masters, Rodrigo's career spanned the last flowering of the Gothic in Spain and the simultaneous development of the Renaissance. As a Gothic master, he directed the two great late cathedrals in that style, Segovia (1526-29 and 1563-77), and Salamanca (1537-77), both begun by Juan. The choir of Segovia is especially remarkable, begun in 1563 following Rodrigo's redesign. He also constructed the choir of the cathedral of Ciudad Rodrigo (1540-49) and was

Rodrigo Gil de Hontañon: College of San Ildefonso, Alcala de Henares, Spain, 1537-53

master at the cathedral of Astorga (1549-59), responsible for transept chapels (1553-57) and the south portal (1551). He was awarded three major works begun by Juan de Alava: the cloister of the cathedral of Santiago de Compostela in 1538, the soaring cathedral of Plasencia in 1544, and the monastery church of San Esteban in Salamanca in 1556. A fine late work is the church of La Magdalena in Valladolid (1566-72). These buildings rank Rodrigo as the most accomplished member of the last generation of Gothic builders in Spain.

Rodrigo was also among the foremost Plateresque masters, epitomizing the Castillian Renaissance style. The facade of the college of San Ildefonso at the university in Alcalá de Henares (1537-53) is perhaps his best work, combining Gothic geometric proportions with Renaissance forms. The three-story central doorway resembles French designs, such as the entrance gate of Château Gaillon or the Golden Gate at Fontainebleau of Gilles le Breton, as well as rare Italian examples, such as the arch of Alfonso II in Naples, the church of Santa Maria dell'Anima in Rome attributed to Giuliano da Sangallo, or the church of San Bernardino in l'Aquila by Cola dell'Amatrice, begun 1525.

However, many Spanish Mudéjar, Gothic and Early Renaissance facades also have triple-story portals: Lorenzo Vázquez's college of Santa Cruz in Valladolid (circa 1485) is an important example. Rodrigo's facade probably was not directly influenced by foreign models, but manipulated native ideas into a coherent expressive whole.

The unfinished palace in Salamanca of Don Alonso de Acevedo y Zúñiga, count of Monterrey, designed in 1539 with Fray Martín de Santiago, is equally noteworthy. Based on Milanese models, its design was a vast quadrilateral with four wings and corner towers plus two projecting rear wings. Less than half was completed. Also in Salamanca is the eclectic palace for Alonso de Fonseca, juxtaposing Late Gothic, Islamic and Brunelleschian wings in its courtyard. Other important Plateresque palaces are the U-shaped Casa Rodrigo de Ulloa in Mota del Marqués, begun in the early 1540s, and the splendid Casa Guzmanes in Leon, begun circa 1558, completed by Rodrigo's disciple Juan del Ribero Rada.

Rodrigo used this synthetic style in ecclesiastical work, as in the church for Las Bernardas in Salamanca, contracted in

1552. It has a Late Gothic single nave and a classicizing square sanctuary with shell-shaped squinches supporting a shell-shaped semidome. He also spearheaded the transformation of northern Spanish hall churches to the Renaissance style, as at San Sebastián in Villacastín (begun 1529) San Martín at Mota del Marqués (begun before 1534), and Santiago in Medina de Rioseco, designed in 1533.

Rodrigo's unusual grasp of the two conflicting styles makes him the most important architect of the transitional period in Spain. His work is as fine and inspired as that of Pedro de Machuca, Diego de Siloe, Andrés de Vandelvira, or even Juan de Herrera, whose restrained classicism ultimately supplanted Rodrigo's style in official favor.

Despite an extremely busy and peripatetic career, Rodrigo found time to jot down notes for an architectural treatise. His original text and illustrations, apparently kept at the cathedral of Salamanca, are lost, but parts were copied about 1681 by Simón García, a Salmantine architect, as part of a Baroque architectural compendium.

Rodrigo's booklet illuminated the last formulaic development of Gothic tradition, and introduced classical ideas into it. The booklet presented proportioning and structural formulae to be followed by an architect designing a temple. Although Rodrigo apparently did not use them in his designs, they would have simplified repetitive tasks in a large architectural practice. Two proportioning systems were based on square and circle (geometry) and on human proportions (analogy). A system based on a musical canon of octaves and fifths was discussed briefly. The chapters on classical orders in Simón García's manuscript are not by Rodrigo, and it seems unlikely he would have included such a topic in his original writings.

Gothic spatial geometric planning, undoubtedly reflecting his father's teachings, seemed unfashionable to Rodrigo, who included it for those who might not understand human proportions. Analogy was his favorite method. Aisle widths of churches were proportioned using body width, arm length to elbows, or forearm and hand lengths. Elevations of three-aisled hall churches were like a body without a head. Elements such as windows, pediments, stairs and towers fit into the large human figure whenever possible. For example, nave windows could be sized and placed using the head of the upright body regulating the transverse section. For other details, *homunculi* were embedded into the fabric so that human proportions were repeated at a small scale. Human analogy or geometry were used only to control interior spaces. Structural components were normally sized by independent structural formulae. Only the ribs of Late Gothic vaults were proportioned by analogy, using fingernail measurements. Pier buttresses were sized by five arithmetic and geometric formulae. Another formula for the correct weight of a keystone in a vault or arch was a unique discussion of this problem in 16th-century architectural literature. Also unique was a condensed step-by-step description of the construction of a rib vault and the empirical methods used to solve stereotomic problems.

With human proportioning, Rodrigo created churches typologically similar to geometrically constructed Gothic ones. Differences between geometric and human proportions are small, so Vitruvius' opinion that the human figure is extracted from the circle and the square was confirmed. Nonetheless, the generator of the form changed from an abstract geometric diagram to a living body, suggestive of the idea of the creation of man by God in his own image, a cosmological analogy between architect and God current since the 13th century.

—SERGIO L. SANABRIA

GILL, Irving

American. Born in Syracuse, New York, 1870. Died in Carlsbad, California, 7 October 1936. Married Marion Breashears, 1929. Worked as a draftsman for Adler and Sullivan, Chicago, 1890-93; opened own office, San Diego, California, 1895; worked in partnership with W. S. Hebbard, San Diego, 1898-1906, and with his nephew, Louis J. Gill, 1914-16; also maintained office in Los Angeles.

Chronology of Works
All in the United States
† *Work no longer exists*

1904-06	George Marston House, San Diego, California (with William S. Hebbard)
1906	Burnham House, San Diego, California (with Hebbard)
1907	Laughlin House, Los Angeles, California
1908	Wilson Acton Hotel, La Jolla, California
1908-09	Holly Sefton Memorial Hospital for Children, San Diego, California†
1908-10	Scripps Institution of Oceanography, La Jolla, California
1909	Bentham Hall, Bishop's School, La Jolla, California
1910	Lewis Courts, Sierra Madre, California
1910	Scripps Hall, Bishop's School, La Jolla, California
1911	Timken House, San Diego, California†
1912	Banning House, Los Angeles, California
1913	Women's Club, La Jolla, California
1914	Recreation Building, La Jolla, California
1914-16	Dodge House, Los Angeles, California†
1915	Ellen Scripps House, La Jolla, California
1916	Gilman Hall, Bishop's School, La Jolla, California (with Louis J. Gill)
1919	Horatio West Court, Santa Monica, California
1927	First Church of Christ Scientist, Coronado, California
1929	City Hall, Oceanside, California (with John Siebert)
1931	Kindergarten, Oceanside, California (with Siebert)

Publications

ARTICLES BY GILL

''The Home of the Future: The New Architecture of the West—Small Homes for a Great Country.'' *Craftsman* 30, (May 1916): 140-151.

BOOKS ABOUT GILL

GEBHARD, DAVID, and WINTER, ROBERT: *A Guide to Architecture in Los Angeles and Southern California.* Santa Barbara, California, 1977.
JORDY, WILLIAM H.: ''Craftsmanship as Reductive Simplification: Irving Gill's Dodge House.'' In *American Buildings and Their Architects: Progressive and Academic Ideals at the Turn of the Twentieth Century.* Garden City, New York, 1972.
KAMERLING, BRUCE: *Irving Gill: The Artist as Architect.* California, 1979.
McCOY, ESTHER: *Five California Architects.* New York, 1960.
McCOY, ESTHER: *Irving Gill 1870-1936.* Exhibition catalog. Los Angeles, 1958.
STARR, KEVIN: *Americans and the California Dream.* New York, 1973.

ARTICLES ABOUT GILL

"Irving Gill's Dodge House 1916-65." *Arts and Architecture* (September 1965).

*

Irving Gill's legacy is an American architecture of the frontier Southwest whose sources lay in the Spanish mission and 20th-century technology. He was an untrained architect whose father was a builder, and his lifelong interest rested more firmly in construction methodology than in building styles. Though Gill was born in New York state and learned his craft with the Chicago school, his architecture is rooted in southern California in type and locale. His desire to work in a structurally clear, unadorned cubist format was wedded to the regional factors of the West Coast; the result was a modernist architecture that reflected the climate, topography and heritage of the site. Aspects of his works reflect European currents of the time, especially the work of C. F. A. Voysey in England and Charles Rennie Mackintosh in Scotland. However, Gill's puritan ethos and democratic philosophies define him as an American idealist in the vein of Walt Whitman.

Gill went to Chicago in 1890 and worked initially in the office of J. Lyman Silsbee. Within six months, he joined the firm of Adler and Sullivan as a draftsman for the Transportation Building for the 1893 World's Columbian Exposition. In 1892 he arrived in San Diego, where he found an "unwritten page" in need of an architectural identity. His tenure in Louis Sullivan's office with Frank Lloyd Wright left him with the idea of a democracy in architecture, a rejection of the Beaux-Arts traditions rooted in Rome and the Renaissance, and an interest in and respect for modern materials.

Gill saw Sullivan's appreciation for the sheer walls of African architecture paralleled in the southwestern adobe. The low hills and broad expanse of desert combined with the Spanish and Native American cultural history inspired a local style that would be tempered with technology. Gill's eventual aim was a middle-class architecture incorporating his own sober aesthetics, cost efficiency and regionalism. Function, simplification and sanitation were the keys to his design process and led to his gradual involvement with reinforced concrete, prefabricated building construction and an architecture seen as avant-garde.

Gill's early commissions in the San Diego area gave little indication of his fully developed style. They included a normal school (1895, demolished); the Pickwick Theater, based on Sullivan's Transportation Building; and a fountain in San Diego Plaza. From 1898 to 1906 he worked in partnership with W. S. Hubbard, a San Diego architect. They designed a number of houses in San Diego and Coronado in the popular brick-and-shingle and half-timber styles, notable for their redwood interiors. Gill went east in 1902 to design a Newport mansion for Albert Olmsted, the son of landscape architect Frederick Law Olmsted. Between 1906 and 1912 Gill experimented with the Prairie style, building structures typified by strong horizontals and broad sheltering roofs. The respectful use of wood and an incipient angularity relate these works to the Arts and Crafts movement. Gill's objectives were always more scientific than the Craftsmen's, and like Wright, he was fascinated by the potential of the machine and modern building methods.

In 1907 he began building structures with concrete and hollow tile. These include the Loughlin house in Los Angeles (1907) and the five-story Wilson Action Hotel in La Jolla (1908), his only multistory structure. Gill's interiors became more minimal, and he adopted the mission arch for his edifices. As his structures became increasingly simplified, the relationship of exterior and interior space was expressed through outside walls, pergolas, terraces and courtyards. The undecorated surfaces allowed for the play of nature, which was emphasized through landscape design.

The Holly Sefton Memorial Hospital in San Diego (1908) and the Scripps Institute in La Jolla (1908) are early examples of Gill's mature Style. Both are cost-efficient utilitarian buildings of monolithic concrete construction. Their surfaces are devoid of ornament and projections, and the roofs are flattened. The Scripps Institute anticipated the well-lighted factory of the 1930s in its fenestration and box-like form. The Timkin House, San Diego (1911, demolished), went a step further in its refinement of interior and exterior relationship and its use of abstract design elements. It is considered an earlier prototype for the Dodge House in Los Angeles.

In 1911 Gill's nephew, Louis, joined the firm. At that time Gill began to experiment with tilt-slab construction, an early method of building prefabrication, using equipment purchased from the United States government. The wall began as a platform tilted by jacks at a 15-degree angle. Concrete was poured over hollow tile and steel bars used as reinforcement. Windows and doors were integrated into the form. After the concrete cured, walls up to 60 feet long were lifted into place. The Women's Club, La Jolla (1913), is the most successful example of the process.

The morality of Gill's work was based on a social concern for the individual, manifested in housing for the unemployed, and barracks for the laborer and the company town. Lewis Courts, Sierra Madre (1910), a low-cost housing project, is a square plan of single units arranged around a large central court. Each unit has its own entry and a private garden. Later, Gill's plans for the laying out of the industrial town of Torrance, California (1913), were never completed according to his designs because of opposition from labor and public opinion.

Gill published no formal treatises, but in a *Craftsman* article (May 1916) he stated that the four sources of architectural strength were the straight line, the arch, the cube and the circle. The arch was espoused as one of the most imposing architectural features. Gill displayed a masterful sense of geometry and form in the Luther Dodge House, Los Angeles (1914-16, demolished 1970). He massed cubic forms horizontally in a U-plan, and punctured them with frameless windows. The sprawling plan was typified by an interweaving of inner and outer space. Reinforced concrete was treated with the monumentality of stone.

The Dodge House formally relates to Adolf Loos' Secessionist Steiner House in Vienna (1910). Both reflect principles put forth by Otto Wagner in *Moderne Architektur* (1895) in their frank expression of a progressive, rationalist approach, but any evidence of influence on Gill's work is inconclusive.

Gills' reputation suffered with the blacklash against modernism between the wars. His linear interpretation of the Spanish mission was rejected in favor of the heavily baroque Mission Revival style introduced by Bertram Goodhue at the Pan-Pacific Exposition in 1915. Gill's last projects were civic and commercial buildings for Coronado and Oceanside.

Gill was a notable regional architect who emerged as part of the first wave of modernism in this country at the turn of the century. As a romantic realist, his visions were executed in terms of function and quality. In the 1930s Frank Lloyd Wright acknowledged Gill's contribution to architecture (Wright's son Lloyd worked as a draftsman in Gill's office), resulting in a revived interest in Gill's work. The vocabulary of "California modern" that Gill established is still used today, and can be seen throughout southern California.

—SUSAN GUILES-CURRAN

GILLY, Friedrich.

German. Born near Stettin (now Szczecin, Poland), 1772. Died in Karlsbad (now Karlovy Vary, Czechoslovakia), 1800. Father was the architect David Gilly, at whose architecture school Friedrich studied. Summoned with his father to Berlin to work for Frederick the Great, 1788; inspector in the Royal Buildings Department, 1788; surveyor in the Schwedt region, 1790; traveled to France, England, southern Germany and Vienna, 1797-99; appointed professor of optics and perspective at the new Bauakadem ie, Berlin, 1799.

Chronology of Works
All in eastern Germany
† *Work no longer exists*

1792-94	House, 14 Jägerstrasse, Berlin†
1795	Schloss, Schwedt (remodeling)
1796-97	Monument to Frederick the Great (competition entry)
1797	Church, Paretz
1797	Grave of Duchess Maltzahn, Dyherrnfuhrt
1799	House, 30 Bruderstrasse, Berlin
1799	Theater, Königsberg
1799	Villa Molter, Tiergarten, Berlin†
1800	Farm Buildings and Tahitian Hut, Schloss Bellevue, Berlin†

Publications

BOOKS BY GILLY

Schloss Marienburg in Preussen. With Friedrich Frick. 1799-1803. Reprint: Düsseldorf, 1965.

ARTICLES BY GILLY

"Beschreibung des Landhauses Bagatelle bey Paris" and "Beschreibung des Landsitzes Rincy unweit Paris." In DAVID GILLY (ed.): *Sammlung nützlicher Aufsätze und Nachrichten die Baukunst betreffend.* 1799.

BOOKS ABOUT GILLY

DOEBBER, ADOLF: *Heinrich Gentz: Ein Berliner Baumeister um 1800.* Berlin, 1916.
Friedrich Gilly und die Privatgesellschaft junger Architekten, 1777-1800. Exhibition catalog. Berlin, 1984.
GILLY, DAVID: *Handbuch der Landbaukunst.* 2 vols. Berlin, 1797-98.
GILLY, DAVID: *Praktische Anweisung zur Wasserbaukunst.* Berlin, 1809-18.
GILLY, DAVID: *Sammlung nützlicher Aufsätze und Nachrichten die Baukunst betreffend.* 1797-1805.
GILLY, DAVID: *Über Erfindung: Construction und Vortheile der Bohlen-Dächer.* Berlin, 1797.
HEDERER, OSWALD: *Klassizismus.* Munich, 1976.
HERRMANN, WOLFGANG: *Deutsche Baukunst des 19 und 20. Jahrhunderts.* Basel, 1932.
KAUFMANN, EMIL: *Von Ledoux bis Le Corbusier: Ursprung und Entwicklung der autonomen Architektur.* Vienna, 1933.
LAMMERT, MARLIES: *David Gilly: Ein Baumeister des deutschen Klassizismus.* Berlin, 1964.
LEVETZOW, KONRAD: *Denkschrift auf Friedrich Gilly.* Berlin, 1801.
ONCKEN, ALSTE: *Friedrich Gilly: 1772-1800.* Berlin, 1935.

RIETDORF, ALFRED: *Gilly: Wiedergeburt der Architektur.* Berlin, 1940.
SCHMITZ, HERMANN: *Berliner Baumeister vom Ausgang des achtzehnten Jahrhunderts.* 2nd ed. Berlin, 1914.
SIMSON, JUTTA VON: *Das Berliner Denkmal für Friedrich den Grossen.* Frankfurt, 1976.
WATKIN, DAVID, and MELLINGHOFF, TILMAN: *German Architecture and the Classical Ideal 1740-1840.* London and Cambridge, Massachusetts, 1987.

ARTICLES ABOUT GILLY

ADLER, FRIEDRICH: "Friedrich Gilly, Schinkels Lehrer." *Zentralblatt der Bauverwaltung* No. 1 (1881).
FLESCHE, HERMAN: "Friedrich Gilly." In *Fünf Deutsche Baumeister.* Braunschweig, 1947.
JOHANNES, HEINRICH: "Das Denkmal Friedrichs des Grossen von Gilly." *Kunst im Deutschen Reich* 6 (1942): 156-164.
KLINKOTT, MANFRED: "Friedrich Gilly, 1772-1800" and "Fünf Architekten des Klassizismus in Deutschland." *Dortmunder Architekturheft* 4 (1977): 11-41.
NEUMEYER, ALFRED: "Monuments to 'Genius' in German Classicism." *Journal of the Warburg and Courtauld Institutes* 2 (1938): 159-163.
PEVSNER, NIKOLAUS: "Karl Friedrich Schinkel." *Studies in Art, Architecture and Design* 1 (1968): 174-195.
RIEMER, H.: "Friedrich Gillys Verhältnis zum Theaterbau." Ph.D. dissertation. University of Berlin, 1931.
SCHMITZ, HERMANN: "Friedrich Gilly." *Kunst und Künstler* 8 (1910): 506-512.

*

Architectural taste in the German lands during the second half of the 18th century tended to be dominated by French exemplars and practitioners, yet there was a strong native Baroque and Rococo tradition that created some of the most delightful architecture in all Europe. In addition, English Palladianism influenced some developments, especially in Protestant Prussia and Saxony, while the cult of the picturesque and an enthusiasm for the English garden made their marks. By the 1790s, however, many German intellectuals were seeking some sort of cultural identity of their own within the *Aufklärung,* and turned to a stripped, pure classicism based on antiquity (and therefore uncorrupted by French, English or Italian interpretations) in a longing for an architectural style suited to growing national aspirations. The architecture of antiquity, and especially the architecture of ancient Greece, was felt to be more truthful, humane and suited to ideals of freedom: it was untainted with absolutism, superstition or the stylistic preferences of other nations. Dignity and simplicity were to be the watchwords of a virtuous, serious-minded and honorable Germany.

Friedrich Gilly was one of the most remarkable of young Prussian architects to experiment with a pure, stripped, Greek neoclassicism. Born near Stettin, Gilly (as his name suggests) came from a line of Huguenot refugees who had found sanctuary in enlightened Prussia. Young Gilly received his early training from his father, David, and by 1788 was appointed an inspector at the Königliche Baubehörde. He also continued his studies at the Akademie der Bildenen Künste in Berlin under such towering figures as Friedrich Wilhelm von Erdmannsdorff, Carl Gotthard Langhans and Gottfried Schadow, and imbibed the writings of Winckelmann and Goethe. His architecture became more and more severe, stripped, primitive and elemental as a result, with all the gravity of antiquity, and especially of Greek antiquity.

When the Akademie announced an architectural competition for a monument to Frederick the Great in 1796, Gilly found the ideal vehicle to demonstrate his flair, and in 1797 he produced a stunning design consisting of a massive plain podium in which the sarcophagus of the king was to lie under a vault crowned by a wreath of stars. On this plinth stood a Greek Doric temple in which would be a statue of Frederick illuminated from above, so the architecture was to be powerful in its lighting effects and would convey strong emotions through its mysteriousness and sublime nobility. From the steps of the temple, there would be views over the royal city, so the siting was important in that the works of the king were to be seen from his monument. The temple on its podium was to stand within a precinct entered through a triumphal arch of the starkest plainness: this arch is shown on the drawings with a battered base in which are loculi-like niches, and with a coffered vault set over primitive Greek Doric colonnades. Here, then, was the triumphal arch and ceremonial gateway transformed, using a similar architectural language to that of Claude-Nicolas Ledoux and Etiénne-Louis Boullée, made monumental, tough and solemn. Here was the architectural equivalent of Mozart's *Maurerische Trauermusik,* or the darkly heroic funeral march from Beethoven's Third Symphony.

Obelisks were to stand sentinel before and behind the temple podium, while *couchant* lions in the Egyptian style were to double as fountains. The vast empty space, with its stark Greco-Egyptian character, was therefore to have a strongly funereal flavor enhanced by the loculi, by the crushing power of the podium and blank walls (the *architecture parlante* of desolation and terror of death), and by the obelisks. A further funereal touch was to be given by the neoclassical sarcophagus lids set around the circular carriageway. Yet there are no carriages on the drawing, no people, nothing but a dreamlike emptiness of sublime terror, still and almost surreal.

Gilly stressed that his design would convey indestructability in its powerful scale, and that its immensity and uniqueness would be unforgettable in the image. The monument would convey concepts such as honor and would commemorate not just the king, but mankind, an idea with pronounced Masonic overtones.

The impact that this scheme made on a whole generation of Prussian architects was immense, and the design was all the more seductive because of the accomplished draftsmanship of its author. Gilly's genius with the pencil, pen and color gained him a travel bursary, which he used to see buildings in England, France and Central Europe from 1797 to 1799. In France he made many drawings, and recorded such neoclassical essays as the Rue des Colonnes and the Barrières of Ledoux, but he also made perceptive drawings and notes of prerevolutionary buildings he admired.

For the last year of his short life, Gilly designed a number of villas, town houses, garden buildings and incidental structures, as well as a mausoleum, part of which survives near Wroclaw, Poland. His most brilliant project of that period was his unrealized design for a National Theater in Berlin, which has two hemicycles on either side of a large cubic form, a primitive Doric unpedimented portico and Diocletian windows. Some modernists claim this *esquisse* as a pioneering "functional" building, but the second hemicycle does not express what is within it. On the contrary, the National Theater project is a typical piece of stripped classicism, absolutely of its time, and recalls aspects of Ledoux's Besançon Theater (1775). It is still a fine piece of work, but there are other parallel designs with which it can be compared.

In 1799 Gilly was appointed professor of optics and perspective at the Bauakademie in Berlin, in which year he produced his remarkable drawings for a mausoleum employing monoliths devoid of all references to the orders: the effect is primitive in the extreme, like an 18th-century rationalist interpretation of a Stonehenge.

That Gilly's work had a profound effect on several architects of genius who were either of his generation or who came after is not in doubt. Leo von Klenze, Karl Friedrich Schinkel, Friedrich Weinbrenner and Heinrich Gentz are only a few names that can be mentioned in this context. It is one of the great tragedies of European art that Gilly's life was cut off at an even earlier age than that of Mozart, and that so little of his work survives, most of it on paper only. If a monument to the humane and noble aspirations of those who dreamed of German unity in the 18th and early 19th centuries is ever built, Gilly's marvelous design for Frederick the Great's memorial should be realized in a renewed Berlin of the future.

—JAMES STEVENS CURL

GINSBURG, Moisei.

Russian. Born in Minsk, Russia, 1892. Died in Moscow, 1946. Graduated from the Academy of Arts, Milan, Italy, 1914, and received an engineering degree from the Rizhsky Polytechnic, Moscow, 1917. Private practice in the Crimea, 1918-21; professor, Vkhutemas (State Higher Art and Technical Studios), Moscow, and instructor, Moscow Institute of Higher Technology, from 1923. Founding member, Association of Contemporary Architects (OSA), 1925; editor of the journal of the Moscow Architectural Socie ty, *Arkhitektura*, 1923; founder and editor, with Aleksandr Vesnin, of the journal of the Society of Contemporary Architects (OSA), *Sovremennaia arkhitektura*, 1926-30.

Moisei Ginsburg: Narkomfin Apartments, Moscow, Russia, 1927-29

Chronology of Works
All in the Soviet Union [Russia]

1927-29	Narkomfin Apartments, Moscow (with I. F. Milinis and S. Prokhorov)
1927-31	Courts of Justice, Alma-Ata (with Milinis)
1928-29	Type F. Residential Block, Sverdlovsk (with A. Pasternak)
1929-34	Administration Building, Turkestan-Siberia Railway, Alma-Ata
1932	Low-rise Housing, Chenigo Industrial Area (with M. Bartshch)
1935-37	Ordjonikidze Sanatorium, Kislovodsk

Publications

BOOKS BY GINSBURG

Ritm v arkhitekture. Moscow, 1923.
Stil' i epokha. Moscow, 1924; as *Style and Epoch*. Cambridge, Massachusetts, 1982.
Zhilishche. Opyt piatiletnei raboty nad problemoi zhilishcha. Moscow, 1934.
Arkhitektura sanatoriia NKTP v Kislovodske. Moscow, 1940.

ARTICLES BY GINSBURG

"L'architecture contemporaine." *VOKS Bulletin*, Nos. 42-44 (7 November 1927): 26-31.
"Mass-Production Housing Proposals in the USSR." *Architectural Association Journal*, Vol. 59 (November-December 1944): 114-116.

BOOKS ABOUT GINSBURG

CHAN-MAGOMEDOV, S. O.: *Moisej Ginzburg*. Milan, 1975.
DE FEO, V.: *URSS: Archittetura 1917-1936*. Rome, 1963.
KOPP, ANATOLE: *Town and Revolution: Soviet Architecture and City Planning 1917-1935*. New York and London, 1970.
LISSITZKY, ELEAZAR: *Russia: An Architecture for World Revolution*. Cambridge, Massachusetts, 1970.
SHVIDKOVSKY, O. A.: *Building in the USSR: 1917-1932*. London, 1971.

ARTICLES ABOUT GINSBURG

KHAN-MAGOMEDOV, S. O.: "M. Y. Ginzburg, 1892-1946." *Architectural Design*, No. 2 (1970): 92-94.
KHIGER, R.: "M. Ia. Ginzburg. Put teoretika i mastera." *Sovetskaia arkhitektura*, No. 15 (1963): 117-136.
KRIUKOV, M. V.: "God borby na stroitelnom fronte." *Stroitelstvo Moskvy*, No. 11 (1930): 9-12.
PASTERNAK, A.: "Novye sotsialnye tipy zhilishcha." *Stroitelstvo Moskvy*, No. 5 (1929): 9-16.
SOKOLOV, N.: "Mastera sovetskoi arkhitektury." *Arkhitektura SSSR*, Nos. 17-18 (1947): 79-96.
VLASOV, ALEKSANDR V.: "Nash put. Vsesoiuznoe soveshchanie sovetskikh arkhitektorov." *Arkhitektura SSSR*, No. 6 (1937): 23-25.

*

Moisei Yakovlevich Ginsburg received a part of his architectural education in Milan and later was awarded a degree in engineering in Moscow. He was the son of an architect, and the family's professional lineage has continued, with both his son and grandson becoming architects, too. A practitioner and educator, Ginsburg became the theorist and propagator of the Russian constructivist movement. He authored the important book *Style and the Epoch* (1924) and edited the magazine *Contemporary Architecture*. In his writings, Ginsburg analyzed the evolution of the new forms, stressing their technical basis. He strongly upheld what he called "the mechanization of life"—the integration of scientific and technological discoveries into the process of rational, artistic creation. As a leading proponent of constructivism, Ginsburg had also worked on theoretical explanations of the style in comparison with past architectural canons. He presented a set of drawings showing the lawful process in the development of architectural forms: the formal evolution of architectural styles analyzed throughout history culminated in architectural constructivism.

The architects of the revolutionary period in Russia knew that their fundamental task was housing. To satisfy the great demand for flats, research was aimed toward standardization and industrialization of housing construction. The proposed collective way of life, with its concentration of state-owned public services, led architects to invent a *dom-komuna*, or house-commune, which was practically a dormitory for workers. A house-commune was to be equipped with all facilities for living, and as all land had become public, planners were free to expand the facilities as needed. The house-communes or blocks of flats were designed to be tall and compact, with surrounding land left wide open, available for recreation.

Few of these plans were realized. But the ideas of the constructivists concerning the organization of a housing complex had a significant impact on later work abroad as well as in Russia. Designs of new dwellings, housing ensembles, city districts and towns were inspired by constructivist experiments in housing. The influence was especially evident in the work of Le Corbusier and in certain housing schemes in Scandinavia, England and East Central Europe.

The constructivist concept of housing was based on the search for a social condenser—a new way of living, a tool for molding social transformation. One would shake off all associations with the old by the very act of living in a new environment. In practical terms, the Soviet architect was given the task of establishing a new type of building, not intended for single individuals but for the masses.

The major criterion for the new housing type was to foster the breakdown of the family structure. The family, as originally conceived by the Communist society, was not significant as a unit. A woman, as the equal of a man in this society, was to be freed from all household duties. The constructivist's radical innovation, meant to facilitate this way of life, was the house-commune. A house-commune was a complex for dwelling, recreation, education, entertainment and sport. It contained individual sleeping units, but kitchens, dining rooms, bathrooms, living rooms and club rooms were all communal. In fact, a house-commune contained very few private spaces.

Ginsburg had been heavily involved in the research and design of housing. His most important project is also a significant landmark of constructivist architecture. He designed the Narkomfin apartments in collaboration with Ignaty Milinis and S. Prokhorov in 1927-29. The house-commune for the People's Commissariat for Finance, a governmental agency, was built on Novinsky Boulevard in Moscow.

In the Narkomfin development, housing units were grouped in a six-floor building block on pilotis. All the communal facilities were in another five-story block linked to the first by a covered gallery on the second floor. It was thus a complex that grouped housing units and facilities separately, whereas collective facilities were usually scattered across a whole district.

The six-story living wing has eight two-story, two-bedroom units with kitchen, dining area, full bath and a two-story living room. There are 16 one-and-a-half-story, one-bedroom units with half bath, kitchenette and one-and-a-half-story living room, and five atypical two-story, two-bedroom "end of the building units." In addition, the living wing has a two-story penthouse and a roof terrace, and on the ground floor there is a unit for the house manager. The innovative maisonette-type housing units give its inhabitants views out from two opposite sides of the building, provide for cross ventilation and save floor area because only two corridors serve the entries to the five floors of apartments.

This project combined units of the F type developed by the Stroikom office (construction committee dealing with communal-housing design), which were intended for small families of childless couples, with units of the K type consisting of three rooms on two levels. The F-type unit had only a kitchenette in an alcove, but the K type unit had a kitchen of about four square meters. Since this traditional type of housing was designed as an instrument to educate and prepare people for collective life without making such a way of life compulsory, there was no obligation to use the communal facilities provided in these buildings. Rudimentary individual kitchens therefore continued to exist in both types of units, although in the later communal houses these were to disappear completely. In order to encourage a collective way of life, buildings of the Narkomfin type put many collective facilities at the inhabitants' disposal, among them communal kitchens and dining rooms, laundries, cleaning services, kindergartens, gymnasiums, libraries and rooms for "intellectual work," and summer dining rooms on the roof.

Architecturally speaking, the Narkomfin building was a good example of the constructivists' functional method. All the usual elements of Modern Movement architecture were also present, among them ribbon windows, freestanding columns and roof terraces. It provided its inhabitants with what constructivists, like modern architects in the West, considered the indispensable human environment: air, sun and greenery. But the Narkomfin project, like the other experimental blocks built following Stroikom's research, was merely a stage on the road to that total collectivization of the way of life which would be affected by the communal houses.

The Narkomfin project met the principal requirements of modern architecture as outlined in the 1920s by Le Corbusier in his "Five Points of Architecture": 1. The housing wing sits on pilotis, thus allowing nature to flow beneath the building without interruption. 2. The roof terrace replaces the area of the land taken up by the footprint of the building. 3. The structural system of columns and slab construction allows for a free layout of partitions and the enclosure of the building. 4. Continuous ribbon windows and large expanses of glass are possible because of the independence of the building's enclosure and the building's supporting structure. 5. A horizontal ribbon window allows maximum daylight into a room, in contrast to the punched-type openings in a traditional bearing-wall system of support and enclosure. Ironically, Le Corbusier did not get to build a project based on the "Five Points of Architecture" until later, when in 1947-52 the Unité d'Habitation collective-housing project was executed in Marseilles, France.

Ginsburg did not submit to the political pressures of the 1930s, when constructivism was condemned by the Soviet conservative architectural establishment as a style influenced by capitalism and, as such, politically undesirable. His entry for the competition of the Palace of the Soviets in the early 1930s was a clear solution of pure volumes expressed by contemporary materials.

After that competition, which was unsuccessful for him as well as for the whole constructivist movement, he spent most of his time on theoretical work—a criticism of eclecticism. Ginsburg tried to persuade his colleagues to study the problems of standardization instead of imitating past forms.

—PETER LIZON

GIULIO ROMANO.

Italian. Born Giulio Pippi, in Rome, Italy, ca. 1499. Died in Mantua, 1 November 1546. Chief assistant to Raphael, ca. 1514-20: worked on Stanza dell'Incendio frescoes, Vatican, and on Sala di Constantino, then completed some of Raphael's unfinished works; also worked in Genoa; settled in Mantua, 1524. Appointed Superiore Generale of public buildings in Mantua, 1526.

Chronology of Works
All in Italy
* *Approximate dates*
†*Work no longer exists*

1520*-24	Palazzo Maccarani, Rome
1521	Giulio Romano House, Rome†
1523	Villa Lante al Gianicolo, Rome (completion of work begun by Raphael)
1524-38	Castle, Marmirolo (additions)†
1525-32	Palazzo del Tè (villa and stables for the Gonzaga family), Mantua
1530*	Pescheria, Mantua
1530*	12-13 Piazza Broletto, Mantua
1530*	22 Via Carlo Poma, Mantua
1530*	2 Via Solferino, Mantua
1531	Palazzina della Paleologa, Mantua†
1533-49	Porta della Cittadella, Mantua
1538-39	Estivale, Palazzo Ducale, Mantua
1538-44	Giulio Romano House, Mantua
1540-46	Abbey of San Benedetto al Polirone, near Mantua (restoration)
1542	Palazzo Thiene, Vicenza (completed by Andrea Palladio)
1544-46	Cathedral, Mantua (restoration)

Publications

BOOKS ABOUT GIULIO

Giulio Romano. Milan, 1989.

HARTT, FREDERICK: *Giulio Romano*. 2 vols. New Haven, Connecticut, 1958.

VERHEYEN, EGON: *The Palazzo del Tè in Mantua: Images of Love and Politics*. Baltimore, 1977.

ARTICLES ABOUT GIULIO

GOMBRICH, ERNST: "Zum Werke Giulio Romanos." *Jahrbuch der kunsthistorischen Sammlungen in Wien* (1934-35): 79-104; 121-150.

MAGNUSSON, BØRJE: "A Drawing for the Façade of Giulio Romano's House in Mantua." *Journal of the Society of Architectural Historians* 47 (June 1988): 179-184.

PALLUCCHINI, R.: "Giulio Romano e Palladio." *Arte veneta* (1958): 234-235.

PALLUCCHINI, R.: "Andrea Palladio e Giulio Romano." *Bollettino del Centro Internazionale di Studi 'Andrea Palladio'* (1959): 38-44.

STILLER: "Palazzo del Te." *Allgemeine Bauzeitung* 49.

*

Giulio Romano, as a native Roman, was able to develop a refined knowledge of ancient art that served him well in both his paintings and architecture. He was a gifted assistant of Raphael, working as early as 1514 on the master's fresco paintings in the Vatican's Stanza dell'Incendio. Giulio was also involved with Raphael's architectural projects, such as the Villa Madama, and helped to decorate Baldassare Peruzzi's Villa Farnesina. He eventually became the dominant figure in Raphael's studio before the master's death in 1520; he completed Raphael's Villa Lante three years later.

Giulio's Palazzo Maccarani in Piazza Sant'Eustachio (circa 1520-24) was his most important architectural statement in Rome. His use of a rusticated base with paired classical orders on the five bays of the palace's main floor recalls Bramante's Palazzo Caprini. Giulio set the windows of the *piano nobile* on a string course, however, and omitted capitals from the third-story pilasters that meld with part of the entablature to create a flat wall in a manner that Michelangelo later used for the Campidoglio's Palazzo dei Conservatori. Such practices hint at Giulio's willingness to depart from classical usage in a way never found in Bramante's architecture.

In 1524, the marchese of Mantua, Federigo Gonzaga (1500-40, duke in 1530) invited Giulio to Mantua, where he embarked on a construction project involving a villa and stables that became his architectural masterpiece. This was the complex of buildings and gardens at Federigo's stud farm on a T-shaped island outside the city walls of Mantua.

Giulio's initial project was to transform a portion of the Gonzaga stables into an unpretentious villa. The walls of the *stalle* on the west and south, which had to be included in his designs, determined the plan's final rectangular shape, although not its size or the internal arrangement of rooms. The wide perimeter of walls around an enormous open courtyard makes the palace look grander than it is. Giulio achieved great visual interest in the play of the upright pilasters against the busy Doric architrave and in the rusticated sprawl of the window surrounds.

Several major halls had been decorated in 1527-28, the windows of which were in place and restricted by the in situ fresco decoration, so that when Giulio later replaced the plaster wall of the exterior with orders, spacing of the facade windows became a problem. Giulio tried to compensate for their off-center placement in each bay by partially masking their positions with rusticated window surrounds. These asymmetries have been remarked upon as Giulio's willful departure from classical canons and, therefore, as reflective of a Mannerist approach to architecture. If his idiosyncratic approach to symmetry can now be understood as having a rational basis, no such explanation is forthcoming to explain his practice of dropping the Doric triglyphs in two of the garden facades. He might have intended these, too, as distractions to those elements over which he had no control, so that anomalies became consistencies, yet each slipped triglyph occurs over a window or cavity, thus underscoring the classical intervals between solid and void.

In the interior, Giulio's Sala dei Cavalli depicts the champions of the Gonzaga stud farm in fresco paintings on the walls. The family's horse breeds had been winners of races throughout the Italian peninsula and were similarly commemorated in other Gonzaga palaces. In the adjacent Sala di Psiche, Giulio painted in warm colors across two adjacent walls the splendid wedding feast of Cupid and Psyche with nymphs, deities and other mythical creatures in attendance. The heavily framed ceiling coffers depict isolated scenes of the loves of the gods.

The most popular of Giulio's fresco decorations are in his Sala dei Giganti. Painted after 1530 in anticipation of the second visit of Emperor Charles V to Mantua, the squarish room has a domed ceiling with a throne of Jupiter beneath a canopy at its apex. On the four walls, presumptuous Titans, rebuffed in their attempts to scale Mount Olympus, tumble to the earth as their caves collapse about them.

Giulio also left his signature in the ducal palace in 1538-39, when he designed the heavily textured, seven-bay *cortile* facade, accented by the spiral fluting of Doric columns.

Federigo had been quickly impressed by Giulio's talents and had honored him by appointing him *superiore generale* of public buildings in August 1526. He also awarded him a home and Mantuan citizenship, and at the end of that year gave Giulio the post of *superiore delle strade* with an annual stipend of 500 ducats.

Giulio's only work with religious structures came after Duke Federigo's death in 1540. This work included the cathedral of Mantua and the abbey church of San Benedetto Po near Mantua. Although the labor involved merely projects of renovation, the labor was extensive; yet in Giulio's articulation of interior space, his interest in contrasts was defeated by the scale of the structures.

He was more successful with his own house in Mantua, which was also a renovation project. His contributions were the fresco decorations of the living quarters and the masking of the old exterior with a screening facade.

Giulio's facade of modest dimensions, 20 meters long by 12 deep, has two stories with a rusticated base and attic. A string course that separates *piano nobile* and ground floor rises as a gable above the central portico, above which is a niche and statue of Mercury serving as a sign of Giulio's profession, of his antiquarian interests and of his Roman origins. The windows of the *piano nobile* resting on the string course are set within round-headed arches.

Within the structure, Giulio depicted fresco personifications of Minerva, goddess of wisdom, prudence and the arts, and Mercury, god of eloquence. Apollo and Prometheus flank the fireplace, as the hearth stresses Giulio's Roman origins.

Titian's splendid portrait of Giulio from circa 1536 is preserved in London, Giulio's self-portrait in the Uffizi. In the latter he holds a drawing of a central-plan structure thought to be a church project for a Gonzaga pantheon.

—EDWARD J. OLSZEWSKI

GIURGOLA, Romaldo.

American. Born in Rome, Italy, 2 September 1920; immigrated to the United States, 1954; naturalized, 1959. Married Adelaide F. Bercivenga, 1952; one daughter. Studied at the School of Architecture, University of Rome, 1945-49, B.Arch. 1949; Columbia University, New York, 1949-51, M.Arch 1951. Partner, with Ehrman B. Mitchell, Mitchell/Giurgola Architects, Philadelphia, 1958-88; since 1980, partner, Mitchell/Giurgola and Thorp Architects, Canberra, Australia; offices established in Sydney, 1988, and Singapore, 1989. Assistant professor of architecture, Cornell University, Ithaca, New York, 1952-54; professor of architecture, University of Pennsylvania, Philadelphia, 1954-67; chairman of the Department of Architecture, 1967-72, Ware Professor of Architecture, 1972-91, and since 1991, professor emeritus of architecture, Columbia University, New York. Fellow, American Institute of Architects, 1975, and Royal

Australian Institute of Architects, 1983; Gold Medal, American Institute of Architects, 1982; Gold Medal, Royal Australian Institute of Architects, 1988.

Chronology of Works
All in the United States unless noted

1962	Philadelphia Life Insurance Company Office Building addition, Philadelphia
1963	White House, Chestnut Hill, Pennsylvania
1965	American Institute of Architects National Headquarters, Washington, D.C. (competition project)
1970	Dayton House, Wayzata, Minnesota
1971	United Fund Headquarters, Philadelphia, Pennsylvania
1972	Mission Park Residential Houses, Williams College, Williamstown, Massachusetts
1972	Adult Learning Research Laboratory, MDRT Foundation Hall, American College, Bryn Mawr, Pennsylvania
1973	Columbus High School, Columbus, Indiana
1973	Worship Assembly Building, Benedictine Society of St. Bede, Peru, Illinois
1973	Lang Music Building, Swarthmore College, Swarthmore, Pennsylvania
1975	Penn Mutual Life Tower, Philadelphia, Pennsylvania
1975	Liberty Bell Pavilion, Philadelphia, Pennsylvania
1976	Tredyffrin Public Library, Tredyffrin Township, Strafford, Pennsylvania
1977	Sherman Fairchild Center for the Life Sciences, Columbia University, New York
1977	Master plan for the future development of the United States Capitol, Washington, D.C. (design consultant; with Wallace, McHarg, Roberts and Todd)
1981	Technical High School, Maniago, Italy
1981	Elementary School, Aviano, Italy
1981	Concert Theatre renovation and reconstruction, C.W. Post Center, Long Island University, Greenvale, New York
1981	Wainwright State Office Complex, St. Louis, Missouri (with Hastings and Chivetta)
1982	College of Health Sciences Technology and Management Building, and Health Services Building, Massachusetts Institute of Technology, Cambridge (with Gruzen and Partners)
1983	Knoll International Assembly and Shipping Facility, phase I, East Greenville, Pennsylvania
1984	AB Volvo Corporate Headquarters, Göteborg, Sweden
1985	Walter Royal Davis Library, University of North Carolina, Chapel Hill (with Leslie N. Boney)
1988	Parliament House of Australia, Canberra, Australia
1989	St. Thomas Aquinas Parish Church, Charnwood, ACT, Australia
1990	IBM Palisades Advanced Business Institute, Palisades, New York
1992	ANA Hotel, The Rocks, Sydney, Australia

Publications

BOOKS BY GIURGOLA

Louis I. Kahn. With Jaimini Mehta. Zurich and Boulder, Colorado, 1975.

Romaldo Giurgola: Parliament House of Australia, Canberra, Australia, 1988

ARTICLES BY GIURGOLA

"Architecture in Change." *Journal of Architectural Education* (November/December 1962).
"Reflections on Buildings and the City: The Realism of the Partial Vision." *Perspecta* 9/10 (1965).
"Forces Shaping Current Design." *American Institute of Architects Journal* (May 1979).
"The Producing Moment." *Inland Architect* (January/February 1981).
"Notes on Buildings and Their Parts." *Harvard Architectural Review* (Spring 1981).
"Reflections on the Order of the City and the Order of the Land." *Architect* (Melbourne, December 1983).
"A. S. Hook Address." *Architecture Australia* (November 1988); reprinted in *Space Design* (February 1989).
"Parliament House, Canberra." *Architecture Australia* (November 1988).
"Issues 2000." *Steel Profile* (March 1991).
"In Pursuit of Technology's Elusive Heart." *Steel Profile* (June 1991).

BOOKS ABOUT GIURGOLA

BECK, HAIG (ed.): *Parliament House, Canberra: A Building for the Nation.* Sydney, 1988.
Mitchell/Giurgola Architects. New York, 1983.

ARTICLES ABOUT GIURGOLA

"Australian Parliament House." *Progressive Architecture* (August 1988).
"Giurgola: Eight Recent Works of Mitchell/Giurgola Architects." *Space Design* (August 1986).
"Mitchell/Giurgola and Thorp Architects: Parliament House in Canberra." *Architecture and Urbanism* (May 1989).
Process: Architecture, special issue (March 1989).

Romaldo Giurgola is a native of Italy with offices in Philadelphia and New York. His architectural roots, however, are in the Philadelphia school of the 1960s under the influence of Louis I. Kahn. Mitchell/Giurgola Architects, founded in 1958 with Ehrman B. Mitchell, operates as a collaborative firm. Although the firm has many affinities with Kahn's work—plan geometries, articulation of light and materials—Mitchell/Giurgola has increasingly taken a more contextual approach to design, emphasizing context in favor of Kahn's monumentality. "We thus make our buildings . . . [acquire] their measure not only through their role of evoking human activities or presences but also through their relative relationship to other elements of the environment," explains Giurgola, implying both the built and the natural.

Some early contextual gestures seem compromised by a brutal monumentality. The firm's second-place entry for the Boston City Hall (1963) opened the building mass to a huge public square, a feature lacking in Kallman McKinnell and Knowles' aloof winner. Both projects were high Brutalist design, making the Mitchell/Giurgola entry the lesser of two urbanistic evils. The firm's ill-fated American Institute of Architects Headquarters project, a precariously sloping design of similar style, shared this weakness as it seemed ready to devour the dainty Octagon it so willfully acknowledged.

With the brutal monumentalism toned down, subsequent projects better resolved abstract form and contextual responsibility. The highly sculptural Worship and Assembly Building of the

Benedictine Society of St. Bede, with its diagonally placed square assembly hall and four triangular light monitors (to make a cross-shaped plan), acts as a landmark without visually alienating the rest of the campus. It helpfully extends both the campus plan and brick palette, establishing a meaningful procession and a convenient automobile dropoff. Such bold but cooperative form is a hallmark of Mitchell/Giurgola's mature work.

Penn Mutual Life Tower in Philadelphia shows similar qualities in high-rise form, defying the glass prisms of its time through sculptural response to urban issues. The 22-story tower completes a symmetrical composition behind Independence Hall, while also preserving an 1830s facade within its own glass skin. A slim 12-story indentation echoes a nearby cornice height, and an adjoining articulated elevator shaft leads to a concrete observation deck as distinguished public element. A cast-in-place concrete screen on the west acts as a scale-changing element, sun block and abstraction of the Egyptian Revival facade. The architecture succeeds by giving architectonic form to contextual, not arbitrary, gestures.

Having shaken the self-centered monumentalism of early works, Mitchell/Giurgola proved it could find organization and expressive richness in tight sites and tough programs, such as in Fairchild Center at Columbia University. Building organization distinguishes clearly between servant and served, technical and social spaces, while a screen wall acts as a major formal device. These elements, traceable to Kahn, take on their own life in this work. A structurally required lightness, emphasized in the screen wall by individually articulated panels, replaces Kahn's monumentality. This screen reduces glare, articulates a crystalline staircase and creates immediate exits for extensive lab exhausts.

Another project, the Walter Royal Davis Library at the University of North Carolina in Chapel Hill (1985), is a similarly accommodating problem solver, lending neighborly scale to a deceptively packed program, expressed in structural brick. Likewise, projects such as the Volvo Headquarters (1985) or the IBM Palisades Business Institute (1989) both establish a dialogue with their surroundings—in these cases, the untouched landscape.

Mitchell/Giurgola has succeeded in elaborating Kahn's formal and organizational principles, but less so his buildings, as is attested by their ill-received proposed addition to Kahn's Kimbell Museum in Fort Worth, Texas. The design, a literal extension of Kahn's modular cycloid arches, was killed by professional outcry.

The firm may be best remembered by its largest project, Australia's Parliament House in Canberra. On a sprawling site, two monumental parabolic retaining walls back to back organize the Parliament House, holding between them a mound of earth. The mound attaches to a grand entry court to the north and the executive wing to the south, burying a long axis of public spaces in between. At the apex of this mound are an 80-meter stainless-steel mast structure supporting a huge Australian flag; an overlook to Walter Burley Griffin's Canberra master plan; and a glass pyramid topping the members' hall, opening governmental machinations to public view. To the east and west are the considerable low-rise buildings of the House and the Senate, embraced by the curving retaining walls.

This bold design form posits itself as a geographic center in plan and location, yet it is defiantly antimonumental. Although it contains some imperfect details, it is refreshingly alien. It embodies Mitchell/Giurgola's axial plans and close relationship with the environment played out here in a compelling mannerist extreme.

—CHARLES ROSENBLUM

GOČÁR, Josef.

Czechoslovakian. Born in Semin, Bohemia (now Czech Republic), 13 March 1880. Died in Prague, 10 August 1954. Married; son was the architect Jiři Gočár. Studied at Technical School for Building, Prague, 1903-08. Served in Austrian Army, 1917-24. In private practice, Prague, 1908-45. Dean, Academy of Fine Arts, Prague, 1924-28; president, Czechoslovak Association of Architects.

Chronology of Works
All in Czechoslovakia unless noted

1909-10	Wenke Department Store, Jaromir
1910	Concrete Stairway, Marienkirche, Hradec Králové
1910	Kralovo House, near Brno
1911-12	House of the Black Mother of God, Prague
1911-12	Health Spa, Bohdaneč
1912	Černa Matka Bozi, Department Store, Prague
1921-23	Czechoslovak Legion Bank, Prague
1923-24	Tannery School, Hradec Králové
1924-27	School Complex, Hradec Králové
1924-25	Czechoslovak National Pavilion, Exposition Internationale des Arts Décoratifs, Paris, France
1925-26	Agricultural Education House, Prague
1926-27	Ambrož Choir, Hradec Králové
1927-32	Czechoslovak Rail Administration, Hradec Králové
1928-30	St. Wenceslas Catholic Church, Prague
1932-33	Three villas, Czechoslovak Werkbund Housing Estate, Baba District, Prague
1935	Regional Administration, Hradec Králové

Publications

BOOKS BY GOČÁR

Tschechische Bestrebungen um ein modernes Interieur. With P. Janak and F. Kysela. Prague, 1915.
Hradec Králové. Prague, 1930.

BOOKS ABOUT GOČÁR

BENEŠOVÁ, MARIE: *Josef Gočár.* Prague, 1958.
HERBENOVÁ, OLGA: *Josef Gočár.* Jaromer, 1983.
WIRTH, Z.: *Josef Gocár.* Geneva, 1930.

*

Josef Gočár belonged to that generation of architects who greatly influenced the course of Bohemian architecture during the early years of the 20th century. His architectural education was in the spirit of the Viennese architect Otto Wagner, with whom Gočár's teacher, Jan Kotěra, had studied. Kotěra played an important role in Prague in overcoming the historicism that had been so prevalent in the 19th century; in that respect, he can be compared to Wagner in Vienna and H. P. Berlage in Amsterdam. In his early projects, Gočár worked in a number of different idioms as he sought to develop his own style. The Wanke Department Store in Jaroměř (1909-10) exhibits an almost neoclassical discipline and a modern use of materials. However, he also tried a monumental sculptural approach, as, for instance, in his competition entry for the Prague Town Hall (1910).

Gočár's indecisiveness was a consequence of his discontent with the architectural conceptions of Wagner and his followers. Gočár and a few of his colleagues found the architecture of Wagner and Kotěra too rational and too socially oriented, too little interested in the artistic and spiritual aspects of architecture. It is possible to see a parallel here with the attitude of the Amsterdam school toward the work of Berlage, who was also accused of ignoring architecture's artistic aspects. Cubism offered Gočár and his group the way out of this dilemma. Cubism, which had effected drastic changes in existing painterly norms, seemed to offer the requisite conditions for the "spiritualization" of architecture in Prague.

Architects and painters, united in the group Skupina Výtvarných Umělcú (Group of Visual Artists), quickly appropriated the forms of French cubism and interpreted them further (from 1911 to 1915). It was chiefly Gočár and his fellow architect Pavel Janák who translated cubist concepts into an architectural language. The key traits of this architecture are rhythm and tension in the building mass, "the visual conquest of matter." Between 1911 and 1912 Gočár created two most characteristic examples of the new architecture: the Sanatorium in Bohdaneč and the House of the Black Mother of God in Prague. Gočár achieved rhythm and tension in the facades through the use of angled planes and prismatic forms, which were specifically analogous to the decomposed picture planes of analytical cubist painting.

Shortly before the end of World War I, Gočár's architectural idiom underwent a change, however. The prismatic forms were replaced by round and cylindrical elements, and their composition became more static and hierarchical. In addition, Gočár also turned to flat, polychrome decoration. For a brief time after 1918, this development in cubist architecture, known as "rondocubism," became a national style in the new Czech Republic. The best example of the style is Gočár's Legiobank in Prague (1921-23). In the mid-1920s, under the influence of Dutch architecture—the Amsterdam school and Willem Dudok in particular—Gočár abandoned this decorative cubism, which by then had proven to be an architectural dead end.

Gočár demonstrated his new, more functionalist, orientation in his Czech Pavilion at the 1925 Exposition des Arts Décoratifs in Paris and in a few school buildings in Hradec Králové. The schools were commissioned in conjunction with his urban planning for the town: Gočár planned the town's expansion, also creating numerous individual structures. Gočár's schools for Hradec Králové made his development toward functional architecture apparent. The first schools had facades of plain tiles (a Dutch influence) with still-abstract classical lines, but the following schools were planned in strong cubic forms. The last building, the Kindergarten (1926-27), already had all the characteristics of contemporary whitewashed functional architecture. In the late 1920s and throughout the 1930s, Gočár designed a few government buildings and villas in this manner; notable are his four villas in Prague's well-known villa colony "Baba" (from 1933). He also remained active in the realm of urban planning, and his proposals for ideal housing settlements for the Bata firm are especially interesting. He attempted to synthesize the old idea of a workers' settlement around a factory with concepts of modern urban planning in these proposals.

Despite the development of his architectural style, Gočár's approach remained basically classical. This is most apparent in the careful balance of proportions and in his ground plans, most of which are symmetrical arrangements around a main axis. Gočár's preference for the expressive and sculptural qualities of architecture ended with his cubist period. Only in St. Wenceslas Church in Prague (1928-30) did he show his capacity for expressive, though subdued, dynamic designs again. Not the least important of Gočár's accomplishments was his activity as a professor at the Academy of the Arts in Prague: in 1924 he succeeded Jan Kotěra, and in 1928 he became rector. Although

Maximilian Godefroy: Unitarian Church, Baltimore, Maryland, 1817-18

the number of architecture students at the academy was limited, Gočár became very influential through his teaching.

—OTAKAR MÁCEL
Translated from the German by Marijke Rijsberman

GODEFROY, Maximilian.

American. Born in France, ca. 1765. Died in 1840. Sailed to America, 1805; instructor in architectural drawing and military engineering at the College de Baltimore (later known as St. Mary's Seminary), Baltimore, Maryland, 1805; moved to London, England, 1819; returned to France, 1839-40.

Chronology of Works
All in the United States
* Approximate dates
† Work no longer exists

1806-08	St. Mary's Chapel, Baltimore
1812-13	Commercial and Farmers Bank, Baltimore†
1812-13	St. Thomas' Church, Bardstown, Kentucky
1812-22	Masonic Hall, Baltimore†
1813-15	First Presbyterian Churchyard, Baltimore (gates and vaults)
1814	Fort McHenry, Baltimore (sallyport)
1815-25	Battle Monument, Baltimore
1816*	Courthouse, Richmond, Virginia†
1816-30	Capitol Square, Richmond†
1817-18	Unitarian Church, Baltimore
1825-26	Catholic Charities School, London, England†
1829-33	Palais de Justice, Laval, France (restoration and new wing)
1829-36	Hospice des Aliénés, Nayenne, France
1831-40	Préfecture, Laval, France (entrance, auxiliary buildings and restoration)

Publications

BOOKS ABOUT GODEFROY

ALEXANDER, ROBERT L.: *The Architecture of Maximilian Godefroy.* Baltimore, 1974.

ARTICLES ABOUT GODEFROY

ALEXANDER, ROBERT L.: "The Drawings and Allegories of Maximilian Godefroy." *Maryland Historical Magazine* 53 (1958): 17-33.
ALEXANDER, ROBERT L.: "The Public Memorial and Godefroy's Battle Monument." *Journal of the Society of Architectural Historians* 17 (1958): 19-24.
DAVIDSON, CAROLINA V.: "Maximilian Godefroy." *Maryland Historical Magazine* 29, No. 3 (September 1934): 1-20, 175-212.
HOYT, WILLIAM D.: "Eliza Godefroy, Destiny's Football." *Maryland Historical Magazine* 36, No. 1 (March 1941).
QUYNN, DOROTHY M.: "Maximilian and Eliza Godefroy." *Maryland Historical Magazine* 52 (March 1957): 1-34.
RUSK, WILLIAM SENER: "Godefroy and Saint Mary's Chapel, Baltimore." *Liturgical Arts* 2 (June-September 1933): 140-145.

On coming to America in 1805, Maximilian Godefroy possessed considerable knowledge of recent and contemporary French architecture. His buildings testify to a commitment to work in what he considered a correct, modern style to produce designs of lasting merit and international acclaim. With that knowledge, he was able to build works that gave Americans a new conception of the public building.

From the *ancien régime* he learned that buildings should possess character, especially the character to be projected by a building according to its function in a broad sense. Not for him was the *architecture parlante* of Claude-Nicolas Ledoux's House of the Director of the River Loue, but rather the more general character defined by Jacques-François Blondel in the mid-18th century. For his chapel for St. Mary's Seminary in Baltimore (1806-08), Godefroy employed smooth surfaces without strong projecting parts, over which he deployed a series of curves in the Neo-Gothic doors, windows and niches. This was Blondel's formula for a building that was both religious and feminine, appropriate for a dedication to the Virgin.

Similarly, Godefroy sought a masculine character in his masterpiece, the Unitarian Church in Baltimore (1817-19). The parts are fewer, larger and bolder, and cast prominent shadows over the surfaces. Although he followed Blondel in the evocation of character, his architectural forms speak of the revolutionary generation that succeeded Blondel, especially as their work was codified and spread by J.-N.-L. Durand. The building is basically a cube with the hemisphere of the dome rising from its top. Its triple-arched entry, topped by a pediment, advances before the wall plane and opens into a recessed vestibule, all set between two massive corner piers. The building resembles works of a generation earlier in France, the period of Ledoux and Etienne-Louis Boullée, who designed expressions of the power of the central government then still reigning. The church, however, received its masculine character in order to express the power of reason and the seriousness of the religious activities practiced there.

In addition to the metaphorical character, Godefroy sought to make meaning more specific through allegory. The smooth, rusticated masonry and battered walls of the podium of the Battle Monument in Baltimore (1815-25) express strength, all right, but the 18 courses of masonry represent the states of the union at the time of the battle. Differing from the slightly older revolutionary generation, to achieve this specificity Godefroy depended heavily on figural sculpture, usually allegorical and occasionally narrative. Reliefs on the fascial shaft (itself a timely symbol of unity and strength) report details of the battle at North Point, while the allegorical figure at the top, wearing a mural crown, holding a laurel wreath and rudder, and accompanied by an eagle and a cannonball, refers specifically to Baltimore's victory over a naval siege during the War of 1812. Not only did the public of the time appreciate such an allegorical character, but Godefroy's program, interpreting each detail of the composition, shows that he was conscious of it. Again, St. Mary's Chapel was to have the 12 apostles in the niches across the top of the facade, and an angel in glory holds an inscription, "To the One God," in the pediment of the Unitarian Church. Godefroy's use of figural sculpture on buildings far exceeded that of Benjamin Henry Latrobe and younger architects, such as Robert Mills, and probably was owed to his French origins.

Godefroy's pre-Romantic eclecticism gave his buildings another source of meaning. In the forms and interior disposition of the chapel, Godefroy, like Latrobe, alluded to the sublime that was seen in the great vaulted Gothic cathedrals. On the monument, Egyptoid aspects included the battered wall of the podium and its cavetto cornice with winged sun-disks, and they symbolized eternal commemoration for those who died in

defense of Baltimore. The Italian Renaissance forms of the entrance arcade, doors, interior and furniture of the church were symbols of learning and reason. All of these older styles achieved new interest and appreciation at the time in Europe, especially in France, and thus show Godefroy's continuing awareness of architectural activities there.

Godefroy is usually considered a professional architect, although his preparation in construction was weak. Upon his arrival in America, his experience apparently was limited to a small amount of work in hydraulic (canal building) and military engineering, whereas he was a creditable draftsman. He corresponded to the gentleman-architect as Latrobe defined the type in 1806, long in theoretical and book knowledge, but short in the experience of building, or as Thomas Jefferson put it, more experienced on paper. For Godefroy part of the process of making himself a professional consisted of mastering structural processes through experience. Re-using builders in whom he developed confidence and asking for help from others, such as Latrobe, Godefroy learned while building. His late drawings show the growth in his abilities as he made details of foundations and other structural elements to guide the builders.

Public buildings, rather than domestic, comprised the large part of Godefroy's work. For permanence as well as impressiveness, they were built of stone or had the appearance of stone—brick and rubble construction covered with stucco, then lined to imitate ashlar masonry; an example is the Unitarian Church. For St. Mary's Chapel, of brick with stone ornament, he had a recipe from Latrobe to give the appearance of stone, and the Battle Monument has a marble veneer over brick.

The material was important both in Godefroy's conception of significant architecture and for his patrons who wanted buildings not only to house urban activities, but also to make the city modern in order to attract business. Engaged in international trade, the merchant class held both political and cultural leadership and was involved in all of his commissions, except for St. Mary's Chapel, built for Sulpician refugees from revolutionary France. Although his completed works were few in number and his career success was small, Godefroy, like Latrobe and others of his generation, provided buildings that showed a way beyond the domestic, and toward monumentality.

—ROBERT L. ALEXANDER

GOFF, Bruce.

American. Born in Alton, Kansas, 8 June 1904. Died in Tyler, Texas, 4 August 1982. Married Evelyn Hall, 1926 (divorced). Apprenticed with and worked for the firm of Rush, Endacott, Rush in Tulsa, Oklahoma, 1916-30; partner, Endacott and Goff, Tulsa, 1930-33; private practice, Park Ridge, Ifi01935; director of design, Libbey-Owens-Ford Glass Company, Toledo, Ohio, 1935-36; private practice, Chicago, Illinois, 1936-42; served with United States Navy construction batallion, 1942-45; private practice, Berkeley, California, 1945-56; private practice, Bartlesville, Oklahoma, 1956-64; private practice, Kansas City, Missouri, 1964-69; private practice, Tyler, Texas, 1970-82. Professor, 1947-55, and director, 1948-55, School of Architecture, University of Oklahoma, Norman.

Chronology of Works
All in the United States
† *Work no longer exists*

1919	Graves Summer House, near Los Angeles, California
1923-26	Robinson Studio, Tulsa, Oklahoma

1926-29	Boston Avenue Methodist-Episcopal Church, Tulsa, Oklahoma
1928-29	Riverside Studio, Tulsa
1938-39	Elin House, Northfield, Illinois
1939-40	Cole House, Park Ridge, Illinois
1940	Unseth House, Park Ridge, Illinois
1940-41	Colmorgan House, Glenview, Illinois
1944-45	Camp Park Military Facilities, Camp Parks, California
1947-48	Ledbetter House, Norman, Oklahoma
1948-50	Ford House, Aurora, Illinois
1949-50	Cox House, Boise City, Oklahoma
1949-50	Hopewell Baptist Church, near Edmond, Oklahoma
1950-55	Bavinger House, near Norman, Oklahoma
1951-52	Wilson House, Pensacola, Florida
1956-58	Price House, Bartlesville, Oklahoma
1957-58	Pollock House, Oklahoma City, Oklahoma
1958-59	Jones House, Bartlesville, Oklahoma
1958-60	Gutman House, Gulfport, Mississippi
1964-65	Dace House, Beaver, Oklahoma
1965	Hyde House, Kansas City, Kansas
1965-67	Duncan House, near Cobden, Illinois
1965-67	Nicol House, Kansas City, Missouri
1970-72	Glen Harder House, near Mountain Lake, Minnesota
1970-72	Second Plunkett House, Lake Village, near Tyler, Texas
1970-73	Jacob Harder House, Mountain Lake, Minnesota
1974-76	Second Barby House, Tucson, Arizona
1978-88	Shin'Enkan Museum of Japanese Art, Los Angeles County Museum of Art, Los Angeles, California (completed by Bart Prince)

Publications

BOOKS BY GOFF

Bruce Goff, Architect. Portfolio. Chicago, 1978.

ARTICLES BY GOFF

"A Declaration for Independence." *Western Architect* (January 1930).

"Notes on Architecture." *Bauwelt* 4 (January 1958): 88.

"Absolute Architecture." *Architecture d'aujourd'hui* (June/July 1962).

"Goff on Goff." *Progressive Architecture* (December 1962): 102-123.

"Architecture as Art." *Progressive Architecture* (December 1962).

"Frank Lloyd Wright: le roi des étoiles." *Architecture d'aujourd'hui* (April/May 1964).

"Originality and Architecture." In TAKENOBU MOHRI (ed.): *Bruce Goff in Architecture.* Tokyo, 1970.

"A Young Architect's Protest for Architecture." *Perspecta* 13/14 (1971): 330-357.

BOOKS ABOUT GOFF

COOK, JEFFREY: *The Architecture of Bruce Goff.* London and New York, 1978.

DeLONG, DAVID G.: *The Architecture of Bruce Goff: Buildings and Projects 1916-1974.* 2 vols. New York, 1977.

DeLONG, DAVID G.: *Bruce Goff: Toward Absolute Architecture.* Cambridge, Massachusetts, and London, 1988.

JENCKS, CHARLES: *Late Modern Architecture.* London, 1980.

MOHRI, TAKENOBU (ed.): *Bruce Goff in Architecture.* Tokyo, 1970.

MURPHY, WILLIAM, and MULLER, LOIS (compilers): *Bruce Goff: A Portfolio of the Work of Bruce Goff.* New York, 1970.

ARTICLES ABOUT GOFF

"Bruce Goff." *Inland Architect* Special issue (December 1979).

"Bruce Goff." *Architecture d'aujourd'hui* Special issue (June 1983).

CANADY, JOHN: "Pavilions on the Prairie." *Horizon* (November 1961).

COOK, JEFFREY, and ALAN, H.: "The Loner." *Inland Architect* (September/December 1982).

DeLONG, DAVID G.: "Bruce Goff 1904-1982." *Progressive Architecture* (September 1982).

LYALL, SUTHERLAND: "The Diversity of Bruce Goff." *Building Design* (13 October 1978).

McCALLUM, IAN: "Bruce Goff." *Architectural Review* (May 1957).

McCOY, ESTHER: "Bruce Goff." *Arts and Architecture* No. 3 (1983).

PARK, BEN ALLAN: "The Architecture of Bruce Goff." *Architectural Design* 27 (May 1957): 151-174.

PLESSIX F. DU, and GRAY, C.: "Bruce Goff, Visionary Architect." *Art in America* (February 1965): 82-87.

SERGEANT, JOHN, and MOORING, STEPHAN (eds.): "AD Profiles 16: Bruce Goff." *Architectural Design* 48, No. 10, special issue (October 1978).

THOMAS, G. S.: "Bruce Goff: Architecture Without Style." *Baukunst und Werkform* (July 1953).

TROXEL, LINDA, and OMINSKI, JULIAN: "Principles of Design: A Seminar with Bruce Goff." *Kansas Engineer* (Lawrence, Kansas, March 1964).

WAECHTER, H. H.: "Architecture of Bruce Goff." *American Institute of Architects Journal* (December 1959): 32-36.

*

Bruce Goff, whose work is still virtually unknown to a majority of the public and many architects alike, operated outside of the mainstream of modern architecture, within a fantasy world of his own making. The Kansas native began his career at the age of 12 as an apprentice with the firm of Rush, Endacott and Rush in Tulsa, Oklahoma, educating himself as best he could from the selection of books and periodicals that were available in that office, and in the local library. Goff was especially interested in the work of Aubrey Beardsley, Gustav Klimt and Erté, as well as the architecture of Erich Mendelsohn, Josef Hoffmann and Bruno Taut, and the combined influence of all these sources is eventually traceable in most of his work.

The most profound influence of all, however, was a periodical that was dedicated exclusively to the work of Frank Lloyd Wright. After reading it, Goff wrote to Wright for more information and received a coveted Wasmuth portfolio by return mail. This portfolio, which had already caused a sensation in Europe, became a catalog for the forms that Goff began to develop, and he soon assimilated the personality of Wright as his alter-ego. While the similarities between the work of the two men have frequently been dismissed as a young man's homage to a more talented master, or even more unkindly as a simple copying of forms, there are several interesting parallels: although Wright was born 37 years before Goff, both men shared the same birthday, and they bore a striking resemblance to one another. Each man had also determined to become an architect at an early age, cutting short formal education to enter into an apprenticeship with a well-established firm, which allowed them both to have a great deal of responsibility on large projects.

They also share a visceral, almost sacred, view of natural materials, deriving highly geometric forms from biological sources, and to the extent that they both responded sensitively to topographical as well as environmental prerogatives, each can be classified as an organic architect. While both men demonstrated an indefinable, midwestern character in their work, Goff was far more mainstream and less highbrow in his approach, incorporating much of the popular culture into his work. Because of the Depression, Goff took a job with Libby Ford Glass Company in 1936, eventually becoming director of design. Because of his experience there and his exposure to other industrial products, his work eventually took on a far more eclectic character than that of his mentor.

After serving in World War II, Goff joined the University of Oklahoma at Norman in 1947, beginning a very productive phase in his career. The Ledbetter and Ford houses of that period both show his love of large expanses of rough-hewn local materials, innovative serpentine structures and open, uncluttered plans. The Bavinger house, which was built near Norman in 1950, also repeats many of these design features in a more primitive way.

Goff left the University of Oklahoma in 1956 and appropriately set up an office in Wright's Price Tower in nearby Bartlesville. At that point his work became what can only be called phantasmagorical, as can be seen in the Gutman, Gryder, Dace and Nicol houses, which were built between 1958 and 1964. Each of these houses is characterized by central, stepped and carpeted "conversation pits," high, triangular spaces and polychromatic interiors.

The Price house, which he began in 1956, and which was commissioned by the same client that had built the Bartlesville office tower designed by Wright, was added to in stages as the needs of the family increased and may be considered most typical of Goff's highly personal style. Called "Starview Farm," the house spirals outward in characteristically Wrightian geometry, but its interiors far surpass the eccentric combination of even that eccentric architect's later years.

Whereas Wright was respected for his genius and skill but distrusted by the Modern Movement because of his emphasis on context and his search for regional as well as historical prototypes in his Prairie houses, Goff did not fare as well. His populism, use of color and unlikely combinations of materials, along with his unpredictability, placed him in another category altogether, even making him a figure of contempt. With a change in architectural direction today and the prevalence of more pluralistic attitudes, however, his work—and the inventiveness that is integral to it—is being reassessed. As a result, it seems that history will be far kinder to him and that a more objective analysis of what he has achieved can now be made. Given the varied directions that architecture is taking, it is certain that that analysis will be meaningful.

—JAMES M. STEELE

GOMEZ DE MORA, Juan.

Spanish. Born in Madrid, Spain, ca. 1580. Died in Madrid, 28 February 1648. Father was the painter Juan Gómez de Mora. Student of his uncle, Francesco de Mora, whom he succeeded in 1611 as court architect of King Philip III.

Chronology of Works
All in Spain
* Approximate dates
† Work no longer exists

1611-16	Encarnacíon Church, Madrid
1616ff.	Clerecía Jesuit College, Salamanca (not completed until the mid-18th century)
1617-19	Plaza Mayor, Madrid (facades; since rebuilt)†
1619-27	Alcázar Palace, Madrid (south front)†
1621	Casa del Campillo, El Escorial park
1625ff.	Colegio del Rey ('de Santiago'), Salamanca (expansion; completed after his death by others)
1640ff.	Ayuntamiento Palace, Madrid (completed after his death by José de Villareal)

*

As *maestro mayor* of the royal palaces in Madrid and El Pardo from 1611 until his death, Juan Gómez de Mora held the highest position possible for a Spanish architect and builder. Although not responsible for far-reaching innovations, he influenced Spanish court architecture during the entire first half of the 17th century. As a result of the court's dynastic connections with the Netherlands, his architecture also found a rich following in what is now Belgium. Gómez de Mora succeeded Juan de Herrera in the office of court architect, but his style was influenced rather by the work of his uncle Francisco de Mora, who combined Herrera's strict vocabulary of form with a greater formal freedom. Gómez de Mora's works moved between a Mannerist and Early Baroque idiom, and remained clearly within the Spanish tradition, in spite of his thorough knowledge of Italian architectural theory concerning the treatment of surface and volume.

Gómez de Mora's first important work was the Church of the Royal Convent of the Encarnación in Madrid (1611-16). Built on a Latin-cross plan, the church has a single nave and a crossing dome. The three-story facade, which is crowned by a triangular gable, opens up to a narthex by means of three arcades in the lower story. That element in the design may have been inspired by Counter-Reformation architecture. Windows arranged to form V shapes alternate with barely accentuated wall surfaces in the two upper stories, which, despite a certain coolness, endows the facade with a pictorial effect. Proportion and articulation of the facade are closely related to Francisco de Mora's Church of San José in Avila (1608-15), but they have been simplified and made less playful. The Encarnación Church became an important example for numerous later churches of the monastic orders.

In 1616 Gómez de Mora took over the planning and construction of the Clerecía in Salamanca, a Jesuit college founded by Philip III. Although the complex was completed only in the mid-18th century, the plan and substantial parts of the church are Gómez de Mora's work. The elaborate U-shaped ensemble, which consists of a church, monastery and college, is laid out around two courtyards in a functional design. Most likely the layout was derived from the Collegio Romano in Rome, with which the Jesuits were familiar. Whether the design of the church, as a wall-pier construction with galleries and a crossing dome, was inspired by Giacomo Barozzi da Vignola's Church of Il Gesú, also in Rome, remains unclear, since Spain itself had a tradition of buildings of this type.

Between 1617 and 1619 Gómez de Mora worked on the Plaza Mayor in Madrid, a project considered to be of overwhelming importance since the 15th century. Continuing Herrera's work,

Juan Gomez de Mora: Plaza Mayor, Madrid, Spain, 1617-19

he designed a large rectangular square (about 100 by 200 meters), surrounded on all sides by four-story buildings with arcades at ground level. Only the Casa de la Panadería (the city's bread market, from where court delegations witnessed autos-da-fé) is distinguished from the other buildings, by the order of its columns and the gable. The square was destroyed by fire several times, and its present appearance goes back to the neoclassical reconstruction by Juan de Villanueva.

Gómez de Mora's reconstruction of the Alcázar in Madrid (1619-27) also fell victim to a fire, but a wooden model of the building has survived. He gave the traditional fort-like type of a four-wing structure with corner towers a portal on the southern side, and articulated both upper stories with pilasters and triangular gables. The Alcázar scheme—in diminished form, it must be noted—also asserts itself in the exterior of the Cárcel de Corte, the former national prison. In the layout with two courtyards divided by staircases a connection with hospital architecture is also visible. The decorative brickwork is within the Spanish tradition. On the other hand, the gradual stepping of the columns around the gabled central projection, which creates a strong impression of depth and movement, is unusual for Spanish architecture. Gómez de Mora did the designs for the prison, but it is not known whether he took part in its construction.

The Church of the Bernardine Nuns in Alcalá de Henares, an oval structure obviously deriving from Roman examples, was once attributed to Gómez de Mora, but is now rightly assigned to Sebastián de la Plaza.

Even though Gómez de Mora was the leading architect in early-17th-century Spain, his work came at the end of an epoch rather than at the beginning of a new one. His early work

demonstrated a slow but uninterrupted distancing from the severity of Herrera's design principles, as well as the development of a personal style, as in the Encarnación Church. The turn toward Baroque forms, at least in the realm of court architecture, was hesitant and superficial, however. After the middle of the century, new centers of building activity arose in Granada, Seville, Salamanca and Santiago de Compostela, which took a leading role in the development of Baroque architecture in Spain. Gómez de Mora's buildings became objects of aesthetic interest once more only with the rise of academic classicism and the return to indigenous architectural traditions.

—BARBARA BORNGÄSSER KLEIN
Translated from the German by Marijke Rijsberman

GONDOUIN, Jacques.

French. Born in St. Ouen-sur-Seine, France, 7 June 1737. Died in Paris, 29 December 1818. Studied with Jacques-François Blondel; won royal pension for four years of study in Rome, where he met Giovanni Battista Piranesi; traveled to Holland and England; returned to France, 1764; appointed as royal architect, 1766, and as designer of furnishings for the crown, 1779. Member of the Académie d'Architecture Royale, 1774; member, Institut, 1795, and of the Conseil des Bâtiments Civils; appointed to the commission on royal buildings, 1808.

Chronology of Works
All in France
* Approximate dates

1769-75	École de Chirurgie (now École de Médecine), Paris
1780s	Villa, *Les eaux vives*, near Paris (not completed)
1805*	Caduceus Fountain, Place de l'École de Médecine, Paris†
1806-12	Column, Place Vendôme, Paris (with J.-B. Lepère)

Publications

BOOKS BY GONDOUIN

Description des Ecoles de Chirurgie. Paris, 1780.

BOOKS ABOUT GONDOUIN

BRAHAM, ALLAN: *The Architecture of the French Enlightenment.* Berkeley, California, and Los Angeles, 1980.

ARTICLES ABOUT GONDOUIN

ADHÉMAR, JEAN: ''L'Ecole de Médecine.'' *Architecture* 47, No. 3 (Paris, 1934): 105-108.

Jacques Gondouin was an architect in France in the second half of the 18th century, known now most for his design of the École de Chirurgie, or School of Surgery, in Paris. His father was a gardener who, from the humblest of beginnings, ended as the *jardinier du roi (king's gardener),* a favored servant of Louis XV, and was responsible for the gardens at Choisy, the king's favorite château. As a student in the school of Jacques-François Blondel, Gondouin competed for three successive years for the Prix de Rome without winning first prize. But since he was a protégé of the king, Gondouin was able to go to Rome anyway; there he spent four years sketching and studying, admiring in particular the landscape of the city and the classical ruins that were to be seen everywhere. At one moment, the story goes, he conceived of buying the land of Hadrian's Villa to study it more closely and reconstruct its original appearance. In the end he had to be content, on a second trip to Rome, with the designs he made of the site, which he presented to his friend Giovanni Battista Piranesi.

Gondouin returned to Paris in 1764, via Holland and England, and his first works on returning were done for the postal administration. He also was appointed inspector of the king's furniture, *inspecteur des meubles de la couronne;* it was in that position that Gondouin produced a number of designs for the royal cabinetmakers, making wax models for the approval of the king and queen, one or two of which have survived. But it was also at that time that Gondouin came to know Germain Pichaut de la Martinière, surgeon to the king since 1747, a forceful personality who was concerned with improving the status and repute of surgeons. In 1750 an independent Academy of Surgeons had been established, and in the act of ratification it was stressed that a new anatomy theater was required; an older theater, built earlier in the century on the rue des Cordeliers, is known from an engraving in one of Blondel's volumes.

Gondouin's plan for the new school was arranged in the manner of a large town house, with three wings set around a courtyard and a screen of columns at the front. The main focus, appropriately enough, was for a huge hemispherical anatomy theater that could hold some 1,200 people, emphasized on the exterior by a portico of grand, freestanding Corinthian columns. At the front of the whole plan was a screen of Ionic columns across the entrance, patterned in part on the model of a triumphal arch, yet set at the same scale as the portico at the anatomy theater; a second floor extended from the portico to this screen. On the street side, the screen featured a long relief panel by Pierre-François Bernier. The panel showed Louis XV, followed by Minerva and surrounded by the sick, ordering the building of the anatomy-theater complex, while the Genius of Architecture presented the plan, and Surgery, accompanied by Vigilance and Prudence, guided the king in his actions.

The amphitheater was the most complex part of the design, being partly like an antique theater, yet with a vaulted, semicircular ceiling like that of the Pantheon. The advantages of this were clear: earlier theaters, like that on the rue des Cordeliers, had been completely circular, yet this new arrangement gave all the spectators a far better view of the demonstration, and the oculus at the top, in shape like that at the Pantheon but larger in diameter, gave the room far better illumination; this plan, it should be noted, was later used for debating chambers. On the wall behind the place for the demonstration there was a semicircular lunette that served to establish, as did the relief on the entrance screen, the meaning of what was done there. Famous surgeons were depicted, including La Martinière, and the king was seen encouraging and rewarding them in their progress, as the gods transmitted the principles of anatomy.

Additional service areas in the complex included a smaller theater for the instruction of midwives, a chemistry laboratory and a small hospital, and on the left side, a public hall and a room for experiments. The second floor contained a library, a room for the display of instruments, and the administrative offices. The building was inaugurated in 1775 and received with approval. Luc-Vincent Thiéry described it in 1780 as marking ''a new epoch in architecture.'' Jena-François Blondel remarked that in its articulation it was ''superior to anything [he] had seen newly completed in Paris,'' noting only what he called a ''meanness'' in the approach to the complex, where Gondouin's project for a square in front was never completed. This, as we know from his engraving of the scheme, would have contained a small prison, from which doubtless the corpses for the anatomy classes would have come. Gondouin designed the prison in a very striking style, with a blank, heavily rusticated wall surface, with a few unframed openings and a fountain in the center.

The École de Chirurgie was essentially all that Gondouin built. He began to design a villa for himself, Les Eaux Vives, in the 1780s on the banks of the Seine, in the manner of Andrea Palladio, but that project was never finished. But it was there, sometimes in the guise of a gardener, that Gondouin survived the most dangerous years of the Revolution, though he suffered financially. Soon after the Revolution he was appointed to the Conseil des Bâtiments Civils, becoming a member of the Institute in 1795. In 1807 he prepared a project for the restoration of Versailles, and from 1806 to 1812 he was in charge of the commission for the building of the Colonne Vendôme. In 1814, at the age of 77, Gondouin married a young woman of 17, who died shortly after the birth of a son; Gondouin himself died in 1818, three years after the restoration of the monarchy.

—DAVID CAST

GOODHUE, Bertram Grosvenor.

American. Born in Pomfret, Connecticut, 1869. Died on 21 April 1924. Educated at Russell's College in New Haven, Connecticut. Worked for James Renwick, New York, 1884; worked in office of Ralph Adams Cram and Charles Francis Wentworth,

Boston, 1891; partnership with Cram and Frank W. Ferguson as Cram, Goodhue and Ferguson, Boston, 1897; established own office, New York, 1914.

Chronology of Works
All in the United States unless noted

1892-1913	All Saints' Church, Ashmont, Massachusetts (with Ralph Adams Cram and Frank W. Ferguson; completed in 1941)
1899	Deborah Cook Sayles Public Library, Pawtucket, Rhode Island
1901	Public Library, Nashua, New Hampshire
1902	Gillespie House, Montecito, California
1903-10	United States Military Academy, West Point, New York (with Cram and Ferguson)
1905	La Santissima Trinidad Church, Havana, Cuba (with Cram and Ferguson)
1906-13	St. Thomas Church, Fifth Avenue, New York City (with Cram and Ferguson)
1909-12	First Baptist Church, Pittsburgh, Pennsylvania (with Cram and Ferguson)
1911-15	Panama-California Exposition Buildings, San Diego, California
1914-18	St. Bartholomew's Church, New York City
1914-19	Church of St. Vincent Ferrer, New York City
1916-18	Marine Corps Base and Naval Air Station, San Diego, California
1918-27	Rockefeller Chapel, University of Chicago, Chicago, Illinois
1919-24	National Academy of Sciences Building, Washington, D.C.
1920-24	Sterling Memorial Library, Yale University, New Haven, Connecticut
1920-32	State Capitol, Lincoln, Nebraska
1922-26	Central Public Library, Los Angeles, California

Publications

BOOKS BY GOODHUE

A Book of Architectural and Decorative Drawings. New York, 1914.

BOOKS ABOUT GOODHUE

OLIVER, RICHARD: *Bertram Grosvenor Goodhue.* Cambridge, Massachusetts, 1983.
WHITAKER, CHARLES H. (ed): *Bertram Grosvenor Goodhue, Architect and Master of Many Arts.* New York, 1925.

ARTICLES ABOUT GOODHUE

"The Nebraska State Capitol." *American Architect* 145, entire issue (1934).
SCHUYLER, MONTGOMERY: "The Works of Cram, Goodhue and Ferguson." *Architectural Record* 29, special issue (1911): 1-112.

When the "city beautiful" movement headed into the American West, the cavalcade of architects was led by Bertram Grosvenor Goodhue. In 1891 Goodhue became a partner with Ralph Adams Cram, eventually forming the Boston firm of Cram, Goodhue and Ferguson, with Frank W. Ferguson. During his career,

Goodhue was responsible for the design of the Rice University campus, in Houston, Texas; the 1911-15 Panama-California Exposition, in San Diego, California; and the State Capitol of Nebraska.

The commission for Rice was awarded in response to the firm's successful campus plan for the United States Military Academy (USMA) at West Point, New York. The USMA scheme won critical acclaim because it skillfully accommodated numerous pre-existing buildings on the campus while lending an overall vision for continued growth of the institution. Cram and Goodhue's choice of a "military-gothic" style amplified the natural fortress-like qualities of the Hudson River site. To execute this large commission, Goodhue and Cram decided to open an office in Manhattan to facilitate better communications during construction. Cram continued to head up the operations of the Boston office, while Goodhue took charge of the New York office and supervised construction of the academy.

When the firm was requested to submit schemes for the William Rice University in Houston, the Boston office sent three choices, while the New York office sent only a single scheme. The New York scheme, authored by Goodhue, was eventually chosen because of its ease in phasing and superior organization. The campus was to be formed around a central east-west axis that would be punctuated by a series of subordinate north-south cross axes. The buildings were sited so as to give a sense of completion during development of the campus. Goodhue saw that the flaws in many campus schemes were rooted in the necessity for the plan to be completed in a single building campaign, rendering further additions impossible. Goodhue also saw that the development of the landscape was particularly important to the success of the plan. Elegant alleys of live oaks were planted to provide protection against the intense Texan sun. At the heart of the campus, Goodhue located a large, well-proportioned, and selectively planted quadrangle defined by a series of harmonious Mediterranean Gothic classroom buildings. While the Boston office executed many of the architectural commissions on the campus, Goodhue influenced the character of the future development of the campus through the design of a domed auditorium building which, had it been built, would have been located at the western end of the campus' main axis. The Rice plan represents a masterful synthesis of Beaux-Arts planning strategies, response to regional character, and practical concerns.

Success in Houston, coupled with Goodhue's love of Spanish and Mexican architecture, made the architect a natural choice for the Panama-California Exposition of 1911-15. Local businessmen proposed an exposition to celebrate the opening of the Panama Canal and in an attempt to establish San Diego as the first and most important port in the United States north of the canal. Prior to Goodhue's involvement, the landscape architects Frederick Law Olmsted and his son, Frederick, Jr., had been engaged to design Balboa Park, the proposed location for the fair. When Goodhue made counter proposals for the location of fair buildings, the Olmsteds withdrew from the project on the grounds that their authority had been compromised. Goodhue orchestrated a picturesque group of buildings organized along an axis running perpendicular to an *arroyo* near the center of the park. The architect anchored the "village" of Spanish-Baroque-style buildings around a forecourt, perching the entire group upon the edge of the *arroyo*. The ensemble was given access by a dramatic multiarched bridge over the ravine. Continuing along the axis formed by the bridge and the forecourt, Goodhue designed a broad promenade that gave form to the grouping of numerous fair buildings. The architect had intended that only the bridge spanning the *arroyo* and the forecourt setpiece be preserved for posterity. A testament to the architect's popularity was demonstrated by the citizens of San Diego, who became attached to the Spanish village and funded the dismantling and eventual reconstruction of the fair's temporary buildings in permanent materials. The continued presence of Goodhue's masterpiece in southern California exerted influence over generations of architects in the regions.

Near the end of his career, Goodhue was awarded the first prize in the competition for the State Capitol of Nebraska (1920). The jury selection of the scheme was, according to one juror, made simple by the refinement of the scheme and the memorable quality of the building's primary design element—the tower. The proposal represented a radical departure from what had become a tradition in state capitol building design. Prior to the Goodhue building, the accepted solution to the monumental program of a state capitol building was to emulate the paradigm set by the domed United States Capitol building, in Washington, D.C. Throughout the nation, statehouses became icons of the government centered in the nation's capital city. For those who could not make the journey to Washington, a trip to the state capital might offer an approximation of the experience. Goodhue was aware of the flatness of the Nebraskan plains and saw that a 400-foot tower would act as a forceful image in that context. Selectively ornamented and skillfully massed, the Goodhue building defies stylistic placement. Neither possessing solely the attributes of classical architecture, nor exclusively that of any other particular fashion, the building represents a synthesis of many different styles in a form well suited to its location on the nation's Great Plains.

Goodhue put his civic-design talents to use in the master plan for the California Institute of Technology in Pasadena, and the Los Angeles Public Library. The architect was also noted for his designs of numerous ecclesiastical buildings. Among his most widely recognized church designs are: the United States Military Academy Chapel at West Point; the elegant and asymmetrically balanced St. Thomas Church and the Byzantine St. Bartholomew's Church, both in New York City; and the Rockefeller Chapel at the University of Chicago.

—BRIAN KELLY

GRAVES, Michael.

American. Born in Indianapolis, Indiana, 9 July 1934. Studied at the University of Cincinnati, Ohio, 1954-58, B.Arch.; Harvard University, Cambridge, Massachusetts, 1958-59, M.Arch.; American Academy in Rome, 1960-62 (Prix de Rome; Brunner Fellowship). Private practice in Princeton, New Jersey, since 1964. Lecturer, 1962-63, assistant professor, 1963-67, associate professor, 1967-72, and Schirmer Professor of Architecture, since 1972, Princeton University, New Jersey; has also taught at University of Texas, Austin; University of Houston; New School for Social Research, New York; University of California, Los Angeles. Fellow, American Institute of Architecture.

Chronology of Works
All in the United States unless noted

1967	Hanselmann House, Fort Wayne, Indiana
1967	Urban County Nature and Science Museum, Mountainside, New Jersey
1969	Benacerraf House, Princeton, New Jersey
1971-73	Alexander House, Princeton, New Jersey
1972	Snyderman House, Fort Wayne, Indiana
1974	Claghorn House, Princeton, New Jersey
1975	Newark Art School, Newark, New Jersey (renovation)
1976	Crooks House, Fort Wayne, Indiana
1976	Schulman House, Princeton, New Jersey
1977	Fargo-Moorhead Cultural Center Bridge, between Fargo, North Dakota, and Moorhead, Minnesota
1983	Regional Library, San Juan Capistrano, California
1983	Humana Corporation Headquarters, Louisville, Kentucky
1983-84	Civic Center, Portland, Oregon
1985-	Whitney Museum of American Art, New York (addition)
1985	Disney Company Corporate Headquarters, Burbank, California
1986-90	Walt Disney World Dolphin and Swan Hotels, Lake Buena Vista, Florida
1987	Portside Apartment Tower, Yokohama, Japan
1987	Momochi District Apartment Building, Fukuoka, Japan
1988	Daiei Office Building, Yokohama, Japan
1988	2121 Pennsylvania Avenue Office Building, Washington, D.C.
1988	Tajima Office Building, Tokyo, Japan
1988	Arts and Sciences Building, University of Virginia, Charlottesville, Virginia
1988	Hotel New York, Euro Disneyland, Paris, France
1988-	Lenox Stores and Galleries: Tysons Corner, Virginia; Palm Beach Gardens, California; Bloomingdale's, New York City; B. Altman's, New York City; Costa Mesa, California; Gaviidae Common, Minneapolis, Minnesota; Bloomingdale's, Boca Raton, Florida; Cherry Creek Mall, Denver, Colorado; Bloomingdale's, White Plains, New York; Bloomingdale's, Chestnut Hill, Massachusetts; Castner-Knott, Nashville, Tennessee; Macy's, Herald Square, New York City; Wanamaker's, Philadelphia, Pennsylvania
1989	Town Hall, Onjuku, Japan
1989	Museum of Art and Archaeology, Emory University, Atlanta, Georgia (addition)
1989	Tulips and Elms Apartment Building and Hotel, Brussels, Belgium
1989	500 Forest Guest House, Susono City, Japan
1990	Newark Museum, Newark, New Jersey (renovations)
1990	Private Residence, Sherman Oaks, California
1991	Makuhari International Market, Makuhari, Japan
1991	Denver Central Library, Denver, Colorado

Publications

ARTICLES BY GRAVES

"The Swedish Connection." *Journal of Architectural Education* (Fall 1975).
"Elusive Outcome, Mental Mise-en-scene." *Progressive Architecture* (May 1977).
"The Necessity of Drawing: Tangible Speculation." *Architectural Design* (June 1977).

BOOKS ABOUT GRAVES

ARNELL, PETER; BICKFORD, TED; and WHEELER, KAREN: *Michael Graves: Buildings and Projects 1966-1981.* New York, 1983.
COLQUHOUN, ALAN: *Michael Graves.* London, 1979.
FRAMPTON, KENNETH, and ROWE, COLIN: *Five Architects: Eisenman, Graves, Gwathmey, Hejduk, Meier.* New York, 1972.

JENCKS, CHARLES: *The Language of Post-Modern Architecture*. London, 1977.

————: *Kings of Infinite Space: Frank Lloyd Wright and Michael Graves*. London and New York, 1983.

NICHOLS, K.; BURKE, P.; and HANCOCK, C. (eds.): *Michael Graves, Buildings and Projects 1982-1989*. Princeton, New Jersey, 1990.

STERN, ROBERT A. M.: *New Directions in American Architecture*. New York, 1977.

ARTICLES ABOUT GRAVES

CARL, PETER: "Towards a Pluralist Architecture." *Progressive Architecture* (February 1973).

"Encore Graves." *Progressive Architecture* (July 1983).

"The Enigma of Michael Graves." *Architects' Journal* (14 March 1984).

GANDELSONAS, MARIO: "On Reading Architecture: Eisenman and Graves: An Analysis." *Progressive Architecture* (March 1972).

HATAE, TAKEO: "Rockefeller House and Keeley Guest House" and "About Michael Graves." *Architecture and Urbanism* (March 1974).

"Interview with Michael Graves." *Architecture and Urbanism* (December 1982).

McKEAN, JOHN: "The Architect as Intellectual Artist." *Building Design* (10 October 1975).

"Michael Graves: Evolving a Language." *Fifth Column* (Montreal, Fall 1980).

"Michael Graves Talks on His Works." *Architecture and Urbanism* (December 1983).

"Robert Stern and Michael Graves." *Fifth Column* (Montreal, Fall 1983).

Space Design, special issue (April 1983).

STEPHENS, SUZANNE: "Living in a Work of Art." *Progressive Architecture* (March 1978).

"Three by Graves." *Building Design* (17 June 1983).

*

"In memory of the Man that was; in lamentation of the Collective that wasn't; in the celebration of The Institution that subsists." The architecture of Michael Graves is a memorial to the unknowable soldier who perished in the Cold War. It is a cenotaph of the collectivity stillborn despite the labors to create it. The strengths and weaknesses of Graves' mature works are the emblems, the images, the invisible traces, the coat-of-arms of each one of us who perished sometime between 1967 and 1991. Equally, they are funerary mausolea for the kinds of collective action we dreamt of engaging in during the same period. Thus, this architecture is neither about the individual nor about the collectivity, but rather about the institution after the extinction of the individual and the bankruptcy of the collectivity.

Like its economic and political emanations, the Cold War period in architecture produced an unbreakable deadlock and standoff. No resolution could be found between "self-expression" (the individual) and socially conscious architecture (the collectivity)—neither the architecture of the individual nor that of the collectivity could emerge victorious from this standoff. A resolution had to be found, and that is the neo-laissez faire institution which finally triumphed in Graves' 1988 Copa Banana Lounge Tabletop and coincidentally in the election of George Bush, the collapse of communism, and the end of the welfare state.

Although one can never predict what the "next" thing is that a living architect like Graves might do, his present architecture has remained stylistically static since 1980 when the Portland Building ushered in the Reagan Era and began to usher out the Cold War. What Graves' last decade of work has accomplished is the identification of an architectural language which erases the subject, mocks the collectivity, and glorifies the "institution." The subject has already been erased: "In memory of the Man that was." The avenue elevation of the Portland Building. "In lamentation of the Collective that wasn't." Graves memorializes and ironically elevates "The Institution" which has survived the extinction of the subject and the bankruptcy and corruption of the commonwealth. This is done without nostalgia, whining or breastbeating: The Institution is revealed as the only viable force in a world now bereft both of people and of governments.

No contemporary architect has been more successful in finding a form-language that provides a client with a stronger ironic and "artistic" image and yet really offends absolutely no one. Absolutely no one because with the collapse of Troy, with the end of the Trojan War, collectivity has no voice. The very repetition of the "same" project, time after time, is an indication both of the ease and the contemptuousness, the inoffensiveness of this language. "A Fanfare for The Winner!"

One may well say that in this sense Graves has succeeded Philip Johnson as the premiere ironic image maker of this generation of architects. But image maker of what?

The Institution whose image is made is revealed in the Lenox Identity Program (also 1988). Architect as image maker: "The Lenox china company commissioned Graves to design a new corporate identity program, packaging for its china, glassware and giftware, and several retail stores and boutiques. Included in the identity program and packaging are a new logotype, development of a color palette to be used in a variety of ways, and graphic design of corporate stationery and related items." What I have elsewhere described as Morris Lapidus' trinity of Power, Profit and Fun achieves its apotheosis in the bridal registry tent of the Lenox store at the Gardens Shopping Mall in Palm Beach Gardens, Florida (and yet again also 1988): the color palette and the logotype, the package and the contents, the bride and her attendants, the registry and the reginasty.

In the age of the Cold War, when there were still individuals and governments, the Power, Profit and Fun Trinity was always an underground, semisubmerged countermovement. It took the Reagan Era to liberate this new trinity and to allow it to surface as a publicly proclaimed credo for the emerging "new world order." This is architecture as logotype: In the Dolphin and Swan Hotels in Walt Disney World Florida (witty and fond, and indebted—tongue-in-cheek—to Lapidus' Fontainebleau) or certainly in the aforementioned Copa Banana Lounge tabletop, Graves succeeded in ways that Lapidus, Andy Warhol or Robert Venturi never could—in making kitsch-pop art architecture part of the "serious" mainstream. Graves is America's great architect; Reagan was succeeded by Bush as president; irony progressed from *succès de scandale* to *succès d'estime* and finally to *succès fou*. Another fanfare for the winner, Maestro!

—JOSEPH B. JUHASZ

GREENE, Charles and Henry.

American. Charles Sumner Greene: Born in Brighton, Ohio, 12 October 1868. Died in Carmel, California, 11 June 1957. Married Alice Gordon White, 1901; five children. Studied at Massachusetts Institute of Technology School of Architecture, Cambridge, 1888-91. Worked for Winslow and Weatherall and other

Charles and Henry Greene: David B. Gamble House, Pasadena, California, 1908

Boston architects, 1891-94; partner with Henry Mather Greene, Pasadena, California, 1894-1903, Los Angeles, 1903-06, and Pasadena, 1906-22; practiced independently, in Carmel, California, from 1922.

Henry Mather Greene: Born in Brighton, Ohio, 23 January 1870; died in Altadena, California, 2 October 1954. Married Emeline Augusta Dart, 1899; four children. Studied at Massachusetts Institute of Technology School of Architecture, Cambridge, 1888-91. Worked for Stickney and Austin, then for Shepley, Rutan and Coolidge, Boston, 1891-94; partner, with Charles Sumner Greene, Pasadena, California, 1894-1903, Los Angeles, 1903-06, and Pasadena, 1906-22; practiced independently, in Pasadena, from 1922.

Chronology of Works
All in the United States
† Work no longer exists

1896-97	Kinney-Kendall Building, Pasadena, California
1900	John C. Bentz Building, Pasadena, California
1901	Charles S. Greene House, Pasadena, California
1902	James A. Culbertson House, Pasadena, California
1903	Arturo Bandini House (''El Hagar''), Pasadena, California†
1903	Mary R. Darling House, Claremont, California
1903	Josephine Van Rossem House, Pasadena, California
1903	Martha, Violet and Jane White House, Pasadena, California
1904	Mrs. James A. Garfield House, Pasadena, California
1904	Henry M. Greene House, Pasadena, California
1904	Jennie A. Reeve House, Long Beach, California
1904	Adelaide M. Tichenor House, Long Beach, California
1904	Charles W. Hollister House, Hollywood, California†
1904	Freeman Ford House, Pasadena, California
1905	Henry M. Robinson House, Pasadena, California
1905	South Pasadena Realty and Improvement Company Bridge, Pasadena, California
1906	John C. Bentz House, Pasadena, California
1906	John A. Cole House, Pasadena, California
1906	Caroline S. DeForest House, Pasadena, California

1906	F. W. Hawks House, Pasadena, California
1906	Theodore M. Irwin House, Pasadena, California
1906	James W. Neill House, Pasadena, California (additions and alterations)
1906	Z. A. Robinson House, Pasadena, California
1906	Robert Pitcairn Jr., House, Pasadena, California
1907	Robert R. Blacker House, Pasadena, California
1907	Freeman A. Ford House, Pasadena, California
1908	David B. Gamble House, Pasadena, California
1909	Earle C. Anthony House, Beverly Hills, California
1909	S. S. Crow (Edward S. Crocker) House, Pasadena, California
1909	Charles M. Pratt House, Ojai, California
1909	William R. Thorsen House, Berkeley, California
1911	Nathan Bentz House, Santa Barbara, California
1911	Cordelia A. Culbertson House, Pasadena, California
1913	William M. Ladd House, Ojai, California
1915	Nathan H. Williams House, Altadena, California
1918-23	D. L. James House, Carmel Highlands, California
1920s	Charles S. Greene House, Carmel, California
1923	Charles S. Greene Studio, Carmel, California
1924	Thomas Gould, Jr., House, Ventura, California
1927	Mortimer Fleishhacker Estate, Woodside, California (water garden)
1928	Martin Flavin House, Carmel Highlands, California (library addition and alterations)
1929	Walter L. Richardson House, Porterville, California

Publications

BOOKS ABOUT GREENE AND GREENE

FRAMPTON, KENNETH, and FUTAGAWA, YUKIO: *Modern Architecture: 1920-1945*. New York, 1983.

JORDY, WILLIAM H.: "Craftsmanship as Structural Elaboration: Charles and Henry Greene's Gamble House." In *American Buildings and Their Architects: Progressive and Academic Ideals at the Turn of the Twentieth Century.* Garden City, New York, 1972.

MAKINSON, RANDELL L.: *A Guide to the Works of Greene and Greene.* Salt Lake City, 1974.

MAKINSON, RANDELL L.: *Greene and Greene.* 2 vols. Salt Lake City, Utah, 1977-79.

McCOY, ESTHER: *Five California Architects.* New York, 1960.

RUSSELL, FRANK (ed.): *Art Nouveau Architecture.* London, 1979.

STRAND, JANANN: *A Greene and Greene Guide.* Pasadena, California, 1974.

ARTICLES ABOUT GREENE AND GREENE

"Architecture West." *Progressive Architecture* (November 1972).

BANGS, JEAN MURRAY: "Greene and Greene." *Architectural Forum* 89 (October 1948): 80-89.

BANGS, JEAN MURRAY: "Prophets Without Honor." *American Institute of Architects Journal* (July 1952).

BLOOMFIELD, ANNE: "The Evolution of a Landscape: Charles Sumner Greene's Designs for Green Gables." *Journal of the Society of Architectural Historians* 47 (September 1988): 231-244.

"California: The Emergence of a Tradition." *Architectural Record* (May 1956).

CURRENT, WILLIAM: *Greene and Greene: Architects in the Residential Style.* Fort Worth, Texas, 1974.

"Greene and Greene." *American Preservation* (April/May 1978).

"Greene and Greene: David B. Gamble House, Pasadena, California, 1908." *Global Architecture* (1984).

HARRIS, HARWELL HAMILTON: "The Brothers Greene." *Architectural Record* (November 1975).

JODIDIO, PHILIP: "Greene and Greene." *Connaissance des arts* (December 1977).

LANCASTER, CLAY: "My Interviews with Greene and Greene." *American Institute of Architects Journal* 28 (July 1957): 202-206.

LANCASTER, CLAY: "Some Sources of Greene and Greene." *American Institute of Architects Journal* 34 (August 1960): 39-46.

MAKINSON, RANDELL L.: "Greene and Greene." *Approach* 10 (Spring 1975).

MAKINSON, RANDELL L.: "The Gamble House by Greene and Greene." *Prairie School Review* No. 4 (1968): 1-31.

McCOY, ESTHER: "Notes on Greene and Greene." *Arts and Architecture* (July 1953): 27-38.

McCOY, ESTHER: "Recent Books on Greene and Greene." *Progressive Architecture* (January 1976).

McCOY, ESTHER: "Roots of California Contemporary Architecture." *Arts and Architecture* (October 1956).

"The Morphology of Los Angeles." *Architectural Design* No. 8/9 (1981).

"A Parting Salute to the Fathers of the California Style." *House and Home* (August 1957).

YOST, L. MORGAN: "Greene and Greene of Pasadena." *American Institute of Architects Journal* (September 1950).

YOST, L. MORGAN: "Greene and Greene of Pasadena." *Journal of the Society of Architectural Historians* 9 (March 1950): 11-19.

*

In the opening years of the 20th century, Charles Sumner Greene and Henry Mather Greene created residences that have been called the "ultimate bungalows" of the American arts and crafts movement. Developing a unique regional response to the arroyo area of southern California, the Greene brothers established a standard of craftsmanship, structural expression in carpentry and refined detailing in wood joinery that was unsurpassed in their generation of builders of "craftsman homes."

Greene and Greene's handcrafted houses continued a long-standing tradition of expressive American carpentry reaching back to 17th-century New England frame houses, to 19th-century board-and-batten Gothic Revival cottages in the A.J. Downing tradition, and to the later Stick Style of the 1860s and 1870s. But theirs was a personal synthesis of American craftsman and traditional Japanese constructional expression that effected a transformation of the framing of simple southern California bungalows from mere building to the fine art of architecture.

Working with craftsman Peter Hall, moreover, the brothers Greene produced furnishings and decorative arts for their finest homes, designing objects ranging from exquisite built-in cabinet pieces and bookcases to chairs and side tables, and (for the Gamble House living room) a piano, piano bench and sectional carpets designed by Charles Greene. Wall sconces, recessed lights and frames for windows connecting internal rooms were crafted in hand-rubbed mahogany boards, joined with teak pegs, and filled with opalescent glass in the style of Tiffany's New York studio glass; light fixtures suspended from ceilings by leather straps provided some of the firm's most noteworthy objects of decorative art.

Born in Cincinnati, the Greenes were raised close to nature, on a farm in West Virginia. They attended high school in St. Louis, where their father had opened a medical practice. There, a formative influence on their developing attitude toward the building crafts emerged in the figure of Calvin Milton Woodward, a follower of John Ruskin and William Morris, and founder and director of the Manual Training School of Washington University. At Woodward's school, in addition to following a normal high school curriculum, the Greenes were required to spend two hours daily at manual training, the first year devoted to carpentry and woodworking, with an emphasis on developing an appreciation and understanding of the inherent characteristics of wood. Later training at the Massachusetts Institute of Technology's two-year program in architecture and brief apprenticeships in prominent Boston-area architectural firms set the stage for the Greenes' careers in architecture.

Called to Pasadena by their parents, who had moved there for health reasons, the Greenes traveled to California in 1893. On the way, they stopped in Chicago, host city of the World's Columbian Exposition, where they visited the Japanese exhibit and saw the Ho-o-den pavilion. Japanese architecture reinforced the attitudes promoted in Woodward's wood workshop: an appreciation of, indeed, a reverence for wood, for the craft of building and for expressive detailing. A subsequent visit to the Japanese teahouse and garden at the San Francisco Mid-Winter Exposition confirmed the Greenes' appreciation for Oriental constructional "tectonics" and the "materiality" of building. Stylistically most explicitly evidenced in the Long Beach house for Adelaide M. Tichenor (1904), this synthesis of Oriental influences and craftsman bungalow expression reached its climax with the houses for Robert R. Blacker (1907) and David B. Gamble (1908) in Pasadena, for Charles M. Pratt (1909) in Ojai, and for William R. Thorson (1909) in Berkeley.

After a decade of experimentation, a "Greene and Greene aesthetic" had emerged by 1904 in the Jennie A. Reeve House in Long Beach. A simple, shingled bungalow, the Reeve House combined multiple-gabled overhanging roofs, expressive wood framing, rounded projecting rafters and support beams, open sleeping porches and terraces, and a full range of coordinated landscape features: walkways, fences and garden gates, and cobblestone mixed with brick masonry terrace walls. Inside, furniture and decorative arts, including leaded-glass designs for lanterns, doors and windows, and a complete array of decorative accessories, created a total work of art.

At about the same time, the brothers built two important regionally responsive houses: El Hagar for Arturo Bandini (1903) and a U-plan house of noteworthy restraint and "vernacular" simplicity for Charles W. Hollister (1904). These houses, both now demolished, expressed a "critical regionalist's" response to native colonial and Spanish building traditions, to climate, and to the environment and way of life of southern California. This was achieved through open central courtyard plans and a direct access to the out-of-doors, opening single-room-deep wings to sheltered walkways that enclosed a patio.

With the Robert Blacker House, the firm established a new standard of craftsmanship. The house embodied the Greenes' belief that a wooden house should express the honesty and individual identity of each separate part, that no detail should be ignored, and that finely crafted furnishings, fixtures and structural features should be coordinated with beauty ever in mind. When it was completed, the Blacker House exhibited a structurally expressive and finely detailed staircase whose wood joinery was unprecedented, and the house was ornamented with a rich assortment of stained glass—in the bay window on the staircase landing, in the front door and transom lights of the

garden doors, and in hanging lanterns throughout the house. It appeared the house could not be surpassed.

But it is the David Gamble House, with its dramatically overhanging eaves, its enveloping terraces and porches, and its carefully detailed wood joinery and shingle exterior, that remains the acknowledged masterpiece of the firm. Expressing full confidence in the Greenes based on their recently completed handcrafted homes, the Gambles signed a contract in early 1908 for a house to be completed in less than 10 months. The Greenes employed the full panoply of materials and architectural elements: articulated wood structure, shingle surfaces, Gunite-surfaced foundations, clinker-brick and cobblestone terrace walls, masonry chimney stacks and brick walkways. Inglenook fireplaces, enriched by ornamental tiles and metal hoods, provided backdrops for Greene and Greene furniture, carpets and lamps, and interior surfaces were characteristically enhanced by fine wood joinery, carved friezes and structural expressiveness. Laminated stained-glass-filled transoms, door frames, and sidelights of the front door, whose multiple lights composed, in a single composition, an image of a gnarled tree silhouetted against a sunset of opalescent yellow glass. The Gamble House front door is the masterpiece of craftsman Emile Lange (formerly of the Tiffany Studios in New York).

After an intense but brief period of production of the masterful Greene and Greene bungalows, demand for the refined artisan handiwork of the brothers and their craftsmen slowed, and the partnership dissolved in 1922. Charles Greene had executed alone the best work of his late career, the D.L. James House, Carmel Highlands (1918), and he built his own studio nearby in 1920, effectively abandoning southern California for the coastal region of Carmel. The James House is a unique work in local stone, sensitive to its cliffside site, and a masterpiece of "critical regionalist" architecture. While some independent work continued after 1922, Henry and Charles Greene's generation had passed. Receipt in 1952 of a citation of the American Institute of Architects recognized them as "sensitive and knowing builders" and as "formulators of a new and native architecture." They were, as thousands of bungalows throughout America attest, among our country's singularly most influential architects.

—ROBERT M. CRAIG

GRIFFIN, Walter Burley.

American. Born in Maywood, Illinois, 24 November 1876. Died in Lucknow, India, 11 February 1937. Married the architect Marion Mahony, 1911. Attended University of Illinois, Urbana, 1895-99, B.A. Worked for several Chicago architects, 1899-1901, and for Frank Lloyd Wright, Chicago, 1901-05; private practice, Chicago, 1905-14; associated with Barry Byrne, 1913-14; moved to Australia, where he was director of design and construction for the new federal capital at Canberra, 1913-20; private pract ice, Australia, 1915-35; worked in Lucknow, India, 1935-37. Designed and patented the Knitlock system of construction, 1917.

Chronology of Works
All in the United States unless noted

1901-02	William H. Emery House, Elmhurst, Illinois
1908	Orth Houses, Kenilworth, Illinois
1908	Bovee House, Evanston, Illinois
1909	Sloan House, Elmhurst, Illinois
1909-10	Gunn House, Chicago, Illinois

1910	Carter House, Evanston, Illinois
1911	Ricker House, Grinnell, Iowa
1912	Hurd Comstock House, Evanston, Illinois
1912	Melson House, Mason City, Iowa
1912	Page House, Mason City, Iowa
1912-13	Plan for the Capital City of Canberra, Australia
1913	Stinson Memorial Library, Anna, Illinois
1913	Blythe House, Mason City, Iowa
1921	Walter Burley Griffin House, Eaglemont, Victoria, Australia
1921	Johnson House, Parapet, Castlecrag, New South Wales, Australia
1922	Cheong House, Parapet, Castlecrag, New South Wales, Australia
1924	Capitol Theater, Melbourne, Australia
1934	Incinerators, Willoughby and Pyrmont, New South Wales, Australia
1939	Pioneer Press Building, Lucknow, India

Publications

BOOKS BY GRIFFIN

The Federal Capital. Melbourne, 1913.
The U. P. Industrial and Agricultural Exhibition, Lucknow. Lucknow, India, 1936.

BOOKS ABOUT GRIFFIN

BIRRELL, JAMES: *Walter Burley Griffin.* Brisbane, 1964.
BROOKS, H. ALLEN: *The Prairie School: Frank Lloyd Wright and His Midwest Contemporaries.* Toronto, 1972.
DONNELL, COURTNEY GRAHAM: *Prairie School Town Planning 1900-1915: Wright, Griffin, Drummond.* New York, 1974.
DRAP, ALBERT J, JR., and HEINZ, THOMAS A.: *Walter Burley Griffin: Comprehensive Subdivision Planning in the Midwest.* Urbana, Illinois, 1972.
JOHNSON, DONALD LESLIE: *The Architecture of Walter Burley Griffin.* Melbourne, 1977.
PEISCH, MARK L.: *The Chicago School of Architecture: Early Followers of Sullivan and Wright.* New York, 1964.
VAN ZANTEN, DAVID (ed.): *Walter Burley Griffin: Selected Designs.* Palos Park, Illinois, 1970.

ARTICLES ABOUT GRIFFIN

PURCELL, WILLIAM GRAY: "Walter Burley Griffin, Progressive." *Western Architect* 18 (1912): 93-95.
VAN ZANTEN, DAVID: "The Early Work of Marion Mahony Griffin." *Prairie School Review* 3, No. 3 (1966).
WESTLAKE, GRAEME: "Walter Burley Griffin's Final Days in India." *Inland Architect* 33, No. 1 (January/February 1989): 64-67.

*

In approaching Walter Burley Griffin's work, it is well to remember that much of it was the product of a collaboration with his wife, Marion Mahony, who was a talented renderer and designer of decoration. Mahony has been dismissed as a designer of details, not an architect or planner. Yet many contend that Marion Mahony was the author of more than half the underlays for the Wasmuth publication *Ausgeführte Bauten und Entwürfe von Frank Lloyd Wright* (Berlin, 1910), one of the most influential treatises of the 20th century. Mahony was effectively the chief designer in Wright's Oak Park Studio from 1898 to 1909. Wright minimized her contribution as a renderer, notably in the Wasmuth publication. Like the fabulous mythical beast, Griffin, both in his personal and professional life, was really two creatures joined, so much so that it is well nigh impossible to isolate the relative contributions of husband and wife following their marriage in 1911.

As a human being and architect, Griffin was deeply committed to spiritual and intellectual principles. The influence of Theosophy and, later, of the Rudolf Steiner movement of Anthroposophy can be seen in his commitment to uniting architecture and settlements with the natural realm in an organic totality. Griffin's metaphysical concerns profoundly shaped his work as a designer and land planner. In Australia, a country where pragmatic considerations dominated, Griffin was an exception.

Griffin's outstanding contribution remains his ability to conceive his buildings and relate them to other buildings as an ensemble. He bound all—buildings, their elements, streets, spaces between, planting, the natural terrain—into a convincing, organic whole. The built environments that Griffin produced in the midwestern United States, Australia and India are more impressive than his individual building designs—not that the latter should be ignored, for Griffin could on occasion create magnificent effects, though he was not comparable in his genius to Wright. In addition to his plan for the capital of Australia, Canberra, which has suffered from the over-formal geometry of its plan, Griffin designed a number of neighborhoods at Rock Glen in Mason City, Iowa, and the Trier Center neighborhood in Winnetka, Illinois, as well as the suburbs of Eaglemont, Victoria, and Castlecrag, Sydney, including plans for the cities of Griffith and Leeton, in Australia.

In his emphasis on ecology and the preservation of the natural environment, Griffin was well ahead of his time and anticipated many of the principles in such matters that gained recognition only in the 1960s. Griffin was influenced by the planning ideas of Frederick Law Olmsted (1822-1903), Ebenezer Howard's (1850-1928) garden city movement, the sociological approach of Patrick Geddes (1854-1932), and the revival of classical planning principles occasioned by the Chicago World's Columbian Exposition in 1893.

Griffin's plan for Canberra in Australia re-applied the lessons of Pierre Charles L'Enfant's (1754-1825) plan for Washington, D.C., and, in particular, Cass Gilbert's (1859-1934) plan of 1900, as well as elements of Edwin Lutyens's (1869-1944) plan for New Delhi. Griffin retained the axiality of main boulevards focusing on points or nodes to generate a concentric interlocking geometric web of streets. It was typical of Griffin that these axes were tied to existing topographic elements such as local mountains and river systems.

The question of the relative influence of Griffin on Wright and vice versa is one that may never be satisfactorily answered. This is further complicated by the fact that Marion Mahony spent some fourteen years in Wright's Oak Park studio (1895-1909) before aligning her career with Griffin's. It has been previously pointed out that many of Wright's beautiful renderings from those years were really from the hand of Mahony. It is possible that Griffin's Emery House in Elmhurst, Illinois (1901-02), may have encouraged Wright to try a more informal geometry in his own Prairie houses. But, while Griffin was, without question, an important member of the Chicago school of architecture, he does not rank with Wright, neither in terms of inventiveness nor originality, and the contrast is even greater when it comes to the mastery and orchestration of spatial form. Griffin's houses are more classical and conventional; he was attracted to such Palladian motifs as linked pavilions, symmetry and rusticated base stories.

Griffin's houses in Australia are smaller, less spacious and meaner than his American ones. They lack the earlier sophistication and feel cramped by comparison. His best work is to be found among these fine American examples: in particular, the Emery, Sloan (1909) and Bovee (1908) houses in Chicago; and the Ricker (1911), Melson (1912) and Blythe (1913) houses in Mason City.

Among the most distinguished of his Australian designs are Newman College at the University of Melbourne (1917); the supremely beautiful interior of the Capitol Theatre in Melbourne (1924); Griffin's own house (1921) and the T. R. Wilson houses (1921) at Castlecrag; the "knitlock" building system (Creswick House, Castlecrag, 1926); and his incinerator buildings, notably those at Pyrmont and Willoughby (1934).

From 1935 until his death in February 1937, Griffin worked in Lucknow, India, on a bizarre series of projects. The Pioneer Press Building and Shanti Devi House display the same horizontal lines, now with squarish proportions, a generally squat silhouette and rusticated surface expression consistent with his previous Australian works. But in India, Griffin felt constrained to impose a blend—not always with success—of decorative motifs derived from the transitional architecture of the Nawab period.

Griffin's influence in Australia was imperceptible, and he is chiefly admired as a member of the important Chicago school of architecture and for his connection with Wright. In the 1960s, there was a renewed appreciation of the important environmental example set by his architectural designs and planning of neighborhoods. He inspires more because of his attachment to principle than by his actual buildings, although these occasionally rise to considerable artistic heights. He was foremost a creator of environments that, to a greater extent than the individual work, must be regarded as his real goal and achievement.

—PHILIP DREW

GROPIUS, Walter.

German. Born in Berlin, Germany, 18 May 1883. Died in Boston, Massachusetts, U.S.A., 5 July 1969. Studied architecture, Technical High Schools, Charlottenburg and Munich, 1903-07. Worked in Peter Behrens office, Berlin, 1907-10. Started practice, Berlin, 1910; director, Staatliche Bauhaus, Weimar, 1919; private practice, Berlin, 1928; Vice-President, CIAM, 1929-57; joined Maxwell Fry practice, London, 1934; professor of architecture, Harvard University, Cambridge, Massachusetts, 1937; chairma n, department of architecture, Graduate School of Design, Harvard University, 1938; practice with Marcel Breuer, 1938-43; formed The Architects' Collaborative (TAC), Cambridge, Massachusetts, 1945.

Chronology of Works

1906-09	Workers Houses, Janikow, near Dramburg, Germany
1911	Fagus-Werk, Alfeld-an-der-Leine, Germany (with Adolf Meyer)
1913	Diesel Railway Car, Königsberg, Germany
1913	World's Fair, Ghent, Belgium (interiors)
1913-14	Werkbund Exhibition, Cologne, Germany (with Meyer)
1921	Adolf Sommerfeld House, Dahlem, Berlin, Germany
1922	Memorial Sculpture, Weimar, Germany
1922	Chicago Tribune Building (competition entry)
1923-24	State Theater, Jena, Germany (renovation; with Meyer)
1924	Auerbach House, Jena, Germany (with Adolf Meyer)
1925	Director's House at the Bauhaus, Dessau, Germany
1925	Gropius Residence, Dessau, Germany
1925-26	Bauhaus Building, Dessau, Germany
1926	Müller Factory, Kirchbraach, Germany
1926	Terrace Houses, groups I and II, Törten, Dessau, Germany
1927	Terrace Houses, group III, Törten, Dessau, Germany
1926-27	Weissenhof Houses (two), Stuttgart, Germany
1927	Zuckerkandd House, Jena, Germany
1927-28	Dammerstock Housing, near Karlsruhe, Germany
1927-28	City Labor Office (Arbeitsamt), Dessau, Germany
1928	Lewin House, Zehlendorf, Berlin, Germany
1928	Co-operative Store, Törten, Dessau, Germany
1928	Terrace Houses, group IV, Törten, Dessau, Germany
1929	Feder Furniture Stores, Berlin, Germany
1929	Am Lindenbaum Housing Development, Frankfurt, Germany
1929	Spandel-Haselhorst Housing Development, Berlin, Germany
1929-30	Siemensstadt District, Germany (supervising architect; with Bartning, Forbat, Häring, Henning, and Scharoun)
1930	Werkbund Exhibition, Paris, France
1931	Copper Houses, Finow, Germany
1931	Beinert Tomb, Dresden, Germany
1931-33	Stoves, Frank Ironworks, Hannover, Germany
1931	Building Exhibition, Berlin, Germany
1933	Bahner House, Berlin, Germany
1933	Maurer House, Dahlem, Berlin, Germany
1935	Apartments, St. Leonard's Hill, Windsor, Berkshire, England (with E. Maxwell Fry)
1936	London Film Productions Film Laboratories, Denham, Buckinghamshire, England (with Fry)
1936	Donaldson House, Sussex, England (with Fry)
1936	Levy House, Chelsea, London (with Fry)
1936	Impington Village School, Cambridgeshire, England (with Fry)
1937	Gropius House, Lincoln, Massachusetts, U.S.A. (with Marcel Breuer)
1938	Professor J. Ford House, Lincoln, Massachusetts, U.S.A. (with Breuer)
1938	Hagerty House, Cohasset, Massachusetts, U.S.A. (with Breuer)
1939	Chamberlain House, Sudbury, Massachusetts, U.S.A. (with Breuer)
1939	Frank Mansion, Pittsburgh, Pennsylvania, U.S.A. (with Breuer)
1941	Housing Development, New Kensington, Pennsylvania, U.S.A. (with Breuer)
1941	Abele House, Framingham, Massachusetts, U.S.A. (with Breuer)
1945	Catholic Church, Torreon, Mexico (with J. Gonzales Rejna)
1948	Junior High School, Attleboro, Massachusetts, U.S.A. (with The Architects' Collaborative)
1949-50	Harvard University Graduate Center, Cambridge, Massachusetts, U.S.A. (with TAC)
1953	Wherry District Housing, Quonset, Rhode Island, U.S.A.
1955	Interbau Apartment, Berlin, Germany (with TAC)
1956	United States Embassy, Athens, Greece (with TAC)
1957	Pan American Building, New York City, U.S.A. (with Pietro Belluschi)

Walter Gropius: Fagus-Werk, Alfeld-an-der-Leine, Germany, 1911

1957	University, Baghdad, Iraq (with TAC)
1958	Temple Oheb Shalom, Baltimore, Maryland, U.S.A. (with TAC)
1959	Academic Quadrangle, Brandeis University, Waltham, Massachusetts, U.S.A.
1960	Office and Apartment Building, London, England (with TAC)
1962	School, Berlin, Germany (with TAC)
1963	Rosenthal Ceramics Factory, Selb, Germany (with TAC)
1967	Thomas Glass Factory, Amberg, Germany (with TAC)
1967	Tower East Office Building, Cleveland, Ohio, U.S.A.
1968	Huntington Gallery, Huntington, West Virginia, U.S.A. (with TAC)
1968	John F. Kennedy Federal Office Building, Boston, Massachusetts, U.S.A.

Publications

BOOKS BY GROPIUS

Programm des Staatlichen Bauhauses. Weimar, 1919.
Idee and Aufbau des Staatlichen Bauhauses. Munich and Weimar, 1923.
Neue Arbeiten in Bauhauswerkstätten. Editor. Munich, 1925.
Internationale Architektur. Munich and Weimar, 1925.
Bauhausbauten. Munich and Dessau, 1928.
The New Architecture and the Bauhaus. London, 1935.
Bauhaus 1919-1928. With Herbert Bayer and Ise Gropius. New York, 1938.
Rebuilding Our Communities. Chicago, 1945.

Architecture and Design in the Age of Science. New York, 1952.
The Scope of Total Architecture. New York and London, 1955.
Architektur: Wege zur optischen Kultur. Frankfurt and Hamburg, 1956.
Katsura: Tradition and Creation in Japanese Architecture With Kenzo Tange and Y. Ishimoto. New Haven, Connecticut, 1960.
The Architects Collaborative (1945)-1965. Editor, with others. New York, 1966.
Vertical City. Urbana, Illinois, 1968.
Apollo in the Democracy: The Cultural Obligation of the Architect. New York, 1968.
Town Plan for the Development of Selb. With TAC. Cambridge, Massachusetts, 1970.
Walter Gropius: Das Spätwerk. Exhibition catalog. Darmstadt, 1970.
Walter Gropius: Buildings, Plans, Projects 1906-1969. Exhibition catalog, with introduction by James Marston Fitch. Washington, D.C., 1973.

BOOKS ABOUT GROPIUS

ARGAN, GIULIO CARLO: *Walter Gropius e la Bauhaus*. Milan, 1951.
BANHAM, REYNER: *Theory and Design in the First Machine Age*. New York, 1960.
BAYER, HERBERT: *Bauhaus: 1919-1929*. New York, 1938.
BERDINI, PAOLO: *Walter Gropius*. 1983.
BUSIGNANI, ALBERTO: *Gropius*. Florence, 1972; London 1973.

CURTIS, WILLIAM J. R.: *Boston: Forty Years of Modern Architecture*. Exhibition catalog. Boston 1980.

FITCH, JAMES MARSTON: *Walter Gropius*. London and New York, 1960.

Four Great Makers of Modern Architecture: Gropius, Le Corbusier, Mies van der Rohe, Wright. A symposium. New York, 1963.

FRANCISCONO, MARCEL: *Walter Gropius and the Creation of the Bauhaus in Weimar*. Urbana, Illinois, 1971.

GAY, PETER: *Art and Act: On Causes in Art History—Manet, Gropius, Mondrian*. New York and London, 1976.

GIEDION, SIGFRIED: *Walter Gropius*. Paris, 1931.

GIEDION, SIGFRIED: *Walter Gropius: Work and Teamwork*. New York, 1954.

HERBERT, GILBERT: *Gropius, Hirsch—The Saga of the Cooper Houses*. Haifa, Israel, 1980.

HERBERT, GILBERT: *The Dream of the Factory-Made House: Walter Gropius and Konrad Wachsmann*. Cambridge, Massachusetts, 1984.

HERBERT, GILBERT: *The Synthetic Vision of Walter Gropius*. Johannesburg, 1959.

HERDEG, KLAUS: *The Decorated Diagram: Harvard Architecture and the Failure of the Bauhaus Legacy*. Cambridge, Massachusetts, 1984.

HESSE, FRITZ: *Erinnerungen an Dessau*. 2 volumes. Hannover, Germany, 1964.

HOAG, EDWIN and JOY: *Masters of Modern Architecture: Frank Lloyd Wright, Le Corbusier, Mies van der Rohe, and Walter Gropius*. Indianapolis, Indiana, 1977.

HÜTER, KARL HEINZ: *Das Bauhaus in Weimar*. Berlin, 1976.

INTERNATIONAL HOUSE OF JAPAN: *Gropius in Japan*. Tokyo, 1956.

KOYAMA, MASAKAZU: *Walter Gropius*. Tokyo, 1954.

KURATA, CHIKATADA: *Walter Gropius*. Tokyo 1953.

LANE, BARBARA MILLER: *Architecture and Politics in Germany: 1918-1945*. Cambridge, Massachusetts, 1968.

NERDINGER, WINFRIED: *The Architect Walter Gropius*. Berlin, 1985.

NERDINGER, WINFRIED (ed.): *The Walter Gropius Archive: The Collection of the Busch-Riesinger Museum, Vol.s 1,2,3*. New York, 1990.

PEVSNER, NIKOLAUS: *Pioneers of Modern Design from William Morris to Walter Gropius*. Harmondsworth, England, 1949.

PREISICH, GABOR: *Walter Gropius*. Berlin, 1982.

SCHEIDIG, WALTHER: *Crafts of the Weimar Bauhaus: 1919-1924*. New York, 1966.

SHARP, DENNIS (ed.): *The Rationalists, Theory and Design in the Modern Movement*. 1978.

WEBER, HELMUT: *Walter Gropius und das Faguswerk*. Munich, 1961.

WILHELM, KARIN: *Walter Gropius Industriearchitekt*. Braunschweig, 1983.

WINGLER, HANS MARIA: *The Bauhaus: Weimar, Dessau, Berlin, Chicago*. Cambridge, Massachusetts, 1979.

YAMAWAKI, MITIKO and IWAO: *Bauhaus: Weimar, Berlin*. Tokyo, 1954.

ARTICLES ABOUT GROPIUS

BERDINI, PAOLO: "Gropius in England." *Controspazio* (July/December 1981).

BURNS, JOHN ALLEN, and BURNS, DEBORAH STEPHEN: "The Bauhaus as You've Never Seen It." *American Institute of Architects Journal* (July 1981).

FLAGGE, INGEBORD: "Bauhaus Back to Berlin." *Architectural Review* (December 1979).

FRY, E. MAXWELL: "Walter Gropius." *Architectural Review* (March 1955).

GORDON, BARCLAY F.: "The Fagus Factory: Contemporary Design Seventy Years Later." *Architectural Record* (July 1981).

HOEBER, FRITZ: "Das neue Bauhaus in Weimar." *Der Architekt.*, no. 22 (1919).

HOLFORD, WILLIAM: "Gropius 1952." *Architectural Review* (July 1952).

JAEGER, FALK: "The Bauhaus Building in Dessau." *Deutsche Kunst und Denkmalpflege* no. 2 (1981).

JENCKS, CHARLES: "Gropius, Wright, and the International Fallacy." *Arena: Architectural Association Journal* (June 1966).

LABATUT, JEAN: "Labatut on Gropius." *Architectural Forum* (August 1952).

MORSE, CLIFFORD H. and BRUNATI, MARIO: "Gropius e TAC: Lavori Recenti." *Casabella* (September 1967).

PEVSNER, NIKOLAUS: "Gropius and Van de Velde." *Architectural Review* 133 (March 1963): 165-168.

RICHARDS, J. M.: "Walter Gropius." *Architectural Review* (August 1935).

RUDOLPH, PAUL (ed.): "Walter Gropius et son école." Special number, *Architecture d'aujourd'hui* (February 1950).

SCHEFFAUER, H. G.: "The Work of Walter Gropius." *Architectural Review* (August 1924): 50-54.

SCOTT, STAN: "The True Relevance of Walter Gropius." *Royal Institute of British Architects Journal* (March 1974).

STEIN, RICHARD G.: "The Legacy of Walter Gropius." *Architectural Design* no. 7/8 (1982).

SUMMERS, NEIL: "Analyzing the Gropius House as Energy-Conscious Design." *American Institute of Architects Journal* (February 1977).

*

"I gathered that some of them must have had a sort of nightmare idea about me as a man composed out of steel tubes," wrote Walter Gropius to a friend in 1937; one can only note how insightful the man was in observing then what is still today a prevailing opinion. Many students of architecture continue to read Gropius, as well as his oeuvre, as the archetypal cubist-functionalist automaton that made modernism so "cold." This, however, is a serious misreading, for what modernism meant to Gropius, and Gropius to modernism, was a profoundly humane idealism, a true belief in the dignity of the proletariat and the worker's right to a decent environment. All of this was to be manifested through the purged aesthetic of the utopian will to form of the early 20th century.

In a 1934 address to the Royal Institute of British architects, Gropius spoke of the "true mission of the architects of my generations," and expressed his desire to bridge "the disastrous gulf between reality and idealism." He was an idealist by nature, a pragmatist by circumstance; the most significant formative period of his career was spent amidst the chaos of two world wars and terrible social conditions in Germany. Having founded the avant-garde Bauhaus in 1923, both in theory and in building, he was forced out by the Nazi regime by 1931, and he began a refugee sojourn that was to take him from Germany to England, and from England to America, by 1937. Through more than a decade of turmoil, what sustained Gropius and his work was the consistency of form and beliefs that were his Bauhaus legacy.

While at the Bauhaus, Gropius had written the first of a series of *Bauhaus Bücher, Internationale Architektur,* perhaps the earliest published compendium of modernism and protomodernism, the book that should be credited with identifying the emerging aesthetic that would later be called the International Style. From such seminal works as the classical AEG factories of his mentor, Peter Behrens, and Frank Lloyd Wright's Larkin building, to revolutionary works such as Erich Mendelsohn's Hat factory, Gerrit Rietveld's Schroeder house, Le Corbusier's Citrohan house, and his own design for the *Chicago Tribune* building, Gropius as early as the writing of this book in 1924 had selected the landmark modern designs that continue to be influential today, proving his vision of the 20th century to be timeless. Next to these works, he transposed the unconscious architecture of the American grain silo, and the sophisticated skyline of Manhattan, which he had seen on a visit during the 1920s. He was one of the first Europeans to grasp fully the vast American potential for modernism.

It was through Gropius that Le Corbusier acquired the photographs of grain silos that were to become a major motif of "l'Esprit Nouveau." Whereas for Le Corbusier, industrial motifs remained just that, aesthetic gestures, for Gropius, the machine, in all its gritty reality as well as in metaphor, became a cornerstone of his work. In Gropius' elegant Model Factory for the Werkbund Exhibition (1914), in his early Fagus Factory (1911) and even in his entry for the Chicago Tribune (1922), one perceives Gropius' desire to give artistic form to the emerging type of the modern world, the factory. For example, of all the major entries in the Chicago Tribune Competition, only in Gropius' design was the office tower not only integrated with the preexisting factory, but inspired by its tough gridded facade. For Gropius, reality and metaphor were one in the factory, and the factory was beautiful. Particularly in the Fagus Factory he set the standard for functional beauty, designing the glass curtain wall, the unsupported glass corner and the sculptural concrete, extruded glass-encased stairway, all of which used the new materials of the industrial world that became emblematic of early modernism. Gropius brought the machine aesthetic to its apotheosis as architectural form.

In addition to the factory, Gropius also made significant contributions to the typologies of mass housing, or *siedlungen,* and to the modern open-plan school; his works can be studied for their primary emphasis on either social or aesthetic concerns. Outstanding among the socially significant works to which he was so committed would certainly be the Siemensstadt Siedlung (1929), the finest of Gropius' German *wohnungstyp* for the working man, a complex that included the light, air and individual balconies and common open space of his theoretical housing designs of the 1920s and early 1930s in a fully unified, sleek white design on a monumental scale. Also in the category of socially inspired works was the English Impington Village College (1936, with Maxwell Fry), a school and community center that became a demonstration project for the social benefit of the common man, sponsored by an elite band of British liberal architects and intellectuals who had brought Gropius to their country as a refugee in 1934. To visit this extant work in rural Cambridgeshire today, one hardly believes that it is more than 50 years old, so prescient was the loose, constructivist-influenced design of Gropius and his English collaborators.

In purely aesthetic terms, the undisputed masterwork of Gropius was, of course, the Dessau Bauhaus, for that work was not simply a building but an idea embodied. There, Gropius was architect not only of the building, but architect of the spirit, as well. Its famous spinning-pinwheel plan can be interpreted as symbolic of Gropius' philosophy of "unity in diversity," as each of the functional units of the complex maintains its disparateness while "spinning" centrifugally about the unity of the composition. Aesthetic dialectics are inherent in the design as well, as the giant curtain of the workshop wing is juxtaposed against the cubic solidity of the administrative wing. The building is thus a constant polemical play of precariously counterbalancing aesthetic elements.

The building, furthermore, was just a part of that which was meant by "Bauhaus," for the Bauhaus was a school, a methodology, a generator of industrial prototypes, and the Bauhaus was a way to live, free in the spirit of the modern world. Gropius, as founder and director, brought to the Bauhaus such figures as Marcel Breuer, Laszlo Moholy-Nagy, Ludwig Mies van der Rohe and so many other modern masters that long after its brief history, its influence on the architecture and design of the 20th century has been pervasive.

Although throughout his long career Gropius was a great sponsor of other artists and a master synthesizer of ideas, it would be untrue to say that as an artist Gropius himself was consistently creative, for it is quite apparent that his earliest German period, the time from the Werkbund to the Bauhaus, exceeded the remainder of his career aesthetically. Many artists have periods of creativity and of quiescence, but for Gropius, the schism was more obvious and more lasting. This likely was due to the intense political conflicts of his career and the difficulty of repeated enforced emigration. Gropius had suffered greatly as director of the Bauhaus, personifying an institution that had become particularly unpopular with the fascist regime in his own country. At the same time he became something of a cult figure to the outside world, which would eventually rescue him, offering refuge in Britain and the United States. Those painful years took their toll, however, and Gropius, though outwardly strong, seemed to find the strife creatively enervating.

For a lesser man, or for an architect whose work depended on flamboyant display, this might have been devastating. For Gropius, however, there were personal and professional resources that others did not have, and these were the sustenance of his career after the early period. After all, his personal philosophy had never been a romantic one, and his mature work did not emphasize idiosyncratic personal expression; on the contrary, the individualism of architecture for Gropius was always constrained by the common good, and the aesthetic by the social. These strengths, as made manifest in the *typisierung,* or typeforms, of architecture and industrial design, gave him endurance, and these were the strengths he carried with him as a refugee.

Even in America, Gropius continued to live his life surrounded by the objects of the Bauhaus, and the house he designed for himself in Lincoln, Massachusetts (1937), today bears witness to his Bauhaus past. This house, and its predecessor, the Director's House at the Dessau Bauhaus (1925), form an interesting chronology of his development, chronicling aesthetic metamorphoses that parallel changes in the architect's life. For if the German house boldly stands out for its directness, its stark dialectical modernism, the American work in the Wood's End Colony has been modulated, softened by Gropius' appreciation of the American vernacular, as well as by the fact that this house represented, for Gropius, an architect's refuge in America.

Though Gropius continued to practice in America, first with Marcel Breuer, and later with his Cambridge firm, The Architects Collaborative, his primary interest turned to educating another generation of architects in his own philosophy at Harvard University. As his creative output waned, Gropius relied increasingly on his previously conceived typeforms, or generic solutions to architectural problems, with his creativity reaching its former level only in rare exceptions. In addition to his own house in Lincoln, the high points of Gropius' late career were his designs with TAC for the German industrial concern Rosenthal Glass and Porcelain (1967-69), works which, interestingly, completed the circle of his life. For Rosenthal he was again at home, working in Germany, in his intuitively comprehended factory milieu, again designing, as at the Bauhaus, his industrial prototypes. It is not surprising that the elegant pyramidal form of the Rosenthal Factory harks back to a visionary unbuilt project of Gropius' of 1928, a utopian ziggurat-like design that must have remained unrealized in his consciousness until the last years of the architect's life.

The white-hot years of his Bauhaus cubic forms and giant glass curtains had cooled, but like images reflected in the great sheets of glass, Gropius' architectural vision never clouded, was never compromised. Walter Gropius was a man who had made the modern world, but there was something of the ancient tragic hero in him, too. After all the travails, he remained the architect of the proletariat and the true believer of *internationale Architektur*.

—LESLIE HUMM CORMIER

GROSCH, Christian Heinrich.

Danish. Born in Copenhagen, Denmark, 21 January 1801. Died in Oslo (formerly Christiania), Norway, 4 May 1865. Father was the painter and engraver Heinrich August Grosch (1763-1843). Studied with his father at the Academy of Art in Oslo, 1819/20; further education at the Academy, Copenhagen, 1820/24. Worked for C. F. Hansen, then for G. F. Hetsch; teacher at the Academy of Art, Oslo, from ca. 1825, and director from 1827; appointed city architect of Oslo, 1828; inspector of buildings, 1833.

Chronology of Works
All in Norway
* Approximate dates

1830*	Houses, Oslo (formerly Christiania)
1830*	Bank of Norway, Oslo
1826-30	Stock Exchange, Oslo
1827	Immanuel Church, Halden, Østfold
1842	Government Hospital, Oslo
1850*	Theater, Oslo
1840-53	University Buildings, Oslo (in consultation with Karl Friedrich Schinkel)
1840-59	Bazaar (market complex), Oslo
1850*	Observatories, University, Oslo
1850*	Public Buildings, Fredrikshald, near Oslo
1850*	City Church, Arendal am Skagerak
1850*	Fire Station, Oslo
1850*	City Church, Tönsberg, near Oslo
1856	Canvas Factory, Oslo

Publications

BOOKS ABOUT GROSCH

BUGGE, ANDERS: *Arkitekten Stadskonduktor Chr. H. Grosch.* Oslo, 1928.

*

In the first quarter of the 19th century Oslo (then called Christiania), like Helsinki, suddenly became a capital city and, also like Helsinki, was fortunate in having the service of an architect equal to the need for some new and distinguished buildings. Christian Heinrich Grosch was a young lad when the city became the capital of Norway on the dissolution of the centuries-old union with Denmark in 1814. Norway was then united politically with Sweden—independent, but under the Swedish crown. In the first years of the new relationship, however, architectural ties did not shift to Sweden but remained with Denmark.

Grosch's father, Heinrich August Grosch, had in fact been born in Germany but moved to Copenhagen to study painting in the Royal Academy of Fine Arts. Becoming interested in painting the Norwegian landscape, he moved his family to Frederikshald in Norway in 1811, and founded a school of drawing and painting. In 1817 he moved to Oslo, where he taught in the newly founded Royal Drawing School. Christian therefore grew up in an artistic household, and in 1819 he entered the school himself. A year later he went to Copenhagen to study in the Academy, where he was trained in drawing, perspective and carpentry. Probably even more important than the formal schooling was his work as a draftsman for Christian Frederik Hansen. The great Danish neoclassical architect had recently completed the new Town Hall and Law Courts, and was then in the midst of rebuilding Christiansborg Palace and Vor Frue Kirke, which had been destroyed in the fires of 1794 and 1795. The young Grosch therefore had direct and invaluable experience with a mature architect in charge of major projects for the Danish capital city. Grosch evidently did well in all his work, for he was awarded both the large and small silver medals from the Academy in 1824.

That year, he returned to Oslo and found employment with Hans D. F. Linstow, who was then just beginning the construction of the Royal Palace, since an Oslo residence had to be provided for the Swedish king. The hilly site for this had been chosen by King Karl XIV Johan himself, and the palace still dominates the long boulevard leading down toward the old city. Grosch did not remain long with this project, and started teaching in the Royal Drawing School in 1827. A year later he became city architect for Oslo, and in 1833 inspector for buildings in and around Oslo. As an architect for public buildings, including churches, his output was enormous. He also had an eye for design possibilities in some of the historic styles other than those of Greece and Rome.

Grosch's early works, however, revealed his Danish neoclassical training. A Børs, or Exchange, was needed for the expanding commercial interests of Norway and was begun to his designs in 1826. Although later enlarged, it still has the severe Greek Doric portico before the simple block of the original building, much in the manner of Hansen's grander Ionic portico for the Town Hall in Copenhagen. Similarly, Grosch's Immanuel Church at Halden in Østfold (1827) echoes the cubical exterior of Hansen's Vor Frue Kirke. There Grosch had also to provide a Latin School and a new Town Hall, a fire having devastated the town in 1826.

Buildings for a university in Oslo gave Grosch his greatest opportunity to design a formal group in the neoclassical style. In 1838 the plans were sent to the German architect Karl Friedrich Schinkel, whose suggestions may have helped to soften the severity characteristic of Grosch's earlier works. The site chosen was on the north side of Karl Johan Gate, down the hill from the Royal Palace. Grosch set three buildings around a plaza: a library, museum and academic building, all two-story blocks with central temple fronts. The portico of the central building has freestanding Ionic columns, while those on either side consist of pilasters on shallow projections. The group is Grosch's most monumental work of planning.

Although these buildings, along with many others, established Grosch as the leading neoclassical architect in Norway, his total output was not exclusively in this style. While the university buildings were under construction, from 1840 to 1853, Grosch was also designing a market complex on the slope back of the cathedral. Built in sections from 1840 to 1859, the Bazaar is a unique two-story structure, sweeping around in a great curve, with corridors and arcades linking the individual market stalls. For this Grosch chose Romanesque motifs, carried out in red brick, a much more exotic approach than that for the Børs, and appropriate for the small merchants and craftsmen. He also gave a distinct Romanesque flavor to the Canvas Factory in Oslo in 1856. There, in what was for him a rare industrial project, Grosch used roundheaded windows, pilasters running through two and three stories, and elementary applied arcades to give a suggestion of the Middle Ages to this modern building.

One other stylistic possibility occupied Grosch's attention from about 1846 to 1853: several proposals for wooden churches inspired by Norway's stave churches. He had, after all, been trained in carpentry, and economy had dictated that some of his projects be carried out in wood rather than stone, as he might have wished. Considerable interest in the stave churches had been aroused by the painter Johan Christian Dahl, who was then leading efforts to protect those still remaining. Some of the most interesting of Grosch's wooden church designs were never built and are known only through drawings.

Grosch was younger than Hansen and Carl Ludwig Engel, the architect for the other new Scandinavian capital in Helsinki, and outlived them both by 20 years. While, like them, he made significant contributions in neoclassical architecture, he also went on to explore other possibilities, although his earlier works are generally considered to be his finest achievements.

—MARIAN C. DONNELLY

GRUPPO 7

Italian. Luigi Figini, born in Milan, 1903; Gino Pollini, born in Rovereto, Trentino, 1903. Both graduated, Milan Polytechnic (Figini in 1926, Pollini in 1927). Founded Milanese *Gruppo 7,* 1926.

Chronology of Works
All in Italy

1927-29	Novocomum Apartment Block, Como (architect: Terragni)
1928	First Exhibition of Rationalist Architecture, Rome
1932	Facade for the Exhibition of the Fascist Revolution, Rome (architect: Libera)
1932-36	Casa del Fascio (now Casa del Popolo), Como (architect: Terragni)
1934	Aviation and Fascism Room, Exhibition of Aeronautics, Milan (architect: Baldessari)

Publications

BOOKS BY GRUPPO 7 ARCHITECTS

FIGINI: *Il Piano regolatore della Valle d'Aosta.* With Gino Pollini, BBPR, Piero Bottoni and others. Ivrea, Italy.

FIGINI: *L'Elemento verde e l'abitazione.* Milan, 1950.

POLLINI: *Elementi di architettura.* Milan, 1966.

POLLINI: *Il piano regolatore della Valle d'Aosta.* With Luigi Figini, BBPR, Piero Bottoni and others. Ivrea, Italy 1943.

POLLINI: *La residenza: esperienze di progettazione.* Palermo, Sicily 1973.

ARTICLES BY GRUPPO 7 ARCHITECTS

See the issues of *Rassegna italiana* published from 1926-27.

ARTICLES ABOUT GRUPPO 7 ARCHITECTS

SHAPIRO, ELLEN R.: "Architecture I. Architecture II: The Foreigners—Il Gruppe Sette." *Oppositions* 6 (Fall 1976):85-88

SHAPIRO, ELLEN R.: "Architecture III. Unpreparedness-Incomprehension-Prejudices. Architecture IV: A New Archaic Era." *Oppositions* 12 (Spring 1978): 88-90.

SHAPIRO, ELLEN R.: "The Emergence of Italian Rationalism." *Architectural Design* 51 (1981): 5-8.

The Gruppo 7 was an alliance of recent graduates of the Milan Politecnico who banded together in 1926 with the aim of forging a modern Italian architecture. The group's members, Ubaldo Castagnoli (who left after several months and was replaced by Adalberto Libera), Luigi Figini, Guido Frette, Sebastiano Larco, Gino Pollini, Carlo Enrico Rava and Giuseppe Terragni, set forth the principles of rationalism in architecture in a four-part manifesto. These lengthy writings, which appeared in the unillustrated journal *Rassegna Italiana* from 1926 to 1927, constitute the theoretical foundation of Italian rationalism.

The Gruppo 7's first article was clearly influenced by the wording and message of Le Corbusier's *Vers une Architecture.* Both writings speak of the advent of a new spirit in architecture. The Gruppo 7 architects were careful, however, to distinguish their pronouncements from those of Antonio Sant'Elia, whom they considered too radical in his call for the abolition of all aspects of traditional Italian culture. A certain amount of chauvinism was in fact part of the elements of Gruppo 7's aesthetic. The key to a truly modern Italian architecture, the group insisted, was the establishment of a few fundamental types, even if the Gruppo 7's conception of type was at times nebulous.

In their second article, Gruppo 7 discussed recent international architectural currents and insisted on the national character of each. Interestingly, they considered Le Corbusier both an innovator and traditionalist, but did not share that architect's unequivocal admiration for the machine aesthetic. Instead, they pointed to their "desire for truth, logic, order and Hellenic lucidity."

The group's third article criticized contemporary architectural training in Italy. They inveighed against an outmoded Beaux-Arts teaching system, lamenting the failure of the curriculum to integrate the "practical-scientific" and the "artistic." In addition, they decried their professors' failure to foster respect for a technical aesthetic. This sense of frustration is evident as well in the last article. Comparing themselves to the architects of the archaic period in ancient Greece, the Gruppo 7 declared the existence of a new archaic era. Both epochs, they reasoned, were characterized by a renunciation of individuality and the creation of fundamental types.

These articles, then, constituted the theoretical basis of rationalism. Soon after the publication of their theories, the Gruppo 7 began to gain exposure internationally. They reached a wide audience through their participation in exhibitions in Monza, Milan, Bolzano, Rome, Essen, Stuttgart, Budapest and New York from 1927 to 1931, and through their connection with

CIAM (Congrès Internationaux d'Architecture Moderne), especially during CIAM's meeting in 1933 aboard the *S. S. Patris* in Athens, whose theme was the "Functional City."

The Third Monza Biennale of 1927 was particularly significant, for it provided the first important exposure of the group's design work. Giuseppe Terragni's Gas Works, clearly inspired by certain aspects of constructivism, and Luigi Figini and Gino Pollini's Garage for 500 Automobiles were typical of the exhibited projects' emphasis on industrial and commercial buildings. But because of the youth and inexperience of the Gruppo 7 members, their participation in Monza was limited to renderings and models of unbuilt works.

Soon, however, works of Italian rationalism began to appear. One of the first built works by a Gruppo 7 member was Terragni's Novocomum apartment block in Como (1927-29). The building provoked a scandal when Terragni abandoned his original facade design, a novecento-inspired classical design, in favor of a clearly rationalist composition, replete with smooth surfaces, flat roof and a daring corner solution, where a glass cylinder was embedded in a harsh, right-angular mass.

Pivotal to the Gruppo 7's success was the First Exhibition of Rationalist Architecture in Rome in 1928. In the show's catalog, Gaetano Minnucci and Adalberto Libera wrote a rhetorical preface that proclaimed the fascist spirit of the new architecture. Indeed, the inclusion in the exhibition of a project by Alberto Calza Bini, head of the Union of Fascist Architects and a proponent of monumental classicism, is proof that the rationalists wished to ingratiate themselves with the political and architectural establishment. Indeed, it must be remembered that most members of the group were in fact avowed supporters of fascism, with Terragni among the most committed.

By the time of that exhibition, the group included young rationalist architects from all over Italy. As at Monza, the participation of these architects was limited mostly to projects on paper. However, the presence of more than 40 architects testified to the growing importance of the rationalist movement. In 1930, in fact, the rationalists decided to create an official national organization, the MIAR (Italian Movement for Rationalist Architecture), with Libera as its secretary.

Soon afterward, in March 1931, the MIAR sponsored the Second Exhibition of Rationalist Architecture in Rome at the gallery of P.M. Bardi. In addition to projects, the exhibition featured Bardi's *Table of Horrors,* a photomontage attacking recent aspects of traditional Italian culture, including works by the architect Marcello Piacentini. Bardi's contribution set the polemical tone of the exhibition and prompted the powerful Piacentini to engage in a spirited attack on many aspects of rationalist theory and practice, including the exclusion of ornament, the flat roofs and wide expanses of windows, citing these last two attributes as unsuitable to the Italian climate. In spite of the presence of Mussolini at the exhibition and Bardi's "Report on Architecture for Mussolini," which called attention to the true traditional character of the new architecture, the MIAR ceased to exist six months after the opening of the exhibition.

By that time, however, the rationalists had carved a niche for themselves in the architectural culture of Italy, and both their private and government commissions increased in the 1930s. Terragni's Casa del Fascio in Como (1932-36), Luciano Baldessari's "Aviation and Fascism" room at the Exhibition of Aeronautics, Milan (1934), and Libera's facade of the Exhibition of the Fascist Revolution, Rome (1932), as well as the participation of many progressive architects in the regime-sponsored University of Rome (Città Universitaria) campus testify to the success of the rationalists, for whose enterprise the Gruppo 7 had provided the underpinnings in the late 1920s.

—ELLEN R. SHAPIRO

GUARINI, Guarino.

Italian. Born Camillo Guarini in Modena, Italy, 17 January 1624. Died in Milan, 6 March 1683. Joined the Theatine order in Modena, 1639; subsequently studied in Rome, and was ordained as a priest in 1648; appointed bookkeeper and director of construction at the Church of San Vincenzo, Modena, 1648; became professor of philosophy at Theatine convent in Modena, 1650; elected superior of the convent in 1655; resigned due to conflicts with the court there, and during the next several years taught mathematics and philosophy in Parma, Gustalla and Messina, Italy, and in Paris, France; moved to Turin, ca. 1666.

Chronology of Works
All in Italy unless noted
* Approximate dates
† Work no longer exists

1660	Santissima Annunziata, Messina (facade)†
1662-67	Ste.-Anne-la-Royale, Paris, France (not completed)†
1667-69	San Lorenzo, Turin
1667-82	Santissima Sindone Chapel, Turin
1667ff.*	Castello di Racconigi (not completed)
1673-77	Immacolata Concezione, Turin (completed in 1696)
1674-79	Porta del Po, Turin†
1675-80	Santa Maria d'Araceli, Vicenza (design altered)
1678-1703	La Consolata, Turin
1679ff.	Collegio dei Nobili, Turin (not completed)
1679-85	Palazzo Carignano, Turin
1681-83	Madonna di Loreto, Montanaro, near Turin

Publications

BOOKS BY GUARINI

La pieta trionfante. Messina, 1660.
Placita philosophica. Paris, 1665.
Modo di misurare le fabbriche. Turin, 1674.
Compendio della sfera celeste. Turin, 1675.
Euclides adauctus. Turin, 1676.
Trattato di fortificazione, che hora si usa in Fiandra, Francia et Italia. Turin, 1676.
Leges temporum et planetarum. Turin, 1678.
Coelestis mathematicae. Milan, 1683.
Disegni d'architettura civile ed ecclesiastica di Guarino Guarini e l'arte del maestro. Turin, 1686.
Architettura civile. Turin, 1737.

BOOKS ABOUT GUARINI

ANDEREGG-TILLE, MARIA: *Die Schule Guarinis.* Winterthur, Switzerland, 1962.
BRINCKMANN, ALBERT E.: *Theatrum Novum Pedemontii: Ideen, Entwürfe und Bauten von Guarini, Juvarra, Vittone wie anderen bedeutenden Architekten des piemontischen Hochbarocks.* Düsseldorf, 1931.
BRINCKMANN, ALBERT E.: *Von Guarino Guarini bis Balthasar Neumann.* Berlin, 1932.
BUSCALIONI, PIETRO: *La consolata nella storia di Torino del Piemonte.* Turin, 1938.
CREPALDI, GIUSEPPE M.: *La real chiesa di San Lorenzo in Torino.* Turin, 1953.
MARINI, GIUSEPPE LUIGI: *L'architettura barocca in Piemonte: La provincia di Torino.* Turin, 1963.

MEEK, H. A.: *Guarino Gurarini and His Architecture*. New Haven, Connecticut, 1988.

MIDANA, A.: *Il Duomo di Torino e la real cappella della SS. Sindone*. Turin, 1929.

PASSANTI, MARIO: *Nel mondo magico di Guarino Guarini*. Turin, 1963.

POMMER, RICHARD: *Eighteenth Century Architecture in Piedmont: The Open Structures of Juvarra, Alfieri, and Vittone*. New York, 1967.

PORTOGHESI, PAOLO: *Guarino Guarini*. Milan, 1956.

SANDONNINI, T.: *Del Padre Guarino Guarini*. Modena, Italy, 1890.

SOLERO, S.: *Il Duomo di Torino e la real cappella della Sindone*. Pinerolo, Italy, 1956.

TAMBURINI, LUCIANO: *Le chiese di Torino dal rinascimento al barocco*. Turin, 1968.

VIALE, VITTORIO (ed.): *Guarino Guarini e l'internazionalità del barocco: Atti del convegno internazionale promosso dall'Accademia delle Scienze di Torino (30 September-5 October 1968)*. 2 vols. Turin, 1970.

WITTKOWER, RUDOLF: *Art and Architecture in Italy: 1600-1750*. 4th ed. Harmondsworth, England, 1980.

ARTICLES ABOUT GUARINI

ARGAN, GIULIO CARLO: "Per una storia dell'architettura piemontese." *Arte* 36 (1933): 391-397.

BATTISTI, EUGENIO: "Note sul significato della Cappella della Santa Sindone nel Duomo di Torino." *Atti del X congresso di storia dell'architettura* (Rome, 1959).

BRINCKMANN, ALBERT E.: "La grandezza di Guarino Guarini e la sua influenza sull'architettura in Germania nel '700." *Atti della società piemontese di archeologia e bella arte* 15 (1933): 348-374.

CARBONERI, NINO: "Guarini." In VITTORIO VIALE (ed.): *Mostra del barocco piemontese*. Turin, 1963.

CARBONERI, NINO: "Vicende delle cappelle per la Santa Sindone." *Bollettino della società piemontese di archeologia e belle arti* 18 (1964): 95-109.

CAVALLARI MURAT, AUGUSTO: "Alcune architettura piemontese del settecento in una raccolta di disegni del Plantery, del Vittone, e del Guarini." *Torino* 21 (1942): 7-11.

CHEVALLEY, GIOVANNI: "Il Palazzo Carignano a Torino." *Bollettino della società piemontese di archeologia e belle arti* 5 (1921): 4-14.

CHEVALLEY, GIOVANNI: "Vicende costrutive della chiesa di S. Filippo Neri in Torino." *Bollettino del centro di studi archeologici ed artistici del piemontese* 2 (1942): 63-99.

COFFIN, DAVID: "Padre Guarino Guarini in Paris." *Journal of the Society of Architectural Historians* 15 (May 1956): 3-11.

FRANZ, HEINRICH GEBHARD: "Guarini und die barocke Baukunst in Böhmen: Ein Beitrag zur Frage nach dem Verhältnis der regionalen zu den universalen Europäischen Kunstströmungen." Vol. 2, pp. 121-129 in *Actes du 22 Congrès international d'histoire de l'art*. Budapest, 1972.

HAGER, WERNER: "Guarini: Zur Kennzeichnung seiner Architektur." Vol. 16, pp. 418-428 in *Miscellanea Bibliothecae Hertzianae*. Munich, 1961.

HAGER, WERNER: "Guarini." *Kunstchronik* 7 (1954): 266.

HAGER, WERNER: "Guarinis Theaterkassinade in Messina." In *Das Werk des Künstlers Hubert Schrade zum 60. Geburtstage*. Stuttgart, 1960.

HAGER, WERNER: "Zum Verhältnis Fischer-Guarini." *Kunstchronik* 10 (1957): 206-208.

MARCONI, PAOLO: " 'Vortuti fortuna comes,' Guarino Guarini e il caduceo ermetico." *Ricerche di storia dell'arte* 1-2 (1976): 29-44.

MIDANA, ANTONIO: "Il duomo di Torino e la real cappella della SS. Sindone." *Italia sacra* (1929): 50.

MILLON, HENRY A.: "Guarino Guarini and the Palazzo Carignano in Turin." Ph.D. dissertation. Harvard University, Cambridge, Massachusetts, 1964.

MORGANSTERN, J.: "Guarino Guarini: The Church of the Padre Somaschi for Messina." M. A. thesis. New York University, New York, 1964.

OECHSLIN, WERNER: "Osservazioni su Guarino Guarini e Juan Caramuel de Lobkowitz." *Atti del convegno su Guarino Guarini e l'internazionalità del barocco*. Turin, 1970.

OLVERO, EUGENIO: "Gli scritti del P. Guarino Guarini." *Il duomo di Torino* No. 2 (June 1928).

OLVERO, EUGENIO: "La Madonna di Loreto in Montanaro." *Bollettino del centro di studi archeologici ed artistici del Piemonte* 1 (1940): 5-11.

OLVERO, EUGENIO: "La vita e l'arte del P. Guarino Guarini." *Il duomo di Torino* No. 2 (May 1928).

PASSANTI, MARIO: "La cappella della Santa Sindone in Torino." *Architettura* No. 66 (1961).

PORTOGHESI, PAOLO: "Il tabernaco Guariniano dell'altare maggiore della chiesa di San Nicolo a Verona." *Quaderni dell'Istituto di Storia dell'Architettura* 17 (1956): 16-20.

PORTOGHESI, PAOLO: "L'architetto Guarini." *Civiltà delle machine* 4 (1956): 57-61.

RAMIREZ, JUAN ANTONIO: "Guarino Guarini, Fra Juan Ricci and the 'Complete Salmonic Order.' " *Art History* 4 (1981): 175-185.

RIGOTTI, GIORGIO: "La chiesa dell'Immacolata Concezione." *Bollettino della società piemontese di archeologia e belle arti* 16 (1932): 56-73.

SANDONINI, TOMASO: "Del Padre Guarini Guarino." *Atti e memorie della deputazione di storia patria per Modena e Parma* Series 3, No. 5 (1890): 488-533.

SCHMERBER, HUGO: "Einige Nachrichten über Guarino Guarini." *Monatsberichte für Kunstwissenschaft und Kunsthandel* 2 (1902): 286-287.

TERZAGHI, ANTONIO: "Origini e sviluppo delle cupola ad arconi intrecciati nell'architettura barocca del Piemonte." *Atti del X congresso di storia dell'architettura* (Rome, 1959).

*

The 17th-century Italian monk Guarino Guarini had active careers as a theologian, mathematician and natural scientist in addition to his career as an architect. Born in Modena, he followed his older brother into the ranks of the Theatine order, the only avenue open to someone of his station with academic aspirations. His considerable intellect was acknowledged by his contemporaries, as is evidenced by his election as head of the chapter in Modena soon after the completion of his novitiate, and through his numerous treatises on natural science, mathematics, architecture, fortifications, astronomy and construction. However, this intellectual prowess was not matched by congeniality or tact; he was exiled from his native Modena for an unspecified reason, but later complaints about his hypochondriac personality suggest personal difficulties with colleagues and superiors, a problem that would follow him throughout his career. This exile forced Guarini into a life of travel: he lived in Sicily and France, and conflicting evidence suggests he may have traveled in Spain and Portugal as well, before he settled in the capital of the Duchy of Savoy, the current Turin.

Guarino Guarini: San Lorenzo, Turin, Italy, 1667-69

After his removal from Modena in 1656, he appeared briefly in chapter records in Parma, Guastalla, and back in Modena in 1657. From that point on, there is no record of his whereabouts until his publication of a drama in 1660 in Messina, although some have proposed travels on the Iberian peninsula during this undocumented period. While in Messina, Guarini completed the facade of Santa Annunziata and a small, unidentified chapel, both of which works were destroyed by earthquakes. In 1662 Guarini was transferred to Paris, where he designed and built portions of Ste. Anne-la-Royale. In late 1666 Guarini left amid charges and countercharges of mismanagement of funds, the portions built by him later destroyed in the aftermath of the French Revolution. In contrast, Guarini's work is well represented in Turin by several churches and palaces.

Guarini's invitation to stay in Turin was a fortuitous occasion for him. The Savoyan court in Turin needed significant architectural upgrading to compete on a cultural level with Paris and Vienna, and Guarini needed a respite from the controversy that embroiled him in Paris. In 1667 Guarini began redesigning the chapel of Santa Sindone (construction of which had already been under way for 10 years) and soon after redesigned San Lorenzo. In subsequent years he began construction on La Consolata (1678-1703), Castello di Racconigi (1667-), Palazzo Carignano (1679-85), the Collegio dei Nobili (1679-) and perhaps the Immacolata Concezione (1673-77, 1694-96). As Guarini's reputation increased during the 1670s and early 1680s, he was asked to supply designs for churches outside of Turin: San Gaetano in Vicenza, the church of the Padri Somaschi in Messina, San Filippo Neri in Casale, Santa Maria Ettinga in Prague, Santa Maria della Divina Providence in Lisbon, the Sanctuary at Oropa and perhaps Santa Maria degli Araceli in Vicenza. With the exception of the last, none of these churches was

built, but Guarini's drawings of these projects, engraved and published posthumously in 1686, had a wide circulation and influence.

Guarini's architecture owes a great deal to Francesco Borromini, whose architecture he knew firsthand from his eight-year novitiate in Rome. However, Guarini's architecture was neither a copy nor a continuation of Borromini's work. Instead, Guarini's architecture was based on complex geometries, optical perceptions of the human eye, and on architectural traditions he encountered during his travels. Chief among these were northern European Gothic architecture, known to Guarini during his stay in Paris, and Islamic architecture, certainly seen by Guarini while he lived in Messina and perhaps known to him through travels in Spain.

Guarini's interest in geometric design motifs derived from his extensive training in mathematics. He possessed the skill to manipulate complex geometric figures, and more important, he was able to visualize their three-dimensional form in space. These complex geometries are evident in his ground plans, where circular and oval spaces interpenetrate with adjacent spaces to create dynamic interiors. It is in Guarini's vaulting, however, that his geometric skill is best appreciated. Guarini stated in his architectural treatise, ''Vaults are the principal part of buildings . . .'' (Tratt. III, Cap. 26), and his numerous church designs and relatively few secular commissions each demonstrate this hierarchy. Guarini introduced vaults based on conic sections which, he proudly pointed out, had been used only by him and were notable for their beauty and strength. Conic sections—ellipses, parabolas and hyperbolas—were used by Guarini as profiles for his domed vaults. This use of conic sections was not prompted by knowledge of Desargues' and Pascal's work on conic sections in Paris as is sometimes alluded, nor did Guarini possess special mathematical skills enabling him to calculate the structure of his domes. He did, however, creatively combine elements of his wide range of interests with great success.

That geometry was not the basis of his designs, even for his centrally planned churches, is clear from his architectural treatise. Primary for Guarini was the aesthetic impact of form and the way the eye perceives it in natural light. He included two chapters in his architectural treatise (Tratt. III, Cap. 21 & 22) dealing with optical illusions and how designers might either correct them or take advantage of them. With respect to conic vaults, it is clear that Guarini's selection of elliptical domes for San Lorenzo, San Gaetano and the church of the Padri Somaschi was based on what he perceived as the flat appearance of hemispherical domes because of the lack of light reflected in the crown of the vault. The elliptical profile of his domes is taller than a hemispherical dome, and Guarini lit dark areas of the domes through perforations, avoiding shadows that would have made the domes appear lower. Even in designs using more conventional vaulting shapes, he used light to enhance dramatically the interior volumes.

Guarini's travels were unusual for an Italian architect of the mid-17th century; his openness to other architectural traditions, furthermore, set him apart from all Italian contemporaries. His residence at the Theatine chapter in Paris enabled him to experience firsthand the High Gothic of the Île-de-France, and he described it in his architectural treatise in admiring terms. One of the things he singled out was the technical ability of Gothic architects whose aim was "to build very strong, but also to look weak, so that it would seem a miracle, how they remain standing" (*Architettura civile,* Tratt. III, Cap. 13, Oss. 1). Guarini assimilated this aesthetic and applied it to his own designs, most notably in San Lorenzo, where false pendentives that visually support the dome are hollowed out and terminated in torsional arches demonstrably too weak to support the large dome above. His use of ribbed domes, too, must have been influenced by Gothic ribbed vaulting.

The architect's relationship to Islamic architecture is difficult to assess. There is a startling similarity between the geometry of the dome of San Lorenzo and domes around the mihrab of the mosque of Cordoba, Spain, a basis for speculation about Guarini's alleged travels through Spain, but similar geometries are found in English Gothic structures, early Romanian churches, as well as Spanish Gothic churches. In addition, the Islamic domes are much smaller than Guarini's ribbed domes, with the lower surface of the ribs oriented toward the ground plane instead of following a geometric solid of revolution. If Guarini was directly influenced by Islamic architecture, it was in the general handling of light and volume, and not specific geometric motifs.

Guarini's influence was not limited to the Piedmont region surrounding Turin, but extended to Bavaria and Bohemia as well. Bernardo Vittone is the best-known follower of Guarini in Piedmont, and indeed it was Vittone who was commissioned to complete Guarini's architectural treatise, left unfinished at his death. Vittone built many small chapels, which adapted some of the rib geometries and scenographic effects used by Guarini. The late Baroque of the German-speaking sections of Catholic Europe was also much influenced by Guarini. Johann Lucas von Hildebrandt knew Guarini's work firsthand and designed a close copy of Guarini's San Lorenzo in Gabel. However, it was probably the 1686 publication of Guarini's designs, *Dissegni d'architettura civile et ecclesiastica,* that was most influential in central Europe. His use of interpenetrating volumes was developed further by Christoph Dientzenhofer and Balthasar Neumann, who introduced these dynamic spaces into

the naves of their churches. Although Guarini completed only a portion of the designs he created, through his architectural publications he was able to reach an audience far beyond the Duchy of Savoy, his architecture serving as a bridge between Baroque Rome and early 18th-century architecture in central Europe.

—ELWIN C. ROBISON

GUAS, Juan.

Spanish. Born in Lyons, France ca. 1433. Died in Toledo, Spain, ca. 1497. Married Marina Alvarez, 1459. Trained in Toledo. Master mason of Avila Cathedral, 1471; principal architect of the Royal Works, from 1472.

Chronology of Works
All in Spain
* Approximate dates
† Work no longer exists

1472	Old Cathedral, Segovia (cloister)
1472-75	Hieronimite Monastery of Santa María del Parral, Segovia
1475-79	Castle of El Real de Manzanares, Province of Madrid
1477-96ff.	Franciscan Monastery of San Juan de los Reyes, Toledo
1478-85	Dominican Monastery of Santa Cruz, Segovia
1480-83	Palace of El Infantado, Guadalajara
1483-85	Cathedral, Segovia (cloister portal)
1484	Monastery of El Paular, Segovia (porch and portal of chapel)
1485	Church of Santa Cruz, Segovia (west portal)†
1487-89	Dominican College of San Gregorio, Valladolid (chapel)
1494	Church of the Parral, Segovia (sacristy portal)†

Publications

BOOKS ABOUT GUAS

CHUECA GOITIA, FERNANDO: *Historia de la Arquitectura Española, Edad Antigua y Edad Media.* Madrid, 1965.
HERRERA CASADO, ANTONIO: *El Palacio del Infantado en Guadalajara.* Guadalajara, Spain, 1975.
LAYNA SERRANO, FRANCISCO: *El Palacio del Infantado en Guadalajara.* Madrid, 1941.

ARTICLES ABOUT GUAS

AZCARATE, JOSÉ MARIA DE: "La Obra Toledana de Juan Guas." *Archivo Español de Arte* 29 (1956): 9-42.

*

During the reign of Queen Isabella I of Castille and Ferdinand V of Aragon, a unified Spain saw the rise of buildings in a rich and exotic new style proclaiming the monarchs' power and an end to the anarchy that had prevailed under Isabella's brother, Henry IV of Castille. Juan Guas in Toledo and Simón de Colonia in Burgos were the two major artists and their cities the centers from which the Isabelline style spread. Guas and Simón created

Juan Guas: Palacio del Infantado, Guadalajara, Spain, 1480-83

a Spanish Gothic style, joining disparate ornamental and aesthetic principles from Islamic and Gothic art into wild works carried out with extraordinary verve. This style delighted in extreme, colorful contrasts, yet remained architectural in its sharp distinction between support and decoration. Riotous ornament was applied to every allowable surface, but piers, walls and arches retained their integrity and independence. One senses an architectonic priority, simple structures designed to receive exuberant tapestries of ornament at carefully allotted places.

Juan Guas' father, Pedro, was a Breton mason and sculptor who moved to Toledo in the 1440s as member of a Flemish atelier directed by Hanequin of Brussels, newly appointed master mason of the cathedral. Juan probably was born abroad in the early 1430s, but he was educated and trained in Toledo. His independent work began around 1470, imitating Hanequin's Flamboyant Gothic style, but influenced already by Islamic motifs. In 1471 he was master mason of the cathedral of Avila, responsible for a new west portal, destroyed in 1779. In January 1472 then-Princess Isabella interviewed him, beginning an association that ultimately made him the principal architect of the royal works.

In 1472 Guas began the first of an important group of works in Segovia and its province. The church of the Jeronimite monastery of Santa María del Parral, originally intended as a mausoleum for Henry IV, had been started with a single-nave, Latin-cross plan. Guas, working with Martín Sánchez Bonifacio, new master at Toledo, redesigned the east end, giving each transept and the sanctuary identical trapezoidal plans with splayed walls flaring toward the crossing, focusing on the central space where the unexecuted tomb was to be placed. This east-end arrangement was widely imitated, the earliest copy being at San Francisco in Medina de Rioseco of 1491. Guas' doorways at the

Parral were like Hanequin's, with jambs projecting as pinnacles above the outer archivolts of a central ogee, but a portal in the south transept already exhibited a brilliant play of opposing forces and forms, with an inverted heart-shaped pointed arch above the main arch, the whole framed by a complex *alfiz,* a rectangular molding of Islamic inspiration. Vaults were all different, an unusual feature at the time, with elaborate rectilinear rib patterns of tiercerons and liernes. Guas' other Segovian work included the old cathedral cloister, moved to the new cathedral in 1524, the church of the monastery of Santa Cruz, an attribution, and the cloister of the monastery of Santa María del Paular in the Sierra de Guadarrama.

For the Mendoza family, Guas produced two major residences, the castle of Manzanares el Real, and the palace of the second Duke of the Infantado in Guadalajara, one of his best works. Manzanares el Real, begun before 1475, was serviceable as a castle, but it was intended as a luxurious dwelling, and much effort was devoted to its ornamentation. The parapets and gallery are supported by a remarkable cornice of trefoil arches on rolled corbels imitating *muqarnas* (Islamic stalactite vaults). The Flamboyant Gothic arcade of the belvedere gallery is embellished with a diamond-shaped diaper pattern of Mudejar origin. The walls of the turrets above the towers are ornamented with projecting balls set in a triangular grid, originally backed by a plaster diaper pattern similar to that in the gallery. Here Guas was trying to translate to stone, using Gothic forms, the fantastic plaster enrichments of a Mudejar palace.

This development reached maturity in the palace of the Infantado, perhaps the finest Spanish work of medieval civil architecture. Its main approach is an imposing west facade enriched systematically with diamond-shaped projections in a rhomboid grid, and crowned with a splendid arcaded gallery and seven projecting turrets, elaborating a theme at Manzanares el Real. The asymmetrically placed portal, dated 1480, marks Guas' stylistic liberation from Hanequin. The handsome mixtilineal arch of the door is set into a larger pointed arch, the whole flanked by columns with shafts decorated in a diamond-and-ball diaper pattern used also at Manzanares el Real. Huge sculptures of savages holding the Mendoza arms capped the composition, but were shifted in an insensitive 16th-century alteration. The palace is organized internally around a monumental two-story square courtyard. Spirally twisted columns, taller below, supported mixtilineal arcades, but in the 16th century the ground was raised and squat Tuscan columns were substituted below. The spandrels of the arches were densely inhabited by rampant lions and griffins, diaper patterns, coats of arms and pinnacles. The eye can find no resting place, other than at a larger scale in the finely proportioned symmetrical whole, an effect partly lost due to the alterations.

Guas' most important work is the church and king's cloister in the Franciscan monastery of San Juan de los Reyes in Toledo. A royal commission, this was Isabella's most lavish foundation, intended as a royal pantheon. The church as a four-bay single nave with side chapels between buttresses, a square crossing with a lantern tower, shallow transepts and an octagonal sanctuary. The exterior is relatively simple, its decoration limited to blind arcades framed by *alfices* and Flamboyant pinnacles and roof balustrades. It gives few clues to the richness of the interior.

The interior nave elevation is two stories; a frieze with a continuous inscription divides arcade and clerestory. The piers between bays are extremely complex and varied, their execution perhaps due to different hands. Nave vaults are unusual. They lack diagonal ribs and have central reserve panels with a rotated square. This is a Bohemian vault type used by the Parlers of Prague, brought to Toledo by Hanequin. The crossing lantern also has an unusual variant of this vault, very reminiscent of an Islamic type invented at the 10th-century Capilla de Villaviciosa in the Mosque of Cordoba.

The transepts are the richest work of Guas, with royal coats of arms endlessly repeated on north and south walls, and crossing piers supporting corbelled pulpits of almost indescribable ornamental complexity. Such concentration of decoration was meant, as at El Parral, to focus attention on the crossing where the tombs were to be placed. Two superb portals in Guas' late style lead from the south transept and a south chapel to the king's cloister. Both have doorways with flat basket-handle arches enframed by *alfices*, set into larger mixtilineal arches, with sculptured tympana in between.

The two-story king's cloister is Guas' most refined design. Vaulted below and with a Mudejar wooden roof above, superimposition of Islamicizing forms over Flamboyant Gothic is a major theme. The lower pointed arcades have a handsome simplified version of the tracery patterns of the cloister of the cathedral of Segovia, while upper mixtilineal arches are fully enframed by *alfices*. Deep wall buttresses with Flamboyant rotated pinnacles at the lower level are reduced to thinner enframing diagonal projections at the second story. A superb parapet and projecting pinnacles crown the elevation. The interior jambs are decorated with vines of great variety, equal to the best Romanesque ensembles. There are scenes from everyday life and mythology. Children, nude and clothed, hunt and play. There are even vulgar, burlesque scenes, such as a monkey dressed as a monk reading while seated in a urinal.

Juan Guas was the oldest and also the most daring and inventive of the Isabelline masters. He used the Flamboyant Gothic forms he learned from Hanequin as a starting point from which to play a complex game of themes and variations inspired by Islamic forms. His doorways, for example, with inverted arches

and broken *alfices,* are reminiscent of those at the Aljaferia in Zaragoza. But despite his often unstable-looking structures, there is also an almost classical sense of balance and repose in his creations. His is a highly sculptural architecture, in which sculpture is used to give a sense of direction, order and focus to larger architectonic intentions.

—SERGIO L. SANABRIA

GUIMARD, Hector.

French. Born in Lyons, France, 1867. Died in New York City, 1942. Trained at the École des Arts Décoratifs and the École des Beaux-Arts, Paris; traveled in England and Belgium, 1894-95. Taught at the École des Beaux-Arts, Paris. Moved to the United States in the 1930s.

Chronology of Works
All in France
† Work no longer exists

1888	Restaurant du Quai d'Autueil, Paris
1889	Pavilion de l'Electricité, Exposition Universel, Paris
1891	House, 34 rue Boileau, Paris
1892	Victor Rose Tomb, Batignolles Cemetery, Paris
1893	House, 63 avenue de Clamart, Issy-les-Molineaux
1893	Villa, 41 rue Chardon-Lagache, Paris
1894	Devos-Logie Family Tomb, Gonards Cemetery, Paris
1894-98	Castel Béranger, 14-16 rue de La Fontaine, Paris

Hector Guimard: Castel Béranger, Paris, France, 1894-98

1895	École du Sacré-Coeur, 9 avenue de la Frillière, Paris
1895	House, 1 rue Molitor, Paris
1895	House, 39 Boulevard Exelmans, Paris
1896	House, 72 avenue de Montesson, Le Vessinet, Paris
1897-1901	Humbert de Romans Auditorium, rue Saint-Didier, Paris†
1898	House, 9 and 9 bis Hameau-Boileau, Paris
1898-1900	Maison Copilliot, 14 rue de Fleurus, Lille
1899	Villa La Houle, Hermanville, Calvados
1899	House, 18 rue Alphonse de Neuville, Garches
1899-1900	Castel Henriette, Sèvres (ruins)
1899-1905	Métro station entrances, Paris
1902-03	House, rue de Meulières Chaponval, near Anvers-sur-Oise
1903-05	Apartment Building (Jassedé Block), 142 avenue de Versailles, Paris
1904-07	House, 8 Villa de la Réunion
1905	Castel Orgeval, 2 avenue de la Marc Tambour, Villemoisson
1908	Chalet Blanc, 2 rue du Lycée, Sceaux
1908	House, 16 rue Jean Doyon, Eaubonne
1909-12	Guimard House, 122 avenue Mozart, Paris
1910-11	Mezzara House, 60-62 rue de La Fontaine, Paris
1910	Apartment building, 11 rue François Millet, Paris
1913	House, 3 rue de Crillon, St. Cloud (altered)
1919	Office building, 10 rue de Bretagne, Paris
1921	Albert Adès Tomb, Montparnasse Cemetery, Paris
1922	House, 3 Square Jasmin, Paris
1925	Town Hall of a French Village, Exposition des Arts Décoratifs
1925-26	Apartment building, 18 rue Henri Heine, Paris
1926	Apartment building, 2 Villa Flore, Paris
1927-28	Apartment building, 36 rue Greuze, Paris
1928	Villa Guimard, Vaucresson† (not completed)
1928-29	Apartment building, 38 rue Greuze, Paris

Publications

BOOKS BY GUIMARD

Le Castel Béranger. Paris, 1899.
Fontes artistiques pour constructions, fumisterie, articles de jardins et sepultures, style Guimard. Paris, 1907.

ARTICLES BY GUIMARD

"An Architect's Opinion of 'l'Art Nouveau.' " *Architectural Record* 12 (1902): 127-133.

BOOKS ABOUT GUIMARD

BARILLI, RENATO: *Art Nouveau*. London, 1969.
BRUNHAMMER, YVONNE, and NAYLOR, GILLIAN: *Hector Guimard*. London, 1978.
DUNSTER, DAVID: *Hector Guimard*. London, 1978.

*

Hector Guimard is synonymous with the creation of an architectural style in France that gave expression to the art nouveau movement that swept through Europe in the late 19th and early 20th centuries. Known as *"le style nouveau"* (though Guimard himself referred to it as *"le style Guimard"*), its aim was to visualize the forces of nature through the rhythmic repetition of flowing line. The concept of organic form in Guimard's architecture was stabilized and supported by architectonic structural theory taken from the writings of Eugène-Emmanuel Viollet-le-Duc. His buildings in and around Paris stood as a counteraction to what was perceived as the static classicism of the French academic tradition as set forth by the École des Beaux-Arts, which had defined the national character of French architecture for generations. Guimard is best remembered today for his colorful designs for the stations and entryways of the Paris Métro system, completed in 1901.

Born in Lyons, Guimard went to Paris at age 15. He spent three years at the École des Arts Décoratifs and four more at the École des Beaux-Arts. He left before taking a diploma to work for a construction firm as an architect and on-site craftsman.

The writings of Viollet-le-Duc had a profound impact on the students at the École des Beaux-Arts in the 1880s; Guimard left the academy as a disciple of the theories put forth in *Entretiens sur l'architecture* (1863). In it, Viollet-le-Duc extolled asymmetry, studied ground plans and elevations in terms of form, and recommended the use of new materials, especially cast iron. The design projects in this architectural treatise would provide the direct inspiration for two of Guimard's most original works, the École du Sacré-Coeur and the Humbert de Romans Concert Hall.

Guimard's earliest structures were built in the Auteuil quarter of Paris (16th arrondissement), a rural area that was being heavily developed by the bourgeoisie. The commissions were residential, asymmetrical, eclectic designs incorporating Gothic and picturesque styles. They are more sentimental than logical and display an interest in surface texture and polychromy. Although of lesser architectural importance, they contain many elements of his later, more important works.

In 1894 Guimard went to England, and in 1895 he traveled to Belgium. In Brussels he saw Victor Horta's Tassel House being constructed. Prior to visiting Belgium, Guimard had begun plans for the Castel Béranger, an apartment building made up of moderately priced flats. Upon his return, the plans were revised. While the facade was not greatly changed, the exterior detailing and the interiors were radically altered.

The use of two-tone bricks above a granite base maintained a compatability with neighboring houses, but decoration based on medieval and Japanese forms was applied freely to the structure. Iron was used inside for structural support, sinuously wrought for the entry gate and cast into novel forms for exterior trim. The interior avoids sharp angles, and its lines simulate forms found in nature.

While working on the Castel Béranger, Guimard built a school in Paris, L'École du Sacré-Coeur, which was directly based on the design for the market hall in the *Entretiens sur l'architecture*. Style was determined by function and structure. The two-story school was raised like the market hall on cast-iron, V-shaped pilotis. The pilotis supported an iron girder running the length of the building and supporting the floor above.

Between 1897 and 1901 Guimard adapted another theoretical project proposed by Viollet-le-Duc in his treatises. The Humbert de Romans Concert Hall, which was part of a larger commission, the École Humbert de Romans, was based on the project for a concert hall published in the *Entretiens*. The auditorium was an elongated octagon in plan. The elaborate framework of the roof was steel, clad in mahogany. The main branches supported a rather high cupola, which was pierced like the sides with bays filled with pale yellow stained glass; the effect was said to have been like a Druidic forest.

In 1896 a competition was launched in Paris to design the new Métropolitain (subway) system. Guimard did not enter but was awarded the commission in 1889 when the results of the competition were overridden. The Métro commission was a fusion of art, design and technology. Guimard's interpretation expressed his convictions regarding the integration of form, decoration and structure. The Paris Métro system exhibited the potential and virtuosity of cast iron and connected symbolic and practical functions. Aesthetically, the Architecture appeared to be free-form in design, yet everything was of standardized dimensions. The stations were modular, which necessitated mass producing the parts in molds. They were done in dazzling colors—bright green ironwork with orange panels on the inside. A later attempt to promote his designs for building components in collaboration with the foundry that produced most of his own work failed. Guimard was the only client for these designs that he continued to use throughout his career.

Guimard saw himself as an inspired rationalist, whose aim was to demonstrate logic, harmony and sentiment in his work. His definition of sentiment in architecture was that "which partaking at the same time of logic and harmony, is the complement of both, and leads by emotion to the highest expression of art." He believed, like John Ruskin, in a national architecture, but felt that it should be of the period that needs it. One should look to science and nature, rather than classical precedent, for the language and logic of structure, he believed. He was eclipsed in the 1920s when art nouveau fell out of favor. His later works attempted to incorporate the more progressive principles of 20th-century cubism, but lacked the spirit of his earlier architecture as well as the conviction of the Modern Movement. The art nouveau phenomenon was short-lived, lasting approximately 15 years.

Guimard moved to the United States with his American wife, Adele Oppenheimer, in 1938. He died in obscurity, and most of his architectural plans and drawings were destroyed in World War II. In the past 25 years a renewed interest in the art nouveau movement has brought his name back into architectural study.

—SUSAN GUILES-CURRAN

GWATHMEY, Charles.

American. Born in Charlotte, North Carolina, 19 June 1938. Married Bette Ann Henderson, 1974. Studied at the University of Pennsylvania, Philadelphia, 1956-59, and Yale University School of Architecture, New Haven, Connecticut, 1959-62, M.Arch.; awarded William Wirt Winchester Traveling Fellowship, 1962; Fulbright Fellow in France, 1962-63. In private practice, New York City, 1964-66; partner, Gwathmey-Henderson, 1966-70, and Gwathmey-Henderson-Siegel, 1970-71, both in New York City; partn er, with Robert Siegel, Gwathmey Siegel and Associates, New York City, since 1971. Fellow, American Institute of Architects, 1981. Has taught and lectured widely in the United States.

Chronology of Works
All in the United States unless noted

1966 Gwathmey House and Studio, Amagansett, New York (with Richard Henderson)
1968 Steel House I, Bridgehampton, New York (with Henderson and Robert Siegel)
1969-72 Dormitory, Dining and Student Union Building, State University of New York, Purchase (with Henderson and Siegel)

The following works are in association with Robert Siegel:

1970-72 Whig Hall, Princeton University, New Jersey (renovation)
1971 Cogan House, East Hampton, New York
1976 East Campus Student Housing and Academic Center, Columbia University, New York City
1979 Library and Science Building, Westover School, Middlebury, Connecticut
1978-81 Taft House, Cincinnati, Ohio
1980 First City Bank Building, Houston, Texas
1980-84 De Menil House, East Hampton, New York
1981 Arango Apartment, New York City
1983 Spielberg Apartment, New York City
1983 International Design Center Showroom Buildings, Long Island City, New York
1983 Garey House, Kent, Connecticut
1984-90 School of Agriculture Building, Cornell University, Ithaca, New York
1985 Academic and Multi-Purpose Building, Eugenio Maria de Hostos Community College, Bronx, New York
1985 Spielberg House, East Hampton, New York
1985 Opel House, Shelburne, Vermont
1985-90 Fieldhouse and Basketball Arena, Cornell University, Ithaca, New York
1985-92 Solomon R. Guggenheim Museum, New York City (addition)
1986 College of Architecture Building, University of North Carolina, Charlotte
1988-90 College of Engineering Theory Center Building, Cornell University, Ithaca, New York
1989-92 Disney Convention Center, Walt Disney World, Orlando, Florida

Publications

BOOKS ABOUT GWATHMEY SIEGEL

ABERCROMBIE, STANLEY: *Gwathmey Siegel.* New York, 1981.
ARNELL, PETER, and BICKFORD, TED (eds.): *Charles Gwathmey and Robert Siegel: Buildings and Projects 1964-1984.* New York, 1984.
BRESLOW, PAUL and KAY: *Charles Gwathmey and Robert Siegel: Residential Architecture.* Tokyo, 1976.
FRAMPTON, KENNETH, and ROWE, COLIN: *Five Architects: Eisenman, Graves, Gwathmey, Hejduk, Meier.* New York, 1975.
GOLDBERGER, PAUL: *The Houses of the Hamptons.* New York, 1986.
ROSA, JOSEPH (ed.): *Charles Gwathmey and Robert Siegel: Buildings and Projects 1982-1992.* New York, 1993.

ARTICLES ABOUT GWATHMEY SEIGEL

Architecture and Urbanism, special issue (April 1989).
BOLES, DORALICE D.: "Update on the Guggenheim." *Progressive Architecture* (May 1986).
CROSBIE, MICHAEL J.: "Single Stroke Pays Multiple Dividends: Westover School Addition." *Architecture* (May 1988).
DIETSCH, DEBORAH K.: "Close Encounter of the Modern Kind." *Architectural Record* (Mid-April 1988).
DIXON, JOHN M.: "No Easy Symbolism." *Progressive Architecture* (February 1987).
GANDEE, CHARLES: "A Bridge Too Far." *Architectural Record* (June 1986).

GUNTS, EDWARDS: "Contextual Modernism." *Architecture* (January 1991).

"In Praise of Modernism: De Menil Residence at East Hampton." *Domus* (February 1984).

MAYS, VERNON: "Beyond Convention." *Architecture* (January 1992).

PEARSON, CLIFFORD A.: "Design for Learning." *Architectural Record* (November 1991).

"Residences." *Architecture and Urbanism* (July 1980).

"Three Projects by Gwathmey Siegel." *Architecture and Urbanism* (October 1974).

*

Charles Gwathmey achieved acclaim early in his career for pristine modern houses. While still known today as an architect of exceptional single-family residences, Gwathmey's practice, with partner Robert Siegel, is more diverse and less dogmatic than earlier work, but still equally thorough. A looser formal vocabulary and more specific contextual nods have kept Gwathmey-Siegel's precise modernism current and relevant.

Charles Gwathmey burst most forcefully onto the architectural scene with the Gwathmey House and Studio of 1966. Two obstinate little neo-Corbusian cubes trumpeted reinvigorated modernism to the Long Island beachfront through rigorous geometry and intricate multistory spaces. Based on his Fulbright Fellowship research, Gwathmey comprehensively pursued a Le Corbusier-based modular proportioning system, a fundamental practice in all of his work.

Although Gwathmey's earliest partnership was with Richard Henderson, Robert Siegel joined the practice in 1968 and became sole partner in 1970. Since then, their design collaboration has been nearly inseparable.

Gwathmey's reputation as the architect of immaculate houses was sealed by the Museum of Modern Art's "Five Architects" exhibition and publication of 1972. It placed Gwathmey in a group with formal ties to Le Corbusier, begging the question of ideological coherence in a group that included both arcane theorists and unapologetic practitioners. Occasionally catty critical reception nonetheless characterized Gwathmey as a legitimate neo-Corbusian, building splendid modern houses without leaks.

Through their subsequent development, Gwathmey-Siegel houses have evolved in form and palette, maintaining their spatial intricacy, proportional rigor and, quite often, their beachfront locations. With works such as the Cogan Residence (1971), floor plans grew to greater bulk. Later houses such as the Taft Residence (1978-81) and the de Menil Residence (1980-84) handled burgeoning scale through a new compositional approach. These houses, with separate greenhouse-like components and detached *brises-soleil,* are accretions of forms, showing separation, but not fragmentation, among components. Though contrasting with the singularity of earlier works, these houses are unmistakable in their grid-based design and multistory spaces.

Such opulent residential commissions should not overshadow Gwathmey-Siegel's prominent work in other building types.

The firm's first academic commission came in 1972 with the Dormitory Dining Hall and Student Union complex for the State University of New York at Purchase. The low-rise building is resolute in its rectilinearity, but not unreasonably so for the sloping site. Floor plans of the three residential wings are livelier than expected, and the triangular multiuse building is a compelling spacecraft. The complex is an effective example of hard-edged campus modernism, with close ties to the early houses.

Gwathmey's renovation of Princeton University's Whig Hall, also of 1972, completely reconstructed the Roman temple's interior floors. Leaving the primary facade and building envelope intact, Gwathmey created an abstract modern facade for the new side entry, a memorable metaphor for the peaceful coexistence of classical and modern.

Amid these successes, the firm has shown occasional shortcomings in large-scale projects. East Campus, an academic and residential building at Columbia University in New York City, placed a sleek courtyard at the foot of 20 floors of ingeniously gracious duplex residences. The contrasting slab building exterior, however, is crisp but reticent, lacking the humanity of expression that would find its way later into most large-scale institutional works.

In addition to campuses, Gwathmey-Siegel found easy entree into residential and commercial interiors through ongoing embrace of their modular proportional system. Extensive chair rails, wainscots and transoms provided ample fodder for the architects' grid, while the diminished architectural opportunities led to a rise in the use of color, a welcome addition upon arrival in larger projects.

Such color and freer forms have flourished in Gwathmey-Siegel's work, such as the Center for Theory and Simulation in Science and Engineering, one of three Gwathmey-Siegel buildings completed at Cornell University, Ithaca, New York, in 1990. A narrow, curving, seven-story slab with an off-center interlocking drum and cylindrical stair towers at each end, this is their best example yet of large-scale form making, complete with road-hugging shape and contextual colors. However, whether it commands or blocks views of the adjacent gorge depends on where one stands.

The 1990s may well judge Gwathmey-Siegel by their Guggenheim Museum addition and renovation, set to open in 1992. Because additions to landmark museums are notoriously thankless commissions, Gwathmey-Siegel's early major redesign comes as no surprise. As it stands, the downsized, muted, but elegant northeast building mass is a smaller target for criticism than was the original scheme, while adding some of the desperately needed space that spawned the addition in the first place. With the reopening of Frank Lloyd Wright's seventh floor and the promise of Gwathmey-Siegel's multistory galleries, most criticism will undoubtedly turn to praise.

Gwathmey's earliest works were much too strident for the sensitivity of the Guggenheim commission; however, the propriety and efficacy of the project serve as a strong argument for modernism against those who would prefer decorated sheds or deconstructed structures.

—CHARLES ROSENBLUM

H

HADFIELD, George.

American. Born in Leghorn (now Livorna), Italy, 1767. Died on 2 May 1826. Studied architecture at the Royal Academy, London; trained in office of James Wyatt. Superintendent of the construction of the Capitol Building, Washington, D. C., 1796; established own firm, Washington, D.C.

Chronology of Works
All in the United States
† Work no longer exists

1796-97	Treasury Department Building, Washington, D.C.†
1798-1800	War Department Building, Washington, D.C.†
1801-02	Washington Jail, Washington, D.C.†
1801-03	Marine Barracks, Washington, D.C.†
1801-03	Marine Commandant's House, Washington, D.C.
1802-17	Custis-Lee Mansion, Arlington, Virginia
1803	Arsenal, Washington, D.C.†
1816-19	Commodore David Porter House, Washington, D.C.
1820-50	City Hall, Washington, D.C. (wings and center)
1822	Assembly Rooms, Washington, D.C.†
1824	Second Bank of the United States, Washington, D.C. (branch office)†
1826	John Peter Van Ness Mausoleum, Oak Hill Cemetery, Washington, D.C.

Publications

BOOKS ABOUT HADFIELD

GOODE, JAMES M.: *Capital Losses: A Cultural History of Washington's Destroyed Buildings.* Washington, 1979.
HAMLIN, TALBOT: *Greek Revival Architecture in America.* New York, 1944.
MADDEX, DIANE: *Historic Buildings of Washington, D.C.* Pittsburgh, 1973.
NELLIGAN, MURRAY HOMER: *Custis-Lee Mansion, the Robert E. Lee Memorial, Virginia.* Washington, D.C., 1962.
REIFF, DANIEL D.: *Washington Architecture, 1791-1861: Problems in Development.* Washington, D.C., 1971.
TOWNSEND, GEORGE A.: *Washington Outside and Inside.* Hartford, Connecticut, 1873.

ARTICLES ABOUT HADFIELD

CUNNINGHAM, H. F.: ''The Old City Hall, Washington, D.C.'' *Architectural Record* 37 (March 1915): 268-273.
GOODFELLOW, G. L. M.: ''George Hadfield.'' *Architectural Review* 138 (July 1965): 35-36.
HUNSBERGER, G.: ''The Architectural Career of George Hadfield.'' *Columbia Historical Society Records* 51-52 (1955): 46-65.
RICHMAN, MICHAEL: ''George Hadfield (1763-1826): His Contribution to the Greek Revival in America.'' *Journal of the Society of Architectural Historians* 33 (1974): 234ff.

*

Little remains of George Hadfield's architectural output, which seems to have been concentrated in the city of Washington. Textural and visual documentation of his known and attributed buildings is sparse, making a full evaluation of his work difficult. Trained at the Royal Academy in London, he won both silver and gold medals for his designs, the latter in 1784. In 1790 he was awarded the academy's first traveling fellowship to study in Rome; his reconstruction drawing of Praeneste is still on display at the Royal Institute of British Architects library.

At the age of 31, on the recommendation of the painter John Trumbull, Hadfield was invited by George Washington to take charge of building the U.S. Capitol according to William Thornton's premiated design. Hadfield conceived of his job at the Capitol as that of a responsible architect making whatever practical and design changes he deemed necessary as construction progressed. The city commissioners disagreed, and he was dismissed in 1798. Benjamin Henry Latrobe considered Hadfield one of the best designers in the country and attributed his failure at the Capitol to inexperience in dealing with the often-conflicting needs of workmen and clients. The only aspect of the extant Capitol attributable to Hadfield seems to be the guilloche frieze that separates the basement from the main story.

In compensation, Hadfield was asked to design the Treasury Building contiguous to the White House; his three-story, long rectangular structure in the late Georgian style was eventually replicated for the other three executive-department office buildings flanking the president's house. More *retarditaire* than the residence they were meant to complement, they were nonetheless simple and elegant brick structures with giant porticoes facing north and south, and double-ramped staircases serving their longitudinal circulation spines.

Most of Hadfield's known public and private works in the city were destroyed or substantially altered before the advent of photography. The ghost of his Marine Barracks survives on the same site on Capitol Hill. Built by 1803, an elegant Marine Commandant's House was at the head of a range consisting of a smaller officers' residence flanked by a long, single-story cadets' dormitory fronted by an arcade. Its sponsorship by President Thomas Jefferson and arrangement suggests that it may have acted as an embryonic stimulus for Jefferson's subsequent University of Virginia design. Between 1901 and 1906 the complex was rebuilt; its incipient spatial organization of double ranges of officers' quarters and dormitories was completed in an arts and crafts style. The Commandant's House was enlarged by the addition of a single bay (creating an asymmetrical composition) and a mansard roof, but two finely proportioned and detailed semicircular bays survive nearly intact.

Arlington House, George Washington Parke Custis' residence, now located in Arlington National Cemetery, was completed in 1820. The two-story central section is flanked by lower wings articulated by tall, arched windows set within sunken blind arches. Its most arresting feature is its massive hexastyle Doric portico designed as a stage set so that it would be visible from the federal city on the opposite shore of the Potomac. The whole is stuccoed brick, with the columns marbleized to increase their sense of power and solidity.

Hadfield's most significant building, the Washington City Hall (1820), still stands but has undergone numerous alterations, including a sandstone refacing in the 1930s that is probably more refined and detailed than the original. Hadfield's design was never completely executed, as he had planned for a colonnaded rotunda capped by a low saucer dome to project in front of the north-facing courtyard of his H-shaped building. As built, it was a typical five-part, E-shaped building with a hexastyle Ionic portico joined to wings by three bays of tall arched windows set within blind arches, a fenestration pattern that seems to have been Hadfield's leitmotif. The untouched interior marble stairhall demonstrates the delicate refinement of Hadfield's sensibility at its best.

In 1824 Hadfield designed the Second Bank of the United States, a hipped-roof cube that stood opposite the Treasury Building until the late 1890s. (It can be seen on the back of ten-dollar bills.) The purity of its form is complemented by a simple, round-headed door set within a broad arch, and wide tripartite windows topped by sunken blind arches on the main story. Hadfield's last documented work was the Van Ness Mausoleum (now in Oak Hill Cemetery), a circular Ionic tempietto derived from the Roman Temple of Vesta and completed in 1826, the year of his death. A decade later, Hadfield's only known pupil, William Parker Eliot, submitted Hadfield's design to the competition for the Washington National Monument, but its form and style are unknown.

The disappearance of Hadfield's papers and drawings is a major loss to the study of American Architecture. He brought a level of sophistication to buildings that may have influenced many American-born and trained architects, but our paucity of knowledge of them prevents us from truly evaluating their impact.

—PAMELA SCOTT

HAMILTON, Thomas.

Scottish. Born in Glasgow, Scotland, 11 January 1784. Died in Edinburgh, Scotland, 24 February 1858. Married in 1813. Apprenticed to his father, the builder Thomas Hamilton, 1801-17. Burgess of Edinburgh, 1819; worked independently; architect to the Edinburgh Improvement Commission, 1827-34. Fellow, Institute of British Architects, 1836-46; cofounder and treasurer, Royal Scottish Academy, 1826; Gold Medal, Paris International Exhibition, 1855.

Chronology of Works
All in Scotland
† Work no longer exists

1820-23	Burns Monument, Alloway, Ayrshire
1825-29	Royal High School, Edinburgh
1827-30	Arthur Lodge (formerly Salisbury Cottage), Dalkeith Road, Edinburgh [attributed]
1827-30	Assembly Rooms and Steeple, Ayr
1827-31	King's Bridge, Edinburgh
1827-34	George IV Bridge, Edinburgh (and associated town planning)
1830-32	Burns Monument, Edinburgh
1831-33	Dean Orphanage, Edinburgh
1834	Earl Gray Pavilion, Royal High School Playground, Edinburgh†
1844-46	Royal College of Physicians, 9 Queen Street, Edinburgh

Publications

PUBLICATIONS BY HAMILTON

Observations Explanatory of the Two Designs for Completing the College of Edinburgh. Edinburgh, 1816.
''Proposal for Forming a Communication Between the North and South Sides of the City of Edinburgh, by Means of a Bridge Entering the Lawn Market, Nearly Opposite Bank Street. Illustrated by a Plan.'' *Scots Magazine* (March 1817): 163-165.
Attestations Referred to in Letter to the Lord Provost of Edinburgh from Thomas Hamilton Junior, Relative to His Qualifications for Filling the Office of Superintendent of Public Works in the City of Edinburgh. Edinburgh, 1819.
A Report Relative to Proposed Approaches from the South and West of the Old Town of Edinburgh. With William Burn. Edinburgh, 1824.
A Report Relative to the Proposed Improvements on the Earthen Mound at Edinburgh. Edinburgh, 1830.
Men and Manners in America. Edinburgh, 1833.
A Letter to Lord John Russell on the Present Crisis Relative to the Fine Arts in Scotland, with Plans and Perspective Views of the Proposed Galleries on the Mound. Edinburgh, 1850.

BOOKS ABOUT HAMILTON

CROOK, J. MORDAUNT: *The Greek Revival.* London, 1972.
YOUNGSON, A. J.: *The Making of Classical Edinburgh: 1750-1840.* Edinburgh, 1966.

ARTICLES ABOUT HAMILTON

FISHER, IAN: ''Thomas Hamilton of Edinburgh: Architect and Town Planner (1784-1858).'' Thesis. Christ Church College, Oxford, 1965.
HUGHES, T. HAROLD: ''Great Scottish Architects of the Past. No. 7: Thomas Hamilton.'' *Quarterly Illustrated of the Royal Incorporation of Architects in Scotland* 20 (1926): 97-115.
MEARS, F. C.: ''Measured Drawings of Lawnmarket and Castlehill Made by Thomas Hamilton, Architect'' *Book of the Old Edinburgh Club* 12 (1923).

*

Thomas Hamilton was probably the most creative and imaginative of the small group of Scottish Greek Revival architects, including William Playfair and William Burn, who contributed to the earning for Edinburgh of the soubriquet the ''Athens of the North.'' In his ability to manipulate the elements of Hellenic architectural vocabulary and apply them to complex new building types that were unknown in antiquity, Hamilton was surpassed in Scotland only by the Glasgow architect Alexander Thompson.

Like Playfair and Burn, Hamilton came from a family that was professionally involved with architecture and building. His father, to whom he became apprenticed, was a wright and cabinetmaker, and his uncle, from whom he also received training, was a builder. Hamilton was born into a lower social level than his famous contemporaries, both of whom served as pupils under successful architects of the day (Robert Smirke in the case of Burn, and William Stark in the case of Playfair). He was nevertheless probably the finest architect of the three, and his relatively humble origins may be the explanation for why he was responsible for many fewer buildings than either Burn or Playfair. His access to potential clients may well have been limited.

The works by which Thomas Hamilton is chiefly remembered are the Royal High School, the Dean Orphanage and the Royal College of Physicians, all in Edinburgh, and two monuments to the Scottish poet Robert Burns, one in Edinburgh and one in Alloway, Ayrshire. He was also something of a town planner and played a significant part in the planning of major road developments in Edinburgh, which contributed to the successful development of the city in the first half of the 19th century.

Hamilton's masterpiece was the Royal High School of Edinburgh (1825), a building that has been described by Sir John Summerson as "... the noblest monument of the Scottish Greek Revival." This building is situated on the steeply sloping side of Calton Hill, one of several areas of high ground close to the center of the city that were successfully exploited by Edinburgh architects in the early 19th century in the creation of a "picturesque" townscape. The Royal High School is one of a number of buildings and monuments clustered on and around the top of the hill.

The centerpiece of Hamilton's building is the school hall, in the form of a Doric temple modeled on the Theseion in Athens. This hall is flanked by wings containing classrooms, which appear as stoa-like colonnades terminating in massive rectangular block pavilions. Except in the case of the latter, clerestory lighting has been used to avoid the need for windows on the front elevation. The whole building sits on a massive two-tiered base, the lower tier of which conforms to the curving line of the road that sweeps around the south side of Calton Hill. A pair of pedimented gateways provide access to the building from this road through the base wall, and the base wall itself is terminated by small prostyle temples with unfluted columns. The latter do not quite face each other, as they are inclined outward, following the sweep of the roadway. The whole assembly is a fine example of picturesque composition in which the various parts of the building are fitted together to provide a well-resolved whole, while at the same time accommodating the planning requirements of a 19th-century institutional building. Whether viewed squarely from the front from the Royal Mile of Edinburgh, one mile away across the valley that separated the Old from the New Town, or more closely from the curving road around its base, in which case the features of the building are revealed in stages, the building is satisfying, both as an architectural composition in its own right and as a significant element in the townscape.

Like his contemporaries, Hamilton could turn his hand to other styles besides that of the Greek Revival. His Dean Orphanage (1831), a large institutional building in its own wooded grounds, is a much restrained version of Vanbrughian Baroque, almost neoclassical in feeling. In the Royal College of Physicians building in Edinburgh (1844), Hamilton produced an unusual and original essay in neoclassicism. His attempts at Gothic and Romanesque were less successful, however.

As a town planner, Hamilton made a significant contribution to the final appearance of the city of Edinburgh. The early 19th century was a time of rapid expansion of the city, and an important aspect of this was the provision of roads and bridges to link the various parts of this city of hills, ridges and valleys. Hamilton contributed a number of articles and reports to the debate concerned with how the various thoroughfares should be sited. He also served as architect to the Edinburgh Improvement Commission, which was set up by an act of Parliament in 1827 to oversee the execution of these vital public works. His ideas were crucial to the final layout of the city, and he was personally responsible for the architectural aspects of two important bridges, the Kings Bridge and George IV Bridge, both of which were important constituents of the city's network of communications. The fact that the layout of the center of Edinburgh remains more or less unchanged is an indication of the quality of Hamilton's thinking. Had it been necessary to alter his arrangements significantly to accommodate the traffic of the 20th century, it is likely that severe damage would have been inflicted on the historic city center.

Despite his undoubted skills as a city planner, however, Hamilton is chiefly remembered as one of the principal architects of the Greek Revival in Scotland. His achievement in that respect was all the more remarkable in view of the fact that he was untraveled. He acquired his knowledge of Hellenism entirely from books, because so far as is known, he never left his native Scotland.

—A.J. MACDONALD

HANSEN, C. F.

Danish. Born Christian Frederik Hansen in Copenhagen, Denmark, 29 February 1756. Died at Villa Rolighed near Copenhagen, 10 July 1845. Studied with C. F. Harsdorff at the Academy, Copenhagen, where he won numerous honors, 1772-79; study trips to Italy and Germany; appointed state architect for Holstein, 1783; professor at the Academy, 1791, and eventually director; elected to the Academy, 1785; chief inspector of buildings, Holstein, 1808-44.

Chronology of Works
All in Denmark unless noted

1789-92	Cesar Godeffroy House, Nienstedten, Germany
1790-96	Peter Godeffroy House, Blankenese, Germany
1792-94	Orphanage, Altona, Germany
1794-95	J. Blacker House, Blankenese, Germany
1795-1804	Houses, Palmaille, Altona, Germany
1798	Manor House Perdol, Holstein, Germany†
1792-1803	City Hall, Oldesloe, Denmark
1802	Søholm House, Copenhagen, Denmark
1803-16	City Hall and Law Courts, Copenhagen
1803-28	Christiansborg Palace, Copenhagen (re-erected)†
1810-16	Gymnasium, Metropolitanskolen, Copenhagen
1810-26	Chapel, Christiansborg Palace, Copenhagen
1810-29	Our Lady Cathedral, Copenhagen
1818-20	Hospital, Schleswig, Germany
1820-23	Church, Hørsholm, Denmark
1828-34	Church, Neumünster, Germany
1829-33	Church, Husum, Germany

Publications

BOOKS BY HANSEN

Sampling af forskjellige og private Bygninger. Kjöberbaun, Denmark, 1825-ca. 1840.

C. F. Hansen: City Hall and Law Courts, Copenhagen, Denmark, 1803-16

BOOKS ABOUT HANSEN

JAKSTEIN, WERNER: *Landbaumeister Christian Friedrich Hansen.* Neumünster, Germany, 1937.

LANGBERG, HARALD: *Omkring C. F. Hansen.* Copenhagen, 1950.

LUND, HAKON, and KÜSTER, CHRISTIAN L.: *Architekt Christian Frederik Hansen, 1756-1845.* Exhibition catalog. Hamburg, 1968.

LUND, HAKON: *Christiansborg Slot.* Copenhagen, 1975.

LUND, HAKON: *Nogle tegninger af C. F. Hansen.* Copenhagen, 1975.

RUBOW, JØRN: *C. F. Hansens arkitektur.* Copenhagen, 1936.

WEILBACH, FREDERIK: *C. F. Hansens Christiansborg.* Copenhagen, 1935.

WIETEK, GERHARD (ed.): *C. F. Hansen 1756-1845.* Neumünster, Germany, 1982.

ARTICLES ABOUT HANSEN

JAKSTEIN, WERNER: ''C. F. Hansens Rat- und Arresthaus.'' *Wasmuths Monatshefte für Baukunst* 10 (1926): 222-239.

C. F. Hansen was one of the most influential architects of his day. His career stretched over two generations, from 1784, when he took up the surveyorship of Holstein, until 1844, when he retired from his various posts. He was responsible for some of the most important projects in the kingdom during that long period; as professor at the Art Academy from 1808 and as chief inspector of buildings from 1808 to 1844 he was central, both as arbiter and master of architectural taste. He was, however, not just a good civil servant, administrator and teacher, but a gifted architect, in whose works the spirit of his age speaks its clear language. His inquiring, unbending interpretation of neoclassicism propagated the new European aesthetic.

Hansen was the son of a shoemaker from Schleswig. His mother had been wet-nurse to the later King Christian VII, and under royal patronage his training began early. He was enrolled at the Academy when only 10, and at 16 advanced to the School of Architecture there. Like many of his fellow students, he also served apprenticeships as a carpenter and bricklayer. His teacher Caspar Frederick Harsdorff (1735-99) not only introduced Hansen to the newest European architectural currents but gave him the opportunity to apply his studies, as clerk of works at Frederik

V's Chapel in Roskilde Cathedral. In 1779 Hansen won the Major Gold Medal, normally accompanied by a six-year travel scholarship; lack of funds, however, restricted his time abroad to a year and a half, from 1782 to 1784, most of which he chose to spend in Rome. Immediately upon his return Hansen took up the position of surveyor in Holstein, which he had been awarded in preference to older and more experienced colleagues.

Very little is known of Hansen's first years in government employment: the only project known is the orphanage in Altona (1792-94; destroyed in 1944). The Danish town of Altona, a suburb of independent Hamburg, had enjoyed rapid economic and cultural expansion after a Dano-Russian treaty of 1768 consolidated the surrounding Danish duchies of Schleswig and Holstein; wealthy businessmen and merchants were busy establishing their position through the construction of imposing residences. Rather than allowing aristocratic domesticity to provide models for their own, they turned their attention to the architecture of revolutionary France. In the young and obscure C. F. Hansen they found someone who could meet their expectations of a modern and tasteful home. His first was a country house for the merchant Johann Cesar Godeffroy in Dockenhuden, on the Elbe River (1789-92). Its neo-Palladian antecedents are clear in the characteristically recessed entrance flanked by two giant Doric columns, the lower side wings and the flat roof profile. The smooth planes of the walls, broken only by sharply defined window openings, and the restrained decoration—pedimented aedicules around the two windows on each side of the entrance—leave a predominant impression of a geometric solid. In the semicircular projection on the garden front the building accommodates the land and the river. Romanticism's appreciation for the landscape played an important role there; notwithstanding the house's stringent axiality and symmetry, one approaches it by meandering paths under the spreading crowns of freely planted trees. The house set the tone for a number of others built for great Hamburg merchants on the north bank of the Elbe. For Hansen, any frustrations arising from their relatively small scale and the demand for economical building materials would have been offset by permission to experiment. J. Blacker's country house in Blankenese (1794-95) was surrounded by no fewer than 28 freestanding columns: from the top of Krähenberge it crowned the fishing village like an acropolis. Gebauer's House in Othmarschen (1806-08), a circular building with a conical straw roof, paraphrased contemporary speculation about the primitive hut.

On Altona's old bowls alley, the Palmaille, Hansen built, from 1795 to 1804, nine private houses which turned the street into the town's fashionable promenade. At Palmaille 116 he also built, in 1803, his own house. These formal town houses, on restricted and often awkward sites, met the neo-Palladian demand for axiality and symmetry, but the interiors, with their enchantingly shaped rooms, often surprise. Gathered in a relatively small area, these houses have an impressive cumulative effect, a sympathetic example of a neoclassical streetscape. Differences in size and shape do not preclude an harmonious whole, an elegant and evidently relaxed, but always moderate neoclassicism that served to characterize its occupants as cosmopolitan citizens of the world, hard-working and modest, but with sure taste. Even the Palmaille offers nature—rows of trees and similarly disciplined grass, as well as views over the Elbe.

In 1794 Copenhagen Castle burned down; the next year a great part of the city was destroyed in another fire. Hansen, who had by then made his name, was called to the capital by the commission appointed to supervise the rebuilding of the Town Hall; he was also invited to submit a proposal for the best way to turn the castle ruins into a new royal residence.

Hansen's projects for the reconstruction of both buildings were approved in 1803. His town hall-courthouse on Kongens Nytorv presents, with the adjoining prison (completed in 1815), what is probably his most romantic design, a fine example of *architecture parlante* inspired by Giovanni Battista Piranesi's prison fantasies and Jacques François Blondel's character theory. The courthouse invites respect: its giant Ionic portico with stairs behind, unbroken wall planes and the low roof profile were by then to be expected of Hansen, but here they are on a new, larger scale. The prison is sombre. The heavily rusticated socle, which gives weight to the building, has *oeil-de-boeuf* openings brought down from their traditional place on the mezzanine; rusticated, barred windows left no doubt as to the misery of the prison's inhabitants. Two arched, covered overhead walkways join the prison and the courthouse over the narrow Slutterigade; the evocative and picturesque result inspired various painters with its associations, not entirely coincidental, of the famed Bridge of Sighs in Venice.

Hansen was more restricted at Christiansborg Palace (completed in 1828; burned down in 1884), both by the older building's foundations and by a tight budget that required him to recycle some building materials. Hansen reoriented the palace by demolishing the wing on the riding yard and replacing it with a great colonnade; he smoothed and redecorated the walls in a neoclassical way, accenting them only with pediments and, in front of the center pavilion, another colonnade.

A freer hand was possible with the reconstruction of the adjoining Palace Chapel (completed in 1826). The arrangement of a high cupola over a rectangular body was inspired by Frederik V's chapel in Roskilde. The thermal windows, projecting portico with five Ionic columns and the low roof, which partly obscures the rise of the cupola, reveal Hansen's interest in Roman models: among his drawings can be found careful studies of the Pantheon and another showing Giacomo Barozzi da Vignola's Sant'Andrea in Via Flaminia. The attribution of the latter drawing to Hansen, in the 1950s, confirmed his long-suspected interest in Vignola's church.

Many Copenhagen buildings were again destroyed in 1807, when the English bombarded the city. One was Vor Frue Kirke, now Copenhagen's cathedral, whose tall spire had been a well-loved landmark. This time Hansen's reconstruction constituted an entirely new building. Vor Frue Kirke (completed in 1829) is the work of his maturity, and the most antique of his designs: to this point and no further could neoclassicism be taken. The church presents itself like an Early Christian basilica; an Italianate campanile rises over the great temple front. Inside, light enters from above, through the cassettes of a barrel vault supported by Doric columns that Hansen allowed himself to leave smooth, without fluting. Apostle figures sculpted by Bertel Thorvaldsen stand in front of the arcade below, and the space culminates in Thorvaldsen's giant statute of Christ, which had first been intended for the Palace Chapel.

Concurrently with these large and demanding commissions Hansen continued to work as the surveyor for Holstein, which he visited once a year to supervise construction. His mental hospital in Schleswig (completed in 1820) was the first purpose-built asylum in what was then Denmark; a symmetrical complex of a rural, cloistered character, it deservedly aroused interest in European medical circles. Hansen further explored the problems of church design and particularly the placement of the tower in churches for Neumünster (1828-34) and Husum (1829-33), examples of his churches for smaller towns.

At the time of his death the style that Hansen created was dead too. Aesthetic absolutes were no longer viable; antiquity, as the only acceptable model, had to retreat in the face of other models that were closer in both time and space. For a long time

Hansen's work was judged to be cold and alien. It was only at the beginning of the 20th century, with the advent of modernism, that Hansen won new recognition as one of functionalism's forerunners: with his mastery of a simple and strong formal language and his technical skill in dealing with complex problems, he was again recognized as a unique and original creative artist, who worked quite freely with his sources of inspiration.

—WIVAN MUNK-JØRGENSEN
Translated from the Danish by Christine Stevenson

HANSEN, [Hans] Christian.

Danish. Born in Copenhagen, Denmark, 20 April 1803. Died in Vienna, Austria, 2 May 1883. Brother was the architect Theophilus Hansen. Studied with G. F. Hetsch at the Academy of Architecture in Copenhagen, where he won the gold medal in 1829; traveled to Rome in 1831, to Naples in 1833, and then to Sicily and Greece; in Athens, excavated and reconstructed the Temple of Athena Nike on the Acropolis, with Ross and Schaubert (that work published in *Die Akropolis von Athen*, 1839); appoi nted professor at the Academy, Copenhagen, 1857.

Chronology of Works

1834-36	Mint, Athens, Greece
1836-42	Civil Hospital (now the Cultural Center), Athens, Greece
1836-64	University, Athens, Greece
1838	St. Paul's, Piraeus, Greece
1841	Anglican Church, Athens, Greece (with Charles R. Cockerell and others)
1847-54	Ophthalmos, Athens, Greece
1853-57	Austrian Lloyd Steamship Company Arsenal, Trieste, Italy
1859-61	Observatory, Copenhagen
1859-63	City Hospital, Copenhagen, Denmark
1863-70	Zoological Museum, Copenhagen
1869-72	Church, Holbaek, Copenghagen, Denmark
1870-71	Christiansdal Convent, Copenhagen, Denmark
1873-75	St. Josef's Hospital, Copenhagen

Publications

BOOKS ABOUT HANSEN

HAUGSTED, IDA and BENDTSEN, MARGIT: *Arkitekten Christian Hansen i Grækenland 1833-50*. Exhibition catalog. Copenhagen, 1986.

MPIRES, KOSTOS E.: *Ai Athenai apo tou 19ou eis ton 20oun aiona*. Athens, 1966.

RUSSACK, H. H.: *Deutsche bauen in Athen*. 1942.

TAVLOS, J.: *Neo-classical Architecture in Greece*. Athens, 1967.

ARTICLES ABOUT HANSEN

AKERSTROM-HOUGEN, G.: ''Den nyklassiska Arkitekturen i Grekland.'' *Konsthistorisk Tidskrift* (1972).

[Hans] Christian Hansen: City Hospital, Copenhagen, Denmark, 1859-63

HAUGSTED, IDA: "The Architect Christian Hansen and the Greek Neo-classicism." *Scandinavian Studies in Modern Greek* (1980).

LINDHØLM, SVEN: "Brodrene Christian og Theophilus Hansens vaerker i Athen." *Arkitekten Manedshaefte* 57, nos. 4-5 (1955): 69-74.

STROMSTAD, P.: "Kommunehospitalets opførelse." In *Kobenhavns hospitalsvoesen 1863-1963.* Copenhagen, 1963.

VILLADSEN, VILLADS: "Kobenhavns Universitets bygninger." Vol. 4, pages 240-260 in Sv. Ellehoj and L. Grane (eds.), *Kobenhavns Universitet.* Copenhagen.

VILLADSEN, VILLADS: "Studien über den byzantinischen Einfluss auf die europäische Architektur des 19. Jahrhunderts." *Hafnia* (1978): 43-77 (1978).

*

When Christian Hansen was born, progressive Danish artists dreamed of Attica, of making Copenhagen the new Athens; it was a vision tinged with some bitterness after the Napoleonic Wars, which left the country desperately poor. But it was Denmark which, with Bavaria, had most to do with rebuilding the old Athens. In 1834 Hansen, for whom there could be little work in his homeland, was named architect to the newly independent Greek court (under Otto, son of Ludwig of Bavaria, king of Greece from 1832 to 1862); and Christian's more famous brother Theophilus Hansen (1813-91), known for his later work in Vienna, collaborated with him from 1838 to 1846 in Athens, where Theophilus himself designed important buildings. In Greece, Christian Hansen was equally important as an archaeologist, preservationist and teacher, often working under difficult and dangerous conditions.

Hansen's training at the Royal Academy of Art in Copenhagen, under G. F. Hetsch (1788-1864) and his namesake C. F. Hansen (1756-1845), culminated in his winning the Large Gold Medal in 1829. The prize included a travel scholarship. Hansen left Denmark—for 26 years, as it turned out—in August 1831, reaching Rome, where he would spend 14 months, at the end of the year. Impressed as he inevitably was with Roman antiquity, it was his months en route, in the German lands, which were more important for his later architecture and intellectual interests. In Dresden, Hansen met the architect Joseph Thürmer (1789-1833), an expert on Greek antiquity; and in Munich, he met Leo von Klenze (1784-1864) and Friedrich von Gärtner (1792-1847), architects to King Ludwig of Bavaria, who would both usurp projects close to Hansen's heart: Klenze with his town plan for Athens (1834) and Gärtner with the Royal Palace there (1836-41).

Above all, the monumental buildings that Karl Friedrich Schinkel (1781-1841) had designed for Berlin made an enormous impression on Hansen. The plain geometry, interrupted only by simplified classical pilasters, entablatures, and window and door surrounds of Hansen's Civil Hospital (1836-42, now the Cultural Center) on Solanos Street in Athens is very Schinkelesque. Beneath and behind vibrant Greek Revival detailing, the smooth planes of Hansen's Athens University building (1836-64)—on which Theophilus collaborated and which was finished by the Greek L. Kaftantzoglou (1812-85)—are punctuated by trabeated windows and porticoes that owe as much to Schinkel's rationalism as to archaeological observation. A letter Christian Hansen wrote in 1834 from Athens to Theophilus, still an architectural student in Copenhagen, emphasized the rationality of the Greeks: "Learn the Greek style first. When you understand it, seize the feeling with which the Greeks did everything, then you'll more easily comprehend the Gothic, the Florentine, or any other sort of architecture, for the same philosophy works for them all."

Hansen's reaction to Greece, which he reached in 1833, was mixed: the wild, wooded and mountainous landscape was pleasantly unlike Denmark's, and it was filled with fascinating ruins whose cumulative effect was, however, rather depressing. While still on his scholarship and after gaining his appointment, he measured and drew these assiduously, comparing them with classical remains he had seen in Rome. His official duties included the surveying, and recommendation for preservation, of the remnants of Athens' classical, Byzantine and even Ottoman Turkish past. With his friend and longtime collaborator Eduard Schaubert (1804-60) and the chief archaeologist Ludwig Ross (1806-59), Hansen published a survey of the Temple of Nike on the Acropolis (Berlin, 1839); with Schaubert and the Hungarian Joseph Hoffer (ca. 1810-before 1851), he made the measurements that led to Hoffer's pioneering account, published in 1838, of horizontal curvature in classical Greek temples. Most delightful to Hansen, however, was the realization that classical Greek architecture had been brightly colored, a question still controversial at that time in Europe but which his own observations confirmed. The white marble of the Athens University building is brilliantly set off by gilt and polychromy.

In 1850 Hansen left Greece for Trieste, where he spent several years working on the Lloyd's Steamship Company's shipyards (1853-57), a major project for which he prepared with 18 months' studying shipyards all over Europe. It was in the "Greco-Byzantine" style that dominated his later career. Hansen was a sympathetic and gifted interpreter of Byzantine architecture, of which fine examples were to be seen in Athens. He understood it to represent the admixture of late classical and early medieval Greek architecture; it is possible that when in Germany he had discussed the attractive theory, then current, that the Romanesque architecture of the Rhineland had been strongly influenced by Byzantium and as such marked the transition between the Byzantine and Gothic styles. After his return to Denmark in 1857, much of Hansen's time was taken up with the restoration of medieval ecclesiastical buildings, work which he possibly considered in that light.

The Byzantine style was obviously suitable for hospitals, that institution born of Early Christian *caritas.* One of Hansen's last buildings for Athens was the Ophthalmos (1847-54), a delightful little eye hospital (1847-54) and a modest prefiguration of Copenhagen's Kommunehospital (1859-63), his major work in Denmark, whose sheer size rather offsets the delicacy of its colored brick patterning.

—CHRISTINE STEVENSON

HANSEN, Theophilus.

Danish. Born in Copenhagen, Denmark, 13 July 1813. Died in Vienna, Austria, 17 February 1891. Brother was the architect [Hans] Christian Hansen. Married the daughter of the Viennese architect/planner Ludwig Förster, in 1851. Studied with G. F. Hetsch at the Academy of Architecture, Copenhagen, 1824-37; traveled to Germany and Italy, then to Athens, Greece, where he was a technical instructor; moved to Vienna at the invitation of Ludwig Förster, 1846; worked independently in Vienna.

Theophilus Hansen: Austrian Parliament Building, Ringstrasse, Vienna, Austria, 1874-83

Chronology of Works

All in Austria unless noted
† Work no longer exists

1858	Fleischmarkt, Vienna
1858	Chapel of the Protestant cemetery, Vienna
1859-60	Palace of Baron Sina, Hohe Markt, Vienna
1860	School, near the Polytechnikum, Vienna
1861	Greek Academy of Sciences, Athens, Greece
1864-68	Palace for the Archduke Wilhelm, Vienna
1872-77	Academy of Fine Arts, Vienna
1874-77	Exchange, Schottenring, Vienna (mostly†)
1874-83	Austrian Parliament Building, Ringstrasse, Vienna

Publications

BOOKS ABOUT HANSEN

EGGERT, KLAUS: *Die Ringstrasse*. Vienna and Hamburg, 1971.

MIGNOT, CLAUDE: *Architektur des 19. Jahrhunderts*. Stuttgart, 1983.

NIEMANN, J. and FELDEGG, F. VON: *Theophilus Hansen und sein Werk*. Vienna, 1893.

WAGNER-RIEGER, R.: *Wiens Architektur im 19. Jahrhundert*. Vienna, 1970.

WAGNER-RIEGER, R., and KRAUSE, W. (eds.): *Historismus und Schlossbau*. Munich, 1975.

WANZENBÖCK, H., and SCHIEFER, H.: *Die Ringstrasse: Als Wien zur Weltstadt wurde*. Vienna, 1988.

ARTICLES ABOUT HANSEN

FISCHER-HÖLZL, M.: "Theophilus Hansen, Leben und Frühwerke." Ph.D. dissertation. Graz, Austria, 1946.
GANZ, J.: "Theophil Hansens 'hellenische' Bauten in Athen und Wien." *Österreichische Zeitschrift für Kunst und Denkmalpflege* (1972).
WAGNER-RIEGER, RENATE: "Der Architekt Theophil Hansen." *Anzeiger der österreichischen Akademie der Wissenschaften* 114 (1977): 260-76.

*

During his training in Copenhagen, Theophilus Hansen was influenced by French classicism and by the work of Karl Friedrich Schinkel. Hansen's early work, therefore, was a synthesis of different tendencies in Schinkel's architecture with a greater reliance on painting and sculpture. As a result, he achieved a new conception of classicist motifs in the framework of the romantic *Gesamtkunstwerk*. Later modifications of his style resulted from his long stay in Athens, where he studied Greek antiquity, and came to grips with Hellenic and particularly Byzantine architecture. Hansen arrived in Vienna in 1846, embarking upon a collaboration with the architect and patron Ludwig Förster (1797-1863). During Hansen's early Viennese years, a richly ornamented late classicism with a strong orientation to color dominated his work. As an independent architect Hansen turned to a romantic historicism, building in a Byzantine and late Gothic style. Among the chief works of his early period are the Vienna Fleischmarkt (1858), the palace of Baron Sina on the Hoher Markt (1859-60), the chapel of the former Protestant cemetery (1858), the Protestant School next to the Polytechnikum (1860) and the Greek Academy of Sciences in Athens (1861).

His participation (anticipated since the early 1860s) in the Ringstrasse expansions provided him with an opportunity to build in a neo-Renaissance style. He soon became a leader in the architectural utilization of polychromy, following Gottfried Semper's conception of the *Gesamtkunstwerk*. By the same token, he became one of the leading exponents of the so-called Vienna style. One of his contributions was the development of a new monumental residential building type, first realized in the Heinrichshof (1861-62), for the brick manufacturer Heinrich von Draschke. These three apartment buildings in the style of the Italian Renaissance exercised a powerful influence on Viennese architecture. The three buildings were conceived as one unified block with an emphasis on the central building. The palatial exterior reinforced the buildings' appearance of a single monumental palace. Hansen designed the Musikverein on the Karlsplatz in the same High Renaissance style. Hansen's inclusive organic design integrated a monumental clarity with graceful precision, and created an overarching unity out of a diversity of elements. Hansen's achievement rests in the synthesis of independent, freestanding monumental buildings, and their simultaneous harmonious integration into the surrounding urban landscape.

Although done at almost the same time, Hansen's palace for Archduke Wilhelm (1864-68) shows a relaxation of his formal idiom. Great clarity in the articulation of the facade is combined with a highly individual treatment of form in the entire building. This style, which Hansen himself called "Greek Renaissance," also governed the design of the Academy of Fine Arts (1872-77). The four-story building with heightened corner bays is

especially noteworthy for its festive interiors, particularly those of the freestanding staircase, the auditorium and the columned hall, the latter with a ceiling painting by Anselm Feuerbach (1829-80). Particularly rich furnishings accompany the great diversity of pictorial and sculptural ornamentation.

These built works of the 1860s and Hansen's unexecuted competition design for the Vienna Museum [1866, in collaboration with Karl Hasenauer (1833-94) and Gottfried Semper (1803-79)], prepared for Hansen's masterpiece, which was also the mature result of his studies in Greece: the Austrian Parliament Building (1874-83) on the Ringstrasse. The exterior of this monumental structure, designed in the spirit of Greek antiquity, already symbolizes the political system based on two parliamentary houses, by means of the double division in the facade. A central structure inspired by ancient temple architecture is set between the two side buildings. It functions both as divider and as architectural connector of the two main blocks. The central section has a portico treated like an independent space, which was Hansen's preferred central motif. This design unifies the side sections as the more important building elements. The portico is modeled on the Erechtheion gate on the Acropolis, and has a bronze portal. The two parliamentary wings end in corner pavilions. Eight statues of antique historians and four horsebreakers accompany the powerful double ramp leading to the central portico.

Behind the main entrance of the portico, disposed along the central east-west axis, are the entrance hall, the vestibule with Ionic columns, the atrium and the central hall, which is spatially defined by a peristyle. The sequence ends with two more great halls. Greek elements, such as the three orders, define the interior design. The temple-like central hall, with its 24 colossal red columns, is conceived along the lines of central spaces in classical architecture. It is one of the most important interiors in Austria, particularly for its successful visualization of the nature and idea of government. The chamber of the former House of Representatives, which has a plan in the form of a heightened semicircle, is inspired, on the other hand, by the architecture of classical Greek theaters. The walls recall the antique stage with colonnades, entablature, gables and figural ornamentation. The vertical articulation of all spaces is determined by columns, pilasters, pillars and pilaster strips that reach from floor to ceiling.

At the same time as the Parliament Building, Hansen built the Exchange on the Schottenring (1874-77). The Exchange, with its freestanding staircase and the columns set in front, is a classicist Renaissance structure recalling Roman architecture. As a composition made up of different building elements it represents a kind of *Gruppenbau* (group construction), organized on the basis of opposed internal directions, particularly in the portico. The magnificent main hall of the Exchange, which was destroyed in a fire in 1956, has half columns, large side windows and a coffered ceiling ornamented with stucco made to resemble marble. The wealth of color in the pressed terra-cotta slabs and the rich figurative decoration contribute to the splendor of the room. Hansen himself was responsible for the ornamentation throughout the interior. With his participation in design drawings and the modeling of the smallest decorative details, Hansen stimulated a regeneration of the arts and crafts in Vienna.

In the first half of the 1870s Hansen built several private palaces in Vienna (Tedesco, Ephrussi, Epstein), in which he continued his work with the reconception of traditional residential building types begun with the design of the Heinrichshof. Until 1890 he was occupied with several important projects, among others the Royal Palace in Athens and the town halls of Copenhagen and Hamburg. In 1882 Hansen entered the competition for the Berlin Reichstag, participating in the competition for plans to develop the Berlin Museum Island in 1884-86.

Hansen's stylistic changes during his career spanning almost 40 years may be considered on three different levels, following R. Wagner-Rieger's account. First, there is the eye-catching change in the use of different historical styles, which he never simply copied but always integrated with his own design principles. Second, there are certain constants to be found in Hansen's work, which he applied at all times, and which remain easily recognizable despite all the stylistic changes. Examples of such constants are the grid-like divisions of the plans (e.g., orthogonal support systems); the closed, partly interconnected building blocks without courtyards; and the closed courtyards which are conceived like closed hypaethral interior spaces. Third, Hansen modified larger forms in the course of his career, moving, for instance, between the use of a centralized emphasis and an emphasis on sides and corners. His oeuvre is accordingly characterized by a rhythmical alternation of compositions. The interplay of constants and stylistic modifications in the choice of historical styles forms the basis of Hansen's personal style. His work emphasized the creative personality of the architect, and also made him one of the principal founders of the so-called Vienna style, along with Heinrich von Ferstel, Friedrich von Schmidt and Karl von Hasenauer.

—CAROLIN BAHR
Translated from the German by Marijke Rijsberman

HARDOUIN-MANSART, Jules.

French. Born in Paris, France, 16 April 1646. Died in Marly, near Paris, 11 May 1708. Great-uncle was the architect François Mansart, with whom he trained. Worked for Libéral Bruant at the Hôtel des Invalides, Paris, 1670; worked at Versailles, 1671; commissioned by King Louis XIV to design the Château du Val, 1672; Royal Architect, 1675, Premier Architect, 1685, and Surintendant des Bâtiments, 1699-1708, all under Louis XIV. Involved in the reorganization of the Royal Academy of Architecture, 1699.

Chronology of Works
All in France
† Work no longer exists
* Approximate dates

1666*	Petit Hôtel de Conti, Paris†
Before 1670	Hôtel de Lorge, Paris†
Before 1670	Hôtel de Noailles, St.-Germain†
1670	Hôtel des Invalides, Paris (with Libéral Bruant)
1673*	J. Hardouin-Mansart House, Rue de Tournelles, Paris
1673-79	Château for Madame de Montespan, Clagny†
1674	Château du Val, St.-Germain†
1675	Château, Dampierre
1675	Hôtel de Ville, Arles
1676	Pavilions for the Grove of Fame, Versailles
1678-89	Palais, Versailles (renovations and additions, including the Hall of Mirrors)
1679	Château, Marly†
1679ff.	Dôme des Invalides, Paris
1684-86	Place des Victoires, Paris
1685	Colonnade, Versailles
1685	Château, St.-Cloud
1685	Pont Royal, Paris (with Jacques Gabriel)
1685-1700	Place Vendôme, Paris
1689-98	Chapel, Versailles (with Robert de Cotte; not completed until 1710)

Publications

BOOKS ABOUT HARDOUIN-MANSART

BLUNT, ANTHONY: *Art and Architecture in France: 1500-1700.* 2nd ed. Harmondsworth, England, 1973.
BOURGET, PIERRE, and CATTAUI, GEORGES: *Jules Hardouin-Mansart.* Paris, 1960.
Hardouin-Mansart et son école. Paris, 1946.
HAUTECOEUR, LOUIS: Pp. 527-688 in *Le règne de Louis XIV.* Vol. 2 in *Histoire de l'architecture classique en France.* Paris, 1948.
MARIE, ALFRED and JEANNE: *Mansart à Versailles.* 2 vols. Paris, 1972.
MARIE, ALFRED: *Versailles au temps de Louis XIV. Mansart et de Cotte.* Paris, 1976.

ARTICLES ABOUT HARDOUIN-MANSART

JESTAZ, B.: "Jules Hardouin-Mansart et l'église des Invalides." *Gazette des beaux-arts* (1965).
MAROT, PIERRE: "Jules Hardouin-Mansart et le plan de la primatiale de Nancy." *Le pays lorrain* (Nancy, 1930).

*

The architecture of Jules Hardouin-Mansart epitomizes the grand epoch of Louis XIV, whom he served as royal architect in 1675, premier architect in 1685, and later, from 1699 to the year of his death in 1708, superintendent of buildings (*surintendant des bâtiments*). His contributions to the ongoing expansion of the royal château of Versailles, the most visible architectural achievement of Louis XIV's reign, established a stage for the pageantry, formality and grandiosity of the court of the Sun King of France in the late 17th century. As primary architect of the era, Hardouin-Mansart also designed other châteaux throughout the country as well as town houses, city squares and major churches in Paris.

Hardouin-Mansart, who had the confidence of Louis XIV and was awarded noble titles in 1683 and 1693, was a victim of jealousy among his contemporaries. Louis de Rouvroy, duke of Saint-Simon, a visitor to the late court of Louis XIV, was particularly vitriolic in his criticism of both the king and the royal architect, and asserted that Hardouin-Mansart kept a team of architects hidden in a back room producing designs for his projects. This negative view survives in some modern criticism, such as that of Richard Blomfield, who criticized Hardouin-Mansart for not going to Italy and stressed what he perceived as the architect's absence of taste, lack of scruples and sycophancy about his architectural achievements. This claim that the best of Hardouin-Mansart's architecture was not his own does not seem credible, because it does not take into account his grand vision for the era of Louis XIV. As chief architect in charge of creating an extensive complex of monuments that defined the reign and reflected the absolute monarchy of Louis XIV, Hardouin-Mansart placed his own distinctive stamp upon the architecture of the era and required a large staff to accomplish the king's desires.

Hardouin-Mansart was the great-nephew of François Mansart, the famous classical architect of the early 17th century, and assumed the last name of his great forebear. He also inherited

Jules Hardouin-Mansart: Dôme des Invalides, Paris, France, 1679ff.

the older architect's enormous collection of plans and drawings and, from that array of material, apparently gleaned many ideas that he later expressed in his own work. He was influenced also by his contemporaries, including the royal landscape architect André Le Nôtre and the royal painter Charles LeBrun. From such diverse sources, Hardouin-Mansart amassed ideas that he synthesized into his own grand style.

He began his extremely successful career by designing a house at Clagny from 1673 to 1678/1679 for Madame de Montespan, mistress of the king, after being introduced to her by Le Nôtre. The house, which was destroyed after 1769 but is known from engravings, demonstrates the imposing scale on which Hardouin-Mansart worked from the inception of his architectural practice.

While he was at work at Clagny, Hardouin-Mansart became acquainted with the king, who then brought him to Versailles. The architect's earliest works there were garden projects. In 1676 he designed two classical pavilions for the Grove of Fame (*Bosquet de la Renommée*), later the Grove of the Domes (*Bosquet des Domes*), north of the Royal Walkway (*Allée Royale*), which was constructed to honor Louis XIV's recent military victories. These domed pavilions with pedimented facades, which were destroyed later, flanked a statue of Fame enclosed within a double balustrade and lent an architectural character to Le Nôtre's landscape. In 1685 Hardouin-Mansart designed and built one of the most distinctive of the garden features, the Colonnade, a circular arcade of alternating blue and pink marble Corinthian columns in the Colonnade grove south of the Royal Walkway.

In 1678 Hardouin-Mansart became involved with the remodeling of the château, to which Louis Le Vau had added an enclosure (*envellope*) on the garden side in 1668-69 to provide essential space for the increasingly crowded court. Early drawings reveal that Hardouin-Mansart's original plans were to add extra floors, but he lengthened the north and south walls of the garden front instead. Inside, he reconstructed the main floor and transformed the Grand Apartment of the king into an enfilade of elaborately decorated rooms, which Louis XIV decided to designate his new state apartment. The king then chose a part of the old structure for his own private apartment. Hardouin-Mansart also completed the famous King's Staircase, begun by François d'Orbay and Le Vau, which as decorated by LeBrun became the Ambassadors' Staircase (*Escalier des Ambassadeurs*), which was destroyed in 1752.

On the exterior, Hardouin-Mansart enclosed Le Vau's balcony to form the Hall of Mirrors (*Galerie des Glaces*) and enlarged the north and south walls of the garden side to encompass the expanded interior space. He also placed round arched windows in Le Vau's enclosure to conform with those of his new gallery. On the court side, he rebuilt the walls of the marble court and joined four small pavilions to form two wings of the Ministries (1683); and he added new arches to the windows and redesigned the attic of the marble court.

In 1683 Hardouin-Mansart constructed two very practical structures for the château. To house and feed the households of the king and queen, he built the Grand Commun, a large classical building south of the projecting court pavilion. Facing the court, across the Place d'Armes, he built the new horse stables (Grand Écurie and Petite Écurie), whose inner curving walls face the court of the château and anticipated Hardouin-Mansart's later projects of city planning by creating the effect of a unified city space.

His masterpiece on the interior of the château is the Hall of Mirrors. To provide proper lighting for LeBrun's painted glorification of Louis XIV as a military leader on the vaulted ceiling, Hardouin-Mansart designed large arched windows on the garden side balanced by large reflecting mirrors from Venice on the inner wall. To build the adjoining rooms, he had to suppress two rooms of the old royal apartment. In these end rooms, he continued the military theme. In the Room of War (*Salon de la Guerre*), north of the gallery, the bellicose king ruled in war; however, in the Room of Peace (*Salon de la Paix*), the first room of the Queen's Apartments, the king who excelled in war now presided over peace. In another room of the new state apartments, the Room of Abundance (*Salon d'Abondance*), Hardouin-Mansart established a strong architectural character in what was typically a matter of interior decoration by creating an architectural decoration over the door. His frame is an archivolt formed by the curving of the entablature.

Controversy surrounds one of Hardouin-Mansart's new buildings in the park. In 1679-80 he replaced Le Vau's Orangery (*Orangerie*) with a larger structure, whose vaulted interior is massive and simple. Some contemporary sources, however, credit Le Nôtre as the designer, but Hardouin-Mansart's biographers Pierre Bourget and Georges Cattaui dispute this claim. The massive scale of the building, its simplicity and its purely architectural character argue more for authorship by the architect Hardouin-Mansart, who brought order and simplicity to Le Nôtre's quasi-architectural groves in the gardens, than by the landscape architect.

In 1687 Hardouin-Mansart rebuilt the royal retreat in the village of Trianon, Le Vau's Porcelain Trianon (*Trianon de Porcelaine*). The plan of Hardouin-Mansart's Grand Trianon is an asymmetrical configuration of rooms designed to provide views of all the features of the formal garden that Le Nôtre had designed around the old house and continued around the new building. An L-shaped extension, including a long gallery and a pavilion named the Trianon-in-the-Woods (*Trianon-sous-Bois*) because it exceeds into the woods, adds to the unusual character of the pink and yellow marble building.

Late in Louis XIV's reign, in 1689-98, with the assistance of his protégé and brother-in-law Robert de Cotte, Hardouin-Mansart began the permanent chapel the king insisted on building despite economic and political crises and against the advice of many at court, including his morganatic wife Madame de Maintenon. The chapel, however, is a sterling example of classical beauty at Versailles. Built on a simple plan, it consists of a lower chamber, whose massive piers support an upper gallery for the king to hear Mass. Freestanding Corinthian columns support the entablature on the upper level. The decoration, planned by Hardouin-Mansart and de Cotte, is a combination of white and other light colors and reflects stylistic changes at the late court of Louis XIV. On the exterior, a high roof gives the building a Gothic appearance, although its classical detail on the side facing the court echoes the style of the interior. Hardouin-Mansart did not live to finish the chapel, which was completed in 1710, two years after his death.

In Paris, Hardouin-Mansart designed the new church of the Invalides Hospital complex, begun by Liberal Bruant. The Church of St. Louis by Bruant was already part of the complex, but in 1679 Hardouin-Mansart began a second church to honor the king. His structure, often referred to as the Dome of the Invalides, has a square plan divided into four chapels at the corners. Massive central piers support the dome, which is notable for its three sections, the first of its kind. A low, masonry dome opens into a second masonry dome. On the Place Vauban, the church facade is distinguishable by the height of the dome, which is twice the length of each side of the square. Its vertical thrust links its symbolism with the national French Gothic tradition, but its classicism aligns it with contemporary churches, such as St. Paul's Cathedral in London.

Other projects in Paris were two city squares: the octagonal Place Vendôme (1685-1700), a harmonious space created by surrounding an equestrian statue of Louis XIV with classical houses; and the Place des Victoires (1684-86), a less successful venture of a circular space of houses around an equestrian statue. That square was not finished and was altered drastically with time.

Hardouin-Mansart also designed the royal château at Marly, a country-house complex that influenced the style of institutional planning. There, in 1679, he built a house for the king and surrounded it on two sides with six small pavilions on each side of a sunken court. Marly absorbed large sums of money and was destroyed during the Revolution of 1789.

In a career that spanned the second half of Louis XIV's reign, Hardouin-Mansart created many significant monuments of the period and directed a large ensemble cast in the immense production starring Louis XIV as a still-youthful Sun King in the beginning, then the mature military warrior, and an aging, religious fanatic at the end. Not only did Hardouin-Mansart represent the age of Louis XIV, but he and the king were near contemporaries who concluded their long and brilliant careers with a single focus on a permanent chapel for Versailles. It was finished two years after the death of Hardouin-Mansart and five years before the death of the king; that chapel was perhaps Hardouin-Mansart's finest work and the crowning architectural achievement of both the royal architect and the royal patron.

—JOYCE M. DAVIS

HÄRING, Hugo.

German. Born in Biberach, Württemberg, Germany, 22 May 1882. Died in Göttingen, West Germany, 17 May 1958. Studied at Technische Hochschule, Stuttgart, 1899-1901, and Technische Hochschule, Dresden, 1901-02. Served in the German Army, 1914-15, 1917-18. Practiced privately in Ulm, 1903-04, then in Hamburg, 1904-14; worked as architect for the rebuilding of East Prussia, 1915-16; private practice in Berlin, 1918-43, and Biberach, 1943-58. Secretary, Der Ring, Berlin, 1926-33; founder memb er of CIAM (Congrès Internationaux d'Architecture Moderne), 1929; head of the Reimann (Kunst und Werk) School of Art, Berlin, 1935-43.

Chronology of Works
All in Germany unless noted

1916-18	Manor House, Gr'Plauen, East Prussia
1916-19	Hans Römer House, Neu-Ulm
1917	Reimann Shop and Living Quarters, Allenburg, East Prussia
1922	Gaffre Guinle Hospital, Rio de Janeiro, Brazil
1923	Gut Garkau Agricultural Building, near Lübeck
1924	Auction Rooms, Lübeck
1925	Tobacco Goods Factory, Neustadt, Holstein
1926	Terrace Housing, Zehlendorf, Berlin
1927	Max Voythaler Building, Lankwitz, Berlin
1928	Art Exhibition Hall, Tattersalle, Berlin
1928	Adler Weekend House, Wansee Country Club, Berlin
1928-29	Frenzel House, Elbing, East Prussia
1930	Behrendt House, Berlin
1930	Karlshorst Housing Development, Treskowallee, Berlin
1930	Rodenstrasse Housing Development, Lichtenberg, Berlin
1930-31	Beck/Segmehl House, Biberach

1932	Eichkamp Housing Development, Berlin
1937-41	Von Prittwitz Building, Tutzing
1938	Open-air school, Torbole sul Garda, Italy
1942	Kunst and Werk School, Berlin
1949-52	Werner Schmitz House, Biberach

Publications

BOOKS BY HÄRING

Vom neuen Bauen. Über das Geheimnis der Gestalt. Berlin, 1957.
Die Ausbildung des Geistes. Zur Arbeit an der Gestalt. Fragmente. Berlin, 1968.

ARTICLES BY HÄRING

"Probleme des Bauens, Parts 1-3." *Neubau* No. 17 (10 September 1924).
"Probleme des Bauens, Part 4." *Neubau* No. 13 (10 February 1925).
"Wege zur Form." *Form* No. 1 (October 1925). English translation: "Approaches to Form." *Architectural Association Quarterly* 10, No. 1 (1978).
"Geometrie und Organik." *Baukunst und Werkform* No. 9 (1951).
"Beispiel einer Wohnung." *Deutsche Architektur* (East Berlin, July 1967).
"Two Cities—a Study on Urban Planning Problems." *Daidalos* (15 June 1982).

BOOKS ABOUT HÄRING

JOEDICKE, JÜRGEN (ed.): *Das andere Bauen.* Stuttgart, 1982.
LAUTERBACH, HEINRICH, and JOEDICKE, JÜRGEN (eds.): *Hugo Häring: Schriften, Entwürfe, Bauten.* Stuttgart, 1965.

ARTICLES ABOUT HÄRING

BEHR, ADALBERT: "Hugo Häring on his 100th birthday." *Architektur der DDR* (East Berlin, May 1982).
JOEDICKE, JÜRGEN: "Häring at Garkau." *Architectural Review* 127 (May 1960): 313-318.
JOEDICKE, JÜRGEN: "Hugo Häring." *Arts and Architecture* 83 (February/March 1966): 8-12.
JOEDICKE, JÜRGEN: "Hugo Häring: Zur Theorie des organhaften Bauens." *Bauen und Wohnen* No. 11 (November 1960): 419-422.
JONES, PETER BLUNDELL: "Hugo Haring." *Architectural Review* (April 1982).
KREMER, SABINE: "Hugo Haring on his 100th birthday." *AIT* (May/June 1982).

*

Hugo Häring was one of several important architects of the 20th century whose philosophy of organic architecture has gone relatively unrecognized. His basic interest was in the development of housing, an evolution that he understood as the foundation of being.

When Häring was studying at the Technische Hochschule of Stuttgart, the historicism of the 19th century was still predominantly there. The presentation of different historical styles had little meaning for him, and he developed an aversion to the accepted meaning of "architecture." In the years after his studies until 1921, Häring worked with several architects in Germany. In 1921 he moved to Berlin, where he met Ludwig Mies van der Rohe. During that time Häring, who sublet office space from Mies, recognized the fundamental difference between his forms and those of Mies. Mies' architectural vocabulary was based on geometry, Häring's on the organic understanding of form. In the mid-1920s Häring became a member of the association Der Ring, which included Mies and the architects Peter Behrens, Walter Gropius, Bruno Taut, and Erich Mendelsohn. The goal of Der Ring was to unify all the progressive elements of that time, with the intention of reshaping the architectural profession from the inside as well as from the outside.

In the years after World War I, the crushing demand for workers' housing became one of the main tasks for architects. Häring worked on the Gross-Siedlung Fischtalgrund in Berlin-Zehlendorf (1926-27) and at the Gross-Siedlung Siemensstadt in Berlin (1928-31). He was interested in the development of minimized dwellings with flat roofs and, in 1932, was the only German architect who was invited by Josef Frank to participate in the International Werkbund Exhibition in Vienna. He also participated for a short time at the Weissenhof Exhibition in Stuttgart, but left the exhibition when he recognized that the overall development moved from the individual to the International Style.

In 1935 Häring became the principal of the Reimann School in Berlin, which was a private school for art and industrial design. The school was in constant struggle with the government and with the Nazi regime. In addition to the existing problems, Häring hired faculty such as George Muche, Joost Schmitt and others who were not appreciated by the ruling regime. That struggle in general was something that occupied much of Häring's life.

Häring's view of history was based upon the conceptions of the 18th, 19th and early 20th centuries. He used those ideas and developed his own understanding of history, taking portions from traditional theories and recombining them. This undertaking should be understood as a contribution to the process of clarifying architectural history. He saw architectural history as a sequence of classical and Gothic epochs, a theory that believes in cycles and stands in opposition to the 18th-century belief in a constant progression. Häring's ideal society was one in which the predominance of the individual person was the most important part. Häring defined as his goal for the individual, as for the political society, the development of the mind for the creation and development of form. He did not look at architecture and architectural history from an artistic or expressive point of view, but from the viewpoint of structure. Häring understood structure as a principle that dictates an order system in space and time. This principle could be divided into the organic and geometric structural systems. Häring viewed organic structures as a system of fulfillment of life as a whole, in space and time. The function and task of the individual elements are responsible for their shape in space. Tools and machines are designed to fulfill a function, and their expression is secondary, in analogy to natural organisms, which are created for their function, not for their aesthetic expression.

The geometric structural systems, which Häring considered to be purely intellectual, also demand an order of space and time, but not as a life-fulfilling goal. Their goal for Häring was the creation of forms that follow the pressure of geometry.

This fundamental difference was also the difference between Häring's understanding of the German "*neues Bauen*" and the French "*architecture moderne.*" The German word "*neu*" referred to a search for new beginnings in Häring's view, whereas the French word "*moderne*" was concerned only with superficial change. The *neues Bauen* therefore began with the essence of creating and a new interpretation of the act of building, and followed a principle that existed before the discovery of any geometry. For Häring the organic principles in architecture that were the essence of the *neues Bauen* had nothing to do with imitating organic nature. It was rather the concept that form and shape of things is not derived from the exterior but is found in the essence of the object itself.

Häring saw the *neues Bauen* as the continuation of the principles of the Gothic—the belief that the end of the geometrical, classical architecture finally had arrived. In his discussion about *neues Bauen,* Häring used the contrasting points of geometry and the organic, with respect to both classical and Gothic architecture, an idea that is equivalent to Johan Wolfgang von Goethe's (1749-1832) basic understanding of history. Goethe turned against an understanding that architecture imitates nature, but also mentioned that the genius would build like nature. Goethe's point of view about Gothic as German architecture was taken up by several authors, including Georg Wilhelm Friedrich Hegel (1770-1831) and Friedrich von Schlegel (1772-1829).

Häring did not build as many projects as some of his colleagues, but the few projects he executed, such as Gut Garkau in Holstein (1922-26) and Haus Werner Schmitz in Biberach (1950), were important for the idea of organic architecture, not only in Germany but in Europe as a whole. The shapes and forms of the buildings of Gut Garkau were driven from the goal of finding a solution that could fulfill the demands of a building in a simple and direct way. The logical sequence of functions that had to be accommodated dictated the shapes of the buildings. These buildings documented Häring's understanding of the *neues Bauen* and became guidelines for subsequent generations of architects.

—UWE DROST

HARRISON and ABRAMOVITZ.

American. Wallace K. Harrison: Born in Worcester, Massachusetts, 28 September 1895. Died in New York City, 2 December 1981. Married Ellen Hunt Milton, 1926; one daughter. Studied at Columbia University, New York City, 1916-17, and at the École des Beaux-Arts, Paris, 1923-24. Worked in New York City: for McKim, Mead and White, 1916-17; for Bertram Goodhue, 1920-21; as partner in Corbett, Harrison and MacMurray, 1929-34; as partner with André Fouilhoux, 1935-41, with Fouilhoux and Max Abramovitz, 1941-45; partner with Max Abramovitz, 1945-76; private practice, 1976-81. Taught at Columbia University, 1926-27, and Yale University, New Haven, Connecticut, 1938-41; Gold Medal, American Institute of Architects, 1957. Max Abramovitz: Born in Chicago, Illinois, 23 May 1908. Married Anne Mary Casy, 1937 (divorced, 1964); one daughter; married Anita Zeltner Brooks, 1964. Studied at the University of Illinois, Champaign-Urbana, 1925-29, at Columbia University, New York City, 1929-31, and at the École des Beaux-Arts, Paris, France, 1932-34. Partnership with Wallace K. Harrison, 1945-76; partner in Abramovitz, Harris, Kingsland, 1976. Associate professor of fine arts, Yale University, New Haven, Connecticut, 1939-42.

Chronology of Works
All in the United States unless noted
† *Work no longer exists*

1929-74 Rockefeller Center, New York City (with Raymond M. Hood, L. A. Reinhard and Henry Hofmeister,

Harvey Wiley Corbett, William H. McMurray and
André Fouilhoux)
1939-40 Perisphere and Trylon, World's Fair, New York
City†
1947-53 United Nations Buildings, New York City (with Le
Corbusier, Oscar Niemeyer, Sven Markelius and
others)
1950-53 Alcoa Building, Pittsburgh, Pennsylvania
1953-58 First Presbyterian Church, Stamford, Connecticut
1959-60 Time-Life Building, New York City
1959-68 Lincoln Center for the Performing Arts, New York
(Harrison as project coordinator and architect of Metropolitan Opera House; Abramovitz as architect of
Avery Fischer Hall)
1960-64 Phoenix Mutual Life Insurance Building, Hartford,
Connecticut
1963-78 South Mall, New York State Capital, Albany
1967-71 United States Steel Building, Pittsburgh, Pennsylvania

Publications

BOOKS ABOUT HARRISON and ABRAMOVITZ

HARRISON, HELEN A.: *Dawn of a New Day: The New York
World's Fair 1939/40.* New York, 1980.
KRINSKY, CAROL: *Rockefeller Center.* New York and London,
1978.
NEWHOUSE, V.: *Wallace K. Harrison, Architect.* New York,
1989.
YOUNG, EDGAR B.: *Lincoln Center: The Building of an Institu-
tion.* New York, 1980.

ARTICLES ABOUT HARRISON and ABRAMOVITZ

"Alcoa Complete: Pittsburgh's 30-Story Aluminum Waffle is
America's Most Daring Experiment in Modern Office Build-
ing." *Architectural Forum* 99 (November 1953): 124-131.
KRINSKY, CAROL: "St. Petersburg-on-the-Hudson: The Al-
bany Mall." In *Art the Ape of Nature.* New York, 1981.
"The Secretariat a Campanile, a Cliff of Glass, a Great Debate."
Architectural Forum 93 (November 1950): 93-113.

*

Harrison and Abramovitz was one of the most renowned architectural firms in the United States, responsible for such large
complexes as the United Nations Building and the Lincoln
Center for the Performing Arts in New York City, and the Mall
in Albany, New York.

In 1926 Wallace K. Harrison had married Ellen Milton, the
sister-in-law of Abby Rockefeller, and by 1929 he was one of
the many advisers to Rockefeller Center, serving in this capacity
from its very beginnings through the expansion to Sixth Avenue
in the 1940s and beyond. The plan is as extraordinary as the
design of the individual buildings, the style a form of art deco,
caught in Indiana limestone and embellished with details of
ornament and decoration of a very high quality. The plan, which
was perhaps modeled on the schemes of Roman imperial architecture, became internationally famous, with a sunken plaza,
an underground concourse, the famous Radio City Music Hall
and landscaped terraces. It is one of the great urban spaces of
this century; none of the later plans Harrison was involved with
seemed to be as successful.

In 1939-40 the firm was chosen to design the Perisphere and
the Trylon theme building for the World of Tomorrow Fair in
New York City. The war intervened, but then in 1947, responsibility for the completion of the design of the United Nations
Headquarters in New York after the work by Le Corbusier,
Oscar Niemeyer and Sven Markelius was given to Harrison, to
be assisted by Max Abramovitz. The result, if perhaps less
inventive than the first scheme of Le Corbusier, was a delicate
and elegant skyscraper. Built in 1949-50, it was one of the first
glazed curtain-wall structures in the city.

In the early 1960s the firm received the commission for the
Lincoln Center for the Performing Arts, a project conceived
some 25 years earlier at the time of the beginning at Rockefeller
Center, but not possible until a site large enough, some 18 acres,
was made available on the west side of Manhattan when blocks
of slums were demolished. The buildings, done between 1959
and 1964, are grouped around a large plaza. Though each building is different in design, all are clad in travertine in a style—
with its ranges of stripped columns—that can be called a loose
version of neoclassicism; Harrison was the coordinator for the
whole center and architect of the Metropolitan Opera House,
with Abramovitz responsible for what is now Avery Fisher
Hall. The whole plan, for better or worse, became the model
for the many cultural centers built throughout the United States
in the 1960s.

Harrison's last great commission was for the Albany South
Mall, a complex of some nine buildings of various shapes and
sizes, including a 44-story office building and an egg-shaped
Performing Arts Center, made of marble and concrete, grouped
upon a platform of promenades, garages and storage spaces,
the whole based in part on an idea Governor Nelson Rockefeller
had borrowed from the Palace of the Dalai Lama in Lhasa,
Tibet. It was a scheme years behind its time, and both the design
and the vast costs of the project were much criticized.

Abramovitz, meanwhile, became involved in other projects
in the Midwest and in France, and in 1978 formed a new
partnership with Michael Harris and James Kingsland, designing among other projects, the Banque Rothschild Building in
Paris. Their work is not now perhaps to our taste, but in their
time, both architects were much honored. In 1957 Harrison
received the Gold Medal of the American Institute of Architects,
the highest award possible.

—DAVID CAST

HARRISON, Peter.

American. Born in Yorkshire, England, 14 June 1716. Died 30
April 1775. Married Elizabeth Pelham. Presumably trained by
William and John Etty of York. Worked in Mercantile Business,
Newport, Rhode Island, 1762; settled in New Haven, Connecti-
cut, 1766; appointed Collector of Customs in New Haven.

Chronology of Works
All dates are approximate
All works either destroyed or altered

1737-39 Drayton Hall Plantation, near Charleston, South Carolina
1749 St. Paul's Church, Halifax, Nova Scotia
1752 Winthrop House, New London, Connecticut
1759 Touro Synagogue, Newport, Rhode Island
1764 Morris House, New York City
1765 Battersea Plantation, Petersburg, Virginia
1770 Trinity Church, Brooklyn, Connecticut
1772 Brattle Congregational Church, Boston
1774 Baptist Meeting House, Providence, Rhode Island
n.d. Christ Church, Cambridge

Peter Harrison: Redwood Library, Newport, Rhode Island, 18th century

n.d.	St. John's Church, St. John's, Newfoundland
n.d.	Cozzens House, Newport, Rhode Island
n.d.	State House, Charleston, South Carolina
n.d.	St. George's Chapel, New York City
n.d.	St. George's Church, Dorchester, South Carolina (steeple)
n.d.	Vassall House (now Longfellow House), Cambridge, Massachusetts
n.d.	St. Paul's Chapel, New York City
n.d.	St. Paul's, Falmouth, Maine
n.d.	Brick Presbyterian Church, New York City
n.d.	Governor Shirley's House, Nassau, Bahamas
n.d.	Virginia Statehouse
n.d.	N. Stuyvesant House, New York City
n.d.	Woodland's Plantation, near Charleston, South Carolina
n.d.	Redwood Library, Newport
n.d.	King's House, Spanishtown, Jamaica

Publications

BOOKS ABOUT HARRISON

BRIDENBAUGH, CARL: *Peter Harrison: First American Architect.* Chapel Hill, North Carolina, 1949.

PIERSON, WILLIAM H., JR.: *American Buildings and Their Architects: The Colonial and Neo-Classical Styles.* Garden City, New York, 1970.

ARTICLES ABOUT HARRISON

BACH, R. F.: "Peter Harrison: Pioneer American Architect." *Architectural Record* 43 (June 1918): 580-81.

COOLIDGE, J.: "Peter Harrison's First Design for King's Chapel, Boston." In *De Artibus Opuscula XL: Essays in Honor of Erwin Panofsky,* edited by M. Meiss. New York, 1961.

KIMBALL, S. F.: "Colonial Amateurs and Their Models: Peter Harrison." *Architecture* 53-54 (June-July 1926): 155-60; 185-90.

METCALF, P.: "Boston Before Bulfinch: Harrison's King's Chapel." *Journal of the Society of Architectural Historians* 13 (March (1954).

NEWCOMB, REXFORD G.: "Peter Harrison, Early American Classicist." *Architect* 10 (June 1928): 315-18.

SCHLESS, N. H.: "Peter Harrison, the Touro Synagogue, and the Wren City Church." *Winterthur Portfolio 8* (1973): 187-200.

*

Peter Harrison has been called both the "First American Architect" and merely a talented but regional amateur with only about eight buildings to his credit. He was neither: Governor Nathaniel Butler was probably the first American architect as early as 1620, when he designed the Statehouse at St. George, Bermuda, in what he thought was the latest Italian style; and Harrison, with 18 documented and 88 less-than-fully documented designs from Newfoundland to Barbados, was hardly regional or amateur.

Thanks to his training (presumably by William Etty of York, 1675-1734, and his son John Etty, 1705-1738), Harrison was equally at home with two supposedly antithetical architectural styles: the restrained English Late Baroque of James Gibbs, John Vanbrugh, Edward Jerman and William Etty, and the neo-Palladianism of the Earl of Burlington, William Kent, Colen Campbell and Henry Flitcroft. Harrison made an admirable synthesis of the two styles.

Like many of his contemporaries, Harrison frequently gleaned ideas from his ample library of architectural pattern books by Gibbs, Campbell, William Halfpenny, Edward Hoppus, Kent, Batty Langley, Robert Morris, William Pain, William Salmon, Abraham Swan and Isaac Ware, among others. Unlike some architects, Harrison never slavishly copied buildings straight from a book, but always had the self-confidence and talent to improve on what he found and weld disparate elements into a vital, unified entity.

Similarly, he was not ashamed to take ideas from existing buildings and express them in his own way. Thus, Vanbrugh's Castle Howard (where Harrison may once have worked) was reflected in Shirley Place; Etty's York Mansion House reappeared at the Brick Market, Newport; the burned-out Virginia Statehouse was reshaped into the Statehouse of Antigua; the paired-column arrangement that Harrison saw under construction at Nicolas Nicole's Church of Ste. Madeleine in Besançon,

France, was introduced at King's Chapel, Boston; Colonel Verrier's unexecuted plan for a two-story cupola on the King's Bastion at Louisbourg, Nova Scotia, bore fruit atop Harrison's St. Paul's Church, Halifax; details from Etty's Holy Trinity Church, Leeds, appeared at Harrison's Christ Church in Cambridge, Massachusetts, and the Brattle Congregational Church in Boston; the arrangement of pillars and galleries at Trinity Church, Newport (1723ff), was reused at St. Paul's in Halifax, Trinity Church in Brooklyn, Connecticut, and probably St. John's Church in St. John's, Newfoundland; and the dark yellow color that Harrison saw on his tour of Andrea Palladio's works in the Veneto in 1748 presumably caused him to specify that his buildings be painted yellow with cream trim, whether they were constructed of stone, brick or wood.

While Harrison was amazingly inventive, even when he was being derivative, he was not above repeating parts of designs that worked well: the elevation for the Cozzens House in Newport, Rhode Island, was recycled for the South Carolina Statehouse; St. George's Chapel in New York City was repeated in only slightly altered form for St. Michael's Church in Charleston, South Carolina, although the local committee subsequently made substantial changes; the tower and steeple of St. James' Church, Lancaster, Pennsylvania, reappeared with slightly different proportions for St. George's Church, Dorchester, South Carolina; the Winthrop House, New London, Connecticut, with its surprisingly unacademic gambrel roof, was repeated with minor changes in five other houses just north of Boston; the Vassall (now called Longfellow) House, Cambridge, Massachusetts, was the first of nine variations of a theme using applied giant Ionic pilasters; St. Paul's Chapel, New York City, and the Baptist Meeting House, Providence, were two different interpretations of a Gibbs design, and further variations of the same theme appeared at St. Paul's in Falmouth, Maine, the Brattle Congregational Church in Boston, and the Brick Presbyterian Church in New York City; the theme of a wide, astylar, pedimented breakfront was introduced in no fewer than 18 buildings, and similar one-bay breakfronts were given to a further seven.

Harrison's innovations included the first true dome in British America (Governor Shirley's House, Nassau); the first double-decked, neo-Palladian portico in America (Drayton Hall, near Charleston, followed by the new Virginia Statehouse, the N. Stuyvesant House in New York, and Battersea Plantation, Petersburg, Virginia); the first giant porticoes on American buildings other than churches (Woodlands Plantation, near Charleston; Redwood Library, Newport; the King's House, Spanishtown, Jamaica; and Morris House, New York). Harrison's most famous invention was rusticated wooden siding (what George Washington called "rusticated boards"), occasioned by Governor Shirley not being able to afford to build Harrison's design in stone for Shirley Place in 1746. This was the first American architectural invention to travel to Europe.

Harrison had also been well grounded in military architecture, which enabled him to understand the Louisbourg fortifications in 1744. His unexecuted plan for Fort George, Newport, was completely up to date with the latest European theories of how best to use a site like Goat Island to protect Newport. The plan is one of only three of his drawings that survive, and all three show him to have been an excellent draftsman.

Harrison took good advantage of opportunities offered to him. When he was ready to begin his own architectural career at age 21, Britain had entered a slump that provided little work even for experienced architects. Accordingly, he signed on to work on a ship commanded by his older brother, Joseph. When Joseph's ship stopped at various American ports, Peter began seeking out architectural commissions in those ports (Drayton Hall, near Charleston, and Stratford Hall, Virginia, probably being among his first—an impressive start). He continued this procedure after he had been promoted to captain of his own ship.

In 1744 he was captured at sea by the French and taken prisoner to the fortress at Louisbourg, Nova Scotia, where he quickly made friends with Colonel Verrier, the fortress architect. Surreptitiously, Harrison copied Verrier's plans of the fortress and harbor, and, upon his release in a prisoner exchange, presented the plans to Massachusetts Governor William Shirley. Shirley used the plans to persuade his reluctant legislature to support his planned attack on Louisbourg, which he did successfully in April 1745. The purpose of the attack was to draw out French General d'Anville, who had planned to invade British America from France in June of that year; without the Louisbourg distraction, the French doubtless would have captured all of British America (including the West Indies), which lay completely undefended while Britain used its soldiers and fleets to defend Britain against Bonnie Prince Charlie's French-financed invasion. At the 1748 peace conference, France traded nearly all of British India it had just captured in exchange for Louisbourg, so Harrison's initiative may fairly be said to have preserved both North America and India for the British Empire.

Shirley rewarded Harrison for his invaluable part in scuttling the French plans by commissioning him to design a fabulous mansion outside Boston, Shirley Place; by suggesting to other British colonies that they show their gratitude by hiring Harrison to design any important buildings they might need; and by encouraging Harrison to visit France while Shirley was attending the peace conference. Once in France, Harrison may have joined Verrier for a tour of Besançon and for a firsthand look at Palladio's buildings in northern Italy.

Before his departure for Europe, Harrison had married Elizabeth Pelham, a relation both of Mrs. Shirley and of the British prime minister; she was the wealthiest heiress in Newport. The family settled at Leamington Farm in Newport in a handsome villa designed by Harrison. The house still stands on Harrison Avenue, but in unrecognizable shape. Matching portraits of Peter and Elizabeth Harrison by Nathaniel Smibert are in a private collection, but copies are on view at the Redwood Library in Newport. In 1766 Harrison moved to New Haven, Connecticut, where he was given the post of royal customs collector after the resignation of his brother Joseph. Shortly before Harrison's death in late April 1775, a protest mob broke into his house and destroyed the contents, including the entire priceless collection of his designs, which has made it much more difficult for researchers to follow Harrison's career.

Harrison designed more than 100 buildings (including 24 churches and 23 public or government buildings) in every major British colony from Newfoundland to Barbados. If Harrison had remained in Britain, he might have achieved the kind of status accorded someone like John Carr of York. In his career in America, however, Harrison stands head and shoulders above any other architects who lived in America in his lifetime, based on the scope, sophistication and imagination of his designs.

—JOHN F. MILLAR

HARRISON, Thomas.

British. Born in Richmond, Yorkshire, England, 1744. Died in Chester, 29 March 1829. Studied in Rome, 1769-76. Worked independently as architect and bridge builder, Chester; county surveyor, Cheshire, 1815.

Chronology of Works

All in England unless noted
† Work no longer exists

1783-88	Skerton Bridge, Lancaster
1786-99	Lancaster Castle, Lancaster (completed by J. M. Gandy in 1802-23)
1788-93	St. Mary's Bridge, Derby (rebuilding)
1788-1822	Chester Castle, Cheshire
1791-97	Stramongate Bridge, Kendal (rebuilding)
1793-94	Kennet House, Clackmannanshire†
1796-99	Broomhall, Fife, Scotland
1800-03	Lyceum, Liverpool
1802-06	Portico Library, Manchester (altered in 1922)
1805-09	Exchange, Manchester†
1808-10	North Gate, Cheshire
1810	Moel Fammau Monument, Denbighshire, Wales†
1811-15	Church of Our Lady and St. Nicholas, Liverpool (steeple)
1814-16	Lord Hill Column, Shrewsbury (original design by Edward Haycock)
1816-17	Anglesey Column, Plas Newydd, Wales
1821-23	St. Martin's Lodge, Chester
1824-25	Hawkstone Citadel, Shropshire
1827-29	Grosvenor Bridge, Cheshire (not completed until 1831)

Publications

ARTICLES ABOUT HARRISON

CROOK, J. MORDAUNT: "The Architecture of Thomas Harrison." *Country Life* 149 (15 and 22 April, 6 May 1971): 876-879, 944-947, 1088-1091.
OCKRIM, M. A. R.: "The Life and Work of Thomas Harrison of Chester, 1744-1829." Ph.D. dissertation. University of London, Courtauld Institute, 1988.
OCKRIM, M. A. R.: "Thomas Harrison and the Rebuilding of Chester Castle: A History and Reassessment." *Chester Archaeological Society Journal* 66 (1983): 57-76.
PIROTTA, LUIGI: "Thomas Harrison architetto inglese accademico di San Luca per sovrana motu proprio." *Strenna dei romanisti* 21 (1960): 257-263.
STILLMAN, DAMIE: "British Architects and Italian Architectural Competitions, 1758-1780." *Journal of the Society of Architectural Historians* 32 (1973): 43-66.

*

In all of Thomas Harrison's work his strength was the understanding and handling of pure masonry forms; C.R. Cockerell noted that "it is in the great intelligence of the masonry that Harrison's merit lies" and Reginald Blomfield later praised him as "almost, if not quite, the first architectural genius in the kingdom, with a more clear apprehension of the principles of the art and a more accurate knowledge of the structural department of it than, perhaps, any man of his day."

Harrison's most important work, which he won in competition in February 1786, was the rebuilding of Chester Castle in an innovatory Greek Revival style. The exterior is distinguished by its sobriety, long low silhouette and powerful handling of masonry. It included felons' and debtors' jails, shire hall and offices, armory, barracks and grand propylaeum, and occupied him for almost 30 years (1788-1815). The polygonal plan of the felons' jail, an outstanding solution to the design of the reformed prison, was based on William Blackburn's Northleach Bridewell, Gloucestershire (1785); the shire hall portico was the first large-scale application in Britain of a baseless, unfluted, primitivistic Greek Doric order, here modeled freely on the Tuscan order as described by Vitruvirus, and remarkable for its gigantic proportions. The interior hemicycle was inspired by Jacques Gondoin's École de Chirurgie, Paris (1769-75), though Harrison introduced a simplified Ionic Ilissus order.

At about the same time, in 1786-99, he was working on the reconstruction of Lancaster Castle in a Gothic style to complement the existing building. The shire hall (circa 1791-92) was a Gothic rendering of Chester, and the male felons' prison (1792-93) was a hybrid of the polygonal and radial jail plans used by Blackburn. Harrison's reputation as a public architect was made with these structures and others such as the Liverpool Lyceum (1800-03), and Portico Library (1802-06) and Exchange (1805-09) in Manchester, all early instances of Greek Revival buildings.

Before he designed the public buildings, however, Harrison had established himself as a bridge builder, exercising his engineering skills as well as his architectural talents; again, his strength was in the understanding of masonry construction and the handling of massive forms. Following seven years of study in Rome (1769-76), Harrison had stayed briefly in London before returning to Richmond, from where he sent some exhibits to the Royal Academy: a national monument (1779) and two elevations of a bridge across the Thames (1780). His architectural career was launched in 1783 when he won the competition for the Skerton Bridge, Lancaster. From then on, bridge building occupied him throughout his career.

The Skerton Bridge (completed in 1788) had elliptical arches and a level surface across the river, a device never before used in England on a large scale, but pioneered in France by Jean-Rodolphe Perronet at his celebrated Neuilly-sur-Seine, Paris (1768-74). Probably because of the Skerton Bridge's success, Harrison was commissioned to rebuild St. Mary's Bridge, Derby (1788-93), and the Stramongate Bridge, Kendal (1791-97); both were more modest interpretations of the same theme. In addition, Harrison held an unofficial appointment as bridge master of Lancashire (1792) and worked on several Cheshire bridges from 1800 to 1805. He received the county surveyorship of Cheshire in 1815, after having carried out the duties for 15 years. He also experimented with laminated timber constructions of his own devising at Warrington (1812, demolished) and Cranage (1816, demolished). Although neither was a practical success, they were daring works and the first of their type to be built in England; such structures were not developed until John Green considered them for his Tyne Bridge, Scotswood, in 1827-28.

Harrison's final and greatest work of engineering was the Grosvenor Bridge, Chester, begun 1827 and not completed until 1833, after his death. It was then—at 200 feet—the largest single-span masonry arch in the world. It appears almost too weak to bear its load, but the beautiful proportions are a merit rather than a defect. Harrison's opinions were respected, and he was consulted in several important commissions, including the Eden Bridge, Carlisle (1805), the Strand (later known as the Waterloo) Bridge (1809) and the Ouse Bridge, York (1810). This made him known to engineers—the Rennies, William Jessop, Jesse Hartley and Thomas Telford—as well as to architects.

Domestic architecture was a small but important part of his practice. His houses, apart from the triangular, castellated Hawkstone Citadel, Shropshire (1824), were generally of two types: a plain, fashionable style like that of Samuel Wyatt, characterized by finely cut masonry, minimal motifs, tripartite windows and domed bows, e.g., Kennet House, Clackmannanshire (1793-94, demolished); and the idyllic stucco villa with wide eaves, resembling the work of John Nash and Henry

Holland, e.g., St. Martin's Lodge, Chester (1821-23, for himself). His plans developed from the villa type favored by Robert Adam and the Wyatts into more asymmetrical arrangements of the principal rooms. His only large house was Broomhall, Fife (1796-99, for Thomas, seventh earl of Elgin), and his suggestion that Elgin use his embassy to Constantinople to gather details of Greek architecture and sculpture resulted in the eventual acquisition of the "Elgin marbles."

Harrison was the leading Greek Revivalist of the northwest of England, pioneering the baseless Doric and a simplified Ionic order with great assurance. His public works are characterized by their constructive aspects, pure geometrical shape, and refinement and simplification of a limited number of motifs. His domestic works are of great external simplicity.

Harrison's abilities and professional character were respected and admired by his contemporaries. He was an architect of national stature, but because of his retiring nature remained in the northwest, where his major works ensure his reputation.

—MOIRA RUDOLF

HAUSSMANN, Georges-Eugène.

French. Born in Paris, France, in 1809. Died in Paris, 9 January 1891. Studied at the Lycée Henri IV, College Bourbon, and at the University of Paris Law School. Secretary-general of the prefecture of the Department of the Vienne in western France, 1830-70; prefect, Department of the Var, 1849; prefect, Department of the Yonde, 1850; prefect, Department of the Gironde, 1851; involved with the rebuilding of Paris under Napoleon III during the 1850s and 1860s.

Publications

BOOKS BY HAUSSMANN

HAUSSMANN, GEORGES-EUGÈNE: *Mémoires du Baron Haussmann.* 3 vols. Paris, 1890-93.

BOOKS ABOUT HAUSSMANN

CHAPMAN, J. M., and CHAPMAN, BRIAN: *The Life and Times of Baron Haussmann: Paris in the Second Empire.* London, 1957.
DES CARS, JEAN, and PINON, PIERRE: *Paris-Haussmann.* Paris, 1991.
EARLS, IRENE A.: *Napoleon III: L'architecte et l'urbaniste de Paris.* Levallois, France, 1991.
GAILLARD, JEANNE: *Paris la ville: L'urbanisme parisien à l'heure d'Haussmann: Des provinciaux aux parisiens; La vocation ou les vocations parisiennes.* Paris, 1977.
HALL, P.: *Cities of Tomorrow.* London, 1988.
LAMEYRE, G.: *Haussmann, préfet de Paris.* Paris, 1958.
LAROZE, G.: *Le Baron Haussmann.* Paris, 1932.
LAVEDAN, PIERRE: *Histoire de l'urbanisme à Paris.* Paris, 1975.
MALET, HENRI: *Le Baron Haussmann et la rénovation de Paris.* Paris, 1973.
PINKNEY, DAVID H.: *Napoleon III and the Rebuilding of Paris.* Princeton, New Jersey, 1958.
REAU, LOUIS; LAVEDAN, PIERRE, et al.: *L'oeuvre du Baron Haussmann, préfet de la Seine, 1853-1870.* Paris, 1954.
SAALMAN, HOWARD: *Haussmann: Paris Transformed.* New York, 1971.

Georges-Eugène Haussmann: Boulevards, Paris, France, 1853ff.

Georges-Eugène Haussmann, a prefect of the Department of the Seine River, was solely responsible for the construction and rebuilding of Paris during the 1850s and 1860s. He worked initially under the decree of Emperor Napoleon III in this project, which proved to be one of the most audacious, dynamic and time-consuming.

Haussmann's background was aristocratic and Bonapartist. He received his education at the Lycée Henri IV, the College Bourbon and the University of Paris Law School. After the Revolution of 1830, he was appointed prefecture of the Department of the Vienne which he held from 1831 to 1870. There followed after the Revolution of 1848 his being elevated to the post of prefect of the Department of Var. And in 1850 he was involved in the Department of the Yonne and the next year made prefect of the Department of the Gironde. These appointments were made possible through his allegiance to Louis-Napoleon Bonaparte.

By 1853 the emperor summoned him to design, renovate and rebuild Paris. He wanted Haussmann to make Paris the seat of his complete imperial power; to model the city to adjust and fit into the concepts, modes and population growth brought on by the industrial revolution; and to create a city that would exemplify a strong, central government.

To these dictums Haussmann devoted his energy for the following 17 years. First, he had old buildings razed, had some 90 miles of private and civic structures constructed and streets newly dug; 4,400 acres of parks and gardens were designed—the most noted were the beauteous Bois de Boulogne and Bois de Vincennes. In addition, he created a plan to bring in 33 million gallons of spring water and construct some 354 miles of sewers. The latter put an end to the discharge of waste water into the Seine River, demonstrating Haussmann's ecological farsightedness.

Most interesting were his designs for city planning. He used concepts, ideas and classic-appearing elements adopted from the École des Beaux-Arts, that is, mathematically oriented streets with exact perspectives and straight lines, and buildings that were the same in height and physical appearance. His avenues, such as the Boulevard Voltaire and Boulevard de Sebastopol, were picturesque and innovative, as they emphasized buildings such as Charles Garnier's Opéra. Haussmann's eight avenues that radiated outward from the Arc de Triomphe and Place de l'Etoile and Avenue de l'Opéra proved to be innovations in "radial" city-planning.

Haussmann characteristically designed buildings that stood four stories in height, and showed pilasters of the Corinthian order and round rooflines. These were seen on noted thoroughfares such as the Place du Théâtre-François, Place de l'Opéra and Place Saint-Michel.

As France evolved into the Second Empire period, classically inspired structures appeared under Haussmann's direction. Noteworthy were the Palaise de Justice (1857-68), whose west facade was designed by Louis-Joseph Duc, and the Tribunal de Commerce (1860-65) built by Antoine-Nicolas Bailly. These, plus numerous schools, hospitals, *maines* and army barracks echoed classic motifs. There even followed Haussmann's use of new industrial materials, including iron and glass, which were employed by his former *confrère* and schoolmate, Victor Baltard. This was observed in market pavilions from 1854 to 1866.

Haussmann will always remain a controversial architect. Those opposing him have condemned his razing of old Paris' historical buildings, his ultimate failure to relieve the city's overpopulation of congested areas, and his creation of confusing traffic patterns in his designs of converging avenues, boulevards and streets. Yet, his undaunted desire to plan beautiful and picturesque parks and physical open spaces of landscape within a crowded city's matrix was a positive characteristic for which he will be remembered.

Haussmann had the capacity of not destroying or wiping away the old and tried. His plans kept alive and blended the new with the old as he combined architecture of the 13th century with that of the 19th. His far-reaching designs and ideas spread to other French cities—Avignon, Toulouse and Lyons, and even to outside metropolises such as Rome, Brussels, Mexico City and Philadelphia. He was, in essence, the quintessential designer and theoretician, whose ideas, though considered brazen and revolutionary at their time, did herald an expression that inspired many modern architects and city planners.

—GEORGE M. COHEN

HAVILAND, John.

American. Born in Somerset, England, 15 December 1792. Died on 2 March 1852. Trained in office of architect James Elmes, London. Established own practice, Philadelphia, 1816. Professor at the Franklin Institute, Philadelphia, 1824-30.

Chronology of Works
All in the United States unless noted
* Approximate dates
† Work no longer exists

1812-13	Chapel of St. John the Evangelist, Chichester, England
1819-20	Moses Moody Villa, Haverhill, Massachusetts

1820-22	First Presbyterian Church, Philadelphia, Pennsylvania†
1821-37	Eastern State Penitentiary, Philadelphia
1822-24	St. Andrew's Episcopal Church (St. George's Greek Orthodox Church), Philadelphia, Pennsylvania
1824-26	Pennsylvania Institution for the Education of the Deaf and Dumb (Philadelphia College of Art), Philadelphia, Pennsylvania
1825-26	Franklin Institute (Atwater Kent Museum), Philadelphia, Pennsylvania
1825-28	Arcade, Philadelphia, Pennsylvania†
1826-27	Arcade, New York City†
1826-33	United States Naval Hospital, Port Nelson, Virginia
1827-28	Walnut Street Theater, Philadelphia, Pennsylvania (remodeling)
1828	Chinese Pagoda and Labyrinthine Garden, Philadelphia†
1830	Colonnade Row, Philadelphia†
1830-31	Miner's Bank, Pottsville, Pennsylvania†
1831-33*	Independence Hall, Philadelphia, Pennsylvania (restoration of Assembly Room)†
1833-36	Missouri Penitentiary, Jefferson City, Missouri
1833-36	New Jersey Penitentiary, near Trenton, New Jersey
1834-37*	Rhode Island Penitentiary, Providence, Rhode Island
1835-38	Halls of Justice and House of Detention (The Tombs), New York City
1836	Essex County Court House and Jail, Newark, New Jersey†
1837-38	Whig and Cliosophic Society Buildings, Princeton University, Princeton, New Jersey†
1838	Arkansas Penitentiary, Little Rock, Arkansas†
1838	Pennsylvania Fire Insurance Company, Philadelphia, Pennsylvania
1838-41	Philip Syng Physick (Roberts) House, Philadelphia, Pennsylvania†
1846-48	Berks County Prison, Reading, Pennsylvania†
1848-51	Lancaster County Prison, Pennsylvania
1848-51	Pennsylvania State Insane Asylum, Harrisburg, Pennsylvania†
1850	Metropolitan Hotel (Brown's Hotel), Washington, D.C.†

Publications

BOOKS BY HAVILAND

The Builder's Assistant. With Hugh Bridport. 3 vols. Philadelphia, 1818-21.
Young Carpenter's Assistant (ed.). Text by Owen Biddle. Philadelphia, 1830.
An improved and enlarged edition of Biddle's The Young Carpenter's Assistant; . . . Revised and corrected with several additional articles and forty-eight new designs . . . by John Haviland, Architect. Philadelphia, 1837.

BOOKS ABOUT HAVILAND

CARROTT, RICHARD: *The Egyptian Revival: Its Sources, Monuments and Meaning, 1808-1858.* Berkeley, California, 1978.
CRAWFORD, WILLIAM: *Report on the Penitentiaries of the United States.* London, 1834.
HAMLIN, TALBOT: *Greek Revival Architecture in America.* New York, 1944.
HITCHCOCK, HENRY-RUSSELL: *American Architectural Books.* New York, 1976.

John Haviland: Eastern Penitentiary, Philadelphia, Pennsylvania, 1821-37

TEETERS, NEGLEY K., and SHEARER, JOHN D.: *The Prison at Philadelphia.* New York, 1957.

A View and Description of the Eastern Penitentiary of Philadelphia. Philadelphia, 1830.

ARTICLES ABOUT HAVILAND

BAIGELL, MATTHEW ELI: "John Haviland in Pottsville." *Journal of the Society of Architectural Historians* 26 (1967): 307-309.

BAIGELL, MATTHEW ELI: "John Haviland in Philadelphia, 1818-1826." *Journal of the Society of Architectural Historians* 25 (1966): 197-208.

BAIGELL, MATTHEW ELI: "John Haviland." Ph.D. dissertation, University of Pennsylvania, Philadelphia, 1965.

GILCHRIST, AGNES ADDISON: "John Haviland before 1816." *Journal of the Society of Architectural Historians* 20 (1961).

JOHNSTON, NORMAN B.: "John Haviland: Jailor to the World." *Journal of the Society of Architectural Historians* 23 (May 1964): 101-105.

NEWCOMB, REXFORD G.: "John Haviland, Early American Architectural Specialist." *Architect* 11 (December 1928): 285-288.

TEETERS, NEGLEY K.: "The Early Days of the Eastern State Penitentiary." *Pennsylvania History* (October 1949).

*

Of the many notable architects practicing in Philadelphia in the early 19th century, few were more innovative than John Haviland, as the range of his commissions demonstrated. Like his contemporaries, he was influenced, but not confined, by the revival of classicism; in his best-known work, the Eastern Penitentiary, he abandoned the style of the Greek Revival altogether. Exhibited in his works was a willingness to experiment with materials as well as styles. The familiarity with both neoclassicism and various means of construction can be traced to the years before his arrival in the United States.

As an apprentice to James Elmes in London, young Haviland learned the vocabulary of neoclassicism and supervised the construction of the Chapel of St. John the Evangelist in Chichester—a church whose design was inspired by the Tower of the Winds in Athens and whose gallery was supported by cast-iron pillars. Further exposure to this means of construction was afforded by his employment in the Imperial Corps of Engineers in Russia. Only after his arrival in Philadelphia in 1816, however, did his practice flourish.

Among his first contributions to the architecture of the New World was the publication of *The Builder's Assistant,* whose illustrations of the Greek orders undoubtedly aided the spread of the popularity of the Greek Revival. Included were comments on the relationship between domestic architecture and its site, a hallmark of the picturesque; his attention to this topic has been cited as an early introduction of this taste in the United States.

Two of his early works—the Cridland Villa in Roxborough, Pennsylvania, and Moody Villa in Haverhill, Massachusetts—exhibited the influence of the Greek Revival, but on his own terms: careful observance of proportions, an emphasis on the rectangular and horizontal in the composition of the villa, and the manner in which the facade revealed the disposition of interior space have been cited as examples of his interpretation of Greek architecture; the influence of the picturesque was revealed in the inclusion of porches and greenhouses, which were attached to the villas.

Yet Haviland was willing to imitate closely models from antiquity, as his two designs in an exhibition in 1817 at the Pennsylvania Academy of the Fine Arts, "A Proposed Design for a National Bank" and "Ground Plan of a National Bank," reportedly did. Two designs for churches shortly thereafter likewise indicated this inclination. For his designs of the First Presbyterian Church in 1820 and St. Andrew's Episcopal Church in 1822, both in Philadelphia, he relied upon the Temple on the Ilissus in Athens and the Temple of Dionysus at Teos, respectively. The First Presbyterian Church boasted the first facade adopted from a Greek temple on a church in Philadelphia and joined St. John's Cathedral in Boston as the earliest example of this type of facade on a religious institution in the United States. That status did not deter his critics, who observed that the intercolumniations failed to provide the proper proportions. However, the proportions of St. Andrew's were faithfully copied from the Temple of Dionysus, according to Haviland, a fact doubly significant to him, as that temple had been cited as the best example of its type by Vitruvius.

That imitation of the Ionic portico was followed by the simplification of the Doric portico for the Pennsylvania Institution

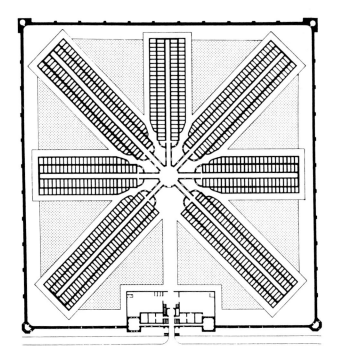

for the Deaf and Dumb in 1824. With little precedent to guide him, Haviland successfully accommodated the program and, moreover, offered a facade, which, although not as archaeological in its representation, exhibited uniformity in its combination of forms. His readiness to experiment was further illustrated in his design for the Franklin Institute in 1825: although he relied upon the Choragic Monument of Thrasyllus as a model, he increased the number, as well as the width, of the piers; the facade was austere and, in spite of its confined site, monumental. That same year yielded the design of the Philadelphia Arcade to house offices and accommodate various commercial activities. Gone was the device of a massive facade, replaced by a screen of arches. Yet a sense of unity remained, as did clarity of organization and restraint in the treatment of ornament—a feature this piece did not share with its source of inspiration, Samuel Ware's Burlington Arcade in London.

For his design of the Eastern Penitentiary, constructed between 1823 and 1829, Haviland chose to abandon the Greek Revival and adopt features inspired by the Gothic Revival and prisons in Britain—turrets, crenellation and a lack of ornament. Widespread in its influence, particularly on the Continent, the radial plan was soon preferred instead of the panopticon; its reception firmly established the architect's reputation.

The works that followed the penitentiary and arcade signaled a shift in style. Characteristics, which have been cited as typical, included the manner in which ornament was displayed more freely on facades, the disparity in the relationship between facade and interior space, and the differentiation between elements of the facade. Two examples were the renovations of the Blight House and the Walnut Street Theater. Experimentation with materials and styles continued, however, with the erection of the first iron facade in the United States on the Miners' Bank in Pottsville, Pennsylvania, and the appearance of motifs from Egyptian architecture on the facade of the Pennsylvania Fire

Insurance Company in Philadelphia and in the details of the Halls of Justice in New York.

—JED PORTER

HAVLÍČEK, Josef.

Czechoslovakian. Born in Prague, Czechoslovakia, 5 May 1899. Died in Prague, 30 December 1961. Studied at the Czech Technical University, Prague, 1916-23, and at the Academy of Fine Arts, Prague, 1923-26; apprenticed with Josef Gočár, Prague 1925-26. In partnership with Karel Honzík, Prague, 1928-36; private practice, Prague, 1936-61. Founder of the Devětsil group, 1920; member of Manes, Sdruzeni architeku, SIA and CIAM (Congrès Internationaux d'Architecture Mode rne); Czechoslovakia's delegate to the Committee of Architects for the United Nations Building, New York, 1947.

Chronology of Works
All in Czechoslovakia

1924-25	Apartment Block, Smíchov, Prague
1926-28	Villa, Smíchov, Prague (with Karel Honzík)
1926-28	Dilo Apartment Block, Štěpánská, Prague (with Honzík)
1926-28	Chicago Department Store, Narodní Trída, Prague (with Jaroslav Polívka)
1927-28	Habich Apartments, Offices and Department Store, Stepánská, Prague (with Polívka)
1929	Villa U Dívcích Hrado, Prague (with Honzík)
1929-34	State Pensions Institute, Žižkov, Prague (with Honzík)
1930	KOL-DOM collective apartment project, Prague
1936	Sanatorium, Poděbrady
1937	Apartment Block, Letná, Prague
1938	Apartment Block, Letohradská, Prague
1950	Regional Dairy and Milk Processing Plant, Strakovice
1952-58	Vitezného Unora Redevelopment, Kladno-Rozdělov (with K. Neumann, V. Hilsky, N. Konerza and E. Kovarík)

Publications

BOOKS BY HAVLÍČEK

Stavby a plány. Prague, 1931.
Návrhy a stavby: 1925-1960. Prague, 1964.

ARTICLES BY HAVLÍČEK

"Economy and Architecture." With Karel Honzík. *Kvart* (1935).
"High Rise Buildings in Boxframe Construction." With K. Neumann. *Architekt*, No. 23 (1958).

BOOKS ABOUT HAVLÍČEK

HONZIK, KAREL: *Architektura vsem.* Prague, 1956.
HONZIK, KAREL: *Cestou k socialistické architekture.* Prague, 1960.
KOLAR, V.: *Skyscrapers.* Prague, 1946.
KOULA, J. E.: *A Book about Czech Architecture.* Prague, 1943.

KREJCAR, JAROMIR (ed.): *L'architecture contemporaine en Tchécoslovaquie*. Prague, 1928.

TEIGE, KAREL: *Contemporary International Architecture*. Prague, 1929.

ARTICLES ABOUT HAVLÍČEK

"Josef Havlícek—Oeuvres." *Cahiers d'Art* (1926).

NAGAO, SHIGETAKE and TOMINAGA, YUZURU: "House at Prague, 1929." *Space Design* (May 1977).

PAGANO, GIUSEPPE: "Storia dell'architettura funzionale." *Casabella* (April 1942).

"The Question of Monumentality." *Architekt SIA*, No. 8 (1944).

SETNICKA, J.: "Modern Architecture in Czechoslovakia." *Vedag* (1931).

"The Work of Josef Havlíček." *Perspective* (Canada) (1948).

"The Work of Josef Havlíček." *Architektura CSR*, No. 4 (1959).

*

Josef Havlíček was one of the leading architects of Czechoslovakia when functionalism reigned there in the 1920s. It was at that time that the architectural language of aesthetic purism began to show functionalist aspects, in layouts, structure and construction techniques, with massing, form and composition more and more determined by a conscientious consideration of a building's functions. The architectural avant-garde in Prague and Brno associated with the Devětsil—a society of progressive writers, artists and architects influenced by the socialist ideals of Soviet constructivism—started producing work comparable to that of Le Corbusier, the Bauhaus, De Stijl and Soviet constructivism. It was amid those developments that Havlíček embarked on his career as an architect.

Havlíček, after studying at the Czech Technical University and the Academy of Fine Arts in Prague, began working in the office of Josef Gočár in 1925. In 1926 he entered a design in the Prague City Hall Competition, and in 1927 he designed an entry for the Nusel Valley Bridge Competition. Havlíček's bridge design is notable for the nine housing towers which serve to hold up the span of the roadway. Among Havlíček's early executed designs in Prague were the Chicago Department Store (1926-28) in the Narodní Třída and the Habich Department Store (1927-28) in the Štěpanska Street. Both buildings were done in collaboration with Jaroslav Polívka. Reinforced-concrete skeletons offered a free plan, and made it possible to use a curtain-wall system and ribbon windows in these buildings. At the Habich store, the facade is articulated with balconies and a section set back from the front. This play of solid and void and of light and shadow gives the building a dynamic appearance.

From 1928 to 1936, Havlíček collaborated with Karel Honzík. Their most important project was the Pensions Institute (1929-34). The design for this building went through several changes during the development stages, particularly in the disposition of volumes. However, the basic cruciform footprint blocks of offices flanked by two residential and commercial wings was retained from the original concept. The complex follows the slope of its site. The Pensions Institute has all the attributes of a functionalist building: a uniform modular system, a well-defined entry, expressed vertical circulation, a roof terrace, and ribbon windows bringing maximum daylight into the free-plan interiors. Shadows are crisp on the pristine white ceramic tiles of the exterior. The building has a bold silhouette, standing out among the red roofs and steeples of historic Prague. The Pensions Institute met with considerable resistance from Prague's older inhabitants, who felt a modern high-rise was out of place in the picturesque old town.

Housing was an important concern for functionalist architects, and the architects in the Devětsil group produced studies of communal housing in the late 1920s and early 1930s. Havlíček was no exception in this regard. The functionalist search for the ideal inexpensive family home emphasized functional layouts and a healthy environment. Sun and air were brought into the houses by means of large openings. Balconies, verandas and roof terraces were designed to extend family life outdoors.

Havlíček designed a tenement house for the Czech Werkbund at the Exhibition of Contemporary Culture held at Brno in 1928. This building exemplified the new functionalist conception of low-income housing. Working with his partner Honzík, Havlíček also applied functionalist principles in the design of Villa U Dívčích Hrado in Prague (1929). The stereotomic volume of the building is lightened by a carved-out loggia, ribbon and porthole windows, and a sculptural circular staircase connecting the living level with the house garden. In 1930 Havlíček and Honzík designed the KOL-DOM, a complex of high-rise collective housing units complete with services and amenities, which was to provide equality in housing. Each unit consisted of two blocks of apartments joined by vertical circulation cores. The blocks were elevated on pilotis, and featured continuous ribbon windows.

In the postwar period, Havlíček intensified his search for the simplification of architectural mass to elementary forms. He also became interested in the design of tall buildings. The 1947 competition design for the United Nations Headquarters in New York City and the Toronto City Hall Competition entry (1958) both explore a pyramidal tripod mass. A central core with three sloped wings to provide structural stability is designed to maximize natural lighting, through the increase in the exterior surface. His continuing research into the architecture of tall buildings was implemented in the series of point towers at a public-housing complex in Kladno-Rozdělov, designed and executed between 1952 and 1958. "We design high-rise housing," Havlíček explained, "so we save the land and the dwellers can use the open space for recreation." The 1958-59 study for a high-rise hotel in the Tatra Mountains and the 1958 study for a library tower exemplify Havlíček's continuing search for a unified expression of structure and architectural form.

Throughout his career, Havlíček adhered to the functionalist dictum that "form follows function," so eloquently expressed first by Louis Sullivan. Sullivan's vision was fully realized in functionalist architecture, and particularly in the work of Josef Havlíček.

—PETER LIZON

HAWKSMOOR, Nicholas.

British. Born in Nottinghamshire, England, ca. 1661. Died in Millbank, Westminster, 25 March 1736. Married Hester Hawksmoor; daughter was Elizabeth Hawksmoor. Clerk for Samuel Mellish, Doncaster; clerk for Christopher Wren; supervisor, Winchester Palace, 1683; clerk of works, Kensington, 1689; clerk of works, Greenwich Hospital, 1698; clerk of works, Whitehall, 1715; secretary to the Board of Works, 1715; senior official, Royal Works; surveyor to the Commissioners of Sewers for Westminster, 1696; surveyor, Fifty New Churches Commission, 1711; Surveyor to Westminster Abbey, 1723; Comptroller of Works, 1721.

Nicholas Hawksmoor: St. Mary Woolnoth, London, England, 1716-24

Chronology of Works
All in England
* Approximate dates
† Work no longer exists

1692-95	Christ's Hospital Writing School, London†
1695-96	King's Gallery, Kensington Palace, London
1695*-1710	Easton Neston, Northamptonshire (later altered)
1699-1707	King William Court, Greenwich Hospital, London (south and west ranges)
1700-03	Queen Anne Block, Greenwich Hospital, London (east range)
1704-05	Orangery, Kensington Palace, London [attributed]
1711-12	Kensington Charity School, London†
1712-13	Old Clarendon Building, Oxford
1712-18	St. Alfege, Greenwich, London
1714-29	Christ Church, Spitalfields, London
1714-29	St. Anne, Limehouse, London
1714-29	St. George-in-the-East, Wapping, London
1716-17	Queen Anne Block (court Loggias), Greenwich Hospital, London
1716-17	St. James's Palace, London (stable yard arcade)
1716-24	St. Mary Woolnoth, London
1716-30	St. George, Bloomsbury, London
1716-35	All Souls College, Oxford (north quadrangle)
1718-24	St. Michael, Cornhill, London (tower)
1722-25	Blenheim Palace, Oxfordshire (Long Library, southeast rooms, Woodstock Gate)
1727-33	St. John, Horselydown, Bermondsey, London (with John James)†
1727-33	St. Luke, Old Street, Finsbury, London (with James)†
1728	Pyramid, Castle Howard, Yorkshire
1729-36	Mausoleum, Castle Howard, Yorkshire (not completed until 1742)
1730*	Carmire Gate, Castle Howard, Yorkshire
1731-35	Temple of Venus, Castle Howard, Yorkshire†
1733-36	Queen's College, Oxford (screen and gateway)
1734-36	Westminster Abbey, London (west towers and gable; not completed until 1745)

Publications

BOOKS ABOUT HAWKSMOOR

COLVIN, H. M. (ed.): *The History of the King's Works, 1660-1782*. London, 1976.
DOWNES, KERRY: *English Baroque Architecture*. London, 1966.
DOWNES, KERRY: *Hawksmoor*. London, 1959.
GOODHART-RENDEL, H. S.: *Nicholas Hawksmoor*. London, 1924.
GREEN, DAVID: *Blenheim Palace*. London, 1951.
SERVICE, ALASTAIR: *The Architects of London*. London, 1979.

ARTICLES ABOUT HAWKSMOOR

CAST, DAVID: ''Seeing Vanbrugh and Hawksmoor.'' *Journal of the Society of Architectural Historians* 43 (December 1984): 310-327.
DE LA RUFFINIERE DU PREY, PIERRE: ''Hawksmoor's 'Basilica after the Primitive Christians': Architecure and Theology.'' *Journal of the Society of Architectural Historians* 48 (March 1989): 38-52.

LANG, S.: "Vanbrugh's Theory and Hawksmoor's Buildings."
    Journal of the Society of Architectural Historians 24 (May
    1965).
LANG, S.: "By Hawksmoor out of Gibbs." *Architectural Review*
    (April 1949).
WEBB, GEOFFREY: "The Letters and Drawings of Nicholas
    Hawksmoor Relating to the Building of the Mausoleum at
    Castle Howard." *Walpole Society* 19 (1931): 111-164.

*

Nicholas Hawksmoor, an English architect active in the early
18th century who was the associate, friend and colleague of John
Vanbrugh, is known now especially for his London churches, the
most famous of which may be Christ Church, Spitalfields. Like
Vanbrugh, Hawksmoor worked in a style that was in its forms
essentially classical. However, the designs of Vanbrugh and
Hawksmoor openly played on the emotions also, in a way
classical architecture never had. He incorporated historical references to Gothic and Elizabethan architecture into his secular
work, and, in the churches, allusions both to the older ecclesiastical buildings of England and also the basilican forms of early
Christianity.

Like Vanbrugh, and for the same artistic reasons, Hawksmoor
was criticized for his designs, especially by Lord Burlington
and the classicizing architects around him who came to power in
England in the 1720s and 1730s; they condemned Hawksmoor's
work for the variety of motifs and for what could always be
called its mixed and individual style. But Hawksmoor escaped
some of the abuse Vanbrugh incurred, because he was a far less
social or political figure and more a simple working architect.

He was engaged, for most of his career, not by private patrons
but by public bodies such as the universities of Oxford and
Cambridge and the church commissioners in London. He did
produce a number of designs for private patrons for new or
remodeled houses, but only at Easton Neston, Northamptonshire, does any of that work survive. There, Hawksmoor
designed the exterior for a building executed in the 1690s by
the general office of Christopher Wren.

Hawksmoor was born in Nottinghamshire, the son of a yeoman farmer of some standing. Little is known of his early
education, but around 1680 he entered the service of Wren as
what was called his domestic clerk. From about 1684 onward,
he was clearly associated with nearly all of Wren's works, most
notably at St. Paul's Cathedral, where he is considered to have
been responsible for the design of the two west towers. It was
Wren who led Hawksmoor to his first projects, at Easton Neston,
St. Mary's in Warwick (unexecuted), and at the Writing School
for Christ's Hospital in London. And it was through Wren that
Hawksmoor obtained his several offices at Kensington Palace,
where he was made clerk of works in 1689, at Winchester
Palace in 1683, at Chelsea Hospital and at Greenwich, where
he was clerk of the works for some 37 years. After his association with Wren, Hawksmoor enjoyed the support of Vanbrugh,
working with him at Castle Howard and at Blenheim; after
Vanbrugh's dismissal from Blenheim in 1716, Hawksmoor took
his place and saw the building through all its later stages. On
the one side, Hawksmoor was able to lend to Vanbrugh a level
of technical and practical experience that, as Vanbrugh knew, he
lacked. Yet to Wren, Hawksmoor was able to suggest, especially
after 1700, a range of imagination and drama that his more
disciplined master had never realized.

It was in 1711, on the passing of the act of Parliament for
the building of 50 new churches in London, that Hawksmoor
was appointed one of the surveyors, together with John James.
It was from that position that he supervised the building of the
famous London churches: St. George, Bloomsbury; St. George-
in-the-East, Wapping, Stepney; St. Mary Woolnoth; St. Alphege, Greenwich; and St. Anne, Limehouse. All are extraordinary and individual designs.

St. Mary Woolnoth, the smallest, which was the church of
the lord mayor of London, has a front articulated with steps of
columns and bands of heavy rustication so disposed that they
allude both to the details of the church that was replaced but
also, despite the classical forms, to the fronts of medieval
churches with two small facing towers. St. Anne, Limehouse,
has an apparently more freestanding front, the whole looking
not unlike the mix of Gothic and classical forms and plan that
Wren had been able to work out so well for all of his London
churches. But as a note from Hawksmoor confirms, the tower
and steeple were carefully based on the description of the Tower
of the Winds in Athens; he filled out the sides and the east end
with window elements taken from the work of Hugh May, and
for the great eastern end, Hawksmoor relied on his knowledge
of the triumphal arches of the Romans. St. Alphege, Greenwich,
had in its first plan a buttressed, octagonal lantern of the kind
Hawksmoor used later at St. George-in-the-East. The portico,
which has an arch within it, recalls the first design by Wren
for the portico at St. Paul's.

Christ Church, Spitalfields, has elements taken from the work
of Leon Battista Alberti and from classical porticoes and the
spires of Gothic churches. And at St. George-in-the-East, with
its corner towers and the rising belfries, there are elements
borrowed from Sebastiano Serlio, Giacomo da Vignola and
an earlier design for St. Mary-le-Bow by Wren. St. George,
Bloomsbury, has for its main front another great portico, this one
hexastyle and based on the Pantheon. The steeple is modeled,
through a reconstruction of the design by Wren, on the Mausoleum of Halicarnassus, topped here by a statue of the new king,
George I.

These are the record and the iconography of the details. The
plans of all these churches seem to be based on the basilican
form which Hawksmoor could have known from a text such as
Joseph Bingham's *Origines Ecclesiasticae* (1708). On occasion,
however, as at Christ Church, Hawksmoor also incorporated a
hint of the centralized church plans of the Renaissance, which
he would have known from Alberti and Andrea Palladio. Hawksmoor could think in many modes. If necessary he could work
very soberly, and in his designs for Greenwich Hospital, the
Clarendon Building in Oxford and the mausoleum at Castle
Howard, he approached a style that was as grave and grand as
anything the Romans had built. At other times he worked in
the Gothic style, less happily perhaps at All Souls College,
Oxford, but more delicately at Beverly Minister, Yorkshire, and
at Westminster Abbey, London, where he designed the two
west towers. Then, at some of the garden structures built at
Castle Howard—the Pyramid, the Carrmire Gate and the so-
called Four Faces—where he was free to be imaginative, he
displayed a variety of invention in both Gothic and classical
styles that was extraordinary. Perhaps nobody in English architecture has understood the disposition of form better than Hawksmoor.

Hawksmoor did not travel to France or Italy; he read very
widely, however, and it was from that reading and from the
plans included in the many recent archaeological books that
were appearing all over Europe that he was able to build for
himself a rich and wide language of classical forms. Hawksmoor
said very little about his own work, but in a comment that
scholars have studied very carefully, he referred to a design by
Vanbrugh as being based, as he put it, both on "Strong Reason"
and "Good Fancy." The term "Reason" is not unusual here;

Wren would have said as much about the sources of his architecture. But the word "Fancy" is new and interesting, for it connects Hawksmoor, however directly or indirectly, to a set of artistic concerns and opinions spoken of a few years earlier by the philosopher Thomas Hobbes. Hobbes recognized what judgment is: the reasoning process by which, to the artists of the Renaissance, all art should be judged. But perhaps from his essential materialism, Hobbes came to think of art not as the imitation of an idea so much as a type of mere resemblance, based then not on reason alone but on the mobile and even irrational constitutive faculty of Fancy, which ranges, as he put it, over the forms of a work of art as a spaniel might over the fields, tracking for meanings and tying to what it sees any number of accidental associations and allusions. It was this notion, rather than the older principles of propriety and order—though Hawksmoor did use the phrase "Good Fancy"—that encouraged Hawksmoor to embody in his architecture the forms and associations of history. His designs for the churches newly named for the queen or then the patron saint of England alluded to the older buildings of England and, in those allusions, could stand as symbols of the whole program of redefinition that the Church of England was engaged with in those years. No Palladian would ever have tried so much.

The work that Hawksmoor produced was, for these very reasons, inimitable, and apart from Henry Joynes, who worked with him for many years, he had no pupils and no followers. The end of Hawksmoor's career was not as successful as its beginning. Some of his proposals for Castle Howard and Blenheim, in the changing tastes of the 1720s, were modified to suit his Palladian critics. At Oxford and Cambridge, where he did a little work, Hawksmoor was gradually supplanted by the new architect, James Gibbs, who worked in a more traditional, Italianate manner. In 1718 Hawksmoor lost his position in the Royal Works, and in 1729 Thomas Ripley was appointed in his place as surveyor at Greenwich Hospital. Early on in his career, Hawksmoor had had Vanbrugh to support him and advance his claims when he was not bold enough to do so himself; but Vanbrugh died in 1726, and there was nobody left to help him.

All of Hawksmoor's greatest work was done, however, and most of it—being for such public bodies as the church commissioners and the universities—survived, if sometimes neglected, to be rediscovered by architects and critics at the beginning of this century. More than 500 of Hawksmoor's drawings are known, scattered among the major collections in England, and many of them were published in the volumes of the Wren Society, especially the text devoted to Greenwich Hospital. The extensive and interesting correspondence between Hawksmoor and the earl of Carlisle about the modifications in the design for the mausoleum at Castle Howard was printed in the Papers of the Walpole Society.

Hawksmoor's interest in town planning was notable, too, though nothing came of his schemes; designs survive for both Oxford and Cambridge, and in 1736, the year of his death, he put out a pamphlet with a proposal for a new bridge at Westminster. In the end, the bridge first built there between 1739 and 1747 was designed by the Swiss engineer Charles Labelye.

—DAVID CAST

HEJDUK, John.

American. Born in New York City, 19 July 1929. Married Gloria Fiorentino, 1951; two children. Studied at Cooper Union College of Art and Architecture, New York City, 1947-50; University of Cincinnati, Cincinnati, Ohio, 1950-52, B.Arch.; Graduate School of Design, Harvard University, Cambridge, Massachusetts, 1952-53, M.Arch. Worked for I. M. Pei, New York City, 1947-52; chief designer, A. M. Kinney Associates, 1960; private practice in New York City, since 1965. Instructor in architectural de sign, University of Texas, Austin, Texas, 1954-56; assistant professor of architecture, Cornell University, Ithaca, New York, 1958-60; critic in architectural design, Yale University, New Haven, Connecticut, 1961-64; professor of architecture, from 1964, and dean of the School of Architecture, from 1975, Cooper Union, New York City. Fellow, American Institute of Architects, 1979.

Chronology of Works
All in the United States unless noted

1960   Demlin House, Locust Valley, Long Island, New York
1974-75   Foundation Building restoration, Cooper Union, New York
1986   The Collapse of Time, design and construction of clock element from "Victims" project, Architectural Association School of Architecture, London, England
1988   Tegel Housing and Kreuzberg Tower and Wings, IBA Social Housing, Berlin, Germany
1990-91   House of the Suicide/House of the Mother of the Suicide (elements from the "Lancaster/Hanover Masque"), at Georgia Institute of Technology, Atlanta (1990), and at Prague Castle, Prague, Czechoslovakia (1991)

Publications

BOOKS BY HEJDUK

Three Projects. New York, 1969.
Projects/John Hejduk Exhibition catalog. Paris, 1972.
Fabrications. New York, 1974.
Mask of Medusa: Works 1947-83. New York, 1985.
Victims. London, 1986.
The Collapse of Time and Other Diary Constructions. London, 1987.
Bovisa. New York, 1987.
Vladivostock, Riga, Lake Baikal. New York, 1989.
John Hejduk, Lancaster/Hannover Masque. London, 1989.

BOOKS ABOUT HEJDUK

DIAMONSTEIN, BARBARALEE: *American Architecture Now II.* New York, 1985.
FRAMPTON, KENNETH, and ROWE, COLIN: *Five Architects: Eisenman, Graves, Gwathmey, Hejduk, Meier.* New York, 1972.
John Hejduk, Architect. Zurich, 1973.

ARTICLES ABOUT HEJDUK

"Five on Five." *Architectural Forum* (May 1973).
TEYSSOT GEORGES: "Conversation with John Hejduk." *Lotus* 44/4 (1985).
VAN DEN BURGH, WIM: "John Hejduk's Masques." *Forum* (May 1988).
VIDLER, ANTHONY: "John Hejduk: Vagabond Architecture, Reveries of a Journeyman Architect." *Lotus* 68 (1991).

Principally known as an author and educator, and often seen as a poet and visionary, John Hejduk is an architect whose interests are largely theoretical, and lie in the investigation of form and space. His career as a practicing architect was established primarily through the restoration of one building, that of the Cooper Union Foundation, in 1974-75, as the majority of his projects remain unbuilt. While he has published numerous design projects, his most significant contribution to the architectural field has been in his role as dean of the school of architecture at Cooper Union in New York City, a position he has held since 1975. His open, individualized approach to the teaching of architecture has earned the school a reputation as one of the most progressive institutions for the study of architecture. Emphasizing the concurrent study of such subjects as painting, music and philosophy, Hejduk encourages students to view architecture as part of the fabric of society. In 1988 Hejduk's commitment to quality education was acknowledged by the American Institute of Architects and the Association of Collegiate Schools of Architecture when he was awarded the Topaz Medal for excellence in education.

Born in New York City, Hejduk studied at Cooper Union, then earned his professional degree in architecture at the University of Cincinnati and a master's degree at Harvard. A Fulbright scholarship enabled him to travel to Rome in 1953-54, and upon his return to the United States he was offered a teaching position at the University of Texas, Austin. While in Texas, he produced a number of designs for houses based on Palladian concepts of harmonious space and geometric balance. These experiments established the basis for future design projects. Hejduk saw his time in Texas as personally fruitful; it was there that he met fellow architect Colin Rowe and painter Robert Slutzky, who provided him with inspiration and a supportive environment for his architectural investigations. Prior to settling at Cooper Union in 1964, Hejduk taught at Cornell from 1958 to 1960 and at Yale from 1961 to 1964.

Hejduk's subsequent phase of development again related to domestic planning, and included the design of the "Diamond" Houses. The Diamond Houses, dating from the late 1960s, involved the transformation of a cubist space into architectural terms. Inspired by the De Stijl work of Piet Mondrian and Theo van Doesburg, Hejduk's houses featured a square plan within which the axis had been rotated 45 degrees, questioning traditional notions of frontality and organization. Typically, Hejduk rendered these ideas using axonometric projections, which lent a sculptural, dynamic quality to his drawings.

During the late 1960s Hejduk became associated with a group of architects that included Peter Eisenman, Michael Graves, Charles Gwathmey and Richard Meier, who were known collectively as the New York Five, or simply "the Whites." The Five had all been educated during the 1950s, when the views of the major European architectural figures working in the International Style, such as Le Corbusier, Ludwig Mies van der Rohe and Walter Gropius, prevailed. Although the work of the New York Five was stylistically diverse, the underlying motivation was the same: all five sought to come to terms with the modernist philosophies in which they had been trained. The New York Five published a book in 1972, titled *Five Architects,* which was critically attacked in the press by a second group of architects as being abstract and overly intellectual.

Hejduk's 1974-75 restoration of the Cooper Union Foundation Building, a New York City landmark dating to 1859, perfectly embodied the ideas of the New York Five. As described by *Progressive Architecture* magazine shortly after its completion, the project was really neither an adaptive reuse nor a restoration, but rather a "purification"—a direct reference to its new, sweeping expanses of clean white walls. While the other members of the New York Five, with the possible exception of Peter Eisenman, went on to become allied with the postmodern movement, incorporating referential color and symbols into their designs, Hejduk's work has remained in a fairly consistent modernist vein, and has begun increasingly to incorporate disciplines beyond the world of architecture.

For instance, his recent work is a mix of architectural and sculptural ideas, and includes a series of "masques." Contemporary versions of the dramatic enactments popular during the 16th and 17th centuries, Hejduk's masques include projects such as the 1986 erection of a large-scale public clock in Bedford Square, London, in conjunction with the Architectural Association School of Architecture. The clock, termed "an experimental masque," was composed of monumental numbers arranged vertically in descending order and set within a movable frame, to suggest perhaps the transitory nature of time. The elaborate act of assembly associated with Hejduk's masques emphasizes the notion that process can be as compelling as product.

In the 1980s Hejduk created a series of masques for cities throughout the world, such as his Berlin Masque (1980-81) and the Lancaster/Hanover Masque (1982-83). Envisioning these masques as a novel, imaginative approach to town planning, Hejduk created dwellings for a variety of inhabitants, such as The Retired Actor, The Widow, and The Master Builder, which were never actually executed, but in some way physically referenced the psychology of their proposed occupants.

Hejduk's first built work since the restoration of the Cooper Union Foundation was a villa and a housing complex erected in Berlin in the late 1980s. Part of a larger complex for the International Building Exhibition (IBA), Hejduk's units, although simple in design and free from historical quotation, nevertheless seem to refer to medieval German building traditions through the use of steeply pitched rooflines. The critical success of Hejduk's work in Berlin has proven to the public that he is more than just a paper architect.

—MEREDITH ARMS BZDAK

HENNEBIQUE, François.

French. Born in Neuville-St.-Vaas, near Arras, France, in 1842. Died in 1921. Apprenticed as a stone mason. Worked as an independent contractor, from 1867; established offices in Paris and Brussels, Belgium, as a consulting engineer; opened office in the rue Danton, Paris, 1899. Received patent for reinforced concrete, 1892.

Chronology of Works
All in France unless noted

1894	Refinery of St.-Ouen, Paris
1895	Large Mills, Nantes
1895	Spinning Mill, Tourcoing
1896	Barrois Spinning Mill, Lille
1896	Justice Building, Verviers, Belgium
1897	Bank, Basel, Switzerland
1897	Canal Bridge, Evilard
1897	Flon River Bridge, Lausanne, Switzerland
1897	Frings Spinning Mill, Hellemmes, Lille
1898	Coal Silo, Aniche Mines
1898	Echez River Bridge, Tarbes
1898	Fontaine Workshops, Boulogne-sur-Seine
1899	Lys River Bridge, Ghent, Belgium
1899	Vienne River Bridge, Châtellerault

1900	Grand Palais, Paris
1900	Palais des Lettres, Sciences et Arts, Paris
1900	Petit Palais, Paris
1902	Bormida River Bridge, Millesimo, Italy
1904	Hennebique House, Bourg-la-Reine
1905	Meuse River Bridge, Liège, Belgium
1906	Ill River Bridge, Feldkirch, Austria
1906	Loire River Bridge, Decize
1907	Rhone River Bridge, Pyrimont
1907	Loire River Bridge, D'Imphy
1907	Viaduct, Dewine-Merxem

Publications

BOOKS BY HENNEBIQUE

The Hennebique Armored Concrete System. New York, 1908.

ARTICLES BY HENNEBIQUE

Numerous articles in *Le béton armé* (Paris, 1898-1921) and *Ferro-Concrete* (1909).

BOOKS ABOUT HENNEBIQUE

BILLINGTON, DAVID P.: *The Tower and the Bridge: The New Art of Structural Engineering.* Princeton, New Jersey, 1983.
CHRISTOPHE, PAUL: *Le Béton Armé.* Paris, 1902.
COLLINS, PETER: *Concrete: The Vision of a New Architecture. A Study of Auguste Perret and His Predecessors.* London, 1959.
MARSH, CHARLES F.: *Reinforced Concrete.* New York, 1904.
PEVSNER, NIKOLAUS: *Sources of Modern Design.* London, 1968.

ARTICLES ABOUT HENNEBIQUE

CUSACK, PATRICIA: "Architects and the Reinforced-Concrete Specialist in Britain 1905-1908." *Architectural History* 29 (1986): 183-196.
GUBLER, JACQUES: "Prolégomènes à Hennebique." *Etudes de lettres* 4 (1985): 63-159.
MAILLART, ROBERT: "Das Hennebique-System und seine Anwendungen." *Schweizerische Bauzeitung* 37 (1901).
RITTER, WILHELM: "Die Bauweise Hennebique." *Schweizerische Bauzeitung* 33 (1899).
TWELVETREES, W. NOBLE: "François Hennebique: A Biographical Memoir." *Ferro-Concrete* 13 (1921): 119-144.

*

François Hennebique is one of the modern architects whose place in architectural history has been secured at least as much by his contribution to construction as by his talents in design. Hennebique actually made two important technical contributions to modern architecture: first, he pioneered the design of reinforced concrete structures; second, he pioneered the business of reinforced concrete construction on a large scale.

It was through the second of these contributions that the true significance of the first was realized. Numerous others, such as Joseph Monier in France, may lay legitimate claim to having invented reinforced concrete. It was Hennebique, however, who systematically investigated the possibilities of reinforced concrete construction, developed a complete system of reinforced concrete structural design through sustained empirical experiment, and finally devised the means for using this system in the construction of an extremely large number of buildings throughout the world. Few contemporary careers paralleled his own, as those of Gustave Eiffel, Auguste Perret and Rafael Guastavino y Moreno did in many respects; and even fewer had such a lasting impact on 20th-century architecture, heavily dependent as it has proven on the use of reinforced concrete.

The story of Hennebique's career is the stereotypical story of a self-made man, exploiting all opportunities but mostly just persevering in a single direction. It is probably significant that he grew up in northern France and worked early on in Belgium, both heavily industrialized areas where experimental building in new materials had gone on for decades. Working as a contractor, he believed concrete to be a material potentially attractive to his clients, resistant as it was to fire. In the course of actual building projects, he carried out concerted practical experiments in putting this material to use. Significantly, he paid particular attention to the placement of reinforcing iron bars in the concrete to carry shear and tensile forces. While later engineering research has not found all of Hennebique's calculations to have been absolutely correct, his general approach seems to have been quite sound. Indeed, by this approach he laid the foundation for later work in the theoretical design of concrete frames. Hennebique patented his designs, and the methods for carrying them out, in 1892.

It was at that point that Hennebique began to make his contribution to the development of the modern construction business. Ceasing to work directly as a contractor, he began to function more as an engineer. He eventually employed dozens of draftsmen and professional engineers to specify the structural requirements of buildings under design by or for client architects and developers. Meanwhile, he contracted with agents in various countries to arrange for the correct execution of his plans by certified, licensed contractors. One such agent was L. G. Mouchel, who represented Hennebique in the United Kingdom.

The success of Hennebique's enterprise—and hence, to a great extent, the success of reinforced concrete construction itself—depended not only on the quality of his products but on the vigorousness with which he advertised his services. Hennebique's finished structures were undoubtedly his best advertisements, especially in the early years when reinforced concrete construction was still extremely rare, or when a building was unusually large or prominent. Thus his mills at Nantes, Lille and Tourcoing (1895-96) afforded his firm considerable visibility among precisely the class of entrepreneurs likely to call upon its services. In 1905, in a calculated publicity stunt, Hennebique built a fanciful villa for himself at Bourg-la-Reine, in which good taste was entirely sacrificed to the incorporation of a maximum number of features in reinforced concrete. In order to realize the full advertising value of all such projects, Hennebique featured the most prominent of them in a house journal, *Le Beton Armé* (1898-1921).

Although his importance has been recognized by historians of architecture and construction for many decades, Hennebique remains something of a historiographic challenge. Tracing his career has proven difficult not only because of the worldwide geographic distribution of his production, but because of the sheer quantity of the archives remaining from his company.

—ALFRED WILLIS

HENRY of REYNS.

British. Died ca. 1253. Probably active from the 1230s until his death. Master of king's masons at Windsor Castle; adviser at York Castle, 1245; master of the works at Westminster Abbey, London, 1245-53.

Chronology of Works

All in England

1245   York Castle (as advisor on the new fortifications)
1245-53   Westminster Abbey (rebuilding)

*

Master Henry of Reyns is known primarily as the first master of the works of Westminster Abbey. He was an important master mason who rose to the top of his profession in England and whose work can be verified by unsurpassed documentation, namely, the English royal building accounts. Because Westminster Abbey combines many undoubtedly French features with its equally undoubtedly English ones, critical discussion of Master Henry has focused until recently almost exclusively on his nationality—was he English or French? Such an evaluation no longer seems as pressing; in an important respect, the question of Master Henry's nationality ignores the obvious fact that he was familiar with aspects of both the English and French masonry traditions. Consideration should focus rather on the nature of his activities at Westminster and elsewhere and the special nature of the royal works at the Abbey.

Known simply as Master Henry in the royal accounts, he is first mentioned in December 1243, when it would appear that he was "master of the King's masons" at Windsor Castle, where in 1240 King Henry III had initiated the construction of new royal apartments, including a new Chapel of St. Edward, which was being roofed late in 1243 but was probably completely finished only in 1245-46. On 13 March 1245, the king sent Master Henry all the way to York to advise on the new fortifications he had ordered at the castle there during the previous summer. Work was begun in that year, and by 1262, Clifford's Tower had been erected on a heightened motte, and a curtain wall with two gateways and five towers had been built.

Most of the references to Master Henry in the royal accounts, however, relate him to the work of rebuilding Westminster Abbey, which began in July 1245. He was master of the works there until 1253, which must have been near the time of his death. He was certainly dead by March 1261, when his son Hugh, also a mason, donated land which he had received from his father to the Abbey. In this document, Henry is called, uniquely, *"magistri Henrici de Reyns."* While Reyns could, in fact, refer to Raynes in Essex, it is much more likely that it is Reims in France. But this does not necessarily mean that Master Henry was from Reims; he could equally well—or, in fact, more probably—simply have worked or been trained there.

As master of the works at Westminster Abbey, Master Henry was part of an administration that King Henry III had created especially for his project of rebuilding the church and most important monastic buildings. A special exchequer was created to handle the financing of construction, and Edward, son of Odo the goldsmith, was appointed as keeper of the works and one of the treasurers of the exchequer. A representative of the abbot and convent also sat on the exchequer. In fact, Master Henry also acted as a keeper of the works at times. Beyond these arrangements, it is also clear that King Henry III took a personal and lasting interest in the project and certainly cannot be considered a passive figure in major design decisions. Thus, Master Henry would have had to work closely with, and sometimes on, the exchequer, keeping closely in touch with its monastic representative, and, most importantly, he had constantly to please a king who wanted a work of regal sumptuousness and was impatient to see it finished.

All of these relations would have affected the design of the building, but undoubtedly it was Master Henry, as master of

the works, who was responsible for presenting many of the specifically architectural possibilities and putting everything together into a coherent whole. His position also required him to purchase materials, and he would often have had to travel to quarries, for instance, in order to do so. He was also in charge of the laborers and craftsmen, who in 1253 numbered on average 300 men. They were mostly English, but significantly, there are a few probably French names in the accounts, and at least one hand among the sculptors in the church has been identified stylistically as French. In addition, these French masons appear to be among the few at Westminster who were paid by taskwork, which appears not to have been as common in England at that time as in France; most of the workmen were paid by day rate, as appears to have been more usual in England.

Master Albericus, in particular, who was paid by taskwork for tracery in the cloister and chapter house vestibule, may have been French. It must be stressed that it was unusual for one "master" to be serving under another on building sites at that time; indeed, this is the first recorded instance. It may, in fact, have been Master Henry's ability to oversee such subsidiary masters by setting them specific taskwork, which could also be budgeted more easily than day-rate labor, that inspired King Henry III to create the centralized position of king's master mason in charge of all royal works south of the Trent. This position was, in fact, first taken up by Master Henry's successor at Westminster, John of Gloucester, in 1256. More germanely to Westminster, it also means that Master Henry need not have been the architecturally schizoid personality that the nationality debate has made him out to be. He must certainly have had a cosmopolitan perspective on matters of architectural style and practice on both sides of the Channel. An ability to delegate specific technical tasks, such as the cutting of bar tracery, to trusted senior associates such as Master Albericus would have considerably increased the scope of his own activities; resulted in a flexible and diverse building team capable of effects and techniques outside the expertise of a single "workshop"; and also have speeded the project along, as the design process and major tasks were delegated downward. It is certainly possible, for instance, that Master Albericus at least helped Master Henry to design the tracery he was cutting.

Such a situation can help to explain how French *tas-de-charge* vault springings can combine with typically English cell-filling techniques and ridge ribs. It can also throw considerable light on the nature of the French elements in the design of Westminster. The Rayonnant "system," as Jean Bony calls it, was not imported wholesale. Rather, a "mixed package" of French features found a place in the design, and many of those were a generation old. The more up-to-date Rayonnant work is mostly limited to the chapter house and cloister, as we have seen in the work of Master Albericus, and in the church's transept roses, which postdate Master Henry's involvement in the project. Thus, Master Henry apparently made use of a personal experience of French architecture, which he gained before entering the king's service, while relying on a few "imported" associates for the more contemporary French references at Westminster.

The meager remains of the Windsor chapel are stylistically consistent with the work at Westminster, and there seems little doubt that this, too, is Master Henry's work. In fact, it may have been at Windsor, rather than Westminster, that Master Henry introduced bar tracery to England, certainly his most important contribution to English architecture. It is unlikely that Master Henry was also responsible for the west window at Binham; it probably was inserted after his death. It is impossible to ascertain how much Master Henry might have contributed to the design of the works at York castle, but Clifford's Tower

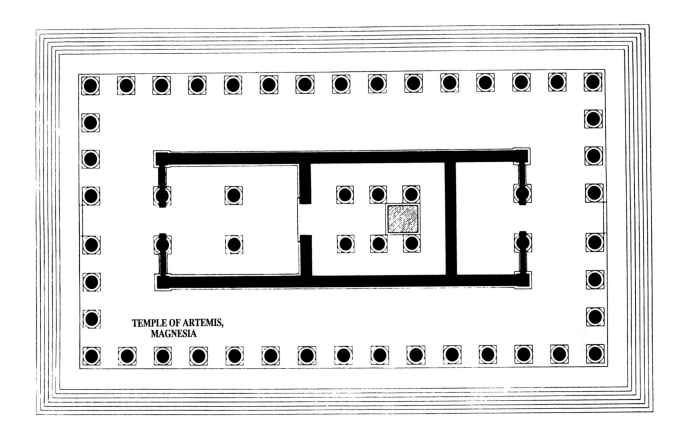

TEMPLE OF ARTEMIS,
MAGNESIA

was designed as a quatrefoil-plan keep, certainly aligning it with northern French precedents (Etampes, Amblény).

Altogether, it would seem likely that Master Henry was English, with some French training, but if this was so, it certainly cannot be seen, as many proponents of the nationalist argument believe, as a win for the home team. That so many French features found a place in Westminster Abbey reflects a great enthusiasm for French accomplishments. It is a credit to Master Henry's creative and administrative abilities that he was able to understand, combine and synthesize with current English practice the international tastes and piety of his employer, the king, into an amalgam which, in however piecemeal a fashion, exercised an enormous influence on subsequent English architecture.

—JAMES BUGSLAG

HERMOGENES.

Greek. Active ca. 150-130 B. C.

Chronology of Works
All in Asia Minor (now Turkey)
All works date from around the middle of the 2nd century B. C.

Temple of Dionysos, Teos
Temple of Zeus Sosipolis, Magnesia
Temple of Artemis Leucophryene, Magnesia
Altar of the Temple of Athena, Priene
Altar of the Temple of Artemis, Magnesia

Publications

BOOKS ABOUT HERMOGENES

DINSMOOR, W. B.: *The Architecture of Ancient Greece.* London, 1950.
LAWRENCE, A. W.: *Greek Architecture.* Harmondsworth, England, 1974.

ARTICLES ABOUT HERMOGENES

HOEPFNER, W.: "Zum ionischen Kapitell bei Hermogenes und Vitruv." *Athenische Mitteilungen* (1968).
SCHLIKKER, W.: "Hellenistische Vorstellungen von der Schönheit des Bauwerks nach Vitruv." *Athenische Mitteilungen* (1968).
VON GERKAN, A.: "Das Altar des Artemistempels in Magnesia am Mäander." *Athenische Mitteilungen* (1968).

*

Endowed with a dialectical sensitivity for tradition and innovation, Hermogenes was a key figure in promoting a new spirit in Hellenistic architecture. Judging from the range of his influence in prefiguring some of the characteristic features of Roman architecture such as spaciousness and frontality, it is most probable that he worked around 150-130 B.C. Ascribing Hermogenes to the second rather than to the end of the third century B.C., as suggested by some writers, is also corroborated by stylistic evidence.

From Vitruvius we gather that Hermogenes was not only a progressive practitioner but also a brilliant theoretician who left a treatise on architecture, now lost. In his studies of the Ionic order he devised a new canonic system of ideal proportions in which he favored the eustyle principle with wider-spaced columns. He was not the inventor of the pseudodipteros (omitting the inner row of columns). By promoting its use, however, he catapulted the architecture of his age into a more space-conscious mentality.

Several of his built works are still extant and may be visited in Asia Minor today. These include the temples of Dionysos at Teos and the Temple of Zeus Sosipolis at Magnesia on the Meander, both given a date in the second quarter of the second century B.C.; the Temple of Artemis Leucophryene, also at Magnesia, which belongs to the third quarter of the century; and the altars of the Temple of Athena at Priene and of the Temple of Artemis at Magnesia, attributed to Hermogenes. As a corpus, these buildings present a stage-by-stage crystallization of Hermogenean principles. Chronologically, they represent touchstones in the organic development and aesthetic refinement of the Ionian temple.

Hermogenes eschewed the use of the Doric order in temple design, and even changed one of his temples from the Doric to the Ionic order during construction. However, the Ionian style itself had reached a stalemate in the beginning of the Hellenistic period. Ionian monumental temples such as the Temple of Artemis at Ephesus, which was reconstructed on a larger scale during that time, for the most part repeated archaic design schemes without substantial change. Pytheos had cautiously attempted a different approach in his Temple of Athena at Priene (340 B.C.). However, with the exception of its canonic proportions and deep pronaos, the new plan was unable to counteract the widespread use of Doric principles and did not have a lasting impact.

As the primacy of religious factors dwindled in favor of civic institutions during the latter part of the Hellenistic era, the way was paved for vigorous experimentation to meet new architectural requirements in new building types. This exuberant social and cultural ambiance and the economic boom that followed no doubt fostered the emergence of Hermogenes as a pioneer in sacral design.

Stylistically, the small Temple of Zeus Sosipolis, with a tetrastyle prostyle front and a rear porch distyle *in antis,* appears to be among the earliest works of Hermogenes. Although its deep and emphatic porch prefigures Roman frontality, the persistence of the bulky Anatolian Ionian base and the lack of frieze reliefs on the entablature point to an early date of construction. However, the eustyle principle involving a wider spacing of columns is successfully applied, even though there is no pseudodipteros due to the type of plan.

A further stage of development in Hermogenean principles is seen in the hexastyle Temple of Dionysos at Teos, not far from Magnesia. Fully conforming to the eustyle principle, new features include the use of the Attic frieze and base. Trapped in strict symmetry, the cavernous pronaos has become almost as deep as the naos indicating a greater space awareness. Despite these progressive features, however, the plan lacks the spacious pseudodipteros, echoing instead the anachronistic peripteral form in the Temple of Athena at Priene.

According to Vitruvius, the octastyle Temple of Artemis Leucophryene, with 15 columns on the flanks, represents a peak in sacral design due to its pseudodipteral plan. Indeed, wide, airy corridors all around the temple evoke a Roman notion of space. Simplified profiles in architectural details, with crisper outlines allowing an exquisite play of light and shade, perpetuate the traditional importance of the exterior in the Greek temple. The tripartite perforation of the pediment serves not only to reduce the visual and structural mass of the temple front, but

in conjunction with both vertical and horizontal symmetry generates continuity in the overall design.

In a secular age of prolific building, Hermogenes appears to have made his reputation in sacral architecture, specializing in temples and altars. Although he followed Pytheos in some respects, he was not fettered by stubborn technicism or revivalist sentiment, and his well-practiced reinterpretation of Ionic temple design survived into the Roman age.

—SUNA GÜVEN

HERRERA, Juan de.

Spanish. Born in Maliano, near Santander, Spain, in 1530. Died in Madrid, in 1597. Married Marid de Alvaro, 1571 (died in 1576). Married Ines de Herrera (his niece), 1582. Studied at the University of Valladolid; also studied in Brussels. In Italy, 1553. Worked with Juan Bautista de Toledo, 1562-67; worked as architect to King Phillip II, 1567-87 (officially from 1579); courtier in charge of palace furnishings, from 1579; directed the Academy of Mathematics, Madrid, from its founding in 1584.

Chronology of Works
All in Spain

1563-84 San Lorenzo El Escorial Royal Monastery, near Madrid (after general plans by Juan Bautista de Toledo and others)
1571-85 Alcázar, Toledo (reworking of the main staircase design; southern facade design; with Geronimo Gilli)
1571-86 Royal Palace, Aranjuez (main facade and the atrium)
1580-85 Cathedral, Valladolid (completed later by others)
1582-98 Exchange, Seville
1590-97 El Escorial (sanctuary of the basilica)

Publications

BOOKS BY HERRERA

Sumario y Breve Declaracion de los Diseños y estampas de la fabrica de San Lorençio el Real del Escurial, Madrid, 1589. Madrid, 1954.
Tratado del Cuerpo Cúbico, conforme a los principios y opiniones del "Arte" de Raimundo Lulio. Madrid, 1935.

BOOKS ABOUT HERRERA

CERVERA VERA, LUIS: *El "Ingenio" creado por Juan de Herrera para cortar hierro.* Madrid, 1972.
CERVERA VERA, LUIS: *Inventario de los Bienes de Juan de Herrera.* Valencia, Spain, 1977.
CERVERA VERA, LUIS: *Las estampas y el sumario de el Escorial por Juan de Herrera.* Madrid, 1954.
CHUECA GOITIA, FERNANDO: *Arquitectura del Siglo XVI.* In *Hispaniae XI.* Madrid, 1953.
CHUECA GOITIA, FERNANDO: *La Catedral de Valladolid.* Madrid, 1947.
El Escorial 1563-1963. 2 vols. Madrid, 1963.
IÑIGUEZ ALMECH, FRANCISCO: *Las Trazas del Monasterio de S. Lorenzo de El Escorial.* Madrid, 1965.
KUBLER, GEORGE and SORIA, MARTIN: *Art and Architecture in Spain and Portugal and Their American Dominions, 1500-1800.* Baltimore and Harmondsworth, England, 1959.

KUBLER, GEORGE: *Building the Escorial*. Princeton, New Jersey, 1982.

LLAGUNO Y AMIROLA, EUGENIO and CEAN BERMUDEZ, JUAN AGUSTIN: Vol. 2 in *Noticias de los arquitectos y arquitectura de Espana desde su restauración*. Genoa, Italy, and Madrid, 1977.

LOPEZ SERRANO, MATILDE: *Trazas de Juan de Herrera y sus seguidores para el Monasterio del Escorial*. Madrid, 1944.

RUIZ DE ARCAUTE, AGUSTIN: *Juan de Herrera*. Madrid, 1936.

SANCHEZ CANTON, FRANCISCO JAVIER: *La Librería de Juan de Herrera*. Madrid, 1941.

SIGÜENZA, FRAY JOSE DE: *Historia de la Orden de San Jerónimo, Madrid, 1600*. Madrid, 1907-09.

ARTICLES ABOUT HERRERA

KUBLER, GEORGE: "Galeazzo Alessi e l'Escuriale." In *Galeazzo Alessi e l'Architettura del Cinquecento*. Genoa, Italy, 1975.

RODRIGUEZ Y GUTIÉRREZ DE CEBALLOS, ALFONSO: "Juan de Herrera y los Jesuitas." *Archivum Historicum Societatis Iesu* 35, No. 25 (1966): 285-321.

TAYLOR, RENE: "Architecture and Magic: Considerations on the Idea of the Escorial." In HOWARD HIBBARD (ed.): *Essays in the History of Architecture Presented to Rudolf Wittkower*. London, 1967.

In 1584 Juan de Herrera wrote a memorandum to Philip II, to which he attached a curriculum vitae. This document provides precise information about his training and professional qualifications. Important for his activities as court architect of Philip II were his studies of geometry and mathematics in Valladolid and Brussels. Between 1547 and 1559 he lived outside of Spain. Of particular importance was his stay in Italy, where he arrived as a soldier, in 1553. The study period in Brussels and his time in Italy gave him the opportunity to familiarize himself with the architecture of those locales.

His training in, and knowledge of, European architecture led to his promotion, in 1559, to the position of assistant to Philip II's court architect, Juan Bautista de Toledo. During Philip's reign, supervision and completion of all royal and state projects were in the hands of a court architect, who could carry out his commissions only in the closest consultation with Philip himself. It was in this manner that the court dictated architectural style.

After the death of Juan Bautista de Toledo, Herrera took over supervision of all of the king's construction works, first as *"criado de nuestra casa"* and finally as *"Architecto General de su Mgestad, y Aposentador de su Real Palacio."* His first commission in that capacity was the alteration, expansion and completion of the monumental complex of El Escorial.

The palace was situated on a cliff that was more than 1,000 meters high, in the Sierra Guadarrama, northwest of the new capital of Madrid. Construction of the multifunctional complex had been begun to designs by Toledo. Herrera had been assistant to Toledo for the construction of El Escorial. The close collaboration between the king and the two architects was part of a tradition fostering close contact between the monarch and his courtiers. Herrera had already experienced such contact during the time of his studies in Valladolid, and as a young courtier at Brussels and later at the court of Emperor Charles V in Yuste.

For 17 years Herrera supervised the construction of El Escorial and effected many changes in plan during that time. However, he was not independently active, but collaborated with Giovanni Battista Castello from Bergamo, Italy. Herrera's talent and his fruitful relationship with the king finally led to his being given sole responsibility for the project in 1572.

Herrera first rationalized the organization of the construction work, which made it possible to carry this gigantic complex— 161 to 204 meters, with foundations 10 meters deep, and with a church dome 90 meters high—to completion on 13 September 1584. Herrera's strict organization determined work hours and construction teams, and rationalized construction methods. Many of these innovations had been suggested in Andrea Palladio's theoretical writings, with which Herrera may have been familiar, and all had positive economic consequences. The complicated technical organization of the gigantic construction site, the preparation of new designs for the church and the alteration of the southwest corner were Herrera's principal contributions after 1572. The construction of the roof and the two-story addition to the western facade were also executed under his supervision.

The severe, unornamented facade of the complex is only barely interrupted by the entrances of the northern and western sides, three to each side. Although the entrances function as thoroughfares, they do not invite the visitor to enter. That is no less true for the western facade, even though the portals have profiles and frames there (begun in 1576). An alternation of niches and windows characterizes the main portal, which thus points to the Italian architect Palladio. This central portal is framed by the two-story facade, whose Doric order in turn recalls Sebastiano Serlio's theories. The entrance leads to the forecourt of the church. The emphasis achieved by means of placing a facade in front of a church designates it as the principal visitors' entrance.

The Church of El Escorial was the last building of the complex to be constructed. The original plans by Toledo were revised at the behest of Philip II. The church was finally built on a square, centralized plan, with a crossing dome and low corner spaces, to a design by Herrera. It is evident, then, that the architect took into account the criticisms of Toledo's design that had been made at the king's invitation by another architect, Francesco Paciotto. The dome had seemed too high to Paciotto, and Herrera lowered it. Nevertheless, the interior space is dominated by the dome, still 90 meters high, and supported by four monumental pillars. Herrera's entry area, with a narthex and a loggia, and the mausoleum located under the Sacrament Chapel determined the direction religious architecture in Spain was later to take. Herrera finally widened the galleries in the choir, which continue into the transept. These galleries, then, are located on the level of the *piano nobile* of the royal apartments. This solution satisfied Philip's wishes for the greatest possible unity between residential, governmental and church buildings. On 30 August 1584 the Church of San Lorenzo el Real was dedicated.

In the middle of the east-west axis of the two cloisters of El Escorial, Herrera constructed the first "imperial" staircase. The monumental design constitutes an independent construction element in the overall complex. Although it begins as a single flight, the stairway splits into two flights at the landing. Both of these flights double back to a gallery over the entrance area. This three-pronged staircase later became the indispensable symbol of power in the monumental secular Baroque. Staircases equaling the grandeur of the one at El Escorial were not found before the 17th and 18th centuries, however, in Italy and Germany. Even though there was a tradition of open staircases in Spanish architecture (at Toledo and Salamanca), there was no immediate model for this dramatic imperial design anywhere in Spain or Italy.

By means of his contribution, Herrera endowed the complex of El Escorial with a sense of order, proportion and geometry in the layout. Similar basic forms are symmetrically arranged. The parallel lines and straight angles had a long-lived influence on Spanish architecture. They form the basis of the *"estilo desornamentado,"* which is at the opposite extreme of the Plateresque style it replaced. Basic elements like the great square stone slabs, which enclose spacious open rooms, and the treatment of detail create the cool and severe effect typical of the "Herrera style."

As a multifunctional building with a church, monastery, palace, gravesite, library and museum, the complex also influenced the *"maniera grande,"* which was widely used during the Baroque.

As court architect to Philip II, Herrera was in charge of all royal architecture and other important secular buildings. In 1571 he worked on the southern facade of the Alcázar by Toledo, a work based on the principles of the Italian Giacomo Barozzi da Vignola. Herrera added a rusticated base, a superposed order combined with brick, and a crowning gallery in the Plateresque tradition. Further projects, some unexecuted, destroyed or unfinished, in Toledo (Santo Domingo el Antifuo) and Madrid (Plaza de Mayor, bridge over the Manzanares) can be attributed to Herrera.

Valladolid Cathedral was another important project. He constructed the building between 1580 and 1585. It was later finished by Alberto de Churriguera, and its plan was to be widely imitated (Salamanca, Mexico City, Lima).

Herrera designed the Exchange (Lonja) of Seville in 1582. The entire complex is built on a square plan surrounding a square courtyard, which has a two-story Doric gallery on all sides. Stone and brick are combined in the manner of Vignola in the low-relief facade, which has small projecting elements.

The simple idiom of Herrera was gradually disseminated throughout Spain. Churches, palaces, town halls and residential buildings came to follow Herrera's principles like an academic recipe.

The royal summer residence at Aranjuez was another important project. Philip II undertook the alteration of the monastic building into a royal country residence in 1564, when Toledo submitted designs for the chapel. After Toledo's death, Herrera submitted designs for the residence itself, but that building remained unfinished at Philip's death. Drawings by Juan Gómez de Mora, now in the Vatican, provide information about the design. The two domes and the 90-degree grid of the walls again point to an Italian influence. Herrera integrated these elements into a total design which, though discreet in exterior ornamentation, has a noble, introverted and monumental effect.

With the construction of the monastic royal residence of El Escorial in the heart of Spain, Juan de Herrera created a monumental symbol of established power for Philip II. The isolation of the site of the monastery-palace and its uninviting character connect the building to the medieval traditions of Christian Spain, whose spirit was best expressed in castles. All but the most indispensable decoration was banned from Herrera's severe, impersonal Renaissance style. The naked structure was to speak through its monumentality only. This new state style, also called the "Herrera style," determined Spanish architecture in the 16th century.

—KATHARINA PAWELEC
Translated from the German by Marijke Rijsberman

HERTZBERGER, Herman.

Dutch. Born in Amsterdam, Netherlands, 6 July 1932. Married Hans van Seters, 1959; three children. Graduated from Technical University, Delft, 1958. Private practice in Amsterdam, since 1958. Instructor, Academy of Architecture, Amsterdam, 1965-70; professor, University of Delft, since 1970; professor, University of Geneva, Switzerland, since 1986; chairman, Berlage Institute, Amsterdam, since 1990; has taught and lectured widely in the United States and Canada. Editor of *Forum*, Amsterdam (with Aldo van Eyck), 1959-63. Honorary member, Académie Royale de Belgique, 1975; honorary Fellow, Royal Institute of British Architects, 1991.

Chronology of Works
All in the Netherlands unless noted

1959-66	Students Residence, Weesperstraat, Amsterdam
1960-66	Montessori School, Delft (extensions in 1970 and 1981)
1964-74	De Drie Hoven Home for the Elderly, Amsterdam-Slotervaart
1968-72	Centraal Beheer Office Building, Apeldoorn (with Lucas and Niemeijer)
1969-70	Eight experimental houses (Diagoon type), Delft
1972-74	De Schalm Neighborhood Center, Deventer
1973-78	Vredenburg Music Center, Utrecht
1978-80	Forty houses, Westbroek, near Utrecht
1978-82	Haarlemmer Houttuinen, Amsterdam (urban renewal)
1979-82	Kassel-Dönche Housing Project, Kassel, Germany
1979-90	Ministry of Social Welfare and Employment Office Building, The Hague
1980-83	Amsterdamse Montessori School and Willemspark School, Amsterdam
1980-84	De Overloop Housing for the Elderly, Almere-Haven
1982-86	LiMa Housing Project, Berlin-Kreuzberg, Germany
1984-86	De Evenaar Kindergarten and Elementary School, Amsterdam
1986-89	Het Gein Housing Project, Amersfoort
1989-90	Private house/studio 2000, 16 houses in the Muziekwijk area, Almere

Publications

BOOKS BY HERTZBERGER

Herman Hertzberger: Buildings and Projects 1959-1986. With Arnulf Lüchinger. The Hague, 1987.

ARTICLES BY HERTZBERGER

"Some Notes on Two Works by Schindler." *Domus* (September 1967).

"Looking for the Beach under the Pavement." *Royal Institute of British Architects Journal* (1971).

"Homework for More Hospitable Form." *Forum* 3 (1973).

"A Lesson from St. Peter." *Spazio e societa* (September 1980).

"The Tradition behind the 'Heroic Period' of Modern Architecture and the New Formalism." *Spazio e societa* (March 1981).

"The Mechanism of the 20th Century and the Architecture of Aldo van Eyck." In *Aldo van Eyck*, edited by A. van Roijen-Wortmann and F. Strauven. Amsterdam, 1982.

"Building Order." In *Via 7*. Cambridge, Massachusetts, 1984.

"L'espace de la maison de verre." *Architecture d'aujourd'hui* 236 (1984).

Herman Hertzberger: Vredenburg Music Center, Utrecht, Netherlands, 1973-78

BOOKS ABOUT HERTZBERGER

CONTINENZA, ROMOLO: *Architetture di Herman Hertzberger.* Calabria, 1988.

EMBLETON, N.: *The Works of Aldo van Eyck and Herman Hertzberger.* Thesis, University of Newcastle, England, 1978.

HAAGSMA, IDS (ed.): *Amsterdamse Bouwen, 1880-1980.* Utrecht and Antwerp, 1981.

OFFERMANN, KLAUS: *Architekten: Herman Hertzberger.* Stuttgart, 1987.

REININK, WESSEL: *Herman Hertzberger, Architect.* Rotterdam, 1990.

VAN DER KEUKEN, J.: *Herman Hertzberger, six architectures photographiées.* Milan, 1985.

ARTICLES ABOUT HERTZBERGER

Architecture and Urbanism, special issue (March 1977).
Architecture and Urbanism, extra edition (April 1991).

"Herman Hertzberger: Musical Architecture." *Architects' Journal* (April 1976).

"Hertzberger's Variations." *Progressive Architecture* (July 1980).

LÜCHINGER, ARNULF: "Strukturalismus: Architektur als Symbol der Demokratisierung." *Bauen und Wohnen* (May 1974).

LÜCHINGER, ARNULF: "Strukturalismus: Eine neue Stromung in der Architektur." *Bauen und Wohnen* 1 (1976).

MENZIES, WALTER: "Little Things Mean a Lot: The Philosophy of Herman Hertzberger." *Building Design* (April 1976).

VAN DIJK, HANS: "Herman Hertzberger: Architectural Principles in the Decade of Humanism." *Dutch Art and Architecture Today* 6 (December 1979).

*

Herman Hertzberger is part of a strong tradition in 20th-century Dutch architecture whose contributors, from J. J. P. Oud and Johannes Duiker to Aldo Van Eyck and J. B. Bakema, have spawned such seminal groups as CIAM (Congrès Internationaux d'Architecture Moderne) and Team 10. Team 10 participants Bakema and Van Eyck edited the influential Dutch journal *Forum*. The young Hertzberger joined *Forum's* editorial meetings and thus became intimately acquainted with ongoing progressive architectural ideas.

Dutch modernism has always been underpinned by a powerful theoretical base, and Hertzberger has maintained that tradition. His buildings are supported by written agendas of great clarity, which are a development of Team 10 ideas. Central to Team 10 thinking was the "sense of place," which was an attempt to break through the limitations of CIAM's "space-time." Consequently, Hertzberger's oeuvre on the one hand develops the broad principles of Team 10 to produce a widely accessible architecture for "everyman" but on the other, supports such theories with clear formal architectural statements.

Hertzberger's work adheres to a movement that has been described as structuralism, a portmanteau expression that has its origins in the writings of Claude Lévi-Strauss. It is an attitude that eschews the determinism of the functionalist camp and is best characterized by Hertzberger's own account of "polyvalent" space in 1963: "... in place of prototypes which are collective interpretations of individual living patterns are prototypes which make individual interpretations of the collective patterns possible...." Hertzberger therefore reinterprets the social commitment of modernism, now underpinned by active user-participation in the design process and also by commissions directed toward the masses rather than an elite. In this sense his oeuvre has, like its functionalist forebears, a strong political undercurrent.

Hertzberger, although a prolific writer, has said little about the powerful architectural language which his buildings so consistently express. Nevertheless, it is a language that supports the wider theoretical stance in that it permits a range of interpretation. Any analysis of Hertzberger's major works at once reveals the fundamental aspects of his architectural language: all respond to the imposed order of a structural grid; all have an overt sense of "structure" and "infill"; all employ ingenious prefabrication to a greater or lesser extent; all use a limited range of materials, concrete (*in situ* and precast) with blockwork and glazing of varying translucency.

All these devices are evident at his Centraal Beheer Building in Apeldoorn (1974). A regular tartan grid of concrete columns interacts with an irregular arrangement of 7.5-metre-square working platforms. Top-lit spaces separate these platforms, producing a building of enormous visual complexity, heightened by Hertzberger's mastery of daylighting from both rooflights and conventional windows.

Similar themes are explored at the Home for the Elderly in Amsterdam-Slotervaart (1974). There, the order of a limited range of repetitive prefabricated components is expressed externally and internally to heighten the inside/outside relationships, another central theme in Hertzberger's architecture.

The Utrecht Music Centre (1978) harnessed Hertzberger's design philosophy to a large and complex civic building sited within an historic city. It is a masterwork where, again, repetitive structural elements (circular concrete columns with massive square cushion capitals) provide an orderly framework for the insertion of two auditoria, a restaurant, shops and offices, to produce an infinite variety of "in-between spaces" for associated uses. It is these spaces with balconies and rooflighting which are at once intimate and yet integrated with the whole; they permit the variety of interpretation so central to the "structuralist" ethos. Again, the palette of materials is limited to concrete, and blockwork with glass blocks. However, small-scale incident is provided by Hertzberger's ingenious metalwork

interventions in the form of balustrades and a range of beautifully wrought purpose-made light fittings. Richness is imparted to the auditoria by redwood in unlipped ply and lush red seating. Predictably, the architectural vocabularies of inside and outside are identical, so that the discipline of structure and infill is similarly expressed internally and externally.

Hertzberger has emerged as a giant of late 20th-century architecture, and a fitting inheritor of a worthy Dutch tradition. His work is an ample reminder that modernism so adapted and developed is a more fitting response to society's needs in the late 20th century than the superficial manifestations of postmodernism.

—A. PETER FAWCETT

HILBERSEIMER, Ludwig.

American. Born in Ludwig Karl Hilberseimer Karlsruhe, Germany, 14 September 1885; immigrated to the United States, 1938; naturalized, 1944. Died in Chicago, Illinois, 6 May 1967. Studied at the Technische Hochschule, Karlsruhe, 1906-11. Architect and planner in various European cities, mainly Berlin, 1918-38; in private practice as a town planner, Chicago, Illinois, 1938-67. Founder and Director of the City Planning Department at the Bauhaus, Dessau, Germany, 1929-32. Professor and director o f the Department of City and Regional Planning, 1938-57, and professor emeritus, 1957-67, Illinois Institute of Technology, Chicago. Fellow, American Institute of Architects.

Chronology of Works
All in Germany unless noted

1925-27	Housing Estates, Adlergestellstrasse, Adlershofstrasse, Dörpfeldstrasse, Berlin
1926	Rheinlandhaus Building, Belleallianceplatz, Berlin
1927	Shops, Kreuzbergstrasse, Mehringdammstrasse, Obentrautstrasse, Berlin
1927	Town House, Weissenhofsiedlung, Stuttgart
1932	Housing, Zehlendorf Estate, Berlin
1935	Housing, Rupendorn Estate, Berlin
1955-63	Lafayette Park Development Plan, Detroit, Michigan
1956	Hyde Park Development Plan, Chicago

Publications

BOOKS BY HILBERSEIMER

Gross-stadtbauten. Hannover, 1925.
Gross-stadtarchitektur. Stuttgart, 1927.
Beton als Gestalter. With Julius Vischer. Stuttgart, 1928.
Internationale neue Baukunst. Stuttgart, 1928.
Hallenbauten. Leipzig, 1931.
The New City: Principles of Planning. Chicago, 1944.
The New Regional Pattern. Chicago, 1949.
The Nature of Cities: Origin, Growth and Decline. Chicago, 1955.
Ludwig Mies van der Rohe. Chicago, 1956.
Contemporary Architecture: Its Roots and Trends. Chicago, 1963.
Entfaltung einer Planungsidee. Berlin, 1963.
Berliner Architektur der 20 Jahre. Mainz and Berlin, 1967.

ARTICLES BY HILBERSEIMER

"Reichstagerweiterung und Platz der Republik." *Form* (1 July 1930).
"Neue Literatur über Städtebau." *Form* (15 October 1930).
"Vorschlag zur city Bebauung." *Form* (15 December 1930).
"Die Wohnung unserer Zeit." *Form* (15 July 1931).
"Entwurf für die Stadthalle Nürnberg." *Form* (15 October 1931).
"Die Bewohner des Hauses Tugendhat äussern sich." *Form* (15 November 1931).
"Haus Dr. B. in Berlin-Zehlendorf." *Form* (15 November 1932).
"Reflections on a Greek Journey." *Inland Architect* (February 1967).

BOOKS ABOUT HILBERSEIMER

In the Shadow of Mies. Chicago, 1988.
LAMPUGNANI, VITTORIO M.: *Visionary Architecture of the 20th Century*. Stuttgart and London, 1982.
RAVE, ROLF, and KNÖFEL, HANS-JOACHIM: *Bauen seit 1900 in Berlin*. Berlin, 1968.

ARTICLES ABOUT HILBERSEIMER

ACHILLES, ROLF: "Ludwig Hilberseimer: Recent Views." *Inland Architect* 33, No. 1 (January/February 1989): 44-48.
MALCOMSON, REGINALD F.: "Elementos de la nueva ciudad: la obra de Ludwig Hilberseimer." *Hogar y arquitectura* (May/June 1968).
"Plan d'urbanisme de Chicago." *Architecture: formes et fonctions* (1957).
"Profile: Ludwig Hilberseimer." *Aufbau* (March 1959).
RASCH, BODO: "The Development of the Weissenhof Estate in Stuttgart." *Deutsche Bauzeitung* (November 1977).
REINER, JAN: "The New City: Social Planning Is a Social Task." *Architect and Engineer* (June 1945).
"Siedlung Lafayette Park, Detroit." *Bauen und Wohnen* (November 1960).
WINTHROP, HENRY: "Modern Proposals for the Physical Decentralization of Community." *Land Economics* (Madison, Wisconsin, February 1967).

*

In an interview shortly before his death, Ludwig Karl Hilberseimer was asked what he had accomplished in his professional lifetime. His laconic reply: "Almost nothing." It was not that Hilberseimer was modest or self-effacing. Rather, given a lifetime of teaching and writing about architecture and city and regional planning, in his opinion, he had succeeded in changing very few minds or in realizing few of his proposals for restructuring the urban environment and how mankind might live in such an environment.

Educated as an architect at the Technische Hochschule in Karlsruhe, Hilbs, as he was invariably known to friends, associates and students alike, pursued a productive career in architecture well into the 1920s. His work, at first strongly influenced by Karl Friedrich Schinkel (1781-1841), Germany's leading neoclassical architect in the 19th century, is marked by a clarity and logic, an economy of means, simple surfaces and ample light that place him firmly in the Modern Movement in architecture. His house for the Weissenhofsiedlung in Stuttgart (1927) is, to our eyes, an eminently livable residence. Concern for convenience, light and air are everywhere in evidence. The design of the house is a logical outgrowth of Hilbs' exhaustive analysis of the problems confronting both modern architecture and architects.

As early as 1925, with publication of *Gross-stadtbauten,* there was a conceptual shift in his work from architecture, that is, isolated buildings, to large-scale planning, the integration of architecture and the urban fabric. Through his essays and technical writings, Hilbs sought to inform a larger audience as to the value of and necessity for approaching the solution of modern social and architectural problems without the prejudice of an historical perspective. It was his view that each problem should be approached with a fresh outlook, without preconceptions, with logic and intense analysis of the problem itself. Such an open, "modern" attitude attracted the attention of Walter Gropius (1883-1969), then director of the Bauhaus. In 1929 Hilbs was appointed to the Bauhaus faculty by Hannes Meyer (1889-1954), Gropius' successor; there Hilbs was responsible for developing a curriculum in planning studies as well as teaching architecture and construction design. Although he continued to practice architecture, teaching at the Bauhaus afforded him an opportunity to test his ideas about a new urban structure predicated on, but not dominated by, the automobile, whose impact was beginning to be felt. In the sometimes spirited proving ground of the classroom, Hilbs refined his thinking, clarified his intentions, and became a model of intellectual rigor for his students.

While at the Bauhaus, he continued his friendship and association with Ludwig Mies van der Rohe (1886-1969), that institution's last director (1930-33). Their relationship, while based on mutual respect, was not without difficulty. For Hilbs, Mies' work was sometimes not pragmatic enough. To him, Mies sometimes allowed aesthetic concerns to influence his judgment. For Hilbs, the strength of any solution to a problem lay in the internal logic and consistency of the solution. As he quickly made clear to his students, Hilbs believed that "Principles do not change with a change in scale. Nor do they change with the number of stories," a criticism he leveled against Mies' work. There is no question that he applied the same stringent criteria to his own work. Nowhere is this more evident than in his rejection of his project from the mid-1920s for a high-rise city. While the logic of the proposal is very clear, Hilbs came to realize that his "Metropolis" was, according to his own evaluation, "more a city for corpses than for living people." In examining every idea and every proposed solution with the same rigor he applied to his own work as well as the work of others, he hoped to convince even his strongest critics of the virtue of his proposals, of the essential rightness of the work to be considered on its own terms.

Commencing at the Bauhaus, Hilbs' association with Mies continued during their time in the United States, where they arrived in 1938. Mies became director of architecture at the Armour (later Illinois) Institute of Technology in Chicago. His responsibilities included developing a new curriculum in architecture. To assist him and to develop the planning curriculum, Mies asked Hilbs to join the IIT faculty. Hilbs' approach to the curriculum as well as to planning in general can be summarized in a word: holistic. Such an approach places him firmly in the tradition of European planning beginning with Arturo Soria y Mata (1844-1920), continuing with Ebenezer Howard (1850-1928) and Tony Garnier (1869-1948), and including the work of Benton MacKaye (1879-1975) and Lewis Mumford (1895-1990). While Hilbs' thinking had not been limited by national boundaries, the move to the United States allowed him to approach planning problems beyond such arbitrary boundaries, at the scale of the region as defined by watersheds, physical resources, economic possibilities, and the overriding need for ordered growth as related to transportation systems, employment opportunities and annual rainfall.

Arguably, it was this clarity of intention that reinforced and strengthened his long collaboration with Mies. The first of these joint ventures was their proposal to redevelop (with Herb Greenwald, 1915-59) Chicago's Hyde Park neighborhood (1956). The ideas contained in this project were later realized in their proposal to redevelop Detroit's Lafayette Park (1955-63). On the 78-acre site, already cleared of existing structures and with the existing pattern of streets removed, what Hilbs and Mies proposed was nothing less than a new structure for urban life, one combining the density of the large city with the open greenspace of the country. A 19-acre park, accessible to the pedestrian but closed to automobile traffic, separates the mixture of high-rise apartments, two-story row houses and one-story court houses. The housing units are connected with each other by footpaths running through the greenspace. Hilbs further subjugated the automobile by placing surface parking four feet below the level of housing. Although Lafayette Park is not large enough to fully demonstrate the validity of Hilbs' approach to planning cities, it does suggest the possibilities such a comprehensive approach offers.

His planning works contain a reasoned examination of the means whereby an ordered balance might again be achieved between man and nature, between urbanism and the countryside. In the final analysis, Hilbs' work is essentially conservative, i.e., it is predicated on the intelligent use of resources over time, the reduction of loss and waste. His lasting contribution to planning and planning theory is his pedestrian-scaled neighborhood settlement unit, for this is a means whereby growth and reform might be accomplished over time, within limits, and on an actual site. As Hilbs presented his ideas, they are a statement of intentions, a philosophical construct as to how mankind might live: humanistically and in harmony with nature.

Throughout his life, Hilbs continued to publish his ideas. In addition to *Gross-stadtbauten*, his other important works in German include: *Gross-stadt Architektur* (1927), *Internationale neue Baukunst* (1928), *Entfaltung einer Planungsidee* (1963) and *Berliner Architektur der 20er Jahren* (1967). In English his important works include *The New City* (1944), *The New Regional Pattern* (1949), *The Nature of Cities* (1955), *Mies van der Rohe* (1956) and *Contemporary Architecture; Its Roots and Trends* (1964).

The Association of Collegiate Schools of Architecture recognized Hilbs' contributions to education by awarding him its Citation of Excellence in Teaching in 1958. Dia Mundial del Urbanismo de la Asociacion de Ingenieros y Arquitectos de México gave Hilbs an honorary diploma (1962/1963). In 1962, he was awarded an honorary Doctor of Laws degree by the Western Reserve University, Cleveland, Ohio. The next year he was awarded an honorary Doktor-Ingenieur degree by the Technische Universität, Berlin, and was named to the Akademie der Künste, also in that city. Lastly, the Alumni Association of the Illinois Institute of Technology named Hilbs to its Hall of Fame (posthumously, in 1985).

—DAVID A. SPAETH

HILDEBRANDT, Johann Lukas von.

Austrian. Born in Genoa, Italy, 14 November 1668. Died in Vienna, Austria, 16 November 1745. Father was German; mother was Italian. Married Francisca Johanna Perpetua Geist, 1706; eight children. Studied architecture in Genoa and continued in Rome, 1690; early training as military engineer; studied under Carlo Fontana in Rome. Architecture career began in Italy, 1693-95; military engineer, 1695; Councillor to the Court in Vienna, 1698; appointed court architect, 1700; enobled by Hapsburg Cou rt, 1720; Named first court architect after the death of Fischer von Erlach, 1723.

Chronology of Works
All in Austria unless noted
* Approximate dates
† Work no longer exists

1697-1715	Palais Schwarzenberg (originally Mansfeld-Fondi Garden Palace), Vienna (completed by J.B. and J.E. Fischer von Erlach)
1699	Triumphal Arch Gateway, Kohlmarkt, Vienna
1699-1711	Dominican Church of St. Lawrence, Gabel, Bohemia
1700-23	Belvedere, Vienna (Lower Belvedere completed 1714-15; Upper Belvedere, 1720-23)
1707-11	Harrach Estate, Halbthurn, Burgenland
1701-1717	Ráckeve Palace, Czepel, Hungary
1702, 1708-09, 1723-24	City Palace of Prince Eugen of Savoy, Vienna (interiors and additions)
1703	Sarcophagus for the Archduchess Maria Josefa, Capucine Church, Vienna
1703-17	Saint Peter's Church, Vienna
1704-09	Loretto Chapel, Rumburg, Bohemia
1705	Castrum doloris for Leopold I, Augustine Church, Vienna
1705	Schreyvogel House, Breslau, Silesia†
1705-06	Starhemberg-Schönburg Garden Palace, Vienna (completed by Franz Jänggle, 1711; interior completed by others, 1721)
1705-11	Schönborn Garden Palace, Vienna
1707-11	Harrach Estate, Bruck-an-der-Leitha
1709-10	Archbishop's Residence, Salzburg
1709-11	Harrach Estate, Aschach-an-der-Donau†
1710-13	Schönborn Country House, Göllersdorf
1711	Liechtenstein Estate, Guntramsdorf†
1711-15	Weissenstein Palace (stair pavilion and central pavilion), Pommersfelden, Germany
1712	Sarcophagus of Joseph I, Capucine Church, Vienna
1713-16	Daun-Kinsky City Palace, Vienna
1714-17	Parish Church, Pottendorf
1715	Church of Maria Loretto, Göllersdorf
1715*-25	Schönborn Chapel, Würzburg, Germany
1716-46	Church of Maria Treu, Vienna (completed by Mathias Gerl, 1751)
1717	Seminary Church of the German Order of Knights, Linz
1717-19	Austrian State Chancellery, Vienna
1720	Bartolotti von Partnfeld House, Vienna
1720-25	Poor House and Soldier's Hospital, Alser
1720-44	Prince-Bishop's Residence, Würzburg, Germany (with Johann Balthasar Neumann)
1721-27	Mirabell Palace, Salzburg (later altered)
1724	Parish Church, Georgswalde, Bohemia
1724-39	Monastery of Göttweig, Göttweig (east and north wings and stairhall)
1725	St John of Nepomuk Shrine, Augarten Bridge, Vienna†
1725*-30	Garden House, Siebenbrunn Palace
1725-32	Schlosshof Estate, Marchfeld
1727	Parish Church, Seelowitz, Moravia
1727-30/ 1734-35	Harrach Garden Palace, Vienna

Johann Lukas von Hildebrandt: Belvedere, Vienna, Austria, 1700-23

1730	House, 3 Teifer Graben, Vienna
1730	Merklein House, Vienna
1730	Teubelhof House, Vienna
1731	Marian Column, Göllersdorf
1732-45	Werneck Palace, Franconia, Germany (with Johann Balthasar Neumann)
1733	Parish Church, Aspersdorf
1733	Parish Church, Strazendorf
1733	Saint John of Nepomuk Shrine, Schönborn Estate, Göllersdorf
1736	Castrum doloris for Prince Eugen of Savoy
1740-41	Parish Church, Göllersdorf
1746*	Monastery of Klosterbruck, Near Znaim

Publications

BOOKS ABOUT HILDEBRANDT

AURENHAMMER, HANS: *J. B. Fischer von Erlach*. London, 1973.

BRINCKMANN, ALBERT E.: *Von Guarino Guarini bis Balthasar Neumann*. Berlin, 1932.

FRANZ, HEINRICH GERHARD: *Studien zur Barockarchitektur in Böhmen und Mähren*. Brno, Czechoslovakia, 1943.

FREEDEN, M. H. V.: *Balthasar Neumann, Leben und Werk*. 2nd ed., Munich, 1963.

GRIMSCHITZ, BRUNO: *Das Belvedere in Wien*. Vienna, 1946.

GRIMSCHITZ, BRUNO: *Johann Lucas von Hildebrandt*. Munich and Vienna, 1959.

GRIMSCHITZ, BRUNO: *Johann Lucas von Hildebrandts Kirchenbauten*. Vienna, 1924.

GRIMSCHITZ, BRUNO: *Wiener Barockpäläste*. Vienna, 1944.

HAGER, WERNER: *Die Bauten des deutschen Barocks: 1690-1770*. Jena, Germany, 1942.

HAUTTMANN, MAX: *Geschichte der kirchlichen Baukunst in Bayern, Schwaben und Franken: 1550-1780*. Munich, 1921.

HEGEMANN, HANS W.: *Die deutsche Barockbaukunst Böhmens*. Munich, 1943.

HEMPEL, EBERHARD: *Baroque Art and Architecture in Central Europe*. Baltimore, 1965.

HOFMANN, WALTER: *Schloss Pommersfelden*. Nuremberg, Germany, 1968.

KERBER, OTTMAR: *Von Bramante zu Lucas von Hildebrandt*. Stuttgart, Germany, 1947.

KNOPP, NORBERT: *Das Garten-Belvedere*. Munich, 1966.

McKAY, DEREK: *Prince Eugene of Savoy*. London, 1977.

SEDLMAIER, RICHARD and PFISTER, RUDOLF: *Die Fürstbischöfliche Residenz zu Würzburg*. Munich, 1923.

SEDLMAYR, HANS: *Johann Bernhard Fischer von Erlach*. 2nd ed., Vienna, 1976.

SEDLMAYR, HANS: *Österreichische Barockarchitektur: 1690-1740*. Vienna, 1930.

WENZEL, WERNER: *Die Gärten des Lothar Franz von Schönborn*. Berlin, 1970.

ARTICLES ABOUT HILDEBRANDT

AURENHAMMER, HANS: ''Ikonographie und Ikonologie des Wiener Belvederegartens.'' *Wiener Jahrbuch für Kunstgeschichte* 17 (1955): 86-108.

KELLER, HARALD: ''Das Treppenhaus im deutschen Schloss- und Klosterbau des Barock.'' Unpublished Ph.D. dissertation, University of Munich, 1936.

WAGNER-RIEGER, RENATE: "Die Piaristenkirche in Wien."
Wiener Jahrbuch für Kunstgeschichte 17 (1955): 49-62.

*

Johann Lukas von Hildebrandt's father was a captain in the army and his mother an Italian, and Italian remained his first language for the rest of his life. He received his early training as a military engineer (as did Johann Balthasar Neumann), and studied under Carlo Fontana (1638-1714) in Rome, where he imbibed a wide and informed knowledge of Baroque architecture; there he became familiar with the works of masters such as Francesco Borromini (1599-1667), from which he derived his love of elliptical plans, undulating facades and interpenetration of space. In Italy he also became familiar with the work of Guarino Guarini (1624-83), the Theatine monk who was himself greatly influenced by Borromini's designs, and who was to take the complicated geometries of vaulting and centralized spaces even further than did the Roman master.

Fontana himself had a great influence on architecture at the time, for he was a celebrated teacher who numbered among his pupils not only Hildebrandt, but Johann Bernhard Fischer von Erlach (1656-1723), Hildebrandt's great contemporary and rival. In fact, Hildebrandt and Fischer von Erlach were to become the most important Baroque architects in Austria.

During the 16th century and for most of the 17th century, Austria and Vienna were really cultural backwaters, subservient to the domination of Italian influences, yet at the end of the 1690s Vienna became once more a place of enormous cultural importance. Hildebrandt and his rival contributed no small part to this tremendous renaissance of art and architecture, and it is a significant part of the story to understand how this came about.

After the calamitous Thirty Years' War (1618-48), the emperor's position in the Holy Roman Empire had become weak, and indeed almost untenable, for the empire itself was in reality nothing more than a very loose federation, complicated by the religious divide that left a huge part of the territories Protestant, under Protestant princes and even Protestant electors. Apart from the religious divide, which weakened the cohesion of the empire, the Hapsburg realms were threatened on the west by the ambitions of the French, and of King Louis XIV in particular. With a cynicism that was breathtaking in its self-centered lack of scruple, Louis XIV supported the Turks and the Hungarians in their designs on the Holy Roman Empire, thus threatening Christian control of Europe and, indeed, Christendom itself. At that time, Islam was once more in an expansionist mood, and in 1683 a huge Turkish army attacked the eastern territories of the empire and laid siege to Vienna itself. It was a long and unpleasant business, but the emperor found strong allies in John III Sobieski, king of Poland, and in the electors of Bavaria and Saxony. Financial aid was given by the papacy, Savoy, Tuscany, Genoa, Spain and Portugal, and the emperor's allies ultimately drove the Turks deep into Hungary. Louis XIV's annexation of German territory in the west pushed the German princes of the empire into a closer relationship with Vienna, and in 1689 Great Britain and the Netherlands concluded the Grand Alliance with the emperor against the ambitions of Louis XIV: the pope himself was partly instrumental in bringing this about in order to keep the French monarch under control. One of the first allied victories was the defeat of the French and Jacobite forces at the Battle of the Boyne in 1690. The Allies won many military successes, and in 1697 the emperor appointed Prince Eugen of Savoy as commander-in-chief of the imperial forces, and the Turks were decisively defeated in the east. The Peace of 1699 brought Hungary, Transylvania and a large part of Slavonia into the empire. Thus Austria became a great power, and Kaiser Leopold I restored the empire to its imperial status, with enlarged territories, a new sense of confidence in his lands, and the removal of external threats, notably that of Islam. At the end of the 17th century, then, Austria, and above all its capital, Vienna, became centers of artistic endeavor. A new sense of security enabled the art of architecture to flourish, and that art was to glorify the Hapsburgs, the Church and the ruling castes of the empire.

In 1696 Hildebrandt settled in Vienna with an eye, no doubt, to the main chance. From 1697 to 1715 he was involved in the building of the Palais Schwarzenberg in Vienna, in which the influence of Borromini and Guarini is apparent. In the Dominican Church of St. Laurenz in Gabel, North Bohemia (1699), Hildebrandt demonstrated his familiarity with Guarini's style, for he employed a complex plan of two ellipses separated by a circle with chapels set in the diagonals, and used concave corners with convex balconies. He also developed arcuated systems that recall Guarini in their complicated geometry. The facade, with its towers and bowed front, anticipated that of the Peterskirche in Vienna.

In the same year in which he built the Gabel church, Hildebrandt applied for the post of *Hofbaumeister* (court architect), to which he was appointed in 1700, and from then on he appears to have intrigued for commissions against his rival, the older Fischer von Erlach. He succeeded Fischer as first court architect on the latter's death in 1723, and was knighted by the emperor in 1720.

From 1702 to 1708 Hildebrandt worked on the designs for the Peterskirche in Vienna, a collegiate and parish church with a plan consisting of a long ellipse separating two rectangular compartments, with an apsidal choir. There is a cupola over the center, and the facade has twin towers three stages high set at angles on plan that flank the bowed front, which seems to be compressed between the towers, an effect that is enhanced by the buckled appearance of the entablature. It is an extraordinary achievement, this marvelous Baroque church that nestles in a small space in the dense urban fabric of the Old Town only a short distance from the great Cathedral of St. Stephen. In fact, the design of the Peterskirche in some ways anticipated Fischer von Erlach's altogether more grand and imperial Karlskirche of some years later (began 1716), but the front of the Karlskirche is stretched out, while that of the Peterskirche is almost painfully compressed. The plan of the Peterskirche was used again for the little Seminarkirche in Linz (1717-25), which again has a boldly modeled, bowed front.

From 1716 Hildebrandt worked on the designs for the Piaristenkirche of Maria Treu in Vienna, the monastic church of the Piarist order: this has an octagonal rotunda with the north and south sides extended as side chapels, but the plan is similar to that of the Laurenzkirche at Gabel. The walls sway inward on convex curves, and the church is by far the lightest and most joyous in a city where Baroque tends to be somber. Chapels are again set on the diagonals of the octagon. The influence of Borromini is very apparent in this church. The two towers are very slender, and the composition has a lightness not usual in Viennese churches.

Hildebrandt seems to have enjoyed the patronage of Prince Eugen of Savoy from around 1701, and for the prince he designed the Schloss Ráckeve in Hungary, a summer palace consisting of a series of low pavilions with a central block over which is an octagonal cupola. He also cultivated other patrons, among them the powerful Schönborn family, prince-bishops of Würzburg. For Lothar Franz von Schönborn he designed a country house at Göllersdorf in 1710-13, and much later, 1740-41 the parish church in the same village.

All this time, Hildebrandt was developing his contacts with the princely members of the court, and from 1713 to 1716 he designed and built the Palais Daun-Kinsky in Vienna, which is a town palace, seven windows wide, but two courtyards deep. The street façade has a giant order of very tall slender pilasters, the central four of which are tapered, like inverted obelisks, set on a rusticated ground floor, and there are windows in the frieze of the crowning entablature. The building is entered through an exuberant portal with its atlantes and swaying open pediment. The *Treppenhaus* (staircase) of the palace is situated on one side, with an opening to the second floor and with a gallery that leads back to the front facade. The balustrade is inventive and lively, while the vaulting and arches are treated with such freedom and plasticity that they almost defy analysis. There Hildebrandt displayed his mastery of perspective and of complex geometries, especially in his staircase designs, while the spatial relationships and the illusory effects are breathtaking in their ingenuity, especially on such a cramped site.

Hildebrandt further developed the staircase theme at Schloss Weissenstein, Pommersfelden, where Lothar Franz, Graf von Schönborn, arch-chancellor of the Holy Roman Empire, elector and archbishop of Mainz, prince-bishop of Bamberg and canon of Würzburg, determined to build himself a palace worthy of such a prelate. The architect was Johann Dientzenhofer, but the famous *Treppenhaus* in the huge central block was designed partly by Lothar Franz and partly by Hildebrandt. This stunning stair rises up, surrounded by three stories of galleries, and is one of the most felicitous of many wonderful staircases in Baroque central Europe.

Hildebrandt's greatest work is unquestionably the Belvedere in Vienna, the town palace of Prince Eugen of Savoy. Work began in 1700, and the Lower Belvedere was completed in 1714-15. The Upper Belvedere, that extraordinary dream of a palace, with its fantastic roof silhouette and its magically elegant facades, was built between 1720 and 1723. The two palaces were linked by a series of terraced gardens, with statuary and planting. The Lower Belvedere is a central pavilion with wings extending on either side, and the Upper Belvedere is a grander version of this arrangement, set on a terrace far above the smaller building. This layout derives from the narrow garden with a house at one end and an eye-catching pavilion at the far end, a scheme that Hildebrandt had used at the Göllersdorf palace. The Upper Belvedere contains the most celebrated of all Hildebrandt's staircases, with its mighty vaulting, sculptures and theatrical spatial effects that derive from Borromini and Guarini. For Schloss Mirabell in Salzburg (1721-27) he also designed the airy and delightful staircase, with its urns and *putti*.

From 1720 to 1723 and again from 1729 to 1744 Hildebrandt, through his Schönborn connections, collaborated with Johann Balthasar Neumann (1687-1753) on the design of the Residenz for the prince-bishop of Würzburg. Hildebrandt contributed designs for the pediments and the upper works of the great central pavilion, which are similar to those of the Upper Belvedere in Vienna. He also made designs for the interiors of the Kaisersaal and the chapel, both of which are among his finest achievements.

Hildebrandt was involved in the reconstruction of Stift Göttweig. His designs were very ambitious, and the proposals were never completed, but the handsome staircase building containing the *Kaiserstiege* (Emperor's Stair, 1738), with its celebrated ceiling fresco by Paul Troger, is as noble as anything Hildebrandt achieved. The balustrade has garlanded urns set on the pedestals, and the stair rises up symmetrically within a space that is airy and light, as only the best of Baroque rooms can be.

Hildebrandt paid great attention to the details of his buildings, and the decorative treatments he used make his work unmistakable. His architecture was conceived as plastic forms, and his massing was designed to look good from every angle. He fused his elements and often created extraordinary silhouettes using parts that were themselves disparate, but which he put together with unerring flair.

　　　　　　　　　　　　　　　—JAMES STEVENS CURL

HIPPODAMOS of MILETOS.

Greek. Lived ca. 500-440 B.C. From Miletos in Asia Minor (now Turkey). Involved with plans for Miletos (which had been destroyed), after 479 B.C.; in Athens from 470 B.C.

Chronology of Works
* *Approximate dates*

475 B.C.*	Town Plan, Miletos, Asia Minor
470 B.C.*	Town Plan, Peiraios, Greece
443 B.C.*	Town Plan, Thurii, Italy

Publications

BOOKS ABOUT HIPPODAMOS

ARISTOTLE: *The Politics.*
CASTAGNOLI, FERDINANDO: *Orthogonal Town Planning in Antiquity.* Cambridge, Massachusetts, and London, 1971.
CASTAGNOLI, FERDINANDO: *Ippodamo di Mileto e l'urbanistica a pianta ortogonale.* Rome, 1956.
EGLI, ERNST: *Geschichte des Städtebaus.* Vol 1. Zurich and Stuttgart, 1959.
GIULIANO, ANTONIO: *Urbanistica delle citta greche.* Milan, 1966.
MARTIN, ROLAND: *L'urbanisme dans la Grèce antique.* Paris, 1956.
VON GERKAN, A.: *Griechische Städteanlagen.* Berlin, 1924.
WARD-PERKINS, JOHN B.: *Cities of Ancient Greece and Italy: Planning in Classical Antiquity.* New York, 1974.

ARTICLES ABOUT HIPPODAMOS

ERDMANN, M.: 'Hippodamos von Milet und die symmetrische Städtebaukunst der Griechen.'' *Philologus* 42 (1883).
McCREDIE, J. R.: ''Hippodamos of Miletus.'' In P. G. MITTEN, J. G. PEDLEY and J. ASCOTT (eds.): *Studies Presented to George M. A. Hanfmann.* Mainz, Germany, 1971.

　　　　　　　　　　　　　　　*

Hippodamos is known to us principally from brief comments about him in Aristotle's treatise on politics (1267b): ''Hippodamos invented the division of cities and cut up (*sic*) the Piraeus.'' His theories about the division of cities, as described by Aristotle, were social rather than architectural, and if it were not for the passing reference to Piraeus, the harbor town of Athens, he would have been known not as a town planner but more as a philosophical theorist, concerned with the distinction between classes, their location in the community and the means of supporting them. His association with the planning of Piraeus dates him fairly securely to the second and third quarters of the fifth century B.C. There is a possibility, therefore, that he was also involved in the planning of the Athenian colony of

Thurii in southern Italy, probably founded in 443 B.C. But when Strabo (xiv 654) tells us that the new town of Rhodes was founded (toward the end of the fifth century) by the same architect "it is said," as with Piraeus the uncertainty and vagueness make it more likely that this was a town laid out on Hippodamian principles, rather than by Hippodamos himself. The fact that Aristotle, writing in the fourth century B.C., knew the theory behind the planning suggests that Hippodamos wrote a treatise on town planning; but if he did, nothing of it survives. We are therefore dependent on the evidence of Piraeus in assessing his achievement, which is less than adequate.

The idea of developing Piraeus as a fortified harbor town was universally attributed in antiquity to the Athenian statesman Themistokles, who initiated a naval policy as the only hope for effective resistance against the threat of Persian attack (derived from earlier similar, partially successful policies at Samos and Miletos). It is clear from the history of the Persian invasion of Greece in 480-479 B.C. that the development of Piraeus as a fortified base had not been achieved by that time. Hippodamos' activity there must, therefore, postdate the invasion. Archaeological investigation, though seriously hampered by the modern redevelopment of the town, shows that Piraeus was laid out on a grid plan of streets. Descriptions of the town indicate that there was a designated commercial area (*emporikon*) by the principal harbor enclosed within the line of fortification, the two smaller harbors serving as bases for warships, with the necessary dockyard and arsenal buildings.

An area excavated in the late 19th century has been reinterpreted recently as part of a sequence of modest houses of regular arrangement, suggesting the possibility of a region set aside for a relatively humble section of the population, perhaps in accordance with the class-distinction theories of Hippodamos. If so (and this is highly speculative), Aristotle's phraseology may indicate that the words "cut up" refer to Hippodamos' division of the town into distinct social areas, rather than the routine arranging of streets in a grid plan.

Hippodamos' position in the history of town planning within the ancient world is thus somewhat uncertain. Clearly he achieved a distinct reputation, but through lack of real understanding it is almost impossible to see what exactly he propounded or achieved. The arrangement of planned Greek towns with streets forming a regular rectangular grid is often loosely described as "Hippodamian," but, though he undoubtedly used a grid at Piraeus, earlier examples of grid plans (as in the Greek colonies of Sicily) show that the grid was well known before his time, and was, indeed, already the normal way of assigning plots of land for whatever purpose within planned cities. The division of Greek cities into defined areas—political and religious, commercial and industrial, as well as socially distinctive residential areas—is one which occurred naturally in those communities that were not planned. Miletos itself, totally destroyed by the Persians in 494 B.C. and rebuilt to a new grid plan after 479 B.C., was perhaps the natural place (given the intellectual attitudes known to have existed there in the sixth century) for the development of speculation about the ideal arrangement for cities, and Hippodamos is best interpreted in this context, as an observer and interpreter of Greek practice, but also as a planner who seems to have been prepared to put his theorizing to the test of practical application.

—R. A. TOMLINSON

HITTORFF, Jacques Ignace.

German. Born in Cologne, Germany, 1792. Died on 25 March 1867. Studied at the École des Beaux-Arts, Paris, under Charles

Percier, from 1811. Appointed *sous-inspecteur* under François Belanger as architect of the Bourbon Restoration, 1815; study tours to England, 1820, Germany, 1821, and Italy, 1822-24; held government post of *architecte du Bois de Boulogne et des Champs Elysées*, Paris, 1852-55. Elected to Académie des Beaux-Arts, 1853.

Chronology of Works
All in France
† Work no longer exists

1818	Decorations for the funeral of the Prince de Condé, Paris†
1820	Decorations for the funeral of the duc de Berry, Paris†
1821	Decoration for the baptism of the duc de Bordeaux, Notre Dame, Paris†
1824	Decorations for the funeral of Louis XVIII, Basilica of St. Denis†
1825	Decoration for the coronation of Charles X, Cathedral, Reims†
1825	Salle Favart, Paris†
1825-30	Tuileries Palace, Paris (interior decorations)†
1827-28	Théâtre de l'Ambigu-Comique, Paris
1832-40	Place de la Concorde, Paris
1833-48	Church of St.-Vincent-de-Paul, Paris (completion)
1834-40	Restaurant Pavilions, Panorama and Circus on the Champs-Elysées, Paris
1847-50	*Mairie* of the Fifth Arrondissement, Paris (completion)
1851-52	Cirque Napoleon (Cirque d'Hiver), Paris
1852-55	Houses, Place de l'Etoile, Paris (with Charles Rohault de Fleury)
1853-55	Institut Eugénie-Napoleon, Paris
1854-55	Temple of the Muses, Paris (with J. A. D. Ingres)
1855-61	*Mairie* of the First Arrondissement, Paris
1856-59	Hôtel du Louvre, Paris (with Charles Rohault de Fleury, Auguste Pellechet, and Alfred Armand)
1858-66	Gare du Nord, Paris

Publications

BOOKS BY HITTORFF

Description des cérémonies et des fêtes qui ont eu lieu pour le baptême de son altesse royale Monseigneur Henry-Charles-Ferdinand-Marie-Dieudonné d'Artois, duc de Bordeaux. With Jean Lecointe. Paris, 1827.
Architecture antique de la Sicile. With Ludwig Zanth. Paris, 1827.
Architecture moderne de la Sicile. With Ludwig Zanth. Paris, 1835.
Restitution du temple d'Empédocle à Selinonte; ou, l'architecture polychrome chez les grecs. Paris, 1846-51.

ARTICLES BY HITTORFF

"Eglise de la Madeleine." *Journal des artistes* Nos. 20-22 (1834).
"Mémoire sur Pompeii et Pètra." Vol. 25, part 2, pp. 377-416 in *Mémoires de l'Academie des inscriptions et belles-lettres.* Paris, 1866.

BOOKS ABOUT HITTORFF

BEULÉ, CHARLES ERNEST: *Eloge de Hittorff*. Paris, 1868.
HAMMER, KARL: *Jakob Ignaz Hittorf: Ein Pariser Baumeister, 1792-1867*. Stuttgart, 1968.
HAUTECOEUR, LOUIS: *Histoire de l'architecture classique en France*. Paris, 1955.
Hittorff: un architecte de XIXième siecle. Paris, 1987.
MIDDLETON, ROBIN D. (ed.): *The Beaux-Arts and Nineteenth Century French Architeture*. London, 1982.
SCHNEIDER, DONALD: *The Works and Doctrine of Jacques Ignace Hittorff (1792-1867)*. New York, 1977.

ARTICLES ABOUT HITTORFF

BROWNLEE, DAVID: "Neugriechisch/Néo-Grec: The German Vocabulary of French Romantic Architecture." *Journal of the Society of Architectural Historians* (March 1991): 18-21.
NORMAND, ALFRED: "Notice sur la vie et les oeuvres de J. I. Hittorff, artiste français." *Moniteur des architectes* Series 2, 2 (1867): 113-121, 145-148.

The career of Jacques-Ignace Hittorff spanned the middle third of the 19th century and encompassed a variety of buildings, ranging from churches to train stations. The strength of his professional reputation rests on the number of projects he executed in Paris, where he lived from 1811 until his death in 1867. Originally from Cologne, Hittorff was one of many art and architecture students who went to study in the capital of the French Empire. Upon his arrival in Paris in 1811, he came under the tutelage of the famed Empire Style interior decorator and architect, Charles Percier. From Percier, Hittorff gained an interest in classical antiquity and a theoretical base in architecture. Percier's "liberal classicism" called for inventive use of classical elements tempered by concerns for contemporary taste and local sensibilities. The inherent flexibility of this theory led to the eclecticism that characterizes Hittorff's oeuvre.

Hittorff approached eclecticism empirically: he plundered Western architectural history for specific elements that suited the needs of his projects. In *Architecture Polychrome chez les Grecs* (1851), he stated, "I never made use of an element from antiquity because I had seen it used by Greek or Roman artists, but because I had judged it to be well-applied by them and [because] its new use had to lead to a satisfying result independent of its origin." Hittorff sought a synthesis of seemingly disparate architectural motifs in his work. Not surprisingly, his eclectic aesthetic colored his assessment of works by others. The neoclassicism of Pierre Vignon's Madeleine was unacceptable to him because it was nearly a facsimile of a Roman type rather than a creative synthesis of various historical elements.

Hittorff's most characteristic work is the Church of St. Vincent-de-Paul (1824-44). Originally commissioned to his father-in-law, Jean-Baptists Lepère, the church is a synthesis of Greek, Gothic and Byzantine elements, described by Charles Garnier as "*néo-Grec*." This term derived from the contemporary German architectural aesthetic, with which Hittorff surely came into contact in his travels to Germany in 1821. Similar churches in the *néo-Grec* mode were constructed in Munich by Hittorff's rival, Leo von Klenze, such as the Apostelkirche (1818-26) and the Residenzkapelle (1827-37). Hittorff's eclecticism was nurtured by this German background as well as by Percier's teachings.

The facade of St. Vincent-de-Paul combines a Greek Ionic portico with double towers reminiscent of Gothic prototypes. Hittorff blended two disparate sources such as these with finesse: he applied classicizing pilasters to the towers and perched four acroterion figures representing the four evangelists atop the attic. Another element from classical antiquity was the application of polychromy to the facade. Thirteen painted enameled panels depicting the life of Christ were executed by a student of Gros, Pierre-Jules Jollivet, but they were eventually taken down due to clerical charges of impropriety.

The interior of the church also recalls several sources. The exposed beams of the ceiling are painted in red, blue and gold, the same colors of the painted beams in the cathedrals at Messina and Monreale, which Hittorff saw during his stay in Sicily. The frescoes above the Ionic colonnade, executed by J. H. Flandrin, depict a procession of Jerusalem pilgrims in the style of the Panathenaic procession.

The use of the Ionic order in St. Vincent-de-Paul demonstrates Hittorff's method of eclectic architecture. The interior was originally designed in the Corinthian order by Jean-Baptiste Lepère, yet the lower colonnade was changed to the Ionic by Hittorff in 1830. According to Hittorff, the Ionic was singularly suited to Christian architecture because one could apply Christian symbols such as crosses, wheat stalks and bunches of grapes on the banding below the volutes of the capital and in the continuous frieze above. In this way, Hittorff rationalized his use of eclecticism in order to reach a satisfying synthesis. The case of St. Vincent-de-Paul displays an intensely personal approach in Hittorff's eclecticism.

In the mayor's office for the first arrondissement of Paris (1857-60), Hittorff incorporated eclectic elements into a generalized Gothic scheme. The project was under the jurisdiction of his nemesis, Baron Georges Eugène Haussmann, who antagonized Hittorff as being against the spirits of the replanning of Paris, or in other words, too conservative. Haussmann issued directives to Hittorff on the general appearance of the building. According to the prefect, the *mairie* had to serve as a pendant to the Gothic Church of St. Germain-L'Auxerrois on the Place du Louvre. The reception of Hittorff's building was overwhelmingly negative, for it was thought that the *mairie* diminished the value of the Gothic facade of the church. Its brand of eclecticism was also attacked as being a "pastiche" and "caricature." Nevertheless, others viewed the *mairie* as praiseworthy for its references to the linkage of civil and religious life: for example, the rose window of the marriage room complements that of the church. The *mairie* follows Hittorff's idea that a building must strive to be a melange of styles within a homogenous scheme. In St. Vincent-de-Paul, eclectic elements are blended into a classical scheme; in the *mairie,* the general theme is Gothic with classicizing motifs.

The facade of Hittorff's last project, the Gare du Nord, is largely eclectic in its mixture of classical, Gothic and Baroque styles. Yet the train station is also characteristic of Hittorff's interest in structural innovation and use of new materials, such as metal. This interest stemmed from the influence of François-Joseph Bélanger, for whom Hittorff apprenticed during the construction of the cupola of the Halle au Blé in 1811. Hittorff executed the interior support system of the train shed in metal, yet he sabotaged the potential modernity of the building by clothing the outer structure in stone. Similarly, Hittorff used a metal support system totally masked by masonry for St. Vincent-de-Paul. He derived this system from his studies of the Temple of Zeus Olympus at Agrigento in 1823.

Hittorff's most innovative applications of metal construction were in the Panorama, a building intended specifically for the viewing of circular perspective paintings, and the circuses for

Jacques Ignace Hittorff: Church of St. Vincent-de-Paul, Paris, France, 1833-48

the Champs-Elysées. In these buildings, Hittorff revealed the metal construction because of the relative informality of the functions, which allowed for greater experimentation. Consequently, Hittorff directly applied the lessons learned from Bélanger: in the Panorama, the iron structure acts as ornament, which is also the case in the Halle au Blé. The Panorama and the circuses established Hittorff's reputation as an architect and engineer.

Hittorff also excelled in developing iconographic programs for his works. He began as an architect of ceremonial and festive decorations, working in the style of his master, Percier. From that experience he learned the importance of a lucid, unified

decorative program. He was responsible for the decorative program of St. Vincent-de-Paul. In the Gare du Nord, the iconography is inherent in the structure and use of materials. The Gare du Nord aspired to be the equivalent of a temple to transportation and technology, where the tripartite arched stone facade is glazed, reminiscent of Gothic rose windows. Hittorff referred to the "nave" and "side aisles" of the interior, which refers to the basilical structure of the design. But his most successful iconographic program was the project for the embellishment of the Place de la Concorde, executed for King Louis-Philippe between 1832 and 1835. The eclectic inclusion of rostral column lamps, fountains, statues of personified French commercial cities arranged by geographic location, and the famed obelisk of Luxor are due to Hittorff's project. Through these decorations, Hittorff created a nationalistic iconography that referred to technological and commercial progress, in keeping with the mood of the July monarchy.

Hittorff is well remembered for his architecture but also for his part in the polychromy controversy of the 1830s, which caused a dispute between him and Desiré Raoul-Rochette, who represented the opinion of the *secrétaire perpetuel* of the École des Beaux-Arts, Antoine-Chrysostome Quatremère de Quincy. Hittorff's studies of the polychromy of Greek temple ruins clashed with the aesthetic of Quatremère, who adhered to the idea of the pristine whiteness of Greek architecture as described by the German archaeologist Johann Joachim Winckelmann. Additionally, the generally accepted view of the polychromy of Greek architecture was politically charged at the time due to its use as a tool to rebel against the Académie by young architecture students, such as Henri Labrouste. Hittorff's objectives were more academic than revolutionary; he merely wished to indicate that polychromy served to articulate the orders and to express the character of the building. In *Architecture Polychrome chez les Grecs,* Hittorff vindicated his position on ancient polychromy by reconstructuring the Temple of Empedocles from disparate geographic locations and cultures, testimony once again to the extent of his eclecticism.

—CYNTHIA ELMAS

HOFFMANN, Josef.

Czechoslovakian. Born in Pirnitz, Moravia, now Brtnice, Czechoslovakia, 15 December 1870. Died in Vienna, Austria, 8 May 1956. Married Anna Hladik, 1903. Married Karla Schmatz, 1925; one son. Studied architecture at the Academy of Art, Vienna, 1892-95; awarded the Rome Prize, 1895. Worked in the studio of Otto Wagner, Vienna, 1896-97; private practice in Vienna, 1898-1956. Taught at the Vienna School of Applied Arts, 1899-1936; founder member, the Sezession Group, 1897; founder (with Kolomon Moser and Fritz Wärndorfer) of the Wiener Werkstätte, 1903; director (with Gustav Klimt) of the Kunstschau, Vienna, 1908-09; cofounder and director, Austrian Werkbund, Vienna, 1910; director, Künstlerwerkstätte, Vienna, 1943-56.

Chronology of Works
All in Austria unless noted

1898	Ver Sacrum Salon, *Sezession Exhibition*, Vienna
1899	Apollo Candle Shop, Vienna
1899-1902	Exhibition designs for the Sezession, Vienna
1901-03	Moser and Moll Houses, Hohe Warte, Vienna
1903-11	Ast House, Vienna
1904-06	Sanatorium, Purkersdorf, near Vienna
1905-11	Palais Stoclet, Brussels, Belgium
1911	Austrian Pavilion, Rome, Italy
1913	Primavesi House, Winkelsdorf, North Moravia, Czechoslovakia
1913-14	Austrian Pavilion, Werkbund Exhibition, Cologne, Germany
1913-15	Skywa (Panzer) House, Heitzing, Vienna
1918	Pazzani Palace, Vienna
1920-22	Berl House, Freudenthal (now Bruntal), Czechoslovakia
1925	Austrian Pavilion, Exposition des Arts Décoratifs, Paris, France
1928	Altmann and Kuhne Pastry Shop, Vienna
1929	Design of the Austrian Werkbund Exhibition, Vienna
1930	Austrian section, International Exhibition, Stockholm, Sweden
1930	Otto Wagner Monument, Vienna
1932	Four low-cost terraced houses, Werkbund Estate, Vienna
1934	Austrian Pavilion, Biennale, Venice
1950	Public housing, Blechturmgasse, Vienna
1952	Public housing, Silbergasse, Vienna (with Josef Kalbac)
1954	Public housing, Heiligenstätterstrasse, Vienna (with Kalbac)

Publications

BOOKS ABOUT HOFFMANN

BARONI, DANIELE: *Josef Hoffmann e la Wiener Werkstatte.* Milan, 1981.

BORSI, FRANCO, and PERIZZI, ALESSANDRA: *Josef Hoffmann: tempo e geometria.* Rome, 1982.

GEBHARD, DAVID: *Josef Hoffmann: Design Classics.* Exhibition catalog. Fort Worth, Texas, 1983.

GRESLERI, GUILIANO (ed.): *Josef Hoffmann.* New York, 1985.

MEYER, CHRISTIAN (ed.): *Josef Hoffmann: Architect and Designer, 1870-1956.* Vienna and New York, 1981.

MÜLLER, DOROTHÉE: *Klassiker des modernen Möbeldesign: Otto Wagner, Adolf Loos, Joseph Hoffmann, Koloman Moser.* Munich, 1980.

SEKLER, EDUARD F., and CLARK, ROBERT JUDSON: *Josef Hoffmann 1870-1956: Architect and Designer.* Exhibition catalog. London, 1977.

SEKLER, EDUARD F.: *Josef Hoffmann: The Architectural Work.* Princeton, New Jersey, 1985.

VERONESI, GIULIA: *Josef Hoffmann.* Milan, 1956.

ARTICLES ABOUT HOFFMANN

BEHRENS, PETER: ''The Work of Josef Hoffmann.'' *Architecture* (Journal of the Society of Architects, London) 2 (1923): 589-599.

BIRKNER, OTHMAR: ''Josef Hoffmann 1938-1945.'' *Werk* (Zürich, October 1967).

EISLER, MAX: ''Josef Hoffmann 1870-1920.'' *Wendingen* Series 3, Nos. 8/9, special issue (1920): 4-20.

FREY, DAGOBERT: ''Josef Hoffmann zu seinem 50. Geburtstage.'' *Architekt* 23 (1920): 65-72.

GIRARDI, VITTORIA: ''Josef Hoffmann, maestro dimenticato.'' *Architettura* (October 1956).

''Josef Hoffmann und seine Schule.'' *Moderne Bauformen* No. 26 (1927).

MANSER, JOSE: ''Hoffmann at Liberty.'' *Building Design* (26 October 1979).

Alte und Moderne Kunst special issue (November/December 1970).

VERO, PETER: ''Little Square Hoffmann.'' *Architectural Review* (December 1977).

VILADAS, PILAR: ''Josef Hoffmann Revisited.'' *Interiors* (September 1979).

VOGELGESANG, SHEPARD: ''The Work of Josef Hoffmann.'' *Architectural Forum* 49, No. 4 (1928): 697-712.

Joseph Hoffmann: Purkersdorf Sanatorium, Vienna, Austria, 1904-06

Viewed within the context of the Modern Movement, Josef Hoffmann was a conservative revolutionary. Although the radically pared-down geometric style he developed just after the turn of the century presaged the rise of the International Style in the 1920s, Hoffmann, like most of his Viennese contemporaries, was unwilling to make a decisive break with history. Despite the extraordinary scope of his formal inventiveness, he continued to experiment with historical forms throughout his long career, seeking ways to reconcile traditional architecture with the needs and concerns of modern life.

In contrast to his mentor, Otto Wagner, who focused his creative energy on large monumental structures, Hoffmann built relatively few public buildings. Instead, he concentrated his attention on the domestic sphere, designing a series of houses and interiors for the wealthy Viennese middle class. Much of Hoffmann's oeuvre—like that of his nemesis Adolf Loos—was an exploration of the possibilities of dwelling. During the nearly 60 years of his active life he produced a virtually endless string of variations on the home, its furnishings and the objects contained within it.

At the center of Hoffmann's endeavors, however, remained a steady preoccupation with form and style. In common with other architects of *fin-de-siécle* Vienna, Hoffmann stressed the importance of the surface, of facade, symbol and ornament—the language of building—rather than more expressly architectonic issues. Even after World War I, when most of his contemporaries turned their attention to architecture's social dimensions, he continued to show an unusual degree of concern for formal and stylistic problems.

As a student of leading Ringstrasse architect Carl von Hasenauer, Hoffmann infused his early work with the formal and symbolic language of late Viennese historicism. After Otto

Wagner replaced Hasenauer at the Academy of Fine Arts in 1894, Hoffmann, inspired by Wagner's call for a modern aesthetic, became one of his most devoted followers. Over the course of the next several years Hoffmann worked in Wagner's office on the *Stadtbahn* (city railway) producing designs consistent with the Wagner school.

In the late 1890s, however, Hoffmann came under the powerful spell of Joseph Maria Olbrich and began to experiment with curvilinear art noveau. The sinuous shapes and rich vegetal decoration which he exhibited in works such as the Apollo Candle Shop and the interiors for the fourth and fifth Secession exhibitions earned him comparisons with Antoní Gaudi, Hector Guimard and Victor Horta.

After 1901, Hoffmann's stylistic mode began to change once more. Inspired by the crisp geometric works of Glasgow designers Charles Rennie Mackintosh and Margaret Macdonald, he gradually abandoned Olbrich's curvilinear style in favor of a new idiom based on rectilinear forms. During that period he also stripped away much of the ornament from his designs and restricted his palette primarily to black, white and gray. This so-called purist phase of Hoffmann's work, evident already in the four houses he designed for friends and fellow artists on the Hohe Warte just after the turn of the century, reached its apotheosis in the Purkersdorf Sanatorium, a building which in many ways anticipated the rise of the International Style 20 years later.

Even before the Purkersdorf Sanatorium was completed, however, Hoffmann began exploring the possibilities of a decorative style based on a rich ornamentality. His most successful and complete realization of this vision was the Palais Stoclet in Brussels, commissioned by a wealthy Belgian who imposed virtually no budgetary limits. Hoffmann, working in concert with the artisans of the Wiener Werkstätte, oversaw every aspect of the house's planning and construction, producing the consummate example of the Viennese ideal of the *Gesamtkunstwerk,* or total artwork.

After 1905, Hoffmann again began to change directions, moving away from the Jugendstil toward a new historicism based on classical motifs. This return to classicism, already manifest in the Palais Stoclet, reached its apex in the Primavesi House and the pavilions he designed for the exhibitions in Rome (1911) and Cologne (1914). The stripped classicism of these and other works of that period left a deep impression on many younger architects—among them Robert Mallet-Stevens—and prefigured in important ways the rise of art deco in the 1920s.

After World War I Hoffmann designed a series of housing complexes for the city of Vienna. But the focus of his work continued to be on private residences and interiors for the wealthy bourgeoisie. Many of his works of the early postwar years—for example the Berl, Ast and Knips houses—show a strong interest in folk motifs, which Hoffmann combined with a stripped classicism to create a unique decorative style.

Hoffmann's designs of the late 1920s and early 1930s, many of which he produced jointly with his young assistant Oswald Haerdtl, are marked by an attempt to come to terms with the changing face of the Modern Movement. Several of these works, among them the Altmann Store and the model houses at the 1932 Vienna Werkbund exhibition, closely approximated the image of the reigning *Neue Sachlichkeit.*

But by the 1920s Hoffmann was becoming increasingly out of step with the Modern Movement. At a time when most of the modernists were placing growing emphasis on designing goods for mass production, he continued to pour much of his time and energy into the craft-based Wiener Werkstätte. Despite his experiments with the formal language of the International Style, he continued even in the 1940s and early 1950s to churn out highly decorative designs.

After his death in 1956, Hoffmann was largely forgotten. Little was written about him in the standard histories of the Modern Movement, and many of his works were significantly altered or destroyed. Hoffmann's rediscovery in recent years owes much to the revival of interest in ornamentalism. His true importance, however, lies less in his role as a form-giver than in the specific role he played within the Modern Movement. In his search for an acceptable modernism, Hoffmann suggested important ways for maintaining a dialogue between the present and the past, a legacy which no doubt should grow in importance in the future.

—CHRISTOPHER LONG

HÖGER, Fritz.

German. Born in Beckenreihe, Germany, 1877. Died in 1949. Studied at the Baugewerkschule (School of Architecture), Hamburg, Germany, 1897-99. Worked for the architectural firm of Lund and Kallmorgen, Hamburg, 1901-05; private practice, Hamburg, 1906-49.

Chronology of Works
All in Germany

1912-13	Klöpperhaus Department Store, Hamburg
1920	Administration Offices, Schleswig-Holsteinischenstrom A. G., Rendsburg
1923-24	Chilehaus Block, Hamburg
1926	Grosse Bliechen, Broschek & Co. Publishing House, Hamburg
1926-28	Curschmannstrasse Gymnasium, Hamburg
1926-29	Reemtsma Building, Cigarette Factory, Hamburg-Wandsbek
1927-28	Anzeiger Building, Hannover
1927-28	Leder-Schüler Works, Hamburg
1927-28	Scherk Perfume Factory, Berlin
1927-43	Sprinkenhof Kontorhaus, Hamburg
1928	Administration Offices, Bentheimer Railway A. G., Bentheim
1928	Flughafen Estate, Hamburg-Fuhlbüttel
1928-29	Town Hall, Wilhelmshaven-Rustringen
1930	City Hospital, Delmenhorst
1931-33	Evangelist Church, Hohenzollernplatz, Berlin-Wilmersdorf
1935-38	Siebetsburg Housing Estate, Wilhelmshaven

Publications

BOOKS ABOUT HÖGER

BERKENHAGEN, EKHART (ed.): *Fritz Höger: Baumeister—Zeichnungen.* Berlin, 1977.

KAMPHAUSEN, ALFRED: *Der Baumeister Fritz Höger.* Neumünster, 1972.

PEHNT, WOLFGANG: *Expressionist Architecture.* New York and London, 1973.

WESTPHAL, CARL J. H. (ed.): *Fritz Höger, der niederdeutsche Backsteinbaumeister.* Lübeck, Germany, 1938.

ARTICLES ABOUT HÖGER

BOYKEN, V. IMMO: "Fritz Högers Celler Martin-Luther-Kirche vom 'Wesen und Wert der Gotik' in seinen Werk." *Architectura* No. 1 (1989): 76-93.

BOYKEN, V. IMMO: "Fritz Högers Kirche am Hohenzollernplatz in Berlin—Architektur zwischen Expressionismus und 'Neuer Sachlichkeit'." *Architectura: Zeitschrift für Geschichte der Baukunst* 15, No. 2 (1985): 179ff.

FUESS, H.: "Die Celler Höger-Kirche." *Celler Heimatkalender* 16 (1950).

"Kirche am Hohenzollernplatz in Berlin-Wilmersdorf." *Bauwelt,* 24, No. 16 (1933).

"The Rathaus at Rüstringen, Germany." *Architectural Review* 69 (February 1931).

*

Fritz Höger was trained at the Baugewerkschule in Hamburg, where he practiced from 1907 into the 1930s. Hamburg, situated midway between Amsterdam and Copenhagen on the North Sea, shared with those cities a long historical tradition of brick architecture. The city architect of Hamburg from 1907 until 1920 was Fritz Schumacher, who developed a faintly eclectic expression of the traditional brickbuilders' idiom (*Backsteinbau* in German) related to that of such contemporaries as H. P. Berlage in the Netherlands and Martin Nyrop in Denmark, and perhaps best described as a species of National Romanticism. Höger inherited that tradition, as can be seen in his Klöpperhaus Department Store (1912-13), built of brick with a traditional copper-clad roof. The Klöpperhaus, with its rational pier module filled with swelling window bays, compares favorably with such contemporaries as Alfred Messel's Wertheim Store in Berlin and Joseph Maria Olbrich's Tietz Store in Düsseldorf. It was not yet expressionistic, however, in either form or detail.

Following World War I, Höger became the best known expressionist of the Hamburg school, developing the *Backsteinbau* tradition beyond the conservative National Romanticism of the prewar period. His best-known work is the Chilehaus (1923-24), a vast business block (*Kontorhaus*) filling two city blocks in the Messberg quarter of Hamburg Altstadt. Höger's sources for the Chilehaus are seemingly diverse, including Schumacher's Finanzbehörde (1918), the Scheepvaarthuis in Amsterdam (1912-16) and the work of such German contemporaries as Hans Poelzig (Grosses Schauspielhaus in Berlin) and Peter Behrens (I. G. Farben Headquarters at Hoechst). As in those earlier works, Höger manipulated the brick detail into an expressive and evocative form, transcending the earlier eclecticism of the National Romantic tradition. The undulating wall plane and the prow-shaped corner suggest—perhaps even symbolize—the functions of a maritime shipping office. The Chilehaus is not an isolated monument, however, but part of an intensive colony of such *Kontorhäuser,* including Höger's own adjacent Sprinkenhof of 1927-28, with streamlined wings added in the 1930s. All are expressionistic in the sense that they manipulate brickwork in original ways, rejecting the eclecticism of the earlier National Romantic tradition, but not repudiating ornamental detail, unlike the new sensibility being pursued by the emerging International Style.

Höger's architecture retained the same concern with expressive brick in other programmatic contexts. At the Anzeiger Hochhaus in Hannover, he applied expressionist brick detail to one of the dwarf high-rises then beginning to appear in Europe. Actually the nine-story Anzeiger Hochhaus is one story shorter than the Chilehaus, but its narrower street frontage and pyramidal massing make it appear high in relation to the Hannover streetscape. The stepped profile of the street-level shopping arcades recalls similar forms from the Paris Exposition des Arts Decoratifs of 1925, suggesting a possible cross-fertilization between expressionism and the modernistic tradition.

In his office block for the Leder-Schüler Works (1927-28), however, Höger chose to dramatize the vertical dimensions of a dwarf high-rise by layering the building masses and emphasizing pier lines. The work of Frank Lloyd Wright, recently published in *Wendingen,* the journal of the Amsterdam school, was a possible influence. A Dutch connection is also suggested at the Lilienthalplatz Housing Estate in Hamburg, where Höger's articulation of corners with variations of fenestration and materials recalls contemporaneous practices in the Amsterdam school. This is at variance with the more straightforward detailing of the new Hamburg *Siedlungen* at Jarrestadt and Dulsburg supervised by Fritz Schumacher, who had returned to Hamburg as *Oberbaudirector* in 1923.

On the Curschmannstrasse Gymnasium (1926-28), Höger employed pitched roofs and latent Gothic windows to relieve the otherwise cubistic masses of the functional plan, and developed the entrance tower with a variety of picturesque details. The closest contemporary analogy would be to the schools W. M. Dudok was designing for Hilversum in the 1920s, once again reinforcing the sense of affinity between the Amsterdam and Hamburg schools. Unlike Dudok, however, Höger did not seem to be evolving toward functionalism. The essentially expressionist treatment of the Curschmannstrasse Gymnasium, with its decorative details, also stands at odds with Schumacher's Meerweinstrasse School in the Jarrestadt Siedlung (1928-30), in which modern structure rather than crafted detail is expressed.

Finally, at the Church on the Hohenzollernplatz in Berlin (1931-33), Höger disciplined his obsessive concern with constructed detail in a powerfully massed contemporary expression of ecclesiastical character. Throughout the decade since the Chilehaus, however, Höger had remained fundamentally an expressionist, largely unaffected by then-current tendencies in German architecture toward functionalism or the International Style. As the Nazis rejected expressionism as decadent even as they spurned international modernism, 1933 brought to an end Höger's effective career as a formgiver in German architecture.

—JAY C. HENRY

HOLABIRD and ROCHE.

HOLABIRD, William.
American. Born in New York, 1 September 1854. Died in Evanston, Illinois, 18 July 1923. Son was John Holabird, architect. Educated at West Point Military Academy. Draftsman, office of William Le Baron Jenney, Chicago; established firm with Ossin Simmons and Martin Roche, Chicago, 1880; firm became Holabird and Roche, 1883. Member of the old Western Association of Architects; fellow, American Institute of Architects, 1889.

ROCHE, Martin.
American. Born in Cleveland, Ohio, 1 August 1853. Died on 6 June 1927. Attended Art Institute of Chicago. Worked for William Le Baron Jenney, Chicago; partner, Holabird and Roche, Chicago, 1883. Member, old Western Association of Architects; fellow, American Institute of Architects.

Chronology of Works
All in the United States

1887-89	Tacoma Building, Chicago, Illinois†
1891	Pontiac Building, Chicago
1893-94	Old Colony Building, Chicago
1893-95	Marquette Building, Chicago
1898	Gage Group, Chicago
1898	Williams Building, Chicago
1898-99	Cable Building, Chicago†
1899-1900	McClurg Building, Chicago
1900-05	Mandel Brothers Store Annex, Chicago
1903	Champlain Building, Chicago
1904	Chicago Building, Chicago
1904-09	Republic Building, Chicago†
1908-09	LaSalle Hotel, Chicago†
1909-10	Brooks Building, Chicago
1911	City-County Building, Chicago
1911-12	Rand McNally Building, Chicago
1920	Crear Library, Chicago
1923-27	Palmer House, Chicago
1924-26	Roanoke Tower, Chicago
1925-27	Stevens Hotel, Chicago
1927-28	333 North Michigan Avenue Building, Chicago

Publications

BOOKS ABOUT HOLABIRD and ROCHE

BRUEGMANN, ROBERT: *Holabird & Roche, Holabird & Root: An Illustrated Catalog of Works.* 3 vols. New York, 1991.
CONDIT, CARL W.: *American Building Art: The Nineteenth Century.* New York, 1960.
CONDIT, CARL W.: *Chicago, 1910-29: Building, Planning, and Urban Technology.* Chicago, 1973.

Holabird and Roche: Marquette Building, Chicago, Illinois, 1893-95

CONDIT, CARL W.: *The Chicago School of Architecture: A History of Commercial and Public Building in the Chicago Area, 1875-1925.* Chicago, 1964.

HOLCOMB, PAUL: *Depreciation and Obsolescence in the Tacoma Building.* Chicago, 1929.

MUJICA, FRANCISCO: *History of the Skyscraper.* Paris, 1929.

RANDALL, FRANK A.: *History of the Development of Building Construction in Chicago.* Urbana, Illinois, 1949.

ZUCKOWSKY, JOHN (ed.): *Chicago Architecture 1872-1922: Birth of a Metropolis.* Exhibition catalog. Chicago, 1987.

ARTICLES ABOUT HOLABIRD and ROCHE

WEBSTER, J. CARSON: "The Skyscraper: Logical and Historical Considerations." *Journal of the Society of Architectural Historians* 18 (1959): 126-139.

WINKLER, FRANZ: "Some Chicago Buildings Represented by the Work of Holabird and Roche." *Architectural Record* 31 (1912): 313-387.

*

The architectural firm of Holabird and Roche is best known for its contribution to the development of the tall office building. The firm occupies an important place within the history of the Chicago school. William Holabird and Martin Roche, the firm's founders, both worked in the office of William Le Baron Jenney, whose engineering was paramount in the development of the steel-frame structure in Chicago architecture. From 1883, when Roche and Holabird became partners, until the death of William Holabird in 1923, the two men collaborated in successful partnership.

Contemporary with the exceptional Chicagoan firms of Adler and Sullivan, and Burnham and Root, Holabird and Roche contributed to a period of great building and innovation in architecture. The Holabird and Roche buildings are distinguished by their balance of innovation and conservatism and their synthesis of new techniques and materials with classical ornamentation. Essentially a pragmatic firm, Holabird and Roche's functional architectural theory is to be found in the buildings themselves. The firm's continued success, even extending to the next generation of Holabird and Root, lay in the architects' understanding of the importance of this type of balance for creating good architecture, both public and private.

The architectural promise of Holabird and Roche was first recognized in the Tacoma Building (1887-89). The Tacoma (demolished in 1929), a 12-story office structure, had an L-shaped plan and projecting bay windows designed for the practical function of providing light and air in the office space. The projecting windows also expressed the skeletal frame beneath the terra-cotta sheathing of the two street facades. The innovation of the iron-and-steel framing expressed in the facade of the building drew the attention of 20th-century historians, because it set a stylish precedent for modern skyscraper design. Holabird and Roche's progressive use of materials was combined with a traditional interest in classical composition. The Tacoma, like most of the Holabird and Roche buildings, maintained a tripartite exterior, with the three divisions still clearly defined.

While the basic elements of Holabird and Roche's skyscraper style were established in the Tacoma, it was really in the Marquette Building (1893-95) that the style became a working formula for multistory office structures. Holabird and Roche received that commission from the land developer Peter Brooks. Carl Condit's research has revealed that Brooks and his lawyer, Alan Aldis, were actively involved in the projects they commissioned and often set forth a number of requirements for the architects. In regard to the Marquette, Aldis and Brooks formulated the functional aspects for the commercial office structure. Their requirements included the need for well-lit office spaces, an impressive entrance and first-floor lobby area, efficient upkeep, minimum operating expenses, and planning to maximize the number of tenants. Holabird and Roche's E-shaped plan and bay-wide windows successfully maximized both space and light. The elevators were grouped around the middle prong of the E, thus utilizing the darkest part of the building and providing a central circulating area. It was partially their talent for creating efficient, functional spaces that established Holabird and Roche's reputation for multistory office buildings and generated similar commissions.

The balanced proportions, direct expression of the steel cage and an impressive entrance imbue the Marquette with stylish sophistication, making it one of the firm's most acclaimed buildings. In designing the Marquette building, Holabird and Roche replaced the projecting bay windows of the Tacoma with a flattened surface, more directly communicating the structure beneath. Of the 16 stories, the bottom two form a "base" for the building. This lower portion of the building features true Chicago-style windows, large horizontal glass panes divided by thin mullions to form a central panel with small flanking panels. Three Ionic columns articulating the main entrance provide the structure with elegance and monumentality.

The middle section, composed of 12 of the 16 stories, is dominated by expansive windows, which regularly delineate the cells of the steel cage. Unbroken piers and recessed spandrels are also arranged to articulate the structural framing and express the verticality of the building.

The uppermost stories of the Marquette are distinguished from the lower stories by moldings. The heavy cornice and the 15th and 16th stories mark the "capital" of the base-shaft-capital design which forms the style of the building.

During that early period in skyscraper history, architects were searching for a style that would be appropriate to the new techniques that allowed buildings to soar high into the sky. Holabird and Roche, more than any other firm in Chicago, worked out a style using the basic elements established in their Marquette Building. The trademarks of their style are functional spaces, Chicago-style windows arranged regularly across the steel structure, a tripartite division and classical ornamentation. Notable examples of this style in the work of Holabird and Roche are the Cable Building (1898-99, demolished in 1961), the Republic Building (1905, 1909, demolished in 1961), the Mandel Brothers Annex (1900, 1905) and the Brooks Building (1909-10).

Also significant is the McClurg Building (1899-1900). The building has been praised for its extremely simple exterior, dominated by large Chicago windows. The terra-cotta sheathing was reduced to a minimum, so that the windows hardly appear to be separate divisions. Instead, there is a sense of the "glass box" of later skyscrapers. It has been noted, however, that the McClurg Building, unlike the Marquette, was a loft building, far from the center of the business district. It was designed, therefore, to be a simpler structure than a downtown office building. Nevertheless, it did anticipate some of the later skyscrapers in which the glass and steel framing became the articulation of the facade.

In the second decade of the 20th century, Holabird and Roche began to explore different possibilities for the skyscraper style using a combination of Gothic and classical details. The Chicago Tribune competition in 1922 demonstrated this new trend in skyscraper design. The Holabird and Roche design for the tower won third place in the international competition. The design incorporated a large Gothic arch marking the main entrance, a multistory shaft for office space and an enormous Gothic niche for a sculpture above the central shaft. Although this building was not executed, the Chicago Temple Building (1922-23) reiterated the Gothic nature of the Tribune entry. Commissioned by the First Methodist-Episcopal Church, the structure incorporated a chapel at street level and 20 stories of office space above. The religious function of the building is expressed by the Gothic ornamentation, in particular an eight-story spire that tops the building.

Also notable in Holabird and Roche's œuvre is the City Hall and County Building in Chicago (1911). The structure required a design that would express governmental stature and function as an office building. The solution for Holabird and Roche was to clothe the office building in a base, giant six-story columns and a story-high entablature. The building was criticized for not allowing the facade to express the structure of the building; nevertheless, it does express the nature of governmental power.

The success of Holabird and Roche continued its momentum into the second generation. In 1927, following the death of Martin Roche, William Holabird's son John joined John W. Root to continue the firm as the partnership of Holabird and Root. Many of the buildings of Holabird and Roche and Holabird and Root remain in use today because of their emphasis on function, utility and a conservative taste that has survived for almost a century.

—MELISSA CARD

HOLDEN, Charles.

British. Born in Bolton, Lancashire, England, 12 May 1875. Died in London, 1 May 1960. Married Margaret Macdonald, 1913 (died in 1954). Studied at Manchester Institute of Technology, 1893-96, Manchester School of Art, 1896-97, and Royal Academy School of Architecture, London, 1898-99.tant to architect Jonathan Simpson, Bolton, 1896; articled to E. W. Leeson, Manchester, 1896-97; articled to C. R. Ashbee, London, 1898; worked for H. Percy Adams, with whom he formed partnership in 1907; w orked from 1912 with John Loughborough Pearson as Adams, Holden and Pearson; lieutenant in Royal Engineers during World War I; appointed to Imperial War Graves Commission after war; began collaborating with London Passenger Transport Board, 1923. Gold Medal, Royal Institute of British Architects, 1936; refused knighthood.

Chronology of Works
All in England unless noted

1900-03	Belgrave Hospital for Children, Kensington, London
1901-02	British Seamen's Hospital, Istanbul, Turkey
1902-04	Law Society, Chancery Lane, London (extension)
1903-06	King Edward VII Sanatorium, Midhurst, Sussex
1904	Tunbridge Wells General Hospital, Kent
1905-06	Central Reference Library, Bristol
1906-12	Royal Infirmary, Bristol
1907-08	British Medical Association (now Zimbabwe House), London
1908	Women's Hospital, Soho Square, London
1911-29	Sutton Valence Public School, Kent
1914-23	King's College for Women, Kensington, London
1918-26	War cemeteries in France and Belgium
1922	War Memorial Gateway, Clifton College, Bristol
1924-29	Underground Stations (Piccadilly Circus, Leicester Square, etc.), London (rebuilding)
1925-26	Underground Stations, Northern Line, London
1927-30	London Transport Headquarters, 55 Broadway, London
1931-33	Underground Stations, Piccadilly Line, London
1931-37	Senate House and buildings for London University, Bloomsbury, London
1933	National Library of Wales, Aberstwyth, Wales
1952-58	Birkbeck College, Students' Union and Warburg Institute, London University, Bloomsbury, London

Publications

BOOKS ABOUT HOLDEN

SERVICE, ALASTAIR: *The Architects of London.* London, 1979.
SERVICE, ALASTAIR (ed.): *Edwardian Architecture and Its Origins.* 1975.
STAMP, GAVIN, and HARRIS, JOHN: *Silent Cities.* London, 1977.

ARTICLES ABOUT HOLDEN

HANSON, BRIAN: "Singing the Body Electric with Charles Holden." *Architectural Review* 158 (December 1975): 349-356.
HUTTON, CHARLES: "Dr. Charles Holden." *Artifex* 3 (1969): 35-53.
MAYER, MARTIN: "Underground Architect." *Building Design* (11 April 1975).
MIDDLETON, GRAHAME: "Charles Holden and his London Underground Stations." *Architectural Association Quarterly* 8, No. 2 (1976).
PEVSNER, NIKOLAUS: "Patient Progress—The Life and Work of Frank Pick." Pp. 190-209 in *Studies in Art, Architecture and Design: Victorian and After.* Princeton, New Jersey, 1968.

*

Charles Holden's reputation rests today primarily on the work that he did in the 1930s for London Transport and for the University of London. Because he was so feted for the former, and often criticized for the monumentality of the latter, they have tended to obscure the rest of his long, prolific and often brilliant career. Regardless of scale or type, all his buildings share certain leitmotifs that form a continuum throughout his career. It is not a continuum defined by style, but by Holden's attitudes toward architecture and building, most particularly his attention to craftsmanship and detailing, his desire for a collaboration with artists and sculptors, and by his very personal handling of massing.

Already in 1902, Holden's genius has been recognized. C. R. Ashbee cited him, together with such masters as G. F. Bodley, Philip Webb, W. R. Lethaby and Henry Wilson, as "one of the real architects [that] can be numbered on the fingers of one's two hands." It is in his early work that one first sees Holden going beyond the stylistic confines of the time, and creating a very personal architecture—an architecture founded, not on style or ideology, but on the pillars of "truth, order and clarity," combined with the strength that Holden drew from the rough-hewn poetry of Walt Whitman, by which he, like Louis Sullivan and Frank Lloyd Wright, was so influenced. Holden first encountered Whitman in his native Bolton, which was one of the great centers of Whitmanic culture in England. At the epicenter of the movement was J. W. Wallace and the "loving comrades" of the Eagle Street College. It was in 1898, at a time when Holden had reached an impasse in his search to find an appropriate solution for the RIBA Soane Medallion competition, that Wallace declaimed to Holden Whitman's "Laws for Creation." As Holden said in later life, it was the hearing of this poem that allowed him to start thinking for himself and to create a design that was "his confession of faith, his confession of his poverty of imagination even—but it was his own, bald, bleak perhaps, but naked and unashamed." This desire for the "naked and unashamed" is an important leitmotif in Holden's work, and is the source for his aphorism of "When in doubt, leave it out."

In 1905 Holden published, anonymously, two pieces in the *Architectural Review,* the first titled "If Whitman had been an architect," and the second, "Thoughts for the Strong." Both were a chastisement of contemporary architecture, and were a call to action: "Come, you Modern Buildings, come! Throw off your mantle of deceits; your cornices, pilasters, mouldings, swags, scrolls; behind them all, behind your dignified proportions, your picturesque groupings, your arts and crafts prettiness and exaggerated techinques; behind and beyond them all hides the one I love." The ones Holden loved were those that "shall be as naked as [they] choose," and were to be found "in a measure, in our mills, our warehouses, our back elevations (they are not as godless as we thought them)." This was surely a reference to the warehouses and mills that so dominated the landscape of turn-of-the-century Lancashire, and in turn to the "back elevations" of some of Holden's own œuvre.

Although Holden's language and criticisms seem a little strong for such a modest man, it must be remembered that by 1905, although he was only 31, he had built some of his most important buildings. Among them were the Belgrave Hospital for Children, London (1899-1901); the British Seaman's Hospital, Constantinople (1901-02); the extension to the Incorporated Law Society, London (1902-04); and, most important, the Bristol Central Reference Library (1902-06). Although these and some of his other buildings are today almost forgotten, at the time they were among the most seminal of the age. As Percy Thomas, the president of the RIBA in 1936, said when awarding Holden that institution's Gold Medal: "Those early works of Holden gave the younger architects of his time the same inspiration which the modern young architect appears to obtain from Mendelsohn and Corbusier." A case in point is the Bristol Central Reference Library, which was the source for the west facade of Charles Rennie Mackintosh's Glasgow School of Art, as well as being an inspiration to Edwin Lutyens at Castle Drogo and to many other architects of lesser standing.

But if one is to search for Holden's monument, one must ride the Underground. It is for his headquarters building for London Transport and the fifty-odd Underground stations that Holden will be best remembered, because these are not only very fine and elegant buildings, but were also perceived as being not only modern but also within the context of English tradition.

—EITAN KAROL

HOLL, Elias.

German. Born in Augsburg, Germany, 28 February 1573. Died in Augsburg, 6 January 1646. Father, Hans Holl, was a mason, as were grandfather, Sebastian Holl, and great-grandfather, Jakob Holl. Married Maria Burckhart, 1595 (died in 1607); eight children. Married Rosina Reischlen, 1610 (died in 1635); 13 children. Trained as a mason with his father; visited Italy, 1600-01. City mason of Augsburg, 1602-31, and served also during the Swedish occupation, 1632-35.

Elias Holl: Town Hall, Augsburg, Germany, 1614-20

Chronology of Works
All in Germany
† Work no longer exists

1601	Foundry, Augsburg†
1602	Baker's House, Augsburg
1602	St. Anna's Tower, Augsburg
1602-07	Zeughaus (Armory), Augsburg
1605	Siegelhaus, Augsburg†
1605	Wertachorugger Tor, Augsburg (alterations)
1609	Slaughterhouse, Augsburg
1609	Barfüsserbrücke, Augsburg (substructure preserved)
1613	St. Anna Gymnasium, Augsburg
1614	Neue Bau, Augsburg†
1614-20	Town Hall, Augsburg
1622	Klinkertor, Augsburg†
1622	Rotes Tor, Augsburg
1625-30	Heilig Geist Spital, Augsburg

Publications

BOOKS BY HOLL

Selbstbiographie des Elias Holl. Edited by Christian Meyer. Augsburg, 1873.

BOOKS ABOUT HOLL

BAUM, JULIUS: *Die Bildwerke des Elias Holl.* Strasbourg, 1908.
BLENDINGER, FRIEDRICH: *Elias Holl: Augsburger Stadtbaumeister 1573-1646.* Exhibition catalog. Augsburg, 1973.
CHRISTOFFEL, U.: *Augsburger Rathaus.* Augsburg, 1929.

HIEBER, HERMANN: *Elias Holl: Der Meister der deutschen Renaissance.* Munich, 1923.

HITCHCOCK, HENRY-RUSSELL: *German Renaissance Architecture.* Princeton, New Jersey, 1981.

INSTITUT FÜR STÄDTEBAU UND ARCHITEKTUR DER BAUAKADEMIE DER DDR (ed.): *Grosse Baumeister 2.* Berlin, 1990.

LEYBOLD, LUDWIG: *Das Rathaus der Stadt Augsburg.* Berlin, 1886-88.

MEYER, CHRISTIAN: *Die Hauschronik der Familie Holl.* Munich, 1910.

ROECK, BERND: *Elias Holl: Architekt einer europäischen Stadt.* Regensburg, 1985.

SCHÜRER, OSKAR: *Elias Holl: Der Augsburger Stadt Werkmeister.* Berlin, 1938.

STANGE, ALFRED: *Die deutsche Baukunst der Renaissance.* Munich, 1926.

VON BEZOLD, G.: *Die Baukunst der Renaissance in Deutschland.* Leipzig, 1908.

WALTER, RENATE VON: *Das Augsburger Rathaus: Architektur und Bildgehalt.* Augsburg, 1972.

ARTICLES ABOUT HOLL

ALBRECHT, INGEBORG: "Elias Holl, Stil und Werk des 'Maurmaisters' und der Augsburger Malerarchitekten Heinz und Kager." *Münchner Jahrbuch der bildenden Kunst* 12 (1937): 101-136.

HAGER, WERNER: "Vergleichendes zu Elias Holl." *Aachener Kunstblätter* 41 (1971): 231-236.

LIEB, NORBERT: "Augsburger Baukunst der Renaissancezeit." Pp. 229-247 in HERMANN RINN (ed.): *Augusta 955-1955: Forschungen und Studien zur Kultur- und Wirtschaftsgeschichte Augsburgs.* Munich, 1955.

PFISTER, RUDOLF: "Die Augsburger Rathaus-modelle des Elias Holl." *Münchner Jahrbuch der bildenden Kunst* 12 (1937): 85-100.

STANGE, ALFRED: "Zur Bibliographie des Elias Holl." *Münchner Jahrbuch der bildenden Kunst* 4 (1927): 20-22.

ZIMMER, JÜRGEN: "Das Augsburger Rathaus und die Tradition." *Münchner Jahrbuch der bildenden Kunst* 28 (1977): 191-218.

*

Elias Holl was one of the leading German architects of the first half of the 17th century. Holl was born in Augsburg in 1573, and died there in 1646. His career was terminated by Counter-Reformation politics in 1635.

Holl's work characterizes him as one of the principal architects of the transition between Late Renaissance and Early Baroque. In his creative development of indigenous traditions, he achieved a form a architectural expression which is difficult to associate firmly with either one of these styles. His principal buildings in Augsburg, such as the Zeughaus, Slaughterhouse and Town Hall display innovative, and unrepeated, design solutions in facades and interiors.

Holl came from an Augsburg family of architects. His father, Hans Holl, made a name for himself as building master for Jacob Fugger. Elias Holl served his apprenticeship with his father, and worked for him as a journeyman until the father's death in 1594. In 1596 he himself became a master in Augsburg, and was accepted into the guild. As a consequence of his involvement with the alteration of a private house in 1599/1600, he met the city councilman Anton Graf, who had commissioned the project. Graf invited him for a trip to Venice (18 November

1600 to 31 January 1601). The style of Holl's later work indicates that Holl made a particular study of the architecture of the three great Renaissance masters Jacopo Sansovino (1486-1570), Michele Sanmicheli (1484-1559) and Andrea Palladio (1508-1580) when he was in Venice. Holl was also familiar with the teachings of Vitruvius, Leon Battista Alberti and Palladio through the publications, engravings and woodcuts that were widely available in the 16th century. The basis of Holl's architecture was already laid out in the work of these theorists, particularly such concepts as harmony, variation in tectonic form and solidity of execution.

In 1602 Holl was made city architect of Augsburg to replace Jacob Eschay (died in 1606). In the same year he received his first great commission—to alter and expand the Zeughaus on Zeughausplatz, situated southwest of the St. Moritz Church. An older, 16th-century building was to be connected at straight angles to a new north wing. Special art historical significance resides in the principal facade of the eastern side of the new, main wing. Holl created this facade in collaboration with the painter and architect Josef Heintz the Elder (1564-1609). The painter Mathias Kager (1575-1634) also worked for Holl.

Built according to a simple layout, the Zeughaus facade displays distinctly Baroque features, such as a diversity of forms and pictorial dynamism. Stylistically, the facade stands between Mannerism and Baroque. Holl did not match the dynamism of the Zeughaus in any of his numerous later buildings. The location of the two-wing building is also significant from an urban-planning perspective. With the addition of the north wing, Holl simultaneously created a public square and shaped the Augsburg urban landscape.

Besides the work on the Zeughaus, Holl completed a great number of other commissions. These included houses, a castle, and a variety of religious and civic buildings for the independently governed city of Augsburg, such as guildhouses and towers for the city's fortifications.

In 1605 Holl built the municipal Siegelhaus, which displays a recognizable kinship to the Zeughaus in the articulation of the facade. However, a tendency toward the later simplification of the dynamic articulation and the unification and reduction of the diversity of forms is already in evidence in this building. The city Slaughterhouse (1609) exemplifies Holl's later development even more clearly. An independent architectural sensibility that maintains close ties to tradition asserts itself in the design. The further development of elements of late medieval residential architecture became central to Holl's work.

His early buildings were so popular that, in 1607, the emperor Rudolf II paid Holl 50 guilders for the drawings for the Zeughaus, the Siegelhaus and the Beckenhaus.

Holl's most mature achievement was his design for the Augsburg Town Hall. The dynamic articulation of the early work gave way in this facade to a massing of "Palladian" simplicity, in which the articulation of the exterior expresses the organization of the interior. The Town Hall is a unique creation of the Late Renaissance, a fusion of the Italian palazzo and German hall architecture. The Augsburg Town Hall is one of the most mature creations of early-17th-century German architecture.

Besides his activity as city architect, Holl designed buildings for prominent patrons outside Augsburg, and he was also active as a consultant. Holl's significance lies not only in his architectural work, however, but also in his achievements in urban planning in the city of Augsburg. He transformed the medieval city into a modern urban landscape determined by sequences of streets and squares, principally through the felicitous insertion of monumental hinged building complexes.

In 1609 Holl took over the systematic renovation of the city's fortifications and the water-supply and drainage systems, in addition to renovating the towers at the Klinkertor and the Frauentor. In the alteration of the Wertachbrugger Tor (1605), he had already furnished proof of his ability in the area of modern fortifications. Holl thus had an extremely wide-ranging career in the service of the city, in many areas of architecture and urban planning. He built residential structures, warehouses, guildhouses, market halls, towers and gates for the fortifications.

As a Protestant, he was adversely affected by the religious wars, and in 1630 was removed from office on the basis of the Counter-Reformation's "Edict of Restitution." After Swedish troops occupied Augsburg in 1632, these measures were undone, and he was restored to his position as city architect. In those years, he was active mostly as a military engineer for the Swedish army, occupied with the further expansion of the city's defensive system. After the departure of the Swedes in 1635, Holl was fined and again removed from office.

In 1898 the architect's "Hauschronik des Augsburger Stadtbaumeisters Elias Holl" first saw the light of day. It is an autobiographical document of great art-historical value, providing information about the architectural and urban-planning activities of a man whose work stood on the threshold between the Late Renaissance and the Early Baroque.

—PETRA LESER
Translated from the German by Marijke Rijsberman

HOLLAND, Henry.

British. Born in London, England, 7 June 1745. Died in London, 17 June 1806. Father was Henry Holland, master builder. Married Bridget Brown, daughter of the landscape gardener Lancelot Brown, 1773; five children. Trained at his father's yard in Fulham. Joined Lancelot Brown as partner, 1771; worked with John Sloan and Charles Tatham, 1772-78; appointed clerk of works at the Royal Mews at Charing Cross, 1775; surveyor to Bridewell and Bethlehem Hospitals; employed as architect by the Prince of Wales, 1782-93.

Chronology of Works
All in England unless noted
* Approximate dates
† Work no longer exists

1770	Hale House, Hampshire
1770	Hill Park, near Westerham, Kent (for the First Earl of Hillsborough)
1770-71	Battersea Bridge, Middlesex†
1771-74	Claremont House, Esher, Surrey (with Lancelot Brown)
1774-75	Benham Place, Newbury (with Brown)
1775-78	Cadland, Hampshire (with Brown)†
1775-78	Trentham Hall, Staffordshire (remodeling, with Brown)†
1776-78	Brook's Club, St. James's Street, London
1777	Cardiff Castle, South Wales (restoration with Brown)†
1777ff.	Hans Town, London (including development of Sloane Street, Hans Place, Cadogan Place, Holland's House)
1778-81	Berrington Hall, Herefordshire
1779-80	The Crown Inn, Stone, Staffordshire (new front to street)
1779-82	Chart Sutton Church, Kent (rebuilt except for tower)

1781-82	Nuneham Park, Oxfordshire (alterations with Brown)†
1783-96	Carlton House, London (rehabilitation)†
1786-87	Marine Pavilion, Brighton, Sussex
1787	York House, Whitehall, London (additions; now Dover House)
1787	Knight's Hill, Norwood, Surrey (for the 1st Lord Thurlow)†
1787	Stanmore House/Park, Middlesex (alterations)†
1787-89	Althorp, Northamptonshire (remodeling)
1787-1802	Woburn Abbey, Bedfordshire (alterations)
1788-92	Broadlands, Hampshire
1791-94	Drury Lane Theater, London†
1792	Covent Garden Theater, London (remodeling)†
1792	Swan Hotel, Bedford†
1794-1800	Outlands House, Weybridge, Surrey (for Frederic Duke of York)
1795	Theater, Marischal Street, Aberdeen, Scotland†
1795	Debden Hall, Essex†
1796-1800	Southill House, Bedfordshire
1796*	Park Place, near Henley-on Thames, Berkshire (remodeled 1871)
1799-1800	East India House, Ledenhall Street, London (completion)†
1799-1800	Warehouses, East India Company, London (following modified version of designs by Richard Jupp)
1800	Wimbledon Park House, Surrey†
1803-04	Albany Chambers, Piccadilly, London
1805	Hertford Castle (alterations to Gatehouse)
1807	Assembly Rooms, Ingram Street, Glasgow, Scotland†

Publications

BOOKS ABOUT HOLLAND

STROUD, DOROTHY: *Henry Holland: His Life and Architecture.* London, 1966.

ARTICLES ABOUT HOLLAND

HODSON, H. B.: "Holland the Architect." *Builder* 13 (1855): 437.

*

Henry Holland, like George Dance the Elder (1695-1768), George Dance the Younger (1741-1825) and Robert Taylor (1714-88), had close connections with the city of London: Holland's father, also Henry (1712-85), was master of the Tylers' and Bricklayers' Company, and had a business as a master builder in Fulham. Young Henry seems to have learned his skills in his father's yard, but in 1771 he branched out as an architect, having already carried out alterations at Hale House, Hampshire, in 1770: works for the first earl of Hillsborough at Hill Park, near Westerham in Kent, in the same year; and Battersea Bridge, designed also in 1770-71. In 1771, in fact, he joined Lancelot "Capability" Brown (1716-83) in an informal partnership arrangement, and worked on the erection of Claremont House, near Esher in Surrey, for the first Lord Clive, between 1771 and 1774. Brown had employed the elder Holland to execute many of his architectural commissions, and, as Brown's confidence in young Holland grew, he was able to hand over the architectural side of his practice to him. In 1773 young Holland married Brown's daughter, Bridget, and grew so much in his father-in-law's esteem that he was named as an executor of Brown's will in 1779.

Through Brown, Holland developed his contacts with a very large and aristocratic clientele, and his involvement in the building of Brooks' Club-House at 60 St. James's Street in London in 1776-78 introduced him to many members of the Whig aristocracy who were to be so important to him in the future.

Holland's architectural style was strongly influenced by French exemplars culled from the published works of Marie-Joseph Peyre, Pierre Patte and Jacques Gondoin, and he actually employed a French assistant, J.-P. Trécourt, as well as numerous French craftsmen on his many jobs. Holland's work, therefore, was infused with a strong neoclassical flavor, and his architecture was comparable to that of the Adam brothers in its delicacy and fashionable elegance, from which much of the outmoded Palladianism had been expunged.

Through his Whig contacts Holland was employed as an architect by George, Prince of Wales (later King George IV), for whom he carried out major works at Carlton House between 1783 and 1796, including the handsome Corinthian portico, Ionic screen and sequence of elegant interiors. Carlton House also included a forecourt that was strongly reminiscent of a Parisian *hôtel,* and indeed may have owed something to the designs by Pierre Rousseau for the Hôtel de Salm. At Carlton House and Berrington Hall, Herefordshire (1778-81), Holland designed very spacious and lovely staircases, the spatial effects of which were greatly admired at the time. Berrington, fortunately, can still delight us today.

Holland employed the young John Soane (1753-1837) from 1772 to 1778 at a salary of £60 per annum: Soane claimed afterward that he himself was responsible for the design of the finished entrance hall at Lord Clive's Claremont House, which had been designed by Holland with "Capability" Brown. Another formidable talent also employed as a draftsman in Holland's office, Charles Heathcote Tatham (1772-1842) joined Holland in 1789, staying there until he left for a tour of Italy (which Holland helped to finance) in 1794. Tatham's drawings for details at Carlton House and elsewhere were exquisite, and some survive in the Drawings Collection of the Royal Institute of British Architects.

Like his father, Holland engaged in speculative developments, and from 1771, with capital put up by the older Holland, he leased land in Chelsea from Lord Cadogan, and erected Hans Town, comprising Sloane Street, Sloane Place, Cadogan Place and Hans Place on the site from 1777.

Holland's work has certain affinities with that of William Chambers (1723-96), especially in his use of French neoclassical precedents, but, unlike Chambers, Holland did not eschew things Greek, and in this respect his work had more in common with that of the Adam brothers. Holland, however, did not travel very much outside England, and in fact only visited France for the first time on the eve of the Revolution: he was content to study his architecture through published works.

Holland appears to have been a man who disliked the limelight, who valued his independence and who kept the world at a distance. What public notice he had was unwelcome to him, and he never exhibited his works at the Royal Academy. He was a district surveyor, and a clerk of the works at the Royal Mews at Charing Cross, an Office of Works appointment he obtained in 1775. He became surveyor to the Honourable East India Company in 1799, and was also surveyor to the Bridewell and Bethlehem Hospitals from 1782 to 1793. He published a report on the causes of fires in buildings in 1793, and wrote two interesting papers: one was on the construction of workers' cottages (1797), and the other was on the use of *pisé* in building (also 1797). Both papers were published in the *Communications*

of the Board of Agriculture. Indeed, Holland seems to have been responsible for the introduction of pisé as a building material in England, and his work on the subject was again derived from French precedent and publications.

Much of Holland's oeuvre has been destroyed, including what was probably his masterpiece, Carlton House, but Berrington Hall gives an excellent flavor of his refined and elegant style. Unfortunately, most of his drawings and other papers were also destroyed by his executors after his death.

—JAMES STEVENS CURL

HOLLEIN, Hans.

Austrian. Born in Vienna, Austria, 30 March 1934. Studied at the Department of Civil Engineering, Bundesgewerbeschule, Vienna, 1949-53, then at the School of Architecture, Academy of Fine Arts, Vienna, 1953-56, Dip.Arch.; studied in the United States: architecture and planning at the Illinois Institute of Technology, Chicago, 1958-59; M.Arch., College of Environmental Design, University of California, Berkeley, 1960. Worked in various architectural offices in the United States, Sweden and Germany; private practice in Vienna, since 1964; consultant designer to various corporations in Austria, France, Italy, Japan and the United States, since 1966. Professor of architecture, Academy of Fine Arts, Düsseldorf, Germany, since 1967; head of the School and Institute of Design, since 1976, and leader of the master class in architecture, since 1979, at the Academy of Applied Arts, Vienna; visiting professor, Yale University, New Haven, Connecticut, since 1979; editor of *Bau,* Vienna, 1965-70 . Pritzker Prize, 1985.

Hans Hollein: Haas Haus complex, Vienna, Austria, 1985-89

Chronology of Works

All in Austria unless noted

1965	Retti Candle Shop, Vienna
1970-75	Siemens Headquarters Building, Munich, Germany
1972	Media-Line at Olympic Village, Munich, Germany
1972-82	Städtiches Museum, Abteiberg, Mönchengladbach, Germany
1973	Museum of Modern Art, Villa Strozzi, Florence, Italy
1974	Schullin Jewelry Shop I, Vienna
1976-79	Austrian Tourist Bureau Central Branch Office and three Branch Offices, Vienna
1977-78	Museum of Glass and Ceramics, Teheran, Iran
1981	Beck Department Store, Munich, Germany
1981	Museum of Applied Art, Vienna (extension)
1981-82	Schullin Jewelry Shop II, Vienna
1981-83	Beck Shop at Trump Tower, New York City, USA
1983	National Museum of Egyptian Civilization, Cairo, Egypt
1985-89	Haas Haus complex, Vienna
1987-	Banco Santander Headquarters, Madrid, Spain
1989-	Fukuda Motors Building, Tokyo, Japan

Publications

BOOKS BY HOLLEIN

GA 47: Otto Wagner. Ed. by Yukio Futagawa. Tokyo, 1978.
Design: Man Transforms. Vienna, 1989.
Paolo Piva: Design und Architektur. With Wilhelm Holzbauer and Sergio Polano. Salzburg, 1991.

ARTICLES BY HOLLEIN

"Rudolf M. Schindler—ein Wiener Architekt in Kalifornien." *Aufbau* (March 1961).
"Transformations." *Arts and Architecture* (May 1966).
"Architecture." *Aujourd'hui art et architecture* (May/June 1966).
"Neue Konzeptionen aus Wien." *Bau* 2/3 (1969).
"All is Architecture." *Architectural Design* (February 1970).
"Messages." *Japan Architect* (June 1976).
"Position and Move." *Space Design* (April 1976).

BOOKS ABOUT HOLLEIN

BODE, PETER M., and PEICHL, GUSTAV: *Architektur aus Österreich seit 1960.* Salzburg, 1980.
ESHERICK, JOSEPH: *Hans Hollein/Walter Pichler, Architektur.* Exhibition catalog. Vienna, 1963.
Hans Hollein: Work and Behavior, Life and Death, Everyday Situations. Exhibition catalog. Vienna, 1972.
MACKLER, C.: *Hans Hollein.* Aachen, West Germany, 1978.
PETTENA, GIANNI: *Hans Hollein: opere 1960-1988.* Milan, 1988.

ARTICLES ABOUT HOLLEIN

COOK, PETER: "Stirling and Hollein." *Architectural Review* (December 1982).
DAVEY, PETER: "Hollein in Munich." *Architectural Review* (June 1981).
"Hans Hollein." *Space Design* (May 1973).
"Hans Hollein: A Biographic Interview." *Arquitecturas bis* (November 1975).

"Hans Hollein's 'architecture parlante'." *Architectural Review* (October 1980).
"A View of Contemporary World Architecture: Hans Hollein." *Japan Architect* (July 1970).

Hans Hollein may be classified as an artist, furniture and exhibit designer, and graphic designer, but mostly as an architect. He resembles the city in which he was born, Vienna—a city that is rich in its plurality of form as a result of its numerous political and social changes. Similarly, Hollein's core of architectural work fails to reflect a recognized doctrine, just as Vienna lacks a pronounced national style of architecture.

His predecessors, Richard Neutra and R. M. Schindler, aspired to the development of the functionalist "modern" architecture which valued technology, circulation and efficiency in its meaning. Their understanding and expression of architecture became just a vein of Hollein's design vocabulary. He felt that the directive approach of his countrymen needed to achieve more in the social realm. Society had become more complex with a greater base of cultural, economic and personal differences. He realized a disjunction between the elites who create the environment and the masses who inhabit and use it. Hollein would progress toward the ideals of the Arts and Crafts movement of total design or total work of art. His intention would be to communicate with the public and the profession through work based on both modernity and conventionality.

This transitional approach emphasized the city context, the value of the users and architectural expression through ornament. Hollein observed the great advances of other disciplines and their response to the physical and emotional needs of people. Throughout his career, Hollein has developed a philosophy and architectural vocabulary, detailing that most objects in life can be classified as architecture. This means that the man-made elements around each one of us can have a distinct effect on our sensory capabilities.

The other pronounced aspect of Hollein's work involves the metaphors or content of irony in his aesthetics of building. His use or combination of modern and common materials translates into buildings that seldom proclaim their functions. His use of ornament contradicts the building form. It is not applied in a manner subservient to structure or imitative of nature, but is purposely constructed for its own independent validity. It states clearly the distinction between what is merely on the surface of objects and what they are in reality. The composition of these differing building elements creates a sense of tension that unites the appearance. Whether the commission is large or small, the budget open or constrained, Hollein not only solves the program but makes a distinct aesthetic architectural statement.

Hollein began his architectural career with small urban infill projects. One of the most notable was the Retti Candle Shop in Vienna (1965), a design that exemplifies a structure that fails to indicate its function. The street-side facade of polished aluminum, which is inset into the typical Viennese stucco surroundings, does not indicate the housing of soft, warm candles. Despite the modern exterior, the building does not solicit itself on this street of exclusive shops. Hollein did not feel that the use of neon signs or large expanses of display windows was necessary to merchandise the product. Instead, he created pedestrian interest through small, sweeping object windows that protrude into the plane of the walkway. These two clever devices convey the contents of the store to passersby on both sides of the street—but in a subtle manner. The plan of the building consists of two interlocking geometric rooms with walls of aluminum and mirror finish. The combination of these design elements creates a movement and pulsation in the space, which makes it appear larger than it is and maximizes the circulation within.

The Media-line design at the Olympic Village in Munich was completed in 1972. This project incorporated Hollein's belief that everything can be considered and treated as architecture. The Media-line is a metal framework that networks throughout the business district of Munich, working as a transportation depot and information center for citizens as well as visitors. Hollein's development of the structure not only answered the program but also dealt with the senses and behavior of its users. The network provides environmental conditioning against the changeable weather, using subsurface heating systems and canopies that are attached above the structure to screen users from the elements. Waterways and waterjets along the Media-line also provide a cooling effect and audio pleasure at the seating and gathering areas. Hollein provided designated locations for audio-visual information displays, orientation-locator signage with abundant security lighting throughout the complex. The Media-line project serves as testimony that simple building programs could be expanded to address a broad range human needs.

The Schullin Jewelry Shop I in Vienna (1974) portrays the architect's use of irony and iconography in his expression. The shopfront relates semiotically to the function of the store. The various emblems employed through material usage create a series of related associations that illustrate the building's function. Like the Retti Candle Shop, Hollein avoided using signs that would clutter the street appeal. Hollein selected shiny marble for the front facade and set back the entrance door from the building periphery and the walkway. The color and proportion of the street elevation agree contextually with the surrounding buildings. Hollein achieved the prementioned icon through a fissure of brass sheets layered in an organic form splitting the clean marble plane. He placed protruding randomly end-lit brass and chrome tubes within that form (providing supply and return air for the mechanical equipment, with the lights obstructing their being seen from below). The aesthetic provides an image of geology, archaeology and machinery associated with gemology. Once again, Hollein used a visual technique in an entranceway to draw attention to his structure. Through a unique composition of materials he also made the storefront appear larger than it actually is.

Unlike many other architects who limit themselves to the aesthetic of layered drywall and a paint palette in their ornamental elements of architecture, Hollein exhibits extraordinary skill in detailing finishes (granite, brass, chrome, plastic, fabric, wood, paper) of dissimilar nature and properties with cohesive effects that are clean and elegant. He also displays exemplary skill in lighting through various techniques learned from outside his architectural practice. Through a combination of task lighting, he has created desirable reflections on the merchandise as well as on the clientele.

The Städtliches Museum, Mönchengladbach, Germany, was Hollein's largest commission when it was completed in 1982. The complex lies at the edge of the main district atop undulating brick terraces that step down with the topography. The siting prohibits a competition in scale and in material usage with context with the historic structures nearby. The layout of the museum takes the form of a variegated colony of buildings in compliance with the form of this city of medieval heritage. The coordination of spaces takes the shape of the orthogonal and the organic, and is not a preordained tectonic pattern as is typical of most civic structures. The building volumes are of different shapes and materials: the exterior of the administrative building is composed of stone and a faceted setback of curtain wall that reflects the masonry wall forms below, the gallery tents are made of zinc-coated and sandstone panels with roof lights, and the entrance pavilion is constructed of white marble and chrome elements. The visual disparity of the buildings evokes a tension between the volumes that seems to pull the collage together.

The function of the project lies between the traditional gallery and the modern, open, free-plan gallery. Art with special needs is housed under controlled conditions of the protected gallery while more modern works and sculpture preside in larger and naturally lit spaces. The use of daylight in these spaces is beneficial in terms of viewing the art as well as being psychologically desirable for visual contact with the outside environment. The museum is integrated with the site in order to provide indoor/outdoor use. The surface courtyards are given over to the public for open-air museum functions and provide several vantage points for viewing the modern art. The outside circulation patterns also allow the observer to interpret the expressiveness of the buildings from several perspectives. The large expanses of fenestration in some of the enclosed galleries allow the passerby to view certain portions of the collections after museum hours. Overall, Hollein has presented a sensitivity to context and the history of an area. He has designed with the past, present and toward the future with the employment of modern technology and the consideration of flexibility in design for the public response.

The Haas-Haus in Vienna, completed in 1989, faces the southwest corner of St. Stephen's Cathedral. The site of this building is one of the most historic in Vienna. It was the locale of a Roman *castrum* at one time and survived massive destruction during the air raids of World War II. Hollein reflected this historic precondition with the use of a curved building line that imitates the spirit of the Roman structure and medieval street. Hollein desired historic reference that would be reminiscent of medieval city planning, and gave the outline of the Haas-Haus plan an oriel tower at the terminus of the street intersection. This play of building volume would provide a vista that separates the cathedral plaza from the extended promenade of the Graben. The projection was lifted one story above ground line because of the existing location of the subway below.

Hollein envisioned that the projection in the building form could also be the origin of a future arcade that would articulate the storefronts along the Stephansplatz. The arcade would allow a means of incorporating the new structure with the existing building fabric through its proportions, and provide a covered area for the public at this popular city square. The street level of the facade on the Graben reflects the typical canopied Viennese storefronts in the shopping district of elegant, diminutive shops. The remainder of the elevation consists of diagonal panels of light-green amazonite stone facing, which rests on a one-and-a-half-story colonnade of pink pilotis that begins at the tower.

The squared rationalism and simple perforated facade are indicative of traditional house structures and are an allusion to the Roman fortified corner. However, the heaviness of the masonry bearing down on the slender profile of the implied pilotis suggests an irony by the architect and illustrates an appliqué condition. The interplay of color with the heavy stone panels being visually supported by the airy pink columns emphasizes the image. Hollein aspires to his concern for iconographic inversions on this occasion. As the elevation bends toward the Stephensplatz, a tilted stone cube element marks a transition in building materials. The aesthetic changes to a steel-and-glass wall system with a juxtaposed roofline, which includes a concrete diving-board canopy that offsets the neighboring traditional rooftop decoration. The work is reminiscent of the modernism of Le Corbusier and Ludwig Mies van der Rohe. The highly articulated elevation represents modernity and the current use of the building.

The overall structure consists of eight floors, five levels of shopping from ground level through the fourth floor, with office space up through the sixth level. A café shares the sixth level with office space, in the form of the oriel projection located below it. A restaurant with accompanying café and terrace occupies the seventh floor. The café and restaurant are oriented toward the cathedral plaza, along with the rest of the Stephensplatz elevation and its glazed envelope, and have a splended view of the historic district. Between the entrance and the atrium lies a typical Hollein rotunda rendered with a gilded ceiling.

The shopping area of the Haas-Haus is divided by a vertical well of staggered steps and escalators rendered in light-yellow limestone with accents of red and green marble. The space is capped by a translucent artificially backlit domed atrium that casts a range of light intensity, from daylight conditions, to twilight, to an evening blue halo. On the crest of the shopping pavilion is a red Chinese bridge with tree set against sky-blue walls. This imagery is countered with a one-person lookout, cantilevered out over the atrium, to peer downward at the happenings below. Hollein through this imagery has created a feeling of openness and the freedom to explore.

Hollein has orchestrated various types of interior lighting throughout the transparent portion of the building. The distribution of light casts a rich energy into the square and the neighborhood. In the Haas-Haus, Hollein has used materials in building that reflect the surroundings, as well as the content and functions of the building. Hollein has related the old with the new, modernism with tradition, rather than reject the one for the other.

Like many cities, Vienna has no coherent or national architectural style; it is historically pluralistic and atypical. Hollein believes that architecture needs not only to reflect the essence of urban life and history but also to incorporate modern materials and methods in building to anticipate change in the future. He is an architectural collagist who attempts and usually succeeds with the integration of art, technology and architecture in his designs. Hollein employs a universal grammar and syntax though classical elements—the columns, arches, domes and methods of joinery and ornament—and gains a creative impetus from society and technology. He creates a certain ambiguity in his work that is complex and idiosyncratic, and which can be illuminating or troubling to the observer. Hollein succeeds in his atypical method of design because of his ability to detail precisely a collage of building materials and to create visual intrigue in a contextually sensitive way.

—ROBERT FERKIN

HOOD, Raymond M.

American. Born in Pawtucket, Rhode Island, 29 March, 1881. Died in Stamford, Connecticut, 14 August 1934. Studied at Brown University, Providence, Rhode Island, and at Massachusetts Institute of Technology, Cambridge, Massachusetts, B.S., 1903; trained in offices of Cram, Goodhue and Ferguson, Boston, and Palmer and Hornbostle, Pittsburgh; diploma in architecture, École des Beaux-Arts, Paris, France, 1911. Opened office with Henry Hornbostle, Pittsburgh, 1911; established own office, New Y ork, 1914; joined by J. André Fouilhoux, 1920; elected member of the Board of Design at the Century of Progress Exposition, Chicago, 1933. Fellow, American Institute of Architects, 1934; president, Architectural League of New York, 1929-31.

Chronology of Works
All in the United States unless noted

1922-25	Chicago Tribune Tower, Chicago, Illinois (with John Mead Howells)
1924	American Radiator Building, New York City
1924	St. Vincent de Paul Asylum, Tarrytown, New York (with J. André Fouilhoux)
1925	Raymond Hood House, Stamford, Connecticut
1926	Bethany Union Church, Chicago, Illinois
1927	McCormick Mausoleum, Rockford, Illinois
1927	Morris House, Greenwich, Connecticut
1927	National Broadcasting Company Studios, New York
1928	Apartment House, 3 East 84th Street, New York City (with Howells)
1928	National Radiator Building, London, England (with J. Gordon Reeves)
1929	Masonic Temple and Scottish Rite Cathedral, Scranton, Pennsylvania (with Frederick Godley, Fouilhoux and H. V. K. Henderson)
1930	Beaux-Arts Apartments, New York City (with Kenneth M. Murchison, Godley and Fouilhoux)
1930	Daily News Building, New York City (with Howells)
1930	Joseph M. Patterson House, Ossining, New York (with Howells)
1930-33	Rockefeller Center, New York City (with L. A. Reinhard and Henry Hofmeister, Harvey Wiley Corbett, Wallace K. Harrison and William H. McMurray, and Fouilhoux)
1931	McGraw-Hill Building, New York City (with Godley and Fouilhoux)
1931	Rex Cole Showroom, Bay Ridge, New York
1931	Rex Cole Showroom, Flushing, New York
1933	Electricity Building, Hall of Social Science and Radiator Pavilion, Century of Progress Exhibition, Chicago, Illinois

Publications

ARTICLES BY HOOD

"The Chicago Tribune Competition." *Architectural Record* (February 1923).
"Exterior Architecture of Office Buildings." *Architectural Forum* 41 (September 1924).
"The American Radiator Company Building, New York." *American Architect* 126 (19 November 1924).
"The National Broadcasting Studios, New York." *Architectural Record* (July 1928).
"Business Executive's Office." *Pencil Points* (March 1929).
"The Spirit of Modern Art." *Architectural Forum* (November 1929).
"Beauty in Architecture." *Architectural Forum* (November 1930).
"The News Building." *Architectural Forum* (November 1930).
"Three Visions of New York." *Creative Art* (August 1931).
"The Design of the Rockefeller Center." *Architectural Forum* (January-June 1932).
"The Apartment House Loggia." *Architectural Forum* (January 1934).

BOOKS ABOUT HOOD

KILHAM, WALTER H.: *Raymond Hood, Architect; Form Through Function in the American Skyscraper.* New York, 1973.

NORTH, ARTHUR T.: *Raymond Hood*. New York and London, 1931.

SCHWARTZMAN, JOHN B.: *Raymond Hood: The Unheralded Architect*. Charlottesville, Virginia, 1962.

STERN, ROBERT A. M., and CATALANO, THOMAS P.: *Raymond Hood*. New York, 1982.

ARTICLES ABOUT HOOD

CORBETT, HARVEY WILEY: "American Radiator Building." *Architectural Record* (May 1924).

"McGraw-Hill Building." *Architectural Record* (April 1931).

"New York Daily News Building." *Architectural Record* (December 1930).

"Raymond Hood." *Progressive Architecture* (July 1974).

The architecture of Raymond M. Hood will always be remembered through his philosophy of concept and design, when he stated: ". . . I could never build the same building twice." Unlike his contemporaries, this shy, small-in-stature man created powerful, energetic structures that transcended their Gothic-inspired ancestors—all of which turned his designs into elegant skyscrapers that soured majestically above the skylines of Chicago and New York City.

After receiving his degree in architecture from the Massachusetts Institute of Technology, Hood became an apprentice draftsman in the architectural firm of Cram, Goodhue and Ferguson in Boston. It was from Cram and Goodhue that he followed the Gothic Revival style.

By 1905 Hood was in Paris, where he pursued courses in architecture at the École des Beaux-Arts. The following year, he returned to the firm of Cram, Goodhue and Ferguson, and then entered the architectural office of Henry Hornbostel in Pittsburgh. Dissatisfied with the course of his career at that time, he returned to the École, where in 1910 he was awarded a degree in architecture. After a year of travel in Europe, where he was exposed to historical styles, Hood reentered the firm of Hornbostel. In 1914 he went to New York and established a firm with another architect, Rayne Adams. There, for eight years he received few commissions, working only for other architects or as a consultant.

However, in June 1922 the course of Hood's career changed. He had read an announcement in the *Chicago Tribune* for an international competition to design ". . . the world's most beautiful office building." The New York architect John Mead Howells asked him to enter the competition, an entry on which they collaborated. From over 263 submitted designs, Hood and Howells won first prize ($50,000). The result was the Tribune Building (1924). It was Gothic in appearance, with a logical mass and projecting tower. Some said it was this structure that put an end to the Chicago school, for already tastes were shifting to what was called a "Woolworth Gothic" manner, named for Cass Gilbert's Woolworth Building in New York City (1910-13).

There followed the American Radiator Building in Chicago (1924). Its unique block-brick mass and "punched-in" appearance from the street produced a tower-like effect. Although based on Gothic lines, its guilded details in the upper stories, with flood lights at night, gave a romantic effect to its soaring vertical mass.

The success of these projects brought much work to Hood's firm. There followed the French-appearing St. Vincent de Paul Asylum, Tarrytown, New York (1924), and the Gothic mode of the Masonic Temple and Scottish Rite Cathedral, Scranton,

Pennsylvania (1929). He even designed, with J. Gordon Reeves, a black brick building in London known as the National Radiator Building (1928).

Following the principles of Hugh Ferris' zoning law of 1916, the *Daily News* Building in New York (1930) was set back from the street. Along with Howells, he designed its structure with vertical, cubistic-like precision. White bricks set between vertical window strips accentuated its exterior, only to have its top cut off dramatically. This style was thereupon to affect the manner of New York skyscrapers for the next 30 years. Also, it marked the absolute end of the Gothic style for high-rise structures.

Other projects followed—the Beaux-Arts Apartments, New York (1930), with the assistance of Kenneth Murchison; two General Electric Showrooms, in Flushing and Bay Ridge, New York (1931); and his General Electric Pavilion at the Chicago World's Fair of 1933, of whose board of design he was a member.

Yet the most memorable commission came in 1930 when three architectural firms—L. A. Reinhard and Henry Hofmeister; Harvey Wiley Corbett, Wallace K. Harrison and William H. MacMurray; and Hood and Jacques André Fouilhoux—became involved with the Rockefeller Center project. Hood assumed more of a consulting role. He was, though, quite instrumental in designing the RCA Building within the center. Its appearance reflected his earlier *Daily News* Building.

The final major project was Hood's designs for the McGraw-Hill Building, New York (1931). With the assistance of Godley and Fouilhoux, he created what is called a "light-shell structure," which appeared to be hung on a steel frame. Color was also introduced. Blue-green glazed terra-cotta blocks were placed between window bands. All was graded in hue from top to bottom. The structure put an end to the skyscraper as a vertical mass of brick, stone and glass. Ultimately, it paved the way for the Bauhaus International Style, whereby glass walls were placed like curtains on a steel frame.

Although Hood was not the most dominating architect of his era, he did leave his mark as a "pathfinder" for the skyscraper style that was typically American in manner, mode and spirit.

—GEORGE M. COHEN

HORTA, Victor.

Belgian. Born in Ghent, Belgium, 6 January 1861. Died in Brussels, 11 September 1947. Studied at Ghent Academy, 1874-77; Académie des Beaux-Arts, Brussels,1881. Worked in the office of the architect Jean Dubuysson, Paris, 1878-80; assistant architect, office of Alphonse Balat, Brussels, 1884-85; in private practice, Brussels, 1886-1915; lived in London, 1915, and in the United States, 1916-18; resumed practice in Brussels, 1918-47. Head of the architecture department, 1892-97, and professor, 1897-1915, Université Libre, Brussels; professor from 1912, and director, 1927-31, Académie des Beaux-Arts, Brussels.

Chronology of Works
All in Belgium unless noted
† *Work no longer exists*

1889	Lambeaux Sculpture Pavilion, Brussels
1890	Mattyn House, Brussels
1892-93	Tassel House, Brussels
1893	Autrique House, Brussels
1894	Frison Town House, Brussels
1894-1903	Winssinger House, Brussels
1895-1900	Hôtel Solvay, 224 avenue Louise, Brussels

Victor Horta: Horta House, Brussels, Belgium, 1898

1896-98	Maison du Peuple, Place Emile van de Velde, Brussels†
1897-1900	Van Eetvelde House, Brussels
1898	Horta House (now Musée Horta), Brussels
1901-03	L'Innovation Department Store, rue Neuve, Brussels†
1902	Belgian Pavilion, International Exposition of Decorative Arts, Turin, Italy
1902	Monument to Brahms, Vienna
1903	Grand Bazaar Department Store, Frankfurt, Germany (with the sculptor Van der Stappen)†
1903-05	Waucquez Department Store, Brussels
1903	Hallet House, Brussels
1903-28	Musée des Beaux-Arts, Tournai
1906	Wolfers Building, Brussels
1906-26	Brugmann Hospital, Jette, Brussels
1914-52	Halle Centrale, Main Railway Station, Brussels (construction begun in 1924; completed by Maxim Brunfaut)
1920-28	Palais des Beaux-Arts, Brussels
1925	Belgian Pavilion, Exposition des Arts Décoratifs, Paris, France

Publications

BOOKS BY HORTA

Considérations sur l'art moderne. Brussels, 1925.
L'enseignement architectural et l'architecture moderne. Brussels, 1926.

BOOKS ABOUT HORTA

Art Nouveau: Belgium/France. Exhibition catalog. Houston, 1976.
BORSI, FRANCO, and PORTOGHESI, PAOLO: *Horta.* New York, 1991.
DELEVOY, ROBERT L.: *Victor Horta.* Brussels, 1958.
FRAMPTON, KENNETH, and FUTAGAWA, YUKIO: *Modern Architecture: 1920-1945.* New York, 1983.
Guimard, Horta, Van de Velde. Exhibition catalog. Paris, 1971.
HENRION-GIELE, SUZANNE: *Victor Horta.* Exhibition catalog. Brussels, 1973.
HOPPENBROUWERS, A.; VANDENBREDEN, J.; and BRUGGEMANS, J.: *Victor Horta architectonographie.* Brussels, 1975.
MADSEN, S. TSCHUDI: *Sources of Art Nouveau.* New York, 1956.
PUTTEMANS, R., et al.: *Victor Horta.* Brussels, 1964.
RUSSELL, FRANK (ed.): *Art Nouveau Architecture.* London, 1979.

ARTICLES ABOUT HORTA

"Hôtel van Eetvelde and Atelier Victor Horta." *Global Architecture* No. 42.
"Lettura di Victor Horta." *Archittetura* Special edition, Nos. 23-29 (1958).
MADSEN, S. TSCHUDI: "Horta: Works and Style of Victor Horta before 1900." *Architectural Review* 118 (December 1955): 388-392.
THIEBAULT-SISSON: "The Innovator: Victor Horta." *Art et décorations* Vol. 1 (January-June 1897): 11-18. Republished

in BENTON, T. and C., and SHARP, D.: *Form and Function.* London, 1975.

"Victor Horta." *Rythme* Special issue, No. 39 (Brussels, April 1964).

*

From the Hôtel Tassel (1892) to Gros Waucquez (1903-05) in a decade that encompassed the turn of the century, Victor Horta left a legacy of extraordinary art nouveau architecture for later generations to enjoy or to be offended by, to interpret and reinterpret. This compact, rich, airy volume of work still remains an enigma, always more complex than any web of words thrown over it—always elusive of users', renovators' or critics' attempts at control.

Within Horta's life oeuvres, the decade of his art nouveau accomplishments is framed by early neo-Renaissance work on the one side, and a characteristic pre- and postwar rationalism on the other. At the fin de siècle he turned on the twists of a romantic floral organicism really as but a stage between two "classical" styles. But it is this foray into the lush, artificial, sepulchral Winter Garden that correctly remains as the source of his just fame and eminence.

"And this also has been one of the dark places of the earth." In looking at Horta's architecture of this period one is not reminded as strongly of the "decadents" like Oscar Wilde or Aubrey Beardsley, to whom he of course had a strong affinity, as of Joseph Conrad, specifically of *The Heart of Darkness* (1897). For this is not really the architecture of a decadent and artificial organicism that it is often perceived to be. Rather, these are buildings in the mode of irony—an architecture that expresses pain, despair, cynicism, a wounded idealism: a view of a sepulchral Europe feasting on and being seduced by its exotic, lush, jungle-infested, narcotizing dreams of being the colonist of esoteric dark continents. Not a poppy or a lily in a medieval hand as much as a plastic and architectural expression of the anguish, the scream of Hermann Obrist's golden-silk embroidery upon its gray woolen-cloth ground: whiplash-cyclamen.

"[I]t is like a running blaze on a plain, like a flash of lightning in the clouds. We live in the flicker." Here is fin de siècle architecture, then, as an ironically punned and darkly ambiguous "stage," as production, as interior furnishing. The stage is threshold and transition, theater and artifice, artifice protected by the fourth wall.

"The snake had charmed me." First and foremost, Horta's work is ironic—itself and its cynical negation a single phase, plant, motif, figure. The Winter Garden's iron is tortured, cobbled, wrought and beaten into plant forms. On a wooden inkblot-inkstand made for the Hôtel Solvay, stone softens itself into roots at the demands of flora. A lightbulb as bulb and filament is presented as the electric anther and stigma of a fireplace and yet is enfolded in gilded bronze petals.

Within the language of its own irony, this architecture is cynical—not just superficial, clever-cynical but deeply and darkly crystal. It is deeply and ironically cynical first of all of the possibility of progress—moral, material, aesthetic. It is ironic and cynical about the self-congratulatory liberalism of those who "selflessly" assume the white man's burden.

The most modern materials are twisted around to a crafted organic, prehuman representation of the "natural." Out of the booty of five continents a treasure trove of amulets, hallucinatory images, fetishes, opium dreams, botanical illustrations and fetid jungle flowers has been created. But if this language does not accept the illusion of "progress," then it also is not a language of decadence; this is not a return to the prehuman

scarab existence nor a deevolution into plants or apes, not a progress toward an angelic or at least Pre-Raphaelite "better tomorrow." This is, rather, a cyclonic vortex around an unfathomably dark center or inner core: the pseudo-Roman-era mosaics on the ground floor of the Hôtel Tassel.

"[T]he tranquil waterway leading to the uttermost ends of the earth flowed sombre under an overcast sky—seemed to lead into the heart of an immense darkness." Within its ironic, self-referential cynicism, Horta's work is also negatory, negativistic: not old art—new art; not old art—young art; not sober art—intoxicated art—Bacchic art; not dynamic art—accelerating art. Each "statement" begets its own negation and each negation supersedes the contradictories.

This is an art that pursues the goal of eluding the historical categories, of eluding analyses, of eluding words and theories—an art that slips through the grasp of the critic and comes back to haunt the waking viewer with nightmares and spectral apparitions from the other side. It is a puzzle or perhaps more accurately a set of interconnected and intertwined labyrinths that function as a rebus or an enigma.

"[T]he only thing for it was to come to and wait for the turn of the tide." Horta's art nouveau architecture then marked not the end of the 19th century—but the beginning of the 20th; nor yet the beginning of the 20th century but the end of the 19th. This architecture—neither beginning nor end—was perhaps an interlude, a satyr play between two acts of a classic tragedy. Finally there is a brief and passing theatrical moment when the actors gambol on the stage in a moment of release but not of catharsis: Apocalypse Now (at the Winter Garden).

Horta was not typical; to him the meaning of an episode was not inside like a kernel, but outside, enveloping the tale which brought it out only as a glow brings out a haze, like a misty halo made visible by the spectral illumination of moonshine.

—JOSEPH B. JUHASZ

HOWE, George.

American. Born in Worcester, Massachusetts, 17 June 1886. Died in Cambridge, Massachusetts, 16 April 1955. Married Maritje Patterson, 1907. Studied at Harvard University, Cambridge, Massachusetts, graduated 1907; École des Beaux-Arts, Paris, 1908-12. Served as a Lieutenant in the Corps of Interpreters, United States Army, as assistant military attaché at Bern, Switzerland, 1917-19. Worked for Furness, Evans and Company, Philadelphia, 1914-16; partner, Mellor, Meigs and Howe, 1916-28; established own office, Philadelphia, 1928; partner, with William Lescaze, Howe and Lescaze, 1929-34; in private practice, 1935-40; in partnership with Louis I. Kahn, 1941, and with Kahn and Oscar Stonorov, 1942-43; supervising architect, 1942-44, and deputy commissioner for design and construction, 1944-45, Public Buildings Administration, Federal Works Agency; in private practice, 1945-48; in partnership with Robert Montgomery Brown, 1949 until his death in 1955. Chairman of the Department of Architecture, Yale University, New Haven, Connecticut, 1950-54; established the architectural journal *Perspecta*, Yale University, 1952. Fellow, American Institute of Architects; Gold Medal, American Institute of Architects, 1922 and 1939.

George Howe: Philadelphia Saving Fund Society Building,
Philadelphia, Pennsylvania, 1931

Chronology of Works
All in the United States
† *Work no longer exists*

1914-17	High Hollow, Philadelphia, Pennsylvania
1924	Willowbrook Farms (Page House), Paoli, Pennsylvania (with Walter Mellor and Arthur I. Meigs)
1924-28	United States Coast Guard Memorial, Arlington National Cemetery, Virginia (with the sculptor Gaston Lachaise)
1929	Oak Lane Country Day School, Philadelphia (with William Lescaze)†
1931	Philadelphia Saving Fund Society Building, Philadelphia (with Lescaze)
1932-34	Square Shadows, Whitemarsh, Pennsylvania
1937-39	Fortune Rock, Mount Desert Island, Maine
1940-42	Pine Ford Acres, Middletown, near Harrisburg, Pennsylvania (defense housing; with Louis I. Kahn)
1941-43	Carver Court Housing, Coatesville, Pennsylvania (with Louis I. Kahn and Oscar Stonorov)
1954-55	*Evening and Sunday Bulletin* Building, Philadelphia (with Robert Montgomery Brown)

Publications

BOOKS BY HOWE

The Work of Mellor, Meigs and Howe. New York, 1923.
A Modern Museum. With William Lescaze. Springdale, Connecticut, 1930.

ARTICLES BY HOWE

"Functional Aesthetics and the Social Ideal." *Pencil Points* (April 1932).
"Two Architects' Credos: Traditional Versus Modern." With William A. Delano. *Magazine of Art* (April 1940).
"New York World's Fair." *Architectural Forum* (July 1940).
"The Meaning of Art Today." *Magazine of Art* (May 1942).
"Low-Cost Houses." *Architectural Forum* (November 1942).
"Monuments, Memorials, and Modern Design—An Exchange of Letters." *Magazine of Art* (October 1944).
"Relation of the Architect to Government." *Michigan Society of Architects Bulletin* (31 July and 7 August 1945).
"Master Plans for Master Politicians." *Magazine of Art* (February 1946).
"Statement by George Howe at Princeton University's Bicentennial Celebration." *Michigan Society of Architects Bulletin* (24 June 1947).
"A Lesson from the Jefferson Memorial Competition." *American Institute of Architects Journal* (March 1951).
"Old Cities and New Frontiers." *American Institute of Architects Journal* (January 1952).
"Training for the Practice of Architecture." *Perspecta* No. 2 (1953).

BOOKS ABOUT HOWE

JORDY, WILLIAM H.: "The American Acceptance of the International Style: George Howe and William Lescaze's Philadelphia Saving Fund Society Building." In *American Buildings and Their Architects: The Impact of European Modernism in the Mid-Twentieth Century*. Garden City, New York, 1972.
STERN, ROBERT A. M.: *George Howe: Toward a Modern American Architecture*. New Haven, Connecticut, and London, 1975.

WEST, HELEN HOWE: *George Howe, Architect, 1886-1955*. Philadelphia, 1973.

ARTICLES ABOUT HOWE

BROOKS, H. ALLEN: "PSFS: A Source for Its Design." *Journal of the Society of Architectural Historians* 27 (December 1968).

HITCHCOCK, HENRY-RUSSELL: "Howe and Lescaze." In *Modern Architecture: International Exhibition*. New York, 1932.

JORDY, WILLIAM H.: "Philadelphia Saving Fund Society Building: Its Development and Its Significance in Modern Architecture." *Journal of the Society of Architectural Historians* 21 (May 1962): 47-83.

"New Waves in American Architecture." *GA Houses* Special issue (May 1982).

ROBIN, A.: "Howe and Lescaze." *Architecture d'aujourd'hui* No. 4, special issue (November/December 1933).

STERN, ROBERT A. M.: "Philadelphia Saving Fund Society Building: Beaux-Arts Theory and Rational Expressionism." *Journal of the Society of Architectural Historians* 21 (May 1962): 84-102.

TATMAN, SANDRA L.: "A Study of the Work of Mellor, Meigs and Howe." Master's thesis. University of Oregon, Eugene, Oregon, 1977.

WRIGHT, HENRY: "Philadelphia Saving Fund Society Building." *Architectural Forum* (May 1964).

ZEVI, BRUNO: "George Howe: An Aristocratic Architect." *American Institute of Architects Journal* (October 1955).

ZEVI, BRUNO: "George Howe." *Metron* No. 25 (1948).

*

George Howe's importance in 20th-century American architecture is that he acted as a catalyst for various aspects of the Modern Movement. He brought into the firm of Howe and Lescaze the commission for the Philadelphia Saving Fund Society (PSFS) building, a landmark of the movement. He published numerous articles forwarding the cause of the movement through the pages of the Philadelphia *T-Square Club Journal*. As architect to the federal government from 1942 to 1945, he managed to move the administration away from classical expression in public architecture. He both wrote the program and helped to judge the Jefferson Memorial Competition (1948). He served as a very successful chairman of the Department of Architecture at Yale University from 1950 to 1954, revising the program, and establishing *Perspecta* (1952), the first and still the most prestigious student architectural magazine.

Howe graduated in the fine arts from Harvard (1907), traveled in Italy for a year and then enrolled in the Paris École des Beaux-Arts in 1908. Returning to the United States in 1913, he worked for Furness, Evans and Company, built his own house called High Hollow at Chestnut Hill (1914-17), and became a partner in the firm of Mellor, Meigs and Howe (1915-28), which specialized in residential architecture. Howe's designs tended to be romantic and picturesque but Beaux-Arts in their considerations of site, organization and materials. Two books, *A Monograph of the Works of Mellor, Meigs and Howe,* and *An American Country House* by Arthur Meigs, published in 1923 and 1925, respectively, illustrated the work designed by the firm. From 1923 to 1927, Howe was responsible for a series of small Beaux-Arts branch banks for PSFS, and in 1926 he prepared a design for a high-rise office building, including a branch bank at ground level, at Market and Twelfth streets in Philadelphia.

This scheme had the appearance of a conglomeration of elements taken from entries submitted for the Chicago Tribune competition of 1922.

During that period, Howe gradually became aware of European developments in modern architecture, causing him to reconsider his own approaches to design. While in Paris for the Exposition Internationale des Arts Décoratifs in 1925, he encountered the work of Le Corbusier. From 1927, numerous examples of European modernism and a few American examples were published in the *Architectural Record* under the editorship of A. Lawrence Kocher. During 1928 Howe left the office of Mellor, Meigs and Howe and set up an independent practice in Philadelphia, taking George Daub and Louis McAllister with him. In March 1929 James Willcox, president of PSFS, asked Howe to proceed with a design for the Market and Twelfth streets site. Although Howe prepared four schemes during March 1929, he knew that he needed a partner trained in the ideals of the Modern Movement, someone who had successfully practiced in that idiom. That person was the Swiss-born architect William Lescaze, who had emigrated to the United States in 1920 and practiced in New York City since 1923.

Howe met Lescaze in January of 1929. They signed articles of copartnership in May 1929, stating that Howe was to be responsible for business contacts and Lescaze for the architectural designs of the partnership. These dates are important because a controversy exists concerning the authorship of the building. Howe met Lescaze in January 1929, made designs of PSFS in March, and signed articles of agreement in May. He therefore knew Lescaze prior to his preliminary designs of PSFS. Lescaze claimed that he never saw these preliminary drawings as he proceeded to design PSFS. The partnership of Howe and Lescaze lasted three years, although as a legal entity it continued until 1935. Howe brought into the partnership the PSFS commission, the most significant building with which either architect was ever involved. All negotiations with and presentations to James Willcox were made by Howe, while Lescaze and his capable assistants worked on the building and its details, down to the coat hooks and pepper and salt shakers.

Howe later joined forces with Louis Kahn at a period when a series of publicly funded housing projects were a major concern in the United States. Later the firm was known as Howe, Kahn and (Oscar) Stonorov. Howe unsuccessfully attempted to associate professionally with the product designer Norman Bel Geddes, and he maintained offices at some time with his former assistant Louis McAllister and at another time with Robert Montgomery Brown.

Howe died in 1955, a year after leaving his administrative post at Yale. His lasting contribution there had been to lead a team of innovative designer-critics, including his old friend and partner Louis Kahn, both a part of what is sometimes termed the "Philadelphia School."

—LAWRENCE WODEHOUSE

HOWELLS, John Mead.

American. Born in Cambridge, Massachusetts, in 1868. Died in 1959. Father was the novelist William Deane Howells. Graduated from Harvard University, Cambridge, Massachusetts, 1891; graduated from the École des Beaux-Arts, Paris, France, 1897. In partnership with I. N. Phelps Stokes, 1897-1917; also worked with Raymond M. Hood.

Chronology of Works
All in the United States

Howells and Phelps Stokes:

1898	Madison Square Church Mission House, New York City
1901	Woodbridge Hall, Yale University, New Haven, Connecticut
1901	Horace Mann School, New York City
1905	Stock Exchange Building, Baltimore, Maryland
1905-06	St. Paul's Chapel, Columbia University, New York City
1906-09	Royal Insurance Buildings, New York City, San Francisco, California, and Baltimore, Maryland
1908	Frankl Building, New York City
1909	First Congregational Church, Danbury, Connecticut
1913-16	Paine Hall (music building) and Dudley Hall, Harvard University, Cambridge, Massachusetts
1916	Turk's Head Office Building, Providence, Rhode Island
1916	Cobb Building, Seattle, Washington
1916	Metropolitan Theater, Seattle, Washington

John Mead Howells:

1920	Corona Building, New York City
1922-25	Chicago Tribune Tower, Chicago, Illinois (with Raymond M. Hood)
1928	Beekman Tower, New York City (originally Panhellenic House)
1929-30	Daily News Building, New York City (with Hood)
1930	Title Guarantee and Trust Company, New York City
1934	Colonel Stuart House, Charleston, South Carolina (restoration)

Publications

BOOKS BY HOWELLS

Lost Examples of Colonial Architecture. New York, 1931.
The Architectural Heritage of the Piscataqua. New York, 1937.
The Architectural Heritage of the Merrimack. New York, 1941.

BOOKS ABOUT HOWELLS

BUNTING, BAINBRIDGE and NYLANDER, ROBERT H.: *Survey of Architectural History in Cambridge, Report Four: Old Cambridge.* Cambridge, Massachusetts, 1973.
GOLDSTONE, HARMON H. and DALRYMPLE, MARTHA: *History Preserved: A Guide to New York City Landmarks and Historic Districts.* New York, 1974.
WHITE, NORVAL and WILLENSKY, ELLIOT: *American Institute of Architects Guide to New York City.* New York, 1978.

ARTICLES ABOUT HOWELLS

STOKES, I. N. PHELPS: "Random Reflections of a Happy Life." Privately printed. New York, 1941.
WEISMAN, WINSTON R.: "A New View of Skyscraper History." Pp. 115-160 in Edgar Kaufmann (ed.), *The Rise of an American Architecture.* New York, 1970.

John Mead Howells, perhaps best known as joint designer of the Tribune Tower in Chicago, was born in Cambridge, Massachusetts, the son of accomplished writer and editor William Dean Howells and Elinor Mead Howells. His uncle was William Rutherford Mead, one of the founding partners of the noted architectural firm McKim, Mead and White. In 1883 Howells worked briefly in the office of McKim, Mead and White, and again in 1891-92, after his graduation from Harvard. He entered the École des Beaux-Arts, Paris, in 1892 and was awarded the *diplôme* in 1897. Upon returning to the United States, he settled in New York City and established an office with I. N. Phelps Stokes in 1897.

Isaac Newton Phelps Stokes, known as Phelps Stokes or I. N. Phelps Stokes, was born in New York City to an extremely wealthy family. Raised in gracious luxury, he was also trained in the family tradition of enlightened philanthropy. Upon graduation from Harvard in 1891, in accordance with his father's wishes, he entered the banking business; however, by 1893 he had persuaded his family to let him study architecture. He began general studies at Columbia University and then, in 1894, he too enrolled at the École des Beaux-Arts in Paris. In 1897 he returned to the United States and joined Howells. That year they submitted the winning design of the University Settlement building. The next year, 1898, they built the Madison Square Church Mission House on Third Avenue in New York City.

In the following years, the partners developed a successful practice and designed a number of notable buildings. Their work was generally restrained in character, employing a stylistic eclecticism that reflected the use or context of each building. Several of their commissions came from the unmarried sisters of Phelps Stokes—Olivia and Caroline Stokes. One of the earliest of these was Woodbridge Hall at Yale University (1901). Given to commemorate the 200th anniversary of Yale, Woodbridge Hall is a French academic classic *hôtel* in limestone, named in honor of one of the founders of Yale. The style of the building and its material were selected in conjunction with the adjoining bicentennial building complex by Carrère and Hastings, so that the three buildings would form a coordinated quadrangle. Another commission from the sisters was St. Paul's Chapel at Columbia University in New York City (1905-06). For this building, one of the few on the Columbia campus not designed by McKim, Mead and White, Howells and Stokes used a modified Italian Renaissance style, with strong references to the work of Filippe Brunelleschi, but they built with red brick to integrate the chapel with the Columbia campus. Also among their early buildings was the Horace Mann School, near Columbia University (1901).

Their significant business buildings included the Stock Exchange Building, Baltimore, Maryland (1905), a series of office blocks for the Royal Insurance Buildings in New York City, Baltimore and San Francisco (1906-09), and the Frankel Building, New York City (1908). Other office blocks included the Turks' Head Office Building, Providence, Rhode Island (1916). In 1913-16 the firm built Paine Hall (the music building) and Dudley Hall at Harvard University.

Howells' detailed study of American Colonial architecture found expression in the firm's First Congregational Church, Danbury, Connecticut (1909), inspired by early-18th-century prototypes. The partners were not always successful in competitions, but their entries for the New York Historical Society (1904), the New York City Municipal Building (1908) and the Washington State Capitol in Olympia (1911) were published in the architectural press. Outside of the Northeast, Howells and Stokes completed several buildings in Seattle, Washington, including the Cobb Building and the Metropolitan Theater (1916).

The partnership was dissolved in 1917, when the partners started practicing separately. Stokes devoted himself to housing reform for the working classes, an interest he had long held. As early as 1896 Stokes had submitted a design in a model tenement house competition sponsored by New York's Improved Housing Council. In 1898 he helped to form the Charity Organization Society's Tenement House Committee, which in turn led to the creation of the Tenement House Commission by then-governor Theodore Roosevelt. Attacking the cramped conditions of the ubiquitous "dumb-bell" apartment, Stokes developed an alternative apartment block design, realized in the construction of the Tuskegee Houses, a six-story apartment block intended for African-Americans, built in 1901 and financed by the Stokes sisters. Also in 1901, he wrote the draft of the New York Tenement House Law. His innovative Dudley model tenement block in New York City, built in 1910, met resistance from the city's Tenement House Department. Thereafter he focused his energy (1911 through 1937) on lowering the cost of workers' housing through the Phelps-Stokes Fund created by his sisters in 1911. He continued to believe that the most practical solution to housing reform lay in making construction of improved apartment units profitable for private speculators, and hence he criticized the federal government's housing programs of the 1930s as impractical and utopian.

Aside from Stokes' early work with Howells, and his efforts at housing reform, he is also remembered for his interest in the history of Manhattan Island. After 1908 he actively collected old prints of the city and conducted historical research. The result was a massive six-volume illustrated work, *The Iconography of Manhattan Island, 1498-1909* (1915-28). This remains unparalleled as a source of information about Manhattan.

After 1917, Howells independently produced several country houses on Long Island, and the Corona Building in New York City (1920). The resurgence of Howells' career came in 1922 when, in association with the younger Raymond Hood (1881-1934), he won first prize in the celebrated design competition for "the world's most beautiful skyscraper," the Chicago Tribune Tower (1922-25). Inspired by the Tower of Butter on the west front of the Cathedral of Rouen, France (1485), Howells and Hood developed a slender tower in three parts, with a two-story base set off by Flamboyant Gothic crenellation, a tall central section of offices with emphasized vertical piers (and stripped of the horizontal banding found at Rouen), and terminating in a crown in which the flying buttresses of the model allowed for a graduated setback in accordance with the city's new zoning ordinances.

Following that, Howells and Hood continued to work together periodically, as in their competition entry for a courthouse in Providence, Rhode Island (1924), on an apartment house on 84th Street in New York City (1928-29), and most notably, on the Daily News Building in New York City (1929-30). Nonetheless, Howells maintained an independent practice, designing the acclaimed Panhellenic House (now Beekman Tower) in New York City (1928), whose strikingly abstract art deco modeling shows Howell's study of Eliel Saarinen's second-place design in the Tribune Tower competition.

A careful student of early American architecture, Howells put his research to practical use in restoring buildings of that style, especially in Portsmouth, New Hampshire, and Charleston, South Carolina, where, in 1934, he purchased and restored the Colonel Stuart House originally built in 1767. Like his father, Howells was an active writer, and was a frequent contributor to *Harper's Magazine* and the *Century,*

as well as to architectural journals. He also published three books: *Lost Examples of Colonial Architecture* (1931), *The Architectural Heritage of the Piscataqua* (1937) and *The Architectural Heritage of the Merrimack* (1941).

—LELAND M. ROTH

HUNT, Richard Morris.

American. Born in Brattleboro, Vermont, 1827. Died on 31 July 1895. Son was the architect Richard Howland Hunt. Trained at M. Lafuel's atelier and the École des Beaux-Arts, Paris, France. Worked as inspector of construction at the Louvre and Tuileries, Paris, 1854; established own office, New York, 1857. Co-founder, American Institute of Architects (president, 1883).

Chronology of Works
All in the United States
† *Work no longer exists*

1855-57	Thomas P. Rossiter House, New York City†
1857-58	Studio Building, New York City†
1861-63	J. N. A. Griswold House, Newport, Rhode Island
1867-69	Scroll and Key Society Clubhouse, New Haven, Connecticut
1867-73	Seventh Regiment Monument Pedestal, New York City
1868	Matthew C. Perry Statue Pedestal, Newport, Rhode Island
1868-72	Presbyterian Hospital, New York City†
1869-70	Academic Hall, Hampton Normal and Agricultural Institute, Hampton, Virginia†
1869-70	Martin L. Brimmer Houses, Boston, Massachusetts†
1869-70	East Divinity Hall, Yale Divinity School, New Haven, Connecticut†
1869-70	Stuyvesant Apartments, New York City
1869-79	George P. Wetmore Mansion, Newport, Rhode Island (alterations)
1870	Charlotte Cushman House, Newport, Rhode Island†
1870-71	Thomas G. Appleton House, Newport, Rhode Island
1870-71	Marquand Chapel, New Haven, Connecticut†
1870-71	Travers Block, Newport, Rhode Island†
1870-71	George Waring House, Newport, Rhode Island
1870-72	Stevens Apartment House (Victoria Hotel), New York City†
1870-77	Lenox Library, New York City
1871-72	Howland Circulating Library, Beacon, New York
1871-72	Van Rensselaer Building, New York City†
1871-73	Marshall Field House, Chicago, Illinois†
1872-73	Henry G. Marquand House, Newport, Rhode Island†
1872-74	Virginia Hall, Hampton Normal and Agricultural Institute, Hampton, Virginia
1873-74	Roosevelt Building, New York City
1873-76	Delaware and Hudson Canal Company Building, New York City†
1873-76	Tribune Building, New York City†
1876-79	Lenox Library, Princeton, New Jersey†
1878-80	William K. Vanderbilt Mansion, Oakdale, New York†

1878-82	William K. Vanderbilt Mansion, New York City†
1879-80	Saint Mark's Chapel and Rectory, Islip, New York
1880-81	Second Academic Hall, Hampton Normal and Agricultural Institute, Hampton, Virginia
1880-82	Marquand Chapel, Princeton, New Jersey†
1880-84	Yorktown Monument, Yorktown, Virginia (with Henry Van Brunt)
1881-82	Guernsey Office Building, New York City†
1881-83	Association Residence, New York City
1881-84	Henry G. Marquand House, New York City†
1881-86	Statue of Liberty Pedestal, New York City Harbor
1881-90	Horace Greeley Statue Pedestal, New York City
1882-83	Lafayette Statue Pedestal, Burlington, Vermont
1883	Washington Statue Pedestal, New York City
1884-85	Pilgrim Statue Pedestal, New York City
1884-86	James W. Pinchot Mansion (Grey Towers), Milford, Pennsylvania
1884-87	James Garfield Monument Pedestal, Washington, D.C.
1884-89	William Borden Mansion, Chicago, Illinois†
1884-89	Vanderbilt Mausoleum, Moravian Cemetery, Staten Island, New York (with Frederick Law Olmsted)
1885-87	Ogden Mills Mansion, New York City†
1885-91	Chemical Laboratory, Princeton, New Jersey
1886-87	Levi P. Morton Mansion (Ellerslie), Rhinecliff-on-Hudson, New York†
1886-89	Archibald Rogers Mansion (Crumwold Hall), Hyde Park, New York
1887-88	New York Free Circulating Library, New York City
1887-93	United States Naval Observatory Buildings, Washington, D.C.
1888-91	Henry Ward Beecher Statue Pedestal, Brooklyn, New York
1888-92	Odgen Goelet Mansion (Ochre Court), Newport, Rhode Island
1888-92	William K. and Alva Vanderbilt Mansion (Marble House), Newport, Rhode Island
1888-95	George W. Vanderbilt Mansion (Biltmore House), Asheville, North Carolina
1889-91	Joseph R. Busk Mansion (Indian Spring), Newport, Rhode Island
1889-92	Clark Hall, Adelbert College (Case Western Reserve University), Cleveland, Ohio
1889-93	Gymnasium, United States Military Academy, West Point, New York†
1889-95	Academic Building, United States Military Academy, West Point, New York
1890-91	William V. Lawrence Mansion, New York City†
1890-94	Trinity Church, New York City (doors)
1891-93	Administration Building, World's Columbian Exposition, Chicago, Illinois
1891-94	Oliver H. P. Belmont Mansion (Belcourt Castle), Newport, Rhode Island
1891-94	Elbridge T. Gerry Mansion, New York City†
1891-95	Mansion for Mrs. William B. Astor and John Jacob Astor IV, New York City†
1892-95	Cornelius Vanderbilt II Mansion (The Breakers), Newport, Rhode Island
1893-95	Fogg Museum (Hunt Hall), Harvard University, Cambridge, Massachusetts†
1894-1902	Metropolitan Museum of Art, New York City (Wing "D," completed by Richard Howland Hunt)

Publications

BOOKS BY HUNT

Designs for Gateways. New York, 1866.

ARTICLES BY HUNT

"A Paper on the Architectural Exhibit of the Centennial Exhibition." *Proceedings of the American Institute of Architects* 10 (1876): 34-38.

BOOKS ABOUT HUNT

ANDREWS, WAYNE: *Architecture, Ambition and Americans.* New York, 1964.
BAKER, PAUL R.: *Richard Morris Hunt.* Cambridge, Massachusetts, 1980.
FERREE, BARR: *Works of Richard Morris Hunt.* New York, 1895.
STEIN, SUSAN (ed.): *The Architecture of Richard Morris Hunt.* Chicago, 1986.
VAN PELT, JOHN VREDENBURGH: *A Monograph of the William K. Vanderbilt House: Richard Morris Hunt, Architect.* New York, 1925.

ARTICLES ABOUT HUNT

BURNHAM, ALAN: "The New York Architecture of Richard Morris Hunt." *Journal of the Society of Architectural Historians* 11 (May 1952): 9-14.
COLES, WILLIAM A.: "Richard Morris Hunt and His Library as Revealed in the Studio Sketchbooks of Henry Van Brunt." *Art Quarterly* 30 (1967): 224-238.
FERREE, BARR: "Richard Morris Hunt: His Art and Work." *Architecture and Building* 23 (7 December 1895): 271-275.
GASS, JOHN B.: "American Architecture and Architects, with Special Reference to the Works of the Late Richard Morris Hunt and Henry Hobson Richardson." *Journal of the Royal Institute of British Architects* 3 (6 February 1896): 229-332.
LANDAU, SARAH BRADFORD: "Richard Morris Hunt, the Continental Picturesque, and the 'Stick Style'." *Journal of the Society of Architectural Historians* 42 (October 1983): 272-289.
PARIS, WILLIAM FRANCKLYN: "Richard Morris Hunt: First Secretary and Third President of the Institute." *Journal of the American Institute of Architects* 24 (December 1955): 243-249; 25 (January 1956): 14-19; 25 (February 1956): 74-80.
SCHUYLER, MONTGOMERY: "The Works of the Late Richard Morris Hunt." *Architectural Record* 5 (October-December 1895): 97-180.
VAN BRUNT, HENRY: "Richard Morris Hunt: A Memorial Address." *American Architect and Building News* 50 (2 November 1895): 53-56.
VAN BRUNT, HENRY: "Richard Morris Hunt." *Journal of the American Institute of Architects* 8 (October 1947): 180-187.
WALLIS, FRANK E.: "Richard Morris Hunt, Master Architect and Man." *Architectural Review* 5 (1917): 239-240.

*

Richard Morris Hunt was long accorded the status of dean of American architects by his peers; his eminence resulted from his being the first American to study at the prestigious École des Beaux-Arts in Paris and from the importance of his trendsetting designs.

Hunt was born in Brattleboro, Vermont, the son of a highly prosperous lawyer, banker and congressman. After his father's death in 1832, his mother, Jane Maria Leavitt Hunt, took her sons William and Richard first to New Haven, Connecticut, and Boston, Massachusetts, and then to Europe when William's health suffered. Following a visit to Italy, William decided on a career as an artist, prompting Mrs. Hunt to move the family to Italy and then to Paris. The younger son, Richard, began to study architectural drawing with Samuel Darier in Geneva.

In 1845 Richard decided on a career as an architect, whereupon the family settled in Paris. In 1845 Richard was accepted into the atelier of Hector Martin Lefuel (1810-80) and in 1846 he entered the École des Beaux-Arts. In 1851 he was advanced to the level of first class and continued his studies until 1854. During his years at the École, Hunt also traveled extensively in Europe and the Middle East. His success in Lefuel's atelier was such that when Lefuel was placed in charge of building additions to the Louvre palace, Lefuel asked Hunt to serve as inspector of works. Hunt also assisted Lefuel in the design of the Pavillion de la Bibliothéque.

In September 1855 Hunt decided to set himself up in practice in New York City, but in his first commission, a combination house-studio (1855-57) for his artist-friend Thomas P. Rossiter, Hunt encountered American building customs with which he was unfamiliar. The house was being paid for by Rossiter's father-in-law, Dr. Eleazer Parmly, who had already supervised construction of a number of speculative houses he built in Manhattan. Parmly felt Hunt's charges for his services were too high, especially for supervising construction. Parmly refused to pay, whereupon Hunt took Parmly to court. The verdict, in Hunt's favor, established a standard fee schedule for trained architects as distinct from carpenter-craftsmen, and brought Hunt the reputation as a champion of architects' rights. Commissions, however, were scarce, prompting Hunt in 1856 to work briefly for Thomas Ustick Walter in Washington, D.C., on the extensions to the United States Capitol.

Hunt returned to New York in 1857, where he was instrumental in organizing the American Institute of Architects, which at first encompassed only greater New York City, but became a national organization. He also built the Studio Building on Tenth Street in New York (1857-58), a brick structure of two stories with extremely large windows. Hunt occupied one of the studios, and the others quickly filled with some of the most progressive artists in the city. In his studio Hunt organized an atelier, based on his experience in Paris, and gathered around him a group of students who went on to become some of the most important architects at the end of the century, among them George B. Post (1837-1913), Henry Van Brunt (1832-1903), William R. Ware (1832-1915) and Frank Furness (1839-1912).

In 1861, the year Hunt married Catherine Clinton Howland of New York, he designed a summer house for J. N. A. Griswold in Newport, Rhode Island (1861-63), beginning the great period of summer-house construction there. The irregular rambling plan of the Griswold House, its boldly patterned slate roof, encircling porches and elaborate stick-like framing defined what historian Vincent Scully later called the "Stick Style," which flourished in Newport and other coastal resorts after the Civil War. Hunt's later Travers Block of Shops in Newport (1870-71) further developed this style. Shortly after 1863, the Hunts began an extensive period of travel and study in Europe; there the couple's first child was born—Richard Howland Hunt, who also became an architect.

Following Hunt's return to the United States in 1867, his designs became more Gothic in character (inspired by contemporary French sources) as demonstrated in the Presbyterian Hospital, New York City (1868-72), and the East Divinity Hall,

Yale University, New Haven, Connecticut (1869-70). Gothic details were used for Hunt's Stuyvesant Apartments in New York City (1869-70); the internal planning, based on French prototypes, made apartment dwelling respectable among New York's social elite.

In many respects the epitome of that portion of Hunt's career was represented by his soaring Tribune Building, New York City (1873-76); the tower of that office block reached 260 feet and was for a number of years the tallest business building in the world. In construction, the Tribune Building was structurally conservative, using massive masonry piers in the outer walls, with an internal structure of brick partition walls carrying wrought-iron beams and wooden floor decks. The fact that the exterior stone-and-brick piers were structural was clearly expressed, and Hunt introduced broad segmental arches to distribute the loads. This and the overscaled geometric ornamental motifs revealed another French influence on Hunt, that of the so-called *néo-grec* movement. This expression of masonry structure came in use in Paris in the 1840s and continued through the mid-19th century. Among other concerns, it aimed at creating an expression of load and support in masonry construction that would be as clear and direct as that seen in Greek temple construction. In particular, shallow segmental arches were favored across openings, since they were interpreted as expressing the action of masonry more truthfully than hidden lintel beams. This same expression already had been used by Hunt in the broad arched windows of the Tenth Street Studio.

Néo-grec structural expression also was used for the large Lenox Library (1870-77), which Hunt built at Fifth Avenue and 70th Street, one of several libraries that later would be combined to form the nucleus of the New York Public Library (see Carrère and Hastings; the Lenox Library was later destroyed to make way for the classical French town house of Henry Clay Frick, now the Frick Museum, built by Carrère and Hastings in 1914). The Lenox Library also had the bold, overscaled, geometric decorative motifs that came to characterize Hunt's version of *Néo-grec*.

By 1879 Hunt was developing a very different stylistic idiom (although still drawn from French sources), but his last essay in *Néo-grec* structural expression is also his best known. In 1877 Hunt was selected to design the base for the gigantic Statue of Liberty then being completed under the direction of sculptor Frédéric-Auguste Bartholdi in Paris. The site, donated by the federal government, was Bedloe's Island in New York Harbor, once the site of a harbor fortification with a star-shaped fort. Hunt decided to integrate the fortifications into his base design. Following advice from Bartholdi, Hunt designed an immense truncated pyramid of concrete, faced with huge blocks of granite whose emphatic rustication, overscaled rondels and classically derived details matched in scale the huge copper statue. Hunt's base also provided a double anchoring system for the internal steel-and-wrought-iron truss frame, designed by the French bridge engineer Gustave Eiffel, supporting Bartholdi's outer shell of hammered copper and resisting the great lateral forces generated by winds sweeping across the harbor.

Student of the École that he was, Hunt worked with a number of sculptors, designing enclosing stone frames and pedestals. Most of his collaborations were with John Quincy Adams Ward (1830-1910). For Ward, Hunt designed bases and settings for figures of William Shakespeare (1866), the Seventh Regiment Memorial (1874), Commodore Perry Monument (1868), Major General John F. Reynolds Monument (1872), and the George Washington Monument on the steps of Federal Hall on Wall Street (1883), all in New York City; the Yorktown Monument in Yorktown, Virginia (1880-84); the William Earl Dodge Statue in New York City (1885); the James A. Garfield Monument in

Washington, D.C. (1887); the Horace Greeley Statue in New York City (1890); and, perhaps the best, the base for Ward's imposing bronze figure of Henry Ward Beecher, Brooklyn, New York (1891). Particularly innovative was Hunt's bronze base for Franklin Simmons' (1839-1913) equestrian figure of General John A. Logan, erected in Iowa Circle, Washington, D.C. (completed in 1901). Many of Hunt's late collaborations were done with sculptor Karl Bitter, including the interiors of Biltmore House (1895) and bronze doors for Trinity Church (1894-96). It was particularly fitting that Hunt would himself later be commemorated by a collaborative monument built at the edge of Central Park, facing the Lenox Library, designed jointly by architect Bruce Price (1843-1903) and sculptor Daniel Chester French (1850-1931).

In 1879 Hunt's work and his career took a decisive turn when he was given the commission for a grand new urban residence to be built on New York's Fifth Avenue by William Kissam Vanderbilt. Completed in 1882, it was the setting for an eagerly awaited ball. As intended by Vanderbilt and Hunt, the exquisitely detailed limestone château, inspired by those along the Loire River in France, was the means by which the nouveau riche Vanderbilt family was admitted into the inner circles of New York society. Thereafter, Hunt was called upon by other members of that select and extremely wealthy group to design residences, including those for Ogden Mills (1885-87) and Mrs. William Astor (1891-95), both in New York City. Another more compact Loire château was built in Chicago for William Borden (1884-89). For William K. and Alva Vanderbilt, Hunt built a grand but restrained 18th-century classical French palace, Marble House, in Newport, Rhode Island (1888-92). The sons of William K. Vanderbilt also went to Hunt. For Commodore Vanderbilt II, Hunt designed the largest of the Newport "cottages," the Italian palace called the Breakers (1892-95). Most imposing of all was the sprawling Loire château built in Asheville, North Carolina, for George Washington Vanderbilt, Biltmore House (1888-95), set in garden terraces by Federick Law Olmsted, and surrounded by 120,000 acres of forest.

Hunt's career ended with two large buildings signifying the important public role he believed architecture should play. One was a temporary building, the tall domed Administration Building that formed the focal point of the Court of Honor at the World's Columbia Exposition in Chicago (1892-93), a commission that was given to Hunt by the other architects working on the fair as a gesture of the esteem in which they held the man they called the "dean" of American architects. The second, and the last building begun by Hunt, was a grand Beaux-Arts classical structure encasing the earlier wings of the Metropolitan Museum of Art in New York City, and presenting a formal arcaded public entry to Fifth Avenue. Designed by Hunt in 1894-95, it was built under the direction of his son, Richard Howland Hunt, and completed in 1902.

Richard Morris Hunt provided a professional model for architects at the end of the 19th century. His work, bridging the move from High Victorian Gothic to formal classicism, similarly provided models in diverse areas, ranging from apartment complexes, spacious residences for the wealthy, public libraries, collaborative works of sculpture and major art museums.

—LELAND M. ROTH

HURTADO, Francisco.

Spanish. Born Francisco de Hurtado Izquierdo in Spain, 1669. Died in 1725. Master joiner at the Church of San Lorenzo, Córdoba, Spain, 1696; chief architect, Córdoba Cathedral, 1697;

royal tax commissioner for the town of Priego, 1712; founded a workshop for decorators and craftsmen in Priego.

Chronology of Works
All in Spain
* Work no longer exists

1693	Camarín, Mausoleum of the Counts of Buenavista, Málaga [attributed]
1696	San Lorenzo, Córdoba (retable)
1699	La Fuensanta Antechamber, Córdoba (reconstruction of stairway)
1700	Houses, calle del Baño (now calle de Céspedes), Córdoba
1701-03	Hospital of the Destitute, Córdoba
1703	El Carpio (vaulting of side aisles)
1703	Parish Church, Belalcazar (first story of the belfry)
1703-20	Cartuja of Granada (sacristy, executed posthumously)
1703ff.	Cathedral, Córdoba (sacristy)
1704	Capilla Mayor of Church of La Magdalena, Córdoba (divisionary steps)
1707	Santiago (retable)
1713	Cathedral, Granada (marble pulpits)
1719*-25	Cartuja of Nuestra Señora del Paular, Rascafría (sacristy; not completed until 1770*)

Publications

BOOKS ABOUT HURTADO

BONET CORREA, ANTONIO: *Barock in Andalusien.* Barcelona, 1982.
GALLEGO Y BURIN, ANTONIO: *El barroco granadino.* Granada, 1956.
KUBLER, GEORGE: *Arquitectura de los siglos XVII y XVIII (Summa Artis 24).* Madrid, 1957.
KUBLER, GEORGE, and SORIA, MARTIN: *Art and Architecture in Spain and Portugal and Their American Dominions, 1500-1870.* Harmondsworth, England, and Baltimore, 1959.
OROZCO DIAZ, EMILIO: *La Cartuja de Granada.* Leon, 1987.
PITA ANDRADE, JOSÉ MANUEL: *Capilla Real y Catedral de Granada.* Leon, 1981.
SCHUBERT, OTTO: *Historia del barroco en España.* Madrid, 1924.

ARTICLES ABOUT HURTADO

TAYLOR, R. C.: "Francisco Hurtado and His School." *Art Bulletin* 32 (March 1950): 25-61.
TAYLOR, R. C.: "La Sacristía de la Cartuja de Granada y sus autores." *Archivo español de arte y arqueología* 35 (1962): 135-172.

*

Francisco de Hurtado Izquierdo, an architect, sculptor and decorative artist from Andalusia, is important most of all for his ornamentation of church interiors and for his retables and tabernacles. Working almost exclusively for religious patrons, he created a form of religious Baroque art in which different media

Francisco Hurtado: Cartuja of Granada, Granada, Spain, 1703-20

all contribute to a single unified effect. To contemporaries, Hurtado's work came to seem the artistic embodiment of devotion. His decorative forms, covering clearly articulated surfaces, were derived from classical elements, prismatically broken and multiplied. Hurtado's style influenced the development of Baroque architecture in Andalusia for decades, and even asserted itself in the architecture of the colonies.

Although he was held in very high esteem by contemporaries, Hurtado's art fell into disrepute in the late 18th century, during the classical era. His work was held up as the prime example of architectural corruption and degradation of taste, primarily by Antonio Ponz, an important Spanish art critic. This lack of appreciation obstructed a proper understanding of Hurtado's work until the beginning of this century. The critical task of reevaluation is made more difficult by the fact that Hurtado often did not himself carry his designs to completion. The possibility of changes in the original designs by a different hand is always to be reckoned with.

After serving in the Spanish army, Hurtado was active in Córdoba as *"maestro de ensamblador,"* that is, as a specialist in the manufacture of retables, reliquaries and other religious accouterments. Undoubtedly that experience had an influence on his later architectural work. In 1697 he signed himself *"maestro mayor"* of Córdoba Cathedral, and worked from then on for the cardinal and archbishop, Don Pedro de Salazar y Góngora. In Salazar's service he erected the Sacristy, in a style appropriate to the significance of the cathedral, and the archbishop's tomb. The latter was inspired by the work of Giovanni Lorenzo Bernini, and was Hurtado's only purely sculptural (and hardly convincing) work. The Sacristy nevertheless clearly indicated the future development of Hurtado's architectural-decorative style. The upper level, and the pendentives and ribs of the crowning dome of this octagonal, clearly articulated centralized structure are entirely covered with stucco ornamentation. Vegetable forms, grotesques and heads of cherubs dissolve the upper surfaces into filigree, clothing the classical elements of articulation without obscuring them. The interaction of architectural and decorative elements became the hallmark of Hurtado's art.

Hurtado also may have been involved at that time in the design of the so-called *camarín* (a richly decorated reliquary of a form quite common in Spain) at the Virgen de la Victoria at Malaga. The almshouse in Córdoba, also founded by Salazar, on the other hand, has a simple, functional structure and sparing ornamentation. In 1699 Hurtado married Mariana de Gamiz y Escobar at Priego, but returned to Córdoba, where he received a series of minor commissions as an architect. At that time he established a relationship with the Carthusian order, which was the decisive turn in his career and prompted his move to Granada.

Hurtado's first work for the order was the alteration of the Sagrario Chapel of the Carthusian Monastery at Granada, which had been begun in 1702 but was finished only much later. After lengthy discussions about the structure's support system, Hurtado designed a square domed space supported by lateral oratories, and by two Corinthian columns set on each side of a niche with sculptures of saints in each corner. The tabernacle is set in the center, on twisted, black, Solomonic columns. Finished in rich, projecting sculptural forms, the tabernacle dominates the space. Round windows in the lateral chapels, set at the level of the column bases, afford a view of the structure. The effect of the chapel as a whole is determined by its balanced proportions, but even more by the tabernacle's polychrome marble cladding, which was not yet common in Spain at the time, and which lend a sense of drama to the structure. Gilded capitals and stringcourses form a contrast to the pink, green,

black and gray stone, whose nuances are also taken up in the ceiling paintings by Antonio Palomino.

In 1704 designs were first made for another Sagrario, this one for Granada Cathedral. From 1706, Hurtado signed himself *"maestro mayor"* responsible for its construction. Construction of this independent complex, which is located on the southern side of the cathedral, dragged on for decades—like most of Hurtado's buildings—and was only finished by Hurtado's assistant José de Bada. The structure, on a square plan with an inscribed Greek cross, has a central dome and four side domes. This classically proportioned building stands in stark contrast to the style of the Córdoba Sagrario. Elements of the composite order of Diego de Siloe's columns in the cathedral itself are integrated into the powerful compound piers of the Sagrario crossing, which may be explained by the fact that the chapter desired a stylistic harmony between the Sagrario and the cathedral. The sparing decoration was later executed by José de Bada. The exterior of the building is given a monumental appearance by the use of a triumphal arch and gigantic pilasters. These motifs followed the design of Alonso Cano's west facade. The Sagrario of Granada Cathedral demonstrates the extent to which Hurtado's art was rooted in classical forms, despite the decorative exuberance of the designs. Hurtado also created the St. Jacob's Altar for the cathedral and two marble pulpits after Italian models. He modified the pulpits to such a degree as to provide the displeasure of the chapter, however.

In 1712 Hurtado was made royal administrator of Priego, through the mediation of the prior of El Paular. The office assured him financial independence as an artist. Several years later he founded an important school for decorators and artisans, who disseminated his style throughout Andalusia. He himself took over the decoration of the *camarin* of Priego, modernizing the original design.

In 1718 Hurtado received another commission from the Carthusians, this time to build the Sagrario of the Carthusian Monastery of Nuestra Señora del Paular, located in the mountains near Segovia. Undoubtedly, admiration for the Sagrario at Granada had prompted the order to commission a similar work of art for the complex at El Paular. However, Hurtado was also unable to complete this commission. The design may be ascribed to him, but the actual construction must largely be credited to his assistant Teodosio Sánchez de Rueda. This Sagrario is a rare example of Andalusian art in other parts of Spain. The sanctuary consists of a small cruciform space, and a larger one. The latter is square on the exterior, but in the interior has been fitted out with three chapels on the axes of a Greek cross and four chapels in its corners. The marble and jasper tabernacle, set in the center of the cruciform space, is an architectural caprice: it has four levels, and an inner and an outer ring of supports. The space behind it is illuminated by circular windows set above the cornice. The lighting, together with the gilding of the retable, creates a dramatic contrast with the darker inner sanctum. The transition between the spaces is formed by a gold and red portal, whose Moorish accents cannot really be associated with Hurtado's art.

The Sacristy of the Cartuja, Granada (1713-42), surely the most imposing and artistically most mature of the works associated with Hurtado, has posed riddles to researchers thus far. Although rich documentation about the works at the complex is available, no information concerning the construction of this particular building has been found. Nevertheless, the design can be ascribed to Hurtado, following the findings of R. C. Taylor and Gallego Burín. Supervision of the construction may to a large extent have been the work of Hurtado's assistants Luís de Arevalo, Luís Cabello and José de Bada. It seems that Hurtado, as the principal architect of the Carthusian order, was attracted to do the design for this structure. His responsibility for the plans is not in doubt. Construction itself was not begun, significantly enough, until 1732, when the Sagrario of El Paular was finished.

The Sacristy of the Cartuja in Granada is a masterwork of the Spanish Baroque, representing the Andalusian version of the style in highest quality. The compact single nave, which is divided into four alternating wide and narrow bays, is finished with a rare example of a transept-like wing, which has a niche for the altar and retable in the eastern end. The nave is covered with a shallow barrel vault, which is pierced with windows at the base. The transept has a drumless, elliptical dome. The simple design of this church-like space is alive with the sculptural decoration of its structural elements, which remain clearly visible in spite of the rich stucco decor. The pilasters of the Sacristy, for example, as Taylor has pointed out, are composed of no fewer than 45 decorative motifs: capital elements, moldings, volutes, candelabras and the so-called "pig-ears" (diagonally placed segments of arches). All of these elements are to be found in other works by Hurtado, and are derived from the traditional artistic repertoire of Córdoba. The same is true for the sculptural decoration of the vaults. The main cornice is chamfered over the capitals of the pilasters, and curves up and down across the wall surfaces. Its lines are taken up by numerous flattened profiles. Together with the lighting, the decorative elements create an impression of filigree. In contrast to Hurtado's other buildings, there are no figurative elements in the sacristy, which is only insufficiently explained by the function of the space.

Hurtado's later style constituted the beginning of a second phase in Spanish Baroque architecture, which concentrated on the decoration of upper surfaces. This trend was particularly clearly manifested in retable architecture, in which the dominant Solomonic columns were replaced by linear forms such as pilasters and *estípites* (a kind of inverted pyramid). The emphasis on flat decorative elements and their integration into Baroque architecture is especially convincing in the Andalusian style, since the tradition of the *yeserías* (Moorish stuccowork) had survived there.

Hurtado's style was adopted by his assistants and his students, most of all by José de Bada, and disseminated throughout the Andalusion region, where it held sway until the arrival of classicism. The close relationship of Mexican retables to works in Córdoba and Granada is a remarkable phenomenon. In spite of numerous speculations concerning a possible influence from the New World on the art of the mother country, it is more likely that Hurtado's style was taken to the overseas colonies by the members of his circle.

—BARBARA BORNGÄSSER KLEIN
Translated from the German by Marijke Rijsberman

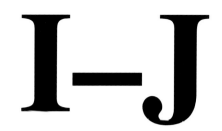

I–J

IKTINOS.

Greek. Active in Greece, ca. 450-400 B. C.

Chronology of Works
All in Greece
All dates are approximate

447-437 B.C.   Parthenon (partially destroyed and rebuilt), Athens
437 B.C. ff.   Telesterion, Eleusis
429-400 B.C.   Temple of Apollo Epikourios, Bassae

Publications

BOOKS ABOUT IKTINOS For English translations of the classical texts refered to, see the editions in the Loeb Classical Library, Cambridge, Massachusetts, and London.

BERVE, HELMUT and GRUBEN, GOTTFRIED: *Greek Temples, Theatres and Shrines.* New York, 1963.
CARPENTER, RHYS: *The Architects of the Parthenon.* Harmondsworth, England, 1970.
COOPER, FREDERICK A.: *The Temple of Apollo at Bassai: A Preliminary Study.* New York, 1978.
DINSMOOR, W. B.: *The Architecture of Ancient Greece: An Account of its Historic Development.* London, 1950.
HOFKES-BRUKKER, CHARLINE and MALLWITZ, ALFRED: *Der Bassai-Fries.* Munich, 1975.
MYLONAS, GEORGE E.: *Eleusis and the Eleusinian Mysteries.* Princeton, New Jersey, 1961.
NOACK, FERDINAND: *Eleusis.* Berlin and Leipzig, 1927.
PAUSANIAS: *Description of Greece.* Book 8,Chapter 41,sections 7-9.
PLUTARCH: *Perikles.* Book 13, Chapters 4-5.
ROBERTSON, D. S.: *A Handbook of Greek and Roman Architecture.* 2nd ed. rev., 1964.
ROUX, GEORGES: *L'architecture de l'Argolidé aux IVe et IIIe siècles avant J. C.,* Paris, 1961.
STRABO: *Geography.* Book 9, Chapter 1, sections 12, 16.
TRAVLOS, JOHN: *Pictorial Dictionary of Ancient Athens.* New York.
VITRUVIUS: *De architectura.* Book 7, Praef., 12, 16.

ARTICLES ABOUT IKTINOS

DINSMOOR, W. B.: "The Temple of Apollo at Bassae." *Metropolitan Museum Studies.* 4 (1932-33): 204-227.
ECKSTEIN, F.: "Iktinos, der Baumeister des Apollontempels von Phigalia-Bassae." In F. ECKSTEIN (ed.): *Festschrift für W. H. Schuchhardt.* Baden-Baden 1960.
FRANTZ, ALISON: "Did Julian the Apostate Rebuild the Parthenon?" *American Journal of Archaeology* 83 (1979): 395-401.

HAHLAND, WALTER: "Der Iktinische Entwurf des Apollontempels in Bassae." *Jahrbuch der deutschen archäologischen Instituts* 63/64 (1948/1949): 14-39.
KNELL, H.: "Iktinos: Baumeister des Parthenon und des Apollontempels von Philaglia-Basse?" *Jahrbuch des Deutschen Archäeologischen Institute.* 83 (1968):100-117.
MALLWITZ, A.: "Cella und Adyton des Apollontempels in Bassai." *Mitteilungen des Deutschen Archäologischen Instituts, Athenische Abteilung* 77 (1962): 140-177.
MARTIN, R.: "L'atelier Ictinos-Callicratès au temple de Bassae." *Bulletin de Correspondance Hellénique* (1976): 427-442.
McCREDIE, JAMES R.: "The Architects of the Parthenon." In *Studies in Classical Art and Archaeology.* Locus Valley, New York, 1979.
PANNUTI, U.: "Il Tempio di Apollo Epikouriosa Bassai (Phigalia): Storia, struttura et problemi." *Atti della Accademia Nazionale dei Lincei: Memorie—Classe di Scienze morali, storiche e filologiche.* Rome. Series 8, Vol. 16,4 (1971): 171-262.
RIEMANN, H.: "Iktinos und der Tempel von Bassae." *Jahrbuch des Deutschen Archäologischen Instituts* (1968).
WESENBERG, B.: "Wer Erbaute den Parthenon?" *Mitteilungen des Deutschen Archäologischen Instituts, Athenische Abteilung* 97 (1982): 99-125.
WINTER, F. E.: "Tradition and Innovation in Doric Design III: The Work of Iktinos." *American Journal of Archaeology* 84 (1980): 339-416.

*

Iktinos is perhaps the most famous of all ancient Greek architects. His name is linked with three extraordinary Doric temples built during the High Classical period, circa 450-400 B.C.: the Parthenon (Vitruvius, Strabo, Pausanias, Plutarch, Ausonius), the Telesterion in Eleusis (Vitruvius, Strabo), and the Temple of Apollo Epikourios at Bassae (Pausanias).

The Periklean Parthenon is the first known building attributed to Iktinos, which he worked on together with Kallikrates under the supervision of Pheidias (Plutarch, *Perikles* 13). In designing the Parthenon, Iktinos and Kallikrates had to satisfy several conditions: as much material as possible from the first (unfinished) Parthenon had to be reused in the new temple, and they had to provide a wider-than-normal cella to contain the new colossal ivory and gold statue of Athena planned by Pheidias. As with Michelangelo nearly 2,000 years later, such restrictions did not hamper these two great architects, but inspired them to create one of the most magnificent structures ever built.

The Periklean Parthenon is remarkably similar to its predecessor in plan, and yet Iktinos and Kallikrates introduced several significant changes. They widened and shortened the temple, bringing it into line with the new canon exemplified by the Early Classical Temple of Zeus at Olympia. They increased the number of columns across the front from six to eight, and those

Parthenon

of the flanks from 16 to 17; the prostyle columns standing before the truncated porches were accordingly increased from four to six. As a result, the width of the temple is greater in proportion to its height, and the horizontal and vertical measurements of the short sides (excluding the cornices and pediments) conform to a ratio of 9:4. This ratio is one that is especially pleasing to the human eye and is found throughout the Parthenon.

The octastyle facade of the Parthenon, together with its unusually wide cella, excessively narrow *pteroma,* densely packed columns and pronounced angle contraction, gives it a breadth, solidity and majesty not found in other Greek temples. At the same time, the Doric columns of the peristyle are more slender than ever before, imparting a sense of lightness to the structure. The temple thus mirrors in abstract form the spiritual nature of Athena herself, a goddess who embodied both masculine and feminine characteristics.

The "refinements" built into the Parthenon by its architects infused the temple with an organic quality, giving it an everlasting impression of freshness (Plutarch, *Perikles* 13), even in its ruined state. Among these refinements, the slight upward curvature of the stylobate, which is transmitted up through the entablature, the slight inward tilting of the columns and lower entablature, and outward tilting of the corona give the temple a soaring quality. At the same time, the downward curvature of stylobate and entablature toward the corners, the slight thickening of the corner columns, and the excessive angle contraction create the impression of strong, solid corners, rooted to the rock, containing the vital mass of the temple within. The result is a kind of fine-tuned architectural *contrapposto,* comparable to that achieved in contemporary sculpture by Polykleitos.

As with most Greek temples before it, the exterior aspect of the Parthenon is its most important, but one detects also an

awakening interest in interior spaces, which occupied Iktinos for the remainder of his career. The Periklean Parthenon had two cellas, an unusual feature retained from the first Parthenon. The main cella was exceptionally spacious, with a double-tiered ·-shaped colonnade of Doric columns, which, aside from its structural function, served as a frame for the cult statue. In the secondary cella, entered from the west, the expected double-tiered Doric arrangement was replaced by four tall Ionic columns, thus creating a unified space. In using Ionic elements within Doric structure (there was also an Ionic frieze which ran at the top of the outer cella wall), Iktinos and Kallikrates followed Attic precedent, in particular that of the old Temple of Athena Polias which stood on the north side of the Acropolis.

The Parthenon was finished save for some of its sculptural adornment by the year 437 B.C., at which time Iktinos apparently went to Eleusis to redesign and enlarge the existing Telesterion, which had grown too small for its purposes. Located on the rocky limestone acropolis, the Telesterion, a large hall sacred to Demeter and Persephone in which mystery rites were carried out annually, was unique among Greek temples. Its interior design was of the utmost importance, its exterior, in contrast, insignificant.

As with the Parthenon, Iktinos had to reuse as much of the earlier Telesterion as possible. He doubled the size of the temple, transforming it from a rectangle to a square, thus placing the *anactoron* (a narrow rectangular room that served as the holiest of the holies), which hitherto had been to one side of the temple, in the center for the first time. Twenty widely spaced columns arranged in rows were planned to support the roof, and a series of seats lined the four walls; those on the northwest, carved from living rock, are still visible today. On three sides two evenly spaced doorways gave access to the temple. The result was "the first real centrally planned space of antiquity." Iktinos planned an exterior peristyle, but its exact shape is disputed. The temple was altered and essentially completed by Coroebus, Metagenes and Xenokles (Plutarch, *Perikles* 13). They nearly doubled the number of interior supports, creating a forest of columns comparable to those of earlier Telesterions. The portico, when built, was restricted to the eastern side, imparting a frontal emphasis to the structure at odds with its otherwise centralized arrangement.

Shortly after the death of Perikles in 429 B.C., Iktinos went to Bassae, a remote mountainous site in Arcadia, to build a new temple of Apollo Epikourios (Pausanias 8.41.9). Once again he had to work within certain constraints. The new Doric temple was to be erected "on the rebuilt underpinnings" of its Archaic predecessor, a long, narrow temple that faced north-south (instead of east-west). A local hard gray limestone served as the primary building material. Using the laws of linear perspective, well known to contemporary scene painters, Iktinos mitigated the long Archaic proportions of the plan by means of several refinements, which included an outward curvature of the *krepidoma,* and a slight widening of the temple toward the rear.

The truly revolutionary aspect of the Bassae temple, however, is the design of its interior. Iktinos divided the narrow cella into two parts, a cella proper and an adytum. He thus achieved a length-to-width ratio of 9:5 for the cella proper, remarkably close to the ideal ratio of 9:4 employed in the Parthenon. Inside the temple Iktinos abandoned the normal double-tiered arrangement of Doric columns and used instead Ionic half columns, engaged to short spur walls, leaving as much space as possible in the center. For these columns, which carried a full Ionic entablature (including a carved frieze), Iktinos designed unusually dynamic, flaring bases, and three-faced volute capitals with fat, convexly curved cushions. To separate the cella from the adytum he set the last two Ionic columns on diagonal spur walls, and placed between them a single Corinthian column, the earliest known example of its kind. Thus the adytum could be seen and entered from the cella proper. The temple at Bassae marked the first time in Greek architecture that a Doric temple harbored a completely Ionic interior, and it was there that Iktinos' interest in interior spaces, which was hinted at in the Parthenon, and developed in the Telesterion, came to full fruition.

After Bassae, the design of temple interiors grew increasingly important. Fourth-century architects followed Iktinos' lead, using the Ionic/Corinthian order within Doric temples, often reducing the interior colonnades to engaged columns decorating the cella walls, leaving the cellas uncluttered. Another aspect of Iktinos' design at Bassae reached beyond the fourth century and into the Hellenistic era in its influence. There Iktinos created a sense of controlled spaces drawing the visitor in from the bright sunshine through the deep, shadowy pronaos, and into the semidarkness of the cella to behold the epiphany of Apollo himself in the sunlight that flooded the adytum beyond through a doorway in the eastern wall. The axial progression, the passage through light and dark, and the element of surprise, all of which appeared together for the first time at Bassae, were later exploited by Hellenistic architects.

Throughout his career, Iktinos showed himself to be a highly innovative architect, turning preexisting conditions into stunning, original architectural solutions. He played a crucial role in the creation of the Parthenon, introduced the Corinthian capital into Greek architecture, a form which had lasting influence from the Romans to the present day, and developed the interior of the Greek temple as a space in its own right. In so doing, he left his lasting mark on generations to come.

POSTSCRIPT: The career of Iktinos, like that of Kallikrates, is highly controversial. Some scholars believe Kallikrates alone designed the Parthenon, others (based on Plutarch *Perikles* 13) that Iktinos never worked in Eleusis, and still others that the temple at Bassae is not by his hand. While ancient testimonia regarding Iktinos abounds, it is often conflicting, and to date archaeologists have unearthed no surviving inscription(s) bearing his name. For a full understanding of these issues the reader is directed to the accompanying bibliography.

—PATRICIA MARX

ISOZAKI, Arata.

Japanese. Born in Oita City, Japan, 23 July 1931. Married the sculptor Aiko Miyawakiin, 1972. Studied at the University of Tokyo, Faculty of Architecture, Dip.Arch., 1954. Worked with Kenzo Tange's Team and Urtec, Tokyo, 1954-63; director of Arata Isozaki and Associates, Tokyo, since 1963. Has taught widely in the United States. Gold Medal, Royal Institute of British Architects, 1986.

Chronology of Works
All in Japan unless noted

1962-66	Oita Prefectural Library, Oita
1964	Nakayama House, Oita
1967-70	Festival Plaza, Expo '70, Osaka
1968-71	Fukuoka City Bank Headquarters, Fukuoka
1971-74	Museum of Modern Art, Takasaki, Gunma
1973-74	Kitakyushu Central Library, Kitakyushu, Fukuoka
1973-75	Yano House, Takaishi, Tama-ku, Kawasaki
1975-77	West Japan General Exhibition Center, Kitakyushu, Fukuoka
1976-78	Kamioka Town Hall, Gifu
1979-83	Tsukuba Center Building, Tsukuba Science City, Ibaragi
1981-86	Museum of Contemporary Art, Los Angeles, California, USA
1983-85	Palladium Club, New York City, USA
1983-90	Sant Jordi Sports Hall, Olympic Ring, Barcelona, Spain
1985-89	National Museum of Egyptian Civilization, Cairo (interior design and installation)
1986-90	Art Tower Mito, Mito, Ibaragi
1986-	Brooklyn Museum, Brooklyn, New York, USA (addition)
1987-89	Bond University, Administration/Library/Humanities Building, Queensland, Australia
1987-90	Disney Building, Lake Buena Vista, Florida, USA
1987-90	Kitakyushu International Conference Center, Kitakyushu, Fukuoka
1988-90	International Friendship Pavilion, Expo '90, Osaka
1989-90	JR Yufuin Railway Station, Oita
1989-	Kashii Twin Towers, Fukuoka
1990-	Izu Museum of Contemporary Art, Ito

Publications

BOOKS BY ISOZAKI

Kukan-e (collected writings 1960-69). Tokyo, 1971.
Shuho-ga (collected writings 1969-78). Tokyo, 1979.
Kenchiku-no-Chiso (critical essays). Tokyo, 1979.

Architectural Pilgrimage to World Architecture. With photographs by Kishin Shinoyama. 12 vols. Tokyo, 1980-92.
MOCA Drawings 1981-83. Tokyo, 1983.
Post-modern Genron (The Principles of Post Modernism). Tokyo, 1985.
Ima, Mienai Toshi (Now, the City Invisible). Tokyo, 1985.
Post-modern no Jidai to Kenchiku (The Post-Modern Era and Architecture). Tokyo, 1985.
Katsura Villa, The Ambiguity of Its Space. New York, 1987.
Barcelona Drawings. Barcelona, 1988.
Kenchiku no Seijigaku (The Politics of Architecture). Tokyo, 1989.
Image Game. Tokyo, 1990.
Seikimatsu no Shiso to Kenchiku (Thoughts and Architecture at the Turn of the Century—Dialogue with Koji Taki). Tokyo, 1991.

ARTICLES BY ISOZAKI

"About My Method." *Japan Architect* (August 1972).
"The Metaphor of the Cube." *Japan Architect* (March 1976).
"Rhetoric of the Cylinder." *Japan Architect* (April 1976).
"A Metaphor Relating with Water." *Japan Architect* (March 1978).
"On Formalism." *Japan Architect* (January 1979).
"Ma: Japanese Space-Time." *Japan Architect* (February 1979).
"When the King Was Killed." *GA Document Special Issue 1* (August 1980).
"A Rethinking of Spaces of Darkness." *Japan Architect* (March 1981).
"The Ledoux Connection." *Architectural Design* (January/ February 1982).
"Of City, Nation and Style." *Japan Architect* (January 1984).
"Architecture With and Without Irony." In *New Public Architecture: Recent Projects by Fumihiko Maki and Arata Isozaki*, New York, 1985.
"The Paradox of Tradition." In *Kagu: Mobilier Japonais*, Angers, France, 1985.
"The Current State of Design." In *International Design Yearbook 4*, New York, 1988.
"Notes on the Works 1985-1991." *Space Design* (October/ November 1991).

BOOKS ABOUT ISOZAKI

BARATTUCCI, BRUNILDE, and DI RUSSO, BIANCA: *Arata Isozaki: Architecture 1959-1982.* Rome, 1983.
BOGNAR, BOTAND: *Contemporary Japanese Architecture.* New York, 1985.
BOGNAR, BOTAND: *The New Japanese Architecture.* New York, 1990.
DREW, PHILIP: *The Architecture of Arata Isozaki.* New York and London, 1982.
The Prints of Arata Isozaki 1977-83. Exhibition Catalog. Tokyo, 1983.
STEWART DAVID B., and YATSUKA, HAJIME: *Arata Isozaki: Architecture 1960-1990.* New York, 1991.

ARTICLES ABOUT ISOZAKI

AARON, BETZY: "Arata Isozaki Architecture and the Unreal City." *Artspace* (Summer 1991).

"Arata Isozaki 1976-1984." Special issue of *Space Design* (January 1984).
Architectural Design, special issue (January 1977).
COOK, PETER: "On Arata Isozaki." *Architectural Design* (January 1977).
FILLER, MARTIN: "The Recent Work of Arata Isozaki, Parts 1 and 2." *Architectural Record* (October 1983; May 1984).
FRAMPTON, KENNETH: "Arata Isozaki's MOCA." *Domus* (November 1986).
GOLDBERGER, PAUL: "Arata Isozaki." *Architectural Digest* (March 1989).
HOLLEIN, HANS: "Position and Move." *Space Design* (April 1974).
Japan Architect, special editions (March and April 1976).
MILLER, NORY, and CASS, HEATHER: "Arata Isozaki: Exploring Form and Experience." *American Institute of Architects Journal* (November 1979).
RASTOFER, D.n: "Isozaki: The Art of Construction." *Architectural Record* (January 1988).
SUZUKI, HIROYUKI: "The Dismantling of History." *Space Design* (October 1991).
TAYLOR, JENNIFER: "The Unreal Architecture of Arata Isozaki." *Progressive Architecture* (September 1976).
VILADAS, PILAR: "On MOCA." *Progressive Architecture* (November 1986).

*

Arata Isozaki is recognized as one of the world's most compelling architects. Postmodern in his aesthetic stance, Isozaki is a rigorously unsentimental architect, and radically innovative in his juxtaposition of masses and materials. He utilizes an unerring sense of classical form and monumentality, with a clear commitment to architecture's ability to evoke and communicate social and psychological meaning. His compositions are baroque and asymmetrical, often ironic, sometimes witty, always serious. Among his more controversial works to date is his New Tokyo City Hall, Shinjuku, Tokyo (1985-86), wherein he transformed a traditional Western building form into a technologically advanced, highly symbolic structure.

Isozaki's work has been known outside Japan since the early 1980s, when major architects of several highly developed capitalist countries began receiving commissions worldwide. These architects have been in individual revolt against the formal purity of the International Style for the last two decades. Isozaki refers to the group, of which he is a part, as the "new architectural mafia." It includes, among others, Michael Graves, James Stirling, Peter Eisenman, Richard Meier and Hans Hollein. As postmodern architects, they reassert the use of metaphor, symbol and content as being as basic to architecture's nature as its formal invention. They share concerns with mass, surface colors and textures, and the use of unorthodox materials. These architects are also vigorously eclectic, utilizing design motifs from architectural history, as well as from each other. They favor a pared-down classical vocabulary of circles, squares, cubes and pyramids. Except for their revolt against International Style orthodoxy, they share no ideology. Their styles are distinctly different, heterogeneous.

There are good reasons why Isozaki, an architect from Japan (rather than a Japanese architect), has risen to unique prominence. His work has been termed schizophrenic, possessed of multiple dualities. The special tensions between East and West among the formal, sensual and historical elements in his work give Isozaki's architecture a particular resonance for our time. He was 15 years old when World War II ended, 23 when he graduated from architecture school at the University of Tokyo

Arata Isozaki: Tsukuba Center Building, Tsukuba Science City, Ibaragi, Japan, 1979-83

in 1954 and joined the architectural firm of Kenzo Tange. This was a firm strongly influenced by Le Corbusier's Brutalism of the 1950s, its style of mass and monumentality already providing alternatives to the International Style. Isozaki was 32 when he left Tange to establish Arata Isozaki and Associates in 1963; his work through the 1960s continued to show the influence of Le Corbusier, as well as that of Karl Friedrich Schinkel, another classical architect working in a period of rapid change. The bare-bones classicism of Isozaki's Gunma Prefectural Museum of Fine Art in Takaseki (1971-74) recalls the distilled serenity common to both architects.

Coming of age amid the atomic devastation of western Japan near the destroyed cities of Nagasaki and Hiroshima, Isozaki reached artistic maturity, however, in a visually, physically and morally deconstructed world. He said in 1985: "For the first twenty years of my career as a professional architect, I believed that architecture could only be accomplished by irony. Architecture was an unfulfilled wish, a mourning for what was lost— Hiroshima, Holocaust. To bridge over the gap, a style of wit, a sense of humor and paradox were adopted." The trauma of loss was directly expressed in "Electric Labyrinth" (1968, the Milan Triennale), an altered photograph of a blasted city dominated by two huge mutant forms of skeletal architecture. Japan's remarkable entry into the electronic world followed, however, and Isozaki's robot-activated "cybernetic environment" in Festival Park, Osaka, for Expo '70 was the beginning of his current experimentation with the hypertechnologies of the future.

It is with his architecture of metaphor, nonetheless, that Isozaki has created his most influential work. His most perverse example of architecture as metaphor is expressed in his Tsukuba Civic Center (1980-83), a commission whose aim was to provide a center for a Japanese new town, a center for science and technology. The irony is that the literary metaphors and architectural allusions Isozaki used are all from Western culture, from Roland Barthes' linguistics, to Mannerist Guilio Romano and French Classicists Claude-Nicolas Ledox and Etienne-Louis Boullée, to J. B. Fischer von Erlach. All are utilized in providing a noncenter for the complex of buildings: cubes, squares and cylinders which house a hotel, community center and concert hall around a central shopping plaza.

Isozaki then took Michelangelo's great pointed oval from the Campidoglio, and sunk it below that central plaza. Water flows down into this space from a fragmented waterfall, producing a kind of nonfountain. Toshiaki Nagasawa's sculpture of a bronze laurel tree wrapped in a gold tunic (symbol of Daphne's transformation near a river) stands in a natural grassy area at the top of the waterfall. Thoroughly Western in origin, the sculpture is also a symbol of absence, and may allude to the universal need for myths of transformation. Disparate materials—finely crafted ceramic tile, glistening aluminum, rough and smoothly cut stone—are all juxtaposed in both buildings and plaza, unified by variations of the colors gray, tan and gold, and with patterns of light and water Isozaki has given architectural expression to ambiguity: to the idea of an empty center as metaphor for the absence of leadership essential to the autonomy of science. The Tsukuba Civic Center suggests as well the idea that the Japanese are at their most characteristic when learning from others.

Isozaki also said in 1985, "After twenty years of practical experience, I am now going to find a method to create architecture without irony." And it is an architecture without irony, rich in metaphor and virtuoso synthesis, that Isozaki has achieved in the late 1980s. The Los Angeles Museum of Contemporary Art (1981-86) and the Art Tower Mito, Ibaragi, Japan (1986-90), are both bold compositions of daringly disparate elements unified with evocative wit and harmony.

—ANN CROWE

JACOBSEN, Arne.

Danish. Born in Copenhagen, Denmark, 11 February 1902. Died in Copenhagen, 24 March 1971. Studied at the Academy of Arts, Copenhagen, Dip.Arch., 1928. In private practice, Copenhagen, 1930 until his death in 1971; also designed textiles and furniture from 1943. Professor of architecture, Academy of Arts, Copenhagen, 1956-71.

Chronology of Works
All in Denmark unless noted

1929	House of the Future, Exhibition in Forum, Copenhagen (with Flemming Lassen)
1931	Rothenborg House, 37 Klampenborgvej, Copenhagen
1932	Bellevue Seaside Development, Copenhagen
1933-34	Bellavista Housing, Bellevue, Copenhagen
1937-38	Stelling House, Gammel Torv 6, Copenhagen
1937-42	Town Hall, Aarhus (with Erik Møller)
1942	Town Hall, Søllerød (with Lassen)
1943	Smokehouse, Odden
1950	Søholm Terraced Housing, Strandvejen, Klampenborg, near Copenhagen
1952-56	Munkegaard School Vangedevej, Gentofte
1955	Town Hall, Rødovre
1955	Jespersen and Son Office Building, Copenhagen
1957	Carl Christensen Factory, Aalborg
1958-60	SAS Royal Hotel and Air Terminal, Copenhagen
1960-62	Tom's Chocolate Factory, Ballerup
1961-65	St. Catherine's College, Oxford, England
1961-78	National Bank of Denmark, Copenhagen (with Hans Dissing and Otto Weitling)
1966-69	Hamburg Electricity Supply Company Headquarters, Hamburg, Germany (with Weitling)
1966-77	Town Center, Castrop-Rauxel, Germany (with Weitling)
1970-73	Town Hall, Mainz, Germany (with Weitling)
1972-76	Danish Embassy, London, England (with Dissing and Weitling)

Publications

BOOKS ABOUT JACOBSEN

Arne Jacobsen: Architecture, Applied Art. Exhibition catalog. London, 1959.
FABER, TOBIAS: *Arne Jacobsen.* New York and London, 1964.
KASTHOLM, JøRGEN: *Arne Jacobsen.* Copenhagen, 1968.
PEDERSEN, JOHAN: *Arkitekten Arne Jacobsen.* Copenhagen, 1954.
RUBINO, LUCIANO: *Arne Jacobsen: opera completa.* Rome, 1980.
SKRIVER, POUL ERIK: *Arne Jacobsen: A Danish Architect.* Copenhagen, 1972.

ARTICLES ABOUT JACOBSEN

"Danish Embassy in London." *Deutsche Bauzeitschrift* (Gutersloh, July 1980).
GENTILI, E.: "Evoluzione di Jacobsen nella moderne architectura danese." *Casabella* (September/October 1956).
HACKNEY, R.: "Arne Jacobsen: Architecture and Fine Art." *Leonardo* (Oxford, Autumn 1972).
"Recent Buildings by Arne Jacobsen." *Zodiac* No. 5 (1959).

Arne Jacobsen: Town Hall, Rodovre, Denmark, 1955

SKRIVER, POUL ERIK: "L'oeuvre d'Arne Jacobsen." *Architecture d'aujourd'hui* (December 1960/January 1961): 42-53.
SKRIVER, POUL ERIK: "Royal-Hotel-Copenhagen." *Arkitektur* 4, No. 6 (December 1960): 209-248.

A leading proponent of modern architecture in Denmark, Arne Jacobsen combined in his work the precision of Ludwig Mies van der Rohe with the traditional humanity seen in the work of his Nordic mentors, Erik Gunnar Asplund and Alvar Aalto. In seeking simple and logical solutions to architectural and design problems, he further exhibited the Danish sensitivity in use of materials. These qualities not only made Jacobsen a successful competitor in numerous architectural competitions, but informed all levels of his practice. Jacobsen was equally interested in both the small detail and the larger conception, for his furniture, flatware, glass and fabric designs were as well known and appreciated as his architecture.

Though his early work was in the austere Nordic classicism of the post-World War I period, as witnessed in a 1927 villa design and the award-winning project for the National Museum in Klampenborg (1928), his work from the end of the 1920s on was uncompromisingly modern. In the "House of the Future" competition of 1929, Jacobsen's award-winning entry, done with Flemming Lassen, exploited all aspects of contemporary industrial technique. Man had become motorized and effective; a car garage, boat house and landing pad for a small helicopter were integrated into the form of the house. Labor-saving areas for women allowed time for employment and sunbathing on the roof terrace.

This modernity infused all his subsequent works. The Rothenborg House in Klampenborg (1931) lay as a ship or machine on its verdant site. The Bellavista housing estate in Klampenborg (1933) incorporated the white cubic forms and machine imagery associated with the Weissenhofsiedlung in Stuttgart, while orienting itself to the favorable views from the site. Other works done in the Bellevue development, in the northern Copenhagen suburb of Klampenborg, contained numerous influences from Walter Gropius' Bauhaus complex. In the Bellevue development Jacobsen not only integrated landscape and building design, but also designed the furniture and fixtures for the theater, restaurant and lido. He added other buildings to this complex throughout his career. The Stelling Building (1937), an urban work in downtown Copenhagen, also demonstrated the simplicity and clarity of modernist expression that Jacobsen sought to achieve.

In the early 1940s, like many Scandinavian contemporaries, Jacobsen moved toward a more tactile, expressive form of modernism, incorporating a richer material vocabulary and more traditional forms of expression. In exemplary works such as the Fish Smokehouse in Odden Harbor (1942), the Aarhus Town Hall (1939-42, done in collaboration with Erik Møller), and the Søllerød Town Hall (1940-42, done in collaboration with Flemming Lassen), the expressed programmatic clarity of modernism was combined with the more associative formal vocabulary and use of materials found in traditional Nordic architecture. Traditional norms softened modernist austerity to provide more corporeal substance and regional character to the architecture. Jacobsen began to incorporate traditional pitched-roof forms, brick, tile and stone cladding, and smaller, punched window openings into his compositions.

In 1943, as a result of the German occupation of Denmark, Jacobsen sought refuge in Sweden. During that period he collaborated with his wife to produce a number of floral textile designs, and continued to pursue furniture and applied designs, including flatware and glassware.

Returning to Denmark after the war, Jacobsen won the competition for the Søholm housing complex. The complex was of brick, and not only demonstrated a sensitivity to texture and human scale, but set the precedent for Danish housing design in the postwar era. Most of Jacobsen's work of the 1950s and 1960s infused influences from the United States with European industrialized design values. The Rødovre Town Hall (1955) owes a debt to Eero Saarinen's General Motors Technical Center, while the SAS Royal Hotel (1958-60) was certainly influenced by Skidmore, Owings and Merrill's Lever House design. In both cases, though, Jacobsen's personal interpretation is obvious. For the hotel, he designed the furniture, tableware and light fixtures. One of these designs, his popular bent-wood chair the "Violin," is still being produced today. Jacobsen designed and produced, during that period, a series of chair designs for Fritz Hansen, office desks for S.O.O.L., and lamps and clocks for Louis Poulsen.

In complexes like the Jespersen and Son Office Complex (1955), the Tom's Chocolate Factory (1961) and the National

Bank of Denmark (1961-71, done with H. Dissing and O. Weitling), Jacobsen combined the simplicity and precision of industrially produced buildings with the tactility of traditional masonry construction. Other works of a more tactile, vernacular quality include the factory for Carl Christensen in Aalborg (1957), the Munkegaard School in Gentofte (1952-56), and a number of very expressive single-family residences in the suburbs of Copenhagen. Late in his career, Jacobsen collaborated with Otto Weitling on a number of large projects in Germany: the Hannover Concert Hall (1965), the Hamburg Power Company Headquarters (1966-69),the City Hall in Mainz (1970-73), a grammar school in Hamburg, and a recreation center in Fehmarn. The City Hall in Mainz, in particular, is an excellent essay in the experimental qualities achieved from juxtaposing precise Miesian detailing against large masonry masses. These qualities hallmarking Jacobsen's postwar practice are also found in his best later works: St. Catherine's College at Oxford University (1961-65), the National Bank of Copenhagen (1971), the American Express Bank in Copenhagen and the Royal Danish Embassy in London (1972-76).

A modernist's modernist, Arne Jacobsen provided a legacy of works which were exemplary in their use of materials, integration of furnishings and overall design control. He is considered to have set the standard for what the world recognizes as ''Danish modern.''

—WILLIAM C. MILLER

JAHN, Helmut.

American. Born in Nuremberg, Germany, 4 January 1940. Married Deborah Ann Lampe in 1970. Studied at the Technische Hochschule, Munich, Germany, 1960-65, Dip.Ing./Arch.; Illinois Institute of Technology, Chicago, Illinois, 1966-67. Worked with P. C. von Seidlein, Munich, Germany, 1965-66; joined C. F. Murphy Associates, Chicago, 1967: assistant to Gene Summers, 1967-73; partner, director in charge of planning and design, and executive vice-president, 1973-81; principal, from 1981, president, si nce 1982, and chief executive officer, since 1983, Murphy/Jahn Associates, Chicago. Has taught at University of Illinois at Chicago, Harvard University and Yale University.

Chronology of Works
All in the United States unless noted

1970	McCormick Place, Chicago, Illinois (convention center)
1974	Kemper Arena, Kansas City, Missouri
1977	Athletic Facility, St. Mary's College, Notre Dame, Indiana
1978	La Lumière Gymnasium, La Porte, Indiana
1978	Rust-Oleum Corporate Headquarters, Vernon Hills, Illinois
1980	Xerox Centre, Chicago, Illinois
1980	De La Garza Career Center, East Chicago, Indiana
1982	Support Facility, Argonne National Laboratories, Argonne, Illinois
1982	First Source Center, South Bend, Indiana
1982	One South Wacker Office Building, Chicago, Illinois
1982	Board of Trade, Chicago, Illinois (addition)
1983	Office Building, 11 Diagonal Street, Johannesburg, South Africa
1983	O'Hare Rapid Transit Station, Chicago, Illinois

Helmut Jahn: United Airlines Terminal, Chicago, Illinois, 1987

1984	Agricultural Engineering Science Building, University of Illinois, Champaign
1984	Office Building, 701 Fourth Avenue South, Minneapolis, Minnesota
1985	State of Illinois Center, Chicago, Illinois
1986	Office Building, 362 West Street, Durban, South Africa
1986	Park Avenue Tower, New York City
1986	Northwestern Rail Terminal, Chicago, Illinois
1987	United Airlines Terminal, O'Hare International Airport, Chicago, Illinois
1987	One Liberty Place, Philadelphia, Pennsylvania
1989	750 Lexington Avenue, New York City
1989	Cityspire, New York City
1989	Messe Frankfurt Convention Center, Frankfurt, West Germany
1990	Barnett Bank Headquarters, Jacksonville, Florida

Publications

ARTICLES BY JAHN

''Architectural Form.'' With James Gottsch. *Bauen und Wohnen* (December 1975).

BOOKS ABOUT JAHN

BLASER, WERNER: *After Mies.* New York, 1977.
BLASER, WERNER (ed.): *Helmut Jahn Airports.* Basel and Boston, 1991.
CASARI, MAURIZIO, and PAVAN, VINCENZO: *New Chicago Architecture.* New York, 1981.

DIAMONSTEIN, BARBARALEE: *American Architecture Now II.* New York, 1985.

GLIBOTA, ANTE: *Helmut Jahn.* Paris, 1987.

GOLDBERGER, PAUL: *The Skyscraper.* New York, 1981.

JOEDICKE, J. A.: *Helmut Jahn: Design of a New Architecture.* New York, 1987.

MILLER, NORY: *Helmut Jahn.* New York, 1986.

PORTOGHESI, PAOLO: *Postmodern: The Architecture of the Postindustrial Society.* New York, 1984.

SAXON, RICHARD G.: *Atrium Buildings—Development and Design.* London, 1983.

ARTICLES ABOUT JAHN

Architecture and Urbanism, extra edition (June 1986).

"Analysis of Planned and Completed Projects by C. F. Murphy Associates." *Bauen und Wohnen* (September 1974).

BRUEGMANN, ROBERT: "High Flight." *Inland Architect* 32/5 (September/October 1988).

"The Building of the Year 2,000." *Inland Architect* (May 1980).

"Chicago, Chicago." *Building Design* (25 July 1980).

"Chicago on the Drawing Boards." *Horizon* (September 1978).

"The Chicago Seven." *Architecture and Urbanism* (June 1978).

"The Constructional Ideas of Helmut Jahn." *Inland Architect* (January/February 1988).

"Contemporary Architects: Helmut Jahn." *Architecture and Urbanism* (July 1978).

"Facade at Right Angles." *Progressive Architecture* (December 1980).

"A Grand Gateway" and "United Airlines Terminal." *Progressive Architecture* (November 1987).

"Grand Stuctures." *Techniques et architecture* (May 1976).

"Helmut Jahn/Murphy Associates." *Controspazio* (Bari, Italy, April/June 1981).

"Helmut Jahn Topples the Box." *Architect and Builder* (Cape Town, South Africa, June 1982).

"Helmut Jahn's Tall Buildings." *Art* (October 1990).

"High Tech Expansion: United Airlines Terminal 1 Complex, O'Hare International Airport and O'Hare Rapid Transit Extension Station, Chicago, Illinois." *Architectural Record* (May 1985).

INGRAHAM, CATHERINE: "On Visibility, Travel and Transformation: The Questions of North Western Atrium." *Inland Architect* 32/3 (May/June 1988).

"Jahn Wacker." *Architectural Review* (April 1981).

"Kemper Arena." *Domus* (April 1976).

MARLIN, WILLIAM: "Missing Mies." *Architectural Record* (July 1979).

MILLER, NORY: "Architecture: Helmut Jahn." *Architectural Digest* (March 1984).

"Minnesota II." *Progressive Architecture* (January 1979).

"One South Wacker, Chicago." *GA Document* (Summer 1980).

"Panoply of Images: State of Illinois Center, Chicago." *Progressive Architecture* (February 1981).

"Romantic Hi-Tech" [interview]. *Planning and Building Developments* (Braamfontein, South Africa, March/April 1983).

"St. Mary's Athletic Facility." *Industria delle costruzioni* (February 1979).

"Three Designs by Murphy Jahn." *Architectural Record* (December 1981).

"Works: Helmut Jahn of Murphy Jahn." *Architecture and Urbanism* (November 1983).

The *wunderkind* of Chicago architects in the 1980s, Helmut Jahn is a scion of Ludwig Mies van der Rohe's powerful legacy. His work in the United States, Europe and Africa represents an adaption of Mies' principles of austerity, clarity and elegant precision to a world of corporate theatrics, historical self-consciousness and formal flamboyance.

Jahn's work is related to a second modernism, a mannerist extension of a more orthodox modernism. The expression of structure is a primary theme in these buildings; in addition, however, his work explores the expressive possibilities of color and reflective surfaces. Dynamic spaces and formal complexity distinguish his work from earlier modernism, as well.

The German-born Jahn graduated from the Technische Hochschule in Munich in 1965 and worked for Peter C. von Seidlein the next year. He went to Chicago in 1966 to pursue graduate studies at the Illinois Institute of Technology (IIT), where the curriculum still reflected the teaching and design philosophies of Mies. At IIT he studied with Myron Goldsmith and Fazlur Khan and developed a sense of the expressive potential of structure. He joined C. F. Murphy Associates in 1967 and was an assistant to Gene Summers until 1973, when he became executive vice-president and director of planning and design. In 1981 the firm became Murphy/Jahn.

In almost all of his designs, Jahn employs structure as a form-giving element; furthermore, he explores technology as an appropriate component of contemporary ornament. In his tall office buildings, there are frequently interlocking geometries; in this aspect, his work exhibits its clearest reaction to the prismatic formal purity of Mies and his disciples. Jahn also experiments with color and the effects of transparency in contrast with reflectivity and translucency.

The body of Jahn's work can be grouped loosely into four phases: low-rise pavilions (not unlike Mies' interest in this form as seen in Crown Hall at IIT and the Farnsworth House); early tall office buildings, for example, the Xerox Centre in Chicago; mixed-use facilities, such as the State of Illinois Center in Chicago; and later tall office buildings, for example, One Liberty Place in Philadelphia. In this latter phase, he has explored his interest in the complexity of interlocking geometries, the impact of the building on the skyline by means of its accompanying reinforced top, and the relation of the building to the street as made emphatic by reinforced entries and covered walkways.

Representing the first phase, Kemper Arena in Kansas City, Missouri, completed in 1974, employs an oval to reduce the structural span, as well as to provide proximity to events for the maximum number of spectators. The structural concept relates directly to Mies' solution at Crown Hall, where the roof is suspended from deep steel girders on the exterior of the building. At the arena, the roof is suspended from three tubular space-frame trusses, also on the exterior. White metal panels, softened by curved corners, enclose the space. While less diaphanous and jewel-like than Crown Hall, Kemper Arena is clearly indebted to its Miesian antecedent.

At St. Mary's College Athletic Facility in Notre Dame, Indiana (1977), the structural members are painted in bold colors, and trusses support the roof cantilever at both ends over the corridors. A thin membrane of translucent fiberglass panels encloses this facility for tennis, volleyball and basketball. One of the most direct and elegant designs from this phase is the La Lumière Gymnasium in La Porte, Indiana (1978), a single vault of thin, corrugated, galvanized steel sheeting, suppressed into the ground with no intermediate supports. At the Rust-Oleum Corporation National Headquarters, a two-story office building in Vernon Hills, Illinois (1978), parking is located in an open structure beneath the building. Above ground, a glazed, shed-roofed hall extends the length of the building, in which the ducts and tubes for mechanical equipment are exposed. On the exterior, aluminum paneling and horizontal bands of windows prefigure the treatment of the enclosure of the Xerox Centre.

In the De La Garza Career Center in East Chicago, Indiana (1980), the structural elements, trusses supported by tubular columns, are painted bright green, and yellow enclosure panels contrast with interior brick partitions. The Argonne Program Support Facility at Argonne National Laboratories in Argonne, Illinois (1982), served as a pilot project for the passive collection of solar energy: the plan is a circle (the smallest amount of material required for an enclosure) with a segment truncated for future solar collectors. The arc of the circle is completed by a lake that reflects the sun's rays into the building.

Representing the second phase, the Xerox Centre in Chicago (1980) is distinguished by its round corner, related perhaps to Louis Sullivan's corner hinge at Carson Pirie Scott department store to the north and east, and by a ground-level facade that undulates inward, exposing round columns. The corner extends above the roof to form a circular penthouse. The proportion of glazing in relation to the tight membrane of coated aluminum panels increases the amount of light admitted on the north side of the building. Diagonal lines provide a playful decorative element in the arrangement of lighting fixtures on the first two stories, diagonal strips of asphalt on the roof, and expansion joints in the paving of the ground plane.

A mixed-use development in South Bend, Indiana, the First Source Center (1982), sets two buildings at angles to create a trapezoidal courtyard. The prismatic quality of the two forms, along with their sloped tops, relates the buildings to Philip Johnson's Pennzoil Place in Houston.

At One South Wacker Drive (1982), a 40-story office building in Chicago, Jahn began his exploration of the effects of colored glass. Set back twice, with sloped atria at each of those points, the building's facade presents an overlay of a colossal columnar order, created by contrasting deep gray and pink glass. In a conjunctive addition to Holabird and Root's Board of Trade in Chicago, he adapted that firm's earlier form, incorporating in part a limestone veneer, setbacks, reentrant corners and a pyramidal cap.

Representing the third phase of the work, 11 Diagonal Street in Johannesburg, South Africa (1983), projects a double-glazed curtain wall, taut and almost seamless, from the floor plan of a diamond with notched ends and beveled corners. The State of Illinois Center in Chicago (1985) places a similar emphasis on the plastic qualities of the curtain wall. The plastic treatment of glass is also central to the design of the O'Hare Rapid Transit Station in Chicago (1983), in which a back-lit, undulating glass-block wall encloses both sides of the concourse.

The fourth phase of Jahn's work might be seen as beginning with 701 Fourth Avenue South in Minneapolis (1984) and 362 West Street in Durban, South Africa (1986); both forms consist of two concentric octagons. In the former, the inner octagon is surrounded by a stepped-down ring; in the latter, an exoskeleton for the treatment of the outer ring is employed.

A selection of the most recent tall buildings reveals the introduction of masonry to the facade. In the Park Avenue Tower in New York City (1986), glass and granite sheathe this 35-story obelisk, with chamfered corners and an open pyramidal crown. In One Liberty Place in Philadelphia (1987), a stone base supports a curtain wall articulated by reentrant corners and stepped-back intersecting gables. This design was clearly the precedent for Loebl Schlossman Hackl's Prudential Plaza addition in Chicago.

Restoring a concern for the picturesque possibilities of the top of a tall building, Jahn designed both 750 Lexington Avenue and Cityspire in New York City (1989) with prominent caps. In the former, a rectangular base supports an octagonal center, from which a glass cylinder with a stepped-back conical top springs. In the latter, a 70-story, mixed-use development, glass-enclosed wings sit beside an octagonal, stone-clad tower with a ribbed, copper-clad dome.

Jahn's later buildings break away from Mies' austere minimalism and, with their reinforced entrances, stepped-back forms and impact on the skyline, recall the picturesque urbanity of skyscrapers of the 1930s. Whether the materials he has selected will wear as gracefully, and whether the details through which he assembles those materials will prove equally durable, remains to be seen.

—PAUL GLASSMAN

JAPELLI, Giuseppe.

Italian. Born in Venice, Italy, 18 May 1783. Died in Venice, 8 March 1852. Studied at the Accademia Clementina, Bologna. Entered the studio of Giovanni Antonio Selva, 1803.

Chronology of Works
All in Italy

1816-31	Caffé Pedrocchi, Padua
1817ff.	Villa dei Conti Cittadella Vigodarsene, near Saonara (chapel and gardens)
1821	Meat Market, Padua
1825	Hotel Reale Orologio, San Lorenzo (facade)
1827	Villa Gera, Conegliano
1828	Theater, Cittadella (facade)
1829	Restaurant, Acqua Raineriana
1837	Caffé Pedrocchi, Padua (Il Pedrocchino wing)
1840s	Greenhouse, Villa Torlonia
1842	Caffé Pedrocchi Casino, Padua
1847	Teatro Nuovo, Padua (remodeling)
1848	Museo Atestino, Este (gardens)

Publications

BOOKS ABOUT JAPELLI

DAMERINI, GINO: *Un architetto veneziano dell'ottocento: Giuseppe Japelli*. Venice, 1934.
FIOCCO, GIUSEPPE: *Giuseppe Japelli: Architetto*. Padua, Italy, 1931.
LAVAGNINO, EMILIO: *L'arte moderne dai neoclassici ai contemporanei*. Turin, Italy (1956) 1961.
MEEKS, CARROLL L. V.: *Italian Architecture: 1750-1914*. New Haven, Connecticut, 1966.
SELVATICO, PIETRO ESTENSE: *Scritti d'arte*. Florence, 1859.

ARTICLES ABOUT JAPELLI

MANTIGLIA, ROBERTO C.: "Giuseppe Japelli architetto." *L'Architettura* 1 (1955): 538-52.
ROWAN, A.: "Japelli and Cicogarno." *Architectural Review* (March 1968): 225-28.

*

Giuseppe Japelli was an Italian architect of the first half of the 19th century, and may have been—as Carroll Meeks has said—the most original North Italian architect of his generation. He

Giuseppe Jappelli: Caffé Pedrocchi, Padua, Italy, 1816-31

is most known for the design of the Caffé Pedrocchi in Padua (1816-31).

Japelli was born in Venice and educated first at the Accademia Clementina in Bologna. In 1803, when he was 20, he entered the studio of Giovanni Antonio Selva, to whom much in Japelli's eclecticism and interest in the architecture of other countries can be traced. In those years Japelli traveled extensively in Germany, Belgium, England and France, making himself fully knowledgeable about the latest works of the leading European architects.

At the beginning of his career he was involved with a number of projects of hydraulic engineering. But in 1816 he began work on the Caffé Pedrocchi, a small, private club in Padua that was owned and run, like the clubs in London, by an individual proprietor. The plan of the *caffé* is triangular, with three large Doric porches on each of the corners, the main entrance being at once square and U-shaped, the projections being two of these porches. The central body of the building is, in the normal Palladian tradition, made up of a giant Corinthian order over a rusticated ground floor. The porticoes, however, with their baseless, Doric columns supporting a massive entablature, were perhaps taken from the recently completed designs by Luigi Cagnola for the Porta Ticinese in Milan (1801-14), which was the first instance in Italy of the archaeological yet romantic classicism long known in France and England, examples of which Japelli would have seen on his travels.

The interior decoration at the Caffé Pedrocchi came from many different sources, including an Egyptian lodge room, an Empire-style ballroom and a Gothic suite. In 1837, after traveling again to England, Japelli added a wing, "il Pedrocchino";

it was designed in the neo-Gothic style after such English examples as Strawberry Hill and Arbury Hall.

Japelli built much in and around Padua: a Meat Market (1821) in the Greek Revival style, a neoclassical facade of the Theater at Cittadella (1828) and a remodeling, in the Empire and Rococo styles, of the Teatro Nuovo (1847). His most extensive and notable design, after the Caffé Pedrocchi, was for the main building and gardens of the Villa dei Conti Cittadella Vigodarsene, near Saonara, begun in 1817. The chapel near the gate is Palladian, the cylindrical base and low dome recalling the church at the Villa Barbaro at Maser, though in its small size it is more like one of the garden pavilions by Lord Burlington at Chiswick House in England.

The villa itself is vast and plain, perhaps like the design by Palladio at the Villa Gondi, but built on a scale reminiscent of Somerset House in London. The central motif of seven bays and the end wings of four bays are all covered by a weighty and unbroken hipped roof; there is no ornament. All this stands in a fashionably romantic park where the once-ordered avenues were changed into English meadows, with an artificial lake and dotted clumps of trees. As in all the English gardens, there were grottoes, temples and a Gothic cellar, sweetly melancholic. The success here led to Japelli receiving a number of other such garden commissions, perhaps the most interesting of these being for the Museo Atestino in Este.

After his death, Japelli was praised particularly by Pietro Estense Selvatico in 1856 for having led Italian design away from a simple imitation of cinquecento architecture toward a more appropriate Gothic, Lombard style. From force of tradition, Italy had lagged behind other countries in acknowledging that style, and Selvatico was pleased to be able to praise Japelli for his first studies of Lombard and arcuated styles, of which, for all its indebtedness to England, "il Pedrocchino" could stand as an example.

—DAVID CAST

JEFFERSON, Thomas.

American. Born in Albemarle County, Virginia, 13 April 1743. Died at Monticello, near Charlottesville, Virginia, 4 July 1826. Educated at College of William and Mary, Williamsburg, Virginia. Self-taught in architecture. Governor of Virginia; United States Minister to France, 1785; Secretary of State, 1790-93; Vice President of the United States, 1797-1801; President of the United States, 1801-09.

Chronology of Works
All in the United States
* Approximate dates
† Work no longer exists

1755-97	Montpelier, near Orange, Virginia (remodeled 1797-1812)
1768-82	Monticello, near Charlottesville, Virginia (remodeled 1796-1809)
1785-99	Virginia State Capitol, Richmond, Virginia
1793	Woodbury Forest, near Charlottesville, Virginia
1795ff.	Belle Grove, near Charlottesville, Virginia
1797*	Edgemont House, near Charlottesville, Virginia
pre-1798	Edgehill House, near Charlottesville, Virginia (second house, 1828)
1802-08	Farmington House, near Charlottesville, Virginia (addition)
1806-12	Poplar Forest House, Bedford County, Virginia
1809	House, Farmington, Kentucky
1817-22	House, Barboursville, Virginia (now in West Virginia)
1817-26	University of Virginia, Charlottesville, Virginia
1818	Botetourt County Courthouse, Fincastle, Virginia†
1820	House, Oakhill, Virginia (now in West Virginia)
1821	Buckingham County Courthouse, Buckingham, Virginia†
1824-26	Christ Church, Centerville, Virginia

Publications

BOOKS BY JEFFERSON

The Writings of Thomas Jefferson. Edited by Andrew A. Lipscomb. 20 vols. Washington, D.C., 1905.
Autobiography. New York, 1959.
Thomas Jefferson's Architectural Drawings. Compiled and with Commentary and a Checklist by Frederick Doveton Nichols. Rev. and enl. 4th ed. Boston, 1978.

BOOKS ABOUT JEFFERSON

ADAMS, WILLIAM H. (ed.): *Jefferson and the Arts: An Extended View.* Washington, D.C., 1976.
ADAMS, WILLIAM H.: *Jefferson's Monticello.* 1983.
ADAMS, WILLIAM H.: *The Eye of Thomas Jefferson.* 1976.
BERKELEY, FRANCIS LEWIS, and THURLOW, CONSTANCE E. (compilers): *The Jefferson Papers of the University of Virginia.* Charlottesville, Virginia, 1950.

BERMAN, E. D.: *Thomas Jefferson Among the Arts, an Essay in Early American Aesthetics.* New York, 1947.
BETTS, E. M. (ed.): *Thomas Jefferson's Garden Book 1766-1824.* Philadelphia, 1944.
BOYD, JULIAN P. (ed.): *The Papers of Thomas Jefferson.* 19 vols. Princeton, New Jersey, 1950-.
EAMES, CHARLES: *The World of Franklin and Jefferson*, Exhibition catalog, Los Angeles, 1976.
FRARY, IHNA T.: *Thomas Jefferson, Architect and Builder.* Richmond, Virginia, 1931.
GUINESS, D., and SADLER, J. T.: *Mr. Jefferson, Architect.* New York, 1973.
HAMLIN, TALBOT: *Greek Revival Architecture in America.* New York, 1944.
KIMBALL, FISKE: *Thomas Jefferson, Architect.* Boston, 1916. Reprint: New York, 1968.
KIMBALL, FISKE: *Domestic Architecture of the American Colonies and of the Early Republic.* New York, 1922.
KIMBALL, FISKE: *Thomas Jefferson and the First Monument of the Classic Revival in America.* Harrisburg and Washington, D. C., 1915. Reprinted from the *Journal of the American Institute of Architects*, vol. III, Nos. 9-11 (September-November 1915).
LAMBETH, WILLIAM ALEXANDER and MANNING, WARREN H.: *Thomas Jefferson as an Architect and a Designer of Landscapes.* Boston and New York, 1913.
LEHMAN, KARL: *Thomas Jefferson, American Humanist.* New York, 1947. Reprint: Chicago, 1980.
MALONE, DUMAS: *Jefferson and His Time.* 6 vols. Boston, 1948-81.
MAYO, BERNARD (ed.): *Jefferson Himself: The Personal Narrative of a Many-Sided American.* Charlottesville, Virginia, 1942. Reprint: 1970.
McLAUGHLIN, J.: *Jefferson and Monticello. The Biography of a Builder.* New York, 1988.
MORRIS, ROBERT: *Select Architecture: Being Regular Design, of Plan and Elevation Well Suited to Both Town and Country.* 1757. Reprint: New York, 1973.
NEVINS, D., and STERN, ROBERT A. M.: *The Architect's Eye: American Architectural Drawings, 1799-1978.* New York, 1979.
NICHOLS, FREDERICK D., and GRISWOLD, R. E.: *Thomas Jefferson, Landscape Architect.* Charlottesville, Virginia, 1978.
NICHOLS, FREDERICK D. (compiler): *Thomas Jefferson's Architectural Drawings.* 4th ed. rev. Boston, 1978.
NICHOLS, FREDERICK D., and BEAR, JAMES A.: *Monticello.* Monticello, Virginia, 1967.
NORTON, PAUL F.: *Latrobe, Jefferson and the National Capitol.* New York and London, 1977.
O'NEAL, W. B.: *A Checklist of Writings on Thomas Jefferson as an Architect.* Charlottesville, Virginia, 1959.
O'NEAL, W. B.: *Jefferson's Buildings at the University of Virginia.* Charlottesville, Virginia, 1960.
O'NEAL, W. B.: *Jefferson's Fine Arts Library: His Selections for the University of Virginia Together with His Own Architectural Books.* Charlottesville, Virginia, 1976.
PADOVER, SAUL K. (ed.): *Thomas Jefferson and the National Capital.* Washington, D.C., 1946.
RYAN, W., and GUINESS, D.: *The White House: An Architectural History.* New York, 1980.
SCHOULER, J.: *Thomas Jefferson.* New York, 1919.
VAUGHAN, J. and GIANNINY, O.: *Thomas Jefferson's Rotunda Restored, A Pictorial Review 1973-1976 with Commentary.* 1981.

WHITE, MORTON and LUCIA: *The Intellectual Versus the City, from Thomas Jefferson to Frank Lloyd Wright.* New York, 1962.

ARTICLES ABOUT JEFFERSON

ACKERMAN, JAMES S.: "Il Presidente Jefferson e il Palladianesimo Americano." *Centro Internazionale di Studi d'Architettura Andrea Palladio Bollettino* no.6, part 2 (1964): 39-48.

ADAMS, WILLIAM H.: "Thomas Jefferson and the Art of the Garden." *Apollo* 104 (September 1976): 190-197.

BARNWELL, J.: "Monticello: 1856." *Journal of the Society of Architectural Historians* 34 (December 1975): 280-85.

BEAR, J. A., JR.: "Furniture and Furnishings of Monticello." *Antiques* 102 (July 1972): 113-123.

BEISWANGER, W.: "Jefferson's Designs for Garden Structures at Monticello." *Journal of the Society of Architectural Historians* 35 (December 1976): 310-312.

BINNEY, I. M.: "University of Virginia." *Country Life* 163 (12 January 1978): 74-77.

BOYD, JULIAN P.: "Thomas Jefferson and the Roman Askos of Nïmes." *Antiques* 104 (July 1973): 116-124.

BROWN, GLENN: "Letters from Thomas Jefferson and William Thornton, Architect, Relating to the University of Virginia." *Journal of the American Institute of Architects* 1 (1913): 21-27.

BUTLER, J. F.: "Competition 1792: Designing a Nation's Capitol." *Capitol Studies*, special issue 4 (1976).

CHASE, D. B.: "The Beginnings of the Landscape Tradition in America." *Historic Preservation* 25 (January 1973): 34-41.

CLARK, D. P.: "History in Houses: Farmington, in Louisville, Kentucky." *Antiques* 93 (February 1968): 224-29.

DAVIS, J. F. (ed.): "Landscape and the Traveller's Eye." *Journal of the Society of Architectural Historians* 35 (December 1976): 308-315.

DONNELLY, M. C.: "Jefferson's Observatory Design." *Journal of the Society of Architectural Historians* 36 (March 1977): 33-35.

FILLER, M.: "Charles Moore: House Vernacular." *Art in America* 68 (October 1980): 105-112.

FITCH, JAMES MARSTON: "Architects of Democracy: Jefferson and Wright." In *Architecture and the Esthetics of Plenty.* New York, 1961.

FLEXNER, J. T.: "Great Columbian Federal City." *American Art Journal* 2 (Spring 1970): 30.

GARRETT, W. D.: "Bicentennial Outlook: The Monumental Friendship of Jefferson and Adams." *Historic Preservation* 28 (April-June 1976): 28-35.

HELLENBRAND, H. L.: "The Unfinished Revolution... The Thought of Thomas Jefferson." Ph.D. dissertation. Stanford University, 1980.

HORAT, HEINZ: "Thomas Jefferson: Intellectual Architecture." *Architectura* No. 1 (1989): 62-75.

HOWARD, S.: "Thomas Jefferson's Art Gallery for Monticello." *Art Bulletin* 59 (December 1977): 583-600.

ISHAM, N. M.: "Jefferson's Place in Our Architectural History." *American Institute of Architects Journal* 2 (May 1941): 230-35.

KIMBALL, FISKE: "Form and Function in the Architecture of Jefferson." *Magazine of Art* 40 (1947): 150-53.

KIMBALL, FISKE: "Jefferson and the Public Buildings of Virginia." *Huntingdon Library Quarterly* 12, Nos. 2-3 (February and May 1949): 115-120, 303-310.

KIMBALL, FISKE: "Jefferson and the Public Buildings of Virginia: I—Williamsburg, 1770-1776." *Huntington Library Quarterly* XII (February 1949): 115-120.

KIMBALL, FISKE: "Jefferson and the Public Buildings of Virginia: II—Richmond, 1779-1780." *Huntington Library Quarterly* XII (May 1949): 303-310.

KIMBALL, FISKE: "Thomas Jefferson and the First Monument of the Classical Revival in America." *Journal of the American Institute of Architects* 3 (1915): 10.

LAMBETH, WILLIAM ALEXANDER: "Thomas Jefferson and the Arts." *American Institute of Architects Journal* 12 (October 1924): 454-455.

LANCASTER, CLAY: "Jefferson's Architectural Indebtness to Robert Morris." *Journal of the Society of Architectural Historians* 10 (March 1951): 3-10.

LE COAT, G.: "Thomas Jefferson et l'architecture métaphorique: le village académique à l'Université de Virginie." *Revue d'art canadienne* 3, Part 2 (1976): 8-34.

LERSKI, H.: "The British antecedents of Thomas Jefferson's architecture." Dissertation. Johns Hopkins University, Baltimore, 1957-58.

LEWIS, D.: "Il classicismo romantico in America: Il tempio nella sua forma complete." *Bollettino di Centro Internazionale di Studi di Architettura Andrea Palladio* 13 (1971): 299-309.

MAYOR, A. H.: "Jefferson's Enjoyment of the Arts." *Metropolitan Museum Bulletin* New Series 2 (December 1943): 140-166.

MILLER, S. F.: "Mr. Jefferson's Passion: His Grove at Monticello." *Historic Preservation* 32 (March-April 1980): 32-35.

NEWCOMB, REXFORD G.: "Thomas Jefferson, the Architect." *Architect* 9 (January 1928): 429-432.

NICHOLS, FREDERICK D.: "Belle Grove, A Jeffersonian Jewel in the Valley of Virginia." *Arts in Virginia* 18 (Winter 1978): 8-19.

PICKENS, B.: "Mr. Jefferson as a Revolutionary Architect." *Journal of the Society of Architectural Historians* 34 (December 1975): 257-279.

PIERSON, WILLIAM H., JR.: "American Neoclassicism, The Idealistic Phase: Thomas Jefferson." In *American Buildings and Their Architects: The Colonial and Neo-Classical Styles.* Garden City, New York, 1970.

REPS, JOHN W.: "Thomas Jefferson's Checkerboard Towns." *Journal of the Society of Architectural Historians* 20 (October 1961): 108-114.

RICE, H. C.: "A French Source of Jefferson's Plan for the Prison at Richmond." *Journal of the Society of Architectural Historians* 12 (December 1953): 28-30.

ROBERSON, S. A.: "Thomas Jefferson and the Eighteenth-Century Landscape Garden Movement in England." Dissertation. Yale University, New Haven, Connecticut, 1974.

RODMAN, W. S.: "Lighting Schemes of Thomas Jefferson." *Transactions of the Illuminating Engineering Society* 12 (1917): 105-121.

SCULLY, VINCENT, JR.: "American Houses: Thomas Jefferson to Frank Lloyd Wright." In EDGAR KAUFMANN, JR. (ed.): *The Rise of American Architecture.* New York, 1970.

SHONTING, D. A.: "Romantic Aspects in the Works of Thomas Jefferson." Dissertation. Ohio University, Athens, Ohio, 1977.

SMITH, G. M.: "Belle Grove's Olmstead Papers." *Historic Preservation* 24 (January 1972): 24-27.

STAPLEY, M.: "Thomas Jefferson, the Architect: A Tribute." *Architectural Record* 29 (January 1911): 178-185.

Thomas Jefferson: Monticello, near Charlottesville, Virginia, 1768-82

STEWART, P. L.: "The American Empire Style: Its Historical Background." *American Art Journal* 10 (November 1978): 97-105.

WADDELL, GENE: "The First Monticello." *Journal of the Society of Architectural Historians* 46 (March 1987): 5-29.

WATERMAN, T. T.: "Thomas Jefferson: His Early Works in Architecture." *Gazette des Beaux-Arts* Series 6, 24 (August 1943): 89-106.

*

Of his many accomplishments, Thomas Jefferson wished to be remembered for three: authorship of the Declaration of Independence; writing the Statute of Virginia for Religious Freedom, which was the model for the national bill of religious freedom; and as the father of the University of Virginia.

In 1782 the Marquis de Chastellux, a French visitor to the new American nation, wrote, "Let me describe to you a man, not yet forty, tall, with a mild and pleasing countenance, but whose mind and attainments could serve in lieu of all outward graces—after having played a distinguished role on the stage of the New World—the first American who has consulted the Fine Arts to know how he should shelter himself from the weather!"

Although Jefferson was educated at the College of William and Mary as an attorney, his interests and vigors and activities expanded greatly beyond the practice of law. He was a legislator in the king's government, a leader in the American Revolution, author of the Declaration of Independence, governor of Virginia, a minister of the new United States to France, secretary of state, vice-president and then third president of the nation.

Among the fine arts, Jefferson's greatest devotion was, in his words, for the "elegant and useful art" of architecture. He wrote, "Architecture is my delight, and putting up and pulling down one of my favorite amusements." He studied the classics of the times as published by Andrea Palladio and Vincenzo Scamozzi, which influenced his first designs of Monticello (begun in 1768). The construction of the home was interrupted by his election as the Virginia delegate to the Continental Congress, and in 1779 by his election as governor of Virginia.

From 1784 to 1789 Jefferson was United States minister to France. During that period he observed firsthand his old "friends" from his books, the important Roman monuments in southern France and northern Italy. A prolific correspondent, while in Nîmes, France, in 1787, he wrote to the comtesse de Tessé, "Here I am, Madame, gazing whole hours at the Maison Carrée, like a lover at his mistress." Other Jefferson favorites were the Paris municipal grain market, by Jacques Molinos, which he described as "the most superb thing on earth," and Claude-Nicolas Ledoux's Hôtel Guimard.

Shortly after Jefferson arrived in Paris, the Virginia committee for public buildings requested that he design the new state capitol. The foundations for the building had already been constructed, forcing development of plans and a plaster model before additional work could be done. The United States having recently won independence from Great Britain, Jefferson proceeded directly to the classic antiquities of Rome for his architectural images. His favorite ancient Roman building was the Maison Carrée at Nîmes; thus, his finest interpretation for the first public building in America was patterned on the image of a Roman temple.

He returned from France with 80 crates of furniture, architecture books, wine, a French cook, and the desire to modify and enlarge his Monticello. It appears that at that time his vision of architecture included the dome and rotunda, and the introduction of an octagon in the building plan. His fascination with geometric forms matured at that time, giving him an understanding and mastery of the triangular pediment, squares and rectangles, domes and especially octagons, and the ability to incorporate them into sophisticated massing compositions. Jefferson's buildings from then on included these elements as prominent design forms. Isaac Coles, a friend, wrote, "He is a great advocate of light and air—He was for—octagons. They were charming. They gave you a semi-circle of air and light."

In 1789 Jefferson was appointed secretary of state, which presented responsibilities for the plan and design of the United States' new capital city. Pierre Charles L'Enfant, a French surveyor, was given the task of laying out the city of Washington. Jefferson provided him with plans of other major cities, including Amsterdam, Bordeaux, Karslruhe, Lyons, Marseilles, Milan, Montpelier, Orléans, Paris and Turin.

On completion of his term as secretary of state, Jefferson decided to enlarge Monticello. The smaller houses of Paris influenced his architectural thinking, and he began dismantling the original roof and porticoes. He wrote, "All the new and good houses are of a single story, that is of the height of 16 or 18 f[eet] generally, and the whole of it given to the rooms of entertainment. But in the parts where there are bedrooms they have two tiers of them from 8 to 19 f[eet] high each, with a small private staircase." At that time, Jefferson constructed the octagonal dome as the visitors' bedrooms for the house. Through careful fenestration, by designing the second-floor windows at floor level and behind an ornamental balustrade, he gave the house the appearance of a single-story structure.

Jefferson was elected to the presidency in 1800 and took office in 1801, the first president to be inaugurated in Washington. After his term as president ended in 1809, he began work on a new, more private home, at a considerable distance from Monticello. Poplar Forest, in Bedford County, Virginia, became his greatest search for form with the octagon and the dome.

The plan is a domed octagon with elongated octagonal rooms within the envelope, having square stairwells and porticoes on the four opposite faces of the octagon. The two outbuildings were also configured as octagons with domed roofs.

Other residences in Virginia that Jefferson is credited with designing or modifying are Farber near Charlottesville, Bremo in Fluvanna County, Montpelier (home of James Monroe), James Madison's home in Orange County, Oak Hill in Loudoun

County and Barboursville in Orange County. Using the octagon and the dome and concepts from Palladio, Jefferson designed a governor's mansion for Richmond, Virginia, and a President's House in Washington. These were never constructed.

Jefferson designed several public buildings in Virginia, including Botetourt Courthouse (1818), Buckingham Courthouse (1821), Charlotte Courthouse (1821-23) and Christ Church, Charlottesville (1824). All but the Charlotte Courthouse have been burned or destroyed. His influence through his workmen contributed to a number of other public and private buildings throughout Virginia.

One of the three accomplishments for which Jefferson wished to be remembered was the founding of the University of Virginia. He had considered the establishment of a state university of Virginia. He had considered the establishment of a state university since 1800, and described his work as "the Hobby of my old age." His concepts in education were forerunners of modern higher education in the classics, sciences and technology.

The university was chartered in 1819 as a product of Jefferson's genius and untiring efforts. He secured the funding for the construction and operations from private individuals and from the Virginia General Assembly, selected the site for the university, developed the plan, designed the buildings and prepared the specifications, supervised the construction, devised the curriculum, selected the faculty, served as the university's first rector and, finally, served as a member of the Board of Visitors.

The plan was a simple rectangle approximately 200 feet wide and without determined length. Jefferson placed the most important building, the domed temple library and administration building (the Rotunda), as the focus of the central axis, with two rows of buildings facing onto a common lawn, parallel to the center axis. Temple-shaped pavilions equally separated by student quarters and joined together by classical colonnades facing the lawn separated the two rows. Each pavilion housed faculty quarters on the second floor and classrooms on the first floor. Two additional rows of student quarters were built behind the center rows, with enclosed gardens between and separated transversely by serpentine walls. Six "hotels," for the purpose of dining and exchange in foreign language during meals, were located in the second row of student quarters.

Jefferson described the ideal organization of a university in a letter in 1810 to the founders of the University of Tennessee: "It is infinitely better to erect a small and separate lodge for each separate professorship, with only a hall below for his class, and two chambers above for himself joining these lodges by barracks for a certain portion of the students, opening into a covered way to give a dry communication between all schools. The whole of these, arranged around an open square for grass and trees, would make it, what it should be in fact, an academic village."

Jefferson's attention to classical details, including temple forms, capitals, columns, bases, entablatures, dentiles, moldings and fenestration, introduced the new architecture to the United States. In his design of the University of Virginia, his standard was to shape the pavilions into a "model of chaste and correct architecture, and of a variety of appearance, no two alike so as to serve as specimens for the architectural lecturer."

Jefferson's creative talents guided the classical image of the university's architecture; however, he intelligently relied on some of the most knowledgeable and well-known architects and manuscripts of the time to advise on specific details for the pavilions. The Doric order of Pavilion I was modeled from plates in Roland Fréart de Chambray's *Parallèle de l'Architecture Antique et de la Moderne* (1650; English edition by John

Evelyn, 1723). The Doric order of Pavilion IV was taken from Chambray's plate of the Temple of Albano in Rome. The Ionic order of Pavilion VI and the Doric order of Pavilion X were from his plate of the Theater of Marcellus in Rome, and the Corinthian order of Pavilion VIII was from his plate of the Baths of Diocletian in Rome. Pavilions II and IX were modeled on the Ionic order shown in Giacomo Leoni's plates of the Temple of Fortuna Virilis in Rome. Pavilion III's Corinthian capitals were also designed from Leoni's drawings, as were the Ionic order of Pavilion V and Doric order of Pavilion VII. William Thornton and Benjamin Latrobe advised on Pavilions VII and VIII, respectively.

Jefferson used Hadrian's Pantheon, the circular and domed temple in Rome, as his model for the Rotunda at the university. He scaled the building to one half of the Roman Pantheon, and designed simplified Corinthian capitals and entablature. This dominant statement is the visual terminus of the university grounds.

Jefferson wrote, ''You see I am an enthusiast on the subject of the arts. But it is an enthusiasm of which I am not ashamed, as its object is to improve the taste of my countrymen, to increase their reputation, to reconcile them to the respect of the world, and procure them its praise!''

—GORDON ECHOLS

JENNEY, William Le Baron.

American. Born in Fairhaven, Massachusetts, 1832. Died in Los Angeles, California, 1 June 1907. Studied engineering at Lawrence Scientific School, Cambridge, Massachusetts; diploma from École des Beaux-Arts, Paris, France, 1856. Fought in the Civil War, 1861: Major-General in United States Army under General U. S. Grant. Established own architectural office, Chicago, 1866; organized Jenney, Schermerhorn and Bogart firm; partner, Jenney and Mundie office, 1891. Fellow, American Institute of Architects; delegate to International Congress of Architects, Madrid, Spain, 1901.

Chronology of Works
All in the United States
† Work no longer exists

1872	Portland Building, Chicago, Illinois†
1879	First Leiter Building, Chicago†
1884-85	Home Insurance Building, Chicago†
1889-90	Manhattan Building, Chicago
1889-91	Second Leiter Building, Chicago
1890-91	Sears, Roebuck and Company Store, Chicago
1891	Central Young Men's Christian Association Building, Chicago
1891	Ludington Building, Chicago
1891	Manhattan Building, Chicago
1891-92	Fair Store (Montgomery Ward and Company Store), Chicago
1892-93	Isabella Building, Chicago
1893	Horticultural Building, World's Columbian Exposition, Chicago†
1896	Morton Building, Chicago
1904-05	Chicago Garment Center, Chicago

Publications

BOOKS BY JENNEY

Principles and Practices of Architecture. Chicago, 1869.

ARTICLES BY JENNEY

''Construction of a Heavy Fireproof Building on Compressible Soil.'' *Engineering Record, Building Record and Sanitary Engineer* 13 (1885): 32-33.
''Chicago Construction, or Tall Building on a Compressible Soil.'' *Inland Architect and News Record* 18 (1891): 41.

BOOKS ABOUT JENNEY

CONDIT, CARL W.: *The Chicago School of Architecture: A History of Commercial and Public Building in the Chicago Area, 1875-1925.* Chicago, 1964.
MUJICA, FRANCISCO: *History of the Skyscraper.* Paris, 1929.
RANDALL, FRANK A.: *History of the Development of Building Construction in Chicago.* Urbana, Illinois, 1949.
TURAK, THEODORE: *William Le Baron Jenney, A Pioneer of Modern Architecture.* Ann Arbor, Michigan, 1986.

ARTICLES ABOUT JENNEY

TURAK, THEODORE: ''Jenney's Lesser Works: Prelude to the Prairie Style?'' *Prairie School Review* (Third Quarter, 1970).
TURAK, THEODORE: ''The École Centrale and Modern Architecture: The Education of William Le Baron Jenney.'' *Journal of the Society of Architectural Historians* 29 (1970): 40-47.
WEBSTER, J. CARSON: ''The Skyscraper: Logical and Historical Considerations.'' *Journal of the Society of Architectural Historians* 18 (1959): 126-139.
WOLTERSDORF, ARTHUR: ''The Father of the Skeleton Frame Building.'' *Western Architect* 33 (1924): 21-23.

*

Both engineer and architect, William Le Baron Jenney was the founder of the Chicago school and helped to develop and formulate the steel-frame skyscraper. In Chicago, he created buildings of iron and later steel skeleton whose powerful exteriors related to their underlying structures. Jenney abandoned the old method of medieval-revival philosophy for new, ''functional'' aesthetics that became known as modern architecture. As a mentor, he paved the way for future skyscraper designers such as Louis Sullivan, Martin Roche, William Holabird and Daniel Burnham.

Born in Fair Haven, Massachusetts, Jenney's family owned whaling ships. Perhaps, it was there that young Jenney developed a fascination with the craft of building as he watched local shipbuilders put together these mighty vessels that braved the sea.

He first attended Phillips Academy, Andover (Mass.) and then enrolled, in 1850, at the Lawrence Scientific School at Harvard University. Not satisfied with Harvard's scientific/engineering program, he thereupon entered, in 1853, the well-known and highly prestigious École Centrale des Arts et Manufactures in Paris and graduated three years later. It was by the designer-theorist Jean Nicolas Louis Durand that Jenney was most impressed, through his erudite lectures on structure and physical stress. Durand remained an influential factor in Jenney's later designs.

William Le Baron Jenney: Second Leiter Building, Chicago, Illinois, 1889-91

During the years between his graduation from the École and his return to Paris found him serving as an engineer for the Tehuantepec Railroad Company in Mexico. Jenney's stay in Paris from 1858 to the end of the following year found him gaining practical experience. He especially noted later the warehouses of St. Ouen Docks (1865-66), which were the first-known many-story, concrete-floored, iron-frame structures that had curtain walls and were deemed entirely fireproof—all elements that Jenney would later incorporate into his skyscrapers in America.

In 1861 he enlisted in the Union armies and fought in the Civil War. He was a captain, under General U. S. Grant, in the Mississippi campaign, and under General William T. Sherman in Tennessee. In 1866, he was discharged with the rank of major. In 1868 Jenney opened an office in Chicago, and from 1870 to 1871 he was a landscape engineer for the West Park District there.

Jenney's first major work came in 1879, when he designed the first Leiter Building, at 280 West Monroe Street (it still exists). The cage-like building showed pillars of brick for its exterior walls and wide glass windows, which forecast the "Chicago windows" of Louis Sullivan. Its interior had a cast-iron frame construction, especially noted in the columns.

Then came the Home Insurance Building (1884-85, demolished in 1929). It was planned, with the help of the engineer George B. Whitney, as a skyscraper. The original design was to be nine stories high, and in 1891 was elevated to 11 stories. There, columns of both cast and wrought iron were used, and its floor beams and girders were made of wrought iron (to the sixth floor) and so-called spandrel girders of steel from the seventh to 11th floors. The building not only marked the first

use of steel in America but was the initial skyscraper to display a fully metal skeleton-frame construction (iron and steel). All this led to his second Leiter Building (1889) and the Manhattan Building (1891). The latter, showing unique "bay windows" designed with the assistance of the engineer Louis E. Ritter, had a full skeleton frame which supported the walls, roof and floors, as well as being windproof. Characteristic of its exterior, Jenney used bay windows to catch sunlight despite its location on narrow Dearborn Street.

From then on, Jenney designed only ferrous-metal buildings, exploiting the combinations of iron, wrought iron and steel. This was realized in two Chicago department stores: the Sears, Roebuck and Company Store (1890-91) and the Fair Store (1891-92). The Sears building, although clothed in granite, revealed beneath this masonry skin a metal skeleton, and displayed delicate, ornamental details to alleviate its otherwise monotonous, block-like appearance. On the other hand, the nine-story Fair design showed a pronounced emphasis of a "revealed" skeleton. Its first two stories were almost pure glass made to suit its owners, who wanted a large display area for their merchandise.

Later works—all in Chicago—of the skeleton variety were: the Ludington Building (1891), the Morton Building (1896), and the Chicago Garment Center (1904-05).

Jenney eventually retired to Los Angeles in 1905 and died there two years later.

The legacy Jenney left was one of courage and imagination. Louis Sullivan, who worked for a short time in his studio in 1873, said that he was ". . . more a connoisseur than an architect." Truly, Jenney's buildings were important as "innovations" and for their use of metals in a creative way. Yet, he will best be remembered as a "catalytic architect" who stimulated and made possible for the younger generation of Chicago school designers a new approach in creating architecture.

—GEORGE M. COHEN

JENSEN-KLINT, Peder Vilhelm.

Danish. Born in Denmark, 1853. Died in 1930. Trained as an engineer at the Polyteknisk Læreanstalt; studied painting at the Painting School of the Royal Academy of Art, Copenhagen.

Chronology of Works
All in Denmark

1896	Holm Villa, 27 Sofievej, Copenhagen
1897-98	Gymnasium, 51 Vodrofsvej, Copenhagen
1905-06	Rodsten Villa, 12 Onsgaardsvej, Copenhagen
1907	Aagard House, Ryslinge
1907-09	Vodskov Church, Aalborg
1913-40	Grundtvigs Church and surrounding housing, Copenhagen (not begun until 1921, after Jensen-Klint's death; completed by his son, Kaare Klint, in 1940)
1914	Annas Church, Bjelkes Allé, Copenhagen
1921	St. Hans Tveje Church, Odense
1923	Young Men's Christian Association Building, Odense

Publications

BOOKS BY JENSEN-KLINT

Bygmesterskolen. Copenhagen, 1911.

BOOKS ABOUT JENSEN-KLINT

FRAMPTON, KENNETH, and FUTAGAWA, YUKIO: *Modern Architecture: 1920-1945.* New York, 1983.
JELSBAK, JENS (ed.): *Grundtvigs Kirke.* Copenhagen, 1977.
MARSTRAND, JACOB: *Grundtvigs Mindekirke paa Bispeberg.* Copenhagen, 1932.
MILLECH, KNUD: *Danske Arkitektur stromninger: 1850-1950.* Copenhagen, 1951.

ARTICLES ABOUT JENSEN-KLINT

FISKER, KAY: "Den Klintske skole." *Arkitektur* 7, No. 2 (special issue, April 1963): 37-80.
MILLECH, KNUD: "P̊ Bjerget, Grundtvigs Kirke." In HARALD LANGBERG (ed.): *Hvem byggede hvad.* 3 vols. Copenhagen, 1968-71.

*

Though P. V. Jensen-Klint found his creative path relatively late, it was a wide one, including most kinds of art. He trained first as an engineer, qualifying in 1877 at the Polyteknisk Læreanstalt, and worked for a few years as an engineer and teacher before turning to art. In those early years he worked in several genres of painting and sculpture; he trained at the Painting School of the Royal Academy of Art in Copenhagen. In the mid-1890s he began the architectural work that would occupy the rest of his life. His first independent commission was the gymnasium at Vodroffsvej 51, Copenhagen. It was a fluid

period for architecture, when historicism was about to be overtaken by a more inquiring, empirical approach; a mixture of styles in a single building was becoming more common, and increasingly acceptable. Jensen-Klint himself was then preoccupied by the national version of historicism, the so-called "Herholdt line," after the architect D. Herholdt, who could manage a happy combination of historicist elements with native building traditions. Jensen-Klint's favorite material was brick, with its long roots in Danish tradition, and in his most important works, all ecclesiastical, he aligned himself squarely with Danish brick Gothic construction.

Most of Jensen-Klint's buildings are houses and churches; he made a significant contribution to the development of the so-called Danish "smaller house," a type that had begun to attract the attention of architects. A sudden enlargement in the country's housing stock at the turn of the century, in part caused by an economic boom, lasted until the bank crisis of 1908. After several years of attempts, Jensen-Klint in 1912 established the Building School as an option available at the technical colleges: such training was to improve the craftsman's chances of being able to work with aesthetic independence and with a sharper eye to quality. Jensen-Klint was also a force behind the formation of the association Bedre Byggeskik, which offered courses of study as well as plans and models for smaller houses. Though he did not work much on this minor scale himself, Jensen-Klint was an extremely important figure to an entire generation of younger socially conscious architects such as Ivar Bentsen and Povl Baumann, who in 1909 founded Den fri Arkitektforening (The Free Association of Architects) in opposition to the established Akademisk Arkitektforening (Academic Association of Architects). A good example of Jensen-Klint's

Peder Vilhelm Jensen-Klint: Grundtvigs Church and surrounding housing, Copenhagen, Denmark, 1913-40

own version of the "smaller house" was the so-called Smith's House, shown at the Agricultural Exhibition in Århus in 1909.

His villas are distinctive for their use of red brick and the powerful, slightly heavy forms, influenced by the Baroque Revival, particularly as it had taken shape in England: the house at Onsgaardvej 12, Copenhagen (1905-06), is typical in this respect. For the composer Aagaard he built in 1907, in Ryslinge, a house whose mixture of Gothic and Baroque elements verges on the fantastic; a happier example of Jensen-Klint's experiments with brick is his competition project for the Frederiksberg Fire and Police Station of 1915.

As a convinced Grundtvigian, Jensen-Klint's faith played an important part in his church designs, which he developed with unusual intensity and care; Vodskov Church, Aalborg, is from 1907-09, and Annas Church on Bjelkes Allé, Copenhagen, is from 1914.

The work of his maturity is the church dedicated to the memory of N. F. S. Grundtvig, at Bispebjerg, Copenhagen, for which Jensen-Klint prepared the first proposal in 1913. Construction began after his death, in 1921, under the direction of his son, Kaare Klint; Grundtvig's Church was consecrated in 1940. This is the medieval Danish parish church translated to a grand scale. Money for its construction came from private individuals, as well as from the state. Yellow brick was used inside and out, and it is on account of the uniform crafting and application of this material that the church presents a beautiful example of the revival of older Danish construction techniques. The great stepped gable, with its brick patterning continued in the tower and the west front, looms over the houses of Bispebjerg and gives the building the character of both monument and church. In designing the tower Jensen-Klint tried to create an impression of breadth and unity with the rest of the building; the result is extremely untraditional and, seen from behind, the tower can appear like a screen. Behind it rises the choir with buttresses and the crow-stepped chapel gables, a configuration well known from Danish medieval churches.

The interior of Grundtvig's Church is an imposing unity, an enchanting artistic tour-de-force whose great expanses of unplastered wall and vault are built up from the little module, the brick. It is a successful space, redolent of tradition, but avoiding decorative details and adhering to great forms as it does, it expresses modernity and functionalism too. Kaare Klint designed the inventory, pews, organ and the great pulpit. The low houses around the church, "the town on the hill" ("Bispebjerg" literally means "bishop's hill"), was P. V. Jensen-Klint's idea; only some of those he projected were built. His own evaluation of Grundtvig's Church can be found in the book *Den lidettroende i sin bekendelse (Little of Faith in his Confession)*, where he wrote, "I got the feeling, but not the will, the life." The church's strength lies precisely in the feeling, and in the consummate handling of materials; it suggests a transitional architect, an isolated romantic who was nevertheless aware of social currents that were leading the way to a new and more broadly based Danish culture.

—WIVAN MUNK-JØRGENSEN
Translated from the Danish by Christine Stevenson

JOHNSON, Philip.

American. Born in Cleveland, Ohio, 8 July 1906. Studied at Harvard University, Cambridge, Massachusetts, 1923-30, A.B.; Harvard Graduate School of Design, 1940-43, B.Arch. Founder/director, Department of Architecture, Museum of Modern Art, New York, 1930-36 and 1946-54; private practice, Cambridge, Massachusetts, 1942-46; partnership with Landis Gores, 1946-53; private practice, New York City, 1954-64; partnership with Richard Foster, New York City, 1964-67; partnership with John Burgee, New York City, 1967-87; consultant to John Burgee Architects, since 1987. Fellow, American Institute of Architects, 1963. Pritzker Prize, 1979.

Chronology of Works
All in the United States unless noted

1943	Philip Johnson House, Cambridge, Massachusetts
1949	Philip Johnson Glass House, New Canaan, Connecticut
1950	John de Menil House, Houston, Texas
1950	Mrs. John D. Rockefeller III Guest House, New York City
1951	Hodgson House, New Canaan, Connecticut (with Landis Gores)
1951	Oneto House, Irvington, New York (with Gores)
1952	Davis House, Wayzata, Minnesota
1953	Abby Aldrich Rockefeller Sculpture Garden, Museum of Modern Art, New York City (landscape architect, James Fanning)
1953	Wiley House, New Canaan, Connecticut
1953-56	Kneses Tifereth Israel Synagogue, Port Chester, New York
1956	Boissonnas House, New Canaan, Connecticut
1956	Leonhardt House, Lloyd's Neck, Long Island, New York
1957	University of St. Thomas, Houston, Texas (auditorium and classroom buildings)
1958	Seagram Building, New York City (with Ludwig Mies van der Rohe)
1959	Four Seasons Restaurant, Seagram Building, New York City
1960	Museum, Munson-Williams-Proctor Institute, Utica, New York
1960-64	Nuclear Reactor, Rehovot, Israel
1960	Roofless Church, New Harmony, Indiana
1961	Amon Carter Museum of Western Art, Fort Worth, Texas
1962	Philip Johnson Pavilion, New Canaan, Connecticut
1963	Museum for Pre-Columbian Art, Dumbarton Oaks, Washington, D.C.
1963	Sheldon Memorial Art Gallery, University of Nebraska, Lincoln
1964	Boissonnas House, Cap Benat, France
1964	Kline Geology Laboratory, Yale University, New Haven, Connecticut (with Richard Foster)
1964	Museum of Modern Art, New York City (East Wing, Garden Wing, remodeled Sculpture Garden and Upper Terrace)
1964	New York State Pavilion, Flushing, New York (with Foster)
1964	New York State Theater, Lincoln Center, New York City (with Foster)
1965	Epidemiology and Public Health Building, Yale University, New Haven, Connecticut
1965	Philip Johnson Painting Gallery, New Canaan, Connecticut
1965	Kline Science Center, Yale University, New Haven, Connecticut (with Foster)
1965	Henry L. Moses Institute, Montefiore Hospital, Bronx, New York
1968	Bielefeld Art Gallery, Bielefeld, West Germany
1970	John F. Kennedy Memorial, Dallas, Texas

Philip Johnson: Johnson Glass House, New Canaan, Connecticut, 1949

| 1970 | Philip Johnson Sculpture Gallery, New Canaan, Connecticut |

1970 Philip Johnson Sculpture Gallery, New Canaan, Connecticut
1971 Albert and Vera List Art Building, Brown University, Providence, Rhode Island
1972 Andre and Bella Meyer Hall of Physics (facade) and Tisch Hall, New York University, New York City (with Foster)

The following projects in association with John Burgee:

1972 Art Museum of South Texas, Corpus Christi, Texas
1972 Burden Hall, Harvard University, Cambridge, Massachusetts
1972 Neuberger Museum, State University of New York, Purchase, New York
1973 Boston Public Library, Boston, Massachusetts (addition)
1973 IDS Center, Minneapolis, Minnesota
1974 Niagara Falls Convention Center, Niagara Falls, New York
1975 Fort Worth Water Garden, Fort Worth, Texas
1975 Morningside House, Bronx, New York
1976 Avery Fisher Hall, Lincoln Center, New York City (interior)
1976 Pennzoil Place, Houston, Texas
1976-81 Post Oak Central I, II & III, Houston, Texas
1977 Century Center, South Bend, Indiana
1977 Fine Arts Center, Muhlenberg College, Allentown, Pennsylvania
1977 General American Life Insurance Company Building, St. Louis, Missouri
1977 Thanks-Giving Square, Dallas, Texas

1978 80 Field Point Road, Greenwich, Connecticut
1979 Terrace Theater, Kennedy Center for the Performing Arts, Washington, D.C.
1979 1001 Fifth Avenue, New York City (facade)
1980-82 Peoria Civic Center, Peoria, Illinois
1980-84 AT&T Corporate Headquarters, New York City
1980 Garden Grove Community Church (''Crystal Cathedral''), Garden Grove, California
1984 Pittsburgh Plate Glass (PPG) Corporate Headquarters, Pittsburgh, Pennsylvania
1984 RepublicBank Center (NCNB Center), Houston, Texas
1985 Transco Tower and Park, Houston, Texas
1985 One United Bank Center Plaza, Denver, Colorado

Publications

BOOKS BY JOHNSON

Modern Architects. With others. New York, 1932.
The International Style. With Henry-Russell Hitchcock. New York, 1932.
Machine Art. New York, 1934.
Mies van der Rohe. New York, 1947; 2nd ed., 1953; 3rd ed., 1978.
Writings. Edited by Robert A. M. Stern. New York, 1978.
Writings of Philip Johnson. Introduction by Peter Eisenman. New York, 1979.
Deconstructivist Architecture. With Mark Wigley. New York, 1988.

BOOKS ABOUT JOHNSON

DIAMONSTEIN, BARBARALEE: *American Architecture Now II.* New York, 1985.

HITCHCOCK, HENRY-RUSSELL: *Philip Johnson: Architecture 1949-1965.* New York and London, 1966.

JACOBUS, JOHN M.: *Philip Johnson.* New York, 1962.

JENCKS, CHARLES: *Late-Modern Architecture.* London, 1980.

MILLER, NORY: *Johnson/Burgee: Architecture.* London, 1980.

NOBLE, CHARLES: *Philip Johnson.* Tokyo, 1968; London, 1972.

Philip Johnson/John Burgee: Architecture 1979-85. New York, 1985.

Philip Johnson: Processes. Exhibition catalog. New York, 1978.

STERN, ROBERT: *New Directions in American Architecture.* New York, 1977.

ARTICLES ABOUT JOHNSON

Architecture and Urbanism, special issue 6 (1979).

"Behind the Mirror: On the Writings of Philip Johnson." *Oppositions* (Fall 1977).

"California Trio." *Building Design,* special issue (17 February 1984).

FUJII, WAYNE: "Philip Johnson on Philip Johnson." *GA Document* (Summer 1980).

HITCHCOCK, HENRY-RUSSELL: "Current Work of Philip Johnson." *Zodiac 8* (1961).

HITCHCOCK, HENRY-RUSSELL: "Philip Johnson." *Architectural Review* (April 1955).

"Interview with Philip Johnson." *Archetype* (Winter 1983).

"Johnson/Burgee." *Progressive Architecture,* special issue (February 1984).

"New Directions: Paul Rudolph, Philip Johnson, and Buckminster Fuller." *Perspecta 1* (1952).

"Philip Johnson: Modern or Post-Modern?" *Casabella* (April 1981).

*

Philip Johnson has been a figure of nearly steady consequence in the world of international architecture during the final two-thirds of the 20th century. An uncommon combination of intelligence, erudition and restlessness of temperament, reinforced by the privileges of wealth and station, has made him exceptionally quick to sense major shifts in architectural thought and theory at the global level, then to articulate them, then to promote them publicly, and at last to give them up as soon as they fade and others take their place. If the arts of the 20th century have been notable for pluralism and volatility, few men have matched him in recognizing that identity and contributing to it.

In short, his genius is critical rather than creative, an observation that applies not only to his accomplishments as a writer and museum curator, but to the architecture he has designed himself. The latter is greater in quantity than the former, but it is a function primarily of judgment and advocacy, only secondarily of invention. Two of his most celebrated buildings, one early, one late, suffice to illustrate the point. He himself has characterized his Glass House of 1949 as an elaborate response not only to Ludwig Mies van der Rohe's Farnsworth House but to historical stimuli as diverse as the works of Claude-Nicolas Ledoux, Karl Friedrich Schinkel, Le Corbusier and Kasimir Malevich. The AT&T Building of 1984 is famous mostly as a monumental validation of the postmodernist aesthetic. Neither work was original in form or meaning, but both are effective as summations and critiques of the forms and meanings they represent.

Born in 1906 to a well-to-do family in Cleveland, Johnson took his undergraduate training at Harvard University, majoring in classics and philosophy. He graduated in 1930, by which time he had struck up a friendship with the young director of the newly opened Museum of Modern Art, Alfred Barr, who drew him into the arts. Barr encouraged Johnson's newly found interest in architecture, which the latter pursued under the further tutelage of another brilliant young contemporary, the historian Henry-Russell Hitchcock. Johnson and Hitchcock toured Europe in 1930, studying the modernist modes pioneered during the 1920s by J.J.P. Oud in Holland, Mies van der Rohe and Walter Gropius in Germany, and Le Corbusier in France. In 1932 Johnson collaborated with Hitchcock and Barr in an epochal exhibition at the Museum of Modern Art, "Modern Architects," which effectively introduced the new architecture to the United States and turned the term "International Style" into a virtual synonym for the Modern Movement. Later in 1932 Johnson was formally installed as the first director of the museum's Department of Architecture, where he organized several other important shows, including "Machine Art" in 1934.

His constitutional restlessness manifested itself most dramatically when he resigned his museum post late in 1934 to launch a career in right-wing/populist politics. After trying unsuccessfully to attach himself to the Louisiana demagogue Huey Long, he found his way into the orbit of the "radio priest," Rev. Charles Coughlin, whose anti-New Deal pronouncements of the late 1930s grew increasingly sympathetic with the cause of Nazi Germany. Johnson's own published articles of the time were close to fascism in outlook. With the onset of World War II, however, he recognized the folly of his political adventure and committed himself again (and for good) to the arts, enrolling in the Harvard architecture school in 1940 and studying with Gropius and Marcel Breuer. He graduated in 1943. After a stint in the U.S. Army, he returned in 1946 to New York, to resume his position at the Museum of Modern Art and to set up his own practice.

Since his first encounter with architecture, Johnson had regarded Mies van der Rohe as the greatest of the European moderns, a conviction evident not only in the 1947 Mies retrospective he staged at the museum, accompanied by the first monograph on that master's work, but in Johnson's own architecture. The Glass House, built for his estate in New Canaan, Connecticut, was followed by a group of residential designs, e.g., the Hodgson (1951), Oneto (1951) and Davis (1952) houses, that followed, gracefully but faithfully, the geometric reductivism of the Miesian manner. His apparently natural tendency toward eclecticism came to the fore in his 1953-54 design for the Kneses Tifereth synagogue, in which a Miesian rectilinear box was qualified by an ovoid entrance reminiscent of Ledoux and an interior vault that recalls John Soane. His collaboration with Mies in the latter's Seagram Building of 1958 was his last close contact with his erstwhile hero.

By the end of the 1950s Johnson was already acting out the statement he became famous for: "You cannot not know history." Several of his buildings, like the Amon Carter Museum (1961) and the Sheldon Memorial Art Gallery (1963), harked back to classicism in their arches and axialities, while others were based on a variety of historical sources: the Roofless Church (1960) on Indian stupas and Norwegian stave churches, the Nuclear Reactor in Israel (1964) on the undulating domes of Francesco Borromini, the 1964 painting gallery at his New Canaan estate on Mycenaean beehive tombs.

Johnson's partners have included Landis Gores (1946-53), Richard Foster (1964-67) and perhaps most prominently, John Burgee (1967-88). This last relationship resulted in Johnson's largest commercial works, nearly all of them marked by an exuberant plundering of the past. Historicism tinctured with an urban irony—a hallmark of postmodernism—is evident in the Pittsburgh Plate Glass Building (1984), the Republicbank Center (1984) and the Transco Tower (1985). Even so, Johnson could just as easily shift back to modernism, as in his use of an immense space frame to produce the all-glass exterior of the Crystal Cathedral (1980). Indeed, as the momentum of postmodernism began to wane in the later 1980s, his interest gravitated to an international group of architects who, largely through his own propagandizing efforts at the Museum of Modern Art, have come to be known as the deconstructivists.

Throughout a career of close to 60 years, Johnson's very mercuriality has been, paradoxically, one of his most consistent character traits. So is his unwavering belief in architecture as a formal artistic discipline, its social and philosophical aspects of only secondary importance to him or of no importance at all. This point of view, with its overtones of elitism, has earned him as many detractors as admirers. Still active in his mid-80s, he remains one of the pivotal figures of contemporary architecture.

—FRANZ SCHULZE

JONES, Inigo.

British. Born in London, England, 1573. Died on 21 June 1652. Apprentice to a joiner, St. Paul's Churchyard; painter, 1603; designer to Queen Anne of Denmark, 1605-40; architectural consultant, Hatfield House, 1609; surveyor to Henry, Prince of Wales, 1610; surveyor of the King's Works, 1613; surveyor-general, 1615; Member of Parliament, 1621.

Chronology of Works
All in England
* Approximate dates
† Work no longer exists

1608*	Lady Cotton Monument, Norton-in-Hales, Shropshire
1609	Hatfield House, Hertfordshire (modifications of south front) [attributed]
1615*	Houghton House, Bedfordshire (frontispieces) [attributed]
1615-17	Newmarket Palace, Suffolk (brewhouse, stables, ridinghouse, doghouse)
1616-35	Greenwich Palace (Queen's House; completed by others), Kent
1617*	Byfleet House, Surrey (remodeling) [attributed]
1617-18	Oatlands Palace, Surrey (great park gate, silkworm house, vineyard gate)
1617-18	St. James's Palace (Prince's Buttery), Westminster, London
1617-18	Somerset House, Strand, London (hall lantern)
1618	Arundel House, Strand, London (gateway and probably the Sculpture Gallery)
1618*	Edward Cecil's House, Strand, London (entrance)
1619*	Fulke Greville's House, Strand, London
1619-20	Whitehall Palace, London (Marquess of Buckingham's lodgings)
1619-21	Newmarket Palace, Surrey (Prince's lodging and clerk of work's house)
1619-22	Whitehall Palace, London (Banqueting House)
1620-21	Whitehall Palace, London (Countess of Buckingham's lodgings)
1621	Beaufort House, Chelsea, London (gateway)

1623	Thoebalds Palace, Hertfordshire (stable)
1623	Westminster Palace, London (House of Lords)
1623-24	Greenwich Palace, Kent (remodeling of chapel and great park gate)
1623-25	St. James's Palace, Westminster, London (Queen's Chapel)
1624	Whitehall Palace, London (park stairs)
1625	Thoebalds Palace, Hertfordshire (Banqueting House)
1626	Somerset House, Strand, London (Queen's Cabinet Room)
1626	St. James's Palace, Westminster, London (Sculpture Gallery)
1629	Whitehall Palace, London (Cockpit Theatre)
1630s*	Ascott House, Buckinghamshire (wing and apartment)
1630-35	Somerset House, Strand, London (Queen's Chapel)
1631	Bagshot Park, Surrey (lodge)
1631	Oatlands Palace, Surrey (garden arbor)
1631	St. James's Palace, Westminster, London (park gate)
1631-32	Hale Church, Hampshire [attributed]
1631-37	St. Paul's Church, Covent Garden, London (burned 1795; rebuilt 1795-98 by Thomas Hardwick)†
1633-42	St. Paul's Cathedral, London (restoration)†
1634-35	Hyde Park Lodge, London
1635	Oatlands Palace (balcony to Queen's lodging), Surrey
1635	Somerset House, Strand, London (Cross Gallery)
1636-37	Barber Surgeon's Hall Anatomy Theatre, London
1637	Somerset House, Strand, London (new Cabinet Room)
1637	Whitehall Palace, London (new Masquein Room)
1637-38	Cathedral, Winchester (choir screen; remnant in Museum of Archaeology, Cambridge)†
1640-41	Wimbledon House, Surrey (additions)

Publications

BOOKS BY JONES

Inigo Jones on Palladio (facsimile of Jones's annotated Palladio). Ed. B. Allsopp. 2 vols. (1970).
The Most Notable Antiquity of Great Britain, Vulgarly Called Stone-Heng. 3rd ed. London, 1725.

BOOKS ABOUT JONES

SERVICE, ALASTAIR: *The Architects of London.* London, 1979.
CUNNINGHAM, P.: *Inigo Jones: A Life of the Architect.* London, 1848-49.
GOTCH, JOHN A.: *Inigo Jones.* London, 1928.
HARRIS, JOHN: *Catalogue of the Drawings Collection of the Royal Institute of British Architects: Inigo Jones and John Webb.* Farnborough, England, 1972.
HARRIS, JOHN, and TAIT, A. A.: *Catalog of the Drawings by Inigo Jones, John Webb, and Isaac De Caius at Worcester College, Oxford.* London, 1979.
HARRIS, JOHN; ORGEL, STEPHEN; and STRONG, ROY: *The King's Arcadia: Inigo Jones and the Stuart Court.* Exhibition catalog. London, 1973.
KENT, WILLIAM: *Designs of Inigo Jones.* London, 1727.
LEES-MILNE, JAMES: *The Age of Inigo Jones.* London, 1953.
LOFTIE, W. J.: *Inigo Jones and Wren: or the Rise and Decline of Modern Architecture in England.* London, 1893.
ORGEL, STEPHEN, and STRONG, ROY: *Inigo Jones: The Theatre of the Stuart Court.* 2 vols. London, 1973.

Inigo Jones: Greenwich Palace, Greenwich, London, England, 1616-35

RYKWERT, JOSEPH: *The First Moderns: The Architects of the Eighteenth Century.* 1980.

STRONG, ROY: *Festival Designs by Inigo Jones.* London, 1967.

SUMMERSON, JOHN: *Architecture in Britain: 1530-1830.* 6th. ed. rev. Harmondsworth, England, 1977.

SUMMERSON, JOHN: *Inigo Jones.* Harmondsworth, England, 1966.

VARDY, JOHN: *Some Designs of Mr. Inigo Jones and Mr. William Kent.* London, 1744. Reprint: Farnborough, England, 1967.

WARE, ISAAC: *The Designs of Inigo Jones.* London, 1756.

ARTICLES ABOUT JONES

BELL, C. F.: "Portraits of Inigo Jones." *Journal of the Royal Institute of British Architects* (11 September 1937): 1007.

DE BEER, E. S.: "Notes on Inigo Jones." *Notes and Queries* (30 December 1939, 27 April and 4 May 1940).

GORDON, D. J.: "Poet and Architect: The Intellectual Background to the Quarrel between Ben Jonson and Inigo Jones." *Journal of the Warburg and Courtauld Institutes* 12 (1949).

GOTCH, JOHN A.: "The Original Drawings for the Palace at Whitehall Attributed to Inigo Jones." *Architectural Review* (June 1912).

GOTCH, JOHN A.: "Inigo Jones's Principal Visit to Italy in 1614: The Itinerary of His Journeys." *Journal of the Royal Institute of British Architects* Series 3, 46 (21 November 1938): 85-86.

HARRIS, JOHN: "Inigo Jones and the Prince's Lodging at Newmarket." *Architectural History* 2 (1959).

HARRIS, JOHN: "A Prospect of Whitehall by Inigo Jones." *Burlington Magazine* 109 (February 1967): 89.

HARRIS, JOHN: "Inigo Jones and His French Sources." *Metropolitan Museum Bulletin* 19 (May 1961): 253-264.

HARRIS, JOHN: "Inigo Jones and the Courtier Style." *Architectural Review* 154 (July 1973): 17-24.

HARRIS, JOHN: "The Link Between a Roman Second-Century Sculptor, Van Dyck, Inigo Jones, and Queen Henrietta Maria." *Burlington Magazine* 115 (1973): 526-530.

KEITH, WILLIAM GRANT: "Some Hitherto Unknown Drawings by Inigo Jones." *Burlington Magazine* 22 (1913): 218-226.

KEITH, WILLIAM GRANT: "A Theater Project by Inigo Jones." *Burlington Magazine* 31 (1917): 61-62, 105-111.

KEITH, WILLIAM GRANT: "Inigo Jones as a Collector." *Journal of the Royal Institute of British Architects* Series 3, 33 (1925-26): 94-108.

MILLAR, OLIVER: "Dobson's portrait of Inigo Jones." *Burlington Magazine* 104 (1952): 207.

ROWE, COLIN: "The Theatrical Drawings of Inigo Jones, Their Sources and Scope." M. A. thesis, University of London, 1947.

SIMPSON, P., and BELL, C. F.: "Designs by Inigo Jones for Masques and Plays at Court." *Walpole Society* 12 (1924).

SKOVAARD, J. A.: "Inigo Jones and Christian IV [of Denmark]." In *A King's Architecture.* 1973.

SMITH, JOAN SUMNER: "The Italian Sources of Inigo Jones's Style." *Burlington Magazine* 94 (July 1952): 200-206.

STONE, LAWRENCE: "Inigo Jones and the New Exchange." *Archaeological Journal* 114 (1957): 106-121.

SUMMERSON, JOHN: "Inigo Jones." *Proceedings of the British Academy* 50 (1964): 169-192.

SUMMERSON, JOHN: "The Surveyorship of Inigo Jones." In HOWARD COLVIN (ed.): *The History of the King's Works.* London, 1975.

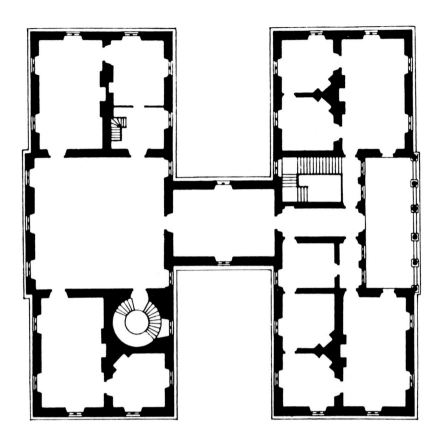

TAIT, A. A.: "Inigo Jones—Architectural Historian." *Burlington Magazine* 112 (1970): 235.

WEBB, GEOFFREY: "Inigo Jones Tercentenary." *Country Life* (20 June 1952).

WHINNEY, MARGARET: "An Unknown Design for a Villa by Inigo Jones." In HOWARD COLVIN and JOHN HARRIS (eds.): *The Country Seat*. London, 1970.

WHINNEY, MARGARET: "Inigo Jones: A Revaluation." *Journal of the Royal Institute of British Architects* Series 3, 59 (1952): 286-289.

WHINNEY, MARGARET: "John Webb's Drawings for Whitehall Palace." *Walpole Society* 33 (1942-43): 45-107.

WICKHAM, GLYNNE: "The Cockpit Reconstructed." *New Theatre Magazine* 7 (1967): 2ff.

WITTKOWER, RUDOLF: "Inigo Jones, Architect and Man of Letters" *Journal of the Royal Institute of British Architects* Series 3, 60 (January 1953): 83-90.

WITTKOWER, RUDOLF: "Inigo Jones, Puritanissimo Fiero.' *Burlington Magazine* 90 (1948): 50-51. Reprinted in *Palladio and English Palladianism*. London, 1974.

*

It is commonplace that architecture reflects the form and state of society at given periods of history. This reflection is usually revealed when society is stable and the mirror image undistorted. It is therefore all the more remarkable that, emerging from the confusion following the ascension of James VI, king of Scotland, to be James I of England, there should have arisen an artist who in the course of his career epitomized Renaissance man and almost singlehandedly brought the Renaissance in art and architecture to England. This was Inigo Jones, who was born in 1573 and died in 1652.

One of the fascinating aspects of considering the career of a great artist is to identify and attribute the influences of his formative years. Jones ranks among the greatest of British architects, yet remarkably, little is known of his early life. Indeed, when his whole career is reviewed, it is his achievements that catch attention, while the personality and character of the man are but rarely revealed. This is not to argue that there is deliberate concealment. We have knowledge of incidents, in particular the famous quarrel with Ben Jonson, which demonstrates that Jones could be forceful in demanding public recognition when he felt it was due. Nevertheless, there are few private documents remaining. The information about him is drawn largely from writings of his pupil and eventual successor, John Webb.

The mystery of Jones' early years can be contrasted with the sudden prominence he assumed at the age of 31 at the court of James I. In youth he was apprenticed to a joiner in St. Paul's churchyard. With hindsight, this is significant in that he was not trained in the conventional tradition of the London Mason contractors of the time. He is also reported to have traveled in Italy in the latter part of the 16th century. This rests on the tradition that, early in the 17th century, he was "sent for out of Italy" by Christian IV of Denmark to assist the intellectual and artistic movement which was a feature of that monarch's reign. The clear implication is that he had something to offer the Danish court. The likelihood is that, apart from his curiosity in observing and recording classical design, he could transmit the ideas of prominent scholars in northern Italy to nascent intellectual groups in England, the best-known example of which was that gathering around Francis Bacon. Indeed, Jones later developed a reputation for philosophy as well as aesthetic authority in the intellectual circles within the courts of James and Charles.

Jones could not have been in the service of the Danish king for long, as he was engaged by Oxford University in 1605 to assist in the staging of entertainment for James I by providing "rare devices," but he is reputed to have produced very little of what was expected. Indeed, his early work shows little evidence of the mastery of the classical idiom that was such an important feature of his later work. An example is his design for the facade of the New Exchange. John Summerson has observed that although delicately drawn, "it is nevertheless obviously the work of someone who had had little to do with architecture and nothing with building." The inconsistency of design is also seen in his design for the upper stages of the tower of Old St. Paul's Cathedral, which again shows lack of appreciation of both structure and composition. There are several opinions about the curious combination of elements in this design. It may have arisen naturally out of the romanticism and unreality of his work on stage settings for the masques that occupied much of his time at court. A more positive aspect may have been that he was beginning to recognize the importance of silhouette in the architecture of the Late Elizabethan builders and of the picturesque forms of the great houses in France. His duties at the court of James I involved visits to that country. He rapidly acquired patronage. This was highlighted by his appointment as surveyor to the Prince of Wales in 1610. There is, however, little to show from that period, as the prince died in 1612. Jones was soon once more engaged on the great masques devised to celebrate the wedding of the daughter of James I, Elizabeth, to the heir apparent to the throne of Bohemia. Jones was with the party that traveled to Heidelberg, and he also traveled on with the earl of Arundel to Italy. That period, 1613-14, can be seen to be of importance in Jones' development as an architect. From his papers there is evidence that he studied the work of Sebastiano Serlio and Giacamo Barozzi da Vignola, and met Vincenzo Scamozzi, then an old man, in Venice in 1614.

The metamorphosis that Jones underwent during his visit to Italy was one of the most startling events in aesthetic history. Gone was the tentative mixture of old and new, with uncertainty of technical control, to be replaced by mastery of the classical idiom. Once more we grasp a glimpse of the man behind the design. He kept a sketchbook and in a note he suggested that the Mannerism rife in Italy at the time was inappropriate to "solid architecture." The latter term included facade design, although he allowed that ornamentation had a place in interiors and garden features. This development of Jones' personal philosophy was based on the discipline of an architecture designed according to rules of proportion, and masculine in character. We know he was a strong personality. Was his work the sublimation of personality to the precise expression of a mature classical style?

While recognizing the significance of Jones' assimilation of Renaissance values, one must see other important events as influential at that critical point in his career. First, the intellectual circles, both at the court of James I and in Europe, were demanding change so as to make a final break from the medievalism and the "magic" of the Elizabethan age. The Rosicrucian manifestos published between 1612 and 1614 were widely seen to challenge the pope and the reactionary Catholicism that had been deployed to restrict the acceptance of early scientific ideas. The English court was caught up in the excitement of the times. The marriage of James I's daughter, Elizabeth, to the putative king of Bohemia was seen as a catalyst in gathering support for the Protestant cause in Europe. The tragedy that was to lead

to the Thirty Years' war was not apparent, nor even, at that time, was there hint of the civil war in England that was to cast a shadow over Jones' later career. The time was ripe for radicalism, and suddenly the opportunity arose: The king's surveyor died in 1615, and Jones was the natural choice to be successor.

Then followed the work that marked the English architectural Renaissance. The Queen's House at Greenwich was begun in 1616, was delayed by the death of Queen Anne in 1619, but was completed for Henrietta Maria in 1635. In 1617 Jones designed a new Star Chamber, but a shortage of public funds, presaging the tension that led to the Civil War, caused the building plans to be canceled. The Banqueting Hall at Whitehall was destroyed by fire. Its replacement was Jones' most famous creation, and epitomized the geometric control that was a feature of much of his later work. Jones used a cube as basic element in control of proportion. A double cube generated the proportion of the major rooms. From this basic discipline, classical rules took care of the proportion and articulation of surfaces both external and internal. The Queen's Chapel at St. James Palace is a double cube bounded by the entablature, which allowed for a coved, barrel-vaulted ceiling above the cornice. The extra height in the end wall allowed Jones to use the device, in the window design at the end of the church, of raising an arch in the center of the three lights and returning the cornice over intermediate columns. This feature, derived from Vincenzo Scamozzi, has been used to identify Jones' hand in the design of the south facade of Wilton House.

Jones' duties as the king's surveyor probably meant that a great deal of work not directly linked to his official duties had to be left to others who carried out detailed design and supervision work on site. An example is the development at Covent Garden. There, the Earl of Bedford wished to develop a residential quarter, which became the first essay in urban design in England. Overdevelopment in London had meant a ban on new building except on old foundations. Jones, as official surveyor, was drawn into the scheme to ensure "Uniformity and Decency." It had been realized that a church would add respectability to the scheme, but according to Walpole, the Earl made it clear that it had to be economic: "I would not have it better than a barn." Jones replied, "Well then, you shall have the handsomest barn in England!" The relationship of the chapel and the redispersed houses allowed two piazzas to be formed. One model for Covent Garden may have been the development at Leghorn in northern Italy, which probably fueled the rumor that Jones had been involved in the design of the church there. But again, his youth and his architectural inexperience upon his return to England make this improbable. The Place Royale in Paris (1608), which he would have seen on his visits, would have been a more appropriate influence. The chapel portico uses the Tuscan order, which even today adds a heroic sense of scale to the composition, and suggests Jones' desire to achieve a personal and durable adaption of classicism.

Upon the ascension of Charles I in 1625, William Laud, bishop of London (1628-1633) and later archbishop of Canterbury, revitalized the restoration of St. Paul's Cathedral, which James I had initiated in 1620. The Laudian revolution was remarkable for changes in the liturgical layout of Anglican churches. Jones was closely involved with the Laudian movement. He was, therefore, one of the commissioners for the work at St. Paul's and honorary architect until the Civil War, when the work was stopped. Jones' contribution was to the west front, for which he prepared designs in 1631, of which one was built (1634-42). This design showed the command of scale and style that was later commended by Christopher Wren, and showed a maturity in merging old and new work missing from Jones' early (1608) attempt at this subject. The cathedral suffered during the Civil War and was finally destroyed in the Great Fire of London.

What can be surmised about Jones the man? He lived and worked in a period of conflict and religious tension. The penalties for dissent could be barbarously cruel. It behooved public figures to be careful, and they often used metaphysical and allegorical language. That Jones could steer a circumspect course shows a highly developed sense of preservation, in some ways similar to the careful statesmanship of his royal master James I.

Jones' later designs indicate a growing sense of his wish to work on a massive scale, possibly as an extension to the desire to impose a personal stamp on discussion, as seen at Covent Garden. The first plan for Whitehall Palace, of which the present Banqueting Hall was to form a minor part, shows a scheme of the greatest scale, greater than any comparable development in Europe. Yet even there, in the disposition of buildings arranged around courtyards, Jones showed himself to be aware of the need to achieve a character that was peculiarly English. It may be that Jones in his later career felt that he could impress himself on the political scene to an extent, while in his formative years he had had to be circumspect. His own religious position was hidden behind the public persona. Wren later assumed him to be a Catholic, but the papal agent who wrote to Rome on the completion of the Somerset House chapel in 1636 noted the unreligious stance of the architect. Jones' association with Archbishop Laud exposed him to puritan fury at the outbreak of the Civil War. His involvement with the masques also were a source of irritation. He was captured by commonwealth troops in 1644. His remarkable sense of self-preservation served him well; his life was saved, and even his estate, though threatened, was preserved. Upon payment of a substantial fine, he was, in fact, pardoned in 1646.

Jones had occupied an eminent but lonely position. Whether or not this isolation was intentional is not known. The danger of relying upon one man was clear to the establishment, and Jones was charged with the training of his assistant, John Webb. Jones must receive tribute for guiding his chief assistant into the position of authority that Webb later occupied. The later architect was thus in a natural position to write upon Jonesian concepts and to extrapolate on topics that were ascribed to Jones himself.

As a former royalist, Jones had no official position. Webb reported on Jones' advice on construction at Wilton and for the great palace at Whitehall while Charles was awaiting execution, but that seems to have been the extent of Jones' work during the last years of his life.

—K. H. MURTA

JONES, Owen.

British. Born in London, England, 1809. Died in 1874. Married Isabelle Wild, 1842. Apprenticed to Lewis Vulliamy (1791-1871), 1825; traveled in Greece, Egypt and Spain, 1830-34. Joint architect (interior decoration), London 1851 Great Exhibition. Published *Grammar of Ornament*, 1856. Gold Medal, Royal Institute of British Architects, 1857.

Chronology of Works
All in England
† *Work no longer exists*
* *Approximate dates*

1843-47	8 Kensington Gardens, London†
1845-49*	24 Kensington Palace Gardens, London
1852-54	Courts in Crystal Palace, Sydenham, London†
1855-58	St. James's Concert Hall, Piccadilly, London†
1858	Crystal Palace Bazaar, London
1859-62	Osler's Glass Shop, London
1865-70	16 Carlton House Terrace, London (interiors)
1872*	Abbotsfield House, Somerset
1872	Eynsham Hall, Oxford

Publications

BOOKS BY JONES

Plans, Elevations, Sections, and Details of the Alhambra. With Jules Goury. 2 vols. London, 1842-45.
The Illuminated Books of the Middle Ages. London, 1844.
The Polychromatic Ornament of Italy. London, 1846.
An Apology for the Colouring of the Greek Court at the Crystal Palace. London, 1854.
The Grammar of Ornament. London, 1856.
Lectures on Architecture and the Decorative Arts. London, 1863.

BOOKS ABOUT JONES

DARBY, MICHAEL, and PHYSICK, JOHN: *'Marble Halls': Drawings and Models for Victorian Secular Buildings.* London, 1973.

ARTICLES ABOUT JONES

DARBY, MICHAEL: ''Owen Jones and the Oriental Influence in Nineteenth Century Design.'' Ph.D. dissertation. Reading University, Reading, England, 1974.
DARBY, MICHAEL, and VAN ZANTEN, DAVID: ''Owen Jones's Iron Buildings of the 1850s.'' *Architectura* (1974): 53-75.

*

As a student on grand tour through Egypt, Turkey, Greece and Spain in the 1830s, Owen Jones entered into contemporary debates concerning the character and extent of architectural polychromy on ancient buildings, carefully measuring and studying the ruins to gather evidence. Above all, it was this experience that led him to spend his career formulating correct principles of design, color and ornament, and working out their application in Victorian architecture and interior design. Non-European decoration, particularly the Moorish ornament of the Alhambra in Granada, Spain, was the main source of his inspiration, as he addressed the problem of re-creating an Eastern experience of brilliant color and geometrical ornament in a form acceptable to a British audience.

It was the task of measuring and drawing the Alhambra that allowed him to study closely the principles underlying Moorish decoration, and it was the publication of these drawings as *Plans, Elevations, Sections, and Details of the Alhambra* (1842-45) that established his reputation as an expert on Islamic architecture. This sumptuous and expensive two-volume work featured large-scale chromolithographs printed by Jones himself, which emphasized the importance of color in architecture, and displayed his reconstruction of the polychromy of the Alhambra to best advantage. Described as ''the most influential book on Islamic architecture and decoration to appear in Britain,'' it revealed the intricacy and vibrant coloring of Moorish patterns, and demonstrated their derivation from a series of grids.

His first attempts to adapt these principles used by the Moors in the Alhambra to the needs of architecture in Britain met with limited success, when he undertook the design and decoration of 8 and 24 Kensington Palace Gardens, London (1843 and 1845), as part of a speculative scheme for the entrepreneur and terra-cotta manufacturer John Marriott Blashfield. The designs are an uncertain, yet somehow charming amalgamation of European architecture and exotic detailing; they are Italianate in style with vaguely Moorish ornamentation and balcony walls and parapets pierced with fretwork.

It was in the realm of interior design rather than architecture that Jones met with his initial success. His designs for James Wild's Christ Church, Streatham (1841), and Lewis Vulliamy's All Saints, Ennismore Gardens, London (1840), employed a Byzantine style of decoration, and received favorable reviews in the press. Subsequently, it was interior design that brought Jones to the forefront as a professional designer. Through the influence of Henry Cole, organizer with Prince Albert of the London 1851 Great Exhibition, he was appointed joint architect of that exhibition, developing a scheme for the interior decoration of Joseph Paxton's iron-and-glass exhibition building, the Crystal Palace. Jones idea to paint the interior of the structure using primary colors separated by white in the ratio blue 8 / red 5 / yellow 3 drew on his experience with color at the Alhambra and the contemporary color theories of the French chemist Michel Eugène Chevreul and Field. This brilliant scheme was calculated so that the viewer, looking down the length of the nave, would experience bright colors merging into neutrality in the distance. Although this scheme met with much skepticism at first, after its completion it was applauded vigorously; one contemporary likened the effect to "... the hazy indistinctness which Turner alone can paint."

Through his successful work at the Crystal Palace, Jones strengthened his ties with Henry Cole and consequently was actively involved in the establishment of the Department of Practical Art, set up to administer the Government Schools of Design. His involvement with the Cole circle was critical for the continued refinement of Jones ideas concerning correct principles of design, and it was during that period that Jones produced his definitive statement of design principles, *The Grammar of Ornament* (1856). Intended for use as a handbook in the provincial Schools of Design, *The Grammar* formed an integral part of Cole's campaign to raise the standards of High Victorian design and thus boost British trade. The folio included 100 chromolithographic plates illustrating ornament from a variety of cultures, together with commentary on 37 principles of correct design. Derived to a large extent from his study of Moorish ornament, Jones' principles stressed "colour," "fitness," "harmony," "proportion," and the "repose" that these could engender. Widely regarded as the leading Victorian book on ornament, *The Grammar* found an international audience, playing a formative role in structuring the thinking of architects such as Louis Sullivan, Frank Llyod Wright and Le Corbusier. Although *The Grammar* was intended as a study of correct principles of design, it was widely employed by architects and designers as a pattern book, being particularly valuable for its large number of plates devoted to non-European decoration, including examples of Egyptian, Indian, Islamic, Persian and Hindoo [*sic*] ornament.

Success at the Crystal Palace brought architectural commissions. During the late 1850s, Jones designed a series of iron-and-glass buildings and their interiors for nouveau-riche, middle-class capitalists in London, including St. James Hall (1858), the Crystal Palace Bazaar (1858) and a showroom for Messrs. Osler's (1859). Jones had advocated the use of new materials in architecture as early as 1835; in a lecture titled "On the Influence of Religion in Art," he argued for the use of iron and glass in formulating an appropriate architecture for a new age. The interior of the display gallery for Osler's, a well-known Victorian glass manufacturer, illustrates how he was in a position to combine these views with his ideas concerning color and correct design principles. The roof of the gallery was divided into 14 compartments, each containing stained glass set in geometric panels of fibrous plaster. Large mirrors along the walls created the effect of extended space, while pendant gas burners completed the transformation of the whole into a phantasmagoric Victorian version of an Eastern bazaar. According to one author, this was "an attempt to make permanent the effects which Jones had succeeded in achieving in the Great Exhibition."

Jones' late interiors for private homes continued to draw on effects of color and geometrical ornament. Between 1865 and 1870, Alfred Morrison hired him and the firm of Jackson and Graham to decorate the ground and first floors of 16 Carlton House Terrace, London. There, Jones worked with a combination of Greek and Moorish designs, setting off ceilings and walls with brilliant areas of red, green and gold. This strikingly lavish series of interior spaces illustrated his dictum that "form without color is like a body without a soul," and demonstrated once again his success in translating an Eastern experience of color and form into Victorian terms.

—ELLEN A. CHRISTENSEN

JUVARRA, Filippo.

Italian. Born in Messina, Sicily, in 1678. Died in Madrid, Spain, 31 January 1736. Worked in the studio of Carlo Fontana, Rome, 1703-14. Appointed First Architect to the King, 1714.

Chronology of Works
All in Italy unless noted

1708-10	Antamoro Chapel, San Girolamo della Carità, Rome
1715	Santa Cristina, Turin (facade)
1715-36	San Filippo Neri, Turin (not completed until later by others)
1716	Palazzo Birago di Borgaro, Turin
1716	Palazzo Martini di Cigala, Turin
1716	Quartieri Militari, Turin
1717-31	Church and Monastery, Superga, near Turin
1718	Santa Croce, Turin
1718	Castello Reale, Rivoli (not completed)
1718-21	Palazzo Madama, Turin (remodeling)
1720	Campanile, Cathedral, Turin
1720	Scala delle Forbici, Palazzo Reale, Turin
1720-29	Venaria Reale Stables and Citroneria
1728*	Sant' Andrea, Chieri†
1729	Piazza Vittoria, Turin
1729-33	Stupinigi Hunting Lodge, near Turin
1720s	Royal Palace, Turin (remodeling of theater)
1730	Palazzo Guarene, Turin (facade)
1732-35	Chiesa del Carmine, Turin
1735	Royal Palace, Madrid, Spain (executed in a reduced form)
1736	La Granja Palace, Sant'Ildefonso, Spain (garden facade; not executed until later by others)

Filippo Juvarra: Superga, Turin, Italy, 1717-31

Publications

BOOKS ABOUT JUVARRA

BARONI DI TAVIGLIANO, G.: *Modello della Chiesa di S. Filippo per li PP. dell'Oratorio di Torino, inventato e disegnato dall'abate e cav. Don Filippo Juvarra, primo architetto di S. M.* Turin, 1758.

BERNARDI, MARZIANO: *La palazzina di caccia di Stupinigi.* Turin, 1958.

BOSCARINO, SALVATORE: *Juvarra architetto.* Rome, 1973.

BRINCKMANN, ALBERT E.: *Theatrum Novum Pedemontii: Ideen, Entwürfe und Bauten von Guarini, Juvarra, Vittone wie anderen bedeutenden Architekten des piemontischen Hochbarocks.* Düsseldorf, 1931.

CARBONERI, NINO: *La reale chiesa di Superga di Filippo Juvarra.* Turin, 1979.

CAVALLARI MURAT, AUGUSTO: *Forma urbana ed architettura nella Torino barocca.* 3 vols. Turin, 1968.

GRISERI, ANDREINA: *Le metamorphosi del barocco.* Turin, 1967.

HAGER, HELLMUT: *Filippo Juvarra e il concorso di modelli del 1715 bandito da Clemente XI per la nuova sacrestia di S. Pietro.* Rome, 1970.

MALLÉ, LUIGI: *Le arti figurative in Piemonte.* Turin, 1962.

MALLÉ, LUIGI: *Palazzo Madama in Torino.* Turin, 1970.

MALLÉ, LUIGI: *Stupinigi un capolavoro del settecento europeo tra barocchetto e classicismo: architettura, pittura, scultura, arredamento.* Turin, 1972.

MARCONI, PAOLO; CIPRINANI, ANGELA; and VALERIANI, ENRICO: *I disegni di architettura dell'archivio storico dell'Accademia di San Luca.* 2 vols, Rome, 1974.

MARINI, GIUSEPPE LUIGI: *L'architettura barocca in Piemonte: La provincia di Torino.* Turin, 1963.

MILLON, HENRY A.: *Filippo Juvarra.* New York, 1984.

MYERS, MARY L.: *Architectural and Ornament Drawings: Juvarra, Vanvitelli, the Bibiena Family and other Italian Draftsmen.* New York, 1975.

PLAZA SANTIAGO, FRANCISCO DE LA: *El palacio real nuevo de Madrid.* Spain, 1978.

POMMER, RICHARD: *Eighteenth-Century Architecture in Piedmont: The Open Structures of Juvarra, Alfieri, and Vittone.* New York and London, 1967.

ROVERE, LORENZO; VIALE, VITTORIO; and BRINCKMANN, ALBERT E.: *Filippo Juvarra.* Turin, 1937.

TELLUCCINI, AUGUSTO: *L'arte dell'architetto Filippo Juvarra in Piemonte.* Turin, 1926.

VIALE FERRERO, MERCEDES: *Filippo Juvarra, scenografo e architetto teatrale.* Turin, 1970.

VIALE, VITTORIO (ed.): *Mostra di Filippo Juvarra, architetto e scenografo.* Exhibition catalog. Messina, Italy, 1966.

WITTKOWER, RUDOLF: *Art and Architecture in Italy: 1600-1750.* 3rd ed. Harmondsworth, England, 1973.

ARTICLES ABOUT JUVARRA

ACCASCINA, MARIA: "La formazione artistica di Filippo Juvarra." *Bollettino d'arte* 41:38-52; 42:50-60, 150-162 (1956-57).

BATTISTA, EUGENIO: "Juvarra a San Ildefonso." *Commentari* 9, No. 4 (1958): 273-297.

BENEDETTI, SANDRO: "Una quasi sconosciuta opera Juvarriana: La costruzione settecentesca del palazzo pubblico di Lucca." *Palladio* 23 (1973): 145-183.

CHEVALLEY, GIOVANNI: "La formazione della personalità artistica di Filippo Juvarra." *Bollettino della società piemontese di archeologia e bella arti* 1 (1947): 72-82.

CHEVALLEY, GIOVANNI: "Vicende costruttive della chiesa di San Filippo Neri in Torino." *Bollettino storico-bibliografico subalpino* 44 (1942): 63-99.

FICHERA, FRANCESCO: "Juvarra tra Bernini e Borromini." *Quadrivio* 49 (1935).

GRISERI, ANDREINA: "Il classicismo Juvarriano." Pp. 153-172 in VITTORIO VIALE (ed.): *Bernardo Vittone e la disputà fra classicismo e barocco nel settecento*. Turin, 1972.

LUSTIG, R.: "Filippo Juvara scenografo." *Emporium* (1926).

MASINI, LEONARDA: "La vita e l'arte di Filippo Juvarra." *Atti della società piemontese di archeologia e belle arti* (1920): 9-197ff.

MILLON, HENRY A.: "The Antamoro Chapel in S. Girolamo della Carità in Rome: Drawings by Juvarra and an Unknown Draftsman." Pp. 261-288 in HENRY A. MILLON (ed.): *Studies in Italian Art and Architecture, 15th through 18th Centuries*. Cambridge, Massachusetts, 1980.

MILLON, HENRY A.: "Vasi Piranesi, Juvarra." Pp. 345-363 in *Piranèse et les français*. Rome, 1978.

MISCHIATE, OSCAR, and VIALE FERRERO, MERCEDES: "Disegni e incisione di Filippo Juvarra per edizioni romane del primo settecento." *Atti accademia delle scienze di Torino* 110 (1976): 211-274.

OECHSLIN, WERNER: "Bildungsgut und Antikenrezeption des frühen Settecento in Rom." In *Studien zum römischen Aufenthalt Bernardo Antonio Vittones*. Zurich and Freiburg im Breisgau, 1972.

PINTO, JOHN: "Filippo Juvarra's Drawings Depicting the Capitoline Hill." *Art Bulletin* 62 (1980): 598-616.

PREIMESBERGER, RUDOLF: "Entwürfe Pierre Legros für Filippo Juvarras Capella Antamoro." *Römische historische Mitteilungen* 10 (1966-67): 200-215.

ROBOTTI, C.: "Rivoli—il castello." *Restauro* 23 (1976): 17-24.

TAVASSI LA GRECA, BIANCA: "Il decennio romano di Filippo Juvarra." *Storia dell'arte* 41 (1981): 21-30.

WITTKOWER, RUDOLF: "Un libro di schizzi di Filippo Juvarra a Chatsworth." *Bollettino della società piemontese di archeologia e bella arti* 3 (1949). Reprinted in *Studies in the Italian Baroque*. 1975.

WITTKOWER, RUDOLF: "Un libro di schizzi di Filippo Juvarra a S. Pietro a Roma." *Bollettino della società piemontese di archeologia e bella arti* 3 (1949): 158-161.

*

Toward the end of the 17th century, architecture in Italy divided into two different stylistic approaches. The first of these, "Late Baroque classicism," was a classicizing trend that was transitional between Baroque and neoclassicism. Although abandoning the more plastic forms and spaces of the Baroque, it remained varied and rich and full of unorthodox details. It was also deliberately scenographic in approach. It was the style favored by the Church and the courts. In contrast, Italian Rococo, characterized by free and imaginative decoration, a

reduction of emphasis upon the orders as a decorative ordering system, and a rich play of curvilinear shapes and spatial complexities, was the favored style of the aristocracy and the rich bourgeoisie. Although the *rocaille* decoration that is employed in Italian Rococo architecture certainly derives from French precedent, it is Late Baroque classicism that is most influenced by France. French classicism as developed by François Mansart, Louis Le Vau, Jules Hardouin-Mansart and others, was disciplined by stringent rationalism that produced architecture which was emphatic, unambiguous, carefully proportioned and easily readable; it became the world's model of stately imperial architecture.

Although he followed the great Guarino Guarini in Turin, Filippo Juvarra's work shows little connection to Guarini's. It was shaped instead by a 10-year stint in the studio of Carlo Fontana in Rome (1703-14) during which time he not only worked on Fontana's projects designed in an academic classical Late Baroque manner, but also studied the entire Roman historical building inventory, paying particular attention to the works of Michelangelo and the architects of the Roman Baroque era. His boldest, most creative accomplishments during that period came from commissions from Cardinal Ottoboni for stage sets for his theater in the Cancelleria. Juvarra also found time for numerous design exercises for everything from coats of arms and book illustrations to vast urban redesign schemes.

King Vittorio Amedeo II of Savoy's great building schemes were placed in Juvarra's charge after he was appointed "First Architect to the King" in 1714. In this capacity he designed four town palaces, four royal residences and five churches, all in or near Turin. In addition, he was responsible for the third major extension to the city, designing the Via Del Carmine-Corso Valdocco and Via Milano-Piazza Emanuele Filiberto quarters.

No single architectural style characterizes these projects. Juvarra used different styles for different projects, eclectically selecting in each case that style he considered most appropriate for the project at hand. This free eclecticism shaped the design of his four most important projects. The town palace for the queen mother is modeled upon Versailles, the Church of San Filippo Neri borrows from Borromini's Oratory and De Re Magi Chapel, the design of the Stupinigi Hunting Lodge reveals complete assimilation of Rococo models, and the Chiesa del Carmine reinterprets the German hall church.

Juvarra's career was short—he died in 1736, only 22 years after assuming his position in Turin—but he produced an astonishing amount of work. In addition to the projects in the Piedmont, he worked for Emperor Joseph I of Austria, King John V of Portugal, August the Strong of Saxony and Philip V of Spain. In 1720 he traveled to London and Paris. In London, he became acquainted with Lord Burlington, to whom he dedicated a volume of designs for architectural fantasies.

The design of the facade of the Palazzo Madama was based upon the garden front of the palace of Versailles. However, Juvarra transformed and improved the French prototype. Juvarra shortened, strengthened and simplified the base story by eliminating the round window heads and expressing the bay divisions by means of prominent rusticated piers. These piers carry the collosal order of Corinthian pilasters and columns that organize the second and third floors into a single *piano nobile* story.

The great space behind the new facade is devoted entirely to a foyer-staircase hall. Each end of the barrel-vaulted space is filled with a stair which doubles back on itself to reach a central bridge that leads to the state apartments of the palace. No stair nearly so grand as this had been built in Italy, and very few of comparable magnificence had been built elsewhere. Its plan is French but its decoration is Italian; it recalls the decorative details of Pietro da Cortona and Francesco Borromini. Exuberant, naturalistic motifs appear next to flat, almost neoclassical features.

In contrast, the Stupinigi Hunting Lodge (1729-33) is based upon the Italian star-shaped plan in which corresponding units are grouped around a central core. However, the scale of Stupinigi is so vast that the result is vastly different from the smaller villa prototypes. In appearance and decorative exterior detail, Stupinigi presents the simplest classical design of any of Juvarra's works. Its main salon is among the finest examples of Italian Rococo.

Stupinigi's central pavilion and the diagonal arms that it generates are the focus of a vast landscape layout that skillfully manipulates form, rhythm and enclosure to masterful effect. All exterior spaces interpenetrate in a manner similar to Guarini's interior spaces, creating a pulsating dynamic sequence.

The *salone delle feste* at Stupinigi is truly festive indeed. A cage structure made up of four piers carrying a saucer dome is inserted into this oval space. The inner structure is connected to the outer one by undulating mezzanine balconies and apparently weightless ceiling vaults. The color scheme—white and bright pastel hues—and the painted decoration dematerialize the mass and make the structure seem weightless.

From the first days of the Renaissance onward, Italian architects had been fascinated with the problems posed by the centrally planned domed church. Juvarra was no exception to this rule. His masterpiece, the Superga (1717-31), an immense monastery dominated by a votive church, located on a mountain overlooking the plain of Turin and the Alps beyond, is the most important of his experiments with this form.

Entry to the church is by means of a large, square, pedimented porch with four Corinthian columns to the side. The major axis proceeds through alternating large and small spaces to the high altar—porch, narthex, circular nave, a connecting link comparable to the narthex, octagonal choir and oval sanctuary. The octagonal choir is actually the center of a Greek cross; its chamfered piers support pendentives carrying a dome that is not visible from the exterior.

In the main body of the church, eight columns carry a circular entablature that supports the drum of the dome. There is no pendentive zone and the columns carry a continuous circular entablature. Juvarra combined in the Superga two different forms of the centralized church: a Greek-cross choir and sanctuary, and a Pantheon-type nave. There is nothing of Guarini's pioneering interpenetration of dynamic spatial units in this building; Juvarra returned to the carefully proportioned, individually articulated spaces of northern Italian Renaissance tradition.

The most innovative of Juvarra's buildings is the Chiesa del Carmine (1732-35). It is a Late Baroque/Rococo reinterpretation of the German Gothic hall church—a church with piers that divide aisle and nave spaces that are of the same height. For its nave, as in the festival salon at Stupinigi, Juvarra created a cage structure independent of the outer enclosing architectural envelope. Light is filtered into the nave from aisle windows in the galleries behind the tall wall piers and into the chapels below through oval apertures in their diaphanous vaults. This lighting system gives the church a mystical religious feeling.

The wall piers are tenuously connected to the exterior wall by the chapel and gallery vaults, which are hardly more than pendentives carrying oval openings. They are connected to each other by arches that support sculptural ensembles featuring *rocaille,* doubly-curving segmental pediments. The piers rise through the gallery level to become the supports for ribs that cross the nave and define the units of its barrel vault. The vault segments between the ribs seem weightless; they end, tent-like, as crisp-edged arches that are intersections with the equally weightless gallery vaults. All is rendered in stucco painted in a luscious cream, rose, green and gray color scheme.

Because neither the hall-church form nor the use of galleries was part of Italian tradition and because Juvarra did not share Guarini's interest in Gothic structural systems, it seems apparent that in the case of the Chiesa del Carmine, Juvarra was borrowing from central European Baroque and Rococo churches rather than directly from Gothic prototypes or from Italian architectural tradition.

From the end of the 17th century on, architects borrowed freely from both the great work of the Roman Baroque masters, the older traditions of the 16th century, and even from classical antiquity itself. Juvarra studied, doing measured drawings, the works of Brunelleschi, Michelangelo, Sanmicheli, Bernini, Borromini and of ancient Rome. From these studies he extracted a traditional architectural language that underlay his personal style. Although he chose widely from the repertory of precedent, his selections were related to the particular circumstances of the commission at hand, and were always shaped in new and exciting ways.

—C. MURRAY SMART, JR.

KAHN, Albert.

American. Born in Rhauen, Westphalia, Germany, 2 March 1869. Died on 8 December 1942. Apprenticeship, Mason and Rice Office, Detroit, 1884; established own office, Detroit, 1902. Gold Medal, International Exposition of Arts and Sciences, Paris, 1927; Chevalier of the Legion of Honor, France.

Chronology of Works
All in the United States unless noted
† *Work no longer exists*

1903	Conservatory and Aquarium, Belle Isle, Michigan
1903	Packard Motor Car Company Plant, East Grand Boulevard, Detroit
1903	Engineering Building, University of Michigan, Ann Arbor, Michigan
1905	Packard Motor Car Company Building No. 10, Detroit
1906	George N. Pierce Company Automobile Plant, Buffalo, New York
1907	Grabowsky Power Wagon Company Plant, Detroit
1907	Trussed Concrete Building, Detroit
1907	Mergenthaler Linotype Company Plant, Brooklyn, New York
1907	George G. Booth House (now Cranbrook House), Bloomfield Hills, Michigan
1908	Casino Building, Belle Isle, Michigan
1909	Ford Motor Company Main Building and Machine Shop, Highland Park, Michigan
1910	Packard Motor Company, Forge Building, Detroit
1910	National Theater, Detroit
1910	Dodge Brothers Corporation Plant and Office Building, Hamtramck, Michigan
1910	Hudson Motor Car Company Plant and Office Building, East Jefferson Avenue, Detroit
1913	Ford Motor Company Plant Expansion, Highland Park, Michigan
1913	Hill Auditorium, University of Michigan, Ann Arbor
1913-15	Detroit Athletic Club, Detroit
1917	Laboratory Building, U.S. Aviation School, Langley Field, Virginia
1917	Ford Eagle Plant, Ford Rouge River Complex, Detroit
1917-25	General Motors Building, Detroit
1919	Buick Motor Car Company Plant, Flint, Michigan
1921	Fisher Body Company Plant, Cleveland, Ohio
1922	Detroit Institute of Arts, Detroit
1922-24	Glass Plant, Ford Rouge River Complex, Detroit
1923	Job Foundry, Ford Rouge River Complex, Detroit
1924-25	Motor Assembly Building, Ford Rouge River Complex, Detroit
1925	Ford Motor Company Engineering Laboratory, Dearborn, Michigan
1925	Pressed Steel Building, Ford Rouge River Complex, Detroit
1927-29	Fisher Building, Detroit
1928	Chrysler Corporation, Plymouth Plant, Detroit
1929-32	Kahn Branch Office, Moscow, Chelyabinsk Tractor Plant, Kuznetsk and Stalingrad (Ford) Assembly Plants, etc., Soviet Union [Russia]
1929-39	Glen Martin Plant, Middle River, Maryland
1931	Hudson Motor Company Office Building, Detroit
1933	Ford Motor Company, Rotunda Building, Dearborn, Michigan
1935	Chevrolet Motor Division, Commercial Body Plant, Indianapolis
1936	Chrysler Corporation Press Shop, De Soto Division, Detroit
1936	Republic Steel Corporation Hot and Cold Strip Mills, Cleveland, Ohio
1936-41	De Soto Division Press Shop, Detroit
1937	Chrysler Half-Ton Truck Plant, Detroit
1937	General Motors Corporation Manufacturing Plant Diesel Engine Division, Detroit
1938	Chrysler Corporation, Half-Ton Truck Plant Assembly Building, Dodge Division, Warren, Michigan
1938	Burroughs Adding Machine Company, Office and Factory, Plymouth, Michigan
1939	Ford Exposition Building, World's Fair, New York City†
1941	American Steel Foundries, Cast Armor Plant, East Chicago, Illinois
1941	Curtiss-Wright Corporation Airport Plant, Buffalo, New York
1942	Chrysler Tank Arsenal, Warren Township, Michigan
1942	Amertorp Corporation, Ordnance and Torpedo Plant, Chicago, Illinois
1942-43	Willow Run Bomber Plant, Ford Motor Company, Ypsilanti, Michigan

Publications

BOOKS BY KAHN

Architecture. With others. New York, 1948.

BOOKS ABOUT KAHN

The Legacy of Albert Kahn. Exhibition catalog. Detroit, Michigan, 1970.
HILDEBRAND, GRANT: *Designing for Industry: The Architecture of Albert Kahn.* Cambridge, Massachusetts, 1974.
NELSON, G.: *The Industrial Architecture of Albert Kahn.*
ROTH, LELAND M.: *A Concise History of American Architecture.* New York, 1979.

ARTICLES ABOUT KAHN

"Albert Kahn, Architect, 1869-1942." *Architectural Record* 93, No. 1 (1943): 14-16.

*

Albert Kahn's career was marked by strongly divergent currents. Known as a capable architect who could produce a fine, historically influenced residential or commercial building, Kahn also was respected for his revolutionary industrial architecture.

Kahn's familiar and capable Beaux-Arts style grew directly out of his training as an apprentice in the Detroit office of Mason and Rice in 1884. Within a 12-year period, he progressed from working as a mere apprentice to the firm's chief designer. In 1890 Kahn received the *American Architect and Building News* scholarship for study abroad. In Europe he explored the buildings of the past as well as modern Beaux-Arts designs. These European travels provided the necessary finish to Kahn's Beaux-Arts education. Back in Detroit, Kahn returned to his previous employer, where he remained until 1896.

For the next six years Kahn worked as a principal in a variety of partnerships, and in 1902 he became an independent architect. Kahn was eventually joined in practice by his brothers Julius and Moritz.

When Julius joined the firm in 1903 as chief engineer, he brought with him an interest in the fledgling science of concrete construction. Upon Julius' arrival, Kahn's firm began work on the Engineering Building for the University of Michigan in Ann Arbor. That construction experience made Julius aware of defects in the then-current empirical system of designing concrete reinforcement. After having made conclusive tests, Julius designed a scientific system of reinforced concrete, called the Kahn bar. Together Albert and Julius made the office an unparalleled force in reinforced-concrete design. Soon Julius set up an independent company to supply reinforced concrete, the Trussed Concrete Steel Company.

Armed with an ability to appreciate the elegant engineered solution to an architectural problem and with his brother's expertise, Albert Kahn soon began to tackle the challenging need for industrial design in the burgeoning commercial Detroit community. In 1903 Kahn also was commissioned by the Packard Motor Car Company to create a factory where the manufacturing processes would be organized in a logical and progressive pattern. Kahn designed a "hollow" square building brightened with windows on all of the exterior surfaces. Although the first buildings designed for Packard were of conventional wood-frame construction, Kahn soon realized that he could employ his brother's trussed concrete steel to great advantage, creating larger unobstructed spaces. The overall use of concrete also solved the problem of oil-soaked wooden floors common during the fabrication and assemblage of machinery. The Packard No. 10 Building (1905), was the first factory building of reinforced-concrete construction in Detroit. It had a column spacing of 32 by 60 feet.

Few architects regarded factory design as a suitable challenge to their abilities early in the 20th century; with the steady growth of industry, however, a need to provide architecturally engineered factory complexes had developed by the 1920s. Albert Kahn, Inc., was soon known as the American architectural firm that specialized in this new form. Kahn assembled a team of designers who expertly utilized each building's program and the economics of the situation to create a structure that would serve the client's need. They were careful to create spaces that could easily be modified with the changing needs of the owners. This style of industrial design was evident as early as 1910, when the Ford Motor Company began production in Kahn's Highland Park Plant near Detroit.

Ford purchased the site in Highland Park with the intention of building an entire plant under one roof to replace earlier, inadequate plants. The four-story main building was 840 feet long by 140 feet wide, and it was of reinforced-concrete slab-and-beam construction throughout. Industrial steel sash windows, imported from England, also were used for the first time in the United States, making this a thoroughly modern building. Adjacent to the plant was a one-story machine shop with a sawtooth skylight roof, as well as an office building of concrete construction finished in a more formalized Beaux-Arts style. Between 1912 and 1915, the continuously moving assembly line was perfected at Ford's Highland Park plant, and in 1918 a six-story reinforced-concrete building was added to the complex. This building was accessed directly by rail lines, which allowed deliveries straight into the site. An overhead traveling crane in the skylit center of the building conveyed materials from the railroad cars to the various floor levels, via cantilevered reinforced-concrete balconies. Kahn continued to design buildings and complexes for Ford through the 1920s, including the famous River Rouge Plant in Dearborn, Michigan.

In April 1929 a committee from the Soviet Union was in Detroit making a tour of automobile factories. The visitors found that Albert Kahn was the architect of most of the factories, and they approached him to design a tractor plant. At first the work was done in Kahn's Detroit office; eventually his brother Moritz moved to Moscow with a staff of 25 people and opened a branch office. Kahn agreed to train Russian architects and engineers in industrial design. The Kahn office trained more than 1,000 Russians and participated in the creation of 521 factories, large and small, within the Soviet Union.

Albert Kahn prophesied that the new materials would eventually be seen as beautiful in themselves, creating a new aesthetic. About formed concrete he said, "Gradually we shall accustom ourselves to form marks, we shall not only accept them, but take advantage thereof." Through the use of modern materials—concrete, steel and glass—and construction design and techniques, Kahn brought industrial architecture into the modern age. Concerned with making a good product that fulfilled the needs of the owner and the industry, Albert Kahn fathered a revolution in industrial design.

—JOYCE K. SCHILLER

KAHN, Ely Jacques.

American. Born in New York City, 1 June 1884. Died in New York City, 5 September 1972. Married Elsie Paut, 1913; married Beatrice Sulzberger, 1939; married Liselotte Hirshman, 1964. Studied at Columbia University, New York, B.A., 1903; B.Arch., 1907; studied at the École des Beaux-Arts, Paris, DPLG, 1911. Worked in several architectural offices in Paris and New York, 1911-17; architect, Buchman and Fox, New York, 1917-19; partner, Buchman and Kahn, New York, 1919-29; in private practice, New York, 1930-40: worked with Robert Allan Jacobs, from 1938; in partnership with Robert Allan Jacobs, Kahn and Jacobs, New York, from 1940 until his death in 1972. Professor of design, Cornell University, Ithaca, New York, 1915; lecturer in architecture, Metropolitan Museum of Art, New York, 1929-34; director of the department of architecture, Beaux Arts Institute of Design, New York, 1931; instructor in design, New York University, 1932. Fellow, American Institute of Architects.

Chronology of Works

All in the United States

† *Work no longer exists*

1924-27	2 Park Avenue Office Building, New York City
1926	Furniture Exchange Building, New York City
1926-27	Insurance Center Building, New York City
1927	Court Square Building
1927	Bergdorf Goodman Store Building, New York City
1928	Federation Building, New York City
1929	Film Center Building, New York City
1929	Allied Arts Building, New York City
1929	Squibb Building, New York City
1929	Yardley and Company Offices, New York City
1930	Bonwit Teller Store, New York City
1930	Holland Plaza Building, New York City
1930-31	Buildings at 1400 and 1410 Broadway, New York City
1931	Continental Building, New York City
1939	Maritime Transportation Building, World's Fair, Flushing, New York†
1944	Fort Greene Houses, Section 2, Brooklyn, New York
1944	Service Station prototype, New York City (project)
1945	Savings and Loan Office prototypes (projects)
1947	Universal Pictures Building, New York City
1955	Mile High Center Building, Denver, Colorado (with I.M. Pei and associates)
1969	One Astor Plaza, New York City

Publications

BOOKS BY KAHN

Design in Art and Industry. New York, 1935.
A Building Goes Up. New York, 1969.

ARTICLES BY KAHN

"Do Architects Want Criticism?" *American Architect* (April 1930).
"Contemporary Design in Architecture." *American Institute of Architects Journal* (April 1948).
"American Office Practice." *Architect and Building News* (15 August 1957).
"Tall Buildings in New York." *Royal Institute of British Architects Journal* (October 1960).

BOOKS ABOUT KAHN

KIMBALL, FISKE: *American Architecture.* Indianapolis and New York, 1928.
MOCK, ELIZABETH (ed.): *Built in U.S.A. 1932-1944.* New York, 1944.
Ely Jacques Kahn. New York and London, 1931.
SEXTON, R. W.: *The Logic of Modern Architecture: Exteriors and Interiors of Modern American Buildings.* New York, 1929.

ARTICLES ABOUT KAHN

"Designing the Bonwit Teller Store." *Architectural Forum* (November 1930).
"Home Loan Headquarters." *Architectural Record* (January 1945).
"Office Building, 120 Wall Street, New York City." *Architectural Record* (April 1931).

SAYLOR, HENRY H.: "Ely Jacques Kahn." *Architecture* 64 (1931): 65-70.
"Service Station." *Pencil Points* (August 1944).

*

Ely Jacques Kahn was one of the lesser-known progressive-minded American architects working in the first half of the 20th century. His fame rests on a large number of art deco skyscrapers in New York City, built in the 1920s and 1930s. This style, with classicist undertones, was his preferred design mode. He espoused a modernist position, emphasizing a functionalist design theory and running his professional practice as a model of efficiency. To be modern for Ely Kahn was to represent one's own time. His aim was not to be remembered as an intellectual, but to serve his clients.

This pragmatic outlook seemed to result from his education in the Parisian École des Beaux-Arts. As with many other modern masters, this sound training produced the efficiency for which Kahn was well known. His architectural designs were diverse. He worked mostly in the field of the tall commercial building. He began his career at the beginning of skyscraper development in New York, with steel-framed, stone-clad structures. In the mid-1920s, he began using the setback formula required by New York City's 1916 zoning ordinance. It was in that period that he formed his characteristic volumetric solutions. These consist of simple masses, arranged in stacked cubical volumes, influenced by ancient ziggurats. This phase saw the decline of his use of traditional ornamentation, which was replaced by incidents in the form and shapes of a building. Kahn then went on to become one of the influential art deco designers. After World War II, he combined the setback form with slick International Style exteriors, attempting to make his designs compatible with both contemporary and earlier skyscrapers. Kahn's office served as associate architect for the Seagram Building.

Kahn's design theory was progressive and he was adamant about adhering to modern ideas. Such concerns included honesty in design and materials, and a preference for functional solutions. He saw architectural design as problem solving, and the honest solution as its goal and result. He had an uncanny ability to analyze the fundamentals of a problem and subsequently express them clearly and openly. While his was the modernist expression, he accepted it neither as a style nor as a vehicle for the personal expression of the artist. Common sense, engineering instinct, cost and income calculations were the parameters that needed to be followed to achieve a beautifully solved problem. His designs were practical, economical, highly organized and technically competent. Kahn was a complete designer, quite capable of integrating shape, decoration and color. He was of the opinion that every designer must be aware of the functions of an object and the characteristics of the materials used. He was primarily influenced by the Decorative Arts Exhibition in Paris of 1925, the Vienna Secession and his passion for Oriental art and architecture. Especially his early ornament has the linear, subdued and elegant quality of the art nouveau style.

Kahn's designs are not garish, but rather aim to create a quiet, comfortable atmosphere. He could be inventive, even if his buildings had to accommodate zoning and financial limitations. The sound methodology Kahn had been exposed to in his academic and conservative training enabled him to cope admirably with the changes in technology and taste occurring during the first half of the 20th century. His overriding concern for functional feasibility produced a variety of architectural solutions. His skyscraper designs became influential, since he was a leading proponent of art deco commercial buildings. This style was revealed primarily in the shapes of his skyscrapers, as they became more polygonal than before.

Since Kahn was interested in all aspects of architecture and its allied arts, his ornamental treatments were usually original, and he produced especially opulent entrance lobbies in his buildings. While he felt that a skyscraper should be the direct economic expression of materials and plan, he also aimed at more, namely a combination of structure and feeling. This was usually achieved through his ornamentation. The huge masses of his skyscrapers were relieved by lively decoration, which, however, had to be more than an assemblage of "dead leaves." Kahn saw decoration not necessarily just as ornament. Ornamentation was for him rather the combination of shape, proportions, color and texture. He valued above all the impact of extra-architectural disciplines on architectural design, the study of architectural history and craftsmanship in the decorative arts. His interest in structure and decoration led to the study of novel materials and their applicability for architectural and ornamental purposes. However, he called the use of extraneous materials and mere picturesque patterns absurd. In addition to his architectural practice, he also organized exhibitions of interior and industrial design.

Kahn's ultimate goal was to correlate architecture with both present and future requirements. His lifelong quest was for the "natural" form required of the buildings of his time. Characteristics of this form were the optimal usability of the plan, its adaptability to changing future needs, the greatest accommodation of the user's comfort, and the use of the best available structural material. Accepting function as the basis of design raised these characteristics to the criteria of fitness, not of stylistic correctness. He was adept at using materials alone to create beautiful ornamentation, especially in the form of stringcourses and machicolations. Decoration was primarily created from a desire to enrich a surface with a play of light and shadow. His artistic ideal was "the beauty of a plain surface, relieved by the artist." He believed that aesthetic values are created not through historicist copying or imaginary experimentation, but rather through fine proportion, a balance of mass, and agreeable colors of materials. He was quite conscious of the fact that decoration for the tall building had to be original and could not just consist of blown-up patterns from smaller buildings. Decoration had first and foremost to serve its particular purpose, and could not be taken simply from a pattern book.

—HANS R. MORGENTHALER

KAHN, Louis I.

American. Born Louis Isidore Kahn on the Island of Saarama, Estonia, 20 February 1901; immigrated to the United States, 1905; naturalized, 1915. Died in New York City, 17 March 1974. Married Esther Virginia Israeli, 1930; one daughter. Studied at the University of Pennsylvania, Philadelphia, 1920-24, B.Arch. In private practice, Philadelphia, 1937-74. Gold Medal, Royal Institute of British Architects, 1972.

Chronology of Works
All in the United States unless noted
† Work no longer exists

1944-46 Psychiatric Hospital, Philadelphia (with Oscar Stonorov).
1951-53 Yale Art Gallery, Yale University, New Haven, Connecticut

1952-62 Mill Creek Public Housing, Philadelphia (with others)
1954-59 Bath House and Master Plan, Jewish Community Center, Trenton, New Jersey
1957-64 Richards Medical Research Building, University of Pennsylvania, Philadelphia
1958-61 Tribune Review Building, Greensburg, Pennsylvania
1959-65 Salk Institute Laboratory Buildings, La Jolla, California
1959-67 Unitarian Church, Rochester, New York
1962-74 New national capital, Dacca, Bangladesh
1962-74 Institute of Management, Ahmedabad, India
1965-74 Theater of the Performing Arts, Fine Arts Center, Fort Wayne, Indiana
1966-70 Olivetti-Underwood Factory, Harrisburg, Pennsylvania
1966-72 Kimbell Art Museum, Fort Worth, Texas
1967-72 Library and Dining Hall, Phillips Exeter Academy, Exeter, New Hampshire
1969-74 Center for British Art and Studies, Yale University, New Haven, Connecticut

Publications

BOOKS BY KAHN

Louis I. Kahn: Talks with Students. Houston, Texas, 1969.
The Louis I. Kahn Archive. Personal Drawings in Seven Volumes from the Kahn Collection on Permanent Loan to the University of Pennsylvania. New York, 1990.
The Notebooks and Drawings of Louis I. Kahn. Edited by Richard Saul Wurman and Eugene Feldman. Cambridge, Massachusetts, 1973.
Why City Planning Is Your Responsibility. With Oscar Stonorov. New York, 1942.
Writings, Lectures, Interviews. New York, 1991.
You and Your Neighborhood. With Oscar Stonorov. New York, 1944.

ARTICLES BY KAHN

"Order and Form." *Perspecta* 3 (1955): 47-63.
"Architecture Is the Thoughtful Making of Spaces." *Perspecta* 4 (1957).
"Remarks." *Perspecta* 9-10 (1965): 303-335.
"Structure and Form." *Royal Architectural Institute of Canada Journal* (November 1965).
"Architecture: Silence and Light." In ARNOLD TOYNBEE (ed.): *On the Future of Art.* New York, 1970.
"Harmony Between Man and Architecture." *Design* (Bombay, March 1974).

BOOKS ABOUT KAHN

GIURGOLA, ROMALDO, and MEHTA, JAIMINI: *Louis I. Kahn.* Boulder, Colorado, 1975.
KOMENDANT, AUGUST E.: *Eighteen Years with Architect Louis I. Kahn.* Englewood Cliffs, New Jersey, 1975.
LOBEL, JOHN: *Between Silence and Light: Spirit in the Architecture of Louis I. Kahn.* Boulder, Colorado, 1979.
RONNER, HEINZ; JHAVERI, SHARAD; and VESELLA, ALESSANDRO (eds.): *Louis I. Kahn: The Complete Works 1935-1974.* Boulder, Colorado, 1977.
SCULLY, VINCENT J., JR.: *Louis I. Kahn.* New York, 1962.

TYNG, ALEXANDRA: *Beginnings: Louis I. Kahn's Philosophy of Architecture.* New York, 1984.

WURMAN, RICHARD S. (ed.): *What Will Be Has Always Been, The Words of Louis I. Kahn.* New York, 1986.

ARTICLES ABOUT KAHN

BLAKE, PETER (ed.): "The Mind of Louis Kahn." *Architectural Forum* 137 (1972).

BLAKE, PETER (ed.): "Louis I. Kahn." *Architecture & Urbanism,* special issue (1973).

BONNEFOI, C.: "Louis Kahn and Minimalism." *Oppositions,* 24 (1981): 3-25.

EMERY, M. (ed.): "Louis I. Kahn." *Architecture d'aujourd'hui,* special issue, No. 142 (February-March 1969).

FRAMPTON, KENNETH: "Louis Kahn and the French Connection." *Oppositions* (Fall 1980).

FUTAGAWA, YUKIO (ed.): "Yale University Art Gallery; Kimbell Art Museum, Fort Worth." *Global Architecture* No. 38 (1976).

FUTAGAWA, YUKIO (ed.): "Richards Medical Research Building, Pennsylvania; Salk Institute for Biological Studies, California." *Global Architecture* No. 5 (1977).

KATAN, E. and R.: "Louis Kahn." *Architecture d'aujourd'hui* 105 (1962-63).

"Louis I. Kahn." Special issue of *Architectural Forum* (July/August 1972).

SMITHSON, ALISON: "Review of Recent Work: Louis Kahn." *Architectural Design* (August 1973).

SMITHSON, PETER: "Thinking of Louis Kahn." *Architecture and Urbanism* (September 1975).

*

Louis Kahn played a pivotal role in the history of postwar American architecture. Many view him as the inheritor of the mantle passed from Thomas Jefferson to Frank Lloyd Wright—of embodying for a generation the legatee of "architecture in the American grain." Others view his significance to be as the major precursor or even as the initiator of a new direction in architecture: postmodernism—the last legatee, the first legate. If both of these statements are true, then his architectural oeuvres themselves constitute a turning point. I shall attempt to describe how his work joins two strands that are the striate soma of American architecture.

The easiest way to label and thereby perceive this pivot point is to say that it constitutes a shift, a change of direction from "architecture for the people" to "architecture for architecture." From the very inception of the republic, the contradictions between Jeffersonian and Hamiltonian visions have haunted the American landscape. A superficial but accurate simplification about these tendon-like strands might be that the Jeffersonian-Wrightian USonian vision covers the reality of the Hamiltonian-anonymous, truly functional, grain-silo, steel-plant, atomic-bomb-factory architecture. The latter is the "architecture" of industry, urbanism and division of labor. The argument would go that until postmodernism, for "high architecture" Hamiltonian reality was covered with a veneered overlay of images of rural independent and decentralized husbandry, suburbia and craftsmanship. This "veneer," this "architecture of the guilty conscience" is the "people's architecture" whose "humanism" survives in Kahn's architectural vision.

The manifestations of Jeffersonianism in Kahn's architecture include the veritable workshop of natural light in the age of artificial illumination, the worship of brick, marble and wood in the age of glass, steel and concrete. In terms of the "institutions" that Kahn designed, his conflicts with clients and users amount to an affirmation of individual entrepreneurial research in the age of purposeful atomic-age division of knowledge. In reference to the practice of architecture, Kahn's work constitutes a rearward-looking individual architectural practice in and age of mass, anonymous architectural corporate practices based on production, profit and surplus design value that is alienated both from the building and the architects. In short, Kahn's practice was a nostalgic look back to an imagined "rugged individualism" in the face of the division and dissolution of the labor of the artistic avant-garde.

The turn toward postmodern architecture exposes the absurdity of the coverup of the "real" architecture of production by the superficial urban and suburban architecture of consumption. The turning point in American architecture toward this kind of exposure can be attributed to some of Kahn's key institutional projects. Architecture for architecture, finally, because if architecture remains high art it cannot escape the fate of art to represent: once function as coverup is exposed, the only retreat is to self-reference. This self-reference is to what Kahn called the "idea": the want, the desire, disembodied of its "form" and finally bereft of the actual physical design, the construction, the program. In Kahn's most distinguished and personal projects "form" is but the imperfect "footprint" of the "idea" "behind" it. We can trace this development in Kahn's work as the progression from the Richards Medical Research Building, through the Salk Institute to its final apotheosis in the Kimbell Art Museum.

Kahn's work thus signals a turning from "bourgeois architecture"—from bourgeois art—toward a self-referential, ironic, perhaps even narcissistic "spiritual" dream-world of two-dimensional, ice-cold, conceptual postarchitecture—an architecture which feeds upon the images of previous architectures. This new-fashioned Hamiltonianism is the worship of the idea of the means and methods of production: the progress of institutions as "idea" in the absence or perhaps in contradiction to the humans who work on or possibly even "benefit" from these productive assets. The veneration of the disembodied stock, the spiritualized asset itself, the signal, the icon, the underlaying idea, the percept, the appearance, of the act of perception. The turning is toward a "formalism" in which Idea, pure Form, transcends mere design, self-declared "humanism" or "democracy" and becomes and end in itself—*purity of essence.*

In Kahn's pronouncements this is a straightforward if mystical and impractical architectural Neoplatonism (yet bereft of the irony that it later begot): "I think of Psyche as a kind of benevolence—not a single soul in each of us—but rather a prevalence from which each one of us always borrows a part. . . . And I feel that this Psyche is made of immeasurable aura. . . . I think that Psyche prevails over the entire universe. . . . I sense that the psychic Existence Will calls on nature to make what it (Psyche) wants to be." Inserting the seed of desire into an architecture of need, inserting idea and Form into an architecture of "designing for human needs," inserting Psyche into an architecture of Will—ironically indeed—begot an architecture of deadly, diseased, viral, genetically engineered, sardonic and tortured spectral shades: but an architecture of purity that surpassed Ludwig Mies van der Rohe's most dust-free fantasies. Finally, the reverence of the disembodied *institution.*

The iciness and frigidity, the flatness and thinness, the tenebrous and spectral spirituous esterification of the American grain is perhaps best seen in the rigid interplay of concrete slab shadow-casters which characterize Kahn's mature work. For example, in the Salk Institute's massing and fenestration, the

Louis I. Kahn: Salk Institute Laboratory Buildings, La Jolla, California, 1959-65

oblique wood inserts into the concrete grid which constitute the frames for the windows have transformed the quest for "natural" light to a cave dweller's hunger for the transitional cool monochromatic murky and shadowy refraction of the sun. The shorelight is filtered into a directionless and achromatic diffuse moonlit Californian on-location "night" Western movie-chase set.

Yukio Futagawa's powerful photography, which has become the classic "representation" of this project, has the contrast and the visual intensity of the "moonlit" desert chase scenes of high-1950s Saturday-matinee Hoppie Westerns. Father Sun as presence has been veiled and erased as have all traces of humans (save for the occasional carefully placed, unoccupied director chair as a kind of empty mold for the Californian bodies [not yet made]).

As we penetrate into the office complexes, "individual" though they be, we have nonetheless entered an internalized City of Perpetual Mist. Here, at the edge of the deep Pacific Ocean live and work these fog-bound Cimmerian biomedical researchers; in their move to California, the wide-open windows of the Richards Research Building have become deeply lidded

and socketlike receptacles gouged into the concrete skeleton of The Institute: foreshadowing the vaulted daylight-illuminators of the Kimbell Art Museum.

The transition point between the old and the new, the humanist and the organizational, the modern and the postmodern, becomes, arrogates to itself, a place in time and a dynamism in motion to be celebrated and emphasized: between and betwixt. Fully both this-and-that: "I put the glass between the structure members and the members which are not of structure because the joint is the beginning of ornament. And that must be distinguished from decoration which is simply applied. Ornament is the adoration of the joint." Not without tongue in check is there a self-reference in this quotation about the Kimbell to the Kahn lurking within and beneath it: the joint between and betwixt—the "both" and the "and." I imagine, within his lights, also the legatee and the legate.

The new world of the Kimbell or the Salk is truly a dreamworld both inside and out: with each foray into the place of shades a turn of the spiral around a nodal point: the pivot, the pin of the hinge, the shaft of the joint. In this postmanifestation of historical Hamiltonianism reality is the progressive irrelevance, abstraction and anonymity of the human being: a planned obsolescence that can Now be Shown and Proclaimed. The dreamworld turned into reality, a reality in which the past is preserved and frozen into immobility—it is now as if the two periods of "waking" that bracket the night's "events" are frame and door where reality is on the shady side of the windows. The barred steel gates afore each courtyard of the Salk Institute seem designed to keep the shady inmates in more than the fleshy plebs out: to confine that which may perhaps prove to be a source of pollution after all.

The barred institutional gates of this last resort turn on the hinges of sleep. The sleeping self burrows into the depths of its experience, foresees the post-nuclear, biochemical morrow and thus prepares for it. This architectural morrow is finally the two-dimensionalization of architecture itself, whether in the Roman Numeral Houses of Peter Eisenman, of the Piranesian phallocentric nightmares of Lerup's Texas Zero or No Family House, or indeed of the sacrificial altar into which is buried the fallout shelter for the Nuclear Human Family: the hidden Labyrinth of Libera's (or was it Malaparte's?) Malaparte house on Capri.

—JOSEPH B. JUHASZ

KALLIKRATES.

Greek. Active in Greece during the third quarter of the fifth century B. C.

Chronology of Works
All in Greece
All dates are approximate
† Work no longer exists

465-460 B.C.   South Acropolis Wall, Athens [attributed]
465-449 B.C.   Parthenon, Athens ('Kimonian phase') [attributed]†
450-447 B.C.   Temple of Athena Nike, Athens (first project)†
448-442 B.C.   Temple of Hephaistos, Athens [attributed]
447-438 B.C.   Parthenon, Athens
447-446 B.C.   Acropolis, Athens (enclosure works)†
445-443 B.C.   Middle Long Wall, Athens†
442-438 B.C.   Temple of Poseidon, Sounion [attributed]
438-434 B.C.   Temple of Ares, Athens [attributed]†
434-432 B.C.   Temple of Nemesis, Rhamnous [attributed]†
430 B.C.   Temple by the Ilissos, Athens [attributed]†
425-423 B.C.   Temple of Athena Nike, Athens [attributed]
425-417 B.C.   Athenian Temple of Apollo, Delos [attributed]†
421-405 B.C.   Erechtheion, Athens [attributed]

Publications

BOOKS ABOUT KALLIKRATES

CARPENTER, RHYS: *The Architects of the Parthenon.* Harmondsworth, 1970.

ARTICLES ABOUT KALLIKRATES

CHILDS, WILLIAM A. P.: "In Defense of an Early Date for the Frieze of the Temple on the Ilissnos River." *Mitteilungen des Deutschen Archaeologischen Instituts: Athenische Abteilung* 100 (1985): 207-251.
MARK, I. S.: "Nike and the Cult of Athena Nike on the Athenian Acropolis." Dissertation, New York University, 1979.

MATTINGLY, H. B.: "The Athena Nike Temple Reconsidered." *The American Journal of Archaeology* 86 (1982): 381-385.
MILES, M. M.: "The Date of the Temple on the Ilissos River." *Hesperia* 49 (1980): 309-325.
PICON, C. A.: "The Ilissos Temple Reconsidered." *American Journal of Archaeology* 82 (1978) 47-81.
SHEAR, I. M.: "Kallikrates." *Hesperia* (1963): 375-424.
WESENBERG, B.: "Wer Erbaute den Parthenon?" *Mitteilungen des Deutschen Archaeologischen Instituts: Athenische Abteilung* 97 (1982): 99-125.
WESENBERG, B.: "Zur Baugeschichte des Niketempels." *Jahrbuch des Deutschen Archaeologischen Instituts* 96 (1981): 28-54.

---

*

Kallikrates was an architect of fortification walls and of temples. Perikles gave him the task of building the third (i.e., middle) long wall from Athens to Piraeus (Plutarch, *Perikles* 13), which, along with the other two long walls, was designed to prevent Athens from being cut off from its harbor in time of war. Kallikrates' name also appeared on an Athenian decree of about 450 B.C. (*IG* I² 44, *SEG* X 32, XXV 16) in connection with a repair to the Acropolis wall to "prevent thieves and runaway slaves from gaining access to the citadel."

Plutarch named both Kallikrates and Iktinos as architects of the Periklean Parthenon, but other ancient sources mentioned Iktinos and not Kallikrates in this context (Strabo, Pausanias, Ausonius and Vitruvius). A number of ingenious explanations have been proposed for this apparent discrepancy, but it seems best to accept Plutarch's statement as accurate. Plutarch studied in Athens as a youth, and must have seen the names of both architects inscribed in stone on the Parthenon construction decree and expense accounts. Unfortunately, the decree is lost, and the expense accounts exist today only in small fragments, the names of the architects missing. Even if we had proof that Kallikrates worked on the Parthenon, it would be impossible to be certain what his particular contributions were to that magnificent structure.

In a decree of about 448 B.C. (*IG* I² 24) Kallikrates was given the commission to design a temple and a stone altar for the precinct of Athena Nike, and to provide the precinct itself with a door or gate. As both the southern wing of Mnesikles' Propylaea and the new bastion for the Nike temple had to be built first, it was circa 424 B.C. before the marble Nike temple could be completed.

Set high on its lofty bastion, the tiny temple of Athena Nike, dedicated to Athena as Victory, beckons the visitor to the Athenian Acropolis. Both temple and bastion are slanted slightly inward with respect to the Propylaea, and together they embrace the visitor, inviting him upward through the gateway. Working within the constraints of the small precinct and of Greek religious tradition, which dictated that the temple face east with its altar before it, Kallikrates placed the temple in the extreme western portion of the precinct. Perched near the edge of the bastion, like a winged Victory poised for flight, the temple seems to soar upward—the result of certain subtle "refinements" introduced by Kallikrates (a batter to the side walls and the steps, a rise in the *krepidoma* toward the center, and an inward inclination of the columns), while at the same time it is held in check by a heavier-than-normal entablature (partly missing today). The Ionic columns are slightly stocky, and the lower torus moldings of their bases are squashed, further giving the impression of the muscles of a winged creature contracted in readiness to spring forth into the air. (In ancient times the Nike parapet, added to the edges of the bastion in 410 B.C., obscured

Nike Temple, Acropolis

the column bases in all but the eastern aspect of the temple). Like the Parthenon with its more numerous "refinements," the temple of Athena Nike seems to reach toward the sky while at the same time being rooted firmly to the spot.

Two other temples—an Ionic temple on the Ilissos River and the Doric Temple of the Athenians on Delos—can be assigned to Kallikrates on the basis of their striking similarity to the Nike temple in plan, proportions, elevation and decorative details. All three are small amphiprostyle temples lacking an opisthodomos and having an unusually wide, nearly square, cella, which gives extra emphasis to their colonnaded facades, while deemphasizing the plain ashlar faces of their northern and southern exposures. The tetrastyle Ilissos temple is more traditional in its proportions and plan than the Nike and Delos temples, suggesting that it is the oldest of the three. Situated on a small hill above the banks of the Ilissos river not far from the precinct of Zeus Olympios, where it could be seen from the nearby Athenian Acropolis, the Ilissos temple has a length-to-width ratio of 2.2, the fifth-century norm, and a deep pronaos. Its deity is unknown, and it exists today in sorry ruins. The hexastyle Athenian Temple on Delos, also in ruins, was dedicated to Apollo in 417 B.C. It lay on the right-hand side of the sacred way "squeezed between the archaic Ionic temple and the unfinished platform of a large temple." Despite room to expand lengthwise, the Delos temple is short, its length-to-width ratio of 1.76 foreshadowing a fourth-century trend. The Nike temple is the most compact of the three. Lacking both a pronaos and an opisthodomos, and with a length-to-width ratio of only 1.5, it resembles a *naiskos*. Like a *naiskos* the eastern end of the cella is left open.

In these three temples Kallikrates introduced several innovative features: piers *in antis*, pilasters and windows. By using piers *in antis* in the Nike temple he was able to suggest, in one

bold stroke, both the expected wall with a door which normally closes off the eastern end of a temple cella, and the columns *in antis* normally found at the front of a temple pronaos. On the Delos temple, windows were cut into the eastern cella walls, and four piers *in antis* spanned the entrance to the pronaos. Pilasters articulated the exterior rear wall of the cella, echoing the piers of the pronaos, and serving to remind one of the piers that would have stood in the opisthodomos had it existed.

The Ilissos and Nike temples also bear witness to Kallikrates' contributions to the development of the Ionic order. They both have the earliest known version of the Attic Ionic base (with a scotia between two tori), and toichobate moldings that match the column bases. They are also the first Athenian Ionic buildings with the exterior Ionic architrave divided into three fasciae in the Asian manner, and have more plastically rendered Ionic capitals than had hitherto been employed in Athens.

The temples by Kallikrates discussed above have several things in common with the Parthenon: a wider-than-usual cella (which in the Parthenon was created to accommodate the large cult statue of Athena being prepared by Pheidias), and certain "refinements" that leave few true vertical and horizontal surfaces. Kallikrates may have been responsible for these aspects of the Parthenon, as well as the truncated porches, or he may have learned them from his association with Iktinos, and applied them to his later temple architecture.

Kallikrates, then, along with Pheidias, Iktinos and Mnesikles, was responsible, in part, for one of the greatest achievements of Western architecture—the fifth-century Athenian Acropolis, whose buildings have, even in their ruined state, an unsurpassed grandeur and beauty, and a "bloom of eternal freshness" that "preserves them from the touch of time, as if some unfading spirit of youth, some ageless vitality had been breathed into them" (Plutarch, *Perikles* 13). For his contribution to this magnificent architectural ensemble alone, Kallikrates deserves to be remembered for all time.

POSTSCRIPT: Nearly every aspect of Kallikrates' career is hotly contested in modern scholarship. It is not the purpose of this essay to summarize or entertain those arguments. For a fuller understanding of the controversies surrounding the career of Kallikrates the reader is directed to the accompanying bibliography. Other temples occasionally attributed to Kallikrates (on less secure grounds) include the Erechtheion, and the series of mid-fifth-century Attic temples by the so-called Hephaisteion architect.

—PATRICIA MARX

KARFÍK, Vladimír.

Czech. Born in Idrija, Yugoslavia, 1901. Studied architecture at the Technical University, Prague; apprenticed with Le Corbusier, Paris, 1924-25. Worked in office of Holabird and Root, Chicago, and then for Frank Lloyd Wright, 1926-29; chief architect for the Baťa Company, Zlin, 1930-46; professor of architecture, Slovak Technical University, Bratislava, 1946-71. Honorary member, American Institute of Architects.

Chronology of Works
All in Czechoslovakia unless noted

1930   Baťa Department Store, Brno
1931   Baťa Department Store, Bratislava

Vladimír Karfík: Baťa Enterprise Offices, Zlin, Czechoslovakia, 1932

1931	Baťa Department Store, Liberec
1932	Baťa Enterprise Offices, Zlin
1932	Hotel, Zlin
1937	Baťa Department Store, Amsterdam, Netherlands
n.d.	Housing for Baťa factory workers, Belcamp, Maryland, U.S.A.
n.d.	Housing for Baťa factory workers, East Tilbury, Thurrock, England

Publications

BOOKS BY KARFÍK

Administratívne budovy. Bratislava, 1975.
Nové smery vo výstavbe škôl. With others. Bratislava, 1963.

ARTICLES ABOUT KARFÍK

ŠLACHTA, ŠTEFAN: "Prof. Ing. arch. Vladimir Karfík 75—rocny." *Projekt* yearbook 18, 202, No. 10 (1976): 56-58.
ŠLACHTA, ŠTEFAN: "Zlín architecture." *Archithese* 6 (1980): 41-43.

*

Vladimír Karfík, a member of the CIAM (Congrès Internationaux d'Architecture Moderne), perhaps the most important personality of the second generation of the architectural avant-garde in Czechoslovakia, is the architect of a number of buildings in the functionalist style. The style has been synonymous with the industrial look of the cities and industrial complexes founded by the Czechoslovak industrialist Thomas Baťa. The so-called Zlín architecture, developed by Karfík in the 1930s, is evident in many residential, institutional, administrative, recreational, educational and industrial structures and ensembles in Czechoslovakia, including in the cities of Zlín, Partizanske, Svit and Otrokovice. These cities, centered around the shoemaking industry, were developed by Baťa from an idea into reality.

After Karfík graduated in architecture in Prague, he first apprenticed at the office of Le Corbusier in Paris in 1924-25. There he collaborated on the project "Plan Voisin de Paris." Then, in 1926-29 he traveled to the United States, where he worked for the Chicago firm Holabird and Root, and later joined the office of Frank Lloyd Wright. Karfík began working at the Taliesin East office in Wisconsin, and then he witnessed the design and construction of Taliesin West in Arizona. Karfík's best-known work from that period is his perspective drawing of Wright's project for the Gordon Strong Automobile Object and Planetarium, Sugar Loaf Mountain, Maryland (1929).

From 1930 to 1946 Karfík worked as the head of the architecture department of the Baťa Company. His office initiated and established the imagery of the Baťa Company buildings, referred to as the Zlín architecture. The architectural aesthetics of the imagery were based on the industrial look: exposed concrete skeleton of round columns with red brick infill, large expanses of glass and flat roofs. In fact, the rhythm of repeated structural bays on the building facade was achieved through standardized modular systems of a typical floor plan layout. The basic Zlín module measured 6.15 by 6.15 meters and 6.15 × 7.5 meters. The Baťa new towns of Zlín, Partizanske, Svit and Otrokovice were designed as garden cities with buildings submerged in green. The contrast of the red brick and light-gray concrete architecture on the background of the green is very effective. The Baťa new towns were designed with comprehensive services and amenities for their populations. In his 16 years as head of the Baťa Company's architectural office, Karfík designed and built a number of schools, churches, sports buildings, theaters, hotels, apartment houses and single family houses, all in the Zlín style.

The 16-floor central administration building, completed in 1938, was at the time the tallest office building in Czechoslovakia. It was designed and built with the standard Zlín module in an open office-floor concept. The service cores were located on the outside of the office block. A unique feature of this building design was the office of the president of the company. The six-by-six-meter office was an elevator car complete with its own air-conditioning system, a sink with running water and communication system. The idea behind the elevator office was that time was saved when the president of the company had to see his employees who worked on different floors of the 16-story building.

The Baťa Company trademark department stores were also designed by Karfík with the standard Zlín module. However, the exterior finish was different. A glass curtain wall was employed, with floor-to-ceiling continuous ribbon windows. The structural concrete slab and the floor assembly were expressed in horizontal bands of white opaque glass.

In 1946 Karfík moved to the city of Bratislava, where he was appointed a professor of architecture at the Slovak Technical University. As an educator, for 25 years he influenced his students with utilitarian aims in architectural design under the credo of functionalism: form follows function. While teaching and writing, he continued to design housing, educational buildings, offices, and other structures—highly acclaimed buildings based, as always, on rational principles, economy and architectural typology.

—PETER LIZON

KENT, William.

British. Born in Bridlington, Yorkshire, England, ca. 1685. Died 12 April 1748. Worked as a painter in Rome, 1714, and at Burlington House, 1719; master carpenter, Board of Works, 1726; master mason and deputy surveyor, 1735; appointed inspector of paintings in the Royal Palaces, 1727; portrait painter to the king, 1739. Member, Tuscan Academy in Florence, 1713.

Chronology of Works

All in England

* *Approximate dates*

† *Work no longer exists*

before 1727	Burlington House, Piccadilly, London (decoration)
1725-38	Chiswick House, Middlesex (decoration and garden works)
1726	Houghton Hall, Norfolk (decorations)
1728	Sherbourne House, Gloucestershire (decoration and furniture)
1730*	Pope's Villa, Twickenham
1730	Richmond Gardens, Surrey
1730*	Stanwick Park, Yorkshire [attributed]
1730-40	Stowe House, Buckinghamshire (garden buildings and decoration)
1731	Kew House, Surrey (including garden works and State Barge)
1731	Raynham Hall, Norfolk (decoration)
1731	Royal Mews, London
1731	York Minster, York (pavement)
1732	Esher Place, Surrey (decorations)
1732	Hampton Court Palace, Middlesex
1733	Treasury Buildings, Whitehall, London
1734	Devonshire House, London
1734	Holkham Hall, Norfolk
before 1735	Claremont, Surrey (garden works)
before 1735	Shotover Park, Oxfordshire (garden works)
1735	Aske Hall, Yorkshire (Gothic Temple)
1735	Easton Neston, Northamptonshire (decoration)
1736	St. James's Palace, London (Queen's Library)†
1738	Rousham House, Oxfordshire
1739	Westminster Hall, London (Gothic screen)
1740*	Worcester Lodge, Badminton, Gloucestershire
1741	22 Arlington Street, London
1741	Gloucester Cathedral (choir screen)
1741	York Minster, York (Gothic pulpit and furniture)
1742*	16 St. James's Place, London
1742-44	44 Berkeley Place, London
1744	Euton Hall (The Temple), Suffolk
1746	Banqueting House, Euton Hall, Suffolk
1748*	Wakefield Lodge, Northamptonshire
1749	Horse Guards, Whitehall, London
n.d.	Oatlands House, Surrey (garden buildings)

Publications

BOOKS BY KENT

Designs of Inigo Jones. London, 1727.

BOOKS ABOUT KENT

HUNT, J. D.: *William Kent: Landscape Design Gardener.* New York.
JOURDAIN, MARGARET: *The Work of William Kent.* London, 1948.
LEES-MILNE, JAMES: *Earls of Creation.* London, 1962.
RYKWERT, JOSEPH: *The First Moderns, The Architects of the Eighteenth Century.* Cambridge, Massachusetts, and London, 1980.
SERVICE, ALASTAIR: *The Architects of London.* London, 1979.
VARDY, JOHN: *Some Designs of Mr. Inigo Jones and Mr. William Kent.* London, 1744. Reprint: Farnborough, England, 1967.
WILSON, MICHAEL I.: *William Kent.* London, 1984.
WITTKOWER, RUDOLF: *The Earl of Burlington and William Kent.* York, 1948.

ARTICLES ABOUT KENT

BEARD, GEOFFREY: "William Kent and the Cabinet-makers." *Burlington Magazine* (December 1975).
BRYANT, JULIAS: "Chiswick House: The Inside Story." *Apollo.* 136 (July 1992): 17-22.
COX, TRENCHARD: "William Kent as Painter." *Artwork* 7 (1931).
EICHHOLZ, J. P.: "William Kent's Career as Literary Illustrator." *Bulletin of the New York Public Library* 70 (1966): 620-646.
HONOUR, HUGH: "John Talman and William Kent in Italy." *Connoisseur* (August 1954).
JOURDAIN, MARGARET: "Early Life and Letters of William Kent." *Country Life* (25 August 1944).
KIMBALL, FISKE: "William Kent's Designs for the Houses of Parliament." *Royal Institute of British Architects Journal* 39 (6 August and 10 September 1932).
MIDDELDORF, U.: "William Kent's Roman Prize in 1713." *Burlington Magazine* (April 1957).
WITTKOWER, RUDOLF: "Lord Burlington and William Kent." *Archaeological Journal* 102 (1945). Reprinted in *Palladio and English Palladianism.* London, 1974.
WOODBRIDGE, K.: "William Kent as Landscape-Gardener: a Re-Appraisal." *Apollo* (August 1974).
WOODBRIDGE, K.: "William Kent's Gardening: the Rousham Letters." *Apollo* (October 1974).

*

Today's consideration of William Kent as one of England's most extraordinary multifaceted 18th-century artistic personalities rests not only on a reappraisal of his diverse oeuvre (primarily in the 1730s), but also on the deserved high professional status he attained during his lifetime. Kent's unique style stemmed from his innovative, yet always acceptable, manipulative use of decoration. He often interlaced somewhat flimsy Gothic and flamboyantly rendered Baroque details with classical elements, integrating them with complimentary spatially planned settings.

Kent's humble beginnings precluded neither his entrance into the world of royalty and the cognoscenti nor recognition as an artist, architect, landscape gardener and designer of sculpture,

silver and furniture. This incredible range of expertise coalesced
in an equally impressive progression of projects for a comprehensive assemblage of clients. These projects ranged from designs for members of the court, the prestigious Houses of Parliament (erected posthumously) and an extravagant royal barge,
to those in ranks below, a sensational staircase at 44 Berkeley
Square, London, and fanciful drawings for Edmund Spenser's
The Faerie Queene.

Kent's ease in different mediums was congruent with his
ebullient personality. Despite his unpolished ways, this conviv-
ial man, who ate and drank too much, was at ease with others,
even those far above his social station. The relaxed and imaginative Kent had the ability to complete projects simultaneously,
visiting them only periodically. All these qualities enabled him
to become an ongoing and crucial link in the Palladian group,
espousing the architectural principles of symmetry, harmony
and proportion advocated by Andrea Palladio (1508-80), and
originally dictated by Vitruvius.

This elite fraternity, composed of second-generation Whigs,
led by Horace Walpole, was ushered into power by the accession
of George I and the beginning of a prosperous economic period.
Most of its members were ready to accept the purer, revitalized
Palladian forms and, with the exception of Kent, discard the
oppressive ingredients of the Baroque style manifested by Christopher Wren, John Vanbrugh and Nicholas Hawksmoor. Many
Whigs also belonged to another privileged group, the Burlington
Circle headed by Richard Boyle, third earl of Burlington, Kent's
mentor and key patron.

The moral aspects of this connection between politics and
society were expressed in the writing of Lord Shaftesbury, and
provided an excellent environment in which Kent could flourish.
This also nurtured the reappearance of the Palladian style that
had emerged 100 years earlier in the work of Inigo Jones (1573-
1652), the first professionally sanctioned English architect, who,
like Kent, began his career as a painter. The drawings of these
two exponents were later brought together and reproduced by
Kent's disciple John Vardy in *Some Designs of Mr. Inigo Jones
and Mr. William Kent.* However, the most salient impetus for
the second, more enduring 40-year phase of this revival was
the 1715 publication of the first installment of Giacomo Leoni's
(ca. 1686-1746) English translation of the *Four Books of Architecture* by Palladio, and the first volume of *Vitruvius Britannicus*
by Colen Campbell (1676-1729). Campbell interpreted principles illustrated from these books into designs for the now-
demolished Wanstead, and the extant Mereworth, thus initiating
the format for the English Palladian villas and Kent's architectural work beginning at Chiswick for Lord Burlington.

The measure of Kent's contribution versus Burlington's, both
at Chiswick and at Holkham for the first earl of Leicester, has
often been argued. More important, Kent with Burlington, and
later Kent on his own, incorporated Palladian elements on exterior surfaces, including centrally positioned domes resting on
colonnaded porches, and *piano nobiles* reachable by outside
staircases. The employment of this formal staccato approach
extended from pedimented and arched fenestration to rusticated
ground stories. Kent's individual invention was in rendering an
aesthetic sense of contrast between the design of a severe and
solemn exterior and a sumptuous, florid interior.

Vividly painted coffered ceilings, whose individual compartments were laden with geometric and allegorical figures, were
complemented below in similarly solid-colored furnishings.
These striking surfaces, sometimes including walls, were covered with richly textured silk damasks and velvets, and interrupted by elaborate pedimented doors and chimneypieces, gilt-
framed paintings and, in plainer areas, niches for statuary. This
coordinated startling interior decor, the first by a native-born

Englishman, anticipated the later, more expansive neoclassical
work of James Stuart and Robert and James Adam. Consisting
primarily of ceremonial-type seating pieces and tables, Kent's
furniture designs echoed Italian prototypes. Massive and architectonic, they were often profusely embellished, ornamented
with gilt overscaled animal and merfolk representations, anticipating the even more masculine and more symbolically correct
early-19th-century Regency designs of Thomas Hope. Kent
never personally upholstered any furnishings, but called upon
the services of cabinetmakers James Moore, Benjamin Goodison and John Gumley. Kent also designed smaller silver accouterments, such as a chandelier, a centerpiece, cream jugs, and
a 22-karat gold cup for his good patron, Colonel James Pelham.
Sadly, only a few of these items survive today in their original
settings, such as the suites of seating furniture at Holkham and
Houghton, a framed bed surmounted with an immense scallop
shell design, also at Houghton, and a less documented settee
at Wilton.

All these interior trappings acted as a foil to Kent's more
informal manipulation of external areas, often reminiscent of his
debt to Alexander Pope's contemporary garden at Twickenham.
Both men were precursors for succeeding themes in this vein
by Lancelot "Capability" Brown and Humphry Repton. Even
Kent's conceptions for garden structures used divergent contrasts, whether in temples suggesting contemplation or more
rustic conceits inviting restful pursuits. Their invention had
another side; they were often harmoniously positioned axially
to the main house, and frequently engineered to startle the
beholder. This exhilarating element of surprise was attained
through abrupt placement of cascading water and thickets, while
similar devices were applied to produce opposing, more natural
effects and uninterrupted views visible from different vantage
points. Ponds, irregular paths and clumps of trees, which would
change with maturity, were intermittently placed to introduce
a tranquil effect not present in Kent's interior designs. The
overall arcadian ambiance, present in a fully mature fashion at
Carleton House, is better known at Stowe. This atmospheric
quality was not entirely due to his recreation of the picturesque
quality Claude Lorrain and Gaspard Poussin produced in their
paintings, but somewhat to an outgrowth of his own architectural
development. This axiom appears analogous to Kent's outlook
on his own integral professional performance, seemingly
prompted more by confidence in his own creative genius than
by looking over his shoulder for guidance.

Kent's potential might never have been realized but for his
earlier 10-year Italian sojourn. During that apprenticeship period
he received instruction in drawing and painting in the manner
of the old masters, and traveled with John Talman, a well-
known connoisseur of arts. However, his initial accomplishment
in painting, and a much later appointment as painter to the
Crown, did not evoke success; he was ultimately considered a
second-rate artist. His royal connections won him the animosity
of James Thornhill (1675-1734), from whom he snatched the
commission for decorating a new suite of state rooms at Kensington Palace. This incident antagonized William Hogarth, the
moral artist and Thornhill's son-in-law, who thereafter carica-
tured Kent.

While in Italy Kent procured objects of virtu for well-to-do
clients. This task, seemingly unimportant to Kent's future at
the time, familiarized him with the monetary value of antiquities
and their importance as symbols of status and a reverence for
the past. These elite men often amassed works of art while on
the grand tour, as they absorbed the artistic heritage and culture
of the Continent. Returning home, they became the arbiters of
taste who bestowed patronage on the artisans who built or

renovated their London town houses and country villas to accommodate their newly acquired treasures. Kent won the blessing of one of these benefactors, Lord Burlington, whom Kent had met on his second grand tour.

In the 18th century patronage was de rigueur, and a key component to the development of English cultural life. Burlington "The Apollo" and Kent as "his Proper Priest" personify two key figures in this unregulated but highly cohesive system in which mutual respect prevailed between benefactor and creator, regardless of class. Kent's and Burlington's participation in this type of arrangement was even more unique, as their professional and social relationships were almost indivisible. Neither Burlington's marriage nor his umbrella of patronage and hospitality, which intermittently included the composer George Frideric Handel, the poet John Gay and the sculptor Giovanni Guelfi, ever came between their close platonic friendship. For 30 years the unflappable Kent subtly maintained a favored position in Burlington's household. However, Chiswick was not created as a permanent dwelling place but for entertaining and displaying Burlington's works of art. Although continually plagued by custodial and restoration problems, and devoid of most furniture, it stands as a diminutive memorial to them both.

The spirit of Kent's legacy can be found in today's antique gallery, where his designs are reproduced on console tables, their pedestals exposing compelling portrayals of eagles. More significant is his bequest advocating a unified decorative scheme, which, though commonplace in the 1990s, was a startling innovation in the early 18th century.

—ELIZABETH MICHELSON

KLEIHUES, Josef-Paul.

German. Born in Rheine, Westphalia, Germany, 11 June 1933. Married Sigrid Müller in 1961; four children. Studied at the Technical University, Stuttgart, 1955-57, and Berlin, 1957-59, Dip.Ing.; at the École Nationale Supérieure des Beaux-Arts, Paris, 1959-60. In private practice, as architect and town planner, Berlin, since 1963; since 1973, professor of design and architectural theory, and, since 1984, chair for architectural and urban design, Dortmund University. Editor, *Dortmunder Architekturhefte*, since 1975; initiator and director, Dortmunder Architecture Days, 1975-83; director, International Building Exhibition (IBA), Berlin, 1979-87; has also taught at Cooper Union, New York, and at Yale University, New Haven, Connecticut.

Chronology of Works
All in Germany unless noted

1960-66	Westend Neurological Hospital, Berlin (with Peter Poelzig)
1964-65	Housing and pedestrian area, Gropiusstadt, Berlin (with H. H. Moldenschardt)
1967	Senior Citizens Club, Berlin-Schäfersee (withMoldenschardt)
1968-74	Kleihues Studio, Berlin-Schlachtensee
1969-83	Main Workshops, Municipal Sanitation Department, Berlin-Tempelhof
1971-77	Block 270 Housing Development, Vineta Platza, Berlin-Moabit (with M. Schonlau)
1973-81	Neukölln Hospital, Berlin (with J. König)
1975-80	Town Center Housing and Commercial Development, Wulfen New Town (with U. Falke)
1976-82	Heimat Museum, Blankenheim
1978	Ephraim Palais reconstruction (with Jewish Museum

	extension), Berlin (with M. Baum, U. Falke and R. Hauser)
1978-82	German Steel Museum, Solingen (with M. Baum)
1985-89	Museum of Pre- and Early History, Frankfurt
1986	Municipal Gallery, Sindelfingen
1986-88	Residential Building (House 7, Block 7), Berlin
1987-88	Henninger Museum and Municipal Art Gallery, Kornwestheim
1988-89	Art Exhibition Halls, Hamburg
1989	Hamburger Bahnhof, Berlin (renovation as Museum of Contemporary Art)
1989	Deichtorhallen, Hamburg (renovation as exhibition center)
1991-	Museum of Contemporary Art, Chicago, Illinois, U.S.A.
1991-	Office Building and Four Seasons Hotel, Block 208, Berlin

Publications

BOOKS BY KLEIHUES

Berlin Atlas zu Stadtbild und Stadtraum. Berlin, 1974.
Park Lenne: Eine innerstädtische Wohnform. Berlin, 1977.
Dortmunder Architekturhefte 15: Museumbauten—Entwürfe und Projekte seit 1945 (ed.). Exhibition catalog. Dortmund, West Germany, 1979.
International Building Exhibition Berlin 1987, Examples of a New Architecture (ed., with H. Klotz). New York, 1986.

ARTICLES BY KLEIHUES

"Siedlung Dahlhauser Heide" (with Spiegel and Boennighausen). *Dortmunder Architekturhefte* 12 (1978).
"Building in Berlin." *Domus* (June 1980).
"Architecture Needs to Be Cared for by All of Us." *Bauen und Wohnen* (January/February 1981).
"German Federal Republic." *Architectural Review* (June 1981).
"1984: The Berlin Exhibition." *Architectural Association Quarterly* (January/June 1982).
"Kleihues, Walker, and Ungers talk about their work at AIR." *Architect* (The Hague, March 1982).

BOOKS ABOUT KLEIHUES

COSTANZO, MICHELE, and GIORGI, VINCENZO: *Josef Paul Kleihues Architetture museali.* Milan, 1991.
O'REGAN, JOHN (ed.): *Josef Paul Kleihues.* Dublin, 1983.
SHKAPICH, KIM (ed.): *Josef Paul Kleihues: Museum Projects.* New York, 1989.

ARTICLES ABOUT KLEIHUES

Architecture and Urbanism, special issue (October 1986).
BRANDOLINI, S.: "Josef Paul Kleihues: due progetti recenti." *Casabella* 50 (December 1986).
DOUBILET, S.: "Modernism Embracing the Gothic." *Progressive Architecture* 71 (May 1990).
"J. P. Kleihues: Recent Work." *Lotus International* 15 (1977).
"Junge Berliner Architekten." *Deutsche Bauzeitung* 8 (1968).
KNOBEL, LANCE: "Kleihues Complexities." *Architectural Review* (July 1981).
LAMPUGNANI, V. M.: "Towards a Poetic Rationalism" [interview]. *Domus* (September 1991).
"Landesgalerie Düsseldorf." *Domus,* No. 4 (1976).

"The Museum of Ancient History in Frankfurt." *Casabella* (June 1982).

2C *Construccion de la Ciudad*, special issue (Barcelona, June/September 1977).

"Work by J. P. Kleihues." *Space Design* 10 (1977).

*

Josef-Paul Kleihues is the most prominent German exponent of rationalism, together with Oswald Mathias Ungers. He describes himself as a "poetic rationalist." Clarity of forms, strict principles of order, purist geometry, a functional approach, contemporary materials and a technological idiom are reconciled in his work with an unusual spatial sensibility, respect for the spirit of place, symbolic content and an at-times narrative loquacity. All these characteristics are to be found in a general context of calm, humor and a certain playfulness, so that Kleihues, unlike Ungers, is never at risk of succumbing to the constraints of his own architectural systematics.

While his early work displayed a preoccupation with the ideas of New Brutalism and structuralism, Kleihues developed a more individual architectural language at the end of the 1960s. For all its originality, however, Kleihues' personal style pursues a further development of modernism—albeit in a critical manner—and attempts to integrate the modernist style with the classical tradition. It must be noted, however, that Kleihues' understanding of classical architecture is less the product of a direct encounter with antiquity, with Palladio, or with Mediterranean culture, than it is the product of his admiration for the great masters of classicism, first and foremost Karl Friedrich Schinkel (1781-1841). It is undoubtedly possible to find a line of development from Palladianism and the so-called "architecture of the Revolution" through romantic classicism and its exponents, such as Friedrich Gilly, Schinkel and the Schinkel school, through the reception of Schinkel's work by Peter Behrens and German neoclassicism at the beginning of the 20th century, and even through Ludwig Mies van der Rohe, all the way down to Kleihues. Kleihues is well aware of his historical distance from classical architecture. Even so, his work pursues a coherence of form and content. Kleihues has the artistic consciousness of a postmodernist architect, without actually being a postmodernist.

Kleihues' relationship to Prussian classicism and to Berlin modernism is most clearly demonstrated in the main plant of the Berlin Sanitation Department (1969-76, 1970-83). The long facades of the three-aisle halls—with their formula of paratactically sequenced pillars—recall Behrens' industrial buildings, but also Schinkel's Bauakademie. The severity of all individual elements, down to the machinery, creates an almost cultic aura.

Again and again, Kleihues has made the serial connection of equal units into a theme. His museum designs for Hannover (1972) and Düsseldorf (1975) are notable examples of this. The museum projects demonstrate precisely Kleihues' sensitivity to a given urban context or an already existing structure. The design for the Heimat Museum at Blankenheim (1976-82), with its richly varied building blocks constructed out of steel framework set on a natural stone base, demonstrated respect for the normative formal range of village architecture with its timber-frame construction. The Museum of Pre- and Early History in Frankfurt (1985-89) self-consciously incorporated the former Carmelite Convent. The unpretentious Municipal Gallery in Sindelfingen (1986), with its octagonal tower, mediates between the old Town Hall and the newer library. The Municipal Gallery in Kornwestheim (1987) successfully reorganized the heterogeneous urban environment. In the transformation of the former Hamburger Railway Station in Berlin (1989) into the Museum of Contemporary Art, Kleihues went back to neo-Renaissance

pavilion architecture in the use of differently gridded building blocks. The historic arrivals-and-departures hall, preserved as an enormous exhibition space, is enclosed by other building elements. At the same time, Kleihues transformed the Deichtorhallen in Hamburg into an exhibition center.

Kleihues, whose drawings are of great beauty, is one of those architects whose designs on paper have influenced the international architectural scene almost as much as their realized buildings. As was the case with the admired masters of romantic classicism, Kleihues treats his drawings as an independent medium in which to solve architectural problems under the conditions of artistic autonomy.

One of the most important aspects of Kleihues' architecture is his revision of principles of urban planning. In the final analysis, these revisions amount to a rejection of the doctrine of the Athens Charter, the set of urban-planning ideals produced by CIAM (Congrés Internationaux d'Architecture Moderne) under the influence of Le Corbusier in 1933. The residential complex on the Vineta-Platz in Berlin-Moabit (1971-77) was the beginning of Kleihues' work in urban planning. He originally planned four freestanding residential blocks around an open courtyard on a rectangular site. Later those initial ideas were reworked into a closed complex, in part under the influence of Leon Krier, who worked in Kleihues' office at the time. The resulting square block was balanced by a second block, and the principle of a continuous border of houses, underlined by rows of trees, took shape in a new form along the corridor of the street. The preferred planning model of modernism—open rows of houses—had thus been rejected in demonstrative fashion. The project for the Park Lenné quarter in Berlin (1977), with its six similar residential complexes, radically espoused the idea of residential blocks. This project did not exhibit Kleihues' usual respect for the historic urban context of Berlin, however, particularly not in scale or in the normative technological treatment of the construction materials.

Having been made program director of new construction for the "International Architecture Exhibition Berlin 1984-87" (IBA), Kleihues was able further to develop his concept of circumspect renewal and critical reconstruction under the motto "Living in the Inner City." Berlin was a particularly significant context for these efforts, since it had not only suffered wholesale wartime destruction and a postwar division, but had also collected the urban-planning sins of modernist architecture like no other city. Confirming the historically grown city plan and the traditional Berlin tenement architecture, Kleihues realized a string of blocks of buildings by inserting new structures and filling in gaps. Mostly green inner courtyards enhance the quality of life in Kleihues' residential buildings.

Kleihues has also made a name for himself as a teacher and theorist, and also through his exhibitions and other publicity work. As professor of architecture at the University of Dortmund, he has been active in implementing the so-called "Dortmunder Modell," which seeks to integrate the different disciplines associated with architecture. He has also been a visiting professor in the United States. The exhibitions conceived by Kleihues, the Dortmunder Architecture Days founded by him, and the IBA events have become international forums of contemporary debate in architecture and urban planning.

—MICHAEL HESSE
Translated from the German by Marijke Rijsberman

KLENZE, Leo von.

German. Born in Bockenem bei Hildesheim, Germany, 29 February 1784. Died in Munich, 27 January 1864. Trained in Berlin

Leo von Klenze: Walhalla (Temple of Fame), Munich, Germany, 1830-42

under Friedrich Gilly, 1800-03. Went to Paris and worked in office of Percier and Fontaine, 1803; became court architect at Kassel, 1807; went to Munich, 1813; court architect to Crown Prince Ludwig, 1816-23; traveled to southern Italy and Sicily, 1823; travelled to Greece for King Ludwig I, 1834; went to Russia and worked for Czar Nicholas I, 1839 and later.

Chronology of Works
All in Germany unless noted

1812	Court Theater, Wilhelmshöhe
1816-21	Leuchtenberg Palace, Munich
1816-31	Glyptothek (museum of ancient sculpture), Munich
1823-25	National Theater, Umbau, Munich (rebuilding)
1826-30	Ministry of War, Munich
1826-35	Residenz, Königsbau, Munich
1826-36	Pinakothek (painting gallery), Munich
1826-37	Residenz, Allerheiligen-Hofkirche, Munich
1830-42	Walhalla (Temple of Fame), Munich
1832-42	Residenz, Festsaalbau, Munich
1832-52	Hermitage, St. Petersburg, Russia (addition)
1836	Törring Place, Munich (rebuilding)
1842-63	Befreiungshalle (Hall of Liberation), Kelheim, Bavaria
1843-54	Ruhmeshalle (Hall of Fame), Munich
1846-60	Propyläen, Munich

Publications

BOOKS BY KLENZE

Sammlung architektonischer Entwürfe für die Ausführung bestimmt oder wirklich ausgeführt. 10 parts. Munich, 1830-50.
Anweisung zur Architektur des christlichen Cultus. Munich, 1822; 1833.
Die Walhalla in artistischer und technischer Beziehung. Munich, 1843.

BOOKS ABOUT KLENZE

BOTTGER, P.: *Die alte Pinakothek in Munchen.* Munich, 1972.
HEDERER, OSWALD: *Leo von Klenze—Persönlichkeit und Werk.* Munich, 1981.
Klassizismus in Bayern, Schwaben und Franken. Architekturzeichnungen, 1775-1825. Munich, 1980.
LIEB, NORBERT, and HUFNAGEL, F. (eds.): *Leo von Klenze: Gemälde und Zeichnungen.* Munich, 1979.
WATKIN, DAVID, and MELLINGHOFF, TILMANN: *German Architecture and the Classical Ideal.* Cambridge, Massachusetts, and London, 1987.

ARTICLES ABOUT KLENZE

KIENER, HANS: "Leo von Klenze." Ph.D. dissertation. University of Munich, 1922.

Leo von Klenze was responsible for creating many of the finest buildings in Bavaria, and for giving a new image to the capital, Munich. He was an architect of genius who, in Crown Prince (later King) Ludwig (1786-1868), found the ideal patron, but he was also a gifted painter who chose topographical, architectural and landscape subjects, a writer of many works about architecture, and an archaeologist who specialized in ancient Greece.

Ludwig had a passion for the south, especially for Greece and Italy, and, with his architect, transformed Munich in an image of those countries. Klenze had trained in Berlin under Friedrich Gilly, and knew Karl Friedrich Schinkel while in the Prussian capital. Klenze imbibed much from his teachers and contemporaries in Berlin, and saw in Greek architecture great possibilities for the future. He wrote that just as Andrea Palladio had adapted Roman architecture to the needs of his own time and country, so he (Klenze) would attempt to do the same with Greek architecture adapted for Germany.

In 1803 he went to Paris, where he was influenced by J. N. L. Durand and worked in the office of Percier and Fontaine. He then became court architect at Kassel, where Napoleon's brother Jérôme was king from 1807, and designed the Court Theater at Wilhelmshöhe in 1812, his first building to be realized. After the fall of Jérôme in 1813 Klenze went to Munich, where he met Prince Ludwig.

In 1815 Ludwig invited Klenze to submit designs for a new sculpture gallery—to be called the Glyptothek—in a planned modern square. This square was named the Königsplatz to celebrate the creation of the kingdom from the old electorate in 1806. Ludwig had acquired the sculpture from the temple at Aegina and was determined to give the antique remains a worthy setting. In 1816 the foundation stone of Klenze's Glyptothek was laid, and the architect moved to Munich. It was the beginning of a fruitful relationship, and Klenze was appointed *Hofbaumeister* (court architect) in the same year. The Glyptothek, with its unfluted Greek Ionic order, Hellenistic and Renaissance elements, and richly colored interior, was perfectly matched to its contents. Klenze believed that splendor and color were essential to make even undistinguished antique sculpture look fresh, pure and at its best.

Also in 1816 came Klenze's design for the Leuchtenberg palace, the first building in the new Ludwigstrasse (which was to extend from the Residenz north of the old city). The Leuchtenberg Palace, with its echoes of the Palazzo Farnese in Rome, was the first Italianate Renaissance revival building in 19-century Germany. Klenze was to design the facades for the Ludwigstrasse, and all of them had to be approved by Ludwig. Florentine Renaissance elements began to appear.

In 1822 Klenze designed the Pinakothek, built 1826-36, to house the royal collection of paintings. This superb gallery has elevations based on the Palazzo Cancellaria in Rome and on the Belvedere *cortile* in the Vatican, but the plan, with its seven galleries along the center of the first floor illuminated from above, and its windows lighting the loggia-like corridor, was ingenious and influential. On the north side was a series of small chambers, balancing the corridor on the south. Unfortunately, the sumptuous interiors, like those of the Glyptothek, have not been restored after war damage.

When Ludwig ascended the throne in 1825, Klenze was commissioned to add various buildings to the Residenz. These were the Königsbau, or south wing (1826-35), that faces the Max-Joseph Platz; the Allerheilgenhofkirche (1826-37) on the east; and the remodeling of the north front, the Festsaalbau (1832-42). The Königsbau facade mixed elements of the Palazzo Pitti in Florence with the sunken-pilaster theme from Leon Battista

Alberti's Palazzo Rucellai in Florence, but the sumptuous interiors had a strong Empire flavor in addition to the Italian Renaissance themes. Opposite the Königsbau in the square is the post office, which Klenze added in 1836: It is based on the Ospedale degli Innocenti in Florence.

The Italianate aspects are strongly represented in the Allerheiligenhofkirche as well, for the building is based on the Palatine Chapel at Palermo, with quotations from San Marco in Venice, and a north Italian Romanesque form for the exterior.

Klenze's greatest buildings, however, are his public monuments, which are an eloquent testimony to his love of and understanding of Greek antiquity. One of his finest works is the Walhalla, built between 1830 and 1842 on a platform high above the Danube. This platform alludes to images of antique buildings such as the Solomonic temple podium, ziggurats, and even the Tower of Babel. The Walhalla is a Greek temple, based on the Parthenon, that commemorates distinguished Germans. It is in a sense a secular place of pilgrimage, celebrating national pride and achievement. It was intended to remind Germans of their nationality as Germans, and its architectural image derives from Gilly's proposed monument to Frederick the Great of Prussia. The temple employs the Doric order outside, but the Ionic (both volute and Caryatid) order is used in the rich polychrome marble interior, which is itself an original conception derived from the naos of a Greek temple. Lighting is from above, in the manner of C. R. Cockerell's reconstruction of the Temple of Apollo Epicurius at Bassae. The glowing, colored walls set off the white marble portrait busts (mostly by Christian Daniel Rauch, Johann Gottfried Schadow and J. L. Tieck) that stand on corbels, and a statue by Andreas Schwanthaler of King Ludwig I dressed in a Roman toga oversees the arrangement. The crowning entablature of the interior is carried on antae and 14 caryatids (also by Schwanthaler), which are not quite like the Greek originals, for they wear drapes of bearskins and represent the Valkyries who carried the dead heroes to Valhalla in Teutonic mythology.

The lower entablature of the interior is decorated with reliefs by J. M. von Wagner depicting the historical and legendary past of the Teutons, from the time of their supposed departure from the Caucasus to the proclamation of Christianity by St. Boniface. Thus, links were established between the Greece of antiquity and modern Germany. Outside, the tympana, carved by Schwanthaler, show the defeat of the Romans by Arminius, and Germania surrounded by the provinces lost but regained between 1813 and 1815. So a parallel was proposed between German unity and the Greek victory over the Persians leading to Greek unity.

Klenze's Walhalla has something of the character of a tomb or cenotaph, and it is certainly one of the finest monuments of neoclassicism in the world.

Links between Bavaria and Greece were forged when Otto, Ludwig's son, was offered the newly created throne of Greece. Klenze prepared plans to beautify Athens, unfortunately unexecuted, although some of his proposals for conserving ancient sites were adopted. Klenze also designed the Hermitage Museum (1832-52) in St. Petersburg for Czar Nicholas I; it is probably one of the very finest neoclassical buildings ever erected.

In Munich, the links with Greece were celebrated in the Propyläen (1846-60), the gateway to the city and the Königsplatz from the west and from the Nymphenburg palace. The Propyläen was suggested by the Brandenburg Gate in Berlin, but is in the purest Greek, with Doric porticoes and massive pylons of a strong Greco-Egyptian character.

As soon as he had ascended the throne, King Ludwig I had approached Klenze for designs for a Ruhmeshalle (Hall of

Fame) to be erected in Munich, but nothing further happened until 1833, when the king requested Friedrich von Gärtner, Klenze, J. D. Ohlmüller and G. F. Ziebland to make proposals for the Ruhmeshalle on a new site above the Theresienwiese just outside the city. Klenze was duly appointed, and from 1843 to 1854 a Greek Doric colonnade, rather like a stoa, terminating at each end in pedimented projecting wings, was erected on a high podium. In form it is very like the great Hellenistic altar at Pergamon, now in Berlin, but which in 1843 had not been discovered. Schwanthaler carved the tympana and metopes, which are allegories of the Arts, Peace, Trade and War. Schwanthaler also modeled the huge bronze statue of Bavaria that stands in front of the Ruhmeshalle: this colossal allegorical figure is placed on the central axis of the composition, is accompanied by the Bavarian lion, and holds a wreath aloft.

Essentially, the Ruhmeshalle is a shelter for portrait busts of eminent Bavarians, set against the wall behind the noble Doric colonnade. It is therefore a variation on the Walhalla theme.

On a tall hill above the Danube near Kelheim, Klenze built the Befreiungshalle (1842-63), the monument to the wars of liberation against the French. It is a solemn and moving building, wonderfully colored and sited, with no windows penetrating its walls. It is basically a cylinder surrounded by 18 buttresses on which are allegorical figures representing the German states; the upper part of the drum has a Roman Doric colonnade. The interior is polychromatic and features an arcade of segmental arches, in front of which are angels with shields. Above the arcade are the names of the German generals, and a Tuscan colonnade carries the massive coffered ceiling. The Befreiungshalle has the character of a mausoleum mingled with the Pantheon theme. It is a moving work of the purest architecture, noble and still in its stunning setting.

Leo von Klenze is of great importance as an architect because his work is a wonderful synthesis of neoclassical and renaissance motifs, with forays into the *Rundbogenstil* of Early Christian, Romanesque and Florentine Renaissance prototypes. His vision of Greece transformed Munich into a great European capital city, with some of the very finest neoclassical buildings in the world.

—JAMES STEVENS CURL

KNOBELSDORFF, Georg Wenzeslaus von.

German. Born on the Kuckädel Estate in Crossen (now Krosno Odrzanskie, Poland), 17 February 1699. Died in Berlin, Germany, 16 September 1753. Sophie Charlotte Schöne was his common-law wife; two daughters. Studied painting at the Berlin Academy under Antoine Pesne, and, after 1729, architecture under A. von Wangenheim and Johann Gottfried Kemmeter. Joined the Prussian army in 1714, reaching rank of *Hauptmann* (captain), but retired because of ill health in 1729. Toured Italy with Crown Prince Frederick of Prussia, 1736-37. Appointed *Oberintendant* (superintendant) of royal palaces and gardening when Frederick became king of Prussia, 1740; sent to Dresden and Paris, 1740; also served as theatrical and musical director, 1740-42.

Chronology of Works
All in eastern Germany
† Work no longer exists

1735   Temple of Apollo, Amalthea Garden, Neuruppin, Brandenburg (later altered)

1737-40   Schloss Rheinsberg, Brandenburg (rebuilding)
1740-42   Schloss Monbijou, Berlin (remodeling and extensions)†
1740-43   Schloss Charlottenburg, Berlin (new wing)
1741-43   Opera House, Berlin (later altered, enlarged, reconstructed)
1744-46   Schloss, Zerbst, Saxon Anhalt
1744-51   Stadtschloss, Potsdam (remodeling)†
1745-47   Schloss Sanssouci, Potsdam
1747   Schloss, Dessau (reconstruction; only partly built)†
1747-73   St. Hedwig's, Berlin (executed by Johan Bouman the Elder, later reconstructed in altered form)
1750   Lehmann House, Old Market, Potsdam
1751-52   House of the Equestrian Bodyguard, Potsdam
1751-53   Neptune Grotto and Deer Park Colonade, Sanssouci Park, Potsdam
1752   French Church, Potsdam (later damaged)

Publications

BOOKS ABOUT KNOBELSDORFF

EGGELING, TILO: *Studien zum friderizianischen Rokoko: Georg Wenceslaus von Knobelsdorff als Entwerfer von Innendekorationen.* Berlin, 1980.
HEMPEL, EBERHARD: *Baroque Art and Architecture in Central Europe.* Harmondsworth, England, 1965.
KNOBELSDORFF, WILHELM VON: *Georg Wenceslaus von Knobelsdorff.* Berlin, 1862.
KÜHN, MARGARETE: *Georg Wenceslaus von Knobelsdorff.* Berlin, 1953.
KÜHN, MARGARETE: *Schloss Charlottenburg.* Berlin, 1955.
KURTH, WILLY: *Sanssouci: Ein Beitrag zur Kunst des Deutschen Rokoko.* Berlin, 1970.
STREICHHAN, ANNALIESE: *Knobelsdorff und das friderizianische Rokoko.* Burg bei Magdeburg, Germany, 1932.
WEISE, A.: *Sanssouci und Friedrich der Grosse.* Jena, 1925.

ARTICLES ABOUT KNOBELSDORFF

GIERSBERG, HANS JOACHIM: "Studien zur Architektur des 18. Jahrhunderts in Berlin und Potsdam." Ph.D. dissertation. Humboldt Universität, Berlin, 1975.

*

At the beginning of the 18th century the dominant architectural style in Berlin (then a comparatively small town on the Spree) was Baroque: The two great masterpieces of that style were the Royal Palace by Andreas Schlüter (ca. 1664-1714) and the Zeughaus by Johann Arnold Nering, Schlüter and Jean de Bodt. It is a tragedy of European dimensions that Schlüter's great Schloss was wantonly destroyed for doctrinaire political reasons by the East German regime after World War II.

With the Enlightenment (or *Aufklärung,* as it is known in Germany) came an interest in architectural developments in France and England, and in Prussia under King Frederick II (1712-86), French and English influences dominated taste. It is particularly true that in parts of the German-speaking lands where Protestantism was the favored religion, a Palladian Revival derived from England occurred, although this was sporadic.

George Wenzeslaus von Knobelsdorff: Schloss Sanssouci, Potsdam, Germany, 1745-47

Frederick's enthusiasms for things French, Italian and English meant that no style was de rigueur, and themes were developed simultaneously. The brilliant king attracted men of genius to his court, and many talents contributed to the provision of architecture of considerable variety.

Unquestionably the most important of these men with extraordinary ability and creative imagination was Georg Wenzeslaus von Knobelsdorff (1699-1753), a Prussian aristocrat and army officer, who retired from the army with the rank of *Hauptmann* in 1729 because of ill health. He studied painting with the gifted Antoine Pesne (1683-1757), and architecture under Wangenheim and Kemmeter at the Royal Academy in Berlin. A friendship developed between Knobelsdorff and the young Crown Prince Frederick, one of the first fruits of which was a delightful and sensitive portrait of the prince by his new friend. In 1735 Knobelsdorff designed and built the charming circular Temple of Apollo in the prince's gardens of Amalthée at Neuruppin. This little garden temple has engaged Tuscan columns and a low dome over it, and is sometimes referred to as the *Temple d'Amalthée* in what frederick referred to as his *cher jardin de Ruppin.*

After a period of study in Florence, Rome and Venice in 1736-37, Knobelsdorff returned to Prussia, where he provided designs for the water front of Schloss Rheinsberg that employed the paired columns so favored in French architecture from the time of Claude Perrault's east front of the Louvre. This Frenchifying of the dour castle Frederick called Remusberg (from the improbable legend that Remus was buried on an island in the nearby lake) was so successful that it was said that to go from the castle at Wusterhausen to Rheinsberg was to step from a Rembrandt into a Watteau.

When the crown prince became king in 1740, Knobelsdorff was immediately appointed *Oberintendant* of buildings and gardens, and dispatched to see the architecture of Dresden and Paris: the new king expected his architect to be up-to-date in his studies.

Soon Frederick required Knobelsdorff to prepare drawings for a new Opera House on the Unter den Linden in Berlin. This fine building, the first example of Palladian Revival in Prussia, was commenced in 1740. The design clearly derives from Colen Campbell's Wanstead of the second decade of the 18th century, which had been illustrated in *Vitruvius Britannicus* Volumes I and III of 1715 and 1725, respectively (copies of which were in Frederick II's library). The hexastyle portico at *piano nobile* level and the treatment of the pedimented window openings are both quotations from Wanstead, although at Berlin Knobelsdorff placed the Corinthian portico in the short Unter den Linden elevation, and treated the longer elevations with centerpieces of hexastyle unpedimented projections that are closely modeled on Wanstead minus the pediment. In fact, Wanstead's presence is overwhelming in this great and noble building, which merged court ceremonial with operatic performances. A conscious emulation of the lavish spectacles of the Saxon court at Dresden was obvious, for the Opera House was partly a temple of Apollo that served also as dining room and vestibule to the house, and the auditorium could have its floor adjusted to convert it into a ballroom.

Knobelsdorff was not only an accomplished neo-Palladian, for soon after designing the Opera House he created a new wing at Schloss Charlottenburg: in deference to Frederick's Francophile temperament the interiors were in the most delicate Rococo style. Then followed the enchanting palace of Sans Souci at Potsdam

(1745-47), one of the most delicious masterpieces of Rococo ever created, the plans of which were worked up by Knobelsdorff after sketches by the king himself. It is a single-story building with an elliptical Marmorsaal in the center of the composition. Instead of pilasters or columns on the garden elevation, the bays are marked by means of paired terms, the satyr figures of which struggle in the liveliest fashion to support the weight of the entablature above. There can be no question but that these marvelous creations are based on the sculptures by Balthasar Permoser on Matthaeus Pöppelmann's Zwinger Palace in Dresden, which Frederick had seen when crown prince, and which Knobelsdorff had recently studied. Sans Souci is sited at the top of a slope, and the falling ground is terraced. These terraces are filled in with glass, to form conservatories, and the effect is that this delightful little palace seems to stand at the top of a series of cascades. The one problem is that when viewed from the bottom of the slope (where there is a large pool with a fountain) the facade of Sans Souci is partly obscured, and seems to be cut in half. Knobelsdorff realized that would be the case, and wanted to create a podium on which the palace would stand, but Frederick wanted to step straight out of the windows onto the terrace, and overruled his architect. In spite of this design fault the ensemble at Sans Souci is among the most felicitous in all Europe. On the north side of the palace the entrance court is embraced by two arcs of a screen of paired columns, suggesting once again a pronouncedly French classical theme. Framed between the ends of this curved screen are the sham ruins on a distant eminence terminating the vista from the court.

The Rococo interiors of Sans Souci are among the finest creations of that style in Germany and, with their spiders' webs, porcelain delicacy and charming coloring, survive to enchant us today. Rococo the Marmorsaal is not, however: this has coupled Corinthian columns, giving the room a definite French classical flavor, yet the shape, elliptical on plan, is a familiar Baroque theme from Rome, and alludes to a derivation from the Pantheon itself. The overall effect is grave and gay, antique and modern, and encapsulates Knobelsdorff's ability to pull many themes together in his designs, and thus suggest a wide eclecticism of culture and learning.

Knobelsdorff was also responsible for the more sedate Stadtschloss in Potsdam (1744-51), which also combined classical and Rococo architectural motifs. After 1746, however, he quarreled with the king, probably in relation to Sans Souci, and ceased to be involved in the royal building projects. Nonetheless, in 1753 Frederick composed a funeral elegy in which he referred to the architect's love of "noble simplicity" and knowledge of antique precedent.

Main influences on Knobelsdorff, apart from those of Andrea Palladio and the neo-Palladians, were the Baroque of Dresden and the classicism of France. He derived his facility for design in the Rococo mode from the work of Juste-Aurèle Meissonier (1695-1750) and Jacques de Lajoue (1686-1761), both of whom were masters of the Rococo style at its most light and inventive. The Rococo that Knobelsdorff introduced to Berlin was confident, brilliant and strongly influenced by the French masters. Knobelsdorff as a furniture designer worked with Johann August Nahl (1710-85), who, as *Directeur des Ornements* under Knobelsdorff, realized much of the interior design at Charlottenburg and at the Stadtschloss and Sans Souci at Potsdam. In 1746 he also ceased work at Potsdam and went to Strasbourg to get away from the outrageous demands of the king on his life and energy. Nahl was succeeded by Johann Christian Hoppenhaupt (1719-1786), who worked with his elder brother Johann Michael (1709-69). Both Hoppenhaupts contributed to the detailing of furnishings and decorations for Knobelsdorff's buildings.

—JAMES STEVENS CURL

KOTĚRA, Jan.

Czechoslovakian. Born in Brno, Czechoslovakia, 1871. Died in Prague, 1923. Studied at the Baugewerbeschule in Plzeu; graduated in 1897 from the Academy of Fine Arts, Vienna, where he studied with Otto Wagner; traveled to the Netherlands and England in 1905. Professor, School of Industrial Design, Prague, 1898-1911; professor, Academy of Fine Arts, Prague, 1911-23. Member of the 'Siebener Club,' Vienna, and chairman of the Mánes group, Prague.

Chronology of Works
All in Czechoslovakia unless noted

1899-1900	Peterka House, Venceslas Square, Prague
1901-02	S. V. U. Mánes Exhibition Pavilion, Auguste Rodin Exhibition, Prague
1902	Mácha House, Bechyně, Prague
1902-03	Trmal House, Prague-Strasnice
1904	Sucharda House, Prague
1905-06	Tonder House, St. Gilgen, Austria
1905-07	National House, Prostějov
1906-07	Water Tower, Prague-Michle
1906-12	Municipal Museum, Hradec Králové
1907-08	Chamber of Commerce and Trade Pavilion, Jubilee Exhibition, Prague
1908-09	Laichter Apartment House, Prague
1908-09	Jan Kotera House, Prague
1908-09	Kratochvíl House, Černošice
1909-13	Worker's Garden Colony, Louny
1911	Tomáš Bată Residence, Gottwaldov-Zlín (reconstruction)
1911-12	Slávia Bank, Sarajevo, Yugoslavia
1911-13	Mandelík Mansion, Radboř
1912-13	Mozarteum (Urbanek Department Store), Prague
1913-14	Lemberger Palace, Vienna, Austria
1921	Štenc Summer Villa, Všenory

Publications

BOOKS BY KOTĚRA

Prace me a mych zaku, 1898-1901 (German edition: *Meine und meiner Schüler Arbeiten: 1898-1901*). Vienna, 1902.

BOOKS ABOUT KOTĚRA

FUCHS, BOHUSLAV: *In margine uměleckého odkazu Jana Kotěry*. Brno, 1972.
MADL, KAREL B.: *Jan Kotěra*. Prague, 1922.
NOVOTNY, OTAKAR: *Jan Kotěra a jeho doba*. Prague, 1958.
RUSSELL, FRANK (ed.): *Art Nouveau Architecture*. London, 1979.
ŠLAPETA, VLADIMIR, and MAREK, PAVEL: *Národní dum v Prostějově*. Prostejov, 1978.
WIRTH, Z.: *Jan Kotěra 1871-1923*. Exhibition catalog. Prague, 1926.

*

At the turn of the century, Czech architecture, along with French, English, German, Austrian, Hungarian and Russian architecture, entered the era of a new artistic movement: art nouveau. Called "Secession," as in Austria, the Czech art nouveau was not merely an effort to dispense with historicism, but sought to create original and independent principles of form and decorative elements of a new style.

Prague architect Jan Kotěra, a pupil of the Viennese modernist architect Otto Wagner, accomplished in his designs the application of a functional layout and volume to counter the aesthetics of eclecticism. Simultaneously, Kotěra asserted the requirement of truthfulness in architecture; to counter a slavish respect for the tradition and imitation of historical motifs, he required a creative search for the new. Finally, to counter the prevalent interest in treatment and embellishment of a facade, Kotěra's design principles asked for consideration of a building's purpose and volume, whose structural elements are not to be concealed. In 1910 Kotěra was appointed professor of architecture at the Academy of Fine Arts in Prague. His teaching greatly influenced the new generation of architects in Bohemia.

In the midst of the development of art nouveau, which spread rapidly in European architecture, the evolution of modern Czech architecture was characterized by individual architects forming a homogeneous group noted for its marked rationalism. Apart from the work of Kotěra, this is seen in the designs of the rest of the pioneers of Czech modernism: Otakar Novotný, Josef Gočár and Pavel Janák. Their familiarity with contemporary European art enabled them to be in touch with the progressive ideas of Otto Wagner, Adolf Loos, H. P. Berlage, Henry van de Velde, Tony Garnier, Auguste Perret and Peter Behrens. The architectural ideas of layout, volume, structure and form were developed in an entirely original manner. Thus Kotěra consistently enhanced serviceability and simplicity of form using traditional building materials.

The first significant art nouveau design by Kotěra, the Peterka House (1899-1900) on the Wenceslas Square in Prague, is a mixed-use row-building whose functions are clearly expressed on the front elevation. Other notable art nouveau projects are the National House in Prostejov, the Chamber of Commerce Pavilion at the exhibition in Prague, held in 1908, and the Municipal Museum in Hradec Králové (1906-12), one of the best examples of the building type in Czechoslovakia.

Kotěra's significant residential architecture includes his own villa (1908-09) and the Laichter Apartment House (1908-09), both in Prague. The massing of his house consists of three boxes of a different height. The most voluminous box is roofed with a pyramidal form. The flat roof of the circulation "tower" is crowned with an octagonal lantern. The lowest box top is occupied by a large terrace. The aesthetics of the villa lie in the balance of the asymmetrical composition of the three boxes, in a careful placement of fenestration, and in the brick and stucco finishes of the elevations. Similarly, in the Laichter Apartment House, the materials for the five-story structure are brick and stucco. Devoid of any embellishment, the asymmetrical composition of the building layout and the corresponding front feature the offset cantilevered mass of a piece of the third floor supported by piers organized in a strong vertical rhythm. This vertical rhythm is then counteracted by a rhythm of horizontal lines at the top of the building. The restraining simplicity and the lack of decor in these designs borders on artistic asceticism.

The Mozarteum (Urbanek Department Store) in Prague (1912-13) is a strict symmetrical composition separated from its neighbors by a rectangular concrete frame topped by a triangular gable. The bottom commercial part has the storefront on the ground floor and a second-floor ribbon fenestration. The upper residential part consists of three progressively upward recessed bays of brick infill framed into stepped concrete verticals. This dynamic facade was a precedent to Kotěra's cubist period. His 1913 entry in the competition for a monument to the historical Bohemian general Jan Žižka on the Vitkov Hill in Prague represents an articulate application of the cubist language, which

was widely accepted among Czech modernists. In this design, he collaborated with the sculptor Jan Stursa. Kotěra also used Stursa's sculptures in the Mozarteum.

Czech cubism is the only case in the world in which a stylistic language translated from painting and sculpture was successfully applied to architecture. Czech cubism was an attempt, as a part of the effort for national self-determination, to create a "national" architectural style.

After the 1918 foundation of the Czechoslovak Republic, Jan Kotěra experienced a crisis in his design activity. Architectural aesthetics were changing, his projects for the Prague University did not progress, and Kotěra was disappointed that the new republic did not commission from him any significant projects.
—PETER LIZON

KRIER, Leon.

Luxembourg. Born in Luxembourg, 7 April 1946; moved to England, 1968. Attended the University of Stuttgart for six months, 1967-68. Assistant to James Stirling, London, 1968-70 and 1973-74; project partner, with J. P. Kleihues, Berlin, 1971-74; private practice, London, since 1974. Lecturer, Architectural Association School, London, 1973-76, Royal College of Art, London, 1977, and Princeton University, New Jersey, 1977; Jefferson Professor of Architecture, University of Virginia, Charlottes ville, 1982.

Chronology of Works

1980-83 Strada Novissima facade, Corderie dell'Arsenale, Venice, Italy
1989 House, Seaside, Florida, U. S. A.

Publications

BOOKS BY KRIER

Buildings and Projects of James Stirling (ed.). Stuttgart and London, 1974.
Projects on the City—Projects of Unit 10 Students, Unit Master Leon Krier. Exhibition catalog. London, 1975.
Rational Architecture Rationale. Brussels, 1978.
The Reconstruction of the European City. Brussels, 1978.
The City within the City (ed.). Rome, 1979.
Analisi e progetto per una citta in pericolo. Exhibition catalog. Rome, 1979.
Contreprojets Controprogetti Counterprojects. With Maurice Culot. Brussels, 1980.
Südliche Friedrichstadt. With Maurice Culot. Boissano, Italy, 1981.
Leon Krier Drawings 1967-1980. New York, 1981.

ARTICLES BY KRIER

"Progetti di Leon Krier 1968-72." *Controspazio* 10 (1972).
"Projects on the City." *Lotus* 11 (1976).
"The City within the City." *Architectural Design* (March 1977).
"Cities within the City: Projects on London and Paris." *Architecture and Urbanism* (November 1977).
"The Blind Spot." *Architectural Design* (April 1978).
"The Lesson of the Urban Block." *Lotus* 18 (1978).
"The Consumption of Culture." *Oppositions* 14 (1978).
"The Fable of the Spoon and the Fork." *Architectural Design* 2 (1979).

"A Proposal for the Motorway—Athens/Piraeus" and "The Berlin Tiergarten." *Lotus* 31 (1981).

"Look Back in Anger: Architects and the Fear of Architecture; or, 'Forward, Comrades, Let's Go Back'." *Domus* (December 1981).

"Classical Architecture and Vernacular Building." *Architectural Design* 52 (1982).

"Krier on Speer." *Architectural Review* (February 1983).

"The Love of Ruins, the Ruins of Love." *Modulus* 16 (1983).

"Communities versus Zones" and "A Small Fertile Island." *Lotus* 36 (1983).

"The Reconstruction of Vernacular Building and Classical Architecture." *Architects' Journal* (12 September 1984).

"The Reconstruction of the European City: Outline for a Charta." In *Acts of the Seventh Congress of UIA*, Cairo, 1985.

"Completion of Washington." *Lotus* 50 (1986).

"House at Seaside." *Architectural Design* 8 (1986).

"Architecture of Desire." *Architectural Design* 4 (1986).

BOOKS ABOUT KRIER

FRIEDMAN, MILDRED S. (ed.): *City Segments*. Exhibition catalog. Minneapolis, Minnesota, 1980.

KLOTZ, HEINRICH: *The History of Postmodern Architecture*. Cambridge, Massachusetts, 1988.

KRIER, ROB: *Urban Space*. London, 1979.

Leon Krier, La ricostruzione della citta europea. Exhibition catalog. Verona, 1980.

QUATTROCCOLO, FULVIO: *50 disegni di architettura*. Exhibition catalog. Bra, Italy, 1980.

ARTICLES ABOUT KRIER

DUTTON, THOMAS A.: "Cities, Cultures, and Resistance: Beyond Leon Krier and the Postmodern Condition." *Journal of Architectural Education* (Winter 1989).

EISENMAN, PETER: "Interview with Leon Krier." *Skyline* (February 1983).

GRUMBACH, ANTOINE: "Les Frères Krier." *Architecture d'aujourd'hui* (July 1975).

JAMES, SUSAN P.: "Leon Krier: Theory, Practice." Thesis. Washington University, St. Louis, Missouri, 1978.

KOENIG, G. K.: "Projects in a Bottle." *Casabella* (November 1972).

"Leon Krier, Houses, Palaces, and Cities." *Architectural Design* Profile 54 (September 1984).

MAXWELL, ROBERT: "Culot-Krier." *Architectural Design* (March 1977).

MURPHY, J.: "A Gate at the Seaside." *Progressive Architecture* (December 1989).

*

No one can accuse Leon Krier of standing in the shadow of his older brother Rob. While their earlier works shared many similarities—understandable given their relationship and close association—Leon Krier has evolved into one of the leading theoreticians of his generation, in many ways epitomizing the post-1968 attitude with his dictum "I can only make Architecture, because I do not build; I do not build, because I am an Architect" (*Leon Krier; Drawings 1967-1980*).

From the mid-1960s to the early 1970s, Leon Krier became acquainted with the work of O. M. Ungers, where Rob Krier was working, and worked with James Stirling on such projects as the Siemens AG proposal (1969) and Derby city center (1970),

and with Josef-Paul Kleihues on the Berlin-Wedding housing block (1971). His foundation thus coincides with the reawakening critique of the role of history and the traditional city, that one also finds in the writings of Aldo Rossi and the Tendenza architects.

But Leon Krier was above all investigating an architecture aligned with Maurice Culot and the ARAU in post-1968 Bruxelles which declared war on modern capitalist architecture and its destruction of the city: "As far as we are concerned . . . the problem of urban form cannot be treated separately from the urban struggle" (M. Culot, "The Counter-Projects," *Contre-projets*). Indeed, Krier was involved in "a global strategy for the reconstruction of the European city" which called for a city again based on streets, squares and urban quarters, one which integrated all functions of urban life in pedestrian-scale areas. Leon Krier's proposals, like Culot's counterprojects, rely on a typology and morphology structures and spaces not unlike those of Rob Krier or Ungers. But there is an adamant demand that preindustrial forms be used, and above all Krier champions a return to a classicism in architecture. Krier believes that "the rejection of Classical Architecture has entailed a renunciation of the universal and human principles on which architecture has been founded for thousands of years. . . . The real point is that architecture can be good or bad, just as there is a human and an inhuman way of producing and using architecture. . . . Architecture is not politics: it is being used for political ends" (L. Krier, "Look back in anger," *Domus* 623). By advocating a retrogressive stand, "Leon Krier thus moved on to a solitary reconstruction of the universe, resting the answer to the failure of modernist aspirations on a classicism idealized by archaeology. So his city has become an idealized replica—rather like the restoration work of Viollet-le-Duc—of a theoretical Gothic-classical city" ("Imitating the city," *Lotus International 33,* 3).

From his proposal for extending the Willibrord Abbey in Echternach, Luxembourg (1970), and for making sense out of the Kirchberg plateau in Luxembourg City (1978), to his ruminations for the reconstruction of the Mall in Washington, D.C. (1986), and his proposal for the Poundbury development in Dorchester, England (1989), the Krier approach always entails the definition of streets, squares and monuments. His works are often criticized for their repetitiveness, yet one cannot fail to recognize that inherent in this repetitiveness and predictability—that is, a stubborn use of parallel charts in the manner of J. N. L. Durand to illustrate the appropriateness of a Krier plan versus other alternatives, or his use of pseudo-Tuscan motifs with oversized pilasters, heavy timber trusses and billowing curtains—is simply an attempt to discredit vestiges of an industrial society which Krier opposes.

What makes Krier's arguments very seductive is the manner in which they are presented. He relies on exquisitely crafted Piranesi-like ink drawings. His imagery evokes a freshness and breeziness. Similar to Le Corbusier's freehand drawings, Krier's sketchy renderings include stout figures (here clothed), streamlined biplanes, winged dirigibles and Tuscan landscapes. If one were to ignore these and other scalar indicators, the principal spaces that he proposes would appear to possess medieval qualities, what one finds for instance in San Gimigniano's narrow alleys and human-scaled open plazas. But the reality is another, as the political agenda for reinventing preindustrial craft conflicts with the images of gigantic public loggias found in the "Roma Interrota" and Bremen-Teerhof projects, structures that require all of postindustrial technology's gymnastics. As one can see in the proposal for his hometown of Echternach (1970), Krier is not above altering scale for his own means. What is too small is shown larger, what would be large is indicated smaller.

Krier summarizes his explorations in simple categories such as "The Three Models to Conceive Urban Spaces," "Parallel of Cities—Quarters-Wards; the Measure, 10 Minutes on Foot" or "The Building-Block and its Specific Size," because, as Colin Rowe writes, "to attract attention of even a small public requires the exercise of a relentless simplification. The message must be direct and elementary. It should involve much reiteration and a minimum of fastidious reservation" (C. Rowe, "The Revolt of the Senses," *Architectural Design* 54:7/8, p. 7). The appeal of Krier's approach, according to Thomas A. Dutton, is that it involves "a search for authenticity," but he warns that it "is not a search grounded in reality, but in a retreat from reality, in the fantasy world of idealism" (*Journal of Architectural Education,* 4).

Until his recent tower house in the exclusive resort town of Seaside, Florida (1989), Krier had not built, save for the "Strada Novissima" portico at the 1980 Venice Biennale, an intervention full of satire and irony reflecting ". . . his programmatic statement that progress in architecture ought not to be equated with technical progress" (Heinrich Klotz, *The History of Postmodern Architecture,* p. 300). His current forays under royal tutelage in Dorchester may indeed result in urban experiments that satisfy Krier's quest for classically conceived pedestrian precincts, but without the political agenda of his formative investigations.

—GERARDO BROWN-MANRIQUE

KRIER, Rob.

Luxembourg. Born in Grevenmacher, Luxembourg, 10 June 1938; settled in Vienna, Austria, 1975. Married Gudrun Schnitzer, 1964. Studied at the Lycée Classique, Echternach, Luxembourg, 1951-59; Technical University, Munich, 1959-64, Dip.Ing.Arch. Worked in the offices of O. M. Ungers, Cologne and Berlin, 1956-66, and Frei Otto, Berlin and Stuttgart, 1967-70. Assistant instructor, University of Stuttgart, 1973-75; guest professor, École Polytechnique Fédérale, Lausanne, 1975; pro fessor, and head of Design Institute, since 1976, and dean of architecture and interior design, 1979-81, Technical University, Vienna. In private practice as architect and urban planner, Vienna, since 1976.

Chronology of Works

1968-70	Siemer House, Warmbronn, Stuttgart, Germany
1974-75	Dickes House, Bridel, Luxembourg
1977-80	Social Housing, Ritterstrasse South, Kreuzberg, Berlin, Germany
1977-82	Social Housing, Ritterstrasse North, Kreuzberg, Berlin, Germany
1978-84	Social Housing, Spandau, Berlin, Germany
1980-84	Social Housing, Wilmersdorf, Berlin, Germany
1982-87	Social Housing, Rauchstrasse, Tiergarten, Berlin, Germany
1982-88	Social Housing, Breitenfurter Strasse, Vienna, Austria
1983-86	Social Housing, Hirschstettenerstrasse, Vienna, Austria
1983-87	Social Housing, Schrankenberggasse, Vienna, Austria
1985-89	Social Housing, Forellenweg, Salzburg, Austria
1986-88	Social Housing, Schinkelplatz, Kreuzberg, Berlin, Germany
1986-88	Facade for a hotel, Salzburg, Germany
1987-89	Quartier Saint-Germain, Amiens, France
1988-91	Altendorf, Mühlheim an der Ruhr, Germany
1990-92	Apartment building, Bilbao, Spain

Publications

BOOKS BY KRIER

Stadtraum in Theorie und Praxis. Stuttgart, 1975; as *Urban Space,* New York and London, 1979.
Notizen am Rande: Sketch Book. Berlin, 1975.
On Architecture. London, 1982.
Rob Krier: Urban Projects 1968-1982. New York, 1982.
Architectural Composition. London, 1985.

ARTICLES BY KRIER

"City Divided into Building Plots: Dwelling on the Ritterstrasse, Berlin, South Friedrichstadt, 1977-1980" and "South Friedrichstadt: Scheme for an Ideal Project for the Friedrichstadt Zone." *Lotus* 28 (1980).
"The White House." *Architectural Design* 52 (January/February 1982).
"Ritterstrasse Housing." *Lotus* 41 (1984).

BOOKS ABOUT KRIER

KLOTZ, HEINRICH: *The History of Postmodern Architecture.* Cambridge, Massachusetts, 1988.

ARTICLES ABOUT KRIER

"Projekte für die Internationale Bauausstellung Berlin 1984." *Schriftenreihe zu IBA.* Vol. 2. Berlin, 1981.
"Rauchstrasse Berlin." *Architectural Review* (March 1986).
"Rob Krier: Interview." *Stadtbauwelt* (December 1983).
"Rob Krier: Projects." *Space Design* (October 1978).
"Rob Krier: Urban Space." *Architectural Design* 18 (1978/79).
"The Work of Rob Krier." *Architecture and Urbanism* (June 1977).
"The Work of Rob Krier." *Nueva forma* (Madrid, April 1973).
"The Work of Rob Krier." *Nueva forma* (Madrid, February 1975).

---

*

The architecture of Rob Krier is characterized by its unabashed reliance on variations. Whether it is the design of a dwelling's central space, exterior facades or the composition of buildings around a public space, Krier begins by investigating all possible alternatives, and then adamantly using any number of them in preparing the specific proposals. One finds this in many housing complexes which he has been able to realize in Berlin and elsewhere, but especially in the urban design schemes which Krier has prepared since the mid-1970s.

Krier was influenced early in his career by O. M. Ungers, in whose office he worked in the mid-1960s. Ungers was at the time preparing such seminal proposals as the T. H. Twente dormitory complex in Enschede and the Grünzug-Süd project in Cologne-Zollstock; the seeds of building typology and urban

Rob Krier: Social Housing, Breitenfurter Strasse, Vienna, Austria, 1982-88

morphology, the bases for Ungers' proposals, were implanted then. Krier later put forth his own theories in *Stadtraum in Theorie und Praxis,* written primarily between 1967 and 1970. It was than that his brother Leon joined him in discussions, a period when their theoretical positions seemed to merge.

By the time *Stadtraum* was published, Rob Krier had built two small projects, the Siemer House near Stuttgart (1968) and the Dickes House in Bridel, Luxembourg (1974), rather modest structures which hinted at his future course. But as Kenneth Frampton has observed, ''Krier is at his best at the urban scale, where minimum space standards find their compensation in the generosity and clarity of the urban space'' (K. Frampton, ''Krier in Context,'' *Rob Krier: Urban Projects 1968-1982,* p. 7). In *Stadtraum,* Krier included his 1975 proposal for the reconstruction of the center of Stuttgart based on an ''archaeologically informed rehabilitation of urban 'wastelands' '' (Heinrich Klotz, *The History of Postmodern Architecture,* p. 296); it was an investigation and application of urban space design in the tradition of Camillo Sitte, ''an unreflecting use of historical patterns in urban planning, their phenomenological use, so to speak, as a self-contained aesthetic system; historicism without historical consciousness . . . (working) outside history insofar as [Krier] uses its products as material, as the aesthetic deposits of unreflecting processes, as a treasure-chest of unprocessed experience'' (Friedrich Achleitner, ''On Rob Krier,'' in Rob Krier, *On Architecture,* pp. 7-8). In Krier's hand, these are rooms as those inside a house, and their diversity and definition are paramount in the design and renovation of the city. Krier himself explains it another way: ''The 1960s revealed the need for a more coherent theoretical approach in the social sector. It is now time for architecture to consolidate the theoretical foundation of its own long-established craft, the art of building,

to re-discover the basic elements of architecture and the art of composing with them'' (''On My Profession,'' *On Architecture,* p. 10.).

Of significance are his scheme for the Royal Mint competition (1973-74), the urban designs for the Renweg in Vienna (1977), and his proposal for the Südfriedrichstadt area of Berlin (1977), which was prepared as one of the investigations in anticipation of the Internationale Bauausstellung Berlin 1984/87 (IBA). This last proposal was a particularly Sittesque vision for a major 19th-century neighborhood. Krier used figural space as the centering element of his urban composition, conceived as series of major and minor public spaces formed by strongly defined urban blocks.

The Südfriedrichstadt area was one of the major sites for the IBA. Its urban design incorporated Krier's vision and has become a reality, fomented by his two interventions, the earlier Ritterstrasse South (''The White House,'' 1977-80) and ''Schinkelplatz'' (Ritterstrasse North, 1977-82) with the reconstituted 1829 Feilner House by Karl Friedrich Schinkel. Krier prepared the master plans for both, more successfully implemented in the IBA component than in its neighbor to the south. Both reveal another important intention of Krier's: ''I have proposed the division of the edge of the block into quite separate sites for the following reasons, the first of which is the most vital: 1) so that a number of jobless architects, including myself, may find work and put an end to the production of mass-produced dwellings, nearly always designed by just one architect; 2) so as to produce once more small residential units for 8-10 families who will get to know one another'' (Rob Krier, ''The White House,'' *Architectural Design* 52:1/2, p. 67). Krier defined the general characteristics of the blocks, inviting several young architects to assure architectural diversity within normative restraints for the urban blocks, recalling the subtle richness of Berlin's 19th-century bourgeois neighborhoods and avoiding the monotony of functionalist architecture.

The design of the "White House" reveals the dialectic nature of Rob Krier's aesthetics. While programmatically it is an exploration in building and unit typologies, and while it owes much to Corbusian design, there are quirks introduced which deviate from this clarity, for "despite his public commitment to a Rationalist typology, Krier constantly betrays through his drawings a highly Romantic temperament, and with this, his affinity for the ethos and grain of Expressionism" (Kenneth Frampton, "Krier in Context", *Rob Krier: Urban Projects 1968-1982,* p. 3). In addition, Krier's unit plans, while developed from innumerable typological variations, are still rather limited and awkward. His designs are highly structured and hierarchical groupings of spaces. Even within the restrictiveness of German housing standards, where every square centimeter ought to be usable space, Krier insists on introducing nonorthogonal spaces as central halls, devoting a large percentage of the available floor space to a difficult volume.

However, the Rauchstrasse complex on the southern edge of the Tiergarten (1980; built 1982-87), also for the IBA, manifests the breadth of Krier's skills as an urban designer and his evolving sensibilities for building. There the appropriate response from Krier was a complex of urban villas that recall the previous structures in the area. He incorporated the still-standing former Norwegian mission into the plan, using it to develop the regulating cube for two rows of freestanding structures, and closed the whole with a bridge-building. Krier diversified his tectonic palette with a variety of materials, not just white stuccoed masonry.

What is most satisfying in Krier's recent projects is that for him theory and practice of architecture do converge. In the manner in which he develops his proposals, Krier is able to satisfy the intellectual desire for objectivity and rationality while preserving the heart and soul of architecture, the idiosyncrasies of the particular, of the romantic. And the results are well above the norm.

—GERARDO BROWN-MANRIQUE

KROLL, Lucien.

Belgian. Born in Brussels, Belgium, 17 March 1927. Married Simone Marti, 1965. Studied at the École Normale Supérieure de la Cambre, Brussels, Dip.Arch. 1951; studied city planning at the Institut Supérieur de la Cambre, the Institut Supérieur International d'Urbanisme, Brussels, and at the School of Gaston Bardet, Brussels, 1951. In partnership with architect Charles Vandenhove, Brussels, 1951-57; in private practice, Brussels, since 1957; established Atelier Kroll, with other s, in Brussels. Professor of architecture, École Saint-Luc de St.-Gilles, Brussels, 1970-71; professor, U. P. A., Grenoble, 1979-81; visiting professor, Miami University, Oxford, Ohio, 1980. Founder/member, Institut d'Esthetique Industrielle, Brussels, 1956.

Chronology of Works
All in Belgium unless noted

1952-53	Chapel of Pont-de-Bonne, Modave Highway, Huy, Modave (with Charles Vandenhove and G. Watelet)
1957	Crafts Workshops (remodeled from barn), Abbey of Maredsous
1960-63	Chapel, Linkebeek
1961	Chapel, Waharday
1961-63	Abbey of Gihindamuyaga, near Butare, Rwanda, Africa
1961-65	Housing Complex, 20 Avenue Louis Berlaimont, Auderghem, Brussels (with participation of future inhabitants)
1962	Electronic Instruments for MBLE, Belgium (projects)
1963-65	Dom Lambert Bauduin Ecumenical Center, Abbey of Chevetogne
1965-66	La Maison Familiale Primary School, 150 Chausée Bara, Braine-l'Alleud
1966-70	Ministry of Commerce, Industry and Mines, and the President's Palace, Kigali, Rwanda, Africa
1967-69	Agricultural Cooperative Administration Center, Nyabisindu, Rwanda, Africa
1968-69	Church, Biesmeree, Namur
1968-77	Medical Faculty Buildings Complex, Catholic University of Louvain, Woluwé, Belgium
1970-75	Master plan for the new capital city of Kimihurura, Rwanda
1974-75	Convent for the Dominican Sisters, rue de Renivaux, Ottignies
1975	Dominican House, Froidmont, Rixensart
1978	City Center redevelopment plan, Witten, Germany (as project consultant)
1979	Académie d'Expression par le Geste et la Parole alterations, Utrecht, Netherlands
1981	Housing, Laroche-Clermault, France
1982	Station Alma, University of Woluwé, Belgium
1989	Home for the elderly, Ostende
1989	Social housing, Haarlem, Netherlands
1989-91	Housing complex, Bordeaux-l'essac, France

Publications

BOOKS BY KROLL

Composants. Brussels, 1983.
The Architecture of Complexity. London, 1986.

ARTICLES BY KROLL

"Le stand d'esthétique industrielle." *Bouwen en Wonen* 6 (1956).
"La vocation de l'industrial designer." *Relève* 3 (1965).
"Réponse architecturale à une attitude non directive." *Neuf* 8 (1967).
"Industrial design en Grande Bretagne" and "Archigram." *Maison* 4 (1968).
"L'Institut de l'environnement." *Maison* 3 (1970).
"Why I Could Build Woluwe." *Wonen TA/BK* (June 1977).
"Construire et participer." *Combat Nature* 34 (1978).
"Can Architecture Be Taught?" *Journal of Architectural Education* (Fall 1981).
"Architecture 80: Doctrines et incertitudes." *Cahiers de la recherche architecturale* (October 1980).
"Our Friends the Rationalists." *Architectural Design* (December 1981).
"Rehabilitation of Perseigne." *Architectural Association Quarterly* (July/December 1982).
"L'architecture et l'usager: pour une démilitarisation de l'acte de bâtir." *Art Press* (June/August 1983).
"Method and Practice: the Alma Subway Station." *Space Design* (May 1984).

Lucien Kroll: Medical Faculty Buildings Complex, Woluwé, Belgium, 1968-77

BOOKS ABOUT KROLL

BEKAERT, GEERT, and STRAUVEN, FRANCIS: *La construction en Belgique 1945-1970*. Brussels, 1971.

DANTEC, J. P.: *Enfin, l'architecture*. Paris, 1984.

JENCKS, CHARLES: *The Language of Post-modern Architecture*. New York, 1977.

MIKELLIDES, BYRON: *Architecture for People*. London and New York, 1980.

MILLER, GEOFF A.: *Kroll at Woluwé-St.-Lambert: A New Perspective*. Thesis. University of Newcastle, England, 1983.

PEHNT, WOLFGANG: *Lucien Kroll: Buildings and Projects*. New York, 1987.

ARTICLES ABOUT KROLL

"Atelier Lucien Kroll." *Architecture française* 39 (1977).

"Bauen und Wohnen: Die Architektur des Lucien Kroll." *Basler Magazin* 11 (1982).

"Lucien Kroll." *Art d'eglise* (January/March 1976).

"Quelques réalisations religieuse de Lucien Kroll." *Art d'eglise* (July/September 1970).

"The Ideas of Lucien Kroll." *Architecture* (April 1977).

DEBUYST, FRÉDÉRIC (ed.): "Trois réalisations communautaires de Lucien Kroll." *Art d'eglise* 174 (1976).

GODEBSKI, NICOLAS: "Lucien Kroll: Architecture et participation." *CREE* 45 (December 1976).

HUNZIKER, CHRISTIAN: "Portrait de Lucien Kroll." *Architecture d'aujourd'hui* (January/February 1976).

STRAUVEN, FRANCIS: "The Anarchitecture of Lucien Kroll." *Architectural Association Quarterly* 9/2 (1976).

WILLIAMS, STEPHANIE: "The Ecological Architecture of Lucien Kroll." *Architectural Review* (February 1979).

*

Robert Venturi and Lucien Kroll are true counterparts, although their architecture has nothing obviously in common. Both architects emerged as important figures in the early 1960s, after a decade of intellectual and artistic evolution that involved candidly assessing the good and bad points of modern architecture, and questioning many of its fundamental assumptions. Their mature designs, developed in both cases in conjunction (rather than in parallel) with their theories, transcend modernism without either rejecting it entirely or pastiching premodern compositions. As Venturi is the prime theoretician of postmodern architecture in America, Kroll is the preeminent theoretician—indeed, the conscience—of postmodern architecture in Europe.

Kroll's career in the 1950s was a quiet excursion, through a somewhat ugly period, made in good company: that of his partner from 1951 to 1957, Charles Vandenhove. Kroll designed a number of fairly modest houses and churches, using simple materials such as brick and wood. His plans show a predilection for irregular polygons, shared by many architects of the period.

What seems most remarkable in retrospect is how continuous Kroll's evolution has been since that time, as compared with, say, Vandenhove's rather episodic development from abstract modernist to postmodern historicist. Kroll has remained faithful to his complex geometries involving irregular polygons, to a straightforward use of materials, and to a commitment to finding modest (even startlingly modest) solutions to the real architectural problems of his clients.

Kroll's maturity may be dated to the years 1961 to 1966, and specifically to three projects: a cooperative housing complex in Auderghem, including the architect's own quarters (1961-65), the Ecumenical Congress Center at Chevetogne (1963-65), and the Family House boarding school at Braine-L'Alleud (1965-66). Also of importance to Kroll's intellectual development was his involvement during that same period with several projects in Rwanda, the former German colony and Belgian trust territory in central Africa. If situationists like Yona Friedman and participationists like Ralph Erskine did not actually influence Kroll at that time (as John Habraken certainly did), at the very least it may be said that they were contemporaries traveling very similar paths.

In the Auderghem housing complex, Kroll brought to fruition a technique of closely involving clients in making the key decisions in the design process. The problem was, first, to get people to come to terms clearly with their own living needs, and second, to get them to negotiate those needs with their neighbors in such a way that their architect could formulate a feasible design. Probably the most important lesson learned from this project was that the diversity of social requirements can be a cheap source of formal diversity in a work of architecture created to satisfy those needs. (Venturi might have noted that "complexity and contradiction" need cost no more than a "dull sameness.")

In building the Ecumenical Conference Center and the Family House boarding school, Kroll refined his techniques for enabling direct client involvement in design, and settled finally upon the rich vocabulary of forms and materials (including many which he had been using for more than a decade) that he was to exploit to astounding effect in his masterpiece, the Social Zone of the Medical Faculty, Catholic University of Louvain (begun in 1968).

Kroll's experience in Rwanda gave him a profound sense of the effects of colonialism upon any population. This sense surely colored his view of modern architecture in the early 1960s, which he characterized as a "neo-colonial gesture" among all the other cultural manifestations of the dominant forces in Western society (*La Revue Nouvelle*, No. 7-8, 1969, p. 5).

Kroll's Social Zone for the new campus of the Catholic University of Louvain in Woluwé-Saint-Lambert, a suburb of Brussels, brought him to the attention of the international community of architects and earned him a largely undeserved reputation as a "bad boy" of postmodernism—a promoter of a kind of "anarchitecture" that looked something like a traditional cityscape put through a giant food grinder. To be sure, the partisans of environmental authoritarianism (Kroll's "neo-colonials," including the university authorities and the orthodox modern architects they had hired to design the rest of the campus) did not like it, and indeed Kroll never really wanted it to appeal to them. The Social Zone was designed for, and with, the students who would live, eat, relax and sleep in it. The dormitories were designed to allow easy transformation of interior spaces by removing partitions to various positions on a modified SAR grid. Their radical exterior appearance thus resulted from literally expressing the diversity of the students' requirements in the (mutable) design and actual construction of their buildings. Throughout the complex was planted, or rather let grow, an "anarchist" garden whose maturity in recent years has considerably muted the original sharpness of Kroll's structures, and makes the Social Zone an ever-more-delightful, half-urban, half-rural environment.

Since achieving the notoriety he gained with the construction of the Social Zone in Woluwé, Kroll has been challenged by a number of projects in Belgium, the Netherlands and France. These projects have involved the creation of viable new neighborhoods, often in areas blighted by the presence of dreary, high-rise apartment blocks. By working with the actual and future inhabitants of the neighborhoods involved, Kroll has developed many promising solutions to particularly difficult urban design problems. His infill housing scheme for Alençon, France (1978), for instance, is an exemplary conversion of a welfare housing project into an attractive, viable community.

—ALFRED WILLIS

L

LABROUSTE, Henri.

French. Born in Paris, France, 1801. Died in 1875. Brother was the architect Théodore Labrouste. Studied at the École des Beaux Arts; Premier Grand Prix, 1824; studied at the French Academy in Rome, 1824-30. Director of an independent atelier, Paris, 1830-56.

Chronology of Works
All in France

1843-50   Bibliothèque Sainte-Geneviève, Paris
1854-75   Bibliothèque Nationale, Paris (reading room)

Publications

BOOKS BY LABROUSTE

Les temples de Paestum. Vol. 3 in *Restaurations des monuments antiques par les architects . . . de l'Académie de France à Rome.* Paris, 1877.

BOOKS ABOUT LABROUSTE

BAILLY, ANTOINE-NICOLAS: *Notice sur M. Henri Labrouste.* Paris, 1876.
DELABORDE, HENRI: *Notice sur la vie et les ouvrages de M. Henri Labrouste.* Paris, 1878.
DREXLER, ARTHUR (ed.): *The Architecture of the Ecole des Beaux-Arts.* Cambridge, Massachusetts, 1977.

GIEDEON, SIGFRIED: *Henri Labrouste.* Paris, 1960.
HOFMANN, WERNER, and KULTERMANN, UDO: *Modern Architecture in Color.* New York, 1970.
LABROUSTE, LÉON: *La Bibliothèque Nationale.* Paris, 1885.
LABROUSTE, LÉON: *Esthétique monumentale.* Paris, 1902.
Labrouste, architecte de la Bibliothèque Nationale de 1854-1875. Paris, 1953.
MIDDLETON, ROBIN D. (ed.): *The Beaux-Arts and Nineteenth-Century French Architecture.* London, 1982.
MILLET, EUGENE: *Henri Labrouste, sa vie, ses oeuvres.* Paris, 1882.
SADDY, PIERRE: *Henri Labrouste, architecte, 1801-1875.* Paris, 1977.
Souvenirs d'Henri Labrouste: Notes recueillées et classées par ses enfants. Fontainebleau, France, 1928.
VAN ZANTEN, DAVID: *Designing Paris: The Architecture of Duban, Labrouste, Duc, and Vaudoyer.* Cambridge, Massachusetts, 1987.

ARTICLES ABOUT LABROUSTE

LEVINE, NEIL A.: "Architectural Reasoning in the Age of Positivism: The Neo-Grec Idea of Henri Labrouste's Bibliothèque Ste.-Geneviève." Ph.D. dissertation. Yale University, New Haven, Connecticut, 1975.

*

Henri Labrouste is considered one of the pioneers of modern architecture. The search for meaningful architecture that could

Henri Labrouste: Bibliothèque Sainte-Geneviève, Paris, France, 1843-50

represent his time was the guiding force throughout his life. This concern eventually paved the way for further explorations that took place during the Modern Movement.

To best understand Labrouste we must place ourselves in early 19th-century France, when political, social and especially technological circumstances were redefining the role of architecture. At that time, architecture was being approached by two fundamentally different points of view, those of the academic architect and the civil engineer. The École des Beaux-Arts was the leading force of the academic architects. Their main aim was the pursuit of beauty, their concerns compositional. They proclaimed a neoclassical idealism based on Vitruvian and Renaissance treatises. For them, the search for beauty was universal and was inherent in the Roman classical orders. The academic architects proclaimed monumental architecture as the highest form of art. They considered cut stone and masonry the only noble materials worthy of such expression.

The gap between the academic architects and the engineers grew as new materials of construction were developed. The concerns of the engineers were more specific in nature. They embodied issues such as utility, structural economy and efficiency, and required a more scientific understanding of the materials. The École des Beaux-Arts regarded those concerns as irrelevant when weighed against the emblematic responsibility of monumental architecture.

Labrouste, aware of the dilemma confronting architecture, tried to bridge the gap between the two views. He attempted to combine in his architecture classical principles through a rational approach toward technology and materials. He was trained at the École des Beaux-Arts, and since his early years showed a keen awareness of the stale conservatism and narrow-minded approach of the academy. Having won the Grand Prix in 1824, Labrouste was sent to the French Academy in Rome to further his studies in classical Roman orders. He decided, however, to restore three pre-Roman temples at Paestum for his fourth-year project. This initial selection of greek temples as well as the conclusions obtained in his reconstruction presented a direct confrontation to the strict classical truths promoted by the academy. He proclaimed the Greek order as a higher form of art than the Roman order. He analyzed these temples with a specific view of their construction. His reconstruction not only dealt with the stone structure, but also expanded into the impermanent nature of materials such as wood and stucco, which gave detail, life and overall meaning to these buildings. The formal or conceptual framework of the building was, in his view, related to the social and cultural program it was to fulfill. He concluded through his observations that one of the three temples he was analyzing was not a religious building but a civil assembly hall. The Temple of Hera I had a row of columns along its central axis, which implied to him a concern for structural economy, in its smaller spans, that was civic in character. This denied a previous reconstruction accepted by the academy. Labrouste's project was highly criticized in Paris, and from that moment he became an outcast at the École des Beaux-Arts.

His rational approach to the understanding of the temples at Paestum generated a design philosophy that he was to follow throughout his career. For Labrouste form was not predetermined from established rules, but rather was attained through a logic that included a local response to materials, as well as cultural and functional necessities of the work.

As Neil Levine pointed out in his chapter "The Romantic Idea of Architectural Legibility," meaningful expression was the real issue facing the 19th-century architect. This quest for meaning became even more urgent with Victor Hugo's warning in "Notre Dame de Paris," where he argued that the printed word had replaced architecture as the highest form of human expression. Literature, by the new accessibility of books brought about by the printing press, was undermining architecture of its power of expression.

Labrouste's response to these 19th-century concerns can be found in his first important building, the Bibliothèque Sainte-Geneviève. He established a rigor of design in his decision-making process that illustrated his philosophies throughout the project. The building was meant to be read syntactically as structural and nonstructural elements became synthesized. Labrouste engaged the user in an intellectual procession that began in an austere, solid exterior and culminated in the Reading Room, where cast iron was used as the main structural element. It was the first time cast iron was used in a monumental building.

In the severe simplicity of the exterior, much criticized at the time, exists a modern transparency that reveals the internal organization of the building. The building is comprised of two stories: a continuous horizontal base at the ground floor that supports on the second floor a repetitive series of arches. These arches are filled with windows and panels that bear engraved names of 810 authors arranged chronologically from Moses to the Swedish chemist Jöns Jakob Berzelius, thus narrating the historical evolution of the world from Judaism to modern science. A simple, unadorned entrance leads into a compressed vestibule. This room resembles a hypostyle hall of solid masonry columns using very light cast-iron elements as decoration. In between the columns are busts of literary figures in a background of pictorial landscapes reminiscent of the historical past. The stairwell at the end is lit from above, creating a dramatic effect that draws the inhabitor toward the source of light. In the center of the stairwell is a monument to Ulrich Gering, who brought the printing press to Paris. The final destination is a very light and open room. A row of thin cast-iron columns occupies the longitudinal center of the room and gives support to two barrel vaults defining the non-hierarchical quality of the space. It resembles the Civil Assembly Hall at Paestum. There is a gracious balance between the iron structure and the masonry exterior of the room.

Books and light become the significant elements in defining the enclosure of the room, as the introduction of "technology" brings them together. This assemblage, expressed through the development of parts, reveals the act of learning as a progressive discovery implicit in the conceptual framework of the building.

Labrouste further explored these ideas in the Reading Room and book stacks of the Bibliothèque Nationale, where he achieved a delicate balance between a reassessed understanding of classical architecture and the technology of his time.

Labrouste's legacy lies in a comprehensive attitude toward design. Departing from the previous premise that the modern architect could not rely solely on predetermined classical form to convey meaning, he proposed a new way of understanding and projecting architecture. Form would only acquire meaning when reflecting the relation to its context through the orchestration of its structure, materials, and purpose. Only then would the physiognomy of a work take on a life of its own.

—ANNABEL DELGADO

LAFEVER, Minard.

American. Born in Morristown, New Jersey, 10 August 1798. Died on 24 September 1854. Self-taught as architect; began career as a carpenter. Established own firm, New York, 1828.

Chronology of Works

All in the United States
* Approximate dates
† Work no longer exists

1831-33	Sailors' Snug Harbor, Staten Island, New York [attributed]
1834-35	First Reformed Dutch Church, Brooklyn, New York (with James Gallier, Sr.)†
1839-40	New Dutch South Reformed Church, Washington Square, New York City†
1841-42	First Baptist Church, Broome Street, New York City†
1842-44	Church of the Saviour (First Unitarian Church), Brooklyn, New York
1843-44	Pierrepont Street Baptist Church, Brooklyn, New York†
1843-44	Whalers' Church (First Presbyterian Church), Sag Harbor, New York
1844-45	Church of the Divine Unity, New York City†
1844-47	Church of the Holy Trinity, Brooklyn, New York
1845	Tomb Monument for Ada Augusta Shields, Brooklyn, New York
1846-47	Brooklyn Savings Bank, Brooklyn, New York†
1846-48	Episcopal Church of the Holy Apostles, New York City
1846-48	Second Presbyterian Church, Richmond, Virginia
1847	Monument to George Washington, New York City (not completed)†
1847*-53	Arched Bridge and Terrace, Brooklyn, New York†
1848-50	Church of the Neighbor, Brooklyn, New York†
1848-50	First Baptist Church, Syracuse, New York†
1848-50	First Presbyterian Church, Syracuse, New York†
1849-50	First Dutch Reformed Church, Syracuse, New York†
1850-51	Dutch Reformed Church on the Heights, Brooklyn, New York†
1851-52	Pearl Street Congregational Church, Hartford, Connecticut†
1851-52	Dutch Reformed Church, Kingston, New York
1851-52	Strong Place Baptist Church, Brooklyn, New York
1854	Munro Academy, Elbridge, New York†
1854-56	Packer Collegiate Institute, Brooklyn, New York

Publications

BOOKS BY LAFEVER

The Young Builder's General Instructor. Newark, New Jersey, 1829.
The Modern Builder's Guide. New York, 1833.
The Beauties of Modern Architecture. New York, 1835.
The Modern Practice of Staircase and Hand-Rail Construction . . . With Plans and Elevations for Ornamental Villas. New York, 1838.
The Modern Builders' Guide. New York, 1855.
The Architectural Instructor. New York, 1856.
The Complete Architectural Instructor. New York, 1857.

BOOKS ABOUT LAFEVER

BROWN, ROSCOE C. E.: *Church of the Holy Trinity, Brooklyn Heights in the City of New York, 1847-1922.* New York, 1922.

HAMLIN, TALBOT: *Greek Revival Architecture in America.* New York, 1944.
LANDY, JACOB: *The Architecture of Minard Lafever.* New York, 1970.

ARTICLES ABOUT LAFEVER

LANDY, JACOB: "The Washington Monument Project in New York." *Journal of the Society of Architectural Historians* 28 (1969): 291-297.
McKEE, HARLEY J.: "Minard Lafever in the Syracuse Area." *Straight Edge* 9 (1956): 3-5.
SHEPHERD, BARNETT: "Sailor's Snug Harbor Reattributed to Minard Lafever." *Journal of the Society of Architectural Historians* 35 (1976): 108-123.

*

Minard Lafever, a self-taught architect who began his career as a carpenter, was an important American participant in the romantic revivals of the first half of the 19th century. Practicing architecture and publishing builder's guides during a period of national expansion, Lafever was an exemplar in the architectural field of a type enshrined in American mythology: the self-made man who succeeds through talent, ambition and hard work. His Brooklyn and Manhattan churches assured Lafever a prominent place in the history of the American Gothic Revival, while his published Greek Revival designs helped spread that movement across the country.

From his arrival in New York City from the Finger Lakes region of New York state in the late 1820s until his death in 1854, Lafever had an active architectural practice. The architect's early work in the Greek Revival mode was exemplified by the temple-form Brooklyn First Reformed Dutch Church (1834-35, demolished) and Building C of Sailors' Snug Harbor on Staten Island (1833), a retirement home for mariners. After achieving success with Gothic churches, Lafever late in his career began to employ Renaissance forms as well, notably in the New York Church of the Holy Apostles (1846-48) and the Brooklyn Savings Bank (1846-47). The stylistic diversity of Lafever's designs suggests that he was a true eclectic. Like many of his colleagues in the first half of the century, he employed a range of styles, making his choices based on current taste and the associations of a particular style.

Lafever, along with Richard Upjohn and James Renwick, inaugurated the mature Gothic Revival in American church architecture. In a series of Brooklyn and New York Churches of the 1840s and 1850s, Lafever took an inventive approach to Gothic forms, often freely mixing Early English, Decorated or Flamboyant, and Perpendicular elements in a single edifice. Characteristic of Lafever's Gothic churches were rugged, rock-faced masonry exteriors with cut stone trim and picturesque roof lines achieved through turret buttresses, towers, spires and crenelated parapets. While the exteriors typically relied on English Perpendicular precedents, Lafever's church interiors were usually Decorated, incorporating fanciful curvilinear tracery in the windows, lierne ribs in the vaults, and original designs for bosses, capitals, corbels and finials. Lafever considered Gothic, as well as Norman, architecture to be especially appropriate for ecclesiastic structures, but declined to toe the line of archaeological and structural purity advanced by the English and New York ecclesiological societies. His distinctly personal Gothic churches were never exact copies of medieval or contemporary

English Gothic Revival structures, and they employed decorative plaster vaults rather than stone vaulting.

The Episcopal Church of the Holy Trinity (now St. Ann's and the Holy Trinity) in Brooklyn Heights (1844-47), capstone of Lafever's career as an architect, amply displays his inventiveness as a Gothic designer. Although the overall composition is probably indebted to A. W. N. Pugin's design for an ideal parish church, either directly or as reworked by Upjohn at Trinity Church on Wall Street, the ornamental details reveal the creative imagination Lafever applied to Gothic sources. Inspired by English curvilinear Decorated and French Flamboyant examples, he achieved particularly opulent effects in Holy Trinity's interior. The church's plaster vaults are lavishly articulated with lierne ribs and lushly foliated bosses, and the exceptional flame-shaped Flamboyant tracery of the chancel and vestibule windows contains the stained glass designs of William Jay Bolton.

Lafever forged his career as an architect at a time when the profession in America was just beginning to emerge. He received practical training in his years as a carpenter and builder, and learned his architectural history from the books and prints in the library of the firm of Town and Davis. Having endured the unrewarding labor of supplying detail drawings to builders early in his professional life, Lafever fought consistently for the professional standing of architects, insisting that they work directly with clients in determining building design. His concern for professionalism made him an early member of the American Institution of Architects, forerunner of the American Institute of Architects.

Lafever's most significant impact on American architecture came from his five builder's guides published from 1829 through 1856. Carpenters and builders in New York state, the South and the old Northwest relied heavily on *The Young Builder's General Instructor* (1829), *The Modern Builder's Guide* (1833) and *The Beauties of Modern Architecture* (1835) for the classical orders and Greek Revival details. Lafever was a master at reworking the Greek decorative vocabulary of rosettes, anthemion bands, modillions, scrolls and moldings into sophisticated new designs that could be realized in wood or plaster in American buildings. His Greek Revival details, like his Gothic ornament, were far from archaeological and often disregarded classical proportions. The architect's successive publications demonstrate consistent growth in the refinement and inventiveness of the designs, those in *The Young Builder's General Instructor* being rough and unsophisticated compared with later ones.

Builders used Lafever's published designs for exterior doorways, parlor doors, mantels, cornices and ceiling rosettes in numerous houses and commercial structures built east of the Mississippi from the 1830s until the Civil War. To cite just one example, the frieze and cornice of the entrance to Diamond Point in Harrodsburg, Kentucky (1840), were closely adapted from a design for a parlor door in *The Beauties of Modern Architecture*. Builders used the guides more for details than for house forms, although two winged, temple-form houses from *The Modern Builder's Guide* were widely imitated, as in the Mackay House in Willeysville, New York, and the Baldwin House in Auburn, New York (1838). Manufacturers of wood and plaster ornament also adapted Lafever's designs for their mass-produced pieces.

Lafever's career coincided with the period of the intensive settlement of the trans-Appalachian West, when new communities needed large numbers of buildings of all types. That the young American republic achieved a degree of elegance in its architecture, even in areas scarcely a generation removed from frontier status, is due in large measure to the influence of the builder's guides of Minard Lafever and a few others.

—ROBERT W. BLYTHE

LANGHANS, Carl Gotthard.

German. Born in Landeshut, Silesia (now in Poland), 15 December 1732. Died in Gruneiche, near Breslau (now Wroclaw, Poland), 1 October 1808. Son was the architect Carl Ferdinand Langhans. Studied law before turning to architecture. Began architecture career in Breslau, 1764; traveled to Italy, 1768-69; visited France, the Netherlands and England, 1775; appointed director of the Royal Office of Buildings, 1788; won competition for a monument to Frederick the Great of Prussia, 1797 (not built). Taught at the Bauakademie, Berlin.

Chronology of Works
All in eastern Germany (Polish names noted of areas now in Poland)
† *Work no longer exists*

1764-72	Protestant Church, Gross-Glogau (Głogów)†
1766-86	Palais Hatzfeld, Breslau (Wroclaw)
1767	Deanery and Curiae, Cathedral, Breslau
1771	Sugar Refinery, Breslau†
1773	Friedrichstor, Breslau (remodeling)†
1777-79	Poorhouse, Kreuzburg (Kluczbork), Silesia†
1780	Barracks, Brieg (Brzeg)
1782	Old Theater, Breslau†
1785	Protestant Church, Gross Wartenburg (Barczewo)
1785	Protestant Church, Waldenburg (Walbrzych)
1785-87	Pachaly House, Breslau
1787	Marienkirche an Neuen Markt, Berlin (tower)
1787	Opera House, Berlin (rebuilding)
1787	Schloss Charlottenburg Park, Berlin (Theater)
1788	Belvedere, Schloss Charlottenburg Park, Berlin (Tea House)
1788-89	Hauptwache, Breslau†
1789	Mohrenstrasse Colonnades, Berlin
1789-90	Veterinary School, Berlin
1789-94	Brandenburg Gate, Berlin
1791	Orangery, Marmorpalais, Potsdam
1794-95	Royal Palace, Breslau (extension)
1795	Protestant Church, Reichenbach (Dzierzoniów)
1800-02	Royal (National) Theater, Berlin (rebuilt by Karl Friedrich Schinkel after a fire in 1817)†
1802-08	Protestant Church, Rawitsch (Rawicz) (since rebuilt)

Publications

BOOKS ABOUT LANGHANS

BAUCH, KURT: *Das Brandenburger Tor.* Cologne, Germany, 1966.
HINRICHS, WALTHER: *Carl Gotthard Langhans: Ein schlesischer Baumeister, 1733-1808.* Strasbourg, France, 1909.
WERNER, PETER: *Pompeji und die Wanddekoration der Goethezeit.* Munich, 1970.

ARTICLES ABOUT LANGHANS

GRUNDMAN, GÜNTHER: "Die Richtungsänderung in der schlesischen Kunst des achtzehnten Jahrhunderts." In HANS TINTELNOT (ed.): *Kunstgeschichtliche Studien.* Breslau, Poland, 1943.

Carl Gotthard Langhans: Brandenburg Gate, Berlin, Germany, 1789-94

Carl Gotthard Langhans is known to have worked in Breslau from around 1764 (when he would have been in his early thirties). There, he designed a new wing for the Palais Hatzfeld in a conservative style, which is what one would expect from someone who was at that time very much a provincial. In fact, Langhans showed every symptom of being a late developer.

He was able eventually to travel to Italy in 1768-69, but not until 1775 did he manage to visit France, the Netherlands and England. Those voyages stood him in good stead, and clearly enlarged his horizons very considerably beyond his Silesian background. In 1788 he took the fateful step of moving to Berlin, where he was appointed *Oberhofbaurat*—it is clear that by that time he had powerful connections. In his new and important capacity he designed the Dissection Theater for the Veterinary College (1789-90): in this work he demonstrated that he had imbibed the architectural ideas emanating especially from France and from England. He used a primitive Doric order, massive stereometrically pure forms and a mighty dome in his composition. Clearly, his work derived from the Halle au Blé dome in Paris by Jacques Legrand and Jacques Molinos of 1783, and from the work of Alexandre Théodore Brongniart, then very much a rising star. In fact, the Brongniart influence and Langhans' rise in Prussia point to a Masonic connection. With the Dissection Theater and the Brandenburg Gate, Langhans helped found a new style of architecture, a starkly simple style, linking the end of the 18th century with the Greece of antiquity, and joining aspirations of German nationalism with the concept of the free peoples of ancient Greece. Langhans, in short, was a founder of German neoclassicism.

His most celebrated building is the Brandenburg Gate in Berlin (1789-94), which was based on the Athenian Propylaea, and which was the first important monument of the Greek

Revival in Germany. Yet the order is not Greek Doric, but Roman, and Langhans must have derived the basic form of his design from Julien David Le Roy's *Ruines des plus beaux monuments de la Grèce,* published in Paris in 1758. With the Brandenburg Gate, Johann Joachim Winckelmann's championship of Greek art was perceived as having triumphed at last. But the Gate is not all Greek, as the quadriga on top of the composition is Roman, and the position on the axis of the Unter den Linden owes more to the Roman triumphal arch than to any Greek propylaea.

In spite of its lack of purity, however, the Brandenburg Gate was important in many ways, not least as the prototype of several Doric gateways, of which Leo von Klenze's great work in the Königsplatz, Munich (1846-60), must be counted the most successful. The Brandenburg Gate was also significant because it was seen by Thomas Hope, who liked it so much that 10 years later he advocated that the style of Greek antique architecture should be adopted for Downing College, Cambridge, and that the Brandenburg Gate should be the exemplar for the entrance to the college. Perhaps the nearest versions of the Brandenburg Gate were Klenze's first design for the Propyläen, Munich, of 1817, and Thomas Harrison's gateway to Chester Castle, built 1811-13.

It is a curious feature of Langhans' architecture that it could be startlingly original and memorable, as in the case of the Brandenburg Gate; severe and stark, as in the Gate and the Veterinary College Theater; but that more often it was conservative, even dull. He designed some very fine interiors for the Niederländischen Palais in Potsdam (1787), and he produced an *esquisse* in the Baroque mode for the Belvedere at Schloss Charlottenburg, Berlin. His austerely neoclassical interiors of 1790 for Karl von Gontard's Marmor Palais, Potsdam, were severely antique in style, with an entrance vestibule unquestionably derived from Robert Wood's *Ruins of Palmyra* of 1753, but for the Theater at Schloss Charlottenburg (1788-89) he reverted to an Anglo-Palladian style, influenced no doubt by G. W. von Knobelsdorff's Opera House on the Unter den Linden in Berlin. More adventurous, perhaps, was Langhans' State Theater at Potsdam (1795), the facade of which sat on a tall blank podium punctured only by three plain arched openings. Above this podium was a tetrastyle *in antis* arrangement of Ionic columns carrying a plain entablature, over which the attic contained a relief in the antique style in a panel. This attic was crowned by a plain pediment.

Langhans built the Royal Theater in the Gendarmenmarkt, Berlin (1800-02), an unadventurous structure with an Ionic portico, which burned down in 1817 and was replaced by Karl Friedrich Schinkel's Schauspielhaus. Langhans also won the competition in 1797 for a monument to Frederick the Great of Prussia: his design was in the form of a monopteral temple sheltering a statue of the king, but it was far less impressive than Friedrich Gilly's stunningly memorable and original entry. Like Gilly's design, it was never realized.

The curiously brilliant Langhans, who could be so old-fashioned and uncertain at times, yet a trend setter and promoter of a startlingly new phase of neoclassicism at others, was also a teacher at the Bauakademie, and shared the instruction of practicalities with David Gilly. He was therefore an influence on some of the greatest German neoclassicists, including Schinkel and Klenze. Furthermore, with the reunification of Germany, his famous Brandenburg Gate has acquired a new potency as a symbol two centuries after it was built.

—JAMES STEVENS CURL

LASDUN, Denys.

British. Born in London, England, 8 September 1914. Studied at the Architectural Association School, London, 1931-34. Served as a Major in the Royal Engineers, British 2nd Army, 1939-45: M. B. E. Married Susan Virginia Bendit, 1954; three children. Worked with Wells Coates, 1935-37; joined Berthold Lubetkin's Tecton team, 1937-38; rejoined Tecton after World War II, until group's dissolution in 1948; principal, Denys Lasdun and Partners, 1960-78; Lasdun, Redhouse and Softley, 1978-85, and, since 1986, Denys Lasdun, Peter Softley and Associates. Has taught at University of Manchester, 1961, and at University of Leeds, 1962-63. Member of the Council, Architectural Association, since 1974. Gold Medal, Royal Institute of British Architects, 1977.

Chronology of Works
All in England unless noted

1937-38	House, 32 Newton Road, Paddington, London
1948	Hallfield Housing, Paddington, London (with Tecton)
1951	Hallfield Primary School, Paddington, London
1952	Usk Street Cluster Block Housing, Bethnal Green, London
1955	Claredale Street Cluster Block Housing, Bethnal Green, London
1958	Flats, 26 St. James' Place, London
1958	Peter Robinson Store and Offices, Strand, London (now London headquarters of the New South Wales Government)
1959	Fitzwilliam College, Cambridge

1960	Royal College of Physicians, Regent's Park, London
1962-68	University of East Anglia, Norwich
1963	Sports Center, University of Liverpool
1963	Charles Wilson Social Center, University of Leicester
1965	Comprehensive redevelopment for the University of London: School of Oriental and African Studies; Institute of Education; Institute of Advanced Legal Studies
1966	Residential building, Christ's College, Cambridge
1967-76	National Theatre, Waterloo Bridge Site, London
1973	European Investment Bank (EEC Headquarters Building), Luxembourg, Belgium
1978-84	IBM Central London Marketing Centre, South Bank, London
1980-85	City of London Real Property Company Offices, Fenchurch Street, London
1986	Milton Gate Offices, Chiswell Street, London
1990	European Investment Bank (EEC Headquarters Building), Luxembourg, Belgium (additional buildings)

Publications

BOOKS BY LASDUN

Architecture in an Age of Scepticism. London, 1984.

ARTICLES BY LASDUN

"Housing in London." In *Architects Yearbook*, London, 1951.
"Impressions of American Architecture." *Architectural Association Journal* (June 1954).
"Le Corbusier's Maison Jaoul." *Architectural Design* (March 1956).
"LCC Housing Scheme: Picton Street, Camberwell." *Architectural Association Journal* (June 1956).
"Thoughts in Progress." Monthly discussions with J. H. V. Davies. *Architectural Design* (December 1956 to December 1958).
"MARS Group 1953-1957." *Architects' Yearbook* 8 (1957).
"Means not Ends." *Royal Institute of British Architects Journal* (June 1961).
"Process of Continual Cooperation." *The Financial Times* (2 August 1961).
"Seven Keys to Good Architecture." *20th Century* (Winter 1962/63).
"An Architect's Approach to Architecture." *Royal Institute of British Architects Journal* (April 1965).
"Le Corbusier." *Architecture d'aujourd'hui* (September/November 1965).
"A Sense of Place and Time." *Listener* (17 February 1966).
"The National Theatre." *Listener* (22 February 1968).
"Random Thoughts on Creativity." *Royal Institute of British Architects Journal* (May 1977).
"Architectural Aspects of the National Theatre." *Royal Society of Arts Journal* (November 1977).
"Architecture, Continuity and Change." *Royal Institute of British Architects Transactions* 2 (1982).

BOOKS ABOUT LASDUN

CURTIS, WILLIAM J.R., et al.: *A Language and a Theme: The Architecture of Denys Lasdun and Partners.* London, 1976.
CURTIS, WILLIAM J.R.: *Modern Architecture since 1900.* London, 1982.

Denys Lasdun: National Theatre, London, England, 1967-76

JACKSON, ANTHONY: *The Politics of Architecture*. London, 1970.

MAXWELL, ROBERT: *Neue englische Architektur*. Stuttgart, 1972.

SAUNDERS, ANNE: *Art and Architecture in London*. London, 1984.

SERVICE, ALASTAIR: *The Architects of London*. London, 1979.

SHARP, DENNIS: *A Visual History of Twentieth Century Architecture*. London, 1972.

SMITH, G. E. KIDDER: *The New Architecture of Europe*. New York and London, 1961.

WEBB, MICHAEL: *Architecture in Britain Today*. London, 1969.

ARTICLES ABOUT LASDUN

"Denys Lasdun, His Approach to Architecture." *Architectural Design* (June 1965).

"Evolution of a Style." *Architectural Review* (May 1969).

BUCHANAN, PETER: "Lasdun Landmark." *Architectural Review* (November 1981).

CANTACUZINO, SHERBAN: "New Buildings for London University, Bloomsbury." *Architectural Review* (March 1980).

CURTIS, WILLIAM J. R.: "University of East Anglia." *Archithese* 14 (1975).

JORDAN, ROBERT FURNEAUX: "Denys Lasdun: England." *Canadian Architect* (September 1962).

SHARP, DENNIS, and DAVIES, COLIN: "Denys Lasdun: A New National Role." *Building* (17 September 1976).

*

Uniquely, for a contemporary British architect, Denys Lasdun can claim a direct lineage from the pioneering days of English modernism, and therefore indirectly from the heroic period of continental modernism. He worked with Wells Coates, founder of the MARS Group (pejoratively referred to as the "Martians" by G. B. Shaw), from 1935, but in 1937 joined Tecton, where he was influenced by Berthold Lubetkin's powerful modernist architectural language. That language had many strands, not least being a formal clarity which owed much to Le Corbusier's exposition of the "Five Points," but also the notion that a modernist vocabulary could serve new concepts of urbanism, allied to real social purpose.

Modernism had largely been a continental phenomenon, and assured examples of the genre by indigenous English architects were few. However, when just 23, Lasdun was able to demonstrate with remarkable maturity his mastery of the new architecture in a house designed in 1937 at 32 Newton Road, Paddington, London. It owed much to Le Corbusier's Maison Cook of 13 years earlier in its sectional organization, strip windows, pierced parapets to the roof terrace, and the interplay of curved and planar forms.

After war service and shortly before Tecton was dissolved (a dissolution precipitated by Lubetkin's appointment as chief architect at Peterlee New Town, Durham), Lasdun designed Hallfield Housing, Paddington, where the imagery of balcony-access multistory slab blocks emerging from a lush landscape remains as the first postwar example of Le Corbusier's "Ville Radieuse."

Lasdun's commitment to a social program was more clearly elicited in his "cluster block" housing at Claredale Street, Bethnal Green (1955). There, dwellings with optimum aspect for sunlighting were equipped with generous balconies and clustered around a central core of services and vertical circulation, in an attempt to regenerate the rich social contact associated with the 19th-century housing it replaced. However, the flats at 26 St. James' Place, London (1958), show Lasdun equally committed to designing houses for a wealthy bourgeoisie, where the *béton brut* of Bethnal Green inspired by Le Corbusier's Unité d'Habitation gave way to bronze and polished granite. The section, with its double-height living space and associated balcony, is archtypically Corbusian with implied Unité references: the external expression in its clear stratification is inspired by another Corbusian icon, Maison Domino, and was a prelude to Lasdun's most productive and mature phase during the 1960s.

With hindsight, critics tend to assume the orthodox stance of denigrating the architecture of this "devil's decade." Lasdun's work, however, has withstood such onslaughts, while much of the work of lesser contemporaries has justifiably succumbed. In Lasdun's words, the St. James' flats, and even more spectacularly, the Royal College of Physicians, Regent's Park, London (1960), "tried to put back into architecture its links with the city while remaining within the tradition of modern architecture," something which most contemporary English "brutalist" buildings manifestly failed to do. Like the St. James' flats, the Royal

College of Physicians respected the acute sensitivity of its physical context and "accorded with the Nash terraces without aping them." The building further developed Lasdun's expressive theme; the ceremonial area not only celebrates the route through a complex series of spaces, but is a stark, stratified pavilion with huge overhanging soffits and clad in white mosaic, sited at the park's edge. Pilotis at ground level and the plastic eruption of service towers at roof level further underpin Lasdun's debt to Le Corbusier. In contrast, the auditorium is expressed as a battered, curved enclosing wall of blue engineering brick, while the "office" element of the building emerges as a self-effacing infill to the street. The building is in one sense a modernist manifesto responding at once to the needs of the city, and to a hierarchy of uses embodied in the building program.

The massive expansion of British universities in the 1960s was served well by Lasdun's practice. Most notable was the new University of East Anglia (1962-68) outside the historic city of Norwich. A mainstream solution for the time, an elevated pedestrian spine served on the one hand a continuous "wall" of teaching accommodation, and on the other, gave access at high level to cascading ziggurats of student accommodation which responded to the lush, mature landscape.

This stepped section, affording generous balconies associated with each study bedroom, and accommodating service areas in the "undercroft," was refined further (by Lasdun's then-assistant, Edward Cullinan) at Christ's College, Cambridge (1966). However, the massive intrusion of the rear of this single-aspect building at King Street was less than happy.

The decade also saw contributions to the provincial universities; a sports center for Liverpool (1963), was set incongruously and ironically alongside the earlier Georgian terraces of Liverpool's School of Architecture at Abercrombie Square, while the Charles Wilson Senior Common Room at Leicester University of the same year reverted to the well-established theme of the stratified pavilion responding to a park.

Lasdun's considerable work for the University of London (schools of Oriental Studies, Education and Law) of 1965 coincided with the beginnings of the long gestation of his prime commission, the National Theatre, and returned to his theme of the city, the Bloomsbury context allowing for "making the building contribute to the street's language."

Although initiated in the mid-1960s, the National Theatre on London's South Bank was not completed until 1976. It remains as a manifesto for Lasdun's attitudes toward architecture and the city. Hugely complex in its program of user and technical requirements, the central theme of strata addressing the river—surmounted by contrasting fly towers and service towers—achieves its definitive expression. The foyer spaces spill out onto riverside terraces, removing the traditional delineation between internal and external spaces. Not that Lasdun's work is uninformed by tradition—he maintains an acute awareness not only of the classical tradition, but also of the modernist tradition to which he has keenly adhered throughout his career. It is this rigor and clarity which have sustained the authority of Lasdun's work, where lesser contemporaries have succumbed to the pressures of architectural fashion.

—A. PETER FAWCETT

LATROBE, Benjamin H.

American. Born Benjamin Henry Latrobe in Fulneck, England, 1 May 1764. Died in New Orleans, Louisiana, 3 September 1820. Educated at University of Leipzig, Germany; studied architecture with Samuel Pepys Cockerell, London. Established

own office, Philadelphia, Pennsylvania, 1798; appointed Surveyor of Buildings, Washington, D.C., 1804.

Chronology of Works
All in the United States unless noted
* Approximate dates
† Work no longer exists

1791*	Hammerwood Lodge, East Grinstead, Sussex, England
1792*	Ashdown House, London, England
1797	Richmond Penitentiary, Richmond, Virginia†
1798	Bank of Pennsylvania, Philadelphia, Pennsylvania†
1799	Waterworks, Philadelphia†
1799	Sedgeley, Philadelphia†
1801-02	Edward S. Burd House, Philadelphia†
1803	Nassau Hall, Princeton, New Jersey
1803	'Old West' Building, Dickinson College, Carlisle, Pennsylvania
1803-17	United States Capitol, Washington, D.C. (with others)
1804-18	Roman Catholic Cathedral, Baltimore, Maryland
1805	Adena, Chillicothe, Ohio (now restored)
1805	University of Pennsylvania Medical School, Philadelphia†
1807-09	United States Customhouse, New Orleans, Louisiana†
1808	Bank of Philadelphia, Philadelphia†
1808	Christ Church, Washington, D.C.
1808-10	John Markoe House, Philadelphia†
1811	John Pope House, Lexington, Kentucky
1811	Long Branch, Clarke County, Virginia
1811-20	Waterworks, New Orleans, Louisiana†
1813	Henry Clay House (Ashland), Lexington, Kentucky
1814	United States Arsenal, Pittsburgh, Pennsylvania
1816	St. John's Church, Washington, D.C.
1816-17	John Peter Van Ness House, Washington, D.C.†
1816-18	Exchange, Baltimore, Maryland†
1817	Stephen Decatur House, Washington, D.C.
1818	Brentwood, Washington, D.C.†
1820	Louisiana State Bank, New Orleans, Louisiana

Publications

BOOKS BY LATROBE

The Journal of Latrobe; Being the Notes and Sketches of an Architect, Naturalist and Traveler in the United States from 1796 to 1820. Edited by J. H. B. Latrobe. New York, 1905. Reprint: 1971.
The Engineering Drawings of Benjamin Henry Latrobe. Edited by Darwin H. Stapleton. New Haven, Connecticut, 1980.
The Correspondences and Miscellaneous Papers of Benjamin Henry Latrobe. Vol. 1, 1784-1804. Edited by John C. Van Horne. New Haven, Connecticut, 1984.
Impressions Respecting New Orleans by Benjamin Henry Boneval Latrobe; Diary and Sketches 1818-1820. Edited by Samuel Wilson, Jr. New York, 1951.
The Virginia Papers of Benjamin Henry Latrobe 1795-1798. Edited by Edward C. Carter II. 2 vols. New Haven, Connecticut, and London, 1977.
The Papers of Benjamin Henry Latrobe. Edited by Edward C. Carter II. Clifton, New Jersey, 1976.
The Journals of Benjamin Henry Latrobe, 1799-1820: From Philadelphia to New Orleans. Edited by Edward C. Carter

II, John C. Van Horne and Lee W. Formwalt. New Haven, Connecticut, 1980.

BOOKS ABOUT LATROBE

BROWN, GLENN: *History of the United States Capitol*. 2 vols. Washington, D.C., 1900-03.
BRYAN, WILHEMUS B.: *A History of the National Capital*. 2 vols. New York, 1914-16.
HAMLIN, TALBOT: *Benjamin Henry Latrobe*. New York, 1955.
HAMLIN, TALBOT: *Greek Revival Architecture in America*. New York, 1944.
NORTON, PAUL F.: *Latrobe, Jefferson and the National Capitol*. New York, 1977.
SEMMES, J. E.: *Latrobe and His Times, 1803-1891*. Baltimore, 1917.

ARTICLES ABOUT LATROBE

ADDISON, AGNES: "Latrobe vs. Strickland." *Journal of the American Society of Architectural Historians* 2, No. 3 (July 1942): 26-29.
FAZIO, MICHAEL W.: "Benjamin Latrobe's Designs for a Lighthouse at the Mouth of the Mississippi River." *Journal of the Society of Architectural Historians* 48 (September 1989): 232-247.
FITZ-GIBBONS, COSTEN: "Latrobe and the Centre Square Pump House." *Architectural Record* 62 (July 1927): 18-22.
FORMWALT, LEE W.: "Benjamin Henry Latrobe and the Development of Internal Improvements in the New Republic, 1796-1820." Ph.D. dissertation. Catholic University, Washington, D.C., 1977.
KIMBALL, FISKE: "The Bank of Pennsylvania, an Unknown Masterpiece of American Classicism." *Architectural Record* 44, No. 2 (August 1918).
KIMBALL, FISKE: "Benjamin Henry Latrobe and the Beginnings of Architectural and Engineering Practice in America." *Michigan Technic* 30 (1917): 218-223.
KIMBALL, FISKE: "Latrobe's Designs for the Cathedral of Baltimore." *Architectural Record* (December 1917; January 1918).
KIMBALL, FISKE: "Some Architectural Designs of Benjamin Henry Latrobe." *Library of Congress Quarterly Journal* (May 1946).
KIMBALL, FISKE, and BENNETT, WELLS: "The Competition for the Federal Buildings." *Journal of the American Institute of Architects* (January-December 1919).
LATROBE, F. C.: "Benjamin Henry Latrobe: Descent and Works." *Maryland Historical Magazine* 33 (1938): 247-261.
LATROBE, JOHN H. B.: "Construction of the Public Buildings in Washington, D.C." *Maryland Historical Magazine* (September 1909).
NEIL, J. MEREDITH: "The Precarious Professionalism of Latrobe." *Journal of the American Institute of Architects* 53 (May 1970): 67-71.
NEWCOMB, REXFORD G.: "Benjamin Henry Latrobe, Early American Architect." *Architect* 9 (November 1927): 173-177.
PIERSON, WILLIAM H., JR.: "American Neoclassicism, The Rational Phase: Benjamin Latrobe and Robert Mills." In *American Buildings and Their Architects: The Colonial and Neo-Classical Styles*. Garden City, New York, 1970.
RUSK, WILLIAM SENER: "Benjamin H. Latrobe and the Classical Influence in His Work." *Maryland Historical Magazine* 31 (1936): 126-154.
RUSK, WILLIAM SENER: "William Thornton, Benjamin H. Latrobe, Thomas U. Walter and the Classic Influence in Their Work." Ph.D. dissertation. Johns Hopkins University, Baltimore, Maryland, 1933.

*

Benjamin Henry Latrobe transformed American architecture from a provincial endeavor into one of international importance. A child of European Enlightenment rationalism, Latrobe found that while the philosophical and political context of the new republic suited him perfectly, the architectural situation was parochial. Arriving coincident with nascent programs of internal improvement and an increasing need for monumental building construction in both the public and private sectors, he had to contend with gentleman-amateur architects and pattern-book-inspired carpenters in a professional context far less advanced than that of his native England.

Latrobe spent at least as much time on fortune-making schemes and engineering projects as on his architectural practice. These ventures included canal development, pumping systems, rolling mills, textiles manufacture, steamboats and real estate speculation. They reveal him as an early developer-architect ever more anxious throughout his career to invest capital in his own work.

Impeccably educated in the most liberal and progressive European circles, Latrobe developed acute powers of observation, speculation and synthesis. Comfortable with rapidly changing social and scientific circumstances, he introduced advanced architectural theories, technologies and practices to America. From these he evolved an architecture of international significance.

Born in Yorkshire of Moravian parents and attending Moravian schools in England and then Germany from 1776 to 1784, Latrobe received both classical and modern liberal-arts training. Traveling extensively in France, Germany and Italy, he assumed a freethinking posture that eventually yielded distinctive ideas about architecture. Returning to England, he entered a sophisticated intellectual and social circle of artists, writers and theologians. He sought out the best engineering and architectural training in an environment where both were rapidly achieving professional status. Latrobe's years of architectural training and practice in England are obscure yet vitally important for an understanding of his later career. His apprenticeship with the celebrated engineer John Smeaton (1724-92) encompassed a wide range of work, including river navigation and canal building, and has been credited for the later sophistication of his American engineering projects. His training with architect Samuel Pepys Cockerell (1753-1827), however, has not been adequately assessed. Entering Cockerell's office in about 1787-88, Latrobe, in effect, entered a firm begun by Robert Taylor (1714-88), who had mentored Cockerell and then taken him into partnership. Cockerell succeeded to many of Taylor's unfinished projects, and Latrobe undoubtedly worked on some of them.

Architect to the Bank of England, Taylor was one of the giants of his generation. He forged a distinctive Palladian style emboldened by the geometry of giant projecting bays and characterized by great austerity. Cockerell's work was less bold than Taylor's but more ingenious in its planning and spatial organization. The effect on Latrobe of this Taylor-Cockerell inheritance is especially obvious in his earliest American designs. Latrobe also knew the work of George Dance, Jr. (1741-1825), James Wyatt (1746-1813), Robert Adam (1728-92) and the early work of John Soane (1753-1837). While his travel and training gave Latrobe a significant advantage in his new-world context, he eventually came to see himself as a European gentlemen ill prepared for the rough-and-tumble of laissez-faire capitalism in America.

In his youthful European years Latrobe embraced liberal and progressive Enlightenment thinking, which envisioned an ideal society, in harmony with nature, and built upon the natural rights of man translated into democratic freedom for the individual. The United States provided a political climate suitable to Latrobe's liberalism and offered him an escape from both the emotional distress associated with the death of his wife and financial difficulties leading to bankruptcy in England.

Like his friend Thomas Jefferson, Latrobe saw in America the opportunity to create an appropriate architecture for a new political system. Both his social theory and his familiarity with European neoclassicism predisposed him to favor forms of Grecian austerity and simplicity. Yet Latrobe's American architecture by no means merely reiterates the experiments of European employers and counterparts. His buildings are more creative than those of Cockerell and are without the guile exhibited by Soane. While his French predecessor Claude-Nicolas Ledoux posited revolutionary classicism as a rhetorical tool within an old-world monarchical context, Latrobe, in an already-established democracy, advanced a more natural and unself-conscious form of neoclassicism free from the burden of revolutionary rhetoric.

Latrobe acknowledged that public buildings played a didactic role that warranted the use of monumental exterior features and demanded the rational use of vaulted construction. In his domestic architecture he de-emphasized the exterior in favor of the plan. His domestic interiors displayed a spatial variety reflecting the geometries of vaulted construction but often were built predominantly of wood and plaster. Within apparently simple neoclassical structures he eventually developed sophisticated picturesque sequences of space and light, as in the John Pope House at Lexington, Kentucky (1811).

Latrobe was at once conversant with European design and with the American need to express a newfound nationalism. In addition, he carefully observed and recorded American colonial buildings, from Virginia country houses to the architecture of French New Orleans. This wide-ranging perspective allowed him to synthesize international, national and regional forms and ideas in a manner far beyond that of native designers. Grounded in the Enlightenment theories of art and architectural history as taxonomies of forms, types and styles, he was the first architect in America to introduce consciously the concept of historical revivalism, using Greek, Roman and Gothic elements when they seemed appropriate to building type or functional program. His Bank of Pennsylvania (1798) represented a new mode of expression, both more bold and accurate than Jefferson's early temple experiments and more compellingly Grecian than its European counterparts. To the building committee of the Baltimore Cathedral (1804-18), he offered alternative classical and Gothic schemes. He invented ''American orders'' for the United States Capitol (1803-17) by using tobacco and corn in place of traditional classical flora. His creative and subdued historical revivalism set the tone for the next two generations of American architects, who, however, were often more literal and archaeological than their predecessor.

Latrobe confronted the paradox between a nonexistent American engineering profession and the need for engineering knowledge to mobilize and consolidate eastern population increases and westward expansion. This circumstance placed great demands on his knowledge of English methods of surveying and mapmaking, flood and navigation control, and design and construction for transportation and industry. The 1808 national report on internal improvements, on which he collaborated with Secretary of the Treasury Albert Gallatin, offers the most dramatic evidence of his vision for physically transforming the American continent.

Before leaving England, Latrobe built at least two major country houses there and extensively remodeled several more. Though the work of a young designer, his English projects show the plain, geometric taste of a neoclassical purist and exhibit more consistency and maturity than have generally been recognized. During his voyage of immigration, Latrobe lost his architectural drawings and library at sea. Upon arrival in the United States, his initial settlement in Virginia offered him a local aristocracy as clients for whom he produced an array of revealing designs for houses. The notable exception to these domestic designs is his Virginia State Penitentiary, which illustrates social theories in advance of those in Europe and which offers an initial connection to Thomas Jefferson, who had championed penal reform as Virginia's governor.

Seeking a more sophisticated and populous environment, Latrobe settled on Philadelphia, then the nation's capital and cultural center. His Ledouxesque waterworks pump house and its related water-supply system synthesized and transcended European architectural and engineering thinking. Latrobe planned the Bank of Pennsylvania as an Adamesque sequence of imaginative interior volumes announced on the exterior by subtle projections of the wall plane. The bank introduced to the United States a fully developed Grecian neoclassicism, masonry vaulted fireproof spaces and a striking Greco-Roman color palette.

Connections to the Federal Government through Jefferson eventually drew Latrobe to Washington, D.C., where he became surveyor of public buildings. There he salvaged William Thornton's amateur beginnings at the U.S. Capitol and built its great interior spaces, including the monumental Hall of Representatives, based upon a Greco-Roman theater. He resurrected the President's House from its fire-damaged neopalladian pallor. His Greek-cross St. John's Episcopal Church near the White House illustrates his preference for geometric purity and a system of interior surface articulation similar to that of Soane in England, and offers his solution to the ideal church program posited by Italian Renaissance designers. His Baltimore Exchange, designed in a stormy collaboration with Maximilian Godefroy, illustrates Latrobe's ability to conceive of completely new building types serving a capitalist economy. His Roman Catholic Cathedral in Baltimore presents his response to another organizational problem that had transfixed western designers for 400 years: the central-longitudinal plan amalgamation. A commission wrested from Thornton, by then his antagonist, its integration of space, structure, function and exterior form offers the most intact evidence of Latrobe's mature style. Comparable in its spatial openness and interlocking volumes to Jacques-Germain Soufflot's Panthéon in Paris, it is the work of an international designer of the first order.

The end of Latrobe's career in New Orleans presents a microcosm of his lifelong interests and compulsions. Drawn there to make a fortune by supplying the city with water, he conceived of the cityscape in urban design terms, designing the waterworks pump house as a set piece whose portico faced incoming shipping; a Custom House amalgamating national and regional design idioms; a new tower for St. Louis Cathedral, grafting international neoclassical elements onto provincial French and Spanish stock; and the Bank of Louisiana, whose masonry vaulted construction reveals that he created a unique fireproof plan through the interlocking of domed and cross-vaulted spaces. His lighthouse for the mouth of the Mississippi River combined the most advanced neoclassical design theories with engineering innovations to produce a structure that had no equal in Europe.

Throughout his American career Latrobe struggled against both carpenter-builders, who provided "design" services as a part of a construction contract, and gentleman-architects, who usually advised their friends as a favor and seldom supervised construction. In place of this duality Latrobe sought to establish architecture as a legitimate profession based upon the English model of professional conduct. Ironically, he frequently violated his own principles by waiving his fees for philanthropic reasons or to cultivate clients, and by taking on so many commissions and at such great distances that he could not adequately supervise their construction.

Latrobe's architectural and engineering drawings are one area in which his professional standards remained impeccable, and through which he had great impact on American architecture. An extremely talented delineator, he recognized his superiority and used drawings to impress his American clients, to explain his structural innovations, and to insure the accurate realization of his avant-garde ideas. Latrobe's orthographic drawings show buildings in an analytical-neoclassical manner, divorced from their physical context. His perspectives, on the other hand, were the first American architectural drawings to show buildings within complete urban and landscape settings. The impact of his drawings was attested by Charles Bulfinch when, in 1818, he succeeded Latrobe as architect of the U.S. Capitol and surreptitiously wrote: "At the first view of [Latrobe's] drawings, my courage almost failed me."

Latrobe introduced to America the English system of architectural training through apprenticeship. His pupils, Robert Mills and William Strickland, became the first generation of professionally trained native American architects. Latrobe's letters to and about his pupils reflect ambivalence; often impulsively warm and cordial, he could nevertheless be painfully supercilious and critical of his protégés' design abilities. When Mills and Strickland, with their less mercurial and intractable demeanors, began to gain the confidence of American clients and to capture commissions and competitions from Latrobe, he reacted with predictable amazement and outrage. While Latrobe disdained to concede the talents of his collaborators and students, he established genuinely cordial relationships with his craftsmen. He had an uncanny ability to discover and train loyal and competent artisans. Though the subsequent careers of these craftsmen were not so carefully documented as those of his pupils, they had perhaps as important an impact on American architecture.

—MICHAEL FAZIO AND PATRICK SNADON

LAUGIER, Marc-Antoine.

French. Born in Manosque, France, in 1713. Died in Belgrade, formerly Yugoslavia, 15 April 1769. Entered novitiate of the Jesuits in Avignon, 1727; transferred to colleges in Lyons, 1730; took final vows, Paris, 1744. Became known as an art critic and left the Jesuit Order in 1756; elected to academies in Angers, Marseille, and Lyons, 1759-60.

Publications

BOOKS BY LAUGIER

LAUGIER, MARC-ANTOINE: *Essai sur l'Architecture.* Paris, 1753; reprint in English, as *An Essay on Architecture*, Los Angeles, 1977.

LAUGIER, MARC-ANTOINE: *Jugement d'un amateur sur l'exposition des tableaux.* Paris, 1753.
LAUGIER, MARC-ANTOINE: *Apologie de la musique française contre M. Rousseau.* Paris, 1754.
LAUGIER, MARC-ANTOINE: *Oraison funèbre de... Louis Auguste de Bourbon...le 18 Décembre 1755 par le R. P. Laugier, de la Compagnie de Jésus.* Trevoux, France. 1756.
LAUGIER, MARC-ANTOINE: *Histoire de la République de Venise, depuis sa fondation jusqu' à present.* Paris, 1759-1768.
LAUGIER, MARC-ANTOINE: *Observations sur l'architecture.* The Hague and Paris, 1765.
LAUGIER, MARC-ANTOINE: *Histoire des négociations pour la paix conclue à Belgrade...1739.* Paris, 1768.
LAUGIER, MARC-ANTOINE: *Manière de bien juger des ouvrages de peinture par feu M. l'Abbé Laugier.* Paris, 1771.

BOOKS ABOUT LAUGIER

BRAHAM, ALLAN: *The Architecture of the French Enlightenment.* Berkeley, California, and Los Angeles, 1980.
FICHET, FRANÇOISE (ed.): *La théorie architecturale à l'age classique.* Brussels, 1979.
FRANKL, PAUL: *The Gothic.* Princeton, New Jersey, 1961.
GERMANN, GEORG: *Einführung in die Geschichte der Architektur theorie.* Darmstadt, Germany, 1980.
HERMANN, WOLFGANG: *Laugier and Eighteenth Century French Theory.* London, 1962.
MIDDLETON, ROBIN D., and WATKINS, DAVID: *Neo-Classical and Nineteenth Century Architecture.* New York, 1980.
PETZET, MICHAEL: *Soufflots Sainte-Geneviève und der französische Kirchenbau des 18. Jahrhunderts.* Berlin, 1961.
ROBSON-SCOTT, W. D.: *The Literary Background of the Gothic Revival in Germany.* Oxford, 1965.
RYKWERT, JOSEPH: *On Adam's House in Paradise.* New York, 1972.
RYKWERT, JOSEPH: *The First Moderns.* Cambridge, Massachusetts, 1980.
UGO, VITTORIO (ed.): *Laugier e la dimensione teorica dell'architettura.* Bari, Italy, 1990.
WIEBENSON, DORA: *The Picturesque Garden in France.* Princeton, New Jersey, 1978.
WILTON-ELY, JOHN: *The Age of Neo-Classicism: Catalogue of the 14th Exhibition of the Council of Europe.* London, 1972.
WILTON-ELY, JOHN: *The Mind and Art of Giovanni Battista Piranesi.* London, 1978.

ARTICLES ABOUT LAUGIER

ZMIJEWSKA, HELENE: "La Critique des Salons en France avant Diderot." *Gazette des Beaux-Arts*, Series 6, 76:1-144 (1970).

*

The major contribution of Abbé Marc-Antoine Laugier to the history of architecture was his essay on the subject, first published in 1753. In the *Essai sur l'architecture,* he set out his position clearly by saying, "It is the same in architecture as with all of the other arts, its principles are founded on nature itself, and in the processes of nature are to be found clearly indicated, all of the rules of architecture." He stated three observations that he thought would help formulate those rules. These were: the existence of an absolute beauty which he believed to be "independent of the habitude of the senses," the realization that architectural composition is highly susceptible to "all of the operations of the mind that are capable of disorder," and the acceptance of the fact that regardless of the natural genius or talent of the designer, all design ought "nevertheless be subjected and confined by strict laws."

The remainder of Laugier's *Essai* is devoted to his efforts to derive principles for architecture similar to the systematic techniques then being incorporated into scientific procedure, and to thc three categories of commodity, firmness and delight used by Vitruvius as general guidelines for these principles. In the course of his argument for the establishment of immutable, systematic theories of architecture, Laugier made an inspired and memorable allusion to the circumstances that he imagined may have surrounded the construction of the first primitive hut, and that image has since become indelibly associated with his name. In making that allusion, he was echoing sentiments that were also then being expressed in the writings of Jean Jacques Rousseau about the basic integrity of "the noble savage," as well as being acted out by Marie Antoinette, who tried to escape from the artifice of court by having a peasant cottage built behind the Petit Trianon at Versailles, which she used to visit dressed as a milkmaid. The serious intention behind Laugier's use of the idyllic metaphor of the primitive hut, however, was an attempt to reduce the elements of construction down to essentials in order to establish once and for all what was and was not to be considered decoration.

By drawing the conclusion that art should closely imitate the simplicity of nature, Laugier was not only placing himself in direct opposition to the main stylistic direction of the time, but also was elaborating on Plato's ideas regarding the need of aesthetics to serve also a utilitarian purpose. Although classical texts were then available, direct knowledge of ancient Greek architecture itself was extremely limited, as surveys of the temples at Selinus, Paestum and Agrigentum had just begun to be published between 1726 and 1746. A detailed study of the Pantheon by the French archaeologist Julien-David Le Roy did not appear until five years after the first printing of Laugier's *Essai,* coinciding with the rising popular interest in classical architecture toward the later part of the 18th century. Another study, carried out by the English neoclassicist Robert Adam in 1756 and published under the title *The Ruins of the Palace of the Emperor Diocletian at Spalato,* also contributed greatly to this interest. Such limited firsthand knowledge of classical monuments may explain Laugier's extended praise of the Maison Carrée in Nîmes, France, which was the one tangible example that he could examine, as well as his idealized view of the Classical period in general.

Laugier's deep belief in the need for a return to a less complicated architecture, as well as his sermons to the king about the dangers of excess, eventually brought him both official and professional censure, and ultimately prevented him from having a wider audience in his lifetime. Following publication of his *Essai,* Laugier attempted to start a periodical called *L'État des arts en France* (*The State of the Arts in France*), which would have covered both art and architecture and would have been the first review of its kind, but his effort was thwarted by several influential practitioners. In spite of such resistance, Laugier did manage to complete a second book, *Observations sur l'architecture* (1765), which was an extension of the ideas first put forward in his essay of 12 years before.

The relevance of Laugier's work today stems primarily from his dedication to the true expression of physical laws within any structure, and his cross-reference to classical Greek architecture as an example of that truth. Through his argument, he not only paved the way for the neoclassical movements that followed but, by extension, also foresaw the inclusion of this principle in the doctrine of the 20th century's Modern Movement. Laugier's vigorous reaction against the extreme superficiality of the state architecture of the *ancien régime* in 18th-century France, and

Luciano Laurana: Palazzo Ducale, Urbino, Italy, 1466-72

his desire to substitute scientific principles for what he called the "caprice" that he saw around him, also anticipated rationalism. This splinter group of modernism, which was formed just prior to World War II and resurfaced under the name of "Tendenza" afterward, has also sought typologies, but has not shown any of Laugier's poetic vision in the process.

—JAMES STEELE

LAURANA, Luciano.

Italian. Born in 1420/25. Died in Pesaro, in 1479. Trained in Venice. Employed by the Gonzaga family in Mantua and by the Sforza family in Pesaro, ca. 1465.

Chronology of Works
In Italy

1466-72   Palazzo Ducale, Urbino (major sections; palace built between 1455-82)

Publications

BOOKS ABOUT LAURANA

HEYDENREICH, LUDWIG and LOTZ, WOLFGANG: *Architecture in Italy: 1400-1600.* Harmondsworth, England, 1974.
ROTONDI, PASQUALE: *Il Palazzo Ducale di Urbino.* 2 vols. Urbino, Italy, 1950-1951; as *The Ducal Palace of Urbino.* London, 1969.

ARTICLES ABOUT LAURANA

SAALMAN, HOWARD: "The Ducal Palace of Urbino." *Burlington Magazine* 113, No. 814 (1971): 46-51.
WESTFALL, CARROLL W.: "Chivalric Declaration: The Palazzo Ducale in Urbino as a Political Statement." In MILLON, HENRY, and NOCHLIN, LINDA (eds.): *Art and Architecture in the Service of Politics*. Cambridge, Massachusetts, 1978.

*

Luciano Laurana's stature as an architect is insured by the seminal Palazzo Ducale of Urbino, which Baldassare Castiglione called "the most beautiful that can be found in all Italy." Modern historians acknowledge its fundamental importance for later palace architecture. Built between 1455 and 1482, the Palazzo Ducale is notable for a refined classicism based on proportional relationships, and suggestive of a new monumentality. Laurana's contribution, which dates from 1466 to 1472, should be weighed against that of his patron, Federigo da Montefeltro. The ducal role was recognized by Giovanni Santi in his account of the arts at the humanist court, a literary work presented to the Duke's son Guidobaldo in about 1492.

For nearly three decades, Urbino was ruled by Duke Federigo da Montefeltro, a distinguished patron of the arts and letters. Federigo directed the construction of his palace during its 30-year evolution on an imposing hilltop site. There is every indication that he participated in the actual design process, selecting the plan and supervising the decoration of the interior. Federigo's "Lettera patente" to Luciano Laurana of 1468 contains an illuminating account of a humanist's views on architecture: ". . .founded on the arts of algebra and geometry which belong to the seven free and essential arts. . . and that [architecture] is an art that requires both science and genius." Vespasiano da Bisticci's biography of the duke paints the picture of a humane and learned prince, a patron of noble ideals and rational values. As his architect, Laurana gave physical form to these beliefs in a harmonious, classically inspired building.

Construction of the Palazzo Ducale progressed in three stages, the first and final ones conducted without the participation of Laurana. The Florentine architect Maso di Bartolommeo directed work on the old palace complex from 1450 to 1465, but the shape and style of the new building may have resulted from the intervention of Leon Battista Alberti, a frequent visitor to Urbino. The grandly conceived palace moreover reflected the pattern then emerging in Rome. When Laurana entered the employ of the duke in 1465, the design of the palace expanded to include new wings, an enclosed courtyard and refined facades. Laurana, an accomplished builder of fortifications, lent valuable technical expertise to the project as well as a coherent aesthetic design. In 1476 he was replaced by his younger assistant, Francesco di Giorgio Martini, who continued to work until 1482, ostensibly completing Laurana's plan. In that final phase, di Giorgio finished the upper story of the courtyard and the garden, adding a connecting wing to the old castle to the north, and continued the revetment of the facade in marble.

Laurana imposed a fundamental symmetry on the plan while simultaneously exploiting the landscape setting. He created a principal axis, which runs from the public piazza through a vaulted entrance to the heart of the palace, the spacious courtyard. The city facade has three portals and windows on the *piano nobile* defined by classical molding and partially executed limestone revetments. Another facade rises over the steep hillside to the west, housing the ducal apartments—elegant suites of rooms opening to a three-story loggia flanked by turrets. There was a garden terrace in the adjacent area which was intended to hold the ducal mausoleum, a tempietto, in a loggia.

The ensemble forms a stunning tableau, visible from the western approach to the city. Laurana also designed the interior spaces— the vaulted throne room, the monumental double staircase, private living rooms—as well as the architectural detailing in the marble facing for portals and chimneypieces.

The symbolic and literal core of the palace is the courtyard— a spacious, light-filled area bounded by arcades of Corinthian columns and corners marked by stacked pillars. Along the upper story, shallow pilasters alternate with square-headed windows centered over the lower arcades. (The attic story added in the 16th century obscures the original scheme). Both upper and lower entablatures, carved from white travertine like the other architectural members, contain a commemorative inscription in humanist lettering. The colorism, elegant detailing and pleasing proportions work in harmony to endow the courtyard with a sense of refined classicism unequaled in quattrocento design.

The formal values expressed in the architecture of the Palazzo Ducale find their counterpart in the paintings of Piero della Francesca. As the artist was in Federigo's employ during these years, an exchange of ideas between painter, patron and architect seems likely, resulting in such original conceptions as the Cappella del Perdono and the Tempietto delle Muse. Moreover, three panel paintings (now in Urbino, Baltimore and Berlin) share the sensitivity to space, light and proportion found in Laurana's Palazzo Ducale. The architectural perspectives, scenes without subjects, have been attributed to Laurana on the further grounds of his work in wooden intarsia. The marquetry designs in the interior of the palace also employ architectural vistas, devoid of historical and narrative allusions. While there is no evidence that Laurana was active as a painter, he surely devised spatial compositions which could be projected on a two-dimensional surface.

Laurana influenced a younger generation of architects who had contact with his architecture or trained in his workshop. Among those who were crucial for the development of Renaissance Rome were Baccio Pontelli and Donato Bramante, while the latter, along with Francesco di Giorgio, helped to shape the theory and projects of Leonardo da Vinci.

A native of Dalmatia, Laurana must have studied local buildings of ancient origin before training in Venice. It is presumed that he later worked in Florence, and by 1465, he was employed by the Gonzaga family in Mantua and concurrently by the Sforza family in Pesaro. He also produced, during that same year, a model for the Palazzo Ducale at Urbino before he was engaged officially as an architect. His expertise in military architecture earned him the post of artillery master at the Castel Nuovo in Naples from 1472 to 1474; he also may have designed the entrance arch. He is last documented from 1476 to 1749 at the Rocca Costanza in Pesaro, where he made his will.

—EUNICE D. HOWE

LAVES, Georg Friedrich.

German. Born Georg Ludwig Friedrich Laves in Uslar, near Hanover, Germany, 17 December 1788. Died in Hanover, 30 April 1864. Studied at the Kassel Kunstakademie, 1804-07, and at the University of Göttingen, 1807-09. Appointed architect to the royal court in Hanover, 1814.

Chronology of Works
All in Hanover, Germany

1816	Montbrillant Summer Palace (remodeling)
1816-32	Victory Column

1817-22   Laves House I
1817-23   Bibliothek-pavilion (originally gardener's residence), Herrenhausen Garden
1822-24   Laves House II
1823-24   Kaspar von Schulte Villa (''Bella Vista'')
1824-27   Hanover Aegidien Church (remodeling)
1829-33   Georg von Wangenheim Palace (with Georg Moller)
1830   Friedrich Eisendecher Villa (''Villa Rosa'')
1830-42   Leineschloss (renovation)
1843-52   Hanover Opera House

Publications

BOOKS ABOUT LAVES

HOELTJE, G.: *Georg Ludwig Friedrich Laves*. Hanover, 1964.

*

Georg Ludwig Friedrich Laves was among the last generation of German neoclassical architects, his career marking the stages of 19th-century classicism, from the severe and heroic revolutionary architecture of his youth to the more florid Renaissance forms of mid-century. Born in 1788 in Uslar near Hannover, he enjoyed a superlative architectural education at the Kassel Kunstakademie (1804-07), where he studied with his uncle, the architect Heinrich Jussow. There he learned the austere Greek and Roman classicism that stamped his life's work. After two years at the University in Göttingen, he received in 1809 a position in the state building office in Kassel, then under French occupation. In 1814 he was appointed architect to the royal court in Hannover, serving there until his death a half century later.

Laves' early works were strongly stamped by his training, his first projects including a monumental victory column to commemorate Waterloo (1816-32), his own house in Hannover-Linden (1817-22) and the Bibliothek-pavilion, originally the gardener's residence, in the royal Herrenhausen garden (1817-23), the last of which was typical of his style. Distinguished by a neoclassical clarity of composition, it consisted of a simple arrangement of visually detached geometric volumes: a domed cylinder, inserted into a rectangle, which was marked in turn by cubical end pavilions. Laves' sheer wall surfaces were characteristically relieved by a sparing and judicious application of ornament, typically a Greek meander fret, a frieze of garlands, or a profiled string course.

Political events prejudiced Laves' career. Although reestablished as a kingdom in 1815, Hannover was still ruled in absentia by the English monarch and languished as a backwater. While contemporaries such as Karl Friedrich Schinkel in Berlin and Leo von Klenze in Munich prospered, raising monumental public buildings in cut stone, Laves worked for financially strapped patrons, generally working in modest stuccoed half-timber and often simply adding onto existing buildings. Besides remodeling the royal summer palace of Montbrillant (1816), he undertook a major renovation of the royal residence, the 17th-century Leineschloss in Hannover, which, though planned since 1816, was not undertaken until 1830 and completed in 1842. Although the centerpiece of the new Leineschloss was a superbly detailed monumental portico in Roman Corinthian form, much of the rest of his work was cramped by the need to match the French Baroque style of the existing parts. In contrast to his generally spartan exteriors, Laves' interiors were graceful Empire essays, whose cloth hangings and gilt furnishings demonstrated his close knowledge of the Parisian work of Napoleon's architects Percier and Fontaine.

Laves built a number of important houses in and around Hannover, including his own second house (1822-24), the Kaspar von Schulte villa Bella Vista (1823-24), and the Villa Rosa for Friedrich Eisendecher (1830), all of them variations on the same simple geometric theme of a cube fronted by a pedimented block. The culmination of his domestic work was the Georg von Wangenheim palace (1829-33), its design arrived at in consultation with Georg Moller. An extended 11-bay front, the design was a tripartite composition, rising two stories above a rusticated base and marked by a pedimented central section and a colonnaded portico. No other house by Laves showed so well his preferred block-like and cubic compositional character as well as his tasteful, always scrupulously archaeological, ornament.

By 1837, when Hannover again had its own king, an enthusiastic architectural patron, Laves' neoclassicism was out of fashion. Nonetheless, when building his masterpiece, the Hannover Opera House (1843-52), he avoided the Renaissance models that were then fashionable. Composed of visually distinct blocks—a main block crowned by a pedimented gable, a projecting portico, two lower side wings for rehearsal rooms and a small concert hall—his opera house instead reprised the sober and rigorously antique mode of the early 19th century. It was Germany's last major neoclassical monument.

With so many of his architectural projects frustrated, Laves found his most lasting achievements in the field of city planning. Throughout his career, he prepared and revised plans for the expansion of Hannover beyond its medieval core. These generally had a neo-Baroque cast, converging several long axes at central points marked by public monuments or buildings. But Laves also acknowledged the changing nature of the German city with its rising bourgeoisie, and he soon moved beyond the mere coordination of street axes with royal and civic monuments. His plans for the Hannover Ernst-August expansion (1841-43) ingeniously placed the new railroad as the centerpiece of the modern city, providing the generously scaled public spaces and broad commercial streets that remained exemplary in German city planning until the end of the century.

Laves was also interested in construction, experimenting with cast-iron columns in his remodeling of the Hannover Aegidien Church (1824-27) and publicizing a curved iron truss for bridge construction (1834), although it was charged that he plagiarized the latter design. In later years he tried in vain to exploit Hannover's traditional close ties to England. He submitted a fireproof iron design for the Crystal Palace competition (1850) and a *Rundbogenstil* project for the English Foreign Office competition (1857).

—MICHAEL J. LEWIS

LE BRUN, Charles.

French. Born in Paris, France, 24 February 1619. Died in Paris, 12 February 1690. Son of the sculptor Nicolas Le Brun; brother of the painter/engravers Nicolas and Gabriel Le Brun. Studied under François Perrier; in Simon Vouet's studio from age 11, and commission from Cardinal Richelieu at age 15; in Rome, 1642-46, and associated with Poussin and Pietro da Cortona; co-founder of the French Academy, 1648 (and served as rector, chancellor and director); in charge of the Gobelins school for tapestries and furniture, 1662, and co-founder of the Academy of France in Rome, 1666; with Colbert's protection and sponsorship, the most influential artist in France; worked at Versailles, Vaux-le Vicomte and Fontainebleau; knighted, 1662, and created First Painter to King Louis XIV.

Chronology of Works

All in France
† Work no longer exists

1660	Amphitheatre, Place Dauphine (for the wedding of Louis XIV and Marie-Therese), Paris
1663	Louvre, Paris (design for a French Order in the Galerie d'Apollon)
1667	Louvre, Paris (east facade; with Claude Perrault)
1670ff.	Country house, Montmorency†
1678	Palais de Versailles (design for a French Order in the Galerie des Glaces)

Publications

BOOKS ABOUT LE BRUN

Charles Le Brun 1619-1690. Catalogue of the exhibtion held at Versailles (1963).
JOUIN, H.: *Charles Lebrun et les arts sous Louis XIV.* Paris, 1889.

ARTICLES ABOUT LE BRUN

BERGER, R. W.: "Charles Le Brun and the Louvre Colonnade." *Art Bulletin* (December 1970).
KIMBALL, F.: "Mansart and Lebrun in the Genesis of the Grande Galerie de Versailles." *Art Bulletin* XXII (1940).
WILDENSTERN, D.: "Les OEuvres de Lebrun." *Gazette des beaux-arts* 11 (1965).

*

The notion of artistic autonomy, central to 19th-century thought, still influences our understanding of Charles Le Brun. Le Brun the painter is clearly visible, at the expense of a proper view of his role as director of artistic activity in different media during the age of absolute monarchy in France. That he was also active as an architect is little known, in spite of the fact that his varied activity as draftsman of ornamentation, arts and crafts designer, but most of all as the person responsible for the decoration of numerous palaces required a long-lasting involvement with architecture. Le Brun himself described architecture, painting and sculpture as intimately connected art forms. His artistic doctrine envisioned them as responsive in equal measure to the "Idea" (*dessin intellectuel*), and grouped them all under the heading of drawing (*dessin pratique*). Consequently, Le Brun was not concerned primarily with the disposition of masses and organization of space in his architectural work, but with contour and surface articulation. All the same, Le Brun's competence as an architect led to his nomination as a member of the Académie Royale d'Architecture by Louis XIV.

In an architectural context, the different artistic pursuits came together particularly in Le Brun's ephemeral works, such as his decorations and accessories for royal celebrations and occasions of mourning. Le Brun designed the amphitheater at the Place Dauphine in Paris for the wedding of Louis XIV and the Spanish infanta Marie-Thérèse in 1660. He fitted out the triangular space opening toward the Pont-Neuf with a grandiose gate, a mixture of triumphal arch and obelisk. He thus created a kind of interior

space. This celebratory architecture not only carries a complex iconographic program, but even gives the equestrian statue of Henri IV inside the arch a pictorial appearance.

The project for a triumphal monument for Louis XIV gives the impression of an occasional architecture built out of durable materials. It was first destined for the courtyard of the Louvre, but was later placed in modified form in the forecourt of the royal palace. The monument shows the influence of Giovanni Lorenzo Bernini's work. Le Brun designed a central pyramid, set inside a fountain arrangement representing the eight main rivers of France, and crowned by the figure of the king, whose deeds are represented on the pyramid.

The triumphal arch for the Place du Trône, commissioned by the royal minister Jean Baptiste Colbert, was also a monument to Louis XIV. Besides Louis Le Vau, Claude Perrault and other architects, Le Brun submitted designs for the structure in 1668-69. The high attic story became the substructure consisting of base and pedestal of an equestrian memorial in these designs. The measured classical forms show the distance of the Louis Quatorze style from the Roman High Baroque. The powerful measurements and the important, weighty sculptural program articulate the claim to a qualitative and quantitative surpassing of both antique and modern examples, which was typical of the age of the Sun King. Perrault's version of the monument was actually constructed, but the similarity of his design to that of Le Brun serves as evidence of the close collaboration between the two artists.

Le Brun had already collaborated with Perrault and Le Vau on the Petit Conseil du Louvre, which was a team of artists called together by Colbert, and charged from 1667 with the creation of the Louvre's new eastern facade after the programmatic rejection of Bernini's design. With that facade, the young Louis XIV wished to clarify to the world France's claim to political and cultural hegemony. The significance of the facade for the history of architecture cannot be overstated. It suffices to think of the reapplication of columns as members of the support system after the manner of the antique temple that pointed the way to classicism. The fusion of French pavilion architecture with the horizontality and widening of facades of Roman palaces, together with the use of the colossal order at the podium, gives physical expression to the idea of absolute monarchy. Over the simple zone symbolizing the subjects rises the richly ornamented sphere of the ruler. This truly royal facade design became a leitmotif of the Ancien Régime, and still has an effect today in the design of countless government buildings. Le Brun's contribution to the planning of construction at the Louvre can no longer be precisely determined. However, it was undoubtedly Le Brun who first related the iconography of colonnade architecture to Louis XIV as the Sun King. Le Brun's design for the paintings of the dome room at Vaux-le-Vicomte shows Apollo, enthroned in the center of a gathering of the gods, in front of the Sun Palace as mentioned by Ovid. This Sun Palace anticipated the design of the Louvre facade: both have a central triumphal arch flanked by rows of double columns set on a base.

The Petit Conseil was active again in 1668, when the apartments of the king in the Seine wing of the Louvre were to be furnished. The new southern facade repeats the motif of the eastern facade—a pilaster order on a podium—but set back into the surface of the wall. This design prepared for the garden facade at the Palace of Versailles and the facades of the Place Royale.

National and dynastic claims and a consciousness of modernity are evident in Le Brun's designs for a French order, first for the Galerie d'Apollon at the Louvre (1663) and later in the framework of Colbert's competition for the third story of the

Charles Le Brun: Galerie des Glaces, Palais de Versailles, Versailles, France, 1678

Louvre courtyard (1671). The latter was finally used for the Galeries des Glaces at Versailles. Le Brun's French order was in fact simply a variation of the Corinthian order by the insertion of suitably French motifs in the capital, such as the Gallic cock, the fleur-de-lis of the Bourbons and the royal sun. To contemporary minds the design was more significant, however, involving the "invention" of a sixth order, as a national addition to the classical canon.

Besides the actual paintings and the disposition of sculpture and ornament in the decorations of royal palaces, the architectural articulation of the ceilings also fell to Le Brun. His most famous creations include the Galeries d'Apollon at the Louvre (1663), the Escalier des Ambassadeurs (1671) and the Galerie des Glaces (1678) at Versailles. All these were done in close collaboration either with Louis Le Vau or Jules Hardouin-Mansart. Le Brun's repertoire of motifs shows the special influence of Pietro da Cortona's art, although Le Brun developed the division of the ceilings out of the articulation of the walls. A system of ornamented frames cancels out any possible *trompe l'oeil* effect in these works. The paintings present themselves as framed images containing a distant reality of their own. The decoration is not designed merely to overwhelm the viewer, but, in its particular combination of allegory, myth and history, invites the educated visitor to decipher the complex symbolic program.

Le Brun's numerous preserved facade decorations and designs may in many cases be explained with reference to their affinity to the artist's primary medium, painting. Le Brun, as a member of the congregation of the Church of St.-Nicolas-du-Chardonnet in Paris, had been in charge of construction at the church since 1662. He submitted a design for the principal facade, and created the transept facade in 1669. In 1688 Le Brun made a wooden model of his design for the western facade at the Church of St.-Eustache, in which he adapted the five classical orders to the Gothic structure of the existing building.

Collaborating closely with Hardouin-Mansart, Le Brun created the facades of the Pavillon du Roi and the other pavilions at Marly. The frescoes, imitating Italian graffiti, create the illusion of a polychrome articulation system made up of architectural forms and decorative motifs in an antique manner.

The transformation of the sanctuary at St.-Séverin in Paris testifies to altar architecture and choir decoration to designs by Le Brun. Shortly after 1684, the Late Gothic supports were transformed into classical pillars and the pointed arches made round, by covering the old elements in marble and stucco worked to resemble marble. The Baroque marble altar and bronze canopy were executed by Jean-Baptiste Tuby.

Le Brun's most original architectural work was surely his country seat at Montmorency, expanded from 1670, but not preserved. The building itself was unusual. Two massive building blocks flanked an entrance hall, after the model of the Villa Aldobrandini at Frascati near Rome. The weightless, two-story column architecture with a serliana at the upper level formed an open "*salle à l'italienne*" as it were. In a second building phase, this design was preserved only on the eastern garden side, which faced a large reflecting pond. During the alteration a series of rooms was laid out on the western side, toward the courtyard, enhancing the complex with a monumental entrance between two bays. All the arts worked together to create an enchanted isle, which seems to have anticipated 18th-century architecture. The house became the refuge of the aging artist, who had lost his patron with the death of Colbert in 1683.

—MICHAEL HESSE
Translated from the German by Marijke Rijsberman

LECHNER, Ödön.

Hungarian. Born in Pest, Hungary, 27 August 1845. Died in Pest, 10 June 1914. Grandfather was the architect István Lechner; son was the painter Ödön Lechner (1874-1910), and nephews included the architects Jenö Lechner and Loránd Lechner. Studied at the Polytechnical Academy, Pest, 1856, and the Academy of Architecture, Berlin, 1866-68; also traveled to Italy and studied in England. Worked in Paris for Clément Parent, 1875-79.

Chronology of Works
All in Hungary
† *Work no longer exists*

1870-80	Apartment House, 43 Bajcsy Zsilinszky Road, Budapest
1871	Bela Mandel House, Budapest
1882-84	City Hall, Szeged
1883-84	Beniczky-Odescalchi House, Zsámbokrèt†
1883-84	Hungarian State Railways Pension Office, Budapest
1883-84	Miko House, Szeged
1889	Thonet House, Budapest
1893-96	City Hall, Kecskemét
1893-97	Museum of Applied Arts, Budapest
1894	Parish Church, Köbánya, Budapest
1898-99	Post Office Savings Bank, Budapest
1898-1902	Geological Institute, Budapest
1905-08	Balas Sipeki Villa, Budapest
1913	Church of St. Elizabeth, Pozsony, Bratislava

Publications

BOOKS ABOUT LECHNER

KISMARTY-LECHNER, JENO: *Lechner Ödön.* Budapest, 1961.
KOOS, JUDITH: *Style 1900. A szecesszió iparmüvészete Magyarországon.* Budapest, 1979.
PEVSNER, NIKOLAUS, and RICHARDS, J. M. (eds.): *The Anti-Rationalists.* London, 1973.
VAMOS, FERENC: *Lechner Ödön, I-II.* Budapest, 1927.

ARTICLES ABOUT LECHNER

VAGO, JOSEF: "Lechner." *Bildende Künstler* 12 (1911): 549-596.
VAMOS, FERENC: "Lechner Ödön." *Architectural Review* (July 1967): 59-62.
VARGA, LASZLO: "Lechner Ödön (1845-1914): Halalanak felevszazados evfordulojan." *Magyar Épitomüvészet* 4 (1964).

*

A thousand years ago nomadic horsemen from Asia settled in East Central Europe and began the history of Hungary (in Hungarian *Magyarorszag*). Despite the turbulent past and prolonged suffering under the Turks and the Austrians, the Magyar people survived as a national group. Through the centuries, they have kept and strengthened their national identity and language. Surrounded by people speaking Slavic, German and Romance

Ödön Lechner: Post Office Savings Bank, Budapest, Hungary, 1898-99

languages, the 10.7 million Hungarians speak an Ugro-Finnic language which is linguistically unique and unrelated to the languages of their neighbors.

As in other cultural areas, Hungary's architecture also expresses the national tradition and quest for self determination. This is exemplified most vividly in turn-of-the-century works by Ödön Lechner. His desire to create a national Hungarian style in architecture, which would embody and represent the struggle and the unity of the nation throughout the centuries of its existence, started a movement of National Romanticism based on the vernacular material culture. While Lechner and his followers were at first concerned with two-dimensional design, the new generation under the leadership of Karoly Kos broke away from surface ornamentation and learned from indigenous Hungarian builders the asymmetrical massing, exuberant roof lines and articulation of structural elements.

The first modernist buildings in Budapest were designed by Béla Lajta. He was in his early years, influenced first by Lechner and then by Kos. His urban buildings lost the "country look" of National Romanticism. Their massing is simple and the reference to the Hungarian vernacular tradition war retained only in the details of stylized ornaments of the building trims.

The first attempt at designing a building in the Hungarian style was the Vigado (Municipal Concert Hall) in Budapest (1859-64) by architect Frigyes Feszl. The search for a characteristic and unique Hungarian style was a reaction against the influence of German culture at that time. The 1880s brought a rediscovery of Hungarian folk art by the Hungarian intelligentsia. Research into the origins of the Magyars stressed the importance of their relationship to Asia. Lechner, in his declaration of architectural faith—"We shall not rediscover a Hungarian form, we shall make one"—stressed the significance of a distinctive means of expression for the national culture. He wanted to realize such a means of expression through an innovative use of form, structure and building materials.

In 1890 Lechner won the competition for the City Hall in Kecskemet. Built in 1893-96, it was the first public building where he implemented his credo of the Hungarian style. Another prime example of National Romanticism in Hungary is the Budapest Museum of Applied Arts (1893-97), resplendent with its brightly colored glazed ceramic-tile roofs. The white interior of the main exhibition room is filled with light that comes in through the stained glass roof, and filters and bounces among steel beams that are perforated with cutout floral ornaments.

The other two remarkable public buildings by Lechner in Budapest also stand out because of their colorful ceramic-tile roofs. The Geological Institute (1898-1902) and the Post Office Savings Bank (1898-99) display many features of the new style of art nouveau that began at about the same time in Paris, Brussels, Munich and Vienna. For example, it was very natural for Lechner to incorporate curvilinear elements into his designs. The quest for a Hungarian style in the period of National Romanticism continued into the period of the *Szecesszio*, as the Secession or art nouveau was named in Hungary. Most characteristic of Lechner's *Szecesszio* style is the Balas Sipeki family villa in Budapest (1905-08). The asymmetrical, highly articulated front features a half cylinder covered with a half-dome steel-and-glass greenhouse. The play of the solid and void of the mass and the flatness and relief of the surface brings the form to life.

Inspired by Hungarian folklore and traditional Indian and Persian ornamentation, Lechner created his unique architectural language. Behind the fairy-tale look facades lie a clear organization of spaces and a creative use of new materials and structural systems. The high-quality ceramic materials from the Zsolnay Factory—a trademark of his designs—add a stylistic emphasis to the roof ridges, friezes, gables and entryways of his buildings.

Lechner was a trendsetter who was understood by few, but followed by many. Early modernists such as Béla Lajta and the Vago brothers apprenticed in Lechner's office.

—PETER LIZON

LE CORBUSIER.

French. Born Charles-Édouard Jeanneret, La Chaux-de-Fonds, near Neuchâtel, Switzerland, 6 October 1887. Died at Cap Martin, France, 27 August 1965. Immigrated to France, 1917; naturalized, 1930. Adopted the surname Le Corbusier, 1920. Studied engraving at the School of Applied Arts, La Chaux-de-Fonds, under L'Eplattenier, 1900-05. Worked in the office of the architect Josef Hoffman, Vienna, 1907, Auguste Perret, Paris, and, with Walter Gropius and Mies van der Rohe, in the office of Pet er Behrens, Berlin, 1910. Worked as a painter and lithographer from 1912; in private practice as an architect, Paris, 1917-65: in partnership with his cousin Pierre Jeanneret, 1922-40; collaborated with the architect Charlotte Perriand, 1927-29; practiced as ATBAT (Atelier des Bâtisseurs), from 1942. Founder-editor, with Amédée Ozenfant and Paul Dermée, *L'Esprit nouveau*, Paris, 1919-25; founder-member, CIAM, 1928. Lectured extensively in Europe and the United States, 1921-56. Gold Meda l, Royal Institute of British Architects, 1959.

Chronology of Works
All in France unless noted
† Work no longer exists

1905-07	Villa Fallet, La Chaux-de-Fonds, Switzerland
1907-08	Villa Jaquemet, La Chaux-de-Fonds, Switzerland
1907-08	Villa Stotzer, La Chaux-de-Fonds, Switzerland
1912	Villa Jeanneret, La Chaux-de-Fonds, Switzerland
1912-13	Villa Favre-Jacot, Le Locle, Switzerland
1914	Maison Domino (project)
1916	Cinéma La Scala, La Chaux-de-Fonds, Switzerland
1916	Villa Schwob, La Chaux-de-Fonds, Switzerland
1917	Water Tower, Les Landes
1920	Citrohan House (first project)
1920-22	Studio House, Amédée Ozenfant, Paris
1922	Villa Besnus, Vaucresson
1922	Citrohan House (second project)
1922	Contemporary City for 3 Million People, Salon d'Automne, Paris (exhibition project)
1923-25	Villa La Roche-Jeanneret (now Fondation Le Corbusier), 8-10 Square du Docteur Blanche, Paris
1923-25	Jeanneret House, 21 Route Lavaux, Corseaux-Vevey, Switzerland
1924	Villa Lipchitz and Villa Miestschaninoff, Boulogne-sur-Seine
1924	Tonkin House, Bordeaux
1925	Pavillon de L'Esprit Nouveau, Exposition Internationale des Arts Décoratifs, Paris†
1925	Housing Development (Cité Fruges), Pessac
1926	Maison Cook, Boulogne-sur-Seine
1926	Maison Ternisien, Boulogne-sur-Seine
1926	Maison Guiette, Antwerp, Belgium
1926	Salvation Army Building, Paris
1927	Villa Planeix, Paris
1927	Villa Stein-de Monzie (Les Terraces), Garches
1927	Two buildings for the Weissenhofsiedlung Exhibition, Stuttgart, Germany
1928	Villa Baizeau, Carthage, Tunisia
1928	Villa Church, Ville d'Avray†

Le Corbusier: Chapel Notre-Dame-du-Haut and pilgrims' hostel, Ronchamp, France, 1951-55

1928	Demountable Exhibition Pavilion for Nestlé, Paris
1928-31	Villa Savoye, Poissy
1929	Maison de M.X., Brussels, Belgium
1929	Work at the Airport of Bourget, Paris
1929-33	Cité de Réfuge, Salvation Army, Paris
1929-34	Centrosoyus Building, Moscow, Russia
1930	De Beistégui Apartment, Paris
1930	Villa de Mandrot, Le Pradet
1930-32	Apartment House Immeuble Clarté, Geneva, Switzerland
1930-32	Swiss Students' Hostel, Cité Universitaire, Paris (now altered)
1932-37	Pavillon des Temps Nouveaux, Exposition Internationale de Paris†
1933	Apartment House (including Le Corbusier's own unit), 24 rue Nungesser-et-Coli, Paris
1935	Villa on the Atlantic, Les Mathes
1935	Weekend House, La Celle St.-Cloud
1937	Pavillon des Temps Nouveaux, World's Fair, Paris
1937-43	Ministry of Education and Health, Rio de Janeiro (now the Palace of Culture; with Lúcio Costa, Oscar Niemeyer, Alfonso Eduardo Reidy, and Jorge Machao Moreira)
1946	Factory Claude et Duval, Ste.-Dié
1946-52	Unité d'Habitation, Marseilles
1948	Villa Currutcher, La Plata, Argentina
1951-55	Chapel Notre-Dame-du-Haut and pilgrims' hostel, Ronchamp
1951-56	High Court, Chandigarh, India
1951-57	Museum, Ahmedabad, India
1952-53	Unité d'Habitation, Rezé-les-Nantes

1952-54	Mill Owners Association Building, Ahmedabad, India
1952-55	Villa Sarabhai, Ahmedabad
1952-56	Maisons Jaoul, Neuilly-sur-Seine
1952-56	Secretariat, Chandigarh, India
1953-59	Convent La Tourette, Eveux-sur Arbresle
1953-63	Palace of the Assembly, Chandigarh, India
1956	Villa Shodan, Ahmedabad, India
1956-58	Unité d'Habitation, Berlin-Charlottenburg, Germany
1956-58	Philips Pavilion, International Exhibition, Brussels, Belgium†
1956-59	Museum of Occidental Art, Tokyo, Japan
1956-65	Youth and culture building (Maison des Jeunes), Firminy
1957	Unité d'Habitation, Briey-en-Forêt, Briey
1957-69	Brazilian Pavilion, University City, Paris (with Lúcio Costa)
1958-64	Sukna Dam, Chandigarh, India
1959-62	Sluice buildings, Kembs-Niffer
1960-63	Carpenter Center for the Visual Arts, Harvard University, Cambridge, Massachusetts, U.S.A.
1962	Church, Firminy (unfinished)
1962-65	Unité d'Habitation, Firminy (not completed until 1968)
1963-65	Nautical Club, Chandigarh, India
1963-65	Exhibition Pavilion (Maison de l'Homme), Zurich, Switzerland (not completed until 1967)
1964-65	Museum and Art Gallery, Chandigarh, India (not completed until 1968)
1965-69	Stadium, Firminy (not completed until 1969)

Publications

BOOKS BY LE CORBUSIER

Feuille d'avis de La Chaux-de-Fonds. La Chaux-de-Fonds, Switzerland, 1911.

Étude sur le mouvement d'art décoratif en Allemagne. Paris, 1912.

Amédée Ozenfant. Paris, 1918.

Architecture d'époque machiniste. With Amédée Ozenfant. Paris, 1918.

Vers une architecture. Paris, 1923; revised ed, 1924, 1928; as *Towards a New Architecture*, 1931.

Urbanisme. Paris, 1925; as *The City of Tomorrow and Its Planning*, London, 1929.

L'Art décoratif d'aujourd'hui. Paris, 1925, 1959.

La Peinture moderne. With Amédée Ozenfant. Paris, 1925.

Almanach d'architecture moderne. Paris, 1927.

Une Maison—un palais. Paris, 1928.

Précisions sur un état présent de l'architecture et de l'urbanisme. Paris, 1930.

Croisade; ou, le crépuscule des académies. Paris, 1932.

La Ville radieuse. Paris, 1935; as *The Radiant City*, New York, 1935.

Aircraft. Paris, London, and New York, 1935.

Quand les cathédrales étaient blanches. Paris, 1937; as *When the Cathedrals were White*, New York, 1947.

Des Canons, des munitions?—Merci! Des Logis... S. V. P.! Paris, 1938.

Destin de Paris. Paris, 1941.

Sur les quatres routes. Paris, 1941; as *The Four Routes*, London, 1947.

Les Constructions Murondins. Paris, 1941.

La Maison des hommes. With François de Pierrefeu. Paris, 1942; as *The Home of Man*, London, 1948.

Entretien avec les étudiants des écoles d'architecture. Paris, 1943; as *Le Corbusier Talks with Students from the Schools of Architecture*, New York, 1961.

La Charte d'Athenes. Paris, 1943, 1957.

Les trois établissements humains. Paris, 1944.

Propos d'urbanisme. Paris, 1946; as *Concerning Town Planning*, London, 1947.

UN Headquarters. New York, 1947.

La Grille CIAM d'urbanisme. Paris, 1948.

Le Modulor 1948. Paris, 1950; London, 1954.

Poésie sur Alger. Paris, 1950.

L'Unité d'Habitation de Marseille. Paris, 1950; as *The Marseilles Block*, London, 1950.

Une Petite Maison 1923. Paris 1954.

Modulor 2. Paris, 1955; London, 1958.

Le Poème de l'angle droit. Paris, 1955.

Architecte du bonheur. Paris, 1955.

La Chapelle Notre-Dame-du-Haut à Ronchamp. Paris, 1956; as *The Chapel at Ronchamp*, London, 1957.

Les Plans de Le Corbusier de Paris 1922-1956. Paris, 1958.

Le Poème électronique. With others. Brussels, 1958.

L'Atelier de la recherche patiente. Paris, 1960.

Petites Confidences. Paris, 1960.

My Work. London and Stuttgart 1960.

Mise au point. Paris, 1966.

Gaudi. Barcelona, 1967.

Les Maternelles. Paris and New York, 1968.

The Journey to the East. Cambridge, Massachusetts, 1989.

The Le Corbusier Archive From The Foundation Le Corbusier, Paris. New York, 1990.

Oeuvre complète. Ed. by W. Boesiger. 8 vols. Zurich, 1930-61; published in London and New York, 1929-65.

BOOKS ABOUT LE CORBUSIER

ALAZARD, JEAN: *Le Corbusier.* Florence 1951, New York 1960. ALAZARD, JEAN, and HERBERT, JEAN-PIERRE: *De la fenêtre au pan de verre dans l'oeuvre de Le Corbusier.* Paris, 1961.

ANZIVINO, CIRO LUIGI and GODOLI, EZIO: *Ginerva 1927.* Florence, 1979.

Ausstellungsgebaude von Le Corbusier in Zürich. Düsseldorf, 1970.

BAKER, G. H.: *Le Corbusier and the Articulation of Architectural Elements.* Newcastle, 1971.

BAKER, GEOFFREY H.: *Le Corbusier: An Analysis of Form.* New York and London, 1984.

BANHAM, REYNER: *Theory and Design in the First Machine Age.* New York, 1960.

BARDI, PIETRO MARIA: *A Critical Review of Le Corbusier/ Leitura critica de Le Corbusier.* São Paulo, 1950.

BENTON, TIM: *Les Villas de Le Corbusier et Pierre Jeanneret 1920-1930.* Paris, 1984.

BESSET, MAURICE: *Le Corbusier.* New York, 1976.

BESSET, MAURICE: *Qui était Le Corbusier?.* Geneva, 1968.

BESSETT, MAURICE: *Le Corbusier: To Live with Light.* New York, 1987.

BLAKE, PETER: *Le Corbusier: Architecture and Form.* Baltimore and Harmondsworth, England, 1960.

BLAKE, PETER: *Master Builders, Le Corbusier, Mies Van Der Rohe, Frank Lloyd Wright.* New York, 1960.

BOESIGER, WILLY: *Le Corbusier.* Zürich and New York, 1972.

BOUDON, PHILIPPE: *Pessac de Le Corbusier.* Paris, 1969.

BOUDON, PHILIPPE: *Lived-in Architecture: Le Corbusier's Pessac Revisited.* Cambridge, Massachusetts, 1972.

BRADY, DARLENE: *Le Corbusier.* New York, 1990.

BRADY, DARLENE: *Le Corbusier, An Annotated Bibliography.* New York, 1985.

BROOKS, H. ALLEN (ed.): *Le Corbusier Archive.* 32 vols. New York, London, and Paris, 1982-84.

BROOKS, H. ALLEN: *Le Corbusier: The Garland Essays.* New York, 1990.

CALI, FRANÇOIS: *Architecture of Truth.* London, 1958.

CHOAY, FRANÇOISE: *Le Corbusier.* New York and London, 1960.

CLAIR, JACQUES: *Que Repose Le Corbusier.* Paris, 1946.

COLLI, LUISA MARTINA: *Arte, artigianato e tecnica nelle poetica dei Le Corbusier.* Rome 1982.

CURTIS, WILLIAM J. R.: *Le Corbusier: Evolution of His Architecture.* London, 1975.

CURTIS, WILLIAM J. R.: *Le Corbusier: Ideas and Forms.* London and New York, 1986.

DARIA, SOPHIE (ed.): *Le Corbusier: présentations, choix de textes, bibliographie, portraits, facsimiles.* Paris, 1964.

DARIA, SOPHIE (ed.): *Le Corbusier: Sociologue de l'urbanisme.* Paris, 1964.

DE CARLO, GIANCARLO: *Le Corbusier.* Milan, 1945.

DE FUSCO, RENATO: *Le Corbusier: Designer Furniture (1929).* Woodbury, New York, 1977.

DE PIERREFEU, FRANÇOIS: *Le Corbusier et Pierre Jeanneret.* Paris, 1932.

DI PUOLO, MAURIZIO; FAIOLO, MARCELLO; MODONNA, MARIA LUISA: *La Machine à s'asseior: Le Corbusier, Charlotte Perriand, Pierre Jeanneret.* Exhibition catalog. Rome, 1976.

EARDLEY, ANTHONY: *Le Corbusier and the Athens Charter.* New York, 1973.

EARDLEY, ANTHONY and JULLIAN DE LA FUENTE, GUILLERMO: *Atelier rue de Sèvres 35.* Lexington, Kentucky, 1975.

EARDLEY, ANTHONY, and OUBRERIE, JOSÉ: *Le Corbusier's Firminy Church.* New York, 1981.

EVENSON, NORMA: *Chandigarh.* Berkeley, California, 1966.

EVENSON, NORMA: *Le Corbusier: The Machine and the Grand Design.* New York and London, 1969.

FISHMAN, ROBERT: *Urban Utopias in the Twentieth Century: Ebenezer Howard, Frank Lloyd Wright, and Le Corbusier.* New York, 1977.

Fondation Le Corbusier. Paris, 1970.

Four Great Makers of Modern Architecture: Gropius, Le Corbusier, Mies van der Rohe, Wright. A symposium. New York (1963).

FRAMPTON, KENNETH, and FUTAGAWA, YUKIO: *Modern Architecture: 1920-1945.* New York, 1983.

FUTAGAWA, YUKIO (ed.): *Le Corbusier: Villa Savoye.* Tokyo, 1973.

FUTAGAWA, YUKIO, and DOSHI, B. V.: *Global Architecture 32: Sarabhai House, Shodhan House.* Tokyo, 1974.

FUTAGAWA, YUKIO, and FRAMPTON, KENNETH: *Millowners Building; Carpenter Centre.* Tokyo, 1975.

FUTAGAWA, YUKIO, and MEIER, RICHARD: *Global Architecture 13: Villa Savoye, Poissy.* Tokyo, 1972.

FUTAGAWA, YUKIO and YOSIZAKA, TAKAMASA: *Global Architecture 30: Chandigarh.* Tokyo, 1974.

FUTAGAWA, YUKIO and YOSIZAKA, TAKAMASA: *Chappelle Notre-Dame-du-Haut, Ronchamp.* Tokyo, 1971.

FUTAGAWA, YUKIO and YOSIZAKA, TAKAMASA: *Global Architecture 11: Couvent Sainte Marie de la Tourette.* Tokyo, 1971.

FUTAGAWA, YUKIO and YOSIZAKA, TAKAMASA: *Global Architecture 18: Unité d'Habitation, Marseilles; Unite d'Habitation, Berlin.* Tokyo, 1972.

GABETTI, R. and OLMO, C.: *Le Corbusier e "L'Esprit Nouveau".* Turin, 1975.

GANS, D.: *The Le Corbusier Guide.* Princeton, New Jersey, 1989.

GANTHER, JOSEPH: *Revision der Kunstgeschichte: Prolegomena zu einer Kunstgeschichte aus dem Ceiste der Gegenwart, mit einer Anhang "Semper und Le Corbusier".* Ganther, Vienna, 1932.

GARDINER, STEPHEN: *Le Cobusier.* London and New York, 1974.

GATTI, ALBERTO: *L'Abitardie nell'architettura di Le Corbusier.* Rome, 1933.

GAUTHIER, MAXIMILEN: *Le Corbusier; ou, l'architecture au service de l'homme.* Paris, 1944.

GEROSA, PIER GIORGIO: *Urbanisme et mobilité.* Basel and Stuttgart, Germany, 1978.

GIEDION, SIEGFRIED: *Le Corbusier and Contemporary Architecture.* Paris, 1930.

GIRSBERGER, HANS: *Im Umgang mit Le Corbusier.* Zürich, 1981.

GRESLIERI, GIULIANO (ed.): *50 Disegni di Le Corbusier.* Exhibition catalog. Bologna, 1977.

GRESLERI, GIULIANO: *L'Esprit nouveau. Le Corbusier: costruzione e ricostruzione di un prototipo dell architettura moderna.* Milan, 1979.

GRESLERI, G., and MATTEONI, D.: *La Città Mondiale: Anderson, Hebrard, Otlet and Le Corbusier.* Venice, 1982.

GUADARRAMA, LEONIDES: *Le Corbusier en la historia.* Mexico City, 1966.

GUIDO, ANGEL: *La Machino-Latrie de Le Corbusier.* Rosario, Argentina, 1930.

GUITON, JACQUES: *The Ideas of Le Corbusier on Architecture and Urban Planning.* New York, 1981.

HENZE, ANTON and MOOSBRUGGER, BERNHARD: *La Tourette: The Le Corbusier Monastery.* New York, 1966.

HENZE, ANTON: *Le Corbusier.* Berlin, 1957.

HENZE, ANTON: *Ronchamp: Le Corbusiers erster Kirchenbau.* Recklinghausen, Germany, 1956.

HERDEG, KLAUS: *The Decorated Design: Harvard Architecture and the Failure of the Bauhaus Legacy.* Cambridge, Massachusetts, 1984.

HERVÉ, LUCIEN: *Le Corbusier as Artist, as Writer.* Neuchâtel, Switzerland, 1970.

HESSE-FELLINHAUSEN, HERTA (ed.): *Briefwechsel Le Corbusier-Karl Ernst Osthaus.* Hagen, 1972.

HILPERT, THILO: *Die funktionelle Stadt: Le Corbusiers Stadtvision.* Braunschweig, Germany, 1978.

HOAG, EDWIN and JOY: *Masters of Modern Architecture: Frank Lloyd Wright, Le Corbusier, Mies Van Der Rohe, and Walter Gropius.* Indianapolis, Indiana, 1977.

HUSE, N.: *Le Corbusier in Selbstzeugnissen und Bilddokmenten.* Hamburg, Germany, 1976.

IZZO, ALBERTO and GUBITOSI, CAMILLO: *Le Corbusier: Dessins, Drawings, Disegni.* Rome, 1978.

JARDOT, MAURICE: *Le Corbusier: Dessins.* Paris, 1955.

JENCKS, CHARLES: *Le Corbusier and the Tragic View of Architecture.* London and Cambridge, Massachusetts, 1973.

JORAY, MARCEL: *Le Corbusier: Artist and Writer.* New York, 1970.

JORDAN, ROBERT FURNEAUX: *Le Cobusier.* New York and London, 1971.

JULLIAN DE LA FUENTE, GUILLERMO: *The Venice Hospital Project of Le Corbusier.* Houston, Texas, 1968.

KAUGMANN, EMIL: *Von Ledoux bis Le Corbusier: Ursprung und Entwicklung der autonomen Architektur.* Vienna and Leipzig, 1933.

Le Corbusier's Firminy Church. New York, 1981.

MAN, FELIX H.: *Eight European Artists.* London, Melbourne, and Toronto, 1953.

MATHEY, M. FRANÇOIS: *La Couvent Sainte Marie de la Tourette, construite par Le Corbusier.* Paris, 1960.

MOORE, RICHARD A.: *Le Corbusier: Image and Symbol.* Exhibition catalog. Atlanta, Georgia, 1977.

MÜLLER-REPPEN, FRITHJOF (ed.): *Le Corbusier's Wohneinheit "Typ Berlin.",* Berlin, 1958.

NAGY, E.: *Le Corbusier.* Budapest, 1977.

PALAZZOLO, CARLO and RICCARDO, VIO (eds.): *In the Footsteps of Le Corbusier.* New York, 1991.

PAPADAKI, STAMO (ed.): *Le Corbusier: Architect, Painter, Writer.* New York, 1948.

PARDO, VITTORIO FRANCHETTI: *Le Corbusier.* Florence, 1966; Paris, 1968; New York and London, 1971.

PAUL, JACQUES: *Einige deutsche Vorfahren zu Le Corbusier Proportionstheorie.* Nuremberg, 1971.

PAULY, DANIELE: *Ronchamp, lecture d'une architecture.* Paris, 1980.

PAWLEY, MARTIN: *Le Corbusier.* New York, 1970.

PERRUCHOT, HENRI: *Le Corbusier.* Paris, 1958.

PETIT, JEAN: *Le Corbusier, dessins.* Geneva, 1968.

PETIT, JEAN: *Le Corbusier lui-même.* Geneva, 1970; New York, 1971.

PETIT, JEAN: *Le Corbusier parle.* Paris, 1967.

PETIT, JEAN: *Un Couvent de Le Corbusier.* Paris, 1961.

PIERREFEU, FRANÇOIS DE: *Le Corbusier et Pierre Jeanneret.* Paris, 1932.

Projects d'architecture de Le Corbusier. Paris, 1977.

RIBOUD, J.: *Les erreurs de Le Corbusier et leurs conséquences.* Paris, 1968.

RISSELADA, M. (ed): *Raumplan Versus Plan Libre: Adolf Loos and Le Corbusier 1919-1930*. New York, 1988.

ROHNA, KARL ANTON: *Besuch in Ronchamp*. Nuremberg, 1958.

ROTH, ALFRED: *Begegnung mit Pionieren*. Basel, 1973.

ROTH, ALFRED: *Zwei wohnhäuser von Le Corbusier und Pierre Janneret*. Stuttgart, 1927.

ROWE, COLIN; SLUTZKY, ROBERT; and HOESLI, BERNHARD: *Transparenz*. Basel, 1968.

ROWE, COLIN: *Mathematics of the Ideal Villa and Other Essays*. 1976.

SARTORIS, ALBERTO: *Gli elementi dell'architettura funzionale; sintesi panoramica dell'architettura moderna*. 2nd ed., Milan, 1936.

SEGAUD, MARION: *Mythe et idéologie de l'espace chez Le Corbusier*. Paris, 1969.

SEKLER, EDUARD F. and CURTIS, WILLIAM: *Le Cobusier at Work: The Genesis of the Carpenter Center for Visual Arts*. London and Cambridge, Massachusetts, 1978.

SEKLER, MARY PATRICIA MAY: *The Early Drawings of Charles-Eduoard Jeanneret (Le Corbusier): 1902-1908*. New York, 1977.

SERENYI, PETER: *Le Corbusier in Perspective*. New York, 1975.

SHARMA, M.: *Diskussion über Chandigarh: Antworten zu Fragen Europäischer Architekten*. Zurich, 1968.

SOMMERSCHILD, HENRIK: *Le Corbusier*. Oslo, 1966.

TAYLOR, BRIAN BRACE: *Le Corbusier: The City of Refuge, Paris 1929/33*. Chicago, 1987.

TAYLOR, BRIAN BRACE: *Le Corbusier at Pessac: The Search for Systems and Standards in the Design of Low Cost Housing*. Cambridge, Massachusetts, 1972.

TENTORI, FRANCESCO: *Vita e opere di Le Corbusier*. Bari, Italy, 1979.

TROEDSSON, CARL BERGER: *Two Standpoints Towards Modern Architecture: Wright and Le Corbusier*. Göteborg, Sweden, 1951.

TURNER, PAUL VENABLE: *The Education of Le Corbusier*. New York, 1977.

VAN DE ERVE, W. S.: *Le Corbusier: Idealistisch Architect*. Utrecht, Netherlands, 1951.

VENEZIA, FRANCESCO: *La torre d'ombre o l'architettura delle apparenze reali*. Naples, 1978.

VON MOOS, STANISLAUS: *Le Corbusier: Elements of a Synthesis*. Cambridge, Massachusetts, 1979.

WALDEN, RUSSELL (ed.): *The Open Hand: Essays on Le Corbusier*. London and Cambridge, Massachusetts, 1977.

WEST, JOHN PETIT: *Four Compositions of Le Corbusier*. New York, 1967.

*

Arguably *the* architect of the 20th century, Le Corbusier was born Charles Edouard Jeanneret in 1887 at La Chaux-de-Fonds in the Swiss Jura mountains. He was of Huguenot stock, and a Calvinist ethos together with a strong sense of Jura regionalism were powerful influences in his early life; another was that of his teacher at the local art school, L'Eplattenier, an influence which Le Corbusier acknowledged throughout the rest of his distinguished career.

Although initially apprenticed to an engraver (La Chaux-de-Fonds was a noted center for engraving associated with the Swiss watch industry), Jeanneret soon withdrew all aspirations toward watch engraving on account of inadequate eyesight. Instead, he studied, under his mentor L'Eplattenier, decoration and ornament—and architecture.

Le Corbusier: Unité d'Habitation, Marseilles, France, 1946-52

It was through L'Eplattenier that the 17-year-old Jeanneret received his first architectural commission, the Villa Fallet at La Chaux-de-Fonds, completed in 1907. The result was a modest house displaying strong regionalist vernacular overtones but embodying much internal and external decoration emanating from Jeanneret's art school studies.

At that early stage in his career the 20-year-old Jeanneret set off on a five-year voyage of self-discovery before returning to his native La Chaux. His travels embraced the major European capitals, notably Paris, Vienna and Berlin, and he was able to acquaint himself firsthand with major developments in contemporary European art and architecture. For example, he worked in Auguste Perret's atelier in Paris, absorbing the newly emerged technology of reinforced concrete and spending his afternoons studying philosophy, mathematics and architecture in Parisian libraries. A spell in Peter Behrens' office in Berlin imbued Jeanneret not only with the Deutsche Werkbund philosophy but introduced him to Walter Gropius and Ludwig Mies van der Rohe, both of whom worked for Behrens. Before returning home to La Chaux in 1912, where he was to receive more commissions for private houses (and a cinema), Jeanneret visited Greece and the eastern Mediterranean, by which time the attitudes which were to shape the subsequent half century's oeuvre were formed; mathematical proportion, classical order, reinforced-concrete technology and references to Mediterranean vernacular forms were to recur throughout his ensuing career.

During World War I, Jeanneret stayed in La Chaux, engaging in practice and incidentally in Jura regionalist political activity. His most celebrated built work from that period was the Villa Schwob (1916), a Perretesque design in reinforced concrete with stripped classical detail but incorporating that typically Corbusian device, the double-height living room with balcony.

More significant was his project for low-cost prefabricated housing (a theme which would recur), the celebrated Maison Domino, a clever amalgam of *domus* and a reinforced-concrete column grid which reflected the pattern of a domino piece from the eponymous game. Maison Domino was to emerge as one of the great icons of modern architecture.

After the war, Jeanneret returned to Paris, and stayed (save for a sojourn in the Pyrenees during World War II) for the rest of his life. He engaged in the Parisian avant-garde café culture, devoting much of his time to painting and to a brief flirtation with an advanced form of brick manufacture. At that time he met the postcubist painter Amédée Ozenfant, and together they formulated Purism. This theoretical stance in painting attempted to reestablish the primacy of the object, disposing those objects on the canvas according to *"traces régulateurs,"* a proportioning device with Golden Section origins, and depicting those objects within the limited palette of Purist color theory. The nature of the objects was specific: they were common objects whose definitive form had been refined over the centuries: the wine bottle, briar pipe, violin, and these were defined as *"objets types"* within the code of Purist philosophy.

During those years in Paris, Jeanneret developed his skill as arch-publicist of his own work, and *Après le cubisme,* first in pamphlet form and then as the eponymous exhibition at Galerie Thomas, brought Purist painting to a wider audience. This was consolidated a year later in 1919 by the publication of *L'Esprit nouveau,* a journal edited (and largely written) by Jeanneret, Ozenfant and the poet Paul Dermée. Publication ceased in 1925, but a compilation of Le Corbusier's articles reappeared in the seminal *Vers une architecture,* first published in 1923. It was to be arguably the single most influential text upon subsequent generations of architects, extolling in its uniquely messianic style an architecture embracing on the one hand the latest technology but also the definitive lessons of antiquity.

Even by 1922 Le Corbusier's views on the city and the home were fully formed. His Ville Contemporaine for three million people had been exhibited at the Salon d'Automne, Paris, 1922, while the Citrohan House project (a pun on Citroën, France's most progressive mass producer of automobiles), an early manifestation of the *machine à habiter* concept incorporating the Corbusian double-height living space, appeared in the same year.

Allusions to contemporary industrial buildings were manifested in the sawtooth glazed roof of the Ozenfant House, 1922, a Parisian studio for his Purist partner. Ironically, the rift between Le Corbusier and Ozenfant was to be precipitated by a commission to build a house and gallery for the wealthy Swiss banker and art collector Raoul La Roche. Ozenfant had accused Le Corbusier of claiming authorship of Purist theory, but the partnership met dissolution over disagreements on hanging La Roche's cubist and postcubist art collection at the completed Maison La Roche in 1925. Apart from its role as catalyst in severing the Ozenfant influence, the La Roche house demonstrated Le Corbusier's concern for the architectural promenade, a theme which would recur in every subsequent major commission.

The rest of the decade saw not only a restatement of Le Corbusier's theoretical stance in the Pavillon de L'Esprit Nouveau at the 1925 Exposition des Arts Décoratifs, but also a series of domestic commissions of varying scale spawned from his contacts with not only the artistic community but also a wealthy Parisian bourgeoisie. The Pavillon de L'Esprit Nouveau took the *machine à habiter* notion a stage further, suggesting an idealized apartment form replete with double-height living space and gallery, generous external balcony, and furnished with Purist *objet-types* and postcubist art. Also exhibited was

the Voisin plan for Paris, sponsored by the eponymous automobile and aeroplane manufacturer, and in essence a reworked version of Ville Contemporaine which had appeared three years previously.

Of the domestic commissions, Maison Cook completed in 1926 demonstrated Le Corbusier's notion of *les cinq points* (Five Points), incorporating *pilotis,* a roof garden, the strip window, the open plan and the free facade with clarity and authority. *Les cinq points* were to serve as an accessible and seductive paradigm for the new architecture.

Maison Cook and the much grander Les Terraces, Garches (1927), commissioned by the de Monzie family but inhabited by the brother of Gertrude Stein, also demonstrated the importance of Le Corbusier's activity as a painter. The curved "forms brought together in light" which had appeared five years previously in Purist paintings now emerged as dynamic elements within a mature architectural vocabulary and served to reinforce the *cinq points* theory by appearing as curved freestanding partitions which willfully avoided the grid of structural columns. The primacy of Le Corbusier's position as a form giver was also demonstrated by his contribution to the Weissenhofsiedlung, Stuttgart (1927), where three houses brilliantly expressed *les cinq points* and, incidentally, occupied the best sites within the exhibition area.

This mature vocabulary of architectural form also appeared in a series of major commissions which enabled Le Corbusier to realize in microcosm his town-planning theories. The Centrosoyus Building, Moscow, and the Salvation Army Hostel, Paris, La Cité de Refuge, were both commissioned in 1929 and embraced the five points in buildings of urban scale. Both, unsuccessfully in the event, attempted to find a solution to the glazed curtain wall, the Salvation Army hostel incorporating a crude and equally unsuccessful form of air-conditioning. An embittered Le Corbusier was disqualified on a trivial technicality from the League of Nations competition in 1927, and sadly an early opportunity to realize a building of international significance was lost. The wound inflicted by this crass rebuff from the architectural establishment was never to heal.

However, one of the truly seminal buildings in the annals of modern architecture, the Villa Savoye, Poissy, appeared in 1931. In its interpretation of *les cinq points,* its formal language, its incorporation of the promenade, and in its linkage of internal and external spaces, Villa Savoye encapsulated an authoritative image for a mature 20th-century architecture, and remains as perhaps the single most influential building from its period.

Another major commission, a hostel for Swiss students at the Cité Universitaire, Paris, the Pavillon Suisse, expressed an idealized vision of urban life which had appeared in the Ville Radieuse project two years earlier in 1930. Its incorporation of natural materials (a curved rubble wall for the common room) and its massive concrete *pilotis* heralded a change in Le Corbusier's architectural vocabulary suggesting a move away from the machine aesthetic. Such shifting concerns of form and texture predictably had also appeared in his paintings, which increasingly depicted the female form with massive torso and baluster-like limbs.

Travel had always been central to Le Corbusier's career, and visits to South America and to New York were to have a profound influence during the years preceding World War II. The former produced the Ministry of Education and Health Building at Rio de Janeiro (begun in 1937 with Lucío Costa and Oscar Niemeyer), while the latter inspired his book *Quand les cathédrales étaient blanches,* published in 1937.

A growing threat of war and an attendant economic slump substantially reduced the flow of commissions to Le Corbusier's atelier, but the late 1930s saw increased activity in painting and writing together with a curiously ambivalent political involvement with the Syndicalist group, which had fascist affiliations. Overtures via the Syndicalists to the Vichy Government continued after the German occupation of Paris, by which time Le Corbusier had left for the Pyrenees, where he was to stay until the liberation.

After the war Le Corbusier set about the task of rebuilding a wartorn France with visionary zeal. He was commissioned by the Port of Marseilles, Saint Dié and Saint-Gaudens. While an unstable postwar political milieu in France rendered most of these commissions abortive, nevertheless the Marseilles patronage produced the celebrated Unité d'Habitation, completed in 1952 and first of a small series of such buildings in France (and Berlin). For the second time in his career, Le Corbusier produced a truly seminal building, the Unité not only serving as a utopian model for postwar mass housing, but giving architects a new architectural language, *béton brut*, which eschewed the machine aesthetic held so sacred two decades previously.

While engaged on the design for the Unité, Le Corbusier joined, as French delegate, the commission to design the headquarters of the newly founded United Nations. Memories of the League of Nations debacle were still acute and only served to heighten Le Corbusier's deep resentment at Wallace Harrison's appointment as architect. However, a moral victory ensued, for the building emerged as Corbusian in its three-dimensional organization.

The Marseilles Unité had originally been designed with a steel frame as a support structure for accommodating factory-produced apartments. In the event, acute steel shortages in postwar France dictated a shift to reinforced-concrete construction, upon which Le Corbusier capitalized with his architecture of *béton brut*. Board-marked concrete and *la brise soleil* were to characterize most of Le Corbusier's postwar output, but the Unité was the first vehicle for *le modulor*, a universal proportioning system based (like *traces régulateurs*) on the Golden Section and devised during Le Corbusier's wartime exile. The Unité apartments embodied a deep plan with narrow frontage affording dual aspect and a typically Corbusian double-height living space with bed balcony. In accordance with his views concerning an idealized autonomous community, Le Corbusier incorporated a shopping street, gymnasium, crèche and running track within the building, providing, incidentally, a dazzling assembly of plastic forms at roof level.

The Marseilles Unité model was repeated at Nantes in 1955, Berlin, Meaux and Briey-en-Fôret in 1957. However, it was the English who were to absorb most wholeheartedly the Corbusian ethic. *La ville radieuse* had been published in 1945, but was not realized in built form in its native France: the huge powers invested in a postwar British Labour government enabled building of the Ville Radieuse idea on a grand scale in several mass-housing schemes, notably at Roehampton Park by the London County Council Architects' Department.

To some, the Notre-Dame-du-Haut Chapel at Ronchamp (1955) in the Vosges mountains represented a dramatic shift in Corbusier's oeuvre. Its plastic form apparently lacking in structural integrity seemed an antirationalist gesture, nevertheless justified on Le Corbusier's part by an unswerving adherence to *le modulor*. The church was originally devised in steel mesh with a sprayed-on concrete cover (Gunnite), but Le Corbusier was persuaded by Maxwell Fry among others that a more permanent solution was called for. The resultant concrete frame was in the event infilled with rubble from the ruin of the previous medieval church, and the final form with huge battered walls and splayed window openings was sprayed with Gunnite to achieve the desired result, owing everything to Le Corbusier's previous painterly investigations.

The other compelling ecclesiastical work from that most intensive period of his career (he was then 66 years of age) was the Monastery of Sainte-Marie-de-la-Tourette near Lyon, which encapsulated all the long-held Corbusian attitudes in microcosm: the expression of the individual within an autonomous collective community, the dramatic juxtaposition of nature and man-made artifact, the exploitation of "forms brought together in light." Le Corbusier understood monastic life based on an influential visit to the Tuscan Charterhouse of Ema in 1907, and La Tourette triumphed from his utter comprehension of a finite brief.

In 1950 the Punjabi government was looking to build a new capital city at Chandigarh in the Himalayan foothills. First approaching Maxwell Fry in London, they were directed to Le Corbusier's atelier in Paris, and a master plan emerged which encapsulated all the Corbusian hallmarks evidenced in every town-planning project since *La ville contemporaine*. A series of authoritative and monumental buildings emerged, all designed according to *le modulor*, all embracing the *béton brut* architectural vocabulary. As with most of Le Corbusier's *grands projets*, Chandigarh attracted criticism. Like Edwin Lutyens' New Delhi of some three decades previously (and indeed Louis Kahn's subsequent Bangladesh capital at Dacca) Chandigarh was heavily criticized for its imposition of western architectural forms upon an alien culture. Furthermore, *béton brut* seemed an inappropriate building technology for such climatic conditions.

Le Corbusier's influence was universal but nowhere more intense than in Britain. Much of the postwar public housing program in Britain inspired by an egalitarian Labour government espoused Ville Radieuse principles. English architects of international renown, such as Denys Lasdun, Peter Moro and Basil Spence, adhered to Corbusian models for a rich variety of architectural commissions during the 1960s and 1970s. Ironically, given the British profession's adulation of Le Corbusier culminating in the Royal Institute of British Architects' Gold Medal in 1959, Britain was to be denied a Corbusian building, but North America saw one such example, the Carpenter Center for the Visual Arts, Harvard University (1964).

Le Corbusier died in 1965, drowning after a heart attack while swimming at his Cap Martin retreat. As a form giver, he had been the single most influential figure in the development of 20th-century architecture, and accordingly has met with detractors. None deny the brilliance and authority of his individual buildings, particularly where there existed a well-prescribed brief. Rather their criticism has been leveled, albeit with some justification, at his deterministic view of town planning. In any event, to blame Le Corbusier for the abject failure of much postwar mass housing remains a grotesque caricature and does nothing to undermine his primacy in 20th-century architectural history.

—A. PETER FAWCETT

LEDOUX, Claude-Nicolas.

French. Born in 1736. Died in Paris, France, 19 November 1806. Student of Jacques-François Blondel.

Chronology of Works
All in France
* Approximate dates
† Work no longer exists

1762	Café, rue St. Honoré, Paris (interior decoration)
1762*-64*	Cathedral of St. Germain, Auxerre (choir)

Claude-Nicolas Ledoux: Customs Houses, Paris, France, 1784-89

1762*-64*	Château de Maupertuis, Paris (restoration)
1762*-64*	Château de Montfermeil, Paris
1764	Pavillon Hocquart, Chausée d'Antin, Paris
1764*-70*	Château de Bénouville, Normandy
1766	Hôtel d'Hallwyl, Paris
1768	Hôtel d'Uzès, rue Montmartre, Paris (reconstruction)
1770	Hôtel Montmorency, Paris
1771-73	Château for Madame Du Barry, Louveciennes
1771-73	Pavillon Guimard, Paris
1771-73	Pavillon Tabary, Paris
1771-73	Pavillon Termant de St. Germain, Paris
1771-73	Theater (apartment of Madame Guimard), Paris
1771-73	Theater, Besançon
1775-80	Salt Works, Arcs et Senans
1778-81	Hôtel de Thélusson, Chausée d'Antin, Paris†
1780	Pavillon, Attily
1780	Pavillon d'Espinchal, Paris
1784-89	Customs Houses, Paris
n.d.	Hôtel Pradeau de Chemilly, Paris

Publications

BOOKS BY LEDOUX

L'architecture considérée sous le rapport de l'art, des moeurs, et de la législation. Vol. 1: Paris, 1804. Vol. 2 (edited by Daniel Ramée): London, 1846.
L'oeuvre complete. Edited by Daniel Ramée. 2 vols. Paris, 1847.

BOOKS ABOUT LEDOUX

BRAHAM, ALLAN: *The Architecture of the French Enlightenment.* Berkeley, California, and Los Angeles, 1980.
CHRIST, Y.: *Ledoux, architecte du roi.* Paris, 1961.
GALLET, MICHEL: *Ledoux et Paris.* Paris, 1980.
HAUTECOEUR, LOUIS: *Histoire de l'architecture classique en France.* Paris, 1948.
ISOZAKI, ARATA: *Les Salines Royale de Chaux.* Vol. 10 in the *Architectural Pilgrimage to World Architecture* series. Tokyo, 1980.
KAUFMANN, EMIL: *Architecture in the Age of Reason: Baroque and Post-Baroque in England, Italy, France.* Cambridge, Massachusetts, 1955.
KAUFMANN, EMIL: *Three Revolutionary Architects: Boullée, Ledoux, and Lequeu.* Philadelphia, 1952.
KAUFMANN, EMIL: *Von Ledoux bis Le Corbusier: Ursprung und Entwicklung der autonomen Architektur.* Vienna and Leipzig, 1933.
LEMAGNY, J. C.: *Visionary Architects: Boullée, Ledoux, Lequeu.* Austin, Texas, 1990.
LEVALLET-HAUG, GENEVIEVE: *Claude-Nicolas Ledoux.* Paris and Strasbourg, 1934.
MOREUX, JEAN-CHARLES, and RAVAL, MARCEL: *Claude-Nicolas Ledoux: Architecte du roi.* Paris, 1945.
OZOUF, MONA: *L'école de la France: Essais sur la Révolution, l'utopie et l'enseignement.* Paris, 1984.
RITTAUD-HUTINET, JACQUES: *La vision d'un futur: Ledoux et ses théâtres.* Lyons, 1982.
ROSENAU, HELEN: *Ledoux and Utopian Architecture.* 1977.

ROSENAU, HELEN: *The Ideal City and Its Architectural Evolution.* New York (1959) 1975.

VIDLER, ANTHONY: *Claude-Nicolas Ledoux: Architecture and Social Reform at the End of the Ancien Régime.* Cambridge, Massachusetts, 1990.

Visionary Architects: Boullée, Ledoux, Lequeu. Houston, 1968.

ARTICLES ABOUT LEDOUX

GALLET, MICHEL: "Un ensemble décoratif de Ledoux: Les lambris du Café Militaire." *Bulletin carnavalet* 25 (1972).

GALLET, MICHEL: "La jeunesse de Ledoux." *Gazette des beaux-arts* 75 (February 1970): 1-92.

GALLET, MICHEL: "Ledoux et sa clientèle parisienne." *Bulletin de la Société de l'Histoire de Paris* (1974-75): 131-173.

HERRMANN, WOLFGANG: "The Problem of Chronology in Claude-Nicolas Ledoux's Engraved Work." *Art Bulletin* 42, No. 3 (1960): 191-210.

ISOZAKI, ARATA: "The Ledoux Connection." *Architectural Design* (January/February 1982).

LANGNER, JOHANNES: "Claude-Nicolas Ledoux: Die erste Schaffenszeit, 1762-74." Dissertation. Freiburg i. B., 1959.

LANGNER, JOHANNES: "Ledoux und die 'Fabriques': Voraussetzungen der Revolutionsarchitektur im Landschaftsgarten." *Zeitschrift für Kunstgeschichte* 26, No. 1 (1963): 1-36.

LANGNER, JOHANNES: "Ledoux' Redaktion der eigenen Werke für die Veröffentlichung." *Zeitschrift für Kunstgeschichte* 23, No. 2 (1960): 136-166.

OZOUF, MONA: "L'image de la ville chez Claude-Nicolas Ledoux." *Annales, Economie, Société, Civilisation* 21 (November-December 1966): 1273-1304.

VIDLER, ANTHONY: "The Architecture of the Lodges: Ritual Form and Associational Life in the Late Enlightenment." *Oppositions* 5 (Summer 1976): 76-97.

VIDLER, ANTHONY: "The Rhetoric of Monumentality: Ledoux and the Barriers of Paris." *Architectural Association Files* 7 (September 1984).

*

Claude-Nicolas Ledoux's critical fortunes have fluctuated since his own time. His contemporaries recognized him as brilliant but unconventional in his distortion of the French classical tradition, or as financially ruinous and megalomaniacal. Some modern scholars, like Emil Kaufmann, saw in Ledoux a precursor of the 20th-century modern sensibility. Other scholars have undervalued his writings. However, Ledoux's work has been reexamined.

Ledoux's patronage played an important role in his successful career. As an architect to the king, he gathered clients from the court as well as from the middle class. Unfortunately, the Revolution brought an end to his successes.

Ledoux assimilated the teaching of Jacques-François Blondel, who admired the more traditional forms of French classical architecture. Although Ledoux never went to Rome, he knew the work of the French *Prix de Rome* students who admired the monumental architecture of imperial Rome: Marie-Joseph Peyre, Charles de Wailly and Pierre-Louis Moreau-Desproux. Ledoux's first *hôtels* echoed this contemporary taste for antiquity. In the Hôtel d'Uzès (a reconstruction of 1768), he offered a version of antiquity reinterpreted within traditional French domestic architecture. Freestanding Doric columns flanked a triumphal gateway decorated with antique torsos, trophies and arms. The whole composition honored the military exploits of the duc d'Uzès. In the same free manner, at the Hôtel d'Hallwyl

(1766), Ledoux introduced a personal interpretation of a Roman atrium in the rear garden court that also has French precedents.

Ledoux borrowed from a wide variety of sources, including Sebastiano Serlio and Jacques Androuet du Cerceau the Elder, but his work in the 1760s was increasingly influenced by Andrea Palladio. Interest in Palladio, which arose in France around the mid-1750s, was first stimulated by the archaeological approach to Palladio's engravings of monumental Rome, and then by the English and Italian Palladian revivals. Inspired by Palladio's treatise, Ledoux created his own method of composition that is dictated by a symmetry in plan and by the interpenetration of simple volumes in space. The whole elevation is a compact block in which a portico and horizontal elements of cornice, architrave and rustication are stressed. He also borrowed Palladian motifs such as the serlian window.

With this method of composition, Ledoux created numerous formal variations. His engravings, reworked many times even after the completion of the buildings, show a general simplification and absolute regularization of the construction. Such geometrical simplification homogenizes the entire architectural work of Ledoux within a single aesthetic in which his early buildings are presented as prototypes.

The pavilion became one of Ledoux's favorite leitmotifs in his domestic architecture. With it, he adapted Palladio's villa to contemporary French life style. In Mlle. Guimard's pavilion (1771-73), Ledoux displayed a great talent for internal distribution and for inventiveness in the various rooms' shapes. The whole distribution combined comfort, convenience and display as endorsed by J.F. Blondel. In the interior decoration, Ledoux acknowledged the effect of architectural space on the senses, an idea advocated by Jean F. de Bastide (1753) and Nicolas le Camus de Mézières (1780). He imagined elaborate decorative programs for each room in relation to the owner's personality.

In his pavilions built in the outskirts of Paris, Ledoux expressed his interest in nature and in the new picturesque garden. The latter was the visual outcome of a new literary sensibility that considered nature a source of aesthetic emotion. The Hôtel de Thélusson (1778-81) had a remarkable picturesque garden decorated with various motifs—grottoes, exterior boulevards, bridges, viaducts and half-buried antique ruins. The late-18th-century critics were at once pleased and disconcerted by its unorthodox composition and theatrical setting. Today the Hôtel de Thélusson is considered one of Ledoux's most successful private buildings, in which the architect masterfully reinterpreted the French *hôtel* type with a Palladian plan, Roman motifs and a picturesque garden.

Ledoux used his domestic architecture as a laboratory to develop his personal definition of a building's character. The notion of character is another of Ledoux's personal debts to Blondel, for whom each different type of building needed to show its purpose. Blondel based his entire system on rigid social conventions that respected rank and use, but Ledoux broke with that hierarchy imposed by Blondel and explored the notion of character in relation to sensation. Using both observable nature and its inherent principles, Ledoux manipulated geometric masses and light for emotional effect.

With his design for the saltworks at Arc-et-Senans (1775-80), Ledoux extended his art of characterization to encompass new building types. Because Ledoux infused aesthetics into a utilitarian project, he flouted the Académie's rules of *convenance* and suitability of genres by introducing a Tuscan order into an industrial complex. He imagined new symbols that could speak for the saltworks. Rustication and urns spewing saltwater in carved stone were metaphors for the architecture's purpose.

Building forms also spoke of their functions, such as the pyramidal shape of the furnaces. And since within the overall semicircular plan of the saltworks Ledoux placed the working buildings under the symbolic surveillance of the director, who was the defender of the king's interest, the plan was also representative.

But a different reading of the plan also exists. A main axis extends beyond the entrance gate and projects into the chapel that is inside the director's house, which Anthony Vidler maintains creates a metaphysical path between nature, industry and spirituality. According to Vidler, this metaphor was probably inspired by Ledoux's interest in the Masonic movement of the early 1770s. Ledoux's reforms in the saltworks paralleled physiocratic economic reforms in this underdeveloped French region. Sharing the Enlightenment's interest in hygiene and rationalization, Ledoux tried, not always with success, to improve on the organization of previous saltworks.

With the Théâtre at Besançon (1771-73), Ledoux developed another building type. Although he drew his sources from Greco-Roman, Gallo-Roman, Palladian and contemporary theaters, he ingeniously rethought the different components of a theater: acoustics, optics, ventilation, heating and spatial organization. Ledoux's reforms were also social: the architect located the spectators' seats in such a way that all audience members could enjoy the performances equally, but social hierarchy was maintained with the division between loges and seats. Ledoux worked with economy and restraint; he avoided decoration that would distract the eye from the essential forms. The exterior walls were bare, and the emphasis was on the beauty of the cut and the lay of the masonry blocks. For the interior of the theater, Ledoux considered the public to be the main ornament, always changing, always colorful, always on stage. Especially in the 18th century, public architecture was believed to assume an ethical role: the *Encyclopedie* described architecture to be "influential on the people's manners." Ledoux shared that belief and imagined that the moral tableaux enacted on the stage should educate the public.

All Ledoux's other public buildings were conceived with the same care for masses, decoration, function and symbolism. With the customs houses (*barrières*) in Paris (1784-89), Ledoux offered further variations on the combination of geometric masses. With great ingenuity, he was able to produce more than sixty different versions of the customs house, inspired by French and Italian traditions of the 16th century and antiquity. He designed buildings which despite their small size appeared monumental: noncanonical proportions, openings that seemed to be carved into the masses, and varied stone cuttings all contributed to the monumental effect of each of these landmarks.

In 1804 Ledoux published the first volume of what he planned as a series titled *L'Architecture Considérée sous le Rapport de l'Art, des Moeurs et de la Législation*. From its publication, the text was controversial. Considering Ledoux's prose obscure and hermetic, some scholars dissociated Ledoux the writer from Ledoux the architect, an opinion which Mona Ozouf has disproved.

L'Architecture is not didactic, but it appears to be Ledoux's rethinking of his architectural work. According to some of his biographers, with this publication Ledoux attempted to recoup his fame after the Revolution interrupted his brilliant career; therefore, he gathered plans and engravings to demonstrate his genius. The first volume, the only one that he published, contains a description of the ideal city of Chaux (an extension of his previous saltworks) and other built and unbuilt projects. The text includes his meditations and reflections on the current preoccupations of the late 18th century, such as hygiene, morality, pedagogy and economy. The role of the architect is clearly

Jacques Lemercier: Church of the Sorbonne, Paris, France, 1629ff.

stated: he, as recommended by Vitruvius, should be learned in many sciences.

With his utopia, the city of Chaux, Ledoux attempted to bring order to society: the right for everybody to be housed decently, to benefit from light, air and space. Order in society is maintained through specific buildings such as the Panarétéon, the Pacifère and the Temple of Memory. All these buildings educate the individual in the virtuous life. And Ledoux sought new and better functional arrangements. He endorsed the English example of farming in order to demonstrate an ordering of nature. Industry, placed in the core of the rural city, suggests its growing importance for society. This utopia may be seen as the triumph of French rationalism, but, as Ozouf noticed, it is not a vision for the future, but a description of the current obsessions of the late 18th century.

—ANITA POLETTI-ANDERSON

LEMERCIER, Jacques.

French. Born in Pontoise, France, c.1585. Died in Paris, 4 June 1654. Came from a family of masons. Studied in Rome, c.1607-1612.

Chronology of Works
All in France
† *Work no longer exists*

1623	Hôtel de Liancourt, Paris (enlargement)†
1624ff.	Louvre, Paris (rebuilding of the Square Court)
1624-36	Palais Cardinal, Paris (later the Palais Royal)
1629ff.	Church of the Sorbonne, Paris

1631ff.	Château and Town of Richelieu, Poitou
1663ff.	Château and Gardens, Rueil (enlargement) †
1636	Hôtel d'Effiat, Paris†
1639	Theater for Palais Cardinal, Paris
1641	Pavillon de l'Horloge, Louvre, Paris (completion)
1646	Church of the Val-de-Grâce, Paris (supervision of construction of a church designed by François Mansart)

Publications

BOOKS ABOUT LEMERCIER

BLOMFIELD, REGINALD: *History of French Architecture*. New York, (1911) 1974.

BLUNT, ANTHONY F.: *Art and Architecture in France: 1500-1700*. Rev. ed. Harmondsworth, England, 1977.

CRAMAIL, ALFRED: *Le château de Ruel et ses jardins sous le cardinal de Richelieu et sous la duchesse d'Aiguillon*. Fontainebleau, France. 1888.

MAROT, JEAN: *Recueil des plans, profils et élévations de plusieurs palais, chasteaux, églises, sépultures, grotes et hostels bâtis dans Paris*. Farnborough, England (c.1655) 1969.

ARTICLES ABOUT LEMERCIER

BLUNT, ANTHONY F.: "Two Unpublished Drawings by Lemercier for the Pavillon de l'Horloge." *Burlington Magazine* 102 (1960): 447-448.

SAUVEL, TONY: "De l'hôtel de Rambouillet au Palais-Cardinal." *Bulletin monumental* 118 (1960): 169-190 .

SAUVEL, TONY: "Le Palais Royal de la mort de Richelieu à l'incendie en 1763." *Bulletin monumental* 120 (1962): 173-190.

*

Jacques Lemercier was a key figure of the early French Baroque, as first architect to the king and private architect to Cardinal Richelieu, who for all intents and purposes controlled the government from 1624 until 1642. Little of Lemercier's work survives, and his oeuvre is known today primarily through the engravings of Jean Marot and Gabriel Pérelle. Lemercier, who grew up in a family of masons, studied in Rome from about 1607 until 1612, and his work was a flexible if not always successful combination of French and Italian idioms.

The strongest evidence of Lemercier's debt to Roman architecture lies in his ecclesiastical buildings; as with painting, the French public found the Italian style in art more acceptable when it treated a religious subject. The Church of the College of the Sorbonne, designed in 1629, was Lemercier's first major ecclesiastical work, and part of a larger project initiated by Richelieu to construct a new college and garden. It was the first public religious building sponsored by Richelieu, who became an important patron of the French Catholic revival.

Lemercier based the design of both the plan and dome on San Carlo ai Catinari (1611) by the Roman architect Rosato Rosati, with whom he may have studied. Lemercier's version in turn affected Baroque church design outside France, for example, at J. B. Fischer von Erlach's Kollegienkirche in Salzburg (1696-1707). The interior is reminiscent of the Early Christian Basilica of Constantine.

Unlike Rosati's church, the Sorbonne had two principal entrances; both contrasted with French religious facades in the early part of the century, such as that of St. Gervais by Salomon de Brosse (1616). The courtyard facade to the north—the first independent portico applied to an ecclesiastical building in France—may have been inspired by Carlo Maderno's facade for St. Peter's, which was under construction while Lemercier was in Rome. It was more purely antique and in the long run more revolutionary; nevertheless, the west front had more immediate impact. There Lemercier presented a pedantic and sober interpretation of Giacomo della Porta's facade for Il Gesù, a novelty in France, preceded only by the simpler experiments of the Jesuit architect Etiènne Martellange. Lemercier preserved the classical separation of stories and wings, but broke the entablature and introduced a rhythm of coupled columns and pilasters that demonstrate an awareness of the need for a larger organization. Some contemporaries criticized the ordonnance and openings, and Lemercier continued to refine this Roman facade type at the chapels of Richelieu and Rueil, at the entrance pavilion to Richelieu, and in his modifications to François Mansart's initial designs for the Val-de-Grâce.

In contrast, Lemercier's early domestic architecture reveals little Italian influence. Commissioned by the Duc de Liancourt to enlarge the Hôtel de Bouillon begun by Salomon de Brosse, Lemercier worked within a predominantly French tradition. The Hôtel Liancourt incorporated basic elements of the early French *hôtel* derived from the Château de Bury, yet encompassed new features, such as an exaggerated axial differentiation and an expansion of living space, which were important to future Baroque town houses. Although the Hôtel de Bouillon exhibits slightly more unified massing, the facade retains the French decorative lexicon of controlled rustication, quoins, and a limited use of the classical orders.

Lemercier may also have been responsible for the Château de Liancourt, built for the same patron, which has a typical château plan and a severe reduction of the orders. The garden is an important example of the regularity and order of early French Baroque landscape design.

In 1624 Louis XIII appointed Lemercier to continue the rebuilding of the Square Court of the Louvre. Although construction was limited for more than a decade due to economic reasons, it was renewed just after Richelieu's establishment of the Académie Française (1635) and Sublet de Noyer's appointment as sûrintendant des bâtiments (1638). From the beginning Lemercier was guided and restrained by the idiom of Pierre Lescot's venerated facade. He duplicated the earlier elevation on the opposite side of a new pavilion-frontispiece; this Pavillon de l'Horloge incorporated Lescot's decorative system for its three lowest stories, and developed the classicizing overlay upward with an additional attic story supported by caryatids, a complicated pediment and a square dome. Lemercier's work at the Louvre is important not only because it demonstrates an Early Baroque architect operating within a 16th-century French ornamental context, but because it provided him with a vocabulary of forms and motifs to exploit in his private work for Cardinal Richelieu.

Lemercier created three residences for Richelieu: the Palais Cardinal (later the Palais Royal), the Château Richelieu and the Château Rueil. In them Lemercier used the palace type as a vehicle to develop an architectural iconography reflecting Richelieu's personal vision of French government and culture.

Lemercier began the Palais Cardinal the same year that Richelieu regained his position on Louis XIII's state council (1624), and Richelieu himself took an active role in its design. The magnitude of this collection of old and new buildings escalated along with the patron's status, ambition and wealth, and is frequently criticized for its general confusion and impracticality. The palace and gardens did, however, establish a new axis perpendicular to the Louvre and superimposed a more regular grid over the existing urban order. Lemercier typically applied a system of major and minor axes in his landscape design. His work was a notable link between the projects of Henri IV and Louis XIV.

Lemercier's attempts to embody a specific symbolic program are most obvious in his expansion of the château and village of Richelieu, in the cardinal's childhood home in Poitou. The plan of the palace was conventional, but its scale and system of interrelated forecourts harkened back to the vast plan of Charleval designed by Jacques Androuet du Cerceau. The Château de Richelieu is frequently dismissed by modern scholars as additive, retardative and a largely inept reworking of the type, but merely stylistic criticism ignores Lemercier's attempts to create a visual expression of Richelieu's own understanding of his status as an individual and his role in an evolving modern state. The château's garden facade, for example, while an awkward arrangement of unrelated modules, is also a carefully simplified and vernacular restatement of Lemercier's design for the entrance front of the Louvre. Moreover, much of the decorative sculpture on the exterior and at least one of the painting programs of the interior specifically link the cardinal to the ancient hero Hercules, and thus to the concept of [political] virtue and its attendant rewards of prosperity and plenty.

While not on the level of François Mansart and Louis Le Vau, Jacques Lemercier is noteworthy for his attempt to assimilate Italian design of the Renaissance and Baroque into an essentially French manner of building, in order to establish an iconography and hierarchy within French architectural design.

—PATRICIA LYNN PRICE

L'ENFANT, Pierre Charles.

French. Born in Paris, France, 2 April 1754. Died in Maryland, 2 June 1825. Served as officer of French Colonial troops; sailed to America early in 1777 to help the Colonies in their fight for independence; served under George Washington as military engineer; established residence and began architectural practice in New York, 1784.

Chronology of Works
All in the United States
† Work no longer exists

1782	Dauphin Celebration Pavilion, Philadelphia, Pennsylvania†
1787	St. Paul's Chapel, New York City
1788	Federal Constitution Parade Pavilion, New York City†
1788-89	Federal Hall, New York City (remodeling)†
1791	Plan for Washington, D.C.
1794-96	Robert Morris House, Philadelphia, Pennsylvania†

Publications

BOOKS ABOUT L'ENFANT

CAEMMERER, HANS PAUL: *The Life of Pierre Charles L'Enfant.* Washington, D.C., 1950.
KITE, ELIZABETH S. (ed.): *L'Enfant and Washington 1791-1792.* Baltimore, 1929.
REIFF, DANIEL D.: *Washington Architecture, 1791-1861: Problems in Development.* Washington, D.C., 1971.
REPS, JOHN W.: *Monumental Washington: The Planning and Development of the Capital Center.* Princeton, New Jersey, 1967.

ARTICLES ABOUT L'ENFANT

JENNINGS, J. L. S.: "Artistry as Design: L'Enfant's Extraordinary City." *Library of Congress Quarterly Journal* (Summer 1979).
KIMBALL, FISKE: "Origin of the Plan of Washington, D.C." *Architectural Review* New series 7 (September 1918): 41-45.
"L'Enfant's Memorials" and "L'Enfant's Reports to President Washington." *Columbia Historical Society Records* 2 (1899).
PARTRIDGE, WILLIAM: "L'Enfant's Vision: A Discussion of Development from a City on Paper to a City in Actuality." *Federal Architect* 7 (1937): 103-107.
PEETS, ELBERT: "The Genealogy of L'Enfant's Washington." *Journal of the American Institute of Architects* 15 (1927): 115-119, 151-154, 187-191.
PEETS, ELBERT: "Washington as L'Enfant Intended It." In PAUL SPREIREGEN (ed.): *On the Art of Designing Cities: Selected Essays of Elbert Peets.* Cambridge, Massachusetts, 1968.
SIMPSON, SARAH H. J.: "The Federal Procession in the City of New York." *New York Historical Society Quarterly* 9 (1925): 39-57.
"The Story of L'Enfant." *Western Architect* 14 (August 1909): 14-16.

*

Pierre Charles L'Enfant is regarded as among the first professional designers in the United States. His most significant accomplishment was the plan for the new capital, Washington, D.C., begun in 1791. Perhaps influenced by the time he had spent at Versailles as a youth, the scheme superimposed a Baroque layout of grand diagonal boulevards and urban squares over a utilitarian street grid. Major edifices were located on high points in the city, such as the "Congress House" on Jenkins Hill and the "President's Palace" on a knoll facing south to the Potomac River. The ambitious scale of the project was suggested by the (mile-and-a-half-long) embassy and garden promenade L'Enfant envisioned to the west of the Capitol (today's Mall from the Capitol to the Washington Monument), the 160-foot width of major avenues and the eight-square-mile area detailed in the scheme.

Although L'Enfant never designed any buildings for the capital, clues to what he might have imagined architecturally emerge from his renovation of New York City's Federal Hall. The structure, a modest seven-bay, two story structure with three arched openings inset between two wings at ground level, had been the home of the Continental Congress. On 30 April 1789, however, it was to be the site of George Washington's presidential inauguration, an event that required a more commanding profile. Given the unique historic circumstances, it seems reasonable to assume that L'Enfant incorporated in that commission something of his aspirations for the architecture of the new nation.

Stylistically, he balanced a chaste classicism with selectively delicate and often symbolic details. He lifted the silhouette of the Federal Hall with a tall octagonal cupola and a steep roof that absorbed the wings of the structure. Hierarchy was expressed in a second story that was made to appear taller than the lower level. And to highlight the actual location of the inauguration, a good portion of the depth of the center three bays was left open, a formal exterior space marked by a pediment decorated with the American eagle and other insignia, and supported by four Tuscan piers on the ground level and subdivided by four Doric columns on the second story. Overall (with the exception of some lacy grillwork and panels), the composition—while not original—was unified and balanced, and clearly expressed function, strength and pride, if on a somewhat smaller scale than was the norm in Europe. No doubt, in Washington, D.C., L'Enfant felt there was an opportunity to expand and elaborate on this vocabulary, and he went so far as to write President Washington requesting a budget of $1.2 million to cover the first year's construction expenses in the capital.

In terms of reality, L'Enfant's vision outpaced the economic and political situation of those early years in the United States. In a dispute with the city commissioners about the building of a residence across one of the District's proposed streets, he was dismissed before the plan was completed and subsequently refused compensation, because he believed the $2,500 offered him was inadequate. Moreover, this kind of disappointment haunted him throughout his professional career. While in the army during the Revolution, it took more than a year to secure his promotion to major. When he designed the medal and diploma for the Society of the Cincinnati (open to officers who had served in the Revolution and their male descendants), he went over budget and was never fully reimbursed. His 1792 plan for the industrial city of Paterson, New Jersey, was never realized, as strikes and funding problems precipitated the scheme's demise. A lavish house designed for a client in Philadelphia remained embarrassingly half finished when the patron went bankrupt.

In more than four decades of energetic work in the United States, L'Enfant's pride was frequently bruised, as he was seldom able to match the breadth of his proposals to the resources available for projects. Fortunately—and particularly with respect to the plan for Washington, D.C.—this pain never interfered with his pioneer spirit and his ability to articulate and aim for the highest possible design standards.

—THOMAS WALTON

LE NÔTRE, André.

French. Born in Paris, France, 12 March 1613. Died in Paris, 15 September 1700. Grandfather was Pierre Le Nôtre, gardener to Catherine de' Medici at the Tuileries. Studied painting in the studio of Simon Vouet. Served as royal architect to Louis XIII; royal landscape architect under Louis XIV at Versailles.

Chronology of Works
All in France unless noted
All are landscaping projects

1656-61	Château de Vaux-le-Vicomte
1661-87	Château de Versailles
1662	Gardens, Greenwich, England
1662-87	Château de Fontainebleau
1663-73	Château de Saint-Germain-en-Laye
1663-88	Château de Chantilly
1664-79	Palais de Tuileries, Paris
1665-78	Saint-Cloud
1666	Hôtel de Condé, Paris
1670-87	Trianon de Porcelaine and Grand Trianon, Versailles
1673	Château de Conflans
1673-77	Château de Sceaux
1674	Palais Royal
1674-76	Château de Clagny
1675-78	Château de Maintenon
1679-80	Château de Meudon†
1685ff.	Convent School, Saint-Cyr
1691-92	Château de Gaillon
1693-98	Château de Pontchartrain

Publications

BOOKS ABOUT LE NÔTRE

ADAMS, WILLIAM HOWARD: *The French Garden 1500-1800.* New York, 1979.
BERRALL, JULIA S.: *The Garden: An Illustrated History.* New York, 1978.
BOYCEAU DE LA BARAUDERIE, JACQUES: *Traité du jardinage selon les raisons de la nature et de l'art.* Paris, 1638.
CORPECHOT, LUCIEN: *Parcs et jardins de France.* Paris, 1937.
DE SERRES, OLIVIER: *Théâtre d'agriculture.* Paris (1600) 1804-1805.
FOX, HELEN M.: *André Le Nôtre, Garden Architect to Kings.* New York, 1962.
The French Formal Garden. Vol. 3 in Dumbarton Oaks Colloquium on the History of Landscape Architecture. Washington, D.C., 1974.
GANAY, ERNEST DE: *Andre Le Nôtre, 1613-1700.* Paris, 1962.
GOTHEIN, MARIE LUISE: *A History of Garden Art.* London, 1928.
GUIFFREY, JULES: *André Le Nostre.* Paris, 1912.
HAZLEHURST, F. HAMILTON: *Gardens of Illusion: The Genius of Andre Le Nostre.* Nashville, Tennessee, 1980.
JELLICOE, GEOFFREY and SUSAN: *The Landscape of Man: Shaping the Environment from Prehistory to the Present Day.* London, 1987.
PFNOR, RODOLPHE: *Le château de Vaux-le-Vicomte.*

*

André Le Nôtre, landscape architect extraordinaire in the service of Louis XIV, elevated the practice of gardening to the level of prestige accorded art and architecture, while providing an outdoor stage for the glorification of the Sun King as a complement to the architectural interiors created for the royal court by Louis Le Vau and Jules Hardouin-Mansart.

Le Nôtre's training and education included instruction in art and architecture, in addition to apprenticeship in landscape architecture under the tutelage of older professional gardeners. Further, his study of technical treatises on proportions and illusionism contributed to the grand architectural scale and perspectival views of his landscape vistas at Versailles and Vaux-le-Vicomte, as well as numerous other French châteaux, and enabled him to rein in potentially uncontrollable expansions of these gardens with natural boundaries of trees, shrubs and pools, which, in his hand, were transformed into shapes of architectural form and character. Following the advice of an early mentor, Le Nôtre studied painting in the studio of Simon Vouet, premier painter to Louis XIII, and architecture with an architect not yet identified, although possible choices suggested by Le Nôtre's biographer Hamilton Hazlehurst include François Mansart and Jacques Lemercier. And, at the height of his career, in 1679, Le Nôtre made an official trip to Italy for the king and absorbed many ideas in classical Rome for French gardens.

Like Hardouin-Mansart, Le Nôtre was rewarded with many royal honors and titles during his career, but he avoided the petty envy and jealousy aroused by the royal architect. Le Nôtre was regarded highly by the king, who often sought his opinion on artistic and architectural projects; however, he probably was eased out of his prominent position at court late in his career and forced into premature retirement by the Marquis de Louvois, who succeeded Jean-Baptiste Colbert as superintendant of buildings (*Surintendent des Bâtiments.*)

Le Nôtre's early works include the design of the gardens of the Tuileries Palace in Paris while he served as royal architect to Louis XIII, the continuation and culmination of the masterful landscape begun by Claude Mollet for Nicholas Fouquet at Vaux-le-Vicomte, and additional projects for members of the royal family and a number of private patrons. Then, at some point between 1661 and 1662, he began designs for the expansion of the gardens of Louis XIII's hunting lodge at Versailles, which Louis XIV began to expand after reaching his majority. Other projects for Louis XIV included the gardens at Marly, revisions of the gardens at Fontainebleau and St. Germain-en-Laye, and additional changes at the Tuileries Palace in Paris. Also, Le Nôtre designed gardens for members of the king's family and entourage. Among these were Chantilly for the Grand Condé, cousin of the king; Sceaux for Colbert; Meudon for Louvois; and a number of small gardens for the town houses of Parisian patrons.

At Vaux-le-Vicomte, Le Nôtre, already a veteran in the design and redesign of complex landscape schemes, was prepared to leave his own distinctive artistic signature in the landscape. There, in a long, open vista, Le Nôtre, following the general lines of Mollet's earlier scheme for the garden, established a strong main axis that bisects the domed oval salon of the château designed by Louis Le Vau. Symmetrical arrangements of pools (*parterres d'eau*) flowerbeds (*parterres*), grass plots (*parterres de gazon*) and geometric arrangements of trees flank the central axis (*allée*) in a harmonious arrangement of linear perspective leading to some invisible vanishing point well beyond the view of the château from either the garden or court entrance side. The garden setting at Vaux that so clearly signifies the knowledge Le Nôtre had acquired during his earlier studies of art, science and optics is also evocative of the great gardens of the Renaissance in Italy. All over the entire park, Le Nôtre, borrowing from Renaissance precedents, employed a point and counterpoint of pools and grass plots, fountains and flowerbeds, and dramatic surprises of water in unexpected places. The delight and surprise of mysterious water sources presented yet another aspect of dramatic Baroque theater in the 17th century. Throughout the complex scheme of the expansive park, Le Nôtre carefully arranged its components and set them apart from the château so that the building is clearly visible at all times. The geometric configuration of landscape elements enhances the château but never obscures a view of it from either the court or the garden side. And, like the elements of a perspectival view in a Renaissance landscape, the trees at the outer edges of the park fade away into the distance as if blurred by the haze of atmospheric perspectival effects.

Louis XIV was captivated by the grandiose setting of the gardens at Vaux-le-Vicomte when he attended Fouquet's celebrated fête in August 1661, and he took Le Nôtre into his service soon afterward. From that point onward, Le Nôtre served the Sun King until both monarch and landscape architect were old men.

At Versailles, Le Nôtre employed pools, fountains, grass plots and flowerbeds to enhance the grandeur of the young king and to highlight the architectural allure of the expanding château. Although now fixed permanently in the public consciousness by the passage of time because of their familiarity, Le Nôtre's gardens changed often during his tenure. Transformations occasionally occurred daily, while new architecturally oriented landscape fantasies accompanied major events and celebrations at Versailles.

André Le Nôtre: Château de Versailles, Versailles, France, 1661-87

The garden at Versailles, like that at Vaux-le-Vicomte, has a dominant main axis that leads from the center of the city of Versailles, which belonged to the king and was thus subject to the transformation by royal decree, through the center of the château and the main royal walkway (*Allée Royale*) to the terminus of the Grand Canal at the end of the park. Radial streets fan outward into the city of Versailles and the park on the garden side of the château like the orthogonals of a Renaissance perspective scheme in what is known as a goose-foot arrangement (*patte d'oie*), while two major cross axes intersect the main axis. The north *parterre* (*Parterre du Nord*), which was developed late in the program, creates an asymmetrical balance with the new Orangery (*Nouvelle Orangerie*) by Hardouin-Mansart, which replaced an earlier one by Le Vau on the south side of the château. A second cross axis leads to the Trianons north of the château.

In the early years of the reign of Louis XIV, Le Nôtre created numerous temporary garden designs for fêtes and celebrations. Many of these elaborate decorations at Versailles, built at great expense and through extensive efforts of Le Nôtre and his assistants, were characteristic of the early days of the reign of the youthful king when Versailles was still only a hunting lodge. With the development of the château and the decision to move the court to Versailles, Le Nôtre devoted his efforts to permanent creations within the park. Some of these celebrated the king's amorous relationships and did not survive after the alliances ended. Other creations in the park were transformed by later stylistic changes in garden tastes, but Le Nôtre's major grand scheme for the entire network of the garden is still intact.

Le Nôtre's primary focus at Versailles was the theme of Louis XIV as Apollo, and the theme of the sun god dominates the long central axis. In the circular Basin of Latona (*Bassin de Latone*), Apollo's mother appeals to his father Zeus, who punishes those who do not treat Latona properly by turning them into frogs. In the large Apollo Basin (*Bassin d'Apollon*), the Grand Canal extends outward to the edge of the park and terminates the main axis.

As the château, changed during its expansion, Le Nôtre was obligated to transform his gardens to reflect the increasingly grandiose scale of Le Vau's envelope (*enveloppe*). He developed a number of plans for the garden plot directly in front of the château. And, in his final transformation of the garden side, he created two simple, crystal-clear pools (*miroirs d'eau*) to reflect the Hall of Mirrors (*Galerie des Glaces*) that Hardouin-Mansart created by enclosing the central balcony of Le Vau's envelope. These reflecting pools, which are visible from the long reception room, unite the external world of Le Nôtre's gardens with Hardouin-Mansart's grand internal stage.

Le Nôtre's permanent garden embellishments at Versailles had a decidedly architectural character, such as the Ballroom Grove (*Salle de Bal*) and the Grove of the Triumphal Arch (*Arc de Triomphe*). And, although officially attributed to Hardouin-Mansart, the new Orangery has been described in many contemporary sources as based on an idea by Le Nôtre. The issue, which cannot be reconciled without further documentation because Hardouin-Mansart's biographers attribute it to him, merely confirms the strong interest Le Nôtre had in architecture and the respect paid him by his contemporaries.

For the Porcelain Trianon (*Trianon de Porcelaine*), a house built beyond the main axis by Le Vau from 1670 to 1672 as a royal retreat, Le Nôtre designed a formal, symmetrical garden similar to that of the main château. It differed from the main garden, however, in that flowers were a more significant part of the decoration than in the gardens of the main château. Le Nôtre planted a variety of flowers there that were admired as much for their bouquet as for their appearance. In 1687 Hardouin-Mansart replaced Le Vau's deteriorating Porcelain Trianon with the Grand Trianon of pink and yellow marble, but Le Nôtre's garden arrangement remained relatively the same, and was seen to its best advantage from rooms planned by Hardouin-Mansart for their views of the flowers. There, Le Nôtre again established linear perspectival views of the house from parts of the garden to enhance the appearance of the house.

Le Nôtre borrowed from numerous sources and expanded an incipient formal garden tradition in France to define the grand formal garden style of the second half of the 17th century. His garden masterpieces in France led to a vogue throughout the rest of Europe for formal geometric gardens.

—JOYCE M. DAVIS

LEONARDO DA VINCI.

Italian. Born Leonardo di Ser Piero da Vinci, 15 April 1452. Died in Amboise, France, 2 May 1519. Self-taught in architecture; studied painting with Verrocchio in Florence. ca. 1470-77. Member of the Florence guild, 1472; lived in Verrocchio's house, 1476; set up his own studio, late 1470s; worked for Lodovico Sforza, Milan, ca. 1482-99; worked in Florence, 1500-06; worked for Louis XII of France, 1507-19, as painter and engineer; lived in Amboise (but was in Rome, 1513-16).

Publications

BOOKS BY LEONARDO

Notebooks. Edited by Edward MacCurdy. 2 vols. London, 1938; edited by Pamela Taylor, New York, 1960.
Fragments at Windsor Castle from the Codex Atlanticus. Edited by Carlo Pedretti. London, 1957.

BOOKS ABOUT LEONARDO

ARATA, GIULIO ULISSE: *Leonardo architetto e urbanista.* Milan, 1953.
BARONI, C.: *Leonardo as Architect*, Exhibition catalog. Milan, 1939.
BELTRAMI, LUCA: *Leonardo da Vinci negli studi per il tiburio della cattedrale di Milano.* Milan, 1903.
CALVI, I.: *L'architettura militare di Leonardo da Vinci.* Milan, 1943.
DOUGLAS, R. LANGTON: *Leonardo da Vinci, His Life and Pictures.* Chicago, 1944.
FIRPO, L. (ed.).: *Leonardo: Architetto e urbanista.* Turin, 1963.
GALUZZI, P. (ed.): *Leonardo da Vinci, Engineer and Architect.* Montreal, 1987.
HEYDENREICH, LUDWIG H.: *Leonardo da Vinci.* London and New York, 1954.
HEYDENREICH, LUDWIG H.: *Die Sakralbau-Studien Leonardo da Vincis.* Rev. ed., Munich, 1971.
HEYDENREICH, LUDWIG H.: *Leonardo Studies.* New York, 1987.
KEMP, M.; ROBERTS, J.; and STEADMAN, P.: *Leonardo Da Vinci.* New Haven, Connecticut, 1989.
MARANI, P. C.: *L'architettura fortificata negli studi di Leonardo da Vinci.* Florence, 1984.
MÜNTZ, EUGENE: *Leonardo da Vinci, Artist, Thinker, and Man of Science.* London, 1898.

PEDRETTI, CARLO: *A Chronology of Leonardo's Architectural Studies after 1500.* Geneva, 1962.

PEDRETTI, CARLO: *Leonardo, Architect.* 1985.

PEDRETTI, CARLO: *Leonardo da Vinci: The Royal Palace at Romorantin.* Cambridge, Massachusetts, 1972.

ARTICLES ABOUT LEONARDO

BRIZIO, A. M.: "Bramante e Leonardo alla corta di Lodovico il Moro." In *Studi Bramanteschi: Atti del Congresso internazionale.* Rome, 1970.

DEGENHART, BERNHARD: "Dante, Leonardo und Sangallo." *Römisches Jahrbuch für Kunstgeschichte* 7 (1955): 101-292.

FERGUSSON, FRANCES D.: "Leonardo da Vinci and the tiburio of the Milan Cathedral." *Architectura* 7 (1977): 175-192.

GUILLAUME, J.: "Léonard de Vinci et l'architecture française." *Revue de l'Art* XXV (1974): 71.

LANG, S.: "Leonardo's Architectural Designs and the Sforza Mausoleum." *Journal of the Warburg and Courtauld Institute* 31 (1968): 218-233.

MALTESE, CORRADO: "Il pensiero architettonico e urbanista di Leonardo." In *Leonardo Saggi e Ricerche.* Rome, 1954.

MURRAY, PETER: "Leonardo and Bramante: Leonardo's Approach to Anatomy and Architecture and Its Effect on Bramante." *Architectural Review* 134 (1963): 346-351.

PEDRETTI, CARLO: "Newly Discovered Evidence of Leonardo's Association with Bramante." *Journal of the Society of Architectural Historians* 32 (1973): 223-237.

PEDRETTI, CARLO: "The Original Project for S. Maria delle Grazie." *Journal of the Society of Architectural Historians* 32 (1973): 30-42.

PEDRETTI, CARLO: "The Sforza Sculpture." *Gazette des beaux-arts* 69-70 (1977-78).

*

Leonardo da Vinci was not a practicing architect, nor did he leave a body of work from which his importance and his influence can be judged and measured. Indeed, Leonardo never produced any work of architecture that was actually constructed. Rather, he produced a large number of plans, schemes, drawings, elevations, proposals and concepts, ranging from the intimate to the monumental. His inquiry into the possibilities offered by architecture, as both an art and a science, produced plans for churches, chapels, public buildings, palaces and cities and even plans for the regulation of entire regions. It is entirely on the basis of these never-executed proposals that Leonardo da Vinci, as architect, must be appraised; it is in his influence on subsequent architects, and in his influence on their architecture, that he must be considered as contributing to the development of Italian and Western architecture.

Leonardo was among the greatest artists and thinkers of the Italian Renaissance. His wide-ranging intellect examined architecture along with the other arts, fine and natural, and the sciences. His approach to architecture was aesthetic as well as pragmatic, as he was concerned not only with the appearance of a building, but also with its construction and its structure.

In 1487, while in Milan, he submitted a model for a dome to cover the crossing of that city's vast Gothic cathedral, a scheme that was never executed, but which brings to mind the similar, executed project for the crossing of the cathedral in Florence, to which his solution refers and to which it is indebted. During his last years, at Amboise in France, Leonardo produced a scheme for a new city and an imposing royal palace at Romorantin, but this scheme, too, was never executed. It is to his notebooks, then, that one must turn to gain a broad understanding of his immense, if concealed, influence on subsequent architects, such as Bramante, Raphael and Palladio, and their architecture.

Continuing the tradition begun by Filippo Brunelleschi, Leonardo experimented with a large number of central-plan churches. His schemes envisioned endless variations on the theme of the church composed of a central room; plans with circular chapels ringing the central area; plans with alternating chapels ringing the central space creating Greek-cross plans with infilled arms; plans alternating satellite chapels and towers at each corner. The underlying themes seem often to be the circle set in a square, or the circle set in a Greek cross, or the circle set in intersecting squares. Leonardo proposed churches on two levels, with a lower crypt and chapel, and an upper domed church. His plan for a cross-shaped church with a central domed crossing (Paris MS Bf 57) shows a striking resemblance to the plan Donato Bramante was to develop for his new St. Peter's in Rome, as does a plan (Paris MS Bf 18, 19r) which shows the repetition of smaller Greek-cross-shaped chapels around a central space at the crossing of a large, domed Greek-cross plan. In a proposal for a church facade (Venice, Accademia), Leonardo anticipated not only Michelangelo's proposal for the facade of San Lorenzo in Florence, but also the church facades of Andrea Palladio and the later Baroque facades of Carlo Maderno and Giovanni Lorenzo Bernini.

In civil architecture, Leonardo's plan for a palace facade (CA f 885r/322r-b) clearly anticipated not only Bramante's Roman palace style, but Raphael's as well. Leonardo spoke not the language of the Florentine Renaissance of Brunelleschi and Leon Battista Alberti, but rather the fully developed, classically inspired language of the High Roman Renaissance of Bramante.

In urban planning, the extension of architecture into the larger environment, Leonardo proposed schemes that, though never executed, have had a profound influence on the history of urban planning. His proposal for the rebuilding of that area of Florence between San Lorenzo and San Marco would have created a rectangular princely city centered on the Medici palace on the Via Larga (Via Cavour). The scheme was reinterpreted by Giorgio Vasari for his replanning of the area between the Palazzo Vecchio and the Arno River, centering the new Uffizi on the tower of the then-Palazzo Ducale, and thereby creating a new princely city out of the core of republican Florence. This same striking regularity is apparent at the aforementioned Romorantin, with its broad parallel streets intersected at right angles by short, wide cross-streets. Leonardo there introduced the use of urban canals as part of the city's gridded street system. A long, straight canal bisects the city, and shorter canals, following the cross-streets, cross it at right angles, connecting the central canal to a system of ring canals that encircle the town and act as a defensive moat. This clearly articulated scheme, both utilitarian and salubrious, anticipated not only the "water gardens" of the Italian and French Baroque, but also the regularly planned canal and street system of Amsterdam of some 200 years later.

Leonardo's plans for a city center to be built on two levels, with a series of tunnels below ground carrying wagon, cart and horse traffic as well as waste material, and an upper level consisting of a series of arcaded structures framing interconnected public squares and pedestrian walkways, forecast urban forms that did not make their practical appearance until the present century. Leonardo envisioned a city of cleanliness and convenience that would promote the well-being of its inhabitants even in the midst of the dense crowding typical of the Late Medieval-Early Renaissance cities of Italy. Leonardo as architect and urban planner must be considered not in regard to the actual structures he designed and built, but rather in the design of numerous structures, churches and palaces, which had a deep, lasting, profound and beneficial effect on architecture both in

Italy and abroad, on architects in his immediate following, and on subsequent architects from the High Renaissance onward.

Other than the facades, plans, elevations and urban schemes found in his notebooks, Leonardo left no other record of his architectural thinking except in some of his frescoes, and it is to this limited source that one must turn to broaden the understanding of his architectural vocabulary and his contribution to the art of architecture.

Though not displaying a full facade, or even a distant view of a complete structure, the architectural backdrop behind the annunciate Virgin in his early *Annunciation* (Uffizi), reveals an approach to the treatment of the wall which finds no parallel in the palace architecture of the Early Renaissance in Florence. Both the partially glimpsed doorway and the angled corner enframing the Virgin are rendered in fine finished ashlar or marble quoins set in an otherwise unarticulated wall. Above the head of the Virgin, a small tabernacle-like window rests on a *cyma recta* molding and seems to have a marble sliding panel in place of a plane of glass. What is most impressive in this early work (ca. 1475) is the appearance of monumental white quoins, which serenely define the extent of the wall. There is in this treatment a subtle contrast between the beautifully rendered quoins and the smooth, painted stucco surface of the wall. It is a treatment of the wall not found in the works of Brunelleschi or Alberti, who often used heavily rusticated quoins to enframe a rusticated wall, pronouncing the quoining by raising these stones out from the surface of the facade. Leonardo's treatment of this architectural element would seem to prefigure the use of quoins, in this manner, in the works of Giacomo da Vignola, as at the Villa Giulia, Rome, or in the facade of the Palazzo Farnese, Rome, in its original configuration by Antonio da Sangallo the Younger, and in the palace facades of the Roman Baroque, which quite often contrasted the stone texture of the quoins to the smooth surface of the stuccoed wall.

The Adoration of the Magi (1481) is perhaps the most unusual piece of fictive architecture conceived during the last phase of the Early Renaissance, that prefigurement of the High Renaissance (1480-1500) which may be called the "proto-High Renaissance." In this work, Leonardo created an architectural background that is both difficult to describe and even more difficult to comprehend. Several stairways built over arched passageways ascend to an upper terrace, which in the preparatory drawing for the work is shown crowded with spectators, but in the unfinished final work is rendered as a blank wall connected to a series of broken arches and vaults. The scale of this stair wall, its prominent location and its enigmatic quality all seem to point to the architectural ambiguities of Mannerism. Though less convoluted than the lava-like stairs at the Laurentian Library, Florence, for which Michelangelo prepared a design in 1525, these stairs seem to be completely unfunctional and unusable, posing a number of questions as to their symbolic significance and narrative intent. They do, however, serve as inspiration for the many such stairways which ascend and descend in shallow dizzying, dangerous flight in the frescoes of Mannerist artists, such as those produced by Giorgio Vasari at the Vatican and in the Palazzo Vecchio in Florence.

The "proto-Mannerism" of the architecture of the *Adoration* was replaced by the almost pure Palladianism of the setting of the *Last Supper* in Milan (1495-97). This perfectly proportioned interior, reflecting perhaps the perfection of the Divinity contained therein, seems to have been worked out using mathematical formulas as well as perspective construction. The sharply inclined side walls, which illusionistically continue the side walls of the refectory, are divided by four evenly spaced rectangular panels set in an unarticulated wall; the closing rear wall contains three windows (symbolic of the Trinity), of which the central one is larger than the two sidelights, whose lintels are set somewhat below the upper level of the panels of the side walls. The center window is crowned by a segmental pediment that also serves as a sort of half-halo above the head of the Christ. The purity, simplicity and geometric precision of this interior seem to predict the coolly classical interiors of Palladio's villas in the Veneto.

With an attempt to understand Leonardo's fictive architecture, it may be possible to understand the protean nature of this architectural imagination, which seems to encompass in his painted works the development of Italian architecture from Bramante through Palladio.

It may also be argued that the fictive architecture of Leonardo, especially in his complex geometric plans for central churches, looks forward to the imaginative complexity of the Baroque; and that the fantasy of Guarino Guarini's Santa Sindone is prefigured in the *horror vacui* of many of Leonardo's church designs. The multiplication of domes, half-domes, turrets and towers, apses and niches, and the complex patterning of the walls in which every surface is covered with excrescences also recall the Italo-Byzantine churches of Padua and the Veneto, the Byzantine of San Vitale at Ravenna and even the Byzantine churches of Russia and the Moslem mosques of Turkey. An investigation of Leonardo's church designs presents a confounding paradox, as they are capable of being interpreted both as forerunners of future developments and as syntheses of past accomplishments. His treatment of wall surfaces was, at times, both classical and anticlassical: he employed the vocabulary of the classic orders as redefined by Alberti and others, but he employed them without a sense of interval, allowing order to tell against wall and one space to tell against another. In this, his treatment of wall approached the complexity of Mannerism, and his treatment of mass prefigured the ambiguity of Mannerism and the geometric convolution of the Baroque.

Leonardo possibly never intended for these domed structures to really rise from the ground; rather, he may have been experimenting, as he did with so much else, with the problem of uniting the material and the spiritual by the integration of "perfect" geometric forms, the square and the circle. (Think of his drawing of a man astride a circle set in a square.) The centralized church plan had exercised the imaginations of architects throughout the quattrocento, and had found expression in such works as Santa Maria della Consolazione at Todi. Leonardo, in the application of his ever-fertile imagination to such schemes, moved quite rapidly from the realm of the real and the possible to that of fantasy and pure invention. One need but look at the elevation for a centralized church (MS B, the Bibliothèque of the Institut de France) to realize that the structural problems involved in this design, of a church bearing a central high dome ringed by eight smaller domes all set on drums upon a cross-in-square base, would have been enormous. The piers needed to support the superstructure would have invaded the space below the dome, if adequate, or would have proven inadequate if restricted to the small area allowed them. One need but think of the problem Bramante confronted in building the piers for the dome of the new St. Peter's, based, in large measure, on a plan similar to that found in Leonardo's notebook.

One also wonders if the impression presented by the interflowing spaces of these church interiors would have seemed too fluid to be intelligible, too interpenetrating to present a comprehensive reading of the whole through the parts and of the parts within the whole. It is interesting that in his treatment of secular structures, Leonardo relied on the standard vocabulary of Early Renaissance architecture to articulate his walls and on the geometric arrangement of space which had become standardized for palaces and public buildings. In these works, his imagination was more concerned with the matter of sitting, communication, hygiene, convenience and utility, rather than purely formal problems of design. Indeed, some of his urban plans prefigured elements that did not appear in city planning until well into the 19th century. It is possible, therefore, to detect a strong separation in Leonardo's designs between the sacred and the secular. His imagination tended toward the practical and the utilitarian in matters secular, and toward the theoretical and speculative in matters sacred.

One is left, then, with a problem of enormous complexity in attempting to evaluate the architecture of Leonardo da Vinci, which is as ambiguous as the master himself. Of prime consideration is the simple, undeniable fact that the master never built a building, so that, to evaluate his architectural contribution, one must rely on the plans, elevations, schemes and proposals found in his notebooks, drawings, and even paintings. His intentions, therefore, cannot be compared with a finished, built version, so it his intentions alone which must be evaluated. Like the man himself, they reflect a wide-ranging intellect brought to bear on the most complex of the noble arts, and an intellectual curiosity which ranged from the known to the unknown, from past to future, from the practical to the theoretical. These strengths produced a literate architecture that encompassed the traditions of Tuscany and Lombardy and the Veneto, the advances of the quattrocento, the monumentality of Rome, on the one hand; and which foretold the classical perfection of the cinquecento, the ambiguity of Mannerism and the complexity of the Baroque, on the other. To evaluate Leonardo's architecture, then, is to evaluate Leonardo, truly, as an architect's architect.

—DONALD FRICELLI

LESCAZE, William.

Swiss. Born in Geneva, Switzerland, 27 March 1896. Died in New York City, 9 February 1969. Immigrated to the United States, 1923. Studied at the École des Beaux-Arts, Geneva, 1914-15; Eidgenössische Technische Hochschule, Zurich, under Karl Moser, 1915-19, M.A. Worked for Henri Sauvage, Paris, France, 1919-20; worked for Hubbell and Benes, Cleveland, Ohio, 1921-22, and in the office of Walter R. MacCormack, Cleveland, 1922; in private practice, New York City, 1923-29; in partnership wit h George Howe, Philadelphia, 1929-34; principal, William Lescaze and Associates, 1934 until his death in 1969.

Chronology of Works
All in the United States unless noted
† *Work no longer exists*

1929	Oak Lane Country Day School, Philadelphia†
1929-32	Philadelphia Saving Fund Society Office Building, Philadelphia (with George Howe)
1930-31	Frederick V. Field House, Hartford, Connecticut
1930-32	Headmaster's House (Curry House), Dartington Hall, Totnes, Devon, England
1933-34	William E. Lescaze House and Office, New York City
1934	Raymond Kramer House, New York City
1936-37	Alfred Loomis House, Tuxedo Park, New York
1936-38	Columbia Broadcasting System Studios and Offices, Hollywood, California (with E. T. Heitschmid)
1937-39	Aeronautics Pavilion, World's Fair, New York City†
1940-41	Edward A. Norman House, New York City
1959	Swiss Embassy Chancellery, Washington, D.C.
1961	Christian Peace Building and Chapel, United Nations Headquarters, New York City
1969	One Oliver Plaze, Pittsburgh, Pennsylvania

Publications

BOOKS BY LESCAZE

A Modern Museum. With George Howe. Springdale, Connecticut, 1930.
On Being an Architect. New York, 1942.
A Citizens' Country Club or Leisure Center. New York, 1944.
Uplifting the Downtrodden. New York, 1944.

ARTICLES BY LESCAZE

"The Classic of Tomorrow." *American Architect* (December 1935).
"Why Modern Architecture." *Royal Architectural Institute of Canada Journal* (1937).
"America's Outgrowing Imitation of Greek Architecture." *Architectural Record* (August 1937).
"The Meaning of Modern Architecture." *North American Review* (Autumn 1937).
"Marginal Notes on Architecture." *Virginia Quarterly Review* (Spring 1939).
"The Correlation of the Arts." *American Institute of Architects Journal* (November 1952).
"Another Look at PSFS." *Architectural Forum* (June 1964).
"Thoughts on Art and Architecture." *Art International* (February 1968).

BOOKS ABOUT LESCAZE

HUBERT, CHRISTIAN, and SHAPIRO, LINDSAY STAMM: *William Lescaze*. IAUS Catalog No. 16. New York, 1982.
JORDY, WILLIAM H.: "The American Acceptance of the International Style: George Howe and William Lescaze's Philadelphia Saving Fund Society Building." In *American Buildings and Their Architects: The Impact of European Modernism in the Mid-Twentieth Century*. Garden City, New York, 1972.

ARTICLES ABOUT LESCAZE

HITCHCOCK, HENRY RUSSELL: "Howe and Lescaze." In *Modern Architecture: International Exhibition*. New York, 1932.
Journal of the Society of Architectural Historians 21 (May 1962). Special issue on the PSFS Building.
PICA, AGNOLDOMENICO: "Lescaze." *Domus* (July 1969).
ROBIN, A.: "Howe and Lescaze." *Architecture d'aujourd'hui* No. 4, special issue (November/December 1933).

*

William Lescaze was the most significant modern architect practicing in the International Style on the East Coast of the United States during the 1930s. Only Richard Neutra on the West Coast was as important.

Lescaze had trained in Zurich under Karl Moser, and after working for a brief period for Henri Sauvage in France, emigrated to the United States in August 1920. Lescaze initially settled in Cleveland, where all the modern arts seem to have flourished in the early 1920s, but on receiving his first independent commission in 1923, he moved to New York. For the remainder of the 1920s, he experimented in a wide variety of idioms in the design of restaurants, nightclubs, showrooms, stores, apartment interiors, exhibition kiosks, educational buildings and a bus terminal, all small commissions of a temporary nature.

In 1929 Lescaze was introduced to George Howe, an École des Beaux-Arts trained architect of the prestigious Philadelphia firm of Mellor, Meigs and Howe. Howe wanted to practice in the modern idiom but needed a partner conversant with the Modern Movement, and Lescaze provided the answer by signing articles of copartnership. It was agreed that Howe would be the business partner and would negotiate with clients, and Lescaze would design. Howe brought into the partnership a commission for the Philadelphia Saving Fund Society (PSFS) building, for which he had already made some initial studies, but the design of the building and its details, down to the inkwells and coat pegs, was under the direction of Lescaze. Because PSFS was located in the shopping and transportation hub of Market and Twelfth streets, Lescaze incorporated stores at ground level. The banking hall is situated on the second level, and is expressed on the exterior by a huge aluminum window curving around the corner and set in a wall plane of polished charcola-colored granite. Eighteen-foot deep steel trusses span 63 feet across the banking floor to support the tower above, and in turn are supported on steel columns going down to caisson foundations below basement level. Immediately above the banking hall were three floors for bank offices, above which was rentable space slightly cantilevered out over Market Street. A penthouse suite for bank executives and an observatory (now a television station) topped the building. On plan the office tower is the downstroke of a T, while the service core at the rear of the site forms the cross bar. The tower was clad in buff-colored limestone, the same material used for the columns. Brick was used below sill level for the spandrels on all floors of the tower. The partnership of Howe and Lescaze ended with the completion of the PSFS in 1932, when both architects went their separate ways.

Lescaze's share of the commission from PSFS enabled him to purchase a brownstone at 211 East Forty-eighth Street (1932-33), which he demolished, rather as one would remove an old book from a shelf and insert a new one in its place. Its narrow site made internal planning tight, but Lescaze managed to design both an office and residence in this space. Externally the new house consisted of painted stucco, load-bearing glass blocks and aluminum handrails. There was no attempt at contextualism, since architects working in the modern idiom dismissed the past as being historical and thus irrelevant to modern architecture, which was "original" in that it did not look backward. Planning had to be functional, structure logical, and the delight of architecture resulted, in theory, from function and structure. If the old and new married well, it was because both were of good design for their respective periods. Ada Louise Huxtable considered the Lescaze residence "the first modern house built in the United States." Its success led to similar houses for Raymond Kramer at 32 East Seventy-fourth Street (1934) and Edward Norman at 124 East Seventieth Street (1941). Lescaze was equally adept at designing houses on open sites, such as the Frederick Vanderbilt Field house on Red Hill at Hartford, Connecticut (1930-31). Curved walls, spiral external stairs, experimental materials and tubular furniture made it very much part of the International Style. Other houses by Lescaze were illustrated in architectural magazines of international repute, together with those of Walter Gropius, Marcel Breuer and Richard Neutra.

The musical conductor Leopold Stokowski commissioned Lescaze to design the nursery extension (1929) to the Oak Lane County Day School in Philadelphia. Its flat roof acted as an open sun room and playground for children, the large classroom window brought light into the play area, floors were of cork to cushion the falls of children, wall corners were rounded off, and all furniture and fittings, including toilet fixtures, were reduced to a size that children could readily use. William Curry, English headmaster of the new school, was exceedingly impressed with his new primary school, so when he became director of the educational experiment at Dartington Hall in Devonshire, England, he persuaded Leonard and Dorothy Elmhirst, the owners, to use the services of Lescaze for faculty, children and worker's housing, a gymnasium and offices, all built in the International Style.

During the remainder of the 1930s, Lescaze designed other schools, individual houses and housing complexes, movie theaters, CBS studios, exhibition buildings, unbuilt projects for the Museum of Modern Art, and housing at Chrystie-Forsyth streets in New York City.

In 1942 he published *On Being An Architect,* in which he expressed his ideas and philosophy of architecture. The career of Lescaze from 1929 to 1942 was a success story for the modern idiom in architecture, but the war broke his stride; he was approaching 50 at its end. When, thereafter, large, prestigious commissions from real estate developers brought him financial success, he was designing in the same "contemporary" manner as the average architect would. Even his Number One Oliver Plaza, Pittsburgh (1969), is a Miesian takeoff and has none of the originality of PSFS. It is PSFS for which Howe and Lescaze will always be remembered. According to Philip Johnson, PSFS is "the most interesting piece of architecture in the country . . . unique in modern architecture of the world."

—LAWRENCE WODEHOUSE

LESCOT, Pierre.

French. Born in 1500/1510. Died in Paris, France, 10 September 1578. Studied architecture and mathematics; studied painting at Fontainebleau. Became director of the buildings of the Louvre and overseer of the king; worked under Kings François I, Henri II, François II, Charles IX and Henri III.

Chronology of Works
All in France
† Work no longer exists

1541-44	Alter, St. Germain l'Auxerrois, Paris (with Jean Goujon)†
1545-50	Hôtel de Ligneris (now the Musée Carnavalet; with Jean Bullant)
1546ff.	Château du Louvre, Paris (additions)
1551	Petit-Pont, Paris (as consultant)
1578	Pont-Neuf, Paris (as consultant)

Publications

ARTICLES ABOUT LESCOT

BATIFFOL, L.: "Les premières constructions de Pierre Lescot au Louvre." *Gazette des beaux-arts* 11 (1930).

HAUTECOEUR, L.: "Le Louvre de Pierre Lescot." *Gazette des Beaux-Arts* (1927).

THOMPSON, D.: "A Note on Pierre Lescot, the Painter" *Burlington Magazine,* CXX (1978).

Pierre Lescot: Château du Louvre, Paris, France, 1546ff.

Pierre Lescot brought the idea, concept and philosophy of classical architecture to France. A Parisian of wealthy and noble heritage—he was titled Seigneur de Clagny—Lescot learned architecture and mathematics when he was about twenty, and also did painting at Fontainebleau. There is also evidence that he might have sojourned to Rome in 1556. However, Lescot is most noted as "director of the buildings of the Louvre" and as the "overseer of the king." He worked under Francis I, Henry II, Francis II, Charles IX and Henry III.

Lescot's collaboration with the architect/sculptor Jean Goujon is noted in a now-destroyed altar for Saint Germain l'Auxerrois, Paris (1541-44), and the Fontaine des Innocents (1547-49).

From 1545 to 1550 he and Jean Bullant designed a town house, the Hôtel de Ligneris (called the Carnavalet) in Paris. Lescot contributed, in part, to the Château de Vallery, Paris, and served as consultant for the designs of two Paris bridges, Petit-Pont (1551) and Pont-Neuf (1578).

There followed his work, in 1546, under Francis I to erect "... a great *corps d'hostel* on the site of the present grand ballroom" of the Château du Louvre. This was located on the west wing of the old château. There, he incorporated the existing earlier walls of Charles V's castle from medieval times. Also, for the king he designed, for the west wing, a two-level *corps-de-logis* which displayed a central staircase. This staircase was later moved to the north end of the wing, allowing the ballroom to take up the whole first floor. Then, pavilions were built at each end to create a balanced appearance. Also in 1550, with the assistance of Goujon, the Salle des Caryatides was begun, and a tribune for musicians was added on the south side of the ballroom. Six years later (1556), Lescot designed a third level for the facade to conform with the Pavilion du Roi which faced the Seine River.

There followed the so-called "grand design" for the Louvre under Henry II. This entailed the completion of a court to enclose the extended wings. Although there still remains much controversy as to the true designer of this area, Lescot is given much credit in deploying the initial plans of the quadruple-square courtyard that unites the Louvre to the Tuileries.

Lescot's contributions will be remembered, as he was the first French architect to abolish the Gothic manner for a classical formula. He introduced an ornamental taste that was grand, yet ordered—simple and beautiful. His love for the Corinthian and

Composite orders was coupled with ornamental moldings, double-mullion fenestration and capped by his characteristic curved and triangular pediments. As a result of this, the Louvre is marked by a complexity of design so non-Italian and typically French in style.

Lescot was wary that sculpture would play a dominant role in defining his architecture. Although the fusion of architecture and sculpture recalled medieval French manners, it was given a new bent through the introduction of classical Italian motifs and figural influences—thanks to the talent of Goujon and the tastes of Francis I, whose quest was to create an entirely French artistic expression by incorporating Italian aesthetic ideas. Lescot served as this important "artistic bridge" that completed the philosophy of the king and others to follow.

—GEORGE M. COHEN

LETHABY, William Richard.

British. Born in Barnstaple, Devon, England, 1857. Died in London, 1931. Studied at Royal Academy Schools. Completed articles, Barnstaple; senior assistant to Richard Norman Shaw (1831-1912), Leicester. Opened office, 1891; president, Arts and Crafts Society; founded Central School of Arts and Crafts, 1894; joint principal, Central School of Arts and Crafts, 1894-1911; professor of design, Royal College of Art, 1900.

Chronology of Works
All in England unless noted

1891	Avon Tyrell, Christ-church, Hampshire
1893-94	The Hurst, Hartopp Road, Four Oaks, Warwickshire†
1898-1900	Melsetter House, Hoy, Orkney Islands, Scotland
1898-1901	High Coxlease, Lyndhurst, Hampshire
1898-1900	Eagle Insurance Buildings, Birmingham
1900	Gatehouse, Hoy, Orkney Islands, Scotland
1900	Rysa Lodge, Hoy, Orkney Islands, Scotland
1900	SS. Colm and Mary Chapel, Hoy, Orkney Islands, Scotland
1901-03	All Saints Church, Brockhampton

Publications

BOOKS BY LETHABY

Architecture, Mysticism and Myth. London, 1892. Later rewritten for the *Builder* (1928) and published as *Architecture, Nature and Magic.* London, 1956.
The Church of Sancta Sophia Constantinople: A Study of Byzantine Building. With Harold Swainson. London, 1894.
Mediaeval Art. London, 1904.
Architecture: An Introduction to the History and Theory of the Art of Building. London, 1912.
Form in Civilisation. London, 1922.
Londinium Architecture and the Crafts. London, 1923.
Philip Webb and His Work. London, 1935.

BOOKS ABOUT LETHABY

MACLEOD, ROBERT: "Lethaby as a Key to Mackintosh." In PATRICK NUTTGENS (ed.): *Mackintosh and His Contemporaries in Europe and America.* London, 1988.
NAYLOR, GILLIAN: *The Arts and Crafts Movement.* London, 1990.

POSENER, JULIUS (ed.): *Anfänge des Funktionalismus: Von Arts and Crafts zum Deutschen Werkbund.* Frankfurt-am-Main, 1964.
RICHARDSON, MARGARET: *The Craft Architects.* London and New York, 1983.
RUBENS, GODFREY: *William Richard Lethaby, His Life and Work 1857-1931.* London, 1986.

ARTICLES ABOUT LETHABY

PEVSNER, NIKOLAUS: "Lethaby's Last." *Architectural Review* 130 (1961): 354-357.
ROBERTS, A. R. N.: "The Life and Work of W. R. Lethaby." *Journal of the Royal Society of Arts* 105 (1957): 355-371.
ROOKS, NOEL: "The Works of Lethaby, Webb, and Morris." *Journal of the Royal Institute of British Architects* 57 (1950): 167-175.
RUBENS, GODFREY: "William Lethaby's Buildings." In ALASTAIR SERVICE (ed.): *Edwardian Architecture and Its Origins.* London, 1975.
WALKER, FRANK ARNEIL: "William Lethaby." *Architectural Association Quarterly* 9, No. 4 (1977): 45-53.

*

It is much less for his work as a practicing designer than for his activities in design theory and education that William Richard Lethaby may be regarded as perhaps the most percipient architectural thinker in Edwardian England. In these latter respects his writings drew on a long tradition of subversion—A. W. N. Pugin, John Ruskin, William Morris—which, at first religious, even hieratic, later political and revolutionary, finally emerged with modest but compelling clarity in a reasoned critique that was empirical, scientific in a pragmatic sense and "intensely real." Ironically, Lethaby's down-to-earth ideas about the nature of art and architecture, and his theoretical intimations about what "The Modern Position" ought to be, came too late for any English response. By the time his thoughts had matured into a reformist program in the decade or so before the outbreak of World War I Germany was, as he put it, "racing"; the Werkbund had been formed, and Henri van de Velde, Peter Behrens, Bruno Taut and Walter Gropius were all engaged in giving form to the creative alliance of art, craft and industry.

Out of the historical cosmological preoccupations of his first book, *Architecture, Mysticism and Myth* (1891), Lethaby's thinking progressively distilled an increasingly abstract, even materialist, view, rejecting the "magic" of the styles for those "true mysteries of reality" that were grounded in function and necessity. Books such as his studies of Sancta Sophia and Westminster Abbey, where from 1906 he served as surveyor for 22 years, testified to a conviction that it was neither symbolic allusion nor proportional rule that shaped architecture, but "sound common-sense building and pleasurable craftsmanship." The anti-fine-art legacy of William Morris was clear—art, indeed, was for Lethaby simply a matter of operative "skill, experiment and adventure"—while, anticipating Gropius, he deplored the polarization of art and science, regarding them as mutually necessary aspects of all creative work. In this respect, architecture, that is to say building, ought to be understood no differently from, say, seamanship or farming or, even, setting a table.

But like Gropius, too, Lethaby had to come to terms with the industrialization of the building process. There was no dismissal of craftsmanship, but a recognition of the machine's inevitability both as the eliminator of onerous "Mechanical Toil" and, in a more optimistic sense, as the harbinger of

William Richard Lethaby: All Saints Church, Brockhampton, England, 1901-03

"glorious new worlds." What this might mean in concrete terms was less clear. Neither of Lethaby's two best-known commissions—Eagle Insurance Buildings, Birmingham (1898-1900), and All Saints Church, Brockhampton (1901-03)—went much beyond the tentatively unconventional in form, though the latter did have a rough-boarded concrete roof vault—albeit thatched on the outside. Considerable claims have been made for both buildings—Robert Macleod called the Eagle Insurance project "the quietest revolution in architectural history," while Nikolaus Pevsner detected the beginnings of architectural expressionism at Brockhampton—but the part they played in determining the significance of Lethaby's legacy was certainly overshadowed by his writing and teaching.

First at the LCC Central School of Arts and Crafts, where he had been made joint principal in 1896, and later at the Royal College of Art as professor of design from 1900, Lethaby attempted to bring the 19th-century workshop community into a more effectual relationship with manufacturing industry. It was not that Lethaby's program instituted the methods and conditions of mechanized production, but rather that he directed his students away from historicist or eclectic precedent toward "basic design." This curriculum was grounded first, in drawing from nature rather than casts; second, in a critical study of history and tradition that evaluated form as a product of specific unrepeatable social and economic constraints; and third, in the exercise of craft skills. Only from such a foundation integrating designing and doing, and from a knowledge of the new structural disciplines of steel and reinforced concrete design that belonged to what Lethaby called "modern scientific building," would it be possible for the machine to be controlled. It was, in effect, an adumbration of the approach that was followed at Weimar first by van de Velde and later by Gropius.

Despite this practical educational policy and a corresponding theoretical elaboration which, in Lethaby's essays and books, gradually took the shape of a protofunctionalist argument—houses should be "as efficient as a bicycle"—his ideas went largely unexplored in Edwardian Britain. The problem was that his necessary demythologizing of architecture had not been accompanied by any strong iconic initiative, at least not in his own oeuvre. He spoke of the modern way of building being antipicturesque, "flexible and vigorous, even smart and hard," but that was as close as he came to any image of what the new architecture might look like. Some of his contemporaries did provide clues to this missing link, notably C. F. A. Voysey and Charles Rennie Mackintosh, but in realizing a genuinely modern architecture it was on continental Europe that real progress would be made. Lethaby's achievement was to think through the radical consequences of 19th-century English theory: as he wrote at the end of his 1912 book, *Architecture: an Introduction to the History and Theory of the Art of Building,* "Much has to be done, it is a time of beginning as well as of making an end."

—FRANK A. WALKER

LE VAU, Louis.

French. Born in Paris, France, in 1612. Died in Paris, 11 October 1670. Son of the master mason Louis Le Vau, from whom he received initial training. First architect to King Louis XIV, from 1654.

Chronology of Works
All in France
* Approximate dates
† Work no longer exists

1634-37	Hôtel de Bautru, Paris†
1637-40	Hôtel de Gillier, Paris
1638-40	Hôtel de Bretonvilliers, Paris (completion)†
1639-42	Hôtel Sainctot, Paris†
1640-42	Hôtel Le Vau, Paris
1640-44	Hôtel Lambert, Paris
1640*-44*	Hôtel Hesselin, Paris†
1640*-45*	Château du Raincy†
1642-46	Hôtel Tambonneau, Paris†
1649-50	Hôtel d'Aumont, Paris (continuation of earlier work)
1654*-57*	Château de Meudon (remodeling)†
1654-61	Château de Vincennes (King's and Queen's pavilions)
1656-57	Hôtel de Lauzun, Paris
1656ff.	Hôpital de la Salpêtrière, Paris
1657-61	Château de Vaux-le-Vicomte
1659-66ff.	Tuileries, Paris (remodeling)†
1660-63	Louvre, Paris (south facade I)†
1661-64	Louvre, Paris (Galerie d'Apollon)
1662-64	Hôtel de Lionne, Paris†
1662-74	Collège des Quatre Nations, Paris
1662-70	Ménagerie, Versailles†
1667-70	Louvre, Paris (east facade; colonnade with Charles Le Brun and Claude Perrault)
1668ff.	Louvre, Paris (south facade II; with others)
1668-70	Versailles (enveloppe; not completed until 1673 or 1674)
1670	Trianon de Porcelaine, Versailles†

Publications

BOOKS ABOUT LE VAU

PFNOR, RODOLPHE: *Le château de Vaux-le-Vicomte.*

ARTICLES ABOUT LE VAU

ELANDE-BRANDENBURG, A.: "Les Fouilles du Louvre et les projets de Le Vau." *La vie urbaine* (1964): 241.
HAUTECOEUR, L.: *L'Histoire de l'architecture classique en France* Vol. III (1950).
TOOTH, CONSTANCE: "The Early Private Houses of Louis Le Vau." *Burlington Magazine* 109 (1967).
WHITELEY, MARY, and BRAHAM, ALLAN: "Louis Le Vau's Projects for the Louvre and the Colonnade." *Gazette des beaux-arts* (1964).

*

Louis Le Vau was born in Paris to a father, also named Louis Le Vau, who was a master mason. It is assumed that this is where Le Vau received his initial training. He rose to the position of first architect to Louis XIV and was involved directly in the great projects of the day at the Louvre and Versailles. As first architect to the king (from 1654), he necessarily headed a huge team of architects, artists and artisans. One of Le Vau's great strengths was his creation of magnificent Baroque effects through team effort.

Louis Le Vau: Versailles, France, 1668-70

Le Vau's architectural career began in the 1630s when he started designing hotels for the upper bourgeoisie in Paris. The most important of these commissions were for the development of the Île-St.-Louis, where he incorporated river views into the designs; for instance, at the Hôtel Lambert (begun 1640) he extended the main-floor gallery away from the main block toward the river. The way to the gallery exploited the new Baroque concern for the drama of the view through a succession of effects. Ascending the staircase, the visitor emerges from dark into light, enters an oval vestibule, looks down the enfilade through the vestibule and gallery, and out to the Seine.

During that period Le Vau adapted and developed many such ideas of spatial extension from the Italian Baroque. On the exterior of the Hôtel Lambert, access to the house is through a facade curved at each side to round off the corners and express Baroque movement. The curving also expresses the interior plan. The abovementioned oval vestibule is fitted into one curve, while an octagonal room is located at the other.

At Vaux-le-Vicomte (1657-61) built for Nicolas Fouquet, minister to the king, Le Vau designed a country house of a grandeur not seen before in France. It was so grand, in fact, that when Louis XIV saw his minister's house, he confiscated it and had Fouquet arrested for embezzlement. An oval domed salon dominates the structure inside and out. Le Vau had used this feature before at the château Le Raincy (designed before 1645). The salon, which is two stories high and placed on the garden facade, dominates the facade by its size, its distinctive roof and its degree of projection forward. By these means, Le Vau established not only the prominence of this magnificent feature, but also the reach out into the vista of gardens designed

by André Le Nôtre. The theme of the house, which is the focus of an extensive spatial vista, was established there. Vaux was also the initiation of an enormously successful collaboration by Le Vau with his two associates, the painter Charles Le Brun, and the landscape architect Le Nôtre. Le Vau and Le Brun had worked together before, for example, at the Hôtel Lambert, but with this project all three became a team. The success of this collaboration indicates that the three thought in concert, producing an entirety at Vaux which is much greater than its architecture, interior decoration or garden taken in themselves. Critics have considered the garden facade at Vaux flawed due to a careless use of both the colossal and superposed orders. This trait has in fact been important as an identifying characteristic in the attribution of other works by Le Vau.

The east facade of the Louvre (1667-70) was the first of the two renowned palaces Le Vau worked on with the other noted architects, Le Brun and Claude Perrault. What each contributed to the project, famed for its Baroque classical colonnade, is still disputed. Giovanni Lorenzo Bernini, as the greatest contemporary Roman architect, had been invited to submit designs for finishing the Louvre, which had been under construction and alteration for more than 100 years since the initial decision to enlarge substantially the medieval palace. However, Bernini's designs were all rejected after they had been given due consideration, probably because they were so far from the traditions of French architecture. His final design was too plastic, too tall and heavy-appearing for the rest of the building.

Le Vau's work on the Louvre's east facade was not his first involvement with the palace's rebuilding, but this project marked his change from Italianate Baroque to a classical Baroque style. The logic, discipline and austerity of the latter style, which created an appropriate sense of magnificence, were espoused in the dictates of the Académie d'Architecture when it was founded in 1671. The Académie disapproved, by contrast, of the markedly Italianate curved walls and shaped spaces found frequently in Le Vau's earlier period. The Italianate flat roof suited the French emphasis on precision of articulation and massing of simple forms, so this import could be used without criticism.

In the same building phase, the team refaced Le Vau's south facade of 1660-63 to match the east facade. But it is the east facade with its famous colonnade that is the Louvre's most recognizable feature. The long range of two-story double, free-standing columns dominates the facade, moving almost the entire length of the building. This facade has been compared to the peristyle of a Roman temple flattened to a single plane. The central pavilion is narrow and pedimented. It and the end pavilions project only slightly. A balustrade caps the entire length. The supporting basement is high and very plain with an ashlar finish.

From 1662 to 1674 the Collège des Quatre Nations was constructed to Le Vau's design. He sited it on the opposite bank of the Seine, directly across from the Louvre, and intended it to be part of the same grand complex. Le Vau had designed a bridge to join both structures visually, though it was not constructed until the 19th century. The chapel, which dominates the group, has a tall dome over an oval nave. On the main facade, two-story wings curve forward and out to join the chapel to the pavilions at its side. These curving shapes, inside and out, were mainly the influence of the Italian architects Pietro da Cortona, Francesco Borromini and Bernini, who often used such shapes.

The team that constructed Vaux-le-Vicomte established the basis of what is Versailles today. Much of what Le Vau created at Versailles has been greatly altered or destroyed, but the garden facade (1669) designed under his direction remains the focus of Le Nôtre's vistas, despite major alterations. The design of the garden facade continued Le Vau's stylistic change to the classical Baroque. There, as with the east facade of the Louvre, Le Vau broke with the traditional French roof design that dictated a separate steep roof for each section. Instead, he designed a projection forward or stepped-back and created a pavilion. His construction for the château is actually an "enveloppe" surrounding an existing building, which Louis XIV wanted enlarged and made more formal. Today the facade is three full stories high across its entire length. Originally, the central section of 11 bays above the basement level was recessed to create a terrace. Jules Hardouin Mansart altered the exterior, starting in 1678, by filling in the terrace and adding enormous stepped-back wings to each side for housing the court, following Louis XIV's decision to make Versailles the permanent palace. The Hall of Mirrors now stands where the terrace once was. The entire building constructed by Le Vau became merely the central pavilion in a gigantic complex.

One of the most noted features of the palace until it was destroyed in later renovations was the Escalier des Ambassadors (begun 1671 after Le Vau's death). Designed as an interior ceremonial entrance to the king's suite, it was a magnificent feature meant to impress upon foreign visitors the power of the French king. The stair began at a landing, which split to become two stairs in opposite directions along the wall, making skillful use of a long, narrow area. Lit from above by a skylight, the walls were decorated with patterns of colored marbles and illusionistic paintings designed by Le Brun.

Le Vau's actual architectural role at the court of Louis XIV is controversial in great part because it was deliberately obscured by the king's minister and superintendent of the king's buildings, Jean-Baptiste Colbert. Colbert did not want any one particular architect's name associated with a given building; instead, the structure was to be referred to as the "king's work." In the case of Versailles, Le Vau's chief assistant, François d'Orbay, is credited by some with the actual design of the "enveloppe," partly because at Versailles the superposed order is used alone. For earlier designs of garden facades, Le Vau had used the colossal order only or combined it with superposed orders. Some critics have considered this usage, along with other questions of detailing, as reason for leaving the attribution open.

Versailles, in plan and detail, was imitated by courts all over Europe. Features such as the Escalier des Ambassadors and the tall domed salon at Vaux-le-Vicomte made their appearance in both southern and northern Europe. Le Vau's influence on the architecture of the aristocratic and wealthy is incalculable.

—ANN STEWART BALAKIER

LEVERTON, Thomas.

British. Born in Woodford, Essex, England, in 1743. Died in London, 23 September 1824. Father was the builder Lancelot Leverton. Worked independently; surveyor to the Grocers' Company; surveyor to the Phoenix Fire Insurance Company, London; architect, Land Revenue Office, 1809.

Chronology of Works
All in England unless noted
† *Work no longer exists*

1771	Woodford Hall, Essex†
1772	65 Lincoln's Inn Fields, London
1775-81	1, 6, and 13 Bedford Square, London
1776	Boyles Court, Great Warley
1777-82	Woodhall Park, Hertfordshire
1780	Plaistow Lodge, Bromley, Kent
1783	Commemorative arch (for the American Revolutionary War), Parlington House, Yorkshire
1784-94	Phoenix Fire Insurance Company Office and Fire Engine House, London†
1798-1809	Grocers' Livery Hall, London†
1803	Scampston Hall, Yorkshire
1803	'Sugar' House, New York City, U.S.A.
1806	Hamilton Place, London†

Publications

BOOKS ABOUT LEVERTON

HUSSEY, CHRISTOPHER: *English Country Houses: Mid-Georgian, 1760-1800.* 2nd ed. London, 1963.

NEWMAN, JOHN: *The Building of England: West Kent and the Weald.* Harmondsworth, England, 1969.

OLSEN, DONALD J.: *Town Planning in London: The Eighteenth and Nineteenth Centuries.* New Haven, Connecticut, and London, 1964.

RICHARDSON, GEORGE: *The New Vitruvius Britannicus.* 2 vols. London, 1802-1808.

SUMMERSON, JOHN: *Georgian London.* London, 1945; 1978.

ARTICLES ABOUT LEVERTON

HUSSEY, CHRISTOPHER: "No. 1 Bedford Square." *Country Life* 71 (1932): 150-156.
OSWALD, ARTHUR: "Scampston Hall, Yorkshire." *Country Life* 115 (1954): 946-949, 1034-1038.

*

Thomas Leverton was the son of Lancelot Leverton, a builder of Woodford, Essex, from whom he learned the principles of construction. He was able later to "perfect himself in architecture" through the munificence of "influential patrons." Little is known about his training or career until 1771, when he appeared with the first of his 34 designs exhibited at the Royal Academy until 1803. Although he was "extensively employed in the erection of dwelling houses in London and the country," Leverton was not singled out for praise during his lifetime. The pioneering nature of his work is not explained by his qualities of "integrity, industry and true benevolence" noted in his epitaph at Waltham Abbey.

Leverton may have been responsible for the planning and design of Bedford Square, London (1775-80); the principal agent, Robert Palmer, who had property interests in Essex, may have employed him for the technical side of the business. In 1797 Leverton recorded that he (himself) had "a principal concern in promoting the finishing of Bedford Square, and built among other houses in it that of the Lord Chancellor (Loughborough, Nos. 6 and 6A), besides several on my own account, in one of which I now reside" (No. 13). The exterior has similarities with James Adam's work in Portland Place, London (1776), and may owe something to Joseph Bonomi, who had joined Leverton's office (from that of the Adams brothers) in the 1770s. The north and south-side pilaster porticoes have an odd number of columns, an eccentricity of Bonomi's later work.

Leverton's chief strength was the brilliant handling of small-scale interiors, often incorporating motifs which would be innovative in the work of George Dance, Jr., Thomas Harrison of Chester and John Soane more than a decade later. No. 1, Bedford Square has a remarkable interior: an entrance hall with a shallow dome resting on thin decorated bands rather than cornices, opens to lobbies in two directions. The Etruscan Hall at Watton Wood Hall (now Woodhall Park), Hertfordshire (1777-82, for Sir Thomas Rumbold), has a dome carried by flat segmental arches—a Leverton invention later reflected in the work of Thomas Harrison and John Soane.

Leverton's early work at Woodhall Park (1777-82) and Plaistow Lodge (1780, for Peter Thelluson, now Quernmore School), Bromley, Kent, incorporated a number of Adam motifs, while Scampston House, Yorkshire (1803, remodeled for W. T. St. Quintin), reflects the work of the Wyatts.

In his house plans Leverton followed the current fashion of using interlocking curves to link the sequence of rooms, though in "a large house in the country" he is said to have forgotten the staircase. Interiors are generally simple and refined without rich decoration. Many of his buildings have been demolished, hindering assessment of his mature style.

Leverton was surveyor to the Grocers' Company, "to the theatres royal in London" and to the Phoenix Fire Insurance Company, for whom he built offices in Lombard Street, London (ca. 1787), and a fire-engine house at Charing Cross (ca. 1830). He may have assisted John Marquand at the Department of Land Revenue (of the Office of Works); when the latter retired in 1809, Leverton and his pupil Thomas Chawner were appointed joint architects. In 1811, when Marylebone Park reverted to the Crown, Leverton and Chawner submitted an uninspired scheme for its development in which they made no provision for the new street (later Regent Street), but merely extended the formal pattern of Bloomsbury squares north. Not surprisingly, John Nash's more imaginative scheme was preferred and partly executed.

—MOIRA RUDOLF

LIENAU, Detlef.

German. Born in Holstein, Germany, 1818. Died on 2 August 1887. Son was the architect J. August Lienau. Studied at Royal Architectural College, Munich, 1841-43; trained under Henri Labrouste, Paris, 1842-47. Partner with Henri Marcotte, New York, 1848; established own office, New York; associate and teacher of Henry J. Hardenbergh (1847-1918).

Chronology of Works
All in the United States unless noted
* Approximate dates
† Work no longer exists

1850-52	Hart M. Shiff House, New York City†
1850-53	Grace Church, Jersey City, New Jersey
1852	Beach Cliffe (DeLancey Kane Villa), Newport, Rhode Island†
1852	Nuits (Francis Cottenet Villa), Dobbs Ferry, New York
1853*-59	William C. Schermerhorn House, 49 West 23rd Street, New York City†
1859	Mechanics and Traders' Bank, Jersey City, New Jersey†
1859-60	Langdon Estate Loft Buildings, 577-581 Broadway, New York City
1862-70	F. O. Matthiessen and Weichers Sugar Refinery, Jersey City, New Jersey†
1863-64	French and Belgian Plate Glass Company, Howard and Crosby Streets, New York City
1864*	First National Bank, Jersey City, New Jersey†
1864*-68	Elm Park (LeGrand Lockwood Mansion), South Norwalk, Connecticut
1865*	New York Life and Trust Company Building, New York City†
1867-69	Edmund H. Schermerhorn House, 45-47 West 23rd Street, New York†
1868	Odenheimer Hall, Saint Mary's Hall, Burlington, New Jersey†
1869-70	Townhouses for Rebecca Colford Jones, Fifth Avenue and Fifty-fifth Street, New York City
1870-71	Schermerhorn Apartments, Third Avenue, New York City†
1871	Boeraem Row, Jersey City, New Jersey†
1871-72	Grosvenor House, New York City†
1871-73	Suydam Hall, General Theological Simnary, New Brunswick, New Jersey
1872	Schloss Düneck, Ueterson, Germany
1872-73	Cruickston Park, Blair, Ontario, Canada
1873-74	DeLancey Kane Loft Building, 676 Broadway, New York City
1873-74	Sage Library, General Theological Seminary, New Brunswick, New Jersey
1873-76	Hodgson Hall, Savannah, Georgia
1879	Tenement House, 162 Elm Street, New York City†
1881-82	Daniel Parish Estate Office Building, 67 Wall Street, New York City†

1880-82 Panorama Building, Seventh Avenue, New York City†
1885-86 Telfair Academy of Arts and Sciences, Savannah, Georgia (alterations)
1886-87 Houses, 48-54 West 82nd Street, New York City

Publications

ARTICLES ABOUT LIENAU

HARTMANN, SADAKICHI: "A Conversation with Henry Janeway Hardenbergh." *Architectural Record* 19 (1906): 376-380.

KRAMER, ELLEN W.: "Detlef Lienau, an Architect of the Brown Decades." *Journal of the Society of Architectural Historians* 14 (March 1955): 18-25.

KRAMER, ELLEN W.: "The Domestic Architecture of Detlef Lienau, a Conservative Victorian." Ph.D. dissertation. New York University, New York, 1958.

SCHAACK, MARGARET DONALD: "The Lockwood-Matthews Mansion." *Interior Design* 38 (March 1967): 155-163.

SCHUYLER, MONTGOMERY: "Works of Henry J. Hardenbergh." *Architectural Record* 6 (January-March 1897): 335-336.

*

During the 1850s New York surpassed Philadelphia as the architectural capital of the United States. In part this was the result of New York's commercial and financial ascendancy, but it was also the legacy of a small but dynamic group of architects who eventually helped to found the American Institute of Architects in 1857. Among this cadre, which included Richard Upjohn, James Renwick and Leopold Eidlitz, the German architect Detlef Lienau played a major role. Having enjoyed an especially sophisticated European architectural education, Lienau was trained in the whole range of architectural history and was superbly poised to work in the vast variety of historical and eclectic styles permitted in the decades following the stylistic monopoly of the Greek Revival. His work set the standards for New York domestic architecture in the 1850s and 1860s, and helped make the city a leader in American architectural taste.

A native of Holstein, then part of Denmark, Lienau was schooled in Stettin and at the Städtische Gewerbeschule in Berlin, later making in Berlin and Hamburg the necessary apprenticeship in the building trades generally required for admission to a German architectural school. In 1841-42 he attended the Königliche Baugewerksschule in Munich. Between 1842 and 1847 Lienau was in Paris, working in the office of Henri Labrouste, where he was steeped in architectural history and theory, based in part on the systematic study from Labrouste's own travel drawings. Lienau was in the process of establishing himself in practice when the revolution of 1848 and subsequent war in Schleswig-Holstein prompted him to emigrate to the United States, where his brother lived. After a brief partnership with Henri (or Leon) Marcotte, he opened his own office in New York, which he maintained until his death, working for a clientele of wealthy French and German immigrants.

Germany taught Lienau to build, but France taught him to design. It is ironic that although a course of training such as Lienau's was intended to prepare an architect for a career designing for the state, he built no major public buildings in the United States. His work was usually private, comprising a large number of domestic and commercial commissions, generally classical in conception, with rich interior decorative schemes based on Renaissance or antique prototypes. As a result, his rigorous training was reflected not so much in any bold stylistic experiments or in a strongly theory-based practice, but in the quality of his detail and the ease with which he moved among the historical styles. Lienau's first major work was his Hart M. Shiff House at Fifth Avenue and Tenth Street in New York (1850-52), whose mansard roof marked the beginning of the French Second Empire style in New York. Built of brick with a brownstone base and trim, its walls crisply articulated by shallowly projecting bays, the Shiff house was widely imitated in the 1850s.

Lienau's portfolio of European drawings was the treasure trove from which he extracted much of his early work. He plundered drawings of Swiss and Tyrolean houses for his brother's house in Jersey City (1849), medieval stained glass windows for his brownstone Grace Church in the same city (1850-53), and reprised the newest *Rundbogenstil* buildings of Munich for his church designs. But his preferred style was a florid Renaissance mode, seen in his palazzo-like commercial buildings. Lienau soon came to the attention of the public with a series of lavish suburban villas, including that of De Lancey Kane (1852) at Newport, Rhode Island, 2nd Nuits for Francis Cottenet at Dobbs Ferry (1852), New York, an Italianate villa built of Caen stone and overlooking the Hudson River.

While these early suburban houses were symmetrical in conception, with asymmetrical touches restricted to projecting bays or rear ells, his later houses showed a growing freedom in their planning. The greatest of his suburban houses was the LeGrand Lockwood mansion in South Norwalk, Connecticut, begun in 1866. Built of granite and marble, the house was a sprawling composition, animated below with projecting wings, bays and a porte cochere, but unified above by its steep mansard. Unlike so many of its Second Empire contemporaries, with their boxy Italianate volumes crowned by plump mansards, the Lockwood mansion was a disciplined essay in the 16th-century French Renaissance. In the wake of the Civil War, the reign of Second Empire fashion favored Lienau, and he was among the few architects then practicing in New York who by training understood the grammar and nuances of the style; his work was among the best of the era in New York. His masterpieces were the Edmund Schermerhorn house, 45-47 West 23rd Street (1868), and the eight townhouses built as a unified block for Rebecca Colford Jones, Fifth Avenue and 55th Street (1869-70).

Lienau was blessed with a training in design which, for all its exposure to the historical styles, was based on principles rather than styles, and he adapted better than many of his contemporaries to the rapidly changing taste of the 19th-century. The modern classicism of Labrouste's neo-Greek learned three decades earlier served Lienau well in post-Civil War America, and he was able to apply its details to the eclectic architecture of the era. Some of his commercial and industrial designs of that period, built in severe brick with incised detail and crisp neo-Greek moldings, were among his finest work, such as the Mrs. Colford Jones loft, 21 Bowery. Lienau always had a large practice in industrial design, a specialization dating to his earliest work in Europe, and much of his later work consisted of factories and commercial lofts. This became more important as his well-known domestic style fell from favor. But Lienau's final work, if not inspired, always remained tasteful and confident. His final major work, the store and loft for the Daniel Parish estate, 860 Broadway (1880-82), reprised the Neo-Renaissance theme and impeccable ornament that distinguished his entire career.

—MICHAEL J. LEWIS

Pirro Ligorio: Casino of Pius IV, Rome, Italy, 1558-65

LIGORIO, Pirro.

Italian. Born in Naples, Italy, 1513/14. Died in Ferrara, 30 October 1583. Moved to Rome in 1534; employed as a painter and met Palladio. Served as personal architect to the Cardinal of Ferrara, from 1549. Made an honorary citizen of Rome, 1560; succeeded Michelangelo as architect of St. Peter's, 1564.

Chronology of Works

All in Italy

* Approximate dates

† Work no longer exists

1550-72	Villa d'Este, Tivoli
1557-65	Vatican Palace, Rome
1558-65	Casino of Pius IV, Rome
1560-65	Belvedere Court, Rome
1560-65	Tower of Paul III, Rome (revisions and corridor)†
1560*	Lancellotti Palace, Rome
1561	Pantheon, Rome (restoration)
1561-64	Palazzetto of Pius IV, Rome
1564	San Giovanni in Laterano, Rome (north transept)
1564-65	St. Peter's in the Vatican, Rome
1564-65	Sapienza, Rome
1564*	Cenci Palace, Rome
1574	arches for entry of Henry III, Ferrara†

Publications

BOOKS ABOUT LIGORIO

ACKERMAN, JAMES S.: *The Cortile del Belvedere*. Rome, 1954.
COFFIN, DAVID R.: *The Villa d'Este at Tivoli*. Princeton, New Jersey, 1960.
COFFIN, DAVID R.: *The Villa in the Life of Renaissance Rome*. Princeton, New Jersey, 1979.
LAMB, CARL: *Die Villa d'Este in Tivoli*. Munich, 1966.
MANDOWSKY, E., and MITCHELL, C.: *Pirro Ligorio's Roman Antiquities*. London, 1963.
SMITH, GRAHAM: *The Casino of Pius IV*. Princeton, New Jersey, 1977.
VENTURI, ADOLFO: Vol. 11, No. 2, pages 977-988 in *Storia dell'arte italiana*. Milan, 1939.

ARTICLES ABOUT LIGORIO

ANCEL, RENÉ: "Le Vatican sous Paul IV: Contribution à l'histoire de palais pontifical." *Revue Bénédictine* 24 (1908): 48-71.
CASTAGNOLI, P. L.: "Pirro Ligorio topografo di Roma antica." *Palladio* (1952).
COFFIN, DAVID R.: "Pirro Ligorio on the Nobility of the Arts." *Journal of the Warburg and Courtauld Institutes* 27 (1964): 191-210.

*

Although he designed some of the most enchanting structures in Italy in the Late Renaissance, Pirro Ligorio is perhaps the period's most neglected architect. A native of Naples, he went to Rome in about 1534, where he was employed as a painter. There he met Andrea Palladio, and also became a member of the Congregation of the Virtuosi al Pantheon. His career as an architect developed during the papacy of Julius III (1550-55).

Ligorio served as the personal archaeologist to the cardinal of Ferrara, Ippolito II d'Este (1509-72), from 1549. When his patron became governor of Tivoli the following year, Ligorio began his transformation of an old Franciscan monastery into the magical Villa d'Este (1550-72). He explored the ruins of Hadrian's grand villa in Tivoli, and in 1553 published a little treatise on the antiquities of Rome. Ligorio was a facile draftsman and modified his drawing style to capture the petrified flavor of the ancient monuments that he recorded.

When Paul IV assumed the papacy in 1555, he exiled the governor of Tivoli, interrupting progress on the Villa d'Este, but he also appointed his fellow Neapolitan to be architect of the Vatican Palace (1557-65). Ligorio designed a chapel in the pope's Belvedere apartments, and began construction of a casino (1558-65); the casino construction was interrupted briefly by the pontiff's death, but was revived in mid-1560 by his successor, Pius IV (1559-65), from whom the Casino Pio eventually took its name. A complex of great charm, intimacy and visual appeal, originally placed in elegant seclusion, it is visible today from the Vatican corridors in the verdant setting of the papal gardens. Its isolation offered the pope the opportunity of restorative retreat from the daily pressures of courtly commerce in the ancient tradition of *otium.* Modeled on the antique Roman garden house or *diata,* the four-structure complex contains a two-story casino with an open loggia and fountain, and two little gatehouses around an oval court, with the gatehouses placed at the extremities of the oval's long axis.

Ligorio's profuse surfaces give the casino the preciousness of a jewel box. He found inspiration in Pliny's first-century description of his own villa, Laurentina. Ligorio's decorations include stucco reliefs, statuary, inscriptions, escutcheons, festoons and grotesques. Personifications of the Hours, Seasons and Muses accompany Apollo. There are aquatic motifs as well as references to a return of the Golden Age under Pius IV. Biblical fresco decorations in the interior, painted by Federico Barocci, Federico Zuccaro, Santi di Tito and others, involve the themes of papal primacy and church triumph important for the Counter-Reformation reign of Pius IV.

Ligorio was made an honorary citizen of Rome in 1560. At that time he pursued various activities in the Vatican palace as well as the continuation of Bramante's Belvedere court. For the Capitoline Hill, he reconstructed the elevated corridor which had been taken down by Paul IV between the Palazzo Venezia and the tower raised by Paul III at the Franciscan monastery of Santa Maria in Aracoeli, adding a loggia to the new tower. This was demolished in the 19th century for the erection of the monument to Vittorio Emmanuele. Ligorio also worked on the facade and court of the Lancellotti Palace on the south end of the Piazza Navona.

In 1561 Ligorio added a little palace (1561-64) to Pope Julius III's Villa Giulia, which had been given to Federigo and Cardinal Carlo Borromeo, the same year that he restored the bronze doors and lead sheathing of the dome of the Pantheon. Three years later he was paid for a design for the facade of the north transept of the Lateran basilica. Although Ligorio succeeded Michelangelo in 1564 as architect of the Basilica of St. Peter, joined by Giacomo Barozzi da Vignola as his assistant, his work there was limited, as was his reconstruction of the court for the Sapienza at the University of Rome.

Ligorio was briefly imprisoned in 1565 when Guglielmo della Porta accused him of fraud, but he was soon cleared. When Pius V died a few months later, Ligorio returned to Tivoli to complete his work on the villa's sophisticated complex of fountains and gardens. These depended on natural hydraulic pressure to create one of the most memorable spectacles of European architecture. Ligorio's lavish expanse of gardens on a sloping site, his witty display of fountains, and his complicated iconographic program in statuary and architecture turned the villa's terraced grounds into the epitome of Late Renaissance landscape design in Italy. This was accomplished in spite of the fact that Ligorio's designs gave the grounds no dramatic focus or sweeping vista.

Although Ligorio's plan provided axes of demarcation, he forced the visitor to dwell and to deviate from direct routes. By offering no large, inviting portals or panoramas, his gardens invite their guests to linger within geometrical settings. Their expanse is not experienced as a whole, and their pleasures in Ligorio's aesthetic are sequential and cumulative. Views are indirect and gradual, as the villa's beauty is the result of an Aristotelian summation of parts.

Fountains of great variety range from architectural structures with grand basins, to a water organ, to pools, sprays and faucets. Ligorio added lanes of fountains, channels and rivulets, with one set representing the Anio, Albuneo and Erculaneo, the three rivers which unite at Rome to form the Tiber. Ligorio's grottoes contain heroic scenes, both dynastic and mythological. Their statues turn them into onomastic references to the patron, Cardinal Ippolito, as they deal with Hippolytus and his patrons, Diana, the goddess of chastity, and Minerva, the goddess of wisdom. Ligorio also featured Hercules, who, as the patron deity of Tivoli and the mythical ancestor of the Este family, symbolized moral choice. The villa's garden thus became associated with the Garden of the Hesperides, the golden apples of which symbolized Hercules' virtues. On the death of the last Este cardinal in 1586, the villa was inherited by the ambitious collector Cardinal Alessandro Farnese.

Ligorio retired to Ferrara in 1569 as antiquarian to Alfonso II, duke of Ferrara, where he finished his life compiling his encyclopedic studies of antiquities.

—EDWARD J. OLSZEWSKI

LODOLI, Carlo.

Italian. Born in Venice, Italy, in 1690. Died in 1761. Became a Franciscan Novice, Dalmatia, 1706-08; studied theology in Rome, 1708-12. Taught in Verona, 1715-20; in the monastery of Vigna, 1720-28; taught in Venice, ca. 1730; in charge of pilgrims visiting the Holy Land, 1739-45; semi-retirement after 1749 due to poor health.

Publications

BOOKS ABOUT LODOLI

KAUFMANN, EMIL: *Architecture in the Age of Reason: Baroque and Post-Baroque in England, Italy, France.* Cambridge, Massachusetts, 1955.
MEMMO, ANDREA: *Elementi d'architettura Lodoliana ossia l'arte del fabbricare con solidità scientifica e con eleganza non capricciosa.* Milan, 1833-34.
TORCELLAN, GIANFRANCO: *Una figura della Venezia settecentesca: Andrea Memmo.* Rome and Venice, 1963.
VICENTINI, ULDERICO: *Necrologio dei frati minori della provincia veneta.* Venice, 1955.

ARTICLES ABOUT LODOLI

COMOLLI, ANGELO: ''Elementi dell'Architettura Lodoliana.'' Vol. 4, pages 50-84 in *Bibliografia Storico-Critica dell'architettura civile ed arti subalterne.* Milan (1792) 1964-1965.
KAUFMANN, EMIL: ''Piranesi, Algarotti and Lodoli: A Controversy in XVIII Century Venice.'' *Gazette des beaux-arts* 46 (1955): 21-28.
KAUFMANN, EMIL: ''Memmo's Lodoli.'' *Art Bulletin* 46, No. 2 (1964): 159-175.
RYKWERT, JOSEPH: ''Lodoli on Function and Representation.'' *Architectural Review* (July 1976).

*

Until recently, Fra Carlo Lodoli was known in the literature for advocating the radical notion in his day of prioritizing function over aesthetic in architectural design, and he had been hailed by many as an 18-century forerunner to the modern rationalists. This characterization is reductive, and hence misleading. In his day, Lodoli was concerned with large societal reforms, of which architecture formed only a part, reforms that were based on a scholarly reevaluation of history, and in the case of architecture, on the history of architecture. To counter what he identified as untruthful architectural forms, he called for new rules of building that would be informed by an extensive study of statics, mechanics and materials. He did not, however, wish to abandon ornament or the classical orders in favor of severe rational forms.

Lodoli was an eloquent Franciscan whose reputation for his caustic but entertaining wit allowed him to travel in Venetian and Veronese aristocratic circles despite a debilitating illness that caused unsavory lesions on his face. He subsequently became teacher to the sons of that aristrocracy in about 1730, and that insured the widespread dissemination of his innovative ideas. However, the exact nature of those ideas is difficult to identify, as all that survives of Lodoli's writings is an outline for a two-volume treatise on architecture recently translated and published by Edgar Kaufmann, Jr. The friar's theories are best determined by a critical assessment of these and of two other sources: a short—but in its use of sarcasm, often misrepresentative—essay by his pupil, the count Francesco Algarotti, and a dense, at times overly anecdotal work by a younger follower, the aristocrat Andrea Memmo.

According to Memmo, to persuade his students and critics, the master identified why reform was needed in architecture, and then stated the principles on which such reform was to be based. As such, Lodoli encouraged that a whole body of historic architecture and the literature on that architecture—by Vitruvius, Leon Battista Alberti, Sebastiano Serlio and Claude Perrault, to name a few—be reassessed by using common sense and visual analysis. Lodoli judged harshly architectural forms that deceptively represented their structural or functional properties; in particular, he found the Greek appropriation of the forms of wood to create the classical orders in stone, as recorded by Vitruvius, to be untruthful. For example, he condemned as false the dentils below the Doric frieze whose stone forms resembled wooden joist fasteners. (Algarotti overstated Lodoli's rejection of this Vitruvian tenet as a rejection of all Vitruvian thought; it was obvious that Algarotti neither understood nor accepted what he perceived were Lodoli's beliefs.) Lodoli also was critical of such historical forms as the well-proportioned but incommodiously high stairs surrounding Greek temples, and the decorative but functionally unnecessary cornices between the superimposed orders on the facade of the Theater of Marcellus in Rome, and in the interiors of many of Andrea Palladio's buildings.

It is clear that Lodoli believed, in accordance with Vitruvius, that architecture is a science and therefore must be founded on certain principles. Architectural forms must address demonstrated human needs for soundness of solidity, convenience or commodity, and last, ornament or beauty. Algarotti made widespread his most unique principle in what has become Lodoli's famous quote, "quanto è in rapresentazione, deve essere sempre in funzione," which some modern scholars present as informing Louis Sullivan's dictate, "form . . . follows function." Memmo's examples of what Lodoli praised and condemned make it clear what the master more subtly intended by this phrase: function—and here in the sense of structural integrity or apparent usage of architectural elements—should not be contradicted by the form used to represent that function. Lodoli did not reject the use of applied ornament, but rather believed its use should be informed by the function of the architectural form it adorns.

Nearly 30 years ago, Antonio Foscari brought to the public's eye a monument designed by Lodoli which helps exemplify how the friar believed his theories could be converted into practice. These are two window frames in a courtyard facade in San Francesco della Vigna in Venice. Their design addresses the problem of how to build a strong, waterproof building facade. The window openings are spanned by catenary arches; the properties of this arch were then being explored coincidentally by Gottfried Wilhelm Leibniz, Isaac Newton and Lodoli's friend Marchese Giovanni Poleni, and Lodoli considered it statically most perfect. Most remarkable to the modern eye about the windows, however, are the sills and the pediments, where ordinarily classical elements have been transformed for functional purposes.

The sill is tripartite, with the largest central section as wide as the window so as to bear as little weight as possible. The bulk of the weight then is carried through the jambs to two shorter sections joined to the central sill by dovetails, in order to insure that the sill would not deform. In response to the need for deflecting water away from the sill, the middle element in one of the windows was tilted outward and a central channel for the runoff created. The pediment is also tripartite, again to prevent the weight of the wall above from falling solely on one structural member. The pediment's apex was left open to avoid the gaping that would occur during the settling of the building. Despite the fact that these facade windows were ridiculed in their day, as Memmo's written defense of them suggests, they coincide with Lodoli's belief that functional problems such as the distribution of weight and the technical problem of water seepage should be addressed in architectural design without sacrificing altogether architectural ornament.

Among those who inspired Lodoli were Francis Bacon and Galileo, two thinkers whose works the friar taught and whom he admired for their willingness to experiment to discover truth. From Giambattista Vico, Lodoli learned the importance of reevaluating history; he unsuccessfully attempted to publish Vico's *Scienza Nuova* in Venice. Among the many who carried away some enlightened knowledge from the great teacher were Francesco Milizia, architect and author of *Principii di architettura civile* (first published in Genoa, 1781), who absorbed the concern with resolving new demands of a changing society with new forms for civic architecture, and Giovanni Battista Piranesi, author and graphic illustrater of numerous books on various aspects of historic architecture, who caught the fascination with the technical aspects of the buildings he portrayed.

—SUSAN M. DIXON

LOMBARDO, Pietro.

Italian. Born in Carona, Italy, ca. 1435. Died in Venice, June 1515. Settled in Padua, 1564/67; moved to Venice, started own workshop, primarily as sculptor, 1474. Capomaestro of the Doge's Palace in Venice, from 1498.

Chronology of Works
All in Italy
* *Approximate dates*

1471-85	Chancel of San Giobbe, Venice (ornamentation)
1481-89	Santa Maria dei Miracoli, Venice
1487ff.*	Scuola di San Marco, Venice (facade)

Publications

BOOKS ABOUT PIETRO LOMBARDO

BONI, G.: *Santa Maria dei Miracoli.*
McANDREW, JOHN: *Venetian Architecture of the Early Renaissance.* Cambridge, Massachusetts, and London, 1980.
PAOLETTI, PIETRO: *L'architettura e la scultura del rinascimento in Venezia.* Venice, 1893-97.
PLANISCIG, LEO: *Venezianische Bildhauer der Renaissance.* 1921.

ARTICLES ABOUT PIETRO LOMBARDO

BANDELLONI, ENZO: "Pietro Lombardo, architetto nella critica d'arte." *Bollettino del Museo Civico di Padova* 51, No. 2 (1962): 27ff.
MARIACHER, GIOVANNI: "Pietro Lombardo a Venezia." *Arte Veneta* 9 (1955): 36-53.

MOSCHETTI, ANDREA: "Un quadriennio di Pietro Lombardo a Padova (1464-67)." *Bollettino del Museo Civico di Padova* 16 (1913): 1-99; 17 (1914): 1-43.

SEMENZATO, CAMILLO: "Pietro e Tullio Lombardo architetti." *Bollettino del Centro Internazionale di Studi di Architettura "Andrea Palladio"* 6/2 (1964): 262-270.

TRAMONTIN, SILVIO: "La chiesa di S. Maria dei Miracoli." *Venezia sacra* 1 (1959).

*

Pietro Lombardo was a Venetian sculptor and architect, a member of the Solari family, who were known in Venice as the Lombardi. His most memorable design was for the Church of Santa Maria dei Miracoli in Venice. Pietro was born in the 1430s in Carona, a town on Lake Lugano that produced a remarkable number of sculptors, most notably Andrea Bregno. After at least one visit to Florence and perhaps one also to Bologna, Pietro settled in Padua between about 1464 and 1467. He then moved to Venice, where he acquired his own workshop in 1474.

He began work as a sculptor, with the tomb of Doge Pasquale Malipiero (SS. Giovanni e Paolo, Venice, 1464), that of Antonio Roselli (Santo, Padua, 1467) and, most important and individually, that of Doge Pietro Mocenigo (SS. Giovanni e Paolo, Venice, 1481), all of which showed his knowledge, acquired first-hand, of Florentine sculpture and architecture. This work, encompassing as it did the language of classical architecture, led quite easily to sculptural architectural ornament, most notably the capitals Pietro designed for the interior columns at the Scuola di San Marco (1490s); like all his decorative work, these capitals are marked by extraordinary delicacy of detail, flowers, plants, lizards and—since Venice is a seaport—marine creatures, all executed in the standard forms of medieval and classical ornament.

Pietro was assisted in his sculptural and architectural commissions by his workshop, and especially by his sons, Antonio and Tullio. The concept of an independent master was understood less in Venice, in theory or practice, than in Florence, so Pietro often was a collaborator in his architectural projects. That was the case at the Church of San Giobbe, Venice, at the outer end of the Cannaregio Canal. The building had been established in 1450, but the project was expanded in the 1470s, with Pietro being brought in to work on all the decorative areas of the church—the front doorway, the east end of the church, the presbytery behind the lavish archway of the choir. This presbytery is a modest element, a square covered by a dome on pendentives, and is close in style to Filippo Brunelleschi's Pazzi Chapel in Florence. Everything else, especially in the 1480s when Pietro was so busy elsewhere, was finished by his studio. That work included the decoration around the flanking chapels and the main portal, some parts, like the dome, are clearly reminiscent of Brunelleschi's work, in this case at the Church of San Lorenzo in Florence. Pietro also worked on the facade of the Scuola di San Marco, rebuilt after about 1487. This building is a lively, picturesque composition, full of what has been called "an insouiance of proportions," which make it one of the richest compositions in Venice.

But Pietro is remembered most for the Church of Santa Maria dei Miracoli. This project, a nunnery church built between 1481 and 1489, was his particular and special responsibility. The form fits its function. The interior is a hall, with a coffered barrel vault which leads to a choir that is raised to form a gallery, which is domed, like that at San Giobbe, and ends in a semicircular apse. Rich decoration was added, marble facing of remarkable quality, arranged in an ornamental pattern that follows the grain of the marble; all of this makes the space, which is small (about 110 feet by 38 feet), seem even monumental.

The exterior is like the interior. There are two orders on the facade, the lower with a horizontal entablature, the upper with arches distributed, in the Florentine manner, in a symmetrical pattern. The semicircular pediment, which fits the barrel vault inside, works well to crown this facade. The side that faces the canal is decorated for simple visual effect, as is the choir with its dome and turrets, like minarets, that are faced in white. This church was a much-praised building, and one English visitor in 1494 described it as "the fairest of any Nunnery, for the beauty and rare stones, the walls covered with marble."

Pietro was active in a number of projects from the late 1490s until his death in 1515. From 1498 he was *capomaestro* of the Doge's Palace in Venice. In 1501 he was in Treviso, and in 1502 in Cividale, working there in the cathedral. In 1506 he was involved with the Capella Zen in the Church of San Marco, Venice. Beyond these other works, it is clear that his design of Santa Maria dei Miracoli, an aisleless church with a domed choir, was copied in many variants in Venice—perhaps in San Rocco, and then in Santa Maria della Visitazione by Giorgio Spaventa, and San Sebastiano by Lo Scarpagnino.

It is not easy to make one simple story out of Pietro's career. But like his contemporary, Mauro Coducci (ca. 1440-1504), with whom he worked at the Scuola di San Marco, Pietro was engaged in elaborating a sort of Venetian formal idiom; based in part on Florentine design, in part on the traditions of northern Italy, this precedent was to be of immense value to the architects of the next generation in the Veneto.

—DAVID CAST

LONGHENA, Baldassare.

Italian. Born in Venice, Italy, in 1598. Died in Venice, 18 February 1682. Trained initially as a sculptor; trained in architecture with Vincenzo Scamozzi.

Chronology of Works
All in Italy unless noted
* Approximate dates
† Work no longer exists

1616-20	Villa Contarini, River Brenta, Mira†
1619	San Giorgio dei Greci (Severo Monument), Venice
1620-23	Palazzo Giustiniani-Lolin, Grand Canal, Venice
1621-46*	Palazzo Widmann, San Canciano, Venice
1622-44	Palazzo da Lezze, Misericordia, Venice
1624-74	Santa Maria, Chioggia
1629-33	Santo Stefano (D'Alviano Monument), Venice
1629-46	Spirito Santo (Paruta Monument), Venice [attributed]
1630-82	Santa Maria della Salute, Venice (not completed until 1687)
1633ff.*	Levantine Synagogue, Venice [attributed]
1633ff.*	Spanish Synagogue, Venice [attributed]
1634	House at Santi Filippo e Giacomo, Venice†
1635-38	San Giorgio Maggiore (Michiel Monument, Civran Monument), Venice
1636-40	Santa Giustina, Venice (facade)
1636-82	San Antonio, Venice (rebuilding)
1640-63	Procuratie Nuove, Piazza San Marco, Venice (completion of Vincenzo Scamozzi's design)
1641-82	Benedictine Monastery of San Giorgio Maggiore, Venice

Baldassare Longhena: Santa Maria della Salute, Venice, Italy, 1630-82

1644-49   Palazzo Morosini dal Giardin, Venice†
1648-60* Palazzo Belloni-Battagia, Grand Canal, Venice
1648-70   Villa Pesaro (completed 1680/1710 by Antonio Gaspari), Este
1649   Giardino Valmarana, Vicenza (loggia)
1649-54   San Pietro di Castello, Venice (high altar)
1649-73   Carmelite Monastery of the Scalzi, Venice (partially †)
1649-82   Palazzo Pesaro on the Grand Canal, Venice (completed 1682/1710 by Gaspari)
1653-58   Scuola del Santissimo Nome di Dio, Santi Giovanni e Paolo, Venice
1654-64   Vendramin Chapel, San Pietro di Castello, Venice

1655   Church of the Beata Vergine del Soccorso (Santa Maria Rontonda; campanile not completed until 1769/93), Rovigo
1656-64   Prisons, Vicenza (executed by Antonio Pizzocaro)†
1658-75   Santa Maria Assunta, Lorto, Venice
1659-69   Santa Maria Gloriosa dei Frari (Pesaro Monument), Venice
1661-72   San Nicolò di Tolentino, Venice (high altar)
1664-74   Dominican Monastery of Santi Giovanni e Paolo, Venice (completed in 1682 by Giacomo Piazzetta)
1665-70   Palazzo Zane at San Stin, Venice (facade)
1667ff.   San Giorgio Maggiore (Venier Monument), Venice
1667-78   Ospedaletto of Santi Giovanni e Paolo, Venice

1667-82 Palazzo Bon, Venice (later Palazzo Rezzonico; continued 1682*-1712 by Gaspari; completed 1750*-58 by Giorgio Massari)

1668-70 Scuola dei Carmini, Venice (project; executed with changes by Girolamo Viviani and Sante Barbiere)†

1669 San Marco, Venice (Catafalque for François de Beaufort)†

1670-82 Somascan Monastery of Santa Maria della Salute, Venice (completed 1682-1705* by Domenico Mazzoni and others)

1671-78 San Basso, Piazzo dei Leoncini, Venice

1672-73 Basilica of Sant' Antonio (Cornaro Monument), Padua

1670s Villa Lezze, Rovarè (San Biagio di Callalta)†

1670s-82 Seminary at San Antonio di Castello (Ospedale di Gesù Cristo), Venice

1676-78 Scuola di San Nicolo and Collegio Flangini, Venice (both executed 1678-88 by Alessandro Tremignon)

1678-79 Ospedale di San Lazzaro dei Mendicanti, Venice (decorative arch and wellhead)

1678-82 Villa Rezzonico, Bassano (not completed until after 1687)

1681-82 Dominican Convent at Ospizio delle Muneghette, Venice

Publications

BOOKS ABOUT LONGHENA

CRISTINELLI, GIUSEPPE: *Baldassare Longhena, architetto del '600 a Venezia*. Padua, Italy, 1972.

HOWARD, DEBORAH: *The Architectural History of Venice*. New York, 1981.

LEWIS, DOUGLAS: *The Late Baroque Churches of Venice*. London and New York, 1967; rev. ed., 1979.

SEMENZATO, CAMILLO: *L'Architettura di Baldassare Longhena*. Padua, 1954.

TEMANZA, TOMMASO: *Zibaldon de' Memorie Storiche*. Venice and Rome (1738) 1963.

ARTICLES ABOUT LONGHENA

BASSI, ELENA: "Baldassare Longhena." In *Architettura del Sei e Settecento a Venezia*. Naples (1962).

MURARO, MICHELANGELO: "Il tempio votivo di Santa Maria della Salute in un poema del Seicento." *Ateneo Veneto* New series 11 (1973): 87-119.

WITTKOWER, RUDOLF: "Santa Maria della Salute." In *Studies in the Italian Baroque*. London and New York, 1963.

*

Baldassare Longhena's architecture is essentially Venetian, and it is important to understand it in relation to that context. By the 17th century, Venice was economically more secure than it had been for at least a century, and far less vulnerable to the effects of war, piracy and storms at sea. The Venetian Church stood out forcefully against the Pope; at sea Turkish and Spanish power in the Mediterranean was beginning to wane; and despite the loss of Crete in 1669, Venice was mostly successful in naval battles with the Ottoman Empire. Venetian survival depended, however, on preserving the finely balanced political situation in which the republic found itself, and this fact encouraged a political conservatism—a conservatism which, despite superficial appearances, can be discerned in Longhena's architectural production.

Longhena was born in Venice, in the parish of San Severo, the son of a successful stonemason from Ticino. Initially, Baldassare followed his father and trained as a sculptor. The effect of that early training can be seen throughout Longhena's career in his attention to sculptural architectural ornament, exploiting light and shade in relation to mass and texture (perhaps above all at Palazzo Rezzonico).

Like Francesco Borromini, Longhena shifted decisively from sculpture to architecture. His work as an architect began under the guidance of Vincenzo Scamozzi, through whom he became acquainted with 16th-century Venetian architectural traditions, especially the work of Jacopo Sansovino, Andrea Palladio and Michele Sanmicheli, which were enduring influences. Longhena's early domestic works, such as Palazzo Giustiniani Lolin (ca. 1623) and Palazzo da Lezze (ca. 1624), were much influenced by Scamozzi. Sansovino's influence became more apparent in ecclesiastical architecture, as at the Duomo in Chioggia (1633), but Longhena's longlasting fondness of playing with light in spaces and on walls stemmed in considerable measure from Sansovino. Longhena's resultant use of light in his architecture in Venice enhances the lighting effects of that city.

Longhena exploited brilliant white and gray surfaces in much the same way as did Palladio, using gray stone to articulate structural architectural elements and to contrast dramatically with the delicate white sheen of decorative or subordinate parts. This skill is best seen at Longhena's most spectacular work, Santa Maria della Salute (ca. 1630), which is also most reminiscent of Palladio's churches, such as San Giorgio Maggiore or Il Redentore, just across the Giudecca Canal.

An important break occurred in Longhena's career in 1640, as a result of his close association with Scamozzi and his useful influential Venetian connections, when he was appointed *proto* to the *de Supra* branch of the Procuracy of St. Mark's, which charged him with the completion of the Procuratie Nuove, the procurators' houses left unfinished by Scamozzi in the central, most prestigious square in Venice. Scamozzi had already continued Sansovino's Library of St. Mark's elevation down the north of Piazza di San Marco, adding an extra story to provide more space. Longhena finished this wing and built the section at the west end of the piazza, joining the Procuratie Nuove with the Procuratie Vecchie, and embracing the Church of San Gimini-ano in the middle. All this work was demolished in 1807.

In his two most significant palace commissions, at Palazzo Pesaro (1652-1700), for the rich patrician Giovanni Pesaro, and Palazzo Rezzonico, commissioned in 1667 by Filippo Bon, Longhena developed the schemes of Sansovino and Sanmicheli, exploiting large atmospheric spaces, defined by columns, single or coupled, on a dramatically rusticated base. Despite Longhena's having to make restrictive economies, such as re-using the foundations of three earlier palaces at Palazzo Pesaro, his palaces are dramatic and charged, as a result of his unusually free juxtaposition of mass, space, surface and depth in facade (developing Palladio's more superficial concern with line and geometry). An unexecuted early design for Palazzo Pesaro shows what astounding effects Longhena would have created internally, with the use of grand central staircases, had financial restraints not reined him in. Ca' Rezzonico develops the Pesaro theme, with greater restraint and less indulgent decorative carving. The huge keystone heads, animal masks and fanciful balustrades of Palazzo Pesaro reappear here, but more rigorously synthesized and subordinated to the design as a whole. Indeed, this facade resorts more closely to Sansovino's Palazzo Corner than it draws on the exuberant Ca' Pesaro. The resulting lightness combined with massive solidity and substantiality, as at Palazzo Pesaro, was an eloquent form for the Venetian aristocracy, few of whom at that time had the resources for building vast new palaces. The shift in mood from Pesaro to Rezzonico can be interpreted as a sign of a growing conservatism and caution among the Venetian aristocracy, who were increasingly financially cowed and politically insecure. Despite—or more probably as a result of—this apparently reactionary shift, Longhena's vast palaces, which were at once imposing and elegant, outward-looking and confident, traditional and modern, exerted considerable influence in Venice and abroad.

Longhena's Baroque handling of space is best seen at Santa Maria della Salute and in his work for the Benedictine Monastery of San Giorgio Maggiore, particularly in his imposing double staircase there. Derived in essence from Mauro Coducci's Scuole di San Marco staircase, this breaks away from Coducci's claustrophobic tunnel vistas: the ramps do not converge at the top, but instead diverge at the bottom and rise on opposite sides of the vaulted staircase hall. The whole is surprisingly akin to Michelangelo's Laurentian Library staircase in Florence, though released from that work's tension.

Longhena's architecture stands out brilliantly from that of his 17th-century Venetian counterparts. Ironically, this is at least in part because he worked happily within the Venetian tradition, and did not seek to impose new fashions emanating from Baroque Rome. He skillfully managed to continue the very Venetian tradition of turning inward to the Venetian past, while appearing to be outward-looking and progressive.

—HELEN HILLS

LOOS, Adolf.

Czechoslovakian. Born in Brünn (now Brno, Czech Republic), 10 December 1870. Died in Vienna, Austria, 23 August 1933. Studied architecture at Dresden Polytechnic. In private practice, Vienna, 1897-1922; lived in Paris, 1922-28; returned to practice in Vienna, 1928-33. Journalist, *Neue Freie Presse*, 1897-1900. Founder-director, Free School of Architecture, Vienna.

Chronology of Works
All in Austria unless noted
† *Work no longer exists*

1898	Goldman and Salatsch Shop, Vienna
1899	Café Museum, Vienna
1904-06	Karma Villa, Montreaux, Switzerland
1907	American Bar, Vienna
1907	Steiner Plume and Feather Shop, Vienna
1909-13	Knize Store, Graben, Vienna
1910	Steiner Villa, Vienna
1910	Goldman and Salatsch Building (Loos House), Michaelerplatz, Vienna
1912	Scheu House, Vienna
1913	Café Caupa, Vienna
1913	Northartgasse House, Vienna
1913	Bellatz Apartment, Vienna
1913	House, Northartgasse/Sauragasse, Vienna
1913	Paul Mayer Apartment, Vienna
1914	Emil Lowenbach Apartment, Vienna
1915	Gymnasium, Schwartzwald School, Semmering, Vienna
1918-19	Rohrbach Sugar Refinery Factory and Director's House, near Brno, Czechoslovakia
1919	Peter Altenberg Tombstone, Central Cemetery, Vienna
1922	Steiner House, Vienna (reconstruction)
1926-27	Tristan Tzara House, Paris, France

Adolf Loos: Goldman and Salatsch Store, Vienna, Austria, 1898

1928	Moller House, Potzleinsdorf, Vienna
1929	Josef Vogl Apartment, Plzen, Czechoslovakia
1929	Hans Brummel Apartment, Plzen, Czechoslovakia
1930	Leo Brummel Apartment, Plzen, Czechoslovakia
1930	Eisner Apartment, Plzen, Czechoslovakia
1930	Müller House, Prague, Czechoslovakia
1931	Semi-detached House, Werkbund Exhibition, Vienna
1931	Willy Kraus Apartment, Plzen, Czechoslovakia
1931	Small Timber House for Mitzi Schnabel, Vienna
1931	Babi Workers' Estate, near Nachod, Czechoslovakia

Publications

BOOKS BY LOOS

Das Andere. Vienna, 1903.
Wohnungswanderungen. Vienna, 1909.
Richtlinien für ein Kunstamt. Vienna, 1919.
Ins Leere Gesprochen. Paris, 1921 (2nd ed., Innsbruck, 1932). English edition: *Spoken into the Void, Collected Essays 1897-1900.* Cambridge, Massachusetts, 1982.
Trotzdem 1900-1930. Innsbruck, 1931.
Schriften von Adolf Loos. 2 vols. Innsbruck, 1931-32.
Sämtliche Schriften. 2 vols. Edited by Franz Glück. Vienna, 1962.

BOOKS ABOUT LOOS

CZECH, H., and MISTELBAUER, W.: *Das Looshaus.* Vienna, 1976.
DREW, JOANNE (ed.): *The Architecture of Adolf Loos.* 1985.
GRAVAGNUOLO, BENEDETTO: *Adolf Loos: Theory and Works.* New York, 1982.

KULKA, HEINRICH (ed.): *Adolf Loos: Das Werk des Architekten.* Vienna, 1931.

LOOS, E. ALTMAN: *Adolf Loos, der Mensch.* Vienna and Munich, 1968.

MARILAUN, A.: *Adolf Loos.* Vienna, 1922.

MÜNZ, LUDWIG, and KÜNSTLER, GUSTAV: *Adolf Loos: Pioneer of Modern Architecture.* New York, 1966.

RISSELADA, M. (ed): *Raumplan Versus Plan Libre: Adolf Loos and Le Corbusier 1919-1930.* New York, 1988.

RUKSCHCIO, BURKHARDT, and SCHACHEL, ROLAND L.: *Adolf Loos: Leben und Werk.* Salzburg, 1982.

WORBS, D., et al.: *Adolf Loos 1870-1933.* Exhibition catalog. Berlin, 1984.

ARTICLES ABOUT LOOS

"Adolf Loos." *Casabella* special issue, No. 233.

BANHAM, REYNER: " 'Ornament and Crime,' the Decisive Contribution of Adolf Loos." *Architectural Review* (February 1957): 85-88.

RYKWERT, JOSEPH: "Adolf Loos: The New Vision." *Studio International* (July-August 1973): 17-21.

*

Long hailed as one of the pioneers of modern architecture, Adolf Loos remains an elusive and frequently misunderstood figure. He is most often remembered for his celebrated essay "Ornament and Crime" and for the series of strikingly austere villas he designed on the eve of World War I. Yet Loos, despite numerous assertions to the contrary, never called for the systematic eradication of all ornament. And the blank facades of his prewar houses, repeatedly cited as harbingers of the International Style, conceal sumptuous interiors sharply out of character with his reputation as a modern ascetic.

Although Loos' works and ideas had a significant impact on the Modern Movement of the 1910s and 1920s, he maintained a carefully measured distance from the modernist mainstream and was often highly critical of many of its ideological premises and aims. While he shared with the radical modernists the rejection of historicism and outmoded 19th-century social values, Loos refused to subscribe to their call for a wholesale break with history. Like Otto Wagner, who had a profound impact on his intellectual formation, Loos instead sought to reestablish the link with history, to reconcile tradition with the dictates of modern life.

After studying briefly at the Technical University in Dresden, Loos journeyed to the United States in 1893 to view the World's Columbian Exposition in Chicago. Impressed less by the monumental Beaux-Arts architecture of the exhibition than by the simple, utilitarian structures he saw, he prolonged his stay for three years, traveling around the country while earning his way with a series of odd jobs.

The years Loos spent in America and a later stay in England left him with a lifelong admiration for Anglo-Saxon attitudes, and for American and English clothing and household furnishings. After returning to Vienna in 1896, he began to publish a series of polemical articles in the city's leading newspapers decrying the state of contemporary Viennese art and society, and celebrating the worldliness and matter-of-factness of English and American design. In 1903 he founded his own journal, *Das Andere* (The Other), subtitled "A Newspaper to introduce Western Culture into Austria," in which he promoted Anglo-Saxon culture in articles, reviews and advertisements for clothes, accessories and plumbing equipment.

Loos' own design attitudes first found concrete expression in a series of small commissions for interiors he executed around the turn of the century. Among his most important works from that period was the interior of the Cafe Museum (1899); Loos stripped away virtually all conventional decoration to create a simple, austere elegance which contrasted dramatically with the elaborate ornamental style popular in turn-of-the-century Vienna.

After 1900 Loos began to distance himself from the other Viennese modernists. In a series of articles and public speeches, he assailed the tyranny of the *Gesamtkunstwerk* (the total work of art) and the attempts of Josef Hoffmann and the other Secessionists to impose a new, modern decorative style. The attacks culminated in an address Loos presented in 1910 entitled "Ornament and Crime," in which he condemned conventional decoration as a symbol of degeneracy, and argued that superfluous ornament was not only an aesthetic problem, but also an economic and ethical one since it represented the exploitation of the craftsman.

But despite the essay's stridency, Loos did not call for the complete eradication of ornament, only that which was mimetic or used merely as surface decoration. In an essay published in the 1920s, he attempted to clarify his position: "I never meant, as the purists have reiterated *ad absurdum,* that ornament should be systematically and completely abolished. Only that when its time has passed should one not revive it. . . ." Loos' continuing use of ornament is vividly demonstrated in the tiny Kärntnerbar of 1907, in which he used richly veined marbles as well as wood paneling and mirrors to create a sumptuous, yet strikingly modern, effect.

In 1910 Loos received his first major commission, to design a large urban block for the tailor firm of Goldman and Salatsch on the Michaelerplatz. In keeping with his belief that architects should create works which serve their purpose in the simplest and most literal fashion, Loos designed the building with unadorned window openings and a blank facade on the upper stories.

The building's "mute" walls caused a storm of controversy, but largely unnoticed was its innovative interior plan. Loos divided up the space to create a series of rooms of different heights, proportional to their function and importance. The main hall, for example, was two stories high, while the tailor's work area and the fitting room were less than a full story. The result, which Loos' assistant Heinrich Kulka named the *Raumplan,* or spatial plan, was a radically new way of conceiving of interior space. In place of the traditional floor plan, Loos introduced the idea of the building as volume, presaging Le Corbusier's *plan libre* and the open plans of the De Stijl architects.

During the years just prior to and after World War I, Loos designed a series of innovative villas—among them the Steiner, Scheu and Rufer houses—in which he developed many of his ideas. As with the upper portion of the Goldman and Salatsch Building, Loos stripped the facades of these houses down to their barest elements, creating large cubic masses that anticipated the mature International Style. For Loos, the exterior house served merely as a container to conceal the complex assembly of volumes within. The blank surfaces of the houses' exteriors contrast dramatically with the inside: Loos used traditional English forms—inglenooks, unplastered brick fireplaces, wood paneling and exposed ceiling beams—which he combined with richly veined marble and mirrors to achieve a warm, comfortable and strikingly elegant effect.

After World War I, Loos turned his attention to the problem of mass housing, and in 1920 he was appointed chief architect of the Vienna housing office. In addition to overseeing the planning and construction of a number of housing settlements, he also designed a series of innovative solutions for solving the city's housing problem, including a scheme for a "row house with one wall," which he patented. Most of Loos' plans, however, remained unrealized. Disgruntled by bureaucratic interference and disappointed by a lack of private commissions, he moved to Paris in 1924. He was warmly received by the Parisan avant-garde, but the prestigious commissions he hoped for failed to materialize, and he was able to complete only one major work, a villa for Dadaist Tristan Tzara.

Loos returned to Vienna in 1928, and during the last few years of his life concentrated on domestic architecture. In his most important works of that period, the Moller House in Vienna and the Müller House in Prague, he again took up the theme of the *Raumplan,* creating his two most complex and accomplished experiments in spatial planning.

After his death Loos was celebrated as one of the great modernist form-givers. In reality his position with respect to modernity was highly ambivalent. Indeed, a large portion of Loos' work and writings was a reaction to what he viewed as the excesses of the radical modernists. Loos' continuing interest in the architecture of classical antiquity—demonstrated most powerfully by his famous entry for the *Chicago Tribune* Tower, a 35-story skyscraper in the form of a gigantic Doric column—shows how far he stood apart from many of his contemporaries. While he exercised a profound influence on 20th-century architecture, in the end Loos was a transitional figure with his feet planted firmly on both sides of the modernist divide.

—CHRISTOPHER LONG

LOUIS, Victor.

French. Born Louis-Nicholas Louis in Paris, France 10 May 1731. Died in Paris, 3 July 1800. Studied architecture in Rome and Paris.

Chronology of Works
All in France
† Work no longer exists

1761	Chapel, Abbey of Notre Dame de Bon Secours, Paris (decoration)
1765	Chapel of Ames-du-Purgatoire, Paris (decoration)†
1766	Cathedral, Chartres, France (remodeling)
1770	Vauxhall of Senor Torré, Paris†
1770-76	Intendance (Governor's Residence), Besançon
1773	Hôtel of Duke of Richelieu, Paris (entrance and courtyard)
1774	Château de Virasel, near Marmande†
1774-80	Hôtel Boyer-Fonfrède, Bordeaux
1774-80	Hôtel Saige, Bordeaux
1774-80	Lamolère House, Bordeaux
1774-80	Legrix House, Bordeaux
1774-80	Rolly House, Bordeaux
1775	Hôtel Nairac, Bordeaux
1775-80	Grand Théâtre, Bordeaux
1776-79	Cathedral, Noyon (remodeling)
1781-84	Enclosure for the Palais Royal, Paris
1782-83	Théâtre des Petits Comédians, Paris
1786-90	Gobineau House, Bordeaux
1786-90	Théâtre du Palais Royal (now the Comédie Française), Paris
1791-93	Théâtre National, Paris†
1797	Hôtel Titon, Paris (redecoration)

Publications

BOOKS BY LOUIS

La Salle de Spectacle de Bordeaux. Paris, 1782.

BOOKS ABOUT LOUIS

BRAHAM, ALLAN: *The Architecture of the French Enlightenment.* Berkeley, California, and Los Angeles, 1980.
CHAMPIER, VICTOR, and SANDOZ, G. ROGER: *Le Palais Royal d'après les documents inèdits (1629-1900).* 2 vols. Paris, 1900.
GALLET, MICHEL: *Les demeures parisiennes: L'epoque Louis XVIe.* Paris, 1964.
HAUTECOEUR, LOUIS: *Histoire de l'architecture classique en France.* Vol. 4. Paris, 1952.
KALNEIN, WEND GRAF, and LEVEY, MICHAEL: *Art and Architecture of the Eighteenth Century in France.* Harmondsworth, England, 1972.
LORENTZ, S.: *Victor Louis et Varsovie.* Exhibition catalog. Bordeaux, 1958.
MARIONNEAU, CHARLES: *Victor Louis, architecte du théâtre de Bordeaux. Sa vie, ses travaux et sa correspondance.* Bordeaux, 1881.
PARISET, FRANÇOIS GEORGES: *Victor Louis, 1731-1800: Dessins et Gravures.* France, 1980.
PRUDENT, HENRI, and GAUDET, PAUL: *Les salles de spectacle construites par Victor Louis à Bordeaux, au Palais Royal et à la Place Louvois.* Paris, 1903.
RABREAU, DANIEL: *Victor Louis et le théâtre: Scénographie, mise-en-scène et architecture théâtrale aux XVIIIe et XIXe siècles.* Paris, 1982.

ARTICLES ABOUT LOUIS

BLANCHET, LOUIS, and LAPLACE, ROSELYNE: "L'architecture de la Comédie Française." *Monuments historiques de la France* 4 (1978): 35-48.
FOUCART-BORVILLE: "Les projets de Charles de Wailly par la gloire de la cathédrale d'Amiens et de Victor Louis pour le maître-antel de la cathédrale de Noyen." *Bulletin de la Société de l'Histoire de l'Art Français* (1974): 131-144.
OTTOMEYER, HANS: "Autobiographies d'architectes parisiens: 1759-1811." *Bulletin de la Société de l'Histoire de Paris et l'Ile de France* (1971): 141-206.
PARISET, FRANÇOIS GEORGES: "L'architecte Victor Louis et la fille de Diderot." *Archives de l'art français* (1950-57): 270-279.
PARISET, FRANÇOIS GEORGES: "Les découvertes du professeur S. Lorentz sur Victor Louis à Varsovie." *Revue historique de Bordeaux et du Département de la Gironde* (1956).
PARISET, FRANÇOIS GEORGES: "Notes sur Victor Louis." *Bulletin de la Société de l'Histoire de l'Art Français* (1959): 40-55.

*

Victor Louis was a key representative of the neoclassical, sometimes called classic revival, style that gained favor in France in the late 18th century in reaction against the elaborate Rococo style. Neoclassical architecture, with its emphasis on cubic shapes, simplicity of surface and continuity of design, is evident in the building that is considered his masterpiece, the Grande Théâtre at Bordeaux (1775-80), in southwest France. Louis was one of the second generation of architects carrying on the neoclassical movement, whose pioneers were Ange-Jacques Gabriel (1698-1782) and Jacques-Germain Soufflot (1713-80).

Louis' architectural style first became evident in his unexecuted designs for remodeling the royal palace in Warsaw. Stanislaw August Poniatowski, the last king of Poland, had brought the architect to Warsaw in 1765. The style influenced a generation of architects who worked in Poland, including Dominik Merlini and Jan Chrystian Kamsetzer.

Louis' design for the Warsaw palace anticipated his work on the Bordeaux theater. It was only the second freestanding theater built in France and is generally considered the first great modern theater; it remained the model for theaters for more than 100 years. A portico of 12 giant Corinthian columns fronts the rectangular stone building. Inside, it has a high, rectangular vestibule and a striking symmetrical staircase. Louis' emphasis on this part of the building was new in theater design; his staircase hall was the prototype for the one Charles Garnier designed for the Paris Opera, built a century later, and its influence shows in numerous other public buildings of the 19th century. In the auditorium, there are 10 giant columns, four of which support the ceiling, a shallow dome. The auditorium is a truncated circle, with balconies and box seats. There also is a small concert hall above the vestibule. The ancillary rooms were developed far beyond those of France's first freestanding theater, built at Lyons in the 1750s.

The architect designed many important town houses near the Bordeaux theater, and several country houses as well. A particularly ambitious design, however, was never built—a hemicycle of linked houses along the Garonne River in Bordeaux. Louis' Bordeaux studio produced two architects, Louis Combes and Jean Baptiste Dufart, who continued designing in his style into the 19th century.

Returning to Paris, Louis designed an enclosure for the Palais Royal gardens. The enclosure, built from 1781 to 1784, consists of long wings, articulated with large pilasters—rectangular columns—over a loggia, making a popular public meeting place.

Also in Paris, Louis designed his next theater, a replacement for the Opéra, which had been on the right-hand side of the Palais Royal entrance until it burned in 1781. In the new theater (1786-90), built on the opposite side of the entrance, Louis' use of fireproof materials was notable. Theater fires were common at that time: candles and lamps used for lighting often set fire to scenery and costumes, which in turn set fire to the wooden buildings. Galleries and roofs often caved in. To fireproof the new theater's roof, Louis used wrought-iron trusses and hollow clay blocks set in concrete. With this, he was combining the concepts of Jacques Soufflot—who had designed iron trusses and put them into the roof of the Louvre palace in Paris in 1780, making it one of the first iron roofs in the world—and Eustache St. Far, who had first used hollow clay blocks in a fireproof floor in 1785. The theater was called the Théâtre du Palais Royal, and later became the home of the Comédie Française.

Louis' theaters were not his only influential designs. An important work, and an early one, came in 1763, when he designed a church chapel—the Chapelle des Âmes du Purgatoire in the Church of Ste. Marguerite-de-Charonne, Paris. The design incorporated a *trompe l'œil* painting that gave the appearance of rows of Ionic columns supporting a horizontal entablature. The painting was by Paolo Antonio Brunetti; along with his father, Gaetano, and Charles Joseph-Natoire, Brunetti was known for painting a scene of ruins on the walls of an earlier chapel in the Enfants-Trouvés. Contemporary observers hailed the beauty and novelty of Louis' chapel. Subsequent churches

incorporating similar design elements included St.-Philippe-du-Roule, Paris; St. Symphorien, Versailles; and St.-Louis, in St.-Germain-en-Laye.

—TRUDY RING

LUBETKIN, Berthold.

British. Born in Tiflis, Georgia (formerly U.S.S.R.), 16 December 1901. Died in 1990. Immigrated to England, 1931. Studied in Moscow; traveled to Warsaw and Vienna; studied at the École des Beaux-Arts, Paris; worked for Auguste Perret; opened own office in Paris before 1927; formed the Tecton Group (Anthony Chitty, Lindsey Drake, Michael Dugdale and Val Harding; Denys Lasdun joined later) in London, 1932; partner in the Tecton Group, 1932-48; partner in the firm Skinner, Bailey and Lubetk in, London, 1948-52. Gold Medal, Royal Institute of British Architects, 1982.

Chronology of Works
All in England unless noted

1928-31	Apartment Building, 25 Avenue de Versailles, Paris, France (with Jean Ginsberg)
1932	Gorilla House, London Zoo, Regent's Park, London
1933-34	Penguin Pool, London Zoo, Regent's Park, London
1933-35	Highpoint I Flats, Highgate, London
1934	Beach House, Bognor, West Sussex
1934	House, Haywards Heath, Sussex
1934	House (with Pilichowski), Plumstead, Kent
1934-35	Giraffe and Elephant Houses, Whipsnade Zoo, Bedfordshire
1934-36	Berthold Lubetkin House, Whipsnade, Bedfordshire
1935	House, Farnham Common, Surrey
1935	Six Pillars House, Dulwich, London
1935	House, Sydenham Hill, London
1935-38	Finsbury Health Center, London
1936-38	Highpoint II Flats, Highgate, London
1937-39	Penguin Pool and Giraffe House, Dudley Zoo, Worcestershire
1937-51	Priory Green Housing Estate, Finsbury, London
1938-46	Spa Green Housing Estate, Finsbury, London
1942	Lenin Memorial Monument, Holford Square, Holborn, London
1948-50	Peterlee New Town Plan, County Durham (project)

Publications

BOOKS BY LUBETKIN

Opening of Finsbury Health Centre. London, 1938.
Planned A.R.P. London, 1939.
Report to Finsbury Borough Council on Structural Protection for People Against Aerial Bombardment. London, 1939.
Spa Green Estate. London, 1952.
La modernité, un project inachevé. With others. Paris, 1982.

ARTICLES BY LUBETKIN

"The Builders." *Architectural Review* (May 1932): 201-14.
"Town and Landscape Planning in Soviet Russia." *Journal of the Town Planning Institute,* Vol. 19 (February 1933): 69-75.
"Modern Architecture in England." *American Architect and Architecture* (February 1937): 29-42.

"Soviet Architecture: Notes on Developments from 1917 to 1932." *Architectural Association Journal* (May 1956): 260-64.

"Soviet Architecture: Notes on Developments from 1932 to 1955." *Architectural Association Journal* (September-October 1956): 85-89.

BOOKS ABOUT LUBETKIN

ALLAN, JOHN S.: *Lubetkin and Tecton: the Modern Architecture of Classicism*. London, 1981.

CHASLIN, F.; DREW, J.; GARCIAS, J. C.; and MEADE, M. K.: *Berthold Lubetkin*. Brussels, 1981.

COE, PETER and READING, MALCOLM: *Lubetkin and Tecton: Architecture and Social Commitment*. London and Bristol 1981.

COE, PETER; READING, MALCOLM; COHEN, JEAN-LOUIS: *Berthold Lubetkin: un moderne en Angleterre*. Exhibition catalogue. Brussels and Liege, Belgium 1983.

CURTIS, WILLIAM J. R.: *Modern Architecture since 1900*. London, 1982.

ESHER, LIONEL: *A Broken Wave: The Rebuilding of England 1940-1980*. London, 1981.

JACKSON, ANTHONY: *The Politics of Architecture*. 1970.

SERVICE, ALASTAIR: *The Architects of London*. London, 1979.

SHARP, DENNIS (ed.): *The Rationalists: Theory and Design in the Modern Movement*. London, 1978.

ARTICLES ABOUT LUBETKIN

CARROLL, R.: "Berthold Lubetkin and Ove Arup: A Study of a Unique Partnership." Thesis. University of Newcastle, 1976.

COX, A.: "Highpoint Two, North Hill, Highgate." *Focus* 11 (1938): 79.

CURTIS, WILLIAM J. R.: "Berthold Lubetkin on 'Socialist' Architecture in the Diaspora." *Architèse* 12 (1974).

CURTIS, WILLIAM J. R.: "Berthold Lubetkin." *Architectural Association Quarterly* 7, No. 3 (1976): 33-39.

DIEHL, TOM: "Lubetkin—Theory and Practice in Highpoint I and II." Thesis. Architectural Association, London, 1982.

GARDINER, STEPHEN: "Apostle of the Concrete Curve." *Observer Magazine* (16 December 1979).

GLANCEY, JONATHAN: "Lubetkin at Last." *Architectural Review* (April 1982).

JORDAN, R. FURNEAUX: "Lubetkin." *Architectural Review* (July 1955): 36-44.

LAMBERT, SAM: "Historic Pioneers: Architects and Clients." *Architects' Journal* (11 March 1970).

LUDER, OWEN: "Good Dreams Gone Wrong." *Building Design* (22 May 1981).

LYALL, SUTHERLAND: "Thoroughly Modern Architect." *New Society* (14 January 1982).

MANN, C. W. N.: "Discursive Notes on Berthold Lubetkin." Thesis. University of Liverpool, 1975.

SHARP, DENNIS: "High Points." *Building* (5 June 1981).

*

At the age of 30, Berthold Lubetkin arrived in London already with firsthand experience of Russian constructivism (he had studied under Alexander Rodchenko, Vladimir Tatlin and Alexander Vesnin in Moscow), of the classical tradition (Warringer in Berlin and Auguste Perret in Paris), and of the Parisian postcubist revolution.

A year later, in 1932, he formed the celebrated architectural practice Tecton, which was to emerge as the greatest protagonist of continental modernism in Britain, attracting to it such notable talents as Denys Lasdun and Peter Moro. It is indicative of British caution toward the new architecture that Tecton's first commission, the Gorilla House at London Zoo (1933), was for animals rather than people. This small building was not only a prelude to a whole series of zoo buildings at London, Whipsnade and Dudley, but was to characterize that practice's analytical approach to design. The building attempted to simulate the gorilla's natural habitat while affording maximum scope for public viewing. The same principles surrounded the design of the celebrated Penguin Pool at London Zoo, where the ingenious interlocking ramps, designed in association with the engineer Ove Arup, have since become a metaphor for the Modern Movement in England.

If the Penguin Pool owed its formal resolution to the Russian constructivists (Naum Gabo was soon to be resident in England), then the High Point flats, Highgate, London (1933-35), were a potent image of socialist architecture that also might have emanated from Russia, particularly in its provision of communal spaces. The familiar analytical inquiry prefaced the design in that optimum layouts for daylighting and privacy were evolved. This building also furthered the brilliant career of Arup, the engineer who developed the innovative sliding-shutter system for erecting the reinforced concrete walls. High Point 1, the first English interpretation of Le Corbusier's Ville Radieuse, and lauded on that architect's London visit, was followed by the adjacent High Point 2 (1936-38), where lavish space standards and, for example, the provision of maids' rooms at ground-floor level suggested a departure from the socialist ideals that had underpinned the design of High Point 1.

Lubetkin's socialist aspirations met architectural fulfillment, however, with an enlightened public client, the borough of Finsbury. It was fitting that progressive movements in health care and public housing should espouse similarly avant-garde movements in architecture as an expression of their ideals. The Finsbury Health Centre (1935-38), in its Beaux-Arts axiality, demonstrates Lubetkin's deep understanding of the classical tradition but also of the brief: the central pavilion denotes the fixed, immutable functions, while the flanking wings can adapt to change during the building's life.

Lubetkin completed both Priory Green Estate (1937-51) and Spa Green Estate (1938-46) after the war, when the Tecton practice had been disbanded. Both demonstrate Lubetkin's commitment to high-quality mass housing on Ville Radieuse principles. The subsidy system prevalent under the 1936 Slum Clearance Act demanded very high densities (more than 200 persons per acre) for the initial designs, much amended for postwar implementation. Sadly, much of the communal amenity envisaged in the prewar scheme was eroded by a prevailing postwar austerity.

Alongside this social program of work that was to provide prototypical solutions for many postwar progressive idealists, Lubetkin produced a series of distinguished one-off houses during the 1930s. Notable was Six Pillars at Dulwich for S. Leakey (1935), which owed much to Corbusier's villa at Garches for its formal expression. This house, the speculatively built Beach House at Bognor (1934) and the Whipsnade houses (1936), one of which Lubetkin inhabited himself, explored the themes of access via external routes incorporated within the structural grid, of transitions from low-circulation spaces to the climactic major spaces of the house, and of the relationships between habitable rooms and external balconies and terraces. All owed much to Corbusier's "Five Points" for their architectural language; all were beautifully fashioned and immaculately

Berthold Lubetkin: Highpoint I Flats, London, England, 1933-35

detailed, and demonstrated the speed with which Lubetkin's work reached a profound maturity.

Lubetkin's influence upon a growing group of young progressive modernists was immense, but was interrupted by war. Those architects returned from military service to a war-torn Britain and Clement Attlee's progressive socialist government; it appeared that their prewar aspirations for a new architecture serving a new egalitarian society could be realized.

The New Town movement that emerged from the 1947 New Towns Act seemed to provide just that potential for Lubetkin; he was appointed chief architect to Peterlee New Town Development Corporation in 1948, and set about his task with revolutionary zeal. The design of Peterlee was to reflect the traditional solidarity of the northeastern mining community for which it was designed, a dense and compact town, formally organized, in stark contrast to the sprawling Mark One New Towns that encircled London. However, such a high-density concept proved impossible in a coal-mining area that still depended upon working mines to support its economy. In the event, the increasingly entrenched positions of the newly nationalized National Coal Board, the Ministry of Town and Country Planning, and the Board of Trade led to virtual impasse, an intolerable position for Lubetkin, which precipitated his resignation in March 1950.

Disillusioned, Lubetkin retreated to farming in Gloucestershire, and Britain's greatest progressive talent was lost to architecture. However, the spirit of Lubetkin and Tecton lived on in the work of Lasdun, Moro, and Ryder and Yates.

Ironically, it was the identification of postmodern tendencies in the 1970s that again attracted Lubetkin to the architectural limelight more than three decades after his departure from Peterlee. Postmodernism emerged as a catalyst for a reassessment of mainstream modernism, and Lubetkin reemerged as a leading commentator on that reassessment. The most visible vindication of his tragically short architectural career, however, is the listing and subsequent meticulous restoration of his seminal prewar works.

—A. PETER FAWCETT

LUDOVICE, João Frederico.

German. Born in Swabia, Germany, 1670. Died in Lisbon, Portugal, 18 January 1752. Trained as a goldsmith. Served in the imperial armies, Augsburg. Went to Rome, 1697; worked under Andrea Pozzo at the Gesù Church. Married an Italian woman and changed his name from Ludwig to Ludovice, 1700. Moved to Lisbon, 1701.

Chronology of Works
All in Portugal

1716-23   University Library, Coimbra
1716-29   Cathedral, Évora (apse)
1717-30   Convent-Palace, Mafra, Near Lisbon

Publications

BOOKS ABOUT LUDOVICE

DE CARVALHO, A.: *D. João V e a arte do sen tempo*. Lisbon, 1962.

João Frederico Ludovice: Convent-Palace, Mafra, Portugal, 1717-30

KUBLER, G. and SORIA, M.: *Art and Architecture in Spain and Portugal and their American Dominions, 1500-1800.* Harmondsworth, 1959.

ARTICLES ABOUT LUDOVICE

KELLENBENZ, H.: ''Johann Friedrich Ludwig, der Erbauer der Klosterresidenz in Mafra.'' *Württembergisch Franken*, N. F. 32 (1958) (1962).

*

The German goldsmith-architect João Frederico Ludovice was the primary transmitter of the Italian Baroque to Portugal and the leading architect of the Portuguese 18th-century. His masterpiece, the convent-palace at Mafra near Lisbon (1717-30), was the most ambitious and monumental architectural undertaking of the Portuguese Baroque. Financed with the gold extracted from Portugal's colony Brazil, Mafra is the premier example of the Italianate *estilo joanino* (Joanine Style) favored by King João V (1706-50) and his Austrian queen. It was in the *chantiers* of the ''school'' at Mafra that Ludovice trained the generation of architects that reconstructed the Portuguese capital of Lisbon after the great earthquake of 1755.

Ludovice's style derived from his German and Italian background, and reflected the decorator's special talent for synthesizing European Baroque traditions and Portuguese decorative practices in an architecture of rich imported marbles and fine finishes and trims. Born in 1670 in Swabia, Johann Friedrich Ludwig was trained as a goldsmith and served in the imperial armies in Augsburg before going to Rome in 1697. There he

worked as a goldsmith under Andrea Pozzo for the Jesuits on the decoration of Il Gesù with the Gaap family of Augsburg goldsmiths. He was known for his virtuosity in the handling of metal, which he demonstrated in his casting of bronze reliefs and a silver figure of Saint Ignatius for the altar of Il Gesù church. In 1700 he married an Italian woman and changed his name to Ludovice. Although there is little documentation on his early career in Augsburg and Rome, he may have heard the lectures of Carlo Fontana and probably received some formal training in architecture before going to Lisbon in 1701 to serve the Jesuits there, still as a goldsmith. After several years of carrying out work exclusively for the Jesuit order, Ludovice received the Mafra commission in 1711 on the strength of his recommendations from the Jesuits and the favor of the queen. The appointment was probably conditioned as well by the lack of a more-capable architect in Portugal at the time.

The design and style of the convent-palace and church at Mafra illustrate the Joanine synthesis of forms and ideas deriving from the central European, Roman Baroque and Jesuit sources to which Ludovice was exposed during his career. The relationship of the convent, with its spacious courtyards and axial corridors, to the palace, which stretches all along the west front and is broken only in the middle by the church facade, recalls the planning of late 17th- and 18th-century Austrian and German abbeys such as Weingarten and Einsiedeln, Stift Gottweig and Melk. The axial layout in which convent buildings are arranged behind a twin-towered monumental church facade rising at the center of an extended palace block is also found in Carlo Fontana's plan for the Jesuit college at Loyola, Spain (1682). The relationship between the church and the palace at Mafra is similar to the arrangement of Sant'Agnese in Piazza

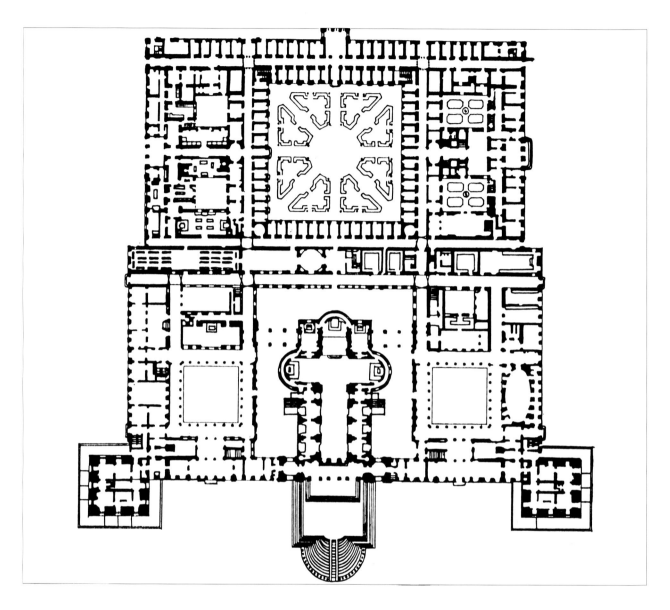

Navona and the Palazzo Pamphili in Rome. While the composition of Ludovice's palace facades recalls the Palazzo Montecitorio by Bernini and Fontana, the church itself—the facade, its loggia and the nave—recalls St. Peter's in Rome. The concavely curved, high-drummed dome derives from the Roman works of Pietro da Cortona and Francesco Borromini, and the star ornaments in the window reflect the architect's preference for the detailing of the latter. The bulbous cupolas and the fortress-like end pavilions introduce Germanic Late Baroque elements in a building that is otherwise Roman in treatment. The compositional heaviness and excessive width of Ludovice's church facade, with its pronounced layering of columns, pilasters and niches, and its placement of statues over voids, reflects his decorative training as a goldsmith, his experience with the Jesuits, and his familiarity with the manneristic Baroque of the Gesù and St. Peter's facades.

Perhaps the greatest significance of Ludovice and his work at Mafra was the opportunity they gave Portuguese builders to observe the refined adaptation of the Roman Baroque in a Portuguese context. In the *chantiers* of Mafra, Portuguese military engineers learned what the Lisbon military academy did

not teach: how to erect and decorate a building with carefully cut stone, tastefully executed ornament, and high-quality finishes of imported and Portuguese marbles and painted plaster. Because the architectural design component of the Academia Militar curriculum was very limited, many Portuguese engineers naturally looked to Mafra to supplement their training in fortifications and military science. Several of the major Lisbon military engineers who were involved in the reconstruction of Lisbon after the earthquake, including Mateus Vincente de Oliveira and Reinaldo Manoel, worked as Ludovice's assistants at Mafra. Ludovice's work anchored them in a rich Baroque tradition which, in supplementing the disciplined training of the military academy, gave the functional ''Pombaline'' architecture of post-earthquake Lisbon a special traditional flavor.

The basilica at Mafra influenced church design in both Lisbon (the Basilica da Estrela) and the Brazilian colony (the church of the Candelária in Rio de Janeiro). Mafra was, in short, the only true school of architecture in pre-earthquake Lisbon and the measuring rod of good design for 18th-century architecture in both Portugal and Brazil. In addition to Mafra, Ludovice also built the apse of the cathedral at Évora (1716-29) in the

Mafra manner and the University Library at Coimbra (1716-23), in a richer, more plastic mode. His distinctive achievements and important place in the architecture of Portugal were celebrated by the Portuguese king, who gave him the honorary title *arquiteto do rei* (royal architect).

—DAVID K. UNDERWOOD

LURÇAT, André.

French. Born in Bruyères, Vosges, France, 27 August 1894. Died in Sceaux, Hauts-de-Seine, 10 July 1970. Married to Renée Michel. Studied at the École Municipale des Beaux-Arts, Nancy, 1911-13; École Nationale Supérieure des Beaux-Arts, Paris, 1913-14 and 1918-23. Served in the Infantry, French Army, 1914-18. In private practice, Paris, 1923-34; immigrated to Russia: professor of Town Planning, Institute of Architecture, Moscow, 1934-35; returned to France: in private practice, Paris, 1937-70. Founder-member, CIAM (Congrès Internationaux d'Architecture Moderne), 1928.

Chronology of Works
All in France unless noted

1924-25	Jean Lurçat Studio-House, Paris
1925	Georg and Gromaire House, Paris
1925-26	Villa Seurat, Paris
1925-26	Michel House, Versailles
1926-27	Guggenbuhl House, Paris
1927	Apartment Block, Bagneux
1930-31	Hôtel Nord-Sud, Calvi, Corsica
1930-33	Karl Marx School Complex, Villejuif
1932	Werkbund Houses, Vienna, Austria
1946-60	Unité de Quartier Fabien Housing, Saint-Denis
1949-58	Cité Paul Eluard Housing, Saint-Denis
1951	Leduc House, Sceaux

Publications

BOOKS BY LURÇAT

Architecture. Paris, 1929.
Projets et Réalisations. Paris, 1929.
Urbanisme et architecture. Paris, 1942.
Formes, Composition et Lois d'Harmonie; éléments d'une science de l'esthétique architecturale. 5 vols. Paris, 1953-1957.
Oeuvres récentes I. Paris, 1961.

BOOKS ABOUT LURÇAT

André Lurçat, architecte. Exhibition catalog. Paris, 1967.
STEINMANN, MARTIN (ed.): *CIAM: Dokumente 1928-1939.* Basel and Stuttgart, 1979.

ARTICLES ABOUT LURÇAT

Architecture, mouvement, continuité, special issue, 40 (1976).
SHAND, P. MORTON: "Andre Lurçat's Architecture." *Architects' Journal* 29 April 1931).

*

To say that André Lurçat was one of the great French architects of the 1920s is to make a statement so simply factual as to be banal. His designs for villas and studio houses, in the severe style of Adolf Loos and Le Corbusier, were widely known and published in some of the most prestigious architectural magazines. Such was his reputation that in 1928 at La Sarraz, he became a founding member of the *Congrès Internationaux d'Architecture Moderne* (CIAM). By any standards of judgment, he was quite the equal of Robert Mallet-Stevens, J. J. P. Oud, or any number of the modern architects represented at the Weissenhof housing exhibition of 1927.

But to say simply that Lurçat was a great modern architect is also to stop quite short of the truth. Lurçat was, in fact, a revolutionary modern architect—an architect who saw the promotion of modern design as bound up inextricably with the advancement of socialism. Already during World War I he had been a member of the *Étudiants Revolutionnaires,* and after the war displayed his Communist sympathies over more plainly, both through his writings and through his architecture. From 1934 to 1936 he worked in the Soviet Union, and in the close atmosphere that incubated the theory of socialist realism actively participated in the debates of the time concerning the proper nature of proletarian architecture and the importance of monumentality to its expression. His voluminous treatise, *Formes, Composition et Lois d'Harmonie* (1953-57), drew attention to the fundamentally material nature of the architectural work and attempted to reconcile the principles of modern design to the dictates of Stalinist aesthetics, through the discovery of compositional strategies common to great buildings of all periods and styles.

Lurçat's development as an architect closely paralleled the evolution of his political ideals and his artistic theories. In the 1920s, in a series of designs for artists' studios, bourgeois villas and apartment blocks, and working-class housing estates, he investigated the options of the progressive architect in a class society. These designs were mainly for sites on the outskirts of Paris. Notable for their functional as well as formal elegance, they also reveal a taste for monumentality that made Lurçat particularly receptive to the Soviet ideas to which he was later exposed. Two buildings epitomize Lurçat's work of this period: the row of town houses—not quite modest enough to be working-class, not quite luxurious enough to appeal to the upper bourgeoisie—he contributed to the Werkbund housing exhibition in Vienna in 1932, and the Karl-Marx School at Villejuif, one of the "red suburbs" of Paris (1930-33).

Lurçat won the commission for the Karl-Marx School in competition, with a design elaborated in close collaboration with specialists in education and hygiene. It is a long, multistory block with large windows illuminating spacious classrooms, and a protected playground behind. The construction of this building was a matter of great pride to the citizens of Villejuif, and its financing something of a political feat for the municipal administration. The school was, and remains, a symbol of Communist aspirations and achievements. It has never been merely a symbol, however, since it was built to respond to very real community needs (a dramatic increase in the number of children enrolled in public education programs) and was designed, using a method that married positive social research with artistic adventure, to meet those needs as fully and as straightforwardly as possible. The Karl-Marx School may therefore fairly be regarded as the preeminent example of functionalist modernism in France.

The remaining years of the 1930s were, for Lurçat, a period of theory building. Although he built nothing in the Soviet Union, his experiences deepened his commitment to a proletarian architecture and strengthened his conviction that the creation of that architecture must be part and parcel of the revolutionary movement.

After World War II, Lurçat was one of the architects most heavily involved in the reconstruction of France. It is hard to qualify any of his later works, which included many housing schemes and public buildings, as an indubitable aesthetic success. Certainly, nothing in his later career ever equaled his achievement at Villejuif. Nevertheless, these works are notable as the practical applications of Lurçat's mature theory of architectural design and production. Providing modest dwellings and public accommodations, they met definite functional (usually quite basic) requirements in economical ways. At the same time, the architect gave each of them a certain monumental character, intended to affirm the social worth and political autonomy of the populations they served. In these respects, Lurçat's later buildings have very much the same spirit, if not the same formal quality, as those built between the wars. Lurçat never abandoned his mission as a socially engaged architect, but merely adapted his work toward that mission to the changed material circumstances of revolutionary praxis.

In the Cold War period, the low aesthetic merit of Lurçat's later work did nothing to mitigate the increasingly unfashionable status of Lurçat's overtly left-wing political position. Probably due in large part to that factor, and despite the importance of his early contributions, a cloud settled over his entire career. Only occasionally in the literature of modern architectural history do some of his brightest achievements—the Hotel Nord-Sud at Calvi (1930-31), the Werkbund houses in Vienna, the Karl-Marx School—shine through the obscurity.

—ALFRED WILLIS

LUTYENS, Edwin.

British. Born Edwin Landseer Lutyens in London, England, 29 March 1869. Died in London, 1 January 1944. Married Lady Emily Lytton (daughter of the viceroy of India), 1897; five children. Studied at the South Kensington School of Art (Royal College of Art), London, 1885-87. Worked for Ernest George (1839-1922), 1887-88; opened own office in Surrey, 1889; private practice, London, 1890-1944; appointed chief architect for imperial capital at New Delhi, India, 1912; principal architect, Imperial War Graves Commission, London, 1916-44. Gold Medal, Royal Institute of British Architects, 1921; Gold Medal, American Institute of Architects, 1924; president, Royal Academy, 1938; knighted, 1918.

Chronology of Works
All in England unless noted

1890	Crooksbury Lodge, Farnham, Surrey
1893-95	Chinthurst Hill, Surrey
1896	Warren Lodge (Warren Mere), Thursley, Surrey (rebuilding)
1896	Munstead Wood, Godalming, Surrey
1897-98	Le Bois des Moutiers, Varengeville, France
1897-1908	The Pleasaunce, Overstrand, Norfolk (alterations)
1899-1902	Deanery Gardens, Sonning, Berkshire
1899	Tigbourne Court, Witley, Surrey
1901-04	Marsh Court, Stockbridge, Hampshire
1901-12	Folly Farm, Sulhampstead, Berkshire (additions)
1902	The Hoo, Willingdon, Surrey (Alexander Wedderburn House), alterations and gardens
1902	Blackburn House, Little Thakeham, Sussex
1903-04	Papillon Hall, Leicestershire
1903-07	Lindisfarne Castle, Holy Island, Northumberland (conversion)
1904-07	Heathcote, Ilkley, Yorkshire
1905-08	Nashdom, Taplow, Buckinghamshire
1906	Hestercombe House, Somerset (garden)
1908	Plan for Hampstead Garden Suburb, London (with Raymond Unwin)
1909-11	St. Jude's Church, Hampstead Garden Suburb, London
1910-30	Castle Drogo, Drewsteignton, Devon
1911	The Salutation, Sandwich, Kent
1912-31	Viceroy's House, New Delhi, India
1924	Marsh Court, Stockbridge, Surrey (great hall addition)
1925-28	Memorial to the Missing of the Royal Air Force, Arras, France
1927-28	British Embassy, Washington, D.C., U.S.A.
1927-32	Monument to the Missing of the Somme, Thiepval, France
1928	Edward Hudson House, Plumpton Place, Sussex (cottages, entrance gate and bridge)

Publications

BOOKS ABOUT LUTYENS

AMERY, COLIN; LUTYENS, M.; et al.: *Lutyens: The Work of the English Architect Sir Edwin Lutyens.* London, 1981.

BROWN, JANE: *Gardens of a Golden Afternoon: The Story of a Partnership, Edwin Lutyens and Gertrude Jekyll.* Harmondsworth, England, 1982.

BUTLER, A. S. G.: *The Architecture of Sir Edwin Lutyens.* 3 vols. London, 1950.

FAWCETT, JANE (ed.): *Seven Victorian Architects.* University Park, Pennsylvania, 1976.

GHOSH, BIJIT, et al.: *The Making of New Delhi.* New Delhi, 1980.

GRADIDGE, R.: *Edwin Lutyens: Architect Laureate.* London, 1981.

HUSSEY, CHRISTOPHER: *The Life of Sir Edwin Lutyens.* London, 1950.

INSKIP, P.: *Edwin Lutyens.* London and New York, 1980.

IRVING, ROBERT G.: *Indian Summer: Lutyens, Baker, and Imperial Delhi.* New Haven, Connecticut, 1982.

JEKYLL, FRANCIS: *Gertrude Jekyll: A Memoir.* London, 1934.

LUTYENS, MARY: *Edwin Lutyens: A Memoir by His Daughter.* London, 1980.

LUTYENS, ROBERT: *Sir Edwin Lutyens: An Appreciation in Perspective.* London, 1942.

O'NEILL, DANIEL: *Edwin Lutyens: Country Houses.* London and New York, 1980.

RICHARDSON, MARGARET: *The Craft Architects.* London, 1983.

SERVICE, ALASTAIR: *The Architects of London.* London, 1979.

STAMP, GAVIN: *Silent Cities.* London, 1977.

WEAVER, LAWRENCE: *Houses and Gardens by Edwin Lutyens.* London, 1913.

ARTICLES ABOUT LUTYENS

BRYON, ROBERT: "New Delhi." *Architectural Review* 69 (1931): 1-30.

GOODHART-RENDEL, H. S.: "The Work of the Late Sir Edwin Lutyens, O. M." *Journal of the Royal Institute of British Architects* March (1945): 123-131.

Edwin Lutyens: Munstead Wood, Surrey, England, 1896

GREENBERG, ALLAN: "Lutyen's Architecture Restudied." *Perspecta* 12 (1969): 129-152.

*

Edwin Lutyens' roots are in the Surrey of his birth. The village of Thursley, where his father had retired to take up painting and where young Ned was raised, remains a picturesque hamlet of half-timbered and brick medieval houses. Meandering Surrey byways, a village church on the Thursley hill, and rambling rural cottages adorned with cottage gardens became the seedbed for an enduring traditionalism in residential architecture which became the essential image of the Lutyenesque. Marrying local materials, regional forms and established constructional methods, Lutyens displayed an unlimited virtuosity in designing houses, great and small, which seemed to have grown out of the ground itself and which were built in the spirit of olden times. Before Lutyens, England's masterworks in residential architecture were the great country houses whose history reached back to Tudor manorial estates. After Lutyens started building for the middle class, observers from Hermann Muthesius to Gavin Stamp would recognize the essential contribution of Lutyens in creating a new type of English house, the "house in the country" which, in turn, influenced the suburban commuter house.

Lutyens' first house, Crooksbury (1890), is a less assured exercise in Richard Norman Shaw's Old English Style; it mixes tile hanging, brick and half-timber construction, sculptural Tudor chimneystacks, rambling roof forms and picturesque siting—all of which had marked such earlier Shavian works as Leyswood (1868-69) or Grimsdyke (1870-72). Less accomplished than later work, Crooksbury is, however, not without significance, for it was there that the young Lutyens encountered for the first time the gardener Gertrude Jekyll. The meeting was fortuitous, for it was Jekyll who would have the greatest impact on Lutyens' early architectural development, not only because of her already-established client contacts, but especially because of her infectious sensitivity to the Surrey landscape. As Daniel O'Neill has noted, the Lutyens-Jekyll partnership would establish an ideal of Edwardian country life, the Lutyens house in a Jekyll garden, a residential image distinctly different from that of the behemoth Victorian country house.

The promotion of just such an image of the smaller "house in the country" was an intention of *Country Life* magazine publisher Edward Hudson, whose regular features on Lutyens houses helped with the architect other work. After seeing Crooksbury published in *Country Life,* Herbert Johnson commissioned Marshcourt (1901-04); Papillon Hall (1903, now demolished) was built by Lutyens following similar contacts. Hudson himself provided continuous patronage, commissioning new work or renovation at Lindisfarne Castle (1903), No. 15 Queen Anne's Gate in London (1906), Plumpton Place (1927-8), and the *Country Life* Offices (1904). One of the architect's best-known early houses, Deanery Gardens (1901), was built for Edward Hudson.

The Lutyens contribution to a new Surrey vernacular is especially associated with Munstead Wood, the house designed for Gertrude Jekyll herself. This was her home and garden workshop, for ongoing experiments with plantings; moreover,

Munstead was Lutyens' garden for cultivating his own architectural elements within an indigenous, traditional aesthetic: honest construction in stone, oak casement windows, tall chimney masses sculpted to balance the simple formal massing of the house, plain tile roofs, and limited bargeboard and fascia moldings to sharpen the house profile. In all, the house belonged to the landscape of Surrey, and it was this very Lutyenesque character that confirmed the professional relationship between the old-fashioned cottage gardener and her architect.

Although her house was new in 1896, Jekyll remarked in her *Home and Garden* (1900) that it did not look new. "It is designed and built in the thorough and honest spirit of the good work of old days, and the body of it . . . has . . . taken to itself the soul of a more ancient dwelling place. . . . It almost gives the impression of a comfortable maturity of something like a couple of hundred years." Yet, as Jekyll acknowledged, this was no pastiche of historic quotation, "nothing sham old about it," but simply a house conducive to a restful serenity of mind and body. The collection of cottages and gardens built by Lutyens for Jekyll at Munstead beginning in 1894 contributed to a regional Lutyens aesthetic in rural Surrey that by the end of the decade would include Chinthurst Hill (1893-95), Warren Mere (1896), High Hascombe (1896), Fulbrook (1897), and the best of the group, Orchards (1898) and Tigbourne Court (1899).

But Lutyens, as a traditionalist, or even as the consummate craft-architect of the Arts and Crafts movement, would offer limited interest on the basis of his formal aesthetic and handling of materials alone. Certainly, it was more than the recognized merit of a handful of houses in rural Surrey that prompted Lutyens' first biographer, Christopher Hussey, to describe Lutyens as the greatest architect of British history, Christopher Wren and other notables notwithstanding. On the other hand, in assessing significant contributions during the first 40 years of the 20th century in his *Outline of European History* (1943), however, Nikolaus Pevsner dismissed Lutyens and his entire generation, writing that "no British name need here be mentioned." If Lutyens, with his rejection of structural advances, modern materials and modernist dogma, offered nothing to an historian who had recently published *Pioneers of the Modern Movement* (1936), he would offer more to a postmodern generation willing and able to understand his sophisticated planning, his wit, his "complexities and contradictions in architecture."

It is in the more-sophisticated architectural devices in planning, in relating the house to the garden, and in his extraordinary juxtapositions of style, form and material that Lutyens may be viewed as one of the most accomplished and articulate architects in British history. Lutyens orchestrated a series of contradictory elements, which both enhance and enlarge the experience of his traditional houses. At both Orchards and Berrydowne Court (the latter built between Ashe and Overton in Hampshire, 1897), Lutyens presented rural farmhouse architecture and formal, geometric courtyard design, in sequences which at Orchards draws one past a tithe-barn-inspired farm wing to a formal court, and through a cloister arcade to a picturesque, informal house and garden beyond. At Berrydowne, the farm wall along a rural road opens to an enclosed, grid-planted orchard leading to a formal entry courtyard beyond (echoing Orchards), and finally to an American Shingle-Style-inspired garden elevation of tile hanging whose textured materials and forms do not seem to be a part of the same house just experienced. Deanery Gardens, enveloped by an ancient brick wall in the heart of the small Berkshire village of Sonning, combines the vernacular simplicity of a medieval great hall and the studied asymmetry of a manorial garden facade with the geometric order of an enclosed courtyard, entry vistas, radiating garden paths, and an axial rill bisecting a terraced and enclosed southwest garden. Lutyens'

use of geometry brings order to his most architectonic garden layouts, the finest of which is Hestercombe (1903), near Taunton.

At Folly Farm (1901, 1906, 1912) a depressed rose garden is ordered by geometry, and hedge-enclosed terraces create outdoor rooms which architectonically link house and garden. Such an enclosed "room" is experienced in the sunken garden at Marshcourt; similarly, pergolas serve to define garden corridors in numerous Lutyens gardens. The rotunda at Hestercombe is an anteroom within the garden, designed to orchestrate perambulations while remaining as architecturally ordered as an interior room in one of Lutyens' houses. Hedges and terraces define outdoor rooms in the Italian gardens at Ammerdown Park and Heywood (1906), which offer object lessons in linking garden and house, whether the house was designed by Lutyens or not. (Ammerdown Park is a James Wyatt house of 1788).

Lutyens was similarly a master of "fictitious history," employing various devices to suggest a history his newly crafted houses never had. Changes in architectural style, when extensions were made to existing farm structures at Folly Farm, including a Dutch wing (1906), whose formal facade offers a William and Mary era "Wrenaissance" elevation, and a pool and cloister connection to a neovernacular wing (which again recalls the English tradition of Norman Shaw, even as American Shingle Style architects transformed it). Marshcourt's juxtapositions of Tudor manor forms and classic interior details promote a reading of (fictitious) improvements and alterations through various generations of owners. Even haphazard mixtures of red tile, gray flint and Hampshire chalk along the base of an exterior wall suggest changes through time, as though age, weathering and decay had peeled away a layer of revetment to disclose contrasting materials beneath; such devices imply changes over time, which brought 20th-century Marshcourt a history it never had.

In a masterful synthesis at Homewood, Lutyens presents a sophisticated design of stylistic contradictions, spatial complexity and wit. A favorite device of multiple gables, with their weatherboards and simple frame windows, announces a vernacular farm aesthetic. This image of the commonplace is immediately denied by the classical arched entry with its witty, free-floating keystoned lintel. The sheltering roof of the garden elevation (vernacular) wraps round an erupting classical villa (academic), whose pilastered facade is painted white and stuccoed. Classicism appears to extend from the ground between open pavilions, sprouting pilasters like spring tulips, forcing the roof surface back and creating a garden elevation marked by tension, energy and contradictory imagery. The retention of a hint of the dark clapboarding peeping through this layering of the ordinary and sophisticated is a delightful touch of irony and wit.

From the beginning in Lutyens' work, classicism appeared (as at the Homewood stuccoed villa) as an ever-present force, offering stability and order to his passionate love of organic building, and bringing discipline and order to his manipulations of space and form. Heathcote (1906) is a weighty and compact composition in the "high game of Palladio" but played with an English, Hawksmoor-inspired flair whose grandiloquence is deflated by Lutyens' willingness to poke fun at the very game he plays. His Georgian houses, such as Ednaston Manor (1912-13) and the Salutation, are dignified and more restrained. Geometry offered Lutyens a controlling discipline evidenced as readily by garden layout as in his house plans; Papillon Hall was a tour-de-force of geometric manipulation. Similarly, classicism disciplined his elevations, from his earliest exercise in Wrenaissance design for Crooksbury's east from (1898) to the enobled facades of Gledstone Hall (1922-25), his last stately country house.

Certain late Lutyens works suggest a development toward what has been called an "elementaries"—a restrained classicism seen in his cenotaphs for Whitehall (1919) and Manchester (1923), and monumentalized in such master works as the Memorial to the Missing, Thiepval, France (1923), the noblest of his fine series of war memorials. Most of his later life was devoted to the layout of New Delhi, India, and the building of its monumental Viceroy's House (begun in 1912). This was the architect's crowning achievement. It may also be the final Lutyenesque contradiction—an embodiment of imperial classicism which had marked a tradition of colonialism, now humanized by the restraint and repose which had colored his English country houses. Soon to be the official residence of the president of the Republic of India, the Viceroy's House was for India both culmination and fulfillment as well as a work of transition (much like Lutyens' life's work), from Victorian to Edwardian, from the Raj to Mountbatten, from the harshness of high noon to the repose of a "golden afternoon."

—ROBERT M. CRAIG

M

MACKINTOSH, Charles Rennie.

Scottish. Born in Glasgow, Scotland, 7 June 1868. Died in London, England, 10 December 1928. Studied at Glasgow School of Art; pupil of John Hutchinson. Joined Honeyman and Keppie firm, 1889; partner, 1901; left Honeyman and Keppie firm, 1913; private practice, alternatively as painter and architect, 1913-28.

Chronology of Works
All in Scotland unless noted
† Work no longer exists

1890	William Hamilton House, Glasgow (Redclyffe), Springburn
1893	Glasgow Herald Building Tower, Glasgow (with John Keppie)
1894-96	Queen Margaret's Medical College, Glasgow (with Keppie)
1895	Martyrs' Public School, Glasgow (with Keppie)
1896	Buchanan Street Tearooms, Glasgow (mural decorations)†
1896-97	Argyle Street Tearooms, Glasgow (furniture)
1896-99	Glasgow School of Art, Glasgow (eastern section)
1897-99	Queen's Cross Church of Scotland, Glasgow
1898	Brüchmann Dining Room, Munich, Germany
1898	Ruchill Street Church Halls, Glasgow
1899-1901	William Davidson House (Windy Hill), Kilmacolm
1900	Mackintosh Apartment, 120 Mains Street, Glasgow (furnishings and decoration)†
1900-12	Ingram Street Tearooms, Glasgow (some interiors and furnishings survive)
1901	Daily Record Offices, Glasgow, Scotland
1902	Scottish Section, International Exhibition of Modern Decorative Art, Turin, Italy†
1902-04	W. W. Blackie House (Hill House), Helensburgh
1902-06	Wärndorfer Music Salon, Vienna, Austria (with Margaret Mackintosh)
1903-10	Cochrane House (Hous'hil), Nitshill
1903-19	Willow Tearooms, Glasgow† (restored without furniture in 1979-80)
1904	Holy Trinity, Bridge of Allan, Stirlingshire (chancel furniture)
1904	Scotland Street School, Glasgow
1905	Ball Dining Room, Berlin, Germany
1906	H. B. Collins House (Mosside), Kilmacolm
1906	Mackintosh House, 78 Southpart Avenue, Glasgow
1906	F. J. Shand House (Auchinibert, now Cloak), Killearn
1906-09	Glasgow School of Art, Glasgow (redesign of western section, including library)
1908	Lady Artists' Club, Glasgow (doorway and furnishings)
1916-20	W. J. Bassett-Lowke House, 78 Derngate, Northampton, England (interiors and furniture)
1917-20	Dugout, Glasgow (interior)
1920	Harold Squire Studio House, Glebe Place, Chelsea, London, England

Publications

BOOKS ABOUT MACKINTOSH

ALISON, FILIPPO: *Charles Rennie Mackintosh as a Designer of Chairs.* London, 1974.

BILLCLIFFE, ROGER: *Architectural Sketches and Flower Drawings by Charles Rennie Mackintosh.* London, 1977.

BILLCLIFFE, ROGER: *Charles Rennie Mackintosh, The Complete Furniture, Furniture Drawings and Interior Designs.* London, 1979.

BILLCLIFFE, ROGER: *Mackintosh Textile Designs.* London, 1982.

BLISS, D. P. (ed.): *Charles Rennie Mackintosh and the Glasgow School of Art.* Glasgow, 1961.

C. R. Mackintosh, Haus eines Kunstfreundes. Darmstadt, Germany, 1902.

COOPER, JACKIE (ed.): *Mackintosh Architecture: The Complete Buildings and Selected Projects.* London, 1978.

DOAK, A. (ed.): *Architectural Jottings by Charles Rennie Mackintosh.* Glasgow, 1968.

EADIE, WILLIAM: *Movements of Modernity: The Case of Glasgow and Art Nouveau.* New York, 1990.

HOWARTH, THOMAS: *Charles Rennie Mackintosh and the Modern Movement.* London, 1952.

MACLEOD, ROBERT: *Charles Rennie Mackintosh, Architect and Artist.* London, 1968.

NUTTGENS, PATRICK (ed.): *Mackintosh and His Contemporaries in Europe and America.* London, 1988.

ROBERTSON, PAMELA (ed.): *Charles Rennie Mackintosh: The Architectural Papers.* Glasgow, 1990.

YOUNG, A. H.: *Charles Rennie Mackintosh (1868-1928): Architecture, Design and Painting.* Exhibition catalog. Edinburgh, 1968.

ARTICLES ABOUT MACKINTOSH

BILLCLIFFE, ROGER, and VERGO, PETER: "Charles Rennie Mackintosh and the Austrian Art Revival." *Burlington Magazine* 119 (1977): 739-746.

KOSSATZ, HORST-HERBERT: "The Vienna Secession and Its Early Relations with Great Britain." *Studio International* (January 1971): 9-20.

PEVSNER, NIKOLAUS, and RICHARDS, J. M. (eds.): *The Anti-Rationalists.* London, 1973.

PEVSNER, NIKOLAUS: ''Charles Rennie Mackintosh.'' In *Studies in Art, Architecture and Design: Victorian and After*. Princeton, New Jersey, 1968.

SMITH, W. J.: ''Glasgow: 'Greek' Thomson, Burnet and Mackintosh.'' *Quarterly Review of the Royal Incorporation of Architects in Scotland* (August 1951): 56-60.

*

The active architectural career of Charles Rennie Mackintosh was a relatively short one packed into little more than two decades spanning the turn of the century. Almost everything he did, not only in building but in the varied fields of the decorative arts, was carried out in and around his native city of Glasgow. It is true that, after leaving Glasgow in 1914, Mackintosh did complete a few projects in England, most notably the precociously art deco conversion of Derngate in Northampton (1916), but by the World War I years, circumstances or choice seem to have led him to abandon architectural practice and turn his creative artistic attention to painting, a pursuit that he continued, principally at Port Vendres in the south of France, until his death in 1928.

The innovative intensity of his architectural output, during twenty years or so, and its pivotal fin-de-siècle context and content have made Mackintosh not only perhaps the best-known representative of a nation whose particular and most remarkable historical cultural expression might well be architectural, but a designer whose wider role in the transformation of architectural order and imagery has assured him a place on the world stage. Indeed, it is the intriguing interplay between national and international influences, and between the rooting continuities of tradition and the liberating possibilities of the future, that characterize his special genius. In terms of his significance in the history of art and in what Nikolaus Pevsner called ''the geography of art,'' Mackintosh is a major figure.

From the early 1890s this dialectic was present. On the one hand, as a member of ''The Four'' group at the Glasgow School of Art, along with Herbert MacNair and the Macdonald sisters, Margaret and Frances, he was infected by European symbolism and art nouveau. Mystical, attenuated forms insinuated themselves through his graphic design work into the decorative detailing of his early buildings. This new visual language drawn from nature effectively released Mackintosh from the historicism of his student designs, though it did not provoke the same structural consequences as in France or Belgium, remaining confined to the incidental realm of architectural ornament. On the other hand, from the indigenous tradition of Scottish Baronial architecture, he drew more solid architectonic lessons. Lighting a Ruskinian lamp to power, he was led by an admiration for sheer mass in building to cast doubt on those ''rose-tinted hallucinations'' vested by some in the Crystal Palace. More significant, however, was the functional moral he found in the direct response of the Scottish tower house and castle to the practical needs of material and use; this he forcefully applied to the issues raised by his own commissions. In a number of buildings a unique synthesis—never wholly resolved but all the more tense and vital for that—began to appear.

At Martyrs' School, Glasgow (1895), where the plan organization is relatively conventional, there is both an incipient addiction to art nouveau in the detail and a bold honest exposure of the roof construction trusses. At Queen's Cross Church, Glasgow (1897-98), in a broadly Gothic setting, the same combination is evident: flowing naturalistic forms cut into timber and stone but, above, are ruthlessly revealed the riveted steel joist ties that cross the church below the timber-boarded vault over the nave. But it was in his competition-winning project for the Glasgow School of Art (1897-99; 1907-9) that Mackintosh most brilliantly exploited the interactive potential of these two influences.

Moreover, it was in this astonishing building—partly perhaps because it was built in two historically separate phases, a delay that allowed other factors such as the rectilineal elegance and cool sense of space derived from Japanese and Viennese sources to make their impact—that Mackintosh's mature style emerged.

The School of Art is unexceptional in plan—an E configuration laid along the north side of a city block sloping abruptly to the south—but its elevational appearance, though of course not without its varied roots, is, in the final aggregation, dramatically original. To the east and south, the memory of the tall gaunt walls of 16th- or 17th-century Scottish castles is never distant; to the north, it is the overriding functional need for north light to the great studios that dominates the formal concept; to the west, the last part of the building to be designed, an unprecedented rippling curtain of stone and glass rises above the steep street to catch the glow of the evening sun. Inside, the interiors are endlessly rich in spatial pleasures and decorative invention: studios have a severe, almost Japanese, austerity; the library glows with mystical complexity.

Throughout the long realization of the School of Art, Mackintosh's architectural ideas were developing under the influence of other commissions and events. In 1899 he built his first significant house, Windyhill at Kilmacolm (1899-1901), in which he was able to adduce his knowledge and admiration of Scottish architecture to the task of bourgeois domestic design. The Hill House at Helensburgh (1902-3) followed. Both are white-harled L-plan houses, unquestionably Scottish in formal idiom but, at the same time, provocatively untraditional: both have bare but calmly composed elevations to the garden, yet both present oddly agitated fenestration on the opposite sides of the building. Evidently Mackintosh was using the functionalist moral of the national tradition to challenge his own manipulative skill with the immediate and contingent needs of the plan. At Scotland Street School, Glasgow (1904-6), the symmetry of the brief prevented such audacity; nonetheless, the conically capped staircases became transparent cylinders, still somehow recognizably Scottish, but radically transformed from the solid historically familiar drums at Holyrood, Falkland or Tolquhon.

At the center of the rear elevation of Scotland Street is a thoroughly geometricized version of the thistle, Scotland's national emblem. While this, too, illustrates the phenomenon of transformation, it indicates particularly that parallel formal change that had affected Mackintosh's use of the language of art nouveau. This process found its clearest expression in the sequence of four Glasgow tearoom projects for which he was engaged by the formidable Kate Cranston. Beginning in Buchanan Street (1896), where he contributed only a mural decoration of whirling plant-like motifs, and ending with the Willow Tea-Room (1903-4), where his involvement was comprehensive, Mackintosh developed a series of progressively more abstract, spatially intriguing and preciously caparisoned interiors.

The impetus for this abstraction came in part from Japan, but more directly from Vienna, where Mackintosh and his wife Margaret Macdonald had visited to great acclaim when in 1900 they and their coterie of Glasgow designers had exhibited furnishings and decorative art at the Eighth Exhibition of the Viennese Secession. There, contact with Josef Hoffmann, Joseph Olbrich, Karl Moser and others seems to have directed Mackintosh into a more geometrical decorative mode. Most of his subsequent work, especially that carried out in the second phase of the Glasgow School of Art, eschewed the more overtly naturalistic ornament of earlier years, while a corresponding abstraction began to affect his architectural conceptions so that, although the white, almost cubic, quality of the Scottish tradition of building persisted, its more historically identifiable forms did not. Typical were several designs of 1901, e.g., the crisp pyramid-roofed Auchenbothie Lodge at Kilmacolm, the white glazed-brick walls of the Daily Record offices in Glasgow, and the unbuilt Haus eines Kunstfreundes competition project promoted by the Darmstadt publisher Alexander Koch—a design, only now finally constructed in Glasgow (1989-90), which seems to herald the International Style of the 1920s and 1930s.

The events in Vienna and Darmstadt signaled European recognition for Mackintosh. His work was published abroad; his furniture went on show in Turin (1902) and Moscow (1903). Minor commissions in Munich and Vienna came his way. But Mackintosh's career failed to ignite like that of his Austrian contemporaries. At first it seemed, however, that Glasgow could sustain his talent, and for as long as the School of Art was building, there was work. But by the end of the decade the picture had changed. Problems with colleagues and clients built up; commissions dried up. Finally Mackintosh left Glasgow. Understandable disillusionment, self-inflicted decline, mid-life crisis? It is impossible to say.

This sentimental lure of tragedy too readily leads away from balanced criticism. Latter-day emulators too easily traduce the distinctive "Glasgow Style" into kitsch. But Mackintosh's architectural achievement cannot be obscured. Some have seen him as a pioneer of the Modern Movement, others as "a last and remote efflorescence of a vital British tradition." He was neither; yet he was both. For it was an ability to engross the dichotomies of his time—national and international, tradition and innovation, craft and art, nature and geometry—and thus invest his work with a creative and lasting ambivalence that marks his paradoxical greatness. Mackintosh was at once a part of his age and apart from it.

—FRANK ARNEIL WALKER

MADERNO, Carlo.

Italian. Born in Capolago, Italy, in 1556. Died in Rome, 30 January 1629. Worked as a master of stucco decoration in the workshop of his uncle, Domenico Fontana, 1570s. Appointed architect of St. Peter's, Rome, 1603.

Chronology of Works
All in Italy
* *Approximate dates*
† *Work no longer exists*

1586	Obelisk, Vatican City, Rome (with Domenico Fontana)
1587	Obelisk, San Giovanni in Laterano, Rome
1587	Obelisk, Santa Maria Maggiore, Rome
1589	Obelisk, Santa Maria del Popolo, Rome
1593-1603	Santa Susanna, Rome (new facade and remodeling)
1595*	Palazzo Salviati, Rome (completion)†
1598-1617	Palazzo Mattei di Giove, Rome
1600	Cappella Salviati, San Gregorio Magno, Rome
1600	Santa Maria in Aquiro, Rome
1600*-08*	San Giacomo degli Incurabili, Rome (facade)
1602-05*	Capella Aldobrandini, Santa Maria sopra Minerva, Rome (completion)
1603	Santa Lucia in Selci, Rome
1603-20*	Villa Aldobrandini, Frascati
1605-06	St. Peter's, Rome (first temporary baldachin, choirscreen and wooden ciborium)
1607-12	St. Peter's, Rome (facade)
1608*-12*	Santa Maria della Vittoria, Rome
1608-15	San Giovanni dei Fiorentini, Rome (crossing, drum, and dome)
1608-28*	Sant' Andrea della Valle, Rome (completed nave, began facade and built crossing, drum and dome)
1609	Fountain, Vatican Belvedere, Rome (now altered)
1609-16	St. Peter's, Rome (nave)
1611-13	Borghese Garden Palace on Quirinal (Palazzo Rospigliosi-Pallavicine), Rome (with others)
1611-14	Cappella Rivaldi, Santa Maria della Pace, Rome
1612-14	Aldobrandini Chapel, Cathedral, Ravenna
1612-14	Palazzo Borghese, Rome (addition)†
1613-17	Quirinal Palace, Rome (completion)
1614	Fountain, Piazza di San Pietro, Rome
1617	Convent, Santa Maria Maddalena dei Convertini, Rome†
1617-24	Palazzo Barberini, Castelgandolfo, Rome
1618-25	Palazzo di Monte di Pietà, Rome
1622	Palazzo Aldobrandini, Rome
1622	Villa Ludovisi, Frascati (water theater)
1622	Villa Lodovisi, Rome
1622-23	Palazzo Ludovisi, Rome (Chigi-Odescalchi; later remodeled)
1625	Castelgandolfo, Rome (new construction)
1625	Palazzo-Peretti (Fiano-Almagià), Rome
1626	Pantheon, Rome (campanili)†
1626	Sant 'Ignazio, Rome (built by others)
1626-28	Palazzo Barberini, Rome (completed by Bernini, with Borromini and perhaps Cortona)

Publications

BOOKS ABOUT MADERNO

BAGLIONE, GIOVANNI: *Le vite de' pittori, scultori, architetti, ed intagliatori.* Rome, 1642; 1935.
CAFLISH, NINA: *Carlo Maderno.* Munich, 1934.
DONATI, U.: *Carlo Maderno.* Lugano, 1957.
HIBBARD, HOWARD: *Carlo Maderno and Roman Architecture: 1580-1630.* University Park, Pennsylvania, 1971.

ARTICLES ABOUT MADERNO

BERGER, ROBERT W.: "Garden Cascades in Italy and France: 1565-1665." *Journal of the Society of Architectural Historians* 33, No. 4 (1974): 304-322.
BLUNT, ANTHONY: "The Palazzo Barberini: the Contributions of Maderno, Bernini and Pietro da Cortona." *Journal of the Warburg and Courtauld Institutes* 21 (1958): 256-287.
FAGIOLO DELL'ARCO, M.: "Villa Aldobrandina Tuscolana." *Quaderni dell'Istituto di Storia dell'Architettura*, Rome, 1960.
KIRWIN, W. CHANDLER: "Bernini's Baldacchino Reconsidered." *Römisches Jahrbuch für Kunstgeschichte* 19 (1981): 143-71.
LEFEVRE, RENATO: "Della Porta e Maderno a Palazzo Chigi." *Palladio* 21 (1971): 151-58.
WADDY, PATRICIA: "The Design and Designers of Palazzo Barberini." *Journal of the Society of Architectural Historians*, 35, No. 3 (1976): 151-85.
WHITMAN, NATHAN T.: "Roman Tradition and the Aedicular Façade." *Journal of the Society of Architectural Historians* 29, No.2 (1970): 108-123.

Carlo Maderno: St. Peter's, Rome, Italy, 1607-12

Carlo Maderno, an architect who worked in Rome in the generation before Francesco Borromini, Pietro da Cortona and Giovanni Lorenzo Bernini and the full Baroque, is perhaps best known for one of his earliest works, the facade of St. Peter's. The model of strong columnar architecture that Maderno articulated there was to become a part of the tradition of design in Rome for all of the architects who came after him. He was also praised for his practical expertise, being in charge, as it were, of the Tiber for many years, building along its length aqueducts, embankments and bridges and several other forms of hydraulic control.

Maderno was born into a family of architects; his uncle Domenico Fontana was architect for Pope Sixtus V. Maderno seems to have been in Rome by the mid-1570s, rising in power in Fontana's workshop, and when Fontana, charged with the embezzlement of papal funds, was exiled from Rome in 1594, Maderno quickly emerged as the leading architect in the city.

His first achievement was a remodeling, from 1593 to 1603, of the older church of Santa Susanna in the Quirinal for Cardinal Girolamo Rusticucci, who knew him from his own connections with Fontana. The plans for expansion there, which followed the establishment in that neighborhood of the new aqueduct by Sixtus V, the Acqua Felice, required a whole new area to be built and the church itself to be redone. All the interior details were removed, with the nave becoming an unbroken space with a coffered wooden ceiling and spaces for new frescoes on the walls. Yet the most striking and influential detail of the church was the facade, which, like many of the period, was essentially a separate architectural feature. It has five bays, continuing the wings at the side, but the surface moves from the engaged columns at the ends to the almost freestanding ones at the center. It is this movement that lends the whole front a sculptural force

that few facades before had embodied, though hints of such a design can be seen in the facade of Il Gesù by Giacomo Vignola. The upper story continues the pattern below; above the pedestal runs a balustrade which—to the horror of neoclassical critics—picked up balustrades at the wings. The whole facade has a simplicity and richness that Maderno was hardly able to equal for all the power of his later work at St. Peter's and Sant'Andrea della Valle.

By the time Santa Susanna was done, Maderno had been appointed architect to St. Peter's, and in 1605 he received the commission from Pope Paul V to complete the still-unfinished building. The opinion of the more powerful cardinals was that a nave should be appended to the centralizing structure of Bramante and Michelangelo, but another group in the church was concerned with preserving the appearance of what those architects had done. Maderno worked out a striking balance of these requirements, together with new details required by the pope, most obviously a loggia for benediction, which entailed making the facade a screen with a narthex portico inside; then, after the design was done, the pope in 1612 ordered that the facade be flanked by two bell towers or *campanili*. There, all of Maderno's practical experience was necessary, for water was discovered under the site at the south end; wells were constructed and piles, bricks, tiles and sandbags were poured into the foundation. Maderno's design did not rise above the attic; later, Giovanni Lorenzo Bernini, in an unwise move that almost ruined his career, attempted to add a tower on the south end, and the whole structure began to crack.

The interior of St. Peter's provided equal challenges; though the nave, until the 19th century one of the largest spaces in European architecture, is essentially based on what was there, the piers and arches follow the previous design in a way that suggests a simple, unified space. It is characteristic of Maderno's quiet skill that, even with these extensions, there is still a sense inside of a unified, centralized church. The aisles are narrow, each opening upward into oval domes with lanterns that bring in light and avoid the darkness found in many churches of that time. Maderno was also in charge of decorating the crossing, and if Bernini's later work was in the end responsible for what we see now, it is possible some of the details of his design were suggested by Maderno, most notably the idea of the twisted, Solomonic columns—an idea for the baldachin borrowed, or so Francesco Borromini was to say, from Maderno. For the piazza, there was less planned, though Maderno had the idea of a fountain pool around the obelisk; this was something else Bernini used when in the 1650s he built the present piazza.

All this work at St. Peter's did not prevent Maderno from working for other patrons; on occasion he even worked outside Rome, most successfully at the church of San Domenico in Perugia. He also designed a number of ecclesiastical projects in Rome, including some notable chapels—completing a project by Giacomo della Porta for the Aldobrandini Chapel in Santa Maria sopra Minerva (1602) and adding the high-altar chapel to Santa Maria della Pace (1611-14).

In 1608 Maderno began work on the completion of the church of Sant'Andrea della Valle, the mother church of the Theatine Order, which had been begun, perhaps to the plan of Giacomo della Porta, in 1591. The first patron died when only the nave had been built, but finally Cardinal Alessandro Peretti, a nephew of Sixtus V, agreed to finish what was there, employing the family's firm, by then headed by Maderno. The architect then finished the nave, transepts and chancel, and began work on the drum in 1620, making in that year a model for the dome that envisaged a structure second only in scale to that of St. Peter's. Sant'Andrea does not stand on clear space, so Maderno planned this dome as a separate entity and as something to be seen separately, announcing the church perhaps, but not intended to match any other part of what was there. In designing the dome Maderno was helped by his new assistant, Borromini, and if parts of the detail seem to stem from what was at St. Peter's—most notably the paired Ionic columns on the corners of the octagon that alternate with windows in the intervening bays, in the lantern where the paired columns share a single capital—we see signs of the style of this younger architect. Inside, there was a series of clustered pilasters, and Maderno continued these around the apse; also, the drum was given eight windows, making the interior lighter. Maderno also designed a grand front; this was begun in the 1620s but was left unfinished, to be completed some 40 years later by Carlo Rainaldi.

Maderno also did a great deal of work on secular buildings. In 1612-14, he added a wing to the Palazzo Borghese (demolished in the 19th century), with hanging garden and loggias that faced the port of Ripetta, a delicate recollection of the life of the villa, attached to a city building. He also built a city garden for Cardinal Borghese next to the palace of the popes on the Quirinal, above the baths of Constantine, and was probably responsible for the wonderful Casino dell'Aurora (1612), named after the famous painting there by Guido Reni. He also built the fourth wing of the Quirinal Palace (1613-17), most notably the large Capella Paolina and the Sala dei Corrazzieri, supervising in addition, in ways we cannot now untangle, the garden and the decorations placed in them (his earliest work, notably, had been in stucco decoration). His last such work, and it is very difficult for us now to reconstruct this, was the Palazzo Barberini, which he began in 1626-28 and which was completed after his death by Bernini with the help of Borromini and perhaps even Cortona.

The Barberini, concerned after the election of Urban VII in 1623 with building for themselves a family residence, purchased an old palace near the Quirinal on the site of a garden owned once by Cardinal Rodolfo Pio of Carpi, a noted collector and scholar. Domenico Fontana had worked on the older structure, and in Maderno's final plan, which came about only after many turns and changes, the old left wing was attached to this new building, the scheme being for an H-shaped palace, not unlike the kind of villa suggested in the Palazzo Borghese. Much has been changed, but the design of the Palazzo Barberini, like all of Maderno's work, shows elements both old and new. The facade is essentially that of the Palazzo Farnese; yet in other details it seems close to the Palazzo Borghese, or even to the Quirinal Palace, though it must be remembered that some of the parts there now may depend as much on Bernini and Borromini as on Maderno.

Maderno was clearly a great architect, but he was followed by Bernini and Borromini, both of whom in their differings ways seem to have had a far richer architectural imagination. But it was Maderno who introduced a new and particular type of grand architecture to Rome, and the influence he exerted on Borromini was very important, above all perhaps an encouragement for which Borromini was extremely grateful and which perhaps led to his insistence on being buried in Maderno's grave in San Giovanni dei Fiorentini.

—DAVID CAST

MAEKAWA, Kunio.

Japanese. Born in Niigata City, Japan, 14 May 1905. Studied at the University of Tokyo, Department of Architecture, graduated 1928; trained in Le Corbusier's office, Paris, 1928-30; trained in Antonin Raymond's office, Tokyo, 1930-35. In private practice, Tokyo, since 1935.

Chronology of Works
All in Japan

1952	Nihon Sōgo Bank Main Office, Tokyo
1954	Kanagawa Prefecture Music Hall, Yokohama
1958	Harumi Cooperative Apartments, Tokyo
1960	Cultural Hall, Kyoto
1960-64	Gakushin University Buildings, Tokyo
1961	Metropolitan Festival Hall, Tokyo
1971	Saitama Prefecture Museum, Ohmiya
1974	Tokyo Kainjō Insurance Company, Tokyo
1982	Kumamoto Prefectural Concert Hall and Theater, Kumamoto
1983	Kunitachi College of Music Concert Hall, Kunitachi
1983	Yokohama Municipal Office of Naka-Ward, Yokohama
1983	Hirosaki Municipal Funeral Hall, Hirosaki
1985	Niigata Municipal Museum, Niigata
1986	Ishigaki Municipal Auditorium, Ishigaki

Publications

ARTICLES BY MAEKAWA

"Thoughts on Civilization and Architecture." *Architectural Design* (May 1965): 229-230.

"Formes et Fonctions." *Architecture: Formes et Fonctions* No. 13 (1967).

Kunio Maekawa: Metropolitan Festival Hall, Tokyo, Japan, 1961

"L'Humanisme et l'Architecture." *Architecture: Formes et Fonctions* No. 14 (1968).
"Hommage à Sakakura." *Architecture d'aujourd'hui* (October/November 1969).
"La Décadence Psychologique des Architectes." *Architecture: Formes et Fonctions* No. 15 (1969).
"Vom Tod der Architektur." *Kölner Stadt-Anzeiger* (5 December 1977).

BOOKS ABOUT MAEKAWA

ALTHERR, ALFRED: *Three Japanese Architects: Mayekawa, Tange, Sakakura.* Teufen, Switzerland, 1968.

ARTICLES ABOUT MAEKAWA

Space Design, special issue (April 1992).

*

Of the first generation of Japanese architects who advocated modern architecture, Kunio Maekawa clearly was the leader. He was fortunate in his education and training, which provided him with a knowledge of the Modern Movement unparalleled among his Japanese contemporaries. He added his own considerable abilities in design to create architecture which was memorable in its progressive and innovative approach. His buildings revealed a standard of excellent quality which was widely accepted by a public bound by a traditional culture.

Upon his graduation from Tokyo University in 1928, Maekawa traveled to France to study and work in the studio of Le Corbusier. After two years in Paris and five years in Antonin Raymond's office in Tokyo, Maekawa opened his own architectural business in 1935. While in the offices of Le Corbusier and Raymond, Maekawa strengthened his confidence in handling reinforced concrete, and he began to perfect his concept of architecture. Though he appreciated the niceties of traditional Japanese architectural design, the appearance of his first buildings echoed the International Style as practiced by Le Corbusier. Maekawa learned the value of Japanese design when blended with modern architectural concepts when he worked under Raymond's guidance. As a result, when he opened his office, he was already a mature designer.

Japan, however, had become increasingly nationalistic, and Western ideas were politically unpopular. Maekawa nonetheless entered several design competitions using modernist solutions, with the result that his proposals were judged to be "decadent." His lack of success did not deter him from continuing to be an outspoken proponent of Western architectural philosophy in spite of the risk of endangering his career.

While the military increasingly demanded the services of Japanese architects, the private sector was severely restricted in new construction. Consequently, Maekawa was forced to accept military commissions for projects in which very little imagination was required or even tolerated. By the end of World War II, however, he had acquired valuable experience in the logistical and engineering problems of architecture. Moreover, he had used that time to analyze further his own philosophy of design.

Freed from the restrictive military control of the war years, Maekawa emerged as the leading architect of Japan. The rebuilding of Japan allowed him to design major buildings in the functional and efficient style that he had earlier advocated. The optimistic viewpoint of the Japanese for a new and modern Japan made his buildings timely and appropriate. The architecture that he produced was in definite contrast to the traditional Japanese models and the early Western styles which were familiar to the Japanese populace. Though his practice centered on civic buildings needed in the 119 cities destroyed during the war, Maekawa did not ignore the problem of public housing. His office designed a prefabricated house available in a variety of plans. This design proved to be too costly, so another solution to housing was investigated—the multistory apartment building.

The Harumi Apartments in Tokyo (1958) offered the first high-rise solution to the housing problem in Japan. Maekawa made use of his training under Le Corbusier: The relationship between the Harumi Apartments and Le Corbusier's Unité d'Habitation in Marseilles is certainly evident, especially in concept. Some details such as the sculptural units on the roof recall the work of Maekawa's former master. Maekawa's design reveals an interesting texture on the facade of the massive building. This is achieved by the interplay of projecting and receding planes enframed by strong vertical surfaces. Though outdistanced by later housing complexes, the Harumi Apartments were highly lauded and formed the prime example to later Japanese architects faced with similar projects.

The Gakushuin University school building (1960) and the library (1964) in Tokyo represent a further influence of Le Corbusier, but in a much lesser degree than that seen in the Harumi Apartments. Some elements remain, such as the oversized sculptural ramps, the roof sculpture and the eccentric pyramidal form of the lecture hall. In addition, there are elements which are ascribed to Maekawa, such as the contrast between the planes of the building facades and the superb finish given to the external and internal surfaces of the buildings. The use of sculptured land between the buildings enlivens the space. The definition of the pyramid from its base is clearly shown and is reminiscent of roofs sometimes seen in traditional Japanese rural architecture.

The Tokyo Metropolitan Festival Hall (1961) is the most praised and publicized of Maekawa's designs. The building's considerable mass was minimized by a powerful horizontal roof form emphasized by large recessed entry areas. This concept is seen in many examples of traditional Japanese architecture. The concrete forms of the Festival Hall are sheeted with marble to provide a fine finish. Only an echo of Le Corbusier's influence remains in this design when one considers the Japanese qualities of space, mass and finish which are drawn from castle and *minka* (farm house) buildings. The Festival Hall also benefits from the sculptured landscaping around the building.

In the later years of his career, Maekawa relied more and more on the younger architects in his office to provide the exciting designs for which his firm was noted. Strongest of these coworkers were Masato Otaka, Ryuichi Miho and Riuchi Hamaguchi. Kenzo Tange too had worked in Maekawa's office, in 1938.

Because of the quality of design in his buildings, the influence that he had on his contemporaries and the younger members of the Japanese architectural profession, and the recognition that he received by virtue of the numerous international honors and awards granted to him, Kunio Maekawa surely can be regarded as the father of Japanese modern architecture.

—JAMES P. NOFFSINGER

MAIANO, Giuliano da.

Italian. Born near Florence, Italy, in 1432. Died in Naples, 17 October 1490. Brother was the architect and sculptor Benedetto da Maiano, with whom he often collaborated. Began his career as a woodworker. Possibly worked and studied with Rossellino at Pienza, 1459-64. Appointed capomaestro of the Florence Cathedral, 1477. Called to Naples by King Ferrante, 1485.

Chronology of Works
All in Italy
† *Work no longer exists*

1461-66	Palazzo Antinori, Florence [attributed]
1462	Palazzo Strozzino, Florence (completion of second story)
1466-68	Chapel of Santa Fina, Collegiata of San Gimignano
1470	Church of Santissima Fiore e Lucilla, Arezzo
1472	Pazzi Chapel, Church of Santa Croce, Florence (completion of work begun by Filippo Brunelleschi)
1472	Palazzo del Capitano, Sarzana (mostly †)
1473	Palazzo Spannocchi, Siena
1474ff.	Cathedral, Faenza (not completed until 1513)
1481	Santa Maria, Loreto, Naples (mostly †)
1485	Porta Capuana, Naples
1487-92	Villa of Poggioreale, Naples†

Publications

BOOKS ABOUT MAIANO

CENDALI, L.: *Giuliano e Benedetto da Maiano*. Florence, 1926.
FABRICZY, CORNELIUS VON: *Giuliano da Maiano architetto del Duomo di Faenza.*
HERSEY, GEORGE L.: *Alfonso II and the Artistic Renewal of Naples, 1485-1495*. New Haven, Connecticut, 1969.
HEYDENREICH, LUDWIG H., and LOTZ, WOLFGANG: *Architecture in Italy 1400-1600*. Harmondsworth, England, 1974.

ARTICLES ABOUT MAIANO

FABRICZY, CORNELIUS VON: "Giuliano da Majano." *Jahrbuch der königlich-preussischen Kunstsammlungen* 24, supplement (1903): 137-176.
FABRICZY, CORNELIUS VON: "Giuliano da Majano in Macereta." *Jahrbuch der königlich-preussischen Kunstsammlungen* 26 (1905): 40ff.
FABRICZY, CORNELIUS VON: "Giuliano da Majano in Siena." *Jahrbuch der königlich-preussischen Kunstsammlungen* 24 (1903): 320ff.
GOLDTHWAITE, RICHARD A.: "The Building of the Strozzi Palace: The Construction Industry in Renaissance Florence." *Studies in Medieval and Renaissance History* 10 (1973): 94-194.

*

The son of Leonardo di Antonio, a stonecutter and building materials supplier from the community of Maiano north of Florence, Giuliano began his artistic career as a woodworker and intarsia craftsman. Although he continued to practice that trade, he became more and more involved in architecture and is best recognized for his work in this field. His architectural style is typified by a decorative lightness found throughout the arts of late quattrocento Florence, as well as by a reworking of the motifs found in the vocabularies of earlier Renaissance masters such as Brunelleschi, Michelozzo and Bernardo Rossellino.

Giuliano's first essay into architecture appears to have been the completion of the second story of the Palazzo dello Strozzino in Florence (1462), in which he utilized a design based on the model of Michelozzo's Medici Palace. Closely related to this project is the Palazzo Pazzi-Quaratesi (1462-72), one of Florence's most significant domestic buildings. Although this palace often has been attributed to Giuliano da Maiano, Howard Saalman has offered persuasive arguments favoring Giuliano da Sangallo. More assuredly associated with Giuliano da Maiano is the Palazzo Antinori, originally built (circa 1461-66) for Giovanni di Bono Boni. This elegantly detailed building features an exterior of finely defined masonry blocks, divided into three stories by crisply classical molding strips. The off-centered portal with a typically pointed framework communicates with one of the city's most pleasing courtyards, executed in the best tradition of Michelozzo and Rossellino.

From 1466 to 1468, Giuliano was engaged in the renovation of the medieval Collegiata (cathedral) of San Gimignano. The most significant survivor of that intervention is his Chapel of Santa Fina, for which he designed an architectural framework based on that of the Rossellino shop's Chapel of the Cardinal of Portugal at San Miniato, Florence; he collaborated with his younger brother, Benedetto, on the execution of the altar.

Giuliano's Palazzo Spannocchi in Siena dates from 1473. Again, one is reminded of the Medici Palace of Michelozzo, but a closer model is that of the Palazzo Piccolomini-Todeschini in Siena, designed about 1460 by Rossellino for the nephew of Pope Pius II, and constructed between 1469 and 1509. Ambrogio Spannocchi was one of the Piccolomini pope's treasurers, and that association suggests some relationship between Giuliano and the Rossellino workshop. Giuliano could have worked under Rossellino at Pienza (1459-64), perhaps executing the inlaid woodwork in its cathedral, and could even have received architectural instruction from Rossellino. This conjectured relationship is strengthened by the fact that his younger brother, Benedetto de Maiano, received training as a sculptor in the shop of Bernardo Rossellino's brother Antonio. The Palazzo di San Galgano in Siena, similar in style to that of the Spannocchi, also has been attributed to Giuliano. His possible involvement in the construction of the Piccolimini Palace at Bagno Vignoni, locally given to Bernardo Rossellino, remains uninvestigated.

Back in Florence, Giuliano intervened in two projects originally initiated by Brunelleschi. At the Pazzi Chapel at Santa Croce, Giuliano was responsible for the inlaid wooden door to the chapel and may even have directed the completion of the portico. At Santo Spirito in 1486, Giuliano sided with the monks in forcing the alteration of Brunelleschi's four-door entry to a more conventional three-door system. That change, made despite the strong objections of Giuliano da Sangallo, severely revised the intended spatial arrangements of the interior. In 1477 Giuliano da Maiano was given the by-then largely ceremonial title of *capomaestro* of the Florence Cathedral, a title he held until his death.

Giuliano's talents were frequently in demand outside of Florence, and he played an important role in disseminating the architectural style of the Florentine Renaissance to the other regions of Italy. Little remains from his Palazzo del Capitano in Sarzana (1472), and only the two-story loggias (reminiscent of Rossellino's Spinelli Cloister at Santa Croce, Florence) of the cloister of the Badia in Arezzo survive.

In 1474 Giuliano was called to Faenza in the Romagna region of northern Italy to work on the cathedral (completed in 1513). Giuliano's design produced one of the most significant Renaissance churches in the region and a possible influence on the later church plans of Biagio Rossetti in Ferrara. The Latin-cross plan of the Faenza Cathedral features a nave of square bays with alternating piers and columns, flanked by paired side aisles, bays and chapels. The cathedral clearly employs Brunelleschian devices, including the use of sail vaults.

At Macereta, in the Italian Marches, Giuliano may have designed the Loggia dei Mercanti (sometimes dated to 1485-91), with its arcuated openings and corner piers. In nearby Recanati, he has been credited (now disputed) for work on San Domenico (1481) and San Agostino (1484), providing the portals for both churches. Only the courtyard and portions of the facade of his Palazzo Venier-Garalli in Recinati survive. From 1481 to 1486 Giuliano served as architect for the fortified Sanctuary of the Santa Casa of Loreto, but how much remains from his participation is unclear. That he was involved in programs of military architecture is supported by his earlier (1471) work at the fortress of Montepoggiolo.

Giorgio Vasari's mid-16th-century *Lives* credits Giuliano with a number of Roman projects, including the famous Benediction Loggia at the Vatican, and the construction of the Palazzo Venezia and the associated Basilica of San Marco. Modern scholarship has denied the Roman attributions, with the design of those structures most recently being given to Francesco del Borgo. Vasari's testimony concerning Giuliano's activity in Naples seems better founded. Giuliano was called to Naples in 1485 by King Ferrante and rebuilt the Porta Capuana for him and, if we are to believe Vasari, "also designed many fountains with beautiful and ingenious inventions for the houses of nobles and for the piazzas." One of those houses was the villa of La Duchesca (destroyed), built for the wife of Prince Alfonso. His role in designing the Palazzo Como (1488-90) is uncertain.

Giuliano's most significant Neapolitan project, as well as what probably was his greatest architectural contribution, was at Prince Alfonso's villa at Poggioreale, begun in 1487. Inspired in large measure by the villa descriptions of Pliny, this country estate (destroyed in the 19th century) featured a rectangular plan with corner tower pavilions, projecting like bastions, and a two-story articulated elevation. The use of gardens, aqueducts and fountains as principal components of the design heralded a new and more open villa design, looking forward to the programs of Baldessare Peruzzi at the Farnesina in Rome or Peruzzi and Antonio da Sangallo at Caprarola. Shortly before his death in Naples in 1490, Giuliano may have returned to Florence, where he entered the competition sponsored by Lorenzo de' Medici for the completion of the front of the cathedral.

Giuliano's younger brother Benedetto (1442-97) was a frequent collaborator, and the two often functioned as a team, with Giuliano having primary architectural responsibility and Benedetto completing the sculptural components. On his own, Benedetto may have had some involvement with the construction of the Strozzi Palace in Florence, although a major role in the project has been convincingly denied by Richard Goldthwaite and reattributed to Giuliano da Maiano. Benedetto's most significant architectural accomplishment remains the broad portico with its Brunelleschian suggestions erected by him in the late 1490s in front of the church of Santa Maria della Grazie outside of Arezzo.

—CHARLES R. MACK

MAKI, Fumihiko.

Japanese. Born in Tokyo, 16 September 1928. Married Misao Matsumoto, 1960; two children. Studied in Kenzo Tange's Research Laboratory, University of Tokyo, 1948-52, B.Arch. 1952; studied at Cranbrook Academy of Art, Bloomfield Hills, Michigan, 1952-53, M.Arch. 1953; studied at Harvard Graduate School of Design, Cambridge, Massachusetts, 1953-54, M.Arch. 1954. Designer with Skidmore, Owings and Merrill, New York, and Josep Lluis Sert, Jackson and Associates, Cambridge, 1954-56; founder-memb er, Metabolism Group, Tokyo;

Fumihiko Maki: Municipal Gymnasium, Fujisawa, Japan, 1984

lecturer, Department of Urban Design, 1965-79, and professor
of architecture, 1979-89, University of Tokyo; has also taught
in the United States.

Chronology of Works
All in Japan unless noted

1960	Toyota Memorial Hall, Nagoya University, Nagoya
1960	Steinberg Arts Center, Washington University, St. Louis, Missouri, U.S.A.
1963	Memorial Hall, Chiba University, Chiba
1968	Rissho University, Kumagaya
1969-78	Hillside Terrace Apartment Complex, Tokyo
1972	St. Mary's International School, Tokyo
1972	Osaka Prefectural Sports Center, Sakai, Osaka
1974	Center for the School of Art and Physical Education, Tsukuba University, Ibaraki Prefecture
1975	Low-cost experimental housing, Lima, Peru
1975	Embassy of Japan, Chancellery and Ambassador's Residence, Brasília, Brazil
1976	Austrian Embassy, Chancellery and Ambassador's Residence, Tokyo
1979	Iwasaki Museum, Kagoshima Prefecture
1981	New Library, Keio University, Minato Ward, Tokyo
1982	Maezawa Garden House/YKK Guest House, Kurobe, Toyama Prefecture
1983	Dentsu Advertising Company Offices, Kita Ward, Osaka
1984	Municipal Gymnasium, Fujisawa, Kanagawa Prefecture
1985	Wacoal Art Center (Spiral Building), Minato Ward, Tokyo
1986	National Museum of Modern Art, Kyoto
1988	Tsuda Hall, Shibuya Ward, Tokyo
1989	Nippon Convention Center (Makuhari Messe), Chiba Prefecture
1989	TEPIA Science Pavilion, Minato Ward, Tokyo
1990	Tokyo Metropolitan Gymnasium, Shibuya Ward, Tokyo
1991	Keio University Shonan Fujisawa Campus, Fujisawa, Kanagawa Prefecture
1992	Yerba Buena Gardens Visual Arts Center, San Francisco, California, U.S.A.

Publications

BOOKS BY MAKI

Metabolism 1960. Tokyo, 1960.
Investigations in Collective Form. St. Louis, Missouri, 1964.
Movement Systems in the City. Cambridge, Massachusetts, 1965.
Translation of *Communitas* by Paul and Percival Goodman. Tokyo, 1967.
What Is Urban Space? with Kawazoe Noboru. Tokyo, 1970.
The City of the Unseen. Tokyo 1980.
Translation of *The Architect: Chapter in the History of the Profession* by Spiro Kostof. Tokyo and New York, 1981.

BOOKS ABOUT MAKI

BOGNAR, BOTAND: *Contemporary Japanese Architecture: Its Development and Challenge.* New York, 1985.
————— : *The New Japanese Architecture.* New York, 1990.

SALAT, SERGE (ed.): *Fumihiko Maki: An Aesthetic of Fragmentation*. New York, 1988.

ARTICLES ABOUT MAKI

Architecture mouvement continuité, special issue (March 1985).
"Fumihiko Maki's Recent Thought." *Japan Architect* (February 1982).
Japan Architect, special issues (May 1979; March 1983; March 1987).
Japan Echo, special issue (November 1979).
"Japan Through the Looking Glass." Special issue of *Domus* (June 1981).
Space Design, special issues (June 1979; January 1986).

*

After more than three decades of teaching and practice, Fumihiko Maki, over 60 years old and at the peak of his career, is more active and creative than ever. His achievements are amply proven by his numerous outstanding projects, which include museums, educational and sports facilities that are among the finest of public architecture in Japan. Now his office is also busy with several foreign projects, including the Yerba Buena Visual Arts Center in San Francisco (1992). Educated both in Tokyo and the United States, Maki in his designs fuses the influences of Japanese Oriental and Western cultures in a most successful way, while never yielding to trivial or formalistic historicism. His increasingly sophisticated work can be characterized by a rationality of design, modular dimensioning, the use of industrialized materials, components and structures, yet also by a growing sensibility to details, craftsmanship and, most important, to the experiential qualities of space, or rather, place.

Maki first became known as a member of the so-called Metabolism Group in the early 1960s. The metabolist movement, which dominated Japanese architecture for more than a decade, was preoccupied primarily with the systematization of design and the extensive application of industrial technology in both architecture and urbanism. Prefabricated and mass-produced elements, units and even capsules supported by various megastructures were utilized to assure functional and spatial flexibility, change and growth and operational efficiency in the congested city. Maki's strong interest and work in new modes of urban design brought him in close association with the metabolists, yet he never really shared their technological phantasmagoria, obsession with mechanical changeability in their aim at futuristic and/or utopian cities. He was more inclined to approach the issue of urban flexibility from a more realistic, "down-to-earth" position: first, by his refusal of the master-planning practice of the modernist, second, by trying to implement in his actual work the diverse viewpoints of the citizens.

Therefore, even his early projects, such as the Nagoya University Toyota Memorial Auditorium (1960), the Chiba University Memorial Auditorium (1963), and especially the Rissho University Kumagaya Campus Buildings (1968), while displaying some of the insignia of metabolist architecture—massive, unfinished reinforced-concrete structures, the emphasis on vertical circulation shafts—all made initial but significant steps toward mediating between inside private and outside public spaces, and so establishing continuity between architecture and urbanism. Eventually Maki departed toward a mode of design that was inspired more by the urban context than merely by technology. His investigations of the part-and-whole relationship as the basis of collective urban forms provided a well-founded theoretical background to his contextualist architecture unfolding in the 1970s.

As opposed to a modernist "compositional form" and the metabolist "maga-form," Maki promoted a "group form," an organizational system wherein between parts and the whole a reciprocal relationship is maintained. In such systems, while the whole supports the existence and development of the elements, the elements themselves constitute, in various ways, the "collective" whole, and are not simply determined or ruled by it. For Maki, such reciprocity also implied that, in responding to the qualities of the surrounding built environment, works of architecture acquire some basic attributes of urban formations. In this regard, the most successful early work of Maki is the Hillside Terrace Apartment Complex in Tokyo (1969-76, 1987) which, through its porous matrix of formal disposition and spatial fluidity, mediates between two adjacent yet sharply divergent urban areas.

Since the early 1980s Maki has gradually enriched his architecture by extending his concerns beyond the physical aspects of the built environment to include also the cultural, social and technological landscape or milieu. In short, in addition to the place-character of an architectural setting, the images of "primary landscapes" retained in the collective memory of the Japanese have come to play a significant role in his works, best shown in the YKK Guest House in Kurobe (1982) and the Keio University Hiyoshi Library in Yokohama (1985). In any case, however, Maki has managed to evoke such primary landscapes without reverting to postmodernist, historicist cliches.

Rather than reusing a formal tradition, Maki has begun to respond more noticeably to the layered, collage-like quality of the heterogeneous Japanese city by articulating his buildings with sequentially layered spaces that, similar to traditional architecture and gardens, involve the intricate arrangement of surfaces and, in so doing, the conjuring up of a phenomenological depth (*oku*). Accordingly, building envelopes of Maki's works have become gradually "detached" from the tectonic body and, acquiring a certain sign quality, freely manipulated, as best exemplified by the Spiral Building (1985) and Tepia Science Pavilion (1989), both in Tokyo, and the National Museum of Modern Art in Kyoto (1986).

Although Maki has remained faithful to the abstract vocabulary of modernism, he has departed from its compositional ideals in several ways, most importantly in respect to its standard notion of integrated whole (synthesis of form), inasmuch as Maki's works have attained throughout the years an increasingly fragmentary quality. Such quality is well demonstrated by the Spiral Building, but can be observed even in such cases where, as at the Fujisawa Municipal Gymnasium (1984) and the Tokyo Metropolitan Gymnasium (1990), tectonic or structural considerations had to play a primary role in shaping the buildings. In the Fujisawa Gymnasium, for example, Maki seems to have made every attempt to undermine the continuity and unity of its form. In so doing, however, Maki has been able not only to recollect better the fragmentary and collaged nature of the Japanese city, but also to broaden the range of the building's references; the stainless-steel-plate-covered and curving surfaces, like an elusive, surrealist vision, can remind one equally of an ancient samurai warrior helmet, a mask, the shape of the wooden gong in Buddhist temples, as well as a spaceship or UFO and many other futuristic images, yet never at the expense of brilliant structural engineering and overall workmanship.

Recognizing the significance of both advanced technology and the dynamism and diverse nature of contemporary urban society, Maki continues to pursue an architecture that is properly multifaceted and superbly fit for our age of pluralism.

—BOTOND BOGNAR

MANSART, François.

French. Born in Paris, France, in 1598. Died in Paris, 23 September 1666. Trained by his brother-in-law Germain Gaultier.

Chronology of Works

All in France
* *Approximate dates*
† *Work no longer exists*

1623	Château of Berny†
1623	Church of the Feuillants, Paris (facade)†
1624	Church of St. Martin-du-Champs, Paris (altar)†
1626	Château of Balleroy, near Bayeux
1628	Notre-Dame, Paris (Altar of the Virgin)†
1632	Church of Ste. Marie de la Visitation, Paris
1635	Château of Blois (Orléans Wing)
1635	Hôtel de la Vrillière, Paris†
1642	Château de Maisons, near Paris
1642	Hôtel de Chavigny, Paris
1645	Church of the Val-de-Grâce, Paris
1645*	Château de Fresnes (chapel)†
1648	Hôtel de Jars, Paris†
1648	Hôtel de Guénégard, Paris (remodeling)†
1650s-60s	Château of Gesvres†
1653*	Hôtel de Guénégard (des Brosses), Paris
1655	Hôtel de Carnavalet, Paris (alterations)
1657	Church of the Minimes, Paris (portal)†
1665	Hôtel d'Aumont, Paris (staircase)†

Publications

BOOKS ABOUT MANSART

BLUNT, ANTHONY: *François Mansart and the Origins of French Classical Architecture*. London, 1941.
BLUNT, ANTHONY: *Art and Architecture in France 1500-1700*. 4th ed. rev. Harmondsworth, England, 1982.
BRAHAM, ALLAN, and SMITH, PETER: *François Mansart*. 2 vols. London, 1973.
HAUTECOEUR, LOUIS: pp. 20-76 in *Le règne de Louis XIV.* Vol. 2 in *Histoire de l'architecture classique en France.* Paris, 1948.
STERN, J.: *Le château de Maisons*. Paris, 1934.

ARTICLES ABOUT MANSART

BRAHAM, ALLAN, and SMITH, PETER: ''Mansart Studies I-V.'' *Burlington Magazine* (1963-65).

*

François Mansart was perhaps the first great Renaissance architect in France. Certainly something of his later reputation can be gauged by the fact that, though he was not the first to use it, a particular form of roof was named after him. Mansart worked most of his life for a group of newly enriched patrons and financiers and government officials. His life was not without its problems, though, for he was arrogant and touchy by character, losing several commissions for this reason. Yet for him part of this account may also be—as it was for his near-contemporary

François Mansart: Château de Maisons, near Paris, France, 1642

in England, Inigo Jones—a symptom of his idea of the status he deserved in a culture, Italianized though it was, that was not yet accustomed to the idea of the intellectual and independent architect.

We know very little about Mansart's training. His father was a master carpenter who died when he was young, and Mansart was trained by his brother-in-law, Germain Gaultier, who had worked with Salomon de Brosse; it must have been from this knowledge that Mansart, who never visited Italy, acquired his knowledge of classical design. If indeed Mansart was born in 1598, as some sources say, his career began very early, for by 1623 he was at work on the facade of the Church of the Feuillants in Paris; there he used a type of design, with flat wall panels, outlined with sharp reveals, borrowed from architects such as Giacomo Barozzida Vignola and Donato Bramante, that he employed all his life. He worked on other ecclesiastical projects, of which only the Church of Ste. Marie de la Visitation (1632) and the Val-de-Grâce (1645) still stand. These show a gradual move in style from a simple classicism to what is in some of their parts a richer, Baroque manner.

It was in the area of domestic design, however, that Mansart showed his most individual invention, establishing, on the basis of the work of earlier architects like Jacques Androuet du Cerceau and Salomon de Brosse, a form of classical design that fit the social expectations of his new clients and could then be used easily by architects working in the same type after him. Of his first such design, a château at Berny (1623), only a fragment survives; this is competent enough, for the project involved the remodeling of an older building. But the result was a design essentially in separate blocks, and the details, though hinting at the type of classicism Mansart was to work with later, retained a number of Mannerist touches. The next building, Balleroy (1626), near Bayeux, is more successful: Mansart was able to combine what he had learned from de Brosse or du Cerceau and use it with the older French idea of brick and stone architecture. The profile of the building rises in simple masses to a central block, strongly vertical in direction, crowned with a sharp roof and a cupola.

The son of the owner of Balleroy, Jean de Choisy, was chancellor to Gaston, duc d'Orléans, the brother of Louis XIII, and it was by that connection that in 1635 Mansart received the commission to rebuild the château at Blois. Only a part of his project there was completed, but the part built is remarkable and was accommodated by Mansart to all the irregularities of the site. The courtyard facade is marked by a central projecting element that is stepped back very delicately through its three stories, and like the rest of the block is articulated with paired, unfluted pilasters framing the window bays, each layer being emphasized by deep cornices. The roof is only lightly pierced by smaller dormer windows at the crest, and the chimneys are set at the extreme ends, the whole section there becoming a simple, unbroken block, massive, yet delicate. The rest of the design was not built; if it had been, the four facades would all have been different, with the interior containing several chambers of a curved plan. At the northwest facade, Mansart suggested a domed entrance pavilion, part of which was reminiscent of Carlo Maderno's design for Santa Susanna in Rome.

A few years after that, in 1642, Mansart began work on the Chateau de Maisons, in the forest of Ste. Germain, for René de Longeuil, a wealthy government official who gave Mansart a free hand in the design. In some ways, it was a smaller version of Blois, though it looked back also to the kind of massing Mansart had done at Berny and Balleroy. The main block, of a broad U-shaped plan, sits on a moated terrace. The centerpiece is like that of Blois, but narrower and taller, the top story being framed against a truncated pyramid, topped, as at Balleroy, with a small cupola. Beyond that, as at Balleroy, the other elements of the plan were each given their own separate forms. The design below the roof is horizontal, the first and second floors divided by a strong cornice; the wings on the garden front have freestanding columns; and elsewhere the window bays and niches, like those at Blois, are framed by paired shallow pilasters. Parts are severe, perhaps, but the other forms, the recesses and projections, seem to soften the effect of the whole, while keeping a proper sense of decorum. And the roof, in its height and pitch, fits the scale of the building as satisfyingly as in any of Mansart's other designs. The interior decoration at the Château de Maisons has been preserved. In the center, in the entrance vestibule, everything is somewhat severely done in stone, the balustrade being made up of wonderfully interwoven stone arcs, carrying leaf capitals, that then support the heavy stone railing. But elsewhere the decoration is more colorful, in some ways anticipating, so it seems, the style of Louis XVI just before the Revolution. The estate, it must be noted, was broken up at the end of the 19th century, and in place of the terraced gardens Mansart designed are now roads and houses; however, the effect of the building remains, a perfectly classical design, as perfect, as so many have said, as any building erected in France.

It was in those years also, 1640 to 1645, that Mansart began a number of private houses in Paris. His first such house had been done in 1635 for Louis de Vrillière, and there he established the type of building that he continued to use, namely a large block and garden, one side flanked by what was termed a gallery block. There, as often elsewhere, the exteriors were severe, any exuberance being reserved for inside. Among the most notable of these private buildings was that of the Hôtel de Jars (begun in 1648), where because of the narrowness of the site, Mansart set the rooms in two ranges, with the staircase at the right on the courtyard side. This he followed with the design of the Hôtel Carnavalet (1655); in another later design, perhaps his last, that for the Hôtel d'Aumont (1665), he was able to increase the sense of the size of the space he had to work in by using an unusual staircase design attached to the walls, and preceded by a vestibule with transverse niches that seemed to expand its size.

Toward the end of his life, Mansart was one of the architects commissioned by Jean-Baptiste Colbert, first minister to Louis XIV, to submit designs for the completion of the Louvre and for a funeral chapel for the Bourbons at the Church of St. Denis. For St. Denis, Mansart suggested a centralized building that seems to hark back to the designs for churches by Leonardo da Vinci, the main space being covered with a high dome with smaller ones clustered around it. The chapel was not built. For the Louvre project, known only through drawings, the problem was that of harmonizing the old with the new, while making the whole appear as grand and stately as possible. What Mansart suggested was a design that moved with bold and strongly stated masses; that approach worked well because of his skill at such massing and the organization he gave to the rhythms of the various parts of the elevations. Beyond that, he livened up the simple and rectangular plan that was there by placing pavilions at the corners and entrances, and adding short wings at these corners. And the vast bulk of the structure was broken up, as were the walls at Blois, by a rich pattern of solids and voids, all of which made the plan seem lighter than might have been expected.

Mansart rose from comparatively humble origins to become the great designer of French 17th-century classicism, something he achieved without any formal schooling. He did own copies of Vitruvius and some of the designs of Vignola; it is interesting that he avoided, so it seems, the work of Sebastiano Serlio, which so many of his contemporaries found appealing. Unlike

Serlio, Mansart believed that the orders were not sacrosanct, but to be used as freely as needed. The one regret of Mansart's career was that he never acquired royal patronage. And it is an historical fact that much of what he did build was treated quite badly—only about one third of what he built survives—when the original owners were forgotten or disgraced. Then there was his temperament, which may have precluded any complete success. But Mansart's particular influence was continued through the efforts of his great-nephew Jules Hardouin, who took his uncle's name, thereby beginning a dynasty of French architects with the various names Mansart, Hardouin and Gabriel that lasted well into the 18th century.

Mansart's work was not classical in the severe sense, perhaps, of Poussin or Corneille; his patrons were not as restrained in their appetites as that. But his style, as Anthony Blunt put it, was the equivalent in architecture of the style of classicism "which grew suddenly to dominate French culture in other fields during the minority of Louis XIV." It was perhaps Mansart and his building at Maisons of which Voltaire was thinking when he wrote of the eye, satisfied by a structure it could see, "never surprised and always enchanted." That is the classical ideal of architecture.

—DAVID CAST

MARCHIONNI, Carlo.

Italian. Born in Rome, Italy 10 February 1702. Died in Rome, 28 July 1786. Apprenticed to Filippo Barigioni. Entered the service of Cardinal Alessandro Albani, 1740s. Became supervising architect of St. Peter's, Rome, 1773.

Chronology of Works
All in Italy unless noted
* Approximate dates
† Work no longer exists

1734	Collegiate Church, Nettuno
1738	Cardinal Alessandro Albani Villa, Anzio (later altered)
1739	Santa Maria Sopra Minerva, Rome (monument to Benedict XIII; execution of sarcophagus relief with representation of Lateran Council; statue of angel with Orsini family coat of arms)
1741	Santa Maria Maggiore, Rome (statue of unidentified pope)
1742	San Giovanni, Montecelio (decoration of lateral chapels)
1743	Santa Croce in Gerusalemme, Rome (monument to Benedict XIV)
1745*	Palazzo di Propaganda, Rome (vestibule busts)
1746	Santa Maria Sopra Minerva, Rome (temporary interior decoration)†
1747	San Crisogono, Rome (monument to Cardinal Giacomo Milli)
1747	San Rocco, Lisbon, Portugal (relief in the Chapel of St. John)
1748	Sant'Apollinare, Rome (statue of Sant'Ignazio)
1748	Cathedral, Siena (relief in the Cappella della Madonna del Voto)
1755-62	Villa Albani, Rome (casino; coffeehouse, temples, fountains)
1756*	Molo Clementino of the Harbor, Ancona
1763-86	Piazza del Plebiscito, Ancona
1763-86	San Domenico, Ancona
1764	Catafalque (for King Augustus III of Poland and Saxony)†
1765ff.	Chiesa della Maddalena, Messina
1773	Catafalque (for King Emanuele III of Savoy)†
1776-83	St. Peter's, Rome (sacristy)

Publications

BOOKS ABOUT MARCHIONNI

ACCASINA, MARIA: *Profilo dell' Architettura a Messina dal 1600 al 1800*. Rome, 1964.

BELLI BARSALI, ISA: *Ville di Roma: Lazio*. Milan, 1970.

BLUNT, ANTHONY: *Sicilian Baroque*. London, 1968.

CANCELLIERI, FRANCESCO GIROLAMO: *Sagrestia Vaticana eretta dal Regnante Pontefice Pio Sestoe*. Rome, 1784.

CARRERAS, PIETRO: *Studi su Luigi Vanvitelli*. Florence, 1977.

COUDENHOVE-ERTHAL, EDUARD: *Carlo Fontana und die Architektur des römischen Spätbarocks*. Vienna, 1930.

ELLING, CHRISTIAN: *Rome: The Biography of Her Architecture from Bernini to Thorvaldsen*. Boulder, CO (1967), 1975.

FERRARI, GIOVANNI: *Le Bellezze Architettoniche per le feste della chinea in Roma*. Turin, Italy, 1920.

GAMBARDELLA, ALFONSO: *Architettura e Committenza nello Stato Pontificio tra Barocco e Rococcò*. Naples, Italy, 1979.

GAUS, J.: *Carlo Marchionni: Ein Beitrag zur römischen Architektur des Settecento*. Cologne and Graz, Austria, 1967.

HAGER, HELLMUT: *Filippo Juvarra e il Concorso di modelli del 1715 bandito da Clemente XI per la Nuova Sacresita di S. Pietro*. Rome, 1970.

JACOB, SABINE: *Italienische Zeichnungen der Kunstbibliotek Berlin: Architektur und Dekoration 16. bis 18. Jahrhundert*. Berlin, 1975.

JUSTI, CARL: *Winckelmann und seine Zeitgenossen*. 3rd ed. Cologne, Germany 1898 (1956).

LEWIS, LESLEY: *Connoisseurs and Secret Agents in Eighteenth-century Rome*. London, 1961.

MANCINI, CLAUDIO M.: *S. Apollinare: La Chiese e il palazzo*. Rome, 1967.

MARCONI, PAOLO: *Giuseppe Valadier*. Rome, 1964.

MATTEUCCI, ANNA MARIA and LENZI, DEANNA: *Cosimo Morelli e l'architettura delle legazioni pontificie*. Imola, Italy, 1977.

MITCHELL, HERBERT and NYBERG, DOROTHY (eds.): *Piranesi: Drawings and Etchings at the Avery Architectural Library, Columbia University*. New York, 1975.

ORTOLANI, SERGIO: *Santa Croce*. Vol. 106 in *Le Chiese di Roma Illustrate*. Rome, 1924 (1969).

PORTOGHESI, PAOLO: *Roma Barocca*. Cambridge, Massachusetts, 1966 (1970).

RICCOBONI, ALBERTO: *Roma nell' arte: La scultura nell'evo Moderno; dal Quattrocento ad oggi*. Rome, 1942.

SALERNO, LUIGI: *Palazza di Spagna*. Naples (1967).

SCHIAVO, ARMANDO: *La Fontana di Trevi e le altre opere di Nicola Salvi*. Rome, 1956.

STAMPFLE, FELICE: *Giovanni Battista Piranesi: Drawings in the Pierpont Morgan Library*. New York, 1978.

VANVITELLI, LUIGI: *Vita di Luigi Vanvitelli a cura di Mario Rotili*. Galantina, Italy, 1975 (1976)-1977.

WITTKOWER, RUDOLF: *Art and Architecture in Italy: 1600-1750*. 3rd ed. Harmondsworth, England, 1973.

Carlo Marchionni: Villa Albani, Rome, Italy, 1755-62

ARTICLES ABOUT MARCHIONNI

BERLINER, RUDOLF: "Zeichnungen von Carlo und Filippo Marchionni." *Münchner Jahrbuch der bildenden Kunst* 9-10 (1958-59).

A contemporary of Ferdinando Fuga and Luigi Vanvitelli, Carlo Marchionni was one of the most imaginative of the 18th-century Roman architects. Throughout his lengthy career, his works exhibited a wit and playfulness, and a fascination with the scenographic quality of design which historians have classified as signifying an 18th-century revival of the High Roman Baroque. His work often consciously recalls that of 17th-century architects such as Giovanni Lorenzo Bernini, to whom he is linked because of his apprenticeship with Filippo Barigioni, student of Carlo Fontana, who in turn was a follower of Bernini's. Marchionni was also a highly versatile designer, at various times fulfilling the role as architect, engineer, designer of decorative interiors and temporary structures, as well as landscape architect and caricaturist. (He was also a sculptor, and his works are competent but not distinguished in that area.) Furthermore, he had an uncanny ability to address creatively, preexisting site conditions when composing his designs. The diversity and character of Marchionni's work were as symptomatic as they were indicative of the situation in Rome, with its limited available architectural projects.

Marchionni first displayed his love of scenography in his design and rendering of an early project, a piazza for a seaport.

In that submission to the 1728 Accademia di San Luca competition, for which he won first prize, Marchionni conceived of an elegant open space which faced out to the sea. It was defined by a semicircular pileup of arcades, all topped by cornices adorned with statuary. In his presentation of the design, Marchionni captured the dramatic effects of light and shade under a tumultuous skyline. He carried this drama to almost self-mocking limits; the composition, which displays a fiery shipwreck in the foreground, was contained within an artfully conceived *trompe-l'oeil* enframement. Such a love of perspectival effects Marchionni converted to the third dimension, as in his contribution to the revitalization of the port city of Ancona for Pope Clement XII Corsini. There Marchionni was expert in framing an architectural vista on a small urban scale when he designed the facade of the Church of San Domenico (1763-86). Keeping in mind the steeply sloping site on which the church stood, Marchionni created a curvilinear facade at the summit of a carefully positioned staircase so that the facade, and the statue of Clement XII before it, could be viewed to advantage. Thus, his design for the facade and its square helped situate the church into the predetermined site visually as well as physically.

The same creative spirit is displayed in Marchionni's designs for minor structures, including those for memorial events and for garden adornment. His temporary catafalque for King Augustus III of Poland and Saxony (1764) is dramatically composed. It was designed so as to hold aloft a medallion of the deceased's portrait by means of frond-like ribs. Marchionni deliberately played with organic forms, which suggested the transitory nature of life appropriate for a funerary monument.

In this design in particular, Marchionni's absorption of the lessons of Bernini is most clearly exemplified.

A theatrical sensitivity typifies Marchionni's most noted works, those executed for the famous 18th-century patron of the arts, Cardinal Alessandro Albani. Entering Albani's service in the 1740s, Marchionni designed many villas for him, including one in Nettuno (1750s) and one in Castel Gandolfo (early 1740s). His most famous architectural works, however, were within Albani's villa in Rome. While questions of attribution are still being debated in the secondary literature, it is commonly agreed that Marchionni was responsible for the Villa Albani's garden layout and the casino situated at one end. The casino was a long, rectangular, open portico with a closed story above the central bays. The structure faced and addressed a semicircular coffeehouse set opposite it on the one short, curved boundary of the basically rectangular garden. Marchionni's placement of the buildings in relationship to one another created a series of framing elements in the garden, while other garden buildings either marked points of visual or physical termination or highlighted transitions between sections of the garden.

At the ends of the garden casino, Marchionni situated two little temple buildings, one dedicated to, and housing the statue of, Diana of Ephesus, and the other using ancient caryatids as temple-front columns. Also, he is often cited as the one responsible for an artificially ruined garden monument. Because he borrowed classical Greek forms in these works and displayed a fascination with the ruin, Marchionni, despite the affinity in many of his works for the Roman Baroque, has often been termed a forerunner of the neoclassical. It is true that architectural projects of an ephemeral nature often were the media in which architects experimented with new ideas and forms. However, Marchionni's works should foremost be characterized for their scenographic quality.

In his day, Marchionni had a reputation as a competent architect. He succeeded Luigi Vanvitelli as supervising architect (*architetto soprastante*) of St. Peter's in Rome at the latter's death in 1773. At the cathedral, Marchionni completed a work for which he is less known, the new Sacristy, which is sandwiched between the basilica and the Porta di Santa Marta (1776-83). For this he designed a tall, domed, octagonal space flanked by smaller lateral rooms. The manner in which Marchionni succeeded in creating an autonomous structure which compositionally respects the major monument is impressive. The Sacristy is connected to the basilica by means of two corridors which, despite substantial level changes, were designed so as to appear from the outside as an appendage to St. Peter's. Marchionni used Michelangelo's facade as a prototype for his own design so that the two adjacent buildings would be perceived as one design. However, the Sacristy is distinguished by a dome and cupola that mark it as an autonomous space. There, then, Marchionni demonstrated his ability to work skillfully with preexisting structures.

Lastly, Marchionni is also well known for his interior designs, especially those for the Villa Albani in Rome. The extant drawings for doors, overdoors, cornices, entablatures, wall decorations, fireplaces, consoles, keystones, trophies and Albani arms show not only Marchionni's facility, but also his exuberance for creating imaginatively lively surface decoration. Furthermore, there was a playful way in which he rendered his drawings. For example, in the drawing of the placement of the Antinous relief—one of the many antiquities that were housed in the villa—above the fireplace, Marchionni inserted an 18th-century character who carries on a witty dialogue, both verbal and visual, with the ancient Antinous. There, as in Marchionni's larger dramatic compositions, the architect embellished the perception of reality.

Marchionni was a versatile, but not a minor, designer. In his work, he demonstrated that he had strong technical abilities. Elaborating on the work of Vanvitelli, Marchionni proposed and built a jetty in the port of Ancona, called the Molo Clementini for the pope who commissioned it (ca. 1756). In fact, Marchionni's varied oeuvre is a testimony to a genius who rose to the task of responding to the enormous range of responsibilities demanded of architects of the mid-18th century in Rome.

—SUSAN M. DIXON

MARKELIUS, Sven Gottfrid.

Swedish. Born in Stockholm, Sweden, 25 October 1889. Died 27 February 1972. Studied at Stockholm Technical College, then at the Academy of Fine Arts. Married Karin Simon, 1938. Worked in office of Ragnar Östberg, Stockholm, 1915; private practice, Stockholm, concentrating on urban planning and building standardization for the Stockholm City Council, 1915-31; director of Planning Department, Stockholm Building Institute, 1938-44; director of city planning, Stockholm, 1944-54. Member, Consul tants Group for the United Nations Building, New York, 1947. Taught at the Stockholm Polytechnic and in the United States. President, Federation of Swedish Architects, 1953-56; Gold Medal, Royal Institute of British Architects, 1962.

Chronology of Works
All in Sweden unless noted
* Approximate dates

1925	Pavilion and Urban Complex, *Byggo och Bo* exhibition, Lidingo
1926	Elementary School, Sundsvall (competition project)
1926-32	Concert Hall, Hälsingborg
1928-30	Villa Markelius, Nockeby
1929	Students Club Building, Stockholm Polytechnic (with Uno Åhrén)
1930	House designs for Stockholm Exhibition
1935	Kollektivhus, Stockholm
1937	Contractors Association Building, Stockholm
1939	Swedish Pavilion, World's Fair, New York, U.S.A.
1945	Markelius Villa, Kevinge
1953-54	Trades Union Center, Linköping
1955	Trades Union Center, Stockholm
1965*	Hötorget Development
1965	Ör (Sundyberg) Housing Project

Publications

BOOKS BY MARKELIUS

Acceptera. With Erik Gunnar Asplund, Wolter Gahn, Gregor Paulsson, Eskil Sundahl and Uno Åhrén. Stockholm, 1931.
Vallingby, Stockholm. The New Self-Supporting Neighbourhood. Stockholm, 1955.

ARTICLES BY MARKELIUS

''Town Planning in Stockholm—Housing and Traffic.'' With Göran Sidenbladh. *Svenska arkitekters riksförbund* (1949): 62-78. In JACOBSON (ed.): *Ten Lectures on Swedish Architecture.* Stockholm, 1949.
''Local Environment.'' Council for Planning Action, *Symposium* 1 (1949): 28-30.

"Town Planning Problems of Stockholm." *Architects' Year Book* 3 (1949): 64-75.

"Relation of Dwelling Type and Plan to Layout of Residential Quarters." In *Papers of the International Federation for Housing and Town Planning, 20th Congress, Lisbon* (Amsterdam, 1952).

"Swedish Land Policy." *Secretariat* (1952): 128-142.

"Stockholms Struktur." *Byggmästaren* 35, No. A3 (1956): 49-76.

"Architecture in a Social Context." *Architectural Record* 135 (April 1964): 153-164.

BOOKS ABOUT MARKELIUS

RAY, STEFANO: *Il contributo svedese all'architettura contemporanea e l'opera di Sven Markelius*. Rome, 1969.
RUDBERG, EVA: *Sven Markelius, 1889-1972*. Stockholm, 1990.
SMITH, G. E. KIDDER: *Sweden Builds*. London, 1957.

ARTICLES ABOUT MARKELIUS

"Redevelopment in Stockholm." *Architect and Building News* (24 January 1962).
"The New Empiricism—Sweden's Latest Style House at Kevinge." *Architectural Review* (June 1947): 199-201.
HAMLIN, TALBOT F.: "Sven Markelius." *Pencil Points* 20 (June 1939): 357-366.
RICHARDS, J. M.: "Stockholm's new commercial centre." *Architectural Review* (August 1961).
ROSENTHAL, R.: "Vallingby Town Centre Stockholm." *Architectural Design* (October 1956).
SHEPHEARD, PETER: "Sven Markelius." *Modern Gardens* (1953).

*

Sven Markelius, a contemporary and friend of both Erik Gunnar Asplund and Alvar Aalto, was among the most active Swedish polemicists for functionalism, as modernism was termed in Scandinavia. More than most architects of his generation, Markelius' commitment to modernist social programs influenced his entire career and all of his work. Yet he remains somewhat of an enigmatic figure outside the Nordic region.

During World War I, Markelius worked as Ragnar Östberg's assistant on the Stockholm City Hall. He then traveled to Italy with Asplund in 1920, and his early work—the Simrishamn Cemetery project (1923-25), *Bygge och Bo* (*Building and Living*) exhibition house (1925) and Sundsvall elementary school (1926)—was characteristic of the austere classicism executed throughout Scandinavia during the 1920s. This classicism had two sources of inspiration: first, the simple vernacular architecture of northern Italy, and second, the work of the Nordic neoclassicists C. F. Hansen, Gottlieb Bindesbøll, Nicodemus Tessin and Carl Ludwig Engel. Exploration of the relationship between architecture and the landscape can be seen in Markelius' 1926 site planning project for the environment surrounding the island town of Visby.

Markelius' most important work of that period, the Hälsingborg Concert Hall, indicates more clearly than any other of his buildings the dissolution of Nordic classicism in favor of functionalism. His competition projects between 1926 and 1928 were explicitly neoclassical, with Schinkelesque volumetrics and Pompeian interiors. The completed work of 1932, on the other hand, demonstrates a clear expression of functionalist elemental organization: the circular entry foyer, linear promenade to the concert hall and the cubic concert hall are discrete

forms articulated through shaping and structural expression. Within the large cubic volume floats the oval music hall, with its flat ceiling, raked seating and suspended sound reflector. Gone are the neoclassic references and Asplundesque Egyptian doorways and detail qualities. In their stead are the planar surfaces and industrially inspired detailing of modernism.

The Villa Markelius at Nockeby (1928-30) continued the modernist qualities seen in the concert hall, as did the Le Corbusier-inspired Student Union for the Institute of Technology in Stockholm of 1929 (designed with Uno Åhrén). Markelius traveled extensively during that period, making contact with the leaders of the Modern Movement and visiting their exemplary works. He, along with Aalto and other Scandinavian architects, actively participated in meetings held by CIAM (Congrès Internationaux d'Architecture Moderne). Following the success of Asplund's 1930 Stockholm Exhibition, Markelius joined Asplund and four other architects in authoring *Acceptera*, a radical manifesto supporting functionalist architecture.

Among the more successful of Markelius' functionalist works was the "Kollektivhus" in Stockholm (1935). Designed to answer the needs of working parents (especially single-parent families), the complex contained flats, a restaurant and a nursery for children. The flats, though modest in size, were open-planned and contained large exterior balconies with planters. Mixed-use projects like the Contractors Association Headquarters in Stockholm (1937) and proposals for housing estates—specifically for families with children—were a specialty of Markelius. The design sensitivity exhibited in these works and their expression of social concerns transcend the institutional quality so often associated with modernist works. Markelius's Swedish Pavilion for the 1939 New York World's Fair cemented his international reputation. Like many of his contemporaries during the early 1940s, he built a suburban villa for himself that incorporated more traditional architectural qualities and materials, and had a more integrated relationship with the surrounding landscape.

Markelius is also known for his planning, as he was division head of the National Board of Building and Planning from 1938 to 1944, and director of city planning in Stockholm for the next nine years. His reputation placed him on the international consulting group for the United Nations Headquarters in New York City, and the advisory committee for the UNESCO Building in Paris. In his capacity as planning director for Stockholm, Markelius initiated the policy of establishing satellite towns on the outskirts of the city to prevent haphazard suburban growth. From his planning dictates came the developments of Farsta, Vallingby and Högdalen—all suburban communities heralded at the time as exemplary architectural designs. Markelius was also instrumental in making downtown Stockholm more amenable to pedestrian traffic, as seen in the developments for Nedre Norrmalm in the 1950s and for the Hötorget during the 1960s.

From today's perspective, those same developments have been subject to certain criticisms. The suburban communities are now cited for demonstrating all the negative attributes of welfare state design. They bear witness to the expressive doldrums of a vapid modernism. Similarly, the city center redevelopments are criticized for their austerity and lack of the traditional scale and texture of a European city. More successful, especially with respect to social concerns, are Markelius' contemporaneous housing developments. The high-density design for the Ör housing complex in Sundyberg is an interesting solution to a difficult situation.

An unbuilt project, the new Municipal Theater in Stockholm (1956-70), had an expressive and complex, even Aalto-like, quality to it. It indicates that Markelius' inventiveness as a designer lasted to the end of his career. He was, without doubt, one of the most productive and outstanding Scandinavian architects and planners of this century. For though his work ranged from single-family residences to housing complexes for up to 6,000 inhabitants, and from theaters to large, intercity redevelopments, Markelius continually strove to base his designs on sound social principles, and to be responsive to the particulars of locale. He was a "modern architect" in the most positive sense of the term.

—WILLIAM C. MILLER

MATTHEW, Robert Hogg.

Scottish. Born in Edinburgh, Scotland, 1906. Died in 1975. Studied at Melville College, Edinburgh, and at the Edinburgh School of Art. Worked for the Department of Health, Scotland, 1936; chief architect, 1945; chief architect to London County Council, 1946-53; partnership with Stirrat Johnson-Marshall, 1953; professor of architecture, Edinburgh University, from 1953.

Chronology of Works
All in England unless noted

1951	Royal Festival Hall, London
1958	Alton West Housing, Roehampton
1963	New Zealand House, London
1968	York University, York
1970	Royal Commonwealth Pool, Edinburgh, Scotland
1974	Stirling University, Stirling, Scotland
n.d.	Bath University, Bath
n.d.	University of Coleraine, Northern Island

Within the architectural profession, Robert Matthew made an unrivaled impact upon postwar Britain, being at once supremely able as architect, administrator and academic. No one within his generation (which includes some formidable figures) could boast success in such wide-ranging activity, nor could they lay claim to such a lasting effect on the environment.

The son of an architect, Matthew was educated at Melville College and at the Edinburgh School of Art, where he proved to be a brilliant student. His first architectural post was in public practice in 1936 with the Department of Health in Scotland, where after nine years he reached the post of chief architect. This presaged a distinguished career as chief architect to London County Council which terminated in 1953 upon his entry concurrently into academic life as professor of architecture at Edinburgh University and partnership with Stirrat Johnson-Marshall to produce, under largely public patronage, one of Britain's most formidable architectural practices.

At London County Council, Matthew had the prescience to appoint a team of dedicated enthusiasts; Leslie Martin, as deputy, added a powerful theoretical regime which complemented Matthew's pragmatism, and assistants like Peter Moro and William Howell were to become internationally renowned in their own right. During that period such seminal works as the Royal Festival Hall (1951) and Alton West Housing, Roehampton (1958) were produced, signaling a triumph for postwar public architecture in Britain.

Matthew's first major commission in private practice was New Zealand House, London (1963), quite the best example, for its period, of a scaled-down and Anglicized version of the American prestige office building with podium and tower, based on the Skidmore, Owings and Merrill model. Although criticized at the time for its intrusion, particularly into St. James' Park, it remains a building of immense authority detailed with great care and precision. It served as a prototype for a whole spate of less rigorous multistory office buildings conceived in Britain during the 1960s.

Matthew's architectural practice grew alongside enormous expansion in the public sector. The New Town Movement, particularly in Mark Two guise, the New Universities and expansion of existing higher-education establishments, public housing and key civic buildings all came within Matthew's ambit and collectively represented a prodigious body of work.

Most prominent among the new universities following the Robbins Report on higher education was York, completed in 1968. Like most of its contemporaries, York adhered to the fashionable campus model rather than redevelop a rundown inner city, a course that would have found favor two decades later. The benefits were, however, obvious, and a (now mature) landscape has absorbed the teaching and residential buildings that were constructed using CLASP components, albeit with a precast concrete cladding system especially developed for York. The outcome was an egalitarian, unself-conscious "background" architecture entirely appropriate to the spirit of the new universities. The one-off auditorium and library, which could not lend themselves to CLASP (a system developed for secondary schools in the 1950s), provided a necessary counterpoint to the relaxed informality of system-built stock.

At Stirling University, Scotland, completed in 1974, Matthew eschewed system building, but repeated the successful juxtaposition of lush landscape and an appropriately discreet architecture informally arranged around a lake and yet related to an existing mature wood. Least successful was Bath University, where the opportunity to promote a "town and gown" ethos was lost by the decision to locate some two miles from the city center. Another unfortunate decision was the employment of a pedestrian "deck" above ground level forming a concourse for access to departments free from vehicular traffic. Thus the potential of the landscape's intervention so cleverly harnessed at York and Stirling was unfulfilled.

Northern Ireland was well served by Matthew's practice; the new university at Coleraine, although modest in scale, demonstrated the same concern for unpretentious buildings set in the landscape, and Craigavon New Town took to Ireland already well-established principles of neighborhood planning. That both enterprises failed cannot be attributed to Matthew but to the bias of political and sectarian chicanery for which the province is noted.

A host of distinguished civic buildings ran in parallel. Most notable was the Royal Commonwealth Pool, Edinburgh (1970). The building is wonderfully assured in its exaggeratedly stratified composition externally and in the clarity of its internal planning. Like all of Matthew's buildings, it is confident without a trace of the mannerist tendencies of his contemporary, Basil Spence. Here was a building with an international role (built when the Commonwealth merited more than token status) utilizing an appropriate development of the International Style.

Matthew's practice during a decade and a half of frenetic activity produced consistently robust but self-effacing buildings: architectural "panegyrics" were left to more flamboyant contemporaries. Significantly, after his death in 1975, his practice receded into a fashionable and eclectic pastiche totally at variance with the principles established by Matthew in a long and distinguished career.

—A. PETER FAWCETT

MAY, Hugh.

British. Born in Sussex, England, 1621. Died in London, 21 February 1684. Servant to the Duke of Buckingham; paymaster of the works, 1660; surveyor of the works, 1666; comptrollership, 1668; clerk of the recognizances in the courts of common Pleas; King's Bench; inspector of French and EnglisPWfi0(rs at Whitehall, St. James, Greenwich and Hampton Court; comptroller of the works, Windsor, 1673; architect to Windsor Castle.

Chronology of Works
All in England
† Work no longer exists

1663-68	Cornburg House, Oxfordshire (rebuilding and additions)
1664	Eltham Lodge, Kent
1665	Berkeley House, London
1675-84	Windsor Castle (remodeling upper ward; with others)†
1677-84	Cassiobury Park (not completed until 1780)†
1682-83	Chiswick, Middlesex

Publications

BOOKS ABOUT MAY

DOWNES, KERRY: *English Baroque Architecture.* London, 1966.
HILL, OLIVER, and CORNFORTH, JOHN: *English Country Houses, Caroline, 1625-1685.* London, 1966.
REDDAWAY, T. F.: *The Rebuilding of London after the Great Fire.* London, 1940.

ARTICLES ABOUT MAY

WEBB, GEOFFREY F.: ''Baroque Art.'' *Proceedings of the British Academy* 33 (1947).
WEBB, GEOFFREY F.: ''The Architectural Antecedents of Sir Christopher Wren.'' *Royal Institute of British Architects Journal* 27 (May 1933).

*

Hugh May, together with Balthazar Gerbier and Roger Pratt, was one of a number of architects active in England in the 1660s and 1670s after the restoration of Charles II. It is not easy to measure his achievement, for much of what he did is gone now, most obviously the remodeling at Windsor Castle and the great house at Cassiobury Park. The style of his designs, when set against the earlier innovations of Inigo Jones or the range and power of John Vanbrugh and Nicholas Hawksmoor after him, seems to speak more perhaps of a way of designing that was to come than anything fully realized in itself. But he was a significant and influential figure.

We have no records of his training and no identified drawings from his hand. But that he was well versed in the practices of architecture is clear not only from his work, but from a comment by John Aubrey that it was May who had invented ''the Staff-mouldings on solid right Angles,'' something Aubrey said became very popular. And as comptroller of the works and architect to Windsor Castle, May became a well-known figure at the court, for whom many of the houses he designed were built. These are for us his most tangible legacy, built on simple, regular plans with a straightforward style of ornament, the whole design rendered with a sense of modesty and frugality, borrowed

from the example of Dutch architects like Pieter Post and Jacob van Campen; that simplicity matched the taste of his patrons, many of whom, like May, had spent the years of Oliver Cromwell in Holland.

May was born in Sussex 1621, the son of a landed gentleman, and it seems, from a report he gave to Samuel Pepys, that he spent his early years in the service of the duke of Buckingham. We know also that in 1656 he went to Holland with the artist Peter Lely, staying there for some four years. But in 1660, with the return of Charles II, May was appointed paymaster of the works, which gave him financial supervision of the royal palaces.

His rise after that through the architectural bureaucracy of the court was not without mishaps. But in 1673, when Christopher Wren was appointed architect to St. Paul's, May succeeded Hartgill Baron as comptroller of the works at Windsor. It was then that he took charge of reconstructing the whole complex, remodeling some 25 rooms in the upper ward of the castle. All that work was destroyed in a subsequent remodeling in the early 19th century, but visual records that survived show that what May did there was in the grandest of styles. The Chapel Royal, in particular, seems to have had a rich, absolutist interior that was almost the match of the apartments of Louis XIV at Versailles.

All the while, May was at work for his patrons at the court, rebuilding part of Cornbury House, Oxford, for the first earl of Clarendon; adding a chapel and stables, Eltham Lodge, Kent, for Sir John Shaw, Bart.; Berkeley House, Piccadilly, for the first Lord Berkeley of Stratton; Burlington House, also on Piccadilly, for the first earl of Burlington; Cassiobury Park, Hertfordshire, for the first earl of Essex; Morr Park, Hertfordshire, for the duke of Monmouth; and one house in Ireland, Kilkenny Castle, County Kilkenny, for the first duke of Ormonde. Some of these houses were perhaps a little grandiose; John Evelyn noted that at Berkeley House, beyond the main front, there were quadrant colonnades that linked the central block to the service wings on the Piccadilly frontage ''in imitation of a house described by Palladio.''

Both Berkeley House and Burlington House, being in London, were well known. But for us Eltham Lodge, the one clear surviving work of May, is his most important building. It is smaller and simpler, a double-pile plan—the term is that of Roger Pratt—borrowed perhaps from examples printed in Philip Vingboons' *Gronden en afbeeldsels der voornaamste gebouwen* (1648), with a simple cornice below the roof line in place of a frieze, and the facade rendered in brick with simple Ionic pilasters in stone, the whole done with an economy and modesty that was at once practical and socially appropriate. And the use of brick, in place of a grander stone, was particularly fitting, since in England, as in Holland, brick had long been an important building material.

May's success as an architect can be measured by the fact that, for years afterward, much of his work, like that of Roger Pratt, was attributed to Christopher Wren, from whom all that was good in 17th-century architecture was supposed to have come.

—DAVID CAST

MAYBECK, Bernard.

American. Born Bernard Ralph Maybeck in New York City, 7 February 1862. Died in Berkeley, California, 3 October 1957. Married Annie White, 1890. Apprentice cabinet-maker tot he firm of Pottier and Stymus, New York City, 1879-81; studied under Jules André, École Nationale et Spéciale des Beaux-Arts, Paris, 1882-86; studied at special courses of the University of

Bernard Maybeck: First Church of Christ, Scientist, Berkeley, California, 1910

California, Berkeley, 1894-96, 1898-1900; also attended the École des Beaux-Arts, Arts et Métiers, Louvre and Sorbonne, Paris, 1896-98. Worked with the architects John M. Carrere and Thomas Hastings, New York City, 1886-88; partner, Russell and Maybeck, Kansas City, 1888; worked for Ernest Coxhead, San Francisco, California, 1889-90, and for A. Page Brown, San Francisco, 1891-94; in private practice, Berkeley, California, from 1894. Instructor in drawing, University of California, Berkeley, 1894-97, and director of architectural studies, Mark Hopkins Institute of Art, San Francisco, 1895-97; manager of the Phoebe A. Hears t Competition for the architectural design of the University of California campus, 1896-1900; instructor in architecture, University of California, Berkeley, 1898-1903 (devised first complete curriculum in architecture); opened San Francisco office in 1902; retired from active practice, 1938. Gold Medal, American Institute of Architects, 1951.

Chronology of Works
All in the United States

1886	Ponce de Leon Hotel, St. Petersburg, Florida (with Thomas Hastings)
1892-1902	Bernard Maybeck House, Berkeley, California†
1894	Keeler House, Berkeley, California
1896	Mining Building, University of California, Berkeley
1896	Lawson House, Berkeley, California†
1896	Hall House, Berkeley, California†
1897	Davis House, Berkeley, California†
1899	Hearst Hall, University of California, Berkeley†
1899	Town and Gown Club, Berkeley, California (with later additions by other architects)
1900	Bridgeman House, Berkeley, California
1900	McCrea House, Berkeley, California
1900	Men's Faculty Club, University of California, Berkeley
1901	Flagg House, Berkeley, California
1902	Wyntoon, Phoebe Apperson Hearst residence, McCloud River, California†
1902	G. H. Boke House, Berkeley, California
1902	Stockton House, Berkeley, California†
1902	Keeler Studio, Berkeley, California
1902	Dresslar House, Berkeley, California†
1904	Gates House, San Jose, California
1905	Outdoor and Clubhouse, Mill Valley, California
1906	Hopps House, Ross Valley, California
1906	Hillside Club, Berkeley, California†
1907	Lawson House, Berkeley, California
1909	L. L. Roos House, San Francisco, California
1910	First Church of Christ Scientist, Berkeley, California
1910	Randolph School, Berkeley, California
1913	Chick House, Berkeley, California
1913-15	Palace of Fine Arts, Panama Pacific International Exposition, San Francisco, California
1917	Bingham House, Montecito, California
1917	Clyde Hotel, Clyde, California
1919	Forest Hills Association Club Building, San Francisco, California

1920	James J. Fagan House, Portola Drive, Woodside, California
1921	Alpine Glen Springs Resort buildings, El Dorado County, California
1921	Clark House, Berkeley, California
1923	R. H. Mathewson House, Berkeley, California
1924	O. K. McMurray House, Berkeley, California
1924-38	Principia College, Elsah, Illinois
1925	Hearst Memorial Gymnasium, University of California, Berkeley (with Julia Morgan)
1926	Packard Automobile Showroom, San Francisco, California
1927	R. I. Woolsey House, Kensington, Contra Costa County, California
1927	Earl C. Anthony House, Los Angeles, California
1927-29	First Church of Christ Scientist, Berkeley, California (additions, with Henry Gutterson)
1928	Packard Automobile Showroom, Oakland, California†
1933	Wallen W. Maybeck House No. 1, 2751 Buena Vista Way, Berkeley, California
1940	Aikin House, Berkeley, California

Publications

BOOKS BY MAYBECK

"The Planning of a University." In *Blue and Gold* (University of California Yearbook). Berkeley, California, 1900.
Hillside Building. Booklet. Berkeley, California, 1907.
Palace of Fine Arts and Lagoon. San Francisco, 1915.
The Principia College Plans. St. Louis, Missouri, 1927.

ARTICLES BY MAYBECK

"A Dream That Might Be Realized." *Merchants Association Review* (San Francisco, November 1903).
"House of Mrs. Phoebe A. Hearst in Siskiyou County, California." *Architectural Review* (Boston, January 1904).
"Palace of Fine Arts." *Transactions of the Commonwealth Club of California* (San Francisco, August 1915).
"Fine Arts Palace Will Outlast Present Generation." *Architect and Engineer* (November 1915).
"Reflections on the Grauman Metropolitan Theatre, Los Angeles." *Architect and Engineer* (June 1923).

BOOKS ABOUT MAYBECK

CARDWELL, KENNETH H.: *Bernard Maybeck: Artisan, Architect, Artist*. Santa Barbara, California, 1977.
CHENEY, SHELDON: *New World Architecture*. London, 1930.
JORDY, WILLIAM H.: "Craftsmanship and Grandeur in an Architecture of Mood: Bernard Maybeck's Palace of Fine Arts and First Church of Christ Scientist." In *American Buildings and Their Architects: Progressive and Academic Ideals at the Turn of the Twentieth Century*. Garden City, New York, 1972.
LONGSTRETH, RICHARD W.: *On The Edge of The World, Four Architects in San Francisco at the Turn of the Century*. Cambridge, Massachusetts, 1989.
McCOY, ESTHER: *Five California Architects*. New York, 1960.
SARGEANT, WINTHROP: *Geniuses, Goddesses and People*. New York, 1949.

ARTICLES ABOUT MAYBECK

BANGS, JEAN MURRAY: "Bernard Ralph Maybeck, Architect, Comes into His Own." *Architectural Record* 103 (January 1948): 72-79.
BANHAM, REYNER: "The Plot Against Bernard Maybeck." *Journal of the Society of Architectural Historians* 43 (March 1984): 33-37.
"Bernard Maybeck: Factory Products for a Romantic Architecture." *AC: International Asbestos Cement Review* (October 1979).
"Churches." *Architectural Record* (December 1956).
CRAIG, ROBERT M.: "Bernard Ralph Maybeck and the Principia: Architecture as Philosophical Expression." *Journal of the Society of Architectural Historians* (Philadelphia) October 1972).
"The Dream Made Permanent." *Progressive Architecture* (February 1968).
GRANDEE, CHARLES K.: "Two Houses with links to the past." *Architectural Record* (March 1980).
HARRIS, JEAN: "Bernard R. Maybeck." *American Institute of Architects Journal* (May 1951).
HAYS, WILLIAM C.: "Some Interesting Buildings at the University of California: The Work of Bernard Maybeck, Architect." *Indoors and Out* 2 (1906): 70-75.
"How to Embalm a Building." *Architectural Forum* (November 1967).
"Maybeck: The Work of a Grass-Roots Visionary." *Interiors* (January 1960).
NICHOLS, F. D.: "A Visit with Bernard Maybeck." *Journal of the Society of Architectural Historians* (October 1952).
RICE, RICHARD B.: "Bernard Maybeck: Experiments with Cellular Concrete." *LA Architect* (Los Angeles, May 1981).
SMITH, THOMAS GORDON: "Bernard Maybeck's Wallen II House." *Fine Homebuilding* (April-May 1981).
WURSTER, WILLIAM W.: "San Francisco Bay Portfolio." *Magazine of Art* (December 1944).

*

Bernard Maybeck's work reflects three dimensions of the architect's professional preparation, design intentions and artistic outlook. Maybeck was first, and foremost, an artist whose goal was the creation of beauty. He spoke of "painting pictures" in brick and stone, and while such pictorialism encouraged a level of historicist pastiche in some of his work, even his most romantic excursions are vigorous arrangements, detailed and crafted into quintessentially "Maybeckian" compositions. Second, he was a builder-craftsman; his lineage extends to the medieval artisan-builder who combined local materials and simple construction, directly expressed; his handiwork was in the tradition of the Arts and Crafts movement. Maybeck's best work is tectonically expressive, honest and simple. Third, Maybeck as architect was interested in total, environmental design. His breadth of outlook encouraged him to look beyond individual college building's to master plans, and beyond single Berkeley houses to an environmental philosophy for the entire hillside community. Working during a period which revered "functionalism" as the chief determinant of a universalized modern architecture, Maybeck focused his attention on client needs, viewing each client as unique and reflecting in each building individual purpose, spirit and character.

Educated at the École des Beaux-Arts in Paris, Maybeck joined the ranks of the leading academic architects of his day, yet his work was frequently marked by a naïveté and innocence that appeared uncontaminated by scholarly rule and traditional historicism. While his concept and methods of crafting buildings spring from various sources, what he never lost from his Paris training was the Beaux-Arts vision of *planning*. Five years of study under Jules André at the École instilled in Maybeck a classicist's appreciation for scale and proportion, and the beauty of pattern and rhythm of elements contributing to a balanced plan or orderly composition.

French rationalism and monumentality were always to be qualified, however: by the site (the softening of natural forms in the landscape) and by the emotion (the evocative associations of style as well as color, including those local or national forces contributing to an American or regional style). These ideas informed Maybeck's architectural production from the very beginning, when he served as a draftsman and decorator for Carrère and Hastings at their Beaux-Arts-composed Ponce de Leon Hotel in St. Augustine, Florida (1888). Maybeck's stamp is evident, although his precise contributions are not documented. The hotel's "regionalist" style (Spanish Renaissance with a Moorish spirit), its innovative concrete construction based on traditional coquina (shell) composite building materials, and its exuberant, witty and eclectic decorative schemes would find more in common with what Maybeck would subsequently design than with Carrère and Hastings' restrained academic classicism.

When Maybeck embarked on his own academic design, he created monumental works of "Beaux-Arts classical" architecture considered to be masterpieces of the American academic tradition. At the University of California in Berkeley, Maybeck designed (with Julia Morgan) the Hearst Memorial Gymnasium (1925), with its projected but unexecuted Memorial Auditorium. But his best-known work in this tradition was the Palace of Fine Arts (1915) for the Panama-Pacific Exposition. Both designs were accomplished compositions displaying a hierarchy of form and spatial organization governed by axis, order and geometry. But the Palace of Fine Arts was not merely an exhibition hall for paintings and objects d'art. Maybeck's architecture was to be an architecture of theater: procession, climax, drama and beauty were to mark the experience of the fair-goer whose psychological and emotional state of mind would inform the evocations linking building and spectator. As a transition from the "crass commercialism" of the exposition's central axis, and closing its vista, Maybeck's monumental rotunda, with its embracing colonnade, stood at the edge of an informal landscaped lagoon. A spirit of melancholy and a hushed mood of contemplation characterized Maybeck's domed pavilion, where he sought to evoke a sense of "sadness, modified by the feeling that beauty has a soothing influence." His stage set would ready the exposition visitor for the fine arts on display in the steel-framed building behind; no copyist's exercise in the classical revival could be so evocative.

For Maybeck, architecture was not merely piling stone on stone, but involved the embodiment of spiritual ideas in construction. Both feelings and building blocks were his materials. His own experience in visiting the medieval church of St. Germain des Pres in Paris is recorded: only when the music began did Maybeck experience the "life" of the forms, the emotional quality in the church itself. He spoke of the sincerity of medieval builders, and for him architecture was spiritual. Whatever his architectural language, Maybeck was never prosaic, and at the Palace of Fine Arts, Maybeck translated the epic poetry of monumental classicism to an architecture of mood.

Maybeck is best known as the father of the Bay Region tradition, and in his collection of redwood houses, sited naturally into the hills of Berkeley, Maybeck joins the brothers Charles and Henry Greene, Frank Lloyd Wright, C. F. A. Voysey and Edwin Lutyens as the great "craft architects" of their generation. His first private client was Charles Keeler, a poet and naturalist best known for his authorship of *The Simple Home*, written in 1904 when he was president of the Hillside Club. Dedicated to Maybeck, *The Simple Home* embodies Maybeck's own ideas about architecture, suggesting a Boswell-Johnson relationship between these two arbiters of artistic taste within the hillside community. Keeler envisioned an environmentally sensitive aesthetic utopia of Berkeley homeowners living in Maybeck houses and leading an Arts and Crafts life-style; his (and Maybeck's) architecture equated art and life. A simple standard of living would provide time to enjoy nature, family and culture. If Keeler's book set forth the call, Maybeck's turn-of-the-century Berkeley houses provided the model. Maybeck's designs for his own Berkeley houses (1892-1902, altered; 1909, destroyed in 1923), as well as for Keeler's several houses and studios there (1894, 1902, 1907), the Hillside Club (1906, destroyed in 1923), and various other Berkeley houses and institutions embodied these ideas of natural building. They employed simple ceiling trusses, exposed posts, and expressive framing with redwood panels inside and shingles outside left uncovered and unpainted; the artisan houses nestled comfortably into the hillside "as though they have been there for all time."

The juxtaposition of the monumentality of the Beaux-Arts projects and the intimate domesticity of the Berkeley houses announces a theme which unified Maybeck's varied and eclectic life's work: the coexistence of grandeur and intimacy. Indeed, the architecture of Bernard Maybeck is full of contradictions that give evidence of a fertile, imaginative mind willing to learn from any source and eager to apply various architectural styles and construction methods to the creation of beautiful buildings. His masterpiece, the First Church of Christ Scientist, Berkeley (1910), has been described as evidencing an "eclecticism with vengeance," and except for Antoní Gaudi's eccentric manipulations of historic form and structure, or Frank Furness' exaggerated tensions and collisions of form and materials, few comparable examples of architectural eccentricity rival Maybeck's.

History was a resource from which associationist images could be drawn both for pictorial effect and as a means to convey a particular character in Maybeck's architecture. The architect sought to embody, in the Maybeckian Tudoresque of Principia College, Elsah, Illinois (1924-38), a spirit of friendliness and home. Deep in the primeval setting of the forested country estate of Phoebe A. Hearst on the McCloud River in California, moreover, Maybeck composed "an enchanted castle" in a "pearly" landscape, a baronial retreat known as Wyntoon (1902, destroyed by fire in 1933). Similar theatrics color the Spanish castle, Hollywood-style built to enable a Packard dealer "to enact life's dramas"; the Earl C. Anthony House, Los Angeles (1927) is a stage set of historical quotations for an auto baron whom Maybeck called a 20th-century "merchant Prince." Anthony also commissioned Maybeck to design a series of automobile showrooms, and Maybeck responded with equal panache: his San Francisco (1926) and Oakland Packard Agencies (1928, demolished) presented splendidly anachronistic moods of imperial classical grandeur and medievalism (respectively) for the display of modern horseless chariots. At Oakland, Maybeck's baronial architectonic shroud fronts a utilitarian garage, a cosmetic facelift which, reflected in the tree-lined lake, recalls the painterly sham castles of the early 19th century.

It is easier to see the artist in Maybeck through these more pictorial and historicist buildings, but in every project the architect drew upon his trained and cultivated aesthetic sense (but also common sense), to inform his search for Beauty. He trusted his on-site laborers to build solid, well-crafted structures, and he relied on his studied knowledge of his clients to insure that the building functioned for those who commissioned them. His individuality, his regional responsiveness, his expression of the

American spirit in architecture were all encouraged, from the start, by his Beaux-Arts mentor Jules André, who had taught Henry Hobson Richardson the same thing, and, in assessing Maybeck's life work, André would have approved.

—ROBERT M. CRAIG

McINTIRE, Samuel.

American. Born in Salem, Massachusetts, 1757. Died on 16 February 1811. Married Elizabeth Crowninshield. Came from a family of carpenters. Practiced independently, Salem, Massachusetts.

Chronology of Works
All in the United States
† Work no longer exists

1780	Elias Hasket Derby House, Salem, Massachusetts
1782-1801	Peirce-Nichols House, Salem, Massachusetts
1782-89	F. Boardman House, Salem, Massachusetts [attributed]
1785-86	Courthouse, Salem, Massachusetts†
1786	Second Elias Hasket Derby House, Salem, Massachusetts (renovation)
1793	Nathan Read House, Salem, Massachusetts
1793-94	Derby Summer House, Danvers, Massachusetts
1793-98	T. Lyman House, Waltham, Massachusetts
1795	William Orne House, Salem, Massachusetts [attributed]
1795-99	Fourth Elias Hasket Derby House, Salem, Massachusetts†
1796	Assembly House, Salem, Massachusetts
1800-01	Oak Hill, Peabody, Massachusetts [attributed]†
1803-04	South Congregational Church, Salem, Massachusetts†
1804-05	John Gardner House, Salem, Massachusetts
1804-06	C. Crowninshield House, Salem, Massachusetts [attributed]
1805-07	Hamilton Hall, Salem, Massachusetts
1808-09	G. Tucker House, Salem, Massachusetts

Publications

BOOKS ABOUT McINTIRE

COUSINS, FRANK, and RILEY, PHIL M.: *The Wood-Carver of Salem.* New York, 1916.

DYER, WALTER A.: *Early American Craftsmen.* New York, 1915.

KIMBALL, FISKE: *Mr. Samuel McIntire, The Architect of Salem.* Portland, Maine, 1940.

Samuel McIntire: A Bicentennial Symposium, 1757-1957. Salem, Massachusetts, 1957.

WARD, GERALD W. R.: *The Assembly House.* Salem, Massachusetts, 1976.

WARD, GERALD W. R.: *The Gardner-Pingree House.* Salem, Massachusetts, 1976.

WARD, GERALD W. R.: *The Peirce-Nichols House.* Salem, Massachusetts, 1976.

Samuel McIntire: John Gardner House, Salem, Massachusetts, 1804-05

ARTICLES ABOUT McINTIRE

ALLEN, GORDAN: "The Vale, Lyman House, Waltham." *Old-Time New England* 42 (April 1952): 81-87.

DOWNS, JOSEPH: "Derby and McIntire." *Metropolitan Museum of Art Bulletin* New Series 6 (October 1947): 73-81.

DYER, WALTER A.: "Samuel McIntire, Master Carpenter." *House Beautiful* 37 (February 1915): 65-69.

KIMBALL, FISKE: "Furniture Carvings by Samuel McIntire." *Antiques* 18-19 (1930-31): 388-392, 498-502; 30-32, 116-119, 207-210.

LITTLE, NINA FLETCHER: "Cornè, McIntire, and the Hersey Derby Farm." *Antiques* 101 (1972): 226-229.

NEWCOMB, REXFORD G.: "Samuel McIntire, Early American Architect." *Architect* 9 (October 1927): 37-43.

PRATT, R. H.: "McIntire, the Colonial Carpenter." *House and Garden* 51 (February 1927).

SWAN, MABEL: "A Revised Estimate of McIntire." *Antiques* 20 (1931): 338-343.

SWAN, MABEL: "McIntire Vindicated." *Antiques* 26 (1934): 130-132.

SWAN, MABEL: "McIntire: Check and Countercheck." *Antiques* 21 (1932): 86-87.

WALKER, AMROSE: "Samuel McIntire—A Sketch." *Essex Institute Historical Collections* 68 (1932): 97-116.

*

Considering his humble background, his complete lack of formal training in any of the arts, and the scarcity of colleagues in his profession as architectural planner and decorator, it is remarkable that Samuel McIntire's performance had in it strains of greatness, if not genius. His rise to this status was slow, starting as it did in the family trade of carpentry. Grandfather, father and two brothers were all carpenters living and working among the other artisans of Salem, Massachusetts, but something impelled Samuel McIntire to succeed in several ways that his relatives and friends did not, or could not.

Generally known today as an architect and wood-carver, McIntire was actually less of an architect and more of an architectural and furniture decorator, for his fundamental designs for buildings were mainly traditional, and his furniture was designed and built by others and only decorated by him. McIntire's only progressive designing came from using recent English builder's books, such as the *Practical House Carpenter* by William Pain (London, 1788 and later, and the first American edition, 1796), and in imitating the recent work of Charles Bulfinch of Boston. In the period of his best work, from 1800 until his death in 1811, McIntire still could be called a follower of the Robert Adam school of decorative work, but in the United States no one else did Adamesque work as well as he did. And if one places English work beside McIntire's, it will be readily seen that McIntire did in fact not copy directly. Instead, he preserved the general feeling and scale, while carving his own patterns and details. Carved roses were his particular love.

Although he influenced the work of designers in many parts of the country, McIntire's own work, with just a few exceptions, is to be found only in Salem. A sufficient number of his house designs have survived, in the streets of the city and in his drawings in the possession of the Essex Institute, to allow a comprehensive view of his entire career. His early work is best represented by the Peirce-Nichols House (1782), designed when he was only 25. The facade is loaded with architectural decoration against a clapboard background. Considerable monumen-

tality is derived from the giant Doric pilasters framing each side. The cumbersome windowsills and architraves project boldly, as does the heavy cornice that carries a balustrade. The entrance portico, also Doric, projects beyond any other feature to establish a point of introduction to the house. It is reached through a street gateway that is an extension of the house plan and was also designed by McIntire. Examined individually, the details, both inside and out, are somewhat crude and are adopted from previous architectural work. As an ensemble the house is very attractive and served to establish McIntire as a carpenter of high quality in Salem.

In the early 1790s McIntire visited Boston, apparently for the express purpose of studying some house designs by Charles Bulfinch, because he returned to Salem with drawings of two Bulfinch houses. He must have admired Bulfinch's drawing technique and mode of presenting drawings to clients, for as soon as he made his own new designs, McIntire shifted from the rough, inexact drawings of his early years to a superior kind that only professional architects used. Bulfinch, though not strictly professional, had already made a similar conversion after having traveled to England in search of architectural knowledge.

In that middle period McIntire designed his most notorious work, the mansion for Elias Hasket Derby (1795-99), the richest merchant in Salem and one of the great world traders of the era. Since cost was of little consequence, McIntire could lavish the fruits of all his newly gained knowledge of Adam decoration and planning upon the Derby drawings. The result was the construction of a costly and famous house covered with decorative effects, containing a grand staircase and an oval reception room looking out upon more than an acre of garden in the center of Salem. Perhaps even Derby was a little perturbed when the construction bills were calculated, as the house was built of wood rather than brick. It no longer survives (demolished in 1815), owing to the inability of younger members of the family to support such a luxurious mansion.

The change in McIntire's status as the new century arrived was marked by his no longer working, as his brothers continued to do, for daily wages. He began to do piecework, taking orders only for special jobs. These were making full plans for buildings, but not working at the construction of them, or carving a set of chair backs or ornaments for a chest. He even carved a few portrait busts in wood. His best architectural designs occurred then in such works as the Gardner House (1805). The house facade was most carefully composed for the precise use of well-laid brick. The particular delight of the exterior is the entrance portico, the idea for which probably derived from Bulfinch's Otis House in Boston, whose semicircular portico was in place by 1801. The interior rooms have mantels and fireplace surrounds, door architraves and a variety of moldings in McIntire's finest manner. Many of these were made by carving a mold into which a mixture called composition was pressed. On removal the composition was glued to the wooden surface as decoration.

In addition to his major career activities, McIntire spent much time with music for the North Church. He played the bass viol, wrote compositions and directed the church choir. Although he wrote no treatises, and only one short letter of his survives, his handwriting is clear and spelling equal to any but the most learned.

Proof of McIntire's value to his community is at his grave, where the slate tombstone bears this inscription: "He was distinguished for Genius in Architecture, Sculpture, and Musick: Modest and sweet Manners rendered him pleasing: Industry and Integrity respectable: He professed the Religion of Jesus in his entrance on manly life; and proved its excellence by virtuous Principles and unblemished conduct."

—PAUL F. NORTON

McKIM, MEAD and WHITE.

McKIM, Charles Follen.
American. Born in Isabella Furnace, Pennsylvania, 24 August 1847. Died in St. James, New York, 14 September 1909. Studied at Lawrence Scientific School, Harvard University, Cambridge, Massachusetts; apprentice, Russell Sturgis office; pupil, Atélier Daumet of the Ecole des Beaux-Arts, Paris. Draftsman, Gambrill and Richardson office, New York, 1870; organized McKim, Mead and Bigelow firm, New York City, 1878; organized McKim, Mead and White firm, New York City. Fellow, American Institute o f Architects; Gold Medal, Royal Institute of British Architects, 1903; American Institute of Architects Gold Medal, 1909.

MEAD, William Rutherford.
American. Born in Brattleboro, Vermont, 1846. Died in Paris, France, 21 June 1928. B.A. degree, Amherst College, 1867; trained in Russell Sturgis office, New York. Partner, McKim and Mead; partner, McKim, Mead and White Office, New York. Fellow, American Institute of Architects.

WHITE, Stanford.
American Born in New York, 9 November 1853. Died in New York, 5 June 1906. Son was Lawrence Grant White, architect. Graduated, University of New York, 1871. Student draftsman, Gambrill and Richardson office, New York, 1872; partner, McKim, Mead and White, New York, 1880.

Chronology of Works
All in the United States unless noted
† *Work no longer exists*

1876-77	Moses Taylor House, Elberon, New Jersey
1879-80	Short Hills Casino, Short Hills, New Jersey
1879-80	Casino, Newport, Rhode Island
1880-83	Cyrus McCormick House, Richfield Springs, New York†
1881-97	Shaw Memorial, Boston, Massachusetts
1882-84	American Safe Deposit Company Building, New York City†
1882-85	Charles L. Tiffany House Group, New York City†
1882-85	Henry Villard House Group, New York City
1882-86	H. A. C. Taylor House, Newport, Rhode Island†
1883-87	First Methodist (Lovely Lane) Church, Baltimore, Maryland
1883-88	John F. Andrew House, Boston, Massachusetts
1885-88	Church of the Ascension, New York City (chancel remodeling)
1886-87	William G. Low House, Bristol, Rhode Island†
1887-90	New York Life Insurance Company Building, Kansas City, Missouri
1887-90	New York Life Insurance Company Building, Omaha, Nebraska
1887-91	Madison Square Garden, New York City†
1887-95	Public Library, Boston, Massachusetts
1889-90	Johnston Gate, Harvard University, Cambridge, Massachusetts
1889-91	Century Club, New York City
1889-91	Hotel Imperial, New York City†
1890-92	Amory-Olney Double House, Boston, Massachusetts
1891-92	King Model Houses, New York City
1891-93	Agriculture Building, New York State Pavilion, and other buildings, World's Columbian Exposition, Chicago, Illinois†
1891-94	Metropolitan Club, New York City
1891-94	Walker Art Gallery, Bowdoin College, Brunswick, Maine
1891-94	Whittemore Memorial Library, Naugatuck, Connecticut
1892-1904	State Capitol, Providence, Rhode Island
1892-95	Herald Building, New York City†
1892-95	Power Houses and Echota Housing, Niagara Falls, New York†
1892-96	Three Houses for H. A. C. Taylor, New York City†
1892-1901	Five Buildings, New York University, New York City
1893-1913	Columbia University, New York City
1893-1915	Brooklyn Institute (now Brooklyn Museum), Brooklyn, New York
1893-1916	Harvard Club, New York City
1895-97	George A. Nickerson House, Boston, Massachusetts
1895-99	Frederick W. Vanderbilt House, Hyde Park, New York
1896-1900	University Club, New York City
1896-1907	Rotunda (restoration) and Four Buildings, University of Virginia, Charlottesville, Virginia
1897-99	Gymnasium, Radcliffe College, Cambridge, Massachusetts
1897-1902	Herman Oelrichs House, Newport, Rhode Island
1898-1900	State Savings Bank, Detroit, Michigan
1900-03	Joseph Pulitzer House, New York City
1900-05	Bank of Montreal, Montreal, Quebec, Canada (additions)
1901-04	Knickerbocker Trust, New York City†
1901-04	Interborough Rapid Transit Powerhouse, New York City
1902-03	White House, Washington, D.C. (restoration)
1902-07	J. Pierpont Morgan Library, New York City
1902-09	Payne Whitney House, New York City
1902-10	Pennsylvania Station, New York City†
1902-14	New York Public Library, New York City (14 branch facilities)
1903-06	Tiffany's, New York City
1903-13	Bellevue Hospital, New York City (11 sections)
1904-26	Metropolitan Museum of Art, New York City (eight sections and additions)
1906-08	Mackay School of Mines, University of Nevada, Reno, Nevada
1906-12	Percy Pyne House, New York City

Publications

BOOKS ABOUT McKIM, MEAD AND WHITE

BALDWIN, CHARLES C.: *Stanford White.* New York, 1931.
GRANGER, ALFRED H.: *Charles Follen McKim: A Study of His Life and Work.* New York, 1913.
HILL, FREDERICK P.: *Charles F. McKim: The Man.* Francestown, New Hampshire, 1950.
MOORE, CHARLES: *The Life and Times of Charles Follen McKim.* New York, 1929.
REILLY, CHARLES H.: *McKim, Mead and White.* New York, 1924.
ROTH, LELAND M. (ed.): *A Monograph of the Work of McKim, Mead and White 1879-1915.* With an introductory essay, ''McKim, Mead & White Reappraised'' and notes on the

plates. New York, 1974 (original ed., 4 vols., New York, 1915-20).

ROTH, LELAND M.: *The Architecture of McKim, Mead and White, 1870-1920: A Building List*. New York, 1978.

ROTH, LELAND: *McKim, Mead and White, Architects*. New York, 1983.

Sketches and Designs by Stanford White. Edited by Lawrence Grant White. New York, 1920.

WILSON, RICHARD GUY: *McKim, Mead and White*. New York, 1983.

WODEHOUSE, LAWRENCE: *White of McKim, Mead, and White*. New York, 1990.

ARTICLES ABOUT McKIM, MEAD AND WHITE

ANDREWS, WAYNE: "McKim, Mead and White: New York's Own Architects." *New York Historical Society Quarterly* 35 (1951).

DESMOND, HARRY W., and CROLY, HERBERT: "The Work of Messrs. McKim, Mead and White." *Architectural Record* 20 (1906): 153-246.

MOSES, LIONEL: "McKim, Mead & White: A History." *American Architect* 121 (1922): 413-424.

RAMSEY, STANLEY C.: "The Work of McKim, Mead and White." *Journal of the Royal Institute of British Architects* 25 (5 November 1917): 25-29.

ROTH, LELAND M.: "Three Industrial Towns by McKim, Mead, and White." *Journal of the Society of Architectural Historians*. 38 (1979): 317-347.

STURGIS, RUSSELL: "The Work of McKim, Mead and White." *Architectural Record* No. 1 (1895).

*

The architecture of McKim, Mead and White was widely influential in the first third of the 20th century because of several factors. One was the sheer number of their buildings in nearly every major city north of Virginia and east of Kansas City. Another was the breadth of building types for which they created identifiable images at the turn of the century, most notably shingled country houses, public libraries both small and large, as well as collegiate campuses. Another was the extremely high construction quality of their buildings, which set a standard for public buildings through 1940. Yet another was the role played by the office as a training ground for young architects, serving in effect as a kind of atelier for scores of young men who formed partnerships in the drafting rooms, won major competitions for public buildings, and were thus launched on their own independent careers in cities from Boston to San Francisco.

The success of the firm was due to the complementary nature of the three partners—McKim the idealist, Mead the pragmatist, and White the sensualist. McKim's ardent idealism and adherence to universal principles were shaped by the example of his father, a leading activist and fund raiser for the abolitionist cause. McKim's idealism was also strengthened by his short period in the office of Russell Sturgis, a champion of Ruskinian principles. McKim's adherence to universal architectural types was further nurtured by three years of study at the École des Beaux-Arts in Paris. Mead was the realist of the trio, serving as in-house engineer (until other specialists were added to the firm, in particular Teunis J. Van der Bent), supervising the office staff and managing the finances of the partnership. White was the firebrand, eager to break precedent, to use new materials, to experiment with building form and enrich visual perception by employing a coordinated variety of colors, textures and materials. The high professional ideals of both McKim and White were developed during several years as assistants in the office of Henry Hobson Richardson.

The merging of McKim's search for clear geometries and White's penchant for picturesque variety resulted in the Shingle Style houses and country clubs for which the firm first became known in the early 1880s. In addition to their studied irregularity and inventiveness, these shingled buildings incorporated many elements derived from the partners' close study of American colonial architecture; as McKim's geometries became more and more abstract, there was an increasingly correct use of 18th-century classical forms. The year 1882-83 is significant for the start of three separate houses, each using classical forms appropriate to its contextual setting. For the urban six-house complex for Henry Villard in New York (1882-85), McKim and White employed correct quattrocento Italian elements; for the John F. Andrew house in Boston (1883-88), McKim and White used Federalist motifs and a bowed front evoking the architecture of Charles Bulfinch and Beacon Hill; and in Newport, Rhode Island, McKim drew upon local colonial sources for a summer house for H. A. C. Taylor (1882-86, demolished). This redirection toward classical sources demonstrates both the delayed effect of a sketching trip of 1877 in which the partners studied previously denigrated Colonial buildings, and the influence of Joseph Morrill Wells, the major draftsman in the office, who was a champion of Italian Renaissance formalism.

McKim, Mead and White were also leading proponents of the integration of all the visual arts into their work, calling upon painters, sculptors and mosaicists to participate in the embellishment of their buildings. The resulting unity of expression can be seen in the interiors of the Villard house, the chancel of the Church of the Ascension in New York (1885-87), and most especially in the mosaics, sculpture and murals of the imposing Boston Public Library (1887-95). This public building propelled the firm to the forefront of the profession and for a generation served as the model for other public and collegiate libraries. Models for public museums and libraries in smaller towns were provided by the firm's Walker Art Gallery at Bowdoin College in Brunswick, Maine (1891-94), with four murals, and by the diminutive Whittemore Memorial Library in Naugatuck, Connecticut (1891-94). It was the partners' desire to unify the arts that prompted both McKim and White to design enveloping settings for sculptures by Augustus Saint-Gaudens and Daniel Chester French, and for White to design picture frames for painters such as Thomas Dewing and Everett Shinn.

Another field in which the firm excelled was the design of building groups. To a certain extent the success of the ensemble of the buildings comprising the World's Columbian Exposition in Chicago (1893) can be credited to changes suggested by McKim. As the buildings of the exposition were being developed in 1892-93, the firm was simultaneously engaged in designing two major college campuses, a smaller campus, and the augmentation of a fourth campus. The principal endeavors were the master plan and initial buildings for Columbia University at Morningside Heights (northern Manhattan) in New York (McKim) and the plan and initial buildings for the New York University campus in the Bronx (White). Both plan schemes focused on commanding domed library structures placed in the center of the composition or on the principal governing axis. Meanwhile, McKim was engaged in devising a compact centralized plan and the first building (a gymnasium) for Radcliffe College in Cambridge, Massachusetts. And in 1895 White was commissioned by the regents of the University of Virginia to rebuild Jefferson's Library Rotunda, recently destroyed by fire; the regents also instructed White to place three new classroom buildings at the foot of Jefferson's Lawn, thereby closing the original composition. The culmination of the firm's interest in planning was McKim's participation in the Senate Park Commission, Washington, D.C., in 1901-02, which restored the orthogonal clarity of Pierre L'Enfant's plan for the national capital city.

By the end of the 1880's, the firm had evolved a pattern of stylistic allusions, in which a severe High Renaissance or augustan Roman classicism (in stone or marble) was employed for governmental and public buildings such as the Boston Public Library; the Knickerbocker Bank, New York (1901-04, demolished); or the Morgan Library, New York (1902-07). Georgian or Federalist classicism (in brick) was employed for urban houses, clubs, or collegiate buildings such as the Harvard College gates (1889 ff.); the Harvard Club, New York (1883 ff.); the Amory-Olney houses, Boston (1890-02), or the Rhode Island State House, Providence (1892-1904). A highly ornamented and colorful North Italian/Spanish Renaissance style (in brick with terra-cotta trim) was developed for public buildings of a more festive nature such as Madison Square Garden (1887-91, demolished), the New York *Herald* Building (1892-95, demolished), and the Century Club (1889-91). The severe Roman work was most commonly McKim's, and the festive White's. Deviations from this associational formalism were rare.

The work of McKim, Mead and White is notable for its wide diversity, ranging from elegant, private urban town houses and more informal country retreats to decorous public buildings, churches and libraries, and industrial buildings (such as the powerhouses for the Niagara Falls Power Company station in Niagara Falls, 1892-95 [demolished], and the Interborough Rapid Transit Powerhouse in New York, 1902-04). The firm also designed housing for industrial workers ("Echota" in Niagara Falls, 1893-95). Although the firm didn't seek out such commissions, it responded skillfully to requests for urban tenements (such as for James Miller on 47th Street, New York, 1886-87) and for a large group of speculative middle-class townhouses in Harlem (the David H. King Model Houses or "Striver's Row," New York, 1891-92).

Nonetheless, as the modern commercial high-rise office building was being perfected in Chicago in the 1880s and 1890s, McKim, Mead and White in New York deliberately shunned such commissions whenever possible. Although they were skilled planners and designers of horizontal buildings and building groups (as admirably illustrated in their complex organization of the multilevel Pennsylvania Station in New York), McKim, Mead and White chose not to explore the expressive potential of the vertical office building, which McKim, especially, viewed with apprehension. The exceptions to this were their early H-shaped twin office blocks for the New York Life Insurance Company in Kansas City, Missouri, and Omaha, Nebraska (1887-90).

An important characteristic of McKim, Mead and White's work was their reference to local building traditions and stylistic idioms as seen in the additions and alterations they made to the Bank of Montreal (1900-05); their sensitive restoration of the White House in Washington, D.C. (1902-03), which has been remained relatively untouched by later renovations; and their additions to the Metropolitan Museum of Art in New York (1904-26).

The building that best illustrated how McKim, Mead and White could use traditional forms in the service of modern engineering was Pennsylvania Station in New York (1902-10, demolished), whose carefully separated traffic patterns led to large public spaces adjusted in breadth and height to the volume of traffic. Everything focused on a vaulted waiting room and a glass-covered concourse inspired by the huge public spaces of the Baths of Caracalla in Rome. The station was spacious, but divided into easily perceivable parts; it provided what turn-of-the-century critics viewed as an appropriately formal and grand entrance into the city. Penn Station incorporated formal clarity and technological ingenuity, comparable to the celebration of business profits in the skyscraper, but laid horizontally to serve both commerce and the public. Its demolition in the mid-1960s did much to crystallize the American movement toward architectural preservation.

Like the firms of Adler and Sullivan and Burnham and Root in Chicago, McKim, Mead and White sought a uniquely modern and American architecture based on the spirit of place and people. For McKim, Mead and White, who built in some of the oldest cities along the eastern seaboard, that tradition and spirit were seen as best expressed in Colonial classical buildings, balanced in composition and harmonious in their ensemble. Thus, McKim, Mead and White championed a reinvigorated classicism, shaped by a discerning eclecticism that drew upon the Georgian and Renaissance sources of early American architecture. McKim's greater formal training and innate sobriety gave to the firm's work a clarity and *gravitas*, which White lightened with a richness of texture and inventive ornamentation. Within the context of late-19th-century idealized formalism and associational references to the past, the work of McKim, Mead and White represented a generous realization of the Vitruvian triad of commodious planning, sound construction and visual delight.

—LELAND M. ROTH

MEIER, Richard.

American. Born in Newark, New Jersey, 12 October 1934. Studied at Cornell University, Ithaca, New York, 1953-57, B.Arch. Worked for Frank Grad and Sons, New Jersey, 1957; worked for Davis, Brodie and Wisnieski, and then for Skidmore, Owings and Merrill, New York, 1958-60; worked for Marcel Breuer, New York, 1960-63; principal, Richard Meier and Associates, New York, since 1963 (firm name Richard Meier and Partners, Architects, since 1980). Adjunct instructor, 1963-66, assistant professor, 196 6-69, and adjunct professor of architecture, 1969-73, Cooper Union, New York; also visiting professor/lecturer at numerous American universities. Fellow, American Institute of Architects. Pritzker Prize, 1984; Gold Medal, Royal Institute of British Architects, 1989.

Chronology of Works
All in the United States unless noted

1962	Lambert Beach House, Fire Island, New York
1965	Mr. and Mrs. Jerome Meier House, Essex Falls, New Jersey
1967	Smith House, Darien, Connecticut
1969	Saltzman House, East Hampton, Long Island, New York
1970	Westbeth Artists' Housing, New York
1971	House, Old Westbury, New York
1972	Twin Peaks Northeast Housing, Bronx, New York
1973	Museum of Modern Art, Villa Strozzi, Florence, Italy
1973	Douglas House, Harbor Springs, Michigan
1976-77	Bronx Developmental Center, New York
1978	Aye Simon Reading Room, Guggenheim Museum, New York
1978-79	Atheneum, and Pottery Shed, New Harmony, Indiana
1981	Hartford Seminary, Hartford, Connecticut
1982	Elementary School, Columbus, Indiana

Richard Meier: Museum für Kunsthandwerk, Frankfurt, Germany, 1984

1983	Giovanitti House, Pittsburgh, Pennsylvania
1983	High Museum of Art, Atlanta, Georgia
1984	Siemens Office and Laboratory Complex, Munich, Germany
1984	Des Moines Art Center, Iowa
1984	Museum für Kunsthandwerk, Frankfurt, Germany
1984-86	Ackerberg House, Malibu, California
1984-88	People's Bank Headquarters, Bridgeport, Connecticut
1984-88	Grotta House, Harding Township, New Jersey
1985	J. Paul Getty Center, Brentwood, California
1986	City Hall and Central Library, The Hague, Netherlands
1986	Exhibition Building, Ulm, Germany
1987	Royal Dutch Paper Mills Corporate Headquarters, Hilversum, Netherlands
1988	Museum of Contemporary Art, Barcelona, Spain
1989	Museum of Ethnology, Frankfurt, Germany
1990	Fox Studios, Los Angeles, California (expansion and renovation)

Publications

BOOKS BY MEIER

Recent American Synagogue Architecture. Exhibition catalog. New York, 1963.
Richard Meier, Architect: Buildings and Projects 1966-1976. New York, 1976.
Richard Meier: Drawings of Four Objects, A Post Card Book 1976. New York, 1977.
On Architecture (lecture paper). Cambridge, Massachusetts, 1982.
Richard Meier, Architect. With introduction by Joseph Rykwert. 2 vols., New York, 1984-91.
Richard Meier Collages. London, 1990.

ARTICLES BY MEIER

"Planning for Jerusalem." *Architectural Forum* (April 1971).
"Strategies: Eight Projects." *Casabella* (May 1974).

"Tre Recenti Progetti." *Controspazio* (Bari, Italy, September 1975).

"Dialogue." With Arata Isozaki. *Architecture and Urbanism* (August 1976).

"General Remarks."*Japan Architect* (December 1976).

"Olivetti Prototypes." *Architecture d'aujourd'hui* (December 1976).

"On the Spirit of Architecture." *Architectural Digest* (June 1981).

"Remembering Breuer." *Skyline* (October 1981).

BOOKS ABOUT MEIER

BLASER, WERNER (ed.): *Richard Meier: Buildings for Art.* Boston and Basel, Switzerland, 1990.

DIAMONSTEIN, BARBARALEE: *American Architecture Now.* New York, 1980.

DIAMONSTEIN, BARBARALEE: *American Architecture Now II.* New York, 1985.

FRAMPTON, KENNETH and ROWE, COLIN: *Five Architects: Eisenman, Graves, Gwathemy, Hejduk, Meier.* New York, 1972.

IZZO, FERRUCCIO: *Richard Meier: Architecture/Projects 1986-1990.* Florence, 1991.

ARTICLES ABOUT MEIER

BRANCH, MARK ALDEN: "Bridgeport Center." *Progressive Architecture* (July 1989).

FRAMPTON, KENNETH: "Richard Meier: The European Dimension." *Architecture Today* (March 1991).

GALLOWAY, DAVID: "A Heightened Urbanity: The Recent Works of Richard Meier." *Architecture and Urbanism* (March 1988).

GOLDBERGER, PAUL: "Architecture: Richard Meier." *Architectural Digest* (September 1978).

HOYT, CHARLES: "Four Projects by Richard Meier: Change and Consistency." *Architectural Record* (March 1975).

HOYT, CHARLES: "Richard Meier: Public Space and Private Space." *Architectural Record* (July 1973).

JENCKS, CHARLES: "Richard Meier and the Modern Tradition." In *The New Moderns*, London, 1990.

RYKWERT, JOSEPH: "The Very Personal Work of Richard Meier and Associates." *Architectural Forum* (March 1972).

RYKWERT, JOSEPH: "Richard Meier: Two New Houses in USA." *Domus* (March 1987).

"Spatial Structure: Richard Meier." *Architecture and Urbanism*, special issue (April 1976).

STEPHENS, SUZANNE: "The Individual: Richard Meier." *Progressive Architecture* (May 1977).

STEPHENS, SUZANNE: "Malibu Modernism." *Progressive Architecture* (December 1987).

"White Existence—Richard Meier 1961-77." *Space Design*, special issue (January 1978).

*

Richard Meier is the most distinguished of those Americans working within the traditions of the Modern Movement. At a time when most American architects of his generation were exploring forms outside the Modern Movement, Meier's work remained consistent, rooted in the practicalities and the poetry of program and construction. His international reputation was built on a series of wonderful private houses, developing the language of the Parisian villas built by Le Corbusier in about 1930. Le Corbusier's villas had been concrete, or cement rendered to look like concrete; Walter Gropius and Marcel Breuer had taken that language and translated it into American construction in a series of houses in New England with white cubes in timber constructed with bold external chimneys. Meier took that development and combined it with a return to the more flamboyant forms and double-height spaces of Le Corbusier. Later in his career, with larger projects, the scale became too great for the Corbusian villa, so Meier extended the vocabulary and faced the buildings in metal panels. White is always the favorite color.

Meier studied at Cornell and then worked for New York firms, first Davis, Brodie and Wisnieski, then Skidmore, Owings and Merrill, and, finally, three years with Marcel Breuer. While at the Breuer office, he executed his first independent commission, the Lambert Beach House on Fire Island in Long Island Sound. A simple holiday home built in timber, it has two characteristics which foreshadow Meier's mature work—a beautiful plan and an interest in construction. Because of its location, the Lambert Beach House was prefabricated so that only nine days' work on site was needed. This concern with construction became so important that most publications of Meier's work have included reproductions of the production drawings. Meier has said that he wishes to be thought of as a master builder rather than as an artist, but his frequent collaboration with Frank Stella shows that the artistic side of an architect's work is also of supreme importance to him.

In 1963 Meier left Breuer to open his own office in New York City. Like many young architects, he found his first important clients in his own parents, and the Mr. and Mrs. Jerome Meier House was completed in Essex Falls, New Jersey, two years later. A thick, heavy parapet to a flat roof placed over regular masonry walls gives the house a weighty serenity; the serenity was to continue into his later work, but he never again was in love with weight.

In 1967 Meier completed his first masterpiece, the Smith House in Darien, Connecticut. Lightly perched on a beautiful, well-treed site with a rocky foreshore to Long Island Sound, the Smith home was an image of pure magic; it was published worldwide and made its architect a star. Behind the image, Meier had worked out his direction—a white painted house with simple plan and complicated section. A line of small rooms with load-bearing stud walls is on the entrance side; the visitor walks through this restricted space into a high, glassy, steel-framed living volume with the fireplace on axis with the entrance, and with the Sound beyond. Corbusian ramps and curbed half landings are combined with windows of enormous sheets of glass which would not have been practical in Le Corbusier's day.

The Smith House was followed by a series of houses. In the Saltzman House at East Hampton, New York, Meier took many of the ideas of the Smith House, but made the forms more complicated and interesting in response to a less interesting site. The large house at Old Westbury, New York, allows the exploitation of features not possible in a smaller house, such as the use of long ramps as a major part of the experience of moving through the house, and the incorporation of top lights to add to the play of light in the interior. The 1973 completion of the Douglas House at Harbor Springs, Michigan, marked the high point of Meier's work as a designer of single-family houses. Perched on a steep slope overlooking Lake Michigan, the entrance is from a bridge at the top of the slope leading to the upper floor, where the visitor eventually emerges at the highest level of a three-story living room. From there, dizzying staircases lead to the lake.

In 1975 a book was published in New York. Called simply *Five Architects,* it illustrated houses by Peter Eisenman, Michael Graves, Charles Gwathmey, John Hejduk and Richard Meier. Immediately dubbed the "New York Five," these architects received great publicity. In general the houses were white and involved explorations in geometry, and it did appear, briefly, that these five talented architects had much in common. But not for long. No sooner was the book published than the five started going in different directions. The Smith and the Saltzman houses of Meier are illustrated and clearly show that he and Gwathmey are the two architects most concerned with the realities of program and construction.

By the mid-1970s Meier was obtaining larger commissions. In 1977 the completion of the Bronx Developmental Center demonstrated that he had passed one of an architect's greatest tests—making the jump from designing elegant houses to constructing major buildings. The Developmental Center is a home for mentally disabled people, and as the surroundings are so poor it turns inward onto courtyards. The cladding is of silver metal panels with round-cornered openings punched in them, very much in the manner pioneered by Jean Prouvé in France.

The Atheneum at New Harmony, Indiana, completed in 1979, set the style and material for Meier's big buildings. Acting as a visitor center for an idealistic settlement, the Atheneum, with its seductive curves, its extensive ramped circulation inside and out, and its impeccable white cladding, reinforced modernism at the moment of its greatest rejection. The Hartford Seminary (1981) and the High Museum in Atlanta (1983) followed, confirming and refining the ideas and techniques used at the Atheneum.

A hard architecture of white metal might be expected to ignore context. But Meier has shown a sensitivity to his surroundings, not in terms of style but in terms of their underlying geometry. His 1973 project for a Museum of Modern Art at the Villa Strozzi in Florence, Italy, used the geometry of the remaining facades of the old villa as a starting point. The 1978 Aye Simon Reading Room within New York's Guggenheim Museum is a jewel-like space owing much to Frank Lloyd Wright, but with no sense of parody. This contextual skill emerged on a larger scale in the Kunsthandwerk Museum at Frankfurt-am-Main; that building has the white metal panels and the ramped circulation of a typical Meier building, but the plans took their geometry from a slight shift in alignment of the adjacent roads, and the elevations took their geometry from the Villa Metzler, a neoclassical house that forms a key part of the complex and to which Meier has given pride of place.

With the completion of the museums at Atlanta and Frankfurt, Meier's position as one of the world's leading architects was assured. The extensive Getty complex in southern California and many prestigious projects around the world followed those successes and have enabled the architect to take his chosen language to a greater richness and larger scale.

—JOHN WINTER

MELNIKOV, Konstantin.

Russian. Born Konstantin Stepanovich Melnikov in Moscow, 1890. Died in Moscow, 1974. Studied painting, 1905-11, then switched to architecture, 1912-17, at the Moscow School of Painting, Sculpture and Architecture. Worked for the Moscow City Soviet after the 1917 Revolution; taught at Vkhutemas (Higher State Art and Technical Studios), Moscow, 1921-23, and at the Moscow Architectural Institute, 1930s; discredited

Konstantin Melnikov: Soviet Pavilion, Exposition des Arts Décoratifs, Paris, France, 1925

as an architect by the government in 1937, and returned to painting.

Chronology of Works

All in Russia unless noted
† *Work no longer exists*

1917	Main building of AMO (now Likhachev) automobile works, Moscow (facade)
1917	Factory structures, AMO automobile works, Moscow (with A. F. Loleidt)
1923	Makhorka Pavilion, All-Union Agriculture and Cottage Industries Exhibition, Moscow†
1924	Sarcophagus for V. I. Lenin, Red Square, Moscow
1924	Sukharevka Market Bar/Administrative Building, Moscow
1925	Display kiosks, Torgsektor Exhibit, Paris, France
1925	Soviet Pavilion, Exposition des Arts Décoratifs, Paris, France†
1926	Baldachin for funeral of Leonid Krasnin, London, England
1926	Leyland Bus Garage, Moscow
1927	Frunze Workers' Club, Moscow
1927	Kauchuk Workers' Club, Moscow
1927	Rusakov Workers' Club, Moscow
1927-28	Pravda Workers' Club, Dulevo
1927-28	Svoboda (now Gorky) Workers' Club, Moscow
1927-29	Melnikov House, Moscow
1928	Kauchuk Factory Cafeteria, Moscow
1929	Burevestnik Workers' Club, Moscow
1929	Gosplan parking garage, Moscow (with V. I. Kurochkin)

1929	Stormy Petrel Workers' Club, Moscow
1930	Moscow Chamber Theater, Moscow (reconstruction)
1934	Heavy Industry Commissariat, NKTP, Moscow
1949	Central Department Store, Saratov (interior)

Publications

ARTICLES BY MELNIKOV

"Arkhitekture pervoe mesto." *Stroitelstvo Moskvy* No. 1 (1934): 9-13.

"Arkhitekturnoe osvoenie novykh materialov." *Arkhitektura SSSR* No. 3 (1934): 37.

"Tvorcheskoe samochuvstvie arkhitektora." *Arkhitektura SSSR* No. 9 (1934): 10-11.

BOOKS ABOUT MELNIKOV

LUKHMANOV, N.: *Arkhitektura kluba*. Moscow, 1930.

STARR, S. FREDERICK: *Melnikov: Solo Architect in a Mass Society*. Princeton, New Jersey, 1978.

STRIGALEV, A., and KOKKINAKI, I. (eds.): *K. S. Melnikov*. Moscow, 1985.

WORTMANN, A. (ed.): *The Muscles of Invention*. Rotterdam, 1990.

ARTICLES ABOUT MELNIKOV

"Vosmidesiatiletie Konstantina Stepanovicha Melnikova." *Arkhitektura SSSR* No. 11 (1970): 68-69.

BYKOV, V.: "Konstantin Melnikov i Georgi Golts." *Sovetskaia arkhitektura* No. 18 (1969): 59-67.

GERCHUK, I.: "Konstantin Melnikov." In SHVIDKOVSKY, O. A. (ed.): *Building in the U. S. S. R. 1917-1932*. London, 1971.

ILIN, MIKHAIL A.: "Dva novykh kluba." *Stroitelstvo Moskvy* No. 10 (1931): 15-16.

KARRA, A. I.: "Dva klubnykh zdaniia." *Stroitelstvo Moskvy* Nos. 8-9 (1930): 24-28.

KHAN-MAGOMEDOV, S. O.: "Kluby segodnia i vchera." *Dekorativnoe iskusstvo SSSR* No. 9 (1966): 2-6.

KHIGER, R.: "Arkhitektor K. S. Melnikov." *Arkhitektura SSSR* No. 1 (1935): 30-34.

LUKHMANOV, N.: "Tsilindricheskii dom." *Stroitelstvo Moskvy* No. 4 (1929): 16-22.

STARR, S. FREDERICK: "Konstantin Melnikov." *Architectural Design* 7 (1969).

ZHEITS, V.: "O tsilindricheskom dome arkhitektora Melnikova." *Stroitelstvo Moskvy* No. 10 (1929): 18-19.

*

Konstantin Stepanovich Melnikov was one of the acknowledged and influential leaders of the new direction of Soviet architecture in the 1920s. A prolific designer, in a decade he entered all important architectural competitions and carried out numerous commissions. Among the realizations were six clubs for workers, four garages and his own house. In 1922-23 he took part in three major architectural events with competition entries for the Palace of Labor, a workers' dwelling complex and the executed Makhorka (Tobacco) Pavilion at the Agricultural Exhibition in Moscow. His designs for the sarcophagus in the Lenin Mausoleum and the Novo-Sukharevsky Market in Moscow were executed in 1924. He won the competition for the Soviet Pavilion at the 1925 International Exhibition of Decorative Arts in Paris. The pavilion established Melnikov as an architectural innovator and presented to the world the exuberant designs of the Soviet avant-garde. In appreciation for the successful show in Paris, the Soviet government gave Melnikov a parcel of land on which to build his house. The fashionable area of Arbat in Moscow was chosen for the lot.

Melnikov completed his education in the spring of the revolutionary year 1917. He began as a painter, then later transferred to architecture. Melnikov was very particular in his ideas about architecture, which he shared in polemics with his contemporaries. In the first half of the 1920s he also taught architecture at Moscow's Vkhutemas School (the Higher State Art and Technical Studios) and in the 1930s at the Moscow Architectural Institute. Discussion was fierce and disagreement about the theory and philosophy of the new architecture was heated at times. The architects grouped in associations to form their ideological platforms, and to define views on design and the role of the architect in society. The mainstream movement named constructivism had the greatest following. Melnikov, however, never joined the constructivists (lead by Aleksandr Vesnin and Moisei Ginsburg). His artistic position was perhaps closer to that of the rationalists (lead by Nikolai Ladovsky). He became a member of the ASNOVA group (Association of New Architects), but his association with that group was brief. Consequently, as an architect with a markedly individual approach, he did not regard himself as belonging to any particular trend.

Throughout his career in architectural design, Melnikov was preoccupied with curves, and especially with the circle. His 1923 entry for the Palace of Labor competition is an asymmetrical composition organized from a circular colonnaded plaza. Both the large and small auditoriums conjure images of large sloped megaphone-like forms. A rotating series of curved sections stacked in a vertical cylinder, which was to constantly change the building silhouette, was used in the entry for the Leningrad Pravda competition in 1924.

Experimenting and searching for new forms, Melnikov evolved a method of combining a set of intersecting cylinders. He used this strategy in a number of designs for housing and public buildings and in the house he designed for himself. A direct connection to the geometry of the house is evident in the 1927 competition design for the Zuyev Factory Workers' Club. It is a linear composition of two pairs of intersecting cylinders. Also, the design for the Burevestnik Workers' Club (1929) features a four-story cylinder defining the plaza of the main entry to the building. The four floor-to-ceiling glass bays open the cylinder to the natural light and to the views from the street as well. In the 1930 invited competition for the Frunze Military Academy, Melnikov's design consisted of 12 cylinders organized in three rows, like soldiers in a military parade.

The design of his house is composed of two cylinders joined at one third of their volume, which forms a footprint of the numeral 8. The exterior brick bearing wall is 50 centimeters thick. The brick of the two cylinders is laid in a diagonal system of a diamond-shaped pattern, which forms a series of diamond "openings." Half of these diamond "openings" make room for placing of the hexagonal windows and the other half of the "openings" are "covered" to create the air-cushion thermal insulation pockets in the wall. The floors of the house are designed as a system of two-way wood coffered joists. The sturdy two-way structural system of the floors was used because of the nine-meter clear span from the perimeter bearing walls of the two cylinders. In using masonry construction for the cylinder walls, Melnikov took advantage of the traditional skills of Russian masons who had built numerous central-plan churches throughout the country. Concrete and steel were scarcely available in the Soviet Union at the time, and the architect knew that Russian construction workers were experienced in building with bricks and wood.

Melnikov succeeded in breaking away from tradition, from the eclecticism of the 19th-century bourgeois house. His design was for a new family, liberal and intellectual, whose life-style required different spatial arrangements of house functions. The ensuing architectural image reflected also the social and political changes and the advancement of technology and science of the 20th century. The form was devoid of any decoration, embellishment or ornament. The aesthetic strength was in the direction and truthful expression of structure, functions and building materials, of how the sun entered the interior spaces, how fenestration framed the views and the multiple images of the outside world, and how solid and void and light and shadow played on the architectural form.

The young artists who became the heralds of the revolutionary society were searching for a new language in architecture to express the ideals of the new social and political order established in the country. Architectural constructivism, as the movement of the Russian avant-garde came to be known in the West, was established as a dynamic, articulated, machinistic vocabulary of forms full of high contrasts.

From the early 1930s on, when all creative activity was channeled by decrees into a governmentally dictated socialist realism, until his death, Melnikov was denied any commissions. He could not compromise his progressive beliefs and design the pompous edifices of the "Stalinist Gothic," and remained condemned by both the political and architectural establishments as a "formalist."

—PETER LIZON

MENDELSOHN, Erich.

German-born American. Born Erich Mendelsohn in Allenstein, East Prussia, Germany (now Olsztyn, Poland), 21 March 1887. Died in San Francisco, California, 15 September 1953. Immigrated to England, 1933; naturalized, 1938; immigrated to the United States, 1941; naturalized, 1946. Married Louise Maas, 1915. Studied at the Technische Hochschule, Berlin, and Technische Hochschule, Munich (under Theodor Fischer), 1907-11. Independent architectural practice in Munich, 1911-14; war service with German army, 1917 -19; in partnership with Serge Chermayeff, London, 1933-39; executed commissions in Palestine, 1934-41; moved to New York, 1941; in private practice, San Francisco, California, 1945 until his death in 1953.

Chronology of Works
All in Germany unless noted
† Work no longer exists

1911	Chapel, Hebrew Cemetery, Allenstein (now Olsztyn, Poland)
1919-23	Hat Factory, Steinberg, Herman & Co., Luckenwalde
1919-24	Einstein Tower, Potsdam
1921-23	Berliner Tageblatt Building, Berlin
1921-22	Weichman Silk Store and Offices, Gleiwitz (now Gliwice, Poland)
1923	Sternfeld House, Heerstrasse, Berlin
1926-27	Schocken Department Store, Nuremberg
1926-27	Jewish Cemetery, Königsberg (destroyed by Nazis)
1926-28	Schocken Department Store, Stuttgart†
1927-28	Universum Cinema, Kurfürstendamm, Berlin
1928-29	Schocken Department Store, Chemnitz
1929-30	Mendelsohn House, Rupenhorn, Berlin
1929-30	Hebrew Youth Center, Essen
1930-32	Columbus House, Berlin†

1933-35	De La Warr Pavilion, Bexhill-on-Sea, England (with Serge Chermayeff)
1935-36	Weizmann Residence, Rehovot, Palestine (Israel)
1935-36	Schocken Residence and Library, Jerusalem, Palestine (Israel)
1937-38	Hadassah University Medical Center, Mount Scopus, Jerusalem, Palestine (Israel)
1937-38	Government Hospital, Haifa, Palestine (Israel)
1937-38	Anglo-Palestine Bank, Jerusalem, Palestine (Israel)
1937-38	Trade School, Jagur, Palestine (Israel)
1939	Agricultural Institute, Rehovot, Palestine (Israel)
1946-50	B'nai Amoona Temple and Community Center, St. Louis, Missouri, U.S.A.
1946-50	Maimonides Health Center, San Francisco, California, U.S.A.
1946-50	Temple and Community Center, Cleveland, Ohio, U.S.A.
1948-52	Emanu-El Temple and Community Center, Grand Rapids, Michigan, U.S.A.
1950-51	Russell House, Pacific Heights, San Francisco, California, U.S.A.
1950-54	Mount Zion Temple and Community Center, St. Paul, Minnesota, U.S.A.
1951-53	Atomic Energy Commission Laboratories, Berkeley, California, U.S.A.

Publications

BOOKS BY MENDELSOHN

Erich Mendelsohn: Structures and Sketches. London, 1924.
Amerika: Bilderbuch eines Architekten. Berlin, 1926.
Russland, Europa, Amerika: Ein architektonischer Querschnitt. Berlin, 1929.
Neues Haus—Neue Welt. Berlin, 1931.
Der Schöpferische Sinn der Krise. Berlin, 1932.
Three Lectures on Architecture. Berkeley, California 1944.
Erich Mendelsohn: Letters of an Architect. Edited by Oskar Beyer. New York and London, 1967.

ARTICLES BY MENDELSOHN

"Architecture of Our Own Times." *Architectural Association Journal* (June 1930): 5-18.
"Background to Design." *Architectural Forum* (April 1953): 105-108.
"The 3-Dimensions of Architecture: Their Symbolic Significance." In *Symbols and Values.* New York, 1954.

BOOKS ABOUT MENDELSOHN

PEHNT, WOLFGANG: *Die Architektur des Expressionismus.* Stuttgart, 1973; as *Expressionist Architecture,* London, 1973.
ROGGERO, M. F.: *Il contribuo di Mendelsohn alla evoluzione dell'architettura moderna.* Milan, 1952.
SCHILLER, LOTTE (ed.): *Eric Mendelsohn: Catalog of Sketches.* Mill Valley, California, 1970.
SHARP, DENNIS: *Modern Architecture and Expressionism.* London, 1966.
VON ECKARDT, WOLF: *Eric Mendelsohn.* New York and London, 1960.
WHITTICK, ARNOLD: *Eric Mendelsohn.* London, 1940.
ZEVI, BRUNO (ed.): *Erich Mendelsohn: Opera completa. Architettore e imagini architettoniche.* Milan, 1970.
ZEVI, BRUNO: *Erich Mendelsohn.* New York, 1985.

ARTICLES ABOUT MENDELSOHN

BANHAM, REYNER: "Mendelsohn." *Architectural Review* (August 1954): 84-93.

"Disegni di Eric Mendelsohn." *Architettura* Nos. 79- . Complete publication of sketches began with this issue.

"Erich Mendelsohn." *Architectural Forum* (April 1953): 105-121.

"Erich Mendelsohn." *Architecture vivante* Special issue (Autumn/Winter 1932).

MORGENTHALER, HANS: "The Early Sketches of Erich Mendelsohn: The Search for an Industrial Metaphor." *Avant Garde* 2 (Summer 1989).

PALTERER, DAVID: "Traces of Mendelsohn." *Domus* (January 1984).

POSENER, JULIUS: "Mendelsohn." *Architecture d'aujourd'hui* (May 1932).

SCHILLER, H.: "The Last Work of a Great Architect." *Architectural Forum* (February 1955): 106-117.

SHAPIRO, IRVING D.: "Erich Mendelsohn." *American Institute of Architects' Journal* (June 1958).

ZEVI, BRUNO (ed.): "Eric Mendelsohn: An -ism for a Man." *Architettura* 9, No. 95, Special issue (September 1963).

ZEVI, BRUNO: "Eric Mendelsohn." *Metron* No. 49/50 (1954).

*

Erich Mendelsohn's creative span extended over four tumultuous decades, vibrant with change. Uprooted by cruel fate from his native Germany, he had to reestablish himself, again and again, in different countries: England, Palestine and the United States, and to adapt to very disparate environments and cultures. Moreover, he was a man divided within himself: when he called himself an East-Prussian Oriental, he pointed with irony to that deep chasm, in terms of his roots, affinities and emotional loyalties, which separated Mendelsohn the acculturated German from Mendelsohn the atavistic Jew. As a consequence, to perhaps a greater degree than any other major architect of his tragic generation, his life was disrupted by the traumas of the times—not only two world wars and political and economic turmoil, but the ever-present threat of anti-Semitism, virulent with the rise of the Nazis in Germany, latent but feared in his adopted Britain—resulting in a professional career characterized by an essential discontinuity. In addition, from inward impulses, his architecture also underwent a process of evolution: developing, changing, maturing. However, if in a sense there were thus several different Mendelsohns, there was also at the core one essential creative personality, enduring through every transformation.

The first Mendelsohn emerged from the Great War, his architecture a personal catharsis: the utopian dreamer of dreams, the creator of visionary prototypes, the quintessential expressionist. In these dynamic early sketches Mendelsohn called out to a new world in the making. Unlike others of his generation, Mendelsohn's expressionism was not a negative reaction, not a sad cry of despair, but rather an exuberant song of hope. If there is passion in these imaginary drawings, it lies in a joyous vision of the grand harmonies of the future, coupled with an almost-mystic belief in the architect's own all-conquering creative power to shape his world. For Mendelsohn, this force derived not only from an affirmation of faith in the future, but also from the nourishing roots of an ancient past. These sketches were at once evocations of a brave new world, bravura displays of an explosive artistic ego, and monumental altars to ancestral gods. "Whatever work I did," he wrote in 1933, "especially my nonrealistic outbursts in sketches and conceptions, got its strength from the biblical simplicity which fulfills itself and embraces the whole world at the same time." This Mendelsohn, who saw every design as simultaneously expressive of the specific/now and the universal/timeless, is the enduring Mendelsohn, no matter how much his architecture changed in character, form and aspect.

Every Mendelsohn project began with a conceptual sketch, and these sketches were always expressive, in their dynamic form and character. The buildings as actually constructed, however, although inherently faithful to the initial concept, were inevitably transmuted into an architecture which was more controlled, more disciplined and more realistic, in the sense of being translatable into the real world of economics, building materials and construction processes. In other words, they were as much a product of the intellect as of the heart, a synthesis sought by Mendelsohn ever since, in Holland in 1923, he was confronted by, and felt compelled to reject, the opposed and destructive extremisms (all fire or ice) of Amsterdam and Rotterdam. Therefore, with the exception of the Einstein Tower in Potsdam, at the beginning of his professional career, the architecture of Mendelsohn's German period (1919-33), contrary to accepted wisdom, should not be classified as expressionist. True, it is a contrapuntal and dramatic architecture, often with dynamic features: a sweeping bay, a tautly curved facade, a vigorous imposed rhythm of horizontal lines or bands; but these are allusions to forms canonized in his sketches, mere metaphors of expressionism rather than its impassioned spirit.

The heart of Mendelsohn's practice, the buildings actually executed, was commercial, for hard-headed, albeit enlightened, clients. It consisted mainly of a series of notable department stores and office buildings: the stores for Schocken at Nuremberg, Stuttgart and Chemnitz, for Deukon at Berlin and Cohen-Epstein at Duisburg, finally the Columbushaus in Berlin. Each in its way is a first-class all-round product: original in conception, strikingly composed, stylistically sophisticated, immaculately detailed and functionally planned. In these characteristics lies the essential difference between the ephemeral visionary sketch and the enduring art of architecture; this may be a diminution of architectural power, but it is also its proper consolidation and consummation in real terms. That these were qualities desired by Mendelsohn, and not merely reluctantly accepted, can be seen in his own house at Am Rupenhorn, whose essential characteristics are simplicity, clarity, rationality, and—surprisingly—not dynamic expressionism but classic repose. This is the second Mendelsohn: still the imaginative architect, but also the complete professional.

Between 1933, when he fled Germany, and 1941, when he settled in the United States, Mendelsohn's most significant work (with the exception of the Bexhill Pavilion, with Chermayeff) was to be found, not in England, "an interregnum," but in Palestine (Eretz Israel), "the true soil desired by my blood and my nature." In a series of outstanding buildings, such as the Weizmann House, the library for his old client Zalman Schocken, or the Hadassah Hospital on Mount Scopus, yet another Mendelsohn emerged, graver perhaps and more restrained. Architecturally sensitive to the indigenous cultural milieu in which he was now building, its cubic forms and massive materials, his designs responded as well to the natural environment—its climate, topography, flora—and, at a deeper level, to its brooding biblical immanence. Burdened by the millenia-long and tragic history of his people, and inspired by its efforts to create a better future, the fire of Zionism burned bright in Mendelsohn the Jew, although not without ambivalence, for Mendelsohn the sophisticated European was never completely at ease in Palestine's brave and blunt new world.

There was no such hesitancy about the architecture of his Palestine period, however: it belonged, rooted unambiguously and inevitably in time and place.

The final Mendelsohn is that of the American period, from 1941 until his death in 1953. In a sense, this was his least productive phase, a period of alienation and disjunction, out of touch with his present surroundings and severed from all that was meaningful in the past. The Maimonides Hospital in San Francisco was a lyrical interlude in an otherwise less distinguished succession of designs, mainly for synagogues, which desperately attempted to recapture the brio of his early sketches in built form. While the talent and creativity of Mendelsohn is always present, even in these works, they are too self-conscious, they try too hard, to be entirely convincing. Utopia is lost, gravitas set aside, and pathos terribly near: a sad ending to the career of one of modern architecture's greatest figures.

—GILBERT HERBERT

MICHELANGELO.

Italian. Born Michelangelo Buonarroti in Caprese, Italy, 6 March 1475. Died in Rome, 18 February 1564. Apprenticed to Ghirlandaio in Florence at age 13; also studied anatomy; patronized in Florence by the Medici (worked briefly in Bologne, ca. 1495); in Rome, 1496-1501; then in Florence; again in Rome, 1505: worked for Pope Julius II in the Sistine Chapel and on his tomb; in Florence, 1522-34; then in Rome, from 1534: worked for Leo X, Clement VII, and Paul III.

Chronology of Works
All in Italy
* Approximate dates
† Work no longer exists

1505-40s	Monument to Pope Julius II, San Pietro in Vincoli, Rome
1514	Chapel of Pope Leo X, Castel Sant'Angelo, Rome (facade)
1517ff.	San Lorenzo, Florence (facade)
1519-34	Medici Funeral Chapel, San Lorenzo, Florence
1524-34	Biblioteca Laurenziana, San Lorenzo, Florence (not completed until 1571 by Niccolò Tribolo, Giorgio Vasari, and Bartolommeo Ammannati according to Michelangelo's designs)
1525-33*	Sant'Apollonia, Florence (portal)
1527-29	Fortifications, Florence†
1539	Base for the Equestrian Statue of Marcus Aurelius, Capitol, Rome
1539-64	Piazza del Campidoglio, Rome (not completed until later by others)
1540s	Palazzo del Senatore, Rome (stairway)
1546-49*	Palazzo Farnese, Rome (cornice design; completion of facade and courtyard)
1546-64	Palazzo Nuovo, Rome (Museo Capitolino)
1546-64	St. Peter's, Rome (dome not completed until 1590 by Giacomo della Porta and Domenico Fontana from Michelangelo's model; building not completed until 1626 by Carlo Maderno)
1550-51	Vatican Palace, Rome (stairway in the upper garden of the Cortile del Belvedere)
1560*	Cappella Sforza, Santa Maria Maggiore, Rome (not completed unitl 1573 by della Porta)
1561-64	Porta Pia, Rome
1561ff.	Santa Maria degli Angeli, Rome (interior)

Publications

BOOKS BY MICHELANGELO

Michelangelo: A Record of His Life as Told in His Own Letters and Papers. New York, 1976.
RAMSDEN, E. H. (ed.): *Michelangelo, Letters.* 2 vols. Stanford, California, and London, 1963.

BOOKS ABOUT MICHELANGELO

ACKERMAN, JAMES S.: *The Architecture of Michelangelo.* Harmondsworth, England, and Baltimore, 1961; rev. ed., 1971.
BLANC, CHARLES: *L'oeuvre et la vie de Michel-Ange.* Paris, 1876.
BONELLI, RENATO: *Da Bramante a Michelangelo.* Venice, 1960.
CLEMENTS, ROBERT J.: *Michelangelo's Theory of Art.* New York, 1961.
CONDIVI, ASCANIO: *The Life of Michelangelo.* Baton Rouge, Louisiana, 1976.
DE MAIO, R.: *Michelangelo e la controriforma.* Bari, Italy, and Rome, 1978.
DE TOLNAY, CHARLES: *Michelangelo.* 5 vols. 2nd ed. Princeton, New Jersey, 1969-70; one-volume edition, 1975.
FREY, DAGOBERT: *Michelangelo Buonarroti architetto.* Rome, 1923.
FROMMEL, CHRISTOPH L.: *Der römische Palastbau der Hochrenaissance.* 3 vols. Tübingen, Germany, 1973.
GOLDSCHEIDER, L.: *Michelangelo: Paintings, Sculpture, Architecture.* New York, 1954.
HIBBARD, HOWARD: *Michelangelo: Architect.* 2nd. ed., 1985.
HIRT, M.: *Michelangelo and His Drawings.* New Haven, Connecticut, 1988.
MARIANI, VALERIO: *Michelangelo e la facciata di San Pietro.* Rome, 1943.
MILLON, H. A. and SMYTH, C. H.: *Michelangelo, Architect: The Facade of San Lorenzo and the Drum and Dome of St. Peter's.* Milan, 1988.
MURRAY, LINDA: *Michelangelo.* New York and London, 1980.
PAPINI, G.: *Vita di Michelangelo.* Florence, 1949.
PORTOGHESI, PAOLO, and ZEVI, BRUNO (eds.): *Michelagniolo architetto.* Turin, 1964.
REDIG DE CAMPOS, D.: *Raffaello e Michelangelo.* Rome, 1946.
SCHIAVO, ARMANDO: *Michelangelo architetto.* Rome, 1949.
SCHIAVO, ARMANDO: *La vita e le opere architettoniche di Michelangelo.* Rome, 1953.
SUMMERS, DAVID: *Michelangelo and the Language of Art.* Princeton, New Jersey, 1981.
THODE, H.: *Michelangelo: Kritische Untersuchungen über seine Werke.* 3 vols. Berlin, 1908-13.
VASARI, GIORGIO: *La vita di Michelangelo nelle redazioni del 1550 e del 1568.* Naples, Italy, 1962.
VON GEYMÜLLER, HEINRICH: *Die Architektur der Renaissance in Toskana.* Vol. 8. Munich, 1904.
WILDE, JOHANNES: *Michelangelo.* Oxford, 1978.
WITTKOWER, RUDOLF: *La cupola di San Pietro di Michelangelo.* Florence, 1964.
ZANGHIERI, GIOVANNI: *Il Castello di Porta Pia di Michelagniolo (1564) al Vespignani (1864) e ad oggi.* Rome, 1953.

ARTICLES ABOUT MICHELANGELO

ASKEW, P.: "The Relation of Bernini's Architecture to the Architecture of the High Renaissance and of Michelangelo." *Marsyas* V (1950).

Michelangelo: St. Peter's, Rome, Italy, 1546-64

BARDESCHI-CIULICH, LUCILLA: "Documenti inediti su Michelangelo e l'incarico di San Pietro." *Rinascimento* 17 (1977): 235-275.

ELAM, CAROLINE: "The Site and Early Building History of Michelangelo's New Sacristy." *Mitteilungen des kunsthistorischen Instituts in Florenz* 23 (1979): 155-186.

FASOLO, VINCENZO: "Disegni architettonici di Michelangelo." *Architettura e arti decorative* 6 (1926-27): 385-401, 433-455.

GULDAN, ERNST: "Die jochverschleifende Gewölbedekoration von Michelangelo bis Pozzo." Dissertation. Göttingen, Germany, 1954.

HAGELBERG, L.: "Die Architektur Michelangelos in ihren Beziehungen zu Manierismus und Barock." *Münchner Jahrbuch der bildenden Kunst* N. F., 8 (1931): 264-280.

MACDOUGALL, ELIZABETH: "Michelangelo and the Porta Pia." *Journal of the Society of Architectural Historians* 19 (1960): 97-108.

"Michelangelo als Architekt." Vol. 2, pages 3-70 in *Stil und Überlieferung in der Kunst des Abendlandes*. Berlin, 1967.

POPP, ANNY E.: "Unbeachtete Projekte Michelangelos." *Münchner Jahrbuch der bildenden Kunst* New series, 4 (1927): 389-477.

SAALMAN, HOWARD: "Michelangelo: S. Maria del Fiore and St. Peter's." *Art Bulletin* 7, No. 3:374-409 (1975).

SCHOTTMÜLLER, FRIDA: "Michelangelo und das Ornament." *Jahrbuch der kunsthistorischen Sammlungen in Wien* N. F., 2 (1927): 219-232.

SCHWAGER, KLAUS: "Die Porta Pia in Rom." *Münchner Jahrbuch der bildenden Kunst*. Series 3, 24:33-96 (1973).

SUMMERS, DAVID: "Michelangelo on Architecture." *Art Bulletin* 54, No. 2 (1972): 146-257.

TAFURI, MANFREDO: "Michelangelo architetto." *Civiltà delle machine* 20 (1975): 49-60.

THOENS, CHRISTOF: "Bemerkungen zur St. Peter-Fassade Michelangelos." In *Munuscula Discipulorum*. Berlin, 1968.

WALLACE, WILLIAM E.: " 'Dal disegno allo spazio': Michelangelo's Drawings for the Fortifications of Florence." *Journal of the Society of Architectural Historians* 46 (June 1987): 119-134.

WITTKOWER, RUDOLF: "Michelangelo's Biblioteca Laurenzia." In *Idea and Image*. London, 1978.

ZEVI, BRUNO: "Michelagniolo e Palladio." *Bollettino del Centro Internazionale di Studi di Architettura "Andrea Palladio"* 6, No. 2:13-28.

*

Michelangelo Buonarroti, whose artistic conceptions and creations towered over the High Renaissance and Mannerist eras of Italian art, was a sculptor, painter, poet and architect of herculean talent and output. His architectural enterprises, which included at least 29 projects and commissions, were extremely varied; they included designs for religious and secular buildings, city plans and fortifications. Yet for all of this activity, no "finished" architectural drawings by his hand exist, and no building ever was completed precisely as Michelangelo had intended. Throughout the progress of a commission, Michelangelo was consistently challenged by the evolution of his ideas and designs; just as he metaphorically drew life from stone in the creation of his sculpted figures, so too, in the more abstract manner which is the sensibility of architecture, Michelangelo designed buildings and spaces with a kinship to life itself.

During and shortly after his lifetime, Michelangelo's architectural designs received mixed reviews. To the Vitruvian purists, whose unforgiving adherence to classical norms left them bereft of any appreciation of inventiveness, Michelangelo's compositional judgment was characterized by randomness and capriciousness. Such criticisms found particular support in the sober intellectual climate of Counter-Reformation Rome, which condemned the artistic license evident in the creation of grotesque ornament and in Pirro Ligorio's vehement attacks on Michelangelo's architecture, which censured his designs for lacking decorum. Giorgio Vasari, who was not unaffected by this constrictive atmosphere, asserted that it was Michelangelo's superior judgement which allowed for his deviation from classical norms. In discussing Michelangelo's architectural designs for the New Sacristy of San Lorenzo in Florence, Vasari wrote in 1568 that "he departed not a little from the work regulated by measure, order, and rule, which other men did according to a common use and after Vitruvius and the antiquities, to which he would not conform. That license has done much to give courage to those who have seen his methods to set themselves to imitate him, and new fantasies have since been seen which have more of the grotesque than of reason or rule in their ornamentation. Wherefore, the craftsmen owe him an infinite and everlasting obligation, he having broken the bonds and chains by reason of which they had always followed a beaten path in the execution of their works." Vasari's remarks, however laudatory, were balanced by a cautious conservatism; he observed that Michelangelo's architectural designs strode a tenuous line between confusion and the fullest liberation of art.

Contemporary and succeeding generations of artists possessed a clear appreciation for Michelangelo's inventive creations. Benvenuto Cellini praised Michelangelo's transformation of the classical orders, while Ascanio Condivi, Michelangelo's friend and biographer (1553), expressed the view that Michelangelo had equaled, if not surpassed, ancient classical architects. In a passage defining the relationship between Michelangelo and Pope Julius III, Condivi wrote, "Michelangelo did nevertheless make a design at the request of His Holiness for the facade of a palace which he had in mind to build in Rome; it is something unusual and new to whoever sees it, indebted to no style or rule either ancient or modern. The same is true of many of his other works in Florence and in Rome, proving that architecture was not treated by the ancients so exhaustively that there is not room for new invention no less charming or beautiful."

Michelangelo himself, with his usual ironic modesty, denied that architecture was his profession, vowing simply, "I shall do what I can. . . ." Condivi reinforced Michelangelo's constant disclaimer, but noted that Michelangelo did not "content himself merely with the knowledge of the principal elements of architecture, but he also insisted on knowing everything which in any way pertained to that profession . . . in which he became as proficient perhaps as those who have no other profession." It was, however, the master of Italian Baroque art a century later, Giovanni Lorenzo Bernini, who gave us the most succinct and appropriate critique of Michelangelo's architecture, noting that as "architecture is pure *disegno,* Michelangelo was a divine architect."

By the mid-16th century, *disegno,* a uniquely rich artistic concept which joined the creative idea with its manifestation through draftsmanship, was viewed as the nourishing source of the arts of painting, sculpture and architecture. Michelangelo's activity as an architect, which was related to his approach to sculpture and painting, was not out of the ordinary in the Renaissance. Architects trained solely in the profession, such as Antonio da Sangallo, were few; artists who became architects, bringing with them an established pictorial or sculptural sensitivity, such as Raphael, Giulio Romano and Michelangelo, were more the rule. Michelangelo's earliest architectural designs were

Michelangelo: Piazza del Campidoglio, Rome, Italy, 1539-64

linked directly, through the genesis of *disegno,* to sculpture and painting. The initial plan for the Tomb of Julius II (1505) was to combine approximately 40 sculpted figures with a three-level, freestanding architectural support. The heroic figures of the Sistine Chapel ceiling are set within an illusory architectural framework, and his novel plan of the facade of San Lorenzo in Florence (commissioned 1517) was to be, in his words, "the mirror of architecture and sculpture of all Italy." In his final design for the San Lorenzo project, Michelangelo proposed a palace-like facade with two stories of the same width, thus offering a new and inventive solution to the problems posed by the varying roof levels of the Christian basilica. The facade was to be a field for sculpture, but even more, the entire facade itself was to be developed in relief. The energy of the sculpted figures would have been bound, through *disegno,* to the three-dimensional activity of the facade.

Michelangelo understood architecture in terms of sculpture and painting, and he understood sculpture and painting in terms of the human figure. For Michelangelo, the human figure, which possessed the fullest considerations of the microcosmic/macrocosmic tradition since antiquity, was the apex of creation, and, as such, it was the center of his artistic invention. At different times in his life, Michelangelo dissected cadavers in the belief that the revelations of anatomy would be a guidepost for his art. While we more easily understand these associations with his figural works, they also underlie his architectural designs.

Michelangelo wrote little of what would be considered art theory; one compelling passage concerning architecture is found in a letter to a church dignitary. In the letter, Michelangelo discusses the relationship between the architectural plan and its various parts and adornments, noting that a change in the form of the plan necessitates a change in the corresponding parts and adornments. He based this knowledge on an analogy with the human figure. Michelangelo demonstrates how the parts of the body relate to the whole by stating that "the nose, that is in the middle of the face, is neither obligated to one nor the other eye, but one hand is altogether obligated to be like the other, and one eye like the other, with respect to the sides and of the corresponding parts. Because it is a certain thing, that the members of architecture derive from the members of man. Who has not been or is not a good master of the human body, and most of all of anatomy, cannot understand of it."

We should not confuse Michelangelo's organic conception of architecture with the earlier tradition which associated the parts and proportions of a building with those of the human body. Michelangelo defined the relationship between the whole of a plan and its parts as an organic association governed by symmetry. Symmetry here is not simply a mode of composition; it is rooted in the physical structure of living creatures. In this way, symmetry becomes one basis for our empathetic response to a building. But for Michelangelo, the goal of art was more than the mere representation of the figure; the goal was to create figures which, as Vasari described, possessed "motion and breath." The application of these concepts to architecture was grounded not only in Michelangelo's power of artistic invention, but also in his creative imagination and judgment.

As has been established above, Michelangelo took liberties with the classical aesthetic, yet he utilized elements of the vocabulary of classical architecture. In his first architectural commission, the exterior of the Chapel of Leo X in the Castel Sant'Angelo in Rome (1514), Michelangelo's creative imagination *(fantasia)* foils our expectations of the classical temple front. The pediment and temple front advance from the "facade," breaking the expected planarity, and the typical screen of columns, which is called for by the pediment, has given way to a central pillar, surmounted by a bracket instead of a capital, which is flanked by two circular openings. The development of the chapel front in spatial dimensions, the inventive and imaginative use of classical elements to suggest an anthropomorphic quality, and the adherence to symmetry are all ruled by the freedom of expression gained by the mastery of *disegno*.

Just as the finger relates to the hand, the hand to the arm, and so on, and all the body parts are interwoven into a complete figure, so too Michelangelo's treatment of the individual components of the design bears the same poetic license which applies to the plan as a whole. Preparatory drawings reveal Michelangelo's *fantasia*: profile studies, in places, suggest an organic, muscular quality, while in another drawing a column base is capriciously resolved into a grotesque head. Viewing the wall tabernacles of the vestibule of the Laurentian Library, for example, we are met by apparent contradictions of form and function. The framing pilasters, which are only partially fluted, taper downward, and the capitals, which do not owe allegiance to Vitruvian standards, are reduced in size from the top of the pilasters. The contradictions evident here and elsewhere are, in a microcosmic way, characteristic of the vestibule design as a whole. The recessed columns, set above the floor and visually mounted on brackets, pose questions of adornment and structure, while the independence and monumentality of the sculpturally massed staircase effect a conflict of implied motion.

Vasari's acknowledgment that Michelangelo had "broken the bonds and chains" which had fettered artists to the conservative weight of tradition, written in reference to the Medici Chapel, also part of San Lorenzo, is equally applicable here. In the vestibule, the architectural forms themselves begin to possess the "motion and breath" of Michelangelo's sculpted figures. With plan and adornments liberated by invention and imagination, yet ruled by judgment, Michelangelo, who earlier approached architecture in sculptural terms, now viewed architecture with the plasticity of sculpture itself.

Michelangelo took charge of the construction of the new St. Peter's in 1546. Already, major architectural commissions were overshadowing those for sculpture and painting. During his remaining years in Rome, until his death in 1564, Michelangelo turned almost exclusively to architecture as a vehicle of personal expression. But the *fantasia* which Michelangelo had lavished on earlier architectural designs now gave way to a monumental simplicity which defined mass and space in a manner analogous to a living organism. The use of the giant order on the Campidoglio palaces and at St. Peter's created a new lucidity and cohesive unity for the architectural forms. At St. Peter's, paired giant pilasters establish rhythmic accents and create underlying walls that sheath the building like muscle and flesh over bone. The inner structural core of the building, like a skeleton, both defines the exterior design and confers vitality upon it. But having achieved a monumental grandeur of mass and space which rivaled ancient Roman architecture, Michelangelo continued to probe, elucidate and advance his architectural concepts.

Although still governed by invention, imagination, judgment and symmetry, Michelangelo's last architectural designs present a final paradox. In the Porta Pia (1561 onward) the elements of a personal, subjective fantasy, reaching back to the Middle Ages yet simultaneously beyond the Renaissance, again are given liberal rein. At the same time, at Santa Maria degli Angeli, built into the ancient ruins of the Baths of Diocletian, Michelangelo reduced interior adornment to lessen the effect of mass, de-emphasizing the physical structure of the building. In the Porta Pia the capacity of imagination is celebrated; at Santa Maria degli Angeli the transcendental is promoted.

Michelangelo's late architectural designs in turn fed the imagination of Baroque architects. But the authority of Michelangelo's architecture always has remained uniquely his own. As in his sculptures and paintings, Michelangelo's artful conception transformed the classical tradition of architecture into a personal exaltation.

—BERNARD SCHULTZ

MICHELOZZO DI BARTOLOMEO.

Italian. Born in Florence, Italy, 1396. Died in Florence: buried 7 October 1472. Trained as a goldsmith; worked with Ghiberti on bronze doors for Florence Baptistery, ca. 1417-24 (also worked with Ghiberti in 1437-42); in partnership with Donatello, 1425-ca. 1438. Succeeded Brunelleschi as architect of Florence Cathedral, 1446.

Chronology of Works
All in Italy unless noted
* Approximate dates

1422	Villa at Trebbio, Mugello
1422*-26	Church of Bosco ai Frati, Mugello
1425*	San Girolamo, Volterra
Before 1427	Villa at Careggi, Mugello
1437*	Sant'Agostino, Montepulciano (facade)
1437*-52	San Marco, Florence
1440	Palazzo Communale, Montepulciano
1442*-57	San Lorenzo, Florence
1444-55	Santissima Annunziata, Florence
1444-59	Palazzo Medici, Florence
1444ff.*	Palazzo Vecchio, Doganna, Florence
1445ff.*	Santa Croce, Florence
1446-52	Cathedral, Florence
1452	Santa Maria delle Grazie, Pistoia
1452*	Villa at Cafaggiolo, Mugello
1454	San Bartolomeo at Monte Oliveto, Florence
1454-58	Palazzo Vecchio, Florence (cortile)
1458*-61	Villa Medici, Fiesole
1459	San Paolo dei Convalescenti Hospital, Florence
1461-64	City Walls and Fortifications, Dubrovnik (formerly Yugoslavia)

Publications

BOOKS ABOUT MICHELOZZO DI BARTOLOMEO

CAPLOW, HARRIET McNEAL: *Michelozzo*. New York and London, 1977.

GORI-MONTANELLI, LORENZO: *Brunelleschi e Michelozzo*. Florence, 1957.

HYMAN, ISABELLE: *Fifteenth Century Florentine Studies: The Palazzo Medici and a Ledger for the Church of San Lorenzo*. New York, 1977.

LIGHTBOWN, R. W.: *Donatello and Michelozzo: An Artistic Partnership*. London, 1980.

MORISANI, OTTAVIO: *Michelozzo architetto*. Turin, 1951.

VASARI, GIORGIO: *Le opere di Giòrgio Vasari, con nuove annotasioni e commenti*. 9 vols. Florence (1568), 1973.

Michelozzo di Bartolomeo: Palazzo Vecchio, Florence, Italy, ca. 1444ff.

ARTICLES ABOUT MICHELOZZO DI BARTOLOMEO

CAPLOW, HARRIET McNEAL: "Michelozzo at Ragusa: New Documents and Revaluations." *Journal of the Society of Architectural Historians* 31, No. 2 (1972): 108-119.

FABRICZY, CORNELIUS VON: "Michelozzo di Bartolomeo." *Jahrbuch der Königlich Preussischen Kunstsammlungen* 25 (1904): 34-110.

GOMBRICH, E. H.: "The Early Medici as Patrons of Art." In *Italian Renaissance Studies: A Tribute to the Late Cecilia M. Ady.* London, 1960.

HEYDENREICH, L. H.: "Die Tribuna der SS. Annunziata in Florenz." *Mitteilungen des Kunsthistorischen Institutes* 3 (1931): 268-285.

HEYDENREICH, L. H.: "Gedanken über Michelozzo di Bartolomeo." In *Festschrift Wilhelm Pinder.* Leipzig, 1938.

LOTZ, WOLFGANG: "Michelozzos Umbau der SS. Annunziata in Florenz." *Mitteilungen des Kunsthistorischen Instituts in Florenz* 5 (1940): 402-422.

MARCHINI, G.: "Aggiunto a Michelozzo." *Rinascita* 7 (1944): 24-51.

SAALMAN, HOWARD: "Michelozzo Studies." *The Burlington Magazine* CVIII (1966): 242-50.

SAALMAN, HOWARD: "Tommaso Spinelli, Michelozzo, Manetti, and Rossellino." *Journal of the Society of Architectural Historians* XXV (1966): 151-160.

SAALMAN, HOWARD: "Michelozzo Studies: The Florentine Mint." In *Zeitschrift Ulrich Middeldorf.* Berlin, 1968.

SAALMAN, HOWARD: "The Palazzo Comunale in Montepulciano." *Zeitschrift für Kunstgeschichte* 28 (1965): 1-46.

In the first half of the 15th century, the economy of the Florentine Republic expanded in an unprecedented manner. The Portinari family—which owned the Medici bank headquartered in Milan—were patrons of Florentine art and culture, and contributed greatly to the dissemination of Florentine culture. The enlightened politics of Cosimo de'Medici strongly encouraged cultural exchange and consolidated relations with the more powerful countries of the time. As a result, Florentine culture spread far and wide, penetrating even the Venetian sphere.

In the early 15th century, Florence became an inexhaustible fount of artistic genius. Florentine artists of that period were particularly noted for their ability to define an independent role, and to determine the course of action necessary for artistic success in that role. Michelozzo di Bartolomeo Michelozzi stood out among his fellow artists as a skilled artisan, particularly in demand for his skill in working marble and casting bronze. His talent for work on the grand scale, most suitable for architectural work, was apparent early in his career.

Michelozzo also enjoyed the good fortune of being preferred over Filippo Brunelleschi by Cosimo the Elder for the design of the Palazzo Medici. Brunelleschi had produced an initial cube-shaped design for the palace to be positioned in front of the Church of San Lorenzo, a design rejected by Cosimo. According to Giorgio Vasari, Brunelleschi created a kind of architecture "too sumptuous and magnificent, which bore him envy among the citizens." (Brunelleschi's resentment at Cosimo's decision prompted him later to build a palace for Luca Pitti—Cosimo's adversary—on the Boboli Hill, though on a grander scale than the Medici property could accommodate.) Michelozzo created a masterful interpretation of the geometric principles of the new architecture, producing an alternative vision of the perspective plan devised by Brunelleschi.

Originally, the corner created by the intersection of the two vertical planes of the facades of the Palazzo Medici was reinforced by the void of the loggia at ground level. Meanwhile, the rhythm of the mullioned windows, each with two lights, is intensified by the acceleration of the perspective lines toward the vanishing point. That horizontal dynamic is set against the movement of the fascias. The lower rustication diminishes by gradation up to the smooth top floor, which is surmounted by projecting cornices supported by sturdy corbels. The interior courtyard has an open gallery far from Brunelleschi's clear linearity. Its chiaroscuro tonality is evocative of the Middle Ages. While Brunelleschi observed the past in order to project his work into the future, Michelozzo's designs celebrated the past, particularly the epoch of Arnolfo di Cambio (ca. 1245-ca. 1310). Nevertheless, Michelozzo's pictorial sense, supported by the lyricism of the archaeological remains embedded in the courtyard walls, created an environment in which Renaissance culture could flourish.

His friendship and admiration for Cosimo motivated Michelozzo to follow him during his exile to Venice. During that period Michelozzo had the opportunity to work on both new constructions and reconstructions. He demonstrated a particular talent for altering existing buildings to suit the needs and taste of his own time. He revised the designs for the Palazzo dei Rettori in Ragusa. For the design of the Palazzo Comunale facade at Montepulciano, he took evident clues from the larger works of Arnolfo di Cambio in Florence, applying these on a reduced scale. The facade seems a little squat, since certain minimal technical and functional requirements had to be met in spite of the scale reductions. The facade, fusing Florentine and Roman Renaissance elements, achieves a harmonious and homogeneous symbiosis with the main square, which it faces. The facade of the Church of San Agostino in Siena, on the other hand, vaguely recalls Brunelleschian motifs in the lower part flowing up to the sculptural splendors of the niches and the tympanum.

Michelozzo's talent was fully expressed in his design for the Portinari Chapel at the Sant'Eustorgio complex in Milan. The chapel is a masterpiece, harmonizing all the different forces of the Florentine Renaissance. Again a Brunelleschian influence is perceptible, in the rhythm of the Sacristy of San Lorenzo in Florence. The diminishing arches produce a nearly telescopic effect, which directs the gaze to the ark. A similar technique was adopted for the tabernacle Michelozzo placed in the Crucifix Chapel at the Church of San Miniato al Monte, that Florentine masterpiece of Romanesque art. The tabernacle has a solemnity that echoes the work of Leon Battista Alberti.

One of Michelozzo's most rewarding commissions was the reconstruction of the courtyard and the creation of new rooms at the Palazzo Vecchio in Florence. The palace had been enlarged, and therefore made heavier, since its original construction. It was decided to re-lay the foundations for Arnolfo di Cambio's seriously damaged columns, and to substitute them with more massive ones. The upper part of the building was lightened in a way similar to the Palazzo Medici courtyard. Functionally diverse new rooms were added at the top, which were connected with steps and grand staircases. Michelozzo also strengthened the tower, which had cracked as a result of the weight deflected on the corbels. Michelozzo's alterations to the Palazzo Vecchio, enhancing its splendor, also made it appear more like a fortress than a palace.

Michelozzo also expanded the San Marco convent, located in an area of Florence undergoing rapid expansion. Building a complex of the highest order around the old cloister, he substantially enriched the cityscape. With its lowered arches and the upper dormitories lit by tiny windows, the structure exudes a medieval atmosphere of prayer and meditation. The library, standing out from the rest of the building, is dominated by slender columns, which divide the space into three naves. The central nave is covered with a barrel vault, the lateral ones with cross vaults. The movement in the perspective, generated by the columns and the gentle curves of the arches, imparts a vibrant dynamic to the extraordinary transparency of the space. It is that kind of architecture that produced painters like Fra Angelico: the splendid transparency and the attenuated, luminous colors of the scenery in his paintings seem directly influenced by it.

Benefiting from his connection to the Medicis, Michelozzo designed a number of splendid villas around Florence for wealthy Florentines. Particularly noteworthy was the Villa Medici in Fiesole, which was, unfortunately, later altered. Its neo-medieval tendencies, particularly evident in the use of a corner tower, also characterize the Villa Careggi, which stands out for its crenelated roof resting on the close-set corbels without a break in continuity. The spirit of the Villa Careggi—favorite residence of Lorenzo the Magnificent, who entertained Marsilio Ficino's "Platonic Academy" there—reflects the nearness of the city, in its lesser elevation and in the frequency of the window openings. The Castle of Cafaggiolo, on the other hand, was a symbol of Medici power with its more pronounced brackets, its elongated corbels and its door set in the tower. The tower itself was an innovation, projecting from the facade, which it divides into two. That design endowed the essentially medieval scheme with a new kind of movement. It became an imposing new element of representation, which added to the building's significance.

—GIULIANO CHELAZZI
Translated from the Italian by Terri L. Stough

MIES VAN DER ROHE, Ludwig.

American. Born in Aachen, Germany, 27 March 1886. Died in Chicago, Illinois, 17 August 1969. Immigrated to the United States, 1938; naturalized, 1944. Studied at the Domschule, Aachen, 1897-1900; Aachen Trade School, 1900-02. Apprentice to Bruno Paul, Berlin, Germany, 1905-07; joined Peter Behrens office, 1908-11; in private practice, Berlin, 1911-14; served in the German Army, 1914-18; returned to private practice, Berlin, 1919-37; in private practice, Chicago, 1938-69. Founded Der Ring, Ber lin, 1925; vice-president, Werkbund, 1926; director, Bauhaus, Dessau and Berlin, 1930-33; director of architecture, Illinois Institute of Technology, Chicago, 1938-59.

Chronology of Works
† *Work no longer exists*

1907	Riehl House, Neubabelsberg, Berlin, Germany
1911	Perls House (later Fuchs House), Zehlendorf, Berlin, Germany
1913	House, Heerstrasse, Berlin, Germany
1914	Mies van der Rohe House, Werder, Germany
1914	Urbig House, Neubabelsberg, Berlin, Germany
1919-21	Kempner House, Berlin, Germany
1924	Mosler House, Neubabelsberg, Berlin, Germany
1925	Municipal Housing Development, Afrikanischestrasse, Berlin, Germany
1925-26	Wolf House, Guben, Germany

Ludwig Mies van der Rohe: Crown Hall, Illinois Institute of Technology, Chicago, Illinois, 1950-56

1926	Monument to Karl Liebknecht and Rosa Luxemburg, Berlin, Germany†
1927	Apartment House, Werkbund Exposition, Stuttgart, Germany
1927	Weissenhofsiedlung, Stuttgart, Germany
1927	Silk Exhibit, Exposition de la Mode, Berlin, Germany (with L. Reich)
1928	Fuchs House, Zehlendorf, Berlin, Germany (addition)
1928	Esters House, Krefeld, Germany
1928	Lange House, Krefeld, Germany
1928-30	Tugendhat House, Brno, Czechoslovakia
1929	German Pavilion and Industrial Exhibits, International Exhibition, Barcelona, Spain†
1931	Model House and Apartment, Berlin Building Exposition, Germany†
	Illinois Institute of Technology, Chicago, Illinois, U. S. A.:
1939-41	Master Plan
1942-43	Metals Research Building (with Holabird and Root)
1944-46	Engineering Research Building (with Holabird and Root)
1945-46	Alumni Memorial Hall (with Holabird and Root)
1945-46	Chemistry Building
1945-46	Metallurgical and Chemical Engineering Building (with Holabird and Root)
1945-50	Boiler Plant
1950-56	Crown Hall (with others)
1945-51	Farnsworth House, Plano, Illinois, U. S. A.
1946-49	Promontory Apartments, Chicago, Illinois, U. S. A. (with others)

1948-51	860 and 880 Lake Shore Drive Apartments, Chicago, Illinois, U. S. A. (with others)
1953-56	Commonwealth Promenade Apartments, Chicago, Illinois, U. S. A. (with others)
1954-58	Cullinan Hall, Museum of Fine Arts, Houston, Texas, U. S. A. (with others)
1954-58	Seagram Building, New York City, U. S. A. (with others)
1955-56	Lafayette Park Housing Development, Detroit, Michigan, U. S. A.
1957-61	Bacardi Office Building, Mexico City, Mexico, U. S. A.
1959-73	Federal Center, Chicago, Illinois, U. S. A. (with others)
1960-63	American Federal Savings and Loan Association, Des Moines, Iowa, U. S. A. (with others)
1962-68	New National Gallery, Berlin, Germany
1963-69	Toronto-Dominion Centre, Toronto, Ontario, Canada (with others)

Publications

BOOKS BY MIES VAN DER ROHE

Bürohaus. Berlin, 1923; revised as *Der moderne Zweckbau,* Munich, 1926.
Industrielles Bauen. Berlin, 1924.

ARTICLES BY MIES VAN DER ROHE

"Frank Lloyd Wright: An Appreciation." *College Art Journal* (Autumn 1946).
"Mies Speaks." *Architectural Review* (December 1968): 451-452.
"Arbeitsthesen," "Die neue Zeit," "Technik und Architektur" and "Über die Form in der Architektur." In ULRICH CONRADS (ed.): *Programmes and Manifestoes on 20th Century Architecture*. London and Cambridge, Massachusetts, 1970.

BOOKS ABOUT MIES VAN DER ROHE

BILL, MAX: *Ludwig Mies van der Rohe*. Milan, 1955.
BLAKE, PETER: *The Master Builders: Le Corbusier, Mies van der Rohe, Frank Lloyd Wright*. New York and London, 1960.
BLAKE, PETER: *Mies van der Rohe: Architecture and Structure*. New York, 1960.
BLASER, WERNER: *After Mies: Mies van der Rohe—Teaching and Principles*. New York, 1977.
BLASER, WERNER: *Mies van der Rohe: The Art of Structure*. New York, 1965.
BONTA, J. P.: *Mies van der Rohe: Barcelona 1929—An Anatomy of Architectural Interpretation*. Barcelona, 1975.
CARTER, PETER: *Mies van der Rohe at Work*. London and New York, 1974.
DREXLER, ARTHUR (ed.): *The Mies van der Rohe Archive Part I: 1907-1938. An Illustrated Catalogue of the Mies van der Rohe Drawings in the Museum of Modern Art*. New York, 1990.
DREXLER, ARTHUR: *Ludwig Mies van der Rohe*. New York and London, 1960.
FRAMPTON, KENNETH, and FUTAGAWA, YUKIO: *Modern Architecture: 1920-1945*. New York, 1983.
GLAESER, LUDWIG: *Ludwig Mies van der Rohe: Drawings in the Collection of the Museum of Modern Art*. New York, 1969.
GLAESER, LUDWIG: *Ludwig Mies van der Rohe: Furniture and Furniture Drawings*. New York, 1977.
HARRINGTON, KENNETH: *Mies van der Rohe, Architect as Educator*. Exhibition catalog. Chicago, 1986.
HILBERSEIMER, LUDWIG: *Contemporary Architecture: Its Roots and Trends*. Chicago, 1964.
HILBERSEIMER, LUDWIG: *Ludwig Mies van der Rohe*. Chicago, 1956.
HOAG, EDWIN and JOY: *Masters of Modern Architecture: Frank Lloyd Wright, Le Corbusier, Mies Van Der Rohe, and Walter Gropius*. Indianapolis, Indiana, 1977.
HOCHMAN, ELAINE S.: *Architects of Fortune: Mies van der Rohe and the Third Reich*. New York, 1988.
JOHNSON, PHILIP: *Mies van der Rohe*. New York, 1947; 3rd ed., New York, 1978.
NEUMEYER, FRITZ: *The Artless Word: Mies van der Rohe on the Building Art*. Cambridge, Massachusetts, 1991.
PAPI, LORENZO: *Ludwig Mies van der Rohe*. Florence, 1975.
PAWLEY, MARTIN: *Mies van der Rohe*. London 1970.
SCHULZE, FRANZ (ed.): *Mies van der Rohe: Critical Essays*. Cambridge, Massachusetts, 1990.
SCHULZE, FRANZ (ed.): *The Mies van der Rohe Archive; Part II: The American Years 1938-1969. An Illustrated Catalogue of the Mies van der Rohe Drawings in the Museum of Modern Art*. New York, 1990.
SCHULZE, FRANZ: *Mies van Der Rohe: A Critical Biography*. Chicago and London, 1985.
SCHULZE, FRANZ: *Mies van der Rohe: Interior Spaces*. Exhibition catalog. Chicago, 1982.

SMITHSON, ALISON and PETER: *Mies van der Rohe: Veröffentlichungen zur Architektur*. Berlin, 1968.
SMITHSON, ALISON and PETER: *Without Rhetoric*. London, 1973.
SPAETH, DAVID: *Ludwig Mies Van Der Rohe: An Annotated Bibliography and Chronology*. New York, 1979.
SPAETH, DAVID: *Mies van der Rohe*. New York and London, 1985.
SPEYER, JAMES and KOEPER, FREDERICK: *Mies van der Rohe*. Exhibition catalog. Chicago 1968.
SWENSON, A. and CHENG, P.: *Architectural Education at IIT 1938-1978*. 1980.
TEGETHOFF, WOLF: *Mies van der Rohe: The Villas and Country Houses*. Cambridge, Massachusetts, 1985.
ZUKOWSKY, JOHN (ed.): *Mies Reconsidered: His Career, Legacy and Disciples*. Exhibition catalog. Chicago, 1986.

ARTICLES ABOUT MIES VAN DER ROHE

BLAKE, PETER: "Ludwig Mies Van Der Rohe." *Architectural Forum* 87 (November 1947).
CADBURY-BROWN, H. T. (ed.): "Ludwig Mies van der Rohe." *Architectural Association Journal*, special issue (July/August 1959).
CARTER, PETER (ed.): "Mies van der Rohe." *Architectural Design*, special issue (March 1961).
DREXLER, ARTHUR: "Seagram Building." *Architectural Record* (July 1958).
GROPIUS, WALTER: "Ludwig Mies van der Rohe." *Bauen und Wohnen* (May 1966).
HONEY, S.: "Mies at the Bauhaus." *Architectural Association Quarterly* 10, No. 1 (1978): 51-59.
JOHNSON, PHILIP: "Schinkel and Mies." In ROBERT A. M. STERN (ed.): *Writings/Philip Johnson*. New York, 1979.
LOHAN, DIRK: "Mies van der Rohe: Farnsworth House, Plano, Illinois, 1945-50." *Global Architecture Detail*, No. 1 (1976).
MELISI, PAOLO: "Mies, or Architecture in Enchained Liberty." *Domus* (November 1982).
MONEO, RAFAEL: "Un Mies menos conocido." *Arquitecturas bis* 44 (July 1983): 2-5.
MUMFORD, LEWIS: "The Lesson of the Master." *New Yorker* (13 September 1958).
NORBERG-SCHULZ, CHRISTIAN: "Interview with Mies van der Rohe." *Architecture d'aujourd'hui* (September 1958).
SERENYI, PETER: "Mies' New National Gallery." *Harvard Architecture Review* (Spring 1980).
STERN, ROBERT A. M.: "Mies and the Closing of the Bauhaus." *Nation* (22 September 1969).
VON BEULWITZ, D.: "The Perls House by Mies van der Rohe." *Architectural Design* (November-December 1983): 63-71.
WESTHEIM, P.: "Mies van der Rohe: Entwicklung eines Architekten." *Kunstblatt* 2 (February 1927): 55-62.
WESTHEIM, P.: "Das Wettbewerb der Reichsbank." *Deutsche Bauzeitung* (1933).
WINTER, JOHN: "The Measure of Mies." *Architectural Review* (February 1972): 95-105.
ZERVOS, C.: "Mies van der Rohe." *Cahiers d'art*, 3 (1928): 35-38.

*

By consensus one of the several greatest architects of the 20th century, Ludwig Mies van der Rohe enjoyed two careers, each of roughly 30 years, in Germany and America respectively. He exerted a powerful impact on the building art of both cultures,

Ludwig Mies van der Rohe: Farnsworth House, Plano, Illinois, 1945-51

and in his later years, the 1950s and much of the 1960s, he was arguably the most influential architect in the world.

Mies' spare, understated manner of design, by which he reduced structure and space to geometric abstraction, then submitted the results to meticulously proportioned refinements, qualified him in some respects as the quintessentially symbolic figure of the Modernist Movement. Normally square-cut, clearly articulated and scrupulously free of all historicizing ornament, the buildings of his mature years were conceived more often than not as pure formal objects, maximally generalized in function and independent of context. Such attributes are consistent with much of the modernist aesthetic, especially as it came to be understood in the United States following World War II. Thus Mies became the most visible and most obvious target of the postmodernist rebellion of the later 1960s that not only revived interest in historicist form but elevated concern for context to a major architectural virtue.

Ironically, he was not admired universally by the modernists of the 1920s in Europe, where a widespread belief in functionalism and in the related social obligations of the building art led to criticism of him for his very personal devotion to formal elegance, precision of detailing and expensive materials. Certainly these last qualities were central to the best of his European built efforts, e.g., the German Pavilion at the Barcelona International Exposition of 1929 and the Tugendhat House, completed a year later. His American masterpieces, the Farnsworth House (1951), Crown Hall (1956) and the Seagram Building (1958), depend more than any of the European works on the steel more readily available to him in an American environment, but their excellence derives no less from a richness of effect combined with a temper of patrician restraint.

Mies was born in 1886 in Aachen, at a time when German architecture as a whole was guided by a taste for ostentation. Thus, coming of age in the first decade of the 20th century, he formed his consciousness of the art just when a counterspirit of sobriety began to inform it. Moving to Berlin in 1905, he worked briefly for the designer-draftsman-architect Bruno Paul, whose influence may be discerned in the directness and simplicity of Mies' first independent design, the Riehl House (1907). From 1908 to 1912 Mies was in the atelier of Peter Behrens, whose commercial work had established him as the leading progressive architect in Germany, but whose residential designs betrayed a profound respect for the neoclassical master Karl Friedrich Schinkel. It was the latter aspect of Behrens that moved Mies, most obviously in the major project of his early years, the Kroeller-Mueller residence (1912). Meant to accommodate both the owners and their art collection, the house bowed not only to Schinkel but, in its interlocking massing, to Frank Lloyd Wright, whose work Mies knew from its 1910-11 publication in Berlin.

Since the Kroeller-Mueller House was never built, moreover since Mies served with the German army in World War I until 1918, he was little known at the outset of the 1920s. He adapted readily enough, however, to the modernist thought that swept postwar Berlin, and between 1921 and 1924 he designed five projects whose audacity of concept and mastery of form stamped him as one of the more promising members of the younger German generation. The first of these works was a pair of radical high-rise buildings, one (1921) roughly triangular in plan, the other (1922) more nearly amoeboid, but both undifferentiated in the richly reflective glass surfaces of their elevations. The hint of expressionism apparent in them was replaced in his third project by a mood closer to *die neue Sachlichkeit.* His 1922-23 design for an office building in reinforced concrete featured cantilevered slabs closed by parapets in an alternating rhythm with ribbon windows, the latter device in one of its earliest uses. The last of the five projects were residences. The pinwheel-shaped plan of the 1923 Concrete Country House, which reflected antecedents in Russian constructivism, reached out eagerly to its surrounding spaces, assuming a form quite unlike the more compacted *prisme pur* associated with most modernist houses of the time. The Brick Country House of 1924 was notable especially for the use of interior walls as space-defining rather than space-enclosing elements. There is a suggestion of influences from the painters of the De Stijl movement and again from Wright, but Mies' plan was more fluid in its openness and more centrifugal in its movement than anything the American master had done in his Prairie years.

Not until 1926, with the Wolf House, did Mies see any of his stylistically advanced designs built. By then he owed his growing reputation not only to the products of his drawing board but to his activities as a propagandist for the modernist cause. Between 1923 and 1925 he was chairman of the Novembergruppe, named after the month of the 1918 liberal revolution in Germany. He was also one of the founders, in 1923, of the avant-garde journal *G* and, in 1924, of Der Ring, a group of reform-minded German architects. The attention of the international architectural community was drawn to him when, at the invitation of the Deutscher Werkbund, he supervised the organization and construction of the Weissenhofsiedlung, a housing colony in the modernist style that opened in Stuttgart in 1927. The visible unity of the buildings there, together with the reputations of such participating designers as Le Corbusier, Walter Gropius, J. J. P. Oud, Behrens and Mies himself, seemed to many observers to signal ''the triumph of the new architecture,'' as one critic, Walter Curt Behrendt, called it.

Toward the end of the 1920s Mies was notably less involved with architectural politics, concentrating instead on his own work and producing, most notably, the Barcelona Pavilion and the Tugendhat House. Both works relied for support on a columnar grid that largely freed the interior walls of that function, thus introducing a dynamic flow of space, as proposed earlier in the Brick Country House. A lavish use of glass walls at Barcelona and large glass windows in the Tugendhat House amplified the interplay of interior and exterior space. In several other plans for houses (e.g., the Berlin Building Exposition House and the Gericke House project, both of 1931) he continued to explore the possibilities of the open plan.

Some changes in his work after 1933 tempt speculation of a causal connection with the Nazi accession in Germany in that year. The project for the Reichsbank, while modernist in elevation, was huge in scale and symmetrical in plan, suggesting not only a return to the classicizing tendencies of Mies' pre-World War I work, but a possible partial accommodation to the Nazi taste for monumentality. At the same time, in a group of courthouse projects he persisted with his open, asymmetrical plans, but enclosed the houses in walled courts, as if to sequester them from the outer world.

By then, 1934, he had watched in frustration as the Bauhaus, which he had served as director since 1930, gradually collapsed under pressure of right-wing elements in Germany. Previously supported by the city of Dessau, where it had been located since 1925, the school was closed in 1932 when the municipal council surrendered to the demands of its radical rightist faction. Mies thereupon reopened the Bauhaus as a private institution in Berlin, but in the summer of 1933, following another forced shutdown, this time by the Nazis, the faculty voted to disband for good.

Mies' personal professional fortunes languished for several more years in the antimodernist atmosphere of Hitler Germany. In 1938, however, he accepted the offer to head the architectural school of the Armour Institute of Technology (later Illinois Institute of Technology) in Chicago, and his American career was launched. During World War II he taught more than he designed, but after 1945 much of his 1939-40 plan for the campus of IIT—the first wholly modern campus design in America—was realized.

The two principal building forms that most occupied him in the remaining two decades of his active life were the high-rise building and the clear-span pavilion. While both were distinguished by the same exacting expression characteristic of his European work, they tended toward a compactness of mass and a symmetry of plan that marked the American Mies as a designer closer to the classicist tradition than he had been in the 1920s. His first major tall buildings were the twin apartment towers at 860-880 Lake Shore Drive in Chicago, in which the steel frame with floor-to-ceiling glass infill demonstrated the identification of structure and expression with near-maximal clarity. The 860-880 towers are standardly regarded as the work that most influenced the rectilinear silhouettes of America urban skylines during the 1950s and 1960s. It is also widely agreed that his Seagram Building of 1958 was the greatest built example in his own corpus of the tall glazed prism, a building, moreover, whose vast forecourt likewise inspired the widespread use of the plaza in city architecture during the third quarter of the century.

Mies claimed that his clear-span pavilions fulfilled his belief that a unitary space made function flexible, since function would thus be unimpeded by any permanently fixed interior parts. Since he was drawn as much to abstracted space as to abstracted structure, this view may have been a rationalization as much as a rationale. In several of his most impressive pavilions, Crown Hall at IIT, the Convention Hall project of 1953, and even the jewel-like Farnsworth House, the openness of the spaces works to the disadvantage of multiple simultaneous functions. (Alternatively, in his great project for the Mannheim National Theater of 1953, the interior is taken up by two theaters and their auxiliary spaces fixed and relatively inflexible; the building envelope is less an arena than a shelter.)

These criticisms of Mies are overshadowed by another, pertinent to his high-rise buildings: the very authority of his reductivist solutions resulted in a sameness of appearance, if not to say style, in his later examples of the form. Worse still, the criticism goes, the army of architects who followed his lead and the corporate clients who profited economically from the simplifications of his design approach only contributed further to a monotony in the American urban landscape.

In a sense, then, Mies was fortunate to depart the scene just as the postmodernist countermovement began to assert itself. The ''PoMo'' revolution, however, has developed its own set of clichés in the meantime, and as the century draws to a close, Mies' own reputation has begun to rise again. The difference between him and his epigones is now clearer than ever. In his best works a singular artistic sensibility was at work; the Modern Movement can claim no finer monuments to itself and none more certain to secure a lasting place in history.

—FRANZ SCHULZE

MILLS, Robert.

American. Born in Charleston, South Carolina, 12 August 1781. Died on 3 March 1855. Studied at the College of Charleston; studied architecture under James Hoban, Washington, D.C.,

Robert Mills: County Record Building (Fireproof Building), Charleston, South Carolina, 1821-27

1799; taken into Thomas Jefferson's home, Monticello, as architectural student; returned to Washington, D.C., 1803, to study under Benjamin Latrobe; established own office, Philadelphia, 1808.

Chronology of Works
All in the United States
* Approximate dates
† Work no longer exists

1804-06	Circular Church, Charleston, South Carolina†
1807-12	First Presbyterian Church, Augusta, Georgia
1808-10	Prison, Mount Holly, New Jersey, (now Burlington County Prison Museum)
1809-10	Franklin Row, Philadelphia, Pennsylvania†
1809-12	State House, Philadelphia, Pennsylvania (wings)†
1809-16	Washington Hall, Philadelphia, Pennsylvania†
1811-12	Sansom Street Baptist Church, Philadelphia, Pennsylvania†
1812-13	Octagon Unitarian Church, Philadelphia, Pennsylvania†

1812-17	Monumental Church, Richmond, Virginia
1813-14	Upper Ferry Bridge, Philadelphia, Pennsylvania (cover)†
1814-42	Washington Monument, Baltimore, Maryland
1816*-18	Brokenbrough House, Richmond, Virginia
1816-18	First Baptist Church, Baltimore, Maryland†
1816-19	Waterloo Row, Baltimore, Maryland†
1817-22	First Baptist Church, Charleston, South Carolina
1818*-20	Potts House, Frederick, Maryland
1821-22	Hoffman House, Baltimore, Maryland†
1821-23	Bethesda Presbyterian Church, Camden, South Carolina
1821-23	Jail, Lancaster, South Carolina
1821-23	Jail, Union, South Carolina
1821-25	Courthouse, Winnsboro, South Carolina
1821-26	Powder Magazine, Charleston, South Carolina†
1821-27	County Record Building (Fireproof Building), Charleston, South Carolina
1822-24	Courthouse, Georgetown, South Carolina
1822-24	Jail wing, Charleston, South Carolina†
1822-25	Courthouse, Kingstree, South Carolina

1823-25	Second Ainsley Hall House, Columbia, South Carolina
1823-25	Courthouse, Conway, South Carolina
1824-27	De Kalb Monument, Camden, South Carolina
1825-30	Courthouse, Camden, South Carolina
1831-34	Marine Hospital, Charleston, South Carolina
1833-55	Washington National Monument, Washington, D.C. (not completed until 1884)
1836-40	Patent Office Building, Washington, D.C.
1836-42	Treasury Building, Washington, D.C.
1838-39	Courthouse, Alexandria, Virginia†
1838-40	South Carolina Library, Columbia, South Carolina
1839-41	Jail, Washington, D.C.†
1839-42	Post Office Building, Washington, D.C.

Publications

BOOKS BY MILLS

A Model Jail of the Olden Time: Designs for 'A Debtors Gaol and Work-House for Felons,' for Burlington County, State of New Jersey. New York, 1928.
Some Letters of Robert Mills, Engineer and Architect. Columbia, South Carolina, 1938.

BOOKS ABOUT MILLS

BROWN, GLENN: *History of the United States Capitol*. 2 vols. Washington, D.C., 1900-03.
BRYAN, JOHN MORRILL: *Robert Mills, Architect, 1781-1855*. Columbia, South Carolina, 1976.
ELDER, WILLIAM VOSS: *Robert Mills' Waterloo Row, Baltimore 1816*. Baltimore, Maryland, 1971.
GALLAGHER, HELEN PIERCE: *Robert Mills, Architect of the Washington Monument, 1781-1855*. New York, 1935.
HAMLIN, TALBOT: *Greek Revival Architecture in America*. New York, 1944.
RAVENEL, BEATRICE ST. JULIEN: *Architects of Charleston*. Charleston, South Carolina, 1945.
WADDELL, GENE, and LISCOMBE, R. WINDSOR: *Robert Mills's Courthouses and Jails*. Easley, South Carolina, 1982.

ARTICLES ABOUT MILLS

ALEXANDER, ROBERT L.: "Baltimore Row Houses of the Nineteenth Century." *American Studies* 16 (1975): 65-76.
AMES, KENNETH: "Robert Mills and the Philadelphia Story." *Journal of the Society of Architectural Historians* 27 (1968): 140-146.
BRYAN, JOHN MORRILL, and JOHNSON, JULIE M.: "Robert Mills' Sources for the South Carolina Lunatic Asylum, 1822." *Journal of the South Carolina Medical Association* 75, No. 6 (1979): 264-268.
CLARK, A. C.: "Robert Mills, Architect and Engineer." *Columbia Historical Society Records* 40-41 (1940): 1-32.
"Daily Journal of Robert Mills, Baltimore, 1816." *Maryland Historical Magazine* 30 (1935): 257-271.
GALLAGHER, HELEN PIERCE: "Robert Mills, America's Finest Native Architect." *Architectural Record* 65-66 (April, May and July 1929): 387-393; 478-484; 67-72.
HALL, LOUISE: "Mills, Strickland and Walter: Their Adventures in a World of Science." *Magazine of Art* 40:226-271 (November 1947).
HOYT, WILLIAM D.: "Robert Mills and the Washington Monument in Baltimore." *Maryland Historical Magazine* 34-35 (1939-40): 144-160; 178-189.

"The Journal of Robert Mills, 1828-1830." *South Carolina Historical and Genealogical Magazine* 52:133-139, 218-224; 53:31-36, 90-100 (1951-52).
"Letters from Robert Mills." *South Carolina Historical and Genealogical Magazine* 39 (1938): 110-124.
MASSEY, JAMES C.: "Robert Mills Documents, 1823: A House for Ainsley Hall in Columbia, S. C." *Journal of the Society of Architectural Historians* 28 (1963): 228-232.
MILLER, J. JEFFERSON: "The Designs for the Washington Monument in Baltimore." *Journal of the Society of Architectural Historians* 23 (March 1964): 19-28.
NEWCOMB, REXFORD G.: "Robert Mills, American Greek Revivalist." *Architect* 9 (March 1928): 697-699.
PIERSON, WILLIAM H., JR.: "American Neoclassicism, The Rational Phase: Benjamin Latrobe and Robert Mills." In *American Buildings and Their Architects: The Colonial and Neo-Classical Styles*. Garden City, New York, 1970.
WADDELL, GENE: "Robert Mills' Fireproof Building." *South Carolina Historical Magazine* 80 (1979): 105-135.
WASHBURN, W. E.: "Temple of the Arts; National Collection of Fine Arts and National Portrait Gallery." *American Institute of Architects Journal* 51 (1969): 54-61.
WILLIAMS, GEORGE W.: "Robert Mills' *Contemplated Addition to St. Michael's Church*, and *Doctrine of Sound*." *Journal of the Society of Architectural Historians* 12, No. 1 (1953): 23-31.

*

Robert Mills' 55-year career spanned the half century during which architecture in America underwent its first crucial stage of professionalization. He was profoundly influenced by the two greatest architectural thinkers and practitioners of his day in America, Thomas Jefferson and Benjamin Henry Latrobe. Mills' father took him from South Carolina to Washington to apprentice with James Hoban, who had won the competition for the White House. There, Jefferson fostered the young Mills' development by giving him access to his architectural library and introducing him to Latrobe. Under the joint tutelage of Latrobe and Jefferson (informal on the latter's part), Mills learned that architectural design as a product of the mind was a more valuable accomplishment than involvement in the building trades, and that public architecture offered the widest opportunities. His period of training and apprenticeship under Latrobe was fairly short, beginning in 1803 and ending about 1808, when the two men began to compete for the same buildings.

Little remains of Mills' early row houses and churches in Philadelphia, Baltimore and Charleston. However, several important buildings that survive from his first decade as an architect exhibit all the major architectural concerns of his later career. In its plan, the Jail in Mount Holly, New Jersey (1808-10), demonstrates Jefferson and Latrobe's liberal social attitudes concerning a healthful and secure environment for the reformation of incarcerated humans. Mills' still-extant Lunatic Asylum in Columbia, South Carolina (1822), greatly expanded on this theme. Both were built to be fireproof, constructed with brick vaults, a technique Mills learned as Latrobe's apprentice, and which he later successfully applied to all of his monumental public buildings.

In 1812 Mills won the competition for Monumental Church, the memorial honoring Richmond's leading citizens who had died in a major theater fire. The church was octagonal in plan, as were his contemporaneous Sansom Street Baptist Church and First Unitarian Church in Philadelphia (both demolished). Mills designed large, open spaces to accommodate preachers and the large crowds they attracted, as one of his major interests was developing an architectural prototype that worked well acoustically. Although not all of his design was built, Monumental Church stands alone among Mills' designs in retaining much of his symbolic decoration. In his American order he introduced stars (for immortality) in a variant of the Ionic. He invented a second order on the interior, composed of an eclectic mixture of ancient funerary symbols. The church's open porch shelters the monumental urn under which the ashes of the dead are buried. Three sets of Doric columns derived from the Temple of Apollo at Delos are set *in antis* on the church's exposed sides, an order which Mills used repeatedly in his mature style.

Mills won his second major competition in 1814. The Baltimore Washington Monument as built differs considerably from the eclectic design that was selected, which had seven balconies (with medieval details) from which visitors could view the relief-sculpted surfaces of the column. Mills intended the monument to be a sculptural and architectural document recounting the major events of George Washington's civic and military career. He continued to view monuments in this didactic light into the 1850s with his design for the Virginia Washington Monument. The Baltimore Washington Monument was repeatedly simplified throughout its 30-year construction history, resulting in a Doric column with a cubic basic topped by a standing figure of Washington. At 170 feet it is the tallest commemorative column in the world, a fact noted at the time in European publications of it. Thirty years after Mills designed that monument, his proposal for the Washington National Monument was selected, partly because it would be the world's tallest structure.

Mills spent the decade of the 1820s in his native South Carolina, where he built several important buildings as part of a statewide public improvements program. These included numerous courthouses and jails (many of which are extant), which were designed according to a limited number of models. They represent a retrenchment, where Mills turned to strictly classical models after having some of his earlier innovative designs ridiculed. His two greatest works from that period, the Columbia Asylum (1822-27) and the Public Records Office ("Fireproof Building," 1824-26) in Charleston, demonstrated his personal interpretation of giant Palladian porticoes with doubled curved staircases attached to stark, solid, fireproof structures. Mills' finest work of domestic architecture, Ainsley Hall House (1823-25) in Columbia, is a spacious and innovative American interpretation of an English Regency plan with apsidal-ended parlors set back to back and entered from the garden through a great niched doorway.

In 1830 Mills settled in Washington, where he spent the last quarter century of his life. It was there that he built his greatest works and designed government buildings to be erected in many parts of the country. Four New England custom houses attest to the maturity of his style, where boldness of outline and detail accompanied solidity of construction. Granite walls and brick vaulted interiors formed an integral unity seemingly sculpted in place. Marine hospitals for Charleston, Key West and New Orleans, as well as a prototypical design used for hospitals along the inland waterways, represent a building type requiring repetitive series of rooms, an architectural solution Mills applied to his contemporaneous office buildings.

In 1836 Mills secured two major government commissions, the design and construction of the Treasury Building, and the construction of the Patent Office Building, which closely followed his own design entry into the limited competition. Their scale, function and location within the federal city mandated their important architectural treatment. Both were vaulted structures following the plan found in embryo at Mills' Charleston Fireproof Building, with a central barrel-vaulted corridor flanked by groin-vaulted offices. The major architectural feature of the Treasury Building is its 466-foot Ionic colonnade along its street facade, a vastly expensive feature for which Mills sacrificed interior spaciousness. The Patent Office has a massive Doric portico which projects from a long rectangular building on the model of Leo von Klenze's Glyptothek in Munich (1816-31). The Patent Office building served as museum as well as office building, and its interior spatial arrangement was designed to serve both functions; half the main story and the entire top floor were open to their full widths through combinations of groin and barrel vaulting. In both buildings Mills used circular geometrical stairs copied from those erected by Latrobe at the Capitol, but he placed them more prominently and fully exploited their cantilevered and corbeled construction to achieve a sense of weightlessness. In 1839 construction of Mills' design for the General Post Office began. Much smaller than the two earlier buildings, it was modeled on the compact shape of a Renaissance palazzo, the first major building in America to adopt this new revival style. Its Corinthian pilasters were based on those of the Temple of Jupiter Stator, the first marble temple in Rome. The Post Office was the first marble building in Washington.

Mills was unsuccessful in getting major commissions during the next 15 years but his designs were nonetheless very influential on the buildings eventually erected, particularly the Smithsonian Institution Building (for which Mills was the associate architect) and for the extensions to the United States Capitol. In 1845 he secured his last major commission, the Washington National Monument. Its present form is a mere outline of what Mills intended. Designed in two parts, the 600-foot obelisk was to serve as a monument to George Washington, while the 250-foot-diameter colonnaded base was to honor all the heroes, civic and military, of the Revolutionary era. Thirty Doric columns represented the states in the union in 1845, and statues of the signers of the Declaration of Independence stood in niches behind them. History paintings and statues of the fathers of the Revolution were to ornament the interior. Due to political forces and a depleted treasury, construction was halted in 1854 and did not resume until 1876. When completed in 1884, the 555-foot obelisk was shorn of any ornament whatsoever, so Mills gained the reputation as an architect whose taste was for stark geometric forms.

In addition to his architectural career, Mills was an accomplished engineer, involved in canals, road surveys, railroad lines and numerous mechanical inventions. He was the only American architect of his generation to author several books, including the landmark *Atlas of South Carolina* (1822) and its companion volume, *The Statistics of South Carolina* (1826), in which one small part of his knowledge of the history, physical geography and natural resources of the country was displayed. Mills was not a brilliant designer like his mentor Latrobe, but he understood and responded to American architectural needs from the mundane (he designed privies for the Treasury Department) to the sublime. The common thread throughout his work was his desire to create uniquely American architectural forms, which, he told Jefferson, he hoped would not be considered inferior to European architecture. He left no specific written record of his design theory, but examination of his complete oeuvre suggests that its key was the eclectic mixture of architectural forms and motifs derived from a wide range of historical periods, making him an early practitioner of what was to become the leitmotif of American architecture.

—PAMELA SCOTT

MNESIKLES.

Greek. Active in Greece during the second half of the fifth century B. C.

Chronology of Works
All in Greece

437-431 B.C.	Propylaia, Athens
n.d.	Erechtheion, Athens [attributed]
n.d.	Stoa Basileios (Stoa of Zeus Eleutherios), Athens [attributed]

Publications

BOOKS ABOUT MNESIKLES

BUNDGAARD, J. A.: *Mnesicles.* Stuttgart, 1957.
DINSMOOR, W. B. JR: *The Propylaia to the Athenian Acropolis I: The Predecessors.* Princeton, New Jersey, 1980.

WAELE, JOS DE: *The Propylaia of the Akropolis in Athens: The Project of Mnesikles.* Amsterdam, 1990.

ARTICLES ABOUT MNESIKLES

DINSMOOR, W.B. JR: "Preliminary Planning for the Propylaia by Mnesikles." In *Le dessin d'architecture dans les sociétés antiques: Actes du colloque de Strasbourg 26-28 janvier 1984.* Leiden, 1985.
EITELJORG, H.: "New Finds Concerning the Entrance to the Athenian Acropolis." *Archaiologika Analekta ex Athenon* 8 (1975): 94-95.
EITELJORG, H.: "A Computer's-Eye View of the Acropolis Gateway." *Biblical Archaeology Review* 17 (July-August 1991): 62-63.
HELLSTRÖM, PONTUS: "The Planned Function of the Mnesiklean Propylaia." *Opuscula Atheniensia*, vol. 17 (1988): 107-21.

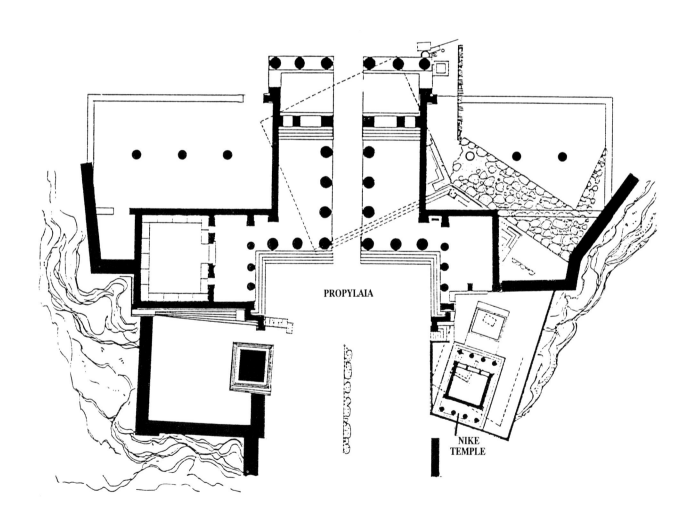

PROPYLAIA

NIKE
TEMPLE

Were it not for a brief mention in Plutarch (*Perikles* 13), who credits him with the Periklean Propylaia, Mnesikles' name would not have been preserved for posterity. He is mentioned in no other extant literary source, nor in any known inscription. Although two other buildings—the Erechtheion and the North-West Stoa of the Athenian Agora (i.e., the Stoa Basileios or Stoa of Zeus Eleutherios)—occasionally have been ascribed to him by modern scholars, his most certain work remains the Periklean Propylaia, undertaken as soon as the Parthenon was essentially complete in 437 B.C.

Gateways in Greek sanctuaries, which marked off the holy precinct within from the profane outside, had evolved during the course of the sixth century B.C. from simple openings in a temenos wall, to more elaborate structures with porticoes resembling pedimented temple fronts, and were thus themselves transformed into sacred architecture. When Mnesikles was called upon to provide a new gateway for the Athenian Acropolis, to match the grandeur of the newly finished Parthenon, he created a Propylaia of monumental size and complexity, reflective of the grandiose ambitions of Periklean Athens. Skillfully adapted to the rising and uneven terrain, through terracing and ingenious design, Mnesikles' Propylaia spans the western side of the Acropolis. In the center, dominating the design, large hexastyle porticoes front the long, wide entrance passage on east and west, their Doric columns echoing those of the Parthenon in proportion, spacing and profile, and like the columns of the Parthenon pronaos and opisthodomos they are set in a prostyle arrangement. A pair of low, horizontal wings flank the central passage on the west, and project forward, embracing the visitor, drawing him upward and inward. The intent is the same as the giant colonnades of St. Peter's Square built in Rome 2,000 years later by Giovanni Lorenzo Bernini, who likened his colonnades to "the outstretched arms of the Church welcoming the faithful." Although the wings, with their tristyle-in-antis porches, give the illusion of perfect symmetry, the south wing is, in truth, only a facade, its western anta transformed into a freestanding pillar, and its length sharply curtailed so that it would not encroach on the tiny precinct of Athena Nike. Mnesikles planned these wings as dining halls for the celebration of sacrificial feasts, hence the asymmetrical placement of the doorway in the North Wing, which, in the end, served this function alone. Here the walls above the dining couches were either hung with panel paintings or painted with frescoes (Pliny *N.H.* 35.101; Pausanias 1.22.6); consequently, this wing is often referred to as the "Pinakotheke."

The western aspect of the Propylaia is pulled together into one harmonious unit by a simple but ingenious device. All three porticoes, despite the glaring differences in column size, rest on a four-stepped --shaped krepidoma of white Pentelic marble, save the lowermost step beneath the wings, which is of blue Eleusinian limestone. When looking at the ensemble as a whole, or the central portico by itself, the eye sees a majestic four-stepped base, but when gazing upon one of the individual wings alone, the eye picks out only the three marble steps. Thus differences in scale are acknowledged within the established hierarchy of form without sacrificing the unity of the whole. In ancient times, a second pediment—which marked the gate wall and the transition to the eastern third of the porch—was visible behind and slightly higher than the first. To insure that this back pediment formed part of a harmonious interlocking design, Mnesikles raised the western roof slightly, by placing Ionic columns inside the western porch, and kept the eastern roof as low as possible by placing the eastern portico on a mere two-stepped krepidoma, and making its columns almost a foot shorter than those on the west. Since the western portico is seen from a foreshortened angle, the difference in size between the two porticoes is not readily apparent. As a result of these careful adjustments to the roof levels, the abrupt upward surge of the Acropolis rock is evident only at ground level, where the gate wall, pierced by five doorways, rests on a pair of five steep steps. A wide central ramp—built to accommodate the Panathenaic Procession and its attendant sacrificial animals—splits the krepidoma of the central passage in two, leaving an extra-wide central intercolumniation, with three metopes and two triglyphs in the frieze course above, instead of the usual two and one arrangement. Here Mnesikles used a double cantilever to relieve stress on the architrave below. And he concealed iron beams in the delicate Ionic architraves inside the porch, giving them the strength to support a splendid, coffered, marble ceiling, greatly admired in antiquity (Pausanias 1.22.4).

The eastern aspect of the Propylaia is unsatisfactory in its present state. Mnesikles had planned two halls flanking the central passage to serve as dining rooms for the consuming of the sacrificial meat at the Panathenaic festival; between them the eastern portico would have projected slightly forward in the center. These halls were never built, and to this day the marble courses on the eastern faces retain their lifting bosses and last layers of protective stone, which would have been carved smooth upon completion of the structure. Work stopped on the Propylaia in 431 B.C. at the outbreak of the Peloponnesian Wars, and was never resumed due to the objection that Mneskles' design would have necessitated demolition of more of the remaining Mycenaean fortification wall on the south, and also would have intruded on the precinct of Artemis Brauronia. Without its flanking halls, the central passage of the Propylaia projects too forcefully onto the Acropolis, making one keenly aware of its incomplete state.

We do not know for certain what other buildings Mnesikles may have designed or had a hand in designing. On the basis of his splendid Propylaia alone, he deserves a place in architectural history as one of the great, innovative architects of Classical Athens, whose gateway to the Athenian Acropolis was without parallel in ancient times.

—PATRICIA MARX

MONTUORI, Eugenio.

Italian. Born in Pesaro, Italy, 1907. Trained in Rome; degree in architecture, 1931. Assistant professor of city planning, Polytechnic Institute, Rome.

Chronology of Works
All in Italy

1931ff.	Sabaudia, near Rome
1934	Concourse, Venice
1936	Plans for Bolzano
1940	Plans for Carbonia
1947ff.	*Stazione Termini*, Rome

*

Eugenio Montuori is an Italian designer, one of the most experienced and successful architects to practice in Rome in the past 50 years. He is known most for his reconstruction of the railway station, the Stazione Termini.

Montuori was born in Pesaro and trained in Rome, and his first designs were for buildings at the University of Rome (1933) and for a project for the Palazzo Littorio (1934). But it was in

Eugenio Montuori: Stazione Termini, Rome, Italy, 1947ff.

1934 that Montuori, together with a group of other young architects who were all part of the rationalist architectural movement in the north of Italy associated with Giuseppe Terragni, won the competition for the design of Sabaudia, one of five new towns planned by the Fascist regime as part of the reclamation of the Pontine marshes south of Rome. The foundation stone for Sabaudia—the town's name was derived from the family name of the king of Italy, Savoia—was laid in 1931, and the town center was inaugurated by the king and queen of Italy the following year.

The project called for a municipality of 20,000 persons, 5,000 in the town center; the solution was for a plan around a group of grid-like streets, set in a concave, angled profile, with the public buildings in a square to the west. The program was well designed, but what contributed to the subsequent fame of the city, like that also of the contemporary train station in Florence by Giovanni Michelucci, was the particular style of the architecture: stark and clean, it stood out very clearly from the more traditional architecture to be seen elsewhere. This new architecture was based on a functionalism that—necessarily for the architects—Mussolini also supported as the proper style for the new Italy.

The public buildings at Sabaudia were completed first, to suggest an idea of Fascist efficiency, and that helped a certain organic growth in the city, rather than the pattern of separate zones so often seen in other new cities in Europe. Among the most notable buildings, all designed by the group of which Montuori was a member, is the Town Hall, emblazoned with a relief showing an image of "Marching Victory," and the 600-seat cinema, modeled on the section of a circle to maximize visibility within.

Montuori subsequently designed a number of other projects for the Fascist government, including the concourse for the railway station at Venice (1934), several other plans for cities, including Bolzano (1936) and Carbonia (1940), and buildings at the Piazza Imperiale in Rome. The fall of Mussolini in 1945 did little to limit Montuori's practice, and in 1947 he and a group of architects including Angelo Mazzoni and the engineer Leo Calini entered the competition for the remodeling of the main railway station in Rome. Various plans had been afoot since 1931 when Mussolini, feeling that the old station built in the 1870s was not appropriate as an entrance to his new, grand capital, announced a competition for a new complex. Building

was begun, but was stopped under the pressure of war; hence the 1947 competition, which required in its program the preservation of the old Agger Serviano at the western corner of the site, and a range of offices and facilities for employees of the railroad. Montuori's plan met these requirements.

The station itself comprises a building wrapped around some 22 tracks, the right-hand part being used for suburban services, the rest for express and mail trains. The central block of offices and services, marked by thin, horizontal windows that serve to emphasize the scale, and about five stories in height and 2,000 feet long, faces the Baths of Diocletian; below is a street of shops opening up at both ends to the avenues beyond. In front of this is the entrance, a glass and metal screen, protected by a floating cantilevered roof, welcoming the commuters.

After the station's completion in 1950, Montuori worked, most notably, with many of his old associates, on a plan for a block of offices on pilotis in the Via Po (1963). But it is on the design for the Stazione Termini that his fame will rest. Henry-Russell Hitchcock called the station "one of the largest and finest of the post-war buildings in Italy." For others, skeptical now of the stylistic implications of the design, the station is of a type, like the buildings of the Brazilian Oscar Niemeyer, that is difficult to accept, a vision of the future rapidly becoming what has been called "an anachronistic image of the past." History alone will tell.

—DAVID CAST

MOORE, Charles.

American. Born Charles W. Moore in Benton Harbor, Michigan, 31 October 1925. Studied at the University of Michigan, Ann Arbor, 1942-47, B.Arch.; Princeton University, New Jersey, 1954-57, M . F. A., Ph. D. Served in the U. S. Army Corps of Engineers, United States, Japan and Korea, 1952-54: lieutenant. Partner, Moore Lyndon Turnbull Whitaker, Berkeley, California, 1962-65, and MLTW/Moore Turnbull, Berkeley, 1965-69; principal, Charles W. Moore Associates, Essex, Connecticut, 1970-75; partner, Moore Grover Harper, Centerbrook, Connecticut, 1975-85; partner, Moore Ruble Yudell, Los Angeles, since 1976; principal, Charles W. Moore, Architect, Austin, Texas, since 1985. Has taught at numerous universities, including University of California, Berkeley, Yale University, University of California, Los Angeles, and, since 1984, University of Texas, Austin. Fellow, American Institute of Architects, 1968.

Chronology of Works
All in the United States unless noted

1957	Hubbard House I, Monterey, California
1959-60	Hubbard House II, Corral de Tierra, California
1961	Jobson House, Palo Colorado Canyon, California
1961-62	Bonham House, Boulder Creek, California
1962	Moore House, Orinda, California
1963	Jewell House, Orinda, California
1964-65	Sea Ranch Residential Resort, north of San Francisco, California
1965	Johnson House, Sea Ranch, California
1965-66	Lawrence House, Sea Ranch, California
1965-74	Kresge College, University of California, Santa Cruz,
1966	Faculty Club, University of California, Santa Barbara,
1968	McElrath House, Santa Cruz, California
1968	Church Street South Housing, New Haven, Connecticut
1969	Naff House, Pajaro Dunes, California
1969	Klotz House, Westerly, Rhode Island
1970	Housing Project, Orono, Maine
1973-76	House, near New York City
1975-78	Piazza d'Italia, New Orleans, Louisiana
1979	Rodes House, Kenter Canyon, Los Angeles, California
1979	Riverfront Landing, Dayton, Ohio
1982	St. Matthew's Episcopal Church, Pacific Palisades, California
1985	Hood Museum of Art, Dartmouth College, Hanover, New Hampshire
1985	Tegel Harbor Housing, Berlin, Germany
1988	Drummond Island Hotel, Drummond Island, Michigan

Publications

BOOKS BY MOORE

The Place of Houses. With G. Allen and D. Lyndon. New York, 1974.
Dimensions. With G. Allen. New York, 1976.
Body Memory and Architecture. With K. C. Bloomer. New Haven, Connecticut, 1977.
The Poetics of Gardens. With William J. Mitchell. Cambridge, Massachusetts, 1988.

ARTICLES BY MOORE

"You Have to Pay for the Public Life." *Perspecta* 9/10 (1965).
"Creating of Place." *Image* 4 (1966).
"Plug It in, Rameses, and See If It Lights Up, Because We Aren't Going to Keep It Unless It Works." *Perspecta* 11 (1967).
"Schindler: Vulnerable and Powerful." *Progressive Architecture* (January 1973).
"After a New Architecture: The Best Shape for a Chimera." *Oppositions* (May 1974).
"Where Are We Now, Vincent Scully?" *Progressive Architecture* (April 1975).
"Southerness." *Persepecta* 15 (1975).

"Self-Portrait." *Architecture d'aujourd'hui* (March 1976).
"A Personal View of Architecture." *Arquitectura* (July/August 1980).

BOOKS ABOUT MOORE

JOHNSON, EUGENE J. (ed.): *Charles Moore, Buildings and Projects 1949-86*. New York, 1986.
LITTLEJOHN, DAVID: *Architect: The Life and Work of Charles W. Moore*. New York, 1984.

ARTICLES ABOUT MOORE

Architecture and Urbanism, special issue (May 1978).
"Charles Moore and Company." *GA Houses* 7 (1980).
"Dossier: Charles W. Moore." *Architecture d'aujourd'hui* 184 (1976).
FILLER, MARTIN: "Charles Moore: House Vernacular." *Art in America* 68 (October 1980).
"Interview One: Charles Moore." *Transition* (St. Kilda, Victoria, June 1981).
MISAWA, HIROSHI; EHIRA, KANJI; and SUGAWARA, MICHIO: "Charles Moore and His Partners." *Japan Architect* 112 (September 1965).
"Space, Time and Practice: Charles Moore, a Teacher Par Excellence." *Progressive Architecture* (October 1987).

*

If the boot fits, put it on: if this is not Charles Moore's architectural motto, it ought to be. Although Moore takes the architecture of the satirical put-on perhaps further than any contemporary architect—confronting client, user, architectural critic, historian, and the profession of architecture in turn—it has at least to be admitted that he has been and remains his own primary client, user, historian, critic and connoisseur audience.

He has consistently been willing to be first to wear the boots he has designed for others. Moore's architectural genius has been most consistently exercised in the design of his own homes; it is as if his external "work" were but preparatory exercises to the really serious put-on of his only truly worthy opponent: himself. It is as if the succession of Moore houses are the work for which all his other projects are but simply practice. We feel that the nonhome work will surely come to fruition in the next Moore house.

Moore's "homes" rely for their success on the carefully cultivated illusion of providing each of us with our own special keyhole through which to watch the Master: from Morley Baer's photo of the bath of the Orinda House (1962), through Norman McGrath's revealing photo of the interior of the bedroom of the New Haven House (1966), to the pillow details drawn into the plan of the Austin House (1985)—it is as if we were being whispered to: I have put my genius into my life; I have only put my talent into my works. A blending of business and pleasure; the business of revealing pleasure; the pleasure of doing business—stage business, theatrical business, business that is put on.

There is a special ambiguity in this staged self-revelation: an ambiguity that is not inertly suggestive but actively insinuating, but nevertheless still delicious, voluptuous fun. It is after all, of course, a hoax, but it nevertheless rises above the merely vulgar in that both the confidence man and the John know and enjoy the masque, the charade: one can certainly not accuse the builder-of-homes-for-the-architect Moore of the public scandal of washing his clean linen in public.

What elevates Moore's homework above some titillating "fan mag" concoction, some sordidly depressing "confessional" revelations about thinly disguised country *garçonnières?* To begin with, the black humor in these homes is always first and foremost directed at himself. If the satirical put-on hurts, and if he fears to smile at his own jokes, it is because it is his own lips that are chapped. It is this courage that is the first act that makes his work both redemptive and artistic. As we gaze on the photographs of Moore's homes, we confront, we witness, we are confronted by a *mise-en-scène* for an allegory, a masque, with the theme: "The courage of self-destruction."

As Mishima showed, self-destruction is redemptive and artistic only as a public act. The second act, therefore, is the ability to translate the farce of "self-expression" unto the physical public theater. Moore's work reaches if not its culmination then its catharsis in a supreme moment of autoerotic suicide: in a carefully staged, lit, produced and rehearsed, a superbly put-on *auto-da-fé.*

The making public not of the photo but of the object—the Piazza d'Italia: New Orleans at the boot of Italy, at the aboveground burial among the *ragazzi* of the Italian interment clubs of New Orleans, after the careful study of faux marble, of historicist farce facade, paint and makeup, the tragedy of the mirror-self revealed as makeup, as so much face powder, as a Garbo-Camille with a heart of gold—he had the courage and the talent to show us our own forbidden colors and thereby to bring the Moment to its crisis.

The Piazza d'Italia is an instant monument: it decayed and became a compost pile of itself the very instant that it was "finished." For Moore, the third act of turning self-revelation into high art was to accept the reality of decay. There, in his supreme moment as public architect, Moore dared to be less: he touched the City lightly, and like a delicate banana blossom, it was touched, and having materialized, and having been touched, the bloom is now quite gone. But a mask remains. As he touched the City, he touched us at the center of our role-determined social reality: he showed us with a special puckish playfulness that, in truth, we live in an age of surfaces.

We walk about the ruins of the Piazza d'Italia, and we realize that the Bomb has already gone off. We are but spirits inhabiting a barren land wiped clean and free by a plague of our own making, by a past no longer available for redemption. Moore reveals "the truth of masks." When I was last at the Piazza d'Italia I watched: as the architectural students set up their medium-format cameras on the tripods, a vagrant carefully set a fire under himself: was this Moore, bereft of the funerary mask of himself, gazing over his left shoulder?

TABLEAU.

CURTAIN.

The special power of the satirical put-on is that it is able to expose the underside of reality by holding a mirror firmly and brutally to our feet. Though in these liberated times, the home does seem to be the proper sphere for the man, the mock epic of the Piazza d'Italia liberates the long-buried and chained Father long enough to give him space to pick his head above the muck for the moment, and scarf just one or two of the remaining, though contaminated, cucumber sandwiches. If the boot fits, put it on.

—JOSEPH B. JUHASZ

MOOSBRUGGER, Caspar.

Austrian. Born at Au in the Austrian Vorarlberg, 22 July 1656. Died at Einsiedeln, Switzerland, 26 August 1723. Came from

Caspar Moosbrugger: Benedictine Abbey, Einsiedeln, Switzerland, 1674-1723

a family of architects and craftspeople from the region of Bregenz at the eastern end of the Bodensee. Began training as a stonemason, 1670. Began independent practice, 1673; worked as a stonemason under Johann Georg Kuenin at the Benedictine Monastery, Einsiedeln, Switzerland, 1674-81; entered the Benedictine order, 1682; worked for the Benedictines of Muri, from 1684; wo rked for the Benedictine Monastery at Disentis, 1680s and 1690s; worked on the monastery buildings of Einsiedeln, 1705-13. Moosbrugger family members Andreas and Peter Anton I produced Rococo stuccoworks in the 1770s and 1780s.

Chronology of Works
All in Switzerland

1674-1723	Benedictine Abbey, Einsiedeln (various projects and complete rebuilding from 1702; not completed until 1735 by others)
1685	Abbey Church, Fischingen
1687	Monastery Church, Sarnen (enlargement)
1690-1711	Chapel of St. Ulrich, St. Urbain (completed by others)
1691-93	Chapel of St. Anne, Mariastein
1694-98	Benedictine Abbey Church, Muri (rebuilding)
1696-1712	Benedictine Abbey Church, Disentis [attributed]
1703	Carthusian Monastery Church, Ittingen
1714-24	Benedictine Abbey Church, Weingarten
1720-21	Benedictine Abbey Church, St. Gallen (early projects; latter projects carried out by other Moosbruggers, e.g., the neoclassical altar by J. S. Moosbrugger, 1810)

Publications

BOOKS ABOUT MOOSBRUGGER

BIRCHER, L.: *Die Kunstdenkmäler der Schweiz (KDM), Kanton Schwyz I.* Basel, 1927.

BIRCHER, L.: *Einsiedeln und sein Architekt Bruder Caspar Moosbrugger.* Augsburg, Germany, 1924.

KUHN, P. ALBERT: *Der jetzige Stiftsbau Maria-Einsiedeln.* Einsiedeln, Switzerland, 1880-81; 1913.

LIEB, N. and DIETH, F.: *Die Vorarlberger Barockbaumeister.* Munich, 1960.

OECHSLIN, WERNER (ed.): *Die Vorarlberger Barockbaumeister: Katalog der Ausstellung in Einsiedeln und Bregenz.* Einsielden, Switzerland, 1973.

SANDNER, OSCAR: *Die Kuen-Bregenzer Baumeister des Barock.* Konstanz, Germany, 1962.

ARTICLES ABOUT MOOSBRUGGER

DONIN, R. K.: "Kaspar Mosbrugger und die Vorarlberger Bauschule." *Mitteilungen der Gesellschaft für vergleichende Kunstforschung in Wien* 5 (1952).

REINLE, A.: "Die Doppelturmfassaden der Vorarlberger Meister." *Montfort* 2 (1966): 342ff.

REINLE, A.: "Ein Fund barocker Kirchenund Klosterpläne." *Zeitschrift für Schweizerische Archäologie und Kunstgeschichte* 11 (1950-51).

SAUERMOST, H. J.: "Schema und Eigenbrödler: Eine Analyse der Vorarlberger-Forschung." *Unsere Kunstdenkmäler* 20 (1969): 310ff.

*

It was a characteristic of architecture in southern Germany during the 18th century that much of it was produced by family teams: the brothers Zimmermann and Asam are two famous examples, but there are instances of several generations of architects, stuccators, sculptors and painters who were prominent in certain regions of the German-speaking lands. The Benedictine monk Caspar Moosbrugger (1656-1723) belonged to a celebrated family of architects and craftsmen who hailed from the area in the region of Bregenz at the eastern end of the Bodensee. This family was connected by marriage and through professional contacts with other septs and families involved in architecture and building crafts in what is now southern Germany, Switzerland and Austria. The Moosbruggers, with the Beers and the Thumbs, can be considered as among the chief protagonists of the Vorarlberg school of south German architects and craftsmen of the Baroque and Rococo era.

Caspar Moosbrugger's two greatest achievements are the vast and grand Benedictine Abbey churches of Weingarten near Ravensburg, some 30 kilometers north of Lindau-am-Bodensee (1714-24), and Einsiedeln, some 10 kilometers south of Lake Zurich, in Switzerland, although the precise nature of his contributions is still the subject of much debate. At Weingarten, Einsiedeln and St. Gallen (the latter some 30 kilometers west of Bregenz, and south of the Bodensee), Moosbrugger's name occurs very early in the history of the genesis of the designs, and in the case of St. Gallen we can date his involvement to 1720-21, only two years before his death.

Moosbrugger was one of the first architects in central Europe to experiment with breaking the mold of basilican arrangements by means of large polygonal, elliptical or circular spaces as early as the 1680s. Born at Au in the Austrian Vorarlberg, he became a lay-brother at Einsiedeln in 1682, but little is known of how he acquired his architectural knowledge; yet we are aware that he prepared drawings that were reasonably accomplished. At Weingarten, the west front features a giant order of pilasters, and consists of a convex front held between twin towers: the obvious precedent is J. B. Fischer von Erlach's Kollegienkirche in Salzburg (1694-1707). Behind the convex facade is a three-bay nave, then a crossing with apsidal transepts very like those of Salzburg Cathedral (begun 1614 to designs by Santino Solari, but based on an earlier scheme by Vincenzo Scamozzi), a dome over the crossing, and a two-bay sanctuary with apsidal east end. The clarity of the plan and the remarkably unbasilican form of the interior, where each bay is vaulted and the side aisles are merely vestigial spaces, makes this great church an unusual achievement.

Even more extraordinary is Einsiedeln, where Moosbrugger himself lies buried. This huge monastery, in plan not unlike the Escorial, was rebuilt in 1704-19 to designs by Moosbrugger, and the church itself was begun in 1719. Moosbrugger prepared many drawings, starting with those he made when he first arrived at Einsiedeln, but the final version of the plan is one of the strangest in all the German-speaking lands. The west end of the church is remarkably like that of Kloster Weingarten, with its twin towers flanking a convex front in which giant orders play their part. In each case there is an attic over the center of the facade with a central niche and crowning groups of statuary, although Moosbrugger was probably not responsible for the design of these attics.

It is the nave arrangement behind the facade that is extraordinary, and it is this which marks Moosbrugger as an architect of genius. Around 1617 Santino Solari (whose work at Salzburg has been noted above) designed a solemn shrine in which was placed the *Gnadenbild,* or picture of the Black Virgin of Einsiedeln. Some distance to the east was a chancel which was erected in the 17th century to supersede that of the earlier, medieval church. Moosbrugger designed a building that joined these parts in a strange and brilliant composition. He placed the shrine of the Virgin in a new, approximately octagonal space, to the east of which were two square nave-bays (each covered by a low domical ceiling) with rectangular aisle-bays on each side. Now the oddest thing about the great western space, intended as a setting for the shrine and for the accommodation of pilgrims, is that two piers rise from the shrine itself to carry the ends of the radiating arches of the vaulting, so that the geometry and the spatial relationships are disturbingly complex. To the east of the nave is a narrower three-bay sanctuary approached from steps. Thus the overall effect of the interior, looking east from the large space to the narrow sanctuary, is one of great length, exaggerated by the tricks of perspective. The geometry is of extreme complexity, and we are in the world of Baroque illusion, where techniques of stage-scenery are in evidence.

Moosbrugger's plans were realized by his brother-in-law, Michael II Rüf, and later by Michael's cousin, Johann II Rüf, and the sense of theater was enhanced when the brothers Asam began work there in 1724, and transformed an already complicated architecture into a fantasy of riotous decorative effects.

Einsiedeln is a development of the church at Muri, not far from Zurich, which was originally a Romanesque Benedictine abbey, remodeled by Moosbrugger in 1694-98. He rebuilt and extended the cruciform twin-towered basilica, leaving the towers and the low choir. He then created an octagonal space with transeptal chapels to the west. The building was realized, as with much of Moosbrugger's work, by another architect.

At St. Gallen, Moosbrugger had been responsible for early projects (from 1720) which showed two domed crossings, but a third design had a centrally planned nave with an elliptical form at the crossing. It seems likely that the great central space of St. Gallen as built was at least suggested by Moosbrugger's ideas.

Other members of the family, Andreas and Peter Anton I Moosbrugger, were still producing Rococo stucco works during the 1770s and 1780s: Andreas was responsible for the stucco decorations at the church of Horgen (1780-81), and J. S. Moosbrugger designed the neoclassical high altar at St. Gallen (1810), demonstrating a family connection with the area and with specific buildings over a long period. As late as 1845-46 Hieronymus Moosbrugger carried out some neo-Baroque work in Vienna.

Caspar Moosbrugger, although in some ways a shadowy figure, was a designer of spatial complexities rather than a decorator of surfaces. Indeed, from what we know of his designs, his work is at least as interesting as that of the more celebrated Balthasar Neumann.

—JAMES STEVENS CURL

MORGAN, Julia.

American. Born in San Francisco, California, 1872. Died in 1957. Studied at the University of California, Berkeley, degree in engineering; studied at the École des Beaux-Arts, Paris. Worked on projects for William Randolph Hearst over a period of 25 years.

Chronology of Works
All in the United States
† Work no longer exists

1902-10 Phoebe Apperson Hearst Hacienda (Hacienda del Pozo de Verona), Pleasanton, California (alterations and additions)
1903-04 Bell Tower, Mills College, Oakland, Calif
1905-06 Library, Mills College, Oakland, California
1905-07 Goddard Cottages, Berkeley, California
1906 Cole House, Berkeley, California
1907 Playter House, Piedmont, California
1907-08 Gymnasium, Mills College, Oakland, California
1908-10 St. John's Presbyterian Church (now Julia Morgan Center for Performing Arts), Berkeley, California
1909 Kapiolani Rest Cottage, Mills College, Oakland, California
1913-15 Young Women's Christian Association, Oakland, California
1913-15 Young Women's Christian Association, San Jose, California
1913-28 Asilomar Conference Center, Pacific Grove, California
1915 Panama-Pacific International Exposition Women's Building, San Francisco, California†
1915-18 Williams and Mitchell House, Berkeley, California
1916 Social Center, Mills College, Oakland, California
1919-38 San Simeon (for William Randolph Hearst), California
1920 Elliott House, Berkeley, California
1920-21 Hayfield (Goodrich) House, Saratoga, California

Julia Morgan: San Simeon, California, 1919-38

1921-22	Emmanu-el Sisterhood Residence, San Francisco, California
1925	Hearst Cottage, Grand Canyon, Arizona†
1925-26	Phoebe Apperson Hearst Memorial Gymnasium and Pool, University of California, Berkeley, California (with Bernard Maybeck)
1926-27	Young Women's Christian Association, Honolulu, Hawaii
1926-27	Young Women's Christian Association, Salt Lake City, Utah
1928	Williams House, Berkeley, California
1929-30	Berkeley Women's City Club (now Berkeley City Club), Berkeley, California
1929-30	Young Women's Christian Association, San Francisco, California
1933-41	Hearst Estate, Wyntoon, McCloud, California

Publications

BOOKS ABOUT MORGAN

AIDALA, THOMAS R., and BRUCE, CURTIS: *Hearst Castle, San Simeon*. New York, 1984.

BEACH, JOHN: *Julia Morgan, an Architect from Oakland*. Oakland, California, 1976.

BOUTELLE, SARA HOLMES: *Julia Morgan, Architect*. New York, 1988.

LONGSTRETH, RICHARD: *Julia Morgan, Architect*. Berkeley, California, 1977.

MURRAY, KEN: *The Golden Days of San Simeon*. New York, 1971.

TORRE, SUSANA (ed.): *Women in American Architecture: A Historic and Contemporary Perspective*. New York, 1977.

WINSLOW, CARLETON: *The Enchanted Hill*. Milbrae, California, 1980.

WOODBRIDGE, SALLY: *Bay Area Houses*. Salt Lake City, Utah, 1988.

ARTICLES ABOUT MORGAN

BOUTELLE, SARA HOLMES: "The Woman Who Built San Simeon." *California Monthly* 86, No. 6 (April 1976): 12-14.

BOUTELLE, SARA HOLMES: "Women's Networks: Julia Morgan and Her Clients." *Heresies* 11, No. 3 (1981): 91-94.

LONGSTRETH, RICHARD: "Julia Morgan: Some Introductory Notes." *Perspecta* 15 (1975): 74-86.

STEILBERG, WALTER: "Some Examples of the Work of Julia Morgan." *Architect and Engineer of California* 55 (1918): 39-107.

*

Julia Morgan's life work combined the Continental sophistication of her Beaux-Arts training (she was historically the École's first woman graduate), the engineering skills of an accomplished builder, and the environmental sensitivity of a craftswoman who practiced in her native California. Born in San Francisco in 1872, she came into contact early with two of the most formative influences of her career, her mentor, Bernard Maybeck (1862-1937), and her most renowned client, William Randolph Hearst (1863-1951). In the tradition of Maybeck and his circle, Morgan developed a respectful approach to the building of natural, simple houses positioned harmoniously on their sites, well-crafted handmade buildings, and regionally expressive and colorful structures. Her formal Parisian education in the fine art of architecture prepared her to offer capable and polished

design skills to that great collector of cultural artifacts, William Randolph Hearst, for whom she built her best-known work, the enchanted hillside castle, San Simeon. It is the duality of the California vernacular, with its native materials and forms and Arts and Crafts approach to making buildings, juxtaposed with the competence and urbanity of the Beaux-Arts tradition which characterizes the life work of Julia Morgan.

The best of several Morgan churches in the San Francisco Bay region was St. John's Presbyterian (1908-10), a small wood-frame structure in the tradition of an Arts and Crafts church. St. John's set the stage for the domesticized Gothic of Maybeck's Christian Science Church in Berkeley, which immediately followed (1910); historically, Morgan's church bridged the gap between Richard Upjohn's expressive board-and-batten Stick Style country churches of 19th-century America and the recent vernacular barn-inspired structural expressionism of E. Fay Jones' Thorncrown Chapel in Eureka Springs, Arkansas (1980). At St. John's, Morgan's fusion of domestic gables, exposed rafter ends, and windows of residential scale, in a work composed with a Romanesque-inspired structural simplicity and expressiveness, created a masterpiece of American urban church architecture.

The promise of that early work was fulfilled at Asilomar, a conference center at Pacific Grove underwritten by Phoebe Apperson Hearst, William Randolph's mother, for whom Maybeck earlier had directed the Hearst Competition for the University of California campus plan at Berkeley (1898-99). Asilomar's Administration Building (1913), Chapel (1915), Crocker Dining Hall (1918) and Merrill Hall (1928) all display an Arts and Crafts framework of exposed timbers, unpainted redwood construction and local stone. Built with an economy of means amid Monterey pines, the buildings appear to have grown naturally from their sites; Asilomar constitutes one of the most important collections of Arts and Crafts architecture anywhere.

Morgan's women's buildings make up another significant body of related work; these range from the Emmanu-el Sisterhood Residence in San Francisco (1921-22) to the Berkeley Women's City Club (1929-30) to the many YWCA (Young Women's Christian Association) buildings which Morgan designed for diverse sites from Pasadena, California (1921), to Honolulu, Hawaii (1926-27). Earlier, Morgan's Mission-style campanile (1903) for Mills College had established an expressive cultural regionalism as a central theme in the architect's California work; similarly, at the YWCAs, the designer's sensitivity to scale and to place, as well as the YWCAs' various cultural references, help to bring character to these buildings. For instance, Morgan's use of color, decorative tile, flaring roof eaves and pierced ornamental window grilles (with their references to *lou chuang*) define the image of the Chinese YWCA and its adjacent Residence (1929-30) in San Francisco. Honolulu's YWCA (1926-27) displays a more restrained provincial classicism, Oakland's YWCA (1913-15) the more urbane monumentality of an Italian Renaissance palazzo. Oakland's sophisticated style, moreover, anticipated the Hearst Memorial Gymnasium and Pool for Women (built 1925-26), which Morgan and Maybeck jointly planned as part of a monumental Beaux-Arts classical complex whose theater, music building and museum were never built. What unified such eclectic work by Julia Morgan was her conviction that each commission was unique and that she had to reflect the individuality of each client's program in the building.

That approach was similarly evidenced in Morgan's residential designs, which were as varied as her clients. Her Arts and Crafts homes range in character from the Voyseyesque Orsamus Cole House, Berkeley (1906), and the Playter House, Piedmont (1907), to the redwood-shingle cottages in the Maybeckian and

Joseph Worcester tradition (Goddard Cottages, Berkeley, 1905-07, and the Williams and Mitchell House, Berkeley, 1915-18). English neo-Georgian and other Edwardian images are reflected in Morgan's Elliott House, Berkeley (1920), and her Hayfield (or Goodrich) House, Saratoga (1920-21). The Williams House, Berkeley (1928), is especially rich in medieval-inspired stone and wood carvings, murals and noteworthy Venetian Gothic windows, loggias and porch arcades.

Morgan's best-known residential works are undoubtedly those built for her most renowned clients, Phoebe and William Randolph Hearst. From 1902 through 1910, Morgan made additions to the Hearsts' Hacienda del Pozo de Verona, which had been designed by A. C. Schweinfurth in 1895. Her medieval and at times playful guest cottages at Wyntoon (Maybeck's 1902 castle there for Phoebe Hearst had burned in 1930) were built from 1933 to 1941 to form a "Bavarian Village" along the McCloud River. The carved wood and stone decorations, decorative hardware and murals at Wyntoon offer Hollywood translations of the spirit of William Burges at Castles Cardiff and Coch in Wales. The whole of Wyntoon became an amalgam of Tudor, Gothic and Walt Disney imagery culminating a remarkably eclectic architectural career with a fairy-like ensemble of Fantasy buildings.

But nothing in the Morgan oeuvre approaches the dream world made real of Hearst's San Simeon project (although Hearst's abortive plan to transport the monastic church of Santa Maria de Ovila, Spain, to Wyntoon for use as a swimming pool comes close). At San Simeon, Morgan worked steadily from 1919 through 1938 on the creation of her (and Hearst's) masterpiece, the Enchanted Hill with its castle, guest cottages, swimming pools, zoo and extraordinary collection of art. Antiques and architectural fragments were gathered there for display and to form a stage set for Hearst's royal Hollywood lifestyle. Morgan's piecing together of this cultural jigsaw puzzle provided a setting for Hearst's variegated art collection ranging from Egyptian sculpture, Chinese and Greek vases, clerical vestments, wall hangings, exotic carpets and ceiling paintings (or imported whole painted ceilings). The castle offered, among its 127 rooms, a medieval refectory for dining, billiards played against a backdrop of mille-fleurs tapestry, an outdoor Neptune swimming pool, and (beneath two tennis courts) an indoor Roman pool awash with sumptuous mosaics and classical statuary. The project cost between $25,000 and $30,000 per month during the early 1920s, and ultimately such expenditures contributed to the collapse of the Hearst empire—but not before Julia Morgan had crafted her most renowned work, the Enchanted Hill of San Simeon.

—ROBERT M. CRAIG

MORRIS, William.

British. Born in Walthamstow, Essex, England, 24 March 1834. Died 3 October 1896. Married Jane Burden, 1859; two daughters. Studied at Marlborough College, Wiltshire, 1848-51; Exeter College, Oxford, 1853-55, B.A., 1856, M.A., 1875. Articled to G. E. Street's architectural firm, Oxford and London, 1856; worked as a painter, 1857-62; friend of Edward Burne-Jones, Dante Gabriel Rossetti, Ford Madox Brown and others in the Pre-Raphaelite Brotherhood; founder, with Burne-Jones, Rossetti, Brown an d others, Morris Marshall Faulkner and Co. design firm, London, 1861-74, subsequently Morris and Co., 1874-96; public lecturer on art, architecture and socialism, 1877-96; founder, Kelmscott Press, Hammersmith, 1890-96. Examiner, South Kensington School of Art, later Victoria and Albert

Museum, London, 1876-96; founding member and secretary, Society for the Protection of Ancient Buildings, 1877.

Publications

BOOKS BY MORRIS

A Dream of John Ball. London, 1888.
News from Nowhere. London, 1891.
Gothic Architecture. London, 1893.
Arts and Crafts Essays (ed.). London, 1893.
Collected Works of William Morris. Edited by May Morris. 24 vols. London, 1910-15.
The Letters of William Morris to His Family and Friends. London, 1950.
The Unpublished Lectures of William Morris. Detroit, Michigan, 1969.
Political Writings of William Morris. Edited by A. L. Morton. New York, 1973.

BOOKS ABOUT MORRIS

BRADLEY, I.: *William Morris and His World.* London, 1978.
DRINKWATER, JOHN: *William Morris.* London, 1912.
HENDERSON, PHILIP: *William Morris: His Life, Work, and Friends.* New York and London, 1967.
LETHABY, WILLIAM: *Philip Webb and His Work.* London, 1935.
MACKAIL, JOHN W.: *The Life of William Morris.* 2 vols. London, 1899.
MARSHALL, RODERICK: *William Morris and His Earthly Paradises.* 1981.
MORRIS, MAY: *William Morris: Artist, Writer, Socialist.* 2 vols. Oxford, 1936.
NAYLOR, GILLIAN: *The Arts and Crafts Movement.* London, 1990.
NAYLOR, GILLIAN (ed.): *William Morris by Himself.* London, 1988.
PEVSNER, NIKOLAUS: *Pioneers of the Modern Movement from William Morris to Walter Gropius.* Harmondsworth, England, 1936.
RICHARDSON, MARGARET: *The Craft Architects.* London and New York, 1983.
SEWTER, A. C.: *The Stained Glass of Morris and His Circle.* 2 vols. New Haven, Connecticut, and London, 1974-75.
STANSKY, P.: *Redesigning the World: William Morris, the 1880s and the Arts and Crafts.* Princeton, New Jersey, 1987.
THOMPSON, E. P.: *William Morris, Romantic to Revolutionary.* London, 1955.
THOMPSON, PAUL: *The Work of William Morris.* New York and London, 1967.
VALLANCE, AYMER (ed.): *The Art of William Morris.* London, 1897.
WATKINSON, RAY: *William Morris as Designer.* New York and London, 1967.

ARTICLES ABOUT MORRIS

MACLEOD, ROBERT: "William Morris and Philip Webb." In *Style and Society: Architectural Ideology in Britain: 1835-1914.* London, 1971.
PEVSNER, NIKOLAUS: "William Morris and Architecture." *Royal Institute of British Architects Journal* 3rd series, 64 (1957). Reprinted in *Studies in Art, Architecture and Design: Victorian and After.* Princeton, New Jersey, 1968.

PEVSNER, NIKOLAUS: "William Morris, C. R. Ashbee and the Twentieth Century." *Manchester Review* 7 (1956): 437-458.

ROOKS, NOEL: "The Works of Lethaby, Webb, and Morris." *Journal of the Royal Institute of British Architects* 57 (1950): 167-175.

*

In the century since his death, William Morris has been honored widely as a designer, craftsman, publisher, poet and social theorist, especially for his views on the relationship between art and society. He has also come to occupy a place in the standard history of architecture, which needs some explanation, considering that it is based mainly on one sizable house, which was designed for him by his friend Philip Webb on the occasion of Morris' marriage. Moreover, Morris lived in it for only five years, partly due to the effect on his health of its peculiar orientation, with its major rooms facing north and its corridors and services to the south.

The explanation of Morris' importance in architecture is suggested by two books. Bringing the merits of the English house to the attention of the German public at the beginning of the 20th century (*Das englische Haus,* 13 vols., 1904-05), Hermann Muthesius cited Morris' Red House as "the first private house of the new artistic culture, the first house to be conceived and built as a unified whole inside and out, the very first example in the history of the modern house."

A generation later, in 1936, Nikolaus Pevsner was to update and generalize this assessment in his influential book *Pioneers of the Modern Movement from William Morris to Walter Gropius,* which went through various editions and is still in print. In it, Pevsner endorsed Morris' thesis that art should be part of ordinary life, and that this harmony had been destroyed by the excesses of industrialization. However, he rejected Morris' belief that art was a natural product of a person's labor, and insisted that it could be supplied by a trained intermediary who would inject "good design" into the mass production of a society's artifacts. Hence the reference to Gropius, who elevated the common factory to a symbol of the new era.

In this revised scenario, which was to become the standard interpretation of the period, Morris was of considerable importance because he could be used to bolster a line of reasoning that would show why the modern style was inevitable, at a time when its advocates were still attempting to establish its legitimacy. Conversely, the current disillusionment with the modern style allows a reassessment of Morris' theoretical positions.

Morris' critique of society stemmed from his dislike for the products of his day. But far from being representative of any broad social group, his taste was not even shared by other educated persons. George Bernard Shaw quipped that Morris did not join the Fabians because he could not stand the ugliness of the furniture where they met. Rather than being a man of the people as he thought, Morris with his "stained glass attitudes" was more rightly included among the aesthetes in Gilbert and Sullivan's parody of them in *Patience.* As Muthesius had suggested, what Morris helped create was a new art style, later known as Arts and Crafts.

The "people" bought decoration, naturalism, sentiment, the qualities of design that Morris dismissed as "cheap and nasty." The aesthetes" offered them designs based on ethical strictures and abstracted patterns that appealed only to a small "cultivated" clientele. The paternalism of the stance that Morris adopted, that people should take what they were given or do without, is more obvious today now that the social pretensions of modern architecture have dropped away and revealed its "art for art's sake" underpinning. The notion that, after the social revolution, everyone would have Morris' taste was just one of his conceits.

This also applied to Morris' ideal of a just and beautiful society. Such noble aspirations are not easy to question, but their pursuit was to have adverse consequences. Although of the commercial middle class himself, Morris looked to the working class for the salvation of civilization. It did things with its hands, just like his heroes of the Middle Ages; its obvious loss of innocence was the fault of its ruthless employers. In contrast, his despised fellow entrepreneurs sought only money and power. It was this caricature of the new industrial classes that encouraged the Modern Movement to impose its vision on the "deserving poor." And, even now that Western nations are largely middle class in outlook, the same contempt for its value is still proclaimed by architects to justify their attempts to exclude it from any participation in the design of its own buildings.

Morris also disliked what architects produced, especially those who worked in the neoclassical style, but the connection he drew between architecture and craft was largely irrelevant. Architects have traditionally intervened as designers between their clients and their buildings. Even houses have been constructed by specialized trades for many centuries. The only difference between the "good old days" and then was, presumably, that builders might have been closer to their public, or might have taken more pride in their work, both unlikely assumptions. Furthermore, while the notion of enriched construction might be a useful design strategy, it is by no means the only one, and decoration or content can be just as readily applied, as is obvious from the history of architecture itself.

More to the point was Morris' rediscovery of the merits of vernacular architecture. Generations of architectural theorists had tried to separate architecture, with its metaphysical pretensions, from building, which was spurned as mere utilization construction. By praising barns and cottages, Morris reversed the equation, making it possible even for people with good taste to prefer visiting ordinary old buildings than the latest architectural event. It is this perception, that the meaning inherent in the reality of our everyday artifacts is more significant than the meaning imposed upon them by architects, which strengthens today's conservation movement.

And, of course, Morris founded the Society for the Protection of Ancient Buildings. Outraged by the alteration of historical buildings under the guise of restoration, Morris argued instead for their preservation, resulting in 1882 in the initial Ancient Monuments Protection Act, which gave the British nation the power to take care of its most venerable sites and buildings.

The conclusion must be that in spite of any dissension concerning its specific merits, Morris' life's work was so wide in its scope and ideas that it can still be used as a catalyst for current beliefs and actions.

—ANTHONY JACKSON

MOSER, Karl.

Swiss. Born in Baden, Switzerland, 10 August 1860. Died in 1936. Studied in Zurich, 1878-82; studied at the École des Beaux-Arts, Paris, 1883-84. In private practice, Baden, from 1885; professor, Technische Hochschule, Zurich, 1915-28; elected first president of CIAM, 1928.

Chronology of Works

* Approximate dates

1891-93	St. John's Church, Berne, Switzerland
1896-97	Villa Boveri, Baden, Switzerland
1898-99	Villa Römerberg; Baden, Switzerland
1898-1901	St. Paul's Church, Basel, Switzerland
1900*	Christ Church, Karlsruhe, Germany
1902-05	St. Paul's Church, Berne, Switzerland
1905	St. John's Church, Mannheim, Germany
1906	Luther Church, Karlsruhe, Germany
1907-10	Kunsthaus, Zurich, Switzerland
1908	St. Anton's Church, Zurich, Switzerland
1909-11	Prostestant Church, Flawil, Switzerland
1911-12	St. Paul's Church, Lucerne, Switzerland
1911-14	University of Zurich, Zurich, Switzerland (main building)
1912	Savings Bank, Aarau, Switzerland
1912-13	Badischer Bahnhof, Basel, Switzerland
1918-20	Fluntern Church, Zurich, Switzerland
1925-26	Kunsthaus, Zurich, Switzerland (addition)
1925-31	St. Antonius Church, Basel, Switzerland

Publications

BOOKS BY MOSER

Die Pauluskirche in Basel. With Hans Curjel. Basel, 1962.

ARTICLES BY MOSER

"Neue holländische Architektur: Bauten von W. M. Dudok, Hilversum." *Werk* 9 (1922): 205-214.

BOOKS ABOUT MOSER

KIENZLE, HERMANN: *Karl Moser 1860-1936.* Zurich, 1937.

ARTICLES ABOUT MOSER

BIRCHLER, LINUS: "Karl Moser und moderne katholische Kirchenbau." *Schweizer Rundschau* 36, No. 8 (1936): 633-639.
EESTEREN, CORNELIUS VAN; GIEDION, SIEGFRIED; LE CORBUSIER; and SCHMIDT, GEORG: "Karl Moser and 28 February 1936." *De 8 en opbouw* 7, No. 8 (1936): 85-96.
PLATZ, GUSTAV: "Architekt K. Moser in der baukünstlerischen Entwicklung seiner Zeit." *Schweizerische Bauzeitung* (1930).

*

Karl Moser's impact on architecture was exerted both as a designer and a teacher. His work began in late-19th-century historicism and ended in 20th-century modernism. In his last years, he became a mentor of the International Style, especially in his native Switzerland. His prolific design activity produced churches, schools, banks, hotels, office buildings, villas and railway stations.

Moser began his architectural career as a child of his time. During his studies in Zurich, in a program still under the influence of Gottfried Semper, he was indeed impressed with courses on the history of architecture. After transferring to the École des Beaux-Arts, he complained the education was dominated by depressing conventions and empty formalism. However, he found Paris an exciting city and was impressed by its urban plan and some of the recent public buildings. These influences accounted for Moser's honesty and authenticity as an architect. And too, already as a young boy, he was an excellent draftsman with a particular flair for perfection and exactness of depiction.

Moser began his design career as an eclectic. He first followed the widely practiced Romanesque Revival, possibly influenced by H. H. Richardson's work in the United States. However, he was not interested in symbolic aspects. Rather, his focus was on the spatial quality of this stylistic mode, with emphasis on the handling of proportions and details. The eclectic choices were, thus, not motivated by ideological considerations. The important goal of his designs was the achievement of a unified overall form. Details and decoration were usually subordinated under the organic conception of the whole building. In essence, Moser considered the organic treatment of space the primary goal of design: his understanding of architecture was sculptural. Even when his designs combined elements from various styles, their assembly achieved an honest feeling of space, derived from a free grouping of volumes and a clear spatial organization.

In his second phase, Moser embraced the art nouveau style. He especially followed the planar emphasis of the Vienna Secession architects. There lay the germ for Moser's conception of a building as a *Gesamtkunstwerk.* He encouraged the collaboration of artists in architectural design, and considered painting and sculpture integral parts of a building. His designs of that period were characterized by smooth, and slightly curving, wall and facade surfaces, as well as large-scale details. His work occupied the middle ground between the floral profuseness of art nouveau and the literalness of historicism. He combined the art nouveau style with the novel construction technology that became a hallmark of the later International Style. His designs are part of monumental art nouveau.

In his third stylistic phase, Moser adopted neoclassicism. The stylistic features, however, were not displayed in literal form. At the Zurich Kunsthaus, the pitched roof took the place of the temple pediment. Moser proved quite adept at moving from one style to another. He also aligned himself with the mainstream of post-World War I architecture. Moser advocated neoclassicism not for its simplicity of form, but for its capacity to establish a harmonic, national style. It came out of a need for principles.

In his final creative period, Moser demonstrated his courage to develop independently of his own tradition. In his last buildings, the interiors began to assert themselves, push out, stretch details and structures and dominate the exterior appearance. Finally, his designs expressed a true spatial feeling. Moser began to design from inside to outside, focusing much attention on the layout of the ground plan. Again in the Kunsthaus in Zurich, lighting questions, the hanging of artworks, and the distribution of libraries and auditoriums were accepted as important elements of design. This approach can be called functionalist. The allusions to past styles were substituted by a trend toward organic configuration.

Moser became a promoter of the International Style, a highly publicized move because of his support for Le Corbusier's submission to the Palace of the League of Nations competition. He also designed the first concrete church in Switzerland, St. Anton's in Basel (1925-31), as questions of use became more important than problems of representation. Nevertheless, heeding symbolic questions prevented Moser from becoming as abstract as his younger pupils. In that period, materials and construction were no longer tied to a national tradition, but became usable everywhere, became international. Moser again formulated the International Style in his own terms,

Karl Moser: Kunsthaus, Zurich, Switzerland, 1907-10

by initiating his own dispute with it. Nevertheless, that phase presented quite an abrupt break with his earlier stylistic phases. It was propelled by Moser's conviction that the International Style could solve all problems of architecture. He became quite radical in his last creative period. The artistic element, as an individual expression of the art nouveau style, was replaced by an objective quality, subjecting the artist to external control.

Moser was among the few architects who bridged the long passage from historicism to the International Style. He was an eclectic capable of handling a variety of styles. However, he possessed a humanist conception of architecture. He was always capable of imposing his own authenticity as an artist on his creations. This was especially apparent in his understanding of a building as a collaborative product. He deemed the contributions of painters and sculptors to be important attributes of a building. Architecture, painting and sculpture were united to create a representative work of art. His conception of architecture was that of a sculpture: the building had to form an organic whole. Blind, literal imitation was not his trademark. Thus, he could even conceive using the most up-to-date technology with historicist details. Historicist vocabulary went together with the open expression of the building material.

Moser was always capable of imbuing a building with a monumental quality, so that his designs were noticed beyond their regional domain. An art museum became a temple of art, as well as a demonstration of contemporary materials, technologies and stylistic concerns. Ultimately, Moser's career gave expression to an awareness which registered the problems of the age critically, and enabled the architect to respond with ever-changing solutions to the changing requirements of the time.

—HANS R. MORGENTHALER

MULHOLLAND, Roger.

Irish. Born in County Londonderry, Ireland, 1740. Died in 1818. Married and moved to Belfast in 1770. Worked as a carpenter and general builder, then as an architect; founder of Linenhall Library, 1788.

Chronology of Works
All in Northern Ireland
† Work no longer exists

1779	First Presbyterian Church, Dunmurry, County Antrim
1782	First Presbyterian Church, Rosemary Street, Belfast
1780-90	Housing on Donegall Street, Academy Street, William Street, Church Street, Dunbar Street, Gordon Street, Robert Steet, Hill Street, Belfast†
1783-85	White Linen Hall, Belfast†
1787	Belfast Castle, Belfast (coach house)†
1790	Houses on Linenhall Street, Belfast (now Donegall Place)†
1796	Bridge over Reed's Strand, Belfast (repairs)†
1805	House of Correction, Belfast†

Publications

BOOKS ABOUT MULHOLLAND

BRETT, C. E. B.: *Buildings of Belfast 1700-1914*. London, 1967.
BRETT, C. E. B.: *Roger Mulholland, Architect of Belfast, 1740-1818*. Belfast, 1976.

*

Roger Mulholland was a native of County Londonderry, but by 1770, when he married, he was settled in Belfast (then a small town), and seems to have worked as a carpenter and general building contractor until 1786, when he was described as an "Architect." Yet there is evidence that he was designing buildings with architectural pretensions earlier than that.

He appears to have been a man of some cultivation, for he subscribed to a book of *Views of Dublin* in 1780, and in 1788 was one of the founders of the Linenhall Library, to which he presented a set of Colen Campbell's *Vitruvius Britannicus;* this would suggest that he was no mere jobbing builder or carpenter, but an architect, interested in the niceties of architectural design and composition.

His early years are shrouded in mystery, but he may have been at least influenced by the Londonderry architect Michael Priestley, who designed Lifford Court House, Port Hall near Londonderry, and the church of Clondahorkey or Ballymore near Sheephaven, all in County Donegal. Priestley may also have designed Prehen, a small house of about 1740, situated on the south side of the River Foyle near Londonderry.

Priestley favored Gibbsian surrounds and other motifs culled from pattern books. Gibbs surrounds are strongly evident in the Ballymore church, and again at the First Presbyterian Church at Dunmurry in County Antrim of 1779, a decent little preaching-box with two doors, one for men and the other for women. It is highly likely that the architect for this charming building was Roger Mulholland. The survival of the Gibbs surrounds can be explained by the provincialism of Ireland and by the curious time warp which meant that until the later part of the 19th century, taste tended to lag behind that of England, and especially behind London.

Mulholland's most active years as an architect were during the 1780s, the period during which the policies of improvements to the town of Belfast evolved by the impecunious earl of Donegall were encouraging the granting of building leases in some quantity. From 1781 Mulholland was involved in the design of a new Presbyterian church at Rosemary Street, Belfast, which is unquestionably his best work. The building committee determined that the plan of the new church should be an ellipse, and Mulholland's proposals for the design were accepted. At one stage, Francis Hiorne (1744-89), the Warwick architect who had designed the church of St. Anne in Belfast for Lord Donegall (completed 1776 and demolished 1900), was consulted about the design of the pews, but it was Mulholland who seems to have designed the galleries, pews and other furnishings, as well as the church itself.

Rosemary Street Presbyterian Church, with its marvelous box-pews, gallery that seems to sway backward and forward with convex and concave curves within the elliptical plan, rather like the best of Rococo work in Germany, elegant Corinthian columns supporting the gallery, and exquisite proportions, is one of the loveliest creations of Irish Nonconformist architecture, and was completed in 1783. Projecting from one of the narrow ends of the ellipse was a two-story rectangular structure containing the entrance vestibule, stairs to the galleries, and the vestry above the entrance. This projection was rusticated on the ground floor and had semicircular-headed arches over the

two windows and central door (the latter complete with fanlight), while the first floor had an order of pilasters and three aediculated windows, the central one of which had a triangular pediment and the two side ones segmental pediments. The composition was crowned with a large pediment, giving to the facade the character of a temple front on a high podium. Unfortunately, Mulholland's elegant facade was altered in 1833 when a new front was created to give improved access to the galleries: the stuccoed facade was less robust and somewhat hesitant in its composition.

Much of Mulholland's work at the time was involved in the creation of houses. He carried out various developments in the vicinity of the new church of St. Anne, including the large three-story vicarage, completed in 1789.

Mulholland may have been the architect of the White Linen Hall, which had many Gibbsian features used by Priestley. It was a handsome ensemble of buildings, and Mulholland may also have had a hand in the design and erection of some of the Late Georgian houses in Donegall Square and the vicinity of the White Linen Hall. He certainly designed three substantial houses in Linenhall Street (now Donegall Place), and he was responsible for Lord Donegall's Agent's House on the site of Belfast Castle: this was a five-window-wide front with a central doorway with Gibbs surround.

His last major building appears to have been the House of Correction, erected at the corner of Howard Street and Fisherwick Place, opposite the site of what is now the Grand Opera House. The design seems to have been finalized around 1811, and in 1817 one James Boyd contracted to build it. This was *architecture parlante* indeed, for the blank walls, broken only by massive piers at regular intervals, and by a gate set within a stark blind arch surmounted by a plain pediment, made the exterior aspect worthy of C.-N. Ledoux or George Dance the younger at their most forbidding. The house itself, which stood inside the walled enclosure, had a tall pedimented centerpiece with semicircular-headed windows, two lower wings punctured only by lunettes, and two pedimented plain end pavilions. The central block was surmounted by a squat clock-tower. The total effect was extraordinarily grim, like John Vanbrugh's work stripped of ornament, Dance at his most severe, and Ledoux at his most admonitory, all mixed together. This was the town jail until the building of Lanyon's Crumlin Road Prison in 1843-45.

As far as we know, therefore, we have only the Dunmurry and Rosemary Street churches remaining of Mulholland's oeuvre. The White Linen Hall was demolished to make way for Brumwell Thomas' Baroque City Hall of 1896-1906, the last of his many houses have been destroyed in recent decades, and his House of Correction survived for only a couple of generations. Research into Mulholland is bedeviled by the fact that so many records in Ireland were destroyed in the 1920s and at other times, while the destruction of Georgian Belfast by the Victorians and their successors, not to mention recent damage by bombs, has accounted for the loss of much of the gracious fabric that a sensitive and cultivated local architect created during Belfast's period of most felicitous growth.

—JAMES STEVENS CURL

MULLETT, Alfred B.

American. Born Alfred Bult Mullett in Taunton, England, 7 April 1834. Died on 20 October 1890. Studied at an Ohio college (now University of Cincinnati); studied in European schools. Sons were the architects Thomas A. Mullett and Frederick M. Mullett. Worked in Isaiah Rogers' office, Cincinnati,

Alfred B. Mullett: Old Executive Office Building, Washington, DC, 1971-89

Ohio, 1860; supervising architect of the United States Treasury Department, Washington, D.C., 1865-74.

Chronology of Works
All in the United States
† Work no longer exists

1850-79 Customhouse, Charleston, South Carolina
1865-67 White House, Washington, D.C. (alterations)†
1866-69 Courthouse and Post Office, Springfield, Illinois†
1866-70 State Museum (Mint), Carson City, Nevada
1867-69 Treasury Building, Washington, D.C. (north wing extension)
1867-71 Appraisers' Stores, Philadelphia, Pennsylvania†
1867-71 Courthouse and Post Office, Des Moines, Iowa†
1867-71 Courthouse and Post Office, Madison, Wisconsin†
1867-72 City Hall (Customhouse and Post Office), Cairo, Illinois
1867-72 Courthouse and Post Office, Portland, Maine†
1867-73 Customhouse, St. Paul, Minnesota†
1867-73 Marine Hospital, Chicago, Illinois†

1868-72 Customhouse, Portland, Maine
1868-72 Old Customhouse, Wiscasset, Maine
1869-73 Customhouse, Astoria, Oregon†
1869-74 Mint, San Francisco, California
1869-75 Pioneer Courthouse, Portland, Oregon
1869-80 Courthouse and Post Office, New York City†
1871-72 Community Services Administration (Customhouse and Post Office), Machias, Maine
1871-74 City Hall (Courthouse and Post Office), Columbia, South Carolina
1871-74 East Tennessee Historical Center (Courthouse and Post Office), Knoxville, Tennessee
1971-89 Old Executive Office Building (State, War and Navy Building), Washington, D.C.
1873-84 Customhouse and Post Office, St. Louis, Missouri
1874-79 City Hall (Courthouse and Post Office), Lincoln, Nebraska
1874-79 Courthouse and Post Office, Parkersburg, West Virginia†
1874-79 Century Station Post Office, Raleigh, North Carolina
1874-81 Apppraisers' Stores, San Francisco, California†

1874-84   Post Office and Courthouse, Philadelphia, Pennsylvania†
1874-85   Customhouse and Post Office, Cincinnati, Ohio†
1885-86   Sun Building (now American Bank Building), Washington, D.C.
1887-88   Central National Bank, Washington, D.C.
1888-89   William A. Hammond House, Washington, D.C.†

Publications

BOOKS ABOUT MULLETT

CONDIT, CARL W.: *American Building*. Chicago, 1968.

HILLS, W. H., and SUTHERLAND, T. A. (compilers): *A History of Public Buildings under the Control of the Treasury Department*. Washington, D.C., 1901.

HOPKINS, GRIFFITH MORGAN: *A Complete Set of Surveys and Plats of Properties in the City of Washington, District of Columbia*. Philadelphia, 1887.

HOPKINS, GRIFFITH MORGAN: *Real Estate Plat-book of Washington, D.C., Comprising the Entire North-west Section from the Original Plats of Squares and Subdivisions*. Philadelphia, 1892-1896.

Illustrated Washington: Our Capital. New York, 1890.

JENNINGS, J. L. SIBLEY: *Massachusetts Avenue Architecture*. Washington, D.C., 1975.

MADDEX, DIANE: *Historic Buildings of Washington, D. C.* Pittsburgh, 1973.

SCHWARTZ, NANCY B. (compiler): *District of Columbia Catalog: Historic American Buildings Survey (1974)*. Charlottesville, 1976.

SMITH, D. M.: *A. B. Mullett: His Relevance in American Architecture and Historic Preservation*. Washington, D. C.

ARTICLES ABOUT MULLETT

WODEHOUSE, LAWRENCE: "Alfred B. Mullett and His French Style Government Buildings." *Journal of the Society of Architectural Historians* 31, No. 1 (1972): 22-37.

WODEHOUSE, LAWRENCE: "Alfred B. Mullett's Court Room and Post Office at Raleigh, North Carolina." *Journal of the Society of Architectural Historians* 26, No. 4 (1967): 301-306.

Although an architect in the private sector prior to the Civil War and after 1875, Alfred Bult Mullett is most famous as a public architect, working for the United States government as supervising architect to the Treasury Department from 1865 to 1874. During that period, he designed and constructed about $50 million worth of work, ranging from post offices costing a few thousand dollars in small New England towns, to the State, War and Navy Building (now the Executive Office Building), which cost well over $10 million.

Mullett trained for two years at what is now the University of Cincinnati, worked for Isaiah Rogers, traveled widely, and designed in what can broadly be termed the Beaux-Arts idiom, emanating from the École des Beaux-Arts in Paris. Mullett did not train there as some of his contemporaries did, but his buildings were "rational," that is, the plans were ample and straightforward, the construction and structure were simple, and the buildings were made to appear truthful and effective. His buildings had to express their use. Site conditions, location and climate were carefully considered, and Mullett took special care in provide lighting, ventilating, heating and other building services. While utility was an important aspect of his design, it was more important that the buildings had aesthetic appeal, which for a Beaux-Arts building meant classically derived design. Beauty came through one of a variety of classical styles, ranging from revivals of the Roman neoclassical, the Italian Renaissance, and an extension of 17th-century French Renaissance architecture revived in France under Louis Napoleon and known as the Second Empire style. (In the United States the Second Empire style was more popularly termed the "General Grant" style because it paralleled the president's popularity and his demise.)

Little is known of Mullett's architecture prior to 1865, but as supervising architect of the Treasury Department he designed a marine hospital, assay offices, mints, appraiser's stores and federal buildings for many cities. In those intense federal buildings, the post office would occupy the ground floor, the customs offices would be located on the second floor, and the tall federal courtroom would fill the third, extending into the roof space. Some of Mullett's designs followed in the tradition of Ammi Burnham Young (1798-1874), who was supervising architect of the Office of Construction within the Treasury Department from 1852 to 1861. Both used the neoclassical Roman Revival style usually consisting of an end portico or pavilion on the building, accessed by a flight of steps. The Roman Revival San Francisco Mint, built on a whole city block, had corner pavilions and a central portico on its main facade. Young also utilized the style of High and Late Renaissance Italian palaces of the 16th century as modified into the Renaissance Revival in London by Charles Barry, and this Mullett also continued. Mullet often capped his Renaissance Revival buildings with mansard roofs typical of the Second Empire style, making the detailing of his elevations bolder and more three-dimensional than Young's. Perhaps the best example of this style was the Federal Building in Madison, Wisconsin (1867-70), now demolished. The most elaborate and expensive of all Mullett's Second Empire designs were the federal buildings for Boston, Cincinnati, New York, Philadelphia and St. Louis, and the State, War and Navy Building in Washington.

Mullett was overworked, underpaid and always the butt of those who saw influential employees of the federal government as corrupt. A combination of these factors led to his resignation from governmental service in 1874. Thereafter he worked in New York as an architect, an adviser to the Department of the Navy and to those seeking patents. Returning to Washington, he set up practice with his sons and applied for a total of 32 building permits between 1884 and 1887.

Mullett was inventive in many fields, as his numerous patents attest. He designed concrete foundation rafts on wooden piles for problem site conditions in San Francisco and St. Louis, and developed metal roof structures covered in heavy slates to be weatherproof and effective covers on his buildings. He experimented with new techniques for heating, ventilation and insulation, utilized fireproof construction for structure and building elements such as shutters and doors, and was concerned with interior details, including elaborate fittings for courtrooms, furniture, lighting fixtures, post-office boxes and even the design of door handles and hinges.

Mullett was an architect who considered all aspects of the building process in detail, including construction, services, organization of the parts of a building, and the aesthetic appearance, in a day and age when that was not always the case.

—LAWRENCE WODEHOUSE

N

NASH, John.

British. Born in London, England, 1752. Died in East Cowes Castle, 13 May 1835. Married Mary Ann Nash. Draughtsman, Sir Robert Taylor Office; association with Samuel Saxon; established own firm, London, 1796; partnership with Humphry Repton; architect to the Department of Woods and Forests, 1806; surveyor-general of the works, 1813.

Chronology of Works
All in England unless noted
* Approximate dates
† Work no longer exists

1789-92	Jail, Carmarthen
1791-93	St. David's Cathedral, Abergavenny (rebuilding of west front)
1792-93	Jail, Cardigan
1795-98	Jail, Hereford
1797	Casina, Dulwich†
1797	Southgate Grove, Middlesex
1798ff.*	East Cowes Castle, Isle of Wight†
1800-04	Luscombe Castle, Dawlish, Devonshire
1801*-03	Killymoon Castle, County Tyrone, Ireland
1808*	Cronkhill, near Shrewsbury
1808*	Longner Hall, Shropshire
1805	Sandridge Park, Stoke Gabriel, Devonshire
1806*	Garnstone Castle, Herefordshire†
1806-13	Childwall Hall, Lancashire†
1808	Aqualate Hall, Staffordshire†
1808*	Caerhayes Castle, Cornwall
1808*	Ravensworth Castle, County Durham†
1809*	Knepp Castle, West Grinstead, Sussex†
1810	Rockingham House, County Roscommon, Ireland†
1810-11	Blaise Hamlet, Bristol
1811	Lough Cutra Castle, County Galway, Ireland
1812-27	Terrace Facades and Lodges, Regents Park, London
1813-14	Carlton House, London (suite of rooms on lower ground floor)†
1813-15	Langham House, London†
1813-16	Royal Lodge, Windsor†
1815-21	Royal Pavilion, Brighton (remodeling and extension)
1815-30	Facades, Regent Street, London†
1818-19	Shanbally Castle, County Tipperary, Ireland†
1819	Harmonic Institution, Regent Street, London†
1820-21	Nash House, 14 Regent Street, London†
1822-24	Royal Mews, Pimlico, London
1823	Suffolk Street Gallery, London
1822-25	All Souls Church, Langham Place, London
1824ff.	Park Village West and Park Village East, Regents Park, London†
1824-30	Buckingham Palace, London (rebuilding)
1826-27	St. Mary's Haggerston, London†
1826-28	United Services Club, Pall Mall, London
1827-33	Carlton House Terrace and Carlton Gardens, London

Publications

BOOKS BY NASH

Views of the Royal Pavilion. London, 1991.

BOOKS ABOUT NASH

COLVIN, HOWARD (ed.): Vol. 6 in *The History of the King's Works.* London, 1973.
DAVIS, TERENCE: *John Nash, the Prince Regent's Architect.* Newton Abbot, England, 1973.
DAVIS, TERENCE: *The Architecture of John Nash.* London, 1960.
HOBHOUSE, HERMIONE: *A History of Regent Street.* London, 1973.
MANSBRIDGE, MICHAEL: *John Nash: A Complete Catalogue.* New York, 1991.
MUSGRAVE, CLIFFORD: *Royal Pavilion: An Episode in the Romantic.* London, 1959.
ROBERTS, HENRY D.: *A History of the Royal Pavilion, Brighton.* London, 1939.
SERVICE, ALASTAIR: *The Architects of London.* London, 1979.
SMITH, H. CLIFFORD: *Buckingham Palace: Its Furniture, Decoration and History.* London and New York, 1931.
SUMMERSON, JOHN: *The Life and Work of John Nash, Architect.* Cambridge, Massachusetts, and London, 1980.
SUMMERSON, JOHN: *John Nash: Architect to King George IV.* 2nd ed. London, 1949.
TEMPLE, NIGEL: *John Nash and the Village Picturesque.* Gloucester, 1979.

ARTICLES ABOUT NASH

McKENDRY, JENNIFER: ''The Attitude of John Nash Toward the Gothic Revival Style.'' *Journal of the Society of Architectural Historians* 47 (September 1988): 295-296.

*

John Nash was an architect and developer in England at the end of the 18th and the beginning of the 19th century. His career was marked by many changes of interests and of fortune; he was first an architect of what is called the ''picturesque'' style; he developed Regent Street and Regent's Park in London in the 1820s, and he was also the architect of George IV, remodeling for him both Buckingham Palace and the Royal Pavilion in Brighton.

Nash was probably born in London, but of a Welsh family. His father was an engineer and millwright in Lambeth. When Nash was 14 he was apprenticed to Robert Taylor, one of

John Nash: Terrace Facades and Lodges, Regent's Park, London, England, 1812-27

London's leading architects, and he worked in Taylor's office for eight years. But in 1774 he left Taylor, married and began a series of speculative developments in London, of which some houses in Bloomsbury Square and Great Russell Street, dating from about 1777, still survive. But those ventures failed, and by 1783 Nash was bankrupt and proceeding with a divorce. He left London for Carmarthen in South Wales, leaving architecture behind and following several business enterprises. However, a visit by Samuel Pepys Cockerell, a fellow pupil in Taylor's office, rekindled Nash's interest in architecture, and he soon acquired a commission from a local landowner to build a bathhouse on the latter's estate. That commission began a revival of his career as an architect.

In the next few years Nash worked on several public commissions in the area, for jails at Carmarthen (1789-92), Cardigan (1795-98) and Hereford (1797). By then he was once again established as an architect of repute; he returned to London, marrying in 1798 and building for himself a large house on Dover Street. He had become a country-house architect, working from London, and in the next few years, in company with the landscape gardener Humphry Repton, he worked with remarkable success; Nash followed Repton's large practice throughout England, building about eight houses and many cottages and lodges. All these were done in a delicate, varying form of classicism, with towers and irregular silhouettes, modeled in part on the picturesque spirit of the house Richard Payne Knight had designed for himself at Downton Castle, Herefordshire (1774-78). In 1802, however, the partnership with Repton broke up, as Nash was too demanding. But by then he was so well established as an architect that the commissions kept flowing in, and he designed in the next 10 years some 30 houses in Ireland and England.

The style of these houses varied; some were castles, like Luscombe Castle, Devonshire (1800-04), and Lough Cutra Castle, Galway (1812-27); some were in the Italian style, like Cronkhill, Salop (1802), and Sandridge Park, Stoke Gabriel (ca. 1805). The plans were either for enlarged versions of the conventional villa, but irregular, or for more original arrangements whereby the main rooms were all placed, again irregularly, on each side of a long gallery, open from the ground to the roof, with balconies projecting at the second-floor level. Detail was not important there, as Nash's main concern was with the pattern of massing and the silhouette of the buildings when seen, as in the picturesque manner, at a distance. It was also in this manner that he built a number of cottages and lodges, including a whole estate of cottages for pensioners at Blaise Castle, near Bristol (1811), where earlier he had designed a thatched dairy and a conservatory.

In 1806 Nash had been appointed architect to the Office of Woods and Forests, and though this was not an immediately lucrative position, it was one full of opportunities. For example, in 1811 the 500 acres of Marylebone Park, which had been leased to the duke of Portland, would revert to the Crown, and it had long been decided, that this park would be developed as a new residential area. Proposals had been solicited in 1793, but nothing came of them. In 1810, however, the commissioners of the Office of Woods and Forests and the Office of Land Revenue instructed Nash and Thomas Leverton, a builder and surveyor, to prepare plans for residences and for a street to allow access from this area to the centers of Charing Cross and Westminster. Leverton's plan was prosaic, a checkerboard pattern like that of the piecemeal development of the west of London. Nash preserved a large part of the parkland and scattered the houses among the trees, suggesting a gigantic double circus—not unlike what John Wood had designed earlier at Bath—making all this a vision of what has been called semirural picturesqueness. Nash's equally original idea for the street was based on a careful appraisal of the land values; he suggested that the street be continued beyond the park into the poorer section of Soho, with the line shifting at what is called the Quadrant so that the street would then cross Piccadilly and run down into Pall Mall. This project was built during the next few years, with Nash as general supervisor for the Commission of Woods and Forest. Builders would apply for individual building leases along the route, and Nash would suggest the proper elevation for each building.

The houses in the park followed, though the number of individual villas was reduced from the original 50 to 26; twelve lines of terraces were built at the outskirts between about 1812 and 1827, again by speculative builders, and again with their designs approved beforehand either by Nash or by Decimus Burton on Nash's authority. Those buildings too were designed more for general effect than for detail; the most complex, that at Cumberland Terrace at the east end of the park, is a three-part composition, with a central portico of 10 Ionic columns, behind which runs a great pediment filled with sculpture. One further detail there was a canal (filled up in 1942), which was to serve both as a commercial route into the park and as the source for waters to be used in the ornamental ponds that were part of the overall design of the park. For this Nash formed a company and raised the appropriate capital, investing very heavily himself in the offering.

But all that time, he was also developing a closer relationship with the prince regent. His first work for him had been the enlargement of a cottage in Windsor Great Park (1813) to house the prince regent before he could occupy Windsor Castle itself. A year later Nash built a new suite of rooms at Carlton House, and in 1815 he was asked to work on improvements at the royal residence on the south coast at Brighton, the Royal Pavilion. That building had been built by Henry Holland some 30 years earlier as a modest, classicizing house, but in 1804 William Porden had added a huge, domed stable block, purportedly in the Indian style. That planted a seed, and the prince suggested that such a style—familiar from the work of topographical painters such as William and Thomas Daniell—be used in all future renovations. There is as much Chinese decoration as Indian, and the result is a design striking in effect and original in detail, most of it done by Frederick Crace. Some new materials and techniques were used, most notably in the central onion dome, which is framed and covered with iron sheeting.

In 1820 the prince regent succeeded to the throne as George IV, and talk was immediately heard about building a new royal palace. But palaces were not a part of the English tradition, and Nash suggested, in place of a new building, the reconstruction of Buckingham House, a building of the previous century that was well situated at the southwest end of St. James' Park. Work on Buckingham Palace began in 1824, and nothing was to be preserved of the old house, except the brick frame. At that point Carlton House was demolished, and the site on which it stood was developed for housing, the result being Carlton House Terraces; the park in front was replanned to be a proper foreground, and the mall recreated to make a formal avenue on the axis of Buckingham Palace. This was Nash's last triumph, for the rebuilding of Buckingham Palace was not successful architecturally, and its costs soon far exceeded what was expected. And when George IV died in 1830, Nash was dismissed from his office as architect to the Board of Works, and was required to explain the various expeditious, if almost improper, financial arrangements he had made during the rebuilding of Buckingham Palace. A year earlier, in 1829, Nash had suffered a mild stroke,

and in 1834 he decided to leave London and retire to East Cowes in the Isle of Wight.

At his death Nash was troubled by financial difficulties since the real estate market in which he had invested so heavily was in a recession. Also, his type of architectural eclecticism was in great disrepute among the younger architects, who were speaking of such matters as purity and truth to materials. But Nash had been a highly inventive and successful architect, the first since Christopher Wren to suggest a major replanning of London. And as John Summerson has put it, Wren's proposal failed, but that of Nash succeeded.

—DAVID CAST

NERVI, Pier Luigi.

Italian. Born in Sondrio, Lombardy, 21 June 1891. Died in Rome, 9 January 1979. Married Irene Calosin, 1924; three children. Studied at Bologna University, Dip.Ing., 1913. Officer in the Engineering Corps of the Italian Army, 1915-18; engineer with the Società per Costruzioni Cementizie, Bologna, 1913-15 and 1918-23. In private practice, Rome, from 1923: partner, Nervi and Nebbiosi, 1923-32; president, Ingg. Nervi and Bartolia, from 1932; partner with sons Antonio, Mario and Vittorio, Studio Nervi, 1960 until his death in 1979. Professor of Technology and Technique of Construction, Architecture Department, University of Rome, 1947-61. Gold Medal, Royal Institute of British Architects, 1960.

Chronology of Works
All in Italy unless noted
† *Work no longer exists*

1927	August Cinema, Naples
1929-32	Municipal Stadium, Florence†
1935/40	Aircraft Hangars for the Italian Air Force, Orvieto
1942-43	Cargo Boat
1948-50	Exhibition Halls, Salone B and Salone C, Turin
1953-58	UNESCO Secretariat Building and Conference Hall, Paris, France (with Bernard Zehrfuss and Marcel Breuer)
1955-59	Pirelli Tower, Milan (with Gio Ponti and others)
1956-57	Palazzeto dello Sport, Rome (with Annibale Vitellozzi)
1957-59	Flaminio Stadium, Rome (with Antonio Nervi)
1958-59	Palazzo dello Sport, Rome (with Marcello Piacentini)
1958-60	Corso Francia elevated road, Rome
1958-61	Railway station, Savona
1960-61	Palace of Labor, Turin
1960-62	Bus Terminal, New York City, U.S.A.
1961-63	Burgo paper manufacturing plant, Mantua
1961-67	Australia Square Tower, Sydney, Australia
1962-66	Place Victoria Tower, Montreal, Canada
1963-68	Risorgimento Bridge, Verona
1966-71	St. Mary's Cathedral, San Francisco, California, U.S.A.
1966-71	Papal Audience Hall, Vatican City

Publications

BOOKS BY NERVI

El lenguaje arquitectonico. Buenos Aires, 1950.
Arte o scienza del costruire? Rome, 1954.

Pier Luigi Nervi: Palazzo dello Sport, Rome, Italy, 1956-59

Costruire correttamente. Milan, 1955. English ed.: *Structures*. New York, 1956.

Concrete and Structural Form. London, 1955.

Nuove strutture. Milan, 1963. English ed.: *New Structures*. London and Stuttgart, 1963.

Aesthetics and Technology in Building. Cambridge, Massachusetts, and London, 1965.

ARTICLES BY NERVI

"Arte e technica del costruire." *Quadrante* (June 1931).

"Precast Concrete Offers New Possibilities for Design of Shell Structures." *American Concrete Institute Journal* (February 1953).

"The Place of Structure in Architecture." *Architectural Record* (July 1956).

"Reinforced Concrete Construction." *Progressive Architecture* (September 1957).

"Critica delle strutture." *Casabella* (January, February, March and April 1959).

BOOKS ABOUT NERVI

ARGAN, GIULIO CARLO: *Pier Luigi Nervi*. Milan, 1955.

BILLINGTON, DAVID P.: *The Tower and the Bridge: The New Art of Structural Engineering*. Princeton, New Jersey, 1983.

DESIDERI, PAOLO; NERVI, PIER LUIGI; and POSITANO, GIUSEPPE: *Pier Luigi Nervi*. Bologna, 1979.

HUXTABLE, ADA LOUISE: *Aesthetics and Technology in Building*. Cambridge, Massachusetts, 1965.
HUXTABLE, ADA LOUISE: *Pier Luigi Nervi*. New York, 1960.
JOEDICKE, JÜRGEN, and ROGERS, ERNESTO NATHAN: *The Works of Pier Luigi Nervi*. Stuttgart and London, 1957.
MAJOR, MATE: *Pier Luigi Nervi*. Budapest 1966, Berlin 1970.
PICA, AGNOLDOMENICO: *Pier Luigi Nervi*. Rome, 1969.

ARTICLES ABOUT NERVI

KATO, AKINORE (ed.): "Pier Luigi Nervi." *Process: Architecture* special issue (April 1981).

Pier Luigi Nervi once said, "By education and by choice, I am an engineer." Despite that declaration, he is considered one of the greatest architects of the 20th century. He created structures with the aesthetic eye of an artist and the scientific scrutiny of an engineer, generating what he called "a creative synthesis of structure and design."

Although Nervi's closest stylistic parallels were his predecessors Robert Maillart and François Hennebique, he was unaware of most of their projects until he had been practicing for 15 or 20 years. Nervi did not look to his contemporaries for solutions to his architectural challenges; he merely looked deeper into the problems themselves. While many architects, both in Italy and around the world, designed minimal rectilinear structures in line with the International Style, Nervi created architecture in a flowing and organic manner.

He was frugal and honest in his structural design, allowing no force to take an inefficient route to its goal. He called this the "Truthful Style," and it gave his structures a logical simplicity that made them easy to build. "When I approach a project," he said, "I first reject all solutions which do not seem to be economically valid." Nervi's work was the product of an engineer's search for the most efficient solution to, and most aesthetic expression of, a spatial problem: "I have never found this relentless search for economy an obstacle to achieving the expressiveness of form I desired. On the contrary, the technical factor, like the static one, has often been a source of inspiration."

With the strength of Fascism in the 1920s, Italian rationalism became the most important interwar architectural movement. Giuseppe Terragni, for example, through buildings like his Casa del Fascio (1932-36), attempted a compromise between the outright nationalism of Italian classicism and the increasingly compelling structural logic of the machine age. Nervi too was influenced by machine-age logic, as well as by the writings of Le Corbusier; however, he never aligned himself with any group or movement, and his work remained stylistically independent of passing trends.

After his 1913 graduation from the school of Civil Engineering in Bologna, Nervi spent 15 years working for the Società per Costruzioni Cementizie. As he supervised construction sites and researched reinforced concrete, Nervi became fascinated by its properties. He wrote: "Mankind has never before had a material of such expressive potential and so adaptable to solutions of the technical and social problems of our times. . . . A new material and new times call for a new architecture."

From 1932 onward he headed his own company, Società Inggenieure Nervi e Bartoli, working as engineer, architect and contractor on all his projects. He insisted that "the collaboration of architect, engineer and builder is absolutely necessary." Controlling all aspects of the building process, Nervi kept efficiency high and could invent new methods of construction to help him realize his architectural visions.

In 1935 he created his first true masterpiece, a series of airplane hangars at Orbeletto for the Italian Air Force. Each hangar had a roof of crisscrossing solid concrete arches, the whole of which rested on Nervi's famous leaning columns. The end result was overwhelming, yet gracefully refined. Then, in 1940 he improved upon that design with a second set. To simplify the construction process he precast the roof in manageable truss-like sections. This saved the time, labor and wood of a giant formwork, making the structures quicker and cheaper to build. The second hangar project marked the beginning of Nervi's use of precast members, a practice he later developed into an artistic and stylistic signature.

Nervi invented a new construction material called "ferrocemento," which permitted him to create his flowing patterns. Ferro-cemento consisted of wire mesh with about three quarters of an inch of concrete sprayed on top. It could be made in any shape without formwork and was sturdy enough to be a structural member even in his most massive projects.

For example, in 1948 Nervi won a commission to replace an exhibition hall in Turin, but had only eight months to do so. Known as the "Salone B," this new hall had to be 310 feet by 243 feet, with no interior supports. Nervi designed it as a long, low, transversely corrugated vault made of hundreds of identical prefabricated ferro-cemento pieces. Later, they were covered with a thin layer of reinforced concrete to bond them into a monolithic whole. Nervi then continued to use this process, bonding small, light ferro-cemento parts into enormous thin-shell structures like the Palazzo dello Sport for the 1960 Olympic Games in Rome.

Throughout his life Nervi wrote and lectured as much as possible. His major theme was "correctness" in construction, which included criteria like stability and ease of use. Most important, though, was the naturalness, comprehensibility and efficiency of a structure's static scheme. Like any good engineer, Nervi insisted that designers focus on the efficient solution of structural problems, after which the design would easily unfold.

Because of their "correctness," industrial revolution engineering feats such as the Firth of Forth Bridge and the 1889 Hall of Machines were among Nervi's greatest influences. Apart from that era of large-scale engineering advances, he believed that "the Gothic was the highest expression of a true art of building." Great Gothic cathedrals, like Notre Dame de Paris, most closely followed his requirement of static efficiency, being, as he put it, a "fusion of aesthetics and technology so complete that one cannot separate construction from architecture." Nervi sought just that, the fusion of aesthetics and technology, and he achieved it.

—DAVID PLUMMER

NESFIELD, W. Eden.

British. Born William Eden Nesfield in 1835. Died in 1888. Father was the landscape gardener William Andrews Nesfield (1793-1881). Studied with William Burn (1789-1870), 1851-53; studied with his uncle, Anthony Salvin (1799-1881), 1853-56; toured Europe, 1857-58. Opened own office, 1858; partnership with Richard Norman Shaw (1831-1912), 1866-68; continued to work independently until his retirement in 1880.

Chronology of Works

All in England unless noted

† *Work no longer exists*

1860-61	Farm buildings, Shipley Hall, Derbyshire
1861-62	Croxteth Hall, Lancashire (cottages)
1863	Sproughton Manor, Suffolk
1863-65	Combe Abbey, Warwickshire (addition)†
1864	Lodge, Regent's Park, London†
1864-68	Cloverley Hall, Shropshire†
1865	Estate cottage, Crewe Hall, Cheshire
1867	Lodge, Kew Gardens, London
1870	Southampton Lodge, Broadlands, Hampshire
1871-74	Kinmel Park, Denbigh, Wales
1872-74	Bodrhyddan, Flintshire, Wales
1872-75	Barclays Bank, Saffron Walden, Essex
1872-78	Holy Trinity, Calverhall, Shropshire
1873-74	Plas Dinan House, Montgomeryshire, Wales
1877-78	Babbacombe Cliff, Devon
1877-80	Gwernyfed Park, Brecon, Wales
1878	Loughton Hall, Essex
1878	Grammar School, Newport, Essex

Publications

BOOKS BY NESFIELD

Specimens of Mediaeval Architecture. London, 1862.

BOOKS ABOUT NESFIELD

DIXON, ROGER, and MUTHESIUS, STEFAN: *Victorian Architecture.* New York and Toronto, 1978.

SAINT, ANDREW: *Richard Norman Shaw.* New Haven, Connecticut, 1976.

SERVICE, ALASTAIR (ed.): *Edwardian Architecture and Its Origins.* London, 1975.

ARTICLES ABOUT NESFIELD

BRYDON, J. M.: "William Eden Nesfield." *Architectural Review* 1 (1896-97): 235-247, 283-295.

CRESWELL, H. B.: "William Eden Nesfield, 1835-1888: An Impression and a Contrast." *Architectural Review* 2 (1897): 23-32.

FORSYTH, JAMES: "William Eden Nesfield." *Architectural Association Notes* 16 (August 1901): 109-111.

HEBB, JOHN: "William Eden Nesfield." *Journal of the Royal Institute of British Architects* Series 3, 10 (1903): 396-400.

SPIERS, R. P.: "Development of Modern Architecture." *Magazine of Art* 21 (1898): 83-88.

*

Although William Eden Nesfield, with his partner, Richard Norman Shaw, is best known as the creator of the Old English style, his earliest buildings were all Gothic in style, done in the muscular High Victorian manner of William Butterfield and George Edmund Street. Nesfield first demonstrated his genius in the design of the sumptuous wing at Combe Abbey in Warwickshire (1863-65), where his Gothic became a personal idiosyncratic style several years before William Burges had built Castell Coch or Cardiff Castle. In style, the Combe Abbey wing combined Norman, Gothic and Tudor with perfect ease; it was a masterly composition. Its arches were round, not pointed, and its major architectural theme was the English late-medieval window-wall of huge windows divided by stone tracery into many rectangular lights. It was the boldest step yet among Gothic revivalists away from stylistic purity, and it suggested the eclectic Old English style to come.

Nesfield's experiments at Combe Abbey led him, after 1862, to evolve his own variant of the new Old English style. It was just another stylistic possibility for him, one he thought most appropriate for small cottages, but of doubtful value for large houses. His Regent's Park Lodge (1864) gave London its introduction to the revived vernacular style. The lodge was typical of the cottages and lodges Nesfield designed for patrons throughout the country. It was picturesque like the Regency cottages of John Nash, but designed with greater finesse and built with more careful craftsmanship. All of Nesfield's buildings were lovingly adorned with all manner of willful eclectic detail borrowed from sources as diverse as Japanese classical architecture and vernacular farmhouses—incised work, carved bargeboards, tongue-shaped wall tiling, turned balusters, heraldry, dates and monograms.

Other domestic architects produced eclectic work, but Nesfield outshone all at fusing disparate elements into coherent new styles. Nesfield's first major work, Cloverly Hall (1864-68) enlarged upon and refined the ideas of Combe Abbey. It features two-inch brickwork, split-level planning, massive use of concealed structural ironwork, slate-hanging, a stable tower with penthouse, and much refined ornament, much of which is of Japanese derivation. Its central feature is a tall great hall, and the amount of window exceeds that at Combe Abbey.

Elsewhere Nesfield's style was very different. Kew Gardens Lodge and Kinmel Park, also designed in the 1860s, were among the first recognizably Queen Anne buildings to appear in England. They were inspired by the Dutch House at Kew and Christopher Wren's Hampton Court block, respectively. The Kew Gardens Lodge of 1867 is particularly charming. It is small and simple, rectangular in plan, but deliberately asymmetrical. It features brickwork done in an early-18th-century manner and a two-story design made to appear to be a story-and-a-half by means of a very steep roof and gigantic dormers. It plays asymmetrical elements—an off-center entrance and dormers on the front and one side—against a traditional classical form. The Queen Anne style has been described as a "Classical style without Classical laws of proportion" (*Victorian Architecture,* p. 27). In fact the Queen Anne style follows no laws at all; it attempts solely to be attractive, simple and homely. The Kew Gardens Lodge is a perfect example.

So is Nesfield's masterpiece, Kinmel Park, Denbighshire (1871-74), which is one of the most grandiose exercises in the Queen Anne style ever constructed. The house is actually a remodeling and expansion of an existing Greek Revival house. An additional story was added, but many features were determined by what was there. The existing window openings were retained in most instances, and the shifted axis between front and garden entries was also kept. Nesfield added a steep pitched roof to contain the new third floor, a two-bay terminal pavilion at the north end, a centered entry pavilion on both sides, and an extensive service wing to connect the stables to the house on the south. The main body of the house would appear to be a French château such as François Mansart might have designed in brick for an English gentleman. Only the asymmetrical chimney placements disturb the symmetry. It is surprising, therefore, to discover that classical symmetry and axial planning play no part in the shape and arrangement of rooms. What clearly establishes the house as a great Victorian mansion is the vast picturesque service and stable wing, which is treated as a totally free composition. It is testimony to Nesfield's compositional genius that the two parts create an harmonious unity.

The house is generously decorated throughout. Brick and stone alternate to form quoins on all pavilion corners. Window and door frames are stone; richly carved stone friezes cap each story. Nesfield's "pies," borrowed from Japanese sunburst patterns, and the sunflowers associated with the Aesthetic movement decorate both interior and exterior.

Nesfield, like many others of his day, was fascinated by Japan. His decorative patterns invariably include overlapping and free-floating pies, incised cement plasterwork or woodwork in circular Japanese patterns. But he borrowed as freely from the medieval and classical traditions as well. For him, these eclectic borrowings, which he used to decorate his work between 1865 and 1880, symbolized the architect's claim to a wider freedom of stylistic choice. That is what the Aesthetic movement was all about—the liberation of art from ethical values. Anything that looked good was good. For Nesfield, style was a matter of simple choice and personal preference to be decided upon almost whimsically. Other than his unfailing compositional judgment, he used no rules or guidelines to shape his designs; yet he invariably produced sensitively proportioned, gracefully detailed, light-filled domestic buildings that remain, today, pleasant environments for living.

—C. MURRAY SMART, JR.

NEUMANN, Johann Balthasar.

German. Born January 1687. Died in Würzburg, Germany, 18 August 1753. Apprenticed as a foundryman, ca. 1700. Settled in Würzburg to work in the foundry of Ignaz Kopp, 1711; trained in architecture, 1711-13; worked on a map of Würzburg, 1714-15; worked for the chief architect of Würzburg, Josef Gretsing, from 1715; appointed architect of a new Grand Palace in Würzburg by the Prince-Bishop Johann Philipp Franz, 1719; became first architect of Würzburg, by 1724; appointed *baudirektor*, 1729; consultant for military and civil building in Trier, 1733.

Chronology of Works
All in Germany
† Work no longer exists

1717-53	Residenz, Würzburg (not completed until 1776)
1721-36	Schönborn Chapel, Würzburg
1723-33	Fortifications, Würzburg
1726	Inn 'Zum Hirschen' (now Dresdner Bank), Würzburg
1726-30	Benedictine Priory Church, Holzkirchen (roof incorrectly replaced)
1727-43	Benedictine Abbey Church, Münsterschwarzbach†
1728-50	Saint Damiansburg Palace, Bruchsal†
1729	Fortifications, Ehrenbreitstein
1730-33	Chapter House, Bamberg
1730-39	Parish and Pilgrimage Church of the Holy Trinity, Gössweinstein
1731-33	Seminary (now City Hall), Bamberg
1732-34	Würzburg Residenz Church, Würzburg
1733-44	Schloss Werneck (Schönborn Summer Palace), Werneck
1734-45	Werneck Summer Palace Chapel, Werneck
1734-53	Collegiate Church of St. Paulin, Trier (not completed until 1754)
1737-53	Market Place, Stores, Theaterstrasse, Würzburg
1738-40	Cathedral, Worms (high altar)
1738-40	Rombach Palace, Würzburg
1738-53	Parish Church of St. Peter, Bruchsal (not completed until the 1770s)
1739-53	Parish and Mortuary Church of Sts. Cecilia and Barbara, Heusenstamm (not completed until 1756)
1740-45	Parish Church of the Holy Cross, Gaibach
1740-45	Parish Church of the Holy Cross, Kitzingen
1740-48	Schloss Augustusburg, near Brühl (grand staircase)
1740-52	Pilgrimage Church of the Visitation of Mary, Würzburg (called the Käppele; later additions 1761-81)
1741-53	Dominican (now Augustinian) Church, Würzburg (not completed until 1771)
1742-46	Jesuit Church of St. Ignatius, Mainz†
1742-53	Premonstratensian Monastery, Oberzell (facade, convent; stair, completed 1760)
1743-53	Pilgrimage Church of the Assumption of Mary, Vierzehnheiligen (not completed until 1772)
1743-53	Benedictine Abbey Church of the Holy Cross, Neresheim (not completed until the 1790s)
1745-51	Holy Stairs, Bonn
1749	Cathedral, Würzburg (alterations and additions)
1751-53	Pilgrimage and Parish Church of the Visitation of Mary, Limbach am Main (not completed until the 1760s)
1752	Monastery, Banz (front wings; constructed by J. J. M. Küchel)
1753	Palace, Veitshöchheim (additions and stair)

Publications

BOOKS ABOUT NEUMANN

BACHMANN, E.: *Residenz Würzburg*. Munich, 1970.

Balthasar Neumann in Baden-Württenberg. Exhibition catalog. Stuttgart, 1975.

Balthasar Neumann, Leben und Werk: Gedächtnisschau zum 200. Todestage. Exhibition catalog. Würzburg, 1953.

BLUNT, ANTHONY (ed.): *Kunst und Kultur des Barock und Rokoko: Architektur und Dekoration*. Freiburg, 1979.

BOLL, WALTER: *Die Schönbornkapelle am Würzburger Dom: Ein Beitrag zur Kunstgeschichte des XVIII. Jahrhunderts*. Munich, 1925.

BRINCKMANN, ALBERT E.: *Von Guarino Guarini bis Balthasar Neumann*. Berlin, 1932.

HANSMANN, WILFRIED: *Balthasar Neumann: Leben und Werk*. Cologne, 1986.

HIRSCH, FRITZ: *Das sogenannte Skizzenbuch Balthasar Neumanns: Ein Beitrag zur Charakteristik des Meisters und zur Philosophie der Baukunst*. Nendeln, Germany, 1912; 1978.

HITCHCOCK, HENRY-RUSSELL: *Rococo Architecture in Southern Germany*. London, 1968.

HOTZ, JOACHIM: *Katalog der Sammlung Eckert aus dem Nachlass Balthasar Neumanns im Mainfränkischen Museum Würzburg*. Würzburg, 1965.

KELLER, JOSEPH: *Balthasar Neumann: Eine Studie zur Kunstgeschichte des 18. Jahrhunderts*. Würzburg, 1896.

KNAPP, FRITZ: *Balthasar Neumann—Der grosse Architekt seiner Zeit*. Bielefeld, Germany, 1937.

KORTH, THOMAS, and POESCHKE, JOACHIM (eds.): *Balthasar Neumann. Kunstgeschichtliche Beiträge zum Jubiläumsjahr 1987*. Munich, 1987.

LOHMEYER, KARL: *Die Briefe Balthasar Neumanns an Friedrich Karl von Schönborn*. Saarbrücken, Germany, 1921.

LOHMEYER, KARL: *Die Briefe Balthasar Neumanns von seiner Pariser Studienreise 1723*. Düsseldorf, 1911.

Johann Balthasar Neumann: Schloss Augustusburg, Brühl, Germany, 1740-48

NEUMANN, GÜNTHER: *Neresheim*. Munich, 1947.

NORBERG-SCHULZ, CHRISTIAN: *Architektur des Barock*. Stuttgart, 1975.

NORBERG-SCHULZ, CHRISTIAN: *Architektur des Spatbarock und Rokoko*. Stuttgart, 1975.

OTTO, CHRISTIAN F.: *Space into Light: The Churches of Balthasar Neumann*. Cambridge, Massachusetts, and London, 1979.

REUTHER, HANS: *Die Kirchenbauten Balthasar Neumanns*. Berlin, 1960.

SCHENK, CLEMENS: *Balthasar Neumanns Kirchenbaukunst*. Würzburg, 1939.

SEDLMAIER, RICHARD, and PFISTER, RUDOLF: *Die fürstbischöfliche Residenz zu Würzburg*. 2 vols. Munich, 1923.

TEUFEL, RICHARD: *Balthasar Neumann: Sein Werk in Oberfranken*. Lichtenfels, Germany, 1953.

TEUFEL, RICHARD: *Vierzehnheiligen*. Lichtenfels, Germany, 1936; 2nd ed., 1957.

Verzeichnis der Bücher, Kupferstiche und Handzeichnugnen aus der Verlassenschaft. Würzburg, 1804.

VON FREEDEN, MAX HERRMANN: *Balthasar Neumann als Stadtbaumeister*. Würzburg, 1937; 1978.

VON FREEDEN, MAX HERRMANN: *Balthasar Neumann: Leben und Werk*. 2nd ed. Munich and Berlin, 1963.

ARTICLES ABOUT NEUMANN

ANDERSEN, LISELOTTE: ''Studien zu Profanbauformen Baltha-
    sar Neumanns: Die grossen Residenzprojekte für Wien,
    Stuttgart und Karlsruhe.'' Unpublished Ph.D. dissertation,
    University of Munich, 1966.
BACHMANN, E.: ''Balthasar Neumann und das Mittelalter.''
    Stifter-Jahrbuch, III (1953).
BRUNEL, GEORGES: ''Würzburg: Les Contacts entre Balthasar
    Neumann et Robert de Cotte.'' *Actes du XXII Congrès Inter-
    national d'Histoire de l'Art (Budapest, 1969)*. Budapest,
    1972.
FRANZ, HEINRICH GEBHARD: ''Die Klosterkirche Banz und
    die Kirchen Balthasar Neumanns in ihrem Verhältnis zur
    böhmischen Barockbaukunst.'' *Zeitschrift für Kunstwis-
    senschaft* 1 (1947): 54-72.
FRANZL, LUDWIG: ''Balthasar Neumann: Dachwerke seiner
    Landeskirchen.'' Dissertation. Technische Universität, Ber-
    lin, 1982.
HEGEMANN, HANS WERNER: ''Die Altarbaukunst Balthasar
    Neumanns.'' Ph.D. dissertation, University of Marburg, Ger-
    many, 1937.
REUTHER, HANS: ''Die Landkirchen Balthasar Neumanns.''
    Zeitschrift für Kunstgeschichte 16 (1953): 154-170.
REUTHER, HANS: ''Nachtrag zum Balthasar Neumann-Jubi-
    läumsjahr 1953.'' *Kunstchronik* 7 (1954): 35-37.
REUTHER, HANS: ''Neues Schrifttum über Balthasar Neu-
    mann.'' *Kunstchronik* 6 (1953): 209-221.

*

Balthasar Neumann was one of the most important German architects of the early 18th century, the traditional period when the Late Baroque started to give way to the Rococo. Neumann's career was closely linked with the two prince-bishops von Schönborn—Johann Philipp Franz and Friedrich Carl—whose preferred architect he was. Under Friedrich Carl von Schönborn he became responsible for all military, religious and civic architecture of the independent districts of Würzburg and Bamberg, besides the prince-bishop's private houses, including gardens. He also became architectural consultant to all the princes of southern Germany, excepting Bavaria. Neumann's oeuvre is typified most of all by its diversity. He received commissions for religious and for secular buildings, and was in that respect an exception among the architects of his time.

Born to a clothmaker in Bohemia in 1687, Neumann embarked in about 1700 on an apprenticeship as a foundryman specializing in bells and cannon. In 1711 he came to Würzburg, where he met the engineer Andreas Müller. Müller encouraged him to give up his profession to study the theory of civil and military architecture. In 1714 Neumann joined the personal staff of the prince-bishop, quickly climbing the ranks in the following years. Soon, he was made the Würzburg prince-bishop's chief engineer, and took part in military campaigns in the Balkans and in northern Italy. He also accompanied the prince-bishop's chief architect, Josef Greising, on inspection tours in those years. In 1719 Neumann was made the prince-bishop's architectural director, and in the same year he began work on designs for the prince-bishop's Residenz in Würzburg, also coordinating the work of the other architects involved in the project. The Würzburg Residenz was his lifework: he coordinated the design process, supervised construction from 1720 to 1744, and collaborated on the ornamentation until 1753. His three-month trip to Paris was related to his work on that palace.

Between 1723 and 1729, Neumann began designs for the Priory Church at Holzkirchen near Würzburg, and the Benedictine Abbey Church at Münsterschwarzbach. He also collaborated on designs for the St. Damiansburg Palace at Bruchasal. From 1729 to 1746, Friedrich Carl von Schönborn was his most important patron. Neumann designed Schloss Werneck (1733-44), the Würzburg Residenz Church (1732-34), the Cathedral Chapter House at Bamberg (1730-33), the Parish and Pilgrimage Church at Gossweinstein (1730-39), the Augustinian Church at Würzburg (1741-44), the high altar for Worms Cathedral (1738-40), and the grand staircase for Schloss Augustusburg near Brühl (1740). His designs for the expansions of the Vienna Hofburg were also done during that period. In 1749 he again became chief architectural director in Würzburg, under the prince-bishop Carl Philip von Greifenclau. From 1743 onward, Neumann worked on the plans and designs of his two completed late works: the Pilgrimage Church at Vierzehnheiligen and the Benedictine Abbey at Neresheim.

Besides churches and houses for the nobility, he designed fortifications (Würzburg 1723-33; Ehrenbreitstein, 1729), bridges, mills, streets, and numerous civic buildings and houses. Already in 1715, an intensive grappling with problems of urban planning was apparent in his work. The broad range of his architecture indicates numerous influences from the architectural traditions of Austria, Bohemia, France and Italy. Neumann never copied architectural models, however, but absorbed them into his own style. As a consequence, direct models are rarely to be found for any of his buildings. Nevertheless, Neumann himself pointed out how important engravings and firsthand experiences from his travels were to him.

The earliest known designs by Neumann, for the Würzburg Residenz (1717) and for the Schönborn Chapel at Würzburg Cathedral (1721), already showed the characteristics of his formal idiom. The characteristic disposition of the wings of the residence around large courtyards, and the principle of enclosing one room within another were already in evidence there. During the design of the Schönborn Chapel and the Residenz Church, Neumann came up against the most important architect of the Austrian Baroque, Johann Lukas von Hildebrandt (1688-1745). Competing with Hildebrandt, Neumann also responded to his work. In the process, he achieved greater clarity in spatial expression, gained a sense of proportion and dynamics, which contributed to the expressive wealth of his work. Neumann also adopted Hildebrandt's signature motif, a large curved and scalloped gable with a relief field, making it his own. In the 18th century, that was not so much plagiarism as the recognition of a rival's artistic ability.

During the construction of the Würzburg Residenz Church, Neumann began his experimentations with different vault systems. In later years he pursued the idea of intersecting vaults as well as the concept of interior structures unrelated to the shell of the walls. The Werneck Summer Place Chapel (design process begun in 1734, construction completed in 1744-45), for instance, has an oval vault, supported by downward-tapered pillars with round niches set between them. The vault, it must be noted, covers a trapezoidal room.

Because of his technical proficiency in the construction of vaults, Neumann achieved exceptional designs with the grand staircases at Schloss Augustusburg near Brühl (1743-48) and at the Würzburg Residenz (1752-53). The latter, decorated with frescoes by Giovanni Battista Tiepolo, may be considered one of the most impressive Baroque interiors.

Neumann was also known for his ability to save muddled designs, of which the Pilgrimage Church at Vierzehnheiligen is a good example. The designs submitted in 1742 called for a church with a Latin-cross plan. The abbott of the Cistercian monastery to which the church belonged chose a building master who was to realize the construction according to Neumann's design. However, the builder independently changed the plan, shortening the choir in such a way that the altar came to be situated at the end of the nave, in front of the crossing rather than in the crossing, as Neumann had planned it.

Since the foundation had already been laid, Neumann had to work out a new design incorporating the changes. When construction work was resumed in 1744, Neumann used a principle he had also employed in the Würzburg Residenz Church. He situated a long, oval vault not over the crossing but over the altar in the eastern part of the nave, and set smaller oval vaults at each end of the long one. The disposition of the vaults and the use of the pilaster order or the pillar-column motif create a clear spatial organization with a focus on the altar.

Neumann often used new motifs, introducing variations or further developments of them. Again and again, he returned to procedures used years before, treating these in the same way. The development of his buildings, from the first designs to completion of construction, never was a linear process with Neumann. Ideas of the early design phases, set aside in favor of others, were often retrieved later for new applications. Such a design process preceded the construction of the Abbey Church at Neresheim, one of his most successful buildings. Neumann's integration of a prominent rotunda within a rectangular design is one of the greatest achievements of Late Baroque spatial organization.

The great diversity of Neumann's design solutions shows the extent to which his work again and again engaged fundamental tectonic problems. The problem of reconciling a dominant circular shape with a basic longitudinal plan was especially important to him. In the churches at Vierzehnheiligen and Neresheim he created the most beautiful solutions. Neumann was also greatly interested in double endings of interior spaces, in which the structural skeleton is clearly distinguished from the outer wall. In his most important buildings the problems of interior space were solved by an interpenetration of rooms. Neumann's churches are distinguished by a unique and harmonious monumentality. As a consequence of the rich interior ornamentation (frescoes, sculptures, stucco, marble), often finished only after his death, his buildings became exemplary instances of Late Baroque and Rococo *Gesamtkunstwerke*.

—PETRA LESER

Translated from the German by Marijke Rijsberman

NEUTRA, Richard.

Austrian. Born in Vienna, Austria, 8 April 1892. Died in Wuppertal, Germany, 16 April 1970. Trained at Technische Hochschule, Vienna, graduated 1918. Worked in Berlin; moved to the United States, 1923; worked in New York and Chicago before settling in southern California. In private practice, Los Angeles, from 1925: in partnership with Robert Alexander, 1949-58, and with his son Dion in Richard and Dion Neutra and Associates, Los Angeles, 1965-70.

Chronology of Works
All in the United States unless noted

1927	Jardinette Apartments, Los Angeles, California
1927-29	Lovell Health House, Los Angeles, California
1931	Office Building for Universal-International, Los Angeles, California
1932	Van Der Leeuw House (Neutra House), Silverlake,

Los Angeles (destroyed by fire 1963; rebuilt by Neutra, with his son Dion, 1964)

1934	Corona Avenue School, Los Angeles, California
1934	Sten House, Los Angeles, California
1935	Beard House, Altadena, California
1935	Von Sternberg House, San Fernando Valley, California†
1936	Plywood Model House, Los Angeles, California
1936	California Military Academy, Los Angeles, California
1937	Brown House, Fisher's Island, New York
1937	Kraigher House, Brownsville, Texas
1937	Kun House, Los Angeles, California
1937	Miller House, Palm Springs, California
1937	Strathmore Apartments, Los Angeles, California
1937	Beckstrand House, Palos Verdes, California
1938	Lewin House, Los Angeles, California
1939	National Youth Administration Centers, Sacramento and San Luis Obispo, California
1939	Amity House, Compton, California
1940	Kahn House, Telegraph Hill, San Francisco, California
1940	Evans Plywood Building, Lebanon, Oregon
1941	Avion Village, Texas
1942	Kelton Apartments, Westwood, Los Angeles, California
1942	Channel Heights Housing, San Pedro, California
1942	Nesbitt House, Los Angeles, California
1944	Rural School Buildings, Puerto Rico
1946	Desert House, Palm Springs, California
1948	Tremaine House, Montecito, California
1951	Hinds House, Los Angeles, California
1951	Price House, Bayport, New York
1952	Moore House, Ojai, California
1957	Slavin House, Santa Barbara, California
1959	Licoln Memorial Museum, Gettysburg, Pennsylvania
1959	United States Embassy, Karachi, Pakistan
1961	Glen House, Stamford, Connecticut
1961	Hall of Records, Los Angeles, California
1964	Rentsch House, Wenger, Switzerland

Publications

BOOKS BY NEUTRA

Wie baut Amerika? Stuttgart, 1926. English ed., edited by Thomas Hines. Los Angeles, 1979.
Amerika. Vienna, 1930. English ed., edited by Thomas Hines. Los Angeles, 1979.
National Planning Methods of Mass Housing. With the editors of the International Congress for New Building. London, 1930.
House and Home. With others. New York, 1935.
Circle: Routes of Housing Advance. With others. London, 1938.
Preface to a Master Plan. With others. Los Angeles, 1942.
New Architecture and City Planning. With Paul Zucker. New York, 1945.
Architecture of Social Concern in Regions of Mild Climate. São Paulo, 1948.
Mystery and Realities of the Site. New York, 1951.
Survival Through Design. New York and London, 1954.
Life and Human Habitat. Stuttgart, 1956.
Life and Shape (autobiography). New York, 1962.
Auftrag für Morgen. Hamburg, 1962.
World and Dwelling. Stuttgart, 1962.
Building with Nature. New York, 1970.

Richard Neutra: Desert House, Palm Springs, California, 1946

Pflänzen, Wasser, Steine, Licht. With Dion Neutra. Berlin, 1974.
Bauen und die Sinneswelt. Dresden, 1977.

BOOKS ABOUT NEUTRA

BOESIGER, WILLY (ed.): *Richard Neutra: Buildings and Projects.* Vol. 1. Zurich and London, 1923-66.
DREXLER, ARTHUR, and HINES, THOMAS S.: *The Architecture of Richard Neutra: From International Style to California Modern.* Exhibition catalog. New York, 1982.
EXNER, H.; NEUTRA, D.; HAMERBACHER, H. (eds.): *Richard and Dion Neutra: Pflanzen, Wasser, Steine, Licht.* Berlin and Hamburg, West Germany 1974.
HINES, THOMAS: *Richard Neutra and the Search for Modern Architecture.* New York and Oxford, 1982.
McCOY, ESTHER: *Richard Neutra.* New York, 1960.
McCOY, ESTHER (ed.): *Vienna to Los Angeles: 2 Journeys—Richard Neutra and Rudolph M. Schindler.* Santa Monica, California, 1979.
NEUTRA, DIONE, (ed): *Richard Neutra, Promise and Fulfillment 1919-1932.* 1986.
PAL, MATÉ: *Richard Neutra.* Budapest 1970.
PAWLEY, MARTIN: *Richard Neutra.* London, 1971.
SPADE, RUPERT: *Richard Neutra.* New York and London, 1971.
WRIGHT, FREDERICK: *Richard Neutra: Is Planning Possible?* Los Angeles, 1958.
ZEVI, BRUNO: *Richard Neutra.* Milan, 1954.

*

Born in Vienna in 1892, Richard Neutra grew up in the city at the time of its greatest architectural creativity. As a teenager he met Adolf Loos, saw his buildings and imbibed the notion that ornament was crime. Loos had lived in the United States for three years and communicated his enthusiasm for the new world to the young Neutra, so when the Wasmuth publications of Frank Lloyd Wright appeared in 1911, Neutra greeted them with enthusiasm. For most of the architects of the European avant-garde, admiration for the houses of Frank Lloyd Wright was mixed with dismay at their remoteness, their suburbanism and their lack of commitment to simple geometric form. Neutra was young, open-minded and naturally inclined to appreciate things American; he understood much of what Wright was doing and longed to see the buildings on the ground. Wright remained the greatest influence on Neutra for his entire working life.

But thoughts of transatlantic travel had to be postponed until the coming of peace and prosperity. For a time Neutra worked in Switzerland on landscape and city planning projects. After World War I the public offices of German cities became exciting and sometimes revolutionary places for architects to work, and Neutra was employed by the municipality of Luckenwalde. In 1922 he moved to Berlin and became familiar with those architects who can be seen, in retrospect, to have been the key architects of the time: Ludwig Hilberseimer, Arthur Korn, Ludwig Mies van der Rohe, Erich Mendelsohn. Sometimes Neutra collaborated with them, and occasionally he would receive a direct commission for a house and would set himself up in one of their offices. In 1923 Mendelsohn and Neutra were partners for the winning entry for a competition for a business center in Haifa, Israel.

Berlin in the early 1920s was an exciting place for a young architect. It was a great world of ideas, and a few significant buildings were being built. But for Neutra America beckoned; for a long time he had seen it as the land of opportunity, and in 1923 he crossed the Atlantic with his wife, Dione. The attraction of America was not the commerce and skyscrapers of New York, but the more spacious, open world of Flank Lloyd Wright, so it was to the Midwest that the Neutras went.

Neutra found work with Holabird and Roche, a large Chicago commercial architectural firm that had built pioneer framed structures during the heroic age of Chicago architecture 30 years previously. Before long he achieved his ambition and worked with Wright at Taliesin, Wisconsin. Neutra had first known Wright's work through books; now he was in close contact with the man himself. Even though Neutra eventually was to have a famous practice of his own, through all these phases his admiration and affection for the older architect remained unchanged.

Parallel with his love of architecture, Neutra had another interest, the relation of man with nature. He coined the expression "biorealism" in contrast to "dollars-per-square-foot realism." Today we would call this interest "ecology," but such concerns were not fashionable during Neutra's lifetime, and many who admired his buildings were embarrassed when they heard him talk, dismissing his ideas as "cranky." Neutra's book *Survival through Design,* written in 1954, was not well received at the time, but looking back it can be seen as a step toward the environmental concerns of 30 years later. In 1926 it seemed to the Neutras that southern California, with its sympathetic climate, offered the opportunity to construct buildings for human use closest to the nature in which our species evolved. It so happened that much of Wright's work at the time was in Los Angeles, and Wright's man on the spot was another Viennese architect, Rudolph Schindler, five years older than Neutra. So the Neutras made their final move.

In 1926 Schindler and Neutra shared an office in Los Angeles. Their relationship over the years was a stormy one, but they collaborated in the early years and in 1927 submitted a joint entry for the League of Nations Competition. At the time of the Neutras' arrival in Los Angeles, Schindler was just completing his most important work, the Lovell House on Newport Beach, the first sophisticated International Style house on the West Coast. Two years later Neutra won over Dr. Philip Lovell as a client for himself and built the Health House.

Neutra's Health House, on a canyon site at Griffith Park, was a masterpiece, comparable with its contemporary, Le Corbusier's villa at Garches, France. In Dr. Lovell, Neutra found a client sympathetic to his developing ideas on biorealism, and the house has numerous features intended to promote physical fitness—a swimming pool, a basketball court, an open-air gymnasium and sleeping porches. The house is constructed with a steel frame with large steel windows that accentuate the frame, but solid parts are white painted plaster in the manner of the European Modern Movement, but also in the manner of earlier Los Angeles architects such as Irving Gill. So the house combines Californian traditions with those of European modernism; it sets up a desirable, healthy lifestyle, and its long horizontal lines sit with great beauty on the hillside. It became one of the best known and most visited modern houses in America and made Richard Neutra's name famous around the world.

The Health House was followed by other houses, often of exquisite quality, but lacking the high drama of the Health House. However, they often involved experiments in construction. The Van Der Leeuw House by Silver Lake, finished in 1932, used timber, but the Beard House at Altadena, completed two years later, was entirely of steel, with wall units made of exposed H. H. Robertson pressed metal panels used structurally, a concept 50 years ahead of its time; the hollows in the metal construction were filled with hot air to form a radiant panel in the heating season, an illustration of Neutra's ability to rethink the requirements of building from first principles. The Beard House was followed by Neutra's most famous sheet-steel house, the Sternberg House in San Fernando. Beautifully planned on a generous scale, with curved external walls of aluminum-coated steel, the Sternberg house had a friendly, almost sensuous feel that distanced it from the modern work being built in Europe at that time. This was clearly an architecture that could have popular appeal.

Concurrent with these houses was the Corona School at Bell. Single-story, with outside teaching spaces to each classroom, it became a model for schools the world over. When the war put a stop to private house building, Neutra used that experience for other social projects, notably the schools in Puerto Rico and the Channel Heights' wartime housing development at San Pedro, one of the few American successes in the field of low-cost housing.

The five years following the war marked a high point in Neutra's career as a designer of elegant houses and as the creator of a most enviable lifestyle. It was America's great moment of confidence, and Neutra made the most of it. The 1946 Desert House in the Badlands of Cordillera set down the good life— including pool—in the most hostile surroundings. Sitting elegantly on the desert floor, this structure cooled by iced water was perhaps the first postwar building of quality. In the next year, the Tremaine house in Santa Barbara set the good life in the more congenial landscape of a grove of mature oaks; the reinforced concrete frame wanders informally in the landscape, creating cool internal and outdoor spaces for the occupants' pleasure.

Success brought fame, and fame brought numerous and larger commissions. In 1949 Neutra took Robert Alexander into partnership, and later worked with his own son, Dion. Many projects of elegance and inventiveness flowed from the larger office, but the work no longer matched the world quality of the precious period.

—JOHN WINTER

NIEMEYER, Oscar.

Brazilian. Born in Rio de Janeiro, Brazil, 15 December 1907. Married Annita Baldo, 1929. Studied at the Escola Nacional de Belas Artes, Rio de Janeiro, 1930-34, Dip.Arch. Worked in the architectural studio of Lúcio Costa and Carlos Leão, Rio de Janeiro, 1935, and the studio of Le Corbusier, Paris, 1936; architect, Departmento de Patrimonio Historico e Artistico Nacional, Rio de Janeiro, 1936-37; in private practice, Rio de Janeiro, 1937-56; chief architect, NOVACAP (Government Building Authority), Brasília, 1956-61 (architectural adviser since 1961); returned to private practice, Rio de Janeiro, 1961. Lecturer, School of Architecture, Federal University of Rio de Janeiro, since 1968. Founder editor, *Modulo,* Rio de Janeiro, 1955. Pritzker Prize, 1988.

Chronology of Works
All in Brazil unless noted

1937	Obra do Berço Nursery and Maternity Clinic, Rio de Janeiro
1937-43	Ministry of Education and Health, Rio de Janeiro (with Le Corbusier, Lúcio Costa, Jorge Machado Moreira and Afonso Eduardo Reidy; now the Palace of Culture)
1939	Oswald de Andrade House, São Paulo
1939	Brazilian Pavilion, World's Fair, New York City, U.S.A. (with Le Corbusier)

Oscar Niemeyer: Brasília, Brazil, 1957-64

1941	National Stadium, Rio de Janeiro
1941	Water Tower, Rio de Janeiro
1942-46	Pampulha Development, with the Church of São Francisco de Assisi, Yacht Club, and Restaurant, Minas Gerais, near Belo Horizonte
1942	Oscar Niemeyer House, Gavea, Rio de Janeiro
1943	Kubitschek House, Pampulha, Minas Gerais
1944	Prudente de Morais Neto House, Rio de Janeiro
1944	Recreation Center, Rodrigos de Freitas Lagoon, Rio de Janeiro
1945	Yacht Club, Rio de Janeiro
1947-52	United Nations Building, New York City, U.S.A. (with international team of architects, including Le Corbusier and Sven Markelius—Wallace K. Harrison, chairman)
1950	COPAN Office Building, São Paulo
1953	Oscar Niemeyer House, Rio de Janeiro
1957-64	Brasília (all major government buildings, the cathedral, the university, the National Theater, and a housing complex)
1966	Manchete Headquarters, Rio de Janeiro
1967-72	Communist Party Headquarters, Paris, France
1968	Ministry of Defense, Brasília
1968-75	Mondadori Building, Milan, Italy
1969-78	University of Constantine, Algeria
1972	Gomes House, Rio de Janeiro
1983	Samba Stadium, Rio de Janeiro
1984	Sixty schools, State of Rio de Janeiro
1988	Memorial da América Latina, São Paulo
1989	Nove de Novembro Monument, Volta Redonda

Publications

BOOKS BY NIEMEYER

Minha experiência em Brasília. Rio de Janeiro, 1960.
Textes et dessins pour Brasilia. Paris, 1965.
Viagens: Quase memorias. Rio de Janeiro, 1966.
Oscar Niemeyer. Milan, 1977.
A forma na arquitetura. Rio de Janeiro, 1978.
Rio—de Província a Metrópole. Rio de Janeiro, 1980.
Como se faz arquitetura. Rio de Janeiro, 1986.
Brasília. Rio de Janeiro, 1986.

ARTICLES BY NIEMEYER

Numerous articles in *Modulo* (Rio de Janeiro).

BOOKS ABOUT NIEMEYER

BRUAND, Y.: *Arquitetura contemporâno no Brasil*. São Paulo, 1981.
FILS, ALEXANDER (ed.): *Oscar Niemeyer: Selbstdarstellung, Kritiken, Oeuvre*. West Berlin, 1982.
LUIGI, GILBERT: *Oscar Niemeyer: une esthétique de la fluidité*. Marseille, 1987.
MINDLIN, HENRIQUE: *Modern Architecture in Brazil*. New York, 1956.
PAPADAKI, STAMO: *The Work of Oscar Niemeyer*. New York, 1954.
PENTEADO, H., et al.: *Oscar Niemeyer*. São Paulo, 1985.

ARTICLES ABOUT NIEMEYER

Architectural Review, special issues (March 1944; October 1950; October 1954).

Architecture d'aujourd'hui, special issues (September 1947; October 1952; October/November 1958; January/February 1974).

Progressive Architecture, special issue (April 1947).

South America's leading architect and the most celebrated and dynamic practitioner of Brazilian modernism, Oscar Niemeyer occupies a controversial position in the history of modern architecture. In 1936, at the very start of his career, he demanded that his mentor Lúcio Costa include him in the Brazilian team then being formed to collaborate with Le Corbusier on the design of the new Ministry of Health and Education Building in Rio de Janeiro. Profoundly influenced by Le Corbusier, Niemeyer subtly transformed the building's Corbusian design idea into the first monumental statement of Brazilian modernism in Rio. In 1945, following upon his collaboration with Costa on the Brazilian Pavilion at the 1939 New York World's Fair and his more important independent commissions in Pampulha (a suburb of Belo Horizonte) for future Brazilian president Juscelino Kubitschek, Niemeyer proclaimed himself a communist. He received political prisoners freed by the government and allowed his office to become the headquarters of the Metropolitan Committee of the Brazilian Communist Party.

His communist sympathies notwithstanding, in 1947 Niemeyer was invited to serve on the advisory committee for the design of the United Nations Headquarters in New York City. There he was accosted on a street corner by his old teacher Le Corbusier, who, perceiving the developing talents of the young Brazilian, quickly proposed that they collaborate on the assignment. Even though Le Corbusier has often been credited with the design of the original United Nations complex, the final "collaborative" project Nos. 23-32 perhaps owes more to Niemeyer's design No. 32 than to Le Corbusier's design No. 23. At a lunch in Paris several years later, Le Corbusier reportedly told Niemeyer during a conversation about the designs: "Oscar, you are a generous man." On the strength of his United Nations performance, Niemeyer was invited that same year to teach at Yale, but the land of the free refused him a visa, presumably because of his communist affiliations.

The polemics of Niemeyer's *oeuvre* and the criticisms of it have centered on his conception of architecture as a plastic art freed from all traditionalism by the technical and material advances of modern society. But for Niemeyer, Brazil's status as an underdeveloped nation has severely limited that freedom, so that only a few can truly practice it: the country has lacked the broad political, cultural and educational basis for a "social architecture," that is, an architecture that serves the masses of Brazil. In the absence of such a basis, the only alternative for the socially conscious architect is to make the best use of the modern technological developments by creating a lyrical, dynamic architecture that symbolizes Brazil's aspirations to modernity. Niemeyer argues that the architect is not primarily a social reformer, that architecture cannot fundamentally transform society. Rather than being shackled by social preoccupations he cannot control, the architect must be free to create bold, plastic forms of great expressive power, made possible primarily by the technical exploitation of structural reinforced concrete.

Niemeyer's early work is characterized by subtle refinements to the formal system of Le Corbusier. The essence of Niemeyer's contribution to the Ministry of Education Building, for example, was essentially twofold: the manipulation of Le Corbusier's squat pilotis into taller and more slender forms, and the transformation of Le Corbusier's idea of fixed sun-breakers (*brise-soleil*) into a system of movable, louvered slats (*quebra-sol*) that could be adjusted to the angle of the sun from inside. Niemeyer's thin, 10-meter-tall pilotis not only increased the building's sense of structural lightness and called attention to its vertical monumentality, they also increased the spaciousness of the ground-level public terrace beneath. At the same time, the linear pattern of the *quebra-sol* system resulted in a horizontally unified tall office building with a visually interesting surface texture deriving from the variations of the angles of the individual slats. Niemeyer used the system again in his first independent commission, the Obra do Berço (Public Nursery School) in Rio (1937), and again in the Banco de Boavista, this time with the slats oriented vertically. Later, in the Copan Building in São Paulo and in a similar apartment complex in Belo Horizonte (Minas Gerais state), he monumentalized the fixed horizontal slat form to give compositional unity and plastic richness to the two buildings' dramatically curving facades.

A second, formally richer phase of Niemeyer's career was launched in the early 1940s, in the designs for the major buildings of Pampulha, a new suburb of Belo Horizonte. The Pampulha projects, commissioned by Belo Mayor Juscelino Kubitschek, the future president of Brazil and Niemeyer's patron in Brasília, brought Niemeyer recognition as a leading international practitioner of "free-form modernism." While Le Corbusier continued to experiment with the rectangular concrete slab in his work on the Unité d'Habitation at Marseilles, Niemeyer was already seeking more daring alternatives to the rectilinear compositions of the International Style. His masterpiece at Pampulha is unquestionably the small Church of São Francisco de Assisi (1943), a poetically lyrical statement using parabolic vaults and *azulejo* (blue ceramic tile) murals. (The *azulejos* were the work of Candido Portinari, who also did panels for the Ministry of Health Building in Rio.) Niemeyer's outspoken love for the free-form curve has led to many innovative creations and nearly as many vituperous criticisms (most notably from the architect and artist Max Bill). But for Niemeyer, pure functionalism is undesirable for architecture because it reduces building to a consideration of mere technical problems; like Costa, he has never abandoned the conception of architecture as first and foremost an expressive, plastic art.

After about 1954 and the second Biennial de São Paulo, and especially after a trip to Europe in 1955, Niemeyer moved into a third phase, a period of critical reflection characterized by a retrospective defense of his ideas through writing. Although it did not lead to a fundamental change in his style or principles, this reflection did prepare the way for the greater formal simplicity and compositional equilibrium of his mature work in Brasília. In this period he sought a purification and variation of the plastic inventions achieved in Pampulha.

Beginning in 1957, Niemeyer was commissioned by his friend and former patron, the then-president Kubitschek, to design all the main buildings for the new capital, Brasília. His work in Brasília is of two major types: the government complex and public buildings that form part of the city's monumental axis, and the public-housing projects for the city's inhabitants. Niemeyer produced not only a large corpus of multifamily dwelling units but also a rich repertoire of public buildings, such as the Cathedral and the Congress and Secretariat complex in the Plaza of the Three Powers. To some critics, these bold works have been more successful as urban sculptures than as functioning buildings. Yet Niemeyer's love of curving forms and ramps, the dynamism of the light and dangling structure, the treatment of buildings as plastic entities with a life of their own—these features are displayed to their fullest richness in Brasília, where they were interrelated urbanistically for the first time.

In 1964, in the wake of a right-wing military coup, Niemeyer exiled himself to France and began another, very productive phase of his career. The late 1960s and early 1970s saw the construction of some of his favorite works: the Communist Party Headquarters in Paris and the Mondadori Building in Milan. Back in Rio in the 1970s, he undertook an urban development project with Costa, in the Zona Sul suburbs in Rio Novo and the Barra de Tijuca. In 1988 he was awarded the Pritzker Prize for architecture (with Gordon Bunshaft). Although the right-of-center reformist regime of President Fernando Collor de Mello recently cut Niemeyer from the government payroll, he energetically continues to turn out designs from his office overlooking Copacabana Beach. His most recent works—most notably the Samba Stadium and "Brizolão" public schools in Rio de Janeiro, the Memorial Nove de Novembro in Volta Redonda, and the Memorial da América Latina in São Paulo—all illustrate his interest in the popular culture of Latin America and his persisting utopian vision of a better world for the region's peoples. Even if Niemeyer denies that social reform is not the primary responsibility of the architect, these recent works seem to reflect Niemeyer's ambivalence about this issue: as he himself has stated, given the opportunity and proper resources, the architect can foster, or at least call for, an improved society through socially conscious design.

But in the end, what often seems to be most important for Niemeyer is good form, and more specifically, the sweeping arc and the flowing curve. Understanding the source of his love for curvilinear forms leads us to a deeper appreciation of this highly sensual artist. As he wrote: "It is not the right angle that attracts me, nor the straight line, hard and inflexible, created by man. What attracts me is the free and sensual curve—the curve that I find in the mountains of my country, in the sinuous course of its rivers, in the clouds in the sky, in the body of the woman who is loved. The entire universe is made of curves—the universal curve of Einstein." But the bow to Einstein notwithstanding, Niemeyer and his creations are above all children of Rio de Janeiro. To "understand" Niemeyer's parabolic vaults, flowing curves and arcing lines, perhaps one need look no further than the natural architectures of Sugar Loaf Mountain and Copacabana Beach.

—DAVID K. UNDERWOOD

NOLLI, Giovanni Battista.

Italian. Born in Montronio, near Como, Italy, ca. 1692. Died in Rome, 3 July 1756. Trained as a surveyor in Milan, graduated 1722. Worked as a goeometrician to the Cesarea Real Giunta: made various plans of Milan and surroundings; worked under the King of Sardinia in Piedmont, 1729-31. In Rome, 1735/36; worked on a plan of Rome which was published in 1748.

Chronology of Works
In Italy

1751-56   Santa Dorotea in Trastevere, Rome

Publications

BOOKS BY NOLLI

Nuova pianta di Roma. Rome, 1748.
The Nolli Map of Rome. Princeton, New Jersey, 1989.

BOOKS ABOUT NOLLI

EHRLE, FRANCESCO (ed.): *Roma al tempo di Benedetto XIV: La Pianta di Roma di Giambattista Nolli del 1748.* Rome, 1932.

ARTICLES ABOUT NOLLI

FACCIOLI, CLEMENTE: "Gio. Battista Nolli (1701-1756) e la sua gran 'Pianta di Roma' del 1748." *Studi Romani* 14 (1966):415-442.
"S. Dorotea in Rom und verwandte Kitchenbauten." *Architectura* 4 (1974): 165-180.
ZANKER, JURGEN: "Die 'Nuova Pianta di Roma' von Giovanni Battista Nolli (1748)." *Wallraf Richartz* 35 (1973): 309-342.

Giovanni Battista Nolli, an architect and surveyor, is best known for a vast plan of Rome published in 1748. Born in Montronio, near Como, he was trained in Milan as a surveyor. His first position was as geometrician to the Cesarea Real Giunta, with the task of making various plans and maps in and around Milan. That position lasted until 1724; between 1729 and 1731 he worked in the Piedmont, serving under the king of Sardinia as "*Mensure Générale du Duché de Savoye.*" By 1735-36 he was in Rome, engaged already with his plan.

But Nolli was also an architect, his one building of significance being the Church of Santa Dorothea in Trastevere, begun in 1751 and finished, after his death, in 1756. It is a simple design, occupying the site of an earlier church, done for the order of the Minori Conventuali. The plan is octagonal, with an emphasis on the longitudinal axis; the articulation on the exterior, with a concave facade that fits nicely into the street, is bare and cleanly ordered. The cupola is reminiscent of work by Nolli's contemporaries Luigi Vanvitelli (1700-73) and Nicola Salvi (1697-1751), but the forms were toned down for the simple order commissioning the church. It is possible that Nolli worked also, in the late 1740s, in the gardens for a villa around the Porta Salaria, now the Villa Albani.

His most important achievement, however, remains the plan of Rome, *La Pianta Grande di Roma*, published in 1748; the engravings were done by Carlo Nolli, his son, with the help of Rocco Pozzi and Pietro Campana, with vignettes by Stefano Pozzi. A famous plan of Rome had been produced in 1551, two centuries earlier, by Leonardo Bufalini, and Nolli undoubtedly knew of that work. And in 1742 he restored the famous *Forma Urbis*, a marble plan of ancient Rome. But the city had grown and changed much in the intervening years, and by the beginning of the 18th century there was demand for a new mapping of Rome. Nolli began in 1736, under the support of a fellow Milanese, Padre Diego de Revillas. By 1742 the essential work had been done, as can be seen in the drawing for this, known as the Scaccia-Scarafoni plan, which is now in the library of the Palazzo Venezia in Rome. This version reproduced a plan of the whole city, within the area defined by the walls, with the buildings being seen in plan, all numbered.

The printed plan is similar, the one difference being that in the drawing, open areas and portions of the open areas are also noted; this may have been a reference to the divisions of properties, information possibly to be included in the final plan if a full index had also been printed. Six years later, in 1748, the plan was published, with a dedication to Pope Benedict XIV. It was paid for by Gerolamo Belloni, a rich banker ennobled by the pope. The plan measures about 1.87 meters by 1.65 meters, and is made up of 16 separate printed sections. The patterns of the buildings are sharply defined with darkened areas, churches and palaces are marked out carefully with the full plans, porticoes and chapels all visible, and the names of squares and open spaces are inscribed above them at the appropriate place; also attached was an alphabetical list of *rioni*, or areas of the city.

Beyond this, Nolli also published in 1748 a smaller version of the plan, known immediately as the *Pianta piccola*; a simple reduction to one plate, about 69 centimeters by 47 centimeters, the smaller plan was engraved by Carlo Nolli and Giovanni Battista Piranesi, and dedicated to Cardinal Alessandro Albani. The large plan was offered for sale, even as far away as London, but it did not sell well. The absence of an accompanying book may have hindered its usefulness. Nolli died poor and alone in 1756, and was buried in Santa Dorothea, the church he had built; his tomb may have been destroyed in restorations done there in 1926.

—DAVID CAST

NOTMAN, John.

American. Born in 1810. Died in 1865. Co-founder, Pennsylvania Institute of Architects, 1861 (forerunner of the American Institute of Architects Philadelphia Chapter).

Chronology of Works
All in the United States
* Approximate dates
† Work no longer exists

1836-39	Laurel Hill Cemetery, Philadelphia
1837-38	Nathan Dunn's Cottage, Mount Holly, New Jersey†

John Notman: Athenaeum, Philadelphia, Pennsylvania, 1845-47

1839	Riverside, Burlington, New Jersey†
1839-40	Academy of Natural Sciences, Philadelphia†
1845-46	New Jersey State House, Trenton, New Jersey (redesign and enlargement)
1845-47	Athenaeum, Philadelphia, Pennsylvania
1845-47	Chapel of the Holy Innocents, Burlington, New Jersey
1845-48	New Jersey State Lunatic Asylum (now Trenton Psychiatric Hospital), Trenton, New Jersey
1847-52	St. Mark's Church, Philadelphia, Pennsylvania
1848	Hollywood Cemetery, Richmond, Virginia
1850-60*	Capitol Square, Richmond, Virginia
1851-52	Prospect Villa, Princeton, New Jersey
1851-52	St. Peter's Church, Pittsburgh, Pennsylvania
1851-57	Cathedral of St. Peter and St. Paul, Philadelphia (facade)
1853*-55	Fieldwood Villa (now Guernsey Hall), Princeton, New Jersey
1855-59	Nassau Hall, Princeton, New Jersey
1855-59	St. Clement's Church, Philadelphia, Pennsylvania
1856-59	Holy Trinity Church, Philadelphia, Pennsylvania
1857-58	Cathedral of St. John, Wilmington, Delaware

Publications

BOOKS ABOUT NOTMAN

GREIFF, CONSTANCE M.: *John Notman, Architect.* Philadelphia, 1979.
GREIFF, CONSTANCE M.; GIBBONS, MARY W.; and MENZIES, ELIZABETH G. C.: *Princeton Architecture.* Princeton, New Jersey, 1967.
JACKSON, JOSEPH: *Early Philadelphia Architects and Engineers.* Philadelphia, 1923.
SMITH, ROBERT C.: *John Notman and the Athenaeum Building.* Philadelphia, 1951.
TATUM, GEORGE B.: *Penn's Great Town.* Philadelphia, 1961.

ARTICLES ABOUT NOTMAN

DALLETT, FRANCIS JAMES: "John Notman, Architect." *Princeton University Library Chronicle* 20, No. 3 (1959): 127-139.
FAIRBANKS, JONATHAN: "John Notman: Church Architect." M. A. thesis. University of Delaware, Newark, 1961.
SMITH, ROBERT C.: "John Notman's Nassau Hall." *Princeton University Library Chronicle* 14, No. 3 (1953): 109-134.

*

It is the great irony in the career of John Notman that a man best known for his architectural works came to prominence via a project of landscape design. In winning the 1836 competition for the design of Laurel Hill Cemetery in Philadelphia, he firmly established his reputation as an up-to-date designer, since Laurel Hill was only the second rural cemetery in romantic style to be built in the United States. That commission, which included architectural features as well, such as the classical entry portal and Gothic chapel, launched Notman into a series of acquaintanceships that placed his work squarely in the forefront of American design. Through J. Jay Smith, noted editor and one of the directors of the cemetery, he met Andrew Jackson Downing, considered the premier mid-century design critic and landscape designer. With his works published and praised by Downing, Notman could have done little else but be a success.

Although his earliest architectural works, such as the New Jersey State House and the Chapel of the Holy Innocents in Burlington, New Jersey, were in classical or then-ascendant Gothic styles, it was for his early use of Renaissance Italian precedents that he is best remembered. At residences, such as Riverside in Burlington, he used a robust Italianate style with asymmetrical plan and openly connected rooms. His architectural work is also noteworthy for innovations in structural design and in the behavioral aspects of design. For an atypically uninspired plan at the Academy of Natural Sciences in Philadelphia, Notman used iron for structural members, rather than merely as ornament, while in plans for the New Jersey State Lunatic Asylum at Trenton he demonstrated great skill in adapting new theories about the role of physical settings in treatment of the mentally ill, providing light, air and as home-like an atmosphere as possible in the institution.

At other times his work was revolutionary not for the use of modern materials and means, but for a return to historically accurate construction. At St. Mark's Anglican Church in Philadelphia, often considered his foremost nonresidential design, he supported a roof resting upon structural timber with solid stone walls. This construction technique presaged the structural authenticity of the Romanesque Revival in the late 19th century. Perhaps much of the construction and detail quality of Notman's buildings can be attributed to his often serving as contractor as well as designer. Early training in building crafts, particularly the stonework that his father and brother had practiced at home in Scotland and his own training as a carpenter, assured that designs carefully resolved on paper were executed with equal care.

Notman's landscape architectural commissions were as varied in type and style as those in architecture. His reputation as the designer of Laurel Hill won him several major commissions elsewhere, including ill-fated work on a plan for Spring Grove Cemetery. There the proprietors did not find his tightly packed, geometrically based roads and paths to be as suitable to the rolling landforms of Cincinnati as they had been on the bluffs above the Schuylkill. The cemetery board implemented little of this plan before hiring, first, Howard Daniels and, later, Adolph Strauch for redesigns.

In his home region in the mid-Atlantic Notman remained as popular a landscape designer as ever, as evidenced by a string of commissions in Virginia in the late 1840s. Of those, his design for Capital Square in Richmond stands out as one of the first uses of a park-like romantic design in a public place, the success of which may have influenced President Millard Fillmore's decision a little over a year later to employ Downing to develop a plan for the Mall in Washington, D.C. Equally important, and certainly more appealing to the modern eye, was Notman's plan for Hollywood Cemetery, also in Richmond, hallowed after the Civil War as the resting place of many Confederate dead and site of the principal southern monument to war dead. Hollywood is Notman at his most sensitive and a rural cemetery at its most romantic, with sinuous roads tucked into the landform and rocky brooks defining scenic open areas.

In his lifetime and in modern histories, perhaps due to his eclectic design interests, Notman has been overshadowed by contemporaneous architects and landscape architects, such as Alexander Jackson Davis, Richard Upjohn, Adolph Strauch, and the firm of Copeland & Cleveland. Some of this lack of attention may also be due to a modern interpretation of his work as relying excessively on English examples of his day. While he did copy details, like those for a tracery window in St. Mark's, in the broader view his work translated and expanded upon these examples, rather than using them uncritically as did many who merely copied from pattern books and periodicals.

Such an assessment also belies the unique contributions that he did make, particularly in introducing a greater variety of historically derived architectural styles and as one of the first to design large-scale public landscapes in North America.

—NANCY J. VOLKMAN

NOWICKI, Matthew.

American. Born Maciej Nowicki in Chita, Russia, of Polish parents, 26 June 1910. Died 31 August 1951. Immigrated to the United States, 1922. Married Stanislawa Sandecka, 1936. Studied at the Art Institute of Chicago, 1922; Gerson School of Design, Warsaw, Poland, 1925; Warsaw Technological University, 1929-36, M.Arch. In private practice, Warsaw, 1936-39; served as a Lieutenant in the Polish Army Artillery, 1939; participated in the Warsaw Insurrection, Home Army, 1944; taught underground clas ses in architecture and town planning during the Nazi occupation, Warsaw, 1939-45; design chief, Capital Rebuilding Bureau (BOS), Warsaw, 1945-46; cultural attaché, Polish Consulate, Chicago, 1946; Polish representative, United Nations Site and Building Committee, New York, 1946-47. Senior professor of architecture and acting head of the School of Design, North Carolina State College, Raleigh, 1948-51; employed by the architectural firm of Mayer and Whittlessey, New York, to begin firm's study for Chandi garh, the new capital city of the Punjab, India, 1949 until his death in an airplane crash in 1951.

Chronology of Works
All in the United States
† Work no longer exists

1939	Polish Pavilion, World's Fair, New York City†
1948-53	Dorton Arena, North Carolina State Fair, Raleigh, North Carolina
1949	Building for Brandeis University, Waltham, Massachusetts

Publications

BOOKS BY NOWICKI

The Writings and Sketches of Matthew Nowicki Compiled by Bruce Harold Schafer. Charlottesville, Virginia, 1973.

BOOKS ABOUT NOWICKI

BARUCKI, TADEUSZ: *Maciej Nowicki.* Warsaw, 1980.
JOEDICKE, JÜRGEN: *Geschichte der Modernen Architektur.* Stuttgart, 1958.
MUMFORD, LEWIS (ed.): *Roots of Contemporary American Architecture.* New York, 1952.
WISLOCKA, IZABELLA: *Polish Avant-Garde Architecture 1918-1939.* Warsaw, 1970.

ARTICLES ABOUT NOWICKI

HRYNIEWIECKI, J.: "Matthew Nowicki 1910-1951." *Projekt* (Warsaw) no. 1 (1957).
"Matthew Nowicki." *Architectural Forum* (October 1950).
"Matthew Nowicki." *Architecture d'aujourd'hui* (September (1957).

"Matthew Nowicki." Special issue of the *North Carolina State College School of Design Student Publication* (Raleigh, Winter 1951).

MUMFORD, LEWIS: "The Life, Teaching and Architecture of Matthew Nowicki." *Architectural Record* (June/August 1954).

WOOD, ERNEST: "A Radical settles down in Raleigh, North Carolina." *American Institute of Architects Journal* (September 1980).

*

Maciej Nowicki was born in Siberia before Polish independence. He immigrated to the United States in 1922, when still a child, and began his high school education there. When he returned to Poland in 1925, he entered the Gerson School of Design in Warsaw. He continued his education at Warsaw Technological University's School of Architecture, and received his degree in 1936. Even before graduating, Nowicki entered designs in a variety of competitions and won two: one for a mosque in Warsaw and the other for a housing complex.

After concluding his studies, Nowicki taught at his alma mater until the school was shut down by the Germans upon the beginning of World War II. For the next four years, he carried on his teaching of architecture in secret.

In 1936 Nowicki married Stanislawa Sandecka, and the next year the two won the Gold Medal for their graphic art at the Paris Exposition. In 1939 Nowicki received the second prize for his design of the Polish Pavilion at the New York World's Fair.

After the end of the war, in 1945 and 1946, Nowicki was stationed in Chicago as the cultural attaché at the Polish consulate. In 1947 he sat on the United Nations Headquarters Building Committee, and later served as a consultant to Wallace K. Harrison, who was in charge of the building's construction. He was visiting scholar at the Pratt Institute in New York in 1948, and over the next two years he headed the Department of Architecture of the School of Design at Raleigh (now the University of North Carolina). He reformed the educational program at the School of Design, and his innovative teaching became the basis for curriculum changes in architectural schools throughout the United States.

His outstanding ability, versatile European education and analytical stance, coupled with a lively imagination and artistic sensitivity, assured Nowicki a leading role in the postwar architectural avant-garde. As a student, he had been fascinated by the work of Le Corbusier (1887-1965; pseud. for Charles Édouard Jeanneret), but he turned away from formalism as he matured. His professional philosophy became rather closer to the pragmatism of the older generation of French architectural modernists as represented by Auguste Perret (1874-1954). Any attempt to classify Nowicki with postwar architectural trends is misleading, as he always remained highly original both in his intellectual approach and in practical design solutions. Simply put, Nowicki's architectural vision was a constant search for truth. In "Composition in Modern Architecture" (*Magazine of Art*, 42), he wrote, "Truth in composition is not the exact disclosure of the inside functions of the building on its exterior, nor is it the frank expression of its construction. Both functionalism and construction must be ordered by the truth of unity and the diversity within it; in other words by the basic laws of the universe, the expression of which man calls beauty."

In Nowicki's opinion, the dominant intellectual tendencies of the day impose limits on originators, but within such limits there is considerable variation caused by differences in temperament, imagination and individual sensitivity. Achieving a balance between order and creative temperament is the subject and goal of architectural design. Architecture must not be evaluated only in terms of aesthetic criteria, according to Nowicki. Appraisals must include an analysis of the rationality of form, which should be based on a conscious intellectual, philosophical vision. As Nowicki wrote in the abovementioned article, "Order is the creation of an intellectual approach, and unity based on order always has a classical flavor. Diversity is the expression of creative temperament, imagination and emotion and therefore is a factor of what we may call romanticism. Again the two forces exist side by side, one incomplete without the other, and we may conclude that the search for a balance between them is the objective of composition in modern architecture." Nowicki's design practice and teaching expressed this approach.

Nowicki found ideal conditions for the development of his talents in the United States. His best-known work, Cow Palace (later renamed the Dorton Arena), is located in Raleigh. The design demonstrates the architect's thorough understanding of construction technique and building materials. He deployed the material unerringly, achieving an optimal functional solution, balanced proportion and great beauty of detail. Two gigantic interpenetrating arches of reinforced concrete support a steel-cable suspension roof. The Dorton Arena was the first building to employ suspension techniques—until then found only in bridges—for its roof construction. With the application of this bold and innovative design concept, Nowicki introduced a new era of modern design. Offering great formal variety, the suspension roof is also the most economic covering for sports arenas and other large public structures.

Nowicki worked closely with Eero Saarinen (1910-61) on the development of the master plan for the Brandeis University campus. He collaborated with Clarence Stein (1882-1975) on the Columbus Circle design for New York City and on designs for the commercial center in Los Angeles. In this last project, Nowicki used the suspension construction again: an enormous steel structure was raised on four posts. An unprecedented area of usable space was created as a result of the elimination of all supports except at the corners.

Nowicki's last design, undertaken in collaboration with many eminent modern architects, for Chandigarh, India, was left unfinished at his untimely death in an airplane crash in 1950. Nowicki maintained that mature architecture is like art, and may be interpreted as a sculptural shaping of function in space. In a posthumously published article (*Magazine of Art*, 44), Nowicki wrote, "Art may be one, but it has a thousand aspects. We must face the dangers of the crystallizing style, not denying its existence but trying to enrich its scope by opening new roads for investigation and future refinements."

—JERZY ANDRZEJ STARCZEWSKI

NYROP, Martin.

Danish. Born in Denmark, 11 November 1849. Died in Copenhagen, 18 May 1921. Trained as a carpenter. Studied at the Copenhagen Academy of Art, 1870-76; traveled on fellowship to Italy, Greece and France. Professor, 1906, and director, 1908, Copenhagen Academy of Art.

Chronology of Works
All in Denmark

1884   Gymnastics Building, Volkshockschule, Vallekilde, Själland

Matthew Nowicki: Dorton Arena, North Carolina State Fair, Raleigh, North Carolina, 1948-53

1888	Agriculture and Art Buildings, Exposition of Industry, Copenhagen
1889	Frants Henningsen House, Hellebäk, Själland
1889-91	Villa, Rungstedvej 47, near Copenhagen
1889ff.	Villas Solvang and Hytten, Vallekilde
1891-92	Landesarchive, Copenhagen
1892-1905	City Hall, Copenhagen
1899-1900	Bridge, Frederiksholm Canal, Copenhagen
1903-04	Church, South Jutland
1903-04	Church, Stenderup
1903-04	Church, Sundeved
1905-06	Lyngebäksgaard, near Nivaa, Själland
1906-08	Elias Church, Copenhagen
1907	Volkshochschule, Vallekilde (remodeling and additions)
1908-13	Bispebjerg Hospital, Copenhagen
1914-18	Luther Church, Copenhagen (with J. Smith)
1916-18	Bispebjerg Hospital, Copenhagen (additions)
1918-19	Martin Nyrop House, near Gentofte, Själland
1919-21	Villa Bjerrelide, Ordrup
1920	Landsarchiv, Copenhagen (additions)

Publications

BOOKS ABOUT NYROP

BECKETT, FRANCIS, et al.: *Arkitekten Martin Nyrop*. Copenhagen, 1919.

FABER, TOBIAS: *Dansk Arkitektur*. 2nd ed. Copenhagen, 1977.

FUNDER, LISE: *Arkitekten Martin Nyrop*. Copenhagen, 1979.

HANSEN, HENNING: *Martin Nyrop*. Copenhagen, 1919.

LANDBERG, HARALD, and LANGKILDE, HANS ERLING: *Dansk Byggesaet omkring 1792 og 1942*. Copenhagen, 1942.

LUND, HAKON, and MILLECH, KNUD: *Danmarks Bygingskunst fra Oltid til Nutid*. Copenhagen, 1963.

MILLECH, KNUD: *Danske Arkitekturstrømninger 1850-1950*. Copenhagen, 1951.

RASMUSSEN, STEEN EILER: *Nordische Baukunst*. Berlin, 1940.

*

One of late-19th-century Denmark's best and most versatile architects, Martin Nyrop is known internationally for the Copenhagen Town Hall (1892-1905), the first of a great trio of "traditionalist" European civic buildings that also includes the Stockholm City Hall (1909-23) of Ragnar Östberg (1866-1945), who had studied Nyrop's building, and the Amsterdam Exchange (1893-1903) of H. P. Berlage (1856-1934). Berlage, Östberg and Nyrop were fascinated by building materials, whose visual and structural properties they infused with a range of sociological and historical significances; and they all envisaged their buildings not just as enclosures, but as satisfyingly sculptural and ornamented solids. But the younger architects, unlike Nyrop, gravitated to an increasingly sober, planar ahistoricism during the design process: the Copenhagen Town Hall, once popularly acclaimed, is today more difficult than the other buildings to admire, and to place historically.

In Denmark, Nyrop's reputation rests on broader foundations, which include the originality, beauty and functional integrity of such buildings as the gasometer for the Østre Gasværk (1880), the Elias (Elijah) Church (1906-08) and the Bispebjerg Hospital

(1908-13), all in Copenhagen, and, in an inordinately domesticated culture, his skill and influence as a designer of houses. Above all, his intense patriotism infused both his fascination with Nordic vernacular architecture, and his involvement with such social programs as the Folk High School Movement and the improvement of national standards of house construction: in both respects, his career anticipated the concerns of Carl Petersen and other members of the ''new classicist'' generation.

Nyrop's first house design, for Bakkehave, Hørsholm (1879), is effectively Italianate, with hints of the Nordic in the painted wood and the design of the metal fittings. The villa he designed for his sister Agnes (Rungstedvej 47, north of Copenhagen, 1889-91) is even simpler, symmetrical and rectangular under its big single-pitched roof, whose giant eaves form the veranda and sheltered entrance. Nyrop was striving to reach the truly vernacular, the essential and necessary forms of wood building. The villas Solvang and Hytten in Vallekilde, both begun in 1889, are more luxurious manifestations of Nyrop's interest in pre-industrial architecture, which had narrowed to the happy search for a common Nordic language, whose vocabulary could be borrowed from the brightly painted houses of Dalarna, Sweden, for example, or the sophisticated wooden construction of medieval Norwegian stave churches. The roofs were good Danish thatch, the half-timbering filled in with air-dried bricks and boarded with planks painted golden yellow, red and green. It was highly rational construction, devised with Nyrop's customary professionalism, and no expense spared for the intelligentsia seeking respite in the purity and simplicity of rural material culture.

Nyrop, who had been concerned that such villas should blend with the local vernacular, later turned his attention to the actual material circumstances of the rural population. The pressing need for cheap and healthy housing, especially for the farming smallholder, became steadily more evident after the turn of the century. Architects, among whom Nyrop took a leading role, working with the Ministry of Agriculture, met the need with free advice, plans and the construction of model homes. Such apothegms as ''Avoid unnecessary decoration, but give things

that are necessary an attractive and suitable form'' (in Nyrop's introduction to a book of model plans published in 1909) suggest that for the age-old preference for cheap imitations of metropolitan high styles, the architects would substitute a vernacular that had itself become a high style. However, this education, later extended to modest suburban dwellings, in the ''natural'' beauty, unconnected with ornament, of the traditional manmade environment—a well-made, well-proportioned window, for example—contributed much to the high standards of domestic design to which Danes have since become accustomed.

In 1887 a sketch competition was organized to design a replacement for C. F. Hansen's Copenhagen Town Hall (1805-15), which had become crowded during the course of the 19th century. Nyrop, then at work on his flamboyantly Nordic buildings for the Copenhagen Industrial Exhibition of 1888, shared first prize for a design not much different from the completed building: the brief was detailed, and specified, for example, exteriors of unplastered brick and the inclusion of the glass-roofed internal courtyard, as well as the accommodation required by various departments. The stylistic clarity of Nyrop's project contrasts sharply with the overheated distillations of the German Gothic, French Renaissance and Rosenborg (Danish 17th-century) styles submitted by the other architects. Nyrop managed an extremely idiosyncratic synthesis of the Italian Middle Ages—Siena's Palazzo Pubblico comes to mind immediately, a comparison sharpened by the off-center placement of the tower—and, more subtly, the Baltic brick urban vernacular. Ferdinand Meldahl (1827-1908) compared the gabled back facades, for example, to a row of old warehouses, which is exactly right, though not meant as a compliment. The building is a huge rectangle enclosing two internal courtyards separated by a transverse wing; its internal arrangements are reflected with precision on the facades. But the Copenhagen Town Hall is best seen at close quarters: it abounds with beautifully finished decoration telling the story of the city, and the country, that Nyrop loved so well.

—CHRISTINE STEVENSON

O

O'GORMAN, Juan.

Mexican. Born in Mexico City, Mexico, 6 July 1905. Died in Mexico City, January 1982. Married Helen Fowler, 1941. Studied at National University of Mexico, Dip.Ing., 1926; apprenticed to Carlos Obregón Santacilia, 1927; studied painting with Antonio Ruiz, Ramon Alba Guedarrama and Diego Rivera. Worked in the architectural offices of José Villagrán García, Carlos Tarditi and Carlos Contreros, Mexico City, 1927-29; chief draftsman, office of Carlos Obregon Santacilia, 1929-32; head, Mexico City Department of Building Construction, 1932-34. In private practice, Mexico City, from 1934. Cofounder, School of Architecture, 1932, and professor of Architecture and Architectural Composition, 1932-48, National Polytechnic Institute, Mexico City. Founder, Workers' Housing Study Group, Mexico City, 1936.

Chronology of Works
All in Mexico
† *Work no longer exists*

1929-30 Juan O'Gorman House I, Mexico City
1929-30 Diego Rivera House and Studio, Mexico City
1931 Tomás O'Gorman House, Mexico City
1932-34 Technical School, Mexico City
1932-34 Twenty-eight primary schools throughout Mexico, for the Ministry of Education
1934 Castellaños House, Mexico City
1936 Electricians' Union Building, Mexico City
1944-45 Museo Anahuacalli, Mexico (as consultant; with Diego Rivera)
1952-53 National Library, State University of Mexico, Mexico City
1953-56 Juan O'Gorman House II, Mexico City†

Publications

BOOKS BY O'GORMAN

El arte util y el arte artistico. Mexico City, 1932.
Autobiografia, antologia, juicios criticos y documentacion exhaustiva sobre su obra. Mexico City, 1973.

BOOKS ABOUT O'GORMAN

MYERS, I. E.: *Mexico's Modern Architecture.* New York, 1952.
SMITH, CLIVE BAMFORD: *Builders in the Sun: Five Mexican Architects.* New York, 1967.

ARTICLES ABOUT O'GORMAN

"Biblioteca y Hemerocteca Nacional." *Arquitectura* (Mexico City, September 1952).

"Federal Schools of Mexico." *Architectural Record* (May 1934).
GOERITZ, MATHIAS: "Juan O'Gorman." *Arquitectura* (Mexico City, December 1960).
"Jardines del Pedregal da San Angel." *Arts and Architecture* (August 1951).
McCOY, ESTHER: "The Death of Juan O'Gorman." *Arts and Architecture* (August 1982).
"Mexico City University: Its New Campus and Buildings." *Northwest Architect* (Minneapolis, September/October 1952).
"Modern Mexican Architecture." *Process: Architecture* special issue (July 1983).
"Mosaics." *Arts and Architecture* (February 1959).
"O'Gorman House." *Architectural Design* (September 1970).

*

The architectural career of Juan O'Gorman can be separated into two distinct phases, each seeming to negate the claims of the other, and each having an approximately equal impact upon the Mexican scene. In the 1920s and 1930s O'Gorman built some of the earliest and most radically utilitarian structures in the country. Suddenly in the mid-1930s, distraught by what he saw as the aesthetic impoverishment of his own work and that like it, he withdrew from architecture and devoted most of his energies to painting. When he returned to building a decade later, it was with a regional style whose ornamental richness he himself termed "baroque."

O'Gorman was one of a number of students at the National Academy of San Carlos (later the National School of Architecture) who in 1926 were present for Jose Villagran Garcia's first classes in functionalist theory. Upon graduation he worked in the offices of Villagran, Carlos Obregon Santacilla and other "progressives." These were transitional years for Mexican architecture, and "progressive" still meant the stripped-down rationalism and Beaux-Arts symmetry of Villagran's Hygiene Institute (1925) and Tuberculosis Sanatorium (1929). By the late 1920s, however, Mexican functionalism could be seen branching into two divergent factions: the more conservative "integralistas" like Villagran, who spoke of building as both science and art, and emphasized beauty as an outgrowth of material and structural integrity and a form's fitness to function; and the "radicals," who viewed architecture as a branch of engineering in which aesthetic considerations should have no role at all. The radicals advocated functionalism as a means of breaking with historical styles and the despised colonial past they evoked, and of answering the social imperatives of a poor, underhoused, undereducated country, struggling amidst the devastation brought by a decade and a half of revolution.

With his second independent commission (his father's 1929 house in San Angel—often cited as the first pure functionalist structure in Mexico) O'Gorman proved himself a leader among the radicals and an ardent disciple of Le Corbusier. Despite his

Juan O'Gorman: Juan O'Gorman House II, Mexico City, Mexico, 1953-56

claims that his work of this period was based solely on utilitarian considerations—and his later distaste for it because of this—a house such as that built in 1930 for painter Diego Rivera, with its nautical detailing, sawtooth roofline, cantilevered projections and highly sculptural exterior spiral staircase is a most visually satisfying variation on Le Corbusier's purist themes of the early 1920s. Anyone who had read *Vers Une Architecture* four times before the age of 20, as O'Gorman claimed to have, should hardly have missed the comments on art and beauty standing alongside those regarding structural and material rationalism. A house may well be "a machine to live in," but it should also involve "the masterly, correct and magnificent play of volumes brought together under light."

While O'Gorman's "communist style," as it was dubbed by some conservative critics, did not meet with universal approval, it did gain government sympathy under the administrations of Presidents Calles and Cardenas. In 1932, at the urging of Secretary of Public Education Narciso Bassols, O'Gorman (with Jose Cuevas) founded the functionalist-based School of Construction. Between 1932 and 1935, under Bassols' sponsorship, he built a technical school and at least 24 primary schools, and carried out the renovation of 29 existing schools—all within the astonishingly modest budget of one million pesos (about $500,000). Considering the 52 million pesos spent by the government a decade earlier for just eight neocolonial-style schools, O'Gorman's reinforced-concrete-and-glass structures— "stripped for action," in Esther Born's phase—must have seemed the only logical choice were Mexico to keep pace with a rapidly industrializing world.

It is notable that nearly all of O'Gorman's exteriors of this functionalist period were brightly painted in colors like red, green, blue and orange. Le Corbusier in the 1920s had often tinted walls in an effort to manipulate the perception of spatial depth. O'Gorman's colors, however, were far more highly keyed. On a practical level these colors, as opposed to white, could be said to reduce glare in the bright tropical light. But these are also colors found in Mexican folk art and architecture, and their use in O'Gorman's work should be seen in part as an early attempt to "localize" the International Style. The idea for this probably came from Diego Rivera, then deeply involved with Mexican folk art and employing many of its motifs in his own painting. O'Gorman's house for Rivera was painted a brilliant shade of blue—called "azul anil"—often used on village exteriors in the belief that it helps ward off evil spirits.

O'Gorman's first architectural project after his 10-year hiatus was as consultant for Rivera's Mayan-revival style Anahuacali Museum of Pre-Columbian art (1944-45). By then O'Gorman had taken a far broader view of functionalism, seeing his earlier "puritanism," as he called it, as the antithesis of traditional Mexican form. "Functionalism," he said, "has been distorted in practise . . . So today the task is to try to produce an architecture which, irrespective of all functional rules, will be more functional, that is to say, with a better adaptation to climate, to customs and to site. . . . Architecture must become a work of art, an expression of man's deepseated need to achieve harmony with his surroundings and with his fellow men. . . . We need for Mexico a Mexican architecture. . . ." In his exchange of utilitarianism and "academic abstraction" for a "people's" regional style, O'Gorman was making a move related to that of Mexican painters like Rivera, who around 1920 abandoned European avant-garde styles for the clear figurative didacticism of their famous murals.

The two most significant works of O'Gorman's second phase were the Central Library of the University City and his own home in El Pedregal. It is worth noting that, although he did not refer explicitly to these works as "surrealist," he did count among the primary influences upon them two great surrealist ancestors: Antonio Gaudí and Ferdinand Cheval. Both of these structures are marked by elements of myth and magic comparable to those which pervade O'Gorman's painting. The 10-story library tower—originally conceived as a truncated pyramid with translucent onyx windows, but made cubic to better fit the character of the other campus buildings—was covered with mosaics made of stones gathered from all parts of Mexico. The almost four-and-one-half thousand square yards of mosaics depict a history of ideas in Mexico: Pre-Hispanic, colonial and modern. According to O'Gorman, the use of mosaic allowed an organic integration of painting, sculpture and architecture, comparable to that found in medieval cathedrals, "a complete plastic art, of our time, in our tradition, and expressing the aspirations of the people of Mexico." As the most widely discussed building of the University City complex, the library—along with Luis Barragán's earlier Gardens of El Pedregal, which O'Gorman dismissed as a cosmetic forgery—served to announce the emergence of a distinctive, post-International Style, Mexican modern architecture.

The architect's own home, partly excavated from a natural grotto and covered inside and out with mosaics, provided him with even greater freedom in exploring these ends. O'Gorman called it his "most complete and satisfying work" and one of only "three examples of modern Mexican architecture" (the others being the stadium and fronton courts of the University City). The near-perfect integration of the house into the rugged volcanic landscape was also the source of its dysfunction, unfortunately. O'Gorman's wife complained of leaks and dampness, and of the difficulty of keeping the lava interiors clean. The house did have an atavistic strangeness that marked it as the product of a unique imagination and brought it wide praise, but its many idiosyncrasies, functional shortcomings and relatively high construction and maintenance costs prevented it from being picked up as a basic model for a Mexican regional style. O'Gorman's disappointment in this regard was driven near the breaking point when an unsympathetic new owner, against promises made to the architect during the time of sale, tore it down in 1970.

—KEITH EGGENER

OLBRICH, Joseph Maria.

Austrian. Born in Troppau, Austrian Silesia, 1867. Died in Düsseldorf, Germany, 1908. Assistant to Otto Wagner, Vienna. Opened own office, Vienna, 1898. Co-founder, Austrian Sezession.

Chronology of Works
All in Germany unless noted
† *Work no longer exists*

1897-98	Secession Building, Vienna, Austria
1898	Max Friedmann House, Hinterbrühl, Austria (completion)
1899-1900	Hermann Bahr House, Vienna, Austria
1899-1900	Hermann Stöhr House, St. Pölten, Austria
1899-1901	Ernst Ludwig House, Darmstadt
1900	Christiansen House, Darmstadt
1900	Habich House, Darmstadt
1900	Glueckert House, Darmstadt
1900	Bosselt House, Darmstadt
1900	Keller House, Darmstadt
1900	Deiters House, Darmstadt
1900	Gauss House, Darmstadt
1900-01	J. M. Olbrich House, Darmstadt
1901	Entrance Portal, Artists' Colony Exhibition, Darmstadt
1901	Exhibition Gallery, Artists' Colony Exhibition, Darmstadt
1901	Restaurant, Artists' Colony Exhibition, Darmstadt
1901-02	Joseph Stade House, Darmstadt†
1901-02	Gustav Stade House, Darmstadt†
1901-03	Albert Hochstrasser House, Kronberg im Taunus
1902	Carl Kuntze House, Berlin†
1902	Playhouse for Princess Elizabeth of Hess, Wolfsgarten Castle
1903-04	Triple House Group, Darmstadt
1903-04	Fountain Court, Louisiana Purchase International Exposition, St. Louis, Missouri, U.S.A.†
1904	Edmund Olbrich House, Troppau, Austrian Silesia (facade)†
1905	Color Gardens, Darmstadt†
1905-06	Der Frauenrosenhof, Cologne
1905-08	Wedding Tower and Exhibition Building, Darmstadt
1906-07	Erwin Silber House, Bad Soden bei Salmünster
1906-08	Old Castle, Giessen (interiors)†
1906-09	Leonhard Tietz Department Store, Düsseldorf
1907-08	Luisplatz Fountains, Darmstadt
1907-08	Opel Worker's House, Darmstadt†
1907-08	Upper-Hessian House, Darmstadt
1907-09	Hugo Kruska Houses, Cologne†
1908	Max Clarenbach House, Wittlaer
1908-09	Theodor Althoff Store, Gladbeck†
1908-09	Walter Banzhaf House, Cologne†
1908-09	Joseph Feinhals House, Cologne

Publications

BOOKS BY OLBRICH

Ideen. Vienna, 1900.

Architektur von Professor Joseph Maria Olbrich. 3 vols. Berlin, 1901-04. Reissued with commentaries, Tübingen, Germany, 1988.

BOOKS ABOUT OLBRICH

CLARK, R. J., et. al.: *J. M. Olbrich: Das Werk des Architekten.* Darmstadt, Vienna and Berlin, 1967.

FRAMPTON, KENNETH, and FUTAGAWA, YUKIO: *Modern Architecture: 1920-1945.* New York, 1983.

HAIKO, PETER, and KRIMMEL, BERND: *Josef Maria Olbrich Architecture.* New York, 1988.

LATHAM, IAN: *Joseph Maria Olbrich.* London, 1980.

LUX, JOSEPH A.: *Josef Maria Olbrich.* Vienna, 1919.

RUSSELL, FRANK (ed.): *Art Nouveau Architecture.* London, 1979.

SCHREYL, K. H.: *Joseph Maria Olbrich: Die Zeichnungen in der Kunstbibliothek Berlin.* Berlin, 1972.

SEKLER, EDUARD F.: "Gli schizzi el viaggio in Italia di Josef Hoffmann e Josef Olbrich." In *Artisti austriaci a Roma.* Rome, 1972.

VERONESI, GIULIA: *Joseph Maria Olbrich.* Milan, 1948.

ARTICLES ABOUT OLBRICH

CLARK, R. J.: "J. M. Olbrich 1867-1908." *Architectural Design* 12 (December 1967).

PEVSNER, NIKOLAUS: "Secession." *Architectural Review* (January 1971): 73-74.

ROETHEL, J.: "Josef Maria Olbrich." *Architekt* No. 7 (1958): 291-318.

*

Joseph Maria Olbrich's career spanned the pivotal years between the rejection of historicism in the early 1890s and the advent of the new functionalist architecture on the eve of World War I. Although he died at age 40, Olbrich played a central role in the beginnings of the modernist revolution, helping to lay the groundwork for what came after.

A student of Carl von Hasenauer, an architect of Vienna's Ringstrasse, Olbrich rejected in his earliest work the neo-Baroque monumentality that characterized late Viennese historicism. Soon after graduating, however, he began to explore the possibilities of creating a new architectural vocabulary that combined past models with a "modern" symbolic language. His remarkable skill as a draftsman—evident already in his student years—attracted the attention of Otto Wagner, and beginning in 1893 he worked as Wagner's assistant on the massive Vienna *Stadtbahn* (city railway) project. During the roughly three years he spent in Wagner's office, Olbrich designed details for many of the *Stadtbahn* stations, including the exterior of the Hofpavilion at Schönbrunn and the famous twin stations on the Karlplatz. His early *Stadtbahn* designs were strongly informed by Wagner's distinctive pared-down classicism. By 1897, however, he began to develop his own stylistic idiom, drawing heavily on French and Belgian art nouveau and the work of Charles Rennie Mackintosh. In place of Wagner's free classical style, Olbrich employed intricate floral motifs and curvilinear geometric forms to create a rich, new decorative language.

The distinctive style that Olbrich developed came to define the early phase of the Austrian Jugendstil, and by the turn of the century his works were widely imitated in Vienna. Even Wagner himself was not immune to Olbrich's influence, as is evident in the floral decoration on the facades of Wagner's two Linke Wienzeile apartment houses, built just before the turn of the century.

But unlike many of his contemporaries, who began around that time to explore the possibilities of a new architecture unfettered by the past, Olbrich continued to draw from a variety of historical sources. In his first major independent commission, the Secession Building (1897-98), he combined elements of Wagner's classical style with Jugendstil and ancient Near Eastern imagery. Olbrich, however, used history not as his basic point of reference (as the historicists had done) but as a source of forms to solve specific problems. Unlike Wagner, who stressed the importance of a building's functional requirements, Olbrich believed that each project should be unique, corresponding to a particular subjective impulse. As a result, most of his works evince an almost boundless range of shapes, forms and colors.

Joseph Maria Olbrich: Wedding Tower and Exhibition Building, Darmstadt, 1905-08

In 1898 Olbrich opened his office and began to design houses and interiors for a number of wealthy patrons. Among the most important of these commissions was the completion of a half-built villa for Max Friedmann (1898). Strongly influenced by the English Arts and Crafts movement and the late-19th-century German ideas of the *Gesamtkunstwerk,* or total artwork, Olbrich designed every feature of the house, from the furniture and lighting fixtures to the wallpaper and textiles. He continued to design silverware, ceramics, textiles and jewelry throughout his career, and these works represent one of the most important aspects of his oeuvre.

During those years he also experimented with combining Jugendstil ornament and vernacular forms. In the Bahr House (1899-1900), for example, he fused the rich, sinuous forms of the early Jugendstil with a typical Austrian country house, creating a style that was widely copied throughout central Europe.

In 1899 Grand Duke Ernst Ludwig of Hesse invited Olbrich to join his artists' colony in Darmstadt, Germany. Olbrich, who was entrusted with overseeing the colony's architectural development, designed a studio and exhibition building, the Ernst Ludwig House (1899-1901), as well as a series of artists' houses. As with his earlier Bahr House, he continued to employ vernacular models, decorating the buildings with a seemingly inexhaustible vocabulary of forms and patterns.

After 1903, however, Olbrich's work began to show a renewed interest in monumentality and historical precedents. This shift was already evident in the Wedding Tower and Exhibition Building in Darmstadt (1905-08), which include elements of both north German medieval architecture and the Biedermeier. Olbrich's continuing reliance on historical models is particularly apparent in his last two major works, the Tietz Department Store in Düsseldorf (1906-09) and the Joseph Feinhals House in Cologne (1908-09). Drawing on a variety of historical sources ranging from the Italian Renaissance to 19th-century German architecture, Olbrich sought to create a new, "modernized" historicism that would reconcile the dictates of a modern society with traditional architecture. But his experiments ended abruptly in 1908, when he died of leukemia.

After his death Olbrich was largely forgotten. In the purist climate of the 1920s and 1930s, the dense, florid ornament and historical allusions of works seemed sadly passé. It was not until the late 1960s, with the renewed interest in ornament, that Olbrich began to be rediscovered. Although Olbrich's later buildings are more restrained than his early designs, all of his works display a multitude of decorative ideas, materials and colors. Indeed, Olbrich's powers of ornamental invention were matched among those of his generation only by Frank Lloyd Wright. While his built works sometimes lack a sense of cohesiveness, Olbrich demonstrated the rich possibilities of architectural and decorative form.

—CHRISTOPHER LONG

OLIVEIRA, Mateus Vicente de.

Portuguese. Born in Barcarena, Portugal, 13 June 1706. Died in Lisbon, ca. 1786. Studied under João Frederico Ludovice. Worked in Queluz, then called to Lisbon, 1758, to assist in the reconstruction of the city after an earthquake.

Chronology of Works
All in Portugal

1747-92   Château, Queluz, near Lisbon
1779-90   Basilica da Estrêla, Lisbon

Publications

BOOKS ABOUT OLIVEIRA

FRANÇA, J.-A.: *Une Ville des Lumières, la Lisbonne de Pombal.* Paris, 1965.

The military engineer and architect Mateus Vicente de Oliveira was the favorite Portuguese designer of the royal court in Lisbon during the second half of the 18th century. A member of the generation of "Pombaline" military engineers who worked for the Portuguese First Minister Pombal in the reconstruction of Lisbon after the great earthquake of 1755, he received his architectural training in the chantiers of João Federico Ludovice's Mafra. From Ludovice he took a deep appreciation of Italian Baroque form and quality workmanship in fine materials. Mateus Vicente's achievement lies in his stylish reworking of the Italianate Baroque traditions of the Portuguese Joanine style of Mafra and in his sensitivity to contemporary fashions and the courtly tastes of his patrons, the royal Bragança family.

His first major project, the Château at Queluz near Lisbon (1747-92), is the premier Portuguese example of the elegant Rococo style that was by then somewhat outmoded throughout most of Europe. Mateus Vicente's design for the main pavilion reflects both his mastery of Ludovice's idiom as well as his application of the Joanine decorative vocabulary to a *château de plaisance* in the French classical manner of the 17th century. Laid out in a formal, symmetrically planned "U" with a main *corps-de-logis,* flanking pavilions and a *cour d'honneur* leading to the gardens, Queluz illustrates the Portuguese military engineer's integration of French formal planning and stylish curvilinear ornament with the same Joanine concern for a quality decorative finish that characterized Ludovice's work at Mafra.

In terms of its style and composition, Queluz is essentially a Portuguese decorative overlay on a château in the Louis XIV mode of Jules Hardouin Mansart's Pavilion at Marly (1679). Stripped of its ornament, Mateus Vicente's main garden facade closely resembles that of Mansart's château. Both facades are two-story compositions with giant pilasters and a three-bay frontispiece crowned by a triangular pediment. The pilasters support straight, unadorned entablatures. In Queluz, however, the composition has been condensed into seven bays, which are more widely spaced than the nine bays of Marly, and which follow a 2-3-2 grouping created by the four pairs of overlapping pilasters that define the frontispiece and the ends of the pavilion. The triangular pediment is carved with the Portuguese royal escutcheon and garlands on each side. A typically Portuguese tile roof is visible behind the balustrade that runs on either side of the pediment. The fenestration is also a key element in the decorative system of the facade. Sculptural ornamentation in the form of floral motifs and cartouches framing *putti* is limited to the tops of the segmental frames around the French doors. On the upper story, these doors open onto grilled balconies with bases defined by a stringcourse which, supported by pairs of consoles, extend the length of the facade. The central door of the main story is framed by paired columns and a curvilinear frame, which is echoed in the frame and rippled pediment (of Joanine derivation) in the French door above. The ochre and pink plaster finishes on the wall surfaces, otherwise unadorned, give dainty Rococo coloring to the whole.

In 1758 Mateus Vicente was called away from Queluz to assist in the reconstruction of earthquake-torn Lisbon, and the French goldsmith Jean-Baptiste Robillion assumed the works on the château. The Portuguese engineer's major post-earthquake work, the monumental Basílica da Estrêla in Lisbon (1779-90), reveals an even closer adherence to the style of his teacher, Ludovice, than does Queluz. The Estrêla's obvious source is the Basílica at Mafra, and Mateus Vicente treated the theme (twin towers framing a monumental, high-drummed dome in the manner of St. Peter's in Rome) with characteristic attention to ornamental details and surface refinement. Within the panorama of Portuguese post-earthquake architecture, the Estrêla is really more Joanine than Pombaline in style: the reductive rationalism of the military engineer is no more in evidence there than in Queluz, perhaps because both the château and the Estrêla were commissions of the Portuguese royal family, whose tastes were aristocratic and *retardataire*. Because of this royal patronage and the strong impact of Ludovice, Mateus Vicente emerged as the most conservative, most characteristically "Baroque" architect of the Pombaline age in Lisbon.

—DAVID K. UNDERWOOD

OLMSTED, Frederick Law.

American. Born in Hartford, Connecticut, 26 April 1822. Died in Waverly, Massachusetts, 28 August 1903. Married Mary Olmsted, 1859; sons were the landscape architects John C. Olmsted and Frederick Law Olmsted Jr. Worked as a surveyor before turning to landscape architecture; in partnership with Calvert Vaux to create Central Park, New York City, 1958; partnership lasted until 1872; continued the practice with his sons.

Chronology of Works
All in the United States

1858	Central Park, New York City (with Calvert Vaux)
1864	Mountain View Cemetery, Oakland, California
1866	Prospect Park, Brooklyn, New York (with Vaux)
1868	Park System, Buffalo, New York (with Vaux)
1868	Riverside Community, Illinois (with Vaux)
1871	State Asylum for the Insane, Buffalo, New York (with H. H. Richardson)
1873	Morningside Park, New York City (with Vaux)
1874	United States Capitol Grounds, Washington, D.C.
1875	Riverside Park, New York City (with Vaux)
1878	Park System, Boston, Massachusetts
1879-81	Ames Memorial Town Hall, North Easton, Massachusetts (with Richardson)
1880-81	Oakes Ames Estate, North Easton, Massachusetts (with Richardson)
1880-83	Crane Memorial Library, Quincy, Massachusetts (with Richardson)
1884	Beardsley Park, Bridgeport, Connecticut (wth John C. Olmsted)
1886	Stanford University, Palo Alto, California (with Shepley, Rutan, and Cooledge)
1887	Niagara Falls Reservation, New York (with Vaux)
1888	Biltmore Estate, Asheville, North Carolina (with Richard Morris Hunt)
1888	Park System, Rochester, New York
1889	Downing Park, Newburgh, New York (with Vaux)
1889	Park System, Milwaukee, Wisconsin
1891	Park System, Louisville, Kentucky
1893	World's Columbian Exposition, Chicago, Illinois (with others)

Publications

BOOKS BY OLMSTED

Walks and Talks of an American Farmer in England. New York, 1852.
A Journey in the Seaboard Slave States. 2 vols. New York, 1904.

ARTICLES BY OLMSTED

"H. H. Richardson." *American Architect* (July 1886).
"Landscape Architecture of the World's Columbian Exposition, 1893." *American Architect and Building News* 41.

BOOKS ABOUT OLMSTED

BARLOW, ELIZABETH: *Frederick Law Olmsted's New York.* New York, 1972.
CONDIT, CARL W.: *American Building Art.* New York, 1960.
FABOS, JULIUS G.; MILDE, GORDON T.; and WEINMAYR, V. MICHAEL: *Frederick Law Olmsted, Sr., Founder of Landscape Architecture in America.* Amherst, Massachusetts, 1968.
FEIN, ALBERT: *Frederick Law Olmsted and the American Environmental Tradition.* New York, 1972.
MITCHELL, BROADUS: *Frederick Law Olmsted.* Baltimore, 1924.
OLMSTED, FREDERICK LAW, JR., and KIMBALL, THEODORA (eds.): *Frederick Law Olmsted 1822-1903.* 2 vols. New York, 1922-28.
ROPER, LAURA WOOD: *FLO: A Biography of Frederick Law Olmsted.* Baltimore, 1973.
SCHUYLER, DAVID, and CENSER, JANE TURNER (eds.): *The Years of Olmsted, Vaux and Company.* Baltimore, 1992.
SUTTON, S. B. (ed.): *Civilizing American Cities: A Selection of Frederick Law Olmsted's Writings on City Landscapes.* Cambridge, Massachusetts, 1971.

ARTICLES ABOUT OLMSTED

KOWSKY, FRANCIS R.: "Municipal Parks and City Planning: Frederick Law Olmsted's Buffalo Park and Parkway System." *Journal of the Society of Architectural Historians* 46 (March 1987): 49-64.
SMITH, G. M.: "Belle Grove's Olmstead Papers." *Historic Preservation* 24 (January 1972): 24-27.
TISHLER, WILLIAM H.: "Frederick Law Olmsted: Prophet of Environmental Design." *Journal of the American Institute of Architects* 44 (December 1965): 31-35.
ZAITZEVSKY, CYNTHIA: "The Olmsted Firm and the Structures of the Boston Park System." *Journal of the Society of Architectural Historians* 32 (1973): 167-174.

*

Like many other 19th-century pioneers in landscape architecture, Frederick Law Olmsted's eclectic, self-initiated, practical education prepared him to integrate the complex of concepts and skills that eventually merged, in large part under his leadership, to define the new profession. Olmsted's experiences as journalist and social critic had allowed him to travel across much of the United States, acquiring practical knowledge of horticulture, geology and hydrology. Equally important for his later practice, these widely read reports, especially the controversial *A Journey through the Seaboard Slave States with Remarks on Their Economy,* made his name known among the educated and affluent, just the people who later became his clients.

Social and geographic experience alone, of course, would not have directly prepared Olmsted for his later profession. Of greater practical use was experience in managing his two scientifically run model farms at Sachem's Head and Staten Island, New York. There his concerns ran the agricultural gamut from animal husbandry to pomology. It was those work experiences, along with his social connections, that provided him access to the most valuable job of his life. In 1857, after a concerted campaign on his behalf by family friends such as Washington Irving, he was appointed superintendent of land clearing for the new park planned for New York City. The intimate site knowledge that this position assured, coupled with a fertile imagination and a fortuitous partnership with Calvert Vaux, all but guaranteed success when a competition for design of the park was announced.

The Central Park competition was not only the pivotal event in Olmsted's career, but also a critical turning point for the profession of landscape architecture. Without the notoriety of the competition and the success of the winning ''Greensward'' design, it is questionable whether the then-named profession of ''landscape gardening'' would have ever moved beyond the garden scale of estate work and cemetery design to embrace comprehensive environmental planning in which social, ecological, functional and aesthetic concerns were all equally relevant. At Central Park the designers demonstrated that even undistinguished sites could be completely transformed to create the illusion of naturalistic landscapes; that parks had an important social function in offering places of release for urban residents with no access to the countryside; and, of great interest to politicians, that these ends could be achieved without cost to the city, since parks generated more in increased tax revenues from surrounding property than their actual cost.

Olmsted could easily have built a very successful practice by exploiting these concepts across the continent. Almost every large city sought his expertise and for a few he, either alone or with a partner, did develop plans, such as those for Prospect Park in Brooklyn, Mount Royal Park in Montreal, and Seneca Park in Rochester, New York. When forced to turn down commissions, he exploited his reputation to further promote the fledgling profession, as well as other practitioners by suggesting men like H. W. S. Cleveland or Jacob Weldenmann for the project. As a leader in a new and often misunderstood profession, Olmsted sought to define its philosophy through his work and writing, while his quandary regarding the identity of the profession was clearly revealed in correspondence with Vaux. There he pondered an appropriate name for this innovative discipline, which combined aspects of fine art, horticulture, natural science, social science and architecture, but surpassed them all in scope.

The diversity of projects in which Olmsted engaged during his professional life attests to his devotion to those social and environmental missions that remain the philosophical underpinnings of landscape architecture. Parks planning was to him a form of progressive city planning through which human moral character could be uplifted, while improving urban health and safety. His scheme for the park system in Boston, the famed Emerald Necklace, best illustrated this twin mission. Originally intended to form a continuous crescent from the Common to the Neponset River, this system located recreational areas close to neighborhoods throughout the city, while at the same time managing problems of flooding and sewage pollution. The most important gem on the necklace, Franklin Park, was to be a bit of country in a stressful city.

Besides all of the cities and towns that were permanently improved through his skill and perseverance, Olmsted's greatest achievement was establishing a professional firm that trained future leaders of landscape architecture, such as Warren Manning and Henry Hubbard, and perpetuated the sound principles upon which his practice had been built. After ending his partnership with Vaux in the 1870s, Olmsted worked informally with other designers, including Weidenmann, until his son John C. Olmsted became a partner. It was John and his younger brother Frederick Law Olmsted, Jr. who eventually perpetuated the firm, which existed into the 1950s as Olmsted Brothers. Throughout Olmsted's later years, as mind and body began to fail under the strain of almost 50 years of hard field work, his thoughts were constantly on continuation of the firm and advancement of the profession. It was as though he knew that the physical works of design to which he had dedicated his energy were minor achievements compared to the multifaceted discipline for which he, in large measure, could take credit for pioneering.

—NANCY J. VOLKMAN

OPPENORD, Gilles-Marie.

French. Born in Paris, France, 27 July 1672. Died in Paris, 13 March 1742. Son of a Dutch craftsman who settled in France. Studied at the French Academy in Rome, 1692-99. Chief architect, St. Sulpice, Paris, 1725-31.

Chronology of Works
All in France

1704	St.-Germain-des-Prés, Paris (altar)
1706	Abbey of St. Victor, Paris (choir)
1709	Cathedral, Amiens (Altar of St. Jean)
1712	St. Jacques de la Boucherie, Paris (altar)
1714	Hôtel de Pomponne, Paris (interior)
1716	Château de Bonn (interior)
1716-20	Palais Royal, Paris (remodeling)
1719-29	Hôtel d'Assy, Paris (interior)
1720-21	Hôtel du Grand Prieur de Temple, Paris
1723-24	Hôtel de St. Albin, Paris
1723-30	Hôtel Crozat, Paris
1725-40	St. Sulpice, Paris
1729	Cathedral, Meaux (choir screen and altars)
1731-49	Hôtel Gaudion, Paris
1732-40	Eglise de l'Oratoire, Paris

Publications

BOOKS ABOUT OPPENORD

HAUTECOEUR, LOUIS: Vol 2 in *Histoire de l'architecture classique en France.* Paris, 1948.

KALNEIN, WEND GRAF, and LEVEY, MICHAEL: *Art and Architecture of the Eighteenth Century in France.* Harmondsworth, England, 1972.

ARTICLES ABOUT OPPENORD

MALBOIS, EMILE: "Oppenord et l'église Saint Sulpice." *Gazette des Beaux Arts* 69 (1928): 34-46.
"Watteau and Oppenord." *Burlington Magazine* 97 (1955).

*

Gilles-Marie Oppenord was a French architect active during the French Regency and important for the development of the Rococo style in Europe. His father, a Dutch craftsman who had settled in France, was mentioned in 1684 as living in the studios of the Louvre, where he worked as *ébéniste royale* to the king. This connection was extremely important, for the younger Oppenord became a protégé of the superintendant of buildings, Edouard Colbert (the marquis de Villacerf); it was through his help that in 1692 Oppenord was allowed to be attached to the French Academy in Rome, where, two years later, he became an official pensioner. Much was made of his talents, and during his seven years in Italy he evidently worked hard, studying both antique sculpture and the work of more modern figures like Giovanni Lorenzo Bernini and Francesco Borromini. It was from what might be called his digestion of the Italian Baroque that Oppenord was able to make a particular contribution to the evolution of the French Rococo.

On his return to Paris, Oppenord was not taken up in the royal works, his patron de Villacerf having been replaced by Jules Hardouin-Mansart. But Oppenord kept busy designing engravings for books and proferring designs for whatever commissions were available. In 1704 the new altar for the church of St. Germain-des-Prés was done from his designs; an early, unbuilt version had included the twisted columns and the rich superstructure of Bernini's *baldachino* at St. Peter's, and the final version, even with its plain columns, was completely Baroque in its details, most notably in the two angels on volutes who hold the medieval reliquary.

Other ecclesiastical projects followed: a design in 1706 for an altar for the Abbey of St. Victor, tomb monuments and the Altar of St. Jean in a chapel in the Cathedral of Amiens and, in 1712, the high altar for the Church of St. Jacques de la Boucherie in Paris.

The altar at Amiens, done in 1709, shows how much Oppenord used Italian Baroque elements, for the shape, with the entablature protruding at either side, yet supported by columns with elaborate capitals, is that of the altar by Borromini at Sant'Agnese in Agone in Rome. Yet the central portion, with what was originally a painting in the middle, is enclosed by a frame with laurel sprays and garlands lipping over the corners that seems typically French. Oppenord continued to work for ecclesiastical authorities, and in this area perhaps his most important work was that, done quite late in life, at the Church of St. Sulpice, where he was chief architect from 1725 to 1731.

In 1715 Louis XIV died. This worked to the immediate advantage of Oppenord, for his protector, the duc d'Orléans, was appointed regent of France until 1723, when the new king would reach majority. This led to a remarkable range of commissions for Oppenord. The first was for the remodeling of the Palais Royale, a vast project for the duc d'Orléans, which we now know only from drawings. Oppenord began with the apartments of the *duchesse* on the ground floor and those of the regent in the left wing. The following year he rebuilt the picture gallery with a chimneypiece with pilasters, consoles, an immense mirror

and Victories pulling aside heavy curtains that seem to have come from Borromini; the end wall was filled with a magnificently ornamented oval hemicycle.

Oppenord's fame grew, and in 1716 he was even asked by the elector of Cologne to design doors, paneling and chimneypieces for his palace in Bonn. It was at that time that Oppenord was at his busiest as a designer, and many examples of his work are known through engravings and drawings for a whole range of furniture, such as tables, clocks, frames, candelabra and chimneypieces. In 1723 Oppenord was asked by Pierre Crozat, a notable collector, to remodel the gallery of the Hôtel Crozat in Paris and design an orangery for this château at Montmorency. And from 1731 until his death 11 years later, Oppenord lived in an apartment in the Hôtel Crozat, where he became friendly with other artists of the time, most notably Rosalba Carriera and Antoine Watteau.

One other notable commission, perhaps never carried out, was for the Hôtel Gaudion in the Marais in Paris; the designs were done when Pierre-Nicolas Gaudion was *garde du trésor royal* between 1731 and 1749, and are now in the Musée des Arts Decoratifs in Paris. Following Oppenord's death, more than 2,000 of his drawings were purchased by the publisher Gabriel Huquier and published, in the late 1740s, in three volumes of *Oeuvres*. Known familiarly as the *Petit, Moyen* and *Grand Oppenord,* these books ensured Oppenord's immortality and made possible the use of his models throughout Europe by any artist who was concerned, as he was, with formal decorations.

—DAVID CAST

ÖSTBERG, Ragnar.

Swedish. Born in Vaxholm, Sweden, 14 July 1866. Died in Stockholm, 1945. Studied at the Royal Institute of Technology, Stockholm, 1885-88, and Royal Academy of Arts, Stockholm, 1888-91. Worked in the office of the architect Isak Gustaf Clason, early 1890s. Traveled to the United States in 1893, and to France, Italy, Greece, England and Spain, 1896-99. Taught at the Klara Architectural School, 1910-11, and the Royal Academy of Art, Stockholm, 1922. Editor, *Arkitektur,* 1908-12. Gold Medal, Royal Institute of British Architects, 1926.

Chronology of Works
All in Sweden

1901-03	Ebbagården, Tureberg
1905	Villa Pauli, Stockholm
1905	Villa Ekarne, Stockholm
1906	Theatre, Umea
1906-10	Östermalms School, Stockholm
1907	Villa Larsson, Storangen, Nacka
1907-23	Stockholm City Hall, Stockholm
1909	Villa Nedre Manilla, Stockholm
1909-11	Villa Bonnier, Stockholm
1910	High School (Östermalms Läroverk), Stockholm
1911	Villa Elviksudde, Stockholm
1911-13	Odd Fellows' Building, Stockholm
1911-21	Patents' Office, Stockholm
1918	Carl Eldh Atelier, Stockholm
1924-28	Helsingborg Crematorium, Helsingborg

1927-33	Kalmar Grammar School, Kalmar
1930	Industry Center, Stockholm
1930	Students' Club, Uppsala
1930	Värmland National House, Uppsala
1931-34	Swedish Maritime Museum, Stockholm
1939	Zoorn Museum, Mora

Publications

BOOKS BY ÖSTBERG

Auswahl von schwedischer Architektur der Gegenwart. Stockholm, 1908.
En architekts anteckningar. Stockholm, 1928.
The Stockholm Town Hall. Stockholm, 1929.

BOOKS ABOUT ÖSTBERG

AHLBERG, HAKON: *Swedish Architecture of the Twentieth Century.* London, 1925.

ARTICLES ABOUT ÖSTBERG

"Crematorium Halsingborg." *Architect and Building News* (8 January 1932): 44-46.
ROBERTSON, HOWARD: "Ragnar Östberg." *Royal Institute of British Architects Journal* (6 November 1926): 15-23.
ROBERTSON, HOWARD: "Naval Museum, Stockholm." *Architect and Building News* (17 January 1936).
"The Stadshus at Stockholm." *Architectural Review* (January 1924): 1-6.

*

During the first third of the 20th century, Ragnar Östberg occupied a prominent and influential position among Swedish architects. In addition to an active practice, he taught at both the independent Klara Architectural School (1910-11) and the Royal Academy of Art (1922), edited the journal *Arkitektur* (1908-12), and was awarded the Gold Medals of the RIBA (1926) and the AIA (1932). Though he was often labeled a romantic eclectic, Östberg's work was of vital importance to the development of Swedish classicism during the 1920s. And while no contemporaneous Swedish architect enjoyed a comparable international reputation, it was founded primarily upon one building: the Stockholm City Hall (1907-23).

Creator of an architecture that was highly personal yet simple, original yet eclectic, Östberg was among the Swedish architects who, in the early years of the 20th century, called for a modern, national architecture. Beginning his practice as a designer of domestic villas, Östberg incorporated influences from English and continental Jugendstil sources, as well as from Swedish vernacular building. His early houses combined the informality of English interior spatial planning with the Scandinavian preference for a symmetrical facade, a response to both Nordic climate and tradition, coupled with the demands of modern domestic living. The Villa Pauli in the Stockholm suburb of Djursholm (1905), and the Villa Bonnier in Stockholm (1909-11), exemplify these qualities. The villas influenced the work of younger Swedes like Erik Gunnar Asplund, Elis Benckert and Sigurd Lewerentz, not to mention a generation of Nordic designers.

In the same period, Östberg was invited by a group of younger architects to teach at the independent Klara School. At that time a conflict had developed between the more neoclassic-based teaching at the Royal Academy of Arts in Stockholm and a group of young designers interested in incorporating influences from traditional Swedish architecture, handicrafts and applied designs in their work. Östberg, along with the other faculty, brought a romantic sensibility that acknowledged the influences of these sources.

European medieval architecture influenced Östberg's larger projects, as seen in the more somber, dark red brick volumes of the Östermalms Läroverk School in Stockholm (1910) and the Stockholm City Hall (1907-23). Though Östberg received the City Hall commission in 1907, he had been studying the site since 1901 through a series of design proposals for a new law courts building. The City Hall forms itself around two courtyards, one exterior and one interior (known as the Blue Room), and is of red brick with a copper roof. Claiming a prominent point on Lake Mälaren, thus gathering in the surrounding elements of the city, the complex has both a romantic compositional quality and a classical lightness. Despite the continued refinement over the course of the project, and the historical influences seen in its detail elements, the work achieves a striking architectural unity, contains interiors of special quality, and responds convincingly to the urban setting. It is truly one of the finest public works of this century.

As the source of his international fame, the Stockholm City Hall occupies a strange position in Östberg's oeuvre. The long period of design and building caused him to redefine and refine the project several times. Yet he never fully departed from his original ideas, and many features, including the two courts, never left the scheme. Qualities of the art nouveau were integrated into the composition along with directly picturesque elements, as were direct references to Italian classical and Swedish vernacular sources. Despite the reputation Östberg received from abroad as a result of this work, he received few Swedish commissions during that period.

Often labeled a romantic eclectic, Östberg was nonetheless of vital importance to the development of Swedish classicism that occurred immediately after World War I. Over the course of the design of the Stockholm City Hall, classical influences gained an increasing foothold in his work, particularly in the interiors and furniture. This is particularly true of the Prince's Gallery. In his later work Östberg did not embrace totally a pure neoclassicism, but, as seen in his Villa Elviksudde (1911), he incorporated Nordic vernacular elements and motifs in the designs. The Patent and Registration Office (1911-21) and the Carl Eldh's Atelier (1918), both in Stockholm, continued this trend. The atelier is a small, simply formed wooden building, with a rotunda-shaped reception area and pedimented south studio space being the classical elements. The rotunda reappeared in the Helsingborg Crematorium (1924-28) as the apex of the chapel. The light marble columns supporting the dome contrast the solid, plain exterior forms of the building. Uncompromisingly classical works include the Kalmar Grammar School (1927-33) and the Swedish Maritime Museum (1931-34), located in Ladugardsgärdet in Stockholm. The curved form of the Maritime Museum responds to the wide terrace steps of the amphitheater left from Asplund's 1930 Stockholm Exhibition. While classical in inspiration, with its dominant entry rotunda and rhythmic window placement, the building has an austere "modernist" quality to its exterior.

With the 1930 Stockholm Exhibition the trend toward functionalism, as modernism was called in the Nordic countries, emerged as the dominant force in Swedish architecture. The Industry Center in Stockholm (1930) is the only Östberg building exhibiting functionalist sensibilities. Basically, Östberg remained opposed to the Modern Movement, preferring to continue as a classicist for the remainder of his career. Though receiving much international acclaim for his work, Östberg ended his career somewhat isolated from his colleagues. Yet today we look to Ragnar Östberg as one who was able to blend international and local sources into a powerful and creative architecture.

—WILLIAM C. MILLER

OTTO, Frei.

German. Born in Siegmar, Saxony, Germany, 31 May 1925. Married Ingrid Smolla, 1952. Studied at the Schadow School, Berlin-Zehlendorf, 1937-43; Technical University of Berlin, 1948-52, Dip.Ing., 1952; Dr.Ing., 1954. In private practice, Zehlendorf, Berlin, since 1952; member of the Studio Warmbronn, Germany, since 1968. Founder, Development Center for Lightweight Construction, Berlin, 1957. Professor and director of the Institute for Lightweight Structures, since 1964; has taught extensively i n Europe and the United States.

Chronology of Works
All in Germany unless noted

1955	Bandstand, Federal Garden Exhibition, Kassel
1957	Entrance Arch and Dance Pavilion, Federal Garden Exhibition, Cologne
1963	Wave Hall, International Horticultural Exhibition, Hamburg
1964	Snow and Rocks Restaurant Pavilion, Swiss National Exhibition, Lausanne, Switzerland
1965-67	West German Pavilion, World Exposition, Montreal, Canada
1967-72	Roofs for Olympic Stadium and Arenas, Olympic Park, Munich (with Behnisch, Bubner, and Leonhardt)
1967-68	Retractable roof for the Open-Air Theater, Bad Hersfeld, Hessen (with Romberg and Bubner)
1971	Mobile large umbrella roofs for the Music Pavilion, Cologne
1972-74	Hotel and Conference Center, Mecca, Saudi Arabia
1974-75	Multi-purpose Hall and Restaurant, Mannheim
1975-78	Sports Hall, King Abdul Aziz University, Jeddah, Saudi Arabia (with Gutbrod, Henning, Arup and Happold)
1980	Great Aviary, Hellabrunn (with Happold)
1980-85	Diplomatic Club, Riyadh, Saudi Arabia (with Omrania and Happold)
1988	Hook Park, England (with ABK)
1989	Ceremony Tent, Bamberg (with Dörrer and Happold)
1990	Okohaus IBA, Berlin (with Kendel and others)

Publications

BOOKS BY OTTO

The Suspended Roof. Berlin, 1954. .
Structures: Traditional and Lightweight. New Haven, Connecticut, 1961.
Tensile Structures. 2 vols. Cambridge, Massachusetts, and London, 1969.
Natürliche Konstruktionen. With others. Stuttgart, 1982.
Schriften und Reden 1951-1983. Edited by B. Burkhardt. Braunschweig and Stuttgart, 1984.
Gestaltwerdung: zur Formentstehung in Natur, Technik und Baukunst. Cologne, 1988.

Frei Otto: Diplomatic Club, Riyadh, Saudi Arabia, 1980-85

ARTICLES BY OTTO

"Vom Nest zu modernen Wohnstadt." *Architekt* 3/12 (1954).

"Vom ungeheizt schön warmen Haus und neuen Fenstern." *Deutsche Bauzeitschrift* 3 (1955).

"Bauten für morgen?" *Bauen und Wohnen* 3 (1955).

"Die Stadt von morgen und das Einfamilienhaus." *Baukunst und Werkform* 12 (1956).

"Les toitures suspendues et les voilures." *Architecture d'aujourd'hui* (March 1956).

"Formes, techniques et constructions humaines." *Architecture d'aujourd'hui* 78 (1958).

"Imagination et architecture." *Architecture d'aujourd'hui* 102 (1962).

"Contribution à l'architecture pneumatique." *Architecture d'aujourd'hui* (June 1962).

"Villes futures." *Architecture d'aujourd'hui* 115 (1964).

"Ein Interbau und ein Spinnerzentrum." *Deutsche Bauzeitung* (September 1970).

"Die neue Zeit der vielen Architekturen." *Deutsche Bauzeitung* (December 1972).

"Die Europastadt." *Deutsche Bauzeitung* (December 1973).

"Creation, Creativity and Architecture." *Architectural Design* 7 (1975).

"Mit Leichtigkeit gegen Brutalität." *Deutsche Bauzeitung* (January 1976).

"Les formules qui mènent l'architecture." *Architecture* 396 (1976).

"Widernatürliche Architektur." *Universitätnachrichten* 50 (1977).

"Wie weiter?" *Schweizerische Bauzeitung* 16 (1977).

"Der Pneu, Bauprinzip des Lebens." *Bild der Wissenschaft* 15 (1978).

"Das Aesthetische." *Mitteilung des Instituts für leichte Flächentragwerke* 21 (Stuttgart, 1979).

"Biologie und Bauen." *Durchblick* 6 (1980).

"Bauen in Natur und Technik." In *Forschung in der BRD*. Weinheim, West Germany, 1983.

BOOKS ABOUT OTTO

DREW, PHILIP: *Frei Otto: Form and Structure*. London, 1976.

GLAESER, LÜDWIG: *The Work of Frei Otto*. Exhibition catalog. New York, 1971. Revised as *Leichtarchitektur: Frei Otto and His Teams 1955-1976*. 1975.

JOEDICKE, JÜRGEN (ed.): *Documents of Modern Architecture: Shell Architecture*. Stuttgart and London, 1963.

KLOTZ, HEINRICH: *Architektur in der Bundesrepublik—Gespräche mit Günther Behnisch, Wolfgang Döring, Helmut Hentrich, Hans Kammerer, Frei Otto, Oswald Mathias Ungers*. Frankfurt, 1977.

ROLAND, CONRAD: *Frei Otto: Spannweiten, Ideen und Versuche zum Leichtbau*. Berlin, Frankfurt and Vienna, 1965.

ROLAND, CONRAD: *Tension Structures*. New York, 1970.

ROLAND, CONRAD: *Frei Otto*. London, 1972.

ARTICLES ABOUT OTTO

DREW, PHILIP: "Frei Otto—Search for a Minimal Architecture." *Architect* (February 1980).

"Frei Otto at Work." *Architectural Design* (March 1971).

"Frei Otto: Biographical and Bibliographical Notes." *Zodiac* 21 (1972).

"Frei Otto." *Architecture and Urbanism* (June 1982).

"Frei Otto's New Work." *Mimar* (April/June 1982).

"Frei Otto's Pneumatic Structures." *Architectural Design* (July 1966).

"Frei Otto—Recent Projects." *Architecture d'aujourd'hui* (October 1982).

"Hotel and Conference Centre, La Mecca, Saudi Arabia." *Domus* (June 1979).

"Natural Structure: Ideas and Plans of Frei Otto and His Team." *Deutsche Bauzeitung* (July 1982).

"Otto Biography." *Industrial Design* (June 1971).

"Otto's Desert Tent." *Building Design* (16 January 1981).

ROLAND, CONRAD: "Frei Otto's Pneumatic Structures." *Architectural Design* (July 1966).

SCHUNCK, E.: "Aesthetic Truth." *Architekt* (December 1982).

SEGAL, WALTER: "Frei Otto in Defence of Nature." *Architects' Journal* (9 March 1983).

"Tents as Ideal Buildings." *Japan Architect* (July 1970).

WILLIAMS, STEPHANIE: "When Is a Tent Not a Tent?" *Building Design* (16 January 1976).

"The Work of Frei Otto." *Architecture Canada* (12 June 1972).

*

Throughout his career Frei Otto has kept his design and academic activities separate. He is a complex and, in some respects, contradictory figure who must be counted one of the outstanding innovators and architectural visionaries of the century.

If at first he appears to belong to the rationalist current of the great 20th-century constructors, and to be a structural determinist in his approach to architectural form, this interpretation is far from adequate and only represents a part of the total picture. It ignores Otto's very German romanticism and powerful identification with natural form, which has both an intellectual and an emotional component. Similar preoccupations may be detected in the expressionist fantasies of Bruno Taut, notably in his crystalline temples and *Alpine Architektur* sketches.

For purposes of classification, Frei Otto can be grouped with Felix Candela, R. Buckminster Fuller and Walter Bird, all of them important technical and structural innovators. Otto is considerably more than an inventor and researcher who has expanded the vocabulary of tensile structural form in a systematic, somewhat didactic manner. He is an inventor, for all that, with creative pretensions who is motivated by a concern to find new and efficient modes of creating shelter that are flexible and adaptive and impose themselves on neither the users nor the environment. In this sense, Otto is a conscious environmentalist who very early explored ecologically sound alternatives that offered a means of reducing the stress imposed by building activities on the environment. He was an early advocate of what has come to be called "green architecture" long before this became a fashionable concern.

The tent arose among nomads who had a restricted access to resources, so it was to be expected that Otto would turn to the tent as an efficient and, at the same time, very beautiful model of minimal building that was economical and easily adapted. The modern tent, as distinct from tensile structures originating in suspension bridge technology, is very largely Otto's personal creation.

Traditional Western tents had acquired simple predetermined shapes, and 20th-century engineers favored the practice of mathematically determined surfaces. In the 1950s, at a time when the statistical analysis of such structures was still in its infancy, Otto explored a host of minimal surface shapes, directly using models to generate the forms.

The small Bundesgarten textile pavilions of the 1950s are among Otto's most beautiful and elegant creations—the riverside shelter and dance pavilion at Cologne (1957) and the small star pavilion at Hamburg (1963) are consummate marriages of construction and aesthetics. Prior to 1963, such textile pavilions were comprised of standard membrane elements arranged additively. It was not until after the mid-1960s, when Otto began to collaborate with the Stuttgart architect Rolf Gutbrod, that he began to investigate picturesque asymmetrical roof forms divided unequally by low and high anchorage and support points in their interior. The Pavilion of the Federal Republic of Germany at Expo '67 in Montreal (1965-67) was the earliest and, without question, one of the most stunning applications of such a freely sculpted surface terrain recalling in a poetic manner qualities associated with alpine scenery.

The restaurant pavilions at the Swiss National Exhibition of 1964, at Laussanne, were the first to use cable-nets. Prior to that, all his roofs were fabricated from cotton-canvas for spans between 20 and 30 meters (66 to 98 feet). The combination of membrane and cable-net in one construction introduced a new set of problems which were not properly understood at the time, so the Laussanne pavilions must be seen as transitional structures that anticipate the later mature, large-scale cable-net roofs. With this development, modern tensile roof construction and the modern engineered tent can be said to have come of age, insofar as the technical means used in their construction matched the structural requirements for realizing large tensile surfaces having freely shaped terrains. The roofs over the main sports area in the Olympiapark at Munich (1967-72), built by Günther Behnisch with Otto as roof design consultant, realized a new scale and design sophistication for this type of construction and led, in turn, to the pioneering of purely mathematical, computer-based procedures for determining their shapes.

Otto also developed a type of convertible roof with a variable geometry which enabled the roof to be extended or retracted at will mechanically. Many such roofs have been constructed in Germany, France and elsewhere, but none is so captivating in Germany, France and elsewhere, but none is so captivating as the roof for the Open Air Theater at Bad Hersfeld in Hessen (1967-68). The convertible roof was a logical extension of the fixed-membrane shelter that exploited the innate flexibility of the textile fabric—a self-erecting and self-demounting tent, in effect.

In the decade following the completion of the Munich Olympic Games facility, Otto was engaged in the realization of a quantity of adventurous proposals, among which the umbrella roofs at Cologne (1971), the roofs for the Conference Centre in Mecca, Saudi Arabia (1974), the timber grid shell multipurpose hall and restaurant in Mannheim (1975), a sports complex at King Abdulaziz in Jeddah (1975-78), the Munich Aviary in Munich (1980) and Diplomatic Club in Riyadh (1980-85) must be rated as being the most significant in terms of the advancement of building technique. A number of them were sited in the Middle East and recognized the inspiration and the need for continuity between the new structures and the older traditional forms of the nomad tent shelters.

Since 1972, Otto has concentrated increasingly on the examination and understanding of biological structures as a way of furthering his development of lightweight structures. At the back of all this activity lies the conviction, present from the very first, but now given elevated importance, of identifying the most efficient ways of building using a minimum of material, in order to build in the most sympathetic way with the natural environment. Otto continually has sought out parallels between biological forms and manmade structures in a quest for new inspiration.

Otto must be ranked alongside the likes of Felix Candela, R. Buckminster Fuller and Pier Luigi Nervi as the man, who, more than anyone, succeeded in bringing the tent into line with 20th-century potentialities in terms of materials and technology. He is not an architect as the term is usually understood, but is rather, a creative catalyst who has worked with others and inspired them in his long journey toward more efficient lightweight structural forms appropriate to the 20th century. He is rare insofar as he combines a superb grasp of the beauty of the shapes he works with, with the result that his structures are not only convincing as engineering, but are, at the same time, wonderful pieces of sculpture. This is nowhere more evident than in his convertible or retractable roofs, which are also magnificent kinetic sculptures.

It is Otto's unique gift to his time to see minimal lightweight structure as liberating and a bridge to natural or organic form. His activities have enriched the dictionary of architectural form, while challenging preconceived traditional modes of monumental and style-bound design.

—PHILIP DREW

OUD, J. J. P.

Dutch. Born in Purmerend, North Holland, 9 February 1890. Died in Wassenaar, 5 April 1963. Studied at the Quellinus Arts and Crafts School, Amsterdam; Rijksnormaal School, Amsterdam; Technical University, Delft. Worked in the offices of Cuypers and Stuyt, Amsterdam, and of Theodor Fischer, Munich. In private practice, Purmerend, Netherlands, 1913-14; worked with W.M. Dudok, Leiden, Netherlands, 1915-16; in private practice, Leiden, 1916-18; city architect, Rotterdam, 1918-33; in private pract ice, Rotterdam, 1933-54, and in Wassenaar, near The Hague, 1954 until his death in 1963. Founder-Member, with others, De Stijl Group, Leiden, 1916-20, and, with Theo van Doesburg, *De Stijl* magazine, 1917.

Chronology of Works
All in the Netherlands unless noted
† *Work no longer exists*

1911	Vooruit Cooperative, Purmerend (houses and meeting hall)
1914	Van Bakel House, Heemstede
1914-16	Leiderdorp Housing Estate (with W. M. Dudok)
1915	Van Essen-Vincker House, Blaricum
1917	Villa Allegonda, Katwijk-aan-Zee
1920	Tusschendijken Housing Estate, Rotterdam
1922	Out-Mathenesse Estate, Rotterdam
1924	Café de Unie, Rotterdam†
1925-29	Kiefhoek Housing Estate, Rotterdam
1927	Terraced Housing, Weissenhofsiedlung, Stuttgart, Germany
1938-42	Shell Office Building, The Hague
1947-50	Esveha Office Building, Rotterdam
1948	Dutch Soldiers' Monument, Grebbeberg Cemetery, near Rhenen
1949-56	Lyceum, The Hague
1952-60	Bio Convalescent Resort for Children, Arnhem
1954-61	Utrecht Life Insurance Company Building, Rotterdam
1957-63	Convention Center, The Hague

Publications

BOOKS BY OUD

Het Hofplein van Dr. Berlage. Rotterdam, 1922.
Holländische Architektur. Munich, 1926.
Nieuwe bouwkunst in Holland en Europe. Graveland, Netherlands, 1935.
Il Palazzo B. I. M. Shell. The Hague, 1951.
Zijn er nog architecten? The Hague, 1959.
Mijn Weg in De Stijl. The Hague and Rotterdam, ca. 1960.
Mondriaan. With L. J. F. Wijsenbeek. Zeist, Netherlands, 1962.
Architecturalia voor bouweheren en architecten. The Hague, 1963.
J. J. P. Oud, Architect 1890-1963: Feiten en herinneringen gerangschikt. Edited by Hans Oud. The Hague, 1984.

ARTICLES BY OUD

Numerous articles in *De Stijl* (Leiden), *De 8 en Opbouw* (Amsterdam), *i 10* (Amsterdam), and *De Groene Amsterdammer*.
"Over cubisme, futurisme, moderne bouwkunst." *Bouwkundig Weekblad* 37, No. 20 (16 September 1916).
"Wohin führt das neue Bauen: Kunst und Standard." *Neue Zürcher Zeitung* (September 1927).
"Architecture and the Future." *Studio* (December 1928): 401-406.
"The European Movement Towards a New Architecture." *Studio* (April 1933): 249-256.
"United Nations Headquarters." *Royal Institute of British Architects Journal* (October 1948).
"Clarity in Town Planning." *Housing and Town and Country Planning* (April 1949).

BOOKS ABOUT OUD

DE GRUYTER, W. JOS: *J. J. P. Oud*. Rotterdam, 1951.
HITCHCOCK, HENRY-RUSSELL: *J. J. P. Oud*. Paris, 1931.
JAFFÉ, H. L. C.: *De Stijl 1917-1931*. London, 1956.
STAMM, GUNTHER: *The Architecture of J. J. P. Oud 1906-1963*. Exhibition catalog. Tallahassee, Florida, 1978.
VERONESI, GIULIANA: *J. J. P. Oud*. Milan, 1953.
WIEKART, K.: *J. J. P. Oud*. Amsterdam, 1965.

ARTICLES ABOUT OUD

"Building at The Hague." *Architectural Review* (April 1948).
"J. J. P. Oud." *Forum* Nos. 5-6 (1951): 114-148.
MAGDELIJNS, HANS: "Architect Oud and Melody in Architecture." *Bouw* (15 and 29 October 1983).
POLANO, SERGIO: "Notes on Oud." *Lotus* (September 1977): 42-49.
STAMM, GUNTHER: "Cubism and De Stijl." *Bouw* (17 March 1979).
VAN DOESBURG, THEO: "L'evolution de l'architecture moderne en Hollande." *Architecture vivante* (Autumn 1925).
VERONESI, GIULIANA: "Jacobus Johannes Pieter Oud, 1890-1963." *Zodiac* No. 12 (1963): 82-105.

*

J. J. P. Oud was, aside from Willem Dudok (1884-1974), probably the best-known Dutch architect before World War II. His reputation as a promoter of modern architecture was established early on, and was due mainly to his activity in Rotterdam. Since 1918 Oud was employed with the Rotterdam housing authority, and he designed five major housing projects in those years.

Some of them—such as Hoek van Holland and Kiefhoek—gained international renown in publications about modern architecture. Oud's work was highly praised among modernist architects and critics, and indeed his invitation to participate in the Deutscher Werkbund's Weissenhofsiedlung exhibition in Stuttgart in the late 1920s was based on those projects.

In his work, Oud achieved a unity of modern architectural expression with the social ideas of the avant-garde of the 1920s. The fact that he held an official position in public service, rather than being an independent architect, also made him an example early on. In Germany, Martin Wagner accepted a similar position in Berlin only in 1924, while Ernst May followed a year later as architect for the Frankfurt building authority. Historically, the only counterpart to Oud's situation existed in Vienna, but the Viennese housing projects were not highly valued by modern architects.

Oud built little during the 1930s, after leaving his position with the Rotterdam housing authority in 1933. This was due not only to the deteriorating economic situation, but also to Oud's reservations about the objectivity of modern architecture. While Oud was viewed as an exponent of modern architecture in the 1920s, the situation changed drastically in the 1930s. In Oud's opinion, architecture "should convey the aesthetic conviction of one person (the architect) to another (the viewer)." He wished to realize this conviction by means of a hierarchical order, symmetry and ornament. It is not surprising, then, that Oud distanced himself from CIAM (Congrés Internationaux d'Architecture Moderne) and from his functionalist colleagues in Holland. Oud's first built work of any significance after the Rotterdam projects was the headquarters building for BIM (later Royal Dutch Shell) in The Hague, designed in 1938.

The question remains whether Oud's work during the 1930s truly represented a fundamentally different approach to architecture. The question is predicated on Oud's portrayal as a functionalist during the 1920s, which is, however, not quite accurate historically. Oud's interest in new architectural purposes developed under the influence of H. P. Berlage, but he was also fascinated by the cubist painters. As a consequence of his interest in cubism, he came into contact with Theo van Doesburg in 1915. Two years later, Oud was one of the founders of the group De Stijl. The claim of the group to be creating a universal but timely art with objective means led to an abstraction of Oud's formal idiom. His design for houses on the Strandboulevard in Scheveningen (1917) displayed the new, abstract rhythm of forms in the street facades. De Stijl's striving after of objective means also led to an interest in the design of industrially produced articles: the precision of such products was interesting not only on formal grounds (for their objectivity of form) but also in rational-organizational terms.

This latter aspect was especially important for the layouts of Oud's houses, and for his pursuit of standardization and normalization of housing construction. Even though the facades of his housing developments were suggestive of industrial production processes, Oud never applied these ideas to the entire designs. He treated the structures, down to the smallest details, as architectural objects going beyond the merely functional. His design of corners, detailing of facades and use of color are proof of his interest in architectural form. In commissions other than the social housing projects, this basic attitude becomes even clearer. The Café de Unie (1925) and the Villa Alegonda (1927) are particularly good examples. Oud's pursuit of a rationalist architecture in the 1920s was a point of departure, not an ultimate goal. Like his friend and colleague Bruno Taut, Oud rejected functionalism without the will to achieve form.

Oud always remained faithful to this basic thought, and for that reason CIAM's rational systematization of the problematics of architecture and urban planning was foreign to him from the very beginning. In the further developments of Oud's architecture in the 1930s, this difference only became more pronounced. The Shell building, which is ornamented and has an almost neoclassical conception of building mass, and the proposal for Hofplein in Rotterdam (1942) illustrate Oud's desperate search for a balance between functionalism and timely formal expression. In those projects, the balance shifted toward hierarchy and monumentalism, which generally corresponded to the social situation of the time.

After World War II, Oud attempted to recapture an equilibrium between the functional and aesthetic aspects of architecture. The influence of the "Delft school," which made itself felt for a brief time in connection with the postwar reconstruction in the Netherlands, also indirectly contributed to Oud's search. Fearing a future return to conservative architecture, he opposed the work of the Delft school with what he called a poetic functionalism, which took up the concerns of the De Stijl period. The Vrijzinnig Christelijk Lyceum in The Hague (1949-56) and the Bioherstellingsoord in Arnhem (1952-60) are examples of the later work. Again Oud attempted to find functional design solutions while also connecting them with an aesthetic value.

—OTAKAR MÁČEL

Translated from the German by Marijke Rijsberman

P

PAESSCHEN, Hans Hendrik van.

Belgian. Born in Antwerp, Belgium, ca. 1515. Died in Antwerp, ca. 1582. Studied in Italy. Worked with the sculptor Cornelis Floris de Vriendt.

Chronology of Works
* Approximate dates

1560*	Duke of Brabant's Palace, Brussels, Belgium [attributed]
1561-66	Raadhuis (Town Hall), Antwerp, Belgium
1564	Hanseatenhuis, Antwerp, Belgium
1564	Burghley House, near Stamford, England (sections)
1566-68	Exchange, London, England
1567	Bachegraig House, near Tremeirchion, Clwyd, Wales
1574	Kronborg Castle, Helsingør, Denmark (enlargement)
1576	Uraniborg, Hven Island, Denmark
1577	Badstuen, Hillerød, Denmark
1577	Fadeburslangen, Hillerød, Denmark

Publications

BOOKS ABOUT PAESSCHEN

MILLAR, JOHN FITZHUGH: *Classical Architecture in Renaissance Europe 1419-1585.* Williamsburg, Virginia, 1987.

*

While Italy was blessed with the architecture of Andrea Palladio (1508-80) and France with that of Philibert de l'Orme (ca. 1505/10-70), northern Europe's leading architects were, for the most part, attempting to modify the Gothic style by increasing the ratio of glass to masonry in a wall. The little classicism that did appear was in poor proportion and heavily encrusted with decorative strapwork. A notable exception to this Mannerist situation was Hans Hendrik van Paesschen from Antwerp, who brought a pure Italian classicism to most of his designs in Flanders, the Netherlands, Germany, Denmark, Norway, Sweden, England and Wales.

Hendrik, almost exactly a contemporary of Palladio and de l'Orme, is today almost unknown, for a variety of reasons. First, many of his better buildings are often wrongly attributed to his friend the Antwerp sculptor Cornelis Floris de Vriendt (1514-75), because the latter was placed in the position of hiring Hendrik to draw the designs while Floris carved the sculpture and addressed the concerns of civic leaders. Second, since Hendrik's work extended through so many countries, it is difficult to find his name spelled the same way twice. He appears as Henri de Pas or de Passe in French, as Hendrik van Paesschen, van de Passe, Paas, Hans Pascha, Hans Fleming, Passaeus and

Paschen in the Germanic countries, and as Henryke in England, among the most popular.

Hendrik's best-known building today is the Raadhuis (Town Hall) in Antwerp (1561-66). At that time, Antwerp was the most prosperous city in northern Europe and thus needed an impressive building for its seat of government. A competition for the design of the building attracted architects from Italy, France and the low Countries, but no winner was declared; Floris was appointed to select an architect and oversee the project. He picked Hendrik.

The Raadhuis is a large four-story building, whose ground floor on the front is of brutal-scale, rusticated stonework pierced by 19 arches. The next two floors are composed of large windows separated by Tuscan and Ionic pilasters, respectively, and the windows of the top floor are largely hidden behind a massive overhanging balcony and the heavy eaves of the high hipped roof. The central three bays above the arcade consist of variations on a theme of loosely paired engaged columns arranged around arches and niches in a four-story confection, the rhythm being similar to—but not slavishly copied from—Donato Bramante's Vatican Upper Court Belvedere loggia design that Sebastiano Serlio had adapted a decade earlier for the courtyard at Ancy, in France. In the middle of the building was a courtyard surrounded by an arcaded loggia, but the courtyard is now covered by a roof.

The Raadhuis, while obviously not an Italian building, is closely related to Italian architectural ideas of the day, such as a courtyard surrounded by an arcaded loggia. Hendrik included a courtyard with arcaded loggia in several of his more important buildings. The largest of these was the Hanseatenhuis, a brick palace built for the Hanseatic merchants at Antwerp in 1564.

Somewhat similar to the Hanseatenhuis was the Royal Exchange in London, commissioned by Elizabeth I's financial genius, Sir Thomas Gresham. Gresham also commissioned a similar building near the exchange as a house for himself, which he left in his will as the home for Gresham College. Gresham further commissioned a country house outside London called Osterley that originally looked much like a brick version of Serlio's Ancy on the outside, but which was unrecognizably altered in the 18th century. Hendrik designed parts of two vast country houses for Elizabeth's lord chancellor, Gresham's friend Sir William Cecil (later Lord Burghley), Burghley House and Theobalds Park. At Burghley, in addition to its loggias (now enclosed from the weather), the courtyard contains a pair of modified Venetian arches, probably the first time this motif appeared in England. Hendrik also used a variant form of the Venetian arch on the Laube attached to the Town Hall in Lübeck, Germany.

Hendrik was strongly attached to Italian forms, proportions and symmetry, but he also quoted local idioms when that seemed appropriate, such as the stepped gables and scrolled gables of northern Europe. Good examples of these can be found at the Badstuen (Bathhouse) and Fadeburslangen (Long Pantry), both at Hillerød; the Brabant Palace in Brussels; the alterations to

Kronborg Castle and Number 76 Stengade, both at Helsingør; and Selsø Castle in Zealand.

One of Palladio's greatest contributions to architecture is said to be the integration of dependencies and ancillary buildings into the overall design of a house. Hendrik was not behind Palladio in this respect, for he successfully integrated dependencies in some of his own designs. At Bachegraig House in northern Wales, the handsome villa (which would not have been out of place had it been designed 150 years later) formed a neat forecourt with the gatehouse and the storage buildings intended for Sir Richard Clough's import business (parts of these buildings, with the marble colonnaded loggia filled in, still stand). Uraniborg on Hven Island, Denmark, built as a residence and observatory for the renowned astronomer Tycho Brahe, as well as dormitory for visiting astronomers, had the design of the house completely integrated with the geometrical gardens and the four dependencies.

Uraniborg was crowned with an elaborate dome, and although it was very different from what Palladio intended at the Villa Capra (La Rotonda), the two should be compared. The domed octagonal church at Willemstad should be compared with others of similar date, including Palladio's chapel at Maser and de l'Orme's four chapels at Anet, Villers-Cotterets, Saint-Léger and Saint-Germain-en-Laye. Other domes that may be attributable to Hendrik are the villa in Moorfields, London (with giant Tuscan pillars at the angles), which is known only from two 16th-century views of London, and the Spanish Gate at Antwerp, designed for the emperor's triumphal arrival; the gate, with its freestanding colonnade in front, may be compared with Serlio's unexecuted project for the Bathhouse at Fontainebleau, although doubtless Hendrik never saw Serlio's drawings for that.

As an Italian-trained architect, Hendrik was expected to know more than merely domes and loggias. His expertise in fortifications was so highly regarded that he was hired to design fortifications at Antwerp, Alvsborg, Willemstad, Klundert, Bohus, Akershus, Dendermonde and Kronborg—some of these being in countries that fought on opposing sides in wars even while he was working for them. Based on what little survives, the fortifications were fairly standard, state-of-the-art designs of the period.

Hendrik was trained in Italy, probably both in Florence and Rome, and he was probably there at the same time as his friend Floris was studying sculpture in Italy. Upon returning to northern Europe, Hendrik may have worked with Sebastiaan van Noyen (a pupil of Antonio da Sangallo the Younger) at Cardinal Granvelle's palace in Brussels. Hendrik was the first to bring the full Italian Renaissance style of architecture to Britain—many years before Inigo Jones was born—and his work left a deep impression on Christopher Wren a century later. Wren, during his architecturally formative years, was resident professor of astronomy at Hendrik's Gresham College, only a stone's throw from Hendrik's Royal Exchange, and echoes of both buildings can be detected in many of Wren's own subsequent works.

In Hans Hendrik van Paesschen, northern Europe had its only contemporary architect whose buildings can be compared to those of Serlio, Palladio and de l'Orme, although it does not seem that he directly copied any of their works.

—JOHN F. MILLAR

PAINE, James.

British. Born in Andover, Hampshire, England, 1717. Died in France, 1789. Father was John Pain, carpenter; married Sarah Jennings; married Charlotte Beaumont; son was James Paine.

Studied under Thomas Jersey; studied at St. Martin's Lane Academy, London. Superintending architect, Nostell Priory; also worked independently; clerk of the works, Queen's House, Greenwich, 1745; clerk of the works, Mews, Charing Cross, 1746; clerk of the works, Newmarket, 1750-1780; clerk of the works, Richmond New Park Lodge, 1758; architect of the works, 1780; high sheriff of Surrey. Member and president, Society of Artists of Great Britain.

Chronology of Works
All in England
† *Work no longer exists*

1737-50	Nostell Priory, Yorkshire (supervision of construction and interior decoration)
1744-45	Heath House, Wakefield
1745-48	Mansion House, Doncaster
1749-50	Wadworth Hall, Doncaster
1750-56	South Ormsby Hall, Lincolnshire
1754	76 St. Martin's Lane, London†
1754-57	Hardwick Hall, County Durham (garden buildings)†
1754-58	Matthew Fetherstonhaugh House (now Dover House), Whitehall, London
1754-68	Alnwick Castle, Northumberland (reconstruction)†
1755-64	Gosforth Hall, Newcastle
1755-78	Middlesex Hospital, London†
1756-64	Chatsworth, Derbyshire (stables, bridge, etc.)
1758	Axwell Park, County Durham
1758-60	Cavendish Bridge, Derbyshire†
1758-63	Stockeld Park, Yorkshire
1759	St. Ives, Yorkshire†
1760	Bywell Hall, Northumberland
1760-66	Gibside Chapel, County Durham
1760-75	Brocket Hall, Hertfordshire
1763-67	Worksop Manor, Nottinghamshire†
1763-68	Sandbeck Park, Yorkshire
1764-70	Thorndon Hall, Essex
1765-70	Weston Park, Staffordshire (temple and bridge)
1765-73	Salisbury Street, London†
1766-70	Lord Petre's House, Park Lane, London†
1768-70	Hare Hall, Essex
1769-71	79 Pall Mall, London†
1769-72	Shrubland Hall, Suffolk
1770-76	Wardour Castle, Wiltshire
1771-72	Society of Artists of Great Britain Exhibition Room, Strand, London†
1773-74	37 King Street, Covent Garden, London
1774-77	Richmond Bridge, Surrey
1779-85	Chertsey Bridge, Surrey
1783	Walton Bridge, Surrey†
1783-89	Kew Bridge, Surrey†

Publications

BOOKS BY PAINE

Plans, Elevations and Sections of Noblemen's and Gentlemen's Houses Executed in the Counties of Derby, Durham, Middlesex, Northumberland, Nottingham and York. 2 vols. London, 1767-83.

ARTICLES ABOUT PAINE

BINNEY, MARCUS: ''The Villas of James Paine.'' *Country Life* (20 and 27 February, 6 March 1969).

James Paine: Wardour Castle, Wiltshire, England, 1770-76

LEACH, PETER: "The Life and Work of James Paine." Unpublished D. Phil thesis, Oxford University (1975).

*

James Paine was one of the most individual and inventive of English architects in the generation which followed that of Lord Burlington and William Kent. Born at Andover in Hampshire, the son of a carpenter, he studied in London at William Hogarth's St. Martin's Lane Academy, and then appears to have begun his career through contact with Lord Burlington's circle. His first commission was to supervise the erection of Nostell Priory, Yorkshire (ca. 1737-50), a large country house designed by James Moyser, a friend and follower of Burlington; from that beginning Paine established a successful country-house practice in the north of England, which during the 1750s he augmented by taking over the north-country practice of Burlington's former assistant Daniel Garrett. As early as 1746, however, Paine returned to live in London, and his work was not confined to the north; the large extent of his work prompted Thomas Hardwick's well-known comment that Paine and Robert Taylor "nearly divided the practice of the profession between them, for they had few competitors till Mr. Robert Adam entered the lists." Paine's position was reflected in the prominent role he played in the Society of Artists of Great Britain, the precursor of the Royal Academy, serving as president in 1770-72 and designing its Exhibition Room in London (1771-72, demolished 1815); while in retirement, he established himself as a country gentleman, serving in 1785 as high sheriff of Surrey.

In 1755-56 Paine visited Italy, his itinerary including Rome and probably the Veneto, but the journey did not play a very significant part in his artistic development. He later criticized the fashion for foreign travel among architects and had little sympathy for the emergent interest in the architecture of antiquity; he emphasized rather the importance of practical convenience rather than the pursuit of "inconsistent antiquated modes," and dismissed the architecture of the Greeks as "despicable ruins." His own explicit expression of the "new and striking" was instead achieved entirely within the framework of English Palladianism. His most important contribution was as a leading exponent of the compact, centrally planned Palladian villa as a country-house form.

Paine was a pioneer in particular in exploiting the practical advantages of the "villa with wings," and in developing the practical and visual potential of the type of top-lit central staircase which became a hallmark of the mature villa-based house. At the same time, he developed a lively and individual elevational style based on the "staccato" manner of Burlington and Kent: early experiments with interlocking pediments on the model of Andrea Palladio's church facades were succeeded by remarkable tripartite compositions derived from the wings of Holkham Hall, while the repertoire of smaller-scale detail included empty niches, splayed window surrounds, open pediments and vestigial cornice strips. These characteristics are illustrated in a memorably rich and varied sequence of houses beginning with his first independent commission as an architect, Heath House, Yorkshire (1744-45), and continued by examples such as Serlby Hall, Nottinghamshire (1754-73); Bedford Hall, Northumberland (1755-56); Stockheld Park, Yorkshire (1758-63); and Bywell Hall, Northumberland (ca. 1760).

Paine's greater houses of a more traditional type were by contrast relatively few in number, the principal examples being Worksop Manor, Nottinghamshire (1763-67, demolished 1843); Sandbeck Park, Yorkshire (ca. 1763-68); and Thorndon Hall,

Essex (1764-70). But at the Gibside Chapel, County Durham (1760-66), he devised an elegant and original reworking of further themes from Palladian ecclesiastical architecture, and his individual manner was also displayed in some of his urban buildings, notably the Middlesex Hospital, London (1755-78, demolished 1925), and his redevelopment of Salisbury Street, London (1765-73, demolished 1923), where in the riverward frontage he ingeniously combined a tripartite grouping with the quadrant form. For his interiors he adopted in his early years the Rococo style of decoration which had been pioneered in circles close to the St. Martin's Lane Academy, but he combined such enrichment with elements of Palladian detail, and in his chimneypieces in particular endowed conventional Palladian formulas with a new lightness and delicacy; examples of this manner are at Nostell Priory, the Mansion House at Doncaster, Yorkshire (1745-48), and Felbrigg Hall, Norfolk (1752). Later, however, conceding that "Palmyra and Baalbec" were "valuable for the ornaments," he devised a variant on the type of neoclassical decoration popularized by Robert Adam, examples of which are in the ballroom at Sandbeck Park and the Temple of Diana at Weston Park, Staffordshire (ca. 1770). Paine also favored the Kentian combination of plasterwork and decorative painting, the most notable instance being the salon at Brocket Hall, Hertfordshire (1771-73).

Paine also established an occasional role as a builder of bridges, particularly in his later years, the finest example being that across the Thames at Richmond, Surrey (1774-77). However, the commission that represented the climax of his career, endowing it with a satisfying symmetry, was the contemporary Wardour Castle, Wiltshire (1770-76). There he used the Palladian villa form for a house of the very largest size—the logical consequence of the progressive development of the villa idea, which at Wardour achieved its most fully realized expression. Drawing together all the principal strands in both his planning and his articulation of the country house, the building is one of English Palladianism's definitive images.

—PETER LEACH

PALLADIO, Andrea.

Italian. Born Andrea di Pietro dalla Gondola, in Vicenza, Italy, 30 November 1508. Died in Vicenza, 19 August 1580. Apprenticed to a stone mason at an early age; worked for the Pedemuro stone shop, Vicenza. Studied in the Academy of Giangiorgio Trissino, ca.1535. Moved to Venice, 1550s.

Chronology of Works
All in Italy
* *Approximate dates*
† *Work no longer exists*

1532-33	San Michele, Vicenza (chapel and tomb of Enrico Antonio Godi; with Pedemuro shop)†
1533	Villa of Enrico Antonio Godi, Lonedo (service building; with Pedemuro shop)
1534-38	Cathedral of Santa Maria Maggiore, Vicenza (high altar, and tomb of Bishop Girolamo Bencucci da Schio; with Pedemuro shop [attributed])
1536	Portal between Basilica and Palazzo del Podestà, Vicenza [attributed]
1537-38	Villa Trissino, Vicenza (with Giangiorgio Trissino and Sebastiano Serlio [attributed])
1537*-42	Villa of Girolamo and Pietro Godi, Lonedo

1539-42	Palace of Giovanni Giacomo and Pier Antonio Civena, Vicenza
1540*-45*	Palace of Monte Da Monte, Vicenza
1541*-43*	Villa of Giuseppe and Antonio Valmarana, Vigardolo
1541-55	Villa of Taddeo Gazoto (called Villa of Girolamo Grimani after 1550), Bertesina
1542-44	Villa of Vettor Pisani, Bagnolo
1542-48	Villa of Marc'Antonio and Adriano Thiene, Quinto Vicentino
1542-58	Palace of Marc'Antonio Thiene, Vicenza
1543	Festival structures for entrance of Cardinal Bishop Nicolò Ridolfi, Vicenza†
1544-55	Villa of Bonifacio Poiana, Poiana Maggiore
1544-64	Villa of Leonardo Mocenigo, River Brenta, Dolo†
1545*-48*	Villa of Biagio Saraceno, Finale di Agugliaro
1546-47	Santo Spirito in Sassia, Rome (baldachin for high altar [attributed])
1546*-57	Palace of Girolamo Chiericati, Vicenza (not completed until 1680*)
1546-59	Villa of Paolo Contarini, Piazzola sul Brenta [attributed]†
1547-52	Palace of Giuseppe Porto, Vicenza
1547-65	Villa of Vincenzo Arnaldi, Meledo Alto (partially preserved)
1547-84	Villa of Giovanni Chiericati, Vancimuglio
1548	Villa of Giacomo Angarano, Bassano (service wings)
1548-53*	Villa of Marco Zen, Cessalto
1548-70	Villa of Michele and Lodovico Caldogno, Caldogno
1549-58	Villa of Daniele and Marc'Antonio Barbaro, Maser
1549*-53	Villa of Nicolò and Alvise Foscari, Malcontenta (Gambarare)
1549*-63	Palace of Giovanni Battista Della Torre, Verona
1549-80	Basilica, Vicenza (not completed until 1617)
1550*-52	Wooden bridge on River Cismone, Cismon del Grappa
1550*-52*	Palace of Floriano Antonini, Udine
1551-53	Villa of Zorzon Cornaro, Piombino Dese
1552-55	Villa of Francesco Pisani, Montagnana
1552-69	Villa of Marc'Antonio Sarego, Santa Sofia di Pedemonte (Verona)
1553-76	Villa of Francesco and Lodovico Trissino, Meledo di Sarego
1554*-56	Villa of Francesco Thiene, Cicogna di Villafranca Padovana (only service building completed)
1555-58	San Pantaleone, Venice (high altar)†
1556/63	Arch in honor of Domenico Bollani, Udine
1556-63	Villa of Francesco Badoer, Fratta Polesine
1556*-66	Villa of Francesco Ripeta, Campiglia†
1557-58	Theatrical settings, Accademia Olimpica, Vicenza [attributed] †
1557-58	Palazzo Municipale, Feltre (ground arcade [attributed])
1557-74	Cathedral of Santa Maria Maggiore, Vicenza (drum and dome of apse)
1558-61	House of Leonardo Mocenigo, Padua
1559-61	Wooden bridge on River Bacchiglione, at Porta Santa Croce, Vicenza†
1559-62	House of Pietro Cogollo, Vicenza
1559*-67	Villa of Leonardo Emo, Fanzolo, Vicenza
1559-80	Stone bridge on River Tesina, Torri di Quartesolo
1560*-62	Villa of Leonardo Mocenigo, Marocoo†

Andrea Palladio: Villa of Leonardo Emo, Vicenza, Italy, 1559-67

1560-65	Almerico portal, Cathedral of Santa Maria Maggiore, Vicenza
1560*-65	Santa Lucia, Venice (Mocenigo Chapel, not completed until 1592; nave built to Palladio's design 1609-11)†
1560-74	Monastery of Santa Maria della Carità, Venice
1560-80	Monastery of San Giorgio Maggiore, Venice
1561-69	Villa of Vettor Pisani, Bagnolo
1561-66	Palace of Bernardo Schio, Vicenza (facade)
1562-64	Palazzo Municipale, Brescia (windows)
1562-69	Villa of Annibale Sarego, Miega di Cologna Veneta†
1563*-66	Villa of Gian Frecesco Valmarana, Lisiera di Bolzano Vicentino (not completed until 1615)
1564-65	Palazzo Pretorio, Cividale del Friuli (executed by others 1565-86)
1565	Festival structures for entrance of Bishop Matteo Priuli, Vicenza†
1565*-70*	San Francesco della Vigna, Venice (facade)
1565-69	Villa of Paolo Almerico (*La Rotonda*), Vicenza (not completed until after Palladio's death)
1565-71	Valmarana Palace, Vicenza
1565*-72	Loggia del Capitaniato, Vicenza
1568-70	Wooden bridge on River Brenta, Bassano (since rebuilt)
1569-75	Palace of Giulio and Guido Piovene, Vicenza [attributed]†
1570-72	Scuola dei Mercanti, Venice [attributed]
1570-75	Palace of Montano Barbaran, Vicenza
1571	Santa Maria della Celestia, Venice (cloister; executed by others)
1572	Harbor at Piazza dell'Isola, River Bacchiglione, Vicenza†
1572	Villa of Giuseppe Porto, Molina di Malo (unfinished)
1572-77	Palace for Orazio and/or Francesco Thiene, Vicenza (completed in 1593 by Vicenzo Scamozzi [attributed])
1574	Arch and loggia for entrance of King Henri III of France, Venice†
1574-80	Ospedaletto di Santi Giovanni e Paolo, Venice†
1574-80	Ducal Palace, Venice (reconstruction and interior decoration)

1575-80*	Tomb of Brunor Volpe, Santa Corona, Vicenza
1575-80	Stone bridge on River Guà, Montebello Vicentino
1576-80	Valmarana Tomb Chapel, Santa Corona, Vicenza (not completed until 1597)
1576-80	Church of the Redeemer, Venice (not completed until 1591)
1578-79	Sanctuary of the Madonna di Monte Berico (Altar for College of Notaries), Vicenza†
1579	Gemona Portal, San Daniele del Friuli
1579-80	Chapel of the Redeemer (Tempietto Barbaro, not completed until 1580-84), Villa of Marc'Antonio Barbaro, Maser
1580	Teatro Olimpico, Vicenza (not completed until 1580-83 by Silla Palladio)

Publications

BOOKS BY PALLADIO

The Four Books of Architecture. 1570. Reprint of 1738 English edition, with introduction by Adolf K. Placzek, New York, 1965.

BOOKS ABOUT PALLADIO

ACKERMAN, JAMES S.: *Palladio.* Harmondsworth, England, and Baltimore, 1966.
ACKERMAN, JAMES S.: *Palladio's Villas.* New York, 1967.
BATTILOTTI, DONATA: *Le ville di Palladio.* Milan, 1990.
BOECKLER, G. A.: *Andreas Palladius, von der Civil- oder Buergerlichen Baukunst.* 2 vols. Nuremberg, 1698.
BORDIGNON FAVERO, G. P.: *La Villa Emo di Fanzolo.* Vicenza, 1970.
BURGER, FRITZ: *Die Villen des Andrea Palladio.* Leipzig, 1909.
BURNS, HOWARD; FAIRBAIRN, LYNDA; and BOUCHER, BRUCE: *Andrea Palladio, 1508-1580: The Portico and the Farmyard.* London, 1975.
CAMPBELL, COLEN: *Andrea Palladio's Five Orders of Architecture.* London, 1728-29.
CONSTANT, CAROLINE: *The Palladio Guide.* Princeton, New Jersey, 1989.
DALLA POZZA, A. M.: *Andrea Palladio.* Vicenza, 1943.
FERRARI, L.: *Palladio a Venezia.* Venice, 1880.

Il Redentore, Venice

FLETCHER, BANISTER F.: *Andrea Palladio: His Life and Works*. London, 1902.

FORSSMANN, E.: *Palladios Lehrgebäude*. Stockholm, 1965.

GURLITT, C.: *Andrea Palladio*. Berlin, 1914.

HARRIS, JOHN: *The Palladians*. 1982.

HOFER, P.: *Palladios Erstling: Die Villa Godi Valmarana in Lonedo bei Vicenza*. Basel and Stuttgart, 1969.

HOWARD, DEBORAH: *The Architectural History of Venice*. New York, 1981.

Inigo Jones on Palladio (facsimile of Jones's annotated Palladio). Edited by Brian Allsopp. 2 vols., 1970.

IVANOFF, N.: *Palladio*. Milan, 1967.

KUBELIK, M.: *Die Villa im Veneto: zur typologischen Entwicklung im Quattrocento*. 2 vols. Munich, 1977.

LEONI, GIACOMO: *The Architecture of Andrea Palladio in Four Books*. London, 1721.

LEWIS, DOUGLAS: *Drawings of Andrea Palladio*. 1981.

LOUKOMSKI, G. K.: *Andrea Palladio, sa vie, son oeuvre*. Paris, 1927.

MAGRINI, ANTONIO: *Memorie intorno la vita e le opere di Andrea Palladio*. Vicenza, 1845.

MAZZOTTI, GIUSEPPE: *Palladian and Other Venetian Villas*. London, 1958.

PANE, R.: *Andrea Palladio*. Turin, 1961.

PÉE, H.: *Die Palastbauten Andrea Palladio*. Würzburg, 1939.

PUPPI, LIONELLO: *Andrea Palladio*. Boston, 1975.

PUPPI, LIONELLO: *Palladio Drawings*. New York, 1990.

ROWE, COLIN: *The Mathematics of the Ideal Villa and Other Essays*. 1976.

SCULLY, VINCENT J., JR.: *The Villas of Palladio*. 1986.

SEMENZATO, C.: *La Rotonda di Vicenza*. Vicenza, 1968.

SPIELMANN, H.: *Andrea Palladio und die Antike*. Munich and Berlin, 1966.

TIMOFIEWITSCH, VLADIMIR: *Die sakrale Architektur Palladios*. Munich, 1968.

TIMOFIEWITSCH, VLADIMIR: *La chiesa del Redentore*. Vicenza, 1969.

WHITEHILL, WALTER, and NICHOLAS, F.: *Palladio in America*. 1978.

WITTKOWER, RUDOLF: *Architectural Principles in the Age of Humanism*. London, 1952.

WITTKOWER, RUDOLF: *Palladio and English Palladianism*. London, 1974.

WUNDRAM, M., and PAPE, T.: *Andrea Palladio 1508-1580: Architect Between the Renaissance and the Baroque*. Cologne, 1989.

ZORZI, GIAN GIORGIO: *I disegni delle antichità di Andrea Palladio*. Venice, 1959.

ZORZI, GIAN GIORGIO: *Le opere pubbliche e i palazzi privati di Andrea Palladio*. Venice, 1965.

ZORZI, GIAN GIORGIO: *Le ville e i teatri di Andrea Palladio*. Venice, 1969.

ZORZI, GIAN GIORGIO: *Palladian Villas*. Venice, 1958.

ARTICLES ABOUT PALLADIO

FRANCO, F.: "L'innovazione del Palladio nelle Logge della Basilica." *Odeo Olimpico* (1968-69): 5-9.

HOWARD, DEBORAH: "Four Centuries of Literature on Palladio." *Journal of the Society of Architectural Historians* 39 (May 1980): 224-241.

HOWARD, DEBORAH, and LONGAIR, MALCOLM: "Harmonic Proportion and Palladio's *Quattro Libri*." *Journal of the Society of Architectural Historians* 41 (May 1982): 116-143.

LOTZ, WOLFGANG: "Three Essays on Palladio." In *Studies in Italian Renaissance Architecture*. Cambridge, Massachusetts, 1977.

MASSON, G.: "Palladian Villas as Rural Centers." *Architectural Review* (1955): 18ff.

MAGAGNATO, L.: "I collaboratori veronesi di Andrea Palladio." *Bollettino del Centro Internazionale di Studi di Architettura "Andrea Palladio"* (1968): 170-187.

"Riflessioni sul tema Palladio urbanista." *Bollettino del Centro Internazionale di Studi di Architettura "Andrea Palladio"* 8 (1966).

ZEVI, BRUNO: "Michelagniolo e Palladio." *Bollettino del Centro Internazionale di Studi di Architettura "Andrea Palladio"* 6, No. 2:13-28.

ZORZI, GIAN GIORGIO: "I desegni delle opere palladiane pubicate ne' *I Quattro Libri* e il loro significato rispetto alle opere eseguite." *Bollettino del Centro Internazionale di Studi di Architettura "Andrea Palladio"* 3 (1961): 12-17.

*

Andrea Palladio was an architect of great skill and equally great fortune. Born Andrea di Pietro dalla Gondola, he was apprenticed at an early age as a stonemason, working his way up through the ranks in the craft tradition. While Palladio was in his late 20s, his employer, the Pedemuro stone shop of Vicenza, began renovations of a villa for Gianogiorgio Trissino, a humanist who headed an academy for the education of young nobles. In fairy-tale-like fashion, Trissino was impressed by the intelligence and talent of the young stonemason, and invited him to join the academy, where he learned Latin, was exposed to humanist theories of architecture and received the new title of Palladio, a celestial messenger in one of Trissino's dramas.

Not only did Trissino educate Palladio, but he served as a mentor and sponsor as well. It was Trissino who first took

Palladio to Rome and doubtless encouraged his measurement and study of ancient ruins there. It was also Trissino who sponsored Palladio's design for the Palazzo della Ragione in Vicenza, an architectural commission which Palladio won over several distinguished architects of the Veneto. And finally, it was through Trissino that Palladio made the contacts enabling him to move to Venice in the 1550s.

Palladio's early design work showed an interest in Mannerist motifs developed by Giulio Romano and others, but even in this early period there was an abstract quality to his architectural ornament that was to become a ''signature'' of his design work. Palladio's mature design was not Mannerist; standard stylistic labels do not help us explain Palladio's architecture except insofar as his study of antique design labels him as Renaissance in spirit. It is not that Palladio worked in a vacuum. His several trips to Rome and possession of many drawings copied or obtained from other architects are ample evidence of his communication with colleagues. However, the fact that he was an independent master with the Pedemuro shop before his association with Trissino may explain his somewhat independent design career.

One of the most important building types Palladio designed was the villa. Many of these commissions were for Venetian patrons who were investing in farm complexes in the Veneto region. Venice had recently expanded its territories on the mainland in order to provide the city with an agricultural hinterland. Investment in agriculture was important both strategically and economically; the investors did not trust such vital interests to hired overseers, but directed much of the work in person. These clients needed functional farm complexes that would provide living quarters appropriate to their station. Palladio accomplished this twofold requirement in many villa designs by linking the farm buildings, or *barchesse,* together with the main residence pavilion to form a single unified complex. The three built villas best exemplifying this form are the Villa Barbaro in Maser, Villa Emo in Fanzolo and Villa Badoer in Fratta Polesine. Each of these villas has symmetrical wings of *barchesse* flanking the raised residence pavilion with its freestanding classical portico. These unified complexes of dwellings and farm structures possess a monumental quality reminiscent of Imperial Rome as well as provide for close supervision of farm production, the ideal design solution for Palladio's humanist clients.

Palladio's continued popularity over the years is partly dependent upon his architectural treatise, *I Quattro Libri de'Architettura (The Four Books of Architecture),* published in Venice in 1570. The impact of this book is aided by the clear and readable woodcuts of antique reconstructions and Palladio's own designs. Earlier treatises on architecture, for example Sebastiano Serlio's, had illustrations that did not ''read'' well on the page. However, Palladio had publishing experience, having produced the illustrations for Daniele Barbaro's annotated translation of *Vitruvius.* That experience aided Palladio in organizing page composition, line weights and shading techniques into graphics with lasting impact.

Scholars have noted discrepancies between the published drawings in Palladio's designs in *I Quattro Libri* and the actual dimensions in his palaces and villas. Part of this stems from the aim of his treatise. Intended neither as an accurate record of designs nor as a collection of ideal prototypes, Palladio's treatise is a didactic work, intended to instruct both client and architect. One of the most studied aspects of this instruction concerns Palladio's use of harmonic proportions, a practice linked to Venetian patronage by Rudolf Wittkower in his fundamental study *Architectural Principles in the Age of Humanism.*

Harmonic proportion is a term referring to both the proportional relationship of a harmonic mean between two numbers (such that $[b-a]/a = [c-b]/c$) and to the proportional relationship between frequencies (or lengths of strings) of musical harmonies. These latter proportions relate simple musical intervals of an octave, 5th, 4th, major 3rd and minor 3rd, to respective ratios of 2:1, 2:3, 3:4, 4:5 and 5:6, and so on. Deborah Howard and Longhair have shown that a majority of plans in *I Quattro Libri* have room dimensions whose ratios equal those of simple musical intervals, but variations in Palladio's built work have caused difficulties in interpretation. The key to understanding Palladio's use of humanist architectural theories is the realization that his theoretical knowledge was an overlay on his considerable craft knowledge of construction and building practices. Several of Palladio's initial sketches for buildings survive, showing simple grids with single lines denoting walls, double hatch marks for doors and windows, and room dimensions. These simple sketches were then adapted to the construction site: inches (and in isolated cases, feet) were added to or subtracted from room dimensions to accommodate the physical thickness of walls, brick modules and structural demands of vaulting. Palladio's application of architectural theory was always tempered by the practical reality of the building site.

Although never able to secure the important architectural post of *proto del sale* in Venice, Palladio nevertheless received several important public commissions: he repaired sections of the Doge's Palace, built sections of the Convento della Carità, designed the facade of San Francesco della Vigna, and designed the churches of San Giorgio Maggiore and Il Redentore. In these church designs Palladio tried to reconcile the interior arrangement with that of the facade, a difficult task because of the inherently different geometries of a Christian basilica section and an antique temple front. Palladio solved this compositional problem by using overlapping temple fronts, one corresponding to the height of the nave, the other to that of the aisle.

Most of Palladio's urban palaces were built in Vicenza. Many were designed to occupy or extend through an entire city block, but these plans were only partially completed. The surviving elements show rusticated bases, colossal orders and sculptural decoration to create a monumental front to the street. However, Palladio was also concerned with the surrounding urban context, striking a balance in design so that his palaces would stand prominently on the street, yet remain a part of the adjacent buildings.

Palladio's treatise was translated and went through several editions in each of the major European languages. The English-speaking world was especially influenced by him, first through Inigo Jones, an English architect who traveled through the Veneto shortly after Palladio's death and introduced Renaissance forms to England. One hundred years later Richard Boyle, the third earl of Burlington, visited Palladio's buildings as Jones did and purchased a great many Palladian drawings. Enamored of Palladio's work, Boyle actively championed his cause, forming what is now called the neo-Palladian school in England in the mid-18th century. Many buildings were designed for (and by) Boyle based on Palladio's designs from his drawings, and Boyle also commissioned treatises illustrating these British buildings. The torch passed to the United States through Thomas Jefferson, a gentlemen architect in addition to statesman, who likewise revered Palladio and actively used his treatise on architecture in his design work; Jefferson's first Monticello design was an adaptation of Palladio's Villa Cornaro in Piombino Dese.

Palladio's popularity continues through studies linking his work with that of Le Corbusier, a major architect of the 20th century, and the abstract quality Palladio gave to his designs, paralleling the aesthetic of the Modern Movement. However, one of the enduring fascinations with Palladio regards the dual nature of his training: carving stone and directing construction, then academic study with the nobility and exposure to ancient and contemporary writings on architecture. In a sense the professional dynamic of Renaissance architecture is embodied in Palladio, for as the medieval master mason was replaced by the Renaissance artist/architect, so Pietro dalla Gondola the craft-trained stonecutter became Palladio, the scholar, author and architect of humanist patrons.

—ELWIN C. ROBISON

PARKER and UNWIN.

PARKER, Barry.
British. Born in the north of England, 1867. Died in 1941. In partnership with his 2nd cousin, Raymond Unwin, Buxton, 1896-1906; partnership dissolved, 1914; continued practicing independently as an architect.

UNWIN, Raymond.
British. Born in the north of England, 1863. Died in 1940. Worked for Stavelley Coal and Iron Company, early 1890s; in partnership with his second cousin, Barry Parker, Buxton, 1896-1906; partnership dissolved, 1914; worked in town planning, London, from 1906.

Chronology of Works
All in England unless noted

Barry Parker:

1895	Campbell Hyslop House, Church Stretton, Shropshire
1902	New Earswick (master plan), near York
1903	Homestead House, Chesterfield, Hertfordshire
1903-04	Rockside Hydropathic Hotel, Matlock, Derbyshire
1907-08	W. E. Steers Home Hilltop, Whitehill, Caterham, Kent
1907-10	Hamstead Garden, near London
1908	Stanley Parker Cottage, Letchworth, Hertfordshire
1914-16	Clock House Estate, West Grinstead, Sussex
1920s-41	Withershawe Estate, near Manchester
1917	Pacaembu, near São Paulo, Brazil (urban planning)

Raymond Unwin:

1905-07	Folk Hall, New Earswick, near York
1911-12	Primary School, New Earswick, near York

Parker and Unwin:

1895	St. Andrew's Church, Barrow Hill, near Staveley, Derbyshire
1896	Macnair House, Hill Crest, Marple, Cheshire
1903	E. R. Woodhead House, near Chesterfield, Derbyshire
1903-04	Goodfellow House, Clayton near Stoke, Stratfordshire
1903-06	Cooperative Housing, St. Botolph's Avenue, Sevenoaks, Kent

1904	Letchworth Garden City, Hertfordshire
1904	H. Vause House, Rugby
1907	Oakdene, Rotherfield, Sussex
1907-09	Whirriestone, Rochdale, Lancashire
1914	Aitken House, Letchworth, Hertfordshire

Publications

BOOKS BY PARKER and UNWIN

The Art of Building a Home: A Collection of Lectures and Illustrations by Barry Parker and Raymond Unwin. London, 1901.
Cottage Plans and Common Sense. London, 1902.
Town Planning in Practice. London, 1909.

BOOKS ABOUT PARKER and UNWIN

Barry Parker & Raymond Unwin, Architects. London, the Architectural Association, 1980.
ASHWORTH, WILLIAM: *The Genesis of Modern British Town Planning.* London, 1954.
CREESE, WALTER L.: *The Legacy of Raymond Unwin.* Cambridge, Massachusetts, 1967.
CREESE, WALTER L.: *The Search for Environment.* New Haven, Connecticut, 1966.
KIESS, WALTER: *Urbanismus im Industriezeitalter: von der klassizistischen Stadt zur Garden City.* Berlin, 1991.
PURDOM, C. B.: *The Garden City: A Study in the Development of a Modern Town.* New York, 1913.
SCOTT, M. H. BAILLIE; UNWIN, R.; ET AL: *Town Planning and Modern Architecture at the Hampstead Garden Suburb.* London, 1909.

ARTICLES ABOUT PARKER and UNWIN

CREESE, WALTER L.: "Parker and Unwin, Architects of Totality." *Journal of the Society of Architectural Historians* 22 (October 1963).
HAWKES, DEAN: "The Architectural Partnership of Barry Parker and Raymond Unwin." *Architectural Review* 163 (1978): 327-332

*

Beginning their partnership at the culmination of the Arts and Crafts movement, Barry Parker and Raymond Unwin shared with their contemporaries, such as M. H. Baillie Scott, C. F. A. Voysey, Frank Lloyd Wright, Ernst May and Hendrik Petrus Berlage, a strong ideological commitment that was based on the social, political and moral writings of John Ruskin and William Morris. Morris established the basic principle of the movement that the arts must be unified. Accordingly, the architect should design every last detail of the house, including the furniture, fixtures and wall coverings, and he should evoke the positive spirit of creation within his work. Morris' book *News from Nowhere* (1890) provided the literary image of the medieval village as the animate symbol of self-expression and community for the Arts and Crafts movement that the partnership would reinterpret in their city plans.

Unwin's professional life was inextricably linked to his political beliefs and involvement in organizations such as the Fabian and Manchester Socialist Societies. His work in housing reform and planning was aimed at minimizing the impact of rapid industrialization on English society, especially byelaw streets of industrial housing, which Unwin described as ''the most dreary, depressing, and hopelessly ugly areas upon the face of the earth.'' Unwin was more politically active than Parker and expressed the need to make art available to all classes. In his essay ''Art and Simplicity,'' he wrote: ''If the love of art did really result in making more and more elaborate collections of beautiful things necessary . . . it [would] be but an added burden, still more terribly dividing those who work from those who enjoy. . . .'' Although Parker was equally passionate about the political and moral ideology of the Arts and Crafts movement, he remained throughout his professional career an architect, designer and aesthetician, while Unwin moved almost exclusively into the realm of town planning after the dissolution of the partnership in 1914.

Parker and Unwin expressed a philosophy that was similar to the credo of ''form follows function,'' but in their actual work they did not allow their designs to break free from fairly conservative styles. One of their objectives was to make art and architecture accessible to everyone. They made this possible through the adaptation of English vernacular architecture, which was familiar to a wide audience. Parker and Unwin made no apologies about deriving their aesthetic inspiration from medieval forms—it was a logical source providing the inherent qualities they sought. Parker stated, ''Many would-be artistic people think that things derive an artistic value simply from being old or old-fashioned . . . at the present time . . . the standard of design is so debased that it would be almost impossible to bring out of the past . . . forms for these which would not surpass in beauty those now current among us. If art in our homes were living and progressive the old and old-fashioned would be the ugly and inartistic.''

The formation of guilds at that time was important as a means of training craftsmen in medieval techniques and exhibiting their work. Exhibits demonstrated the combined talents of artist, architect and craftsman, and symbolized the interdependence of the arts. In 1896, Parker and Unwin's first year together, the Northern Art-Workers Guild was formed by Walter Crane in Manchester. It was for the Guild exhibit in 1903 that Parker and Unwin displayed a town-planning scheme titled ''Cottages near a Town,'' which incorporated a group of cottages arranged around a green in a checkerboard pattern. Each house was situated to take advantage of the sunlight with a front-to-back living room, and each had an inglenook and bay window. The plan for ''Cottages near a Town'' marked the introduction of town planning as a viable medium for the Arts and Crafts designers. In particular, it heralded Parker and Unwin's lifelong interest in the notion of the integral relationship between architecture and town planning—both essential parts of the holistic design process.

Despite their efforts to rationalize their designs on strictly objective grounds, both Parker and Unwin were enamored of things medieval. They chose to incorporate inglenooks, built-in furniture, plain unfinished surfaces, and two-story halls in many of their designs, on the grounds that these features would improve the quality of life and were logical responses to their clients' needs. Likewise, Parker and Unwin's plans for Letchworth and Hampstead Garden Suburb were purportedly inspired by the medieval village, on the basis that such villages grew organically and logically from their surroundings. The medieval model introduced quadrangles, closes and free-form planning. Undoubtedly, the architects also liked these features for their clear association with an idealized medieval past.

Parker and Unwin's design for Letchworth Garden City was viewed critically by some garden advocates because it was too abstract, falling short of its goals by being, as C. B. Purdom claimed, ''based on theory rather than practice. . . . Theories, whether learnt from William Morris or invented for oneself, are good for one's own personal experiments; they are bad to enforce upon others.'' Indeed, were the moral implications and lessons of the Arts and Crafts justifiably imposed on people when dealing with the design of their houses and towns? Followers of the movement did not stop to question the fitness of their principles for others; they considered them to be basic to societal reform and human contentment. Yet, many people could not afford to buy the products, or did not want to subscribe to the principles of the Arts and Crafts movement. Parker and Unwin, however, remained committed to bridging the economic gaps between people by promoting simple, inexpensive cottage designs for all classes throughout their careers.

—SUSAN HOLBROOK PERDUE

PARLER FAMILY.

German. Family of influential architects active in Germany and Bohemia during the 14th century. Most important member was Peter Parler (born 1330/33; died in Prague, 1399). Father was Heinrich of Gmünd, master of the works of the Heiligkreuz Church in Schwabisch-Gmünd; Peter was most likely apprenticed with his father. Traveled extensively in his youth, and worked in Strasbourg and Cologne; appointed master of the works at Prague Cathedral by emperor Charles IV after the death of the architect Matthias of Arras, 1352. Other members of the family included Peter's brother, Michael Parler, who worked as a stonemason at the Cistercian Monastery Goldenkron, in southern Bohemia, and later worked in Prague; Peter's second son Wenceslaus Parler was a stonemason at Prague Cathedral and later master of the works at the Church of St. Stephen, Vienna; Peter's youngest son, John Parler, became master of the works in Prague by 1398. Another branch of the family worked in the upper Rhenish region, and another in the Ulm region.

Chronology of Works
All in Bohemia (Prague)

Peter Parler:

1352ff.   Prague Cathedral (St. Vitus'), Prague (including the Tomb of King Ottokar I, 1377, and numerous vaults)
1357   Stone Bridge over the Vlatva, Prague
1360   St. Bartholomew's Church, Kolin (choir)
1370ff.   All Saints Chapel, Hradcany Castle (choir)

Publications

BOOKS ABOUT THE PARLER FAMILY

BACHMANN, E.: *Peter Parler*. Vienna, 1952.
BINDING, GÜNTHER: *Masswerk*. Darmstadt, 1989.
KLETZL, OTTO: *Peter Parler, der Dombaumeister zu Prag*. Leipzig, 1940.
LEGNER, ANTON (ed.): *Die Parler und der Schöne Stil 1350-1400*. 4 vols. Exhibition catalog. Cologne, 1978.
NEUWIRTH, JOSEPH: *Peter Parler von Gmünd, Dombaumeister in Prag und seine Familie*. Prague, 1891.
NUSSBAUM, NORBERT: *Deutsche Kirchenbaukunst der Gotik*. Cologne, 1985.

Peter Parler: Prague Cathedral, Prague, Czechoslovakia, 1352ff.

REINHOLD, H.: *Der Chor des Münsters zu Freiburg i. Br. und die Baukunst der Parler.* 1929.
SWOBODA, K. M.: *Peter Parler, der Baukünstler und Bildhauer.* Vienna, 1939.

ARTICLES ABOUT THE PARLER FAMILY

BOCK, H.: "Der Beginn spätgotischer Architektur in Prag (Peter Parler) und die Beziehungen zu England." *Wallraf Richartz Jahrbuch* 23 (1961): 191-210.
BRÄUTIGAM, G.: "Gmünd-Prag-Nürnberg. Die Nürnberger Frauenkirche und der Prager Parlerstil vor 1360." *Jahrbuch der Berliner Museen* 3 (1961): 58-75.

In the Luxemburger Charles IV, rival king from 1346 and Holy Roman emperor from 1355 (died in 1378), the German empire, after decades of political uncertainty, once more had a statesman and art patron who had a great influence on the history of architecture. Charles' wish to give architectural expression to his power led to the construction of a great many monumental buildings. These were inspired by French architecture, but also continued German traditions, such as that of the hall church (a church with naves of equal height). Under the House of Luxemburg, the Gothic style was chosen, for the first time in Germany, to signify royal culture. In the development of specific architectural forms to implement Charles' program, the Parler family of architects played the most significant part.

Leaving out of consideration all the legends and speculations that have sprung up around the name, the geographical reach of the Parlers' activities remains truly astounding. Members of this family led the most important workshops of Germany— Schwabisch-Gmünd, Prague, Strasbourg, Freiburg, Basel, Vienna—and from these workshops they influenced the architectural developments in the surrounding regions. The Parlers are the first Gothic architects for whom rich source material provides information not only about their work but also about their lives. For the first time in Germany the architect steps forward in person.

Their influence and their imposing achievements are also evident in the fact that, at the end of the 15th century, both Matthäus Roriczer in his *"puechlein der fialen gerechtigkeit"* ("pamphlet doing justice to pinnacles") and Hans Schmuttermeyer in his pamphlet on pinnacles referred to the Parlers as the guardians of good old architecture. The Prague workshop led by the Parlers at the end of the 14th century was still so famous and respected in the 16th century that one would invoke the name as proof of one's architectural good taste.

Peter Parler, master of the works at St. Vitus' Cathedral in Prague, was the first of the family to use the professional designation as a surname. (A "parlier" was the deputy master of the works in a medieval workshop.) In Cologne at the beginning of the 14th century the name already appeared for a certain Master Arnold and a Walter, who were referred to as "poleyr" and "paleyr," respectively. The use of Parler as a surname in this family, however, is only documented for Peter and two of his sons. The rest of his descendants and the branches of the family in the Upper-Rhenish area and in Ulm did not use the name. It has been demonstrated that a doubly broken angle rod inscribed on sculptures—on the Parler bust at St. Vitus' Cathedral, for instance—was the sign of the Prague and Upper-Rhenish Parlers.

Little is known about the development of the most important member of the Parler family, Peter, until he was made cathedral architect for the cathedral in Prague. He was born in 1330 or 1333 to Heinrich of Gmünd, and most likely he served his apprenticeship with his father. (Heinrich was master of the works of the Heiligkreuz Church in Schwabisch-Gmünd, begun in 1351, for example, which is one of the buildings which introduced the Late Gothic style to Germany.) Peter seems to have traveled considerably early in his career, and worked both in Strasbourg and Cologne. In Cologne he met his first wife, Gertrud, daughter of the stonemason Bartholomäus. On the basis of stylistic comparisons, the hypothesis has been put forward that Peter also participated in the construction of the Frauenkirche in Nuremberg, which was founded by Charles IV. Construction work on this church is documented for 1352, and it was dedicated in 1358.

The emperor Charles IV transferred the supervision of Prague Cathedral to Peter Parler after the death of the architect Matthias of Arras in 1352, as the inscription over Peter's bust in the cathedral's triforium commemorates. Peter Parler would thus have gone to Prague in his early twenties. In Prague he soon received further commissions: he built a stone bridge over the Vltava in 1357, and from 1370 he constructed the choir of the All Saints' Chapel at the Hradčany Castle. He executed the tomb of King Ottokar I of Bohemia in the southern choir chapel of Prague Cathedral, for which he was paid in 1377. He was also involved in the creation of the busts in the Prague Cathedral triforium, which are an important link in the development of European portraiture in the 14th century. In addition he designed the choir of St. Bartholomew's Church in Kolin, which was added to the Early Gothic nave, in 1360. As *"magister fabricae"* (master of the works) he was an employee of the Prague Cathedral chapter, receiving a yearly salary, a winter and a summer wardrobe, free housing and firewood. For consulting and for personally executed pieces of work (such as the tomb of Ottokar) he was paid additional sums. He was held in high esteem in Prague, was a lay assessor, and owned at least five houses on the Hradčany hill until 1383. Peter died in 1399, and was buried in Prague Cathedral.

The city of Prague, situated on the Vltava River, was the focus of the emperor Charles IV's efforts to create an image of magnificence to represent his power. The city was chosen as his principal residence, and in 1344 became the metropolitan seat of government. Construction of Prague Cathedral was begun in the same year. The French architect Matthias of Arras designed the plan after the example of French cathedrals with polygonal chapels, as seen at Narbonne, Rodez and Toulouse. When Matthias died in 1352, large parts of the radial chapels, ambulatory and interior ground-level arcades had been erected. Peter Parler, as his successor, exploited the stylistic possibilities of his age, and developed a multiplicity of new motifs and connections for the cathedral. As a consequence of Peter's work, St. Vitus' Cathedral at Prague became one of the key buildings of the 14th century, and an inexhaustible source of inspiration to generations of architects. In Peter's work, the understanding of architectural and sculptural decoration, and its function in the articulation of facades was fundamentally changed. Single elements were given greater freedom and independence from the overall decor. Instead of the traditional regular spacing and interweaving of similar formal elements, Peter introduced a controlled variation and interlacing of independent forms.

Peter's delight in formal experimentation, in the playful, in contrasts, and in the rupture of harmony in the interconnection of motifs came to be characteristic design methods, distinguishing the German Gothic style of the second half of the 14th century. In the six-part clerestory windows of Prague Cathedral, which were begun in 1374, Peter set the outer windows of the lower part at an inward angle, and crowned them with trefoils. The resulting wave-like pattern makes it seem as though each window has been subdivided once more. This particular achievement, for all its power, was not imitated elsewhere, however.

Particularly eye-catching, as Norbert Nussbaum has remarked, is "the multiplicity of tracery forms, which are put together in ever varied combinations. A lively, almost restless, movement in the upper levels is created. Closed and broken circular tracery forms, combined with each other, are put together with spherical triangles, one of the corners of which seems to bend down and sideways, and with lancette arches carved with crescents. Particularly rich are the bladder ornaments, which are set end to end to form a kind of twin bladder ornament, or rotated and then combined." The twin bladder ornaments became a dominant element in the designs of the great workshops of southern Germany—Vienna, Regensburg and Ulm—and also in buildings in Westphalia, such as the Church of St. Lambert in Münster. In more general terms, it may be observed that, after somewhat hesitant beginnings, the tracery forms developed by the Parlers flourished in the first two decades of the 15th century.

Finally, the Parlers' virtuosity in conceiving vaults must be mentioned. Parallel ribs, combined with intersecting triradiated forms, are set under shallow barrel vaults. Peter's vault covering the choir of St. Vitus' Cathedral (completed in 1385) was the first monumental vault of its kind in central Europe. Before installing the choir vault, he had done the vaults in the Sacristy (1362), the St. Wenceslaus Chapel (1367), the porch of the southern transept portal (1367/68), and the passage through the Altstadter Turm (after 1370)—all with ribs in triradiated patterns.

The exemplary nature of the buildings, the determining influence of the House of the Luxemburgs, and the large Parler family, who were active in three successive generations of architects, contributed to the dissemination of this version of the Late Gothic style. Since the same first names (Heinrich, Johann, Michael) recur again and again, it has not been possible thus far to determine the work of single members of the family with any degree of certainty. Peter's brother, Michael Parler, was first found active as a stonemason at the Cistercian Monastery Goldenkron in southern Bohemia, and later in Prague. Among Peter's children, the eldest son, Nicolas, was a priest in Prague; the second son, Wenceslaus, was a stonemason at Prague Cathedral, and later master of the works at the Church of St. Stephen in Vienna; the youngest son, John, was master of the works in Prague by 1398. Peter's second daughter married the stonemason Michael of Cologne. From the branch of the family living in the Upper Rhenish region came Johann von Gmünd, master of the works at the cathedrals of Freiburg and Basel; Michael of Freiburg, also called of Gmünd, master of the works at Strasbourg Cathedral from 1383; Henry of Gmünd, also called of Freiburg, architect to the margrave of Moravia from 1381, had also worked in Cologne. Another branch of the family was active at Ulm Minster during the last quarter of the 14th century. Since the masters of the Gothic period were generally trained as stonemasons and sculptors; and since the architecture was articulated stone construction, in which tectonic form, sculptural ornament and figures, and glass form a unity, the Parlers had a broad effect not only on architecture. They were also influential as sculptors, and had an enduring effect on the development of style in the second half of the 14th century and the beginning of the 15th century in central Europe. The art of the Parlers constitutes one of the greatest developments in the history of European art.

—GÜNTHER BINDING

Translated from the German by Marijke Rijsberman

PARRIS, Alexander.

American. Born in Hebron, Maine, 24 November 1780. Died in Pembroke, Massachusetts, 10 June 1852. Apprenticeship with Noah Bonney, 1799. Architect and engineer, Boston, 1818.

Chronology of Works
All in the United States

1805	Richard Hunnewell House (Portland Club), Portland, Maine
1805	Richard Boyd House (St. Elizabeth's Home for Children), Portland, Maine
1807-08	Preble House, Portland, Maine
1811-13	John Wickham House, Richmond, Virginia
1819-21	David Sears House, Boston, Massachusetts
1819-21	St. Paul's Church (Episcopal Cathedral), Boston, Massachusetts
1819-29	Charlestown Navy Yard and Harbor, Boston, Massachusetts (dry dock and sea walls)
1824	G.W. Lyman House, Boston, Massachusetts
1824-26	Faneuil Hall Market (Quincy Market), Boston, Massachusetts
1827-28	Unitarian Church (Stone Temple), Quincy, Massachusetts
1827-40s	North and South Market Buildings, Boston, Massachusetts

Publications

BOOKS ABOUT PARRIS

HAMLIN, TALBOT: *Greek Revival Architecture in America.* New York, 1944.
KILHAM, WALTER H., JR.: *Boston After Bulfinch: An Account of Its Architecture, 1800-1900.* Cambridge, Massachusetts, 1946.
KIMBALL, FISKE: *Domestic Architecture of the American Colonies and of the Early Republic.* New York, 1922.
PIERSON, WILLIAM H., JR.: *American Buildings and Their Architects: The Colonial and Neo-Classical Styles.* Garden City, New York, 1970.

ARTICLES ABOUT PARRIS

BISHIR, CATHERINE W., and BULLOCK, MARSHALL: "Mr. Jones Goes to Richmond: A Note on the Influence of Alexander Parris' Wickham House." *Journal of the Society of Architectural Historians* 43 (March 1984): 71-74.
BRYAN, JOHN MORRILL: "Boston's Granite Architecture, ca. 1810-1860." Ph.D. dissertation. Boston University, 1972.
ZIMMER, EDWARD F., and SCOTT, PAMELA J.: "Alexander Parris, B. Henry Latrobe, and the John Wickham House in Richmond, Virginia." *Journal of the Society of Architectural Historians* 41 (October 1982): 202-211.

*

Alexander Parris was raised by his paternal grandfather, a teacher, surveyor, farmer, businessman and town meeting moderator. By the age of 19 Parris had completed his apprenticeship with Massachusetts housewright Noah Bonney, and within a decade had made the transition from talented builder to creative architect. Parris' career developed in New England, and the majority of his architectural works were in the Boston area.

From 1828 (his 48th year) until 1852 his livelihood focused on engineering projects, principally lighthouses and navy yards for the federal government.

Parris' first works, of which two major examples survive, were erected in Portland, Maine. In their cubic forms, delicate proportions, and refined exterior and interior details (including elliptical staircases and plaster groin vaults), the brick Richard Hunnewell House (1805; presently the Portland Club) and the Richard Boyd House (1805; presently St. Elizabeth's Home for Children) are archetypally Federal in style, and owe their main features to the architecture of Charles Bulfinch and Asher Benjamin. By 1807, when his Commodore Edward Preble House in Portland was completed, Parris had begun to think of architecture in spatial rather than structural and decorative terms. The development of two major facades (one facing a garden) and his break with the traditional four-square house plan common during the preceding century in American architecture foreshadowed his two major domestic works, the John Wickham House (1811-13) in Richmond and the David Sears House (1819-21) in Boston.

In 1809 and 1810 Parris was unable to find permanent work in New York and Philadelphia, but he benefited enormously from the range of sophisticated buildings he found in those centers of American avant-garde architecture. Particularly influential was the work of Benjamin Henry Latrobe, whose advanced neoclassicism—abstract and spatial—challenged the ornateness of the prevailing Federal style. Latrobe's use of ancient Greek temple forms with their bold orders and large-scale detail, his emphasis on volumetric spaces and planar surfaces, and his ingenious and complex plans profoundly influenced Parris' future designs. Upon his return to Boston, Parris joined the recently established Social Architectural Library, which gave him ready access to a wide range of architectural books, including recent publications by John Soane and John Plaw (illustrating English examples of works similar to Latrobe's), as well as earlier standard architectural treatises and pattern books.

Parris' domestic masterpiece, the Wickham House, was long attributed to his contemporary Robert Mills. While he was in the process of building it, Parris met Latrobe and received from him a critique of the design. In its final form the Wickham House is a two-story, rectangular structure with a hipped roof, projecting entrance porch and colonnaded garden facade. It is constructed in brick, stuccoed and scored in imitation of ashlar masonry. Five large tripartite windows and an elliptical fanlit central door articulate the main facade, while the Ionic porch follows the profile of a wide central semicircular bow facing the garden. Its plan was unusual because of the layering of space from front to back along the central axis. A rectangular vestibule is separated from the circular stairhall by a wide arch. The flying elliptical stair, constructed in wood, is one of the finest in America from that period. Concentration of the entry and vertical circulation in the front half of the house resulted in three major public rooms opening onto the single-story porch. Parris learned from Latrobe the importance of linking rooms en suite in order to create spatial flow, but he retained his own ornate and beautifully crafted staircase, a hallmark of his work.

In 1819 Parris adapted for a northern clime and stone construction many of the features of the Wickham House for the John Sears House in Boston, placing the two major facades adjacent to, rather than opposite, one another. The design gained a ponderosity and solidity that was to characterize his major works of the next decade, Fanueil Hall or Quincy Market (1824-26) in Boston and the Stone Temple (1827-28) in Quincy.

Faneuil Hall Market (a municipal endeavor sponsored by Mayor Josiah Quincy) is possibly the greatest work of architecture in the Greek Revival style in America. Even in its present incarnation the powerful spatial and formal qualities of the three buildings comprising the complex—originally a central market (with rented stalls) flanked by two ranges of individually owned stores—dominate Boston's old dock area. Vast in extent, yet irregular in form and orientation (due to a variety of political and economic forces), the Quincy granite structures have such strong architectonic qualities that the planning inconsistencies are diminished. The north (520 feet by 55 feet) and south (530 feet by 65 feet) stores were designed as four-story warehouses in the "Boston granite style," in which monolithic slabs of stone quarried on the diagonal were generally used in trabeated construction. At Quincy Market Parris combined arched and trabeated openings, copied from the model of an earlier Boston office building. He concentrated his design energy on the center market, each end of which is terminated by a tetrastyle Doric temple from strongly reminiscent of Inigo Jones' St. Pauls' Covent Garden (1631-34) in London. A central, projecting domed pavilion occupies one-seventh of the market's total length of 535 feet. Its elliptical form, often perceived as round, helps diminish the great length of the market building.

Parris was the architect of numerous churches; fortunately his best survives. John Adams donated the stone quarries to build the Stone Temple (Unitarian Church) in Quincy; his death in 1826 hastened its construction, as it was to serve as his tomb and monument. John Quincy Adams (while president) consulted with Parris on the tower design. As at Quincy Market, Parris combined rock and smooth-faced granite, which contributes to the church's architectonic character. The dressed stone facade, fronted by a hexastyle Greek Doric portico and topped by a cubic clock base and open tempietto bell tower, is sparse, even severe, yet not ponderous . At the Stone Temple Parris displayed mastery in his proportional control of granite, a heavy and difficult material. The shallow, coffered wood dome (with prehensile rosettes) that spans the entire church is one of the lesser-known great ceilings in America.

—PAMELA SCOTT

PAXTON, Joseph.

British. Born in Milton Bryan, near Woburn, England, 1801. Died in 1865. Member of Parliament, 1855-65; knighted, 1851.

Chronology of Works
All in England unless noted
† Work no longer exists

1826-44	Chatsworth Gardens, Chatsworth
1836-39	Farm Buildings, Chatsworth
1836-40	Great Stove, Chatsworth†
1838-42	Village Cottages, Edensor, near Chatsworth
1842-43	Upton Park, Slough
1842-44	Prince's Park, Liverpool
1843-47	Birkenhead Park, Liverpool
1846	Burton Closes, Bakewell (completed by A. W. N. Pugin)
1849-50	Victoria Regia House, Chatsworth
1850-51	Crystal Palace, Hyde Park, London†
1850-58	Lismore Castle, County Waterford, Ireland
1851-54	Mentmore Towers, Buckinghamshire (with G. H. Stokes)
1851-54	Crystal Palace, Sydenham (relocation)†
1852-56	Crystal Palace Park, Sydenham
1853-59	Ferrières (Rothschild House and Gardens), near Paris, France

1854-63 Park and Grounds, Mentmore, Buckinghamshire
1864 Battlesden House, Bedfordshire

Publications

ARTICLES BY PAXTON

"Mr. Paxton's History of the Building for the Great Exhibition of 1851." *Illustrated London News* 17 (19 October 1850): 385-386.

"The Industrial Palace in Hyde Park: Mr. Paxton's Lecture at the Society of Arts." *Illustrated London News* 17 (16 November 1850): 385-386.

"What Is to Become of the Crystal Palace?" *Gardener's Chronicle* No. 27 (5 July 1851): 420-421.

BOOKS ABOUT PAXTON

ANTHONY, J.: *Joseph Paxton: An Illustrated Life, 1803-1865.* Aylesbury, England, 1973.

BERLYN, P., and FOWLER, C., JR.: *The Crystal Palace, Its Architectural History and Constructive Marvels.* London, 1851.

CHADWICK, GEORGE F.: *The Works of Sir Joseph Paxton.* London, 1961.

COWPER, CHARLES, and DOWNES, CHARLES: *The Building Erected in Hyde Park for the Great Exhibition of Industry of All Nations, 1851.* London, 1852.

MARKHAM, VIOLET R.: *Paxton and the Bachelor Duke.* London, 1935.

ARTICLES ABOUT PAXTON

"Another Side to Paxton." *Architectural Review* 110 (October 1951): 262-263.

CHADWICK, G. F.: "Paxton and Sydenham Park." *Architectural Review* 129 (February 1961): 122-127.

CHADWICK, G. F.: "Paxton and the Great Stove." *Architectural History* 4 (1961): 77-92.

FITCH, JAMES MARSTON: "The Palace, the Bridge and the Tower." *Architectural Forum* 87 (October 1947): 88-95.

MARKHAM, VIOLET R.: "Joseph Paxton and His Buildings." *Transactions of the Society of Arts* 99 (1950-51).

MASSINGHAM, B.: "Gardeners of the Past: Sir Joseph Paxton." *Gardener's Chronicle* 157 (2 January 1965).

MAZZUCCHELLI, A. M.: "Da Paxton a Gropius." *Casabella* 8 (March 1935): 8-9.

*

Joseph Paxton epitomizes the self-made Victorian so eulogized in Samuel Smiles' *Self Help.* In a life spent in the service of a great country house (the duke of Devonshire's at Chatsworth), growing from humble gardener to a noted man of affairs, his work reflects with a rare transparency the dominant values and tastes of his age.

Paxton designed remarkable but straightforward glass houses, first on the Chatsworth grounds and then the Crystal Palace ("a greenhouse bigger than ever a greenhouse was built before," in John Ruskin's words) for the Great Exhibition of 1851; he designed a model village on the Chatsworth estate in the utterly unmemorable style of the day, and then a monstrous and tasteless pile at Mentmore, where his client, Baron Meyer de Rothschild, lacked the restraint of economic necessity. In architectural ideas, much of Paxton's simple "associationism" came from that other gardener, common-sense worrier and amateur architect, John Claudius Loudon (1783-1843).

Paxton's taste could perhaps most clearly be seen in the Crystal Palace once it was translated from the original site of the Great Exhibition to Sydenham Hill: bloated in scale, flanked by Isambard K. Brunel's inelegant water towers, symmetrical, vaulted; in place of the direct, three-story, "infinite"—or at least indeterminate—building in Hyde Park, there was a Durandesque, Beaux-Arts composition in stick framing and glass, its vast, five-story form paradoxically more comprehensible and stolid.

Therein Paxton's art reflects his life. In the 1840s he was already a public figure—he was on the board of various railway companies, and he started a newspaper (with Charles Dickens as editor). In the 1850s he became director of the Crystal Palace at Sydenham, and moved to live nearby, but he was increasingly beset by worries and criticisms. He became a member of Parliament, and, caught up in a growing vortex of public and business life, far from his sure ground—in the Chatsworth gardens—he died in 1865.

Paxton's most endearing qualities were his insatiable curiosity—about plant life and human manufacture (between which he drew links when encouraged to theorize). His chief skill was, however, clearly in the marshaling of engineering forces to alter the surface of the land, and in that regard his monument was the first Crystal Palace in Hyde Park.

From his early 20s, Paxton was directing teams to level and drain, build and plant, divert streams, form waterfalls and create fountains. He sent expeditions for exotic Amazonian plants, and built the most economical and daring glass cages to match them. He mounted an amazing outdoor display on the evening of Queen Victoria's visit to Chatsworth in 1843. The duke of Wellington, traveling with the royal party, always a man interested in how things were done, got up the next dawn to find out. He found nothing: gardens perfect and still, all lanterns and equipment gone, charred grass returfed, not a trace of the mass of people from the previous evening. Paxton's regiment of workers had toiled with great organization and efficiency, silently, through the night. "I should like to have had that man of yours," said Wellington to Devonshire, "for one of my generals."

Generals rarely have to count the cost. Paxton's years at Chatsworth encouraged the grandiose and rarely encouraged an economical outlook; yet it was when every penny counted that his best work was produced.

—JOHN McKEAN

PEABODY and STEARNS.

PEABODY, Robert Swain.
American. Born in New Bedford, Massachusetts, 1845. Died in Marblehead, Massachusetts, 3 October 1917. Graduated from Harvard College, Cambridge, Massachusetts, 1866; studied at the École des Beaux-Arts, Paris, France. Partnership with John G. Stearns, Boston, 1870-1917; head of the City Parks Department, Boston. Fellow, American Institute of Architects, 1889; president, Boston Society of Architects.

STEARNS, John Goddard.
American. Born in New York City, 18 May 1843. Died on 16 September 1917. Graduated from Lawrence Scientific School, Cambridge, Massachusetts, 1863; trained in the office of Ware and Van Brunt, Boston. Partnership with Robert Swain Peabody, 1870-1917.

Chronology of Works
All in the United States
† Work no longer exists

1871-72	Glen Eyrie Lodge, Colorado Springs, Colorado†
1872-74	Providence (Park Square) Railroad Station, Boston, Massachusetts†
1873-75	College Hall, Smith College, Northampton, Massachusetts
1874-75	Brunswick Hotel, Boston, Massachusetts†
1874-75	Mutual Life Insurance Company Building of New York, Boston, Massachusetts†
1875	William A. Appleton House, Milton, Massachusetts†
1877-78	Pierre Lorillard House (First Breakers), Newport, Rhode Island†
1877-78	John C. Phillips House, Boston, Massachusetts†
1878-79	Hemenway Gymnasium, Harvard College, Cambridge, Massachusetts†
1879-80	Union League Club Clubhouse, New York City†
1879-81	Wayman Crow, Jr., Museum of Fine Arts, St. Louis, Missouri†
1880-81	Church of the Messiah, St. Louis, Missouri
1880-81	Public Library, Easthampton, Massachusetts
1880-81	United Bank Building, New York City†
1882-83	Antlers Hotel, Colorado Springs, Colorado†
1882-83	Turner Building, St. Louis, Missouri†
1882-84	Catherine Lorillard Wolfe House (Vinland), Newport, Rhode Island
1883	National Bank of Commerce, New Bedford, Massachusetts
1883-84	George Nixon Black House (Kragsyde), Manchester-by-the-Sea, Massachusetts†
1883-84	R. H. White Warehouse, Boston, Massachusetts†
1884-85	Memorial Hall, Lawrenceville School, New Jersey
1884-85	St. Louis Club Clubhouse, St. Louis, Missouri†
1886-87	Easton Beach Pavilion, Newport, Rhode Island†
1886-88	First Parish Church, Weston, Massachusetts
1887-88	James J. Hill House, St. Paul, Minnesota
1887-91	Exchange Building, Boston, Massachusetts
1888-89	Fiske Building, Boston, Massachusetts
1889	Union Church, Northeast Harbor, Maine
1889-90	Jersey City Railroad Station for the Central Railroad of New Jersey, Jersey City, New Jersey
1889-90	Frederick W. Vanderbilt House (Rough Point), Newport, Rhode Island
1890-91	Central Railroad of New Jersey Building, New York City†
1890-91	Security Building, St. Louis, Missouri
1890-91	Union Station, Duluth, Minnesota
1892-93	Machinery Hall, World's Columbian Exposition, Chicago, Illinois†
1892-93	Massachusetts State Building, World's Columbian Exposition, Chicago, Illinois†
1893	John T. Davis House, St. Louis, Missouri
1893	Society for Savings Bank, Hartford, Connecticut
1894	John Sloane House (Wyndhurst), Lenox, Massachusetts
1886-1901	Groton School, Groton, Massachusetts
1896-98	Worcester City Hall, Massachusetts
1897-99	Chamber of Commerce Building, Cleveland, Ohio†
1901	Peabody House (The Fenway), Boston, Massachusetts
1902-04	India Building, Boston, Massachusetts
1902-04	Percival Roberts House (Penshurst), Narberth, Pennsylvania†
1903-08	Simmons College, Boston, Massachusetts
1905-07	Weld Boat Club Boathouse, Cambridge, Massachusetts
1908-09	Town Hall, Clinton, Massachusetts
1909-15	United States Customhouse, Boston, Massachusetts (extension)
1911-14	Public Library, Bangor, Maine
1914-15	Worcester Academy Gymnasium, Worcester, Massachusetts

Publications

BOOKS ABOUT PEABODY and STEARNS

DAMRELL, CHARLES: *A Half Century of Boston's Building.* Boston, 1895.

GOUDY, MARVIN E., and WALSH, ROBERT P. (eds.): *Boston Society of Architects: The First Hundred Years, 1867-1967.* Boston, 1967.

HOYT, EDWIN P.: *The Peabody Influence.* New York, 1968.

MEEKS, CARROLL L. V.: *The Railroad Stations: An Architectural History.* New Haven, Connecticut, 1956.

SCULLY, VINCENT J., JR.: *The Shingle Style and the Stick Style: Architectural Theory and Design from Richardson to the Origins of Wright.* New Haven, Connecticut, 1955.

STURGIS, RUSSELL: *A Critique of the Work of Peabody and Stearns.* Reprint of "Peabody and Stearns." *Architectural Record* 3 (July 1896): 53-97.

ARTICLES ABOUT PEABODY and STEARNS

BOND, ANTHONY: "The Commercial Architecture of Peabody and Stearns in Boston." M.A. thesis. Pennsylvania State University, Philadelphia, 1974.

HOLDEN, WHEATON: "The Peabody Touch: Peabody and Stearns of Boston, 1870-1917." *Journal of the Society of Architectural Historians* 32 (May 1973): 114-131.

SCHUYLER, MONTGOMERY: "The Romanesque Revival in America." *Architectural Record* 1 (1891): 151-198.

SCHWEINFURTH, JULIUS A.: "Robert Swain Peabody: Tower Builder." *American Architect* 130 (1926): 181-191.

*

The firm of Peabody and Stearns was among the preeminent architects active in New England in the late 19th and early 20th centuries. In many ways it was the Boston equivalent of McKim, Mead and White in New York City, for its work influenced that of the entire region and its office served as a training ground for a younger generation of architects.

Robert Swain Peabody was born in New Bedford, Massachusetts, the son of Ephraim Peabody, rector of King's Chapel, Boston. After his graduation from Harvard University in 1866, Robert Peabody spent several months in the office of architect Gridley J. F. Bryant and then moved to the office of William R. Ware and Henry Van Brunt; in those two offices Peabody was exposed to some of the best examples of Second Empire Baroque and High Victorian Gothic architecture then being produced in Boston. In 1867 he traveled to England and then to Paris, where he was admitted to the École des Beaux-Arts. He was in the Atelier Daumet along with Charles Follen McKim (1847-1909), who became his close friend. Both left Paris in 1870, when Peabody returned to Boston and established a partnership with John Goddard Stearns, Jr.

Stearns, born in New York City, graduated from Harvard in 1863 with a degree in engineering. He then entered the office of Ware and Van Brunt in Boston, where, for seven years, he worked closely with Ware, becoming chief draftsman in the office. In the partnership with Peabody, Stearns specialized in engineering and construction superintendence.

Peabody and Stearns obtained numerous early commissions through family contacts and through acquaintances made while in the Ware and Van Brunt office, designing a number of railroad stations and business buildings from the start. One good example was the large Providence Railroad Station, Park Square, Boston (1872-74, demolished). Their work at that time combined elements of High Victorian Gothic color with the classical orders and high mansard roofs of Second Empire Baroque, both then extremely popular styles. One example was their Mutual Life Insurance Company of New York Building in Boston (1874-75). The highly picturesque composition of the High Victorian Gothic was evident in several of their houses of those years, as in a house at Medford, Massachusetts (1877), and in the large wooden summer house for Pierre Lorillard at Newport, Rhode Island, the first "Breakers" (1878, demolished).

Even in the early houses, however, the beginnings of Peabody's interest in classical order was evident, for here and there appeared columns, pediments, and belvederes translated into towers. As with his close friend McKim, Peabody's interest in early Colonial architecture took two directions, one toward the study and emulation of 18th-century classicism and ultimately the embrace of classical architecture entirely, and the other toward the study of geometric order in a more abstract sense. The first and more antiquarian direction resulted in a series of articles by Peabody extolling the beauties of 18th-century houses, published in the *American Architect and Building News* in 1877 and 1878, signed with the pen name "Georgian." This also resulted in a curiously picturesque house at Brush Hill, Massachusetts, with 18th-century classical details such as corner pilasters and a Palladian window (1877-78).

By combining such classical elements in picturesque, asymmetrical compositions, Peabody led the way in creating the American version of free classicism, or the "Queen Anne" style, as demonstrated in the firm's Hemenway Gymnasium, Harvard University (1878-79, demolished), and the even more picturesque New York Union Club (1879-90, demolished), won in competition.

In the other direction, by maintaining careful geometric control in highly original wooden compositions, Peabody simultaneously helped to create the American "Shingle Style," as shown in the large George Nixon Black house, Kragsyde, Manchester-by-the-Sea, Massachusetts (1883-84), perhaps the firm's residential masterwork of the mid-1880s. Even more rigorous in its geometrical order was their Elberon Casino, Elberon, New Jersey (1885).

During the later 1880s, Peabody and Stearns, like so many New England architects, fell under the pervasive influence of Henry Hobson Richardson (1838-86). His massive proportions and rough-faced masonry appeared in Peabody and Stearns' Memorial Hall at the Lawrenceville School, New Jersey (1884-85), and also in the sprawling James J. Hill residence in St. Paul, Minnesota (1887-88).

Along with McKim, Mead and White, and Babb, Cook and Willard in New York City, Peabody and Stearns endeavored to develop a system of masonry construction in tall buildings that expressed the bearing nature of masonry walls, drawing on the ordered hierarchy of classical design. For Peabody and Stearns the result appeared in the heavily proportioned R. H. White Warehouse, Boston, Massachusetts (1882-83), the Fiske Building, Boston (1888-89), with its more medieval steep roofs,

and culminated in the Exchange Building, Boston (1887-91), with its pilastraded base, six-story midsection, and two-story attic level set off by an encircling cornice. In the five-story Pope Manufacturing Company Building, Boston (1894), Peabody used this three-part composition in the broadly glazed ground floor, the midsection of windows grouped in tall arcades, and an attic story with modillion cornice—all of the detail in terra-cotta.

By the time of the World's Columbian Exposition in 1893, Peabody and Stearns had fully adopted classicism in their work, boldly announced in their Machinery Hall in Chicago, with its surrounding colonnades and Roman temple entry porticoes. For the Massachusetts Building in Chicago, the firm created a free interpretation of the Hancock House of 1737 on Boston's Beacon Hill. Peabody's sensitivity toward Georgian and Federal residential design was put to good use in more than 80 town houses he designed in the rapidly developing Back Bay section of Boston, including one of the best, his own residence in The Fenway (1900-01). Perhaps his finest Georgian creation was the red-brick Groton School (1886-1901). Among the firm's most striking classical commercial buildings were the Chamber of Commerce in Cleveland, Ohio (1901), and the soaring Pharos lighthouse tower erected over Ammi B. Young's Greek Revival Custom House, Boston (1911-14).

As the firm's practice grew to include buildings across the United States, Peabody focused his attention on conceptual design and gave his assistants considerable breadth in the development of details. His personality and the quality of his designs drew the best young men to the office. Nearly all were graduates of the Massachusetts Institute of Technology and, as they left the office to establish their own careers, they created a network that spanned North America. This network rivaled that similarly created by McKim, Mead and White—even Joseph Morrill Wells, so important in the office of McKim, Mead and White, began in the office of Peabody and Stearns. Peabody's special interest in Colonial architecture was continued in Boston by Arthur Little. Also active in Boston were former assistants Clarence Blackall and city architect Edmund Wheelwright, among many others. Other more far-flung associates included Theophilus Chandler in Philadelphia, Pennsylvania; Albert H. Spahr and Colbert A. MacClure in Pittsburgh, Pennsylvania; and George Fuller, Charles Frost and Henry Ives Cobb in Chicago, Illinois. Further to the west were William Eames and Thomas C. Young in St. Louis, Missouri, where Pierce Furber also operated the Peabody and Stearns western branch office. Ion Lewis of Whidden and Lewis in Portland, Oregon, was also an alumnus, as was A. C. Schweinfurth in San Francisco, California.

Peabody and Stearns provided some of the most significant private and public architecture in New England at the turn of the 19th century. Important, too, was the atelier they provided in their office, training many younger architects who carried that high-principled professionalism to cities across the continent.

—LELAND M. ROTH

PEARCE, Edward Lovett.

Irish. Born in either Ireland or England, 1699. Died on 7 December 1733. Father was General Edward Pearce, cousin of the architect John Vanbrugh, with whom the younger Pearce may have studied. Married his cousin Anne Pearce; four daughters. Traveled through France and Italy studying architecture, 1723-24. Began his architectural career in Dublin, 1726; elected member of Irish Parliament for Ratoath, 1727; appointed surveyor general for Ireland, 1730. Knighted, 1732.

Edward Lovett Pearce: Parliament House, Dublin, Ireland, ca. 1729

Chronology of Works

All in Ireland
* Approximate dates

1719/22ff.	Castletown, County Kildare (entrance hall, curved colonnades and wings)
1727	Drumcondra House, County Dublin
before 1729	Cashel Palace, County Tipperary (completed by others)
1729*	Parliament House, Dublin (completed after Pearce's death by Arthur Dobbs)
1730*	9 and 10 Henrietta Street, Dublin
1730	Bellamont, Forest, County Cavan
1731*	Summerhill, Enfield, County Meath
1733	Desart Court, Callan, County Kilkenny [attributed]
1733-34	Aungier Street Theatre, Dublin
n.d.	Castle, Dublin (upper castle yard, southeast block)

Publications

BOOKS ABOUT PEARCE

COLVIN, H. M. and CRAIG, MAURICE J. (eds.): *Architectural Designs in the Library of Elton Hall by Sir John Vanbrugh and Sir Edward Lovett Pearce*. Oxford, 1964.
SADLEIR, T. U.: *Sir Edward Lovett Pearce*. Dublin, 1927.

*

Edward Lovett (or Lovet) Pearce came from a Norwich family with close Irish connections: his lineage on the maternal side included a lord mayor of Dublin and a clan chieftain of the O'Mores. His father, General Edward Pearce, was John Vanbrugh's first cousin, and the young Pearce was taught the rudiments of architecture by that master of the Baroque. Although Pearce entered the Army in 1716, he did not pursue his military career: in the early 1720s he was in contact with Lord Burlington's circle, and in 1723-24 traveled in France and Italy to study architecture, having met Alessandro Galilei, who was designing the great house at Castletown, County Kildare (under construction in 1722), for Speaker Conolly. The Conolly connection is significant, for Pearce acted as an agent for Conolly in Italy, and kept in close touch with Galilei. It was through

Conolly that Pearce got the chance to design part of Castletown, and to have his scheme for the Parliament House realized. Pearce's good fortune to be related to many of the families building great houses in Ireland during the 1720s and 1730s doubtless helped his architectural career.

By 1726 Pearce was living in Dublin, and in 1727 he was elected member of the Irish Parliament for the Borough of Ratoath; almost immediately he prepared designs for the new Parliament House in Dublin, which were approved by the king, the viceroy and Parliament in 1728. In this wonderful building, Vanbrughian and Palladian influences merged: from Vanbrugh derived the treatment of corridors, which include sequences of domed compartments on square plans, the great *cour d'honneur* of the front embraced by the projecting wings, and the relationships of the masses; from Palladianism came the stepped Pantheon dome that was not unlike that of Burlington's house at Chiswick, the apsidal-ended rooms derived from Roman *thermae* and villas, and the giant order carrying the continuous entablature. The colonnaded front probably derived in part from Andrea Palladio's Villa Santa Sofia at Pedemonte and from the Palais Bourbon in Paris, while the arcuated motifs set within pedimented aedicules at the ends of the wings derived from Vincenzo Scamozzi and were used later by Roger Morris for the Palladian Bridge at Wilton. However, the most obvious descendant of Pearce's arrangement of the court is Robert Smirke's British Museum, designed a century later. Inside the Parliament House Pearce put the House of Commons in the center under the octagonal dome, while the House of Lords was given a subsidiary position across the corridor to the east. The Lords' chamber survives, with its vestibule, nave and apsidal east end, a plan resembling that of the Temple of Venus and Rome in Palladio's Book IV, Plate XXIII. The giant Corinthian order of pilasters and the smaller Ionic order may have been suggested by Palladio's San Giorgio Maggiore in Venice. Pearce's building is unquestionably one of the most brilliant designs of the 18th century, combining the best of antique, Baroque and Palladian motifs. In 1730 Pearce was appointed surveyor-general of works and fortifications in Ireland, and was knighted in 1732. It was clear he had arrived.

For something less than a decade Pearce was the leading exponent of Palladianism in Ireland. In Henrietta Street, Dublin, he built two adjoining houses, one of which resembled the house Lord Burlington built for Lord Mountrath in Great Burlington

Street in London. Pearce was probably also responsible for part of Upper Castle Yard in Dublin Castle, including the block with the centerpiece (resembling Lord Pembroke's villa in Whitehall), with an octagonal lantern and cupola derived from William Kent's *Designs of Inigo Jones* (1727).

Pearce was known in England, for he made drawings for Heydon Hall in Norfolk, designed extensions to Ashley Park near Walton in Surrey, and prepared a scheme for a large Palladian palace at Richmond for King George II. He also designed a facade for Shadwell Park in Norfolk in 1725. Pearce was assisted in much of his work by Richard Cassels, who came from Hesse-Kassel, and who was steeped in Netherlandish and French classicism derived from Palladio. However, Pearce's first collaboration was not with Cassels, but with Galilei, at Castletown, begun between 1719 and 1722. Galilei designed the main block, a great 13-window-wide, three-story Palladian building over a basement, and sketched the curving colonnades that link the house to the lower wings. Pearce worked on the designs for the colonnades and wings after 1726, and was also responsible for the two-story entrance hall and many of the other rooms. The Castletown hall was the model for many later Irish houses, including Cashel Palace, Castle Dobbs and Castle Ward.

Documentary evidence in Ireland is often infuriatingly scarce, and much of Pearce's oeuvre is attributed rather than certain. Arch House, Wilkinstown, County Meath, for example, is an early-18th-century house with a curved bow in the center and circular wings like towers, with semicircular-headed windows; it is attributed to Pearce, and has idiosyncrasies worthy of Vanbrugh. Pearce may also have played a part in the genesis of Ballyhaise House, County Cavan, for which Cassals was the executive architect.

Bellamont, Forest, Cootehill, County Cavan, was one of the finest Palladian villas in the British isles, built in 1730 for Thomas Coote, who was Pearce's uncle. The immediate antecedents of this splendid design were Palladio's Villa Capra at Vicenza and the Villa Pisani at Montagnana, although the structure is of brick with stone dressings. The exquisite interiors, and especially the modillioned cornices, have all the hallmarks of Pearce as an assured designer of great sophistication. Pearce also appears to have been involved in the design of Cabra Castle, Kingscourt, County Cavan, a Palladian house subsequently engulfed in a Gothick pile. More important was Cashel Palace in County Tipperary, begun for Archbishop Goodwin before 1729, and completed under Archbishop Theophilus Bolton; it is a seven-window-wide symmetrical composition, with a three-window-wide central breakfront. Not unlike this building was Castle Dobbs, Carrickfergus, County Antrim (ca. 1730), which contained a hall similar to that of Speaker Conolly's house at Castletown. Castle Dobbs was by Arthur Dobbs, Pearce's successor as surveyor-general, who also completed the Parliament House in 1739, and who was clearly well versed in Pearce's style. Pearce may have had a hand in the design of Cuba Court, Banagher, County Offaly, which was a perfect Irish Palladian house with a pedimented doorcase and tapering pilasters similar to Vanbrugh's work at King's Weston; the motifs were derived in turn by Vanbrugh from Michelangelo.

Desart Court, Callan, County Kilkenny (1733), a seven-window-wide Palladian composition with wings joined to the central block by surved sweeping elements, was probably designed by Pearce, although the composition of the central block owed much to the Queen's House at Greenwich by Inigo Jones. Pearce designed the two-story pedimented frontispiece with pilastered Venetian window in the upper story at Drumcondra House, County Dublin, around 1727; some of the distinguished interior work there also appears to have been designed by him. In the style of Pearce are Dundrum, County Tipperary, and the

eyecatcher at Gloster, Brosna, County Offaly, the latter for a first cousin of the architect. Pearcian themes recurred at King House, County Roscommon; Rathnally, Trim, County Meath; Lismore, Crossdoney, County Cavan; and Seafield, Donabate, County Dublin. For Hercules Rowley (who shared the representation of County Londonderry with Speaker Conolly), Pearce designed Summerhill, Enfield, County Meath, which was the most dramatic and extraordinary of all Irish Palladian mansions, around 1731. It had a massive central block with four quarter-engaged Corinthian columns set in a recess, two-story quadrants terminating in stone towers with octagonal stone domes, then end pavilions. The house had two pairs of arcaded chimney stacks similar to those of Eastbury Park in Dorset by Vanbrugh.

Pearce's plans for Palladianizing Stillorgan House in County Dublin came to nothing, but the grotto of seven domed chambers, and the obelisk on a rock-work base (the latter derived from Giovanni Lorenzo Bernini's fountain in the Piazza Navona in Rome and intended as a mausoleum for the Allen family of Stillorgan) survive to this day.

Pearce was responsible for regulating under 3 George II c.14 the sizes of bricks manufactured in Ireland, and toward the end of his life he may have designed the Southwell Schools and Almshouses in Downpatrick, County Down. There is no proof of the authorship of the Southwell Schools, but the building is a distinguished design, dating from 1733 (the year of Pearce's death), and the Southwell family's English seat was King's Weston by Pearce's cousin Vanbrugh. The wonderful brick arch at the rear of the Downpatrick ensemble looks distinctly Vanbrughian.

Pearce was a prominent Freemason, and his design for the Stillorgan mausoleum has Masonic allusions (the Allens, too, were Masons). Probably Ireland's greatest architect, Pearce died while still in his thirties, and was buried in Donnybrook church.

—JAMES STEVENS CURL

PEARSON, John Loughborough.

British. Born in England, 1817. Died in London, 1897. Son was the architect Frank Loughborough Pearson. Studied with Ignatius Bonomi, Durham. Worked briefly for Anthony Salvin and Philip C. Hardwick, from 1842. Fellow, Royal Institute of British Architects; Royal Academy; Gold Medal, Royal Institute of British Architects, 1880.

Chronology of Works
All in England unless noted
† Work no longer exists
* Approximate dates

1843-44	St. Ann's Chapel, Ellerker, Humberside
1846-48	St. Mary's Church, Ellerton, Yorkshire
1848-50	Treberfydd House and Church, Brecon, Wales
1849-50	St. Matthew's Church, Landscove, Devon
1849-52	Holy Trinity Church, Bessborough Gardens, London†
1857	Quar Wood House, Gloucestershire (much altered)
1857-59	St. Leonard's Church, Scarborough, North Yorkshire
1858-61	St. Mary's Church, Dalton Holme, Yorkshire
1860	St. Peter's Church, Daylesford, Gloucestershire
1860-64	St. Peter's Church, Vauxhall, London
1863-66	Christ Church, Appleton-le-Moors, Yorkshire
1866-68	St. John the Evangelist Church, Sutton Veny, Wiltshire
1868	Roundwick House, Sussex

1868-73	St. Mary's Church, Vicarage and School, Freeland, Oxfordshire
1871-77*	St. Augustine's Church, Kilburn, London (spire 1897-98)
1874-78	St. John's Church, Holborn, London
1876-85	St. Michael's Church, Croydon, London
1878-97	Truro Cathedral, Cornwall (completed in 1910)
1879-81	St. Alban's Church, Bordesley, Birmingham
1882-84	St. George's Church, Cullercoats, Northumberland
1883-85	St. Agnes' Church, Sefton Park, Liverpool
1884-85	St. Bartholomew's Church, Thurstaston, Cheshire
1887ff.	Brisbane Cathedral, Queensland, Australia (with Frank Loughborough Pearson)
1892-95	2 Temple Place (former Astor Estate Office), Westminster, London
1895-97	St. Theodore's Church, Port Talbot, Glamorgan, Wales

Publications

BOOKS ABOUT PEARSON

DIXON, ROGER, and MUTHESIUS, STEFAN: *Victorian Architecture*. New York and Toronto, 1978.

FAWCETT, JANE (ed.): *Seven Victorian Architects*. University Park, Pennsylvania, 1976.

CLARKE, BASIL F. L.: *Church Builders of the Nineteenth Century*. London, 1938.

QUINEY, ANTHONY: *John Loughborough Pearson*. New Haven, Connecticut, and London, 1979.

ARTICLES ABOUT PEARSON

"The Late Mr. J. L. Pearson, R. A., and His Work." *Builder* 73 (1897): 514.

"The Late John Loughborough Pearson, R. A." *Journal of the Royal Institute of British Architects* Series 3, 5 (1897-98): 113-121.

NEWBERRY, J. ERNEST: "The Work of John L. Pearson, R. A." *Architectural Review* 1 (1897): 1-11, 69-82.

*

John Loughborough Pearson, during his apprenticeship and the early years of his practice, began a serious study of A. W. N. Pugin's architectural philosophy. This study led him to embrace the Gothic style enthusiastically. Interestingly, however, Pearson's Gothic was always tempered with a concern for proportion that he had developed during his classical training in the offices of Ignatius Bonomi, Anthony Salvin, and Philip Hardwick. Although Pearson was responsible for a number of country house designs, notably Treberfydd House in Breconshire and Quar Wood in Gloucestershire, his fame was made primarily by his churches in the neo-Gothic style.

Pearson's experiments during that first decade of practice led him to an understanding of architectural space and form that is rare in any age. He learned how to design churches that were visually solid and satisfying without depending on ornament or unessential buttressing; he also learned how to apply classical proportional systems, particularly the golden section, to Gothic design.

In 1857, with the design for the Church of St. Leonard in Scarborough, North Yorkshire, Pearson entered a new phase of his career. This middle period of Pearson's work was a mature High Victorian phase that lasted until 1870.

Pearson's High Victorian manner was quite different from that of most of his contemporaries. He had no "rogue" tendencies at all; he was much more interested in producing harmonious visual combinations than in being novel or surprising. (Throughout his life his work was characterized by restraint, never by excess.) He used constructional polychromy subtly and sparingly, usually to differentiate structural parts rather than to add pattern. He used decoration lavishly, but he always contrasted it with plain areas; his decoration was more likely to be sculptural and architectural than planar applied work. He utilized High Victorian heavy massing of building components. He never allowed masses to collide, but instead composed and integrated them into a classically ordered composition.

Pearson's masterpiece of the middle period of his career was the church of St. Peter, Vauxhall (1860-64). His earlier churches had all had English plans, and their forms and details had been an interesting stylistic mixture of English Decorated and French Early Gothic styles. In contrast, St. Peter's plan and form are Romanesque, and Italian Romanesque at that!

The church has much in common with G. E. Street's Church of St. James the Less, designed in 1859. Both reflect Italian influence, both are constructed of polychromatic brick, both have interior arcades supported by stumpy circular columns with elaborately, boldly carved capitals, and both use interior painted decoration. Street's church has a detached campanile; Pearson's campanile has been attached very gingerly, with its base joined to the west end of the north aisle wall. Street used a plethora of exterior buttresses for strength and vigor; Pearson eliminated most buttresses in favor of simpler, calmer geometric volumes. The polychromy of St. Peter's is much more restrained than in Street's St. James the Less, but the geometry of the various compositional elements is much stronger and simpler.

The interior of St. Peter's is as powerful and bold as the exterior. St. Peter's combines nave and chancel into a single space and is brick-vaulted throughout. The vaulting there represented Pearson's new commitment to vaulted construction—a commitment that resulted in a series of subsequent vaulted church designs. The visual strength of the brick walls and vaults and the proportions of the spaces give St. Peter's a power and spaciousness that is exceptional. (The proportions throughout the church are based upon the golden section, a ratio of 1:1.6.)

St. Peter's, in its proportioning, planning and vaulting, was a High Victorian prototype for Pearson's Late Victorian churches of the 1870s and 1880s. In these churches Pearson substituted elegance and refinement for St. Peter's boldness and muscularity, but the basic elements that characterized his late work were fully developed in this High Victorian masterpiece. More important in Pearson's development was the discovery made at St. Peter's that a church without much ornament or unessential buttressing could be made to satisfy the most demanding High Victorian critics by combining classical proportioning principles with Gothic design.

The finest work of Pearson's Late Victorian period, St. Augustine, Kilburn Park (1871-77), is, in many ways, the culmination of the experimentation of the previous decade-and-a-half. It is bold, vigorous and richly decorated in the High Victorian manner; yet it possesses a space as complex, majestic, elegant and sublime as any Late Victorian church.

In St. Augustine's, Pearson applied the best characteristics of his earlier churches. There, however, a crispness of parts and edges, and a simplification of forms, replaced the brutal muscularity of Vauxhall. As at Vauxhall, the main body of the church is extremely tall and unbuttressed. Pearson liked sheer walls of brick. Kilburn Park's brick walls are largely monochromatic; the strongly polychromatic diapering of Vauxhall is gone, and the stone dressing is very restrained. The power of the exterior of this church comes not from unorthodox elements, elaborate decoration or constructional polychromy, but from the projection and recession of its major form components.

The great glory of St. Augustine, Kilburn Park, is its interior, however. Pearson used a totally new plan for the church. It is a Latin-cross plan with double aisles, all vaulted. The inner aisles carry galleries. The divisions between the bays of the galleries are wall piers that help absorb the thrust of the major vaults by functioning as interior buttresses. The galleries continue through the transepts (the wall piers change to the slenderest imaginable piers there), establishing the nave and chancel as one great continuously vaulted space. The galleries bridge this space, establishing a rood screen at the entrance to the choir. Light floods in from the transepts to illumine the rood screen. From the nave it is possible to see through the gallery arcades into the spaces of the transepts, suggesting a spatial complexity belied by the simplicity of the major space. The effect is wonderful; the space is as baroque in its richness and complexity as any in English architectural history.

St. Augustine's was the logical culmination of the experiments in spatial interpenetration and classical proportioning that characterized Pearson's early work. In it Pearson established himself as a master of spatial design. Handsome, carefully proportioned space was the hallmark of Pearson's churches throughout his career. There is no question, however, that elegance and restraint, and slender, attenuated forms had replaced the bold, muscular forms of the churches discussed above. In St. Augustine's, Pearson's genius is clearly revealed in a church that combines the boldness of the High Victorian era with the sensitivity of the Late Victorian era. This church represents the artistic zenith of his career; with it he establish himself as the preeminent church architect in England in the 1870s.

—C. MURRAY SMART, JR.

PEI, I. M.

American. Born Ieoh Ming Pei 26 April 1917, in Canton, China; immigrated to the United States, 1935; naturalized, 1954. Married Eileen Loo, 1942; four children. Studied at Massachusetts Institute of Technology, Cambridge, B.Arch., 1940; studied with Walter Gropius at Harvard Graduate School of Design, Cambridge, Massachusetts, M.Arch., 1946. Served on the National Defense Research Committee, 1943-45. Instructor, then assistant professor, Harvard Graduate School of Design, 1945-48; director of architecture, Webb and Knapp Inc., New York, 1948-55; partner, I. M. Pei and Partners, since 1955 (Pei Cobb Freed and Partners, with Henry N. Cobb and James Ingo Freed, since 1989). Pritzker Prize, 1983.

Chronology of Works
All in the United States unless noted

1952-56	Mile High Center, Denver, Colorado
1953-61	Town Center Plaza (stage I), Washington, D.C.
1954-63	Henry R. Luce Chapel, Taunghai University, Taida, Taiwan
1957-62	Kips Bay Plaza, New York City
1959-64	Green Center for the Earth Sciences, Massachusetts Institute of Technology, Cambridge, Massachusetts
1960-61	Government Center, Boston, Massachusetts
1960-70	National Airlines Terminal, Kennedy International Airport, New York City
1961-64	School of Journalism, Newhouse Communications Center, Syracuse University, Syracuse, New York
1961-66	University Plaza, New York University, New York City
1961-67	National Center for Atmospheric Research, Boulder, Colorado
1964-79	John Fitzgerald Kennedy Library, Boston, Massachusetts
1964-70	Dreyfus Chemistry Building, Massachusetts Institute of Technology, Cambridge, Massachusetts
1966-68	Des Moines Art Center, Des Moines, Iowa (addition)
1966-69	Bedford-Stuyvesant Superblock, Brooklyn, New York
1966-71	Cleo Rogers Memorial Library, Columbus, Ohio
1966-77	Municipal Center, Dallas, Texas
1967-70	Air Traffic Control Tower, Federal Aviation Agency (standardized model for various airports in the U.S.)
1967-73	Canadian Imperial Bank of Commerce Complex, Toronto, Canada
1968	Everson Museum of Art, Syracuse, New York
1968-72	Mellon Art Center, Choate School, Wallingford, Connecticut
1968-73	Herbert F. Johnson Museum of Art, Cornell University, Ithaca, New York
1968-78	National Gallery of Art, Washington, D.C. (east wing)
1970	Columbia University Master Plan, New York City
1970	Wilmington Tower, Wilmington, Delaware
1970-76	Overseas-Chinese Banking Corporation Headquarters, Singapore, China
1972-76	Ralph Landau Chemical Engineering Building, Massachusetts Institute of Technology, Cambridge, Massachusetts
1977-81	Museum of Fine Arts, Boston, Massachusetts (west wing)
1977-84	IBM Office Building, Purchase, New York
1978-82	Texas Commerce Tower/United Energy Plaza, Houston, Texas
1978-84	Wiesner Building, Massachusetts Institute of Technology, Cambridge, Massachusetts
1979	Art Museum, Indiana University, Bloomington, Indiana
1979-82	Fragrant Hill Hotel, Beijing, China
1981-92	Mt. Sinai Medical Center, New York City (modernization: Phase I, 1981-89; Phase II, 1989-92)
1982-89	Meyerson Symphony Center, Dallas, Texas
1982-89	Bank of China, Hong Kong
1983-	Le Grand Louvre (including the Pyramide), Paris, France (expansion: Phase I, 1983-89; Phase II, 1989-)
1986-89	Creative Artists Agency Headquarters, Beverly Hills, California
1986-89	Rosemary Hall Science Center, Choate School, Wallingford, Connecticut
1988-90	Sinji Shumeikai Bell Tower, Shiga, Japan
1989-	Regent Hotel, New York City

Publications

ARTICLES BY PEI

"The Nature of Urban Space." In HARRY S. RANSOM (ed.): *The People's Architects.* Chicago, 1964.

"The Two Worlds of Architecture." *American Institute of Architects Journal* (July 1979).

I. M. Pei: Pyramide, Le Grand Louvre, Paris, France, 1983-

BOOKS ABOUT PEI

McLANATHAN, RICHARD (compiler): *East Building, National Gallery of Art: A Profile*. Washington, D.C., 1978.
SUNER, BRUNO: *Ieoh Ming Pei*. Paris, 1988.
WISEMAN, CARTER: *I. M. Pei, A Profile in American Architecture*. New York, 1990.

ARTICLES ABOUT PEI

"About I. M. Pei." *Architecture* (August/September 1981).
American Institute of Architects Journal, special issue (June 1979).
"I. M. Pei Speaking." *Interiors* (July 1980).
"I. M. Pei and Partners." *Architecture Plus* (February 1973).
"Paeans for Pei." *Progressive Architecture* (October 1963).
"Pei Cobb Freed and Partners: Changes for Survival." *Architecture* (February 1990).
"The Third Way: The Architecture of I. M. Pei." *Connaissance des arts* (June 1982).

*

In an age when many architects articulate complex theories of architecture to explain their buildings, I. M. Pei stands out as a notable exception to this trend. As one of the most prolific architects of our time, Pei permits his forms to speak for themselves. His insistently rational, highly sculptural forms have much to say.

The evolution of Pei's career can be divided into three stages of development: his early career with developer William Zeckendorf; his national recognition after receiving the commission for the John F. Kennedy Library; and the Grand Louvre project, which secured his place as one of the foremost architects of his time. Pei's works illustrate his devotion to simple, geometrical forms as well as his meticulous attention to materials and ornamental details. His attention to the individuality and uniqueness of each project, and his sensitivity to the intended use of the structure and site of every design, makes it difficult for us to reduce an understanding of his work to an investigation of his style.

Pei left China in 1935 to study architecture in the United States. After a short stay at the University of Pennsylvania, he went on to the Massachusetts Institute of Technology, where he majored in architectural engineering and graduated in 1940. World War II and the subsequent postwar revolution in China prevented him from returning home. Instead, he began his graduate studies at Harvard, but soon departed to serve with the National Defense Research Committee. In 1944 he returned to the Graduate School of Design at Harvard to study with Walter Gropius and Marcel Breuer. Though at MIT he had gained a firm understanding of advanced technology, it was really at Harvard that Pei was taught the "form-follows-function" tenets of modernism. Not unlike many of his contemporaries, Pei absorbed the Bauhaus idealism and architectural sterility advocated by Breuer and Gropius. Its influence remains evident in even his most mature work.

After completing his master's degree in 1948, Pei was hired by real estate developer William Zeckendorf to work for the architectural division of his contracting firm, Webb and Knapp, Inc. In New York, Pei was immediately thrust into the world of big business, and was given the unusual opportunity to work on large-scale, big-budget projects right at the start of his career. One of his earliest projects, the Gulf Oil Building in Atlanta

(1950-52), shows how even on a small budget Pei could manipulate expensive materials to create the illusion of luxury. In order to give the building a corporate presence, Pei attached nonstructural slabs of marble to the frame of the building, a technique he would use extensively in the East Building of the National Gallery. Although Pei's design for the building was a flat Miesian box, he used the marble veneer to create a prestigious image without going over budget.

Pei's association with Zeckendorf introduced him to large-scale urban revitalization projects such as Mile High Center in Denver (1952-56), the Town Center Plaza in Washington, D.C. (1953-61), and the Kips Bay Plaza in New York (1957-62). In all of these projects, Pei considered the cities as an integrated unit. His sensitivity to how buildings would relate to their site and the entire urban framework became one of Pei's trademarks.

While working at Webb and Knapp, Pei became acquainted with the three architects who would later become partners in his own firm, Henry N. Cobb, Eason H. Leonard and James Ingo Freed. In 1960 Pei formally established I. M. Pei and Associates. This move marked his withdrawal from the Webb and Knapp firm and gave him the independence to build a strong reputation of his own.

Due to his association with Zeckendorf, Pei was initially somewhat shunned by the world of high design. It was only after his break with Zeckendorf and the completion of projects such as the National Center for Atmospheric Research in Colorado (1961-67) that he assuredly began to gain recognition for his unique design style. In the National Center for Atmospheric Research, Pei attempted to integrate architecture and science. This was the first building Pei worked on that was not surrounded by other structures but was instead enclosed within a dramatic natural setting. Pei chose to design a complex of forms which would echo the powerful silhouette of the adjacent mountain peaks rather than compete with them. In order to achieve a greater harmony between environment and architecture, Pei eliminated many conventional scale-defining details and had the concrete mixed with stone quarried from the bordering peaks. These adjustments permitted the buildings to blend visually with their surroundings without being dwarfed by them.

It was the John F. Kennedy Library in Boston (1964-79) that gave Pei the national recognition he had been seeking. Pei's ability to persevere throughout the 15-year construction period tested his ability to be both architect and diplomat. The project went through three different designs and three different sites before its eventual completion. The original proposal included an 85-foot-high truncated glass pyramid, which was ultimately modified. This marked the first use of a form that would remain a constant in his work through the pinnacle of his career in the Louvre project. The finished project shows Pei's developing interest in combining fine materials, bold sculptural forms and elegant interiors. Other projects completed during that period, such as the Dallas Municipal Administration Center (1966-77), illustrate Pei's struggle to balance the relationship between the powerful, abstract forms and the humanitarian component necessary for a public building.

The Kennedy Library and the Dallas Municipal Center represent critical works in the evolution of Pei's architectural idiom, but it is the East Building of the National Gallery in Washington, D.C. (1968-78), that illustrates his mature style. At the time he was commissioned, Pei was already quite experienced in museum design. He had completed the Des Moines Art Center Addition in Iowa (1968), the Johnson Museum of Art at Cornell University (1973) and the Everson Museum in Syracuse, New York (1968). In each, Pei created a unique architectural statement sensitive to its site and to surrounding structures—an important aspect of the East Building project. Pei's design for the building seems to have come in a single stroke of genius. One line divided the trapezoidal plot of land into two triangles. The larger isosceles triangle would house the museum and would share a central east-west axis with the existing building by John Russell Pope. The right triangle would serve as the Center for Advanced Study in the Visual Arts.

In order to unify two seemingly divergent structures (Pope's neoclassical with Pei's modern design), the architect employed both physical and conceptual means. Physically, the buildings share a similar east-west axis, underground concourse level, aboveground plaza and pink Tennessee marble from the same quarries. The genius of Pei's design lies in his subtle sensitivity to site. A similar sensitivity underlies the relationship between the architecture and the artworks inside the museum. The manner in which Pei parallels the hierarchy of spatial distribution from Pope's design permits the architecture of both buildings, although stylistically different, to function harmoniously. This vision, combined with the fine craftsmanship, luxurious materials and the dramatic composition of the masses (with their 19-degree angle on the west end of the study center), has made the East Building the most celebrated of all Pei's works.

It was perhaps Pei's success at the National Gallery that made him a prime candidate for what he would later call "the most important project of his life," the expansion of the Louvre Museum in Paris. During this project, the Grand Louvre Phase I Cour Napoleon and Richelieu Wing Connections (1983-89), Pei encountered all of the problems that existed in previous projects regarding style, site and materials. But there was one significant new feature to be considered there: "*l'esprit du Louvre*." Influenced by 17th-century French landscape design, Pei devised an image that would be both modern and classical in its simplicity—a large pyramidal glass entrance. Although the underground renovations were more costly and extensive than the courtyard, it was the pyramid that received all of the criticism in the press. Despite the initial attack (Charles Jencks labeled Pei a "megalomaniac"), Pei's pyramid would soon become as the Eiffel Tower before it, part of the Parisian tradition of controversial but popular urban structures.

In the fall of 1989, Pei's firm was renamed Pei, Cobb, Freed and Partners. This modification was executed in order to recognize the substantial talent of his partners Henry Cobb and James Freed, who were, respectively, the primary architects for the John Hancock Tower in Boston (1966-76) and the Jacob Javits Convention Center in New York City (1979-86). In addition, this move gave Pei the opportunity to delegate business responsibilities and enabled him to pursue smaller projects on his own. The Sinji Shumeikai Bell Tower in Shiga, Japan (1988-90), illustrates this shift to a more personal architecture. It contains the rigorous geometry typical of Pei, but it also embodies a spiritual quality not apparent in his earlier structures. This new fusion between sculptural forms and increasingly personal designs will doubtlessly be an important feature of Pei's future works.

—LISA VIGNUOLO

PELLI, Cesar.

American. Born 12 October 1926, in Tucuman, Argentina; immigrated to the United States, 1952; naturalized, 1964. Married Diana Balmori, 1950. Studied at the University of Tucuman, 1944-49, Dip.Arch; University of Illinois, Urbana-Champaign,

Cesar Pelli: Pacific Design Center, Los Angeles, California, 1972

1952-54, M.S.Arch. Associate architect, Eero Saarinen and Associates, Bloomfield Hills, Michigan, and Hamden, Connecticut, 1954-64; director of design, DWJM, Los Angeles, 1964-68; partner for design, Gruen Associates, Los Angeles, 1968-76; principal, Cesar Pelli and Associates, New Haven, Connecticut, since 1977. Dean of the School of Architecture, Yale University, New Haven, 1977-84; has taught extensively in the United States and South America.

Chronology of Works
All in the United States unless noted

1966	Worldway Postal Center, Los Angeles, California
1967	COMSAT Laboratories, Clarksburg, Maryland
1967	Kukai Gardens Housing, Honolulu, Hawaii
1969	City Hall, San Bernardino, California
1970	Commons and Courthouse Center, Columbus, Indiana
1972	Pacific Design Center, Los Angeles, California (expansions, 1984)
1972	United States Embassy, Tokyo, Japan
1975	Rainbow Center and Winter Garden, Niagara Falls, New York
1977-84	Museum of Modern Art, New York (residential tower and museum renovation)
1980	Cleveland Clinic, Cleveland, Ohio
1981-87	World Financial Center and Winter Garden, New York City
1982-84	Herring Hall, Rice University, Houston, Texas
1984	Mattatuck Museum, Waterbury, Connecticut
1985	Boyer Center for Molecular Medicine, Yale University, New Haven, Connecticut
1985-89	Norwest Center, Minneapolis, Minnesota
1986	Canary Wharf Tower, Retail and Assembly Building, Light Rail Station, London, England
1987	Nationsbank Corporate Center and Founders Hall, Charlotte, North Carolina
1987	Performing Arts Center, Charlotte, North Carolina
1987-90	Carnegie Hall Tower, New York City
1989	Law and Business Schools Center, Wake Forest University, Winston-Salem, North Carolina
1989	Frances Lehman Loeb Art Museum, Vassar College, Poughkeepsie, New York
1989	Physics and Astronomy Building, University of Washington, Seattle, Washington
1989	Mathematics Building, Institute for Advanced Study, Princeton, New Jersey
1990	NTT Corporate Headquarters, Tokyo, Japan
1991	Ohio Center for the Performing Arts, Cincinnati, Ohio

Publications

ARTICLES BY PELLI

"Open Line City." *Progressive Architecture* (June 1970).
"Third Generation Architects." *Architecture and Urbanism* (March 1971).
"Four Days in May." *Architecture and Urbanism* (September 1974).
"Transparency: Physical and Perceptual." *Architecture and Urbanism* (November 1976).
"Conversation: Cesar Pelli on Architectural Technology." *Architectural Record* (August 1979).

"My Favorite Building: The Crystal Palace." *Architecture and Urbanism* (February 1980).

"Skyscrapers." *Perspecta* (January 1982).

"Architectural Form and the Tradition of Building." *Via* (November 1984).

BOOKS ABOUT PELLI

GANDELSONAS, MARIO, and PASTIER, JOHN (eds.): *Cesar Pelli: Buildings and Projects 1965-1990*. New York, 1990.

ARTICLES ABOUT PELLI

Architecture and Urbanism, special issues (March 1971; November 1976; July 1985; February 1990).

"Cesar Pelli/Gruen Associates." *Global Architecture* No. 59 (Tokyo, 1981).

"A New Phase of Cesar Pelli." *Space Design*, special issue (September 1980).

*

As a contemporary and very active architect, Cesar Pelli's contributions to architectural history are still being established and interpreted. Nevertheless, the impact of this Argentinean-born architect on modern architecture worldwide is evident from his large number of commissions. Many critics have not only acknowledged the integrity and quality of his buildings, but also have observed that Cesar Pelli is one of the few architects whose words seem to match his actions.

In Pelli's architectural discourse, two critical issues emerge. First, he maintains an interest in the materials appropriate to modern building. The modern structure, supported by a steel cage, requires only a lightweight cladding to cover the frame. Pelli has primarily explored the use of glass to express the function of an envelope enclosing the building. In the 1980s, however, more of his buildings explored the possibilities of glass and stone cladding. Second, Pelli is concerned with the role of the building in the context of the city. For Pelli, buildings are not isolated objects meant only to be self-referential, they are part of a larger social and urban context—buildings are what create cities. Therefore, the architect has a responsibility to try to create architecture that is sensitive to its site and its larger urban environment.

While Pelli's interest in materials and new building techniques place him firmly in the context of modernism, his sensitivity to the urban context of architecture also makes him sympathetic to postmodern ideology. In trying to describe and categorize architects like Pelli, critics coined the term "neomodern," or "late modern." The neomodern architect remains true to the technology and materials of modernism, while adding to the vocabulary of modern building forms. Pelli's modern interests, including "speaking" architecture, truth to materials and construction, and variations on the Miesian "glass box," are combined with his concern for the urban fabric. However, Pelli criticizes postmodern architects who subscribe to arbitrary eclecticism and artistic signature to define their works. Rather, he believes that the position of the building in the architect's oeuvre must be subordinate to the position of the building in the context of the city.

One of Pelli's most famous buildings, the Pacific Design Center, which he designed in 1972 while at Gruen Associates, has been labeled both modern and postmodern. The center, located in West Hollywood, has been nicknamed the "Blue Whale" for its enormous size, shape and coloring. The Design Center's requirement for large design display areas was answered by Pelli in the long horizontal structure. The bright color and shape of the building, which resembles a molding used in interior design, reflect the function of the Design Center. The steel frame, sheathed in glass, effectively clothes the building while not visually or physically weighing it down. The bright blue, opaque glass was created by fusing colored ceramic tile to the glass, creating a relatively inexpensive and durable product.

In 1984 Pelli's architectural firm, Cesar Pelli and Associates, began an expansion of the Pacific Design Center. The unique nature of the original structure required a unique solution. Pelli designed two equally unusual shapes, one an upside-down pyramid, and the other an irregular slice of an oval. Pelli used the same opaque glass to sheathe the new structures, but varied the color. The additions rest on a plinth of blue glass matching the original "Blue Whale." The volumetric purity of each form and the modular grid of the skins unify the three buildings. This complex exemplifies Pelli's interest in "speaking" architecture: the bright colors and shapes appropriately express the design function.

The additions to the Pacific Design Center were executed by Pelli's current firm, which was established in New Haven following his acceptance of the position of dean at the Yale School of Architecture in 1977. Shortly after his move to the East Coast, Pelli was selected to be the design architect for the renovation, expansion and residential tower at the Museum of Modern Art in New York City. The commission was accompanied by a number of restrictions and requirements, including the accommodation of the existing museum structure, the visual integration of the tower into the surrounding skyline, and the creation of a new museum space to match the growing international prominence of the museum.

The most striking components of Pelli's solution are the glass-enclosed Garden Hall and his residential tower. The open glass Garden Hall creates both a visual and functional connection between the floors of the museum. The escalators to connect the museum space between floors are located in this glass hall. All the floors are given a full view of the sculpture courtyard, breaking down the barriers between the exterior and the interior, and expanding the exhibition space to the outside.

The design of the residential tower reflects Pelli's concern for the cladding and materials of modern buildings. While still utilizing glass to cover the steel frame, Pelli created an exterior of multicolored ceramic glass and tinted vision glass. The 11 colors of ceramic glass, in brownish grays and blues, were selected to relate to the colors of midtown Manhattan. Thus, while the tower is essentially a modern "glass box," Pelli integrated the structure into its surroundings by his use of color. Without moving away from the materials of modernism, he created a more sensitive building aesthetic.

This new aesthetic is most powerfully stated in his towers for the World Financial Center in the Battery Park City development. The varying heights of the towers stand out against the towers of the neighboring World Trade Center, enhancing the skyline. For Pelli, the city is a work of art to which each architect is responsible and skyscrapers are public monuments because they contribute to the cityscape. By making his buildings shorter, he has given perspective and scale to the height of the World Trade Center towers. The thin membranes of Pelli's towers are a grid of flame-finished granite and glass. This exterior grid expresses the modular grid system of the office spaces contained in the buildings. The proportion of granite to glass in the skins gradually decreases with the buildings' height. This effect, combined with the stepped setbacks of the buildings, creates the illusion of increasing lightness. Copper tops in a variety of shapes crown each building.

Pelli's many other buildings and projects continue this search for new materials and new expressions, which is always tempered by his consideration for the context of the city and the site. The Norwest Center in Minneapolis (1985-89), Herring Hall (1982-84) and Ley Student Center (1984-86) at Rice University, Carnegie Tower (1987-90) and plans for skyscrapers in Chicago reflect Pelli's diversity, sensitivity to site and willingness to explore new options for architecture.

—MELISSA CARD

PERCIER and FONTAINE.

French. Charles Percier born in Paris, France, 22 August 1764; died in Paris, 5 September 1838. Pierre-François-Léonard Fontaine born 1762; died 1853. Both studied at the Ecole des Beaux-Arts. Formed a professional partnership which lasted from 1792 until 1815, with the death of Napoleon Bonaparte. Firm was named Architectes du Louvre et des Tuileries, 1804. Percier taught architecture at the Ecole des Beaux-Arts, 1815-38. Fontaine continued to work privately as an architect, 1815 until his retirement in 1848.

Chronology of Works
All in France

1802ff. Rue de Rivoli buildings, and other projects for unifying the Louvre and the Tuileries palaces
1816-26 Chapelle Expiatoire, Paris (Fontaine)

1829 Palais Royale, Paris (Fontaine; restoration and addition of the Galérie d'Orleans)

Publications

BOOKS BY PERCIER and FONTAINE

Palais, maisons, et autres édifices modernes, dessinés à Rome. Paris, 1798.
Recueil de decorations executées dans l'église Notre Dame et au Champs-de-Mars. Paris, 1807.
Choix des plus célèbres maisons de plaisance de Rome et de ses environs. Paris, 1809-13.
Recueil des décorations intérieures. Paris, 1812.
Résidences des souverains. Paris, 1833.

BOOKS ABOUT PERCIER and FONTAINE

BIVER, M. L.: *Pierre Fontaine, premier architecte de l'empereur.* Paris, 1964.
DUPORTAL, J.: *Charles Percier.* 1931.
FOUCHÉ, M.: *Percier et Fontaine.* 1904.
HAUTECOEUR, LOUIS: *Histoire de l'architecture classique en France.* Paris, 1953.

ARTICLES ABOUT PERCIER and FONTAINE

BOYER, F.: ''Charles Percier, documents inédits.'' *Bulletin de la Société de l'Histoire de l'Art Français* (1962).

Percier and Fontaine: Arc du Carrousel, Paris, France, 1806-08

Charles Percier and Pierre-François-Léonard Fontaine formed a professional partnership in 1792 based on a friendship from their student days at the École des Beaux-Arts. Percier was an introverted, meticulous personality who excelled at decoration and interior design. Fontaine complemented Percier in terms of character and profession: he was the public figure who handled the business aspect of the partnership, and his expertise was the structural aspect of buildings. Their collaboration lasted from 1792, when they started on Parisian set designs, until 1815, the end of the reign of their principal patron, Napoleon I. Afterward, Percier taught architecture at the École des Beaux-Arts until his death in 1838. Fontaine continued to be the *premier architecte* for Louis XVIII, Charles X and Louis-Philippe, until his retirement in 1848.

Percier and Fontaine were famous for the "Empire style" of interior design, which they disseminated within France by refurbishing the palaces at Fontainebleau, Strasbourg and Versailles, among others. It quickly became the official court style throughout Europe, attracting the attention of sovereigns such as Frederick William III of Prussia and Czar Alexander I of Russia. The relative simplicity of the characteristic shrunken ornament on a blank rectangular field of wall or fabric appealed to post-Revolution taste, which shunned the complexity of Rococo arabesque line. The opulence of Percier and Fontaine's interior design lay in their use of colors such as olive green, gold and red, as seen in their work for Empress Josephine at Malmaison in 1802. Antique motifs were placed on brightly colored walls, fabrics and furniture, speaking of the personality of the patron and the purpose of the room. In a "Bed designed for Monsieur T., Paris," taken from their collection of interior-design projects, *Recueils de décorations intérieures* (1812), a militaristic theme is incorporated into a neoclassical decorative vocabulary, with a painted frieze of animal hunting. Also, a bow and arrow hold up the tent-like drapery of the bed. The ornaments for the studio of Jean-Baptiste Isabey (a famed miniaturist) "refer to the arts associated with drawing, identifying the inclinations and talents of the eminent artist for whom they were executed": allegorical figures of Painting, Architecture, Sculpture and Engraving decorate wooden pilasters in the Etruscan style, and a frieze of figures of Fame with garlanded medallions of famous artists lines the upper walls.

Percier and Fontaine's application of neoclassical motifs to interior decoration is relatively superficial in its interest in the appearance of the antique, especially when one considers the moral quality associated with earlier neoclassical works, such as the early paintings of Jacques Louis David. Yet like David, Percier and Fontaine adapted the "revolutionary" style of the previous generation to fit Napoleon's aesthetic, which was based on imperial Roman architecture. As students, Percier and Fontaine were influenced by Etienne Louis Boullée's idea of the sublime in architecture, as is evident from their winning projects for the Prix de Rome in 1785 and 1786. Additionally, Fontaine had immediate exposure to the theory and practice of Claude-Nicolas Ledoux when he aided the older architect with the Barrières project in 1790. Using the Imperial Roman and Italian Renaissance architectural vocabulary they had studied in Italy, Percier and Fontaine were able to transform Boullée's sublimity and Ledoux's creativity into an architecture of grandeur that suited Napoleon's taste, yet often was too expensive to execute. This was the case for the project of the Palace of the King of Rome (Napoleon's son) on the Chaillot hill in Paris, as well as the unification of the Louvre and Tuileries Palace, a problem which plagued them for 30 years.

In their written works, Percier and Fontaine insisted on the interdependence of architecture and decoration. In the *Recueils,* they stated, "The construction of buildings is analogous to the human skeleton. It must be embellished without being completed masked. Construction, according to the country, climate, and type of building dictates the ornamental motif. Construction and decoration therefore are interconnected." Empire style interior decoration does articulate the structural forms of a room more than the amorphous filigree style of the Rococo interior, against which Percier and Fontaine rebelled. In architecture, Percier and Fontaine worked in the neoclassical mode, taking into consideration the problems of cultural and geographic limitations in "construction." In this way, their theory is inherently flexible because it resisted the literalness of Pierre Vignon's brand of neoclassicism, seen in the Madeleine. Consequently, Percier and Fontaine have been labeled as "liberal classicists" because by respecting the contemporary context of their architecture, they avoided the redundancies of neoclassical architecture that replicated antique prototypes.

The theories set forth in the writings of Percier and Fontaine found expression in the Arc du Carrousel in Paris (1806-08). Based on the Arch of Septimius Severus in Rome, the monument commemorates Napoleon's victory at Austerlitz. It is one of the two executed works or Percier and Fontaine's project to unite the palatial complexes of the Louvre and Tuileries. Standing just outside the *cour d'honneur* of the Tuileries, it was meant to mark the entrance of that palace and to be a terminus for a new street aligned with the axes of both palaces. Flat relief decoration depicting battle events covers the entire surface, while columns in red marble emphasize the skeletal construction of the arch. The attic is decorated with reliefs as well, and statues of soldiers of the Grand Armée continue the vertical line of the columns below, relieving the monument of the horizontal heaviness of the attic. Similarly, the proliferation of surface decoration lightens the monument. In contrast, Jean François Chalgrin's Arc de Triomphe emphasizes the perpendicularity of attic versus arch and piers, and isolates the surface relief upon a plain ashlar masonry wall. Consequently, the Arc du Carrousel is reminiscent of Percier and Fontaine's furniture designs. Napoleon himself likened the monument to a pavilion rather than to a triumphal arch.

The other completed project linked to the unification of the Louvre and the Tuileries palaces was the Rue de Rivoli buildings of 1802. The sublimity of the repetition of forms inspired by Boullée was produced by a ground-level arcade with six additional stories. The street was a model for future urban projects in Paris in the 19th century and beyond in its emphasis on repetition as a means to achieve urban grandeur.

The elevation of the Palace for the King of Rome on the Chaillot hill is akin to Boullée's designs for a Temple of Peace atop a hill. The grandiose project was never executed because of the expense of its execution. It was to have been a Parisian, Beaux-Arts version of Versailles, encompassing a palace for Napoleon's son, the future king of Rome, on the right bank, mirrored by a military school complex on the left bank. In a watercolor of the palace by Fontaine, the repetition of levels of colonnades crowning a succession of entrance ramps recalls the scale of Boullée's unexecuted projects and the grandeur of Roman architecture as seen in the Temple of Fortune at Palestrina.

In 1816 Percier and Fontaine ended their collaboration. As Percier disseminated "liberal classicism" to a large number of students at the École des Beaux-Arts, Fontaine continued his professional career. Fontaine's most notable works include the Chapelle Expiatoire (1816-26) and the restoration of the Palais Royale for Louis-Philippe, which included the addition of the Galérie d'Orléans in 1829, the earliest arcaded space to have a glass barrel vault.

—CYNTHIA ELMAS

PERRAULT, Claude.

French. Born in Paris, France, 25 September 1613. Died in Paris, 9 October 1688. Brother of the writer Charles Perrault. Trained as a physician. Practiced medicine in Paris; conducted scientific research as a member of the new Académie des Sciences, from 1666; appointed by Colbert to prepare a translation of Vitruvius, 1666.

Chronology of Works
All in France

1667-70   The Louvre, Paris (east facade)
1667-69   Observatoire, Paris
1669   Arc de Triomphe, Paris (not completed)

Publications

BOOKS BY PERRAULT

Mémoires pour servir à l'histoire naturelle des animaux. Paris, 1671.
Les dix livres d'architecture de Vitruve, corrigez et traduits nouvellement en français avec des notes et des figures. Paris, 1673.
Abrégé des dix livres d'architecture de Vitruve. Paris, 1674. English edition: *An Abridgment of the Architecture of Vitruvius.* London, 1692.
Essais de physique, ou recueil de plusieurs traitez touchant les choses naturelles. 4 vols. Paris, 1680-88.
Ordonnance des cinq espèces de colonnes selon la méthode des anciens. Paris, 1683.
Recueil de plusieurs machines de nouvelle invention. Paris, 1700.
Oeuvres diverses de physique et de mécanique de MMs C. et P. Perrault. Leyden, 1721.
Voyage à Bordeaux. Edited by Paul Bonnefon. Paris, 1909.

BOOKS ABOUT PERRAULT

HALLAYS, A.: *Les Perraults.* Paris, 1920.
HERMANN, WOLFGANG: *The Theory of Claude Perrault.* London, 1973.
SORIANO, MARC: *Le dossier Perrault.* Paris, 1972.

ARTICLES ABOUT PERRAULT

BARCHILLON, JACQUES: "Les Frères Perrault." *Revue du XVII siècle* 56 (1962).
PETZET, MICHAEL: "Claude Perrault als Architekt des Pariser Observatoriums." *Zeitschrift für Kunstgeschichte* 30 (1967): 1-54.
TAFURI, MANFREDO: "*Architettura artificialis*: Claude Perrault, Sir Christopher Wren e il dibatto sul linguaggio architettonico." In *Barocco europeo, barocco italiano, barocco salentino: Atti di Congresso Internazionale sul Barocco* (Lecce, Italy, 1969): 375-398.

Claude Perrault: The Louvre, Paris, France, 1667-70

Claude Perrault's fame as an architect rests on three buildings, all conceived between 1667 and 1670 amid some form of controversy. Although he is best remembered as the designer of the east facade of the Louvre, his claims as its sole designer continue to be disputed. Major changes in the plan of the Observatoire for the Académie des Sciences were forced on him after construction was well under way. Due to the criticisms of the Académie d'Architecture, his Arc de Triomphe commemorating the military victories of Louis XIV never rose far beyond its foundations. While the difficulties which Perrault suffered during his short stint as a practitioner were the result of problems specific to the designs, even more it was the theory of architecture which they embodied that provoked the hostility of the architectural community and represents his significant contribution to the history of 17th-century French architecture. Perrault postulated, on the basis of new scientific methods, a radical definition of beauty that challenged the conceptions of classical architecture inherited from the Renaissance.

Had he never become involved in architecture, Perrault would still be remembered for the highly original scientific work he pursued throughout his entire life. Following training and practice as a medical doctor, he devoted himself to research as a member of the Académie des Sciences. The founding of the academy in 1666 by Louis XIV was a clear signal that the government recognized the revolutionary discoveries taking place in the sciences—not only their contribution to knowledge in general, but also their material impact on society. Perrault's work was primarily in the areas of physiology and anatomy. He was a member and later the leader of the academy's team performing dissections of animals, and its findings are recorded in the publication *Essais de physique* (1680-88). Another interest which Perrault pursued was mechanics, leading to a number of inventions for new machines and instruments, published in 1700.

Perrault's direct involvement with architecture began in 1666 when he was commissioned by Jean-Baptiste Colbert, Louis' finance minister, to make a new, annotated translation of Vitruvius. While there is evidence that he had always had an interest in architecture, Perrault's selection as the official translator probably had more to do with his family connections—his brother Charles, best remembered for recording fairy tales, was secretary to Colbert. Any other intellectual of his education would have had the necessary knowledge of Latin and Greek, a familiarity with classical architecture and its theory, and most likely even a previous exposure to the discussions of materials, construction techniques and mechanical devices contained in the ancient treatise.

Perrault's translation, published in 1763, was immediately received with universal acclaim and became the standard work. It was, most importantly, Perrault's springboard into the realm of theoretical speculation which proved to be highly original and controversial. In the commentary of his *Vitruvius* and later in his architectural treatise *Ordonnance des cinq espèces de colonnes* (1683), Perrault presented a new definition of beauty that reflected new scientific attitudes. These attitudes, which challenged the very basis of Renaissance thought, were the subject of the *Querelle des anciens et des modernes,* a debate in France that revolved primarily around literature, spread to painting and architecture, but ultimately derived from science. On one side were the "ancients," who upheld the humanist idea of the Golden Age of the classical Greeks and Romans, affirming the authority of the ancients and the belief that while they must be forever imitated, they could never be surpassed. On the other side were the "moderns," including Perrault's brother Charles, who challenged ancient authority and its rules. Instead, they proclaimed the greatness of their own age of the Sun-King, and thereby the equality and even superiority of its

literature to ancient texts. Whereas the original scientific debate had been resolved by Perrault's time, there being no question that ancient natural philosophy had been proven wrong and surpassed through the direct study of nature and rational thought of the moderns, the issues proved more difficult in the realms of literature and architecture.

At the Académie d'Architecture, founded in 1671, a version of the *Querelle* was fought between François Blondel, its first director, who took the side of the ancients, and Claude Perrault, who took the side of the moderns. Blondel's position, recorded in the 1675 publication of his lectures at the Académie, upheld the Renaissance view that the rules of good architecture must be established on the authority of Vitruvius and the ancient monuments. They demonstrated that the forms and proportions of the classical orders imitated the human body, the tree and wood carpentry. As in music, the application of the ratios of small whole numbers throughout a building created harmonious relationships which everyone had an inborn ability to appreciate. Therefore beauty in architecture was absolute, real and natural, and in accord with the laws of nature.

Rejecting the "blind adoration of the ancients," Perrault used reason, judgment and experience to prove that there were two kinds of beauty, "positive" and "arbitrary." He demonstrated that the most important arbitrary beauty was proportion by disproving the idea that proportions were absolute. The orders were clearly not based on an exact imitation of nature. While musical harmonies certainly could not be altered without giving offense, many different systems of proportion could be pleasing. Therefore, architectural proportions had nothing agreeable in themselves. They had come to be loved only because of their association with positive beauties—the richness of material and exactness of workmanship, as well as the magnificence and symmetry of the design. These were qualities founded on reason and good sense. Arbitrary beauties, however, were established through custom and changed according to fancy and prejudice.

Perrault's dualistic definition of beauty in architecture not only was the product of the methods of 17th-century science, but also of its interpretation of nature, structuring it according to rational, absolute laws (positive beauties), as well as empirical, relativistic laws (arbitrary beauties). Perrault applied this paradigm to other cultural phenomena, comparing the variety of acceptable architectural proportions to the changing modes of dress and ways of speaking at the court of Louis XIV, as well as to the different national preferences represented by French and Italian music. While the judgment of arbitrary beauties was not based on reason, but on custom, Perrault did not propose to do away with them. Instead, they were the foundation of good taste and must be controlled by an authority.

For architecture, this authority was Perrault himself. In his treatise he presented a new system for the five classical orders, justified by its basis in reason, whole numbers and simple divisions, and, paradoxically, by its basis in ancient precedent. Because he had distilled his proportions from the multitudinous measures of the ancient monuments, Perrault believed that he had rediscovered the original system of Vitruvius, lost due to the negligence of the workmen. Rather than a return to ancient authority, this indicated his recognition of the legitimacy of the classical proportions gained through long-standing custom.

In order further to establish his system as a law, Perrault rejected the most important artistic device of the architect—optical adjustments. According to Vitruvius and Renaissance theorists, these refinements of the proportions, made to correct any visual distortions created by the viewing position, were the surest demonstration of the architect's wisdom and skill. For Perrault, based on contemporary theories of optics, changes to the exact proportions were unnecessary because the eye perceived accurately and the judgment automatically understood any optical illusions. Although the proportions must be fixed, he welcomed inventions as the only means for architecture to change for the better, restricting them, however, to persons of genius and reason, like himself. For the Louvre, Perrault invented the coupled columns of the east facade, as well as a French order, a version of the Corinthian with plumes, fleurs-de-lis and orbs, for the attic story of the Cour Carrée. It would appear that in appropriate situations Perrault accepted certain adaptations of the established forms of the orders as arbitrary beauties that reflected the greatness of the French culture, successor to the Greek and Roman.

Unfortunately, it is difficult to find a clear impact of Perrault's theory either on his own designs, since they were completed before his theoretical writings, or on contemporary practice, since his position seems to have gained no following among practitioners. His theory is highly significant, however, as a demonstration of the intellectual climate of the period. Handpicked by Colbert, Perrault applied the methods and reasoning of science to the phenomenon of architecture. He shocked Blondel and the Académie by formulating a relativistic theory of beauty where proportions were a basis of beauty, not due to any absolute and natural cause, but due to the arbitrary dictates of custom. At the same time, he impeded the creative freedom allowed by custom by calling for a select few to establish the standard of good taste for the entire culture. By this means Perrault reflected and reinforced the inclinations of the culture toward a unified and restrained French form of classicism, the visible manifestation of the progress toward perfection taking place under the absolutism of Louis XIV.

—LYDIA M. SOO

PERRET, Auguste.

French. Born in Brussels, Belgium, of French parents, 12 February 1874. Died in Paris, France, 28 February 1954. Married Jeanne Cordeau, 1902. Studied at the École des Beaux-Arts, Paris, 1891-95. Worked in his father's building construction firm, Paris, 1897-1905; partner, with brothers Gustave and Claude, in the successor company, Perret Frères, from 1905. Professor, École des Beaux-Arts, Paris. Inspector-general of Public Works and National Palaces, France; member, French National Committee for the Reconstruction. Gold Medal, Royal Institute of British Architects, and American Institute of Architects, 1948.

Chronology of Works
All in France unless noted
† *Work no longer exists*

1903-04	Apartments, 25 bis rue Franklin, Paris
1905	Garage, rue Ponthieu, Paris
1910-13	Théâtre des Champs-Elysées, Paris
1922	Société Marseillaise de Crédit Building, 4 rue Auber, Paris
1922-23	Notre-Dame du Raincy, Le Raincy, near Paris
1923	Grand-Quevilly House, near Rouen
1925	Theater and Albert Levy Pavilion, Exposition des Arts Décoratifs, Paris
1925	Crédit Hôtelier Building, rue de la Ville-l'Évêque, Paris
1925	Church of St. Thérèse, Montmagny, Seine et Oise
1925	Observation Tower, Grenoble Exhibition
1926	Cassandre House, Versailles
1926	Chana Orloff House, rue de la Tombe-Issoire, Paris
1926	Aghia House, Alexandria, Egypt
1927	Braque House, rue du Douanier, Paris
1928	Chapel, Arceuil, Seine
1929	Eiffel Monument, Paris
1929	Hure House, Boulogne-sur-Seine, Paris
1929	Oblates Convent, Saint Benoit
1929	Ecole Normale de Musique, Paris
1930	Lange House, avenue Ingres, Paris
1931	Nubar Bey House, Garches
1931	Chapel, Vanves
1932	Apartment Building, 51-55 rue Raynouard, Paris
1932	Marine National Building, Paris
1934	Mobilier National (National Guard) Building, Paris
1935	Pont de l'Arc, Paris
1937	Museum of Public Works, Paris
1945	Master plan for the reconstruction of Le Havre
1952	Church of St. Joseph, Le Havre

Publications

BOOKS BY PERRET

Contribution à une théorie de l'architecture. Paris, 1952.

ARTICLES BY PERRET

"Le Musée Moderne." *Mouseion* (December 1929).
"Architecture: Science et poésie." *Construction moderne* 48 (October 1932).
"L'Architecture." *Revue d'art et d'esthetique* (June 1935).
"Construire un musée." *Encyclopédie française.* Paris, 1938.

BOOKS ABOUT PERRET

CHAMPIGNEULLE, BERNARD: *Auguste Perret.* Paris, 1959.
COLLINS, PETER: *Concrete: The Vision of a New Architecture. A Study of Auguste Perret and His Predecessors.* London, 1959.
JAMOT, P.: *Auguste and Gustave Perret et l'architecture du béton armé.* Paris and Brussels, 1927.
ROGERS, ERNESTO NATHAN: *Auguste Perret.* Milan, 1955.
ZAHAR, MARCEL: *D'une doctrine d'architecture: Auguste Perret.* Paris, 1959.

ARTICLES ABOUT PERRET

"Notre Dame of Le Raincy." *Space Design* (September 1980).
BADOVICI, JEAN: "Auguste et Gustave Perret." *Architecture vivante* (Summer 1925).
GOLDFINGER, ERNO: "The Work of Auguste Perret." *Architectural Association Journal* (January 1955).
GREGOTTI, VITTORIO: "Classicisme et rationalisme d'Auguste Perret." *Architecture mouvement continuité* 37 (November 1975).
PROUVÉ, JEAN, and GREGOTTI, VITTORIO: "Classicism and Rationalism in Perret." *Domus* (May 1974).
RAYMOND, ANTONIN: "The Doctrine of Auguste Perret." *Architectural Record* (January 1954).
VAGO, PIERRE (ed.): "Auguste Perret." *Architecture d'aujourd'hui* 7, special issue (October 1932).

Auguste Perret: Notre-Dame du Raincy, Le Raincy, 1922-23

Auguste Perret searched throughout his architectural career for a true understanding of 20th-century architecture. These concerns stemmed from the rationalist theories of 19th-century France as well as from the direct influence that Julien Guadet, Eugène-Emonvele Viollet le-Duc and August Choisy had on his education. An individual who operated within the spirit of Greek classicism, Perret believed that by pursuing a rigorous analytical path toward a rational comprehension of the materials and methods of construction of the building, he would eventually arrive at an expression of form as essential as that discovered in Greek antiquity. His legacy lies in this rigorous and disciplined undertaking to develop reinforced concrete in order to express modern architecture.

Like the Greeks, who tried to express the basic characteristics of timber construction, he limited his use of structural concrete to the trabeated frame. In a meticulous and restrained manner, he tested his knowledge of reinforced-concrete construction in order to develop, from this technique, the essential qualities of architectural elements. Perret thought that by defining the intrinsic characteristics of the elements of architecture—such as columns, beams, arches and walls—and then arranging them syntactically, poetry would result in a work of architecture. For example, the shape and entasis of a column should express the essential connection that is necessary to provide rigidity in the structural frame. The shape of beams should express an elegant continuity in order to develop refined profiles. Walls should not be poured, but should provide instead a more intimate articulation of smaller parts that would reinforce a sense of scale. Windows in domestic architecture should follow the vertical proportions of the human body in order to provide a sense of scale and orientation.

The technical proficiency of Perret's discoveries paved the way for the explorations of younger architects like Le Corbusier. Perret opposed Le Corbusier's formal expressionism, however, and advocated a more restrained and traditional architectural vocabulary. The purity and rigor of Perret's approach to design enabled him to leave behind built manifestations of his philosophy.

Perret left the École de Beaux-Arts before obtaining an official diploma in order to join his father's construction firm. There he learned hands-on the necessity for economy: maximum effort by minimum means. Without compromising the standards of quality, he was constantly challenged to produce ingenious and efficient solutions for the different problems.

Perret had a very prolific architectural practice. His various projects included industrial, domestic, civic, religious and city planning. Perret treated all his projects, regardless of scale, with the same concern and systematic respect.

Among his first residential projects in reinforced concrete was the notable apartment building on Rue Franklin. Although the concrete surface of the building has a tile cladding, the layout of the tile reinforces the structural frame. Monochromatic tiles follow the frame, while the tiles of the infilling walls are patterned with lighter leaf-like motives recalling the landscape of the surrounding area. The ingenious planning is perhaps the most important aspect of the building. By carving out the front of the building, Perret increased the surface area and allowed all the rooms to be evenly lit. Also very relevant is the substitution of all interior load-bearing partitions with slender columns. This created an internal transparency with remarkable resemblance to future "open plans." Even though the point loads on the interior generated the "Pilotis," Perret did not pursue the pilotis' structural value as an opportunity to define a new kind of internal spatial understanding, but instead continued to adhere to more traditional planning.

Another important building of his early period is a small garage on Rue Ponthieu. This building illustrates an understanding of form and proportion. Its simple appearance presents a refined expression of its material and structure. The concrete structural system is expressed as having a dignity of its own; its rhythm is manipulated beyond structural necessities. The articulation of structure and surface and the subtle manipulation of proportion in this very simple program express his quest to excel beyond the limits of construction.

Notre Dame du Raincy was the first religious building in which Perret continued his explorations with concrete. With very limited funds he managed to create a significant religious monument. Rows of four columns march down a basic rectangular basilica plan to support a shallow longitudinal vault over the nave, with transverse perpendicular vaults over the aisles. The enclosure consists of a continuous screen of perforated precast panels filled with colored glass. This articulation maintains the scale on the exterior of the church, where the structural rhythm is not present, and allows the wall to disappear on the inside in a translucent veil of light. The vaulted ceiling appears to soar over the very slender columns, embracing the audience. The columnar structure and the surrounding non-bearing enclosure are stripped to their bare essence, epitomizing Perret's philosophies.

In the Musée des Travau Publics, Perret achieved utmost sophistication in the use of concrete. Within a traditional plan and spatial organization, Perret perfected the syntactic expression of the building's parts. The fluted columns are tapered toward the bottom, in order to enforce their rigid connection to the beams. The beams are carved on the underside in order to create articulated profiles. The panels set within the structure present a slight differentiation in color, which, combined with the precision of the joints, enhances the effects of light and shadow. The controlled and careful articulation of its parts assigns this building a somber, harmonious quality.

Perret in his method of design would first seek a structural skeleton that could best fulfill the functional necessities of the program. Then, after standardizing the parts of the buildings in the form-work, he would involve himself in a diligent refinement of the way the parts were assembled. Dimensions were adjusted to create optical satisfaction and visual harmony. Aggregates were added to the concrete to express subtle changes of tone and texture. All this was done in an effort to pursue an orderly understanding of classical beauty. Peter Collins, in his book "Concrete," quotes Perret: "There is nothing so precise in all our precise mechanisms, of which we are so proud, as the way the elements for this monument are assembled; yet not one is regular, for the columns are inclined at different angles, the spaces between them vary, and the architraves are arched— all to correct optical distortions to obtain harmony." This quote refers to the Parthenon, but it also illustrates Perret's awareness of the precision necessary in order to create "poetry" from the language of construction.

Perret did not pursue glory through plastic expressionism. In a quiet manner he applied the same methodical rigor to all his buildings, regardless of purpose or scale. His architecture was extremely rational, and although he was innovative in his technique, his spacial explorations were traditional. His concerns for human scale and proportion did not preclude values essential to reinforced concrete as material. Furthermore, notions of stability, permanence and correctness inherent within the assemblage of the concrete system rendered his buildings with an earnest and timeless quality.

—ANNABEL DELGADO

Baldassare Peruzzi: Palazzo Massimo alle Colonne, Rome, Italy, 1533-36

PERUZZI, Baldassare.

Italian. Born in Siena, Italy, in 1481. Died in Rome, 6 January 1536. Moved to Rome, ca. 1505; worked in Carpi, 1514-15; became assistant to Antonio da Sangallo the Younger, Rome, 1520; returned to Siena (after having been captured and released during the Sack of Rome, 1527); became the official architect in Siena, 1527; returned to Rome at the end of his life to work for the Massimo family.

Chronology of Works
All in Italy
* Approximate dates

1505*	Villa le Volte, near Siena [attributed]
1505-11	Villa Farnesina, Rome
1513-15	Ancient Duomo, Carpi (facade)
1513-15	San Nicolò, Carpi (nave)
1520-27	St. Peter's, Rome (nave)
1522	San Michele in Bosco, Bologna (portal)
1520-27	Palazzo Fusconi-Pighini, Rome (aediculae of facade, courtyard)
1525*	Villa Trivulzi-Borromeo, Salone River, near Rome
1527-32	Fortifications, Siena
1531-33	San Domenico, Siena (rebuilding)
1531-36	St. Peter's, Rome (plans for completion)
1533-36	Palazzo Massimo alle Colonne, Rome (completed after his death)
1533-36	Palazzo Ricci, Montepulciano (southern Tuscany)
1535*	Palazzo Vescovo-Pollini, Siena [attributed]

Publications

BOOKS ABOUT PERUZZI

KENT, WILLIAM W.: *The Life and Works of Baldassare Peruzzi of Siena.* New York, 1925.

FROMMEL, C.: *Die Farnesina und Peruzzis architektonisches Frühwerk.* Berlin, 1961.

REDTENBACHER, RUDOLF: *Baldassare Peruzzi und seine Werke.* Karlsruhe, 1875.

WURM, H.: *Der Palazzo Massimo alle Colonne in Rom.* Berlin, 1965.

ARTICLES ABOUT PERUZZI

LOTZ, WOLFGANG: "Entwürfe Sangallos und Peruzzis für S. Giacomo in Augusta in Rom." *Mitteilungen des Kunsthistorischen Instituts in Florenz* 5 (1937-40): 441ff.

MARANI, PIETRO C.: "A Reworking by Baldassare Peruzzi of Francesco di Giorgio's Plan of a Villa." *Journal of the Society of Architectural Historians* 41 (October 1982): 181-188.

*

The painter and architect Baldassare Peruzzi was a native of Siena who established his career as an architect in Rome, where he was patronized by his fellow countryman and papal banker, Agostino Chigi (1466-1520). Peruzzi was a highly inventive draftsman whose designs influenced Sebastiano Serlio, Giulio Romano, Jacopo Sansovino and Andrea Palladio. Peruzzi also worked on stage scenery and pageants. Scores of his drawings survive, among which are one of the earliest uses of an oval church plan and, in the Uffizi, an extraordinary drawing of plan and elevation more like a modern isometric projection. It reveals Peruzzi's concern for the structure's organic unity by visualizing space in terms of the intimate relationship of height, width and depth, and of interior and exterior. Possibly influenced in his early years by the Florentine architect Francesco di Giorgio Martini, he entered the circle of Bramante and Raphael after his arrival in Rome in about 1505.

Sigismondo Chigi's Villa le Volte in Siena (ca. 1505), although not documented, is taken as an example of work from Peruzzi's early career. The villa's lateral wings framing a central loggia is an element in common with his major project in Rome, the Villa Farnesina (1505/6-11), for the more prominent member of the Chigi family, Agostino. Situated on the banks of the Tiber, it is an early example of a suburban villa. The villa plan is extraordinary for its combination of spaciousness and intimacy. It has a two-story elevation with a plan in the shape of a square letter C. The exterior walls were provided with painted fesco decorations, of which but a few traces remain, and had open loggias on two sides. Peruzzi was responsible for the villa's construction and also contributed to its decoration. He painted the allegorical horoscope of his patron on the frescoed ceiling of the Hall of Galatea, as well as the illusionistic loggias and urban views in the grand Hall of Perspective on the second story.

Peruzzi worked in Carpi in 1514 and 1515 for Chigi's neighbor in Rome, Alberto Pio, who was count of Carpi and imperial ambassador. They signed a contract of February 1515 for a facade for the cathedral of Carpi. That same year, Peruzzi also delivered a model for a new structure similar in plan to Bramante's St. Peter's, but with diagonally placed piers supporting a dome.

Peruzzi became assistant to Antonio da Sangallo the Younger on Raphael's death in 1520, and involved himself in the construction of Bramante's Vatican basilica. He was captured in the Sack of Rome seven years later and forced into debt to ransom his freedom; he fled to his native Siena, where he became the republic's official architect on 10 July 1527.

He remained in Siena most of the following years, but returned to Rome before the end of his life to work for members of the Massimo family on the reconstruction of palaces burned in the Sack of Rome. The family's old residential complex was the site of the first books ever printed in Rome, works by Cicero, Pliny and Saint Augustine, and by the Germans Conrad Sweinheim and Arnold Pannartz, in 1467.

The three Massino brothers, Pietro, Angelo and Luca, had their residences on the narrow (12 feet wide), curving Via Papale (a papal procession route, now the Corso Vittorio Emanuele). Begun in 1532, the separate but adjacent palaces occupied an irregular site and were to incorporate portions of the earlier buildings. Thus, Peruzzi's curved facade for Pietro's Palazzo Massimo alle Colonne was dictated by its site, and his use of a Roman portico *in antis* commemorated the facade of the destroyed palace. The portico's asymmetrical placement was in response to a second, similarly narrow street perpendicular to the Palazzo Massimo's facade.

Peruzzi reserved orders for the ground level rather than the main floor (*piano nobile*), but unlike Giuliano da Sangallo's Villa Medici at Poggio a Caiano (1480s), his Doric portico has no pediment. Peruzzi widened the facade at both ends, with the section at the left largely a false front, but he thereby made the loggia appear to be at the palace's center. The facade so extended with its convex center was now more visible from both ends of the street.

Peruzzi emphasized the facade's flatness in the upper three stories to the point of omitting window surrounds and articulation of bays, although he emphasized the *piano nobile* by taller windows with balconies. The broad, flat area of the upper levels risked making the facade seem top-heavy, but Peruzzi compensated for this with smaller window openings, which perforate and lighten the flat surface. He articulated his portico with paired columns changing to a column-pilaster pair at the extremities of the portico, then to paired pilasters at the end bays, retaining the same rhythms throughout. Paired pilasters had appeared in the Roman Cancelleria (1486-96), but in Peruzzi's portico the muscular play of solid and void was more reminiscent of Bramante's Tempietto.

Within the loggia Peruzzi added apses to both ends in mimicry of the ancient Roman basilica. A narrow corridor placed off-center leads to a small *cortile* of two stories of superimposed Doric and Ionic orders and an attic. Peruzzi preserved the original line of the old walls and the former site of the *cortile,* while slightly enlarging the palace area, so in the end the shape and appearance of his palace were the result of an intelligent balance of practical and artistic considerations.

—EDWARD J. OLSZEWSKI

PETERSEN, Carl.

Danish. Born in Copenhagen, Denmark, 17 January 1874. Died in Copenhagen, 19 June 1923. Apprenticed to a carpenter, and studied drawing with Christen Dalsgaard; studied at the Royal Academy of Art, Copenhagen, 1896-1901. Professor at the Royal Academy, Copenhagen.

Chronology of Works
All in Denmark

1912-15   Faaborg Museum, Copenhagen

Publications

BOOKS ABOUT PETERSEN

PAAVILAINEN, SIMO: *Nordisk Klassicism/Nordic Classicism.* Exhibition catalog. Helsinki, 1982.
STEPHENSEN, HAKON: *Arkitekten Carl Petersen.* Copenhagen, 1979.
SWANE, LEO: *Faaborg Museum.* Copenhagen, 1932.

ARTICLES ABOUT PETERSEN

HIORT, ESBJØRN: "Museet i Faaborg og nyklassicism i Norden." In ERLING NIELSEN (ed.): *Ikke bare om Norden.* Copenhagen, 1975.

*

Carl Petersen was a leader among the Nordic architects who after 1900 began to study Renaissance treatises, northern European architecture of the pre-industrial period and vernacular buildings. They were seeking native building traditions, models for a use of materials that was true to their properties, good craftsmanship and the stylistic homogeneity that would result from these, after intense analysis of the proportions of old buildings and their individual components. The result was what the Danes call "new classicism," which, in the eyes of its practitioners, was less a revival of 18th-century neoclassicism than the end of style itself. The new classicism corresponded to contemporary German investigations, those of the Deutscher Werkbund for example, and the historical-prescriptive work of Hermann Muthesius (1861-1927) and Heinrich Tessenow (1876-1950).

To this greater European project, Petersen contributed the Faaborg Museum (1912-15), the most perfect refutation of the criticism that this was an inhumane and programmatic architecture; an acute and highly personal historical sensibility; a genius for polemics and organizing exhibitions; and two key texts. The lectures called "Textures" ("*Stoflige Virkninger,*" 1919) and "Contrasts" ("*Modsætninger,* 1920) aroused interest throughout Scandinavia when published in the journal *Architekten.* Short and unpretentious, they underlined the importance of material effects to our appreciation of form, something Petersen had learned as a ceramist. His lesson, that architects must have complete control over material effects, is still taught to architectural students all over the world through the writings of his admirer Steen Eiler Rasmussen.

Petersen's grandfather had been a distinguished Arctic explorer; his grandmother was half-Greenland Eskimo. Petersen, in whose face the descent showed plainly, was proud of the great hunters among his forefathers. His upbringing was not only in the liberal spirit of Denmark around 1800 (his family decided, for example, that before studying architecture at the Royal Academy of Art in Copenhagen he would have to apprentice himself to a carpenter), but also conducted within a living tradition. Throughout his youth Petersen heard reminiscences of the great figures of the early to mid-19th century, the "Golden Age" of Danish art. At his school, Sorø Academy, itself physically and figuratively a product of the Enlightenment, he was taught drawing by Christen Dalsgaard, a painter active at the end of the Golden Age. Petersen later recalled how a room in Dalsgaard's house was painted cobalt blue, "the purest colour I know" and one he would use to effect in the domed hall at Faaborg. His interest in the architecture of the period was sharpened by an exhibition of M. G. Bindesbøll's drawings for Thorvaldsen's Museum (1839-48) in 1901. From Bindesbøll's museum, Petersen would borrow for his own the brilliant polychromy, the manipulation of the sightlines down the galleries

and their disruption, and the conviction that architects must take what they need from the past without priggish qualms about stylistic "purity."

In 1901, too, Petersen left the Art Academy after five years, calling it "cramped." He could not reconcile himself to the Academy's "style architecture" orthodoxy, which advocated the "correct," i.e., accurate and unadulterated, use of historical styles in modern design, yet simultaneously encouraged each student to find his very own historical style in which to work. The result, castigated by Petersen and his friends as "individualism," was not always bad, but drafting work for Martin Nyrop's Copenhagen Town Hall project (completed in 1905) only strengthened Petersen's commitment to an architecture beyond style, but not beyond national tradition or the appreciation—after some guidance from architects—of its actual users.

Popular education about the future of style began with the "spire affair" of 1909, when the brewer and art patron Carl Jacobsen proposed erecting a spire on the tower of the stringently reductive Vor Frue Kirke (1811-29) in Copenhagen, designed by C. F. Hansen (1756-1845) and long regarded by the "style architects" as the epitome of arid cosmopolitanism and stylistic confusion. Petersen led the opposition in a debate that generated scores of articles and ripostes in the architectural journals and popular press; the debate died down only in 1914, when Jacobsen died. In the meantime, Petersen's friend Hans Koch (1873-1922) inherited an important collection of Hansen's drawings. In 1911 Petersen and Koch mounted a public exhibition of the drawings, which illustrated an architecture that was serviceable, consistent in its presuppositions, simple and serene, and Petersen published a long article whose directness of engagement with and empathy for Hansen as a designer has seldom been matched since.

Petersen's connections with the Danish art world led to the commission for the Museum of Faaborg, on the island of Funen. A frank quotation from the portal of Hansen's Thornton House in Hamburg (1795-96), two Doric columns set *in antis* with a high, narrow arch springing from their capitals, introduces the museum. Hansen, the neoclassicist, had crowned the door of the Thornton House with a pediment; Petersen, the new classicist, let the triangular, tiled hip of the typical Danish roof do the same. Petersen overcame the constraints of the long and narrow site with strong contrasts in colors, lighting, and room shapes and orientation. From a skylit vestibule one passes into a dim, deep-cobalt octagonal domed hall, which receives just enough light to reveal, mysteriously, the statue of the museum's founder. A large, red rectangular gallery waits beyond, and beyond that an *enfilade,* reminiscent of Thorvaldsen's Museum, of smaller rooms. Reminiscent of the older museum, too, is the care with which Petersen and Kaare Klint (1888-1954) designed the mosaic floors, complex patterns different in every room, but whose colors bridge adjacent rooms to distinguish different parts of the museum.

Petersen's later work kept pace with the new classicists' increasing social engagement, their sense of the architect's wider responsibilities. In the aftermath of World War I, in countries that (with the exception of Finland) had managed to stay neutral, social reform, and not least mass housing construction, seemed imminent. In 1919, with Ivar Bentsen (1876-1943), Petersen entered a competition to develop disused railway land in Copenhagen; a tract defended their submission's huge, repetitive facades, entirely unornamented and interrupted only by window and door openings. In the 1920s, it would be concluded that such monumental tidiness was not only undemocratic but unrealistic. In the meantime the new classicism had aroused European interest, which was renewed in the 1970s.

—CHRISTINE STEVENSON

PIACENTINI, Marcello.

Italian. Born in Rome, Italy, 8 December 1881. Died in Rome, 1960. Studied at the Accademia di San Luca, Rome, Dip.Arch., 1904. Served in the Italian Army during World War I. In private practice, Rome, from 1906. Served as the government architect (principal architect to Mussolini). Professor, Scuola Superiore di Architettura, Rome. Editor, *Architettura*, Rome, 1922-43.

Chronology of Works
All in Italy unless noted
† *Work no longer exists*

1910	Italian Pavilion, International Exposition, Brussels, Belgium†
1911	Plans for National Exposition, Rome†
1912	Hotel Roma, Bengasi
1912-28	Palace of Justice, Messina
1914-23	Banca d'Italia, Rome
1915	Italian Pavilion, World Exposition, San Francisco, California, U.S.A.†
1915-17	Cinema al Corso, Rome
1920	Garden City Garbatella, Rome (first stage complete; with Gustavo Giovannoni)
1922	Palace of Justice, Bergamo
1923-30	Triumphal Arch, Genoa
1924-34	Church of Cristo Re, Rome
1924-38	Casa Madre dei Mutilati, Rome
1927	Ambassador Hotel, Rome (with G. Vaccaro)
1928-31	Ministry of Corporations, Rome (with Vaccaro)
1931	Master plan of Rome
1932	City Center and Via della Conciliazione, Rome
1932-33	University of Rome, (with others)
1932-40	Palace of Justice, Milan
1934-36	Banca Nazionale del Lavoro, Rome
1937	Italian Pavilion, Exposition, Paris, France (with Giuseppe Pagano and C. Valle)†
1937-43	Esposizione Universale di Roma, Rome (with others)
1950-51	Chapel, University of Rome
1955-60	Palazzo dello Sport at EUR, Rome (with Pier Luigi Nervi)
1956	Palazzo della Ragione, Ferrara
1957	Palace of Justice, Palermo

Publications

BOOKS BY PIACENTINI

Architettura d'oggi. Rome, 1930.
Volto di Roma. Rome, 1945.

BOOKS ABOUT PIACENTINI

ACCASTO, G.; FRATICELLI, V.; NICCOLINI, R.: *L'architettura di Roma capitale, 1870-1970.* Rome.
CIUCCI, GIORGIO: *Il dibattito sull'architettura e la città fasciste.* Turin, 1982.
DE SETA, C.: *La cultura architettonica in Italia tra le due guerre.* Bari, 1972.
LUPANO, MARIO: *Marcello Piacentini.* Rome, 1991.
PATETTA, LUCIANA: *L'architettura in Italia 1919-1943: Le polemiche.* Milan, 1972.
PICA, A.: *Nuova architettura italiana.* Milan, 1936.
PORTOGHESI, PAOLO: *L'eclettismo a Roma 1870-1922.* Rome, 1969.

ARTICLES ABOUT PIACENTINI

CASCIATO, MARISTELLA: "Radical Abstract and Cerebral." *Wonen-TA/BK* (July 1983).
ZEVI, BRUNO: "Marcello Piacentini mori nel 1925." *Architettura* (1958).

*

Often called Mussolini's Albert Speer, Marcello Piacentini was the most powerful architect in Italy in the 1930s. He was the Accademico d'Italia (like a leading professor), the director of *Architettura* magazine (the official architecture journal of the National Fascist Party) and either the winner of, or chairman of the jury for, most of the important competitions that were held in Italy in the 1930s. Among his most famous works are the new town center for Brescia, the Ambasciatori Hotel in Rome and the street in front of St. Peter's Square (the Via della Conciliazione).

Piacentini is the man normally held accountable for whatever difficulties the rationalist avant-garde ran into, and he is usually blamed for the demise of the Modern Movement in Italy. However, Piacentini was neither as doggedly nor as unreasonably antimodern in his outlook as his reputation would suggest. It is true that he was politically conservative, and defended the conservatism of his class and profession against radicalism and liberalism. It is true that he was authoritarian and domineering, and the allegations that he doled out work like a Mafia don may be correct. But a careful look at his architecture and his writings shows that he has been unfairly condemned on a number of counts.

Piacentini's early work was clearly in sympathy with modernist developments. He played a part in the Roman avant-garde of the immediate post-World War I period, and his Cinema Corso (1925) is still considered a monument of protomodern Italian architecture. Some scholars have argued that it was not until the late 1930s that Piacentini relinquished his modernist sympathies. He lauded many of the attempts of the modernists and later invited some of them to collaborate with him on the University of Rome and the exposition that resulted in Rome's EUR quarter. It may be noted also that his own contributions to these complexes are stylistically indistinguishable from some of the buildings by the more avant-garde architects.

In his 1930 book, *L'Architettura d'oggi,* he published selected buildings by the European avant-garde such as Ludwig Mies van der Rohe's Barcelona Pavilion and the Wolf House (a building of dense brick structure without horizontal windows), and the La Roche/Jeanneret houses by Le Corbusier. The illustrations in this little book are a balanced exposition of both the well-known and the avant-garde. Certainly, Piacentini singled out the "older generation" of modern architects over the young International Style architects for his highest praise: Paul Bonatz, Dominikus Böhm, Ragnar Östberg, Eliel Saarinen and Auguste Perret—architects who, from the 1930s onward, have been considered "transitional" figures in the history of modern architecture. This preference by itself, of course, does not make an antimodernist of Piacentini.

Even if his architecture itself did not justify Piacentini's power and prominence, it must be conceded that his writings are of superior merit, and evince a keen critical eye. Having gained some distance from the debate, we can now see that his attacks on the avant-garde were less unreasonable than they appeared to be at the time, and were in fact mounted from the very viewpoint that the rationalists promoted. His criticisms were often just, and in effect he exposed the "emperor's nudity." Piacentini pointed out the peeling plaster, the underused spaces, leaking roofs and overheated rooms of the modernists'

Marcello Piacentini: University of Rome, Rome, Italy, 1932-33

buildings, and implied, in a reasonable manner, that the essentially symbolic basis of modernist architecture was often realized at the expense of function and efficiency.

In opposition to the international ideals of the Modern Movement, Piacentini espoused a regionalism thoroughly grounded in climatic realism. In *L'Architettura d'oggi,* for instance, he wrote that Italians "ultimately cannot accept the new fixed formulas of completely glass walls and low ceilings; we must defend ourselves against a burning sun and excessive heat six months out of the year. This means we must still use natural and heavy materials, in dimensions that cannot, because of their nature, be differentiated from the old ones." Without attics, Piacentini warned, Italian houses would be unlivable from April to October.

Piacentini also adopted a cultural regionalism which appears less persuasive today than his climatic arguments. Modern architecture was not suitable for Italians because, he claimed, "We need gesture and form; we need stirring words and smiles. We are essentially musical; our art is always a song."

In answer to international modernism, Piacentini formulated a regionalist version of "modernism" of his own—at least he called it that—which would proceed to a kind of stripped classicism. There were some unresolved tensions in Piacentini's work, however, as may be clear from this statement that "Modernism is found in local physiognomy, irreducible individuality, fantasy and artistry in opposition to internationalism, objectivity, pure logic and technology." And many of his own buildings, anything rather than exemplifying a stripped classicism, are encrusted with grotesque caricatures of quasiclassical elements. As much a watchdog against modernist architecture, Piacentini was a shill for eclecticism.

Piacentini seems to have been ambivalent about other issues as well, particularly in relation to the memorable statement, made in 1928, that there should be "two architectures, one in underwear, the other in evening dress." This was an intriguing idea of two kinds of building, a vernacular and a high-style architecture, but it was obviously not new. (This division is reflected also in Piacentini's writings on the symbolism of horizontals and verticals, which he associated not only with old and new architecture, but also with domestic and monumental architecture.) With the underwear/evening dress opposition, Piacentini proposed a variation in the final expression of a building, a cosmetic coding, added to represent the importance a given edifice had in society, rather than a difference of origins or of design process. The idea depends upon a lack of correspondence between tectonic structure and architectural expression, yet elsewhere he had argued in favor of just such a correspondence, and against Ugo Ojetti's insistence on rhetoricism.

The polemic with Ugo Ojetti presents another puzzle. In a series of open letters, Ojetti and Piacentini crossed swords in such a manner that Piacentini sounded almost like a rationalist. Ojetti argued that Italy could regain its architectural status only with a renewed use of arches and columns. Piacentini countered that the modern world militated against rounded forms in windows and doors, and that somewhere a modern style could make itself felt without too much allusion to old forms. At the same time, he argued for the reproduction of standard architectural types, in opposition to the new typology favored by modernist architects, who argued that technology of necessity created its own new types. To Piacentini, however, the most modern technology could be used to support whatever expression the architect wished to achieve.

Piacentini's influence on the avant-garde has not been fully studied to date, but his arguments must be regarded as important. They influenced the direction of Italian architecture in the 1930s, even though Piacentini cannot be held solely responsible for its fate. Other factors, like the Great Depression, Italy's isolation from the West after the war with Ethiopia, and the highly publicized notion of autarchia (self-sufficiency) also played an important part. Piacentini's arguments helped move Italy in the direction of a more accommodating stance toward historical precedent and the traditional values of the period.

Marcello Piacentini survived the war to complete his huge street in front of St. Peter's Square, the Via della Conciliazione, begun under fascism as the commemoration of the reconciliation of the Church with the Kingdom of Italy, the Lateran Pact of 1929. It was finished in 1950. In an irony worthy of Pirandello, one of Piacentini's last works was the curtain-wall surrounding Pier Luigi Nervi's celebrated covering of the Palazzo dello Sport for the 1960 Olympic Games in Rome.

—THOMAS L. SCHUMACHER

PIETILÄ, Reima and Raili.

PIETILÄ, Reima.
Finnish. Born in Turku, Finland, 25 August 1923. Married Raili Paatelainen (see below), 1961; one daughter. Studied at the Institute of Technology, Helsinki, 1945-53, Dip.Arch. Corporal in the Finnish Army, 1942-44. Architect in the City Master Planning Department, Helsinki, 1953-54; worked in the offices of architects Cedercreutz-Railo, and Viljo Revell, Helsinki, 1955-56; in private practice, since 1957, and with Raili Pietilä, Helsinki, since 1960. Professor of architecture, University of Oulu, Finland, 1973-79; has taught at numerous universities in the United States.

PIETILÄ, Raili.
Finnish. Born in Pieksämäki, Finland, 15 August 1926. Married Reima Pietilä, 1961; one daughter. Studied at the Institute of Technology, Helsinki, 1948-56, Dip.Arch. In private practice with Reima Pietilä, since 1960.

Chronology of Works
All in Finland unless noted
Work by Reima Pietilä:

1958	Finnish pavilion, World's Fair, Brussels

Works by Reima and Raili Pietilä:

1966	Kaleva Church, Tampere
1966	Dipoli Congress and Student Center, Otaniemi
1966-69	Suvikumpu Housing Area, Tapiola, Espoo
1972	Swimming Pool, Sauna and Art Gallery, Kittilä, Lapland
1972	Sauna Bath Building, Saarinen Museum, Kirkko-nummi
1975	Master Plan for Cultural Services, Hervanta, Tampere
1978-79	Leisure Time and Congregational Center and Market Hall, Hervanta, Tampere
1978-82	Main Library, Tampere
1979-81	Lutheran Church, Lieksa
1980	Kukkatalo House and Garden Center, Suvikumpu, Tapiola
1981	Council of Ministers Building, Kuwait City, Kuwait
1981	Ministry of Foreign Affairs Building, Kuwait City, Kuwait
1981	Reception Hall, Sief Palace Area, Kuwait City, Kuwait (extension)
1983-84	Home for the Elderly, and Children's Nursery, Pori
1983-84	Malminkartano experimental housing, Helsinki
1983-85	Finnish Embassy, New Delhi, India
1984-92	Official Residence of the President of Finland, Mantyniemi, Helsinki

Publications

BOOKS BY REIMA PIETILÄ

The Morphology of Expressive Form. Helsinki, 1958.
Centres and Noncentres. Helsinki, 1969.
Concept of Visual Entity in Environmental Design. Wagenhingen, Netherlands, 1971.
Architectures "Totales" et "Partielles" dans le contexte d'une image morphologique de l'environnement. Arc-et-Senans, France, 1973.
Notion, Image, Idea: Notes on Architectural Teaching. Otaniemi, Finland, 1974.
Leisure Time Architecture. Helsinki, 1977.

ARTICLES BY REIMA PIETILÄ

"Hobby Dogs." *Arkkitehti* 6 (1967).
"Local—Non-Local." *Arkkitehti* 7/8 (1967).
"Dipoli: Literal Morphology." *Arkkitehti* 9 (1967).
"The Zone." *Arkkitehti* 1 (1968).
"Reima Pietilä." *Arkkitehti* 7/8 (1976).
"Essays on Architecture." *Arkkitehti* 5 (1977).
"Architecture That Directs Its Own Birth." *Arkkitehti* 6 (1977).
"Eight Ways to Break Free from Rabbit-Hutch Architecture." *Arkkitehti* 2 (1979).
"The Architecture of Lieska Church." With Roger Connah. *Arkkitehti* 7 (1983).

BOOKS ABOUT PIETILÄ

BENINCASA, CARMINE: *Il labirinto del sabba: L'architettura di Reima Pietilä.* Bari, Italy, 1979.
BURKLE, THOMAS JOHN: *A Dialectic of Architectural Systems and Poetry: Theory and Works of Reima Pietilä.* Thesis. University of Washington, Seattle, 1983.
CONNAH, ROGER: *Writing Architecture.* Helsinki, Cambridge, Massachusetts, and London, 1989.
QUANTRILL, MALCOLM: *Reima Pietilä: Architecture, Context and Modernism.* New York, 1985.
QUANTRILL, MALCOLM (ed.): *One Man's Odyssey in Search of Finnish Architecture.* Helsinki, 1988.
SALOKORPI, ASKO: *Modern Finnish Architecture.* New York, 1970.
TEMPEL, EGON: *New Finnish Architecture.* New York, 1968.

ARTICLES ABOUT PIETILÄ

HAUSEN, MARIKA: "Reima Pietilä." *Paletten* 4 (1967).
MILLER, WILLIAM: "Pietilä's Step in a Different or New Direction." *Architecture and Urbanism* 5 (1981).
MUTO, AKIRA: "Pietilä in the Seventies." *Architecture and Urbanism* 9 (1974).
"Reima Pietilä and Raili Paatelainen." *Jano arquitectura* 34 (1976).
TREIB, MARC: "Pietilä: Rebel in Finland." *Architectural Forum* (December 1967).

Reima and Raili Pietilä: Main Library, Tampere, Finland, 1978-82

The public library in Tampere, Finland, is affectionately known by its competition name of ''Metso''—ruffed grouse. In less than a decade Metso has become the unofficial symbol of this industrial city in the heart of the lake country; it is featured on a postage stamp, and everyone knows the name of the architects, Reima and Raili Pietilä. A successful library and civic-cultural center, Metso is also a complex, metaphorical work of art that taps the collective memory of some long-forgotten Nordic-Celtic twilight.

Metso inspires myriad recollections of past monuments, but there is no copying, no trite postmodern pastiche. The central dome echoes the Pantheon, Hagia Sophia, the work of Max Berg and Thomas Jefferson, yet it is whimsically canted off horizontal axis; sky blue and lightness on the inside, heavy, copper-coated outside (a cartoonist depicted Reima Pietilä in his trademark wool cap standing in front of Metso, suggesting the true source of the dome). While there is nothing identifiably Roman or classical, the spaces function with Beaux-Arts logicality. The faceted glass entrance with its interior waterfall makes reference to Tampere's *raison d'être* location on a rapids between two lakes.

If any architect's spirit inhabits this spiraling nautilus of metal and rock, it is H. H. Richardson's. Metso and the New England libraries grew from a shared glacial landscape—granite and Romanesque, the material and style adopted by late-19th-century National Romantic architects to assert Finland's artistic and cultural independence from oppressive Russian rulers.

This past-respectful yet astylar architecture is equally apparent in the Pietiläs' Lieksa Church designed a year after Metso. Lieksa's domed Greek-cross plan pays homage to the original 1838 church by Carl Ludwig Engel, which burned, while the cruciform skylight along with the use of copper, granite and wood meld a contemporary Lutheran modern with the Orthodox faith of the Karelian forests. The cave-like quality of Metso, however, is more characteristic of the Pietiläs' geomorphism that appeared 20 years earlier in the flounder-as-filleted-by-Borromini plan of Kaleva Church, also in Tampere. This symbolic expressionism is central to such designs as the unsuccessful competition for Malmi Church and the roman à clef Dipoli Student Center.

Dipoli, undoubtedly the Pietiläs' best-known work, with its huge boulders, copper-sheathed walls and concrete roof, reads as a primeval shelter and the primal cave. From Dipoli onward, the anthropomorphic images flourish—Reima Pietilä outlined a cat asleep on his drafting table to arrive at Malmi's basic configuration. There is also the caterpillar-like plan of the old people's home in Pori, the arctic-horizon roofline of the Finnish Embassy in New Delhi, and Mica Moraine, the home of the president of Finland, where the undulating glass walls reflect the ice age origins of the motherland.

Dipoli provides a dramatic contrast with neighboring buildings by Alvar Aalto and Kaija and Heikki Siren at Otaniemi Institute of Technology, as well as the adjacent, mostly modern garden city of Tapiola. Aalto's early career may have inspired the modernism of so much postwar design in Finland, but his greatest works, like the Pietiläs, are often organic in shape, emphasize natural materials and, most important, are those that reflect the landscape and psyche of Finland.

For the Pietiläs, there is no style, only the problem at hand, yet their unusual, idiosyncratic path to the solution marks them as worthy successors to Aalto. This is not to say that the Pietiläs have been outside the polemical battles that have enlivened Finnish architecture, particularly since Aalto's death in 1976. In fact, in his role as teacher and poet-philosopher, and in his attempt to create a new language of architecture, Reima Pietilä has become something of a cult figure, a designer as known for his theory as for his buildings.

Because the Pietiläs' work is seemingly difficult to comprehend (or perhaps too childlike in its simplicity?), their corpus is relatively small. But beneath and beyond the dazzle of their literary-cerebral aura, the Pietiläs' buildings—slow to be appreciated but already something of counterculture classics—are undeniably original and incredibly powerful.

—WILLIAM MORGAN

Giovanni Battista Piranesi: Santa Maria del Aventina, Rome, Italy, 1764-66

PIRANESI, Giovanni Battista.

Italian. Born in Venice, in 1720. Died in Rome, 9 November 1778. Apprenticed to Matteo Luchessi, then to Giovanni Scalfurotto, Venice.

Chronology of Works
In Italy

1764-66   Santa Maria Aventina, Rome (reconstructions and additions)

Publications

BOOKS BY PIRANESI

Della introduzione e del progresso delle belle arti in Europa ne' tempi antichi, prefazione. See Wilton-Ely, J.
Della magnificenza ed architettura dei Romani. Rome, 1760.
Diverse Maniere d'Adornare i Cammini ed Ogni Altra Parte Degli Edifizi Desunte dall' Architettura Egizia, Etrusca e Greca. Rome, 1769.
Il Campo Marzo dell'Antica Roma, edited by Franco Borsi, Rome, 1958.
Magnificenza ed Architettura de'Romani. 1761-62.
Osservazioni di G. B. P. sopra la Lettre de M. Mariette aux Auteurs de la Gazette Littéraire de l'Europe Inserita nel Supplemento dell'istessa Gazzetta Stampata Dimanche 4 Novembre MDCCLIV. Rome, 1765.
Prima parte di architettura e prospettive. Rome, 1743.

Prisons. With the "Carceri" Etchings. Preface by Aldous Huxley and critical study by Jean Adhémar, London and Paris, 1949.
The Polemical Works edited by J. Wilton-Ely. Farnborough, 1972.
Vasi, Candelabri, Cippi, Sarcophagi, Tripodi, Lucerne ed Ornamenti Antichi Disegnati ed Incisi dal Cav. G. B. Piranesi. Rome, 1778-1791.
Diverse maniere d'adornare i cammini. Rome, 1769.
Le antichità romane. 4 vols. Rome, 1756ff.
Parere su l'architettura. Rome, 1765.
Antichità di Cora. Rome, 1764.
Lettere di giustificazione scritte a Milord Charlemont e a di lui Agenti di Roma dal Sig. Piranesi. Rome, 1757.

BOOKS ABOUT PIRANESI

BACOU, ROSELINE: *Piranèse: Gravure et dessins.* Paris, 1974. English edition: *Piranesi: Etchings and Drawings.* Boston and London, 1975.
BRUNEL, G.: *Piranèse et les français, 1740-1790.* Rome, 1978.
CALVESI, MAURIZIO: *G. B. Piranesi e Francesco Piranesi.* Exhibition catalog. Rome, 1967-68.
CROFT-MURRAY, E. (ed.): *Piranesi: His Predecessors and His Heritage.* Exhibition catalog. London, 1968.
FOCILLON, HENRI: *Giovanni Battista Piranesi, 1720-1778.* Paris, 1918.
FOUCHET, M. P.: *Piranesi: Les prisons imaginaires.* Paris, 1970.
G. B. Piranesi, Etchings. Exhibition catalog. London, 1973.
GIESECKE, A.: *Giovanni Battista Piranesi.* Leipzig, 1911.
HARVEY, MIRANDA: *Piranesi: The Imaginary Views.* London and New York, 1979.

HERMANIN, FEDERICO: *Piranesi, architetto ed incisore*. Rome, 1922.

HERMANIN, FEDERICO; VOLPICELLI, L.; and PERUCCI, C. A.: *Piranesi: Carceri d'invenzione*. Rome, 1966.

HIND, ARTHUR M.: *Giovanni Battista Piranesi: A Critical Study*. London, 1922.

KAUFMANN, EMIL: *Architecture in the Age of Reason: Baroque and Post-Baroque in England, Italy, France*. Cambridge, Massachusetts, 1955.

KELLER, LUZIUS: *Piranèse et les romantiques français: Le mythe des escaliers en spirale*. Paris, 1966.

LEVIT, HERSCHEL: *Piranesi: Views of Rome, Then and Now*. New York and London, 1976.

MAYOR, A. HYATT: *Giovanni Battista Piranesi*. New York, 1952.

MILLER, NORBERT: *Archäologie des Traums: Versuch über Piranesi*. Munich, 1978.

MITCHELL, HERBERT and NYBERG, DOROTHY (eds.): *Piranesi: Drawings and Etchings at the Avery Architectural Library, Columbia University*. New York, 1975.

MORAZZONI, GIUSEPPE: *Piranesi, architetto ed incisore*. Rome, 1921.

MURRAY, PETER: *Piranesi and the Grandeur of Rome*. London, 1971.

PENNY, NICHOLAS: *Piranesi*. London, 1978.

Piranesi: Incisioni-Rami-Legature-Architetture. Exhibition catalog. Venice, 1978.

PRAZ, MARIO, and JANNATTONI, L.: *Piranesi: Magnificenza di Roma*. Milan, 1961.

PRAZ, MARIO: *Piranesi: Le carceri*. Milan, 1975.

REUDENBACH, BRUNO: *Piranesi: Architektur als Bild*. Munich, 1979.

ROBINSON, ANDREW: *Piranesi: Early Architectural Fantasies*. Chicago, 1986.

SCOTT, JONATHAN: *Piranesi*. London and New York, 1975.

STAMPFLE, FELICE: *Giovanni Battista Piranesi: Drawings in the Pierpont Morgan Library*. New York, 1978.

THOMAS, H.: *The Drawings of Giovanni Battista Piranesi*. London, 1955.

VOGT-GÖKNIL, U.: *Giovanni Battista Piranesi: Carceri*. Zurich, 1958.

VOLKMANN, HANS: *Giovanni Battista Piranesi, Architekt und Graphiker*. Berlin, 1965.

WILTON-ELY, JOHN: *The Mind and Art of Giovanni Battista Piranesi*. London, 1978.

ARTICLES ABOUT PIRANESI

FISCHER, M. F.: "Die Umbaupläne des Giovanni Battista Piranesi für den Chor von S. Giovanni in Laterano." *Münchner Jahrbuch der bildenden Kunst* xix (1968).

HARRIS, JOHN: "Le Geay, Piranesi and International Neo-classicism in Rome." In *Essays on the History of Architecture Presented to Rudolf Wittkower*. London, 1967.

KAUFMANN, EMIL: "Piranesi, Algarotti and Lodoli: a controversy in XVIII century Venice." *Gazette des Beaux-Arts* 46 (1955).

KÖRTE, WERNER: "Giovanni Battista Piranesi als praktischer Architekt." *Zeitschrift für Kunstgeschichte* 2 (1933).

MONFERINI, A.: "Piranesi e Bottari." *Piranesi e la cultura antiquaria*. Rome, 1983.

PALLUCCHINI, R.: "Introduzione al Convego." *Piranesi tra Venezia e l'Europa*. Florence, 1983.

RIEDER, W.: "Piranesi's 'Diverse Maniere'." *Burlington Magazine* LXV (1973).

WITTKOWER, RUDOLF: "Piranesi's *Parere sul'architettura*." *Journal of the Warburg and Courtauld Institutes* II, 2 (1938); reprinted in *Studies in the Italian Baroque*. London, 1975.

Giovanni Battista Piranesi's position in the history of architecture is a curious one. Although he received training in the profession as a youth in Venice and referred to himself as an architect all his life, Piranesi did not practice the art until late in his career (Santa Maria del Priorato, Rome). He instead became a skilled engraver and etcher after an apprenticeship with Giuseppe Vasi on his arrival in Rome at the age of 20; Piranesi is best known for an unbridled artistic imagination and vast technical achievements as one of the century's most prolific graphic illustrators. Piranesi's prints represent for the most part architectural monuments, and include *vedute,* maps, *capricci,* archaeological pastiches and reconstructions, and restored or invented antiquities. His mark on the history of architecture, then, is best gauged by his influence on the many, especially French and English architects and designers, with whom he had contact both directly in Rome and via his popular images published and distributed throughout Europe. They borrowed from him a mode of conceiving the built environment which inspired European neoclassical and visionary architecture and design of the late 18th and early 19th centuries.

Piranesi's early works included *vedute*—such as those bound and published together in *Le Vedute di Roma* (1748)—which were created as mementos of Rome and its environs for the many "grand tourists" of his age, and *capricci,* such as his first independent publication, *Prima Parte* (1743), which was conceived as a collection of imaginary grand monuments. In these publications, his images are forceful in that they captured the magnificence of ancient and modern Roman architecture, although not necessarily its accuracies. His grand conception of scale and the value of the effects of light and shade which he conveyed in his prints with the sensibility of a painter informed these and all his works, as did his obsessive fascination with the structure and planes of a building. He retained this same manner of representing the built environment in the plates of *Le Antichità Romane* (1756), a four-volume compendium of the monuments of Rome and the Roman *campagna,* in images that are part souvenir and part archaeological illustration, and of his later archaeological texts of the early 1760s.

Through his images, Piranesi no doubt influenced French neoclassical and visionary architecture. His method of representing architecture, instilling it with character, was transferred via the *pensionnaires* at the Academie di Architecture in Rome, by students such as Louis Le Lorrain, Nicolas Henri Jardin, E. A. Petitot, Charles de Wailly and A. F. Peyre, into the architecture of neoclassicism. Although the promise for generating a new architecture exhibited by these students remained for the most part unfulfilled when they returned to France, the next generations, including Etienne-Louis Boullée, Claude-Nicolas Ledoux, Jean-Fransois de Neufforge and J. N. L. Durand, continued the vision of scale and the transmission of mood in their forms liberated by the vision of Piranesi. Piranesi's contacts and points of interaction with the French neoclassicists were the focus of a conference in 1978; research on the summary influence of Piranesi on the French architects is forthcoming.

Piranesi also played a role in the development of English neoclassicism via the figure of Robert Adam. Adam was associated with Piranesi during his stay in Rome from 1755 to 1757, and their friendship was fruitful. Adam returned to England with a fascination with motifs of past cultures, including those of Greece, Rome and Etruria. Piranesi's publication of two decorative-art books, *Diverse maniere* (1769) and *Vasi, candelabri, cippi, sarcophagi* (1778), informed the later interior decorative schemes of Robert Adam, by supplying motifs to the more literal-minded English, and generated what is termed the Adam style in England.

In the 1760s Piranesi engaged in the theoretic polemics regarding aspects of historical and contemporary design current in mid-18th-century Europe. His scholarly texts were always accompanied by engravings that more potently conveyed his arguments, which tended to be dense and at times inconsistent and personal. There he addressed such issues as the supremacy—both chronological and technical—of Greek versus Roman architecture in his *Della Magnificenza* (1761), responding to the thesis of Julien-David LeRoy. Piranesi's opinions reflected much of the thought of the day, which reflected attitudes toward the past. There Piranesi revealed himself as a figure on the threshold of the modern age in his conception of history and archaeology in the service of architecture. While he was accurate—as accurate as technology allowed—in his archaeological fieldwork, his methods of archaeological research included an acceptance of universal memory and the artistic imagination as a useful means to help reconstruct the past.

—SUSAN M. DIXON

PLATT, Charles Adams.

American. Born in New York, 1861. Died in Cornish, New Hampshire, 12 September 1933. Four sons. Attended the National Academy of Design in New York; studied in Europe, 1882-87; joined the workshop of St. Gaudens, Cornish, New Hampshire, 1887; returned to Europe, 1892; exhibited paintings in Paris. Established architectural practice in New York, 1916.

Chronology of Works
All in the United States

1896-97	Garden, Brandegee Estate, Brookline, Massachusetts
1900	Garden, Larz Anderson Estate, Brookline, Massachusetts
1901	Frank Cheney, Jr., House, South Manchester, Connecticut
1901-04	Winston Churchill House and Garden, Cornish, New Hampshire
1902	Maxwell Public Library, Rockville, Connecticut
1904	John Jay Chapman House and Garden, Barrytown, New York
1904	Herbert Croly House and Garden, Cornish, New Hampshire
1905-06	Studio Building, 131-135 East 66th Street, New York City
1907	Mrs. James Roosevelt Twin Houses, New York City
1907-09	William G. Mather House and Garden, Cleveland, Ohio
1908-17	Harold F. McCormick House and Garden, Lake Forest, Illinois
1909	Josephine Shaw Lowell Fountain, Bryant Park, New York
1910-13	Russell A. Alger, Jr., House and Garden, Grosse Pointe, Michigan
1910-13	John T. Pratt House and Garden, Glen Cove, New York
1911-12	Leader Building, Cleveland, Ohio
1913-18	Freer Gallery, Washington, D.C.
1914	Astor Court Apartment Building, New York City

1915	Eugene Meyer, Jr., House, Mount Kisco, New York
1919	Hanna Building, Cleveland, Ohio
1919-30	University of Illinois Campus and Buildings, Urbana, Illinois
1922	William Fahnestock House, 457 Madison Avenue, New York City
1922	Palmer Library, Connecticut College for Women, New London, Connecticut
1922-33	Phillips Academy Buildings, Andover, Massachusetts
1925	Coolidge Auditorium, Library of Congress, Washington, D.C.
1926-27	Corcoran Gallery of Art, Washington, D.C. (addition)
1928-29	Apartment Buildings, New York City
1929	Lyman Allyn Gallery of Art, New London, Connecticut
1930-32	Deerfield Academy, Deerfield, Connecticut (buildings and grounds)

Publications

BOOKS BY PLATT

Italian Gardens. New York, 1894.

BOOKS ABOUT PLATT

CORTISSOZ, ROYAL: *Monograph of the Work of Charles A. Platt.* New York, 1913.
ISHAM, SAMUEL: *The History of American Painting.* New York, 1927.
MORGAN, KEITH N.: *Charles A. Platt: The Artist as Architect.* 1985.
VAN RENSSELAER, MARIANA GRISWOLD: *American Etchers.* New York, 1886.

ARTICLES ABOUT PLATT

CROLY, HERBERT: "The Architectural Work of Charles A. Platt." *Architectural Record* 15 (March 1904): 181-244.
EMBURY, AYMAR: "Charles A. Platt, His Work." *Architecture* 26 (1912): 130-162.

*

Few students or travelers have benefited as completely from sojourns abroad as did Charles Platt. His field observations of European architecture and designed landscapes influenced not only his personal style, but the work of a generation of designers, as well. It was while in France to study painting, following his youthful successes as an etcher, that Platt first became exposed to the grand Renaissance traditions of architecture and landscapes. Later during his celebrated trip to Italy, which resulted in his only significant written work, *Italian Gardens,* Platt viewed the more compact, human-scale designs of the cinquecento, which refined and crystallized his earlier design concepts. Those images were to inform the works that followed and to regenerate the Renaissance concept of the villa, that is, house, formal grounds, productive areas and distant landscapes as part of one indivisible composition.

In America Platt's design laboratory for these new ideas was the artists' colony at Cornish, New Hampshire, where the dramatic hills and valleys of the Connecticut River Valley provided the kind of natural backdrop that had inspired Italian designers. With immediate contacts through friends in the art world, such as Stephen Parris, Platt was quickly and frequently engaged to develop plans for houses, gardens or both. Even before Italy his designs, such as that for the Walker Residence or for his own home, were characterized by simple, classically derived building facades with equally clear floor plans, quite in contrast to much residential architecture of the late 1880s and 1890s, with its Queen Anne asymmetry and irregular masses. Equally unique was the use of geometric, architectonic spaces in the landscape which up to that time few landscape architects other than Nathan Barrett had favored. In many ways the summer homes of Cornish were diminutive versions of buildings and sites that Platt would design for the rest of his life.

Platt's interest in landscape design focused on site planning, rather than on planting design. Ellen Shipman, a noted designer in her own right, and other landscape architects often worked with Platt on planting aspects of projects. In site planning Platt's great virtuosity was the use of line, whether in formal lines of sight, in naturalistic woodland edges, or in the forms of garden structures or plants. At Gwinn, the Mather estate on Lake Erie in Cleveland, a broad, half-oval retaining wall enveloped a small harbor. This curving edge at the shoreline reinforced the contrast between the natural realm of the lake and the rectilinear forms of the designed estate grounds. An equally affective aspect of his plans was the use of generously scaled outdoor structures, such as pergolas or covered porches, to create transition spaces from indoors to outdoors.

As his work in landscape design evolved, Platt came to rely on compositions which combined three types of spaces, but he always adapted their arrangement and design to local conditions. His design for the Garden of Weld in Brookline, Massachusetts, which a contemporary called ''. . . the most perfect garden in the world,'' illustrated one use of this tripartite arrangement of turf panel, formal floral garden and structured woodland. Where his design duties extended beyond the gardens, he also typically included generously scaled, but simply detailed, parking courts.

Platt's name is most often associated with residential design because his earliest and most publicized works were for estates. After 1910, though, he designed an increasing number of commercial and public buildings, and worked on a large number of monuments and memorials. The Freer Gallery of the Smithsonian Institution in Washington, D.C., is the ''Platt system'' at its most refined. Its classic facade blended well with McMillan Commission proposals for architectural designs on the Mall, while the contrast of smooth and rusticated surfaces both articulated the arched entryway and gave this relatively small structure a presence among its larger and more elaborate neighbors. In plan the building was a massive block punctured by a central courtyard with an enclosing cloister-like arcade, which, as in his residences, blurred the edge between indoors and outdoors. A simple symmetrical room and hall arrangement gave clarity to the order of gallery visitation while at the same time implying separation into wings for different collections.

Less well known than his architectural works and residential landscapes were Platt's institutional site plans. In these he was able to extend Renaissance notions of rationally ordered space to large, complex sites. At the University of Illinois in Champaign-Urbana, he used axiality, symmetricality, sight line reinforcement in the third dimension, and repetition of architectural styles to create a completely unified, hierarchical campus plan. So successful was this scheme that many of its aspects are religiously followed to this day.

It is a testament to the clarity of Platt's original vision of spatial design that the basic organizational and stylistic approaches he developed in the 1890s were used and refined throughout his professional career. Applying his discriminating selectivity, Platt developed building schemes that had clear, simple spatial structures, while at the same time preserving relationships of internal function to facade design. Unlike other designers of formal gardens, such as Fletcher Steele, he envisioned the formal garden as an integrated sequence of spaces, rather than as a mere collection of thematic gardens. Perhaps Platt's most lasting contribution to the world of design was his vision of the interrelatedness of all architecture, landscape architecture, interior design, sculpture and painting as segments of a single circle that would materialize only when all were joined.

—NANCY J. VOLKMAN

PLAYFAIR, William Henry.

Scottish. Born in London, England, 28 August 1790. Died in Edinburgh, Scotland, 19 March 1857. Father was the architect James Playfair (1755-94). Studied with the architect William Stark (1770-1813), Edinburgh. Worked in the offices of James Wyatt (1746-1813) and Robert Smirke (1781-1867), London, 1813; opened own office shortly thereafter.

Chronology of Works
All in Scotland

1818	City Observatory, Calton Hill, Edinburgh
1819-27	Old Quad, Edinburgh University, Edinburgh
1820-23	Royal Circus, Edinburgh
1822-26	Royal Institution (now the Royal Scottish Academy), Edinburgh
1825	Monument to John Playfair, Calton Hill, Edinburgh
1826-29	National Monument, Calton Hill, Edinburgh (not completed)
1827-28	St. Stephen's Church, Edinburgh
1829-32	Royal College of Surgeons, Edinburgh
1831	Monument to Dugald Stewart, Calton Hill, Edinburgh
1838-45	Floors Castle, Roxburghshire (remodeling)
1841-45	Donaldson's Hospital, Edinburgh
1846-50	Free Church College, Edinburgh
1850-54	National Gallery of Scotland, Edinburgh

Publications

BOOKS ABOUT PLAYFAIR

CROOK, J. MORDAUNT: *The Greek Revival.* London, 1972.
DUNBAR, JOHN G.: *Architecture of Scotland.* London, 1966.
HITCHCOCK, HENRY-RUSSELL: *Early Victorian Architecture in Britain.* 2 vols. New York, 1954.
LINDSAY, IAN G.: *Georgian Edinburgh.* Edinburgh, 1948.
MACAULAY, JAMES: *The Gothic Revival, 1745-1845.* Glasgow, 1975.
YOUNGSON, A. J.: *The Making of Classical Edinburgh, 1750-1840.* Edinburgh, 1966.

ARTICLES ABOUT PLAYFAIR

GRAHAM, J. M.: ''Notice of the Life and Works of W. H. Playfair.'' *Transactions of the Architectural Institute of Scotland* 5, Part 4 (1859-61): 13-28.
HUGHES, T. HAROLD: ''W. H. Playfair.'' *Quarterly of the Incorporation of Architects in Scotland* Nos. 17-18 (1926).

William Henry Playfair: Royal Scottish Academy (formerly Royal Institution), Edinburgh, Scotland, 1822-26

It has been argued that Edinburgh, the "Athens of the North," owes its sobriquet not so much to its architecture but to the intellectual climate of the time. But if that climate demanded an intellectual architecture, then it must be that of William Henry Playfair. For although he never visited Greece or Rome, his architecture is infused with great learning, and reflects the intellectual world to which his uncle, Professor John Playfair, introduced him as a child and in which he practiced until poor health forced him into retirement and led to his death at the age of 66. Although his output was less prodigious than that of his rivals, the exacting quality and picturesque prominence of the work have ensured his lasting reputation.

Playfair's early training had been with talented Hellenists, William Stark in Scotland, and James Wyatt and Robert Smirke in London. Thus it is not surprising that, in 1816, Playfair used the Greek in his successful competition entry for the completion of Robert Adam's Roman Doric Old Quad at the University of Edinburgh. Built in 1819-27, these interiors are magnificent and provide that place of learning with a suitably stoic air: but is there not something a little Roman about the great coffered vault of the Upper Library, even a memory of Jean François Chalgrin's St. Philippe de Roule in Paris? Perhaps Playfair saw that building when he visited France in the summer of 1816.

It is possibly the siting of his buildings which makes Playfair's architecture so memorable. His early development of craggy Calton Hill resulted in a picturesque cemetery and a series of great, sweeping terraces which wrap themselves around the hill before descending toward the distant sea. These are Greek, using Doric, Ionic and Corinthian orders, and vast in scale: Royal Terrace is five stories high and 1,200 feet (360 meters) long. But it is the monuments on the top of the hill which stand out: the City Observatory (1818), four hexastyle porticoes

fronting a domed Greek cross; the Playfair Monument (1825), tetrastyle Doric, a lionless Lion Tomb from Cnidos; the Dugald Stuart Monument (1831), taken from the Choragic Monument of Lysicrates in Athens; and the National Monument. The National Monument, which Playfair later described as "proof of the pride and poverty of the Scots," was to be a replica of the Parthenon, built to honor the Scottish soldiers killed in the Napoleonic Wars. Charles Robert Cockerell was employed in 1823 to ensure the accuracy of the reproduction, and Playfair, the next year, to see it built. Work began in 1826, but after three years only 12 Doric columns, stylobate and architrave had been completed. And so it has remained. But if Edinburgh was the poorer for this debacle, then Playfair was the richer, for here, with the guidance of Cockerell and the example of the Parthenon, he had completed his education.

The scale of the National Monument was realized in the two temples Playfair built at the bottom of the Mound. The first, the Royal Institution (now the Royal Scottish Academy), built in 1822-26, was a formidable Greek Doric temple, but after five years Playfair returned to enrich and lengthen the building, adding sphinxes, columns and porticoes. He placed the National Gallery behind and not quite on axis with its giant neighbor, suggesting, perhaps, the irregular arrangement of ancient Greek sites. Originally Doric, the design had become Ionic by 1848 when the building was funded and might even have had picturesque towers on the corners, but those were dispensed with. What resulted was a lighter and more varied elevation than that of the Royal Institution.

Despite their scale, both the Royal Institution and the National Gallery promote a picturesque attitude peculiar to the Greek Revival in Britain. The same might be said of Playfair's Surgeon's Hall (1829-32), which performs the difficult operation of being both a street-front building and a freestanding one. The long, low wall, with its twinned entrances, forms both the street edge and the plinth for the hexastyle Ionic portico above. Thus Surgeon's Hall "floats" above the street, allowing its front and side porticoes every opportunity of expression. This is mature Playfair, and quite Athenian.

Playfair is most remembered for his Greek Revival architecture, but his sensibility to siting, mass and form is perhaps best understood from his works outside the stylistic umbrella of emotive neoclassicism. Donaldson's Hospital (1841) is a large, quadrangular, Jacobethan palace on the Edinburgh skyline. Drawing variously from Burghley, Linlithgow and Audley End, it achieves scale but not at the expense of detail, and remains picturesque without losing any of its formality. Playfair's obituarist in *The Scotsman* was surely right when he noted: "Architecture is an art so extremely apt to go astray that an intense fastidiousness, when it is subservient to powerful genius, is a great safeguard to the Public against permanent structural abomination."

—NEIL JACKSON

PLEČNIK, Jože.

Yugoslav. Born in Ljubljana, formerly Yugoslavia, 23 January 1872. Died in Ljubljana, 1957. Trained in the workshop of his father, a woodworker; continued training as a woodworker at the technical school, Graz, Austria; entered the studio of Otto Wagner, 1894; studied under Wagner at the Academy of Fine Arts, Vienna, 1895-98; won the Prix de Rome, traveled in Italy and France, 1898. Worked in Wagner's studio, 1899-1900; in private practice, Vienna, 1901-11; professor at the School of Applied Arts, Prague, 1911-21; professor at the Polytechnical School, Ljubljana, 1921-56.

Chronology of Works
All in Yugoslavia unless noted

1900	Villa Langer, Vienna, Austria
1901-02	Residential Apartments, Hamburgerstrasse, Vienna, Austria
1903-05	Zacherl House, Vienna, Austria
1910-13	Holy Ghost Church, Vienna, Austria
1920-30	Prague Castle, Prague, Czechoslovakia (restoration)
1920-30	Presidential Villa, Lány, Czechoslovakia
1923-27	Bogojine Church, Slovenia
1925-27	Chamber of Commerce, Ljubljana (interiors)
1926-27	St. Francis Church, Ljubljana
1928-30	Insurance Company Building, Ljubljana
1928-31	Sacred Heart Church, Prague, Czechoslovakia
1931	Shoemakers Bridge, Ljubljana
1931	Three Bridges, Ljubljana
1931-33	Villa Prelovšek, Ljubljana (restoration)
1932-57	Saint Anthony Church, Belgrade
1933-34	Peglezen House, Ljubljana
1937-40	National University Library, Ljubljana
1937-40	St. Michael in Barje Church, Ljubljana
1938-40	Funerary Chapels Ensemble, Ljubljana
1938-40	Zale Cemetery, Ljubljana
1939-42	Market, Ljubljana
1952-53	Monastery of the German Knights, Ljubljana (restoration)

Publications

BOOKS BY PLEČNIK

Napori. With F. Stelè. Ljubjana, Yugoslavia, 1955.
Architectura perennis. With F. Stelè and Anton Trstenjak. Ljubljana, Yugoslavia, 1941.

BOOKS ABOUT PLEČNIK

Architekt Jože Plečnik. Ljubljana, Yugolslavia, 1968.
BURKHARDT, FRANÇOIS (ed.): *Joče Plečnik, Architect—1872-1957.* Cambridge, Massachusetts, 1989.
Jose Plečnik, 1872-1857, Architecture and The City. Exhibition catalog. Oxford, 1983
POZZETTO, MARCO: *Joče Plečnik e la scuola di Otto Wagner.* Turin, Italy, 1968.
PRELOVSEK, DAMJAN: *Josef Plečnik: Wiener Arbeiten 1896-1914.* Vienna, 1979.
STRAJNIC, KOSTA: *Josip Plečnik.* Zagreb, Yugoslavia, 1920.

ARTICLES ABOUT PLEČNIK

BASSETT, R.: "Ljubljana 1925." *Architectural Review* 168 (1980).
BASSETT, R.: "Plečnik in Ljubljana." *Architectural Review* 170 (1981).

*

The work of one of Otto Wagner's most talented students, the Solvenian architect Jože Plečnik, did not receive much attention until recently. Plečnik's removal from the architectural historical milieu of the first half of the 20th century, in which most of his contemporaries were involved, was the result of his refusal to embrace fully the strongly deterministic ideology of modernism. Immersed in the world of his own belief in the individuality of each particular architectural situation, and devoted to the patient research of human scale and historical reference through the built form, Plečnik succeeded in creating an immense and deeply personal body of work in Vienna, Prague and his native Ljubljana.

Born into the modest, hardworking and deeply religious family of a Karst woodworker, Plečnik received his first training in his father's workshop; it was there that he developed a sincere appreciation for craft, an appreciation that would be constantly expressed in his design. He was trained as a woodworker at the technical school in Graz, then a town in the Austro-Hungarian monarchy, and spent several years as a furniture designer, only to become dissatisfied with his profession. He moved in the mid-1890s to the monarchy's capital, Vienna, where he not only witnessed but also actively participated in the events that marked the Viennese *fin-de-siècle*.

Plečnik enrolled in the architecture department at the Academy of Fine Arts in 1895, and studied under Otto Wagner for three years. Although in the beginning Plečnik's lack of formal education was an obvious obstacle, Wagner was instantly aware of the young man's talent, and he accepted him into his studio without hesitation. During that period, as well as several years after it, Plečnik worked in Wagner's office and developed a very close relationship with Wagner. However, Plečnik, the modest, religious and ascetic newcomer to Vienna, and the cosmopolitan Wagner differed in their respective views of the main tasks of architecture. But these differences, though unbridgeable, did not prevent the two architects from continuing to respect each other's work.

Jože Plečnik: Zacherl House, Vienna, Austria, 1903-05

Plečnik graduated in 1898 as one of the best students at the academy, winning the prestigious Rome traveling scholarship. Plečnik's Italian travel would permanently mark his work and his understanding of architectural history. After he returned from an almost yearlong trip, Plečnik continued to work in Wagner's office. Their disagreements became more and more frequent, and Plečnik left Wagner's office in 1900 to set up his own practice. For a short period he was associated with the Viennese Secession movement that had gathered various artists, including painters, sculptors and architects. In the academic year 1911-12, Wagner retired, and Plečnik was unanimously nominated to be his successor by the collegium of the academy (both students and professors), but was three times rejected by Archduke Franz Ferdinand. Plečnik, without bitterness, left Vienna for Prague, where he was appointed to a position at the School of Applied Arts. For the next decade he devoted himself to pedagogical work.

In 1921 he returned to his hometown of Ljubljana to take over the position of head of the department of architecture at the newly established Ljubljana University. The post-World War I liberation of Slovenia from centuries of foreign rule meant not only a resolute break with the imposed Austrian cultural presence, but also an opportunity to express a long-suppressed national identity. Plečnik readily accepted the challenge not only of educating the first generation of Slovenian architects, but also of redesigning the nation's capital, Ljubljana. In a period of only 15 years (until the beginning of World War II), Plečnik, fully aware of the importance of a new image for the city, succeeded in designing numerous projects that would charge Ljubljana with a new, symbolic energy. While it can be noted that his Ljubljana design failed to address fully issues

such as the future growth of the city (as in terms of transportation), through the new, symbolic itinerary it provided the city's inhabitants with a timely and desperately needed sense of unity and dignity.

His numerous built projects in Ljubljana included regulation of the banks of the Ljubljanica River, including several bridges; a market; university library; stadium; cemetery; churches; parks and squares; buildings of public importance, such as an insurance company and a chamber of commerce; and numerous pieces of urban furniture, such as a candelabra, columns and benches. Plečnik's creativity lasted until his death: in 1956, at age 84, he finished the restoration of a former monastery, Krizanke, transforming the courtyard into an open-air theater, with an immense sensitivity for the detail and combination of different materials.

Parallel to his Ljubljana projects, Plečnik worked from the early 1920s until the mid-1930s on another immense project—restoration of Prague Castle. He was appointed as the castle architect by Czech President Tomáš Masaryk, with whom he later became friends. Plečnik's design symbolically proclaims a unity of cultures, that of the Mediterranean and that of central Europe, through the careful and thoughtful combination of historical references. The same attempt can be noted in his design for Ljubljana.

Plečnik's conceptions of history, place and scale were intertwined, and it is necessary to observe them as a whole and not separately from one another. It is in the basic premise of Plečnik's work that history is to be understood as the flow of a living organism, as a rich continuum, and not as a static collection of data, that his shift from Wagner's teaching would become more apparent and, therefore, eventually so would his shift from modernism. Plečnik did not reject the use of historical references, as Wagner had proposed in his highly influential *Modern Architecture,* a textbook he had written for his students. Rather than searching for the universal values that would express the needs of ''modern man'' (a term emphasized by Wagner), Plečnik became more and more concerned about the need to express particularity, the individuality of each architectural situation, exploring the memory of the place through careful use of historical reference.

He also clearly understood the technological aspect of architecture, incorporating the most advanced materials; his two most important Viennese projects, the Zacherl House (1903-05) and the Holy Ghost Church (1910), were among the first examples in central Europe of the use of reinforced concrete. Yet the use of materials or technology never became the dominant element in Plečnik's design; rather, he strove to achieve a specific reconciliation of *genius loci* and *genius temporis* in his buildings.

A passionate devotion to the values of the individual human being, the appreciation of the experience of every single user of his architecture, also played a decisive role in Plečnik's design. He understood human scale as a common denominator; it was reflected in his designs as an elaboration of every detail of the building (and therefore as a means to facilitate, break the perception of the building into multiple experiences for the observer). The examples of the National University Library (1937-40) and Zale Cemetery (1938-40), both in Ljubljana, are especially convincing in that respect. Plečnik, redesigning his native Ljubljana, introduced the issues of human scale, historical reference and memory of place on the level of the city, achieving the complexity and richness of meanings, and therefore enabling Ljubljana's citizens to find their own personal interpretation of different urban situations.

—MAGDALENA GARMAZ

PONTI, Gio.

Italian. Born in Milan, Italy, 18 November 1891. Died September 1979. Married Giulia Vimercati, 1921; four children. Studied at the Milan Polytechnic School of Architecture, Dip.Arch., 1921. Served in the Italian Army, 1916-18. Partner with Emilio Lancia, Milan, 1927-33; partner with Antonio Fornaroli and Eugenio Soncini, Milan, 1933-45; partner with Fornaroli and Alberto Rosselli, Milan, 1952 until he retired in 1976. Professor of architecture, Milan Polytechnic, 1936-61. Founder editor, *Domus* magazine, Milan, 1928-41, 1948-79.

Chronology of Works
All in Italy unless noted

1930-31	Banca Unione, Milan (with E. Lancia)
1931	Villa Bouilhet, Paris, France
1931	Union Bank, Milan (with E. Lancia)
1932	Casa Borletti, Milan (with E. Lancia)
1933	Lictor Tower, Milan (with C. Chiodi)
1934	School of Mathematics, University of Rome, Rome
1934-39	Department of Letters Building, University of Padua, Padua
1935-36	Italian Institute, Vienna, Austria
1936	Montecatini Office Building, Milan (with A. Fornaroli and E. Soncini)
1936	Design for the Catholic Press Exhibition, Vatican City
1938	RAI Offices, Milan
1939	Villa Donegani, Bordighera

Gio Ponti: Pirelli Tower, Milan, Italy, 1956-58

1939	Great Hall and Basilica, Palazzo del Bo, University of Padua
1940	Fiat Building, Milan (with Fornaroli and Soncini)
1944	Casa Barzanti, Milan
1952	Edison Building, Milan (with Fornaroli)
1954	Villa Planchart, Caracas
1955	Town Hall, Cesanatico, Pesaro (with Fonaroli and Rosselli)
1956-58	Pirelli Tower, Milan (with others)
1971	Cathedral, Taranto
1972	Museum of Modern Art, Denver, Colorado, U.S.A.
1974	Shui-Hing Department Store, Hong Kong
1978	Shui-Hing Department Store, Singapore

Publications

BOOKS BY PONTI

La casa all'italiana. Milan, 1933.
Italiani. With Leonardo Sinsigalli. Milan, 1937.
Politica dell'architettura. Milan, 1944.
Verso la casa esatta. Milan, 1945.
L'architettura e un cristallo. Milan, 1945.
Ringrazio iddio che le cose non vanno a mode mio. Milan, 1946.
Paradiso perduto. Milan, 1956.
Milano oggi. Milan, 1957-60.
Amate l'architettura. Genoa, 1957. English ed.: *In Praise of Architecture*. New York, 1960.
Nuvole sono immagini. Milan, 1968.
Gio Ponti: The Complete Works, 1923-78. Edited by Lisa Licitra Ponti. Cambridge, Massachusetts, and London, 1990.

ARTICLES BY PONTI

Numerous articles in *Domus* and *Stile*, Milan, and in other architectural and design periodicals throughout the world.

BOOKS ABOUT PONTI

Cinquante anni di architettura italiana dal 1928 al 1978. Milan, 1979.
DI PATETTA, S. DAMIEN: *Il razionalismo e l'architettura in Italia durante il fascismo*. Venice, 1976.
GENNARINI, P. E.: "Gio Ponti: dell'architettura al disegno per l'industria." *Pirelli* No. 6 (November-December 1951): 8-9.
KAUFMANN, EDGAR, JR.: "Scraping the Skies of Italy." *Art News* (February 1966).
LABO, MARIO: *Ponti Summing Up*. Milan, 1958.
PAGANO, GIUSEPPE: *Tecnica dell'abitazione*. Milan, 1936.
PIACENTINI, MARCELLO: *Architettura d'oggi*. Rome, 1930.
PICA, AGNOLDOMENICO: *Architettura italiana ultima/Recent Italian Architecture*. Milan, 1959.
PLAUT, JAMES S.: *Espressione di Giovanni Ponti*. Milan, 1954.
SHAPIRA, N. (ed.): *The Expression of Gio Ponti*. Minneapolis, 1967.

ARTICLES ABOUT PONTI

BANHAM, REYNER: "Pirelli Building, Milan." *Architectural Review* (March 1961).
"Gio Ponti, 1891-1979." *Domus* (October 1979).
"Gio Ponti, 1891-1979." *Space Design* special issue (May 1981).

*

One of the most influential architects and designers of this century in Italy, Gio Ponti created a uniquely Italian modernism in the fields of interior and industrial design and architecture.

Perhaps his greatest legacy is the journal *Domus,* of which he was founder-director from 1928 to 1979. Ponti used the pages of *Domus* as an effective mouthpiece for his philosophy of the home and his ideas regarding interior design. The household objects he designed for the ceramics firm Richard-Ginori at the Monza Biennale of 1927, for example, were in the designer's own words, "an instance of morality." In these and other early works, the influence of the Wiener Werkstätte is evident.

A lifelong interest in the interior furnishings and architecture of the home was manifested most clearly in Ponti's series of apartment blocks designed for the upper middle class of Milan. In the Casa Borletti (1932, with Emilio Lancia), Ponti worked with a pared-down classical vocabulary that placed him securely in the group of Milanese "Novecento" architects, whose practitioners included Giovanni Muzio and Giuseppe De Finetti. With Emilio Lancia, Ponti later designed a series of residential complexes in Milan in which references to classicism were reduced to decorative touches.

The three connected buildings in the Via De Togni (1934) reveal the architect's turn in the mid-1930s toward a greater use of the vocabulary of rationalism. This group of buildings served as the prototype for other medium-sized apartments, whose interiors often featured "furnished windows" and space dividers, and whose stucco exteriors often were painted in bright colors. The Rasini apartment block and tower (1935, with Lancia) is an example of Ponti's "composition of elements." The tower itself, with its staggered rear profile, is a fusion of the "Novecento" and rationalist languages.

The creation of such apartment blocks and interiors could be considered one of Ponti's most significant design activities of his long career. His first editorial in *Domus* in 1928 was, in fact, titled "La casa all'italiana," in which he outlined his unique philosophy: "The 'casa all'italiana' is not a refuge ... against the ... climate.... Its design does not derive solely from the material necessities of life, it is not only a *machine à habiter*.... Its comfort lies in something higher, in giving us through architecture a measure for our very thoughts...."

Ponti's creation of a uniquely Italian modernism can also be seen in the first Montecatini Building in Milan (1938-39, with Antonio Fornaroli and Eugenio Soncini), one of the first "modern" office buildings in the Lombard capital. The architect himself described the building as reflecting "the coordinated repetition of functions and gestures, of the form and harmony of work," all of which, he believed, dictated the "architectural sameness" of the design. In what had by then become typical of Ponti's aesthetic, the Montecatini Building joined a traditional building material, marble, with a decidedly rationalist facade design. It was this "eclectic modernism" that Ponti had in fact insisted upon earlier, in the selection criteria for the decorative and industrial arts at the Fifth Milan Triennale of 1933, of which he served as director of the executive committee.

The architect put this fusion of classical and rationalist languages to work in one of his most famous buildings, the Mathematics Faculty of the University of Rome (1934). While the front elevation integrated the building into the overall classicizing scheme of the university devised by Marcello Piacentini, the rear elevation was an homage to the rationalist vocabulary, albeit in traditional Roman brick. Its flat roof, ribbon windows and great curved, smooth facade made Ponti's contribution to the new university unique. Ponti designed other significant work in Rome, including the scheme for the Catholic Press Exhibition in Vatican City (1936).

Ponti's best known building, the Pirelli skyscraper in Milan (1956-58, with Antonio Fornaroli, Alberto Rosselli and Giuseppe Valtolina; Pier Luigi Nervi and Arturo Danusso, structural engineers), has been hailed as one of the most original and articulate expressions of skyscraper design of the postwar period. Its tapering sides and bold structural skeleton give the building, once the tallest in Europe, its inimitable profile. It was described in the architectural press soon after completion as "magnificent," "certainly the most impressive, probably the best building" constructed in Milan in the postwar period. Indeed, it is recognized as a brilliant piece of advertising and as a symbol of the economic power and architectural daring of the Milanese industrialists.

Ponti's contributions to Italian and international design continued into the 1960s and 1970s. This work included religious architecture, such as the Cathedral of Taranto (1971), as well as banks, stores and houses in Italy, Holland, Pakistan and Hong Kong. Throughout his life, he contributed actively to the area of industrial design, theater design, city planning and architecture. His notion of modernism, always bound up with the idea of "morality," was central to his work, including his many influential editorials and books. Not only an astute designer, but a theorist as well, Ponti succeeded in fusing the forms and ideas of Italian classical tradition and rationalism. From the classicizing Bouilhet House in Garches, France (1926), to the "Superleggera" chair for Cassina (1955), Ponti never veered from a moderate avant-garde position. His prodigious output has secured him a central role in 20th-century design culture.

—ELLEN R. SHAPIRO

POPE, John Russell.

American. Born in New York City, 2 April 1874. Died in New York City, 27 August 1937. Attended College of the City of New York; studied architecture under William R. Ware, Columbia School of Mines, New York; studied at American Academy, Rome; diploma, École des Beaux-Arts, Paris, 1900. Worked in Bruce Price's office, New York; established own firm, New York, 1903. Member of the Fine Arts Commission, 1917-22 and the Federal Triangle Design Committee (1929-33). Fellow, American Institute of Architects, 1907; chevalier of the French Legion of Honor, 1924; member, Royal Institute of British Architects; member, Beaux-Arts Institute of Design; appointed to National Commission of Fine Arts; president, American Academy, Rome.

Chronology of Works
All in the United States
* Approximate dates

1905	Jacobs Summer Residence, Newport, Rhode Island
1907	McLean Residence, Washington, D.C.
1911	White-Meyer Residence, Washington, D.C.
1911-15	Temple of the Scottish Rite Freemasonry, Washington, D.C.
1919*	Union Station, Richmond, Virginia
1920	Laughlin Residence, Washington, D.C.
1925	Lincoln Memorial, Hodgenville, Kentucky
1925*	Marcus L. Ward Home for Aged and Respectable Bachelors and Widowers, Maplewood, New Jersey
1927	University Baptist Church, Baltimore, Maryland
1927-37	Baltimore Museum of Art, Maryland
1928	Estate of Marshall Field III, Huntington, New York
1928	First Presbyterian Church, New Rochelle, New York
1928-30	John Russell Pope House, Newport, Rhode Island
1929	Constitution Hall of the Daughters of the American Revolution, Washington, D.C.
1929	American Pharmaceutical Building, Washington, D.C.
1930	National City Christian Church, Washington, D.C.
1932	Calhoun College, New Haven, Connecticut
1932	Payne Whitney Gymnasium, Yale University, New Haven, Connecticut
1933-35	National Archives Building, Washington, D.C.
1936	Theodore Roosevelt Memorial, American Museum of Natural History, New York City
1937	American Battle Monument, Montfaucon, France
1937	Duveen Sculpture Gallery, British Museum, London, England
1937	Sculpture Hall, Tate Gallery, London, England
1937-41	National Gallery of Art, Washington, D.C. (completed by Eggers and Higgins)
1937-43	Jefferson Memorial, Washington, D.C. (completed by Eggers and Higgins)

Publications

ARTICLES ABOUT POPE

CROLY, HERBERT: "Recent Work of John Russell Pope." *Architectural Record* 29 (1911): 441-511.

HUDNUT, JOSEPH: "The Last of the Romans: Comment on the Building of the National Gallery of Art." *Magazine of Art* 34 (1941): 169-173

"John Russell Pope." *Journal of the Royal Institute of British Architects* 45 (1937): 102.

STANTON, PHOEBE: "A Note on John Russell Pope, Architect, 1874-1937." Part 2, pp. 60-69 in *Baltimore Museum of Art Annual IV: Studies in Honor of Gertrude Rosenthal.* Baltimore, 1972.

SWALES, FRANCIS S.: "Master Draftsman: John Russell Pope." *Pencil Points* 5 (1924): 64-80.

*

The crowning achievement of the architect John Russell Pope is most certainly the National Gallery of Art in Washington, D.C. By the time of its dedication in 1941, nearly four years after the architect's death, Pope's classical design had provoked a storm of debate, being deemed a white elephant by some critics, while simultaneously being heralded as a tour de force by others. The building's design can be seen as an evolution in the stylistic development of its author and a continuation of the legacy that Pope had inherited from his mentors William R. Ware and Charles Follen McKim.

John Russell Pope was born, the son of a portrait painter, in New York in 1874. Upon completion of his primary and secondary education he enrolled first in City College and later in Columbia University. Pope worked during his second and third years at Columbia under the direct supervision of William R. Ware, the elder statesman of American architectural education. Upon his matriculation from Columbia, Pope won the C. F. McKim Roman Scholarship in 1895 and the Schemerhorn Traveling Scholarship the following year. During his European sojourn, Pope produced a large quantity of accurate and vivid measured drawings of the major monuments of both the Renaissance and classical antiquity. Pope's discipline and self-motivation for the study of architecture led him almost predictably to the École des Beaux-Arts in Paris, where he was awarded the

Jean Le Claire Prize (1898) upon completing the entire course of study in a record time of two years.

Pope worked for Bruce Price upon his return to New York, until he began his own practice in 1903. Pope's practice included a healthy mixture of both public and private patronage. His residential projects accommodated the baronial aspirations of his affluent clients through the design of grand country houses and villas (e.g., Jacobs Summer Residence in Newport, Rhode Island, 1905. In these projects Pope turned to the classical models of Italian and French villas and their gardens for his inspiration. Though the architect is probably best remembered for the restrained and articulate classical style that typifies his country estates and public buildings, Pope was equally capable of rendering a more romantic tone to many of his domestic commissions. Pope's own house in Newport (1928-30) was a rambling display of both ideal and circumstantial form presented in a picturesque composition that suggests and aggregate of buildings assembled over time.

Pope's residential design talents were also tested in urban contexts. In the McLean Residence (1907), in Washington, D.C., Pope presented an inventive interpretation of a Florentine palazzo. The White-Meyer Residence (1911) and the Laughlin Residence (1920), both in Washington, were renditions of Georgian and French neoclassical architecture, respectively. The difficult task of accommodating a gracious promenade suitable for entertaining while simultaneously making provisions for services and conveniences was skillfully handled by means of an ingenious combination of en suite and corridor-loaded planning strategies.

Though Pope was respected for his expertise in residential design, he gained a reputation for being one of the preeminent designers of public buildings. Pope's first significant and most sublime monumental work was the Temple of the Scottish Rite Freemasonry (1911-15), in Washington, D.C. The pyramidal design of the temple was based upon the Tomb of Mausolus at Halicarnassus. Pope fabricated a promenade that was enriched by complex iconographic programs to frame the rituals of the Scottish Rite. The favorable reception of this building established Pope as one of the prime contenders for future commissions in the nation's capital.

Pope also proposed a series of schemes for a memorial to Abraham Lincoln on various sites throughout Washington, D.C. The schemes ranged from those of somber classical temples to those of dramatic funeral pyres that recalled the dramatic designs of Etiénne-Louis Boulée. Though Pope's schemes were not chosen for construction, the architect continued to have a significant influence upon the planning and design of the nation's capital through his involvement in the Fine Arts Commission (1917-22) and the Federal Triangle Design Committee (1929-33). He was to have a direct effect upon the shaping of the Mall and the realization of the ambitions set out by the McMillan Commission through his built designs for the National Archives (1929-33), American Pharmaceutical Building (1929), the Jefferson Memorial (1935-37) and, finally, the National Gallery of Art (1937-41).

By the time the commission for the National Gallery of Art was awarded, Pope had established his credentials as an expert in museum design. He was consulted on the National Gallery of Art in London and the Tate Gallery between 1929 and 1932. The successful Museum of Fine Arts in Baltimore (1929) and additions to the Metropolitan Museum of Art (1930), the Cloisters (1930) and the Frick Collection (1932) in New York City paved the way for Pope's ultimate commission. Pope's professional and technical expertise made him attractive to the institutional client. *Architectural Record* published a version of the "Office Manual of John Russell Pope" between February and

April 1931, citing the architect's attitude toward professional practice as exemplary for contemporary architects. Additionally, Pope's personal style of ornamental restraint, capacity to orchestrate elegant promenades, discretion with materials and mastery of interior illumination made the architect a natural choice for the commission. Changing stylistic sentiments, particularly the gaining of a foothold for International Style modernism in America, caused the Pope design to come into the national spotlight. Much to the benefit of the architect, donor Andrew Mellon preferred a traditional repository for his collection. Mellon's sentiments received support from the conservative Commission of Fine Arts. Pope's later commissions were completed after his death in 1937 by Eggers and Higgins, who had an indepth knowledge of the architect's intentions.

Pope's death marked the close of an era in the history of American architecture. Though Pope was concerned with many of the technical innovations that fascinated the International Style modernists, he maintained equal convictions about the refinement of a stylistic vocabulary which transcended time and the whimsy of fashionable taste. His resolve to remain fundamentally Greco-Roman caused the architect, like so many other "traditional modernists," to be excluded from nearly all of the histories of 20th-century architecture.

—BRIAN KELLY

PÖPPELMANN, Matthaeus D.

German. Born Matthaeus Daniel Pöppelmann in Herford, Westphalia, Germany, ca. 3 May 1662. Died in Dresden, 17 January 1736. Married Catherine Stumph, ca. 1692; sons included Carl Friedrich Pöppelmann (died in 1750), architect and adviser to the court in Warsaw, and the painter Johann Adolf Pöppelmann (1694-1773). Settled in Dresden, 1686; employed by the *Bauamt*, Dresden, 1690; appointed *Baukondukteur*, 1691; in charge of palace rebuilding operations for August the Strong, from 1704; appointed *Landbaumeister* (state architect), 1705; sent on study trip to Prague, Vienna and Rome, 1710; visited Paris and Versailles, 1715; promoted to *Oberlandbaumeister* (senior state architect), 1718.

Chronology of Works
All in Germany unless noted
† *Work no longer exists*

1708-19	Zwinger, Dresden (gardens, alterations and additional pavilions)
1715-33	Dutch Palace (now the Japanese Palace), Dresden (restoration and expansion, with Zacharias Longuelune and Jean de Bodt)
1716-36	Königstein Fortress (various works)
1720-23	Schloss Pillnitz, near Dresden (with Longuelune)
1720-24	Flemish Palace, Dresden†
1722-23	Peterstor, Leipzig†
1722-23	Schloss Graditz, near Torgau
1723-33	Hunting Lodge, Moritzburg (rebuilding)
1723-27	Church, Pillnitz
1727	Augustus Bridge (over the Elbe), Dresden
1728-30	Church, Friedrichstadt, Dresden
1730	Palace for the Saxon Kings of Poland, Warsaw (with Longuelune; only central section built)
1732-39	Dreikönigskirche (Church of the Epiphany), Dresden (completed by Georg Bähr)

Matthaeus D. Pöppelmann: Zwinger, Dresden, Germany, 1708-19

Publications

BOOKS ABOUT PÖPPELMANN

ASCHE, SIGFRIED: *Balthasar Permoser und die Barockskulptur des Dresdner Zwingers*. Berlin, 1966.

ASCHE, SIGFRIED: *Balthasar Permoser: Leben und Werk*. Berlin, 1978.

BACHLER, HAGEN, and SCHLECHTE, MONIKA: *Führer zum Barock in Dresden*. Dortmund, 1991.

DÖRING, BRUNO ALFRED: *Mathes Daniel Pöppelmann, der Meister des Dresdner Zwingers*. Dresden, 1930.

ERMISCH, HUBERT GEORG: *Der Zwinger zu Dresden*. Berlin, 1952.

FRANZ, GERHARD: *Zacharias Longuelune und die Baukunst des 18. Jahrhunderts in Dresden*. Berlin, 1953.

GURLITT, CORNELIUS: *August der Starke: Ein Fürstenleben aus der Zeit des deutschen Barock*. 2 vols. Dresden, 1924.

HARTMANN, HANS-GÜNTHER: *Pillnitz: Schloss, Park und Dorf*. Weimar, 1981.

HECKMANN, HERMANN: *Matthäus Daniel Pöppelmann als Zeichner*. Dresden, 1954.

HECKMANN, HERMANN: *Matthäus Daniel Pöppelmann: Leben und Werk*. Munich and Berlin, 1972.

HECKMANN, HERMANN: *Matthäus Daniel Pöppelmann und die Barockbaukunst in Dresden*. Stuttgart, 1986.

HEMPEL, EBERHARD: *Der Zwinger zu Dresden, Grundzüge und Schicksale seiner künstlerischen Gestaltung*. Berlin, 1961.

HENTSCHEL, WALTER: *Die sächsische Baukunst des 18. Jahrhunderts in Polen*. Berlin, 1967.

LÖFFLER, FRITZ: *Das alte Dresden*. Dresden, 1955.

SPONSEL, JEAN-LOUIS: *Der Zwinger, die Hoffeste und die Schlossbaupläne zu Dresden*. 2 vols. Dresden, 1924.

ARTICLES ABOUT PÖPPELMANN

HEMPEL, EBERHARD: ''Matthaeus Daniel Pöppelmann.'' *Westfällische Lebensbilder* 5 (1937).

*

Matthaeus Daniel Pöppelmann, though a Westphalian, settled in Dresden in 1686, and was appointed to the Landbauamt in 1691. In due course he became architect to the splendor-loving elector of Saxony and king of Poland, August II the Strong (reigned 1694-1733), and obtained the commission to build the Taschenberg Palais in Dresden for one of August's mistresses.

Under August the Strong, Dresden became prominent as a center for the arts. The invention of porcelain by J. F. Böttger in 1709 made Dresden significant in the marketing of fine porcelain, while the curious position of August as a Roman Catholic convert in a Protestant country created a new climate in Saxony. This was because August was hereditary president of the *Corpus Evangelicorum* in the Imperial Diet at Regensburg, thus on his conversion (so that he could be acceptable to the Poles as their new king) the Protestant ethos of Saxony became confused and weakened. The result was that Leipzig became one of the most liberal and enlightened of centers for publishing in all central Europe, as it was inhibited by neither strict Protestant primness nor excessive Papist paranoia.

In 1709 Pöppelmann was required to build a temporary grandstand and amphitheater of timber for a royal occasion, the visit of the king of Denmark to Saxony. August liked the structure so much he decided to replace it with a permanent building of stone to be called the "Zwinger," meaning, in German, a bailey, an outer courtyard, a bearpit or a cage. The Zwinger was intended to be part of a vast new Royal Palace which Pöppelmann was commanded to design: this huge complex would have stretched across to the banks of the River Elbe, and would have been a rival to Versailles in its magnificence, but it was not realized.

To ensure that everything would be as up-to-date as possible, Pöppelmann was sent, in 1710, to study architecture in Vienna and Italy, where he imbibed ideas from the architecture of Johann Lukas von Hildebrandt and J. B. Fischer von Erlach, and the essentials of Roman Baroque, especially the work of Carlo Fontana. In 1715 he also visited Paris and Versailles.

What, therefore, is the fragment (the anterior court only) known as the Zwinger which exists today, restored after war damage? It is partly an orangery, partly a grandstand, partly a nymphaeum and partly a gallery. It was intended to reflect glory on August by alluding to all the elements of Roman *thermae*. It is a large space (106 by 107 meters), with squares off two of the sides terminating in crescents in the centers of which are elaborate pavilions, built 1711-20. The space is enclosed by single-story galleries that link two-story pavilions and a gateway of the most exuberant Baroque style. Three sides were completed, but the fourth was later filled in with Gottfried Semper's picture gallery. On the court, in the corners, are four two-story pavilions between which are the squares terminating in the crescents with the amazing two-story pavilions. The long gallery by the canal has in its center the celebrated Kronentor of 1713. While the galleries are long runs of arched windows with pilasters and piers between, and are relatively plain, the Kronentor and the pavilions are Baroque extravaganzas, flights of fancy unchecked by any mundane notions of mere use, and objects in which architecture and sculpture are perfectly wedded. In the Kronentor broken segmental pediments are set at angles, swaying away from each other as though they had turned their backs, and great pile-ups of *putti,* with royal and electoral emblems and cartouches, rise to a bulbous knob of a climax on which is the crown. On the pavilions in the crescents, terminal figures struggle to carry the profusion of stonework above, and the whole is a wonderful expression of creativity and joyous invention. Everything there is in a state of movement, and the imaginative use of Baroque elements seems inexhaustible in its sheer bursting exuberance. The sculptor was Balthasar Permoser (1651-1732), and there can be no doubt that he and Pöppelmann created at the Zwinger a work that makes Roman Baroque look staid and almost stodgy.

Yet where did this riot of the architectonic imagination originate? Pöppelmann knew Vienna, had seen drawings by celebrated architects in the Vatican, and had access to a set of Andreas Schlüter's designs published in Berlin. Yet the clearest precedent for the Kronentor is the design for an octagonal tabernacle for a 40-hour exposition (plate 60) and the window dressings from San Carlo Borromeo, Milan, with broken pediment and cartouche between (plate 100) in Andrea Pozzo's *Prattica della Perspettiva,* which had come out in a German edition of 1708. The side pavilions, too, owe not a little to the facade of Pietro da Cortona's Santa Maria della Pace in Rome, where segmental curves are used to great effect. This is not to denigrate the freshness and originality with which Pöppelmann treated his architecture, for he transformed his Italian models utterly, and in comparison with the Zwinger, Italian Baroque *does* look rather tame.

Pöppelmann was also responsible for the enchanting Schloss Pillnitz (1720-23), situated on the Elbe near Dresden. This *Wasserpalais* has figures of Chinamen set under the widely overhanging eaves, with roofs also in the Chinese taste (very reminiscent of the central roof of the Upper Belvedere in Vienna). This "Indian"-cum-chinoiserie palace is one of the happiest creations of Saxon Rococo. August also planned an exotic pavilion at Pillnitz in which every room would have been paneled and roofed with porcelain, but the scheme was not executed.

From 1727 Pöppelmann appears to have been involved in designing extensions to the Japanisches Palais in Dresden-Neustadt, which was built to house the elector's collection of eastern porcelain and to show off the products of the Meissen factory. Pöppelmann may have worked on the original building of 1715-17: it also had a wide-eaved concave roof of a Chinese appearance, and the courtyard was decorated with statutes of mandarins. As well as these activities he designed the Dreikönigskirche in Neustadt (1732-39), but, as he was in Warsaw for much of that time, and after 1736 dead, the building was supervised by Georg Bähr, the architect of the brilliantly successful Frauenkirche in Dresden.

In 1728 Pöppelmann collaborated with Zacharias Longuelune (1689-1748), a French-born painter-architect, in designs for a huge new palace for the Saxon kings of Poland in Warsaw, but only the central section was built (1730). This would have been one of the largest palaces ever conceived, and in its complicated geometrical patterns promised even more delights than the Zwinger.

On his death, Pöppelmann's son, Karl Friedrich (died 1750), succeeded him as architect to the court in Warsaw. M. D. Pöppelmann is important as the designer of the Zwinger, one of the most outstanding examples of secular German Baroque architecture, but his scheme for the Warsaw palace certainly would have been as interesting. Schloss Pillnitz is a charming example of the 18th-century interest in exotica of an Oriental sort and falls into the early Rococo period.

—JAMES STEVENS CURL

PORTA, Giacomo della.

Italian. Born near Genoa, Italy, ca. 1532/33. Died in Rome, 1602. Apprenticed to Giudetto Giudetti, Vignola, and perhaps Michelangelo. Became architect of St. Peter's Rome, 1573.

Chronology of Works
All in Rome, Italy unless noted
* Approximate dates
† Work no longer exists

1562-68	Oratorio dell'Arciconfraternita del Santissimo Crocifisso di San Marcello
1564*	Santa Caterina dei Funari (facade)
1564-73	Santa Maria Maggiore (Sforza Chapel)
1565*-71	San Giovanni in Laterano (Massimo Chapel)
1565-84	Conservators' Palace, Capitoline Hill
1571-84	Il Gesù (facade, barrel vault, and completion of construction)
1572-78	Fountain, Piazza del Popolo (now in Piazza Nicosia)
1573*	Palazzo Farnese (upper loggia on the garden side)
1573-79	Senators' Palace, Capitoline Hill (interior)
1574-78	North and South Fountains, Piazza Navona
1574-79	St. Peter's (Chapel of Gergory XIII)
1575	Fountain, Piazza del Pantheon

Giacomo della Porta: Il Gesù, Rome, Italy, 1571-84

1578-85	Cordonata and Piazza, Capitoline Hill
1580*	Palazzo Capizucchi Gasparri, Piazza Campitelli
1580	Palazzo Serlupi-Lovatelli, Piazza Campitelli
1580	Santa Maria ai Monti
1580*-83	Sant'Atanasio dei Greci
1580-84	San Luigi dei Francesi (facade)
1581-84	Fountain, Piazza Colonna
1581-84	Fountain of the Turtles, Piazza Mattei
1582-84	Santa Maria Scala Coeli
1582-88	Fountain of the Egyptian Lions, bottom of the ramp to the Capitoline Hill
1582-91	Palazzo Ruggieri, Corso Vittorio Emanuele
1582-1602	San Giovanni dei Fiorentini (nave)
1583*	Palazzo Maffei-Marescotti, Via dei Cestari
1583*	Trinità dei Monti (facade)
1584-87	Palazzo Aldobrandini-Chigi, Piazza Colnna (initial stage)
1585	Palazzo Crescenzi-Serlupi, Via del Seminario
1586-87	St. Peter's (dome; with Domenico Fontana)
1587-92	Fountain, Piazza San Marco

1588-89	Fountain, Piazza Campitelli
1589	Fountain, Piazza Montanara
1589-90	Fountain, Piazza Ara Coeli
1589-93	Fountain, now in Piazza del Quirinale
1590	'La Terrina' Fountain, Piazza Chiesa Nuova
1591	Fountain, now in Via del Progresso
1951	Sant'Andrea della Valle (nave)
1593*	Palazzo Paluzzi Albertoni, Piazza Campitelli
1593-1602	Senators' Palace, Capitoline Hill (facade)
1594-1601	St. Peter's (Chapel of Clement VIII)
1594-1604	Palazzo Giustini-Piombino (completed by Carlo Lombardi)†
1596-1597	Pucci Tomb, Santa Maria sopra Minerva
1597-1602	San Giovanni in Laterano (transept)
1599	San Nicola in Carcere (facade)
1599	San Paolo alle Tre Fontane
1600	Santa Maria sopra Minerva (Aldobrandini Chapel)
1601	Villa Aldobrandini, Frascati

Publications

BOOKS ABOUT PORTA

ACKERMAN, JAMES S.: *The Architecture of Michelangelo*. Harmondsworth, England, and Baltimore, 1971.

GRAMBERG, W.: *Die Düsseldorfer Skizzenbücher des Giacomo della Porta*. 3 vols. 1964.

HEYDENREICH, LUDWIG H., and LOTZ, WOLFGANG: *Architecture in Italy, 1400-1600*. Harmondsworth, England, 1974.

ONOFRIO, CESARE D': *Le fontane di Roma*. Rome, 1957.

ONOFRIO, CESARE D': *La Villa Aldobrandini di Frascati*. Rome, 1963.

PECCHIAI, PIO: *Il Campidoglio nel cinquecento, sulla scorta dei documenti*. Rome, 1950.

PECCHIAI, PIO: *Il Gesù di Roma descritto ed illustrato*. Rome, 1952.

PROJA, GIOVANNI BATTISTA: *S. Nicola in Carcere*. Rome, 1970.

RUFINI, E.: *San Giovanni dei Fiorentini*. Rome, 1957.

TIBERIA, VITALIANO: *Giacomo della Porta: un architetto fra manierismo e barocco*. Rome, 1974.

WITTKOWER, RUDOLF: *La cupola di San Pietro di Michelangelo*. Florence, 1964.

ARTICLES ABOUT PORTA

ARSLAN, WART: "Forme architettoniche civili di Giacomo della Porta." *Bollettino d'arte* 6 (1926-27): 508-528.

BATTISTI, EUGENIO: "Disegni cinquecenteschi per San Giovanni del Fiorentini." *Quaderni dell'Istituto di Storia della Architettura* 31-48 (1961): 185-194.

FAGIOLO DELL'ARCO, M.: "Villa Aldobrandina Tuscolana." *Quaderni dell'Istituto di Storia dell'Architettura* (1960).

GIOVANNONI, GUSTAVO: "Chiese della seconda metà del cinquecento in Roma." Pp. 177-235 in *Saggi sulla architettura del rinascimento*. Milan, 1935.

HIBBARD, HOWARD: "The Early History of Sant'Andrea della Valle." *Art Bulletin* 43 (1961): 289-318.

LEFEVRE, RENATO: "Della Porta e Maderno a Palazzo Chigi." *Palladio* 21 (1971): 151-158.

SCHWAGER, KLAUS: "Kardinal Pietro Aldobrandinis Villa di Belvedere in Frascati." *Römisches Jahrbuch für Kunstgeschichte* 9-10 (1961-62): 289-382.

SCHWAGER, KLAUS: "Giacomo della Porta's Herkunft und Anfänge in Rom: Tatsachen, Indizien, Mutmassungen." *Römisches Jahrbuch für Kunstgeschichte* 15 (1975): 109-141.

THELEN, H.: "Der Palazzo della Sapienza in Rom." *Miscellanea Bibliothecae Hertzianae* 1 (1961): 258-307.

TIBERIA, VITALIANO: "Alcune note su Giacomo della Porta." *Palladio* 21 (1971): 181-188.

VON HENNEBERG, JOSEPHINE: "An Early Work by Giacomo della Porta: The Oratorio del Santissimo Crocifisso di San Marcello in Rome." *Art Bulletin* 52 (1970): 157-171.

WASSERMAN, JACK: "Giacomo della Porta's Church for the Sapienza in Rome." *Art Bulletin* 46 (1964): 501-510.

*

Giacomo della Porta steadily acquired stature in Roman architectural circles, gaining the title of "Architect to the Roman People" in 1564. The most prolific architect of the last quarter of the 16th century, he demonstrated his mastery of building technique in the most challenging projects of his era. Yet the character of his projects ranged from derivative to innovative. At his best, as in the justifiably famous facade of Il Gesù, he fused conventional elements to produce a dynamic, unified design.

He was born in Porlezza in Lombardy, near Genoa, where his antecedents had been sculptors. When he moved to Rome at mid-century, the burst of building activity coincided with his switch to architecture. His first master was probably Guidetto Guidetti, an able but little-known architect who designed the two-story facade of Santa Caterina dei Funari. Whatever della Porta's formal association with Vignola, their relations must have been strained after della Porta won the competition for Il Gesù in 1571. Furthermore, Vignola belonged to the circle of the Sangallo family, archrivals of Michelangelo, who became della Porta's paradigm. Regardless of whether Giacomo della Porta was ever engaged as his apprentice, the younger architect finished Michelangelo's most significant projects.

Della Porta's fruitful interaction with Michelangelo's architecture is exemplified by the Capitoline Hill. After the master's death in 1564, della Porta took over as architect (or surveyor of works), interpreting and amending the original plans. He completed the Conservators' Palace according to Michelangelo's project, but added a wide central window with a broken pediment to the central bay (1565-84), later duplicated on the Capitoline Palace. The remodeling of the Senators' Palace involved significant changes to the facade project, as della Porta simplified the windows and the central staircase (1593-1601). Della Porta's intervention extended to the piazza and the monumental staircase; nevertheless he remained faithful to the essence of Michelangelo's great urban plan.

In 1573, della Porta succeeded Vignola, who in turn had taken over from Michelangelo, as architect-in-chief of St. Peter's, thereby gaining another opportunity to implement as well as respond to Michelangelo's visionary ideas. As indicated in Michelangelo's plan, a new western arm for the crossing necessitated the demolition of the 15th-century choir. Della Porta oversaw the construction of a tunnel-vaulted arm of greater dimensions, and a monumental elevation on the garden exterior. He completed the Chapel of Gregory XIII (1574-78) and, much later, the Chapel of Clement VIII (1594-1601). The minor domes, which appear in Dupérac's engraving of 1569, derive from Vignola and della Porta, rather than Michelangelo, whose intentions remain unclear. Della Porta vaulted the dome of St. Peter's in 1588-91 with the double-shell construction planned by Michelangelo. However, the attenuated profile of the extant dome resembles the Florentine cupola rather than Michelangelo's hemispherical, classically inspired rotunda.

With his projects for church facades, della Porta contributed to a crucial aspect of architectural planning in the later 16th century. The increasing number of churches constructed on a longitudinal plan demanded alternative, yet consistently harmonious, arrangements for the two-story facade. Della Porta's project for San Luigi dei Francesi (1580-84) included a facade of two stories of equal dimension, with the width articulated by the classical orders. The design derived from Michelangelo's unexecuted plans for San Lorenzo in Florence, where a screen of columns added depth and rhythm to the surface of the facade. Although della Porta simplified his source, he typically found inspiration in the sculptural, dynamic manner of Michelangelo.

Della Porta frequently arranged the two-order facade in a pyramidal form, the type favored by Renaissance architects since Leon Battista Alberti. His winning design for Il Gesù represented a coherent solution to the restrictions imposed by a tall nave flanked by side chapels at the lower level. Unlike Vignola, who submitted a project notable for the equilibrium of its component parts, della Porta emphasized the plasticity of the surface and the monumentality befitting the mother church of the Jesuit order. As a result of della Porta's intervention, the facade acquired a strong central focus, with pilasters and engaged columns massed around the main portal, and with triangular and curving pediments to elevate the eye. Della Porta's patron, Cardinal Alessandro Farnese, ordered a giant barrel vault over the nave, rather than the more conventional wooden roof, with the result that the imposing dimensions of the interior compliment the verticality of the facade. Both the facade and vault were finished in 1577, and della Porta remained as architect-in-charge until the completion of the church in 1584.

Della Porta produced a longitudinal plan and a two-order facade for the Church of Santa Maria at Monti (1580). The plan is smaller and more compact than at Il Gesù, with a rectangular nave, nearly equal in proportion to the crossing, and three chapels to each side. In the interior, the entablature projects over the intervening pilasters, creating the effect of a sculpted, variegated surface that carries over into the vault. Della Porta was also responsible for the system of stucco decoration in the vault, which resulted from his expertise as a sculptor. The facade is one of the more successful of its type, combining the suggestion of Vignola's measured classicism with della Porta's own grasp of design principles.

There was hardly an architectural problem which Giacomo Della Porta did not confront during his long and active career. He continued to refine the interior elevation of the longitudinal church, as in Sant'Andrea della Valle (begun 1591), and he designed an unusual, octagonal plan for the centralized Church of Santa Maria Scala Coeli (1582-84). His variations on the facade included an early example of the use of twin towers at Sant'Atanasio dei Greci (ca. 1580-83) and SS. Trinitá dei Monti (ca. 1583). Some of his most impressive designs were stimulated by the works of other architects, as in the competition with Vignola at Il Gesú. On the other hand, his response to Michelangelo was notable for its subtlety; della Porta sought to merge his own architectural identity with that of the acknowledged master. For example, at the Palazzo Farnese, he built the garden facade (ca. 1573), a pleasing triple-arched loggia with a delicate cornice, set into the massive wall. Giacomo della Porta developed an ability for interpretation and synthesis, thereby laying foundations in the later 16th century for the Baroque.

—EUNICE D. HOWE

POST, George Browne.

American. Born in New York City, 1837. Died in Bernardsville, New Jersey, 28 November 1913. Studied civil engineering at New York University; entered R. M. Hunt's atelier, New York. Partnership with Charles D. Gambrill, 1860; established own firm, New York City, 1867. President, American Institute of Architects, 1896-97; honorary member, Royal Institute of British Architects; chevalier de la Legion d'Honneur, France, 1901; Gold Medal, American Institute of Architects, 1911.

Chronology of Works
All in the United States
† *Work no longer exists*

1868-70	Equitable Life Assurance Company Building, New York City
1872	Troy Savings Bank, Troy, New York
1873-75	Western Union Building, New York City†
1874-75	Chickering Hall, New York City
1875	Williamsburgh Savings Bank, Brooklyn, New York
1875-76	New York Hospital, New York City
1878-79	Long Island Historical Society Building, Brooklyn, New York
1879-80	Smith Building, New York City
1880-81	Post Building, New York City
1881-83	Mills Building, New York City
1881-85	Produce Exchange, New York City
1882-93	Cornelius Vanderbilt House, New York City
1883-85	Cotton Exchange, New York City
1884-85	Hamilton Club, Brooklyn, New York
1888-90	New York Times Building (now part of Pace College), New York City
1889-90	Pulitzer Building, New York City
1889-90	Union Trust Company Building, New York City
1890-93	Erie County Savings Bank, Buffalo, New York
1890-94	C. P. Huntington House, New York City
1891-92	Havemeyer Building, New York City
1893	Manufacturers and Liberal Arts Building, World's Columbian Exposition, Chicago, Illinois
1894	Bank of Pittsburgh, Pittsburgh, Pennsylvania
1895-98	Weld Building, New York City
1896	Park Building, Pittsburgh, Pennsylvania
1896	636-638 Broadway, New York City
1897-99	St. Paul Building, New York City
1897-1908	College of the City of New York, New York City
1901-04	New York Stock Exchange, New York City
1904-07	Wisconsin State Capitol, Madison, Wisconsin
1907-08	Cleveland Trust Company, Cleveland, Ohio
1910-11	334 Fourth Avenue, New York City
1911-12	Hotel Pontiac, Detroit, Michigan
1911-12	Statler Hotel, Cleveland, Ohio
1912	Williamson Building, Cleveland, Ohio

Publications

BOOKS ABOUT POST

CONDIT, CARL W.: *American Building Art, the Nineteenth Century.* New York, 1960.

ARTICLES ABOUT POST

BALMORI, DIANA: "George B. Post: The Process of Design and the New American Architectural Office (1868-1913)." *Journal of the Society of Architectural Historians* 46 (December 1987): 342-55.

MIKKELSEN, MICHAEL A.: "The Wisconsin State Capitol, Madison, Wisconsin." *Architectural Record* 42 (1917): 194-233.

SCHUYLER, MONTGOMERY: "The New Stock Exchange." *Architectural Record* 12 (1902): 413-420.

STURGIS, RUSSELL: "The Warehouse and the Factory in Architecture." *Architectural Record* 15 (January 1904): 1-17.

STURGIS, RUSSELL: "A Review of the Work of George B. Post." *Architectural Record* (June 1898).

"The Union Trust Company's Building, Broadway, New York, N.Y." *American Architect and Building News* 42 (October 1893).

WEISMAN, WINSTON: "New York and the Problem of the First Skyscraper." *Journal of the Society of Architectural Historians* 12 (March 1953): 13-21.

WEISMAN, WINSTON: "The Chicago School Issue." *Prairie School Review* 9 (1972): 6-30.

WEISMAN, WINSTON: "The Commercial Architecture of George B. Post." *Journal of the Society of Architectural Historians* 31 (September 1972): 176-203.

"Where Architects Work: George B. Posts's Workshop." *Architectural Record* 10 (1900): 77-85.

*

George Browne Post has been called the "father of the New York skyscraper," and his importance to the aesthetic and structural development of the tall office building is often underestimated, yet undeniable. One of several important pupils of Richard Morris Hunt—the first American graduate of the École des Beaux-Arts in Paris—Post excelled in the designing of commercial, public and private buildings. As an outstanding member of the "Eastern Establishment," Post contributed to the strong classical revival at the turn of the century in the period known as the American Renaissance. By the time of his death in 1913, he had received the highest honors attainable by an architect, including the AIA Gold Medal in 1911, and was decorated a Chevalier de la Legion d'Honneur in 1901. These and other honors indicate the high respect in which Post was held on both the national and international architectural scenes.

Post established his reputation with the Equitable Life Assurance Building in New York (1868-70) designed in collaboration with Arthur Gilman and Edward Kendall. Post was responsible for the interior structure, which included some use of iron supports and, most important, an elevator. Consequently, the Equitable Life became the first office building to be planned from the start with an elevator, a feature which would revolutionize commercial design. The elevator provided the vertical release for the skyscraper by allowing for greater rental value of the upper floors.

Post's 260-foot-high Western Union Building (1873-75) was one of the tallest buildings in the world, and was considered to be one of the first skyscrapers. The three-part division of the design into base, midsection and top anticipated the formula to be used consistently for the tall office building. The most progressive element of the design was the rational and functional grid-like organization of office space in the midsection of the building. This innovative feature stood in stark contrast to the flamboyant Second Empire roof that capped the composition. This expensive element would soon be abandoned in favor of a clean, flat, unbroken roofline. Although Post designed tall office buildings, he was not active in pushing the skyscraper to soaring new heights. Unlike the Chicago skyscraper pioneer Louis Sullivan, who promoted the vertical growth of the office building, Post believed the commercial buildings should "appear low, to be firmly anchored to the ground." One of Post's greatest structural achievements was his design for the New York Produce Exchange (1881-85). It was there that he came closest to true skyscraper construction. A complete metal skeleton, with cast-iron columns supporting wrought-iron beams, carried the interior load. Post exploited the possibilities of a metal frame by creating a trading room which spanned an incredible 3,200 feet of unobstructed space. The outer walls, however, were self-supporting, becoming a protective screen rather than full skeleton construction. He articulated the exterior of the eight-story building in an elegant "modified Italian Renaissance" style designed in brick and terra-cotta. The structural system employed in the Produce Exchange became inspirational to the skyscraper architects of the Chicago school and their development of full skeleton construction.

With the technical success of the Produce Exchange, Post received the prestigious commission for the Manufacturers and Liberal Arts Building at the World's Columbian Exposition in Chicago in 1893. He was one of three major East Coast architects invited to participate in the fair, and was given the largest structure to design. The interior span of the fair building was an astonishing 368 feet, a few feet larger in clear span than the Machinery Palace at the Paris Universal Exhibition of 1889, considered to be the largest clear span in the world. Keeping with the classical format of the fair, Post provided the exterior of the building with a series of arcades and placed large Roman triumphal arches at the major entrances. He became a major promotor of the strong revival of classicism inspired by the Columbian Exposition. His most famous design in this classical revival style is the New York Stock Exchange (1901-04). This monumental building, with its pedimented facade supported by six Corinthian columns, has become a memorable symbol of America's financial institutions.

In 1906 Post was joined by his two sons, William S. and James O., who entered the firm as equal partners under the name of George B. Post & Sons. This move helped ease the strain of managing one of the largest architectural firms in the country, which has continued to the present day. George B. Post died suddenly in November 1913, ending a long and prestigious career as one of America's pioneers in the development of the modern office building.

—KURT PITLUGA

POST, Pieter.

Dutch. Born in Haarlem, Netherlands, 1608. Died in The Hague, 1669. Worked as assistant to Jacob van Campen; worked as engineer to the statesman Constantijn Huygens; supervisor of works, 1640, and official architect, 1646, for Frederick Henry at Noordeinde Palace, The Hague; also worked independently.

Chronology of Works
All in the Netherlands

1645ff.	Huis ten Bosch, The Hague
1656-64	Town Hall, Maastricht

Publications

BOOKS ABOUT POST

ANDREAE F., HEKKER R. C., and TER KUILE E. H.: *Duizend Jaar Bouwen in Nederland.* Amsterdam, 1957-58.
BLOK, G. A. C.: *Pieter Post.* Siegen, 1937.
KUYPER, W.: *Dutch Classicist Architecture: A Survey of Dutch Architecture, Gardens, and Anglo-Dutch Relations from 1625 to 1700.* Delft, 1980.

Pieter Post worked in several areas of the Dutch Republic in the style of Baroque classicism as a capable but not greatly innovative follower of Jacob van Campen. The style, which was largely shaped in Holland by van Campen, was at its height by the 1630s and flourished there until about 1670. Characterized by a move away from the tall and decorative toward lower, simpler shapes which used the international vocabulary of the classical orders, the Classical Baroque appealed to the Dutch as an expression of greater dignity. Working initially as van Campen's assistant, Post was at the center of the development of this influential style. Post, the son of an artist, was a skilled draftsman and engraver of his own designs.

Post's very active independent career began as an engineer for the Dutch statesman Constantijn Huygens, which meant that he was introduced to court circles early in his career. By 1640

Post was the supervisor of works for the *stadholder* Frederick Henry at Noordeinde Palace, The Hague. In 1646 Post became Frederick Henry's official architect, and held that position and remained at the center of building activity until his death in 1669.

It was in that capacity that Post designed his best-known early work, the Huis ten Bosch, The Hague (begun in 1645), a country house for Amalia van Solms, Frederick Henry's wife. A compact but more complex design than those of van Campen, Huis ten Bosch is organized around a dominant cruciform domed hall, the Oranjezaal. On the exterior, the two-story entrance facade is divided into three sections of equal width with a pedimented central section. Post brought the end sections forward to break the idea of contained form cultivated by van Campen in such small, private structures. (During the 18th century, the exterior was greatly enlarged, and in the process Post's design for the facade was destroyed.) A large and wide, but short, octagonal cupola dominates the roofline and is the only indication of the interior hall.

The hall, which rises from the first story through the cupola, provides a magnificence beyond the small size of the building. In Post's unusual design for the hall, the transition from wall to ceiling and cupola opening is accomplished by means of coving. In a room of such complex shape, cruciform and high for its width, the coving must change direction frequently. The activity this produces in the design—both upward and outward—adds to the magnificence of the room. The walls are covered with rich Baroque allegorical decoration devised by Constantijn Huygens as a memorial to Frederick Henry (who died in 1647) and painted by several Dutch and Flemish artists, principally Jacob Jordaens but including Jacob van Campen.

At the same time Post carried out his royal commissions, he also designed many civic and private works. Among these designs were a great variety of building types, including a town plan for Mauritsstad, Brazil (ca. 1637), whose governor at the time was Prince Johan Maurits. Country houses, a mock castle, townhouses, town halls, churches, assembly halls, weigh houses, almshouses, a powder magazine, covered markets, a gun foundry and interior-decorating projects are among Post's accomplishments.

Among his civic designs, he is best known for the Maastricht Town Hall (1656-64). Reminiscent of the simple mass of van Campen's Amsterdam Town Hall (begun in 1648), Post's taller, narrower structure is equally imposing but designed on a much smaller scale. The building is three stories high and nine bays wide, compared with Amsterdam's five-story, 23-bay structure. In using a three-part elevation, each three bays wide, Post repeated his own success at the Huis ten Bosch. But in the Town Hall it is the central pedimented section, and not the end sections, that Post moved forward. On the main entrance facade, that central section projects farthest forward on the ground floor and progressively less so as the design moves upward. At the attic level, the central three bays capped with a pediment project above the roofline, but their facade is level with the elevation of the main block.

The Maastricht Town Hall's departures from van Campen's Amsterdam design are striking. The roof is more steeply pitched, a feature emphasized by the much greater height of the cupola. Post's cupola begins with the arcade van Campen used, but three stages intervene between it and the hemispherical dome of the type van Campen had used. Post is often regarded as an uninspired follower, but this design demonstrates how original he could indeed be.

—ANN STEWART BALAKIER

POTTER, Edward T.

American. Born Edward Tuckerman Potter in Schenectady, New York, 1831. Died on 24 October 1904. Brother was the architect William Appleton Potter; married Julia Maria Blackford. Apprenticeship, Richard Upjohn office, New York City, 1854-56. Established own firm, Schenectady, New York.

Chronology of Works
All in the United States
* Approximate dates
† Work no longer exists

1858-78	Nott Memorial, Union College, Schenectady, New York
1861-63	First Dutch Reformed Church, Schenectady, New York
1864-75	New England Congregational Church, Chicago, Illinois†
1865-72	All Saints' Memorial Church, Providence, Rhode Island
1867-69	Church of the Good Shepherd, Hartford, Connecticut
1867-73	Trinity Episcopal Cathedral, Davenport, Iowa
1871-72	St. John's Church, Yonkers, New York
1871-73	Harvard Church, Brookline, Massachusetts
1873-81	Mark Twain House, Hartford, Connecticut (with A. H. Thorp)
1894-96	Caldwell Hart Colt Memorial Parish House, Hartford, Connecticut
1901	Tenement Housing, New York City

Publications

BOOKS BY POTTER

A Statement of the Considerations Influencing the Design of the First Dutch Reformed Church, Schenectady, New York. New York, 1868.
World Pictures in Capitals. Philadelphia, 1869.

BOOKS ABOUT POTTER

LANDAU, SARAH BRADFORD: *Edward T. and William A. Potter, American High Victorian Architects.* New York and London, 1979.

*

Like his younger half-brother William Appleton Potter, E. T. Potter was a gentleman architect. In 1856 he married Julia Maria Blackford whose father, a banker, gave her a million dollars in 1863. That meant that although Potter began as a struggling architect, he was wealthy enough not to have to provide for his family through the practice of architecture. Most of his commissions were ecclesiastical, designed at a period when the High Victorian Gothic was the predominant romantic style. He designed few residential and secular buildings, which together with the churches amounted to fewer than 80 projects over a 30-year period of practice.

From 1854 to 1856 Potter served his architectural apprenticeship in the New York office of Richard Upjohn, and during 1857 spent nearly five months in England and France. His first independent architectural design dates from 1855, while he was working for Upjohn, but his first major commission was the First Dutch Reformed Church in Schenectady, New York (1862-63). It continued the Upjohn tradition in the High Victorian

Gothic, having a variety of polychromatic bands in local stone of different hues for the exterior, as advocated by the writings of John Ruskin and G. E. Street and as practiced in England by Street and William Butterfield. It was closest nevertheless to Deane and Woodward's Oxford Museum (begun 1856) in polychromy and sculpture. Potter discussed his philosophy of design for the church in an 1868 publication, and William Gillespie wrote a book in 1864 on the foliated capitals atop its polished granite and marble columns. The naturalistic leaves carved on the 13th-century capitals in the chapter house of Southwell Minster in England were the prototypes for capitals on the wooden screen dividing nave from single transept-like adjoining hall.

Potter was willing to use cast and wrought iron in other church designs, a practice which was frowned upon in Britain and the United States, except by lesser Low Church architects, and which had been rejected by the ecclesiological societies on both sides of the Atlantic after the very early phases of the Gothic Revival. In his travels in England during 1857, Potter had admired the Crystal Palace, which many in England, including Ruskin, had condemned. Ruskin had, however, justified the use of iron columns and ribs in Deane and Woodward's Oxford Museum because he claimed that this was the manner in which medieval builders would have used iron had they known of its structural potential. Potter was one of a small coterie of architects who liked the slenderness of iron columns because they allowed uninterrupted viewing inside the churches. Much later Potter was inspired by the second volume of Viollet-le-Duc's *Entretiens sur l'architecture* (1872), which forwarded the use of iron rather as the medieval builders had used wood frame construction.

Although Potter designed few secular buildings, his Nott Memorial at Union College, Schenectady, is an example of High Victorian Gothic applied to collegiate use. Plans for the college dated back to 1813, when Joseph-Jacques Ramée positioned a Pantheon rotunda at its focal point. Both the North and South colleges proposed by Ramée were actually built, but the more expensive proposed central building was postponed until 1858, when Potter was asked to design a building of unspecified use. His scheme called for a 16-sided, two-story Roman-Romanesque rotunda, the foundations of which were completed in 1859. There was a lapse in construction until 1872, by which time Potter had developed into a mature High Victorian Gothic designer. Internal light-metal supports were constructed during 1874 and 1875, but the rotunda was an awkward space, even though it worked well once William Appleton Potter and Robert Henderson Robertson converted it to a library in 1880.

Although E. T. Potter's early domestic architecture followed the tradition established by A. J. Downing and A. J. Davis, the house for Samuel L. Clemens at Hartford, Connecticut (1873-74), reflected the Stick Style of Richard Morris Hunt in Newport, Rhode Island, with elements transposed from France and elsewhere in Europe. Exterior walls were of a deep orange-red brick, and patterns ranged from brown and yellow to hues of blue. Internally the house relied upon English sources.

Potter's architecture always followed the precedents of others, as the three buildings discussed suggest. His brother, William Appleton Potter, was just as eclectic in his designs, but was more to the forefront in the various phases of 19th-century stylistic developments. E. T. Potter retired from the practice of architecture in 1877. In retirement he became concerned with the squalid and overcrowded conditions of tenement living in New York City. He published numerous suggestions for courtyard tenements, hoping that developers would adopt and build to his ideas. Only one set of tenements was constructed to Potter's designs; they are located at 326-330 East 35th Street and date from 1901.

—LAWRENCE WODEHOUSE

POTTER, William A.

American. Born William Appleton Potter in Schenectady, New York, 1842. Died in Rome, 19 February 1909. Brother was the architect Edward Tuckerman Potter. Graduated, Union College, 1864. Worked with Edward Potter, 1867-74; established own firm, New York City.

Chronology of Works
All in the United States
† Work no longer exists

1871-73	Chancellor Green Library, Princeton University, Princeton, New Jersey
1872-74	John C. Green Science Building, Princeton University, Princeton, New Jersey†
1872-75	South Congregational Church, Springfield, Massachusetts
1874-76	Berkshire Athenaeum, Pittsfield, Massachusetts
1875-76	University Hotel, Princeton, New Jersey (with Robert H. Robertson)†
1875-77	Stuart Hall, Princeton Theological Seminary, Princeton, New Jersey (with Robertson)
1875-77	Witherspoon Hall, Princeton, New Jersey (with Robertson)
1875-79	Courthouse and Post Office, Covington, Kentucky†
1875-79	Customhouse and Post Office, Fall River, Massachusetts†
1875-79	Courthouse and Post Office, Grand Rapids, Michigan†
1875-80	Courthouse and Post Office, Atlanta, Georgia†
1875-82	Post Office and Courthouse, Nashville, Tennessee
1877-78	C. H. Baldwin House, Oyster Bay, New York (with Robertson)
1879-80	E. H. Van Ingen House, Washington, Connecticut (with Robertson)
1881-83	Powers-Washburn Hall, Union College, Schenectady, New York†
1887-89	Christ Church, Poughkeepsie, New York
1887-89	Holy Trinity Church Complex (St. Martin's Episcopal Church), New York City
1891-94	Alexander Hall, Princeton University, Princeton, New Jersey
1892-97	Teachers College, New York City
1895-97	First Reformed Dutch Church, Somerville, New Jersey
1896-97	Pyne Library (East Pyne Building), Princeton University, Princeton, New Jersey

Publications

BOOKS ABOUT POTTER

LANDAU, SARAH BRADFORD: *Edward T. and William A. Potter, American High Victorian Architects.* New York and London, 1979.

William A. Potter: Chancellor Green Library, Princeton, New Jersey, 1871-73

ARTICLES ABOUT POTTER

HITCHCOCK, HENRY-RUSSELL: "Ruskin and American Architecture, or Regeneration Long Delayed." Pp. 166-208 in JOHN SUMMERSON (ed.): *Concerning Architecture: Essays on Architectural Writers and Writing Presented to Nikolaus Pevsner.* London, 1968.
SCHUYLER, MONTGOMERY: "The Work of William Appleton Potter." *Architectural Record* 26 (1909): 176-196.
WODEHOUSE, LAWRENCE: "William Appleton Potter, Principal *Pasticheur* of Henry Hobson Richardson." *Journal of the Society of Architectural Historians* 32 (1973): 175-192.

*

William Appleton Potter practiced architecture during the last quarter of the 19th century in the romantic tradition of Henry Hobson Richardson. Potter evolved from Richardson's High Victorian Gothic into the Richardsonian Romanesque, Queen Anne style, and beyond Richardson to the academic Late Gothic Revival. Potter was not professionally trained, but worked in the architectural office of his half-brother Edward Tuckerman Potter from 1867 to 1874. Potter came from a large and affluent family, and both he and his siblings had distinguished careers in academic, religious and professional fields.

In 1864 William graduated with a degree in chemistry from Union College, where his father was vice-president, and he taught for one year at Columbia prior to travel in Europe. In Edward's office he met his future partner, Robert Henderson Robertson (1849-1919), a graduate of Rutgers who had joined the office in 1872.

While still working for his brother, William obtained his first commissions at the invitation of Princeton University, and in quick succession he designed the Chancellor Green Library (1871-72), Green School of Science (1874), University Hotel (1875-76) and Stuart Hall for the Princeton Theological Seminary (1875-77), all in the High Victorian Gothic. That version of the Gothic no longer looked exclusively to English medieval architecture, but to a wider European spectrum. Structural polychromatic and decorative materials were organized in a variety of patterns and colors, and detailing was bold so that each building design could be an entirely new and original composition, although adapted from a variety of sources. The South Congregational Church at Springfield, Massachusetts (1872-74), was possibly Potter's most significant design in the High Victorian Gothic idiom, although it was strongly reliant upon Richardson's North Congregational Church (1866-69) in the same town. On the exterior, South Congregational is bold but elegant, with a unity of elements, while its interior is spacious and has a generous organization of the plan.

Potter's reputation at Princeton contributed to his being appointed as supervising architect of the Treasury Department, in succession to A. B. Mullett, on January 1, 1875. Potter and Robertson became partners probably late in 1874, a partnership that lasted until 1880, and they continued to accept work while Potter held his government position. Potter was always the major designer within the partnership, although Robertson seems to have contributed several designs in the Queen Anne style.

As supervising architect for 18 months, Potter modified and designed new federal buildings, ranging from the building at Dover, Delaware, costing only $50,000, to his largest at Nashville, Tennessee, costing $400,000. By comparison, Mullett's largest federal buildings cost from $4 million to $10 million. All Potter's designs continued in the High Victorian Gothic, but they were uncharacteristically symmetrical. Internal organization and structure were little different from the designs by Ammi Young or Mullett. In the building at Grand Rapids, Michigan, Potter introduced Romanesque elements, motifs and details, and that led to a similar expression when he returned to private practice. The competition drawings for the symmetrical Metropolitan Opera House in New York (1880) continued the precedents established at Grand Rapids.

Richardson' Trinity Church in Boston (1872-78) and the Richardsonian style in general had a strong impact upon Potter and other members of the architectural profession. This can best be seen on the Princeton campus, where Potter designed Commencement Hall [Alexander Hall] (1892) in the bold polychromatic style. The style was more suited to religious buildings, and three by Potter in New York City illustrate his mastery of the style. St. Agnes Chapel on 92nd Street (1889) and the Madison Avenue Lutheran Church of St. James (1891) are no longer extant and can be studied only from illustrations. This is not the case for Holy Trinity, Harlem (1887-89), now St. Martin's Episcopal Church, with its parish house and rectory. There a rich brown sandstone contrasts with the warm rock-faced granite; the whole is capped by a red tile roof.

Potter had won the competition for St. Agnes while his brother, Henry Codman Potter, was Episcopal bishop of New York. Not wishing to be accused of nepotism, the bishop was determined that his brother would not win the competition for the Cathedral of St. John the Divine, which William had entered in collaboration with Robertson. There was a two-stage competition with the four finalists, including Potter, competing for the first premium. William disqualified himself by submitting late. Had his design been successful, it would have been an excellent example of the Late Gothic Revival. The design was basically a compilation of elements from the English medieval period with strong ties to Lincoln and Peterborough cathedrals, but with a magnificent cluster of four towers capped with spires at the corners of the central crossing, an original touch based upon Spanish medieval examples. This was not Potter's only digression into that late 19th-century phase of the Gothic. He designed several secular buildings in the style, including his last building for Princeton, the Pyne Library (1895-96), a great quadrangular building adjoining the small Chancellor Green Library of a quarter-century earlier. Termed collegiate Gothic, the style was associated academically with Oxford and Cambridge buildings, and although it mimicked the 15th century, Potter's library paralleled what was being built at Oxbridge in the late 19th century. The new library also incorporated the most up-to-date metal structural stack system.

Potter was a major figure in the romantic traditions of the late 19th century and one of the best architects who captured the spirit of H. H. Richardson. He retired to Rome in 1902 and died there in 1909.

—LAWRENCE WODEHOUSE

POZZO, Andrea.

Italian. Born in Trento, Italy, 30 November 1642. Died in Vienna, Austria, 31 August 1709. Trained in north Italy; novice in order of Discalced Carmelites at Convento delle Laste, near Trento, 1661-62; became a Jesuit lay brother, 1665, but encouraged to continue painting by his superiors; worked in Rome, 1681-1702; worked in Vienna, from 1703.

Chronology of Works

All in Italy unless noted
† *Work no longer exists*

1676-79	San Francesco Saverio, Mondovi (high altar and sham cupola)
1681-84	Il Gesù, Frascati (high altar)
1684-85	Sant'Ignazio, Rome (sham cupola)
1685	Il Gesù, Rome (*Quarant'ore*)†
1685	Sant'Ignazio, Rome (left transept altar)†
1685-1701	Sant'Ignazio, Rome (choir)
1695-99	Il Gesù, Rome (altar of Sant'Ignazio)
1697-99	Sant'Ignazio, Rome (altar of San Luigi Gonzaga)
1697-1703	Cathedral, Foligno (high altar)
1699-1725	Sant'Ignazio, Dubrovnik, formerly Yugoslavia
1700-05	Cathedral, Ljubljana, formerly Yugoslavia
1700-11	San Francesco Saverio, Trento
1702	Oratorio di San Bernardo, Montepulciano
1702	Santa Maria dei Servi, Montepulciano
1702(?)	San Sebastiano, Verona (high altar)
1702-04	Collegiata di San Michele, Lucignano d'Arezzo (high altar)
1702-14	Il Gesù, Montepulciano
1703-09	Universitätskirche, Vienna, Austria (high altar and *coretti*)
1704	Chiesa dei Gesuiti, Belluno
1705-10	Santa Maria delle Grazie, Arco, Trento (high altar)
1706	Franziskanerkirche, Vienna, Austria (high altar)

Publications

BOOKS BY POZZO

Perspectiva pictorum et architectorum. 2 vols. Rome, 1693-1700. English edition: *Rules and Examples of Perspective.* Edited by John James. London, 1707.
Significati delle pitture fatte nella volta della chiesa di S. Ignazio. Rome, 1828.

BOOKS ABOUT POZZO

CARBONERI, NINO (ed.): *Andrea Pozzo architetto (1642-1709).* Trento, Italy, 1961.
DE FEO, VITTORIO: *Pozzo: Architettura e illusione.* Rome, 1988.
KERBER, BERNHARD: *Andrea Pozzo.* Berlin and New York, 1971.

ARTICLES ABOUT POZZO

ENGGASS, ROBERT: "The Altar-rail for St. Ignatius's Chapel in the Gesù in Rome." *Burlington Magazine* 116 (1974): 178-189.
WITTKOWER, RUDOLF, and JAFFE, IRMA B. (eds.): *Baroque Art: The Jesuit Contribution.* New York, 1972.

*

Andrea Pozzo is best known for his illusionistic *quadratura* painting, but he also wrote an important treatise on perspective, and worked as an architect in both permanent and ephemeral architecture. His work, especially in architecture, has received comparatively little recent scholarly attention, perhaps because his delight in rich materials and complex, sinuous forms is not shared by many today and partly because his work's geographical dispersion makes it a demanding subject.

Like Francesco Borromini, to whom he was indebted, much of Pozzo's artistic formation was northern Italian. Born in Trento, he worked as a painter there, in Milan and Como before joining the Jesuits as a lay brother in Milan in 1665. Almost all his work was undertaken for the Jesuits, between 1681 and 1702 in Rome, and thereafter in Vienna, where he stayed until his death.

Despite its geographical dispersion and variety, certain themes unite his work. Illusionism, perspective, drama, manipulating light and creating impressions of forbidding majesty were his perennial concerns, mustered in support of Catholic faith and of the Jesuits in particular. He was indebted to the theater: much of his painting exploits theatrical devices and stage requisites, such as the proscenium arch, the curtain, the *quadratura* backdrop, and painted "actors" stepping out from the painted wings. As Rudolf Wittkower has pointed out, Pozzo's *Perspectiva pictorum et architectorum* (two volumes published in Rome, 1693 and 1698), evinces the very close relationship between painting in the grand manner and stage design.

The *Perspectiva* exercised a keen influence on architects throughout Europe (translations were printed in German, English and Flemish, and a manuscript version exists in Chinese). The treatise shows how the orders should be drawn in perspective, as in *sotto in su* painting; designs for altars, tabernacles and ephemeral structures for festivals; and church designs. In characteristic 17th-century fashion, Pozzo suggested that familiarity with perspective and *quadratura* was enough to qualify anyone as an architect. He enjoyed complex curvilinear plans, and towering and dramatic elevations, enlivened by every Baroque element, such as broken and open pediments, and multiplied in a manner reminiscent of Spanish work by Francisco Hurtado Izquierdo.

The painted decoration of the vaults, apse and walls of Sant'Ignazio in Rome (1684-94) is one of the most elaborate programs of religious painting of the period, expounding the whole early history of the Jesuits. The *quadratura* painting of the nave vault, illustrating the Gospel phrase which Saint Ignatius made his own, "Ignem veni mittere in terram," is unusually daring in its illusionism: from a point in the middle of the nave, all the perspective falls into place and the vault opens into the apparent heights of infinity. Foreshortened columns create a continuum between real and unreal architecture, mundane and spiritual experience. Color and light create a limpid iridescent atmosphere in which the universal truth of Jesuit rule is celebrated.

Pozzo designed two closely related and particularly lavish altars for the two principal Jesuit churches in Rome: the altars of Saint Ignatius (ca. 1700) in the left transept of Il Gesù and the Altar of Saint Luigi Gonzaga (built in 1750 from a drawing by Pozzo) in the right transept of Sant'Ignazio. Brilliantly colored and full of movement, the principal architectural structure in both is an aedicule framed by marble Solomonic columns, wound round with gilt bronze vine leaves. The reference is to Solomon's Temple in Jerusalem: both iconographically and formally the altars function in relation to the churches in which they stand.

His paintings and sculptured altars evoke worlds in which human beings are dwarfed by the daunting environment of monumental architecture in which they sit, stand or fall, powerless, fragile, yet fantastically elegant. The result is a nervous tension between subject and mood; a world of impossible contradictions and unattainable absolutes. The combination of apparent inclusion with effective exclusion from his fantastic painted spaces achieves the desired effect of asserting the power and authority of the Jesuit order and overwhelming the worshipper.

Temporary structures must have provided wonderful opportunities for Pozzo to exploit his love of color, illusion, complex structure and propaganda, making their loss all the sadder. His *sepolcro* for the exposition of the sacrament at Easter for Sant'Ignazio, for example, was a grand *tempietto,* providing a formidable setting for the blazing urn containing the sacrament. However, the relationship between his permanent architecture and his ephemeral *apparati* was close. Indeed, once he had designed something pleasing to him, he was ready to apply it to remarkably different functions. Thus the main altar of the Santuario della Madonna delle Grazie is a reworking of his first project for the facade of San Giovanni in Laterano (*Trattato,* II, 83).

Pozzo's fantastic imagination and love of elaborated exuberant decoration were too much for many of his contemporaries, and many of his ideas remained on paper—among the most significant of them being his projects for the Cathedral at Frascati (1696) and for the facade of San Giovanni in Laterano.

—HELEN HILLS

PRANDTAUER, Jacob.

Austrian. Born in Stanz near Landeck, Austria, 1658. Died in St. Pölten, 16 September 1726. Cousin, teacher and colleague of Joseph Mungenast (died 1741). Learned masonry from Hans Georg Asam, 1677; under contract to the Italian Carlones family of masons and sculptors, 1680; studied in Munich, 1683-85. Was a sculptor for Albert Ernst, duke of Courland, on his castle in Thalheim, 1689.

Chronology of Works
All in Austria

1660-1710	Pilgrimage Church of Maria Taerl, near Melk (crossing and part of the cupola)
1689	Benedictine Monastery, Weikendorf (remodeling and completion)
1690	Castle of Thalheim, Schwaighof (chapel and pavillions)
1694-1700	St. Pölten Abbey, Schwaighof
1698	Castle, Ochsenburg (additions)
1702-07	Church, Weikendorf (remodeling)
1702-14	Benedictine Church and Monastery, Melk (new construction and rebuilding by Mungennast after a fire, 1738)
1703	Cellar Extension, Wiesenthal
1706-32	Pilgrimage Church, Sonntagberg
1708-12	Carmelite Church and Monastery, St. Pölten, Schwaighof
1708-15	Garsten Monastery, St. Florian (completion)
1713	Monastery, Klosterneuburg
1714	Monastery, Herzogenburg
1715-26	Church, Ponsee (remodeling)
1716	Refectory, Melk
1717-22	Meierhof, Kremsmünster, Linz
1718-22	Marble Hall, St. Florian
1719-26	Court of Kremsmünster, Linz
1720	Dechantei, St. Florian
1721-22	Church, St. Pölten, Schwaighof
1721-26	Church, Ravelsbach
1724-26	Hohenbrunn
1725	Church, Wullersdorf
1725-28	Monastery, Herzogenburg

Jacob Prandtauer: Benedictine Church and Monastery, Melk, Austria, 1702-14

Publications

BOOKS ABOUT PRANDTAUER

BACHMANN, LUISE GEORGE: *Die andere Schöpfung: Ein Baumeister Roman*. Paderborn, Germany, 1949.

HANTSCH, HUGO: *Jakob Prandtauer: Der Klosterarchitekt des österreichischen Barock*. Vienna, 1926.

HEMPEL, EBERHARD: *Baroque Art and Architecture in Central Europe*. Harmondsworth, England, 1965.

HOTZ, WALTER: *Melk und die Wachbau*. Berlin, 1938.

Jakob Prandtauer und sein Kunstkreis. Exhibition catalog. Vienna, 1960.

KERBER, OTTMAR: *Von Bramante zu Lucas von Hildebrandt*. Stuttgart, Germany, 1947.

MILLON, HENRY A.: *Baroque and Rococo Architecture*. New York, 1961.

RIESENHUBER, MARTIN: *Die kirchliche Barockkunst in Österreich*. Linz, Austria, 1924.

SCHIER, WILHELM: *Das Benediktinerstift Melk a.d. Donau*. Vienna, 1930.

SEDLMAYR, HANS: *Österreichische Barockarchitektur: 1690-1740*. Vienna, 1930.

VOLKSHOCHSCHULE, LANDECK: *Bildner, Planer und Poeten im Oberen Inntal: Fetschrift der Volkhochschule Landeck anlässlich des 300. Geburtstages Jakob Prandtauer's geleitet von Hermann Kuprian*. Innsbruck, Austria, 1960.

*

Jakob Prandtauer (1658-1726) was the cousin, teacher, and later the colleague of Joseph Mungennast (died 1741). Both men came from the Tirol, which is next door to Bavaria, so Bavarian influences were strong in that region. Tirol also had a lively local craft tradition, and Prandtauer, trained as a mason, was steeped in a healthy respect for local craftsmen and their potential creativity.

One of the first buildings on which Prandtauer worked was the Pilgrimage Church of Maria Taferl (1660-1710): it is set on a hill on the north bank of the Danube some eight miles north of Melk. Prandtauer appears to have been responsible only for the crossing and part of the cupola.

Prandtauer's masterpiece is unquestionably the great Benedictine Abbey of Melk, situated on a high rock on the south bank of the Danube, some 50 miles west of Vienna. Nikolaus Pevsner called Melk the "Durham of the Baroque," and there is no reason to quarrel with his assessment. The composition is judiciously calculated to make the greatest impact, and to exploit the possibilities of the splendid site to the full. The large abbey-church with its elaborate twin towers and its high cupola is set back, and two wings of the abbey buildings containing the library and the Kaisersaal project in front of the facade of the church, converging as they approach the edge of the sheer cliff, and seeming to embrace the court in front of the church. The wings sit on a mighty podium, and this is continued in curves from the bases of the wings forming a platform on top. The ends of the curving podium are joined by a huge arch so that the view of the front of the church is uninterrupted from the river. Together, the library, Kaisersaal and church symbolize the trinity and unity of learning, worldly power and faith.

The site is very narrow and long, and the composition, with its great ranges of abbey buildings, its impressive courts and its mighty church, is undoubtedly full of majesty and drama. Prandtauer unified the elements into one huge complex and created a vast axis running through the length of the entire scheme.

Prandtauer's church is of the wall-pier type, with three-bay nave, slightly projecting transepts, and high octagonal drum and cupola over the crossing. The choir is of two bays with an apse. This interior is somber and rich, glowing with warm greens, ochres, reds and golds. Frescoes are by Rottmayr, architectural motifs by Gaetano Fanti, and the pulpit and central groups of statuary on the high altar are by Peter Widerin; the high altar itself is by Antonio Beduzzi. The total effect is very Roman, but given a regional character in much of the detail.

Melk was begun in 1702 and the shell was completed in 1714, while furnishings and finishes were more or less in place in the 1730s. A fire destroyed the superstructures of the original towers, so the elaborate bulbous tops and pinnacles we admire today were rebuilt to designs by Mungennast in 1738.

Melk is such an outstanding composition that it is worth examining possible sources. The celebrated front to the river must derive from the Kirche zu den neun Chören der Engel in Vienna of 1662 by Carlo Antonio Carlone: there, the church front stands back from the square Am Hof, and has two wings projecting on either side of the facade between which, on the *piano nobile,* is a large balcony. It is really a Melk in miniature. The cupola at Melk owes something, perhaps, to the Erhardskirche in Salzburg (1685-89 by Caspar Zugalli), while the tops of the towers are as lavish as any in the Tirol or in Salzburgerland.

At the monastery of St. Florian, Prandtauer built the memorable and very fine open stair of 1708 (in which the symmetrical flights are expressed on the elevation between the composite pilasters of the giant order), and the heroic Marmorsaal or Kaisersaal. He also produced a plan in 1706 for a huge monastery at Klosterneuburg near Vienna, but his designs were altered at the instigation of Graf Althan, and Donato Felice d'Allio was called in to build the fragment that now stands.

At Sonntagberg Prandtauer and Mungennast built the Parish and Pilgrimage Church (again on a hill) in 1706-32. This church is of great magnificence and is much more impressive than Maria Taferl: from it there are stunning views over miles of the surrounding countryside. This is a wall-pier church of a vaguely basilican type with a three-bay nave, slightly projecting transepts, apsidal sanctuary and twin-towered facade. The whole composition is massive, monumental and noble, with more elegantly fashioned external moldings and other details than at Maria Taferl. The center of the facade between the towers is concave, and suggests Francesco Borromini as a source, or even J. B. Fischer von Erlach's Dreifaltigkeitskirche in Salzburg.

Working in the Baroque style at the cathedral (the nucleus of the former monastery of St. Hippolytus, from which the town takes its name) at St. Pölten from 1722, Prandtauer created an interior of overpowering richness, with much gilding, deep browns and reds. The impressive frescoes are by Bartholomeo Altomonte, Daniel Gran and Thomas Friedrich Gedon. Prandtauer also completed Carlone's Pilgrimage Church of Christkindl near Steyr (1708-09), built the miniature Melk of the Parish Church at Ravelsbach near Hollabrunn, the Carmelite Church at St. Pölten, and began the Parish Church at Wullersdorf, completed by Mungennast. Prandtauer collaborated with Mungennast and Matthias Steinl at the Augustinian (now Parish) Church at Dürnstein, the superstructure of the beautiful single tower of which is recalled in a slightly different form at the main facade of Melk.

This remarkable architect also designed several town houses in St. Pölten, where he often exploited rhythms and swinging, curving lines in the treatment of moldings. In his churches the interiors were often somber and powerful, but he never used the ellipse: he favored the wall-pier type of plan arrangement.

Prandtauer would be remembered for Melk alone, and his reputation is soundly based on that great building: it is one of the finest architectural compositions ever created. But he has a further immense importance in that he aided the very considerable reconstruction necessary in Lower Austria after the horrors of the Turkish invasion in the 1680s, and in so doing he established in Austrian Baroque architecture a close link between tradition, local craftsmanship, and the grammar of architectural design, which was its greatest strength and the source of its immense vitality. That grammar was, of course, based on the classical language of architecture, but with Prandtauer and his contemporaries, it was given a distinctive regional flavor, and became a style of Austrian architecture in the 18th century. We are fortunate in having so much of that achievement to delight us today.

—JAMES STEVENS CURL

PRATT, Roger.

British. Born in Ryston, Norfolkshire, England, 1620. Died in Ryston, 20 February 1685. Father was Gregory Pratt; married Anne Monins. Matriculated, Magdalen College, Oxford, 1637; trained at the Inner Circle, London. Worked independently. Knighted.

Chronology of Works
All in England
* Approximate dates
† Work no longer exists

1650*	Coleshill House, Berkshire†
1663	Horseheath Hall, Cambridgeshire
1663	Kingston Lacy, Dorset
1664	Clarendon House, Piccadilly, London†
1669	Ryston Hall, Norfolk

Publications

BOOKS ABOUT PRATT

GUNTHER, R. T. (ed.): *The Architecture of Sir Roger Pratt, Charles II's Commissioner for the Rebuilding of London After the Great Fire.* Oxford, 1928.
LANG, JANE: *Rebuilding St. Paul's.* 1956.
STOYE, J. W.: *English Travellers Abroad.* 1952.
SUMMERSON, JOHN: *Architecture in Britain 1530-1830.* Harmondsworth, England, 1963.

*

Roger Pratt was a scholar and connoisseur of architecture in England in the years after the return of Charles II, an architect also who invented a type of the English country house that, together with the work of Hugh May, established a model of building for many of the architects and gentlemen in the later 17th and 18th centuries.

Pratt was born in 1620 into a family whose seat was at Ryston, near Downham, Norfolkshire. He was trained first as a lawyer at Oxford and at the Inner Temple, London. But in 1640 his father died, leaving him enough income to go abroad in 1643 and spend six years in France, Italy, Flanders and Holland, traveling widely, taking notes on all he saw and, at the end of that time, living in Rome with John Evelyn. He returned to England in 1649 and took up his abode again in the Inner

Temple. But he seems never to have practiced law, devoting himself instead to the world of architecture developing in England in the years of the Restoration. This did not bring him wealth, but it kept him very busy and, for a while, very much in the public eye. And while he never fulfilled his intention of publishing a systematic treatise on architecture, the knowledge he had of both classical and European architecture and his influence among his friends and associates led him to be, as Howard Colvin has put it, "one of the pioneers of classical architecture in England."

Pratt's work as an architect began in 1650 with the commission he received from his cousin, Sir George Pratt, to rebuild his house at Coleshill, Berkshire, which had earlier been badly damaged in a fire. It seems that in taking this on, Pratt was able to persuade his cousin to demolish what had already been done there by John Webb, perhaps even by Inigo Jones. Webb's design was articulated with orders; Pratt's was unadorned either by columns or pilasters, and it was this form of simple, astylar design that Pratt kept to in all his other houses.

The plan, which he reproduced in his succeeding houses, was what he himself called a "double pile." This plan featured a simple, rectangular block divided lengthwise by a corridor with rooms on either side, the central rooms on the short axis being, on the first floor, the staircase hall and the great parlor, and on the second floor, a great dining room and the continuation of the staircase. This design came in part from Inigo Jones and the Queen's House, and there is much also in the detailing of the exterior, the windows and the balustraded platform on the roof that may have come from Jones or from France or even from Italy and the palaces in Genoa. But Pratt made all this his own, giving both stories equal visual importance.

It was this kind of unhierarchical articulation that he repeated in all he did, whether at Horseheath, Cambridgeshire, which he built in 1663 for William, Lord Alington, or even the larger houses that, beyond a central block, had two projecting wings, articulated in the same way, with balustrades extending above them; houses in this style included Kingston Lacy in Dorset, built for sir Ralph Bankes, and Clarendon House in Piccadilly (1664) for Edward Hyde, first earl of Clarendon. Clarendon House was one of the first great classical houses built in London, and John Evelyn called it "without hyperbolies, the best contriv'd, the most usefull, gracefull, and magnificent house in England." Though it was demolished in 1683, only a few years after being finished, it was from its central location very well known and often imitated, the closest surviving imitation being perhaps Belton House in Lincolnshire (1684), built by the mason William Stanton.

After the Restoration, Pratt was called in with Hugh May and Christopher Wren to advise the commissioners for the repair of St. Paul's Cathedral, just before the Great Fire of 1666. After the Fire he was one of the three commissioners appointed by Charles II to supervise the rebuilding of the city of London, something he worked long and hard at, being rewarded in 1668 for his services with a knighthood.

In that year, having married Anne, the daughter of Sir Edmond Monins, Bart., of Waldershare in Kent, he began to rebuild the family house at Royston, which he had inherited from his cousin Edward Pratt in 1664. This was his last piece of architecture; it seems he spent his later years very quietly as a country gentleman. However, there are some notes, dating from about 1672, that are concerned with a palace on the Thames, probably for the duke of York who since 1664 had owned the site of the old royal palace of Richmond. But Pratt's work was done, and the model of building he established with designs like that of Coleshill and Horseheath became so famous that like so much

else of interest in architecture in England in the 17th century, it was for many years attributed to Wren.

—DAVID CAST

PRICE, Bruce.

American. Born in Cumberland, Maryland, 12 December 1843. Died on 28 May 1903. Daughter was Emily Price Post. Architectural trainee with Niernsee and Nelson, 1862. Joint practice with Ephraim Baldwin, Baltimore, 1868; established own office, Wilkes-Barre, Pennsylvania, 1873; established own office, New York City, 1877. President, New York Architectural League, 1877-1879. Fellow, American Institute of Architects, 1890.

Chronology of Works
All in the United States unless noted
† *Work no longer exists*

1866	St. Paul's Evangelical Lutheran Church, Baltimore, Maryland
1871	R. E. Lee Memorial Church, Lexington, Virginia
1876	Woodward Monument, Wilkes-Barre, Pennsylvania
1877	Tick's Drug Store, Wilkes-Barre, Pennsylvania
1879	Union League Club House, New York City
1879	The Craigs, Newport, Rhode Island
1880	Cathedral, Demerara, British Guiana
1883	Seacroft, Seabright, New Jersey
1884	Seaverge, Seabright, New Jersey
1884	Casa Far Niente, Bar Harbor, Maine
1885	First Methodist-Episcopal Church, Wilkes-Barre, Pennsylvania
1885ff.	Village and Gate House, Tuxedo Park, New York
1885	Chamber of Commerce, Cincinnati, Ohio
1885	Parlor car for the Boston and Albany Railroad
1886	Howard House, San Mateo, California
1886-89	Windsor Station, Montreal, Canada
1887	Levey House, Elizabeth, New Jersey
1889	Carisbrooke, Schroon Lake, New York
1889	Osborn Hall, Yale University, New Haven, Connecticut
1892	Jersey Central Railroad Station, Elizabeth, New Jersey
1892-93	Château Frontenac, Quebec, Canada
1893	The Turrets, Bar Harbor, Maine
1894-96	American Surety Building, New York City
1897-98	Georgian Court, Lakewood, New Jersey

Publications

BOOKS ABOUT PRICE

GRAYBILL, SAMUEL: "Bruce Price: American Architect 1845-1903." Ph.D. dissertation. Yale University, New Haven, Connecticut, 1957.

STURGIS, RUSSELL: *The Works of Bruce Price.* New York, 1977.

*

Bruce Price was one of the great American architects of the late 19th century and among the first to win an international reputation. In an age that exalted originality above all else, he balanced his rich architectural imagination with a disciplined work method, forceful composition, sensitive treatment of the details and, above all, strict attention to the plan. Together with Henry Hobson Richardson, Louis Sullivan and McKim, Mead and White, he formed part of that talented generation of architects who began their careers with their faces buried in the publications of English and French architects, and ended them with the situation largely reversed.

The son of a lawyer, in Cumberland, Maryland, Price lacked the benefit of formal architectural training at the French École-des-Beaux-Arts. His education was improvised, consisting of a few months at Princeton University (1862), office training in Baltimore with the Austrian architect John Niernsee (1862-66) and a brief study trip to Europe (ca. 1867). In 1868 he and Ephraim Baldwin formed a partnership in Baltimore, dividing their energies between English Gothic churches and French Second Empire houses, youthful works of particular liveliness and assurance. In 1873 Price struck out on his own, working first for his wife's family in Wilkes-Barre, Pennsylvania, and then in New York City from 1877 until his death. His inlaws were socially well connected and introduced Price to the fashionable society families who sustained his practice to the end. For them he built elaborate houses and hotels at Newport, Rhode Island, Bar Harbor, Maine, and Southampton, New York, as well as New York City.

Against a background of constant stylistic change, Price developed an approach to composition that was largely independent of style. Even in the restless High Victorian period, Price moved more quickly than most toward repose and clarity of massing. Along this trajectory his finest work was done in the middle of his career, between 1880 and 1895. His earlier work, such as an agitated neo-Gothic project for an historical society in Wilkes-Barre (1874), was sometimes precocious and eccentric, while the work of his final decade was often drier and less lyrical. But in between came a series of buildings where he struck a delicate balance between picturesque expressiveness and classical simplicity.

Price's greatest achievement was in the development of the so-called Shingle Style. Talk about devising an architecture that responded to America's climate, materials and society had been common since the 1850s, but Price's generation was the first to approach that ideal seriously. Already in the late 1870s he began to experiment with various stylistic sources to develop a distinctive American domestic architecture, borrowing the shingled construction and the massing of American colonial architecture, the classical details of the English Queen Anne revival, and the additive plan of the Gothic Revival. These disparate elements were still distinct at first, as at ''The Craigs'' at Newport (1879), a superb tribute to Richard Norman Shaw's work in England. But Price merged his influences until by the middle of the decade the separate strands were no longer distinguishable.

This development culminated at the Tuxedo Park resort community in Rockland County, New York, commissioned in 1885 by Pierre Lorillard. In some 40 houses, designed and built in six months, Price produced his most abstract and vigorous designs, based on bold gabled masses, compact silhouettes and shingled surfaces clinging to massive rubble foundations and chimneys. Specific historic reminiscences were banished from these taut buildings, and young Frank Lloyd Wright was so taken with them that he modeled his own house after one.

Half a dozen buildings in Canada—train stations, hotels and houses for the Canadian Pacific Railroad, most of them in Montreal and Quebec—formed the most unusual chapter of Price's career. Here was a rare opportunity for an American architect of the Francophiliac 1890s. Price took as his model the French architecture of the early 16th century, particularly in its bold grouping of masses and animated rooflines. He also saw in the heavy lithic character of Canadian architecture a natural context for Richardson's powerful masonry. The Château Frontenac (1892-93) was the finest of these Canadian works and surely the best of the American essays in the Loire Valley château, which was more at home on a French Canadian hilltop town than on Fifth Avenue in New York City.

Price turned classical, along with virtually his entire generation, in the 1890s, producing such work as the sumptuous Georgian Court, the George Gould House at Lakewood, New Jersey (1897-98). Nonetheless, this late work was less academic than that of his Paris-educated contemporaries. This was the legacy of his training and practice, for Price was hardly a paper designer, preferring to gauge his details and massing according to visual criteria. For this his model was the *neo-grèc* architecture of mid-19th-century France, which emphasized the expressive power of abstract lines. Throughout his career the so-called optical refinements of ancient Greek architecture inspired the details in the most diverse of his works, in classical and medieval designs, houses and skyscrapers. He termed his 1876 George Woodward monument in Wilkes-Barre ''purely Greek'' and referred to the subtle bowing of his shingled houses at Tuxedo Park as ''entasis.'' Even in the American Surety Building (1894-96), a 20-story skyscraper in New York, he recessed each successive window one inch deeper into the wall to suggest classical tapering in a building whose articulation was based on the tripartite members of a column.

Price was at the summit of his reputation at the turn of the century when he was invited to design the Tokyo palace for the Japanese crown prince. Shortly thereafter he became ill, and traveled to Paris to recuperate, where he died in 1903. Price's legacy was as much social as architectural. While the classical character of his late work was continued by his disciple John Russell Pope, his daughter Emily Post was perhaps more influential. As the arbiter of American etiquette in the 20th century, Post codified a language of behavior for the same rarefied clients that her father had served, placing the same value on refinement and unostentatious grace that her father demonstrated in their houses.

—MICHAEL J. LEWIS

PRIMATICCIO, Francesco.

Italian. Born in Bologna, Italy, 1504/05. Died in 1570. Worked with Giulio Romano in Mantua, Italy, 1526-31; moved to France at the invitation of François I, 1532; formed the school of Fountainebleau.

Chronology of Works
All in France
† *Work no longer exists*

1533-36	Palais de Fontainebleau (Chambre du Roi, Chambre de la Reine), Fontainebleau
1543	Grotto, Jarden des Pins, Fontainebleau
1555	Grotto, Château de Meudon
1563	Chapelle des Valois (funerary chapel completed by others after Primaticcio's death), St. Denis, Paris†
1568	Palais de Fontainebleau (Aile de la Belle Cheminée), Fontainebleau

Publications

BOOKS ABOUT PRIMATICCIO

BLUNT, ANTHONY: *Art and Architecture in France, 1500-1700.* 2nd ed. Harmondsworth, England, 1977.
DIMIER, LOUIS: *Le Primatice.* Paris, 1900.
LERSCH, T.: *Die Grabkapelle der Valois in St. Denis.* Munich, 1970.

ARTICLES ABOUT PRIMATICCIO

BAROCCHI, P.: "Precisioni sul Primaticcio." *Commentari* 11 (1951): 203.
GOLSON, LUCILE: "Serlio, Primaticcio and the Architectural Grotto." *Gazette des beaux-arts* 27:96-107.
JOHNSON, W. McALLISTER: "Les débuts de Primatice à Fontainebleau." *Revue de l'art* 6 (1969): 9.

In architecture, painting, sculpture and the decorative arts, Francesco Primaticcio was pivotal in the early transfer to France of Italian Mannerism. One of many Italian artists summoned by French kings, Primaticcio arrived at the Fontainebleau court of Francis I in 1532. He returned to Italy on several occasions, but France remained his home and the focus for his work until his death in Paris in 1570. Although Primaticcio's reputation has been based largely on his painting and work in stucco, his late achievements in architecture are praiseworthy.

Primaticcio's early training was under Giulio Romano (ca. 1499-1546) at the Palazzo del Tè, Mantua, from 1526 until 1532. There, Primaticcio most likely developed the elegant style for which he became noted at Fontainebleau. Although Primaticcio's contribution to the Palazzo del Tè is uncertain, his absorption of the Roman tradition through Giulio was significant. Giulio transferred to Mantua the Roman tradition of mural painting and stuccowork created by his teacher, Raphael (1483-1520). Primaticcio's work at Fontainebleau was greatly indebted to that early experience of the artistic inventiveness and archaeological interests of the Raphael school, and, by extension, Raphael. Significant for the future of French art was the underlying relationship of master and successor between Raphael and Primaticcio. The school of Fontainebleau became, for generations of French artists into the 19th century, an academy where the extended school of Raphael could be studied firsthand on native soil.

Upon his arrival at Fontainebleau, Primaticcio joined Rosso Fiorentino (Giovanni Battista Rosso). During the 1530s and 1540s, both artists, and their many assistants, were involved in the sculptural and painted decoration of the royal palace. Much of that work was subsequently destroyed or restored, thus making attribution difficult. Generally, however, as in the Chambre de la Duchesse d'Étampes (1540-45), scholars attribute to Primaticcio's hand the forms which tend toward a delicacy and ease in contrast to the abruptness and sharpness of Rosso's figures. Indeed, something of the heightened elegance of Primaticcio's designs seems to have been transferred from the figural arts to his work in architecture.

In 1540, Primaticcio traveled to Rome, a city just then recovering from the artistic drought caused by the Sack of 1527. A renewed sense of purpose and a desire for expansion invigorated the great enterprise of Roman redevelopment; this may have inspired Primaticcio to turn his attention to architecture at that time. An early work, the grotto of the Jardins des Pins at Fontainebleau (ca. 1543), incorporates both sculpture and architecture, suggesting that Primaticcio initially approached the two

arts as one. The design of the grotto, giants emerging from the rusticated entry piers of the facade, evokes Giulio Romano's frescoes of the Fall of the Giants in Mantua, executed before Primaticcio left that city in 1532. Primaticcio's use of rusticated blocks and exaggerated keystones at the grotto further underscores references to the Palazzo del Tè.

Primaticcio's continued awareness and utilization of Italian models can be detected in the ceiling design of the Galerie d'Ulysse (ca. 1550), decorated with grotesques and small panels of figures. It has been suggested that Perino del Vaga's (1500/01-47) Salone di Studio of the Palazzo Cancelleria, Rome, was Primaticcio's source. It is more likely, however, that Primaticcio was directly inspired by such designs as the Volta d'Orata of the Golden House of Nero, so well known to Raphael and the Raphael school, and indeed, the source for Perino's design.

Attributed to Primaticcio is the Aile de la Belle Cheminée, an addition to Fontainebleau of 1568. The academic classicism characteristic of the facade has been noted as the influence of Giacomo da Vignola (1507-73), whose work in Bologna Primaticcio no doubt knew from his own visit to the city in 1563. Indeed, in terms of its restricted classical vocabulary the work stands in strong contrast to the grotto. However, the smooth combination of French and Italian elements is in keeping with what his Italian contemporaries were building in France, among them Sebastiano Serlio's Ancy-le-Franc (ca. 1546).

One of the most significant architectural monuments attributed to Primaticcio is the Chapelle des Valois, an addition to the end of the north transept of St. Denis, Paris. The chapel no longer survives, but is known from an engraving by Jean Marot (ca. 1619-79). This circular mortuary chapel was commissioned by Catherine de' Medici by 1561. Six chapels radiate around the tomb of Catherine and Henri II, one for each of their sons, and one each for altar and entrance. The sculpturesque quality of space perceived in the ground plan is akin to the undulating forms modeled by Primaticcio in stucco at Fontainebleau.

Scholars have long debated the authorship of this tomb complex. Giorgio Vasari (*Vite,* 1568), credited the first plan to Primaticcio, an attribution L. Demier (1900) supported. References to Italian models (Donato Bramante's Tempietto [1502?] and Michelangelo's plans for San Giovanni dei Fiorentini [1559], both Rome, as well as Antonio da Sangallo the Younger's designs for the dome of St. Peter's [1538-43]) support the authorship of Primaticcio, whose return to Italy in 1563 no doubt strengthened his ties to the Italian classical tradition.

Primaticcio's architectural and decorative works suggest that his particular talent was as a highly competent and imaginative synthesizer. This is due, in part, to the artist's early training in the workshop of Giulio Romano. Just as important, however, were the needs and international affiliations of the French court at mid-century.

—MARJORIE OCH

PRIOR, Edward.

British. Born Edward S. Prior in 1852. Died in 1932. Studied with Richard Norman Shaw (1831-1912). Opened own practice, 1882. Slade Professor of Fine Art, Cambridge University, 1912-32.

Chronology of Works
All in England

1883	Red House, Byron Hill, Harrow, Middlesex
1884-86	Henry Martyn Memorial Hall, Cambridge
1885	Pier Terrace, West Bay, Bridport

1887-89   Holy Trinity, Bothenhampton
1895-98   The Barn, Exmouth, Devonshire
1897   Lychgate, Brantham, Suffolk
1901-04   Zoological Laboratory, Cambridge
1904-07   St. Andrew, Roker, near Sunderland
1911-14   Greystones, Highcliff-on-Sea

Publications

BOOKS ABOUT PRIOR

RICHARDSON, MARGARET: *The Craft Architects*. London, 1983.

ARTICLES ABOUT PRIOR

GRILLET, C.: "Edward Prior." *Architectural Review* (November 1952): 303-308.

*

In all architectural movements there are those artists whose qualities are not given recognition by contemporary commentators, but who later become important in reconsideration of the genre. This is often because their work is not to be found in the mainstream, being shadowed by the limelight of the leaders. Very often these secondary figures are producing innovative work that is divergent from that of the acknowledged leaders, and it is only when their work is seen from a historical perspective that the significance of their design is seen.

Such a figure is E. S. Prior, whose professional career as a practicing architect was constrained by his appointment as Slade Professor of Fine Art in 1912, at the University of Cambridge. He was an eminent scholar of medieval art and architecture. His published works included *The Cathedral Buildings of England* (1905), *A History of Gothic Art in England* (in association with A. Gardner, 1912) and *An Account of Medieval Figure Sculpture in England* (1932). His interest in Gothic work undoubtedly informed his views on the relationship between design and building, which to some extent caused him to dissent from the professional methods of the early 20th century. The description by Goodhard Rendel of Prior as a rogue architect of the Victorian era is probably much too strong, but it does indicate Prior's individualist view— at variance with professional attitudes at the time—about the divorce of design and building, which he argued reduced the quality of the finished work.

Prior, educated at Harrow and Cambridge, was articled to Richard Norman Shaw in 1872, and although his own practice commenced in 1882, was associated with Shaw until late in 1880s. His contemporaries in Shaw's office included W. R. Lethaby, although the latter arrived only in the year Prior left. Both were heavily involved in the Arts and Crafts Movement, Prior being also a founder member of the Art Workers Guild. It was at this formative stage that his position could be described as being on the revolutionary wing of a radical movement. He argued that the time for the styles was over—"such things are gone by."

His position vis a vis the Arts and Crafts movement was that he accepted the principles of that group but was virtually alone in pursuing them to the logical end. This was the situation in which he is revealed as an innovative designer, a position where the experimenter takes the risks, while others observe and build on the positive virtues that are revealed. Prior's theory was that the architect should act almost as a builder, organizing the work and specifying materials, which should be local. Much of the detailing should be left to the craftsmen on site. This technique later became one of the sophistications of the Arts and Crafts Movement, with Edwin Lutyens and Lethaby, among others, being articulate about leaving detailing to the craftsmen on site within an architectural framework.

Prior, as was his nature, did not compromise as did others, and this deliberate refusal to control the detailed building design set him aside from his fellow professionals. Where he could not be on site himself, he deputed others to act as site architect. His close associate, Randall Wells, took this role at what is now regarded as Prior's finest building, the Church of St. Andrew, Roker, Sunderland (1906-07). This project epitomized Prior's use of traditional, and local, materials and forms, although also his use of experimental structural techniques. The use of reinforced-concrete purlins allowed the spacing of the transverse arches to be greater than was usually found at the time and provided the broad rhythm that is a dominant feature of the church both internally and externally. The interior spatial sense is heightened by the device of piercing the arch bases to allow aisles to run down the side of the church. There was an understanding in the parish that Prior, in designing the great transverse arches, had reflected the forms common in shipbuilding, as some of the world's great shipyards were only a short distance away. The credibility in this story may depend on the fact that the patron for the church was Sir John Priestman, a shipbuilder himself.

Prior's general views on ecclesiastical architecture reflected the principles behind his work. Indeed, he argued that in times of great art, creativity and honesty were expressed equally in all buildings. At St. Andrew's he employed the leading artist-craftsmen of the day. The reredos tapestry was designed by Edward Burne Jones, with Morris & Co. as the weavers. The stained glass was by M. A. Payne, and much of the stonecut lettering by Eric Gill.

Prior had built a church before St. Andrew's, that of Holy Trinity at Bothenhampton (1887-89). The commission for that church followed his terrace of houses and small hotel at Pier Terrace in the same small seaside town. He had originally set up his practice with two small projects in Harrow, the Red House and a house at Harrow Laundry, which was completed in 1887. All encompassed the characteristic Arts and Crafts appearance and thus were in contrast to the prevailing stylistic work of that period.

Prior was an architect whose professional duties prevented him from having greater involvement in practice, while his ethical sense refused to allow him to follow the path taken by many professionals that led to rewarding commissions. His list of completed work is therefore limited. It is difficult to judge what influence he might have had if he had complied with professional attitudes of the day. The answer is probably not great. His drawings for the University of Cambridge Medical Schools and for the Military Medical Schools in Hampshire reflect, presumably, patronal authority and are in the classical idiom. Indeed Prior did not carry out any major work following Roker. It is clear that when he had to compromise, his design suffered.

We can, however, now almost a century later, trace his influence in two areas: first, in manifestations of church architecture later in the century, and second, in his arguments about the relationships between the architect and the building. In church architecture of this century the influence of the liturgical movement has been the outstanding feature. The necessity for spiritual values to be expressed in Christian building was predicted by Prior in the essay which served as his submission for the competition for Liverpool Anglican Cathedral. Prominent church designers such as Eric Gill and George Pace realized the link between austerity and spirituality in built form. Prior's views on the relationship between design and construction were very close to the thoughts of several critics of modern architecture, who argue that the way buildings are made should inform the design. The need for increased quality in our buildings reflects Prior's determination that honesty and durability in construction are necessary attributes, and that the means must be found to allow these characteristics.

His actual methods may be too precious to be universally applied, but in his general principles Prior can be seen as a much more influential figure than the apparent leaders of the Arts and Crafts Movement. His challenge to convention may yet place him as an important figure in the history of architectural development.

—K. H. MURTA

PROUVÉ, Jean.

French. Born in Paris, France, 8 April 1901. Died in Nancy, France, 23 March 1984. Father was the painter Victor Prouvé. Married Madeleine Schott, 1924; five children. Self-taught in architecture; trained as a blacksmith and metalworker, under Émile Robert and Szabo, Paris, 1916-23. Served in the French army, and worked with the Resistance in nancy, 1940-44; mayor of Nancy, after the Liberation, 1945. Established own metal furniture and fittings workshop, Nancy, 1923-40, and in Nancy-Maxéville, 1944-54; director of the Architectural Department, Compagnie Industrielle de Transport, Paris, 1954-66; in private practice as consultant engineer, in Paris and Nancy, 1966 until his death in 1984. Consultant engineer to CNIT and UNESCO, 1957-70. Instructor, Conservatoire National des Arts et Matières, Paris, 1957-71. Founder-member, Union des Artistes Modernes, Paris, 1930. Chevalier, 1950, and Officer, 1975, of the Légion d'Honneur, France.

Chronology of Works
All in France unless noted
† Work no longer exists

1936-37	Roland Garros Aero-Club, Buc†
1937	Pavilion of the Union of Contemporary Artists, World's Fair, Paris†
1938-39	Maison du Peuple, Clichy
1939	Prototypical Emergency Houses
1947-48	Experimental School, Vantoux
1949	Fédération du Bâtiment Building, Paris
1950	Houses, Meudon
1950	Marne Printing Works, Tours
1950-51	Exhibition Hall, Lille
1951	Firehouse, Bordeaux
1951	School Complex, Villejuif
1956	Pump Room, Evian
1958	Luxembourg Pavilion, World's Fair, Brussels, Belgium†
1961	French Atomic Energy Commission Building, Pierrelatte
1961	Library, Chemistry, Natural Science, and Nuclear Physics buildings, Faculty of Sciences, Lyon
1962	Museum and Cultural Center, Le Havre
1963-73	Free University, Berlin, Germany (detailing)
1966	Ermont Youth Center, Val d'Oise, Paris
1966	Two houses at the Air France Center, Arbonne
1967	Exhibition Hall, Grenoble
1967	Houses and School, St.-Michel-sur-Orge
1967-68	School, Orléans
1968	Unesco Building V, Paris
1968-70	Prototypical Total Service Stations
1969-70	École Nationale d'Architecture, Nancy
1976-82	Works at the Forum des Halles, the Vélodrome de Bercy, and in the Quartier de l'Horloge, Paris
1981	Hertz Tower, Ouessant

Publications

BOOKS BY PROUVÉ

Le métal. Paris, 1929.

ARTICLES BY PROUVÉ

"L'habitation de notre époque." *Architectural Association Journal* (December 1965).
"Classicism and Rationalism in Perret." With Vittorio Gregotti. *Domus* (May 1974).

BOOKS ABOUT PROUVÉ

BEEREN, W. A. L.; VAN GEEST, JAN; KANTHAUS, E. W.: *Jean Prouvé, constructeur.* Exhibition catalog. Rotterdam and Delft, 1981.
CLAYSSEN, DOMINIQUE: *Jean Prové: L'idée constructive.* Paris, 1983.
HUBER, BENEDIKT, and STEINEGGER, JEAN CLAUDE (eds.): *Jean Prouvé Prefabrication: Structures and Elements.* London and New York, 1971.
Jean Prouvé. Paris, 1964.
Jean Prouvé: Meister der Metallumformung: Das neue Blech. Cologne, 1991.
MELLOR, C. J.: *Jean Prouvé: Aspects of Innovation.* Thesis. University of Liverpool, England, 1978.

ARTICLES ABOUT PROUVÉ

BANHAM, REYNER: "Jean Prouvé: The Thin Metal Detail." *Architectural Review* 131 (April 1962): 249-252.
CHASLIN, FRANÇOIS: "The Great Tinsmith Jean Prouvé." *Rassegna* (June 1983).
CHOAY, FRANÇOISE: "Jean Prouvé." *Oeil* No. 46 (1958).
"Jean Prouvé." *Esthétique industrielle* (January/February 1957).
"Jean Prouvé." *Architecture* special issue (Brussels, December 1954).
MEADE, MARTIN K.: "Foster, Prouvé and Loos in Paris." *Architects' Journal* (9 March 1983).
NEWTON, NIGEL: "Prouvé, Modern Movement Pioneer." *Building Design* (30 March 1984).
RABENECK, ANDREW: "Jean Prouvé." *Architectural Design* 41 (July 1971).
VERRES, MICHEL: "Jean Prouvé: Architect-Mechanic." *Architectural Review* (July 1983).
"The Work of Jean Prouvé." *Architectural Design* 33 (1963): 511-525.

*

Jean Prouvé had no formal architectural education, having been apprenticed to a well-known metalworker and blacksmith in Paris at the age of nine. This lack of conventional training—a characteristic he shared with a surprising number of other modern masters—was perhaps one of the main reasons for his objectivity, and his talent in being able to point out the failure of contemporary architects to fully utilize the potential of industrialization. Ludwig Mies van der Rohe, who, like Prouvé, also came to architecture through a building trade, repeatedly said that architecture really existed only when technology had reached complete fulfillment, and that the goal of modernism should be to encourage building and industrialization to grow together. Prouvé sought to reach that fulfillment in the medium that he knew best, and his unquestionable success in achieving it has been an inspiration to many others who have attempted to explore the architectural potential of technology ever since.

Serving mostly in the capacity of engineering consultant to other architects throughout his career, Prouvé constantly looked for ways to introduce the techniques of industrial production into the profession, and also to have the building trades benefit from the efficiencies of such techniques. He frequently noted that the contemporary construction process had really changed little since the Middle Ages, depending primarily on separate trades working sequentially rather in unison toward what should be a common goal. He realized that in that process, however, the architect no longer fulfilled the key role of the master builder of the past, being largely separated from the construction sequence once the working-drawing stage had been completed. This division from the actual building phase, in his view, had also been aggravated by the cult of individuality that had been introduced as early as the Renaissance, but accelerated by the Modern Movement, which tacitly encouraged the development of distinct stylistic personalities that looked upon standardization as being anathema to individuality.

As an alternative, Prouvé recommended that architects seek reunion with the building process. As a first step in that reunion, he advocated that they come to have a far better understanding of the materials that they specify, including the way in which these materials are made, in order to more fully appreciate their characteristics. By also becoming familiar with the way the machines that produce those materials operate, Prouvé also believed that architects could utilize them better. He differed from a majority of his contemporaries in this respect, for rather than disdain the lessons of the past and consider historical monuments to be technologically primitive, as might be expected, he saw that each of the best of them was a complete expression of the most advanced physical knowledge and tectonic skill available at the time of their construction. When considered in this way, a megmon, pyramid or Gothic cathedral begin to take on a completely new dimension, reminding us that *techne,* which is the Greek root word in technology, represents craftsmanship, and not electronic wizardry.

When carried out as the combined effort of an entire culture, rather than a single individual, this craftmanship carries a special kind of inspiration in it that Prouvé perceptively identified as being absent in most contemporary architecture, making it dead in a sociological sense. While similar feelings have been expressed by a few enlightened and more traditionally minded architects from the developing world in the past, Prouvé parted company with them in his belief that this lost inspiration will return only when the full potential of industry is realized in architecture. To do this, he proposed that in addition to involving architects in the manufacturing process, they must also be educated differently. In the system he proposed, the conventional pedantic emphasis on methods of construction would be replaced with a stress on the idea of a building as being composed of elements, each of which has infinite variations, much like the parts of an automobile or the notes of a musical scale. While the number of notes on the scale is fixed, the possibilities within that system have been used to create seemingly endless combinations.

Of all his projects, his Maison du Peuple, designed in conjunction with Bodlansky, Beaudouin and Lods in Clichy, near Paris, is possibly the best example of his philosophy that architecture must totally harmonize with the methods of its production. Made up of entirely movable walls, floors and ceiling panels, and wrapped in stressed, spring-loaded metal panels, the building clearly defines what Prouvé meant when he spoke of the need to produce ''conditioned'' building elements that could be far more flexible than those in use. The Sainsbury Centre in Norwich, Norfolk is a direct descendant of this philosophy, and its architect, Norman Foster, perhaps more than any other designer today, seems to personify the new attitude toward technology that Prouvé had in mind.

In the many exhibitions of his work that he organized, Prouvé used the word *constructeur* as a title, rather than architect or engineer. The word is difficult to translate into English, having mixed connotations of contractor, master builder and even mechanic in it. The title is very appropriate for him, as he was all of these, serving as an example of the multidisciplinary talents necessary to cope with today's highly complex construction industry.

—JAMES M. STEELE

PUGIN, A. W. N.

British. Born Augustus Welby Northmore Pugin in London, England, 1812. Died in Ramsgate, Kent, 14 September 1852. Father was the architect Augustus Charles Pugin (1769-1832); married three times: second marriage was to Louisa Burton, 1833, and third marriage to Jane Knill, 1848; son was the architect Edward Welby Pugin (1834-75); converted to Roman Catholicism in 1835.

Chronology of Works
All in England unless noted
† Work no longer exists

1833-37	King Edward VI School, Birmingham (decorative detailing for Charles Barry)†
1835-36	St. Marie's Grange, Alderbury, Wiltshire
1837	Clarendon Park, Alderbury, Wiltshire (gatehouse)
1837	St. James' Church, Reading
1837-38	Oscott College, Sutton Coldfield, Warwickshire (chapel and completion of buildings)
1837-39	St. Marie's Church, Derbyshire
1837-45	Scarisbrick Hall, Lancashire
1837-52	Alton Towers, Staffordshire
1838	Church of Our Blessed Lady and St. Thomas of Canterbury, Dudley, Worcestershire
1838	St. Anne's Church, Keighley, Yorkshire
1838	St. Peter's College, Wexford, Ireland (chapel and interior fittings)
1838-41	St. Alban's Church, Macclesfield, Cheshire
1839	Convent of Mercy, Bermondsey, London†
1839	Loreto Abbey, Rathfarnum, Ireland (alterations and additions)
1839	St. Mary's Church, Uttoxeter, Staffordshire
1839-40	St. Chad's Cathedral, Birmingham
1839-40	St. Marie's Church, Warwick Bridge, Cumberland (now Church of Our Lady and St. Wilfrid's)
1839-42	St. John's Church, Banbury, Oxfordshire (school, presbytery, and decoration of chancel)
1839-42	St. Wilfrid Church, Hulme, Manchester
1839-44	Mount St. Bernard Abbey, Leicestershire

1840	Castle Rock, Leicestershire (entrance and interior details)
1840	St. Winifride's Chapel, Shepshed, Leicestershire
1840-41	Bishop's House, Birmingham†
1840-42	St. Oswald's Church, Old Swan, Liverpool
1840-44	St. Alphonsus' Church, Barntown, Wexford, Ireland
1840-46	St. Giles' Church, Cheadle, Staffordshire
1840-52	St. Cuthbert's College, Durham (completed later by others; Pugin's design altered)
1840ff.	Grace Dieu Manor, Leicestershire (decoration and additions)
1840ff.	St. John's Hospital, Alton, Staffordshire
1841	School, Spetchley, Worcestershire
1841-44	St. Barnabas' Cathedral, Nottingham
1841-47	Convent of Mercy, Liverpool†
1841-47	St. Marie's Church, Liverpool†
1841-48	Oxenford Grange, Surrey (farm buildings, bridge, and gatehouse)
1841-48	Peper Harrow House, Surrey (renovations and additions)
1841-51	Bilton Grange, Rugby, Warwickshire (renovations and additions)
1842ff.	St. Mary's Cathedral, Killarney, Ireland
1843	Ratcliffe College, Leicestershire
1843-44	Gateway for Magdalen College, Oxford†
1843-44	The Grange, Ramsgate, Kent
1844	St. Alphonsus' Church, Barntown, Wexfordshire
1844-52	Houses of Parliament, London (decorative detailing for Charles Barry)
1845-46	Glebe Farm (formerly Rampisham Rectory), Rampisham, Dorset
1845-46	Parish Church, Rampisham, Dorset (restoration of the chancel)
1845-46	St. Marie's Church, Rugby, Warwickshire
1845-46	Woodchester Park, near Stroud, Gloucestershire (completed later by others)
1845-48	St. Peter's Church, Marlow, Buckinghamshire
1845-50	St. Augustine's Church, Ramsgate, Kent
1845-52	St. Patrick's College, Maynooth, Ireland
1847-48	Burton Closes, Bakewell, Derbyshire (additions and interior decorations)
1847-49	St. Oswald's Church, Winwick, Liverpool (chancel)
1847-49	St. Thomas' Church, Fulham, London (church and presbytery)
1847-49	St. Osmund's Church, Salisbury
1848	Manor House (now Manor School), Wiburton
1848	St. Cuthbert's Church, Durham (chapel)
1850	Aston Cemetery Chapel, Birmingham
1850	Leighton Hall, Welshpool, Montgomeryshire (interior decoration)
1850	St. George's Cathedral, Southwark, London (Petre Chantry interior)
1851	Church of Our Lady Star of the Sea, Greenwich, London (decoration)

Publications

BOOKS BY PUGIN

Specimens of Gothic Architecture. London, 1821.
Illustrations of Public Buildings in London. 1825-28.
Gothic Ornaments. London, 1831.
Gothic Furniture 1835. Designs for iron and brass work, 1836. Designs for gold and silversmiths 1836. Details of antient timber houses. 4 vols. 1835-36.
Contrasts. London, 1836.

The True Principles of Pointed or Christian Architecture. London, 1841.
The Present State of Ecclesiastical Architecture in England. London, 1843.
An Apology for the Revival of Christian Architecture in England. Oxford, 1843.
Glossary of Ecclesiastical Ornament and Costume. London, 1844.
Floriated Ornament: A Series of Thirty-one Designs. London, 1849.
A Treatise on Chancel Screens and Rood Lofts. London, 1851.

ARTICLES BY PUGIN

''Doorway of Cloister, Abbey of St. Wandrille.'' *London and Dublin Journal of Useful Knowledge for 1838* (13 March 1838): 161-164.
''Fireplace in the Abbey of St. Amand, Rouen.'' *London and Dublin Orthodox Journal of Useful Knowledge for 1838* (13 March 1838): 193-196.
''Jube of St. Ouen.'' *London and Dublin Orthodox Journal of Useful Knowledge for 1838* (3 March 1838): 129-131.
''Lectures on Ecclesiastical Architecture.'' *Catholic Weekly Instructor* (1, 7, 14 and 21 February 1846).
''Monumental Brass of the Fifteenth Century.'' *London and Dublin Journal of Useful Knowledge for 1838* (12 May 1838): 289-292.
''West Front of St. Lawrence's Church, Nuremberg.'' *London and Dublin Journal of Useful Knowledge for 1838* (26 May 1838): 321-323.
''West Front of Rouen Cathedral.'' *London and Dublin Orthodox Journal of Useful Knowledge for 1838* (17 February 1838): 97-99.

BOOKS ABOUT PUGIN

CLARK, KENNETH: *The Gothic Revival.* Harmondsworth, England, 1928.
DIXON, ROGER, and MUTHESIUS, STEFAN: *Victorian Architecture.* New York and Toronto, 1978.
EASTLAKE, CHARLES: *A History of the Gothic Revival.* London, 1872. FERREY, BENJAMIN: *Recollections of A. N. Welby Pugin and His Father, Augustus Pugin.* London, 1861.
FERRIDAY, PETER (ed.): *Victorian Architecture.* London, 1963.
GWYNN, DENIS R.: *Lord Shrewsbury, Pugin and the Roman Catholic Revival.* London, 1946.
HARRIES, J. G.: *Pugin: An Illustrated Life of Augustus Welby Northmore Pugin, 1812-52.* Aylesbury, England, 1973.
HITCHCOCK, HENRY-RUSSELL: *Early Victorian Architecture in Britain.* 2 vols. New Haven, Connecticut, and London, 1954.
HOUGHTON, WALTER E.: *The Victorian Frame of Mind.* New Haven, Connecticut, 1966.
PORT, M. H. (ed.): *The Houses of Parliament.* New Haven, Connecticut, and London, 1976.
ROPE, EDWARD GEORGE: *Pugin.* Ditchling, England, 1935.
SERVICE, ALASTAIR: *The Architects of London.* London, 1979.
STANTON, PHOEBE B.: *Pugin.* London and New York, 1971.
TRAPPES-LOMAX, MICHAEL: *Pugin: A Medieval Victorian.* London, 1932.
WEDGWOOD, ALEXANDRE: *A. W. N. Pugin and the Pugin Family.* London, 1985.
WHITE, JAMES F.: *The Cambridge Movement, the Ecclesiologists and the Gothic Revival.* Cambridge, 1962.

ARTICLES ABOUT PUGIN

PEVSNER, NIKOLAUS: "A Short Pugin Florilegium." *Architectural Review* 94 (1943): 31-34.
SIRR, HARRY E. G.: "Augustus Welby Pugin: A Sketch." *Journal of the Royal Institute of British Architects* 25:213-226.
STANTON, PHOEBE B.: "Pugin: Principles of Design versus Revivalism." *Journal of the Society of Architectural Historians* 13 (September 1954): 20-25.

*

The name of Augustus Welby Pugin is inextricably associated with the Gothic Revival. As a practicing architect and decorative artist of prodigious energies, and as an architectural theorist and critic of fervent views, Pugin became the leading advocate of Gothic architecture during the second quarter of the 19th century. In a remarkably short period of 17 years (his first building dates from 1835, and he was dead at 40 in 1852), Pugin designed more than 100 buildings. Moreover, in order to ornament them, he established a successful business to produce, from his meticulous designs, stained-glass windows and decorative metalwork. In addition, he wrote eight major books to proselytize his new architectural religion that Gothic was "the only true Christian architecture." His moral pronouncements, rejecting all other architectural styles as heretical, were founded on a substantial achievement as a scholar of medieval art and architecture, and reflected his fervor as a converted (1835) and devout Catholic. He transformed the Gothic Revival from a stylish architectural dress—one of many available in an era of romantic historicism—to a moral commitment, a principled, disciplined language, which it was an architect's Christian duty to employ in building, especially in the building of churches.

Pugin therefore established the theoretical groundwork of the leading architectural school of thought in 19th-century England (and with considerable influence abroad). In his *True Principles of Pointed or Christian Architecture,* published in 1841 (although written a few years earlier), Pugin presented an alternative to "the little more than mere capricious opinion [that has] hitherto [characterized] architectural criticism." Arguing that "the laws of Architectural Composition are based on equally sound principles as those of Harmony and Grammar," Pugin advanced principles intended to "furnish a standard by which the excellence of the antient (*sic*) buildings may be duly appreciated, and the extravagances and inconsistencies of modern styles readily discerned."

Like that of his French counterpart, Eugène Viollet-le-Duc (two years his junior), Pugin's interest in medievalism was not archaeological or antiquarian per se, not a revivalist's interest in style but a modernist's pursuit from the past of lessons applicable to contemporary design. Pugin outlined theories about construction, ornament, materials and function, observing most notably: 1. that all the ornament of true pointed edifices were merely introduced as decoration to the essential construction of these buildings; 2. that the construction of pointed architecture was varied to accord with *the properties of the various materials employed* shown by ancient examples of stone, timber, and metal construction [John Ruskin (1819-1900) would expound on this idea, without acknowledgment of his debt to Pugin, in "The Lamp of Truth," part of *The Seven Lamps of Architecture* (1849).]; 3. that no features were introduced in the antient (*sic*) pointed edifices which were not essential either for convenience or propriety; and 4. that pointed architecture is most consistent as it decorates the useful portions of buildings instead of concealing them. . . . Such ideas link Pugin both to structural rationalism and to modern functionalism, and his influence has been profound.

Pugin's major contribution was his assertion that the quality of architecture reflects the quality (good or bad) of society. His equation of architecture and morality prompted Gothic Revivalists and their successors to attribute moral qualities to buildings: truth in structure; honesty to place, to local conditions, materials and techniques; expression of truth in composition, in which external forms reflected the arrangements of interior spaces and doors and windows were neither classically nor picturesquely disposed, but were placed with a consideration of light, ventilation, access and circulation requirements.

Pugin's ideas were further advanced by the publication in 1843 of *An Apology for the Revival of Christian Architecture in England,* and his influence especially spread through the adoption of his ideas by the Ecclesiological Society, whose organ *The Ecclesiologist* had a major impact on contemporary architecture. When *The Ecclesiologist,* devoted entirely to church design and criticism, prescribed rules for Gothic building, they were principles Pugin articulated. Particularly in evidence was Pugin's emphasis on the administration of the sacraments within the mysterious and holy sanctuary, separated from the nave by altar rail, rood screen and chancel arch. When *The Ecclesiologist* criticized the construction of a new church or the restoration of an old one, the publication's criteria reflected Pugin's ideas: every detail of the church, from plan and form to ornament and fittings, must be appropriate to its function in the religious service or Mass so that architecture expressed the meaning of Christianity. It was only after the Ecclesiological Society prescribed Middle Pointed English (13th-century Decorated) as the only acceptable style (1845), and after John Ruskin's emotional writings on Gothic appeared (*The Seven Lamps of Architecture* [1849] and *The Stones of Venice* [1851-53]), that other Gothic influences began to supplant Pugin's.

Pugin had advanced his medieval prejudices from the start of his career in the mid-1830s. In *Contrasts; or, A Parallel Between the Noble Edifices of the Fourteenth and Fifteenth Centuries, and Similar Buildings of the Present Day; shewing the Present Decay of Taste: Accompanied by appropriate Text* (1836), Pugin made visible the concerns earlier expressed by Thomas Carlyle (1795-1881) regarding the threat of the industrial revolution on society. On facing pages of *Contrasts,* Pugin presented images of medieval, juxtaposed with modern, townscapes as indications of the aesthetic consequences of the new techniques. Rather than the choking smokestacks, factory structures and bridges of the modern engineer, Pugin's medieval townscapes and village scenes of church steeples and decorated architecture were the ideal model for architecture, not because they were more beautiful or more picturesque, but because they were morally right. This model reflected a pre-industrial society of Christian builders whose employment of ancient constructional techniques, building materials and artisan craftsmanship insured an honest expression. Such ideas offered clear implications for William Morris (1834-96) and the Arts and Crafts movement.

As a practicing architect, Pugin dedicated his almost exclusive efforts to religious buildings. St. Barnabas' Cathedral, Nottingham (1841-44), St. Chad's Cathedral, Birmingham (1839-40), and St. Augustine's Ramsgate, Kent (1845-50), are representative. His most renowned church design may be St. Giles', Cheadle, Staffordshire (1840-46). Even Cardinal John Henry Newman, whose preferences were not in favor of the Gothic and who rightly found Pugin argumentative and intolerant, was overwhelmed by St. Giles': "the most splendid building I ever saw."

Scarisbrick Hall, Lancashire (1837-45), and Pugin's work on Alton Towers, Staffordshire, from 1837 to 1852 constituted his major efforts in the field of country-house design. Such work achieved for Pugin a reputation as a decorator which brought him his best-known commission, the Gothic Revival decorative scheme for London's Houses of Parliament (1844-52), whose basic plan is the work of Charles Barry (1795-1860).

Among Pugin's domestic works, it would not be his larger country houses which offered contemporaries his most influential models. Indeed, Scarisbrick Hall, his first major architectural commission, enjoyed the extravagance of a limitless budget but displayed the less-mature handling of detail and form by a young architect. Its flourishes of decoration, although founded on 14th- and 15th-century precedent, were less disciplined by the moral imperative to be "correct," let alone "Christian," and Scarisbrick Hall, in the end, appears more theatrical, picturesque and ornamental than his smaller secular work. His heart and soul were not in the fashionable lifestyle of the country-house set.

But when he designed smaller-scaled vicarages, convents, or his numerous presbyteries and small schools, Pugin frequently found in them a secular complement to his churches, and he developed a dignified and forthright individual style for such buildings. Each was original, comfortable and conveniently composed. Building materials were frankly employed to emphasize honesty of construction and local practice, and roof forms and massing are simple and natural.

Indeed, in his smaller domestic works, Pugin laid the foundation for the modern "well-wrought" house, composed according to convenience and functional need and constructed of local materials in the manner "of olden days." This would characterize William Morris' later definition of his ideal architecture. Pugin planted the seeds. Beginning with his own house near Salisbury, St. Marie's Grange (1835-36) ("the only modern building that is compleat in every part in the antient style"), and ending with his house, the Grange, at Ramsgate (1843-44), Pugin's smaller domestic projects linked medieval vernacular forms to the neovernacular of William Butterfield (1814-1900) at Baldersby St. James (1855) and Philip Webb at the Red House, Bexleyheath (1859-60). While Hermann Muthesius

thought Webb's Red House "unique" and historians have viewed it as the archetypal neovernacular residence inspiring the Arts and Crafts domestic revival, Webb was already indebted to Butterfield, and neither would have been quite the same without Pugin. Pugin's insistence on sound construction, enriched by ornament, and true to traditional methods and local materials, shows him to be the true founder of the Arts and Crafts movement, as his Rampisham Rectory (now Glebe Farm) in Dorset suggests. At Rampisham, Pugin captured the simplicity and anonymity of the medieval mason's handiwork, the careful informality and ordinary (rather than picturesque) asymmetry of organic building.

As the leading exponent of the Gothic in England at midcentury, Pugin was already being rivaled by new leaders of a changing Gothic Revival, architects informed by Pugin's work but bursting from its correctness in a fury of "muscular Gothic" and High Victorian coloration. William Butterfield, George Edmund Street (1824-81), John Loughborough Pearson (1817-97) and William Burges (1827-81) would be the new formgivers, or at least would repattern, resculpt and redecorate established forms. For example, the compact and original massing of Pugin's Bishop's House, Birmingham (1840-41, now demolished) influenced Butterfield's masterpiece, All Saints Margaret Street, London (1850-53), designed as a model church for the Ecclesiological Society and the springboard for a new fury of "permanent polychrome" and "constructional coloration." Butterfield's church would move the Gothic Revival to the High Victorian Gothic and, as Ruskin noted, create the "first piece of architecture . . . built in modern days which is free from all signs of timidity and incapacity." Perhaps Pugin was too "true," but in Ruskin's word, the new Gothic was marked by "force, vitality, and grace of floral ornament, worked in a broad and masculine manner." After 1853, with All Saints Margaret Street complete, Christian Gothic would give way to "muscular Gothic," and the intense religiosity of Pugin, exhausted and put to rest, would influence but not lead a new generation of High Victorian Gothicists.

—ROBERT M. CRAIG

Q-R

QUARENGHI, Giacomo.

Russian. Born Giacomo Antonio Quarenghi in Valle Imagna, near Bergamo, Italy, 20 September 1744. Died in St. Petersburg, Russia, 18 February 1817. Largely self-taught in Architecture; in Rome during the 1760s, and practiced in the studios of Antoine Derizet and Nicola Giansimoni. Moved to St. Petersburg at the invitation of Catherine II, 1779; continued to work there for Paul I and Alexander I.

Chronology of Works
All in Russia unless noted
† Work no longer exists

1769-73	Santa Scholastica, Subiaco, Rome (interior remodeling)
1777	Palace for Lord Hagerston, England
1781-89	English Palace, Peterhof, near St. Petersburg†
1782-83	Foreign Ministry, St. Petersburg
1782-85	Rafael Loggias Building, St. Petersburg
1782-88	Music Pavilion, Tsarskoe Selo (now Pushkin)
1783	Birzha Building, St. Petersburg
1783-84	Prince Bezborodko House, Poljustrowo
1783-84	Count Zavadovsky Estate, St. Petersburg
1783-87	Hermitage Theater , St. Petersburg
1783-89	Academy of Sciences, St. Petersburg
1785-90	State Bank, St. Petersburg
1789-92	Fontanka Palace, St. Petersburg
1789-96	Court Pharmacy, St. Petersburg
1790-1800	Yussupov Palace, St. Petersburg
1790-1805	Gallery of Shops, Moscow
1792-96	Alexandrovsky Palace, Tsarskoe Selo (now Pushkin)
1798-1800	Maltiyskaya Capella (Church of the Knights of Malta), St. Petersburg
1804-07	Konnogvardeisky Manej, St. Petersburg
1806-08	Smolny Institute, St. Petersburg
1814	Narva Triumphal Arch, St. Petersburg
1814-15	English Church, St. Petersburg

Publications

BOOKS ABOUT QUARENGHI

ANGELLINI, L.; CHIODI, L.; and ZAVELLA, V.: *Disegni di Giacomo Quarenghi.* Vencie, 1967.

EGOROV, I. A.: *The Architectural Planning of St. Petersburg.* Athens, Ohio, 1969.

HAMILTON, G. H.: *The Art and Architecture of Russia.* Harmondsworth, England, 1954.

HAUTECOEUR, L.: *L'architecture classique à St. Pétersbourg à la fin du XVIIIe siècle.* 1912.

KOSUNOVA, MILIZA: *Giacomo Quarenghi at the Galleria dell'Accademia in Venice. Master Drawings 7,* No. 3 (1969): 308-310.

*

Giacomo Quarenghi, one of the major Russian architects of the late 18th and early 19th centuries, united in his creative work the development of Russian classicism with the European traditions of Andrea Palladio and the latest discoveries of neoclassicism. Quarenghi spent the first part of his life in Italy, where he built relatively little. The second part of his life was spent in Russia, which truly became his new motherland. Soon after his arrival in St. Petersburg in 1779, Quarenghi embarked on a strikingly intense period of activity which lasted for more than three decades.

A native of Bergamo, in northern Italy, Quarenghi did not receive a formal education in architecture. His views were formed in the atmosphere of artistic life in Rome during the 1760s amid the reigning passion for antiquity. Quarenghi's interest in Palladio's legacy was stimulated by the influence of the Venetian neoclassical school. His first work—the reconstruction of Santa Scholastica, a medieval church in Subiaco, near Rome (1769-73)—was a free paraphrase of the interior of the Church of Il Redentore by Palladio. In addition, Quarenghi was familiar with English architecture, which also based itself on Palladian ideas, as well as with new tendencies in French architecture. His palace for Lord Hagerston (1777) and other projects in England were a response to English neoclassical Palladianism.

When invited to Russia to serve at the court of Catherine II, Quarenghi was already an accomplished master with a rigorously precise architectural credo. Using the classical system of architectural orders as a foundation, he developed a distinctive and mature style by synthesizing the traditions of various European schools. His style took root in Russian soil, and Quarenghi became the leading Russian architect, essentially creating a strict classicism in the 1780s. Along with his contemporaries I. E. Starov and Charles Cameron, Quarenghi created a series of programmatic works in St. Petersburg and environs, which decisively influenced Russian architecture of that time.

Quarenghi's early St. Petersburg buildings revealed an inclination toward monumental grandeur and laconic clarity, a certain coolness and abstractness of design. A Palladian spirit pervades the English Palace in Peterhof (1781-89, destroyed). The center of the main facade was accentuated by an eight-column Corinthian portico with a wide staircase. The projecting, solemn portico stands in opposition to the geometrically austere design of the building and the ascetically even walls. An even sharper contrast between a highly sculptural extended portico and a simple flat facade gave the Academy of Sciences Building (1783-89) an expressive appearance. The large-scale Ionic order was in harmony with the scale of the surrounding cityscape, dominated by the Great Neva River.

In the Foreign Ministry Building (1782-83) and the English Church (1814-15), central porticoes were raised high above ground level and are flush with the wall. The colonnade of the Hermitage Theater (1783-87) is also flush with the facade without accentuating the central axis. The design fulfilled the requirement that the building harmonize with the Emperor's Hermitage ensemble, and was inspired by Palladio's Teatro Olimpico in Vicenza and Claude-Nicolas Ledoux's Théâtre Guimard in Paris. All three buildings evoke the theme of the semicircular amphitheater hall.

The St. Petersburg Bourse (1783) was assigned a significant role in shaping the panorama along the banks of the Neva River. Ellipsoid in plan and with two porticoes, the building was an interesting interpretation of Palladian and ancient Roman techniques. However, the self-contained design was not in keeping with the open river site, and the building was later destroyed. Despite this, Quarenghi's adjacent Gostinny Dvor and warehouse buildings, adorned with large-scale arcades, set the theme for future construction on the Vasilievsky Island arrow.

The arcade was one of the main motifs in Quarenghi's work. The architect used the device of a two-level arcade covering the whole facade for the first time in the Raphael Loggias building (1782-85), which was erected as an addition to the emperor's Hermitage and followed the pattern of Raphael's loggias at the Vatican Palace. Quarenghi later varied the arcade motif in many of his commercial buildings.

The Palladian country-house design received new expression in Prince Bezborodko's country house (1783-84) and in Count Zavadovsky's Lialichi estate (1783-84). Quarenghi attached curved colonnades or arcades to the main buildings to the rear of the courtyards. Prince Jusupov's Fontanka palace (1789-92) has a semicircular courtyard, which is interesting for its original arrangement. The architect also employed the typical layout of a country house in the Gosudarstvenny Bank building. Two colonnaded galleries link the enormous arc of the functional structure from the inside, connecting it to the central administrative building erected in the back of the courtyard.

The Academy of Sciences, Hermitage Theater and Gosudarstvenny Bank were the most significant of Quarenghi's works in the 1780s. The concert pavilion in Tsarskoe Selo stood out among his more intimate structures. The architect composed an effective building by combining an elementary parallelopiped with a portico and rotunda set into the body of the building. Creating a series of grand halls, Quarenghi also proved his worth as a master of interior design.

Alexandrovsky Palace (1792-96) in Tsarskoe Selo became the masterpiece of the next decade. Its plan was unusual. Quarenghi built a small courtyard with two Corinthian colonnades inside the main wide courtyard. The colonnades were a consummate example of the Corinthian order and endowed the building with an appearance of grandeur and splendor. Although the French architects Jacques Gondouin and Ledoux employed such colonnades in their works, the design of Alexandrovsky Palace was unique. Quarenghi also used an extended monumental colonnade for the Ekaterininsky Palace in Moscow and Count Sheremetiev's house. In the center of the latter building, the architect built a light semicircular rotunda formed by two rows of columns. In the Maltiyskaia Chapel (1798-1800), commissioned by Paul I, Quarenghi returned to Palladian precepts. Reminiscent of the Church of San Francesco della Vigna in Venice, the exterior of the building was markedly soft and intimate in form.

In the early 1800s Quarenghi erected the Mariinskaia Hospital for the Ekaterininsky Vospitatelny Institute and the emperor's Cabinet building in the strict classical style. The Smolny Institute Blagorodnyh Devits building (1806-08) became Quarenghi's main work of the decade. The architect once again employed the open courtyard theme. The wide block adorned with pilasters served as a background to the eight-column portico; it softened the contrast between the classical order and the flat surface of the wall. Porticoes, flush with the wall at the ends of the side wings, served to clarify the three axis structure.

In the Horse Guards building (1804-07), Quarenghi turned to ancient Greek architecture for the first time. The sculptural Doric portico with a gable and deep loggia created a light effect designed to enhance the perspective extending along the Admiralty building. Earlier, Quarenghi had contributed to the creation of St. Petersburg's ensemble of central squares by erecting the Fittinghof House. The structure, adorned with a representative colonnade, set the scale for Admiralty Prospekt and Palace Square.

During the reign of Alexander I in the early 19th century, Quarenghi gradually surrendered his leading position to architects of a new generation—A. N. Voronikhin, A. D. Zakharov and Thomas de Thomon. In his last works, Quarenghi employed classical Roman patterns of the imperial age. The Narva Triumphal Arch (1814), erected to commemorate the victory over Napoleon, resembled the ancient Roman arches of Titus and Constantine, as well as Percier and Fontaine's Arc du Caroussel in Paris. For the Memorial Church project in Moscow (1815), Quarenghi recreated the design of the Pantheon, which he had always admired. A return to ancient patterns completed the circle of the architect's search. His oeuvre largely defined the austere and ceremonial appearance of St. Petersburg and the general development of Russian classicism.

Quarenghi entered the history of art not only as an architect, but also as a painter. Many of his drawings,—mostly views of Rome, St. Petersburg, Moscow and other cities—retain both artistic and documentary value.

—BORIS M. KIRIKOV
Translated from the Russian by Konstantine Klioutchkine

RABIRIUS.

Russian. Active in Rome during the first century A. D.

Chronology of Works
In Italy

A.D. 80s-90s Palace of the Caesars on the Palatine, Rome

Publications

BOOKS ABOUT RABIRIUS

CREMA, L.: *L'Architettura Romana* (*Encyclopedia Classica* XII, part I). Turin, 1959.
FINSEN, HELGE: *Domus Flavia sur le Palatin; Aula Regia-Basilica.* Hafniae, Denmark, 1962.
MACDONALD, WILLIAM L.: *The Architecture of the Roman Empire.* New Haven, Connecticut, 1965.

ARTICLES ABOUT RABIRIUS

WARD-PERKINS, J. B.: "Roman Concrete and Roman Palaces." *The Listener* 563 (1956): 701-70.

Roman architects are generally faceless and nameless. Only a handful are known, and only because one of their creations became so famous that the architect is named by historical sources. The architect Rabirius is mentioned twice in the sycophantic sources that praise the accomplishments of the Flavian emperor Domitian. Despite the vicissitudes of history, however, Rabirius' contribution to architectural history is clear: he planned and designed one of the most famous buildings of Roman antiquity, a symbol of luxury and power to later ages, a building innovative in its construction and in its blatant adaptation of architectural form to imperial ideology, a building that became eponymous for its type. The building is the palace on the Palatine, and of all of Rabirius' achievements, his lasting fame results from the fact that the palace became *the* symbol of imperial power in the medieval and Renaissance periods.

The Flavian palace was built on a large expanse of the Palatine hill that dominates the valleys of the Forum Romanum and the Circus Maximus. The complexity of the site resulted in a structure characterized by elaborate terracing and changes in level. The topographical complexity, however, is belied by the axiality of a plan that adheres to the Roman penchant for order and clarity. Rabirius' architecture was innovative in its use of brick-faced concrete to mold both exterior and interior space in a new way. The use of concrete allowed for novel interior effects and vaulting in the public part of the palace, and for smaller but more spatially interesting vaulted and domical spaces in the massive, private part of the palace. The trickiness of the site and the innovative quality of the architecture seem to have pushed Roman construction technology to its limits, for although the palace was considered a marvel by succeeding generations, later emperors had to brace or buttress parts of the structure to avoid collapse.

Rabirius was a leader in the "concrete revolution" of the first century A.D., an architect innovative in his use of new materials to create new interior spatial effects. An equal contribution was his understanding of the ideological needs of the principate and the need for an architectural language that could express power and reflect a fundamental aspect of new empire, the change of the power and stature of the emperor, particularly important to Domitian, to a more-than-human figure, a *dominus et deus*. The division of the Flavian palace into public (conventionally referred to as the Domus Flavia) and private (Domus Augustana) sections reflects these needs.

The public part of the palace was on the highest crest of the hill, placed on high with an imposing facade facing the valley of the republican forum. The processional road that wound its way up from the forum reinforced the symbolism of ascent, a meaning that was not lost on contemporary Romans, judging from the Flavian poet Statius' well-known reference to the palace as "piercing heaven" and "touching the stars." The gentle incline and moderate height of the Palatine hill would hardly warrant such hyperbole if the symbolism of the topography were not evident.

The public spaces of the Domus Flavia consisted of large, lofty reception areas, one clearly a basilica, another a reception hall, the Aula Regia. Reconstruction of the roofing systems used in these spaces is still controversial, but the massive footings and heavy corner buttresses at least suggest the possibility of vaulting. The walls of the reception rooms were richly articulated with deep, aedicular niches. There Rabirius seems to have played with the kind of effects that became popular in second-century architecture in Rome and the provinces, "baroque" effects that changed the planes of the walls into a moving, patterned surface, strongly three-dimensional but still observing the dignity and scale of the rooms. Behind (south of) the reception areas was a large peristyle court and an imperial triclinium (banquet hall). The brilliant decorative and spatial effects of this area have been described, in typical sycophantic style, by Statius. Despite the hyperbole, the effect must have been grand. There the emperor, framed in the curve of a vaulted apse, would have presided over a feast both visual (architecture, sculpture and polychrome marble decoration) and aural (fountains and other hydraulic works).

The private part of the palace, the Domus Augustana, on the other hand, was divided into multiple levels with smaller, more intimate spaces arranged around several multistoried peristyles. The peristyle form evoked the gracious living areas of Roman villas and town houses, the landscaped center around which Roman family life revolved. This introspective space provided an area of retreat for the emperor and his family, a public space where the humanity of the emperor was sheltered from public view. In creating this division of the palace into parts that separated the *res publica* from the *res privata,* Rabirius was following precepts of planning established in late republican villas where the villa itself served as a place for contemplative leisure, *otium,* for public men normally consumed with active pursuit of political and military achievement, *negotium.*

In the smaller spaces of the private part of the palace, Rabirius seems to have varied normal axial planning by creating a series of spaces that once again utilized themes of texture and surface, but on a smaller scale. The walls were varied by multiple niches and exedrae, and succeeding spaces were varied in size, shape and vaulting. The style was playful, sometimes even quirky or frivolous, but very much suited to the private nature of this part of the palace. The most revolutionary rooms were two octagonal nymphea with alternating square and round niches. The play of light, texture, temperature and sound would have mirrored, on a smaller scale, the grand effects of the public peristyle. Rabirius proved himself master of an architecture of impression, sometimes grand and befitting the *dignitas* of the emperor, at other times intimate and playful, but always controlled and always manipulative.

To the south of the Domus Augustana was a large imperial box, set high and virtually suspended over the Circus Maximus, semicircular in shape and designed as much to display the emperor to the Roman people as to allow the imperial family to watch the chariot races below. Further to the east Rabirius planned an enigmatic sunken peristyle garden, shaped like a hippodrome, whose function and symbolism have still not been adequately explained.

The Palatine palace is the only structure that can be safely attributed to Rabirius, despite many attempts to assign other buildings to him on the basis of style. That such attempts are constantly made is testament to his influence and to the fame that accrued from the Palatine complex, a timely building, innovative in construction and planning, subtle in its understanding of the changing political institutions of empire.

—P. GREGORY WARDEN

RAGUZZINI, Filippo.

Italian. Born in Italy, ca. 1680. Died in Rome, in 1771. Settled in Rome, 1724. Worked under Pope Benedict XIII until 1730. Inducted in the Congregazione dei Virtuosi al Pantheon; named Architect of the Roman People.

Filippo Raguzzini: Piazza Sant'Ignazio, Rome, Italy, 1727-36

Chronology of Works
All in Italy
* Approximate dates
† Work no longer exists

1710*	Chapel of San Gennaro, Chiesa dell'Annunziata, Benevento
Before 1724	Palazzetto De Simone, Benevento
1724-25	Chapel of San Domenico, Santa Maria sopra Minerva, Rome
1725-26	Ospedale di San Gallicano, Rome
1725-27	San Sisto Vecchio, Rome (restoration)
1726	Cappella del Crocifisso, Rome (restoration)
1726	Santa Maria del Rosario, Rome
1726-29	San Bartolomeo, Benevento
1727	Palazzo Lercari, Albano (portal and atrium)
1727-28	Cappella Savelli, Santa Maria in Aracoeli, Rome
1727-31	SS. Quirico e Giulitta, Rome (facade)
1727-31	Santa Maria della Quercia, Rome
1727-36	Piazza Sant'Ignazio, Rome
1729	Casino Lercari, Albano
1729-34	Chiesa del Divino Amore, Rome
1731	Spanish Steps, Rome (restoration)
1738-40*	Cappella del Presepio, Santa Maria in Trastevere, Rome
1739-40*	Cappella del Battistero, Santa Maria in Trastevere, Rome
1741-42	Villa Gentili, Rome
1767	Palazzo Terragnoli, Benevento

Publications

BOOKS ABOUT RAGUZZINI

ROTILI, MARIO: *Filippo Raguzzini e il rococò romano*. Rome, 1951.

ROTILI, MARIO: *Filippo Raguzzini nel terzo centenario della nascita*. Naples, 1982.

ARTICLES ABOUT RAGUZZINI

ASHBY, T.: "The Piazza di S. Ignazio, Rome: Its History and Development." *Town Planning Review* 13, No. 3 (1929): 139-148.

BONELLI, MASSIMO: "Per una interpretazione di Filippo Raguzzini." *Capitolium* 49, Nos. 10-11 (1974): 29-33.

CONNORS, JOSEPH: "Alliance and Enmity in Roman Baroque Urbanism." *Römisches Jahrbuch der Bibliotheca Hertziana* 25 (1989): 207-294.

GOLZIO, VINCENZO: "Nuovi documenti su Filippo Raguzzini." *Archivo d'Italia* 2 (1934): 145-149.

HABEL, DOROTHY METZGER: "Filippo Raguzzini, Carlo de Dominicis and Domenico Gregorini: New Documentation." *Paragone* 39, Arte 7, No. 455 (1988): 62-67.

HABEL, DOROTHY METZGER: "Filippo Raguzzini, the Palazzo and Casino Lercari in Albano and the Neapolitan Ingredient in Roman Rococo Architecture." Pp. 230-252 in HELLMUT HAGER and SUSAN S. MUNSHOWER (eds.): *Light on the Eternal City: Recent Observations and Discoveries in Roman Art and Architecture*. University Park, Pennsylvania, 1987.

HABEL, DOROTHY METZGER: "Piazza S. Ignazio, Rome in the 17th and 18th Centuries." *Architectura, Zeitschrift für Geschichte der Baukunst* 11 (1981): 31-65.

LORET, MATTIA: "L'architetto Raguzzini e il rococò in Rome." *Bollettino d'arte* 27 (1934): 313-321.

LOTTI, LUIGI: "La Villa Gentili, oggi Domenici, e la sua attribuzione a Filippo Raguzzini." *Palatino* 6 (1962): 11-15.

LOTTI, PIERLUIGI: "Filippo Raguzzini nel terzo centenario della nascita." *Alma Roma* 21, Nos. 5-6 (1980): 53-59.

MÜLLER, CLAUDIA: "Die Piazza S. Ignazio in Rom. Guarini-Rezeption und Rokoko-Strukturen dei Filippo Raguzzini." *Giessener Beiträge zur Kunstgeschichte* 6 (1983): 138-179.

SCATASSA, ERCOLE: "Benedetto XIII e i suoi artisti beneventani." *Rassegna bibliografica dell'arte italiana* 26:111-119, 156-161; 27:138-141.

VENDITTI, ARNALDO: "Un'opera del Raguzzini: Il Palazzo Terragnoli a Benevento." Pp. 215-226 in *Studi di storia dell'arte in onore di Valerio Mariani*. Naples, 1971.

Dubbed an "architetto gotico e beneventano" by artist and wit Pier Leone Ghezzi (1674-1755), Filippo Raguzzini and his Roman works figured prominently in the development of Roman Rococo architecture. Once attributed by modern historians with the founding of the style, Raguzzini is now more accurately recognized for his refinement of the building types and the decorative motifs associated with this elegant, if modest, style most apparent in Roman architecture dating to the first quarter of the 18th century. Ghezzi's epithet referred to two aspects of Raguzzini's career. On the one hand, the reference to his architecture as "gothic," that is to say, wildly inventive and anticlassical, suggested the affinity of his designs and devices with the 17th-century Roman architecture of Francesco Borromini (1599-1667) to which the adjective had already been applied with some regularity; on the other, the label "Beneventine" marked Raguzzini as one of the stable of bureaucrats and artists called to Rome in the entourage of Pope Benedict XIII Orsini (1724-30), who served as archbishop of the southern Italian town of Benevento. Few of these individuals were actually from Benevento—Raguzzini was born in Naples and Benedict XIII himself hailed from Gravina near Bari—but the label was used indiscriminately by Roman chroniclers in a pejorative sense to identify these papal associates as foreign, and thereby untutored, and, as it turned out, underhanded in their dealings once in Rome. If biting, this characterization of Raguzzini was also telling, for he can be credited with participating in the established taste for the decorative and pictorial details of Borromini's earlier architecture and, more important, with adding to this revival new and somewhat exotic ingredients that derived from the architectural traditions of his native city of Naples.

Raguzzini's earliest works appear to have been undertaken as part of a campaign initiated by Cardinal Vincenzo Maria Orsini, the future Benedict XIII, to rebuild the city of Benevento after the earthquakes of 1688 and 1702. Although the documentation is not solid, Raguzzini's name is associated with two early projects in Benevento, the Cappella di San Gennaro in the Church of the Annunziata (ca.1710) and the Palazzo de Simone (before 1724). Neither of these is of particular note, although in both, motifs that were typical of Raguzzini's work throughout his career appeared for the first time; these included fanciful cartouche-like embellishments to pediments, pilasters and wall surfaces, as well as decorative wall openings of distinctive shapes, such as modified rectangles with semicircular sides and modified quatrefoils.

Of far greater consequence was Raguzzini's Roman work. He appears to have arrived in Rome in 1724, where he assumed the position of leading architect throughout Benedict XIII's reign. In that context he was responsible for numerous official projects, generally a matter of routine repair and maintenance of major papal monuments, including St. Peter's, San Giovanni in Laterano and the papal palaces, and for a series of modest restorations of small churches throughout the city, among them San Sisto Vecchio, SS. Quirico e Giulitta and San Biagio dei Materassai (the Church of Divino Amore).

His greatest opportunities, however, came with a handful of projects for new buildings. Among these, the Ospedale di San Gallicano, Piazza Sant'Ignazio and the church of Santa Maria della Quercia rank as the most noteworthy. This sequence of building projects also documents the "Romanization" of Raguzzini's architectural style, evident in the increasing reduction of florid ornamentation and the growing appreciation of how the planes of his architectural surfaces could carve and animate as well as monumentalize his designs. While the Ospedale di San Gallicano was celebrated in its time for its progressive engineering of sanitary and hygienic devices (especially relative to the ventilation of the wards), it is also a design that in 1726

was unique in the Roman architectural cityscape. The squat proportions of the complex, and especially of the church facade embedded within the main facade of the hospital, were decidedly foreign to Roman tradition; the decorative panels framing the large windows of the hospital facade and the roughened stucco panels applied equally to the wall surfaces and to the pilaster orders of the two stories would have appeared entirely unorthodox. But in all cases the sources for these motifs can be traced to the earlier 17th-century work of the Neapolitan architect Cosimo Fanzago (1591-1678) and to the legacy of his work in the early-18th century architecture of Domenico Antonio Vaccarro (1678-1745) and Ferdinando Sanfelice (1675-1748) in an around Naples.

By comparison, Raguzzini's designs for Piazza Sant'Ignazio and Santa Maria della Quercia eschewed many of these pictorial devices in favor of considerably more tectonic solutions in which the wall planes bend and bulge to carve the surrounding exterior spaces. This is especially evident in Piazza Sant'Ignazio, Raguzzini's most significant contribution to Roman architecture. There, the architect was employed by the Jesuits of the Church of Sant'Ignazio to open the space in front of their massive Baroque church and in so doing to design a cluster of Jesuit-owned rental properties. The result was an ingenious design in which five independent buildings were coordinated to define an impressive, yet intimate, space incorporating the curvilinear lines that appeared in the monumental urban designs for the Porto di Ripetta (1703-05) designed by Alessandro Specchi (1668-1729) and for the Scala de Spagna (1723-26) designed by Francesco de Sanctis (ca.1693-1731) with a delicacy apparent in the scale and the surface treatment of the architecture of the defining structures. Moreover, the defining buildings, perhaps the first modern apartment buildings in the city, were conceived from the first as elegant rental units to house a growing upper-middle-class clientele. Although Piazza sant'Ignazio ignored the tradition of Roman urban design as inherited from the 16th and 17th centuries in which the axis of approach was dominant and priority was assigned to one central monument, usually a church or palace, it certainly combined the Roman attention to an architecture of active planes molding space with the contemporary, early-18th-century Roman taste for delicate ornamentation. This same combination is found at Santa Maria della Quercia, where the swelling curve of the facade, in which the stunted proportions of the facade of San Gallicano reappeared, is marked by the crisp pleating of a multiple pilaster order, lending a decidedly tectonic quality to the whole in spite of the diminutive scale of the building.

If Raguzzini can be considered as having fallen under the influence of traditions of Roman architecture, he can also be credited with influencing his Roman colleagues to indulge in a greater ornamentation of their buildings and in new spatial devices. In his work for private patrons—especially in the palace atrium and casino (1727-29) in Albano for Cardinal Lercari and in the Cappella del Presepio (1738-40) in Santa Maria in Trastevere for Cardinal Fini—Raguzzini remained steadfast to his Neapolitan heritage. In these works, the use of stucco to mold wildly inventive floral frames and wall appliques was distinctive as was, in the case of the palace atrium at Albano, the attention to molding interior spaces, affording rather distinct qualities of light and air. The impact of these qualities on the Roman scene was documented by the works of Raguzzini's Roman associates and especially those of Carlo de' Dominicis (1696-1758), who is documented as having been an assistant to Raguzzini from about 1724 until at least 1731, and Domenico Gregorini (1692-1777).

Raguzzini's work after the death of Benedict XIII in 1730 is difficult to track. He remained active in the Accademia di

San Luca, was inducted into the Congregazione dei Virtuosi al Pantheon and retained the office of Architetto del Popolo Romano until his own death, but the only documented work is the Villa Gentili in Rome (1741-42), although he also entered the competition for the facade of San Giovanni in Laterano in 1732. It would appear that his continued activity took the form of designing various apartment houses in the city and in working for various private patrons. Moreover, the possibility that he continued to work on projects in Benevento—as the Palazzo Terragnoli project (1767) would suggest—and, perhaps, in Naples as well certainly exists inasmuch as his ties to that city remained strong throughout his career.

In the end, however, the taste for Raguzzini's architecture and, indeed, for Roman Rococo architecture in general was supplanted by the academic classicism of Alessandro Galilei (1691-1737), as demonstrated by the selection of his design for the facade of San Giovanni in Laterano as early as 1732, and of Ferdinando Fuga (1699-1782) whose facade for Santa Maria Maggiore was complete by 1743. Raguzzini's work from the later 1720s remains nonetheless a significant document to the vitality and invention of the best of Roman Rococo architecture.

—DOROTHY METZGER HABEL

RAINALDI, Carlo.

Italian. Born in Rome, Italy, 4 May 1611. Died in Rome, 8 February 1691. Trained in the shop of his father, Girolamo Rainaldi. Named architect of the Roman people.

Chronology of Works
All in Rome, Italy unless noted
* Approximate dates

1645-50	Palazzo del Museo Capitolino (with Girolamo Rainaldo, on design of Michelangelo and Giacomo della Porta)
1647-50	S. Maria della Scala (tabernacle and high alter)
1650s	S. Girolamo della Carità (restoration)
1652-53	Sant'Agnese in Piazza Navona (with Girolamo Rainaldi; replaced by Borromini, then recalled to the project in 1657)
1655*-79	S. Maria di Montesanto and S. Maria dei Miracoli, Piazza del Popolo
1656-65	S. Andrea della Valle (facade)
1656-75	S. Maria in Campitelli
1660*	Villa Mondragone, Frascati (*giardino secreto*)
1660*	Cathedral, Ronciglione
1660-87	S. Maria del Sudario (rebuilding)
1663-65	S. Lorenzo in Lucina (convent)
1667	S. Silvestro in Capite (high alter)
1669-75	S. Maria Maggiore (rear facade)
1669-75	S. Maria del Suffragio (rebuilding)
1670*	S. Carlo ai Catinari (Chapel of S. Biagio alter)
1671	S. Lorenzo in Lucina (high alter)
1671	S. Maria Maggiore (monument of Clement IX)
1671-74	Gesù e Maria (facade and interior restoration)
1671-80	Palazzo Borghese (rebuilding, garden facade, and nymphaeum)
1675-90	Palazzo del Grillo (portals)
1677-78	Lateran Baptistry (Oratory of S. Venanzio, Ceva Tombs)
1680-91	S. Silvestro in Capite (interior decoration)
1681	S. Maria in Via (facade completion)
1685*	S. Maria in Montesanto (Aquilante Chapel)

Publications

BOOKS ABOUT RAINALDI

EIMER, GERHARD: *La fabbrica di Sant'Agnese in Navona.* 2 vols. Stockholm, 1970-71.

FAGIOLO DELL'ARCO, MAURIZIO, and CARANDINI, SILVIA: *L'effemero barocco. Strutture della festa nella Roma del '600.* 2 vols. Rome, 1977-78.

FASOLO, FURIO: *L'opera di Hieronimo e Carlo Rainaldi.* Rome, 1961.

FERRAIRONI, FRANCESCO: *S. Maria in Campitelli.* Vol. 33 in *Le chiese di Roma illustrate* series. Rome, n.d.

HEMPEL, EBERHARD: *Carlo Rainaldi, ein Beitrag zur Geschichte des römischen Barocks.* Munich, 1919.

HIBBARD, HOWARD: *The Architecture of the Palazzo Borghese.* Rome, 1962.

KRAUTHEIMER, RICHARD: *The Rome of Alexander VII.* Princeton, New Jersey, 1985.

ORTOLANI, SERGIO: *S. Andrea della Valle.* Vol. 4 in *Le chiese di Roma illustrate* series. Rome, n.d.

WITTKOWER, RUDOLF: *Art and Architecture in Italy 1600-1750.* 3rd ed. Baltimore and Harmondsworth, England, 1973.

ARTICLES ABOUT RAINALDI

ARGAN, GIULIO CARLO: "S. Maria in Campitelli." *Commentari* 11 (1960): 74-86.

FASOLO, FURIO: "Carlo Rainaldi e il prospetto di S. Andrea della Valle a Roma." *Palladio* 1 (1951): 34-38.

HABEL, DOROTHY METZGER: "Carlo Rainaldi's Facade Project for S. Lorenzo in Lucina." *Journal of the Society of Architectural Historians* 43 (March 1984): 65-70.

HAGER, HELLMUT: "La crisi statica della cupola di S. Maria in Vallicella in Roma e i rimedi proposti da Carlo Fontana, Carlo Rainaldi e Mattia di Rossi." *Commentari* 24 (1973): 300-318.

MATTIAE, GUGLIELMO: "Contributo a Carlo Rainaldi." *Arti figurative* 2 (1946): 49-59.

MATTIAE, GUGLIELMO: "Le Porte di Roma in un codice di Carlo Rainaldi." *Capitolium* 22 (1947): 68-72.

NOEHLES, KARL: "Buchbesprechungen: Furio Fasolo: *L'opera di Hieronimo e Carlo Rainaldi.*" *Zeitschrift für Kunstgeschichte* 25 (1962): 166-177.

NOEHLES, KARL: "Die Louvre-Projekte von Pietro da Cortona und Carlo Rainaldi." *Zeitschrift für Kunstgeschichte* 24 (1961): 40-74.

TREVISANI, FRANCESCO: "Carlo Rainaldi nella chiesa di Gesù e Maria." *Storia dell'arte* 11 (1971): 163-171.

WHITMAN, NATHAN T.: "Roman Tradition and the Aedicular Facade." *Journal of the Society of Architectural Historians* 29 (1970): 108-123.

WITTKOWER, RUDOLF: "Carlo Rainaldi and the Roman Architecture of the Full Baroque." *Art Bulletin* 19 (1937): 242-313. Reprinted in RUDOLF WITTKOWER: *Studies in the Italian Baroque.* London, 1975.

*

Modern historians of Roman Baroque architecture have understood the architecture of Carlo Rainaldi to be highly derivative. Following the lead of Rudolf Wittkower (1937), scholars had perceived Rainaldi's idiom as dependent on selective borrowings from the architectural works of his older colleagues, Giovanni Lorenzo Bernini (1598-1680), Francesco Borromini (1599-1667) and Pietro da Cortona (1597-1669), laced with what Wittkower later (1973) identified as a "deliberate return to a

Carlo Rainaldi: S. Maria in Campitelli, Rome, Italy, 1656-75

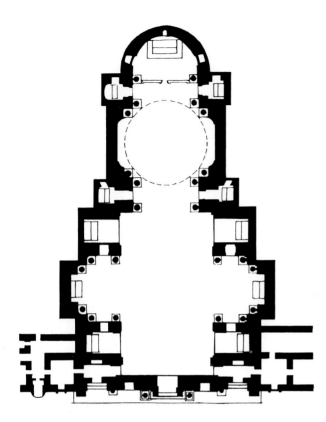

Rainaldi's work on the church of Santa Maria in Campitelli is his most significant. As Architetto del Popolo Romano, he was selected architect for this project because the rebuilding of the church was financed by the city, although it was also a pet project of Pope Alexander VII Chigi (1655-67), who appears to have played no small part in the inception and progress of the work. The building history, as first outlined by Wittkower (1937) and refined by Hellmut Hager (1967-1968), is complex and involved Rainaldi's preparation of a number of projects; most notable of these is a design for an oval church with a two-story, convex facade. By 1662, however, when construction began, a longitudinal plan with a straight facade had been selected.

The church is highly inventive in plan, consisting of a combination of a large Greek cross into which one enters and a smaller, square-domed space to which the semicircular apse beyond is appended. Both centralized forms—the Greek cross and the square—are flanked by small chapels that serve to reinforce the nave-like, longitudinal quality of the interior. In plan, this sequence of spaces, unusual in Roman architecture (Wittkower and others suggest sources in northern Italian architectural traditions), has a telescopic quality that is reinforced by the monumentality of the architecture of the elevation, where freestanding giant columns mark all angles of the geometry of the plan. The result is a bold and active interior in which the columns become the markers by which the plan and the directional telescoping of this are made apparent. In all, the interior of Santa Maria in Campitelli, on the one hand reminiscent of the grand interiors of Roman Counter-Reformatory churches (e.g., Il Gesù, Santa Maria in Vallicella and especially Sant'Andrea della Valle) and on the other quite fresh and even unique in Rome, marks Rainaldi's finest achievement as an independent personality, for here the tradition of a muscular, columnar architecture, traceable to Roman imperial monuments, is fused with a typically Roman preoccupation with spatial manipulation.

The facade of Santa Maria in Campitelli is equally remarkable. Designing within the tradition of the aedicular facade developed in two unequal stories, Rainaldi invested the orders—pilasters at each outer edge, engaged columns in the middle bays, and columns standing free before the wall at the very center—with a monumental force. As plastic units the orders appear to carve deep crevices into the wall, an impression reinforced by the craggy pediments they carry, and as pictorial units, they serve to cast deep shadows and to intensify the bright light that seeps behind the freestanding order of the central bay.

Although the original scheme for the facade of Santa Maria in Campitelli included sculptural decorations that might have softened its overwhelmingly architectural cast, the end result is a significant monument to Rainaldi's ability to fuse the aggressive with the restrained and to the contemporary taste for a balance between these two stylistic alternatives. Other examples of this stylistic duality included the contemporary architectural works of Cortona, such as his design for the facade of Santa Maria in via Lata (1658-62), and Bernini's work at Sant'Andrea al Quirinale (1658-71). This aspect also remained a part of Rainaldi's own work in the 1660s, as evidenced in his design for the facade of Sant'Andrea della Valle and the work on the twin churches of Santa Maria dei Miracoli and Santa Maria di Montesanto at Piazza del Popolo. In all of these designs Rainaldi worked in concert with others. At Sant'Andrea della Valle he was assisted by Carlo Fontana (1638-1714), while his design for the twin churches at Piazza del Popolo, refined by Bernini, was actually carried out under Fontana. In the past, the more restrained classical ingredient as it appeared in Rainaldi's work at that time has been attributed to the influence of Bernini and

Mannerist structure.'' More recent studies, however, have helped to revise our understanding of Rainaldi's architecture as considerably more original. He is now appreciated as a more individual designer whose work merits attention for the strongly Roman flavor of its inventions.

Born in the city of Rome and trained in the shop of his father Girolamo Rainaldi (1570-1655), a conservative architect overshadowed in his own day by Carlo Maderno (1556-1629), Carlo Rainaldi first appeared as a collaborator with his father in the mid-1640s. Carlo's name is associated with many of the major architectural projects of the mid-17th century: he prepared a design for the controversial towers of St. Peter's, for the piazza in front of St. Peter's, for the Spanish Steps and for the rebuilding of the Louvre in Paris. These projects, although never carried out, suggest that Rainaldi was considered a ranking architect along with the more famous Bernini, Borromini and Cortona. His major independent works date to the 1660s, when he established a bold and personal style by combining the more aggressive aspects of the Baroque with a new restraint and reticence symptomatic of the growing classicism of Roman art and architecture that appeared in the second half of the 17th century.

Rainaldi's earliest project of note was his design work at Sant'Agnese in Piazza Navona. Carlo's role in this commission, awarded by Pope Innocent X Pamphili (1644-55) to both Rainaldis in 1652, is difficult to discern inasmuch as they were replaced on the job by Borromini, who was, in turn, dismissed in 1657. At that point Carlo Rainaldi was recalled, although it would appear that he was not given a free hand in the work; Bernini and Cortona both are recorded as consultants. In the end, it is very difficult to appreciate Carlo's contribution to this important building project, although Gerhard Eimer has suggested that he can be attributed with the introduction of the Greek cross plan with heavily decorated piers and with the concave facade, two of the most salient aspects of the design.

Fontana, but this is to deny Rainaldi's strength as a designer, as best demonstrated by his entirely independent work at Santa Maria in Campitelli.

Rainaldi's late work, dating after 1670, showed a decided change in style as the classical component began to far outweigh the more Baroque aspect of his mature work. The rear facade of the basilica of Santa Maria Maggiore and the facade of the Gesù e Maria on via del Corso both date from this late period. In each solution was extremely tame, even dry, compared to his earlier works, and this may have reflected both a growing decline in the economy of Rome and the Papal States as it affected the building industry, as well as a marked shift in taste away from the grand style fostered by Alexander VII and toward a more academic classicism championed by Fontana, heir of Bernini's architectural practice. This late work is disappointing in its seeming lack of personality, but it does serve to highlight the strength of Rainaldi's mature architecture. If overshadowed by the work of his more prodigious colleagues in Rome, Carlo Rainaldi's architecture nevertheless remains an important component of the Baroque city at its height under the reign of Alexander VII.

—DOROTHY METZGER HABEL

RAPHAEL.

Italian. Born Raffaello Santi (or Sanzio), in Urbino, Italy, 6 April 1483. Died in Rome, 6 April 1520. Trained in painting with his father, Giovanni Santi. Commuted between Perugia and Citta di Castello, probably as junior partner to Perugino, 1500-04; based at Florence by 1504, then settled in Rome, 1508. Became artistic supremo in Rome after the accession of Leo X; succeeded Bramante as architect for the new St. Peter's, 1514. Pupils/assistants included Giulio Romano, Giovanni da Udine, Per ino del Vaga, Penni, and Polidoro da Caravaggio.

Chronology of Works
All in Rome, Italy
* Approximate dates
† Work no longer exists

1512ff.*	Memorial chapel for Agostino Chigi, S. Maria del Populo (not finished until 1554)
1514*-18*	Villa Farnesina (stables)
1515	Loggia of San Damaso
1516	Palazzo Banconia dell'Aquila†
1516ff.	Palazzo Pandolfini, Florence (design executed by others)
1518*20	Villa Madama

Publications

BOOKS ABOUT RAPHAEL

AMES-LEWIS, FRANCIS: *The Draftsman Raphael.* New Haven, Connecticut, 1986.

BECHERUCCI, LUISA, et al.: *Raffaello: L'opera, le fonti, la fortuna.* 2 vols. Novara, Italy, 1968.

BONELLI, RENATO: *Da Bramante a Michelangelo.* Venice, 1960.

CAMESASCA, E. (ed.): *Raffaello Sanzio, tutti gli scritti.* Milan, 1956.

CROWE, J. A., and CAVALCASELLE, G. B.: *Raphael: His Life and Works.* 2 vols. London, 1882-85.

CUZIN, JEAN PIERRE: *Raphaël: Vie et oeuvre.* Fribourg, Switzerland, 1983.

DACOS, NICOLE: *Le logge di Raffaello: Maestro e bottega di fronte all'antico.* Rome, 1977.

ETTLINGER, LEOPOLD and HELEN: *Raphael.* Oxford, 1987.

FROMMEL, C. L., et al. (ed.): *Raffaello architetto.* Milan, 1984.

GOLZIO, VINCENZO: *Raffaello nei documenti, nelle testimonianze dei contemporanei, e nella letteratura del suo secolo.* Vatican City, 1936.

GRIMM, HERMANN: *The Life of Raphael.* Boston, 1888.

HOFFMANN, T.: *Raffael in seiner Bedeutung als Architekt.* 4 vols. Zittau, 1904-14.

HOLMES, CHARLES J.: *Raphael and the Modern Use of the Classical Tradition.* London and New York, 1933.

JONES, ROGER, and PENNY, NICHOLAS: *Raphael.* New Haven, Connecticut, 1983.

McCURDY, EDWARD: *Raphael.* London and New York, 1917.

MULAZZANI, GERMANO: *Raffaello.* Milan, 1983.

OBERHUBER, KONRAD: *Raphael.* Milan, 1982.

PASSAVANT, J. D.: *Raphael von Urbino.* 3 vols. Leipzig, 1839-58.

PEDRETTI, CARLO: *Raphael.* Bologna, 1982.

POUNCEY, P., and GERE, J. A.: *Raphael and His Circle.* London, 1962.

QUATREMERE DE QUINCY, M.: *Histoire de la vie et des ouvrages de Raphael.* Paris, 1833.

Raffaels Zeichnungen. Berlin, 1913-41.

RAY, STEFANO: *Raffaello architetto.* Bari, Italy, 1974.

REDIG DE CAMPOS, D.: *Raffaello e Michelangelo.* Rome, 1946.

SALMI, MARIO, et al.: *The Complete Works of Raphael.* New York, 1969.

VENTURI, ADOLFO and LIONELLO: *Raphael.* Milan, 1952.

VOGEL, J.: *Bramante und Raphael.* Leipzig, 1910.

VON GEYMÜLLER, HEINRICH: *Raffaello Sanzio, studiato come architetto.* Milan, 1884.

ARTICLES ABOUT RAPHAEL

MÜNTZ, E.: "Les maisons de Raphael à Rome." *Gazette des beaux-arts* 1 (1880): 353-358.

SHEARMAN, J.: "Raphael as Architect." *Journal of the Royal Society of Arts* (April 1968).

*

Raphael was trained as a painter, and it was more as a painter than as an architect— perhaps not to threaten the preeminence of Michelangelo—that Giorgio Vasari chose to write of Raphael in his book *The Lives of the Artists* (1550), thereby establishing a certain picture of Raphael for all subsequent histories. But in 1514, partly on the advice of Donato Bramante, Raphael was appointed architect-in-chief to St. Peter's. Not only was this position one of evidently extreme authority, but it shows clearly that the pope, Leo X, believed Raphael fully capable of carrying out whatever such a position entailed.

The reckoning by scholars of Raphael's contribution to the history of High Renaissance architecture has varied. On the one hand, it can be said that, unlike his contemporaries Giuliano da Sangallo or il Cronaca, he was not a professional architect, whatever that means in this historical context. On the other hand, as John Shearman has argued, there is also a case for saying that in the last six years of his life, from the appointment in 1514 until 1520, Raphael was, from the evidence of his built and unbuilt designs, "the greatest living and practicing architect (in Italy)." To which the following details must be added: First, for architecture itself, as the career of Bramante shows (he was

Raphael: Memorial Chapel for Agostino Chigi, Rome, Italy, ca. 1512ff.

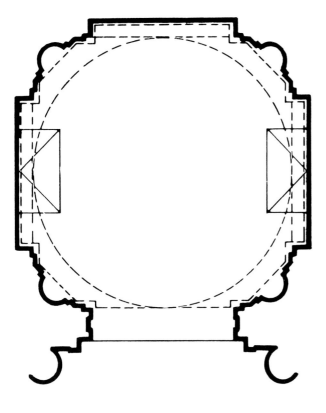

a painter for most of his life), no clear sense existed then of an architectural profession; second, all the arts in the Renaissance were tied together under the idea of drawing, or *disegno,* and so it had been possible, even two centuries earlier, for the painter Giotto to make a design for the Campanile of Florence Cathedral; and third, from his painting *The Marriage of the Virgin* (1504), which has in the background a remarkable 16-sided building, to all the details of the frescoes he did some 10 years later in the Stanza della Segnatura and the Stanza d'Eliodoro, Raphael showed in the representation of space and the background for his figures an extraordinarily rich and complex understanding of what Renaissance architecture was concerned with, and how its parts might be used to new and different effects. As Shearman again notes, almost no studies by Raphael for architecture have survived; this may be a matter of chance, since to early collectors Raphael was important more as a painter. But details are there to be seen on the edges of sheets of drawings for other subjects, and what these show is what we might expect: that Raphael was an extremely skillful and knowing designer.

He had, in a sense, been born to the task, for the Ducal Palace at Urbino was one of the richest monuments of the Early Renaissance style outside Florence. Yet, from being trained first as a painter, Raphael was perhaps free then to embody in his designs elements of a more purely visual effect than architects of a practical tradition would have been comfortable with— like Giuliano da Sangallo, who was passed over for the position at St. Peter's. Raphael's concern with visual possibilities and his interest in remains of classical materials of all subjects and types encouraged him to propose designs and decorations that seemed highly original, and then exerted a strong effect on architecture and interior decoration throughout the remainder of the 16th century.

So far as we know, when he was made *magister operis* at St. Peter's in 1514, Raphael had worked on only two buildings, a memorial chapel for Agostino Chigi in Santa Maria del Popolo and, for Chigi also, the stables in the building known later as the Villa Farnesina. The Chigi Chapel, which even Vasari allowed was by Raphael, was begun perhaps in 1512, the stables certainly by 1514; but if the stables were finished in 1518, the chapel took longer, requiring after Raphael's death that it be finished by a pupil, the whole scheme not being done until about 1554. Both works depended on the model of Bramante: Raphael used in the stables orders derived from what Bramante had done at the Palazzo Caprini, Raphael roofed the chapel with a dome, as Bramante had done at the Tempietto, and arranged then the system of arches and pendentives and entrances in a way that recalls the great first scheme of Bramante for St. Peter's—writ small, of course, in the chapel.

Raphael went beyond Bramante in a number of ways, however, most immediately in that Bramante himself, unlike most of his predecessors, designed his architecture with a single optimal viewing perspective, rather than spatial, effect, Raphael in the Chigi Chapel gave spectators not one, but various such visual opportunities: he required them to look in several directions—inside the space, not outside it as at the Tempietto—to all four corners of the plan, taking in the four statues placed there in the corner niches. And if for Bramante all the parts of the structure were a whole—walls, orders, entablatures—for Raphael there was far less emphasis on the wall between these parts. If any idea remained of the architecture of the building itself, this would function essentially as a form of scaffolding that holds the parts that are so obviously there.

All this demonstrated a remarkable understanding and knowledge of architecture. Raphael must surely have studied the new buildings of Florence very carefully when he was there, so too the buildings of Rome once he arrived in that city. Also with a characteristic thoroughness, he began to study the treatise of Vitruvius, translated for him in 1514 by the humanist Fabio Calvi; he also made some recorded visits to the classical monuments that were all around, once in 1514 in the company of the antiquarian Andrea Fulvio, and then in 1516 to Tivoli with Pietro Bembo, Baldassare Castiglione and other literary figures. In addition to looking at monuments and consulting classical sources, Raphael doubtlessly also turned to every kind of ancient source, from coins to miniatures, to fill out his picture of antiquity. A memorandum we have on the study of the ancient monuments that survives, without date, address or an author identified, is believed to have been written by Raphael to Leo X, perhaps with the help of Castiglione. Emphasized in this correspondence is the importance of drawing and measuring the monuments accurately, and producing representations of them in plan, perspective and cross sections; yet it is also noted that the record of such direct observation should be compared always to literary writers, and especially to Vitruvius.

After the Chigi Chapel, Raphael worked on a number of varied commissions, in 1515 completing the Loggia of San Damaso, and producing designs for the Church of Sant'Eligio degli Orefici and for the Palace of Jacopo da Brescia. The church, which was modified in innumerable ways in the years after, was in its plan a perfect instance of the centrally designed Renaissance church, a Greek cross, with reference to churches such as Giuliano da Sangallo's Santa Maria delle Carceri in Prato and Bramante's Santi Celso e Giuliano. Bramante's work is also a presence in the designs of the Palace of Jacopo da Brescia, not only in the manner of the articulation of the facade, but in the fact that the long facade was arranged to be seen from one privileged position, the distances between the half columns being progressively diminished to allow it to seem, from a point near the square of St. Peter's, to be longer than it was.

In the designs for the Loggie of the Vatican, where he was completing a project of Bramante's, Raphael began to experiment with the range of elements that would appear, a few years later, at the Villa Madama. He did so in a way that fit well with what was there already, and afforded some very proper spaces for the decorative painting then laid in by artists in Raphael's workshop, after Raphael's designs. This, as Vasari tells us, pleased the pope so much that he gave Raphael all the work then being done in the papal palaces. Raphael was also busy at that time outside the Vatican, working, notably, on the Palazzo Branconia dell'Aquila (1516), which was later demolished to allow Giovanni Lorenzo Bernini's columns in front of St. Peter's. The facade there was set in two levels; the ground floor was articulated with an engaged Tuscan order, and on the upper floor, leaving the type of articulation seen at the Cancelleria, Raphael set the windows of the *piano nobile* in a series of boldly molded aedicules with alternating pediments, between which were niches to balance the convex forms below them. This form of articulation was also found at the Palazzo Vidoni-Caffarelli, the design of which has been attributed to Raphael.

The private project he was working on at his death was the Villa Madama, set on Monte Mario, behind the Vatican, and built for Cardinal Giulio de' Medici, later Pope Clement VII. This was a great villa *all'antica:* the center was a large courtyard; terraces were built into the hill on which the villa was set; and in addition to the large living quarters, there was to be a theater, stabling for some 200 horses, a large hippodrome and a garden with highly elaborate fountains. A great open stair led up to the entrance of the villa, rivaling that of the Belvedere Court at the Vatican; throughout its length the villa was finished with forms that recalled antiquity and especially details from Nero's Domus Aurea, newly discovered and known by Raphael. Painting, sculpture and architecture were all at the Villa Madama, serving to express in the building an ideal of the cultured, gracious living to be enacted within its walls. Yet it must be noted that the villa had a troubled history: it was badly damaged, only a few years after it was begun, during the Sack of Rome in 1527; and the gardens were neglected for centuries. What we see there now is largely the result of modern restorations.

A different story of misfortunes attended Raphael's work at St. Peter's, in this case the problem being a lack of interest on the part of the new pope, Leo X. Work proceeded very slowly, yet of great importance for the subsequent history of the church was the institution in 1516 of the office of coadjutor, who was to be responsible for planning and executing the working drawings; Antonio da Sangallo held that office until he succeeded as architect-in-chief of St. Peter's upon Raphael's death. What, in fact, Raphael did at St. Peter's is difficult to reconstruct. Even before his appointment was ratified, however, he had been asked to prepare a new general design and a model; it was this that Sebastiano Serlio later published as being Raphael's final design, together with a comment that Raphael had made use of several parts of Bramante's model, which had been left incomplete.

In its elements the plan is clear enough. An aisled nave of some five bays was set in front of the domed space Bramante had designed, giving the building a longitudinal axis, the facade being a broad, two-story portico. Around the transepts, Raphael added ambulatories and, perhaps for structural reasons, he decided to set the outer walls, which were exposed to the thrust of the dome, nearer to the piers of this dome than had been originally planned. With these ambulatories it was then possible to reduce the distance between the crossing and the apses, and to double the exterior walls of the apse itself; the thrust of the

dome could then be carried over the vaults of the transepts to the line of the ambulatories, and thence to the outer walls. The exterior views of these ambulatories show a Doric order with aedicules and engaged columns, the insignia of Leo X appearing on the metopes.

When it came to Bramante's dome, Raphael kept both its shape and its structure. Yet in the appearance of the church as a whole, Raphael seems to have gone further than Bramante in a kind of classicism, applying to the front a temple facade like the one Leon Battista Alberti had put at Sant'Andrea in Mantua, but making sure the apex of the pediment was the same height as the apex of the vault. This was an enormous project, larger both in scale and grandeur than the design of Bramante, and since the Vatican was under particular financial distress during those years, there was no chance that it could be built quickly. Yet the effect of Raphael's plan was indelibly set on all that came after it, for in following Bramante's older design, Raphael returned the plan of St. Peter's to the traditional T shape of the first basilica; that made his church, like the first, both the record of the burial place of the apostle and the site of a processional way, St. Peter's being both the official residence of the pope, and one of the several pilgrimage churches all visitors to Rome had to see. Raphael combined all this, with characteristic skill, in one great, classical scheme.

Raphael is associated with other projects as well. Vasari tells us that in Florence Raphael designed the palace for the bishop of Troia, now the Palazzo Pandolfini; this was begun in 1516, though all the extant work was executed by Giovanni Francesco and Aristotile da Sangallo, and the full scale of the plan was not built. Also according to Vasari, Raphael participated in 1518 in the competition for the Church of San Giovanni dei Fiorentini in Rome, but nothing else is known of that project. At that time Raphael was also in general charge of a project, carried out in his workshop, for the Palazzo Alberini. In 1519 he sent to Federigo Gonzaga a project for a memorial monument in the shape of a pyramidal tomb, presumably for the marquis of Mantua, Francesco Gonzaga. It is possible also that he was associated with the design of the house of Baldassare Turini, now known as the Villa Lante, in Rome.

Certainly in 1520 he was involved in the design of his own palace on the Via Giulia, though he died only a few days after signing a lease on the property. But the plans were already done, and they seem to stand as a proper ending to his architectural career. The whole design is governed by a sense of optical perspective, all four facades being articulated by giant pilasters, placed carefully at unequal distances from one another to conceal the different dimensions of each side. The plan is in some ways like that of the Villa Madama, yet adapted appropriately to the idea of both a private and urban palace. Everything is gracious and rich and inventive.

When Raphael was buried later that year, his tomb was set, as a token of honor, in the Pantheon. It seems a particularly appropriate choice, for this building was but one of the many classical monuments, perhaps also the most important, from which Raphael had taken so much and to such effect in his work in architecture.

—DAVID CAST

RASTRELLI, Bartolomeo.

Russian. Born Bartolomeo Francesco Rastrelli in Paris, France, ca. 1700. Died in St. Petersburg, Russia, 1771. Father was the architect and sculptor Bartolemeo Carlo Rastrelli (1675-1744).

Studied with his father, and accompanied him to St. Petersburg, 1715; then studied in Paris under Robert de Cotte. Returned to Russia, 1730; appointed court architect, 1736.

Chronology of Works
All in Russia
* Approximate dates
† Work no longer exists

1730*	Annenhof Palace Complex, Moscow†
1732	Third Winter Palace, St. Petersburg†
1736-40	Biron Palace, Mitau
1741-44	Summer Palace, St. Petersburg†
1743-57	Vorontsov Palace, St. Petersburg
1744-50	Anichkov Palace, St. Petersburg†
1747-48	Cathedral of St. Andrew, Kiev
1747-52	Summer Palace, Peterhof, St. Petersburg (renovation)
1748-55	Smolny Convent, St. Petersburg
1749-56	Grand Palace, Tsarskoe Selo (now Pushkin; renovation)
1750	Mon Bijou Pavilion, Tsarskoe Selo (now Pushkin)†
1750-54	Stroganov Palace, St. Petersburg
1754-62	Fourth Winter Palace, St. Petersburg
1755-62	Grotto, Tsarskoe Selo (now Pushkin)

Publications

BOOKS ABOUT RASTRELLI

ARKIN, DAVID E.: *Rastrelli*. Moscow, 1954.

DENISOV, J. and PETROV, A.: *B. F. Rastrelli*. Leningrad, 1963.

GRABAR', IGOR' IMMANULOVICH: Vol.s 3 and 4 in *Istoriia russkago iskusstva*. Moscow, 1910-1914.

HAMILTON, G. H.: *The Art and Architecture of Russia*. Harmondsworth, England, 1954.

LO GATTO, ETTORE: *Gli artisti italiana in Russia*. Rome, 1939.

KOZ'MIAN, GALINS KUZ'MINICHNA: *F. B. Rastrelli*. St. Petersburg, 1976.

Bartolomeo Rastrelli: Fourth Winter Palace, St. Petersburg, Russia, 1754-62

ARTICLES ABOUT RASTRELLI

LUKOMSKI, GEORGIO: "Bartolomeo Rastrelli architetto italiano in Russia." *Architettura e Arti Decorative* 4 (1924-25): 337-358.

*

Italian by origin but born in Paris, Bartolomeo Francesco Rastrelli became the creator and leading master of High Baroque architecture in Russia. He studied the basics of architecture under the guidance of his father, the sculptor and architect Carlo Bartolomeo Rastrelli (1675-1744), with whom he moved to St. Petersburg in 1716. In St. Petersburg, Bartolomeo Rastrelli was appointed court architect and received commissions from the imperial court and aristocracy. His creativity bloomed during the 1740s and 1750s.

Rastrelli's architecture was representative and ceremoniously decorous and made a valuable contribution to the festive appearance of the Russian capital. Rastrelli developed his intensely original style by fusing Western Baroque techniques and forms with the Russian, particularly Muscovian, architectural tradition of the 17th and early 18th centuries. He combined a large scale, clarity and austerity in planning with intricacy of silhouette and facade. The varied decoration was always highly sculptural and dynamic. He employed combinations of contrasting colors to create a picturesque polychromy and to emphasize the facade's ceremonial appearance. The architect widely used order systems, particularly pilasters and three-quarter columns, to intensify wall texture and enrich the light effects of his architecture.

Rastrelli worked during the mid-18th century, the period when construction in and around St. Petersburg reached an unprecedented level of activity. At that time, old imperial residences and aristocratic palaces were reconstructed, and new ones were built. Rastrelli's earliest works, palaces for the governor of Moldavia in St. Petersburg (1721) and for Count Ernst Johann Biron in Ruental (1736-40, 1763) and Mitava were austere, almost severe in form. Elizabeth I's Summer Palace at Tsarskoe Selo became an important stage in the development of Rastrelli's style. The architect abandoned his earlier, outdated Kurland palace plans employing compact compositions. He created a more sophisticated ensemble with an open estate plan. Further development of this tendency led Rastrelli to create city palaces with linear facades.

Following this development, Rastrelli designed palaces for M. I. Vorontsov and S. G. Stroganov in St. Petersburg. He turned away from his earlier passive, flat forms to active, dynamic architecture. Vorontsov Palace's central block was set in the background of a courtyard embraced by extended, low, functional blocks. In building the palace, Rastrelli turned for the last time to the country-estate palace type. Stroganov Palace became a masterpiece of the private palace genre. With facades erected along the street, the palace was a purely urban house-block, not connected to a park, but locked around the inner courtyard. Rastrelli designed an intensely plastic facade, creating an inimitable accent for Nevsky Prospekt, St. Petersburg's main street. He thus endowed the palace with a city-planning significance, as he did with all of his St. Petersburg buildings.

Rastrelli designed many country palaces and residences around St. Petersburg. His park and palace ensembles in Tsarskoe Selo and at Peterhof were marked by a unique individuality. Great Peterhof Palace, reconstructed by Rastrelli from 1749 to 1754, was austere in appearance. It was not a comprehensive expression of the architect's talent or of his vision of a grand palace complex, as he had to preserve the basics of the palace's original early-17th-century design. He enlarged the central tripartite block and the two side blocks. Rastrelli had more freedom to reveal his architectural imagination in reconstructing the side blocks. However, his approach was most radical in the palace interiors, which he created anew. Also a talented painter, Rastrelli designed the interior decorations himself. The palace's formal and private interiors and the church emanate a festive spirit. A seemingly infinite enfilade of grand halls opening from the main staircase comprehensively revealed the architect's interior-planning techniques.

From 1752 to 1756, Rastrelli reconstructed another imperial residence, the Great Palace in Tsarskoe Selo. As at Peterhof, his task was to enlarge the building. The architect fundamentally altered both the layout and facade decoration of the palace. Using a design drawn up by previous architects, Rastrelli created a grand, formal imperial-residence ensemble. At its center he built an enormously extended palace, dominating the courtyard galleries and park. Rastrelli created the splendid Baroque facade by skillfully dividing its segments and distributing architectural accents, which accumulated toward the center. He intricately interfused junctions of columns, pilasters and other decorative elements to enrich the palace's appearance. Creating the palace's festive interiors, Rastrelli revealed his brilliance as a decorator.

The Smolny Monastery (1749-62), the only large-scale Baroque ensemble in St. Petersburg, fully revealed Rastrelli's architectural talent. Although Rastrelli's plan was not carried out completely, the monastery ensemble was unique because its appearance most comprehensively expressed his architectural vision. A cathedral served as a center for the symmetrical composition. In 1749 Rastrelli altered his original project and proceeded to build Smolny Cathedral with a Greek-cross plan and a five-dome superstructure, which Rastrelli reintroduced into Russian architecture after a 50-year period of neglect. Rastrelli combined this feature, characteristic of Russian late-17th-century architecture, with Baroque stylistic elements. Four bell towers with domes were raised closely to the central tower. The pyramidal design's upper structures were marked by a particular lightness, providing the cathedral with a notable verticality. The cruciform cloister composition accentuated the appearance of the centrally positioned cathedral. Five small churches crowned with domes were erected at the corners of the cloister blocks; they corresponded to the five-domed cathedral. Rastrelli built the monastery complex according to the traditional Russian monastery scheme. However, he created an original and unique interpretation of the five-domed Baroque monastery-palace.

Rastrelli most powerfully revealed his architectural brilliance in his most significant work, the Winter Palace (1754-64), whose design and construction concluded his 40-year career. With the Winter Palace, Rastrelli masterfully created a new focal point for the city. Located at the city's center, the palace reigns over St. Petersburg's architecture, and seems to be a magnet attracting the surrounding spaces. Adorned with decorative sculpture, the monumental palace is dimensionally intricate and sophisticated in rhythm. The enormous scale of the Winter Palace required the use of architectural detail larger than that which Rastrelli had previously employed. His inventive treatments of the four facades allow them to be read from many different perspectives. The building was located on the bank of the Neva River, St. Petersburg's "main street." The Winter Palace set the tone for all subsequent building in the center of St. Petersburg.

Rastrelli had to discontinue his architectural activity after Empress Elizabeth's death in 1761, at about the time that the classical style took hold in Russian architecture. For several years, Rastrelli worked in Kurland, at the court of Count Biron, who had been the omnipotent favorite of Empress Anna, and for whom Rastrelli had built palaces in Mitava and Ruental.

Rastrelli died in 1771, but the exact date and place of his interment are unknown.

—MARIA L. MAKOGONOVA
Translated from the Russian by Konstantine Klioutchkine

RAYMOND, Antonin.

American. Born Antonin Rajman in Kladno, Bohemia (now Czech Republic), 10 May 1888; immigrated to the United States, 1910; naturalized, 1914. Died in Langhorne, Pennsylvania, 21 November 1976. Married Noémi Pernissin, 1914. Studied at University of Prague, 1906-10. Served in the United States Army Intelligence Corps, in France and Switzerland, 1917-19. Worked in the office of Cass Gilbert, New York, 1910-12; worked in the office of Frank Lloyd Wright, Chicago, Illinois, and Taliesen, Wisconsin, 1912-17; worked for Wright in Tokyo, assisting on Wright's Imperial Hotel, 1919-20; established American Architect-Engineers, Tokyo, 1920-23; in private practice, Tokyo, 1923-37; returned to the United States via India, 1937: opened an office in New York, 1938, and a design studio in New Hope, Pennsylvania, 1939; in partnership with L.L. Rado, from 1946; returned to Japan and reestablished practice there, 1947. American Institute of Architects Medal of Honor, 1956.

Chronology of Works
All in Japan unless noted

1917	de Vieux Colombier Theater, New York City, U.S.A.
1920	Hoshi School, Tokyo
1921	Women's Christian College
1923	Raymond House, Reinanzaka, Tokyo
1923-33	St. Luke's International Hospital, Tokyo
1934	St. Paul's Church, Karuizawa, Nagano
1934	Kawasaki House, Tokyo
1937-41	Golcond Dormitory, Pondicherry, India
1941	Camp Upton, Long Island, New York, U.S.A. (facilities for three Coast Artillery Regiments)
1945	Long Island Railroad Station, Great River, New York, U.S.A.
1948	Midtown Art Galleries, New York City, U.S.A.
1950-52	Reader's Digest Office, Tokyo
1951	Antonin Raymond House, Tokyo
1952	First National City Bank, Nagoya
1958-61	Gunma Music Center, Takasaki
1959-60	Iran Embassy, Azabu, Tokyo
1960-66	Nanzan University Campus, Nagoya
1961-64	Matsuzakaya Department Store, Ginza, Tokyo
1965	San Carlos University, Cebu, Philippines
1965-66	Shibata Catholic Church, Niigata
1966	International School, Nagoya
1966	Anglican Episcopal Church, Tokyo
1966-69	Pan Pacific Forum, University of Hawaii, Honolulu, U.S.A.

Publications

BOOKS BY RAYMOND

Collection of Antonin Raymond's Work. Tokyo, 1931.
Raymond's House. Tokyo, 1931.
Antonin Raymond: His Work in Japan 1920-1935. Edited by K. Nakamura. Tokyo, 1935.
Architectural Details. With Noémi Raymond. Tokyo, 1938.

Antonin Raymond: An Autobiography. Rutland, Vermont, and Tokyo, 1973.

ARTICLES BY RAYMOND

"Concrete for New Designs." *Architectural Record* (January 1936).
"Working with USHA under the Lanham Act." *Pencil Points* (December 1941).
"Toward True Modernism." *Pencil Points* (August 1942).
"Housing: A Post-War Responsibility and Opportunity." *American Institute of Architects Journal* (December 1945).
"The Spirit of Japanese Architecture." *American Institute of Architects Journal* (December 1953).
"The Doctrine of Auguste Perret." *Architectural Record* (January 1954).
"Some Ideas Regarding an Organized Effort to Provide Public Housing in Japan." *Hisaakira Kano* (12 August 1955).

BOOKS ABOUT RAYMOND

REICHOW, HANS BERNHARD: *Organische Baukunst.* Berlin and Braunschweig, West Germany, 1949.

ARTICLES ABOUT RAYMOND

"Architect Comes Home from Japan." *Architectural Forum* (February 1939).
KILLICK, J. (ed.): "Antonin Raymond, Architect." *Architectural Association Journal* 78 (special issue, August 1962).
MARLIN, WILLIAM: "A Conversation with Ladislav Rado." *Architectural Record* (May 1978).
"A Portfolio of Recent Works by Antonin Raymond." *Architectural Forum* (November 1941).
"Urban School Design." *Progressive Architecture* (March 1967).
"U.S. Architecture Abroad." *Architectural Forum* (March 1953).
"U.S.A. Abroad." *Architectural Forum* (December 1957).

*

Certainly one of the most important foreign architects to practice in Japan was Antonin Raymond, who had a long career which included two phases in Japan. The first phase was before World War II, when Raymond was very influential in the beginning of the modern architectural movement in Japan. The second phase was after the war, when he contributed to the maturation of the Modern Movement.

Of the number of influences on Raymond, an important one stems from his central European derivation. While a student at the University of Prague, he became a follower of Otto Wagner. Wagner's work was almost devoid of ornament, used lucid and powerful compositions employing flexible plans, and expressed a sensitivity to the natural qualities of materials. The architecture thus expressed brought Raymond into contact with the Modern Movement.

Raymond's professional career was initiated in the New York office of Cass Gilbert, where he worked on the Woolworth Building. Although Raymond wrote little about that period of his career, it must have been an exciting experience for the young Czechoslovakian architect in 1910 to be employed in the design of one of the world's most impressive buildings. The broadening environment in which he found himself provided many opportunities, and in 1912 he traveled to Chicago, where he worked for Frank Lloyd Wright.

The philosophy exhibited in Chicago architecture and in Wright's Taliesin studio directly appealed to Raymond, and he eagerly accompanied Wright in 1919 to Japan to assist in the construction of the Imperial Hotel in Tokyo. Japan at that time was rapidly and avidly assimilating radical social changes which had their origins in the late 19th century and were based on European and American models. Cultural tradition, however, was so ingrained that very little modification of those values was popular. Examples of Western-style architecture revealed a mix of historical styles in which few Japanese architects found inspiration. Foreign architects who visited Japan were greatly impressed with the traditional Japanese cultural expression that they encountered. Among those architects were Bruno Taut, Frank Lloyd Wright and Antonin Raymond.

After Raymond had completed his work with Wright on the Imperial Hotel, he established an office in Tokyo. Thus began the strongest phase of his architectural career. Among those who worked in his office were two Japanese, Junzo Yoshimura and Kunio Maekawa, who became prominent architects in later decades. Yoshimura's work was a successful blending of Japanese and Western expression, and resulted in his receiving major commissions and awards. Much of his work was influenced by the basic lessons practiced under Raymond's leadership. The works of Maekawa were so aesthetically and technically advanced that he was considered the leading Japanese architect for years. After completing his formal education, Maekawa worked in Le Corbusier's studio before returning to Japan, where he worked for five years in Raymond's office before opening his own business. Maekawa never abandoned traditional Japanese design principles, but emphasized a reinforced-concrete architecture based on both Le Corbusier's and Raymond's buildings. During the 1920s and 1930s Raymond endeavored to involve a structural engineer in the initial design stages of his projects. As a result, several young Japanese engineers benefited from Raymond's approach to design.

Raymond's office was active for 18 years during the first phase of the architect's career in Japan. During that period the buildings that he produced became more polished and more subtle. The modified International Style that is typical of his work is perhaps exemplified in the Morinosuke Kawasaki House in Tokyo (1934). In this house many cultural considerations were met, including spiritual requirements for the orientation of the house. Modern elements are also apparent: the use of reinforced-concrete construction, steel casement windows, insulation, tile floors, a roof garden and antiseismic construction.

The political environment made it very difficult for foreign businessmen in Japan by 1937, so when the opportunity for Raymond to take a commission in India occurred, he closed his Tokyo office, spent a brief time in India and then returned to New York City to open a new practice. From 1938 to 1948 his office was continually occupied with federal, state and local government contracts for projects such as military camps, housing and airports.

In 1949 Raymond accepted a commission to design the Reader's Digest Building in Tokyo, which prompted the second phase of his career in Japan. Raymond found Japan in dire need of major construction and was immediately employed on important projects. In these buildings he softened the International Style and replaced it with a style which is not as dazzling but is a more relaxed and comfortable solution to architecture. Raymond died in 1976 after spending 43 years practicing architecture in Japan.

Raymond's contributions and influences may be seen in five areas: the Japanese architects and structural engineers who worked in his office and became instrumental in spearheading the Modern Movement in Japan; the architecture produced by his office, which illustrated that a successful blend between modern Western and traditional Japanese design was possible; his anti-seismic structures; his publications, which helped to educate many in the values of Japanese culture; and the many awards and honors that Raymond received.

—JAMES P. NOFFSINGER

REIDY, Affonso.

Brazilian. Eduardo Affonso Reidy Born in Paris, France, 27 October 1909. Died in Rio de Janeiro, Brazil, 10 August 1964. Married Carmen Portinho, 1934. Studied at the Escola Nacional de Belas Artes, Rio de Janeiro, Dip.Arch., 1930. Worked in the Municipal Service Department, Rio de Janeiro, from 1934; chief of the Division of Architecture, Municipal Works Department, Rio de Janeiro, 1934-47. Honorary fellow, American Institute of Architects, 1964.

Chronology of Works
All in Brazil unless noted

1936-43	Ministry of Education and Health (now Palace of Culture), Rio de Janeiro (with Lucío Costa, Oscar Niemeyer, Le Corbusier, Jorge Machado Moreira and others)
1947-52	Pedregulho Housing Project, Rio de Janeiro
1950-52	Gavea Housing Project, Rio de Janeiro
1951	Marechal Hermes Community Theater, Rio de Janeiro
1952	Carmen Portinho House, Rio de Janeiro
1954-60	Museum of Modern Art, Rio de Janeiro
1956	Master Plan for Flamingo Park, Rio de Janeiro (with Roberto Burle Marx)
1957	City Employees Insurance Fund Headquarters, Rio de Janeiro

Publications

BOOKS ABOUT REIDY

BRACCO, SERGIO: *L'architettura moderna in Brasile*. Bologna, 1967.

FRANCK, KLAUS: *The Works of Affonso Eduardo Reidy*. New York and London, 1960.

REICHOW, HANS BERNARD: *Organische Baukunst*. Berlin and Braunschweig, 1949.

SERGE, ROBERTO (ed.): *Latin America in its Architecture*. New York and London, 1981.

ARTICLES ABOUT REIDY

"Affonso Eduardo Reidy." *Baukunst und Werkform* (January 1962).

"Affonso Eduardo Reidy." *Zodiac* No. 6 (1960).

"Brazil: Museum of Modern Art in Rio de Janeiro." *Architecture d'aujourd'hui* (January/February 1954).

"Conjunto Residencial Pedregulho." *Informes de la construccion* (December 1956).

LOWETH, S.: "Some New Architecture in Brazil." *Architects' Journal* (31 January 1946).

NIEMEYER, OSCAR: "Affonso Eduardo Reidy." *Architecture d'aujourd'hui* (September/November 1964).

"Pedregulho: Ein Wohnquartier in Rio de Janeiro." *Werk* (August 1953).

Affonso Reidy: Pedregulho Housing Project, Rio de Janeiro, Brazil, 1947-52

"Rio de Janeiro Museum of Modern Art." *Architectural Review* (May 1954).
"Versicherungsgebäude in Rio de Janeiro." *Bauen und Wohnen* (March 1960).

*

Along with Lúcio Costa and Oscar Niemeyer, Affonso Reidy was one of the leaders and most creative practitioners of the heroic age of Brazilian modernism inaugurated in about 1930. A staunch advocate of Costa's curricular reforms of Rio de Janeiro's Escola Nacional de Belas Artes, he developed an architecture that remained even more faithful to the rationalist principles of Le Corbusier than did the work of his more celebrated Brazilian contemporaries. Reidy's early interest in urban planning and the social aspects of architecture had been stimulated in 1929 by his brief assistantship with the French urbanist Alfred Agache, who introduced the new discipline of urbanism to Brazil and drew up an ambitious master plan for Rio beginning in 1927. Reidy's work reflects a concern for creating a "social architecture" on an urban scale, an architecture that would be responsive to the needs of Rio's inhabitants, both rich and poor. His professional involvement with the city's municipal urbanism and public housing departments provided a stimulating official context for the further development of this career interest. His mature style, reflected best in his public housing complexes at Pedregulho and Gávea (1947-52) and his Brazilian Museum of Modern Art (1954-60), all in Rio, illustrate his successful synthesis of the functional rationalism of Le

Corbusier, the pleasing and clear aesthetic unities of Costa, and the expressive structural plasticity of Niemeyer.

The evolution of Reidy's architecture reflects the immense influence of Le Corbusier, and particularly the European master's six-week stay in Rio de Janeiro in 1936. During that time, Le Corbusier served as consulting adviser on the design of the new Ministry of Education and Health Building (1936-43) and drew up a project for a city university for Rio. It was in the collaborative design context of the Ministry project that Reidy, perhaps more than his colleagues, fell under the Corbusian spell. Although he would subsequently adhere closely to Le Corbusier's principles, Reidy went beyond them to develop a highly personal idiom with a characteristically Brazilian touch, one derived in large measure from his attentiveness to the new vocabulary developed by Costa and Niemeyer.

Reidy's first major project, the Pedregulho residential complex begun in 1950, forcefully launched his career and brought him quickly to international attention. The complex, Reidy's expanded answer to Le Corbusier's Unité d'Habitation program, was for Brazil both a social and architectural manifesto of modernism in reinforced concrete. The project reflected Reidy's interest in achieving social reform through a functionally and aesthetically unified urbanistic ensemble embodying the idea of a complete community that would be sensitive to the essential needs of its inhabitants. Intended for lower-income civil servants employed by the city, the project was rooted in a new and wide-ranging social statistical analysis of the future community, an analysis of the type Alfred Agache had called for as a necessary preliminary in his master plan for Rio.

Reidy's ensemble focused spatially and socially on the community school, the aesthetic masterpiece of the complex as well as the symbol of progress for a largely illiterate Brazilian society. Around it he planned a residential mono-block, serpentine in a plan, a commercial center, and sports and health facilities. Laying out the whole with great sensitivity to the densely forested hillside site, Reidy followed Le Corbusier in using pilotis to raise the structures up off the rugged terrain, thereby significantly cutting the ground preparation costs. Reidy's careful site planning also preserved for the residents a magnificent view of Guanabara Bay below. While the planning of the project is noteworthy for its functional complexity and spatial continuity, the forms themselves are volumetrically simple, clear, and even classic in their Corbusian idealism. For Pedregulho, Reidy appropriately proposed a simplified architectural language for a popular program.

The Corbusian forms and ideas with which Reidy experimented in Pedregulho were the point of departure for the Unidade Residencial de Gávea (1952), an aesthetically more harmonious adaptation of the same theme on a different site. Although the principal facade of its serpentine block illustrates a greater union of aesthetic and functional considerations than its precursor, the project as it was executed did not rise to Reidy's specifications. Poor craftsmanship and the application of a uniformly uninspiring coat of beige paint greatly compromised an otherwise impressive document of artistic progress. Moreover, Reidy's design efforts were thwarted by a lack of official government support for the implementation of a "social architecture." Sadly, he did not live to see the completion of any of his major projects.

Reidy's swan song and his most powerfully plastic work was Rio's waterfront Museum of Modern Art (1954-60). There he achieved a classically composed composition with the sculptural and structural dynamism of Niemeyer, using a skeletal system of repeating, scissor-shaped transverse supports of brute concrete from which the floor of the upper level is effectively suspended.
—DAVID K. UNDERWOOD

RENNIE, John.

Scottish. Born in Phantassie, East Lothian, Scotland, 7 June 1761. Died in London, England, 10 April 1821. His youngest son, John, continued the elder Rennie's practice. Studied at Edinburgh University, 1780-83. Began his career as a bridge/canal builder, 1783; traveled to England and was offered a position with the Scottish inventor James Watt at Staffordshire, 1784; set up business at Blackfriars, 1784. Fellow, Royal Society, 1798; refused knighthood, 1817.

Chronology of Works
All in England unless noted
† Work no longer exists

1784	Bridge, Water of Leith near Stevenhouse Mill, Midlothian, Scotland
1795	Bulk Aqueduct, Lancashire†
1795-97	Dundas Aqueduct, Bath (Limpley Stoke)
1796	Conder Aqueducet, Lancashire
1796	Yarrow Aqueduct, Lancashire
1797	Avoncliff Aqueduct, near Bath
1797	Lune Aqueduct, Lancaster
1798-1800	Wolseley Bridge, near Colwich, Staffordshire
1800	Whiteadder Bridge, Berwickshire†
1800-03	Kelso Bridge, Roxburgh County, Scotland
1803	Musselburgh Bridge, Midlothian, Scotland
1805	Darlaston Bridge, Staffordshire†
1806	East India Docks, London (main entrance)†
1810	Fosdyke Bridge, Lincolnshire†
1812-13	Newton Stewart Bridge, Wigtownshire
1814	Bridge over river Goomtee, Lucknow, India
1814	Newton Stewart Bridge, London†
1815	Stratford on Avon Railway Viaduct, Stratford on Avon (Bancroft Gardens)
1815-16	Chepstow Bridge, Monmouthshire
1815-19	Southwark Bridge, London†
1817	Waterloo Bridge, London†
1817-19	Wellington Bridge, Leeds, Yorkshire
1818	Bridge, Naples, Italy
1818	Stoneleigh Bridge, Warwickshire
1819-21	Bridge of Earn, Perth County, Scotland
1821	Custom House, Entrance Arch and Lighthouse, Holyhead, Anglesey, North Wales
1821	New Galloway Bridge, Kirkcudbrightshire, Scotland
1825-31	London Bridge, London (constructed by his son John; completed, 1831; transferred to United States and rebuilt, 1963)

Publications

BOOKS BY RENNIE

The Autobiography of Sir John Rennie. 1875.

BOOKS ABOUT RENNIE

BOUCHER, C. G. T.: *John Rennie.* Manchester, 1963.
REYBURN, WALLACE: *Bridge Across the Atlantic: The Story of John Rennie.* London, 1972.
RICHARDSON, A. E. and GILL, C. L.: *Regency Architecture of the West of England.* 1924).
RUDDOCK, TED: *Arch Bridges and Their Builders, 1735-1835.* Cambridge, England, 1979.

*

John Rennie was one of several distinguished engineers bred in late-18th-century Scotland. His natural bent for mechanics developed early, and he became a successful millwright, having spent much time in the workshops of Andrew Meikle (1719-1811), millwright and inventor of the drum threshing-machine of 1784. Rennie's savings were sufficiently substantial to ensure that he could study at the University of Edinburgh from 1780 to 1783, and, on arriving, he set up as a general engineer and millwright on his own account, when he introduced cast-iron pinions instead of wooden trundles in some of his machinery. In 1784 he traveled to England to improve his understanding of engineering, and visited James Watt (1736-1819) at Soho in Staffordshire. Watt offered Rennie a post, and after a short spell in Soho, Rennie went to London to supervise the construction of the new machinery for the Albion Flour Mills at Southwark, which Boulton & Watt were making and assembling, including the steam-powered plant. Rennie was responsible for the design of much of this machinery, a feature of which was the use of cast iron for most of the shafting and framing, and the advanced mechanisms he evolved helped to establish his reputation as an engineer.

He then set up his own business as an engineer at Blackfriars, and devoted his attention to the construction of canals. His first undertaking in England was in connection with the building of the Kennet and Avon Canal (for which he built the beautiful, simple and elegant Dundas Aqueduct at Limpley Stoke, which carries the canal of the River Avon [1795-97]), followed by the Rochdale Canal, which passes through very difficult terrain between Rochdale and Todmorden. He was also responsible for the building of the Lancaster Canal, including the Lune Aqueduct, which carries the canal over the River Lune (1794-97), and in 1802 he redesigned the Royal Canal from Dublin to Shannon in Longford, Ireland. He also became engaged in extensive operations to drain the Lincolnshire Fens and to improve the channels of the River Witham.

His works for docks and harbors included the London Docks, the East and West India Docks (including the bridge over the River Lea at East India Dock Road [1809]), Holyhead Harbour, the spectacular Ramsgate Harbour, the dockyards of Sheerness and Chatham, the great breakwater across Plymouth Sound (1811), and the beautiful harbor at Donaghadee in County Down (1821) which was completed by his son in 1834. His experiences in such works led him to evolve improvements in the design of the diving bell, and he also invented the steam-powered dredging machine. He was meticulous in examining local conditions, and his reports and estimates were models of exactitude and professionalism.

He began building bridges early in his career, and it is probably in this role that he is best remembered. One of his first works was the bridge over the Water of Leith near Stevenhouse Mill, Midlothian, of 1784. After the Wolseley Bridge near Colwich in Staffordshire (1798-1800), Rennie constructed his first great masterpiece of bridge building: this was the elegant structure over the River Tweed at Kelso (1800-03), which has half-elliptical arches carried on piers graced with tough Doric columns. It is a robust and handsome piece of work, with assured masonry.

After Whiteadder Bridge, Berwickshire, of 1800; Musselburgh Bridge, Midlothian, of 1803 (which included improvements in the design of the longitudinal section, which was flatter than most bridges previously built); Boston Bridge, Lincolnshire of 1804-07; and other bridges at Virginia Water in Surrey and Darlaston in Staffordshire (both 1805), he began work on the East India Docks, one of a series of schemes for docks and harbors throughout the country.

Following the Fosdyke Bridge in Lincolnshire (1810), he designed the new bridge over the Thames at Somerset House (later called Waterloo Bridge), employing the use of foundations in coffer dams: the bridge was opened in 1817. Then followed the bridge at Newton Stewart in Wigtownshire of 1812-13, a large bridge at Lucknow in India in 1814, and the New Bridge, Grecian Drive, Steleigh Abbey, Warwickshire (1814-15). In 1813 he had designed Southwark Bridge, and this was completed in 1819: it had three cast-iron arches set on stone piers. There were other bridges at Leeds (Wellington Bridge), Naples, Bridge of Earn in Perthshire, Cramond Bridge in Midlothian, New Galloway, and Chepstow in Monmouthshire (a very handsome structure indeed).

In 1821 he submitted designs for a new London Bridge, which was completed under the direction of his son, Sir John Rennie (1794-1874): this was a structure of great nobility and apparently easy simplicity, but it was in fact extremely subtle.

London Bridge was Rennie's last substantial work, and indeed he has been very unfortunate in that many of his best designs have been destroyed. Waterloo Bridge was demolished in 1938, Southwark Bridge in 1920, and London Bridge in 1967 (although the latter was rebuilt in the United States, in Arizona.

Rennie was one of Britain's greatest engineers. He was elected F.R.S. in 1798, and after his death in his house in Stamford Street, London, in 1821, he was buried in St. Paul's Cathedral.

—JAMES STEVENS CURL

RENWICK, James.

American. Born in Bloomingdale, New York, 11 November 1818. Died on 23 June 1895. Attended Columbia College, New York, M.A., 1839. Self-taught in architecture. Engineer, Erie Railroad, 1836; superintendent, Distributing Reservoir of the Croton Aqueduct, New York; worked independently, New York City, from 1843.

Chronology of Works
All in the United States
* Approximate dates
† Work no longer exists

1843	Bowling Green Fountain, New York City†
1843-46	Grace Church, New York City
1846-47	Calvary Church, New York City
1846-47	Church of the Puritans, New York City†
1847	Grace Church Rectory, New York City
1847-49	Free Academy, New York City†
1847-55	Smithsonian Institution, Washington, D.C.
1848-49	South Dutch Church, New York City†
1849-51	James Renwick, Sr., House, New York City†
1849*-51	Second Presbyterian Church, Chicago, Illinois†
1850-51	Clarendon Hotel, New York City†
1850-51	Trinity Church, Washington, D.C.†
1851	Martinstow (Ames House), West Haven, Connecticut
1851*-52	St. Denis Hotel, New York City
1852	LaFarge House, New York City†
1852-54	Longstreet Castle, Syracuse, New York
1853-54	Cruger Mansion, New York City†
1853-54	St. Stephen's Church, New York City
1853-56*	Smallpox Hospital, New York City
1854-55	Clinton Avenue Congregational Church, Brooklyn, New York†
1855	Rowhouses, 37-41 West 9 Street, New York City†
1855-56	Bank of the State of New York, New York City†
1858-61	Island Hospital, New York City
1858-79	St. Patrick's Cathedral, New York City
1859-62	Albermarle Hotel, New York City†
1859-71	Corcoran Gallery, Washington, D.C.
1861-65	Vassar College, Poughkeepsie, New York
1863-64*	Greyston (Dodge House), Riverdale, New York
1863-65	Church of the Covenant, New York City
1865	Winyah Park (Lathers House), New Rochelle, New York†
1867-69	Foundling Hospital, New York City†
1867-69	St. Ann's Church, Brooklyn, New York†
1868*-69	Young Men's Christian Association Building, New York City†
1869	Northwestern Dispensary, New York City†
1869-70	Daniel Willis James House, New York City†
1869-71	New York City Hospital for the Insane, New York City†
1870-71	Appleton Building, New York City†
1871-72	St. Bartholomew's Church, New York City†
1871-74	Second Presbyterian Church, Chicago, Illinois
1877*-78	Gallatin House, East Hampton, New York†
1880-82	Archbishop's House (Catholic), New York City
1880-82	Stock Exchange, New York City† (enlargement)

1881-82	Gallatin House, New York City
1882-83	St. Patrick's Cathedral (rectory), New York City
1882-83	All Saints' Church, New York City
1885-88	St. Patrick's Cathedral, New York City (spires)
1886-87	Protestant Episcopal Diocesan House, New York City†
1887-88	Cathedral, St. Augustine, Florida (enlargement)
1887-88	Warehouse, 808 Broadway, New York City

Publications

BOOKS ABOUT RENWICK

PIERSON, WILLIAM H., JR.: "James Renwick, St. Patrick's Cathedral, and the Continental Gothic Revival." In *American Buildings and Their Architects: Technology and the Picturesque: The Corporate and Early Gothic Styles*. Garden City, New York, 1978.

STEWART, WILLIAM R.: *Grace Church and Old New York*. New York, 1924.

ARTICLES ABOUT RENWICK

CANTOR, JAY E.: "The Public Architecture of James Renwick, Jr." Master's thesis. University of Delaware, Newark, Delaware, 1971.

HUMPHREY, EFFINGHAM: "The Churches of James Renwick, Jr." Master's thesis. New York University, New York, 1942.

McKENNA, ROSALIE THORNE: "James Renwick, Jr., and the Second Empire Style in the United States." *Magazine of Art* 44 (March 1951): 97-101.

McKENNA, ROSALIE THORNE: "A Study of the Architecture of the Main Building and the Landscape of Vassar College, 1860-1970." Master's thesis. Vassar College, Poughkeepsie, New York, 1949.

RATTNER, SELMA: "Renwick's Church for Blacks." *Historic Preservation* 24 (1972): 32-35.

RATTNER, SELMA: "Renwick's Design for Grace Church: Religious Doctrine and the Gothic Revival." Master's thesis. Columbia University, New York, 1969.

James Renwick: Smithsonian Institution, Washington, DC, 1847-55

James Renwick was a self-taught architect whose achievements in architectural theory and engineering remain unique in the development of the Gothic Revival in the United States. Throughout his career, he remained a "purist" in concept, design and building integrity, as well as an innovator in combining traditional motifs with new structural devices and mechanical and technological systems. He always remained true to the Gothic Revival manner, never deviating into an eclectic mode or using shorthand methods to achieve his goals.

The son of a successful merchant and engineer, Renwick was surrounded by influential social aristocracy. It was from his father, the elder James Renwick, that he developed an interest in engineering, art and architecture. Upon graduation from Columbia College in 1836, he obtained an appointment as an engineer for the Erie Railroad, and from 1837 to 1842 was an assistant engineer for the Croton Aqueduct Commission in New York City.

In 1843 he won the commission for the design of Grace Church in New York City. Its design, like that of Richard Upjohn's Trinity Church (1841-46), followed medieval Gothic lines. In fact, it was inspired by Gothic French and English sources, emulating the so-called French Flamboyant and English Decorated styles. Grace Church showed undulating tracery patterns and exhibited the first use in American Gothic Revival architecture of the cruciform plan. The church had a wooden spire (Renwick wanted stone), plaster vaulting and lavish white marble.

There followed in the early 1840s and 1850s (except for the French-derived Romanesque Church of the Puritans in New York City, 1946-47) Gothic churches such as Calvary Church, New York City (1846-47); South Dutch Church, New York City (1848-49); Second Presbyterian Church, Washington, D.C. (1850-51); and his competitive designs, in 1846, for the new Smithsonian Institution in Washington, D.C. (1847-55).

By 1848 Renwick began using the Romanesque—based on the Norman, Lombard or Byzantine, and more commonly known as the "round" style—for his commercial structures, churches, residences and civic monuments. Examples of his Romanesque style were St. Stephen's, New York City (1853-54), and Clinton Avenue Congregational Church, Brooklyn Heights, New York (1854-55). These churches, as well as his parents' home (1849-51), located on lower Fifth Avenue in New York City, displayed an eclectic Romanesque style with their textile-red bricks, heavy cornices, corbels, moldings and pronounced stone tracery.

In the 1850s Renwick designed elegant hotels in New York City. These included the Clarendon (1850-51), with it multicolored brick and terra-cotta facade; the St. Denis Hotel (ca. 1851-52), built for his mother; and the La Farge House (1852; burned in 1854 and rebuilt in 1854-56), with its cast-iron grille and distinctive white Italian marble palazzo.

There followed Renwick's designs in the Second Empire manner. Typical was the Cruger Mansion (1853-54) in the Palladian style, and the famous Corcoran Art Gallery (1859-71), also called the Renwick Gallery, in Washington, D.C.

Renwick's change from the medieval Gothic/Romanesque to the au courant modern French mode was visible in his municipal hospitals located on Blackwell's Island, New York: the Smallpox Hospital (1853-ca. 1856) and the Second Empire Island Hospital (1856-61).

His academic architecture included Vassar College in Poughkeepsie, New York (1861-65). The building resembled the Tuileries palace, which he had seen on a recent trip to Paris.

Renwick's commissions had grown by then to such an extent that he took on two partners, Richard Tylden Auchmuty in 1858 and Joseph Sands in 1860. Also at that time, he began to incorporate fire-retardant materials such as cast iron into his buildings. For example, the Bank of the State of New York in New York City (1855-56) had a complete floor frame of iron as well as iron beams, troughs and girders.

Renwick's most noted design was St. Patrick's Cathedral in New York City (1858-79; spires added in 1885-88). There, he used the exterior twin towers of the cathedrals of Amiens, Reims and Cologne as models, and the cathedrals of Exeter, Westminster and Yorkminster for interior designs. Although the church was regarded as his greatest achievement aesthetically, Renwick was to be disappointed by the lack of funds to complete what he deemed to be the consummate Decorated Gothic Revival building.

There followed St. Bartholomew's in New York City (1871-72). Criticized by many as "Byzantine" and "Lombardo-Gothic," this structure, sometimes called "the Vanderbilt Church" because of a $400,000 gift from that family, was the most noted design shown by Renwick's firm at the Centennial Exhibition in Philadelphia of 1876.

Renwick used a High Victorian English style, in the manner of William Butterfield and George E. Street, at St. Ann's Protestant Episcopal Church in Brooklyn Heights, New York (1867-69), and at the highly acclaimed All Saints' Roman Catholic Church in Harlem, New York (1882-93).

The High Victorian style was epitomized by the million-dollar Booth's Theater in New York City (1867-69). Its sheet-iron roof, mechanical theatric contrivances and elegant interior made it one of the most elaborate and ornamental architectural attractions of post-Civil War America. Also, along those lines, the Young Men's Christian Association (YMCA) Building, New York City (1868-69), further displayed High Victorian motifs of brown stone with yellow stone details. And two more municipal hospitals—the Foundling Hospital on Randall's Island (1867-69) and the New York City Hospital for the Insane on Ward's Island (1869-71)—again revealed the High Victorian mode.

In the 1870s Renwick began a new style for commercial buildings through the introduction of cast iron into facades. In New York City, the Appleton Building (1870-71) and the designs for the front of the New York Stock Exchange (1880-82) displayed this material that allowed for more light via larger allotments for window space.

Renwick was also a designer of country homes. The modest frame cottage (ca. 1877-78) for his friends Amy and Frederic Gallatin, located in fashionable East Hampton, Long Island, New York, showed a refinement of taste and historical styles.

After the death of his partner Joseph Sands in 1880, Renwick introduced to the firm the talents of James Lawrence Aspinwall. And in 1890 Renwick's lengthy career culminated in the design for the National Gallery of History and Art in Washington, D.C. This building, with its reinforced-concrete construction, was to resemble the Parthenon externally and the Taj Mahal in its decorative splendor. Though the structure was never built, the theme became the model for the World's Columbian Exposition of 1893 in Chicago.

—GEORGE M. COHEN

REPTON, Humphry.

British. Born in Bury St. Edmonds, Suffolk, England, 21 April 1752. Died in Essex, 3 March 1818. Married Mary Clarke, 1773; two sons were architects: John Adey Repton (1775-1860) and George Stanley Repton (1786-1858). Early schooling was in Bury and Norwich; went to the Netherlands to learn Dutch,

1764: spent five months in Amsterdam and two years in school in Rotterdam; returned to England, and studied botany and gardening; was self-taught as an architect. Began career as a general merchant, ca. 1773, but failed; met William Windham of Felbrigg through botanical studies; worked as secretary to Windham in Dublin, and began his specialization in botany and landscape gardening, 1783; returned to Essex to work as landscape gardener, 1789; worked in partnership with John Nash (1752-1835), 1795-99; assisted in the architectural business of his own sons, from 1800.

Chronology of Works
All in England
* Approximate dates
† Work no longer exists

1788	Catton, Norfolk
1789	Brandesbury, Middlesex†
1789-1802	Welbeck Abbey, Nottinghamshire (and remodeling)
1790	Cobham, Kent
1790	Bulstrode, Buckinghamshire
1790	Wentworth, Woodhouse, Yorkshire
1791	Sheffield Park, Sussex
1791	Thoresby, Nottinghamshire†
1795	Burley-on-the-Hill, Leicestershire
1795	Warley Hall, Worcestershire (and Doric temple)
1796-1800	Corsham, Wiltshire
1797	Southgate Grove, London
1798	Attingham, Shropshire
1799	Luscombe, Devonshire
1799	Panshanger, Hertfordshire
1800	West Wycombe Park, Buckinghamshire
1802	Brentry House, Avon (also designed house)
1803	Longleat, Wiltshire
1803-07	Stanage, Norfolk (and alterations to house)
1805-13	Uppark, Sussex (and alterations to house)
1810	Endsleigh, Devonshire
1810*	Apsley Wood Lodge, Bedfordshire (small house and garden)
1812-19	Sheringham Bower, Norfolk (also designed house)
1814*	Ashridge, Hertfordshire

Publications

BOOKS BY REPTON

Sketches and Hints on Landscape Gardening. London, 1795.
Observations on the Theory and Practice of Landscape Gardening. London, 1803.
Fragments on the Theory and Practice of Landscape Gardening, Including Some Remarks on Grecian and Gothic Architecture. London, 1816.

BOOKS ABOUT REPTON

HUSSEY, CHRISTOPHER: *The Picturesque.* London, 1924.
HYAMS, EDWARD: *Capability Brown and Humphry Repton.* 1971.
KNIGHT, RICHARD PAYNE: *The Landscape.* London, 1794.
LOUDON, J. C. (ed.): *The Landscape Gardening and Landscape Architecture of the Late Humphry Repton, Esq.* London, 1840.
MALLINS, EDWARD: *English Landscaping and Literature.* London, 1966.
PRICE, UVEDALE: *Essay on the Picturesque.* London, 1794.
STROUD, DOROTHY: *Humphry Repton.* London, 1962.

ARTICLES ABOUT REPTON

HUSSEY, CHRISTOPHER: "Humphry Repton 1752-1818." *Country Life Annual* (1952).
KETTON-CREMER, ROBERT WYNDHAM: "Humphry Repton in Norfolk." In *A Norfolk Gallery.* London, 1948.
PEVSNER, NIKOLAUS: "Humphry Repton: A Horilegium." *Architectural Review* 103 (1948).
STEEGMAN, J.: "Bayham Abbey, Designs for a House and View by Humphry Repton." *Architectural Review* 53 (1936).
STEEGMAN, J.: "Humphry Repton at Blaize Castle." *Architectural Review* 83 (1938).

*

Humphry Repton received his education in schools in Bury and Norwich, to which latter city the family moved in 1762. He went to the Netherlands to learn Dutch in 1764 (a necessary accomplishment for a budding merchant in East Anglia at that time), spent some five months in the household of Zachary Hope in Amsterdam, and some two years at school in Rotterdam. At 16 he returned to Norwich, learned the trade in calicoes and satins, and set up as a general merchant in that city. His business failed, however, and he retreated to the country, where he studied botany and gardening.

In the neighboring parish lived William Windham of Felbrigg (1750-1810), whose library contained a great many books on botanical subjects which Repton studied. In 1783 Windham was appointed chief secretary to the lord lieutenant of Ireland, and Repton accompanied him to Dublin, an experience which seems to have consolidated his determination to specialize in botany and landscape gardening. On his return from Ireland, Repton moved to Hare Street near Romford in Essex, to a house which he altered and improved: he retained the house as his residence for the rest of his life.

Repton lost money on various schemes, including one for the improvement of the conveyance of mail, after which, at the age of almost 40, he was obliged to earn his living, and decided to practice as a landscape gardener. At first, in his *Sketches and Hints on Landscape Gardening* (1795), he supported the ideas of Lancelot "Capability" Brown (1716-83) against the strictures of Richard Payne Knight (1750-1824) and Uvedale Price (1747-1829), the writers on the picturesque, who advocated natural and picturesque beauty and stated that the fashionable mode of Brown was at "variance with all the principles of landscape-painting, and with the practice of all the most eminent masters." In due course, however, Repton abandoned the formalism of Brown and William Kent, adopting a more varied and natural style, which was described as combining "artistical knowledge ... with good taste and good sense." Lancelot Brown died in 1783, having cornered the market in landscape design for many years, and Repton determined to step into the void with schemes that were more naturalistic and more truly in the style of the painters of landscapes than Browns's allusions to Arcady had achieved.

Repton's first significant work in landscape design was realized at Cobham in Kent around 1790, and led to further commissions. It was his remodeling of the east and west fronts of Welbeck Abbey in Nottinghamshire and the laying out of the grounds there in 1790 that made his name, and ensured introductions to eminent persons, including Edmund Burke, William Pitt and William Wilberforce. Since 1781, too, he had been contributing to histories and to other collections, and his output of publications was prolific.

Repton had a facility as a draftsman, and he was able to sell his ideas to clients by means of cleverly composed perspective views with hinged overlays showing the "before" and "after" comparisons. He realized the value of attractive presentation in the marketing of his proposals, and indeed he produced his beautifully drawn and colored schemes in bound form with red morocco covers, the so-called "Red Books," many of which survive. His lavish productions were a form of trademark, and his fame spread quickly: he was mentioned in Jane Austen's *Mansfield Park,* and he received over 200 commissions for works to parks and gardens, to all of which he gave the same meticulous attention.

Repton was self-taught as an architect, and saw architecture as inseparable from landscape gardening. He worked for a brief period with John Nash (1752-1835), who appears to have designed the Home Farm at Burley-on-the-Hill in Rutland in the rustic cottage style when Repton carried out his substantial works on the landscape at that great house. Repton later collaborated with his eldest son, John Adey Repton (1775-1860). However, he was alone responsible for the remodeling of the facades at Welbeck referred to above, and he carried out sundry other architectural works. He designed a number of "neat rustic cottages," including a pair of thatched cottages as entrance lodges to a park, and he was a pioneer of the picturesque cottage style which was such a fashionable feature of many demesnes in the first years of the 19th century.

Repton saw his style as essentially eclectic, containing the best of Brown's ideas and even the earlier works of French masters. He set out his theories in his *Observations on the Theory and Practice of Landscape Gardening* (1803). In this book he demonstrated how the character of buildings could be completely changed by applied ornament: classical styles suggested formality, while Gothic was informal, a factor that could be emphasized by asymmetrical composition. Repton invented a type of Anglo-Indian architectural style in his designs for Brighton Pavilion, and his ideas about the progressive nature of style heralded a wide-ranging 19th-century eclecticism that sometimes became indiscriminate.

Repton's observations on landscape gardening and on architecture were reprinted by John Claudius Loudon (1783-1843) with a memoir by Loudon himself, titled *The Landscape Gardening and Landscape Architecture of the late Humphry Repton,* in 1840. Repton also produced many drawings of country houses set in landscapes "improved" by himself, and these were published in *Peacock's Polite Repository.* He had a very profound influence on the architectural climate of the 1820s, 1830s and 1840s.

From 1811, following a spinal injury, Repton was prevented from carrying out major works of landscape, although he managed to produce his *Fragments on the Theory and Practice of Landscape Gardening, Including Some Remarks on Grecian and Gothic Architecture* in 1816, assisted by his son John. He died at home in Hare Street in 1818, and was buried in Aylsham churchyard in Norfolk.

—JAMES STEVENS CURL

RICCHINO, Francesco.

Italian. Born Francesco Maria Ricchino in Milan, Italy, 1584. Died in Milan, 24 April 1658. Studied with his father, Bernardo Ricchino, a military engineer; studied with the architect Lorenzo Binago, Milan; studied in Rome, 1600-03, at the invitation of Cardinal Federico Borromeo. Became an architect of the Milan

Cathedral under Aurelio Trezzi, 1605; became *capomaestro* of the Milan Cathedral, 1631.

Chronology of Works
All in Milan, Italy

1607	San Giovanni Battista
1607-30	San Giuseppe
1627	Collegio Elvetico (completion of facade)
1631	Palazzo Annoni
1636	Seminario Maggiore (central portal)
1645-48	Palazzo Durini
1651ff.	Pallazo di Breta

Publications

BOOKS ABOUT RICCHINO

BARONI, C.: *L'architettura da Bramante al Ricchino.* Milan, 1941.
CATANEO, ENRICO: *Il San Giuseppe del Richini.* Milan, 1957.
DENTI, GIOVANNI: *Architettura a Milano tra controriforma e barocco.* Florence, 1988.
MEZZANOTTE, PAOLO: *Di alcuni disegni inediti di Francesco Maria Ricchino per la chiesa di S. Maria di Loreto in Milano.* Milan, 1914.
NORBERG-SCHULZ, CHRISTIAN: *Baroque Architecture.* New York, 1971.
WITTKOWER, RUDOLF: *Art and Architecture in Italy: 1600-1750.* 3rd ed. rev. Baltimore and Harmondsworth, England, 1973.

ARTICLES ABOUT RICCHINO

GENGARO, MARIA LUISA: "Da Bramante al Richino." *Arti* 6 (1941).
GENGARO, MARIA LUISA: "Dal Pellegrini al Richino. Costruzioni Lombarde a pianta centrale." *Bollettino d'arte* (November 1936).
MEZZANOTTE, PAOLO: "Apparati architettonici del Ricchino per nozze auguste." *Rassegna d'arte* No. 10 (October 1915).
MEZZANOTTE, PAOLO: "Il Ricchino." In *La Martinella di Milano.* Milan, 1949.

*

Francesco Maria Ricchino was the most prominent Baroque architect working in Milan in the first half of the 17th century. Ricchino and two architects of the previous century, Galeazzo Alessi (1512-72) and Pellegrino Tibaldi (1527-96), were the only Milanese architects to attain national fame in Italian architectural history while maintaining workshops in Milan.

Ricchino studied first with his father, Bernardo Ricchino, a military engineer, and then with Lorenzo Binago (1554-1629), a prominent Milanese architect of the turn of the century. In 1600 Cardinal Federico Borromeo invited Ricchino to Rome to complete his studies. Nothing is known of Ricchino's work in Rome, but an apprenticeship in one of the numerous shops led by Lombard architects would have been assured.

Upon his return to Milan in 1603, Ricchino submitted a number of plans for the facade of the cathedral then under construction, and in 1605 he became an architect of the Milan Cathedral under Aurelio Trezzi. Ricchino must have worked mainly with Trezzi during his early years, as he inherited Trezzi's unfinished work upon the latter's death in 1625. In the first half of Ricchino's career, his rivals included the older

Lorenzo Binago as well as Ricchino's contemporary, Fabio Mangone (1587-1629), but after their deaths in 1629 and the ensuing plague that devastated Milan in 1630, Ricchino rose to unequaled stature.

Ricchino's first independent work was the Church of San Giuseppe, designed in 1607, consecrated in 1616, and completed externally by 1630. This church plan consists of two Greek-cross plans fused together. The large, open interior was accentuated by partially engaged Corinthian columns, resulting in a highly sculptural effect. This profusion of columns in an interior was a native Milanese tradition, seen for example in Tibaldi's Church of San Fedele (begun in 1569). The precedent for the use of a centralized plan derived from Early Christian churches found in large number in Milan, and reappeared only in the seicento in Milan, beginning with Binago's Church of Sant'Alessandro (1602). The exterior of San Giuseppe, a relatively flat facade ornamented with niche sculpture on both levels, was based on Carlo Maderno's Church of Santa Susanna in Rome (1603). The double pediment on the second story was an innovation of Ricchino's, however, and later became a popular Baroque motif in Rome.

While Renaissance Milanese architects preferred the longitudinal church plan based on the teachings of Archbishop Carlo Borromeo of Milan, Milanese architects of the Baroque age showed a consistent preference for the centralized plan. Ricchino's predilection for the centralized plan can also be seen in his 13 projects for the rebuilding of Santa Maria di Loreto, consecrated in 1616. Each plan shows a variation on a Greek cross, oval, or other elongated, centralized plan. A strong transverse axis always appears in these plans, fulfilling Borromeo's practical, liturgical requirement of crossing arms and chapels, yet the superimposed circular format also follows the more ideal iconography of a sanctuary, or sacred space.

Federico Borromeo was instrumental in organizing the restoration of many churches, and founded an institution toward that purpose in 1620. Ricchino renovated and rebuilt a vast number of those churches during that time, many of which have been destroyed. Federico Borromeo also continued his uncle Carlo Borromeo's work of establishing hospitals, libraries, colleges and seminaries in Milan. Ricchino worked for Cardinal Federico on a number of those commissions, such as the building of the Biblioteca Ambrosiana, directed by Lelio Buzzi between 1603 and 1609, and the garden loggia of the Collegio Borromeo in Pavia (1616).

Ricchino also completed the facade of the Collegio Elvetico, founded in 1579 by Carlo Borromeo, and built between 1603 and 1629 by Fabio Mangone, Gerolamo Quadrio and Ricchino. This facade, planned in 1627, was one of the earliest concave palace facades of the Baroque age, underlining Ricchino's dynamic, sculptural style, which anticipated the work of architects such as Francesco Borromini in Rome. Ricchino's design of the central portal of the Seminario Maggiore in Milan (1636) was also highly sculptural, displaying atlantes flanking the entrance, reminiscent of the giant half figures that seem to support the facade of Leone Leoni's Palazzo degli Omenoni in Milan (1565). Ricchino was awarded the highly prestigious position of *capomaestro* of Milan Cathedral in 1631, an acknowledgment of his stature as the most important architect of his day in that city.

Ricchino's private commissions began only in the second half of his career. The plague, as well as economic instability, had prevented palace building for the previous 30 years, while Ricchino had remained occupied working for Federico Borromeo on religious structures until Federico's death in 1631. The first palace built by Ricchino was that of Count Paolo Annoni, begun in 1631. The facade had a simplicity similar to Roman Renaissance palaces, but with a subtle Mannerist accentuation

of sculptural detail. This conservative approach to private architecture continued with Ricchino's later private buildings, such as his most famous palace, built for Giovan Battista Durini, begun in 1645 and completed in three years. The interior cortile features paired columns supporting arches in the colonnade, a clear reminder of Milanese courtyards in the Renaissance, such as in the Palazzo Marini (1557) by Galeazzo Alessi. Alessi's courtyard still remained much more sculptural, however. The dynamic, sculptural approach seen in Ricchino's public and religious commissions did not appear fully in his private works, but could still be found in later public buildings, such as the Palazzo Brera built for the Jesuits in 1651, where Ricchino reintroduced his famous concave facade.

—ALLISON PALMER

RICHARDSON, H. H.

American. Born Henry Hobson Richardson near New Orleans, Louisiana, 1838. Died in 1886. Graduated, Harvard College, Cambridge, Massachusetts, 1859; enrolled in atelier of Louis J. Andre, École des Beaux-Arts, Paris. Draftsman, office of Théodore Labrouste, Paris; employed by Jacques Ignace Hittorff, Paris; partnership with Emlyn Littel, New York, 1867; partner with Charles D. Gambrill (1832-80) in Gambrill and Richardson, New York, 1867. Fellow, American Institute of Architects; member, Society of Arts and Sciences; member, Archaeological Institute of America.

Chronology of Works
All in the United States unless noted
† *Work no longer exists*

1867-69	Grace Church, Medford, Massachusetts
1867-69	Western Railroad Offices, Springfield, Massachusetts†
1869	Hayden Building, Boston, Massachusetts
1869-71	High School, Worcester, Massachusetts†
1870-71	State Asylum for the Insane, Buffalo, New York
1870-72	Brattle Square Church, Boston, Massachusetts
1872	Andrews House, Newport, Rhode Island†
1872-73	Hampden County Courthouse, Springfield, Massachusetts
1872-73	North Congregational Church, Springfield, Massachusetts
1872-77	Trinity Church, Boston, Massachusetts
1874-75	Watts Sherman House, Newport, Rhode Island
1875-76	Cheney Building, Hartford, Connecticut
1875-81	New York State Capitol, Albany, New York
1876-79	Winn Memorial Public Library, Woburn, Massachusetts
1877-79	Ames Memorial Public Library, North Easton, Massachusetts
1878	James Cheney House, South Manchester, Connecticut
1878-80	Sever Hall, Harvard University, Cambridge, Massachusetts
1879	Ames Monument, Sherman, Wyoming
1879-80	Rectory, Trinity Church, Boston, Massachusetts
1879-81	Ames Memorial Town Hall, North Easton, Massachusetts
1880-81	Ames Gate Lodge, North Easton, Massachusetts
1880-82	City Hall, Albany, New York
1880-82	Crane Memorial Public Library, Quincy, Massachusetts

H. H. Richardson: Allegheny County Courthouse and Jail, Pittsburgh, Pennsylvania, 1884-88

1880-84	Austin Hall, Harvard University, Cambridge, Massachusetts
1881-82	Browne House, Marion, Massachusetts
1881-84	Old Colony Railroad Station, North Easton, Massachusetts
1882-83	Ames Store, Kingston and Bedford Streets, Boston, Massachusetts†
1882-83	Sard House, Albany, New York
1882-83	Stoughton House, Cambridge, Massachusetts
1882-85	Ames Store, Washington Street, Boston, Massachusetts
1883	Boston and Albany Railroad Station, Chestnut Hill, Massachusetts
1883-86	Emmanuel Church, Pittsburgh, Pennsylvania
1883-88	Billings Library, University of Vermont, Burlington, Vermont
1884	Baptist Church, Newton, Massachusetts
1884-85	Boston and Albany Railroad Stations in Brighton, Eliot, Waban, Framingham, Woodland and Wellesley Hills, Massachusetts
1884-86	Hay House, Washington, D.C.
1884-88	Allegheny County Courthouse and Jail, Pittsburgh, Pennsylvania
1885-87	Glessner House, Chicago, Illinois
1885-87	MacVeagh House, Chicago, Illinois
1885-87	Marshall Field Wholesale Store, Chicago, Illinois†
1885-87	Union Station, New London, Connecticut
1885-88	Chamber of Commerce Building, Cincinnati, Ohio†
1886-87	Ames Store, Harrison Avenue, Boston, Massachusetts
1886-94	Lululand (Herkomer House), Bushey, Hertfordshire, England

Publications

BOOKS BY RICHARDSON

A Description of Trinity Church. Boston, n.d.

BOOKS ABOUT RICHARDSON

CHESTER, ARTHUR H.: *Trinity Church in the City of Boston: An Historical and Descriptive Account.* Cambridge, Massachusetts, 1888.

CINCINNATI ASTRONOMICAL SOCIETY: *Richardson, the Architect.* Cincinnati, Ohio, 1914.

EATON, LEONARD K.: *American Architecture Comes of Age: European Reaction to H. H. Richardson and Louis Sullivan.* Cambridge, Massachusetts, and London, 1972.

HITCHCOCK, HENRY-RUSSELL: *Richardson as a Victorian Architect.* Baltimore, 1966.

HITCHCOCK, HENRY-RUSSELL: *The Architecture of H. H. Richardson and His Times.* New York, 1936.

LARSON, PAUL CLIFFORD, and BROWN, SUSAN M. (eds.): *The Spirit of H. H. Richardson on the Midland Prairies.* Ames, Iowa, 1988.

MUMFORD, LEWIS: *Sticks and Stones: A Study of American Architecture and Civilization* New York, 1924.

MUMFORD, LEWIS: *The Brown Decades: A Study of the Arts of America, 1865-1895.* New York, 1931.

NORTON, BETTINA (ed.): *Trinity Church: The Story of an Episcopal Parish in the City of Boston.* Boston, 1978.

OCHSNER, JEFFREY KARL: *H. H. Richardson: Complete Architectural Works.* Cambridge, Massachusetts, and London, 1982.

O'GORMAN, JAMES F.: *H. H. Richardson: Architectural Forms for an American Society.* Chicago and London, 1987.

O'GORMAN, JAMES F.: *Henry Hobson Richardson and His Office: Selected Drawings.* Cambridge, Massachusetts, 1974.

O'GORMAN, JAMES F.: *Three American Architects: Richardson, Sullivan and Wright, 1865-1915.* Chicago and London, 1991.

SCULLY, VINCENT J., JR.: *The Shingle Style and the Stick Style: Architectural Theory and Design from Richardson to the Origins of Wright.* New Haven, Connecticut, 1955.

ARTICLES ABOUT RICHARDSON

EATON, LEONARD K.: "Richardson and Sullivan in Scandinavia." *Progressive Architecture* 47 (1966): 168-171.

FRIEDLAENDER, MARC: "Henry Hobson Richardson, Henry Adams and John Hay." *Journal of the Society of Architectural Historians* 29 (1970): 231-246.

HARRINGTON, ELAINE: "Setting a Standard: H. H. Richardson's Glessner House." *Inland Architect* 32, No. 2 (March/April 1988): 55-60.

HITCHCOCK, HENRY-RUSSELL: "Richardson's New York Senate Chamber Restored." *Nineteenth Century* 6 (Spring 1980): 44-47.

HUBKA, THOMAS C.: "H. H. Richardson's Glessner House: A Garden in the Machine." *Winterthur Portfolio* 24 (Winter 1989).

ICKEUS, R. L.: "H. H. Richardson and Basic Form Concepts in Modern Architecture." *Art Quarterly* No. 3 (1940): 273-291.

LARSON, PAUL CLIFFORD: "In Search of the Richardsonians." *Inland Architect* 32, No. 2 (March/April 1988): 61-67.

MUMFORD, LEWIS: "The Regionalism of Richardson." In *Roots of Contemporary American Architecture.* New York, 1952.

OCHSNER, JEFFREY KARL, and HUBKA, THOMAS C.: "H. H. Richardson: The Design of the William Watts Sherman House." *Journal of the Society of Architectural Historians* 51 (June 1992): 121-145.

OCHSNER, JEFFREY KARL: "H. H. Richardson's Frank William Andrews House." *Journal of the Society of Architectural Historians* 43 (March 1984): 20-32.

OLMSTED, FREDERICK LAW: "H. H. Richardson." *American Architect* (July 1886).

SCHEYER, ERNST: "Henry Adams and Henry Hobson Richardson." *Journal of the Society of Architectural Historians* 12 (March 1953): 7-12.

SCHUYLER, MONTGOMERY: "The Romanesque Revival in America" and "The Romanesque Revival in New York." *Architectural Record* 1 (October-December 1891).

STEBBINS, THEODORE E.: "Richardson and Trinity Church: The Evolution of a Building." *Journal of the Society of Architectural Historians* 27 (December 1968): 281-298.

VAN BRUNT, HENRY: "Henry Hobson Richardson, Architect." In WILLIAM A. COLES (ed.): *Architecture and Society: Selected Essays of Henry Van Brunt.* Cambridge, Massachusetts, 1969.

When Louis Sullivan stood before H. H. Richardson's Marshall Field Wholesale Store (1885-87) in Chicago, he described the masterwork as "an oasis in the desert. . .a virile force. . .stone and mortar [which] spring[s] into life. . .a monument to trade, to the organized commercial spirit, to the power and progress of the age." At the scale of the 20th-century city, the building presented one huge block of granite and sandstone masonry forming a "manly" structure devoid of the vulgarities of Victorian commercialism. The Marshall Field Store, filling an entire city block, "[stood] four square and brown. . .in physical fact," a mass as powerful and solid as an 11th-century Romanesque church, yet composed with a simplicity and economy of detail which offered an immediate legacy to modernism. It was the very embodiment of the energy and force of a burgeoning metropolis, the "Hog Butcher for the World. . .the Nation's Freight Handler; Stormy, husky, brawling, City of the Big Shoulders."

Henry Hobson Richardson was America's Architect of the Big Shoulders. He was a solid figure of a man—"how much like your buildings you are," a client once remarked—and his contribution to contemporary builders was vital, powerful and direct. He quite simply taught his contemporaries how to compose at the new urban scale. With the borrowed vocabulary of Romanesque arches, masonry construction and expressive surface textures, Richardson transformed historicist forms to modern expression. Within a conservative, utilitarian language, his commercial buildings were never prosaic. The composed masses of his buildings, their dignified and increasingly restrained details, and the simplicity and largeness of his conceptions evidenced a forceful personality which eventually created a unique Richardsonian Romanesque style. Even more than Louis Sullivan and Frank Lloyd Wright, Richardson was the giant of his age.

Richardson's early life was marked by fortuitous circumstances which served him well as he prepared for his architectural practice. Born in Louisiana, Richardson learned early to speak French. He sought unsuccessfully to qualify for West Point but came north anyway to become a civil engineer. He entered Harvard in 1854, excelled in math, continued his study of drawing (an avocation he had started at age 10), and gave up civil engineering in favor of architecture. All would serve him well when he applied to be the second American student to enter the École des Beaux-Arts in Paris.

Although the symmetrical, hierarchical layout of certain early Richardson works, notably the Buffalo State Hospital (1870-71), would evidence strong Beaux-Arts planning character, the architect, armed with the best professional training available, was not to engage in the conventional exercises of an academic designer. As significant to his training was his exposure to the more picturesque domestic traditions of English design, first viewed when he traveled through the British Isles with college friends (on the way to the École des Beaux-Arts during the summer of 1859). Richardson's knowledge of the Queen Anne Olde English style of Richard Norman Shaw, transmitted through the pages of *The Builder* and other British journals to which Richardson subscribed, is clearly evident in Richardson's domestic architecture of the 1870s (Andrews House, Newport, 1872; James Cheney House project, South Manchester, Connecticut, 1878; and especially the Watts Sherman House, built in Newport in 1874). The "free style" of Shaw encouraged a picturesqueness, textural richness and materially tectonic architecture that was rich, never academically dry, and conducive to a first decisive step out of the historicism of the midcentury.

Indeed, biographers have seen three Richardsons: the Romanesque revivalist, the Victorian designer, and the protomodernist. The more naive historicist borrowings of the language of the High Victorian Gothic at his Worcester (Massachusetts) High School (1869-71) or Hampden County Courthouse in Springfield, Massachusetts (1872-73), looked to George Gilbert Scott and G. E. Street, respectively. His North Congregational Church in Springfield (1872-73) recalled the freer, less dry, style of Shaw, just as his project for a Church in Columbus, Ohio (1871-72), already synthesized the constructional theories of John Ruskin (as embodied by William Butterfield at Baldersby St. James), details from Street at St. James Westminster, and recollections of Émile Vaudremer in Paris.

But it was not this ''Victorian'' Richardson whose mark was to be stamped most significantly on the American landscape. In his masterful transitional project for Trinity Church, Boston, Richardson first brought together the forces that would mark the very best of his work: Romanesque masses compacted in a solid composition of weighty volumes and powerful forms; textural variety of colorful materials directly laid up and juxtaposed in an ornamental tapestry of surface enrichment; craftsmanship evidenced in a building which is both the simple construction of a master mason as well as the handiwork of a team of artisans. In the academic tradition of the American Renaissance (embodied in McKim, Mead and White's Boston Public Library, added the following decade across Copley Square from Trinity), Richardson's building is a total work of art: Augustus St. Gaudens' sculpture adorns the open space outside the north transept and adjacent to Trinity's flanking chapel building; John LaFarge stained glass and murals; William Morris stained glass (three upper north transept windows and bapistry window); and Romanesque capitals and other carvings enrich an added west porch, based on St. Giles du Gard. However, it would be in its restrained pyramidal massing and in its translation of both the Romanesque vocabulary and pictorial surface effects to an almost abstract simplicity that Trinity's impact on subsequent work by the architect would be felt.

Indeed, after Trinity was completed in 1877, Richardson's work would move toward a restrained protomodernism whose Romanesque attenuations were mere shadows of the age's Victorian eclecticism. The architect's library designs give evidence of this evolution. The Syrian arch, Romanesque stair tower, gabled vernacular halls whose separate forms and functional volumes *added up* to create the Richardson suburban library (the Ames Library at North Easton, Massachusetts, 1877, for example) were already *synthesized to an integrated whole* three years later at the Crane Memorial Library, Quincy.

The contrast between the master's fusion of formal elements at the Crane Library and the ''Richardsonian'' quotations and pictorial devices which mark its adjacent annex (not designed by Richardson) is almost as dramatic as the contrast between Richardson's own more historicist pictorialism in his work of the late 1860s and early 1870s compared to his integrated absorption of architectural elements into restrained and simple works after 1880. From the picturesque Queen Anne of the 1870s, Richardson would evolve to create, in the Stoughton House in Cambridge (1882), a masterpiece of restrained Shingle Style domestic design. From the awkward Ames Memorial Town Hall (1879) Richardson would recombine his Richardsonian Romanesque elements to greater success in the Albany City Hall (1880-82) and achieve a final synthesis in the Allegheny County Courthouse and Jail in Pittsburgh (1884-8), a masterwork which he never saw completed. From the small scale of the Chestnut Hill Railroad Station (1883) to the medium scale of his Emmanuel Episcopal Church in Allegheny City (Pittsburgh) (1883) to the large scale of his project for an Episcopal Church in Albany (1883), Richardson's rationalism displays an economy of form and controlled discipline which brings dignity and power to his work. The Chestnut Hill suburban railroad station

is a classic statement of the integration of form and function. The arch determined Chestnut Hill's design as directly as it did the large commercial structures Richardson built during these years in Boston and Chicago.

These developments away from picturesque historicism toward an integrated urban architecture are especially evidenced in Richardson's treatment of elements in the commercial block he built during the two periods. The Cheney Block in Hartford, Connecticut (1875-76), retained the popular Ruskinian polychromatic voussoirs and constructional coloration fashionable during the 1870s, and accented the masses with gables, balustrades and pyramidal turrets. Corner towers, as well as the grouping of single, paired or triple columns along the upper arcade, joined with the changing rhythms of pier supports to compose the urban block. The Cheney Block's devices reappeared at the Ames Library the next year as well as at the Ames commercial buildings in Boston in the early 1880s. But the final integration was achieved at the Marshall Field Wholesale Store in Chicago. Its dignity, economy and strength were, similarly, products of its simple composition, its direct expression of materials, and its pattern of windows and rhythm of embracing arches.

Despite his École training (or more likely because of it, as he, like Bernard Maybeck, had studied in the atelier of Jules André), Richardson's architecture was not ''school music'' but ''bravura music,'' as contemporary critic Montgomery Schuyler observed. When Richardson died in 1886, William LeBaron Jenney had just completed Chicago's first skyscraper and Frank Lloyd Wright was about to build his first house. Although he would not live to witness the rapid changes in both urban and suburban architectural design, in 20 short years Richardson had already made his mark. From his monumental masonry blocks of ''Richardsonian Romanesque'' to the landscape settings of North Easton, Richardson had established a lasting legacy for American architects of the following generation.

—ROBERT M. CRAIG

RIETVELD, Gerrit.

Dutch. Born Gerrit Thomas Rietveld in Utrecht, the Netherlands, 24 June 1888. Died in Utrecht, 25 June 1964. Studied drawing at the Municipal Evening School, Utrecht, 1906-08; architectural drawing with the architect P. Houtzagers, Utrecht, 1908-11; architecture with P.J. Klaarhamer, Utrecht, 1911-15. Worked as apprentice cabinetmaker in his father's business, 1899-1906; draftsman, C.J. Begeer's Jewelry Studio, Utrecht, 1906-11; in private practice as a cabinetmaker, Utrecht, 1911-19, and as an architect, Utrecht, 1919-60: collaborated on architectural and interior projects with Mrs. Truus Schroder-Schrader, Utrecht, 1921-64; partner, with J. van Dillen and J. van Tricht, Utrecht, 1960 until his death in 1964. Instructor in Industrial and Architectural Design, Academie voor Beeldende Kunsten, Rotterdam and The Hague, Academie van Beeldende Kunst en Kunstnijverheids, Arnhem, Netherlands, and Academie voor Baukunst, Amsterdam, 1942-58. Member, de Stijl Group, 1919-31; Co-founder, CIAM (Congrès Internationaux d'Architecture Moderne), 1928.

Chronology of Works
All in the Netherlands unless noted
† *Work no longer exists*

1919   Cornelis Begeer Shop, Oudkerkhof, Utrecht
1920-22 G. Z. C. Jeweler's Shop, Kalverstraat, Amsterdam†

1923	Exhibition Room, Greater Berlin Art Exhibition, Berlin, Germany (with Vilmos Huszar)
1923-25	Schröder House, Prinz Hendriklaan 50, Utrecht
1926-27	Marie Lommen House, Wassenaar
1927-28	Garage and chauffeur's living quarters, Utrecht†
1928	Zaudy Shop, Wesel, Germany†
1930-31	Van Urk House, Zwaluwenweg, Blaricum (with Truus Schröder)
1930-31	Row Houses, Erasmuslaan 5-11, Utrecht (interior with Schröder)
1930-32	Row Houses, Wiener Werkbund Siedlung, Vienna, Austria
1932	Row Houses, Robert Schumannstraat, Utrecht
1932	Music School and House, Henriette van Lyndenlaan 6, Ziest
1934	Row Houses, Erasmuslaan and Prinz Hendriklaan, Utrecht (with Schröder)
1935	Summer House for V. Ravesteyn-Hintzen, Breukelerveen
1936	Cinema, Vreeburg, Uredenburg, Utrecht
1939	Murk Lels Family House, Maarsbergenseweg 3, Doorn
1939	Brandt-Corstius Family House, Petten
1940	Penaat Family House, Tongeren
1940	Pot Family House, Rijksdijk 22, Krimpen Aan Der Lek
1941	Nijland Family House, Bilthoven
1941	Verrijin-Stuart Summer House, Breukelerveen
1951	Stoop House, Velp
1954	Netherlands Pavilion, Biennale, Venice, Italy†
1954	Sculpture Pavilion, Sonsbeek Park, Arnhem†
1954-57	Housing, Hoograven, Utrecht (with van Grunsven and H. Schröder)
1956	Visser House, Bergeyk (with H. Schröder)
1956	Juliana Hall and Entrance, Trade Fair, Utrecht
1956	De Ploeg Textile Factory, Bergeyk
1956-68	Institute for Applied Art (now Gerrit Rietveldacademie), Amsterdam (completed by J. van Dillen and J. van Tricht)
1957-63	Academie voor Beeldende Kunst, Arnhem
1958-59	Van Doel House, Ilpendam
1959-60	De Zonnehof Exhibition Hall, Amersfoort
1961-64	Van Sloobe House, Heerlen
1963-72	Rijksmuseum Vincent van Gogh, Amsterdam (completed by J. van Dillen and J. van Tricht)

Publications

BOOKS BY RIETVELD

Nieuwe zakelijkheid in der nederlandsche architektur. Amsterdam, 1932.
Over kennis en kunst, lezing-cyclus over stedebouw. Amsterdam, 1946.
Rietveld, 1924—Schröder Huis. Amsterdam, 1963.

ARTICLES BY RIETVELD

"Aanteekening bij Kinderstoel." *De Stijl* No. 9 (1919).
"Aspecten van het nieuwe bouwen." *Forum* No. 2/3 (1949).
"De bedoeling van de tentoonstelling." In *Schoonheid in huis en hof.* Amersfoort, Netherlands 1950.
"Die Nachkriegsarchitektur in Holland." *Werk* (Zurich) No. 11 (1951).
"Moord op Utrechts binnenstad: of levensvoorwaarde voor een stad" in *Elseviers Weekblad* (October 1955).

Numerous articles in *De 8 en Opbouw* and *Bouwkundig Weekblad.*

BOOKS ABOUT RIETVELD

BANHAM, REYNER: *Theory and Design in the First Machine Age.* New York, 1960.
BARONI, DANIELE: *Gerrit Thomas Rietveld: Furniture.* London, 1978.
BERTHEUX, WIL: *Gerrit Rietveld, Architect.* Amsterdam, 1972.
BLESS, FRITS: *Gerrit Rietveld, 1888-1964: Een biografie.* Amsterdam, 1982.
BROWN, THEODORE M.: *The Work of Gerrit Rietveld, Architect.* Cambridge, Massachusetts, and Utrecht, 1958.
BUFFINGA, A.: *Gerrit Thomas Rietveld.* Amsterdam, 1971.
DE ROOK, GERRIT JAN, and BLOTKAMP, CAREL: *Rietveld Schröderhuis 1925-1975.* Exhibition catalog. Utrecht, 1975.
The De Stijl Environment. Cambridge, Massachusetts, 1983.
FRIEDMAN, M.: *De Stijl: 1917-1931. Visions of Utopia.* Minneapolis, 1982.
Gerrit Rietveld, Architect. Exhibition catalog. London, 1972.
JAFFÉ, HANS L. C.: *De Stijl, 1917-1931: The Dutch Contribution to Modern Art.* Amsterdam, 1956.
MULDER, BERTUS: *Rietveld Schröder Huis 1925-1975.* Utrecht, 1975.
OVERY, PAUL: *The Rietveld Schröder House.* Cambridge, Massachusetts, 1988.
OVERY, PAUL: *De Stijl.* London, 1969.
PETERSEN, AD (ed.): *De Stijl.* 2 vols. Amsterdam, 1968.
Rietveld tentoonstelling. Exhibition catalog, Utrecht, 1958.
RODIJK, G. H.: *De huizen van Rietveld.* Zwolle, Netherlands, 1991.
SCHAAFSMA, H.: *Gerrit Rietveld: Bouwmeester van ein nieuwe tijd.* Utrecht, 1959.
VAN DEN BROEK, J. H.; VAN EESTEREN, C.; et al.: *De Stijl.* Amsterdam, 1951.
WATTJES, J. G.: *Nieuwe nederlandsche Bouwkunst.* 2 vols. Amsterdam, 1923-26.
YERBURY, F. R.: *Modern Dutch Building.* London, 1931.

ARTICLES ABOUT RIETVELD

BERG, E., and BAK, H.: "Rietveld and His Museum Buildings." *Arkitekten* (12 March 1974).
BLESS, FRITS: "Rietveld: Myth and Reality." *Forum* (July 1981).
"Gerrit Rietveld." *Forum* No. 3, special issue (1958).
"Gerrit Rietveld." *Domus* (September 1965).

*

Gerrit Rietveld is best known for his furniture and as the architect of the Schröder House (1924-25), one of the iconic buildings of early modernism. He was also an innovative designer of shops, made an important contribution to housing, and designed a number of major public buildings in the Netherlands during the last decade of his life.

Trained as a furniture maker, Rietveld began to produce experimental furniture such as the Red Blue Chair (ca. 1918). Probably not painted in its familiar colors until 1923, the chair became a key artifact of De Stijl, a multi-media aesthetic movement with which Rietveld was associated from 1919. In this and other early designs he employed the so-called "Rietveld joint," where the wooden elements from which each piece of furniture is constructed extend beyond the point of juncture, remaining separate and distinct. With its visually independent planes, sliding partitions and ingenious built-in fitments, the Schröder House is closely related to Rietveld's furniture, examples of which were used in the house; a number of new pieces were made especially for it.

Designed in close collaboration with his client Truus Schröder, the house was his first complete building. Schröder, a widow, wanted an austere and intimate living space for herself and her three children. Using inexpensive materials and primary colors, the house was organized inventively. Its upper floor was outfitted with partitions able to be opened or closed to create a variety of living spaces. Included in this space were the children's bedrooms and a dining/sitting area. The bathroom and Schröder's own bedroom were on the same floor but separate. The lower floor had a more conventional layout, including a kitchen, a study, and a space that Rietveld used as an atelier even though it had been designed to be a garage. In an unconventional touch, strips of glass were placed above the walls these rooms shared, creating a sense of intimacy while letting in additional light. The house originally was credited to both Rietveld and Schröder.

Among Rietveld's designs preceding the Schröder House were the Goldsmiths and Silversmiths Company (GZK) shop in Amsterdam (1921) and a surgery for Dr. Hartog in Maarssen (1922), both later destroyed. The GZK shopfront was an asymmetric construction of rectangular glass vitrines to display jewelry and draw the customer into the shop. Hartog's surgery was a combination of specially commissioned furniture and earlier pieces like the Red Blue Chair, set off by colored rectangles and a large red circle painted on the wall. Many of Rietveld's most spectacular shop designs were for German clients in the late 1920s, such as Zaudy in Wesel (1928). There he broke open the 19th-century facade with three floors of furniture showrooms lit by huge windows on the two upper floors and a large setback cubic vitrine on the ground floor, employing neon signs and arrows to draw passersby inside.

In 1927 Rietveld designed the Chauffeur's House in Utrecht using standardized prefabricated concrete planks attached to steel I-beams. There were various technical problems, and the house was extensively remodeled, although it is now in the process of restoration. His subsequent experiments with producing standardized norms for low-cost housing were closer to the "Nieuwe Bouwen," the Dutch version of the International Style, than to De Stijl. The rowhouses and duplex apartments opposite the Schröder House in Erasmuslaan (1930-31; 1934), in collaboration with Schröder, who was also the client, incorporated innovations derived from the Schröder House such as folding or sliding partitions and spaces that could double up as living and sleeping areas.

These ideas were developed in a number of unrealized designs for working-class housing in the late 1920s. Rietveld was able to put some of them into practice in the model rowhouses for the Wiener Werkbund Siedlung in Vienna (1930-32), and a terrace of low-cost speculative dwellings in the Robert Schumannstraat, Utrecht (1934), for the construction company Bredero. The Vienna houses were built to very tight specifications, with four-meter frontages and access to the upper floors from tiny spiral staircases. Large areas of glass, previously considered a sign of status and luxury, were introduced to provide adequate light and circulation of fresh air. Although Rietveld himself did not receive a municipal housing commission in Holland until after World War II—at Hoograven, Utrecht (1954-7), with Van Grunsven and Han Schröder—many of his innovations were incorporated into social-housing schemes in Rotterdam during the early 1930s by architects such as J. H. van den Broek and J. B. Bakema, as well as Jan Brinkman and

L. C. van der Vlugt. Later furniture designs such as the Zig-Zag Chair (1932) and Crate Furniture (1934) were produced in quantity and sold by the Metz Store in the Netherlands.

In a number of private villas designed during the 1930s and 1940s, Rietveld experimented with combinations of flat and pitched roofs and "modern" and "traditional" materials, as in the Verrijn-Stuart Summer House in Breukelerveen near Utrecht (1941), which with its walls of green bargeboarding and roof of reed thatch has an almost postmodern appearance. He also designed many refined and well-planned houses during the 1950s, such as those at Ilpendam (1958-59) and Bergeyk (1956). Rietveld's work was almost entirely on a small scale until the mid-1950s, when modernism became institutionalized and his reputation as a pioneer of early modernist architecture and furniture design was established. He designed the major De Stijl exhibitions for the Stedelijk Museum in Amsterdam (1951), the Venice Biennale and the Museum of Modern Art in New York City (1952).

As a result, he received a number of major public commissions, including the Netherlands Pavilion for the Venice Biennale (1954), the Academy of Fine and Applied Art at Arnhem (1957-63; with his partners, J. H. F. Van Dillen and J. Van Tricht), the Academy of Applied Arts (now the Gerrit Rietveld Academy) in Amsterdam (1956-68), and the Sculpture Pavilion at Arnhem (1954), later rebuilt in the park of the Kröller-Müller Museum in Otterlo. The Van Gogh Museum in Amsterdam (1963-73) was his final work, realized posthumously by his partners Van Dillen and Van Tricht. There the harmonious proportions and skillful use of asymmetry that had been employed on a smaller scale in the Venice pavilion produced a handsome but restrained addition to the museums quarter of Amsterdam. The interior is a light and sober aula with circulation and exhibition areas on the ground floor; the two top floors have hanging space around a central void that provides indirect natural lighting.

—PAUL OVERY

ROBERTS, Henry.

British. Born a British subject in Philadelphia, Pennsylvania, 16 April 1803. Died in 1876. Apprenticed in the office of Charles Fowler (1791-1867), from 1818; joined practice of Robert Smirke (1781-1867), 1825; enrolled at that time in the Royal Academy Schools; traveled abroad, where he saw the Albergo di Poveri (Reclusorio) in Naples, 1829; established his own practice, London, 1830; won competition for Hall for Fishmongers' Company, 1831; appointed architect to Destitute Sailors' Asylum, London, 1834; fellow, Institute of British Architects, 1837; founder-member and architect to the Society for Improving the Condition of the Labouring Classes, 1844; conferences in France, Germany and Switzerland.

Chronology of Works
All in England
* Approximate dates

1831-34	Fishmongers' Hall, London
1836	Glebe House, Southmore, Kent
1838	Escot House, Devon
1839-40	Escot Church, Devon
1839-40*	Peamore House, Alphington, near Exeter
1843	Norton Fitzwarren, Somerset
1844	Model Housing Estate, Bagnigge Wells
1844-46	First London Bridge Station, London†

1850* Workers' Hostel, Drury Lane (conversion of three houses)
1850* Thanksgiving Buildings, Portpool Lane
1849-50 Model Houses for Families, Streatham Street, Bloomsbury
1851 Model Houses for Families Erected by H.R.H. Prince Albert at the Great Exhibition, London

Publications

BOOKS BY ROBERTS

The Dwellings of the Labouring Classes. 1850; rev. ed., 1867.
House Reform; or, What the Working Classes May Do to Improve Their Dwellings. 1852.
The Improvement of the Dwellings of the Labouring Classes. 1859.
Proposed People's Palace and Gardens for the Northern and Midland Counties. 1863.
The Essentials of a Healthy Dwelling, and the Extensions of Its Benefits to the Labouring Population. 1862.
The Physical Condition of the Labouring Classes, Resulting from the State of their Dwellings. 1866.
Efforts on the Continent for Improving the Dwellings of the Labouring Classes. Florence, 1874.

BOOKS ABOUT ROBERTS

CURL, JAMES STEVENS: *The Life and Work of Henry Roberts 1803-76.* Chichester, England, 1983.
SCOTT, GEORGE GILBERT: *Personal and Professional Recollections.* London, 1879.
TARN, J. N.: *Five Per Cent Philanthropy: An Account of Housing in Urban Areas Between 1840 and 1914.* Cambridge, 1973.

ARTICLES ABOUT ROBERTS

FOYLE, A. M.: "Henry Roberts." *Builder* (2 January 1953).
PEVSNER, NIKOLAUS: "Model Houses for the Labouring Classes." *Architectural Review* 93 (May 1943).
PEVSNER, NIKOLAUS: "Early Working Class Housing." In *Studies in Art, Architecture and Design: Victorian and After.* Princeton, New Jersey, 1968.

*

Henry Roberts began his architectural career in the office of Charles Fowler in 1818, and in 1825 joined the progressive practice of Robert Smirke, also enrolling at the Royal Academy Schools. He then traveled abroad, and in 1829 saw the Albergo di Poveri, or Reclusorio, in Naples, the massive six-story model dwellings with workshops for crafts, one of Roberts' first tastes of philanthropic housing.

In 1830 he established his own practice in London, and the next year won the competition to design the new Hall for the Fishmongers' Company in the city of London. This brilliant building, in a scholarly Greek Revival style (where the influence of Smirke was clear), incorporated several innovations, including a concrete-raft foundation and a structure using hollow bricks, brick arches bedded in concrete, and hollow pot-tiles in the vault of the Banqueting Hall, which created an especially felicitous acoustic. Roberts' assistant was the young George Gilbert Scott; the hall was finished in 1840.

In 1834 Roberts was appointed architect to the Destitute Sailors' Asylum near the London Docks, his first venture in the designing of shelter for the poor. He developed his connections with persons of an Evangelical persuasion, and by 1835 was well established in both society and the profession, being a founder-member of the Institute of British Architects (of which he became a fellow in 1837). His connections with the Evangelicals gained him several commissions, including the Glebe House, Southborough, Kent, the distinguished Escot House in Devon, Peamore House at Alphington near Exeter, and Norton Fitzwarren in Somerset. He also designed several churches, but his essays in Gothic and Romanesque were not impressive, and indeed they were subjected to severe criticism by *The Ecclesiologist.* More successful was his design in the Italianate style for the London Bridge terminus for the Croydon, Brighton, and South Eastern Railways.

In 1844 Roberts became a founder-member of the reconstituted Society for Improving the Condition of the Labouring Classes, with which he was to be closely involved as honorary architect for the next decade. One of the principal objects of the Society was to "arrange and execute plans as models for the improvement of dwellings of the labouring classes," and Roberts contributed an enormous amount of energy in promoting the Society's aims, either in tracts, booklets, books or lectures, as well as in the production of designs for model housing of all types.

In the beginning, the Society published plans for model dwellings designed by Roberts, but eventually the committee decided that the best way of making a dent in public opinion was to build actual exemplars through money raised by subscription and loans. The first estate of model dwellings based on designs by Roberts was erected in 1844 at Bagnigge Wells between Lower Road, Pentonville, and Gray's Inn Road. This was followed by a Model Lodging House for Working Men, a conversion of three houses in Drury Lane as a hostel for workers, and Thanksgiving Buildings, Portpool Lane, a block designed to house 20 families and 128 single women.

The next project of the Society was the "Model Houses for Families" in Streatham Street, Bloomsbury, a distinguished design for housing 48 families in a three-sided block, grouped around a court, with access to individual flats by balconies; each flat was self-contained, had its own lobby, and consisted of a main room, two bedrooms, a kitchen, and a water closet, a tremendous advance for the time. A bath- and washhouse was also provided, as were other communal facilities. The entire building was constructed to be as fireproof as possible, the floors and roof being built of hollow-brick arches covered with concrete. The Model Houses were opened in 1850, and were important for many reasons, not the least of which were the changes in the law they heralded. Standards of design, construction and accommodation were generally well ahead of their day, yet the authorities levied window tax on the block. Roberts argued that each gallery access was an elevated street so that each flat, with its independent access, was a separate dwelling, and therefore too small a unit to be assessed for tax. Roberts won his case, and window tax was abolished. By the time Roberts published a new edition of his important and informative book, *The Dwellings of the Labouring Classes,* in 1853, the abolition of window tax was seen as the most important concession made to the public call for sanitary amelioration.

The most celebrated of all Roberts' designs for working-class housing was that for the "Model Houses for Families Erected by H.R.H. Prince Albert" at the Great Exhibition of 1851. The plans derived from several years' experimentation by Roberts, with the mature example of Streatham Street well to the fore. This important exhibit consisted of four flats, each consisting of a living room, bedrooms (each with separate access) and a scullery with sink, plate rack, coal bin, dust shaft and meat safe. There was also a water closet inside each flat. The most important feature of the design was the staircase at the front which gave access to the upper floor. Construction included the use of hollow bricks for "dryness, warmth, durability, security from fire, and deadening of sound." The Model Houses were popular among visitors to the exhibition, and copies of the plans and specifications were sold in quantity. Roberts patented his designs for hollow bricks used in the construction of this distinguished and ingenious scheme (based on plans which could be extended upwards and repeated on either side). In fact the design was the basis of much later work, and established a precedent for minimum accommodation, self-contained, well built, adequately ventilated and fire-resistant.

Roberts greatly extended the influence of the Society and of its aims by writing descriptions of his own designs for publication, by producing many plans for model dwellings of all sorts that were printed and sold by the Society (and realized throughout the British Isles, so they were pattern-book designs on a grand scale), by writing and lecturing on the benefits of sound, dry, ventilated, hygienic and well-planned housing, and by disseminating information on the housing movement throughout Europe. He unquestionably made the most important contribution to the whole question of housing the working classes in the middle decades of the 19th century. He became a respected expert, both nationally and internationally, and, almost alone among his profession, concerned himself with the practical problems of designing cheap and wholesome dwellings for the poor. His visits to France, Germany, Switzerland and international conferences aroused much interest, and he gave many important papers that changed the course of housing history. As a planner, he was skillful and inventive, and his achievements, notably at Streatham Street, at the estate he designed at Windsor, and at the 1851 Exhibition, rose above the utilitarian to heights of real architectural quality. The solid advances pioneered by Roberts in planning, construction, privacy, safety, hygiene and dignity at Streatham Street alone were not to be surpassed in Britain until the London County Council developments at the turn of the century.

His was a life that embodied the chief virtues of the time: prudence in financial matters, a thorough grasp of professional expertise, immense industry, benevolence toward the less fortunate, a willingness to experiment and develop new ideas, ability to give full attention to minutiae and detail, and a deeply felt kinship with humanity based on his Evangelical Christian beliefs.

—JAMES STEVENS CURL

ROCHE, Kevin.

American. Born in Dublin, Ireland, 14 June 1922; immigrated to the United States, 1948; naturalized, 1964. Married Jane Tuohy, 1963; five children. Studied at the National University of Ireland, Dublin, 1940-45, B.Arch.; Illinois Institute of Technology, Chicago, 1948-49. Designer, Michael Scott and Partners, Dublin, 1945-46, 1947-48; architect with Maxwell Fry and Jane Drew, London, 1946, and with the United Nations Planning Office, New York, 1949; associate, Eero Saarinen and Associates, Bloomfield Hills and Birmingham, Michigan, and Hamden, Connecticut, 1950-66 (principal associate in design to Saarinen, 1954-61); since 1966, partner in Kevin Roche, John Dinkeloo and Associates, Hamden, Connecticut. Grand Gold Medal, Académie d'Architecture, France; Pritzker Prize, 1982.

Chronology of Works

All in the United States unless noted
† *Work no longer exists*

1961-68	Oakland Museum, Oakland, California
1962-64	IBM Pavilion, World's Fair, New York City†
1962-67	Richard C. Lee High School, New Haven, Connecticut
1962-69	Administration, Student Union and Physical Education Buildings, Rochester Institute of Technology, Rochester, New York
1963-65	Cummins Engine Company Components Plant, Darlington, Durham, England
1963-68	Ford Foundation Headquarters, New York City
1964-74	Fine Arts Center, University of Massachusetts, Amherst
1965-69	Knights of Columbus Headquarters, New Haven, Connecticut
1965-69	United States Post Office, Columbus, Indiana
1965-71	Power Center for the Performing Arts, University of Michigan, Ann Arbor
1965-72	Veterans Memorial Coliseum, New Haven, Connecticut
1965-73	Creative Arts Center, Wesleyan University, Middletown, Connecticut
1966-72	Aetna Life and Casualty and Computer Building, Hartford, Connecticut
1966-72	Irwin Union Bank and Trust Company, Columbus, Indiana
1967-71	College Life Insurance Company of America Headquarters, Indianapolis, Indiana
1967-85	Metropolitan Museum of Art, New York City (master plan and additions)
1969-75	United Nations Development Corporation Hotel and Office Building (stage I), New York City
1969-77	Federal Reserve Bank of New York, New York City
1970-73	Cummins Engine Company Sub-Assembly Plant, Columbus, Indiana
1970-74	Richardson-Merrell Corporate Headquarters, Wilton, Connecticut
1970-74	Worcester County National Bank, Worcester, Massachusetts
1972	Cummins Engine Company Corporate Headquarters, Columbus, Indiana
1972-81	Indiana and Michigan Power Company, Fort Wayne, Indiana
1973-76	Fiat World Headquarters, Turin, Italy
1973-76	Kentucky Power Company Headquarters, Ashland, Kentucky
1974-79	Denver Center for the Performing Arts, Denver, Colorado
1975-79	John Deere and Company Headquarters, Moline, Illinois
1976-81	International Business Machines Corporation Thomas J. Watson Research Center, Yorktown Heights, New York (addition)
1976-82	J. M. Moudy Building, Texas Christian University, Fort Worth
1976-82	Union Carbide Corporation World Headquarters, Danbury, Connecticut
1977-82	Bell Telephone Laboratories, Holmdel, New Jersey (expansion)
1977-82	General Foods Corporation Headquarters, Rye, New York
1978-82	John Deere Financial Services Headquarters, Moline, Illinois

Kevin Roche: Ford Foundation Headquarters, New York City, New York, 1963-68

1979   United Nations Development Office and Apartment/
            Hotel (stage II), New York City
1980-88   Central Park Zoo, New York City
1980   DeWitt Wallace Museum of Fine Arts, Colonial Wil-
            liamsburg, Virginia
1980   E. F. Hutton Building, New York City
1981   Block One Development, Denver, Colorado
1983   Bouygues World Headquarters, Paris, France
1983   Office Development, 60 Wall Street, New York

Publications

BOOKS ABOUT ROCHE

HARA, HIROSHI: *GA 4: Kevin Roche, John Dinkeloo and Asso-
    ciates*, edited by Yukio Futagawa. Tokyo, 1971.
FUTAGAWA, YUKIO: *Kevin Roche, John Dinkeloo and Associ-
    ates 1962-75.* Tokyo and Fribourg, Switzerland, 1975.
HORUMI, NOBUO: *GA Detail 4: Kevin Roche, John Dinkeloo
    and Associates.* Tokyo, 1977.
O'REGAN, JOHN, and O'TOOLE, SHANE (eds.): *Kevin Roche,
    Architect: The Work of Kevin Roche, John Dinkeloo and
    Associates.* Dublin, 1983.
FUTAGAWA, YUKIO (ed.): *GA 9: Kevin Roche, John Dinkeloo
    and Associates.* Tokyo, 1984.
DAL CO, FRANCESCO (ed.): *Kevin Roche.* New York, 1986.

ARTICLES ABOUT ROCHE

Architectural Forum, special issue (March 1974).
Architecture and Urbanism, extra edition 8 (August 1987).
"Architecture Is a Language" [interview]. *Architectes* (January
    1979).
"A Conversation with Kevin Roche." *Perspecta* 19 (1982).
KEEGAN, EDWARD: "Illusions in Fin de Siècle Chicago: 900
    North Michigan and the Leo Burnett Building." *Inland Ar-
    chitect* 34/1 (January/February 1990).
"Sheer and Shiny: Kevin Roche, Mega-Architect." *Building
    Design* 10 (October 1980).
"Three Buildings by Kevin Roche, John Dinkeloo and Associ-
    ates." *Domus* (February 1976).
"Two Splendid Fine Arts Centers by Roche Dinkeloo and
    Associates." *Architectural Record* (May 1975).
"The Work of Kevin Roche." *Architect and Builder* (Cape
    Town, South Africa, November 1982).

*

Kevin Roche, a native of Ireland with an architecture degree
from the national university, worked in the studios of Maxwell
Fry in London immediately after World War II. After studying
with Ludwig Mies van der Rohe at the Illinois Institute of
Technology, Roche joined Eero Saarinen and Associates in
1950. He served as Saarinen's principal associate from 1954
until 1961.

With Saarinen's untimely death in 1961, the firm followed
through with preexisting plans to move to Hamden, Connecticut.
The firm carried out Saarinen's existing commissions and
earned new ones, continuing as Kevin Roche/John Dinkeloo
and Associates. John Dinkeloo, also a Saarinen veteran, was
partner in the new firm until his death in 1981. Without ever
directing design, he acted as a constant sounding board for
ideas, and lent to all projects his engineering skills and innate
sense of materials. Also carried over from Saarinen was a design
approach based on study models: the construction of many
alternative schemes in three-dimensional form.

Though Saarinen's diverse work could never be considered
singular in style, Roche followed his mentor's innovative, tectonic and open-minded approach to architecture much longer
than professional continuity would have dictated, making it
clearly his own.

Roche's approach to architecture has consistently been, like
Saarinen's, a complete reconception of building type and form
for each commission. These are often highly sculptural designs
which abandon preconceived typologies.

The Oakland Museum in California (1961-68), for example,
appears less as architecture than a horizontal De Stijl composition in landscape placed at the center of Oakland. Three floors
of gallery spaces are nestled into the vast urban site, surmounted
by a multilevel series of interconnected landscaped plazas. Despite the monumentality of many of these works, nature often
plays an important role.

The Ford Foundation Headquarters in New York City (1963-
68) is a similarly unconventional incorporation of landscape in
an urban area: a 12-story office building with a 12-story, one-
third-acre atrium. This building has elements that can be considered Roche's style, if any can: its upper floors have large steel
beams with articulated joints, while the glazing of the lower
nine floors is taut and straightforward. Structural piers are monumental with sharp edges, and glazed openings are large voids,
not punched holes. Roche created, in addition to its tectonic
wonder, one of the great spaces of New York.

Roche carried his formal and structural reconception of building types to the Knights of Columbus Headquarters Building
in New Haven Connecticut (1965-69). Four stout tile-covered
concrete columns at the points of a square support the heavy
horizontal floor beams of the 23-story tower. While the structural beam/*brise-soleil* details recall Saarinen's John Deere
Headquarters in Moline, Illinois, and Roche's later expansion,
this building calls mostly to the highway. It is an early example
of architecture designed for the speeding automobile (of adjacent Interstate 95). The contiguous Veteran's Memorial Coliseum (1965-72) perhaps sacrifices too much to said automobiles.
The 10,000-seat stadium is topped by a four-level parking platform—dramatic from the highway, alienating from town.

A better example of successful freeway-side sculpture is the
College Life Insurance Company of America in Indianapolis,
Indiana. Truncated quarter pyramids in sheer glass have me-
chanicals and elevators in massive L-shaped walls. The three
existing buildings of nine planned are compelling minimal
sculpture seen from the highway, though appropriate to their
suburban location.

Roche's developing work has explored new relationships
with the automobile and with nature, most remarkably in his
Union Carbide Headquarters in Danbury, Connecticut (1982).
With a multilevel parking garage as a core, Roche has in-
termeshed the building with the thick woods through a series
of fractal-like projections that nearly touch the woods, emphasizing nature in the one-quarter-mile-long structure. Roche established a similar relationship at New York's Metropolitan
Museum, where a series of grand but restrained glass halls
serenely juxtapose art and nature.

The General Foods Corporation Headquarters (1988-82), on
the other hand, stands away from nature while hinting at historicism. Specifically, its symmetrical plan, central rotunda and
enormous reflecting pool clearly recall Beaux-Arts architecture,
although the taut masonry and glass ribbons are decidedly
modern.

Similar historicism appeared in the 1980s series of tower
projects which explored conventional base-middle-top articulation schemes. The realized E. F. Hutton Tower in New York
City, like the proposed Morgan Bank Tower, is a pleasant

enough composition, but surprisingly conventional for Roche. Other tower proposals based on abstracted column motifs have been rather ungainly. Roche's contrasting early high-rise designs had defied convention: United Nations Plaza One and Two through a sculptural approach to glass skin, and the proposed Federal Reserve Bank of New York (1969) with its 160-foot, four-column pedestal.

Roche has found balance at the Central Park Zoo in New York City, completed in 1988. He shows his facility with picturesque procession and has created an appropriately scaled arcade for his abstracted columns. Roche is at his best, though, combining a picturesque approach to landscape with heroic structure.

—CHARLES ROSENBLUM

RODRíGUEZ, Ventura.

Spanish. Born in Madrid, Spain, 14 July 1717. Died in Madrid, 26 August 1785. Draftsman at the Royal Palace of Aran Juez, 1731-36, and worked there under Giovanni Sacchetti. Active in the Spanish Academy, Madrid, 1752-85, and director of architecture, 1752; municipal architect, Madrid, 1764.

Chronology of Works
All in Spain
† Work no longer exists

1749-53	Church of San Marcos, Madrid
1750	Church of the Monastery of Santo Domingo de Silos, Burgos
1750	Chapel of the Virgin, Nuestra Señora del Pilar, Zaragoza
1752	San Julían, Cuenca Cathedral (main altar and chapel)
1753	Trasparente, Cuenca Cathedral
1754	San Norberto, Madrid (facade)†
1755	Chapel of San Pedro de Alcantara, Arenas de San Pedro
1755	La Encarnación, Madrid (remodeling of nave)
1759	Convent of the Agustinos Filipinos, Valladolid
1760-63	Royal Palace, Valladolid (restorations)
1761-64	College of Surgery, Barcelona
1761-64	Cathedral, Jaén (sagrario)
1762	Municipal Slaughter and Curing House, Madrid
1763	Infante Don Luis House, Boabdilla del Monte
1767	San Sebastián, Azpeita (facade)
1770	Cathedral, Almería (traschoir)
1771	Collegiate Church, Santa Fe
1772	Chapel of the College of the Poor Damsels of Santa Vitoria, Córdoba (completion and restorations)
1772	Cathedral, Zamora (main altar)
1773	Palace, Liria
1775	La Encarnación, Loja (completion)
1776	Parish Church, Vélez de Benandalla
1777	Fountain of Apollo, Madrid (with M. Alvarez)
1777	Nuestra Senora de la Asunción, Rentería (main altar and presbytery)
1777	Parish Church, Alvia del Taha
1777-84	Parish Church, Larrabezúa
1779	Basilica, Covadonga
1779	Santa María la Mayor, Algarinejo
1780	Parish Church, Cajar
1780	Santos Sebastián e Ildefonso, Olula del Río
1783	Cathedral, Pamplona (facade)
1783	Parish Church, Talará

Publications

BOOKS ABOUT RODRíGUEZ

CALZADA, ANDRÉS: *Historia de la arquitectura española*. Barcelona, 1933.
KUBLER, GEORGE, and SORIA, MARTIN: *Art and Architecture in Spain and Portugal and Their American Dominions 1500-1800*. Baltimore and Harmondsworth, 1959.
REESE, THOMAS F.: *The Architecture of Ventura Rodriguez Tizón in the Development of the Eighteenth Century Style in Spain*. 2 vols. New York, 1976.
SCHUBERT, OTTO: *Historia del barroco en Espána*. Madrid, 1924.

ARTICLES ABOUT RODRíGUEZ

CHUECA GOITIA, FERNANDO: "Ventura Rodríguez y la escuela barroca romana." *Archivo Español de Arte* 15 (1942): 185-210.
INIGUEZ ALMECH, FRANCISCO: "Don Ventura Rodríguez." *Arquitectura* 17 (1935): 75-112.
INIGUEZ ALMECH, FRANCISCO: "La formación de don Ventura Rodríguez." *Archivo Español de Arte* 22 (1949): 137-148.
LORENTE JUNQUERA, MANUEL: "La evolución arquitectónica en España en los siglos XVIII y XIX." *Arte Español* 30 (1946): 74-79.

*

The work of the Spanish architect Ventura Rodríguez exemplifies the transition from academic Baroque architecture to the classical principles of the later 18th century. As a representative of the first generation of *Spanish* architects working under the Bourbons, Rodríguez enjoyed tremendous esteem as court architect until the death of Ferdinand VI, and afterward was a (controversial) professor of the Academy. Of the numerous designs he prepared for the court, the Academy and for private patrons, approximately 50 were realized. While his early work was completely under the influence of the Italian Baroque from Giovanni Lorenzo Bernini to Guarino Guarini, the influence of François Blondel's *L'Architecture Française* became discernible at the end of the 1750s. Blondel's influence led Rodríguez to a form of academic classicism. The discovery of Greek and Roman antiquity, however, also led Rodríguez to a study of the work of Juan de Herrera and of the indigenous architectural heritage.

Ventura Rodríguez received his training as an architect and draftsman from Étienne Marchand in Aranjuez and, from 1735, from Filippo Juvarra and G. B. Sacchetti in Madrid. His first important commission was the Parish Church of San Marcos in Madrid (1749-53). The exterior of the building, remaining strictly within the Baroque style, goes back to Bernini's Church of Sant'Andrea al Quirinale with the concave curve of the facade, which neatly veils an unfavorable site. The design of the interior, with its five overlapping ellipses, recalls Giacomo Bonavia's Church of SS. Justo y Pastor, also in Madrid, and their common source, Guarini's Divina Providência in Lisbon. Rodríguez' church surpasses its predecessors in the scenic arrangement of the spatial sequence. In this design, Rodríguez proves himself one of the few Spanish architects to deviate from the rigid structures of rectangular plans.

In 1750 Rodríguez undertook a very difficult assignment in the reconstruction of the Pilgrimage Church of the Pillar in Zaragoza, which had been begun by Francisco Herrera. The sacrosanct pillar, at which the Virgin Mary had appeared to the

Ventura Rodríguez: Cathedral, Pamplona, Spain, 1783

apostle James, could not be changed, but at the same time a way had to be found to accommodate the needs of the numerous pilgrims. Rodríguez changed the space around the sanctuary on the western side of the central nave, designing a vaulted ellipse with four shells on the axes. Three sides are opened by Corinthian columns, while the fourth, western side is closed as an altar wall. The latter is divided in three by niches, but has the appearance of a triptych as a result of the iconographical program. The mercy statue is not in the center, but in the right-hand exedra. Rodríguez thus achieved a dramatic effect, which is heightened by the marble ornamentation and by the light from the dome above. Although Rodríguez remained faithful

to Baroque principles in this chapel, the design of the interior of the complex is characterized by calm, classicist elements.

In 1755 Rodríguez prepared the first designs for the reconstruction of the interior of the Church of the Encarnación in Madrid. The wide arcade with Ionic pilasters, the continuous stringcourse and the coffered barrel vault signal a definitive break with the Baroque style. The influence of the French architect Blondel and the Italian Carlo Lodoli begins to make itself felt instead. The reconstruction was completed only in 1767.

The Convent Church of the Augustine Missionaries of the Philippine Islands in Valladolid, for which Rodríguez prepared the design in 1760, is characterized by a clear and functional design and by a strictly classical articulation. This centralized building with a flat dome was given a divided lower and upper choir for liturgical reasons, and Rodriguez repeated this motif in several later buildings. The sanctuary itself was integrated into the block-like convent buildings, which present a slender but grand facade to the world. In the severity of the lines and the lack of all ornamentation, the design returns to indigenous Spanish tradition, particularly the architecture of Juan de Herrera.

A project for the Church of San Francisco el Grande in Madrid was rejected in 1761, to the extreme disappointment of Rodríguez and his followers. Rodríguez' design, inspired by St. Peter's in Rome, was a variant of projects for Madrid Cathedral, which had brought him membership in the Academia in 1746. However, a proposal by Francisco de la Cabezas was preferred for San Francisco el Grande, which led to the existing, rather squat, centralized building. The rejection was a further setback after the death of Ferdinand VI had meant the loss of Rodríguez' position at court, limiting the architect to private clients. His position at the Academy was not uncontested either, as is clear from the longlasting controversy with Diego and Juan de Villanueva.

The facade of Pamplona Cathedral (1783) is noteworthy among Ventura Rodríguez' late works. The monumental front, full of pathos, is set before the Gothic building. Projecting far from the central nave wall, its principal elements are two block-like towers and a portico with a triangular gable carried by four Corinthian double columns.

Rodríguez died in 1785, having paved the way for the absorption of classicism in Spain and prepared for the return to indigenous architectural traditions.

—BARBARA BORNGÄSSER KLEIN
Translated from the German by Marijke Rijsberman

ROEBLING, John and Washington.

ROEBLING, John Augustus.
American. Born in Muhlhausen, Thuringia, Germany, 12 June 1806. Died 22 July 1869. Son was Washington Augustus Roebling. Trained at the Royal Polytechnic Institute, Berlin, graduated 1826. Immigrated to the United States, 1831; settled in Pennsylvania. Worked as engineer for the state of Pennsylvania, 1837; invented the twisted-wire cable, 1841.

ROEBLING, Washington Augustus.
American. Born in Saxonburg, Pennsylvania, 26 May 1837. Died 21 July 1926. Father was John Augustus Roebling. Studied at the Rensselaer Polytechnic Institute. Worked at his father's wire factory in Trenton, New Jersey, and assisted in the construction of many bridges. Traveled in Europe, 1867-68. Associate, and later chief engineer, New York Bridge Company, from 1869.

Chronology of Works
All in the United States
John Roebling:

1844-45   Pennsylvania Canal Aqueduct, Allegheny River, Pennsylvania

John and Washington Roebling: Brooklyn Bridge, New York City, New York, 1867-83

1845-50   Rondout, Neversink, Delaware and Lackawaxen Aqueducts, Pennsylvania
1846   Smithfield Street Bridge, Monongahela River, Pittsburgh, Pennsylvania
1851-55   Niagara River Bridge, Niagara Falls, New York
1854   Bridge over the Ohio River, Wheeling, West Virginia (reconstruction)

John and Washington Roebling:

1857-60   6th Street Bridge, Allegheny River, Pittsburgh, Pennsylvania
1856-67   Cincinnati Bridge, Ohio River, Covington, Cincinnati
1867-83   Brooklyn Bridge, New York

Publications

BOOKS BY JOHN ROEBLING

Long and Short Span Railway Bridges. New York, 1869.

BOOKS ABOUT ROEBLING

BILLINGTON, DAVID P.: *The Tower and the Bridge: The New Art of Structural Engineering.* Princeton, New Jersey, 1983.

*

The principal and basic concept of bridge construction developed by John Roebling was that the transmission of all stresses of a continuous, elastic cable should run the length of a structure.

Although the method of suspension-bridge construction was achieved in the 19th century in Europe, it was the isolated genius of John, and later his son Washington, that lent an extra dimension to this type of daring bridge-building.

John came from Mühlhausen in Thuringia, Germany. In 1826 he received a civil engineering degree from the Royal Polytechnic Institute, Berlin. Through Professor Georg Friedrich Hegel, he became interested in metaphysics and wrote a thesis on the suspension bridge at nearby Bamberg, Bavaria.

In 1831 he and his brother Karl moved to the United States. They settled in Pennsylvania, where they took up farming. But agricultural life was not for John. His interests lay in other areas, and in 1837 he became an engineer for the state of Pennsylvania. His duties were to supervise and survey the building of dams, canals and their locks. That experience led to his invention of the twisted-wire cable in 1841. Eight years later, he opened a factory in Trenton, New Jersey, to manufacture this type of wire cable. Previously, wrought-iron chains had been used to support the decks of suspension bridges. The iron was too weak, however, and the wire cable proved to be strong and elastic under adverse conditions. Roebling first used it for a cable-suspension aqueduct for the Pennsylvania State Canal (1844-45), which spanned the Allegheny River. Its success led to four aqueducts erected between 1846 and 1850 over the Delaware and Hudson Canal, which crossed the Delaware River.

Roebling's reputation as a bridge engineer increased. He had a talent for designing large and daring spans over rivers. For example, in 1854 he redesigned Charles Ellet's damaged bridge that crossed the Ohio River at Wheeling, West Virginia. The concept was to create radiating stays that moved outward and downward from towers to points on the panel deck below. This foreshadowed his later aerodynamic devices for bridge stability. Some of his bridges, such as the one that spanned the Allegheny River at Pittsburgh (1857-60), could maintain railroad cars on the deck and still be stable.

The greatest challenge and project in his career occurred in 1856 when he became chief designer-engineer for a bridge to span the East River, connecting New York City to Brooklyn. Tragically, he died as a result of a foot infection before the bridge's completion in 1883. However, the Brooklyn Bridge remains a lasting testimonial to his knowledge of suspension-bridge construction utilizing the device of twisted-wire cable and radiating, interweaving cables suspended from its Gothic pointed towers to the deck below.

John Roebling also will be remembered as a theorist on bridge construction, because of his extensive writings. His treatise, *Long and Short Span Railroad Bridges* (1869), was written in an almost metaphysical manner, as it speculated on imaginary modes of suspension-bridge design.

John's son Washington was also a bridge designer. He attended Rensselaer Polytechnic Institute and initially worked at his father's wire factory in Trenton, New Jersey. By 1860 Washington was working with John on many bridge commissions. His career was interrupted by the Civil War when he, as a Union officer, supervised bridge construction over the Shenandoah and Rappahannock rivers. After the war, he rejoined his father and participated in the completion of the Cincinnati Bridge (1865-67).

After a brief European sojourn (1867-68), Washington became an assistant and later chief engineer for the New York Bridge Company. He took over his father's position in 1869 upon John's death. In 1872 Washington developed caisson disease as a result of being trapped in one of the underwater chamber piles of the Brooklyn Bridge.

During the remainder of his life (after the completion of the Brooklyn Bridge) he was president of his father's firms in New York and Trenton.

The work of John and Washington Roebling paved the way for further advances in wire-cable suspension-bridge construction. Especially through John's efforts, the so-called "long-span" bridge became a physical reality and earmark, if not symbol, of American architectural achievements, as the skyscraper had been in the late 19th century.

—GEORGE M. COHEN

ROGERS, Isaiah.

American. Born in Marshfield, Massachusetts, 19 August 1800. Died on 13 April 1869. Apprenticed to a carpenter, 1816; trained at Solomon Willard office, Boston. Established own firm, Boston, 1826; supervising architect of the United States Treasury, 1863.

Chronology of Works
All in the United States
† Work no longer exists

1822-24	Theater, Mobile, Alabama†
1826	Commercial Wharf, Boston, Massachusetts (since altered)
1826	Masonic Hall, Augusta, Georgia†
1827	Tremont Theater, Boston, Massachusetts†
1828-29	Tremont House, Boston, Massachusetts†
1829-30	Lowell Town House, Lowell, Massachusetts (since altered)
1833	First Parish Church, Cambridge, Massachusetts (alterations)
1833-34	Bangor House, Bangor, Maine (since altered)
1833-36	Suffolk Bank, Boston, Massachusetts†
1834-36	Astor House, New York City†
1835	Bank of America, New York City†
1836-38	Stephen Salisbury House, Worcester, Massachusetts
1836-42	Merchants' Exchange, New York City (since altered)
1837-39	Middle Collegiate Dutch Reformed Church, New York City†
1838-39	Merchants' Bank, New York City†
1839	Benjamin L. Swan House, New York City†
1839-40	Granary Burying Ground Gate and Fence, Boston, Massachusetts
1839-41	Exchange Hotel, Richmond, Virginia†
1840-41	Exchange Bank, Richmond, Virginia†
1840-42	Merchants' Exchange, Boston, Massachusetts†
1841-42	Jewish Cemetery, Newport, Rhode Island (gate and fence)
1842	Touro Synagogue, Newport, Rhode Island (gate and fence)
1843-44	Enoch Reddington Mudge Mansion, Swampscott, Massachusetts†
1844-45	Female Orphan Asylum, Boston, Massachusetts†
1844-45	Astronomical Observatory, Harvard University, Cambridge, Massachusetts (since altered)
1844-45	Quincy Town House, Quincy, Massachusetts
1846	Howard Athenaeum, Boston, Massachusetts†
1847	Astor Place Opera House, New York City†
1849-50	Commercial Bank, Cincinnati, Ohio
1849-50	Tyler Davidson Store, Cincinnati, Ohio†
1849-52	St. John's Episcopal Church, Cincinnati, Ohio†

1850-51	George Hatch Villa, Cincinnati, Ohio
1850-51	Winthrop B. Smith Villa, Cincinnati, Ohio†
1850-52	Phillips House (Hotel), Dayton, Ohio†
1850-56	Louisville Hotel, Louisville, Kentucky†
1851-52	Battle House, Mobile, Alabama†
1852-53	Capital Hotel, Frankfort, Kentucky†
1854	Metropolitan Hall, Chicago, Illinois†
1854	Newcomb Building, Louisville, Kentucky†
1855-56	Commercial Bank of Kentucky, Paducah, Kentucky†
1855-56	W. B. Reynolds Store, Louisville, Kentucky
1855-61	Hamilton County Courthouse, Cincinnati, Ohio (completion)†
1856	Louisville Medical Institute, Louisville, Kentucky†
1861	Hamilton County Jail, Cincinnati, Ohio
1858-61	Ohio State Capitol, Columbus, Ohio (completion)
1859-69	Maxwell House, Nashville, Tennessee†
1862-65	United States Treasury Building, Washington, D.C. (west wing)
1866	Pike's Opera House, Cincinnati, Ohio

Publications

BOOKS ABOUT ROGERS

ELIOT, WILLIAM HAVARD: *A Description of Tremont House.* Boston, 1830.

HAMLIN, TALBOT: *Greek Revival Architecture in America.* New York, 1944 (1964).

KILHAM, WALTER H.: *Boston After Bulfinch.* Cambridge, Massachusetts, 1946.

WILLIAMSON, JEFFERSON: *The American Hotel.* New York, 1930.

ARTICLES ABOUT ROGERS

MYERS, DENYS PETER: ''Isaiah Rogers in Cincinnati.'' *Bulletin of the Historical and Philosophical Society of Ohio* 9 (1951): 121-132.

MYERS, DENYS PETER: ''The Recently Discovered Diaries of Isaiah Rogers.'' *Columbia Library Columns* 16 (1966): 25-31.

*

Most American architects before the third quarter of the 19th century were largely self-taught, gradually learning the formal and theoretical aspects of their profession after mastering its techniques during an apprenticeship with members of the building trades. Few were as talented as Isaiah Rogers. Eleven years after apprenticing with the Boston housewright Jesse Shaw, Rogers designed the Tremont House, Boston's premier hotel, famous in America and Europe for its architectural stylishiness and multiple modern conveniences. Rogers' ambition to be a designer rather than a builder probably accounted for the four years of additional training he underwent with Solomon Willard from 1822 to 1826.

Like the majority of his contemporaries, Rogers' career encompassed proficiency in a wide range of building types, including residences, churches, warehouses, factories, theaters, an observatory and a hospital. He was best known among his contemporaries (and to posterity) as a designer of large and impressive business buildings: hotels, banks and merchants' exchanges. His principal works were clustered mainly around three urgan centers: Boston, New York and Cincinnati. The culmination of his career was a two-year appointment as supervising architect of the Treasury Department (1863-65), the second architect to hold that position.

Rogers practiced a form of historical eclecticism common during the first half of the 19th century in America, frequently choosing stylistic archetypes dependent on the function of the structure. Thus his First Parish Church (1833) in Cambridge, Massachusetts, was Gothic Revival and the Jew's Cemetery Gate (1841-42) in Newport, Rhode Island, was Egyptian Revival. He did not, however, adhere strictly to this historical associationism, as he used the Gothic Revival for a house for Enoch Mudge (1843-44) in Swampscott, Massachusetts, and a theater, the Howard Athenaeum (1846) in Boston.

Until the late 1840s Rogers' public works were characterized by a particularly bold and vigorous Greek Revival style, but during his last twenty years in practice his classically derived designs were in a restrained Italianate mode. This stylistic change coincided with Rogers' move to Cincinnati, the architecturally sophisticated center from which he produced numerous public and private structures in Ohio and Kentucky. During that period, when his commissions outstripped his ability to cope with them, he took Henry Whitestone as a partner (1853-57), his son Solomon Willard Rogers joined the firm in 1855, and Alfred Bult Mullett began his career as a draftsman in 1857, but left to establish his own practice five years later.

Rogers' career, developing from itinerant builder to director of a major architectural firm, and then appointment to the most significant position in public architecture in the country, was the archetypal American success story. Unlike many of his generation of American architects, Rogers never visited Europe. Without formal education or influential family, he achieved professional stature by hard work; his ability to think spatially and design sophisticated and elegantly complex buildings when there were few American examples to guide him bespeaks an unusual talent. His inventive architectural solutions to basic socially oriented problems (in his hotel designs) can probably be attributed to this relative aesthetic isolation.

It is tragic that so little of what he built survives, notwithstanding the solid granite construction of his major works. In 1909 McKim, Mead and White added two stories to his New York Merchants' Exchange, irrevocably altered the facade and destroyed the dome, but Rogers' twelve 30 foot, 8 inch Ionic monoliths (33 tons each) in Quincy granite still exist on Wall Street. The west wing of the U.S. Treasury Building in Washington, D.C. (1863-65), is his only monumental work to survive with integrity, but its exterior pattern had already been established by Thomas U. Walter and does not reflect Rogers' design ethos.

Rogers' reputation was established at the age of 30 upon completion of the Tremont House in 1830. At that stage in his career he showed a particular genius for resolving the inherent dichotomy between irregular sites, ordered and rational plans, and symmetrical elevations. His standard solution was to place a large open space at the core (a rectangular open courtyard at the Tremont House, a giant rotunda at the New York Merchants' Exchange), surround it with minor, irregularly shaped service areas (which might include courtyards and circulation spaces), and line the building's perimeters with a variety of regularly laid-out rooms. The main facade of the four-story, 170-room Tremont House had a two-story tetrastyle Doric portico as its major entrance, but four additional doors opened directly into two pairs of spacious double public rooms. The secondary facade had an entrance into the colonnaded dining room with windows overlooking Beacon Street and an interior garden court. Private hotel rooms disposed along double-loaded corridors above these public rooms were augmented by a third wing entirely given over to bedrooms, including luxurious suites of two and three rooms on the main story.

Modern amenities, such as interior plumbing (eight bathing rooms in the basement, privies in the courtyard and running water in each of the bedrooms), central heating, gas lighting (in public rooms only) and annunciator bells supplemented the large number of public rooms for the use of the hotel's patrons. No other hotel in the world offered this range of amenities. The Tremont House was the first of Rogers' eight hotels; New York's Astor House (1834-36) was the second. His last hotel, the Maxwell House in Nashville, was completed 35 years after the Tremont House.

Although the integration of plan and function of the Tremont House was masterful, its facade did not approach the architectural sophistication of the New York Merchants' Exchange, whose six years of design and construction (1836-42) Rogers oversaw daily. A giant colonnade of 12 Ionic colums above a full basement ranged across the main facade in the same manner as Robert Mills' contemporaneous Treasury Building in Washington, D.C. Both may have been influenced by Karl Friedrich Schinkel's Altes Museum (1824-30) in Berlin. Stairs to the main-story rotunda passed between the monolithic Quincy granite columns set on high plinths, an impressive and unusual entrance to the 80-foot rotunda, whose four sets of double Corinthian columns (41 feet tall in variegated Italian marble) set *in antis* recalled the Roman Pantheon. Rogers designed an iron dome, but it was built in brick, a double dome lit by a cupola framed in iron whose top was 124 feet above the subbasement.

The scale and spatial complexity of Rogers' works were matched by their forceful elegance, almost all unhappily superseded by later generations of American architecture.

—PAMELA SCOTT

ROGERS, Richard.

British. Born in Florence, Italy, of British parents, 23 July 1933. Married the architect Su Brumwell, 1960; Ruth Elias, 1973. Studied at the Architectural Association School, London, 1953-59, Dip.A.A.; Yale University School of Architecture, New Haven, Connecticut, M.Arch., 1962. Served in the British Army, 1951-53. Partner, with Norman and Wendy Foster: Norman Foster, and Su Rogers, Team 4, London, 1963-68, and Richard and Su Rogers, London, 1968-70; partner with Renzo Piano, London, Paris, and Genoa, 1970; chairman, Richard Rogers Architects, London. Royal Institute of British Architects Gold Medal, 1985. Knighted.

Chronology of Works
All in England unless noted

1967	Reliance Controls Ltd. Electrical Factory, Swindon, Wiltshire
1968	Spender House, Utting, Essex (with Su Rogers)
1968	House for Rogers' parents, Wimbledon (with Su Rogers)
1971-77	Centre National d'Art et de Culture Georges Pompidou (Centre Beaubourg), Paris, France (with Renzo Piano and Sir Ove Arup and Partners)
1975	PA Technology Centre Research Laboratories, Workshops and Ancillary Administration Building, near Cambridge (with Renzo Piano)
1978-86	Lloyd's of London Headquarters, London
1985-88	Securities Market, Citibank, Billingsgate, London
1986-	Office Development, World Trade Centre, London
1986-87	Commercial Centre, Nantes, France
1987-88	Reuters Docklands Building and Recreational Facility, London

Publications

BOOKS BY ROGERS

The Building of Beaubourg. With Renzo Piano and others. London, 1979.
Architecture: A Modern View. London, 1990.

BOOKS ABOUT ROGERS

APPLEYARD, BRYAN: *Richard Rogers: A Biography*. London, 1986.
Global Architects 44: Centre Beaubourg. Tokyo, 1977.
COLE, BARBIE CAMPBELL (ed.): *Richard Rogers and Architects*. 1985.
DAVIES, COLIN: *High Tech Architecture*. New York, 1988.
SUCKLE, ABBY: *By Their Own Design*. London, 1980.
SUDJIC, DEYAN: *Norman Foster, Richard Rogers, James Stirling: New Directions in British Architecture*. London, 1986.

ARTICLES ABOUT ROGERS

''Architects' Architecture.'' *Architects' Journal* (28 January 1981).
''Billingsgate Joins Office Space Pool.'' *Building Design* (5 June 1981).
''Centre du plateau Beaubourg: concours d'idées.'' Special issue of *Techniques et architecture* (February 1972).
''Centre Pompidou.'' *Architectural Design* 2 (1977).
''Lloyd's Logic.'' *Building* (February 1980).
''Napp Laboratories, Cambridge.'' *Architecture d'aujourd'hui* (June 1982).
''Piano and Rogers: Architectural Method.'' *Architecture and Urbanism* (June 1976).
''Piano and Rogers: Centre Beaubourg.'' *Architectural Design* (July 1972).
''Piano and Rogers.'' *Architectural Design* 5 (1975).
''Piano and Rogers.'' *Architects' Journal* (21 April 1972).
''Piano and Rogers—Beaubourg.'' *Domus* (October 1971).
''RIBA Discourse.'' *Royal Institute of British Architects Journal* (January 1977).
''Richard Rogers: Interview with Dennis Sharp.'' *Building* (6 April 1979).
''Rogers: Ideal Site.'' *Architects' Journal* (30 January 1980).
''Six British Architects.'' *Architectural Design* 12 (1981).
''Richard Rogers, 1978-88.'' *Architecture and Urbanism* (December 1988).

*

Born in 1933 of English and Italian parentage, Richard Rogers is leader of the architectural movement known as ''hi-tech'' and one of the most important British architects of the late 20th century. His best-known buildings are the Centre Pompidou in Paris and Lloyd's of London.

The completion of an industrial building for Reliance Controls in Swindon in 1967 marked the arrival of a new hard-edged and very competent generation on the English architectural scene. Intellectually and structurally rigorous, it had none of the empiricism and sloppy thinking that characterized English architecture at the time. Just as the critics were deciding that the

Richard Rogers: Centre Georges Pompidou, Paris, France, 1971-77

Modern Movement was played out, here was a stylish modern building by confident young architects who knew where they were going. The architects were called Team 4, and the four included Norman Foster and Richard Rogers, who had already worked together as students at Yale. The previous generation of English modernists had looked to Europe, but with Foster and Rogers the American influence was predominant—the America of Ludwig Mies van der Rohe, of Charles Eames, of the Case Study Houses of California and of Ezra Ehrenkranz's Californian schools.

Reliance Controls was a simple, straightforward steel building, with a Miesian steel frame, but it had diagonal bracing like the Eames House, and the beams projected beyond the columns to imply the possibility of extension. Internally, office space and industrial space were identical in an idealistic and egalitarian program. The white frame and the beautiful proportions set it apart from other industrial buildings.

After Reliance Controls Team 4 broke up. Richard Rogers and his wife Sue designed two houses that developed the big-span, low-building theme of Reliance. The Spender House at Utting in Essex, finished in 1968, has a small house and an artist's studio facing one another across a courtyard; 14-meter-span portals bridge both the house and the studio, spanning each in the long direction. At the same time, a house for Richard Rogers' parents was built in London's suburb of Wimbledon, and there a technological jump was made from the corrugated metal siding used at Swindon and Utting to prefabricated sandwich panels with plastic-coated aluminum facing and neoprene gasket jointing. Rogers' fascination with the cutting edge of advanced building technology was clearly revealed.

There were lean years after the two houses, and then Rogers, teamed up with the Italian Renzo Piano, won the international competition for the Centre Pompidou in Paris. This brought world fame and years of hard work to see the building through to completion in 1977. No other 20th-century building has made so many leaps forward, both technically and intellectually. Probably only relatively young and inexperienced architects would have dared so much—older and more knowledgeable designers would have been frightened off by the difficulties. The building was brought through to its triumphant realization, and its successful impact on the surrounding area set the designers off in a new direction as urban designers. Richard Rogers followed up this direction in his designs for Coin Street and the spectacular Thames Bridge project of 1986, linking London's South Bank with the West End in a series of urban gestures that the capital had not seen since John Nash in the early 19th century.

While the Centre Pompidou was under construction, Piano and Rogers built the first phase of their PA Technology Centre at Melbourn, south of Cambridge. A simple, infinitely changeable building, it had clean, simple facades but an open undercroft, where air-conditioning trunking and other services were joyfully exposed. Centre Pompidou had been a one-off, but at Melbourn the designers proved that they could tackle a routine building type with the same élan.

The new headquarters for Lloyd's of London, completed in 1986, gave Richard Rogers and Partners the chance to build a major urban building within the tight urban grain of the city of London. The building required a vast "Room" for the underwriters, and the solution was to place the largest rectangular room possible on the site and to place staircases, lavatories and service runs in all the leftover spaces around this rectangle. This completely reversed the central-core concept of most modern office buildings, and gave the office a startling new image with lifts and pipes on display so that it was compared, in the popular mind, to an oil refinery. But its very complexity enabled it to sit well in its traditional setting, and the quality of materials and workmanship enabled a conservative client to make it their home.

Lloyd's is, perhaps, the culmination of hi-tech. The Richard Rogers Partnership followed it with a beautifully crafted restoration job at Billingsgate Market, and then subsequently, designs for office buildings on a more modest scale than Lloyd's, at the World Trade Centre opposite the Tower of London and on Grosvenor Road on the North Bank of the Thames. These designs are much less flamboyant than the Centre Pompidou or Lloyd's, and are concerned with sensitively inserting modern buildings into the urban fabric.

The late 1980s in England saw the great debate with Prince Charles attacking modern buildings, good or bad, and making a plea for a return to past styles. The prince used public speeches, television and a book to deliver this message. Many architects lost their nerve under this media onslaught, but Richard Rogers stood firm, answering the prince with his own television program and becoming the mouthpiece for modern architects. This has made him, more than any other architect, a well-known personality with the public at large in the United Kingdom.

—JOHN WINTER

RONDELET, Jean-Baptiste.

French. Born in Lyons, France, 4 June 1734. Died in Paris, 26 September 1829. Studied under Jacques-François Blondel, Paris, 1763. Worked as technical adviser to Jacques-Germain Soufflot at Ste. Geneviève (now the Pantheon), Paris, from 1770; Inspector of Works, Pantheon, 1806-12. Founding member, Commission des Travaux Publics, 1793-94; founding member, Conseil des Bâtiments Civils, from 1795. Created the École Centrale des Travaux Publics (later the École Polytechnique), Pari s, 1795. Taught at the École des Beaux-Arts; inducted into the Institut, 1815.

Publications

BOOKS BY RONDELET

Mémoire sur l'architecture considérée généralment, avec des observations sur l'administration relative à cet art, et le projet d'une école pratique qui serait chargée de tous les ouvrages publics. Paris, 1789-90.
Prospectus d'un traité théorique et pratique sur l'art de bâtir... sollicitant une place à l'Institut. Paris, 1799.
Traité théorique et pratique de l'art de bâtir. 7 vols. Paris, 1802-17.
Commentaire de S. J. Frontin sur les aqueducs de Rome: Traduit du latin avec le texte en regard . . . suivi de la description des principaux aqueducs construits jusqu'à nos jours. Paris, 1820.
Notice historique sur l'église de Sainte-Geneviève. Paris, 1852.

ARTICLES BY RONDELET

Articles in Vols. 1 and 2 in ANTOINE CHRYSOSTHEME QUATREMERE DE QUINCY (ed.): *Encyclopédie méthodique.* Paris, 1788-1820.

BOOKS ABOUT RONDELET

CHEVALIER, PIERRE, and RABREAU, DANIEL: *Le Panthéon.* Paris, 1977.
MATHIEU, MAE: *Pierre Patte: sa vie et son oeuvre.* Paris, 1940.

ARTICLES ABOUT RONDELET

MATHUSEK-BAUDOUIN, MARIE NOELLE: "Biographie de Jean Rondelet." In *Soufflot et son temps.* Paris, 1980.

Despite the relative paucity of built works attributed to him, Jean-Baptiste Rondelet occupies a central position in the history of architecture by virtue of the immense popularity of his treatise, and the broad scope of his powers as member of the government architectural administration in the decades surrounding the French Revolution. Due to the highly practical cast of his *Traité théorique et pratique de l'art de bâtir* (1802-17), and to the technical nature of the expertise he brought to his major building commission, the Pantheon in Paris, Rondelet has often been regarded as a technician among artists, the engineer of the late neoclassical architectural world. However, close scrutiny of his writings and of his diverse contributions to French architecture as government architect reveal the inaccuracy of portraying Rondelet as an augur of the 19th-century split between design and construction (between architecture and engineering). To the contrary, he should be regarded as one of the last and most vociferous advocates of the integration of both realms of knowledge within the single practitioner.

Rondelet challenged what he perceived as an emphasis on "decoration" within the state-sponsored architecture of his time (which, in the hierarchical system of the Académie and Bâtiments du Roi, amounted to virtually all public architecture), arguing that beauty in architecture did not proceed simply from the judicious application of "the orders" or reside in the "paper architecture" pictures premiated by the Académie. According to Rondelet, beauty should emerge rather as the logical result of a rigorous analysis of the functional and constructional problems posed by a given project. Convinced that the latter in particular had been woefully neglected by his compatriots, Rondelet undertook to write a comprehensive treatise on the structural and material bases of architecture. In so doing Rondelet was not arguing a privileged position for the "firmitas" element of the traditional Vitruvian triad of firmness, utility and delight. Rather he was seeking to redress an imbalance caused by a century of superficial striving for a poorly understood "venustas." This was evident in Rondelet's fund-raising appeal to the government, in which he made his case for an expensive "theoretical and practical treatise on the art of building." "I am far from believing that the study of construction alone is sufficient for an architect, for a building can be neither convenient nor attractive despite being very sound and expensively built," he wrote. However, he observed, this particular flaw was rare in contemporary architecture, where it was more common that a "beautiful" exterior would conceal both awkward distribution and unstable structure. Rondelet blamed the government, which devalued the technical education of architects by awarding prizes and encouragements to "extraordinary and often inexecutable projects" by architects preoccupied with decoration, to the utter neglect of function, expense and solidity. His treatise, which the government did initially agree to underwrite, despite later reneging for lack of funds, was a bid for balance, for the reinsertion of technique at the core of the artistic process.

Rondelet's understanding of the technical aspects of architecture was not narrowly conceived, embracing as it did both the "theory" and the practice of the builder's art. In his treatise he gave equal weight to each, presenting both scientific principles and the methods they generate. Rondelet's own experience as inspector of the works at the Pantheon provided him with a wealth of real-life examples of design and construction problems posed and solved. The Pantheon project fueled his special interest in the science of materials as well: Rondelet's sophisticated analyses of the strengths of materials (based on testing mechanisms of his own design) and their optimal combination in construction constitute perhaps the most original and influential contributions made in the treatise. The same research that allowed Rondelet in the 1790s to diagnose the highly publicized cracking of the piers of the Paris Pantheon as a materials problem (thus not a flaw in Jacques-Germain Soufflot's design—negligent workers, he charged, had improperly combined internal mortar and wooden components) led him to question rather heretically the structural instincts of past luminaries from Palladio and Michelangelo to the architects of the Parthenon. In the concise "history of architecture" with which Rondelet introduced his treatise, he identified in both ancient Greek temples and the dome of St. Peter's in Rome the same fatal flaw—improper use of materials. The ancient Greeks, he argued, consigned themselves to a spatial and structural dead-end by emulating in stone an architecture conceived in wood. The Romans, on the other hand, he congratulated for devising an architecture in perfect accord with the strengths and nature of the materials available.

Given that Rondelet regarded structural sophistication as prerequisite for aesthetic success, one is not surprised by his appreciation for Gothic architecture. Rondelet operated well within the prevailing neoclassical mode of the day, in his practice and in his role as architectural adviser to the government. But like his mentor Soufflot, Rondelet found much to admire and to extract from the medieval past. Again the science of materials served as Rondelet's yardstick. To explain the "surprising" and "unheard of" effects attained by Gothic architects, Rondelet invoked their genius for "recognizing and assigning to each material" the role appropriate to its capacities, to yield the most durable result. If this appreciation seems to presage the analyses of Eugène-Emmanuel Viollet-le-Duc, Rondelet's patriotic conclusions confirm the parallel: "One cannot help but be saddened to see abandoned today a constructional system that was so well suited to the resources and nature of our climate."

Rondelet's attitudes toward the architecture of the past and his opinions on its current condition were relevant to a larger audience than that of his own clients and students. As a member of every successive architectural administration from the early days of the French Revolution to the apogee of Napoleon's Empire, Rondelet ruled, in concert with his colleagues in the inner circle, on every public project proposed in France. Rondelet was a founding member of the two revolutionary architectural administrations that replaced the abolished Bâtiments du Roi (the Commission des Travaux Publiques, 1793-94, and the Conseil des Bâtiments Civils, founded 1795). He participated in the creation of the École Centrale des Travaux Publiques (later the École Polytechnique) in 1795, taught at the École des Beaux-Arts, and was honored with induction into the Institut National des Sciences et des Arts in 1815. From this standpoint, Rondelet's was one of the most successful of late-18th-century careers. By negotiating the treacherous territory between royal, revolutionary and imperial systems of governance, he assured a measure of continuity within a profession in crisis, and went on to influence directions taken in the architecture of the 19th century.

—LAUREN M. O'CONNELL

ROOT, John Wellborn.

American. Born in Lumpkin, Georgia, 10 January 1850. Died 15 January 1891. Studied at Oxford College, England; graduated, City College, New York, 1869. Employed by James Renwick; employed by James Snook, Brooklyn, New York; partner, Carter, Drake and Wight firm, Chicago; partner, with Daniel H. Burnham, Burnham and Root, Chicago, 1873; consulting architect, World's Columbian Exposition, Chicago, 1890.

Chronology of Works
All in the United States
† *Work no longer exists*

1874	Sherman House, Chicago, Illinois†
1880-81	Grannis Block, Chicago†
1881-82	Montauk Building, Chicago†
1882-83	Chicago, Burlington, and Quincy General Office Building, Chicago†
1883-86	Rialto Building, Chicago†
1884-85	Insurance Exchange Building, Chicago†
1884-90	Monadnock Building, Chicago (not completed until 1892)
1885-87	Phenix Building, Chicago†
1885-87	Art Institute (later the Chicago Club), Chicago†
1885-88	The Rookery, Chicago (interior light court redesigned by Frank Lloyd Wright in 1905)
1886-87	St. Gabriel's, Chicago
1886-87	Pickwick Flats, Chicago†
1886-88	Board of Trade Building, Kansas City, Missouri†
1887-88	Lake View Presbyterian Church, Chicago†
1887-90	Society for Savings, Cleveland, Ohio
1888-90	Rand-McNally Building, Chicago†
1889-90	Edward H. Valentine House, Chicago†
1889-91	Chicago (Great Northern) Hotel, Chicago†
1889-91	Reliance Building, Chicago (completed according to revised designs by Charles B. Atwood in 1894-95)
1890-91	Masonic Temple, Chicago† (not completed until 1892)
1890-91	Mills Building, San Francisco, California (not completed until 1892)
1890-91	Union Depot, Keokuk, Iowa
1890-91	Woman's Building, Chicago (not completed until 1892)†

Publications

BOOKS BY ROOT

The Meanings of Architecture: Buildings and Writings by John Wellborn Root. Edited by Donald Hoffmann. New York, 1967.

BOOKS ABOUT ROOT

CONDIT, CARL W.: *The Chicago School of Architecture: A History of Commercial and Public Building in the Chicago Area, 1875-1925.* Chicago, 1964.
HINES, THOMAS S.: *Burnham of Chicago: Architect and Planner.* New York, 1974.
HITCHCOCK, HENRY-RUSSELL: *Modern Architecture: Romanticism and Reintegration.* New York, 1929.
HOFFMANN, DONALD: *The Architecture of John Wellborn Root.* Baltimore, 1973.
MONROE, HARRIET: *John Wellborn Root: A Study of His Life and Work.* Boston and New York, 1896.

SCHUYLER, MONTGOMERY: *American Architecture and Other Writings*. Edited by William H. Jordy and Ralph Coe. Cambridge, Massachusetts, 1891; 1961.

TALLMADGE, THOMAS E.: *Architecture in Old Chicago*. Chicago, 1941.

ARTICLES ABOUT ROOT

EATON, LEONARD K.: "John Wellborn Root and the Julian M. Case House." *Prairie School Review* 9 (1972): 18-22.

HOFFMANN, DONALD: "John Root's Monadnock Building." *Journal of the Society of Architectural Historians* 26 (1967): 269-277.

OVERBY, OSMUND R.: "Monadnock Block." Unpublished report, Washington, D. C. (1963).

OVERBY, OSMUND R.: "Rookery Building." Unpublished report, Washington, D. C. (1963).

REBORI, A. N.: "The Work of Burnham & Root, D. H. Burnham & Co. and Graham, Burnham & Co." *Architectural Record* 38, No. 1 (July (1915): 32-168.

ROBERTSON, THOMAS BURNS: "John Wellborn Root, Architect (1850-1891)." Unpublished M. A. thesis. New York University, 1942.

STARRETT, THEODORE: "John Wellborn Root." *Architects' and Builders' Magazine* 13 (1912): 429-431.

*

John Wellborn Root was one of the most inventive American architects at the end of the 19th century, combining artistic sensitivity to form and detail with ingenuity in solving technical problems generated by the new tall office building.

Root's father, Thomas, an aspiring architect as a child, was a native of Vermont who, in midlife, moved to Lumpkin, Georgia. There he operated a dry-goods store and married Permelia Wellborn. The boy's artistic talents emerged early, for John was a precocious musician and artist. When the family moved to Atlanta, Georgia, the boy was given a special studio room. During the Civil War, John was sent to Liverpool, England, to stay with business friends of his father's; there he continued his studies, especially in music. At the end of the war, when John returned home, the family moved to New York City and John entered the University of the City of New York, studying engineering; he graduated in 1869. Since there was, as yet, no architecture school in the United States, Root entered the architectural office of James Renwick, where he studied for a year. He then obtained a job in the office of architect John Butler Snook, who was then building the old Grand Central Station in New York City, with its attached huge shed over the tracks built of light metal trusses and glass. Root's drawings were seen by Peter Bonnet Wight, formerly of New York, but then in Chicago and in partnership with Asher Carter and William H. Drake. Following the disastrous fire in Chicago in 1871, the volume of new construction prompted Wight to invite Root to Chicago to become head draftsman in the office of Carter, Drake and Wight.

In Wight's office Root met another young draftsman, Daniel Hudson Burnham, with whom he felt a special affinity. In 1873 Burnham and Root left to establish their own independent practice, but they received few commissions because a severe economic depression was beginning that lasted until 1878. By working for other architects to pay the rent, and with Root's earnings as organist at the First Presbyterian Church, they survived that difficult period. In 1874 they made the acquaintance of John B. Sherman, an influential businessman, and for him they built a residence that same year. Comparatively restrained

in form and detail, unlike so much of Chicago's florid postfire architecture, that house began to establish the firm's reputation.

In 1880 Root formed an acquaintance with Owen Aldis, a lawyer and agent for Peter and Shepard Brooks of Boston. Aldis managed investment properties for the Brooks brothers, initiating and supervising new commissions for them. Impressed by Root, Aldis gave the firm the commission for a simple office structure, the Grannis Block (1880-81). The straightforward expression of the structural red-brick piers, and the simple integrated floral motifs in matching terra-cotta, revealed Root's debt to Wight's emphasis on structure and to his own reading of French theorist Eugène-Emmanuel Viollet-le-Duc. In the next decade Root became an avid student of other theorists such as Edward Garbett and Gottfried Semper.

In 1881 the Brookses had Burnham and Root design the even simpler and more cost-effective Montauk Block (1881-82). The size of this heavy masonry office block, and the weak bearing capacity of the underlying marshy soil, led Root to develop a radically new foundation type, using a flat grillage of steel railroad rails encased in concrete to spread out the weight and still leave open usable space in the basement. This "floating raft" technique was quickly adopted by other Chicago architects.

Following those early successes, the firm was deluged with commissions for residences, clubhouses, office blocks and railroad stations. These included buildings for the Burlington Railroad and the Santa Fe Railroad as far away as Topeka, Kansas, and a large tourist resort hotel outside Las Vegas, New Mexico. By 1884 the firm's office buildings were reaching 10 stories, and in their outer brick walls Root was clearly seeking an ordered hierarchy inspired in part by the grouping of round-headed Romanesque arches as employed by Boston architect Henry Hobson Richardson (1838-86). A good example is Root's Insurance Exchange Building (1884-85). In 1884 Root made a decisive design innovation, collecting all the intermediate floors of the McCormick Harvesting Machine Company Building (1884-86) into a tall arcade, thus reducing the six-floor facade to three essential parts: a single-story base set off by a strong horizontal cornice, a midsection of four floors merged in the tall brick arcades, and a terminating attic story capped by a heavy corbeled cornice. The impact of this on Richardson, who visited Chicago in 1885, has never been properly evaluated. Even so, the reverse impact of the decorative qualities of Richardson's work on Root was also strong, as is evident in his Art Institute Building, Chicago (1885-87).

The limits caused by the sheer weight and mass of solid masonry construction were quickly becoming apparent to Root. In the long and narrow Phoenix Building (1885-87), Root employed a light metal skeleton for the inside wall, allowing it to be opened up for the maximum use of glass. The best expression of the use of a metal skeleton was in the firm's masterwork of the mid-1880s, the Rookery Building (1885-88), also built for the Brooks brothers. Almost square in plan, and situated at a most important corner in the financial district of Chicago, it has massive stone, brick and terra-cotta structural piers on the outer walls carrying metal lintels, but the rear walls and the walls of the broad inner light court are carried entirely by a metal skeleton resting on broad "floating raft" foundations. The Rookery was quickly acclaimed a great artistic and structural success.

There followed another rush of commissions for apartment blocks, churches, residences and office blocks, including three major buildings in Kansas City, Missouri. Altogether, it has been estimated that in their 14 years of practice, Burnham and Root handled 356 commissions—an average of more than two buildings a month. Particularly interesting among their smaller works of that period was the Lake View Presbyterian Church

(1887-88), covered entirely in wooden shingles. An important office block was the square, 10-story tower of the Society for Savings, Cleveland, Ohio (1887-90), lit by a wide light court open down through its center and covered by a rooftop skylight. This theme was repeated and improved in the Rand-McNally Building, Chicago (1888-90), in which the thin facade piers clearly revealed the presence of the inner steel skeleton. Not only was this the first of the firm's buildings to be entirely supported by a metal frame, but the frame was made entirely of steel. The Rand-McNally Building opened up a broad inner light court, with a skylight over the ground-floor lobby. On its exterior, Root began to develop a more truly personal decorative style, less indebted to Richardson.

The transition from masonry bearing walls to all-metal framing, and what this meant regarding costs and the density of the outer wall, was dramatically illustrated in two of Root's buildings completed almost simultaneously in the 1890s, the Monadnock and Reliance buildings. The first of the two, the Monadnock (1884-92), was another commission from the Brooks brothers. Root began as early as the spring of 1884, but construction was put off until economic conditions improved. The client's instructions were clear: because the site was quite narrow, the building was to be an extremely tall 16 stories; at the insistence of Shepard Brooks, too, the outer walls were to be of solid brick; and ornament was to be most severely restrained. As a result of these design limitations, Root developed a slim design, adapted from an Egyptian pylon, devoid of all projecting ornament. Construction was finally begun in mid-1890 and finished in 1892. Because of the Brookses' conditions, the brick walls had to be made six feet thick at the base where rental shop space was at a premium.

In 1889, while plans for the Monadnock were being completed, Root began designs for the radically different Reliance Building (1889-90, 1894-95) for William E. Hale. Hale envisioned a slender office tower of 15 stories on the small corner lot he owned, but he decided in favor of the new steel framing. This meant that at the ground floor Root was able to open up extremely broad plate-glass display windows, with the steel columns encased in the slenderest panels of granite (although since "modernized," the slender supports are still visible). The upper portions of the building, not completed until 1894-95, have columns encased in slender blocks of white-glazed terracotta designed by Charles B. Atwood, who replaced Root after his untimely death.

The last year of Root's life was extremely busy, for he was not only writing and delivering papers elaborating his design philosophy, but also carrying on his most important commissions, while starting several even larger and more unusual office buildings. One of the latter was the building for the Women's Christian Temperance Union, Chicago (1890-92), a large 12-story block, H-shaped in plan, providing a light court facing the street, and terminating in multistory, tall, hipped roofs punctuated by numerous dormers. The second major building begun that year was the Masonic Temple (1890-92), which filled an entire block and rose to the unprecedented height of 20 stories, topping out at 302 feet. Neither of these survives, but fortunately another of Root's last works does, the massive 10-story block of the Mills Building, San Francisco, California (1890-92), whose three-part facade demonstrates Root's success in designing the first of America's skyscrapers, and which has successfully demonstrated Root's engineering skill by riding out two major earthquakes.

Root, like his contemporary H. H. Richardson, died at the height of his artistic powers. When he died, Root had just begun work on the planning and buildings for the World's Columbian Exposition to be held in 1893. Jackson Park on Chicago's South Side had been selected for the fair site, when, in August 1890, Root was appointed consulting architect for the fair and began sketching out ideas for a great basin of water surrounded by exhibition buildings. A month later, Root's individual appointment was rescinded, and instead the firm of Burnham and Root was appointed consulting architect. As the scope of the gigantic exhibition made it unfeasible for one office to design everything, Burnham recommended that 10 architectural firms from the East and Midwest be selected to design the most important buildings, with Burnham and Root designing the numerous auxiliary buildings. Because the New York architects were apprehensive about the whole undertaking, Root agreed to meet with them on a trip east. He mailed the easterners a sketch of the ground plan in late December 1890, met with them in New York a few days later, traveled on to Atlanta, Georgia, to meet with clients, and returned to Chicago in January 1891, exhausted. The eastern architects had just assembled in the office of Burnham and Root in the Rookery to make final plans for the buildings. Root could not conclude the deliberations, however, for he contracted pneumonia and died only days later, on 15 January.

The buildings on which Root was at work were completed by Charles B. Atwood (1848-95), who was hastily taken on as Root's replacement, and Atwood designed many of the auxiliary buildings of the Columbian Exposition. The experience of the fair and Atwood's presence changed the character of the firm, and thereafter Burnham's work underwent a dramatic shift toward academic classicism.

John Wellborn Root's accomplishment lay in his ability to meet the stringent and exacting demands of his businessmen clients, to develop innovative technical solutions to the problems of building ever higher on Chicago's unstable soil, and to shape a visually engaging envelope around his metal skeletons, inside and out, that drew some inspiration from the past but became increasingly original. A student of contemporary architectural theory, he was also an able speaker and persuasive writer, making clear the basis of his design decisions. He set about shaping a style that grew out of his own times and its conditions; his artistic celebration of untrammeled mercantile capitalism has never really been surpassed.

—LELAND M. ROTH

ROSSELLINO, Bernardo.

Italian. Born Matteo Gamberelli, in Settignano, near Florence, Italy, in 1409. Died in Florence, 23 November 1464. Trained as a stonemason. Worked in Florence until 1451, then traveled to Rome to assist in the revitalization of the city under Pope Nicholas V. Returned to Florence, then engaged in the rebuilding of Pienza under Pope Pius II, from 1459.

Chronology of Works
All in Italy
* Approximate dates

1433-35	Fraternità di Santa Maria della Misericordia, Arezzo (facade)
1436-38	Cloister, The Badia, Florence (with others)
1446	Sala del Consistoro, Palazzo Pubblico, Siena (portal)
1446-48	Tomb of Leonardo Bruni, Santa Croce, Florence (triumphal arch)
1448-52	Palazzo Rucellai, Florence (core and courtyard)
1448-52	Spinelli Cloister, Santa Croce, Florence
1453	Santo Stefano Rotondo, Rome (renovation)
1457-64	San Miniato ai Monte, Florence (renovations)

Bernardo Rossellino: Palazzo Piccolomini, Rebuilding of Pienza, Pienza, Italy, 1459-64

Publications

BOOKS ABOUT ROSSELLINO

CARLI, ENZO: *Pienza, la città di Pio II*. Siena, 1966.
FINELL, LUCIANA: *L'umanesimo giovane: Bernardo Rossellino
a Roma e a Pienza*. Rome, 1984.
HARTT, FREDERICK; CORTI, GINO; and KENNEDY, CLARENCE:
*The Chapel of the Cardinal of Portugal, 1434-1459, at San
Miniato in Florence*. Philadelphia, 1964.
MACK, CHARLES R.: *Pienza: The Creation of a Renaissance
City*. Ithaca, New York, and London, 1987.
PLANISCIG, LEO: *Bernardo und Antonio Rossellino*. Vienna,
1942.
SCHULZ, ANNE MARKHAM: *The Sculpture of Bernardo Rossel-
lino and His Workshop*. Princeton, New Jersey, 1976.
TYSKIEWICZ, MARYLA: *Bernardo Rossellino*. Florence, 1929.

ARTICLES ABOUT ROSSELLINO

FABRICZY, CORNELIUS VON: "Ein Jugendwerk Bernardo Ros-
sellinos und spätere unbeachtete Schöpfungen seines Meis-
sels." *Jahrbuch der königlich preussischen Kunstsammlungen* 21 (1900): 33-54, 99-113.
HEYDENREICH, LUDWIG H.: "Pius II als Bauherr von Pienza."
Zeitschrift für Kunstgeschichte 6 (1937): 105-146.
MACK, CHARLES R.: "Bernardo Rossellino, L. B. Alberti and
the Rome of Pope Nicholas V." *Southeastern College Art
Conference Review* 10 (1982): 60-69.
MACK, CHARLES R.: "Building a Florentine Palace: The Pa-
lazzo Spinelli." *Mitteilungen des Kunsthistorischen Instituts
in Florenz* 27 (1983): 261-284.
MACK, CHARLES R.: "Nicholas V and the Rebuilding of Rome:
Reality and Legacy." Pp. 31-56 in HELLMUT HAGER and
SUSAN S. MUNSHOWER (eds.): *Light on the Eternal City:
Recent Observations and Discoveries in Roman Art and
Architecture*. University Park, Pennsylvania, 1987.
MACK, CHARLES R.: "Notes Concerning an Unpublished Win-
dow by Bernardo Rossellino at the Badia Fiorentina." *South-
eastern College Art Conference Review* 5 (December 1970):
2-5.
MACK, CHARLES R.: "The Rucellai Palace: Some New Propos-
als." *Art Bulletin* 56 (1974): 517-529.
PREYER, BRENDA: "The Rucellai Palace." Pp. 155-228 in F.
W. KENT, et al.: *Giovanni Rucellai ed il suo Zibaldone, II:
A Florentine Patrician and His Palace*. London, 1981.
SAALMAN, HOWARD: "Tommaso Spinelli, Michelozzo, Ma-
netti and Rossellino." *Journal of the Society of Architectural
Historians* 25, No. 3 (1966): 151-164.

SALMI, MARIO: ''Bernardo Rossellino ad Arezzo.'' In MARIA DUPRE DAL POGGETTO and PAOLO DAL POGGETTO (eds.): *Scritti di storia dell'arte in onore di Ugo Proacci.* Milan, 1977.

SANPAOLESI, PIERO: ''Costruzioni del prima quattrocento nella badia Fiorentina.'' *Rivista d'arte* Series 2, 24 (1942): 143-179.

SANPAOLESI, PIERO: ''Precisazioni sul Palazzo Rucellai.'' *Palladio* New Series 13 (1963): 61-66.

*

Bernardo di Matteo Gamberelli, called Rossellino, was born near Florence in the village of Settignano. His father was a quarry owner, and Bernardo and his brothers (Antonio, Giovanni and Domenico) were all trained as stonemasons. There is no record of the master to whom Bernardo Rossellino was apprenticed, and his real teacher seems to have been the experimental atmosphere of Florence in the mid-1420s.

Learning both carving and construction, Rossellino appears to have been captivated by the ''new-wave'' approaches being developed by Filippo Brunelleschi, Donatello, Lorenzo Ghiberti and Masaccio. Perhaps more faithfully than their other followers, Rossellino held true to a classical commitment and assumed a position of leadership in promulgating the sculptural and architectural vocabulary of the Roman revival. Celebrated as a sculptor (the Leonardo Bruni Tomb, the Empoli Annunciation Group, the San Egidio tabernacle), Rossellino gained particular distinction through his expanding role as an architect, achieving lasting fame in this area for his work in Rome under Pope Nicholas V and for the rebuilding of the city of Pienza for Pope Pius II. Part of his artistic importance lay in his entrepreneurial skills, through which he was able to assemble a large and highly successful workshop that dominated the stoneworking field in Florence during the 1450s and 1460s.

Rossellino's personal devotion to ''new-wave classicism'' can be seen in his first commission, at the Misericordia Palace in Arezzo (1433-35). Facing much the same situation as Leon Battista Alberti was to encounter at Santa Maria Novella two decades later, Rossellino and his associates wedded a modern upper story to a Gothic lower in a deft, if still awkward, combination of sculpture and architectural elements, drawn from the most progressive sources available. In his ability to appropriate and reshape the contributions of others, Rossellino displayed a characteristic brand of creative eclecticism which became a hallmark of his style.

Rossellino was back in Florence in 1436 to establish his own workshop and to join a crew of stonemasons then at work at the Aranci Cloister of the Badia. His principal contributions (1436-38) to this project included a handsome door frame and an unusual cross window. He also may have suggested the use of the pilaster strips which, modeled after Brunelleschi's unrealized intentions for the Ospedale degli Innocenti, divide the surfaces of the two-story loggias into a systematic grid. The surviving documents point to a more decisive role for Rossellino at the companion project at Santa Maria alle Campora, whose cloister (1436) rivals that of Michelozzo at San Marco as the first such structure built in the Renaissance style. Documented assignments such as supplying materials for the monastery at San Miniato ai Monte, portions of the galleries for the Florence Cathedral, and the stone frame for a round window installed at the Guild of Magistrates and Notaries exemplify the sort of piecework that occupied his workshop in the 1440s.

Two projects, combining both sculptural and architectural elements, were of particular significance during the 1440s. One, undertaken in the Palazzo Pubblico of Siena (1446) involved the design of a magnificent marble door frame leading into the Sala del Concistoro, a benchmark in early Renaissance design. The other project was the triumphal arch tomb erected in Santa Croce for the Florentine statesman and scholar Leonardo Bruni. That Rossellino received this most important commission attests to the recognition he was achieving among the artists of Florence. In the Bruni Tomb, Rossellino (while building upon the precedents of Donatello and Michelozzo) achieved a standard in classical design emulated in a succession of later sepulchral monuments. A somewhat bland (workshop?) replication of the Sienese portal leads into the cloister yard that Rossellino built for Tommaso Spinelli at Santa Croce from 1448 to 1451. There, the harmonious spirit of the early Renaissance achieves its full flowering in the spacious proportions of the loggias and the careful architectural and sculptural detailing. During the same years, Rossellino was employed by Giovanni Rucellai to remodel several old dwellings into a new family palace. His work for Rucellai, on this occasion, involved internal systematization, and a vaulted passageway leading to a new courtyard and loggia in the rear.

Rossellino's career took an important turn when he traveled to Rome in 1451 to join the vast architectural team then engaged by Pope Nicholas V to revitalize the ancient city. Although his retainer exceeded that of all other stonemasons, he is documented at only two projects, furnishing hoists for the *torre grande* at the Vatican and restoring Santo Stefano Rotondo (windows and door frames, vaulting, pavement). His primary task was, apparently, to draw up plans, under the supervision of Alberti, for rebuilding the Vatican and St. Peter's, projects which, due to the death of the pope in 1455, were never carried out.

His position as a papal architect brought Rossellino renewed success upon his return to Florence. He was commissioned to refurbish San Miniato ai Monte (1457-64), design a palace for Tommaso Spinelli (ca. 1459, featuring a perspectively innovative passageway), work at the Ospedale degli Innocenti (1457-59) and in SS. Annunziata (1462-64), and construct a classical facade for the Palazzo Rucellai (ca. 1462) drawing upon the Roman prototypes of the Colosseum and the Villa le Mura at Anguilaria. His presence at the Fiesole Badia remains speculative. Rossellino's Florentine career peaked in 1461, when he was selected as building superintendent of the Florence Cathedral. Outside of Florence, he designed the Palazzo Piccolomini-Todeschini in Siena (ca. 1460) and a new bell tower for the church of San Pietro in Perugia (1463).

Despite his previous accomplishments, the true measure of Rossellino's architectural worth lies in the extraordinary project he undertook for Pope Pius II Piccolomini at Pienza between 1459 and 1464. There, Rossellino designed the Palazzo Piccolomini for the family, town hall, bishop's palace and canons' house, all set compactly about a trapezoidal square; he also supervised the construction or renovation of palaces for several cardinals and members of the papal curia, and a quantity of houses for the citizenry of Pienza. For the Palazzo Piccolomini, a massive three-story block set about a spacious courtyard, he designed three articulated facades resembling that of the Palazzo Rucellai in Florence (which the Palazzo Piccolomini may well predate), and a garden front of three tiers of loggias. At the cathedral he combined a classicizing exterior with a light-filled ''hall church'' interior. The real significance of Pienza, however, lies not in the considerable merits of the individual units, but in Rossellino's conception of the urban totality, the inspiration for which may have come from the Albertian atmosphere of his earlier experience in Rome. While other architects of the Early Renaissance, Alberti included, were forced to deal with town planning on a theoretical basis, Rossellino was able to confront the problem and to produce one of the most pleasing and harmonious cityscapes in the history of urban design.

—CHARLES R. MACK

ROSSI, Aldo.

Italian. Born in Milan, Italy, 3 May 1931. Studied under Ernesto N. Rogers and Giuseppe Samonà, Polytechnic of Milan, 1949-59, Dip.Arch. Worked in the studios of Ignazio Gardella and Marco Zanuso, Milan, 1956-57; in private practice, Milan, since 1959 (in collaboration with Gianni Braghiera from 1971). Editor, *Casabella-Continuità*, Milan, 1955-64. Has taught extensively in Europe and the United States. Pritzker Prize, 1990.

Chronology of Works
All in Italy unless noted

1969-74	Gallaratese 2 Housing Block, Milan
1971-88	San Cataldo Cemetery, Modena
1972-76	Elementary School, Fagnano Olona
1979	Secondary School, Broni
1983	Apartment Complex, Rauchstrasse, Berlin, Germany
1984-87	Housing Blocks for the *Internationale Bauausstellung Berlin*, Berlin, Germany
1985-88	Commercial center *Centro Torri*, Parma (with M. Baracco, G. Braghieri, P. Digiuni, M. Scheurer
1986	School of Architecture, University of Miami, Coral Gables, Florida, U. S. A.
1987-88	Toronto Lighthouse Theater, Toronto, Canada (with M. Adjmi)
1988	Single-family house, Mount Pocono, Pennsylvania, U. S. A. (with M. Adjmi)

Publications

BOOKS BY ROSSI

Concorso per la ricostruzione del Teatro Paganini di Parma. With Carlo Aymonino. Venice, 1966.

L'Architettura della città. Padua, 1966; as *Architecture of the City*, Cambridge, Massachusetts, 1982.

Scritti selecti sull'architettura e la città. Edited by Rosaldo Bonicalzi. Milan, 1975.

Ugo Carrega. With Maria Teresa Balboni. Rome, 1976.

Giovanni Bocaccio: Il Decameron (ed.). Bologna, 1977.

1977: un progetto per Firenze. With Carlo Aymonino and others. Rome, 1978.

Costruzioni del territorio e spazio urban nel Cantone Ticino. With others. Lugano, Switzerland, 1979.

Teatro del Mondo. With others. Venice, 1982.

A Scientific Autobiography. Cambridge, Massachusetts, and London, 1982.

Il Libro Azzurro: i mei progetti 1981. Zurich, 1983.

Selected Writings and Projects. Dublin, 1983.

ARTICLES BY ROSSI

"Un monumento ai partigiani." *Casabella* 208 (1955).

"L'Habitation et la ville." *Architecture d'aujourd'hui* 174 (1974).

"An Analogical Architecture." *Architecture and Urbanism* (May 1976).

"Architecture and Rationalism." *Construccion de la ciudad 2C* (Barcelona, March 1977).

BOOKS ABOUT ROSSI

ADJMI, MORRIS (ed.): *Aldo Rossi: Architecture 1981-91.* New York, 1991.

Aldo Rossi, Architect. Milan, 1987.

ARNELL, PETER, and BICKFORD, TED (eds.): *Aldo Rossi, Buildings and Projects.* New York, 1985.

BRAGHIERI, GIANNI: *Aldo Rossi.* Bologna, 1981.

FERLENGA, ALBERTO (ed.): *Aldo Rossi, architetture 1959-87.* Milan, 1987.

FRAMPTON, KENNETH: *Modern Architecture: A Critical History.* Revised edition, New York, 1985.

KLOTZ, HEINRICH: *The History of Postmodern Architecture.* Cambridge, Massachusetts, 1988.

SAVI, VITTORIO: *L'Architettura di Aldo Rossi.* Milan, 1977.

ARTICLES ABOUT ROSSI

"Aldo Rossi and 21 Works." Special issue of *Architecture and Urbanism.* (1982).

"Aldo Rossi: The Idea of Architecture." *Oppositions* 5 (1978); *Space Design* (March 1978).

Architecture and Urbanism, special issue, 65 (1976).

BONFANTI, E.: "Elementi e costruzione: note sull'architettura di Aldo Rossi." *Controspazio* 10 (1970).

COLQUHOUN, ALAN: "Rational Architecture." *Architectural Design* 6 (1975).

Construccion de la Ciudad 2C (Barcelona), special issues, 2 (1975); 5 (1976); (December 1979).

MONEO, JOSÉ RAFAEL: "Aldo Rossi: The Idea of Architecture and the Modena Cemetery." *Oppositions* 5 (Summer 1976).

MOSTOLLER, MICHAEL: "Canaletto and Aldo Rossi: The Relationship Between Painting and Architectural Creation." *Modulus* (Charlottesville, Virginia, 1982).

There have been only a handful of architects whose theoretical writings have significantly affected the evolution of architecture since World War II. Among these is Aldo Rossi, whose 1966 treatise *L'architettura della città* clearly countered the tenets of the Modern Movement. The influence of Rossi in particular revolves around the use of building typologies and urban morphologies. He is the leading voice of the Tendenza, the neorationalist movement born in northern Italy and southern Switzerland.

Just as Robert Venturi's *Complexity and Contradiction in Architecture* is a benchmark in the development of postmodernism in architecture in the United States, Rossi's *L'architettura,* as with Giorgio Grassi's *La costruzione logica dell'architettura,* indicates a divergent direction for contemporary architecture. In his role as editor of *Casabella* (1955-64), as teacher in Milan, Venice, Zurich and at various U.S. institutions, and as practitioner with an ever-increasing international catalog of works, Rossi has affected the direction of architecture and design for much of the younger generation. He proposes that city and building are analogous, and the elements of the city (streets, squares and monuments) have corresponding elements in buildings. In this manner Rossi explores compositions based on archetypal elements. One can clearly see this in the elementary school at Fagnano/Olona (1972-76) or the middle school in Broni (1979), miniature cities composed of urban elements: streets, plazas and monuments transliterated to classrooms along single loaded corridors, courtyards and central library or auditorium. The imagery is clear, and the solutions fit their programmatic requirements. Rossi's architecture is purposefully "timeless," devoid of stylistic indicators. According to Kenneth

Frampton, "Rossi has recognized that most modern programs are inappropriate vehicles for architecture and for him this has meant having recourse to a so-called analogical architecture whose referents and elements are to be abstracted from the vernacular, in the broadest possible sense" (K. Frampton, *Modern Architecture: A Critical History,* p. 294). But Rossi's agenda, Frampton continues, calls for a return to the period of revolutionary neoclassicism: "Rossi attempts to evade the twin chimeras of modernity—positivistic logic and a blind faith in progress—by returning to both the building typology and the constructional forms of the second half of the 19th century. . . ." And Rossi carries this down to the design of objects for the tabletop, the "domestic landscape."

Rossi's formative works, particularly those dating immediately from around the time of the "Architettura Razionale" exhibition at the XV Milan Triennale of 1973, are extremely abstract explorations. Principal among these is the Gallaratese 2 housing block in Milan (1969-74). There, Rossi's smaller, single-loaded, hallway-access housing block acts as counterbalance to Carlo Aymonino's three exuberant structures. Concerning the building typology, Rossi states: "[T]here is an analogical relationship . . . that mix[es] freely with both the corridor typology [and] the architecture of the traditional Milanese tenements, where the corridors signify a life-style bathed in everyday occurrences, domestic intimacy and varied personal relationships" (quoted by Frampton in *Modern Architecture,* p. 295). Furthermore, Michael Mostoller writes: "Rossi achieves this poetry of form beyond speech: poetry derived not only from metaphor and analogy, but from repetition. The power of Rossi's eccentric, surreal, personal architecture is the endless repetition and variation of the thing and its essence. The Gallaratese seems as if it has always been there." ("Canaletto and Aldo Rossi," *Modulus,* 1982, p. 83). Of that period is the Salvatore Orrú Elementary School in Fagnano/Olona, particularly criticized because of the imagery and associations attached to its tectonic elements. Its design is based on very simple and elementary components: a central cylindrical volume capped by a transparent conical roof, placed within a rectangular courtyard, from which extend arms containing the classroom spaces. On the side facing the road into town, a pergola leads to a freestanding chimney in front of the central volume of the school. It is the imagery of this latter element that has been the subject of criticism, as it is associated with chimneys of factories (by Rossi) and death camp incinerators (by his detractors).

Most important of the projects of the middle period is the extension of the Cemetery of San Cataldo in Modena (1971-88), "among the paradigmatic designs of Rationalist architecture" (Heinrich Klotz, *The History of Postmodern Architecture,* p. 242). The project by Rossi with G. Braghieri extends the neoclassical cemetery with a new section to the west. In concept, the new cemetery reflects the dimensional definition of the earlier cemetery. It incorporates the Jewish cemetery, built outside the walls of the 1858 complex, which becomes the pivotal element of the overall composition. In Rossi's project, the surrounding structure and a row of trees enclose the new cemetery space with equal rigidity as the original. The architectonic expression of the new "house of death" (*A Scientific Autobiography,* p. 55) is less opulent, in fact barren. The new complex is defined by an external C-shaped and gabled building with three floors of wall burial cells. A two-floor, flat-roofed columbarium is placed within this. On the center axis and between these two buildings is the cubic roofless house, an ossuary whose image speaks about the fragile and transitory nature of life: "I thought of fashioning the cemetery on a Rationalist concept of death, as a disruption of life. I tried therefore to represent it as a deserted house with empty windows and as a factory with a smokestack where work has been disrupted." (Rossi, quoted by Klotz in *The History of Postmodern Architecture,* p. 242). Other elements are the arcade building parallel to the perimeter structure which faces the Jewish and old cemeteries, and the perpendicular building housing the chapels.

In his later work, beginning with the housing blocks for the *Internationale Bauausstellung Berlin* (IBA) of 1984-87, there is an increased use of material as ornament. Like Adolf Loos' Goldman and Salatsch Department Store in Vienna, Rossi's buildings now rely on the differentiation of constructive elements, for example the apartment buildings on Rauchstrasse and Kochstrasse in Berlin, the office building in Turin, the complex in Perugia, the hotel in Osaka, or his first major complex in the United States at the University of Miami in Coral Gables, Florida. But these remain essentially simple structures resolving specific programmatic requirements through the use of archetypal elements, "familiar objects whose form and position are already fixed but whose meanings may be changed . . . whose common emotional appeal reveals timeless concerns" (Aldo Rossi, "An Analogical Architecture," in *A+U,* May 1976, p. 74). Above all, at whatever scale he is working, Aldo Rossi in an inimitable way rationalizes and synthesizes his investigations until he arrives at evocative forms which transcend time.

—GERARDO BROWN-MANRIQUE

ROSSI, Karl Ivanovich.

Russian. Born in Russia, 1775. Died in 1849. Studied with Vinchenco Brenna, and assisted Brenna on the construction of Mikhailovsky Castle, St. Petersburg. Worked independently in Moscow and Tver, 1808-12; returned to St. Petersburg, 1814; became leading member of the Committee of Building and Hydraulics, St. Petersburg, 1814.

Chronology of Works
All in Russia

1817-20	Anichkov's Palace, St. Petersburg
1818-22	Park-Palace Complex, Elagin Island
1819-25ff.	Mikhailovsky Palace
1819-29	Central Headquarters and Ministries Building, St. Petersburg
1826	Nikolaevskie Gate, St. Petersburg
1826-27	Winter Palace, St. Petersburg
n.d.	Alexandrovsky Theater Ensemble, St. Petersburg

Publications

BOOKS ABOUT ROSSI

EGOROV, IURII ALEKSEEVICH: *The Architectural Planning of St. Petersburg.* Athens, Ohio, 1969.
HAMILTON, G. H.: *The Art and Architecture of Russia.* Harmondsworth, England, 1954.
Vseobchtchaia istoria arkhitektury. Moscow, 1963.

*

Karl Rossi was the last great master of Russian high classicism, which was based on the French Empire style. The flowering of his creativity occurred in the period from 1816 to 1832. It was a time of intense architectural exploration, caused by the excitement in Russian society after the victory over Napoleon. It was followed by the degeneration of classicism into a formal,

Karl Ivanovich Rossi: Central Headquarters and Ministries Building, St. Petersburg, Russia, 1819-29

bureaucratic style. Although Rossi built glamorous palaces, park complexes and important administrative and public buildings, city planning became the main focus of his creative work.

Rossi enlarged and brilliantly completed the system of splendid open spaces in St. Petersburg's center. In the capital alone, he created and reconstructed 12 squares and 13 streets. Rossi's talent was to organize large expanses of space, which he endowed with rich perspectives and blended into the existing environment, occasionally using theatrical effects. For him, the center of an ensemble was not a building, but a space surrounded by facades. However, Rossi's striving for total unity held the danger of transforming architecture into large-scale decoration. Thus, symptoms of the crisis in classicism began to develop in his brilliant work.

In Rossi, the architect yielded and became subordinate to the city planner. He was less original in his architectural designs and often borrowed themes from other architects. Rossi's mature style was markedly solemn and representational, exquisite and rich in decoration. It reveals features common to French neoclassicism and Empire, the creative work of A. N. Voronikhin and the work of Giacomo Antonio Quarenghi. Rossi also relied on

a synthesis of the arts, following A. D. Zakharov's Admiralty building (1806-23).

Rossi's teacher Vincenzo Brenna (ca. 1750-1804) largely influenced his development. In the 1790s Rossi became Brenna's assistant during construction of Mikhailovsky (later Engineers) Palace, the new St. Petersburg residence of Paul I. Rossi's city-planning ambitions could already be seen in his early project for the embankment next to the Admiralty, revealing his inclination to gigantism. A grandiose arch with rostral columns was to complete the city center's ceremonial facade on the side of the Neva River.

Rossi began to work independently in Moscow and Tver in 1808. His participation in the Moscow Kremlin reconstruction stimulated an interest in medieval forms, following the terms of the commission. Rossi's Ekaterininskaia Church and Kremlin Nikolskaia Tower were romantic stylizations of medieval architecture, as was his later work, Nilova Pustyn Monastery near Lake Seliger. His concurrent construction of Glazovo village near Pavlovsk introduced a folklore movement in 19th-century Russian architecture, based on traditional models of building. However, Rossi's theater on Arbat Square in Moscow and works in Tver and other cities nearby, revealed an adherence to principles of classicism. Various structures—churches and commercial, administrative and private buildings—were infused with a cool clarity. For the architect, the Moscow and Tver period served as practical training in city planning.

Having returned to St. Petersburg in 1814, Rossi began work in Pavlovsk, where he created a series of park and palace complexes and later the cast-iron Nikolaevsky Gate (1826). His original design for this gate employed the traditional Doric portico with an attic. The use of cast iron allowed him to enlarge the space between column groupings, opening up a wide passage to the street.

Between 1817 and 1820, Rossi reconstructed Anichkov Palace on Nevsky Prospekt in St. Petersburg. Two identical pavilions with semicircular rotundas, arched windows and statues of Russian warriors were the principal elements in the ensemble. For the design of the pavilions, the architect drew on the theme of the Narva Triumphal Arch in St. Petersburg by Quarenghi.

Rossi created a large-scale park and palace complex on Elagin Island (1818-22) for the empress Maria Feodorovna. With terraces, a semicircular rotunda and Corinthian porticoes, the palace served as the focus of the ensemble. Collaborating with the park designer D. Busch, Rossi placed functional buildings and pavilions within the picturesque landscape of the park. The Maslianny Meadow open parterre served as the spatial center of the ensemble.

While working on the Elagin Palace, Rossi demonstrated outstanding talent as a decorator. Rossi did all the interior design work, from the general structure to minute details of decoration and furniture. Working on this project, he perfected the skills he had cultivated during the reconstruction of Prince Oldeburgsky Palace in Tver, and while furnishing the halls of the Pavlovsk, Anichkov and Winter Palaces. Later he continued work on the main imperial residence, the Winter Palace (1826-27), where he created the famous "War of 1812" Gallery.

Rossi played a leading part in the Committee of Building and Hydraulics, which was established in 1814 to supervise construction in St. Petersburg. A large-scale reconstruction of the city to improve city planning was realized through Rossi's projects. He treated every local construction as a means of reorganizing a larger area. In 15 years, Rossi composed a system of interrelated ensembles in the city center. He made a significant contribution to the arrangement of central squares, Nevsky Prospekt and the Neva embankments.

In 1819 Rossi was commissioned to build Mikhailovsky Palace in St. Petersburg. He approached the creation of the ensemble from a city-planning perspective. Besides the main building and park, he created a square and new streets which connected Mikhailovsky Palace with Inzhenerny Castle and Nevsky Prospekt. He also prolonged the adjacent Sadovaia Street toward the Neva, terminating the street in Suvorov Square. At the same time, he laid out alleys and passages around Inzhenerny Castle and built Manej Square in the vicinity.

Notably ceremonial and richly decorated, Mikhailovsky Palace's main facade occupies the background of the courtyard. A Corinthian colonnade with a portico at its center spans the wall between the base and the entablature. The park facade, with a 12-column loggia above the arcade and side porticoes, echoes Ange-Jacques Gabriel's buildings on the Place de la Concorde in Paris. Of all the brilliant interiors, only the main staircase, the church and the white column hall have survived; the rest were destroyed in the 1890s when the palace was remodeled to function as the Russian Museum. Buildings in the square in front of the palace and in Mikhailovskaia Street were erected to Rossi's design. Their modest architecture serves as a background to the main building of the ensemble.

Rossi's most important work was the General Staff building on Dvortsovaia Square (1819-29). The building is 700 meters long. Using some existing structures, Rossi filled the southern side of the square with a unified facade built along a parabolic line. The Corinthian colonnade in the center of the facade softened the contrast between the monotone walls and the gigantic central arch with its 17-meter span, which became the focal point of the whole ensemble. Rich in sculptural forms and crowned with a "Chariot of Glory," the structure was designed as a triumphal arch and dedicated to the military glory of Russia. It was the culmination of the synthesis of the arts in Russia. The theme of the Narva Triumphal Arch by Quarenghi, based on classical Roman models, was again applied to the General Staff building. The double arch hid the turn of the subjacent street, which connected the square to Nevsky Prospekt. The building's side wings with Corinthian colonnades were similar to the facade of the Fittinghoff House on Admiralty Prospekt (also by Quarenghi). The repetition of these designs reinforced the unity of the entire ensemble of central squares.

In the Senate and Synod building (1829-34), Rossi once again drew on the theme of the Narva Triumphal Arch. He also employed the device of the arch above the subjacent street, dividing the building into two parts. The difference in the length of the parts was softened by a rounded corner, which also provided a transition from the square to the Neva embankment. The alternation of wide, columned loggias and projections with painted columns accentuated the expressive plasticity of the facade. However, overburdened with unexpressive ornamentation, the central part of the building looked markedly pompous.

Administrative buildings by Rossi added unity and stature to the appearance of Dvortsovaia and Senatskaia Squares. They also became the official facade of the Russian Empire style. The General Staff building became the monument to Alexander I's reign, while the Senate and Synod building marked the beginning of Nicholas I's rule.

The construction of the Alexandrinsky Theater ensemble was the highest achievement of Rossi's city-planning career. In place of a haphazard group of buildings, Rossi created two unified squares, one facing Nevsky Prospekt, the other facing Fontanka River. The squares were connected by what was then called Theater Street. The square in front of the theater was rectangular in form, its axis coinciding with the direction of Theater Street. The axis was continued on the other side of Nevsky Prospekt by Malaia Sadovaia Street, and the long perspective was terminated by a decorative portico Rossi built on Manej Square.

On the longitudinal sides of this square, the Public Library building was coordinated with the two pavilions of Anichkov Palace. A loggia with 18 columns and statues of ancient philosophers, poets and scientists decorated the Public Library facade. An attic in the center of the colonnade corresponded to Alexandrinsky Theater's loggia and porticoes. The compact theater building, adorned with "Apollo's Chariot" on the main facade, was set in the background of the square. The engineer M. E. Clark used metal constructions for the first time in history in the construction of the theater.

The space of the square flows around the theater and into Theater Street. On opposite sides of the street, Rossi built two identical buildings. The extensions of the facades surround the semicircular square facing the Fontanka River. Rossi also designed three streets radiating from the center of the square.

The Alexandrinsky Theater ensemble was harmonious and unified, austere and grand. However, the strict organization of the viewer's spatial perception and the consistent urge towards uniformity showed signs of the decline of classicism. The street and semicircular square facades were monotonous and schematic.

Rossi's completion of the ensemble ended the classical epoch in Russian architecture. In 1832 Rossi resigned his post on the Building and Hydraulics Committee and did not create anything significant during the remaining 17 years of his life. The death of classicism became his own artistic tragedy.

—BORIS M. KIRIKOV

Translated from the Russian by Konstantine Klioutchkine

ROSSI, Mattia de.

Italian. Born in Rome, Italy, 14 January 1637. Died in Rome, 2 August 1695. Trained in architecture with his father, Marcantonio. Worked as an assistant to Bernini, from 1655. Succeeded Bernini as architect of St. Peter's, 1680. Became president of the Academy of St. Luke, 1681 and 1690-93.

Chronology of Works
All in Italy

1667-69	Casino of Pope Clement IX, near Pistoia
1668	Palazzo Rospigliosi, near Pistoia (free-standing chapel)
1670	Sant'Andrea al Quirinale, Rome (altars, sacristy, and building for the novices)
1675	Santa Bonaventura and Monastery dei Padri delle Scuole Pie, Monterano, near Oriolo
1675	Santa Maria delle Vergini, Rome (remodeling and altars; now Santa Rita)
1675	Palazzo Muti Bussi, Piazza della Pilotta, Rome
1676-79	High Altar, Santa Maria di Montesanto, Rome
1676-86	Monument to Clement X, St. Peter's, Rome
1680	Santa Maria delle Vittoria, Rome (organ loft)
1682-89	San Francesco a Ripa, Rome (remodeling)
1684-86	Santa Galla and Hospice, Rome
1685-90	Capella Zucchi, Santa Maria in Campitelli, Rome
1686-89	Ospizio di San Michele, Rome
1686-95	Collegiata Santa Maria dell'Assunta, Valmontone (not completed until 1698)
1690-95	Cappella Torre, Santa Maria Maddelena, Rome (altar; not completed until 1696 by Carlo Francesco Bizzaccheri)
1691	Catafalque for Alexander VIII, St. Peter's, Rome
1692-95	Sante Croce e Bonaventura dei Lucchesi, Rome (facade not completed until 1696) [attributed]
1694	Dogana di Ripa Grande, Rome (completed by Carlo Fontana)
n.d.	Santa Francesca a Capo le Case, Rome

Publications

BOOKS ABOUT ROSSI

BALDINUCCI, FILIPPO: *Vita del Cavaliere Giovanni Lorenzo Bernini, scultore, architetto e pittore.* 1682. English edition: University Park, Pennsylvania, 1966.

BORSI, FRANCO: *Bernini architetto.* Milan, 1980.

BRAUER, HEINRICH, and WITTKOWER, RUDOLF: *Die Zeichnungen des Gianlorenzo Bernini.* New York, 1931.

CASANOVA, MARIA L.: *S. Maria di Montesanto e S. Maria dei Miracoli.* Rome, 1960.

COUDENHOVE-ERTHAL, EDUARD: *Carlo Fontana und die Architektur des römischen Spätbarocks.* Vienna, 1930.

D'ONOFRIO, CESARE: *Castel Sant'Angelo e Borgo tra Roma e Papato.* Rome, 1978.

FAGIOLO DELL'ARCO, MAURIZIO, and CARADINI, SILVIA: *L'effimero Barucco: Strutture della festa nella Roma del seicento.* 2 vols. Rome, 1978.

FAGIOLO DELL'ARCO, MAURIZIO and MARCELLO: *Bernini: Una inroduzione al gran teatro del barocco.* Rome, 1967.

GAYNOR, JUAN SANTOS, and TOESCA, ILARIA: *S. Sivestro in Capite.* Rome, 1963.

HIBBARD, HOWARD: *Carlo Maderno and Roman Architecture: 1580-1630.* University Park, Pennsylvania, 1971.

MENICHELLA, ANNA: *S. Francesco a Ripa.* Rome, 1981.

PESCI, BENEDETTO: *S. Francesco a Ripa.* Rome, 1959.

WITTKOWER, RUDOLF: *Art and Architecture in Italy, 1600-1750.* 3rd ed. rev. Harmondsworth, England, 1973.

ARTICLES ABOUT ROSSI

HAGER, HELLMUT: ''Bernini, Mattia de Rossi and the Church of S. Bonaventura at Monterano.'' *Architectural History* 21 (1978): 68-78.

HAGER, HELLMUT: ''La crisi statica della cupola di S. Maria in Vallicella in Roma e i rimedi proposti da Carlo Fontana, Carlo Rainaldi e Mattia di Rossi.'' *Commentari* 24 (1973): 300-318.

HAGER, HELLMUT: ''Zur Planungs-und Baugeschichte der Zwillingskirchen auf der Piazza del Popolo: S. Maria di Montesanto und S. Maria dei Miracoli in Rom.'' *Römisches Jahrbuch für Kunstgeschichte* 2 (1967-68).

PINELLI, ANTONIO: ''Bernini a Monterano.'' *Il seicento: Ricerche di storia dell'arte* 1-2 (1976): 171-179.

---

*

Mattia de Rossi was a native of Rome who had trained as an architect with his father, Marcantonio. He spent much of his career from 1655 as a favorite assistant of Giovanni Lorenzo Bernini, accompanying him to Paris in 1665, then supervising construction on a section of Bernini's colonnade for St. Peter's Square. Rossi also assisted him on the construction of Sant'Andrea al Quirinale, on San Tommaso at Castel Gandolfo, and on church projects in Ariccia. He produced finished designs and architectural models for many of Bernini's projects.

For the Franciscans at Monterano, Rossi erected the church of San Bonaventura, which had been commissioned by an adopted cardinal-nephew of Pope Clement X. His roofed dome was a modification of Bernini's intention to erect a visible dome on a high drum. Rossi also remodeled the medieval basilica of San Francesco a Ripa (1682-89).

For his own churches, Rossi preferred oval plans with longitudinal axes, as in Santa Galla (1684-86), and for his major work, the Collegiate Church in Valmontone (1686-95). In plan the latter mimics Santa Maria di Montesanto (1662-75) on the Piazza del Popolo, which was the work of Carlo Rainaldi and Bernini; but Rossi's contribution is to be found in the inviting concave portico with muscular columns set between tall towers.

Rossi's rectangular arrangement of three stories of circular halls for the casino of Pope Clement IX (1667-69) near Pistoia demonstrated an inventive approach to the articulation of interior space, but his major accomplishment in secular architecture was Innocent XI's hospital of San Michele (1686-89). Rossi's design for the Customs House at the Roman port of Ripa Grande (1694) was completed by Carlo Fontana. Rossi displayed a degree of novelty in his Palazzo Muti Bussi of 1675 on the Piazza della Pilotta. This is a structure of three wings with a one-story colonnaded portico which both encloses the courtyard as the building's fourth side and serves as a facade flanked by the lateral wings of the palace. It is a variant of his father's design for the Porta Portese in Trastevere (1643). The balustrade resting on the portico's entablature has its counterpart on the cornice of the palace's taller wings.

Rossi worked for other rulers and princes of the church such as the Principe Marescotti and the Cardinals Benedetto Pamphilij and Rinaldo d'Este. Although he made designs for Rome's Trevi Fountain and the Rometta Fountain for the Villa d'Este in Tivoli, neither was executed. Rossi constructed the catafalque for the funerary ceremonies of Pope Alexander VIII Ottoboni in St. Peter's Basilica in 1691. This was a large, freestanding apparatus with corner columns and numerous candelabra.

Rossi had previously designed the monument to Pope Clement X (1676-86) in the basilica's right transept, which was striking for its more fractionated composition of Bernini's prototypical Baroque tomb of Urban VIII (1628-47) in the apse. Rossi was responsible for the tomb's structural design and supervised its construction. He had acquired previous experience in dealing with structural problems for tomb niches in the piers of St. Peter's during his work with Bernini on the tomb of the Chigi pope, Alexander VII (1671-78). Rossi delegated the tomb's figural carvings to three sculptors, as documented in a contract of 30 September 1682. L. Reti's relief carving commemorating Pope Clement X's opening of the Holy Door for the Jubilee Year of 1675 depicts a kneeling figure holding a vase. Armando Schiavo has suggested that this may be a portrait of Rossi.

Other frequent Baroque activities of a more modest scale involved the construction and renovation of chapels and altars. Rossi designed and constructed a freestanding chapel for the Palazzo Rospigliosi in 1668. He was responsible for all of the altars in the perimeter chapels of Bernini's oval plan at Sant'Andrea al Quirinale. He also saw to the erection of the high altar at Santa Maria di Montesanto (1671-79) and built the organ loft in Santa Maria delle Vittoria. In 1685-1690, he designed the Cappella Zucchi in Santa Maria in Campitelli.

Rossi was highly regarded by his contemporaries. He succeeded Bernini as architect for St. Peter's and superintendent of the Fabbrica in 1680. He also served as president of the Accademia di San Lucca in 1681 and 1690-1693, a vote of confidence that matched the four-year presidency of the esteemed architect-painter Pietro da Cortona earlier in the century.

Rossi was one of the major sources of information for Filippo Baldinucci's biography of Bernini, which Queen Christina of Sweden had commissioned in 1682. The Sieur de Chantelou mentioned Rossi in his diary recording Bernini's visit to Paris, and both he and Baldinucci characterized Rossi as a knowledgeable, charming and highly animated personality. They offer clear accounts of his tact and of his devotion to Bernini. Lione Pascoli published a biography of Rossi in his collection of artists' lives (1730). The Swedish architect Nicodemus Tessin the younger, on his stay in Rome in 1673, considered Rossi to be among the three best architects then in the city.

—EDWARD J. OLSZEWSKI

RUDOLPH, Paul Marvin.

American. Born in Elkton, Kentucky, 23 October 1918. Studied at Alabama Polytechnic Institute, Auburn, 1935-40, B.Arch. 1940; studied at Harvard Graduate School of Design, Cambridge, Massachusetts, under Walter Gropius, 1940-43, 1946-47, M.Arch. 1947. Served as a lieutenant in the United States Navy, 1943-46. Began practice with Ralph Twitchell, Sarasota, Florida, 1948-52; in private practice, Sarasota, and New Haven, Connecticut, 1952-58; chairman, School of Architecture, Yale

University, New Haven, 1958-65; in private practice, New York, since 1965.

Chronology of Works
All in the United States unless noted

1946	Denman House, Sarasota, Florida (with Ralph Twitchell)
1947	Miller House, Sarasota, Florida (with Ralph Twitchell)
1948	Healey Guest House ('Cocoon House'), Sarasota, Florida (with Ralph Twitchell)
1951	Hook Cottage, Siesta Key, Sarasota, Florida
1952	Walker Guest House, Sanibel Island, Florida
1953	Hiss House ('Umbrella House'), Lido Shores, Florida
1954	Taylor House, Venice, Florida
1956	Yanofsky House, Newton, Massachusetts
1957	Blue Cross/Blue Shield Headquarters, Boston, Massachusetts (with Anderson, Beckwith and Haible)
1958	Jewett Arts Center, Wellesley College, Massachusetts (with Anderson, Beckwith and Haible)
1958	Art and Architecture Building, Yale University, New Haven, Connecticut
1959	May Memorial Unitarian Church, Syracuse, New York
1960	Interdenominational Chapel, Tuskegee Institute, Alabama
1962	IBM Complex, East Fishkill, New York (with Walter Kidde)
1962	Mental Health Building and Health, Welfare and Education Building, Government Center, Boston
1963	Southeastern Massachusetts Technological Institute, North Dartmouth, Massachusetts (with Desmond and Lord)
1963	Creative Arts Center, Colgate University, Hamilton, New York
1964	Paul Rudolph Offices, West 57th Street, New York
1968	Government Center, New Haven, Connecticut
1969	Burroughs Wellcome Corporate Headquarters, Durham, North Carolina
1970	Deare House, Great Neck, Long Island, New York
1971	Diaei Company Office Building, Nagoya, Japan
1972	Entrecanales y Tavora Office Building, Madrid
1975	Chapel, Chandler School of Theology, Emory University, Atlanta, Georgia
1979	Marina Centre Developments, Singapore
1982	Pt. Yamano Utama Office Building, Jakarta Pusat, Indonesia
1984	Pavarini House, Greenwich, Connecticut
1984	Tuttle House, Rock Hall, Maryland
1986	Bond Centre, Hong Kong
1987	Colonnade Condominiums, Singapore
1988	Dharmala Sakti Building, Jakarta, Indonesia

Publications

BOOKS BY RUDOLPH

Architectural Education in the United States. Washington, D.C., 1962.
Global Architecture 2: Frank Lloyd Wright—Fallingwater. With Yukio Futagawa. Tokyo, 1970.
Drawings. Edited by Yukio Futagawa. Tokyo, 1972
The Evolving City: Urban Design Proposals. With Ulrich Franzen and Peter Wolf. New York, 1975.

Paul Marvin Rudolph: Art and Architecture Building, Yale University, New Haven, Connecticut, 1958

ARTICLES BY RUDOLPH

"The Changing Philosophy of Architecture." *Architectural Forum* (July 1954).
"The Six Determinants of Architectural Form." *Architectural Review* 120 (1956).
"Regionalism in Architecture." *Perspecta* 4 (1957).
"The Creative Use of Architectural Material." *Progressive Architecture* (September 1959).
"What Is Quality?" *American Institute of Architects Journal* (July 1963).

BOOKS ABOUT RUDOLPH

FUTAGAWA, YUKIO: *Paul Rudolph*. Tokyo, 1968; London, 1971.
MOHOLY-NAGY, SIBYL: *The Architecture of Paul Rudolph*. New York and London, 1970.
SCHWAB, GERHARD: *The Architecture of Paul Rudolph*. New York, 1970.
SPADE, RUPERT: *Paul Rudolph*. London and New York, 1971.

ARTICLES ABOUT RUDOLPH

Architecture and Urbanism, special issue (July 1977).
"Interview: Paul Rudolph." *Progressive Architecture* (December 1990).
Japan Architect, special issue (July 1970).

Paul Rudolph began his advanced architectural studies at the Harvard Graduate School of Design in 1941 after a year of professional practice in Birmingham, Alabama. His studies there, where he was a student of Walter Gropius and Marcel Breuer, were interrupted by three years of military service at the Brooklyn Naval Yard as a supervisor of ship construction.

In 1948, a year after his graduation from Harvard, Rudolph entered a partnership with Ralph Twitchell in Sarasota, Florida. The firm specialized in private residences, and Rudolph first gained national recognition for projects such as the Healy Guest House (1948-49) and the Hook House (1951-52), both in Sarasota. These houses utilized glass doors, translucent screens and bent-plywood vaults to gain the maximum benefits from the climate. The partnership with Twitchell was dissolved in 1952 and Rudolph opened his own practice. He won the Outstanding Young Architect Award in 1954 at an international competition held in Sao Paulo, Brazil, for a house that featured hinged glass panels for walls, the Walker Guest House (1952-53) on Sanibel Island, off the coast of Florida. Although these early designs referred to the formal austerity of the Bauhaus and Gropius' model of three-dimensional, cellular architectural space, the "Harvard box," they also demonstrated Rudolph's understanding of the way two-dimensional surfaces, serving as screens, can sensitively organize space.

In the late 1950s, Rudolph received his first commissions for larger, public buildings, which signaled the beginning of a series of innovations in his architecture and an interest in urban planning. In the Mary Cooper Jewett Arts Center at Wellesley College, Wellesley, Massachusetts (1958-59), Rudolph attempted to harmonize a new brick building with its immediate surroundings—in this case, collegiate neo-Gothic buildings—

signaling a definite break with the training he had received at Harvard. The Jewett Arts Center, although only a partially successful example of Rudolph's new treatment of buildings as space-shaping surfaces, did announce a new trend in architecture by moving away from the standard forms and devices of modernism and influencing the work of many architects, among them Philip Johnson and Eero Saarinen.

Rudolph became the chairman of the department of architecture at Yale University in 1958. The most renowned project he undertook during that period was the university's Art and Architecture Building (1958-63). This structure, a paradigm of Brutalism in its masses of corrugated concrete aggregate, is often viewed as the culmination of Rudolph's work to that date. It marked a change in his approach toward urban form and the way a building relates to its environment. It is an architectural essay in the architect's characteristic vocabulary: an irregular plan, textured surfaces, interlocking forms and bold interior spaces. The building has often been compared to Frank Lloyd Wright's Unity Temple in Oak Park, Illinois (1904-06), and Larkin Building in Buffalo, New York (1904-05), because of the sculptural massing of its towers (which, as in the Larkin Building, house mechanical services) and the provocative manner in which it relates to its environment. The Art and Architecture Building has also been the subject of controversy. Some critics and students have found the building to be unfunctional and the interior overbearing and too inadequately partitioned to be occupied. It was refurbished after several floors burned in 1969.

Rudolph left his position at Yale in 1965 and opened an office in New York, where he has continued to produce innovative designs in both the public and private sectors. The Deane Residence, Great Neck, New York (1970-76), with its compact arrangement of smooth surfaces and linear lattice frames, consciously recalls the Stick Style as well as the work of Wright. In addition, Rudolph began to focus on the problems of urban design and the need for new solutions, an interest which is found in his writings, such as *Evolving Cities* (1976), a book he coauthored with Ulrich Franzen. Two projects from that time, the unbuilt New York Graphic Arts Center and the Boston Government Service Center (1962-71), demonstrate some of his ideas about urban design in the way groups of large towers share a common plaza, which adds human proportions to the complexes, to promote a sense of community.

Three projects commissioned in the 1980s continued these ideas. The Colonnade Condominiums (1980-87), Singapore, are very similar in concept to the unexecuted Graphic Arts Center in the use of modular housing units that resemble Le Corbusier's Domino House Project (1914), but now stacked to form a tower. Rudolph designed the Dharmala Sakti Building, Djakarta (1982-88), in direct response to the climate and traditional Indonesian architecture. Rudolph used cantilevered overhangs, adapted from Indonesian roofs, to shade the glazing. The third project, the Bond Centre in Hong Kong (1984-88), is among the most unusual of Rudolph's buildings because of its glass towers. The exterior walls are not monotonous sheets of glass but have been faceted to enclose cantilevered rooms. In each of these commissions, Rudolph provided an open plaza, which allows the buildings to participate in the public life of the cities. The buildings are also similar in that the first six stories, approximately 120 feet, of each have been given a human scale, above which rises the massive tower. Rudolph has devised this formula in direct response to the inability of the human eye to recognize images beyond 120 feet.

Paul Rudolph has shown a consistently individual interpretation of the architecture and architectural theory of his immediate predecessors, specifically Frank Lloyd Wright, Le Corbusier

and the Bauhaus. He has absorbed and translated many of the architectural developments of his time into his own language. He believes the modular unit is the "brick" of 20th-century architecture. His structures are designed in accord with six general principles: site, function, materials, space, scale and the period. For Rudolph, the renewed probing and articulation of these principles can lead to a successful solution to any architectural problem.

—LORETTA LORANCE

RUSKIN, John.

British. Born in London, England, 8 February 1819. Died 20 January 1900. Married Euphemia Chalmers Gray, 1848 (divorced, 1854). Studied at Christ Church, Oxford, 1836-40, 1842, B.A.; M.A., 1843. Traveled in Europe, especially Italy, on numerous occasions; lived mainly in Venice, 1849-53; lectured throughout England, 1855-70. Drawing teacher, Working Men's College, London, 1850s; first Slade professor of fine art, Oxford University, 1869-79 and 1883-84. Fellow, Royal Institute of British Archi tects.

Publications

BOOKS BY RUSKIN

Modern Painters. 5 vols. London, 1843-60.
The Seven Lamps of Architecture. Kent, England, 1849.
The Stones of Venice. 3 vols. Kent, England, 1851-53.
The Oxford Museum. With Henry Acland. London, 1859.
The Works of John Ruskin. Edited by Edward T. Cook and Alexander Wedderburn. 39 vols. London, 1903-12.
Ruskin's Letters from Venice 1851-1852. Edited by J. L. Bradley. London, 1955.
The Diaries of John Ruskin. Edited by Joan Evans and J. H. Whitehouse. 3 vols. London, 1956-59.
Ruskin Today. Edited by Kenneth Clark. Harmondsworth, England, 1964.
The Correspondence of Thomas Carlyle and John Ruskin. Edited by G. A. Cate. London, 1982.

BOOKS ABOUT RUSKIN

AUTRET, J.: *Ruskin and the French before Marcel Proust.* Geneva, 1965.
BELL, QUENTIN: *Ruskin.* New York and London, 1978.
BLAU, EVE: *Ruskinian Gothic: The Architecture of Deane and Woodward, 1845-1861.* Princeton, New Jersey, 1982.
BRADLEY, ALEXANDER: *Ruskin and Italy.* 1987.
BROOKS, MICHAEL W.: *Ruskin and Victorian Architecture.* 1987.
COLLINGWOOD, W. G.: *The Art Teaching of John Ruskin.* London, 1891.
COLLINGWOOD, W. G.: *The Life of John Ruskin.* London, 1893.
CONNER, PATRICK: *Savage Ruskin.* London, 1979.
COOK, EDWARD T.: *The Life of John Ruskin.* 2 vols. London, 1911.
EASTLAKE, CHARLES: *A History of the Gothic Revival.* London, 1872.
EVANS, JOAN: *John Ruskin.* New York, 1954.
GARRIGAN, KRISTINE O.: *Ruskin on Architecture: His Thought and Influence.* Madison, Wisconsin, 1973.
HEWISON, ROBERT: *John Ruskin: The Argument of the Eye.* Princeton, New Jersey, and London, 1976.

HILTON, TIMOTHY: *John Ruskin: The Early Years*. New Haven, Connecticut, 1985.

KEMP, WOLFGANG: *The Desire of My Eyes: A Life of John Ruskin*. 1991.

LADD, HENRY A.: *The Victorian Morality of Art: An Analysis of Ruskin's Esthetic*. New York, 1932.

LANDAU, G. F.: *The Aesthetic and Critical Theories of John Ruskin*. Princeton, New Jersey, 1971.

MACLEOD, R.: *Style and Society: Architectural Ideology in Britain 1835-1914*. London, 1971.

MUTHESIUS, STEFAN: *The High Victorian Movement in Architecture 1850-1870*. London, 1972.

NAYLOR, GILLIAN: *The Arts and Crafts Movement*. London, 1990.

PEVSNER, NIKOLAUS: *Ruskin and Viollet-le-Duc: Englishness and Frenchness in the Appreciation of Gothic Architecture*. London, 1969.

PEVSNER, NIKOLAUS: *Some Architectural Writers of the Nineteenth Century*. Oxford, 1972.

ROSENBERG, J. D.: *The Darkening Glass: A Portrait of John Ruskin's Genius*. New York, 1963.

SAINT, ANDREW: *The Image of the Architect*. London, 1983.

SHERBURNE, J. C.: *John Ruskin, or The Ambiguities of Abundance*. Cambridge, Massachusetts, 1972.

STEIN, ROGER B.: *John Ruskin and Aesthetic Thought in America, 1840-1900*. Cambridge, Massachusetts, 1967.

SWENARTON, MARK: *Artisans and Architects: The Ruskinian Tradition in Architectural Thought*. New York, 1989.

UNRAU, JOHN: *Looking at Architecture with Ruskin*. London, 1978.

UNRAU, JOHN: *Ruskin and St. Mark's*. London, 1984.

WALTON, PAUL H.: *The Drawings of John Ruskin*. Oxford, 1972.

WHEELER, MICHAEL, and WHITELEY, NIGEL (eds.): *The Lamp of Memory: Ruskin, Tradition and Architecture*. Manchester, 1992.

WIHL, GARY: *Ruskin and the Rhetoric of Infallibility*. 1985.

ARTICLES ABOUT RUSKIN

HITCHCOCK, HENRY-RUSSELL: "Ruskin or Butterfield: Victorian Gothic at the Mid-Century." In *Early Victorian Architecture in Britain*. New Haven, Connecticut, and London, 1954.

HITCHCOCK, HENRY-RUSSELL: "Ruskin and American Architecture, or Regeneration Long Delayed." In JOHN SUMMERSON (ed.): *Concerning Architecture: Essays on Architectural Writers and Writing Presented to Nikolaus Pevsner*. Baltimore and London, 1968.

SEKLER, MARY PATRICIA MAY: "Le Corbusier, Ruskin, the Tree, and the Open Hand." In RUSSELL WALDEN (ed.): *The Open Hand: Essays on Le Corbusier*. Cambridge, Massachusetts, 1977.

*

John Ruskin was at once the greatest and the most influential writer on architecture during the 19th century, his influence extending well beyond the drawing office into the drawing rooms of the burgeoning middle classes. A. W. N. Pugin was his equal as a polemicist, but Ruskin reached a mass audience and, despite the evangelical tone which pervaded his key architectural writings when they were first published in the late 1840s and early 1850s, his views on architecture received the endorsement of the Ecclesiological Society and thus found favor among its preferred architects, including William Butterfield and G. E. Street.

The key to a comprehension of Ruskin's architectural perceptions begins in an understanding of his use of evangelical typology in his writings and its relevance to his 19th-century context. His polymathic writings must also be approached as an adaptable and always growing organic whole. Ruskin cannot be judged in the terms of an architect, because he came to the study of architecture from the outside and was not in any real sense an architectural practitioner. He did collaborate with George Gilbert Scott in the preparation of designs for the stained glass windows at St. Giles, Camberwell, and at Camden Chapel, where the Ruskins were members of the congregation, and he prepared designs for windows at the Oxford Museum, for which his protégé Benjamin Woodward of the architects Deane and Woodward was the designer, but he was not, as common currency would have it in the early 20th century, the designer of virtually every building of the Gothic Revival. Despite this and the fact that his views differed from those of Pugin as well as many in the growing architectural profession, his influence was great. Furthermore, given his propensities, his lack of formal training proved to be more a strength than a weakness in his reading of architecture: he was not weighed down with the baggage of a classical architectural education and was therefore able to exercise his peculiar architectural sensibility to its fullest degree. In the resulting perceptions lie his most lasting legacies.

His introduction to architecture was an associational one influenced by the ideas of William Wordsworth, Sir Walter Scott and the watercolorists, which found satisfactory architectural expression to be in the harmony of a sublime or picturesque association between buildings and the natural landscape. A parallel and developing interest in architecture and geology was encouraged in the young Ruskin by J. C. Loudon, author of the influential *Encyclopaedia of Cottage Farm and Villa Architecture*, and found expression in Ruskin's *The Poetry of Architecture*, first published in London's *Architectural Magazine*, where his preference for the forms and tones of medieval architecture was reinforced.

Ruskin moved from this early associational appreciation of architecture to a visually perceived and optically correct reading which found increasing expression in his drawings after 1845. His key architectural writings produced between 1849 and 1853, *The Seven Lamps of Architecture* and the three volumes of *The Stones of Venice*, show evidence of this evolution in a context founded on his conception of nature in which landscape figured in a material and metaphorical equation with architecture. This had, for Ruskin, found its realization in the medieval cathedrals. In "The Lamp of Beauty" and in the first volume of *The Stones of Venice*, Ruskin argued for an architecture that derives its forms from the contours and proportions most frequently found in nature, while in "The Lamp of Power" he made the equation between majesty in nature and mass in architecture, mass not only of bulk but of light and darkness and color. From nature he also developed the concept of the wall-veil.

Ruskin, like Gilbert Scott, made the distinction between architecture and building, and seemed to equate the former with ornamentation. For this he has been consistently derided both by Victorian and later critics. However, his definition of ornament is the key to an understanding of his reading of architecture and is found in his conception of the orders of ornament. For him these exist in good architecture and are dependent for their perception on viewing distance. The first order viewed from afar is found in the weight and vigor of building mass, which is transmuted to an increasing richness of detail in the second order as the viewer approaches. Increasingly greater detail becomes apparent in the third and fourth orders as the viewer stands beneath the building and then approaches more closely its individual elements. The designer therefore needs to be aware of the modifying effect of detail on visual perception as well as the need for modification of detail to accommodate a changing viewpoint.

Ruskin also argued for the use of color to modify and enhance detail. Coupled with this conception in his writings is evidence of his comprehension of spatial and structural ideas couched in terms that are not technical, and which were more accessible to his general readership than to the architectural profession. Most significantly, he argued for the importance of subliminally perceived relationships and proportions, again at odds with the mathematically generated proportions of the classically trained.

He noted four styles of architecture as precedents that encompassed his ideas, but he came to be wary of the rampant eclecticism he saw around him. However, his eloquent espousal of Venetian Gothic led to the development of a "Ruskinian" style in Victorian architecture, from which he distanced himself. The nearest visual equation with his ideas was achieved by Woodward, in whose work may be found evidence of Ruskin's orders of ornament in forms and details derived from specific dictums of Ruskin's, including the need for a single bounding line and the preeminence of forms derivative of the square and circle. This work also exhibits ornamental detail originating in nature, although without the full degree of abstraction which Ruskin espoused. Of the High Victorian architects, Ruskin spoke favorably of aspects of Butterfield's All Saints, Margaret Street, and of the work of Street.

The study of architecture was the catalyst in Ruskin's work for a shift to the study of social issues; his work in the latter field influenced later theorists and pratitioners in architecture and design, including William Morris, C. R. Ashbee and W. R. Lethaby. In addition to his architectural influence, Ruskin bequeathed in his architectural prose a literary heritage that was to influence a number of writers, including Marcel Proust. His major bequest, however, lies in his description of the architectural experience derived from a unique visual and optical capacity, and its record expressed in words and drawings.

—R. J. MOORE

RUUSUVUORI, Aarno.

Finnish. Born in Kuopio, Finland, 14 January 1925. Died in Helsinki, Finland, February 1992. Married Anna Maria E. Jäämeri, 1970. Studied architecture at the Technical University, Helsinki, 1946-51; Dip.Arch. Established private practice, Helsinki, 1952. Acting professor, 1959-63, and professor of architecture, 1963-66, Technical University, Helsinki. Editor, 1952-55, and editor-in-chief, 1956-57, *Arkkitehtilehti* magazine, Helsinki. Director, Museum of Finnish Architecture, He lsinki, 1975-78, 1983-88. Honorary member, American Institute of Architects, 1982.

Chronology of Works
All in Finland

1961	Hyvinkää Church and Parish Center, Hyvinkää
1964	Huutoniemi Church and Parish Center, Vaasa
1965	Church and Parich Center, Tapiola, Espoo
1964-66	Weilin and Göös Printing Works, Tapiola, Espoo
1970/84	City Hall, Helsinki (renovations; stages I and II)

Aarno Ruusuvuori: City Hall, Helsinki, Finland, 1970/84

1979	Parate Printing Works, Helsinki
1987-	Plan for the National Museum, Helsinki (extensions)

Publications

BOOKS BY RUUSUVUORI

Finland Builds. Exhibition catalog. Helsinki, 1953.
Business Architecture in Finland. Helsinki, 1959.
Single-Family Houses. Helsinki, 1960.
Alvar Aalto. Exhibition catalog. Helsinki, 1978.

BOOKS ABOUT RUUSUVUORI

Finnish Architecture. The Hague, 1975.
KIDDER SMITH, G. E.: *The New Churches of Europe.* London, 1964.
SUHONEN, PEKKA: *Uutta suomalaistra arkkitehtuuria.* Helsinki, 1967.
TEMPEL, EGON: *Neue finnische Architektur.* Stuggart, 1968.

ARTICLES ABOUT RUUSUVUORI

"Aarno Ruusuvouri: Works." *Kentiku* No. 6 (1973).
"Aarno Ruusuvuori: Survey of Works." *Le carré bleu* No. 1 (1984).

*

Aarno Ruusuvuori earned his architectural diploma from the Helsinki University of Technology in 1951 and established an office in 1952. He joined the staff of the Technical University of Helsinki in 1959, and kept in close contact with younger architects, becoming professor of modern architecture in 1963. He was State Artist Professor from 1978 to 1983. Ruusuvuori always took a keen interest in his profession and was editor of the Finnish architectural journal *Arkkitehti* from 1952 to 1957. Work in his practice later left him less time for honorary duties. However, he was twice director of the Museum of Finnish Architecture, in 1975-78 and again in 1983-88. Ruusuvuori consistently encouraged good design as a teacher, a member of assessor panels and design boards, and a founding member of the Architecture Society of Finland. He was made an honorary member of the American Institute of Architects in 1982.

Ruusuvuori's work is distinguished by careful attention to detail and a grasp of structure that almost invariably stamps his buildings with characteristic clean lines, unadorned by decoration. Early success in competitions for the design of parish churches in Hyvinkää (1961) and in Huutoniemi, Vaasa (1964), exhibit unconventional geometric daring.

In the case of Hyvinkää Church, a vast, tentlike roof structure rises on corrugated wall sections such that the smaller structure over the utility areas cuts the taller structure over the triangle-shaped nave, allowing an inverted V-shaped glazed opening to be set into the apex. Light spills indirectly over the interior, reflected from the vertical corrugated wall sections. In the Huutoniemi Church, the monopitch roof slopes upward to the ''prow of the ship'' (a figure of the Church), and light from a high aperture is thrown from the angled ceiling downward to the congregation. The nave in this church is wider than it is long, a clever departure from the traditional mode of church interiors. Each church has support facilities for parish activities generous enough to make a missionary pastor yearn for home leave. These buildings, whose construction was financed by the ambitious Lutheran-Evangelical Church, reveal a strikingly innovative ecclesiastical architecture, different from the Imatra and Seinäjoki churches of Alvar Aalto. Ruusuvuori set a headline for an uncompromising style of church architecture followed since by the many architectural graduates who studied under him.

In 1965 Ruusuvuori won the church competition for the Garden City of Tapiola, a modest commission that he executed without undue ceremony. The concrete blockwork of the cube-shaped interior is relieved by the soft natural light streaming from a deep grid set into the rear wall. The beauty of the building lies in the way a place of worship becomes inconspicuously part of the city fabric. The parish center, isolated from its environment, brings to mind the peace of a convent cloister, and the feeling is enhanced by the tightly knit parish buildings and perimeter wall. Ruusuvuori adorned this building not with images of religious import but with the details of the steel window and door panels, furniture such as the grooved, marble-topped baptismal font, and the restrained belfry. All show his keen perception of functional design. Work on the church by the same office was completed in 1986.

The theory underlying Tapiola Garden City was that a dwelling suburb should be able to provide employment and avoid the commuter wave that hampers traffic flow in big cities. Ruusuvuori designed a two-story industrial building there for Weilin+Göös Printers, built in 1966. The innovative use of independent columns, each carrying 7,850 square feet of intermediate floor, and an equal area of roof suspended from above allowed the use of full-height solid infill panels in external walls at second-floor level and a continuous, glazed arcade at ground-floor level. In virtue of a sloping site, the building was served by ramps to each floor, an important asset for the movement of paper. The W+G Tapiola printing house is a prime example of how a properly designed industrial plant in sylvan surroundings can improve job performance. Ruusuvuori successfully undertook further industrial commissions for Marimekko (1968), Paragon (1973) and Parate (1979).

His restoration work began with Hämeenlinna Church (1964). After winning first prize in the open competition for the restoration of Helsinki's City Hall, he began a long and arduous planning process that caused rejuvenation of the old city center, and improved the viability of older buildings. Ruusuvuori showed exceptional skill in restoring such sensitive areas from the 17th-century town, and achieved a functional and well-designed milieu that attracted the return of both municipal and craft workers.

Ruusuvuori did not neglect the challenge dear to Finnish architects of all schools: to design a successful sauna. His 1966 design for an experimental house for Marimekko, in which tolerances were reduced to the order of 1 millimeter, showed that dimensional exactitude was a reachable target for the manufacture of timber elements. A sauna prototype made from elements appeared in 1968. Transportable to any location, it took only a day to erect. This was a technical breakthrough for the period. The sauna seating could be ordered in abache wood, a slow conductor of heat, so as not to scorch the skin. Floors were covered in sisal mats. Ruusuvuori built an even smaller sauna for his own use near Kerimäki, Eastern Finland. More like a piece of furniture than a building (area 111 square feet), it had three space elements: sauna, vestibule and veranda. The most recent sauna designed by the office Sauna Bonsdorff (1987) is technically exciting, but it lacks the rural simplicity of the above.

The office won a prestigious first prize in an invited competition to plan a suitable extension to the National Museum in Helsinki in 1987. The original building enjoys the status of a national shrine, at least for architects. It was designed by Gesellius, Lindgren, Saarinen, and completed in 1910. The new addition was to provide space for rotating exhibitions, lecture rooms and a conservation department. A solution placing the required accommodation below ground was to be expected, as no work above ground could be reconciled with the formal courtyard. Ruusuvuori cleverly selected the southwest corner of the courtyard as giving the best access to existing underground space. He proposed a new concourse at the lowest level below ground. It had a sloped skylight over an auditorium and several lantern lights strategically placed to give natural light for other functional spaces below ground. He skillfully kept the demands of the brief within three levels of excavation. In comparison with excavations for other museums, excepting the Louvre in Paris, which is larger than most, Ruusuvuori's solution combines a native ingenuity with assurance and restraint in solving what has become a growing problem for museums everywhere.

—DESMOND O'ROURKE

S

SAARINEN, Eero.

Finnish. Born in Kirkkonummi, Finland, 20 August 1910. Died in Ann Arbor, Michigan, 1 September 1961. Father was the architect Eliel Saarinen. Family immigrated to the United States, 1923. Studied sculpture at the Académie de la Grand Chaumière, Paris, 1929-30; studied architecture at Yale University, New Haven, Connecticut, B.F.A. 1934. Joined his father's architectural practice, Ann Arbor, Michigan, 1936; practiced with his father, 1937-41; partner, with his father and J. Robert Swanson, Saarinen-Swanson-Saarinen, Ann Arbor, 1941-47, then, with his father, Saarinen, Saarinen and Associates, Ann Arbor, 1947 until his father's death in 1950; principal of the successor firm, Eero Saarinen and Associates, Birmingham, Michigan, 1950-61.

Chronology of Works
All in the United States unless noted

1937-38	Community House, Fenton, Michigan (with Eliel Saarinen)
1938	Berkshire Music Center, Tanglewood, Massachusetts (with Eliel Saarinen)
1938-40	Kleinhaus Music Hall, Buffalo, New York (with Eliel Saarinen)
1938-40	Crow Island School, Winnetka, Illinois (with Eliel Saarinen; Perkins, Wheeler and Will)
1939-42	Tabernacle Church of Christ, Columbus, Indiana (with Eliel Saarinen)
1941	Houses, School and Community Hall, Center Line, Michigan (with Eliel Saarinen and J. Robert Swanson)
1941-42	A. C. Wermuth House, Fort Wayne, Indiana (with Eliel Saarinen)
1942	Schools, Willow Run, Michigan (with Eliel Saarinen and J. Robert Swanson)
1942	Summer Opera House and Chamber Music Hall, Berkshire Music Center, Tanglewood, Massachusetts (with Eliel Saarinen)
1943	Lincoln Heights Housing Area, Washington, D.C. (with Eliel Saarinen and J. Robert Swanson)
1945-56	General Motors Technical Center, Warren, Michigan (with Smith, Hinchman, and Grylls)
1946-57	Metropolitan Milwaukee War Memorial, Milwaukee, Wisconsin
1948-64	Jefferson National Expansion Memorial (Gateway Arch), St. Louis, Missouri
1953-56	Kresge Auditorium and Chapel, Massachusetts Institute of Technology, Cambridge, Massachusetts (with Anderson and Beckwith)
1953-57	Irwin Miller Residence, Columbus, Indiana (with Alexander Girard and Dan Kiley)
1953-58	Concordia College, Fort Wayne, Indiana
1955-58	Dormitory Complex, University of Chicago, Chicago, Illinois
1955-59	United States Chancellery Building, Oslo, Norway
1955-60	United States Embassy, London, England (with Yorke, Rosenberg, and Mardall)
1956-59	Ingalls Hockey Rink, Yale University, New Haven, Connecticut
1956-60	Law School, University of Chicago, Chicago, Illinois
1956-62	Terminal, Trans World Airways, Kennedy Airport, New York City
1957-60	Dormitory, University of Pennsylvania, Philadelphia, Pennsylvania
1957-61	Thomas J. Watson Research Center, International Business Machines Corporation, Yorktown, New York
1957-62	Bell Laboratories, Holmdel, New Jersey
1957-63	Deere and Company Headquarters, Moline, Illinois
1958-62	Dulles Airport, Chantilly, Virginia (with Ammann and Whitney)
1958-62	Samuel F. B. Morse and Ezra Stiles Colleges, Yale University, New Haven, Connecticut
1960-64	Columbia Broadcasting System Headquarters, New York City

Publications

BOOKS BY SAARINEN

Eero Saarinen on His Work. Edited by Aline B. Saarinen. New Haven, Connecticut, 1962; 2nd ed., 1968.

ARTICLES BY SAARINEN

"The Architecture of Defense Housing." Edited by Edmond H. Hoben, in *National Association of Housing Officials Journal* (Chicago), no. 165 (1942).
"Trends in Modern Architecture." *Michigan Society of Architects Bulletin* (May 1951).
"Our Epoch of Architecture." *Journal of the American Institute of Architects* 18 (1952): 243-247.
"Six Broad Currents of Modern Architecture." *Architectural Forum* (July 1953).
"The Changing Philosophy of Architecture." *Architectural Record* (August (1954).
"Function, Structure and Beauty." *Architectural Association Journal* (July-August 1957): 40-51.
"Campus Planning: The Unique World of the University." *Architectural Record* (November 1960).

BOOKS ABOUT SAARINEN

CLARK, ROBERT JUDSON: *Design in America: The Cranbrook Vision 1925-1950.* Exhibition catalog. New York, 1983.

Eero Saarinen: Terminal, Trans World Airways, Kennedy Airport, New York City, New York, 1956-62

HALL, EDWARD and MILDRED: *The Fourth Dimension in Architecture*. Santa Fe, New Mexico, 1975.

HAUSER, E.: *Saarinen*. Hamburg, 1984.

IGLESIA, E. J.: *Eero Saarinen*. Buenos Aires, 1966.

LARRABEE, ERIC and VIGNELLI, MASSIMO: *Knoll Design*. New York, 1981.

MEYEROWITZ, JOEL: *St. Louis and the Arch*. Boston, 1980.

SPADE, R. and FUTAGAWA, Y.: *Eero Saarinen*. New York, 1968.

TEMKO, ALLAN: *Eero Saarinen*. New York and London, 1962.

ARTICLES ABOUT SAARINEN

Architecture and Urbanism, special issue (April 1984).

CARTER, PETER: "Eero Saarinen 1910-1961." *Architectural Design* (December 1961).

DEAN, ANDREA O.: "Eero Saarinen in Perspective." *American Institute of Architects Journal* (November 1981).

DORFLES, G.: "Eero Saarinen: The TWA Terminal and the American Embassy, London." *Zodiac* 8 (1961): 84-89.

FREEMAN, ALLEN: "The World's Most Beautiful Airport?." *American Institute of Architects Journal* (November 1980).

HALIK, NANCY LICKERMAN: "The Eero Saarinen Spawn." *Inland Architect* (May 1981).

HASKELL, DOUGLAS: "Eero Saarinen 1910-1961." *Architectural Forum* (October 1961).

HEWITT, WILLIAM: "The Genesis of a Great Building and an Unusual Friendship." *American Institute of Architects Journal* (August 1977).

KAUFMANN, EDGAR, JR.: "Inside Eero Saarinen's TWA Building." *Interiors* 121 (1962): 86-93.

LESSING, LAWRENCE: "The Diversity of Eero Saarinen." *Architectural Forum* (July 1960).

LIFCHEZ, RAYMOND: "On Eero Saarinen." *Zodiac* 17 (1967).

McCUE, GEORGE: "The Arch: An Appreciation." *American Institute of Architects Journal* 67 (1978): 57-63.

McQUADE, WALTER: "Eero Saarinen, A Complete Architect." *Architectural Forum* 116 (October 1962): 102-119.

Michigan Society of Architects Bulletin (Detroit), special issue (July 1953).

PAPADEMETRIOU, PETER C.: "Coming of Age: Eero Saarinen and Modern American Architecture." *Perspecta* 21 (1985): 116-141.

"Recent Work by Eero Saarinen." *Royal Institute of British Architects Journal* (November 1960).

"Recent Work of Eero Saarinen." *Zodiac* 4 (1959): 30-67.

TEMKO, ALLAN: "Eero Saarinen: Something Between Earth and Sky." *Horizon* (July 1960).

ZEVI, BRUNO: "Pluralismo e prop-architettura." *Architettura* (September 1967).

*

Ironically, two of this century's modern architects shared a life's work, the same initials and a birthday. Eliel Saarinen was born in 1873 and Eero Saarinen, his only son, in 1910, on August 20. The Saarinens are also the only father-son duo to have received the Gold Medal of the American Institute of Architects. They had careers, and shared careers in partnership, which eluded simple formal classification; in Eero's case, the path to personal realization as an architect was complicated by maturing under his father's shadow.

The United States was their adopted country. Eliel had a promising career in his native Finland by 1910, and had become internationally known as a planner-architect. He maintained an atelier and salon of the cultural arts, including the work of his weaver wife Loja, at Hvitträsk, his home near Helsinki, where the children, Eva-Lisa (known as Pipsan) and Eero, were raised. However, the virtual collapse of the Finnish economy following independence from Russia in 1919 made architectural practice impossible. In 1922 Eliel achieved worldwide notice when he placed second in the international competition for the Chicago Tribune Tower; on that basis, at age 49 he decided to immigrate to the United States. The family joined Eliel in mid-1923, settling briefly near Chicago in Evanston, Illinois, and then in Ann Arbor, Michigan, where Eliel was given a special appointment at the University of Michigan in 1924.

Among Eliel's students were J. Robert F. Swanson, who was to become his son-in-law, and Henry Scripps Booth, son of George G. Booth, publisher of the *Detroit News*. Having been impressed by the elder Saarinen through a study for a Detroit civic center initiated with his students, and sharing a vision of the cultural integration of the arts, Booth retained him to undertake a master plan for a group of educational institutions at his estate, Cranbrook, in nearby Bloomfield Hills. By late 1925 the Saarinens had moved to Cranbrook.

Cranbrook was a comfortable adjustment, a kind of Americanized Hvitträsk, and with Eliel's double role as principal architect and then president of the Cranbrook Academy of Art, the entire family's creative energies were given focus. After apprenticing in the Cranbrook architectural office in 1928 and 1929, Eero left for Paris on the eve of the Great Depression to study sculpture at the Académie de la Grande Chaumière through the spring of 1930, and continued his studies at Cranbrook after his return. By that time, his interests began to turn more definitively toward architecture.

The decade of the 1930s is the period where Eero attempted to define a modern architecture that could recognize the innovations of the International Style, but also retain a comfortable foothold in the past. Such was the case with the most modernistic building at Cranbrook, the Institute of Science (1934-38) whose overall form is abstract and certain details, such as the cantilevered entrance canopy, suggest a modernist disposition, at the same time as its supports are decorative piers more evocative of Eliel Saarinen. In 1931 Eero entered the Graduate School of Fine Arts at Yale University. Upon completion of the program in 1934, he left for Europe and traveled through Egypt and the Near East before returning to Finland to serve as a collaborator on extensions to the Swedish Theater in Helsinki.

Through an opportunity provided by the Yale connection, Eero was invited in early 1938 to serve as a designer in the office of Norman Bel Geddes in New York; it was here that he explored the possibilities of "streamlining" as a designer for the General Motors "Futurama" building at the 1939 World's Fair.

Simultaneously, the Saarinens began to achieve national notice. Eero had placed fifth in a national competition for an art center at Wheaton College, and in the summer of 1938 the team placed second in a campus plan and college library competition at Goucher College. The principal innovations exhibited in both is that of carefully balanced assymmetry and a greater flow between spaces. Several major independent projects were also initiated: the Kleinhans Music Hall (Buffalo, New York 1938-40; Kidd & Kidd, Associated Architects) and the Crow Island (Southwest) School (Winnetka, Illinois 1930-40; Perkins, Wheeler & Will, Associated Architects) and perhaps the most famous, the First Christian Church in Columbus, Indiana (1939-42; E. D. Pierre and George Wright, Associate Architects). Not only were these among the few significant buildings built during the Great Depression, but they were clearly modern, Kleinhans

exhibiting Art Deco streamlining in its interiors. These projects also drew upon a unique wealth of design talent from the graduate program in Architecture at the Academy of Art, which had been initiated by Eliel Saarinen in 1931. By the late 1930s, this was strengthened by Charles Eames as the head of the Design Department, Harry Bertoia in the metal workshop, and Eero being appointed as assistant to his father.

During these years, Eero explored the theme of relating form to the limits of technology, particularly with Charles Eames, who worked on Kleinhans, the Columbus Church, and the Smithsonian, initiating a lifelong friendship. Together they collaborated on the innovative 1939 Faculty Exhibit at Cranbrook using a lightweight tensile system. They developed furniture, such as the "potato chip" chair, using molded plywood techniques which won first prize in the Organic Design in Home Furnishings Competition sponsored by the Museum of Modern Art (1940-41). Eero pursued this direction through the war years, after Eames left for his future career in California.

During the World War II, a national awareness of planning and a resurgence in building activity provided the Saarinen office expanded opportunities. Capitalizing on Eliel's reputation as a planner (his book *The City* appeared in 1943), numerous college campus plans led to actual buildings. Institutional clients followed, of which the most important was the creation of the General Motors Technical Center, beginning in 1945. This was "the" commission that consolidated Eero Saarinen's reputation.

After the partnership was reformed as Saarinen, Saarinen and Associates in 1947, other postwar projects displayed formal themes which might best be characterized as a tentative post-International Style modernism, while the GMTC conveyed a pivotal search for form. The first scheme contained essential Saarinen themes, such as the presence of the lake as a large, unifying formal element and the interplay of horizontal forms punctuated by vertical elements. Eliel had early demonstrated in his 1924 studies for the Chicago Lakefront a willingness to deal with the automobile, and the overall feeling was of a functionalist, industrialized campus organized formally by principles evoked by the 1939 "City of Tomorrow" at Norman Bel Geddes's GM "Futurama," imposing an image which sought a means to express the essence of modernism in a new cultural context.

A second version of the GMTC followed after the project had been stopped for nearly half a year by a major strike, and its revised organization reflected the principles of Mies van der Rohe (1886-1969)—a debt openly acknowledged by Saarinen. In contrast, however, to the more static, nearly neoclassical groupings at the recently designed campus for the Illinois Institute of Technology, the newer version of the Tech Center evidenced a dialectic interplay between objectivity and romantic subjectivity. It should be noted that by 1950 both Kevin Roche, who worked briefly for Mies, and John Dinkeloo, from the Chicago office of Skidmore, Owings and Merrill, were at the Saarinen office. After 1967, the practice was known as Kevin Roche John Dinkeloo & Associates.

The subjective dimension is critical to understanding Saarinen's work, because this allowed it to retain disparate elements within it, from the ability to accept the use of neoclassical order in an industrial building to the development of manufactured products into lyrical design elements, the most notable being the design of the curtain wall construction employing window installation using neoprene gaskets such as those in automobile windshields. In his uses of a refined industrialization, Saarinen suggested in its purity and technological advancement a society which was perhaps the greatest industrialized nation, and GMTC the first monumental exploration of this technology and its cultural meaning. It was the image of the Tech Center plan which formed the background when a portrait of Eero Saarinen appeared on the cover of *Time* magazine, July 2, 1956.

The attraction of the Miesian vocabulary was undoubtedly its minimalism as an aspect of precision and abstraction. Subsequent projects pushed the mute nature of such expression. Notable examples include the International Business Machines manufacturing plant (Rochester, Minnesota; 1956-59) where both glass and solid panels were uniformly of 5/16-inch thickness, neutralizing distinctions between solid and transparent portions of enclosure by an implicit and literal interchangeability, and the Bell Telephone Laboratories Development center at Holmdell, New Jersey (1957-62), whose neutral exterior was a precursor to the all-glass skins of the late 1970s through one of the earliest uses of solar mirror glass. Rochester's aformal nature as a potentially endless system of large and small spatial modular units, combined together as needed, and Bell's finely gridded, blank reflective surfaces in a sense reflected a parallel to the Abstract Expressionists in art, whose neutrality of representation was concerned with *process* rather than content and resulted in an extremely precisionist strain in formal abstraction, as in the art of Josef Albers or Barnett Newman. Related to this abstracted industrialized minimalism is the John Deere and Company Administrative Building (Moline, Illinois; 1957-63), a composition of the repetition of analogous forms and the relationship of parts through the use of standard steel sections in one of the first applications of Cor-Ten steel, whose finish is an arrested self-rusting skin; highly sculptural and articulated, Deere continued the precisionist abstract image of industrialized production, while it metaphorically related to the steel used in the company's tractors and farm equipment.

Another facet of this minimalist trend was the investment of iconic power in pure forms. At the Massachusetts Institute of Technology, the Kresge Auditorium and MIT Chapel (1953-56) extend the ideas of Mies by the pure integrity of structure in the then-largest thin shell roof, a precision of architectural form in the segmented dome on three pendentives and the purity of a brick cylinder. Paradoxically, pure forms also organized difficult sites; the Stephens College Chapel (Columbia, Missouri; 1953-57) was a pure square, the United States Embassy in Oslo, Norway (1955-59) reconciled a difficult urban site into a simple triangular solid and the Irwin Miller Residence (Columbus, Indiana; 1953-57) is a square in a Cartesian landscape.

It is the lack of a clear stylistic progression which has confounded a critical analysis of Saarinen's work, for while exploring the abstracted meaning of technological expression, he was equally willing to expand on pure forms of allegory and allusion. Possibly the greatest public monument produced in the period of modern architecture, Saarinen's entry to the Jefferson National Expansion Memorial Competition in St. Louis (1948-67) synthesized the qualities of abstraction, monumentality and structural daring with a stainless steel arch 630 feet in height derived from a catenary curve, and is also metaphorical in its allusions, consciously symbolizing the idea of the Gateway to the West.

New advances in construction and engineering also facilitated a greater freedom of formal expression and gave Saarinen a means of suggesting, in abstract terms analogous to that occurring in painting, metaphorical allusions. "Action" and "gestural" painting suggested an aesthetic of coherence through a single image. The Trans World Airlines Flight Center at New York's Kennedy Airport (1956-62) was perhaps the most advanced of sculptural forms, providing a continuity of space and shape which facilitated passenger flow, but whose complex curves were allegorically meant to suggest flight. The metaphor

was, as John Jacobus suggested, intended as "an updated *architecture parlante* . . . a literary architecture that would arouse emotions and affect sentiments."

Diversity within unity is a critical characteristic of Eero Saarinen's architectural achievements; never an orthodox modernist, he is best understood as a *heterodox* modernist. In many ways the Dulles International Airport in Chantilly, Virginia, near Washington, D.C. (1958-62) was the synthesis of the multiple directions of the last decade of his career, as it was an indicator of what might have been that career's possible future course. Saarinen's rational method was able to resolve a redefined program without precedent (the first all-jet airport) through the employment of advanced technology in both construction and functional innovation.

The Mobile Lounge of Dulles depicts the development of an industrial design component between gateway and aircraft. Its roof slab was poured integrally with suspension steel cables slung between sloped pylons without the use of scaffolding, creating a clear span of nearly 170 feet. The design combines a rigorous and direct symmetrical organization, at the same time as it is aformal in its acceptance of future growth and indeterminacy. Its visual qualities are essentially abstract and sculptural, yet its monumentality is heroic as a "gateway," and its whiteness evokes a metaphorical connection to Washington, D.C.

Eero Saarinen appeared to be, at the time of his death in September 1961, on the edge of a new point of synthesis, with formal inventiveness which drew on the traditions of the past but, having little interest in repetitive vocabularies, suggested the possibility of an autonomous architecture for each project. As John Jacobus observed, "Stripped of its literary complications, however, it at last becomes a form of universal strength. . . . Eero Saarinen did more than reflect the changing tastes and passion of his time: he truly found himself as an architect and as an individual."

—PETER PAPADEMETRIOU

SAARINEN, Eliel.

Finnish. Born in Rantasalmi, Finland, 20 August 1873. Died in Cranbrook Hills, Michigan, 1 July 1950. Son was the architect Eliel Saarinen. Immigrated to the United States, 1923. Simultaneously studied painting at Helsinki University and architecture at Helsinki Polytechnic, 1893-97: Dip.Arch. Partner with Gesellius and Lindegren, Helsinki, 1896-1905; in private practice, Helsinki, 1907-23, Evanston, Illinois, 1923-24, and Ann Arbor, Michigan, 1924-37; practiced with son Eero in Ann Arbor, 1937-41; partner, with Eero and J. Robert Swanson, Saarinen-Swanson-Saarinen, Ann Arbor, 1941-47; partner, Saarinen, Saarinen and Associates, Ann Arbor, 1947-50. Director, 1925-32, president, 1932-50, and director of the Graduate Department of Architecture and City Planning, 1948-50, Cranbrook Academy of Arts, Bloomfield Hills, Michigan.

Chronology of Works
All in Finland unless noted:

1900	Finnish Pavilion, Paris Exposition, Paris, France
1901-03	Hvitträsk, near Helsinki
1902	Suur-Merijoki, near Viborg
1902-12	National Museum, Helsinki
1904	Nordiska Foreningsbanken, Helsinki
1904	Railway Station, Viborg
1904-19	Helsinki Railway Station, Helsinki

1905-07	Molchow-Haus, Mark Bradenburg, Germany
1909-13	City Hall, Joensuu
1910-15	Munksnas-Haga Plan, Helsinki
1911-12	City Hall, Lahti
1918	Greater Helsinki Plan, Helsinki

All in the United States:

1922	Chicago Tribune Tower (competition entry)
1926-30	Cranbrook School for Boys, Bloomfield Hills, Michigan
1926-41	Cranbrook Academy of Art, Bloomfield Hills, Michigan
1928-30	Saarinen House, Bloomfield Hills, Michigan
1929-31	Kingswood School for Girls, Cranbrook, Bloomfield Hills, Michigan
1929-30	Hudnut House, New York (with Ely Jacques Kahn)
1931	Stevens Institute of Technology, Hoboken, New Jersey
1931-33	Institute of Science, Cranbrook, Bloomfield Hills, Michigan
1937-38	Community House, Fenton, Michigan (with Eero Saarinen)
1938	Berkshire Music Center, Tanglewood, Massachusetts (with Eero Saarinen)
1938-40	Kleinhaus Music Hall, Buffalo, New York (with Eero Saarinen)
1938-40	Crow Island School, Winnetka, Illinois (with Eero Saarinen; Perkins, Wheeler and Will)
1939-42	Tabernacle Church of Christ, Columbus, Indiana (with Eero Saarinen)
1940-43	Museum and Library, Cranbrook Academy of Art, Bloomfield Hills, Michigan
1941	Houses, School and Community Hall, Center Line, Michigan (with Eero Saarinen and J. Robert Swanson)
1941-42	A. C. Wermuth House, Fort Wayne, Indiana (with Eero Saarinen)
1942	Schools, Willow Run, Michigan (with Eero Saarinen and J. Robert Swanson)
1942	Summer Opera House and Chamber Music Hall, Berkshire Music Center, Tanglewood, Massachusetts (with Eero Saarinen)
1943	Lincoln Heights Housing Area, Washington, D.C. (with Eero Saarinen and J. Robert Swanson)
1944-48	Edmundson Memorial Museum, Des Moines Art Center, Iowa

Publications

BOOKS BY SAARINEN

Munksnas-Haga. With Gustaf Strengall. Helsinki, 1915.
The Cranbrook Development. Bloomfield Hills, Michigan, 1931.
The City: Its Growth, Its Decay, Its Future. New York, 1943.
The Search for Form: A Fundamental Approach to Art. New York, 1948; as *The Search for Form in Art and Architecture.* New York, 1985.

BOOKS ABOUT SAARINEN

CHRIST-JANER, ALBERT: *Eliel Saarinen: Finnish-American Architect and Educator.* Chicago, 1948. Rev. ed.: Chicago, 1979.

CLARK, ROBERT JUDSON, et al.: *Design in America: The Cranbrook Vision 1925-1950.* Exhibition catalog. New York, 1983.
DEMKIN, IGOR: *Eliel Saarinen ja'Suur-Tallinn.* Tallinn, Estonia, 1977.
GAIDOS, ELIZABETH (ed.): *The Creative Spirit of Cranbrook.* Bloomfield Hills, Michigan, 1972.
GIEDION, SIGFRIED: *Space, Time and Architecture.* Cambridge, Massachusetts, 1941.
GROPIUS, WALTER: *The New Architecture and the Bauhaus.* London, 1935.
HAUSEN, M.; KIRMO, M.; AMBERG, A.; and VALTO, T. (eds.): *Eliel Saarinen: Projects 1896-1923.* Cambridge, Massachusetts, 1990.
MEURMAN, OTTO: *Asemakaavaoppi.* Helsinki, 1947.
NOYES, ELIOT F.: *Organic Design in Home Furnishings.* New York, 1941.
NYSTROM, PER: *Toly kapitel om Munksnas.* Helsinki, 1945.
SETALA, HELMI: *Kun Suuret Olivat Pienia.* Helsinki, 1911.
SIRÉN, J. S. (ed.): *Eliel Saarinen, Muistonäyttely.* Helsinki, 1955.
Saarinen (1907)-1923. Finnish Museum, 1984.
Saarinen's Interior Design, 1896-1923. Finnish Museum, 1984.
The Saarinen Door. With an introduction by Eva Ingersol Gatling. Bloomfield Hills, Michigan, 1963.

ARTICLES ABOUT SAARINEN

BARKER, KENT: "Eliel Saarinen: An Appreciation." *Journal of the Royal Architectural Institute of Canada* (December 1944).
BLOMSTEDT, AULIUS: "Eliel Saarinen." *Arkkitehti* 11/12 (1943).
"Eliel Saarinen Residence, Cranbrook Academy of Art." *GA Houses* (July 1981).
"Eliel Saarinen." Special issue of *Form Function Finland* no. 2 (1984).
FAYANS, STEFAN: "Baukunst und Volk." *Moderne Bauformen* 8, No. 8 (1909): 337-353.
HAUSEN, MARIKA: "Gesellius-Lindgren-Saarinen." *Arkkitehti* 9 (1967).
HAUSEN, MARIKA: "The Helsinki Railway Station in Eliel Saarinen's first versions 1904." *Taidehistoriallisia Tukimuksia Konsthistoriska Studier* 3 (1977): 57-114.
HUDNUT, JOSEPH (commentator): "Crow Island School, Winnetka, Ill." *Architectural Forum* 75 (1941): 79-92.
HUDNUT, JOSEPH: "Kleinhans Music Hall, Buffalo, N.Y." *Architectural Forum* 75 (1941): 35-42.
HUDNUT, JOSEPH: "Smithsonian Competition Results." *Magazine of Art* 32 (1939): 456-459, 488-489.
JUNG, BERTEL: "Eliel Saarinen." *Arkitekten* 3 (1932).
MIKKOLA, KIRMO: "Eliel Saarinen as the Interpreter of Urban Planning in His Own Time." *Arkkitehti* 4 (1981).
MIKKOLA, KIRMO: "The Finnish Horizon." *Byggekunst* 1 (1982).
MUTO, AKIRA and SANO, KEIBUN: "Railway Station, Helsinki." *Space Design* (November 1982).
ÖHQUIST, JOHANNES: "Ein Finnischer Städtebauer." *Städtebau* 17, Nos. 3-4:21-27.
OSBORN-BERLIN, MAX: "Ein modernes Märkisches Waldschlösschen (Molchow-Haus bei Alt-Ruppin)." *Moderne Bauformen* 7, No. 6:217-239.
REID, KENNETH: "Eliel Saarinen, Master of Design." *Pencil Points* 17 (September 1936): 463-494.
STRENGELL, GUSTAF: "L'Architecte Eliel Saarinen." *Art vivant* (15 October 1928).

SULLIVAN, LOUIS: "The Chicago Tribune Competition." *Architectural Record* 53 (1923): 151-157.

SWANSON, J. ROBERT: "Eliel Saarinen." *Michigan Technic* (Ann Arbor, May 1924).

TILGHMAN, DONNELL: "Eliel Saarinen." *Architectural Record* 63 (May 1928): 393-402.

WANSCHER, VILHELM: "The Chicago Tribune Building." *Arkitekten* 25 (1923): 22-28.

*

Within the tradition of architecture that draws upon numerous histories and memories, Eliel Saarinen was a master. He had the rare ability to synthesize and transform diverse artistic sources, depending on the context, program and symbolic needs of a given project, to create meaningful works of art. While his architecture remains outside of the traditions of modernism as defined by the International Style, it is a remarkable example of an alternative modernism, an architecture which was not intended to be universal in its application but rather a vehicle of specific cultural expressions.

Saarinen first received national, indeed international, attention with the Finnish pavilion for the Paris Exposition of 1900, a building that demonstrated with considerable flair his ability to use architecture to communicate symbolic content. He designed it with his partners, Armas Lindgren and Herman Gesellius, during the last two years of the 19th century, a period when the relative autonomy that Finland had experienced as a Russian grand duchy was under attack. Many prominent artists responded with works that became symbols of national identity and expressions of political protest designed to elicit international support against the czar's policy of Russification. Drawing upon the theories and designs of the English Arts and Crafts movement, the Vienna Secession and the Jugendstil architects, Saarinen and other architects used the forms and details of Finnish medieval castles, stone churches and vernacular log structures to create an architectural language which has come to be called Finnish National Romanticism. In the pavilion, the plan and form recalled Finnish medieval churches while the interior of the central hall was dominated by the frescoes of Akseli Gallen-Kallela illustrating the mythical events portrayed in Finland's national epic, the *Kalevala*. While Finns no doubt recognized the national sources of the pavilion, other visitors would have assumed that it was Finnish by its very contrast to the Beaux-Arts architecture that dominated the exposition. The building, however, was a synthesis of national and international styles and equally indebted to American influences, including the neo-Romanesque architecture of Henry Hobson Richardson.

In addition to the symbolic role of architecture, another theme central to Saarinen's career, if not the guiding principle, is the idea that architecture encompasses all aspects of design. Eero Saarinen, reflecting on his father's career at a Munich congress in 1960, observed: "My father. . .saw architecture as everything from city planning to the ashtray on a living room table." As a total work of art, a *Gesamtkunstwerk*, the architects' Villa Hvitträsk (1901-03) is a masterwork. Situated on a wooded ridge above a lake, the complex included a home for each of the partners and a joint studio arranged around a central courtyard. The exteriors of the original buildings were distinguished by their use of granite and timber, materials indigenous to Finland which had become symbols of national identity during the National Romantic movement. The timber construction, which recalled vernacular farmhouses, continues in the interior of Saarinen's section, for which he designed or selected a rich variety of applied arts. The dining room, for example, includes carved oak furniture, a *ryijy*-rug and metal sconces designed by Saarinen, as well as frescoes and stained glass supplied by other artists.

The Finnish National Museum (1902-12), the last project designed under the auspices of the Gesellius, Lindgren and Saarinen partnership, was the culmination of the National Romantic movement in Finland. The architects won this competition with the argument that each of the museum's departments should be separate and given its own architecturally identifiable form, a concept for which National Romanticism's picturesque and typically asymmetrical style was particularly appropriate. Thus, the ecclesiastical art was housed in a medieval church and the weaponry was placed in a fortress-style tower.

Like the Finnish Pavilion, the Helsinki Railway Station (1904-19) integrates national ideas with international forms. Saarinen's first design for the station was similar in form and detail to the museum. National Romanticism, however, was no longer the potent symbol it once was. With the Russian czar losing power and Germany continuing to grow as a European power, Finland began to look beyond mere cultural autonomy toward political independence. For this expanded context where the symbolism needed to reflect international, not just national, concerns, Saarinen redesigned the station in the rational style as it was developing in Germany and Austria. With its major interior spaces boldly expressed in the exterior form, the building is an important example of early modernism in which architectural form expresses a building's function. Although this approach also formed the basis of the International Style, Saarinen consistently cloaked this formalism with the materials and details of a more traditional regionalism.

The building also is pivotal in Saarinen's career as the first project where the urban context was an important aspect of the design. City planning, for Saarinen the ultimate *Gesamtkunstwerk* and the subject of one of his books, remained a central issue in his career, although for the most part economics and politics prevented the implementation of these theories and plans. In neighborhoods such as those that he proposed for Helsinki's Munkkiniemi-Haaga plan, Saarinen combined intimate squares, based on the historical models developed by Camillo Sitte and implemented by Raymond Unwin in his garden cities, with the classical axes used by Georges-Eugène Haussmann in Paris. His planning on an urban scale is best demonstrated by the Greater Helsinki Project, one of the first large-scale studies of a decentralized plan in which the inner city was ringed by small garden communities linked together by an elaborate system of railways and highways.

It was his entry for the *Chicago Tribune* Competition of 1922 that brought Saarinen critical acclaim in the United States and led him to relocate in the Midwest. The majority of the American entries, including the winning Gothic design of Raymond Hood and John Mead Howells, were overtly historical in their conception, while many of the European entries represented the ideas of the European avant-garde. Saarinen's proposal, which won second place, integrated the strengths of both views. While the building had a vaguely medieval tone, overt historic references were avoided, and ornamentation was minimized to accentuate the building's telescoping form.

As architect-in-residence (1925-50) at the Cranbrook Educational Community and president (1932-46) of its Art Academy, Saarinen was responsible not only for giving physical form to most of the campus but also for helping to shape the program of the academy, one of the most influential art schools in America. Kingswood School for Girls (1929-31) and Saarinen House (1928-30), his own home and studio, are the community's gems. When designing Kingswood he searched for a new architectural vocabulary, one that would express his adopted American heritage. Nestled into the slope of a hill overlooking a lake, the school has a horizontal emphasis and broad, hipped roofs that draw upon the Prairie houses of his friend and midwestern rival, Frank Lloyd Wright, while the stepped forms of the chimneys, recalling the Tribune Tower entry, provide strong vertical accents. The interiors demonstrate the collaboration of Saarinen's family, including his wife Loja (woven textiles), daughter Pipsan (wall and ceiling stenciling) and son Eero (furniture). Ornamental themes were established in architectural elements such as chimneys and columns and repeated in the design of gates, leaded-glass windows and textiles. In Saarinen House, a personal space, the architect combined the clarity and simplicity of modernism with the warmth of his earlier National Romantic interiors. In the dining room, a refined example of art deco, he contrasted the crisp geometries of an octagonal plan, square rug and round table with the soft textures of waxed pine panels, a contemporary Finnish tapestry and velvet portieres. His panache as a designer is evident through the use of brilliant red paint on the interior of four corner niches and a gilded domed ceiling.

Eero proved to be an important influence on his father. The buildings that they designed together during the last decade of Eliel's career demonstrate a synthesis of Eliel's sustained sensitivity to materials and detailing and Eero's desire to create bold sculptural forms. In the Kleinhans Music Hall, Buffalo, New York (1938-40), the large auditorium and small chamber music hall are expressed in the curving forms of the exterior. Although the building is constructed of concrete, it is clad in tan brick and Mankato stone, traditional materials that impart a warmth and human scale to the building. Crow Island School, Winnetka, Illinois (1938-40), expresses the Winnetka Board of Education's progressive educational system through a series of distinctly articulated classrooms. The building became a prototype for the low, spreading elementary schools of the postwar era. In the Tabernacle Church of Christ, Columbus, Indiana (1939-42), the major components, including a freestanding bell tower, are arranged around a sunken garden and defined by pure rectangular forms.

Together, these buildings continued the role Eliel Saarinen established early in his career, forming a bridge between the traditionalists and the avant-garde, and integrating national motifs and international forms to create a modern architecture rich in its detail and meaning.

—GREGORY M. WITTKOPP

SAFDIE, Moshe.

Canadian. Born in Haifa, Israel, 14 July 1938. Moved to Canada, 1955, and acquired Canadian citizenship, 1959. Married Nina Nusynowicz, 1959 (divorced, 1981); married Michal Ronnen, 1981. Studied at McGill University, Montreal, B.Arch.,1961. Worked for Van Ginkel and Associates, Montreal, 1961-62; worked for Louis I. Kahn, Philadelphia, Pennsylvania, 1962-63; section head, Canadian Corporation for the 1967 World Exhibition, 1963-64; private practice in Montreal, since 1964, then in Jerusalem, since 1971, and in Boston, Massachusetts, and Toronto, Ontario, since 1978. Professor of architecture and director of the Desert Architecture and Environment Department, Desert Research Institute, Ben Gurion University, Beersheva, Negev, Israel, 1975-78; professor of architecture and urban design, Graduate School of Design, Harvard University, Cambridge, Massachusetts, 1978-89.

Chronology of Works

1967	Habitat '67, Montreal, Canada
1968-72	Habitat Puerto Rico, San Juan, Puerto Rico
1971-79	Yeshiva Porat Yosuf Rabbinical College, Jerusalem, Israel
1971-81	Master Plan and completion of Housing Stages 1a and 1b, Coldspring New Town, Baltimore, Maryland, U.S.A.
1974	Master Plan for the Western Wall Precinct, Jerusalem, Israel
1979	Paley Youth Wing, Rockefeller Museum, Jerusalem, Israel
1979-81	Cambridge Center Master Plan, Cambridge, Massachusetts, U.S.A
1983-90	Colegio Hebreo Maguen David Campus, Mexico City, Mexico
1984	Ardmore Luxury Condominiums, Singapore
1988	Hebrew Union College Campus, Jerusalem, Israel
1988	National Gallery of Canada, Ottawa, Canada
1988	Musée de la Civilisation, Quebec City, Canada
1989	Esplanade Condominiums, Cambridge, Massachusetts, U.S.A
1990-	Hebrew Union College Cultural Center and Skirball Museum, Los Angeles, California, U.S.A.
1990-	Mamilla Center Master Plan, Jerusalem, Israel
1990-	Ballet Opera House, Toronto, Ontario, Canada

Publications

BOOKS BY SAFDIE

Beyond Habitat. Cambridge, Massachusetts, 1970; revised as *Beyond Habitat by Twenty Years*, 1987.
For Everyone a Garden. Cambridge, Massachusetts, 1974.
Habitat Bill of Rights. Pamphlet. With Sert, Ardalan, Doshi, and Candilis. Teheran, Iran, 1976.
Form and Purpose. Boston, 1982.
Harvard Jerusalem Studio. Cambridge, Massachusetts, 1986.
Jerusalem: The Future of the Past. Boston, 1989.

ARTICLES BY SAFDIE

"On From Habitat." *Design* (October (1967).
"Post Mortem on Habitat: Anatomy of a System." *Royal Institute of British Architects Journal* (November 1967).
"Industrialized Buildings: Variety Within Repetition." *Architecture Canada* (November 1968).
"Habitat '67." In RICHARD KOSTELANETZ (ed.): *Beyond Left and Right.* New York, 1968.
"Presentation of Habitat, Puerto Rico and New York, Fort Lincoln and San Francisco." *Architectural Design* (January 1969).
"New Environmental Requirements for Urban Building." *Zodiac* 19 (1969).
"Collective Consciousness in Making Environment." In *The Frontiers of Knowledge.* New York, 1975.
"Private Jokes in Public Places." *Inland Architect* (November/December 1981).

BOOKS ABOUT SAFDIE

DREW, PHILIP: *Third Generation.* London, 1972.
Habitat '67. Ottawa, 1967.

ARTICLES ABOUT SAFDIE

BLANC, ALAN and SYLVIA: "Rebuilding Jerusalem: The Work of Moshe Safdie's Practice." *Building Design* (10 November 1978).

Moshe Safdie: National Gallery of Canada, Ottawa, Canada, 1988

DAVEY, PETER: "Building a New Jerusalem." *Architects' Journal* (29 November 1978).

"An Interview with Safdie." *Ariel* (Jerusalem, 1973).

KOMENDANT, A. E.: "Post Mortem on Habitat '67." *Progressive Architecture* (March 1968).

LECUYER, ANNETTE: "Safdie Goes Back to Basics." *Building Design* (11 May 1979).

"Moshe Safdie: Building in Context." *Process: Architecture* 56 (1985).

"Preservation and Renewal of Architecture and Urban Space." *Space Design*, special issue (October 1983).

PYKE, ALEXANDER: "Habitat '67." *Architectural Design* (March 1967).

SCHMERTZ, MILDRED F.: "A New Setting for the Western Wall." *Architectural Record* (April 1978).

SHARP, DENNIS: "The National Gallery of Canada." *Architecture and Urbanism* (September 1990).

SHENKER, ISRAEL: "Moshe Safdie." *Horizon* (Winter 1973).

More has been written about Moshe Safdie's Habitat in Montreal than about any other Canadian building in recent memory, and it is indeed the architect's first structure that characterizes his early reputation and development. A student project designed for Expo '67, Habitat distinguished itself as an approach to high-density lodgings that managed to avoid uniformity and monotony despite its reliance on modular components. Habitat was unsuccessful in some respects, but it is understood nonetheless as a creative solution to the monotony of prefabrication, even as it benefited from the standardization such techniques

introduce. Much of Safdie's subsequent work consisted of variations on this theme in related projects for Haifa, Israel; San Juan, Puerto Rico; and New York City. Although he became quite well known around the world, his reputation in Canada faded. This would not have concerned him very much, since he was then affiliated with Harvard University.

Most recently, Safdie has once again been catapulted into the public eye in Canada with two plum commissions for the federal government, neither of which is like his early work. The more ostentatious of the two is the new National Gallery of Canada in Ottawa. Opened in 1988, the structure is mammoth in scale and generally unornamented on the outside, apart from grand crystalline structures rising to great heights at important corners. These are pretty typical of many postmodernist buildings, especially (and ironically) those Taut-like beehives of glass adorning newer shopping malls. The principal beehive rhymes cleverly with the octagonal neo-Gothic library attached to the rear of the parliament buildings directly across the river. Of course, such large expanses of glass create conservation problems for the works inside them, necessitating sun-screens and various other mechanisms for the slit ceilings in exhibition spaces throughout the building. All of the other interior details, from door hardware to bathroom fixtures, have a similar, exquisitely industrial polish.

Access to the exhibition areas is gained by ascending a long ramp in an exceedingly tall and narrow space described in the popular press as megalomaniacal. It is, admittedly, virtually useless as an exhibition hall, but it does provide an exciting architectural overture to the aesthetic experiences presumed to be waiting inside. It has been noted that the walk up this long slope makes the visitor feel like a member of a procession entering a temple, an impression which is surely not accidental. (The exterior walls of the building are placed well within a mostly empty plaza that in retrospect seems almost like a *temenos*.) Elsewhere in the irregular plan is an equally tall, but much wider, grand staircase with treads of such great depth that the whole is really a succession of landings. Like many of the other non-exhibition parts of the building, this area is roofed almost entirely by glass, whereas the walls remain undecorated, aside from the interest inherent in the materials from which they are made. (There is one exception: along one of the walls of a corridor adjacent to the grand staircase are a few sparingly placed panels filled with single, bright blue flowerets.) Here and there are abrupt spatial surprises, such as unexpected balconies around a corner, second stories that do not seem to correspond to the placement of those below, and in one spot a charming, freestanding colonnade in a brilliantly lit atrium. The greatest surprise is the faithful restoration and reconstruction of the entire interior of Rideau Chapel, a local Gothic building with an exciting and elaborate system of fan vaults. Safdie's role here, of course, was simply to afford the city an opportunity to save this endangered historical relic.

Safdie's other recent triumph is the exactly contemporary Musée de la Civilisation in Québec City. Here, too, he has enclosed tradition, as it were, in this case by building around a historical home once belonging to a family by the name of Estèbe. Apart from its proportions—the crystals here are taller and thinner—the building's exterior is much like the National Gallery's. It is, however, jammed right against the narrow streets on all sides, as are most buildings in this picturesque old French provincial quarter. The museum's collection is quite different, too; instead of the sanctified high art of its Ottawa counterpart, it displays the history of "material culture," ranging from cutlery to shoes. Perhaps the ostensible differences between high and low culture also account for the fact that the entrance hall, unlike the aisle at the National Gallery, is a cavernous arrangement of stairs and platforms more suggestive of a public airport than of the cramped streets outside.

—ROBERT J. BELTON

SALVIN, Anthony.

British. Born in Worthing, England, 1799. Died in 1881. Worked for John Nash (1752-1835); set up practice, 1828. Fellow, Royal Institute of British Architects; Gold Medal, Royal Institute of British Architects, 1863

Chronology of Works
All in England unless noted

1828-32	Moreby Hall, Yorkshire
1828-33	Mamhead House, Devon
1830-36	Methley Hall, Yorkshire (restoration)
1831-36	Farham, Sussex
1831-37	Harlaxton Manor, Lincolnshire
1835-43	Scotney Castle, Lamberhurst, Kent
1838-42	Rufford Abbey, Lancashire
1840	Christ Church, Kilndown, Kent (alterations)
1841-43	Church of the Holy Sepulchre, Cambridge (restoration)
1846-48	Penoyre, Brecon
1846-51	Hafod, Dyfed, Wales
1847-50	Peckforton Castle, Shropshire
1849-50	St. Stephen, Hammersmith, London
1853-69	Tower of London, London (restoration and additions)
1854	Gurney Bank (now Barclays Bank), Great Yarmouth, Norfolk
1854-65	Alnwick Castle, Northumberland (rebuilding)
1854-65	Keele Hall, Staffordshire
1856-57	St. Mark, Torquay, Devon
1858-67	Windsor Castle, Berkshire (restoration and additions)
1864-75	Thoresby Hall, Nottinghamshire
1869	Albury House, Surrey
1869-72	Paddockhurst (now Worth Priory), Sussex

Publications

BOOKS ABOUT SALVIN

ALLIBONE, JILL: *Anthony Salvin, 1799-1881*. Columbia, Missouri, 1988.
EASTLAKE, CHARLES L.: *A History of the Gothic Revival*. London, 1872.
GIROUARD, MARK: *The Victorian Country House*. New Haven, Connecticut, and London, 1979.
HITCHCOCK, HENRY-RUSSELL: *Early Victorian Architecture in Britain*. New Haven, Connecticut, and London, 1954.
HUSSEY, CHRISTOPHER: *English Country Houses: Late Georgian, 1800-1840*. London, 1958.
WHITE, JAMES F.: *The Cambridge Movement: The Ecclesiologists and the Gothic Revival*. Cambridge, 1962.

ARTICLES ABOUT SALVIN

"The Late Mr. Anthony Salvin, Architect." *Builder* 41 (1881): 809-810ff.

*

Although Anthony Salvin built the first church directly supervised by the Ecclesiological Society at Kilndown, Kent (1840), his church work is a small part of his oeuvre, and it is less than memorable when compared to the work of the great Victorian architects who specialized in churches. It is for country houses that Salvin is best remembered. Of the five great Early Victorian country-house architects—A. W. N. Pugin, Charles Barry, Blore, William Burn and Salvin—Salvin was one of the most successful; he was also the one most skilled at combining functional planning, scholarly detail and picturesque composition. Although Salvin's specialty was castle architecture, he also designed Elizabethan and even a few classical houses.

During his half century of practice, his production was very large and his reputation as country-house architect was unrivaled. Although his houses were expressive and powerful when a work of military flavor was demanded, his greatest contribution may have been the steadying moderation of his practice on clients able to afford the most fantastic that money could buy. His early houses were his best; his later houses seem cold and mechanical in contrast with the verve and brilliance of his early work. Salvin's most palatial house, Thoresby Hall, is a good example. Mark Girouard says that Thoresby is "a cold house, dead in its handling and dead in detail . . . a depressing decline from Harlaxton built thirty years earlier."

Although a number of Italian Renaissance Early Victorian country houses were constructed (Greek and Roman Revival styles had faded from fashion), the English tended to prefer "English" styles, especially English Gothic and Elizabethan. English Gothic houses invariably featured a great hall as a romantic stylistic feature rather than a functional necessity; it might be used as a banquet hall or a stair vestibule or a billiards

Anthony Salvin: Harlaxton Manor, Lincolnshire, England, 1831-37

room. Salvin was particularly keen on great halls, perhaps because one of his first professional jobs was the restoration of
the great hall at Brancepeth Castle, County Durham. The Jacobean Hall at Harlaxton is particularly impressive.

Salvin's reputation was made by two great houses, Mamhead
Park, Devon (1828-33), and Moreby Hall, Yorkshire (1828-
32)—vast and sumptuous houses completed before Salvin was
30. Moreby Hall introduced a number of elements that became
the norm in Manorial Gothic: square-headed sash windows with
double transoms and stone mullions and frames, roofs pitched
at 45 degrees, chimneys sprinkled picturesquely along the skyline, and servants' wings extending the houses' facades to the
side at smaller scale. Mamhead introduced the English Manorial
Gothic style 10 years or more before it became popular elsewhere.

Scotney Castle, Kent (1835-43), revived the Tudor Gothic
style. Its entrance front is very original in its composition. It
features an irregular mixing of window and blank wall and a
subtle interplay of diagonals that make this composition unlike
anything produced during the Late Georgian period.

The Elizabethan style was particularly popular during the
Early Victorian period; it enabled the architect to combine picturesque composition with rich surface decoration. Harlaxton
Manor is one of the most exuberant examples of this style. Its
exterior is Salvin's and was built between 1831 and 1837. There
is, however, some question about the designer of the Baroque
interior. The owner, Gregory Gregory, sent Salvin to Europe to
study Baroque masterpieces, but he may have been an unwilling
student, for he left Gregory's employ in 1837 or 1838, perhaps
in a disagreement over the Baroque interior design Gregory
demanded. Salvin was succeeded by William Burn, whose other
work suggests that he was incapable of something as fanciful

and ebullient as was produced at Harlaxton. The interior design
is much more characteristic of Burn's chief clerk and later
partner, David Byrce, who designed a number of successful
baroque buildings.

Ingenious planning was always Salvin's forte, and it is nowhere more evident than at Harlaxton. The house was dug into
the slope so that the main rooms on the *piano nobile* level in
front could open directly to the garden in back, and so that
basement service spaces got light and air from the lower front
elevation. Salvin manipulated the skyline and the walls to
achieve a picturesque quality. He was conscious of light and
shade, carefully modeling the surfaces in an extremely plastic
manner, and he used turrets, gables and chimneys to create a
lively skyline. The entrance facade is formal and symmetrical;
the rear facade is informal and asymmetrical. Salvin combined
the Elizabethan house with baroque gates and garden buildings
in a singularly successful eclectic mix; the result was one of
the landmark buildings of the Early Victorian period.

Those not content with a great hall might opt for a castle.
This desire for ultimate medieval fantasy led to the development
of the "castle" style. Salvin's great exercise in the genre was
Peckforton Castle in Shropshire (1847-50). The castle was archaeological in intention and, due to a hilltop site, remarkably
picturesque. The castle was not a sham castle, however, but a
scholarly recreation of a medieval castle with parts designed
to accommodate the 19th-century functions for which they were
to be used; in short, it was both a medieval castle and a Victorian
house, with virtually no conflict between the two. It was a
modern feudal castle from which Lord Tollemache could rule
over his vast estate.

Salvin understood that the essential nature of a castle is
expressed in the manner in which the apartments engage the

interior of the great encircling wall. At Peckforton, in spite of deviations from archaeological correctness, the building retains the essential flavor of the castle form. It is long, low and sober, unlike the flashy sham castles Belvoir and Penrhyn. The sensitivity to form adjustment which results in architecture revealed and enhanced by light that distinguishes Harlaxton is also present here. Massive walls and towers rise above the trees on top of a hill.

The asymmetry of the courtyard allows an extremely functional plan. The main rooms of the house occupy a corner that is the focus of form buildup. This corner is anchored by the great hall on the courtyard side and a great circular tower, containing the dining room, on the exterior side. Formal planning based on the intersection of three axes—two perpendicular to each other, one at the diagonal—organizes the interior. The result is visually successful in both mass and the character of the interior visual sequence. Smooth-cut ashlar interior walls contrast with rusticated stone exterior surfaces, producing an effect of great solidity. No country house in the castle style, before or after, surpassed the strength, power and livability of Peckforton.

—C. MURRAY SMART, JR.

SANGALLO, Antonio da, the Younger.

Italian. Born in Florence, Italy, 1484. Died in Terni, Italy, 28 September 1546. The architects Antonio da Sangallo the Elder and Giuliano da Sangallo were his uncles; his cousins included the architects Giovanni Francesco da Sangallo (1482-1530) and Bastiano da Sangallo (1484-1551), and his nephew was Francesco da Sangallo, son of Giovanni and chief architect of Florence Cathedral, from 1573. Antonio da Sangallo the Younger was probably trained by his uncles; he traveled to Rome with Giulian o in 1503; worked for Donato Bramante, first as carpenter, then as draftsman and supervisor of projects, 1503-14; worked at St. Peter's, Rome, under Raphael, from 1514; developed an independent practice by 1515, and became personal architect to Cardinal Alessandro Farnese at about the same time; architect-in-chief (with Baldassare Peruzzi), from 1520, and then on his own, from 1536, at St. Peter's, Rome; Pope Paul III was his patron from 1534.

Chronology of Works
All in Italy
* Approximate dates

1515*-19*	Castello Farnese, Capodimonte
1515*-19	Palazzo Baldassini, Rome
1515*-46	Palazzo Farnese, Rome
1517	Chapel of the Sacrament, Cathedral, Foligno
1517-18	Serra Chapel, San Giacomo degli Spagnuoli, Rome
1518*-27	Palazzo Ferratini, Amelia
1520*-30*	Santa Maria di Loreto, Rome
1521*-27*	Castello Farnese, Caprarola
1522-27	Palazzo Regis (Le Roy or Farnesina) ai Baullari
1525-27	Zecca (Palazzo del Banco di Santo Spirito), Rome
1526-34	Apostolic Palace, Loreto
1527-35	Pozzo di San Patrizio, Orvieto
1530	Cesi Chapel, Santa Maria della Pace, Rome
1534-36	Fortezza da Basso, Florence
1534-43	Casa Sangello in Via Giulia, Rome
1536*	Palazzo Farnese, Gradoli
1537	Papal Fortress, Ancona
1537-42	Bastione Ardeatina
1538	Santo Spirito in Sassia (facade)
1538-43	St. Peter's, Rome (wood model)
1540-46	Pauline Chapel and Sala Regia, Vatican Palace, Rome
1543-46	Palazzo Sacchetti, Rome (Sangallo)
1543-46	Fortifications of Vatican Borgo and Porta Santo Spirito, Rome

Publications

BOOKS ABOUT SANGALLO

CLAUSSE, GUSTAVE: *Les San Gallo*. 3 vols. Paris, 1900-02.
GIOVANNONI, GUSTAVO: *Antonio da Sangallo il Giovane*. 2 vols. Rome, 1959.

ARTICLES ABOUT SANGALLO

BUDDENSIEG, TILMANN: "Bernardo della Volpaia und Giovanni Francesco da Sangallo." *Römisches Jahrbuch für Kunstgeschichte* 15 (1975): 89-108.
FROMMEL, CHRISTOPHER L.: "Antonio da Sangallos Cappella Paolina." *Zeitschrift für Kunstgeschichte* 27 (1964): 1-42.
LISNER, MARGRIT: "Zum bildhauerischen Werk der Sangallo." *Pantheon* 27 (March 1969): 99-119; (May 1969): 190-208.

*

Antonio da Sangallo the Younger, filling a void created by Raphael's death in 1520, assumed leadership of the competitive world of Roman architecture. For more than two decades he remained the preeminent architect in the city, gaining major commissions and recognition from important patrons. He directed a busy workshop of younger architects who carried out designated duties. With their collaboration, there was hardly an area of architectural activity that Sangallo did not touch. He designed an astonishing number of churches, as well as palaces and villas for private families. He undertook projects on a vast scale which involved urban planning, hydraulics and military fortification, and public works such as hospitals and bath structures. Finally, he was an incessant investigator of ancient theory, the rules of which he amended and applied to his own designs.

The Sangallo family, Florentine in origin, comprised a dynasty of architects spanning three generations. Giuliano da Sangallo (1445-1516) worked for Pope Julius II in Rome and was probably his nephew's first teacher. Antonio the Elder (1455-1534), another uncle, was also active in Rome and Tuscany. As Antonio the Younger became established in his own right, other relatives gravitated toward his workshop. The most prominent were Bastiano (known as Aristotile) da Sangallo (1481-1551), Giovanni Francesco da Sangallo (1482-1530) and Giovanni Battista (known also as Il Gobbo) da Sangallo (1496-1552). Other young architects, such as Guidetto Guidetti, Galeazzo Alessi, Nanni di Baccio Bigio and Bernardo della Volpaia, trained in the highly organized workshop, which stressed the study of the antique and produced such magnificent examples of architectural draftsmanship as the Codex Coner (London, Sir John Soane's Museum). The indefatigable "Sangallo clique," as Michelangelo labeled them, continued some of Antonio's projects after his death.

Antonio da Sangallo the Younger spent his formative years in the Fabbrica of St. Peter's. He was the first to rise through the ranks from carpenter to chief architect of the church. Unlike his peers, Sangallo did not begin his career as a painter, but rather

Antonio da Sangallo, the Younger: Palazzo Farnese, Rome, Italy, ca. 1515-46

trained exclusively in architecture. He worked as a draftsman for Bramante, whose interpretive skill he emulated. Although the architectural drawings generated by Bramante's circle were largely unsigned and highly theoretical, those attributed to the young Sangallo, like the Greek-cross plan of Santi Celso e Giuliano, reflect the master architect's ideas. Raphael, the next architect of St. Peter's, made Sangallo an assistant, teaching him the specialized function of architectural renderings. The plan, cross-section and elevation gradually replaced the perspective views popular with Bramante. In addition, Sangallo acquired knowledge of engineering techniques, for he was entrusted with strengthening the crossing piers begun by Bramante.

Antonio da Sangallo the Younger succeeded Raphael as architect of St. Peter's, triumphing over his longtime colleague, Baldassare Peruzzi, who remained in the Fabbrica as co-architect. Sangallo had mixed success in building the church, both from his point of view and in respect to the definitive design. During the next 25 years, he oversaw the construction of the crossing according to the original plan, but introduced a longitudinal axis by adding an enlarged facade. The latter endeavor earned him the disdain of Michelangelo, whose well-known remark about Sangallo's "wasteful" plan reveals the architect's declining prestige toward the end of his life. Sangallo's project may be reconstructed completely from an engraving of the facade and a wooden model, executed by Antonio Labacco, as well as from various ground plans and interior views. His plan called for a compendium of classical forms with decorative accents in the tall towers, all of which obscured the harmony of Bramante's original design.

It is unfortunate that, with this project, Sangallo is remembered as an architect whose attention to detail outweighed his powers of synthesis. To the contrary, he was engaged consistently with theoretical models. He regarded Vitruvius as the authoritative source, and sponsored a critical study of *The Ten Books of Architecture* in his workshop. In his enthusiasm for the correct classical building vocabulary, he even criticized architectural details of the Pantheon, as well as Raphael and Michelangelo for their interpretation of the antique. It is no wonder that Sangallo successfully integrated classical features—like thermal windows and coffered ceilings—into his buildings.

Among his most interesting designs were centrally planned structures. These grew out of his fascination with ancient prototypes as well as the influence of Bramante, as in the octagonal plan, circumscribed by a square, for Santa Maria di Loreto of the 1520s. His project for San Giovanni dei Fiorentini (ca. 1518), demonstrates an inventive streak. He proposed a circular core surrounded by 16 domed chapels which, in turn, served as internal buttressing for a spacious dome. Jacopo Sansovino won the competition, but construction was entrusted to Sangallo, with his expertise in engineering. He displayed his full, creative powers for the hospital church at San Giacomo degli Incurabili (ca. 1523), in a centralized plan surmounted by a tall dome.

Sangallo's increasing success brought him to the attention of the powerful Farnese family. As early as 1517, Cardinal Alessandro Farnese selected Sangallo as architect for the family palace, initiating a long relationship between artist and patron. Construction of the palace proceeded, but plans were expanded with the papacy of Paul III (1534-49) and were concluded after Sangallo's death. Nevertheless, Sangallo can be credited with the creation of a grand palace type encompassing an entire city block. He designed a central courtyard with a three-story elevation based on ancient prototypes. The superimposed classical orders of the arcades produce a serene, measured effect reminiscent of Bramante. Similarly, the tunnel vault of the entrance, decorated with coffering and supported by massive Doric columns, evokes the grandeur of High Renaissance classicism, as do the interior staircases and spacious halls. The exterior of the Palazzo Farnese is severe, an astylar surface punctuated by string courses and quoins at the corners. Yet, it is likely that this uncompromising adherence to an austere classicism contributed to Sangallo's dismissal as architect and, if one is to believe the histrionics of Giorgio Vasari, to his untimely demise. Dissatisfied with Sangallo's plans, Paul III held a competition for the cornice of the palace in 1546. Michelangelo emerged victorious, designing not only the sculpted cornice, but altering the top story of the interior courtyard and adding a central window to the facade.

Despite this setback and increasing competition from a younger generation of architects, Sangallo retained the title of papal architect until his death in 1546. His stature as a professional architect was unequaled, ensured by his training as well as four decades of architectural practice in the hub of theoretical inquiry.

—EUNICE D. HOWE

SANGALLO, Guiliano da.

Italian. Born in Florence, Italy, 1443. Died in Florence, 20 October 1516. Father was the sculptor Francesco Giamberti, founder of the Sangallo family; brother was the architect Antonio da Sangallo the Elder, and his nephew was the architect Antonio da Sangallo the Younger. Trained by his father in wood sculpture; apprenticed to the military engineer Francesco di Giovanni, with whom he worked on fortifications at the Vatican, from 1465; returned to Florence in the 1470s; worked for Lorenzo th e Magnificent on the Villa Medici, 1480; with the death of Lorenzo in 1492 and the expulsion of the Medici family in 1494, Antonio was deprived of his principal source of patronage; but he found a new patron in Cardinal Giuliano della Rovere (later Pope Julius II), from 1494; appointed chief administrator (with Raphael and Fra Gicondo), St. Peter's, Rome, by Pope Leo X, 1515.

Chronology of Works
All in Italy
* *Approximate dates*

1472*-80*	Palazzo of Bartolomeo Scala (now Ghirardesca), Florence
1480-97*	Villa Medici, Poggio a Caiano
1484-91	Santa Maria delle Carceri, Prato
1489-95	Santo Spirito, Florence (vestibule and sacristy; with Il Cronaca)
1490-1501	Palazzo Gondi, Florence
1492	Santa Maria Maddalena dei Pazzi, Florence (atrium)
1494	Palazzo Rovere, Savona
1495-1513	Fortifications of Poggio Imperial, near Poggibonsi (with Antonio da Sangallo the Elder)
1498	Palazzo Strozzi, Florence
1499-1500	Basilica of the Santa Casa, Loreto (cupola)
1501-03	Fortress, Nettuno (with Antonio da Sangallo the Elder)
1502-03	Fortress, Arezzo (with Antonio da Sangallo the Elder)
1502-05	Fortress, Borgo San Sepolcro (with Antonio da Sangallo the Elder)
1509-12	Fortress, Pisa

Publications

BOOKS ABOUT SANGALLO

CLAUSSE, GUSTAVE: *Les San Gallo.* 3 vols. Paris, 1900-02.
FABRICZY, CORNELIUS VON: *Die Handzeichnungen des Giulano da Sangallo.* Stuttgart, 1902.
FALB, RUDOLF (ed.): *Il taccuino senese di Giuliano da San Gallo.* Siena, 1902.
FOSTER, PHILIP ELLIS: *A Study of Lorenzo de' Medici's Villa at Poggio a Caiano.* New York and London, 1978.
FROMMEL, CHRISTOPHER L.: *Der römische Palastbau der Hochrenaissance.* 3 vols. Tübingen, Germany, 1973.
GIOVANNONI, GUSTAVO: *Antonio da Sangallo il giovane.* Rome, 1959.
HÜLSEN, CHRISTIAN VON (ed.): *Il libro di Giuliano da Sangallo: Codice Vaticano Barberiniano, latino 4424.* 2 vols. Leipzig, 1910.
MARCHINI, GIUSEPPE: *Giuliano da Sangallo.* Florence, 1942.
SEVERINI, GIANCARLO: *Architetture militari di Giuliano da Sangallo.* Pisa, 1970.

ARTICLES ABOUT SANGALLO

BROWN, BEVERLY LOUISE, and KLEINER, DIANA E. E.: "Giuliano da Sangallo's Drawings after Ciriaco d'Ancona: Transformations of Greek and Roman Antiquities in Athens." *Journal of the Society of Architectural Historians* 42 (December 1983): 321-335.
FABRICZY, CORNELIUS VON: "Giuliano da Sangallo: Chronologischer Prospekt." *Jahrbuch der Preussischen Kunstsammlungen* 23 (1902): 1-42.
LISNER, MARGRIT: "Zum bildhauerischen Werk der Sangallo." *Pantheon* 27 (March 1969): 99-119; (May 1969): 190-208.
MIARELLI MARIANI, GAETANO: "La critica del Vasari e la setta sangallesca." In *Il Vasari storiografe e artista: Atti del congresso internazionale (1974).* Florence, 1976.

*

Giuliano da Sangallo was an architect in Florence and Rome in the second half of the 15th century, most known now for his design of the Villa Medici at Poggio a Caiano and the Church of Santa Maria delle Carceri in Prato. His father was Francesco Giamberti, a woodworker and decorator for the Medici, but Giuliano, like all the later members of this family, was always known after about 1481 as Sangallo, this name coming from the district around the Porta San Gallo in Florence where they lived. Giuliano was probably first trained by his father in wood sculpture, something he continued to practice all his life. But very early on he was apprenticed to the military engineer Francesco di Giovanni, il Francone, and about 1465 he went with Francesco to Rome to work on a series of now-unidentifiable projects in the Vatican. By the early 1470s Giuliano was back in Florence, and the style of architecture in which he worked then seems to reflect the experience of Rome and the forms of building he had seen there.

An early commission was for the courtyard of the Palace of Bartolommeo Scala, which was at once like a Florentine *cortile* but also, as appropriate for so learned a patron, a peristyle in the classical manner, with arcades and attached pilasters, a

Giuliano da Sangallo: Villa Medici, Poggio a Caiano, Italy, ca. 1480-97

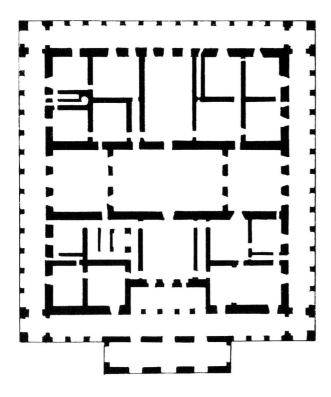

figured cornice and relief ornaments that seem very close to the kind of imaginative reconstructions of antique architecture we can see in Giuliano's sketchbooks. A little later, Giuliano won the competition for the design of the villa of Poggio a Caiano that Lorenzo de' Medici announced in the beginning of the 1480s. The result was what Ludwig Heydenreich has called at once the earliest, and yet perhaps the most perfect, example of the new type of the humanist villa that was, of course, to last so long in Italy. The villa dominates the crest of a gentle hill, the building rising from an arcaded platform terrace that was perhaps derived from the antique idea of the cryptoporticus; the entrance is an Ionic porch with a broad and decorated pediment. The plan is rigorously symmetrical and centers upon a large barrel-vaulted hall that, in details like the carved terra-cotta coffers and the grandeur of its space, evokes very powerfully the grandeur of the interiors to be seen in Roman architecture.

Following this project, and with the continued support of Lorenzo de' Medici, Giuliano received a commission for the Church of Santa Maria delle Carceri in Prato. In essence, this simple, centrally planned church follows the tradition of Filippo Brunelleschi: with its dome on pendentives at the crossing, the barrel vaults and the Greek-cross plan, it is in a sense the Pazzi Chapel writ large. The result, with its strong, ordered interior articulation and the clear pattern of the outside, with coupled pilasters at the ends of the arms, is simple and extremely grand. In a similar manner, Giuliano followed Brunelleschi with the Ionic atrium he designed in 1492 for the church of Santa Maria Maddalena dei Pazzi and with the octagonal sacristy of Santa Spirito (ca. 1489-95), done with the help of il Cronaca.

But a change of circumstances was coming. With the death of Lorenzo in 1492 and the expulsion of the Medici two years later, Giuliano lost his main source of patronage and had to turn elsewhere. In 1494 he designed the Palazzo Rovere in Savona for Cardinal Giuliano della Rovere; when the cardinal became Pope Julius II and went to Rome, Giuliano followed him expecting commissions, only to be disappointed when the pope gave the grandest opportunities for building to Donato Bramante.

Giuliano returned to Florence, where he remained until 1513 and the election of Pope Leo X. He was appointed building administrator of St. Peter's in 1515, together with Raphael and Fra Giocondo, but his contributions to the final design of the church were minor. At the same time, the year before he died, he put forth plans for the facade of the Church of San Lorenzo in Florence that were to have a decided influence on the later projects there of Michelangelo.

Giuliano manifested a fascinating dichotomy in his work. In his designs for the Palazzo Gondi (1490-1501) and the Palazzo Strozzi (1498) he produced elaborations essentially of what Michelozzo had done earlier at the Palazzo Medici, and there was, even in his designs for San Lorenzo, something not quite of the period. But of all the architects in Florence in the 15th century, Giuliano was the one to anticipate most closely the spirit of the architecture of the High Renaissance, and his designs achieved a monumentality few of his contemporaries in Florence were able to accomplish. In addition to Giuliano's buildings, a remarkable collection of his drawings still exists, representing, with those of Francesco di Giorgio, the richest surviving documentation of architectural practice in Florence at the end of the 15th century.

—DAVID CAST

SANMICHELI, Michele.

Italian. Born in Verona, Italy, 1484. Died in Verona, September 1559. Father was the mason Giovanni Sanmicheli; other masons in the family were Giovanni's brother Bartolomeo, his son Paulo, and Paolo's son Giangirolamo (who became Michele's assistant). Michele trained with his father and uncle, and then with Donato Bramante in the papal workshops in Rome, 1500/07. Served as superintendent of works at Orvieto Cathedral, 1509-24; consultant on fortifications of Verona, 1526-27; began lifelong s eries of appointments to create and maintain a network of modern fortresses in the Venetian empire, early 1530s.

Chronology of Works
All in Italy
* Approximate dates
† Work no longer exists

1513-32	Cathedral, Orvieto (partial completion of central gable)
1514-59	Cathedral, Orvieto (spires, not completed until 1590)
1516-23	Crypt Chapel and Chancel Tomb of Girolamo Petrucci, Church of San Domenico, Orvieto (partially†)
1519*	Cathedral, Montefiascone (main body)
1527*-35*	Palazzo Lavezola (Pompei), Verona
1527*-57	Pellegrini Chapel, Church of San Bernardino, Verona
1528-35	Fortifications, Legnago
1528-35	Porta San Martino, Legnago
1530-31	Palazzo Canossa, Verona
1530-31	Barbarigo Bastion, Verona
1532*	Palazzo Bevilacqua, Verona
1532*-37	Palazzo Grimani at San Severo, Venice [attributed]
1533	Palazzo del Podesta, Verona (portal)
1533-51	Porta Nuova, Verona
1534-41	Cathedral, Verona (choir screen)
1535	Faler Bastion, Verona
1535-44	Fort of San Andrea, opposite Lido, Venice
1538	San Bernardino Bastion, Verona
after 1538*	Palazzo Bragadin at Santa Formosa, Venice (portal)
1538-42	Villa Brenzone, Punta San Vigilio del Garda [attributed]
1539-56	Corner Bastion, Padua
1539*-42	Villa Corner, Piombino Dese†
1540	San Zeno Bastion, Verona
1540-51	Villa Soranzo (La Soranza), Treville di Castelfranco†
1541*	Villa Saraceno (Palazzo delle Trombe), Finale di Agugliaro
1542	Palazzo Lando-Corner (Corner-Spinelli), Venice (remodeled main halls and ceiling with Giorgio Vasari)
1544-58	Tomb of Alessandro Contarini, Padua
after 1547	Monument to Cardinal Pietro Bembo, Basilica of Sant'Antonio, Padua
1547-50	Porta San Zeno, Verona
1547-50	Spagna Bastion, Verona
1547-59	Church of Santa Maria in Organo, Verona, (lower order of facade not completed until 1592)
1548	Lazzaretto Hospital, near Verona
1548-56	Palazzo Gussoni at Santa Fosca, Venice [attributed]
1548-59	Porta del Palio, Verona
1551	San Francesco Bastion, Verona
before 1555	Palazzo Roncale, Rovigo [attributed]
1555	Bucintoro Boathouse, Venice (facade) [attributed]
1555	Palazzo Guastaverza, Verona [attributed]
1555-64	Palazzo Corner Molenigo, San Polo, Venice
1557-59	Palazzo Grimani, San Luca, Venice (completed 1561-68 by Gian Giacomo dei Grigi, and 1570-75 by Giannantonio Rusconi)
1558*	Chapel of Villa Della Torre, Fumane
before 1559	Church of San Giorgio in Braida (dome [completed 1604] and Campanile)
1559-61	Church of the Madonna di Campagna, Verona

Publications

BOOKS ABOUT SANMICHELI

FIOCCO, G. (ed.): *Michele Sanmicheli: Studi raccolti dall'Academia di Agricoltura, Scienze e Lettere di Verona.* Verona, 1960.

GAZZOLA, PIERO (ed.): *Michele Sanmicheli.* Exhibition catalog. Venice, 1960.

HOWARD, DEBORAH: *The Architectural History of Venice.* New York, 1981.

LANGENSKJÖLD, ERIK: *Michele Sanmicheli, the Architect of Verona: His Life and Works.* Uppsala, Sweden, 1938.

POMPEI, ALESSANDRO: *Le cinque ordini dell'architettura civile di Michele Sanmicheli.* Verona, 1735.

PUPPI, LIONELLO: *Michele Sanmicheli: Architetto di Verona.* Padua, Italy, 1971.

RONZANI, F. and LUCIOLLI, G.: *Le fabbriche civili, ecclesiastiche e militari di Michele Sanmicheli.* Genoa, 1876.

Michele Sanmicheli: Porta del Palio, Verona, 1548-59

ARTICLES ABOUT SANMICHELI

LEWIS, DOUGLAS: "Un disegno autografo del Sanmicheli."
    Bollettino dei Musei Civici Veneziani 27, Nos. 3-4 (1972):
    7-36.

Michele Sanmicheli and Jacopo Sansovino were the chief importers of the monumental Roman High Renaissance style into Venice and the Veneto. Sanmicheli spent his formative years in Rome, probably training in the papal workshops under Donato Bramante (ca. 1444-1514). Sanmicheli's architecture is a fusion of Bramante's High Renaissance monumentality and clarity, Giulio Romano's (ca. 1499-1546) Mannerist strangeness, and visual devices from the antique. As a northerner, Sanmicheli's own preference for a livelier surface was woven into these sources.

Giorgio Vasari says his friend Sanmicheli left Verona for Rome at the age of 16 (ca. 1500) after having received an excellent technical training from his father and uncle, who were architects. After his Roman training, Sanmicheli spent 17 years (1509-26) as superintendent of works at Orvieto Cathedral, where he is credited primarily with completion of the upper areas of the central gable. His strong technical facility was his most important contribution to the project. During that time, he worked on a myriad of other projects in the area, mostly ecclesiastical. The largest project of the Orvieto period was the design for the main body of the Cathedral at Montefiascone (ca. 1519).

He began a simultaneous career as an engineer of military defenses in 1526 when Clement VII sent Sanmicheli and his friend, the architect Antonio da Sangallo the Younger, to the northern borders of the Papal States to inspect city walls and fortifications. Antonio belonged to a family of architects that had already developed a widely emulated system of fortification design. He must have been the source for some of Sanmicheli's knowledge of the type. Together they inspected existing works and built new ones. The tour was initiated by foreign pressures which culminated in the Sack of Rome in 1527. The subsequent flight of Sanmicheli to Verona was from a Rome that could not for the present afford extensive artistic activity. Thereafter Sanmicheli extensively practiced military engineering in fortification design with distinction for the Republic of Venice, integrating the work with his career as an architect.

Sanmicheli traveled to inspect fortifications throughout the Venetian Republic, spending much time in the Levant gaining firsthand experience with antique architectural remains. Verona itself is rich in Roman ruins such as the Porta de' Borsari. As a result of this contact, as well as from travel for the pope, he was equipped with broader knowledge of the antique than most architects had at their command. The problem with evaluating his oeuvre has always been to find ways of reconciling satisfactorily the engineer with the architect. It is impossible to assess just how Sanmicheli integrated the two approaches and what it was he learned from his military work. Much of this must remain conjectural.

From the time of Sanmicheli's return to his native city, he worked as an official of the Venetian Republic, accepting private commissions at the same time. Due to his presence, Verona became the richest north Italian center of Renaissance architecture after Venice and Vicenza. Following the lead of Donato Bramante and Pope Julius II in Rome in city planning, Sanmicheli transformed whole sections of medieval Verona into a more distinct Renaissance city. Perhaps from his experience with fortification design, he gained a strong spatial sense that allowed him to plan highly successful, sweeping topographical designs. Combining his skills in designing forts and buildings, he designed new city gates within bastions for Verona. The best known of the gates, the Porta Nuova (1533-51) and Porta Palio (1548-59), both display the monumentality of the Roman High Renaissance style. For the Lido in Venice, Sanmicheli designed the Sant'Andrea Fort (1543). These designs appropriately used heavily rusticated stonework for much of the constructions. Many of the columns and piers, treated in a Mannerist vein, are so heavily encased within rusticated blocks that only the capital is visible.

Sanmicheli knew that fortifications must not only be strong; even more important, they must look strong. Giulio Romano's heavy rustication on both stories of the Palazzo del Te, Mantua (1527-34), was the example which seems to have guided his choice. At Te, Giulio also used large, heavily projecting rustication for the voussoirs and keystones as well as the virile Doric order. The impregnable character and richness of this usage was borrowed by Sanmicheli for Verona and Venice. He added his own Mannerist devices to these constructions. A case in point is the cutting back of the top layer of rustication to reveal more rustication on the outer side of the Porta Palio to invest it with an even more rugged character.

Sanmicheli received commissions for ecclesiastical and other civic structures during his career in the Veneto. His use of Bramante's design for the circular Tempietto, Rome (after 1511) for some of these buildings is notable. The Lazzaretto, a quarantine hospital outside Verona (begun 1548), has a rectangular plan with the cells of the patients around the perimeter. At the center stands a small, domed, circular chapel with two concentric circles of Tuscan columns as chancel screen, and an altar in the center. The chapel had no walls, so the patients could watch the Mass from their cells. The Capella Pellegrini, Church of San Bernardino, Verona (begun ca. 1526-27) and the Church of the Madonna di Campagna, Verona (1559-61), are both domed cylinders. The chapel moves Bramante's colonnade inside, while the church retains it on the exterior. Both insert a high base for the dome, unlike Bramante. These additions can be regarded as Mannerist devices which produce a high, narrow silhouette more in keeping with Michelangelo's Mannerist use of the same device in his Medici Chapel, Florence (1519-34).

Sanmicheli's private palazzos in Verona and Venice make use of his vast repertoire of classical elements as well as the other influences already noted. He designed and built three major palazzos in Verona (Palazzo Pompei, 1527?-57; Palazzo Canossa, 1530-31; Palazzo Bevilacqua, before 1532?) and two in Venice (Palazzo Corner-Mocenigo at San Polo, 1555-64; Palazzo Grimani at San Luca, 1557-59). The earliest, the three in Verona, are all based on Bramante's House of Raphael, Rome (ca. 1510), the most important domestic structure of the 16th century in Italy. Every important Renaissance palazzo after that time was modeled on it in some way. A five-bay, two-story structure, it had a rusticated basement with a round-arched arcade supported by piers. The *piano nobile* is balustraded, with two Doric half columns on high bases in each bay and which support a frieze. The window in each bay is pedimented. Sanmicheli used the two-story design, rusticated basement and balustraded *piano nobile* with attached columns for the Veronese houses. Beyond that he played with Mannerist devices and enlivened the surface with a more sculptural treatment. Mezzanine windows have become a row of features in themselves. Brackets support the mezzanine. Keystones are richly sculptured. Windows alternate in size and the smaller ones look squeezed between columns. At the Palazzo Canossa the balustrade has been moved up to the cornice of the roof, and the columns have been replaced by thin, flat piers with a strip running behind them to make them appear even thinner.

The palazzos in Venice were not treated with such marked Roman High Renaissance influence. It has been noted that Roman monumentality was not suited to the canals of Venice because the apparent heaviness would seem to make the buildings sink into the water. The facade of the Venetian palazzo compensated through the development of taller and thinner proportions based on a three-story elevation. Windows were larger with less solid wall between them. Sanmicheli carried the model further, using an attenuated Mannerist approach. The canal facade of the Palazzo Grimani, when seen from an angle, extends above the roofline of the house proper with several feet of false front. The result is a house that appears to be much larger than it actually is, because the site narrows rapidly behind the facade. The Palazzo Corner has three mezzanines, one above each story, which appear as smaller separate stories. Sanmicheli took none of the usual measures to integrate them into the design of the story below. The result is a very tall house. The height is further emphasized by the tall, round-arched window in the center of each of the top stories. The keystones for these openings are at the same height as the corresponding mezzanine windows. Complex sculptural effects further embellish all five of these palazzos, giving them facades enlivened with the effects of chiaroscuro.

Whether Sanmicheli was working as architect or engineer, he developed designs that stamped the cities of Verona and Venice with his own version of the High Renaissance. At the same time, he inspired contemporaries such as Jacopo Sansovino, as well as subsequent generations of architects, including Andrea Palladio.

—ANN STEWART BALAKIER

SANSOVINO, Jacopo.

Italian. Born Jacopo Tatti in Florence, Italy, 1486. Died in Venice, 27 November 1570. Apprenticed to Andrea Contucci (called Andrea Sansovino), Florence, 1502-05; also influenced by Giuliano da Sangallo. Followed Contucci and Sangallo to Rome to work as a sculptor, 1506-11; returned to work in Florence, 1511-18; returned to Rome, 1518-21; finally moved to Venice in 1521, where he spent the rest of his career, aside from a stay in Rome, 1525-27; appointed superintendent of procuracy at St. Mark's, Venice, 1529.

Chronology of Works
All in Italy
* *Approximate dates*
† *Work no longer exists*

1515	Cathedral of Santa Maria del Fiore, Florence (wooden festival facade; with Andrea del Sarto)†
1515	Wooden Triumphal Arch (for entry of Pope Leo X), Porta Sal Gallo, Florence†
1518-21	San Giovanni dei Fiorentini, Rome (with Antonio Da Sangallo the Younger; never completed)†
1518*-30s	Palace of Giovanni Gaddi (Strozzi-Niccolini), Rome
1519-33	Santa Maria sopra Minerva, Rome (Monument of Cardinal Alvise of Aragon)†

1519ff.	San Marcello al Corso, Rome (rebuilding; with Sangallo)
1521*-27	San Marcello al Corso, Rome (Monument of Giovanni Michiel, Cardinal of Sant'Angelo, and Antonio Orso, Bishop of Agen)
1521-31	Villa of Frederico Priuli, Treville di Castelfranco (with others)† [attributed]
1530-32	Chapel of the Assumption and the Monument of Bishop Gelasio Nichesola, Cathedral, Verona
1531	Five Doric Shops, Ponte della Pescaria, Venice
1531-70	Scuola Grande della Misericordia, Venice (not completed until 1589)
1534-70	San Francesca della Vigna, Venice
mid-1530s-42	Santo Spirito in Isola, Venice (facade and choir)†
1535-47	State Mint (Zecca), Venice
1536-40	Santo Croce di Gerusalemme, Rome (Monument to Francisco Quinones, Cardinal of Santa Croce)
1536-60	Library of St. Mark's, Venice (not completed until 1591 by Vincenzo Scamozzi)
1536ff.	Santa Maria Mater Domini, Venice (Altar of the Virgin and other work)
1537-40	Piazza San Marco, Venice (loggetta)
1538	Palazzo Dolfin, Venice
1540*	Villa Garzoni, Pontescale, near Padua
1540*-70	San Martino, Venice (not completed until 1633-53)
1544-62*	Palazzo Moro, Venice
1545-47	Ca' di Dio, Venice
1545*-66	Palazzo Corner (della Ca' Grande), San Maurizio, Venice
1549*-66	San Fantin, Venice (choir) [attributed]
1553-66	San Giuliano, Venice (with Alessandro Vittoria; not completed until 1593)
1554-57	Fabbriche Nuove at Rialto, Venice†
1555-58	Scala d'Oro, Doge's Palace, Venice (with Michele Sanmichele)
1555*-61	San Salvatore, Venice (Monument of Doge Francesco Venier and other work)
1557-58	San Geminiano, Venice (facade, roof, and dome)†
1557-58	San Sebastiano, Venice (Monument of Archbishop Livio Podocataro)
1557-70	Santa Maria dei Crociferi, Venice (now dei Gesuiti; Monument of the Da Lezze Family) [attributed]
1558-66	State Mint, Venice (third story) [attributed]
1565-68	Church of the Incurabili, Venice†
1568	San Basso, Venice (sacristy and high altar)†

Publications

BOOKS ABOUT SANSOVINO

HOWARD, DEBORAH: *Jacopo Sansovino: Architecture and Patronage in Renaissance Venice*. New Haven, Connecticut, and London, 1975.

HOWARD, DEBORAH: *The Architectural History of Venice*. New York, 1981.

LORENZETTI, GIULIO: *Itinerario sansoviniano a Venezia*. Venice, 1929.

MARIACHER, GIOVANNI: *Il Sansovino*. Milan, 1962.

PITTONI, L.: *Jacopo Sansovino scultore*. Venice, 1909.

SAPORI, F.: *Jacopo Tatti, detto il Sansovino*. 1928.

TAFURI, MANFREDO: *Jacopo Sansovino e l'architettura del '500 a Venezia*. Padua, Italy, 1969.

ARTICLES ABOUT SANSOVINO

GALLO, R.: ''Jacopo Sansovino a Pola.'' *Rivista di Venezia* 5 (1926): 255-286.

GIOVANNI, GUSTAVO: ''Un'opera sconosciuta di Jacopo Sansovino in Roma.'' In *Saggi sulla architettura del rinascimento*. 2nd rev. ed. Milan, 1935.

HOWARD, DEBORAH: ''Le chiese del Sansovino a Venezia.'' *Bollettino del Centro Internazionale di Studi di Architettura ''Andrea Palladio''* 19 (1977): 49-67.

LEWIS, DOUGLAS: ''Sansovino and Venetian Architecture.'' *Burlington Magazine* 121 (1979): 38-41.

LEWIS, DOUGLAS: ''Un disegno . . . e la notizia del committente del Sansovino per S. Francesco della Vigna: Nuovi appunti per il mecenatismo artistico del Procuratore Vettor Grimani.'' *Bollettino dei Musei Civici Veneziani* 17, Nos. 3-4 (1972): 7-36.

LOTZ, WOLFGANG: ''Palladio e Sansovino.'' *Bollettino del Centro Internazionale di Studi di Architettura ''Andrea Palladio''* 9 (1967): 13-23.

LOTZ, WOLFGANG: ''The Roman Legacy in Sansovino's Venetian Buildings.'' In *Studies in Italian Renaissance Architecture*. Cambridge, Massachusetts, 1977.

*

Called il Sansovino, Dacopo Tatti trained in his native Florence under Andrea Sansovino, from whom he took his name. Considered by many to have been primarily a sculptor, he achieved a remarkable integration of sculpture and architectural planes. Perhaps his greatest contribution was the introduction of the architectural style of the High Renaissance to Venice, where governmental and private patronage had become more substantial than ecclesiastical patronage; his most important designs were for public buildings and palaces.

Highly skilled in the conservation of ancient sculpture, Sansovino reached his artistic maturity in Rome, where from 1505 he served as sculptor and restorer of ancient statues at St. Peter's, at the peak of Donato Bramante's influence, whose classical tradition he would introduce in Venice. In 1511 or 1512 he returned to Florence and worked there until 1518, when he returned to Rome. With the sack of Rome in 1527, he fled to Venice, where in 1529 the doge commissioned him to repair the main dome of St. Mark's. That year Sansovino became the principal official architect in Venice as well as its leading architect; for the rest of his life, he lived there. Andrea Palladio admired him and emulated several elements of his work.

In 1515 Sansovino earned the commission to design a wooden facade to cover the unfinished 14th-century Church of Santa Maria del Fiore for the entry of Pope Leo X into Florence. Influenced by Giuliano da Sangallo's Santa Casa in Loreto, Sansovino derived the design from the triumphal arch, incorporating paired columns of the Corinthian order with niches and statues.

Having selected Sansovino over several other prominent architects, Leo X subsequently commissioned him to design San Giovanni dei Fiorentini in Rome. Construction began in 1520, but the building was never completed. In Venice, Sansovino began the planning for San Francesco della Vigna in 1534; this church is most noted, however, for the facade that Palladio designed for it beginning in 1562.

Jacopo Sansovino: Piazza San Marco, Venice, 1537-40

Sansovino's most lasting achievement in Venice, however, was the redesign of the Piazza San Marco, one of the most harmonious public spaces in the world; his work there began in 1537. As the mercantile intersection between the East and West, Venice had an architectural tradition endowed with Oriental splendor. In choreographing the ceremonial center of the city, Sansovino assumed the responsibility of giving order and clarity to a collection of buildings from several centuries, including St. Mark's, the campanile, the Doge's Palace and the heraldic columns. The Piazzetta, which links the Piazza with the canal and lies at approximately a right angle to it, channels traffic toward St. Mark's. Sansovino's great opportunity lay with the Piazzetta, in which he introduced to Venice its first High Renaissance buildings, the Mint (Zecca), the Library and the Loggetta. Additionally, he made the campanile independent of the other buildings, emphasizing it as the vertical element at the intersection of the two squares.

Work on the mint, in which the treasury of the republic was safeguarded, began in 1537. Introducing what Giorgio Vasari called the rustic order, Sansovino developed a highly sculptural expression of the Doric order, embellished with heavily banded columns. He incorporated the existing cheese shops into the ground floor and made the building fireproof, since silver was coined in a foundry on the ground floor and gold in another on the *piano nobile*. A long hall separated the foundries in the front section from the courtyard at the rear. In 1558 he began work on the third story. The unmistakable image of fortification relates to Michele Sanmicheli's (ca. 1484-1559) Fortress of Sant' Andrea, begun 15 years earlier. Its ground floor exhibits plain rustication, its *piano nobile* bold rustication of its Doric order in addition to severely projecting lintels, and its upper story a banded Ionic order, pediments and a bracketed cornice.

Originally used as an exclusive meeting place for nobles attending councils of state, the loggetta became in the 17th century a room for the guards of arsenal workers who kept public order during sessions led under the command of a procurator. It is now an entrance to the campanile, where tickets to view the tower are sold. In strong contrast to the medieval campanile, the loggetta displays a system of arches derived from the pattern of the triumphal arch, possibly inspired by Giuliano da Sangallo's project for San Lorenzo in Florence. Having separated the campanile from its adjacent buildings, Sansovino created a triple, overlapping set of triumphal arches directly opposite the Porta della Carta designed by Bartolomeo Bon (or Buon) that leads to the Scala dei Giganti. Surrounded by an engaged bench, a balustrade, added in the 17th century, encloses the forecourt. Red, white and green marble enrich the pilasters and freestanding Corinthian columns, which support a projecting entablature. Bronze sculptures ornament attic and spandrel panels. In the attic panels, Venice is portrayed as Justice and, above the outer arches, Cyprus and Crete, the republic's two conquests, are personified. *Putti* play with classical armor in the four smaller panels above the shell niches. On the side walls, the polychromy delineates roundels and a semicircular relieving arch above a Serlian motif. Within the niches stand Minerva, Apollo, Mercury and Peace.

Three residential designs illustrate the breadth of Sansovino's design abilities. Begun in 1538, the Palazzo Dolfin, later Manin, exhibits the assured and restrained elegance of a mature Renaissance style. The six-bay facade along the waterfront contains, at its ground floor, an open arcade supported by pilastered piers of a Doric order. Ionic engaged columns replace the ground-floor pilasters in the middle story, and a Corinthian order of engaged columns supersedes at the top story. In the upper stories, where the rhythm of columns doubles in the two center bays, the window openings are half the width of the arches below. Antique lion heads hover in the frieze above each column and in the centers of the wider bays. The Villa Garzoni at Pontescale (1540), near Padua, is widely regarded as approaching more nearly the sensibility of an ancient villa than any other in the architecture of the 16th century. Related to the Theater of Marcellus (11 B.C.) and the courtyard of the palazzo Farnese in Rome (1541) by Antonio da Sangallo the Younger, its two-story loggia displays piers with engaged columns. Its U-shaped plan relates to Baldassare Peruzzi's Villa Farnesina in Rome (1509-11), with a courtyard opening to the rear. The Villa Garzoni is admired for its feeling of repose and understatement. From 1545 to 1566 at the Palazzo Corner della Ca' Grande (San Maurizio), Sansovino adapted the Roman prototype of the palace to Venetian requirements.

Sansovino's work in Venice from the 1550s includes a warehouse, sculpture and a church facade. Begun in 1554, the Fabbriche Nuove di Rialto comprised appropriately plain warehouses of white Istrian stone. Above a rusticated waterfront arcade, two stories of pedimented windows align themselves between Doric pilasters in the middle story and Ionic pilasters in the top story. In 1556 Sansovino created large figures of Mars and Neptune for the upper landing of the Scala dei Giganti, adjacent to the Piazza San Marco. Although perhaps overscaled, they show the classical influence of Michelangelo on Sansovino. Returning to the prescription provided by the triumphal arch, he began in 1557 to design a facade for San Geminiano, later demolished under Napoleon I.

At San Giuliano (1553-66) Sansovino designed a large unpartitioned square, with a flat ceiling decorated with corner cartouches and volutes. Rooted in the local tradition, the church does not respond to the influence of the domed, nine-part central plan of St. Mark's. Inside, a central altar is enclosed by a cross vault and is flanked by two lower chapels. A cornice line at the height of these two chapels divides and lends proportion to the walls.

Although not as catholic as that of Palladio, his admirer, Sansovino's influence was nevertheless durable. His handling of form and texture in the Piazza San Marco brought the classical tradition and an energetic classicizing effect to Venice, carrying that group of islands from the Middle Ages into the Renaissance.

—PAUL GLASSMAN

SANT'ELIA, Antonio.

Italian. Born in Como, Italy, 1888. Died in Monfalcone, 1916. Studied at Milan and Bologna. Established firm, Milan, 1912.

Publications

ARTICLES BY SANT'ELIA

"Messagio" and "Manifesto of Futurist Architecture." In ULRICH CONRADS (ed.): *Programs and Manifestoes on 20th Century Architecture*. Cambridge, Massachusetts, 1970.
"Architettura Futurista" (Manifesto, 1914). In G. C. ARGAN, et al.: *Dopo Sant'Elia*. Milan, 1935. English translation in R. CARRIERI: *Futurism*. Milan, 1963.

BOOKS ABOUT SANT'ELIA

APOLLONIO, U.: *Antonio Sant'Elia*. Milan, 1958.
APOLLONIO, U.: *Futurist Manifestos*. London, 1973.
CARAMEL, LUIGI, and LONGATTI, ALBERTO: *Antonio Sant'Elia: The Complete Works*. New York, 1989.
GODOLI, E.: *Il Futurismo*. Rome and Bari, Italy, 1983.
TISDALL, CAROLINE, and BOZZOLLA, ANGELO: *Futurism*. London, 1977.

ARTICLES ABOUT SANT'ELIA

BANHAM, REYNER: "Sant'Elia." *Architectural Review* 117 (1955): 295-301.
BANHAM, REYNER: "Sant'Elia." *Architectural Review* 119 (1956): 343-344.

*

Antonio Sant'Elia is the most well known and highly regarded of the futurist architects even though only two of his futurist projects were realized. The first, designed in December 1913 and since destroyed, was an elaborate cubic-shaped tomb for the Caprotti family of Como. The second, which stands in Como, was an adaptation of one of Sant'Elia's sketches by Enrico Prampolini that was completed by Attilio and Giuseppe Terragni in 1933. Although the monument seems a parody of the massive "Architectural Dynamism" sketches by Sant'Elia from which it was derived, it is a memorial to both Sant'Elia and to others who, like him, died during World War I. Sant'Elia's reputation rests primarily upon his manifesto, *Messagio*, originally published in 1914; his futurist vision of the city as a transportation network and communications center; and the considerable number of drawings illustrating his concept.

Sant'Elia's early work shows the influence of the innovative *stile liberty* architects Raimondo D'Aronco and Giuseppe Sommaruga and of the Viennese Secessionists Otto Wagner, Joseph Olbrich and the younger members of Wagner's architectural school. The Villa Elisi, a country house near Como, commissioned from Sant'Elia in 1911 by the industrialist Romeo Longatti and now drastically altered, featured a frescoed pediment, made in collaboration with the sculptor Gerolamo Fontana, in the style of Gustav Klimt. The potency of these early influences can be seen in two facades Sant'Elia designed during his most futurist period: the enclosure and exterior decorations of a school building in the Via Brambilla in Como (1914-15), and the facade decorations of a building in the Via Cesare Cantu, Como (1915), where Sant'Elia's father, Luigi, ran a barber shop.

The beginnings of Sant'Elia's characteristic architectural style are seen in 1912 when he started to develop his ideas for the Città Nuova (New City), a future utopian metropolis. The Citta Nuova was conceived as a vast urban center of monumental buildings, some with external elevators, connected at several levels by streets and covered passageways. Inspiration for the Citta Nuova came primarily from the technological projects of Otto Wagner for the city of Vienna, and from the skyscrapers and technological developments of modern American cities.

The drawings and sketches for the Citta Nuova were first shown in February 1914 at an exhibition in Milan organized by the Associazione degli Architetti Lombardi. In May of the same year, they were again exhibited in Milan at the first exhibition of the Nuove Tendenze (New Tendencies), a group Sant'Elia had joined in 1912. The Citta Nuova drawings were complemented by Mario Chiattone's designs for "Structures of a Modern Metropolis." The works of both Sant'Elia and Chiattone presented the imagery that was to be associated with futurism, and illustrated the new architecture of the new city as envisioned by the two architects.

Included in the catalog for the Nuove Tendenze exhibition were statements by members of the group and a preface, *Messagio*, by Sant'Elia. *Messagio* contained Sant'Elia's proclamation that a new architecture free from the limitations and restrictions of tradition was possible and necessary. This new architecture would not rely upon a decorative or imitative style, but upon science and technology in its reaction to the requirements and circumstances of modern life. The monumentality and symmetry of the few buildings of the Citta Nuova that were rendered in plan or elevation do not, however, conform to Sant'Elia's claim of a complete split with the architectural traditions of the past.

It was through the Nuove Tendenze exhibition and *Messagio* that Sant'Elia attracted the attention of Filippo Tommaso Marinetti, the leader of the futurist movement. Marinetti was undoubtedly quick to realize the similarities between the ideas Sant'Elia expressed and those of the futurists. Both championed a complete rejection of the values and traditions of the past in favor of a future world dominated by technology and mobility. The wording of *Messagio* indicates that Sant'Elia may have already been familiar with the futurists' ideas before he became associated with them after the Nuove Tendenze exhibition. The degree of his participation and membership in the movement is a matter of debate. Some scholars tend to label Sant'Elia a socialist and dissociate him from Marinetti because of the latter's connection to fascism. Two months after the publication of *Messagio*, a slightly revised version of it, *L'Architettura futurista* (*The Manifesto of Futurist Architecture*, was published by Sant'Elia in the journal *Lacerba*. The alterations, believed to be the work of Marinetti, entailed the insertion of the word "futurist" or "futurism" where possible, and additional sections at the beginning and end. The differences between *Messagio* and the *Manifesto* are essentially stylistic and do not significantly affect the context.

Unfortunately, Sant'Elia's promising career was cut short when he died on the battlefield at Monfalcone in 1916 during World War I. His architecture was distinctive and had very little in common with the other modern architectural movements that were developing. There are correlations with some of Eric Mendelsohn's untitled sketches that explore the dynamics of building types and forms, and with the designs of the Russian constructivists. Despite the principally theoretical aspect of his accomplishments, Sant'Elia's images exerted a significant influence on architecture after World War I. His insistence on the structural possibilities of new materials was influential in the development of rationalism and probably affected the work of Le Corbusier, particularly the 1922 "Ville Contemporaine." Because Sant'Elia's work was so prophetic, he is often regarded as the harbinger of the modern era of architecture.

—LORETTA LORANCE

SANTINI-AICHEL, Johann.

Czechoslovakian. Born in Bohemia (Prague, Czechoslovakia), 1667. Died in Prague, 7 December 1723.

Chronology of Works
All in Bohemia (Czechoslovakia)

1708-10	Chapel of the Name of the Virgin, Mladotice
1710-35	Pilgrimage Church, Křtiny
1711-51	Pilgrimage Church of Mariánské Týnice, near Kralovice
1712-26	Benedictine Church, Kladruby (reconstruction)
1712-36	Premonstratensian Church, Želiv (reconstruction)
1713-14	Černin-Moržin Palace, Prague
1719-21	Pilgrimage Church of St. John Nepomuk, Green Mountain, near Z'dár
1721-23	Karlová Koruna hunting lodge (Karlskrone), near Chlumec
1721-32	Benedictine Church, Rajhrad

Publications

BOOKS ABOUT SANTINI-AICHEL

BACHMANN, E.: "Die Barockgotik Santini-Aichels." In *Barock in Böhmen*, 1964.

FRANZ, H. G.: *Bauten und Baumeister der Barockzeit in Böhmen*. Leipzig, 1962.

ARTICLES ABOUT SANTINI-AICHEL

FRANZ, H. G.: "Gothik und Barock im Werk des Johann Santini Aichel." *Wiener Jahrbuch für Kunstgeschichte* 14 (1950): 65-130.

*

Johann Santini-Aichel was the most important architect in Bohemia besides Christoph and Kilian Ignaz Dientzenhofer, and the principal works of the so-called Baroque Gothic are associated with him. Among Santini-Aichel's few secular buildings was the Černin-Moržin Palace in Prague (1713-14), which further developed the traditional palace facade by means of a triangular composition in the central bay. The central axis has a balcony on the *piano nobile* and at ground level is flanked by portals set in the side axes. The composition of portals at the Thun-Hohenstein Palace (1716), in contrast, was derived from the work of J. B. Fischer von Erlach. The hunting lodge Karlová Koruna (Karlskrone) near Chlumec (1721-23) was a more original design. Three wings, each on a diamond-shaped plan, penetrate a circular central building. Two of the wings enclose the grand staircase. In this highly complex design, Santini-Aichel applied the anticlassical schemata of Mannerist palaces. The building also responded to the bud-shaped mercy chapels typical of Bohemia and to Fischer von Erlach's pleasure-house designs.

Santini-Aichel was in charge of monastic architecture in the province of Bohemia and Moravia. His religious architecture is in the style of Francesco Borromini and Fischer von Erlach, particularly Fischer von Erlach's fanciful early work. In contrast to the Dientzenhofers, Santini-Aichel did not follow Guarino Guarini's style, with its discontinuities between vaults and the spaces they cover, nor the wall pilaster and canopy principle. Interior space, in Santini-Aichel's work, was determined by the walls, while the vaults remained structurally subordinate elements.

The Baroque Gothic of Bohemia is a confusing phenomenon. It definitely cannot be understood as the survival of medieval architectural traditions, since the Thirty Years' War had put an end to all construction work in the wake of the Gothic style. It would also be incorrect to compare Santini-Aichel's churches to movements running counter to normative aesthetics, such as the Gothic Revival, whose relativism toward the classical canon led to historicism. Unlike French adaptations of the Gothic style, the Baroque Gothic of Bohemia was not an effort to come to grips with Gothic construction technique. Furthermore, the influence of the Borromini style, which sought to enrich the classical decorative repertoire by means of an antisystematic application of Gothic forms, was slight. Santini-Aichel's art has little in common with the immanent Gothic style of Guarini, the Dientzenhofers or Balthasar Neumann. Guarini used only the structure of the medieval examples. The Dientzenhofers introduced a development that fused the southern German wall-pilaster church with the Guarini style, until finally, in Neumann's work, the canopy and double-shell wall of the Middle Ages articulated Late Baroque architectural thought in a new way.

The Baroque Gothic of Santini-Aichel must be understood against the background of its functional history. The first phase of the reestablishment of Catholicism in Bohemia after the Battle of White Mountain was expressed architecturally with recourse to Italian examples. The second phase, at the dawn of the 18th century, became more mindful of regional tradition and returned to the pre-Hussite Middle Ages, possibly as a result of the cult of Saint John Nepomuk. The second phase was dominated by the old monastic orders, primarily the Cistercians and Premonstratensians. Their monasteries, which had been destroyed by the Hussites, were then reconstructed. The choice of Gothic forms was therefore less an artistic phenomenon than a programmatic attempt to reconnect with interrupted monastic traditions. The visitor to the reconstructed buildings was to experience the illusion of being in a medieval church. Similar efforts can be found in the older Jesuit Gothic, which sought to repress the historical fact of the Reformation by means of a pseudo-medieval church architecture. Another example of the approach was the reconstruction of Orléans Cathedral, which had been destroyed by the Huguenots.

Santini-Aichel, then, reconstructed a Gothic style with an awareness of the historical distance, and with the goal of overcoming that distance. He saw the Gothic style as a past architectural style with a distinct repertoire of forms, colored by his own Late Baroque sensibility. The medieval appearance of a building was to be achieved by gathering characteristic motifs and decorative elements. The reconstructed Gothic was much less concerned with recreating structure than surface texture. The most striking characteristic of Santini-Aichel's churches is the abundant use of pointed arches, of multiply differentiated stucco rib vaults, but most of all the bizarrely lush compositions of pinnacles and Gothic gable forms in architecture and decoration.

The first building of this nature was the Cistercian Church at Sedlec, which had been burned down in 1421 by the Hussites.

Reconstruction took place from 1703 to 1707. The five-nave church followed the Gothic cathedral scheme. In spite of the Gothicizing net vault with stucco ribs in the central nave, the range of Gothic elements did not yet assert itself in the entire space, but was limited to the wall surfaces and vault elements.

The reconstruction of the Premonstratensian Church in Želiv (1712-36) represented a definite step forward toward spatial unification. Santini-Aichel made use of the unified space of the choir hall and constructed a rib vault over all the naves, following the example of Benedikt Ried's Cathedral of St. Barbara in Kutná Hora. As a consequence, a Baroque dynamic developed in the resulting wall surfaces and vaults. The illumination, achieved by piercing the vaults over the lateral naves in front of the high windows, is also Baroque. The space begins, as it were, to circulate.

The most significant creation of this group was the reconstruction of the Benedictine Church at Kladruby, between 1712 and 1726. The church had also been destroyed during the Hussite and Thirty Years' Wars. The extent to which the Gothic style represented the Middle Ages and pre-Reformation relationships to contemporary minds becomes clear in the Gothic reconstruction of this originally Romanesque church. In place of the three-apse Romanesque complex, a centralized clover-leaf choir was built. A powerful Gothicizing dome rises over the crossing. The lantern holds up the royal crown of Bohemia so as to be visible from afar. In a letter of 1720, the client expressly praised the *"more gotico nondum visa cupula."* Santini-Aichel sought, insofar as the basilican scheme permitted, to unify the different interior spaces by means of the vault ribs. At Kladruby the decoration was also limited to Gothic forms.

Baroque Gothic and indigenous Baroque came together in Santini-Aichel's pilgrimage churches and mercy chapels. The renovation of the sanctuaries, which go back to pre-Hussite times, and the new foundation of pilgrimage places were also part of the program to re-Catholicize Bohemia. The ambulatory around the reliquary is part of the typology of pilgrimage churches. The ambulatory of the pilgrimage churches of Bohemia is not integrated with the main building, but is separate from it, in contrast to Bavarian pilgrimage churches, for instance. Dominikus Zimmermann's churches may serve as a specific example. By building the ambulatory as an independent structure, a courtyard, a kind of sacred realm, was created. Typologically, the design derived from antiquity. The type was brought into Bohemia in the 17th century by Italian architects, and is to be found in a wealth of variants before Santini-Aichel's use of the form. However, in his hands the separate ambulatory design reached its highest form of development.

The Pilgrimage Church of Mariánské Týnice near Kralovice (1711-51) survives heavily damaged. It is a centralized building combining the domed cross plan with the medieval scheme of four half domes. The separate ambulatory consequently stands in communication with the church space, which was a design solution that Santini-Aichel used again and again in varied form. Only one ambulatory of this complex *"ad quadratum"* design was actually realized, however.

The Pilgrimage Church of Křtiny (1710-35), was built to designs by Santini-Aichel and under the supervision of the master mason Franz-Joseph Ritz from Brno. The building rises over a cloverleaf plan, which, in its combination of circle and cross, undoubtedly had symbolic value. The two-story ambulatory has arcades facing the inner courtyard. The appearance of the church exterior is reminiscent of fortifications, with the single tower facade, ambulatory and the towers and bastion-like projections recalling fortification architecture. The pilgrimage place thus presented itself as a celestial stronghold of mercy.

The similarly "fortified" pilgrimage place on White Mountain near Prague may have influenced Santini-Aichel's last work—the Benedictine Church at Rajhrad (1721-32). A series of centralized vaulted spaces, laid out along the central axis behind a narrow transept, forms the transition to the broad and short choir that balances the transept. All the same, the complex discontinuities of the vaults with the basic plan typical of the southern German Late Baroque are not in evidence here. The sculpturally modeled walls determine the interior, while the vault remains curiously unarticulated. The wall architecture loses itself in the illusionistic ceiling paintings.

The mercy chapels of Bohemia with centralized, sometimes irregular layouts combined a range of distinct influences. The symbolic plans associated with the circle of the Dientzenhofers; the mercy chapels of the Alps and, with them, the medieval traditions of devotional architecture; the spiritual spatial combinations of Mannerist polygonal palaces; and the Baroque pleasure- and garden-houses all entered into these designs. The hunting lodge of Karlová Koruna comes to mind again.

An example of such a mercy chapel is the Chapel of the Name of the Virgin at Mladotice (1708-10). The vault of the lantern displays the key element of the building: two opposed triangles forming a hexagon. The mass of the walls is concentrated into pillars at the corners, while the vault is derived from a Gothic three-arm star.

The Pilgrimage Church of St. John Nepomuk on Green Mountain near Ž'dár (1719-21) surpasses all related buildings in artistic influence, formal complexity and symbolic content. The defining themes of Santini-Aichel's art are all present in this church. The commissioned ambulatory achieved a previously unknown independence, but was nevertheless indissolubly connected to the church proper by a highly elaborate systematics. The church itself took the type of the star-shaped mercy chapel to new heights. The leitmotif of the symbolic plan is a five-arm star, referring to the five stars which, according to legend, surrounded the head of the drowned Saint John Nepomuk. All these elements are connected in perfected fashion with Santini-Aichel's Baroque Gothic as he had developed it in the monastic churches of Bohemia.

—MICHAEL HESSE
Translated from the German by Marijke Rijsberman

SCAMOZZI, Vincenzo.

Italian. Born in Vicenza, Italy, 2 September 1548. Died in Venice, 7 August 1616. Father was the surveyor and building contractor Gian Domenico Scamozzi. Visited Rome, 1579-80, then moved to Venice in 1581.

Chronology of Works
All in Italy
* Approximate dates
† Work no longer exists

1568-75*	Villa of Girolamo Ferramosca, Barbano (with Gian Domenico Scamozzi)
1572-93	Palazzo Thiene-Bonin, Vicenza
1574-1615	Villa of Leonardo Verlati, Villaverla
1575	Palazzo Caldogno, Vicenza
1575-78	Rocca Pisani (Vettor Pisani Villa), Lonigo
1576-79	Trissino-Trento (Pierfranceso Trissino Palace), Vicenza (with Gian Domenico Scamozzi)
1580s	Villa of Francesco Priuli, Treville di Castelfranco (north wing)
1580-92*	Villa Capra/La Rotonda, Vicenza (completed construction of Andrea Palladio's structure, and added stables)
1581-86	San Gaetano da Thiene, Padua
1581-99	Procuratie Nuove, Piazza San Marco, Venice (continued with a different interior design by Francesco Smeraldi and completed in 1663 by Baldassare Longhena)
1582*	Palazzo Cividale, Vicenza [attributed]
1582-91	Library of St. Mark's, Venice (completion of Jacopo Sansovino's design)
1584-85	Teatro Olimpico, Vicenza (remodeling of structure by Andrea Palladio)
1587-96	Library of St. Mark's, Venice (antisala)
1588	Villa Cornaro, Poisolo di Castelfranco (reconstruction)
1588-90	Theater (for Duke Vespasiano Gonzaga), Sabbioneta
1590	Villa of Girolamo Contarini, Loreggia (revised in construction)
1590-95	San Nicolò da Tolentino, Venice
1591-94	San Gaetano da Thiene, Padua (monastery)
1591-95	Villa of Girolamo Cornaro, Piombino (completion) [attributed]
1591-97	Villa Duodo and Chapel off San Giorgio, Monselice
1592-1616	Palace of Galeazzo Trissino al Corso, Vicenza
1594-1600	Villa of Valerio Bardellini, Monfumo†
1596	Villa of Girolamo Ferretti, River Brenta, Sambruson del Dolo
1596-97	Villa of Girolamo Cornaro, Piombino (stable)
1597	Villa of Nicolò Molin, Mandria
1597	Villa Priuli, Carrara Padovano†
1597-98	Villa Godi, Sarmego
1601	Palazzo del Bò, Padua (university facade)
1601-06	San Giacomo di Rialto, Venice (altar of Scuola degli Orefici; with Girolamo Campagna)
1601-36	San Lazzaro dei Mendicanti Church and Hospital, Venice
1604-12	Cathedral of Sts. Rupert and Virgil, Salzburg, Austria (completed in 1614-28 by Santino Solari)
1605	Santi Giovanni e Paolo, Venice (sacristy door; with Alessandro Vittorio)
1605-16	Villa Duodo, Monselice (six chapels for Via Romana)
1607-11	San Giorgio Maggiore, Venice (facade)
1607-16	Villa Cornaro al Paradiso, Venice (twin pavilions)†
1609	Domenico Trevisan Villa, San Donà di Piave†
1609-16	Palazzo Contarini, Santrovaso on the Grand Canal, Venice
1614	Palazzo Loredan, Venice (east wing; demolished in 1659 and rebuilt in 1660)

Publications

BOOKS BY SCAMOZZI

Discorsi sopra l'antichità di Roma. Venice, 1582.
Taccuino di vaggio da Parigi a Venezia. Venice, 1600. New edition by Franco Barbieri: Venice and Rome, 1959.
L'idea dell'architettura universale. Venice, 1615.

BOOKS ABOUT SCAMOZZI

BARBIERI, FRANCO: *Vincenzo Scamozzi*. Vicenza, 1952.

DONIN, RICHARD KURT: *Vincenzo Scamozzi und der Einfluss Venedigs auf die Salzburger Architektur*. Innsbruck, Austria, 1948.

HERSEY, GEORGE L.: *Pythagorean Palaces*. Ithaca, New York, 1976.

ARTICLES ABOUT SCAMOZZI

DE LA CROIX, HORST: "Palmanova: A Study in Sixteenth-Century Urbanism." *Saggi e memorie di storia dell'arte* 5 (1966): 23-41.

GALLO, RODOLFO: "Vincenzo Scamozzi e la chiesa di San Nicolò da Tolentino." *Atti dell'Istituto Veneto di Scienze, Lettere e Arti* 117 (1958-59): 103-122.

LEWIS, DOUGLAS: "Girolamo II Corner's Completion of Piombino, with an Unrecognized Building of 1596 by Vincenzo Scamozzi." *Architectura* 7 (1977): 40-45.

PUPPI, LIONELLO and LOREDANA: "Scamozziana—progetti e alcune altre novità grafiche con qualche quesito." *Antichità viva* 13, No. 4 (1974): 54-80.

SCOLARI, F.: *Commentario della vita e le opere di Vincenzo Scamozzi*. Venice, 1838.

TIMOFIEWITSCH, VLADIMIR: "Das Testament Vincenzo Scamozzis vom 2 September 1602." *Bollettino del Centro Internazionale di Studi di Architettura "Andrea Palladio"* 7 (1965): 316-328.

*

Vincenzo Scamozzi was an architect and a writer on architecture, active in Verona in the second half of the 16th century, perhaps the most important figure there between Andrea Palladio and Baldassare Longhena, his one pupil. What is interesting about Scamozzi's education and training is that he seems to have modeled it, very self-consciously, around the idea of the gentleman and artist, of the humanist even, rather than as anything more specifically practical. His father, Gian Domenico Scamozzi, is documented in Vicenza as a successful surveyor and building contractor, though so far as architectural design is concerned, he is described as a carpenter; this trade, as we know from several other similar records in the Renaissance, often led toward the higher profession of architecture.

The younger Scamozzi's first documented commission, a villa for Girolamo Ferramosco in Barbano (ca. 1520), was done with his father; a few years later, with the Villa Verlati in Villaverla and the Palazzo Caldogno in Vicenza (both ca. 1575), Scamozzi gave clear evidence of his skill in design, while needing his father still for practical advice. And it was with his father helping him that Scamozzi produced what was perhaps his most imposing building, the Palazzo Thiene-Bonin (1572-1593), a retreat for Vettor Pisani from the plagues in the city. It was a perfect Palladian villa, set in the form of a cube on a high hill, and dominated on three sides by a Palladian window and at the front by an open loggia with a simple screen of columns and a pediment. Inside is a domed circular hall, lit by an oculus, the building being fed by the airy spaces of the corner rooms so that everything is cool and light. The forms throughout are articulated simply and solidly; the success of this design led Scamozzi to repeat it in variations, some twenty years later at the Villa Molina at Mandria and then at the Villa Cornaro al Paradiso (1607-1616), where he set a pair of matched pavilions in the design, something suggested perhaps by the model of the Villa Lante at Bagnaia, but in its effect a feature that seems to announce the richness of the forms of the Baroque.

When Scamozzi arrived in Venice in 1581, he received very quickly the commission for his largest and most prominent work, that of the Procuratie Nuove on the Piazza of San Marco, a project that in the end took some 80 years to be finished; it was completed in 1663 by Longhena. The two lower stories of this facade follow exactly those of Jacopo Sansovino's Library of San Marco; above these Scamozzi added a third floor, derived from a Palladian project of 1578 for the Palazzo Ducale in the city. The result was to provide what might be called a continuous screen for the houses of the procurators of San Marco, each one joined to the next and taking up some five bays of the whole.

This design made Scamozzi's reputation, and for the next few years he was very busy. In 1588 he built a theater for the Gonzagas at Sabbionetta, their new town outside Mantua; this followed Scamozzi's remodeling in 1584-85 of Palladio's Teatro Olimpico at Vicenza, but it varied from that great example in being lower and more narrowly shaped, the stage at the end of the axis being like a perfect, distant scenographic illusion, set carefully for the view of the seats and the ducal throne at the back.

After this, for Scamozzi there were problems, designs offered but not completed; the record we have shows instance after instance of his arrogance and also, to his discredit, expressions of the intense rivalry he felt for Palladio, though interestingly it was he who completed the construction of Palladio's Villa Rotonda and added the stables there. In 1595 Scamozzi was dismissed from work for the Church of the Theatines, the plans he produced for the Theatines and for their principal church in Venice being simplified by the brothers. And the great commission he received in 1604 to design a cathedral for the bishop of Salzburg, Wolf Dietrich von Raitenau, was not done as Scamozzi had planned it, being reduced when a competing architect was asked to finish it.

Yet Scamozzi's career ended with one further moment of glory, the commission for the Palazzo Contarini at San Trovaso on the Grand Canal in Venice (begun ca. 1610). However, for all its novelty it is a slightly dry building, with thinly articulated orders and a style of fenestration, with deeply elongated windows, that seems closer to the Gothic proportions of the neighboring palace than anything strictly classical.

Scamozzi had been to Rome several times, and after his first visit between 1579 and 1580, he published two engravings of classical buildings there. On his return to Venice in 1581 he published 40 commentaries and three introductory chapters for a set of topographical prints of Rome by Giambattista Pittoni, put out as the *Discorsi sopra le Antichità*. Some time after that, Scamozzi began his treatise on architecture, *L'Idea della architettura universale*, in six books, published first in 1615, the year before he died. There, as perhaps everywhere, Scamozzi had ideas beyond his talents; the text is extremely dense, and the general effect of what he wrote, beyond the plates, was minimal. The sixth book on the orders, however, was taken out and translated into several languages. For centuries it was one of the standard handbooks on design for both architects and craftsmen.

—DAVID CAST

SCARPA, Carlo.

Italian. Born in Venice, Italy, 2 June 1906. Died in Sendai, Japan, 28 November 1978. Married Onorina Lazzari, 1934; one son. Studied architecture at Accademia de Belle Arti, Venice, 1920-25; Dip.Arch. Served in the Italian Army, 1926. In private practice as architect, designer and graphic artist, in Venice,

Carlo Scarpa: Brion Cemetery, Verona, Italy, 1970-78

1927-62, in Asolo, 1962-72, and in Vicenza, 1972 until his death in 1978. Design consultant for the Venice Biennale, from 1941. Assistant instructor, 1926-29, 1932-33, professor, 1933-76 , emeritus professor, 1976-77, and director, 1970-78, Istituto Universitario di Architettura, Venice; head of design course, Istituto Artistico Industriale, Venice, 1945-47; head of visual studies course, Istituto Superiore di disegno Industriale, Venice, 1960-61.

Chronology of Works
All in Italy unless noted

1927-47	Glassware for Venini Company, Murano
1936-37	Ca Foscari, University, Venice
1941	Tomb of Rizzo Family, Cemetery of San Michele, Venice
1941	Design of the Biennale, Venice; design of subsequent exhibitions at the Venice Biennales of 1949 (Paul Klee); 1950 (Pavilion of the Art Book); 1952 (Tiepolo); 1956 (Venezuelan Pavilion); 1960 (Erich Mendelsohn); 1968 (Pursuit of New Structures)
1947-56	Museo dell'Accademia, Venice
1953	Antonello di Messina Exhibition, Town Hall, Messina
1953-54	Palazzo Abatellis, Palermo, Sicily
1953-60	Museo Correr, Venice
1953-61	Veretti House, Udine
1954-56	Galleria degli Uffizi, Florence (with others)
1957-58	Olivetti Showroom, Venice
1957-64	Museo di Castelvecchio, Verona (restoration)
1960	Frank Lloyd Wright Memorial Exhibition, Triennale, Milan
1961	Sense of Color and Mastery of Water Exhibition, Italia '61, Turin
1964-68	Zentner House, Zurich, Switzerland
1967	The Poem Exhibition, Italian Pavilion, Expo '67, Montreal, Canada
1970-78	Brion Cemetery, San Vito d'Altivole
1973-78	Banca Popolare di Verona, Verona
1975-78	Ottolenghi House, Bardolino
1975-78	Housing blocks, Vicenza

Publications

BOOKS BY SCARPA

Memoriae causa (ed.). Verona, 1977.
Carlo Scarpa, Venezia 1906-Sendai 1978: I sette foglie giapponesi. Edited by G. Scarpa. Venice, 1979.

BOOKS ABOUT SCARPA

ALBERTINI, B., and BAGNOLI, A.: *Carlo Scarpa: Architecture in Details.* Cambridge, Massachusetts, 1989.
Carlo Scarpa—architetto poeta. Exhibition catalog. London, 1974.
Carlo Scarpa: Drawings for the Brion Family Cemetery. Exhibition catalog. New Haven, Connecticut, 1984.
CRIPPA, MARIA A.: *Carlo Scarpa, Theory, Design, Design Projects.* New York, 1986.
DAL CO, FRANCESCO, and MAZZARIOL, GIUSEPPE (eds.): *Carlo Scarpa: The Complete Works.* New York, 1986.
FRACASI, M.: *The Carlo Scarpa Guide.* Princeton, New Jersey, 1989.

LATOUR, ALESSANDRA: *Carlo Scarpa 1906-1978.* Exhibition catalog. New York, 1986.

ARTICLES ABOUT SCARPA

BETTINI, S.: "L'architettura di Carlo Scarpa." *Zodiac* 6 (1960): 140-187.
"Carlo Scarpa." *Progressive Architecture* 62, special issue (May 1981).
"Carlo Scarpa." *Space Design* special issue (June 1977): 7-162.
PORTOGHESI, PAOLO: "Cemetery Brion-Vega, S. Vito, Treviso, Italy, 1970-1972." *Global Architecture* No. 50 (1979).
SANTINI, PIER CARLO: "Olivetti Showroom, Querini Stampalia and Castelvecchio Museum." *Global Architecture* No. 51 (1979).
ZAMBONINI, G.: "Process and Theme in the Work of Carlo Scarpa." *Perspecta* 20 (1983): 21-42.
ZEVI, BRUNO: "I premi nazionali di architettura e urbanistica a Carlo Scarpa e Ludovico Quaroni." *Architettura* No. 15 (1957).

*

Carlo Scarpa's architecture reflects tradition as well as the modernist and rationalist vocabulary of Adolf Loos, Le Corbusier and Walter Gropius that was imported into Italy in the late 1920s. His traditionalism is not a matter of postmodernist ironic quotation but rather represents a dedication to humanist ideals of scale, quality and the possibility of a poetics of form. His "modernism" did not lead him to theoretical debates about the social or cultural agency of architectural form. Instead, his architecture is a parable of passages between places, materials and structural elements. His architectonic of transition involves a complexity that moves forms off axis, separating them at the moment of contact to produce an unexpected dazzle of sensuous detail. Even his architectural renderings, so much a part of his otherwise limited production, contain layers of changes and thoughts. They cohere, not from a unifying plan, but from sheer visual richness. It is a richness dedicated to materials and to Venetian craftsmanship, functioning not merely as ornament but as a metaphor bespeaking a modern though fragmented urban life.

Scarpa's lifelong commitment to visual richness is obvious in his early designs for Angelo Venini's glassworks in Murano (begun in 1933) which are indebted to Pablo Picasso, Fernand Léger and Paul Klee. The severe geometries, animation and rhythm of Piet Mondrian and Alvar Aalto influenced the design of the glazed wall in his early restoration of the Ca' Foscari in Venice (1936-37).

It was in small-scale restorations and his designs for the Venice Biennali from the years 1946 to 1961 that Scarpa achieved a mature style inspired by Frank Lloyd Wright. His design for an exhibition of Klee's small oil paintings at the 1948 Biennale, a masterwork of sensitivity, acknowledged the scale of those paintings. The arrangement of panels fractured space in clear harmony with the spatial logic of the paintings themselves. Scarpa's adoption of a new spatial freedom was evident in the Pavilion of the Art Book, at the 1950 Biennale, and more pointedly in the Venezuelan Pavilion at the 1956 Biennale. There space was defined in a series of geometrically simple yet ornamented cubes, springing in a nonhierarchical fashion from a central focal point. Wright's geometric vocabulary and theoretical concerns also influenced Scarpa's domestic architecture during that period. The Veritti House in Udine (1953), with its multiplication of cylindrical forms in plan and elevation, pool and enclosed winter garden, clearly demonstrates this.

The transition to an autograph style occurred in Scarpa's designs for the Pavilion of the Veneto region at the Italia '61 Exhibition in Turin. In this pavilion, Scarpa's obsessive use of a simple geometric form (the square), varied by scale and color, overlapped and juxtaposed, adding shimmer and animation to both surface and space; his use of water as a symbol and a reflective boundary, and the use of architectural form for poetic purpose prefigured his most important later works: the restoration of the Castelvecchio in Verona (1957-64), the Brion Cemetery in San Vito d'Altivole (1970-72) and the Banca Popolare in Verona (1973-81).

Scarpa's association with the Museo Civico di Verona, the Castelvecchio, built by the Scaligeri in 1354 with Napoleonic additions in 1806, began with exhibition designs in 1958 and continued beyond the major restorations of 1962-64. Faced with the problem of designing a modern museum space within an historical structure, Scarpa chose to concentrate on the points of intersection—of architectural form, space and time. Windows and doorways retain exterior profiles but are covered with rectangular glazed screens on the interior; floor tiling is not drawn flush to the walls; a hole in the floor allows visual access to a Roman foundation, while others capture views of the Adige River. The keystone of the architectural composition is the 14th-century statue of Cangrande della Scala. Perched on an inaccessible platform of wood and copper-clad beams, the statue sits at the intersection of the medieval and Napoleonic wings. Scarpa designed a richly layered and overdetermined space— no one view clarifies its structure, yet every view is united at the same focal point, the statue of Cangrande.

The Brion Cemetery, commissioned in 1969 for the tombs of Giuseppe and Onorina Brion, is a formalized landscape but not a city of the dead in the grand Italian manner. The L-shaped plan consists of a pavilion and chapel, each on a pond, and two sarcophagi huddled under an archway reminiscent of an arcosolium in the catacombs. A visitor experiences this landscape as a journey through a symbolic narrative. Of obvious but uncertain symbolism are the tile-rimmed intersecting rings in the entryway, the visible mechanism of a doorway leading to the pavilion, sarcophagi which lean toward each other in private dialogue, the watercourse which leads from the tombs to the pavilion pond with its floating cross, and the carefully articulated cubic masses of the chapel. Scarpa has suggestively controlled and articulated boundaries and horizon lines, whether at the surface of the ponds or at the sloping outer walls. He has obsessively piled exquisitely detailed rectangles—squares within squares. They define the chapel, dive into the surrounding pond, and arch over the tombs. He has achieved meaning without reference in an intensely poetic and private space.

Scarpa's career ended in 1978 just as he was receiving increased public recognition. The Banca Popolare in Verona, completed posthumously in accord with his voluminous drawings, suggests the direction he might have followed. The bank building is an uneasy juxtaposition of a classical tripartite facade with an independent inner glazed screen. Heavy stepped cornices and stringcourses reminiscent of the Brion Chapel are interrupted, joints are again avoided or undermined, and geometry is evaded in the slightly off-round facade windows. The structure comments on the incommensurability of disparate structures, materials and forms. It evokes the problems Scarpa faced in fitting a modern building into the tight Roman grid of Verona, and perhaps offers a metaphor for the uneasy juxtaposition of the fragments of modern urban life.

—RICHARD PALEY

SCHAROUN, Hans.

German. Born in Bremen, Germany, 20 September 1893. Died in West Berlin, 25 November 1972. Studied at the Technical High School, Charlottenburg, Berlin, 1912-14. In private practice, Insterburg, Germany, 1919-25; in partnership with Adolf Rading, Berlin, 1926-28; in private practice, Berlin, 1932 until his death in 1972. Professor of Architecture, Academy of Arts and Crafts, Breslau (now Wroclaw, Poland), 1925-32; senior professor of town planning, Technical University, Berlin, 1946-58; head, Institute of Building Studies, Berlin, 1947-51. President, Berlin Academy, 1955-68.

Chronology of Works
All in Germany unless noted

1913	Kruchen House, Buch, near Berlin (with Paul Kruchen)
1917	Community Hall, Kattenau, East Prussia
1917-18	Farmhouse, Thierfeld, near Gumbinnen, East Prussia
1920	Two houses, Pregelstrasse, Insterburg, East Prussia
1920	Kamswyken Housing Development, near Insterburg, East Prussia
1922	Gobert House, Sodehnen, East Prussia
1923-24	Apartment Blocks, Parkring, Insterburg, East Prussia
1924-25	Public Buildings, Bad Mergentheim Spa, Württemberg
1927	Transportable Wooden House, German Garden and Industry Exhibition, Liegnitz
1928-29	Apartment Block, Kaiserdamm, Charlottenburg, Berlin
1929	Single People's Apartment Block, Werkbund Exhibition, Breslau (now Wroclaw, Poland)
1929	Housing, Kaiserstrasse, Bremerhaven
1929-30	Apartment Block, Hohenzollerndamm 35-36, Wilmersdorf, Berlin
1930	Housing Development, Siemensstadt, Berlin
1932	Apartment Block, Hohenzollernring, Spandau, Berlin
1933	Apartment Block, Zwerbruckerstrasse 38-46, Spandau, Berlin
1933	Housing Development, Kladow-Hottengrund, Berlin
1933-35	Schminke House, Löbau, Saxony
1937	Housing, Elbestrasse, Bremerhaven
1937-38	Noack House, Potsdam
1938	Housing, Blessmannstrasse, Bremerhaven
1940	Housing, Kaiserstrasse 240-254, Bremerhaven
1949	Institute of Building Conversion, German Academy of Sciences, Berlin
1954-59	Romeo and Juliet Flats, Zuffenhausen, Stuttgart
1956-62	Geschwister Secondary School, Lunen, Westphalia
1959-63	Berlin Philharmonic Hall, Tiergarten, Berlin
1961-68	School, Marl, Westphalia
1963-71	German Embassy, Brasilia, Brazil
1965-73	City Theater, Wolfsburg
1967-78	State Library, Berlin
1970	Church and Parish Center, Rabenberg, Wolfsburg
1970	German Maritime Museum, Bremerhaven

Publications

BOOKS ABOUT SCHAROUN

FRAMPTON, KENNETH, and FUTAGAWA, YUKIO: *Modern Architecture: 1920-1945.* New York, 1983.

JANOFSKE, ECKEHARD: *Architekture-Raume: Idee und Gestalt bei Hans Scharoun.* Braunschweig and Wiesbaden, West Germany, 1984.

JONES, PETER BLUNDELL: *Hans Scharoun.* London, 1978.

LAUTERBACH, HEINRICH: *Hans Scharoun.* Berlin, 1967.

PEHNT, WOLFGANG: *Expressionist Architecture.* London, 1973.

PFANKUCH, PETER (ed.): *Hans Scharoun: Bauten, Entwürfe, Texte.* Berlin, 1974.

ARTICLES ABOUT SCHAROUN

"Hans Scharoun." *Architecture d'aujourd'hui* 10, Nos. 57-58 (October 1967): 2-61.

FRAMPTON, KENNETH: "Genesis of the Philharmonie." *Architectural Design* (March 1965).

JANOFSKE, ECKEHARD: "Meaning from Contrast: Scharoun's Philharmonic in Berlin." *Daidalos* (14 March 1982).

JONES, PETER BLUNDELL: "Hans Scharoun." *Royal Institute of British Architects Journal* (November 1978).

JONES, PETER BLUNDELL: "Organic versus Classic." *Architectural Association Quarterly* 10, No. 1 (1978): 10-20.

JONES, PETER BLUNDELL: "Scharoun Houses." *Architectural Review* (December 1983).

JONES, PETER BLUNDELL: "Scharoun's Staatsbibliothek: State Library, Berlin." *Architectural Review* 165 (June 1979): 330-341.

LANIER, R. S.: "Acoustics in-the-Round at the Berlin Philharmonic." *Architectural Forum* 120 (May 1964): 98-105.

"Philharmonic Concert Hall, Berlin." *Global Architecture* No. 21 (1973).

SPEIDEL, MANFRED: "Hans Scharoun: State Library, Berlin." *Architecture and Urbanism* (May 1980).

STABER, MARGIT: "Hans Scharoun. Ein Beitrag zum organischen Bauen." *Zodiac* 10 (1962): 52-93.

*

Hans Scharoun, whose extreme position toward theory and buildings deeply influenced generations of architects, was one of the most important architects of the 20th century. Historians generally have dismissed him as a talented but mainly idiosyncratic architect, only to recognize later his fundamental importance for modern architecture. His attitude to domestic planning was close to Hugo Häring's philosophy, although not as extreme. Scharoun was one of the few important architects in Germany to deal successfully with the disruption of World War II.

Scharoun was educated at the Technische Hochschule Berlin-Charlottenburg, where he occasionally worked in the office of Paul Kruchen who was a faculty member. At the outbreak of World War I, Kruchen was appointed district architect for the reconstruction of East Prussia, and he selected Scharoun as his associate for the site management.

After the war Scharoun was strongly affected by the hope and excitement of a new awareness called expressionism. This movement tried to establish a collaboration between the different arts and architecture. But this new awareness was also recognized as an intellectual laboratory for political and social happenings. Germany and its intellectual community became the gathering place for an active exchange of cultural, political and philosophical theories which carried great hopes for architects.

Architects such as Bruno Taut (1880-1938) called for a combined effort of all who had faith in the future. His call did not go unheeded, and in 1918 young artists and architects founded

Hans Scharoun: Berlin Philharmonic Hall, Berlin, Germany, 1959-63

in Berlin the Arbeitsrat für Kunst (Work Council for the Arts) to unify their intentions and to spread their ideas. Scharoun was associated with the Arbeitsrat and was also a member of Taut's Gläserne Kette (''glass chain''), which was founded in 1919 and communicated through the exchange of circular letters and sketches. The contingency with the Gläserne Kette had a deep impact on Scharoun's evolution. He was at that time still in the process of defining his goals and theories, to which he remained faithful during World War II and during his later life. It also was during that time when he developed his socialism and philosophy, which were reflected in his lifelong obligation to the idea of community and its architectural interpretation.

In 1919, after his military service, Scharoun opened a private practice in Insterburg, East Prussia, where he built a few private homes. He directed most of his time and energy between 1919 and 1925 toward several design competitions. Scharoun's first competition success in 1919, the plan for reconstructing the cathedral square at Prenzlau, still showed a classical treatment. The competition entry for the cultural center in Gelsenkirchen in 1920 featured a kind of crystal structure which reflected Scharoun's involvement with the Gläserne Kette and his search with Taut and the brothers Wassili (1889-1972) and Hans Luckhardt (1890-1954) for a new language of form. This phase of crystal structures, with its meager functional appeal, lasted briefly. The projects of that time suggest Scharoun's reaction against classical formalism.

After that phase Scharoun directed his search toward free curves with a conscious abandonment of geometric formalism. Scharoun was intrigued by the notion of using the dynamics of movement to generate architectural form. His drawings at the time were similar in style and approach to Erich Mendelsohn's (1887-1953) drawings. Mendelsohn's sketches, consisting

mainly of buildings in elevation, presented a utopian belief which had only visual meaning. Scharoun combined that theme with his interest in using circulation to generate the plan.

The projects during that time also revealed the strong influence of Hugo Häring on Scharoun's work, particularly on his later output. Häring, a friend of Scharoun's, was one of the most important architects and theorists of the ''Organic Movement.'' His architectural philosophy, which he defined as *''das neue Bauen''* (''new building''), rejected the geometric, intellectual aesthetic and promoted a process through which the form of a building becomes the expression of its function.

In 1925 Scharoun was offered a professorship at the Breslau Arts Academy, which was supervised by Adolf Rading, with whom Scharoun later shared an office in Berlin. In 1926 Scharoun joined the organization Der Ring, which included most of the contemporary architects. One of them was Ludwig Mies van der Rohe (1886-1969) who, as the organizer, invited Scharoun to participate in the 1927 Weissenhof Exhibition for the Deutscher Werkbund in Stuttgart. The single-family house at the Weissenhof Exhibition was Scharoun's first significant building. During the period between 1927 and 1933 he executed a respectable number of buildings, such as an apartment block on the Kaiserdamm, Berlin (1929), an apartment block at the Breslau Werkbund Exhibition (1929), the Siemensstadt housing development, Berlin (1930), and House Schminke, in Löbau, Saxony (1932-33). All of those projects contain a marine imagery which can be traced back to Scharoun's participation at the Weissenhof Exhibition.

Under the pressure of the Nazi regime, the Breslau Academy was closed in 1932. Scharoun lost his professorship and the chance to participate in competitions as well as to attain public commissions. He did not emigrate like many of his colleagues, and was able to build 15 private homes during 1933-43.

After the war Scharoun was appointed the city planning officer of Berlin. He helped to organize and reconstruct the city, and saved many historical buildings from total demolition. The 1950s and 1960s saw the realization of several important buildings by Scharoun, including the Primary School in Darmstadt (1951), the Geschwister Scholl School, Lünen (1958-62), the Philharmonie, Berlin (1958-63), and the Theater in Wolfsburg (1965-73). These projects were evidence of the continuous existence of the ''Organic Movement'' even after the acknowledged worldwide victory of the International Style. The book *Ursprung und Gegenwart* (1949) by the Swiss philosopher Jean Gebser, in which he argues that the human being experiences space and time in a three-step process described as the pre-perspectival, the perspectival and the a-perspectival worlds, seemed to influence Scharoun's vision of space. Scharoun often noted that he understood cultural development also as being dependent on space and time. His understanding tied culture to the materialistic environment of a specific geographical location, and timewise, linked culture to the prevailing consciousness of humanity.

Scharoun's buildings often seem meaningless to those who refuse complexity and irregularity and will not evaluate them on their spatial concepts. Scharoun's spatial understanding allows the observer to recognize the limitations of the orthogonal continuum of space. The interaction of several nonorthogonal systems, which function in Scharoun's buildings as space-defining elements, generates spatial relationships which question any preoccupied experience of space. It is exactly this level of development which documents Scharoun's ultimate goal, to integrate human beings themselves into the creative process.

—UWE DROST

SCHICKHARDT, Heinrich.

German. Born in Herrenberg, Germany, 5 February 1558. Died in Herrenberg, 31 December 1634. Married daughter of Herrenberg's Mayor Grüninger, 1584. Apprenticed to Georg Beer, 1578, with whom he worked on the Lusthaus in Stuttgart, 1580s; also worked independently; court activity, from 1590, and appointed as court architect, 1596; traveled to Italy, 1598 and 1599-1600, one of the first German architects to do so; worked in Mompelgard (now Montbeliard, France), 1600-08, then moved back to Stuttgart.

Chronology of Works
All in Germany unless noted
† *Work no longer exists*

1586	Rathaus, Esslingen
1599	Fortifications, Freudenstadt
1599-1609	Neue Bau, Stuttgart (addition to the Royal Schloss)†
1600-08	Church of St. Martin, Mompelgard (now Montbeliard), France

Publications

BOOKS ABOUT SCHICKHARDT

BAUM, JULIUS: *Die Kirchen des Baumeisters Heinrich Schickhardt.* Stuttgart, 1905.
BAUM, JULIUS: *Heinrich Schickhardt.* Strasbourg, 1916.
FLEISCHHAUER, WERNER: *Renaissance in Herzogtum Württemberg.* Stuttgart, 1971.
HITCHCOCK, HENRY-RUSSELL: *German Renaissance Architecture.* Princeton, New Jersey, 1981.
ROMMEL, H., and KOPP, G.: *Die Stadtkirche von Freudenstadt.* Freudenstadt, 1963.
STANGE, ALFRED: *Die deutsche Baukunst der Renaissance.* Munich, 1926.
VON BEZOLD, G.: *Die Baukunst der Renaissance in Deutschland.* Leipzig, 1908.

ARTICLES ABOUT SCHICKHARDT

SCHWEIKHART, G.: ''Heinrich Schickhardt e il Teatro Olimpico.'' *Bollettino del Centro Internazionale di Studi ''Andrea Palladio''* (1969): 393-398.

*

Although Heinrich Schickhardt was born and died in Herrenburg and built extensively in Württemberg and other parts of Germany, it was perhaps his travels to Italy that weighed most significantly on his architectural career.

Little is known about his apprenticeship, but Schickhardt traveled to Stuttgart in 1578 to work with architect George Beer, undertaking work on the Lusthaus, a public recreational building in Stuttgart. The structure has alternately been attributed to both architects. Beer was serving at that time as the ducal architect, while Schickhardt, even though only 22 years old, had received commissions for two castles for noblemen. Of the Lusthaus' singular large hall with four round corner towers and multistory scrolled gables, only a fragment of the loggia remains today, reerected in a new location.

In 1584 Schickhardt married the mayor's daughter in Herrenburg. He subsequently bought land and a house and became a member of the town council. During the 1580s he worked with Beer in Stuttgart, and also in Wahrend.

The Rathaus at Esslingen (1586) characterizes Schickhardt's work of the period. He extended the existing building, constructing a new facade and interior. The facade of the six-story building places twin arched entries among the simple Doric pilasters. The three-story gable is topped with a lantern and ornamented with scrolls typical of German architecture of the period, but with indentations unique to Schickhardt. The interior includes abbreviated twisted columns of near-Romanesque-style capitals supporting Gothic net vaulting.

In 1590 Schickhardt was called upon by the duke of Württemberg to work on public and ducal buildings for the court in Stuttgart. He was appointed a *Baumeister* for the duke in 1596, putting him in charge of all building.

It was in 1598 that Schickhardt made his first trip to Italy with the duke, with the express purpose of studying new Italian architecture. Schickhardt was one of the first German architects to study Italian Renaissance architecture, traveling again to Italy in 1599 and 1600, that time reaching Rome. His extensive diaries and sketches first appeared in publication in Tübingen in 1603, directly perpetuating the spread of Italian architectural style in the north.

Schickhardt's trip was actually preparation for a specific project: the Neue Bau at Stuttgart (1599-1609), which was to be an addition to the old castle. With the royal stables on the first floor, the building also housed a two-story great hall and an armory at the top. Some details of the building, such as the high hipped roof, were typically German, although some Italian influence appeared, primarily in proportions and occasional appearance of some classical details. Orders decorated the corner towers and the middle of the long facades. The building was removed in 1777.

An example of Schickhardt's Italianate style survives in Mompelgard, now Montbeliard in France, where the architect lived from 1600 to 1608. The Church of St. Martin is a simple rectilinear mass, adorned with simple Doric pilasters with a vertical pedimented window between each pair. Dormer windows are small gables, contributing to a design whose restraint indicates a shift away from Mannerist Gothic architecture and increased influence of Italian design.

As part of Schickhardt's ducal duties, he was responsible for several nonarchitectural tasks, such as planning, surveying and design of fortifications. He redesigned old towns and built completely new towns and their fortifications, such as Freudenstadt, where Schickhardt's design of 1599 survives partially realized. Planned as a square with a huge square *Schloss* turned diagonally in the middle, the town was to have two main avenues and major buildings at the L-shaped intersections of the smaller streets. An unusual L-shaped church survives as a remnant of that remarkable plan, although its almost vernacular articulation owes nothing to Schickhardt's Italian sojourns.

In addition to buildings, Schickhardt built gardens, greenhouses and fountains, bathhouses, water follies, mills and mines. He also designed machinery and regulated rivers. Although the onset of the Thirty Years' War in 1618 curtailed his major architectural commissions, he continued working extensively in surveying and building fortifications. Particularly in his surveying work, Schickhardt was notorious for working exceptionally quickly. He made very precise maps, plans and proposals, some of which were carried out more than 200 years later.

Schickhardt's success in his work brought him wealth and acclaim. He died at 76 after being wounded by looting soldiers of the Kaiser after the Battle of Noeflingen.

—CHARLES ROSENBLUM

SCHINDLER, R. M.

American. Born Rudolf M. Schindler in Vienna, Austria, 5 September 1887; immigrated to the United States, 1914. Died in Los Angeles, California, 22 August 1953. Married Sophie Pauline Gibling, 1919. Studied at the Technical College, Vienna, 1906-11; studied at Vienna Academy of Fine Arts, 1910-13, under Otto Wagner. Worked in Mayr and Mayer office, 1911-13; worked for Ottenheimer, Stern and Reichert, Chicago, 1914; joined the office of Frank Lloyd Wright, 1916, as unsalaried employee; became salaried, 1918; sent by Wright to oversee work on the Barnsdall Houses, in Los Angeles, 1920-21; in private practice, Los Angeles, 1921 until his death in 1953: in collaboration with Richard Neutra and Carol Aronovici, 1925-31.

Chronology of Works
All in the United States

1916	J. B. Lee House, Maywood, Illinois (remodeling)
1917-18	Buena Shore Club, Chicago, Illinois
1920	Director's House, Olive Hill, Los Angeles, California
1920-21	Barnsdall Houses A and B, Olive Hill, Los Angeles (with Frank Lloyd Wright)
1921-22	Schindler/Clyde Chase Double House, Hollywood, California
1923	C. P. Lowes House, Eagle Rock, California
1923	Pueblo Ribera Court, La Jolla, California
1923	O. S. Floren House, Hollywood, California

1924	John C. Packard House, South Pasadena, California
1924-25	Dr. Phillip Lovell Beach House, Newport Beach, California
1925	S. Breacher House, Los Angeles, California
1925	J. E. Howe House, Los Angeles, California
1928	Braxton Gallery, Hollywood, California
1928	Grokowsky House, South Pasadena, California
1928	C. H. Wolfe Summer House, Avalon, Catalina Island, California
1929	Satyr Bookshop, Los Angeles, California
1929	Lingerbrink Cabin, Calabasas, California
1930	R. F. Elliot House, Los Angeles, California
1931	Hans N. Von Korber House, Hollywood Riviera, Torrance, California
1932-34	Sardi's Restaurant, Hollywood, California
1932-36	Veissi House, Hollywood, California
1933	Standard Oil Service Station (prototype)
1934	W. E. Oliver House, Los Angeles, California
1934	John J. Buck House, Los Angeles, California
1934	Bennati Cabin, Lake Arrowhead, California
1934-35	Elizabeth Van Patten House, Silver Lake, Los Angeles, California
1935-36	Ralph C. Walker House, Los Angeles, California
1936	C. C. Fitzpatrick House, Los Angeles, California
1936	McAlmon House, Los Angeles, California
1937	Henwar Rodakiewicz House, Los Angeles, California
1938-41	Apt. Bldg. for A. L. Bubeshko, Los Angeles, California
1938	Guy C. Wilson House, Los Angeles, California
1939	Apt. house for Mrs. S. T. Falk, Los Angeles, California
1940	Alber Van Dekker House, Canoga Park, California
1941	Hilaire Hiller Studio-house, Hollywood, California
1942	Rose L. Harris House, Los Angeles, California
1944	Bethlehem Baptist Church, Los Angeles, California
1945	F. Presuburger House, Studio City, California
1946	M. Kallis House, Studio City, California
1946-49	Tietz Medical Offices, Los Angeles, California
1946-49	Armon House, Los Angeles, California
1948	R. Lechner House, Studio City, California
1948	Laurelwood Apartments, Studio City, California
1949	Eileen Janson House, Hollywood, California
1949-50	Adolph Tischler House, Bel Air, California
1950	Tucker House, Hollywood, California
1950-51	Ries House, Los Angeles, California
1950-52	Samuel Skolnik House, Los Angeles, California
1952	Schlesinger House, Los Angeles, California

Publications

BOOKS BY SCHINDLER

Collected Papers. Los Angeles, 1948.

ARTICLES BY SCHINDLER

"A Manifesto 1912." In T. and C. BENTON and D. SHARP (eds.): *Form and Function.* London, 1975.

"A Cooperative Building." *T-Square* (February 1932).

"Space-architecture." *California Arts and Architecture* (January 1935).

"Furniture and the Modern House." *Architect and Engineer* (December 1935 and March 1936).

"Architect—Post War—Post Everybody." *Pencil Points* (October and November 1944).

R. M. Schindler: Dr. Phillip Lovell Beach House, Newport Beach, California, 1924-25

''Reference Frames in Space.'' *Architect and Engineer* (April 1946).

BOOKS ABOUT SCHINDLER

BANHAM, REYNER: *Los Angeles: Four Cultures*. New York, 1971.

GEBHARD, DAVID: *Schindler*. London and New York, 1971.

McCOY, ESTHER (ed.): *Vienna to Los Angeles: Two Journeys—Richard Neutra and Rudolph M. Schindler*. Santa Monica, California, 1979.

McCOY, ESTHER: *Five California Architects*. New York, 1960.

SARNITZ, A.: *R. M. Schindler: Architect*. New York, 1989.

ARTICLES ABOUT SCHINDLER

BANHAM, REYNER: ''Rudolph Schindler: A Pioneer Without Tears.'' *Architectural Design* (December 1967).

GEBHARD, DAVID: ''Ambiguity in the Work of R. M. Schindler.'' *Lotus* No. 5 (1968).

HERTZBERGER, HERMAN: ''Some Notes on Two Works by Schindler.'' *Domus* (September 1967).

HITCHCOCK, HENRY-RUSSELL: ''An Eastern Critic Looks at Western Architecture.'' *California Arts and Architecture* (December 1940).

HOLLEIN, HANS: ''Rudolf M. Schindler—ein Wiener Architekt in Kalifornien.'' *Aufbau* 16, No. 3 (March 1961): 102-110.

McCOY, ESTHER: ''Four Schindler Houses of the 1920s.'' *Arts and Architecture* (September 1953).

McCOY, ESTHER: ''Letter of Louis H. Sullivan to R. M. Schindler.'' *Journal of the Society of Architectural Historians* 20 (December 1961).

McCOY, ESTHER: ''Letters between R. M. Schindler and Richard Neutra 1914-1924.'' *Journal of the Society of Architectural Historians* 33 (September 1974).

MOORE, CHARLES: ''Schindler: Vulnerable and Powerful.'' *Progressive Architecture* (January 1973).

O'NEIL, DAN: ''The High and Low Art of Rudolf Schindler.'' *Architectural Review* (April 1973): 241-246.

''Rudolph Schindler.'' *Architecture and Urbanism* special issue (November 1975).

SARNITZ, AUGUST E.: ''Proportion and Beauty—the Lovell Beach House by Rudolph Michael Schindler.'' *Journal of the Society of Architectural Historians* 45 (December 1986): 374-388.

SEGAL, WALTER: ''The Least Appreciated: Rudolph Schindler.'' *Architects' Journal* (19 February 1969).

SISAN, DAVID: ''Aspects of the House—3 Projects by Schindler.'' *Canadian Architect* (February 1981).

TREIBER, DANIEL: ''Rudolph M. Schindler 1887-1953.'' *Architecture mouvement continuité* (June-September 1981).

*

''The architect has finally discovered the medium of his art: SPACE.'' With that statement, written in 1912, when he was 25 years old, Rudolf Schindler established the scope of his architectural work. Space, not mass, was the primary medium of his architectural designs. The construction of space and its intended perceptual experience became the generators of the forms of his architecture. This particular conception transforms his designs into examples of architectural sculpture. Throughout his career, Schindler generally worked with a vocabulary of volumes. When developed fully, intersecting masses were used to establish the shape of a building. The cubical nature of Schindler's shapes was derived from a tendency toward abstraction and the theory of cladding he was exposed to through his training in Vienna under Otto Wagner and Adolf Loos.

The emphasis on space was influenced above all by Loos' *Raumplan*—the free vertical and horizontal spatial expanse—and Frank Lloyd Wright's use of interrelated, open space as a prime force in developing a domestic typology. Every element in Schindler houses is subordinate to the creation of space: furniture, structure and a modular, proportional system for facade elevations.

Schindler's architectural work proceeded in phases. These are characterized by variations in the relationship between the structural frame of a building and its walls and other elements of enclosure.

In his first phase, Schindler defined architecture as enclosed space. Through monolithic construction—especially using the tilt-slab system—space was scooped out of the universe. The open expression of this structural system served also as exterior decoration. Light formed the core of the house, and space was allowed to flow freely from inside to outside by opening walls through French doors.

The second phase of Schindler's work, exemplified by the Lovell Beach House, was characterized by a clear division between the structural system of the building and the articulation of its volumes. The houses can be characterized as supported spatial enclosures. The structural frame was treated as an independent element of the building. It established a rhythmic exterior articulation not unlike that promoted by the De Stijl movement. In this context, the Lovell Beach House may be the most perfect example of the International Style. Indeed, it marked the beginning of the mature period of Schindler's career. Due to economic restraints, he had to abandon reinforced concrete as his primary building material. In a singular step, that gives excellent testimony to his adaptability, he settled on wood framing as his future structural system. The exteriors were then covered with stucco. Thus, he used a carpenter's technology to produce examples of the International Style. His buildings were shaped by means of shifting vertical and horizontal planes, which were assembled to articulate space. As a result, the interiors consisted of layered space, manipulated in both vertical and horizontal directions.

The last period of his development was distinguished by a renewed focus on the structural system. He continued using wood, but in a much more rustic manner. The balloon frame was transformed into a heavy timber frame forming again the main exterior articulation. The volumes supported by this structure were assembled of varied geometric shapes. Through their heavy forms and details, these architectural elements were clearly distinguished from the spaces they created and appeared to hover above the enclosed interior space. Consequently, this contained space had an aggressive character.

Schindler treated space as the raw material of building. The articulated room was the goal and product of his designs. The general characteristic of his interior arrangements was the separation between private spaces for each individual, and large, communal group spaces. If possible, indoor space was allowed to extend into the surrounding landscape through views and ample glass surfaces.

Elevating space to the primary element of architectural design made Schindler quite a unique figure in the International Style. He was among a group of select architects who did not consider function the most important design rationale.

The variety in form and structure implies that Schindler was not an ideologue clinging to a single design theory throughout his life. His philosophy emphasized above all simplicity. He proclaimed in 1932: "I am not a stylist, not a functionalist, nor any other sloganist." His perennial theme was the "man-made environment."

He managed to shape his own architectural manner out of modern technology. His style was an amalgamation of the most diverse influences: Mission style, Arts and Crafts ideals, the balloon frame, the Jazz Age and De Stijl. These are sources also shared by other masters of the International Style. In Schindler's case, they were subordinated to his space architecture. He was not interested in decoration, but rather in how the materials themselves could be used to create the ornamentation of a building. Working in southern California, Schindler quite consciously integrated climate factors into his designs, especially the sleeping porches of earlier stylistic traditions.

Schindler was not only highly adaptive in the stylistic aspects of design. He proved to be equally absorptive in his design theory. Always ready to modify his ideas, he accepted contradiction as a positive quality. His ideas were shaped under the impact of Otto Wagner, Adolf Loos and Frank Lloyd Wright. He successfully attempted to connect Wright's emphasis on symbolic elements of architecture—above all the expression of a particular understanding of the family—with the purely intellectual concerns of European International Style architects.

Schindler was, thus, a perfect product of his background and training. In addition, he masterfully exploited his environment. The progressive circles of Los Angeles created a client pool and lifestyle that perfectly agreed with Schindler's own architecture and social inclinations. His antihistoricism was, thus, derived from social interpretation. This humanist quality of his buildings allowed Schindler to carve out his own personal niche within the history of 20th-century architecture. The variety of his designs and his openness to all sorts of stylistic and theoretical influences are the qualities that enabled him to create an autonomous style of architecture. In addition, he fully accounted for the context into which his buildings were placed. All the various influences on his style and theory were grafted onto the Los Angeles experience. This mastery of concurrent adaptation to, and exploitation of, diverse influences will remain the lasting contribution of Rudolf Schindler to the design profession.

—HANS R. MORGENTHALER

SCHINKEL, Karl Friedrich.

German. Born in Neuruppin, Germany, 13 March 1781. Died in Berlin, 9 October 1841. Studied at the Gymnasium in Ruppin, 1787-94; continued at the Gymnasium zum Grauenkloster, Berlin, 1794; completed studies with Obersekindareife; studied architecture with David Gilly (father of Friedrich Gilly), from 1798; enrolled in the Bauakademie, 1799. Embarked on a two year study tour, 1803; met Wilhelm von Humboldt in Rome; returned to Berlin, 1805; took up painting during French occupation of Berlin, 1 805-08; Appointed supervisor for civil, royal and religious buildings and controller of historic monuments in kingdom of Prussia, 1809; put in charge of all state and royal building in Berlin following the defeat of Napoleon.

Chronology of Works
All in Germany unless noted
† Work no longer exists

1800-01	Estate Outbuildings, Neu Hardenburg
1800-01	Pomona Temple, Potsdam
1801-03	Schloss Buckow, Kreis Lebus (remodeling)†

Karl Friedrich Schinkel: Schauspielhaus, Berlin, Germany, 1819-21

1802-05	Steinmeyer House, Friedrichstrasse, Berlin†
1803	Bleichause, Quilitz
1803	School, Quilitz
1806	Tilebein House, Züllcow, near Stettin, Poland
1810	Palace of Freidrich Wilhelm III, Berlin (interior renovations)†
1810	Schloss Charlottenburg, Berlin (bedroom of Queen Luise)
1810-40	Mausoleum for Queen Luise, Park Charlottenburg, Berlin (with Heinrich Gentz)
1811	Monument to Queen Luise, Gransee
1812-40	Schloss Ehrenburg, Coburg
1816-17	Prince August's Palace, Wilhelmstrasse, Berlin (interiors)†
1816-20	Cathedral, Lustgarten, Berlin†
1817	Monument to the Fallen, Grossbeeren
1817	Prince Friedrich's Palace, Wilhelmstrasse, Berlin (interiors)†
1817-18	Neue Wache, Unter den Linden, Berlin (royal guard house)
1817-18	Saalbau, Bad Freienwald Oder
1817-18	Barracks, Lindenstrasse, Berlin†
1818-21	Kreuzberg Monument, Berlin (later altered)
1818-24	Zivilkasino, Potsdam†
1819	Neue Wilhelmstrasse, Berlin†
1819-21	Schauspielhaus (theater and concert hall), Berlin
1820	Catholic Church, Marienwerder
1820-23	Schloss Neuhardenburg, Quilitz
1821-24	Nikolaikirche, Magdeburg-Neustadt
1821-24	Schloss Tegel, Berlin (remodeled)
1821-26	Luisenkirche, Charlottenburg, Berlin (tower only)
1822	Schloss Seifersdorf, near Dresden (remodeling)
1822-24	Schlossbrücke, Berlin (now Friedrich Engels Bridge)
1822-24	Antonin Hunting Lodge, near Ostrowo, Poland
1822-25	Gatehouses, Lange Brucke, Potsdam†
1822-25	Schauspielhaus, Achen (theater; plans later reworked by Cremer)
1823	Arts and Crafts School, Charlottenburg, Berlin (remodeling)†
1823	Behrend Landhaus, Charlottenburg, Berlin†
1823-24	Gatehouses, Potsdam Gate, Berlin†
1823-31	Altes Museum, Lustgarten, Berlin
1823ff.	Schloss Stolzenfels, Stolzenfels, Rhine (reconstruction)
1824-25	Ingenieur und Artillerieschule, Berlin (Kriegsakademie facade only)†
1824-25	New Pavilion, Berlin (now Schinkel Pavilion; later rebuilt)†
1824-26	Kavelierhaus (Danziger Haus), Pfaueninsel, Berlin
1824-26	Singakademie, Berlin (altered in execution by Heinrich Ottmer)
1824-26	Royal Schloss (crown prince's apartments), Berlin†
1824-27	Schloss Glienecke, Berlin (including park structures)
1824-33	Scharnhorst Memorial, Invaliden Cemetery, Berlin
1825	Pavilion, Schloss Bellevue, Berlin†
1825-27	Elisen Fountain, Aachen
1825-27	Lighthouse, Arcona, Rügen
1825-27	Theater, Hamburg (Schinkel's design altered in construction by C.L. Wimmel)†
1825-29	Gesellschafthaus, Friedrich Wilhelms Garden, near Magedeburg
1825-30	Friedrich Werder Church, Berlin

1826	Schloss Charlottenhof, Potsdam (remodeling)
1826-28	Unteroffiziersschule, Jägeralle, Potsdam
1827	Konigliches Palais (Royal Chapel), Unter den Linden, Berlin†
1827-28	Prince Karl's Palace, Wilhelmplatz, Berlin (interiors)†
1827-29	Feilner House, Berlin (fragments survive in the Märkisches Museum and the Berlin Museum, Berlin)†
1829-32	Packofgebäude, Berlin†
1829-33	Court Gardener's House, Charlottenhof, Sanssouci, Potsdam
1829-33	Peterhof Palace, near St. Petersburg, Russia (chapel)
1830	Pavilion, Roman Baths, Charlottenhof, Potsdam
1830-33	Prince Albrecht's Palace, Berlin†
1830-34	Elisabeth Church, Invalidenstrasse, Berlin
1830-37	Nikolaikirche, Potsdam (dome added 1843-49 by others, later restored)
1831-33	Hauptwache, Dresden
1831-36	Leipzig University, Leipzig (main building)
1831-36	Bauakademie, Berlin†
1832-34	Nazarethkirche, Wedding, Berlin (later altered and rebuilt)
1832-34	Saint Johannes, Alt Moabit, Berlin (later altered)
1832-34	Saint Pault, Gesundbrunnen, Berlin
1832-35	Observatory, Berlin†
1832-35	Schloss Babelsberg, Potsdam (later extended)
1834	Chauseehaus, Schiffmühle, near Frienwalde
1835-37	Grosse Neugierde, Gleinicke Park, Berlin
1838-40	Schloss Kamenz, Silesia
1840*	Church, Krzeszowica, Poland
1840-45	Town Hall, Zittau (not completed until later by others)

Publications

BOOKS BY SCHINKEL

Dekorationen auf den königlichen Hoftheatern zu Berlin. 5 parts. Berlin, 1819-25.
Sammlung architektonischer Entwürfe. Berlin, 1819-40. Reprint: Chicago, 1981.
Entwurf zu einem Königspalast auf der Akropolis zu Athen. 4th ed. Berlin, 1878.
Sammlung architektonischer Entwürfe: Enthaltend theils Werke welche ausgeführt sind theils Gegenstände deren Ausführung beabsichtigt wurde. 2 vols. Berlin, 1866. Complete English edition published as *Collection of Architectural Designs.* Princeton, New Jersey, 1989.
Vorbilder für Fabrikanten und Handwerker. With Peter Christian Wilhelm Beuth. 3 vols. Reprint: Berlin, 1925.
Werke der höheren Baukunst für die Ausführung erfunden. 2 vols. 1842-48.
Werke der höheren Baukunst. Potsdam, 1848-50.

BOOKS ABOUT SCHINKEL

BEENKEN, H.: *Schöpferische Bauideen der deutschen Romantik.* Mainz, 1952.
BERLIN VERWALTUNG DER STAATLICHEN SCHLÖSSER UND GÄRTEN: *Karl Friedrich Schinkel: Architektur, Malerei, Kunstgewerbe.* Berlin, 1981.
BOETTICHER, CARL: *Carl Friedrich Schinkel und sein baukünstlerisches Vermächtnis.* Berlin, 1857.
BÖRSCH-SUPAN, HELMUT: *Das Mausoleum im Charlottenburger Schlossgarten.* Berlin, 1976.

BÖRSCH-SUPAN, HELMUT: *Der Schinkel Pavillon im Schlosspark zu Charlottenburg.* Berlin, 1970.
DEUTSCHE BAUAKADEMIE: *Über Karl Friedrich Schinkel.* Berlin, 1951.
FORSSMAN, ERIK: *Karl Friedrich Schinkel: Bauwerke und Baugedanken.* Munich, 1981.
FORSTER, KURT: *Karl Friedrich Schinkel.* London, 1982.
GEYER, ALBERT: *Die historischen Wohnräume im Berliner Schloss.* Berlin, 1926.
GIEDION, SIGFRIED: *Spätbarocker und romantischer Klassizismus.* Munich, 1922.
GIESE, LEOPOLD: *Schinkels architektonisches Schaffen: Entwürfe und Ausführungen.* Berlin, 1921.
GRISEBACH, AUGUST: *Karl Friedrich Schinkel.* Leipzig, 1924.
GROPIUS, MARTIN: *Karl Friedrich Schinkel: Dekorationen innerer Räume.* Berlin, 1877.
GRUPPE, OTTO F.: *Carl Friedrich Schinkel und die neue Berliner Dom.* Berlin, 1943.
HENSELMANN, HERMANN, et al.: *Über Karl Friedrich Schinkel.* Berlin, 1951.
JACOBSTHAL, E.: *Rückblicke auf die baukünstlerischen Prinzipien Schinkels und Böttichers.* Berlin, 1890.
KACHLER, KARL GOTTHILF: *Schinkels Kunstauffassung.* Basel, 1940.
Karl Friedrich Schinkel. Exhibition catalog. Berlin, 1961.
Karl Friedrich Schinkel: 1781-1841. Exhibition catalog. Berlin, 1980.
KLOPFER, PAUL: *Von Palladio bis Schinkel: Eine Charakteristik der Baukunst des Klassizismus.* Esslingen, Germany, 1911.
KRÄTSCHELL, JOHANNES: *Karl Friedrich Schinkel in seinem Verhältnis zur gotischen Baukunst.* Berlin, 1892.
KUGLER, FRANZ: *Karl Friedrich Schinkel: Eine Charakteristik seiner künstlerischen Wirksamkeit.* Berlin, 1842.
LEMMER, KLAUS J. (ed.): *Karl Friedrich Schinkel: Berlin, Bauten und Entwürfe.* Berlin, 1973.
LOHDE, LUDWIG: *Schinkels Möbelentwürfe, welche bei Einrichtung prinzlicher Wohnungen in den letzten zehn Jahren ausgeführt wurden.* 3rd ed. Berlin, 1835-37; 1861.
LORCK, CARL VON: *Karl Friedrich Schinkel.* Berlin, 1939.
LORCK, CARL VON: *Schinkel: Reisen in Deutschland.* Essen, 1956.
MACKOWSKY, HANS (ed.): *Karl Friedrich Schinkel: Briefe, Tagebücher, Gedanken.* Berlin, 1922.
MAHLBERG, PAUL: *Schinkels Theater-Dekorationen.* Düsseldorf, 1916.
MEIER, GÜNTER (ed.): *Karl Friedrich Schinkel: Aus Tagebüchern und Briefen.* Berlin, 1967.
NEUMANN, MAX: *Menschen um Schinkel.* Berlin, 1942.
PESCHKEN, GOERD: *Das architektonische Lehrbuch.* Berlin, 1979.
PESCHKEN, GOERD: *Schinkels Bauakademie in Berlin: Ein Aufruf zu ihrer Rettung.* Berlin, 1961.
PLAGEMAN, VOLKER: *Das Deutsche Kunstmuseum, 1790-1870.* Munich, 1967.
POSENER, JULIUS (ed.): *Festreden Schinkel zu Ehren: 1846-1980.* Berlin, 1981.
PUNDT, HERMANN G.: *Schinkel's Berlin: A Study in Environmental Planning.* Cambridge, Massachusetts, 1972.
RAVE, PAUL ORTWIN: *Karl Friedrich Schinkel.* Munich and Berlin, 1953.
RAVE, PAUL ORTWIN, and KUHN, MARGARETE (eds.): *Karl Friedrich Schinkel: Lebenswerk.* 14 vols. Berlin, 1939-68.
RIEMANN, GOTTFRIED, and HESSE, CHRISTA: *Karl Friedrich Schinkel: Architekturzeichnungen.* Berlin, 1991.

RIEMANN, GOTTFRIED (ed.): *Karl Friedrich Schinkel. Reisen nach Italien*. Berlin, 1979.

SCHIEDLAUSKY, GÜNTHER: *Karl Friedrich Schinkel*. Burg b. M., 1938.

Karl Friedrich Schinkels Werk und Wirkungen. Berlin, 1981.

SIEVERS, JOHANNES: *Die Arbeiten von Karl Friedrich Schinkel für Prinz Wilhelm, späteren König von Preussen*. Berlin, 1955.

SNODIN, MICHAEL (ed.): *Karl Friedrich Schinkel: A Universal Man*. New Haven, Connecticut, 1991.

SPRINGER, PETER: *Schinkels Schlossbrücke in Berlin: Zweckbau und Monument*. Berlin, 1981.

STAHL, FRITZ: *Karl Friedrich Schinkel*. Berlin, 1912.

WAAGEN, GUSTAV: *Karl Friedrich Schinkel als Mensch und als Künstler*. Düsseldorf, 1844.

WATKIN, DAVID, and MELLINGHOFF, TILMAN: *German Architecture and the Classical Ideal 1740-1840*. London and Cambridge, Massachusetts, 1987.

WOLZOGEN, ALFRED VON (ed.): *Aus Schinkels Nachlass: Reisetagebücher, Briefe und Aphorismen*. 4 vols. Berlin, 1862-64.

WOLZOGEN, ALFRED VON: *Schinkel als Architekt, Maler und Kunstphilosoph*. Berlin, 1864.

ZADOW, MARIO: *Karl Friedrich Schinkel*. Berlin, 1980.

ZILLER, HERMANN: *Schinkel*. Bielefeld and Leipzig, 1897.

ARTICLES ABOUT SCHINKEL

ADLER, FRIEDRICH: "Friedrich Gilly, Schinkels Lehrer." *Zentralblatt der Bauverwaltung* 1 (1881).

ADLER, FRIEDRICH: "Schinkels Festrede: Die Bauschule zu Berlin von Karl Friedrich Schinkel." *Zeitschrift für Bauwesen* 19 (1869): 463-475.

BAYER, JOSEPH: "Goethe, Schinkel und die Gothik." Pp. 64-85 in ROBERT STIA (ed.): *Baustudien und Baubilder: Schriften zur Kunst, aus dem Nachlass*. Jena, Germany, 1919.

BLOCH, PETER: "Das Kreuzberg-Denkmal und die patriotische Kunst." *Jahrbuch der Stiftung Preussicher Kulturbesitz* 11 (1973): 142-159.

BÖRSCH-SUPAN, HELMUT: "Schinkels Landschaft mit Motiven aus dem Salzburgischen." *Zeitschrift für Kunstgeschichte* 32, Nos. 3-4 (1969): 317-323.

CARTER, RAND: "Karl Friedrich Schinkel's Project for a Royal Palace on the Acropolis." *Journal of the Society of Architectural Historians* 38, No. 1 (1979): 34-46.

EINEM, HERBERT VON: "Karl Friedrich Schinkel." *Jahrbuch der Stiftung Preussicher Kulturbesitz* 1 (1963): 73-89.

ETTLINGER, LEOPOLD D.: "A German Architect's Visit to England in 1826." *Architectural Review* 97 (May 1945): 131-134.

Farbe und Raum 35, No. 3, entire issue (1981).

GRIMM, HERMANN: "Schinkel als Architekt der Stadt Berlin." *Zeitschrift für Bauwesen* 24 (1874): 414-459.

GRISEBACH, AUGUST: "Karl Friedrich Schinkel." *Die Grossen Deutschen* 2 (1956): 548-558.

HITTORFF, JAKOB I.: "Historische Notiz über Carl Friedrich Schinkel." *Zeitschrift für Bauwesen* 8 (1858): 98-106.

JOHNSON, PHILIP: "Schinkel and Mies." In *Writings/Philip Johnson*. New York, 1979.

KAUFFMANN, HANS: "Zweckbau und Monument: Zu Friedrich Schinkels Museum am Berliner Lustgarten." Pp. 135-166 in *Eine Freundesgabe der Wissenschaft für Ernst Hellmut Vits* (1963).

KNOPP, NORBERT: "Schinkel's Idee einer Stilsynthese." In WERNER HAGER and NORBERT KNOPP (eds.): *Beiträge zum Problem des Stilpluralismus*. Munich, 1977.

KOCH, GEORG FRIEDRICH: "Karl Friedrich Schinkel und die Architektur des Mittelalters." *Zeitschrift für Kunstgeschichte* 29 (1966): 177-222.

KOCH, GEORG FRIEDRICH: "Karl Friedrich Schinkels architektonische Entwürfe im gotischen Stil." *Zeitschrift für Kunstgeschichte* 32 (1969): 282-300.

KUNST, HANS-JOACHIM: "Bemerkungen zu Schinkels Entwürfen für die Friedrich Werdersche Kirche in Berlin." *Marburger Jahrbuch* 19 (1974): 241-258.

LIPSTADT, HÉLÈNE, and BERGDOLL, BARRY: "Karl Friedrich Schinkel: Architecture as Alchemy." *Progressive Architecture* 62, No. 10 (1981): 72-77.

MANTEUFFEL, CLAUS ZOGE VON: "Schinkel und Semper-Idee und rationale Grundlage der Stilbildung." In HELMUT BÖRSCH-SUPAN (ed.): *Gottfried Semper und die Mitte des 19 Jahrhunderts*. Basel, 1976.

PESCHKEN, GOERD: "Eine Stadtplanung Schinkels." *Archäologischer Anzeiger* (1962): 861-876.

PESCHKEN, GOERD: "Schinkels nachgelassene Fragmente eines architektonischen Lehrbuchs." *Bonner Jahrbücher* 66 (1966): 293-315.

PESCHKEN, GOERD: "Technologische Ästhetik in Schinkels Architektur." *Zeitschrift des deutschen Vereins für Kunstwissenschaft* Nos. 1/2 (1968): 45-81.

PEVSNER, NIKOLAUS: "Karl Friedrich Schinkel." In *Studies in Art, Architecture, and Design*. Vol. 1. London, 1968.

POSENER, JULIUS: "Schinkel's English Diary." In *From Schinkel to the Bauhaus*. New York, 1972.

POSENER, JULIUS: "Schinkel's Eclecticism and 'the Architectural'." *Architectural Design* 53 (November-December 1983): 33-39.

RAVE, PAUL ORTWIN: "Schinkels Traum von einem Königspalast auf der Akropolis zu Athen." *Atlantis* 6 (1934): 129-141.

RICHARDSON, ALBERT E.: "Karl Friedrich Schinkel: A Study." *Architectural Review* 31 (1912): 61-79.

RIEMANN, GOTTFRIED: "Englische Einflüsse im architektonischen Spätwerk Karl Friedrich Schinkels." *Forschungen und Berichte* 15 (1973): 79-104.

RIEMANN, GOTTFRIED: "Frühe englische Ingenieurbauten in der Sicht Karl Friedrich Schinkels." *Forschungen und Berichte* 13 (1971): 75-86.

SIEVERS, JOHANNES: "Das Vorbild des 'Neuen Pavillons' von Karl Schinkel im Schlosspark Charlottenburg." *Zeitschrift für Kunstgeschichte* 23 (1960): 227-241.

WATKIN, DAVID: "Karl Friedrich Schinkel: Royal Patronage and the Picturesque." *Architectural Design* 49, Nos. 8/9 (1979): 56-71.

WOLZOGEN, ALFRED VON (ed.): "Karl Friedrich Schinkel und der Theaterbau." *Bayreuther Blätter* 10 (1887): 65-90.

*

Karl Friedrich Schinkel was a creative genius; a master of architecture, painting, stage-design, panoramas and draftsmanship; a civil servant who was a friend of royalty; and an intellectual who knew some of the best minds of his day. His output was enormous: his work, rational and poetic, was not stylistically restricted, and he sought the essence of architecture, for the integrity of his designs is absolute.

Schinkel's career spanned a period of great change in architecture, when designers sought a primitive expression of plain forms, stripped of frippery, and turned into the gravity of Greek

Doric. Friedrich Gilly's stunning Greco-Roman-Egyptian monument to Frederick the Great, exhibited in 1797, fired the young Schinkel's desire to become an architect, and in 1798 the latter joined the studio and household of Gilly's father, David (1748-1808). In the following year Schinkel enrolled in the newly opened Bauakademie, where he received a thorough grounding in classicism, and imbibed Alois Hirt's theories of the historical principles of design which later appeared in *Baukunst nach den Grundsätzen der Alten* (1809).

In 1803 Schinkel left for a two-year study tour, and in October met Wilhelm von Humboldt (1767-1835) in Rome. During his *Wanderjahre* in Italy he concentrated on recording the brick buildings of the medieval period, for he felt he was already fully conversant with the classical language of architecture. In 1805 he was back in Berlin, but found lean times as Prussia was threatened with war, although he managed to design and build a country house near Stettin. This ended the first period of his development, which was dominated by the influence of Friedrich Gilly (died 1800).

War broke out in 1806, Prussia was defeated, the royal family retired to Königsberg, and Berlin was occupied by French troops until 1808. There was virtually no building activity, so Schinkel devoted himself to drawing and painting. In 1809, however, he prepared the first of a series of ravishing designs for the remodeling of apartments for the return of the king and queen, and the following year, on the recommendation of the queen and Humboldt, he was appointed supervisor for civil, royal and religious buildings as well as controller of historic monuments throughout the kingdom.

The death of the beloved Queen Luise in 1810 helped to focus patriotic feelings, and Schinkel, with Friedrich Gentz and King Friedrich Wilhelm III, designed the queen's severe Greek Doric mausoleum at Charlottenburg. In that year too Schinkel saw a major exhibition of paintings by Caspar David Friedrich (1774-1840), which had a profound influence on his own work.

In 1813 Prussia declared the War of Liberation, and the king, with Schinkel, designed the Iron Cross. Iron suggested strength, nobility, fortitude, economy and self-sacrifice: it was therefore suitable to the national mood, like the Doric of the queen's mausoleum. One of Schinkel's earliest essays using cast iron was the Gothic shrine to the queen at Gransee of 1811, and for the rest of his life he was to use the material with sensitivity. Indeed his attitude to new technologies and to the problems of industrialization was judicious and intelligent.

Following the *Völkerschlacht,* the defeat of Napoleon and the occupation of Paris, Prussia developed a sense of national pride that was partly to be expressed in architecture. Schinkel was put in charge of all state and royal building commissions in Berlin, and this marked the end of the second phase of his career, in which visionary architecture, landscapes, panoramas and experiments with Gothic were dominant.

Schinkel's influential report on the preservation of national monuments led to state protection of historic buildings throughout Prussia. He also designed many stage sets for the Nationaltheater, the finest of which were the 26 scenes for the production of Mozart's *Die Zauberflöte* given as part of the 1816 victory celebrations: these sets were among the most authoritative ever designed, and showed Schinkel's mastery of color, mood and scholarship. The year 1816 also saw the commission for the Neue Wache in Berlin, completed in 1818, in which discipline, power and strength are suggested by the severe and free interpretation of Greek Doric set against a plain fortress-like block.

A further Gothic essay was realized in his memorial cross that gave Kreuzberg its name; gradually, however, he retreated from Gothic, and most of his buildings are firmly classical or

of the round-arched styles, with the exception of the brick Gothic Friedrich-Werdersche-Kirche (1824-38).

Schinkel's great achievements from 1816 were the master plan for Berlin and the series of splendid civic buildings he created there, starting with the Neue Wache. Following a fire which destroyed Carl Gotthard Langhans' Nationaltheater (and many sets by Schinkel), the latter was instructed to prepare plans for the Schauspielhaus (1819-26). This brilliant work incorporated a Greek Ionic portico and the square mullions that were to be so influential: these were derived from the Choragic Monument of Thrasyllus, but the repetition of this mullion was suggested by ancient Egyptian prototypes recently published in France. The *Schauspielhaus* is sited between the twin churches which Carl von Gontard designed and built in the 1780s, so the new theater reads like a temple anchored between them.

Schinkel published his first portfolio of designs in 1819, the year he built the elegant bridge linking the Lustgarten to the Unter den Linden. In the following year he remodeled Schloss Tegel for Humboldt (completed 1824), and in 1821 began publishing the *Vorbilder für Fabrikanten und Handwerker,* which was probably the first attempt by an architect to raise standards of design for mass-produced articles.

From 1823 to 1831 Schinkel worked on the Museum am Lustgarten (now the Altes Museum), in which Greek orders, a Roman dome and stereometrically pure forms merge. The building has a podium and an Ionic colonnade *in antis,* while the rotunda and dome are held within a cubic form that rises as an attic. The design had an air of indisputable authority and a sense of antique *gravitas.* War damage, vandalism, and ham-fisted and feeble new interiors have left this masterpiece in a sorry state.

Two exquisite miniatures followed in 1824: Schloss Glienicke (with its Kasino and Grecian Belvedere), and the Sommerhaus at Charlottenburg, and then came the momentous visit to France and England in 1826. Schinkel saw the designs for the British Museum, met John Nash, and was astonished by the warehouses and factories. He learned about fireproof construction and gas lighting, both of which he introduced to Berlin on his return.

J.-F. Blondel's *De la Distribution des Maisons de Plaisance* influenced the design of Charlottenhof at Potsdam, a villa beautifully related to its site, with a raised terrace-garden approached directly from the main upper-level rooms: the terrace is bounded by the tetrastyle antique portico, a pergola and an exedra. There can be no villa in the world as charming as this.

Also at Potsdam, the Gärtnerhaus of 1829 (in a round-arched Italianate villa style), joined to a teahouse in the form of an antique temple (the Römische Bäder) of 1833, is a wonderful picturesque ensemble probably inspired by Papworth and Nash and by Schinkel's Italian tour. The group of buildings, steps, loggias, pergolas, water, spaces and asymmetrical composition add up to a stunning performance. In the town center is the Nikolaikirche, which stands out among Schinkel's achievements for its stereometrical purity of forms: a cube with semicircular windows, a great portico and an apse set against the cube, and a dome recalling that of J.-G. Soufflot's Panthéon sum up neoclassical concerns. The church marks the end of the third phase of Schinkel's career, in which he demonstrated his complete mastery of Greek, Roman and Italianate forms.

Shortly after his 50th birthday, in 1831, Schinkel designed the new Bauakademie to house the School of Architecture and his own office and flat. Influenced by German, Italian and English brick buildings, it was one of Schinkel's most perfect creations, and was virtually unclassifiable in terms of style. With its segmental-headed windows, dressed with terra-cotta, it recalled industrial and warehouse architecture, and represents a high point in Schinkel's use of brick, a material he also incorporated in the nearby Friedrich-Werdersche-Kirche. The Bauakademie was damaged in World War II, but to the eternal disgrace of the East German authorities it was demolished in 1961.

Two unbuilt designs for royal palaces must be mentioned here, for they represent the highest achievements of any neoclassical architect: they are the palace on the Athenian Acropolis (1834) and Schloss Orianda in the Crimea (1838), which must rank among the most beautiful works of architecture ever conceived. With the Bauakademie, they mark the last phase of Schinkel's career, in which eclecticism, syncretism and mature classicism combined in a rich mix.

Schinkel died in the Bauakademie in 1841, honored throughout Europe, and was buried in the Dorotheen-Städtischer-Friedhof, where his grave is marked by a Greek stele.

Schinkel was the master of elegant restraint in design, and was steeped in an understanding of geometry, classicism and materials: his drawings have an authority conveyed in the cleanest of lines. In his work technological innovation and historical continuity are beautifully balanced, and his buildings are well arranged and anchored to their sites.

—JAMES STEVENS CURL

SCHLÜTER, Andreas.

German. Born in Danzig or Hamburg, ca. 1660. Died in St. Petersburg, Russian, 20 June 1714. Married Anna Elisabeth Spangenberg, 1694; three children. Studied with the sculptor Saporius in Danzig; sent to study architecture in France and Italy by Elector Friedrich III. Began career as a mason in Danzig, 1696; later became a master sculptor; called to Berlin by Elector Friedrich III, 1693; appointed *Schlossbaudirektor*, 1699; member of Berlin Academy, 1701, and director of the Academy of Arts, 1702-04; dismissed from all official posts, 1707; became director of architecture for the court of Peter the Great in St. Petersburg, 1713.

Chronology of Works
All in Germany unless noted
* Approximate dates
† Work no longer exists

1688*-93*	Cathedral, Olivia, Poland (high altar)
1698-99	Arsenal, Berlin (begun by Johann Arnold Nering, and completed by Jean de Bodt)
1698-1706	Schloss, Berlin (renovation and interior decoration; later expanded and completd by Johann Friedrich Eosander)†
1701-04	Post Office, Berlin†
1701*-06	Münzturm, Berlin†
1703-06	Small Stables, Berlin
1704-07	Lustschloss, Bad Freienwalde, Brandenburg
1705-07	Foundry, Berlin†
1711-12	Landhaus Kamecke, Berlin†
1713-14	Art Gallery, St. Petersburg, Russia (completed by others)
1713-14	Monplaisir Palace, near St. Petersburg (completed by others)
1713-14	Peterhof Palace, near St. Petersburg, Russia (completed by others)

Publications

BOOKS ABOUT SCHLÜTER

GEYER, A.: *Geschichte des Schlosses zu Berlin.* Berlin, 1936.
GURLITT, CORNELIUS: *Andreas Schlüter.* Berlin, 1891.
HAGER, WERNER: *Die Bauten des deutschen barocks, 1690-1770.* Jena, Germany, 1942.
HEMPEL, EBERHARD: *Geschichte der deutschen Baukunst.* Munich, 1956.
HEMPEL, EBERHARD: *Baroque Art and Architecture in Central Europe.* Harmondsworth, England, 1965.
IWICKI, ZYGMUNT: *Der Hochaltar der Kathedrale in Oliva: Ein Werk von Andreas Schlüter.* Freiberg, Germany, 1980.
LADENDORFF, HEINZ: *Der Bildhauer und Baumeister Andreas Schlüter.* Berlin, 1935.
PESCHKEN, GOERD, and KLÜNNER, WERNER: *Das Berliner Schloss.* Berlin, 1982.

ARTICLES ABOUT SCHLÜTER

HALLSTROM, BJÖRN HENRIK: ''Der Baumeister Andreas Schlüter und seine Nachfolge in St. Petersburg.'' *Konsthistorisk Tidskrift* 30 (1961): 95-126.
HUBALA, ERICH: ''Das Berliner Schloss und Andreas Schlüter.'' In *Gedenkschrift Ernst Gall.* Munich, 1965.
KELLER, FRITZ-EUGEN: ''Triumphbogen in der Berliner Architektur des 17. und 18. Jahrhunderts.'' Vol. 1: 99, pp. 103-105 in *Berlin und die Antike.* Berlin, 1979.
KÜHN, MARGARETE: ''Andreas Schlüter als Bildhauer.'' In *Barockplastik in Norddeutschland.* Mainz, Germany, 1977.
PESCHKEN, GOERD: ''Neue Literatur über Andreas Schlüter.'' *Zeitschrift für Kunstgeschichte* 30 (1967): 229-246.

Andreas Schlüter began his career as a mason in Danzig, then became a master sculptor, working on the pediments of the Krasiński Palace in Warsaw for King John Poniatowski during 1689-93. His work in Warsaw is vigorous, and includes reliefs of chariot groups and classical figures in the antique style. In fact, some of these reliefs look almost neoclassical, and could pass for 18th-century sculpture.

In 1693 he was called to Berlin by the elector Friedrich III (1688-1713), who became King Friedrich I of Prussia in 1701 and constituted Berlin a royal residence, uniting the administration of the five parts of the city.

Schlüter was sent to France and Italy to study architecture, and returned to Berlin in 1696. He was employed as a sculptor to embellish the Lange Brücke, the Schloss, and the Arsenal (Zeughaus) designed by Johann Arnold Nering (1659-95). Schlüter's expressive keystones for the windows and doors of the Zeughaus feature the heads of dead and dying warriors. These magnificent and expressive faces are as essential to the success of the Zeughaus as architecture as Balthasar Permoser's sculpture is to the Zwinger in Dresden.

Schlüter is said to have worked on Schloss Charlottenburg, begun in 1695 to designs by Nering, and completed in 1699, the residence of the electress (later Queen) Sophie-Charlotte, wife of Friedrich III. Only the central portion could have had any connection with Schlüter, and it was enlarged by Eosander von Goethe in 1701-07, who added the cupola. Later still it was further extended by Georg Wilhelm von Knobelsdorff. Schlüter appears to have acted more as a clerk of works than as architect. In front of Schloss Charlottenburg today stands Schlüter's heroic equestrian statue (1703) of the Great Elector (1640-88) which is one of the finest of all Baroque sculptures: it formerly stood on the Lange or Kurfürstenbrücke.

Schlüter's greatest architectural work was the Royal Palace in Berlin. There had been a castle on the site since the Middle Ages, but Friedrich III determined to replace the irregular pile of buildings that had been developed piecemeal with a large, uniform structure of imposing proportions in the latest taste; he must have felt Schlüter was equal to the task, for the elector appointed him surveyor general and architect for the new Schloss in 1698. A great Baroque palace, with elevations of monumental severity featuring giant orders of columns in the noble centerpieces and giving the building an air of antique gravity and authority, was erected under Schlüter's direction. The main influences on Schlüter were clearly partly Italian and partly French: Giovanni Lorenzo Bernini's (1598-1680) proposals for the Louvre and Antoine LePautre's (1621-91) *Dessins de plusieurs palais* of 1652 are two obvious sources, but less well known is the fact that Nicodemus Tessin the Younger (1654-1728) (Sweden's royal architect, who adopted a Baroque style reminiscent of Bernini's Louvre project) and Johann Bernhard Fischer von Erlach (1656-1723) visited Berlin while Schlüter was working on his designs, and there are certainly aspects of Fischer's monumental toughness in the Berlin Schloss.

Only the Zweiter Hof was entirely built to Schlüter's designs, and the finest part was the stair in the east wing of this court. The theme of the stair was the "Fall of the Giants," and the figures were based on Michelangelo's heroic sculptures in the Medici Chapel in Florence. The State Rooms, the Schweizer, Elisabeth, Rittersaal and Schwarze Adlerkammer were magnificently decorated with stucco, with powerfully modeled figures set in the corners.

It is a further indictment of the failed Communist regime in what was the German Democratic Republic that the Royal Palace (although partially damaged by bombs in World War II) was razed in 1950 on purely ideological grounds in an attempt to obliterate the past. The destruction of Schinkel's Bauakademie a few years later compounds the crime. The problem is that without Schlüter's great Schloss, the Unter den Linden (that wonderful street lined with masterpieces such as Knobelsdorff's Opera House, Schinkel's Neue Wache and Nering/Schlüter's Zeughaus) simply leads nowhere.

Schlüter also built the Post Office in Berlin in 1701-04, but this, too, was demolished as early as 1889. When the Münzturm, an adjunct at the Royal Palace, had to be pulled down on Schlüter's orders because of structural failure, he was dismissed from all his posts in 1707. Berlin stands on the sands of Brandenburg, and Schlüter was not sufficiently skilled technically to overcome the problems of difficult foundations. However, from 1711 to 1712 he built the charming Villa Kamecke in the suburb of Dorotheenstadt, but it was destroyed by bombing in 1945.

Schlüter reverted to sculpture, and between 1705 and 1714 he designed and made the sarcophagi of the king and queen. When King Friedrich died in 1713 Schlüter left Berlin and settled in St. Petersburg, where he died the following year.

Time has not been kind to Schlüter, and although we have evidence of his designs engraved by his pupil Paul Decker in Berlin, and we have the Zeughaus, war and wanton destruction have removed most of his work. He was undoubtedly one of the most gifted sculptors of his time, capable of a powerful mode of expression and a sureness of touch not always evident in the oeuvre of some of his contemporaries. His creations have almost been as ephemeral as the Münzturm, and the sands of time have been as destructive to his work as have the sands of Brandenburg.

—JAMES STEVENS CURL

SCOTT, George Gilbert.

British. Born in Gawcott, Buckinghamshire, England, 1811. Died in London, 27 March 1878. Married his cousin Caroline Oldrid, 1838. Sons were the architects George Gilbert Scott, Jr. (1839-97), and John Oldrid Scott (1841-1913). Apprenticed with Henry Roberts (1803-76), 1827. Worked for Sampson Kempthorne; partnership with W. B. Moffatt (1812-87), 1835-46; established his own office; appointed surveyor of Westminster Abbey, 1849. Associate, 1855, and member, 1860, Royal Academy; president, Royal Institute of British Architects, 1873-75; knighted, 1872.

Chronology of Works
All in England unless noted
† *Work no longer exists*

1835	Workhouse (now hospital), Old Windsor, Berkshire
1837	Workhouse (now St. Edmund's Hospital), Northampton
1840	Workhouse, Great Dunmow, Essex
1841-42	Christ Church, Turnham Green, London
1841-43	Infant Orphan Asylum (now Royal Wanstead School), Wanstead, Essex
1841-44	Martyrs' Memorial, Oxford
1842-44	St. Giles' Church, Camberwell, London
1842-44	Gaol, Reading, Berkshire
1842-45	St. John the Baptist Church, Westwood Heath, near Coventry
1843	St. Mark's Church, Swindon, Wiltshire
1843-45	St. John the Evangelist Church, West Meon, Hampshire
1844	St. Andrew's Church, Leeds
1844-46	St. Mark's Church, Worsley, Lancashire
1845-60	Nikolaikirche, Hamburg, Germany†
1846ff.	St. John's Cathedral, St. John's, Newfoundland
1847-48	St. Andrew's Church, Bradfield, Berkshire
1847-50	St. Ann's Church, Alderney, Channel Islands
1852-54	Houses, Broad Sanctuary, Westminster, London
1854	Cottages, Ilam, Staffordshire
1854-58	St. George's Church, Doncaster, Yorkshire
1855-59	All Souls Church, Haley Hill, Halifax, Yorkshire
1856-58	St. Matthias' Church, Richmond, Surrey
1856-60	Exeter College Chapel, Oxford
1857	Literary Institute, Sandbach, Cheshire
1857ff.	Cathedral, Lichfield, Staffordshire (restoration)
1857-58	St. Michael's Church, Crewe Green, Cheshire
1857-60	St. Michael's Church, Cornhill, London (restoration)
1858-60	St. Michael's Church, Leafield, Oxfordshire
1858-61	Kelham Hall, Nottinghamshire
1858-62	Walton Hall, Warwickshire
1859	St. Bartholomew's Church, Ranmore Common, Surrey
1861-66	Hafodunos House, Denbigh, Wales
1861-73	Government Offices, Whitehall, London
1862	Town Hall, Preston, Lancashire†
1863-69	St. John's College Chapel, Cambridge
1863-72	Albert Memorial, London
1864-68	Infirmary, Leeds
1865	Sudeley Almshouses, Winchcombe, Gloucestershire
1866	Brill's Baths, Brighton†
1868-71	Glasgow University, Glasgow, Scotland
1868-74	Midland Grand Hotel (St. Pancras Station Hotel), St. Pancras, London
1869-72	St. Mary Abbots' Church, Kensington, London
1874-79	Episcopal Cathedral, Edinburgh, Scotland

Publications

BOOKS BY SCOTT

A Plea for the Faithful Restoration of Our Ancient Churches. London, 1850.
Remarks on Secular and Domestic Architecture, Present and Future. London, 1858.
Design for the New Law Courts. London, 1860s.
Gleanings from Westminster Abbey. London, 1861.
Lectures on the Rise and Development of Mediaeval Architecture. London, 1879.
Personal and Professional Recollections. London, 1879.

BOOKS ABOUT SCOTT

BAYLEY, STEPHEN: *The Albert Memorial: The Monument in Its Social and Architectural Context.* London, 1981.
BURY, SHIRLEY (ed.): *Victorian Church Art.* London, 1971.
CLARKE, BASIL F. L.: *Anglican Cathedrals Outside the British Isles.* London, 1958.
CLARKE, BASIL F. L.: *Church Builders of the Nineteenth Century.* London, 1938.
COLE, DAVID: *The Work of Sir George Gilbert Scott.* London, 1980.
DIXON, ROGER, and MUTHESIUS, STEFAN: *Victorian Architecture.* New York and Toronto, 1978.
FERRIDAY, PETER (ed.): *Victorian Architecture.* London, 1963.
GIROUARD, MARK: *The Victorian Country House.* New Haven, Connecticut, and London, 1979.
HITCHCOCK, HENRY-RUSSELL: *Early Victorian Architecture in Britain.* 2 vols. New York, 1954.
PEVSNER, NIKOLAUS: *Some Architectural Writers of the Nineteenth Century.* Oxford, 1972.
SERVICE, ALASTAIR: *The Architects of London.* London, 1979.
Sir Gilbert Scott (1811-78): Architect of the Gothic Revival. Exhibition catalog. London, 1978.

ARTICLES ABOUT SCOTT

BRIGGS, MARTIN S.: "Sir Gilbert Scott, R. A." *Architectural Review* 24 (1908): 92-100, 147-152, 180-185, 290-295.
COLE, DAVID: "Some Early Works of Scott." *Architectural Association Journal* 66 (1950): 98-108.
FERRIDAY, PETER: "Syllabus in Stone. The Albert Memorial by George Gilbert Scott." *Architectural Review* 135 (1964).
PORT, M. H.: "The New Law Courts Competition: 1866-67." *Architectural History* 11 (1968): 75-93.
STAMP, GAVIN: "Sir Gilbert Scott's Recollections." *Architectural History* 19 (1976): 54-73.

*

George Gilbert Scott was at once the most prolific and the most pragmatic of the important Victorian architects, being active in both the ecclesiastical and the public and commercial fields. The former included participation in the much-criticized church "restorations" of the period. He came to advocate eclecticism, but was not a dogmatic ecclesiologist in the mold of William Butterfield and G. E. Street. He was opportunistic rather than extremist in his choice of commission, and his pragmatism was evident in his establishment of a practice that initially made its name providing workhouses, some 50 in 10 years, under the Poor Law Act of 1834. From these inauspicious beginnings, however, he was to achieve in the 1850s and 1860s an almost unchallenged position at the peak of the architectural profession, albeit in a practice then renowned for its businesslike rather than innovative design skills.

Although his early ecclesiastical work is ordinary when compared with the innovations of Butterfield and Street, some examples show the capacity for safe experimentation which abetted his natural pragmatism. This is evident in his asymmetrical placement of the tower at St. Mark's, Swindon (1843), and the bell turret at St. Andrew's, Leeds (1844). At that time he built the model of what was to become the ubiquitous church type of the next decade in his big, freestanding Gothic St. Giles, Camberwell (1842). It shows his capacity for compromise in design to accommodate his client's ideas and, while the interior does not take advantage of an inherent possibility for spatial manipulation, the building exhibits successful external massing in a form which became the model for Scott and others, and the type of the Early Victorian English church. Scott by then showed the full influence of his conversion to the principles espoused by A. W. N. Pugin, wherein he had renounced much of his earlier work as sham.

A major transformation in Scott's career was heralded in 1845 with his winning competition entry for the Nikolaikirche in Hamburg. Henceforth he became the leading architect for the great body of church clients who did not espouse extreme doctrinal views, clients who preferred an architect who, while competent archaeologically and knowledgeable ritually, was in essence not an aesthete, but a businessman. The resulting body of work marks Scott as an important ecclesiastical practitioner in the Gothic style, but in an Early Victorian, not a High Victorian, mode. His standing was confirmed in 1849 when he was appointed surveyor of the fabric of Westminster Abbey. In the emerging debate that led to the High Victorian Gothic, Scott typically took the middle ground by espousing a 19th-century Gothic Revival that was not mere copying but which allowed for a gradual development of original forms of expression.

In 1855 Scott presented his lecture "On the Pointed Architecture of Italy." Although he predated Street in this, the principles stressed were different and emphasized the manipulation of detached column shafts: in arcades, as decoration for windows, and as contributing to the use of structural color. These ideas were already in evidence in his remodeling of Camden Chapel in Camberwell, the Ruskin family church. This foreshadowed his *Remarks on Secular and Domestic Architecture, Present and Future* (1858), where discussion concerning the distinction between structural and decorative columns and arcades paralleled the traditional discussion in classical and Gothic rationalist debate which argued that the wall arcade must be either clearly decorative in its intent or so united with the wall as to be clearly constructional.

In his *Remarks*, essentially a repetition of his earlier opinions and practice, he also advocated rational planning and construction, an aesthetic of the picturesque and sublime (which is not free from contradiction), and the importance of Gothic motifs for connotations that were at once nationally symbolic and rational. He also argued for principles of decorum and hierarchy in architecture with respect to the treatment of building types, coupled with a stress on the requirements of the new age and a regard for social responsibility. He defined two kinds of utilitarian architecture and argued that important buildings should be decorated and that less important buildings should be left plain. At this distance the most important part of this argument dealt with the "lower" categories of building not then usually considered as architecture meriting an aesthetic of the sublime, but combining straightforward use of materials in buildings of simple outline derived from simple plans and capable of adaptation to most other principles of design.

It was, however, grander forms of secular architecture than the domestic that were to make Scott prominent in the following years. In these buildings he found room for the expression of his principles (and his continuing pragmatism) by emphasizing the sublime in planning, coupled with elements of decoration even richer as the importance of the building increased. This resulted in designs that were in marked contrast to the picturesque qualities of the preceding phase of his work. Scott figured prominently in the competition for the design of new Government Offices, his first design of 1856 emphasizing sublimity in an essentially classical massing elaborated with picturesque Gothic detail and corner treatment, as well as an overall emphasis on the horizontal at the expense of verticality. His design for the Foreign Office was premiated third, that for the War Office not at all, but after much political machination he was awarded the commission, briefly establishing Gothic supremacy in the "Battle of the Styles." The political battle continued, however, and the completed building designed in 1861 was decreed by Prime Minister Palmerston to be in the "Italian" style. The ever-pragmatic Scott eventually acceeded and produced a not-unsatisfactory Renaissance design. Scott's final word on the matter was the preparation for exhibition, also in 1861, of a Gothic version of the final design that he felt was a better essay in that style than his originally premiated scheme.

Scott was prepared to introduce the use of iron and glass into his work, and in the Brighton Baths (1866, since destroyed), he combined their use with that of the dome, an element which he had earlier described as the grandest of architectural features. He always used these modern materials, however, with traditional architectural forms and devices: in the baths, the dome surmounted a two-story arcade that was, loosely, "Ruskinian."

Thwarted by Palmerston in the case of the Foreign Office, Scott was able to achieve a full secular Gothic expression on the grand scale in the most ingenious of his completed works and his major contribution to the High Victorian Gothic, St. Pancras Station Hotel for the Midland Railway. It was paired with the greatest of the iron Victorian railway sheds, W. H. Barlow's St. Pancras Station, and constructed on a site comprising the space left between that shed and Euston Road, a site devoid of right angles or parallel sides. There was also a need to bring users up to the elevated level of the platforms. To achieve this Scott created a huge, sweeping ramp along the Euston Road frontage, and set the body of the building behind this and parallel to the train shed, making only a small projection at the base of the ramp, which is parallel to the road. This divergence creates a considerable visual tension in the street presence of the building, which is complemented by the strongly modeled and hierarchical horizontal arcades and machicolated cornice that define and describe the urban space, and by the Victorian Gothic skyline that announces the building's presence (and the Midland's importance), a symbolic marrying of the industrial revolution and the Gothic Revival. There in a masterly combination of classical uniformity of picturesque detail with sublime but irregular massing inspired by the site, rather than in the contrivance of his well-known Albert Memorial, Scott celebrated the ultimate achievement of the secular in High Victorian Gothic. This is a building that nicely encompasses both his pragmatism and his capacity for innovation—with the latter quality at last dominant.

—R. J. MOORE

SCOTT, Giles Gilbert.

British. Born in England, 1880. Died in 1960. Came from a family of architects: father was George Gilbert Scott, Jr., and his uncle was John Oldrid Scott; grandfather was the noted Victorian architect George Gilbert Scott, Sr.; son Richard Gilbert Scott, also an architect, continued his father's practice. Articled to Temple Moore, a pupil of Giles' father. Knighted, 1924; president of the Royal Institute of British Architects, 1933-35.

Chronology of Works
All in England unless noted

1903-60	Anglican Cathedral, Liverpool (not completed until 1980)
1905-06	Roman Catholic Church of the Annunciation, Bournemouth
1909-12	Roman Catholic Church of St. Maughold, Ramsay, Isle of Man
1909-35	Roman Catholic Church of St. Joseph, Sheringham, Norfolk
1913-15	129 Grosvenor Road, London (with Adrian Gilbert Scott; altered)
1913-16	Anglican Church of St. Paul, Stonycroft, Liverpool
1913-16	Roman Catholic Church of Our Lady, Northfleet
1917-39	Downside Abbey, Somerset (nave of church and new buildings)
1922-27	Charterhouse School Chapel, Godalming
1922-54	Memorial Court, Clare College, Cambridge
1922-60	Ampleforth Abbey and College, Yorkshire (new church and new buildings)
1924-25	Chester House, Clarendon Place, London
1927-56	Roman Catholic Church of Our Lady and St. Alphege, Bath
1927-59	Roman Catholic Church of St. Michael, Ashford
1928-29	Anglican Church of St. Francis, Terriers, High Wycombe
1928-29	Longwall Quad, Magdalen College, Oxford
1929-30	Anglican Church of St. Andrew, Luton
1929-31	Whitelands College, Putney, London
1929-34	Battersea Power Station, London (with Halliday and Agate)
1930-32	Anglican Church of St. Alban, Golders Green, London
1930-34	Library, Cambridge University, Cambridge
1931-32	Lady Margaret Hall, Oxford (chapel and new building)
1931-51	Roman Catholic Cathedral, Oban, Scotland
1933-51	Guinness Brewery, Park Royal, London (with Alexander Gibb and partners)
1935-45	Waterloo Bridge, London (with Rendel, Palmer & Tritton)
1935-46	New Bodleian Library, Oxford
1944-51	Electricity House, Bristol
1944-51	House of Commons, London (rebuilding; with Adrian Gilbert Scott)
1947-48	Rye House Power Station, Hertfordshire (incomplete)
1947-60	Bankside Power Station, London
1950-54	Guildhall, City of London (restoration and new building)
1954-59	Roman Catholic Carmelite Church, Kensington, London

Publications

BOOKS ABOUT SCOTT

REILLY, C. H.: *Representative British Architects of Today*. London, 1931.
STAMP, GAVIN, and HARTE, GLYNN BOYD: *Temples of Power*. London, 1979.

*

Giles Gilbert Scott, the son of George Gilbert Scott, Jr., to whose pupil, Temple Moore, he was articled, was one of the most important architects in Britain during the interwar years. His most famous commission was that for Liverpool Anglican Cathedral which he won in 1903 in the second round of a competition, at the age of 22; this kept him occupied for the rest of his life, the design undergoing continual modifications as the structure rose, the ornament becoming more and more concentrated, the style more monumental and the use of natural light more and more subtle. This led to several other church commissions in the 1920s that Scott carried out in a Romanesque style, as at St. Francis, Terriers, High Wycombe (1928-29), and St. Andrew's, Luton (1929-30), and then later to several commissions for secular buildings such as the university libraries at Oxford and Cambridge. These, based as they were on the academic libraries in the United States, were set in a more modernist tradition, with long, vertical windows and a simple articulation, and were made of reinforced concrete and finished with the most subtle of detailing and beautiful local materials.

Yet these library buildings demonstrate the dilemma Scott faced. He knew of the traditions of modern architecture, but these he tempered with a respect for the older traditions of design and a dislike of novelty, a belief in the evolutionary pattern of architectural history and a skepticism about some of the claims of the pioneers of the Modern Movement. In the disputes of the 1930s, Scott occupied a middle position; in 1933 he was appointed president of the Royal Institute of British Architects, and his address, speaking of tradition and the limits in the past on individualism, is the clearest record of his practical beliefs. After 1945, however, fewer architects were prepared to follow his line. Though he received several commissions, one for the rebuilding of the Houses of Parliament, another for Coventry Cathedral, Scott became more and more isolated, and by the time he died few were taking any note of his work; his cathedral in Liverpool was finished in 1979 in a slightly reduced design.

Among the most complex and controversial of his commissions was that for the exterior of Battersea Power Station. Construction began on the site in 1929; the designs were continually modified, and Scott's participation in the final form of the building, which was likened by those who did not like it to an upturned table, was limited and circumscribed. But the details, a form of restrained and delicate classicism, with fluting and detailed brick moldings, were praised as the appropriate reconciliation of the past with what one critic in 1933 referred to as "Modern architecture for Modern Industry." More commissions followed, most important, the design for the new Guinness Factory at Park Royal (begun in 1934), a slightly asymmetrical grouping of blocks in the style of those at Battersea, but sparer than many being built at that time in the same area; the new Waterloo Bridge over the Thames (begun in 1935), replacing that of John Rennie, a spare, simple and effective design; Electricity House in Bristol (1944-51), and then Rye House Power Station, Hertfordshire (begun in 1947 and unfinished when Scott died), and the Bankside Power Station (1950-54).

However, Scott's most pervasive contribution to the urban landscape of England may have been the designs he produced for the GPO telephone boxes, all now being dismantled. The first went into production in 1926; it had Greek fluting, elegant doors and a dome that was perhaps based on the form John Soane had used in his house at Lincoln's Inn. The second model, so-called No. 6, came out in 1936; it was smaller, the details were simplified, and to compare it to the first design is to see, as one more sympathetic critic put it, the development of Scott's Moderne aesthetic, even though, as his enemies would say, there as in everything he did, on whatever scale, he was fundamentally a traditional and backward-looking architect. The verdict is still out.

—DAVID CAST

SCOTT, M. H. Baillie.

British. Born Mackay Hugh Baillie Scott near Ramsgate, Kent, England, 1865. Died in Brighton, England, 1945. Studied at Worthing; graduated, Royal Agricultural College, Cirencester, 1885. Apprenticed with Charles E. Davis, Bath, 1886. Established own firm, Bedford, 1903; partnership with A. Edgar Beresford, London, 1919.

Chronology of Works
All in England unless noted
† Work no longer exists

1892-93	Red House, Douglas, Isle of Man
1894-96	Bexton Croft, Knutsford, Cheshire
1895-96	Semidetached houses, Douglas, Isle of Man
1897	School and Master's House, Peel, Isle of Man
1897-98	Village Hall, Onchan, Isle of Man
1897-98	Ducal Palace, Darmstadt, Germany (interiors)†
1898-99	Blackwell, Bowness, Westmoreland
1898-99	White Lodge, Wantage, Berkshire
1899-1900	The Garth, Cobham, Surrey
1905	Wertheim Residence, Berlin, Germany (interiors)
1906-07	Bill House, Selsey-on-Sea, Sussex
1907-14	Waldbühl, Uzwil, Switzerland
1908	White Cottage, Biddenham, Kent
1908-09	Undershaw, Guildford
1908-09	Waterloo Court and Multiple Houses, Hampstead Garden Suburb, London
1912	Michaels, Harbledown, Kent
1912-13	Chludzinski House, Laskowicze, Poland
1912-13	The Cloisters, Avenue Road, London
1912-14	Binsse House, Short Hills, New Jersey, U.S.A.
1916-17	White House, Great Chart, Kent
1919-20	Westhall Hill, Burford, Oxfordshire
1920-21	Oakhams, Edenbridge, Kent
1923	The Gatehouse, Limpsfield, Surrey (with A. E. Beresford)
1923	Trunch, Saltwood-in-Hythe, Kent (with Beresford)
1924	House, Mudeford Green, Hampshire (with Beresford)
1928-29	Ashwood, Woking, Surrey (with Beresford)
1931-32	Sandy Holt, Esher, Surrey (with Beresford)
1931-32	Mena House, Walton-on-Thames, Surrey (with Beresford)

Publications

BOOKS BY SCOTT

Haus eines Kunstfreundes. Vol. I. Darmstadt and London, 1902.
Houses and Gardens. London, 1906. Substantially revised as *Houses and Gardens*. With A. Edgar Beresford. London, 1933.
Town Planning and Modern Architecture at the Hampstead Garden Suburb. With Raymond Unwin and others. London, 1909.
Garden Suburbs, Town Planning and Modern Architecture. With others. London, 1911.

BOOKS ABOUT SCOTT

CREESE, WALTER L.: *The Search for Environment: The Garden City Before and After*. New Haven, Connecticut, and London, 1966.
KOCH, ALEX (ed.): *Meister der Innenkunst: Haus eines Kunstfreundes des M. H. Baillie Scott*. Darmstadt, Germany, 1902.
KORNWOLF, JAMES D.: *M. H. Baillie Scott and the Arts and Crafts Movement*. Baltimore and London, 1972.
MEDICI-MALL, KATHARINA: *Das Landhaus Waldbühl von M. H. Baillie Scott: Ein Gesamtkunstwerk zwischen Neugotik und Jugendstil*. Bern, Switzerland, 1979.
MUTHESIUS, HERMANN: *Das englische Haus*. Berlin, 1904-05.
PEVSNER, NIKOLAUS: *Pioneers of Modern Design from William Morris to Walter Gropius*. Harmondsworth, England, 1949.
WHITE, J. P.: *Furniture Made at the Pyghtle Works, Bedford, by John P. White Designed by M. H. Baillie Scott*. London, 1901.

ARTICLES ABOUT SCOTT

BETJEMAN, JOHN: ''Baillie Scott and the 'Architecture of Escape'.'' *Studio* 16 (October 1938): 177-180.
BETJEMAN, JOHN: ''M. H. Baillie Scott.'' *Journal of the Manx Museum* 7 (1968): 77-80.
FISKER, KAY: ''Tre pionerer fra aarhundredskiftet.'' *Byggmästaren* 26 (1947): 221-232.
FRED, W.: ''Der Architekt M. H. Baillie Scott.'' *Kunst und Kunsthandwerk* 4 (1905): 53-73.
MEIER-GRAEFE, JULIUS: ''M. H. Baillie Scott.'' *Moderne Bauformen* 4 (1905): 34ff.
MEYER, PETER: ''Baillie Scott's Waldbühl.'' *Das Werk* 24 (1937): 140-153.
MUTHESIUS, HERMANN: ''M. H. Baillie Scott.'' *Dekorative Kunst* 5 (1900): 5-7, 40-48.
TAYLOR, NICHOLAS: ''Baillie Scott's Waldbühl.'' *Architectural Review* 138 (1965): 456-458.
VON BERLEPSCH-VALENDAS, H. E.: ''Hampstead—Eine Studie über Städtebau in England.'' *Kunst und Kunsthandwerk* 12 (1909): 241-284.

*

M. H. Baillie Scott was an Arts and Crafts architect who was influenced by earlier architects of the period, but who in turn had a universal impact upon the movement, continuing its traditions in his own practice long after the profession had tired of the style and had moved on to other trends.

Scott was born in 1865 at Ramsgate, Kent, and began work as an architectural assistant, in Douglas on the Isle of Man from 1889 to 1893. From 1893 to 1901, he practiced in the same town designing rather small houses, an occasional school, and a village hall. Locating on the Isle of Man did not isolate Scott from the mainstream of the architectural profession, since he read journals including the British periodical *The Builder* and *American Architect*. These journals he considered to be his architectural education, having trained as an estate manager and then worked for the city architect of Bristol, from whom he claimed to have learned nothing. His early residential commissions, small compared to the work of the leaders of the Arts and Crafts movement in England, had more affinity to the Shingle Style of the American East Coast tradition as illustrated in *American Architect*. During the early years of the 20th century, the reverse was true. Then it was Scott who inspired the American Arts and Crafts architects.

His own Red House in Douglas (1892-93) was economically planned without corridors, and was praised by Herman Muthesius in German periodicals and *Das Englische Haus* (1903). *The Studio* also began to publish articles by Scott on his own work, so there was cross-fertilization between C. F. A. Voysey, who influenced him most in the last 1890s, and Scott's later influence on Voysey, especially in decorative cutout design motifs. Scott's style throughout the 1890s ranged widely from small, barn-like houses of half-timbered construction with brick infill inside and out, open timber trusses, inglenooks, floriated leaded windows, boarded doors, large hinges and ironware, and built-in furniture to residences with white roughcast external finishes, well-proportioned elements and a strong horizontality.

In 1897 Ernst Ludwig commissioned Scott to redecorate the dining and drawing rooms of his palace at Darmstadt. This commission boosted Scott's reputation, causing his open plans and simple furniture designs to be more widely known in Europe, most notably to Adolf Loos and Josef Maria Olbrich in Vienna; subsequent commissions came from as far away as Russia and Switzerland. Residential projects came to him from Britain too, such as the White House (1899) on Colquhoun Street in Helensburgh, near Glasgow, a house which had a strong impact upon Charles Rennie Mackintosh and his more famous Hill House further up the hill on the other side of the street.

Scott moved his office to Bedford in 1901, at the beginning of the mature phase of his work when small cottages were still his major contribution. At the high point of their careers, architects frequently write books covering their design philosophies; Scott followed this pattern by publishing *House and Gardens* in 1906.

As the garden city movement progressed in the early 20th century, Scott contributed multiple housing projects, some of which were built at Letchworth, Welwyn and at the Hampstead Garden Suburb. Perhaps his most interesting design was a cooperative community for working women called Waterloo Court (1909) at Hampstead, consisting of 50 apartments arranged around a cloistered court linked to dining and communal facilities.

By about 1907 the Arts and Crafts movement in Britain had lost its drive. Most architects had evolved to other idioms, but Scott remained the most faithful of all architects involved in the movement. In 1905 A. E. Beresford joined Scott and soon took charge of the firm's business dealings and production drawings. He was made a partner in 1919, when Scott moved the office to London. Together Scott and Beresford were responsible for about 130 commissions, the majority of which were built during the 1920s, Scott's most prolific decade. Works included village halls, half-timbered residences, plus those in brick and stone, a war memorial and an apartment house. Scott designed nothing after 1935, and World War II ended the practice in 1939. Henry-Russell Hitchcock, the noted architectural

historian of the 19th and 20th centuries, saw the significance of Scott's earlier work and found it incomprehensible that the later commissions could have come from the same hand. It was the early works, and not the later ones, that established Scott as a major Arts and Crafts contributor to architectural design.
—LAWRENCE WODEHOUSE

SEIDLER, Harry.

Australian. Born in Vienna, Austria, 25 June 1923; immigrated to Australia, 1948, and naturalized as Australian citizen, 1958. Married Penelope A. M. Evatt, 1958. Studied at the University of Manitoba, Winnipeg, Canada, 1941-44, B.Arch.; studied at Harvard University, Cambridge, Massachusetts, under Walter Gropius and Marcel Breuer, M.Arch., 1946. Chief assistant to Marcel Breuer, New York City, 1946-48; worked in office of Oscar Niemeyer, Rio de Janeiro, Brazil, 1948; principal, Harry Seidler and Associates, Sydney, Australia, since 1948. Has taught architecture in Canada, Australia and the United States.

Chronology of Works
All in Australia unless noted

1949-54	Many houses in Sydney (including the Rose Seidler House, now a museum owned by the Historic Houses Trust of New South Wales)
1960	Apartment block, Ithaca Gardens, Elizabeth Bay, Sydney
1960-67	Australia Square, Sydney (with Pier Luigi Nervi)
1961	Lend Lease House Office Building, Sydney
1961	Blues Point Tower Apartment Block, McMahons Point, Sydney
1962	Apartment block, 40 Victoria Street, Potts Point, Sydney
1963-65	Apartment block, 58 Roslyn Gardens, Rushcutters Bay, Sydney
1964	Townhouses and apartment housing, Canberra
1965-68	Space Frame Building, Bourke Road, Alexandria, Sydney
1966-67	Seidler House, Killara, New South Wales
1966-67	Apartment blocks, Edgecliff, Sydney
1967	Apartment blocks, Maloney Street, Rosebery, Sydney
1967-68	Housing project for fellows and research scholars, Australian National University, Canberra
1970	Condominium apartments, Acapulco, Mexico
1970-75	Commonwealth Government Trade Groups Offices, Canberra
1971-73	Seidler and Associates Office Building, Milsons Point, Sydney
1971-77	M.L.C. Centre Office Tower and Theatre Royal, Sydney
1973-77	Australian Embassy, Paris, France
1978-80	Theatre Complex, Ringwood Civic Centre, Melbourne
1980-85	Hong Kong Club and Office Building redevelopment, Hong Kong
1983-87	Riverside Centre and Hilton Hotel, Brisbane
1985-86	Office Building and Headquarters for Capita, Sydney
1985-86	Headquarters for Shell Company of Australia, Melbourne

Harry Seidler: Grosvenor Place, Sydney, Australia, ca. 1950s

1987   Penthouse Apartment and Office Extensions, Milsons Point, Sydney

1987-   QV1 Office Tower and Commercial Centre, Perth

Publications

BOOKS BY SEIDLER

Houses, Interiors, Projects. Sydney, 1954.

Harry Seidler: Houses, Buildings and Projects, 1955-63. Sydney, 1963.

Planning and Building Down Under: New Settlement Strategy and Current Architectural Practice in Australia. Vancouver, British Columbia, 1978.

Internment—The Diaries of Harry Seidler, May 1940-October 1941. London and Boston, 1986.

ARTICLES BY SEIDLER

Since the 1940s, has written extensively for many major architecture periodicals, including *Architecture Design, Architectural Forum, Architectural Review, Architecture and Urbanism, Architecture Australia* and *Arts and Architecture.*

BOOKS ABOUT SEIDLER

Australia Square. Sydney, 1969.

BLAKE, PETER: *Architecture for the New World: The Work of Harry Seidler.* Sydney, 1973.

BLAKE, PETER: *Harry Seidler: Australian Embassy/Ambassade d'Australie, Paris.* Sydney, New York and Stuttgart, 1979.

CLEREHAN, N.: *Best Australian Houses.* Melbourne, 1961.

DREW, PHILIP: *Two Towers, Harry Seidler: Australia Square MLC Centre.* Sydney and Stuttgart, 1980.

FRAMPTON, KENNETH: *Riverside Centre.* Sydney and Stuttgart, 1988.

FREELAND, J. M.: *Architecture in Australia: A History.* Melbourne, 1968.

Towers in the City. Sydney and Milan, 1988.

ARTICLES ABOUT SEIDLER

"Harry Seidler." *World Architecture,* special issue 7 (1990).

*

Born in Vienna in 1923, Harry Seidler studied architecture in England and Canada, and under Walter Gropius at Harvard. He was assistant to Marcel Breuer in New York before settling in Australia in 1948.

Seidler is fully aware of the Australian climate as a form-determinant factor. He advocates solid, heavy buildings with high heat-storage capacity. He suggests the use of predominantly horizontal modulation of windows for daylight admission. He stresses that buildings should be so protected from the sun, wind and rain that the surfaces would last long with minimal maintenance, and be so detailed as not to be disfigured or harmed by the elements. "Modern architecture must learn to grow old gracefully," he argues *(Houses, Buildings and Projects 1955-63).*

Among his multistory apartment blocks, the Blues Point Tower is perhaps the best known. The building has been planned to command a view-arch of 270 degrees from northwest to northeast to capture the view of Sydney's harbor. The apartment block is revolutionary. Seidler introduced elements of structural frames of vertical poured concrete walls as wind bracing and

supports for flat slabs. The building generally retains the rectilinear modulated geometry.

Seidler's European heritage is modified by his sensitivity to the Australian climate. To solve the problem of sun penetration of the Lend Lease House at Sydney Cove (1961, demolished), Seidler devised adjustable horizontal external louvers on the facades. The louvers, giving various patterns on the facades as they were turned by the occupants, were not unlike the bold sun breakers of Le Corbusier.

The building that brought Harry Seidler to international fame is said to be the Australian Square (1961-67). The square, consisting of two buildings, was a bold attempt to give the heart of Sydney's central business district a much-needed open space. A circular form for the tower was devised in order to create desirable relationships with surrounding buildings, to allow maximum available natural lighting into surrounding buildings and streets, and to avoid the "canyon" effect of buildings in the business district. Structural innovation was introduced in the lower rectangular building. The columns supporting the structure were gathered at the ground level by tree-like structural trestles, freeing that level for pedestrian traffic.

The MLC Centre in Sydney (1971-75) is another fine example of urban planning and architectural design. The development aimed to create an urban focal point containing large spaces with open plazas, areas of repose, and other commercial areas and outdoor restaurants, in conjunction with offices. In *Australian Architecture Since 1960,* Jennifer Taylor commented, "The composition of the MLC scheme differs from that of Seidler's previous urban solutions. The buildings of Australia Square are objects placed in accord, but independently, in the area of the site. The MLC buildings form a related totality governed by the curving geometry disciplined by the radials from the centre of the tower."

The Hong Kong Club (1980-84) occupies an expensive site in the heart of Victoria Island in Hong Kong. The club site was developed to accommodate rentable premises and club facilities to realize its full potential. The solution was to provide a two-tier building. The lower tier groups the club's activities around a vertically open and circular space at four levels. The upper tier, a tower of 16 stories, houses the offices.

The western facade, the most prominent of the building, is also the most innovative. This elevation, which faces the well-known Cenotaph Square and is the most seen, called for a span of 34 meters (112 feet) over the entire structure. Massive T-beams with wide flanges were cast *in situ* by a single reusable steel mold, and were used to support the secondary T-beams. The success of the design is due to the integration of structures with architectural design. The logical and rational structural forms provide architectural rhythm and theme.

The Riverside Centre (1983-87) on the Brisbane River bank was awarded the Sir Zelman Cowan Award for nonresidential works in 1987. The site offers fine views up and down the river. The challenge to the architect was to relate the building to its surroundings and to the river. To achieve this, the scheme called for a building without podium. It opened up the ground level to a large plaza of sufficient width to give a sense of identity, making the river part of the space, and a deliberate link between the plaza and the river was made.

The tower is triangular on plan, giving maximum view to the offices and minimizing exposure to the morning sun. The upper stories are heavily textured by aluminum screens, the angles of which are adjusted according to the respective sun angles on the facades.

Internally, Seidler again created clear floor space by linking the central core with the perimeter by deep beams. To reduce the number of supports at the ground level, the columns were gathered to form two massive hyperboloid-shaped buttresses, which were then integrated with the transparent front awning.

A new addition of Seidler's work is the 34-story, reinforced-concrete framed tower in downtown Melbourne, overlooking the well-known Fitzroy Gardens. Seidler devised a free curvilinear form for all the elements—podium, service core and tower. At the street level, the development is approached through a landscaped plaza at a major street corner, and the stone paving extends into the free-form lobby, behind which the curved central core links the podium with the upper floors. The tower is also curved and "floats" around the central core. A sculptured column at the entrance gathers the loads from three columns of upper floors and adds interest to the lobby. The success of the design scheme is in its dramatic presentation in spite of the restrictive site. The building is seen as a stage set in which a variety of activities take place.

Harry Seidler has brought to Australia a new direction in architecture. His linkage with the European tradition gives a sense of precision in architectural design, especially in detailing. There is a sense of consistency and continuity in Seidler's work. He has been able to bring about perfection and excellence in his design through continuous exploration and experimentation within the framework of his architectural ethos.

—B. P. LIM

SEMPER, Gottfried.

German. Born in Hamburg, Germany, 29 November 1803. Died in Rome, Italy, 15 May 1879. Married Bertha Thimmig, 1835; father of the architects Emanuel and Manfred Semper. Studied law and mathematics at the University of Grottingen, 1823-25, and then architecture in Munich with Friedrich von Gärtner, 1825. Fled to France after fighting a duel, 1826. Worked in Paris for Franz Christian Gau and Jacques Ignace Hittorff; traveled to southern France, Italy and Greece, 1830-33; director of the Baus chule of the Royal Academy in Dresden, Germany, 1834-50; exiled to England after participating in an uprising, and taught in the Department of Practical Art at the School of Design, Marlborough House, London, 1851-52; professor and director, Eidgenössische Technische Hochschule, Zurich, Switzerland, 1855; supervised Ringstrasse projects, Vienna, Austria, 1869-76.

Chronology of Works
† *Work no longer exists*

1834-41	Royal Hoftheater, Dresden, Germany†
1847-54	Picture Gallery (completed later by Bernard Kruger and K. M. Hänel), Dresden, Germany
1858-64	Eidgenössische Technische Hochschule, Zurich, Switzerland
1869	Kaiser Forum, Vienna, Austria
1871-78	New Opera, Dresden, Germany (executed by Manfred Semper)
1872-79	Museum of Art History, Vienna, Austria (with Karl Hasenauer; not completed until 1881)
1872-79	Museum of Natural History, Vienna, Austria (with Hasenauer; not completed until 1881)
1873	Burgtheater, Vienna, Austria (executed by Hasenauer in 1874-78)

Publications

BOOKS BY SEMPER

Bemerkungen über bemalte Architektur und Plastik bei den Alten. Altona, Germany, 1834.
Die vier Elemente der Baukunst: Ein Beitrag zur vergleichenden Baukunde. Braunschweig, Germany, 1851. English edition: *The Four Elements of Architecture and Other Writings.* Cambridge, Massachusetts, 1989.
Wissenschaft, Industrie und Kunst. Edited by Hans M. Wingler. Berlin and Mainz, Germany, 1852. Reprint: 1966.
Der Stil in den technischen und tektonischen Künsten; oder praktische Aesthetik—Ein Handbuch für Techniker, Künstler und Kunstfreunde. 2 vols. Munich, 1860-63; 2nd ed., 1878-79.
Kleine Schriften von Gottfried Semper. Edited by Manfred Semper and Hans Semper. Berlin and Stuttgart, 1884.

ARTICLES BY SEMPER

"Development of Architectural Style." Edited and translated by John Wellborn Root. *Inland Architect and News Record* 14 (1890), No. 7: 76-78, and No. 8: 92-94; 15 (1890), No. 1: 5-6, and No. 2: 32-33.

BOOKS ABOUT SEMPER

ETTLINGER, LEOPOLD D.: *Gottfried Semper und die Antike.* Bleicherode, Germany, 1937.
FRÖHLICH, MARTIN: *Gottfried Semper: Zeichnerischer Nachlass an der ETH Zürich, Kritischer Katalog.* Basel, 1974.
GANTHER, JOSEPH: *Revision der Kunstgeschichte: Prolegomena zu einer Kunstgeschichte aus dem Geiste der Gegenwart, mit einer Anhang "Semper und Le Corbusier."* Vienna, 1932.
Gottfried Semper 1803-1879—Baumeister zwischen Revolution und Historismus. Munich, 1979.
HERRMANN, WOLFGANG: *Gottfried Semper: In Search of Architecture.* Cambridge, Massachusetts, 1984.
HERRMANN, WOLFGANG: *Gottfried Semper: Theoretische Nachlass an der ETH Zürich.* Basel, 1981.
LAUDEL, HEIDRUN: *Gottfried Semper: Architektur und Stil.* Dresden, 1991.
PEVSNER, NIKOLAUS: *Some Architectural Writers of the Nineteenth Century.* Oxford, 1972.
QUITZSCH, HEINZ: *Die aesthetischen Anschauungen Gottfried Sempers.* Berlin, 1962.
RYKWERT, JOSEPH: *On Adam's House in Paradise.* New York, 1973.
VOGT, ADOLF M.; REBLE, CHRISTINA; and FRÖHLICH, MARTIN (eds.): *Gottfried Semper und die Mitte des 19. Jahrhunderts.* Basel, 1976.
ZOEGE VON MANTEUFFEL, CLAUS: *Die Baukunst Gottfried Sempers.* Freiburg, 1952.

ARTICLES ABOUT SEMPER

BLETTER, R.: "On Martin Fröhlich's Gottfried Semper." *Oppositions* 4 (October 1974): 146-153.
ETTLINGER, LEOPOLD D.: "On Science, Industry and Art: Some Theories of Gottfried Semper." *Architectural Review* 136 (July 1964): 57-60.
"Gottfried Semper." *American Architect and Building News* 7 (1880), No. 214: 33-47, and No. 215: 43-44.

Gottfried Semper: New Opera, Dresden, Germany, 1871-78

HAMMERSCHMIDT, VALENTIN: "Gottfried und Manfred Sempers Projekt eines Hoftheaters für Darmstadt." *Architectura* 21, No. 2 (1990): 142-159.

HARVEY, LAWRENCE: "Semper's Theory of Evolution in Architectural Ornament." *Transactions of the Royal Institute of British Architects* New Series, 1 (1885).

RYKWERT, JOSEPH: "Semper and the Conception of Style." In *The Necessity of Ornament.* London, 1982.

*

Gottfried Semper is remembered today mainly for his major theoretical work, *Der Stil in den technischen und tektonischen Künsten (Style in the Technical and Structural Arts)* (1860 and 1863). This two-volume text is composed largely of an extensive study of the industrial arts, including textiles, ceramics, carpentry, masonry and metalwork—a study undertaken in order to develop the innovative idea that "... a great part of the forms used in architecture ... originate from works of industrial art.... The works of industrial art therefore very often give the key and basis for the understanding of architectural forms and principles." In *Der Stil,* Semper's concerns are threefold: to fashion a systematic scheme of interpretation for the visual arts, inspired by the comparative anatomy of the naturalist Georges Cuvier (1769-1832); to understand the nonliteral meanings of visual works, mainly architecture; and to give an account of the continuity of artistic tradition. This book earned him a significant place in German art history, and it remains influential today as a pioneering study in nonverbal semiotics.

Although remembered mainly as a theoretician, Semper's contemporary reputation was established initially with the completion of his first major building, the Royal Hoftheater in Dresden. Designed and completed between 1834 and 1841 while he was head of the department of architecture at the Academy of Fine Arts in Dresden, the theater was part of his conception of a cultural center for the city. This conception made ingenious use of the open-ended courtyard of the Baroque Zwinger, which Semper connected to a wide open space extending down to the Elbe River. This space served to relate old and new buildings—the Catholic Hofkirche, parts of the royal palace, a guardhouse by Karl Friedrich Schinkel, and the new theater—and link them to the city as a whole. According to Semper's own account of the project published in 1849, in designing the theater he followed the principle of "... making [the theater's] exterior dependent throughout on the needs of interior organization." The Italian Renaissance-inspired building features a semicircular auditorium with recessed arcaded windows; above this are found upper tiers and a stage house, while pedimented pavilions prominently mark the entrances. The rich interior decor was provided by three leading French designers: Edouard Despléchin, Jules Dieterle and Charles Séchan.

Semper's peaceful and prosperous existence in Dresden was shattered in 1849, when as a republican he participated in an uprising in the city which, ending in defeat, forced him to flee Saxony. Thus began a period of exile that lasted until 1855. Spent mainly in London in the circle of Henry Cole, that period saw the publication of Semper's *Die vier Elemente der Baukunst (The Four Elements of Architecture)* (1851) and other theoretical writings, and was crucial to the formulation of ideas that later would form the basis of *Der Stil.*

Semper initially traveled to London to work with the reformer Edwin Chadwick on a plan to construct a national cemetery. While that plan came to nothing, Chadwick introduced him to Henry Cole, then a leading member of the commission directing the works of the Crystal Palace, Joseph Paxton's iron-and-glass building constructed to house the Great Exhibition of 1851. Through Cole, Semper gained employment in the exhibition building, arranging the exhibits of Canada, Turkey, Sweden and Denmark. Although this work was of relatively minor importance, it afforded him the opportunity to study the exhibition in detail.

There, he saw a wide range of industrial arts, including machines and tools, finished products and works of art. Comparing the machine-produced exhibits of modern nations to the technical arts of so-called "primitive" peoples, he found the latter superior in color and form, only confirming what some of his contemporaries already knew: that the machine had had a detrimental influence on modern production. *Der Stil,* according to one scholar, was Semper's response to everything he had seen in the exhibition: "... the immediate object of the book was to give guidance to contemporary industrial art and to assist it in regaining the quality it lacked most: style."

The formulation of Semper's ideas continued within the context of the Cole circle, when in 1852 he was appointed to a professorship in the department of practical art of the School of Design, headed by Cole. As part of the department's efforts to reform industrial-art education in Britain, Semper conducted classes on the principles and practice of ornamental art applied to metal manufactures. As a professor, he was under obligation to deliver public lectures; it was in those lectures that he began to question the relationship between the industrial arts and architecture as expounded by Owen Jones in the writings of the department: "the decorative arts arise from and should properly be attendant upon architecture."

Inverting Jones' principle, Semper suggested that the forms and rules of architecture could be traced back to those of the practical arts; this would later become the controlling idea of *Der Stil.*

Semper's work in London ended when he accepted a post as professor of architecture at the Eidgenössische Hochschule that was to be established in Zurich. In the following years, he was involved with many large building projects, including the Eidgenössische Technische Hochschule in Zurich (1858-64) and the Kaiser Forum in Vienna (1869) and continued to publish writings of a theoretical nature, the best known of these being *Der Stil.*

In this work, Semper suggested that artifacts and architecture take on meaning, or symbolic interpretation in two principal ways: from the way they are made, and from the purposes that they serve. He drew attention to the most elementary techniques and materials of production in order to investigate the transference of motifs, and thus of meaning, from one material to another and from one context to another. In particular, he was concerned with the way in which traditional forms, especially those of architecture, retain the trace of, and represent earlier structural forms. To that end, he divided artifacts into four main categories by reference to which motifs are defined: textiles, pottery, carpentry and the construction of walls. Architecture is divided into the most elementary forms of building: the hearth, the roof, the floor and space dividing screens or walls. In that way he showed, for example, how walls retain the motif of textiles, which constituted the original wall.

Der Stil has led many scholars to attribute to Semper the view that architecture is the exclusive product of material, technique and function—a view which, it has been convincingly demonstrated by several scholars, was neither held by him nor expounded in *Der Stil.* Elaborating on this point, one scholar has suggested that Semper's idea of the play between "fiction and realization," an idea central to his thought, is the crucial element that has often eluded admirers and critics alike, leading to misinterpretation. Here, visual meaning is seen as dependent on the play between fiction—the suggestion of what is not there, or the masking of what is there—and realization—the bringing out of aspects of the material or construction, thus imparting value to them.

Parts of Semper's work were read with interest by modern architects such as H. P. Berlage, Otto Wagner and Louis Sullivan, although considering the confusion of interpretation, one wants to know exactly what was read and how it was interpreted. Semper's work continues to be influential today; as one scholar notes, "Semper belongs to the circle of those pioneers who recognized the nonverbal sign and its own specific nature and began to interpret it." As such, Semper's work remains suggestive for the future.

—ELLEN A. CHRISTENSEN

SERLIO, Sebastiano.

Italian. Born in Bologna, Italy, 6 September 1475. Died at Fontainebleau, France, ca. 1555. Father was the painter Bartolomeo Serlio. Trained in painting and then in architecture. Worked in Pesaro, Italy, 1511-14; worked in Rome at Vatican workshop under Donato Bramante, Raphael and Baldassare Peruzzi, 1514-27; after the Sack of Rome, moved to Venice in 1527, where he worked independently as an architect and painter, and printed his books; moved to France in 1541, and was appointed consultant for architecture and decoration of the palace at Fontainebleau.

Chronology of Works
All in France unless noted
† *Work no longer exists*

1537-38	Villa Trissino, Cricoli, Vicenza, Italy (remodeling)†
1541-47	Merchants Square, Lyons†
1541-47	Stock Exchange, Lyons†
1541-47	Salle du Bal, Fontainebleau (completed by Philibert de l'Orme in 1548)
1541-48	Castle, Rosmarino†
1541-48	Grand Ferrare, Fontainebleau†
1541-50	Castle of Ancy-le-Franc, Burgundy

Publications

BOOKS BY SERLIO

Tutte l'opere d'architettura. First complete edition, Venice, 1584. Reprint: Ridgewood, New Jersey, 1964.

BOOKS ABOUT SERLIO

AMORINI, ANTONIO BOLOGINI: *Elogio di Sebastiano Serlio: Architetto Bolognese.* Bologna, 1823.
CHARVET, LEON: *Sebastiano Serlio, 1475-1554.* Lyons, 1869.
HOWARD, DEBORAH: *The Architectural History of Venice.* New York, 1981.
ROSCI, M.: *Il Trattato di Architettura di Sebastiano Serlio.* Milan, 1966.
ROSENFELD, MYRA NAN: *Sebastiano Serlio on Domestic Architecture.* New York and Cambridge, Massachusetts, 1979.

Sebastiano Serlio: Castle of Ancy-le-Franc, Burgundy, France, 1541-50

ARTICLES ABOUT SERLIO

ARGAN, GIULIO CARLO: "Sebastiano Serlio." *Arte* (1932): 183-199.

CARUNCHIO, T.: "Dal VII libro di S. Serlio 'XXIII case per edificare nella villa'." *Quaderni dell'Istituto di Storia dell'Architettura* 22 (1976).

DINSMOOR, WILLIAM BELL: "The Literary Remains of Sebastiano Serlio." *Art Bulletin* 24 (June 1942): 55-91, 115-154.

GOLSON, LUCILE: "Serlio, Primaticcio and the Architectural Grotto." *Gazette des beaux-arts* 27:96-107.

McKEAN, JOHN M.: "An Introduction to Sebastiano Serlio." *Architectural Association Quarterly* 11, No. 4 (1979).

OLIVATO, L.: "Per il Serlio a Venezia. Documenti nuovi e documenti rivisitati." *Arte Veneta* (1971): 284-291.

ROSCI, M.: "Sebastiano Serlio e il Manierismo nel Veneto." *Bollettino del Centro Internazionale di Studi Andrea* (1967): 330-336.

WILINSKI, S.: "Sebastiano Serlio." *Bollettino del Centro Internazionale di Studi Andrea* (1965): 103-114.

*

Sebastiano Serlio, a primary source in both the scholarship and practice of architecture, is best known through his systematic masterwork *L'Architettura*. The son of a Bolognese ornamental painter and scene designer, he trained as a painter and became an architect. His father Bartolomeo's instruction—especially in perspective—was invaluable in the multidisciplined artistic field from which architecture emerged as a distinct profession. Serlio was critical to that transformation.

Contemporaries whom Serlio knew well—Michelangelo (1475-1564), Baldassare Peruzzi (1481-1536), Raphael (1483-1520) and Giulio Romano (1492-1546)—were also trained first as painters, as had been the previous generation of Bramante (1444-1514) and Leonardo (1452-1519). Perspective was among their distinctive skills.

Perspective was that technical invention of presentation of the Early Renaissance that characterized the new humanist view of man in the world. As in Serlio's stage set designs, the physical world could be rationalized when its appearance was fixed from a prescribed static viewpoint. The perception was of a coherent and harmonious universe understood through informed intelligence. Serlio codified that intelligence in *L'Architettura* as definitely as its powerful singular title.

Serlio moved to Pesaro in 1511, then worked in Rome from about 1514 until the Sack in 1527. There Peruzzi was his acknowledged master. Serlio was his heir, and some of Peruzzi's drawings illustrated his books. By 1528 Serlio was in Venice, a place most critical to his publication ambitions. In 1541, at the age of 64 with a young family, he moved to France and practiced, wrote and published under the patronage of François I, who died in 1547. Serlio died in Fountainebleau penniless and broken, his major dream, *L'Architettura*, incomplete with only five of the projected seven books published. But he pioneered international practice and brought the systematization of Renaissance architecture to Europe.

The master plan for *L'Architettura* was included in the publication of Book 4 in 1537, the first to appear. Serlio proposed the first comprehensive definition of the field of architecture, a modern and practical counterpart to Vitruvius. Because printing and publishing in any field was still a new invention, Serlio issued the parts as they were ready and as he could find sponsors, accounting for the books' complex publication history. After the 1521 illustrated Como edition of Vitruvius, Serlio's Book 4 was the first book on architecture to be in a living vernacular language. Like the prior landmark, Serlio in his smaller format also designed handsome pages. Title pages were often brilliantly inventive. But by going beyond discourse, Serlio invented a new kind of architecture book and pioneered the illustrated book for all fields. Copious woodcuts communicated the message graphically, often using numbered sequences and sets of illustrations. Text was supportive to visual information. Often text did not fill the space opposite a full-page illustration. Discourse was subordinate to demonstration.

Serlio's familiarity with both construction and buildings made his understandable publications both practical and popular. They became the reference standard for beginning any library in the field. Thomas Jefferson owned the posthumous 1575 edition of Book 7, with its parallel texts in Latin and Italian. Serlio's treatise was a cosmopolitan best seller, with original or pirated editions also in French, Flemish and English. His was the first book on architecture in German. By favorably including medieval and Roman practices as well as regional variants, he expanded the Italian definition of current humanist theory as represented in Leon Battista Alberti. He thus confirmed the discipline as a living and vital profession, not just an academic or philosophic study. Serlio avoided both pedantic idealism and medieval fumbling with his austerity and directness. He provided a documentary clarity that made Renaissance architecture accessible internationally while allowing for local interpretation.

His own life and practice were less accomplished. From what little we know, there was some quirk of personality that kept him from getting major commissions and from settling productively in one place. Serlio married late in life, argued with his clients, and became embittered from professional disappointments. Yet he was often vitally close to the center of architectural events. Through persistence and mobility, he capitalized his ambition in illustrated books that were professionally convincing, rich in content and diverse in origin. In Rome he had worked in the Vatican studio. In Venice in 1533 he designed a timber ceiling for the library of San Marco. In 1534 he participated in the debate on proportions to alter Jacopo Sansovino's design for the church of San Francesco della Vigna, although harmonic proportioning was absent from his commitments in his books. In 1539 for Vicenza, Serlio teamed with Giulio Romano and Michele Sanmicheli in the design competition to renovate the Basilica. What was built by the winner, Andrea Palladio, was very similar to the Serlio project illustrated in Book 4.

Serlio's acknowledged buildings were not without their own merit, although only a few survive. More interesting is how they too became prototypical or provided linkages in the invention of the new age and in the transfer of powerful ideas. Thus if Serlio advised Giangiorgio Tressino on rebuilding his villa at Cricoli, Vicenza (1537-38), the connections to Palladio are multiplied. Serlio's château near Ancy-le-Franc (1541-50), while too Italian in its *maniera antica* for French tastes, became a modernizing model with the clarity of its smooth-faced courtyard and the regularity of the square corner towers. Serlio's Grand Ferrare (1541-48, destroyed) became the prototype for the urban hotel or French town house, with its main block and wings defining a gated courtyard.

Serlio's reputation has escalated recently with the publications of his missing Book 6, *On Domestic Architecture*, from a Munich manuscript in facsimile in Milan 1967, and of the Avery Library manuscript with analyses by Rosenfeld in 1978. Serlio provided four types of rural dwelling and five urban types, each with variations, "from the meanest hovel to the most ornate palace." His concern with the design of housing related to the spectrum of economic and social classes. Thus he assumed a modern sense of responsibility for the accommodation of the poor and working classes, as well as those moneyed or noble.

With Book 4 in 1537 Serlio codified the five orders and the appropriate embellishment of surfaces. With Book 3 in 1540 he illustrated the Roman antiquities and their modern counterparts with Bramante, Raphael and Peruzzi. It included results of a long journey through Istria, Dalmatia and Umbria, as well as his time in Rome. Serlio's dimensioned drawings were accepted as definitive until the publication of accurately measured surveys by Desgodez in 1682. Books 1 and 2 were published together in 1545 and included geometry, optics and perspective. They concluded with the author's wooden theater for the Porto palaces at Vicenza and with the celebrated three stage settings with their deep one-point perspective: the images of comedy and tragedy as urbane, and satire as rustic were environmental fixes that directed the evolution of Renaissance theatrical literature as well as architecture. With Book 5 in 1547 Serlio described temples and churches. Their centralized plans were influential for generations. Although called Book 6, the 1551 publication of *Libre Extraordinaire* with 50 woodcuts on the construction of doorways, with a preference for heavy Doric orders and rusticated stonework, was indeed an *extra*. In particular it became a copy book for outlandish ornamental and manneristic details in England and France, often inserted into conventional buildings.

Thus even without the original book on habitation, Serlio had within his productive lifetime published a prototypical curriculum and vast repository. He initiated the great convention of exposition followed by Palladio, Scamozzi, Vignola and a succession of comprehensive authorities that was essentially unbroken until the 20th century. All continued to expand the thesis that design solutions correctly evolve from prototype and precedent based ultimately on classical architecture, as modified by sensitivity to local conditions. In Britain and the former colonies, Serlio's writings influenced the lineage through Palladio to Inigo Jones, Christopher Wren, Colen Campbell and the earl of Burlington to 18th-century Palladianism. Internationally Serlio also pioneered that union of practice and publication that has celebrated and promoted every leading architect through to our own time.

—JEFFREY COOK

SERT, Josep Lluís.

Spanish. Born in Barcelona, Spain, 1 July 1902. Died in Barcelona, 15 March 1983. Married Ramona Longás, 1938; one daughter. Studied at the Escuela Superior de Arquitectura, Barcelona, M.Arch, 1929. Worked in Le Corbusier and Pierre Jeanneret office, Paris, France, 1929-30; established own office, Barcelona, 1929-37, then worked in Paris, 1937-39; partnership with Paul Lester Wiener and Paul Schulz in Town Planning Associates, New York City, 1939-57; private practice, Cambridge, Massachusetts, 1957-58; partnership with Huson Jackson and Ronald Gourley in Sert, Jackson and Gourley, Cambridge, Massachusetts, 1963-1983. Professor of architecture and dean of the Graduate School of Design, Harvard University, Cambridge, Massachusetts, 1953-69 (emeritus 1969-83). President, CIAM (Congrès Internationaux d'Architecture Moderne), 1947-56. Fellow, American Institute of Architects; Gold Medal, Académie d'Architecture, Paris, 1975; Gold Medal, American

Josep Lluís Sert: Peabody Terrace for Married Students, Harvard University, Cambridge, Massachusetts, 1963-65

Institute of Architects, 1981; Gold Medal, St ate Government of Catalunya, Spain, 1981.

Chronology of Works

1931	Apartment House, Calle Muntaner, Barcelona, Spain
1933	Master Plan, Barcelona, Spain (with others)
1934	Casa Bloc, Paseo Torras y Bages, Barcelona, Spain (low-rent apartments; with others)
1937	Spanish Pavilion, World's Fair, Paris, France (with Luis Lacasa)
1945	Motor City Plan, Brazil
1949	Plan for Medellin, Colombia
1951	Plan for Bogotá, Colombia (with Le Corbusier)
1955	Studio for Joan Miró, Palma, Majorca
1955	Presidential Palace, Havana, Cuba
1955	United States Embassy, Baghdad, Iraq
1958	Center for the Study of World Religions, Boston, Massachusetts, U.S.A.
1958	Health and Administration Headquarters, Boston, Massachusetts, U.S.A.
1959	Museum of Contemporary Art, St. Paul de Vence, France (with others)
1960	Boston University Buildings, Boston, Massachusetts, U.S.A. (with others)
1963-65	Peabody Terrace for Married Students, Harvard University, Cambridge, Massachusetts, U.S.A.
1966	Martin Luther King Elementary School, Cambridge, Massachusetts, U.S.A.
1969	Carmelite Convent Carmel de la Paix, Cluny, France
1970	Undergraduate Science Center, Harvard University, Cambridge, Massachusetts, U.S.A.
1972-75	Joan Miró Center for the Study of Contemporary Art, Barcelona, Spain (with others)
1974	Les Escales Park Housing, Barcelona, Spain (with others)
1977	Cultural Center and Offices, Barcelona, Spain

Publications

BOOKS BY SERT

Solutions. Cambridge, Massachusetts, and London, 1942.
The Heart of the City: Towards the Humanisation of Urban Life (ed.). With Jaqueline Tyrwhitt and Ernesto Nathan Rogers. New York and London, 1952.
The Shape of Our Cities (ed.). With Jaqueline Tyrwhitt. Cambridge, Massachusetts, 1957.
"The Architect and the City." In H. WARREN DUNHAM (ed.): *The City in Mid-Century.* Detroit, 1957.
Cripta de la Colonia Güell de Antoni Gaudí. Barcelona, 1969.

ARTICLES BY SERT

"The Changing Philosophy of Architecture." *Architectural Record* 116 (August 1954).
"Architecture and the Visual Arts." *Harvard Foundation for Advanced Study and Research Newsletter* (31 December 1954).
"What Became of CIAM?" With Walter Gropius, Le Corbusier and Sigfried Giedion. *Architectural Review* (March 1961).
"Remembering Le Corbusier." *American Institute of Architects Journal* (November 1965).
"Sert: Obras y proyectos 1929-1973." *Cuadernos de arquitectura y urbanismo* 93 (special issue, 1972).
"Below the Alhambra." With Frank Woods. *Architectural Review* (March 1980).
"The Lucid Vanguard." *Quaderna* (May/June 1982).

BOOKS ABOUT SERT

BASTLUND, KNUD (ed.): *José Luis Sert: Architecture, City Planning, Urban Design.* New York, 1966.
BORRAS, MARIA LLUISA (ed.): *Sert: Mediterranean Architecture.* Barcelona and Paris, 1974.
FREIXA, JAUME: *Josep L. Sert.* Barcelona, 1979.
ZEVI, BRUNO: *Sert's Architecture in the Miró Foundation.* Barcelona, 1976.

ARTICLES ABOUT SERT

ANDERSON, STANFORD: "Sert's Concept of Living." *Architectural Design* (August 1965).
BOHIGAS, ORIOL: "Jose Lluis Sert—Persevere and Criticise." *Casabella* (July/August 1983).
CAMPBELL, ROBERT: "Homage to a Catalonian." *American Institute of Architects Journal* (February 1981).
DEAN, ANDREA O.: "The Urbane and Varied Buildings of Sert, Jackson and Associates." *American Institute of Architects Journal* 66 (May 1977): 50-58.
DONATO, EMILIO: "In Memoriam: Jose Lluis Sert's House at Harvard." *Arquitectura* (March/April 1983).
DULAC, MARIE: "Towards a Housing Manifesto." *Architecte* (June 1976).
FERRER, DAVID: "The Last Works of J. L. Sert in Barcelona." *Arquitectura* (March 1975).
HALE, JONATHAN: "Ten Years Past at Peabody Terrace." *Progressive Architecture* (October 1974).

JOLY, PIERRE: "Miró and Sert in Barcelona." *Oeil* (September 1975).

"Jose Lluis Sert, 1.7.1902-15.3.1983." *Q* (special issue, April 1983).

MACKAY, DAVID: "Sert for Miró." *Architectural Review* (July 1976).

MAKI, FUMIHIKO, et al.: "Josep Lluis Sert." *Process: Architecture* (special issue, December 1982).

MURRAY, PETER: "A Certain Feeling: Interview with J. L. Sert." *Building Design* (23 May 1975).

SCHMERTZ, MILDRED F.: "Hommage to Catalonia—Fundación Joan Miró." *Architectural Record* (March 1977).

"Sert: Works and Projects 1929-1973." *Cuadernos de arquitectura* (special issue, November/December 1972).

VON MOLTKE, WILLO: "Jose Lluis Sert 1902-1983." *Progressive Architecture* (June 1983).

*

Josep Lluis Sert, a native of Barcelona, emigrated to the United States in 1939, after practicing in Spain and working with Le Corbusier and Pierre Jeanneret in France prior to World War II. He was responsible for organizing the first group of architects with the Congrès Internationaux d'Architecture Moderne (CIAM) in Barcelona, serving as one of the leading proponents of architecture in city planning. Sert played a significant role in the development of new planning theories in the Modern Movement through his writings, speeches, practice and teaching.

Between 1941 and 1958, in association with Paul Lester Wiener and Paul Schultz, he undertook commissions to develop plans for Havana and Varadero, Cuba; Bogotá, Cali, Medellin and Tumaco, Colombia; Chimbota and Lima, Peru; and Brazil Motor City, near Rio de Janeiro. From 1947 until 1956 he served as president of CIAM, was appointed dean of the faculty and professor of architecture at the Harvard Graduate School of Design in 1953, and opened his Cambridge, Massachusetts, practice in 1955. His writings are extensive.

Sert's architectural concepts were closely affiliated with the integration of the urban environment, fostering strong interaction among the urban designer, the city planner, the artist and the architect. His writing and his urban design applications placed emphasis on the public spaces, the arts, human scale, accessibility, major movement routes, and the treatment of the concept of privacy and community. Sert fostered the principles of form and space, juncture of forms, animation of architecture with natural light, and insisted on the treatment of maintaining human scale. Architecture, according to Sert, is to provide exciting interior and exterior spaces, using the arts, people and furnishings to integrate bold color and excitement within space.

Sert's practice most appropriately followed his concepts of modern architecture. His schooling and participation in the arts and architecture endowed him with a thorough knowledge of the genius of past masters. He shared this knowledge with the most sophisticated artists of the 20th century. His associations with Le Corbusier, Walter Gropius, Joan Miró, Georges Braque, and other leading architects and artists of the times offered the opportunities to associate with the finest talents of the Western world. His work furthered the principles of the atrium house, new concepts in privacy and open space in density housing, and a search for new orders in form, mass and space in architecture.

Sert's leadership as dean of faculty of the Graduate School of Design enabled him to introduce new directions in curriculum development, integrating architecture, the arts, landscape architecture and urban design. The pedagogic process was pursued through actual urban and architectural problem-solving approaches, and he invited visiting faculty from the international scene to stimulate new and innovative thought in these disciplines.

His establishment of the curriculum, along with the selection of the faculty and his collaboration with Le Corbusier for the design and construction of the Carpenter Center for the Visual Arts within the School of Design, was an innovative catalyst in focusing on the integration of the arts and architecture. He introduced the first program in urban design in the Graduate School of Design, incorporating graduate faculty and students in the planning, architecture and landscape architecture disciplines.

Sert's architectural practice was a direct response to his theories of integration of the arts in public spaces, treatment of architecture with a spirit of light and space, clear definitions of form and their massing. During his residence in the United States, he continued his work as an international practice, designing and overseeing the construction of new orders, forms and the treatment of space and light in architecture. Sert was one of the few architects who maintained a truly international practice, incorporating his cosmopolitan background in Europe and the Americas. This capacity reflected positively on his leadership of the Graduate School of Design through his contacts and his abilities to attract a highly qualified international faculty.

The important buildings he produced include the United States Embassy in Baghdad and, at Harvard, the Center for World Religions, Holyoke Center, Peabody Terrace for Married Students, Carpenter Center for the Visual Arts (with Le Corbusier as supervisory architect) and Undergraduate Science Center. Other works in the United States are the New England Gas and Electric Association Headquarters, and Martin Luther King Elementary School, both in Cambridge, Massachusetts; Charles River Campus for Boston University in Boston; and the urban renewal plan for the central business district of Worcester, Massachusetts. In Canada, he designed the Dormitory, Library, Dining and Activity Center at Guelph University, Ontario. His European work included the Museum of Contemporary Art for the Maeght Foundation and the residence for Georges Braque, both in Saint-Paul-de-Vence, France; six houses, Punta Martinet, Ibiza, Spain; Carmelite Convent, Carme de la Paix, Mazille, France; master plan for a resort community on the Friol Islands, Marseille, France; Fundación Joan Miró Study of Contemporary Art, Montjuich Park, Barcelona; Studio for Joan Miró, Palma, Mallorca; Les Escales Park Housing and Caixa d'Estalvis de Catalunya, both in Barcelona.

—GORDON ECHOLS

SHAW, Richard Norman.

British. Born in Edinburgh, Scotland, 1831. Died in Hampstead, London, 17 November 1912. Educated in Edinburgh; attended Royal Academy Schools. Articled to William Burn, London, ca. 1849; won Royal Academy Gold Medal, which allowed him to travel to Belgium, France, Germany and Italy for two years; worked for Anthony Salvin; assistant to G. E. Street, 1858; partnership with W. Eden Nesfield, 1866-68. Gold Medal, Royal Institute of British Architects; member, Royal Academy, 1877. Refused knighthood.

Chronology of Works

All in England unless noted
† *Work no longer exists*

1866-68	Holy Trinity Church, Bingley, Yorkshire
1866-68	Glen Andred, Groombridge, Sussex
1866-69	Leyswood House, Groombridge, Sussex (partly †)
1867-69	English Church, Lyons, France†
1870	Village School, Church Preen, Shropshire
1870-71	West Wickham House, London (remodeling)
1870-72	Grims Dyke, Harrow Weald, London
1870-85	Cragside, Rothbury, Northumberland
1871-73	New Zealand Chambers, Leadenhall Street, London†
1873-75	Lowther Lodge, Kensington Gore, London
1874-76	Convent of Bethany, Hampshire
1874-76	196 Queen's Gate, London
1875-76	8 Melbury Road, London
1875-76	6 Ellerdale Road, London
1875-77	Old Swan House, 17 Chelsea Embankment, London
1876-78	Pierrepoint, Frensham, Surrey
1876-81	Adcote, Shropshire
1877-80	Work including 24-35 Woodstock Road and Tabard Inn, Bedford Park, London
1878-79	St. Margaret's Church, Ilkley, Yorkshire
1878-83	Flete, Devon
1879-82	St. Michael and All Angels Church, Bedford Park, London
1879-83	Greenham Lodge, Greenham, Berkshire
1879-86	Albert Hall Mansions, Kensington Gore, London
1880-81	Barings Bank, London†
1882-86	Dawpool, Cheshire†
1881-83	Alliance Assurance Offices, London
1883-85	Bolney House, London
1884-85	180 Queen's Gate, London†
1884-85	39 Frognal, London
1884-86	Banstead Wood, Banstead, Surrey
1885-87	All Saints Church, Leek, Staffordshire
1887-89	Holy Trinity Church, Latimer Road, London
1887-1907	New Scotland Yard, London
1888-90	170 Queen's Gate, London
1889-94	Bryanston, Dorset
1890-93	All Saints Church, Richards Castle, Shropshire
1894-95	All Saints Church, Galley Hill, Swanscombe, Kent
1895-98	White Star Offices, 30 James Street, Liverpool (with J. Francis Doyle)
1898-1901	Parr's Bank, Liverpool
1905-08	Piccadilly Hotel, Piccadilly Circus, London

Publications

BOOKS BY SHAW

Architectural Sketches from the Continent. London, 1858.
Sketches for Cottages. With M. B. Adams. London, 1878.
Architecture: A Profession or an Art? Thirteen Short Essays on the Qualifications and Training of Architects (ed., with T. G. Jackson). London, 1892.

BOOKS ABOUT SHAW

BLOMFIELD, REGINALD T.: *Richard Norman Shaw R. A., Architect, 1831-1912.* London, 1940.
DIXON, ROGER, and MUTHESIUS, STEFAN: *Victorian Architecture.* New York and Toronto, 1978.

GIROUARD, MARK: *The Victorian Country House.* New Haven, Connecticut, and London, 1979.
LETHABY, W. R.: *Philip Webb and His Work.* London, 1935.
PETER FERRIDAY (ed.): *Victorian Architecture.* London, 1963.
RICHARDSON, MARGARET: *The Craft Architects.* London, 1983.
SAINT, ANDREW: *Richard Norman Shaw.* New Haven, Connecticut, and London, 1976.
SERVICE, ALASTAIR: *The Architects of London.* London, 1979.

ARTICLES ABOUT SHAW

BRANDON-JONES, JOHN: "The Work of Philip Webb and Norman Shaw." *Architectural Association Journal* 71 (June 1955): 9-21; (July-August 1955): 40-47.
HALBRITTER, N.: "Norman Shaw's London Houses." *Architectural Association Quarterly* 7, No. 1 (1975): 3-19.
PEVSNER, NIKOLAUS: "Richard Norman Shaw: 1831-1912." *Architectural Review* (March 1941): 41-46.
SAINT, ANDREW: "Norman Shaw's Letters: A Selection." *Architectural History* 18 (1975): 60-85.

Richard Norman Shaw was the most influential and successful of all Late Victorian architects in Great Britain; his career dominated the period from 1875 to 1901. Yet analysis of his work does not reveal a talent comparable to that of John Soane or K. F. Schinkel or H. H. Richardson. His work, instead, reflects the uncertainties of the last decades of the 19th century.

Shaw was apprenticed to the noted country house architect William Burn, and was employed by G. E. Street, one of the greatest of the High Victorians. He shared an office with Eden Nesfield from 1835 to 1888, and was briefly his partner. Shaw worked in many different styles during his 35-year career. He began as a High Victorian Goth; the church at Bingley is typical of his early work. His last work, the Piccadilly Hotel in London, is Edwardian Baroque. Together with Nesfield, he pioneered both the Old English and Queen Anne styles of architecture in the late 1860s and early 1870s. Shaw's reputation overshadows that of Nesfield, but both were gifted architects, and it is difficult to say who contributed what to their practice and to the development of these two new architectural styles.

The Old English style of Shaw's early career is a picturesque vernacular style. Shaw based his Old English style on the houses of the Weald of Sussex, with their tall brick chimneys, tile-hanging, and mullioned windows with leaded lights. Shaw's Old English houses featured skillfully composed horizontal forms contrasted with attenuated vertical chimneystacks; they were longer and lower than High Victorian houses. Invariably, numerous gables played against expanses of steeply pitched roof, and solid wall areas contrasted dramatically with areas having extensive fenestration. Most of his country houses contained revived medieval great halls used for various functions, especially for summer sitting rooms. (These great halls marked the beginning of a movement away from the High Victorian practice of providing a sealed-off room for every conceivable function toward more open planning.) His country house plans were additive; Shaw rarely subdivided large simple forms; he preferred instead to build a composition by aggregating elements, as one would build a block house. The great charm of his Old English houses lay more in the variety of spaces they contained than in their picturesque massing; spaces differed greatly in lighting, height, level and shape.

Old English style designers were backward-looking for social and aesthetic reasons, rather than for religious reasons as the neo-Goths had been. This shift in attitude made all preindustrial societies equally attractive as mines for decorative motifs and forms; ideas were borrowed from the whole English vernacular tradition, plus Japan, Greece and Italy. And the style was used for country houses and village schools as well as for churches. A good example of the Old English style applied to school design is Shaw's Church Preen School, Shropshire (1870). In it, tall windows rise into the roof zone as dormers, gables are timber-framed, and the tall brick chimney adds an important vertical accent to the asymmetrical composition.

Leyswood House, Sussex (1866) was Shaw's first important country-house commission. It was designed for the managing director of his brother's shipping line in Shaw's early Old English country house style. It was described at the time as "quaint," but it was also comfortable and convenient. It did not follow the prevailing pattern of a tall block with a lower service block to one side, surrounded by gardens and terraces. It had no garden and was placed on the edge of a ridge in the middle of a wood. Its composition involved the skillful mix of forms of different sizes and heights that made varied references to past styles; it incorporated Gothic arches, Tudor windows, 17th-century chimneystacks, half-timbering and tile-hanging. An inglenook was made a feature of the dining room. Its plan included rooms of different heights at different levels arranged in a compactly planned courtyard scheme. The result was a sophisticated, picturesque ensemble with gabled roofs, varied fenestration and tall chimneys. Much of it was sham—the half-timbering, for example, was applied over brickwork—but it was certainly visually pleasing. Its long banks of casement windows are the prototype for the ribbon windows of architects from C. F. A. Voysey on, and its great mullioned bays are true window-walls. Picturesque entry to the court occurred through an entry-tower portal that suggested and framed the entry of the house proper.

Cragside, Northumberland (1870-1885), is Shaw's most dramatic Old English house. Its design follows the Leyswood formula, but greatly enlarged. It is dramatically sited on a ledge toward the top of a steep hill above a ravine, and is approached by way of a long, winding drive through a forest. The house appears dramatically at the last moment. It has the aspect of a fortified village seen against the forest green; it also seems to be composed of a prodigious variety of gabled and crenellated towers, some with half-timbered gables. Like Leyswood, it appears to have been built by accretion. It has a strange, rambling plan that escalated over a period of a decade-and-a-half from its beginning as a small hunting lodge. The owner's expertise in hydraulics led to Cragside being the most advanced house of its time. Electric light, central heating, telephone communication from room to room, and all manner of hydraulic equipment made the house conveniently avant-garde.

Shaw's Old English style evolved into a weightier, more sober, more sophisticated style in four large country houses designed in the late 1870s—Pierrepont, Adcote, Flete and Greenham. These were important houses; the quaintness of the earlier Old English houses was not appropriate. These houses were the most masterful of Shaw's designs. They appear to be country houses that were added to over several periods, but sensitively, not haphazardly. In their taut and controlled organizations, Shaw played compositional games.

At the entrance front at Adcote, the best of the lot, he played four fenestration bays against a three-gabled facade. The plan of the main portion of the house is composed of four interlocking units. Sober stonework is relieved not with half-timbering or tile-hanging, but only with the brickwork of the chimneys, which melts into the stonework of the gables below. The house's

interior features the same powerful stonework used on the exterior. Spaces of different sizes and shapes open up to either side of the axial path through the house from the entry, under the screen at the end of the hall, past the stair, to a vestibule that serves the drawing room, dining room and library. However, there is a coldness about Adcote that the earlier houses did not have.

The other style associated with Shaw, the Queen Anne style, is a classical style without classical laws of proportion and composition. Its "freestyle" features need have no meaning; they do not express structure or composition; they are ornamental only. Shaw preferred to use the Queen Anne style in town and the Old English style in the country. The essence of the Queen Anne style is the combination of Gothic Revival composition, free planning and asymmetry, with design detail drawn from English and Dutch 17th- and 18th-century red-brick architecture. Shaw pioneered the style in two modest houses of the late 1860s—West Wickham House and Banstead Wood. He never built a large country house in the style; he left that for Nesfield. The style was most popular for domestic use, both in town and in the country, although it was also used for smaller commercial buildings. One of the most famous of Shaw's Queen Anne commercial buildings is the New Zealand Chambers (1871-73). Its large, ornate oriel windows were borrowed from the 17th-century Sparrowe's House in Ipswich.

Shaw's Queen Anne houses feature red brick, tile roofs, asymmetrically placed bay windows and gables, sash windows with a multitude of small panes, gabled roofs, white trim and rubbed brickwork. Their classical detail was borrowed from late Elizabethan and 17th-century examples. Lowther Lodge (1873-75), now the Royal Geographical Society headquarters, is a notable early example of a house in this style. Its decorative vocabulary is Late Stuart, yet the romantically complex character of Shaw's Old English country houses is retained in its composition of many gables, two tall bay windows, numerous dormers and tall, fluted chimneystacks. It seems to be a country house come to town; it is a large Queen Anne house on an open site in London. An Aesthetic note is the sunflower motif carved into the brickwork.

Lowther Lodge is transitional; it is not fully Shaw's urbane Queen Anne style, because it retains the artful asymmetries characteristic of his Old English country houses. Its primary facade is basically symmetrical—the house is U-shaped around a courtyard—except that its entrance is in the right wing, and the left wing engages a subsidiary stable wing and has a tall chimney growing out of its gable. In contrast, the garden front is extremely asymmetrical. The house is constructed of special 2-inch gauged and cut brick with no stone dressings at all.

The Old Swan House (1875-77), on the Chelsea Embankment, is an outstanding example of a "Shavian" Queen Anne town house—pretty, urbane, built of red brick with white woodwork. It uses Stuart detail in a non-Stuart composition. It is atypical in its severe symmetry, and its window treatment is unique. On the ground floor are simple sash windows; the *piano nobile* features three oriel windows; the tall third story has very tall and thin windows of alternating flat and projecting design; the fourth floor returns to simple sash windows, but larger than those of the ground story; and there are three dormers projecting above the roof eave. The vertical composition is as follows: 7 bays, 3 bays, 7 bays, 7 bays, 3 bays. The second floor projects out past the first, and the third out past the second. These projections make the delicate oriels seem to be supporting the heavy masonry mass of the third story; they were possible only through the use of iron girders.

Many of Shaw's most charming Queen Anne designs are found in Bedford Park, a new London suburb begun by the speculative land developer Jonathan Carr in 1875. Bedford Park was a wealthy suburb that became the monument of the Aesthetic Movement. The Queen Anne style was chosen because it was considered to express the Aesthetic rejection of the showy and the vulgar. Shaw designed for it a church, an inn, a large house for Carr and numerous Queen Anne houses. These are mainly red brick and two stories with attics but no basements, in a mixture of detached, semidetached and terrace houses.

Shaw's Bedford Park church—St. Michael and All Angels—is a mixture of Gothic and vernacular Renaissance; his other churches are more typically Gothic, except that Shaw preferred rough wall surfaces, blunt outlines and stumpy vertical accents to the vertical linearity favored by other Late Victorian architects working in the Gothic mode.

Although he borrowed forms and details from historical styles, Shaw was quick to utilize technological advances in materials and construction techniques. He often used concealed iron joists and stanchions of iron or Bessemer steel, products which made possible the top-heavy urban facades of his Queen Anne buildings, and the planning of upper stories independent of the layout of stories below. He embraced electric lighting enthusiastically; Cragside of 1880 and the Savoy Theatre of 1881 were both lighted electrically.

Shaw always preferred the eclectic to the scholarly, the vernacular to high style. Although his fame is associated with domestic work, in his late career he designed a number of public buildings—including Albert Hall Mansions, the first really distinguished block of apartments built in London, and the New Scotland Yard for the Metropolitan Police—many in Edwardian neo-Baroque style. Shaw's country houses after 1890 became dramatically classical, losing the free classical quality that had characterized his Queen Anne houses.

—C. MURRAY SMART, JR.

SHCHUSEV, Aleksei V.

Russian. Born in Kishinev, Russia, 1873. Died in 1949. Studied at the Academy of Art, St. Petersburg; won scholarships to travel in Russia, 1894, and abroad, 1897-98. Headed (with Ivan V. Zholtovsky) the architecture studio of Mossovet, 1918-21; taught at the Higher State Art and Technical Studios, Moscow, 1918-24; headed urban design studio, 1921-23; president of Moscow Architectural Association, 1921-29; directed Tretiakov Gallery, 1926-29.

Chronology of Works
All in Russia unless noted
† *Work no longer exists*

1908-12	Church-Museum, Natalevka
1908-12	Troitskiy Cathedral, Pochaevskaya Monastery
1913-14	Russian Pavilion, 11th International Exhibition, Venice, Italy†
1912-48	Kazan Railroad Terminal, Moscow
1918-23	Master Plan for Moscow (with Ivan V. Zholtovsky)
1924	Lenin's Temporary Mausoleum and Lenin's First Mausoleum, Moscow†
1925-27	Master Plan for Tuapse (with Leonid A. Vesnin and A. C. Mukhin)
1926-27	Master Plan for Smolensk
1927-28	Sanatorium, Matsest
1928-30	Narkomzem, Moscow (now the Ministry of Agriculture)
1929-30	Lenin's Permanent Mausoleum, Moscow

1930-34	Military-Transportation Academy, Moscow
1930-35	Hotel Moskva, Moscow (with L. I. Savel'ev and O. A. Stapran)
1933-38	Institute Marx-Engels-Lenin, Tbilisi, Georgia
1933-40	Opera, Tashkent
1933-47	Alisher Navoi Theater, Tashkent, Uzbek
1935-39	Institute for Genetics for the Academy of Science of the Union of Soviet Socialist Republics, Moscow
1945-52	Komsomolskaya Subway Station, Moscow
1946-48	Administrative Building, Dzerzhinskii Square, Moscow

Publications

BOOKS BY SHCHUSEV

Arkhitektura i stroitel'stvo Instituta Marksa-Engelsa-Lenina v Thilisi. Moscow, 1940.

ARTICLES BY SHCHUSEV

"Restavratsiya i raskopka fudamentov tserkvi sv. Vasiliya v Ovruche." *Starye gody* 11 (1905): 132-133.
"Stroitelstvo vystavki." *Stroitelnaia promyshlennost* 2 (1923): 5-7.
"Moskva budushchego." *Krasnaya Niva* 17 (1924): 414-418.
"Proekt vremennogo mavzolea na mogile Vladimira Ilicha Lenina." *Stroitelnaia promyshlennost* 4 (1924): 235.
"Zadacha sovremennoy arkhitektury." *Stroitel'naya promyshlennost* 12 (1924): 760-762.
"Proekt gostnisy v Matseste." *Sovremennaya arkhitektura* 3 (1927): 98-99.
"K voprosu o monumental'nom iskusstve." *Iskusstvo* 4 (1934): 2-20.
"Gostnitsa 'Moskva'." *Stroitel'stvo Moskvy* 17/18 (1935): 3-8.
"Tvorcheskie otchety." *Arkhitektura SSSR* 4 (1935): 45-48.
"Chto my sozdali, chego nam nekhvataet." *Arkhitektura SSSR* 6 (1937): 22-23.
"General'nyy plan Novgorda." With V.A. Lavrov. *Arkhitektura i stroitel'stv* 5 (1946): 3-10.

BOOKS ABOUT SHCHUSEV

BABENCHIKOVA, M. V., and NESTEROVOI, N. M.: *Aleksei Viktorovich Shchusev.* Moscow, 1947.
DRUZHINA-GEORGIEVSKAIA, E. V., and KORNFELD, I. A.: *Zodchii A. V. Shchusev.* Moscow, 1955.
GRABAR, IGOR E.; AFANASEV, K. N.; and BACHINSKY, N. M.: *Proizvedeniia akademika A. V. Shchuseva udostoennye Stalinskoi premii.* Moscow, 1954.
KOPP, ANATOLE: *L'architecture de la période Stalinienne.* Grenoble, France, 1978.
SOKOLOV, N. B.: *A. V. Shchusev.* Moscow, 1952.
STROIANOV, N. N.: *Arkhitektura mavzoleia Lenina.* Moscow, 1950.

ARTICLES ABOUT SHCHUSEV

AFANASEV, K.: "Zodchiy A. V. Shchusev." *Arkhitektura SSSR* 8 (1967): 29-35.
ANTIPOV, I.: "Tvorchestvo A. V. Shchuseva." *Arkhitektura SSSR* 5 (1941): 29-34.
NOVIKOV, I.: "Traditsii natsionalnogo zodchestva v tvorchestve A. V. Shchuseva." *Arkhitektura SSSR* 5 (1953): 15-21.

Aleksei V. Shchusev: Hotel Moskva, Moscow, Russia, 1930-35

VELIKORETSKY, O.: "Aleksei Shchusev." *Sovetskaia arkhitektura*18 (1969): 68-71.

VLASOV, ALEKSANDR V.: "Nash put. Vsesoiuznoe soveshchanie sovetskikh arkhitektorov." *Arkhitektura SSSR* 6 (1937): 23-25.

*

The October Revolution of 1917 changed the social structure of Russia's czarist regime in a fundamental way. However, several established architects of the ancièn regime survived that political earthquake without major consequences. One of them was Aleksei V. Shchusev, who continued to rank as one of the prominent architects of the country. Proof of his standing is the number of commissions he received, many of which were also executed. Late in his career he created the Lenin Mausoleum, which, in political terms, was an important commission. In addition, Shchusev held several important positions, including his positions as chairman of Moscow's architectural union, MAO (1921-29), and as director of the Tretiakov Gallery (1926-29). In the 1930s and 1940s, he played a prominent role among Moscow architects. He even received the Stalin Prize in 1941. Shchusev was widely published, and promoted the establishment of an architectural museum. Such a museum was indeed built in Moscow, and bears his name.

His actual contribution to the development of architecture in the Soviet Union was modest. His most significant work, in terms of architectural history, was done before the Revolution. Although he was trained in the classical manner by L. N. Benoit, Shchusev later worked in the so-called "Russian style." Besides a few churches, he designed the Russian Pavilion for the Venice Biennale (1914) and the Kazan Railway Station in Moscow in

that style. The railway administration's 1910 competition for the Kazan Station, which Shchusev won, had made the Russian style a requirement for the projected building. The facade is a long, asymmetrical composition of different, independently articulated parts, which encompass the station's various functions. The details of the various architectural elements of the facade were designed in the spirit of the monuments along the railroad trajectory.

The Revolution did not hurt Shchusev's position. From 1918 he worked for the city of Moscow and was, among other things, commissioned to lead the reconstruction of the city (1918-23). He also played an important role in the Agricultural Exposition of 1923, for which he was the chief architect. The exhibition was dominated by architects of the previous regime: aside from Shchusev, Ivan Zholtovsky (1867-1959), Ivan Fomin (1872-1936) and Fedor Shekhtel (1859-1926) participated. It is interesting to note that Shchusev interceded on behalf of Konstantin Melnikov (1890-1974), making sure that the young architect would build the Tobacco Pavilion (Makhorka). He was disappointed by Melnikov's modernism, however.

After Lenin's death in 1924, the Communist Party leadership assigned the task of designing a mausoleum for Lenin to Shchusev. The project began as a provisional structure for the funeral, then developed into a semipermanent wooden structure (1924-29), and finally into the monument as we know it today. The starting point for the mausoleum was a stepped pyramid, a historically valued funerary form. The first version of the mausoleum was so elementary and lacking in ornamentation that it resembled a composition by the suprematist artist Kasimir Malevich. In the succeeding two versions, remaining entirely within the spirit of antique funerary architecture, the mausoleum was enlarged and crowned with a temple form. However, the absence of ornamentation gives the building a stark expressiveness.

After 1925, as modern architecture flowered in the Soviet Union, Shchusev reoriented himself. The Sanatorium in Matsest (1927) and the former Centrosoyous Building in Moscow (1928-33) illustrate Shchusev's move toward the modern. His winning entry in the competition for the Moscow Telegraph Administration is also noteworthy, but it was not realized. In this project and in others, Shchusev showed that he could also express himself in the language of modern forms. As early as 1929, however, he returned to a historicizing, neoclassical architectural style. The Hotel Moskva in Moscow (1930-35) is a good example of the later style: the design is characterized by an eclectic utilization of a classical idiom and by subdued exterior ornamentation combined with rich interior decoration. These are the hallmarks of Shchusev's architecture of the 1930s.

The change of the political climate in those years was actually only beneficial for Shchusev. His preference for historical sources of inspiration was supported by the cultural and political doctrine of social realism. In several of his projects, particularly the Opera in Tashkent (1933-40) and the Marx-Engels Institute in Tbilisi, Shchusev took his inspiration from local architectural traditions, achieving a kind of "social regionalism." At the end of the 1930s the prevalent "megalomania" became visible in his work too—he designed several large architectonic ensembles in a classical spirit. One of his last works was the Komsomolskaya Metro Station in Moscow (1945-52). In that project he was able to achieve the integration of architecture and the other arts, which had long been his ideal. The interior of the station, like a Rococo palace, is furnished with mosaics and stucco reliefs.

Striking in Shchusev's career was his ability to change course at the right moment, so that he always appeared "up to date." His adaptability was undoubtedly not free from a certain opportunism. Shchusev was politically moderate and rather played a patriarchal role in Soviet architecture, together with his colleague Zholtovsky. Objectively, Shchusev and a few of his old colleagues carried the line of prerevolutionary historicism through the 1920s into the epoch of social realism.

—OTAKAR MÁČEL

Translated from the German by Marijke Rijsberman

SHEKHTEL, Fedor.

Russian. Born in Saratov, Russia, 1859. Died in 1926. Arrived in Moscow, mid-1870s; worked as an illustrator and theater designer. Taught at the Stroganov School of Applied Art, from 1896.

Chronology of Works
All in Russia unless noted

1893	Morozova House, Moscow
1896	Shekhtel House, Moscow
1898-99	Kuznetsov Store, Moscow
1900-02	Ryabushinsky Mansion, Moscow
1901	Boyarsky Dvor Hotel, Moscow
1901	Russian Pavilion, Glasgow, Scotland
1901-02	Derozhinsky Mansion, Moscow
1902	Moscow Art Theater, Moscow
1902	Yaroslavsky Railway Station, Moscow
1902-04	Stroganov School Apartment House, Moscow
1903	Ryabushinsky Bank, Moscow
1907	'Utro Rossii' Printing Press, Moscow
1907	Patrikeev Villa, Khimki
1909	Moscow Merchants' Society Building, Moscow
1910	Shekhtel House, Moscow
1912	Art Movie Theater, Moscow
1923	Turkestan Pavilion, Soviety Agricultural Exposition, Moscow

Publications

ARTICLES BY SHEKHTEL

"Architecture an Its Relationship to Painting and Sculpture." Vol. 1 in *Masters of Soviet Architecture About Architecture.* Moscow, 1975.

BOOKS ABOUT SHEKHTEL

BORISOVA, ELENA A. and KAZHDAN, TATIANA P.: *Russakaya arkhitektura Kontsa XIX-nachala XX veka.* Moscow, 1971.
BORISOWA, ELENA A. and STERNIN, GRIGORI J.: *Jugendstil in Russland. Architektur, Interieurs, bildende und angewandte Kunst.* Stuttgart, 1988.
KIRICHENKO, ERGENIIA I.: *Fedor Shekhtel.* Moscow, 1975.
KIRICHENKO, ERGENIIA I.: *Moskva na rubezhe stoletti.* Moscow, 1977.
KIRICHENKO, ERGENIIA I.: *Russkaya arkhitektura 1830-1910-kh godov.* Moscow, 1978.

The pioneering achievements of the Soviet avant-garde have taken up such a powerful foreground position that the innovations in Russian architecture immediately preceding the Soviet era have received little attention. That has also been the fate of Fedor Shekhtel's work. At the beginning of the October Revolution, he was 58 years old. Shekhtel was prepared, as a number of other "old masters" were, to cooperate with the new regime, but his influence on architectural developments was small. At that time, he had built little, and he died a few years later, in 1926. Nevertheless, Shekhtel was one of the most important Russian architects of the pre-revolutionary era. His work was a significant contribution to the modern and European orientation of Russian architecture.

Shekhtel's career took a slow start. He was not a trained architect, having left the Moscow School of Painting, Sculpture and Architecture after attending for one year. He came to architecture after starting as an artist. He worked as book designer and illustrator, and designed posters and theater decorations. In 1880 he became an assistant in the architectural firm of M. Tversky and A. Kalshinsky. At the end of the decade, he began to work independently.

Shekhtel first drew attention for his villa designs (*osobnyaki*), an example of which is the Villa Morozov in Moscow (1893). In contrast to the more usual classicistic or eclectic conceptions of such projects, Shekhtel preferred asymmetrical compositions, and rejected the corridor principle in favor of centralized plans with a hall. For both the exterior and interior, he used Gothic elements of form. The free plan, comparable to English "free architecture," and the Gothicizing idiom were part of a general reorientation of Russian architecture, which was anticlassical in spirit and turned to indigenous medieval architecture—specifically to medieval wood architecture in about 1900. Picturesque effects, asymmetry, rhythmical compositions, a relationship with landscape, use of color, and the active incorporation of painting and sculpture offered new possibilities, going beyond classicism. Shekhtel's use of a Gothicizing idiom, however,

Fedor Shekhtel: Ryubashinsky Mansion, Moscow, Russia, 1900-02

created a new link with European architecture, since the Russian Middle Ages did not have a Gothic style.

This so-called Russian style was the harbinger of art nouveau in Russia, and after 1900 both styles were often mixed. This was also true for Shekhtel's work. His Russian exhibition pavilion for Glasgow, Scotland (1901) and the Jaroslav Station in Moscow (1907) combined the typical silhouette of Old Russian wood architecture with the curvilinear elegance of art nouveau. For both commissions the national style had been a requirement, but in private commissions Shekhtel was clearly working in the spirit of the European Jugendstil. The best-known work of that period is the Villa Ryabushinsky in Moscow (1911). The villa's cubic building elements are grouped around a cubic core, but these simple volumes come together into a plastic unity through the use of cast-iron decorations, glazed tiles and floral motifs on the walls. The villa's individual elements of form point to a knowledge of the Vienna Secession and the work of Charles Rennie Mackintosh.

After the decorative period of the *"stil modern,"* as art nouveau is called in Russia, Shekhtel concentrated on the possibilities of the new construction techniques in steel and concrete skeletons. Shekhtel utilized skeleton construction for facades: leaving behind architectural ornamentation, his facades were defined by the alternation of pillars with glazed areas. The almost unornamented building of the print shop Utro Rosy (1907) and that of the Merchants Association (1909), both in Moscow, are examples of Shekhtel's functionalist innovations.

Besides his varied work in architectural design (villas, office buildings, banks, sanatoriums, factories and cinemas), Shekhtel was also important for his other contributions to the profession. In 1896 he had begun teaching the theory of composition at the Stroganov Institute in Moscow, and he also taught from 1919 to 1922 at the VKHUTEMAS (Higher State Artistic-Technical Studies). He was chairman of the Association of Moscow Architects (1908-22), and sat on several committees, the last one the program committee and jury of the competition for the Palace of Labor (1922-23). One of his last works was a neoclassical design for Lenin's Mausoleum (1924).

—OTAKAR MÁČEL
Translated from the German by Marijke Rijsberman

SHINOHARA, Kazuo.

Japanese. Born in Shizuoka, Japan, 2 April 1925. Studied at the Institute of Technology, Tokyo, B.Eng., 1953, D.Eng., 1967. In private practice, Tokyo, since 1954. Instructor, 1953-61, associate professor, 1962-69, and professor of architecture since 1970, Tokyo Institute of Technology.

Chronology of Works
All in Japan

1954	House in Kugayama, Tokyo
1961	Umbrella House, Tokyo
1963	House with the Earthen Floor, Karuizawa
1966	House in White, Tokyo
1970	Incomplete House, Tokyo
1971	Repeating Crevice House, Tokyo
1971	Cubic Forest House, Kawasaki
1974	Tanikawa Residence, Karuizawa
1976	House in Uehara, Tokyo

Kazuo Shinohara: Tokyo Institute of Technology Centennial Hall, Tokyo, Japan, 1987

1976	House in Itoshima, Fukuoka Prefecture
1978	House on the Curved Road, Tokyo
1982	House under the High-Voltage Lines, Tokyo
1983	Higashi-Tamagawa Complex, Tokyo
1987	Tokyo Institute of Technology Centennial Hall, Tokyo

Publications

BOOKS BY SHINOHARA

Residential Architecture. Tokyo, 1964.
Theories on Residences. Tokyo, 1970.
Kazuo Shinohara: 16 Houses and Architectural Theory. Tokyo, 1971.
Theories on Residences II. Tokyo, 1975.
Kazuo Shinohara II: 11 Houses and Architectural Theory. Tokyo, 1976.
Kazuo Shinohara. With Yasumitsu Matsunaga. New York, 1982.

BOOKS ABOUT SHINOHARA

BOGNAR, BOTAND: *Contemporary Japanese Architecture: Its Development and Challenge*. New York, 1985.
BOGNAR, BOTAND: *The New Japanese Architecture*. New York, 1990.
BOGNAR, BOTAND: *Kazuo Shinohara*. New York, 1982.
BOYD, ROBIN: *New Directions in Japanese Architecture*. New York and London, 1968.
STEWART, D. B.: *The Making of a Modern Japanese Architecture*. Tokyo, 1987.

An enigmatic figure and one of the most influential designers in Japanese architecture today, Kazuo Shinohara enjoys a reputation both at home and abroad that can be matched by only a few of his contemporaries. This reputation stems primarily from the fact that during his long career as a designer since the early 1950s he has consistently broadened the architectural discourse in Japan, exploring new horizons with his extraordinary projects, thereby also challenging the prevailing architectural ideologies and trends or fashions of the times. With an attitude uncommon for an established architect, he has radically shifted the focus of his architecture and line of design several times throughout the years, making it possible to identify four distinct phases in his overall work to date. His work has always remained highly conceptual in nature, however. His architecture, particularly from the early 1970s on, had a profound impact on the work of a new generation of Japanese architects including, among others, Kazunari Sakamoto, Itsuko Hasegawa and Toyo Ito, who, within the so-called New Wave were often referred to as the Shinohara school.

First trained as a mathematician before obtaining his degrees in architecture, Shinohara in the early stages of his career became fascinated by and explored the abstract qualities of traditional Japanese architecture. His small houses of the 1950s and 1960s, like the House in Kugayama (1954), the Umbrella House (1961) and the House in White (1966), all in Tokyo, reinterpreted the structural and spatial "simplicity" of historic, wooden residences. While featuring some elements of the Japanese house—tiled roofs, *tatami* flooring, sliding wall panels, etc.—these designs experimented with the symbolic value of the purest themes, such as symmetry/asymmetry and division/connection; by way of simplification they created subtle variations in perceptual qualities. In so doing, Shinohara's architecture became increasingly art-oriented; he even declared that "a house is a work of art." Such statement and intention in the 1960s, the age of industrialized and predominantly technology-oriented Metabolist architecture in Japan, were clearly revolutionary, outside the mainstream of Japanese design.

Shinohara's second phase in the 1970s evolved as he abandoned the traditional formal language he had investigated so far. Abstract geometric forms, shaped of unfinished concrete volumes, began to dominate his works. Even the occasionally used slanting roof was turned into a solid pyramid over hard boxes. His architecture was gradually turned more inward-oriented. Residences such as the Incomplete House (1970) and the Repeating Crevice House (1971) in Tokyo, and the Cubic Forest House (1971) in Kawasaki displayed a manifest disinterest in the volatile and chaotic urban environment; on the other hand, inside they concentrated on spatial compositions that were conceived in a unique, poetic minimalism. Shinohara aimed at the evocation of "naked spaces." The quality of primitive simplicity that characterized his architecture from the very beginning was even more pronounced in these projects. In his Tanikawa Residence, a summer house in the woods (1974), for example, he shaped the floor as hard pounded earth that followed the slope of the site.

Influenced by Claude Lévi-Strauss' structural anthropology and Roland Barthes' linguistic theories, Shinohara, from the mid-1970s on, was to complement his prevailing primitivism with his new concepts of "zero-degree machine" and "progressive anarchy." Two major works, the House in Uehara (1976) and the House on a Curved Road (1978), both in Tokyo, exemplify this phase the best. They were designed with massive, oversized concrete columns and sturdy, diagonal braces or beams which, invading the extraordinary interiors, allude to the quality of the jungle. Slowly the issue of order/disorder (anarchy) with an invisible threshold or a curious "gap" in between them emerged as another theme in Shinohara's architecture. Although the solid and relatively simple volumes of his buildings still rejected the chaotic cityscape, now they were also to deny an overall formal unity; spatial and structural elements started to appear as parts in a machine, which is "a physical system in which objects are simply joined together in a *sachlich* manner." In other words, the objectivity of such "functional" design excluded the need and even the possibility of the "synthesis of form," signaling the beginning of Shinohara's quest for theoretical structures in an architecture of fragmentation.

Along with his growing fascination with such high-tech products as the Tomcat fighter plane and lunar landing module, the primitive machine in Shinohara's architecture acquired a more sophisticated quality. In addition to reinforced concrete, industrially produced materials and elements—glass block, stainless-steel sheets, metallic parts—were utilized in larger quantities. Simultaneously the fragmentary formal articulation of his designs, beyond the anarchy of the jungle, found another analogy in the anarchy of the Japanese city. Accordingly, residences, such as the House under High-Voltage Lines (1982) and the Higashi-Tamagawa Complex (1983), could respond more willingly to the layered, collage-like urban fabric of Tokyo, now often introducing cityscapes to the interiors in a selective manner through carefully shaped and focused openings. In fact, anarchy has been transformed into a creative concept by Shinohara. Thus, what he calls the concept of "progressive anarchy" is an operative model which recognizes and responds to the chaotic nature of the Japanese city while not necessarily endorsing it.

Today Shinohara's theoretical investigations and conceptual designs are put to the test in larger public buildings as well, not only in small, private residences. The most significant of his latest works, the Tokyo Institute of Technology Centennial Hall (1987), is designed with a unique structural system and a formal composition that aspires to a mode of architectural integration without synthesis. It admittedly draws from the chaotic energy, ways and means of perception, as well as the alogic of its urban nexus, but, by way of its appeal to a new machine aesthetic or new-tech (as opposed to the unified machine image of high-modernism), it also opposes the uncontrolled excesses of the existing city, especially by refusing to harmonize with the all-too-trivializing modes of signification and representation of the prevailing consumerist urbanism. And in so doing the Centennial Hall prefigures a new, visionary city, an information-fueled technopolis of the future.

The Centennial Hall epitomizes poignantly Shinohara's career as a relentless course oriented away from the past, and attests to his conviction that "tradition can be the starting point for creativity, but it must not be the point to which it returns."

—BOTOND BOGNAR

SILOE, Diego de.

Spanish. Born in Burgos, Spain, ca. 1495. Died in Granada, 22 October 1563. Trained in sculpture with his father, Gil Siloe. Assistant to the sculptor Bartolomé Ordóñez, Naples, and collaborated with Ordóñez on the Caraccioli Chapel in Naples. Worked in Burgos, 1519-28; moved to Granada, 1528.

Chronology of Works
All in Spain
* Approximate dates

1519	Tomb of Bishop Luis de Acuña, Chapel of St. Anne, Burgos
1519-22	Escalera Dorado (Golden Stair), Cathedral, Burgos
1522	Chapel of St. Anne, Burgos (altarpiece)
1523	Chapel of the Constable, Cathedral, Burgos (with Felipe Bigarny)
1528-43	San Jerónimo, Granada (completion of work begun by Jacopo Fiorentino 'El Indaco' in 1523-26)
1528-63	Cathedral, Granada (not completed until the 17th century)
1529-34	Colegio Fonseca, Salamanca (courtyard)
1563*	Church, Iznalloz (executed by Juan de Maeda , 1566-74)

Publications

BOOKS ABOUT SILOE

CAMON AZNAR, JOSE: *La arquitectura plateresca.* 2 vols. Madrid, 1945.

CHUECA GOITIA, FERNANDO: *Arquitectura del Siglo XVI, Ars Hispaniae XI.* Madrid, 1953.

GOMEZ-MORENO, MANUEL: *Las Aguilas del Renacimento Español.* Madrid, 1941; 2nd ed., 1983.

GOMEZ-MORENO, MANUEL: *Provincia de Salamanca.* 2 vols. Madrid, 1967.

KUBLER, GEORGE and SORIA, MARTIN: *Art and Architecture in Spain and Portugal and Their American Dominions: 1500-1800.* Baltimore and Harmondsworth, 1959.

ROSENTHAL, EARL E.: *The Cathedral of Granada.* Princeton, New Jersey, 1961.

Diego de Siloe: Cathedral, Granada, 1528-63

Diego Siloe, sculptor and architect, is widely regarded as the first great Spanish architect of the Renaissance. He was born in Burgos in about 1495, the son of the wildly imaginative Late Gothic sculptor Gil Siloee, from whom he learned only a taste for dense decorations. As a youth Diego was an assistant in Italy to the sculptor Bartolomé Ordóñez. Diego's later work suggests a familiarity with Tuscan and Lombard models, but his only documentable Italian activity was in Ordóñez' marble retablo at the Caraccioli de Vico Chapel in San Giovanni a Carbonara in Naples.

Diego returned to Burgos in 1519, working first on the alabaster tomb of Bishop Luis de Acuña at the cathedral, and becoming an associate of the French sculptor Felipe Bigarny. Diego's first

architectural commission was the Golden Stair (1519-22) in the north transept of the 13th-century cathedral. The steep site made the north portal about 8 meters higher than the floor level of the transept, while the existing Pellejería portal on the east side of the transept left little interior room for a stair. Within these constraints, Diego created one of the great staircases of the Renaissance, with an axial flight that splits in two, rejoining at the landing of the upper portal. Three arches, two below each lateral flight and one on axis at the first landing, house tombs. The arrangement imitates Bramante's stair at the Vatican courtyard, but is steeper and more somber, richly sculpted with grotesques, and with a gilded iron balustrade by a French smith, Hilaire. The four semicircular lower steps and the volute railings resemble closely Michelangelo's later stair at the Laurentian Library in Florence, and a link between the two does not seem accidental.

In 1527 Bigarny sued Diego, the winner of a competition both had entered for the design of the tower of Santa María del Campo near Burgos, thus ending their collaboration. This, the most impressive Renaissance tower in Castile, was subcontracted to the mason Juan de Salas, who modified the upper parts in 1531. The original design consisted of three superimposed cubic blocks with triumphal arch elevations and a culminating octagon, echoing work of the Sangallos in Italy.

Diego moved to Granada in 1528 to complete the sanctuary of the Church of San Jerónimo. The Italian painter and architect Jacobo Florentino, el Indaco, had worked there the year before his death in 1526. Jacobo inherited a Gothic plan, but altered the elevation, articulating the piers with multiple-layered squat Corinthian pilasters including full entablatures and pedestals. Diego built coffered barrel vaults on the transepts and sanctuary, plus a crossing tower with a novel coffered rib vault on squinches. His renowned stereotomic skill emerged with these vaults. Diego still lacked a sense of classical decorum, and decorated every coffer and surface with sculpture, outdoing Jacobo's rich friezes and unconventional capitals, but Jacobo's pilastered piers taught him how to impose classical order on Gothic structure.

In 1528, shortly after his arrival, Diego received the commission for the cathedral of Granada. Begun in 1523 by the Gothic architect Enrique Egas, its huge five-aisle plan with alternating square and triangular bays in the ambulatory imitated the 13th-century cathedral of Toledo, where Egas was master mason. In 1526 Emperor Charles V decided to be buried at Granada rather than with his grandparents, the Catholic monarchs Ferdinand and Isabella, in the small adjacent Royal Chapel. This made the cathedral a royal pantheon, and increased its importance. Diego probably used this pretext, as well as the Roman sympathies of Archbishop Pedro Ramírez de Alva and Captain General Luis Hurtado de Mendoza, to propose a radical redesign. Diego had to defend his project at the Cortes in Toledo in 1529. It revealed a deeper understanding of High Renaissance ideas than any of Diego's earlier works.

As at San Jerónimo, the elevation of piers was altered, using well-proportioned, classically detailed, layered Corinthian pilasters. To attain sufficient height below the vault springings, an awkward tall attic level was added above the entablature. More critical changes were the insertion of a great rotunda in the sanctuary and a monumental triumphal arch on the east facade of the transept. The white piers of the central nave lead into the colorful rotunda with gilding, stained glass and painted retablos. Earl Rosenthal has interpreted this arrangement, with the royal tombs in high niches around the rotunda, as a reference to the Holy Sepulcher in Jerusalem.

The collision of circular and rectilinear elements created complex stereotomic problems. Splayed rampant barrel vaults were needed over the deep radial tunnels between the rotunda and the ambulatory. Three-dimensionally warped curves were created by the intersection of the triumphal arch with the rotunda wall, and by the clerestory arches piercing the rotunda. Spherical rib vaults, *bóvedas baídas,* a compromise between Gothic and Renaissance structure, were used in the ambulatory bays and rotunda. The cathedral was an important training ground for Andalusian stereotomists. Due to the technical virtuosity and the limited funding, completion of the sanctuary and ambulatory would take Diego's lifetime. The cathedral was not finished until the 18th century, and many details, including the nave vaults and west facade, are not his.

In 1529, while defending his design in Toledo, Diego met Archbishop Alonso de Fonseca, who was then building a great college in Salamanca, dedicated to the Spanish patron saint, Santiago. The college was begun in 1521 by Juan de Álava, who executed most of its chapel and other dependencies. In 1529 Diego was asked to submit designs for the main portal and the courtyard. Both were completed under Álava's direction in 1534. The two-story portal has paired engaged Ionic columns with broken entablatures, and four simple candelabra rising above the upper entablature. Decorative exuberance is limited to well-defined areas, between columns and on three long roundels in the upper level. The large, square, two-story courtyard has eight arches per side, and a horizontal emphasis. Its lower arcade rests on slender square piers with very elongated engaged Corinthian columns. Classical proportions are violated, but the Roman syntax of arches framed by trabeation is followed meticulously. The upper story offers a surprising contrast. There arches are depressed instead of semicircular, and the piers carry elaborate candelabra with capricious composite capitals instead of engaged columns. M. Gómez Moreno ascribed the more restrained, classical aspects of these designs to the sober influence of Pedro Machuca, whose design for the Palace of Charles V in Granada dates from 1527.

In 1536 the emperor's secretary, Francisco de los Cobos, commissioned Diego to design his funerary chapel, San Salvador in Úbeda. A reduced version of the cathedral of Granada, this luxurious church has a single nave of three bays and a terminal rotunda imitating the plan of the Caraccioli chapel in Naples. It was executed by Andrés de Vandelvira and Alonso Ruiz, with the French sculptor Esteban Jamete in residence in 1540-42. Apparently Diego was too busy to attend to the work, and was dismissed in 1539.

The classicizing articulated piers of the cathedral of Granada spread widely in Andalusia and Latin America. Diego himself contributed to this movement in 1541 with the design of two important southern cathedrals, Málaga and Guadix. The sanctuary of Málaga forms half of a decagon, with an ambulatory and rectangular radiating chapels. The hall church elevation, with three aisles of equal height, may have been Andrés de Vandelvira's contribution. In 1549 he and Diego executed a model of the cathedral, of which fragments remain. In the smaller ambulatory at Guadix, Diego repeated the plan of Málaga, but simplified the Granadine elevation, eliminating the attic level. This elegant hall church has *bóvedas baídas* rising over powerful piers. A circular chapel attached to the ambulatory dedicated to San Torcuato again quotes the Caraccioli chapel plan.

Two important works attributed to Diego should be mentioned. One is the graceful courtyard of the Palace of the Chancillería in Granada, begun in the 1530s. It is two stories, with a very light arcade on slender Doric columns below, and an Ionic colonnade with corbels supporting an entablature above, a design first developed by Lorenzo Vázquez in Guadalajara. The other is the Greek-cross-plan Sacristía Mayor at the cathedral of Seville, which Diego inspected in 1535. Its technical sophistication, with a *bóveda baída* over the central square and richly coffered splayed barrel vaults in the arms, suggest that Diego provided the design.

It is far easier to define the style of Diego Siloe's sculpture than of his architecture. Specific motifs such as the pilaster pier, the Caraccioli chapel plan or *bóvedas baídas* recur in his work, but no clear syntactical principles. He was able to alter his approach in different projects, whether using Gothic structure, dressing it in classical garb, following a stricter Italian classical syntax, or emulating Islamic courtyards. Such eclecticism is married to a high technical skill in the cutting of stone, and a sculptor's interest in details. His freedom reflects an aesthetic attitude prevalent in Spain until the gradual imposition of a stricter classicism under Philip II at the Escorial, in the 1560s.

—SERGIO L. SANABRIA

SIMÓN DE COLONIA.

Spanish. Born in Spain, ca. 1450. Died in Burgos, Spain, in November 1511. Father was the German architect Juan de Colonia (ca. 1410-ca. 1481). Master of the Burgos Cathedral, 1481-1511.

Chronology of Works
All in Spain
* Approximate dates
† Work no longer exists

1481-88	Carthusian Monastery, Miraflores, near Burgos (completion of work begun in 1441)
1482*-1511	Funerary Chapel for Don Pedro Fernandez de Velasco (not completed until 1532)
1486-1502	Church of San Pablo, Valladolid
1496-1502	Cathedral, Seville (crossing tower)†
1499*-1511	Cathedral, Palencia
1506ff.*	Church of Santa Maria, Aranda de Duero

Publications

BOOKS ABOUT SIMÓN DE COLONIA

CHUECA GOITIA, FERNANDO: *Arquitectura del Siglo XVI.* Madrid, 1953.
CHUECA GOITIA, FERNANDO: *Historia de la Arquitectura Española, Edad Antigua y Edad Media.* Madrid, 1965.
LAMPEREZ Y ROMEA, V.: *Juan de Colonia.* Valladolid, Spain, 1904.
LOPEX MATA, TEOFILO: *Le Catedral de Burgos.* Burgos, Spain, 1950; 2nd ed., 1966.
TORRES BALBAS, LEOPOLDO: *Arte y Arquitectura Gotica.* Madrid, 1952.

*

Simón de Colonia and Juan Guas were the most brilliant architects of the Spanish Isabelline Gothic. Simón, younger by about 15 years, was the second member of a dynasty of master masons settled in Burgos, the Castillian capital. The Colonias were specialists in lantern towers, pierced spires and openwork vaults. Their reputation seems to have survived even the collapse of their two largest ciboria. Simón's German father, Juan de Colonia, was master of the cathedral of Burgos from before 1442 to 1481. He was responsible for the pierced spires of the west facade, several funerary chapels with rib-vault patterns new in Spain, and a crossing tower that collapsed in 1538 and was redesigned by his grandson, Francisco de Colonia, and Juan de Vallejo. Simón was master of the cathedral of Burgos from 1481 to his death. His crossing tower at the cathedral of Seville of 1496-1502 collapsed in 1511.

Simón inherited the work at the Carthusian monastery of Miraflores near Burgos from his father. The monastery had been founded by Juan II of Castile in 1441 as his pantheon, but work slowed down after his death in 1454 due to the anarchy prevailing under his son, Henry IV. The church was completed by Simón from 1481 to 1488 during the reign of Henry's sister Isabella, who interred there her parents and brother. The church

was conservative, but innovations were the superb Flamboyant parapets and pinnacles crowning its exterior, the polyfoil enrichments of the sanctuary rib vaults, and the large royal coats of arms upheld by rampant lions above the west portal. The most innovative work was the interior *retablos* and royal tombs by Gil Siloée and Diego de la Cruz.

Simón continued his father's series of funerary chapels in the cathedral with a magnificent one for Don Pedro Fernández de Velasco, constable of Castille, and his wife Doña Mencia de Mendoza. This monument was begun after 1482, but work slowed down after the constable's death in 1492 and was not completed until 1532. The off-axis position of the chapel in the ambulatory, its octagonal plan, splendid ostentation, and purpose imitated an earlier chapel in Toledo by Hanequin of Brussels for the constable Don Alvaro de Luna. The Burgalese chapel was larger and more pretentious, its huge external mass vigorously punctuated by eight formidable Flamboyant corner pinnacles. The outer walls display a favorite Isabelline motif, reliefs of savages holding the founders' coats of arms.

The interior is entered diagonally through a vestibule, originally the central 13th-century radiating chapel, but the powerful vertical octagonal space effectively recenters the visitor after the oblique approach. The elevation is three stories. Lower walls display the founders' coats of arms tipped toward the altar. The second level is a shallow gallery under slightly pointed arcades whose outer archivolts form ogees. Inner archivolts sprout a bold naturalistic tracery of angels holding symbols of the Passion, and suns and crosses symbolizing Christ. Larger-than-life savage heralds holding coats of arms stand before Flamboyant parapets. These decorations have been attributed to Siloée, but are probably Simón's. At the clerestory level, vaults spring from crisscrossing curved ribs, a German Late Gothic detail seen at the choir of St. Lawrence in Nuremberg (begun 1439).

Most impressive in this chapel is the vault with 16 intersecting ribs, similar to the 10th-century domes flanking the *mihrab* of the mosque of Cordoba. In its center is an embroidered stone fantasy, an eight-pointed star network of traceried ribs with open webs. There, Gothic forms began to embrace Islamic sensibilities.

Guas' and Siloée's innovations must have impacted Simón when he began work at the church of San Pablo in Valladolid in 1486. There he pushed the ornamental potential of the style to its limits. The west facade is a picturesque riot of sculpture and ornament, with endless variations of arches transfixed by vertical shafts, sculptural groups framed asymmetrically, or heralds holding coats of arms, all set against diaper patterns in a design of barbaric *horror vacui. Alfices,* rectangular frames of Islamic origin, multiplied and thickened, have acquired major importance as architectonic elements; arches have become thin and insubstantial. This capricious, arbitrary composition, far removed from the harmonic facades of the High Gothic, is like a tapestry or an exterior *retablo* with little organic relation to the building it enlivens, intended only to attract the visitor. The regular, dull upper three levels and pediment, by Francisco de Colonia, are untouched by the mad genius of Simón. The three-aisle church is otherwise structurally and spatially conservative.

The church of Santa Maria in Aranda de Duero, east of Valladolid, follows similar principles, and is clearly Simón's. Its south facade is again a tapestry of decoration, although more disciplined and with a clearer formal hierarchy, anchored on a wide pointed arch below. Complex tracery hangs from its inner archivolt as at the chapel of the constable, and arbitrary curves, two *mouchettes* and a stilted ogee, sprout from its outer archivolt. These curves frame sculptural scenes of the Passion of Christ. The upper wall has an imbricated ground displaying royal arms held by lions and eagles.

Simon de Colonia: Church of San Pablo, Valladolid, Spain, 1486-1502

Late in the 15th century, Simón worked at the cathedral of Palencia, where he must have influenced the development of complex curvilinear rib vaults, and helped train a new generation of Late Gothic masters, including Juan Gil de Hontañón and perhaps Juan de Alava.

Simón was more interested in visual activity, linearity and texture than in pure form. Even the grandiose prism of the chapel of the constable dissolves its ponderous mass in an upward flaming pyre of projecting pinnacles, an effect unlike the more tectonic forms favored by Guas. Unlike Guas, who often sacrificed structure to achieve rich but orderly formal effects, Simón's undisciplined decoration respects the structural integrity of the real supports, arches or ribs of his buildings. Simón would sacrifice structural intelligibility for the sake of an expressive structure of signifying components. His richly textured areas always contrast against plain surfaces and draw attention to places where the iconographic programs are displayed, thereby magnifying their impact. Since the structural context of these iconographic-textural displays is ignored, Simón's architecture is ultimately reductive, focusing aesthetic means on the propagandistic ends of his aristocratic and royal patrons.

—SERGIO L. SANABRIA

SINAN.

Turkish. Born in Anatolia, Asia Minor (now Turkey), ca. 1491. Died in Istanbul, 1588. Trained as a carpenter, bridge builder and military engineer. Chief architect of Sultan Süleyman, 1538.

Chronology of Works
All in Asia Minor (now Turkey)

1536-37	Hüsrev Pasha, Aleppo
1539	Haseki Hürrem Külliye, Istanbul
1548	Sehzade Mosque Complex, Istanbul
1550-57	Sülleymaniye Külliye, Istanbul
1562-65	Mihrimah Mosque, Istanbul
1567-74	Selimiye Külliye of Selim II, Edirne

Publications

BOOKS ABOUT SINAN

ASPLANAPA, O.: *Turkish Art and Architecture.* London, 1971.
EGLI, ERNST: *Sinan, der Baumeister osmanischer Glanzzeit.* Zurich, 1954.
GOODWIN, GODFREY: *A History of Ottoman Architecture.* Baltimore, 1971.
GOODWIN, GODFREY: *Ottoman Turkey.* London, 1977.
HOAG, JOHN D.: *Islamic Architecture.* New York, 1977.
KURAN, APTULLAH: *The Mosque in Early Ottoman Architecture.* Chicago, 1968.
STRATTON, ARTHUR: *Sinan.* New York and London, 1972.
ÜNSAL, B.: *Turkish Islamic Architecture.* London, 1973.
VOGT-GÖKNIL, U.: *Ottoman Architecture.* London, 1966.

*

Sinan, chief architect of Sultan Süleyman the Magnificent, developed and perfected classical Ottoman architecture. Although he is little known in the West, Sinan is one of the most important architects of the premodern period.

Sinan was born in about 1491 into a Christian family in Anatolia. At the age of 21, he entered the service of Sultan Selim I and converted to the Islamic religion. It is reported that he attended a palace school in Istanbul, where he trained as a carpenter, bridge builder and military engineer. In 1538, after demonstrating his technical proficiency by building a bridge during an army campaign in Moldavia, Sinan was appointed chief imperial architect by Süleyman. This appointment included supervision of construction and construction supplies within the empire, and the design and construction of such public works as bridges, road systems and waterworks. In the 50 years that he held this position under Süleyman and his successors Selim II and Murat III, Sinan designed and constructed more than 460 structures. The official list of his works, the "Tazkirat al-Abniya," credits Sinan with the design of 84 large mosques, 57 colleges (*medreses*), 52 small mosques, 48 baths, 35 palaces, 22 mausoleums, 20 caravan-saries, 17 public kitchens, eight granaries, 8 bridges, seven Koranic schools, six aqueducts, six storehouses and three hospitals; almost 200 of Sinan's works are still standing. In addition, several autobiographical texts preserve his ideas on architecture and construction. Sinan died in 1588 and was buried in a mausoleum (türbe) of his own design in the cemetery at the Süleymaniye, near the tombs of two of his greatest patrons, Süleyman and Süleyman's wife Haseki Hürrem, commonly known as Roxelana.

The Ottoman tradition of domed architecture was well established by Sinan's time, and his experimentation with the design and engineering of single- and multiple-domed structures—especially mosques, mosque complexes and baths—demonstrates his creativity and his interest in creating a clear, unified interior space. Working within the tradition of the domed mosque and, in Istanbul, with the example of the great domed space of Hagia Sophia always before him, Sinan developed a series of variations on the dome as a centralizing motif surrounded by half domes, piers, curtain walls, galleries and/or aisles. In his best mosques he established a rational harmony between exterior form, interior space and structure. Sinan was an innovator in the use of decoration, especially colored glass and painted Iznik tiles, and in the unification of decorative materials and motifs with the architectural forms as a whole.

Sinan's designs for mosque complexes efficiently and harmoniously incorporated the many utilitarian structures necessary for their functions as intellectual centers and as community centers dedicated to social services. A mosque complex (*külliye*) commissioned from Sinan encompassed the mosque and its entrance courtyard, with a fountain for washing, and could also include one or more *medreses*, a library, dormitory for scholars and students, lower-level Koranic school, baths, clock room, hospice, hospital, public kitchen, bakery, bazaar and garden with cemetery.

The Haseki Hürrem Külliye, built for Süleyman's favorite wife, was Sinan's earliest work in Istanbul. Completed in 1539, the *külliye* is exceeded in size in Istanbul only by those of the earlier Beyazidiye mosque and Sinan's later Süleymaniye mosque. The mosque itself was relatively small until a second room, added in 1612, altered Sinan's design. This *külliye* includes a large *medrese,* a primary school, a hospital and a public kitchen. Sinan's utilitarian structures were so well designed that some have continued in use for centuries; at Haseki Hürrem Külliye, for example, the octagonal hospital is still functioning.

The Sehzade Mosque Complex in Istanbul, completed in 1548 and known as the Mosque of the Prince, was commissioned by Süleyman in honor of his son Prince Mehmet, who died of smallpox when he was 21. The complex includes a large courtyard, a *medrese,* a primary school, a public kitchen, a bakery and a hospice. The exterior of the mosque is ornately decorated,

Sinan: Süleymaniye Külliye, Istanbul, Turkey, 1550-57

and the minarets have geometric designs and intricate balconies. The main body of the mosque has a strictly centralized plan, with the main dome surrounded by four half domes on the main axes; each of these is again flanked by half domes, and smaller domes fill the corner spaces. From the exterior, the regularity of Sinan's combinations of large and small domes and clusters of half domes in several sizes predicts the interior, where the vast unified space, broken only by the intrusion of the four huge supporting piers, demonstrates the clarity of Sinan's design and proportional relationships. The most impressive tomb in the garden is the *türbe* of Mehmet, which has a double fluted dome; it is ornately reveted with inlaid stone and terra-cotta, while the interior is sumptuously decorated with Iznik tiles of

unusual color and design, stained-glass windows and frescoes in the dome.

The Süleymaniye Külliye (1550-57) remains one of the most impressive monuments in Istanbul; the complex originally included four *medreses,* a Koranic school, baths, hospital, market street and other structures. The influence of the axial design of Hagia Sophia is apparent in the two axial half domes, which here emphasize a directional movement toward the *mihrab* niche, but Sinan's plan is more centralized, unified and simplified than that of Hagia Sophia. Sinan eliminated the prototype's galleries, and used wider openings into the aisles to unify the space. At the Süleymaniye, Sinan demonstrated his ability to achieve an illusion of lightness and grace in a monumental domed structure.

Sinan: Süleymaniye Külliye

Iznik tiles decorated with floral and foliage designs emphasize the *mihrab* wall, and marble decorates the *mihrab* and *mimber*. Colorful stained-glass windows offer calligraphy within intricate designs, while the doors and window shutters are inlaid with patterns in ivory and mother-of-pearl. The four slender minarets, each with three balconies, are among the highest in Turkey (64 meters or 210 feet). The entrance into the grand arcaded courtyard presents a view of the mosque that emphasizes a closely massed series of domes and half domes. The octagonal Türbe of Süleyman in the cemetery behind the mosque, Sinan's largest and most highly decorated tomb, is surrounded by a columned portico. The nearby tomb of Roxelana is intentionally plain in contrast.

The Mihrimah Mosque in Istanbul was commissioned by Rüstem Pasha, Sülleyman's grand vizier, in honor of his wife Mihrimah, Süleyman's daughter. Completed between 1562 and 1565, it represents Sinan's continuing innovations in the domed mosque plan. Here, at the highest point within the city walls, he designed a mosque with a single high dome raised above arched curtain walls filled with windows; massive turrets at the corners buttress the dome. Harmony between the internal and external design is achieved through the unusual use of clear glass in the windows and by the pendentives, whose shape is echoed on the exterior.

The Selimiye Külliye of Selim II in Edirne (1567-74), built when Sinan was in his 80s, is usually considered the architect's most important work. Here Sinan returned to the strictly central-ized plan seen at the Sehzade mosque, but he placed the but-tressing half domes in the corners to create an octagonal design. The central dome, as wide as that of Hagia Sophia and 42 meters (138 feet) high, is supported by eight huge piers of marble and granite; here the space of the vast domed interior is completely unified. As at the Süleymaniye, the weight and internal tensions of the structure are hidden in order to produce an airy and elegant effect. The four minarets, the tallest in the Moslem world (83 meters or 272 feet high), enhance the cen-trality of the design. The interior of the mosque is rich in design and pattern, with tiles and gilded calligraphy decorating the *mihrab* and *mimber*.

Smaller projects, such as the Baths of Roxelana, show Sinan's skill in designing multiple-domed structures. The mosque of Rüstem Pasha in Istanbul, one of the most attractive of Sinan's small mosques, is distinguished by its simple plan, intimate scale, and the profuse decoration of the facade and interior with Iznik tiles of the highest quality.

Sinan's earliest certain work is the Hüsrev Pasha mosque in Aleppo (1536-37). Other mosques he designed in Istanbul in-clude the Ibrahim Pasha Cami, the Ahmet Pasha Cami, Sokollu Mehmet Pasha Cami and the Zal Mahmut Pasha Cami. Sinan's other works include the kitchen complex at Topkapi Palace, the market of Ali Pasha at Edirne, mosques for Mihrimah in Üskü-dar and for Rüstem Pasha in Tekirdag, inns (*hans*) for Rüstem Pasha in Istanbul and Edirne, the Sokollu Mehmet Pasha Külliye at Lüleburgaz, the Büyük Çekmece Bridge, the Sinanli Bridge at Alpullu, and the Çinili, Mihrimah and Haseki Baths in Istanbul.

—DAVID G. WILKINS

SITTE, Camillo.

Austrian. Born in Vienna, Austria, 17 April 1843. Died in Vienna, 16 November 1903. Father was the architect Franz Sitte. Studied with his father, then apprenticed to Heinrich von Ferstel, 1863. Director of the State School of Applied Arts, Salzburg, 1875; director of the State School of Applied Arts, Vienna, 1883.

Chronology of Works

1873-74   Mechitaristenkirche, Vienna, Austria
1887   Parish Church, Temesvár, Hungary
1891   Hunting Lodge, near Zbirow, Bohemia, Czechoslo-vakia
1894-99   Marienkirche, Townhall, and Parish House, Oderfur-th-Privoz, Ostrava, Czechoslovakia

Publications

BOOKS BY SITTE

Der Städtebau nach seinen künstlerischen Grundsätzen. 1889. English translation: *City Planning According to Artistic Principles.* London 1965.

BOOKS ABOUT SITTE

Berichte zur Raumforschung und Raumplanung 12, No. 4 (1968), special issue.
COLLINS, GEORGE R. and COLLINS, CHRISTIANE C.: *Camillo Sitte and the Birth of Modern City Planning.* New York and London, 1965.

HEGEMANN, WERNER and PEETS, ELBERT: *The American Vi-truvius: An Architect's Handbook of Civil Art.* New York, 1922.
SCHWARZL, J.: *Franz, Camillo und Siegfried Sitte.* 1949.

ARTICLES ABOUT SITTE

ADSHEAD, S.: "Camillo Sitte and Le Corbusier." *Town Plan-ning Review* 14 (November 1930): 35-94.
FEHL, GERHARD: "Stadtbaukunst contra Stadtplanung: Zur Auseinandersetzung Camillo Sittes mit Reinhard Baumeis-ter." *Stadtbauwelt* 65 (1980): 451-461.
SCHORSKE, CARL E.: "The Ringstrasse, Its Critics, and the Birth of Urban Modernism." Chapter 2, pages 24-115 in *Fin-de-Siècle Vienna: Politics and Culture.* New York, 1980.

*

The expanding, noisy, filthy cities of the first half of the 19th century clearly showed the shadow side of industrialization, which was spreading across North America and Europe. Often the consequences were particularly catastrophic in working-class neighborhoods, an injustice on which Alexis de Tocque-ville and Friedrich Engels reported. In the face of this situation, with its often insoluble problems, the discipline of urban plan-ning gained a new relevance.

Camillo Sitte was active as an architect and city planner first in Salzburg (from 1878) and later in Vienna, his hometown. He set about solving the most important urban-planning prob-lems of the time. His pathbreaking book *Der Städtebau nach seinen künstlerischen Grundsätzen,* which was revolutionary in terms of turn-of-the-century urban planning, appeared in 1889. Sitte's book contained a detailed critique of the planning of metropolitan Vienna, a city shaped by Baroque principles, which had left a legacy of unaccented rows of houses and long, straight streets, and had pushed the individual palaces out of the fore-ground of the cityscape. In Vienna as in Salzburg, classicism had merely filled up the gaps between rows of houses, thus reinforcing the monotony. Sitte rejected "string-straight lines of houses," which he experienced as monotonous and saw as proof of the frightful poverty of city building theories. He also rejected the "search for symmetry," which he labeled a "fashion disease." These phenomena were all characteristic of the Baroque, but Sitte did not reject Baroque planning out of hand. He had a positive appreciation for the theatrical perspec-tives and imposing layouts of open spaces of the Baroque. Together with the straight streets, Sitte rejected the block system resulting from the grid intersections. To him, the result was not only a "depressing ugliness," but most of all "a labyrinthine impossibility of orienting oneself." Sitte thought Chicago the most frightful instance of such planning, in spite of the fact that the city experienced its great period of planning and architectural development in those years.

In opposition to the "proverbial tediousness of modern city plans," Sitte began to search for new principles of composition, with the goal of creating more harmonious results in city build-ing. With that goal in mind, he studied the cities of the Middle Ages and the Renaissance, principally in Italy, believing that those paradigms contained structural principles with which to shape a harmonious modern city. For Camillo Sitte, the Italian art of city planning reached its zenith in the design of open spaces. He saw these as the fulcrum of urban life, accommodat-ing traffic, markets, holiday celebrations and processions, as well as the display of monuments. Sitte drew up a history of the development and function of the public space in the urban context, beginning with the Greek agora through the fora of

Rome and Pompeii, to the architectural ensembles of the High Middle Ages, as they may be found in Florence, Ravenna, Manuta, Modena and Verona. The once-dominant church architecture gained a special relevance in Sitte's analysis, since the cathedrals of Italy almost without exception were integrated into the rows of houses which surrounded the open squares, contributing to the impression of closure of this kind of layout. At the same time, Sitte underlined the structural irregularity creating asymmetrical street openings, which may be observed again and again in Italian medieval city plans. The house frontages consequently overlap, each according to its location, leaving hardly any visible gaps in the ranges along the squares. This irregularity stands in contrast to modern designs, in which open spaces are surrounded with regularly disposed blocks. In addition to the small city centers of northern and central Italy, Sitte studied the city of Rome, not only for its great artistic designs (for example, Giovanni Lorenzo Bernini's St. Peter's Square), but also for the alterations designed to deal with an enormous increase in traffic, which already anticipated modern requirements.

All the same, Sitte did not plead for the exact copying of the asymmetrical, harmonious cityscapes of bygone times as a flight from the present. He pursued a rediscovery of a "freedom of conception," in order to overcome the constraints of a rigid regularity. Unfortunately, Sitte was not able to complete his analysis of the aesthetics of city building with the study of the economic and social foundations of urban planning that he had planned.

The effects of Sitte's work on attempts to solve urban-planning problems must not be underestimated. The magazine *Der Städtebau,* founded in 1904 by Sitte and Theodor Goecke, had a particularly powerful influence. The magazine also inspired Georg Simmel's essay *"Die Großstädte und das Geistesleben."* In addition, Sitte's work played an important role in the urban-planning developments of the first decade of the 20th century. Most important among the works inspired by his ideas were the projects for Berlin, particularly the designs by Werner Hegemann and others for the competition of 1910. Hendrik Petrus Berlage in the Netherlands was also influenced by Sitte.

Scandinavian architects and urban planners proved particularly responsive to Sitte's ideas. The possibility of using medieval structures, as mediated by Sitte, for the development of public spaces already influenced Finnish urban plans around the turn of the century, as the Tööklö-Helsinki plan of 1899 demonstrated. Eliel Saarinen combined the British garden-city approach with Sitte's suggestions in planning for a variety of urban contexts, such as the 1918 master plan for greater Helsinki. The same was true for Swedish urban plans of the turn of the century, particularly for the newly developed urban areas of Göteborg in Sweden. As a consequence, Camillo Sitte's work and the planning inspired by it came to form a defining basis for 20th-century urban planning.

—KUNIBERT BERING

Translated from the German by Marijke Rijsberman

SKIDMORE, OWINGS and MERRILL (SOM).

American. Partnership; established in Chicago, Illinois, by Louis Skidmore and Nathaniel Owings, 1936, and with John Merrill, as Skidmore, Owings and Merrill, 1939; branch offices established in New York, 1937, and subsequently throughout the United States. Partners have included Bruce Graham, Myron Goldsmith, Gordon Bunshaft, Fazlur Khan, Adrian Smith and Joe Gonzalez.

Chronology of Works
All in the United States unless noted

1942-46	Atom City, Oak Ridge, Tennessee
1949-50	Veterans' Administration Hospital, Brooklyn, New York
1949-50	Lake Meadows, Chicago, Illinois
1949-50	Terrace Plaza Hotel, Cincinnati, Ohio
1952	Lever House, New York City
1952-55	United States Navy Postgraduate School, Monterey, California
1954	Manufacturer's Hanover Trust, New York City
1955	Hilton Hotel, Istanbul, Turkey
1957	Connecticut General Life Insurance Company Building, Bloomfield, Connecticut
1957	United States Navy Service School, Great Lakes, Illinois
1958	Inland Steel Company Headquarters, Chicago, Illinois
1959	Crown Zellerbach Corporate Headquarters, San Francisco, California
1959	John Hancock Mutual Life Insurance Company Building, San Francisco, California
1960	PepsiCo Incorporated World Headquarters, New York City
1960	Union Carbide Building, New York City
1960-62	John Hancock Building, New Orleans, Louisiana
1961	Chase Manhattan Bank, New York City
1961	Upjohn Pharmaceuticals Company, Kalamazoo, Michigan
1962	Solar Telescope, Kitt Peak, Arizona
1962	United Airlines Headquarters, Chicago, Illinois
1962	United States Air Force Academy, Colorado Springs, Colorado
1963	Beinecke Rare Book and Manuscript Library, Yale University, New Haven, Connecticut
1965	Banque Lambert Building, Brussels, Belgium
1965	University of Illinois at Chicago Circle, Chicago, Illinois
1965	Brunswick Building, Chicago, Illinois
1965	Civic Center, Chicago, Illinois
1965	Equitable Life Assurance Society of the United States Building, Chicago, Illinois
1965	Library and Museum, Lincoln Center, New York City
1965	Vivian Beaumont Theater, Lincoln Center, New York City
1965	Mauna Kea Beach Hotel, Hawaii
1965	H.J. Heinz Company Ltd. Headquarters, Hayes Park, Middlesex, England
1966	Life Sciences Building, Illinois Institute of Technology, Chicago, Illinois
1967	Hartford Fire Insurance Building, San Francisco, California
1967	Marine Midland Bank, New York City
1968	Alcoa Building, Golden Gate Center, San Francisco, California
1968	Bank of America Headquarters, San Francisco, California
1968	Boots Headquarters, Nottingham, England
1970	John Hancock Center, Chicago, Illinois
1971	Hartford Fire Insurance Company Building, Chicago, Illinois
1971	Lyndon Baines Johnson Library, University of Texas, Austin, Texas
1971	One Shell Plaza Offices, Houston, Texas

1971	Sid W. Richardson Hall, University of Texas, Austin, Texas
1973	W. R. Grace Building, Avenue of the Americas, New York City
1974	Hirshhorn Museum and Sculpture Garden, Washington, D.C.
1974	Philip Morris Factory, Richmond, Virginia
1974	Sears Tower, Chicago, Illinois
1974	Wills Headquarters, Bristol, England
1975	Harris Trust and Savings Bank, Chicago, Illinois
1975	Baxter Travenol Laboratories Headquarters, Deerfield, Illinois
1975	Tour Fiat Building, Paris, France
1976	Washington Mall Plan and Constitution Garden, Washington, D.C.
1976	Ohio National Bank, Columbus, Ohio
1977	Khaneh Center, Teheran, Iran
1977	Apparel Mart and Holiday Inn, Wolf Point, Chicago, Illinois
1977	Art Institute of Chicago, Chicago, Illinois (addition and School of Art)
1978	Miami University Art Museum, Oxford, Ohio
1978	Mayo Clinic Community Medicine Facility, Rochester, New York
1978	New World Center, Hong Kong
1979	National City Bank, Cleveland, Ohio
1980	Arab International Bank, Cairo, Egypt
1980	International Museum of Photography, George Eastman House, Rochester, New York
1982	Haj Terminal, King Abdul Aziz Internationl Airport, Jeddah, Saudi Arabia
1984	National Commercial Bank, Jeddah, Saudi Arabia
1983	Southeast Financial Center, Miami, Florida
1985	LTV Center, Dallas, Texas
1985	Citicorp Plaza, Los Angeles
1987	303 West Madison, Chicago, Illinois
1989	AT&T Corporate Center, Chicago, Illinois

Publications

BOOKS BY SOM ARCHITECTS

KHAN, FAZLUR: *Analytical Studies of Relations Among Various Design Criteria for Prestressed Concrete Beams*. With N. Khachaturian and C. P. Siess. Urbana, Illinois, 1955.

KHAN, FAZLUR: *A Study of Tests on Prestressed Concrete Beams*. Urbana, Illinois, 1974.

OWINGS, NATHANIEL: *The American Aesthetic*. New York, 1969.

OWINGS, NATHANIEL: *The Spaces in Between: An Architect's Journey*. Boston, 1973.

ARTICLES BY SOM ARCHITECTS All by Fazlur Khan

"Proposed Revision of Building Code Requirements for Reinforced Concrete." *American Concrete Institute Journal* (Detroit, November 1962). "Proposed Recommended Practice for Concrete Formwork." *American Concrete Institute Journal* (Detroit, March 1963).

"Computer Design of the 100-Story John Hancock Center." With S. H. Iyengar and J. P. Colaco. *Journal of the American Society of Civil Engineers* (December 1966).

"Effect of Column Exposure in Tall Structures." with Mark Fintel. *American Concrete Institute Journal* (Detroit, August 1966).

"The John Hancock Center." *Civil Engineering* (October 1967).

"The Nature of High-Rise Buildings." *Indian Builder* (Bombay, June 1967); reprinted in *Inland Architect* (Chicago, July 1967).

"Analysis and Design of the 100-Story John Hancock Center in Chicago." With S. H. Iyengar and J. P. Colaco. In *Acier Stahl Steel* (Brussels, June 1968).

"The Chicago School Grows Up." *Architectural and Engineering News* (Philadelphia, April 1969).

"The Future of High Rise in America." *Progressive Architecture* (October 1972).

"The Changing Scale of the Cities." *Consulting Engineer* (April 1974).

BOOKS ABOUT SKIDMORE, OWINGS, and MERRILL

BILLINGTON, DAVID P.: *The Tower and the Bridge: The New Art of Structural Engineering*. Princeton, New Jersey, 1983.

Bruce Graham, Som. New York, 1989.

BUSCHIAZZO, MARIO JOSE: *Skidmore, Owings, and Merrill*. Buenos Aires, 1958.

BUSH-BROWN, ALBERT: *Skidmore, Owings and Merrill: Architecture and Urbanism, 1973-1983*. Stuttgart and New York, 1984.

DREXLER, ARTHUR, and MENGES, AXEL: *The Architecture of Skidmore, Owings and Merrill, 1963-1973*. New York, 1974.

EDELMANN, FREDERIC, and GLIBOTA, ANTE: *150 Years of Chicago Architecture, 1833-1983*. Exhibition catalog. Paris, 1983.

GRUBE, OSWALD W.; PRAN, PETER C.; SCHULZE, FRANZ: *100 Years of Architecture in Chicago*. Exhibition catalog. Chicago, 1976.

HEYER, PAUL (ed.): *Architects on Architecture*. New York, 1966.

HITCHCOCK, HENRY-RUSSELL, and DANZ, ERNST: *The Architecture of Skidmore, Owings, and Merrill 1950-1962*. New York and Stuttgart, 1962; London, 1963.

HUXTABLE, ADA LOUISE: *Will They Ever Finish Bruckner Boulevard?* New York, 1970.

KRINSKY, CAROL HERSELLE: *Gordon Bunshaft of Skidmore, Owings and Merrill*. Cambridge, Massachusetts, 1988.

PETER, JOHN: *Masters of Modern Architecture*. New York, 1958.

Skidmore, Owings and Merrill 1936-1980. New York, 1981.

Skidmore, Owings and Merrill: Architects. New York, 1960.

SLAVIN, MAEVE: *Davis Allen: Forty Years of Interior Design at Skidmore Owings and Merrill*. New York, 1990.

TIGERMAN, STANLEY: *Bruce Graham of SOM*. New York, 1989.

WOODWARD, CHRISTOPHER and FUTAGAWA, YUKIO: *Skidmore, Owings and Merrill*. Tokyo, 1968; New York and London, 1970.

*

Skidmore, Owings and Merrill, or SOM, as it has become known, is a large American practice whose work dominated the commercial architecture of the world during the 1950s, 1960s and 1970s. Their best work, particularly in the 1950s, includes some of the most distinguished modern buildings ever built.

Louis Skidmore and Nathaniel Owings had both worked on the 1933 Chicago "Century of Progress" exhibition, and had learned how to handle government agencies, large-scale contracts and the construction of modern buildings. In 1935, meeting in London, they decided to open a practice together, and in the following year they were joined by the engineer John Merrill. During the war they worked on the construction of Oak Ridge, Tennessee, the town for those working on the atomic bomb, and hence entered the postwar world with a big office and a track record of handling large contracts. Neither of the founding partners was a prima-donna architect, but they were great talent spotters; they brought in young designers, often straight out of architecture school, and gave them big buildings to design with a backup of managers and technicians who could hold the design on course and help it through to completion. It was to prove a winning formula, and within the SOM organization some of the leading architects of the time made their careers—Gordon Bunshaft, Bruce Graham, Walter Netsch, Charles Bassett, Myron Goldsmith and many more.

It was Gordon Bunshaft's work in the New York office that raised the firm to stardom with a series of sleek buildings on prominent sites in Manhattan. The completion of Lever House on Park Avenue in 1952 was breathtaking after the gloom and austerity of the war and postwar years. Taking its regularity from Ludwig Mies van der Rohe, its shininess from Richard Neutra, its slab-on-a-podium concept from Le Corbusier, Lever House somehow contrived to be totally American, and at the same time the fulfillment of the European dream of a modern architecture served by an efficient technology. Lever House became the victim of its own success and was soon surrounded by cruder versions of itself, for not since Palladio had a design been so copied—every city in the world with any sort of claim to a modern culture soon had its versions of Lever House, often badly built and poorly serviced, so that a decade later, there was a reaction against curtain-walled office buildings.

Two years after Lever House, Bunshaft followed up that success with the Manufacturers Hanover Trust Company, a four-story glass cube on Fifth Avenue, with the massive round safe door visible to all passersby and a beautiful banking hall with a sculptured wall by Harry Bertoia; then back up Park Avenue for the Pepsi-Cola Building, but there the relentless grid of mullions at five-foot centers was avoided, large plates of glass were used, and partitions simply butt up to the glass with a neoprene strip. Contemporary with Pepsi-Cola is the Union Carbide tower, where SOM designed the interior as well as the exterior in what must be the most precise, geometric and perfect office interior ever built; then to the Wall Street district with the Chase Manhattan Bank and Marine Midland. This series of buildings showed that Bunshaft and SOM knew where they were going and how to get it done. Thirty-five years later, these remain among the best modern buildings in Manhattan.

At the same time as he was building in New York City, Bunshaft gave form to the out-of-town office building. For Connecticut General Life Insurance, on a site at Bloomfield, Connecticut, a spreading cluster of low buildings of shiny glass and metal set the direction for such buildings around the world, just as Lever House had for its urban cousin. Connecticut General was followed a couple of years later by the Emhart Headquarters on an adjoining site. Other out-of-town headquarters buildings followed—Upjohn in Kalamazoo, Michigan; American Can in Greenwich, Connecticut; Baxter Travenol in Deerfield, Illinois; General Electric in Fairfield, Connecticut.

Perhaps the most distinguished of the out-of-town office buildings was built by Charles Bassett of the San Francisco office for the Weyerhaeuser Corporation, a lumber company in Tacoma, Washington. Placed across a beautiful valley like a dam, the Weyerhaeuser Building is long and low, with roofs as a series of planted terraces to tie the building into the landscape.

The Chicago office of SOM was in the hometown of Mies van der Rohe, and it was natural that his students should dominate that office. The Inland Steel building of 1958 was a version of Lever House but with more Miesian characteristics—a more dominant structure, a clearer plan, a tower that comes down to the ground. Later, the SOM office succeeded Mies as architects to the campus at the Illinois Institute of Technology, where they built a library and a fieldhouse. In the early 1970s, the Chicago office of SOM designed and built two of the tallest buildings in the world—the Hancock Center and the Sears Tower. Both of these towers, true to the Miesian tradition, had based their form on the structure, and owed much to SOM's brilliant engineer, Fazlur Khan.

No one pursued the integration of form and structure with more singlemindedness than Myron Goldsmith. Trained by Mies and by Pier Luigi Nervi, he was invited to join the San Francisco office of SOM to design and build two splendid hangars for United Air Lines. These hangars had beautiful steel and concrete structures, with structural members tapering in accord with the stresses they were designed to resist. They were followed by his masterpiece, the Robert McMath solar telescope at Kitt Peak, Arizona, a beautiful white shaft growing out of the Rampart Mountains. The form of the solar telescope is functional—a diamond shape on section to reduce wind pressure, a white-coated copper cladding to keep heat and wind off the separate telescope support structure within. Moving to Chicago, Goldsmith produced a series of buildings which are an ode to the notion that architecture is the magic of structure; the finest of these is not one of his big-city towers, but a small, single-story printing plant for the *Republic* newspaper in Columbus, Ohio, a simple glazed pavilion giving dignity to the printing of the town's own newspaper.

Architectural fashions changed, and the glassy curtain wall, which had seemed so exciting and all-sufficient in the 1950s, began to pall. Bunshaft designed heavy, massive buildings for the Yale Rare Book Library, for the Lyndon Johnson Library at Austin, Texas, and for New York's Lincoln Center. The Chicago office, on the basis of Netsch's "Field Theory," constructed the University of Illinois with concrete in complex shapes based on octagons.

From its earliest days SOM had built in many countries, and in the early 1950s the Istanbul Hilton and housing for State Department personnel in Bremen marked its international intentions. The out-of-town office building was successfully exported to England with the construction of the Heinz Headquarters at Hayes Park, west of London, Wills Tobacco near Bristol and the beautiful office headquarters for Boots, near Nottingham. In the 1970s SOM consolidated its position worldwide, with offices in many countries. As with many large architectural practices, it was the honeypot of the Middle East that provided work during the recession that followed the oil-price rise. Most of the buildings designed in the Middle East by Western architects during that period were of doubtful quality, and many famous names spoiled their reputations by putting up third-rate buildings. Not so SOM. Bunshaft's 27-story National Commercial Bank in Jeddah, Saudi Arabia, is an attempt to make the office tower work in a very hot country; it is a triangular tower with stone on the outside, but the tower is pierced to open up the interior, and the faces of the building onto these interior spaces are fully glazed. Far more dramatic is the Haj Terminal at Jeddah, a magnificent tented structure in which 80,000 pilgrims can stay protected from the sun by 210 semiconical Teflon-coated Fiberglass roof units, all beautifully engineered by Fazlur Khan; it is a masterpiece, and a fitting swansong to the firm's long allegiance to modern architecture.

The 1980s saw the retirement of the first generation of SOM designers, and a shift in client wishes away from puritanical modernism. The developers of the new office boom regarded the rectangular glass and metal towers as old-fashioned, and the new image of postmodernism coincided with the mood of conspicuous consumption of the Ronald Reagan presidency. Tenants, it was said, wanted space in trendy, postmodern buildings, and in 1983 the New York firm of Kohn Pedersen Fox provided it at Chicago's 333 Wacker Drive. SOM, which had built 70 percent of Chicago buildings of more than 20 stories, was alleged to be out-of-date. The new generation of SOM partners responded with a change of style; David Childs in New York, Adrian Smith and Joe Gonzalez in Chicago made postmodernism SOM's style with buildings such as the AT&T in Chicago's Loop. SOM, which for nearly 40 years had set the trend, was now following others, and as postmodernism is seen to be a passing fad, the future may hold more surprises.

While it may have lost its place on the cutting edge of architecture, SOM has retained its technical and commercial expertise. It has expanded with offices in several countries, continues to grow and to be a byword for contractual skill and technical excellence.

—JOHN WINTER

SLOAN, Samuel.

American. Born in Beaver Dam, Pennsylvania, 7 March 1815. Died in Raleigh, North Carolina, 19 July 1884. Established own firm, Philadelphia, Pennsylvania, ca. 1850. Fellow, American Institute of Architects; editor, *Architectural Review* magazine and *American Builder's Journal.*

Chronology of Works
All in the United States

1851	Bartram Hall, West Philadelphia
1851-66	18 public schools, Philadelphia
1853	Masonic Temple, Philadelphia
1854-61	Longwood Villa, Natchez, Mississippi
1855	Bennett and Company Store (Tower Hall), Philadelphia
1856	Joseph Harrison, Jr., Town Mansion, Philadelphia
1866	Horticultural Hall, Philadelphia

Publications

BOOKS BY SLOAN

The Model Architect. 2 vols. Philadelphia, 1852-53.
City and Suburban Architecture. Philadelphia, 1859
Sloan's Constructive Architecture. Philadelphia, 1859.
Sloan's Homestead Architecture. Philadelphia, 1861.

BOOKS ABOUT SLOAN

COOLEDGE, HAROLD N.: *Samuel Sloan: Architect of Philadelphia, 1815-1884.* 1987.

The evolutionary development of a nation's architecture can be strongly influenced by the work, and personality, of architects who—although well known, even famous, at the height of their careers—are almost forgotten by the time of their deaths, and totally forgotten immediately thereafter. When this is the case, the most significant work of such architects usually falls within a period of major social transition, when an old, familiar corpus

of mores is being revised because it no longer fits the nation's changing economy and social structure.

In such times the architect must meet the demands of a new set of clients, having new mores and new problems, when materials and methods to properly solve those problems may be in only the most elemental stage of development, and the architectural forms to properly symbolize their solution may not yet have been considered. Caught between the means and methods of an old architectural vocabulary and the programmatic demands of new social institutions, the architect may devise new and original solutions to functional requirements—circulation, supply, ventilation, heating and lighting—but be forced, by the uncertain dictates of "taste," to clothe his plans in a pastiche of traditional forms. This has been called "eclecticism," usually an opprobrious term, which it should not be, for it can obscure important contributions that result from its practice.

Samuel Sloan, "Architect of Philadelphia," was such an eclectic, and it is hard to reconcile the volume and variety of his work, the social prominence of his clients, and the breadth of his practice with the complete disappearance of his name from architectural records after 1884.

Beginning his professional life as a carpenter and cabinet-maker, Sloan progressed through the stages of construction superintendent, independent builder and self-taught architect to full professional practice with an office which was, for the decade of the 1850s, among the most important in the nation. In that decade he became the preeminent hospital architect of the United States, collaborating with the alienist Dr. Thomas Kirkbride to produce a design for hospitals for the insane that became the accepted national standard for the next 30 years.

In the same period he created "Mr. Sloan's Plan" for public schools, which the City Council of Philadelphia, and then the State of Pennsylvania, designated as its "official" design. The state published a patternbook of Sloan's school designs and provided all its districts with a copy. At least 10 county courthouses and jails in Pennsylvania, New Jersey, Delaware and North Carolina came from his office. One must say "at least" because Sloan published his designs with great success, and it has been impossible to determine the number of buildings taken from his most popular patternbooks (*The Model Architect*, 1852, reissued four times; *City and Suburban Architecture*, 1859, reissued 1867; and *Sloan's Homestead Architecture*, 1861, reissued three times).

This is particularly true of residential work. His office received more than a hundred documented residential commissions, few of which stand, but the number of residences taken from his books and the designs he contributed to *Godey's Lady's Book* cannot even be estimated. The most ambitious of Sloan's residential commissions—Longwood, the octagonal, "Oriental" villa for Dr. Haller Nutt in Natchez, Mississippi—stands, unfinished. The Civil War interrupted its construction, permanently, but until the building of George Vanderbilt's Biltmore House in the 1890s, Longwood was the largest private "folly" to be attempted in the United States.

In 1868 Sloan became an initial member of the reconstituted American Institute of Architects, and, to provide that organization with a house organ, began the publication of the first architectural periodical in the United States, *The Architectural Review.* Initially successful, the magazine rapidly declined in popularity, and suspended publication in 1870. This was an indication of Sloan's waning "image" with the younger generation of postwar architects. He recognized and resented this change in status, and his confidence was further shaken by the results of the competition for the buildings of the Centennial Exhibition of 1876, in which he received the second prize.

Repeated loss of commissions caused him to move his office to Raleigh, North Carolina, in 1883. From there he supervised his last commissions in North and South Carolina.

What Sloan and other practitioners of his generation, A. J. Davis, for example, failed to understand was that their work was not terminal but, like so much else in the period, transitional. Admittedly his school design was almost 50 years ahead of its time, which caused it to be rapidly modified, but it too was eventually overtaken and surpassed.

Sloan's considerable talent did not so much decline as remain static, while the country, and his profession, grew away from him. As a result, at the time of his death he was considered as "belonging . . . to a school which has ceased to excite commotion in the artistic world" (*American Architect and Building News*, Aug. 2, 1884).

Not for almost a hundred years were his basic innovations in functional design recognized. Sloan occupies a midpoint in the evolution of American creative eclecticism, which reached its climax with the work of H. H. Richardson, Louis Sullivan and Frank Lloyd Wright.

—HAROLD N. COOLEDGE, JR.

SMIRKE, Robert.

British. Born in London, England, 1 October 1780. Died in Cheltenham, London, 18 April 1867. Father was the noted artist Robert Smirke, R.A.; brother was the architect Sydney Smirke (1797-1877); married Laura Freston; one daughter. Studied with John Soane, 1796, then with George Dance the Younger and at the Royal Academy Schools; study tour to France, Germany, Italy and Greece, 1801-05. Opened office in London, 1805; appointed as official architect to the Board of Works, 1805 (along with John Soane and John Nash); architect to Royal Mint, 1807; attached architect, Office of Works, 1813; retired from practice upon appointment to Commission for London Improvements, 1845. Associate, 1808, member, 1811, and treasurer, 1820-50, Royal Academy; honorary fellow, Royal Institute of British Architects; Gold Medal, Royal Institute of British Architects, 1853; knighted, 1832.

Chronology of Works
All in England unless noted
† Work no longer exists
* Approximate dates

1806-11	Lowther Castle, Westmorland†
1808-10	Covent Garden Theatre, London (since rebuilt)†
1809-11	Royal Mint, London (additions)
1810-11	Cirencester Park, Gloucestershire (additions)
1810-12	County Courts, Carlisle, Cumberland
1812-15	Eastnor Castle, Herefordshire
1814-16	Shire Hall, Gloucester
1815-17	Shire Hall, Hereford
1816-19	County Buildings and Jail, Perth, Scotland
1816-19	Landsdowne House, London (additions)
1816-38	Inner Temple, London (additions)
1816*-42	Luton Hoo, Bedfordshire (additions; since altered)
1817-22	Millbank Penitentiary, London (additions)
1818	Whittinghame House, Haddington, Scotland
1820-22	Kinfauns Castle, Perth, Scotland
1821	Normanby Park, Lincolnshire
1821-22	St. George's Church, Bristol
1822-24	St. Anne's Church, London
1822-25	St. Philip's Church, Salford
1822-25	Union Club and Royal College of Physicians, London
1823-29	General Post Office, London†
1823-30	County Courts, Lincoln
1823-46	British Museum, London (completed by Sydney Smirke in 1852)
1824-27	Council House, Bristol
1824-27	Temple Church, London (restoration)
1824-28	County Courts, Maidstone, Kent
1825-27	Custom House, London (rebuilding)
1829-35	King's College, London
1829-35	Somerset House, London (completion of river front)
1829-35	London Bridge Approaches, London (facades)
1830-32	Minster, York (restoration)
1831-35	Drayton Manor, Staffordshire†
1833-36	Carlton Club, London (later rebuilt)
1834-37	Temporary Houses of Parliament, London
1836-37	Oxford and Cambridge Club, London (with Sydney Smirke)
1836-37	Shire Hall, Shrewsbury, Shropshire

Publications

BOOKS BY SMIRKE

Specimens of Continental Architecture. London, 1806.

BOOKS ABOUT SMIRKE

CROOK, J. MORDAUNT: *The British Museum.* London and New York, 1972.
CROOK, J. MORDAUNT: *The Greek Revival.* London, 1972.
FAWCETT, JANE (ed.): *Seven Victorian Architects.* University Park, Pennsylvania, 1976.
SERVICE, ALASTAIR: *The Architects of London.* London, 1979.

ARTICLES ABOUT SMIRKE

CROOK, J. MORDAUNT: "Architect of the Rectangular: Sir Robert Smirke." *Country Life* 141 (13 April 1967): 846.
CROOK, J. MORDAUNT: "Sir Robert Smirke: A Pioneer of Concrete Construction." *Transactions of the Newcomen Society* 38 (1965-66): 5-22.

*

Robert Smirke is best known for his British public buildings. His design capability was only moderate, but he exploited both a patronage network and contemporary developments in engineering and building technique, ran a well-organized office, and kept within his estimates. Through the connections of his father, the well-known artist Robert Smirke Sr., he rapidly acquired an extensive clientele, particularly within the early-19th-century Pittite administrations. Success in castle building and civic architecture made him an obvious candidate for one of the three posts created in 1815 as "Attached Architect" of the government Office of Works, responsible for the care of palaces (including Windsor) and public buildings, and his ministerial contacts secured his appointment at the age of only 33. He thus joined John Soane and John Nash at the head of the architectural profession in Great Britain.

Before commencing practice, Smirke traveled in Italy and Greece, from 1801 to 1805, acquiring a first-hand familiarity with Classical Greek architecture that proved highly valuable, for his professional career opened precisely at the time when

Robert Smirke: British Museum, London, England, 1823-46

the Greek style became the rage in Britain. He called it "the noblest" style, "simple, grand, magnificent without ostentation"; it had "a kind of primal simplicity" appealing to a student of Marc-Antoine Laugier. Hence it was an austere version that he practiced, constantly repeating a very limited range of precedents.

In 1808, commissioned to rebuild the Theatre Royal Covent Garden, he seized the opportunity to give London its first building in pure Doric. The Parthenon (from which the portico and antae of the wings were taken) was an unexpected model for a theater, but Smirke thought a national building should aim at grandeur of effect. Panels of sculpture designed by John Flaxman relieved its severity, while at ground level a series of segmental arches formed an arcade. The facade was widely copied for schools and almshouses. This willingness to adapt archaeological exactitude to modern needs was one element in Smirke's success: let "the style of composition. . . be restored to its original purity," he declared, "and it matters little. . .whether its orders be more or less exactly imitated." His functional outlook earned him the scorn of connoisseurs and the admiration of practical men. Behind its Grecian severity there rose the yet-more-severe geometrical mass of auditorium and stage, relieved only by windows and stringcourses. This cubic style—"the New Square Style of Mr. Smirke," A. W. N. Pugin called it—was the consistent basis of his architecture, whatever decorative style might be applied to it.

Thanks to his father's friend, the elderly architect George Dance the Younger, Smirke has been commissioned in 1806 by the ultrarich Lord Lonsdale to rebuild his principal seat, Lowther Hall, Westmorland. This symmetrical castle was derived from James Wyatt's Kew Palace and Ashridge House, via a design that Dance had made: pyramidal in disposition,

culminating in a central tower housing a staircase hall. Thus it was a compromise with the irregularity expected of the picturesque, retaining the symmetry characteristic of classical architecture. Versions of Lowther followed at Eastnor, Herefordshire (1812), and Kinfauns, Perthshire (1820). Through Lonsdale, Smirke obtained civic commissions at Carlisle, Cumberland, and established a line in county administrative buildings.

Towers and battlements hardly obscured the basically rectangular character of such structures. Smirke's cubism was given clearest expression, however, in his simplified Greek country houses, for example, Whittinghame, East Lothian, and Normanby Park, Lincolnshire, dispensing even with the customary portico. In London, too, he used this style for the new clubhouses demanded in the postwar world by associations of individuals with common interests. Country houses which he built in the Tudor style included Drayton Manor (1831-35) for Sir Robert Peel, but the stylistic difference was superficial.

By 1835 Smirke was the only active "Attached Architect," though the post itself had been abolished as a result of reforms in 1832, when Smirke was knighted. During Peel's brief premiership in 1835, he invited Smirke to design new Houses of Parliament in place of those lately burned down. But the appointment was unpopular and a press campaign led to an open competition, which Smirke declined.

Smirke's role as an expert on construction often led to his employment to report on or restore failed works. As early as 1810 he was using load-bearing cast-iron beams at Cirencester Park. Highly significant, too, was his innovative use of concrete foundations to secure the Millbank Penitentiary (1817). The most celebrated, however, was the new London Custom House. When a large part collapsed in 1825, Smirke was called in. In works costing some £177,000, he again made extensive use of concrete, and rebuilt the central "Long Room" to his own design. Again, as the most utility-minded of the three government architects, Smirke was asked to design a headquarters post office in the city of London, after an open competition failed for want of practicality. In 1829-35 he undertook a major piece of urban design, the facades for the approaches to the new London Bridge.

The most important work of Smirke's career was the rebuilding of the British Museum. In 1823 Smirke drew up plans for a great quadrangular building fronted by a giant colonnade (derived, J. M. Crook suggests, from Edward Lovett Pearce's early-18th-century Parliament House in Dublin) of the Ionic order from Priene, which he had already used at the General Post Office. Carried out progressively over the years, these designs were completed in 1852, after he had retired, at a total cost of some £800,000. Smirke employed concrete extensively in the foundations, and cast iron for the roof girders, some over 50 feet long—"the first beams that were ever introduced into London of so great length and with large openings through the web of the beam." But by the 1850s the Greek Revival had had its day, and its largest and ultimate exemplar in London provided ample scope for captious criticism. However, the King's Library, Smirke's finest work, escaped unscathed. Some 300 feet long, 41 feet wide and 30 feet high, articulated by a center compartment widening to 58 feet with giant monolithic columns of polished red Aberdeen granite and Corinthian capitals of Derbyshire alabaster, it ranks among the world's finest libraries.

Smirke arrived professionally equipped in an England poised to enthuse about his chosen style, with vast wealth looking for architectural expression, national buildings loudly demanded, and still sufficiently controlled by patronage to provide him with the necessary position while he was yet young. His natural bent enabled him to exploit the newly developing technology. His simplified classicism nevertheless won only limited acceptance. A quarter of a century later, Smirke's reticence and refusal to enter competition would doubtless have severely confined his operations.

—M. H. PORT

SMITH, James.

Scottish. Born in Moratshire, Scotland, 1645. Died in Edinburgh, 6 November 1731. Father was James Smith, mason; married Janet Mylne. May have studied at Scots College, Rome, 1671; surveyor or overseer of the Royal Works, 1683; worked independently; commissioner of supply for the County of Edinburgh.

Chronology of Works
All in Scotland
* Approximate dates
† Work no longer exists

1688	Chapel Royal, Holyroodhouse, Edinburgh†
1688-90	Canongate Church, Edinburgh
1690*	Whitehall House (now Newhailes House), Midlothian
1693-1701	Hamilton Palace, Lanarkshire†
1697-1700	Melville House, Fife
1700*-15	Yester House, East Lothian
1702-10	Dalkeith House, Midlothian

Publications

BOOKS ABOUT SMITH

BEDFORD, STEVEN and NEVINS, DEBORAH: *Between Tradition and Modernism.* New York, 1980.
MYLNE, R. S.: *The Master Masons to the Crown of Scotland.* 1893.

ARTICLES ABOUT SMITH

COLVIN, H. M.: "A Scottish Origin for English Palladianism?" *Architectural History* xvii (1974).

James Smith was a Scottish architect, "our first architect," as a laird described him in 1719, responsible for bringing to his country, and perhaps even to England, a strain of Palladianism that fed into the stylistic concerns of other later Scottish architects (such as Colen Campbell (1673-1729), and Robert Mylne (1734-1811).

Smith was the son of a master mason and was first trained for the Church. But at some time, perhaps in the 1670s, Smith was abroad and visited Italy, where, as Mylne noted, "(he) studied his Art." This was an obviously important opportunity; later Smith could describe himself as having had a "liberall (*sic*) education at schools and Colledges (*sic*) at home and abroad and occasion to know the world by travelling abroad." From that and from his social and personal connections with Robert Mylne the Elder, then master mason to the Scottish court, and William Bruce, surveyor of the royal works, Smith was able in 1683, a few years after Bruce was dismissed from the post, to acquire the surveyorship of the royal works in Scotland. His main responsibility was the maintenance of Holyroodhouse. He remained in this post through all the vicissitudes of the revolution and the reign of Queen Anne. Though he was later made surveyor of the Highland forts erected by the Board of Ordnance under George I, this employment ended in 1719 when Andrews Jelfe, an English mason and sometime associate of Nicholas Hawksmoor, was made architect for the fortifications under the board's jurisdiction.

Smith was also working all that time, however, for private patrons, and he is best remembered as a designer of Scottish country houses in the classical style Bruce had introduced. The first of these, even before his appointment as surveyor, was Drumlanrig, done for the duke of Queensbury. The most important of Smith's other houses were Hamilton Place, Lanarkshire (1693-1701); Melville House, Fife (1697-1700); Yester House, East Lothian (1702-15); and Dalkeith House, Midlothian (1702-10). Drumlanrig was a romantic, exotic design, based perhaps on the earlier plans for this house. The others, with their simple pedimented fronts and hipped roofs, were plain, quiet houses, in the manner of Bruce's undemonstrative classical designs. But Smith's story does not end with these houses. Though we know very little about the last 10 years of Smith's life, there is evidence to suggest that he was connected with Colen Campbell, then emerging as a proponent of the new Palladianism that was soon to change all English architecture. The argument runs thus: among the drawings owned by Campbell—and now in the collection of the Royal Institute of British Architects in London—are several, clearly not by Campbell's hand, that are exercises on Palladian subjects; they include designs for villas with centralized plans similar to Palladio's Villa Rotonda, a facade based on the Palazzo Iseppo Porto in Vicenza, and architecture that seems to have been the basis for a house "in the theatrical style" that Campbell used for one of the plates in the second volume of *Vitruvius Britannicus* (1717). How Campbell knew Smith is not clear; Campbell could have been his pupil, or it might be that these drawings were acquired by him when Smith was in some financial difficulties in his later years. In 1720, for example, in a petition to the barons of the Exchequer, Smith mentioned the needs of "his numerous family of 32 children"; in 1706 he had had to sell part of an estate at Whitehill, in Inveresk, and in 1726 he assigned the remainder to his son-in-law as security for a debt. But these Palladian drawings by Smith seem earlier than anything of the kind by Campbell and, as H. M. Colvin has put it, if Campbell's Palladianism preceded that of Lord Burlington, so Smith's Palladian plans have precedence over those of Campbell, coming perhaps from his stay in Italy in the 1670s. It is a fascinating if barely known story of influences.

—DAVID CAST

SMITHSON, Peter and Alison.

SMITHSON, Peter.
British. Born in Stockton-on-Tees, County Durham, England, 18 September 1923. Married Alison Margaret Gill, 1949. Educated at the University of Durham, 1939-42, 1945-48; Royal Academy School, London, 1948-49. Worked in London County Council Schools Division, London, 1949-50; in partnership with Alison Smithson, London, since 1950. Contributor to Team 10.

SMITHSON, Alison.
British. Born Alison Margaret Gill in Sheffield, England, 22 June 1928. Married Peter Smithson, 1949. Studied at the University of Durham, 1944-49. Worked in London County Council Schools Division, London, 1949-50; in partnership with Peter Smithson, since 1950. Contributor to Team 10.

Chronology of Works
All in England unless noted

1949-54	Hunstanton Secondary Modern School, Norfolk
1957	Watford House, Devereux Drive, Watford, Hertfordshire
1960	Caro House, Frognal, Hampstead, London
1961	Iraqi House, Piccadilly, London
1963	Occupational Health Unit, Park Royal Hospital, London
1964	Economist Building, St. James's Street, London
1970	Garden Building, St. Hilda's College, Oxford
1972	Robin Hood Gardens Housing, Robin Hood Lane, London
1972	Ansty Plum Studio, Garage and Store, Wiltshire
1978	Amenity (stage 1), University of Bath, Avon
1981	Second Arts Building, University of Bath, Avon
1984	Amenity (stage 2), University of Bath, Avon
1986	Porch, Bad Karlshafen, Germany
1988	Six East, University of Bath, Avon
1990	Auto Barn, University of Bath, Avon
1991	Yellow Lookout, Tecta, Lauenförde, Germany

Publications

BOOKS BY ALISON AND PETER SMITHSON

Uppercase. London, 1960; revised edition, as *Urban Structuring.* London and New York, 1967.
The Euston Arch. London, 1968.

Alison and Peter Smithson: Economist Building, London, England, 1964

Ordinariness and Light: Urban Theories 1952-60 and Their Application in a Building Project 1963-70. London and Cambridge, Massachusetts, 1970.

Without Rhetoric: An Architectural Aesthetic 1955-1972. London and Cambridge, Massachusetts, 1973.

The Tram Rats: A Story for Adults and Children. London, 1976.

The Heroic Period of Modern Architecture. Milan and London, 1981.

The Shift in Our Aesthetic 1950-78. London, 1982.

BOOKS BY ALISON SMITHSON

Team 10 Primer (ed.). London, 1965.

Portrait of the Female Mind as a Young Girl. Novel. London, 1966.

Feedback. London, 1973.

Places Worth Inheriting. London, 1978.

24 Doors to Christmas. Cambridge, 1979.

Anthology of Scottish Christmas pax Hogmanay. Edinburgh, 1980.

Team 10 out of CIAM (ed.). London, 1982.

AS in DS. Delft, Netherlands, 1983.

Team 10 Meetings 1953-1984 (ed.). New York, 1991.

BOOKS BY PETER SMITHSON

Bath: Walks Within the Walls. London, 1971; Bath, 1980.

ARTICLES BY ALISON AND PETER SMITHSON

The Smithsons have written numerous articles together and individually in many architectural publications, most notably for *Architectural Design* from the mid-1950s to the mid-1970s.

BOOKS ABOUT THE SMITHSONS

VIDOTTO, MARCO: *Alison and Peter Smithson.* Genoa, Italy, 1991.

ARTICLES ABOUT THE SMITHSONS

"Robin Hood Gardens." *Architecture and Urbanism* (February 1974).

BANHAM, REYNER: "The New Brutalism." *Architectural Review* (December 1955).

EISENMAN, PETER: "From Golden Lane to Robin Hood Gardens; or If You Follow the Yellow Brick Road, It May Not Lead to Golders Green." *Oppositions* 1 (1973).

FRAMPTON, KENNETH: "The Economist and the Hauptstadt." *Architectural Design* (February 1965).

JOHNSON, PHILIP: "Comment on School at Hunstanton, Norfolk." *Architectural Review* (September 1954).

McKEAN, JOHN M.: "The Smithsons: A Profile." *Building Design* (6 and 13 May 1977).

*

Even if they leave a paucity of works (built or proposed), some architects can stamp themselves on the image of a generation: the husband and wife teams of Charles Rennie Mackintosh and Margaret Macdonald, and Charles and Ray Eames come to mind. After one or two buildings which seem to stand as a lighthouse, illuminating the washy visual memory of their time, energies may move on elsewhere.

Young turks may leap precociously to an aggressive assurance whose foundations appear increasingly shaky until they vanish by the age of 40 as quickly as they came, victims of the "one-novel author" syndrome. Others chisel a place in our memory by slowly, gropingly carving out an architecture which stubbornly states "I am," until we listen; Louis Kahn was over 50 before his first major buildings began to appear.

How can we place Peter and Alison Smithson (or APS, as they sign themselves)? They burst like a meteor in their youth, and have stood firmly in their maturity, stubbornly unmoving even when the mainstream shifted far away, their heroic, quiet independence enigmatic and strangely attractive. They have produced little more than three, utterly different, major buildings: the strong and harsh Hunstanton School (1954), the powerful and urbane Economist Building (1964), the strangely banal and horrendous Robin Hood Gardens (1972).

It was just when Kahn's Yale University Art Gallery was rising that APS jumped hard and very audibly into view: Hunstanton School was designed when they were 20 and 25 in 1948-49; it won the competition, was slowly built, and Alison Smithson told the *Architects' Journal* (on the couple's being jointly awarded "Man of the Year" for 1954): "We are the best architects in the country."

The Smithsons' typical forthrightness has never endeared them to the English establishment which they have loved to hate; yet no architects are more sensitive to criticism. Their tone is often overstated for effect; yet it can become almost self-mocking. Nearly 40 years after that last comment, Peter Smithson adds: "Our influence on contemporary architecture passed with an aspirin."

So what is or, as Peter Smithson would have it, what was this influence? Certainly, it is not in their buildings, for they have built pathetically little, had too many commissions tantalizingly unrealized (notably the British Embassy in Brasília), lacked patronage (as they would put it), entered and lost many competitions. "The Smithson style is very inappropriate to the rhetoric of competitions," they say, endearingly, quixotically entering them with undimmed enthusiasm—winning a few, including the modest Japanese Shinkenchiku house "ideas" competition in the late 1970s amidst a field of competitors generations younger.

It is the Smithson polemic, always unfashionable for 40 years, which remains. From the ICA Independent Group in the early 1950s through an important series of *Architectural Design* essays during the next 15 years, the influence has been through writing. Here, *Without Rhetoric: An Architectural Aesthetic 1955-1972,* despite its awkwardly self-conscious style, provides the best introduction; it is an essential and undervalued book.

From Peter Smithson's teaching in the 1950s (running the final year at the Architectural Association until 1960), and then, after two decades away from it, through the 1980s at Bath University (and at Giancarlo De Carlo's ILAUD [International Laboratory of Architecture and Urban Design] in Italy each summer), the influence is in teaching.

With Golden Lane (a lost competition of the early 1950s), a new set of notions entered housing thought: analyzing *association* and *identity, cluster* and *mobility,* the Smithsons produced an urban theory involving inherent change. (The italic words became keywords to Team 10 and the generation it influenced.)

The tragedy for APS was that two decades later, when they finally had half a chance to build housing, they were expected—and they tried—to build that at Robin Hood. By then their words had come to focus on a gentle ordering, allowing signs of occupancy, a place for ephemeral decoration. The contrast between those provocative ideas for the early 1970s and Robin Hood reality is almost schizophrenic.

APS talked of a framework without rhetoric, a sense of ordinariness quite different from that colonized by Robert Venturi and Denise Scott Brown in Las Vegas, but a frame strong enough to secure one in the cup of its hand: "The gentlest of styles, which leaves itself open to—even suggests—interpretation without itself being changed." Perhaps Peter Smithson's term of greatest compliment was "cool." APS talked (into the 1980s) of layers and urban palimpsests, of shells and the decoration of fabric by gestures of occupancy.

Through their career, APS have repeated how they distrust theory without practice, being "builders by nature and tend[ing] to be nervous if not suspicious of those who proceed from research to another" (as Alison Smithson once rebuked Christopher Alexander at Team 10). So always close to the surface is the constant pain that, despite their heroic endeavors, the Smithsons have so rarely been able to be architects—in the sense of raising buildings.

But they *are* architect (and not educator) in Peter Smithson's inspiring teaching—unswervingly serious, often interspersed with the mumbled tone of dry Durham wit, but careless of the sensibilities of a student when what is at stake is architectural quality. And they *are* architect (and not critic) in their writing— fragments, rarely directly stated, as the blurb of their 1970 collection honestly stated: "elliptical texts designed to prevent the building up of rigid thought patterns in the minds of readers."

Fiercely committed and defended ideas can be illustrated with bunting and Christmas decorations. When I first met Peter Smithson, many years ago, it was St. Valentine's Day. Pinned to his breast was a large, roughly shaped pink heart inscribed I LOVE ARCHITECTURE. As *Without Rhetoric* concluded: "Things need to be ordinary and heroic at the same time." It remains an elusive, unpopular but fascinating theme.

—JOHN McKEAN

SMYTHSON, Robert.

British. Born in England, ca. 1535. Died in Wollaton, 1614. Son was the mason and architect John Smythson. Worked as principal mason for Sir John Thynne, Wiltshire; later settled in Wollaton.

Chronology of Works
All in England
* Approximate dates
† Work no longer exists

1568-80	Longleat, Wiltshire (completion)
1576-78	Wardour Old Castle, Wiltshire (remodeling)
1580-88	Wollaton Hall, Nottinghamshire
1583	Barlborough Hall, Derbyshire [attributed]
1585*	Heath Old Hall, Yorkshire [attributed]†
1585*	Worksop Manor, Nottinghamshire†
1590-97	Hardwick Hall, Derbyshire
1593-1600	Doddington Hall, Lincolnshire [attributed]
1597	Welbeck Abbey, Nottinghamshire (wing; later remodeled as the Oxford Wing)
1601-10	Burton Agnes Hall, Yorkshire
1602*	Chastleton House, Oxfordshire [attributed]
1610*	Wootton Lodge, Staffordshire [attributed]
1611*	Fountains Hall, Yorkshire [attributed]

Publications

BOOKS ABOUT SMYTHSON

AIRS, MALCOLM: *The Making of the English Country House 1500-1640.* London, 1975.
FRIEDMAN, ALICE T.: *House and Household in Elizabethan England: Wollaton Hall and the Willoughby Family.* Chicago, 1989.
GIROUARD, MARK: *Robert Smythson and the Architecture of the Elizabethan Era.* London, 1966.
GIROUARD, MARK: *Robert Smythson and the Elizabethan Country House.* New Haven, Connecticut, 1983.
LEES-MILNE, JAMES: *Tudor Renaissance.* London, 1951.
SUMMERSON, JOHN: *Architecture in Britain, 1530-1830.* 6th ed. Harmondsworth, England, 1977.

ARTICLES ABOUT SMYTHSON

GIROUARD, MARK: "The Development of Longleat House, 1546-1572." *Archaeological Journal* 116 (1961).
GIROUARD, MARK: "The Smythson Collection of the Royal Institute of British Architects." *Architectural History* 5 (1962): 21-184.

Robert Smythson was the most important architect in England in the 16th century, indeed the only architect of that time known to us with any certainty. Comparatively little has been uncovered of his career, nothing is known of his background, and the only evidence of his birthdate is to be found on a tombstone in the church of Wollaton, dated to 1614, where it is said he died at the age of 79. This tombstone refers to Smythson as "architect and surveyour unto the most worthy house of Wollaton and divers others of great account," and it is from the evidence of a house like Wollaton and the others that can be associated with him that we derive our description of Smythson as one of the great figures of English architecture.

The first building where Smythson was recorded is Longleat, Wiltshire, in 1568, where he worked as principal mason for John Thynne, who had begun to rebuild an earlier house ruined by fire. What Smythson did at Longleat is not clear, but there are many features there that seem characteristic of all he was to do in his later work; the symmetry of the plan, the huge area of wall space taken up by windows, and the whole aspect of what historians refer to as the "extroversion" of the house, the way it looks out to the countryside around it, rather than hovering around a central courtyard in the manner of earlier Elizabethan houses.

Smythson's first independent building was at Wollaton, Nottinghamshire, built in the 1580s for Sir Francis Willoughby, sheriff of Nottingham. If Wollaton has many of the features of Longleat, they are elaborated with far more vigor and boldness. The plan has a central hall in place of a courtyard, rising with clerestory windows above the surrounding apartments to let in both light and air, and comes from the design of Poggio Reale that was built in Naples in the middle of the 15th century for Alfonso V and printed in Sebastiano Serlio's *Libri di architettura* (1550). But the great corner towers also suggest the influence of slightly earlier English structures like Michelgrove, Sussex, or Mount Edgcumbe, Cornwall. The general treatment of the exterior, with its cartouches, strapwork and banded shafts, depends upon the type of Flemish ornamentation found in Vredeman de Vries' *Variae architecturae formae* (1563). It is interesting to see Smythson having recourse to such varied sources. And if the result is, in a sense, a pastiche, it has been carried out with extreme strength and so well that, were it not for the absence of any such names in the account books, we might imagine some of the work there was done by foreign craftsmen.

Smythson settled then in Wollaton, and much of his later work was done in that area of the Midlands: Worksop Manor, Nottinghamshire; Doddington Hall, Lincolnshire; Welbeck Abbey, Burton Agnes, Yorkshire; and Chastleton, Oxfordshire, however little the documentation tying them to Smythson, all seem to bear the marks of his particular way of designing. The best known of Smythson's later houses is Hardwick Hall, built for Bess of Hardwick, to replace an older, smaller home. Hardwick, to quote John Summerson, is a house of great and romantic beauty, the front and back being enlivened by enormous areas of windows, the groups of towers at both ends recalling the power and effect of the skyline at Wollaton. And the interior, which has been preserved with so much of its tapestries and plasterwork and fittings intact, is an extraordinarily rich example of the mixture of both medieval chivalric design and the new classicism available from Serlio. Yet the plan, especially in the placing of the hall on the main axis, seems to come from something like Palladio's design for the Villa Valmarana at Lisiera, and the building as a whole, for all its detailing, has something of the dignity and restraint seen in Smythson's first work at Longleat. Nothing like it was being built anywhere else.

Smythson's son, John Smythson, followed in his father's profession, his best-known work being that at Bolsover Castle, Derbyshire, done for Sir Charles Cavendish. It is through his son's agency that so many of Robert Smythson's drawings have survived, many of them now in the library of the Royal Institute of British Architects in London. Some of these were perhaps known to later architects; certainly his houses were, and it is not surprising then to read of Nicholas Hawksmoor, attracted as he was to the history of English architecture, saying of Wollaton that it contained "some true strokes of architecture." No more need be said.

—DAVID CAST

SOANE, John.

British. Born in Goring-on-Thames, Reading, England, 10 September 1753. Died in London, 1837. Father was John Soane, bricklayer; married Elizabeth Smith. Entered the office of George Dance, city surveyor, 1768; studied at Royal Academy Schools, 1771; king's travelling student, 1778. Assistant, Henry Holland office, Mayfair, 1772; worked for Frederick Hervey, Bishop of Derry; worked independently; surveyor, Bank of England, 1788; clerk of the works, Whitehall, Westminster, and St. James, 1791; deputy-surveyor of H. M. Woods and Forests, 1795; clerk of the works to Chelsea Hospital, 1807; attached architect of Board of Works, 1814; professor of architecture, Royal Academy, 1806. Gold Medal, Institute of British Architects, 1835.

Chronology of Works
All in England
* Approximate dates
† Work no longer exists

1781-83	Hamels, Hertfordshire (alterations, lodges and dairies)
1783-84	Blackfriars Bridge, Norwich
1783-85	Burnham Westgate Hall, Norfolk
1783-89	Letton Hall, Norfolk (lodges and gateways)
1784ff.	Langley Park, Norfolk
1784-85	Earsham Hall, Norfolk (music room)
1784-86	Tendring Hall, Suffolk†
1784-87	Saxlingham Rectory, Norfolk
1785-86	Blundeston, Suffolk
1785-88	Shotesham Park, Norfolk
1785-89	Chillington Hall, Staffordshire
1785-93	Piercefield, Monmouthshire (in ruins)
1786-87	Fonthill House, Wiltshire (picture gallery)†
1788	Wardour Castle, Wiltshire (addition to chapel)
1788-98	Bentley Priory, Middlesex
1788-1833	Bank of England, London (interior altered)
1789	Sydney Lodge, Hamble, Hampshire
1789-94	County Goal, Norwich, Norfolk†
1791-93	Wimpole Hall, Cambridgeshire (alterations and additions)
1792	Caius College, Cambridge (Hall remodeled)
1792-95	Buckingham House, 91 Pall Mall, London
1793-1800*	Tyringham Hall, Buckinghamshire
1797	Cumberland, Hyde Park, London (gate and lodge)†
1798-99	Betchworth Castle, Surrey (additions)
1799-1804	Aynho Park, Northamptonshire
1800-02	Albury Park, Surrey
1800-03	Pitzhanger Manor, Ealing, Middlesex
1802	Bramley Church (Brocas Chapel), Hampshire
1804	Simeon Obelisk, Market Place, Reading, Berkshire
1804-06	Port Eliot, Cornwall
1805-06	Stowe House, Buckinghamshire (Gothic library and alterations)
1807-10	New Bank Buildings, Princes Street, Lothbury, London†
1809-11	Moggerhanger, Bedfordshire
1809-17	Royal Hospital, Chelsea, London (infirmary, Secretary's Office, stables)
1811-14	Dulwich College, London (picture gallery, mausoleum)
1812-13	13 Lincoln's Inn Fields, London
1818-19	National Debt Redemption Office, Old Jewry, London†
1821-22	Wotton House, Buckinghamshire (reconstruction)
1822-25	Law Courts, Westminster, London†
1822-27	Parliament, Westminster, London (House of Lords Royal Entrance, gallery, library, committee rooms)†
1822-28	Pellwall House, Staffordshire
1823-24	Insolvent Debtor's Court, Portugal Street, London
1823-24	St. Peter's Church, Walworth, London
1824-26	Board of Trade and Privy Council Office, Whitehall, London
1826-27	Holy Trinity Church, Marylebone, London
1826-28	St. John's Church, Bethnal Green, London
1828	Freemason's Hall, Great Queen Street, Whitehall, London (council chamber)†
1829-33	Banqueting House, Whitehall, London (restoration)
1830-34	State Paper Office, Westminster, London

Publications

BOOKS BY SOANE

Designs in Architecture. London, 1778.
Plans, Elevations and Sections of Buildings Erected in the Counties of Norfolk, Suffolk, Yorkshire, etc. London, 1788.

Sketches in Architecture, containing Plans and Elevations of Cottages, Villas and Other Useful Buildings. London, 1798.

Designs for Public and Private Buildings. London, 1828.

Description of the House and Museum on the North Side of Lincoln's Inn Fields. London, 1832. Enlarged version, 1835-36.

Memoirs of the Professional Life of an Architect. London, 1835.

BOOKS ABOUT SOANE

BIRNSTINGLE, H. J.: *Sir John Soane.* New York, 1925.

BOLTON, ARTHUR T. (ed.): *The Lectures on Architecture, by Sir John Soane.* London, 1929.

BOLTON, ARTHUR T. (ed.): *The Portrait of Sir John Soane.* London, 1927.

BOLTON, ARTHUR T. (ed.): *The Works of Sir John Soane.* London, 1924.

DONALDSON, T. L. (ed.): *A Review of the Professional Life of Sir John Soane.* London, 1837.

DU PREY, PIERRE DE LA RUFFINIERE: *John Soane: The Making of an Architect.* Chicago, 1982.

KAUFMANN, EMIL: *Architecture in the Age of Reason: Baroque and Post-Baroque in England, Italy, France.* Cambridge, Massachusetts, 1955.

SCHUMANN-BACIA, EVA: *John Soane and the Bank of England.* New York, 1991.

SERVICE, ALASTAIR: *The Architects of London.* London, 1979.

STROUD, DOROTHY: *The Architecture of Sir John Soane.* London, 1961.

STROUD, DOROTHY: *Sir John Soane, Architect.* London, 1982.

SUMMERSON, JOHN: *Sir John Soane, 1753-1837.* London, 1952.

ARTICLES ABOUT SOANE

McCARTHY, MICHAEL: "Soane's 'Saxon' Room at Stowe." *Journal of the Society of Architectural Historians* 44 (May 1985): 129-146.

STROUD, DOROTHY: "The Early Work of Soane." *Architectural Review* (February 1957).

SUMMERSON, JOHN: "The Evolution of Soane's Bank Stock Office." *Architectural History* 27 (1984): 135-149.

TEYSSOT, GEORGES: "John Soane and the Birth of Style." *Oppositions* 14 (1978): 61-83.

*

Little is known of John Soane's early life until 1768, when he joined the office (and household) of George Dance, Jr., surveyor to the City of London, on the recommendation of Dance's assistant, James Peacock. He stayed until 1772, when, to gain more practical knowledge, he became an assistant in Henry Holland's Mayfair office, where he remained until 1778.

Soane was admitted to the Royal Academy Schools in October 1771, and in the following year he won the Silver Medal with a measured drawing of the facade of Inigo Jones' Banqueting House at Whitehall. In 1776 Soane won the Gold Medal with a spectacular design of a triumphal bridge, indebted to Thomas Sandby, Marie-Joseph Peyre and Giovanni Battista Piranesi. Two years later he was introduced to George IV by William Chambers, and was nominated the King's Travelling Student for three years. He went to Rome in the company of Robert Brettingham, where he drew and measured the buildings of antiquity, studied contemporary archaeological discoveries and became aware of the ideas in the French Académie and the Roman Accademia di San Luca. He met many future patrons, including Thomas Pitt, Lord Camelford and the eccentric Frederick Hervey, bishop of Derry (later fourth earl of Bristol and the "Earl Bishop"). Soane remarked, "It was the means by which I formed those connections to which I owe all the advantages I have since enjoyed." His designs before and during his Italian trip already showed some of his architectural strengths and weaknesses; his greatest strength then was an ability to design in the grand manner and a facility with ingenious plans. Hervey invited him to Ireland, but the promises of work at Ickworth, Suffolk and at Downhill were rescinded as soon as he arrived. Soane returned to England in June 1780, low in spirits and without work.

For most of that decade he concentrated on modest country houses, in which he took the standard Palladian villa form, as used by James Wyatt or Henry Holland, and worked into it sequences of shaped and cleverly interlocking rooms. There were important departures from precedent, such as the use of a tribune as an internal circulation space. Exteriors were distinguished by their simple shapes, well-handled plain masonry, minimal details and an often "stripped-down" look.

Soane's architectural career proper began in 1788, when, on the death of Robert Taylor and through the influence of William Pitt, he was appointed surveyor to the Bank of England. His competitors included other well-established architects: James Wyatt, Henry Holland and S. P. Cockerell, as well as Charles Beazley, who was apparently favored by the governors and who had "transacted the whole of the Bank business" for Taylor during the last years of his life.

Soane was one of the most original and idiosyncratic of the younger generation of neoclassical architects. His mature style emerged with the Bank Stock Office (Bank of England) in 1792-93—an interior which owed as much to Robert Taylor's Reduced Annuities Office (1782) (for the circular side-lit lantern) as it did to George Dance's Lansdowne House Library (1788-91) (for the semiconcealed lunettes) and All Hallows, London Wall (1765-67). The latter, with its elided internal entablature and its free interpretation of Marc-Antoine Laugier's rationalist doctrine, probably inspired Soane's reduction of the classical vocabulary to diagrammatic decoration: pilasters as thin strips with rudimentary capitals and entablatures appearing as decorated bands. The primitivistic considerations of utility and construction were also from Laugier: the bank building had to be secure, light and fireproof.

The picturesque nature of Soane's later work can best be appreciated at his own house, 13 Lincoln's Inn Fields (1812), a personal museum crammed with architectural fragments and casts of antiquities, drawings, paintings, sculpture and models. The principal rooms are remarkable for their ambiguous spatial effects and the deliberate blurring of interior and exterior space. It is often difficult to decide on which plane the wall exists (if at all), and the visitor is confused by the use of mirror glass in unconventional places: on doors, shutters and over bookcases. In the Breakfast Room light filters down from a concealed source at each side of the shallow saucer dome, giving the illusion that the ceiling is a thin membrane floating over the space. The tension is increased by the incised decoration; small mirrors are set in the soffits. Soane indicated that these elements together with the colored lighting presented "those fanciful effects which constitute the poetry of architecture." It is as if he attempted to fuse classical motifs with something of the character of Late Gothic. The Dining Room and Library were inspired by Angelo Campanella's colored engravings (published in 1778) of an excavated room at the Villa Negroni; the color of the walls, the metal colonettes and apparent view to spaces beyond all hark back to that source. The extensive use of colored lighting throughout the house may have been borrowed from

Horace Walpole's top-lit "cabinet" at Strawberry Hill, but it was indebted primarily to the *lumière mystérieuse* which Soane had admired in certain French churches.

Soane was a pioneer of the early Greek Revival, though he also used Roman orders and ornaments to the end of his career. At Tyringham, Buckinghamshire (1795), and at Bentley Priory, Stanmore, Hertfordshire (1798), he used stop-fluted Greek Doric columns. He used unfluted primitivistic Greek Doric in 1783 at his bark dairy at Hammels, Hertfordshire, and in a series of lodges: at Langley Park, Norfolk (1786), at Sydney Lodge, Hampshire (1789), and at Tyringham (1792). His chief essay in the primitivistic was, however, at the Dulwich Picture Gallery and Mausoleum (1811-14, restored following bomb damage in 1944), where he discarded the orders in favor of minimalist pilasters and capitals, and placed a grotesque array of sarcophagi and funerary urns on the parapet.

Soane had become an Associate of the Royal Academy in 1795 and a full Academician in 1802; in 1806 he succeeded George Dance as professor of Architecture, beginning his meticulously prepared and beautifully illustrated lectures three years later. These had the result of enriching his own architectural awareness and increasing his vocabulary, although his later buildings continued to use earlier themes.

He also held several public appointments, including clerk of the works at Whitehall, Westminster and St. James's (1791); deputy surveyor of His Majesty's Woods and Forests (1795), and clerk of the works to Chelsea Hospital (1807). When the Board of Works was reorganized in 1814, Soane was appointed one of the three "attached architects," personally responsible for the public buildings in Whitehall, Westminster, Richmond Park, Kew Gardens and Hampton Court Palace. When he retired in 1832 he was knighted. In 1834 he was offered the presidency of the Institute of British Architects (the fledgling RIBA), but was unable to accept because of the Royal Academy's rules. The Gold Medal was presented to him in 1835 by 350 subscribers.

Despite his awkward and exacting temperament, Soane had numerous pupils and assistants. Although influential in his lifetime, he had no serious imitators, and the attempt to create a new architectural language ended with him.

—MOIRA RUDOLF

SOLERI, Paolo.

Italian. Born in Turin, Italy, 21 June 1919. Married Corolyn Woods, 1949 (died); two children. Studied at the Turin Polytechnic School of Architecture, D.Arch., 1946; fellow, Frank Lloyd Wright Foundation, Taliesin West, Scottsdale, Arizona, 1947-48. In private practice, Turin, 1950-55; president, The Cosanti Foundation, since 1956; has worked primarily on the Arcosanti project, an energy-efficient town combining architectural and ecological concepts, since 1970; organized the Minds for History series of dialogues and lectures, Arcosanti, Arizona, 1989.

Chronology of Works
All in the United States unless noted

1949   Dome House, Cave Creek, Arizona (with Mark Mills)
1953   Artistica Ceramica Solimene Ceramics Factory, Vietri-sul-Mare, near Palermo, Sicily, Italy
1956-58   Earth House, Cosanti Foundation, Scottsdale, Arizona
1956-76   Cosanti Foundation, Scottsdale, Arizona

1966   Outdoor Theater, Institute of American Indian Arts, Santa Fe, New Mexico
1970-   Arcosanti, Cordes Junction, Arizona

Publications

BOOKS BY SOLERI

Arcology: The City in the Image of Man. Cambridge, Massachusetts, 1969.
The Sketchbooks of Paolo Soleri. Cambridge, Massachusetts, 1971.
The Bridge Between Matter and Spirit is Matter Becoming Spirit. New York, 1973.
The Omega Seed. New York, 1981.
Fragments. San Francisco, 1981.
Paolo Soleri's Earth Casting For Sculpture, Models and Construction. With Scott M. Davis. Salt Lake City, Utah, 1984.
Technology and Cosmogenesis. New York, 1986.
Arcosanti: An Urban Laboratory? Santa Monica, California, 1987.

BOOKS ABOUT SOLERI

WALL, DONALD: *Visionary Cities: The Arcology of Paolo Soleri.* New York, 1971.

ARTICLES ABOUT SOLERI

"Arcosanti." *Architecture d'aujourd'hui* No. 167 (May 1973): 48ff.
BLAKE, PETER: "The Fantastic World of Paolo Soleri." *Architectural Forum* (February 1960): 104-109.
COOK, JEFFREY: "Paolo Soleri." *Architectural Association Quarterly* 1, No. 1:16-23.
MOHOLY-NAGY, SIBYL: "The Arcology of Paolo Soleri." *Architectural Forum* (May 1970): 70-75.
SHARP, DENNIS: "Paolo Soleri." *Building* 10 (November 1972): 75-82.
SKOLIMOWSKI, H.: "Paolo Soleri: The Philosophy of Urban Life." *Architectural Association Quarterly* 3, No. 1 (1970): 34-42.

*

Architects are not sure he is one. He discourages clients and designs theoretical projects beyond both current forms of reference and possibility for realization. But he has a soaring imagination and is a skilled draftsman, so he must be an artist. Although he sells sketches and sculptures, he eschews conventional art galleries and his artistic objects come with prophetic ministerial admonitions. Thus he must be a theologian. But though he advocates frugality, ceremony and pursuit of "omega," he is very incomplete as a theologian since he promotes no particular religion. And as his exquisite visions of sublimity take the form of buildings, even if in outer space, he must be an architect. Thus he is architect as visionary, in the revolutionary traditions of Sebastiano Serlio, Leonardo and Claude-Nicolas Ledoux, with equally fresh social concepts of human organization.

Soleri arrived at Wright's Taliesin West in January 1947, a recent Dottore in Architettura from the Politecnico di Torino. But his apprenticeship barely lasted through the second summer. His first commission (with Mark Mills), the Dome House at

Paolo Soleri: Arcosanti, Cordes Junction, Arizona, 1970-

Cave Creek, Arizona (1949), was built by the two fledgling architects and their client Leonora Woods, whose daughter Corolyn became Soleri's wife. Although poorly detailed and never quite finished, this well-published house with its desert masonry seemed like a powerful Wrightian essay in the dialogue between an earth-sheltered cave and its rotating glass dome. It anticipated Soleri's continuing concern with "a manly setting within which he can sense the grace of being and becoming," as well as his formal language of domes and apses. As the environment of planet earth has deteriorated, Soleri's verbal language of philosophic analogies has become much more convincing. However, layered and imploding architectural forms, progressively more complex, have not always become clearer.

Soleri spent five years in Italy in the early 1950s, a time during which he attempted to practice design at all scales of the built environment, following Wright's commitment to total integration. He produced tableware, napkins and fabrics himself. His design for the large ceramic factory Ceramica Artistica Solimene (1953) was constructed slowly by a growing family pottery business. The subjective exterior of pot shapes was laid up of individual glazed-pot units thrown by the family. The five floors are a continuous ramp around a great skylit hall, its continuity accommodating the lineal sequential functions of the ceramic process. Soleri returned to the more provident United States in 1955, and to Arizona via Santa Fe.

An attempt at classifying Soleri with Wright or Antoní Gaudi, or even within the organic architects, avoids the obvious. Typically Soleri's buildings lack the refinement, the discipline, the richness or the confidence of many lesser-known architects.

Only in occasional moments, especially at Cosanti, do his buildings glow with a sentient grandeur achieved by the most austere of means. By his own admission his buildings are sketches and potentially his least important contribution.

Soleri has expanded the scope and vision of architectural responsibility and has propagated his visionary messages globally on an unmatched scale. His obsession with the destiny role of architecture has catapulted from "worthiness" through "necessity" to "cosmic inevitability" in the evolution of humanity. His early "biotechnic" house studies are represented conceptually by the Dome House, where two concentric half domes would rotate to provide shade or sun or ventilation or some such combination in response to the panorama and climatic needs of a rural desert site. It was a great crystal, yet sheltering, eye.

His earliest important publication, the powerful "Beast," a study for a long-span bridge in Elizabeth Mock's *The Architecture of Bridges* (Museum of Modern Art, New York, 1948), anticipated the elegant form of structural economy. In the 1980s Soleri designed "Pulse Bridges"—long-span structures that would visibly respond to changing environmental realities, as part of his designs of "ecologic minutiae."

It was his four schemes for the Luxemburg Bridge competition of 1958 that propelled his megastructural direction and his bridge cities. Soleri's idea was that if a structure must be built, why not populate its interstices with the mixed uses of a community? This idea quickly overshadowed his concurrent theoretical City on a Mesa. Dispersed concentrations of residential groupings, business centers, university and ground villages would provide a town for 2 million on a tabletop mountain 22 by 10 kilometers, as well as many idealized design exercises. By 1964 Soleri had abandoned it and focused on single megastructured cities as a higher organic response to the necessities for efficiency through compactness and thickness. He invented the word "arcology" to suggest the ecological unity possible with architecture, and emphasized that the urban intensity implicit in such a concentration would miniaturize man's process and free the earth's surface. In contrast to the "pancake" city, such as the horizontal metropolitan Phoenix where Soleri lives, his densely three-dimensional single-structured city prototypes would be designed for specific settings: to span great valleys, to ride the prairie, to hug the Arctic ridge, to float over great depths, or to rotate orbits in outer space—integrated urbanity without automobiles. His designs for 30 arcologies were published by 1970, the year of a large-scale exhibition that opened at the Corcoran Gallery in Washington, D.C. It was the year he began construction of his "nemises," the smallest arcology—Arcosanti was a "city of the future" for 5,000 people, located 70 miles north of Phoenix and built by apprentices paying for the privilege.

Since 1956 Soleri has been building facilities at Cosanti, "before the thing." The first, the Earth House (1956-58), demonstrated how to build on flat open land without defying either nature or the neighborhood. Set in the land, the Earth House has generous sunken gardens to provide private transition spaces outdoors to balance the cavelike, earth-sheltered interior. As his own client and with the energies of summer student workshops beginning in 1964, he built a series of original and exploratory structures beside his home on five acres in Paradise Valley. Experimental metal shops, residences and workspaces were constructed mostly of silt-cast reinforced concrete. This unique conglomeration embraces crude craft and ecological design. It is an ambulatory experience of inventive desert environments that merge architecture and land. The wind bells that support his enterprise continue to be made there in a series of apse-and-vault shelters that invite the desert to participate.

Soleri's recreative activities of movies, television and cottage handcrafts provide powerful and innately popular inputs to his invention. Avoiding consultants, experts, professionals, researchers and scholars, and even colleagues, he has amputated his potential effectiveness but has maintained his naivity. He has the powerful conviction of individual as institution. Soleri is informed by mass media and by his own hand carving the pot-shaped bells, and by his ball pen writing and sketching continuously in his Leonardo-like notebooks.

The latin roots of Soleri's native language have also provided an inventive verbal language similar to English. Sometimes it is powerfully poetic and dramatically descriptive, as in his question and answer sessions. Sometimes, especially in his books, it is impenetrable. The title "*The Bridge Between Matter and Spirit is Matter Becoming Spirit*" (1973) describes precisely Soleri's position. Further reading, however, does not add to one's understanding.

Soleri is a rebel with a growing cause. He emerged in the euphoria of post-World War II creative architectural optimism. He ascended with the energy-conservation and environmental movement of the 1970s, when he also provided musical events that brought 10,000 in 1978 to the remote mesas of an unbuilt Arcosanti. He initiated many intellectual and other cultural events with less success. Recently the Mind for History series provided unprecedented dialogues among the most influential thinkers of our time. His proposals for Peace in Space have explored the architecture and ecology of the outer gravityless universe.

In the meantime, the fragmentary construction of Arcosanti proceeds with painfully small increments to changing master plans. The energy efficiency has not been visible. But the fact of some materiality has allowed Soleri's dream to become not the substance but the possibility of dreams of others who believe in the future.

—JEFFREY COOK

SOMMARUGA, Giuseppe.

Italian. Born in Milan, Italy, 10 July 1867. Died in Milan, 27 March 1917. Studied at the Brera Academy, Milan, and apprenticed to Luigi Broggi; entered the National Parliament Building competition with Broggi, 1890. Worked in Milan and Rome, 1890-1900; appointed general architect of the Esposizioni Riunite, Milan, 1894. Made an honorary member of the Brera Academy; first president of the National Federation of Italian Architects.

Chronology of Works
All in Italy unless noted
† *Work no longer exists*

1897	Palazzine Aletti, Rome
1901-03	Palazzo Castiglione, Milan
1903-04	Italian Pavilion, World's Fair, St. Louis, Missouri, U.S.A.†
1906	Villa Salmoiraghi, Milan
1906	Villa Comi, Milan
1906-07	Villa Faccanoni, Sarnico
1907	Faccanoni Mausoleum, Sarnico
1908	Comi Tomb, Giubiano
1908-09	Villa Carosio, Baveno
1908-12	Hotel Tre Croci, Campo dei Fiori
1913	Villa Romeo, Milan
1915	Villino Poletti, Portineria

Publications

BOOKS ABOUT SOMMARUGA

MONNERET DE VILLARD, UGO (ed.): *L'Architettura di Giuseppe Sommaruga*. Milan, 1908.
NICOLETTI, MANFREDI: *L'Architettura Liberty in Italia*. Bari, Italy, 1978.
PEVSNER, NIKOLAUS, and RICHARDS, J. M. (eds.): *The Anti-Rationalists*. London, 1973.
RUSSELL, FRANK (ed.): *Art Nouveau Architecture*. London, 1979.

*

Giuseppe Sommaruga was one of the main protagonists of *stile liberty*, or art nouveau, architecture in Italy, along with Raimondo D'Aronco and Ernesto Basile. His work, centered mostly in Milan and environs, reflected the aspirations of a growing upper middle class of Milanese industrialists at the turn of the century. Sommaruga designed not only villas, palazzi and funereal architecture, but also public structures such as exhibition pavilions.

Having studied at the Brera Academy under Camillo Boito, Sommaruga came out of the late-19th-century tradition of eclecticism. Early in his career he apprenticed with Luigi Broggi, and together they submitted a project (later premiated) for the

Giuseppe Sommaruga: Palazzo Castiglione, Milan, Italy, 1901-03

Parliament Building competition in Rome in 1889. It was through Broggi's influence that Sommaruga participated in the First Italian Exposition of Architecture in Turin in 1890. This experience was to serve him well, for in 1894 he was appointed general architect of the Esposizioni Riunite in Milan. Sommaruga thus rose quickly to a position of prominence in the Milanese and national cultural milieu. He was made an honorary member of the Brera Academy, president of the Association of Lombard Architects, and first president of the National Federation of Italian Architects.

His acknowledged masterpiece is the Palazzo Castiglioni in Milan (1901-03), built for the young engineer Ermenegildo Castiglioni. In order to familiarize themselves with the latest European architectural currents, both architect and client traveled to France and England before Sommaruga began his design. Contemporary criticism hailed the Palazzo Castiglioni as an example of the "intense new life which gave classical forms a truly modern expression."

While the plan and elevation of this work display an attachment to classicism, the detailing is typical of the *stile liberty*. Indeed, the Palazzo Castiglioni contains features new to the architectural fabric of Milan: a heightened sense of plasticity achieved through vegetal and figural ornament, loggias and other openings, along with an almost Baroque use of rustication in the lower floors. Some critics have seen echoes of the Vienna Secession in the triple square openings on the lowest part of the facade. The controversial nude female statues by Ernesto Bazzaro that once surrounded the entrance were removed after only a few months, and later became part of the garden decor of Sommaruga's Villa Faccanoni in Milan. The interior of the Palazzo Castiglioni features a dramatic stairway with an abundance of lively ironwork designs.

The Palazzo Castiglioni secured Sommaruga a premier place in the profession. Indeed, soon after the building's completion he won the competition for the Italian Pavilion at the International Exposition in St. Louis, Missouri (executed in 1903-04). The design guidelines had called for a building in the "Roman-classical" style, a directive that Sommaruga translated into a monumental essay in classicism. Recognized by many as an aberration from the livelier vocabulary and massing of his private commissions, the pavilion aroused the critical ire of fellow *stile liberty* architect Raimondo D'Aronco, who called it a "national shame," an example of "backward" architecture in the forward-looking United States.

If civic buildings like the Italian Pavilion in St. Louis showed Sommaruga's more monumental, classicizing side, the many commissions he received for private villas and funerary architecture reflected his talent for designing fluid ornament and lively massing. Indeed, the same industrialists who commissioned private villas and apartment buildings from Sommaruga enlisted his services for their symbolic funerary monuments, which constitute some of his most successful work. The Comi Tomb in Giubiano (1908), with its putti and floral friezes enhancing a lively silhouette, is one of the finest examples.

A villa in Milan of 1906 for the same family is an example of the private commissions that provided Sommaruga the outlet for his most daring designs. City *villine* and country villas allowed him to experiment freely with exuberant wrought-iron and concrete designs, an interplay of different materials on the same facade, and often asymmetrical massing. The Villa Carosio in Baveno (1908-09) shows the architect's predilection for a variety of textures, bold ornamental friezes and general asymmetry.

Finally, the architect completed hotel designs in the area around Varese that demonstrated his ability to work successfully in the *stile liberty* on a grandiose scale. The Hotel Tre Croci (1908-12) in Campo dei Fiori and its restaurant are considered masterpieces of this style.

—ELLEN R. SHAPIRO

SONCK, Lars Eliel.

Finnish. Born in Kelvi̊, Finland, 10 August 1870. Died in 1956. Studied at the Polytechnic Institute, Helsinki, graduated 1894. Practiced independently in Finland; leading member of the Finnish National Romantic Movement.

Chronology of Works
All in Finland

1894	Villa Sonck, Finström, Åland Islands
1895	St. Michael's, Turku
1895	Lasses Villa, Bartsg̊rda, Finström
1896	Villa Skogshyddan, Mariehamn, Åland Islands
1899-1907	Tampere Cathedral (St. John's), Tampere
1903	Town Plan, Töölö District, Helsinki (with Gustaf Nystrom)
1903-05	Telephone Building, Helsinki
1904	Villa Ainola, Järvenpää
1905	Eira Hospital, Helsinki
1907-08	Mortgage Society Building, Helsinki
1907-09	Town Plan, Kulosaari, Helsinki
1908	Town Plan, Eira District, Helsinki (with Armas Lindgren and Bertel Jung)
1909-12	Kallio Church , Helsinki
1910-11	Stock Exchange Building, Helsinki
1913-23	Villa Brakeudd, Hirsala, Kirkkonummi†
1915	Fire Station, Kulosaari, Helsinki
1922	Villa Hornborg, near Kustavi
1923-35	Warehouses, Jätskaari, Helsinki
1927	Mariehamn Church, Åland Islands
1935	Mikael Agricola Church, Helsinki (with Arvo Muroma)
1939	Town Hall, Mariehamn, Åland Islands

Publications

ARTICLES BY SONCK

"Till fragan om restaurering af Abo Domkyrka." *Finsk Tidskrift* (January 1897): 22-28.
"Modern Vandalism: Helsingfors Stadsplan." *Finsk Tidskrift* (1898): 262-287.
"Mikael Agricola Kyrkan i Helsingfors." *Arkitekten* 32, No. 12 (1935): 180-182.
"Maamiehen koti I." *Rakentaja* 1 (1902): 5.
"En arkitekonisk fraga, behandlad pa kyrkostämma i Abo." *Arkitekten* 2 (1904): 17-20.
"Pa orätt spar." *Arkitekten* 8 (1904): 83-84.
"Huru der bygges i Helsingfors." *Argus* 7 (1909): 66-67.
"En segsliten kyrkobygbnadsfraga: Platsen för Borga nya kyrka." *Arkitekten* 2 (1915): 19-23.

BOOKS ABOUT SONCK

KIVINEN, PAULA: *Tampereen Tuomiokirkko.* Porvoo, Finland, 1961.

KIVINEN, PAULA; KORVENMAA, PEKKA; and SALOKORPI, ASKO: *Lars Sonck 1870-1956.* Helsinki, 1981.
RICHARDS, J. M.: *800 Years of Finnish Architecture.* Newton Abbot, England, 1978.
VIKSTEDT, J.: *De finska stadernas byggnadskonst.* Helsinki, 1926.

ARTICLES ABOUT SONCK

SPENCE, RORY: "Lars Sonck." *Architectural Review* (February 1982): 40-49.
TREIB, MARC: "Lars Sonck: From the Roots." *Journal of the Society of Architectural Historians* 30, No. 3 (1971): 225-237.

*

Lars Sonck's name is rightly associated with the Finnish National Romantic Movement, Finland's equivalent of Jugendstil or art nouveau. Although Sonck continued designing into the 1940s, most of his best work was completed by 1912.

His early work was very much a part of the resurgence of national consciousness in the arts in the 1890s and early 1900s, centered around the epic poem *Kalevala* (Land of the Heroes), a collection of folk legends written down, adapted and published as a coherent whole in 1849, by Elias Lönnrot. This national epic was the inspiration for the early music of Jean Sibelius and the paintings of Akseli Gallen Kallela, as well as many other artists and writers. Sonck was one of a group of young architects, including Eliel Saarinen, who enthusiastically studied Finnish medieval churches and the timber vernacular architecture of Karelia, where the *Kalevala* was supposed (mistakenly) to have originated, and which was thought of as the cradle of Finnish culture. Sonck was to have made a study tour of Karelia with two fellow students in 1894, but withdrew after winning a major architectural competition for St. Michael's Church, Turku, while still a student. Although the design for the red-brick St. Michael's was largely dependent on German Gothic Revival architecture, especially the work of Johannes Otzen, the completed building exhibited National Romantic elements, particularly in the proportions of the interior and in the decorative detail, which included Finnish flora and fungi, and gable decoration derived from medieval churches. Even more illustrative of the search for national origins were Sonck's early villas, often of log construction, which, while drawing from "Swiss style" rural villa architecture of the mid-19th century, also used details from the log buildings of Karelia. The first was built in 1894, as a holiday house for Sonck himself on Åland Island, his childhood and spiritual home.

Sonck's major architectural work was part of the culmination of National Romanticism between 1899 and 1905. This fertile period in Finnish culture coincided with and was given special significance by dramatic political events. Finland had been an autonomous grand duchy of Russia since 1809, but from 1899 the new czar, Nicholas II, attempted to effect a closer union with Russia through imperial legislation bypassing the Finnish Senate. Finland's protests were to no avail, but emotions ran high and were expressed in the powerful nationalistic artistic products of the time.

These circumstances reinforced the Europe-wide attempt, in architecture, to break free of period styles, particularly the neoclassical and neo-Renaissance, which were associated in Finland with Russian domination. Finland, however, having no other urban precedents to fall back on, turned for inspiration to the powerful and idiosyncratic architecture of the American Henry Hobson Richardson, who was also attracting attention in other parts of Europe. The ready availability of hard Finnish granite made Richardson's rock-faced stonework peculiarly appropriate for Finland.

Sonck's masterpiece, Tampere Cathedral (1899-1907), built of rock-faced, squared granite rubble, demonstrates his transformation of Gothic Revival, Richardsonian and Finnish medieval sources into a new architecture of great primitive strength and originality. Its interior is a centralized, cross-vaulted space, more appropriate for Lutheran worship than the more traditional, directional form of St. Michael's, Turku. Sonck's Helsinki Telephone Company Building (1903-05) was even more dramatically primitive, the size of its granite lintels recalling Richardson's Allegheny County Courthouse and Jail in Pittsburgh (1884-86). In both of Sonck's buildings, Richardson's Romanesque arches were often replaced by primitive Gothic forms not unlike medieval Finnish examples, and wonderful textural contrasts were introduced between smoothly dressed stonework and the rock-faced main walling. In his private hospital for the Helsinki garden suburb of Eira (1904-05), Sonck applied similar massive, but more rounded, forms to a semidomestic purpose. Above the random rubble base and perimeter wall, the stonework gives way to rendered brick, characteristic of Helsinki's classical tradition, but in this case probably influenced by the English Arts and Crafts domestic revival. The contrasting textures of Tampere Cathedral and the Telephone Company Building were here reversed, with a rock-faced entry surround set off against the smooth render of the wall behind. The irregular forms of National Romanticism seem more appropriate for this varied program of small, domestically scaled rooms than for the larger, more repetitive nature of big-city buildings.

By 1904 there were signs of a new rationalism in Finnish architecture. The more internationally orientated Gustaf Strengell and Sigurd Frosterus, a pupil of Henry van de Velde, published vigorous attacks on National Romanticism. "To use archaic forms without real justification," wrote Strengell, "is as senseless as it would be to go around dressed in skins, eat with the fingers or shoot with a bow and arrow instead of a rifle." Although this led to more ordered, "rational" forms, solutions were generally symmetrical and classically based rather than "representative of an age of steam and electricity" as advocated by Frosterus.

Sonck reflected the new mood in 1906 with his winning competition entry for Kallio Church, Helsinki, a symmetrical design with a powerful composition of central tower, domed semiclassical apse and almost-Palladian wings of ancillary accommodation, closing a major vista leading out of the city center. All traces of specifically medieval character were removed, but the rock-faced squared rubble remained. In Sonck's Finnish Mortgage Society Building (1907-08), the classical references, including a giant order of columns, were more explicit though unconventional in detail, and the smoothly dressed, uncoursed ashlar walls were praised by Frosterus, who designed some of the interiors, for corresponding "more closely to modern mechanical processing than the rustic rubble wall and irregular granite boulders" of other recent buildings. The compositional arrangement of colonnade, flanked by projecting end bays and capped with a more solid attic story, became a standard solution, in various modified forms, for many of Sonck's urban buildings throughout the remainder of his career.

Sonck's last city building of real originality and distinction was his Helsinki Stock Exchange (1910-11), which reduced the facades of the Mortgage Society Building to a refined, classically based but almost abstract play of plain, square-cut vertical piers, set against two strong horizontal stringcourses. Unlike the Mortgage Society Building, there is no classical attic story or strong entablature, and on the end bays the vertical piers

lead the eye skyward with hardly an interruption, creating an indeterminate character which can be seen as a leftover of the verticality of the Gothic Revival or as an anticipation of the dynamism of early modernism, akin to the work of Otto Wagner. The building was planned with offices around a courtyard leading to the Stock Exchange itself on the second floor at the rear. This extraordinary courtyard, with its glazed roof and unplastered brick walls, is an inside/outside space appropriate for the harsh Finnish winters and probably reflects the influence of H. P. Berlage's Stock Exchange in Amsterdam (1897-1903) and Martin Nyrop's Copenhagen Town Hall (1892-1905). It was an idea later to be taken up by Alvar Aalto in his Rautatalo Office Building, Helsinki (1955).

Sonck's later work seldom approached the power of his early buildings. The exception to this, however, was a series of remarkable log villas roofed in orange Swedish tiles, especially his own villa, Brakeudd (1913-23) at Kirkkonummi, near Helsinki, and the Villa Hornborg (1922), on an island near Kustavi. Both houses were planned around courtyards echoing Karelian models and incorporating a beautiful and unusual type of veranda, open on two sides with turned posts supporting the roof, like a roofed bridge linking two parts of the building. In the case of the Villa Hornborg, the courtyard is at first-floor level, anticipating Aalto's Säynätsalo Town Hall (1950-52), and is raised up on a mound enclosed by a battered, stone basement story, and entered via a tunnel and steps under the open veranda. These villas successfully combined Finnish vernacular precedent with touches of Baroque and even Japanese influence in their gable forms and entry gateways.

Sonck's lasting contribution to Finnish architecture lies above all in his powerful, idiosyncratic and sculptural formal invention, coupled with a fine sense of the quality and texture of materials and an economical but effective use of carved ornament. Sonck, Aalto claimed in his obituary of the architect in 1956, "has largely contributed to the birth of an individualism which has prevented provincialism from taking place in Finnish Art."

—RORY SPENCE

SOUFFLOT, Jacques-Germain.

French. Born near Auxerre, France, 22 July 1713. Died in Paris, 29 August 1780. Traveled to Rome, 1731; studied at the French Academy in Rome, 1734-38. Returned to France, 1738, and became chief architect of Lyons; elected to the Académie in Lyons, 1739. Traveled again in Italy, 1750-51.

Chronology of Works
All in France
* Approximate dates
† Work no longer exists

After 1738	Hôtel Lacrox-Laval, Lyons (planning and construction)
1739-48	Hôtel Dieu, Lyons (additions)
After 1742	Église des Chartreux, Lyons (high altar and ciborium; after a design by Giovanni Nicolano Servandoni)
1747-49	Archepiscopal Palace, Lyons (renovation)
1748-50	Loge des Changes, Lyons
1751-52	Perachon House, Lyons
1753-56	Theater, Lyons†
1755-80	Ste. Geneviève, Paris (now the Pantheon; not completed until later by others)
1756-60	Notre-Dame Cathedral, Paris (sacristy)

1765ff. Marquis de Marigny House, Ménars (including garden pavilions)
1769 Marquis de Marigny House, Paris
1774* Bertin Estate, Chatou (nymphaeum)

Publications

BOOKS BY SOUFFLOT

Oeuvres ou recueils de plusieurs parties d'architecture. Paris, 1767.
Suite de plans, coups, etc. de trois temples antiques . . . à Pestum. Paris, 1764.

BOOKS ABOUT SOUFFLOT

BRAHAM, ALLAN: *The Architecture of the French Enlightenment.* Berkeley, California, and Los Angeles, 1980.
MATHUSEK-BAUDOUIN, MARIE NOELLE: *Soufflot et son temps.* Exhibition catalog. Paris, 1981.
MONDAIN-MONVAL, JEAN: *Soufflot: sa vie, son oeuvre, son esthétique, 1730-1780.* Paris, 1918.
PETZET, MICHAEL: *Soufflots Sainte-Geneviève und der französische Kirchenbau des 18. Jahrhunderts.* Berlin, 1961.
TERNOIS, D., and PEREZ, F.: *L'oeuvre de Soufflot à Lyon.* Lyons, 1982.

ARTICLES ABOUT SOUFFLOT

BRAHAM, ALLAN: ''The Drawings for Soufflot's Sainte-Geneviève.'' *Burlington Magazine* 108 (October 1971).
MIDDLETON, ROBIN D.: ''The Abbe of Cordemoy and the Graeco-Gothic Ideal.'' *Journal of the Warburg and Courtauld Institutes* (1962): 178ff.

*

Germain Soufflot was perhaps the greatest of 18th-century French architects. His masterpiece, the Church of Ste. Geneviève (1755-80), now the Panthéon, was praised as the most magnificent building constructed since the Renaissance. It epitomized the return to a serious architecture based on a solid knowledge of the antique, inaugurating a new architectural aesthetic: neoclassicism. Soufflot's august architecture was based on a thorough understanding of antique architecture coupled with an affinity for the masterpieces of French classical architecture of the preceding century as defined by François Mansart and Claude Perrault.

In 1731, at the age of 18, and against his father's wishes, Soufflot traveled to Rome—not Paris—to study architecture. His four-year sojourn in Italy coincided with a flurry of activity sponsored by Pope Clement XI, as witnessed in the completion of the facades of San Giovanni in Laterano and Santa Maria Maggiore as well as the construction of the Trevi Fountain and the Spanish Steps. More important for his subsequent career, Soufflot admired the monuments of Seicento architects, particularly those of Carlo Fontana, which were characterized by their regular geometry, heavier mass and architectonic qualities.

In 1738 Soufflot returned to France and established himself as the chief architect of Lyons, one of the largest cities in France after Paris. The following year, he was elected to that city's Académie, where he regularly delivered lectures providing insight into the formation of his architectural thought. One lecture praised the lightness of Gothic architecture at a time when it was generally reviled, foreshadowing his utilization of the Gothic aesthetic for the Church of Ste. Geneviève.

In addition to his active participation in the Académie in Lyons, Soufflot was busy with important municipal commissions such as the Hôtel Dieu (1739-48) and the Théâtre (1753-56). For the Hôtel Dieu, or hospital, Soufflot was asked to construct a new wing along the Rhône River to conceal previous buildings. He built a long and austere three-story building, composed of three pavilions, with a square dome over the centrally located chapel. He rationally fulfilled the practical requirement that patients be allowed to follow Mass from their rooms. Soufflot suppressed the traditional corner pavilions, marking a radical break from classical French massing. He also reduced the decoration to oval, garlanded windows and severe classical orders, further distancing himself from the florid Rococo decoration of the previous decades. Soufflot's unconventional approach to architecture reflected his relative isolation from contemporary French academic thought, since he had studied antique and Renaissance architecture exclusively in Italy. Accordingly, his work betrays a strong feeling for monumentality and for Italian concepts of mass and regularity.

Soufflot returned in 1750 to the Italian peninsula, accompanied by the influential critic Abbé Le Blanc, a protégé of Mme. de Pompadour; by the engraver Charles-Nicolas Cochin; and by Mme. de Pompadour's brother, M. de Vandieres (later Marquis de Marigny and future *directeur des bâtiments du roi*). The year-long trip, marked by visits to Greco-Roman sites such as Paestum and Herculaneum, crystallized Soufflot's prejudice for pure and austere classicism. It was fortuitous that Soufflot's future patron and supporter, M. de Vandieres, was also present, heralding an official shift in taste as well. This also paralleled architectural thinking at the French Academy in Rome, where the study of classical antiquity became increasingly de rigueur.

On his return to France, Soufflot presented to the Lyons Académie his study of Italian theaters, coincidental with his last important commission for the city, its new theater. Predictably, Soufflot adopted the modern Italian plans he had studied in Turin's new theater, characterized by a horseshoe-shaped auditorium. Soufflot's theater was unusual, however, in that it was freestanding and isolated from the rest of the urban fabric. Yet it was equipped with cafés and a foyer, rare public amenities for that time.

In contrast to traditional festive theater decoration, the Lyons theater was marked by a restrained elegance both inside and out. The exterior facade's chief articulation was its plain, recessed windows. As at the Hôtel Dieu, Soufflot depended on the theater's simple mass, and not on decoration, to give it architectural expression. His ideas were to be fully realized some 20 years later in the Odéon theater in Paris by Charles de Wailly and Marie-Joseph Peyre.

Mid-century, characterized by a renewed interest in monumental architecture, marked a turning point in the reign of Louis XV. The first half of the century, during which neither the state nor the church had sufficient funds for major construction projects, had been marked by small-scale, intimate architecture: the hallmark of the Rococo style. By 1750, Louis XV, an amateur architect himself, embarked on an ambitious building program, under the direction of the *directeur des bâtiments,* the Marquis de Marigny. Monumental buildings such as the École Militaire, the Place Louis XV (later Place de la Concorde) and the Church of Ste. Geneviève were soon commissioned. These great architectural projects were a deliberate attempt by Louis XV to emulate the achievements of his great-grandfather, Louis XIV, and to place his reign, widely perceived as lacking in glory and grandeur, on par with that of his illustrious predecessor.

The building of a new church of Ste. Geneviève fulfilled a promise made by the king after his miraculous recovery from illness. Furthermore, the reconstruction of the abbey church, founded in 508 by Clovis, the first Christian king of France, would assert the legitimacy and continuity of the French monarchy. In January 1755, Marigny provided Soufflot, and not the king's *premier architecte,* Jacques-Ange Gabriel, with the commission to build the church, which would rival the Cathedral of Notre Dame in size. Its construction immediately captivated public attention, on account of its royal patronage and its being commissioned to a young, avant-garde architect from the provinces. Soufflot at once saw a unique opportunity to compete with, and to improve upon, the great ecclesiastical masterpieces of the past, notably St. Peter's in Rome and St. Paul's in London.

As in Lyons, Soufflot once again subverted traditional solutions in designing Ste. Geneviève. Baroque church architecture in France, derived from Roman Jesuit examples, was characterized by a Latin-cross plan consisting of a nave lined with side chapels and defined by heavy piers and pilasters. The exterior was distinguished by flying buttresses supporting the nave wall, and by a main facade which was articulated by superimposed orders. Soufflot abandoned that formula and proposed a Greek-cross plan with a dome at the central crossing, with four arms of equal length, each with its own domed compartments. Soufflot was not looking at Baroque architecture, but further back to the masterpieces of Bramante and Michelangelo. Soufflot's avant-garde, centralized plan did not satisfy the clergy, however, who preferred a more traditional Latin-cross configuration. By the time of its foundation ceremony in 1764, further revisions had been imposed on Soufflot's designs: the nave had been lengthened, with the east end becoming a shallow apse, a crypt had been added, featuring the first use of the Doric order in France, and twin towers framed the facade.

The interior colonnade, composed of freestanding columns that supported a straight entablature, was the most startling innovation of Soufflot's nave design, marking a decisive break with the traditional piers and arcades. The forest of columns dematerialized the wall, and the resulting lightness and spaciousness paralleled the effect of Gothic architecture, which Soufflot had lauded at the Académie in Lyons. Soufflot's utilization of bunched columns to support the dome at the central crossing further amplified this spaciousness, allowing for an uninterrupted vista from one end of the church to the other. In addition, the nave colonnade was the starting point for the vaulting system, which consisted of transverse ribs and intersecting arches rising above the columns. Flying buttresses, hidden from view behind a high parapet, were also utilized to support these vaults.

The facade of Ste. Geneviève was dominated by a hexastyle portico, evocative of the monumentality of the Pantheon in Rome, but even more prodigious since its 24 columns were taller than those of the antique prototype. Soufflot's design was typically French, however, with its two pairs of columns added to the sides. This "corner strengthening," which closed the side elevations and mimicked an independent classical temple front, had already been employed by François Mansart for his Église des Minimes in 1657.

The dome of Soufflot's church reasserted the Montagne Ste. Geneviève on the skyline of Paris. It proved to be a most difficult stylistic and engineering challenge for Soufflot and was the object of great controversy. Soufflot's initial design of 1764 was a complex arrangement of engaged columns with pediments encircling a drum which was capped with cone steps leading to a gigantic statue of Saint Geneviève, alluding to antique prototypes. In 1769 Pierre Patte, defender of Jean-François Blondel in his efforts to conserve the French classical tradition of Mansart and Perrault, criticized Soufflot's design and questioned the dome's stability. During the ensuing decade, the controversy over the dome would epitomize the Enlightenment's belief in progress based on truth and experimentation. Soufflot redesigned the dome along the more traditional lines of the Church of the Invalides, but introduced a severe circular colonnade around the drum, following Christopher Wren's design for the dome of St. Paul's in London. Soufflot's austere tempietto-like dome harkened back to High Renaissance centralized church design and hinted at the importance of the column in the interior of the church.

At its completion, Ste. Geneviève was hailed by the leading neoclassical critic and theorist, Abbé Laugier, as an example of a perfect church. It combined the structural lightness and technical daring of Gothic architecture with the regularity, purity and monumentality of classical architecture. The latter, with its stability and sense of repose, would not upset the contemplative mood of the visitor, as was so often the case with Gothic architecture's soaring vaults upheld by seemingly invisible means of support.

Soufflot died in 1780 without seeing his dome completed, but Marigny remained faithful to his architect's design, allowing Soufflot's protégés, Jean-Baptiste Rondelet, Maximilien Brebion and Soufflot le Romain, his nephew, to complete the dome. In 1806, however, when cracks appeared on the crossing columns, these were strengthened by the insertion of pilasters and masonry in between them. The resulting massiveness of the supporting piers forever altered the sense of lightness so integral to Soufflot's aesthetic, and ruined the uninterrupted vista of the crossing.

More drastic changes to Soufflot's designs occurred after the church was secularized in 1791, during the French Revolution, to become a Temple of Great Men. The sculptor and aesthetic theoretician Antoine-Chrysostome Quatremère de Quincy (1755-1849), a tireless advocate of classical architecture, transformed the church to make it consonant with its new secular function as a repository of France's most illustrious men; the ashes of Voltaire and Rousseau had already been transfered there in 1791 and 1794, respectively. According to the prevailing architectural theories of the last decades of the 18th century, architecture was to be expressive of its function, *"architecture parlante."* Quatremère filled in the numerous nave and transept windows, transforming the once-bright interior into a gloomy and dim environment. Furthermore, what had once been light walls, regularly broken by the rhythm of void and solids, became smooth, monumental walls of unbending severity. Quatremère also eliminated the transept doors as well as the flanking bell towers. New sculptural decoration, replete with republican symbolism, was projected for the new temple, turning it into a great workshop for revolutionary sculpture.

The church's subsequent history is intimately tied to the various political regimes that governed France in the 19th century, as the edifice became a symbol of national aspirations. In 1806, under Napoleon, the church reverted to its original function, reflecting the emperor's conciliatory attitude toward the Catholic Church. Under the Restoration, it ironically became a pantheon once more, only to revert to the Catholic cult during the reign of Napoleon III. In 1885, after the funeral of Victor Hugo, Ste. Geneviève was permanently proclaimed as the nation's Panthéon, a function it still serves today.

—MARC VINCENT

SPENCE, Basil.

British. Born in Bombay, India, of British parents, 13 August 1907. Died in Eye, Suffolk, 19 November 1976. Married Mary Joan Ferris, 1934; two children. Educated at George Watson's

College, Edinburgh, 1920-25; Heriot-Watt University Architectural School, Edinburgh, 1925-29; Bartlett School of Architecture, University College London, 1929-30. Served in the British Army, 1939-45. Worked as an assistant in the office of Edwin Lutyens, London, 1929-30; architect, working with William Kininmonth, in the office of Rowand Anderson and Paul, Edinburgh, 1931-33; partner, Rowand Anderson and Paul, Edinburgh, 1934-37; in private practice, Edinburgh, 1937-39; as Basil Spence and Partners, Edinburgh, 1946-63; partnership divided into Sir Basil Spence, London, 1964-76, Spence Glover and Furguson, Edinburgh, 1964-74, and Spence Bonnington and Collins, London, 1964-70. Professor of architecture, University of Leeds, 1955-56; professor of architecture, Royal Academy, London, 1961-68. Fellow, 1947, and President , 1958-60, Royal Institute of British Architects.

Chronology of Works
All in England unless noted

1938	Spence House, Edinburgh, Scotland (rebuilding)
1950-62	Cathedral, Coventry (restoration and addition)
1951	Heavy Industries Exhibition, Sea and Ships Pavilion, Festival of Britain, London
1951	Sea and Ships Pavilion, Festival of Britain, London
1955	Church, Clermiston, Scotland
1958	Wray House, Wimbledon, London
1958	St. Paul's Church, Ecclesfield, Yorkshire
1959	St. Catherine's Church, Sheffield, England
1959	Thorn House (office building), St. Martin's Lane, London
1960	Undergraduate Housing, Queen's College, Cambridge
1960-73	Buildings for the University of Southampton, Hampshire
1962-75	Buildings for the University of Sussex, Brighton
1965	Chemistry Building, University of Exeter, Exeter
1966	Crematorium, Mortonhall, Edinburgh, Scotland
1970	Household Cavalry Barracks, Knightsbridge, London
1971	Chancery, British Embassy, Rome, Italy
1975	Bank of Piraeus, Athens, Greece
1976	Queen Anne's Mansions Office Development, London

Publications

BOOKS BY SPENCE

Exhibition Design. With others. London, 1950.
The Cathedral of St. Michael at Coventry. London, 1962.
Phoenix at Coventry: The Building of a Cathedral. London, 1962.
Out of the Ashes: A Progress Through Coventry Cathedral. With Henk Snoek. London, 1963.
The Idea of a New University: An Experiment in Sussex. With others. London, 1964.
New Buildings in Old Cities. Southampton, Hampshire, 1973.

ARTICLES BY SPENCE

"The Modern Church." *Journal of the Royal Institute of British Architects* 63 (July 1956): 369-376.

BOOKS ABOUT SPENCE

ESHER, LIONEL: *Broken Wave: The Rebuilding of England, 1940-1980.* London, 1981.

ARTICLES ABOUT SPENCE

CAMPBELL, COLIN: "Sir Basil Spence: An Architect's Appreciation." *Scottish Review* (Spring 1977).
GIBBERD, FREDERICK: "Obituary, Sir Basil Spence." *Architectural Review* (April 1977).
MUMFORD, LEWIS: "Sir Basil Spence." *New Yorker* (10 March 1962).
SHEPPARD, RICHARD: "Obituary, Sir Basil Spence." *Journal of the Royal Institute of British Architects Journal* (January 1977).
WODEHOUSE, LAWRENCE: "Old Guard, Avant-Garde." *Building Design* (23 February 1979).

*

Basil Spence was a key, if controversial, figure in British architecture during the two decades that followed the 1951 Festival of Britain. The Festival was, of course, a watershed in the development of postwar British architecture: modernism had by then assumed the mantle of orthodoxy, an architecture for "everyman," and Spence was a major contributor to that event with his Sea and Ships Pavilion.

The turning point in his career was, however, the successful entry in 1951 for the Coventry Cathedral competition. Heavily criticized at the time (and equally when consecrated in 1962), Coventry Cathedral nevertheless, along with the Festival of Britain, signaled the popular arrival of modern architecture in England. Spence's trump card was the retention of the bombed ruins of the existing church and his ingenious linking of the old with the new by a giant porte cochere. But liturgically, the plan broke no new ground (whereas his competitors, Denys Lasdun and Alison and Peter Smithson undeniably had done so), its innate conservatism appealing to the panel of judges, particularly to Robertson and Maufe. Others criticized the building's lack of rigor; tapered columns were, in the event, hung from the roof structure, anathema to dogmatic modernist observers.

Despite these onslaughts, Coventry Cathedral has stood the test of time remarkably well. Immaculate detailing, with traditional materials of the highest quality, and an overt sense of composition (it must be remembered that Spence had worked in Edwin Lutyens' office) have ensured the building's longevity. That it harbors works of art by Sutherland, Piper and Frink (equally controversial in their day) reinforces its importance in the annals of British architecture.

The controversy surrounding the Coventry competition initially produced a lean period for Spence's practice, but by the mid-1950s commissions, many, not surprisingly, ecclesiastical, appeared in increasing numbers. The result was a series of parish churches and schools throughout Britain, sensibly planned, immaculately detailed and fashioned with a real sense of composition. It was fitting that Sheffield, a center for progressive architectural thinking in the late 1950s, should harbor more than a fair share of Spence's work of the period; Ecclesfield School, Parson's Cross School, St. Paul's Church and St. Catherine's Church are noteworthy examples.

By the end of the decade, Spence was able to demonstrate his assurance in another sphere; Thorn House, St. Martin's Lane, London, was his first major commercial commission, and pointed the way to many subsequent examples of the genre from lesser architects.

Basil Spence: Cathedral, Coventry, England, 1950-62

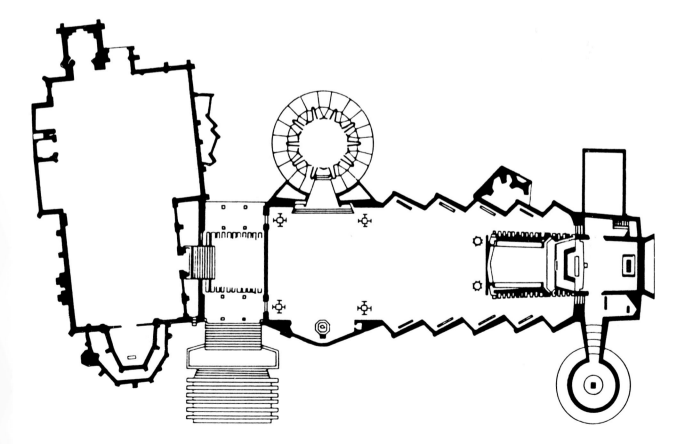

Like many of his contemporaries, Spence contributed hugely to the expansion of the British university system during the 1960s. Most notable was his work at Sussex University from 1965 to 1970, where the barrel vaults and brickwork of Le Corbusier's Maison Jaoul were transformed into a monumental but entirely appropriate collegiate architecture. Spence's work at the University of Southampton demonstrated a quite different approach. There, all eclecticism and thought of picturesque composition were subsumed by the order of the grid and structural expression, demonstrating the influence of his partner, Jack Bonnington.

Bonnington's influence may also be felt in Spence, Bonnington and Collins' design for Sunderland Civic Centre (completed 1970), a rigorously consistent complex adhering to a hexagonal grid, clad throughout in ceramic tile. Other important civic buildings stemmed from the practice, which by the mid-1960s had spawned three separate offices: Basil Spence; Spence, Glover and Ferguson; and Spence, Bonnington and Collins. Hampstead Civic Centre, Library and Swimming Pool (1964) incorporated an ingenious shading device of external vertical concrete fins, which reappeared in 1969 in more assured form at the Municipal Library, Newcastle upon Tyne.

However, alongside Coventry Cathedral, the British Embassy at Rome (completed 1971) must rank as the finest memorial to Spence's talent. Where Coventry had been an inspired response to context, so at Rome Spence used the adjacent Porta Pia by Michelangelo as a key to the scale and proportions of the new chancery. Again the chancery is ample evidence of Spence's mastery of form and composition in the most sensitive of contexts. Although met with criticism at its apparent mannerism when published in 1960, by completion in 1971 such concerns were seen in a more generous light, given that a new, postmodern ethos was gaining momentum.

Equally, the Household Barracks, Knightsbridge, London (completed 1970), and later, the Queen Anne's Mansions office development, London, gave the critics a field day. Spence remained resolute, and both buildings, in retrospect, again demonstrate Spence's facility with an appropriate monumental architecture of its time without recourse to the crass historicism beloved of his successors.

However, his pursuit of the monument could misfire; in his Gorbals housing, Glasgow (1962), his monumental concern seemed to override the need for a socially meaningful housing form.

Spence was never a theorist, and save for his anecdotal and autobiographical work surrounding Coventry Cathedral, his writings on architecture were few, for he was a "doer" in the British pragmatic tradition, and saw no need to theorize about architecture's relationship with the city or, indeed, its social purpose. In that sense, his aspirations were more modest than some of his contemporaries; he could concentrate upon that at which he excelled, the one-off monument in an important and sensitive setting.

Spence never sought accolades from the avant-garde, which, in some measure, may account for a generally hostile reception from his critics. In retrospect, however, his contribution to mid-20th-century British architecture was immense, as his beautifully crafted buildings testify, both technically and aesthetically.

Spence was the sole major British architect of his generation who espoused modernism while accommodating within his brief the English tradition stemming from the Arts and Crafts movement. It was this highly effective marriage which not only gave his work huge popular appeal, but also secured Spence his rightful prominence in the history of postwar British architecture.

—A. PETER FAWCETT

STERN, Robert A. M.

American. Born in New York City, 23 May 1939. Married Lynn Solinger, 1966 (divorced); one son. Studied at Columbia University, New York, B.A. 1960; Yale University, New Haven, Connecticut, M.Arch. 1965. Program director, Architectural League of New York, 1965-66; designer, office of Richard Meier, 1966; urban designer and assistant for design policy, Housing and Development Administration, City of New York, 1967-70; partner, Robert A. M. Stern and John S. Hagmann, Architects, 1969-77; princip al, 1977-89 and principal partner, since1989, Robert A. M. Stern Architects, New York. Has taught at Columbia University, New York, since 1970; professor since 1982. Fellow, American Institute of Architects, 1984.

Chronology of Works
All in the United States unless noted

1965-67	Wiseman House, Montauk, Long Island, New York
1969	Tiffeau-Busch Ltd. Showroom and Offices, New York City
1970	Showrooms for Helen Harper Inc., New York City
1971	William White Jr. Apartment, New York City
1972	Beebe House and outbuildings, Montauk, Long Island, New York
1973-74	Lang House, Washington, Connecticut
1974-76	Residence, Westchester County, New York
1979-81	Residence and Poolhouse, Llewellyn Park, New Jersey
1979-81	Lawson House, Quogue, New York
1979-83	Residence at Chilmark, Martha's Vineyard, Massachusetts
1980-83	Bozzi Residence, East Hampton, Long Island, New York
1982-84	Observatory Hill Dining Hall, University of Virginia, Charlottesville, Virginia
1983-85	Point West Place Office Building, Framingham, Massachusetts
1983-85	Prospect Point Office Building, La Jolla, California
1984-89	Urban Villa, Tegel, West Berlin, Germany
1985-89	Congregational Kol-Israel, Brooklyn, New York
1985-87	Headquarters for Mexx International, Voorschoten, Netherlands
1985-89	Residence on Russian Hill, San Francisco, California
1986-	Brooklyn Law School, Brooklyn, New York (renovation and addition)
1986-93	Center for Jewish Life, Princeton University, Princeton, New Jersey
1986-89	Courtyard Houses, Grand Harbor, Vero Beach, Florida
1986-89	Fine Arts Studio IV, University of California, Irvine, California
1986-91	222 Berkeley Street, Boston, Massachusetts
1987-89	Casting Center, Walt Disney World, Lake Buena Vista, Florida
1987-90	Pasadena Police Building, Pasadena, California
1987-91	Yacht and Beach Club Resorts, Walt Disney World, Florida
1987-91	Ohrstrom Library, St. Paul's School, Concord, New Hampshire
1987-92	Norman Rockwell Museum, Stockbridge, Massachusetts
1988-92	Bartholomew County Hospital, Columbus, Indiana (with additions through 1995)
1988-89	Bancho House, Tokyo, Japan

1988-90	Two Venture Plaza, Irvine Center, Irvine, California
1988-92	Hotel Cheyenne and Newport Bay Club Hotel, Euro Disneyland, Marne-la-Vallée, France
1989-	Roger Tory Peterson Institute, Jamestown, New York
1990-91	Banana Republic, 744 N. Michigan Avenue, Chicago, Illinois
1990-91	Parlor, DIFFA Showhouse, New York City
1990-92	Residence in Hunting Valley, Geauga County, Ohio
1990-92	St. Barnabas Memorial Garden, Irvington, New York
1993-	Tivoli Apartments, Tokyo, Japan

Publications

BOOKS BY STERN

New Directions in American Architecture. New York, 1969; Rev. ed. New York, 1977.

George Howe: Toward a Modern American Architecture. New Haven, Connecticut, 1975.

The Artist's Eye: American Architectural Drawings, 1779-1979. With Deborah Nevins. New York, 1979.

The Anglo-American Suburb. Editor, with John Montague Massengale. London, 1981.

Raymond Hood. With Thomas Catalano. New York, 1982.

East Hampton's Heritage. With Clay Lancaster and Robert Hefner. New York, 1982.

New York 1900: Metropolitan Architecture and Urbanism 1890-1915. With Gregory Gilmartin and John Montague Massengale. New York, 1983.

American Architecture: Innovation and Tradition. Editor, with David G. De Long and Helen Searing. New York, 1986.

Pride of Place: Building the American Dream. Companion volume to the PBS television series. Boston, 1986.

New York 1930: Architecture and Urbanism between the Two World Wars. With G. Gilmartin and T. Melins. New York, 1987.

Modern Classicism. New York and London, 1988.

The House That Bob Built. New York, 1991.

BOOKS ABOUT STERN

The American Houses of Robert A. M. Stern. New York, 1991.

ARNELL, PETER, and BICKFORD, TED (eds.): *Robert A. M. Stern: Buildings and Projects 1965-1980.* New York, 1981.

DIAMONSTEIN, BARBARALEE: *American Architecture Now.* New York, 1980.

DUNSTER, DAVID (ed.): *Robert Stern.* London, 1981.

FUNARI, LUCIA: *Robert A. M. Stern: Modernità e Tradizione.* Rome, 1990.

JENCKS, CHARLES: *Post-Modern Classicism.* London, 1980.

JENCKS, CHARLES: *The Language of Post-Modern Architecture.* London, 1977.

PORTOGHESI, PAOLO: *After Modern Architecture.* New York, 1982.

Robert A. M. Stern: Selected Works. London and New York, 1991.

RUEDA-SALAZAR, LUIS F. (ed.): *Robert A. M. Stern: Buildings and Projects 1981-1986.* New York, 1986.

ARTICLES ABOUT STERN

ASLET, CLIVE: "Architecture: Robert A. M. Stern." *Architectural Digest* 48 (July 1991): 88-95.

GOLDBERGER, PAUL: "Architecture: Robert A. M. Stern." *Architectural Digest* 47 (October 1990): 196-205.

"Recent Works of Robert A. M. Stern Architects." *Architecture and Urbanism* (May 1988): 61-95, 108-150.

"The Residential Works of Robert A. M. Stern." *Architecture and Urbanism*, Extra Edition (July 1982).

*

Robert Stern is a leading postmodernist architect, one of the so-called "Grey" architects, as opposed to the more stringent and theoretical group known as the "Whites," led by Peter Eisenman. Stern is a preeminent exponent of stylistic freedom, responding and responsible to history and to the traditions of design that history can still urge upon us.

Even as a student at Yale in the early 1960s, he showed an interest in eclecticism—in an issue of the journal *Perspecta*, of which he was editor—bringing together the theories and buildings of Robert Venturi, Louis Kahn and Charles Moore. He saw their work as separate instances of a common theme in architecture and its linkage always to tradition. His particular model, as Stern has always acknowledged, was Venturi, and Stern's first major commission, the Wiseman House in Montauk, New York (1965-67) is essentially the Vanna Venturi House writ large; however, as is appropriate for a shore house, it is built out of shingle rather than cement.

In 1969 Stern entered into partnership with John S. Hagmann, and for the next few years their firm produced a range of rich, eclectic and beautifully modulated designs, some—like the Residence, East Hampton, New York (1968-69)—looking back to the Shingle Style, others following the clearer lines of modernist style, especially true of their extensions and remodelings. Other buildings, like the Lang Residence in Connecticut (1973-74), incorporated in one single structure a whole range of styles variously identified as Palladian, Regency and art deco.

In the 1980s Stern's practice was largely confined to residences. As befits someone born in New York City, however, he has always been concerned with the questions of commercial buildings and general housing and if until recently, with some commercial projects, he had no opportunities to practice in these areas, this was not by any choice on his part. He entered the Roosevelt Island Competition, New York, in 1975; in 1976 he designed a beach suburb for Singer Island, Florida; for the Venice Biennale in that same year he began what was called a "subway suburb," a scheme for housing that uses recognizable models from Regency crescents in England and the design of Forest Hills, New York, to lay out a range of moderately priced, single-family homes, which are regular, yet not monotonous. It should be noted, in this connection, that for a while in the early 1970s Stern worked with the city of New York, at one point being a designer in the Housing and Development Administration.

One of his earliest commercial projects was the design, done in 1980, for the D.O.M. Headquarters in Bruhl, Germany, and there, as he acknowledged, he attempted to expand upon the tradition of technically advanced yet classically based buildings of Otto Wagner, Walter Gropius and Adolf Meyer. The following year he produced a large scheme, unfortunately never realized, to revitalize the downtown shopping core of Richmond, Virginia, with massive yet delicate towers to call attention to what was there: galleries, walkways, parking and shops. Perhaps his most successful and well-known commercial building is that of Point West Place, Framingham, Massachusetts (1983-84). West Point Place is a large speculative office building, just off the Massachusetts Turnpike, that has a modern, efficient air, with its slick steel and glass surface. Its colonnaded front marked out with the full weight of stone gives a more traditional account of entrance and the importance of entering a building.

Most recently, Stern has been one of the several architects working for the Disney Organization at Orlando, Florida.

Stern, it should be noted, has always been involved, from his days at *Perspecta*, with criticism and history; he has written innumerable articles, and early on, in 1969, he published a book titled *New Directions in American Architecture* that contained, as such books so often do, an idea of what these new directions should be. He has long been connected with the department of architecture at Columbia University and especially with the Buell Center for Architectural History, which has allowed him to continue his interests in history. His studies of George Howe and Raymond Hood were published in 1975 and 1982, respectively, and several sumptuous volumes on the architecture of New York City, decade by decade, have been compiled under his general editorship.

In 1986 he produced a series of films (and an accompanying book) on American architecture that were shown on television under the title ''Pride of Place.'' That title is significant. Stern has spoken often of his idea of architecture: that it is essentially concerned with what he calls ''the making of a place,'' in which tradition plays an important role. He also argues that architecture is properly an emulation of what is there, whether this is nature or a man-made environment. And yet, he emphasizes, following Venturi, that the modern building—acknowledging tradition yet born inevitably from a set of present circumstances—will reflect a certain tension between the past and the presence of this past. This tension will foster what Stern calls ''a new-old architecture'' that is more resonant than one that is, as he puts it, either ''all about the past,'' or ''all about the present.''

—DAVID CAST

STIRLING, James.

British. Born in Glasgow, Scotland, 22 April 1926; family moved to Liverpool, England, 1927. Died in 1992. Married Mary Shand, 1966; one son, two daughters. Studied at the Liverpool School of Art, 1942; Liverpool University School of Architecture, 1945-50, Dip.Arch.; School of Town Planning and Regional Research, London, 1950-52. Served as a lieutenant in the Paratroops, 1942-45 (in D-Day landing with the 6th Airborne Division, 1944). Worked as senior assistant, Lyons, Israel and Ellis, London, 1953-56; in private practice, London, 1956-92 (partnership with James Gowan, 1956-63; partnership with Michael Wilford, 1971-92 Taught widely in Great Britain and the United States; professor, Düsseldorf Kunstakademie, Germany, from 1977. Royal Institute of British Architects Gold Medal, 1980; Pritzker Prize, 1981.

Chronology of Works
All in England unless noted

1955-58	Low-rise Flats, Ham Common, London
1956	House, Isle of Wight
1958-61	Dining Hall, Brunswick Park Primary School, London
1959-63	Engineering Building, Leicester University, Leicester
1960-64	Home for the Elderly, Blackheath, London
1964-67	History Building, Cambridge University
1964-68	Residential expansion, St. Andrew's University, Scotland
1966-71	Florey Building, Queen's College, Oxford
1967-77	Low-cost Housing Developments, Runcorn New Town
1969-72	Olivetti Training School, Haslemere

1969-76	Low-cost Housing, Lima, Peru
1977-84	Neue Staatsgalerie, Stuttgart, Germany
1979-81	School of Architecture, Rice University, Houston, Texas, U. S. A (extensions)
1979-84	Sackler Museum, Harvard University, Cambridge, Massachusetts, U. S. A
1979-87	Wissenschaftszentrum, Berlin, Germany
1980-86	Clore Gallery (Turner Collection), Tate Gallery, London
1983-88	Performing Arts Center, Cornell University, Ithaca, New York, U. S. A
1986-	No. 1 Poultry, Mansion House, London
1987-	Music and Theater Academies, Stuttgart, Germany
1987-	Palazzo Citterio Art Gallery (Brera Museum), Milan, Italy
1988-	Science Library, University of California, Irvine, U. S. A
1989-	Biennale Bookshop, Venice, Italy

Publications

ARTICLES BY STIRLING

''From Garches to Jaoul.'' *Architectural Review* (September 1955).

''Ronchamp and the Crisis of Rationalism.'' *Architectural Review* (March 1956).

''Regionalism and Modern Architecture.'' *Architect's Yearbook* 8 (1957).

''Anti-Structures.'' *Zodiac* 18 (1969).

''Asian Games.'' *Architectural Design* (January 1975).

''Stirling Connections.'' *Architecture and Urbanism* (February 1975).

''The Monumentally Informed.'' In *Neue Staatsgalerie Stuttgart*. Stuttgart, 1984.

BOOKS ABOUT STIRLING

ARNELL, PETER, and BICKFORD, TED (eds.): *James Stirling: Buildings and Projects*. New York, 1984.

BANHAM, REYNER: *The New Brutalism*. London, 1966.

DREW, PHILIP: *The Third Generation*. Stuttgart, 1972.

JACOBUS, JOHN: *James Stirling*. Stuttgart, 1975.

JENCKS, CHARLES: *Modern Movements in Architecture*. London, 1973.

KLEIHUES, JOSEF PAUL (ed.): *Dortmunder Architekturhefte 15: Museumbauten—Entwürfe und Projekte seit 1945*. Exhibition catalog. Dortmund, Germany, 1979.

KRIER, LEON (ed.): *Buildings and Projects of James Stirling*. Stuttgart and London, 1974.

MAXWELL, ROBERT: *New British Architecture*. Stuttgart, 1972.

POPHAM, PETER: *James Stirling*. London, 1990.

SUDJIC, DEYAN: *New Directions in British Architecture: Norman Foster, Richard Rogers, James Stirling*. London, 1986.

ARTICLES ABOUT STIRLING

BISCOGLI, L.: ''L'opera di James Stirling.'' *Casabella* (June 1967).

COOK, PETER: ''Stirling and Hollein.'' *Architectural Review* (December 1982).

FILLER, M.: ''Architect for a Pluralist Age.'' *Art in America* (April 1981).

FRAMPTON, KENNETH: ''Transformations in Style.'' *Architecture and Urbanism* 5/2 (1975).

James Stirling: Neue Staatsgalerie, Stuttgart, Germany, 1977-84

GIROUARD, MARK: "Florey Building, Oxford." *Architectural Review* 152/909 (1972).

GIROUARD, MARK: "A Modern Neo-Classicist." *Country Life* (May 1974).

"Inside James Stirling." *Design Quarterly 100*, special issue (April 1976).

"James Stirling." *Architectural Design* Profile (1982).

"James Stirling, Michael Wilford and Associates." *Architectural Design* No. 85, special issue (1990).

"James Stirling—Work in Progress." *Casabella* (April 1982).

JODIDIO, P.: "The Dynamic Dissonance of James Stirling." *Connaissance des arts* (November 1981).

KORN, ARTHUR: "The Work of Stirling and Gowan." *Architecture and Building News* (January 1959).

McKEAN, JOHN M.: "Stirling Quality." *Building Design* (14 September 1979).

"Recent Works of James Stirling, Michael Wilford and Associates." *Architecture and Urbanism* (May 1990).

"Stirling since Stuttgart." *Architecture and Urbanism* (November 1986).

*

If one project were to serve as an illustration of the work of James Stirling, it would undoubtedly be the hypothetical "1977 Revisions to the Nolli Plan of Rome," for the *Roma Interrotta Exhibition,* because this project is a condensation of his entire oeuvre. The irreverent English architect opened the introduction to his project by describing his own personality: "Megalomania is the privilege of a chosen few. Piranesi who made his plan in 1762 was surely a Megalomanic Frustrated Architect (MFA) as also Boulee, Vanbrugh, Soane, Sant'Elia, Le Corbusier, etc.,

and it is in this distinguished company as an MFA architect that we make our proposal."

Though, in reality, Stirling is not a megalomaniac, it is important to understand the cynical and often heretical character of the architect. Stirling has always, most certainly, been viewed by critics as a modernist architect. A casual glance at his Cambridge History Faculty or his Queen's College, Oxford, buildings will affirm an admiration of Alvar Aalto, Gunnar Asplund and Le Corbusier. The buildings utilize all of the icons of modern architecture: piloti, roof terraces, ribbon windows and "freed facades, but upon close inspection it becomes apparent that these elements are often manipulated in an unusual manner. Stirling's buildings commonly depart from the modernist ideal by deforming their configurations to create surprisingly traditional urban spaces. This can be viewed in opposition to the presentation of pristine objects within undifferentiated spatial fields, which is so characteristic of modern architecture. Thus the *Roma Interrotta* project became the ultimate opportunity for the architect to demonstrate the ability of his buildings to form urban fabric while fundamentally remaining true to the tenets of 20th-century architecture.

The reason that Stirling's buildings so readily nested within the 1977 version of the Nolli plan is that the architect is equally capable of understanding his own oeuvre in terms of its formal as well as programmatic typology. When the architect writes that some of his buildings have a particularly "wall-like" quality, suitable for forming urban edges and spaces, it is apparent that he subscribes to Leon Battista Alberti's notion of the city that possesses characteristics of a large house, which likewise bears features of the city. It can be asserted that Stirling presents a revisionist view of modern architecture—one that is capable of understanding the critique levied upon the movement, particularly with respect to urbanism, during the second half of the century. Unlike many devout "believers" in the movement who resist questioning the tenets of modern urbanism, Stirling is acutely aware of the tragic failures of 20th-century city planning ideologies and methodologies.

Yet Stirling does not reject the whole thesis of modernism. He selects those aspects of the movement that appear to have provided adequate, often ingenious, solutions to the problems of building. Stirling integrates the reasonable assertions of modern architecture with interpretations of traditional urbanism and indeed more orthodox building configurations. The buildings produced by James Stirling are seldom exercises in clarity and unambiguity. His buildings are often hybrids that combine both "abstract" and "representational" elements.

Stirling regards his early projects such as the Core and Crosswall House as illustrations of the "abstract," whereas the Mavrolean House Project in South Kensington is seen as an example of the "representational" aspects of his work. He notes that in the St. Andrew's University Art Gallery, elements of both the "abstract" and "representational" were combined in his solution. And, in fact, if we are willing to suspend judgment concerning his usage of both of these words (for is not all architecture at once "abstract" and "representational"?), Stirling continued to explore the relationship between these two conceptions in all three of his German museum projects—the projects for Düsseldorf, Cologne and ultimately Stuttgart. In the Neue Staatsgalerie in Stuttgart, we find Stirling making use of "abstract" elements in the form of a series of canopies that mark the entrances to the museum, bold-colored handrails and piano-curved curtain walls. These elements clearly belong to the modernist "mind-set" of the architect, while the stone "chassis" of the building—the primary "representational" element, is indicative of his fascination with tradition.

Since the publication of the *Roma Interrotta* exhibition catalog in 1977, James Stirling has gone on to prove himself to be a major contender in the world of contemporary architecture. He received the Gold Medal of the Royal Institute of British Architects in 1980 and the Pritzker Prize, architecture's answer to the Nobel Prize, in 1981. His unique viewpoint has been useful in ushering the architect past the stylistic and intellectual deadends of poststructuralism (deconstruction, Peter Eisenman, et al.) and postmodern historicism (Michael Graves, Krier and the likes thereof). Stirling is among the group of architects who see the possibilities inherent in allowing modernity and tradition to engage in a meaningful dialogue.

—BRIAN KELLY

STONE, Edward Durell.

American. Born in Fayetteville, Arkansas, 9 March 1902. Died in New York City, 6 August 1978. Married Orlean Vandiver, 1931 (divorced, 1950); married Eleana Torchio, 1954 (divorced); married Violet Campbell Moffat, 1972. Studied at the University of Arkansas, Fayetteville, 1920-23; as apprentice to Henry R. Shepley, Boston, 1923-25; studied at Harvard University, 1925-26; Massachusetts Institute of Technology School of Architecture, 1925-26; Rotch Travelling Scholar,

in Europe, 1927-29. Serve d as a Major in the United States Air Force, 1942-45. Worked with the consortium of architects designing Rockefellar Center, New York City, 1929-35; in private practice, New York City, 1935 until his death in 1978: president, Edward Durell Stone and Associates, New York; offices established in Palo Alto, California, Los Angeles, and Chicago. Instructor in advanced design, New York University, 1935-40; associate professor of architecture, Yale University, New Haven, Connecticut, 1946-52; also lectured at Princeton University and the University of Arkansas, Fayetteville. Fellow, American Institute of Architects; fellow, Royal Society of Arts, London.

Chronology of Works
All in the United States unless noted

1933	Mandel House, Mount Kisco, New York
1936	Henry R. Luce Mepkin Plantation, Moncks Corner, South Carolina
1936-37	House, 4 Buckingham Street, Cambridge, Massachusetts (with Carl Koch)
1939	Museum of Modern Art, New York City (with Philip Goodwin)
1939	Goodyear House, Old Westbury, Long Island, New York
1946	El Panama Hotel, Panama City, Panama
1949	Popper House, White Plains, New York
1951	Fine Arts Center, University of Arkansas, Fayetteville
1954	United States Embassy, New Delhi, India
1956-59	Edward Durell Stone House, New York City (conversion)
1957	Stanford University Medical School and Hospital, Palo Alto, California
1958	United States Pavilion, World's Fair, Brussels, Belgium
1958-65	Huntington Hartford Gallery of Modern Art, Columbus Circle, New York City (now the New York City Department of Cultural Affairs)
1961-64	National Geographic Society Building, Washington, D.C.
1962	State University of New York Campus, Albany, New York
1963	Theater, Loyola University, Los Angeles
1966	Bush Memorial Stadium, St. Louis
1968	General Motors Building, New York City
1969-71	John F. Kennedy Center for the Performing Arts, Washington, D.C.
1970	Eisenhower Hospital, Palm Desert, California
1972	Gerontology Center, University of Southern California, Los Angeles
1972	Law Center, Georgetown University, Washington, D.C.
1973	PepsiCo World Headquarters, Purchase, New York
1974	Standard Oil Building, Chicago, Illinois (with Perkins and Will)
1975	Davidson Conference Center, University of Southern California, Los Angeles

Publications

BOOKS BY STONE

The Evolution of an Architect. New York, 1962.
Recent and Future Architecture. New York, 1967.

ARTICLES ABOUT STONE

DEAN, A. O.: "Cultural Colossi—Kennedy Center at 10." *American Institute of Architects Journal* (August 1981).

"Educational Work of Edward D. Stone." *Architectural Record* (February 1958).

"Edward Durell Stone 1902-1978." *Arts and Architecture* (April/July 1979).

"Genetrix: Personal Contributions to American Architecture." *Architectural Review* (May 1957).

"Minoru Yamasaki and Edward Durell Stone." *Zodiac* No. 8 (1961).

"New Work, Serene and Classic, by Edward Durell Stone." *Architectural Record* (October 1962).

"New York Is the Office of Ed Stone." *Architectural Forum* (October 1961).

"Public Buildings." *Architectural Forum* (November 1971).

"Recent Work by Edward Durell Stone." *Architectural Forum* (July 1941).

"Recent Work of Edward Durell Stone." *Architectural Record* (October 1964).

ROPER, LANNING: "Sculpture in a Broad Landscape." *Country Life* (21 April 1977).

"Theatres." *Progressive Architecture* (October 1965).

"Two California Hospitals by Edward Durell Stone." *Architectural Record* (September 1972).

"The Work of Edward D. Stone." *Architectural Record* (March 1959).

*

Although the architectural quality of his individual buildings is easily and often surpassed by that of works by many other designers, Edward Durell Stone ranks among the most significant American architects of the 20th century. He was one of the earliest American exponents of the International Style, and he had a considerable impact upon architectural education in the United States in the 1950s through his teaching activities at the University of Arkansas and other schools. He is remembered most, however, for being a principal player in the transformation of International Style modernism at mid-century that, by substituting formalism for functionalism as its underlying theoretical basis, laid the foundation for the rise of postmodernism in the 1960s and 1970s. Others, including Morris Lapidus, Philip Johnson and Minoru Yamasaki, also contributed to this transformation. But two factors made Stone's contribution outstanding. First, because his pedigree as an American modernist was equalled only by that of Johnson, his turn to formalism in the early 1950s carried a virtually unmatchable historical weight. Second, because he served throughout his career a clientele drawn from the wealthiest and politically best-connected classes in America, his architecture tended not only to be prominently sited and prominently featured in contemporary publications, but moreover could lay claim to being the official expression of American built culture of the Eisenhower period.

Stone's formalism had deep roots in his Beaux-Arts education at the Massachusetts Institute of Technology and his apprenticeship in the New York office of Schultze and Weaver. With the possible exception of the Albert C. Koch house in Cambridge, Massachusetts (1936), none of his International Style work of the 1930s was informed by so definite a functionalist conviction as that which inspired the contemporary North American work of Juan O'Gorman, Lawrence Kocher or George F. Keck. His work in the International Style showed little influence of Walter Gropius or Le Corbusier, but rather cleverly assimilated motifs from Robert Mallet-Stevens, Richard Neutra and Ludwig Mies van der Rohe.

In a disarmingly frank 1962 autobiography quite possibly inspired by that of Frank Lloyd Wright (which it rivals both in its apparent innocence and its real pomposity), Stone attributed his shift from a relatively severe, though still somewhat decorative, modernism toward the highly ornamental modern formalism of his later career to the taste of his second wife, Maria Torchio, whom he met in 1953. The distinctively feminine quality of most of Stone's work after that date thus probably has a curious but precise historical basis: it was meant as a tribute to a great architect's great romantic involvement.

Although Stone designed houses and public buildings throughout his career, in its later, formalist phase his public structures have an increased relative importance because they more and more frequently were designed to serve institutional and governmental purposes. Such structures included the United States Embassy in New Delhi (1954) and the United States Pavilion at the Brussels World's Fair (1958), both for the U.S. Department of State; the Huntington Hartford Gallery of Modern Art on Columbus Circle in New York City (1958); and the National Geographic Society Building (1961) and the Kennedy Center for the Performing Arts (begun 1959), Washington, D.C. Such buildings generally stand, in typically modernist fashion, as isolated objects in amorphous space. Their interiors are usually arranged on open plans, often with a large multifunctional central space containing isolated geometric elements (such as pools or planters) ringed by smaller enclosed rooms of more definite purpose. Luxurious materials and finishes (marble veneer, gilding, crystal) together with a profusion of fussy decorative details (relief patterns on walls, filigree screens or curtains, neo-Rococo chandeliers) distract attention from often grossly detailed connections. The most distinctive—and the most widely imitated—of the formal devices used by Stone in his late, classicizing designs is the exterior filigree screen or *brise-soleil* (executed in terrazzo in the New Delhi Embassy and in concrete block in the architect's own townhouse in New York City, 1956). While intended to delight, Stone's designs often fail to do so because they were carried out with so much self-conscious seriousness and so little humor, a quality that partially redeems similar work by Lapidus or T. H. Robsjohn-Gibbings, Stone's sometime collaborator on furnishing schemes.

Solemn and obvious, Stone's late architecture responded exactly to the predilection for a vulgar display of tangible wealth that has always characterized middle-class taste in America. At the same time, it also satisfied the equally characteristic American preference for efficiency and straightforwardness. Stone accomplished this simultaneous expression of richness and thrift by wrapping generously proportioned, boxy volumes in glossy or vividly patterned, tactile ornamentation. His eminently likable architecure (featured in *Life*, *Horizon* and other such magazines) quickly became part and parcel of American popular culture, in the same way that the contemporary architecture of Skidmore, Owings and Merrill and Emery Roth and Sons became part and parcel of American corporate culture.

Almost inestimable is Stone's direct and indirect influence not only upon countless architects of little distinction but also upon some of the most prominent ones of a younger generation, such as John Portman. While many of Stone's later buildings were surely in poor taste, none was ever devoid of meaning. In the dumb enormity of these creations, in their frivolous superficiality, in their appealing but ultimately cloying ornamentalism are embedded the historical record of a most important chapter in the development of 20th-century design.

—ALFRED WILLIS

STREET, George Edmund.

British. Born in Woodford, Essex, England, 1824. Died in London, 1881. Married Mariquita Proctor, 1850s; son was the architect Arthur Edmund Street (1855-1938). Articled to architect Owen Browne Carter, Winchester, 1841-44; assistant to George Gilbert Scott, 1844-49; opened office in London, 1849; moved to Wantage, Berkshire, 1850; moved to Oxford, 1852; returned to London, 1856. Gold Medal, Royal Institute of British Architects, 1874; president, Royal Institute of British Architects, 1881; associate, 1866, and member, 1871, Royal Academy.

Chronology of Works
All in England unless noted
† *Work no longer exists*

1847-48	St. Mary's Church, Biscovey, Cornwall
1848-50	St. Peter's Church, Treverbyn, Cornwall
1849-50	Vicarage, Wantage, Oxfordshire
1850	Schools, Inkpen, Berkshire
1852-75	Theological College, Cuddeson, Oxfordshire
1853-54	Vicarage Colnbrook, Buckinghamshire
1854-55	All Saints Church, vicarage, school and cottages, Boyne Hill, Berkshire
1854-61	St. Mary's Convent, Wantage, Oxfordshire
1854-79	St. Peter's Church, Bournemouth, Hampshire
1857-58	St. Thomas' Church, Watchfield, Berkshire
1857-60	St. James' Church, New Bradwell, vicarage and school, Wolverton, Buckinghamshire
1858-65	Church of SS. Philip and James, Oxford
1859-60	St. John the Evangelist Church, Howsham, Humberside
1859-61	St. James-the-Less Church, Westminster, London
1859-66	St. Michael's Church, St. Michael Penkevil, Cornwall (reconstruction)
1860-62	All Saints Church, School and Vicarage, Denstone, Staffordshire
1861-63	Uppingham School Hall, Leicestershire
1861-82	Uppingham School Chapel, Leicestershire
1862-85	St. John's Church, Torquay, Devon
1863-68	Crimea Memorial Church, Constantinople, Turkey
1863-72	All Saints Church, Clifton, Bristol†
1864-90	Convent of St. Margaret, East Grinstead, West Sussex
1865-72	St. Saviour's Church, Eastbourne, East Sussex
1866	Chapel of former workhouse, Shipmeadow, Suffolk
1866-70	St. Mary's Church and School, Westcott, Buckinghamshire
1867-69	St. Margaret's Church and Vicarage, Liverpool
1867-73	St. Mary Magdalene's Church, Paddington, London
1867-81	Holy Trinity Church, Bristol (nave and west facade; not completed until 1888)
1868-78	Christ Church Cathedral, Dublin, Ireland (reconstruction and Synod Hall)
1871-88	St. John the Divine Church, Kensington, London
1872-76	American Episcopal Church, Rome, Italy
1873-76	The Hall (Wigan Rectory), Greater Manchester
1873-76	Holmdale (G. E. Street House), Holmbury St. Mary, Surrey
1873-77	St. Andrew's Church, East Heslerton, North Yorkshire

George Edmund Street: Law Courts, London, England, 1873-82

1873-80	St. James' Church, Kingston, Dorset
1873-82	Law Courts, London
1877-79	St. Mary's Church, Holmbury St. Mary, Surrey
1878	English Church, Müren, Switzerland
1879-81	Misses Monk House, Chelsea, London
1880-87	All Saints' English Church, Rome, Italy
1880-1906	American Church, Paris, France

Publications

BOOKS BY STREET

An Urgent Plea for the Revival of the True Principles of Architecture in the Public Buildings of the University of Oxford. Oxford and London, 1853.

Brick and Marble Architecture in the Middle Ages: Notes on the Tours in the North of Italy. London, 1855.

Some Account of Gothic Architecture in Spain. London, 1865.

Explanation and Illustrations of His Designs for the Proposed New Courts of Justice. London, 1867.

George Edmund Street: Unpublished Notes and Reprinted Papers. Edited by Georgiana G. King. New York, 1916.

ARTICLES BY STREET

"On the Proper Characteristics of a Town Church." *Ecclesiologist* 11 (1852): 247-262.

"On the Revival of the Ancient Style of Domestic Architecture." *Ecclesiologist* 14 (1853): 70-80.

"The Study of Gothic Foreign Architecture and Its Influence on English Art." In ORBY SHIPMAN (ed.): *The Church and the World.* Vol. 1. London, 1866-68.

"Architecture in the Thirteenth Century." In ROBERT H. MARTLEY and R. DENNY URBIN (eds.): *Afternoon Lectures on Literature and Art.* Vol. 4. London, 1867.

"A Lecture Delivered at the Royal Academy Last Session." *Architect* 6 (1871): 299-301, 310-312, 323, 325.

"A Second Lecture Delivered at the Royal Academy Last Session." *Architect* 7 (1872): 78-80, 88-90, 103-104.

BOOKS ABOUT STREET

BROWNLEE, DAVID: *The Law Courts: The Architecture of George Edmund Street.* London, 1984.

CLARKE, BASIL F. L.: *Church Builders of the Nineteenth Century.* London, 1938.

KINNARD, JOSEPH: "G. E. Street, the Law Courts, and the Seventies." In PETER FERRIDAY (ed.): *Victorian Architecture.* London, 1963.

SERVICE, ALASTAIR: *The Architects of London.* London, 1979.

STREET, ARTHUR EDMUND: *Memoir of George Edmund Street, R. A., 1824-1881.* London, 1888.

SUMMERSON, JOHN: "A Victorian Competition: The Royal Courts of Justice." In *Victorian Architecture: Four Studies in Evaluation.* New York, 1970.

SUMMERSON, JOHN: "Two London Churches." In *Victorian Architecture: Four Studies in Evaluation.* New York, 1970.

ARTICLES ABOUT STREET

HITCHCOCK, HENRY-RUSSELL: "G. E. Street in the 1850s." *Journal of the Society of Architectural Historians* 19, No. 4 (1960): 145-171.

JACKSON, NEIL: "The Un-Englishness of G. E. Street's Church of St. James-the-Less." *Architectural History* 23 (1980): 86-94.

PORT, M. H.: "The New Law Courts Competition, 1866-1867." *Architectural History* 11 (1968): 75-93.

SUMMERSON, JOHN: "The Law Courts Competition of 1866-1877." *Journal of the Royal Institute of British Architects* 77, No. 1 (1970): 11-18.

*

George Edmund Street as an architect was, like William Butterfield, a favorite of the High Church but, unlike him, had a considerable secular practice and figured prominently in the architectural competitions of the Victorian period. He was also an architectural archaeologist and noted art theorist who advocated art-architecture. However, any examination of his contribution to High Victorian architecture inevitably begins in a comparison with Butterfield.

In this context, an examination of Street's major churches of the late 1850s and early 1860s—St. James the Less, Westminster, and St. Philip and St. James, Oxford—must include comparison with Butterfield's All Saints, Margaret Street, in London. St. James the Less, like Butterfield's masterpiece, received a range of both positive and negative critical comment. It is an eclectic building, more scholarly in its derivation with the historical sources, including its Italian references, more recognizable; this is a building that more readily reveals in its volume and massing the functional aspects of its design. It is composed of split volumes, as compared with the planar qualities of Butterfield's work. These characteristics may be seen as the physical expression of Street's earlier theoretical writings and the result of his historical and archaeological research. It also exhibits "Ruskinian" qualities especially notable in the design of the detached tower and the building's sense of mass. At St. Philip and St. James, Street created a similar massiveness in masonry, which is modeled in a truly plastic manner.

Street equated Gothic with the constructional qualities of pointed architecture and not with a particular nation or age, and did not consider it essentially church-like or antiquarian. For him it offered constructional benefits that could be coupled with the functional requirements of the age to produce an appropriate aesthetic response. In this he was similar to Butterfield.

Street's eclecticism, however, admitted a greater use of and obvious reference to continental examples, and his influential published works, *Brick and Marble in the Middle Ages, Notes of a Tour in the North of Italy* (1855) and *Some Account of Gothic Architecture in Spain* (1865), reinforced this tendency in his work. The derived aesthetic was a sublime expression of mass exhibiting repose and grandeur through a coherent use of masonry that emphasized the horizontal line. Interior space, three-dimensionally conceived, was modulated by the use of light and shade, which found external expression in the contrast of an unbroken wall with openings punched through its massiveness. This was in a way reminiscent of the importance given by John Ruskin to building mass in all its manifestations. In the middle of Street's career this evolved into a more plastic expression of mass and space, modulated through the use of constructional color in associations of major volumes whose forms encapsulate the activities within.

At All Saints, Butterfield had built the archetypal urban minster, but Street the theorist was the type's written propagandist. In 1850 he proclaimed the unsuitability of planting churches with designs based on rural precedents and executed in rustic materials in urban areas, and argued for a more appropriate urban architecture.

Street is best remembered for his involvement in and eventual design for the new Law Courts fronting the Strand, subject of the most important of the competitions involving the High

Victorian Gothic. His original design, like most of the 11 invited schemes, was conceived as a walled city within the city; at its center it had a great hall lit by clerestories surrounded by lower elements and set within a facade of essentially regular composition using a hierarchy of fenestration to express the building's functions through variety in scale, position, extent and spacing.

The building, whose construction did not begin until 1873 and which was not completed until after Street's death, retained these essentials in an overall composition that is more heavily modeled than his original design, with the hall having direct access from the Strand. Street's influences were Early English forms, a departure from the Italianate nature of his earlier unsuccessful competition proposal for the Foreign Office, which showed the influence of his then-recent travels in northern Italy. Perhaps the respective derivations of the two schemes may be seen as appropriate to the buildings' uses.

With the Law Courts, Street took High Victorian Gothic into the secular world and into the street, designing a building that for all its defects in planning and acoustics shows how this type of architecture can be adapted on a grand scale to the truncated perspective of the urban setting. Although he was also a convincing exponent of ecclesiological ideas and constructional polychromy, his most lasting legacy lies in this adaptation of the style to fit the townscape.

—R. J. MOORE

STRICKLAND, William.

American. Born in 1787. Died on 6 April 1854. Studied under Benjamin Latrobe, 1803-05. Worked independently in Philadelphia, from 1809. President, National Society of Architects, New York, 1836.

Chronology of Works
All in the United States
† Work no longer exists

1808-11	Masonic Hall, Philadelphia, Pennsylvania†
1816-17	Temple of the New Jerusalem (later the Academy of Natural Sciences), Philadelphia, Pennsylvania†
1817	Medical Department, University of Pennsylvania, Philadelphia, Pennsylvania (improvements)†
1818-24	Second Bank of the United States, Philadelphia, Pennsylvania
1820-22	Chestnut Street Theater, Philadelphia, Pennsylvania†
1820-27	Western State Penitentiary, Pittsburgh, Pennsylvania†
1822-25	Mikveh-Israel Synagogue, Philadelphia, Pennsylvania†
1822-23	St. Stephen's Episcopal Church, Philadelphia, Pennsylvania
1824	Musical Fund Society Hall, Philadelphia, Pennsylvania
1824	Triumphal arches for Lafayette's visit to Philadelphia†
1826-33	United States Naval Asylum (later the United States Naval Home), Philadelphia, Pennsylvania
1828	Arch Street Theater, Philadelphia, Pennsylvania†
1828	First Congregational Unitarian Church, Philadelphia, Pennsylvania†
1828	Independence Hall, Philadelphia, Pennsylvania (steeple)
1829-30	Medical and College Halls, University of Pennsylvania, Philadelphia, Pennsylvania†
1829-33	United States Mint, Philadelphia, Pennsylvania†
1830-34	New Almshouse, Blockley Township, Pennsylvania†
1932-34	Philadelphia Merchants' Exchange, Philadelphia, Pennsylvania
1835	Branch Mint, Charlotte, North Carolina
1835-36	Mint, New Orleans, Louisiana
1836-38	Athenaeum, Providence, Rhode Island
1828-40	Delaware Breakwater, off Lewes, Delaware
1836	St. John's Episcopal Church, Salem, New Jersey
1837	Mechanics' Bank (now the Norwegian Seamen's Church), Philadelphia, Pennsylvania
1842	St. Peter's Episcopal Church, Philadelphia, Pennsylvania (tower and steeple)
1845-47	Cathedral of the Blessed Virgin of the Seven Dolors (now St. Mary's Church), Nashville, Tennessee
1845-59	Tennessee State Capitol, Nashville, Tennessee
1848-51	First Presbyterian Church, Nashville, Tennessee
1850	Belmont (now Ward-Belmont School), Nashville, Tennessee
1853	Belle Meade, Nashville, Tennessee [attributed]

Publications

BOOKS BY STRICKLAND

Reports on Canals, Railways, Roads, and Other Subjects. Philadelphia, 1826.
The Public Works of the United States of America. London, 1841.

BOOKS ABOUT STRICKLAND

CARROTT, RICHARD G.: *The Egyptian Revival: Its Sources, Monuments and Meaning, 1808-1858.* Berkeley, California, 1978.
GILCHRIST, AGNES ADDISON: *William Strickland, Architect and Engineer, 1788-1854.* Philadelphia, 1950.
HAMLIN, TALBOT: *Greek Revival Architecture in America.* New York, 1944.
STANTON, PHOEBE B.: *The Gothic Revival and American Church Architecture: An Episode in Taste, 1840-1856.* Baltimore, 1968.

ARTICLES ABOUT STRICKLAND

"Historic Philadelphia: From the Founding Until the Early Nineteenth Century." *Transactions of the American Philosophical Society* 43, Part 1 (1953).
ADDISON, AGNES: "Latrobe vs. Strickland." *Journal of the American Society of Architectural Historians* 2, No. 3 (July 1942): 26-29.
GILCHRIST, AGNES ADDISON: "Additions to *William Strickland, Architect and Engineer, 1788-1854.*" *Journal of the Society of Architectural Historians* 13 (October 1954).
GILLIAMS, E. L.: "A Pioneer American Architect." *Architectural Record* 23 (February 1908): 123-135.
HALL, LOUISE: "Mills, Strickland and Walter: Their Adventures in a World of Science." *Magazine of Art* 40 (November 1947): 266-271.
NEWCOMB, REXFORD G.: "William Strickland, American Greek Revivalist." *Architect* 10 (July 1928): 453-458.

As a prominent architect in the United States during the country's formative years, William Strickland helped shape the image of the new republic through his designs of buildings, including state capitols, banks, theaters, churches and insane asylums. He grew up in Philadelphia, which in the early years of the nation was the most sophisticated city in the United States. There, Strickland was exposed to the arts, including the theater, which enabled him to express his talents as an engraver, painter, scenery designer, surveyor and architect.

Though Strickland is best known for his architectural work, he seems to have had little formal training in the field. His father, a carpenter, obtained an apprenticeship for Strickland with the eminent architect Benjamin Latrobe. Strickland worked in Latrobe's office from 1803 to 1805. Despite his short tenure there, Strickland adopted Latrobe's emphasis on visual clarity and archaeological accuracy.

When Strickland competed with his mentor in the competition for the Second Bank of the United States in Philadelphia, he relied on folios of the parthenon in Stuart and Revett's *The Antiquities of Athens* (1751). To some extent, he merely followed the competition committee's stipulations that the submitted entries be Greek in design and that the building be marble. Strickland's design met these specifications and consequently had a major impact on American architecture; the Second Bank (1818) was one of the earliest copies of the Parthenon built in the country. The only exterior changes that Strickland made were the elimination of the side colonnades. Yet the interior, with its barrel-vaulted banking room on a cross-axis to the facade of the building, expresses an interest in ancient Roman architecture and a manipulation of interior space to match the specific functions of the building as a bank rather than as a Greek temple. Nevertheless, the Second Bank is considered one of the first true examples of the Greek Revival in America.

The Second Bank was not Strickland's first building, but it was his most significant up to that time. The success of that structure led to a number of architectural commissions for public buildings. In 1826 he designed the Greek Revival United States Naval Asylum, which utilized new methods of fireproofing.

His Philadelphia Exchange (1832-34) marked another use of archaeological sources, but in an unusual way. The rectangular structure terminates in a curved portico on the east end, and is topped by an oversized copy of the Choragic Monument of Lysicrates taken from an illustration in Stuart and Revett. This unorthodox mixing of elements appeared later in Strickland's design for the Tennessee State Capitol.

From 1828 to 1833, Strickland designed so many important buildings for Philadelphia that he was generally called the "city architect." Among other structures built in the city were several banks and churches, two theaters, the United States Mint and buildings for the University of Pennsylvania. So much of Strickland's time was occupied by the construction of public buildings that he designed few private houses. However, as a prominent figure in Philadelphia society and a member of such groups as the American Philosophical Society, the Columbian Society of Artists and the Pennsylvania Academy of the Fine Arts, Strickland played a major role in the transformation of the face of the city. He contributed to the gradual professionalization of the architectural field and often exhibited designs at the Pennsylvania Academy of the Fine Arts. In addition, he was the president of the first installation of the short-lived American Institute of Architects, which lasted from 1836 to 1837.

A significant aspect of Strickland's career as an architect was that his ability to create superb architectural drawings was matched by his strong background as an engineer. In 1825 he was sent to England by the Pennsylvania Society for the Promotion of Internal Improvement to obtain information on the construction of railroads. He subsequently worked as an engineer for canal and railroad projects in Pennsylvania and Delaware. Although Strickland's role as an architect focused mostly on the design of buildings, he supervised the construction of some of his most important structures, including the Second Bank, the Naval Asylum, the Philadelphia Exchange and the Tennessee State Capitol.

The Tennessee State Capitol (1845-59, finished posthumously) was Strickland's last work. Again working in the Greek Revival style, he relied on a combination of a Greek Ionic temple topped by a tower sumounted by the Monument of Lysicrates. This time, Strickland carefully scaled his structures to actual Greek proportions, despite his non-Greek combination of a temple and a tower. However, the blend of these two elements brings to mind the national Capitol as well as the Greek ideal of democracy.

Though Strickland was not a very progressive architect in terms of construction techniques, the Tennessee capitol displays Strickland's changing attitude toward the use of iron. In the Second Bank, iron was used in chains encircling the brick piers in the basement as reinforcement only. In Tennessee, however, Strickland used iron as a primary structural material in the rafters of the building to support the central tower.

Although Strickland is remembered for his Greek Revival buildings, he designed in all the major revival styles of the early 19th century. His first building, the Masonic Hall in Philadelphia (ca. 1808) was a Gothic Revival structure, while one of his later buildings, the First Presbyterian Church in Nashville, employed the Egyptian Revival style.

In his interest in revival styles and his adherence to archaeological accuracy, Strickland performed the ultimate service to a national monument in 1824. In that year he restored the steeple of Independence Hall to its original form, probably the first example of Colonial restoration in the United States.

—JULIE NICOLETTA

STUART, James.

British. Born in London, England, 1713. Died in London, 2 February 1788. Married twice; first wife was his housekeeper, had one child who died; married his second wife late in life, had five children. Studied mathematics, geometry, anatomy, and taught himself Greek and Latin. Began his career as a fan painter for Lewis Groupy; traveled to Rome and worked as a tour guide to the English, 1742; went with Matthew Brettingham, Gavin Hamilton and Nicholas Revett to Naples, 1748; went to Greece wit h Revett, 1750; elected member of the Society of Dilettanti along with Revett, 1751; traveled to Constantinople, 1753; fellow of the Royal Society and the Society of Antiquaries of London; painter to the Society of Dilettanti, 1763 (replaced by Joshua Reynolds, 1768); surveyor to Greenwich Hospital, 1768;

Chronology of Works
All in England unless noted
* Approximate dates
† Work no longer exists

1755*   Wentworth Woodhouse, Yorkshire (interior decoration)
1758-59   Doric Temple, Hagley Park, Worcestershire
1759-65   Spencer House, Green Park, London (interiors)
1760-64* Nuneham Park, Oxfordshire (interior decorations and church)

1760-65   Holderness House (later Londonderry House), Hertford Street, London (interior decoration and possibly the original design)†

1763-64   Infirmary, Greenwich Hospital, London (damaged by fire, 1811; now Dreadnought Hospital)

1764-66   Lichfield House, St. James' Square, London (altered by Samuel Wyatt, 1791-94)

1764-70   Shugborough, Staffordshire (interior decoration and park buildings: Arch of Hadrian, 1764-67; Tower of the Winds, 1764; Greenhouse, 1764†; Lanthorn of Demosthenes, 1770)

1770   St. George's Chapel, Windsor Castle, Berkshire (altar-piece)

1775*   Belvedere, near Erith, Kent†

1775*   Wimpole Hall, the "Prospect House", Cambridgeshire†

1775-82   Montagu House (later Portman House), Portman Square, London†

1780*   Temple of the Winds, Mount Stewart, County Down, Ireland

1780-88   Chapel, Greenwich Hospital, London (rebuilding)

Publications

BOOKS BY STUART

The Antiquities of Athens Measured and Delineated by James Stuart and Nicholas Revett. With Nicholas Revett. 4 vols. London, 1762-1816. Reprint: New York, 1968.

BOOKS ABOUT STUART

CALDWELL, A.: *An Account of the Extraordinary Escape of James Stuart.* 1804.

COCKERELL, CHARLES ROBERT: *Antiquities of Athens and other Places of Greece, Sicily, etc.,* supplementary to *The Antiquities of Athens* by Stuart and Revett. London, 1830.

CROOK, J. MORDAUNT: *The Greek Revival.* 1972.

MUSGRAVE, CLIFFORD: *Adam and Hepplewhite and other Neo-Classical Furniture.* 1966.

WATKIN, DAVID: *Athenian Stuart: Pioneer of the Greek Revival.* London, 1982.

WIEBENSON, DORA: *Sources of Greek Revival Architecture.* London, 1969.

ARTICLES ABOUT STUART

BATEY, M.: 'Nuneham Park, Oxfordshire. The Creation of a Landscape Garden.'' *Country Life* (5 September 1968): 540-542.

BOLTON, A. T.: 'Hagley Park.'' *Country Life* (16 October 1915): 520-528.

GOODISON, NICHOLAS: "Mr. Stuart's Tripod." *Burlington Magazine* 114 (1972): 695-704.

HALLEY, J. M. W.: 'Lichfield House.'' *Architectural Review* (May 1910): 273-278.

HARDY, JOHN, and HAYWARD, HELENA: "Kedleston Hall, Derbyshire." *Country Life* 163 (2 February 1978): 262-266.

HARRIS, JOHN: "Early Neo-Classical Furniture." *Journal of the Furniture Historical Society* 2 (1966).

HARRIS, JOHN: "Newly Acquired Designs by James Stuart in the British Architectural Library, Drawings Collection." *Architectural History* 22 (1979): 72-77.

HUSSEY, CHRISTOPHER: 'Shugborough, Staffordshire.'' *Country Life* (25 February; 4-11 March; 15-22 April 1954).

LANDY, JACOB: "Stuart and Revett: Pioneer Archaeologists." *Archaeology* 9 (December 1956): 252-259.

LAWRENCE, LESLEY: 'Greece and Rome at Greenwich.'' *Architectural Review* 109 (1951): 17-24.

LAWRENCE, LESLEY: "Stuart and Revett: Their Literary and Architectural Careers." *Journal of the Warburg Institute* 2, No. 2 (1938): 128-146.

LEWIS, LESLEY: "The Architects of the Chapel at Greenwich Hospital." *Art Bulletin* 29 (1947): 260-267.

NARES, G.: 'Hagley Hall, Worcestershire.'' *Country Life* (19 September 1957): 546-549.

OSWALD, A.: 'Londonderry House.'' *Country Life* (10 July 1937): 38-44.

THORNTON, PETER, and HARDY, JOHN: "The Spencer Furniture at Althorp." *Apollo* 87 (1968): 440-451.

UDY, D.: 'The Furniture of James Stuart and Robert Adam.'' *Discovering Antiques* No. 42 (1971).

*

James Stuart, called "Athenian" in his own lifetime, was the son of a Sottish mariner. He showed an early talent for drawing, and obtained a post with Lewis Goupy (died 1747), a fan painter, who seems to have been responsible for interesting the young man in classical antiquity. While employed by Goupy, Stuart studied mathematics, geometry and anatomy, and soon became a highly skilled draftsman and a gifted painter in watercolor and gouache. He must have been remarkably intelligent and hardworking at that time, for he is also supposed to have taught himself Latin and Greek.

In 1742 he set out for Rome, but unlike many of his contemporaries, he had neither the means nor the patronage to assist him, so he was obliged to earn his living as an itinerant fan painter in order to finance his journey. However, having reached his destination, he was quickly established as a sound judge of pictures, and seems to have acted as a guide for Englishmen on the grand tour as well as operating as an agent for those on the lookout for pictures, antiquities and *objets d'art,* so he was able to raise funds to pay for his stay in Rome as well. In 1748 he set out with Matthew Brettingham (1725-1803), Gavin Hamilton (1723-98) and Nicholas Revett (1720-1804) for Naples, where a plan to visit Greece was formed.

Shortly afterward Stuart and Revett prepared ideas for "publishing an Accurate Description of the Antiquities of Athens," and this proposal interested the British Dilettanti who were then in Italy on the grand tour. With the financial support of the earls of Malton and Charlemont, as well as James Dawkins and Robert Wood, among others, an expedition was mounted, and the party set off for Greece in 1750. The group was delayed in Venice, during which Stuart and Revett were proposed as members of the Society of Dilettanti; they were elected in 1751, in March of which year the young men arrived in Athens.

Greece was then part of the Ottoman Empire, but the party enjoyed special privileges, as the ambassador in Constantinople was a member of the Society of Dilettanti, and gave the project every support; there were several dangerous incidents, however, some of them, at least, provoked by Stuart's splenetic temper. The expedition succeeded in measuring and drawing most of the major monuments of Athenian antiquity, and, after traveling in the Greek archipelago, returned to England in 1755 to commence work on the finished measured drawings and descriptions. In the course of preparation it was decided to devote the first publication to the smaller buildings of Athens, and in 1762 the first volume, *The Antiquities of Athens measured and delineated by James Stuart, F.R.S. and F.S.A., and Nicholas Revett, Painters and Architects,* came out, dedicated to King

George III. This stunningly beautiful book contained accurate illustrations of antique Greek buildings and was the primary sourcebook for that aspect of neoclassicism we call the Greek Revival. The first effects of the publication (which was at once recognized for what it was, namely a major work of scholarship) were less architectural than decorative, for the later volumes containing major buildings such as the temples on the Acropolis were not to appear for some time.

Stuart bought Revett out, even though the latter's name occurs on the title pages of later volumes and Revett was responsible for the beautiful measured drawings that made the first volume such a splendid achievement. Stuart provided the far more general and less useful topographical drawings of the sites.

The Antiquities of Athens made Stuart's name, and thereafter he enjoyed full employment as a painter and as an architect. As the title page states, he was elected a Fellow of both the Royal Society and the Society of Antiquaries of London, and was an eminent member of the Society of Dilettanti. In 1763 he was made Painter to the Society, but, when he failed to honor his obligations to paint portraits of the members, he was replaced by Joshua Reynolds (1723-92) in 1768, in which year Stuart was appointed surveyor to Greenwich Hospital through his Anson connections at Shugborough.

Stuart seems to have become extremely unreliable during the 1760s in that he completed nearly all his commissions with reluctance, and was usually late, if he delivered at all. He was careless in his accounting, bored by administration and generally behaved rather irresponsibly, especially in his relations with artisans. Nearly all his main commissions came from members of the Society of Dilettanti, who appear to have been long-suffering in respect of his attitudes. He preferred conviviality to industry, and it seems that already in the 1760s he may have been an alcoholic.

Nevertheless, Stuart's place in the history of European taste is secure, for he, more than anybody, revealed the glories, dignity and qualities of antique Greek architecture to the world; his influence has been immense, from Russia to America, and from Scandinavia to the Mediterranean Sea. Classical Edinburgh, Karl Friedrich Schinkel's Berlin and Leo von Klenze's Bavaria would not have been created without him.

Architecturally, though, his output was not large. The Doric Temple at Hagley in Worcestershire (1758-59) was the first new building in Europe in which the Greek Doric order was used, while the garden buildings at Shugborough in Staffordshire, including the Arch of Hadrian (1764-67), the Tower of the Winds (1764) and the Lanthorn of Demosthenes (1770, a copy of the Choragic Monument of Lysicrates) were all early examples of the Greek Revival in England. The rebuilding of the Chapel at Greenwich Hospital of 1780-88 was an important early example of the Greek style, while his neoclassical designs for fireplaces, furniture and monuments have secured him a niche in the pantheon of innovators.

Stuart's idleness delayed the publication of the second volume of *The Antiquities,* which eventually came out in 1789 through the efforts of Stuart's widow and of William Newton (1735-90), his assistant and clerk of the works at Greenwich. Volume III appeared in 1795, and in 1816 another volume of papers and drawings was published with a memoir. A final volume came out in 1830, published by C. R. Cockerell (1788-1863) and others.

When Stuart died, his papers were left in great disorder, and were incomplete. Even the executor of his will was one of his boozing companions, and died, mad, in the workhouse. Curiously, Stuart was quite well off when he succumbed to the Demon Drink, as he had acquired a great deal of property,

chiefly on mortgage on new buildings in Marylebone. He was buried in the crypt of St. Martin-in-the-Fields.

—JAMES STEVENS CURL

STURGIS, John Hubbard.

American. Born in Manilla, Philippines, 1834. Died on 13 January 1888. Studied architecture with James K. Colling, London, 1855-57. Moved to Boston, Massachusetts; worked with the architects Gridley J. Bryant and Arthur D. Gilman; in partnership with Charles Brigham, Boston, 1866.

Chronology of Works
All in the United States
† *Work no longer exists*

1862	Ogden Codman, Jr., House (The Grange), Lincoln, Massachusetts
1863	Russell Sturgis House (Sunnywaters), Manchester-by-the-Sea, Massachusetts
1864	Greenvale, Portsmouth, Rhode Island
1864	Samuel A. Ward House (Land's End), Newport, Rhode Island
1866	Edward D. Boit, Jr., House (The Rocks), Newport, Rhode Island†
1867	Henry Cabot Lodge Cottage, Nahant, Massachusetts†
1867	George Abbott James House (Lowlands), Nahant, Massachusetts†
1868	Edward N. Perkins House (Pineband), Jamaica Plain, Massachusetts
1869	Hollis Honnewell House (The Cottage), Wellesley, Massachusetts
1870	Martin Brimmer House, Beverley, Massachusetts
1870-76	Museum of Fine Arts, Copley Square, Boston
1872	Franklin Gordon Dexter House, 55 Beacon Street, Boston
1872	Edward Hooper House, Reservoir Street, Cambridge, Massachusetts
1872	Charles Joy House, 86 Marlboro Street, Boston
1873	Codman Building, 55 Kilby Street, Boston
1874-78	Church of the Advent, Brimmer Street, Boston
1874-86	The Homestead, Geneseo, New York
1876	Boylston House, Brookline, Massachusetts
1876	Warren Delano House, Barrytown, New York
1876	James Lawrence House, 84 Marlboro Street, Boston
1876	Charles Sprague Sargent House, Brookline, Massachusetts†
1880	E. Rollins Morse House, 167 Commonwealth Avenue, Boston
1881	Massachusetts Hospital Life Insurance, 50 State Street, Boston
1882	Frederick L. Ames House, Boston
1882	Arthur Astor Carey House, Cambridge, Massachusetts
1882	Theodore A. Davis House, Newport, Rhode Island
1882	Mrs. Jack Gardner House, 152-154 Beacon Street, Boston
1882	Nathaniel Thayer House, 239 Commonwealth Avenue, Boston
1882	Trinity Church, Independence, Missouri
1882	Young Men's Christian Association, Berkeley Street, Boston
1885	Railway Station, Dedham, Massachusetts

1886	Netherfield, Prides Crossing, Massachusetts
1886	John E. Thayer House, Lancaster, Massachusetts
1886	E. V. R. Thayer House, 17 Gloucester Street, Boston
1887	Boston Athletic Club, Exeter Street, Boston
1887	Railway Station, Stoughton, Massachusetts

Publications

ARTICLES BY STURGIS

"Terra Cotta and Its Uses." *Proceedings of the American Institute of Architects* 5 (1871): 39-43.

BOOKS ABOUT STURGIS

BUNTING, BAINBRIDGE: *Houses of Boston's Back Bay.* Cambridge, Massachusetts, 1967.
KING, MOSES (ed.): *King's Handbook of Boston.* Cambridge, Massachusetts, 1889.
WHITEHALL, WALTER MUIR: *Museum of Fine Arts, Boston: A Centennial History.* 2 vols. Cambridge, Massachusetts, 1970.

ARTICLES ABOUT STURGIS

FLOYD, MARGARET HENDERSON: "John Hubbard Sturgis and the Redesign of the Grange for Ogden Codman." *Old-Time New England* 71 (1981): 41-65.
FLOYD, MARGARET HENDERSON: "Measured Drawings of the Hancock House by John Hubbard Sturgis: A Legacy to the Colonial Revival." In *Architecture in Colonial Massachusetts.* Boston, 1979.
FLOYD, MARGARET HENDERSON: "A Terra Cotta Cornerstone for Copley Square: Museum of Fine Arts, Boston, 1870-1876, by Sturgis and Brigham." *Journal of the Society of Architectural Historians* 32 (May 1973): 83-103.
"The Museum of Fine Arts, Boston." *American Architect and Building News* 8 (1980): 205-215.

*

John H. Sturgis was an international traveler, artist and architect who brought an English taste to American shores. Some say that although he lived most of his life in Boston, he was both aesthetically and philosophically bound to British tastes, manners and mores.

Born in Macao, a son of a well-to-do tradesman in the Orient, especially China, young Sturgis, upon his mother's death in 1873, was sent to the United States and enrolled at the Boston Latin School. Later, his father, Russell Sturgis, settled in London, where John moved in 1850. From 1855 to 1857 he studied architecture in London with James K. Colling. In 1858 he began a career in architecture, working with Colling in Wales and Liverpool.

Sturgis subsequently returned to Boston, where he worked with the architects Gridley J. F. Bryant and Arthur D. Gilman on the so-called "Back Bay" residences located on fashionable Boston thoroughfares such as Beacon Street and Commonwealth Avenue. After those successes, he formed a partnership, in 1866, with Charles Brigham, who was a draftsman in the office of Bryant and Gilman.

Sturgis then returned to England, where he stayed from 1866 to 1870. During that period, he designed buildings on what was called a "transatlantic basis." In 1870, back in Boston, he received his most noted commission—the Museum of Fine Arts, located near Copley Square. He based its design and structure on the South Kensington Museums in London. Here, he employed Gothic ornament with English terra-cotta motifs. There followed his High Anglican Church of the Advent, Boston (1874-78), which exhibited more of the English Gothic terra-cotta decor and foliate ornament. These were ultimately derived from designs by contemporary English craftsmen such as James Brooks, George E. Street and John L. Pearson.

Also during the 1860s, Sturgis created many country and seaside cottages. These were characterized by broken and irregular rooflines that cascaded over broad verandas and chimneys. They all exhibited a polychromatic use of glazed tile, ornate terra-cotta designs and decorative, patterned bricks that were imported from England.

After 1870 Sturgis became influenced by the English architects Richard Norman Shaw, William Eden Nesfield and Bruce Talbert. From them he conceived and introduced to Boston's aristocracy the Queen Anne Revival style. He combined this with earlier architectural manners from the Colonial Georgian and Federal periods, and even remodeled some 18th-century homes. The Edward Hooper House (1872) and the Arthur Astor Carey House (1882), both in Cambridge, Massachusetts, showed these traits and were based on drawings Sturgis had made of the John Hancock House, Boston (1737).

By the 1880s he had become proficient in the design of rich paneling and ornamentation. His Frederick L. Ames House, Boston, (1882), was likened to the first domestic residences by Richard Norman Shaw. Its majestic appearance and intricately carved ornamentation were unrivaled at the time and considered a masterwork in decorative art.

Sturgis will always be remembered as a mentor, scholar and aesthetic influence in the field of interior design and decoration. His drawings and extensive correspondence with notable English architects became important academic sources through their detailed accounts of the Queen Anne and Gothic Revival styles that affected church as well as domestic architectural design in the Boston area.

—GEORGE M. COHEN

STURGIS, Russell.

American. Born near Baltimore, Maryland, 15 October 1838. Died in New York City, 11 February 1909. Graduated, Free Academy (now the College of the City of New York), 1857; studied at Academy of Fine Arts and Sciences, Munich, Germany. Established own firm in New York City, 1865; professor of architecture and design, College of the City of New York, 1878-80. Fellow, American Institute of Architects; secretary, American Institute of Architects, 1867-69.

Chronology of Works
All in the United States
* Approximate dates
† Work no longer exists

1869-70	Farnam Hall, Yale University, New Haven, Connecticut
1870	Durfee Hall, Yale University, New Haven, Connecticut
1871	Henry Farnam House, New Haven, Connecticut
1874-75	Farmers and Mechanics' Bank (now Manufacturers' Hanover Bank), Albany, New York
1874-76	Battell Chapel, New Haven, Connecticut
1875	Plymouth Congregational Church, Minneapolis, Minnesota†
1875-81	First Baptist Church, Tarrytown, New York

1876	Austin Building, New York City†
1884	Charles Farnam House, New Haven, Connecticut†
1885-86	Lawrance Hall, Yale University, New Haven, Connecticut
1898*	Dean Sage House (now St. Louis Senior Citizens' Center), Brooklyn, New York

Publications

BOOKS BY STURGIS

A Dictionary of Architecture and Building. New York, 1901-02.
A History of Architecture.
Homes in City and Country. With others. New York, 1893.

ARTICLES ABOUT STURGIS

"Good Things in Modern Architecture." *Architectural Record* 23 (1908): 92-110.
"Modern Architecture." *North American Review* (April 1871): 370-391.
'Russell Sturgis: Architect, Art Historian and Critic." Produced for the University of Delaware (May 1980).
"School and Practice Designing." *Architectural Record* 19 (1906): 413-418.
"The Warehouse and the Factory in Architecture." *Architectural Record* 15 (January 1904): 1-17.
"The Work of McKim, Mead & White." *Architectural Record*: Great American Architects Series, No. 1. 1895.

BOOKS ABOUT STURGIS

DICKASON, DAVID HOWARD: *Daring Young Men: The Story of the American Pre-Raphaelites.* Bloomington, Indiana, 1953.
STEIN, ROGER: *John Ruskin and Aesthetic Thought in America: 1840-1900.* Cambridge, Massachusetts, 1967.

ARTICLES ABOUT STURGIS

ALEXIS, KARIN M. E.: "Russell Sturgis: A Search for the Modern Aesthetic—Going beyond Ruskin." *Athanor* 3.
ALEXIS, KARIN M. E.: "Russell Sturgis: Critic and Architect." Ph. D. dissertation. University of Virginia, 1986.
HITCHCOCK, HENRY-RUSSELL: "Ruskin and American Architecture, or Regeneration Long Delayed." Pp. 166-208 in JOHN SUMMERSON (ed.), *Concerning Architecture: Essays on Architectural Writers and Writing Presented to Nikolaus Pevsner.* London, 1968.
QUINAN, JACK: "Frank Lloyd Wright's Reply to Russell Sturgis." *Journal of the Society of Architectural Historians* 41 (October 1982): 238-244.
SCHUYLER, MONTGOMERY: "Architecture of American Colleges, II: Yale." *Architectural Record* 26 (1909): 393-416.
SCHUYLER, MONTGOMERY: "Russell Sturgis." *Architectural Record* 25 (1909): 146, 220.
SCHUYLER, MONTGOMERY: "Russell Sturgis." *Scribner's Magazine* 45 (1909): 635-636.
SCHUYLER, MONTGOMERY: "Russell Sturgis's Architecture." *Architectural Record* 25 (1909): 404-410.
WIGHT, PETER BONNET: "Reminiscences of Russell Sturgis." *Architectural Record* 26 (1909): 123-131.

In the architecture and writings of Russell Sturgis there is a struggle between an idealist who loved beauty, refinement and tradition, and an American pragmatist who saw engineers as the great creators of the age and who dreamed of a new and modern style that bespoke of contemporary America and the "new millenium." During a career that spanned half a century, Sturgis, architect, critic and art historian, achieved national and international recognition as a leading force behind the artistic development of American art, architecture and culture in New York and America. As the elder statesman of American architectural criticism during the late 19th and early 20th centuries, he was the most influential critic of his day, with only one rival, his friend Montgomery Schuyler.

Sturgis was a reformer, at times a self-proclaimed "radical," who sought to improve and elevate American art, architecture and culture through his own architecture, scholarship, teaching and criticism, as well as through art institutions and associations that he helped to found. The scope and magnitude of his achievement is impressive, almost staggering: he was a prime mover of many of New York's most important art and cultural organizations, including the Metropolitan Museum of Art, the national body of the American Institute of Architects, the Avery Library at Columbia University, and the Architectural League of New York, and an early promoter of Central Park; he was one of the first generation of European-trained architects, one of the first generation of art educators in New York, an active and popular lecturer in art and architectural history, and one of the first generation of professional art and architectural critics. Sturgis was a prolific writer of articles (more than 600), which appeared in leading newspapers, periodicals (including *Scribner's Magazine, Century* and *The Nation*) and in the professional press of the turn-of-the-century period (he was particularly active in the *Architectural Record*): he was also the author of many books on aspects of art and architectural history, as well as an editor and contributor to many dictionaries and encyclopedias. In particular, he was editor of the monumental *Dictionary of Architecture and Building*, which is still a widely consulted text on architecture and engineering.

Foremost was his contribution as a critic of American architecture. His writings awakened his readers to the realization that Americans had made great contributions in architecture, especially in commercial, industrial and domestic architecture. He identified trends and conflicts in American architecture, and very specifically defined certain characteristics which he linked to an "American style." Sturgis was early to recognize the achievements of H. H. Richardson, Louis Sullivan, McKim, Mead and White, Bruce Price, George Post and Richard Schmidt, among many others, but today he is remembered as little more than a Ruskinian who could not accept the work of Frank Lloyd Wright.

During his formative period of the 1850s and early 1860s in New York, Sturgis was exposed to the medieval revival, eclectic designs and innovations of Richard Upjohn, Richard Morris Hunt, Jacob Wrey Mould, Alexander Jackson Davis, Leopold Eidlitz and James Renwick. He apprenticed with Eidlitz in New York, studied architecture in Munich and traveled in Europe before he established his own practice in New York in 1863. The influence of Eidlitz, John Ruskin and Eugène Viollet-le-Duc, tempered by American pragmatic thought, fostered a reformist philosophy and predisposed Sturgis toward what were viewed as radical solutions found in the Victorian Gothic and creative eclecticism.

Sturgis rose to prominence as one New York's most "fashionable" architects at the forefront of the High Victorian Gothic and romantic rationalism. He received important ecclesiastical, domestic, commercial and academic commissions, but because he and his small staff of one to three assistants emphasized quality, individuality and detailing, his office did not produce huge numbers of works. His buildings for Yale University helped to define the ''collegiate Gothic;'' the Farmers' and Mechanics' Bank in Albany, which revealed a debt to French eclectic and medieval styles, is an example of the architect's determination to use ''modern'' materials (such as cement) and ways of building (modern fireproofing methods); the Scranton Estate in Pennsylvania shows the impact of the French Second Empire; and the Austin Building in New York City, a commercial structure dependent on metal constructive methods, as well as the Roosevelt Houses in New York, and several churches, demonstrate how Sturgis reconciled function, structure and style in his own work. In general, Sturgis' buildings show his desire to modernize traditional styles through simplification, the elimination of ornamentation, and the assertion of consolidated mass. In 1880 Sturgis retired from his active practice, first to recuperate from illness in Europe, and then to dedicate the rest of his life to art and architectural criticism and history.

During the 1860s and 1870s, Sturgis was a prime mover of art and architectural criticism at the inception of the profession. This position allowed him to help direct the course of architectural criticism and to lay the foundation of the professional architectural criticism which flowed in the 1890s. Wedged between the generation of Charles Eliot Norton, J. J. Jarves and Leopold Eidlitz and that of Frank Lloyd Wright, Sturgis, a pivotal figure in defining American progressive architectural theory and criticism, and the most powerful voice among self-proclaimed ''realists'' and ''rationalists,'' played a prominent role in shaping what is now called organic architecture. Sturgis, indebted to romantic rationalism, Viollet-le-Duc, Ruskin and Eidlitz, strove to find ''realistic,'' ''rational'' and ''natural'' architecture, which he associated with ''Practice Designing,'' a method of creation and criticism, as a means to achieve an architecture of equilibrium between engineering and aesthetics by allowing artistic treatment to evolve from the new structural systems of American architecture. When Sturgis condemned the classicism of McKim, Mead and White and the Court of Honor of the World's Columbian Exposition, he was, in theory, reacting against the opposite method, which he called ''School Designing.''

Sturgis' goal as a critic was to direct American architecture toward the ''best'' or ''second best'' designs, and toward a freer system which would reconcile paradoxical elements of science and engineering with art and architecture, utility with beauty, and progressive with tradition. In his search, Sturgis found in the architecture of his contemporaries devastating failures, dead revivalism and disappointing copyism, but also promise and potential, particularly in the works of Louis Sullivan, Bruce Price and George Fletcher Babb, among others. In order to create successful contemporary buildings, Sturgis urged architects to learn from nature, the machine and tradition. The belief in a natural evolution gave credence to the possibility of an American style of architecture. Sturgis told architects that they should be pleased if their works could not be identified as an historic style. Sturgis, who believed an American style was realized in Shingle Style homes and commercial skyscrapers, argued that the architecture of his day represented the ''archaic'' period of a new order in architecture.

Russell Sturgis, architect-reformer, architect-critic and architect-historian, not only profoundly affected American culture, art and architecture of his day, but redirected aspects of art education, art criticism and art history, and defined certain themes which continued to have influence long after his death and which are still of relevance today.

—KARIN M. E. ALEXIS

SULLIVAN, Louis

American. Born in Boston, Massachusetts, 13 September 1856. Died in Chicago, Illinois, 11 April 1924. Studied at the Massachusetts Institute of Technology; studied at Ecole des Beaux-Arts, Paris, France. Draftsman for Furness and Hewitt, Philadelphia; worked for William LeBaron Jenney, Chicago, 1873; partnership with Dankmar Adler, Chicago, 1881-94; practiced privately in Chicago, from 1895.

Chronology of Works
All in the United States
† Work no longer exists

1880-81	Borden Block, Chicago†
1880-81	John Borden House, Chicago†
1881	Rothschild Store, Chicago†
1881-82	Jewelers' Building, Chicago
1881-83	Revell Building, Chicago†
1882	Charles Kimball House, Chicago†
1882	Rosenfeld Building Il, Chicago†
1882-83	Rothschild Flats, Chicago†
1883	Kaufman Store and Flats, Chicago
1883-84	Blumenfeld Flats, Chicago†
1883-85	McVicker's Theater, Chicago (remodeling I)†
1884	Ann Halsted Flats, Chicago
1884	Knisely Building, Chicago†
1884	Charles Schwab House, Chicago†
1884	Morris Selz House, Chicago†
1884	Abraham Strauss House, Chicago†
1884-85	Ryerson Building, Chicago†
1884-85	Scoville Building, Chicago†
1884-85	Troescher Building, Chicago†
1885	Chicago Opera Festival Auditorium, Chicago†
1885	Benjamin Lindauer House, Chicago†
1885-86	Zion Temple, Chicago†
1886	Joseph Diemel House, Chicago
1886	Hugo Goodman House, Chicago†
1886	West Chicago Club, Chicago†
1886-87	Deussenberg Block, Kalamazoo, Michigan
1887	Dexter Building, Chicago
1887-89	Ryerson Tomb, Graceland Cemetery, Chicago
1887-89	Standard Club, Chicago†
1887-90	Auditorium Building, Chicago
1888	Falkenau Flats, Chicago†
1888-89	Walker Warehouse, Chicago†
1888-90	Opera House Block, Pueblo, Colorado†
1889-90	Jewish Training School, Chicago†
1890	Auditorium Banquet Hall, Chicago
1890	Getty Tomb, Graceland Cemetery, Chicago
1890-91	James Charnley House, Chicago (with Frank Lloyd Wright)
1890-91	Chicago Cold Storage Exchange Warehouse, Chicago†
1890-91	Dooly Block, Salt Lake City, Utah†
1890-91	Kehilath Anshe Ma'ariv Synagogue, Chicago
1890-91	McVicker's Theater, Chicago (remodeling II)†
1890-91	Wainwright Building, St. Louis, Missouri
1891-92	Schiller Building, Chicago†
1891-92	Albert Sullivan House, Chicago†
1891-93	Transportation Building, Chicago†
1891-92	Wainwright Tomb, St. Louis, Missouri
1892-93	Meyer Building, Chicago†
1892-93	Union Trust Building, St. Louis, Missouri
1892-94	St. Nicholas Hotel, St. Louis, Missouri†
1893-94	Stock Exchange, Chicago†

Louis Sullivan: Guaranty Building, Buffalo, New York, 1894-96

1894-96	Guaranty Building, Buffalo, New York
1897-98	Bayard Building, New York City
1898-99	Gage Building, Chicago (facade)
1898-1903	Schlesinger and Mayer Department Store (now Carson, Pirie, Scott store), Chicago
1906-08	National Farmers' Bank, Owatonna, Minnesota
1908-09	Henry Babson House, Riverside, Illinois†
1909-10	Harold Bradley House, Madison, Wisconsin
1901-11	People's Savings Bank, Cedar Rapids, Iowa
1910-14	St. Paul's Methodist Episcopal Church, Cedar Rapids, Iowa
1911-14	Van Allen Department Store, Clinton, Iowa
1913-14	Merchants' National Bank, Grinnell, Iowa
1916-18	People's Savings and Loan Association Bank, Sidney, Ohio
1919	Farmers' and Merchants' Union Bank, Columbus, Wisconsin
1922	Krause Music Store, Chicago (facade)

Publications

BOOKS BY SULLIVAN

A System of Architectural Ornament According with a Philosophy of Man's Powers. Washington, D. C., 1924.
The Autobiography of an Idea. New York, 1924.
Kindergarten Chats and Other Writings. Revised version of articles published in the *Interstate Architect* in 1901-02. New York, 1924.

ARTICLES BY SULLIVAN

"Ornament in Architecture." *Engineering Magazine* 3 (1892): 633-644.
"Emotional Architecture as Compared with Intellectual: A Study in Objective and Subjective." *Inland Architect* 24, No. 4 (1894): 32-34.
"The Tall Office Building Artistically Considered." *Lippincott's Magazine* 57 (1896): 403-409.
"The Chicago Tribune Competition." *Architectural Record* 53 (1923): 151-157.

BOOKS ABOUT SULLIVAN

ANDREW, DAVID S.: *Louis Sullivan and the Polemics of Modern Architecture: The Present against the Past.* Urbana, Illinois, and Chicago, 1985.
BUSH-BROWN, ALBERT: *Louis Sullivan.* New York, 1960.
CONDIT, CARL W.: *The Chicago School of Architecture.* Chicago, 1964.
DE WIT, WIM (ed.): *Louis Sullivan: The Function of Ornament.* Chicago, 1986.
DUNCAN, HUGH: *Culture and Democracy: The Struggle for Form in Society and Architecture in Chicago and the Middle West During the Life and Times of Louis H. Sullivan.* Totowa, New Jersey, 1965.
EATON, LEONARD K.: *American Architecture Comes of Age: European Reaction to H. H. Richardson and Louis Sullivan.* Cambridge, Massachusetts, and London, 1972.
ENGLISH, MAURICE (ed.): *The Testament of Stone: Themes of Idealism and Indignation from the Writings of Louis Sullivan.* Evanston, Illinois, 1963.
JORDY, WILLIAM H.: "Functionalism as Fact and Symbol: Louis Sullivan's Commercial Buildings, Tombs, and Banks." In *American Buildings and Their Architects: Progressive and Academic Ideals at the Turn of the Twentieth Century.* Garden City, New York, 1972.
KAUFMANN, EDGAR, JR. (ed.): *Louis Sullivan and the Architecture of Free Enterprise.* Chicago, 1956.
MENOCAL, NARCISO: *Architecture as Nature: The Transcendentalist Idea of Louis Sullivan.* Madison, Wisconsin, 1981.
MORRISON, HUGH: *Louis Sullivan, Prophet of Modern Architecture.* New York, 1935.
O'GORMAN, JAMES F.: *Three American Architects: Richardson, Sullivan, and Wright, 1865-1915.* Chicago and London, 1991.
PAUL, SHERMAN: *Louis Sullivan: An Architect in American Thought.* Englewood Cliffs, New Jersey, 1962.
PEISCH, MARK L.: *The Chicago School of Architecture: Early Followers of Sullivan and Wright.* New York, 1964.
SIRY, JOSEPH: *Carson Pirie Scott: Louis Sullivan and the Chicago Department Store.* Chicago and London, 1988.
TWOMBLY, ROBERT: *Louis Sullivan: His Life and Work.* New York, 1986.
TWOMBLY, ROBERT (ed.): *Louis Sullivan: The Public Papers.* Chicago and London, 1988.
WEINGARDEN, LAUREN S.: *Louis H. Sullivan: A System of Architectural Ornament According with a Philosophy of Man's Power.* New York, 1990.
WEINGARDEN, LAUREN S.: *Louis H. Sullivan: The Banks.* Cambridge, Massachusetts, 1988.

ARTICLES ABOUT SULLIVAN

HITCHCOCK, HENRY-RUSSELL: "Sullivan and the Skyscraper." *Royal Institute of British Architects Journal* (July 1953): 353-361.
KIMBALL, FISKE: "Louis Sullivan: An Old Master." *Architectural Record* 57 (1925): 289-304.
NICKEL, RICHARD: "A Photographic Documentation of the Architecture of Adler and Sullivan." M. A. thesis. Illinois Institute of Technology, Chicago, 1957.
SPRAGUE, PAUL: "The Architectural Ornament of Louis Sullivan and His Chief Draftsmen." Ph.D. dissertation. Princeton University, Princeton, New Jersey, 1968.
TURAK, THEODORE: "French and English Sources of Sullivan's Ornament and Doctrine." *Prairie School Review* 11, No. 4 (1974): 5-30.
WEISMAN, WINSTON: "Philadelphia Functionalism and Sullivan." *Journal of the Society of Architectural Historians* 20, No. 4 (March 1961): 3-19.
WRIGHT, FRANK LLOYD: "Louis H. Sullivan—His Work." *Architectural Record* 56 (July 1924): 28-32.

*

Louis Sullivan, long respected and praised for his critical role in the evolution of the skyscraper and as a pioneer in the application of nontraditional ornamentation, was one of the most crucial figures in American architectural development in the last quarter of the 19th century and into the early years of the 20th. Both in partnership with Dankmar Adler and on his own, he significantly changed the way that clients and the public thought about both the structure and the appearance of their commercial and civic buildings.

In his exhaustive and richly textured writings and speeches, Sullivan damned professional training, the academies and historicism: in the important *Lippincott's* essay of 1896, "The Tall Office Building Artistically Considered"; in his speech to the first convention of the Architectural League of America, "The

Modern Phase of Architecture'' in 1899; in the insightful but dense ''Kindergarten Chats'' of 1901-02; in the poetic and romantic memoir of his early years, *The Autobiography of an Idea* of 1924. Yet he had built the basis for his own success on what he had learned at the École des Beaux-Arts while still a young man. For it was there that he learned to conceptualize his whole design for a project in a way neither his engineering nor college-trained colleagues were ever to equal, there that he learned the approach to developing the design of the ground plan and then working the design up to completion, always keeping the initial preliminary sketch, the *esquisse,* in mind. Though Sullivan's buildings, his writings, and his speeches to young architects increasingly rejected the historical conceits, the traditional orders and decorative schemes, and the conventional forms for building types, the discipline and methodology of his early years remained unchanged. And that approach, admired by many, but replicated only in part by Frank Lloyd Wright and a few others, helped insure against design modification based on merely additive considerations.

Sullivan had studied directly with William Ware, from whom he learned the rudiments of the École method of instruction, before spending a year at the Paris academy itself, but his major influences came from outside the classroom. Seeing the early work of H. H. Richardson had an impact on the young man, and work with the iconoclastic Frank Furness, in 1873, introduced him to both the concepts of verticality and the frank expression of structure in the design process. His half year with William L. Jenny reinforced an opposition to eclecticism and furthered an appreciation for both the role and the appearance of structure in his nondomestic architecture.

Perhaps those predilections attracted him to the work and office of Dankmar Adler, like Jenney, an army-trained engineer. Their ideas, combining a frank admission of the underlying structure of a building, an interest in creating powerful public buildings, and their rejection of historicism for its own sake, with a willingness to attempt audacious solutions to the challenges presented by the new skyscrapers and vast interiors, quickly established their reputation and importance. In building after building, Adler and Sullivan were to make their reputation as engineers and designers of large, uncluttered spaces: from 1880 to 1885 in Chicago there were the Grand Opera House, the Central Music Hall, Hooley's Theater, the remodeling of the Interstate Exposition Building, and McVickers Theater; in Milwaukee, the Exposition Building; and then, of course, from 1886 to 1890 the Auditorium Building in Chicago.

The work of Adler and Sullivan defined the skyscraper, the tall commercial building, in the Wainwright Building in St. Louis, in the Schiller Building and the Stock Exchange in Chicago, in the Guaranty Building in Buffalo, Sullivan alone in the Bayard Building and the Schlesinger and Mayer Department Store in Chicago. Divided into a tripartite arrangement of base, shaft and cornice, each of the major structures, with the appearance of the work of an ever-more-confident Sullivan, became more insistent in its verticality, more likely to reveal the nature of the steel cage construction, and less dependent on the ornamental vocabulary of the historic styles of the past. As Sullivan stated in his famous *Lippincott's* essay, ''If we follow our natural instincts without thought of books, rules, precedents, or any such educational impediments . . . we will in the following manner design the exterior of our tall office building. . . .'' And in his most famous definition of the requirement that the skyscraper admit its height, he declared, ''It must be every inch a proud and soaring thing, rising in sheer exultation.''

Sullivan was not to limit his creative efforts to the skyscraper and the other large commercial structures that came his way. Some of his most notable achievements are found in the design of his three great tombs, Getty, Wainwright and Ryerson, and the small midwestern banks that he produced in the last 25 years of his life. In each of these structures, the design and scale so different from his major structures, he nonetheless created new solutions to traditional uses. Whether in the tombs, freed of both traditional symbolism, or the banks, with uncluttered spaces and devoid of references to classical antiquity, he invented both a new image and a new vocabulary.

Neither to detract from these accomplishments nor to downplay Sullivan's contributions to the great architectural problems of his era, the contemporary observer is still as impressed by the man's sense of design, overall decoration and exuberant ornamentation as were the clients and critics when they first encountered his work. Sullivan may have developed his sense of color first through his exposure to such richly polychromed works of Frank Furness as the Pennsylvania Academy of Fine Arts and even the less flamboyant but equally rich interior of H. H. Richardson's Trinity Church. Though he was influenced by these older men, Sullivan's breathtaking originality, in the combination of gold and light in the Auditorium Building, the floral papers and complex relationships of pattern in the Chicago Stock Exchange, and the flowing, three-dimensional ironwork of the exterior of the Schlesinger and Mayer Department Store, may be equally as important a contribution to American architectural design.

Such contemporaries as Peter Wight also used color as a basic component of their decorative schemes, but Sullivan's combinations of gold and pastel colors, his juxtapositions of geometric and floral forms, and his functional yet startling inclusion of electric lights, particularly in such structures as the Pueblo Opera House and the Chicago Stock Exchange, made him the most admired designer of interior space in the last years of the 19th century. His later work on smaller structures, especially the banks and the tombs, was less dramatic in scale and in the range of design, yet his increased sensitivity to the potential of contrasting textures—brick against plaster against metal—produced effects that are equally important to his enduring reputation. While never a direct rejection of his earlier form of decoration, the later style is, perhaps, a reaffirmation of early American traditions of contrasting materials seen in the colonial period and, in an exemplary fashion, in the restrained classicism of Thomas Jefferson at Monticello. Both on the exteriors—with brick and terra-cotta, with touches of ironwork and even wood—and on the interiors—with marble, brick and glass—Sullivan maximized the decoration effect with a minimum of materials and, often, a magnificently decorated center entrance.

Almost all of Sullivan's work, both those buildings done in partnership with Adler and those completed on his own, received the highest praise when they were built, and his speeches and writings generally received the same level of respect and recognition of their importance when they first appeared. Contemporary peers and the next generation of architects revered him as a pioneer, and the most stringent architectural writers, critics and historians were strong and almost unanimous in their laudatory commentary. A century after his best-known buildings were completed, Louis Sullivan's importance as theorist, designer and decorator remains undiminished. The restored Wainwright Building, the reconstructed Trading Room of the Chicago Stock Exchange, and the grand interior of the Auditorium Theater are as impressive and breathtaking to viewers at the end of the 20th century as they were at the end of the 19th century. The midwestern banks also endure as fresh as when they were designed, attracting our attention and respect by the simple elegance with which they make most later structures look shabby and uninspired.

Sullivan paid little attention to domestic architecture, and the bulk of his buildings served commercial ends in the always evolving and shifting business centers; therefore, many of his greatest buildings have been destroyed to make way for larger structures or those serving different uses, but the very attempts to preserve such structures as the Stock Exchange indicate the importance of his architectural and artistic legacy; the fact that his *Autobiography of an Idea* and his *Kindergarten Chats* are still in print and widely read and quoted is further indication of how highly regarded are the ideas of a man who died destitute and without an architectural practice.

—DAVID M. SOKOL

T

TALMAN, William.

British. Born in West Lavington, Wiltshire, England, 1659. Died in 1719. Comptroller of the king's works, 1689. Worked as architect to William III; also worked independently.

Chronology of Works
All in England
* Approximate dates

1683	Hackwood Park, Hampshire
1684	Blyth Hall, Nottinghamshire [attributed]
1686	Stanstead Park, Sussex
1687	Chatsworth House, Derbyshire (rebuilding of south and east fronts)
1688*-90	Burghley House, Northamptonshire (apartments)
1689	Hampton Court Palace, Middlesex (gardens)
1689	Swallowfield, Berkshire
1690*	Uppark, Sussex
1695	Castle Ashby, Northamptonshire (greenhouse)
1698	Dyrham Park, Gloucestershire
1698*	Kiveton Park, Yorkshire
1699-1702	Hampton Court Palace, Middlesex (state apartments)
1700	Fetcham Park, Surrey
1700*	Dorchester House, Weybridge (garden front)
1700*	Kimberley Hall, Norfolk
1702	Drayton Park, Northamptonshire (south courtyard front)
1705*	Waldershare Park, Kent
1706*	Wanstead House, Essex (garden)

Publications

ARTICLES ABOUT TALMAN

WHINNEY, M. D.: "William Talman." *Journal of the Warburg and Courtauld Institutes* 18 (1955): 123-39.

*

William Talman, a Baroque architect active in England from about 1680 to 1710, was long associated with the court of William III. He has not been well served by history, in part due to his own shortcomings: he was haughty and litigious, and so aware of his own position as a gentleman and an architect that almost all the commissions he took on led to arguments and lawsuits, and many of the projects he began were unfinished or completed later by others. But in his work he also had the misfortune to be overshadowed much of his life by Christopher Wren and then, when Wren faded, by the more sophisticated, if also more talented, figure of John Vanbrugh.

Talman's work was occasionally brilliant, but it was always marked by an eclecticism that makes any chronology of his architecture, or any accounting of his style, very difficult; the many attributions made to him are therefore both questionable and doubtful. There are elements in his attributed work, like the form of Uppark, Sussex, that recall the designs of his predecessors Hugh May and Roger Pratt. Waldershare Park, Kent, seems to evoke the work Wren had just done at Hampton Court. There are also details that come from Europe, as with the plan for Chatsworth, which relates to Giovanni Lorenzo Bernini's design for the Louvre, or the south front, which seems to depend

William Talman: Chatsworth, Derbyshire, England, 1687

on Louis Le Vau's work at Vaux-le-Vicomte. The surviving gateway at Swallowfield, Berkshire, seems to borrow from the architecture of Filippo Juvarra or Guarino Guarini.

Yet it is this very eclecticism that makes some of what he did seem curiously advanced. There were details in his unexecuted designs for Welbeck Abbey and Houghton, both in Nottinghamshire—especially the idea of the main block linked at the corners to pavilions—that looked forward to what was to come in many of the greater 18th-century houses; in the designs he made for Castle Howard, Yorkshire, there were suggestions that very much influenced Vanbrugh when he came to work on his own plans for the house. Yet Kimberley Park, Norfolk, or Fetcham Park, Surrey, or Panton Hall, if these are by Talman, present an austere and unarticulated style that, for all its dependence on Pratt, seems to announce the later sparer designs of Vanbrugh, or even later in the century, those of John Soane.

Talman was the second son of William Talman, a landed gentleman of some means, and inherited property in London upon his father's death in 1663. In 1678, at the age of 28, Talman obtained, perhaps through the help of his patron at the time, the second earl of Clarendon, the sinecure of king's waiter in the port of London. It is not known how he became an architect, but to judge from the character of some of his work, he may have had links with Hugh May. Certainly by 1687 Talman was considered by those in a position to favor him for the contract at Chatsworth expert enough to provide plans for the rebuilding of the south and east fronts.

In 1689 he was appointed comptroller of the King's Works, perhaps through the patronage of the earl of Portland. At the same time he had a seat on the board of works, and it was from that position that, not uncharacteristically, Talman did all he could to undermine Wren's authority as surveyor, accusing him of nepotism and then, when part of the new buildings collapsed at Hampton Court, of gross and particular negligence. When William III died in 1702, the earl of Carlisle, Queen Anne's first lord treasurer, made sure Talman's patent was not renewed, replacing him with Vanbrugh. When in turn Vanbrugh was dismissed in 1713, Talman attempted to regain the comptrollership, but without success.

Talman did much of the work on the interiors of the new buildings erected at Hampton Court for William III. However, he also worked much as a private architect, fulfilling commissions for many of the bureaucrats of the new government; indeed, until the arrival of Vanbrugh, Talman was the leading country-house architect in England. For William Blathwayt, secretary of state, he designed the east front of Dyrham Park, Gloucestershire, modeling this in part on what he had done at Chatsworth. For Sir John Germaine, Bart., at Drayton House, Northamptonshire, he rebuilt the south front in the French manner, articulating it, as John Summerson says, in the liveliest way, "a brilliant study in architectural and ornamental relief." But it was undoubtedly at Chatsworth (from 1686) that Talman did his most important work. The south front, with its great fluted pilasters and the simple, decorated windows with their great keystones that are repeated across the facade, has an authority and dignity no architect after him could afford to ignore.

So far as we know, Talman never traveled to Europe, and the richness of his sources depended, it seems, on reading alone. He acquired a large collection of books and drawings and is on record in 1713 as having stated that he had made "and is still collecting by his son abroad, the most valuable Collection of Books, Prints, Drawings &., as is in any one person's hands in Europe, as all the artists in Towne well know." John Talman, like his father, was an architect, but most of his energies went into preserving, and adding to, the collection of drawings his father had begun. When John Talman died in 1726, the whole group of about 1,600 drawings was sold; some of them found their way into public collections in England, where they can easily be identified by their gilt borders and a triple-T mark.

—DAVID CAST

TANGE, Kenzo.

Japanese. Born in Osaka, Japan, 4 September 1913. Married Toshiko Kato, 1949; married Takako Iwata, 1971. Studied architecture at the University of Tokyo, 1935-38, and graduate school, 1942-45; D.Eng., 1959. Principal, Kenzo Tange Associates, Urbanists and Architects, since 1961. Professor of architecture, 1946-74, and since 1974 professor emeritus, University of Tokyo. Visiting Professor, Massachusetts Institute of Technology, Cambridge, 1959-60, and Harvard University, Cambridge, Massachusetts, 1972. Gold Medal, Royal Institute of British Architects, 1965; Pritzker Prize, 1987.

Chronology of Works
All in Japan unless noted

1949-56	Hiroshima Peace Center, Hiroshima
1952-57	Metropolitan Government Offices, Tokyo
1953	Kenzo Tange House, Tokyo
1955-56	Kurayoshi City Hall, Kurayoshi
1955-57	Shizuoka Convention Hall, Shizuoka
1955-58	Prefectural Government Office, Kagawa
1957-58	Imabari City Hall, Ehime
1958-60	Kurashiki City Hall, Okayama
1959-60	Tokyo Restructuring Plan (project)
1959-64	Ichinomiya Housing Project, Kagawa
1960-62	Nichinan Cultural Center, Miyazaki
1960-64	Tsukiji Redevelopment Plan, Tokyo
1961-64	National Gymnasia for the 1964 Olympic Games, Tokyo
1961-64	St. Mary's Cathedral, Tokyo
1961-67	Yamanashi Communications Center, Yamanashi
1965-66	City Center, Skopje, Yugoslavia (reconstruction)
1965-67	Dentsu Offices, Tokyo
1965-67	University of the Sacred Heart, Taipei, Taiwan
1966-67	Shizuoka Press and Broadcasting Center, Tokyo
1966-68	International School of the Sacred Heart, Tokyo
1966-70	Kuwait Embassy and Chancery, Tokyo
1966-70	Expo '70, Osaka (master plan, trunk facilities, and Festival Plazza)
1967-70	Olivetti Technical Center, Kanagawa
1967-70	Shizuoka and Shimizu Regional Plans, Shizuoka
1969	Central Station, Skopje, Yugoslavia
1970-74	Minneapolis Arts Complex, Minneapolis, Minnesota, U. S. A. (with Parker Klein Associates)
1971	University, Oran, Algeria (hospital and dormitory)
1972-74	Bulgarian Embassy and Chancery, Tokyo
1973-77	University of Tokyo Headquarters, Tokyo
1974	Abbasabad City Center, Teheran, Iran (project; with Louis I. Kahn)
1974	Sacred Garden, Buddha's Birthplace, Lumbini, Nepal
1974-77	Sogetsu Hall and Offices, Tokyo
1975	Iranian Embassy, Tokyo
1976	Institute of Architecture and Urban Planning, Oran, Algeria
1976-78	Hanae Mori Building, Tokyo

Kenzo Tange: National Gymnasium for the 1964 Olympic Games, Tokyo, Japan, 1961-64

1977-82	King's Palace and Crown Prince's Palace, Jeddah, Saudi Arabia
1979	Central Area of New Federal Capital, Abuja, Nigeria
1980-85	Koseinenkin Culture and Service Center, Hiroshima
1980-86	City Telecommunication Center, Singapore
1981	World Square, Sydney, Australia
1981	Federal Buildings, Abuja, Nigeria (National Assembly, Presidential Complex, Supreme Court, Executive Office of the President, Ministry of National Planning)
1981-86	Nanyang Technological Institute, University of Singapore
1982-86	Ehime Culture Center, Matsuyama
1983-88	Kurita Building, Tokyo
1983-88	Yokohama Art Museum, Yokohama
1983-90	American Medical Association Headquarters Building, Chicago, Illinois, U. S. A.
1984	King Saud University Al-Gassim Campus, Riyadh, Saudi Arabia
1984	New World Complex, Singapore
1984-89	Otsu Prince Hotel, Otsu

1984-91	Place d'Italie, Paris, France
1986	New Toyko City Hall Complex, Tokyo
1985-89	United Nations University, phases I and II, Tokyo
1989	Yokosuka Cultural Center, Yokosuka

Publications

BOOKS BY TANGE

Katsura: Tradition and Creation in Japanese Architecture. Tokyo and New Haven, Connecticut, 1960; 1972.
A Plan for Tokyo, 1960. Tokyo, 1961.
Ise: Origin of Japanese Architecture With Noboru Kawazoe. Tokyo, 1962; Cambridge, Massachusetts, 1968.
Japan in the Future. Tokyo, 1966.
Japan in the 21st Century. With the Kenzo Tange Team. Tokyo, 1971.
Architecture and Urban Design. Tokyo, 1975.
Kenzo Tange. Artemis, Switzerland, 1987.

ARTICLES BY TANGE

"Creation in Present Day Architecture and the Japanese Architectural Tradition." *Japan Architect* 31 (1956).

"Architecture and Urbanism." *Japan Architect* 35 (1960).

"Prophecies from Kenzo Tange." *Arquitecto Peruano* (Lima, March/June 1977).

"Architecture and Socio-cultural Development." *Arkitekten* (Copenhagen, March/April 1979).

"Kenzo Tange: Architectonic Autobiography." With Manfredo Tafuri and others. *Plan* (Amsterdam, February 1982).

"After Modernism." With Kazuo Shinohara. *Japan Architect* (November/December 1983).

BOOKS ABOUT TANGE

ALTHERR, ALFRED: *Three Japanese Architects: Mayekawa, Tange, Sakakura.* Teufen, Switzerland, 1968.

BOYD, ROBIN: *Kenzo Tange.* New York and London, 1962.

IKONNIKOV, A. V.: *Kenzo Tange.* Moscow, 1976.

KAWAZOE, NOBORU: *Kenzo Tange.* Tokyo, 1976.

Kenzo Tange 1946-58: Reality and Creation. Tokyo, 1966.

Kenzo Tange 1955-64: Technology and Humanity. Tokyo, 1966.

KULTERMANN, UDO (ed.): *Kenzo Tange: Architecture and Urban Design 1946-1969.* New York, 1970.

KURITA, ISAMU: *Kenzo Tange.* Tokyo, 1970.

NAKA, M.: *Philosophy of Contemporary Architects: Kenzo Tange.* Tokyo, 1970.

RIANI, PAOLO: *Kenzo Tange.* Florence and London, 1969.

ARTICLES ABOUT TANGE

BURCHARD, JOHN ELY: "New Currents in Japanese Architecture." *Architectural Record* 129 (1961).

HOZUMI, NOBUO, and DODD, JEREMY: "Junzo Sakakura, Kunio Mayekawa and Kenzo Tange." *Architectural Design* 35/5 (May 1965).

"Interview with Kenzo Tange." *Architectes* (November 1981).

Japan Architect, special issues (August/September 1976; July/August 1979).

Kenchiku Bunka, special issue (1991).

KULTERMANN, UDO: "Kenzo Tange." *Kunstwerk* (November/December 1960).

Process Architecture, special issue (1987).

Space Design, special issues (January 1980; September 1983; 1987; 1991).

*

Kenzo Tange has been highly praised for the originality, versatility and experimental qualities of his postwar architecture in Japan. His major contributions have been not only in individual buildings but also in the fields of planning, architectural education and publication. Because of his accomplishments, Tange has earned an international reputation as a leader in his profession.

Tange graduated from Tokyo University in 1938 and began his career working in the office of Kunio Maekawa, a disciple of Le Corbusier. Maekawa was instrumental in bringing modern reinforced-concrete architecture to Japan, and became known as the "father of modern Japanese architecture." During World War II Tange enrolled in the postgraduate course at Tokyo University and continued his formal education after the war until he had earned his doctor's degree. For many years Tange has served on the faculty of Tokyo University in the architecture and planning areas, and has accepted positions as visiting lecturer or professor at such universities as the Massachusetts

Institute of Technology. Therefore, he had a direct influence on many students due to his continued interest in education. While Tange was a student during the war, his instructors urged him to enter two design competitions, which he won. Unfortunately, because of war restrictions, neither project was built, and Tange had to wait until after the war to have a major design actually constructed.

The Hiroshima Memorial Peace Center was finished in 1956 and was the result of a successful design that Tange submitted in competition. The prize-winning design, which achieved international acclaim, was a combination of modern concrete construction and a traditional Japanese architectural form which used an elevated platform for the main floor of the building. One example of this form may be seen in the ancient Shosoin (Treasure House) of the Todaiji at Nara. Tange's architecture from this first example throughout his career almost always has had some reference either to rather obvious forms of traditional Japanese architecture or to the guiding principles of that architecture, and is expressed with modern techniques and/or materials.

In the many buildings that Tange has designed, there emerges a pattern of a searching and analytical process, freely using original concepts and experimental techniques in order to provide solutions for modern man. The Kagawa Prefectural Town Hall is an example of concrete construction used in a manner to appear like the traditional post-and-beam technique basic to Japanese architecture. The result is an apparently light tower framework which belies the heaviness of the concrete. This obvious contradiction is an often-used Japanese design practice. Other examples of Tange's experimental buildings include the Shizuoka Convention Hall, which utilizes a hyperbolic paraboloid shell structure; the Kurayoshi City Hall, which uses a new concept by combining city offices with public space; the Kurashiki Municipal Building, which uses a very wide garden space around the building to ease the difference between the new structure and the traditional town buildings; and the Tokyo Olympic Gymnasia, which employ mast-and-cable structures.

The two buildings which form the Tokyo Olympic Gymnasia were completed for the 1964 Olympic summer games and are perhaps the most publicized and most successful of Tange's buildings. The daring structures functioned perfectly and provided a dramatic setting for spectator and competitor. The plans of the buildings allowed for the rapid and efficient handling of crowds. Forms resulting from the structure recall traditional Japanese architecture.

The Shizuoka Shimbun and Broadcasting Building in Tokyo uses a circular tower as a core to contain the infrastructure of the building, such as electricity, plumbing, stairs and elevators. Horizontal cantilevered sections are supported at different levels to provide flexible office space. Since the core tower occupies a small circular space, only a very small area of land was required, resulting in an economical building. Derived from Tange's work on city and regional planning, the design is a three-dimensional essay on one of his ideas.

Tange became noted for his imaginative plans to solve the problems encountered in overcrowded cities. While he was a visiting professor at the Massachusetts Institute of Technology, he and his students studied the possibility of extending the city over Boston Bay. Upon his return to Japan, he continued to study that idea until he had produced a master city and regional plan for Tokyo. The plan contained a "civic axis" which would allow easy and quick movement of vast numbers of people by integrating communication systems with buildings.

Regularly spaced core towers could be attached at any level by spans of bridge-like sections providing multifunctional spaces and freeing the ground or water level for transportation use. This concept could be considered metabolist in that it could grow or diminish according to the functional need by adding or deleting the space bridges between the core towers.

The proposed Tokyo city plan attracted world attention and launched Tange into designing a number of other city and regional plans, including the Hiroshima Master Plan, the Kyoto "Civic Axis," the Morioka City Master Plan and the City Center Project in Skopje, Yugoslavia. The publication of these plans and his architecture led Tange to the publishing of his thoughts on the philosophy of architecture, design, creativity and other topics.

Of Tange's many publications, two major coauthored works focus on the Japanese architectural masterpieces of Ise and Katsura. Much of Tange's philosophical approach to design is revealed in his analysis of these two buildings and their sites.

Without question Kenzo Tange may be considered the genius of Japanese architecture of postwar Japan, especially during the 1960s and the 1970s.

—JAMES P. NOFFSINGER

Bruno Taut: Glass Pavilion, Werkbund Exhibition, Cologne, Germany, 1914

TAUT, Bruno.

German. Born in Königsberg, Germany 4 May 1880. Died in Istanbul, Turkey, 24 December 1938. Married Hedwig Wollgast; one son. Trained in the studio of the architect Bruno Mohring, Berlin, 1900-03; studied at the Technische Hochschule, Stuttgart, under Theodor Fischer, 1903-05. Practiced in Berlin, 1908-21; city architect, Magdeburg, Germany, 1921-23; in partnership with his brother Max Taut and Franz Hoffmann, Berlin, 1923-31; practiced in Moscow, 1932-33, Tokyo, 1933-34, and Ankara and Istanbul, Turkey, 1935 until his death in 1938. Founding member, Arbeitsrat für Kunst.

Chronology of Works
All in Germany unless noted

1910	Tragerverkaufkontors Pavilion, Berlin
1913	Monument to Steel, International Building Trades Exhibition, Leipzig (with Franz Hoffmann)
1914	Glass Pavilion, Werkbund Exhibition, Cologne
1914-22	Public Assembly Hall, Magdeburg
1921-23	Garden City Reform, Magdeburg
1922	Stadt und Land Agricultural Exhibition Hall (now Hermann-Giesler Sports Hall), Magdeburg
1927	Hufeisensiedlung Housing Estate, Britz, Berlin (stage I, with Martin Wagner)
1927	Terraced houses, Westrasse, Johannisthal, Berlin
1927	Workers' apartments, Weissenhofsiedlung, Stuttgart
1928	Housing development, Grellstrasse, Prenzlauerberg, Berlin
1930	Housing development, Buschallee 21-107, Weissensee, Berlin
1931	Forest Housing Development, near Onkel Toms Hütte, Zehlendorf, Berlin (stage I, with Hugo Häring and O. R. Salvisberg)
1938	Bruno Taut House, Ortakoy, Turkey
1938	Ataturk Lyceum, Ankara, Turkey (with Asim Komurcuoglu)
1938	Language and History Faculty Buildings, University of Ankara, Ankara, Turkey
1938	Ministry of Culture Exhibition Buildings, International Exposition, Izmir, Turkey
1938	Kemal Ataturk Catafalque, Ankara, Turkey
1938	High School, Trabzon, Turkey (with Franz Hillinger)

Publications

BOOKS BY TAUT

Monument der Eisens. Leipzig, 1913.
Glashaus: Werkbundausstellung Köln. Cologne, 1914.
Ein Architekturprogramm. Berlin, 1918. Reprinted in ULRICH CONRADS (ed.): *Programmes and Manifestoes on 20th Century Architecture.* London and Cambridge, Massachusetts, 1970.
Alpine Architektur. Hagen, Germany, 1919. English version in DENNIS SHARP (ed.): *Glass Architecture.* London and New York, 1972.
Die Stadtkrone. With Paul Scheerbart and others. Jena, 1919.
Der Weltbaumeister. Architekturschauspiel für symphonische Musik. Hagen, Germany, 1920.
Die Auflösung der Städte, oder die Erde eine gute Wohnung. Hagen, Germany, 1920.
Bauen: Der neue Wohnbau. Leipzig, 1927.
Die neue Baukunst in Europa und Amerika. Berlin, 1929. English ed.: *Modern Architecture.* London, 1930.
Nippon mit europäischen Augen gesehen. Tokyo, 1934.
Architekturlehre: Grundlagen, Theorie und Kritik. Tokyo, 1936.
Frühlicht: Eine Folge für die Verwirklichung des neuen Baugedankens. Berlin, 1963.

ARTICLES BY TAUT

"Für die neue Baukunst!" *Kunstblatt* 1 (1919): 20ff.
"The Nature and Aims of Architecture." *Studio* (March 1929).
"My Siedlungen." *Lotus* (September 1977).
"The Earth—A Good Home." *Oppositions* (Fall 1978).

BOOKS ABOUT TAUT

JUNGHANNS, KURT: *Bruno Taut 1880-1938*. Berlin, 1983.
PEHNT, WOLFGANG: *Expressionist Architecture*. New York, 1973.
PITZ, HELGE, and BRENNE, WINFRIED: *Siedlung Onkel Tom, Zehlendorf, Einfamilienhäuser 1929, Architekt: Bruno Taut*. Berlin, 1980.
UNGERS, O. M., and KULTERMANN, UDO: *Die gläserne Kette: Visionäre Architektur aus dem Kreis um Bruno Taut 1919-1920*. Berlin, 1963.
WHYTE, IAIN BOYD: *Bruno Taut and the Architecture of Activism*. Cambridge, 1982.

ARTICLES ABOUT TAUT

"Bruno Taut." *Forum* 26, No. 6, special issue (1978).
DAL CO, FRANCESCO: "Bruno Taut (1880-1938): Utopia and Hope." *Casabella* (July/August 1980).
MIHARA, T. (ed.): "Bruno Taut." *Space Design* special issue (December 1978).
SCHEFFAUER, HERMAN GEORGE: "Bruno Taut: A Visionary in Practice." *Architectural Review* 12 (December 1922): 154-159.
WAECHTER, H. H.: "Prophets of Future Environments." *American Institute of Architects Journal* 60 (September 1973): 32-37.

*

Bruno Taut was one of the most controversial and influential figures of the expressionist period in Germany. However, his more important, but often overlooked, role is that of one of the best and most active architects of the Modern Movement.

Taut entered the construction trade school at Königsberg at the age of seventeen and worked at the same time as a bricklayer. In 1903 he worked in the office of Bruno Möhring in Berlin, whom he later named as his most influential teacher. During that time Taut was introduced to Theodor Goecke, a friend of Camillo Sitte, whose book *The Art of Building Cities* (1889) was epoch-making. Goecke, who had written the technical-economic part of this book, was the planning commissioner of Berlin and a successful pioneer of urban reforms. He introduced Taut, who attended his lectures, to the problems of urban design and housing development. During his time at Möhring's office, Taut also met the writer Adolf Behne, the painter Max Beckmann and the architect Paul Bonatz.

In 1904 Taut began working at the office of Theodor Fischer in Stuttgart. Fischer at that time was at the peak of his career and known as the leading personality of the "south German" school. At first Taut was completely overwhelmed by Fischer. He lived an isolated life and used his free time to participate in numerous design competitions. At age 28 Taut moved back to Berlin, and in 1909 opened a private practice with Heinz Lassen. Three years later Bruno Taut's younger brother, Max, became a member of that partnership.

Those early years of the 20th century saw an active communication between young artists and writers. Their means of contact in Berlin was a journal and a gallery, both founded by Herwarth Walden, with the name "*Der Sturm*." At that time it was the center of the expressionist movement in Germany. Taut found the basis for his ideas and dreams in that heated and exciting atmosphere, with its links to Goethe's definition of expressionism which celebrated youthfulness and its temporary, substantial nature. That phase in Taut's development, with its confusion and artistic domination, often overshadowed Taut's complex personality as an active architect.

In 1914 Taut built for the glass industry at the Werkbund Exhibition in Cologne a glass pavilion that reflected the first collaboration between architects and artists of the time. Even though it was one of the smallest buildings at the exhibition it was one of the most remarkable. The pavilion was the first manifesto of Taut's glass architecture and was strongly influenced by his friend, the poet Paul Scheerbart. Taut's pavilion featured several types of colored glass which eliminated the exterior from the interior, similar to the glass walls of Gothic cathedrals. This notion of interior reflection, found in Gothic cathedrals, had without doubt some impact on Taut's and Scheerbart's vision of "glass architecture."

During World War I, Taut, who was a dedicated pacifist, continued to work with this idea of a "glass architecture," and he developed numerous drawings which featured "Alpine architecture." The gigantic "Alpine architecture" proposed that "glass architecture" on top of the Alps could symbolize the freedom and reconciliation of the nations encouraged by industry, after stopping the production of war machines. In 1916 Taut proposed the "*Stadtkrone*," which can be understood as the drawn conflict between art and society. The *Stadtkrone* featured an urban order in which religion, the focus of society in the Middle Ages, is substantivized by the social awareness of a future society. The inability of architects at that time to document such an architecture caused them to go back to the precapitalistic city and to the reconstruction of the city of the Middle Ages. This reconstruction took place in the form of garden cities.

Bruno Taut, Hans Poelzig and others tried unsuccessfully with these proposals to overcome the barriers of capitalism. Taut concluded that only a complete spiritual revolution could generate such an architecture, an idea he expressed through the phrase "Revolution of the intellect" and his definition of a "nonpolitical socialism."

In 1918 Taut was also a founding member of the Arbeitsrat für Kunst, which worked to assert the influence of artists in cultural affairs. In December 1919 Taut formed the Gläserne Kette, an organization that communicated by exchanging circular letters and sketches. Both of those organizations broke up in the early 1920s, and the artists and architects realized they would have to wait to execute their phantasmic dreams.

When Taut was elected head of the planning department and building control office in Magdeburg in May 1921, it was the first time a controversial, radical artist was elected in a larger city for a responsible position in the government through the strong support of the workers' unions. Taut, who was well aware of the importance of his position, moved Magdeburg into the spotlight of architectural development in Germany between 1921 and 1924. One of the most remarkable projects of that time was Taut's master plan for the larger Magdeburg area of 1923, for which he proposed a clear separation between industrial, housing and agricultural development. Most of Taut's time in Magdeburg was occupied by projects which were uncertain in their outcome and overshadowed by postwar economic depression.

In 1924 Taut resigned from his position in Magdeburg and moved back to Berlin, where he became the architect of the Housing Development Cooperative of the workers' unions. The growing pressure on the Weimar Republic from the working class resulted in a large commitment to develop a sufficient housing stock. Finally, Taut was able to execute a larger number of buildings. Between 1925 and 1932 he built more than 10,000 dwellings, houses and flats. His work output at that time exceeded that of any modern architect in Germany. The large housing estates in Berlin Britz and Berlin Zehlendorf, among others, brought him worldwide recognition. Most of these buildings still exist and have aged quite well.

In spite of his success, Taut found himself increasingly isolated. His reckless and generous position made him some bitter enemies. The CIAM (Congrès Internationaux d'Architecture Moderne) meeting in 1928 at La Sarraz in Lorraine documented his distance from the trends of the Modern Movement during the second half of the 1920s. The catastrophe of 1933 reinforced his isolation. When most of the well-known modern architects in Germany emigrated to the West, Taut went eastward to Japan and later to Turkey. From 1932 Taut worked in Russia, where he experienced the difficulties of building in a foreign country and of being far removed from the main events in architecture. He also experienced the loss of any response to or influence of his work.

Until his death in 1938, Taut was never a conformist. He spoke out his convictions, unafraid of disagreement. Throughout his life Taut and his beliefs were an irresistible attraction for young people. He clearly cared more for people and their well-being than for dogmatic principles and therefore should not be judged as an avant-garde or guerrilla architect. In his visions and social commitment, Taut was far ahead of his time and remains important to contemporary society.

—UWE DROST

TAYLOR, Robert.

British. Born in Woodford, Essex, England, 1714. Died in London, 27 September 1788. Father was Robert Taylor, a master mason and monumental sculptor; had one son. Apprenticed to sculptor Henry Cheere, 1732; went to Rome on a study tour, and returned to England in 1742. Set up business as a sculptor, 1744; began practice as an architect, 1754; appointed surveyor to the Bank of England, 1764; appointed one of two architects to the Office of Works, 1769; named master carpenter, 1777; named master mason and deputy surveyor, 1780; elected sheriff of London and knighted, 1782; worked as surveyor to estates of duke of Grafton and General Pulteney; appointed surveyor of Greenwich Hospital, the Foundling Hospital and Lincoln's Inn, 1788. Left an endowment to found the Taylorian Institution at Oxford University, for modern language studies.

Chronology of Works
All in England unless noted
* Approximate dates
† Work no longer exists

1753-6	Braxted Park, Essex (rebuilt for Peter Du Cane)
1754-55	35-36 Lincoln's Inn Fields, London†
1754-7	Bishop's Palace, Chester†
1755	Harleyford Manor, near Marlow, Buckinghamshire
1755	Coptfold House, Essex
1756*	70 Lombard Street, Banking House, London†
1756-57	Barlaston Hall, Staffordshire
1760	Grafton House, Piccadilly, London†
1760*-65	Asgill House, Richmond, Surrey
1761*	Ottershaw Park, near Chertsey, Surrey†
1762-67	Danson Hill, Bexleyheath, Kent
1766-88	Bank of England, London (extensive additions)
before 1767	34 Spring Gardens, London†
1768	Chute Lodge, Wiltshire
1768-75	1-14 Grafton Street, London (3-6 survive)†
1770	Purbrook House, Hampshire†
1770*	Sharpham House, Devon
1772	Thorncroft, Leatherhead, Surrey
1772-76	Ely House, 37 Dover Street, London
1772-77	Maidenhead Bridge, Berkshire
after 1772	Porters Lodge, Shenley, Hertfordshire (now a part of Shenley Mental Hospital)
1774-80	Lincoln's Inn, Stone Buildings, London
1775-77	Six Clerks' and Enrollment Offices, Chancery Lane, London
1776	Assembly Room, Belfast, Ireland
1777-90	Gorhambury, Hertfordshire
1778	Long Ditton Church, Surrey†
1778-80*	Heveningham Hall, Suffolk (interiors by James Wyatt)
1788-95	Guildhall, Salisbury, Wiltshire (executed by William Pilkington with some alterations)

Publications

BOOKS ABOUT TAYLOR

SERVICE, ALASTAIR: *The Architects of London*. London, 1979.

ARTICLES ABOUT TAYLOR

BINNEY, MARCUS: "Sir Robert Taylor's Bank of England." *Country Life* 146 (13-20 November 1969): 1244-1248; 1326-1330.
BINNEY, MARCUS: "Sir Robert Taylor's Grafton Street." *Country Life* 170 (12-19 November 1981): 1634-1637; 1766-1769.
BINNEY, MARCUS: "The Villas of Sir Robert Taylor." *Country Life* (6-13 July 1967).

*

Robert Taylor was the son of a master mason, and was apprenticed to the sculptor Henry Cheere (1703-81) in 1714. Once the apprenticeship was completed, young Taylor went to Rome to study, and, on learning of his father's death in 1742, had to travel back through war-torn Europe without valid papers. Having got back safely to England, he found his father had died bankrupt.

Friends rallied round, and Taylor set up in business as a sculptor. By 1744 he was entrusted with the making of the monument to Captain Cornewall in Westminster Abbey for which Parliament had voted funds. In the same year he became free of the Masons' Company by patrimony (his father had been Master), and was commissioned to carve the tympanum of the Mansion House, for which Louis Francois Roubiliac and Cheere had also submitted designs. His finest work of sculpture is generally reckoned to be the Chetwynd monument in Grendon Church, Warwick, and there are many funerary monuments by him listed by Rupert Gunnis.

By the age of 40 Taylor's career changed direction, and he began to practice as an architect. In 1764 he was appointed surveyor to the Bank of England, and in 1769 he was named one of the two architects of the Office of Works. In 1788 he became surveyor of Greenwich Hospital and also surveyor to the Foundling Hospital, to Lincoln's Inn, and to the estates of the duke of Grafton and of General Pulteney. Taylor was elected sheriff of London for the years 1782-83, and was knighted. He died in 1788 from a chill caught while attending the funeral of his friend and client Sir Charles Asgill, and was buried in a vault in the church of St. Martin-in-the-Fields. Much of his very considerable fortune was left to the University of Oxford to establish a foundation for the teaching of European languages, and the Taylorian Institution is his memorial.

Taylor was a very successful and hardworking architect, who numbered S. P. Cockerell and John Nash among his pupils. He was a second-generation Palladian, but his Palladianism was not the result of slavish copying, for his work was varied with great ingenuity. At Purbrook House, Portsdown Hill, Hampshire (1770), for example, he designed a foursquare block consisting of two main stories over a rusticated basement, with attic stories as corner towers having pyramidal roofs, and dormer windows on the sloping roofs between these attics. Four two-story pavilions were linked by quadrant walls to the main block, so the plan owed much to Palladian precedent. In the center of the house, however, was a colonnaded atrium (the earliest known revival of a Roman atrium in England) that was inspired by the excavations at Herculaneum. Also at Purbrook, was a salon in the center of the garden front with one of Taylor's favorite motifs, the canted bay.

At the Bank of England, the Reduced Annuities Office and other works of 1766-88 employed sidelit domes and segmental arches, which anticipated John Soane's later work. Taylor's earliest manner was Baroque, and he favored a variety of Rococo slightly later; by the time he was working on the bank and on Purbrook, however, his style had moved toward an emulation of Roman antiquity, and the Rococo traits had disappeared. With William Chambers (1723-96) and James Paine (1717-89), Taylor can be seen as one of the best architects of his generation between the Palladian revival of Lord Burlington and his circle and the rage for the Adam style.

It is regrettable that most of Taylor's great works of public architecture have been destroyed, but his undoubted gifts as a designer of country houses can still be appreciated, not only in surviving examples, but from the plates of his executed designs published by John Malton, Jr., in 1790-92. One of his finest houses was Sharpham House, Devon (c. 1770), a handsome composition built of superbly finished ashlar, with a rusticated base over which are two stories. The entrance front was designed with a canted bay in the center, behind which, on the *piano-nobile* level, are two bedrooms elliptical on plan linked by means of elliptical vestibules. Behind this extraordinary arrangement (also employed at Harleyford Manor in Buckinghamshire), is a stunning elliptical top-lit space containing the elegant staircase. The entrance hall was designed as an octagon with niches, and contains a circle of Roman Doric columns carrying fragmentary entablatures.

At Asgill House, Richmond, Surrey, (1760-65), the canted bay appears on three of the elevations, but the ingenious composition is a variation on Palladio's pediment-within-a-pediment theme. Other houses where canted bays occurred were Harleyford House, Buckinghamshire, and Coptfold House, Essex (both 1755); Barlaston Hall, Staffordshire (1756-57); Danson Hill, Bexleyheath, Kent (1762-67); and Chute Lodge, Wiltshire (1768). Spectacular Palladian arrangements of subservient pavilions linked to the main block by means of low quadrants occurred at Gorhambury, Hertfordshire (1777-90), Danson Hill and Purbrook House. Gorhambury had a grand showy Corinthian portico set on the podium, but the interiors were not finished according to Taylor's designs. Gorhambury was a mansion, and perhaps even more magnificent was his other very large country house, Heveningham in Suffolk, for which he designed only the shell, the interiors being fitted out by James Wyatt (1746-1813) from about 1780 to 1784 after Taylor was dismissed by Sir Gerard Vanneck, Bart. Heveningham is a powerful and memorable composition with a colonnaded centerpiece seven bays wide on a rusticated, arcaded ground floor,

and an attic story embellished with sculpture. Two-story, five-window-wide ranges link the central block to the pedimented three-bay end pavilions. Heveningham has the air of a palatial terrace house that has wandered from some Late Georgian Bath, London or Edinburgh square and has come to rest in the gentle Suffolk countryside. Certainly the main front has an antique *gravitas* and a pronounced French influence, possibly suggested by Jacques-Denis Antoine's *La Monnaie* (1768-75). The destruction of parts of this great house in the 1980s has been one of the most scandalous architectural losses suffered in England in recent years.

Taylor's references to antiquity also occurred in his designs for the great central Pantheon-like room at Gorhambury, which echoed the Rotunda, or Brokers' Exchange, at the Bank of England. The atrium at Purbrook has been mentioned, and there were several other instances where he used antique motifs with taste and discrimination. The Belfast Assembly Rooms, erected to Taylor's designs at the expense of Lord Donegall in 1776, had an interior of great magnificence, with a segmental vaulted and coffered ceiling, a Corinthian order of pilasters, and plasterwork that certainly suggested something of the elegance of the Adam style, and a great deal of the gravity and dignity associated with antiquity. In this respect, one might wonder if Belfast's handsome Commercial Buildings (1819) by John McCutcheon did not have some connection with Taylor at an early stage of its genesis for in its colonnade at *piano-nobile* level and rusticated, arcaded ground floor, it has a resemblance to Heveningham.

It is probably the fact that so much of Taylor's work has been destroyed that accounts for his architecture being less well known than it might be. He was unquestionably one of the most financially successful, probably one of the most interesting, and undoubtedly one of the most gifted designers of his generation and times.

—JAMES STEVENS CURL

TELFORD, Thomas.

British. Born in Glendinning, Westerkirk, England, 1757. Died in 1834. Apprenticed to a country mason. Journeyman mason, Somerset House, London, 1782; employed by William Pulteney; supervisor, the building of the Commissioner's House, Portsmouth Dockyard, 1784-6; bridge surveyor, Shrewsbury; superintendent, building of County Gaol, 1787; surveyor of public works, Shropshire, 1788. Engineer of the Ellesmere Canal, 1793; engineer to the Commission for Highland Roads and Bridges, 1801-21. President, Institution of Civil Engineers, 1820.

Chronology of Works
All in England unless noted

1787	Shrewsbury Castle (renovations)
1792-94	Church of St. Mary Magdalene, Bridgnorth
1792-96	Church of St. Michael's, Madeley
1793-94	Longdon on Tern Aqueduct, near Shrewsbury
1794-1805	Pont Cyssylte Aqueduct, Wales
1795-96	Buildwas Bridge
1811-12	Bonar Bridge, Scotland
1820-26	Menai Suspension Bridge, Menai Straits, Wales
1823-26	Mythe Bridge, near Tewkesbury
1825-28	Over Bridge, near Gloucester
1827-28	St. Katherine's Docks (warehouses), London
1829-31	Dean Bridge, Edinburgh, Scotland

Thomas Telford: Menai Suspension Bridge, Wales, 1820-26

Publications

BOOKS BY TELFORD

Atlas to the Life of Thomas Telford, Civil Engineer, containing eighty-three copper plates illustrative of his professional Labours. 1838.

The Life of Thomas Telford, Civil Engineer, written by himself; containing a descriptive narrative of his professional labours, ed. J. Rickman. 1839.

BOOKS ABOUT TELFORD

BILLINGTON, DAVID P.: *The Tower and the Bridge: The New Art of Structural Engineering.* Princeton, New Jersey, 1983.

BRACEGIRDLE, B.: *Thomas Telford.* Newton Abbot, England, 1973.

DE SOISSONS, MAURICE: *Telford: The Making of Shropshire's New Town.* Shrewsbury, Shropshire, England, 1991.

GIBB, ALEXANDER: *The Story of Telford.* London, 1935.

HALDANE, A. R. B.: *New Ways through the Glens.* 1962.

PENFOLD, ALASTAIR (ed.): *Thomas Telford: Engineer.* London, 1980.

PROVIS, WILLIAM A.: *An Historical and Descriptive Account of the Suspension Bridge Constructed over the Menai Strait.* London, 1828.

ROLT, L. T. C.: *Thomas Telford.* London, 1958.

RUDDOCK, TED: *Arch Bridges and Their Builders, 1735-1835.* Cambridge, 1979.

ARTICLES ABOUT TELFORD

DE MARÉ, ERIC: ''Telford and the Gotha Canal.'' *Architectural Review* (August 1956): 93-99.

HULBERT, JOHN: ''Thomas Telford: Highland Engineer.'' *Country Life* (8 October 1970).

*

From his beginnings as a stonemason to his founder-presidency of the British Institute of Civil Engineers, Thomas Telford turned his hand to roadbed design, canals, harbor works, bridges, and both church and industrial architecture. Telford began his career intent on becoming an architect, and so thought of himself before he turned to engineering at age 36. Knowledgeable of the architectural authorities of the day, including Colen Campbell, Stuart and Revett, as well as Montfaucon and Gilpin, Telford brought to civil engineering an architectural approach previously lacking.

His career was marked by four overlapping commissions, beginning in earnest when he was appointed surveyor of public works for Shropshire in 1788, possibly through contacts gained as a result of having conducted a "private" excavation of the Roman bath complex at Uriconium, at the behest of Sir William Pulteney, for whom Telford also renovated Shrewsbury Castle. Although primarily responsible for bridges and harbor works in Shropshire, Telford designed two of his more purely architectural projects there, the church of St. Mary's Bridgnorth (1792), having a Tuscan elevation of somewhat ungainly proportions, and St. Michael's Madeley (1792-96), with an unusual octagonal exterior plan masking a severe but interesting oblong interior.

Telford's best-known effort as surveyor is his cast-iron bridge at Buildwas over the Severn (1795). Located a few miles north of the world's first iron bridge at Coalbrookdale (1779), Telford's 130-foot span required only 173 tons of iron, a considerable improvement in efficiency over the Coalbrookdale Bridge's 100-foot length spanned with 378 tons of iron. Telford's bridge remained in use until replaced by a modern steel structure in 1906, and is the premier example of cast-iron treated artistically at the very beginning of this material's structural use.

The second stage of Telford's career came with his appointment as the engineer of the Ellesmere Canal in 1793. There he was responsible for extensive civil engineering works, of which the Pont-y-Cysyllte aqueduct at Llangollen, in Wales, is justly famous. Designed in 1794 and opened in 1805, the aqueduct carried the canal 127 feet above the valley floor, via a 1,000-foot-long cast-iron trough on masonry piers. By being keyed in to the ashlar and brick piers, the flanged cast-iron plates that formed the bed and sides of the aqueduct also tied the side walls against the lateral pressure of the water. Pont-y-Cysyllte was Telford's first major work using his system of hollow piers with cross-wall bracing instead of rubble-filled construction, a method of reducing dead weight he would turn to again for the piers of his Menai Straits Bridge.

At the Port of Ellesmere, Telford's state-of-the-art cargo-handling facilities included three masonry warehouses built over large, voussoired archways providing access for canal boat loading and unloading.

The third and most notable of Telford's positions was as engineer to the Commission for Highland Roads and Bridges, from 1801 to 1821. The Commission was charged with stemming emigration from the Scottish Highlands and sought improved communications to develop fishing and agriculture; Telford proceeded to open the Highlands with 920 miles of new roads and 1,000 bridges spanning everything from culverts to the Spey and Tay rivers. It was there that Telford developed the system of division superintendency over competitively bid subcontracts, which were paid on a periodic basis as work progressed; this was an organizational breakthrough that recognized the changing nature and enlarged scope of civil engineering projects.

Although bridge and canal work took most of his time in the Highlands, Telford also designed some 32 churches in the Hebrides, Orkney and Shetland Islands.

His fourth and last major commission was the London to Holyhead Road, the main route from the capital city to Ireland. Further developing his road-building skills on this 15-year project begun in 1817, Telford also designed standardized tollhouses, tollgates and mileposts along most of the route. These

structures, many of which survive on the modern-day A5 Motorway, must have given an unusual visual cohesiveness to this 250-mile highway.

The capstone of both the Holyhead Road and of Telford's career was the Menai Straits Suspension Bridge (1820-26). Suspension-bridge design overcame three main obstacles: lack of bedrock for mid-channel pier support; the tendency of masonry bridges to act as dams during flooding; and not least, Admiralty requirements that large ships with erect masts should have free passage under any span, and that shipping lanes remain unimpeded, even during bridge construction! This the 580-foot span Menai Straits Bridge provided, giving 100 feet of clear headway, the chains being lifted into place at intervals over a 10-week period when the channel was clear of shipping. The chains were built up of flat wrought-iron links, each nine feet in length, and there Telford introduced the use of alignment jigs to ensure accurately drilled holes for the connections.

Although its unstiffened timber decking was destroyed in a storm only 13 years after completion, replaced first with heavier timber decking and then rebuilt in 1893 in steel, Telford's successful spanning of the Menai Straits gave an important push to suspension-bridge design in Great Britain.

Moving between architecture and engineering was easier in Telford's day—there was less specialization, and the separation of the fine and useful arts was less sharply drawn at a time of fruitful balance between technical mastery and technical constraints. Buried in Westminster Abbey, Telford shall be remembered as a pioneer structural artist for his bold exercises in cast and wrought iron, and as a founding father of modern civil engineering for his organizational innovations and sheer breadth of output over his long career.

—PRESTON THAYER

TENGBOM, Ivar.

Swedish. Born in Vireda, near Jönköping, Sweden, 7 April 1878. Died in Stockholm, 6 August 1968. Married Hjördis Nordin, 1905; married Madeleine Douglas, 1931. Studied at the School of Building, Chalmers Technical College, Göteborg, Sweden, 1894-98; Royal Academy of Arts School of Architecture, Stockholm, 1898-1901 (Royal Gold Medal, 1901), Dip.Arch., 1901. In partnership with Ernst Torulf, Göteborg, 1903-12; in private practice, Stockholm, 1912-62. Architect to the Stockholm R oyal Palace, 1922-59, and to the Drottningholm Royal Palace, 1922-62; Director-General, National Board of Building and Planning, Stockholm, 1924-36. Professor, Royal Academy of Arts School of Architecture, Stockholm, 1916-20. Editor, *Arkitektur* magazine, Stockholm, 1908-11. Gold Medal, Royal Institute of British Architects, 1938.

Chronology of Works
All in Sweden unless noted

1906	A. Brunius Villa, Stockholm
1909	Enskilda Bank, Stockholm
1909-10	Town Hall Borås, Stockholm
1911	Church, Arvika, Stockholm
1911	Sachsska Children's Hospital, Årstalunden, Stockholm
1911-23	Högalid Church, Stockholm

1912-15	Enskilda Bank Headquarters, Stockholm
1913-14	E. Trygger House, Stockholm
1919	Reederei Company Offices, Stockholm
1919	K. Tillberg House, Stockholm
1920-26	Concert Hall, Stockholm
1921	Enskilda Bank, Vänersborg
1921	Sporrong and Company, Stockholm
1925-26	School of Economics, Stockholm
1926-28	Swedish Match Company Headquarters, Stockholm
1928	Skandia Insurance Company, Stockholm (addition)
1928-34	Esselte Building, Stockholm (offices and press)
1930-32	City Palace Building, Stockholm
1930-32	Sydbank, Stockholm (office and apartments)
1933	Church, Höganas
1934	Savings Bank, Örebro
1937-48	Bonnier Publishing House, Stockholm (with Anders Tengbom)
1940	Swedish Institute of Classical Studies, Rome, Italy
1943-44	Åtvidaberg Offices, Stockholm
1948-52	Arvfurstens Palace, Stockholm (restoration and additions)
1949	Bondeska Palace, Stockholm (restoration)
1956-58	Royal Palace, Stockholm (restoration of Museum of Antiquities)
1958	Stockholm Savings Bank, Stockholm (remodeling)

Publications

ARTICLES BY TENGBOM

"How Yesterday Made Possible Today's Swedish Architecture." *American Architect* 140 (August 1931): 32-37, 98-100.

"Aatvidabergs-Huset." *Byggmästaren* 14:239-260.

BOOKS ABOUT TENGBOM

AHLBERG, HAKON: *Swedish Architecture of the Twentieth Century*. London, 1925.

ANDERSSON, HENRIK O., and BEDOIRE, FREDRIC: *Stockholms byggnader*. Stockholm, 1973.

BOKLUND, HARALD (ed.): *Hundra blad svensk byggnadskonst*. Malmö, Sweden, 1923.

BRUNNBERG, HANS; NEUMULLER, HANS-FREDERICK; LONN-ROTH, INGA MARI (eds.): *Trettiotalets byggnadskonst i sverige*. Stockholm, 1943.

LETTSTROM, GUSTAF (ed.): *Nordisk Arkitektur 1946-1949*. Stockholm, 1950.

ÖSTBERG, RAGNAR: *Auswahl von schwedischer Architektur der Gegenwart*. Stockholm, 1908.

PAAVILAINEN, SIMO (ed.): *Nordic Classicism 1910-1930*. Exhibition catalog. Helsinki, 1982.

SMITH, G. E. KIDDER: *Sweden Builds*. New York and Stockholm, 1956.

ARTICLES ABOUT TENGBOM

"Bank in Stockholm Designed by Ivar Tengbom." *Architect and Building News* 193 (1948): 124-125.

"Bonnierhuset" and "Fagersta lasarett." *Byggmästaren* (7 June 1951).

"The Concert House, Stockholm." *Architectural Review* 65 (1929): 184-193.

LINN, BJÖRN: "Ivar Tengbom." In THOMAS HALL (ed.): *Stenstadens arkitekter*. Stockholm, 1981.

NELSON, GEORGE: "Ivar Tengbom." *Pencil Points* (November 1935).

POWERS, ALAN: "The Swedish Influence: Ivar Tengbom." *AA Files* (London, July 1983).

"Swedish Grace: Modern Classicism in Stockholm." *International Architect* No. 8, special issue (1982).

"Swedish Neo-Classicism of the 1920s." *Arkitektur* No. 2, special issue (1982).

*

Among the most successful Swedish architects of his time, Ivar Tengbom was also responsible for some of the most exemplary works of 20th-century Nordic classicism. A confluence of artistic and practical competence, Tengbom's work represents more clearly than that of his contemporaries the emergent new form of the modern professional architect. He not only headed the largest office in Sweden—with a staff of 24 architects as early as 1915—but simultaneously assumed the highest position in the government building authority, the directorship of the Swedish Building Institute (1924-36).

Tengbom's earliest work, done in association with Erik Lallerstedt and then Ernst Torulf, was in the "national realist" style, as national romanticism was called in Sweden. The informal, romantic characteristics of this style can be seen in the villa for the historian A. Brunius in Stockholm (1906), which incorporates vernacular influences; the Högalids Church in Stockholm (1911), which is based upon the medieval cathedral in Visby; and the Arvika church (1911), which draws upon a number of historical Swedish sources. Contributing to Tengbom's leadership position as a theorist for national realism were the two books he edited that documented Swedish vernacular houses and his editorship of the journal *Arkitektur* from 1908 to 1911.

In 1910 Tengbom was one of four practitioners asked to be a tutor at the independent Klara Architectural School by the founding students. At that time a conflict had developed between the more neoclassic-based Royal Academy of Arts in Stockholm and a group of young designers interested in incorporating influences from traditional Swedish architecture, handicrafts and applied designs into their work.

While the other practitioners tutoring at the Klara School were stronger exponents of the picturesque eclecticism of national realism, Tengbom was more the classicist. In time his work become more simplified and restrained, relying on geometrical precision and crisp, classical references. The Stockholm Enskilda Bank (1912), a palazzo-like structure with sumptuous, continentally inspired interiors, marks the beginning of modern classicism in Sweden. As a result of his movement to classicism, Tengbom was appointed court architect in 1922 and directed the restoration work on the royal palaces at Drottningholm and in Stockholm.

Three buildings executed in Stockholm during the 1920s exemplify Tengbom's austere, yet refined and elegant neoclassism: the Concert Hall (1920-26), the School of Economics (1925-26) and the Swedish Match Company (1928). Turning its back to Sveavägen, a major boulevard, and facing the Hötorget market square, the Stockholm Concert Hall is a simple cube rendered in cobalt-blue stucco on brick, and enlivened by an impressive gray granite colonnade. Tengbom chose to have the building face the more quiet square in order to preserve its unique position within Stockholm. The compact, well-planned building holds three auditoria with individual foyers and related public space. The Grand Théâtre in Bordeaux (1777-80) by Victor Louis provided a major source of inspiration for the complex. In addition, Tengbom designed the main auditorium in a classical manner, with a surrounding colonnade supporting galleries, and an illusionistic ''open sky'' on the ceiling. The colonnade created a false perspective which concluded in a temple front that completed the space and acted as a backdrop for the orchestra (the original scene has been destroyed).

The School of Economics forms one edge of the Observatory Hill park, with Erik Gunnar Asplund's Stockholm Public Library forming the other. The L-shaped complex, a response to the urban setting, positions the elongated facade along Sveavägen, with the shorter face addressing the park. The street and park elevations convey an Italianate quality traditionally seen in Swedish public buildings, and are rendered in a severe dark gray color. The interior courtyard is of a French Renaissance character and lighter in expression. The L-shaped composition is accented by a circular, copper-domed tower of rooms which holds the major ceremonial spaces of the building. The position of this element fronts on the park, and commands an excellent view across it.

Three courtyards, of which two are glazed, order the composition of the Swedish Match Company, located in the central business district of Stockholm. The center of the complex is occupied by a semicircular open court, with a granite floor and ground-level walls of marble. This entrance space assumes the role of a traditional *cours d'honneur*, and is based upon the design for the Villa Giulia by Vignola. The interior spaces make use of a number of decorative motifs, to which some of Sweden's most important artists made contributions. The most important of the two glazed courts forms a two-story registration area. The facade, divided into three bays, is rendered in the typical Swedish manner of stucco on masonry. Overall, the Swedish Match Company is among the finest examples of modern classicism in Scandinavia.

These three buildings have an eclectic yet precise quality about them, and incorporate Roman, Renaissance, neoclassical and modernist languages in a highly articulate and original manner. Tengbom's late buildings are rationally planned and can be considered ''functional'' in style, as modernism was termed in Sweden, yet they frequently incorporate a form of stripped classicism internally. Examples include the Esselte House (1928), the City Palace (1932) and the Bonnier House (1937-48), all in Stockholm.

Tengbom was also active in Stockholm's town planning and advocated a form of contextual design which stressed the necessity of continuity in form and materials. In that way, he carried his preference for classicism to the urban level.

—WILLIAM C. MILLER

TERRAGNI, Giuseppe.

Italian. Born in Meda, near Milan, Italy, 18 April 1904. Died in Como, 19 July 1943. Studied at Milan Polytechnic School of Architecture, 1921-26; Dip.Arch. In private practice, with his brother Attilo, Como, 1927-39. Served in the Italian Army, on the Greek and Russian fronts, 1939; repatriated to Italy and died of after-effects of exhaustion. Founder member, with Frette, Larco, Libera, Figini, Pollini, and Rava, Gruppo 7, and MIAR (Movimento Italiano per l'Architettura Razionale), 1926. Founder-editor, with Ciliberti, Lingeri and others, *Valori Primordiali* magazine, Como, 1937.

Chronology of Works
All in Italy

1928	Novocomum Apartment Building, Como
1930	Vitrum Store, Como
1930	Strecchini Tomb, Como
1930	Hair Salon, Como
1932	Sala del'22, Mostra della Rivoluzione Fascista, Rome
1932	War Memorial Erba Incino
1932	Ortelli Tomb, Cernobbio
1932	Tailor's Shop, Monza
1932-36	Casa del Fascio (now Casa del Popolo), Como
1933	Ghiringhelli House, Milan (with Pietro Lingeri)
1933	Toninello House, Milan (with Lingeri)
1933	Artist's Lakeside House, Triennale, Milan (with Gruppo di Como)
1933	Covered Market, Como
1933	War Memorial, Lake Como (with Enrico Pampolini, from a design by Antonio Sant'Elia)
1933	School, Malpensata Quarter, Lecco
1935	Rustici House, Milan (with Lingeri)
1935	Lavezzari House, Milan (with Lingeri)
1935	Post Hotel, Piazza Volta, Como
1935	Sarfatti Monument, Col d'Echele
1935	Pedraglio House, Como
1935-36	Piravano Tomb, Como
1937	Bianca House, Siveso
1937	Casa del Floricoltore, Rebbio
1937	Nuovo Campari Restaurant, Milan (with Lingeri and Alberto Sartoris)
1937	Asilo Sant'Elia, Kindergarten, Como
1937	Danteum, Via dell'Impero, Rome (with Lingeri)
1937	Satellite Quarter, Rebbio (with Sartoris)
1939	Giuliani-Frigerio House, Como
1939	Housing Development, Via Anzani, Como

Publications

ARTICLES BY TERRAGNI

''Architettura.'' With Gruppo 7, in *Rassegna Italiana* (December 1926).
''Gli Stranieri.'' With Gruppo 7, in *Rassegna Italiana* (February 1927).
''Impreparazione, Incomprensione, Pregiudizi.'' With Gruppo 7, in *Rassegna Italiana* (March 1927).
''Una Nuova Epoca Arcaica.'' With Gruppo 7, in *Rassegna Italiano* (May 1927).
''Architettura di Stato?'' and ''Lettera sull'Architettura.'' *Ambrosiano* (February 1931).
''La Costruzione della Casa del Fascio di Como.'' *Quadrante* 35 (1936).
''Discorso ai Comaschi.'' *Ambrosiano* (March 1940).
''Relazione sul Danteum 1938.'' *Oppositions* 9 (1977): 94-105.

BOOKS ABOUT TERRAGNI

ARTIOLI, ALBERTO: *Giuseppe Terragni, La Casa del Fascio di Como*. Rome, 1989.
DANESI, S., and PATETTA, L.: *Rationalisme et architecture en Italie 1919-1943*. Venice, 1976.
EISENMAN, PETER: *Giuseppe Terragni*. Cambridge, Massachusetts, 1985.
FERRARI, L., and PASTORE, D. (eds.): *Giuseppe Terragni: La Casa del Fascio*. Rome, 1982.

FONATTI, FRANCO: *Giuseppe Terragni: Poet des Razionalismo*. Vienna, 1987.

FOSSO, M., and MANTERO, E. (eds.): *Giuseppe Terragni, 1904-1943*. Como, 1982.

GERMER, STEFAN, and PREISS, ACHIM (eds.): *Giuseppe Terragni 1904-43: Moderne und Faschismus in Italien*. Munich, 1991.

LABO, MARIO: *Giuseppe Terragni*. Milan, 1947.

MANTERO, ENRICO (ed.): *Giuseppe Terragni e la città del razionalismo italiano*. Bari, Italy, 1969.

MARIANI, FABIO: *Terragni: poesia della razionalita*. Rome, 1983.

RADICE, M.: *Ritratto di Giuseppe Terragni*. Como, 1949.

SCHUMACHER, THOMAS: *The Danteum: A Study in the Architecture of Literature*. Princeton, New Jersey, 1985.

SCHUMACHER, THOMAS: *Surface and Symbol: Giuseppe Terragni and the Italian Rationalist Movement*. Princeton, New Jersey, 1989.

STUDIO NODO (ed.): *L'Immagine della Ragione: La Casa del fascio di Giuseppe Terragni, 1932/36*. Como, 1989.

VERONESI, GIULIA: *Difficoltà politiche dell'architettura in Italia 1920-1940*. Milan, 1953.

ZEVI, BRUNO: *Giuseppe Terragni*. Bologna, 1980.

ZUCCOLI, L.: *Quindici anni divita e di lavoro con l'amico e maestro Giuseppe Terragni*. Como, 1981.

ARTICLES ABOUT TERRAGNI

ADP: "Terragni." *Domus* (October 1968).

Architettura, special issue (July 1968).

BARDI, P. M.: "Giuseppe Terragni." *Vetro* (July/August 1943).

CACKOVIC, DRAZEN: "Tradition in Modernity: Typology of Architectural Form in the Work of Luigi Figini, Gino Pollini, and Giuseppe Terragni from 1926 to 1943." Ph.D. dissertation. Lehigh University, Bethlehem, Pennsylvania, 1989.

"The Casa del Fascio at Como, Architect Giuseppe Terragni." *Architect and Building News* (July 1937).

COOPER, MAURICE: "Palladio or Terragni?" *Building Design* (22 February 1980).

EISENMAN, PETER: "From Object to Relationship: Giuseppe Terragni." *Casabella* 34 (1970).

"Figurative Paintings and Drawings by Giuseppe Terragni." *Modulus* (Charlottesville, Virginia) 1980/81.

GHIRARDO, DIANE: "Politics of a Masterpiece: The *Vicenda*, of the Decoration of the Facade of the Casa del Fascio, Como 1936-1939." *Art Bulletin* 62 (1980): 466-478.

"Giuseppe Terragni." *Rassegna* special issue (September 1982).

GREGOTTI, VITTORIO (ed.): "Giuseppe Terragni 1904/43." *Rassegna* 11 (1979).

KOULERMOS, PANOS (ed.): "Terragni, Lingeri and Italian Rationalism." *Architectural Design*, special issue (March 1963).

LABO, MARIO: "La Casa del Fascio di Como." *Quadrante*, special issue, 35 (1936).

LINGERI, PIETRO: "Giuseppi Terragni." *Quaderni della Facolta di Architettura* (1945).

MANIERI, CLAUDIO: "Giuseppe Terragni." *Architecture and Urbanism* (September 1976).

"Omaggio a Terragni." special issue, *Arte e architettura*, No. 153 (July 1968).

SCHUMACHER, THOMAS: "From Gruppo 7 to the Danteum: A Critical Introduction to Terragni's *Relazione sul Danteum*." *Oppositions* 9 (1977): 90-93.

SCHUMACHER, THOMAS: "Levels of Meaning in Terragni: The Danteum Project." *Parametro* (May 1976).

SHAPIRO, ELLEN R.: "Architecture I. Architecture II: The Foreigners—Il Gruppe Sette." *Oppositions* 6 (Fall 1976): 85-88

SHAPIRO, ELLEN R.: "Architecture III. Unpreparedness-Incomprehension-Prejudices. Architecture IV: A New Archaic Era." *Oppositions* 12 (Spring 1978): 88-90.

SHAPIRO, ELLEN R.: "The Emergence of Italian Rationalism." *Architectural Design* 51 (1981): 5-8.

"The Subject and the Mask." *Lotus*. no. 20 (1978).

TAFURI, MANFREDO: "Giuseppe Terragni: Subject and Mask." *Oppositions* (Winter 1977).

TEN CATE, GERDA: "Terragni and Italian Rationalism." *Bouw* (Rotterdam, 29 May 1982).

"Terragni." special issue of *2C Contruccion de la Ciudad* (Barcelona) November 1982).

ZEVI, BRUNO (ed.): "Omaggio a Terragni." *Architettura*, special issue, 14 (1968).

*

Widespread international interest in the architecture of Giuseppe Terragni is indeed a recent phenomenon. Although he was acknowledged during his brief professional life (15 years) as one of the leading figures of the Italian Modern Movement— at times considered the most naturally gifted of the lot—interest in Terragni's work ebbed after World War II, not to surface again until the late 1960s. Terragni's work was well known in Italy during the 1940s and 1950s—he was of course included, as were many other Italians, in Bruno Zevi's monumental *Storia dell'Architettura Moderna*, first published in 1953. G. E. Kidder-Smith made brief mention of Terragni in *Italy Builds* (1955), describing the Casa del Fascio in Como as the finest public building in the country, and the Asilo Sant'Elia as the best school. But beyond such brief mention, having little effect (Kidder-Smith published one postage-stamp-size photograph of the Casa del Fascio), Terragni was little known in the English-speaking world.

The little criticism Terragni received in the early postwar period often characterized his work as empty and formulaic, lumping him together with most other Italian modernists working under the Fascist regime. For many scholars the problem with Terragni was the problem with Italy: Fascism. The stench of Italian Fascism still infected the atmosphere of the postwar period. Most Italians preferred to forget the politics of the period—what the philosopher Benedetto Croce described as "the unfortunate episode" of the Fascist era—and foreign architects so closely associated the architecture with the politics that the only acceptable designer was Pier Luigi Nervi (1891-1979), "concealed behind his supposed technical neutrality." In order to disinfect the atmosphere, some of the early postwar writers placed Terragni and the other rationalists outside the politics of the period, or even absolved them of all culpability in the policies of Fascism. The fact that Giuseppe Pagano (1896-1945), Raffaele Giolli, Gianluigi Banfi (1910-45) and Terragni (among others) all died during the war, and some literally were martyred, helped remove them from being judged as part of the mainstream of Fascist politics. For Pagano and Giolli, who had turned against Fascism and paid with their lives, martyrdom was unambiguous. For Terragni, who died during the war under somewhat clouded circumstances, martyrdom had to be established. Further, the fact that these martyrs were also "rational-

Giuseppe Terragni: Casa del Fascio, Como, Italy, 1932-36

ists,'' that is, polemical modernists, made it easier to associate modernism with more liberal causes, even to claim a cultural ''left wing'' for Fascism.

Politics aside, it remains one of the oddities of the Modern Movement that Terragni's reputation should have taken so long to develop outside Italy, especially if one considers the fact that he was the author of some of the finest works of architecture built during the 1930s in virtually every building-type category. His Novocomum Apartment House in Como was the first rationalist building to be built in Italy. His monument to the war dead of World War I (the so-called ''Sant'Elia Monument'') is the best-known monument of its kind in Italy. His Casa del Fascio in Como is the most famous Italian building of the period, bar none. His ''Room of 1922'' (the Sala ''O'') in the 1932 exhibition marking 10 years of Fascism, in Rome, is often considered ''one of the masterpieces of propaganda art in Italy between the world wars.'' His Palazzo Littorio competition (for the National Fascist Party Headquarters) project ''A'' (in collaboration) is widely considered the most intriguing solution to the most important national competition of the period. His Casa Pedraglio in Como displays the first use in Italy of precast concrete facade and balcony elements. And his Casa Rustici in Milan, designed with Pietro Lingeri, is considered a seminal model for housing in a modern urban context.

Even after interest in Terragni increased in the mid-1970s, he was not easily accepted as an important international figure in the Modern Movement, but was depicted as a talented architect from the provinces, a naive country bumpkin. And while some of his projects were recognized as masterpieces, many of his works were disparaged by critics and historians.

Giuseppe Rocchi called him ''an able eclectic, collecting a pile of disparate references.'' Terragni's apparent lack of interest in a ''Corbusian'' elegance of the free plan (shared, incidentally, by architects throughout Europe in the 1930s) has prevented some architects from studying him in depth, even if they admire his ''stylish'' facades. Others still consider him ''non-spatial.'' One of the reasons for this is the fact that Terragni's plans do not seem to be directly reflected in the facades; that is, they do not ''accurately project'' the interior spaces onto the outside. Such an ''exploded-cube'' directive, derived from a narrow reading of Corbusian, De Stijl and Bauhaus principles, was not in fact followed by Le Corbusier himself, but such spatial correspondences have been widely regarded (particularly in England and the United States) as a standard for the International Style.

Opinions about Terragni's oeuvre have oscillated with the times. In the 1930s Pagano condemned him for being too individualistic, even narcissistic. In the 1970s Zevi lauded him for the same trait, extolling his anti-academic Michelangelesque tendencies. Aldo Rossi has acknowledged a debt to Terragni, citing the Danteum project as a particularly important source.

But if the problem of Terragni is the problem of Italy under Fascism, then the same misconceptions about him and his country that attend Modern Movement polemics and first-generation histories (e.g., Sigfried Giedion's *Space, Time and Architecture*) need the same revisions that other Modern Movement architects have received. Significantly, many of the values and directives of the Modern Movement that have come under fire in the last two decades in the wake of the postmodern reaction to modernism are the *same* values and directives that Italians also questioned during the 1920s and 1930s. ''Revisionist'' histories, correcting the excesses of the polemics of orthodox modernism, have been written for many other persons and countries.

—THOMAS L. SCHUMACHER

TESSIN FAMILY.

Swedish. Nicodemus the Elder: Born in Stralsund, Sweden, 7 December 1615. Died in Stockholm, 24 May 1681. Son was Nicodemus Tessin the Younger. Apprenticed to the royal architect, Simon de la Vallée. Became architect of Stockholm, 1661. Nicodemus the Younger: Born in Nyköping, Sweden, 23 May 1654. Died in Stockholm, 10 April 1728. Son was Carl Gustav Tessin. Trained by his father. Toured Europe, 1673-80; in Rome, introduced to Bernini, and studied with Carlo Fontana. Became court architect in Stockholm upon the death of his father in 1681.

Chronology of Works
All in Sweden
* Approximate dates
Nicodemus Tessin the Elder:

1660	Cathedral, Kalmar
1662	Royal Palace, Drottningholm
1671	Caroline Mausoleum, Riddarholms Church, Stockholm (not completed until 1740)
1675-82	Old State Bank Building, Stockholm

Nicodemus Tessin the Younger:

1690s	Nicodemus Tessin the Younger House, Stockholm
1697-1728	Royal Palace, Stockholm (not completed until 1753 by his son, Carl Gustav Tessin, and others)

Publications

BOOKS ABOUT THE TESSIN FAMILY

JOSEPHSON, RAGNAR: *Tessin i Danmark.* Stockholm, 1924.

JOSEPHSON, RAGNAR: *Tessin. Nicodemus Tessin d.y.: Tiden— Mannen—Verket.* 2 vols. Stockholm, 1930-31.

JOSEPHSON, RAGNAR: *L'architecte de Charles XII, Nicodème Tessin, à la cour de Louis XIV.* Paris and Brussels, 1930.

KOMMER, BJÖRN R.: *Nicodemus Tessin der Jüngere und das Stockholmer Schloss.* Heidelberg, 1974.

LINDBLOM, A.: *Sverigs Kunsthistoria.* Stockholm, 1946.

LUNDBERG, E.: *Arkitekturens Formsprak 1629-1715.* Stockholm, 1959.

SIRÉN, OSVALD: *Gamla Stockholmshus af Nicodemus Tessin d. Ae.* 2 vols. Stockholm, 1912.

WRANGEL, FREDRIK ULRIK: *Tessinska palatset: ett bidrag till öfversithllarehusets i Stockholm historia.* Stockholm, 1912.

ARTICLES ABOUT THE TESSIN FAMILY

KÜHN, M.: "Eosander und Tessin." *Sitzungsberichte der Kunstgeschichtliche Gesellschaft zu Berlin* (1952/53).

SIRÉN, OSVALD: "Tessinska palatset." *Ord och Bild* 22 (1913): 385-395.

*

Internationalism in its broadest meaning was brought to Swedish architecture and culture by the Tessin family of architects. The impact of their vision of architecture was so great between 1650 and 1750 that the term "Tessinesque Baroque" is often used to describe Swedish architecture of that period. The Tessins, in particular Nicodemus Tessin the Elder and Nicodemus Tessin the Younger (the family also included Carl Gustav Tessin and Tessin the Elder's stepson, Abraham Svanskold), were to the Swedish Baroque what Giovanni Lorenzo Bernini was to the Italian Baroque and Charles Le Brun to the French Baroque.

The Tessins not only dominated Swedish architecture by receiving many of the most prestigious commissions of the day, but transformed the nature and character of architecture, architectural commissions, architectural practices and the position of the architect in Sweden. They can be credited with (1) defining Swedish Baroque architecture and landscape architecture; (2) achieving an international level of respect for their architecture, thereby elevating Swedish architecture and culture in the eyes of continental designers and patrons; and (3) raising the status of the architect in Sweden. Reminiscent of other highly visible architects of the period, their success was closely linked to royal patronage. Their stature has eclipsed the careers of other architects, casting shadows even upon the work of Simon and Jean de la Vallée, another father and son "dynasty" that profoundly affected the Swedish Baroque.

The architecture and cultural climate shaped by the Tessins facilitated a break from the Swedish Renaissance in the mid-1600s, around the same time Christopher Wren was establishing a full-blown English Baroque. During the 16th and early 17th centuries, geographic proximity, trade relations and the Protestant faith created close political and cultural ties between Sweden and the countries of Germany and Holland. Swedish royalty and nobility imported German and Dutch art and architectural styles, as well as artists, architects and craftsmen. The 17th and early 18th centuries were the "Swedish Age of Greatness," when a policy of aggrandizement initiated by aggressive and fearless warrior kings led to wars with Russia, Poland and Denmark, and culminated in a Swedish Empire centered around the Baltic. The profitable trade and tolls of the Baltic swelled Sweden's financial coffers and offered opportunities for art patronage. Diplomatic ties and occasional alliances with France redirected Swedish politics and culture. During the Baroque, Sweden emerged with full force into the limelight of international influence and prestige.

Born in Stralsund, Nicodemus Tessin the Elder went to Sweden as a young man. Two youthful experiences shaped the direction of his career and architecture: first, an apprenticeship with Simon de la Vallée, the royal architect, and second, a tour of Europe with Simon and his son, Jean de la Vallée. Nicodemus and Jean collaborated on works (such as Carl Gustaf Wrangel's Skokloster on Lake Mälar), employed similar styles, and gained the favor of the monarchy and nobility. They became rivals for the position of leadership after the death of Simon.

During that period, queens with great cultural ambitions for Sweden played a vital role in patronizing the arts. Queen Christina, who fashioned a court after modern European models, brought figures such as Réné Descartes and Sébastien Bourbon to Stockholm, and made Jean de la Vallée her royal architect. Tessin's plan for a new royal palace in Stockholm dating from around 1650 was praised for its individuality, but was not approved. He gained ascendancy during the reigns of Karl X and Karl IX, and was promoted by Queen Hedvig Eleonora. For Karl X, Tessin drew plans for a new palace near Gripsholm, which was never built.

Around the time Tessin received the commissions for Kalmar Cathedral (1660) and Drottningholm (1662), and became the architect of the city of Stockholm (1661), he was the principal royal architect and the undisputed leader of architecture in Sweden. His position gave him the opportunity to redirect royal, domestic and public architecture, which he did mainly through his work at Drottningholm, but also through country and urban estates for the nobility. Other important works were the Wrangel

Tessin Family: Royal Palace, Stockholm, Sweden, 1697-1728

Palace on Riddarholmen, Göteborg Town Hall, Carolean Mausoleum designed as part of Riddarholm Church, and numerous private houses in Stockholm.

His style evolved from an eclecticism, which often combined French, German and Italian elements, toward a purer classical Baroque idiom, as exemplified by Kalmar Cathedral and Drottningholm. Designs such as these show the confidence of a designer who did not merely copy, but interpreted style and adapted the Baroque to Swedish surroundings, materials and economic circumstances. In the process, Tessin "invented" Swedish Baroque styles associated with specific building types: a church type related to Italian precedents and a domestic building type linked to French prototypes. His designs represented a modernization of Swedish architecture, yet they looked out-of-date during the last decade of his life, when his son returned from the Continent with fresh knowledge and inspiration. Tessin the Elder's Old State Bank Building (1675-82) on Järntorg in Gamla Stan, the old city of Stockholm, reflected the influence of modern Italian palaces.

From the day he was carried to the baptismal font by the queen, Nicodemus Tessin the Younger enjoyed the privilege of station, the benefits of his father's training and position, a foundation of architecture built by his father and Simon and Jean de la Vallée, and the support of queens. Hedvig Eleonora sponsored his grand tour of Europe (1673-80), where he spent time in Italy, France and England; Christina received him in Rome, introduced him to Giovanni Lorenzo Bernini, and arranged for him to study with Carlo Fontana, a student of Bernini.

Tessin the Younger's trips to France, where he met Louis XIV and made contacts with leading designers at Versailles, such as André Le Nôtre and Jean Bérain, greatly influenced his approach toward landscape architecture, architectural style and interior design. His friend Bérain, who designed Louis XIV's royal chambers, sent Tessin architectural drawings, including interiors of Parisian hotels, and later designed a lavish royal coach with a silk-fitted interior for the Swedish king.

Upon the death of his father in 1681, Tessin the Younger became the court architect and the leading figure in Swedish architecture and culture. He continued his father's work, completed Drottningholm, received new commissions, expanded the Office of Royal Building, supervised projects in the decorative arts, and planned special events, such as theatrical performances, festivals and funerals. He was an authority on the autocratic life, and a collector of architectural drawings. The arts flourished under the guidance of Tessin the Younger and the patronage of Hedvig Eleonora, who together fostered a cultural atmosphere that competed with France. His son, Carl Gustav, emerged as the cultural leader of the next generation.

Tessin the Younger's experiences in Rome and Paris explain three of the most important aspects of his design: an uncompromising classicism and a bold Baroque manner, Roman grandeur and Baroque monumentalism, and comprehensive Baroque planning and garden design. He lionized French and Italian architecture as the appropriate models for Sweden. His most important commission, the design of the new royal palace in Stockholm, shows how Tessin brought to his work a new vision of architecture, distinct from his father's, and helped to create a "canon" of Swedish Baroque architecture with Italian Baroque exteriors and French Baroque interiors. Furthermore, his formal garden design for Drottningholm, the so-called "Versailles of Sweden," complete with its *parterre* system, perfect axial plan, integrated paths and ways, adornment of sculpture, fountains and pools, reveals the influence of Le Nôtre.

The style, scale and location of Tessin the Younger's own home, the Tessin Palace, expressed the new standing of the architect in Sweden. This handsome, classical palace inspired by Italian styles is ruled by symmetry and centered around a court with a fountain. Its interior was modern French with some ceilings based on drawings of Parisian hotels sent to Tessin by Bérain. Located directly across the street from the Royal Palace in Stockholm, this urban residence is far less grand than its neighbor, but it faces, seemingly addresses the sovereign's palace in the perfect harmony associated with two parts of one design. As his royal commissions were monuments to the Vasa dynasty, his own palace glorified the "Tessin dynasty," and thereby exalted the architect to a status never before experienced in Sweden.

The architecture of the Tessins was made to order for the Swedish monarchs. The Tessins' high-style and fashionable architecture became increasingly "imperial" and laden with symbolism bespeaking absolutism in an age of autocracy. Theirs was an architecture of strength, authority and autonomy, erected by sovereigns who were transfixed by their seeming invincibility, and yet conscious of the peculiar fragility of power. The architecture of the Tessins, particularly of Tessin the Younger, abandoned the Swedish Renaissance and its links to medieval and picturesque styles to create a vision of a continental, international classicism divorced from Swedish architecture of the Vasa Era.

The use of Baroque classicism, an inherently non-Scandinavian style, was justified, for it represented the image of sophistication and internationalism sought by the Swedish monarchs. The language of classicism elevated Sweden through historical associations by ennobling its cultural legacy and historical antecedents. Scholars, most notably Olof Rudbeck the Elder, argued that Sweden was actually Manheim, the oldest civilization on earth, founded by Japheth, Noah's second son. Rudbeck and others asserted that the Goths were Swedish, thereby their conquest of Rome in the fifth century made the Swedes the legal heirs of the empire. This would make Sweden an integral part of Western civilization by directly linking it to the heritage of the Judeo-Christian and classical traditions. Classical symbolism in architecture was used to aggrandize kings, such as King Gustavus II Adolphus, who was represented as a modern-day Augustus Caesar.

When the warrior kings made Sweden a great northern power, the Tessins made Swedish architecture competitive in quality and character with the best of European design. They so transformed the cultural climate of Sweden that we no longer just remember the names of warrior kings and military heroes, but the names of architects.

—KARIN M. E. ALEXIS

TESTA, Clorindo.

Argentinian. Born in Naples, Italy, in 1923. Family returned to Argentina the following year. Degree in architecture, National University, Buenos Aires, 1947; studied painting in Italy, 1949-51. Worked as architect in Town Planning Department, Buenos Aires, 1952-56; private practice in Buenos Aires, since 1956.

Chronology of Works
All in Argentina unless noted

1956-63   Provincial Government House, Santa Rosa, La Pampa (with Boris Dabinovic, Augusto Gaido and Francisco Rossi)

1960-66   Bank of London and South America (now Lloyd's Bank), Buenos Aires (with SEPRA)
1962-84   National Library, Buenos Aires (with Francisco Bullrich and Alicia Cazzaniga de Bullrich)
1970   Central Naval Hospital, Buenos Aires (with Lacarra and Genoud)
1970-75   Bank of Holland, Buenos Aires
1975   Aerolineas Argentinas Building, Catalinas Norte, Buenos Aires (with Lacarra and Rossi)
1976   Presidente Plaza Hospital, La Rioja
1979   Government Hospital, Ivory Coast, Africa
1979   Cultural Center, Buenos Aires (18th-century building conversion, with Jacques Bedel and Luís Benedit)
1982   Paseo de la Recoleta Development, Buenos Aires (with Demaria and Genoud)

Publications

BOOKS BY TESTA

La peste en Ceppaloni (exhibition catalog). Buenos Aires, 1978.

ARTICLES BY TESTA

Hacia una Arquitectura Topologica, with Jorge Glusberg. Lima, 1977.
"A Professional Without Anguish." *Arquitecturas Bis* (January/March 1981).

BOOKS ABOUT TESTA

GLUSBERG, JORGE: *Clorindo Testa, pintor y arquitecto*. Buenos Aires, 1983.
LLIMAS, JULIO: *Clorindo Testa*. Buenos Aires, 1962.

ARTICLES ABOUT TESTA

"Clorindo Testa." *Revista de Arquitectura* 38 (1953).
"Clorindo Testa: The Work of an Artist." Special issue of *Summa* (January/February 1983).
"National Library." *Conescal* (October/December 1979).
World Architecture, special issue, 5 (1990).

*

Clorindo Testa is the leader among current Argentine modernist architects. Initially his buildings seem like works of fantastic architectural daring, yet upon closer examination it becomes clear that in addition to their visual appeal, they are above all skillful solutions to practical problems. Testa's architecture is a humanizing one: his buildings are sympathetic to their inhabitants' needs. Testa emphasizes architecture's ability to serve as a vehicle for human communication, yet he accomplishes this within wonderfully imaginative, sculptural plastic forms.

Testa believes that the architect can be influential in instituting social reform through urban planning and public housing. Argentine architects, however, have not been given the necessary government support to enact such reform. Testa believes that zoning (breaking up a city into separate specialized areas), one aspect of Le Corbusier's theory of urban reform, is an insufficient method for bringing about social reform in Latin America. For Testa, zoning is too specific and isolating, and therefore can accomplish only limited aims. Instead, Testa favors an architecture that is more comprehensive and not so narrowly focused on zoning. Buildings for government and cultural institutions have been among his most important commissions. Thus, for Testa, the idea of the architect as social reformer involves a trickle-down theory; the goal is that the benefits of elite culture will become accessible to the masses, consequently improving the quality of life for all.

While Testa's work is individualistic, his architectural vocabulary reveals the influence of both Le Corbusier and Oscar Niemeyer. Le Corbusier's Chandigarh in India, and Niemeyer and Lucío Costa's Brasília are among the most concerted modern efforts to create "functional" cities. While Testa admires these cities architecturally, he has criticized them as dehumanizing and socially restrictive. Thus Le Corbusier and Niemeyer's influence is more visual than theoretical. Like Le Corbusier and Niemeyer, Testa works primarily in reinforced concrete. Testa also shares Le Corbusier's interest in structure, and his work as a civil engineer is demonstrated by his innovative solutions to structural problems. Finally, Testa, like Le Corbusier, emphasizes the importance of contour and profile, and mass and surface.

The Provincial Government House, Santa Rosa, La Pampa (1956-63), is a long, cubistic mass. Sun breakers arranged in irregular patterns are both aesthetic and functional. They emphasize the cubistic division of the facade, provide variety to the building's rectangular shape and serve as sun protection. The use of sun breakers is not new to Testa; both Le Corbusier and Niemeyer employed them before him. In its use of sun breakers, Santa Rosa resembles Le Corbusier's Secretariat Building at Chandigarh. Yet unlike Le Corbusier, Testa frequently recesses his buildings within a perforated concrete shell, producing a range of increasingly sculptural variations.

In the Bank of London, Buenos Aires (1960-66), Testa carried this idea even further. Testa wanted the bank, located at the intersection of two narrow streets, to blend with and yet stand out from its surroundings. Thus he devised a scheme in which a glass box is recessed within a series of perforated fan-like piers, which serve several purposes. They protect the building from the sun and liven up the building's surface, as do the sun breakers on the Government House. Yet unlike the Santa Rosa house, there is greater dialogue between glass and concrete in the Bank of London. The piers are open so that more of the glass layer is visible from the street. The piers also function as structural elements: the building is essentially hung from them. Yet because Testa places primacy on aesthetic appeal, this structural function is not immediately apparent.

The treatment of the exterior does not prepare the visitor for the interior. Immediately inside is an open transitional space which serves as a covered plaza. Testa modeled this plaza on the Loggia dei Lanzi in Florence. This large open space encourages visitors to congregate in the sunlight diffused by the perforated piers. Just as the glass portion of the building is hung from the piers on the exterior, this idea of hanging also appears inside the building. The bank consists of five stories; the upper three levels hang, suspended from the roof, while the lower two are supported by cantilevered structures. This method of hanging levels and ramps had also been employed by Niemeyer in Brasília, among other works. In the Bank of London, Testa has used structural and functional interior elements for aesthetic purposes. Air-conditioning pipes and ducts are visible. The air-conditioning pipes are painted brightly, enhancing their visual appeal, while the ducts have been incorporated into walkway railings.

Unlike the Bank of London's urban setting, the National Library (1962-84) is located in a wooded area surrounded by water. Testa wanted to incorporate the library into this setting without disturbing the landscape. The library's reading rooms are above ground, while books are shelved on underground levels. This feature is practical, as the underground repository allows for expansion without disturbing the landscape as the library gains more volumes. This design is also sympathetic to the library's patrons, providing them with a pleasant view for conducting their intellectual activities.

Testa used massive piers to raise the aboveground portion of the building. In their sheer mass, these piers are reminiscent of the squat, stocky pilotis Le Corbusier employed in the Unité d'Habitation in Marseilles, France (1946-52). The piloti system creates a covered terrace, which provides shelter from the sun as well as a place for people to congregate. Functionally similar to the entrance hall of the Bank of London, this terrace again illustrates Testa's interest in designing buildings which invite human communication.

The use of reinforced concrete in the National Library is remarkable for its plastic qualities. Testa recessed the library's windows deep within the concrete, creating a rich variety of textures and shadows on the building's exterior. This treatment of windows is another variation on a familiar Testa technique of encasing the windows in a concrete shell, which adds visual appeal as well as sun protection. The rough, brutalist concrete is similar to Le Corbusier's treatment of concrete in the Parliament Building at Chandigarh. Both Le Corbusier and Testa modeled their buildings into bulging, plastic masses. In the National Library, as well as in all his buildings, Testa drew from a language of visual forms to create an imaginative and original work that lacks only the functionalist tendency toward the formulaic.

—PAMELA A. COHEN

THE ARCHITECTS COLLABORATIVE (TAC).

American. Partnership; established, Cambridge, Massachusetts, 1945, by Walter Gropius, Norman Fletcher, Jean Fletcher, John Harkness, Sarah Pillsbury Harkness, Robert McMillen, Louis McMillen, and Benjamin Thompson; TAC International established in 1960; TAC Incorporated, 1964. Current Principals: Norman Fletcher, John Harkness, Sarah Pillsbury Harkness, Louis McMillen, John F. Hayes, Leonard Notkin, Richard Brooker, James E. Burlage, H. Morse Payne, Perry K. Neubauer, Richard A. Sabin, John P. Sheehy, David G. Sheffield, H. Malcolm Ticknor, William Higgins, Sherry Caplan, and Gregory Downes. American Institute of Architects Architectural Firm Award, 1964.

Chronology of Works
All in the United States unless noted

1948	Six Moon Hill, Lexington, Massachusetts
1948-49	Harvard University Graduate Center, Cambridge, Massachusetts
1956-61	United States Embassy, Athens, Greece
1958-63	Pan American Building, New York City (as consultant architects)
1959	Academic Quadrangle, Brandeis University, Waltham, Massachusetts
1964	Hoffman Laboratory of Experimental Geology, Harvard University, Cambridge, Massachusetts
1965	Rosenthal China Factory, Selb, Germany
1967	Rosenthal Glass Factory, Amberg, Germany
1967-70	The Architects Collaborative Headquarters, Cambridge, Massachusetts
1969-73	American Institute of Architects Headquarters, Washington, D.C.
1970-76	Shawmut National Bank, Boston, Massachusetts

1971-79	Bauhaus Archive, Berlin, Germany
1976	Johns-Manville World Headquarters, Jefferson City, Colorado
1978	Kuwait Fund Office Building, Kuwait City, Kuwait
1978-80	Copley Place, Boston, Massachusetts
1978	Institute of Public Administration, Riyadh, Saudi Arabia
1979	South Station Transportation Center, Boston, Massachusetts
1980	Abu Dhabi National Library and Cultural Center, Abu Dhabi
1980	Kuwait Foundation for the Advancement of Science, Kuwait City, Kuwait
1981	Bell Laboratories Telecommunications Facility, Freehold, New Jersey
1983	Noble Research Center, Oklahoma State University, Stillwater
1984	Ministry of Electricity and Water, Kuwait City, Kuwait
1984	O'Neill Library, Boston College, Boston, Massachusetts
1984-89	The Heritage on the Garden Complex, Boston, Massachusetts
1985	Egyptian Museum, Cairo, Egypt (additions and renovation)
1987	A. Alfred Taubman Building, Kennedy School of Government, Harvard University, Cambridge, Massachusetts
1988	State of California Library and Courts Building, Sacramento, California
1988	801 Tower, Los Angeles, California
1988	U.S. Embassy, Cairo, Egypt

Publications

BOOKS BY TAC

Town Plan for the Development of Selb. Cambridge, Massachusetts, 1970.
A Design Manual for Parking Garages. Cambridge, Massachusetts, 1975.
Streets: A Program to Develop Awareness of the Street Environment. Boston, 1976.
Building Without Barriers for the Disabled. New York, 1976.

BOOKS ABOUT TAC

GROPIUS, WALTER (ed.): *The Architects Collaborative 1945-65*. Teufel, Switzerland, 1966.
The Architects Collaborative Inc: TAC 1945-1972. Barcelona, 1972.
The Work of the Architects Collaborative, Vol. 4. New York, 1990.

ARTICLES ABOUT TAC

"The Architects Collaborative." *Architectural Record* (April 1959).
"The Architects Collaborative." *Arts and Architecture* (August 1946).
"The Architects Collaborative." *Baukunst und Werkform* 10 (1957).
"The Architects Collaborative: Recent Works." *Architecture and Urbanism* (July 1978).

MORTON, DAVID: "Bold Discretions: The Work of TAC Interiors." *Progressive Architecture* (September 1978).
"TAC: The Heritage of Walter Gropius." Special issue of *Process: Architecture* (October 1980).

*

The Architects Collaborative was Walter Gropius' American firm, without his name, just as the Bauhaus had been his German school without his name. Though the firm is known as a "collaborative," this is something of a misnomer, as the spirit of Gropius has always dominated, despite the firm's stated policy of "work and teamwork." Every May the *lieber meister's* birthday is celebrated in the TAC courtyard in Harvard Square with wine and toasts, even two decades after his death. They still call him "Grop."

Gropius was a Herculean figure, who throughout his long European and American career surrounded himself with "collaborators," or disciples, with whom he maintained a mentor relationship. He was, in his own words, *"primus inter parus—* first among equals." At the Bauhaus he was director among masters, always he was teacher among students, and later, in the case of TAC, he was renowned architect among partners. Thus the Gropius circle, which lives today in a second generation of architects, evolved. He even chose to live in semicommunal arrangements, at the Bauhaus, in London, and in Lincoln, Massachusetts, and his student-partners followed suit, establishing their own TAC colony in Lexington, Massachusetts, a cluster of modern houses they designed and named Six Moon Hill, where many of the founders still live. The founding partners with Gropius were Jean Fletcher, Norman Fletcher, John Harkness, Sarah Harkness, Robert McMillan, Louis McMillen and Benjamin Thompson.

Writing in *Scope of Total Architecture*, Gropius defined his ideals of architectural collaboration that formed the basis of TAC: *"It is true that the creative spark originates always with the individual, but by working in close collaboration with others toward a common aim, he will attain greater heights of achievement through the stimulation and challenging critique of his teammates, than by living in an ivory tower.* Of course, the creative mind asserts itself usually under any circumstance, even against heavy odds, but if we want to raise the average performance, teamwork becomes essential to sharpen and improve the individual contribution."

Even without Gropius, TAC has survived and prospered. Of the original eight partners, a number have continued to practice, some have accepted emeritus status, and 15 principals were working with them in 1990. A basic tenet of the firm is that each commission is handled by a team led by one of the principals. TAC is today a large, multipurpose American corporate firm, and as such has handled such major projects as the Harvard Graduate Center (1949), the Pan Am Building in New York (1958), the American Embassy in Athens (1961) and the headquarters of the American Institute of Architects in Washington, D.C. (1970).

Though its commissions have been worldwide, the firm is strongly rooted in the Northeast, especially in the Boston-Cambridge area, where its presence is felt architecturally, particularly in buildings for medical facilities and educational institutions, for which the area is known. Representative projects include master plans and construction for Children's Hospital, Boston (1971); the Academic Quadrangle, Brandeis University (1959); the Art and Communication Center, Phillips Academy (1959); and the O'Neill Library, Boston College (1984). Most illustrative of TAC's classic style is the Hoffman Laboratory of Experimental Geology, Harvard University (1964).

Hoffman Lab is a box-like composition of concrete horizontals and verticals offsetting brick panels arranged in a grid pattern, a hovering concrete slab overhanging the box, and thus unifying the structure. Under the umbrage of the overhanging roof is an open-plan, Eames-furnished conference room and deck, from which the blossoms of the campus cherry trees can be seen in spring. These trees, juxtaposed with the rough-hewn modernism, grow within a semi-enclosed courtyard formed by the Hoffman Lab and its predecessor, the University Museum, with which the lab attempts to enter into a contextual relationship through the use of the red brick, which is so much a part of the Harvard landscape. The problem of modern contextualism within a traditional university environment was one with which Gropius himself had previously grappled, in a design similar in configuration to Hoffman Lab—his 1937 plan for Christ's College at Cambridge University in England. Thus one sees here the continuity of Gropius' and TAC's work not only in style, but in architectural issues, as well.

The aforementioned buildings for medical and educational institutions may perhaps seem to have a blandness about them—they are not attention-getting designs. This is not the banality of much knock-off modernism of the 1950s and 1960s, but rather the manifestation of Gropius' design philosophy. Gropius was, after all, the great proponent of the typeform in architecture, having experimented in Europe with open-plan schools as a generic architectural form. These works formed the basis of his later architecture, and TAC actually originated the normative type of American school architecture that became so prevalent during the 1950s postwar American building boom. Many who attended the low, spreading suburban schools of the 1950s owe a part of their childhood experience to the Gropius and TAC model.

Critical opinion of TAC has often held that TAC did not fulfill the creative promise of Gropius' earlier works; however, even if a high design profile has never been the firm's forte, it may not be its intention, either. Instead, TAC has carried on, until quite recently, with Gropius' philosophy of creating a modern idiom for a modern world, a "style of the century," as it was called in Gropius' European days. Since the late 1980s, however, that commitment appears to be undergoing a reevaluation, or one might say, a compromise, as the firm has offered such buildings as Heritage on the Garden, Back Bay, Boston (1989), a new residential development that seeks to be old Boston, in direct conflict with Gropius' ideals of honest modernism. Though not a bad building, it makes one wonder if, as the founding partners retire, and the first-person relationship with Gropius disappears from TAC, will the firm lose its basic stylistic modernism and sustaining philosophy in favor of the expedient and fashionable? Or, as Gropius' own words would have framed the question, "Architect: Servant or Leader?"

—LESLIE HUMM CORMIER

THOMON, Thomas de.

Russian. Born in Nancy, France, 21 December 1754. Died in St. Petersburg, Russia, August 1813. May have studied under Claude Nicolas Ledoux in Paris. Settled in Russia, 1790s. Court architect to Alexander I, 1802.

Chronology of Works
All in Russia
† *Work no longer exists*

1802-05   Great Theater, St. Petersburg†
1803   Theater, Odessa†

1804-05   Warehouses, Salni Embankment, St. Petersburg
1805-08   Memorial Chapel to Paul I, Pavlovsk
1805-11   Column of Glory, Poltava
1805-16   Bourse, St. Petersburg

Publications

BOOKS BY THOMON

Recueil de plans et façades des principaux monuments construits à Saint-Pétersbourg et dans les différentes provinces de l'Empire de Russie. St. Petersburg, 1809.
Traité de peinture précédé de l'origine des arts. St. Petersburg, 1809.

BOOKS ABOUT THOMON

BERCKENHAGEN, EKHART (ed.): *Die Französischen Zeichnungen der Kunstbibliothek Berlin.* Berlin, 1970.
BERCKENHAGEN, EKHART: *St. Petersburg um 1800: Architekturzeichnungen Thomas de Thomon.* Exhibition catalog. Berlin, 1975.
HAMILTON, G. H.: *The Art and Architecture of Russia.* Harmondsworth, England, 1954.
HAUTECOEUR, LOUIS: *L'architecture classique à Saint-Pétersbourg à la fin du XVIIIe siècle.* Paris, 1912.
OSHCHEPKOV, C. D.: *Arkhitektor Thomon.* Moscow, 1950.
VOGT, ADOLF MAX: *Russische und französische Revolutions-Architektur.* Cologne, 1974.

ARTICLES ABOUT THOMON

GRABAR, IGOR: "Les débuts du classisme sous Alexandre et ses sources françaises." *Starye Gody* 13 (1912): 68-96.
LOUKOMSKI, GEORGES: "Thomas de Thomon (1754-1813)." *Apollo* 42 (1945): 297-304.
THOUBNIKOFF, ALEXANDRE: "Thomas de Thomon." *Starye Gody* 9 (1908).

*

Born in Bern, Switzerland, and educated at the Académie Royale d'Architecture in Paris, Thomas de Thomon is known as an outstanding Russian architect of the early 19th century. Together with A. N. Voronikhin and A. D. Zakharov, he shaped the transition of Russian classical architecture to the stage of high classicism. Thomon participated in the founding of a markedly monumental and severe style, characterized by a simple and integrated formal composition, large abstract and lapidary forms, powerful and orderly plasticity and unbroken planes.

Like many of his contemporaries, Thomon was influenced by the artistic discoveries of Claude-Nicolas Ledoux. The architect was guided in his works primarily by the experience of the Paris academic school, by the search for an architecture "on paper" (the famous series of projects in the *"Grand prix d'architecture"*). Thomon addressed the assimilation of antique traditions via French neoclassicism. In Russia he founded the Hellenistic (Neohellenistic) movement. With a bold eye to city planning, he brought the abstract forms of academic architecture and the influences of antique monuments to actual construction projects going on all over St. Petersburg at the time. His Bourse ensemble, located at the confluence of the Neva River arms, not only defined the architectural center of the Russian capital, but also reinterpreted the concept of the spatially open ensemble, linking it to the surrounding urban landscape.

Thomas de Thomon: Bourse, St. Petersburg, Russia, 1805-16

Thomon's creative work can be divided into two periods: the European period (1780-90) and the Russian period (1799-1813). The first saw the development of his talent, the second, the maturation of his artistic credo. After graduating from the Académie Royale d'Architecture in Paris, Thomon was sent to Rome in 1780 for advanced training. In those years he was especially fascinated with painting and graphic design. In 1785 he published a theoretical work, *Traité de peinture,* in which he made use of the judgments of Leonardo da Vinci, Nicolas Poussin and Peter Paul Rubens (the work was reprinted in expanded form in St. Petersburg in 1809). Thomon's landscapes and architectural imaginings are imbued with a romantic spirit and marked by the influence of Hubert Robert and Giovanni Battista Piranesi. He first distinguished himself as a brilliant graphic artist and engraver. Even his early drawings exhibit an attraction to monumental grandeur and severe simplicity in architectural forms.

In the 1790s Thomon worked in Poland, Hungary and Austria and was employed by the Duke of Eszterhazy for several years. His design for G. Eisenstadt's sulphur baths (1795) is distinguished by precise geometrical forms and the prominence of the architect's favorite Doric order. Upon his arrival in Russia in 1799, Thomon had developed a creative vision but lacked practical experience.

Thomon's Russian period witnessed an intense and prolific realization of his amassed potential, enriched by the influence of the St. Petersburg architectural school. Thomon rapidly won recognition. He earned the title of academician and professor of perspective drawing (later, academician of architecture), and in 1802 he was appointed court architect and teacher in the Academy of Arts, then designer in the imperial glassworks.

Thomon entered the design competition for Kazan Cathedral in St. Petersburg in 1800. His design interpreted the devices of French neoclassicism, themes from the ancient Roman Pantheon and the colonnade motif of St. Peter's in Rome but failed to secure him the commission. As early as 1801, Thomon began designing the Bourse ensemble, whose creation brought him world fame. Here, Thomon once again departed from the works of the Paris Académie, creating a variation on the scheme of Pierre Bernard's Bourse. Throughout the ensuing four years Thomon modified and perfected his plan, making use of recommendations from the St. Petersburg Academy of Arts, notably those of Zakharov. By replacing the planned porticoes on the

facades with an unbroken peripheral colonnade, Thomon endowed the Bourse building with a uniquely polished compactness and monumental spaciousness. He enhanced the scale of the rostral columns flanking the square in front of the Bourse, and planned a second, vast square behind the Bourse building. Construction of the ensemble was carried out from 1805 to 1810 (the Bourse opened in 1816).

The organization of the ensemble exhibited Thomon's rare flair for city planning, and his ability to integrate grand and imposing forms and silhouettes into the surrounding setting. With brilliant mastery, Thomon adapted his composition, reminiscent of the designs of the "*Grand prix,*" to the city's topography. His plan called for a man-made, semicircular promontory (Strelka) to be poured behind a granite facing at the tip of Vasilievsky Island. The Bourse building, oriented along the axis of the Strelka, was executed after the fashion of an ancient Greek peripteral temple. The powerful Doric colonnade, with smooth, unfluted shafts, lines a spacious circular gallery on a tall granite stylobate. This building, along with the rostral columns, was an innovative program piece synthesizing architecture and monumental sculpture to portray allegorically the theme of maritime communications. The Bourse ensemble became the central and most important link in the panorama of the Neva watershed.

In 1802 Thomon remodeled the Bolshoi Theater in St. Petersburg in accordance with new theatrical and fireproofing standards (nevertheless, the building burned down in 1811, and was subsequently rebuilt). The architect designed the theater building as a unified block set off by an ascending, eight-column Ionic portico. This structure became a prototype for the Bolshoi Theater in Moscow, built in the 1820s and designed by A. A. Mikhailov and O. I. Boviér. Thomon's theater in Odessa (1804-09) and a hospital he designed for the same city both exhibit a similar scheme of a compact central building with the broad, arching porticoes characteristic of Russian classicism.

Thomon's second masterpiece after the Bourse was the "Salny Buian" (1805-08). The architect endowed this purely utilitarian warehouse with a powerful artistic expressiveness, achieved through simple means: large-scale forms, rustic masonry walls and small, double-column porticoes.

Thomon's smaller structures display the same monumental strength and ceremonial grandeur. Paul I's Mausoleum, a memorial pavilion in Pavlovsk (1805-09), is a variation on the ancient four-column Doric temple. Its stone-block walls and monolithic granite columns accentuate the severe majesty and lyrical grace of the structure. Thomon loved to work with granite, and his fountains on the road from St. Petersburg to Tsarskoe Selo (1807-09) are made out of this material.

The monument to the Battle of Poltava in Poltava (1805-11) had a formative effect on the larger plan of the city. The cast-iron triumphal column is situated in the center of Kruglaia Square, forming a point of perspective for the streets which radiate outward. Thomon also designed a memorial temple on the site of the Poltava battleground (1811), based on a design by Charles Moreau, but enhancing its monumental grandeur and giving it a stark simplicity.

The residential, civic and industrial buildings (1806-07) Thomon designed for various cities throughout Russia were characteristic of his wide compositional range. In his designs for the Institute for the Deaf near the city of Zhitomir and the Institute of the Corps of Communications Engineers in St. Petersburg, Thomon alternated symmetrical and asymmetrical facades. The asymmetrical compositions, with their tranquil rhythm of windows and even-surfaced walls, anticipated the devices of late Russian classicism. The design for a theater on a new, wide square by Nevsky Prospekt in St. Petersburg (1811) is notable for its attention to city-planning objectives.

The Lavalle private residence in St. Petersburg, rebuilt from an earlier structure (1806-09), holds a special place in Thomon's creative work. The facade, with its Ionic colonnade, faces the Neva River. Its delicacy distinguishes it from the stark monumentalism of most of Thomon's works. Notable among the festive front interiors of the residence are a stairwell rotunda, a classical museum hall and a large reception hall.

In little more than a decade, Thomon created a stunning body of work that in many ways defined the character of the center of St. Petersburg. His work anticipated the development of the Russian Empire style. His scope of vision, the artistry of his spatial organization and his sense of large-scale abstract form greatly influenced the final stage of the classical style in Russia.

—BORIS M. KIRIKOV

Translated from the Russian by Gwenan Wilbur

THOMSON, Alexander.

Scottish. Born in Balfron, near Glasgow, Scotland, 1817. Died in Glasgow, 1875. Worked with John Baird ("No. 1," 1798-1859), 1836-49; partnership with John Baird ("No. 2," 1816-93, Thomson's brother-in-law but no relation to the earlier John Baird), 1849-57; partner with G. T. Baird; partner with R. Turnbull.

Chronology of Works
All in Scotland unless noted
† *Work no longer exists*

1846-50	New Campus, University of Glasgow (chief assistant to John Baird)
1849	Warehouse, 3-11 Dunlop Street, Glasgow
1850-56	Twenty small houses, Glasgow
1856	Pollok School, Pollokshaws, Glasgow†
1856	United Presbyterian Church, Caledonia Road, Glasgow†
1856	United Presbyterian Church, St. Vincent Street, Glasgow
1856	Double Villa, Langside, Glasgow
1857	Holmwood Villa, Cathcart, Glasgow
1857	Walmer Crescent, West Ibrox, Glasgow
1857	37-39 Cathcart Road, Glasgow
1857	190-192 Hospital Street, Glasgow†
1857	1-10 Moray Place, Strathbungo, Glasgow
1859	Chalmers Free Church, Glasgow†
1859	126-132 Sauchiehall Street, Glasgow†
1861	Grosvenor Building, Gordon Street, Glasgow
1860	Cairney Warehouse, Bath Street, Glasgow†
1860	249-259 St. Vincent Street, Glasgow†
1863	Buck's Head Warehouse, 63 Argyle Street, Glasgow
1865	Grecian Chambers, Glasgow
1865	27-53 Oakfield Avenue, Glasgow
1866	Northpark Avenue, Glasgow
1867	Great Western Terrace, Kelvinside, Glasgow
1867	Queen's Park Church, Glasgow†
1871	Blackies Printing Works, Glasgow
1871	200 Nithsdale Road, Pollokshields, Glasgow
1871	Ellisland Villa, Pollokshields, Westbourne Terrace, Glasgow
1871	Egyptian Halls, Glasgow
1872	Cowcaddens Cross Building, Glasgow
1875	265-289 Allison Street, Glasgow
1875	87-97 Bath Street, Glasgow
1875	12-24 Norfolk Street, Glasgow

Publications

ARTICLES BY THOMSON

"An Inquiry as to the Appropriateness of the Gothic Style for the Proposed Buildings for the University." *Builder* (19 May 1866): 368-371. Republished in *College Courant* (Glasgow University, 1954) 6:103-115 and 7:14-22.

"The Haldane Academy Lectures, Art and Architecture: A Course of Four Lectures." *British Architect* (1 May, 5 June, 24 July, 30 October and 20 November 1874).

BOOKS ABOUT THOMSON

CROOK, J. MORDAUNT: *The Greek Revival*. London, 1972.

GOMME, ANDOR, and WALKER, DAVID: *Architecture of Glasgow*. London, 1968.

MACFADZEAN, RONALD: *The Life and Work of Alexander Thomson*. London, 1979.

ARTICLES ABOUT THOMSON

BARCLAY, D.: " 'Greek' Thomson: His Life and Opinions." *Architectural Review* 15 (1904): 183-194.

BILLING, J. M. M.: "Alexander 'Greek' Thomson: A Study of the Re-creation of a Style." *Quarterly Journal of the Royal Incorporation of Architects in Scotland* 62 (1939): 20-29.

BLOMFIELD, REGINALD: "Greek Thomson: A Critical Note." *Architectural Review* 15 (1904): 194-195.

BUDDEN, L. B.: "The Work of Alexander Thomson." *Builder* (31 December 1910): 815-819.

EDWARDS, A. T.: "Alexander (Greek) Thomson." *Architects and Builders Journal* (13 May 1914): 350-352.

GILDARD, T.: " 'Greek' Thomson." *Proceedings of the Royal Philosophical Society of Glasgow* 19:191-210; 26:99-107 (1888-94).

GOODHART-RENDEL, H. S.: "Rogue Architects of the Victorian Era." *Journal of the Royal Institute of British Architects* 56 (1949): 251-259.

JOHNSON, N. R. J.: "Alexander Thomson: A Study of the Basic Principles of His Design." *Quarterly Journal of the Royal Incorporation of Architects in Scotland* 43 (1933): 29-38.

LAW, G.: " 'Greek' Thomson." *Architectural Review* 65 (1954): 307-316.

McKEAN, JOHN M.: "The Architectonics and Ideals of Alexander Thomson." *AA Files* No. 9 (Summer 1985).

McKEAN, JOHN M.: "Thompson's Double Villa." *Masters of Building, the Architects' Journal* (19 February 1986).

McKEAN, JOHN M.: "La città di Alexander Thomson." In R. BOCCHI (ed.): *Glasgow: Forma e progetto della città.* Venice, 1990.

SMITH, W. J.: "Glasgow: 'Greek' Thomson, Burnet and Mackintosh." *Quarterly Journal of the Royal Incorporation of Architects in Scotland* (August 1951): 56-60.

The Dictionary of National Biography describes Alexander Thomson as "perhaps the most original architect of modern times." That description might have surprised many who read it in the 1890s, and it might surprise even more a century later. But, with some qualifications, it is essentially true. Thomson, who flourished in Glasgow in the third quarter of the 19th century, was certainly the last and arguably the most original of the few great architects of neoclassicism.

Thomson came from and remained in a provincial city all his life; he had no formal schooling and his architecture was self-taught. Although he worked with the reputable John Baird for thirteen years, he left no *lieber meister* when setting off on his own in mid-century. Yet within a few years he moved from conventional, petit-bourgeois mid-Victorian taste to a refined but personal classicism, in which he produced, between 1856 and 1860, masterworks quite unlike anything known before: the churches at Caledonia Road and St. Vincent Street; the little Moray Place; the Double Villa and Holmwood Villa; and the commercial Cairney Building.

His tight grip then loosened as his projects oscillated between banality and pretentiousness. But between 1867 and 1871, with a second wind, he produced the breath-taking Queen's Park Church and an extravagant commercial block, the Egyptian Halls. Thereafter, despite a reputation now unequaled in his city and spreading fast beyond, he produced little more creative work. It seems his architectural practice survived on twenty-five years of conventional urban building design. But it is remembered for a few spectacular bursts of transformational architecture.

Perhaps it was his self-taught culture and a life bounded by the horizon of a single provincial city which accounts for both his uncanny urban flair and for his most problematic imagery. Unique among his contemporaries, Thomson's oeuvre has an appropriateness and generative power that has stood the test of time. His buildings look quite unlike any Glaswegian precedent; they converse not with individual buildings but with the thrusting, gridded, exploding city. His commercial blocks take their place in the flamboyant downtown grid, while his churches, set in the quieter, more amorphous grid of four-story housing, "build their sites," forming compositions of temple and tower on their acropolis and thus articulating unique forms out of the gridded ground. The Caledonia Road complex, sited where two urban geometries collide, stands like the prow of a city-ship, its diverging sides of uniform four-story housing stretching as far as the eye can see.

Thomson's built terraces and villas and his proposed working-class city-blocks all offered new urban types, each transforming and thus giving definition to the pre-existent city pattern. His buildings clarify, strengthen and make memorable the city form, which generates the *imago urbis*.

Thomson's architectural imagery came from a taste which had many resonances with modernism, but which also needed grandeur, majesty and mystery. Thomson's quest was for the timeless essence of classical architecture onto which he would build his forms for the third quarter of the 19th century. His work is highly inventive technically, but only to further his rhetorical and formal goals, in the manipulation of surfaces and spaces. The range of his invention is remarkable, stretching from endless decorative devices to the formal separation of the planes of structural columns and timber-framed glazing on his facades, from the design of dynamically rhythmical facades and tightly geometric proportions to masterly interior effects of complex spaces through daring use of structure and subtle borrowed light.

His imagery began with the severest, strongest Greek forms (therefore trabeated and windowless where possible); thence he was drawn further to Egypt and to Hinduism. An edifying museum project can resemble nothing so much as the fall of corrupt Nineveh (as depicted by John Martin); Presbyterian churches crouch under Hindu towers; his greatest, Queen's Park Church, an amazing blaze of geometry and polychromy seemingly made for Hollywood, was actually for a congregation of Puritan merchants. Thomson's own strict Calvinist, fundamentalist milieu next to these powerful shadows from Oriental pantheism, or his striving for a timeless architecture amidst the contingent squalor of mid-century Glasgow: such contrasts are seen today in sharp and fascinating relief. His buildings which remain, however, transcend his theorizing or our analysis, displaying a powerful architectonic mastery to justify his reputation as the most original British architect in the century between Soane and Mackintosh.

—JOHN McKEAN

THORNTON, William.

American. Born in Tortola, British West Indies, 20 May 1759. Died in Washington, D.C., 28 March 1826. Graduated, University of Edinburgh, Scotland, 1784. Moved to America, 1787; worked independently.

Chronology of Works
All in the United States
* Approximate dates

1789-90	Library Company Building, Philadelphia, Pennsylvania
1793-1827	United States Capitol, Washington, D.C. (completed by others)
1798-1800	John Tayloe III House (The Octagon), Washington, D.C.
1800*-05	Woodlawn Plantation, Mount Vernon, Virginia
1805*-16	Tudor Place, Georgetown, Washington, D.C.
1817-21	Pavilion VII, University of Virginia, Charlottesville

Publications

BOOKS ABOUT THORNTON

BROWN, GLENN: *History of the United States Capitol.* Washington, D.C. 2 vols. 1900-03.

William Thornton: United States Capitol, Washington, DC, 1793-1827

McCUE, GEORGE: *The Octagon: Being an Account of a Famous House; Its Great Days, Decline and Restoration.* Washington, D.C., 1976.
The Octagon, Dr. William Thornton, Architect. Washington, D.C., 1917.
REIFF, DANIEL D.: *Washington Architecture, 1791-1861: Problems in Development.* Washington, D.C., 1971.
RUSK, WILLIAM SENER: *William Thornton, Benjamin H. Latrobe, Thomas U. Walter and the Classic Influence in Their Work.* Ph.D. dissertation. Johns Hopkins University, Baltimore, Maryland, 1933.
STEARNS, ELINOR, and YERKES, DAVID N.: *William Thornton: A Renaissance Man in the Federal City.* Washington, D. C., 1976.

ARTICLES ABOUT THORNTON

BROWN, GLENN: "Dr. William Thornton, Architect." *Architectural Record* 6 (July-September 1896): 53-70.
BROWN, GLENN: "Letters from Thomas Jefferson and William Thornton, Architect, Relating to the University of Virginia." *Journal of the American Institute of Architects* 1 (1913): 21-27.
BUTLER, JEANNE F.: "Competition 1792: Designing of a Nation's Capitol." *Capitol Studies* 4:63-70.
CLARK, ALLEN C.: "Dr. and Mrs. William Thornton." *Columbia Historical Society Records* 18 (1915): 144-208.
KIMBALL, FISKE, and BENNETT, WELLS: "William Thornton and the Design of the United States Capitol." *Art Studies, Medieval and Modern* 1 (1923): 76-92.
NEWCOMB, REXFORD G.: "Doctor William Thornton, Early American Amateur Architect." *Architect* 9 (February 1928): 559-563.
PETERSON, CHARLES E.: "Library Hall: Home of the Library Company of Philadelphia, 1790-1880." *Transactions of the American Philosophical Society* New Series 43 (1953): 129-147.
RUSK, WILLIAM SENER: "William Thornton, Architect." *Pennsylvania History* 2 (1935): 86-98.

*

Although he was only an amateur architect, Dr. William Thornton played a major role in establishing a national style for public buildings in the United States. In 1792 Thornton submitted a late entry to the competition for the United States Capitol, which was to be built in the newly planned city of Washington in the District of Columbia. Thornton won the first prize for his design of a structure resembling Rome's Pantheon, with its prominent porch of eight Corinthian columns, a plain pediment, and a low dome on a stepped base. Of the winning design, Thomas Jefferson stated, "It is simple, noble, beautiful, excellently arranged" and "had captivated the eyes and the judgment of all."

While Thornton's use of classical sources was not new, particularly at a time when interest in classical learning and the arts flourished, his design of the Capitol possessed the grandeur needed for such a national symbol, but also the simplicity to represent a democracy. Thornton's design was praised by most, but its structural deficiencies required the involvement of a trained architect and engineer, Benjamin H. Latrobe. The burning of the Capitol in 1814 during the War of 1812, the need to expand the building during the 19th century as the country, and consequently the Congress, grew, and the addition of the great dome in the 1860s drastically altered the original structure. Yet Thornton's design set the standard for other public buildings, not only those constructed in the national capital, but those built in state capitals as well.

Architecture was one of many areas which interested Thornton. In his early twenties, he was sent from the West Indies, where he was raised, to England to be trained as a medical doctor. During that time, he became fascinated with science, natural history, government, philosophy, art and architecture. His education and travels in Europe afforded him an excellent opportunity to view a variety of architectural styles, as well as to gain a worldly background, which aided him in his endeavors when he settled in the United States in 1786. At that time, he also became involved with abolition, but though he wrote pamphlets advocating the founding of a free African state, he owned slaves until his death, at which time his will provided for their freedom.

As a gentleman architect, Thornton was better prepared than most of his American counterparts. He read extensively, had traveled widely and was skilled at architectural drawing. Though his fortune was small—his family plantation in the West Indies did not provide an income to match Thornton's lifestyle—he had friends in the top echelon of American society. Among his compatriots were George Washington, Thomas Jefferson and James Madison. These men provided Thornton with numerous jobs, architectural and governmental, throughout his life and furnished him with the necessary social connections to gain more commissions. Washington appointed Thornton as commissioner of the city of Washington in 1794. Although Thornton lost that job in 1801 when the commission became defunct, Jefferson quickly appointed him to two other public offices, one to administer the Patent Office, a post Thornton held until his death in 1828.

Thornton received architectural commissions from this circle as well. In 1800 he built a house for Washington in the District of Columbia. He also designed Woodlawn, near Mount Vernon, for Laurence Lewis, a nephew of the first president. However, such connections did not always help Thornton. In 1800 he lost to his rival Latrobe in the competition for the Baltimore Cathedral. This rivalry had begun with the construction of the Capitol and culminated in a nasty libel suit in 1803. In that year Latrobe was appointed second architect of the Capitol and criticized Thornton's plans for their lack of structural soundness. Thornton, in turn, sent malicious accusations to Latrobe, which were printed in the local newspaper, and consequently Latrobe sued for libel. Although Thornton was defended by the prominent lawyer Francis Scott Key, he lost the case. The incident is an example of Thornton's somewhat fiery temper, which characterized many of his business and social ventures.

Yet Thornton's creativity and lack of formal training as an architect contributed to his conception of a building that is both unique and brilliant. The Octagon (1798-1801), built for Colonel John Tayloe III, was an innovative approach to incorporating a town house in the oddly shaped lots created by Pierre L'Enfant's plan for Washington, consisting of a grid superimposed by radial avenues. Located at the intersection of 18th Street and New York Avenue, N.W., the plot with which Thornton had to work was shaped by a 70-degree angle. The result was a building that followed the line of the corner, with the two flat sides of the structure paralleling the two streets, and the nearly semicircular entry facing the curve of the intersection. The simple early Federal style of the exterior complemented the unusual plan, and the entire project was a highly successful solution to a difficult site.

Through his buildings and his other activities, Thornton participated in the creation and subsequent formation of the United States capital city and its surrounding area. He helped found many societies in the District of Columbia, including the American Society for Colonizing the Free People of Color, and created a model city for this group called "Christopolus." He designed many residential buildings in the city and in Virginia and Maryland, influencing domestic architecture in the region. But most important was the widespread influence of his Capitol, which shaped the type of many subsequent state capitols and, thus, the image of government in the United States.

—JULIE NICOLETTA

THUMB, Michael and Peter.

German. Michael Thumb: born 1640; died 1690. Came from a family of masons and architects; brother was architect Christian Thumb; wife was Christina Feuerstein (whose family was also made up of architects); son was Peter II Thumb, born in Bregau, 1681; died 1766. Peter's grandmother was Barbara Beer (from the Beer family of architects); married Anna Maria Beer, 1707; son Michael (1725-69) was also an architect. Peter apprenticed to Michael Herbig, Mason at Au, 1697; accepted into Au Zunft (guild of masons), 1709. Michael worked in Swabia; his first commissions were from Jesuit Colleges in Landshut and Mindelheim. Peter worked mainly in Southern Germany around Lake Constance; Worked with his father-in-law, Franz Beer, 1720s; settled in Konstanz, 1720; became citizen, 1726; retired in Konstanz, 1758.

Michael and Peter Thumb: Neu Birnau Pilgrimage Church, Germany, 1745-57

Chronology of Works

All in Germany unless noted

Michael Thumb:

1660s	Landshut College
1660s	Mindelheim College
1670-86	Austin Priory, Wettenhausen
1682-86	Pilgrimage Church, Schönenberg, near Ellwangen (completed by Christian Thumb, 1690s)
1686	Premonstratensian Klosterkirche, Obermarchtal
1686-94	Hofen, Friedrichshafen
1686-94	Grafrath, near Fürstenfeldbruck

Peter II Thumb:

1708-12	Ebersmünster Church
1715-22	Abbey Church of St. Trudpert (designed and built nave)
1724-27	Saint Peter's Church, Black Forest
1739-53	Benedictine Library, Saint Peter's, Black Forest
1745-51	Neu Birnau Pilgrimage Church
1758-66	Saint Gall Library and Abbey Church, Switzerland (completed by son Michael Thumb)

Publications

BOOKS ABOUT THE THUMBS

HITCHCOCK, HENRY-RUSSELL: *Rococo Architecture in Southern Germany*. London, 1968.

HOFFMANN, J.: *Der süddeutsche Kirchenbau im Ausgang des Barock*. 1938.

LIEB, NORBERT and DIETH, FRANZ: *Die Vorarlberger Barockbaumeister*. Munich, 1941.

ARTICLES ABOUT THE THUMBS

ULMER, A.: "Übersicht über die Vorarlberger Bauschule und ihre Meister." *Alemania* 3 (1929).

*

The Thumbs were one of several dynasties from the area in the vicinity of Bregenz who, with the Beers and the Moosbruggers, were part of what we now call the Vorarlberg school of architects and craftsmen. This school could boast some of the most original and remarkable creative architectural minds in all southern Germany. The two most celebrated members of the Thumb family were Michael and Peter II Thumb (the latter so called to distinguish him from his grandfather, also of that name); the Thumbs intermarried with the Beers and with other creative septs in the region in the vicinity of the Bodensee.

Michael Thumb, who died at 50 in 1690, worked on several fine churches, including Wettenhausen Abbey Church (1670-87), the Premonstratensian Klosterkirche of Obermarchtal (1686-92), the Pilgrimage Church of Schönenberg near Ellwangen (1682-92), Hofen at Friedrichshafen, and Grafrath near Fürstenfeldbruck (1686-94). All these buildings have a quality that marks them as works of truly distinctive architecture.

At Schönenberg, Obermarchtal and Hofen, Michael collaborated with his brother Christian. Schönenberg is important as a prototype of the *Vorarlberger Münsterschema*, and is defined as a *Wandpfeilerkirche*, or long church with internal buttresses dividing the "aisles" into side chapels: the internal face of each buttress is treated with pilasters, and echoed outside, also by means of pilasters. At Obermarchtal the *Wandpfeilerkirche*

system is also employed, and it is an important precedent for other creations of the Vorarlberg School.

Peter II Thumb's career spanned the first half of the 18th century. Born at Bregau in 1681, he was the son of Michael Thumb and Christiana Feuerstein (whose relatives were also architects and stuccoers), and his grandmother was Barbara Beer, of one of the other famous and brilliant Vorarlberg architectural families. Young Peter Thumb was apprenticed to Michael Herbig, mason, at Au in 1697, where he received a thorough grounding in his craft. In 1707 he married Anna Maria Beer, thus consolidating dynastic links; in 1709 he was accepted into the Au Zunft, or Guild of Masons, when he was already an accomplished architect, for from 1704 to 1711 he supervised the building of Franz II Beer's church at Rheinau in Switzerland. Also in 1709 he carried out works for the Benedictines at St. Trudpert in Baden, and from 1711 to 1715 he acted as executive architect for Beer's Abbey Church at St. Urban. During the years 1707-11 he worked with his older brother Gabriel on the parish church at Lachen in Canton Schwyz, a project begun in 1703 by Caspar Moosbrugger. These family and regional connections sometimes make attributions difficult, and there are certainly times when it is impossible to determine exactly who did what. It is clear, however, that certain themes and ideas were developed by various members of the Vorarlberg school, and that a design by, say, Moosbrugger, might be worked up and incorporated by the Thumbs at some later date.

Most of Thumb's mature work was realized in southern Germany, in that area around Freiburg-im-Breisgau and in Baden. These districts were reached with ease from Konstanz, where Thumb settled from 1720, and of which he became a citizen in 1726.

He designed and built the nave of the Abbey Church of St. Trudpert from 1715 to 1722, a four-bay arrangement with aisle-chapels in the *Wandpfeilerkirche* pattern, and from 1719 he rebuilt the church at Ebersmunster across the Rhine in Alsace.

Thumb's masterpiece is unquestionably the monastery and church of Birnau, set in orchards on the northern shore of the Bodensee. There, he placed two three-story blocks on either side of the church with its single central "western" tower, the body of the church being set behind the long facade. Planning began in 1745, and the shells of the buildings were ready for finishing by 1748.

The interior of the pilgrimage church of Neu-Birnau (as it is known) is unique among all examples of church architecture. The nave is more like a prayer hall, as developed by the Asams at Santa Maria de Victoria in Ingolstadt during the 1730s, but it is far more generous in scale. It has quadrant treatments at the eastern corners and diagonals at the west. "Transepts" are vestigial, segmental on plan, and little more than large recesses, performing as chapels. Vaults are flattened, becoming parts of elliptical curves, and are arranged on complex patterns, giving an elegantly contrapuntal effect to the delicious interior of the church. The plan telescopes to the east, with a square choir having chamfered corners, and an elliptical sanctuary, which comes out as a horseshoe shape on plan. Neu-Birnau has one of the most sumptuous Rococo interiors in all Germany, largely white, but varied by the most subtle of pastel tints and containing rich polychrome decorations at key points in the design.

Thumb ended his career by erecting one of the largest and most magnificent churches of the period, that of the Benedictine Abbey of St. Gallen in Switzerland, where he also designed the fine library. Caspar Moosbrugger produced projects for the new church in 1720-21, but Thumb's involvement, from 1749, began just after the shell of Neu-Birnau had been completed. Thumb was commissioned in 1755 to build the present nave and central domed area, which has certain affinities with ideas developed by Moosbrugger, and is very much a characteristic of the Vorarlberg school. Certainly the central space in the church at St. Gallen is very remarkable and beautiful, and carries the logical development of the *Wandpfeilerkirche* to its glorious, open, centralized conclusion.

Thumb retired to Konstanz in 1758, where he undoubtedly enjoyed that beautiful city and its setting. He was one of the great masters of large centralized church plans, in which variations on the elliptical theme emerged. His designs, notably at Neu-Birnau, are of unusual beauty and harmony, and indeed the grouping of the church and clergy houses is very much happier than in the more celebrated case of Die Wies. With Thumb, however, the Rococo reached its apogee, yet, paradoxically, in some of his later work, notably St. Gallen, the concerns of Baroque architects reemerged. Like other Vorarlbergers, wheels came full circle, themes returned, and elements known to the grandfathers were explored again in the second half of the 18th century.

It is odd that Thumb is not better known outside Germany and Switzerland: his work is at least as interesting as that of the Asams or the Zimmermanns.

—JAMES STEVENS CURL

TIGERMAN, Stanley.

American. Born in Chicago, Illinois, 20 September 1930. Married Judith Richards in 1956, Joann Kinzelberg in 1968, Margaret McCurry in 1979; two children. Studied at Massachusetts Institute of Technology, Cambridge, 1948-49; studied at the Institute of Design, Chicago, 1949-50; studied at Yale University School of Architecture, New Haven, Connecticut, 1959-61, B.Arch. 1960, M.Arch. 1961. Architectural draftsman with George Fred Keck, Chicago, 1949-50, T. David Fitz-Gibbon, Norfolk, Virginia, 1952-54, A. J. Del Bianco, Chicago, 1954-56, and with Milton M. Schwartz, Chicago, 1956-57; designer with Skidmore, Owings, and Merrill, Chicago, 1957-59; architectural draftsman with Paul M. Rudolph, New Haven, Connecticut, 1959-61; chief of design with Harry M. Weese, Chicago, 1962; partner, with Norman Koglin in Tigerman and Koglin, Chicago, 1962-64; principal, Stanley Tigerman and Associates Ltd., Chicago, 1964-82; principal, with Robert Fugman and Margaret McCurry, in Tigerman, Fugman, McCurry Architects, Chicago, 1982-88; since 1988, principal, Tigerman and McCurry, Chicago; professor of architecture, 1965-71, adjunct professor, 1980, and director, School of Architecture, 1985-93, University of Illinois at Chicago; has taught widely in the United States and Europe. Member of the Chicago Seven; fellow, American Institute of Architects.

Chronology of Works
All in the United States unless noted

1962-64	Pickwick Village Townhouses, Chicago
1963-69	Woodlawn Gardens Low-Rise Housing, Chicago
1966-69	Nun's Island Low-Rise Housing, Montreal, Quebec, Canada
1966-76	Five Polytechnics in Bangladesh
1970	Park Place Apartments, Chicago
1970-73	Vollen Barn, Burlington, Wisconsin
1972-73	Frog Hollow, Berrien Springs, Michigan
1972-73	Hot Dog House, Harvard, Illinois
1974	Boardwalk Apartments, Chicago
1974	Richard Gray Gallery, Chicago
1974-78	Illinois Regional Library for the Blind and Physically Handicapped, Chicago

1974-78	Piper's Alley Commercial Mall, Old Town, Chicago
1975-77	Daisy House, Porter, Indiana
1976	Stone-Levin Apartment, Chicago
1976-77	Walner Law Office, Chicago
1976-78	"Animal Crackers" (Blender House), Highland Park, Illinois
1976-78	Ukrainian Institute of Modern Art, Chicago
1976-80	National Archives Center of the Baha'is of the United States, Wilmette, Illinois
1977-79	"Tigerman Takes a Bite out of Keck": Walner House addition, Highland Park, Illinois
1977-79	Anti-Cruelty Society Building, Chicago
1978-81	Pensacola Place Development, Chicago
1979-80	Private House, Highland Park, Illinois
1979-80	Private House II, Highland Park, Illinois
1982	Private House, Highland Park, Illinois
1982	Urban Villa, Berlin, Germany
1982-87	Country House, Washington, Connecticut
1983	Weekend House, Lakeside, Michigan
1983	Helmsley Spear Office Building, Chicago (renovation)
1988-90	Apartment Building, Fukuoka, Japan
1992	Power House Energy Museum, Zion, Illinois

Publications

BOOKS BY TIGERMAN

Versus: An American Architect's Alternatives. With Ross Miller and Dorothy Metzger Habel. New York, 1982.
The Postwar American Dream. Chicago, 1985.
The Architecture of Exile. New York, 1988.

BOOKS ABOUT TIGERMAN

BOISSIERE, OLIVIER: *Gehry, SITE, Tigerman: trois portraits de l'artiste en architecture.* Paris, 1981.
INGRAHAM, CATHERINE: *Stanley Tigerman, Recent Projects.* Chicago, 1989.
UNDERHILL, SARAH (ed.): *Stanley Tigerman: Buildings and Projects 1966-89.* New York, 1989.

ARTICLES ABOUT TIGERMAN

"Architecture: Stanley Tigerman." *Architectural Digest* 45/3 (1988).
"Architecture: Stanley Tigerman." *Architectural Digest* 46/2 (1989).
"Chicago Revisited." *Interior Design*, special issue (December 1974).
"Chicago Seven." *Architecture and Urbanism* (June 1978).
"Eleven Works by Stanley Tigerman." *Architecture and Urbanism* 67 (1976).
"Interview with Stanley Tigerman." *Inland Architect* (September/October 1987).
"Other Architectural Problems and Recent Projects." *Architectural Design* 61 (1991).
"Seven Chicago Architects." *Architecture and Urbanism* (May 1977).
"Stanley Tigerman Pure American." *Architect* (The Hague, May 1979).
"Works of Stanley Tigerman." *Space Design* (October 1978).

In his mercurial architectural career, Stanley Tigerman has constructed buildings and interiors of Miesian purity, historical pastiche, mannered disjunction and vernacular domesticity. He has meanwhile written extensively with an increasingly philosophical bent. Within this variety, he comes across as a shifting but pensive practitioner, a philosopher's Philip Johnson.

As an apprentice, Tigerman worked in Skidmere, Owings and Merrill's Chicago office amid pervasive and unquestioned Miesianism. In a few early designs, he made unrealized forays in this style. At Yale University, Tigerman earned bachelor's and master's degrees under the influence and brief employ of Paul Rudolph. He returned to Chicago, working briefly for Harry Weese and undertaking a two-year partnership with Norman Koglin. Although his partners have included Robert Fugman from 1984 to 1988 and Margaret McCurry from 1988 to the present, Tigerman seems the singular steward of his own career.

Tigerman aptly describes his early-1960s low-rise housing projects Pickwick Village, Pickwick Plaza and Stacked Maisonette Project as both ''De Stijlian'' and ''Rudolphian,'' with their rectilinear planes and didactic brick construction. The architect's perspective renderings also obediently follow Rudolph's hard-edged graphic style.

In his first stylistic turn, Tigerman later completed the purely Miesian Boardwalk Apartment Building, a 28-story reinforced-concrete and glass slab in Chicago,. Seven years later, in 1981, came the nearby Pensacola Place Apartment complex, a similar apartment slab which adds stacked balconies as megacolumns capped by cutouts as Ionic volutes, and topped by a two-dimensional entablature concealing mechanical equipment. Applied clapboard town-house facades cover the base. Tigerman's postmodern one-liner is overt in its self-conscious irony, an appealing aspect of the now-loathed style.

From modernism to postmodernism and beyond, Tigerman frankly catalogs his stylistic meanderings in *Versus: An American Architect's Alternatives* (1982). Through nine styles in just over 20 years, he concludes by invoking Western and Jewish philosophical thought as well as current architectural trendsetters. His architectural search is an Aristotelian and Talmudic dialectic: an ongoing struggle to represent the implicit conflicts of architecture.

Tigerman's writings are more compelling than some of his corresponding buildings. His dialectical juxtaposition of opposites is well-written and pedigreed philosophy, but sometimes gives rise to questionable design. The Baha'i Archives Center project juxtaposes mirror-image building and topiary forms on axis with the existing otherworldly nonagon dome. This is actually one of the more convincing among several designs, either mirrored or cut down the middle.

Tigerman's other stylistic forays have spanned the bizarre, succinct, witty and traditional, finding success in oddly divergent embodiments. A tour through some of his house designs reveals an early (and acknowledged) debt to the work of Gwathmey and Siegel, while his ''Architecture of the Absurd'' sometimes is absurd. However, standouts such as the Hot Dog House, named for its long oval plan, achieve a richness when the dialectic (open/closed, object/dwelling, viewer/viewed) and sight gags (such as in ''House with a Pompadour'') are toned down.

With the Architect's Weekend Retreat (1983), designed in collaboration with partner Margaret McCurry, Tigerman produced an almost folly-like residence of wit and humble sophistication in a play on the farmhouse/granary and basilica/baptistery.

For all his philosophical struggles, Tigerman achieves an unexpected facility with resolved classicizing and vernacular designs. While some of his residences are stripped iterations of Beaux-Arts classicism, other more recent projects are forthrightly historical. The Western Connecticut residence of 1982-87 based on an E. S. Prior Butterfly Plan project, with gables and dormers, is a prime example.

And yet Tigerman's Self-Park Garage in Chicago (1986) *is* a car, from tires to hood ornament. Nor is the architect any easier to pin down in his many interiors and exhibition commissions. They include surrealist landscapes in plastic laminate, straight historical revival, and frantic lattices of intersecting grids.

One certainty is that Tigerman is a serious architectural thinker. His *Architecture of Exile* (1988) is a phenomenal excursion through the ongoing architectural implications of expulsion from the Garden of Eden and subsequent biblical issues. While this may be Tigerman's best work of any kind so far, his *Failed Attempts at Healing an Irreparable Wound* is approaching publication.

Likewise, a recent apartment (1988-90) in Fukuoka, Japan, demonstrates Tigerman's success and increased skill with built metaphor, with tile-covered living units and balconies protruding from and receding behind a 2-meter-square black grid. The six-story building's light court contains an unbroken white grid of one-meter squares. The interior court as ideal and exterior as imperfect realization structure are clear without being heavyhanded, lending meaning to a satisfying form. Tigerman seems to be reconciling rhetoric with built form with increasing success.

Tigerman's view is ''that having more than one view about architecture is not necessarily as arbitrary as is normally thought.'' While the idea is confusing at some levels, the observer is very eager to see what Tigerman does next.

—CHARLES ROSENBLUM

TOLEDO, Juan Bautista de.

Spanish. Born in Madrid, Spain. Died 19 May 1567. Worked at St. Peter's Rome, under Michelangelo. Appointed architect to the court of Philip II, Madrid, 1559.

Chronology of Works
In Spain

1561ff.   El Escorial, Madrid

Publications

BOOKS ABOUT TOLEDO

KUBLER, G. and SORIA, M: *Art and Architecture in Spain and Portugal and Their American Dominions, 1500-1800.* Baltimore and Harmondsworth, England, 1959.
KUBLER, GEORGE: *Building The Escorial.* 1982.

*

Juan Bautista de Toledo was one of the most important Spanish architects, who had a long-lasting influence on the architecture of his country. His name is closely connected with the most important building in Spain, the royal palace El Escorial, situated northwest of Madrid. The palace was designed and constructed in large part during the reign of Philip II, in the 16th century. In contrast to other Spanish architects, who were influenced by the Islamic artists and buildings of Moorish Spain, both the planned and built projects of Juan Bautista de Toledo were based on other structural principles. He had spent some time in Italy, and familiarized himself both with the architecture and the architectural treatises of the Italian Renaissance theorists.

Toledo appears to have been involved in the construction of St. Peter's in Rome, during the tenure of Michelangelo. Later he was active in the employ of the Spanish viceroy in Naples. In 1599 he was called to the court of Philip II in Madrid, in the framework of the court's nationalist and Counter-Reformation policies.

Toledo was made court architect in the same year, and worked on the first designs for the complex of El Escorial. As court architect, Toledo could realize his designs only in the closest consultation with his employer, King Philip II.

After his arrival in Spain, Toledo was occupied in the royal works with alterations, expansions and renovations. The Alcázar in Madrid was one of those projects. It was originally planned as a structure with two courtyards, but was later destroyed. His alteration of the royal apartments at the Palace at Aranjuez, completed only after Toledo's death by Juan de Herrera and J. de Valencia, may serve as another example.

Together with A. Sillero, Toledo undertook the alteration of the Monastery of the Descalzas Reales in Madrid, renovated to accommodate Joanna of Austria. The monastery church, finished in 1564, is attributed to him. It was later extensively altered, however. The simple articulation of the exterior, which is determined by the alternation of fine masonry with stone pilasters and pilaster strips, is in the impersonal style associated with Philip II. It stands in stark contrast to the highly ornamental Plateresque style of the other architecture of the time.

Toledo's principal work is the royal palace El Escorial, a monumental complex which is also the most important architectural work Philip II initiated. The king wanted a mausoleum for his father, Charles V, a large church, a Jeronymite monastery and a palace to accommodate his court, all under one roof. The complex was to express the national character of Spain and its new imperial status. To that end Philip chose the Spanish architect Toledo, with his Italian training, to design the complex and supervise its construction. When Toledo's predecessor, Villalpando, died in 1561, Toledo's responsibilities grew. In the spring of 1562 he developed the layout, laid the foundations and organized the construction work for El Escorial.

Toledo's first plans, never substantially altered, date from 1561. The basic structure is determined by a closed square, which is subdivided by the individual buildings and courtyards to form a kind of grid. The church and forecourt are situated on the axis of the complex. The layout is akin to those of the most important complexes in architectural history, but exploits its characteristics to its own ends. Toledo's plan is comparable to Antonio Filarete's unexecuted design for the Ospedale Maggiore in Milan, the plan of which was derived in turn from the urban villas of the Late Roman era. The layout of such Roman villas was available to Italian Renaissance architects particularly through Diocletian's Palace at Split.

Spanish esteem for Italian architecture was also evident in the fact that the Italian engineer and architect Francesco Paciotto was engaged to solve engineering questions.

Toledo created the southern entry facade and, most important, the two-story Great Cloister, which is also known as the "Patio de los Evangelistas." The cloister also recalls Italian models in its plan, particularly Antonio da Sangallo's Palazzo Farnese.

At Philip's wish, Toledo's original plan for the palace at El Escorial was changed extensively after his death. The western facade in front of the church was heightened by one story, and the two envisioned towers were canceled.

The grid-like plan of the existing buildings in the complex is certainly to be attributed to Toledo, however, which makes him responsible for the fundamental conception of this representative multifunctional complex. His style, both at El Escorial and in the work at Aranjuez, is functionally oriented, and determined by the use of local mouse-gray granite in the facades. This sober style, almost reminiscent of military barracks, was the foundation for the so-called *"estilo desornamentado,"* which was to characterize Spanish architecture for decades.

Even though the present effect of El Escorial is determined by the work of Toledo's successor, Juan de Herrera, the layout creating future possibilities is to be credited to Juan Bautista de Toledo. If the royal palace El Escorial is the expression in stone of the political situation of an entire epoch in Spanish history, it is the achievement of a Spanish architect who planned and partially realized the building, in close collaboration with Philip II. Juan Bautista de Toledo conceived a building that demonstrated the political, religious and spiritual orientation of the Spanish royal house.

—KATHARINA PAWELEC
Translated from the German by Marijke Rijsberman

TOMÉ, Narciso.

Spanish. Born in Spain ca. 1694. Died in Toledo, 13 December 1742. Father was the architect Antonio Tomé, from whom he learned architecture. Brothers were the sculptor Diego Tomé and the painter Andrés Tomé. Reputed to have studied with José de Churriguera in Salamanca. Appointed chief architect of the Cathedral of Toledo, 1721; remained in this post until his death.

Chronology of Works
All in Spain
† *Work no longer exists*

1721-32	Cathedral, Toledo (Transparente)
1731-36	Church of the Convent of Discalzed Carmelites, Madrid (retable)†
1734	Hermitage of Nuestra Señora del Canto, Toro (retable)†
1738	Cathedral, León (retable; built by Simón Gavilán Tomé, 1740-45)†

Publications

BOOKS ABOUT TOMÉ

KUBLER, G.: *Arquitectura española, 1600-1800 (Ars Hispaniae,* vol. XIV). Madrid, 1957.
KUBLER, G. and SORIA, M.: *Art and Architecture in Spain and Portugal and Their American Dominions, 1500-1800.* Baltimore and Harmondsworth, 1959.

ARTICLES ABOUT TOMÉ

"El Transparente de la catedral de Toledo (1721-1732)." *Archivo Español de Arte* (July-September 1969; issued January 1971): 255-288.
"Narciso Tomé's Transparente in the Cathedral of Toledo (1721-1732)." *Journal of the Society of Architectural Historians* (May 1970): 9-23.

The biographical data on Narciso Tomé is scanty, and the records of his activity fragmentary. He was the son of Antonio Tomé (1664-1730), a little-known architect from Toro, a small town in Castile, from whom he learned his profession. It has been frequently stated in critical writings from the 19th century to the present, that Tomé received his architectural training in Salamanca, under José de Churriguera. There is nothing more to substantiate this assumption than the assertions of the neoclassical critics Ponz, Jovellanos and Ceán Bermúdez, who speak of Tomé as belonging to the Salmantine school. This certainly means no more than that his style of architecture was associated with that of the brothers Churriguera and of Pedro de Ribera.

Nothing is known about Narciso previous to 1715, when he appeared working in Valladolid on the central portal of the facade of the university, under the direction of his father and in collaboration with his brother Diego, a sculptor. The role of Antonio Tomé in that enterprise was that of designer, organizer and representative of the family in financial matters; the bulk of the actual work, however, seems to have been carried out by Narciso and his brother.

When, in the last months of 1720, the chapter of the cathedral of Toledo called in the Tomés to develop a design for the Transparente which was to be erected behind the high-altar retable, facing the ambulatory, the situation was quite different; although Antonio is mentioned by name in the first documents pertaining to this commission, it was Narciso who by then had control of the design. The drawings for the Transparente, much as it would be built, were signed by Narciso in June of 1721. His father's name does not appear again in the records, and his brothers, Diego (1696-1732) and Andrés, a painter (1688-1761), worked under his direction to execute his design. On 27 October 1721, Tomé was named *maestro mayor* (chief architect) of the cathedral of Toledo, in temporary substitution of Teodoro Ardemans (1664-1726); upon the latter's death, Tomé acquired the title in property. Work on the Transparente was finished by May 1732, and its altar consecrated on 9 June 1732.

After the completion of the Transparente, Narciso remained as architect of the cathedral until his death, being replaced then by the royal architect Santiago Bonavia (died 1759), the favorite architect of the Bourbon court. In those 10 years, Tomé did not build anything else for the cathedral, although he made drawings (still extant) for the renovation of the 15th-century *trascoro*. His later works, although built, did not survive the 19th century. The high-altar retable for the church of the Convent of Discalced Carmelites of Madrid, known as ''de la Baronesa,'' contracted in 1731 and finished by 1736, is no longer extant; the high-altar retable of the Hermitage of Nuestra Señora del Canto in Toro, commissioned in 1734, was destroyed during the Napoleonic invasion; the high-altar retable for the cathedral of León, commissioned in 1738 to replace the Gothic one, was dismantled in 1880. The retable in Toro, however, is known through paintings and an engraving, and that of León Cathedral, whose fragments were taken to the convent of San Francisco, where they still are, is also known through a painting (Nun's Convent, Villalpando Zamora). Tomé's design for León—built by his nephew, Simón Gavilán Tomé, in 1740-45—was centered on an Assumption of the Virgin, deployed in three tiers. It was as successful as that of the altar in Toledo.

Also in 1740, Tomé made drawings for the potential of the large 15th-century silver monstrance of the cathedral of Toledo, and his last work seems to have been some unidentified change in the altar of Saint Peter in the cathedral. Also attributed to Tomé are the high-altar retable of the Colegiata of Toro, and the retable and 12 lamp-bearing angels in the Chapel of the Holy Sacrament in the Church of San Antonio in Avila. In our day, his artistic fame rests exclusively on Toledo Cathedral's Transparente.

Narciso Tomé is an unusual figure in Spanish architecture, and the origins of his style are difficult to account for. The portal of the University of Valladolid, which presumably illustrates his father's style, in which Narciso was formed, is a rather sober affair when compared with other examples of Spanish late Baroque architecture, such as Pedro de Ribera's portal of the former Hospicio de San Fernando in Madrid (1722-26). The extreme Baroque style of Tomé's Transparente, however, does not reflect study of Ribera's works or of those of the Churriguera brothers. Its design is, in fact, unique in the context of Spanish Baroque architecture, and can only be related to Giovanni Lorenzo Bernini's models of religious monuments in which the three arts were integrated to bring about an illusionistic effect. The Rococo style of the decorative motifs in the Transparente's architecture is easy to refer to sources that were easily accessible to Tomé. His design of an engraved frontispiece for a book on the primacy of the cathedral of Toledo, published in 1726, which shares many ornamental motifs with the Transparente, is a characteristic example of Rococo forms of the kind that were well known in Spain through prints. The overall conception of this elaborate structure, however, cannot have come into being without the study of Bernini's Cathedra Petri in St. Peter's, or the Cornaro Chapel in Santa Maria della Vittoria, Rome. Since there is no indication that Tomé ever traveled to Italy, how Tomé came by his knowledge of Bernini's works can only be surmised. Perhaps, as is the case with Spanish 17th-century painters, it was also through the medium of prints that Tomé learned about major works by important artists abroad.

—NINA A. MALLORY

TON, Konstantin A.

Russian. Born Konstantin Andreevich Ton in St. Petersburg, Russia, 26 October 1794. Died in St. Petersburg, 25 January 1881. Brothers were the architects Alexander Andrejewitsch Ton and Andrej Andrejewitsch Ton. Studied at the St. Petersburg Academy of Arts, 1803-15. In Italy, 1819-28. Returned to St. Petersburg; professor, then rector, St. Petersburg Academy of Arts, from 1831.

Chronology of Works
All in Russia

1829-37	Academy of Arts, St. Petersburg (main halls and chapel)
1830-37	Orthodox Church of St. Catherine, St. Petersburg
1831-34	Dock, Academy of Arts, St. Petersburg
1834-42	Vvedensky Church, St. Petersburg
1838-49	Bolshoi Kremlin Palace, Moscow
1839-83	Church of Christ the Saviour, St. Petersburg
1842-49	Church of the Annunciation, St. Petersburg
1844-51	Armory, Moscow
1844-51	Train Stations for the Russian Railroad Line
1849-55	Church of St. Mironiya, St. Petersburg

*

Konstantin Ton was the leader of the revival movement in Russian church and civil architecture of the 1830s to 1850s. At that time, problems of ethnic distinction, the particularity of the Orthodox spirit and the specific historical path of Russia came into focus in sociopolitical life. Working within governmental guidelines, Ton created an official national style, which embodied the central idea of Nicholas I's reign: the union of autocracy, Orthodoxy and nationality.

Ton's heightened ideological stance predetermined a tendentious, politicized approach to his work. By the late 19th century, democratic journalism was already portraying him as an odious figure; and the majority of his churches were destroyed during the later Soviet struggle against religion. Among the victims of this governmental vandalism was Ton's Church of Christ the Savior, the greatest cathedral in Moscow, which became the proposed site of a Palace of Soviets—a gigantic monument to Joseph Stalin's empire. Ironically, this battle against a national heritage was masterminded in the Great Kremlin Palace, which was also built by Ton.

The beginning of Ton's creative development coincided with the decline of classicism and a forced romantic stylization. Ton emerged as the leading initiator of this trend, which came to be called "Russian Byzantine" or the "Russian style." The essence of this phenomenon was the singleminded manufacture of a purely national retrospective style, based on an interpretation of the devices and forms of ancient Russian architecture. Such an approach was considered an alternative to standard European styles, under the influence of which the Russian architecture of the St. Petersburg era had developed. Ton took a contemporary approach to the ancient Russian heritage. He refracted traditional forms through the prism of academic classicism and transformed construction prototypes with an eye toward new engineering possibilities.

The future father of the Russian style was educated at the St. Petersburg Academy of Arts during the ascendancy of Russian classicism. Ton spent nearly a decade (1819-28) in Italy, where he authored plans for the reconstruction of Fortuna's Sanctuary in Praeneste among others. His work won him recognition and honorary titles in the academies of Rome and Florence.

Upon returning to St. Petersburg, Ton rebuilt the main suite of halls and the chapel in the Academy of Arts (1829-37), thus proving himself an adherent of the classical tradition. He built a monumental dock in front of the Academy building (1831-34), supplementing the unique complex of granite embankments along the Neva River. Two authentic ancient Egyptian sphinxes (15th century B.C.) guard each side of the steps, enhancing the unusual character of the dock.

Throughout his life, Ton remained closely associated with the Academy of Arts. For nearly a quarter of a century after 1831, he was professor, then rector, of architecture, and more than 200 students passed under his tutelage. Ton's pedagogical method combined a theoretical understanding of the historical heritage with a rational approach to practical problems, drawing on achievements in the exact sciences. His key creative principle was the semantically determined selection of compositional and stylistic prototypes which by association expressed a building's function.

Ton first turned to the image of a national past in his plans for the Orthodox Church of St. Catherine in St. Petersburg (1830-37). This program piece is a major work of the Russian style. Despite the obscurity of ancient Russian architectural practices and his own very limited experience with the elaboration of nationalist themes in the works of his predecessors (A. N. Voronikhin, Karl Rossi and V. P. Stasov), Ton found a convincing architectural solution in a compact, five-domed church reminiscent of 15th- and 16th-century Moscow cathedrals. Its distinct interior structure, with four supporting pillars answered by a precise system of vertical architectural divisions on the facades, and onion domes became his favorite devices.

The 1830s witnessed the clearest and most significant period of Ton's career. In the few years following his first piece in the

"national style," he designed churches in Tsarskoe Selo and Peterhof, Vvedensky Church in St. Petersburg and the Church of Christ the Savior in Moscow (all completed, but since destroyed). Each of these buildings varied the five-domed form with its own individual compositional and technical features.

The centralized, symmetrical Vvedensky Church (1834-42) was distinguished by walls of minimal thickness and narrow, diagonally extended sections of supporting pillars. The latter device allowed for an economy of space, improved the interior perspective and contributed to structural stability. The Church of Christ the Savior (designed 1832, erected 1839-83) had a cross-shaped plan. Its massive main bulk was crowned by a wide, illuminated dome with an enormous onion-shaped cupola and four smaller corner bell towers. The cupola, following the example of Filippo Brunelleschi's Florence Cathedral, was erected without falsework. Only the Kremlin was more dominant in the Moscow cityscape than this grand church, which was 102 meters in height. The building was a memorial to the Patriotic War of 1812, and many well-known artists and sculptors participated in its formulation.

This type of centralized, symmetrical five-domed church, created by Ton on the basis of old Muscovite (but not Byzantine) sources, became widespread in mid-19th-century Russian construction. The publication of Ton's works in 1838 and 1844, as well as Nicholas I's approval of his designs as models, helped to increase the popularity of this form. Churches modeled on Ton's designs were built in Piatigorsk, Uglich, Nizhny Novgorod, Saratova, Perm, Krasnoiarsk and other cities.

Features related to late classicism and characteristic of early eclecticism—geometric forms, rigidly symmetrical and regular construction, dry detailing—are all typical of this group of buildings. Subsequently, the architect employed dome and tower ornamentation evocative of 16th- and 17th-century Russian architecture. In the Church of the Annunciation in St. Petersburg (1842-49), the compact five-dome scheme is used with traditional dome tops. Its facades are reminiscent of classicism. The Church of St. Mironiia in St. Petersburg (1849-55) had a vestibule and high, tiered bell tower with a tradital top.

Ton's attention to the themes of national architecture reflected a growing craving for ethnic distinction in Russian society. At the same time, his study of old Russian monuments had its first visible effect on his creative evolution. Traditional roof tops and groups of narrow corner columns showed up for the first time in his design for the gate church of Ipatievsky Monastery in Kostrom (1840), where Ton conducted research and restoration work. Ton may be considered one of the first architect-restorers of the romantic period in Russia. On the basis of his study of wooden folk dwellings, he compiled an atlas of peasant houses and villages for the different climatic zones of Russia (1842).

Ton's most important work after the Church of Christ the Savior was the Great Kremlin Palace (1838-49). The building is the main link in the panorama of the Moscow Kremlin, but does not play a dominant role. The fundamental, massive and extensive form consists of two parts: a wider arcade-like lower level and an upper block with two rows of windows. Its geometry of form, the flatness of its facade and the even, rhythmical order of repeating elements are all features of late classicism, although the shape of the windows and casings and the silhouette of the higher middle section were taken from the neighboring 17th-century Teremny Palace. Details, rather than the building's monotonous composition, endow Ton's palace with its resemblance to the ancient buildings of the Kremlin. The decor of the grand halls, among them the grand Georgian Hall, combines Byzantine, Roman and Renaissance motifs.

Within the same complex as the Great Kremlin Palace, Ton erected a new building, the Armory (1844-51), where famous collections of art works, historical relics, weapons and treasures are stored.

Ton did not consider it categorically imperative to continue following the Russian style. He modeled the two train stations he built for the first Russian railroad line (1844-51) on Western European town halls, keeping the facades in the style of the Italian Renaissance. This compositional and stylistic resolution can be attributed to Ton's understanding of the train stations as public buildings of citywide significance.

The importance of Ton's churches in the larger formation of the city can be measured not only by their place in the existing system of dominant structures, but also by their role in the architectural Russification of the most European city in Russia. The destruction of Ton's churches noticeably impoverished the skylines of large and small Russian cities alike.

—BORIS M. KIRIKOV
Translated from the Russian by Gwenan Wilbur

TORRALVA, Diogo de.

Portuguese. Born in Spain, ca. 1500. Died ca. 1566. Entered the service of the nobleman Beira Litoral, 1529. Married the daughter of the architect Francisco de Arruda, 1534. Appointed master of the works of Alentejo and Évora, by 1587.

Chronology of Works
All in Portugal
All works are attributions; all dates are approximate

1530-60 Augustinian Convent of Santas Maria da Graça, Évora

Diogo de Torralva: Cloister of Joao III, Tomar, Portugal, 1558ff.

1549ff. Pilgrim's Church of Santo Amaro, Alcántara, near Lisbon

1550-60 Bom Jesus de Balverde, near Évora

1558ff. Cloister of João III, Convent of the Order of Christ, Tomar

1560s *Capela-mor* (death chapel), Jeronymite Monastery, Belém, near Lisbon

Publications

BOOKS ABOUT TORRALVA

HAUPT, ALBRECHT: *Die Baukunst der Renaissance in Portugal.* 2 vols. Frankfurt, 1890-95.

KUBLER, GEORGE: *A Arquitectura portuguesa chã. Entre as Especiarias e os Diamantes, 1521-1706.* Lisbon, 1988.

KUBLER, GEORGE, and SORIA, MARTIN: *Art and Architecture in Spain and Portugal and Their American Dominions, 1500-1800.* Harmondsworth, England, 1959.

MARKL, DAGOBERTO: *O Renascimento.* Vol. 6 in *História da arte em Portugal* series. Barcelona, 1986.

SERRÃO, VITOR (ed.): *O Maneirismo.* Vol. 7 in *História da arte em Portugal* series. Barcelona, 1986.

SMITH, R. C.: *The Art of Portugal, 1500-1800.* London, 1968.

SOUSA, VITERBO: *Dicionário histórico e documental dos arquitectos, engenheiros e construtores portugueses.* Lisbon, 1922. Reprint: 1988.

---

*

Diogo de Torralva, an architect active in Portugal, though probably of Spanish extraction, is important for the numerous monumental religious buildings he designed for João III. As court architect of this humanistically inclined king, he played a central role in the dissemination of Italian architecture in Portugal. It is not clear whether Torralva visited Italy himself, but his architecture leaves no doubt that he had a thorough knowledge of the works of Vitruvius, Sebastiano Serlio and Andrea Palladio, which would have been available to him in Spanish and Portuguese translations. His later work makes one think of the drawings and writings of Francisco de Holanda, a contemporary who had been in Rome between 1537 and 1541 at the king's expense, and who had had access to the circle of Michelangelo.

Torralva's style stands between Renaissance and Mannerism, and became the foundation of architectural developments in Portugal up to the end of the 17th century. As early as 1530 a definitive break with the Late Gothic Manueline style had been achieved in Torralva's early work and in the buildings by the brothers João and Diogo de Castilho, who belonged to a slightly earlier generation. It follows, then, that the canon of classical forms was established in Portugal well before it was in Spain, and cannot be ascribed to the influence of the Spanish architects Juan de Herrera (ca. 1530-97) and Filippo Terzi (1520-97). The absorption of Renaissance ideas and forms in Portugal took place independently from Spain, stimulated by the Italian orientation of the court of João III.

Torralva's life and work have not been exhaustively investigated. His oeuvre, as it is known now, consists mostly of attributions, which only in recent years have been more fully described. Little or nothing is known of his origin, birthdate or training. The earliest date about which there is any certainty is 1529, when Torralva entered the service of a nobleman living in Góis (Beira Litoral). Torralva designed a house ''*ao Romano*'' for him and a grave marker in the local parish church. In 1534 he married the daughter of the architect Francisco de Arruda at

Évora, and already he was signing himself "*mestre de obras regias*" (master of the royal works).

The church and cloister of the Augustinian Convent of Santas Maria da Graça at Évora, which were begun in 1530 but not completed until 1560, are ascribed to Torralva. It is possible that his work on these buildings dates from a much later period in his life, however. The convent was founded jointly by João III and the duke of Vimioso, and was intended as a burial site. The design of the complex was entrusted to the foremost artists of the age. The participation of the architects Miguel de Arruda and Diogo de Torralva, and of the sculptor Nicolas Chanterenne is documented, but their exact individual contributions have yet to be determined. The two-level granite facade is unusual in that it has a portico at the lower level. The double-gable motif above the second level recalls Palladio's later churches. The four gigantic atlantes bearing flaming globes, which are set above the corner pilasters, are another unusual feature of the design. Legend has it that they represent the first four sinners condemned by the Santo Oficio. Although the building clearly experiments with classical elements and perspectives, it remains peculiarly wooden and disproportionate. An inscription and certain stylistic features point to a probable date of about 1558.

In about 1540 the Church of Nossa Senhora da Conceição was founded in Tomar, in which similar perspectival effects as at the convent at Évora are deployed. However, this church recalls Roman architecture to a much greater degree, both in its proportions and its articulation. The interior of the three naves is articulated by means of Corinthian columns, an architrave and a barrel vault. A coffered dome is set over the crossing. The cube-like exterior is emphasized by corner pilasters, an entablature and a triangular gable. Portal frames and window surrounds are executed in the classical manner, with considerable foreshortening. Both Torralva and João de Castilho are considered as possible architects.

The small Pilgrim's Church of Santo Amaro in Alcántara near Lisbon (begun in 1549), which is also attributable either to Torralva or João de Castilho, is interesting mostly for its plan. The coffered circular space under the dome has a semicircular gallery opened by wide arcades on the western side. A round altar niche and two side rooms are located on the eastern side. Whether the design of this central plan derives from indigenous tradition or from published designs—for example, by Serlio—has not been determined.

Another church with a central plan is the Bom Jesus de Valverde (1550-60), which is ascribed either to Torralva or to Manuel Pires, an architect active mostly in the Alentejo district. This little-known building, not far from Évora, must be counted among the chief works of Portuguese Mannerist architecture. It is said that Philip II was so impressed with it when he saw it during his trip through Portugal that he had drawings made of it, the better to remember its forms. Its significance lies on the one hand in the consistent use of a single system of proportions applied to every space, on the other hand in the utilization of Palladian motifs in the elevation. The central octagon is defined by columns connected by alternating architraves and archivolts. Four similarly articulated chapels open off the octagon. All spaces have domes, and the dome of the octagon is heightened with a tambour. Every element is consciously related to the others. The church pavement, laid in a pattern of black and white marble squares, is particularly noteworthy. It consists of 351 units, each one square foot in size, which form a consistent grid disclosing the nature of the plan. A grappling with architectural theory is quite obvious.

The principal work of Torralva—who had been knighted and named master of the works of Alentejo and Évora by the time of his involvement with the building—is the so-called cloister of João III in the Convent of the Order of Christ at Tomar. The structure is also called "*dos Filipes*," due to the fact that it was not finished until the Spanish interregnum (Philip II^Philip IV), after 1587. The Castle of the Knights Templar, founded in the 12th century, had been handed over in the early 13th century to the newly founded Order of Christ, who maintained a close relationship with the Crown. As a consequence of Portugal's ascendancy to world power, and the need for an architecture to represent the country's new status, the 12th-century convent was expanded at various times. Torralva's cloister replaced a building by João de Castilho, which may have been dilapidated but more likely was stylistically inadequate for the new times.

Available documents indicate that construction began in 1558 in accordance with the architect's drawings. The wings of the two-story cloister are articulated by rhythmical bays. A Serliana with pilasters rather than columns is set in the upper level, over the wide lower-level arcades. This articulation looks like a combination of two of Serlio's engravings from the *Tutte l'Opere:* the engraving of the Cortile di Belvedere (III, fol. 117v.) and the "*loggie sopra loggie*" (IV, fol. 154r.). These have been transformed into an academic, but nevertheless powerful, architectural idiom. The staircases in the corners seem to be an individual solution by Torralva, although it is possible that they derive from Girolamo Genga's Villa Imperiale in Pesaro (1530). Torralva was familiar with Francisco de Holanda's drawings of that building. On the other hand, in the earlier cloister of the Jeronymite Monastery at Belém, the corners are also unusually strongly underlined, although there the effect is achieved by means of diagonal arcades. In the cloister of Tomar, Torralva convincingly transformed Italian Renaissance architecture into a properly Portuguese style. The forms are heavier, more massive. The contrast between light and dark is more severe and more theatrical than it is in the work of Palladio or his contemporaries. Even so, the building forms a harmonious unity, despite all the stylistic differences, with the rest of the Templars' Castle.

The last work connected with Diogo de Torralva is the *Capela-mor* (literally "main chapel") at the Jeronymite Monastery at Belém near Lisbon, where the artist performed a variety of tasks. The Choir Chapel, which was intended as a pantheon for Manuel I and his descendants, had originally been executed in the Manueline style. It was demolished in 1563 and rebuilt according to a Mannerist design. Construction was completed by Jean de Rouen (Jerónimo de Ruaño), but the design is ascribed to Torralva. The undecorated cube-like exterior expresses the clear, impressive articulation of the interior with projecting Ionic and Corinthian columns, which are continued in the ribs of the coffered vault. The structure of this tunnel-like space had a powerful influence on 17th-century Portuguese architecture.

Torralva died in 1566. His work amounted to a trendsetting contribution to the absorption of Italian Renaissance architecture in Portugal, and founded an independent tradition that lived on until the beginning of the 18th century.

—BARBARA BORNGÄSSER KLEIN
Translated from the German by Marijke Rijsberman

TOWN, Ithiel.

American. Born in Thompson, Connecticut, 1784. Died on 12 June 1844. Studied under Asher Benjamin, Boston, 1804-10. Worked with Captain Isaac Damon, Northampton, Massachusetts, 1814; partnership with Martin L. Thompson, New York, 1827; partner with A. J. Davis, New York, from 1829.

Chronology of Works

All in the United States
* Approximate dates
† Work no longer exists

1810	Botanic Garden House, Harvard University, Cambridge, Massachusetts
1812-15	Center Church, New Haven, Connecticut (built to design by Asher Benjamin)
1813-16	Trinity Church, New Haven, Connecticut
1815	Congregational Meetinghouse, Plainfield, Connecticut
1815	Congregational Meetinghouse, Thompson, Connecticut†
1816	Steamboat Hotel, New Haven, Connecticut†
1825-26	Mrs. Eli Whitney House, New Haven, Connecticut†
1825-27*	Tontine Hotel, New Haven, Connecticut†
1826-27	Jones Court, New York City†
1826-30	Fort Griswold Monument, Groton, Connecticut
1827-28	Christ Church Cathedral, Hartford, Connecticut (with Nathaniel S. Wheaton)
1827-31	Connecticut State House, New Haven, Connecticut†
1828-29	Church of the Ascension, New York City (with Thompson)†
1828-29	City Hall and Market House, Hartford, Connecticut†
1828-30	Samuel Russell House, Middletown, Connecticut

Works with A.J. Davis, as Town and Davis

1829-30	Ralph Ingersoll House, New Haven, Connecticut
1829-30	South Congregational Church, Middletown, Connecticut†
1830-33	General Hospital, New Haven, Connecticut†
1831-32	County Courthouse and Town Hall, Middletown, Connecticut††
1831-32	West Presbyterian Church, New York City†
1831-35	Indiana State Capitol, Indianapolis, Indiana†
1832-35	Cannon Block, Troy, New York
1833-34	Albany Female Academy, Albany, New York†
1833-37	New York University Building, New York City (with Dakin and others)†
1833-40	North Carolina State Capitol, Raleigh, North Carolina (with others)
1833-42	United States Customhouse, New York City (with others)
1835-36	Lyceum of Natural History, New York City†
1835*-37	Ithiel Town House, New Haven, Connecticut†
1836-39	New York Orphan Asylum, New York City (chapel by Davis)†
1836-67	United States Patent Office, Washington, D.C. (with William Parker Elliot and others)
1843-44	Henry H. Elliott House, New York City†
1843-44	Robert C. Townsend House, New York City†

Publications

BOOKS BY TOWN

The Outlines of a Plan for Establishing in New York an Academy and Institution of the Fine Arts. New York, 1835.

BOOKS ABOUT TOWN

HAMLIN, TALBOT F.: *Greek Revival Architecture in America.* New York, 1944.

HITCHCOCK, HENRY-RUSSELL, and SEALE, WILLIAM: *Temples of Democracy: The State Capitols of the U.S.A.* New York, 1976.

KELLY, JOHN FREDERICK: *Early Connecticut Meetinghouses.* 2 vols. New York, 1948.

NEWTON, ROGER HALE: *Town and Davis, Architects: Pioneers in American Revivalist Architecture, 1812-1870.* New York, 1942.

PIERSON, WILLIAM H., JR.: *Technology and the Picturesque: The Corporate and Early Gothic Styles.* Vol. 2A in *American Buildings and Their Architects.* Garden City, New York, 1978.

PIERSON, WILLIAM H., JR.: *The Colonial and Neo-classical Styles.* Vol. 1 in *American Buildings and Their Architects.* Garden City, New York, 1970.

ARTICLES ABOUT TOWN

BROOKS, H. ALLEN: "The Home of Ithiel Town: Its Date of Construction and Original Appearance." *Journal of the Society of Architectural Historians* 13, No. 3:27-28.

DAVIES, JANE B.: "A. J. Davis' Projects for a Patent Office Building, 1832-1834." *Journal of the Society of Architectural Historians* 24 (1965): 229-251.

NEWCOMB, REXFORD G.: "Ithiel Town of New Haven and New York." *Architect* 11 (February 1929): 519-523.

SEYMOUR, G. D.: "Ithiel Town—Architect." *Art and Progress* 3 (September 1912): 714-716.

SIGOURNEY, LYDIA H.: "The Library of Ithiel Town, Esq." *Ladies Companion* 10 (1839): 123-126.

As an architect/engineer, Ithiel Town represents the first generation of professional architects in the United States. His training in the Boston school of Asher Benjamin from 1804 to 1810 provided him with the education to pursue his interest in the romantic archaeological revivals that characterized 19th-century building in the United States. In Boston, Town would have had access to the Boston Athenaeum, founded in 1807, where he undoubtedly would have read such works as Stuart and Revett's *The Antiquities of Athens* (1851). Benjamin's emphasis on classical sources and Town's own strong interest in accurate copies of Greek monuments led to Town's significant role of popularizing the Greek Revival in America.

Yet Town's first building, the First Congregational Church (1812-15, called the Center Church) on the New Haven Green was an amalgamation of elements, deriving primarily from James Gibbs' St. Martin-in-the-Fields. The building shows the influence of Town's mentor, Benjamin; indeed, the records show that the church was based on a plan by Benjamin, while the construction was carried out by Town. However, it is likely that Town made changes as the structure was built. The church went up at the same time as David Hoadley's United Congregational Church next door, and the two buildings are quite similar, with their brick exteriors, Greek temple fronts, and white steeples.

Town's second building, Trinity Church (1813-14), set just south of the Center Church, was dramatically different, and must have been seen as rather revolutionary for its time. The church was built in the "Gothick," a style that was becoming associated with the Episcopal Church to set it apart from the Georgian style of the established Congregational Church. Town's church was one of the first three or four Gothic Revival churches in America. Trinity Church undoubtedly helped establish Town's reputation as a competent architect, yet the majority of his buildings are Greek Revival, and that is the style for which he is known today.

In 1829 Town took on a young partner, Alexander Jackson Davis, and formed one of the first professional architectural firms in America. Together they designed a number of public buildings in the Greek Revival style. The Connecticut State Capitol (1827-31), on the New Haven Green, was designed with the assistance of Davis. Yet the Greek Doric temple with its hexastyle porch shows Town's strong, mathematical interest in the proportions of classic Greek architecture. Like William Strickland's earlier Second Bank of the United States in Philadelphia (1818), the Connecticut Capitol was a near-exact replica of the Parthenon. It established the use of the Greek Revival style for state capitols until Bertram Goodhue's Nebraska State House (1916-28). Although Davis was more eclectic than Town and drawn more to the Gothic Revival than his partner, Town seems to have had the upper hand in the firm's major commissions of the 1830s, for nearly all were Greek Revival structures. These buildings included the state capitols of Indiana, North Carolina, Illinois and Ohio built between 1827 and 1867, the United States Customs House in New York City (1833-42), and insane asylums in New York and Raleigh, North Carolina.

Town's interest in the symmetry of classic Greek architecture was matched by his attention to the engineering aspects of building. His most significant invention was the wooden truss bridge, patented in 1820 and widely used throughout the eastern states for much of the 19th century. The tight lattice-truss design, which allowed for greater spans, anticipated the steel girder construction for bridges by nearly 75 years.

The royalties from the Town truss made the architect a wealthy man. He began collecting art and architectural books as well as medieval manuscripts, prints, paintings and other objects d'art. His library alone eventually numbered more than 11,000 volumes. In his *History of the Rise and Progress of the Arts of Design in the United States* (1834), William Dunlap stated that Town's library was "unrivalled by anything of the kind in America, perhaps no private library in Europe is its equal." Town became increasingly concerned with the education of the artist and the dissemination of knowledge; he provided the New Haven community free access to his library as early as 1834.

Town, who had been a resident of New Haven since 1812, played an active role in the cultural development of the city. He received an honorary degree from Yale University in 1825. In the 1830s, he advocated the formation of a center for the instruction of the fine arts nearly two decades before Augustus Street gave his fine arts building, Street Hall, to Yale.

Perhaps the most telling example of Town's love of knowledge and learning is the house he built for himself in New Haven from 1836 to 1837. The house was designed in the Greek Revival style despite the fact that that mode was being supplanted by the Gothic Revival by the 1830s. While Town did use the Gothic for churches, his reliance on classic Greek architecture was fitting for a home that also served as his own temple of learning. The house was carefully designed, with the preservation of the books in mind; every partition in the house was built of brick to make the library fireproof. Even the interior plastering was put directly on the bricks, with wood lath used only on the ceiling. Such protection did not save the house from the passage of time, however; it was demolished in the 1950s.

To regard Ithiel Town as a force in the development of the architectural profession in the United States, one must thus measure his buildings and his library equally, and conclude that both aspects of his life helped shape not just attitudes toward architecture, but toward learning in general.

—JULIE NICOLETTA

TOWNSEND, Charles Harrison.

British. Born in Birkenhead, Cheshire, England, 1851. Died in 1928. Articled to Walter Scott, Liverpool; apprenticed with T. Lewis Banks, London, 1880s; opened office in London, 1888; joined Art Workers' Guild, 1888.

Chronology of Works
All in England unless noted
* *Approximate dates*

1890	Tourelle, Salcombe, Devon
1892	All Saints, Ennismore Gardens, Knightsbridge, London (west front and alterations)
1892-95	Bishopsgate Institute, London
1892-95	St. Martin's Church, Blackheath, near Guildord
1894*	Blatchfield, Blackheath, Guildford, Surrey
1896	Linden House, Düsseldorf, Germany
1896-1901	Horniman Museum of Ethnology, Forest Hill, London
1897	Cliff Towers, Salcombe, Devon
1899-1901	Whitechapel Art Gallery, London
1900	Dickhurst, near Haslemere, Surrey
1902	Village Cross, West Meon, Hampshire
1902-04	St. Mary the Virgin, Great Warley, Essex
1904	Union Free Church, Woodford Green, Essex
1906	Arbuthnot Institute Hall, Shanley Green, Surrey
1910	Village Hall, Panshanger, Hertfordshire

Charles Harrison Townsend: Bishopsgate Institute, London, England, 1892-95

Publications

ARTICLES BY TOWNSEND

"An Artistic Treatment of Cottages." *Studio* 6 (1896): 24-34.
"The Art of Pictorial Mosaic." *Journal of the Royal Institute of British Architects* Series 3, 8 (1901): 221-241.
"The Royal Institute Library and Some of Its Contents." *Journal of the Royal Institute of British Architects* Series 3, 19 (1912): 429-456.
"The Civic Survey." *Journal of the Royal Institute of British Architects* Series 3, 23 (1916): 177-180.

BOOKS ABOUT TOWNSEND

RUSSELL, FRANK (ed.): *Art Nouveau Architecture*. London, 1979.
SERVICE, ALASTAIR: *The Architects of London*. London, 1979.
SERVICE, ALASTAIR (ed.): *Edwardian Architecture and Its Origins*. London, 1975.

ARTICLES ABOUT TOWNSEND

MALTON, JOHN: "Art Nouveau in Essex." Pp. 159-169 in NIKOLAUS PEVSNER and J. M. RICHARDS (eds.): *The Anti-Rationalists*. London, 1973.
MUSGRAVE, NOEL: "Survival of the Richest: The Whitechapel Art Gallery." *Journal of the Royal Institute of British Architects* 73 (1966): 315.
SERVICE, ALASTAIR: "Arts and Crafts Extremist: Charles Harrison Townsend (1851-1928)." *Architectural Association Quarterly* 6, No. 2 (1974): 4-12.

*

As an architect and a theorist, C. Harrison Townsend advocated the creation of a modern style that was representative of the spirit of the age. Following John Ruskin's advice to the Pre-Raphaelites, Townsend attempted to combine the scientific method of investigation with the cooperative system of the medieval guilds to create a unique vocabulary of design. Townsend compared the design process to scientific experimentation, where the scientist built on the existing body of knowledge in order to create new forms. For Townsend, the methods of architectural design were synthetic and were acquired through an investigation of the past.

Upon arriving in London from Liverpool in 1880, he worked briefly for Eden Nesfield, and certain of Townsend's domestic commissions were essays in the Nesfield/Shaw genre. As late as his design for Blatchfield (ca. 1894), he employed quotations from Richard Norman Shaw's work, such as half-timbering, hanging tiles and the breaking of the facade into sections. Despite a certain amount of copyism, Townsend developed a personal style that emerged between 1883 and 1894.

The major step in Townsend's development was his move to the office of Lewis Banks. The associates in that office showed great enthusiasm for the architecture of H. H. Richardson and the Chicago school. Townsend's continuing interest in the architecture of Richardson was evident in his design for St. Martin's Church at Blackneath and his trip to the United States to see Richardson's work.

The pivotal year in Townsend's career was 1888. In addition to establishing an independent practice and being elected as a Fellow of the Royal Institute of British Architects, Townsend joined the Art Workers' guild. Its publication, *The Studio*, became the medium for Townsend's theories of design. His article

"Value of Precedence" in that journal discussed the merit of studying architectural history as part of the synthesis of design.

His own design process was based on the study of past precedents, and was demonstrated in the design of the Bishopsgate Institution (1892-94). In this commission, Townsend abandoned copyism and employed precedents in an abstract manner. The source for the Bishopsgate facade was an Elizabethan building illustrated in Joseph Nash's *The Mansions of England in Olden Time*. In his design, Townsend retained the twin polygonal towers, the arched entrance, and the band of windows found in Nash's illustration, but he changed the stylistic vocabulary from Elizabethan to Romanesque. For the Tudor arch pictured in the plate, he substituted a broad round arch. The decorative relief above the arch and at the top of the facade were given a treatment reminiscent of Louis Sullivan's work.

The basic themes struck on the facade of the Bishopsgate Institution were developed in the Whitechapel Art Gallery (1897-99). Still present were the twin towers, but they had been reduced in size and no longer dominated the facade. Instead, the off-center arched entrance predominated and served as a foil to the otherwise symmetrical facade. When discussing this building in *The Studio*, Townsend returned to his familiar theme of the use of architectural precedents and presented the Whitechapel Art Gallery as proof that a new style could be derived from the study of older buildings. He offered the gallery as a "building that attempts to strike its own note, to be personal, and to speak 1897, not 1797 or 1597" in spite of its acknowledged historical antecedents.

He underscored the importance of the study of precedent in the reissue of Nash's *Mansions of England* in 1906. In his introduction to the new edition, Townsend described the book as a design tool and instructed architects to reexamine the work. He asserted that the Elizabethans had created a distinctive architectural style through the adaptation of the elements from the architecture of the Italian Renaissance. Instead of copying historic styles verbatim, Townsend challenged architects to follow the example of their Elizabethan predecessors and to adapt the basic styles to meet the current needs of the day. In a lecture to the RIBA on its library, Townsend expanded this argument to the whole of architectural history and encouraged his fellow practitioners to use the RIBA collection as a design resource.

His attempts to reform architectural design were part of his work with the Art Workers' Guild, and he collaborated with its leaders in producing the Guild's major statement on architecture. In 1899, the Art Worker's Guild revived the medieval masque by presenting "Beauty's Awakening" at the London Guildhall. Like the masque, the guild was a medieval institution brought into the present. In both cases, the members of the guild sought to reform architecture by reestablishing the spirit of "medieval" cooperation among artists and craftsmen. The masque demonstrated how a new vision of London could transform the city aesthetically and socially. Townsend wrote the prologue and the epilogue. The significance of his contribution lies in their different depictions of the concept of time. The elderly Father Time speaks the prologue, while the epilogue employs the youthful Spirit of the Age. Inbetween, a vision produced by Clio (history) inspires a renewed architecture. As portrayed in the masque, Father Time and the Spirit of the Age are separated by an instant, but they soon blend into the single entity of history.

As demonstrated through the masque, both Townsend and the guild wanted the architecture of each period to be indicative of its social development, with a new style representing that era's place in history. Townsend and the other architects within the guild developed this theory into the English Free Style, which was based on vernacular architecture and the moral elements of the Gothic Revival. Despite the efforts of Townsend and his associates in the guild, neither the Free Style nor the tenets that it represented survived beyond World War I. Townsend's last major commission came in 1906, and after his service in the war, he returned to a dwindling practice. Townsend's obituary in the *Journal of the RIBA* paid homage to his practice and his dream of a new architecture, both of which had predeceased him.

—DAVID D. MCKINNEY

TRUMBAUER, Horace.

American. Born in Philadelphia, Pennsylvania, 28 December 1868. Died in Philadelphia, 18 September 1938. Married Sara Thompson Williams, 1902. Draftsman for G. W. and W. D. Hewitt, Philadelphia, 1883-1890; private practice in Philadelphia, 1890-1938.

Chronology of Works
All in the United States
† Work no longer exists

1893	W. W. Harrison House (Grey Towers), Glenside, Pennsylvania
1896	George W. Elkins House, Elkins Park, Pennsylvania
1898-1900	William L. Elkins House (Elstowe Manor), Elkins Park, Pennsylvania
1898-1900	P. A. B. Widener House (Lynnewood Hall), Elkins Park, Pennsylvania
1899-1902	Edward J. Berwind House, Newport, Rhode Island
1902-06	Widener Home for Crippled Children, Philadelphia†
1906-08	Racquet Club, Philadelphia
1909-11	J. B. Duke Residence (now Institute of Fine Arts, New York University), New York City
1910-12	Duveen Brothers Building, New York City†
1911-19	Benjamin Franklin Parkway, Philadelphia (with others)
1911-31	Philadelphia Museum of Art (with Zantzinger and Borie)
1912-14	Harry Elkins Widener Memorial Library, Harvard University, Cambridge, Massachusetts
1913-20	Mrs. George D. Widener House, Newport, Rhode Island
1916-21	Edward T. Stotesbury House, Wyndmoor, Pennsylvania†
1917-27	Free Library, Philadelphia (main building)
1923-24	Benjamin Franklin Hotel, Philadelphia
1924-28	Public Ledger Building, Philadelphia
1925-28	New York Evening Post Building, New York City
1925-39	Duke University, Durham, North Carolina
1928-31	Jefferson Medical College and Curtis Clinic, Philadelphia
1932	Wildenstein and Company Building, New York City

Publications

BOOKS ABOUT TRUMBAUER

BRANAM, ALFRED: *Newport's Favorite Architects.* Long Island City, New York, 1976.
MAHER, JAMES T.: *The Twilight of Splendor.* Boston, 1975.

ARTICLES ABOUT TRUMBAUER

"A New Influence in the Architecture of Philadelphia." *Architectural Record* (February 1904).

Everything seemed to militate against success for Horace Trumbauer, yet his corpus ranks among the largest and finest of any American architect from his era. Other architects who reached national prominence near the close of the 19th century came from families of cultural, if not financial, attainment, but he was next to last of six children born to a dry-goods salesman with a wife equally modest. Among the names reflecting the English ancestry of his counterparts, the Pennsylvania Dutch name of this architect strikes its own dissonance. While the rest had been sent to Paris for study at the École des Beaux-Arts, Trumbauer finished school at age 14, his architectural training limited to apprenticeship with the Hewitt Brothers, plus incessant reading. Fame in architecture radiated from New York, but Trumbauer never abandoned his native Philadelphia. Still, these hazards of his life and career helped in fact determine the nature of his works.

Goaded possibly by humble origins, he opened his own office soon after reaching legal age. Right from the start, his clients were primarily the well-to-do, and at age 24 he made his reputation as a mansion builder with Grey Towers. Victorian vestiges lingered, yet were almost wholly swallowed up in Britannic aspirations derived loosely from Alnwick Castle in England. Americans were expressing their new worldliness by importing traditional styles from Europe, but conservative Philadelphia remained under the idiosyncratic sway of Frank Furness until the practice of "working in styles" found an architect ready to make the switch.

Increasing experiments had led Trumbauer to classicized details or occasionally a Colonial-style house, but in 1898 emerged a true classicism suited to his sudden outpouring of mansions. Gilded Age palaces from other architects might seem gawkishly overlarge, yet Trumbauer's lifelong talent for massing let his mansions look at once imposing and compact. Likewise, his decoration was no more elaborate than it was refined. Despite their old-world antecedents, these were not governmental lodgings for an entire court, but modern residences with functional plans and the latest luxuries. Specimens to prove his mastery in the extinct art of creating mansions have sadly grown fewer, although the permanence with which he built exacts a last revenge on those who dare tear them down.

Lack of formal education haunted Trumbauer all his life, not only in his own view of himself, but also through the taunts of his New York competition. Resultant uncertainty caused him to consistently copy the work of other architects. Of course Wren had copied Palladio, and among the other leaders in Trumbauer's period—notably McKim, Mead and White—the practice was commonplace as architects tried to equip their clients with an instant past. Trumbauer went a step further by borrowing from contemporary structures, although even there he was hardly alone. One design was derived from the same Tuxedo Park house by Bruce Price on which Frank Lloyd Wright based his own home in Oak Park. Just as Philip Johnson would later build homages to Ludwig Mies van der Rohe, so did Trumbauer compliment such architects as Richard Morris Hunt by inventing Elstowe Manor as a reduced version of the Breakers, whose entrance hall showed up across the street in Lynnewood Hall. Mostly his copying was a mere point of departure, but when reproducing an entire facade he took advantage of hindsight to improve it.

Reticence about his background helps explain also why he put so much effort into perfecting each detail but so little into publicizing either himself or his practice, even why he allotted himself so little life beyond his more than a thousand works stretching west to Colorado and east to England. Offered an honorary degree from no less than Harvard for designing its library, this man who was forever worried about his untutored state needed coaxing to go accept. Understanding the odd man out let him hire designer Julian Abele, despite staff objections because Abele was black. Other talented designers like Frank Milnor, Charles Rabenold or Frank Seeburger have also been suggested as the genius behind Trumbauer, yet indisputably he was the architect, procuring commissions, deciding how the building would look, overseeing its construction. If—as did Walter Gropius, who had an aversion to holding a pencil—he communicated more through words than drawings, his employees unhesitatingly gave the credit to the "Old Man."

Perhaps best remembered for his mansions, he was not at all a specialist, but erected buildings of all sorts, even pavilions for several amusement parks. Within the prevailing classicism, he likewise moved between ancient, English, French or Early American, sometimes with juxtapositions, as when the Benjamin Franklin Parkway, his magnificent Philadelphia vista based on the Champs Elysées, got crowned with the wholly Greek art museum derived from the Temple of Asclepius on the isle of Cos. He could drift easily into Gothic or Elizabethan; at Duke University, for example, the west campus meant for men is collegiate Gothic, while the east campus for women is brick Colonial.

As the 1920s progressed, such elegant skyscrapers as the Thomas Jefferson Medical College in Philadelphia and the *New York Evening Post* Building in lower Manhattan hinted at modernism, but the Great Depression dried up business before Trumbauer could make another switch. Traditional architects from turn-of-the-century America are at last receiving an honored place in the history of architecture, and when his reputation is similarly rehabilitated, the name Horace Trumbauer may well lead all the rest.

—FREDERICK PLATT

TSCHUMI, Bernard.

French. Born in 1944, of French Swiss parentage. Studied at the Federal Institute of Technology, Zurich, graduated 1969. Taught at the Architectural Association, London, 1970-80; visiting lecturer, Princeton University, New Jersey, 1976-77 and 1980-81; visiting professor, Cooper Union School of Architecture, New York, 1980-83; dean of the Columbia University Graduate School of Architecture; principal, Bernard Tschumi and Associates, New York and Paris. Légion d'honneur, 1987.

Chronology of Works
In France

1983-   Parc de la Villette, Paris

Bernard Tschumi: Parc de la Villette, Paris, France, 1983-

Publications

BOOKS BY TSCHUMI

Architectural Manifestoes. London, 1979.
Manhatten Transcripts. London and New York, 1981.
Architectural Writings 1973-87. London, 1988.
Cinégramme Folie. Princeton, New Jersey, 1987.
Questions of Space: Lectures on Architecture. London, 1990.

BOOKS ABOUT TSCHUMI

The Discourse of Events. Exhibition catalog. London, 1983.
Disjunctions. Exhibition catalog. Berlin, 1987.

ARTICLES ABOUT TSCHUMI

"Bernard Tschumi." *Architecture and Urbanism* (October 1989).
"Deconstruction: A Student Guide." *Journal of Architectural Theory and Criticism*, special issue, Vol. 1, No. 2 (1991).
"Deconstruction III." *Architectural Design* Profile No. 87 (1990): 32-49.
"Parc de la Villette, Paris, France." *GA Document* 26 (May 1990): 38-47.
"Works of Bernard Tschumi." *Architecture and Urbanism* (September 1988).

*

Bernard Tschumi graduated at a time when student revolts in Paris led to the substitution of the Beaux-Arts education by a curriculum which acknowledged the social and economic responsibilities of architects. This rebellious attitude has influenced his work and made him one of the foremost representatives of Deconstruction.

Tschumi considers architecture a tool for social and cultural change. His theoretical foundations lie in early-20th-century artistic movements which questioned existing rules and limits: futurism, dadaism and surrealism. In their wake, he attacked the International Style for favoring intellectual concepts. According to him, the paradox of modern architecture was its inability to mend the split between social reality and utopian beliefs. Instead of acceding to the same objectification of human concerns, Tschumi tried to solve modernism's impossibility of analyzing the essence of space while simultaneously experiencing it. For him the main issue was the difference between real space and mental space. Bridging this paradox between mental construct and sensual experience became his goal. He saw architecture as taking place in the realm between idea and reality, not in semiological/structuralist discourse or in behavioral or sociopolitical problem-solving.

"Transgression" became his central theme. Tschumi's architecture is one of event: events that take place in architecture as well as the event of building. In this respect, Tschumi was influenced by Russian constructivism—architecture as a montage of fragments from reality—and futurism—architecture emerging from literary programs. Tschumi's architectural designs evolved in close connection to his theory. He was interested in establishing an architectural sensitivity which he saw developing at the juncture of aesthetics and language.

His mid-1970s *Advertisements for Architecture* were literally intended to elicit desire for architecture, a desire to uncover architecture behind drawings, words, customs and technology.

They attacked the predominance of intellectual concepts promoted by modern architecture, and aimed to replace them with experiential concerns.

In the *Manhattan Transcripts* (1977-81) Tschumi dealt with the disjunctions between use, form and (social) meaning. He examined what happened to architecture if it was occupied by human events and movements. The *Transcripts* deal with the actual disjunctions of everyday life shown through the discontinuity between human nature and culture. They demonstrate a dynamic conception of architecture. Various devices of transformation are documented, such as compression, insertion and transference. These devices are needed because architectural forms are not derived from functional or material constraints. Photographs, drawings, diagrams and movement schemas are used to tell the story of a murder and a chase taking place in architectural settings.

Tschumi is interested in working at the limits of architecture, where it moves into other fields. In the *Transcripts,* the deconstruction of traditional concepts is performed through documentation. The *Transcripts* are a work of notation, using different notation modes than those traditionally associated with architecture. They question the unity between architectural structures and established meanings. Tschumi questions this unity through the pleasure of tension between what is and is not allowed in an architecture governed by strict rules.

Tschumi began to devise an architecture of space: physical, mental and social. In his Parc de la Villette in Paris (begun in 1982), he has achieved this by deconstructing the structure of the architectural apparatus. The plan is made through superimposing points (pavilions/follies), lines (axes and paths) and surfaces (planes) in an obvious allusion to Wassily Kandinsky's Bauhaus program. A grid establishes a rule which is then disstructured. The axes and paths incorporate human movement, and human nature is further incorporated through different systems of space, articulated as points and planes in the pavilions and open surfaces. In their forms the pavilions for recreational activities treat construction as an event. They derive from a basic cube to which are added parts required by their function. The fragmentation created through juxtaposing various systems and forms produces conflicts, reciprocities and indifference. The Parc de la Villette expresses the dialectic nature of contemporary urban life and culture. Plans and forms are open-ended and subordinated to the program, which is allowed to change. The superimposition of fragments from different orders does not accommodate established conventions, but forces the users to work out their own meanings.

Processes of deconstruction are also used to integrate the contrasting architectural context of a site. Tschumi's design for the County Hall in Strasbourg created new relationships through the fragmentation of the building into geometric forms. Using deconstructivist literary theory, Tschumi also reorganized the program to determine architectural form. For the National Theater, Tokyo, he divided the main activities into strips of program, creating parallel juxtapositions of cultural meanings through the spaces devised for those activities.

Tschumi believes that meaning in architecture is defined by the concepts of dwelling, memory, function and aesthetics. Deconstructing architecture means changing the established semantics of architecture. Tschumi mixes architectural motifs with photographic, cinematographic, choreographic and mythographic writing. With that technique he criticizes existing discourses and concepts, especially those relating social institutions to architecture.

—HANS R. MORGENTHALER

U–V

UNGERS, Oswald Mathias.

German. Born in Kaiseresch/Eifel, Germany, 12 July 1926. Married Liselotte Gabler, 1956; three children. Studied at the Technische Hochschule, Karlsruhe, 1947-50, Dip.Arch. Served in the German Army, 1945-46. In private practice, Cologne, since 1950, Berlin, since 1964, and Ithaca, New York, since 1970. Dean of the faculty of architecture and senator of the Technical University, Berlin, 1965-67 (vice-dean, 1967-68); chairman of the department of architecture, 1969-75, and professor, since 197 5, Cornell University, Ithaca, New York; visiting professor at numerous other institutions.

Chronology of Works
All in Germany unless noted

1951-53	Apartment and Factory Buildings 'Z', Aachener Strasse, Cologne
1953-62	Science Institute, Oberhausen
1955-57	Multi-family housing, Brambach Strasse, Dellbrück, Cologne
1956-69	Student housing 'N,' Lindenthal, Cologne
1957	Multi-family housing, Mauenheimer Strasse, Nippes, Cologne
1957	House ''M'' (two-family house), Dürener Strasse, Cologne
1959	Ungers House, Belvedere Strasse, Müngersdorf, Cologne
1959-60	Apartment Block, Mozart Strasse, Wuppertal
1959-62	Apartment Complex, Jakob Kneip Strasse, Poll, Cologne
1962	Printshop and Publishing House, Braunsfeld, Cologne,
1962-66	Apartment Complex, Märkisches Viertel, Berlin
1963-66	Apartment Complex, New City, Seeberg, Cologne
1974	Masterplan, Fourth Ring Area, Lichterfilde, Berlin
1975-80	Masterplan, Mettenhof, Widdesdorf, Cologne
1978-79	Apartment Building, Schiller Strasse, Charlottenburg, Berlin
1979-83	Housing development, Lützowplatz, Berlin
1979-84	German Architecture Museum, Schaumainkai, Frankfurt
1979-84	Baden State Library, Karlsruhe
1980-82	Multi-family housing, Miquel Strasse, Berlin
1980-83	Galleria and Exhibition Hall 9, Frankfurt
1980-84	Alfred Wegener Institute for Polar and Ocean Research, Bremerhaven
1981-84	Konstantinplatz, Trier
1983-84	High-rise office building, Frankfurt
1989	Residential Development, Salzburg, Austria
1989	Residential Development, Berlin
1990	Bayerische Hypotheken- and Wechselbank, Düsseldorf (reconstruction)

Publications

BOOKS BY UNGERS

Die gläserne Kette: Visionäre Architekturen aus dem Kreis um Bruno Taut 1919-1920. With Udo Kultermann. Exhibition catalog. Leverkusen, 1963.

Die Erscheinungsformen des Expressionismus der Architektur. Cologne, 1964.

Veröffentlichungen zur Architektur (general ed.). 27 vols. Berlin, 1965-69.

Optimale Wohngebietsplanung. With Horst Albach. Wiesbaden, 1969.

Kommunen in der Neuen Welt 1740-1971. With Liselotte Ungers. Cologne, 1972.

Dortmunder Architekturhefte 11: Planungsbeispiel Siedlung Hochlarmark Recklinghausen. With G. Borchers. Dortmund, 1978.

The Urban Garden—Student Projects for the Südliche Friedrichstadt Berlin (ed.). With Hans F. Kollhoff and Arthur A. Ovaska. Cologne, 1979.

Kommentar zum Wettbewerb Kammergericht Berlin. Cologne, 1979.

Architecture as Theme. Milan, 1982.

ARTICLES BY UNGERS

''Zum 'Weltplanungsprogramm' von Buckminster Fuller.'' *Bauwelt* 45 (1961).

''Aus einem Vortrag vor dem Akademischen Architektenverein in Hannover.'' *Baukunst und Werkform* (August 1961).

''Für eine lebendige Baukunst.'' *Bauwelt* (August 1961).

''Insegnamento sviluppo e ricerca.'' *Casabella* 300 (1965).

''Planning and Accident'' and ''Structure—Quality—Dimension.'' *Bau* (June 1967).

''Form in der Gross-stadt.'' *Werk* (November 1967).

''Big Forms in Habitation.'' *Architecture d'aujourd'hui* (May 1969).

''Northwest-Zentrum: Adhoc Heart of a City?'' With Liselotte Ungers. *Architectural Forum* (October 1970).

''Utopische Kommune in Amerika.'' *Werk* (June, July and August 1970; March and August 1971).

''City Problems in a Pluralistic Mass Society.'' *Transparent* (May 1971).

''Early Communes in the U.S.A.'' With Liselotte Ungers. *Architectural Design* (August 1972).

''Towards a New Architecture.'' With Reinhard Gieselmann. In ULRICH CONRADS (ed.): *Programs and Manifestoes in 20th Century Architecture.* Cambridge, Massachusetts, 1972.

''Le Comuni del Nuovo Mondo.'' With Liselotte Ungers. *Lotus* 8 (1974).

''Oswald Mathias Ungers: Theories, Ideas and Proposals.'' With Vittorio Gregotti. *Lotus* 11 (1976).

Oswald Mathias Ungers: Alfred Wegener Institute for Polar and Ocean Research, Bremerhaven, Germany, 1980-84

"Planning Criteria." *Lotus* 11 (1976).
"Designing and Thinking in Images, Metaphors and Analogies." In *Man-trans-Forms*. Exhibition catalog. New York, 1976.
"Cities within the City." *Lotus* 19 (1978).
"A Vocabulary: Oswald Mathias Ungers' Plans for Rebuilding the Town of Marburg" and "Architecture of the Collective Memory." *Lotus* 24 (1979).
"Una teoria trasformazione morfologiche." *Architettura* (January/February 1980).
"Architecture's Right to an Autonomous Language." In *Architecture 1980—The Presence of the Past*. New York, 1980.
"When One Deals with Architecture." *Lotus* 57 (1988).

BOOKS ABOUT UNGERS

KLOTZ, HEINRICH: *O. M. Ungers*. Wiesbaden, 1984.
O.M. Ungers, Works in Progress 1976-80. New York, 1981.
O.M. Ungers, 1951-84: Bauten und Projekte. Braunschweig, 1985.
Oswald Mathias Ungers: Architetture 1951-90. Milan, 1991.
REYNER, BANHAM: *The New Brutalists: Ethic or Aesthetic?* New York, 1966.

ARTICLES ABOUT UNGERS

DAVEY, PETER: "Ungers." *Architectural Review* (June/July 1981).
GREGOTTI, VITTORIO: "O. Mathias Ungers." *Lotus* (January 1976).

O. M. Ungers is one of the more influential architects of the second half of the 20th century, both for his theoretical discourse and his designs. His professional activity is subdivided into two principal periods, formative (from 1950 to 1963) and mature (since 1979), separated by a sojourn in academia when Ungers virtually stopped building, but during which he explored themes and developed positions now prevalent in his work.

His architecture reflects a resolute exploration of alternatives. Ungers steadfastly relies on his encyclopedic knowledge of architecture to refine and alter permutations of previously explored themes such as the house within the house, the city block as an urban archipelago or mini-city, and archaeological layering. More important, his topological and morphological approach recognizes and reinforces the qualities of the place, and presents a positive alternative for current architecture and urban design.

The numerous projects which Mathias Ungers realized during his early period forcefully countered the tenets of modernist orthodoxy of postwar reconstruction. Contextual in their urban disposition, works such as the multifamily complexes on Mauenheimer Strasse in Cologne-Nippes (1957), Brambach Strasse in Cologne-Dellbrück (1955-57) and Mozart Strasse in Wuppertal-Elberfeld (1959) may seem "Brutalist" because of their tectonics, yet as Kenneth Frampton correctly states: ". . . Ungers' expression remained distinct from the New Brutalist *briques apparentes'* manner, since it was not only removed from Corbusian concepts of spatial order but also antithetical to the tradition of the freely manipulated mass . . ." The 1960 essay "Towards a New Architecture," co-authored with Reinhard Gieselmann, explains Ungers' notions: "Architecture is a vital penetration of a multilayered, mysterious, evolved reality.

Its creative function is to manifest the task by which it is confronted, to integrate itself into that which already exists, to introduce points of emphasis and rise above its surroundings. Again and again it demands recognition of the genius loci out of which it grows . . .'' The milestone of that period is Ungers' own family house in Cologne-Müngersdorf, accurately described by Reyner Banham as a ''manifesto-building.'' Recently altered, the Ungers house retains its original expression of interlocking unfinished volumes, which transform the corner of a typical residential street.

Ungers' formative period was followed by one of intense inquiry. In 1963 he accepted an appointment to the Technische Universität in Berlin, where his students explored diverse critical issues related to the rebuilding of the city, while he investigated the assemblage of disparate forms in such proposals as the Grünzug-Süd in Cologne-Zollstock (1963-66), a museums complex in Berlin-Tiergarten (1964), student housing for the T. H. Twente in Enschede, Holland (1964), and the German Embassy to the Vatican (1965). At Enschede, Ungers proposed a mini-city, replete with singular buildings and city blocks, streets and squares; the embassy project alluded to both the archaeological reality of Rome and the diversity of functions to be housed.

Ungers migrated to the United States to serve as chair of architecture at Cornell University (1969-75). He also hoped to do architecture at a grand scale, a possibility that eluded him throughout his tenure. Still, as Peter Davey and others indicated, this was a very important period in his theoretical development, for the ensuing academic debates between the two philosophical leaders, Ungers and Colin Rowe, helped sharpen Ungers' own position. In challenging Rowe's ''pragmatic/humanism,'' based on a reinterpretation of Camillo Sitte's urbanism linked to Le Corbusier's dogma, Ungers advocated a more critical yet positivist approach, which adamantly relies on alternative interpretations of ''images, metaphors and analogies.'' The proposals for Düren-Nord (1973), the Landwehrkanal area of the Tiergarten in Berlin (1973), housing on Roosevelt Island (1975), the Wallraf-Richartz-Museum (1975), Schlosspark area of Braunschweig (1976), housing in Marburg (1976), Hotel Berlin (1977) and the new Courthouse, Berlin (1978-79) are elaborations of themes that Ungers discussed in a series of essays and further expounded in *Architecture as Theme*.

Ungers' mature period began with his return to Germany. During a six-year period, from 1979 to 1984, Ungers saw a number of major projects come to fruition. In Berlin, where his influence is firmly entrenched as former students Dietrich Bangert, Dieter Frowein, Jürgen Sawade, Hans Kollhoff and others make an impact on its cityscape, Ungers executed an apartment building on Schiller Strasse (1978-79), the Lützowplatz housing, which is part of the International Building Exposition (IBA) (1979-83), and the cluster houses on Miquel Strasse in Grünewald (1980-82). Also completed were a new exposition hall, galleria (1980-83) and high-rise office structure (1983-84) at the Frankfurt fairgrounds; the German Architecture Museum (1979-84); in Bremerhaven, a research center for polar exploration (1980-84); in Karlsruhe, the Baden State Library (1979-84); and in Trier, Konstantinplatz (1981-84).

In each project Ungers investigated morphologies and transformations based on divergent and often conflicting sources. For example, the Baden Library not only refers directly to its context, taking cues from works by Friedrich Weinbrenner, including St. Stephen Church across the street, but to the whole tradition of library buildings, from Henri Labrouste's Bibliothèque Ste.-Geneviève to the British Museum reading room. In Trier the new square regularized the open space adjacent to the Roman emperor Constantine's Aula Palatina, permitting this fourth-century structure to be seen relative to its archaeology, as Ungers incorporated evidence of the various elements that once surrounded the building into the paving, and relied on a new loggia to screen the postwar buildings, thus providing a more controlled backdrop for the new space.

At the beginning of the 1990s, Ungers resolutely continues to depend on the square module to control and restrict his work; this has led to criticism, particularly about predictability of the explorations and how they are translated into built form. But the projects, whether a minor commercial block on Venloer Strasse in Cologne or the gargantuan new buildings for the Frankfurt airport and the Berlin fairgrounds, do reflect positively on the collection of Ungers' executed works and reinforce his place in late-century architecture.

In 1990 Ungers was completing the theoretical and aesthetic circle of his lifelong explorations by adding to his residence in Cologne-Müngersdorf. He has placed a highly rationalistic gray cube, stark and foreboding from the outside, in the garden of the original work. It reiterates the theme of ''house within a house'' and is a literal manifestation of this remarkable architect's professional output. An architectural foundation established by Ungers and his wife Liselotte will be located there, and the new insertion will contain his extensive architectural library: a warm envelope of antiquarian books, providing a place for reflection and the study of architecture.

—GERARDO BROWN-MANRIQUE

UPJOHN, Richard.

British. Born in Shaftesbury, England, 22 January 1802. Died on 17 February 1878. Son was Richard M. Upjohn, architect. Draftsman, Samuel Leonard office, New Bedford, Massachusetts, 1828; assistant, Alexander Parris office, Boston, Massachusetts, 1833; established own firm, Boston; partnership with his son, New York, 1851. President, American Institute of Architects, 1857-76; honorary member, Royal Institute of British Architects.

Chronology of Works
All in the United States
† Work no longer exists

1833-36	Houses, Bangor, Maine
1835	Oaklands, Gardiner, Maine
1835-36	St. John's Church, Bangor, Maine†
1839	Kingscote, Newport, Rhode Island
1840-41	Church of the Ascension, New York City
1841-42	Christ Church, Brooklyn, New York
1841-46	Trinity Church, New York City
1844-46	Church of the Holy Communion, New York City
1844-46	Church of the Pilgrims, Brooklyn, New York
1845	Grace Church, Providence, Rhode Island
1845-46	First Parish Church, Brunswick, Maine
1845-55	Chapel and Library, Bowdoin College, Brunswick, Maine
1846	Christ Church, Norwich, Connecticut
1846	St. Mary's Church, Burlington, New Jersey
1846	Trinity Chapel, New York City
1847	Grace Church, Brooklyn, New York
1847	St. James' Church, New London, Connecticut
1847	St. Mary's Church, South Portsmouth, Rhode Island
1847-49	Calvary Church, Stonington, Connecticut
1848	Chapel of the Cross, Chapel Hill, North Carolina
1848	Christ Church, Raleigh, North Carolina

1849-50	St. Thomas' Church, Amenia, New York
1850-51	St. Paul's Church, Buffalo, New York
1850-51	Zion Church, Rome, New York
1851	Church of St. John-in-the-Wilderness, Copake Falls, New York
1851	St. Paul's Church, Brookline, Massachusetts
1851-53	Church of St. John Chrysostom, Delafield, Wisconsin
1852	Rectory, Christ Church, Easton, Maryland
1852	St. Andrew's, Four Mile Point, Tennessee
1852	Taunton Academy, Taunton, Massachusetts
1853	Christ Church, Binghamton, New York
1853	St. Andrew's Church, Prairieville, Alabama
1853	St. Luke's Church, Martin's Station, Alabama
1854	Christ Church, Elizabeth, New Jersey
1854-56	St. Paul's Church, Baltimore, Maryland
1855-56	Low and White Houses, Pierrepont Place, Brooklyn, New York
1855	All Saints Church, Frederick, Maryland
1857	St. Luke's Church, Clermont, New York
1857	St. Luke's Church, Jacksonville, Alabama
1857	St. Thomas' Church, Taunton, Massachusetts
1859-60	Chapel of St. Mary the Virgin, Nashotah, Wisconsin
1859-60	St. Peter's Church, Albany, New York
1861	Greenwood Cemetery, Brooklyn, New York (entrance lodge)
1861-62	Church of St. Philip-in-the-Highlands, Garrison, New York
1865-67	Central Congregational Church, Boston, Massachusetts
1868-70	St. Thomas' Church, New York City†

Publications

BOOKS BY UPJOHN

Upjohn's Rural Architecture. New York, 1852.

BOOKS ABOUT UPJOHN

ANDREWS, WAYNE: *Architecture, Ambition and Americans.* New York, 1964.

PIERSON, WILLIAM H., JR.: "Richard Upjohn, Trinity Church, and the Ecclesiological Gothic Revival." In *American Buildings and Their Architects: Technology and the Picturesque: The Corporate and Early Gothic Styles.* Garden City, New York, 1978.

STANTON, PHOEBE B.: *The Gothic Revival and American Church.* Baltimore, 1968.

UPJOHN, EVERARD M.: *Richard Upjohn, Architect and Churchman.* New York, 1939.

ARTICLES ABOUT UPJOHN

"American Conference of Architects." *Architect* 5 (1871): 179-180.

"American Institute of Architects." *Crayon* (1857-59) 4:182-183; 5:109-111; 199-201; 6:84-89; 97-100.

CHEROL, JOHN A.: "Kingscote in Newport, Rhode Island." *Antiques* 118 (1980): 476-485.

"Church Architecture in New York." *Architect* 8 (1872): 87-88.

LANCASTER, CLAY: *Old Brooklyn Heights.* Rutland, Vermont, 1961.

"New York Church Architecture." *Putnam's Monthly* 2 (1858): 233-248.

Richard Upjohn: Trinity Church, New York City, New York, 1841-46

PATRICK, J.: "Ecclesiological Gothic in the Antebellum South." *Winterthur Portfolio* 15, No. 2 (1980): 117-138.

UPJOHN, H.: "Architect and Client a Century Ago." *Architectural Record* 74 (1933): 374-382

WARE, WILLIAM R.: "Architecture and Architectural Education in the United States." *Civil Engineer and Architect Journal* 30 (1867): 107-109.

*

Richard Upjohn was the paragon in the development of Gothic Revival architecture in the United States. Through his many church designs—some 100—he epitomized what the Gothic Revival manner should be. His book *Upjohn's Rural Architecture* became the bible for those who followed that style. He not only influenced architects of his era, but laid the foundations for later Victorian architecture in the final decades of the 19th century. Upjohn's underlying credo was that "reality" with "truth" must be at the root of design elements, and that each exterior must be an expression of the structure's interior and, ultimately, the raison d'etre of construction.

The English-born Upjohn moved with his family to Newfoundland in 1808, only to return to England the following year. At the age of 17, he became an apprentice to a cabinetmaker, and it was then that he also began to study architecture. Upjohn continued to be an architect even after he opened a cabinetmaking firm at Dorsetshire. There followed his marriage in 1826, and the birth of a son, Richard Michell Upjohn, who also became an architect.

After numerous financial problems in the cabinet business, Upjohn went to the United States in 1828. He first lived in Manlius, New York, and then moved to New Bedford, Massachusetts, in 1833, where he worked with his brother Aaron as a draftsman. The following year, Upjohn settled in Boston, and became associated with the architectural firm of Alexander Parris. There, he designed two Greek Revival houses in Bangor, Maine (1833-36), which were followed by his first Gothic Revival residence, in Gardiner, Maine (1835). The Gardiner House was eclectic and yet revealed Gothic tastes in a refined, simple and generalized manner. The pronounced influence of the Englishman J. C. Loudon's treatise *Farm and Villa Architecture* (1833) was realized at that time.

Then Upjohn made designs for his first church, St. John's in Bangor, Maine (1835-36). That project initiated his own Gothic Revival style. St. John's was based on English church manuals and many drawings of Gothic churches that Upjohn had done while in England. As a result of the church's success, and through his close association with George Washington Doane, bishop of New Jersey, and J. M. Wainwright, the new rector of Trinity Parish in New York City, Upjohn was commissioned to design a new church for the Episcopal clergy. Thus began his most noted endeavor, Trinity Church, which he began in 1841 and finished five years later. There followed another commission, in 1846, for St. Mary's Church in Burlington, New Jersey. Both Trinity Church and St. Mary's firmly established Upjohn's reputation as the foremost American architect of the Gothic Revival.

An influential source for Upjohn's churches was A. W. N. Pugin's *The True Principles of Pointed or Christian Architecture* (1841)—and especially Plate H in that volume, which showed the "perfect" Gothic church. Upjohn used its spire, tower and even nave elevations as a model. And from Plate K he devised the notion of placing a lofty tower-spire at one end of the longitudinal axis of the nave.

Trinity Church became the paragon of the Gothic Revival. Contemporary architects such as Andrew Jackson Downing praised it; he said, "[It] will stand as far above all other Gothic structures of the kind in this country, as a Raphael's madonna before a tolerable sign painting." Even the noted art critic and poet laureate Edgar Allan Poe remarked in the *Broadway Journal* in 1845, "Trinity Church is a very showy building, and it seems to satisfy the sentiment of the promenaders in Broadway very well."

The following year found Upjohn developing and expanding his theories of the Gothic Revival, and between 1844 and 1850 most of his major churches following that mode were built. It was a time in the United States when the Protestant Episcopal communities flourished financially and their congregations were growing in numbers. During that period, Upjohn designed and had erected 20 small and 17 major churches, as well as academic, commercial and domestic structures.

Initially Upjohn's churches, during that epoch, resembled Trinity Church. Both the Church of the Ascension in New York City (1840-41) and Christ Church in Brooklyn, New York (1841-42), have large tower-spires placed above their facades, and a clarity of overall mass. There followed his Church of the Holy Communion, New York City (1844-46). The theme was a parish church, and it was fashioned after designs recommended by his client, the Rev. W. A. Muhlenberg, via the Cambridge Camden Society of England. The result was a smaller church in scale. It displayed an asymmetrical mass with a characteristic steep-pitched roofline. That church began a new mode of Gothic Revival expression in the United States.

From 1844 to 1846 Upjohn was involved with three structures: the Harvard College Chapel, Cambridge, Massachusetts (designed in 1846, but never built); the Church of the Pilgrims, a Congregational church now known as Our Lady of Lebanon, Brooklyn, New York (1844-46); and the Bowdoin College Chapel and Library, Brunswick, Maine (1845-55). The evolvement of these, especially the Bowdoin College project, resulted in his consultation of books about the English Gothic, such as Greg Möller's *Denkmaler der deutschen Baukunst* (1821) and Thomas Hope's *An Historical Essay on Architecture* (1835). Those volumes ultimately brought about another style within Upjohn's architecture—the Romanesque. The Church of the Pilgrims and the Bowdoin College themes reflected that change, which was further enhanced in 1850 when Upjohn traveled to Europe and saw, firsthand, the Lombard Romanesque. Some observers noted that he seemed more comfortable with the Romanesque, especially in his church interiors, with their complex and heavy roof carpentry.

All of that led to a series of small parish churches. An excellent example was the Calvary Church in Stonington, Connecticut (1847-49), which showed a simple and dignified approach to the Gothic.

In 1852 Upjohn wrote *Rural Architecture*. The book contained designs for "country churches and rural houses." The volume set an example for others to follow as it emphasized good proportion, functional planning, intelligent use of materials, and ecclesiastic ornamentation. The result was a series of modest churches that were made of brick and stone. They were simple in design, and had broach spires and double-pitched roofs. These parishes included St. Thomas Church, America, New York (1849-50); Zion Church, Rome, New York (1850-51); and Christ Church, Elizabeth, New Jersey (1854), among others.

For the next 19 years, Upjohn saw the Gothic Revival change into a so-called "High Victorian" manner. His son, Richard Michell Upjohn, became more dominant in his father's architectural firm. Characteristic of the new style were asymmetrical plans, placement of the tower-spire at one end of the axis, less exterior decoration, double-pitched roofs, and more intricate roof carpentry. Typical were St. Peter's, Albany, New York

(1859-60); St. Philip-in-the-Highlands, Garrison, New York (1861-62); and St. Thomas' Church, New York City (1868-70).

Domestic architecture was also an important part of Upjohn's development. It is known that his firm produced more than 75 residences. The most recognized of these was Kingscote, Newport, Rhode Island (1839). Although its mass was once attributed to the influence of Alexander Jackson Davis, the theme suggests Upjohn's knowledge of Loudon's *Encyclopaedia of Cottage, Farm and Villa Architecture* (1800) as a definite source. However, Upjohn modified Loudon's style as he eliminated the oval entry porch, the servant's wing and an anteroom. He added a bay window and changed the kitchen, and put a bedroom above.

For the most part, Upjohn felt that the Gothic style was more appropriate for churches, and not for residences. He said that Gothic made houses appear like ''mini-castles'' in which the exterior disguises the interior space.

Upjohn became the first president of the American Institute of Architects in 1857, and served in that office until 1875.
—GEORGE M. COHEN

UTZON, Jørn.

Danish. Born in Copenhagen, Denmark, 9 April 1918. Married Lis Fenger, 1942. Studied architecture, under Steen Ejler Rasmussen and Kay Fisker, at the Royal Academy of Arts, Copenhagen, 1937-42; Dip.Arch., 1942. Assistant architect in the offices of Paul Hedquist and Gunnar Asplund, Stockholm, 1942-45, and in the office of Alvar Aalto, Helsinki, 1946; private practice, in Copenhagen, 1950-62, in Sydney, Australia, 1962-66, in the United States, Switzerland, and Denmark, since 1966, and in Mallorca, Spain, since 1972; visiting professor, University of Hawaii, Honolulu, 1971-75. Gold Medal, Royal Institute of British Architects, 1978.

Chronology of Works
All in Denmark unless noted

1952-53	House, Holte, near Copenhagen
1952-53	House, near Lake Fureso
1952-53	Jørn Utzon House, Hellebaek, Copenhagen
1954-60	Housing Estate, Elineberg (with E. Andersson and H. Andersson)
1956-68	Opera House, Sydney, Australia (completed by others in 1973)
1957-60	Kingohusene Housing Estate, near Elsinore
1958	Workers' High School, Hojstrup
1959	Melli Bank, Teheran, Iran
1962-63	Danish Cooperative Building Company Housing Development, Fredensborg
1971-73	Jørn Utzon House (''Can Lis''), Porto Petro, Mallorca, Spain
1971-83	National Assembly Complex, Kuwait
1976	Bagsvaerd Church, Copenhagen
1986	Paustian Furniture Building, Copenhagen

Publications

BOOKS BY UTZON

Sydney Opera House. Sydney, Australia, 1962.
Sydney Opera House (booklet with slides). Venice, California, 1975.
GA 61: Church at Bagsvaerd. Tokyo, 1981.
Jørn Utzon, Houses in Fredensborg. 1991.

ARTICLES BY UTZON

''Eget bus ved Hellebaek, Denmark.'' *Byggekunst* 34 (1952).
''Platforms and Plateaus: Ideas of a Danish Architect.'' *Zodiac* 10 (1962).
''Additive Architecture.'' *Arkitektur* 1 (1970).
''Elements in the Way of Life'' [interview]. *Arkkitehti* 2 (1983).
''Can Lis.'' *Living Architecture* 8 (1989).
''Jørn Utzon on Architecture.'' *Living Architecture* 8 (1989).

BOOKS ABOUT UTZON

Third Generation. Stuttgart, 1972.

ARTICLES ABOUT UTZON

Arkitektur (Copenhagen), special issue 1 (1970).
BOYD, ROBIN: ''Utzon: The End.'' *Architectural Forum* (June 1966).
FRAMPTON, KENNETH: ''Jørn Utzon: Bagsvaerd Church, near Copenhagen, 1973-76.'' *Architectural Design* 52, Nos. 7/8 (1982).
GIEDION, SIGFRIED: ''Jørn Utzon and the Third Generation.'' *Zodiac* 14 (1965).
HELMER-PETERSON, K.: ''Jørn Utzon: A New Personality.'' *Zodiac* 5 (1959).
''Intimations of Tactility: Excerpts from a Fragmentary Polemic.'' *Artforum* (March 1981).
KEYS, PETER, and BREWER, COLIN: ''The Sydney Opera House.'' *Architecture in Australia* (December 1965).
Kokusai Kentiku, special issue (November 1965).
NORBERG-SCHULZ, C.: ''La foresta di Utzon a Copenhagen.'' *Casabella* 54 (December 1990).
Quaderns (Barcelona), special issue on Nordic architects (April/June 1983).
''The Sydney Opera House: A Survivor.'' *American Architects Association Journal* (September 1989).
WINTER, JOHN: ''Utzon at Bagsvaerd.'' *Architectural Review* 165 (1979).
World Architecture, special issue, 15 (1991).

*

The development of modern architecture opened the way for the exploration of many different paths, and in one sense, postmodernism is nothing more than a response to this new freedom. One option was a simple and human approach, which emphasized the relationship of form to the landscape and, thereby, made it possible for a convincing identity of building and place to arise. Jørn Utzon extended modern architecture, but he did so in a characteristically Danish fashion that acknowledged the value of ''cultivated intimacy,'' while building on the broad foundation of the Scandinavian tradition marked out by Gunnar Asplund, Arne Jacobsen and Alvar Aalto.

Utzon confirmed, ''I always start from the very beginning, under the actual conditions of place.'' The architectural forms that result are fresh and anonymous; they reach past style to a quality of trueness. Such forms make place meaningful and, in doing so, come to possess the quality of true things.

The key to Utzon's architecture can be found in his confession, ''. . . It meant a lot to me to grow up around shipyards where my father worked.'' Utzon is at his best when designing buildings close to water, as in his own house on the island of Mallorca or the Sydney Opera House on Sydney Harbour. Furthermore, this empathy with the sea is translated into a more general sympathy for the anonymous genius of nature.

Utzon was born in 1918, the same year as the famous Swedish film director Ingmar Bergman. Unlike Bergman, who is very Scandinavian in his anguish and guilt, in his intensely personal angst, Utzon creates sunlit places where people sense tranquility in a world made whole by the act of building.

By and large, Danish architecture is not noted for its high peaks; rather, it is a plateau of uniformly good design. Utzon is the exception. His is an architecture of world stature and significance, but it is an architecture that remains true to its Danish roots, roots which have been enlarged and deepened by extensive travel and a training that gave to this Danish outlook a universal breadth of vision.

Utzon trained at the Academy of Arts in Copenhagen, where he studied under Kay Fisker and Steen Eiler Rasmussen, commencing in 1937 and qualifying in 1942. Following that, he departed occupied Denmark for Stockholm, and spent the remaining war years (1942-45) working with Gunnar Asplund, who made a lasting impression on him. In 1946 Utzon spent several months in Alvar Aalto's Helsinki studio. In 1947-48 he toured Europe, North Africa and the United States, visiting Taliesin West in Arizona, and Mexico a year later. He established a private practice in Copenhagen in 1950, but, except for his own house at Hellebåk (1952) and a house at Holte outside Copenhagen (1952-53), most of his energy went into competitions.

In 1945 Utzon collaborated with Tobias Faber and Mogens Irming on a scheme for the Crystal Palace Development in London. After 1947 he worked with the Norwegian architect Arne Korsmo on a number of competitions for projects in Morocco, Oslo and elsewhere. He was busy on a housing estate at Elineberg in Denmark with E. and H. Anderson, also the result of a competition, when his entry for the Sydney Opera House was awarded first prize in 1956.

Utzon's own house a Hellebåk, on the southern edge of a woods, is an open pavilion with white walls and a white tiled floor, to which a note of warmth was added by the timber-lined flat roof. Its openness, which was new to Denmark at the time, owed a debt to Frank Lloyd Wright, and especially to the Usonian houses, but it was Wright with a Danish inflection. The house at Holte is more Japanese. There Utzon experimented with the articulation of support and the repetition of elements, a theme he was to develop in the Espansiva timber house in 1969.

The Sydney Opera House remains Utzon's best-known work internationally, and with good reason, even considering the fact that the interiors are quite different from what Utzon had envisioned. There is little doubt that the challenge provided by the project stretched Utzon's creative resources and that he was insufficiently experienced, given the experimental nature of the design. His choice of consulting engineer, though understandable, contributed to the corruption of the competition concept.

The shell forms suggest upturned ships' hulls more than sails. The platform, a product of Utzon's Mexican sojourn, recalls the ceremonial steps of Monte Alban. It has been pointed out that the interior wave-ceilings stem from Aalto's Maison Carrée, but, in the event, Utzon transformed his materials so they took on a new meaning specific to the task in hand. The wave-ceilings were subsequently reused in the church at Bagsvård, where they are even freer and support the roof. Many of the ideas for the Sydney Opera House were reapplied in later schemes (Secondary School at Helsingor, Pavilion Complex of the Copenhagen World's Fair, Theatre in Zurich), with such existential symbols as the earth-platforms and cloud-shells used to connote dwelling.

While he was working on the Sydney Opera House, Utzon completed two remarkable housing complexes: the Kingo

Houses at Helsingor and the houses at Fredensborg, both in North Zeeland. In them, he arranged the house units as serpentine chains around central courts, with the houses strung out along the contours of the site to catch the view. There is something very North African about the forms, recalling the additive cubic grouping of Berber houses clustered around platforms and terraces on the High Atlas. However, the L-shaped courtyard arrangement is more Chinese than Moroccan in inspiration, providing outlook and protection, safe enclosure that is not so confining as to be claustrophobic.

In 1971 Utzon built himself a house, which is actually a progression of four anonymous sandstone pavilions, each with its own distinct orientation depending on the view, on the eastern cliffs of Mallorca near Santanyi. The floors and walls are all made from the same honey-colored stone, with irregular, hand-formed vaulted ceilings. On the outside, deep stone frames isolate and fix the views of the Mediterranean from each room. A feeling of peace and tranquility pervades the complex. It is very much like the Palace of Knossos on Crete, with its simple, trabeated masonry forms and its strong attachment to the sea.

The Bagsvård church, completed in 1976, rises from its suburban surroundings like a simple cluster of farm buildings. The rectilinear silhouette of the gray concrete walls and white tile facing, crowned by triangular skylights that step up and down with the walls, contrasts with the rhythmical freedom of the white off-form sprayed-concrete shell inside. The shell surges back and forth in a series of voluptuous swoops and crests coinciding with the 2.2-meter module of supporting elements, before shooting upward in the main meeting hall in a narrow neck that curls over to hide the light source.

At about that time, Utzon won the international competition for the Kuwait National Assembly Complex (1971-79), which was not finished until 1983. The complex consists of two buildings designed to evoke the freedom of a bedouin tent, and to conform to the traditional mode in which Arabs conduct business. The roof of the assembly is draped like a huge concrete tarpaulin, falling in concave folds and mounted along each edge on rounded concrete pylons 15 stories high. It is characteristic of Utzon that he should have chosen vernacular motifs for his Kuwait National Assembly, because it was long considered by English writers and poets in the 19th-century that vernacular speech revealed the genius of a place.

Utzon learned from the places he visited: the Mediterranean, North Africa, Mexico, China. Frequently they were old places on which mankind had left a human imprint. From these experiences he learned about the effect of density, the function of a wall, and other simple, important lessons for the architect. His adoption of an anonymous vernacular-inspired vocabulary has established a closer relationship between his forms and landscape. Because landscape is always different, his architecture is assured of a freshness and uniqueness that are impossible whenever architecture, as happens in mannerism and postmodernism, is reduced to self-consciously repeating itself.

That, finally, may be his greatest contribution to the architecture of this century—the rediscovery of nature and simplicity—in a search for wholeness.

—PHILIP DREW

VALADIER, Giuseppe.

Italian. Born in Rome, Italy, 14 April 1762. Died in Rome, 1 February 1839. Father and grandfather were silversmiths. Studied at the Accademia di San Lucas, Rome. Appointment to the Vatican as *architetto dei sacri palazzi*, 1781; *architetto camerale*, 1786.

Chronology of Works
All in Italy

1784	Villa Pianciani, Terraja (casino and church)
1789	San Crescentino, Urbino (restoration)
1800-18	Villa Poniatowski, Rome
1805	Ponte Milvio, Rome (restoration and reconstruction)
1806	San Pantaleo, Rome (facade)
1811-24	Piazza del Popolo, Cesena
1814-22	Santa Cristina, Cesena
1819-21	Arch of Titus, Rome (restoration)
1819-22	Teatro Valle, Rome (reconstruction)
1820	Colosseum, Rome (restoration)
1823-39	Collegiate Church, Monsampietrangeli (not completed until 1869)
1826-29	Santa Maria ai Monti, Rome (restoration)
1828-29	Sant'Andrea in Via Flaminia, Rome (restoration)
1829-35	Temple of Fortuna Virilis, Rome (restoration)
1832	Palazzo Lezzani, Rome (facade)
1834	San Rocco, Rome (facade)

Publications

BOOKS BY VALADIER

Progetti architettonici. 1807.
Opere di architettura. 1833.

BOOKS ABOUT VALADIER

HOFFMANN, PAOLA: *Il Monte Pincio e la Casina Valadier.* Rome, 1967.
MARCONI, PAOLO: *Giuseppe Valadier.* Rome, 1964.
SCHULZE-BATTMANN, E.: *Valadier, ein klassizistischer Architekt Roms.* Dresden, 1939.

*

Giuseppe Valadier was an Italian architect at the end of the 18th century and in the early years of the 19th century. Perhaps the most important figure in what is considered the second generation of neoclassical architects, Valadier was extremely influential on later architects such as Ippolito Cremona and Antonio Serra.

Valadier was born in Rome, of a family originally from France, and educated there at the Accademia di San Luca. His father had worked for Pope Pius VI, and by the time Giuseppe was only 20 years old, he too was employed by the pope; he was appointed *architetto dei sacri palazzi* in 1781 and, five years later, *architetto camerale.* His most significant project there was the restoration in 1789 of the Cathedral of Urbino, damaged a few years earlier in an earthquake. It was also at that time that he worked on the Palazzo Braschi in Rome, although the design as a whole was probably laid out by Cosimo Morelli. In 1798 the French occupied Rome, and when the pope was forced to flee, Valadier—with his French background—was involved in various activities for them. But by 1800 the new pope, Pius VII, had returned to Rome, and Valadier was recalled as architect in charge of the offices of the Tiber.

He was also busy working for private clients, among them the Torlonia family, for whom in 1806 he built the facade of San Pantaleone, one of his first important designs. It was based on the work of Andrea Palladio, but the rusticated forms extend across an arch around a thermal window above the main door in a way that, in its simplicity, is neoclassical rather than Renaissance or Mannerist. A similar simplicity of forms is also to be seen in his work on the reconstruction of the Ponte Milvio, after severe floods. Taking up the forms there—a simple block with a rusticated arch, surmounted by a second block—Valadier emphasized the massiveness, leaving out any hint of orders; he thus made the whole, in the manner of John Vanbrugh or Claude-Nicolas Ledoux, though without their daring, severe and strong. Windows were allowed only in the upper zone.

In 1810 Valadier was named one of the *direttori dei lavori pubblici di beneficenza.* In the following years he worked on the restoration and systematizing of the Forum, the Colosseum and other areas of Rome, but most important were the Piazza della Rotonda and the Piazza di Trevi; he also supervised the demolition of the Palazetto Venezia and of the *spina* at the Vatican. Valadier included all of that work, and his various other restorations, in a series of volumes he wrote with the help of Filippo Aurelio Visconti, the *Raccolta delle più insigni fabbriche di Roma antica e sue adiacenze* (1813-26).

Valadier's work around the Piazza del Popolo was undoubtedly his most important contribution to urban design. It had been suggested by Leone Pacoli already in 1733 that a church be built at that site to match the Church of Santa Maria del Popolo, and that some buildings be erected to create a cross axis for the piazza. Valadier continued with that idea when in 1793 he proposed that barracks for the papal cavalry and infantry be placed at the east and west sides of the square. Little was done at that time, but in 1811 Valadier elaborated his scheme for the French Commission des Embellissements, parts of which were adapted by the designer Louis Marie Berthault. In 1814, with the return of the pope, the project began again, with Valadier incorporating in his plans the work of Pascoli and Berthault, systematizing the four angles of the piazza and combining the lateral axes with ramps. The south corner of the piazza was embellished with large apartments built for speculation by Giovanni Torlonia and Giuseppe Valenti, the 16th-century fountain in the center was removed and replaced, and a monastery was built on the site of the cloister of the Church of Santa Maria del Popolo. On the other side of the square were built some barracks, the Caserna dei Cherubbinieri. All of this work was completed by 1824.

Further up the Pincian hill, Valadier built the so-called Casino Valadier, a *caffé,* like the famous Caffé Pedrocchi by Giuseppe Japelli in Padua. In this interesting and lively building, each of three different elevations expresses a different function: one for the entrance, one for the terrace, and one for the two sides. The main block rests on a wide terrace, set above loggias in the Doric order. The terrace itself is ringed by what are called "idle" columns of polished granite, set on travertine bases, supporting urns. The whole building is full of detail, inside and out, which the architecture historian Carroll Meeks has characterized as being at once eclectic, picturesque and neoclassical.

In 1818 Valadier was named *ispettore del consiglio d'arte per le fabbriche camerali,* and it was in that role that he worked on the restoration of a number of important ancient buildings, among them the Colosseum (1820) and the Arch of Titus (1819-21). In 1824 he worked on the rebuilding of the Church of San Paolo fuori le Mura, though his design was in the end replaced, after much criticism, by one from Pasquale Belli. Beyond that, Valadier also restored the churches of San Martino ai Monti (1826-29) and Sant'Andrea in Via Flaminia (1828-29), and the Temple of Fortuna Virilis (1829-35). His most important private commissions of that time included the design of the Palazzo Lezzani (1832) on the Via del Corso and the facade of the Church of San Rocco (1834), a rich, almost-Palladian design which was his last work.

Valadier continued publishing his work, too. In 1828 he began the publication of the lectures he had given at the Accademia di San Luca, *L'Architettura Practica,* and in 1838 he published a volume on the building of the Accademia itself, *Cenni sull'origine e sulle stato attuale della insigne Accademia di S. Luca.*

—DAVID CAST

VANBRUGH, John.

British. Born in London, England, January 1664. Died in Whitehall, 26 March 1726. Married Henrietta Maria Yarburgh. Worked for William Matthews in the wire trade, London, 1681; marine captain, 1692; comptroller of His Majesty's Works, 1702; surveyor of gardens and waters, 1716; also worked independently as an architect and was active as a dramatist.

Chronology of Works
All in England
* Approximate dates
† Work no longer exists

1700-12	Castle Howard, Yorkshire
1701	Vanbrugh House, Whitehall, London†
1704-05	Queen's Theatre in the Haymarket (Opera House), London†
1705-16	Blenheim Palace, Oxfordshire (completed by the Duchess of Marlborough and Nicholas Hawksmoor, 1722-25)
1707-10	Kimbolton Castle, Huntingdon (rebuilding)
1708	Audley End, Essex (staircase and screen)
1709-10	Chargate, Surrey†
1710*-14	Kings Weston, Avon
1714	Obelisk, Castle Howard, Yorkshire
1715-20	Claremont, Surrey (mostly†)
1716-17	Great Kitchen, St. James's Palace, London
1718	Pumphouse, Windsor [attributed]
1718-21*	Vanbrugh Castle, Greenwich
1718-26	Eastbury, Dorset†
1719	Pyramid Gate, Castle Howard, Yorkshire
1719*-24	Stowe, Buckinghamshire (rotunda, portico on north front, additions to the house and garden buildings)†
1719-25	Vanbrugh Fields Estate, Greenwich†
1720*	Wellhouse, Skelbrooke, Yorkshire [attributed]
1720-28	Seaton Delaval, Northumberland
1721-22	Lumley Castle, Durham (refacing and remodeling north range)
1722	Somersby Hall, Lincolnshire
1722	Water Tower, Kensington Palace, London [attributed]†
1722-26	Grimsthorpe Castle, Lincolnshire (north range)
1723-25	Newcastle Pew, Esher Old Church, Surrey
1725-26	Temple, Castle Howard, Yorkshire (not completed until 1728)

Publications

BOOKS BY VANBRUGH

The Complete Works. Edited by Bonany Dobrée and Geoffrey F. Webb. London, 1927-28.

John Vanbrugh: Blenheim Palace, Oxfordshire, England, 1705-16

BOOKS ABOUT VANBRUGH

BARMAN, CHRISTIAN: *Sir John Vanbrugh*. 1924.

BEARD, GEOFFREY: *The Work of Sir John Vanbrugh*. London, 1986.

CAMPBELL, COLEN: *Vitruvius Britannicus*. 1715-25. Reprint, New York, 1967.

COLVIN, H. M. (ed.): *The History of the King's Works: V. 1660-1782*. London, 1976.

COLVIN, H. M. and CRAIG, MAURICE J. (eds.): *Architectural Designs in the Library of Elton Hall by Sir John Vanbrugh and Sir Edward Lovett Pearce*. Oxford, 1964.

DOWNES, KERRY: *English Baroque Architecture*. London, 1966.

DOWNES, KERRY: *Vanbrugh*. London, 1977.

DOWNES, KERRY: *Sir John Vanbrugh: A Biography*. London, 1987.

GREEN, DAVID: *Blenheim Palace*. London, 1951.

HUSSEY, CHRISTOPHER: *English Gardens and Landscapes, 1700-1750*. London, 1967.

SERVICE, ALASTAIR: *The Architects of London*. London, 1979.

STREET, A. E.: *Sir John Vanbrugh*. 1891.

WARD, W.: *Sir John Vanbrugh*. 2 vols. London, 1893.

WHISTLER, LAURENCE: *Sir John Vanbrugh, Architect and Dramatist*. London, 1938.

WHISTLER, LAURENCE: *The Imagination of Vanbrugh and his Fellow Artists*. London, 1954.

ARTICLES ABOUT VANBRUGH

CAST, DAVID: "Seeing Vanbrugh and Hawksmoor." *Journal of the Society of Architectural Historians* 43 (December 1984): 310-327.

DOWNES, KERRY: "The Kings Weston Book of Drawings." *Architectural History* 10 (1967): 7-88.

ESDAILE, K. A.: "Sir John Vanbrugh: Some New Historical Facts." *Architect and Building News* (26 March 1926).

HUSEBOE, ARTHUR R.: "Vanbrugh: Additions to the Correspondence." *Philological Quarterly* 53 (1974): 135-40.

KIMBALL, FISKE: "Romantic Classicism in Architecture." *Gazette des Beaux-Arts* Period 6, 25 (1944): 95-112.

LANG, S.: "Vanbrugh's Theory and Hawksmoor's Buildings." *Journal of the Society of Architectural Historians* 24, No. 2 (1965).

McCORMICK, FRANK: "John Vanbrugh's Architecture: Some Sources of His Style." *Journal of the Society of Architectural Historians* 46 (June 1987): 135-144.

ROSENBERG, ALBERT: "New Light on Vanbrugh." *Philological Quarterly* 45 (1966): 603-613.

*

John Vanbrugh, an English architect active in the early 18th century, is most famous as the designer of Castle Howard and Blenheim Palace, two of the grandest and most beautiful buildings in England, yet he is now recognized also for his more modest, more eccentric buildings like Seaton Delaval, Northumberland, and Vanbrugh Castle, Greenwich. His work is rich, complex and often, as John Summerson said of Seaton Delaval, "breathtakingly exaggerated"; many of the later comments about Vanbrugh's designs show how difficult it has been for people to comprehend and like them. And while, like his colleague Nicholas Hawksmoor, he seems never to have lacked work, his whole career was marked by personal and artistic disputes, the most remarkable of those being the arguments that led to his dismissal by the duchess of Marlborough from Blenheim in 1716.

In the years immediately after his death, Lord Burlington and the architects associated with the neo-Palladian movement continually condemned his work and called into question his experience as an architect, his taste and the principles of his design. He used not only forms that were classical in origin—something the neo-Palladians approved of—but elements that alluded to the details of older Gothic and Elizabethan architecture, which were to the other architects completely inappropriate and incorrect. The words used to criticize Vanbrugh's architecture were of a piece: that it was ugly, incoherent and mixed in its forms, or, most interestingly, that it was ponderous, a word that carried with it, beyond any literal significance, a sense of deviating from the truth and order of classical architecture. There were always individual artists who appreciated the forms and effects of Vanbrugh's architecture, like Joshua Reynolds and John Soane. But most people found it unattractive and irritating, and if a building like Blenheim was spared (because it was so public a memorial), there could always be talk—as there was at Grimsthorpe in 1809—of pulling down what Vanbrugh had done and restoring that part to the older style of the house.

It was not until the turn of the 20th century and the attention of Edwin Lutyens that there emerged a more general appreciation of what Vanbrugh had done, based on the very qualities in his work for which earlier he had been condemned. Even so, his house in Whitehall was demolished in 1901. That, however, was the beginning of his restoration. Since then Vanbrugh has been praised by contemporary architects like Robert Venturi, James Stirling and Peter Smithson, and even if this acknowledgment followed the earlier critical and scholarly investigations by Laurence Whistler and Kerry Downes, it has served to establish—in ways that cannot now be shaken an account of Vanbrugh as being, like Hawksmoor, one of the greatest architects of England—inventive, dramatic and highly moral.

Vanbrugh had a rich and interesting life. Born in 1664, his father was the son of a merchant from Haarlem (who had fled Flanders a generation earlier), and his mother was the youngest daughter of Sir Dudley Carleton. Nothing is known of his early life until 1681, when he was recorded as working in London. In 1686 he received a commission in the army with the earl of Huntingdon, and in 1688 he was arrested in France and imprisoned for four years, in Calais first, then at Vincennes, and finally in the Bastille. After his release in 1692 he served in the army once again, in 1698 resuming his position with the earl of Huntingdon.

While in prison in France, however, Vanbrugh had made himself a playwright, and in 1696 his work *The Relapse, or Virtue in Danger,* was produced in London with great success; it was followed, a year later, by the play *The Provok'd Wife,* which was equally successful. In 1704 Vanbrugh built for himself the Queen's Theatre in the Haymarket. This was not a success, and the taste for Vanbrugh's plays was slipping. But by then so too had his interests.

We do not know how he obtained the commission for his first building, Castle Howard, except that it came to him from his social connections with the aristocracy, and especially perhaps from his membership of the Kit-Cat Club, a group of Whigs, of which the earl of Carlisle was also a member.

In 1702, doubtless from these same connections, Vanbrugh was made comptroller of the Royal Works, displacing William Talman, and becoming then the principal colleague of Christopher Wren at the Board of Works. Vanbrugh held that position until his dismissal in 1713 by the new Tory government. However, the Whigs returned, and in 1714 he was restored to the comptrollership, a position he managed to retain—even after both Wren and Hawksmoor had been dismissed from their offices—until the year of his death.

Castle Howard was Vanbrugh's first great work. There he was able to establish the rich, mixed and yet slightly discordant style of architecture he was to work with all his life. But it was in 1704 that he obtained his most important commission, that for the design of Blenheim Palace, near Woodstock, the great monument to England's recent victories over France. Blenheim was an extraordinary tour de force, full of the richest and most inventive architectural ideas. It moved in its styles from the grand, almost French, character of the main north front to the somber articulation on the garden front, and from that to the kitchen court, where double columns, rusticated and surmounted by the lion of old England, stand out in front of an almost totally plain range of windows and portholes, and to the tower at the center with its sequence of arches and reversed volutes ending in four Egyptian pilasters that stand, almost precariously, on four cut stone balls.

The story of the designing of Blenheim was punctuated by arguments and disputes, and in the end much of what is there was put up under the eye of Nicholas Hawksmoor, who, as so often, worked on the site as Vanbrugh's supervisor and professional adviser. Much was always made of Vanbrugh's lack of practical experience, to which many of his critics ascribed what they saw as the failure of Vanbrugh's work. He had read all the proper treatises, however, and was already an artist, if in another medium. Indeed, it was perhaps that very lack of practical experience that might have encouraged him in his inventions and in the way he was able to embody in his designs qualities of effect or feeling that could be found in other realms of art, but were not so openly enunciated in earlier English architecture. His work was often called inconvenient, a term seemingly of practical criticism, but one also about artistic qualities, suggesting a deviation from the order and convenience of true classical architecture.

Vanbrugh designed or rebuilt a number of large houses: at Audley End, Eastbury, Kimbolton, King's Weston, Grimsthorpe and Seaton Delaval. All of them, for all their variations, were intended to capture what Vanbrugh himself, speaking of Kimbolton, called "the Castle Air," or the idea of what he also called "a Noble and Masculine Shew." Details and plans were shot through with historical and affective associations that invited a response quite different from anything intended by Inigo Jones or William Talman before him, or Lord Burlington later. Vanbrugh's smaller designs were similarly original, such as the "Goose-pie House" in Whitehall, or the Belvedere Tower and White Cottage at Claremont, or the various buildings at Greenwich; in these he often used plain brick instead of the more usual stone, freer placements of elements like battlements or oversized keystones, and in some of the plans for these and other projects we can even find the suggestion of an asymmetry that architecture, since the Renaissance, had banished from the world. In the work done when he was supervisor for the Board of Ordnance at the Royal Arsenal, Greenwich, and at Chatham, Plymouth and Upnor—a position he obtained in 1716, probably through the offices of the duke of Marlborough—we see in the simple, plain style and the unashamed use of brick a form of building that would flower in the later 18th and early 19th centuries in the warehouses of designers like D. A. Alexander and Edward L'Anson. But that was not all.

Vanbrugh was not himself a landscape gardener, but he was involved in the planning of two great estates, at Stowe and at Castle Howard, which became renowned both for their plans and their plantings, and for the buildings so carefully and artfully placed within them. In his houses, Vanbrugh could be called an architect of associationism; in his work at Castle Howard and at Stowe he may be seen also as one of the first proponents of what was to be later called the picturesque landscape, England's greatest contribution to the art of Europe.

For all his social activity and correspondence, Vanbrugh spoke very little of his work. And it is perhaps only from a comment Hawksmoor made about one of Vanbrugh's designs for a garden building at Castle Howard that we can begin to understand what Vanbrugh thought of the manner of his architecture. Hawksmoor praised Vanbrugh for having used in that design what he called "Strong Reason" and "Good Fancy"; if the word "Reason" is not unusual in such a context, the use of the term "Fancy," governed or not by the adjective "Good," is interesting and important. What it suggests, as it did also for Hawksmoor, is a connection, however direct or indirect, to a set of artistic concerns and opinions spoken of a few years earlier by the philosopher Thomas Hobbes. Hobbes knew of the Renaissance account of art, that it was the product of Judgment, a reasoning faculty. But materialist as he was, Hobbes came to think of art not so much as the imitation of an idea as much as a mere resemblance, and based then not on reason alone but on the irrational, constitutive faculty of Fancy, which ranged, as he put it, "as a spaniel does over the fields," tracking the forms of art for their meanings and tying what it sees to any number of accidental associations and allusions. It was this, rather than the principles of propriety and order, that encouraged Vanbrugh to embody in what he built something of the forms and associations of the older country houses of England that would suggest to all who saw them what Samuel Johnson was later to call an "historical meditation." This effect, also described by contemporary antiquarians like William Stukeley and Peter le Neve, could be seen in the placement of a large hall at the center of the house, as it had been in medieval buildings; or it was suggested, as at Grimsthorpe, by the placing of a set of portraits in the main room that commemorated the kings of England who had granted lands and titles to the family that owned the house; or it could be embodied in details like battlements or even in a certain looseness in the plan that might recall the gradual, sprawling character of some of the old houses of England, where dwelt—as writers from Jonson to Pope to Jonas Hanway were to proclaim—the true old national virtues of England.

Vanbrugh married only later in life, and he had two sons, one of whom died in infancy, the other at the Battle of Fontenoy in 1745. Vanbrugh's wife, Henrietta Maria, the daughter of Colonel Yarburgh of Heslington Hall, Yorkshire, lived on until 1776, and it was perhaps through her efforts that some of his designs and papers were preserved; the largest collection of his designs is at the Victoria and Albert Museum in London and at Elton Hall in Huntingdonshire, his papers being largely at the Borthwick Institute of Historical Research at York.

—DAVID CAST

VAN BRUNT, Henry.

American. Born in Boston, Massachusetts, 1832. Died in Milton, Massachusetts, 8 April 1903. Educated at Latin School, Boston; graduated, Harvard College, 1854. Partner, Ware and Van Brunt firm, Boston; Department of Architecture chair, Massachusetts Institute of Technology, 1881; partner, with Frank Howe, Van Brunt and Howe, Kansas City, Missouri, 1886. Organizer, Boston Society of Architects, American Institute of Architects; secretary, American Institute of Architects, 1861; Fellow, American Institute of Architects, 1864; president, American Institute of Architects, 1899.

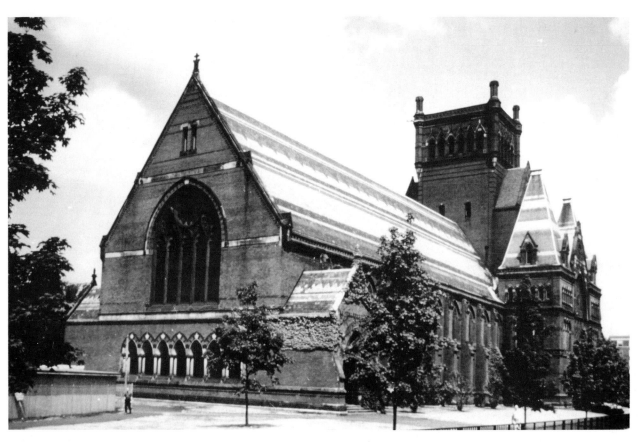

Henry Van Brunt: Memorial Hall, Harvard University, Cambridge, Massachusetts, 1865-78

Chronology of Works
All in the United States
† Work no longer exists

Ware and Van Brunt:

1865-78	Memorial Hall, Harvard University, Cambridge, Massachusetts
1869	First Church, Boston, Massachusetts
1869	Hotel Hamilton, Boston, Massachusetts
1869-80	Episcopal Theological School Buildings, Cambridge, Massachusetts
1871-72	Weld Hall, Harvard University, Cambridge, Massachusetts
1872	St. John's Parish House, Charlestown, Massachusetts
1874	Union Railway Station, Worcester, Massachusetts†
1876-77	Gore Hall (stack addition), Harvard University Library, Cambridge, Massachusetts†
1880	St. Stephen's Church, Lynn, Massachusetts
1880-81	Stone Hall, Wellesley, Massachusetts†
1881-82	Simpson Infirmary, Wellesley, Massachusetts

Henry Van Brunt:

1881-83	University of Michigan Library, Ann Arbor, Michigan†
1882	Billings Music Hall, Wellesley, Massachusetts
1883	Building for Harvard Medical School, Cambridge, Massachusetts
1883	Van Brunt House, Cambridge, Massachusetts

Van Brunt and Howe:

1886-88	Union Pacific Station, Ogden, Utah
1886-88	Union Pacific Station, Cheyenne, Wyoming
1887-89	Rindge Public Library, Cambridge, Massachusetts
1888-89	Kansas City Club, Kansas City, Missouri†
1889	Emery, Bird, Thayer Building, Kansas City, Missouri
1889	Union Station, Lawrence, Kansas
1889-90	Coates House Hotel, Kansas City, Missouri†
1892-93	Electricity Building, World's Columbian Exposition, Chicago, Illinois†
1893	Union Station, Portland, Oregon
1893-94	Kansas City Star Building, Kansas City, Missouri†
1893-94	Spooner Library, Lawrence, Kansas
1895-96	August Meyer House, Kansas City, Missouri
1899	Union Station, Omaha, Nebraska†
1901	S. B. Armour House, Kansas City, Missouri

Publications

BOOKS BY VAN BRUNT

Discources on Architecture. Translation of text by Viollet-le-Duc. 2 vols. Boston, 1875-1881.
Greek Lines. Boston, 1893.
Architecture and Society: Selected Essays of Henry Van Brunt. Edited by William Coles. Cambridge, Massachusetts, 1969.

ARTICLES ABOUT VAN BRUNT

COLES, WILLIAM A.: "Richard Morris Hunt and His Library as Revealed in the Studio Sketchbooks of Henry Van Brunt." *Art Quarterly* 30 (1967): 224-238

HENNESSEY, WILLIAM JOHN: "The Architectural Works of Henry Van Brunt." Ph.D. dissertation. Columbia University, New York, 1979.

PILAND, SHERRY: "Henry Van Brunt of the Architectural Firm of Van Brunt and Howe: The Kansas City Years." M. A. thesis, University of Missouri, Kansas City, Missouri, 1976.

WIGHT, PETER B.: "Henry Van Brunt: Architect, Writer, Philosopher." *Inland Architect and News Record* 23 (1894).

*

In post-Civil-War Boston, when thriving building activity allowed for numerous architectural firms, that of William Robert Ware and Henry Van Brunt had a large share of the business. Their architecture followed the stylistic trends of the times. Their most famous building was one of their earliest: Memorial Hall (1865-78) for Harvard University. Although it is now considered among America's most notable monuments to Ruskinian High Victorian Gothic style, Van Brunt himself, in his Classical Revival phase, regarded it with some ambivalence. After Ware moved to New York and the firm dissolved in 1883, Van Brunt designed some buildings alone, then moved to Kansas City, Missouri, in 1887 to join his new partner, a former employee, Frank Howe (1849-1909). Van Brunt and Howe, which lasted until Van Brunt's death in 1903, became the leading architectural firm west of the Mississippi, with the Union Pacific Railroad as one of its biggest clients, and was the only firm west of Chicago (of five non-Chicago firms) invited to design a building for the World's Columbian Exposition in 1893.

Architectural criticism and peer review were also in their heyday, and Van Brunt actively participated in the movements for architectural education and formation of professional organizations. Around the time that his firm was awarded the Memorial Hall commission in 1865, Van Brunt announced his desire to translate Eugène-Emmanuel Viollet-Le-Duc's *Discourses on Architecture,* which was finally completed in 1881. Like his associate, Ware, Van Brunt's articles and books on architectural criticism were widely read and well regarded.

Ware and Van Brunt attended Harvard College within two years of each other (classes of 1852 and 1854). Both also later separately attended the atelier of Richard Morris Hunt in New York City and began their own apprentice workshop based on the French model, soon after establishing their firm in 1863. Two years later, Ware was invited to form the first professional school of architecture in the United States for the Massachusetts Institute of Technology, which was then in Boston's newly filled Back Bay, and served as its first dean. (He instituted the French atelier system, which spread to other cities' nascent architectural educational institutions, and in 1881 he was asked to form the sixth such school for Columbia University in New York City. Again, he served as its dean.)

Two of Ware and Van Brunt's earliest buildings were the First Church and Hotel Hamilton (both 1869), also in Back Bay. The firm soon became Harvard's favored architects, designing not only Memorial Hall but Weld Hall (1871) and the east wing to Gore Hall (1876-77), the library of Harvard College, which employed French architect Henri Labrouste's stack construction for the first time in America. For the Episcopal Theological School, near Harvard, the firm designed St. John's Chapel (1868) and a quadrangle of buildings reminiscent of a "Flemish village" (1872-80). Additional clients included Episcopal parishes in Massachusetts: St. Stephen's Church, Lynn (1880); St.

John's Parish House, Charlestown (1872); Grace Church, New Bedford; and Stone Hall and Simpson Infirmary at Wellesley College (1880). Ware and Van Brunt also designed houses in and around Boston and in summer communities such as Manchester, Beverly and Gloucester, Massachusetts.

After Ware moved to New York, Van Brunt himself designed Billings Music Hall for Wellesley College (1882), the first building for Harvard Medical School in Boston (1883), and his own Queen Anne house on fashionable Brattle Street in Cambridge (1883).

The commission to Ware and Van Brunt from Charles Francis Adams for the Union Station in Worcester, Massachusetts, in 1874 led to commissions for Van Brunt's subsequent partnership with Howe. Although the predominance of commissions were for buildings in Kansas City such as the Emery, Bird, Thayer Building (1889) and the Kansas City Star Building (1893), the firm turned out numerous passenger terminals for Adams' Union Pacific Railroad: Ogden, Utah (1886); Cheyenne, Wyoming (1886); Lawrence, Kansas (1889); Portland, Oregon (1893); and Omaha, Nebraska (1899). They produced libraries for the University of Michigan and Lawrence, Kansas, as well as hotels and residences. But contact was also maintained in Massachusetts: the H.H. Richardson-inspired Rindge Public Library in Cambridge (1887-89), the Dedham Public Library (1888), and another Episcopal Church (Emanuel) in Shelburne Falls.

Most of Van Brunt's writings were published during those years—articles for *Inland Architect, Architectural Review, Atlantic Monthly,* and two books, *Greek Lines and Other Architectural Essays,* and *Growth of Characteristic Architectural Style in the United States.* William A. Coles credits him with "analytical cogency and historical awareness." However, Van Brunt's writings merely represented the more liberal architectural opinions of his day rather than presenting any cogent or confident architectural criticism, and William A. Jordy also faults Van Brunt's writings for "convoluted abstraction" and for not expressing the lessons of his own practical experience. To Jordy, Van Brunt's opinion in 1899 that Memorial Hall might have had a better chance for permanent standing as a work of art if it had been designed with classical and academic influences is "a perfect paradigm of the shift in conventionally enlightened critical opinion from 1860 through 1890."

Harvard's Gore Hall, with its east wing designed by Ware and Van Brunt, was torn down many years ago. But the historic preservation movement begun in the late 1960s saved Van Brunt and Howe's Union Pacific Depot in Lawrence, Kansas from demolition in 1987. After a period of disfavor and even ambivalence of its worth on Van Brunt's part, and having been called cautiously the "largest and most conspicuous of mature High Victorian Gothic edifices in America" by Henry-Russell Hitchcock, Ware and Van Brunt's Memorial Hall has just undergone extensive restoration of its exterior and stained glass; and after many years of prevailing opinion that the effort was misguided, plans are now under way to replace the tower destroyed by fire in 1956. Originally set on the edge of an open triangle, Memorial Hall was enhanced in the 1970s by the construction of a grassed-over vehicular underpass. Van Brunt's doubts, expressed at the height of the enthusiasm for Classical Revival style, have proved unfounded.

—BETTINA A. NORTON

VAN CAMPEN, Jacob.

Dutch. Born in Haarlem, Netherlands, 1595. Died in 1657. Trained as a painter. Associate of the Dutch humanist Constantijn Huygens.

Jacob Van Campen: Royal Palace (formerly Town Hall), Amsterdam, Netherlands, 1648-55

Chronology of Works

All in the Netherlands
* Approximate dates
† Work no longer exists

1625	Huis Coymans, 177 Keizersgracht, Amsterdam†
1633	Girls' Court, Municipal Orphanage, Amsterdam
1633*	Mauritshuis, The Hague
1638	Accijnshuis, Amsterdam
1638-46	St. Laurens Church, Alkmaar (organ case)
1639-40	Marekerk, Leiden (windows and portico; with Arent van's Gravesande)
1640	Noordeinde Palace, The Hague (rebuilding)
1641-43	Hofwijck, Voorburg (with Constantijn Huygens)
1645-49	Nieuwe Kerk, Haarlem
1648-55	Town Hall, Amsterdam (now Royal Palace, Amsterdam; not completed until 1665)
1655	Laurenskerk (chairs), Alkmaar

Publications

BOOKS ABOUT VAN CAMPEN

FREMANTLE, KATHARINE: *The Baroque Town Hall of Amsterdam.* Utrecht, 1959.
KUYPER, W.: *Dutch Classicist Architecture: A Survey of Dutch Architecture, Gardens, and Anglo-Dutch Relations from 1625 to 1700.* Delft, 1980.
ROSENBERG, JAKOB; SLIVE, SEYMOUR; and TER KUILE, E. H.: *Dutch Art and Architecture 1600-1800.* Harmondsworth, England, 1977.
SWILLENS, P. T. A.: *Jacob van Campen: Schilder en bouwmeester.* Assen, Holland, 1961.
VERMEULEN, FRANS A. J.: *Handboek tot de Geschiedenis der Nederlandsche Bouwkunst.* 3 vols. The Hague, 1928-41.

ARTICLES ABOUT VAN CAMPEN

KLUIVER, J. H.: "De orgelarchitectuur van Jacob van Campen." *Koninklijke nederlandse oudheidkundige bond-bulletin* 73, No. 1 (1974): 1-18.
MEISCHKE, R.: "Amsterdams Burgerweeshuis." *Nederlandse monumenten van geschiedenis en kunst* (1975): 182-183.
MEISCHKE, R.: "De vroegste werken van Jacob van Campen." *Koninklijke nederlandse oudheidkundige bond-bulletin* 65, No. 5 (1966): 131-145.
TERWEN, J. J.: "The Buildings of Johan Maurits van Nassau." In E. VAN DEN BOOGART (ed.): *Johan Maurits van Nassau-Siegen, 1604-1679: A Humanist Prince in Europe and Brazil.* The Hague, 1979.
WEISSMAN, A. W.: "Jacob van Campen." *Oud Holland* 20 (1902).

*

Jacob van Campen, though trained as a painter, became the leading architect of the mid-17th-century classicizing phase of the Dutch Baroque period. His version of the classical Baroque came to symbolize the new independence of the Republic of the United Netherlands when it gained its legal freedom from Spain in 1648. In that same year his masterpiece, the Town Hall in Amsterdam (now the Royal Palace), was begun.

Van Campen, who came from an aristocratic background, was a friend of Constantijn Huygens, a well-known humanist and secretary to the stadtholder, Frederick Henry. Huygens traveled widely and was in constant personal and literary communication with scientific and humanist circles in France and England. He displayed a thorough layman's knowledge through firsthand contact with contemporary architecture in northern European cities. Van Campen must have gained a window on the world through his friend, for, aside from mention in an unreliable source of a trip to Rome, he does not seem to have traveled. Classicizing ideas in architecture were available to van Campen through a variety of sources, especially publications. Van Campen apparently consulted the widely circulated books on architectural theory written by Sebastiano Serlio, Andrea Palladio and Vincenzo Scamozzi. Prints of buildings constructed everywhere in Europe were also widely available. In fact, his designs seem to be derived from classicizing sources rather than from particular antique buildings. They also exhibit a strong northern cast, which argues against his having traveled to Rome. The keeping of diaries was not common among the Dutch in van Campen's day. As a result, many questions of consequence about the works have gone unanswered, such as what van Campen's sources actually were and how he came to know them. In any case, he seems to have assimilated thoroughly the classicizing principles to which he was exposed.

Van Campen's first architectural work was a three-story double house for the Coymans brothers in Amsterdam (1625, not extant). An example of classicizing architecture, remarkable for the date, it was approximately square and therefore had a long street facade. This classical facade lacked gables, a revolutionary architectural idea for the Dutch. The facade had an unclassical even number of bays, eight, but the two doorways dictated such a departure from principle. The bays were separated by single-story pilasters. The four central bays were demarcated with a second pilaster partially visible behind the first. The house retained the steeply pitched traditional Dutch roof.

Van Campen carried out projects for the Dutch court, but because the stadtholder lacked the immense wealth of Spain, France and England, he could not be depended upon as a single source of projects.

The Mauritshuis, The Hague (ca. 1633), built for Johan Maurits van Nassau, who was related to the stadtholder, is the most important domestic structure by van Campen. His skilled use of the color and texture of stone and brick, a particular strength of Dutch architecture, had become established by that time. The two-story house above a basement is freestanding and has a square plan including a courtyard at the front. It fully participates in ideas of classical monumentality. This was the first instance in the Dutch Republic of the application of classical principles and proportions to a ground plan. Except for its steeply pitched and flared roof, which marks it as Dutch, its proportions and decoration, though simplified, display a thorough knowledge of the French version of classical influence. The five bays of the main facade are divided by a giant order of Ionic pilasters. The center bay contains three windows closely spaced. Over the bay is a pedimented gable filled with sculpture. The pedimented entrance is at main-floor level up a short flight of steps. The house is seen from all sides, and van Campen continued the giant order of pilasters around the house to continue on all facades the monumentality he created for the front. The rear facade has five matching bays, with the three central ones projecting slightly forward and maintaining the movement initiated at the front.

Van Campen's largest civic project as well as his masterpiece was the Amsterdam Town Hall (begun 1648). It was created as a symbol of the new republic and was the grandest town hall yet constructed. The main facade, divided into 23 bays, is long and high. The stone exterior is divided vertically by the projection forward of the three bays on each end and of the central seven bays. Subdivisions are created by two rows of Roman and Corinthian pilasters, each two stories high. The central group is capped with a spreading pediment filled with sculpture groups paying homage to the new republic. Vertically the facade is divided into three sections: an almost undecorated ground floor and two parts above. Each section is composed of a stringcourse or architrave and two rows of windows. The windows are treated similarly. This constant repetition of a comparatively small feature magnifies the size of the building, but it also diminishes the building's magnificence through too much subdivision. The ground-floor plan of the rectangular building is designed around two courtyards which flank the high, large Citizen's Hall. To reach this area, the visitor enters at the ground-floor level through a severely plain arcade with seven equal-size doorways meant to express the egalitarian attitudes of the Dutch. The visitor next passes through a narrow corridor which circumvents the Hall of Judgment (where death sentences were pronounced) placed directly in front of the entrances, unavoidably reminding the citizens of the city's judicial power. The roof retains the traditional northern high pitch and punctuation by dormers. An Italianate cupola dominates the roofline.

The relatively small Nieuwe Kerk, Haarlem (1649), was constructed by means of an ingenious variation on the central plan. Though the central plan was not introduced into the Dutch classical Baroque by van Campen, he made skillful use of it: the plan is square with a Greek cross inscribed within it. This simple idea is made visible in a number of ways, all on the interior. The ceiling is composed of wooden barrel cross vaults, with the corners of the ceiling flattened and lowered to the point of the springing of the vaults where they are outlined by architraves. The ceiling supports are Ionic piers and columns.

While van Campen's oeuvre continues to be assessed for the degree of Palladian and other classicizing influences it exhibits as well as traditional usage, there is more certainty concerning the degree of influence his work exerted on other architects in Holland and across the Channel in England. Some English architects of the second half of the 17th century came to know his work directly when they traveled to Holland to escape the effects of the English Civil War. Others saw prints of his designs. Dutch architects working in England were another outlet for his ideas. English architects who incorporated van Campen's influence into their work include such important figures as Hugh May and Christopher Wren. In one of the best-known examples, St. Stephen's Walbrook, London (1672-1717), Wren applied ideas derived from van Campen's Nieuwe Kerk in Haarlem.

—ANN STEWART BALAKIER

VAN DEN BROEK and BAKEMA.

VAN DEN BROEK, Johannes Hendrik.
Dutch. Born in Rotterdam, the Netherlands, 4 October 1898. Died in the Hague, 6 September 1978. Studied at Delft Technical University, Dip.Arch., 1924. In private practice, Rotterdam, 1927-37; in partnership with J. A. Brinkman, 1937-48; principal, with Jacob Bakema, Architectengemeenschap van den Broek en Bakema, rotterdam, 1948-78. Professor of town planning, Technical University, Delft, 1947-64; supervisor, Academy of Architecture, Amsterdam, 1966-76.

BAKEMA, Jacob B.

Dutch. Born in Groningen, the Netherlands, 8 March 1914. Died in Rotterdam, 20 February 1981. Studied at the Academy of Architecture, Amsterdam, 1937-41, Dip.Arch.; Technical University, Delft, 1939-40. Principal, with J. H. van den Broek, Architectengemeenschap van den Broek en Bakema, Rotterdam, 1948-81. Professor of architecture, Technical University, Delft, 1963-80; also taught in Germany and the United States. Member, CIAM, 1947-81, and Team 10, 1963-81.

Chronology of Works

All in the Netherlands unless noted

1948-51	Department Store ter Meulen-Wassen-van Vorst, Rotterdam
1949-53	Shopping Center Lijnbaan, Rotterdam
1950-58	Siedlung Klein Driene, Hengelo (with F. J. van Gool and J. M. Stocla)
1955-60	Montessori School, Rotterdam
1957-60	Dwelling Tower, Hansaviertel, Berlin, Germany
1958-60	Reformed Church, Nagele
1959-61	Shopping Center and Maisonette Dwellings, Bergen
1959-62	Housing Leeuwarden North
1959-68	Housing, Leeuwarden and Kampen
1961-62	Auditorium Center, Technische Hochschule, Delft
1961-62	Office for Postal Services, Arnhem
1963-69	Het Dorp Housing for Handicapped People, Arnhem
1963-72	Town Hall, Terneuzen
1964-69	Hermes (Students' Club), Rotterdam
1969-74	Heineken Brewery, Zoeterwoude

Publications

BOOKS BY BAKEMA

Towards an Architecture for Society. Delft, 1963.
From Doorstep to Town. Zeist, Netherlands, 1964.
Städtebauliche Architektur. Salzburg, 1965.
L. C. van der Vlugt. Amsterdam, 1968.
Team 10 Primer. With others. Edited by Alison Smithson. London, 1968.
Woning en Woonomgeving. 1977.
Thoughts about Architecture. Edited by Marianne Gray. London, 1981.
Architektur der Zukunft, Zukunft der Architektur. With Jürgen Joedicke, Egon Schirmbeck and others. Stuttgart, 1982.

ARTICLES BY BAKEMA

"BFU: Nine Evaluations." With others. *Architecture Plus* (January/February 1974).
"Building in Urban Holland." *Parametro* (April 1979).
"Building with Weathering Steel." *Polytechnische Tijdschrift* (December 1973).
"Bureaucracy Puts Architecture into Cold Storage." *Royal Institute of British Architects Journal* (October 1976).
"Once Again: Two Libraries and Architecture." *Wonen-TA/BK* (June 1979).
"Some Conditions Governing the Current Development of Architecture." *Bauen und Wohnen* (December 1975).
"Trees First, Then Houses." *Bouw* (May 1974).
"Architecture by Planning/Planning by Architecture." *Architects' Year Book* No. 8 (1956): 23-42.
"Dutch Architecture Today." *Architects' Year Book* No. 5 (1953): 67-82.

BOOKS BY VAN DEN BROEK

Woonmogelijkheden in het nieuwe Rotterdam. With Willem van Tijen, Johannes Brinkman and Huig A. Maaskant. Rotterdam, 1941.
Habitations (ed.). Vols. 1-3. Rotterdam, 1945-65.
Creatieve Krachten in de architectonische Conceptie. Delft, 1948.
De Stijl. With Cornelis van Eesteren and others. Amsterdam, 1951.
Beginselen van Kerkbouw. The Hague, 1954.
Gids voor Nederlandse Architectuur. With Meischke and Boot. Rotterdam, 1955.
Scholen. Rotterdam, 1956.

BOOKS ABOUT VAN DEN BROEK and BAKEMA

Bouwen voor een open samenleving. Exhibition catalog. Rotterdam, 1963.
BRINKMAN, J. A.: *Woonmogelijkheden in het nieuwe Rotterdam.* With Willem van Tijen, Huig A. Maaskant, and J. H. van den Broek. Rotterdam, 1941.
GUBIOSTI, CAMILLO and IZZO, ALBERTO (ed.): *Van den Broek/Bakema.* Rome 1976.
JOEDICKE, JÜRGEN (ed.): *Architektur und Städtebau. Das Werk der Architekten van den Broek und Bakema.* Stuttgart, 1963.
NEWMAN, OSCAR: *CIAM '59 in Otterlo: Dokumente der modernen architektur herausgegeben von Joedicke (Jürgen).* Stuttgart, 1961.
SMITHSON, ALISON (ed.): *Team 10 Primer.* London, 1962.

ARTICLES ABOUT VAN DEN BROEK and BAKEMA

BOLTEN, JETTEKE: "Jacob B. Bakema 1914-1981." *Dutch Art and Architecture Today* (December 1981).
DEN HOLLANDER, JORD: "The Architecture of Van den Broek." *Architect* (January 1979).
FUEG, FRANZ: "Van der Broek und Bakema: A Contribution to the History of Architecture." *Bauen und Wohnen* (October 1959).
GRINBERG, DONALD: "Jacob B. Bakema 1914-1981." *Progressive Architecture* (July 1981).
HOUSDEN, B.: "Brinkman, Brinkman, van der Vlugt, van den Broek, Bakema." *Architectural Association Journal*, special issue (December 1960).
NEWMAN, O.: "Jacob Bakema: Holland." *Canadian Architect* (May 1962): 43-50.
PERUGINI, G.: "Costruzioni degli architetti Jacob Bakema e Johannes van den Broek." *Architettura* 5 (September 1959): 324-39.
ROLLING, WIEK: "Jacob B. Bakema: His Destiny and His Enduring Significance." *Bouw* (21 March 1981).
SALOMONS, IZAK: "De Siemensgebouwen in Munich." *Forum* 1 (1980): 15-23.
VAN DE VEN, CORNELIUS: "De laaste werken van de architect-en-gemeenschap van den Broek en Bakema 1970-1980." *Plan* 8 (1980): 14-41.
VAN EYCK, ALDO: "Jaap Bakema 1914-1981." With others. *Forum* (July 1981).
VAN HEUVEL, WIM J.: "Exhibition 'The appropriate architecture of Van den Broek." *Polytechnisch Tijdschrift* (April 1981).
VAN TIJEN, WILLEM: "Het Bureau van den Broek en Bakema" *Forum* (June 1957).

The practice of Van den Broek and Bakema resulted from the analytical and functional approach to design of J. H. Van den Broek being modified by the spatial qualities of J. B. Bakema's tectonic and organic expression. Both architects were central to the development from functionalism to a social attitude toward design in the Netherlands in the postwar period from 1948 to the 1970s. They advanced conceptual ideas on architecture and urbanism in their writings and also in their teaching. The reaction to the historicism that had been the basis of study at the Delft School of Architecture in the 1920s and 1930s was due largely to the influence of Van den Broek and Bakema.

Their firm was a continuation of that of Van der Vlugt and Brinkman. Van den Broek had been brought into the partnership with J. A. Brinkman, following the death of L. C. Van der Vlugt, to become the chief designer. In that capacity he was responsible, in part, for planning proposals for Rotterdam in the postwar years. Jaap Bakema joined the firm in 1948 following a period when he had been influenced by Mart Stam and the De Stijl architect Cornelis van Eesteren. One of the first projects the partnership of Van den Broek and Bakema was responsible for resulted from the regeneration of the central area of Rotterdam. This was the Lijnbaan pedestrian shopping street (1949-53), which formed a basis for similar developments throughout Europe.

Although a meeting with Ernst May and Mart Stam in Frankfurt had a formative influence upon Van den Broek, he did not entirely accept the functionalist ethic. In fact, his reaction to the Dutch version of May's notion of "Existenzminimum," discussed by the Congrès Internationaux d'Architecture Moderne, CIAM, was to soften the concept to the notion of an "optimum" dwelling rather than the "minimum" idea of the Frankfurt CIAM meeting.

Whereas Van den Broek was involved with the International Union of Architects, a more representative body than CIAM, Bakema became involved with the radical groups of CIAM, Team 10 and the Dutch *Forum* group. Bakema was particularly active in the postwar meetings of CIAM. Perhaps that is an understatement, for Bakema's work with the postwar years of CIAM has been compared to that of Walter Gropius in the 1920s and 1930s. However, it is generally accepted that Bakema's work on architecture and urbanism came to fruition with Team 10, of which he was a founder.

The way in which Van den Broek and Bakema's approach to design differed from the previous generation can be seen in the respective positions of Gropius and Bakema. Gropius considered that the architect has a social responsibility to lead society. Bakema, on the other hand, believed that the architect has a moral duty to learn from the society for whom he is designing. Although the work of Van den Broek and Bakema had developed from a functionalist approach, it was criticized by Willem van Tijen who disagreed with the basis of Bakema's organic concept of design allied to the idea of cosmic space and a social attitude toward design. Other critics of Bakema criticized the formal idea of his work, as expressed in his essay "Architecture is the Three Dimensional Expression of Human Behaviour."

Of equal importance to Bakema's work with Team 10 was the formation of the Forum group in the early 1960s. The editorial board of the *Forum* magazine at that time included Aldo van Eyck, Bakema and Herman Hertzberger. The policy of the group showed an artistic and cultural basis for design that included the small of scale and detail of grain. To an extent, the result of *Forum* was the Dutch structuralist approach to design. The ideas of *Forum* were also developed in the "Team 10 Primer," which was based to a fair extent on the work of Bakema and Van Eyck.

Although Van den Broek and Bakema's contribution to the various international groups was significant, their firm also achieved a reputation for architectural expression and urbanism that is recognized in historical studies of the period. The scheme presented at the final meeting of CIAM at Otterlo by Bakema was an urban proposal for Kennemerland (1957-59), an area of North Holland. The project contained neighborhoods, visual groups and a variety in scale of the dwelling units. A good example of this type of scheme is the 't Hool area at Eindhoven.

The wall and spine urban projects influenced by Le Corbusier's Obus scheme for Algiers brought a means of order to Van den Broek and Bakema's sense of urbanity. To a large extent, the significance of the firm lies in the development of urban forms, but there were several architectural projects of note. The design of the Dutch pavilion for the 1970 World's Fair in Osaka, Japan, indicated a possible influence from Metabolism. Arguably, the most successful design was the Town Hall at Terneuzen in Zeeland (1960-68), which had spatial qualities and was designed to allow for flexibility.

Bakema's work continued throughout the 1960s. He was involved in proposals for the Pampusplan. This study was for the development of a linear new town on polders to form an extension to Amsterdam. Bakema also was closely involved with the educational changes at the Delft School, which became known as the "democratization" of the school.

Following the deaths of Van den Broek and Bakema the firm, which became known in the 1980s as the "architectural community" of Van den Broek and Bakema, declined in influence.

—E.S. BRIERLEY

VAN DER VLUGT and BRINKMAN.

VAN DER VLUGT, Leendert Cornelius.
Dutch. Born in the Netherlands, 1894; died in 1936.

BRINKMAN, Johannes Andreas.
Dutch. Born in Rotterdam, the Netherlands, 22 March 1902; died in Rotterdam, 6 May 1949. Studied at the Technische Hochschule, Delft. Worked in the office of his father, Michiel Brinkman, 1921-25; in partnership with Van der Vlugt, Rotterdam, 1925-36; in partnership with Johannes van den Broek, Rotterdam, 1937-48.

Chronology of Works
All in the Netherlands unless noted
† Work no longer exists

1925-26	Theosophical Society Meeting Hall, Amsterdam
1925-27	Van Nelle Tobacco Factory Office Building, Leiden†
1926	Theosophical Society Administration Building, Amsterdam
1926-27	Municipal Housing, Rotterdam
1926-30	Van Nelle Factory, Rotterdam
1927	Heldring and Pierson Bank, Rotterdam
1927	Theosophical Society Administrative Complex, Ommen
1927-28	C. H. Van der Leeuw House, Rotterdam
1927-31	Graansilo Company (grain silo), Rotterdam
1928	Rotterdam Company Workers' Housing, Schiedam
1928-29	Sonneveld House, Rotterdam
1929	Private Chapel and Columbarium, Staverden

Van der Vlugt and Brinkman: Van Nelle Factory, Rotterdam, Netherlands, 1926-30

1929-31	De Bruin House, Schiedam
1929-31	R. Mees and Sons Bank, Rotterdam
1929-31	C. H. Van der Leeuw Summerhouse, Ommen
1930-32	Dutch Postal Service Telephone Booth, Rotterdam
1930-32	Van Stolk and Son Office Building, Rotterdam
1931	Van Ommeren Travel Bureau, Paris, France
1931-38	Van Dam Hospital, Rotterdam (extended by van den Broek and Bakema, 1957-60)
1932-34	Bergpolder Flats, Rotterdam (with Willem van Tijen)
1933	De Maas Grain and Coal Silos, Rotterdam
1933	Rotterdam Golf Club
1934	Holland-American Line Travel Office, Paris, France
1934-36	Feyenoord Stadium, Rotterdam
1934-36	Nuova Tennis Club, Rotterdam
1934-36	Volker Bouwindustria, Rotterdam (middle-class housing)

Publications

BOOKS BY VAN DER VLUGT and BRINKMAN

Woonmogelijkheden in het nieuwe Rotterdam. With Willem van Tijen and Huig A. Maaskant. Rotterdam, 1941.

BOOKS ABOUT VAN DER VLUGT and BRINKMAN

BAKEMA, J. B.: *L. C. van der Vlugt*. Amsterdam, 1968.
BEEREN, WIM; DETTINGMEIJER, ROB; KAUFFMAN, FRANK: *Het Nieuwe Bouwen in Rotterdam 1920-1960*. Delft, Netherlands, 1982.

BENEVOLO, LEONARDO: *The Modern Movement.* Vol. 2 in *History of Modern Architecture*. Translated by H. J. Landry from the 3rd rev. ed. Cambridge, Massachusetts, 1977.
Building for an Open City, Exhibition catalog, Rotterdam (1963).
EIBINK, A., GERRETSEN, W. J., and HENDRIKS, J. P. L.: *Hedendaagsche Architectuur in Nederland*. Amsterdam, 1937.
FANELLI, GIOVANNI: *Moderne architectuur in Nederland 1900-1940*. Translated from the Italian by Wim de Wit. The Hague, 1968.
GRINBERG, DONALD I.: *Housing in the Netherlands*. Rotterdam, 1977.
HAAGSMA, IDS (ed.): *Amsterdamse Bouwen 1880-1980*. Utrecht and Antwerp, 1981.
JOEDICKE, JÜRGEN: *Geschichte der Moderne Architektur*. Stuttgart, 1963.
LEERING, J.: *Bauen '20-40: Der Niederlandische Beitrag zum Neuen Bauen*. Amsterdam, 1971.
MUSEUM BOYMANS-VAN BEUNINGEN: *Bouwen voor een Open Samenleving*. Rotterdam, 1962.
OUD, J. J. P.: *Holländische Architektur*. Mainz, Germany, 1926.
PICA, A.: *Nuova Architettura nel Mondo*. Milan, 1938.
VAN LOGHEM, J. B.: *Bouwen Holland*. Amsterdam, 1932.

ARTICLES ABOUT VAN DER VLUGT and BRINKMAN

De 8 en Opbouw, special issue, 7, No. 10 (1936).
DE HAAN, HILDE and HAAGSMA, IDS: ''A New Social and Cultural Centre—Cinema Becomes a Library.'' *Architect* 6 (1981).

FUEG, FRANZ: "Van der Broek und Bakema: A Contribution to the History of Architecture." *Bauen und Wohnen* (October 1959).

HOUSDEN, B.: "Brinkman, Brinkman, van der Vlugt, van den Broek, Bakema." *Architectural Association Journal*, special issue (December 1960).

"House van der Leeuw, Rotterdam." *Architectural Record* (October 1950).

LIONNI, LEO: "La nuova architettura olandese." *Casabella* (May 1934).

MERKELBACH, B.: "Twee Woonhuizen te Rotterdam van de Architecten Brinkman en van der Vlugt." *De 8 en Opbouw* 11/12 (1934).

PERSICO, EDOARDO and LIONNI, LEO: "Brinkman e van der Vlugt, architetti." *Casabella* (March 1935).

ROTHSCHILD, R.: "Casa popolare a Rotterdam." *Casabella* (December 1934).

"Usines de Tabac, Rotterdam." *Cahiers d'Art*, vol. 4 (1929).

"Van Nelle Factory in Rotterdam." *Architecture* (April 1975).

*

The office of Van der Vlugt and Brinkman owes its reputation to the creative skill of L. C. Van der Vlugt, who is generally recognized as one of the leading architects of the heroic period of modern architecture in the Netherlands. The practice had been founded by Jan Brinkman's father Michiel, who had gained recognition as a designer of social housing, in particular of a block in the Spangen area of Rotterdam that was completed in 1920. This was the block that was especially influential for the members of Team 10 in the 1960s.

When Michiel Brinkman died in 1925, Jan was still a student, but due to his father's work he already had contacts with clients. At that time Van der Vlugt had made a reputation, specifically as the architect of the Technical College building at Groningen, which he had designed with the engineer J. G. Wiebenga, who arguably was the most significant technical influence upon the architects of the Modern Movement in the Netherlands.

Van der Vlugt and Brinkman were in partnership for 12 years, during which time they designed the Van Nelle Factory, the White Houses, including the Van der Leeuw House, and the Feyenoord Stadium in Rotterdam, as well as the administration building for the Theosophical Society in Amsterdam. Van der Vlugt became noted as a leading architect of the "New Objectivity," functionalism and the "New Building." During that period he can be considered in the same context as Gerrit Rietveld, Johannes Duiker, J. J. P. Oud and Mart Stam.

Arguably, the most significant design of Van der Vlugt and Brinkman was that of the factory for Van Nelle (1926-30) in the Spangen district of Rotterdam. The project had many remarkable features, none less than the age of the designers. Van der Vlugt was just in his thirties, Brinkman in his early twenties, and the design architect for the project, Mart Stam, was in his mid-twenties. Stam already had an international reputation of some note. He had collaborated with the Russian constructivist El Lissitzky and had been an editor of the avant-garde, Swiss functionalist magazine *ABC*. The strength of the Van Nelle design was due to Van der Vlugt's formal influence and knowledge of technique, and Stam's will to functionalism. The formal influence is clearly seen in the semicircular rooftop tearoom and the office block, while the functional aesthetic is found in the articulation of the facades and the structural expression.

The concept that was central to Van der Vlugt's architecture at that time was that the building should express a clear unity of aesthetics and technique. Ornament was rejected in favor of sobriety and a minimal approach to design. Space was to be considered as a continuity of interior and exterior space. Le Corbusier praised Van der Vlugt's work of that period for its simplicity of design and vivacity of spirit.

Although the design of factory buildings and offices may be thought of as the appropriate building types for Van der Vlugt's sober architectural style, he also made a significant contribution in the field of housing. Probably in this respect his most accomplished work is to be found in the design of the White Houses in Rotterdam. These were a series of villas in various locations built from reinforced concrete rendered white, with plate glass in steel frames. Van der Vlugt was restrained in the use of color, often expressing his designs in light gray, white and the occasional black area.

Yet, in terms of architectural history the dwelling block associated with Van der Vlugt, which he designed with Willem van Tijen, the leading functionalist architect of that time, is the Bergpolder block of high-rise balcony-access flats (1933-35). It is generally accepted that with the design of this block, the movement toward functionalism achieved recognition. The flats' construction is clearly expressed. The steelwork-supported balconies and access walkways represent a severe form of rational functionalism. In use, the dwellings have proved successful as social housing. The design expresses the functional ideals of an analytical approach to design related to economic constraints.

Other designs by Van der Vlugt contain delightful details and formal devices. In this context should be noted the Diaconessenhuis Hospital on the Westersingel and the Feyenoord Stadium, Rotterdam. Van der Vlugt and Brinkman were also responsible for the Dutch public telephone boxes. One building that veered away from a strictly objective concept of design was that of the administration building for the Theosophical Society in Amsterdam (1925-26). The appearance of the building, of tent-like roof construction, results from the expression of the quarter-circle plan of the design. The strength of the architecture lies in the external formal expression and the sculptural effect of the metal mullions to the windows. The building has now been adapted for use as a library, but fortunately the architectural character and motifs remain.

Although Van der Vlugt's design work is noted for the earnestness and sobriety of the architecture, his personality was a humorous one with a sporting spirit.

—E. S. BRIERLEY

VAN DE VELDE, Henry.

Belgian. Born in Antwerp, Belgium, 3 April 1863. Died in Zürich, Switzerland, 25 October 1957. Studied painting at the Académie des Beaux-Arts, Antwerp, 1882-84, and in Paris, 1884-85. Worked as a painter and interior decorator, Antwerp and Brussels, 1885-94; in private practice as an architect and designer, Brussels, 1895-98, and as Société van de Velde, Brussels, 1898-1900; in private practice, Berlin, 1900-05, Weimar, 1906-14, Switzerland, 1914-21, Wassenaar, near The Hague, 1 921-25, and in Brussels, 1925-47. Founder/director, Kunstgewerbeschule, later the Bauhaus School, Weimar, 1908-14; founder/director, École Nationale Supérieure d'Architecture et des Arts Décoratifs, Brussels, 1925-36. Chair of Architecture, University of Ghent, 1926-35.

Chronology of Works

† Work no longer exists

1895-96   Bloemenwerf House, Uccle, Belgium
1896   Van de Velde House, Avenue Vanderaey, Brussels, Belgium
1898   Keller und Reiner Art Gallery, Berlin, Germany (interiors)
1904   Kunstgewerbeschule, Weimar, Germany
1906   Hohenhof (Karl Osthaus Country House, now houses the Henry van de Velde Gesellschaft), Hagen, Germany
1912   Durkheim House, Weimar, Germany
1914   Theater, Werkbund Exhibition, Cologne, Germany†
1921   Van de Velde House, Wassenaar, Netherlands
1927   Van de Velde House, Tervueren, Belgium
1937   Belgian Pavilion, World's Fair, Paris, France (with I. Eggeriey)
1939   Belgian Pavilion, World's Fair, New York City, U.S.A. (with Victor Bourgeois)
1939   Library, University of Ghent, Ghent, Belgium

Publications

BOOKS BY VAN DE VELDE

Déblaiemant d'art. Brussels, 1894.
L'art futur. Brussels, 1895.
Der neue Stil. Weimar, 1906.
Vernunftsgemässe Schönheit. Weimar, 1909.
Die drei Sünden wider die Schönheit. Zurich, 1918.
Les fondements du style moderne. Brussels, 1933.
Geschichte meines Lebens. Edited by Hans Curjel. Munich, 1962.

BOOKS ABOUT VAN DE VELDE

CURJEL, HANS (ed.): *Henry van de Velde, zum neuen Stil.* Munich, 1955.
DELEVOY, ROBERT, et al.: *Henry van de Velde 1863-1957.* Exhibition catalog. Brussels, 1963.
HAMMACHER, A. M.: *Le Monde de Henry van de Velde.* Paris, 1967.
HÜTER, K. H.: *Henry van de Velde: Sein Werk bis zum Ende seiner Tätigkeit in Deutschland.* Berlin, 1967.
OSTHAUS, KARL ERNST: *Van de Velde, Leben und Schaffen des Künstlers.* Hagen, Germany, 1920.
PLOEGAERTS, LEON, and PUTTEMANS, PIERRE: *L'oeuvre architecturale de Henry van de Velde.* Quebec, 1987.
SEMBACH, KLAUS-JÜRGEN: *Henry van de Velde.* New York and London, 1989.
SHARP, DENNIS, and CULOT, MAURICE (eds.): *Henry van de Velde: Theatre Designs 1904-1914.* London and Brussels, 1974.

*

Architect, painter, decorative arts designer, theorist, writer, lecturer and school administrator were among the professions practiced by Henry van de Velde. This Belgian chemist's son became a painter in early manhood, studying first at a local academy (at which time Vincent Van Gogh was also a student) and afterward in Paris with the academic portraitist Carolus-Duran.

Relatively soon van de Velde made contacts with the nonacademic Impressionists, yet he maintained a strong attachment to the socialist-realist imagery in Jean-François Millet's paintings.

Interest in other movements and individuals followed, including the symbolist poets Stéphane Mallarmé and Paul Verlaine, as well as the composer Claude Debussy. By 1881, van de Velde had returned to Belgium and was soon entranced by the turgid symbolist paintings of Paul Gauguin; then, almost as quickly, he explored Impressionism with zest. To be influenced significantly by both major opposite arms of Post-Impressionism was unusual.

The year 1889 found van de Velde an active member of the Belgian avant-garde exhibition society known as Les XX (Les Vingt). Based in Brussels, Les XX had already sponsored shows by Georges Seurat and fellow Neo-Impressionists such as Paul Signac (an exact contemporary of van de Velde) in 1887. Interestingly, Belgium turned out to be the European country most receptive to Post-Impressionism. Van de Velde's paintings at that time reflected initial influences from Theo van Rysselberghe, Seurat's theories and adoption of certain of the latter's formal painting techniques. Handsome though conservative paintings, such as *Woman at the Window* (1889), represented a phase of settled production. However, self-doubts and then a mental breakdown followed the same year.

During convalescence van de Velde began to explore a broad range of outlets. A serious interest in crafts led him to the work and writings of the English Arts and Crafts movement and its leader, William Morris. Van de Velde responded readily to Morris' insistence on a moral aesthetic rooted in high standards of craftsmanship for all domestic objects. By 1893, apparently recovered, van de Velde was experimenting with craft media and exhibited *Angel Watch,* a tapestry in applique-embroidery—his first effort in that medium. The composition depicts a pastoral quasi-nativity scene, boldly simplified and unified by sweeping energized lines. This quality was already present in certain early paintings and in his first venture into graphic design—a radically reductive, black and white, abstract linear seascape (untitled) for the publication *Dominical.* Both of these works bear influences from Oriental art, the paintings of the French symbolist Maurice Denis, poster art by Jules Cheret, Walter Crane's illustrations and quite possibly Charles Henry's theories addressing human psychological responses to effects of color and line.

Words by van de Velde echoing such diverse art and ideas appeared in his 1894 lecture at Les XX Gallery titled "Déblaiment d'Art," in which he called for the development of a new art. The new art was to be comprehensive and include architecture, applied interior design and graphic design. It was to seek a moral continuity of form and meaning, a design totality resulting in a healthier contemporary environment; a reconciliation of the evocative power of the symbolist movement without allegorical description, yet with a near-total abstract linear language paralleling nature. In *Déblaiment d'Art* (published as a brochure) the phrase "*un art nouveau*" appeared, quite possibly for the first time. Though a brief phrase in an extremely modest publication, it lent itself to what became a highly visible and internationally vital phenomenon in architecture and design from the 1890s to about 1920. It is ironic, moreover, that van de Velde preferred not to use his own term, art nouveau.

Fittingly for van de Velde, Belgium was the birthplace of art nouveau, and in particular Brussels, where Victor Horta's Hôtel Solvay (1894-1903) and Hôtel van Eetvelde (1897-98) were clearly emblematic examples. However, the articulate van de Velde proved to be the mouthpiece for the movement, spreading the call for abstract ornament, expressive line, high craftsmanship, and unified or integrated design.

By 1891 van de Velde had abandoned painting, for reasons unclear, though possibly because he had already achieved an almost irreducible type of abstract composition by the early 1890s. By that time he was also won over to William Morris' social moralism, whereupon he totally immersed himself into domestic and industrial design plus theoretical writing in the same field. For the next several decades he toiled for the new art as an architect, designer, writer and educator, first in Belgium, then in France, Germany, Switzerland and Holland.

In 1895 van de Velde designed and furnished a house for himself near Brussels at Uccle, using it as a model or demonstration for his design theories. About one year later he was visited by Paris art dealer Samuel Bing, who subsequently invited van de Velde to design four rooms for his shop L'Art Nouveau. The designer met the challenge to Bing's satisfaction (though his work was otherwise unevenly received by critics) with unified interiors of furniture stressing abstract ornamentation, tense energy and functional unity. Those rooms and more were sent two years later to an applied-arts exhibition in Dresden, Germany—exposure which in turn led to a variety of additional contacts and commissions. Notable among these were designs and advertising (1897) for Tropon, a dietary-supplement company in Mulheim, a showroom interior (1899) for the Paris shop La Maison Moderne of art critic and dealer Julius Meier-Graefe; the expressionist interior for the Folkwang Museum, Hagen (1902); the position of art educator and administrator for the School of Applied Art, Weimar (from 1907 to about 1914, when as a non-German van de Velde was dismissed at the onset of World War I); cofounder of the Deutsche Werkbund (German alliance between the applied arts and industry) in 1907; and the commission for the sinuously curved theater for that organization's Cologne Exhibition (1914).

Allowed to leave Germany in 1917, van de Velde lived and worked the rest of his life in Holland and Switzerland, where he continued to function variously as an architect and designer, a professor of architecture and a school administrator, for example, as head of the Institut Supérieur des Arts Décoratifs in Brussels from 1925 to 1936. Van de Velde also designed two Belgian oceanliners (1933-34) with distinctive dining rooms and lounges. By 1947 he had settled in Switzerland but was still designing architectural additions to the Kröller-Müller (art) Museum in Otterlo, Belgium, in 1953.

Despite a long career, diverse in its production, van de Velde is perhaps as well known today for his lectures and theoretical writing. From reading representative sections of his extensive opinion, it is fair to observe that he held carefully constructed and often passionate views.

At the center of all mature designs by van de Velde were burning drives and goals: his appeal to reason, that is, to create nothing without reasonable justification for existence; homogeneous, simple-ordered design as opposed to complex, incoherent, unordered design; finding and enhancing the principal focal point of a room to reflect and enhance vital living; and the use of industrial means to implement his elegant and intelligent formulations for a broad audience, the middle class.

Occasionally, van de Velde's views in print were contradicted by his executed designs for buildings or domestic items. Yet overall his desires for the built environment were in step with the advancing Modern Movement during the 1890s-to-1940s period that he helped shape.

—TOM DEWEY II

VAN DOESBURG, Theo.

Dutch. Born Christian Emil Marie Küpper, in Utrecht, the Netherlands, 1883. Died 7 March 1930. Worked in several media,

including design, typography and painting; collaborated on architectural projects with J. J. P. Oud and others; also a critic and a poet, writing Dadaist poetry under the name I. K. Bonset. Founder and editor of the journal *De Stijl*, 1916.

Chronology of Works
All in the Netherlands unless noted
† *Work no longer exists*

1917-18 Villa Allegonda, Katwijk (stained-glass windows, with J. J. P. Oud)

1917-18 Villa De Vonk, Noordwijkerhout, Netherlands (interior decoration, with J. J. P. Oud)

1921 Studies for architectural color application to Terrace Housing and Agricultural School in Drachten (for C. de Boer)

1923 Project for a University Hall, University of Amsterdam (in collaboration with Cor Van Eesteren)

1924-25 Flower Room for Comte de Noailles' Villa, Hyères, France

1926-28 Café L'Aubette, Strasbourg, France (remodeled, with Hans Arp and Sophie Tauber-Arp)†

1929-31 Van Doesburg House and Studio, Meudon, France

Publications

BOOKS BY VAN DOESBURG

Drie Voordrachten over de Nieuwe Beeldende Kunst: haar Ontwikkeling, Aesthetisch Beginsel en Toekomstigen Stijl. Amsterdam, 1919; English translation, *Principles of Neo-plastic Art.* London, 1969.
Klassiek, barok, modern. Antwerp, 1920; French translation, *Classique, baroque, moderne.* Paris, 1921.
Ueber Europäische Architektur. Collected Essays from "Het Bouwbedrijft." 1924-1931. Switzerland, 1990.

ARTICLES BY VAN DOESBURG

"De Nieuwe Beweging in de Schilderkunst." *De Beweging* 8 (August 1916).
"Aantekeningen over Monumentale Kunst: naar Aanleiding van twee Bouwfragmenten." *De Stijl,* vol. 2, No. 1. November (1918).
"Proeve van kleurencompositie in interieur." *De Stijl,* No. 12 (1920).
"Architectuur-Diagnose." *Architectura,* vol. 28, No. 15 (17 May 1924).
"L'Evolution de l'architecture moderne en Hollande." *L'Architecture Vivante,* special issue (Autumn-Winter 1925).
"Schilderkunst: Van Komposite tot Contra-compositie." *De Stijl,* vol. 7, series 13, No. 73/4 (1926).
"Über das Verhaltnis von malerischer und architektonischer Gestaltung." *Der Cicerone,* vol. 19, No. 18 (1927).
"Farben im Raum und Zeit." *De Stijl,* special Aubette number 87-9, series 15 (1928).
"De Beelding van het Interieur." *Het Binnenhuis,* vol. 12, No. 16 (31 July 1930).
De Stijl. Edited by Hans Ludwig Jaffe. 2 vols. Facsimile reprint of the periodical, complete from 1917-1932. Amsterdam, 1968; London, 1970.

BOOKS ABOUT VAN DOESBURG

BALJEU, JOOST: *Theo Van Doesburg*. New York, 1974.

BANHAM, REYNER: *Theory and Design in the First Machine Age*. New York, 1960.

BROWN, THEODORE M.: *The Work of G. Rietveld, Architect*. Utrecht, 1958.

DOIG, A.: *Theo van Doesburg: Painting into Architecture, Theory into Practice*. Cambridge, 1986.

FANELLI, GIOVANNI: *Architettura Moderna in Olanda 1900-1940*. Florence, 1968.

FRIEDMAN, MILDRED (ed.): *De Stijl: 1917-1931. Visions of Utopia*. Oxford, 1982.

HEDRICK, HANNAH: *Theo Van Doesburg, Propagandist and Practitioner of the Avant Garde 1920-1923*. 1980.

JAFFÉ, H. L. C.: *De Stijl—1917-1931. The Dutch Contribution to Modern Art*. Amsterdam, 1956.

LEERING, J.; WIJSENBECK, L. J. F.; and ALTHAUS, P. F.: *Theo van Doesburg 1883-1931*. Eindhoven, Netherlands, 1969.

LEMOINE, SERGE: *Theo van Doesburg*. Paris, 1990.

MANSBACH, STEVEN A.: *Visions of Totality: László Moholy-Nagy, Theo van Doesburg and El Lissitzky*. Ann Arbor, Michigan, 1980.

OVERY, PAUL: *De Stijl*. London, 1969.

PETERSEN, AD (ed.): *De Stijl*. Amsterdam, 1968.

SWEENY, J. J. (ed.): *Theo van Doesburg*. Exhibition catalog. New York, 1947.

VAN DEN BROEK, J. H.; VAN EESTEREN, C.; et al.: *De Stijl*. Amsterdam, 1951.

VAN STRAATEN, E. (ed.): *Theo van Doesburg, 1883-1931; een Documentaire op Basis van Materiaal uit de Schenking Van Moorsel*. The Hague, 1983.

ARTICLES ABOUT VAN DOESBURG

DOIG, A.: "Theo van Doesburg: 'Art/Criticism'." *Modern Dutch Studies* (August 1988).

OUD, J. J. P.: "Glas in lood van Theo van Doesburg." *Bouwkundig Weekblad* (August 1918).

*

The extant architectural works by Theo van Doesburg, some tiled floors and peeling color schemes, some stained-glass windows still in their original position, and a single complete building, would hardly justify the reputation he now enjoys. The difficulty in dealing with him is that he is impossible to contain within the professional or cultural categories of painter, architect, poet, essayist, theorist or performance artist. He was all of these things, and to compound the difficulty, he was a critic too. The voices of his personae were distinct enough to require different names. He was born Christian Emil Marie Küpper, but he abandoned that name completely before his artistic career had properly begun, and he adopted the name Van Doesburg, it seems, in recognition of the man he believed to be his natural father. Aldo Camini was his Futurist persona, and as I. K. Bonset he wrote Dadaist poetry. The difficulty is to find the man among these personae; to find the significant contributions among his inconsistent statements and diverse, often retrospectively and inaccurately dated, works; and to determine the full architectural achievement between the theory and the practice.

To separate these activities and to study them in isolation would give a necessarily false picture; they must be held together in any study as they were held together in the man himself, in a dynamic tension. Still, all of his work was ultimately focused on architecture, as a kind of metaphor for life itself. His activities

as critic and artist led him increasingly toward an architectonic, not to say architectural, painterly manifestation.

Van Doesburg's first direct involvement in architecture came in 1916, on meeting J. J. P. Oud. Besides Oud, he met a number of other artists whom he believed to be moving toward the same principles he himself had been developing in his criticism and his experimentation in painting. In 1926 he looked back over those early years in the introduction to an article in the journal *De Stijl*, "Painting: from Composition to Counter-composition": "In 1912 I published my first drafts concerning the new art under the title 'Specimen for a New Art Criticism.' I attempted to test my own development against the general development of art as objectively as possible and recognised the universal as the new content and the straight line as the new expressive means for the future. These two elements, I thought, must lead to a new style. . . . In 1916, having been released from military service, I founded De Stijl, not without considerable enthusiasm." [vol. VII, series 13, no73/4 (1926) pp.17-27 (p.17)]

There are problems in accepting the artist's own statements about his past—especially when embedded within a strong polemic, as "straight" history, but this was not willful fabrication. What we see here is Van Doesburg's own projection of special significance onto certain selected events. The particular significance and selection are of great interest in any attempt to understand the group dynamics and the resulting works of art and architecture.

In the first place, Van Doesburg looked to his own experience in struggling with the development of a new vocabulary and language of art, then looked to see what the history of art and contemporary developments could tell him (in an almost Hegelian sense) about the new synthesis toward which art was moving. This he understood to be toward the primary elements of art, the universal expressed in the straight line and pure color.

From these conclusions he moved directly to the founding of De Stijl, "in 1916," as he claimed. The journal he founded actually began publication in October 1917. This may have been another inaccurate bit of retrospective dating, but what is more likely is that he was actually referring to the founding of the "group" De Stijl. He recognized in the architects J. J. P. Oud, Jan Wils and Robert van 't Hoff, the painters Piet Mondrian, Bart van der Leck, Vilmos Huszar and Georges Vantongerloo, and the poet Antony Kok, a philosophy similar to his own. There is still debate about the degree to which these men constituted a group or movement. In any case, the seamless front presented by Van Doesburg as editor of the journal *De Stijl* was an illusion. His personal and professional relationships were as changeable as his personae, and the "group" was constantly riven by disagreements.

Van Doesburg's early architectural collaboration with Oud was based on substantial initial theoretical agreement, as can be clearly seen in an article written by Oud, "Concerning Cubism, Futurism, Modern Architecture, etc.," in the professional journal *Bouwkundig Weekblad*: "When painting had escaped the imitation of nature to achieve style, it entered a phase (hopefully it will be less reactionary in a later stage) which is of the utmost importance for architecture because modern painters and modern architects are striving towards one and the same goal, namely the rendering of aesthetic emotion in the purity of means without extraneous elements."

Oud was clearly strongly under the influence of Van Doesburg's developing theory, and on that basis a close collaboration was possible. Between 1917 and 1918 Oud virtually rebuilt Villa Allegonda in Katwijk and designed Villa De Vonk in Noordwijkerhout. Van Doesburg contributed two stained-glass windows to the former, and the tiled floors and color schemes to the latter. In these windows—as in windows he contributed to houses by Jan Wils (the De Lange-Woerden House in Alkmaar and a house in the Sint Antoniepolder, both of 1917), a school by C. de Boer (Drachten, 1919), and in an even more complex way in the tiled floor for De Vonk—Van Doesburg abstracted figures to geometrical arrangements of rectangles of pure color, and then rotated and handed the designs while sometimes varying the color, producing "fugal developments." This sense of movement was even more exaggerated in color schemes for the interiors and especially the exteriors of De Boer's school and (opposite) housing in Drachten.

Painting was, in Van Doesburg's conception, a destabilizing influence on the closed, almost hollowed-out architectural form. In his article "Introducing Two Architectural Fragments (the Hall of a Vacation House [De Vonk] in Noordwijkerhout)" in *De Stijl,* he wrote: "Architecture produces constructive and thus *closed* form. In that it is neutral as opposed to painting which produces *open* form through planar colour images. . . . Architecture connects and binds, Painting loosens and separates. . . . This opposed, yet *complementary* relationship of architecture and painting, or plastic form and planar colour, is the foundation of pure monumental art."

The next major architectural works by Van Doesburg were in collaboration with Cornelis van Eesteren. There was a color scheme of large floating planes of pure primary colors for Van Eesteren's design for a University Hall, and models for a "Maison Particulière" and a "Maison d'Artiste," which were experiments toward the closer identification of architectural color and architectural plane. These works, and much else besides by artists and architects whose names were associated with *De Stijl,* were exhibited in the De Stijl Exhibition at the Galerie de l'Effort Moderne in 1923. The exhibition gave further credence to the existence of a united artistic movement.

By 1919 Van Doesburg had broken with Oud, and from August 1924 collaborative work with Van Eesteren became increasingly strained and was then abandoned. Collaboration collapsed in mutual recrimination and claims over authorship.

Between 1924 and 1925 Van Doesburg produced designs for a small flower room for the villa of the Vicomte de Noailles in Hyères. These designs consisted of planes of pure color again, but this time on the diagonal. This new process played an important part in Van Doesburg's commission to transform the Aubette in Strasbourg into a multifunction entertainment complex. The interior of that 18th-century building was completely transformed, and painting was used to articulate each major space according to its use. Contributions were made by the painters Hans Arp and Sophie Täuber-Arp, but this time Van Doesburg was himself very much in control. His painterly conception of architecture was most fully and successfully achieved in this project. In the "Ciné-dancing" the enormous planes of color were again on the diagonal "in opposition to the natural and architectonic structure," while in the "Café-brasserie" the planes complemented and reinforced the architectonic structure (see "Painting: from Composition to Counter-composition"). The Aubette was reopened in February 1928, but according to Van Doesburg detrimental changes to his designs had begun very soon. He was bitterly disappointed that the public was not ready for his radically new architecture.

Urban design was another area of Van Doesburg's involvement between 1924 and 1929, when he designed a "Ville de circulation." His own house, designed between 1927 and 1929 and built in Meudon, was a prototype for this new area of activity. He died on 7 March 1930, when the house was substantially, though not completely, finished. He had been exhausted by work on the Aubette, and though the house at Meudon was

his first work as a completely independent architect, it was also his last.

Van Doesburg's importance for architecture is not limited by the size of his oeuvre, but is as broad as his influence as a polemicist and as profound as his experiments in a colored architecture.

—ALLAN DOIG

VAN EYCK, Aldo.

Dutch. Born in Driebergen, Netherlands, 16 March 1918. Married Hannie van Roojen, 1943; two children. Studied at the Building School, The Hague, 1938; studied at Eidgenössische Technische Hochschule, Zurich, 1939-43. Worked as an architect in the Public Works Department, Amsterdam, 1946-50; in private practice, The Hague and Amsterdam, since 1952; in partnership with Theo Bosch, 1971-82, and with Hannie van Eyck-van Roojen, since 1982; editor, *Forum* magazine, Amsterdam, 1959-6 3, 1967; professor, Institute of Technology, Delft, since 1968; Paul Philippe Cret Professor of Architecture, University of Pennsylvania, Philadelphia, 1978-83; member, De 8 en Opbouw, Amsterdam, since 1946; member, Team 10, since 1953. Gold Medal, Royal Institute of British Architects, 1990.

Chronology of Works
All in the Netherlands unless noted

1946	Tower Room conversion, Zurich, Switzerland
1947-79	Approximately 650 children's playgrounds, Amsterdam (with the Public Works Department)
1948	Heldring and Pierson Bank, The Hague
1949	Van Eyck Apartment conversion, Amsterdam
1950	Ahoy Entrance Sign, National Maritime Exhibition, Rotterdam
1952	Blue-Violet Room, Stedelijk Museum, Amsterdam
1954	64 houses for the elderly, Amsterdam (with Jan Rietveld)
1955	House, Herman Gorterstraat, Amsterdam (with Gerrit Rietveld)
1955-56	Three schools, Nagele, (with H. P. D. van Ginkel)
1957-60	Children's Home, Amsterdam
1965	Protestant Church, Driebergen
1966	Sculpture Pavilion, Arnhem
1968	Camping sanitary facilities, Loenen a.d. Vecht
1968-70	Roman Catholic Church, The Hague
1969	Visser House, Bergeik (extensions)
1969	Schmela Art Building, Dusseldorf, Germany
1969-70	Housing, Lima, Peru (with Sean Wellesley Miller)
1970	Verberk House, Venlo
1974-76	G. J. Visser House, Retie, Belgium
1975-77	Housing, Zwolle (with Theo Bosch)
1975-79	Hubertus Home (for single parents and their children), Amsterdam (with Hannie van Eyck)
1980-83	Huize Padua Psychiatric Clinic, Boekel (with Hannie van Eyck)
1982-83	Clinic for Drug Addicts, Helmond (with Hannie van Eyck)
1982-83	Siemens AG new buildings, Nuremberg, Germany (with Hannie van Eyck)
1984	Protestant Church for the Moluccan Community, Deventer (with Hannie van Eyck)
1984-86	ESTEC/ESA New Conference Centre and Restaurant, Noordwyk (with Hannie van Eyck)

Publications

ARTICLES BY VAN EYCK

"CIAM 6, Bridgewater: Statement Against Rationalism (1947)." In *A Decade of Modern Architecture* by Sigfried Giedion, Zurich, 1954; reprinted in *CIAM Otterlo* by Oscar Newman, Stuttgart and London, 1961.*IT1*

"Wij Ontdekken Stijl" (We Discover Style). *Forum* 4 (1949).

"De Bal Kaatst Terug" (The Ball Bounces Back). *Forum* 3 (1958).

"Het Verhaal van een Andere Gedachte" (The Story of Another Idea). *Forum* 7 (1959).

"There is a Garden in Her Face." *Forum* 15 (1960-61).

"University College in Urbino by Giancarlo De Carlo." *Zodiac* 16 (1966).

"Dogen." *Forum* (July 1967); reprinted as "The Interior of Time: A Miracle of Moderation," in *The Meaning of Architecture*, ed. by Charles Jencks and George Baird, London 1969.

"The Enigma of Multiplicity." *Harvard Educational Review* 39/4 (1969).

"What Is and Isn't Architecture." *Lotus International* 28 (1980).

"Aldo van Eyck: Annual RIBA Discourse." *RIBA Journal* (April 1981).

"Ex turigo semper alquid novum." *Archithese* (Zurich) 5 (1981).

"Lumière, Couleurs et Transparence." *Architecture d'aujourd'hui* (October 1981).

"R. R. P. (Rats, Posts and Other Pests)." *Architectural Design* 7 (1981).

"By Definition." *Dutch Forum* (June 1982).

BOOKS ABOUT VAN EYCK

Aldo van Eyck, Projekten 1948-1976 (2 vols.). Groningen, Netherlands, 1981-83.

Aldo van Eyck: Hubertus House, with texts by Herman Hertzberger, Francis Strauven and others. Amsterdam, 1982.

EMBLETON, N.: *The Works of Aldo van Eyck and Herman Hertzberger* (thesis). University of Newcastle, England, 1978.

SMITHSON, ALISON: *Team X Primer*. Cambridge, 1968.

STRAUVEN, FRANCIS (ed.): *Aldo van Eyck.* Antwerp, 1985.

————: *Het Burgerweeshuis van Aldo van Eyck: een modern monument.* Amsterdam, 1987.

VAN GEEST, JAN, et al.: *Aldo van Eyck Ax Bax.* Athens, 1983.

ARTICLES ABOUT VAN EYCK

"Aldo van Eyck: architetture e pensieri." *Casabella* (October 1985)

"Architect Ludens: Aldo and Hannie van Eyck." *Architectural Review* (February 1990).

Architecture and Urbanism, special issue (April 1991).

BUCHANAN, PETER: "Street Urchin, Mother's House, Amsterdam." *Architectural Review* (March 1982).

DOUBILET, SUSAN: "Weaving Chaos into Order: Home for Single-Parent Families, Amsterdam." *Progressive Architecture* (March 1982).

GOETHAM, J. VAN: "Casa dei Ragazzi ad Amsterdam, A. van Eyck, Architect." *Architettura* 7 (October 1961).

HERTZBERGER, HERMAN: "The Mechanism of the 20th Century and the Architecture of Aldo van Eyck." In *Aldo van Eyck: Hubertus House*, edited by A. van Roijen-Wortmann and F. Strauven, Amsterdam, 1982.

NICOLIN, PIERLUIGI: "Aldo van Eyck: The Web and the Labyrinth." *Lotus International* 11 (1976).

SMITHSON, PETER: "Church at The Hague." *Architectural Design* 45 (June 1975).

VOELCKER, JOHN: "Polder and Playground." *Architects Yearbook* 6 (1955).

ZEVI, BRUNO: "Children's Home in Amsterdam." *Architettura* 6 (1961).

*

Aldo Van Eyck's long career has not only been characterized by the wide-ranging concerns of theorist, academic and practitioner, but has demonstrated considerable growth. His early work in the idealist tradition of CIAM (Congrès Internationaux d'Architecture Moderne) was tempered in later years by a more recent alternative pluralist vision.

He met with prominence due to his ideas beginning in 1953, when Alison and Peter Smithson led a challenge to the Athens Charter and its strongly functionalist base. The outcome was CIAM 10 held at Dubrovnik in 1956, from which Team 10 emerged. Team 10 effectively signaled the demise of CIAM by establishing a new set of ground rules, to which Van Eyck's contribution was the most radical. Indeed, his views on "hearth" and "threshold" were at variance with mainstream Team 10 thinking, as was, indeed, his rejection of the growing abstraction of international modernism.

This shift of emphasis coincided with a growing interest in anthropology and in the behavioral patterns of children: it is no accident that he designed 650 children's playgrounds. The old guard's obsession for "space and time" was replaced by Van Eyck's "place and occasion" and "articulating the in-between" attitudes, which were manifest in his Children's Home in Amsterdam (1957-60). "A house like a town, a town like a house" was Van Eyck's declared objective when he designed the orphanage. Indeed, the building is a series of repetitive but subtly different pavilions which together combine and interact like the elements of a city. The now familiar repetition of precast concrete dome, circular concrete column, clerestory, glazed wall (often of glass blocks), brickwork and "doorstep" provide a thematic order which Van Eyck breaks down by altering these familiar visual images to suit the range of activities within the building. The plan establishes a hierarchy of accessible semipublic spaces beyond the entrance, whereupon a "bridge" formed by the administration block signals an incursion to more private territory. The echelon planning of the pavilions ensures diagonally disposed circulation areas, which introduce a strong dynamic element. The most-private areas, those for sleeping, are disposed furthest from traffic and the public and are elevated on columns to first-floor level, further emphasizing their remoteness and privacy. The glazed screens of varying transparency allow for constantly varying inside/outside relationships, a concern that has underpinned most of Van Eyck's work. The Amsterdam orphanage was certainly a key work of the 1960s, and was greatly to influence the next generation of Dutch architects, notably Herman Hertzberger and Piet Blom, providing an important formal link between De Stijl and contemporary Dutch architecture.

The orphanage also demonstrated a simultaneous overlay of separate systems: laid out on a repetitive square grid it has diagonal circulation routes and circular elements of large and small scale (sunken play areas or light fittings) which interact with the orthogonal grid. These complex juxtapositions further heighten the potential for a sense of "place," a technique Van Eyck repeated in his competition entry for the Protestant Church at Driebergen, Holland, and again more particularly at his Arnhem Sculpture Pavilion (1966). There a series of four-meter-high parallel walls form not only an ordered backdrop to the exhibits, but interact with drum-like interventions of varying scale to produce surprise and variety.

Compared with many of his contemporaries, Van Eyck has built little, but each completed building has been enormously influential. His Hubertus Home in Amsterdam (1975-79) for single parents and their children is no exception. There, the plan again establishes a carefully contrived hierarchy, from a public face at the street to the intensely private world of children asleep and at play well away from the bustle of urban life. The care over the smallest detail is taken to new lengths: each light fitting, balustrade, even the children's baths are by Van Eyck's hand. No surface or junction is left to chance, and like the orphanage, the Hubertus Home is clear built evidence of Van Eyck's compelling architectural theories.

Van Eyck's place in late 20th-century architecture was further acknowledged when the Royal Institute of British Architects saw fit to award him its prestigious Gold Medal in 1990.

—PETER FAWCETT

VAN OSDEL, John Mills.

American. Born in Baltimore, Maryland, 1811. Died in 1891. Father was John Van Osdel, architect; married Caroline Gailer. Established own firm, Chicago, Illinois, 1844.

Chronology of Works
All in the United States
† *Work no longer exists*

1837	William B. Ogden Mansion, Chicago, Illinois†
1848	City Hall and Market, Chicago, Illinois†
1851	Second Presbyterian Church, Chicago, Illinois†
1853	Court House, Chicago, Illinois
1856	Ironfront Warehouse, Chicago, Illinois†
1872	McCarthy Building, Chicago, Illinois
1872	Peter Page Leather Goods Store, Chicago, Illinois
1873	Kendall Fireproof Building, Chicago, Illinois†
1873	Tremont House Hotel, Chicago, Illinois†

Publications

BOOKS ABOUT VAN OSDEL

CONDIT, CARL W.: *American Building: Materials and Techniques from the First Colonial Settlements to the Present.* Chicago, 1968.
ERICSSON, HENRY: *Sixty Years a Builder.* Chicago, 1942.
John Van Osdel: A Quarter Century of Chicago Architecture. Chicago, 1898.
LOWE, DAVID: *Lost Chicago.* Boston, 1975.
RANDALL, FRANK A.: *A History of the Development of Building Construction in Chicago.* Urbana, Illinois, 1949.
TALLMADGE, THOMAS EDDY: *Architecture in Old Chicago.* Chicago, 1941.

John Mills Van Osdel, described as the first professional architect to work in Chicago, was instrumental in the early development of that fledgling city in the 1830s and 1840s.

Born and educated in Baltimore, Van Osdel was trained by his father, who was a carpenter, cabinetmaker and building contractor. When the elder Van Osdel went to New York City to establish himself there, John, then 14, aided in supporting his family in Baltimore by making simple furniture. Later, when the rest of the family joined the elder Van Osdel in New York, John worked for his father and read architecture books in the Apprentice Library. At age 18, John Van Osdel embarked on his own business as architect and builder. After marrying Caroline Gailer of Hudson, New York, he returned to Baltimore, worked as an architect and builder, and published a handbook on carpentry, *The Carpenter's Own Book* (1834).

Shortly after returning to New York in 1836, Van Osdel met William B. Ogden, a prosperous merchant from Chicago. So impressed was Ogden by the young man that he gave Van Osdel the commission for an elaborate Greek Revival residence in Chicago. The next year Van Osdel went to Chicago to build the Ogden House in a city which then had only several hundred residents. After completing the Ogden residence, Van Osdel returned to New York and for a year was associate editor of the *American Mechanic* (later to become *Scientific American*). He then went back to Chicago, where he built two steamships for lake commerce.

As there were then no other architects in Chicago, Van Osdel's practice grew rapidly. In 1844, when he opened his office, Van Osdel designed a number of residences and blocks of houses, as well as the Greek Revival Rush Medical College. He also designed the first Chicago City Hall that same year. All of those buildings and his second Cook County Court House (1853) were variants of the popular Greek Revival.

During the decade prior to the Civil War, Van Osdel was busy designing a wide variety of buildings in the rapidly growing city, including a number of loft and warehouse buildings. His second Tremont House Hotel (1850) was described in local newspapers as "the chief ornament of the city." The next year, 1851, he entered into a brief partnership with the newly arrived German architect Frederick Baumann (1826-1921). The scale of Van Osdel's output is suggested by the statistics for just one year, 1855, when he is reported to have built in Chicago 19 houses, 10 commercial buildings, three hotels and two schools; while outside Chicago he is said to have built 13 additional buildings, including the original structure housing Northwestern University, Evanston, Illinois (demolished 1973). Just after 1860, in association with George H. Johnson, Van Osdel erected four cast-iron-fronted business blocks on Lake Street, including the Lloyd and Jones Building. After the Civil War, Van Osdel's stylistic range broadened; his Second Presbyterian Church (1869), was Gothic in style. He also designed a number of hotels, including the large Palmer House (1869-70), in the popular Second Empire Style.

When fire swept Chicago in October 1871, Van Osdel dug a pit in the basement of his office building and buried his drawings. After the fire burned itself out, he retrieved his drawings and proceeded to erect more than 8,000 lineal feet of new office and loft buildings. His Kendall Building, begun prior to the fire in 1871, with fireproofing applied by George H. Johnson to the iron internal structure, survived the fire, and demonstrated the effectiveness of fireproofing methods; the building was completed in 1872. Among the many buildings designed by Van Osdel following the fire were the McCarthy Building (1872), the Peter Page Leather Goods Store (1872), yet another Tremont House Hotel (1873) and the imposing third Palmer House (1873-75) in the popular Second Empire Baroque style. Other buildings erected during that busy two-year period included the Oriental Building and the Reaper Block for Cyrus McCormick.

Following ill health in 1873, Van Osdel briefly retired and traveled through the American West, visiting Yosemite in California among other places, and spent the next year in Europe. After 1874 his practice was limited, although around 1886-87 he did design the Law Building, an office block in downtown Chicago in the then-popular Richardsonian Romanesque style. He also designed a new City Hall and County Building (1885), in the High Victorian Gothic style. In 1888-89 he designed the Centennial Baptist Church and an office building for C. C. Heisen. Among his very last works were two large commercial blocks, the Monon Building (1890) and the Terminals Building, (1890), which still stands on South Dearborn Street in Chicago. Also still standing, in Evanston, is another of Van Osdel's last works, the Queen Anne residence for Simeon and Ebenete Farwell, begun in 1890. Both of the latter are believed to have been designed in collaboration with Van Osdel's architect nephew, John Mills Van Osdel II, who carried on his uncle's firm.

Although never a design innovator or particularly interested in experimental building technology, as were many Chicago architects toward the end of his life, Van Osdel was nonetheless very highly regarded by his younger colleagues as the man who introduced the profession to Chicago. Because of the Chicago fire and subsequent periods of vigorous rebuilding in Chicago, today little remains of Van Osdel's contribution, but he was an important source of inspiration to the architects who created the Chicago school in the 1880s and 1890s.

—LELAND M. ROTH

VANVITELLI, Luigi.

Italian. Born in Naples, Italy, 12 May 1700. Died in Caserta, 1 March 1773. Worked in Rome as an architect and builder, 1732-50; moved to Naples, 1750, to work for the Bourbon King Charles.

Chronology of Works
All in Italy
† Work no longer exists

1733-38	Lazaretto and Pier, Ancona
1738	Arch of Clement, Ancona
1739	Church and Cloister of the Olivetani, Perugia
1743	Church of the Gesù, Ancona
1746-50	Cloister of Sant'Agostino, Rome
1749	Santa Maria degli Angeli, Rome (enlargement and addition)
1750	Palazzo Odescalchi, Rome (wings, with Nicola Salvi)
1750	St. Peter's, Rome (decorations for the tribune)
1750-54	Santa Casa, Loreto (campanile)
1752-74	Royal Palace of the Bourbons, Caserta, near Naples
1752-64	Aqueduct to Naples, Caserta
1753-54	Cavalry Barracks, Naples†
1755	Palazzo Calabritto, Naples (facade and stairs)†
1757-63	Foro Carolino, Naples (now Piazza Dante)
1759	Church of San Marcellino, Naples
1761ff.	Church of the Annunziata, Naples (completed by Carlo Vanvitelli in 1782)
1766	Casacalenda Palace, Naples
1772	Perelli Palace, Naples

Publications

BOOKS BY VANVITELLI

Dichiarazione dei disegni del reale palazzo di Caserta. Naples, 1756.
Le lettere di Luigi Vanvitelli della biblioteca palatina di Caserta. Edited by Franco Strazzullo. Galatina, Italy, 1976.

BOOKS ABOUT VANVITELLI

BOLOGNA, F.: *Settecento napoletano.* Turin, 1967.
CAROSELLI, M. R.: *La reggia di Caserta.* Milan, 1968.
CARRERAS, PIETRO: *Studi su Luigi Vanvitelli.* Florence, 1977.
DEFILIPPIS, FELICE: *Il palazzo reale di Caserta e i Borboni di Napoli.* Naples, 1968.
DE FUSCO, RENATO (ed.): *Luigi Vanvitelli.* Naples, 1973.
FAGIOLO DELL'ARCO, MARCELLO: *Funzioni simboli valori della reggia di Caserta.* Rome, 1863.
FICHERA, F.: *Luigi Vanvitelli.* Rome, 1937.
MYERS, MARY L.: *Architectural and Ornament Drawings: Juvarra, Vanvitelli, the Bibiena Family and other Italian Draftsmen.* New York, 1975.
SCHIAVO, A.: *Il Progetto di Luigi Vanvitelli per Caserta e la sua reggia.* 1953.
VANVITELLI, LUIGI, THE YOUNGER: *Vita di Luigi Vanvitelli.* 1823. New edition: Naples, 1975.

*

Luigi Vanvitelli, one of the better-known 18th-century Italian architects, is frequently noted in the secondary literature as a transition figure from the Late Baroque to the neoclassical period. This reputation is substantiated by a formalistic comparison of his early works to his late works. Designs such as the reliquary chapel of San Ciriaco in Ancona (1739) and the Chiesa della Misericordia in Macerata (1735-42)—featuring curvilinear forms, broken entablatures, and surfaces embellished with multicolored marble panels and gilded stucco figurines—place Vanvitelli well within the tradition of the Late Baroque. His position as a neoclassicist, on the other hand, is confirmed by, among other works, the massive architectural complex, the Royal Palace of the Bourbons at Caserta near Naples, which the architect designed late in his career (1752-74). The palace is exemplary of the severe, grand rectilinear forms and clean, unbroken surfaces that characterize the neoclassical movement.

However, the stylistic discrepancies in Vanvitelli's oeuvre alone should not dictate an assessment of the architect's works. It is clear that most of Vanvitelli's built works—regardless of their formal qualities—were guided by an enlightened attitude about the function of architecture. More important than the architect's aesthetic choice of form was his impulse to express clearly the architectural elements' structural function, an impulse related to the growing desire in the 18th century for the understanding and the subsequent study of building mechanics. This new attitude toward architecture also demanded a sensitivity to defining a program that would serve efficiently the building's function. In the case of the Royal Palace at Caserta, that function was to house civic institutions newly established to serve the Neapolitan state under the Bourbon reign.

The program of the Royal Palace at Caserta was forward-looking in this latter respect. Although it has been suggested that the Bourbon king Charles played a large role in determining the arrangement of the palace, historical documents record that the building plan was implemented as designed by Vanvitelli, a native Neapolitan. The palace was created not solely as a

Luigi Vanvitelli: Royal Palace of the Bourbons, Caserta, Italy, 1752-74

royal residence, but as a complex to shelter the many administrative and military offices of the government.

The strictly geometric plan reveals a logic which Vanvitelli believed should dictate the layout of a building. Overall, the palace's form was simple, with four perimeter ranges defining a rectangle bisected by two intersecting interior arms; the configuration as an entity created four internal courtyards that allowed light and air into all parts of the complex. Access to the palace was through a central pavilion on the main facade and into the elegantly vaulted substructure of one of the interior ranges, which provided a grand space to receive and dispense dignitaries. Visitors then proceeded into the palace via an imposing stairway to the left of a central octagonal vaulted pavilion, richly embellished, which was formed at the juncture of the two interior ranges.

The layout of the many rooms on the above stories was well planned to provide for a variety of private and public functions of the royal residence. There was a strict arrangement of the royal apartment in the manner of the French, i.e., enfilade from the public reception room, to the semiprivate camera, and finally to the private garderobe. Connections between the rooms were cleverly calculated to honor the private and public aspect of those rooms. Similarly, offices were hierarchically arranged so that their positions could dictate their use by titled or nontitled dignitaries and functionaries.

Such hierarchical planning was executed in both the small and large scale. For example, apartments and offices were for the most part positioned on the exterior ranges of the complex, while the central ranges, faced on two sides by rows of windows, held such widely accessible spaces as the main stair, the palace chapel and the public theater. These grand elements, designed as almost freestanding structures in a large palace complex,

were situated in such a manner as to impress the casual visitor, but not to disturb the other more private activities performed in the palace. Vanvitelli, then, helped establish a new type of governmental building with his design of Caserta, with its spaces logically arranged to meet the new social and political needs of the expansive Neapolitan governmental system.

Before assuming the commission of the royal palace for Charles, Vanvitelli had a busy, although not flourishing, career in and around Rome. There he executed small-scale commissions, the only type then available in the financially foundering papal state. In that environment, he was active at the same time as Filippo Juvarro and Nicola Salvi, with whom he competed for architectural projects, including two of the more lucrative ones, the facade of San Giovanni in Laterno, and the Trevi Fountain.

In these and in other of his designs, Vanvitelli, like all enlightened architects, was called upon to address the new technical needs of architecture, and he rose to the task. He competed and won—in conjunction with the Marchese Giovanni Poleni, a mathematician best known as codesigner with Isaac Newton and Gottfried Wilhelm Leibniz of the catenary arch—the task of strengthening the unstable dome of St. Peter's designed by Michelangelo (1743-44). Poleni and Vanvitelli suggested encircling the dome with five iron rings, whose form and junctures Vanvitelli designed.

The architect demonstrated other technical abilities throughout his career. He designed the Lazaretto of the port city of Ancona (1733-38). Ancona was in need of a useful pier that would make it a competitive center, given all the foreign commercial ventures operating along the Italian coastline. At the commission of Pope Clement XII Corsini, Vanvitelli, in conjunction with Carlo Marchionni, created a pentagonal-shaped island pier with defensible walls and a prominent bastion on its sea side. It contained a building that housed administrative offices and vaulted storehouses for, among other goods, tobacco. Other technical works for which Vanvitelli was responsible included the aqueduct that supplied the water for the extensive gardens at Caserta. In these projects, Vanvitelli displayed his skills in hydraulics, statics and military engineering.

What underlies all Vanvitelli's architectural designs is the striving for a clarity in expressing structural elements. The substantial enlargement and addition to Michelangelo's transformation of the Roman baths into Santa Maria degli Angeli is one such example (1749). There Vanvitelli accentuated the entablature as a continuous element that wraps around the church, stabilizing the pilasters and columns on which it rests, and sustaining the vaulting that rests on it. It also visually connects the two main disparate chambers of the church. This same clarity was achieved in the Church of the Olivetani in Perugia, where there is a clear demarcation of the vertical elements (1739). The lines of the Corinthian columns and piers extend into the ribs of the vaulting. Large, unadorned panels between the structural elements serve primarily to highlight those elements.

Aside from his architectural achievements, Vanvitelli was an avid letter writer, sometimes writing up to 12 letters a day, many to his family members. His letters, which were published in 1978, give a lively profile of life in the 18th century. For example, in them he vocalized his often-sarcastic opinions of characters both at the Neapolitan court and in the Roman curia, and the intrigues they developed there. More important, he gave an assessment of the architectural profession—to which he clearly devoted much time and energy—at a time when architectural theories were more rampant than projects in Italy.

—SUSAN M. DIXON

VASARI, Giorgio.

Italian. Born in Arezzo, Italy, 30 July 1511. Died in Florence, 27 June 1574. Son of a potter; grandson of the painter Lazzaro Vasari. Married Niccolosa Bacci, 1550. Studied with Il Pollastra in Arezzo and with Pierio Valeriano at the Medici court in Florence; artistic training in Arezzo with Guglielmo da Marcilla (William of Marseilles); frequented the studios of Andrea del Sarto and Baccio Bandelli in Florence, 1524-27; then traveled and worked in Pisa, Bologna, Modena, and Rome, patronized by Cardinal Ippolito de' Medici, 1529-31; worked under the patronage of Duke Alessandro and Ottaviano de' Medici in Florence, 1531-37; traveled extensively during the next 12 years patronized by Bindo Altoviti in Florence, Giovanni Corner in Venice, Cardinal Alessandro Farnese in Rome; then worked in Rome for Pope Julius III, 1550-55 (and a later stint under Pope Gregory XIII, 1573); worked mainly in Florence from 1555: superintendent of the restoration of the Palazzo Vecchio, and designed the Uffizi Palaces; instrumental in founding the Accademia del Sidegno, 1563.

Chronology of Works
All in Italy
† Work no longer exists

1535-37	Cathedral, Arezzo (organ loft)
1537	Triumphal Arch (for the entry of Emperor Charles V), Piazza San Felice, Florence†
1540-48	Giorgio Vasari House, Arezzo
1548ff.	Garden for Cardinal del Monte, Monte Sansovino†
1551-53	Villa Giulia, Rome (with Giacomo Barozzi da Vignola and Bartolomeo Ammannati)
1554	Santa Maria Nuova, Cortona (completion)
1556	Grotta Grande, Boboli Gardens, Florence (facade; completed by Bernardo Buontalenti)
1556-74	Palazzo Vecchio, Florence (renovations)
1559-80s	Uffizi Palaces, Florence
1561-69	Madonna dell' Umilità, Pistoia (cupola)
1562ff.	Piazzo dei Cavaliere, Pisa
1564	Pieve, Arezzo (renovation)
1564	Santissima Flora and Lucilla, Arezzo
1564	Tomb of Michelangelo, Santa Croce, Florence
1565	Santa Croce, Florence (renovation)
1565	Santa Maria Novella, Corridoio (renovation)
1568ff.	Santa Maria della Quercia, Lucignano
1569-72	Madonna della Vittoria, Foiano della Chiana
1570-74	Loggia, Arezzo (not completed until 1596)

Publications

BOOKS BY VASARI

Le opere di Giorgio Vasari, con nuove annotazioni e commenti. 9 vols. Originally published as *Le vite de più eccelenti architetti.* Florence, 1550. Annotated edition by G. Milanesi. Florence, 1878-1906.
Vasari on Technique. New York, 1960.

BOOKS ABOUT VASARI

BOASE, T. S. R.: *Giorgio Vasari: The Man and the Book.* Princeton, New Jersey, 1979.
CARDEN, R. W.: *The Life of Giorgio Vasari.* London, 1910.
HALL, MARCIA B.: *Renovation and Counter-Reformation: Vasari and Duke Cosimo in Santa Maria Novella and Santa Croce 1565-1577.* Oxford, 1979.
KALLAB, W.: *Vasaristudien.* Vienna, 1908.
SATKOWSKI, LEON: *Studies on Vasari's Architecture.* New York, 1979.

ARTICLES ABOUT VASARI

BAROCCHI, P.: "Il Vasari architetto." *Atti dell'Accademia Pontaniana* New series, 6 (1958).
MIARELLI MARIANI, GAETANO: "La critica del Vasari e la setta sangallesca." Pp. 567-585 in *Il Vasari storiografe e artista: Atti del congresso internazionale (1974).* Florence, 1976.
SCHULZ, J.: "Vasari at Venice." *Burlington Magazine* (1961): 500-511.
VENTURI, ADOLFO: "Giorgio Vasari." Vol. 11, Part 2: 385-454 in *Storia del arte italiana.* Milan, 1939.

*

Giorgio Vasari did not, at first, consider himself an architect, nor did he envision a career in architecture. Rather, he clearly and emphatically considered himself a painter, producing a large body of work in that medium throughout his long career. His early interest in painting was fostered by Luca Signorelli, a distant relative who was visiting Arezzo on commission for an altarpiece. Vasari proceeded to study painting in Arezzo under the French stained-glass maker Guilaume de Marcellat. Later, he continued to study painting in Florence and Rome as a member of the traveling court of Cardinal Ippolito de' Medici.

Giorgio Vasari: Uffizi Palace, Florence, Italy, 1559-80s

While in Rome, Vasari became aware of the architectural monuments of that ancient city; in his own "Life" he relates that he spent many long hours in the heat and cold sketching ancient remains in all parts of the city. While in Rome, Vasari fell under the influence of those artists who were to shape the classic monumental architecture of the early cinquecento: Bramante, Raphael, Peruzzi and, above all, Michelangelo. It was also in Rome that Vasari developed his lasting distaste for the architecture of the Middle Ages, the "corrupt" Gothic, which he firmly considered to be a foreign manner of building incompatible with the classic Roman tradition. These forces and concepts were not only to shape his architectural convictions, but actually made him into a "proto-eclectic" architect.

Also influencing his architectural language were the patrons who commissioned works from him. His patronage was drawn largely from the house of Medici, whose members were embarked upon a program of self-glorification and, therefore, desired an architecture based on models ducal, princely, royal, imperial or papal, rather than on forms popular or republican. Due to the source of his major commissions, and in particular the Uffizi Palaces, he was by necessity as well as by inclination constrained to choose architectural forms that fit his clients' aspirations. These forms he then fused into a symbolic language capable of expressing those exalted aspirations.

Vasari began his architectural career in Rome in 1550 at the Villa Giulia, where he helped develop a style that is now generally considered to be "Mannerist." In both Rome and Florence he was awarded several minor commissions, and in his hometown of Arezzo he completed a large structure on the main square that was to prove a forerunner of his major commission.

In 1554 Vasari entered into the service of Duke Cosimo I de' Medici, the first hereditary duke of that line. Vasari's first assignment was the reorganization of the interior of the Palazzo Vecchio in Florence, recently become the Palazzo Ducale; he rebuilt the entrance *cortile,* provided a splendid, intricate stairway to connect the state rooms and private apartments, and completely refurbished the great hall as the throne room for the dukes (later, grand dukes) of Tuscany. In 1559 he was awarded the major architectural commission of his career, the Palaces of the Uffizi. This commission was to prove so difficult to construct that he claimed "... the vast fabric, facing towards the Arno River than which has been built nothing more difficult or dangerous from it being founded over the river and, one might say, in the air."

Vasari, with some justification, may be considered an eclectic architect, as he came to the practice of architecture at that time in its evolution in Italy when artists were forced to acknowledge simultaneously by the revealed legacy of antiquity, the works of the masters of the early cinquecento, the Counter-Reformation and the increasing control of the ruling houses. To satisfy his master and patron, and to demonstrate his knowledge of the works of both the ancients and the moderns, Vasari chose an architectural language that was appropriate, assured, derivative and, paradoxically, original. His many travels throughout Italy to acquire material for his monumental "Lives" had acquainted him with the foremost architectural accomplishments of the moderns, and had also given him a deep understanding of the "rules" as exemplified by the remains of ancient structures. He was aware that his architecture should not only serve its assigned functions, but should also, more importantly, conceal and reveal through architectural language the old order that was being forcibly absorbed into the new state.

Therefore, his design appropriated elements only from those structures that had already been sanctioned as noble: the Piazza

San Marco in Venice, the Belvedere in the Vatican, the remains of the imperial palaces in Rome. His design attempted to avoid references to works either republican or communal. His fusion of elements from such diverse sources as Vitruvian dicta, Roman remains, Florentine quattrocento forms, Michelangelo's oeuvre and the refinements of modern architecture was assured and subtle, working these diverse elements into an architectural composition that seemed to follow all the rules of architecture, while breaking them in ways discernible only to the knowledgeable. It is in this application of the received rules that Vasari can be judged a "derivative" architect. However, in the subtle ways in which he manipulated those rules he may also be adjudged quite an original artist, capable of satisfying the demands of a client and a commission while using the received forms as elements to be applied in a manner both novel and evocative.

As Vasari attempted to refine and define the "Tuscan" style, which had a tendency toward severity and stasis, his mature design for the Florentine palaces advanced that tendency toward intellectual aridity and sophisticated sterility. Yet these same palaces well define in architectural terms the changes in Florentine public life from vibrant republic to submissive duchy. It was Vasari's role, and his genius, to express in architecture that transition, revealing and concealing it while presenting an architectural riddle to the knowing viewer, and an impressive, monumental facade to the casual citizen.

Vasari's finished works bridged the gap between the static perfection of the High Renaissance and the restless energy of the Baroque. It was an architectural expression that looked back to antiquity, to Bramante and to Michelangelo to express the majesty of a ducal state. Vasari's style also advanced into the style of the next century, serving as a model for the Baroque architecture of the nation-states. Vasari was an original eclectic, a synthesizer of the noble art of the past and a progenitor of the coming age of Giovanni Lorenzo Bernini and Francesco Borromini, a bridge between the architecture of the High Renaissance and that of the Baroque, even while he remained faithful to his essential Mannerism.

—DONALD FRICELLI

VAUBAN, Sébastien le Prestre de.

French. Born in France, in 1633. Died in Paris, 30 March 1707. Directed the sieges and fortified the citadels in the wars of King Louis XIV, 1667-1706. More than 120 works are attributed to him, 33 of which were new constructions, the remaining works consisting of renewals and enlargements of older fortifications.

Chronology of Works
All in France unless noted
All dates are approximate

1668	Citadel, Arras
1668	Citadel, Lille
1676	Le Quesnoy
1678-81	*Enceinte*, Maubeuge
1679	Fort de Bellegarde
1679	New City Foundation, Longwy
1679	New City Foundation, Montlouis
1681	*Enceinte*, Soca
1684-85	Aqueduct of Maintenon
1689	*Enceinte*, Belfort
1692	*Enceinte*, Briançon
1692	New City Foundation, Mont Dauphin
1693	Fort Saint Vincent
1694	Fort, Camaret

Publications

BOOKS BY VAUBAN

De l'attaque et de la défense des places. 2 vols. Paris, 1737 and 1828-29.

BOOKS ABOUT VAUBAN

BLOMFIELD, REGINALD: *Sébastien Le Prestre de Vauban: 1633-1707.* London, 1938.
CASSI RAMELLI, ANTONIO: *Sebastiano Le Prestre, Marchese di Vauban.* Rome, 1966.
DUFFY, C.: *The Fortress in the Age of Vauban and Frederick the Great.* 1985.
HALÉVY, DANIEL: *Vauban.* New York, 1923.
KIMBER, THOMAS: *Construction of Vauban's First System of Fortification.* London, 1852.
LAZARD, PIERRE E.: *Vauban: 1633-1707.* Paris, 1934.
LLOYD, E. M.: *Vauban, Montalembert, Carnot: Engineer Studies.* London, 1887.
MICHEL, GEORGES: *Histoire de Vauban.* Paris, 1879.
PARENT, MICHEL, and VERROUST, JACQUES: *Vauban.* Paris, 1971.
RÉBELLIAU, ALFRED: *Vauban.* Paris, 1962.
ROCHAS D'AIGLUN, ALBERT DE (ed.): *Vauban, sa famille et ses écrits, ses oisivetés et sa correspondance.* 2 vols. Paris, 1910.
SAULIOL, RENÉ: *Le Maréchal de Vauban: sa vie, son oeuvre.* Paris, 1924.
TOUDOUZE, GEORGES: *Monsieur de Vauban.* Paris, 1954.

ARTICLES ABOUT VAUBAN

LECOMPTE, CHARLES: "Du service des ingénieurs militaires en France pendant le règne de Louis XIV." *Revue militaire du génie* (1903): 1-163.

*

"Vauban, whose name was Le Prestre," wrote Saint-Simon, "was, at best, a *petit gentilhomme* of Burgundy, but perhaps the most honourable and the most virtuous man of his century and, while he had the highest reputation as the man most skilled in the art of siegecraft and fortification, remained the most simple, the most genuine and the most modest of men."

Sebastian le Prestre de Vauban seems to have been a person who enjoyed taking deliberate risks. At the siege of Maastricht, the marquis de Sourches related, he boldly undertook an "apparently impossible" reconnaissance, after which, to avoid a long detour, he went straight through the enemy lines by night.

Of all military maneuvers, the siege of a town was the one which appealed most strongly to Louis XIV. There was an element of the spectacular about it, and he saw to it that the subjects were fully recorded by his artists. "I have told your son to send a painter," wrote Louis to his minister Jean-Baptiste Colbert on 11 June 1673, "because I believe there will be something beautiful to see."

On 6 June Louis had attacked Maastricht with an army of 25,000. The town was strongly garrisoned under Jacques de Fariaux; he was "a brave man with a good record" and his hopes were high, but he reckoned without Vauban. With a task force of 20,000 peasant laborers, Vauban proceeded to dig his way toward the fortress. The process is described by Christopher Duffy: "Parallel gave way to zig-zag saps, zig-zags to a further parallel and so on until the French were close enough to take the horn work and ravelin of the Tongres Gate by battering and assault.

"The siege parallels had the simplicity of genius . . . the first of the parallels was dug just out of effective cannon range . . . . As further parallels were dug closer to the fortress, so they offered to the besiegers secure sites for their batteries, a defense against sorties and start-lines and supports for assaults. In other words, Vauban assailed the fortress with a marching fortress of his own and stole for the siege attack the tactical advantage which had hitherto been the preserve of defense."

The success was immediate. Fariaux reported from his side that "he who conducted the trenchwork must have been the craftiest man in the world."

It was Vauban's intimate knowledge of the principles of attack which made him master also of the possible methods of defense. His contribution to the military successes of the reign was prodigious. In the first place, his undertakings were on a colossal scale. At Longwy the operation involved the shifting of 640,000 cubic meters of earth and the erection of 120,000 cubic meters of masonry. It was this capacity to think big which lay behind the achievements of the *Grand Siècle*. "We do not live in a reign," wrote Colbert, "which is content with little things. With due regard for proportion, it is impossible to imagine anything which can be too great." Without Colbert's able financial administration, Vauban would never have been able to realize his genius.

The fortification of Lille was Vauban's first great work, and perhaps the most important—"*sa fille aînée dans la fortification*," as he called it himself. The chevalier de Clerville, who was still chief engineer, produced a plan which did not meet with the royal approval. Vauban was given his chance, and he set himself to the task with energy—"*il travaille avec la dernière application*," wrote the marquis d'Humières, governor of Lille.

In plan, Vauban's design for the citadel had the geometrical precision of a snowflake—one five-pointed star superimposed upon another and circumscribed within a 10-pointed star. In section, the three "stars" are seen as three levels, each topping the one in front. Each point to each star was elongated, forming a projection in the shape of a bishop's miter, and the cross fire made possible by the superimposition of those three projections was devastating. The long, sloping parapets enabled the infantry to use their muskets in almost complete safety and to move easily under cover from one position to another. The effect upon morale which such a system must have produced was not the least of its virtues.

From 1667, when he took over from Clerville, to 1706, when he retired, Vauban directed the sieges and fortified the citadels in all of Louis XIV's wars. It has been calculated that he worked on 118 sites, 33 of which were new constructions. Every vulnerable or tactically important point received his attention; the coastal defenses were his fewest; to the south, the Pyrénées formed a sufficient barrier, so it was only at their extremities, at Bayonne and at Perpignan and its surrounding area, that fortresses were needed. In the east, from Antibes to Pignerol, was another line of defenses which gave place to the natural protection of the Alps. But by far the greatest concentration was on the northeast frontier: from Belfort to Calais there were some 60 either built or improved by Vauban.

On his retirement in 1706, Vauban took to philanthropy and espoused the cause of the peasants and the underprivileged, even suggesting a more equitable basis for taxation known as the "*dime royale*." Vauban died shortly after publishing his views. According to Dangeau, Louis was deeply distressed and

stated, "I have lost a man wholly devoted to myself and to the state."

—IAN DUNLOP

VAUX, Calvert.

American. Born in London, England, 20 December 1824. Died on 19 November 1892. Worked in L. N. Cottingham Office, London; draftsman for A. J. Downing, New York City, and partner with Downing, Newburg-on-Hudson, New York; associate, Frederick Law Olmsted office; partner with Frederick Clarke Withers.

Chronology of Works
All in the United States
* Approximate dates
† Work no longer exists

1851-52	William L. Findlay Residence, Newburgh, New York (with Andrew Jackson Downing)†
1851-52	Daniel Parish House, Newport, Rhode Island (with Downing)
1852-53	Francis Dodge House, Washington, D.C. (with Downing)
1852-53	Robert Dodge House, Washington, D.C. (with Downing)
1852-53	Fowler-Moore House, Newburgh, New York (with Downing)
1852*-55	William E. Warren House, Newburgh, New York
1853	Nathaniel P. Willis Residence, Cornwall-on-Hudson, New York
1853*-55	Lydig M. Hoyt House, Staatsburg, New York
1854*-55	Henry H. Chamberlain House, Worcester, Massachusetts (with Frederick C. Withers)
1855*-58	Bank of New York, New York City (with Withers)
1856*-58	Federico Barreda Residence, Newport, Rhode Island
1858-76	Central Park, New York City (with Frederick Law Olmsted)
1865	Eugene A. Brewster House, Newburgh, New York (with Withers)
1865*-66	Charles Kimball Townhouse, Brooklyn, New York (with Withers)
1865*-67	Edwin L. Godkin Townhouse, New York City
1866	Gallaudet College (Columbia Institution for Deaf and Dumb), Washington, D.C. (landscaping, with Olmsted)
1866-73	Prospect Park and Brooklyn Park System, Brooklyn, New York
1867	John James Monell Residence, Beacon, New York (with Withers)
1867-72	Hudson River State Hospital and Grounds, Poughkeepsie, New York (with Withers and Olmsted)
1868-70	Plan of Riverside, Illinois (with Olmsted)
1868-76	Park System, Buffalo, New York (with Olmsted)
1871-73	South Park, Chicago (with Olmsted)
1873-79	Parliament Buildings, Ottawa, Canada (landscaping)
1873-88	Riverside Park, New York (with Olmsted and Samuel Parsons)
1874-76	Henry Baldwin Hyde Residence, Babylon, New York
1874-77	Jefferson Market Courthouse, New York City (with Withers)
1874-77	Museum of Natural History, New York City (with Jacob Wrey Mould)

1874-80	Metropolitan Museum of Art, New York City (with Mould)
1876	George J. Bull Residence, Worcester, Massachusetts
1879-80	Thomas Worthington Whittredge House, Summit, New Jersey†
1879-92	Children's Aid Society, New York City (lodging houses and other structures; some work survives; with George K. Radford)
1881-84	Samuel J. Tilden Townhouse (now National Arts Club), New York City (with Radford)
1881-85	Shearith Israel Cemetery Grounds and Gatehouse, New York City (with Parsons and Radford)
1882-83	Edwin Booth House and Grounds, Middletown, Rhode Island
1887	Morningside Park, New York City (with Olmsted)
1887-94	Downing Park, Newburgh, New York (with Olmsted)
1887-95	State Reservation, Niagara Falls, New York (with Olmsted)
1890-91	Grounds of Wilderstein, Rhinecliff, New York
1894	New York University Grounds, Bronx, New York
1895	New York Botanical Garden, Bronx, New York (with Parsons)

Publications

BOOKS BY VAUX

Villas and Cottages. New York, 1857.

BOOKS ABOUT VAUX

KOWSKY, FRANCIS R.: *The Architecture of Frederick Clarke Withers and the Progress of the Gothic Revival after 1850.* Middletown, Connecticut, 1980.

REED, HENRY HOPE, and DUCKWORTH, SOPHIA: *Central Park, a History and a Guide.* New York, 1967.

SCHUYLER, DAVID, and CENSER, JANE TURNER (eds.): *The Years of Olmsted, Vaux and Company.* Baltimore, 1992.

ARTICLES ABOUT VAUX

DOWNS, ARTHUR CHANNING: "Downing's Newburgh Villa." *Bulletin of the Association for Preservation Technology* 4 (1972): 1-113.

SIGLE, JOHN DAVID: "Calvert Vaux: An American Architect." M.A. thesis. University of Virginia, Charlottesville, 1967.

STEESE, EDWARD: "*Villas and Cottages* by Calvert Vaux." *Journal of the Society of Architectural Historians* 6 (January-June 1947): 1-12.

*

One of the most significant acts of Andrew Jackson Downing's illustrious career was securing English architect Calvert Vaux as partner. Vaux's training in London under Lewis N. Cottingham, a recognized master of Gothic Revival architecture, prepared him to work side by side with Downing in promoting the eclectic, historically derived architecture which both men favored. This partnership with Downing, during which the two collaborated on projects such as Springside, which was Matthew Vassar's estate in Poughkeepsie, New York, and the grounds of the Mall and president's residence in Washington, D.C., was merely the first of a number of productive working relationships through which Vaux influenced 19th-century architectural and landscape architectural design.

It is paradoxical that due to Vaux's collaborative spirit his reputation was obscured, both during his lifetime and in many recent histories. First he worked under the mantle of the renowned Downing, then was overshadowed in the public eye by his partner in the Central Park competition, Frederick Law Olmsted. Vaux was far more significant as a landscape architect than has generally been acknowledged. His particular skill was in structuring outdoor spaces architectonically, but at the same time integrating them with naturalistic designs of the then-prevalent romantic style.

No project illustrated this ability better than did Vaux's conceptual plan for Prospect Park in Brooklyn. There, working alone while Olmsted was in California, Vaux suggested the two major spatial concepts that made Prospect Park's design superior to that for Central Park. First, he recommended that the park site, then divided by Flatbush Avenue, be reconfigured through additional land purchase to avoid unnecessary fragmentation of the landscape. Second, he sketched a clearly delineated entry space for the park—the elliptical plaza that came to be called Grand Army of the Republic Plaza. As the first Beaux Arts-inspired outdoor space in North America, the plaza created a unifying transition between surrounding rectilinear streets and sinuous park roads.

Unfortunately, these significant contributions were overshadowed by Olmsted's greater celebrity, to such an extent that the entire design of Prospect Park was often attributed to him. This may explain, in part, why so few works of landscape architecture by Vaux are known. Those that can be attributed to him demonstrate his fluency with form, topography, materials and spatial sequence. For the Public Grounds of the Canadian Parliament Building in Ottawa, Vaux skillfully resolved a scale problem created when buildings were sited at different levels. By placing Parliament on a terrace linked to the lower level with ramps and staircases, he extended its base line to visually join with that of the lower buildings. This simple, structural solution truly treated landscapes as architecture, rather than as mere accessories to buildings.

His professional projects and collaborations were diverse. With Olmsted he completed plans for park systems in Buffalo, New York, and Chicago, for Downing Park in Newburgh, New York (which the partners designed gratis on the condition that the park be named after their late lamented mentor), for the romantic suburb of Riverside, Illinois, and for Niagara State Reservation, New York. With architectural partners Frederick C. Withers and George K. Radford, he developed details for Central Park, including numerous bridges and the overlook pavilion called the Belvedere, plans for the Bank of New York, and for a president's residence at Gallaudet College in Washington, D.C. Later he specialized in public buildings, designing a series of lodgings for the Children's Aid Society of New York. His last collaborator was landscape architect Samuel Parsons, with whom he designed numerous alterations and additions to Central Park.

From this large body of work two lifelong professional concerns emerged—for quality housing and for preservation of Central Park as a naturalistic park. Vaux's sole individually written book, *Villas and Cottages,* was a treatise and pattern book on well-designed single-family homes. Later, after moving to New York City, he focused on inexpensive housing for middle- and lower-income families. He was an early advocate of multistory apartment construction as a way to provide better housing at lower costs. Facilities designed for the Children's Aid Society were models, in the tenement age, for sanitary, well-lighted group homes.

Vaux viewed the preservation of Central Park as a naturalistic landscape in the heart of the city as an equally socially significant cause to quality housing. During his entire life, in spite of frustrating corruptions of the park due to political intrigue and graft, Vaux remained a steadfast protector of the original plan. Both as a private citizen, through letters to the editor, and during periods of employment as consulting landscape architect, he condemned the unending succession of schemes to add more museums, a speedway or new concessions to the park.

In the midst of this active professional life as architect, landscape architect, site planner and conservationist, Vaux's lifelong personal quest remained to honor the man whom he most admired—Andrew Jackson Downing. His writings referred constantly and lovingly to the "arbiter of taste," in whose honor he pursued every opportunity to establish memorials. He was successful in the park at Newburgh and on the grounds of the Smithsonian Institution in Washington, D.C., for which he designed a commemorative urn with inscription, which now sits in the Haupt Garden. It was most fitting then, although equally tragic, that Vaux should die as Downing had—by drowning. Perhaps it is the highest tribute to Vaux's memory that, like Downing, he too was a great collaborator whose efforts advanced an entire profession, not merely a personal practice.

—NANCY J. VOLKMAN

VAZQUEZ, Lorenzo.

Spanish. Spanish architect, active late 15th and early 16th centuries.

Chronology of Works
All in Spain
* Approximate dates
† Work no longer exists

1488*-92	Palace of Luis de la Cerda y Mendoza, Cogolluda
1489-91	Colegio de Santa Cruz, Valladolid
1489ff.	Franciscan Monastery of San Antonio, Mondéjar†
before 1507	Palace of Antonio de Mendoza, Guadalajara
1509-12	Castle of La Calahorra, Granada (outer walls and doorways) [attributed]

Publications

BOOKS ABOUT VAZQUEZ

CAMON AZNAR, JOSE: *La arquitectura plateresca.* 2 vols. Madrid, 1945.
CERVERA VERA, LUIS: *Arquitectura del Colegio Mayor de Santa Cruz en Valladolid.* Valladolid, 1982.
CHUECA GOITIA, F.: *Arquitectura del siglo XVI (Ars Hispaniae,* vol. XI). Madrid, 1953.
FERNANDEZ GOMEZ, MARGARITA: *Los grutescos en la arquitectura española del Protorrenacimiento.* Valencia, 1987.
KUBLER, G. and SORIA, M.: *Art and Architecture in Spain and Portugal and their American Dominions, 1500-1800.* Baltimore and Harmondsworth, 1959.
LAYNA SERRANO, FRANCISCO: *Historia de Guadalajara y sus Mendozas en los siglos XV y XVI.* 4 vols. Madrid, 1942.
MARTIN GONZALEZ, JUAN JOSE: *Catálogo Monumental de la Provincia de Valladolid (Monumentos Civiles de la Ciudad de Valladolid,* vol. XIII). 2nd ed., Valladolid, 1983.
NADER, HELEN: *The Mendoza Family in the Spanish Renaissance.* New Brunswick, New Jersey, 1979.

ARTICLES ABOUT VAZQUEZ

DIEZ DEL CORRAL GARNICA, ROSARIO: "Lorenzo Vázquez y la casa del cardenal don Pedro González de Mendoza." *Goya* 155 (1980): 280-85.
GOMEZ MORENO, MANUEL: "Sobre el Renacimiento en Castilla: Hacia Lorenzo Vázquez." *Archivo Español de Arte y Arqueología* 1 (1925): 7-40.
SAN ROMAN, F. DEL B.: "Las obras y los arquitectos del Cardenal Mendoza."*Archivo Español de Arte y Arqueología* 7 (1931): 153-61.

*

Little documentation exists about Lorenzo Vázquez, the first non-Italian architect of the Renaissance. Documents call him Segovian. He may have trained in Italy, as he was familiar with Florentine, Bolognese and Milanese models. A recent study by Margarita Fernández suggests instead that he learned of Italian models in books owned by his patrons, members of the Mendoza family. Cardinal Pedro González de Mendoza (1428-95), the powerful confidant of Queen Isabella, was the first of his illustrious family to become interested in classical architecture. He learned about it in 1472 from the papal chancellor Rodrigo Borgia. Cardinal Mendoza's nephew, Íñigo López de Mendoza, second count of Tendilla (1442-1515), led an embassy to Pope Innocent VIII in 1486-88. In Rome, Tendilla must have inspected the architectural projects of Cardinal Borgia while executing a task assigned by his uncle, rebuilding the Church of Santa Croce. He returned to Spain with a deeper understanding of the classical style, and probably with recent editions of the architectural treatises of Leon Battista Alberti (1485) and Vitruvius (1486). He also may have had a copy of Filarete's treatise given to him by King Ferrante I of Naples. Tendilla retained the Milanese humanist Pietro Martire d'Anghiera, and if Vázquez was in Italy, he too could have been hired then.

Cardinal Mendoza's major foundation was the Colegio de Santa Cruz, at the University of Valladolid. The foundation was conceived around 1475; a papal bull of 1479 granted its license and privileges, and it was operating in 1484. In 1486 construction began on a large, rectangular, three-story Gothic building. Its principal facade was asymmetrical, with five irregular bays divided by buttresses, those at the corners canted diagonally. Its interior court was square with seven arcaded bays per side. The cardinal expected a splendidly rich edifice when he visited Valladolid in 1488. His disappointment at the sober, unornamented structure being built led him to stop the work. In 1489 he appointed Vázquez to continue construction, which was completed in 1491. Vázquez's task was largely to embellish with Renaissance details a nearly finished Gothic structure. Vázquez added to the facade a central portal, Corinthian pilasters at the upper buttresses, a Corinthian cornice and a roof balustrade. The central portal occupies the narrowest bay, with an arched door framed by a Corinthian order combining pilasters and engaged columns. Grotesques decorate their shafts and the frieze of the entablature. Another arch decorated with palmettes and dolphins surmounts the entablature. Candelabra flank the upper arch. Faceted rustication fills the rest of the central bay, except for an upper window, and the royal arms and the arms of the founder above. Fernando Chueca has convincingly compared both the doubled arch and the rustication to that of the Palazzo Bevilacqua in Bologna, completed in about 1482. In the interior court Vázquez inserted a classical balustrade in the upper story, and designed several portals. The finest of these gives access to the library, the grandest room in the complex, occupying the upper two stories of the front wing of the college.

Lorenzo Vazquez: Castle of La Calahora, Granada, Spain, 1509-12

The most compelling building by Lorenzo Vázquez is the palace of Luis de la Cerda y Mendoza, duke of Medinaceli, in Cogolludo, Guadalajara (ca. 1488-92). It is a strongly Italianate building with a two-story symmetrical facade, wide and horizontal. The same faceted rustication of the Colegio de Santa Cruz is applied uniformly throughout the wall. It is divided horizontally by a stringcourse, on which rest the six large Isabelline Gothic *biphora* windows of the upper story. The lower story lacks any openings other than the central portal, which is a simplified version of that in Valladolid. Above, a Late Gothic roof balustrade caps a Corinthian cornice. The Medinaceli coat of arms appears repeatedly, in the tympanum above the doorway, in a large roundel above it and on the 15 roof balusters. The juxtaposition of Gothic and Renaissance details recalls Milanese works, Michelozzo's Medici Bank or Filarete's Ospedale Maggiore. The two-story inner court had four by five bays, with a basket-handle arcade on slender Corinthian columns below and a now-ruined trabeated upper level.

In 1489 Tendilla commissioned Vázquez to build the now-ruined Franciscan monastery of San Antonio in Mondéjar, Guadalajara. Its modest church had a Gothic structure with pointed arches and rib vaults, but Ionic pilasters articulated its interior wall elevation. The west portal follows that of Valladolid, with superimposed arches, Corinthian columns, grotesques and candelabra. The upper arch was segmental instead of semicircular, and the lower had multiple archivolts, both Gothicizing traits. A pediment over the upper arch increased the sense of tense superimpositions of this composition.

Vázquez settled in Guadalajara, where he was responsible for several projects, such as the Palace of Cardinal Mendoza, the courtyard of the Dávalos Palace and the courtyard of the Church of Santa María de la Fuente. Most important is the much-altered palace of Antonio de Mendoza, nephew of the cardinal, completed before 1507. Its courtyard with two trabeated stories, which has an unusually rich and slender version of the Tuscan order below, and the Corinthian above, was influential in the development of transitional Spanish courtyards. The grotesque decorations were modeled on drawings from the Codex Escurialensis, owned by Rodrigo Borgia's cousin Diego Hurtado de Mendoza, second son of Tendilla.

The last known work in which Vázquez intervened is the Castle of La Calahorra, Granada (1509-12). It was built for Rodrigo Díaz de Vivar y de Mendoza, marquis of Zenete, illegitimate son of Cardinal Mendoza and his second wife María de Fonseca, whose turbulent love affair and elopement was a famous scandal of the time. In 1510 Michele Carlone of Genoa replaced Vázquez. Vázquez was probably responsible for the outer walls of the castle, and two doorways at the ground level of the court are attributed to him. Carlone expanded the court, adding its famous staircase, and executed most of the remaining decorations, again following models from the Codex Escurialensis.

The work of Lorenzo Vázquez does not exhibit the concern with a regulating order which the best 15th-century Italian architects struggled to achieve. He understood the classical spirit through its decorative devices instead. His work underwent an ongoing development as he refined details, and organized these into increasingly more coherent decorative ensembles. His preferences were certainly prevalent in Spain and France, where Gothic taste was deeply ingrained, and his attitude would continue to mark Spanish Renaissance work for another 60 years.

—SERGIO L. SANABRIA

Robert Venturi: Franklin Court, Philadelphia, Pennsylvania, 1976

VENTURI, Robert.

American. Born in Philadelphia, Pennsylvania, 1925. Married the architect Denise Scott Brown, 1967. Studied at Princeton University, New Jersey, A.B. 1947; M.F.A. 1950; American Academy, Rome, 1954-56. Worked as a designer for the firms of Oscar Stonorov, Philadelphia, Eero Saarinen, Bloomfield Hills, Michigan, and Louis I. Kahn, Philadelphia, 1950-58; partner with Paul Cope and H. Mather Lippincott, Philadelphia, 1958-61; partner with William Short, Philadelphia, 1961-64; partner with John Rauch, 1964-89, and with Rauch and Denise Scott Brown, 1967-89; partner, with Denise Scott Brown, Venturi, Scott Brown Associates, Philadelphia, since 1989. taught at University of Pennsylvania; architect in residence, American Academy, Rome. Instructor, then associate professor of architecture, University of Pennsylvania, Philadelphia, 1957-65; Charlotte Shepherd Davenport Professor of Architecture, Yale University, New Haven, Connecticut, 1966-70; has also taught at Princeton University, Harvard University, and elsewhere in the United States. Fellow, American Institute of Architects. Pritzker Prize, 1991.

Chronology of Works
All in the United States unless noted

1960-63   Guild House, housing for the elderly, Philadelphia, Pennsylvania (with Cope and Lippincott)
1962   Vanna Venturi House, Chestnut Hill, Philadelphia, Pennsylvania
1965-69   Philadelphia General Hospital (renovation and additions)
1973   Trubek and Wislocki Houses, Nantucket Island, Massachusetts
1973   Humanities Classroom Building, State University of New York, Purchase, New York
1973-76   Allen Art Museum, Oberlin, Ohio (renovation and addition)
1974   Four-Bay Fire Station, New Haven, Connecticut
1974   Brant House, Greenwich, Connecticut
1974-77   Pennsylvania State University Faculty Club, State College, Pennsylvania
1975   Tucker House, Mount Kisco, New York

1976	Franklin Court, Independence National Historical Park, Philadelphia, Pennsylvania
1977	Theater Building, Hartford Stage Company, Hartford, Connecticut
1979	Institute of Scientific Information Office Building, Philadelphia, Pennsylvania
1981	Carroll Newman Library, Virginia Polytechnic Institute and State University, Roanoke, Virginia (additions and renovation; with Vosbeck, Vosbeck, Kendrick and Redinger)
1982	Park Regency Condominiums, Houston, Texas
1983	Gordon Wu Hall, Butler College, and alterations to Wilcox Hall, Princeton University, Princeton, New Jersey
1983	Metropolitan Apartment block, Philadelphia, Pennsylvania (conversion of YMCA building)
1985	Lewis Thomas Laboratory for Molecular Biology, Princeton University, Princeton, New Jersey
1986	Natural habitat primate exhibition facility and visitor orientation center, Philadelphia Zoological Gardens, Pennsylvania
1986	Stony Creek office center, Norristown, Pennsylvania (conversion)

Publications

BOOKS BY VENTURI

Complexity and Contradiction in Architecture. New York, 1966; revised edition, 1977.
Learning From Las Vegas. With Denise Scott Brown and Steven Izenour. Cambridge, Massachusetts, 1972; revised edition, 1977.
A View From the Campidoglio, Selected Essays 1953-84. New York, 1985.

BOOKS ABOUT VENTURI/RAUCH/SCOTT BROWN

DIAMONSTEIN, BARBARALEE: *American Architecture Now II.* New York, 1985. DREW, PHILIP: *Third Generation: The Changing Meaning of Architecture.* New York, 1972.
DREXLER, ARTHUR: *Transformations in Modern Architecture.* New York, 1979.
Global Architecture 39: Venturi and Rauch. Tokyo, 1976.
MEAD, CHRISTOPHER (ed.): *The Architecture of Robert Venturi.* Essays by Vincent Scully. Albuquerque, New Mexico, 1989.
PETTENA, GIANNI, and VOGLIAZZO, MAURIZIO (eds.): *Venturi, Rauch and Scott Brown.* Milan, 1981.
SCULLY, VINCENT: *American Architecture and Urbanism.* New York, 1969.
SCULLY, VINCENT: *The Work of Venturi and Rauch.* Exhibition catalog. New York, 1971.
STERN, ROBERT A. M.: *New Directions in American Architecture.* New York, 1969.
Venturi, Scott Brown and Associates on Houses and Housing. London and New York, 1992.

ARTICLES ABOUT VENTURI/RAUCH/SCOTT BROWN

Architecture and Urbanism, special issues (October 1971; November 1974; December 1981; June 1990).
CLIFF, URSULA: "Are the Venturis Putting Us On." *Design and Environment* (Summer 1971).
COHEN, STUART: "Physical Context/Cultural Context: Including It All." *Oppositions* 2 (1974).

COLQUHOUN, ALAN: "Sign and Substance: Reflections on Complexity, Las Vegas, and Oberlin." *Oppositions* 14 (1978).
FILLER, MARTIN: "Learning from Venturi." *Art in America* (April 1980).
JENCKS, CHARLES: "Venturi, Rauch, and Scott Brown." *Architectural Design* (January/February 1982).
MACNAIR, ANDREW: "Venturi and the Classic Modern Tradition." *Skyline* (March 1980).
Progressive Architecture, special issue (October 1977).

As well known as a theoretician as he has been as a designer of buildings, Robert Venturi has been somewhat of an anomaly throughout his distinguished career, consistently outdistancing even the most original thinkers in the architectural avant-garde with the freshness of his ideas.

His first, and perhaps best remembered, surprise for an unsuspecting profession was his book *Complexity and Contradiction in Architecture,* which was published in 1966. The thesis of the book is simply that buildings which are formed out of several complex design criteria are far more interesting than those which are not, and that less, rather than being more, is a bore. As the architectural equivalent of a child's recognition of a king's nakedness in the fable of the emperor's new clothes, this book eventually served to expose the weaknesses of the Modern Movement, and was a critical factor in its decline.

As a dues-paying member himself of what author Tom Wolfe has called the "academic compound," Venturi was able to argue what outsiders had not dared to formulate, and he knew how to structure those arguments most effectively. Originally developed out of a course that Venturi had begun to teach at the University of Pennsylvania in 1957, *Complexity and Contradiction* is organized in a lecture format, with individual graphics arranged sequentially to illustrate the points that are made. As each of the numerous examples is introduced, there is a real, cumulative sense of an irrefutable position being established, and of a limiting intellectual barrier being dismantled, brick by brick.

As such, the book is a legitimate antidote to *Vers Une Architecture,* which was written to proclaim the beginning of the Modern Movement more than four decades earlier, and serves as a self-proclaimed "Gentle Manifesto" set in opposition to that more strident call by Le Corbusier. The proposals put forward by Venturi for an architecture that is complex rather than simple, related to history and context rather than dismissive of it, symbolic and ornamental rather than intentionally codeless, and humorous rather than deadly serious, were all what he called "the circumstantial and ordinary aspects of everyday life."

His recognition of the importance of all of these elements in the significant architecture of the past, as well as in any meaningful direction in the future, elicited an eager response, and eventually served as one of the main building blocks of the postmodern movement that followed.

Rather than being as inclusive as he had hoped, however, postmodernism, in spite of all the convoluted theorizing of its advocates, turned out to be just as restrictive as its predecessor. As Venturi noted in another characteristically penetrating analysis of the situation, appropriately titled "Diversity, Reliance and Representation in Historicism or plus ça change," and published in *Architectural Record* nearly twenty years after *Complexity and Contradiction* had appeared, postmodernism had used different images than modernism, but had retained the same exclusivity and rigity of principles. As such, it had become nothing more than a lock-step sequel to the ideology it had sought to democratize, and had even failed in the relatively simple task of contextual fit that it had set for itself.

In his own work, Venturi has consistently sought to do otherwise, and in the process has managed to convince several generations of architects that the commonplace and everyday built environment cannot be willed out of existence, and is "almost alright." The mere thought of using conventional elements in a building at first shocked many practitioners, but Venturi's handling of such elements eventually convinced even the most reluctant of them that the ordinary could become extraordinary in the right hands. Where the modernists had felt it was necessary to educate and elevate public taste, Venturi and Denise Scott Brown, his wife and partner, have instead convinced architects to accept and improve upon it.

As expressed in his architecture, his original thesis in *Complexity and Contradiction* constantly surfaces as a struggle between the interior requirements of a building and those of its exterior envelope. This, in turn, typically leads to conflict, ending in the separation and eventual divorce of the two. In one of his most famous designs, for his mother's house in Chestnut Hill near Philadelphia, this struggle is acted out between the topographical requirements of a formal, front entry and the main interior stair. Similar confrontations can also be seen as the driving force behind each of his subsequent designs. Following his own "Gentle Manifesto," he has always tried to incorporate what he described in *Learning from Las Vegas* as "double functioning or vestigial elements, circumstantial distortions, expedient devices, eventful exceptions, exceptional diagonals, things in things, crowded or contained intricacies, linings or layerings, residual spaces, redundant spaces, ambiguities, inflections, dualities, difficult wholes, or the phenomena of both-and."

Of all of his work, his most memorable achievement, aside from the written word, may arguably and ironically be a little-known nonbuilding in Philadelphia. When approached by the United States Park Service to restore Benjamin Franklin's long-demolished house on Market Street, which had been adjacent to his printing shop and post office, Venturi found that the only reliable documents of the building that still existed were Franklin's letters to his wife while he was ambassador to France. In those letters Franklin vividly described the house he had in mind, down to the location of windows and doors, and overall dimensions, which match those of the foundation that still survives.

Focusing on the wish expressed in the letters, which did exist, rather than on physical remains, which did not, the architect made a characteristically novel counterproposal to the client, recommending that the outline described by Franklin be ghosted out in brightly colored steel frame, and that quotes from his letters to his wife be commemorated in plaques placed around its base. In Venturi's proposal, which was accepted and built, a museum dedicated to the life and inventions of this highly creative and energetic statesman and diplomat was substituted for the house, and was placed underground so as not to interfere with the image created by the steel frame above.

Instead of presenting a speculative restoration in an all-too-familiar style, the structure allows the public to complete mentally the scene that once existed there, with each image varying according to the background, perception and imagination of the individual viewer. The result is a far more memorable architectural experience than any rebuilding could ever have provided, and tangible proof of Robert Venturi's originality and trust in the general public.

—JAMES STEELE

VESNIN BROTHERS.

Russian. Leonid Vesnin: Born in 1880. Died in 1933. Studied at the Academy of Fine Arts, St. Petersburg, 1901-09. Viktor A. Vesnin: Born in 1882. Died in 1950. Studied at the Institute of Civil Engineering, St. Petersburg. Aleksandr Vesnin: Born in 1883. Died in 1959. Studied architecture at the Institute of Civil Engineering, St. Petersburg. Instrumental in establishing architectural faculty at the State Higher Art and Technical Workshops, 1920. Editor, with Moisei Ginsburg, of the journal of the Society of Contemporary Architects (OSA), *Sovremennaia arkhitektura*, 1926-30.

Chronology of Works
All in Russia [Soviet Union]
† Work no longer exists

1911	Post Office, Myasnitskaya Street, Moscow
1914-15	Sirotkin House, Nizhny-Novgorod
1917	Dynamo Stock Company, Moscow
1919	Karl Marx Monument, Red Square, Moscow†
1924	Pravda Newspaper Building, Leningrad [not built]
1925	Institute of Mineralogy, Moscow
1926-27	Mostorg Department Store, Moscow
1929-30	Dnieper Dam and Hydro-Electric Station
1931-34	Film Actors Club, Moscow
1933-37	Palace of Culture, Moscow

Publications

ARTICLES BY ALEKSANDR VESNIN

"Tvorcheskaia tribuna: problemy sovremennoi arkhitektury." With V. A. Vesnin and M. I. Ginsburg. *Arkhitektura SSSR*, No. 2 (1934): 63-69.
"Tvorcheskii otchet." With V. A. Vesnin. *Arkhitektura SSSR*, No. 4 (1935): 40-44.
"Forma i soderzhanie." With V. A. Vesnin. *Arkhitekturnaia gazeta* (8 April 1935).
"On Socialist Realism in Architecture." *Architectural Design*, No. 1 (1959): 3-6.

ARTICLES BY VIKTOR A. VESNIN

"Menshe 'akademizma'!" *Arkhitekturnaia gazeta* (12 January 1937).
"Ot konstruktivizma k sotsialisticheskomu realizmu." *Arkhitekturnaia gazeta* (23 June 1937).

BOOKS ABOUT THE VESNINS

BARKHIN, MIKHAIL GRIGOREVICH: *Mastera Sovetskoi arkhitektury ob arkhitecture*. Moscow, 1975.
CHINIAKOV, ALEKSEI G.: *Bratia Vesniny*. Moscow, 1970.
DE FEO, V.: *URSS: Archittetura 1917-1936*. Rome, 1963.
ILIN, MIKHAIL A.: *Vesniny*. Moscow, 1960.
KHAN-MAGOMEDOV, S. O.: *Alexander Vesnin and Russian Constructivism*. 1986.
KOPP, ANATOLE: *Town and Revolution: Soviet Architecture and City Planning 1917-1935*. New York and London, 1970.
KROHA, J. and HRŮZA, J.: *Sovetska architektonika avant garda*. Prague, 1973.
LISSITZKY, ELEAZAR: *Russia: An Architecture for World Revolution*. Cambridge, Massachusetts, 1970.
SHVIDOVSKY, O. A.: *Building in the USSR: 1917-1932*. London and New York, 1970.

Vesnin Brothers: Pravda Newspaper Building, Leningrad, Russia, 1924

ARTICLES ABOUT THE VESNINS

"Academician Victor Vesnin." *Royal Institute of British Architects Journal*, 3rd series, Vol. 48 (December 1944): 31-32.

"Arkhitektory—kandidaty v Verkhovnyi sovet SSSR. Viktor Aleksandrovich Vesnin." *Arkhitektura SSSR*, No. 11 (1937): 9-10.

CHINIAKOV, ALEKSEI G.: "Mastera sovetskoi arkhitektury. Bratia Vesniny." *Sovetskaia arkhitektura*, No. 13 (1961): 97-118.

CHINIAKOV, ALEKSEI G.: "Le Korbuze i Vesniny." *Sovetskaia arkhitektura*, No. 18 (1969): 133-143.

ILIN, MIKHAIL A.: "Mastera sovetskoi arkhitektury. Bratia Vesniny." *Arkhitektura SSSR*, No. 1 (1940): 33-49.

KHIGER, R. I.: "V masterskoi arkhitektora. Tvorchestvo bratev Vesninykh." *Arkhitektura SSSR*, Nos. 3-4 (1933): 46-51.

"Victor Vesnin." *American Institute of Architects Journal*, Vol. 4 (August 1945): 47.

VLASOV, ALEKSANDR V.: "Nash put. Vsesoiuznoe soveshchanie sovetskikh arkhitektorov." *Arkhitektura SSSR*, No. 6 (1937): 23-25.

*

The Vesnin brothers generally have been recognized as the founders of constructivism in Russian avant-garde architecture. The Vesnins' design for the Palace of Labor in Moscow became an iconoclastic image of the style to follow. It anticipated the form of Walter Gropius' project for the 1922 Chicago Tribune Tower contest. Further reinforced by ensuing competition entries, such as the Leningrad Pravda offices and the Arcos Company headquarters in Moscow, both designed in 1924, and the Telegraph Office Building in Moscow of 1925 (none of which was built), this imagery was synonymous with the Russian Revolution and symbolized the new social and political order of the country. It was conceived to accommodate the new man who had outlived his past and now lived for a bright future. In aesthetic terms, their project for the Leningrad Pravda Building became a canonical work of constructivism, comparable to Le Corbusier's Ozenfant Studio, Gerrit Rietveld's Schroeder House or Ludwig Mies van der Rohe's glass skyscraper project, all designed during 1922-23.

The Palace of Labor competition for a combined government center and central house of culture was held in 1922-23. The complex was to contain two auditoriums seating 8,000 and 2,500, administrative offices, an observatory, a radio broadcasting center, several museums, a library and a 6,000-seat restaurant. While the results of this competition were to mark the beginning of modern Soviet architecture, the program was also typical of a certain gigantism, which was to reappear throughout the history of the later period, a gigantism that expressed the desire to outdo the capitalist world, even in the scale of its buildings. Though quite impractical, considering the resources available at that time, the program nevertheless reflected an entirely novel conception of what a Soviet building should be, and provided the Vesnin brothers with the basis for a design that, both in functional conception and in architectural forms, opened the way for modern architecture in the Soviet Union. It broke with both classical composition and with symbolic and romantic trends, although these were also represented in the competition.

In spite of the obvious superiority of the Vesnins' design, the first prize went to the architect Nikolai Trotsky, who was later to make a name for himself in Leningrad with supermonumental compositions that borrowed from every period of architectural history. Trotsky's scheme for the Palace of Labor was characterized as an overblown cross of Ledoux with Palladio.

The Vesnin brothers won only the third prize, while Pantelemon Golosov, who joined the constructivists in 1924, obtained fifth prize for a design representing a symbolist trend, a gesture toward machine aesthetics—an enormous mass surrounded by the inevitable spiral inscribed in a gigantic geared wheel.

The Vesnins' design defined the formal vocabulary of architectural constructivism. The composition is asymmetrical both in the plan and the elevations. The exposed reinforced-concrete frame with a vertical emphasis and the superimposed horizontal layers give the building a rhythmic appearance. The larger auditorium, placed in an oval cylinder, is crowned with a set of trussed columns and ventilation tubes. This auditorium's connection-bridge to the main mass of the complex houses the small auditorium. These two auditoriums can unite by means of a movable wall, to raise the seating capacity to 10,500. On top of the complex is a forest of radio-antenna wires for communication with the whole world. Two other features of the design, the meteorological station and the exterior giant digital clock, symbolize another important link of the times: the link from present times to the future.

If this competition marked the beginning of architectural constructivism, it also revealed the influence that the old school still retained, and was to cling to, through the years. The composition of the jury explains why the first prize was awarded to a neo-classicist design. Apart from representatives of the Communist Party, the government and the Moscow Soviet, this jury included Aleksei V. Shchusev, Ivan Zholtovsky and others of the same breed, all of whom had received their training well before the Revolution and in the purest academic tradition.

The constructivist architectural language was manifested through a strong framework of exposed structural elements on a clear stereometric volume that gave forms a rhythmic order. Building entry, circulation and major functions were articulated in the mass so that architecture communicated to observers its use and purpose. Furthermore, the visual paraphernalia connected to the vision of a modern city were organically integrated into a unique and unified artistic expression; these elements included signboards, clocks, antennas, searchlights, loudspeakers, projection screens, public announcements, advertising and shop windows. In other words, a constructivist building was in motion; it was dynamic and animated and designed as a three-dimensional object to be observed at an oblique angle.

Victor, Leonid and Aleksandr Vesnin received their training in Czarist Russia. Aleksandr Vesnin, the youngest of three brothers, was the moving force, the innovator, who gave form to their joint designs. His leadership was equally vigorous in the arena of design philosophy, theory and criticism. In 1925 he founded along with Moisei Ginsburg, the first organization of constructivist architects—the Association of Contemporary Architects. Aleksandr was recognized as the spokesman of the group, and his studio became the training center for the young adherents of the new movement.

A versatile and talented artist, Aleksandr Vesnin first tested the ideas of the new style in painting, graphic design and stage design. He experimented with bold graphics and typography used in poster design and propaganda art, which was intended as the primary means of communication with the largely illiterate masses. The pictorial compositions, integrated with revolutionary slogans, demonstrated the society's thrust forward into the future.

However, it was Aleksandr's contribution to the art of scenography that set him apart from his fellow artists. He created a number of avant-garde stage designs that influenced theater productions worldwide. The realistic and representational approach to scenery imagery was replaced by scaffold-like constructions made of rough wood and metal, exploding the actor's

space in all directions. A stage set consisted, in Vesnin designs, of architectural structural elements such as trusses, columns and beams organized into compositions of towers, bridges, ramps, stairs, elevators and pulleys. This high-technology imagery of the times was further intensified with the use of billboards, signage, neon lights and other elements creating a picture of an exciting and dynamic future world. In fact, the constructivist form vocabulary had been defined in graphic and stage designs before its introduction into architecture.

The Vesnin brothers' contributions to urban design were significant, too. In particular, the concept of the "ribbon city," first envisioned by Nikolai Miliutin and applied by the Vesnins to plans of the cities Stalingrad and Kuznetsk in 1930, laid the foundations of Soviet town-planning principles, which have since been used in hundreds of new towns throughout the Soviet Union.

On 23 April 1932, the Central Committee of the Communist Party passed the historic resolution on the reorganization of literary and artistic associations, which put an end to the cliques and opened the way for the consolidation of all artists on the basis of the creative method of socialist realism. The same year, the All-Union Academy of Architecture was formed. It was declared then that socialist realism was the basic method of Soviet architecture. The Vesnin brothers did not succumb to the political pressure and did not compromise their beliefs. Consequently, they were pushed aside. During the 1930s, the brothers worked mostly on industrial projects. The Dneprostroy hydroelectric power dam on the Dnieper River was the most significant design from that period.

—PETER LIZON

VIGNOLA, Giacomo Barozzi da.

Italian. Born in Vignola, Italy, 1507. Died in 1573 (buried in the Pantheon). Trained in painting in Bologna, then in architecture. Began working as architect for the family of Cardinal Alessandro Farnese, ca. 1530; worked at the Vatican, 1538-39, and appointed as architect to Pope Paul III, 1541; worked at Fontainebleau in France, 1541-43, with Francesco Primaticcio and Sebastiano Serlio; also served as architect at San Petronio, Bologna, 1541-48; worked in Rome for Pope Julius III, 1550-55, then in Piacenza, 1555-59; worked in Caprarola, from 1559; appointed as architect of St. Peter's, Rome: 1564-67 with Pirro Ligorio; 1567-73 by himself.

Chronology of Works
All in Italy
* Approximate dates

1545-55	Palazzo Bocchi, Bologna (unfinished)
1550-53	Sant'Andrea, Via Flaminia, Rome
1551-55	Villa Giulia, Rome (with Bartolomeo Ammannati and Giorgio Vasari)
1558ff.	Palazzo Farnese, Piacenza (unfinished)
1559-73	Palazzo Farnese, Caprarola
1560s	Orti Farnesiani, Rome
1561	Portico dei Banchi, Bologna
1565ff.	Santa Anna dei Palafrenieri, Rome (completed by others)
1566-69	San Maria del Orto, Rome (facade)
1568-73	Il Gesù, Rome (vaulting and facade by Giacomo della Porta)

Giacomo Barozzi da Vignola: Palazzo Farnese, Caprarola, Italy, 1559-73

Publications

BOOKS BY VIGNOLA

La regola dell cinque ordini d'architettura. Rome, 1562.

BOOKS ABOUT VIGNOLA

HEYDENREICH, LUDWIG H., and LOTZ, WOLFGANG: *Architecture in Italy: 1400-1600*. Harmondsworth, England, 1974.

LOTZ, WOLFGANG: *Vignola-Studien*. Würzburg, Germany, 1939.

VASARI, GIORGIO: *Le opere di Giorgio Vasari, con nuove annotazioni e commenti*. 9 vols. Florence, 1550. Reprint edited by G. Milanesi: Florence, 1878-1906.

WALCHER-CASOTTI, M.: *Il Vignola*. 2 vols. Trieste, Italy, 1960.

WILLICH, HANS: *Jacopo Barozzi da Vignola*. Strasbourg, 1906.

ARTICLES ABOUT VIGNOLA

ACKERMAN, JAMES S., and LOTZ, WOLFGANG: "Vignoliana." Pp. 1-24 in LUCY F. SANDLER (ed.): *Essays in Memory of Karl Lehmann*. New York, 1964.

COOLIDGE, JOHN: "Vignola's Character and Achievement." *Journal of the Society of Architectural Historians* 9, No. 4 (1950): 10-14.

KITAO, TIMOTHY K.: "Prejudice in Perspective: A Study of Vignola's Perspective Treatise." *Art Bulletin* 47, No. 2 (1965): 199-229.

LOTZ, WOLFGANG: "Vignola-Zeichnungen." *Jahrbuch der Preussischen Kunstsammlungen* 59 (1938).

PARTRIDGE, LOREN: "Vignola and the Villa Farnese at Caprarola." *Art Bulletin* 52, No. 1 (1970): 81-87.

SCHWAGER, K.: "La chiesa del Gesù del Vignola." *Bollettino del centro di studia architettura "Andrea Palladio"* 19 (1977): 251-271.

*

Giacomo Barozzi, known as Vignola, had a profound impact on the evolution of post-Renaissance architecture in his dual role as a writer and working architect. Overshadowed in his early years by the towering figure of Michelangelo, Vignola came into his own in the 1550s, emerging as the single most influential, if not most prolific, architect of those decades. Both his study of antiquity and his familiarity with earlier Renaissance architecture served as the springboard for flights of experimentation, which were, however, grounded in classicism.

In addition, his literary endeavors altered the character of the standard architectural treatise. Vignola's treatise on the five orders, *Regole delle Cinque Ordini*, was published in 1562, and soon became the standard reference work on the subject. The value of the book lay in the 32 engraved plates illustrating the orders, with each order represented by five or six illustrations. A page showing a pair of columns with architraves appeared first, followed by illustrations of their application as half-columns, including the particulars of moldings, capitals and bases. Measurements appeared as a *modulo*, a standard unit readily transferable to prevailing conventions. Vignola's text was restricted to captions at the bottom of each page so that plates, rather than words, transmitted his message. The accessibility of the treatise contributed to its success among architects whose primary concern was the ready absorption of the classical building vocabulary. The *Regole* remained a best-seller, approximating a textbook, well into the 19th century. An American edition was issued in the early 20th century.

Vignola achieved popularity as an author by diverging from the humanist tradition of architectural theory launched by Leon Battista Alberti after the example of Vitruvius and continued, most notably, by Sebastiano Serlio. Vignola's expertise was similarly grounded in the firsthand study of ancient monuments, but he deliberately directed his treatise to working architects rather than theorists. His approach was selective, for he concentrated on what was "... generally regarded as most beautiful ...," and his purpose was didactic, for he relied on the detailed engravings to convey his points. Such a straightforward approach would have been unthinkable in the early 16th century, before the standardization of architectural practice took place. Moreover, it was not until after Vignola (and in large part because of him) that architects developed a repertoire of motifs for repeated use.

Born in Vignola, Giacomo Barozzi studied painting and architecture in nearby Bologna; his later architecture retained some decorative elements from his Emilian background. He settled in Rome around 1530, probably in the company of the young Cardinal Alessandro Farnese. Vignola remained close to the Farnese family throughout his career, eventually assuming the unofficial position of family architect. He reached maturity during the ascendancy of the Sangallo clan, and thus acquired exposure to the basics of a competent professional practice in the techniques of draftsmanship and construction. Documents of payment show him at work in the Vatican in 1538-39. An unusual interlude in his career occurred in 1541-43 when he traveled to Fountainebleau, "on loan" from the pope to produce bronze replicas of antiquities in the Vatican collections. In France, he also had the opportunity to meet Sebastiano Serlio. From 1541 to 1548 Vignola served as architect of San Petronio in Bologna, for which he produced at least two unexecuted designs for the facade. In Bologna, he also designed the Palazzo Bocchi and a major urban project, the Portico dei Banchi. He faced the task of completing various jobs left unfinished by Michelangelo (died 1564), while contemporaneously refining an individual approach. In 1564 Vignola was appointed architect of St. Peter's, but he shared that post with Pirro Ligorio, at half the salary, before assuming sole authority in 1567. He continued to work around Rome and in central Italy, securing his reputation, with the result that he was buried in the Pantheon.

Vignola made important contributions to the villa design of the Late Renaissance. Built for Pope Julius III, the Villa Giulia in Rome (1551-55) is one of the outstanding examples of a *villa suburbana* of the 16th century. The pope conceived of the project for his *vigna* outside the city walls at the Porta del Popolo and apparently supervised the construction, participating in the design and witnessing the near-completion of the villa before his death. Giorgio Vasari, who mentioned his own role in his *Lives of the Artists*, and Bartolommeo Ammannati were engaged to work with Vignola, a collaborative arrangement that must have fostered frustrations. The result, however, was an imaginative if eccentric fusion of architecture, sculpture and waterworks to create theatrical effects within a landscaped setting.

Vignola designed the palace with a monumental, two-story facade. He employed rustication to articulate the planar surface, and triumphal-arch motifs to emphasize the entrance portal, features suggesting the influence of both Giulio Romano and Sebastiano Serlio. The rear of the palace leads to the semicircular end of the first courtyard. A two-story elevation with a loggia on the ground floor, this austere yet elegant design was

also the creation of Vignola. Ammannati seems to have contributed the three remaining sides of the courtyard as well as the loggia that graces the far end, although perhaps after Vignola's plan. As an extension of the hemicycle, a nymphaeum, fed by waters from the restored Acqua Vergine, occupies a lower level at the center of the second courtyard. Staircases, added later, lead down to the fountain. There, in the inner sanctum of the villa, visitors could observe the play of water, the lavish stucco decoration in shallow relief and ancient sculpture dispersed in niches around the courtyards. The view extends yet further along the main axis, through an open loggia to a garden with classical statuary, seemingly raised to a third story of the villa, but in fact at the upper ground level. The siting of the villa and the deft handling of the architecture produced the artificial construct of a distant vanishing point. However, Vignola's plan for the Villa Giulia was essentially self-contained, a coherent sequence of courtyards fronted by a palace facade notable for its sober classicism.

Vignola's most original work, however, was the immense Palazzo Farnese at Caprarola. Indicative of its singularity is the difficulty encountered when classifying it as a building type. Located at the family seat in the countryside north of Rome, it was hardly an urban residence in the conventional manner of the block-like Renaissance palace. Neither was it a country retreat "ex urbana." As it is constructed on a hill and surrounded by a moat, the freestanding, centralized building resembles a fortress as much as an aristocratic pleasure home. In fact, the unusual pentagonal plan may be due to an earlier commission from Paul III, possibly to Baldassare Peruzzi, for a fortified castle. The papal grandson, Cardinal Alessandro Farnese subsequently engaged Vignola to design a monumental palace on those foundations. Begun in 1559, the resulting construction has a principal facade elevated above connecting ramps and staircases. From this vantage point, the palace presents an imposing yet conventional aspect; its distinctive features come as a surprise to the visitor. The polygonal plan allowed for a symmetrical disposition of rooms, from a large reception hall to a circular staircase on one side (and a round chapel on the other) and then to a series of rectangular precincts, with attention to natural sources of illumination and ventilation. The circular courtyard in the interior has a two-story elevation, which attains a harmonious classicism. The arcade on the upper level is articulated by engaged, Ionic columns of fine proportion, while the rusticated lower level provides an imposing support. The five bastions of the palace project into the surrounding landscape. Whereas formal gardens extended to the rear, an open loggia along the facade overlooked the access road leading to elaborate, terraced ramps—all planned by Vignola.

Vignola's ecclesiastical architecture was no less innovative than his domestic designs. He continued to demonstrate adaptability to his patrons' demands, to draw on his knowledge of classical sources and to exercise independent judgment. He anticipated the Baroque in several plans for Roman churches, while enlarging the repertoire of the later Renaissance. At the same time, his proposals for a Gothic-style facade at San Petronio in Bologna indicate that he was capable of reviving an historical style in an appropriate context.

Given his experience with the prerequisites of a commission, it is surprising to learn of Vignola's one celebrated failure. In 1568 he was commissioned by Cardinal Farnese to design the new Jesuit church for Rome, Il Gesù. Although Vignola's general plan for the church was carried out, his proposals for the facade were rejected in favor of an alternate solution submitted by Giacomo della Porta in 1571. Mario Cartaro's engraving shows that Vignola's design was distinguished by a restrained classicism. He applied measured proportions to compartmentalized planes of the facade in an attempt to balance the width of the church with the height of its nave. In contrast, della Porta proposed a comparatively vertical and centralized design, a dynamic solution preferred by Cardinal Farnese and the Jesuits.

Despite the disappointment at the last stage of his career, Vignola should receive credit for having devised one of the most enduring church plans of the entire century. Il Gesù has a vast, aisleless nave, side chapels, a short transept and a semicircular apse. A tall dome rises over the crossing. The basic form is rectangular, and its simplicity accentuates the monumental scale. Vignola applied his knowledge of the classical orders to the interior elevation. Colossal pilasters are paired in the nave and clustered at the crossing, creating a logical base for the continuous cornice, which in turn serves as the support for the vault. He also allowed for a unified view of the expansive interior. The side chapels are barely visible from the vantage point of the entrance, and the domed crossing both illuminates and elevates the significance of the altar positioned in the apse. In its original state, the surface of the interior vault was covered with whitewash, and the architectural members of the nave were in plain travertine. Il Gesù was both beautiful and functional in its austerity, an appropriate symbol of the Catholic reform of the later 16th century. Although the aedicular facade and the barrel vaulting of the nave were finished by della Porta in 1577, Vignola had realized his patron's vision of a magnificent church with a "single nave, not a nave and aisles," a church "to be entirely vaulted over."

Vignola also played a key role in the evolution of the centrally planned church, expanding the type to include the oval. He experimented with the form throughout his career, as in the plan for an oval chapel for the conclave in the Belvedere Court of the Vatican (ca. 1559), but his two most influential projects date from the beginning and end of his career. The small church of Sant' Andrea in Via Flaminia (1550-53) was built for Pope Julius III, near the papal villa, on the Via Flaminia. The site made the memorial chapel important for pilgrims, who encountered it prior to entering the city at the Porta del Popolo. The interior of Sant' Andrea is oblong in shape, with the long side oriented along the entrance-apse axis. The oval dome springs from a projecting cornice and pendentives; it is illuminated by thermal windows. The facade is composed of a series of interlocking, yet visually distinct, motifs: the pedimental temple front at ground level, the oval drum at the top, and a squared block corresponding to the rectangular ground plan in between. Vignola used flattened pilasters to articulate a triad of bays along the facade, doubling the pilasters at the corners. The upper walls consist of rough masonry, decorated by heavy cornices in the antique manner. The entire design is marked by the inventive combination of ancient and Renaissance motifs, with an emphasis on the distinct parts rather than the synthetic whole.

Santa Anna dei Palafrenieri, begun in 1565, was unfinished at the time of Vignola's death. The architect's son, Giacinto, supervised the construction of a temporary roof in 1583, but completion of the facade and vaulting had to wait until the 18th century. Originally standing free on three sides, the church was encased within rectangular masonry walls. Vignola applied his "signature" flattened pilasters to the exterior in order to create five bays along both the facade and the side elevations. The intercolumniation does not become a standard unit, but instead varies from front to side, along the flattened, rectangular surfaces of the outer walls. Nevertheless, an oval appears in its purest form in the interior of the church. Vignola designed a large, soaring dome set on an entablature supported by eight recessed columns at ground level. Bays of alternating width, housing chapels and entrance portals, enliven the wall elevation.

As a whole, the exterior of Santa Anna dei Palafrenieri bears little relationship to the centralized plan. The disjointedness between interior and exterior and the relative independence of parts distinguish the church from the organically designed central plans of the Renaissance.

Vignola's architecture does not readily submit to stages of a continuous stylistic development. Moreover, his architecture has been characterized alternately as Mannerist and proto-Baroque. Both currents exist in his work, at times simultaneously and even in the same building. Although he was preceded in his interest in the oval church plan by Baldassare Peruzzi, Vignola's highly theoretical approach to the design problem imparts an intrinsic drama to his solutions. Architects of the Italian Baroque, particularly Francesco Borromini, carried his ideas to their logical conclusion.

—EUNICE D. HOWE

VILLAGRAN GARCIA, José.

Mexican. Born in Mexico City, 22 September 1901. Married Concepcion de la Mora, 1935; one son. Attended School of Architecture, National University, Mexico City, 1918-22. Architect for Department of Public Health, Mexico City, 1924-35; practiced privately in Mexico City from 1935; consultant architect to National Committee of the Campaign Against Tuberculosis, 1939-47, and Secretariat of Public Health and Welfare, Mexico City, 1943-45, and to the World Health Organization, Washington, D.C., 1951. Professor of architecture, 1924-57, and director, 1933-35, National School of Architecture, Mexico City.

Chronology of Works
All in Mexico

1925	Institute of Hygiene, Popotla, Mexico City
1929	Tuberculosis Sanatorium, Huipulco, Tlalpam, Mexico City
1929	Children's Health Dispensary Building, Mexico City
1935	José Villagrán García House, Dublin 7, Mexico City
1937	National Cardiological Institute, Mexico City
1941	Apartment Building, Avenida Insurgentes 444, Mexico City
1941	Surgical Block, Huipulco Sanatorium, Tlalpam, Mexico City
1941	Children's Hospital, Mexico City
1942	Chronic Tuberculosis Patients' Block, Huipulco Sanatorium, Tlalpam, Mexico City
1942	Manuel Gea Gonzalez Hospital, Huipulco Sanatorium, Tlalpam, Mexico City
1942	Tuberculosis Sanatorium, Zoquipan, Jalisco
1943	Hospital de Jesus Office Building, Mexico City
1943-46	Hospitals Plan for the Republic of Mexico
1944	Mexico University College, Mexico City
1945-46	Regional Schools Plan for Mexico
1946-50	Condesa Office Building, Mexico City
1951	National School of Architecture Complex, Universidad Nacional de Mexico, Mexico City
1952	Las Americas Cinema and Office Building, Mexico City
1953	National Mission Seminary, Tlalpam, Mexico City
1963	Hotel Maria Isabel, Mexico City
1963	Hotel Alameda, Mexico City
1963	Ford Motor Company Office Building, Mexico City

1976   Complex of 20 buildings for the National Cardiological Institute, Mexico City (Hospital, Outpatients Clinic, Scientific Research Block, Nursing School, Cardiologists' School, Residential Block)

Publications

BOOKS BY VILLAGRAN GARCIA

Panorama de 50 anos de arquitectura mexicana contemporanea. Mexico City, 1950.
Problemas en la formacion del arquitecto. Mexico City, 1964.
Arquitectura y restauracion de monumentos. Mexico City, 1967.
Esencia de lo arquitectonico. Mexico City, 1972.
Estructura teorica del programa arquitectonico. Mexico City, 1972.
El mayor problema de la arquitectura actual. Mexico City, 1974.
La forma en arquitectura. Mexico City, 1975.

ARTICLES ABOUT VILLAGRAN GARCIA

"Children's Hospital, Mexico City." *Architectural Record* (October 1944).
"Hotel Maria Isabel, Mexico City." *Architectural Design* (September 1963).
"José Villagrán Garcia." *Arquitectura* special issue (Mexico City, September 1956).

*

Mexico's Revolution of 1910 involved the overthrow of a native-born autocrat with strong ties to foreign culture and industry (Porfirio Diaz); for many in the arts this was a signal too for liberation from the strictures of the past. Traditional European styles began to be replaced by those of the avant-garde, which if still of foreign origin, at least seemed free of direct colonial associations. The painter Diego Rivera, for instance, between 1910 and 1912 began his experiments with French analytical cubism, and soon moved his subject matter from still lifes and traditional religious themes to imagery which, for the first time since the Spanish conquest, glorified Mexico's native people and traditions.

Entrenched in the Beaux-Arts National Academy of San Carlos, Mexican architects were slower to follow suit. Nevertheless, by 1917 one of the academy's professors, Francisco Zenteno, had introduced students in his theory courses to the rational classicist principles and programmatic analysis of Julian Guadet—Beaux-Arts master of Tony Garnier and Auguste Perret, and through them a major influence on Le Corbusier. Guadet's book *Éléments et théorie de l'architecture* (1902) thus came to Zenteno's star pupil, the man most responsible for bringing modern functionalist architecture to Mexico, José Villagrán Garcia.

With varying degrees of militancy, 20th-century Mexican artists and architects have often presented their work as remedial for the vast social ills of an underdeveloped nation, just recently released from foreign domination. Villagrán's career as builder and educator for nearly six decades was indicative of this trend. By far the greatest share of his built work was in the area of public school and hospital design, where unornamented utilitarian schemes aimed at receiving the highest return from limited financial and material resources. However, in projects like his Hygiene Institute (1925) and Tuberculosis Sanatorium (1929), and even in a late work like the National Cardiological Institute

(1976), the stark forms are laid out with a rigorous classical symmetry that seems strangely at odds with the architect's progressive intent—this type of composition being a direct result of his Beaux-Arts training. But while Villagrán's early buildings were considerably less radical than anything Adolf Loos had done twenty years earlier, for young Mexican designers their arrival seemed both a moral and an aesthetic revelation, a clean and immediate break from an architectural tradition that thus far had suffered few of its European cousin's growing pains.

As an educator, Villagrán began teaching courses in composition and theory in 1924 at the National Academy. His theory and method grew from a profound analysis of Guadet's rationalism, as well as from the more progressive work of contemporary Europeans like Le Corbusier and Walter Gropius. Underlying was a classically Vitruvian recognition of the unity between independent values of structure, function and form. Beauty was the architect's goal, and it remained inextricably linked to truth: the honest expression of structure and materials and, most important, the arrival, through thorough analysis, at forms which best satisfied the complex natures of particular functional programs. Early on Villagrán defined architecture as both "the science and art of building." While this "integralista" position was modified by many of his earliest students—including the "radicals" Juan O'Gorman and Alvaro Aburto, who declared that, theoretically, functionalist architecture should not consider aesthetics at all—Villagrán's teaching was a seminal factor in the development of modernist architecture in Mexico.

From the outset, Villagrán viewed functionalism as a world property, rather than as yet another foreign import. In Villagrán's broad doctrine, the architect was to consider specific variables related to site and user; thus, it seemed to him inevitable that a "native accent"—a particular attitude toward light and proportion—would arise so long as the dictates of truth were carried to their logical ends. He was, however, opposed to the "sectarian and demagogic" radical interpretation functionalism had received from O'Gorman and his followers. In a special issue of *The Architectural Record* in 1937, devoted to Mexico, Villagrán encapsulated his doctrine, defining the "two roles of architecture" as: "1. To set forth reluctantly and to make known the peculiarities of our people. (Unconsciously and without reward, our constructions fulfill this mission.) 2. To take an active and leading part in the evolution of our people. (This is the doctrine of the young architects.)"

So there, intertwined with a pronouncement on the architect's social responsibility, was the call for a regionally expressive form. Villagrán's self-stated reluctance in this regard is nowhere more apparent than in his own buildings, most of which remained formally unremarkable, whatever their functional successes. When, beginning in the 1940s, Mexican architecture did begin to demonstrate distinctive, integrated regional characteristics—in the work of Luis Barragán, O'Gorman and others—Villagrán publicly lamented the "frantic but fruitless pursuit of innovation" that resulted in "antiquated traditionalism." He can easily be imagined discussing his own work . . . when in 1967 he wrote bitterly of "another nationalistic tendency . . . characterized by an attempt to resolve the integral, multiphased architectural problem as it is related not only to form or aesthetics, but also to economics and social considerations, and [which] ignores egocentric preoccupation with the probably outmoded avidity for originality. Such construction which tries to serve the community, reveals a wealth of good intentions coupled with modesty of appearance, and for that reason does not seem to interest critics or commercial magazines, being so obviously related to our real problems, basic and pressing problems which normally are of concern only to us and, among us, to only a few."

Villagrán himself never designed a convincingly regionalistic modern building. But if he hung more tenaciously than most to a rationalist aesthetic, he was nevertheless quite capable of achieving satisfying results. His Hotel Maria Isabel (1962), in collaboration with Juan Sordo Madaleno, combined well-realized utility with an elegant interpretation of the Miesian glass and steel cage—here carried out in clear black glass and anodized aluminum, with structural columns and solid wall areas faced in white Carrara marble.

Architect Max Cetto once suggested that Villagrán perhaps put inordinate emphasis on ideals of truth and logic. Cetto pointed toward a number of Mexican authors who claimed instead that in Mexico, style and fantasy take precedence over truth and rationality. This might have appeared to be the case in the years immediately following World War II, when Mexican modern architecture came into its own by exploring a well of native mysticism. In actual fact though, the most impressive Mexican work of that period achieved a subtle balance between rationality and modernity on one hand, and fantasy and tradition on the other. Villagrán raised the first half of this equation; it remained for others to effect its completion. But if his influence was more in the realm of ideas than building, its significance was nonetheless of the first order.

—KEITH EGGENER

VILLANUEVA, Carlos Raúl.

Venezuelan. Born in Croydon, Surrey, England, 30 May 1900. Died in Caracas, Venezuela, 16 August 1975. Married Margot Arismendi, 1933; four children. Studied at the Lycée Condorcet, Paris, France, and received diploma in architecture from the École des Beaux-Arts, Paris, 1928. Practiced privately in Caracas, 1929-75; architect to the Ministry of Public Works, Caracas, 1929-39; consultant architect to the Banco Obrero, Caracas, 1940-60; founding professor of architecture, University of Venezuela, Caracas, from 1944; founder president, Venezuelan Association of Architects; president, Venezuelan National Board of Historic and Artistic Protection and Conservation; founder director, National Planning Association.

Chronology of Works
All in Venezuela unless noted

1929-30	Church of San Francisco de Yara, Caracas
1931	Bullring, Maracay
1935	Museo de los Caobos, Caracas
1937	Venezuelan Pavilion, World's Fair, Paris, France†
1939	Gran Colombia School, Caracas
1941	El Silencio Quarter, Caracas (redevelopment)
1943-44	General Rafael Urdaneta Housing Development, Maracaibo
1943-45	Dos de Diciembre Housing Development, Caracas (with José Manual Mijares, José Hoffman, and Carlos Branco)
1944-47	Master plan for University City, University of Venezuela, Caracas
1945	Medical Center, University City, Caracas
1950-52	Olympic Stadium, University City, Caracas
1951	Villanueva House, Caracas
1952	Aula Magna (main auditorium), Library, Plaza Cubierto and Walks, and the Botanical Institute, University City, Caracas
1953	Small Concert Hall, University City, Caracas
1954	El Paraiso Housing Development, Caracas (with Carlos Celis and José Manuel Mijares)
1954	Humanities, Science and Physics Buildings, University City, Caracas
1955	School of Dentistry, University City, Caracas
1955-57	23 de Enero High-Rise Housing Development, Caracas (with C. C. Cepero and José Manuel Mijares)
1957	School of Architecture and Urbanism, School of Pharmacy and Olympic Swimming Stadium, University City, Caracas
1958	Villanueva House, Caraballeda
1967	Venezuelan Pavilion, Expo '67, Montreal, Canada (with E. Trujillo)†

Publications

BOOKS BY VILLANUEVA

La Caracas de ayer y de hoy, su arquitectura colonial y la reurbanizacion de "El Silencio." Paris, 1950.
Caracas of Yesterday and Today. Caracas, 1943.
Caracas en tres tiempos. Caracas, 1966.

ARTICLES BY VILLANUEVA

"Nouvelle unités residentielles au Venezuela." *Architecture d'aujourd'hui* 20 (September 1950): 8-13.
"La Ciudad y su historia." *Boletin de Universidad Central* (Caracas, January 1964): 91-96.
"Lettre de Colombia." *Architecture: Formes et fonctions* 12 (1965/66).
"Fonction-Formation-Position." *Architecture: Formes et fonctions* 15 (1969): 9-78.

BOOKS ABOUT VILLANUEVA

BAYON, DAMIAN, and GASPARINI, PAOLO: *Panoramica de la arquitectura latinoamericana.* Barcelona, 1977. English edition: *The Changing Shape of Latin American Architecture: Conversations with Ten Leading Architects.* New York and Chichester, England, 1979.
DAMAZ, PAUL F.: *Art in Latin American Architecture.* New York, 1963.
FRAMPTON, KENNETH, and FUTAGAWA, YUKIO: *Modern Architecture: 1920-1945.* New York, 1983.
HITCHCOCK, HENRY-RUSSELL: *Latin American Architecture since 1945.* New York, 1955.
MOHOLY-NAGY, SIBYL: *Carlos Raúl Villanueva and the Architecture of Venezuala.* New York, 1964.
SERGE, ROBERTO (ed.): *Latin America in Its Architecture.* New York and London, 1981.

ARTICLES ABOUT VILLANUEVA

"Caracas University City." *Arts and Architecture* 71 (November 1954): 14-19.
"Carlos Raúl Villanueva, Hon. FAIA." *Journal of the American Institute of Architects* 64 (1975): 60.
"Housing Projects in Caracas." "La Maison de l'architecte Carlos Raúl Villanueva" and "Unité d'Habitation a Caracas." *Architecture d'aujourd'hui* (October 1956).
"La casa di Villanueva" and "Nuovi quatieri a Caracas." *Domus* (April 1956).
"Three Cubes." *Architectural Forum* (September 1967).

Carlos Raúl Villanueva is to modern architecture in Venezuela what Oscar Niemeyer is to its counterpart in Brazil: the uniquely gifted, preeminent 20th-century designer who spearheaded the synthesis of European modernism and the Latin American artistic traditions of his own country to create a new architecture that is exceptional for its structural dynamism and plastic expressiveness. Four themes stand out in Villanueva's work. The first is his conception of the modern architect as social reformer. The second is his bold experimentation with and eventual mastery of the structural possibilities of reinforced concrete. The third is his synthesis of architecture, planning and the plastic arts. The fourth is his sensitivity to the colonial architectural legacy and special environmental conditions of Venezuela.

Born in London (to a Venezuelan diplomat and French mother) and trained in the École des Beaux-Arts in Paris, Villanueva was more strongly influenced by European eclecticism than was Niemeyer or even Lúcio Costa. His earliest work, the Bullring at Maracay (1931), reflects a structural classicism in concrete that recalls the work of Auguste Perret, and his Museo de Los Caobos in Caracas (1935) contains a Doric peristyle that is remarkable for its precise detailing. Symmetrically disposed around an open garden patio, the museum is the first example of Villanueva's interest in the modernist interpenetration of interior and exterior space. There too he showed for the first time his sensitivity to the sculptural effects created by the strong light contrasts of the tropical sun, and his use of outdoor sculpture to animate the surfaces and spaces of an architectural composition.

Villanueva's vision of the architect as public reformer is reflected in his projects for the Escuela Gran Colombia (1939) and his redevelopment of the El Silencio slum district in Caracas (1941). The first modern elementary school built in Venezuela, the Gran Columbia has been incorrectly called "the curtain raiser for the uniquely Latin American concern with public building projects." The Ministry of Education and Health Building in Rio and Niemeyer's Obra do Berço Nursery School in fact anticipated the Venezuelan development by two years. Still, Villanueva's school was a prototypical achievement in the effort to extend the social benefits of primary education in Latin America. The Gran Columbia represented Villanueva's first conscious attempt to evolve a modernist design vocabulary free of historical references. Boldly cubic in its volumes and asymmetrical in composition, the building recalls the white, streamlined forms created by Le Corbusier and his contemporaries around the time of the 1925 International Exposition in Paris. The gymnasium portico, however, speaks of the building's lingering structural classicism à la Perret, even if only the frames are of *beton*. Concrete frames of masonry thickness and thinner infill panels of hollow brick remained the major construction method in a nation of traditional contractors who did not yet trust the techniques of reinforced concrete.

The rapid and uncontrolled urbanization of Caracas that had begun shortly after the discovery of Venezuelan oil in 1917 created in the capital a housing and infrastructure crisis of unprecedented dimensions. After a period of additional training at the Institut d'Urbanisme in Paris, Villanueva responded to that crisis by collaborating with the Banco Obrero (Venezuelan Workers' Bank) on the improvement of social conditions for the city's laboring classes. The collaboration bore its first fruit in the redevelopment of the El Silencio slum area into a high-density, low-cost housing complex, the first such project to be sponsored and carried out by a Latin American government. Villanueva's effort focused on the reurbanization of the area into a total neighborhood complete with a public plaza (with fountains and colonial-style arcades), pedestrian courts and playgrounds, and apartment blocks with projecting kitchen loggia and balconies to improve ventilation and guarantee residents a view of the play areas and hills beyond. In his General Rafael Urdaneta development (1943) for Venezuela's second-largest city, Maracaibo, Villanueva designed 1,000 single-family houses and several multiple-family structures, laying out the whole following Ebenezer Howard's garden-city concept. The town's elementary school is of interest for its understated evocation of the traditional Spanish colonial patio form.

Villanueva's masterpiece in both planning and architecture, however, is unquestionably his ambitious scheme for the 450-acre campus of the Central University of Venezuela at Caracas (Ciudad Universitária). Though his initial plan for the first building phase (1944-47) was derived from the Beaux-Arts tradition, the complex as it was finally completed 16 years later far surpasses, in its creative exploration of the modernist aesthetic in campus design, Frank Lloyd Wright's project for Florida Southern University. Naturally ventilated through perforated concrete screens and spatially integrated by a series of covered walks and plazas, the campus buildings (of which the Architecture School is one of the most successful) reflect Villanueva's search for a practical, standardized solution to the problem posed by the hot and rainy Caribbean climate. Villanueva conceived of each building as a functionally and expressively unique structure with a special character, plan and set of technical specifications appropriate to the discipline housed within. Variation within unity was the organizing principle he sought, and circulation and the visual experience of the pedestrian were the keys to that unity. Undulating cantilevered canopies and more than a mile of covered walks and screened terraces that are often intertwined with tropical vegetation and accented with modernist sculptures—all this adds plastic richness to the campus and invites the student and visitor to proceed at a casual pace and discover the spaces and buildings on foot.

Also on the campus, the 1952 Olympic Stadium, with its dramatically cantilevered grandstand of V-shaped frames turned on their sides, is a tour-de-force of Villanueva's mastery of the dynamic structural potential and expressive quality of reinforced concrete framing. He also designed a baseball stadium and an Olympic swimming facility for the campus. The sports arenas established Villanueva's reputation as leader of the Venezuelan avant-garde and guaranteed his position as master architect for the university.

One of the major themes expressed in the Ciudad Universitária is the integration of the arts, especially sculpture, mural art and architecture, in the context of the campus' planning. Modernist sculptures by Jean Arp, Antoine Pevsner and others, as well as murals by Fernand Leger and Mateo Manaure add plastic complexity to the campus' spaces and accentuate Villanueva's treatment of the individual buildings as unique sculptural volumes. This unity of the arts is nowhere more dramatically developed than in the interior of the famous Aula Magna (1952), an auditorium that incorporates the work of mobilist Alexander Calder. Calder's "floating clouds," which serve the dual function of pure plastic expression and acoustical regulators or "sails," accentuate the experience of this interior space, defined by the sweeping curve of the ceiling and concrete balcony, as essentially sculptural art. The acoustical, sculptural and spatial sophistication of the Aula Magna represented a breakthrough that would later influence another imposing Venezuelan auditorium: that of the new Caracas Opera House.

Ever firm in his commitment to the improvement of housing conditions for the Venezuelan people, later in his career Villanueva collaborated again with the Banco Obrero in the creation of the El Paradiso (1952) and 23 de Enero (1955) developments in Caracas. Though these complexes have been widely criticized for not having created the sort of modernist paradise implied by the name of the first, they do attest to Villanueva's characteristic, tireless involvement in the search for a solution to Latin America's foremost urban problem.

—DAVID UNDERWOOD

VILLANUEVA, Juan de.

Spanish. Born in Spain, 1739. Died in 1811. Studied at the Accademia di San Luca, Rome, 1759-65. Became architect for the Jeronymite order at the Escorial, near Madrid, 1768; served as royal architect, 1797-1808.

Chronology of Works
All in Spain

1768	Residence of Marqués de Campovillar, El Escorial, near Madrid
1770	Sacristy, Burgo de Osma Cathedral
1770-83	Palafox Chapel, Burgo de Osma Cathedral
1771	Casa de Infantes, El Escorial
1772	Casita de Abajo, El Escorial
1773	Casita de Arriba, El Escorial
1775	Residence of Marqués de Llano, Madrid
1780	House for the Agustinos, Calle de Reloj, Madrid
1781	Entrance to the Botanical Gardens, Madrid
1784	Casita del Prícipe, El Pardo
1787-89	Prado Museum, Madrid
1787-89	Ayuntamiento, Madrid (north facade)
1788-1811	Academy of History, Madrid (not completed until 1847)
1789	Oratory, Church of Caballero de Gracia, Madrid
1789-1808	Royal Observatory, Madrid
1791	Convent of San Fernando, Madrid (reconstruction)
1791	Plaza Mayor, Madrid (restorations)
1809	Cemetery and Chapel, Puerta de Fuencarral;
n.d.	Patio de las Escribanías, Court Prison (now Ministry of Foreign Affairs), Madrid

Publications

BOOKS ABOUT VILLANUEVA

CHUECA GOITIA, FERNANDO, and MIGUEL, CARLOS DE: *La vida y las obras del arquitecto Juan de Villanueva.* Madrid, 1949.
KUBLER, GEORGE, and SORIA, MARTIN: *Art and Architecture in Spain and Portugal and Their American Dominions, 1500-1800.* Baltimore and Harmondsworth, 1959.
GAVILANES, P. M.: *La Arquitectura de Juan de Villanueva: El Proceso del Proyecto.* Madrid, 1988.
SCHUBERT, OTTO: *Historia del barroco en España.* Madrid, 1924.
VEGA, RAMON GUERRA DE LA: *Juan de Villanueva II: Museo del Prado y Jardín Botánico.* Madrid, 1987.

ARTICLES ABOUT VILLANUEVA

CABELLO LAPIEDRA, LUIS: "D. Juan de Villanueva." *Arquitectura* 1 (November 1918): 185-195.

Juan de Villanueva was the key figure in the dissemination of the neoclassical style in Spanish architecture. As architect at the court of Charles III, he was responsible for the expansion of the *sitios reales* of El Escorial, El Pardo and Buen Retiro, as well as for such royal foundations as the Museo del Prado and the Observatorio Astronómico. He designed numerous projects for the Spanish capital in his capacity as *Arquitecto Mayor de Madrid.* Having spent several years in Rome, Villanueva played an important role in bringing the aesthetic theories of the Enlightenment to Spain, which was reinforced by his influence on the teaching at the Academia de San Fernando.

At a young age, Villanueva drew attention with his drawings of old buildings and designs, which earned him a scholarship from the Academia for study in Rome. He stayed in the Eternal City from 1759 to 1763, studying its ancient architecture. At that time, Giovanni Battista Piranesi's *Antichità Romane* appeared, Cardinal Albani had his villa built and furnished in the neoclassical style, and Johann Joachim Winckelmann, as Albani's librarian, postulated the return to Greek Antiquity.

Following a brief stay in Parma, Villanueva returned to Spain, and was soon made an honorary member of the Academia. At the recommendation of the influential Spanish traveler and art critic Antonio Ponz, Villanueva was commissioned to work on El Escorial by the Jeronymite order. As a consequence of that commission, he established a relationship with the Spanish court and the family of Charles III. In the latter's son, the future Charles IV, Villanueva found a patron with a thorough understanding of art and a shared interest in the orders and in classical architecture. Starting in 1770, Villanueva built two smaller residences for the Infantes in the complex of the Villa de San Lorenzo near El Escorial. In 1771 he undertook work on the Casa de Infantes, located opposite the facade of El Escorial. His work at that time was still entirely in the style of Juan de Herrera. In 1772 Villanueva received his first important commission in the planning of the Casita del Principe (or Casita de Abajo) for the Spanish crown prince, and of the Casita de Arriba for the prince's brother, Don Gabriel. Both are variants of the casino type—a country house integrated into the landscape and built in a classical style—which was hardly known in Spain at that time.

The Casita de Abajo was built on a T-shaped plan. The cross bar of the T has a two-story columned portico functioning as the main entrance. The long axis, which ends in a cross-positioned oval hall, has a portico with columns *in antis.* The rustic character of the building is in harmony with the dominant presence of the Doric order and the fasciation of the facade. Single-story annexes flank the symmetrical building, forming a complex of almost independent blocks. In contrast, the Casita de Arriba—a single-story centralized building on a square plan with columned porticoes—uses Palladian motifs and is based on the design of Andrea Palladio's La Rotonda in Vicenza, Italy. The Casita del Principe in El Pardo (1784) is another instance of the casino type, and may be regarded as a prototype for the Museo del Prado. The Casita is divided into five blocks lying crosswise on the long axis. A portico with columns *in antis* emphasizes the long central axis, which is made of square and round main halls and has a facade oriented to the back. The lateral wings terminate in corner pavilions. Red brick and white plaster underline the articulation of the building mass.

At approximately the same time that Villanueva worked on the *casitas reales,* in the course of the 1770s and early 1780s, he submitted designs for the sacristy and the Capilla Palafox for the cathedral at Burgo de Osma. In these designs, he used the motif of a rotunda with freestanding columns, also utilized later at the Prado. Works for the royal family at El Escorial,

El Pardo and Aranjuez are also documented for those years, as are commissions for the nobility and engineering projects.

With Villanueva's appointment as *Arquitecto Mayor de Madrid* to succeed Ventura Rodríguez, in February of 1786, a new phase in the career of the Spanish architect began. The columned galleries of the Casas de Ayuntamiento (1789) and the reconstruction of the Plaza Mayor, which had been destroyed by fire, were among the first of the countless commissions that Villanueva carried out for the city during the rest of his life. From the point of view of architectural history, however, the Museo del Prado and the Observatorio Astronómico hold the greatest significance. Both projects were royal foundations, part of an Enlightenment program of public building, and both must be considered key buildings of Spanish neoclassicism.

The Prado was not originally planned as a picture gallery. After designs by Ventura Rodríguez had been rejected, Villanueva prepared a series of designs for a science museum and the Academy of Sciences in 1785. These projected buildings were to be integrated into the park-like area near Buen Retiro. One of the first sketches called for a central rotunda, connected by means of porticoes and *paseos* to two exedrae. A spacious auditorium was to lie on a second axis, parallel to the first, communicating with the rotunda by means of a narthex. Sequences of rooms would lead out from the auditorium to corner pavilions. The actual building (completely finished in 1819, after it had been damaged during the French invasion) fundamentally retained that original disposition, but was limited to only one cross axis. The *paseos* were transformed into Ionic colonnades at the upper story, while the ground floor is articulated with arcades and square niches. The corner pavilions were enlarged and furnished with internal rotundas. The projecting Tuscan portico provides entrance to a semicircular room at right angles to the facade, which forms the heart of the complex. The exhibition spaces have coffered half-barrel vaults and domes in the style of classical Roman architecture. In the addition of different building blocks, Villanueva referred to his own earlier buildings, such as the Casita del Principe at El Escorial. Typologically and stylistically, the museum designs may be compared to the Museo Pio-Clementino and several Academy examination projects for graduating architects in Paris, Rome and Madrid.

The Observatorio Astronómico, located in the vicinity of the Prado, was Villanueva's last great work. Begun in 1790 and largely completed by 1808, the building has a cruciform plan, and, in spite of numerous interventions, gives evidence of the spread of neo-Hellenistic forms in Spanish architecture. Functionalism and geometrical severity dominate the elevation. The design dramatizes pictorial qualities and oppositions in the contrast of the Corinthian portico to the rotunda that crowns the central salon. These characteristics anticipate the romantic developments of the 19th century. Nevertheless, the building is highly functional: the "tholos" harbors the astronomic observatory and all its equipment.

Villanueva's influence and his numerous superior buildings and designs document the definitive turning away from Baroque principles of design within the Spanish architectural tradition. The requirements of rationality and the self-conscious return to classical traditions led to the victory of neoclassicism, which was accompanied by a reconsideration of the indigenous heritage. Though Villanueva's work must be seen as the preparation for the Enlightenment, in his continuation of the work of Juan de Herrera he was a harbinger of architectural historicism.

—BARBARA BORNGÄSSER KLEIN
Translated from the German by Marijke Rijsberman

VILLARD DE HONNECOURT.

French. Born in Honnecourt-sur-l'Escaut, in northern France, ca. 1180. Died probably in the mid-1230s.

Publications

BOOKS ABOUT VILLARD

BARNES, CARL F., JR.: *Villard de Honnecourt, the Artist and His Drawings.* Boston, 1982.
BECHMANN, ROLAND: *Villard de Honnecourt: la pensée technique au XIIIe siècle et sa communication.* Paris, 1991.
BOWIE, THEODORE (ed.): *The Sketchbook of Villard de Honnecourt.* 3d. rev. ed. Bloomington, Indiana, 1968.
BUCHER, FRANÇOIS: *Architector: The Lodge Books and Sketchbooks of Medieval Architects.* New York, 1979.
ERLANDE-BRANDENBURG, ALAIN, et al.: *Carnet de Villard de Honnecourt.* Paris, 1986.
HAHNLOSER, HANS R.: *Villard de Honnecourt: Kritische Gesamtausgabe des Bauhüttenbuches ms. fr. 19093 der Pariser Nationalbibliothek.* 2nd rev. ed. Graz, Austria, 1972.
LASSUS, JEAN BAPTISTE ANTOINE: *Album de Villard de Honnecourt, architecte du XIIIᵉ siècle, manuscrit publié en facsimilé.* Paris, 1858.
WILLIS, ROBERT (ed.): *Facsimile of the Sketch Book of Wilars de Honecort.* London, 1859.

ARTICLES ABOUT VILLARD

BARNES, CARL F., JR.: "A Note on the Bibliographic Terminology in the Portfolio of Villard de Honnecourt." *Manuscripta* 31 (1987): 71-76.
BARNES, CARL F., JR.: "The Drapery-Rendering Technique of Villard de Honnecourt." *Gesta* 20/1 (1981): 199-206.
BRANNER, R.: "Villard de Honnecourt, Reims and the origin of Gothic architectural drawing." *Gazette des Beaux-Arts* 61 (1963): 129-146.
BURGES, WILLIAM: "An Architect's Sketch-book of the Thirteenth Century." *Builder* 16 (15 and 20 November 1858): 758, 770-772.
GARLING, H.: "Some Remarks on the Contents of the Album of Villard de Honnecourt." *Transactions of the Royal Institute of British Architects, 1858-1859,* 13-20.
LEFRANÇOIS-PILLION, LOUISE: "Un maître d'oeuvre et son album: Villard de Honnecourt." *Maîtres d'oeuvres et tailleurs de pierre des cathédrales.* Paris, 1949.
PIERCE, J.: "The Sketchbook of Villard de Honnecourt." *New Lugano Review* 8-9 (1976): 28-36.
QUICHERAT, J.: "Notice sur l'album de Villard de Honnecourt, architecte du XIII siècle." *Revue archéologique,* ser. 1/6 (1849): 65-80, 164-188, 209-226.
SCHNEEGANS, F. E.: "Über die Sprache des Skizzenbuches von Villard de Honnecourt." *Zeitschrift für romanische Philologie* 25 (1901): 45-70.
SCHULTZ, SIMONE: "Villard de Honnecourt et son 'carnet.'" *Oeil* 123 (1965): 20-29.

*

The portfolio of 33 parchment leaves containing approximately 250 drawings by Villard de Honnecourt now preserved in Paris (Bibl. nat., MS. Fr. 19093) was discovered and first published in the mid-19th century during the height of the Gothic Revival movement in France and England. In that context, Villard's architectural drawings, although they represent only about 16 percent of the total, attracted the greatest attention and writers leapt to the conclusion that the Picard artist was an architect. By the end of the 19th century, during the rampant nationalism following the Franco-Prussian War, French writers were crediting Villard with having "erected churches throughout the length and breadth of Christendom."

This was done without any proof that Villard designed or built any part of any church, or any other type of structure, anywhere. Nor is there any documentation whatsoever that he was in fact an architect. Villard's training may have been in metalworking rather than in masonry; but it may be that Villard was not a professional craftsman of any type, but, rather, simply an inquisitive layman, perhaps "a lodge clerk with a flair for drawing," as Robert Branner put it.

When and why Villard made his drawings is unknown. Nothing he drew can be securely dated after about 1240, so it is reasonable to suppose that he was active in the 1220s and 1230s. If he actually visited the architectural monuments he recorded, rather than knowing some or all of them through drawings such as his own, he visited the cathedrals of Cambrai, Chartres, Laon, Meaux, Reims, and the Abbey of Vaucelles in France; the Cathedral of Lausanne in Switzerland; and the Abbey of Pilis in Hungary.

The assemblage of Villard's drawings is usually called a "sketchbook" in English and an *album* in French, but these terms are misleading. While in Villard's possession, and even when it left his hands to an unknown destination, the leaves were not stitched together or to the portfolio itself. It is thus misleading to imagine that he ever possessed the equivalent of a modern artist's pad of bound blank sheets awaiting sketching.

Codicological analysis of the portfolio, including physical evidence (mainly fragmentary tabs of leaves), textual evidence (two references to drawings now missing), and gaps in 13th-century and 15th-century pagination schemes, demonstrates that the maximum number of leaves that can be *proven* to be lost from the portfolio is 13, with the possible loss of two additional leaves. Eight leaves have been lost since the 15th century; the other five to seven leaves disappeared earlier. The claim that as many leaves have been lost as now survive is untenable and misleading about the original nature and content of the portfolio. The seven quires of drawings are in the sequence Villard himself left them, and within these gatherings the individual folios and bifolios are essentially as he arranged them.

It is difficult to believe, and impossible to prove, that the drawings of Villard de Honnecourt had any effect whatsoever on the architecture of his time. Without exception, his architectural drawings differ from the buildings he drew and suggest he understood very little about stereotomy and the actual design and construction of medieval buildings.

Why, then, is Villard de Honnecourt so frequently credited with having had such importance in the history of medieval architecture? First, his portfolio is a unique survival from the Middle Ages, which makes it impossible to decipher accurately. Inasmuch as there is nothing to compare it to or associate it with, writers have felt free to speculate with unfettered enthusiasm. Second, Villard's drawings profoundly affected the way 19th-century historians thought about Gothic architecture when this specialty of architectural history was in its naive infancy. These early interpreters made several fundamental factual errors on which they based their interpretations. For example, and most notably, they cited the stereotomical formulas on fols. 20r and 20v as proof of Villard's mastery of masonry. But these drawings are, in fact, by a later hand on palimpsests, as was first demonstrated only in 1901.

The 19th-century interpretation of the significance of Villard's drawings is now being reassessed. Since the late 1970s a number of scholars in the United States and in Europe have proposed that Villard was neither an architect nor a mason; and no serious architectural historian any longer claims that Villard's drawings constitute an "encyclopedia of architectural knowledge, encompassing everything a Gothic architect needed to know."

—CARL F. BARNES, JR.

VINGBOONS, Philips.

Dutch. Born in Amsterdam, Netherlands, 1607/08. Died in Amsterdam, 1678. Father was the painter David Vingboons; brothers were the engraver and mapmaker Johannes and the architect Justus Vingboons. Active as a painter and mapmaker, then turned to architecture; became assistant to Jacob van Campen.

Chronology of Works
All in the Netherlands
† Work no longer exists

1638	168 Herengracht, Amsterdam
1639	319 Keisersgracht, Amsterdam
1639	548 Singel, Amsterdam
1639-42	Vredenburg, Beemster, North Holland†
1642	95 Kloveniersburgwal, Amsterdam
1661	New Tower, Kampen
1662	Deventer Townhall, Overijssel (new wing)
1662	364-370 Herengracht, Amsterdam
1664	412 Herengracht, Amsterdam
1664	Vanenburg House, Putten, Gelderland
1669	466 Herengracht, Amsterdam
1670	450 Herengracht, Amsterdam

Publications

BOOKS BY VINGBOONS

Afbeeldsels der voornaemste gebouwen uyt die Philips Vingboons geordineert heeft. Amsterdam, 1648.
De granden...afbeeldingen en beschrijvingen des aldervoornaamste en aldernieuwste gebouwen uyt alle die door Philippus Vingboons geordineert zijn. Amsterdam, 1674.

BOOKS ABOUT VINGBOONS

ANDREAE, F.; HEKKER, R. C.; and TER KUILE, E. H.: *Duizend Jaar Bouwen in Nederland.* Amsterdam, 1957.
OTTENHEYM, K.: *Philips Vingboons (1607-1678) architect.* Zutphen, 1989.
VAN GELDER, HENDRIK E. (ed.): *Kunstgeschiedenis der Nederlanden.* Vol. 2. Rev. ed. Utrecht, 1955.

ARTICLES ABOUT VINGBOONS

KOLLEMAN, G.: "Philip Vingboons en zijn ontwerp voor het Raadhuis op de Dam." *Ons Amsterdam* (1970): 312-315.
KUYPER, W.: "Vingboons' Capitool." *Spiegel Historiael* 11 (1976): 614-622.
VAN BALEN, C. L.: "Het probleem Vinckboons-Vingboons opgelost." *Oud Holland* 56 (1939): 97-112.
VAN EEGHEN, I. H.: "De famile Vinckboons-Vingboons." *Oud Holland* 67 (1952): 217-232.

Philips Vingboons was the second son of the painter David Vinckboons. Before he worked as an architect, Vingboons was active as a painter and a mapmaker. He began his architectural career as an assistant of Jacob van Campen, the most important representative of classicism in the Netherlands during the first half of the 17th century.

One of Vingboons' first commissions was the country house Vredenburg for the wealthy merchant Frederick Alewijn in 1639, in which the influence of van Campen is notable. In addition to the work done by Vingboons, Alewijn asked Pieter Post to work on various projects, and eventually Post's solutions took many elements from Vingboons' designs. Vingboons lost out in another competitive situation, that involving the design of a new Town Hall for Amsterdam; the competition was held in 1639-40, and after years of discussion, the city government chose van Campen's massive project over the more elegant solution of Vingboons.

Many of Vingboons' clients were rich Amsterdam merchants, regents and other industrialists who often wanted big and impressive houses, either in the rapidly expanding city or in the countryside around Amsterdam. One of Vingboons' major clients, almost to be compared with a Maecenas, was Johan Huydecoper, who had made his fortune in the East-India Company and eventually was elected to several terms as mayor of Amsterdam. In 1638 the architect designed an imposing house in Amsterdam for Huydecoper, who in turn recommended Vingboons to many of his friends and relatives. In this large, four-story house on the Singel, Vingboons divided the facade by stacking three different orders of pilasters on top of a basement. (This house was destroyed in 1943.)

Vingboons worked as an architect not only for Amsterdam's many rich patricians, who gave him commissions varying from their own houses to those for the working class, but also for the nobility from other parts of the Netherlands, who frequently commissioned him to design their country houses; he became especially popular after the publication of his designs in 1648.

Vingboons proved to be a talented architect who had a great knowledge of the treatises of Vitruvius, Giacomo da Vignola and Vincenzo Scamozzi, and liked to design according to mathematical principles. Yet he was not at all dogmatic, and knew how to adapt a facade or ground plan to the available space. His approach sometimes led to remarkable projects, which could differ tremendously in style. Whereas the house for Johan Poppen (1642) is severe in its classical composition, other buildings by Vingboons could almost be considered Mannerist—such as the house for Daniel Sohier (1639). This liberty with the classical canons made Vingboons one of the most interesting architects of the 17th century, not only in Holland, but in Europe. Only recently has he received more attention, but many problems are unresolved and need to be investigated. While it is easy to see differences in style as a result of adapting to the building site, they also seem to reflect a general crisis in Dutch society that was expressed in the architectural language.

Another significant change of style occurred after 1660, when Vingboons developed a more sober style through the reduction of ornament and an almost complete elimination of the pilaster orders. The houses of Isaac Nijs (1664) and Joseph Doutz (1669) show the results of that change.

The publication of many of Philips Vingboons' projects in two volumes led to a reputation which went beyond the Netherlands.

Justus Vingboons, a younger brother of Philips, became famous for his Trippenhuis in Amsterdam, a house for two members of the Trip family, who became wealthy in the weapons trade. After having worked in Stockholm, where he was involved in the construction of the Riddarhus, Justus Vingboons

returned to Amsterdam and was commissioned by the brothers Louys and Hendrick Trip to design a double house behind one facade. The most interesting feature of the house is the facade, which is dominated by huge Corinthian pilasters and a rich entablature, both rather uncommon for Amsterdam.

—HERMAN VAN BERGEIJK

VIOLLET-LE-DUC, Eugène Emmanuel.

French. Born in Paris, France, 27 January 1814. Died in Lausanne, 17 September 1879. Married Elizabeth Tempier, 1834. Worked for the architect Marie Huvé, 1830, then for Achille LeClere; taught at the École de Dessin, 1834-50; after extensive travel in Italy, rejoined LeClere at the Conseil des Bâtiments Civils, and then as assistant on the Hôtel des Archives, Paris; became second inspector to the restoration of the Sainte-Chapelle, Paris, 1840; named chef du bureau of the Commiss ion des Monuments Historiques, 1846. Chevalier, Légion d'Honneur, 1849; corresponding member of the Royal Institute of British Architects, 1855. Gold Medal, Royal Institute of British Architects, 1864.

Chronology of Works
All in France unless noted
† Work no longer exists

1840-59	Church of the Madeleine, Vézelay (restoration)
1843-49	Notre-Dame, Paris (sacristy; with J. B. A. Lassus)
1845-64	Notre-Dame, Paris (restoration; with Lassus)
1846-49	H. Courmont House, Paris
1850-75	Cathedral, Amiens (restoration)
1852-58	St. Gimer, Carcassonne
1854-56	Dollfus House (now Maison de Repos Geisbuhl), Dornach
1855-66	Salle Synodale, Sens (restoration)
1856	Durand House, Neuilly†
1856-66	Château de Coucy, Aisne (restoration)
1857	Maignan House, St. Brieuc
1857-58	Constant Troyon House and Studio, Paris†
1857-61	A. Milon House, Paris
1857-65	Griois House (now Château du Tertre), Ambrières les Vallées
1858	Woronzow Tomb, Odessa, Russia
1858-60	École Polonaise, Paris
1858-70	Château de Pierrefonds, Oise (restoration)
1859-61	Chapelle du Petit Séminaire, Paris
1859-63	Sellières Chapel, Cires le Mello
1860-63	Sabatier House (now École Sécondaire d'Agriculture du Prieuré), Pierrefonds, Oise
1860-66	St. Denis de l'Estrée, St. Denis
1860-68	Château de Montdardier, Le Vigan
1860-69	Château de Chamousset, Rhône
1860-71	St. Raymond, Toulouse (restoration)
1860-73	Cathedral, Reims (restoration)
1860-79	Walls, Avignon (restoration)
1861-69	Château de Pupetières, Chabons, Isère
1862-63	Viollet-le-Duc House, Paris
1862-65	Monument to Napoléon and His Brothers, Place du Diamant, Ajaccio, Corsica (with Barye, Thomas, Maillet and V. Dubray)
1862-79	Cathedral, Clermont Ferrand, Puy de Dôme, Avignon (restoration)
1863-65	Sauvage House, Paris
1863-69	Château de la Flachère, St. Verand

1864	Monument to Louis Napoléon and Eugènie, Place Napoléon, Algiers, Algeria
1864-66	Château de Roquetaillade, Mazeres, Gironde (supervised and continued by Duthoit)
1865-66	Tomb for the Duc de Morny, Père Lachaise Cemetery, Paris
1865-67	Château Jacquesson (now part of the Slavia Brewery), Chalons-sur-Marne
1866-67	Notre Dame, Place du Parvis (presbytery)
1868-71	St. Raymond, Toulouse (restoration)
1871-75	Donjon, Toulouse (restoration)
1872-73	Châlet de la Côrte, Le Brévent, Chamonix†
1873-76	Cathedral, Lausanne, Switzerland (restoration)
1874-78	Viollet-le-Duc House (La Vedette), Lausanne, Switzerland†
1874-79	Château d'Eu, Seine Maritime (interior decoration, furniture and outbuildings)
1876-77	Scots Kirk, Lausanne, Switzerland
1879	Millet Tomb, St. Germain en Laye Cemetery, Seine et Oise

Publications

BOOKS BY VIOLLET-LE-DUC

Essai sur l'architecture militaire au moyen age. Paris, 1854.

Dictionnaire raisonné de l'architecture française du XI au XVI siècle. 10 vols. Paris, 1858-68.

Dictionnaire raisonné du mobilier français de l'époque carolingienne à la renaissance. 6 vols. Paris, 1858-75. Selections reprinted in English in *The Foundations of Architecture.* New York, 1990.

Entretiens sur l'architecture. 3 vols. Paris, 1863-79; as *Discourses on Architecture.* Translated by Henry Van Brunt. 2 vols. Boston, 1875-81.

Peintures murales des chapelles de Notre Dame. Paris, 1870.

Histoire d'une fortresse. Paris, 1874.

Histoire de l'habitation humaine depuis les temps préhistoriques jusqu'à nos jours. Paris, 1875; as *Habitations of Man in All Ages.* London, 1876.

Habitations modernes. With Felix Narjoux. 2 vols. Brussels, 1875-77.

Description et historie du château de Pierrefonds. Paris, 1876.

L'art russe, ses origines, ses éléments constitutifs, son apogée, son avenir. Paris, 1877.

Histoire d'un hôtel de ville et d'une cathédrale. Paris, 1878.

Viollet-le-Duc: Voyage aux Pyrénées 1833. Edited by Geneviève Viollet-le-Duc. Lourdes, France, 1972.

The Architectural Theory of Viollet-Le-Duc. Cambridge, Massachusetts, 1990.

BOOKS ABOUT VIOLLET-LE-DUC

ABRAHAM, P.: *Viollet-le-Duc et le rationalisme médiéval.* Paris, 1934.

AUZAS, P. M. (ed.): *Eugène Viollet-le-Duc, 1814-1879.* Exhibition catalog. Paris, 1965.

Catalogue des livres composant la bibliothèque de feu M. E. Viollet-le-Duc. Paris, 1880.

ELLIOTT, SCOTT: *Frank Lloyd Wright and Viollet-Le-Duc, Organic Architecture and Design from 1850 to 1950.*

FOUCART, BRUNO (ed.): *Viollet-le-Duc.* Exhibition catalog. Paris, 1980.

GOUT, PAUL: *Viollet-le-Duc: sa vie, son oeuvre, sa doctrine.* Paris, 1914.

GUBLER, JACQUES (ed.): *Viollet-le-Duc: Centenaire de la mort à Lausanne.* Exhibition catalog. Lausanne, Switzerland, 1979.

PEVSNER, NIKOLAUS: *Ruskin and Viollet-le-Duc: Englishness and Frenchness in the Appreciation of Gothic Architecture.* London, 1969.

PEVSNER, NIKOLAUS: *Some Architectural Writers of the Nineteenth Century.* Oxford, 1972.

SAINT-PAUL, A.: *Viollet-le-Duc, ses travaux d'art et son système archéologique.* Paris, 1881.

ARTICLES ABOUT VIOLLET-LE-DUC

BRESSANI, MARTIN: "Notes on Viollet-le-Duc's Philosophy of History: Dialectics and Technology." *Journal of the Society of Architectural Historians* 48 (December 1989): 327-350.

HOFFMANN, DONALD: "Frank Lloyd Wright and Viollet-le-Duc." *Journal of the Society of Architectural Historians* 28, No. 3 (1969).

MACCLINTOCK, LUCY: "Monumentality versus Suitability: Viollet-le-Duc's Saint Gimer at Carcassonne." *Journal of the Society of Architectural Historians* 40 (October 1981): 218-235.

MIDDLETON, ROBIN D.: "Viollet-le-Duc's Academic Ventures and the Entretiens sur l'architecture." In ADOLF M. VOGT, CHRISTINA REBLE and MARTIN FROHLICH (eds.): *Gottfried Semper und die Mitte des 19. Jahrhunderts.* Basel, 1976.

SUMMERSON, JOHN: "Viollet-le-Duc and the Rational Point of View." In *Heavenly Mansions and Other Essays on Architecture.* London, 1949.

SUMMERSON, J.; PEVSNER, N.; DAMISH, H.; and DURANT, S.: "Viollet-le-Duc." *Architectural Design* profile (1980).

VIOLLET-LE-DUC, GENEVIEVE, and AILLAGON, JEAN JACQUES (eds.): *Le voyage d'Italie d'Eugène Viollet-le-Duc 1836-1837.* Exhibition catalog. Paris, 1980.

*

Eugène-Emmanuel Viollet-le-Duc occupies a unique position in the history of architecture, as an individual who was able to embrace in a single vision the celebration of the past, the incorporation of present technology, and the anticipation of future possibilities. In elaborating a general theory of architecture that could respond flexibly to the infinite variety of local historical traditions, cultural practices and material resources, Viollet-le-Duc offered an alternative in his own day to what he viewed as the ossified precepts of the Académie. Viollet-le-Duc's theory of rationality in architecture was seized upon by a generation of early modern architects at the turn of the century in Europe and the United States; American architects could enjoy his *Lectures on Architecture* in translation as early as 1875 and read analyses in the pages of professional journals. Viollet-le-Duc continues to provide a fecund source of inspiration for architects, historians and critics alike in the late 20th century. His conception of the role of history in design, for example, has much to contribute to current debate.

While his theoretical musings may seem most germane to the architectural practitioner, they represent but a fraction of Viollet-le-Duc's oeuvre. Before the outpouring of revisionist scholarship that attended his centennial in 1979, Viollet-le-Duc was most well known, and generally maligned, for the questionable accuracy of his restorations of medieval monuments in France. His more creative than archaeological approach to the reconstruction of historical buildings found little favor with early historians, and does not accord with contemporary preservation sensibilities. Recent exhibitions and publications have emphasized, however, that Viollet-le-Duc's method, although no longer subscribed to, was grounded in sound theoretical underpinnings. They reveal that Viollet-le-Duc the historian sought, in his imaginative restorations, to "restore" buildings not to some verifiable former condition, but rather to a theoretical stylistic purity, to an ideal completeness that may never have existed in reality. In so doing, he has offered posterity the enjoyment of reclaimed historic fabric, and an instructive representative of a lost episode of cultural history. Recent scholarship stresses above all the debt owed to Viollet-le-Duc for the magnitude of his efforts, as restorer and scholar, on behalf of France's patrimony—at a moment when its value was just beginning to be fully recognized and promoted by the government. He is credited with both the rescue of such monuments as Notre Dame, Carcassonne and Vézelay, and the production of a vast collection of exquisitely rendered drawings, which constitute invaluable historical records of the restoration process and of the condition of buildings prior to his interventions.

Viollet-le-Duc's involvement with the government's effort to salvage an architectural patrimony ravaged by centuries of neglect and destruction was closely linked to his consuming interest in the history of architecture per se. His activities as architect, theorist, preservationist and historian were thoroughly intertwined. Readers of his ostensibly historical works will find them to be suffused with theoretical lessons for contemporary architects, just as the "theoretical" pronouncements of the *Entretiens sur l'Architecture* (1863-72) are replete with historical insights. Readers of the encyclopedic *Dictionnaire raisonné de l'architecture française du XIe au XVIe siècle* (1854-68), for example, will find under the heading "spire" (flèche, V. 5) an historical account of the use of spires in medieval architecture, complete with analytical drawings. The drawings are not purely documentary in nature, however, for they illustrate a set of geometric "laws" the author has extracted from the historical examples, laws which might be applied by contemporary architects to the design of any object silhouetted against the sky. The historical information compiled for the article "church" similarly serves a larger purpose, in this case a political, preservationist one. Viollet-le-Duc offers a complete geographic chronicle of Romanesque churches in France bearing the heading: "worthy of the rank of historic monuments." His approach to history was again an instrumental one—the list is clearly an advocacy document aimed at the French government, argument for official protective designation of the buildings in question.

Viollet-le-Duc's history of Russian art, *L'Art russe, ses origines, ses éléments constitutifs, son apogée, son avenir* (1877), one of his last "histories," is a superbly crafted example of the complex interweaving of historical, theoretical and political principles in his writings. Relying on information provided by a group of Russian scholars with slavophile leanings, he begins with an account of the "origins and development" of Russian architecture before its contamination by Western ideas under Peter the Great. This is followed by his own theoretical program for its future development. Viollet-le-Duc uses the uncharted waters of Russian architecture as a test case for his theory of a "rational architecture," one that would respond "truthfully" to the historical traditions, customs and material capabilities of its sponsors. On these grounds, the only proper course open to contemporary Russian designers, he argues, would be to plumb the depths of their own Muscovite past, and to generate from that reservoir, fertilized with the fruits of modern technology, an architecture expressive of both the Slavic past and the 19th-century present.

In this and other works the "national" component of Viollet-le-Duc's "rationalism" is abundantly clear, and the appropriateness of the narrow label of "structural rationalism," with which he is often associated, is called into question. His theories on the statics of Gothic cathedrals have recently been confirmed by modern scientific analysis, and this has justifiably provided renewed respect for his structural intuition. However, it should be recognized that Viollet-le-Duc's appreciation of the cathedral was not narrowly technical. Indeed his admiration for Gothic architecture was based in part on the conviction that it was a direct expression of the needs, tastes and resources of medieval France, and thus a truly "national" architecture. Nor should the political implications of this assessment be ignored. Long at loggerheads with both the educational and professional establishment in France, Viollet-le-Duc used the "nationality" and the "rationality" of Gothic architecture as ammunition to fuel his campaign against the slavish imitation of "foreign" architectural ideas.

This abhorrence of "servile imitation" of nonnative sources constitutes the cornerstone of Viollet-le-Duc's theories of rationality and nationality in architecture. And it is in his conception of the architect's choice and use of precedent that Viollet-le-Duc is most germane to contemporary architectural concerns—"If a Pompeiian house is charming under the Naples sky," he writes, "for people who lived 2,000 years ago, it does not follow that it would be appropriate to our time and to our climate." (*Histoire de l'habitation humaine,* 1875). In Viollet-le-Duc's view, the architect should consult indigenous sources (or, ideally, nature itself), and interpret rather than copy them.

Throughout his life he railed against the Greco-Roman and Renaissance predilections of his contemporaries at the Académie. Protesting their undigested mimicry of borrowed forms, he argued that the architect must study not the letter of history but its lessons, not the forms, but the principles that inspired them. "Our monuments are covered with imitations of Roman ornament," he wrote (*Dictionnaire,* V), "which is but a misunderstood copy of Greek . . . we copy copies, and at great expense."

As ever he proposed the Gothic paradigm—noting the relationship between the Gothic sculptor and his "model"—nature itself, in the form of native flora. Instead of laboriously copying the details of a given plant, the sculptor discerns certain "organic laws" that define such characteristics as the relationship between stem and leaf and the direction of growth. He then uses those laws to generate his own distinct forms. The resulting ornamentation will emerge "like a natural vegetation of the structure," just as forms generated in accordance with the traditions and talents of a given nation will exhibit a natural integrity.

The preference for emulation over imitation, and for "truthful" response to the whole array of practical and spiritual needs, found echo in his American admirers such as Frank Lloyd Wright, and are no less relevant today.

—LAUREN M. O'CONNELL

VITRUVIUS.

Roman. Born Marcus Vitruvius Pollio. Roman architect, active in the first century B.C. Served under Julius Caesar in the African war, ca. 46 B.C. Built the Basilica of Fano, and was employed in Augustus' program to rebuild Rome. Author of an influential treatise on architecture in ten books.

Publications

BOOKS BY VITRUVIUS

I Dieci Libri dell'Architettura di M. Vitruvio Tradutti e Commentati da Monsignor Barbaro eletto Patriarca d'Aquileggia. Venice, 1556.

Les Dix Livres d'Architecture de Vitruve, Corrigez et Traduits Nouvellement en François avec des Notes et des Figures. Translated and edited by Claude Perrault. Paris, 1673; second edition, 1684.

Vitruvius, The Ten Books of Architecture. Translated by Morris Hickey Morgan. Cambridge, Massachusetts, 1914; 1960.

Vitruvius on Architecture. Translated by Frank Granger. Cambridge, Massachusetts, 1955-1956.

BOOKS ABOUT VITRUVIUS

BECCATTI, G.: *Arte e gusto negli scrittori latini.* Florence, 1951.

BEYEN, HENDRIK GERARS: *Die pompejanische Wanddekoration vom zweiten bis zum vierten Stil.* 2 vols. The Hague. 1930; 1960.

BOETHIUS, A.: *Vitruvius and the Roman Architecture of His Age.* 1939.

BULLANT, JEAN: *Reigle générale d'Architecture des cinq manières de colonnes à scavoir, Tuscane, Dorique, Ionique, Corinthe, & Composite, à l'exemple de l'antique suivant les reigles & doctrine de Vitruve.* Paris, 1564; 2nd ed., 1619.

CARRINGTON, ROGER CLIFFORD: *Pompeii.* Oxford, 1936.

CESARIANO, CESARE: *Di Lucio Vitruvio Pollione de Architectura.* 1521. Reprint: New York and London, 1968.

DRACHMANN, AAGE GERHARDT: *The Mechanical Technology of Greek and Roman Antiquity.* Copenhagen, 1963.

EBHARDT, BODO: *Die zehn Bücher über Architektur des Vitruv.* Berlin, 1918.

GROS, PIERRE: *Aurea Templa: recherches sur l'architecture religieuse de Rome à l'époque d'Auguste.* Rome, Bibliothèque des écoles françaises d'Athènes et de Rome, 1976.

MARSDEN, E. W.: *Greek and Roman Artillery: Technical Treatises.* New York, 1971.

MAU, AUGUST: *Pompeii, Its Life and Art.* New York, 1899; 1904.

PLOMMER, H.: *Vitruvius and Later Roman Building Manuals.* Cambridge, 1973.

SCHEFOLD, KARL: *Die Wände Pompejis.* Berlin, 1957.

ARTICLES ABOUT VITRUVIUS

CERUTTI, STEVEN, and RICHARDSON, L., JR.: "Vitruvius on Stage Architecture and Some Recently Discovered Scaenae Frons Decorations." *Journal of the Society of Architectural Historians* 48 (June 1989): 172-179.

HOEPFNER, W.: "Zum ionischen Kapitell bei Hermogenes und Vitruv." *Athenische Mitteilungen* (1968).

KRAUTHEIMER, RICHARD: "Alberti and Vitruvius." *Acts of the 20th International Congress of the History of Art* 2 (1961): 42-52.

KRINSKY, CAROL HERSELLE: "Seventy-eight Vitruvius Manuscripts." *Journal of the Warburg and Courtauld Institutes* 30 (1967): 36-70.

RUSSELL, JAMES: "The Origin and Development of Republican Forums." *Phoenix* 22 (1968): 304-336.

SCHLIKKER, W.: "Hellenistische Vorstellungen von der Schönheit des Bauwerks nach Vitruv." *Athenische Mitteilungen* (1968).

VAGNETTI, LUIGI (ed.): "2000 anni di Vitruvio." *Studi e documenti di architettura* No. 8, special issue (1978).

WATZINGER, C.: "Vitruvstudien." *Rheinisches Museum* 64 (1909).

For more than five centuries architects and classical archaeologists have attempted to comprehend Greek and Roman architecture, often with frustration, by using Vitruvius and his text *De Architectura*. Being the sole surviving architectural text from classical antiquity and deriving its sources from Italy, Greece and Asia Minor, the treatise was the main authority for several Renaissance writers, such as Leon Battista Alberti, Sebastiano Serlio and Andrea Palladio, in spite of its confusing character as a source of reference vis-a-vis the buildings themselves. Quite apart from its documentary aspect, however, the text is important for its visionary message, which contains regional as well as universal values that hold true even today.

Marcus Vitruvius Pollio was officially employed in the program for rebuilding Rome under Augustus, the first emperor of the Romans, but the official title of the emperor is never mentioned in the treatise. Hence, it was probably finished before 27 B.C. when the title was granted. Consequently, it is clear that Vitruvius had already written his treatise before the familiar characteristics of Roman architecture as we know it today, the structural revolution in concrete and the accompanying metamorphosis in interior space conception, had had a chance to complete their evolution. In other words, there is no critical assessment of these issues, very little on arches, even less on domes and next to nothing on problems arising from the widely used combination of trabeated and arcuated systems. However, it is interesting to note that during the first to the fourth centuries, when Roman architecture had reached its zenith in structural developments, Vitruvius was still very much remembered, and his *De Architectura* was used as a handbook, occasionally at least, as can be inferred from the facts that Pliny and Frontinus refered to him, and that M. Caetius Faventinus and Palladius Rutilius copied from his treatise.

De Architectura consists of 10 books, frequently prefaced in a tortuous and grandiloquent style. Vitruvius is apologetic about the shortcomings of his vernacular Latin: "I request, Caesar, both of you and of those who may read the said books, that if anything is set forth with too little regard for grammatical rule it may be pardoned. For it is not as a very great philosopher, nor as an eloquent rhetorician, nor as a grammarian trained in the highest principles of his art, that I have striven to write this work, but as an architect who has had only a dip into those studies" (I.1.17). It is therefore evident that an accurate reading of Vitruvius depends firstly on careful linguistic decipherment and, secondly, on keeping in mind the *ancient* understanding of concepts such as symmetry, proportion and balance.

Each one of the 10 books belongs to a coherent, planned order, which Vitruvius takes pains to explain. After defining the function and range of architecture and the training of the architect in the first book, the various uses and properties of building materials like brick, sand, lime, *pozzolana*, stone and timber are treated in the second. The third, fourth, fifth and sixth books are reserved for the buildings themselves: a discussion of temples and their orders, and buildings for public use, including the forum, basilica, treasury, prison, senate building, theater, baths and harbors, is followed by a descriptive enumeration of various dwelling types and their characteristics. Floors, walls, vaults and their polished finishings, stuccowork, the sources and manufacture of natural and artificial colors are treated in the seventh book, while the eighth book deals entirely with water, its varieties, uses, control and transportation. The ninth book is devoted to a lengthy astrological discourse on the zodiac, the courses of the sun and the moon and the making of sundials and water clocks. Finally, the subject of the tenth book is machines of every kind. These include hoisting devices, engines, waterwheels and pumps, and the hodometer, catapults, ballistae and siege machines, to be used in times of peace and war, respectively. In this manner, Vitruvius claims to have covered all the branches of architecture in his treatise.

From the range of subjects constituting the 10 books, the text appears to be a profusely detailed manual containing time-tested prescriptions in the practice of architecture, rather than an axiomatic discourse on theoretical issues. In light of its universal message, however, the book is not primarily an *ars* or *techne* either, nor is it a repository of canned information. Nor does it fit any acceptable norm as a variety of building history. Vitruvius' historical consciousness, sometimes as a firsthand observer and often through the eyes of Greek writers whose works are now lost, cannot be overlooked. But he is not an encyclopedic compiler in the traditional sense, since he enriches the commentaries on contemporary and historical buildings by adding his own technical know-how based on his personal experience as a master. In other words, he seeks perfection in the art of building by setting for himself the standard of exemplary works in the past: "I began to write this work for you, because I saw that you have built and are now building extensively, and that in the future also you will take care that our public and private buildings shall be worthy to go down to posterity by the side of your other splendid achievements. I have drawn up definite rules to enable you, by observing them, to have personal knowledge of the quality both of existing buildings and of those which are yet to be constructed. For in the following books I have disclosed all the principles of the art" (I.3).

Here, Vitruvius' architectural ethics and professional attitude assume the responsibility of an ideological mission. Like Virgil, who rewrote Roman history for Augustus, Vitruvius yearns for an architecture that will reveal the greatness of the new empire. In the *Res Gestae* of Augustus, architectural accomplishments are proudly put beside military and other deeds, which proves the importance of architecture in a state-controlled propaganda machine. (Much later, Justinian and Charlemagne also associated architecture with the court and its elitist tradition.) Hence, the grandeur of the Roman state will be reflected in the *auctoritas* and *decor* of its buildings. "The races in Italy, most perfectly constituted in bodily form and mental activity . . . situated by divine intelligence in a peerless . . . country . . . to acquire the right to command the whole world . . ." (VI.1.11) deserve nothing less. This lofty conception embodies all aspects of architecture, such as ensuring a steady water supply (VIII.6.2) or providing appropriate accommodations for different classes of people (VI.5.2)

Although Vitruvius is not a dogmatic reactionist against all innovation, his puritanic preference for the good old ways reflects caution more than anything else. During his era, the Roman evolution in concrete had not yet attained the capacity to fill the architectural vacuum left by the unresolved crisis of the Greek-influenced post-and-lintel system. Consequently, he failed to appreciate the potential of *pozzolana* even though he was aware of its "astonishing" properties (II.6.1). Concerning the far-reaching qualities of the Sanctuary of Fortuna Primigenia at Praeneste or the Tabularium in Rome, for example, it is inconceivable that Vitruvius was unaware of them. Yet there is no comment, reactionary or otherwise, on these contemporary monuments. In a bustling age when upstarts "grabbed" commissions, there may be a hint of sour grapes, Vitruvius being denied the laurels of success, in his beetle-browed denunciation of certain fashionable innovations, as in fresco painting.

On the whole, however, Vitruvian criticisms are not narrow-minded and static. He seeks the truth, verified through reasoning and applied again and again, in order to attain the "highest refinement of learning" (VII.1). Architecture for him is not a profession like any other, but a science that represents learning in many different fields. In this way he aims to bridge the gap between practice and theory by imposing on the architect the moral obligation to write. As he reels off the names of Greek architect-writers one after the other, he wistfully criticizes Roman architects, like Cossutius, who did not leave treatises to explain the great works that they built (7.15). (It is interesting that the basilica at Fano is the only building in Vitruvius' name.) Curiously enough, it is only through Vitruvius that we are informed today of treatises written by Greek architects. Among the latter are books on the reformulation of the Ionic order by Hermogenes, on the Mausoleum at Halicarnassus (one of the seven wonders of the world) by Pytheos and Satryus, on the *tholos* at Delphi by Theodorus of Phocaea, and on the Temple of Artemis at Ephesus by Chersiphron of Crete and his son Metagenes.

While Vitruvius emphasizes the nature of the dynamic dialectic between practice and theory, he simultaneously—and without contradiction—gives equal treatment to philosophers like Socrates, Plato, Aristotle, Zeno and Epicurius on the one hand, and to scientists such as Thales, Democritus, Anaxagoras and Xenophanes on the other. By doing so, he attempts to combine "rules for the conduct of human life" (VII.2) with empirical observations. Through this unorthodox endeavor, which forms the basis for objective reasoning, Vitruvius has succeeded in maintaining his universal relevance throughout the ages.

In copying from Greek sources, knowingly or unknowingly, Vitruvius also touches upon the epistemological importance of language in the transmission of knowledge. At a stage when the cultural identity of Roman society was still under Greek influence, the abundance of Greek architectural terms in *De Architectura* need not be surprising. Nevertheless, the dissonance between Greek and Latin technical terms, particularly in the passage on the Greek house (VI.7.5-6), is striking. In some extreme cases, Vitruvius does not hesitate to state openly that Latin fails to convey knowledge derived from Greek sources: "Harmonics is an obscure and difficult branch of musical science, especially for those who do not know Greek. If we desire to treat of it, we must use Greek words, because some of them have no Latin equivalents" (V.4.1). Regarding this problem almost 1,500 years later, Alberti, in his *De Re Aedificatoria,* which was based on *De Architectura,* rejects the Greek terminology of Vitruvius in a radical gesture, in order to form a scientific language in his own tongue.

Vitruvius' *De Architectura* attempts to define good architecture and at the same time emphasizes the need for thorough training, technical expertise, wide-ranging cultural knowledge and social responsibility in the architect who is to create it. By realistically assessing the many difficulties that face the true architect, he depicts an internally consistent picture of the society in which he lived and worked.

—SUNA GÜVEN

VITTONE, Bernardo.

Italian. Born Bernardo Antonio Vittone in Turin, Italy, 1702. Died in Turin, 1770. Uncle was Gian Giacomo Plantery, with whom Vittone probably studied architecture; also trained under Filippo Juvarra, and at the Accademia di San Luca, Rome, 1731-33. Worked independently in Turin, 1733-70. Elected to Accademia di San Luca, 1732.

Chronology of Works
All in Italy
† *Work no longer exists*

1730	Parish Church, Pecetto
1737	Ospedale di Carità, Casale Monferrato
1738	Capella della Visitazione, Valinotto
1738?	Collegio delle Provincie, Turin
1738	Gonzaga, Corteranzo
1740	San Gaetano, Nice
1740	Santi Vincenzo e Anastasio, Cambiano†
1740-44	San Bernardino, Chieri
1741	Santa Maria Maddalena, Foglizzo
1741-42	Santi Marco e Leonardo, Turin†
1742	Santa Chiara, Bra
1742	Santa Chiara, Turin
1744-49	Albergo di Carità, Carignano
1750	Assunta, Grignasco
1750	Santa Maria di Piazza, Turin
1754	Church, Casotto, Certosa
1754-56	Santa Chiara, Vercelli
1755	San Croce (now Santa Caterina), Villanova Mondoví
1755	San Salvatore, Borgomasino
1757-64	Santi Giovanni e Vincenzo, Sant'Ambrogio di Torino
1758	San Michele, Rivarolo Canavese
1761	Assunta, Riva di Chieri
1769	Chapel of San Secondo, Asti, San Secondo
1770	San Michele, Borgo d'Ale

Publications

BOOKS BY VITTONE

Istruzioni elementari per indirizzo de'giovanni allo studio dell'architettura civile. Lugano, Switzerland, 1760-66.

BOOKS ABOUT VITTONE

BRINCKMANN, ALBERT E.: *Theatrum Novum Pedemontii: Ideen, Entwürfe und Bauten von Guarini, Juvarra, Vittone wie anderen bedeutenden Architekten des piemonteischen Hochbarocks.* Düsseldorf, 1931.

CARBONERI, NINO, and VIALE, VITTORIO: *Bernardo Vittone architetto.* Exhibition catalog. Turin, 1967.

OLVERO, EUGENIO: *Le opere di Bernardo Antonio Vittone.* Turin, 1920.

POMMER, RICHARD: *Eighteenth-Century Architecture in Piedmont: The Open Structures of Juvarra, Alfieri, and Vittone.* New York and London, 1967.

PORTOGHESI, PAOLO: *Bernardo Vittone, un architetto tra illuminismo e rococò.* Rome, 1966.

VIALE, VITTORIO (ed.): *Bernardo Vittone e la disputà fra classicismo e barocco nel settecento.* 2 vols. Turin, 1972-74.

WITTKOWER, RUDOLF: *Art and Architecture in Italy: 1600-1750.* 3rd ed. Baltimore and Harmondsworth, England, 1973.

ARTICLES ABOUT VITTONE

CARBONERI, NINO: "Appunti sul Vittone." *Quaderni dell'istituto di storia dell'architettura* Nos. 55-60; 59-74 (1963).

CAVALLARI MURAT, AUGUSTO: "L'architettura sacra del Vittone." *Atti e rassegna tecnica* 10 (1956): 35-52.

GOLZIO, VINCENZO: "L'architetto Bernardo Antonio Vittone urbanista." *Atti del X congresso di storia dell'architettura Torino* (1959): 101-112.

MILLON, HENRY: "Alcune osservasioni sulle opere giovanili di Bernardo Antonio Vittone." *Bollettino della società piemontese di archeologia e belle arti* 12-13 (1958-59): 144-153.

OECHSLIN, WERNER: "Bildungsgut und Antikenrezeption des frühen Settecento in Rom." In *Studien zum römischen Aufenthalt Bernardo Antonio Vittones.* Zurich and Freiburg im Breisgau, 1972.

PORTOGHESI, PAOLO: "La Chiesa di Santa Chiara a Bra nell'opera di B. A. Vittone." *Quaderni dell'istituto di storia dell'architettura* No. 54 (1962): 1-22.

PORTOGHESI, PAOLO: "Metodo e poesia nell'architettura di Bernardo Antonio Vittone." *Bollettino della società piemontese di archeologia e belle arti* 14-15 (1960-61): 99-114.

*

After Guarino Guarini and Filippo Juvarra, Bernardo Antonio Vittone is the third great master of Piedmontese Baroque architecture. Vittone consciously assimilated the lessons of his earlier compatriots with deliberate nationalistic intent, assembling architectural motifs derived from theirs. In the endeavor, he created a highly imaginative style characterized by light enclosures and light-filled spaces, a style that was distinct from that of the built work of his fellow Piedmontese.

Vittone perfected what has been termed the "open structure" (Richard Pommer, *Eighteenth-Century Architecture in Piedmont*), which he most evidently employed in his churches designed after 1740. These churches are conceptually akin to Juvarra's work wherein the surfaces of the structural enclosures were deliberately eroded. However, Vittone surpassed Juvarra in that he exploited the open structure to its fullest. Interior enclosing forms of the churches are dematerialized chiefly by puncturing architectural elements—such as the dome, the pendentive, the column capital, the pier—to reveal other elements which too have been dematerialized. In this way, an elaborate and playful screen system of multiple levels and layers was created in Vittone's architecture that allows for the diffusion of light throughout his spaces. The surfaces through which light penetrates and on which it is refracted, were enlivened by highly energetic and equally ethereal decorations created for the most part out of stucco and paint.

Despite the visual complexity and playfulness of Vittone's designs, geometry governs the planning of his open structures. It is in this rigid planning that Vittone best exhibits his appreciation for, if not the complete understanding of, the works of Guarini. The skeletal structure, sustaining the perforated enclosures in many of his works, has a sharp clarity. For example, the delineation of vertical elements from the pier or column through the ribbed dome to the lantern is continuous—as at Santa Chiara in Turin (1744-49) and Santa Maria dell'Assunta in Grignasco (1750)—or is terminated in an open-weave ribbed dome as at the Cappella della Visitazione in Valinotto (1738).

One of Vittone's early churches, Santa Chiara in Bra (1742), exemplifies well the open structure. In the central crossing, the skeletal structure is accentuated, from the piers articulated with paired orders, up through the ribs of the dome. Arched openings are cut into the drum on two levels, on the lower level to allow light in from a subsidiary space, and again above, into the skin of the dome itself, to reveal a lit gallery—itself a space perforated in a variety of ways—encircling that dome. The effect is one of light flooded through the lightest of vessels.

In his desire to appropriate the work of Guarini and Juvarra, Vittone was experimental and introduced original formal motifs such as the gouged-out pendentive and the perforated gallery. The gouged-out pendentive was used in the churches of the 1750s, such as in Santa Maria de Piazza in Turin, in the vault of the presbytery. Introduced a decade earlier in the punctured pendentive in San Bernardino in Chieri (1740-44), such a device served to introduce unexpected light into the central domed space, as well as to denigrate the appearance of the dome's solidity by dematerializing its support. A well-lit gallery circling the skeletal base of the dome was also a form exploited by Vittone. This he employed, among other places, at San Bernardino and at Santa Chiara in Bra. It, too, was intended to create the impression of light and lightness.

Although the majority of Vittone's architectural works were built for parishes or religious orders in Piedmont, his career was initiated, somewhat late in life, by his study at the Accademia di San Luca in Rome from 1731 to 1733. There he gained an appreciation of Roman 17th-century architecture, most blatantly evidenced in his volumes of copies of Carlo Fontana's drawings then in the possession of Cardinal Alessandro Albani, a patron influential in the establishment of the neoclassical style. On returning to Turin, Vittone showed his admiration for the work and thought of another 17th-century architect, that of his countryman Guarini, by preparing for publication the latter's treatise *Architettura Civile,* which was published in 1737.

While in Rome, Vittone had also composed some designs which exemplify his knowledge of the published archaeological reconstructions of Johann Bernard Fisher von Erlach—then the rage in Rome. Fisher von Erlach's compilation of antique motifs such as triumphal arches, curved porticoes and dome articulations must have appealed to Vittone. In his own work, Vittone combined architectural forms—those of Guarini and Juvarra—seeing the creative potential of joining familiar forms in a variety of stimulating ways. While Vittone exploited this potential in his interior designs, it is best exemplified in one of his exterior designs—the dome lanterns and campanile for Santa Chiara at Bra.

Aside from being an architect, Vittone was a prolific writer. He published his own architectural treatises, *Istruzione elementari per indirizzo de' giovani allo studio dell'architettura civile* (two volumes) in 1760 and *Istruzione diverse concernanti l'officio dell'architettura civile* (two volumes) in 1766, and other of his writings remained in manuscript form. His written works deal with subjects eclectically compiled in a manner akin to that of his built works. Compared to the exuberant quality of his architecture, however, his writings are largely repetitive and unoriginal. The published works contain encyclopedic repertoires of architectural elements, such as doors, windows and vaults, and architectural types, such as churches and theaters. He supplied pragmatic suggestions for good architectural design, and included plans and sections of his built projects.

For the most part, Vittone's writings show that he was not a revolutionary thinker. For example, Vittone adhered to the history of architecture as recounted by Vitruvius, then being reevaluated and often rejected by architects and architectural theorists alike. However, there are aspects of his texts which display enlightened thinking. He was preoccupied with such contemporary concerns of the day as the education of the architect, and the establishment of typologies for civic architectural monuments. His own work in this latter area included two early projects: the Ospedale di Carità in Casale and the Albergo di Carità in Carignano. These institutional buildings, the hospital and the poorhouse, were well planned to accommodate greater and more clearly defined societal needs.

One way in which academic theory informed Vittone's architecture was in the creation of forms with intentionality. For example, in reference to the three-tiered dome of the chapel at Valinotto, Vittone suggested that each of the superimposed vaults was pierced with openings so that the viewer could see and understand "the variety of the [heavenly] hierarchies represented in these vaults." These spheres were guarded by the Holy Trinity, whose image appears above the dome structure, in the lantern. To Vittone, then, his architecture not only evoked, but represented the triune nature of God, because of the characteristics of its form and decoration.

The significance of Vittone's writings should not be underestimated, for he verbalized what often is implied in the making of architecture, that in form there is meaning. Thus, it is in the simple statements about his complex built works of this great Piedmontese architect that historians have found a legitimization for assigning meaning to architectural form.

—SUSAN M. DIXON

VOYSEY, Charles F. A.

British. Born Charles Francis Annesley Voysey in Hessle, near Hull, Yorkshire, 28 May 1857. Died in Winchester, 12 February 1941. Married, 1885. Educated by private tutor, Dulwich; articled to John Pollard Seddon (1827-1906), 1874; worked for Henry Saxon Snell (1830-1904); worked for George Devey (1820-86), 1880; opened office in London, 1882. Gold Medal, Royal Institute of British Architects, 1940.

Chronology of Works
All in England unless noted
† *Work no longer exists*

1888-89	The Cottage, Bishop's Intchington, Warwick
1890	Cazalet Walnut Tree Farm, Castlemorten, Malvern
1891	W. E. F. Britten Studio, West Kensington, London
1891	J. W. Forster House, Bedford Park, London
1891-92	Grove Town Houses, Kensington, London
1893	Wilson House, Colwell
1895	Wentworth Arms Inn, Elmesthorpe, Hinckley, Leicestershire
1895	Annesley Lodge, Platts Lane, Hampstead, London
1896	Sturgis House and Stables, Hog's Back, near Guildford, Surrey
1897	Dixcot, North Drive, Tooting Common
1897	Norney, Shackleford, Surrey
1897	New Place, Haslemere, Surrey
1898-1900	Broadleys and Moor Crag, on Lake Windermere, Cartmel Fell, Lancastershire
1899	H. G. Wells House, Spade House, Sandgate
1899	Cottage Hospital, Beaworthy, Devon
1899	Pavilion, Oldbury Park, Birmingham
1900	Prior's Garth, Puttenham, Surrey
1899-1900	The Orchard, Chorley Wood, Hertfordshire
1902	Vodin, Pyrford Common near Woking
1903	White Cottage, Lyford Road, Wandsworth
1903	Dr. Fort House, Chorley Wood, Hertfordshire
1904	Lady Somerset House, Higham, Woodford, Essex
1904	Myholme Convalescent Home for Children, Merry Hill Lane, Bushey
1904	Housing and Institute, Whitwood Colliery, Normanton, Yorkshire

1905	White Horse Inn, Stetchworth, near Newmarket
1905	Holly Mount, Knotty Green, Beaconsfield
1905	The Homestead, Frinton, Essex
1906-07	Littleholme, Guildford, Surrey
1909	St. Winifred's Quarry, Combe Down, near Bath
1909	Holiday Cottage, Slindon, Barnham Junction, Sussex
1911	R. Hetherington House, Malone Road, Belfast, Northern Ireland
1912	Memorial to the Earl of Lovelace, Ashley Combe, Somerset
1912	Lady Lovelace House, Lilycombe, Porlock, Somerset
1920	Memorial, Manor House, Tonbridge School

Publications

BOOKS BY VOYSEY

Individuality. London, 1915.
Reason as a Basis of Art. Pamphlet. London, 1906.

BOOKS ABOUT VOYSEY

BRANDON-JONES, JOHN (ed.): *Charles Francis Annesley Voysey, Architect and Designer: 1857-1941*. London, 1978.
DURANT, S.: *The Decorative Designs of C. F. A. Voysey*. New York, 1991.
GEBHARD, DAVID: *Charles F. A. Voysey, Architect*. Los Angeles, 1975.
PEVSNER, NIKOLAUS: *Pioneers of Modern Design From William Morris to Walter Gropius*. Harmondsworth, England, 1949.
RICHARDSON, MARGARET: *The Craft Architects*. London and New York, 1983.
SIMPSON, DUNCAN: *Charles Francis Annesley Voysey, and the Architecture of Individuality*. London, 1979.

ARTICLES ABOUT VOYSEY

"C. F. Annesley Voysey: The Man and His Work." *Architect and Building News* 117 (21 January; 4, 11 and 18 February 1927).
JOHNSON, A.: "C. F. A. Voysey." *Architectural Association Quarterly* 9, No. 4 (1977): 26-35.
PEVSNER, NIKOLAUS: "C. F. A. Voysey." *Elseviers Maandschrift* (1940): 343-355. Reprinted in *Studies in Art, Architecture and Design: Victorian and After*. Princeton, New Jersey, 1968.

*

Among the architects of his generation, Charles Francis Annesley Voysey was an enigmatic individualist, difficult to categorize by style, theoretical position or movement. His work is characterized by a restraint of form (visible in the plain white roughcast exteriors of his houses) and by a stark, almost abstract simplicity in his domestic interiors. His individuality, in a generation liberating itself from the historicism of the 19th century, is further evidenced by economic forms and by a bold flatness in decorative arts designs, including ornamental (sometimes playful) hinges, pierced cutouts or outlines on furniture, and floral wallpaper patterns. Voysey's signature heart motif pierces chair splats, shapes strap hinges, and frequently gains increased interest and delight when the architect positions a bird in silhouette within the heart outline. This childlike Voysey joins Voysey the builder and maker of houses to provide the more complete view of C. F. A. Voysey as a "craft architect."

Historians such as Nikolaus Pevsner have focused on Voysey's formal simplicity and sometimes abstract planarity to force a view of Voysey as a pioneer of modernism. From this point of view, Voysey's studio house at No. 14 South Parade, Bedford Park (1888-1891, addition 1894), is, according to Pevsner, a pivotal work of the avant-garde: its bare walls and precision of detail offer an intentional and remarkable contrast to surrounding redbrick houses built by Richard Norman Shaw and others in Bedford Park and styled in the "free" Queen Anne image of an earlier generation. The scale and something of the austerity of Voysey's Bedford Park studio are echoed in other of his smaller houses, notably the studio at 17 St. Dunstan's Road, Hammersmith (1891), and (especially the garden elevation of) Lowicks, near Frensham, Surrey (1894).

But these houses serve to point to the eccentric individualism of Voysey (and, joining others of his design, to his diversity), not to an intentional emerging body of modernist "pioneer" works by the architect. Indeed, Lodge Style, a house built near Bath for T. S. Cotterell as late as 1909 is self-consciously historicist; it is modeled on Merton College, Oxford (by client demand), and forms a cloister surrounded by purposefully feudal Gothic forms. More typically finding inspiration in vernacular traditions (with respect to both material and type) rather than in specific historic models, Voysey in general presented a free style of craft building which was simple and direct in its style and adaptable to client need and locale. In the end, Voysey's simple roughcast gabled walls evoke traditions of yeoman cottages, and place Voysey in a generation critically responsive to native English sources more than to an emerging "international style." His craft buildings belong in the tradition of makers of architectural form more than shapers of architectural space.

Thus, a more appropriate critical position focuses on Voysey as craftsman and builder. Such a position emphasizes that his work draws on the theoretical foundation of the Gothic Revivalist A. W. N. Pugin (1812-52) calling for a building to express an honesty of construction, to reflect on its exterior, its interior planning, and to embody a Christian morality—a moral architecture both contributing to and reflective of a moral society. Voysey's restrained, almost childlike traditionalism, is an indigenous embodiment of such ideas linked to the Gothic Revival and to the Arts and Crafts movement.

He was, however, less tied to place and to local materials than were others among his English contemporaries; rather, Voysey built distinctive and similar houses in a recognizable Voysey image, whether sited in the Lake District or the suburbs of London, in Surrey or the Malvern Hills. If modernists looked back on this uniform work to find a planar abstraction suggesting a styleless functionalism devoid of ornament—i.e., a protomodernism—it was certainly not Voysey's intention to replace English traditions with a modern international aesthetic, nor did he accept assertions by critics that he had done so.

The characteristic Voysey domestic vernacular image was established in designs dating as early as 1885; a variation of earlier unexecuted schemes was executed in 1888 for M. H. Lakin in his cottage at Bishop's Itchington, Warwickshire, and foreshadowed Voysey's mature aesthetic. Voysey's first major house, Perrycroft at Colwell, Herefordshire (1893-94), retained in the half-timbered tower of the servants' wing a more explicit traditionalism which marked the architect's first designs, in contrast to the more restrained and simple (and better known) main Perrycroft elevation. There, the characteristic Voysey style emerges: a single volume under hovering hipped roof, white roughcast surfaces, banded leaded windows arranged under overhanging eaves, exaggerated chimneys, broad gables (sometimes sweeping nearly to the ground), and the ubiquitous corner battered buttresses. These elements continued to be combined in well-crafted, though often inconveniently planned, and beautifully sited houses. Most typical of Voysey are his rudimental, grouped windows under overscaled gables (untutored shapes as though drawn by a child) as evidenced at Tilehurst (Miss E. Somers House, Bushey, 1904) or at the architect's own house, The Orchard, built in 1899 at Chorleywood; both sites are in Hertfordshire. More mannered forms accent Norney (now Norney Grange, Shackleford, Surrey, 1897) whose prominently bulging, arched entry porch and plastic chimney and buttress masses give evidence of the individualist Voysey. These features join great gable-capped bays in the garden elevation as historic echoes of Norman Shaw. Most idiosyncratic are the grotesques and caricatures, supposedly clients' profiles, which adorn New Place (originally Hurtmore) at Haslemere, Surrey (1897), as well as Lowicks and Norney.

Among Voysey's most published and influential houses are two masterpieces at Lake Windermere, Broadleys (1898) and Moor Crag (1898-99). Indeed, from the start, Voysey was highly successful at getting his work published in the contemporary press. His influence on English contemporary architects is readily seen in the work of M. H. Baillie Scott (1865-1945) and Walter Cave (1863-1939). The domestic image of such early-20th-century new towns as Letchworth, Hertfordshire (1904), and such suburban communities as Hampstead Garden Suburb (from 1905) helped to universalize the Voysey aesthetic. Further, Voyseyesque forms were widely disseminated in housing estates such as those built by the London County Council Architects' Department at Totterdown Fields, Tooting (1903-11).

Ultimately the Voysey image transformed the English semi-detached (duplex) suburban house; hundreds of roughcast Voyseyesque frontal gables and bay windows align "A" roads leading out of major urban centers throughout England. His smaller-scaled domestic structures ranged from stables and cottages adjoining his larger houses, to studios and suburban houses. At the edge of town and country, Voysey's most notable suburban houses are Hollymount at Knotty Green (suburban Beaconsfield, Buckinghamshire, 1905) and Brooke End, at the edge of Henley-in-Arden, Warwickshire (1909). Both of these residences helped to establish the increasingly reduced scale of pre-World War I English housing, and provide links to the "period houses" of American garden suburbs of the 1920s and 1930s.

—ROBERT M. CRAIG

WAGNER, Otto.

Austrian. Born in Penzig, near Vienna, Austria, 1841. Died in Vienna, 1918. Educated in Vienna; studied at the Polytechnic Institute, Vienna, 1857-59; studied at Royal Academy of Building, Berlin, 1860-61; studied at Vienna Academy, 1861-63. Professor, Vienna Academy, from 1894.

Chronology of Works
All in Austria unless noted

1869	Apartment House, 4 Bellariastrasse, Vienna
1871	Synagogue, Budapest, Hungary
1877	Apartment House, 23 Schottenring, Vienna
1880-81	Apartment House, 3 Rathausstrasse, Vienna
1882-83	Apartment House, 6-8 Stadiongasse, Vienna
1833-84	Länderbank, Vienna
1886-88	First Villa Wagner, 26 Hüttelbergstrasse, Vienna
1888	Apartment House, 12 Universitätsstrasse, Vienna
1890	Palais Wagner, 3 Renweg, Vienna
1894-98	Nussdorf Dam, Danube Works, Vienna
1894-99	Stadtbahn System, Vienna (Karlsplatz Station with J. M. Olbrich)
1895	Anker Building am Graben, Vienna
1895	Neumann Department Store, Kärntnerstrasse, Vienna
1898-99	Apartment Houses, 38-40 Linke Wienzeile, Vienna
1898-1904	Quayside Installations, Danube Canal, Vienna
1902	*Die Zeit* Telegraph Office, Vienna
1904-08	Kaiserbad Dam, Vienna
1904-12	Postal Savings Bank Office, Vienna (first and second stages)
1905-07	Church of St. Leopold, Am Steinhof, Vienna
1909-10	Apartment House, 40 Neustiftgasse, Vienna
1910-13	Lupus Sanatorium, Vienna
1912	Apartment House, 4 Döblergasse, Vienna
1912-13	Second Villa Wagner, 28 Hüttelbergstrasse, Vienna

Publications

BOOKS BY WAGNER

Einige Skizzen: Projekte und ausgeführte Bauwerke. 4 vols. Vienna. 1895- 1914.
Wagnerschule: Projekte, Studien und Skizzen aus der Spezialschule für Architektur des Oberbaurats Otto Wagner (1902)-1907. Leipzig, 1910.
Die Grosztadt: Eine Studie über diese. Vienna, 1911.
Die Qualität des Baukünstlers. Leipzig and Vienna, 1912.
Die Baukunst unserer Zeit. 4th ed. Vienna, 1914. Originally published with the title *Moderne Architektur*, 1895.

Otto Wagner: Sketches, Projects, and Executed Buildings. New York, 1987.

BOOKS ABOUT WAGNER

ASENBAUM, PAUL; HAIKO, PETER; LACHMAYER, HERBERT; and ZETTL, RAINER: *Otto Wagner: Möbel und Innenräume.* Salzburg and Vienna, 1984.
BERNABEI, GIANCARLO: *Otto Wagner.* 1983.
FRAMPTON, KENNETH, and FUTAGAWA, YUKIO: *Modern Architecture: 1920-1945.* New York, 1983.
GERETSEGGER, HEINZ, and PEINTNER, MAX: *Otto Wagner, 1841-1918: The Expanding City and the Beginning of Modern Architecture.* New York, 1979.
GIUSTI BACULO, ADRIANA: *Otto Wagner: Dall'architettura di stile allo stile utile.* Naples, 1970.
GRAF, OTTO A.: *Die vergessene Wagnerschule.* Vienna, 1969.
LUX, JOSEPH A.: *Otto Wagner.* Munich, 1914.
MÜLLER, DOROTHÉE: *Klassiker des modernen Möbeldesign: Otto Wagner, Adolf Loos, Joseph Hoffmann, Koloman Moser.* Munich, 1980.
OSTWALD, HANS: *Otto Wagner: Ein Beitrag zum Verständnis seines baukünstlerischen Schaffens.* Baden, Germany, 1948.
PEICHL, G.: *Die Kunst des Otto Wagner.* Vienna, 1984.
RUSSELL, FRANK (ed.): *Art Nouveau Architecture.* London, 1979.
TIETZE, H.: *Otto Wagner.* Vienna, Berlin, Munich and Leipzig, 1922.
TREVISIOL, ROBERT: *Otto Wagner.* Bari, Italy, 1990.
WAGNER, WALTER: *Die Geschichte der Akademie der Bildenden Künste in Wien.* Vienna, 1967.

ARTICLES ABOUT WAGNER

CZECH, H.: "Otto Wagner's Vienna Metropolitan Railway." *Architecture and Urbanism* (July 1976): 11-20.
"Post Office Savings Bank and St. Leopold, by Otto Wagner." *Global Architecture* No. 47 (1978).
TAFURI, MANFREDO: "Am Steinhof, Centrality and Surface in Otto Wagner's Architecture." *Lotus* 29 (1981): 73-91.

*

Despite his traditional academic training at the Vienna Academy of Fine Arts, Otto Wagner was a precursor of modern architecture in a career spanning for more than 50 years. A professor of architecture at the Academy, he had an enormous impact on several generations of students, among them a first generation which formed the Vienna Secession (1887) and a later generation which formed the Austrian Werkbund (1913). Both of these groups looked upon him as a mentor, an inspiration and a colleague in theory and practice. Trained in the historicist and

Otto Wagner: Church of St. Leopold, Am Steinhof, Vienna, Austria, 1905-07

even archaeological approach to architecture, Wagner always drew upon the rich resources of the great historical styles, but in a free and inventive way, while also instinctively placing engineering and modern technology at the service of his buildings.

Under the reign of Emperor Franz Josef, Vienna's population was growing rapidly, demanding expansion of the city as well as modernization. In 1892 an international competition was held for an adviser to the Vienna Transport Commission who would be responsible for designing a new railroad and providing for expanded river canal traffic. The Transit Commission's choice of Wagner permitted him an unparalleled opportunity to plan the entire railroad system, the stations below and above ground, more than 30 pavilions, and a wide range of viaducts and bridges. Between 1894 and 1900 the stations and pavilions were completed, all in a relatively uniform style.

Wagner supervised the design of these railroad pavilions, products of a new age and technology, with enormous sensitivity to the surroundings in which they were to be placed. Most notable is the pavilion at the Karlsplatz, which, with its arched entrance and vaulted roof, plays off against the imposing forms of the Karlskirche just across the square. In like manner, Wagner designed a special entrance pavilion to the railroad just outside the grounds of Schönbrunn Palace. Designed specifically for the use of the royal family when they might choose to ride the railroad, it is crowned with a neo-Baroque dome consonant with the style of the palace itself. But these striking pavilions reveal more than aesthetic sensibility to placement of new structures into an already established architectural environment. Wagner believed in functional style, his motto being: Necessity is the sole mistress of art. Drawing upon the latest discoveries in engineering and technology, he championed the use of iron in a truthful manner, where inner structure is revealed through the arrangement of exterior elements. Wagner expected that new types of buildings would naturally produce new architectural forms—a kind of architectural Darwinism.

In pavilions such as that at the Karlsplatz, the framework is iron and expressed as such, yet the exterior is clad in marble—a juxtaposition of new and traditional materials. The pavilion forms a large rectangular block, yet within the controlling geometry, there is ample decoration. Sunflowers, leaves, stems and buds adorn the surfaces of the marble slabs, along with grilles of wrought iron in shapes derived from or suggestive of nature. These two elements are at the heart of Wagner's style—the combination of geometry and natural motifs resulting in a building that is functional and attractive. The lavish patterns, derived from nature, are contained within a clearly defined classical organization. Even in this railroad pavilion the facade is divided into base, midsection and roof line with frieze and cornice. This definitive classical organization marks all of Wagner's work, even his most fanciful and free-spirited efforts such as the Majolica House of 1898.

Wagner's use of motifs drawn from nature and applied to the exterior wall surface in flat, decorative, nonsculptured patterns exemplifies the Jugendstil, an Austrian version of art nouveau. Clearly Wagner was in sympathy with the group of young artists who formed the Vienna Secession, seeking to free art from the restraints of blind historicism, hoping to champion greater freedom of inspiration in all the arts. In 1899 Wagner scandalized his more traditional colleagues by openly joining the Secession, in association with Gustav Klimt, Josef Olbrich and Koloman Moser, to name but a few of the group.

No structure better exemplifies Wagner's combination of new technology and materials with traditional forms and organization than his Church of St. Leopold at Steinhof, built on a hill on the grounds of the Vienna State Mental Asylum. It is surely the finest example of church architecture in the Jugendstil and one of the most exceptional buildings in Wagner's long career. The church is composed of two basic and substantial volumes—a large cube, forming the church itself, and a huge cupola or sphere that crowns it. These two volumes reflect and announce the reality of a vast, open, spacious, brightly lighted interior capable of seating 800 patients with unobstructed view. The basic cube of the building, massive and solid, is divided into three zones. The base is articulated by the use of heavy, rusticated stone, standing in sharp contrast to the polished white marble-clad facade above. Finally the roof line is defined by a cornice and frieze, divided into sections by the repeating motifs of wreath and cross. While the wreaths suggest the rounded sphere of the dome, the crosses mirror the floor plan of the church itself.

An entrance canopy of copper and glass introduced "new" materials into this otherwise traditional facade of marble and rusticated stone. Thin wrought-iron columns supporting the canopy play off against the massive marble columns behind them. The highly polished marble slabs of the facade are held in place by copper bolts, clearly visible. Thus there are various contrasts of elements—marble and rusticated stone, marble and copper bolts, large and small elements, the massive and the slender, cube and sphere. The dome, traditional in exterior appearance, is supported by a concealed metal skeleton. A sophisticated framework of iron holds insert panels which totally hide the framework from the view of the congregation seated below.

Every detail of the interior was designed by Wagner or one of his associates working in close collaboration with him. Their major consideration was one of hygiene in this church designed for hospital patients. Wagner's Church of St. Leopold is a magnificent example of how *Necessitas* dictates every detail of this *Gesamtkunstwerk*. Thus all is white, supposedly to permit easy detection of any dust or dirt. But the openness and lightness of the interior, flooded by sunlight filtering through the cupola, have also been reinforced and increased by the choice of white. Walls are clad with marble halfway up so as to permit cleaning by hosing down the interior. The floor slopes down toward the sanctuary, not only to permit a better view to patients at the rear, but also to allow water to drain off when the walls have been hosed down. Almost one third of the interior, at the rear, is without pews to permit placement of patients in wheelchairs. Confessionals, also designed by Wagner, lack the traditional curtains since they could collect dust and harbor infection. Even the holy-water fonts are designed to dispense water into the hand at the touch of a button—much more hygienic than permitting visitors to dip their hands into a common fount—thus reducing the risk of contagion.

Yet beyond these technical, hygienic, scientific aspects of the interior, decoration is richly employed, as in the extraordinary stained glass windows by Koloman Moser, beautiful in color and design, and sophisticated in iconography. The stained glass above the entrance depicts the expulsion of Adam and Eve from paradise, while the two windows of the transept walls depict the spiritual and corporal works of mercy as a means of regaining paradise only temporarily lost. Fine mosaics cover the wall behind the altar, and the baldachino is of gold filigree. Wagner himself designed the Mass vestments, chalices, lighting fixtures, monstrance and altar bells in the tradition of the *Gesamtkunstwerk*. The church's interior is light, bright, uplifting, lavish in decorative detail, yet sleek and modern, all achieved by taking advantage of technical advances in metal construction.

It is no surprise that as late as 1913 the students of the Deutsche Werkbund looked to Otto Wagner as a model and inspiration, as had the young rebels of the Secession in 1897.

—FRANCIS J. GREENE

Thomas U. Walter: United States Capitol, Washington, DC, 1850

WALTER, Thomas U.

American. Born Thomas Ustick Walter in Philadelphia, Pennsylvania, 1804. Died in 1887. Son was Thomas Walter, architect. Studied under William Strickland, 1819, 1822. Teacher, Franklin Institute, Philadelphia, 1829; opened own office, 1830; professor of architecture, Franklin Institute, 1841; Federal Government architect, 1861. Secretary, American Institution of Architects, 1836; president, American Institute of Architects, 1872; president, board of managers, Franklin Institute, Philadelphia, 1846.

Chronology of Works
All in the United States unless noted
† *Work no longer exists*

1831	Bricklayer's Hall, Philadelphia, Pennsylvania†
1831	Portico Square, Philadelphia, Pennsylvania
1831	Wills Hospital for the Blind and Lame, Philadelphia, Pennsylvania
1831	Presbyterian Church, West Chester, Pennsylvania
1831-35	Philadelphia County Prison (Moyamensing)†
1833	Amity Street Baptist Church, New York City†
1833-48	Girard College for Orphans, Philadelphia, Pennsylvania
1834	Cohen's Bank, Baltimore, Maryland†
1835	Matthew Newkirk House, Philadelphia, Pennsylvania†
1835	Third Dutch Reformed Church, Philadelphia, Pennsylvania†
1836	Chester County Prison, West Chester, Pennsylvania†
1837	Merchant's and Mechanic's Bank, Wheeling, West Virginia†

1838	James Dundas House, Philadelphia, Pennsylvania†
1838	St. James Episcopal Church, Wilmington, North Carolina
1839	Eleventh Baptist Church, Philadelphia, Pennsylvania
1839	First Baptist Church, Richmond, Virginia
1839	Norfolk Academy, Norfolk, Virginia
1841	Presbyterian Church, Petersburg, Virginia
1843-45	Breakwater, Laguaria, Venezuela
1846	Chester County Courthouse, West Chester, Pennsylvania
1847	City Hall, Norfolk, Virginia
1848	Beth Israel Synagogue, Philadelphia, Pennsylvania†
1848	University of Lewisburg (now Bucknell University), Lewisburg, Pennsylvania
1849	Pennsylvania Medical College, Philadelphia, Pennsylvania†
1850	Patent Office, Washington, D.C. (extension)
1850	United States Capitol, Washington, D.C. (extension)
1851	Hewlings House (Ingleside), Washington, D.C.
1851	Tysen House (Glenelg), Ellicott City, Maryland
1852	Library of Congress (in the United States Capitol), Washington, D.C.†
1852	United States Government Hospital for Insane (St. Elizabeth's), Washington, D.C.
1852	United States Treasury Building, Washington, D.C. (extension)
1855-65	United States Capitol, Washington, D.C. (dome)
1856	General Post Office, Washington, D.C. (extension)
1857	Marine Barracks, Pensacola, Florida
1858-59	Marine Barracks, Brooklyn, New York
1861	Thomas Ustick Walter House, Germantown, Pennsylvania†
1868-70	Eutaw Place Baptist Church, Baltimore, Maryland

Publications

BOOKS BY WALTER

Two Hundred Designs for Cottages and Villas. Philadelphia, 1846.
A Guide to Workers in Metal and Stone. Philadelphia, 1846.

BOOKS ABOUT WALTER

BROWN, GLENN: *History of the United States Capitol.* 2 vols. 1900-03. Reprint: New York, 1970.
DUNLAP, WILLIAM: *A History of the Rise and Progress of the Arts of Design in the United States.* New York, 1834 (1965).
ENNIS, ROBERT B.: *Thomas U. Walter, Arhcitect, 1804-1887.* 2 vols. Philadelphia, 1982.
HAMLIN, TALBOT: *Greek Revival Architecture in America.* New York, 1944.
JACKSON, JOSEPH: *Early Philadelphia Architects and Engineers.* Philadelphia, 1923.
TATUM, GEORGE B.: *Penn's Great Town: 250 Years of Philadelphia Architecture Illustrated in Prints and Drawings.* Philadelphia, 1961.

ARTICLES ABOUT WALTER

BANISTER, TURPIN C.: "The Genealogy of the Dome of the United States Capitol." *Journal of the Society of Architectural Historians* 7, Nos. 1-2 (1948): 1-31.
ENNIS, ROBERT B.: "Thomas U. Walter." *Nineteenth Century* 5, No. 3 (1979): 59-60.

GILCHRIST, AGNES ADDISON: "Girard College: An Example of the Layman's Influence on Architecture." *Journal of the Society of Architecural Historians* 16, No. 2 (1957): 22-25.

HALL, LOUISE: "Mills, Strickland, and Walter: Their Adventures in a World of Science." *Magazine of Art* 40 (November 1947): 226-271.

LISCOMBE, R. WINDSOR: "T. U. Walter's Gifts of Drawings to the Institute of British Architects." *Journal of the Society of Architectural Historians* 39, No. 4 (1980): 307-311.

NEWCOMB, REXFORD G.: "Thomas Ustick Walter." *Architect* 10 (August 1929): 585-589.

RUSK, WILLIAM SENER: "Thomas U. Walter and His Works." *Americana* 33, No. 2 (April 1939): 151-179.

RUSK, WILLIAM SENER: "William Thornton, Benjamin H. Latrobe, and Thomas U. Walter and the Classic Influence in Their Work." Ph.D. dissertation. Johns Hopkins University, Baltimore, Maryland, 1933.

*

Thomas U. Walter of Philadelphia, who was trained in his father's firm as an apprentice bricklayer and stonemason, became one of the leading architects of the United States, mainly associated with the Greek Revival style of the 19th century. His contributions to that period were the primary determinant in Philadelphia's becoming the home of the Greek Revival movement in America.

Walter declared that his early education was "liberal but not collegiate," in response to the family trade. He served as an apprentice architect in the office of William Strickland, and later received formal education at a small, private institution and at the newly founded Franklin Institute. He studied mathematics, physics, architecture, landscape painting and "the several branches of mechanical construction connected with buildings." In 1829 he became a teacher at the Franklin Institute, and in 1841 was appointed professor of architecture, giving lectures on the history and philosophy of architecture. He continued his association with Strickland's office, and opened his own practice in 1830.

His first commission was the Presbyterian Church in Louisville, Kentucky (1831). Other commissions of that year included numerous residences in Philadelphia. The most important was his Egyptian Revival Philadelphia County Prison, Moyamensing (1831-35).

Walter gained his most significant early commission through a competition to design the Girard College for Orphans (1833-48). The plan of Founder's Hall, the primary building, was required, according to Stephen Girard's will, to have "four fifty-foot-square vaulted classrooms and two vestibules on each of three floors." Walter was sent to Europe by the building committee of Girard College to examine the architecture of Italy, France, England and Ireland to prepare for the design development of Founder's Hall. He designed a white marble building in a peripteral octastyle Corinthian temple form derived from the Church of the Madeleine, then being constructed in Paris. The Corinthian peristyle was based on James Stuart and Nicholas Revett's scaled engravings of the Choragic Monument of Lysicrates. Although the external Corinthian peristyle form has little relation to the building's three-story plan, Founder's Hall is considered one of the finest Greek Revival buildings in the United States.

During the 1840s Walter experimented with applications of cast iron to architecture. In 1846 he published two books dedicated to his interests of the time, *A Guide to Workers in Metals and Stone* and *Two Hundred Designs for Cottages and Villas.*

Despite personal, financial and professional disappointments, he became the leading architect of Philadelphia and was continually making new contributions to American taste, style and architecture. His interests centered on simplicity and clarity of form and mass. His pursuit of the traditional geometric Greek temple forms became a mark of his design. He was invited to build a number of churches, including St. George's Episcopal Church in New York, the Presbyterian Church in Lexington, Virginia, and the facade for the Roman Catholic Cathedral of Sts. Peter and Paul in Philadelphia.

In December 1859 Walter presented his entry to the United States Capitol competition, which sought designs for wings for the Senate and House of Representatives to be added to the original building. His design won, and he was appointed designer and architect for the new wings at the Capitol.

His most known work was the design and construction of the Capital dome (1855-65). The old wooden dome was demolished in 1855, and erection of the new cast-iron dome begun. Again, Walter was influenced by European architecture of the day: he based the new dome on A. A. Montferrand's concept for St. Isaac's Cathedral in Leningrad.

Walter executed other work for the United States government, including the design and construction in cast iron of the central room of the recently burned Library of Congress (1852); extensions to the Patent Office (1850), Treasury (1852) and Post Office (1856) buildings; and the Hospital for the Insane (1852), all in Washington, D.C.; and the Marine Barracks in Pensacola, Florida (1857), and Brooklyn (1858-59).

Walter's designs for the Capitol wings and dome were widely influential, and set new standards for architectural expression in American public buildings for the next century. His Capitol is considered by many to be the introduction to Classical Revival federal architecture that uses icons from the past to symbolize democratic government.

Walter also played a role in the professionalization of architecture in America. He was involved with the establishment of the American Institution of Architects in 1836-37, and then with the founding of the American Institute of Architects in 1857, which elected him as its first vice-president. He helped establish the Philadelphia Chapter of the AIA, which was chartered in 1872. Walter served as national president of the AIA from 1876 until his death in 1887.

—GORDON ECHOLS

WANK, Roland.

Austrian. Born Roland Anthony Wank in Austria, 1898. Died 1970. Arrived in New York City from Vienna, 1924. Worked for Fellheimer and Wagner; worked for the Tennessee Valley Authority (TVA), 1933-44.

Chronology of Works
All in the United States

1929-30   Grand Street Housing, New York City
1933-44   Sixteen dams and powerhouses for the TVA, Tennessee

Publications

ARTICLES BY WANK

"Culture Returns to Main Street." *Architectural Record* 90 (September 1941): 76-80.

Roland Wank: Norris Dam, Tennessee, 1933-36

"Architecture in Rural Areas." *New Pencil Points* 23 (December 1942): 47-53.
"Planned Communities: A Speculative Survey of Their Future." *Architectural Record* 93 (February 1943): 44-48.
"The Architecture of Inland Waterways." In PAUL ZUCKER (ed.): *New Architecture and City Planning*. New York, 1944.
"Democratic Planning." In THOMAS H. CREIGHTON (ed.): *Building for Modern Man*. Princeton, New Jersey, 1949.
"The Architect's Place on the Bridge Design Team." With Fred N. Severud. *Progressive Architecture* 35 (September 1954): 89-101.

BOOKS ABOUT WANK

HUXLEY, J.: *TVA: Adventure in Planning*. London, 1943.

*

Roland Wank is one of the lesser known architects of the Modern Movement because so much of his professional life was spent in large offices where individual contributions were often not recognized publicly. Nevertheless, he has been hailed by Reyner Banham as one of the most consequential American practitioners in the International Style, and he is justifiably celebrated for the powerful modernist expression he contributed to the dams and powerhouses constructed by the Tennessee Valley Authority from 1933 to 1944. Throughout his career, Wank showed a willingness to collaborate with engineers and landscape architects on large-scale projects that had a strong commitment to social betterment. At the TVA, for example, Wank not only established the modern idiom, but also insisted that the powerhouses be designed to receive visitors so that local people could have an idea of the better future that lay ahead.

While many European architects of the early Modern Movement were interested in using industrial materials in design, improving social housing and working on building types not generally considered to be "architecture," Wank was unusual because he devoted the better part of his professional life to these issues. The first building for which he claimed credit was the Grand Street Housing (1929-30) in New York City, built for the Amalgamated Clothing Workers to replace slums on the lower East Side. His concern for efficiency, economy and social amenities, together with fresh air and sunlight, were incorporated into a design praised by contemporary critics for its forward-looking qualities.

While in the office of Fellheimer and Wagner, he worked on the Union Terminal in Cincinnati, demonstrating his ability to integrate architectural design with demanding engineering in a very complex project. In the 11 years he served as chief architect at the Tennessee Valley Authority, he designed both large-scale permanent structures (dams and powerhouses) and small-scale temporary ones (workers' housing) with an innovative approach to materials and their fabrication. For the New Jersey Turnpike, one of the first modern high-speed engineered roads in the nation, he collaborated on the design of buildings, bridges, rest areas and even signage as part of a complete environmental design effort.

The series of demountable houses Wank designed for TVA construction workers perhaps best illustrate his continuing commitment to ideals of the International Style. "I could never become interested in designing grand homes for the few who can afford them," Wank observed. "I always wanted to feel that my work was of some public interest, and that it will add to the comfort and enjoyment of the many.'' From the first, these houses were factory-built to minimize on-site costs and permit reuse at different sites, and through experiments, the truckable unit design was found to be most cost-effective. Added to the constraints of weight and highway clearances were wartime shortages of building materials, leading to experiments with sandwich panels for walls and painted canvas for roofs. First by the hundreds and then by the thousands, these two-section demountable houses were manufactured not only for workers at dam sites but also for house scientists, engineers and technicians of the Manhattan Project in Oak Ridge. Expanded versions composed of additional modular sections were proposed to ease the anticipated postwar housing crisis, but the scheme was not a commercial success.

Wank is best remembered for his pioneering designs of TVA dams and powerhouses. Working closely with the project engineers, he was able to bring powerful sculptural expression to their massing, and impart elegance and refinement to their architectural details. Norris (1933-36) was the first TVA dam, and the reworking of its initial Corps of Engineers design into the serenely modern statement by Wank set the pattern for the 15 dams to come, seven on the main Tennessee River and eight on tributary rivers. In all these projects, Wank attempted ''to make the dams look as functional as the engineers have designed them.'' Exterior concrete retained the texture of its formwork, rough-sawn boards set in a checkerboard pattern with raked joints between panels. Interior concrete was left smooth and unpainted as a foil for the subdued industrial colors and materials used in the generator rooms: matte gray and soft green paint on exposed steel, terra-cotta quarry tile flooring, brushed aluminum hardware and trim, and ribbed glass. Large-scale shadow study drawings survive to indicate how carefully the architect considered the placement and proportions of design elements such as bridge supports, railings and lettering. As a result, the dams convey a feeling of permanence, dignity, efficiency and modernity that the passage of half a century has not diminished.

—MARIAN SCOTT MOFFETT

WARCHAVCHIK, Gregori.

Brazilian. Born in Odessa, Russia, 2 April 1896. Died in São Paulo, Brazil, 22 July 1972. Immigrated to Brazil in 1923 (naturalized in 1930). Married Mina Klabin, 1927; three children. Studied architecture at the University of Odessa, at the Reale Istituto Superiore di Belle Arti, Rome, Italy. Worked for Marcello Piacentini, Rome, 1920-23; practiced in São Paulo, Brazil, 1923-31, and with Lucío Costa, Rio de Janeiro, 1931-33; returned to São Paulo, from 1934. Member of CIAM (Congrès Internationaux d'Architecture Moderne), 1929-42.

Chronology of Works
All in Brazil
† *Work no longer exists*

1927-28	Gregori Warchavchik House, São Paulo
1930	First Modern House Exhibition, São Paulo
1930	Luiz da Silva Prado House, São Paulo
1932	Alfredo Schwartz House, Rio de Janeiro (with Lucio Costa)†
1932	Manoel Dias Penthouse Apartment, Rio de Janeiro (interiors)
1938	Apartment Building for CIA de Melhoramentos Gropouva, São Paulo
1939	Apartment Building, Alameda Barão e Limeira, São Paulo
1943	Raul Crespi Beach House, Guaruja
1943-44	Apartment House, Avenida do Estado, Guaruja
1946	Mrs. Jorge Prado Beach Pavilion, Guaruja

Publications

ARTICLES BY WARCHAVCHIK

''Acerca de Arquitectura Moderna'' [The 1925 Manifesto]. *Correio da manha* (Rio de Janeiro, 1 November 1925). Numerous articles in Brazil's major newspapers, 1925-61.

BOOKS ABOUT WARCHAVCHIK

FERRAZ, GILBERTO: *Warchavchik e la introdução da nova arquitectura no Brasil, 1925 a 1940*. São Paulo, 1965.
Gregori Warchavchik: Retrospective. São Paulo, 1975.
MINDLIN, HENRIQUE: *Modern Architecture in Brazil*. Rio de Janeiro and Amsterdam, 1956.
SERGE, ROBERTO (ed.): *Latin America in Its Architecture*. New York and London, 1981.

ARTICLES ABOUT WARCHAVCHIK

FLOUQUET, PIERRE LOUIS: ''L'architecture moderne au Brésil.'' *Chantiers* (Brussels, October 1947).
''Habitations individuelles au Brésil.'' *Architecture d'aujourd'hui* (June 1948).
SARTORIS, ALBERTO: ''Les origines de l'architecture nouvelle a l'amerique latine.'' *Architecture: Formes et fonctions* (1958).

*

As Brazilian modern architecture has long been best known for its distinctively regionalistic approach, it is perhaps unsurprising that Gregori Warchavchik, a foreigner who introduced International Style modernism to that country, should be relegated to the background. Born in Odessa in the Ukraine, Warchavchik began his architectural studies there and continued in Rome, where he worked under the classicist Marcello Piacentini. In 1923 Warchavchik moved to São Paulo to assume a position with the Companhia Construtora de Santo. The year before, leftist intellectuals in São Paulo, in an effort to introduce modern art and its revolutionary implications into the stifling colonial atmosphere of Brazil, had organized there the now famous ''Modern Art Week.'' Warchavchik quickly became associated with the organizers of that event, who had had among them no previous architectural representation, and in 1925 he published his first article in an Italian-language São Paulo paper. Recalling, perhaps, lingering currents in the Rome of his student days, his Corbusian-fueled statement was titled ''Futurism?'' Later that same year a Rio de Janeiro paper translated the article to Portuguese with the new title ''Apropos of Modern Architecture,'' and so in Brazil's two major cities a lively, if limited, debate ensued.

The debate grew more heated in 1927 with Warchavchik's establishment of an independent office and the commencement of his own cubistic white house in São Paulo—the first modernist building in Brazil. To gain approval for the project from local authorities, the architect submitted drawings showing a more highly ornamented facade than he actually intended. The house he then built, even with its stark, classically symmetrical street facade and wrought-iron art deco gates, was seen as radically minimalist. This facade, in fact, cloaked a far more radical open, asymmetrical plan and rear elevation. The unavailability in Brazil at the time of suitable materials forced Warchavchik to import steel, cement and other components from Europe and the United States. Moved perhaps by such expressions as Gilberto Freyre's *Regionalist Manifesto* (Recife, 1926), however, Warchavchik was by no means oblivious to local materials and conditions: a red tile-roofed terrace at the rear of the house opened it to the first of many tropical palm and cacti gardens designed by his wife Mina. Visiting in 1929, Le Corbusier cited the house as being among "the best adaptations of modern architectural . . . tendencies in the tropical landscape."

By 1929 Warchavchik had established a workshop, where local workmen trained by him turned out his own designs for furnishings and fixtures. Along with introducing new industrial techniques, this workshop also made Warchavchik's building practice considerably more cost-effective. Working as his own contractor (a role typical at that time for Latin American architects), he began a series of economical functionalist houses that adhered closely to Le Corbusier's "five points." Characteristic of these houses were their roughly stuccoed white walls and minimal fenestration (against the tropical sun and the high cost of imported glass, and in sympathy with the Ibero-American tradition of the closed facade), cantilevered canopies, asymmetrically "functional" massing, and gardens integrated with the houses via terracing and garden walls that echoed those of the houses themselves. The 1930 model house at Rua Itapolis, site of the "First Modernistic House in São Paulo Exhibition," was among the most elegant of these. More than 30,000 people attended the exhibition, and saw Warchavchik's house filled with his own modern furniture and the work of contemporary Brazilian and European artists like Constantin Brancusi and Jacques Lipchitz. Though opinions on the event were mixed, the critical reaction it provoked in the Brazilian press served to spread throughout the country the news of modernism's arrival.

Modern architecture as a physical presence arrived in Rio the next year, with the opening of the "First Modern House in Rio Exhibition" at Rua Toneleros. One of Warchavchik's largest and most lavish, this house resembled Richard Neutra's Lovell Beach House of 1927 in the way its ribbon-windowed "view" facade cascaded down the steep hillside on which it was built. This exhibition attracted attention which equaled, if not outdistanced, that of the previous year's event in São Paulo. Among the many distinguished visitors was Frank Lloyd Wright, then on the trail with his "Princeton" lectures, which he delivered to the crowd over the course of several days.

Warchavchik had by that time been appointed South American delegate to the Congrés Internationaux d'Architecture Moderne (CIAM) at the urging of Le Corbusier. In that capacity in 1931 he published an article in *Cahiers d'Art,* in which he introduced Europe to modern Brazilian architecture. That article (which featured illustrations of several of his own houses) and others written concurrently for Brazilian papers set the course for later regionalist experiments, arguing as they did for a functionalism based on site-specific variables of climate, geography, light, vegetation and culture.

Warchavchik frequently concentrated his practice on low-income housing, and in so doing, he stood at the forefront of a generation of Latin American-based architects who linked functionalist architecture to social reform. Following the 1930 revolution led by Getulio Vargas, modern architecture was adopted and advanced by the state toward this same end, and the young Lucio Costa, whose strong modernist sympathies had yet to find built expression, was named director of the National School of Fine Arts in São Paulo. Warchavchik was brought

in as a professor there, and despite the commute (he remained based in São Paulo), the firm of Warchavchik-Lucio Costa was soon founded. Though their joint activity was limited, what did get done (e.g., the Alfredo Schwartz House in Rio, 1932) comprised the first built modernist work not only of Costa, but also their young draftsman Oscar Niemeyer and landscape architect Roberto Burle Marx.

An economic downturn following the abortive 1932 Constitutionalist counter-revolution in São Paulo forced the Warchavchik-Costa firm to dissolve in 1933. Warchavchik built little for the remainder of the 1930s, and watched his European contacts wither with Adolf Hitler's rise to power. Meanwhile, Costa allied himself more closely with Niemeyer and other young Brazilians. Their efforts crystallized in the landmark Ministry of Education and Health Building in Rio (1937-43); under the influence of Le Corbusier, who returned for a month in 1936 to consult on the project, Brazilian architecture there began to develop the expressively plastic form for which it became known. A São Paulo apartment house (1939) by Warchavchik shows how he worked with the possibilities of this new plasticity: at one end of the small building's facade, balconies swell outward with a curve reminiscent of Moderne streamlining. The small apartments within were thus given a greater sense of space and openness.

Warchavchik experimented with a variety of solutions throughout the 1940s and 1950s, including such adaptations of vernacular form and materials as found at the thatch-roofed Prado Beach Pavilion at Guaruja (1946). Aside from the openness of the plan, however (this too a characteristic of the vernacular type on which it was based), this simple structure bore little connection to the architect's earlier work; instead of purist idealism, this was a wealthy client's sanitized fantasy of the rustic good life.

Unable to effect a convincing synthesis of the international and the indigenous, or to secure a major public commission, Warchavchik soon fell into the shadows of his former associates. Such seminal studies as Philip Goodwin's *Brazil Builds* (1943) all but ignored his pioneering role. But as native Brazilian architects went on to their distinctive formal achievements, they did so on ground laid open to them by Warchavchik.

—KEITH EGGENER

WATERHOUSE, Alfred.

British. Born in Liverpool, England, 1830. Died in Yattendon, Berkshire, England, 1905. Married Elizabeth Hodgkin, 1858; son was the architect Paul Waterhouse (1861-1924), who became his partner in 1891. Articled to Richard Lane, Manchester, 1848-53; traveled in Britain, France, Italy, Switzerland and Turkey, 1853-54. Set up office in Manchester, 1854; opened office in London, 1865. Gold Medal, Royal Institute of British Architects, 1878; president, Royal Institute of British Architects, 1888-91.

Chronology of Works
All in England unless noted
† *Work no longer exists*

1854	Hothay Holme (now the Lakes District Council Offices), Ambleside, Cumberland
1856	Fryer and Binyon Warehouse, Manchester†
1856	Hinderton House, Neston, Cheshire
1857	Bradford Banking Company (now the Midland Bank), West Yorkshire
1858	Barcombe Cottage, Fallowfield, Manchester†

1859-64	Assize Courts, Manchester†
1861	Royal Insurance Building, King Street, Manchester†
1862-64	Market and Public Offices, and Barclays Bank, Darlington, Durham
1864-66	Clydesdale and North Scotland Bank, London†
1864-66	Hutton Hall, Guisborough, Yorkshire
1865-66	New University Club, London†
1865-73	Grammar School, Reading
1866	Foxhill, Whiteknights Park, Reading, Berkshire
1866	University Union, Cambridge
1866-68	Strangeways Gaol, Manchester
1867-70	Allerton Priory, Allerton Road, Liverpool
1867-71	Lime Street Station Hotel, Liverpool
1867-77	Balliol College, Oxford (master lodge and south front)
1868-69	St. Matthew's Church, Vicarage, School and Cottages, Hampshire
1868-70	Jesus College Detached Range, Cambridge
1868-70	Gonville and Caius College Tree Court, Cambridge
1869-77	Town Hall, Manchester
1869-88	Owen's College (now Owen's University), Manchester
1870-73	Blackmoor House, Hampshire
1870-83	Eaton Hall, Cheshire (partly †)
1871	Market Hall and Town Hall, Knutsford, Cheshire
1871-74	Pembroke College, Cambridge (additions)
1871-74	Seamen's Orphan Institution (now the Park Hospital), Anfield, Liverpool
1872-75	Town Hall, Reading, Berkshire
1872-76	Girton College, Cambridge
1873-81	Natural History Museum, London
1874-77	New Hall, Oxford
1877-1908	Yorkshire College of Science (now Yorkshire University), Leeds
1878	Iwerne Minster House (now Claycsmore School), Dorset
1878	Assize Courts, Bedford
1878	Alfred Waterhouse House, Yattendon Court, Berkshire†
1878-1905	Prudential Assurance Company Headquarters, Holborn, London
1879-82	Town Hall, Hove, East Sussex
1880	1 Old Bond Street, London
1881	Prudential Assurance Building, Manchester
1881-83	Turner Memorial Home, Toxteth, Liverpool
1881-84	St. Paul's School, Hammersmith, London (master's house survives)†
1882-83	St. Elizabeth, Reddish, Lancashire
1883	Lyndhurst Road Congregational Church, Hampstead, London
1884-87	National Liberal Club, Victoria Embankment, London
1885	Prudential Assurance Building, Queen Street, Nottingham
1886	Prudential Assurance Building, Dale Street, Liverpool
1886	Royal Infirmary, Liverpool
1887-89	University Engineering Building and Victoria Building, Liverpool
1888	Hotel Metropole, Brighton
1889-91	King's Weigh House Chapel (now the Ukrainian Catholic Cathedral), Duke Street, London
1891	Lloyd's Bank, Cambridge
1893	St. Mary's Hospital, Manchester
1893-1913	Refuge Assurance Building, Oxford Street, Manchester (with Paul Waterhouse)
1894-97	St. Margaret's Clergy Orphan School, Bushey, Hertfordshire
1895	Prudential Assurance Building, Edinburgh, Scotland
1896-98	Royal Institution of Chartered Surveyors, London
1897-1906	University College Hospital, London
1901-03	Staple Inn Buildings North, London

Publications

BOOKS BY WATERHOUSE

Courts of Justice Competition: General Description of Design. London, 1867.

ARTICLES BY WATERHOUSE

"A Short Description of the Manchester Assize Courts." *Papers of the Royal Institute of British Architects* (1864-65): 165-174.

"Description of the Town Hall at Manchester." *Sessional Papers of the Royal Institute of British Architects* (1876-77): 117-131.

"The President's Address to Students: Colour in Architecture." *Journal of Proceedings of the Royal Institute of British Architects* Series 2, 7 (1890-91): 121-126.

"Architects." In *Unwritten Laws and Ideals of Active Careers.* Edited by E. H. Pitcairn. London, 1899.

BOOKS ABOUT WATERHOUSE

AXON, WILLIAM E. A.: *An Architectural and General Description of the Town Hall, Manchester.* London and Manchester, 1878.

DIXON, ROGER, and MUTHESIUS, STEFAN: *Victorian Architecture.* New York and Toronto, 1978.

GIROUARD, MARK: *Alfred Waterhouse and the Natural History Museum.* New Haven, Connecticut, and London, 1981.

MALTBY, SALLY, et al.: *Alfred Waterhouse, 1830-1905.* London, 1983.

SERVICE, ALASTAIR: *The Architects of London.* London, 1979.

SMITH, STUART ALLEN: "Alfred Waterhouse: Civic Grandeur." In JANE FAWCETT (ed.): *Seven Victorian Architects.* London, 1976.

ARTICLES ABOUT WATERHOUSE

COOPER, THOMAS: "Alfred Waterhouse, R.A., LL.D." *Journal of the Royal Institute of British Architects* Series 3, 12, No. 19 (1905): 609-618.

GIROUARD, MARK: "Blackmoor House, Hampshire: The Property of the Earl of Selborne." *Country Life* 156 (1974): 554-557; 614-617.

JENKINS, FRANK: "The Making of a Municipal Palace: Manchester Town Hall." *Country Life* 141 (1967): 336-339.

*

Although Alfred Waterhouse received his training as an apprentice under Richard Lane, an architect who worked in the classical style, he became an early supporter of the Gothic Revival. After a year of travel spent studying the Gothic architecture of Europe, he set up his office in Manchester in 1854. His practice was established in 1859 when he won the competition for the design of the Manchester Assize Courts. This building revealed Waterhouse's special genius for combining the picturesque with the classical. It featured Gothic facades and a striking skyline, yet was organized by a rational classical plan. The entrance led to a large public hall, flanked on each side by identical courts. The courts building was greatly admired, even by John Ruskin, who found little to like in contemporary Gothic. It established Waterhouse as an architect who could plan large, complex buildings in a convenient way without sacrificing romanticism in appearance.

The facade of the courts building was composed of a central pavilion rising well above the main roof line, flanked by identical wings culminating in pavilion terminals, all dressed up in polychromatic Gothic detail. In its steep roofs and pavilion elements, French Gothic influence was apparent. Unfortunately, the building was razed after it was heavily damaged in the bombings of World War II; however, its impact on Waterhouse's later designs is clearly apparent. In its symmetrical distribution of forms that other High Victorian architects might dispose in picturesque, asymmetrical compositions, the Assize Courts building was a harbinger of Waterhouse's great works to come, especially the Manchester Town Hall and the Museum of Natural History in London. Even the garden facade of the principal apartments of Eaton Hall, the great country house in the French Gothic style that he designed for the duke of Westminster, was composed in this manner.

A bank building commission and the desire to participate in the upcoming competition for the design of the Royal Courts of Justice led Waterhouse to move his office to London in 1865. He felt, justifiably, that the success of the Manchester Assize Courts placed him in a fortuitous position to receive one of the great commissions of the century. After all, had not his ability been recognized when he had been asked to develop the program to be used in the competition? Waterhouse's optimism was not justified. Although he was invited to participate in the limited competition for the design of the Law Courts, and his scheme was generally recognized by the legal community as the best one submitted, the prize was awarded to G. E. Street. Waterhouse's award of the commission to carry out Francis Fowke's design for the Museum of Natural History was, in effect, a consolation prize. The museum that Waterhouse produced is his opus magnum.

Waterhouse's architecture has been criticized as heavy-handed and lacking in sophistication and craftsmanship, but it is unsurpassed in its planning. His Manchester Town Hall is an excellent example of his ability as a planner. It was begun in 1869, 10 years after the Assize Courts, at a time when the Gothic style was being replaced by the Second Empire style as the dominant mode for large public buildings. It is exemplary of Waterhouse's skill in the organization of the plan, in three-dimensional composition and in the bold detailing of materials. It occupies a difficult triangular site. The entrance facade on the main town square is virtually symmetrical in relation to the great tower that rises above the entrance porch located on the central axis, and it ends in similarly scaled but differently fenestrated pavilion terminals. On each side of the entry a large hall leads to a courtroom. Beyond the entry the axis shifts almost imperceptibly—much as it does in Baldassare Peruzzi's Palazzo Massimo in Rome—to accommodate the city hall's great public functions, which stands as an almost-independent structure within the triangular court in the center of the building. Corridors around the court give borrowed light to the offices that ring the exterior of the plan. A variety of windows and decorative details add life and variety to the building. The sophisticated manner in which Waterhouse turned the acute corners of the plan reveals his genius with form.

Waterhouse approached the design of commercial office buildings in much the same way as he did the design of public buildings. He combined detail, classical planning and composition, and the utilization of new materials and building techniques in extremely creative ways. In his 1856 warehouse in Manchester for the Fryer and Binyon Company, he opened up the first story of a building clearly modeled on the Doge's Palace in Venice by means of coupled iron columns. Who else of his generation would have been willing to combine the new and the old in such an unorthodox way?

The London headquarters of the Prudential Assurance Company, begun in 1878 at the corner of Brook and Holborn streets, is the most important example of his commercial work. The building is French Gothic in style. Its major facade is symmetrically arranged around a central entrance pavilion. It balances the strong horizontal expression of its three-and-one-half stories with vertical emphasis provided by a towered entrance pavilion, end pavilions, intermediate pavilions on each side of the central pavilion, and facade modules that rise unbroken to culminate in gabled dormer projections. All was constructed of red-orange terra cotta, a material that contributed unity to the design and gave the building its uniquely Victorian appearance.

Waterhouse used brick and terra cotta copiously. The epithet "red brick university," used in denigrating reference to universities other than Oxford and Cambridge, originated in response to the red-brick and terra cotta universities in the Gothic style that Waterhouse designed for cities in the north of England. These include the Yorkshire College of Science and Liverpool College.

Unlike other great architects of the High Victorian period such as William Butterfield, G. E. Street, J. L. Pearson and William Burges, Waterhouse was never associated with the Anglo-Catholic High Church movement in Britain. This was due in part to his Quaker background, in part to his hard, no-nonsense approach to design, in part to his classical training and in part to his desire to make his buildings modern through the use of materials such as iron and terra cotta. Instead of focusing on church design, Waterhouse devoted his energies to developing a large, extremely successful commercial practice that produced many public buildings, schools, country houses and insurance offices that stand as monuments of Victorian wealth and exuberance.

—C. MURRAY SMART, JR.

WEBB, Aston.

British. Born in London, England, 1849. Died in London, 1930. Father was the noted watercolorist Edward Webb; son was the architect Maurice Webb. Articled to the firm of R. R. Banks and Charles Barry, Jr. (1823-1900), London; traveled to Europe for a year. Established own office, 1873; became partners with E. Ingress Bell (1837-1914). President, Royal Institute of British Architects, 1902-04; knighted, 1904; Gold Medal, Royal Institute of British Architects, 1905; member, Royal Academy.

Chronology of Works
All in England unless noted

1875	St. John's Church, Kingston Blount, Oxfordshire
1879	House, 60 Bartholomew Close, London
1885-97	St. Bartholomew the Great Church, Smithfield, London (restoration)
1887-91	Victoria Assize Courts, Birmingham
1888	House, 23 Austin Friars, London

Aston Webb: Victoria and Albert Museum, London, England, 1891-1909

1890	Metropolitan Life Assurance Company Building, Moorgate, London
1893	French Protestant Church, Soho Square, London
1893-95	Royal United Services Institution, Whitehall, London
1893-1902	Christ's Hospital, Horsham, Sussex
1891-1909	Victoria and Albert Museum, London (Cromwell Road front)
1897	Yacht Club, Yarmouth, Isle of Wight
1899-1905	Royal Naval College, Dartmouth, Devon
1900-06	Imperial College of Science and Technology, London
1901	Birmingham University, Birmingham
1901-13	The Mall/Queen Victoria Memorial, London
1903	Law Courts, Hong Kong
1903-10	Admiralty Arch, London
1903-10	St. Michael's Court, Caius College, Cambridge
1907	Offices of Grand Trunk Railway of Canada, Cockspur Street, London
1908	Webb Court, King's College, Cambridge
1908	Bright's Building, Magdalene College, Cambridge
1909-13	Royal School of Mines, South Kensington, London
1912	Buckingham Palace, London (refacing of the east front)
1913	George V Gateway, Leys School, Cambridge

Publications

BOOKS ABOUT WEBB

SERVICE, ALASTAIR (ed.): *Edwardian Architecture and Its Origins*. London, 1975.
SERVICE, ALASTAIR: *The Architects of London*. London, 1979.

ARTICLES ABOUT WEBB

"Sir Aston Webb's Record: Public Buildings and Churches." *Architects Magazine* 5, No. 57 (1905).
CRESSWELL, H. B.: "A Backward View." *Architect and Building News* 208 (11 August 1955): 172-173.
CRESSWELL, H. B.: "Seventy Years Back." *Architectural Review* 124 (December 1958): 403-405.
LUCAS, WILLIAM: "The Architecture of Sir Aston Webb P. R. A." *Building News* 118 (1920): 63-64.

By the end of the 19th century, Aston Webb was a brilliantly successful Establishment architect, with one of the largest architectural practices in Britain. Although his work embraced a wide range of architectural types, including country houses and churches, the staggering reputation that he came to enjoy was based particularly on his designs for myriad government commissions won in competition. Webb was highly regarded for government structures exhibiting solid construction and clarity of planning, and his approach to design—a free adaptation of historical styles, incorporating sculpture as an integral part of the work—was considered tasteful and appropriate for public buildings. His work has been aptly compared to the majestic, imperial compositions of the Edwardian composer Edward Elgar: "Like Elgar's music, the sweep, thrust and movement of Webb's architecture speaks of solemnity, grandeur, and security."

Webb began building his considerable reputation for government work of the largest kind in the 1880s, particularly after

he and partner Edward Ingress Bell won the 1885 competition for the Victoria Assize Courts, Birmingham. Built between 1887 and 1891 on Corporation Street, the structure was constructed of brick and terra-cotta—materials considered appropriate for Birmingham—in a free Francois I manner. There, the small-scale detailing of the ornamental terra-cotta work by W. Aumonier lends richness, elegance and a pleasurable liveliness to the structure.

From that promising beginning, Webb went on to gain a host of government commissions in different parts of the country, particularly in London. In 1891 he won a limited competition for the principal block of the Victoria and Albert Museum, the newly planned extension of the South Kensington Museum. Opened in 1909, the building is a prime example of Webb's ability to produce architecture that was perceived as particularly sensitive to the government's diverse needs, both structurally and ideologically.

Described stylistically by *The Builder* as ". . . a rich variety of Romanesque," the building exhibits an astonishing amalgamation of classical and medieval elements, as if to signal the variety, age and opulence of the art and design contained within. The perimeter of the site is defined by massive, four-story stone blocks housing side-lit galleries on three stories, and a top-lit gallery on the fourth. The structure boasts an impressive skyline: each block is marked by a dome or a dome and lift tower, while a rather muscular central tower, topped by an open stone crown, rises above the arched entrance. Webb confidently asserted that this combination of domes and towers would provide the structure with ". . . a crown of towers almost unique in Europe." The building is adorned further with an extensive sculptural program provided by academician sculptors, which celebrates the glorious achievements of British artists through the ages, clothing the building in the garb of strident nationalism. A statue of Queen Victoria stands above the great arched entrance, and on either side of the arch are found carved figures symbolizing Truth, Beauty, Imagination, Knowledge, and the four arts: painting, sculpture, architecture and the crafts. In addition, single sculpted figures placed along the facade represent well-known British artists such as Christopher Wren, Josiah Wedgwood and J. M. W. Turner. The treatment of the interior is equally adept: the plan of the structure is striking in its simplicity and clarity, comprising a rectangle linked to the levels of the old building. Upon entering the museum, one quickly leaves the vestibule to enter an elegant domed central hall, which forms a point of repose before one enters the numerous top-lit halls and vaulted courts of various sizes and shapes housing the vast museum collections.

This skillful work was so successful in the eyes of the government that it led to Webb's appointment as architect for two other government buildings in the South Kensington Museum area: the Imperial College of Science and Technology (1900-06) and the Royal School of Mines (1909-13).

Webb's career reached an enviable peak when he won the 1901 limited competition to transform the Mall approach to Buckingham Palace into a memorial to Queen Victoria, a scheme intended as an impressive representation of the power and influence of the British Empire. The final design features a *rond-point* immediately outside the gates of Buckingham Palace, with Thomas Brock's massive statue of Queen Victoria enthroned as *Regina Imperatrix* at its center, gazing authoritatively down the Mall toward Trafalgar Square and Whitehall. Encircling this ensemble Webb placed formal gardens and elaborate gilded iron gates representing Canada, Australia and the African colonies, embellished with statuary by Alfred Drury and Derwent Wood symbolizing a host of smaller British colonies and protectorates. The Mall was widened to form a stately processional way for government ceremonials, ending in Admiralty Arch, a triumphal arch leading to Trafalgar Square. The arch, which also served to house the Admiralty, was designed in a heavy, rusticated classical manner, with concave surfaces on both faces, thus brilliantly concealing the awkward shift of axis from the Mall to Trafalgar Square. Decorated with Brock's sculpture depicting navigation and gunnery, the arch represents the military underpinnings of the British empire—Britian's maritime strength. To complete the project, the government authorized Webb to reface Buckingham Palace, which he redesigned in a delicate French classical manner. The scheme, for which he was knighted in 1904, was hailed enthusiastically by the government as an example of modern town planning comparing favorably in magnificence, although not in scope, with Baron Haussmann's rebuilding of Paris as an imperial capital.

Webb gained government commissions not only within Britain, but also in a variety of British colonies, dominions and protectorates. During the 1880s, he and Bell were appointed consulting architects to the Crown Agents for the Colonies, under whose aegis they were responsible for designing colonial buildings as well as sending young architects, some of whom were members of Webb's office staff, to work in colonial public works departments. His colonial architecture was truly architecture by mail, as he never saw the sites.

Compared with Webb's English work, for example, the Law Courts in Hong Kong (1903) appear rather bland, and were described by a contemporary critic as ". . . of the English school with details of a Greek character. It is a fifteen-bay long main facade with Ionic columns and a large central dome rising above a pediment."

Webb's achievements throughout his career were firmly grounded in energetic participation in the institutional structures of the London architectural scene. He served as president of the Architectural Association, the Royal Academy and the Royal Institute of British Architects, and as a distinguished member of the profession he won many prestigious awards from these institutions as well as their counterparts abroad.

Despite a glowing contemporary reputation, Webb's work is little appreciated by historians today. Nonetheless, as an immensely successful Establishment architect, he produced tasteful monumental government building throughout Britain and the colonies, and according to a radical reassessment of his architecture which has just barely begun, Webb indeed might best be termed ". . . the architectural Elgar of his age."

—ELLEN A. CHRISTENSEN

WEBB, Philip Speakman.

British. Born in Oxford, England, 1831. Died in Worth, Sussex, England, 1915. Educated at Aynho, Northhamptonshire; apprenticed with John Billing, Reading. Worked for George Edmund Street, Oxford; opened office in London, 1856; established own firm, London, 1859; joined firm of William Morris, 1861; founded (with Morris) the Society for the Protection of Ancient Buildings.

Chronology of Works
All in England unless noted
† *Work no longer exists*

1859-60	Red House, for William Morris, Bexley Heath, Kent
1860	Sandroyd (now Benfleet Hall), Fairmile, near Cobham, Surrey
1861-63	91-101 Worship Street, Shoreditch, London (shops and houses)
1863	Arisaig, near Fort William, Inverness-shire, Scotland
1864-65	Prinsep House, Kensington, London
1865-67	Washington Hall, Durham
1868	19 Lincoln's Inn Fields, London
1868-69	35 Glebe Place, Chelsea, London
1868-73	Howard House, 1 Palace Green, Kensington, London
1868-70	Trevor Hall (Church Hill House), East Barnet
1872-73	Joldwynds, near Dorking, Surrey
1872-76	Rounton Grange, Yorkshire†
1874-78	St. Martin, Brampton, Cumberland
1876-78	Four Gables, Brampton, Cumberland
1877-79	Smeaton Manor, Yorkshire
1878	New Place, Welwyn
1879-86	Clouds House, East Knoyle, Wiltshire
1889-90	Bell Brothers Offices, Zetland Road, Middlesbrough, Yorkshire
1891-94	Standen, near East Grinstead, Sussex
1892	Great Tangley Manor, Yorkshire
1902	Cottages at Kelmscott, Lechlade, Gloucestershire

Publications

BOOKS ABOUT WEBB

CURRY, ROSEMARY J., and KIRK, SHEILA: *Philip Webb in the North.* Exhibition catalog. Middlesborough, England, 1984.

FERRIDAY, PETER (ed.): *Victorian Architecture.* London, 1963.

FRAMPTON, KENNETH, and FUTAGAWA, YUKIO: *Modern Architecture: 1851-1919.* New York, 1983.

GIROUARD, MARK: *The Victorian Country House.* New Haven, Connecticut, and London, 1979.

HOFMANN, WERNER, and KULTERMANN, UDO: *Modern Architecture in Color.* New York, 1970.

LETHABY, WILLIAM RICHARD: *Philip Webb and His Work.* London, 1935.

NAYLOR, GILLIAN: *The Arts and Crafts Movement.* London, 1990.

RICHARDSON, MARGARET: *The Craft Architects.* London and New York, 1983.

ARTICLES ABOUT WEBB

ASLET, C.: "Forthampton Court, Gloucestershire." *Country Life* 166 (1979): 938-941.

BLUNDELL JONES, PETER: "Red House." *Architect's Journal* 183, No. 3 (15 January 1986): 36-56.

BRANDON-JONES, JOHN: "Letters of Philip Webb and His Contemporaries." *Architectural History* 8 (1965): 52-72.

BRANDON-JONES, JOHN: "Notes on the Building of Smeaton Manor." *Architectural History* 1 (1958): 31-58.

BRANDON-JONES, J.: "The Work of Philip Webb and Norman Shaw." *Architectural Association Journal* 71 (June 1955): 9-21; (July-August 1955): 40-47.

JACK, GEORGE: "An Appreciation of Philip Webb." *Architectural Review* 38 (1915): 1-6.

JACKSON, NEIL: "A Church for SPAB." *Architectural Review* 162 (1977): 69-71.

LUTYENS, EDWIN: "The Work of the Late Philip Webb." *Country Life* 37 (1915): 618.

MACLEOD, ROBERT: "William Morris and Philip Webb." Pp. 40-54 in *Style and Society: Architectural Ideology in Britain: 1835-1914.* London, 1971.

McEVOY, M.: "Webb at Brampton." *Architects' Journal* 190, No. 17 (25 October 1989): 40-63.

MORRIS, G. H.: "On Mr. Philip Webb's Town and Work." *Architectural Review* 2 (1897): 199-208.

Philip Speakman Webb: Standen, Sussex, England, 1891-94

PEVSNER, NIKOLAUS: "Colonel Gillum and the Pre-Raphaelites." *Burlington Magazine* 95 (1953): 76-81.

ROOKS, NOEL: "The Works of Lethaby, Webb, and Morris." *Journal of the Royal Institute of British Architects* 57 (1950): 167-175.

SMITH, H.: "Philip Webb's restoration of Forthampton Court, Gloucestershire." *Architectural History* 24 (1981): 92-102.

SPENCE, T. R.: "Philip Speakman Webb." *Catalogue of the Drawings Collection of the Royal Institute of British Architects.* (1984): 142-199.

SWENARTON, MARK: "Philip Webb: Architecture and Socialism in the 1880's." Pp. 32-60 in *Artisans and Architects.* London, 1989.

YOKOYAMA, TADAMI: "Trip to 'Epoch Making' Red House." *Global Architecture Houses* 1 (1976): 4-17.

*

Philip Webb's architecture can be properly understood only through an examination of his attitudes toward society, which were nurtured by the cultural circles in which he moved, and in particular the ideas of William Morris and John Ruskin. He shared Morris and Ruskin's rejection of 19th-century commercial values and what they saw as the inevitable vulgarity of its artistic products, and, like Morris, he hoped for a new society brought about through revolutionary socialism. These antiestablishment attitudes were reinforced by his own modest and retiring character and his hatred of pretentiousness and fashion. Webb's architectural training in the Gothic Revival tradition, especially his years with George Edmund Street, introduced him to A. W. N. Pugin's legacy, which was also taken up by Ruskin—the concern for architectural truth, honesty and sincerity, which paralleled the concerns of European realists.

Like Morris, Webb particularly valued vernacular architecture, with its seemingly endless local variations of form, construction and materials, an appreciation of which had grown up within the Gothic Revival tradition. However, he was more concerned about encouraging the continuation or reintroduction of traditional local materials and constructional methods, especially local patterns and textures of walling, than reviving vernacular forms wholesale, in a naive attempt to reestablish a genuinely vernacular architectural tradition. Moreover, he would not, as he told his protégé, W. R. Lethaby, "take refuge in baldness"; he realized that vernacular forms alone were insufficient to deal with the scale of a large building.

Webb and Morris' historical sense, manifested in the philosophy of the Society for the Protection of Ancient Buildings, which they founded in 1877, led them to distrust any notion of artificial stylistic revival. It is instructive to compare Webb with his contemporary Richard Norman Shaw. Whereas Shaw's interest in the vernacular was largely nostalgic, concentrating on its picturesque qualities, Webb looked more deeply at the relationship between building and place. This is most clearly demonstrated in the siting of their respective houses. Shaw would site his houses on prominent rises, to create dramatic and picturesque visual effects, especially on arrival. Webb, on the other hand, generally followed vernacular precedent, siting his houses in positions sheltered from prevailing winds. At Standen, East Grinstead, Sussex (1891-94), for instance, a prominent site had already been chosen and leveled by the client when Webb was called in, but Webb insisted on locating the new building close to an old farmhouse behind the hill, in the lee of the woods. He also characteristically retained the farmhouse and barn, and meticulously underpinned an old granary, as a starting point for his own design.

Webb rapidly outgrew, except in church work, the explicit Gothic Revival forms of Red House, his first independent commission for Morris, in favor of a more eclectic use of historical precedent which evades easy stylistic classification. He was one of the instigators of the Queen Anne Revival, the return to simple vernacular forms of the English classical tradition. However, he avoided the more literal revival of historical detail typical of the mainstream Queen Anne Revival, which he called the "dilettante picturesque," in favor of a plainer, but more robust and idiosyncratic, character. This was partly a legacy of the High Victorian delight in deliberately awkward conjunctions of forms, characteristic of the work of William Butterfield, whom Webb greatly admired. Webb also developed the sense of constructional integrity and richness in Butterfield's work. In Webb's later buildings, external ornament was generally replaced by a rich and complex layering of traditional local techniques and materials. Brick and stone, weatherboard and tile-hanging, were frequently combined in the same elevation, notably at Clouds, Wiltshire (1879-86) and Standen.

Beginning with Trevor Hall, Barnet (1868-70), Webb increasingly moved toward basically symmetrical, economically planned compact blocks, for the principal parts of his houses, usually roughly square in plan and often with a central hall, perhaps influenced by John Vanbrugh's work. In his move toward more classically based compositions, he seems to have departed from Morris' essentially anticlassical stance. He expressed great admiration for the architecture of Michelangelo and, closer to home, even C. R. Cockerell's Ashmolean Museum, Oxford (1841-45). However, he always tried to preserve a certain primitive vitality that he called the "barbaric" or "gothic" element, which he recognized in work of many different periods and styles. This almost awkward quality in Webb's work was probably also due to his determination to avoid the glibness and nostalgic artificiality of fashionable revival architecture. George Jack, his assistant for many years, perspicaciously observed that in Webb, "a very inventive imagination was at all times struggling with an austere restraint which feared unmeaning expressions." Webb's work thus became, in a sense, an architecture of avoidance. In his own words, the task was "how to build less badly."

The symmetry of much of Webb's later buildings was generally underplayed. it was often deliberately contradicted by elevational irregularities, the central focus was sometimes underscaled or denied, and compositional duality was frequently employed. It was as if Webb used symmetry as an ordering system for larger buildings but wished at the same time to undermine its implications of social hierarchy and power. This simultaneous use and abuse of classical form is nowhere more apparent than in his largest house, Clouds, which is a strange amalgam of vernacular and high-style elements from both the medieval and classical traditions.

In his interiors, Webb moved away from mid-Victorian richness and literal stylistic revivalism toward a more original eclectic combination of elements freely adapted from the past. He severely limited the extent of ornamental detail, and what remained was often drawn directly from his own painstaking studies of nature. Increasingly, he lightened his interiors by using plain, unmolded white-painted paneling, and white walls and ceilings, though he sometimes used darker colors in one or two rooms, such as the serene gray-green dining room at Standen. Following the ideas in Ruskin's chapter "The Nature of Gothic" in *The Stones of Venice* (1851/53), which became a kind of architectural manifesto for the Morris circle, Webb tried to find independent creative craftsmen to carry out special decorative detail, in the medieval manner. However, the irony was that creative craftsmanship was considered to be in such a parlous state by Morris and Webb that Webb usually felt obliged to design the overall scheme in some detail, while carefully noting that the work could be varied by the craftsman and the workmanship should not be too mechanical. Webb was extraordinarily and unusually meticulous in the detailing of his buildings, for the period, so that he could control the quality of every part. He therefore completed relatively few buildings, mostly country houses—ironic for a socialist—and retired in 1900 to a humble rented cottage in Sussex.

Webb's high ethical principles and sensitive treatment of old buildings had a great impact on a younger generation of Arts and Crafts architects, including W. R. Lethaby, Ernest and Sydney Barnsley, Ernest Gimson, and C. C. Winmill and John Hebb of the early London County Council Architects Department. Equally influential on these men were the humility of his architectural philosophy, derived from the anonymity and subtlety of vernacular traditions, and his builderly approach, whereby richness was gained through acute sensitivity to and control of traditional materials and methods. This sensitivity to materials and local traditions was clearly very important for Edwin Lutyens, who, in his 1915 obituary of Webb, acknowledged Webb's influence on his early work.

Webb's work represents one of the most fascinating of late-19th-century attempts to generate a modern architectural language from a vigorous and critically eclectic approach to architectural history, transforming found motifs into a new, highly idiosyncratic personal style, melding vernacular and high-style elements.

—RORY SPENCE

WEINBRENNER, Friedrich.

German. Born in Karlsruhe, Germany, 24 November 1766. Died in Karlsruhe, 1 March 1826. Father was Johann Ludwig Weinbrenner (1729-76), one in a line of carpenters from Untermünkheim, near Schwäbisch-Hall; Friedrich married his cousin Margarete Arnold, 1798. Originally trained as a carpenter in his father's shop; worked in Switzerland, 1787-89; traveled to Vienna, Dresden and Berlin, 1790-91, then to Italy, spending time in Rome to study classical architecture, 1792-97; returned to Karlsruhe and was appointed *Bauinspektor*, 1797; worked briefly in Strasbourg and Hannover, then returned to Karlsruhe in 1800; appointed *Baudirektor* for the state of Baden, 1801, and in addition to his building-design activities, conducted archaeological work; visited Paris, 1806; promoted to *Oberbaudirektor* for Baden, 1807. Founded school of architecture, 1800. Member of the Academies of Art, Berlin and Munich.

Chronology of Works
All in Germany
† *Work no longer exists*

1797-1800	Wohnlich House, Karlsruhe
1798	Synagogue, Karlsruhe†
1800-05	Von Beck House, Karlsruhe
1801	Weinbrenner House, Karlsruhe†
1803-13	Margraves' Palace, Rondell-Platz, Karlsruhe
1803-14	Church of St. Stephen, Karlsruhe
1804-08	Infantry Barracks, Karlsruhe†
1805-25	Town Hall, Karlsruhe
1806	Military Barracks, Heidelberg
1806-17	Church, Kleinsteinbach, near Karlsruhe
1806-20	Protestant Church and School, Karlsruhe
1807-08	Court Theater, Karlsruhe†
1808	Palais Hamilton, Baden-Baden
1810-12	Church, Scherzheim, near Kehl
1813-14	Museum Fridericianum, Karlsruhe
1814-16	Chancellery, Karlsruhe
1817	Municipal Theater, Leipzig (remodeling)
1821-24	Konversationshaus, Baden-Baden
1826-27	Mint, Karlsruhe (completed after his death)

Publications

BOOKS BY WEINBRENNER

Architektonisches Lehrbuch. Vols. 1-3. Tübingen, Germany, 1810-19.
Friedrich Weinbrenner, Denkwürdigkeiten. Edited by A. von Schneider. Karlsruhe, 1958.

BOOKS ABOUT WEINBRENNER

BROWNLEE, DAVID: *Friedrich Weinbrenner, Architect of Karls-
    ruhe, A Catalogue of the Drawings in the Architectural
    Archives of the University of Pennsylvania.* Philadelphia,
    1986.
ELBERT, C.: *Die Theater Friedrich Weinbrenners. Bauten und
    Entwürfe.* Karlsruhe, 1988.
Friedrich Weinbrenner 1766-1826. Exhibition catalog. Karls-
    ruhe, Germany, 1977.
KOEBEL, M.: *Friedrich Weinbrenner.* 1922.
VALDENAIRE, ARTHUR: *Friedrich Weinbrenner: Sein Leben
    und seine Bauten.* Karlsruhe, 1919.
VON SCHNEIDER, A. (ed.): *Friedrich Weinbrenner, Denkwür-
    digkeiten.* Karlsruhe, 1958.
WATKIN, DAVID, and MELLINGHOFF, TILMAN: *German Archi-
    tecture and the Classical Ideal.* Cambridge, Massachusetts,
    1987.

ARTICLES ABOUT WEINBRENNER

DELIUS, H.: "Vitruv und der deutsche Klassizismus: Carl
    Friedrich Schinkel und Friedrich Weinbrenner." *Archi-
    tectura* 1 (1933).

*

Friedrich Weinbrenner was one of a group of important German neoclassicists belonging to the generation immediately preceding that of Leo von Klenze and Karl Freidrich Schinkel.

Born in Karlsruhe, Weinbrenner came from a family of carpenters and joiners, so from childhood was familiar with aspects of design, construction and building. He traveled in Switzerland, and later studied mathematics and architecture in Vienna. During the 1790s he was in Berlin, where he prepared many designs, including a version of the Pantheon using the Greek Doric order. Baseless Doric, in its most primitive form as used at Paestum, was seen as appropriately modern for the period. Weinbrenner, like many of his contemporaries, was influenced by Le Camus de Mézières's *Le Génie de l'Architecture, ou l'Analogie de cet Art avec nos Sensations* (Paris, 1780), and later in a German version in Gottfried Huth's *Allgemeines Magazin für die bürgerliche Baukunst* of (1789). Le Camus insisted that form and architecture could arouse sentiments and emotions appropriate to the use of the building, so that architecture could speak of its function (*architecture parlante*).

Weinbrenner knew Carl Gotthard Langhans, Janus Genelli and David Gilly, and around 1792 he traveled to Italy with the artist Asmus Jacob Carstens. He then spent some five years in Rome, where several young German architects were eagerly taking on board the stark neoclassical ideals of the French Academy in that city, and imbibing the latest archaeological discoveries of Roman and Greek buildings. By that time architectural students were obliged to visit the Greek remains at Paestum, and returned home fluent in a language of design using stereometrically pure forms, a sparse and stripped geometry, and severe Greek Doric columns, often made even more primitive in their shapes than those of the historical precedents themselves.

During his stay in Italy, Weinbrenner drew the illustrations for Alois Hirt's *Die Baukunst nach den Grundsätzen der Alten,* published in Berlin in 1809. This was an important study of architecture "according to the principles of the ancients." Weinbrenner also designed many *esquisses* for the usual array of neoclassical building types: mausolea, prisons, monuments and public buildings. These essays were all in the most severe and stripped manner, while his draftsmanship owed something

to both G. B. Piranesi and Carstens. In 1797 Weinbrenner returned to Karlsruhe, where he found his ideal patron in the margrave of Baden, a civilized prince who, like many of his generation, had been attracted by the publications of Piranesi, and so saw in Weinbrenner's work much to his taste.

Weinbrenner was duly appointed *Bauinspektor,* and one of his first jobs was to design the new synagogue: he chose a Greco-Egyptian form with Gothic openings in the center, a suitably exotic piece of eclecticism intended to display lack of bias and devotion to the *Aufklärung.* Following the creation of the duchy of Baden in 1806, and the growing importance of Karlsruhe as a capital city, Weinbrenner was able to realize some of his grander neoclassical transformations of the Baroque town that had been centered on the palace and the 32 avenues radiating from it. South of the palace a civic center was proposed, but not until after 1797 was Weinbrenner able to arrive at his scheme for the center, with its Protestant church and school (built 1806-20) set on the opposite side of the Marktplatz from the Town Hall (built 1807-14). These groups of buildings were to be placed on either side of the main axis leading to the palace (the Schloss-Strasse), while across the northern side of the Marktplatz at right angles to the main axis was the Langestrasse, which effectively drew a line between the palace and its grounds and the newer town to the south. In the center of the upper part of the Marktplatz was the pyramid of red sandstone, one of the most remarkable and most pure of all neoclassical monuments, dating from 1825, and commemorating the Margrave Karl Wilhelm of Baden-Durlach, the founder of Karlsruhe.

The Marktplatz was only one of many visually agreeable spaces on the Schloss-Strasse, which extended south from the palace to the severe Doric Ettlinger Tor (1803), north of which is the Rodellplatz, an octagonal urban space surrounded with palatial buildings, including the New Palace (1803-14), with its grand antique portico.

To the west, in the Friedrichsplatz, is the Roman Catholic church of St. Stephen by Weinbrenner (1803-14), a severe Pantheon-like form with quotations from the Roman *thermae* (complete with Diocletian windows) and a *Rundbogenstil* campanile.

The brilliant town plan, superimposed on the radiating Baroque avenues, created peculiar V-shaped sites at junctions which Weinbrenner developed with verve and *élan.* He also designed model dwellings to be erected throughout the scheme, and founded an important school of architecture in his own house in 1800. This establishment, recognized by Goethe as very significant in the promotion of true architecture, was given ducal patronage, and in due course became part of a new polytechnic, founded on the French model.

Weinbrenner's most original scheme for Karlsruhe was not realized: it dated from 1808, and involved the creation of a stark, plain, unmolded arcade on piers rising three stories, and capped by a continuous cornice. This variation on the Rue des Colonnes in Paris (where the arcade, however, is only one-story high) has had a profound effect on later architects, notably Giorgio Grassi, whose project for colonnaded lodgings for students at Chieti in Italy (1976) recalls Weinbrenner's severe Franco-Prussian essay in sublime repetition and unmolded architecture.

Weinbrenner was one of the most important and influential architects and town planners in all Germany in the first three decades of the 19th century, although by the time his projects for Karlsruhe were completed in the 1820s, his style was becoming less favored by his successor Heinrich Hübsch and other younger men. Today, however, now that the pendulum of taste enables us to appreciate the neoclassical world of the revolutionary, Napoleonic and post-Napoleonic periods, Weinbrenner's remarkable contribution can be seen as original, steeped in the ideas of the Enlightenment, full of Freemasonic allusions, and of a very sophisticated quality.

—JAMES STEVENS CURL

WHITE, Stanford.

American. Born in New York City, 9 November 1853. Died in New York City, 5 June 1906. Father was Richard Grant White; son was Lawrence Grant White, architect. Graduated, University of New York, 1871. Student draftsman, Gambrill and Richardson office, New York, 1872; partner, McKim, Mead and White, New York, 1880.

Chronology of Works
All in the United States unless noted
† *Work no longer exists*

1877-81	Farragut Memorial, New York City (base only; sculpture by Auguste Saint-Gaudens)
1879-80	Casino, Newport, Rhode Island
1880-87	Deacon Chapin Monument, Springfield, Massachusetts
1882-83	Goelet Cottage, Newport, Rhode Island
1884?	Stanford White House, Gramercy Park, New York City
1885-1905	Schools, Library, Bank, Church, Fountain and Three Houses, Naugatuck, Connecticut
1886-87	William G. Low House, Bristol, Rhode Island†
1887-91	Madison Square Garden, New York City†
1887-98	Boston Public Library, Boston, Massachusetts
1888-93	Judson Memorial Church, Washington Square South, New York City
1889-90	Johnson Gate, Harvard University, Cambridge, Massachusetts
1889-92	Washington Memorial Arch, New York City
1890-91	Brown and Meredith Apartment Block, Boston, Massachusetts
1890-95	New York City Herald Building, New York City
1891-92	King Model Houses, New York City
1892-94	Metropolitan Club, New York City
1891-1903	State Capitol, Providence, Rhode Island
1892	Stanford White Estate, St. James, New York
1892-1903	New York University Buildings, Bronx, New York City
1892-1901	Symphony Hall, Boston
1893-95	Bowery Savings Bank, New York City
1893-1902	Seven Buildings, Columbia University, Morningside Heights, New York City
1894-95	Factory and Housing, Roanoke Rapids, North Carolina
1895-99	Frederick W. Vanderbilt House, Hyde Park, New York
1896-1900	University Club, New York City
1896-1907	Rotunda (restoration) and Four Buildings, University of Virginia, Charlottesville
1897-99	Gymnasium, Radcliffe College, Cambridge, Massachusetts
1897-1900	Stuyvesant Fish House, New York City
1897-1902	Herman Oelrichs House, Newport, Rhode Island
1898-1900	State Savings Bank, Detroit, Michigan
1898-1907	James Breece House, Southampton, Long Island
1899-1901	Union, Harvard University, Cambridge, Massachusetts
1900-03	Joseph Pulitzer House, New York City
1900-05	Bank of Montreal, Canada (additions)
1901-04	Interborough Rapid Transit Powerhouse, New York City
1902	White House, Washington, D. C. (restoration)
1902-06	J. Pierpont Morgan Library, New York City (not completed until 1907 by others)
1903-06	Tiffany Building, New York City
1904-06	Colony Club, New York City (not completed until 1908 by others)
1904-06	Madison Square Presbyterian Church, New York City

Publications

BOOKS ABOUT WHITE

ANDREWS, WAYNE: *Architecture, Ambition and Americans.* New York, 1964.
BAKER, PAUL R.: *Stanny: The Gilded Life of Stanford White.* New York and London, 1989.
BALDWIN, CHARLES: *Stanford White.* New York, 1931.
A Monograph of the Work of McKim, Mead & White, 1879-1915. 4 vols. New York, 1915-20.
REILLY, C. H.: *McKim, Mead, and White.* 1924.
ROTH, L. M.: *McKim, Mead & White, Architects.* New York, 1983.
ROTH, L. M.: *The Architecture of McKim, Mead, and White, 1870-1920: A Building List.* New York, 1978.
SCULLY, VINCENT: *American Architecture and Urbanism: A Historical Essay.* New York, 1969.
SCULLY, VINCENT: *The Shingle Style.* New Haven, Connecticut, 1955.
Sketches and Designs by Stanford White. New York, 1920.
WHITE, LAWRENCE GRANT: *Sketches and Designs by Stanford White.* New York, 1920.
WILSON, R. G.: *McKim, Mead & White, Architects.* New York, 1983.
WODEHOUSE, L.: *White of McKim, Mead, and White.* New York, 1990.

ARTICLES ABOUT WHITE

ANDREWS, WAYNE: "McKim, Mead and White: New York's Own Architects." *New York Historical Society Quarterly* 35 (1951).
DAVIS, RICHARD H.: "Stanford White." *Collier's Magazine* 37 (1906): 17.
DESMOND, HARRY W. and CROLY, HERBERT: "The Work of Messrs. McKim, Mead & White." *Architectural Record* 20 (1906): 153-246.
MOSES, LIONEL: "McKim, Mead & White: A History." *American Architect* 121 (1922): 413-424.
RAMSEY, STANLEY C.: "The Work of McKim, Mead and White." *Journal of the Proceedings of the Royal Institute of British Architects* 25 (1917): 25-29.
STURGIS, RUSSELL: "The Work of McKim, Mead & White." *Architectural Record*: Great American Architects Series, No. 1 (1895).
YETTER, G. H.: "Stanford White at the University of Virginia: Some New Light on the Old Question." *Journal of the Society of Architectural Historians* 40 (December 1981): 320-25.

Within the New York architectural firm of McKim, Mead and White, Charles Follen McKim, one of the two designers, was a bold Roman classicist. The other designer was Stanford White, whose work was just as classical as McKim's, but it had an 18th-century delicacy about it comparable to the work of Robert Adam. McKim and White were responsible for more than one thousand commissions.

Both McKim and White had worked for Henry Hobson Richardson, White from 1872 to 1878, when Trinity Church in Boston was being built. From this Richardsonian building came White's love of the Romanesque, which he adopted mainly, but not exclusively, in early projects of the firm. White did not evolve from one style to another, but used all styles as he felt the need. He had visited French Romanesque architecture, including Saint-Gilles-du-Gard in Provençe, and used it for the porch (1901-03) of St. Bartholomew's Church in New York City (1872 by Renwick and Sands), built as a memorial to Commodore Vanderbilt and designed in collaboration with sculptors James O'Connor, Herbert Adams and Philip Martiny.

Earlier, White had introduced the Second Renaissance Revival of the 19th century (as opposed to the first of the 1850s) in the Villard House (1883-85), a building that later had five residences added to it around a courtyard on Madison Avenue. Interiors of the Villard House incorporated paintings, relief sculptures and elaborate detailing; house cost more than $1 million. The style was based upon Roman palazzi of the 16th century, buildings used by Renaissance merchants for business transactions, so White adapted the style to several clubhouses where gentlemen could meet. This was the justification for the Metropolitan Club (1892-94) on Fifth Avenue at Sixtieth Street, established by J. P. Morgan and his wealthy friends as an exclusive club.

As an extension and variation of the Italian Renaissance, White admired the decorative motifs of the Spanish Renaissance, and he used the Giralda tower (1568) at Seville as the model for his Madison Square Garden (1887-91), a large entertainment and convention center originally located on Madison Square. Even though the financial backing by J. P. Morgan, P. T. Barnum and others was generous, the building could not be constructed of stone. Instead terra-cotta was used for the elaborate detailing together with a buff-colored brick. The tower became the base for the copper sculpture *Diana* by Augustus Saint-Gaudens, a lifelong friend with whom White collaborated on numerous works.

Once Renaissance influences had reached England during the 16th and 17th centuries, the styles was then transported to the colonies, including those 13 along the Atlantic seaboard. It is therefore not surprising that 19th-century American architects who had previously looked to Europe for precedents in their design began looking back to their own roots in Colonial architecture, basing designs upon extant examples such as George Washington's Mount Vernon or the New England work of such architects as Samuel McIntire. Many of White's wealthy clients were not willing to live in the limited accommodations that a Colonial house would provide. White therefore designed large spreads in the country for wealthy businessmen, six times the area of an 18th-century residence, but by extending different functions into wings, using the site to maximum advantage, and judicious planting, White was able to break up large compositions into separate pavilions as in the James Breece House at Southampton, Long Island (1898-1907), making it appear authentically Colonial.

Another classical style adopted in the United States was the Greek Revival, of which the Roman Revival was an extension. Thomas Jefferson expertly handled the Roman idiom in several Virginia buildings, including the campus of the University of Virginia. There Jefferson's Pantheon-inspired library burned in 1895, and since White admired the architecture of Jefferson, he was considered the architect to rebuild the library and add new buildings to the lawn. Jefferson's architecture then became the precedent for White's New York University in the Bronx (1892-1903), where the library, as the centerpiece of the campus, was based upon Jefferson's library but with delicate Adamesque terra-cotta detailing. White used the same neoclassical revival again in one of his most successful designs, the Bowery Savings Bank (1893-95) where classical detailing ties the exterior porticoes to the internal columns surrounding the banking hall. There the marriage of interior with exterior scale and detail was enhanced by pedimental sculptures by Frederick Macmonnies.

White was a successful proponent of many other idioms, including the Shingle style, Chateauesque and French provincial, Venetian, French and German Renaissance, and mixed variations of these and other styles. He designed funerary mausolea and pedestals for figures carved by his sculptor friends, high-rise and commercial structures, churches and power stations. He was an interior designer, mixing furniture and fittings from a wide variety of sources, since all would have a common denominator in good design of the period from which they came. He designed a yacht, trophies, bookcovers, picture frames, and was, in fact, a total designer. He was, as Cass Gilbert, a pupil and later successful architect, said at the beginning of the 20th century,"... one of the few men of our time who had genius."

—LAWRENCE WODEHOUSE

WILKINS, William.

British. Born in Norwich, England, 31 August 1778. Died in Cambridge, 31 August 1839. Father was William Wilkins, architect. Educated at Norwich Grammar School; graduated, Caius College, Cambridge, 1800; traveling scholarship, 1801; Fellow of Caius, 1803; Master of Perse School, 1804-06. Established practice, Cambridge, 1804; established office in London, 1809. Member, Society of Dilettanti, 1809. Surveyor to East India Company, 1824. Professor of architecture, 1837.

Chronology of Works
All in England unless noted
* Approximate dates
† Work no longer exists

1805-06	Oberton House, Nottinghamshire
1805-09	East India Company College, Haileybury, Hertfordshire
1805-22	Downing College, Cambridge (not completed)
1807-09	Nelson Pillar, Dublin, Ireland†
1808-09	Lower Assembly Rooms, Bath†
1808*-09	The Grange, Hampshire
1810*-11*	Pentillie Castle, Cornwall (later additions with William Wilkins, Sr.)
1814-17	Nelson Column, Great Yarmouth, Norfolk
1814-19	Dalmeny House, West Lothian, Scotland
1815-18	Tregothnan, Cornwall
1817-19	Freemasons' Hall, Bath
1820-22	Dunmore Park, Stirlingshire†
1820-24	New Norfolk County Jail and Shire House
1821-22	St. Paul's Church, Nottingham†
1821-27	New Court, Trinity College, Cambridge
1822-26	New Quadrangle, Corpus Christi College, Cambridge

William Wilkins: University College London (formerly London University), London, England, 1827-28

1822-26	United University Club, London (with J. P. Gandy-Deering)†
1823-28	New Buildings and Screen, King's College, Cambridge
1825-26	Theater Royal, Norwich†
1826-28	St. George's Hospital, London
1827-30	Yorkshire Philosophical Society Museum (York Museum)
1827-28	University College London (with J. P. Gandy-Deering; formerly London University), London
1832-38	National Gallery and Royal Academy, London

Publications

BOOKS BY WILKINS

The Antiquities of Magna Graecia. Cambridge, England, and London, 1807.
The Civil Architecture of Vitruvius. London, 1813.
Atheniensia, or Remarks on the Topography and Buildings in Athens., London, 1816.
Report on the State of Repair of Sherborne Church. Sherborne, England, 1828.
A Letter to Lord Viscount Goderich on the Patronage of the Arts by the English Government. London, 1832.
An Apology for the Designs of the Houses of Parliament Marked Phil-Archimendes. London, 1836.
Prolusiones Architeconicae; or, Essays on Subjects Connected with Greek and Roman Architecture. London, 1837.

BOOKS ABOUT WILKINS

CROOK, J. MORDAUNT: *Haileybury and the Greek Revival: The Architecture of William Wilkins.* Hoddesdon, England, 1964.
CROOK, J. MORDAUNT: *The Greek Revival.* London, 1972.
LISCOMBE, R. WINDSOR: *William Wilkins 1778-1839.* London, 1980.
SERVICE, ALASTAIR: *The Architects of London.* London, 1979.

ARTICLES ABOUT WILKINS

CROOK, J. MORDAUNT: "Grange Park Transformed." In COLVIN, HOWARD M. and HARRIS, JOHN (eds.): *The Country Seat.* London, 1970.
LITTLE, BRYAN: "Cambridge and the Campus." *Virginia Magazine of History and Biography* 74 (1971): 190-201.
MARTIN, GREGORY: "Wilkins and the National Gallery." *Burlington Magazine* 113 (1971): 318-329.
WALKLEY, GAVIN: "William Wilkins." *Country Life* 30 (December 1939).

*

William Wilkins was, along with Robert Smirke, the principal advocate of the Greek Revival among British architects at the opening of the 19th century. Son of a self-taught architect who also became proprietor of a number of theaters, Wilkins was trained in architecture by his father, William Wilkins (1751-1815), while studying mathematics at Cambridge, where he became a fellow of his college. In 1801-4 a travel scholarship enabled him to visit Greece and Turkey as well as Italy; the fruits of his thorough study of Greek architecture appeared in *Magna Graecia* (1807) which established him as an authority, and in subsequent books. Wilkins had already commenced architectural practice immediately upon his return to Cambridge in 1804. There, with the help of Henry Hope, he promptly won the first significant victory for the Greek Revival, displacing James Wyatt, the leading architect of the day, in a struggle for designing a new college, Downing. At the same time, he wrested the commission for a new East India College at Haileybury from the East India Company's surveyor, Henry Holland, with a campus design similar to his Downing College.

In these works, as R. Windsor Liscombe has pointed out, Wilkins took major Athenian monuments and adapted their scale and function to contemporary needs, giving the purified orders their proper dominance. His growing reputation brought him further commissions, most notably one from Henry Drummond "to show the country a real portico" at Grange Park, Hampshire. Drummond's enthusiasm for recreating Arcadia in the Itchen Valley enabled Wilkins to transform the old house into a domestic version of the Athenian Theseion, with a deep six-columned Doric portico, standing on a monumental terrace which, C. R. Cockerell declared in 1823, "gives it that which is essential to the effect of Grecian architecture and which no modern imitations possess." Wilkins' variations from his antique models, however, earned Cockerell's criticism.

Even Wilkins' adaptation of archaeological exactitude for modern purposes did not secure him a market for Greek Revival country houses. Five major commissions in the second decade of the century had to be designed in Tudor Gothic. The first, Pentillie, Cornwall, in collaboration with his father, included the two-storied porch (derived from East Barsham Manor, Norfolk) that was to become a hallmark of his Tudor houses. However, Dalmeny, West Lothian (1814), for the earl of Rosebery was more significant: it brought domestic Tudor into the country-house design catalog. Its Tudor detail was relatively authentic; its planning more regular and designed rather for comfort than display—"a new kind of house in Scotland" (J. Macaulay), which was widely and rapidly imitated. But Dalmeny's elevating terrace, general horizontality and regular south front derived from Wilkins' Grecian work.

Domestic Tudor proved acceptable also in the phase of new building undertaken by Cambridge colleges in their expansion of the 1820s. Wilkins was asked for designs for a new court at Trinity in 1821, and at Corpus Christi in 1822; he won an open competition for extensions to King's College in 1823. The screen at King's, carefully assimilated to the great chapel but contrasted in scale and mass, is a brilliant piece of urban architecture, which at once gives privacy to the college without concealing its interior and embellishes and defines the street.

In contrast to his rival Grecian, Smirke, who advanced his career through a connection of patrons, Wilkins throughout his career was a keen competition entrant. For Downing and Haileybury he offered designs against the entrenched architect, but increasingly it became the practice to choose an architect by means of an advertised competition, as at King's College. Wilkins was successful in a number of competitions for memorials of the Napoleonic Wars (Nelson's Pillar, Dublin, 1807; the Army or Waterloo Monument, 1817, to cost £200,000 (not executed); the Nelson Column, Great Yarmouth, 1815), though he lost to Smirke the Dublin Wellington Testimonial. Wilkins also won the competition for a new jail and courts at Norwich in 1820 (castellated Tudor). Defeated for the new Westminster Hospital (Tudor), he won St. George's Hospital, Hyde Park Corner, London, with a well-planned, subtle but inexpensive Greek design (1826), which showed that simplicity need not

bar originality; the portico of the east front employs square pillars instead of columns.

It was again through competition that Wilkins won the commission for his masterpiece, London University (now University College London). This Benthamite institution set forth its claims with great magnificence, with a 10-column portico (taken from the Olympieion at Athens) unique in England, deriving further importance from a high, stepped basement of complex form, and crowned with a dome rising behind it. Adding Roman elements to his Greek, Wilkins achieved a triumph of picturesque architecture, though the wings he designed were not executed.

If this work crowned his career, Wilkins' success in a limited competition for a National Gallery may be said to have discredited him. Wilkins attempted to repeat his London University triumph, employing the same elements (an eight-column portico this time) slightly differently composed. Wilkins there sought to achieve picturesque functionalism: a picture gallery had to be sky-lighted, so the height was necessarily limited, and the upper walls adorned with niches instead of windows. But he was denied the extent of sculpture he sought to relieve the building's severity. Changing taste was demanding a richer treatment, and critics immediately attacked it savagely, and have done so frequently since.

An architect of distinction who missed the first rank, Wilkins was fortunate in that he flourished at a period when public buildings were newly in demand, a function for which his preferred style was well suited. His considerable skill in planning met the needs of private as well as public clients. Always scholarly, his designs were more effective in the parts than in the whole. His weakness in large-scale handling of the increasingly rich forms sought in the 1830s was shown even more devastatingly in his Houses of Parliament competition entry (1835) than in the National Gallery.

—M. H. PORT

WILLIAM of SENS.

French. From Sens, France. Died on 11 August 1180, in France. Trained as a mason. Worked as supervisor at Canterbury Cathedral, 1174-77.

Chronology of Works

1174-77 Cathedral, Canterbury (choir remodeling)

Publications

BOOKS ABOUT WILLIAM of SENS

BOASE, T. S. R.: *English Art, 1100-1216.* Oxford, 1953.
WEBB, GEOFFREY: *Architecture in Britain: The Middle Ages.* 2nd ed. Harmondsworth, England, 1965.

ARTICLES ABOUT WILLIAM of SENS

BONY, JEAN: "French Influences on the Origins of English Gothic Architecture." *Journal of the Warburg and Courtauld Institutes* 12 (1949): 1-15.
CHARTRAIRE, ETIENNE: "Sens and Canterbury." In *The Cathedral of Sens.* Paris, (1921) 1926.
DRAPER, PETER: "William of Sens and the Original Design of the Choir Termination of Canterbury Cathedral." *Journal of the Society of Architectural Historians* 42 (October 1983): 238-248.

GERVASE OF CANTERBURY: "Tractatus de combustione et reparatione Cantuariensis ecclesiae." Vol. 1: 3-29 in STUBBS, WILLIAM (ed.): *The Historical Works of Gervase of Canterbury*. London, 1879.

*

William of Sens traditionally has been credited with introducing the French style of Gothic architecture into England after being selected as architect at the Cathedral Church of Canterbury following a fire there in September 1174. Nikolaus Pevsner went so far as to claim that William of Sens "initiated [at Canterbury] a . . . revolution by importing the Early Gothic style of the Île-de-France [into England]."

This is something of an oversimplification. Most of William's "special features" at Canterbury—use of paired columns supporting the main arcade arches in the choir, use of dark Purbeck marble to contrast with light-colored Caen limestone, and use of six-part vaults—were all known in England before 1174. However, it has recently been persuasively demonstrated that William employed germinal flying buttresses in part of his work at Canterbury, the earliest known use of this structural feature in England.

What William did do was to combine these features in a way that was then novel in Britain in that he sought to emphasize height as well as length and breadth in his work. And, in Pevsner's words, ". . . it was the enormous prestige of Canterbury that ensured the swift spread of the new style throughout the country."

William of Sens' use of Caen stone shows his familiarity with native French building materials, and his work at Canterbury reveals that he was conversant with recent architectural trends in Northern France. The claim that his work at Canterbury reflected work at the Cathedral of Saint-Etienne at Sens in France does not hold up. William may have been born in Sens, or may have worked there as a young man, but his architectural antecedents at Canterbury reflect more recent developments in other areas. The traditional view is that William had worked in the region now comprising the Départments du Nord and du Pas-de-Calais. Yet more recently it has been proposed that he may have been more familiar with buildings in the Paris-Mantes-Provins area.

William's activities at Canterbury, the only building project with which he can be associated, was documented in an account of the fire and subsequent reconstruction of the cathedral by a monk at the abbey, one Gervase who died at Canterbury in 1210. While Gervase's account is one of the most detailed, building-season-by-building-season accounts of a construction program surviving from the Middle Ages, it is also significant for its larger implications for the way Gothic architects were selected and what their duties and limitations were.

William of Sens was selected by the monks of Canterbury from a number of candidates interviewed for the job, in part due to his "good reputation," meaning that his work must have been known by his new clients. William at first withheld from the monks the extent of the work required, waiting until they were emotionally better able to commit themselves to the virtual total reconstruction of the choir of their church. William began preparations of "all things needful for the work, either of himself or by the agency of others," suggesting that certain tasks were subcontracted. He arranged for stone to be shipped from France, and "constructed ingenious machines for loading and unloading ships, and for drawing [i.e., carting] cement and stones. He delivered molds [i.e., templates] for shaping the stones to the sculptors who were assembled, and diligently prepared other things of the same kind."

William participated actively in the work until 13 September 1178, when scaffolding on which he was standing collapsed, seriously injuring him in a 50-foot fall. For the remainder of the building season of 1178 William directed the work from his sickbed, having put the monk who was overseer of the masons in charge (and in the process engendering envy of other monks). That William could direct construction without being able to climb to the upper portions of the building means either that all the stones had been cut to size for assembly or that templates had been cut before his accident. It also implies that there may have been drawings of the work remaining to be completed before winter set in, although it is believed that architectural drawings came into general use in Gothic architecture only about half a century later.

When winter came, William's condition had not improved, and he "gave up the work, and crossing the sea, returned to his home in France." Nothing more was ever heard of him. He was succeeded at Canterbury by a different architect, an Englishman also named William, who completed the work on the choir.

—CARL F. BARNES, JR.

WILLIAMS, Owen.

British. Born in Tottenham, London, England, 1890. Died 23 May 1969. Married Gladys Tustian (died in 1947), 1915; two children. Married Doreen Baker, 1947; two children. Studied at University of London, B.S., 1911; apprentice, Electric Tramways Company, London, 1905-11. Worked as architect/engineer for the Trussed Concrete Company (Truscon), London, 1911-12; chief airplane designer, Wells Aviation Ltd., London, 1913; private practice as architect/civil engineer, London, 1919-39; consulting engineer to the British Empire Exhibition, London, 1922-24; partnership with T. S. Vandy, London, 1939-69; consulting engineer for motorway construction to the Ministry of Transport, London, 1945-69. Knight Commander, Order of the British Empire, 1924.

Chronology of Works
All in England unless noted

1914-18	Concrete ships
1921-24	British Empire Exhibition, Wembley, London
1925-30	Montrose Bridge, Scotland
1930	Cumberland Garage, near Marble Arch, London
1932	Boots Factory, Beeston, Nottingham
1931-32	Daily Express Building, London (consulting engineer with Ellis and Clarke)
1933	Cement factory, Thurrock, Essex
1933-35	Pioneer Health Center, Peckham, London
1934	Empire Swimming Pool and Sports Arena, Wembley, London
1937	Synagogue, Dollis Hill, London
1937	Daily Express Building, Glasgow (consulting engineer)
1939	Daily Express Building, Manchester (consulting engineer with Ellis and Clarke)
1939-45	Concrete ships
1945	Motorway design for the United Kingdom Ministry of Design (consulting engineer; stage I completed 1959; stage II completed 1967)
1968	Midland Link Motorways

Owen Williams: Daily Express Building, London, England, 1931-32

Publications

BOOKS BY WILLIAMS

The Philosophy of Masonry Arches. London, 1927.
The Design and Construction of the M1. With O. T. Williams.
London, 1961.

BOOKS ABOUT WILLIAMS

COTTAM, DAVID: *Sir Owen Williams, 1890-1969*. London,
1987.

ARTICLES ABOUT WILLIAMS

"BOAC Headquarters." *Builder* (4 November 1955).
"The Pioneer Health Centre, St. Mary's Road, Peckham, London." *Architectural Record* 77, No. 6 (1935): 437-444.
ROSENBERG, STEPHEN; CHALK, WARREN; and MULLIN, STEPHEN: "Sir Owen Williams." *Architectural Design* 39 (July 1969).
SHARP, DENNIS: "Utopian Engineering: Sir Owen Williams' 'New Architecture'." *Architecture and Urbanism* 3 (1985): 33-46.

*

Owen Williams was a distinguished British engineer. He approached construction with a functionalist attitude and a knowledge of concrete construction; in the 1930s these interests coincided with those of architects, and Williams built a series of major buildings that were regarded as being at the forefront of architectural development.

Williams worked as an engineer for the Trussed Concrete Steel Company and for the Indented Bar and Concrete Engineering Company, two American firms that were promoting the use of reinforced concrete in English building. During World War I he worked on the construction of reinforced-concrete ships, and until the 1920s there was no evidence of interest in architecture, or in design except in functional terms.

During the period 1921-24, with Maxwell Ayrton as architect in charge, Williams was involved in the construction of the British Empire Exhibition at Wembley. It was a great responsibility for a young man, and he was probably brought in because of his knowledge of concrete. The buildings were large and undoubtedly helped to develop the concrete industry, but architecturally they were disappointing, with arches and rusticated joints introduced in an attempt to give concrete the appearance of stone. This work was followed by a series of concrete bridges in Scotland, mostly in collaboration with Ayrton; however, the most dramatic one Williams did on his own, a 216-foot-span reinforced-concrete suspension bridge over the River Esk at Montrose.

From 1929-30 Williams was involved in the design of the Dorchester Hotel in London's Park Lane, but the design was plagued by arguments as to the propriety of having an engineer, and not an architect, in charge of such a building on a prominent site. The original architect wanted a Lutyenesque design and was ousted by Williams; however, when construction had reached first-floor level, there was concern about the functionalist concrete building that was arising, and the architect Curtis Green was appointed. Williams resigned, but the form was set, and all Green could do was to change the shape of the windows and add decoration.

The Boots Buildings at Beeston (1930-32) near Nottingham, are Williams' masterpieces. Straightforward, elegant, unhampered by architectural irrelevancies, they remain important pioneer buildings of the Modern Movement. One can only guess what Williams himself made of the architects who so admired them, seeing the stark beauty of a brave new world in the buildings that Williams claimed as functionalist.

The Daily Express Building (1931) built in London's Fleet Street gave Williams the chance that had eluded him at the Dorchester, that of seeing a design through to completion. The original architects had proposed a conventional short-span steel structure, which made the placing of machines difficult; Williams swept their design aside and marginalized the architects, proposing a reinforced-concrete frame with larger spans, which appealed to the newspaper proprietors on practical grounds. But the drama of the building is the cladding—London's first glass box.

Pilkington had introduced "Vitrolite," an opaque glass, and the shiny black Vitrolite cladding with thin metal jointing produced a sensation at the time, and has not suffered the weathering problems of other new materials. The *Daily Express owners* were so delighted that they commissioned Williams to design two further buildings for them, without architects. Both of these subsequent buildings were clad in black Vitrolite. The Manchester building is superior to Fleet Street, with the Vitrolite used to clad and to emphasize a regular frame. At Glasgow the building is a simple and elegant facade.

Williams' connection with the British Empire Exhibition at Wembley made him an obvious choice to design the Empire Pool, built in the old exhibition grounds in 1933-34. Without Ayrton to impose a traditional architecture, Williams created a dramatic structure. The pool is 200 feet by 60 feet and 4,000 spectators can be seated around it. Reinforced-concrete portals span 236 feet 6 inches, and each has an enormous concrete fin in the outside of the building as a counterbalance.

The Peckham Health Centre (1933-35) combined a radical social program with Williams' radical building techniques. The promoters were doctors, and the intention was to combine recreation, sport, health and research into a building that people would enjoy using. Planned around a swimming pool, the building is entirely reinforced concrete and glass, with eight-foot cantilevers along the long sides terminating in three stories of sliding-folding doors so that the interior could be thrown open to the outside, in accordance with the idealistic health concepts of the promoters.

During World War II, as in World War I, Williams worked on the design and construction of reinforced-concrete ships; several of these were built, ranging in size up to the 2,500-ton *Lady Kathleen.* At the end of the war he designed prefabricated houses in concrete and in aluminum, his only excursion into that material. None of the house designs went into production.

At the end of the 1940s Williams' firm was appointed to design the first British motorway. This led to growth of the firm, acquisition of partners, and a shift away from architecture to civil engineering. The London-to-Birmingham M1 was built in 1951-59; the heavily stylized bridges were severely criticized, and the next length was built with much simpler bridges. Williams' last motorway commission, ''Spaghetti junction'' to the north of Birmingham, was not finished until after his death.

Williams' postwar buildings do not have the impact of his prewar structures. The best is the British Airways maintenance hangar at Heathrow, with a 336-foot span in reinforced concrete, balanced by an office building acting in the same way as the concrete fins at the Empire Pool.

—JOHN WINTER

John Wood the Younger: Royal Crescent, Bath, England, 1767-75

WOOD FAMILY.

WOOD, John (the Elder).
British. Born in Bath, England, August 1704. Died on 23 May 1754. Father was George Wood, builder; son was the architect John Wood. Educated at Blue Coat School, Bath. Worked independently, London and Yorkshire, 1725-27; worked independently, Bath, from 1727.

WOOD, John (the Younger).
British. Born in Bath, England 1728. Died in Batheaston, 16 June 1781. Father was the architect John Wood, with whom he trained. Worked in Liverpool; worked independently, Bath, 1754; magistrate, Somerset. Member, Ugly Face Clubbe, Liverpool, 1751.

Chronology of Works
All in England
* *Approximate dates*
† *Work no longer exists*

John Wood the Elder:

1722-24	Bramham Park Gardens, Yorkshire
1727-28	Ralph Allen House, Lilliput Alley, Bath (enlargement) [attributed]
1727-30	St. John's Hospital, Chapel Courthouse and Chandos Buildings, Bath
1728	Tiberton Court, Herefordshire†
1728-30	Lindsey's (later Wiltshire's) Assembly Rooms, Bath†
1729-36	Houses on Wood Street, John Street and Old King Street, Bath
1729-36	Queen Square, Bath
1732-34	St. Mary's Chapel, Bath†
1734	Belcombe Court, near Bradford-on-Avon, Wiltshire
1734-52	Llandeff Cathedral, Glamorganshire, Wales†
1735-48	Prior Park, near Bath
1738	Lilliput Castle, Lansdown, near Bath
1738-42	General (now Royal Mineral Water) Hospital, Bath
1740	North and South Parades, with Pierrepont and Duke Streets, Bath
1741-43	Exchange and Market, Corn Street, Bristol
1746	The Spa, Bathford, Somerset†
1748-49	Titanbarrow Logia (now Whitehaven), Kingsdown Exchange (now Town Hall), Liverpool
1750ff.*	Gay Street, Bath
1754*	The Circus, Bath (completed by John Wood the Younger)

John Wood the Younger:

1754*	The Circus, Bath (completion of work begun by John Wood the Elder)
1755-57	Buckland House, Berkshire
1760-61	Bitton Church, Gloucestershire
1766	Standlynch (now Trafalgar) House, Wiltshire (wings only)
1767*	Brock Street, Bath
1767-71	The Infirmary, Salisbury, Wiltshire
1767-75	Royal Crescent, Bath
1769-71	New Assembly Rooms, Bath
1770*	Rivers Street, Bath
1772-76	Alfred Street, Bennett Street and Russell Street, Bath [attributed]

1773*	Margaret Chapel, Brock Street, Bath
1773-74	Tregenna Castle, near St. Ives, Cornwall
1773-77	Hot Bath (now the Old Royal Baths), Bath
1779	Hardenhuish Church, Wiltshire (date given is that of consecration)
1780*	Catherine Place, Bath
before 1781	Almshouses, St. Ives, Cornwall

Publications

BOOKS BY JOHN WOOD THE ELDER

The Origin of Building, or the Plagiarism of the Heathens Detected. 1741.
A Description of the Exchange of Bristol. 1745.
Choir Gaure, Vulgarly Called Stonehenge, on Salisbury Plain, Described, Restored, and Explained. Oxford, 1747.
An Essay towards a Description of Bath. 2nd ed., 1749. Reprint, Bath, 1969.
Dissertation Upon the Orders of Columns and their Appendages. 1750.

BOOKS BY JOHN WOOD THE YOUNGER

A Series of Plans for Cottages of Habitations of the Labourer. 1781. 3rd ed., 1806. Reprint, Farnborough, England, 1972.

BOOKS ABOUT THE WOODS

DAKERS, W. S.: *John Wood and his Times.* Pamphlet. Bath, 1954.
GREEN, MOWBRAY A.: *The Eighteenth Century Architecture of Bath.* Bath, 1904.
ISON, WALTER: *The Georgian Buildings of Bath.* London, 1948.
MOWL, TIM, and EARNSHAW, BRIAN: *John Wood—Architect of Obsession.* Bath, 1988.
SUMMERSON, JOHN: *Architecture in Britain: 1530-1830.* 6th ed., revised. Harmondsworth, England, 1977.

ARTICLES ABOUT THE WOODS

BROWNELL, CHARLES E.: "John Wood the Elder and John Wood the Younger: Architects of Bath." Ph.D. thesis. Columbia University, New York, 1976.
COATES, A. BARBARA: "The Two John Woods." Thesis. Royal Institute of British Architects, London, 1946.
HUSSEY, CHRISTOPHER: "No. 9, The Circus, Bath." *Country Life* 102 (1947): 978-981, 1026-1029.
ISON, WALTER: "John Wood the Elder, of Bath." *Journal of the Royal Institute of British Architects* 61 (July 1954): 367-369.
LITTLE, BRYAN: "Wood of Bath." *Architect and Building News* 205 (1954): 499-500.
"Some Original Drawings by John Wood." *Architect and Building News* (4 November 1927).
STROUD, DOROTHY: "The Assembly Rooms, Bath: Their History, Restoration, and Re-opening." *Country Life* 84 (1938): 402-406.
SUMMERSON, JOHN: "John Wood and the English Town-Planning Tradition." In *Heavenly Mansions and Other Essays on Architecture.* London, 1949.
WITHERS, MARGARET: "No. 1 Royal Crescent." *Architect and Building News* 6, No. 7 (1970): 74-77.

WITTKOWER, RUDOLF: "Federigo Zuccari and John Wood of Bath." *Journal of the Warburg and Courtauld Institutes* 5 (1943): 220-222.

*

It was once thought that John Wood the Elder came from Yorkshire, where he certainly worked for a time in his early years. It is now known that he was born in Bath in 1704, the son of a local builder. He attended Bath's Blue Coat Charity School, but as an architect he was essentially self-taught. He was apprenticed to a joiner, perhaps in London. (In 1721 he leased some land in London from the second earl of Oxford, and may have built a house on it.) In 1724 and 1725 he was employed in London, and became familiar with the main elements of Palladian design, as these were displayed in a scheme for one side of Grosvenor Square. In those years Wood was also at Bramham near Tadcaster in Yorkshire, designing a Palladian stable block for a wealthy lawyer, the first Lord Bingley.

In 1725 Wood worked out his scheme for the transformation of Bath, which was necessitated by a rising demand for lodgings, resulting from Bath's immense popularity as a resort. Wood planned a sequence, in three different directions from the ancient center of the city, and on land belonging to various owners, of a square, a grand circus, and an "Imperial Gymnasium," the latter to be used for "medicinal exercises." The gymnasium was never built, however, its plans being replaced by a crescent of lodging houses. At the end of 1725, Wood presented his scheme to one of the landowners concerned. A crucial factor, which encouraged Wood in his projects for Bath, was the decision to make the Avon River navigable from Bristol to Bath, which meant that building materials to supplement the locally available stone could conveniently be transported to Bath.

Queen Square, whose northern side comprises the elder Wood's best Palladian terrace in Bath, was begun in 1727 and finished by 1737. The northern side, inspired by the Palladian block on Grosvenor Square, is given the appearance of a unified palace, even though it is a row of separate houses. Wood himself lived in the middle house, below the blank pediment. Each side of the square, laid out on a sloping site, was individually designed. St. Mary's Chapel was built near one of its corners.

Various houses were built to Wood's designs in the area of the Hospital of St. John the Baptist in Bath. Among his public buildings in Bath are Dame Lindsey's Assembly Rooms and the Royal Mineral Water Hospital. The latter was begun in 1738, on a site originally intended for a theater. Wood's works on the outskirts of Bath included a channel in the Avon to improve navigation, and several buildings for Ralph Allen, the local quarry owner. He designed the great mansion of Prior Park for Allen, and cottages for his quarrymen and river workers. (Wood also designed Allen's town house near the center of the city.) Outside the city Wood designed medium-sized houses at Bathford and near Bradford-on-Avon. He also built a house for a rich clothier at Chippenham, the facade of which has been reerected in recent years on one end of a terrace in Bath.

In other cities, Wood the Elder's buildings include the Exchange at Bristol and the Exchange at Liverpool, which is now the Town Hall. Wood reconstructed part of Llandaff Cathedral, just outside Cardiff, Wales, in a Palladian style. He also did the woodwork for an apse behind the Communion Table of the church of Tyberton in Herefordshire.

John Wood the Elder died in Bath, in 1754, at the age of 49. He had already designed some houses around the Circus, but these were actually built by his son.

John Wood the Younger was born in Bath in 1727-28, and trained with his father. In 1749 the younger Wood was at Liverpool supervising work on the Exchange designed by his father. Soon after the elder Wood's death in 1754, John Wood the Younger completed the Circus. The imposing facades of its houses display a very ornate Roman Doric order on the ground floor. In the metopes there is a wide range of carvings, such as faces, masonic signs, heraldry and other devices based on 17th-century emblems. Ionic pairs of half columns adorn the first floor, while the top story uses the Corinthian order. This combined use of the three orders had some Roman and Renaissance precedents, notably in the Colosseum at Rome.

From the Circus, Brock Street leads to the Royal Crescent (1767-75), one of the younger Wood's masterpieces. The ground floor is simple, and has plain doorways. The Crescent's main effect lies in the plain sweep along its entire length of the Ionic three-quarter columns, which are continued through the height of two stories. The middle section is marked by two closely spaced pairs of columns, and by a middle window larger than the others.

Houses attributed to the younger Wood in other streets in that part of Bath, such as Rivers Street, are a rather pedestrian continuation of the Palladian tradition.

Wood also designed a number of public buildings at Bath. The fine Upper Assembly Rooms (1769-71) were gutted by bombing in 1942, but they were recently restored in Wood's idiom. The Hot Bath for the City Corporation (1772-73) was relatively simple, and had Doric porticos. He departed from the neoclassical style in his design of the Margaret Chapel, off Brock Street, which was a mainly Gothic building, destroyed by bombing in World War II.

Wood also used Gothic for the mansion of Tregenna Castle at St. Ive's in western Cornwall. He designed the brick Infirmary at Salisbury (1767-71), and added wings to the country mansion of Standlynch, near Salisbury. This estate later passed to members of the Nelson family, and is now called Trafalgar House. The compact little classical church of Hardenhuish (pronounced Harnish) near Chippenham was also by Wood, and was finished in 1779.

Wood was a Somerset magistrate for several years and died in 1781 at Batheston, near Bath, at the age of 53.

—BRYAN LITTLE

WREN, Christopher.

British. Born at East Knoyle, Wiltshire, England, 20 October 1632. Died in London, 25 February 1723. Father was Rev. Christopher Wren; married Faith Coghill; married Jane Fitzwilliam; sons were Gilbert, Christopher, William; daughter was Jane. Educated at Westminster School, 1645; B.A., Wadham College, Oxford, 1650; M.A., Oxford, 1653; Fellow of All Souls, 1654; D.C.L., Oxford, 1661. Professor of Astronomy, Gresham College, London, 1657; Savilian Professor of Astronomy, Oxford, 1661; surveyor-general of the King's Works, London, 1669; surveyor, Greenwich Palace, 1696; commissioner for Building Fifty New Churches, London. Member, Royal Society; president, Royal Society, 1681-3; member, Council of the Hudson's Bay Company.

Chronology of Works
All in England
† Work no longer exists

1663-65	Pembroke College Chapel, Cambridge
1664-69	Sheldonian Theatre, Oxford
1668-72	Emmanuel College Chapel and Gallery, Cambridge
1669-71	Custom House, London†
1670-73	Temple Bar, London (moved to Theobalds, Hertfordshire) [attributed]
1670-74	St. Mary Aldermanbury, London
1670-77	St. Mildred, Poultry, London†
1670-79	St. Olave, Old Jewry, London (tower extant)†
1670-81	St. Benet Fink, London†
1670-81	St. Lawrence Jewry, London
1670-85	St. Dionis Backchurch, London†
1670-87	St. Michael, Wood Street, London†
1670-95	St. Mary-at-Hill, London
1670-1703	St. Bride, Fleet Street, London
1670-1707	St. Edmund, Lombard Street, London
1671-74	Williamson Building, Queen's College, Oxford
1671-76	The Monument, London
1671-78	St. Nicholas, Cole Abbey, London
1671-79	St. George Botolph Lane, London†
1671-80	St. Mary-le-Bow, London
1671-1706	St. Magnus, London
1672-17	St. Stephen Walbrook, London
1674-77	St. Stephen, Coleman Street, London†
1674-81	St. Bartholomew, Exchange, London†
1675-76	Royal Observatory, Greenwich, London
1675-1710	St. Paul's Cathedral, London
1676-81	St. James, Piccadilly, London
1676-84	Library, Trinity College, Cambridge
1676-87	St. Michael, Queenhythe, London†
1676-1712	St. Michael Bassishaw, London†
1676-1717	St. James Garlickhythe, London
1677-82	All Hallows the Great, Thames Street, London†
1677-84	All Hallows, Watling Street, London†
1677-85	St. Benet, Paul's Wharf, London
1677-86	St. Martin Ludgate, London
1677-86	St. Swithin, Cannon Street, London†
1677-1704	Christ Church, Newgate Street, London (tower extant)†
1678-87	St. Antholin, Budge Row, London†
1679-1703	St. Mary Aldermary, London
1680-82	St. Clement Danes, London
1680-96	St. Augustine, Watling Street, London (tower extant)†
1681-82	Tom Tower, Christ Church, Oxford
1681-86	St. Matthew, Friday Street, London†
1681-87	St. Benet, Gracechurch Street, London†
1681-87	St. Mary Abchurch, London
1681-87	St. Mildred, Bread Street, London†
1682-89	St. Alban, Wood Street, London (tower extant)†
1682-91	Royal Hospital, Chelsea, London
1683-85	Winchester Palace, Hampshire†
1683-87	St. Clement, Eastcheap, London
1683-87	St. Mary Magdalene, Fish Street, London†
1684-1702	St. Margaret Pattens, London
1684-1704	St. Andrew, Holborn, London
1684-1714	St. Michael, Crooked Lane, London†
1685-88	Whitehall Palace, London (Privy Garden Range and Roman Catholic Chapel)†
1685-94	St. Andrew, Wardrobe, London

Christopher Wren: St. Paul's Cathedral, London, England, 1675-1710

Christopher Wren: Royal Hospital, Greenwich, London, England, 1682-91

1686-94	All Hallows, Lombard Street, London (tower extant; rebuilt at Twickenham, Middlesex)
1686-94	St. Mary Somerset, London (tower extant)†
1686-99	St. Margaret Lothbury, London
1686-1717	St. Michael Royal, London
1687-90	Tring Manor, Hertfordshire (recased)†
1688-93	Whitehall Palace, London (Queen's Apartments)†
1689-96	Kensington Palace, London
1689-1700	Hampton Court Palace, Middlesex
1695-1702	St.-Dunstan-in-the-East, London (tower)
1695-1712	St. Vedast, Foster Lane, London
1696-1716	Royal Naval Hospital, Greenwich, London
1699-1702	Winslow Hall, Buckinghamshire

Publications

BOOKS ABOUT WREN

BEARD, GEOFFREY W.: *The Work of Christopher Wren*. London, 1987.

BENNETT, J. A.: *The Mathematical Science of Christopher Wren*. Cambridge and New York, 1982.

BOLTON, ARTHUR T. (ed.): *The Wren Society*. 20 vols. London, 1924-43.

BRIGGS, M. S.: *Wren the Incomparable*. London, 1953.

DEAN, C. G. T.: *The Royal Hospital, Chelsea*. London, 1950.

DOWNES, KERRY: *The Architecture of Wren*. 2nd rev. ed. Reading, Engalnd, 1988.

DOWNES, KERRY: *Christopher Wren*. London, 1971.

ELMES, JAMES: *Memoirs of the Life and Works of Sir Christopher Wren*. London, 1823.

FÜRST, VIKTOR: *The Architecture of Sir Christopher Wren*. London, 1956.

HUTCHINSON, H. F.: *Sir Christopher Wren: A Biography*. New York and London, 1976.

LANG, JANE: *Rebuilding St. Paul's after the Great Fire of London*. 1956.

LINDSAY, JOHN: *Wren, His Work and Times*. London, 1951.

LITTLE, BRYAN: *Sir Christopher Wren: A Historical Biography*. London, 1975.

LOFTIE, W. J.: *Inigo Jones and Wren: or the Rise and Decline of Modern Architecture in England*. London, 1893.

MILMAN, L.: *Sir Christopher Wren*. London, 1908.

MINNS, E. H., and WEBB, M.: *Sir Christopher Wren*. London, 1923.

PEVSNER, N.: *Christopher Wren 1632-1723*. New York, 1960.

PHILLIMORE, L.: *Sir Christopher Wren, His Family and His Times*. London and New York, 1881.

POLEY, ARTHUR F. E.: *St. Paul's Cathedral, London, Measured, Drawn and Described*. 2nd ed. London, 1932.

REDDAWAY, T. F.: *The Rebuilding of London after the Great Fire*. 1940.

RYKWERT, JOSEPH: *The First Moderns: The Architects of the Eighteenth Century*. 1980.

SEKLER, E. F.: *Wren and His Place in European Architecture*. London, 1956.

SERVICE, ALASTAIR: *The Architects of London*. London, 1979.

STRATTON, A. J.: *The Life, Work, and Influence of Sir Christopher Wren*. Liverpool, 1897.

SUMMERSON, JOHN: *Sir Christopher Wren*. London, 1953.

WEAVER, L.: *Sir Christopher Wren, Scientist, Scholar and Architect*. London, 1923.

WEBB, G.: *Wren*. London, 1937.

WHINNEY, MARGARET: *Christopher Wren*. London, 1971.

WHITAKER-WILSON, C.: *Sir Christopher Wren: His Life and Times*. London and New York, 1932.

WREN, CHRISTOPHER, JR.: *Parentalia, or Memoirs of the Family of Wrens*. London, 1750; as *Life and works of Sir Christopher Wren from the Parentalia, or Memoirs by His Son Christopher,* edited by Ernest J. Enthoven. London and New York, 1903.

Wren Memorial Volume. London, Royal Institute of British Architects, 1923.

ARTICLES ABOUT WREN

BENNETT, J. A.: "A Study of Parentalia, with Two Unpublished Letters of Sir Christopher Wren." *Annals of Science* 30 (1973).

BENNETT, J. A.: "Christopher Wren: Astronomy, Architecture and the Mathematical Sciences." *Journal for the History of Astronomy* 6, Part 3 (1975).

BENNETT, J. A.: "Christopher Wren: The Natural Causes of Beauty." *Architectural History* 15 (1972): 5-22.

COLVIN, H. M.: "Roger North and Sir Christopher Wren." *Architectural Review* (October 1951).

DOWNES, KERRY: "Wren and Whitehall in 1664." *Burlington Magazine* (February 1971).

HAMILTON, S. B.: "The Place of Sir Christopher Wren in the History of Structural Engineering." *Newcomen Society's Transactions* 14 (1933).

HARVEY, P. D.: "A Signed Plan by Sir Christopher Wren." *British Museum Quarterly* 25 (1963).

HUXLEY, G. H.: "The Geometrical Work of Sir Christopher Wren." *Scripta Mathematica* 25 (1960).

JONES, H. W.: "Sir Christopher Wren and Natural Philosophy." *Notes and Records of the Royal Society* 13 (1958).

KIMBALL, FISKE: "Wren: Some of His Sources." *Architectural Review* 55 (1924).

LAW, W. T.: "Notes on the Wren Pedigree." *Genealogist* New Series 6, (1889): 168-171.

SCHLESS, N. H.: "Peter Harrison, the Touro Synagogue, and the Wren City Church." *Winterthur Portfolio 8* (1973): 187-200.

SOO, LYDIA M.: "Reconstructing Antiquity: Wren and his Circle and the Study of Natural History, Antiquarianism, and Architecture at the Royal Society." Ph.D. dissertation. Princeton University, Princeton, New Jersey, 1989.

SUMMERSON, JOHN: "Drawings of London Churches in the Bute Collection: A Catalogue." *Architectural History* 13 (1970): 30-42.

SUMMERSON, JOHN: "Sir Christopher Wren, P. R. S." *Notes and Records of the Royal Society* 15 (1960).

SUMMERSON, JOHN: "The Mind of Wren." In *Heavenly Mansions and Other Essays on Architecture*. London, 1949.

SUMMERSON, JOHN: "The Penultimate Design for St. Paul's." *Burlington Magazine* 103 (1961): 83-89.

TAFURI, MANFREDO: "*Architettura artificialis*: Claude Perrault, Sir Christopher Wren e il dibatto sul linguaggio architettonico." In *Barocco europeo, barocco italiano, barocco salentino: Atti di Congresso Internazionale sul Barocco.* Lecce, Italy, 1969.

WEBB, GEOFFREY F.: "The Architectural Antecedents of Sir Christopher Wren." *Royal Institute of British Architects Journal* (27 May 1933): 582.

When Christopher Wren began to practice architecture at the age of 30, going on to create the large body of work which has made him famous, he was enjoying a successful career as a scientist. Even at a young age he was recognized for his "marvelous gifts" in mathematics and mechanics, subjects which invigorated his otherwise conservative High Church upbringing and humanist education at Westminster School. As an undergraduate at Wadham College at Oxford, fellow at All Souls, and then professor of astronomy at Gresham College in London, Wren conducted the research in mathematics, astronomy and experimental philosophy which forms his other important legacy to history. In 1660, the year of the Restoration, he played a critical role in the institutionalization of the New Science, joining with a small number of colleagues from Oxford and London to found the first English scientific institution, the Royal Society. The next year, when he returned to Oxford as Savilian Professor of Astronomy, Wren began to take on architectural work, in eight years rising to the height of his new profession to become surveyor general. Since he had completed only three buildings by that time, his appointment probably represented a recognition less of his blossoming talent than of his family's steadfast loyalty to the royalist cause through the Civil War. Nevertheless, it was his exceptional abilities, proven in the rapid succession of designs and completed projects for city churches, St. Paul's Cathedral, royal palaces and other public works, that ensured his success and continuance in that post almost to the end of his long life. At the same time, however, Wren did not cease his scientific activities. He remained an active participant in the Royal Society, serving a term as president, although his scientific contributions became more and more limited as his duties as surveyor increased.

Wren's new career as an architect constituted more of a change in employment than in intellectual orientation. Because of his skills in geometry and mechanics, applicable to technological matters in architecture, he was offered his first commissions—to supervise the construction of the fortification at Tangier, which he declined, and to repair Old St. Paul's Cathedral. In formal and stylistic matters he was self-taught, mastering the rules of classical design primarily by using architectural treatises, his firsthand knowledge being limited to the works of Inigo Jones and the early Baroque buildings in Paris that he observed during his brief trip of 1665-66. Wren studied these sources, however, as a scientist, applying the attitudes, methods and knowledge propagated through the Royal Society's Baconian program of study. As a result he formulated a new approach to architecture that challenged Renaissance conceptions on the basis of 17th-century science. His theory, written from around 1675 as "Tracts on Architecture" and posthumously published in the *Parentalia* (1750), comprises a version of the origin and history of architecture and a definition of beauty that begin to explain the relationship between the new scientific values and the particular use of style, form and structure in his buildings.

In accordance with Francis Bacon's program for the reform of learning, Wren and his colleagues rejected all received knowledge in favor of the direct observation of nature and verification by experiment. Recent discoveries proved that the ancients were fallible; therefore, the moderns had to reject their work and surpass it. In architecture, skepticism and empirical procedure led Wren to reexamine the rules presented by the ancient writer Vitruvius and exemplified in the classical remains. Finding "great Differences" among the forms and measures of the orders, he suggested that they had been "arbitrarily used" by the ancients.

At the same time, the Royal Society provided new architectural evidence that led Wren to question inherited notions of classical architecture. The society's early program involved constructing a Baconian history of nature and the mechanical arts, necessary for making new discoveries and formulating hypotheses, which included the mechanical art of architecture. Building materials and structural systems, such as Wren's roof truss used at the Sheldonian Theater, presented in 1663, were not the only architectural matters considered. Out of an interest in practices used in foreign lands and in past ages, the society became aware of certain material remains, accurately described and drawn in reports and published travel books, which seemed outside the accepted development of architecture. In the New World and the Near and Far East there were primitive dwellings of all kinds, as well as monumental forms of building, including Islamic and Chinese architecture. In the former territories of the Egyptian, Persian and Roman empires there were remains that had classical attributes but clearly constituted other modes of building. The most conspicuously inexplicable evidence was found among the material antiquities of Great Britain, examined by society fellows at firsthand and recorded by John Aubrey in his unpublished *Monumenta Britannica*. Whereas Roman antiquities, including the finds made in London by Wren during the rebuilding after the Great Fire, could be placed within recorded history, primitive megalithic structures, such as the stone circles at Stonehenge, Avebury and other sites known to Wren, were another matter.

Given his scientific training, Wren could not ignore the new evidence proving that the inherited precepts of architecture were neither absolute nor universal. But as in the study of nature, he was confident that the true laws of a phenomenon would ultimately be revealed after gathering and analyzing as large a body of data as possible. In his Tracts, therefore, Wren went back to the origin and early history of architecture in an attempt to give "a larger Idea of the whole Art, beginning with the reasons and progress of it from the most remote Antiquity," that is, to discover what he called "the Grounds of Architecture" or first principles.

In formulating a new account of the origin and history of architecture, Wren could not proceed entirely on the basis of the limited archaeological evidence available at the time, and used two well-known literary sources: Vitruvius and the Bible. This may seem to contradict his avowed skepticism, but in fact it is a reflection of the particular nature of 17th-century science. Although Vitruvius' text was ancient, and therefore suspect, Wren accepted it, not just because it was the only surviving ancient architectural treatise, but because scientific tests proved it to be a reliable record: "*Vitruvius* hath led us the true Way to find the Originals of the Orders." At the same time, he could not ignore, as Renaissance theorists had, the conflicting source of the Bible. Wren was among the scientists of the 17th century who, despite their skepticism, were Christians who accepted the authority of the Bible, often describing how in the search for knowledge there were two books to read: Nature and Scripture, both revealing divine laws. Vitruvius and the Bible were considered equally accurate historical documents of indisputable authority, which Wren conflated and amended to create a single chronological framework that would include all known architecture and reveal first principles.

As a sequel to Vitruvius' account of the original primitive dwelling, made out of natural materials to provide protection from the elements, Wren hypothesized on the origin of the first temple, where, according to Vitruvius, the orders had developed. He rejected, however, Vitruvius' demonstration that the orders were based on the forms and proportions of the human body, and focused instead on his implication that the first column was a tree. "The first Temples were, in all Probability, in the ruder Times, only little *Cellae* to inclose the Idol within . . . in the

southern Climates, a Grove was necessary . . . to shade the Devout. . . .'' Due to their uneven growth and eventual decay, the trees surrounding the cella were later replaced by stone pillars with ornaments that recalled the original "Arbour of spreading Boughs." Wren agreed with Vitruvius that the details of the orders followed not only nature's forms, but also its structural laws, since the pillars supported a roof of wood carpentry that was later exactly replicated in stone. Wren called the first primitive and thick column based on the mature tree the Tyrian or Phoenician order because it was used by workers from Tyre, a city in Phoenicia, to build the Temple of Solomon. Thus, the order had not only an origin in nature but also a divine origin, the design of the Temple of Solomon having been dictated by God. Wren believed that this order was used in other monuments of Biblical antiquity, and later adopted by the Greeks, who refined it into the more slender Doric, Ionic and Corinthian orders.

While the idea of a protoclassical, Solomonic order, reconciling Vitruvian and Biblical authority, was first proposed by the exegetical writer Giovanni Battista Villalpando in his famous 1604 reconstruction of the Temple of Solomon, Wren's order had a new form. He rejected Villalpando's Corinthian order of palm leaves, as well as the 17th-century tradition that the temple had spiral or twisted columns, an idea based on the columns originally located at Old St. Peter's in Rome which since the late Middle Ages were thought to be from the Temple of Solomon. Instead, Wren's rude order may have been influenced by recent discoveries of preclassical remains. He stated that after its origin in the remote past, the Tyrian order was transferred from the Egyptians to the Babylonians, to the Phoenicians (from whom it derived its name), and then to the Greeks. Since the Renaissance, scholars had accepted the Egyptians as the precursors of Greek culture, the diffusion of knowledge taking place through one or more of the other ancient eastern empires. Wren knew monuments of these early civilizations, including Egyptian obelisks and columns and the thick, nonclassical columns at Persepolis, the capital of the Persian Empire. Similar in form were the huge megalithic columns of the stone circles in Britain, which were thought to be built by the Romans using a Tuscan/Ionic order (Inigo Jones, 1655), or by Phoenician colonists (Aylett Sammes, 1676), or even by the Druids, the priests of the ancient Britons or perhaps really Old Testament patriarchs, to replace the groves of trees where they had once worshiped (John Aubrey, *Monumenta Britannica*). Many of these ideas are reflected in Wren's hypothesis of the Tyrian order, which, in turn, could account for the existence of these and other prehistoric monuments.

Wren went on to demonstrate the development of the classical style, from the Tyrian to the Greek and Roman, in his chronology of the monuments of Biblical and early classical antiquity. Although contemporary travelers sometimes claimed to record the remains of several of these buildings, Wren depended primarily on evidence of ancient writers whom he assessed as authentic and reliable. The most important were the Bible and Josephus, recording monuments during Old Testament times, and classical writers, including Pliny and Herodotus, providing the only descriptions of famous monuments of early antiquity, such as the Seven Wonders of the World. Using their diverse evidence, Wren attempted to establish a logical form, layout and structure for the buildings, often making drawn reconstructions. He began with the monuments cited in Genesis: the first city of Enos, Noah's Ark, the Tower of Babel and the pyramids of Egypt. Next he described several Tyrian monuments cited in the Bible: the Temple of Dagon destroyed by Samson, the Sepulcher of Absalom and the Temple of Solomon. These were followed by early classical buildings: the Tyrian tomb of the Etruscan king Porsenna, the Mausoleum of Halicarnassus, using the Doric order, and the Temple of Diana at Ephesus, the first building to use the Ionic. Finally, Wren discussed the "Temple of Peace" (Basilica of Maxentius) and the Temple of Mars Ultor.

Because of the scientific viewpoint of his investigation, Wren's account constitutes the first history of architecture, expressing an understanding of each monument as the product of a particular time and place. This nascent historical consciousness led him to formulate principles of architecture that challenged, but did not completely abandon, the Renaissance ideal of the perfection and timelessness of the classical style. While he proved its eternal validity by demonstrating the natural and divine origin of the Tyrian order, he recognized that the subsequent modifications, resulting in many kinds of classical orders—"not only *Roman* and *Greek,* but *Phoenician, Hebrew,* and *Assyrian*"—were legitimate inventions created by the wisdom, wealth and skill of particular civilizations. While he accepted the Vitruvian tripartite definition of architecture, he altered it using the epistemology of 17th-century science: "Beauty, Firmness, and Convenience, are the Principles; the two first depend upon geometrical Reasons of *Opticks* and *Staticks...*" For structure, Wren attempted to determine principles on the rational basis of statics, proposing true geometrical laws for the form and abutment of arches and vaults. He approached beauty, however, from an empirical rather than rational basis, and thus broke from the classical ideal of absolute beauty, his scientific outlook making it possible for him to recognize the influence of individual perception and cultural norms.

"Beauty is a Harmony of Objects, begetting Pleasure by the Eye," he wrote. For Wren beauty was an optical effect—an appearance, not a reality—that was triggered by two kinds of outside stimuli which he called "causes." The natural causes are geometry, uniformity and proportion, which derive from the quality of the object itself. Wren also noted that "Geometrical Figures are naturally more beautiful than . . . irregular; in this all consent as to a Law of Nature." Whereas the classical definition considered geometry and proportion as real and innate qualities, determined by the rational laws of mathematics, Wren was concerned only with a geometrical appearance, determined by the "geometrical Reasons of *Opticks,*" that is, the empirical laws of perception. In order to ensure the appearance of geometry and proportionality, the architect must be "well skilled in Perspective," making optical adjustments in terms of the building's surroundings and the angle and distance of the principal viewing positions. At the same time, relativism in the perception of beauty was also the result of the customary causes. These were outside influences that disturb the intellect: "Familiarity," "novelty," "particular inclination" and "custom." They "breed a Love to Things not in themselves lovely," causing us to see beauty in objects that have no true qualities of geometrical beauty in them. In this case "Fancy blinds the Judgment," that is, the reason is overruled by the imagination that works without rules or authority. Certain physical aspects of objects are accepted as beautiful, although they are only "Modes and Fashions" that for the moment come to form the "Taste" of a particular individual or society. As a result of the customary causes, there are variations in style and form found in different cultures and eras.

Wren did not mean to eliminate the role of the fancy or imagination, but believed it must be carefully controlled and not left to the individual. Standards of taste had to be established according to the authority of the architect, who, governed by a reason and imagination informed by an understanding of history as well as the first principles of architecture, rejected

the customary causes, and the transcended current fashion to build, as Wren wrote, "for Eternity."

In his own architecture Wren attempted to achieve an appropriate standard of beauty using an empirical approach to design. Because he believed that "the true Test is natural or geometrical Beauty," all of his buildings are characterized by a strong clarity of geometry which is classical in proportion. Wren usually articulated these forms using the classical orders, because for him they constituted a historical form of architecture which, although a product of certain societies, had natural and divine origins and therefore continued to be valid for the present. At the same time, because he recognized that beauty was based on taste and custom, Wren felt free to choose the Gothic style when the project called for it. Based on his study of Gothic cathedrals and speculation on their history, Wren recognized that the "Saracen style"—invented by the Arabs and then brought to Western Europe by the returning Crusaders—was, because it resulted from certain cultural conditions, just as valid as the classical. Because of the priority of natural beauty, however, when Wren completed or made additions to Gothic buildings, he united a series of geometrical, classically proportioned forms to create a Gothic whole. At Tom Tower, the entrance gate at Christ Church College in Oxford (1681-82), Wren created a "Gothic" tower by vertically arranging three classical elements—a cubical stage, another based on an octagonal plan, and finally a dome—and overlaying the whole with Gothic ornament to conform with the older structure. The Warrant Design for St. Paul's (1675), with its Latin-cross plan, high nave, low side aisles, and crossing tower, was also an assemblage of various geometrical and horizontal parts. It was accepted as following the traditional Gothic cathedral form, although it was decorated in the classical style and many of its elements were modeled on classical buildings, including the Basilica of Maxentius for the nave and the Pantheon for the crossing. Not only the Warrant Design, but the entire series of schemes for St. Paul's demonstrate the almost arbitrary nature of Wren's use of historical forms. Wren consciously selected models and motifs from all history, but altered them and combined them to suit the needs of the project without regard to the meaning or formal integrity of the original source. As a result, it is difficult to recognize the Basilica of Maxentius as the source for the plan of St. Mary-le-Bow and the various ancient models used in the development of the design of St. Paul's.

Because of his empirical approach, the geometrical clarity of Wren's architecture is oftentimes a visual effect, created for each of the primary "perspectives" of the building, separately from the formal implications of structure and function, as well as from one another. The final design of St. Paul's (1675-1710) appears as a two-story classical block, articulated by superimposed pilasters and crowned by a hemispherical dome. This was achieved by using a screen wall that hides the Gothic interior—a high nave with low sides—and the Gothic flying buttresses that support the nave vaults. The geometry of the dome was created using three shells, only the hidden, inner brick cone having a structural role. At Trinity College Library at Cambridge (1676-84) the courtyard facade, divided into two equal arcaded stories, does not reveal that the upper reading room is a tall space with clerestory lighting. It is located not at the level of the first-floor entablature but at the level of the imposts, making it necessary to fill the lunettes of the lower arcades. The result of Wren's concern with separate geometrical appearance was often a discontinuity throughout the building as a whole, which deviated from the unity and harmony sought in Renaissance architecture, but was consistent with Wren's empirical approach.

By using the values of 17th-century science to analyze and redefine architecture, Wren undermined the foundations of Renaissance classicism. While he reaffirmed the priority of the classical style by giving it a Biblical as well as natural origin, he also developed a historical consciousness that led him to accept the validity of the changes made to that style by different cultures, the legitimacy of other styles such as the Gothic, and the ultimate authority of the architect and society to select and even create a style. While he reaffirmed the priority of geometry in architecture, according with the laws of nature, he did so on an empirical basis that led him to view the building as a series of unrelated appearances, concealing the true form of the structure and the functional plan. This new understanding of architecture, derived from scientific thought and demonstrated in Wren's buildings, saw its ultimate consequences in the historical revivalism and new aesthetic categories of the next centuries.

—LYDIA M. SOO

WRIGHT, Frank Lloyd.

American. Born in Richland Center, Wisconsin, 8 June 1867. Died in Taliesin West, Arizona, 1959. Married Catherine Lee Tobin, 1889 (separated, 1909; subsequently divorced); five children, including the architect Lloyd Wright; left family to live with Mrs. Mamah Bortwick Cheney, 1909 until her death in the Taliesin fire, 1914; married Miriam Noel, 1915 (separated, 1924; died, 1927); married Olgivanna Lazovich, 1925. Studied at the University of Wisconsin School of Engineering, Madison, 1885-87. Worked as a junior draftsman for Allen D. Conover, Madison, 1885-87, and for Lyman Silsbee, Chicago, 1887; assistant architect, 1888-89, and head of planning and design, 1889-93, Adler and Sullivan, Chicago; in partnership with Cecil Corwin, Chicago, 1893-96; in private practice in the Chicago suburb of Oak Park, 1896-97, and in Chicago, 1897-1909; traveled with Mrs. Cheney to Europe and stayed in Fiesole, near Florence, 1909-11; built first Taliesin house and studio, and resumed practice, Spring Green, Wisconsin, 1911; re-opened Chicago office, 1912; Taliesin partially destroyed by fire and rebuilt as Taliesin II, 1914; established office in Tokyo in conjunction with work on the Imperial Hotel, 1915-20; Taliesin II partially destroyed by fire and rebuilt as Taliesin III, 1925; built Taliesin West, Paradise Valley, near Scottsdale, Arizona, 1938; continued to practice in Wisconsin and Arizona until his death, 1959. Gold Medal, Royal Institute of British Architects, 1941; Gold Medal, American Institute of Architects, 1949.

Chronology of Works
All in the United States unless noted
† Work no longer exists

1887	Hillside Home School, Spring Green, Wisconsin
1889-1911	Frank Lloyd Wright House and Studio, Oak Park, Illinois
1891	Charnley House, Astor Street, Chicago, Illinois (with Louis Sullivan)
1892	Twin Houses for Thomas H. Gale, Oak Park, Illinois
1892	Blossom House, Chicago, Illinois
1893	Winslow House, River Forest, Illinois
1893	Walter Gale House, Oak Park, Illinois
1893	Municipal Boathouse, Madison, Wisconsin
1894	Roloson Row Houses, Chicago, Illinois†
1895	Francisco Terrace Apartments, Chicago, Illinois†
1895	Moore House, Oak Park, Illinois (remodeled by Wright in 1923)
1895	Chauncey K. Williams House, River Forest, Illinois
1898-1901	River Forest Golf Club, River Forest, Illinois†
1899	Husser House, Chicago, Illinois†
1900	Bradley House, Kankakee, Illinois
1900	Hickox House, Kankakee, Illinois
1902	Heurtley House, Oak Park, Illinois
1902	Hillside Home School Buildings, near Spring Green, Wisconsin
1902	Willits House, Highland Park, Illinois
1902	Francis W. Little House, Peoria, Illinois
1903	Barton House, Buffalo, New York
1903	Dana House, Springfield, Illinois
1904	Cheney House, Chicago, Illinois
1904	Larkin Company Administration Building, Buffalo, New York†
1904	Martin House, Buffalo, New York
1905	Glasner House, Glencoe, Illinois
1905	Hardy House, Racine, Wisconsin
1905	Smith Bank, Dwight, Illinois
1906	Unity Temple, Oak Park, Illinois
1907	Hunt House, La Grange, Illinois
1907	Tomek House, Riverside, Illinois
1908	Bitter Root Inn, Stevensville, Montana
1908	Browne's Bookstore, Chicago, Illinois†
1908	Isabel Roberts House, River Forest, Illinois
1908-12	Coonley House and Annexes, Riverside, Illinois
1909	Mrs Thomas H. Gale House, Oak Park, Illinois
1909	Baker House, Wilmette, Illinois
1909	Robie House, Chicago, Illinois
1909	Stewart House, Montecito, California
1909	Thurber Art Gallery, Chicago, Illinois†
1910	Universal Portland Cement Exhibition Stand, New York City†
1911	Taliesin, near Spring Green, Wisconsin (major remodelings in 1914 and 1925)
1913-14	Midway Gardens, Chicago, Illinois†
1915	Bach House, Chicago, Illinois
1915-22	Imperial Hotel, Tokyo, Japan†
1916	Richards House, Milwaukee, Wisconsin
1917	Allen House, Wichita, Kansas
1917-20	Barnsdall House and Annexes, Los Angeles, California
1921	Mrs. Thomas H. Gale Summer Cottages, Whitehall, Michigan
1921	Jiyu Gakuen School of the Free Spirit, Tokyo, Japan
1922	Lowe House, Eagle Rock, California
1923	La Miniatura (Millard House), Pasadena, California
1923	Little Dipper (Barnsdall Kindergarten), Los Angeles
1923	Storer House, Los Angeles, California
1923	Ennis House, Los Angeles, California
1923	Moore House, Oak Park, Illinois (rebuilding)
1923	Millard House, Pasadena, California
1924	Freeman House, Los Angeles, California
1927	Biltmore Hotel, Phoenix, Arizona (with Albert McArthur)
1927	Martin House, Derby, New York
1928	Ocatillo Desert Camp, near Chandler, Arizona†
1929	Jones House, Tulsa, Oklahoma
1933	Taliesin Fellowship Complex, Spring Green, Wisconsin (addition to Hillside Home School)
1934	Broadacre City model and exhibition plans
1934	Willey House, Minneapolis, Minnesota

Frank Lloyd Wright: Robie House, Chicago, Illinois, 1909

1936	Roberts House, Marquette, Michigan
1936-46	S. C. Johnson and Son Company Administration Building and Annexes, Racine, Wisconsin
1936-39	Fallingwater (Kaufmann House), Bear Run, Pennsylvania
1937	Wingspread (Johnson House; The Last Prairie House), Racine, Wisconsin
1937	Edgar J. Kaufmann, Sr., Offices, Pittsburgh, Pennsylvania
1937	Hanna House, Stanford, California
1937	Jacobs House I, Madison, Wisconsin
1937	Kaufmann Office, Victoria and Albert Museum, London, England
1938	Taliesin West, near Scottsdale, Arizona
1938	Midway Farm Buildings, Taliesin, Spring Green, Wisconsin
1938	Rebhuhn House, Great Neck, Long Island, New York
1939	Guest House for Falling Water, Bear Run, Pennsylvania
1939	Armstrong House, near Gary, Indiana
1939	Schwartz House, Two Rivers, Wisconsin
1939	Sturges House, Brentwood Heights, California
1939	Goetsch-Winckler House, Okemos, Michigan
1939	Rosenbaum House, Florence, Alabama
1939	Suntop Homes, Ardmore, Pennsylvania
1940	Baird House, Amherst, Massachusetts
1940	Pauson House, near Phoenix, Arizona†
1940	Pope House, Mount Vernon, Virginia (moved in 1964)
1940	Bazett House, Hillsborough, California
1940	Christie House, Bernardsville, New Jersey
1940	Community Church, Kansas City, Missouri
1940	Euchtman House, Baltimore, Maryland
1940	Lewis House, Libertyville, Illinois
1940	Manson House, Wausau, Wisconsin
1940	Pew House, Madison, Wisconsin
1940	Sondern House, Kansas City, Missouri
1940	Auldbrass Plantation, near Yemassee, South Carolina
1940-59	Florida Southern College, Lakeland, Florida
1941	Affleck House, Bloomfield Hills, Michigan
1941	Oboler Gatehouse and Retreat, Malibu, California
1941	Richardson House, Glenridge, New Jersey
1941	Snowflake (Wall House), Plymouth, Michigan
1944	Solar Hemicycle (Jacobs House), Middleton, Wisconsin
1944	S. C. Johnson Research Tower, Racine, Wisconsin
1945	Friedman Vacation Lodge, Pecos, New Mexico
1945	Taliesin Dams, Spring Green, Wisconsin
1946	Griggs House, Tacoma, Washington
1947	Grant House, near Cedar Rapids, Iowa
1947	Jacobs House II, Middleton, Wisconsin
1947	Unitarian Church, Shorewood Hills, Wisconsin
1948	Lamberson House, Oskaloosa, Iowa
1948	Morris Gift Shop, San Francisco, California
1948	Mossberg House, South Bend, Indiana
1948	Walker House, Carmel, California
1948	Walters House, Quasqueton, Iowa
1949	Anthony House, South Bend, Indiana
1949	Laurent House, Rockford, Illinois
1950	Berger House, San Anselmo, California
1950	Carr House, Glenview, Illinois
1950	Gillin House, Dallas, Texas
1950	Keys House, Rochester, Minnesota
1950	Muirhead House, Plato Center, Illinois
1950	Smith House, Bloomfield Hills, Michigan
1950	Wright House, Phoenix, Arizona
1950	Zimmerman House, Manchester, New Hampshire
1952	Price Tower, Bartlesville, Oklahoma
1953	Cooke House, Virginia Beach, Virginia
1953	Price House, Bartlesville, Oklahoma
1953	Wright House, Bethesda, Maryland
1954	Beth Sholom Synagogue, Elkins Park, Pennsylvania
1954	Hoffman Automobile Showroom, New York City
1954	Price House, Paradise Valley, Arizona
1955	Dallas Theater Center, Dallas, Texas
1955	Hoffman House, Rye, New York
1955	Rayward House, New Canaan, Connecticut
1956	Annunciation Greek Catholic Church, Milwaukee, Wisconsin
1956	Solomon R. Guggenheim Museum, New York City
1957-66	Marin County Civic Center, San Raphael, California

Frank Lloyd Wright: Taliesin West, Scottsdale, Arizona, 1938

Publications

BOOKS BY WRIGHT

Ausgeführte Bauten und Entwürfe von Frank Lloyd Wright (the Wasmuth Portfolio). Berlin, 1910. With introduction by C. R. Ashbee. English editions include: *Buildings, Plans and Designs*. New York, 1963. *Frank Lloyd Wright: The Early Work*. New York, 1968. *Studies and Executed Buildings by Frank Lloyd Wright*. Edited by Vincent J. Scully, Jr. 1986.

The Japanese Print: An Interpretation. Chicago, 1912.

Experimenting with Human Lives. Los Angeles, 1923.

The Life Work of the American Architect Frank Lloyd Wright. Edited by H. Th. Wijdeveld. Sandport, Netherlands, 1925. From special issues of *Wendingen* about Wright. Reissued: New York, 1965.

Modern Architecture. Princeton, New Jersey, 1931.

Two Lectures on Architecture. Chicago, 1931.

An Autobiography. New York, 1932. Reissued with additions, London and New York, 1979.

The Disappearing City. New York, 1932. Revised editions: *When Democracy Builds*. Chicago, 1945. *The Living City*. New York, 1958.

Architecture and Modern Life. With Baker Brownell. New York and London, 1937.

An Organic Architecture: The Architecture of Democracy. London, 1939.

Frank Lloyd Wright on Architecture: Selected Writings 1894-1940. Edited by Frederick Gutheim. New York, 1941.

Genius and the Mobocracy. New York, 1949.

The Future of Architecture. New York, 1953.

The Natural House. New York, 1954.

An American Architecture. Edited by Edgar Kaufmann. New York, 1955.

The Story of the Tower. New York, 1956.

A Testament. New York and London, 1957.

Drawings for a Living Architecture. New York, 1959.

The Solomon R. Guggenheim Museum. New York, 1960.

Frank Lloyd Wright: Writings and Buildings. Edited by Edgar Kaufmann, Jr., and Ben Raeburn. New York, 1960.

Architecture: Man in Possession of His Earth. Edited by Iovanna Lloyd Wright and Patricia Coyle Nicholson. New York, 1962.

The Drawings of Frank Lloyd Wright. Edited by Arthur Drexler. New York, 1962.

Frank Lloyd Wright: His Life, His Work, His Words. Edited by Olgivanna Lloyd Wright. New York, 1966.

Architectural Essays from the Chicago School. With others. Chicago, 1967.

In the Cause of Architecture: Essays by Frank Lloyd Wright for the Architectural Review 1908-1952. Edited by Frederick Gutheim. New York, 1975.

Letters to Apprentices. Frank Lloyd Wright. Edited by Bruce Brooks Pfeiffer. Fresno, California, 1982.

Letters to Architects. Frank Lloyd Wright. Edited by Bruce Brooks Pfeiffer. Fresno, California, 1984.

The Guggenheim Correspondence. Edited by Bruce Brooks Pfeiffer. Fresno, California, 1986.

Frank Lloyd Wright: Letters to Clients. Edited by Bruce Brooks Pfeiffer. Fresno, California, 1986.

Modern Architecture: Being the Kahn Lectures for 1930. Carbondale, Illinois, 1990.

ARTICLES BY WRIGHT

"In the Cause of Architecture." *Architectural Record* (March 1908): 155-221.
"In the Cause of Architecture: Second Paper." *Architectural Record* (May 1914): 405-413.
"Architecture and Life in the USSR." *Architectural Record* 82 (October 1937): 58-63.

BOOKS ABOUT WRIGHT

ALOFSIN, ANTHONY: *Frank Lloyd Wright: An Index to the Taliesin Correspondence.* New York, 1990.
BARDESCHI, MARCO: *Frank Lloyd Wright.* London and New York, 1972.
BLAKE, PETER: *The Master Builders: Le Corbusier, Mies van der Rohe, Frank Lloyd Wright.* London and New York, 1960.
BOLON, CAROL R.; NELSON, ROBERT S.; and SEIDEL, LINDA (eds.): *The Nature of Frank Lloyd Wright.* Chicago, 1988.
BROOKS, H. ALLEN: *Frank Lloyd Wright and The Prairie School.* 1984.
BROOKS, H. ALLEN: *The Prairie School: Frank Lloyd Wright and His Midwest Contemporaries.* Toronto, 1972.
BROOKS, H. ALLEN (ed.): *Writings on Wright: Selected Comments on Frank Lloyd Wright.* Cambridge, Massachusetts, 1983.
CARY, JAMES: *The Imperial Hotel: Frank Lloyd Wright and the Architecture of Unity.* Rutland, Vermont, 1968.
CONNORS, JOSEPH: *The Robie House of Frank Lloyd Wright.* Chicago, 1984.
DE FRIES, HEINRICH: *Frank Lloyd Wright.* Berlin, 1926.
DONNELL, COURTNEY GRAHAM: *Prairie School Town Planning 1900-1915: Wright, Griffin, Drummond.* New York, 1974.
EATON, LEONARD K.: *Two Great Architects and Their Clients: Frank Lloyd Wright and Howard Van Doren Shaw.* Cambridge, Massachusetts, 1969.
FARR, FINIS: *Frank Lloyd Wright: A Biography.* New York, 1961.
FISHMAN, ROBERT: *Urban Utopias in the Twentieth Century: Ebenezer Howard, Frank Lloyd Wright, and Le Corbusier.* New York, 1977.
FORESEE, ALYSEA: *Frank Lloyd Wright: Rebel in Concrete.* Philadelphia, 1959.
FUTAGAWA, YUKIO (ed.): *Houses by Frank Lloyd Wright.* Tokyo, 1975.
GILL, BRENDAN: *Many Masks: A Life of Frank Lloyd Wright.* New York, 1987.
GURDA, JOHN: *New World Odyssey: Annunciation Greek Orthodox Church and Frank Lloyd Wright.* 1986.
HANKS, DAVID: *The Decorative Designs of Frank Lloyd Wright.* New York, 1979.
HANNA, P. R., and HANNA, J. S.: *Frank Lloyd Wright's Hanna House.* Carbondale, Illinois, 1990.
HEINZ, THOMAS A.: *Frank Lloyd Wright.* New York and London, 1982.
HENKEN, DAVID and PRISCILLA: *Realizations of Usonia, Frank Lloyd Wright in Westchester.* 1985.
HEYMAN, M., and TAYLOR, R.: *Frank Lloyd Wright and Susan Lawrence Dana, Two Lectures.* 1985.
HITCHCOCK, HENRY-RUSSELL: *In the Nature of Materials: The Buildings of Frank Lloyd Wright, 1887-1941.* New York, 1942.

HOAG, EDWIN and JOY: *Masters of Modern Architecture: Frank Lloyd Wright, Le Corbusier, Mies van der Rohe, and Walter Gropius.* Indianapolis, Indiana, 1977.
HOFFMANN, DONALD: *Frank Lloyd Wright: Architecture and Nature.* New York, 1986.
HOFFMANN, DONALD: *Frank Lloyd Wright's Fallingwater: The House and Its History.* New York, 1978.
HOFFMANN, DONALD: *Frank Lloyd Wright's Robie House.* New York, 1984.
IZZO, ALBERTO, and GUBITOSI, CAMILLO: *Frank Lloyd Wright: Three Quarters of a Century of Drawings.* London, 1979.
JACOBS, HERBERT, with JACOBS, K.: *Building with Frank Lloyd Wright.* Carbondale, Illinois, 1990.
JACOBS, HERBERT: *Frank Lloyd Wright: America's Greatest Architect.* New York, 1965.
JAMES, C.: *The Imperial Hotel.* Rutland, Vermont, and Tokyo, 1968.
JENCKS, CHARLES: *Kings of Infinite Space: Frank Lloyd Wright and Michael Graves.* London and New York, 1983.
KAUFMANN, EDGAR, JR.: *Taliesin Drawings: Recent Architecture of Frank Lloyd Wright.* New York, 1952.
KAUFMANN, EDGAR, JR.: *Nine Commentaries on Frank Lloyd Wright.* Cambridge, Massachusetts, 1990.
KAUFMANN, EDGAR, JR.: *Fallingwater, A Frank Lloyd Wright Country House.* 1986.
LIPMAN, JONATHAN: *Frank Lloyd Wright and the Johnson Wax Buildings.* 1986.
MANSON, GRANT C.: *Frank Lloyd Wright to 1910: The First Golden Age.* New York, 1958.
MEEHAN, PATRICK J.: *Frank Lloyd Wright: A Research Guide to Archival Sources.* New York, 1990.
MEEHAN, PATRICK J. (ed.): *The Master Architect: Conversations with Frank Lloyd Wright.* Somerset, New Jersey, 1984.
MEEHAN, PATRICK J. (ed.): *Truth Against the World: Frank Lloyd Wright Speaks for an Organic Architecture.* Somerset, New Jersey, 1987.
MUSCHAMP, HERBERT: *Man About Town: Frank Lloyd Wright in New York City.* Cambridge, Massachusetts, and London, 1983.
O'GORMAN, JAMES F.: *Three American Architects: Richardson, Sullivan, and Wright, 1865-1915.* Chicago and London, 1991.
PAWLEY, MARTIN: *Frank Lloyd Wright: Public Buildings.* London, 1970.
PEISCH, MARK L.: *The Chicago School of Architecture: Early Followers of Sullivan and Wright.* New York, 1964.
PFEIFFER, BRUCE BROOKS, and NORDLAND, GERALD (eds.): *Frank Lloyd Wright: In the Realm of Ideas.* Carbondale and Edwardsville, Illinois, 1988.
PFEIFFER, BRUCE BROOKS (ed.): *Treasures of Taliesin, 76 Unbuilt Designs.* 1985.
QUINAN, JACK: *Frank Lloyd Wright's Larkin Building.* Cambridge, Massachusetts, 1987.
RANSOHOFF, DORIS: *Frank Lloyd Wright: Living Architecture.* Chicago, 1962.
SCULLY, VINCENT, JR.: *Frank Lloyd Wright.* New York, 1960.
SCULLY, VINCENT, JR.: *The Shingle Style and the Stick Style: Architectural Theory and Design from Richardson to the Origins of Wright.* New Haven, Connecticut, 1955. Reprint: 1971.
SCULLY, VINCENT, JR.: *Frank Lloyd Wright, Master of World Architecture.* 1983.
SECREST, MERYLE: *Frank Lloyd Wright.* New York, 1992.
SERGEANT, JOHN: *Frank Lloyd Wright's Usonian Houses: The Case for Organic Architecture.* New York, 1976.

SERGEANT, JOHN: *Usonian Houses, Designs for Moderate-Cost One-Family Homes.* 1984.

SHARP, DENNIS (ed.): *The Rationalists: Theory and Design in the Modern Movement.* London, 1978.

SMITH, NORRIS KELLY: *Frank Lloyd Wright: A Study in Architectural Content.* Englewood Cliffs, New Jersey, 1966.

SOERGEL, HERMANN: *Wright, Dudok, Mendelsohn.* Munich, 1926.

SPRAGUE, PAUL E.: *Guide to Frank Lloyd Wright and Prairie School Architecture in Oak Park.* Chicago, 1983.

STEINER, FRANCES: *Frank Lloyd Wright in Oak Park and River Forest.* 1983.

STORRER, WILLIAM ALLIN (compiler): *The Architecture of Frank Lloyd Wright: A Complete Catalogue.* Cambridge, Massachusetts, 1978.

SWEENEY, ROBERT L.: *Frank Lloyd Wright: An Annotated Bibliography.* Los Angeles, 1978.

TAFEL, EDGAR: *Apprentice to Genius: Years with Frank Lloyd Wright.* London and New York, 1979.

TANIGAWA, MASAMI: *Measured Drawing: Frank Lloyd Wright in Japan.* Tokyo, 1980.

TEDESCHI, ENRICO: *Frank Lloyd Wright.* Buenos Aires, 1955.

TROEDSSON, CARL BERGER: *Two Standpoints Towards Modern Architecture: Wright and Le Corbusier.* Göteborg, Sweden, 1951.

TWOMBLY, ROBERT C.: *Frank Lloyd Wright: His Life and His Architecture.* New York, 1979.

TWOMBLY, ROBERT C.: *Frank Lloyd Wright: An Interpretive Biography.* New York, 1973.

WHITE, MORTON and LUCIA: *The Intellectual Versus the City, from Thomas Jefferson to Frank Lloyd Wright.* New York, 1962.

WILLARD, CHARLOTTE: *Frank Lloyd Wright.* New York, 1972.

ZEVI, BRUNO: *Frank Lloyd Wright.* Milan, 1954.

ARTICLES ABOUT WRIGHT

ADAMS, RICHARD: "Architecture and the Romantic Tradition: Coleridge to Wright." *American Quarterly* 9 (1957): 46-52.

Architectural Forum special issues (January 1938, January 1948 and June 1959).

BERLAGE, H. P.: "Frank Lloyd Wright." *Wendingen* No. 11, special issue (1921).

CHAITKIN, W.: "Frank Lloyd Wright in Russia." *Architectural Association Quarterly* 5, No. 2 (1973): 45-55.

CRANSHAWE, R.: "Frank Lloyd Wright's Progressive Utopia." *Architectural Association Quarterly* 10, No. 1 (1978): 3-9.

CRAWFORD, ALAN: "Ten Letters from Frank Lloyd Wright to Charles Robert Ashbee." *Architectural History* 13 (1970): 64-76.

FERN, A. M.: "The Midway Gardens of Frank Lloyd Wright." *Architectural Review* (August 1963): 113-116.

FITCH, JAMES MARSTON: "Architects of Democracy: Jefferson and Wright." In *Architecture and the Esthetics of Plenty.* New York, 1961.

Global Architecture issues: No. 1, Johnson Wax; No. 2, Fallingwater; No. 15, Taliesin; No. 25, Oak Park and River Forest; No. 36, Guggenheim Museum and Marin County Civic Center; No. 40, Florida Southern University and Beth Sholom Synagogue; No. 53, Imperial Hotel.

HITCHCOCK, HENRY-RUSSELL: "Frank Lloyd Wright and the Academic Tradition." *Journal of the Warburg and Courtauld Institutes* No. 7 (1944).

HOFFMANN, DONALD: "Frank Lloyd Wright and Viollet-le-Duc." *Journal of the Society of Architectural Historians* 28, No. 3 (1969).

JENCKS, CHARLES: "Gropius, Wright, and the International Fallacy." *Architectural Association Journal* (June 1966).

JORDY, WILLIAM H.: "The Organic Ideal: Frank Lloyd Wright's Robie House." In *American Buildings and Their Architects: Progressive and Academic Ideals at the Turn of the Twentieth Century.* Garden City, New York, 1972.

KOCH, ROBERT: "Glass as Ornament: From Richardson to Wright." *Record of the Princeton University Art Museum* 34 (1975): 28-35.

KOSTA, R.: "Frank Lloyd Wright in Japan." *Prairie School Review* 3, No. 3 (Autumn 1966): 5-23.

LEVINE, NEIL: "Landscape into Architecture: Frank Lloyd Wright's Hollyhock House and the Romance of Southern California." *AA Files* No. 3 (London, January 1983).

MANSON, GRANT C.: "Sullivan and Wright: An Uneasy Union of Celts." *Architectural Review* 118 (November 1955): 297-300.

MANSON, GRANT C.: "Wright in the Nursery: The Influence of Froebel Education on the Work of Frank Lloyd Wright." *Architectural Review* (June 1953): 349-351.

O'GORMAN, JAMES F.: "Henry Hobson Richardson and Frank Lloyd Wright." *Art Quarterly* 32 (Autumn 1969): 292-315.

PEVSNER, NIKOLAUS: "Frank Lloyd Wright's Peaceful Penetration of Europe." *Architects' Journal* 89 (1939): 731-734. Reprinted in DENNIS SHARP: *The Rationalists.* London, 1978.

SCULLY, VINCENT J., JR.: "Wright, International Style, and Kahn." *Arts Magazine* 36, No. 6 (1962): 67-71.

SCULLY, VINCENT J., JR.: "American Houses: Thomas Jefferson to Frank Lloyd Wright." In EDGAR KAUFMANN, JR. (ed.): *The Rise of American Architecture.* New York, 1970.

SEVERENS, KENNETH: "The Reunion of Louis Sullivan and Frank Lloyd Wright." *Prairie School Review* 12, No. 3 (1975): 5-21.

SPENCER, ROBERT C., JR.: "The Work of Frank Lloyd Wright." *Architectural Review* 7 (June 1900): 61-72.

STILLMAN, S.: "Comparing Wright and Le Corbusier." *American Institute of Architects Journal* 9 (April-May 1948): 171-178, 226-233.

"The Studio Home of Frank Lloyd Wright." *Architectural Record* 33 (January 1913): 45-54.

TSELOS, D.: "Frank Lloyd Wright and World Architecture." *Journal of the Society of Architectural Historians* 28, No. 1 (1969).

TSELOS, D.: "Exotic Influences in the Architecture of Frank Lloyd Wright." *Magazine of Art* 46 (April 1953): 160-169.

*

Frank Lloyd Wright has had more written about him and his work than any artistic figure since Michelangelo, and has earned the reputation of being both America's greatest architect and the most important architect of the 20th century. The consistently high quality of his designs over a period of some 60 years, his astonishing innovations in the use of technology and materials, and his integration of all aspects of a building into what he called "organic" architecture are the three major foundations of that reputation.

A prolific author and magnetic speaker who helped establish and define the form of the dialogue as to the meaning and role of architecture, Wright presented a combination of clearheaded defenses and explanations of his own work, and totally unworkable and impractical visionary schemes for reorganizing the entire United States into planned communities (Broadacre Cities) under the benevolent dictatorship of master architects like himself. And, like many creative people before him, especially his teacher Louis Sullivan, Wright used his autobiographical writings to create his artistic development as he wished it to be, denying all influences but those he felt the need or desire to acknowledge. Primarily a designer of single-family homes, for which he had an almost mystical veneration as the center of the family and related values, he nonetheless built one of the earliest integrated office buildings, the Larkin Building; one of the most aesthetically satisfying industrial symbols, the Johnson's Wax Building; several impressive and advanced buildings for religious worship, including possibly the most important church of the 20th century, Unity Temple; and our most innovative art museum, the Guggenheim.

Influenced toward a career in architecture by his mother, who hung his room with prints of English cathedrals and introduced him, as a child, to the Froebel gift blocks, the young boy alternated between winter schooling in Madison, Wisconsin, and summers with his relatives in the rural area where he was eventually to build his own home, Taliesin. After some university training in engineering and work in the office of the dean of engineering at the University of Wisconsin, Allen Conover, Wright left for Chicago and a position in the draufting office for J. Lyman Silsbee. Although Wright was to minimize the value of his work in that office, he learned and absorbed a great deal about residential architecture and the use of materials in the brief time spent there. After several quick changes of position, he ended up in the office of Adler and Sullivan, the most progressive and important architectural firm in Chicago, and developing a nationwide reputation in those years.

The only domestic architecture Adler and Sullivan designed was for their major business clients, and it appears that Wright's experience with Silsbee made him the in-house specialist when there were homes to be built. Nonetheless, Wright learned a great deal about decoration and design principles from Louis Sullivan, and probably developed his approach to solving such difficult engineering problems as those of the Imperial Hotel on what he had learned from Dankmar Adler's example on the Auditorium Building. In the five years he remained in their office, he was exposed to the great era of Chicago building, the birth of the skyscraper, and saw the rise of suburban domestic building in his own Oak Park and the other collar suburbs of Chicago.

His early domestic work shows the influence of both Silsbee's awareness of the eastern Shingle and Stick styles, in terms of wood construction, open plans and high pitched roofs, and the heavier and more imposing hand of H. H. Richardson (filtered through Sullivan), in his use of stately facades with strongly articulated entrances, in both urban and the suburban buildings. Within a decade of going out on his own, Wright had designed an extraordinary series of houses in and around Oak Park, collectively known as Prairie houses. Incorporating many of the elements already described, but usually built of stucco and wood, the houses had irregular plans of interpenetrating spaces increasingly stretched out horizontally, with continuous bands of often brilliantly colored fenestration and porches that both literally and visually extended the living spaces to the outside. In addition, the architect came to believe in designing as many of the interior elements of the house as possible, adding built-in furniture, his own plans for lamps and other fixtures, and even the textile materials, whenever he could persuade a client to allow him the authority and the budget to do so. Much of Wright's later domestic architecture, including both Taliesin East and West, his small Usonian houses of the 1930s to the 1950s, and even such mansions as Fallingwater, still incorporated many of his design touches, and his belief in a unified and "organic" architecture.

Reversing the order of business at Adler and Sullivan's office, Wright was led to several of his major commercial and public commissions by the clients for whom he had designed homes. As early as 1904, after designing houses for the Martin brothers of Oak Park and Buffalo, Wright was given commissions for their E-Z Polish factory in Chicago and one of the century's most carefully thought-out office buildings, the Larkin Administration Building in Buffalo, New York. While engaged in these major projects, he also designed his first major religious building, Unity Temple. In these public structures, concrete or masonry replaced the wood and stucco of the smaller domestic buildings, and space, of necessity, became more ordered. However, even in the geometrically and modularly conceived Unity Temple, clearly defined adjacent spaces were enclosed only on several sides, permitting an easy flow of the eye from one area to another. And though the functions of both the Midway Gardens in Chicago and the Imperial Hotel in Tokyo were more diverse and complex, and the structures were much larger, a similar combination of spacial developments and organic design could be found in those mature works as well.

Wright always enjoyed being the center of attention, lived expansively and well, and enjoyed the cultural and sophisticated pleasures to be enjoyed in such big cities as New York and Chicago (though he was uninterested in and even hostile to modernist developments in the visual arts, literature and music), but both his writings and the designs for projected and completed domestic buildings reveal him to be an essentially antiurban Jeffersonian. Whether in the early Prairie homes, the California homes on cliffs or the various stages of Taliesin and Fallingwater, Wright preferred to have the house function in and as part of the landscape, with as little view of any other built environment as possible. Clearly, when given the chance, he was a master of incorporating the building into its setting, whether on the desert at Taliesin West, in and on the hill at Taliesin East, or, in perhaps his best-known and widely photographed example, Fallingwater, utilizing the relationship with the waterfall to a stunning and dramatic effect. Even in the smaller Usonian homes designed for people of more modest means, he sealed off the walls that faced other buildings and turned all windows toward the inner yard. The writings, particularly and most emphatically *The Broadacre City* volume and the many speeches he gave from the 1930s on, reinforced the concept of an individual in an industrialized world, but on his own acre of land; certain functions of both the state and production would be shared, but a Monticello-like self-sufficiency would be the desired norm. In his "Square Papers," written during the early years of World War II, the architect also exhibited his antiurban bias, suggesting that, if there were no cities, no centers of power, finance and communication, there would be no targets for enemies to bomb or occupy.

One of the great contradictions in Wright's philosophy, though one that helped him accomplish as many major projects as he did during the busiest parts of his later career, was the creation of the Taliesin Fellowship. Combining an apprentice system with many of the attributes of a large working office, yet operated with the apprentices living and working on the grounds of the architect's home and studio, it was a more highly developed and integrated form of the studio practice he'd built, near the turn of the century, at his Oak Park setting. And though many of his "daytime" apprentices and employees went on to significant careers and substantial reputations on their own, few of the Taliesin fellows ever were able to reach the same level of critical recognition. With the Fellowship still operating as a going business within a not-for-profit foundation, more than 30 years after the master's death, it is difficult to assess the impact of his training and example on individuals within the group.

Perhaps not surprisingly, this complex and contradictory man often felt betrayed when his apprentices and protégés broke loose, established their own careers, and achieved success through the design lessons they learned so well from the master.

Part of Wright's genius lay in his bifurcated view of the world, building for the individual on his self-contained piece of property on one hand, and introducing startling technological innovations on the other. The same Usonian house that turned its back on its neighbors contained such innovations as heating conducted through the floor and sandwiched board construction that subsumed both the interior and exterior walls; the Larkin Building, built in the middle of an industrial setting, had open space and such impressive features as a central cleaning system, wall-hung toilets, and furniture specifically designed to maximize the cleanest possible environment for the office staff. Wright, the nature worker and distrustful of institutions, nonetheless built some of the most impressive religious structures of the 20th century, from Unity Temple near the start of his independent career to Beth Shalom Synagogue completed just after his death some 50 years later; there were others of substantial aesthetic merit, in between, as well.

Wright built hundreds of individual homes, scores of major civic and religious structures, and had his designs published in Germany before he reached the age of 45, yet the Imperial Hotel was his only major commission abroad, and the generations of architects and critics who wrote so admiringly of his buildings failed to develop an interest in seeing a Wright building in their own setting. Nor, for all of his writings and lectures, did the master ever seem to feel left out of the international scene: he was far more rankled by the lack of public commissions in his home state and in New York City or Washington. Though his work was heavily concentrated in the Midwest and California, he did live to see his designs come to life throughout the country, many of them in the active last two decades of his life.

Most amazing among Wright's many accomplishments and artistic and technical innovations was the way he kept developing new design solutions over such a long career. For even when he returned to a design of his early years, it was either because he had never fully explored its potential or a client was in no position to accept or afford the solution Wright would have preferred to offer. While maintaining a backward-looking nostalgia for an agrarian past of individual home ownership and seeking to defy the boundaries of the world in which he created, he brought undiminished creativity and vigor to the homes, religious structures, and the variety of civic buildings that issued so coherently and imaginatively from his studio. It is a testament to his genius that the design solutions to the structures he was completing in his nineties were as far from those of his sixties as they were from his thirties. Though Wright was more open to influences than he would ever admit, there has probably never been an architect who has produced such a variety and number of well-designed and individualized buildings, without much repetition, without formula, and without direct recourse to the work of others or himself.

—DAVID M. SOKOL

WYATT, James.

British. Born in England, 1746. Died on 4 September 1813. Father was Benjamin Wyatt. Sons were Benjamin Dean, Philip, Matthew, Charles. Studied under Antonio Visentini, Venice, 1762. Worked in association with family firm, England, 1768; surveyor to Westminster Abbey, 1776; architect to the Board of Ordnance, 1782/83; surveyor-general and comptroller of the Office of Works, 1796. Member, Society of Antiquaries, 1797; member, Royal Academy of Arts, 1785; president, Royal Academy, 1805; member, Architects' Club, 1791.

Chronology of Works
All in England unless noted
* Approximate dates
† Work no longer exists

1768-74	Gaddesden Place, Hertfordshire
1769-72	Pantheon, London†
1771-72	Beaudesert (remodeling)†
1771-73	Town Hall, Burton, Staffordshire†
1772	Heaton Hall, Lancashire
1775*-87*	Sheffield Park, Sussex
1776-94	Radcliffe Observatory, Oxford
1778-80	Bryanston House, Dorset†
1780*-84	Heveningham Hall, Suffolk (interior, orangery and lodges)
1783*-84	Mausoleum, Cobham
1783*-90	Lee Priory, Kent
1786-96	Cathedral, Hereford (restoration)
1787-92	Cathedral, Salisbury (restoration)
1787-93	Cathedral, Lichfield (restoration)
1787-94	Library, Oriel College, Oxford
1787-94	Mausoleum, Brocklesby Park, Lincolnshire
1787-1806	Goodwood House, Sussex
1790-97	Castle Coole, County Fermanagh, Ireland
1795-97	Doric Colonnade, Stowe Park, Buckinghamshire
1795-1805	Cathedral, Durham (restoration)
1796-1813	Dodington Park, Gloucestershire
1796-1813	Fonthill Abbey, Wiltshire†
1799	Norris Castle, Isle of Wight
1799-1813	Belvoir Castle, Leicestershire
1800	Pennsylvania Castle, Portland
1800-08	House of Lords, Westminster Palace, London
1800-11	Kew Palace, Surrey†
1800-13	Royal Apartments, Windsor Castle, Berkshire (remodeling)
1808-13	Ashridge Park, Hertfordshire
1813	Chicksands Priory, Bedfordshire

Publications

BOOKS ABOUT WYATT

DALE, ANTONY: *James Wyatt, Architect.* Oxford, 1956.

EASTLAKE, CHARLES: *A History of the Gothic Revival.* 1872; edited by J. Mordaunt Crook, 1970.

LINSTRUM, D.: *Catalogue of the Drawings Collection of the Royal Institute of British Architects: the Wyatt Family.* Farnborough, 1973.

ROBINSON, JOHN MARTIN: *The Wyatts: An Architectural Dynasty.* London, 1979.

TURNOR, REGINALD: *James Wyatt, 1746-1813.* London, 1950.

ARTICLES ABOUT WYATT

"James Wyatt." *Universal Magazine* 20 (1813): 342-343.

DALE, ANTONY: "James Wyatt and His Sons." *Architect and Building News* 193 (1948): 294-296.

FERGUSSON, FRANCES: "James Wyatt and John Penn, Architect and Patron at Stoke Park, Buckinghamshire." *Architectural History* 20 (1977): 45-55.

FERGUSSON, FRANCES: "The Neo-classical Architecture of James Wyatt." Ph.D. dissertation. Harvard University, Cambridge, Massachusetts, 1973.

FREW, JOHN: "Richard Gough, James Wyatt, and Late 18th-century Preservation." *Journal of the Society of Architectural Historians* 38 (1979): 366-374.

FREW, JOHN: "Some Observations on James Wyatt's Gothic Style." *Journal of the Society of Architectural Historians* 41 (May 1982): 144-149.

ROBINSON, JOHN MARTIN: "The Evolution of the Wyatt Style." *Country Life* (20 December 1973).

"Short Memoirs of the Life of James Wyatt, Esq." *Gentleman's Magazine* 83 (1813): 296-297.

SUMMERSON, JOHN: "The Classical Country House in 18th-Century England." *Journal of the Royal Society of Arts* 107 (July 1959): 539-587.

*

Architecture, like music, often runs in families. The largest dynasty of this profession in England were the Wyatts, who produced more than 20 architects in 200 years. They were a Staffordshire family hailing from the village of Weeford. The most distinguished member and the first to achieve notice was James Wyatt. Born in 1746, he was the sixth of the seven sons of Benjamin Wyatt, who practiced as a builder and architect. James was educated locally and then spent six years studying architecture in Italy—four years in Rome and two in Venice, where he was a pupil of Antonio Viscentini.

He returned to England in 1768 at the age of 22 and found the fashionable world in transports over the work of the brothers Robert and James Adam, who had been in practice in England since 1759. Wyatt was later to allege that he found the public taste "corrupted" by the Adams, but this was probably no more than the disparagement of a rival. In any case, he had no need to apologize, for he was soon to show that he could produce work of the same kind as the Adams, and of equal quality.

In 1770 he won the competition to rebuild the Pantheon in Oxford Street. When that building opened in 1772, Wyatt burst upon the world as a new light. He became so fashionable that his fame even reached Russia: Catherine the Great invited him to come and work for her. In fact, all his life he had more work than his dilatory habits could cope with, and clients were constantly to complain of his delays in carrying out their work.

One of his earliest works in what has come to be called the Adam style was Heaton Hall, Manchester (1772). But probably the finest example was the severely elegant interior of Heveningham Hall in Suffolk (1776-84). The same years saw the building of the Radcliffe Observatory at Oxford. He turned his attention quite early to the Gothic style and at first used this in the revivalist "Gothick" manner, as at Sheffield Park (1776) and Sandleford Priory (1780). In 1782 he designed Lee Priory in Kent in a "Gothick" manner similar to that used by Horace Walpole at Strawberry Hill. In fact, Walpole pronounced it "a child of Strawberry prettier than the parent."

From 1787 to 1797 Wyatt was employed by the ecclesiastical authorities in restoring several cathedrals and buildings of similar status: Lichfield, Salisbury, Hereford, Durham cathedrals and Westminster Abbey, and St. George's Chapel at Windsor. That work, rightly or wrongly, earned Wyatt a bad reputation and the name "Wyatt the destroyer," chiefly as the result of the protests of the antiquary John Carter. He seems to have applied a limited number of ideas such as the removal of rood screens and sometimes also reredoses. But the title was not really deserved, and it is doubtful whether today we should be any better pleased with the work of any other contemporary architect in those distinguished buildings.

During the process of restoration, Wyatt came to study Gothic architecture seriously, as he had studied classical architecture in Rome as a youth. He emerged from his studies as the first serious architect of the Gothic Revival. A good example of this serious Gothic work is East Grinstead Church in Sussex (1796).

But his greatest original Gothic building was Fonthill Abbey near Salisbury, which he designed for the eccentric millionaire William Beckford (1796-1800). The grandiose ideas of his client enabled Wyatt to design a house with an enormous cross plan, of which the north and south wings were 312 feet long and the central tower 120 feet high. But Beckford was in such a hurry and Wyatt so seldom in attendance that the foundations were ill laid, and the central tower collapsed in 1825.

Wyatt designed several castles in the first decade of the 19th century: Norris Castle on the Isle of Wight (1799), Pennsylvania Castle in Portland (1800) and Belvoir Castle in Leicestershire (1801). But his finest surviving Gothic house is in Ashridge in Hertfordshire, which he worked on from 1808 and which was completed after his death by his nephew, Jeffry Wyatt (who later changed his name to Wyatville).

Meanwhile, James Wyatt's classical work continued, though he turned away from the Adam style in favor of a simpler classicism. Probably the best such works of the last 20 years of his life were Dodington House, Gloucestershire; Stoke Poges House, Buckinghamshire; and Castle Coole, Fermanagh, in Ireland.

Wyatt was appointed surveyor general to the Office of Works in 1796. That brought him into constant contact with the royal family, and he did a lot of work for George III, including the building of a new Gothic palace at Kew; built of cast iron, the building was never finished due to the king's illness, and was demolished by George IV. For Queen Charlotte, Wyatt built the charming classical house Frogmore, on the grounds of Windsor Castle, which, happily, still exists.

—ANTONY DALE

WYATVILLE, Jeffry.

British. Born Jeffry Wyatt in Burton-on-Trent, England, 3 August 1766. Died in London, 18 February 1840. Father was Joseph Wyatt; married Sopia Powell; son was George Geoffrey. Apprenticed to Samuel Wyatt, London, 1784/5-1791/2. Worked under his uncle, the architect James Wyatt, London, 1792; partner with John Armstrong, 1799; established own firm, London, 1803. A.R.A, 1822; member, Royal Academy of Arts, 1824; fellow of the Royal and Antiquarian Societies.

Chronology of Works
All in England unless noted
* Approximate dates

1800*	Woolley Park, Berkshire
1800*-13	Longleat House, Wiltshire
1801*-23	Wollaton Hall, Nottinghamshire
1802-06	Nonsuch Park, Surrey
1806-07	Hyde Hall, Hertfordshire
1810-16*	Endsleigh, Devonshire
1814*-17	Ashridge Park, Hertfordshire
1814-17	Dinton Park (Philipps House), Wiltshire
1815*	Bretton Hall, Yorkshire
1817-21	Banner Cross, Yorkshire
1818-41	Chatsworth House, Derbyshire (additions and alterations)
1824-40	Windsor Castle, Berkshire (restoration and remodeling)
1826-30	Lilleshall, Shropshire

1826-37   Golden Grove, Carmarthen, Wales
1828-29   Fort Belveder, Berkshire

Publications

BOOKS BY WYATVILLE

Illustrations of Windsor Castle by the Late Sir Jeffry Wyatville. 1841.

BOOKS ABOUT WYATVILLE

LINSTRUM, D.: *Catalogue of the Drawings Collection of the Royal Institute of British Architects: the Wyatt Family.* Farnborough, 1973.
LINSTRUM, D.: *Sir Jeffry Wyatville: Architect to the King.* Oxford, 1972.
ROBINSON, JOHN MARTIN: *The Wyatts: An Architectural Dynasty.* London, 1979.

*

Jeffry Wyatville (until 1824 Wyatt, but for clarity consistently Wyatville here) established an extensive country-house practice in early 19th-century England. He was a master of picturesque effect, whatever style he worked in. Apprenticed in building to his uncle, Samuel Wyatt, and partner from 1799 in a major timber-contracting and carpentry enterprise, he knew the trade intimately. A second apprenticeship in the 1790s with another uncle, James Wyatt, the leading architect of the time, had familiarized him with a wide range of styles. He was thus well equipped to supply fashionable designs at realistic prices.

Wyatville's first major opportunity was modernizing a famous Tudor mansion, Longleat, Wiltshire, from about 1800; it was one of the earliest examples of the serious revival of Elizabethan architecture, which by the 1820s was widely appreciated for its picturesque qualities. He removed a maze of small offices and courts, created an internal circulation system of corridors and a new great stair, added a homogeneous new north front, providing an improved service range, and remodeled the state rooms in an eclectic style with ceilings "Elizabethan in intent" (Linstrum) and classical woodwork (most of which was destroyed in the 1870s). The surviving staircase vault, corridors and library woodwork exhibit features reminiscent of John Soane's work.

Not long after Wyatville had begun his Longleat designs, he was similarly employed to revise the interior of Wollaton Hall, another famous Elizabethan prodigy house. His modernizing skill was again requisitioned at Woolley Park, Bedfordshire, his first important classical house. He converted the plain brick house of 1690 into a typical Wyatt-style villa, with columned bow crowned by shallow dome on one front, and a Greco-Roman Doric loggia on the other. A year or two later, in the conversion of Hyde Hall, Hertfordshire, the influence of Soane was more marked than that of Wyatville's uncles, and was to remain an important element in Wyatville's work.

During the 1800s such conversions, together with additions, remained the staple of Wyatville's practice. In 1810, however, he made a notable advance with his Endsleigh Cottage, Devon, for the duke of Bedford. A cottage *orné* on the grandest scale, Endsleigh extends for more than 200 feet in an irregular butterfly-wing plan that separates the children's quarters, as well as the offices, from the main house. Although again basically a work of conversion of "an irregular farmhouse," Wyatville's Endsleigh is a major contribution to the picturesque, a building accommodated to the scenery such as Uvedale Price had demanded in his *Essays on the Picturesque* (1798). Endsleigh lacks the conventional prettiness of the genre, having something of the harshness of neighboring Dartmoor in its heavy stone walling and roofs, despite the trimmed tree trunks that support the veranda roofs. But Endsleigh was without comparable sequel.

The unexpected death of James Wyatt in 1813 opened up opportunities for Wyatville, who stepped into his uncle's shoes at Ashridge, Hertfordshire, the most important surviving "mixed Gothic" mansion of the period. By the addition of a family wing and a huge stable wing, he transformed a predominantly regular mansion into an irregular, picturesque pile. The work itself is of a superior character: his stalls in the chapel are some of the best Gothic Revival work of the day. In his classical designs, too, Wyatville showed an increased skill in handling internal space, developing a concept already roughed out at Hyde Hall: a central space related to the main stair, crowned with a shallow dome and glazed lantern. At Dinton Park (Philipps House), Wiltshire, a reductionist exercise in Ionic, the upper walls of the stair hall are pierced fore and aft, opening up the corridors beyond. Yet more dramatic is his handling of a major extension of Bretton Hall, Yorkshire, where the wall at the head of the stairs dissolves into a square Soanic vestibule rising to a large octagonal lantern.

Another Wyatville feature was the wing lying at an obtuse angle to the main house, first used at Endsleigh to create picturesque irregularity; towers, gables and high chimneys completed the picturesque vision, as at Lilleshall, Shropshire, and Golden Grove, Carmarthenshire (both from 1826). Another feature of Endsleigh with which Wyatville was to make great play, most notably at Windsor, was the bay window. An alternative version of the picturesque is found at the great ducal classical mansion of Chatsworth. From 1818 he built a new asymmetrical north wing some 400 feet long, reconstructed the east and north fronts, and created (as at Longleat) an improved circulation. Wyatville's additions, although well integrated with the original mansion, nevertheless transformed it, by their scale and terminal tower (the duke's suggestion), into a palace from a Claude Lorrain landscape. Topped by a loggia open to the winds, the tower is seen by Linstrum as the prototype for Charles Barry's towers of the 1830s and 1840s.

At Windsor, where he was recommended by Chatsworth's owner, Wyatville likewise modernized the royal castle and made it truly picturesque. His uncle James' work there in the previous reign had never been completed, and Wyatville's task was once again to provide a convenient circulation, modern offices and rooms to suit the taste of the day. But never before had he had a task of such magnitude or difficulty, or so much in the public eye. So rotten was the old castle that he had sometimes to dig 25 feet to establish secure foundations. The specifications were drawn for him by Sir Charles Long (later Lord Farnborough), George IV's artistic adviser: new entrances to the inner ward and to the state apartments; a communication corridor around two sides; raising the Round Tower to create a "predominant feature"; adding battlements to the towers; Gothicizing the 17th-century windows; and a number of internal improvements. This program occupied Wyatville throughout the rest of his life. His work there has been criticized for coarseness of detail, but praised for its general effectiveness in realizing the romantic vision of a castle.

Wyatville may thus be seen essentially as a "house doctor" employed to give a new lease on life to old worn-out frames, but contemporaries admired his good eye for picturesque composition.

—M. H. PORT

Y–Z

YAMASAKI, Minoru.

American. Born in Seattle, Washington, 1 December 1912. Died in 1987. Married Teruko Herashiki, 1941; three children. Studied at the University of Washington, Seattle, 1930-34, and then at New York University, New York City, 1934-35. Worked as designer, Githens and Keally, New York City, 1935-37; designer, draftsman and job captain, Shreve, Lamb and Harmon, New York City, 1937-43; designer, Harrison and Fouilhoux, New York City, 1943-44; designer, Raymond Loewy Associates, New York City, 1944-45; chief architect and designer, Smith, Hinchman and Grylls, Detroit, Michigan, 1945-49; partnership with Joseph Leinweber, Detroit, Michigan, and with Leinweber and George Hellmuth, St. Louis, Missouri, 1949-55; principal, Minoru Yamasaki and Associates, Troy, Michigan, 1949-87. Instructor of watercolor, New York University, 1935-36; instructor of architectural design, Columbia University, New York City, 1943-45.

Chronology of Works
All in the United States unless noted

1951-56	Terminal Building, Lambert Airport, St. Louis, Missouri
1955-58	McGregor Memorial Community Conference Center, Wayne State University, Detroit, Michigan
1955-59	Reynolds Metals Regional Sales Office, Southfield, Michigan
1958	American Concrete Institute, Detroit, Michigan
1959	United States Pavilion, World Agricultural Fair, New Delhi, India
1959-61	Dhahran Air Terminal, Dhahran, Saudi Arabia
1959-62	Federal Science Pavilion, World's Fair, Seattle, Washington
1961-64	Northwestern National Life Insurance Company, Minneapolis, Minnesota
1961-66	Century Plaza Hotel, Century City, Los Angeles, California
1962-76	World Trade Center, New York City
1963	Michigan Consolidated Gas Company, Detroit, Michigan (architectural design and detailing)
1965	Woodrow Wilson School of Public and International Affairs, Princeton University, New Jersey
1968-74	Temple Beth-El, Bloomfield Township, Michigan
1968-75	Century Plaza Towers, Century City, Los Angeles, California
1973-76	Performing Arts Center, Tulsa, Oklahoma
1973-82	Saudi Arabian Monetary Agency Headquarters, Riyadh, Saudi Arabia
1978-83	Founders Hall, Shinji Shumeikai, Shiga Prefecture, Japan

Publications

BOOKS BY YAMASAKI

A Life in Architecture. Tokyo and New York, 1979.

ARTICLES BY YAMASAKI

"Notes in Passing." *Arts and Architecture* (July 1959).
"Humanist Architecture for America and Its Relation to the Traditional Architecture of Japan." *Royal Institute of British Architects Journal* (January 1961).
"The Present State of Architecture." *Dicta* (St. Louis, January 1963).
"A Philosophy." *Design* (Bombay, January 1972).
"Architecture East and West." *Architect and Builder* (Cape Town, February 1976).
"Shinji Shumei-kai Temple." *Japan Architect* (September 1983).

BOOKS ABOUT YAMASAKI

Minoru Yamasaki: The Architect and His Use of Sculpture as an Integral Part of Design. Exhibition catalog. Bern, Switzerland, 1967.

ARTICLES ABOUT YAMASAKI

"Airports." *Architectural Record* (August 1970).
"The Architecture of Minoru Yamasaki." *Architectural Record* (May 1957).
"Bearing Wall Expressed in a Skyscraper" and "Natural, Appropriate Use of Concrete Shells." *Architectural Record* (February 1965).
BOURNE, RUSSELL: "American Architect, Yamasaki." *Architectural Forum* (August 1958).
"The Century Plaza: A Resort in Mid-City." *Architectural Record* (August 1966).
"A Conversation with Yamasaki." *Architectural Forum* (July 1959).
HUXTABLE, ADA LOUISE: "Minoru Yamasaki's Recent Buildings." *Art in America* (Winter 1962).
"Minoru Yamasaki and Edward Durell Stone." *Zodiac* No. 8 (1961).
"Minoru Yamasaki Designs His Own Office." *Architectural Record* (September 1968).
"Minoru Yamasaki: Projets et réalisations récents." *Architecture d'aujourd'hui* (April/May 1960).
"Minoru Yamasaki." *Architectural Record* (September 1964).
"Minoru Yamasaki." *Architecture d'aujourd'hui* (April 1958).
"The Morality of Modern Architecture." *Architectural Forum* (May 1956).
"Profilo di un architetto americano: Minoru Yamasaki." *Architettura* (November 1956).

Minoru Yamasaki: World Trade Center, New York City, New York, 1962-76

"Recent Work of Minoru Yamasaki." *Casabella* (January 1966).

"Six New Projects by Yamasaki." *Architectural Record* (July 1961).

"Soaring Ribbed Vaults to Dominate Yamasaki's Design for Seattle Fair" and "Yamasaki's New Expression of 'Aspiring Verticality'." *Architectural Record* (August 1960).

"Structure Plays Leading Role in Latest Yamasaki Designs." *Architectural Record* (December 1963).

"Tradition Rekindled." *Architectural Record* (June 1983).

"Works of Minoru Yamasaki." *Informes de la construccion* (Madrid, October 1974).

"Yamasaki's Dhahran Airport." *Architectural Record* (March 1963).

"Yamasaki's First Tower." *Architectural Forum* (May 1963).

*

Minoru Yamasaki was an American architect who achieved fame in the late 1950s with his sensuous, textile-like structures, and who later changed the Manhattan skyline with the two towers of the World Trade Center.

Born in Seattle, Washington, in 1912, Yamasaki studied architecture at the University of Washington, graduating in 1934. It was during the Great Depression, a bad time for architects, and the young Yamasaki moved to New York City, looking for work. After a year spent doing menial jobs, he obtained a place with the architectural firm of Githens and Keally, later moving to Shreve, Lamb and Harmon, architects for the Empire State Building. From there he joined the architects of Rockefeller Center, Harrison, Fouilhoux and Abramovitz. He then spent a year working with Raymond Loewy Associates, a firm better known for its industrial design than for its architecture. Finally, Yamasaki moved to Detroit to take charge of design in the office of Smith, Hinchman and Grylls. All of these experiences added up to a very thorough grounding in the workings of big projects and big offices.

In 1949 Yamasaki set up his own practice, in partnership with various architects he had known at Smith, Hinchman and Grylls. Early jobs were mostly small, the houses and refurbishments that are the lot of fledgling architectural practices. Yamasaki's working experience had not equipped him for that type of work, but he learned fast, and soon larger jobs came into the practice. A surgery in Detroit and the Adams Junior High School in Wayne, Michigan, were typical of the early work of the firm; simple, hard-edged and very Miesian, the surgery in particular is an exquisite little building, but the early buildings gave no hint of the flamboyance that was to come.

International fame came with the completion of the St. Louis Airport in 1953. Designed by the firm of Yamasaki, Hellmuth and Leinweber, the airport consisted of three great shells, separated from one another by glazing, and gave a stunning image at night. By placing service functions below the main concourse level, the architects achieved a simple, breathtaking space uncluttered by baggage handling and the mundane functions which clutter up so many airports.

After the completion of the St. Louis Airport, Yamasaki developed in a direction of his own. He found that the hard-edged, unyielding emphasis on unadorned structure began to pall, and he searched for more decorative effects. In this he hit the popular mood, and for a short period he was regarded as an architect of world significance. Three buildings in Detroit mark the change to his new decorative mode: the American Concrete Institute, the Reynolds Metals Company offices and the McGregor Memorial Building for Wayne State University. All three of these buildings, completed in the late 1950s, have a lacelike decorative quality at odds with the severe architecture of the preceding decade. The American Concrete Institute has a folded-plate concrete roof of such delicate thinness that it looks like folded paper, giving a lightness and a sense of exquisiteness to the design. The Reynolds Building is enclosed by screens built up of gold-colored metal circles to give shading to the glass. The screens are held out beyond the face of the building, putting a gauze over structure and glazing alike, and having the functional advantage of reducing solar glare and hence lightening the air-conditioning load. The building at Wayne State University has thin, marble-clad steel columns supporting an upper floor and a roof of triangular concrete box beams; these box beams have triangular ends on plan as well as section to give the design the rhythmic complexity the architect was seeking at the time. All three buildings have internal courtyards with glass roofs, and the theme of the outside is repeated on the interior.

The Federal Science Building at the Century 21 World's Fair in Seattle (1962) took the preferred lacelike structure to a tall, open, Gothic structure. The same direction was followed in the Woodrow Wilson School of International Affairs at Princeton, New Jersey, where slender concrete columns look more like decoration than structure.

After that foray into a world of jewel-like richness, Yamasaki returned to an architecture based on structure and on a regular grid. The Michigan Consolidated Gas Company, Detroit, completed in 1963, is a pure white concrete tower, and the Northwestern National Life Insurance Building, completed in Minneapolis in the following year, makes no concessions to the decorative mode—its outer shell is supported on columns at the four corners, with the 19-storey wall plane acting as a beam between them.

Yamasaki used the hull-core structural technique again at his last pair of buildings. Completed in 1976, with Emery Roth as joint architect, the World Trade Center changed the New York skyline with two slim towers of great purity of form. The outer structure is steel, played straight until the tower reaches the ground, where the mullions merge in sinuous curves that once again remind one of the Gothic.

—JOHN WINTER

YEVELE, Henry.

British. Born in Derbyshire, England, ca. 1320-30. Died ca. 1400. Trained as a mason, probably between 1335 and 1350. Worked as a mason in London, from 1353; appointed as disposer of the king's works of masonry at the Palace of Westminster and Tower of London, 1360.

Chronology of Works
All in England
All dates are approximate

1370	Quadrangle College, Cobham, Kent
1381ff.	New College, Oxford (sections)
1395	Hall of Westminster Abbey, London
1395	Canterbury Cathedral (nave)

Publications

BOOKS ABOUT YEVELE

HARVEY, JOHN: *Henry Yevele: The Life of an English Architect.* London, 1944.
HARVEY, JOHN: *Henry Yevele Reconsidered.* London, 1952.
SERVICE, ALASTAIR: *The Architects of London.* London, 1979.

*

Henry Yevele was a mason active in many capacities in the 14th century in England. He worked especially for two kings, Edward III and Richard II, who gave particular attention to buildings. Yevele was born in about 1320 in Derbyshire (if his name is a guide, probably at Yeavely), the son of Roger de Yevele, who also may have been a mason. He received his first training between about 1335 and 1350 in works going on in the area, perhaps at Lichfield Cathedral, Stafford Castle and Uttoxeter.

Details of his early life are vague, but Yevele survived the Black Death, and by 1353 he had been admitted to the freedom of the City of London, soon becoming one of the leaders of the crafts in the city. In 1357 he was appointed mason to the Black Prince; in 1360 he was a disposer of the king's works of masonry at the Palace of Westminster, and documents from later that year mention him as the king's devisor of masonry, which implies that he was recognized as being what we would now term an architect. He simultaneously served as contractor; for example, in 1365 he supplied the tiles for courtyards of the Palace of Westminster, and in 1376 he was granted the wardship of the manor of Langton in Purbeck, which enabled him to obtain large quantities of that area's valuable building stone.

While supplying materials, Yevele was nonetheless also involved in the design of the projects in which these materials were used—at the Clock Tower at Westminster Palace, at Rochester Castle, at Gravesend and at Leeds Castle, Kent. He is also known to have designed various tombs: that of the earl of Arundel and his deceased wife, Eleanor (1374-75); that of John

of Gaunt, duke of Lancaster, and his wife Blanche; and later, when King Edward III died in 1377, his tomb in Westminster Abbey. Commissions also came from other clients, most notably John, Lord Cobham, for whom in about 1370 Yevele built the Quadrangle College at Cobham, Kent, and then from William of Wykeham, for part of New College, Oxford, begun in about 1381.

At about that time, Yevele began work on remodelings in the nave and on the exterior at Westminster Abbey. In about 1395 he worked on the Hall of Westminster, although the extraordinary hammer-beam roof was built by the carpenter Hugh Herland. The style of his work at Westminster Abbey was somewhat old-fashioned, as the new buildings fit in with the parts of the church that had been built more than a century earlier by Henry of Reyns. But when Yevele came to his next project, the nave of Canterbury Cathedral, the design seems much newer, the proportions being much taller, the piers more slender; Yevele may have been following there the delicate manner of the new French architecture. Of all the English Gothic naves, so John Harvey has written, Canterbury is the most satisfying in its design and its proportions, standing as the paragon of the Perpendicular style that had first been introduced to England at Gloucester Cathedral a century earlier.

Yevele was associated also with several other projects; he may have worked in the 1380s at Arundel Castle in Sussex, at Meopham Church in Kent, in 1383 at the gatehouse at Saltwood Castle in Kent, and also at the new church and college at Maidstone in Kent (founded in 1395 and completed after Yevele's death by Stephen Lote). In addition, there are several other buildings where his style may be detected: St. Katherine-by-the-Tower in London (ca. 1351), Arundel Church, the south front of St. Mary's Church in Hitchin (ca. 1360-90), and the former west front of St. Mary Overy, Southwark.

Yevele's career is interesting and historically important, for in an age before the title of the architect was known, he was the closest figure to satisfy such an ideal; scholars have been led to say that Yevele was to his century what Christopher Wren was to his. There are difficulties, of course, with any such account, but the parallel is not without point.

—DAVID CAST

YORKE, Francis.

British. Born Francis Reginald Stevens in Stratford-upon-Avon, England, 1906. Died in London, 1962. Studied at the Birmingham School of Architecture and Town Planning at Birmingham University. Founding member and secretary, MARS (Modern Architecture Research) Group; private practice with Marcel Breuer, 1935-37; practice with Eugene Rosenberg and Cyril Mardall, 1944-62; editor, *Specification*, 1935-62.

Chronology of Works
All in England

1933	Gidea Park Housing, Essex (with William Holford)
1936	Exhibition House, Royal Show, Bristol (with Marcel Breuer)
1936	Ganes House, Clifton, Bristol (with Breuer)
1936	House, High Street, Iver, Buckinghamshire
1937	Sea Lane House, East Preston, Sussex (with Breuer)
1939	Cottages, Stratford upon Avon (with F. W. B. Yorke)
1939-44	Government Deports, Camps and Factories (with William Holford)
1940	Flats, Camberwell, London (with Arthur Korn)
1947	Luccombe House, Isle of Wight

1948	Sigmund Pump's Factory, Gateshead, Durham
1950	Barclay Secondary School, Stevenage, Hertfordshire
1957	Gatwick Airport, Sussex (stage I)
1960	United States Embassy, London (with Eero Saarinen)
1960	Leeds Polytechnic, Leeds (stage III)
1961	YRM and Norwich Union Insurances Societies Offices, Greystoke Place, London

Publications

BOOKS BY YORKE

A Key to Modern Architecture. With Colin Penn. London, 1939.
Flooring Materials. With C. Roy Fowkes. London, 1948.
The Modern Flat. With Frederick Gibberd. London, 1937.
The Modern House in England. London, 1937.
The Modern House. London, 1934.
The New Small House. With Penelope Whitting. London, 1954.

ARTICLES BY YORKE

"Modern Architecture in Czechoslovakia." *Review* 3 (1943).

BOOKS ABOUT YORKE

The Architecture of Yorke, Rosenberg, Mardall 1944-72. London, 1972.

ARTICLES ABOUT YORKE

DAVIES, COLIN: "Modern Masters: Yorke, Rosenberg, Mardall." *Building* (20 March 1981).
FRY, M.: "F. R. S. Yorke: A memoir." *Architectural Review* (July 1962).

*

Known as "K" Yorke to his friends, the architect F. R. S. Yorke was one of the elite few of the British Modern Movement in the 1930s, and he followed this early success in the postwar years by founding a large and distinguished firm, Yorke, Rosenberg and Mardell.

The 1934 Modern Homes Exhibition in East London's Gidea Park gave a chance for several young architects to build houses without the usual constraints. Yorke, in partnership with Holford and Stephenson, built a semidetached pair. They were a spartan white cube of rendered brickwork, large sliding windows and a first-floor projection supported on steel columns. The houses were tentative in form and conventional in plan, but they were a start and gave the English public a notion of what the European Modern Movement was all about. Next year saw the construction of a much more sophisticated house at Nast Hyde, Hatfield: built with reinforced concrete walls carefully made so that the white paint was the only external finish, it had an imaginative layout incorporating glass blocks, double-height living room, and roof terraces, a repertory of modern themes executed with panache and skill. Sadly, this house was demolished in the 1980s; however, the Gidea Park houses remain in good condition.

In 1935, Yorke formed a partnership with Marcel Breuer, a refugee from Nazi Germany and the most famous student of the Bauhaus. The partnership produced exciting projects, particularly the Cement and Concrete Association's Garden City Project of 1936, which foreshadowed so much postwar construction, especially in the United States. But it is built work that is most important, and the Breuer/Yorke partnership has left us with a

few houses that are among the treasures of that heroic period. In the mid-1930s, modern architecture in continental Europe was running out of steam and was being suppressed, and American modernism barely existed; it was the English moment, and it lasted only four or five years before the war killed it.

Modern architecture of the time was characterized by white cubes and an absence of natural materials. It was a doctrinaire stance, with each building seen as a manifesto. Breuer had been brought up in the Modern Movement and felt no need to shout; he was relaxed enough about his architecture to reintroduce traditional materials, and the Breuer/Yorke houses were a significant step for architecture in that respect.

The Ganes House, built in Bristol in 1936, was an exhibition house for a furniture retailer. It had an inventive plan, free-flowing, and using curves and a pergola. Walls were either completely glass or of rough Cotswold stone. It was the English counterpart of Le Corbusier's stone house at Le Pradet. In 1937 came a return to the white cube and the pilotis of the International Style in a house at Angmering-on-Sea, with rooms raised up above an open ground level so that they have the benefit of the spectacular sea views. This lighthearted house was followed by two houses for masters at Eton that are perhaps the most civilized and livable modern houses built in England. The Eton houses have the hard geometry, the regular structural bays and the pergolas of the International Style, but all has been executed in soft handmade brick, and now that the gardens have matured the houses have acquired a gentle, smiling and very English appeal.

Breuer went to the States, and Yorke worked with other partners. A small block of flats in South London was designed with Arthur Korn, another German emigré, and then, in partnership with F. W. B. Yorke, a row of seven cottages on Birmingham Road, Stratford-on-Avon. Built of brick and stone, with simple windows and a single pitch roof of corrugated asbestos-cement sheeting, these houses were of instant appeal and were very cheap to construct. They became the icon for social housing, and their influence is to be seen in every postwar English new town.

The war stopped construction. But Yorke had written *The Modern House* and *The Modern House in England* and coauthored *The Modern Flat*. Republished during the war years, these books had immense influence. Nonacademic and nonintellectual, but written with a reasoned fervor, they gave to a whole generation an architectural ideal. To have one's work included was a guarantee of fame; when building started again, it was to these books that architects turned, but sadly postwar shortages, restrictions or simply lack of talent meant that the standard set in the books was rarely achieved.

After the war, Yorke built one more house in his prewar mode, a long, low house on the Isle of Wight. Finished in 1947, it was the only British postwar house to have any of the quality of the work of the 1930s. But Yorke's real contribution at that time was to expand the scale of his office and his work.

The young architects who went to war as revolutionaries came back as establishment figures, and it was to them that the creators of the new "welfare state" turned. Yorke teamed up with a Czech and a Finn to form Yorke, Rosenberg and Mardell, later simply referred to as YRM.

Postwar England was a dreary place except in the world of ideas, and architecture was no exception. The completion of Yorke, Rosenberg and Mardell's industrial building at Gateshead for Sigmund Pumps had a precision totally lacking from other English work at the time. But it was in school building that the firm made its postwar mark.

The Barclay Secondary School at Stevenage was the showpiece postwar school. Completed in 1950, it embodied all the theories of the day, classrooms lit on two sides, light steel frame and concrete cladding; while so many schools of the time were repetitive and dull, Barclay had style. It also contrived to have a large Henry Moore sculpture. Throughout the 1950s, the office kept building elegant schools, the major building type of the first part of the decade.

Late in the 1950s the practice expanded and new partners made their impact, notably David Allford and Brian Henderson. The workload became more diverse, but the architecture less so. The firm became known for fine detailing and sharp edges. This penchant flourished in two directions: at Gatwick Airport a practical, down-to-earth Miesian style ran parallel with a particular YRM development, the white tile facing. The tile facing designed and executed with the same precision as the firm's Miesian steel buildings came to fame with the firm's own offices in Greystoke Place, London, completed in 1961. It was a manifesto building setting down the firm's commitment to an impeccably detailed, pure, spare architecture. When Yorke died the following year, he left behind a firm that knew where it was going.

—JOHN WINTER

YOUNG, Ammi B.

American. Born Ammi Burnham Young in Lebanon, New Jersey, 1798. Died in Washington, D.C., 4 March 1874. Father was Samuel Young, a carpenter and builder, to whom Ammi was apprenticed; self-taught as an architect. Federal architect, Washington, D.C., 1836; first supervising architect for the United States Treasury, 1852-62.

Chronology of Works
All in the United States

1827-28	Thornton and Wentworth Halls, Dartmouth College, Hanover, New Hampshire
1828	Congregational Church, Lebanon, New Hampshire
1832	St. Paul's Episcopal Church, Burlington, Vermont
1833-38	Vermont State Capitol, Montpelier, Vermont
1834-41	Shaker Great Family Dwelling House, Enfield, New Hampshire
1837-47	Customhouse, Boston, Massachusetts
1839	Reed Hall, Dartmouth College, Hanover, New Hampshire
1855-58	Customhouse and Post Office, Windsor, Vermont
1855-60	United States Treasury Building, Washington, D.C. (south wing)
1857-60	Customhouse and Post Office, Portsmouth, New Hampshire

Publications

BOOKS BY YOUNG

Plans of Public Buildings in Course of Construction, under the Direction of the Secretary of the Treasury, including the Specifications Thereof. Washington, D.C., 1855.

ARTICLES ABOUT YOUNG

MORAN, GEOFFREY P.: "The Post Office and Custom House at Portsmouth, New Hampshire, and Its Architect, Ammi Burnham Young." *Old-Time New England* 57 (1967): 85-102.

WODEHOUSE, LAWRENCE: "Ammi Burnham Young: 1798-1874." *Journal of the Society of Architectural Historians* 25 (1966): 268-280.
WODEHOUSE, LAWRENCE: "Architectural Projects in the Greek Revival Style by Ammi Burnham Young." *Old-Time New England* 60 (1970): 73-85.

---

*

Like his father Samuel and brother Dyer, Ammi Burnham Young was a carpenter-builder of Lebanon, New Hampshire, but he expanded his practice locally prior to moving to Boston, where he designed the Custom House. This led to his appointment as architect to the United States government, a pinnacle for a rural carpenter-builder.

Young's early work was provincial and derivative. It included the Lebanon Congregational Church (1828), based upon the prototypical Late Colonial architecture of Asher Benjamin; two houses in the town; an observatory; and three halls known as "Old Row" at Dartmouth College. Dartmouth Hall had stood since 1791, and Young added Wentworth, Thornton and Reed halls between 1828 and 1840. These simple rectangular boxes were utilitarian neoclassical buildings, with windows punched into the walls and gable ends in the form of pediments. Young's design for the Vermont State Capitol at Montpelier (1833-38) was also neoclassical, with its portico based upon the Theseion in Athens and its dominant (but no longer extant) dome modeled on the Pantheon in Rome. Many such structures of the early 19th-century are termed Greek Revival because the architectural elements are from Greek temples, although Roman space was the source for the interiors. At Montpelier, the dome was designed solely as an external feature, in no way reflecting the internal space arrangements of the house and senate chambers on the second floor or their galleries on the third. At that period of his life, Young was a competent designer, but not an articulate architect.

Young built several structures in Burlington, Vermont, including the Gothic Revival St. Paul's Episcopal Church (1832), prior to moving to Boston, where he came into contact with a group of cosmopolitan architects including Alexander Parris, under whom Young may have gained some instruction. Thereafter, his works became more sophisticated, as may be seen in his most articulate neoclassical building, the Boston Custom House (1837-47), built at a cost of more than $1 million, an expensive structure for the 1840s. End elevations and central porticoes on the long sides of this rectangular building were based on the Theseion in Athens. All 32 exterior Doric columns, 32 feet high and more than five feet in diameter, were turned granite monoliths rather than layered stone drums, as in the Greek original. The use of such expensive construction methods was peculiar to Boston at that time. The porticoes on the long sides gave direct access into a central rotunda or Great Room, 63 feet in diameter and of the same height, capped by a Pantheon dome and oculus, the external appearance of which was reflected in the internal space. (The Great Room was destroyed when a 500-foot tower was added to the building in 1915 by Peabody and Stearns.) In this building Young reached a level of competence and professionalism rare in carpenter-builders who aspired to become architects.

The Boston Custom House began Young's association with the United States government, and led to his being appointed supervising architect of the Office of Construction within the Treasury Department in 1852. Together with Captain Alexander

Bowman as engineer in charge of construction, Young designed approximately 80 federal buildings, most to house the postal and customs services and the federal courts. Five volumes of lithographs illustrating these designs were published as *Plans of Public Buildings in Course of Construction for the United States of America Under the Direction of the Secretary of the Treasury* (Washington, 1855-56).

Several of Young's buildings were built in the Roman Revival tradition, while others were typical of the 1850s Renaissance Revival style, being smaller versions of 16th-century Italian Renaissance palaces known in the United States from the London clubhouses of Charles Barry. Young's Renaissance Revival federal buildings were boxy, built either of brick or stone, and were two or three stories high, depending upon their use. Pedimented windows on each level sat on string courses, and each building was crowned by a cornice. During the mid-1850s, Bowman introduced iron fireproof construction into these buildings, with wrought-iron beams and brick segmental arches. Young detailed the same buildings using cast-iron doors, windows, shutters, quoins, cornices and other classical details and elements. A good example of this type of construction is the Post Office and Courtroom at Windsor, Vermont (1855-58).

Escalating costs on government buildings led to Young's dismissal; he was, for example, spending $5,000 for each monolithic column on the extension to the Treasury Department Building. Little is known of his subsequent career, although he may have maintained a private practice. According to an entry in Alfred Bult Mullett's diary, Bartholomew Oertly of the Construction Branch worked for Young, but other than that reference, nothing is known of the last 15 years of his life.

—LAWRENCE WODEHOUSE

ZAKHAROV, Adrian D.

Russian. Born Adrian Dmitrievich Zakharov in 1761. Died in 1811. Studied at the Academy of Sciences, St. Petersburg. Apprenticed with Jean François Chalgrin, Paris, 1782-86; traveled in Italy, then returned to practice in St. Petersburg, 1794. Professor at the Academy of Sciences; main architect for the Admiralty Department, 1805.

Chronology of Works
All in Russia

1798-1801	Gatchina Residence Buildings, St. Petersburg
1802-03	Standardized Administrative Buildings for Russian Cities
1806-08	Warehouses on the Neva, St. Petersburg
1806-11	Church of St. Andrew, Kronstadt
1806-11	Admiralty, St. Petersburg (restructuring; not completed until 1823)
1809	Gatchina Educational Settlement for Children, St. Petersburg

Publications

BOOKS ABOUT ZAKHAROV

ARKIN, D. E.: *Zakharov i Voronikhin.* Moscow, 1953.
EGOROV, IURII ALEKSEEVICH: *The Architectural Planning of St. Petersburg.* Athens, Ohio, 1969.
GRABAR, IGOR; LAZAREV, V. N.; and KEMENOV, V. S. (eds.): Vol. 8, Part 1 in *Istoriya russkogo iskusstva.* Moscow, 1963.
GRIMM, G. G.: *Arkhitektor Andreyan Zakharov.* Moscow, 1940.
HAMILTON, G. H.: *The Art and Architecture of Russia.* Harmondsworth, England, 1954.
HAUTECOEUR, L.: *L'architecture classique à St. Pétersbourg à la fin du XVIIIe siècle.* 1912.

ARTICLES ABOUT ZAKHAROV

LANCERAY, N.: "Adrien Zakharov et l'Amirauté à St. Pétersbourg." *Starye Gooy* 12 (1911): 3-64.
MILNER-GULLAND, ROBIN: "Art and Architecture in the Petersburg Age, 1700-1860." In ROBERT AUTY and DIMITRI OBLENSKY (eds.): *An Introduction to Russian Art and Architecture.* 1980.

*

The St. Petersburg architect Adrian Zakharov's creative life began at the end of the 18th century, during the strict classical period inspired by Palladian traditions and open to European neoclassicism. The rapid rise of the architect's career coincided with the development of high classicism in the French Empire style in the first decade of the 19th century. Influenced by contemporary French architecture, Zakharov created a new version of the classical style. Monumentality, ceremonial appearance, arrangement of large expanses of space in unified complexes and interaction between architecture and monumental decorative sculpture were characteristic of high classicism. The Admiralty in St. Petersburg as reconstructed by Zakharov became the accepted standard for the style. As the author of this masterpiece, Zakharov joined the masters of European classical architecture.

Educated at the St. Petersburg Academy of Sciences, Zakharov remained closely connected to his alma mater. In 1783 he received a grant from the Academy and went to study in Paris. For three years, he was an intern under the important French architect Jean François Chalgrin, who held the ability of his student in high esteem. On his return to Russia, Zakharov became a professor at the Academy of Sciences and remained in that position for almost 25 years, until his death. For a short time, he also worked as an architect for the Academy buildings.

Zakharov studied architecture until 1800, when he actually started to build. The architect drew on Russian classical sources, especially those of I. E. Starov and Giacomo Quarenghi, and on the innovations of French architects, particularly Chalgrin, Claude-Nicolas Ledoux, Étienne-Louis Boullée and Moitte. Having critically reassessed the peculiarities of these schools, Zakharov created his own method, which was defined by general geometrical forms, large-scale designs and extensive layouts. As the unsurpassed master of large, classical designs, Zakharov continued to employ canonical order types.

Several buildings for the Gatchina (1798-1801), the favorite residence of Paul I, were the earliest of Zakharov's works. The application of Gothic motifs at St. Harlampy Monastery and St. Paul Finnish Church were in accord with the emperor's romantic disposition. However, a return to the Empire style was obvious in the Poultry Building design, based on the opposition of geometric forms in the horizontal block and the adjacent cylindrical towers. A loggia adorned with Doric columns centrally divided the long arcade of the facade. Limestone was used as a building material; this and large-scale details endowed the fairly small building with a monumental appearance. A tendency toward clarity and abstraction of geometric form was evident in the projects for Paul I's Mausoleum (1801-05). In

Adrian D. Zakharov: Admiralty, St. Petersburg, Russia, 1806-11

one of the designs, influenced by the works of Ledoux and Friedrich Gilly, the mausoleum was treated as a truncated pyramid with a Doric portico at the entrance.

Zakharov combined monumentality with plasticity of detail in his church buildings, which were later destroyed. Alexandrovskaia Factory Church and Andreevsky Cathedral in Kronstadt used a Latin-cross plan and were built in austere forms—cubes, parallelopipeds, cylinders and semispheres. Large porticoes extending out into space contrasted to the flat wall surfaces. The Alexandrovskaia Factory Church was similar to the Church of St. Philippe du Roule in Paris by Chalgrin. The original bell tower had a spire similar to that of the Admiralty building, and served as a vertical reference point for Kronstadt. In 1805

Zakharov became the chief architect for the Admiralty Department. A comprehensive reconstruction of the gigantic Admiralty complex in St. Petersburg's center was carried out according to Zakharov's design. The old structure, erected in the first half of the 18th century, contained the Admiralty Department and a shipyard. The building was at the heart of the central squares system, and its tower served as the reference point for the main radiating streets.

Zakharov preserved the old structure, which consisted of two rectangular buildings with a 407-meter-long facade and two wings embracing the shipyard. However, he turned the prosaic, functional structure into a magnificent ceremonial composition. A rhythmical alternation of accents and neutral parts, and a contrast between portico colonnades and flat wall surfaces endowed the long facade with an extreme plasticity of expression. The main part of the structure was the central tower, which consisted of a massive cubic base with a slender colonnade on top, and crowned with a gilded spire. Zakharov alternated the motif of a cubic segment with an arch in the symmetrical facades facing the Neva River. The architect organized the side facades and the side wings according to the three-axis principle. They had wide porticoes in the center and column groupings at the corners. The repetition of elements gave the gigantic building unity and harmony. Working with the best Russian sculptors—F. F. Shchedrin, I. I. Terebenev, S. S. Pimenov and V. I. Demuth-Malinovsky—Zakharov created a brilliant *Gesamtkunstwerk,* setting the standard for Russian architecture. The sculptural program elaborated on the theme of Russia as a naval power. Zakharov's Admiralty became the basic element in the central squares ensemble, which was completed in the first half of the 19th century.

A tendency for city planning was a strong trait of Zakharov's creative method. He contributed to the creation of the St. Petersburg Bourse ensemble, correcting Thomas de Thomon's designs. Zakharov also suggested that the buildings of the Academy of Sciences should be unified into a harmonious classical composition corresponding to the Bourse ensemble.

At the same time, the architect designed projects for standardized administrative buildings in Russian cities (1802-03). A combination of simple blocks with porticoes accentuating the central axis was characteristic of this series. Sixty buildings following these standardized designs have been preserved. In Poltava, they formed the Kruglaia Square ensemble, setting the tone for future construction. These structures were significant for city planning. The hospital in Herson (1808-13) became Zakharov's most notable work in the provinces.

As Admiralty Department architect, Zakharov designed a series of important city-planning projects for St. Petersburg during the last years of his life (1806-11). He worked on these with extreme intensity, as if making up for lost time. Zakharov organized the Proviantsky Island territory and designed the warehouse facades facing the Neva. He turned functional buildings into a unified ensemble, remarkable for its powerful stature and calm clarity. Reconstructing the Admiralty barracks, the architect created an extended block of buildings, expressive in rhythm and silhouette. He also enlarged the Navy Hospital complex and improved the layout of the adjacent area.

The plan for the St. Petersburg Grebnoi Port in Galernaia Harbor was comparable in scale to a small city project. Zakharov divided the large area into three segments according to function. Greenbelts separated the administrative, industrial and residential parts. The architect rhythmically organized the complex by repeating several structural types. The design for the Gatchina Educational Settlement for Children (1809) was similar in approach to the Grebnoi Port complex. The spatial center was the semicircular square with a church. Zakharov arranged the residential area in a large semicircle with identical houses between radiating streets. In this project his city-planning ideas corresponded to those of Claude-Nicolas Ledoux for the project for the city of Chaux.

Zakharov died at the height of his creative activity and failed to see his projects for the Admiralty, Kronstadt and Alexandrovskaia Factory Cathedrals completed. Still, his works decisively influenced the architects of the Russian high classical period (1810-30). The scope of Zakharov's city-planning ideas and ensemble approach to architecture foreshadowed the creative work of Karl Rossi, the brilliant master of the classical ensemble.

—BORIS M. KIRIKOV

Translated from the Russian by Konstantine Klioutchkine

ZIMMERMANN BROTHERS.

German. Dominikus Zimmermann: born in Gaispoint near Wessobrun, Bavaria, 30 June 1685. Died in Wies, Bavaria, 16 November 1766. Married Therese Zöpf, 1708. Johann Baptist Zimmermann: Born in Gaispoint, 3 January 1680. Died in Munich, February 1758. Married. Their father, Elias, was a mason and stuccoist; both brothers were trained as stuccoists at the Abbey of Wessobrunn; both studied under Johann Schmuzer, a leading stuccoist and architect. Dominikus' career was concentrated in Bavarian-Swabian area of Germany; he settled in Landsberg, 1716, where he was elected to the town council, 1734, and eventually became mayor, 1749. Johann Baptist began his career in Bavaria; worked in Munich under the patronage of Max Emanuel and Carl Albrecht, 1720, until his death.

Chronology of Works
All in Germany unless noted
* Approximate dates
Dominikus Zimmermann:

1708-09	Iddakapelle, Benedictine Abbey, Fischingen, Switzerland (five altars, including high altar)
1709-12	Carthusian Monastery Church, Buxheim (stucco and altars)
1715	Parish Church, Birkland (high altar)
1716-18	Dominican Nunnery Church, Mödingen (design, stucco)
1718	Town Hall, Landsberg am Lech (facade and interiors)
1721	Parish Church, Landsberg am Lech (rosary altar)
1724-25	Dominican Monastery Church, Schwäbisch-Gmünd
1725	Parish Church, Buxheim (architect, stucco)
1726-33	Dominican Nunnery Church, Siessen (design, stucco)
1727-35	Wallfahrtskirche Steinhausen, near Biberach in Württemberg
1728-33	High Altars, Ochsenhausen
1733-39	Cloister, Carthusian Monastery, Buxheim (including Annakapelle)
1736-41	Parish Church, Günzenburg
1739	Pilgrimage Chapel, Pöring
1741	Johanniskirche, Landsberg-am-Lech (not completed until 1752)
1744-54	Pilgrimage Church, Die Wies (design and stucco)
1748-54	Church of Maria Himmelfahrt, Schongau (reconstructions)
1754-61	Library, Premonstratensian Abbey of Schussenreid, Swabia
1755-76	Church, Gutenzell (modernization)
1756-57	Parish Church, Eresing (remodeling)

Johann Baptist Zimmermann:

1709-12	Carthusian Monastery Church, Buxheim, near Memmingen (frescoes)
1712-14	Parish Church, Schliersee (stucco, frescoes)
1714-19	Benedictine Abbey, Ottobeuren (stucco)
1716	Cathedral and Cloister, Freising (stucco and frescoes)
1719-20	Dominican Nunnery Church, Mödingen (frescoes and stucco)
1720-26	Neues Schloss, Schleissheim (stucco)
1726-33	Dominican Nunnery Church, Siessen, (frescoes)
1727-36	Wallfahrtskirche Steinhausen, near Biberach in Württemberg (with Dominikus)
1728-30	Ahnengalerie, Residenz, Munich (stucco)

1728-33 Pilgrimage Church, Steinhausen (frescoes)
1733-37 Schatzkammer and Reiche Zimmer, Residenz, Munich (stucco)
1734-39 Nymphenburg, Amalienburg (stucco)
1743-44 St. Michael's Church, Berg-am-Lain, Munich
1743-44 Augustinian Abbey Church, Dietramszell (stucco and frescoes)
1746-54 Pilgrimage Church, Die Wies (frescoes)
1751-55 Benedictine Abbey Church, Andechs (design, stucco, frescoes)
1754-56 Premonstratensian Abbey Church, Schäftlarn (stucco and frescoes)
1756 Neustift, Freising (stucco and frescoes)
1755-57 Neuer Festsaal, Nymphenburg, Munich (stucco and frescoes)

Publications

BOOKS ABOUT THE ZIMMERMANNS

FEULNER, ADOLF: *Bayerisches Rokoko*. Munich, 1923.
GÜNTHER, E.: *Die Brüder Johann Baptist und Dominikus Zimmermann*. 1944.
HAGER, LUISA: *Nymphenburg*. Munich, 1955.
HITCHCOCK, HENRY-RUSSELL: *Rococo Architecture in Southern Germany*. London, 1968.
HITCHCOCK, HENRY-RUSSELL: *German Rococo: the Zimmermann Brothers*. Baltimore, 1968.
KASPER, ALFONS and STRACHE, WOLF: *Steinhausen, ein Juwel unter den Dorfkirchen*. Stuttgart, 1957.
LAMB, CARL: *Die Wies*. Munich, 1948. Reprint: 1964.
LAMPL, SIXTUS: *Johann Baptist Zimmermanns Schlierseer Anfänge*. Schliersee, Germany, 1979.
MUCHALL-VIEBROCK, T.: *Dominikus Zimmermann*. 1912.
RUPPRECHT, BERNHARD: *Die Bayerische Rokokokirche*. Kallmünz, Germany, 1959.
SCHNELL, HUGO: *Die Wies*. Munich, 1934; rev. ed., 1981.
THON, CHRISTINA: *Johann Baptist Zimmermann als Stukkator*. Munich, 1977.

*

Dominikus Zimmermann was born in Wessobrunn, at that time the center of one of the most vital schools of workers in stucco in all Europe; indeed, he began his career as a stuccoer before he developed his talents as one of the greatest Rococo architects working in southern Germany in the first half of the 18th century. He settled first at Füssen, and from 1716 lived in Landsberg-am-Lech, of which town he later became mayor. His relatively small output is confined to southwestern Bavaria and Württemberg, yet his reputation stands high because of the quality and originality of his designs. He often collaborated with his older brother, Johann Baptist Zimmermann, a painter of genius who was also an accomplished stuccoer.

Dominikus Zimmermann's first building was the Dominican conventual church at Mödingen near Dillingen (1716-18), with frescoes and stucco by J. B. Zimmermann. The pulpit, of the 1720s, is especially fine, bursting forth with its tester in a riot of color and gesticulating *putti* from the plain white surfaces behind.

The Zimmermanns were masters of craftsmanship as well as inventive designers of an inexhaustible range of motifs and themes. J. B. Zimmermann contributed the frescoes in two of the greatest churches by his brother: in their joint work is a great homogeneity of design, both of detail and the various parts. The brothers created works of architecture in which lightness and elegance are preeminent, and their works were rarely paralleled, let alone surpassed, by other contemporaries. Delicacy, slenderness and a wonderful sense of balance pervade their creations. They had a lightness of touch and a faultless sense of scale and proportion, so that in their marvelous and perfect interiors a serene gaiety is ever present.

Dominikus Zimmermann was less successful with his exteriors, for at Steinhausen and Die Wies the towers relate very unsatisfactorily to the mass of the churches. His windows, however, are unmistakable and incredibly elegant, for they are often tripartite, and have wide tops, like musical notations.

Following the work at Mödingen, Dominikus Zimmermann designed the Parish Church of Buxheim near Memmingen (1725): it has characteristic windows, but the frescoes are by Georg Hermann rather than by J. B. Zimmermann.

The mature Rococo style of the Zimmermanns was first clearly expressed at Wallfahrtskirche Steinhausen near Biberach in Württemberg (1727-35), a commission by the Premonstratensians of Schussenried for a Pilgrimage Church of Our Lady of Sorrows. In this great building, which is basically a large ellipse with two rectangular elements set at each end of the long axis, the mystical indirect lighting associated with the Baroque architecture of the Asams was abandoned for direct lighting and a color scheme in which white and gold predominate. Throughout this marvelous church Marian symbolism was used in profusion, especially in the great ceiling fresco by J. B. Zimmermann, probably the very finest of his great achievements in terms of composition, architectural effect and color.

From 1736 to 1741 Dominikus Zimmermann built the Frauenkirche, the Parish Church of Günzburg on the Danube, some miles downstream from Ulm. The nave looks rectangular from the outside, but, by means of judiciously placed columns and curving elements swaying inward and out, Zimmermann gave the impression of an elliptical space, accentuated by the positions of the side altars: the choir is narrow with square outer walls but with splayed corners inside.

The third great church by Dominikus Zimmermann is "Die Wies," built in 1744-54 not for imperial or ecclesiastical patrons, but for the local farming community. Many commentators regard this Pilgrimage Church of Christ Scourged as the triumph of south-German Rococo. It stands among the fields and woods in the foothills of the Bavarian Alps northeast of Füssen, hence its familiar name "Die Wies," or "Wieskirche" (*Wies* meaning "field").

As in Steinhausen, Zimmermann created a great central space surrounded by an aisle, but at Wieskirche the chancel is long and rectangular, while at the other end of the church is a small vestibule behind the convex wall of the entrance front. This time the body of the church is not in fact an ellipse, but two semicircles attached to a rectangle. Instead of the piers of Steinhausen, the "nave" is separated from the processional way by means of paired columns, giving a supremely light and elegant effect.

The single tower is set behind the chancel, and is joined to the clergy house. At the junction between the tower and chancel the latter's walls curve inward, forming an apsidal end behind the high altar, and there is a narrow chancel aisle formed of slender columns, making the chancel seem longer and narrower still. The entrance front is embellished with sweeping gables built on curves and tall stone columns detached from the walls behind so that the entablature moves dramatically outward over each column, and the scale of the facade is made more dramatic and the emphasis more vertical by means of the subdivision into panels by means of the columns. Over the vestibule behind this front is the organ, set on a gallery. Freely shaped windows give some indication of the volume of the church inside.

Die Wies has an interior of extraordinary lightness, brilliance and delicacy: the resemblance to Meissen porcelain is again strong. The great fresco is by J. B. Zimmermann, and depicts the moment before the Last Judgment, when Christ is on the rainbow, and has not taken his position on the throne. To the east is the "Mercy Seat," and to the west the "Gate of Heaven."

Coloring is again largely white. As the main body of the church is entered from the small vestibule, the pulpit on the left seems to jump out into the space; it is one of Dominikus Zimmermann's most remarkable creations, and is colored with many reds, dark greens, silver and gold. Above the tester is the "Eye of God" and the "Descending Dove," while Faith, Hope and Charity are represented, as are the attributes of the Evangelists carried by lively white *putti*. At the base of the pulpit a youth holds a fish. Opposite, and balancing the pulpit with that cunning asymmetry which is such a feature of German Rococo, is the grilled loge of the abbot of Steingaden.

The choir, that tall, narrow, deep, rectangular space, is illuminated by high double windows surmounted by single *oeil de boeuf* windows set behind a vestigial gallery. Pilasters are gray and pink scagliola, and the columns of the choir are white and blood-red scagliola, reminding us of Christ's blood at his scourging. The Evangelists (by Egidius Verhelst the Elder) surrounding the altar have their books open at the scourging. The fine figures of the Latin fathers of the Church are by Anton Sturm, and are lively, full of nervous tension, displaying all the dramatic gestures of Rococo at its best.

It has not been proved if Zimmermann worked on the Parish and Pilgrimage Church of Maria Steinbach, but there are similarities when it is compared with Steinhausen and Die Wies, both inside and out. The long choir, with its two-tiered high altar, strongly suggests the Wieskirche in its design and reddish coloring.

Dominikus Zimmermann modernized the church at Gutenzell in 1755-76, designed the high altars at Ochsenhausen (1728), the Neumünster in Würzburg, and Waldsee (1714), and reconstructed the church of Maria Himmelfahrt at Schongau in 1748-54. Between 1754 and 1761 he also created the beautiful library at the Premonstratensian Abbey of Schussenried in Swabia, which is all white, pink, gray and light blue, with gold, and has a gallery of the utmost porcelain-like delicacy on which *putti* support candelabra. The columns carrying the balcony are of pink scagliola.

J. B. Zimmermann carried out the brilliant frescoes at Bergam-Laim (1740s), the fresco of the life of St. Norbert (founder of the Premonstratensian Order) in the church of SS. Peter and Paul at Freising-Neustift of 1756, the stuccowork and frescoes at Schäftlarn (again featuring St. Norbert) of 1754-56, the stucco scrollwork and frescoes at Andechs, the stucco at Raitenhaslach, the frescoes in the nave and choir of the Neumünster in Würzburg, the stucco at Beyharting, frescoes and painting of the Assumption at Maria Himmelfahrt, Dietramzell (1741), the splendid frescoes and stucco ornament for the Cistercian monastery at Landshut-Seligenthal (1732-34), the stucco decorations and fresco (1734) at Wallfahrtskirche Vilgertshofen, the stucco and painting at the Pilgrimage Church of Wemding (1752-54), and the stucco and frescoes at Weyarn (1729).

Johann Baptist's work is lyrical and always lively, and is free from formalism, obtrusive architectural pileups, and even very original, virtually untouched by external influences, except perhaps a dash of French lightness. His designs are beautifully serene, and his great fresco at Die Wies is cheerful, humane and entirely unmenacing. One has a strong sense of a simple, uncomplicated, sunny faith, untarnished by gloomy introspections or notions of hellfire. There is a freshness about his visions that leaves the spirits uplifted: there is merriment aplenty in his

charming compositions. As a colorist he was a genius, using yellows, soft greens, ultramarines and the gentlest of harmonious tints, bathing his work in a clarity and a golden glow.

The Zimmermanns are important because their work has a refreshing sense of delight that comes from their own fecund inventiveness and the certainty of their faith. They succeeded in merging the Rococo style (of which they were masters), which is often associated with courtly decorations, with a long tradition of country craftsmanship linking their own time with the Middle Ages. In their work the world of Hans Sachs comes into the sunlight of the Mozartian 18th century, but with the tradition of inventive creativity and craftsmanship undiminished in the transformation.

Dominikus Zimmermann produced two of the most successful centrally planned churches ever designed, in which the elliptical themes evolved in Roman Baroque architecture in the previous century came to a glorious new interpretation, lifted to realms of fantasy and frothy delight. Two of his interiors, Steinhausen and Wieskirche, are masterpieces by any standards, and his unrealized project for Ottobeuren (1732), again featuring a spacious elliptical rotunda, would have been the largest scheme he ever tackled, but the job went to Simpert Krämer and then to J. M. Fischer, although certain elements from Zimmermann's design survived.

The Zimmermanns, working in a relatively small geographical area in southern Germany, were steeped in their local craft traditions, and in the piety (one of Dominikus' daughters was a nun) of their Roman Catholicism, the symbolism of which was simple, unaffected and direct, and thus capable of being interpreted by unsophisticated craftsmen unspoiled by metropolitan and international veneers. While elements of Baroque forms undoubtedly found their way across the Alps from Italy, the work of the Zimmermanns is unmistakably of its region, and it an safely be said that they, and some of their great craftsmen-artist contemporaries such as the brothers Franz Xaver and Johann Michael Feichtmayr and Johann Georg Üblhörr, invented a south-German Rococo that was one of the most delicious and elegant styles ever evolved.

At their best, the brothers produced interiors where it is difficult to discern where the "architecture" and the "decoration" end or begin, for they created a true synthesis where the plan, the three-dimensional form, the stucco embellishments, the statuary and the coloring combined in a satisfying and harmonious whole.

Finally, their work can only be enjoyed to the full, and fully understood, when the visitor to their great buildings has done his or her homework: the meaning of color, the symbolism of the saints, and especially the Marian imagery need to be known and recognized before the work of the Zimmermanns can be completely absorbed.

—JAMES STEVENS CURL

ZUCCALLI, Enrico.

German. Born in Roveredo, Grisson, Bavaria, 1642. Died 1724. Father was Giovanni Zuccalli, a stuccoist; brother Dominikus Christophorus Zuccalli (died in 1702) was a builder; brother-in-law Kaspar Zuccalli (1629?-1728) was an architect and master mason at the court in Munich; Enrico's nephew Johann Kaspar (1667?-1717) also was an architect. Enrico probably trained with Kaspar. Appointed court architect at Munich, 1673; rose to become most prominent Bavarian architect from 1679 to 1704 under the elector Max Emanuel, but lost his official posts during Max Emanuel's exile to France from 1704 to 1714; reinstated upon Max Emanuel's return to Munich in 1714, but

Enrico Zuccalli: Schloss Lustheim, Munich, Germany, 1684-88

soon after relinquished his position to the architect Joseph Effner.

Chronology of Works
All in Germany unless noted
† *Work no longer exists*

after 1670	Palais Wahl, Munich†
1672-84	Heilige Kapelle, Altötting (administrative buildings)
1674-92	Theatinerkirche St. Cajetan, Munich
after 1678	Palais Au, Munich†
1679-1701	Residenz, Munich (Kaiserzimmer, Alexandersimmer, Sommerzimmer)†
1684-88	Schloss Lustheim, Munich
1688ff.	Palais Kaunitz-Liechtenstein, Vienna, Austria
1691-95	Kloster der Englischen Fräulein, Munich†
1691-1706	Schloss Aurolzmunster, northern Austria [attributed]
after 1692	Palais Törring-Seefeld, Munich†
1693-94	Palais Fugger-Portia, Munich
1693-1701	Schloss Schleissheim, Munich
1695ff.	Palais des princes-évêques, Liège, Belgium (renovation)
1697-1703	Residenz, Bonn (expansion)
1701	Schloss Nymphenburg, Munich (expansion)
1709-26	Benedictine Monastery, Ettal, upper Bavaria (renovation)

Publications

BOOKS ABOUT ZUCCALLI

EBHARDT, MANFRED: *Die Salzburger Barockkirchen im 17. Jahrhundert: Beschreibung und kunstgeschichtliche Einordnung.* Baden-Baden, Germany, 1975.

HAGER, LUISA: *Nymphenburg: Schloss, Park and Burgen.* Munich, 1955.

HAGER, LUISA and HOJER, GERHARD: *Schleissheim: Neues Scloss und Garten.* Munich, 1965; 4th ed., 1977.

HAUTTMANN, MAX: *Geschichte der Kirchlichen Baukunst in Bayern, Schwaben und Franken, 1550-1780.* Munich, 1921.

HEMPEL, EBERHARD: *Baroque Art and Architecture in Central Europe.* New York, 1965; 2nd ed., 1977.

LIEB, NORBERT: *Münchener Barockbaumeister: Leben und Schaffen in Stadt und Land.*, Munich, 1941.

LIEB, NORBERT: *Barockkirchen zwischen Donau und Alpen.* Munich, 1953; 4th ed., 1976.

PAULUS, RICHARD: *Der Baumeister Henrico Zuccalli am Kurbayerischen Hofe zu München: Ein kunstgeschichtlicher Beitrag zur Entwicklung des Münchener Barock und beginnenden Rokoko.* Strasbourg, 1912.

RIEDEL, DORITH: *Henrico Zuccalli: Planung und Bau des Neuen Schlosses Schlessheim.* Munich, 1977.

ZENDERALLI, ARNOLDO: *Graubündner Baumeister und Stukkatoren in deutschen Landen zur Barock un Rokokozeit.* Zurich, 1930.

ARTICLES ABOUT ZUCCALLI

HUBALA, ERICH: "Schleissheim und Schönbrunn." *Kunstchronik* 10 (1957): 349-353.

HUBALA, ERICH: "Das Schloss Austerlitz in Südmähren." *Adalbert-Stifter-Jahrbuch* 5 (1957): 174-200.

HUBALA, ERICH: "Henrico Zuccallis Schlossbau in Schleissheim: Planung und Baugeschichte, 1700-1704." *Münchner Jahrbuch der bildenden Kunst*, Series 3, 17 (1966): 161-200.

PETZET, MICHAEL: "Unbekannte Entwürfe Zuccallis für die Schleissheimer Schlossbauten." *Münchner Jahrbruch der bildenden Kunst*, Series 3, 22: 179-204.

*

After the end of the Thirty Years' War in 1648, Germany experienced a rapid economic expansion. A shortage of native German artists led to the influx of numerous architects and artisans from northern Italy and Graubünden in eastern Switzerland. Among these were several members of the Zuccalli family, of whom Enrico Zuccalli achieved the greatest significance. He followed his older brother-in-law Gaspare Zuccalli to Munich, where Enrico Zuccalli became court architect to the elector Ferdinand Maria in 1673. At that time he was occupied with plans for the expansion of the Heilige Kapelle at Altötting and the redesign of the surrounding square. The project was only partially realized.

Only the foundations of the monumental pilgrimage church, planned as an imposing centralized structure with an ambulatory, were completed. Zuccalli wrote two studies in connection with the Altötting project, in which he paraphrased two churches by Giovanni Lorenzo Bernini (Santa Maria dell'Assunzione in Ariccia and Sant'Andrea al Quirinale in Rome). The documents, preserved in the state archives at Munich, are the earliest studies done in Bavaria of the centralized designs of the Roman High Baroque. The Dechanthof at Altötting (completed in 1678) shows a severe formal idiom in the classical style, which was characteristic not only of Zuccalli's work but also of that of the other masters from Graubünden.

In 1674 Zuccalli was commissioned to complete the Theatine Church of St. Cajetan in Munich. The building, modeled after the Church of Sant'Andrea della Valle in Rome, had been begun by Agostino Barelli in 1663. Even before Zuccalli's involvement with the project, it had been decided to construct a two-tower facade—perhaps at the instigation of the Theatine priest Antonio Spinelli. Zuccalli's contribution to the project was limited to the construction of the dome and the design of the facade. Zuccalli's facade differed from Barelli's in that he reduced the ornamentation while making the articulation elements more prominent. The facade was completed only after 1765 by François Cuvilliés the Elder.

Between 1684 and 1688, Zuccalli built Schloss Lustheim at Oberschleissheim near Munich for the elector Max Emanuel. The building, in Zuccalli's characteristic style, consists of a number of connected cube-like blocks. The clear and severe articulation of the western facade is limited to classical forms (pilaster strips, pilasters, triangular and segmented gables). The ornamentation is very spare, and is utilized only to emphasize the central zone with the portal.

In 1701 the so-called "new Schloss Schleissheim" was erected across from Schloss Lustheim, at the other end of a long canal, which forms the long axis of a large park. A planning phase of more than 10 years preceded the construction of the building. Zuccalli's first designs concerned the alteration and expansion of "Old Schleissheim" (begun in 1597). The three "oval designs" with an elliptical (lengthwise or crosswise) central hall also belong to the early planning phase. These early designs may be compared to the works of Johann Bernhard Fischer von Erlach, particularly Schloss Engelhartstetten (Niederweiden) in southern Austria, which was begun in 1693. Fischer von Erlach's designs for a number of "pleasure houses" influenced Zuccalli's work at Schleissheim as well. In designs dating from the second half of the 1690s, Zuccalli planned gigantic three- or four-wing structures. The compositions of the later designs are more closed, possibly in response to Fischer von Erlach's Schloss Schönbrunn in Vienna (begun in 1696). In the end, only one wing connected to two pavilions by means of low galleries was actually built at Schleissheim. Schloss Aurolzmunster in northern Austria (formerly Bavaria), built between 1691 and 1706 for Count von der Wahl, is similar to Schleissheim. Aurolzmunster has traditionally been ascribed to the Salzburg court architect Giovanni Gaspare Zuccalli, but was most probably the work of Enrico Zuccalli.

Enrico Zuccalli also supplied the designs for the expansion of the castle at Bonn (begun in 1697) and of Schloss Nymphenburg in Munich (1701). At Nymphenburg, two-story galleries and stepped pavilions were added to the main building. The principle of loosely connected building blocks may be traced to Daniel Marot the Elder's palace Het Loo (1685-87) near Apeldoorn in the Netherlands, which Zuccalli may have seen during a trip in 1693. The complexes at Bonn, Schleissheim and Nymphenburg were completed following the War of the Spanish Succession, after 1715. At that time, some changes were made in Zuccalli's designs.

Of Zuccalli's numerous palaces, only the city palace of Kaunitz-Liechtenstein in Vienna (begun in 1688) and the Munich Portia Palace (begun in 1693) have been preserved, though in slightly altered form. The facade of the palace in Vienna clearly shows the influence of Bernini's Palazzo Chigi-Odescalchi in Rome, construction of which was begun in 1664.

Zuccalli's last important work was the alteration of the Benedictine Monastery Ettal in Upper Bavaria. He received the commission in 1709, but construction was concluded only long after Zuccalli's death. The facade of this centralized Gothic church has a concave and a convex curve, and may be traced to Bernini's first design for the eastern facade of the Louvre in Paris (1664). The architecture of Bernini was the most important influence on Zuccalli throughout his career, while the influence of Fischer von Erlach and of the Dutch model was limited to single buildings. Zuccalli's significance resides most of all in his introduction of the formal idiom of the Roman High Baroque to Bavaria.

—HANSJÖRG WEIDENHOFFER
Translated from the German by Marijke Rijsberman

BUILDING INDEX

A

B

D

G

H

I

J

K

L

N

P

Q

R

S

T

U

W

X

Y

Z

NOTES ON CONTRIBUTORS

ADAM, Bernd. Academic adviser, Institute for Architecture and Art History, University of Hannover, Germany. Leader of a project for the investigation of the history of the old town halls in Hannover. **Essay:** Hannover: Altes Rathaus.

ADAMS, David. Director, Center for Architectural and Design Research, Grass Valley, California. Author of essays and booklets on art and architecture, with special emphasis on American stained glass and German expressionist architecture. Contributor to *Journal of the Society of Architectural Historians.* **Essay:** Dornach: Goetheanum.

ALEXANDER, Robert L. Emeritus professor of art history, University of Iowa, Iowa City. Senior editor, *The Papers of Robert Mills.* Author of *The Architecture of Maximilian Godefroy,* 1974; *The Architecture of Russell Warren,* 1979; *The Sculpture and Sculptors of Yazilikaya,* 1986; numerous articles and lectures on architectural history. **Essay:** Maximilian Godefroy.

ALEXIS, Karin M. E. Art and architectural historian, Center for Advanced Study in the Visual Arts, National Gallery of Art, Washington, D.C. Coordinator of the Smithsonian Institution's Art History Series Certificate Program. Author of numerous articles on art and architecture. **Essays:** Russell Sturgis; Tessin Family; Kalmar Cathedral; Stockholm: Drottningholm; Stockholm: Royal Palace.

ANDREOTTI, Libero. Assistant professor of architecture, Georgia Institute of Technology. Assistant editor, *Journal of Architectural Education.* Author of a book on Italian art and architecture during fascism (in progress); numerous lectures and articles on Italian Rationalism and architectural theory and criticism. **Essay:** Como: Casa del Fascio.

ARMS, Meredith. Doctoral candidate in American art and architectural history, Rutgers University. Historic preservation consultant, Sullebarger Associates, Oldwick, New Jersey. **Essays:** Pietro Belluschi; John Hejduk; James Gallier, Sr.; Houston, Texas: Indeterminate Facade Showroom.

BADENOCH-WATTS, Teresa S. Assistant professor of

art history, Potsdam College, State University of New York. Author of *The Works of Johann Heinrich Müntz (1727-1798)* (catalogue exhibition), 1992. Contributor to journals. **Essays:** Charles De Wailly; Simon Du Ry; Richard Boyle, Third Earl of Burlington; Kassel: Löwenburg; London: Chiswick House.

BAHR, Carolin. Formerly affiliated with Institute for Art History, Justus-Liebeg-Universität, Giessen. Author of articles in *Gießener Kunstweg* and *Wege zur Kunst.* **Essays:** Heinrich von Ferstel; Theophilus Hansen.

BALAKIER, Ann Stewart. Associate professor of art history, University of South Dakota, Vermillion. Author of *The Newton Connection* (in preparation). **Essays:** Lieven De Key; Louis Le Vau; Pieter Post; Michele Sanmicheli; Jacob Van Campen; Berkshire: St. George's Chapel, Windsor.

BARNES, Carl F., Jr. Professor of art history and archaeology, Oakland University, Rochester, Michigan. Author of *Villard de Honnecourt, the Artist and His Drawing: A Critical Biography,* 1982. Former president of International Center of Medieval Art and Association Villard de Honnecourt for the Interdisciplinary Study of Science, Technology and Art. **Essays:** Villard de Honnecourt; William of Sens.

BELTON, Robert J. Faculty member, McMaster University, Hamilton, Ontario, Canada. **Essays:** Ernest Cormier; Moshe Safdie; Montreal: Habitat (Expo '67).

BERING, Kunibert. Instructor, Ruhr-Universität Bochum, Germany. Author of *Fra Angelico,* 1984; *Baupropagand der Frührenaissance in Florez-Rom-Pienza,* 1984; *Kunst und Staatsmetaphysik des Hochmittelalters in Italien,* 1986; numerous articles about art and architecture in the Middle Ages and the 20th century. **Essays:** Camillo Sitte; Amsterdam: Herengracht.

BINDING, Gunther. Professor of art history, University of Cologne, Germany. Author of numerous books and articles about architecture, including *Ordensbaukunst in Deutschland,* 1985; *Architektonische Formenlehre,* 1987; *Masswerk,* 1989; *Deutscher Fachwerkbau,* 1989; *Das Dachwerk,* 1991; *Baubetrieb im Mittelalter,* 1993. **Essays:**

Parler Family; Würzburg: Residenz.

BLYTHE, Robert W. Historian, National Park Service, Atlanta, Georgia. Past treasurer of Chicago chapter, Society of Architectural Historians. **Essays:** Charles Bowler Atwood; Minard Lafever; Washington, D.C.: Lincoln Memorial.

BOGNAR, Botond. Professor of architecture, University of Illinois at Urbana-Champaign. Architectural essayist, critic and photographer. Correspondent for *Architecture and Urbanism,* Tokyo, Japan. Author of *Contemporary Japanese Architecture: Its Development and Challenge,* 1985; *The New Japanese Architecture,* 1990. **Essays:** Tadao Ando; Fumihiko Maki; Kazuo Shinohara.

BOHAN, Peter. Professor and chair of Department of Art History, State University of New York, College at New Paltz. Formerly gallery director, College at New Paltz, and assistant curator, Yale University art gallery. Author of *Early American Gold,* 1963; articles on James Burton. **Essays:** Decimus Burton; James Burton.

BOKER, Hans J. Contributor. **Essay:** Cologne Cathedral.

BORNGÄSSER-KLEIN, Barbara. Specialist in Iberian architecture, Ibero-Amerikanisches Institut Preussischer Kulturbesitz, Berlin, Germany. **Essays:** Juan Gomez de Mora; Francisco Hurtado; Ventura Rodríguez; Diogo de Torralva; Juan de Villanueva; Alcobaça: Abbey Church; Belém: Jeronymite Monastery; Madrid: Museo del Prado; Tomar: Christo Church.

BOYLE, Bernard M. Professor of architecture, Arizona State University, Tempe. Editor, *Materials in the Architecture of Arizona, 1870-1920,* 1976; *Blain Drake: Forty Years of Architecture in Arizona,* 1992. Author of articles on Roman and modern architecture; numerous lectures on architecture and historic preservation. **Essays:** Pietro da Cortona; Herculanuem; Nîmes: Maison Carrée; Nîmes: Pont du Gard; Rome: Forum Romanum; Rome: Palazzo Barberini; Rome: Theater of Marcellus.

BRIERLEY, E. S. Senior lecturer in architecture, De Montfort University, Leicester. Author of *De Stijl and the Amsterdam School,* 1979; *J. L. M. Lauwerik's Proportional Systems and Geometrical Structure Drawings,* 1980; *J. B. Bakema, An Architect's Social Attitude to Design,* 1985; numerous lectures and articles on 20th-century European architecture and urbanism. **Essays:** Michel De Klerk; Van den Broek and Bakema; Van der Vlugt and Brinkman; Amsterdam: Eigen Haard Housing.

BROTHERS, Leslie A. Scholar of art history and museum studies. Formerly assistant to curator of photography, Virginia Museum of Fine Arts. Contributor of reviews to *New Art Examiner.* **Essay:** Moscow: Metro Stations.

BROWN-MANRIQUE, Gerado. Professor of architecture, Miami University, Oxford, Ohio. Formerly visiting critic at University of Oregon. Author of *The Ticino Guide,* 1989; *Words and Works: Writings and Projects,* 1989; numerous essays and research presentations on design and parallel issues, and the work of contemporary architects, including O. M. Ungers and the Tendenza architects. **Essays:** Leon Krier; Rob Krier; Aldo Rossi; Oswald Mathias Ungers; Karlsruhe: Marktplatz; Berlin: Altes Museum; Berlin: Gross-Siedlung Siemensstadt; Berlin: IBA.

BUGSLAG, Jim. Visiting assistant professor, University of Victoria, British Columbia. Author of several lectures and articles about medieval stained glass and design. **Essays:** Henry of Reyns; Gloucester Cathedral; Bourges: House of Jacques Coeur; Carcassonne: City Walls and Fortifications; Centula: St. Riquier; Caernarvonshire: Caernarvon Castle; Oxford: Christ Church College; Oxford: Queen's College; Paris: Hôtel de Cluny; Périgueux: St. Front; York: Minster; Vézelay: La Madeleine.

ČAČKOVIĆ, Dražen. Architect, Arex Corporation, Pleasantville, New York. Assistant professor of art and architecture, Lehigh University, Bethlehem, Pennsylvania, and Kansas State University. Formerly coeditor, *Architecture Update.* Author of *Il Gruppo 7: A Bibliography of Periodical Literature,* 1987; *Luciano Boldessari: A Bibliography of Books and Periodical Literature,* 1989; articles and lectures on contemporary architecture. **Essay:** Banfir, Belgiojoso, Peresutti and Rogers (BBPR).

CAMERON, K. C. Reader in French and Renaissance studies, University of Exeter. Editor, *Montaigne and His Age,* 1981; *From Valois to Bourbon,* 1989. Author of *Henri III, a Maligned or Malignant King: Satirical Iconography of Henri de Valois,* 1978; numerous articles on late 16th-century satirical iconography. **Essays:** London: Mansion House; Paris: Madeleine; Paris: Sacré Coeur; Paris: Val de Grâce; Reims Cathedral; Vaux-le-Vicomte: Château.

CARD, Melissa. Graduate student in art history, Rutgers University. **Essays:** Holabird and Roche; Cesar Pelli; New York City: Battery Park City.

CAST, David. Professor of the history of art, Bryn Mawr College, Bryn Mawr, Pennsylvania. Former president of Philadelphia chapter of Society of Architectural Historians. Author of *The Calumny of Apelles,* 1981. **Essays:** Franco Albini; Galeazzo Alessi; Jacques-Denis Antoine; François-Joseph Bélanger; Jacques-François Blondel; Alexandre-Théodore Brongniart; Bernardo Buontalenti; Charles Cameron; Carlo Castellamonte; Mauro Coducci; P. J. H. Cuypers; Robert de Cotte; Hendrik De Keyser; Peter Ellis; Il Filarete; Jacques Gondouin; Harrison and Abramovits;

Nicholas Hawksmoor; Johann Lukas von Hildebrandt; Guiseppe Japelli; Pietro Lombardo; Carlo Maderno; François Mansart; Hugh May; Eugenio Montuori; John Nash; Giovanni Battista Nolli; Gilles-Marie Oppenord; Roger Pratt; Raphael; Giuliano da Sangallo; Vincenzo Scamozzi; Giles Gilbert Scott; James Smith; Robert Smythson; Robert A. M. Stern; William Talman; Giuseppe Valadier; John Vanbrugh; Henry Yevele; London: British Museum; London: Christ Church, Spitalfields; London: Westminster Hall, Houses of Parliament; London: St. Stephen's Chapel, Houses of Parliament; London: Paddington Station; London: Regent's Park; Milan Cathedral; Milan: Santa Maria Delle Grazie; Naples: Castle Nuovo; Naples: San Francesco di Paola; Pavia: Certosa; Rome: Palazzo Della Cancelleria; Rome: Sant' Andrea Della Valle; Rome: Tempietto; Rome: Villa Madama; Yorkshire: Castle Howard.

CHELAZZI, Giuliano. Architect in private practice, Florence, Italy. Contributor to *Pan Arte, Deutsche Bauzeitung* and *L'Architettura.* **Essays:** Arnolfo di Cambio; Filippo Brunelleschi; Michelozzo; Florence: Cathedral; Florence: Ospedale Degli Innocenti; Florence: Palazzo Pitti.

CHRISTENSEN, Ellen A. Doctoral candidate in art history, Northwestern University, Evanston, Illinois. Author of *Government Architecture and British Imperialism: Patronage and Imperial Policy in London, Pretoria and New Delhi (1800-1931)* (thesis: Northwestern University), in preparation; lectures and articles on Edwin Lutyens and Frank Lloyd Wright. **Essays:** Herbert Baker; Owen Jones; Gottfried Semper: Aston Webb.

CLARKE, Timothy. Writer in London, England. Author of numerous articles on architecture and design. **Essays:** London: Battersea Power Station; Paris: La Défense.

COHEN, George M. Professor of art history, Hofstra University, Hempstead, New York. Contributor to *American Artist, Art Voices, Arts Magazine, Art International, College Arts Journal* and other periodicals. Author of *A History of American Art,* 1971. **Essays:** James Bogardus; Charles Bulfinch; Georges-Eugène Haussmann; Raymond M. Hood; William Le Baron Jenney; Pierre Lescot; James Renwick; John A. and Washington Roebling; John Hubbard Sturgis; Richard Upjohn; New York City: St. John the Divine.

COHEN, Pamela A. Graduate student in art history, Rutgers University. **Essay:** Clorindo Testa.

CONDIT, Carl W. Emeritus professor of history and art history, Northwestern University, Evanston, Illinois. Author of books and articles on the history of architecture, building technology and urban technology, published from 1948 to 1982. **Essay:** New York City: Woolworth Building.

COOK, Jeffrey. Regents' professor of architecture, Arizona State University, Tempe. Founding editor, *Passive Solar Journal.* Author of *The Architecture of Bruce Goff,* 1978; *Award Winning Passive Solar Buildings,* 1984; *Passive Cooling,* 1989; *Anasazi Places,* 1992. **Essays:** Sebastiano Serlio; Paolo Soleri.

COOLEDGE, Harold N., Jr. Emeritus professor of art and architectural history, Clemson University, Clemson, South Carolina. Author of *Lusitania,* 1978; *Samuel Sloan, Architect of Philadelphia, 1815-1884;* articles on mid-19th-century architecture and the work of Samuel Sloan. **Essay:** Samuel Sloan.

CORMIER, Leslie Humm. Faculty of Fine Arts, Harvard University Extension, Boston, Massachusetts. Author of articles and lectures on European emigre modernism and its synthesis with American idiom. **Essays:** Walter Gropius; E. Maxwell Fry; The Architects Collaborative (TAC); Lincoln, Massachusetts: Gropius House.

CRAIG, Robert M. Associate professor of architectural history, Georgia Tech, Atlanta. Author of *Guide to Atlanta Architecture,* in preparation. Contributor to *Southern Home.* **Essays:** Charles Sumner and Henry Mather Greene; Edwin Landseer Lutyens; Bernard Maybeck; Julia Morgan; A. W. N. Pugin; Henry Hobson Richardson; Charles Francis Annesley Voysey; Atlanta, Georgia: Hyatt Regency Hotel; Surrey: Tigbourne Court, Hambledon.

CROWE, Ann Glen. Assistant professor of art history, Virginia Commonwealth University, Richmond. Contributor of reviews for *Artpapers.* Author of *The Art of Goya and the Duchess of Alba (1792-1802),* (dissertation: Stanford University). Past president, Ibero-American Society for Eighteenth-Century Studies. **Essays:** Frank Gehry; Arata Isozaki; Los Angeles, California: Museum of Contemporary Art.

CURL, James Stevens. Professor of architectural history, De Montfort University, Leicester, England. Formerly architectural editor, *The Survey of London.* Formerly architect to the Scottish Committee for European Architectural Heritage Year. Author of *A Celebration of Death,* 1980; *The Egyptian Revival,* 1982; *The Life and Work of Henry Roberts (1803-76), Architect,* 1983; *The Londonderry Plantation, 1609-1914,* 1986; *Victorian Architecture,* 1990; *The Art and Architecture of Freemasonry,* 1991; *Classical Architecture,* 1992; *Encyclopaedia of Architectural Terms,* 1992; *Gregorian Architecture,* 1993; numerous articles on architecture, planning, music and the environment. **Essays:** Osvald Almqvist; Asam Brothers; Georg Bähr; George Basevi; John Francis Bentley; Colen Campbell; William Chambers; François Cuvilliés; George the Elder Dance; Dientzenhofer Brothers; Kilian Ignaz Dientzhofer; Friedrich Wilhelm von Erdmannsdorff; Josef Anton Feuchtmayer; Johann Michael Fischer; Johann Bernhard Fischer von Erlach; James

Gandon; Friedrich von Gärtner; Friedrich Gilly; Henry Holland; Leo von Klenze; Georg Wenzeslaus von Knobelsdorff; Carl Gotthard Langhans; Caspar Moosbrugger; Roger Mulholland; Edward Lovett Pearce; Matthaeus D. Pöppelmann; Jacob Prandtauer; John Rennie; Humphry Repton; Henry Roberts; Karl Friedrich Schinkel; Andreas Schlüter; James Stuart; Robert Taylor; Michael and Peter Thumb; Friedrich Winbrenner; Dominikus and Johann Baptist Zimmerman; Berlin: Brandenburg Gate; Berlin: Neue Wache; Dublin: Custom House; Lübeck: Marktplatz; Munich: Amalienburg; Munich: Königsbau; Munich: Propyläen; Munich: St. John Nepomuk; Munich: Michaelskirche; Potsdam: Nikolaikirche; Potsdam: Palace of Sans Souci; Salzburg: Schloss Mirabell; Steinhausen: Pilgrimage Church; Vienna: Hofburg; Vienna: Karlskirche; Vienna: Piaristenkirch; Vienna: Schloss Schönbrunn; Vienna: Belvedere; Vierzehnheiligen: Pilgrimage Church; Weingarten: Abbey Church.

DALE, Antony. Author of *James Wyatt, Architect,* 1956. **Essay:** Frank Lloyd Wright.

DAVIS, Joyce M. Associate professor of art, Valdosta State College, Georgia. Formerly associate professor of architecture and art, Southern University, Baton Rouge, Louisiana. Author of *Lakeland's Unique Architectural Heritage,* 1987; articles on Lakeland, Florida, women artists, African-American women artists. **Essays:** Lancelot "Capability" Brown; Jules Hardouin-Mansart; André Le Nôtre; London: Banqueting House, Whitehouse; Middlesex: Syon House, Isleworth; Nottinghamshire: Wollaton Hall; Oxfordshire: Blenheim Palace; Paris: Panthéon (Ste. Geneviève); Paris: Place des Vosges; Paris: Place Vendôme: Paris: St. Sulpice; Rome: San Giovanni in Laterano; Rome: Trevi Fountain; Versailles: Park.

DELGADO, Annabel. Architect and president, Architectural Design Consultants, Miami, Florida. Coeditor of *New City Journal.* Formerly visiting lecturer in design, University of Miami, Coral Gales, Florida. Cofounder of Miami Design Alliance. Contributor of book reviews to periodicals. **Essays:** Henri Labrouste; Auguste Perret; Le Raincy: Church of Notre Dame; Paris: Bibliothèque Nationale.

DEWEY, Tom II. Associate professor, University of Mississippi. Author of numerous exhibition catalogues. **Essays:** Henry Van de Velde; Bear Run, Pennsylvania: Fallingwater; Brussels: Palais Stoclet.

DIXON, Susan M. Scholar of the history of art. Formerly teaching assistant, Cornell University. **Essays:** Ferdinando Fuga; Alessandro Galilei; Carlo Lodoli; Carlo Marchionni; Giovanni Batitista Piranesi; Luigi Vanvitelli; Bernardo Antonio Vittone.

DOIG, Allan. Assistant curate, St. Helen's Church, Abingdon, England. Formerly lecturer in history and

theory of Art, University of Kent. Author of *The Architectural Drawings Collection of King's College, Cambridge,* 1979; *Theo van Doesburg: Painting into Architecture, Theory into Practice,* 1986. **Essays:** Theo Van Doesburg; Amsterdam: Stock Exchange.

DONHAUSER, Peter L. Doctoral candidate in fine arts, New York University. Assistant museum educator, Metropolitan Museum of Art. Author of articles, lectures and reviews on architecture. **Essay:** New York City: Metropolitan Museum of Art.

DONNELLY, Marian C. Emeritus professor of art history, University of Oregon, Eugene. Fellow of Royal Society of Arts, London. Past president of Society of Architectural Historians. Author of *New England Meeting Houses of the Seventeenth Century,* 1968; *A Short History of Observatories,* 1973; *Architecture in the Scandinavian Countries,* 1992. **Essays:** Carl Fredrik Adelkrantz; Carl Ludwig Engel; Christian Heinrich Grosch; Copenhagen: Amalienborg; Copenhagen: Bourse; Copenhagen: Rosenborg Palace; Helsinki: Senate Square.

DREW, Philip. Architectural historian and critic, Sydney, Australia. Australian correspondent, *Architecture and Urbanism.* Author of *Third Generation: The Changing Meaning of Architecture,* 1973; *Frei Otto: Form and Structure,* 1976; *Tensile Architecture,* 1979; *Two Towers,* 1980; *The Architecture of Arata Isozaki,* 1982; *Leave of Iron: Glenn Murcutt, Pioneer of an Australian Architectural Form,* 1985; *Harry Seidler: Four Decades of Architecture,* 1992; *Veranda: Embracing Place,* 1992; *Real Space: Martorell, Bohigas, Mackay, Puigdomenech,* 1993; numerous articles and lectures on tensile, contemporary and Australian architecture and criticism. **Essays:** Walter Burley Griffin; Frei Otto; Jørn Utzon; Sydney: Opera House.

DROST, Uwe. Assistant professor of architecture, University of Maryland, College Park. Director, International Forum of Young Architects; president of Office of Independent Architecture; president of INTERFACE Consulting. Numerous lectures on contemporary urban design and contemporary German architecture. **Essays:** Günther Behnisch; Egon Eiermann; Hugo Häring; Hans Scharoun; Bruno Taut; Cologne: Werkbund Exposition, 1914; Munich: Olympic Games Complex.

DUNLOP, Ian G. D. Vicar and canon, Salisbury Cathedral. Author of *Versailles,* 1956, 1970; *Châteaux of the Loire,* 1969; *Palaces and Progresses of Elizabeth I,* 1982; *Royal Palaces of France,* 1985; *Burgundy,* 1990. **Essays:** Sébastian le Prestre de Vauban; Beauvais Cathedral; Blois: Château; Chambord: Château; Chartres Cathedral; Dumfriesshire: Drumlanrig Castle; Paris: Louvre; Paris: Nortre-Dame Cathedral; Salisbury Cathedral; Versailles: Palace; Versailles: Petite Trianon;

Versailles: Grand Trianon.

EARLY, James. Professor of English, Southern Methodist University, Dallas, Texas. Author of *Romanticism and American Architecture,* 1965; *Colonial Mexico: Architecture in the Society of Vice Regal New Spain* (in preparation). **Essay:** Mexico City: Cathedral.

ECHOLS, Gordon. Professor of landscape architecture, Urban Planning and Architecture, Texas A&M University, College Station, Texas. Author of *The Early Indigenous Architecture of Texas,* 1993; numerous articles on Spanish colonial planning and architecture. **Essays:** Churriguera Family; Thomas Jefferson; Josep Lluís Sert; Thomas U. Walter; Paris: Eiffel Tower; Paris: Unesco Headquarters; Richmond, Virginia: Virginia State Capital; Siena: Palazzo Pubblico; Venice: Piazza San Marco.

EGGENER, Keith. Doctoral candidate in history of art, Stanford University, Stanford, California. Author of lectures and articles on Mexican modernist architecture. **Essays:** Luis Barragán; Felix Candela; Juan O'Gorman; José Villagran Garcia; Gregori Warchavchik; Mexico: University City.

EISENMAN, H. J. Professor of history, University of Missouri—Rolla. Author of article on Frank Lloyd Wright in *Great Lives from History: American Series,* 1987. **Essay:** Chicago, Illinois: Marshall Field Wholesale Store.

ELMAS, Cynthia. Graduate student in art history, Rutgers University. **Essays:** Jacques Ignace Hittorff; Percier and Fontaine.

ERDMANN, Biruta. Associate professor of art history, East Carolina University, Greenville, North Carolina. Author of introduction to *The Architectural Heritage of Greenville, North Carolina,* 1988. **Essay:** Leopold Eidlitz.

FAWCETT, Peter. Architect. Professor of architecture and head of Department of Architecture and Planning, University of Nottingham, England. Contributor to *Ulster Architect;* numerous lectures and articles on interwar and postwar British architecture. Exhibitor of architectural drawings at national exhibitions. **Essays:** Mario Botta; Johannes Duiker; Frederick Gibberd; Herman Hertzberger; Denys Lasdun; Le Corbusier; Berthold Lubetkin; Robert Hogg Matthew; Basil Spence; Aldo Van Eyck; Liverpool: Metropolitan Cathedral; Marseilles: Unité d'Habitation; London: London Zoo (Penguin Pool/Gorilla House); London: National Gallery Competition; Poissy: Villa Savoye.

FAZIO, Michael W. Professor of architecture, Mississippi State University. Coeditor of *Arris,* the journal of the Southeast Society of Architectural Historians. **Essay:** Benjamin H. Latrobe (with Patrick Snadon).

FERKIN, Robert. Registered interior designer. Author of paper "Harwell Hamilton Harris: His Legacy in American Architecture." Member of Society of Architectural Historians. **Essay:** Hans Hollein.

FRANK, Suzanne S. Associate adjunct professor of architectural history, New York Institute of Technology. Member of Society of Architectural Historians. Author of *Michel DeKlerk (1884-1923): An Architect of the Amsterdam School,* 1984; *House 6—Peter Eisenman's Dream House Revisited* (forthcoming). **Essays:** Peter Eisenman; Columbus, Ohio: Wexner Center for the Visual Arts.

FRICELLI, Donald. Assistant professor of art history, Fordham University, New York City. Formerly assistant professor, Adelphi College, Garden City, New York. Lecturer in Italian art and architecture. Author of *The Architecture of Giorgio Vasari's Uffizi.* **Essays:** Bartolomeo Ammannati; Leonardo da Vinci; Giorgio Vasari; Florence: Uffizi; Rome: Città Universitaria.

GARMAZ, Magdalena. Assistant professor of architecture, Auburn University, Alabama. Formerly architect in Yugoslavia. Author of articles and lectures on Jože Plečnik. **Essay:** Jože Plečnik.

GENSHIEMER, Thomas. Doctoral candidate in architectural history, University of California, Berkeley (dissertation on medieval Islamic cities of East Africa). **Essays:** Cordoba: Cathedral/Mosque of Cordoba; Granada: Alhambra.

GLASSMAN, Paul. Director, Morris-Jumel Mansion, New York City. Contributor to *Inland Architect.* Formerly assistant director, The Frank Lloyd Wright Home and Studio Foundation and visiting lecturer in architectural history, school of Art Institute of Chicago. Past vice president, Chicago Society of Architectural Historians. **Essays:** Daniel Hudson Burnham; Helmut Jahn; Jacopo Sansovino; Chicago: State of Illinois Center; Venice: Library of St. Mark's; Venice: Palazzo Corner.

GLEYE, Paul H. Head of experimental workshop, Bauhaus, Dessau, Germany, and member of Architecture faculty, Montana State University. Author of *The Architecture of Los Angeles,* 1981. **Essay:** Los Angeles: Lovell Health House.

GOODSTEIN, Ethel S. Associate professor of architecture, University of Arkansas, Fayetteville. Formerly associate professor of architecture, University of Southwestern Louisiana. Author of articles in *International Journal of Canadian Studies, American Review of Canadian Studies* and *Critical Studies in Mass Communication;* numerous papers on 19th- and 20th-century North American and British architecture. Member of southeast chapter of Society of Architectural Historians. **Essays:**

Arthur Erickson; Mississauga City Hall; Ottawa: Dominion Parliament Buildings; Toronto: University College.

GOY, Richard J. Author of *Chioggia and the Villages of the Venetian Lagoon,* 1985; *Venetian Vernacular Architecture,* 1988; *The House of Gold: Building a Palace in Medieval Venice,* 1993; numerous articles on the history and architecture of Venice. **Essays:** Venice: Ca' D'Oro; Venice: Doge's Palace; Vicenze: La Rotonda.

GREENE, Francis J. Professor in Department of Languages and Fine Arts, St. Francis College, Brooklyn Heights, New York. Author of articles on French culture and literature. Member of Society of Architectural Historians; member of board of directors, The United Nations Association. **Essays:** Cuthbert Brodrick; Otto Wagner; Liverpool: St. George's Hall; Vienna: Majolica House; Vienna: Postal Savings Bank.

GUILES-CURRAN, Susan. Doctoral candidate in art history, Rutgers University, New Brunswick, New Jersey. **Essays:** Irving Gill; Hector Guimard.

GUISE, David E. Emeritus professor of architecture, City College of New York. Former visiting adjunct professor at University of Pennsylvania and Columbia University. Author of articles on progressive architecture, published in *New York Times* and *Encyclopaedia Britannica Yearbook.* **Essay:** New York City: Seagram Building.

GÜVEN, Suna. Associate professor of architectural history and chair of Department of Architecture, Middle East Technical University, Ankara, Turkey. Member of editorial board of *Journal of the Faculty of Architecture.* Author of articles on Roman architecture. **Essays:** Hermogenes; Vitruvius; Aspendos; Miletos.

HABEL, Dorothy Metzger. Associate professor of art history, University of Tennessee, Knoxville. Author of numerous articles on 17th- and early 18th-century architecture and planning in Rome. **Essays:** Giovanni Antonio De Rossi; Filippo Raguzzini; Carlo Rainaldi.

HAWKINS, Richard L. Security supervisor, Monticello, the home of Thomas Jefferson, Charlottesville, Virginia. **Essay:** Charlottesville: University of Virginia.

HENRY, Jay C. Professor of architecture, University of Texas at Arlington. Author of *Architecture in Texas, 1895-1945,* 1993; numerous papers on Texas and American architecture and European modernism. **Essays:** Fritz Höger; Amsterdam: Scheepvaarthuis; Hamburg: Chilehaus.

HERBERT, Gilbert. Mary Hill Swope Professor of Architecture and Town Planning, Technion: Israel Institute of Technology, Haifa. Formerly teacher at University of Witwatersrand, Johannesburg, and University of Adelaide, South Australia. Author of *The Synthetic Vision of Walter Gropius,* 1959; *Martienssen and the International Style: The Development of Modern Architecture in South Africa,* 1975; *Pioneers of Prefabrication: The British Contribution in the Nineteenth Century,* 1978; *The Dream of the Factory-Made House: Walter Gropius and Konrad Wachsmann,* 1984. **Essays:** Erich Mendelsohn; London: St. Pancras Station and Hotel; Stuttgart: Schocken Department Store.

HESSE, Michael. Professor of history of art, Universität Heidelberg, Germany. Author of *Von der Nachgotik zur Neugotik,* 1984; *Studien zu Renaissance und Barock,* 1986; numerous articles and lectures on modern and contemporary architecture and the fine arts. **Essays:** Dominikus Böhm, Josef-Paul Kleihues; Charles Le Brun; Johann Santini-Aichel.

HILES, Timothy W. Assistant professor of art history, University of Tennessee, Knoxville. Author of articles on Morris Louis; lectures and papers on fin de siècle painting and sculpture. **Essay:** Paris: Métro Stations.

HILLS, Helen. Lecturer in art history, Keele University. Author of *Marmi Mischi in Seventeenth-Century Palermo* (in press). **Essays:** Baldassare Longhena; Andrea Pozzo; Palermo: Piazza Vigliena; Venice: Santa Maria Della Salute.

HOLDER, Philancy N. Emeritus professor of art history, Austin Peay State University, Clarksville, Tennessee. Author of *Cortona in Context, the History and Architecture of an Italian Hill Town,* 1992; numerous articles and lectures. **Essays:** Rome: Villa Giulia; Vicenza: Palazzo Chiericati.

HOLLIDAY, Peter J. Assistant professor of art history, California State University, San Bernardino. Editor of *Narrative and Event in Ancient Art,* 1993. Author of numerous articles on classical art and architecture. **Essays:** Rome: Arch of Constantine; Rome: Arch of Titus; Rome: Temple of Fortuna Virilis.

HORNIK, Heidi J. Assistant professor of art, Baylor University, Waco, Texas. Author of exhibition catalogues; papers on Michele di Ridolfo del Ghirlandaio. **Essay:** Florence: Santa Maria Novella.

HOWE, Eunice D. Associate professor of art history, University of Southern California, Los Angeles. Author of *The Hospital of Santo Spirito and Pope Sixtus IV,* 1978; *Andrea Palladio, the Churches of Rome,* 1991; numerous lectures and articles on Roman urbanism, Italian painting, papal patronage and guidebooks to Rome. **Essays:** Donato Bramante; Giacomo Del Duca; Luciano Laurana; Giacomo della Porta; Antonio da Sangallo the Younger; Giacomo Barozzi da Vignola; Rome: Il Gesù; Rome: Vatican.

HURLEY, Kent C. Associate professor of architecture and

assistant dean, Technical University of Nova Scotia. Former editor for Tech Press. Lecturer in architectural conservation and the English country house. **Essay:** Norfolk: Holkham Hall.

HÜTTEL, Richard. Author of *Kustos Graphische Sammlung; Spiegelungen einer Ruine-Leonardos Abendmahl im 19. und 20. Jahrhundert,* 1993; numerous articles about Leonardo's *Last Supper,* capital town and symbolism of a ground plan. **Essays:** Gottfried Böhm; Nancy: Place Royale (Place Stanislas).

ISTVANFI, Gyula. Professor of history of architecture, Technical University of Budapest, Hungary. **Essays:** Budapest: East Railway Station; Budapest: St. Stephen's Basilica; Budapest: University Church.

JACKSON, Anthony. Formerly professor of architecture, Technical University of Nova Scotia, Halifax, Canada. Author of *The Politics of Architecture,* 1970; *A Place Called Home,* 1976; numerous articles on theoretical aspects of architecture. **Essays:** William Morris; New York City: Grand Central Terminal; New York City: Lever House.

JACKSON, Neil. Architect and architectural historian. Lecturer in architecture, University of Nottingham. Author of *F. W. Troop, Architect,* 1985; *Nineteenth Century Bath Architects and Architecture,* 1991; numerous articles on 19th- and 20th-century architecture. **Essays:** William Adam; William Bruce; William Henry Playfair; Aberdeenshire: Craigievar Castle; Edinburgh: Holyroodhouse.

JAMES, Warren A. Architect. Principal, James & Associates, New York City. Formerly designer at Robert A. M. Stern Architects, New York, and Ricardo Bofill/Taller de Arquitectura, Barcelona and Paris. Author of *Ricardo Bofill/ Taller de Arquitectura: Buildings and Projects, 1960-1988,* 1988; *Kohn Pederssen Fox: Architecture and Urbanism, 1986-1992,* 1993; numerous articles on contemporary architects and architecture. Member of American Institute of Architects, National Institute for Architectural Education and Architectural League. **Essays:** Ricardo Bofill; New Canaan Connecticut: Johnson Glass House; New York City: AT&T Building; Barcelona: German Pavilion.

JUHASZ, Joseph B. Associate professor of architecture and planning, University of Colorado, Boulder. Author of *Environments: Notes and Selections on Objects, Spaces and Behavior* (with Steven Friedman), 1974. **Essays:** Michael Graves; Victor Horta; Louis Kahn; Charles W. Moore; Brussels: Hôtel Tassel; Fort Worth: Kimbell Art Museum; Philadelphia: Richards Medical Research Building.

KARGE, Henrik. Assistant professor of art history, University of Kiel, Germany. Author of *Die Kathedrale*

von Burgos und die Spanische Architektur des 13. Jhs., 1989; *Spanische Kunstgeschichte. Eine Einführung,* 2 vols., 1992; numerous lectures and articles about Spanish art and architecture, German gothic architecture, 19th-century historiography of art and architecture. **Essays:** Burgos Cathedral; León Cathedral.

KAROL, Eitan. Partner of Louis Karol Architects International. Formerly curator of Charles Holden exhibition. **Essay:** Charles Holden.

KELLY, Brian. Principal, Brian Kelly-Matt Bell, Architecture-Urban Design. Assistant professor of architecture, University of Maryland. **Essays:** Bertram Grosvenor Goodhue; John Russell Pope; James Stirling; Stuttgart: Neue Staatsgalerie; Washington, D.C.: National Gallery of Art.

KILINSKI, Karl II. Professor of art history, Southern Methodist University, Dallas, Texas. Author of *Classical Myth in Western Art,* 1985; *Boeotian Black Figure Vase Painting of the Archaic Period,* 1990; numerous articles in *American Journal of Archaeology, Antike Kunst, Arts Magazine, Hesperia* and *Greek, Roman and Byzantine Studies.* President and national trustee, Texas chapter of Society for the Preservation of the Greek Heritage. **Essays:** Delphi; Mycenae.

KIRIKOV, Boris M. Art critic. Vice-director, State Museum of History, St. Petersburg. Lecturer in history of art, St. Petersburg University. Author of several books, pamphlets and articles on 19th- and 20th-century architecture of St. Petersburg, history of church architecture, charity and necropolis of St. Petersburg. **Essays:** Giacomo Quarenghi; Karl Ivanovich Rossi; Thomas de Thomon; Konstantin A. Ton; Adrian D. Zakharov; St. Petersburg: Admiralty.

KOBAK, Aleksandr. Historian and chief expert, St. Petersburg Cultural Foundation; author of several books and numerous articles on 19th- and 20th-century architecture of St. Petersburg, history of church architecture, charity and necropolis of St. Petersburg. **Essays:** St. Petersburg: Exchange; St. Petersburg: St. Isaac's Cathedral.; St. Petersburg: Kazan Cathedral.

KOERBLE, Barbara. Free-lance writer, Fort Worth, Texas. Author of numerous articles on architecture. **Essays:** Edward Larrabee Barnes; Deer Isle, Maine: Haystack School; Oklahoma City: Mummers Theater.

KOSTAREVA, Irena. Historian and senior researcher, State Museum of the History of St. Petersburg. **Essays:** St. Petersburg: Peterhof Palace.

KRINSKY, Carol Herselle. Professor of fine arts, New York University, New York City. Past president, Society of Architectural Historians. Author of *Vitruvius de* *architectura, 1521—,* 1969; *Synagogues of Europe: Architecture, History, Meaning,* 1985; *Gordon Bunshaft of Skidmore, Owings and Merrill,* 1988; numerous articles and lectures on American and European architecture and urbanism. **Essay:** New York City: Rockefeller Center.

LEACH, Neil. Lecturer in architecture, University of Nottingham, England. Translator of Leon Battista's *On the Art of Building in Ten Books* (with others), 1988. **Essays:** Florence: San Lorenzo—New Sacristy; Florence: San Lorenzo—Old Sacristy.

LEACH, Peter. Author of *James Paine,* 1988; articles on aspects of 17th- and 18th-century English architecture. **Essays:** John Carr; James Paine; Derbyshire: Kedleston Hall.

Le ROY, Christian. Professor of ancient history, University of Paris I. Editor-in-chief, *Revue Archéologique.* Author of *Fouilles de delphes; Les Terres cuites architecturales;* numerous articles on archaeology, epigraphy and ancient history. **Essay:** Pergamon.

LESER, Petra. Assistant professor of art history, University of Cologne, Germany. Author of *Der Architekt Clemens Klotz (1886-1969),* 1991. **Essays:** Elias Holl; Johann Balthasar Neumann; Augsburg: Zeughaus; Ottobeuren: Abbey Church.

LEVETO-JABR, Paula D. Formerly instructor at Georgia State University and Indiana University, Bloomington. Member of archaeological excavations. Author of articles on Byzantine art. **Essays:** Aachen: Royal Chapel; Milan: San Lorenzo; Rome: Colosseum; Rome: Pantheon; Rome: Santa Costanza; Rome: Santa Maria Maggiore.

LEWIS, Michael J. Historiographer, Canadian Centre for Architecture, Montreal, Quebec. Author of *The Collected Works of Frank Furness* (with others), 1991; *The Politics of the German Gothic Revival: August Reichensperger,* 1993; various articles on American and German architecture. **Essays:** Georg Ludwig Friedrich Laves; Detlef Lienau; Bruce Price.

LIM, B. P. Professor and head of School of Architecture and Industrial Design, Queensland Institute of Technology, Brisbane, Australia. Editor of *The Indoor Environment of Buildings,* 1989. Author of *Architectural Detailing for the Tropics* (with E. Lip), 1988. **Essays:** John Andrews; Harry Seidler; Oak Park, Illinois: Unity Temple.

LITTLE, Bryan. Author of *The Building of Bath,* 1948; *The Life and Works of James Gibbs,* 1955; *Bath Portrait,* 1961; *English Historic Architecture,* 1964; *Catholic Churches since 1623,* 1966; *English Cathedrals,* 1972; *Sir Christopher Wren: A Historical Biography,* 1975; *Bristol: An Architectural History* (with Andor Gomme and Michael Jenner), 1979. **Essays:** James Gibbs; Wood Family; Bath:

Circus/Crescent/Square; Bristol: St. Mary Redcliffe; Cambridge: King's College; Canterbury Cathedral; London: St. Martin-in-the-Fields; Oxford: Radcliffe Library.

LIZON, Peter. Professor of architecture, University of Tennessee. Coauthor of *Handbook of Architectural Design Competitions,* 1981; and *American Institute of Architects Guidelines for the Management of Quasi-Competitions,* 1982. Author of *Smyrna Airport Design Competition,* 1992; *The Palace of the Soviets: The Paradigm of Architecture in the U.S.S.R.,* 1993; numerous articles on practice, theory and criticism of architecture and planning. **Essays:** Moisei Ginsburg; Josef Havlíček; Vladimír Karfík; Jan Kotěra; Ödön Lechner; Konstantin Melnikov; Vesnin Brothers; Brno: Villa Tugendhat; Moscow: Rusakov Workers' Club; Moscow: G.U.M. Department Store; Moscow: Melnikov House; Moscow: Palace of the Soviets (Competitions); Prague: National Theater.

LONG, Christopher. Researcher, Texas State Historical Association. Formerly teaching assistant, University of Texas at Austin. Contributor to *Austin American-Statesman.* **Essays:** Josef Hoffmann; Adolf Loos; Joseph Maria Olbrich; Vienna: Secession Building.

LORANCE, Loretta. Doctoral candidate in art history, City University of New York. Formerly affiliated with The Metropolitan Museum of Art, New York City. **Essays:** R(ichard) Buckminster Fuller; Paul Marvin Rudolph; Antonio Sant'Elia; New York City: Haughwout Building.

LOWERSON, J. R. Reader in history, University of Sussex. Former editor of *Southern History.* Author of *A Short History of Sussex; Sport and the English Middle Classes, 1870-1916;* numerous historical papers. **Essays:** Amiens Cathedral; Bradford-on-Avon: St. Lawrence; Brighton: Royal Pavilion; Paris: La Sainte-Chapelle.

LUKER, Maurice S. III. Architectural historian in Campus Planning Office, Cornell University. Member of College Art Association. **Essays:** Philibert De L'Orme; Anet: Château.

MACDONALD, A. J. Senior lecturer in architecture, University of Edinburgh, Scotland. Author of *Wind Loading on Buildings,* 1975. Founding member, Edinburgh Center of Architectural History. **Essays:** William Burn; Thomas Hamilton; Edinburgh New Town.

MÁČEL, Otakar. Associate professor of history of architecture, University of Technology, Delft, Holland. Author of *Stühle aus Stahl,* 1980; *The Museum of the Continuous Line* (with J. Van Geest), 1986; *Eiu Stuhl macht Geschichte* (with W. Möller), 1992; articles on modern architecture and design. **Essays:** Peter Behrens; Bohuslav Fuchs; Josef Gočár; J. J. P. Oud; Aleksei V. Shchusev; Fedor Shekhtel; Berlin: AEG Turbine Factory;

Moscow: Kazan Railway Station.

MACK, Charles R. Professor of art history and William J. Todd Professor of the Italian Renaissance, University of South Carolina, Columbia. Author of *Pienza: The Creation of a Renaissance City,* 1987; *Paper Pleasures,* 1992; numerous lectures and articles on Renaissance art and architecture. Past president and board member of southeast chapter of Society of Architectural Historians and Southeastern College Art Conference. **Essays:** Leon Battista Alberti; Lorenzo Ghiberti; Giuliano da Maiano; Bernardo Rossellino; Paestum; Florence: Palazzo Rucellai; Florence: Palazzo Strozzi; Florence: Santa Croce/Pazzi Chapel; Mantua: Sant' Andrea; Rome: Santo Stefano Rotondo.

MADIGAN, Brian. Assistant professor of art history, Wayne State University, Detroit, Michigan. Author of articles on Greek, Roman and late-Antiquity art and archaeology. **Essay:** Thomas Archer.

MAKOGONOVA, Maria. Art critic. Curator of architecture section, State Museum of the History of St. Petersburg. Lecturer in the history of architecture, St. Petersburg Institute of Culture. **Essays:** Bartolomeo Francesco Rastrelli; St. Petersburg: Smolny Monastery; Tsarkoe Selo: Pushkino Palace; St. Petersburg: Winter Palace.

MALLORY, Nina A. Professor of art, State University of New York at Stony Brook. Author of *Bartolomé Esteben Murillo,* 1983; *El Greco to Murillo: Spanish Painting in the Golden Age, 1556-1700,* 1990; numerous articles on Spanish architecture and painting. **Essays:** Narciso Tomé; Toledo: Transparente, Cathedral of Toledo.

MANNELL, Joanne. Assistant professor of art history, Montana State University. Bozeman, Montana. Author of articles on Roman architecture and architectural ornament. **Essays:** Split: Imperial Palace of Diocletian; Tivoli: Hadrian's Villa.

MARX, Patricia A. Adjunct professor of art history, American University. Member of Archaeological Institute of America. **Essays:** Iktinos; Kallikrates; Mnesikles; Athens: Acropolis; Madrid: El Escorial; Nîmes: Amphitheater.

McCLINTOCK, Kathryn Marie. Part-time instructor in art history, The Pennsylvania State University, University Park. Author of *The Sculpture of San Nicola at Bari* (dissertation). **Essays:** Bari: San Nicola; Milan: Sant' Ambrogio; Syria: Krak des Chevaliers.

McKEAN, John. Designer and critic. Head of Interior Architecture, University of Brighton, England. Formerly head of History Unit, University of North London School of Architecture and Interior Design. Author of *Learning*

from Segal, 1988; *The Royal Festival Hall,* 1992; *The Crystal Palace,* 1993. **Essays:** Joseph Paxton; Alison and Peter Smithson; Alexander Thomson; Leicester: Engineering Faculty Building; London: Crystal Palace; London: Royal Festival Hall.

McKINNEY, David D. Program development associate, John F. Kennedy Center for the Performing Arts, Washington, D.C. Author of numerous articles and lectures on Horace Walpole and 18th-century English architecture. **Essays:** Charles Harrison Townsend; Middlesex: Strawberry Hill, Twickenham.

McNEUR, Lorna Anne. Lecturer in architecture, Cambridge University. Formerly design teacher at Carleton and Waterloo universities, Canada. Contributor to journals. **Essays:** New York City: Central Park; Rome: Piazza del Popolo.

MICHELSON, Elizabeth Munch. Free-lance writer on decorative arts and architecture. Curator, New Milford Historical Society, Connecticut. M.A., Cooper Hewitt Museum Master's Program, Parson School of Design. **Essay:** William Kent.

MILLAR, John F. Architectural historian and former museum director. Author of *The Architects of the American Colonies,* 1968; *Classical Architecture in Renaissance Europe, 1419-1585,* 1987; *A Handbook on the Founding of Australia 1788,* 1988; *The Harrison Guide* (in preparation). **Essays:** Peter Harrison; Hans Hendrik van Paesschen; Charleston: Drayton Hall.

MILLER, William C. Professor of architecture and dean, University of Utah. Author of *Alvar Aalto: An Annotated Bibliography,* 1984; numerous articles on Aalto and Finnish architecture. **Essays:** Alvar Aalto; Erik Gunnar Asplund; Kay Fisker; Arne Jacobsen; Sven Markelius; Ragnar Östberg; Ivar Tengbom; Paimio: Tuberculoisis Sanatorium; Stockholm: City Hall; Stockholm: Public Library; Seinäjoki: Civic Center.

MILNER-GULLAND, R. R. Reader in Russian studies, University of Sussex, England. Author of *Introduction to Russian Art and Architecture* (with J. E. Bowlt), 1980; articles on Russian, Byzantine and medieval English art and architecture. **Essays:** Vasili Ivanovich Bazhenov; Moscow: Andronikov Monastery; Moscow: Kremlin.

MOFFETT, Marian Scott. Professor of architectural history, University of Tennessee, Knoxville. Coeditor, *Arris.* Author of *A History of Western Architecture* (with Lawrence Wodehouse), 1989; *East Tennessee Cantilever Barns* (with Wodehouse), 1993; articles and lectures on vernacular architecture. **Essays:** Roland Anthony Wank; Conques: Church of Ste. Foy; Shropshire: Iron Bridge.

MOORE, R. J. Senior lecturer in architectural history, University of Newcastle, New South Wales, Australia. Numerous articles and lectures on Ruskin and Victorian architecture. Member of Society of Architectural Historians of Australia and New Zealand. **Essays:** William Butterfield; John Ruskin; George Gilbert Scott; George Edmund Street.

MORGAN, William. Professor of fine arts, University of Louisville, Kentucky. Formerly architecture critic, *Courier-Journal.* Author of *The Almighty Wall,* 1983; *Collegiate Gothic,* 1989; numerous articles on architecture. **Essay:** Reima and Raili Pietilä.

MORGENTHALER, Hans R. Assistant professor of architecture, University of Colorado at Denver. Author of *The Early Sketches of German Architect Erich Mendelsohn (1887-1953): No Compromise with Reality,* 1992; articles and lectures on Erich Mendelsohn and contemporary architecture. **Essays:** August Endell; Ely Jacques Kahn; Karl Moser; Rudolf M. Schindler; Bernard Tschumi.

MUNK-JØRGENSEN, Wivan. Contributor. **Essays:** Michael Gottlieb Bindesbøll; C. F. Hansen; Peder Vilhelm Jensen-Klint; Copenhagen Cathedral.

MURTA, K. H. Professor of architecture, University of Sheffield. Member of Ecclesiastical Architects and Surveyors; chairman of Board of Architectural Education. Contributor to *Architectural Review; Architects Journal; RIBA Journal.* **Essays:** John Ninian Comper; Inigo Jones; Edward S. Prior; Northumberland: Seaton Delaval.

NEW, Anthony. Architect in private practice, London. Consultant architect to Derby Cathedral and numerous churches. Fellow of Society of Antiquaries and Royal Institute of British Architects. Author of *Observer's Guide to Cathedral,* 1972; *Cathedrals of Britain,* 1980; *The Abbeys of England and Wales,* 1985; *The Abbeys of Scotland,* 1988. **Essays:** Amsterdam: Westerkerk; Durham Cathedral; Exeter Cathedral; Laon Cathedral; Lincoln Cathedral; London: St. James the Less, Westminster; London: St. Mary Woolnoth; London: Tower of London; London: Westminster Abbey; Middlesex: Hampton Court Palace; Rome: Spanish Steps.

NICOLETTA, Julie. Doctoral candidate in history of Art, Yale University. Author of *Structures for Communal Life: Shaker Dwelling Houses at Mount Lebanon, New York* (thesis; in progress). Member of Society of Architectural Historians and Vernacular Architecture Forum. **Essays:** Henry Austin; Charles Bridgeman; William Strickland; William Thornton; Ithiel Town.

NOFFSINGER, James P. Emeritus professor of architecture, University of Kentucky. Taught at Kansas University, University of Minnesota and Insitut Teknologie Bandung (Indonesia). Architect for U.S. Commission of Fine Arts and Historic American Building Survey of U.S. Department of the Interior. Past national director of Society of Architectural Historians. Author of numerous bibliographies on Japanese architects. **Essays:** Kunio Maekawa; Antonin Raymond; Kenzo Tange.

NORTON, Bettina A. Writer and historian, Cambridge, Massachusetts. Formerly director of Cambridge History Society and registrar of print collection, Essex Institute. Author of *History of the Boston Naval Shipyard, 1800-1974,* 1974; *Edwin Whitefield: Nineteenth-Century North American Scenery,* 1977; *Trinity Church: The Story of an Episcopal Parish in the City of Boston,* 1977; *To Create and Foster Architecture: The Contributions of the Boston Architecture Center,* 1989. **Essays:** Asher Benjamin; Henry Van Brunt.

NORTON, Paul F. Emeritus professor of art history Program, University of Massachusetts, Amherst; past chair, for thirteen years, of Department of Art. Formerly editor of *Journal of the Society of Architectural Historians.* Author of *Amerhert, A Guide to its Architecture,* 1977, and *Latrobe, Jefferson and the National Capitol,* 1977; numerous articles on architects and architecture. **Essays:** Samuel Pepys Cockerell; Samuel McIntire; Boston Public Library; Boston: Trinity Church.

OCH, Marjorie. Independent scholar. Author of essays on Italian medieval and Renaissance art, architecture and 19th-century American painting and illustration. **Essays:** Francesco Primaticcio; Florence: Palazzo Vecchio; Florence: San Miniato al Monte; Pisa Cathedral; Ravenna: Sant' Apollinare in Classe; Ravenna: Sant' Apollinare Nuovo; Rome: Palazzo Farnese; Rome: Santa Maria Degli Angeli.

O'CONNELL, Lauren M. Assistant professor of art history, Ithaca College. Author of numerous lectures on French revolutionary architecture, Viollet-le-Duc and 19th-century nationalism. **Essays:** Jean-Baptiste Rondelet; Eugène Emmanuel Viollet-le-Duc.

OLSZEWSKI, Edward J. Professor of art history, Case Western Reserve University, Cleveland, Ohio. Formerly president of Midwest Art History Society. Author of *Giovanni Battista Armenini, on the True Principles of the Art of Painting,* 1977; *The Draftsman's Eyes,* 1981. **Essays:** Giovanni Lorenzo Bernini; Carlo Fontana; Giulio Romano; Pirro Ligorio; Baldassare Peruzzi; Matti Rossi; Mantua: Palazzo del Tè; Rome: Palazzo Chigi; Rome: Villa Farnesina.

O'ROURKE, Desmond. Consulting architect in Washington, D.C., and Helsinki, Finland. Author of articles and lectures on Finnish architecture. Member of Finnish Association of Architects. **Essays:** Erik Bryggman; Aarne Ervi; Aarno Ruusuvuori; Tampere: Kaleva Church.

OVERY, Paul. Lecturer in history of art and design, Goldsmiths College, University of London. Art critic, *Times,* London. Author of *De Stijl,* 1969; *The Rietvel Schröder House* (coauthor), 1988; *Kadinsky: The Language of the Eye,* 1991; numerous lectures and articles on early 20th-century art, architecture and design. **Essays:** Gerrit Thomas Rietveld; Utrecht: Schröder House.

PALEY, Richard. Graduate student in art history, Rutgers University. **Essay:** Carlo Scarpa.

PALMER, Allison. Doctoral candidate in art history, Rutgers University, New Jersey. **Essays:** Cosimo Fanzago; Francesco Ricchino; Rome: Palazzo Massimo; Rome: Piazza Navona.

PAPADEMETRIOU, Peter. Professor, New Jersey Institute of Technology. Author of articles on Eero Saarinen. **Essays:** Eero Saarinen; Chantilly: Dulles International Airport.

PAWELEC, Katharina. Assistant professor of art history, Justus-Liebig-Universität, Giessen, Germany. Author of *Medieval Art,* 1990; *Die Aachener Bronzegitter; Studien zur Karolingischen Ornamntik Um 800.;* several lectures and articles about Karolingian architecture and minor arts. **Essays:** Juan de Herrera; Juan Bautista de Toledo.

PERDUE, Susan Holbrook. Scholar of architectural history, with an emphasis on early 20th-century American architecture and landscape design. **Essay:** Parker and Unwin.

PINCUS, Lisa L. Received master's degree from New York University. **Essay:** Chicago: 860-880 Lake Shore Drive Apartments.

PITLUGA, Kurt. Doctoral candidate, Pennsylvania State University. Formerly teaching assistant in art history. Author of *The Collegiate Architecture of Charles Z. Klauder* (dissertation). **Essay:** George Browne Post.

PLATT, Frederick. Writer on American life between the Civil War and World War I. Author of *The Architecture of Horace Trumbauer* (in preparation). **Essays:** Horace Trumbauer.

PLUMMER, David. Masters candidate in architecture, University of Texas at Austin. **Essay:** Pier Luigi Nervi.

POLETTI-ANDERSON, Anita. Doctoral candidate, University of Virginia, Charlottesville. Formerly writer and researcher at Université Catholique de Louvain's centre d'Histoire de L'Architecture et de Bâtiment. **Essays:** Etiènne-Louis Boullée; Claude-Nicolas Ledoux.

PORT, M. H. Emeritus professor of modern history, Queen Mary and Westfield College, University of London. Formerly editor of *The London Journal;* editor of *The Commissions for Building Fifty New Churches,* 1986. Author of *Six Hundred New Churches,* 1961; *History of the King's Works, vol. VI, 1782-1851* (with others), 1973; *The Houses of Parliament* (with others), 1976; numerous articles on 19th-century British architecture. **Essays:** Charles Barry; Robert Smirke; William Wilkins; James Wyatt; Jeffry Wyatville; Berkshire: Windsor Castle; London: Houses of Parliament; London: Law Courts; London: Reform Club; London: St. John, Bethnal Green; London: St. Pancras Church; London: Somerset House.

PORTER, Jed. Assistant professor of architecture, University of Kentucky. Member, Society for Industrial Archeology. **Essays:** John Haviland; Philadelphia: Eastern Penitentiary.

PRICE, Patricia Lynn. Doctoral candidate in architectural history, University of Virginia, Charlottesville. Dissertation topic concerns Renaissance architectural theory in Italy and France. **Essays:** Germain Boffrand; Du Cerceau Family; Jacques Lemercier.

PTACEK, Robin. Assistant professor in visual arts department, University of Maryland, Baltimore. **Essays:** Kutna Hora: Cathedral of St. Barbara; Prague: St. Vitus' Cathedral; Prague: Černín Palace; Prague: St. Nicholas; Prague: Vladislav Hall; Tabor: Zizka Square.

RATTNER, Donald M. Director, Institute for the Study of Classical Architecture, New York Academy of Art, New York City. Author of numerous articles and lectures on classical architecture. **Essays:** Athens: Choragic Monument of Lysicrates; Athens: Tower of the Winds.

RIJSBERMAN, Marijke. Multilingual free-lance writer and editor, Chicago. **Essays:** Salomon De Brosse; Caprarola: Palazzo Farnese; Fontainebleau Palace; Monreale: Cathedral of Santa Maria La Nuova; Siena Cathedral; Vienna: St. Stephen's Cathedral.

RING, Trudy. Free-lance writer and editor, Chicago. **Essays:** Victor Louis; Bordeaux: Grande Théâtre.

ROBERTS, Ann. Associate professor of history of art, University of Iowa, Iowa City. Contributor of articles on Netherland's art of the late middle ages to *Art Belletin, Oud Holland* and *Burlington Magazine.* **Essay:** Bruges: Town Hall (Stadhuis).

ROBISON, Elwin C. Associate professor of architecture and environmental design, Kent State University. Book review editor, *Architronic: The Electronic Journal of Architecture.* Author of *Architectural Technology before the Scientific Revolution* (with others), 1993; numerous lectures and articles on Guarini, Palladio and early skyscrapers. **Essays:** Guarino Guarini; Andrea Palladio; Chicago: Home Insurance Building; Chicago: Monadnock Building;

Chicago: Reliance Building; Maser: Villa Barbaro; Turin: Palazzo Carignano; Turin: San Lorenzo.

ROSENBLUM, Charles L. Free-lance writer. Doctoral candidate in history of architecture, University of Pittsburgh, Pennsylvania. Formerly public relations coordinator in New Haven, Connecticut. **Essays:** Gustave Eiffel; Romaldo Giurgola; Charles Gwathmey; Kevin Roche; Heinrich Schickhardt; Stanley Tigerman.

ROTH, Leland M. Marion Dean Ross Professor of Architectural History, University of Oregon, Eugene. Former member of board of directors, Society of Architectural Historians. Author of *A Concise History of American Architecture,* 1979; *McKim, Mead and White, Architects,* 1983; *Understanding Architecture,* 1992; several articles and book chapters on planning and industrial workers' housing and vernacular house design from 1860-1920. **Essays:** Carrère and Hastings; Ralph Adams Cram; Ernest Flagg; Cass Gilbert; John Mead Howells; Richard Morris Hunt; McKim, Mead and White; Peabody and Stearns; John Wellborn Root; John Mills Van Osdel; Boston: Massachusetts State House; Chicago: World's Columbian Exposition, 1893; New York City: Lincoln Center; New York City: Pennsylvania Station; Portland: Portland Building.

RUDOLF, Moira. Art historian, special trustees for St. Thomas's Hospital, London. Author of articles for *St. Thomas's Hospital Gazette* and various journals. Member of Society of Architectural Historians of Great Britain. **Essays:** Joseph Bonomi; Thomas Harrison; Thomas Leverton; John Soane; Liverpool: Anglican Cathedral.

SAINT, Andrew. Architectural historian, London. Two-time winner of Alice Davis Hitchcock Medallion of Great Britain Society of Architectural Historians. Author of *Richard Norman Shaw,* 1976; *The Image of the Architect,* 1983; *Towards a Social Architecture,* 1987. **Essays:** London: Sir John Soane's Museum; Strasbourg Cathedral.

SANABRIA, Sergio L. Associate professor of architecture, Miami University, Oxford Ohio. Numerous lectures and articles on 16th-century Spanish architect Rodrigo Gil de Hontañón. **Essays:** Antonio Gaudí; Rodrigo Gil de Hontañón; Juan Guas; Diego de Siloe; Simón de Colonia; Lorenzo Vazquez; Barcelona: Casa Milá; Granada: Palace of Emperor Charles V in the Alhambra; Metz Cathedral; Seville: Cathedral.

SAUNDERS, Ann Loreille. Historian. Fellow of University College, London and Society of Antiquaries of London. Honorary editor to London Topographical Society and Costume Society. Author of *John Bacon R. A.,* 1961; *Regent's Park,* 1969, 1981; *Art and Architecture of London,* 1984, 1988, 1992. **Essay:** London: Hampstead Garden Suburb.

SCHILLER, Joyce K. Lecturer, St. Louis Art Museum, St. Louis, Missouri. Author of numerous lecture and articles on 19th- and 20th-century art and architecture. **Essays:** Albert Kahn; St. Louis: Wainwright Building.

SCHULTZ, Bernard. Professor of art history and chair of division of art, West Virginia University. Author of *Art and Anatomy in Renaissance Italy,* 1985; *Art Past/Art Present* (with David G. Wilkens), 1990; lectures and articles on interdisciplinary relationships between art and medical history. **Essays:** Michelangelo; Florence: San Lorenzo—Laurentian Library; Rome: Piazza del Campidoglio.

SCHULZE, Franz. Professor of art, Lake Forest College. Contributing editor, *Art News* and *Inland Architect;* corresponding editor, *Art in America.* Author of *Fantastic Images: Chicago Art Since 1945,* 1972; *One Hundred Years of Architecture in Chicago,* 1976; *Ames van der Rohe: A Critical Biography,* 1985. **Essays:** Philip Johnson; Ludwig Mies van der Rohe.

SCHUMACHER, Thomas L. Professor of architecture, University of Maryland, College Park. Author of *The Danteum,* 1985; *Surface and Symbol: Giusseppe Terragni and the Architecture of Italian Nationalism,* 1991; numerous articles on modern architecture and urbanism. **Essays:** Marcello Piacentini; Giuseppe Terragni.

SCOTT, Pamela. Visiting lecturer, Cornell University, Washington, D.C. Editor of *The Papers of Robert Mills, 1781-1855* (microfilm edition), 1990. Author of *Buildings of the District of Columbia* (with others), 1993; numerous lectures and articles on Washington, D.C., architecture and early American iconography. **Essays:** George Hadfield; Robert Mills; Alexander Parris; Isaiah Rogers; Washington, D.C.: United States Capital; Washington, D.C.: United States Treasury; Washington, D.C.: Washington National Monument.

SEBESTA, Judith Lynn. Professor of classics, University of South Dakota. **Essay:** Ostia Antica.

SENARCLENS DE GRANCY, Antje. Contributor. **Essay:** Paris: Institut de Monde Arabe.

SHAPIRO, Ellen R. Assistant professor of art history, Massachusetts College of Art, Boston. Former associate editor, *Assemblage.* Author of numerous articles on Italian architecture of the 1920s and 1930s. **Essays:** Ernesto Basile; Gruppo 7; Gio Ponti; Giuseppe Sommaruga.

SHEVCHENKO, Olya. Doctoral candidate, City University of New York. **Essay:** Moscow: Lenin State Library.

SILBERBERG-PEIRCE, Susan. Assistant professor of art history, Colorado State University, Fort Collins, Colorado.

Consultant and photo archival specialist, documentation of Roman wall painting, The Getty Center; photographer of ancient Roman architecture. Author of numerous lectures on Greek and Roman art and architecture. **Essays:** Segesta; Rome: Baths of Diocletian.

SMART, C. Murray, Jr. Professor of architecture, University of Arkansas, Fayetteville. Member of editorial board, *Victorians Institute Journal.* Author of *Muscular Churches,* 1989; numerous articles on 19th-century British architecture. Past president, Southeast Society of Architectural Historians. **Essays:** George Frederick Bodley; Francesco Borromini; William Burges; C. R. Cockerell; Deane and Woodward; Filippo Juvarra; W. Eden Nesfield; John Loughborough Pearson; Anthony Salvin; Richard Norman Shaw; Alfred Waterhouse; London: Natural History Museum; London: New Scotland Yard; Oxford: Keble College; Rome: San Carlo Alle Quattro Fontane; Rome: Sant'Ivo Della Sapienze; Turin: Superga; Turin: Palazzo Madama; Turin: Plazzina Stupinigi.

SMITHSON, Peter D. Architect in private practice. **Essay:** Oxfordshire: Rousham Park.

SMYTH-PINNEY, Julia M. Registered architect. Associate professor of architecture, University of Kentucky. Numerous lectures on the Italian Renaissance and baroque architecture. **Essay:** Rome: Sant' Andrea al Quirinale.

SNADON, Patrick. Associate professor of architecture, Mississippi State University. Author of articles on A. J. Davis, B. H. Latrobe and 19th-century American architecture and interiors. **Essays:** Alexander Jackson Davis; Benjamin H. Latrobe (with Michael W. Fazio).

SOKOL, David M. Professor of history of architecture, University of Illinois at Chicago. Former chair of Oak Park Historic Preservation Commission; former vice president of Unity Temple Restoration Foundation. Editor, Cambridge Monographs on American Artists. Author of *American Architecture and Art,* 1976; *American Decorative Arts and Old World Influences,* 1980; *Life in Nineteenth-Century American,* 1981; *Otto Neumann,* 1988; numerous articles on Frank Lloyd Wright, American landscapes and Chicago architecture. **Essays:** George Grant Elmslie; Louis Sullivan; Baltimore: Catholic Cathedral; Buffalo: Larkin Building; Chicago: Auditorium Building; Chicago: Schlesinger and Mayer Store; New York City: Guggenheim Museum.

SOLOMONSON, Katherine M. Assistant professor, College of Architecture and Landscape Architecture, University of Minnesota. Formerly architectural historian, San Mateo County Historic Resources Inventory. Author of book in progress on Chicago Tribune Tower Competition; articles and book reviews on medieval and modern topics. **Essays:** Chicago: Marquette Building; Chicago: Tribune

Tower Competition; Santiago de Compostela: Cathedral.

SOO, Lydia M. Assistant professor of architecture, Ohio State University, Columbus. **Essays:** Claude Perrault; Christopher Wren; London: Royal Hospital, Greenwich; London: St. Mary-le-Bow; London: St. Paul's Cathedral; London: St. Stephen Walbrook.

SPAETH, David Anthony. Professor of architecture, University of Kentucky, Lexington. Author of *Ludwig Mies van der Rohe: An Annotated Bibliography and Chronology,* 1979; *Ludwig K. Hilberseimer: An Annotated Bibliography,* 1981; *Mies van der Rohe,* 1985; numerous articles and lectures. **Essays:** Charles O. Eames; Tony Garnier; Ludwig Karl Hilberseimer; Chicago: Illinois Institute of Technology; Dessau: Bauhaus; Stuttgart: Weissenhofsiedlung.

SPENCE, Rory. Lecturer in architecture, University of Tasmania, Launceston, Australia. Formerly architect and writer in London, England, and Sydney, Australia. Author of *Catalogue of the Drawings Collection of the Royal Institute of British Architecture, T-2,* 1984; articles on contemporary Australian architecture. **Essays:** Lars Eliel Sonck; Philip Speakman Webb; Helsinki: Telephone Company Building; Tampere Cathedral.

SPIESER, Jean-Michel. Professor of history of art, Université des Sciences Humaines de Strasbourg, Strasbourg Cedex, France. Author of *Thessalonique et ses monuments du IVeau VIe s.,* 1984; *Caričin Grad II; Le quartier sud-ouest de la ville haute* (with others), 1990; articles on early Christian and Byzantine art and archaeology. **Essays:** Instanbul: St. Irene; Instanbul: Church of Christ in Chora; Instanbul: SS. Sergius and Bacchus; Rome: San Paolo Fuori Le Mura; Thessalonica: St. Demetrios.

STARCZEWSKI, Jerzy Andrzej. Assistant professor of architecture, Drury College, Springfield, Missouri. Formerly senior faculty, Warsaw Technological University, Warsaw, Poland. Formerly participated in reconstruction of historic buildings in Poland. Author of *Budownictwo Ogólen* (with others), 1965-75; numerous papers on architecture and building. **Essays:** Matthew Nowicki; Gdansk: Church of St. Mary; Kraków: Sigismund Chapel, Wawel Cathedral; Malbork: Castle of the Teutonic Knights; Poznan: Town Hall; Torun: Town Hall; Warsaw: Old Town Reconstruction; Warsaw: Wilanow Palace; Wroclaw: Church of the Most Blessed Virgin Mary.

STEELE, James M. Associate professor of architecture, Texas Tech University, Lubbock. Formerly architect in private practice, Doylestown, Pennsylvania. **Essays:** Raimondo D'aronco; Bruce Goff; Marc-Antoine Laugier; Jean Prouvé; Robert Venturi; Athens: Agora; Ephesos; Prienne; Ravenna: San Vitale; Rome: St. Peter's Rome: St. Peter's Square.

STEVENSON, Christine. Lecturer in the history of art, Reading University, Reading, England. Editor of *Architectural History.* Author of articles about C. F. Hansen, John Wood the Elder, Danish painting and industrial design around 1800 and the design of 18th-century hospitals and lunatic asylums. **Essays:** Robert Adam; George the Younger Dance; [Hans] Christian Hansen; Martin Nyrop; Carl Petersen.

SULLEBARGER, Beth. Principal, Sullegargers Associates (consulting firm in historic preservation). Editor, *Historic Preservation: Forging a Discipline.* President Emerita, Preservation Alumni, Inc. **Essays:** Othmar Ammann; James H. Dakin.

SUNDT, Richard A. Associate professor of art history, University of Oregon, Eugene. Author of articles on Mendicant architecture. Treasurer, Association Villard de Honnecourt for the Interdisciplinary Study of Science, Technology and Art. **Essay:** Batalha: Monastery of Santa Maria da Vitória.

TATE, Robert B. Corresponding fellow of Institut d'Estudis Catalans, Barcelona and Real Academia de la Historia, Madrid. Fellow of British Academy and Royal Historial Society, London. **Essays:** Lluís Domenèch; Barcelona: Sagrada Familia.

THAYER, Preston. Doctoral candidate, University of Pennsylvania. Project coordinator of *Buildings of the United States* series, Society of Architectural Historians. **Essays:** Isambard K. Brunel; Thomas Telford.

THOMAS, Christopher. Staff member at University of Western Ontario. **Essay:** Henry Bacon.

THOMAS, George. Professor, University of Pennsylvania, Philadelphia. Author of *The Architecture of Frank Furness* (with James O'Gorman and Hyman Myers), 1973; *Frank Furness: The Complete Works* (with Jeffrey Cohen and Michael Lewis), 1991. **Essays:** Frank Furness; Philadelphia: Library of the University of Pennsylvania.

TOMLINSON, R. A. Professor of ancient history and archaeology and head of department, University of Birmingham, England. Chairman of managing committee, British School at Athens. Author of *Argos and the Argolid,* 1972; *Greek Sanctuaries,* 1976; *Greek Architecture,* 1989; *The Athens of Alma Tadema,* 1991; *From Mycenae to Constantinople,* 1992. **Essays:** Hippodamos; Akragas; Syracuse; Tiryns.

TURAK, Theodore. Emeritus professor of art history, American University, Washington, D.C. Author of *William Le Baron Jenney: A Pioneer of Modern Architecture,* 1986; numerous articles on the Chicago School of Architecture and French influences on American architecture. **Essays:** J. N. L. Durand; Paris: Les Halles Centrales.

UNDERWOOD, David K. Assistant professor of art history, Rutgers University, New Brunswick, New Jersey. Author of articles on Brazilian architecture. **Essays:** Aleijadinho; Roberto Burle Marx; Lucio Costa; João Federico Ludovice; Oscar Niemeyer; Matteus Vicente de Oliveira; Affonso Eduardo Reidy; Carlos Raúl Villanueva; Brasília: Federal Capital Complex; Queluz: Royal Palace; Rio de Janeiro: Ministry of Education and Health.

URBAS, Andréa. Assistant professor of architecture, Ball State University. Formerly historical architect, State Historic Preservation Office, Arizona and Illinois. **Essays:** A. J. Downing; Porec: Euphrasius Basilica; Pula: Amphitheater; Gračanica: Monastery Church; Trogir: Trogir Cathedral; Zadar Cathedral; Zadar: Church of St. Donato.

VAN BERGEIJK, Herman. Free-lance architectural historian. Visiting professor at various European and American universities. Author of *M. P. Berlage: Architettura, estetica, urbanistica,* 1985; *W. M. Dudok: Architect and Urbanist,* 1994; numerous lectures and articles on Italian, German and Dutch architecture. **Essays:** Hendrik Petrus Berlage; Willem Marinus Dudok; Philips Vingboons.

VAN SCHOUTE, Roger. Director of Archaeology and History of Art, Catholic University of Louvain, Belgium. **Essays:** Louvain: Town Hall (with Monique Van Schoute); Tournai Cathedral (with Monique Van Schoute).

VIGNUOLO, Lisa. Graduate student in art history, Rutgers University. **Essays:** I. M. Pei; Paris: Louvre, Pyramide.

VINCENT, Marc. Doctoral candidate in history of art, University of Pennsylvania. Author of lectures and articles on Louis Kahn and Paul Cret. **Essays:** Jean-François-Thérèse Chalgrin; Paul Philippe Cret; Ange-Jacques Gabriel; Charles Garnier; Jacques-Germain Soufflot; Paris: Arc de Triomphe; Paris: Les Invalides; Paris: Opéra; Paris: Place de la Concorde.

VOLKMAN, Nancy J. Associate professor of landscape architecture, Texas A&M University, College Station, Texas. Specialist in landscape history and historic landscape preservation. Coauthor of *Landscapes in History: Design and Planning in the Western Tradition,* 1993; numerous articles on 19th-century landscape architect H. W. S. Cleveland. Member of State Board of Review for National Register of Historic Places. **Essays:** John Notman; Frederick Law Olmstead; Charles Adams Platt; Calvert Vaux.

VOLPE, Gianni. Architect. Author of numerous essays on architecture of the Italian Renaissance. Member of Accademia Rafaello di Urbino. **Essays:** Francesco di Giorgio; Urbino: Ducale Palace.

WALDEN, Russell. Reader in history of contemporary architecture, Victoria University, Wellington, New Zealand. Formerly senior lecturer, Birmingham School of Architecture, England. Author of *Voices of Silence: The Chapel of Futuna,* 1986. **Essay:** Ronchamp: Notre-Dame-du-Haut.

WALKER, Frank Arneil. Professor of architecture, University of Strathclyde, Glasgow, Scotland. Author of architectural guides, including *South Clyde Estuary,* 1986; *Central Glasgow,* 1989; *Glasgow,* 1992; *North Clyde Estuary,* 1992; numerous articles on architecture and urban form. **Essays:** William Richard Lethaby; Charles Rennie Mackintosh; Glasgow School of Art.

WALTON, Thomas. Associate professor of architecture and planning, Catholic University of America, Washington, D.C. Editor, *Design Management Journal.* Author of articles on design. **Essays:** Pierre Charles L'Enfant; Washington, D.C.: City Plans.

WARDEN, P. Gregory. Associate professor of art history, Southern Methodist University, Dallas, Texas. Consulting scholar, The University Museum, Philadelphia. Formerly editor of *Perspective.* Author of *The Extramural Sanctuary of Demeter and Persephone at Cyrene, Libya. Final Reports IV,* 1990; numerous lectures and articles on Etruscan and Roman art and archaeology. President, Dallas chapter of Archaeological Institute of America. **Essays:** Apollodorus of Damascus; Rabirius; Pompeii.

WEIDENHOFFER, Hansjörg. Free-lance art historian in Graz, Austria. Author of *Der Salzburger Hofbaumeister Giovanni Gaspare Zuccalli,* 1987; *Sakramentschäuschen in Österreich,* 1991. **Essay:** Enrico Zuccalli.

WHITE, Charles W. Associate professor of architecture, Texas A&M University, College Station. Formerly staff member of Aphrodisias archaeological expedition in Turkey. Author of papers and articles on Hellenistic architecture in the Near East. **Essays:** Baalbek; Palmyra.

WILKINS, Ann Thomas. Lecturer in classics, University of Pittsburgh and Duquesne University, Pittsburgh, Pennsylvania. Formerly faculty member at Vassar College and the University of Michigan. Author of *Hero or Villain: Sallust's Portrayl of Catiline,* 1993; numerous lectures on ancient art, architecture and literature. **Essays:** Epidauros; Olympia.

WILKINS, David G. Professor of the history of art and architecture, University of Pittsburgh. Author of *Donatello* (with Bonnie A. Bennett); *History of the Duquesne Club* (with Mark Brown and Lu Donnely); *Art Past/Art Present* (with Bernard Schultz and Katheryn Linduff). Founding member of Preservation Pittsburgh. **Essays:** Sinan; Florence: Ponte Vecchio (with Rebecca L. Wilkins); Instanbul: Yerebatan Cistern (with Rebecca L. Wilkins);

Instanbul: Hagia Sophia; Moscow: Lomonosov University; Moscow: St. Basil's.

WILLIS, Alfred. Architecture librarian, Kent State University. Author of numerous lectures and articles on Belgian architecture, architectural drawings and architectural literature. **Essays:** François Hennebique; Lucien Kroll; André Lurçat; Edward Durrell Stone; Antwerp: Grote Markt; Antwerp: Town Hall; Brussels: Grand' Place.

WINTER, John. Architect in private practice, London. Council member of London Architectural Association. Formerly visiting professor at Cambridge University, Yale University, Syracuse University and Toronto University. Author of *Modern Architecture,* 1969; *Industrial Architecture,* 1970. **Essays:** Ove Arup; Marcel Breuer; Serge Ivan Chermayeff; Wells Coates; Ralph Erskine; Norman Foster; Richard Meier; Richard Neutra; Richard Rogers; Owings and Merrill Skidmore (SOM); Owen Williams; Minoru Yamasaki; F. R. S. Yorke; Nottinghamshire: Boots Factory, Beeston; Chicago: John Hancock Center; Chicago: Sears Tower; Hong Kong Bank; London: Lloyd's of London; New York City: United Nations Headquarters; Paris: Centre Georges Pompidou.

WITTKOPP, Gregory M. Curator of Collections, Cranbrook Academy of Art Museum, Bloomfield Hills, Michigan. Director of restoration of Saarinen House (Eliel Saarinen's home and studio) at Cranbrook Academy of Art. Formerly curator of exhibitions, Saginaw Art Museum, Saginaw, Michigan. **Essays:** Eliel Saarinen; Helsinki: Railway Station and Administration Building.

WODEHOUSE, Lawrence. Professor of architectural history, University of Tennessee, Knoxville. Coeditor, *Arris.* Author of *Ada Louise Huxtable: A Bibliography,* 1981; *White of McKim, Mead and White,* 1988; *The Roots of International Style Architecture,* 1989; *A History of Western Architecture* (with Marian Scott Moffett), 1989; *East Tennessee Cantilever Barns* (with Moffett), 1993; numerous articles on 19th- and 20th-century American architecture. **Essays:** C. R. Ashbee; Joseph Emberton; George Howe; William Lescaze; Alfred B. Mullett; Edward Tuckerman Potter; William Appleton Potter; M. H. Baillie Scott; Stanford White; Ammi B. Young; Boston: City Hall; Philadelphia: Philadelphia Saving Fund Society Building.

WOJTOWICZ, Robert. Assistant professor of art history, Old Dominion University, Norfolk, Virginia. Author of several articles on Lewis Mumford. **Essays:** New York City: Brooklyn Bridge; Philadelphia: Merchants' Exchange.

WOLNER, Edward W. Assistant professor of architectural history, Ball State University, Muncie, Indiana. Author of *Walter W. Ahlschlager: American Architecture and Urban Society in the 1920s,* (in progress);

numerous conference papers and articles on the relationship between Chicago architecture and Chicago's development between 1835 and 1910 and on 1920s skyscrapers in midwest American cities. **Essays:** Milan: Galleria Vittorio Emanuele II; Milan: Central Railway Station; New York City: Chrysler Building; New York City: Empire State Building; Venice: Il Redentore; Venice: San Giorgio Maggiore.

YARWOOD, Doreen. European consultant. Writer and artist. Author of *Robert Adam,* 1970; *Architecture of*

Europe, 1974, 1983; *English Interiors,* 1984; *Chronology of Western Architecture,* 1987.

ZABEL, Craig. Associate professor of art history, Pennsylvania State University. Previously taught at Dickinson College, University of Virginia and University of Illinois at Urbana-Champaign. Coeditor, *American Public Architecture: European Roots and Native Expressions.* Author of articles on George Grant Almslies, Prairie School bank buildings, public architecture, recent American architects, Eadweard Muybridge and Anselm Kiefer. **Essay:** Owatonna: National Farmers Bank.

PHOTO CREDITS

PHOTOGRAPHS AND ILLUSTRATIONS APPEARING IN *INTERNATIONAL DICTIONARY OF ARCHITECTS AND ARCHITECURE,* VOLUME 1, WERE RECEIVED FROM THE FOLLOWING SOURCES:

E. Makinen/The Museum of Finnish Architecture: **p. 2;** Robert M. Craig: **pp. 6, 30, 45, 78, 109, 114, 131, 164, 177, 195, 232, 291, 299, 333, 348, 362, 370, 375, 412, 435, 438, 444, 457, 477, 503, 513, 517, 537, 543, 550, 558, 573, 579, 583, 599, 602, 611, 637, 640, 659, 661, 664, 730, 741, 764, 793, 812, 851, 871, 894, 905, 918, 921, 938, 970, 972, 977, 980, 989, 992, 993, 999, 1007;** Bildarchiv Foto Marburg/Art Resource, N.Y.: **pp. 13, 49, 67, 75, 91, 107, 152, 180, 198, 200, 213, 223, 243, 268, 328, 338, 402, 419, 481, 492, 527, 590, 597, 608, 624, 644, 651, 677, 740, 822, 875, 886, 895, 927;** Courtesy of Brazilian Embassy, Washington, DC: **pp. 16, 613, 722;** Archiv Alinari/Art Resource, N.Y.: **pp. 18, 34, 79, 273, 432, 553, 715, 750, 781, 845;** Italian Government Travel Office, Chicago, IL: **pp. 22, 280, 289, 449, 488, 577, 604, 670, 680, 776, 936;** Reproduced by permission of Botond Bognar: **pp. 25, 545, 548, 820;** Courtesy of Contemporary Architects: **p. 36;** G. Fredricksson: **p. 41;** South African Consulate General, Chicago, IL: **p. 51;** Reproduced by permission of Sergio L. Sanabria: **pp. 53, 89, 97, 118, 158, 171, 256, 313, 347, 495, 498, 673, 686, 712, 774, 778, 825, 827, 828, 943, 949;** Courtesy of Keith Eggener: **pp. 56;** Courtesy of the British Tourist Authority: **p. 59, 835;** Rosenthal Art Slides, Inc.: **pp. 73, 143, 144, 154, 165, 174, 282, 287, 295, 311, 439, 561, 581, 666, 692, 709, 725, 758, 772, 810, 837, 858, 879, 913, 923, 988;** Courtesy of Flemming Skude/Danish Government: **pp. 81, 355, 357, 428;** Giraudon/Art Resource, N.Y.: **pp. 85, 394, 507;** (c) Inge and Arved von\ der Ropp: **p. 94;** Photograph by Pino Musi: **p. 99;** Courtesy of Jonathan S. Liffgens: **pp. 104, 345, 521, 525, 575, 639, 787, 843;** Courtesy of Leeds City Council Department of Planning: **p. 111;** Courtesy of Randall J. Van Vynckt: **pp. 124, 182, 359;** Courtesy of Irish Tourist Board: **pp. 128, 293;** Architectural Review: **p. 156;** Courtesy of Universite de Montreal: **p. 169;** Courtesy of James Stevens Curl: **pp. 192, 210, 221, 258, 308, 465, 468, 501, 515, 684, 695, 795, 808, 968, 162;** Courtesy of Maurice S. Luker III: **pp. 203, 204;** Kevin Fitzsimons/Wexler Center for the Arts: **p. 234;** Courtesy of Museum of Finnish Architecture: **p. 241;** Timothy Hursley/Arthur Erickson Architects: **p. 244;** Reproduced by permission of Desmond O'Rourke, DipArch SAFA: **p. 249;** OFVW: Austrian Government Tourist Office: **pp. 253, 262, 263, 389, 396, 473, 679;** Architectural Association Slide Library: **p. 265;** Richard Davies/Sir Norman Foster and Associates: **p. 271;** Courtesy of Peter Lizon: **pp. 278, 317, 460, 493, 568, 817, 819, 947;** Courtesy of George E. Thomas: **pp. 284;** Courtesy of Frederick Gibberd: **p. 306;** Austrian Foreign Affairs and Trade Department: **p. 321;** Courtesy of Enoch Pratt Free Library, Baltimore, MD: **p. 324;** Courtesy of John T. Hopf: **p. 367;** Architectenburo Herman Hertzberger: **p. 385;** Neg. number ICHi-19052; Chicago Historical Society: **p. 399;** Atelier Hans Hollein: **p. 405;** Belgian Tourist Office: **p. 410;** Photograph by Anthony Kersting: **pp. 423, 459;** (c) Yas Ishimoto: **p. 426;** Courtesy of Murphy/Jahn Architects: **p. 429;** Courtesy of Philip Johnson: **p. 441;** Courtesy of Lucien Kroll: **p. 475;** Courtesy of Denys Lasdun & Partners: **p. 483;** Courtesy of Berthold Lubetkin: **p. 532;** Courtesy of Portuguese National Tourist Office: **pp. 533, 902;** Ezra Stoller (c) Esto: **p. 566;** Scala/Art Resource, N.Y.: **pp. 588, 884;** (c) Hearst Monument/John Blades: **p. 592;** North Carolina State University, Raleigh: **p. 619;** Courtesy of Atelier Frei Otto: **p. 630;** Photograph by Koji Horiuchi, courtesy of Pei Cobb Freed & Partners: **p. 655;** (c) Aker Photography, Houston, TX: **p. 657;** Courtesy of Raili and Reima Pietila, Architects: **p. 672;** Courtesy of Dmitry Vilensky: **pp. 718, 754, 891, 1012;** Courtesy of Kevin Roche John Dinkeloo & Associates: **p. 737;** Courtesy of French Government Tourist Office: **p. 745;** Reproduced by permission of Fiona Spalding-Smith: **p. 770;** Saska/Art Resource, N.Y.: **p. 790;** Courtesy of Harry Seidler and Associates: **p. 805;** Courtesy of Waltraud Krase: **p. 855;** Buffalo & Erie County Historical Society, Buffalo, NY: **p. 867;** Courtesy of Osamu Murai: **p. 873;** Thierry/French Government Tourist Office: **p. 908;** (c) Dieter Leistner: **p. 911;** (c) Mark Cohn: **p. 944;** National Monuments/Art Resource: **p. 985;** Architectural Press: **p. 998;** Courtesy of Hansjorg Weidenhoffer: **p. 1016.**